Peterson's Scholarships, Grants & Prizes

2009

PETERSON'S
A nelnet COMPANY

PETERSON'S

A nelnet COMPANY

About Peterson's, a Nelnet company

Peterson's (www.petersons.com) is a leading provider of education information and advice, with books and online resources focusing on education search, test preparation, and financial aid. Its Web site offers searchable databases and interactive tools for contacting educational institutions, online practice tests and instruction, and planning tools for securing financial aid. Peterson's serves 110 million education consumers annually.

For more information, contact Peterson's, 2000 Lenox Drive, Lawrenceville, NJ 08648; 800-338-3282; or find us on the World Wide Web at www.petersons.com/about.

Stephen Clemente, President; Fern A. Oram, Content Director; Bernadette Webster, Operations Director; Roger S. Williams, Sales and Marketing; Mark D. Snider, Production Editor; Michael Haines, Copy Editor; Jennifer Fishberg, Research Project Manager; Helen L. Hannan, Research Associate; Phyllis Johnson, Programmer; Ray Golaszewski, Manufacturing Manager; Linda M. Williams, Composition Manager

ISBN-13: 978-0-7689-2624-8
ISBN-10: 0-7689-2624-6

Printed in the United States of America

10 9 8 7 6 5 4 3 2 1 10 09 08

Thirteenth Edition

OTHER RECOMMENDED TITLES

Peterson's College Money Handbook
Peterson's Paying for College: Answers to All Your Questions About Financial Aid, Scholarships, Tuition Payment Plans, and Everything Else You Need to Know

Contents

A Note from the Peterson's Editors

Billions of dollars are given to students and their families every year to help pay for college. Last year, private donors made available more than $7 billion in financial aid to help undergraduate students pay for college. Yet, to the average person, the task of finding financial aid awards in this huge network of scholarships, grants, and prizes appears to be nearly impossible.

For nearly forty years, Peterson's has given students and parents the most comprehensive, up-to-date information on how to get their fair share of the financial aid pie. *Peterson's Scholarships, Grants & Prizes* was created to help students and their families pinpoint those specific private financial aid programs that best match students' backgrounds, interests, talents, or abilities.

In *Peterson's Scholarships, Grants & Prizes,* you will find more than 4,000 scholarship/grant programs and prize sources that provide financial awards to undergraduates in the 2008–09 academic year. Foundations, fraternal and ethnic organizations, community service clubs, churches and religious groups, philanthropies, companies and industry groups, labor unions and public employees' associations, veterans' groups, and trusts and bequests are all possible sources.

For those seeking to enter college, *Peterson's Scholarships, Grants & Prizes* includes information needed to make financing a college education as seamless as possible.

The **How to Find an Award That's Right for You** section paints a complete picture of the financial aid landscape, discusses the connection between honors students and scholarship eligibility, provides important tips on how to avoid scholarship scams, and offers insight into how to make scholarship management organizations work for you.

Also found in **How to Find an Award That's Right for You** is the "How To Use This Guide" article, which describes the more than 4,000 awards included in the guide, along with information on how to search for an award in one of eleven categories.

If you would like to compare awards quickly, refer to the **Quick-Reference Chart.** Here you can search through "Scholarships, Grants & Prizes At-a-Glance" and select awards by highest dollar amount.

In the **Profiles of Scholarships, Grants & Prizes** section you'll find updated award programs, along with information about the award sponsor. The profile section is divided into three categories: *Academic Fields/Career Goals, Nonacademic/Noncareer Criteria,* and *Miscellaneous Criteria.* Each profile provides all of the need-to-know information about available scholarships, grants, and prizes.

Finally, the back of the book features thirteen **Indexes** listing scholarships, grants, and prizes based on award name; sponsor; academic fields/career goals; civic, professional, social, or union affiliation; corporate affiliation; employment/volunteer experience; impairment; military service; nationality or ethnic heritage; religious affiliation; residence; location of study; and talent/interest area.

Peterson's publishes a full line of resources to help guide you through the college admission process. Peterson's publications can be found at your local bookstore, library, and high school guidance office, and you can access us online at www.petersons.com.

We welcome any comments or suggestions you may have about this publication and invite you to complete our online survey at www.petersons.com/booksurvey. Or you can fill out the survey at the back of this book, tear it out, and mail it to us at:

Publishing Department
Peterson's, a Nelnet company
2000 Lenox Drive
Lawrenceville, NJ 08648

Your feedback will help us make your educational dreams possible.

Be sure to take full advantage of the many real opportunities that have been opened up to students and their families by the many organizations, foundations, and businesses that can help you with the burden of college expenses.

The editors at Peterson's wish you the best of luck in your scholarship search efforts!

How to Find an Award That's Right for You

All About Scholarships

Dr. Gary M. Bell
Dean, University Honors College, Texas Tech University

During the next four (or more) years you will spend earning your college baccalaureate degree, think of the learning task as your primary employment. It is helpful to think of a scholarship as part of the salary for undertaking your job of learning. One of your first inquiries as you examine a potential college setting is about the type of assistance it might provide given your interests, academic record, and personal history. Talk to a financial aid officer or a scholarship coordinator at the school. At most schools, these are special officers—people specifically employed to assist you in your quest for financial assistance. Virtually all schools also have brochures or publications that list scholarship opportunities at their institution. Get this literature and read it carefully.

Also, visit either your local bookstore or your local public library and get books that have several hundred scholarships listed in different categories. These books are inexpensive and can be found in the reference section. Excellent information is also available on the Web at http://www.petersons.com/finaid.

Last, high school counselors often have keen insight into resources available at colleges, especially the schools in your area. These people are the key points of contact between institutions of higher education and you.

In general, it is not a good idea to use a private company that promises to provide you with a list of scholarships for which you might be eligible. Such lists are often very broad, and you can secure the same results by using available high school, university, Web based, and published information. The scholarship search you perform online will probably be more fruitful than what any private company can do for you.

What do we mean by the word "scholarship" anyway? In the very broadest sense, scholarships consist of outright grants of monetary assistance to eligible students to help them attend college. The money is applied to tuition or the cost of living while in school. Scholarships do not need to be repaid. They do, however, often carry stringent criteria for maintaining them, such as the achievement of a certain grade point average, the carrying of a given number of class hours, matriculation in a specific program, or membership in a designated group. Scholarships at many schools may be combined with college work-study programs—where some work is also required. Often, scholarships are put together with other forms of financial aid so that collectively they provide you with a truly attractive financial aid package. This may include low-interest loan programs to make the school of your choice financially feasible.

Scholarships generally fall into three major categories: *need-based scholarships*, predicated on income; *merit-based scholarships*, based on your academic and sometimes extracurricular achievements; and *association-based scholarships*, which are dependent on as many different associations as you can imagine (for instance, your home county, your identification with a particular group, fraternal and religious organizations, or the company for which a parent may work). The range of reasons for which scholarships are given is almost infinite.

Most schools accommodate students who have financial need. The largest and best grant programs are the U.S. government-sponsored Federal Pell Grants and the Federal Supplemental Educational Opportunity Grants, which you might want to explore with your financial aid counselor. There is also the Academic Competitiveness Grant (ACG) that is open to Pell Grant recipients who have attended a "rigorous" high school program. Also inquire about state-sponsored scholarship and grant programs.

Merit-based scholarships can come from a variety of sources—the university, individual departments or colleges within the university, state scholarship programs, or special donors who want to assist worthy students. This fact should be remembered as you meet with your financial aid officer, because he or she knows that different opportunities may be available for you as a petroleum engineering, agriculture, accounting, pre–veterinary, or performing arts major. Merit-based scholarships are typically designed to reward the highest performers on such precollege measures as standardized tests (the SAT or ACT) and high school grades. Since repeated performance on standardized tests often leads to higher scores, it may be financially advantageous for you to take these college admission tests several times.

Inquire about each of these three categories of scholarships. The association-based scholarships can sometimes be particularly helpful and quite surprising. Employers of parents, people from specific geographic locations, or organizations (churches, civic groups, unions, special interest clubs, and even family name associations) may provide assistance for college students. Campus scholarship literature is the key to unlocking the mysteries of association-based financial assistance (and the other two categories as well), but personal interviews with financial officers are also crucial.

There are several issues to keep in mind as you seek scholarship assistance. Probably the most important is to determine deadlines that apply to a scholarship for which you may be eligible. It's wise to begin your search early, so that your eligibility is not nullified by missing a published deadline. Most scholarship opportunities require an application form, and it is time well spent to make sure the application is neat, grammatically correct, and logical. Correct spelling is essential. Have someone proofread your application. Keep in mind that if applications require essays, fewer students typically take the time to complete these essays, giving those students who do a better chance of winning that particular scholarship. Always be truthful in these applications but, at the same time, provide the most positive self-portrayal to enhance your chances of being considered. Most merit-based and association-based scholarships are awarded competitively.

Finally, let the people who offer you assistance know whether or not you will accept their offer. Too many students simply assume that a scholarship offer means automatic acceptance. This is not the case! In most instances, you must send a letter of acknowledgement and acceptance. Virtually all schools have agreed that students must make up their minds about scholarship acceptance no later than May 1. But earlier deadlines may apply.

As you probably know, tuition at private schools is typically higher than tuition at state colleges and universities. Scholarships can narrow this gap. Many private institutions have a great deal of money to spend on scholarship assistance, so you may find that going to a private college will cost no more than attending a state-supported college or university. Take note, a substantial scholarship from a private school may still leave you with a very large annual bill to cover the difference between the scholarship amount and the actual cost of tuition, fees, and living expenses.

When you evaluate a scholarship, factor in your final out-of-pocket costs. Also consider the length of time for which the school extends scholarship support. Be cautious about schools that promise substantial assistance for the first year in order to get you there, but then provide little or nothing in subsequent years. The most attractive and meaningful scholarships are offered for four to five years. The scholarship search should not be abandoned once you are enrolled at the school of your choice. There are often a number of additional scholarship opportunities for you once enrolled, especially as you prove your ability and interest in a given field.

A Strategy for Finding Awards

Private scholarships and awards can be characterized by unpredictable, sometimes seemingly bizarre, criteria. Before you begin your award search, write a personal profile of yourself that will help establish as many criteria as possible that might form a basis for your scholarship award. Here is a basic checklist of fifteen questions you should consider:

1. **What are your career goals?**
   Be both narrow and broad in your designations. If, for example, you have a career aim to be a TV news reporter, you will find many awards specific to this field in the *TV/Radio Broadcasting* section. However, collegiate broadcasting courses can be offered in departments or schools of communication. So, be sure to also consider *Communications* as a relevant section for your search. Consider *Journalism,* too, for the same reasons. Then look under some more broadly inclusive but possibly relevant areas, such as *Trade/Technical Specialties.* Or check a related but different field, such as *Performing Arts.* Finally, look under marginally related basic academic fields, such as *Humanities, Social Sciences,* or *Political Science.* We make every attempt to provide the best cross-reference aids, but the nuances of specific awards can be difficult to capture with even the most flexible cross-referencing systems. So you will need to be broadly associative in your thinking in order to get the most out of this wealth of information.

   If you have no clear career goal, browsing through the huge variety of academic/career awards may well spark new interest in a career path. Be open to imagining yourself filling different career roles that you previously may not have considered.

2. **In what academic fields might you major?**
   Your educational experiences to this point or your sense about your personal talents or interests may have given you a good idea of what academic discipline you wish to pursue. Again, use both broad and narrow focuses in designing your search and look at related subject fields. For example, if you want to major in history, there is a *History* section. Also, be sure to check out *Social Sciences* and *Humanities* and, maybe, *Area/Ethnic Studies. Education,* for example, could have the perfect scholarship for a future historian.

3. **In which jobs, industries, or occupations have your parents or other members of your immediate family been employed? What employment experiences might you have?**
   Individual companies, employee organizations, trade unions, government agencies, and industry associations frequently set up scholarships for workers or children or other relatives of workers from specific companies or industries. These awards might require that you study to stay in the same career field, but most are offered regardless of the field of study you wish to undertake. Also, if one of your parents worked as a public service employee, especially as a firefighter or police officer, and most especially if he or she was killed or disabled in the line of duty, there are many relevant awards available.

4. **Do you have any hobbies or special interests? Have you ever been an officer or leader of a group? Do you possess special skills or talents? Have you won any competitions? Are you a good writer?**
   From bowling to clarinet playing, from caddying to ham radio operating, there are a host of special interests that can win awards for you from groups that wish to promote and/or reward these pursuits. Many scholarships are targeted to "student leaders," including sports team captains, yearbook or newspaper editors, student government officers, and club, organization, and community activists.

5. **Where do you live? Where have you lived? Where will you go to college?**
   Residence criteria are among the most common qualifications for scholarship aid. Local clubs and companies provide millions of dollars in scholarship aid to students who live in a particular state, province, region, or section of a state. This means that your residential identity puts you at the head of the line for these grants. State of residence can—depending on the sponsor's criteria—include the place of your official residence, the place you attend college, the place you were born, or any place you have lived for more than a year.

6. **What is your family's ethnic heritage?**
   Hundreds of scholarships have been endowed for students who can claim a particular nationality or racial or ethnic descent. Partial ethnic descent frequently qualifies, so don't be put off if you do not think of your identity as fully tagged as a specific "ethnic" entity. There are awards for Colonial American, English, Welsh, Scottish, European, and other backgrounds that students may not consider to be especially "ethnic." There is even one for descendants of signers of the Declaration of Independence, whatever ethnicity that might have turned out to be some ten generations later.

7. **Do you have a physical disability?**
   There are many awards given to individuals with physical disabilities. Of course, commonly recognized impairments of mobility, sight, communication, and hearing are recognized, but, also, learning disabilities and chronic diseases, such as asthma and epilepsy, are criteria for some awards.

8. **Do you currently or have you ever served in a branch of the armed forces? Or, did one of your parents serve? In a war? Was one of your parents lost or disabled in the armed forces?**
   There are hundreds of awards that use one of these qualifications. There are even awards for descendants of Confederate soldiers.

9. **Do you belong to a civic association, union, or religious organization? Do your parents?**
   Hundreds of clubs and religious groups provide scholarship assistance to members or children of members.

10. **Are you male or female?**

11. **What is your age?**

12. **Do you qualify for need-based aid?**

13. **Did you graduate in the upper half, upper third, or upper quarter of your class?**

14. **Do you plan to attend a two-year college, a four-year college, or a trade/technical school?**

15. **In what academic year will you be entering?**

Be expansive when considering your possible qualifications. Although some awards may be small, you may qualify for more than one award, and these can add up to significant amounts in the end.

Scholarship Management Organizations

Richard Woodland
Former Director of Financial Aid, Rutgers University, Camden

The search for private scholarships can be confusing and frustrating for parents and students. Many families feel they just don't know how to go about the process, so they either hire a private scholarship search company or simply give up. The success rate of many scholarship search firms is not good, and college financial aid professionals always warn parents to be skeptical of exaggerated claims.

The process also confuses many donors. A corporation may want to help its employees or the children of its employees or may want to offer a national scholarship program to its customers or the general public. Unfortunately, the corporation may not want to devote valuable administrative time managing a scholarship program. Similarly, there are many donors who want to target their funds to a particular group of students but simply do not know how.

Stepping in to help are scholarship management organizations. Although many have been around for a long time, the majority of the general public knows very little about them. The reason for this is that scholarship management organizations often do not administer scholarship funds directly to students. Rather, they serve as a clearinghouse for their member donor organizations. Today, savvy parents and students can go online to find these organizations and the scholarship programs they administer.

Two of the largest scholarship management programs are the National Merit Scholarship Corporation™ and Scholarship America™. The National Merit Scholarship Corporation sponsors a competitive scholarship program that seeks to identify and reward the top students in the nation. High school students who meet published entry/participation requirements enter these competitions by taking the Preliminary SAT/National Merit Scholarship Qualifying Test (PSAT/NMSQT®), usually as juniors. A particular year's test is the entry vehicle to a specific annual competition. For example, the 2008 PSAT/NMSQT was the qualifying test for entry into competitions for scholarships to be awarded in 2010. For more information, visit http://www.nationalmerit.org.

Another major player is Scholarship America™, which has distributed more than $1.5 billion dollars to more than 1.5 million students since its founding nearly fifty years ago, making it the nation's largest private-sector scholarship and educational support organization. By involving communities, corporations, organizations, and individuals in the support of students through its major programs, Dollars for Scholars® and Scholarship Management Services™. Whether it is working with national leaders in response to the September 11th tragedy, or with corporations such as Kohl's and Best Buy, Scholarship America is an important organization that helps thousands of students every year. For more information, go to www.scholarshipamerica.org.

In addition to the National Merit Scholarship Fund and Scholarship America, there are other organizations that raise funds and administer scholarships for specific groups of students. Some of these organizations include:

- American Indian College Fund **www.collegefund.org**
- Hispanic Scholarship Fund Institute **www.hsfi.org**
- United Negro College Fund **www.uncf.org**
- Organization of Chinese Americans **www.ocanational.org**
- National FFA Organization (Future Farmers of America) **www.ffa.org**
- Gates Millennium Scholars **www.gmsp.org**

These are just a few of the many scholarship sources available on the Web. In addition to using scholarship search engines, think broadly about yourself, your background, your interests, your family connections (work, religious, fraternal organizations), and your future career plans. Then spend some time browsing the Web. We hope that some of the sources mentioned here will help. Remember, the key is to start early (junior year in high school is best) and be persistent.

Scholarship Scams: What They Are and What to Watch Out For

Several hundred thousand students seek and find scholarships every year. Most students' families require some outside help to pay for tuition costs. Although most of this outside help, in the form of grants, scholarships, low-interest loans, and work-study programs, comes either from the state and federal government or the colleges themselves, scholarships from private sources are an extremely important component of this network. An award from a private source can tilt the scales with respect to a student's ability to attend a specific college during a particular year. Unfortunately, for prospective scholarship seekers, the private-aid sector is virtually without patterns or rules. It has, over many years, become a combination of individual programs, each with its own award criteria, timetables, application procedures, and decision-making processes. Considerable effort is required to understand and effectively benefit from private scholarships.

Regrettably, the combination of an urgency to locate money, limited time, and this complex and bewildering system has created opportunities for fraud. It has been estimated that for every 10 students who receive a legitimate scholarship, one is victimized by a fraudulent scheme or scam that poses as a legitimate foundation, scholarship sponsor, or scholarship search service. Every year, an estimated 350,000 families are cheated in various scholarship scams, totalling more than $5 million.

These fraudulent businesses advertise in campus newspapers, distribute flyers, mail letters and postcards, provide toll-free phone numbers, and have Web sites. The most obvious frauds operate as scholarship search services or scholarship clearinghouses. Another segment sets up as a scholarship sponsor, pockets the money from the fees that are paid by thousands of hopeful scholarship seekers, and returns little, if anything, in proportion to the amount it collects. A few of these scams inflict great harm by gaining access to individuals' credit or checking accounts with the intent to extort funds.

A typical mode of operation is for a fraudulent firm to send out a huge mailing to college and high school students, claiming that the company has either a scholarship or a scholarship list for the students. These companies often provide toll-free numbers. When recipients call, they are told by high-pressure telemarketers that the company has unclaimed scholarships and that for fees ranging from $10 to $400 the callers get back at least $1000 in scholarship money or the fee will be refunded. Customers who pay, if they receive anything at all, are mailed a list of sources of financial aid that are no better than, and are in many cases inferior to, what can be found in *Peterson's Scholarships, Grants & Prizes* or any of the other major scholarship guides available in bookstores and libraries or on the Web. The "lucky" recipients have to apply on their own for the scholarships. Many of the programs are contests, loans, or work-study programs rather than gift aid. Some are no longer in existence, have expired deadlines, or set eligibility requirements that students cannot meet. Customers who seek refunds have to demonstrate that they have applied in writing to each source on the list and received a rejection letter from each of them. Frequently, even when customers can provide this almost-impossible-to-obtain proof, refunds are not given. In the worst cases, the companies ask for consumers' checking account or credit card numbers and take funds without authorization.

The Federal Trade Commission (FTC) warns students and their parents to be wary of fraudulent search services that promise to do all the work for you.

"Bogus scholarship search services are just a variation of the 'you have won' prize-promotion scam, targeted to a particular audience—students and parents who are anxious about paying for college," said Jodie Bernstein, former director of the FTC's Bureau of Consumer Protection. "They guarantee students and their families free scholarship money . . . all they have to do to claim it is pay an up-front fee."

There are legitimate scholarship search services. However, a scholarship search service cannot truthfully guarantee that a student will receive a scholarship, and students almost always will fare as well or better by doing their own homework using a reliable scholarship information source, such as *Peterson's Scholarships, Grants & Prizes,* than by wasting money and more importantly time with a search service that promises a scholarship.

The FTC warns scholarship seekers to be alert for these seven warning signs of a scam:

1. **"This scholarship is guaranteed or your money back."**

   No service can guarantee that it will get you a grant or scholarship. Refund guarantees often have impossible conditions attached. Review a service's refund policies in writing before you pay a fee. Typically, fraudulent scholarship search services require that applicants show rejection letters from each of the sponsors on the list they provide. If a sponsor no longer exists, if it really does not provide scholarships, or if it has a rolling application deadline, letters of rejection are almost impossible to obtain.

2. **"The scholarship service will do all the work."**

   Unfortunately, nobody else can fill out the personal information forms, write the essays, and supply the references that many scholarships may require.

3. **"The scholarship will cost some money."**

   Be wary of any charges related to scholarship information services or individual scholarship applications, especially in significant amounts. Some legitimate scholarship sponsors charge fees to defray their processing expenses. True scholarship sponsors, however, should distribute money, not make it from application fees. Before you send money to apply for a scholarship, investigate the sponsor.

4. **"You can't get this information anywhere else."**

   In addition to Peterson's, scholarship directories from other publishers are available in any large bookstore, public library, or high school guidance office. Additional information on private scholarship programs can be found at www.petersons.com/finaid.

5. **"You are a finalist"—in a contest you never entered, or "You have been selected by a national foundation to receive a scholarship."**

   Most legitimate scholarship programs almost never seek out particular applicants. Most scholarship sponsors will only contact you in response to an inquiry. Most lack the budget and mandate to do anything more than this. If you think that there is any real possibility that you may have been selected to receive a scholarship, before you send any money investigate to make sure the sponsor or program is legitimate.

6. **"The scholarship service needs your credit card or checking account number in advance."**

   Never provide your credit card or bank account number over the telephone to the representative of an organization that you do not know. A legitimate need-based scholarship program will not ask for your checking account number. Get information in writing first. **Note:** An unscrupulous operation does not need your signature on a check. It schemes to set up situations that allow it to drain a victim's account with unauthorized withdrawals.

7. **"You are invited to a free seminar (or interview) with a trained financial aid consultant who will unlock the secrets of how to make yourself eligible for more financial aid."**

   Sometimes these consultants offer some good tips on preparing for college, but often they are trying to get you to sign up for a long-term contract for services you don't need. Often these "consultants" are trying to sell you other financial products, such as annuities, life insurance, or other financial services that have little to do with financial aid. By doing your own research with books from Peterson's or other respected organizations, using the Web, and working with your high school guidance office and the college financial aid office, you will get all the help you need to ensure you have done a thorough job of preparing for the financing of your college education.

In addition to the FTC's seven signs, here are some other points to keep in mind when considering a scholarship program:

- Fraudulent scholarship operations often use official-sounding names containing words such as federal, national, administration, division, federation, and foundation. Their names often are a slight variation of the name of a legitimate government or private organization. Do not be fooled by a name that seems reputable or official, an official-looking seal, or a Washington, D.C., address.

- If you win a scholarship, you will receive official written notification by mail, not over the telephone. If the sponsor calls to inform you, it will follow up with a letter in the mail. If a request for money is made over the phone, the operation is probably fraudulent.

- Be wary if an organization's address is a post office box number or a residential address. If a bona fide scholarship program uses a post office box number, it usually will include a street address and telephone number on its stationery.

- Beware of telephone numbers with a 900 area code. These may charge you a fee of several dollars a minute for a call that could be a long recording that provides only a list of addresses or names.

- A dishonest operation may put pressure on an applicant by claiming that awards are on a first-come, first-served basis. Some scholarship programs give preference to early applicants. However, if you are told, especially over the telephone, that you must respond quickly, but you will not hear about the results for several months, there may be a problem.

- Be wary of endorsements. Fraudulent operations claim endorsements by groups with names similar to well-known private or government organizations. The Better Business Bureau (BBB) and other government agencies do not endorse businesses.

If an organization requires that you pay something for a scholarship and you have never heard of it before and cannot verify that it is a legitimate operation, the best advice is to pay nothing. If you have already paid money to such an organization and find reason to doubt its legitimacy, call your bank to stop payment on your check, if possible, or call your credit card company and tell it that you think you were the victim of consumer fraud.

To find out how to recognize, report, and stop a scholarship scam, contact:

Federal Trade Commission
Consumer Response Center
600 Pennsylvania Avenue, N.W.
Washington, D.C. 20580
Web site: www.ftc.gov

The Better Business Bureau (BBB) maintains files of businesses about which it has received complaints. You should call both your local BBB office and the BBB office where the organization in question is located; each local BBB has different records. Call 703-276-0100 to get the telephone number of your local BBB or log on to www.bbb.org for a directory of local BBBs and downloadable BBB complaint forms. The national address is:

The Council of Better Business Bureaus
4200 Wilson Boulevard, Suite 800
Arlington, VA 22203-1838

There are many wonderful scholarships available to qualified students who spend the time and effort to locate and apply for them. However, we advise you to exercise caution in using scholarship search services and, when you must pay money, always use careful judgment when considering a scholarship program's sponsor.

Searching for Scholarships, Grants & Prizes Online

Today's students need all the help they can get when looking for ways to pay for their college education. Skyrocketing tuition costs, state budget cuts, and diminished personal savings have combined to make financing a college education perhaps the number one concern for parents. College sticker shock is driving many families away from college. No wonder. The "purchasing power" of all aid programs from federal, state, and institutional sources has declined over the past two decades. And it's not only lower-income families who are affected. Some fear they make *too much* money to qualify for financial aid. Regardless of their situation, most families struggle to make sense of the college financial aid process and to decide which aid package is the right one for them.

Despite the confusion, students and parents can and should continue to research as many sources as they can to find the money they need. The Internet can be a great source of information. There are many worthwhile sites that are ready to help you search and apply for your fair share of awards, including Peterson's comprehensive financial aid site at www.petersons.com/finaid.

PETERSON'S "PAY FOR SCHOOL"

Peterson's Pay for School financial aid Web site at www.petersons.com/finaid provides families with a wealth of information on college funding for every step of their college admission process.

Expert Advice

By logging on to www.petersons.com/finaid you gain access to comprehensive articles that describe the ins and outs of federal and state funding; tips for filing the FAFSA and the CSS/PROFILE®; step-by-step advice on what you should be doing junior and senior year of high school; and an audio clip of an interview with a real live financial aid expert. Links to state programs and agencies help you connect directly to those resources. You can also access articles on specific topics, such as advice on 529 Plans, loans and payment plans, scholarship scams, the military, and international students. There is also a section called "Financial Aid This Month," which contains the latest-breaking news on government programs and other college funding topics.

Scholarship Search

Peterson's free **Scholarship Search** connects you to millions of scholarships, grants, and prizes totaling nearly $7 billion and lets you do an individualized search for awards that match your financial and educational needs. In just three easy steps you can register; complete a customized profile indicating your scholastic and personal background, intended major, work experience, and a host of other criteria; and access a list of scholarships that match your needs. Each scholarship is described in detail, including eligibility and application requirements and contact information with links to its e-mail address and Web site. Finding money for college couldn't be easier!

Interactive Tools

When it's time to get to the nuts and bolts of your college financial planning, Peterson's has the tools to help. You can

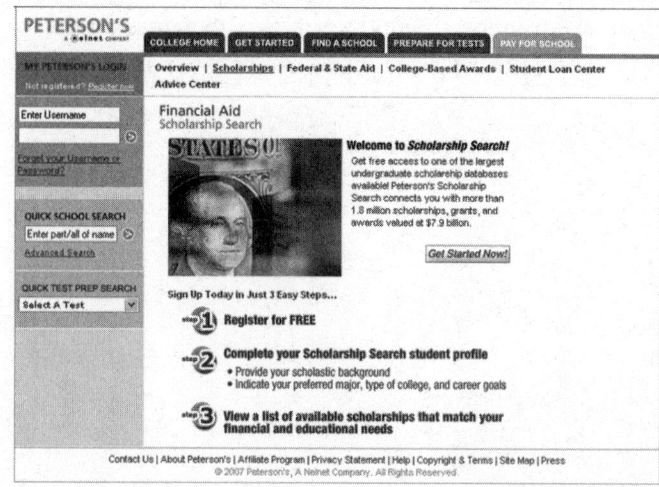

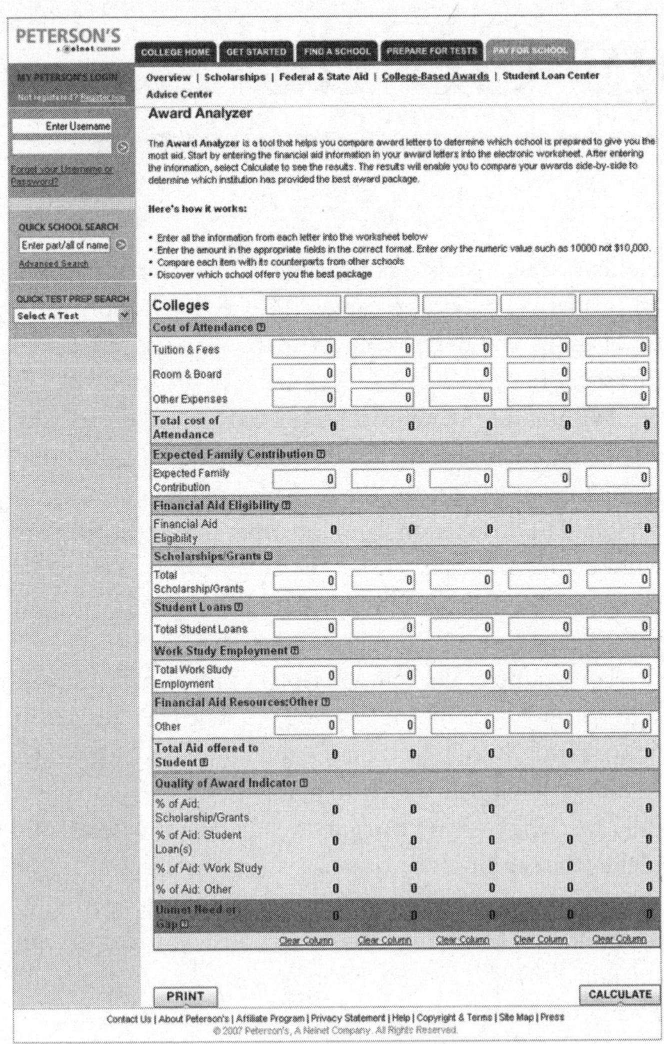

access a calculator to find your Estimated Family Contribution (EFC) as well as a **College Financial Planning Calculator** that lets you figure out your own personal savings plan. After you have received award letters the colleges you've applied to, you can use the **Award Analyzer**, which helps you compare award letters to determine which school is prepared to give you the most aid. You simply enter the information from each award letter you received, press the Calculate button, and you discover which school has offered you the best package.

Searching and applying for financial aid is a complicated process. The resources and tools available to you on www.petersons.com/finaid can help you get your fair share of the financial aid pie. So, what are you waiting for? Log on! Free money for college may be just a mouse click away.

How to Use This Guide

The more than 4,000 award programs described in this book are organized into eleven broad categories that represent the major factors used to determine eligibility for scholarships, awards, and prizes. To build a basic list of awards available to you, look under the broad category or categories that fit your particular academic goals, skills, personal characteristics, or background. The categories are:

- **Academic Fields/Career Goals**
- **Civic, Professional, Social, or Union Affiliation**
- **Corporate Affiliation**
- **Employment/Volunteer Experience**
- **Impairment**
- **Military Service**
- **Nationality or Ethnic Heritage**
- **Religious Affiliation**
- **Residence/Location of Study**
- **Talent/Interest Area**
- **Miscellaneous Criteria**

The **Academic Fields/Career Goals** category is subdivided into 125 individual subject areas that are organized alphabetically by the award sponsor. The **Military Service** category is subdivided alphabetically by branch of service. All other categories are simply organized A to Z by the name of the award sponsor.

Full descriptive profiles appear in only one location in the book. Cross-references to the name and page number of the full descriptive profile are made from other locations under the other relevant categories for the award. The full description appears in the first relevant location in the book; cross-references at later locations. You will always be referred toward the front of the book.

Your major field of study and career goal have central importance in college planning. As a result, we have combined these into a single category and have given this category precedence over the others. The **Academic Fields/Career Goals** section appears first in the book. If an academic major or career area is a criterion for a scholarship, the description of this award will appear in this section.

Within the **Academic Fields/Career Goals** section, cross-references are made only from and to other academic fields or career areas. Cross-references are not provided to this section from the other ten categories. You will be able to locate relevant awards from nonacademic or noncareer criteria through the indexes in the back of this book.

For example, the full descriptive profile of a scholarship for any type of engineering student who resides in Ohio, Pennsylvania, or West Virginia might appear under *Aviation/Aerospace,* which happens to be the alphabetically first engineering category heading in the **Academic Fields/Career Goals** section. Cross-references to this first listing may occur from any other relevant engineering or technological academic field subject areas, such as *Chemical Engineering, Civil Engineering, Electrical Engineering/Electronics, Engineering/Technology, Engineering-Related Technologies, Mechanical Engineering,* or *Nuclear Science.* There would not be a cross-reference from the **Residence** category. However, the name of the award will appear in the Residence index under Ohio, Pennsylvania, and West Virginia. You will always want to check the indexes relevant to your search to get the most out of the guide's listings.

Within the major category sections, descriptive profiles are organized alphabetically by the name of the sponsoring organization. If more than one award from the same organization appears in a particular section, the awards are listed alphabetically under the sponsor name, which appears only once, by the name of the first award.

HOW THE PROFILES ARE ORGANIZED

Here are the elements of a full profile:

Name of Sponsoring Organization

These appear alphabetically under the appropriate category. In most instances acronyms are given as full names.

However, occasionally a sponsor will refer to itself by an acronym. Thus, we present the sponsor's name as an acronym.

World Wide Web Address

Award Name

Brief Textual Description of the Award

Academic Fields/Career Goals (only in the Academic Fields/Career Goals section of the book)

This is a list of all academic or career subject terms that are assigned to this award.

Award

Is it a scholarship? A prize for winning a competition? A forgivable loan? For what type and for what years of college can it be used? Is it renewable or is it for only one year?

Eligibility Requirements

Application Requirements

What do you need to supply in order to be considered? What are the deadlines?

Contact

If provided by the sponsor, this element includes the name, mailing address, telephone and fax numbers, and e-mail address of the person to contact for information about a specific award.

USING THE INDEXES

The alphabetical indexes in the back of the book are designed to aid your search. Two indexes are name indexes. One lists scholarships alphabetically by academic fields and career goals. The other nine indexes supply access by eligibility criteria. The criteria indexes give you the page number of the descriptions of relevant awards regardless of the part of the book in which they appear.

These are the indexes:

Award Name
Sponsor
Academic Fields/Career Goals
[125 subject areas, from Accounting to Women's Studies]
Civic, Professional, Social, or Union Affiliation
Corporate Affiliation
Employment/Volunteer Experience
Impairment
Military Service
Nationality or Ethnic Heritage
Religious Affiliation
Residence
Location of Study
Talent/Interest Area

In general, when using the indexes, writing down the names and page numbers of the awards that you are interested in is an effective technique.

DATA COLLECTION PROCEDURES

Peterson's takes its responsibility as a provider of trustworthy information to its readers very seriously. The data on the award programs in this guide were collected by a third-party data provider between February and April 2008 through an online survey, Internet research, and/or phone interviews with the sponsoring organizations. In addition, Peterson's research staff makes every effort to verify unusual figures and resolve discrepancies. Nonetheless, errors and omissions are possible in a data collection endeavor of this scope. Also, facts and figures, such as number and amount of awards, can suddenly change or awards can be discontinued by a sponsoring organization. Therefore, readers should check with the specific sponsoring agency responsible for administering these awards prior to the time of application to verify all pertinent information.

CRITERIA FOR INCLUSION IN THIS BOOK

The programs listed in this book have the primary characteristics of legitimate scholarships: verifiable sponsor addresses and telephone numbers, appropriate descriptive materials, and fees that, if required, are not exorbitant. Peterson's assumes that these fees are used to defray administrative expenses and are not major sources of income.

Quick-Reference Chart

Scholarships, Grants & Prizes At-a-Glance

This chart lists award programs that indicate that their largest award provides more than $2000. The awards are ranked in descending order on the basis of the dollar amount of the largest award. Because the award criteria in the "Academic/Career Areas and Eligibility Requirements" column may represent only some of the criteria or limitations that affect eligibility for the award, you should refer to the full description in the award profiles to ascertain all relevant details.

Award Name	Page Number	Highest Dollar Amount	Lowest Dollar Amount	Number of Awards	Academic/Career Areas and Eligibility Requirements
SME Family Scholarship	278	$80,000	$ 5000	1–10	Engineering/Technology.
Careers Through Culinary Arts Program Cooking Competition for Scholarships	203	$78,000	$ 1000	88–95	Culinary Arts; Residence: Arizona, California, District of Columbia, Illinois, Massachusetts, New York, Pennsylvania, Virginia.
Terry Foundation Scholarship	812	$76,000	$19,000	208–650	Residence: Texas; Studying in Texas; Talent/Interest Area: leadership.
Boettcher Foundation Scholarships	590	$50,000	$40,000	40	Employment/Volunteer Experience: community service; Residence: Colorado; Studying in Colorado; Talent/Interest Area: leadership.
Davidson Fellows	390	$50,000	$10,000	15–20	Literature/English/Writing, Mathematics, Music, Philosophy, Science, Technology, and Society.
Intel International Science and Engineering Fair	845	$50,000	$ 500	1	Talent/Interest Area: science.
Miss America Organization Competition Scholarships	837	$50,000	$ 2000	70	Talent/Interest Area: beauty pageant.
Young Epidemiology Scholars Competition	299	$50,000	$ 1000	120	Environmental Health, Health and Medical Sciences, Public Health.
National Academy of Television Arts and Sciences John Cannon Memorial Scholarship	181	$40,000	$ 1000	1–10	Communications, TV/Radio Broadcasting.
Ron Brown Scholar Program	592	$40,000	$10,000	10–20	Employment/Volunteer Experience: community service; Talent/Interest Area: leadership. Limited to Black (non-Hispanic) students.
Science, Mathematics, and Research for Transformation Defense Scholarship for Service Program	85	$39,000	$22,000	200	Applied Sciences, Engineering-Related Technologies, Engineering/Technology, Mathematics, Physical Sciences and Math.
Montgomery GI Bill (Active Duty) Chapter 30	653	$37,224	$ 1101	varies	Military Service: General.
U.S. Army ROTC Four-Year College Scholarship	638	$35,000	$ 5000	700–5000	Military Service: Army, Army National Guard.
Freeman Nurse Scholars Program	439	$34,000	$ 7500	49	Nursing; Studying in Vermont.
Los Alamos Employees' Scholarship	770	$30,000	$ 1000	50	Residence: New Mexico.
South Carolina Police Corps Scholarship	383	$30,000	$ 7500	20	Law Enforcement/Police Administration.
University and Community College System of Nevada NASA Space Grant and Fellowship Program	119	$30,000	$ 2500	1–20	Aviation/Aerospace, Chemical Engineering, Computer Science/Data Processing, Engineering/Technology, Physical Sciences and Math; Residence: Nevada; Studying in Nevada.
Voice of Democracy Program	850	$30,000	$ 1000	59	Talent/Interest Area: public speaking, writing.
Two-, Three-, Four-Year Army ROTC Green to Gold Scholarship Program	637	$27,000	$10,000	190–200	Military Service: Army.
Queen Elisabeth Competition	416	$26,749	$ 1337	varies	Music; Talent/Interest Area: music, music/singing.
AXA Achievement Scholarship	587	$25,000	$10,000	52	Employment/Volunteer Experience: community service.

SCHOLARSHIPS, GRANTS & PRIZES AT-A-GLANCE

Award Name	Page Number	Highest Dollar Amount	Lowest Dollar Amount	Number of Awards	Academic/Career Areas and Eligibility Requirements
Princess Grace Scholarships in Dance, Theater, and Film	308	$25,000	$ 5000	15–20	Filmmaking/Video, Performing Arts.
Sons of Italy National Leadership Grants Competition General Scholarships	700	$25,000	$ 5000	8–14	Nationality: Italian.
Illinois Restaurant Association Educational Foundation Scholarships	203	$24,000	$ 750	50–70	Culinary Arts, Food Science/Nutrition, Food Service/ Hospitality, Hospitality Management; Employment/ Volunteer Experience: food service, hospitality; Residence: Illinois.
Environmental Protection Scholarships	132	$22,700	$15,500	1–4	Biology, Earth Science, Environmental Science, Natural Resources, Natural Sciences; Studying in Kentucky.
American Academy of Chefs Chaine des Rotisseurs Scholarship	202	$21,000	$ 1000	10	Culinary Arts, Food Service/Hospitality.
Tuition Exchange Scholarships	612	$21,000	$10,000	3400–4000	Employment/Volunteer Experience: teaching.
Accenture American Indian Scholarship	672	$20,000	$ 2000	5	Limited to American Indian/Alaska Native students.
Coca-Cola Scholars Program	855	$20,000	$10,000	250	Must be in high school.
Gates Millennium Scholars Program	672	$20,000	$ 500	150	Talent/Interest Area: leadership. Limited to American Indian/Alaska Native students.
George and Mary Newton Scholarship	585	$20,000	$ 500	5	Corporate Affiliation.
Glaxo Smith Kline Opportunities Scholarship	814	$20,000	$ 5000	1–5	Residence: North Carolina; Studying in North Carolina.
Horatio Alger Association Scholarship Programs	864	$20,000	$ 2500	1200	Must be in high school.
HSF/McNamara Family Creative Arts Project Grant	98	$20,000	$ 5000	4–8	Art History, Arts, Communications, Fashion Design, Filmmaking/Video, Graphics/Graphic Arts/Printing, Literature/English/Writing, Music, Performing Arts, Photojournalism/Photography, TV/Radio Broadcasting; Nationality: Hispanic, Latin American/Caribbean, Mexican, Nicaraguan, Spanish. Limited to Hispanic students.
Kermit B. Nash, Jr. Academic Scholarship	627	$20,000	$ 5000	1	Disability: physically disabled.
Primary Care Resource Initiative for Missouri Loan Program	212	$20,000	$ 5000	100	Dental Health/Services, Health and Medical Sciences, Nursing; Residence: Missouri; Studying in Missouri.
Samsung American Legion Auxiliary Scholarship	648	$20,000	$ 1000	98	Military Service: General.
Samsung American Legion Scholarship	650	$20,000	$ 5000	98	Military Service: General.
Verizon Foundation Scholarship	586	$20,000	$ 5000	250	Corporate Affiliation.
Washington Crossing Foundation Scholarship	472	$20,000	$ 1000	5–10	Political Science, Public Policy and Administration.
Maryland Association of Private Colleges and Career Schools Scholarship	146	$19,950	$ 500	50	Business/Consumer Services, Computer Science/Data Processing, Dental Health/Services, Engineering/ Technology, Food Science/Nutrition, Home Economics, TV/Radio Broadcasting, Trade/Technical Specialties; Residence: Maryland; Studying in Maryland.
American Legion Department of Kansas High School Oratorical Contest	824	$18,000	$ 150	4	Talent/Interest Area: public speaking.
American Legion National High School Oratorical Contest	826	$18,000	$ 1500	54	Talent/Interest Area: public speaking.
WICHE Professional Student Exchange Program	458	$17,000	$13,300	14	Optometry, Osteopathy; Residence: Washington; Studying in Washington.
Great Expectations Award	861	$16,000	$ 4000	17	
Air Force ROTC College Scholarship	630	$15,000	$ 9000	2000–4000	Military Service: Air Force.
Armenian Relief Society Undergraduate Scholarship	673	$15,000	$13,000	varies	Nationality: Armenian.
Blade Your Ride Scholarship Program	870	$15,000	$ 5000	3	
Elks Most Valuable Student Contest	834	$15,000	$ 1000	500	Talent/Interest Area: leadership.

Award Name	Page Number	Highest Dollar Amount	Lowest Dollar Amount	Number of Awards	Academic/Career Areas and Eligibility Requirements
First in Family Scholarship	766	$15,000	$12,500	10	Residence: Alabama; Studying in Alabama.
Illinois Future Teachers Corps Program	231	$15,000	$ 5000	1150	Education; Residence: Illinois; Studying in Illinois.
Jesse Brown Memorial Youth Scholarship Program	596	$15,000	$ 5000	12	Employment/Volunteer Experience: community service, helping handicapped.
Lowe's Educational Scholarship	602	$15,000	$ 1000	375	Employment/Volunteer Experience: community service; Talent/Interest Area: leadership.
McFarland Charitable Nursing Scholarship	439	$15,000	$ 1000	3–5	Nursing.
National Beta Club Scholarship	544	$15,000	$ 1000	213	Civic Affiliation: National Beta Club.
National FFA College and Vocational/ Technical School Scholarship Program	544	$15,000	$ 1000	1750	Civic Affiliation: Future Farmers of America.
Texas 4-H Opportunity Scholarship	813	$15,000	$ 1500	225	Residence: Texas; Studying in Texas; Talent/Interest Area: animal/agricultural competition.
Tribal Priority Award	686	$15,000	$ 2500	1–5	Limited to American Indian/Alaska Native students.
Howard P. Rawlings Educational Excellence Awards Guaranteed Access Grant	774	$14,800	$ 400	1000	Residence: Maryland; Studying in Maryland.
Arkansas Health Education Grant Program (ARHEG)	82	$14,600	$ 5000	258–288	Animal/Veterinary Sciences, Dental Health/Services, Health and Medical Sciences, Osteopathy; Residence: Arkansas.
DeVry Dean's Scholarships	860	$13,500	$ 1500	varies	Must be in high school.
Department of Education Scholarship for Programs in China	227	$12,000	$ 2000	8–15	Education; Talent/Interest Area: foreign language.
Humane Studies Fellowships	179	$12,000	$ 2000	120	Communications, Economics, History, Humanities, Law/Legal Services, Literature/English/Writing, Political Science, Social Sciences.
Massachusetts AFL-CIO Scholarship	775	$12,000	$ 250	100–150	Residence: Massachusetts; Studying in Massachusetts.
Scholarship For Service (SFS) Program	868	$12,000	$ 8000	1	
Law Enforcement Personnel Dependents Scholarship	591	$11,259	$ 100	varies	Employment/Volunteer Experience: police/firefighting; Residence: California; Studying in California.
Seneca Nation Higher Education Program	700	$11,000	$ 6000	varies	Limited to American Indian/Alaska Native students.
SPIE Educational Scholarships in Optical Science and Engineering	87	$11,000	$ 1000	150	Applied Sciences, Chemical Engineering, Electrical Engineering/Electronics, Engineering-Related Technologies, Engineering/Technology, Materials Science, Engineering, and Metallurgy, Sports-Related/ Exercise Science.
Frank O'Bannon Grant Program	810	$10,992	$ 200	48,408–70,239	Residence: Indiana; Studying in Indiana.
Vermont Incentive Grants	816	$10,600	$ 500	varies	Residence: Vermont.
Tupperware U.S. Inc. Scholarship	576	$10,500	$ 1000	varies	Corporate Affiliation.
A Legacy of Hope Scholarships for Survivors of Childhood Cancer	628	$10,000	$ 1000	1–6	Disability: physically disabled; Residence: Arizona, California, Colorado, Montana.
AG Bell College Scholarship Program	614	$10,000	$ 1000	5–20	Disability: hearing impaired.
Alton and Dorothy Higgins, MD Scholarship	343	$10,000	$ 5000	varies	Health and Medical Sciences. Limited to Black (non-Hispanic) students.
American Legion National Headquarters Eagle Scout of the Year	522	$10,000	$ 2500	4	Civic Affiliation: American Legion or Auxiliary, Boy Scouts; Employment/Volunteer Experience: community service.
Annual Essay Contest on Ayn Rand's "Atlas Shrugged"	829	$10,000	$ 50	49	Talent/Interest Area: writing.
Annual Essay Contest on Ayn Rand's Novel, "The Fountainhead"	829	$10,000	$ 50	235	Talent/Interest Area: writing.
Blogging Scholarship	833	$10,000	$ 1000	3	Talent/Interest Area: writing.
California Junior Miss Scholarship Program	737	$10,000	$ 500	25	Residence: California; Talent/Interest Area: beauty pageant, leadership, public speaking.
California Masonic Foundation Scholarship Awards	737	$10,000	$ 1000	57	Residence: California.

Award Name	Page Number	Highest Dollar Amount	Lowest Dollar Amount	Number of Awards	Academic/Career Areas and Eligibility Requirements
Christianson Grant	864	$10,000	$2500	8	
Cystic Fibrosis Scholarship	618	$10,000	$1000	40–50	Disability: physically disabled.
DC Tuition Assistance Grant Program	750	$10,000	$2500	7000	Residence: District of Columbia.
Department of Human Resources Federal Stafford Loan with the Service Cancelable Loan Option	451	$10,000	$4000	1	Nursing; Residence: Georgia; Studying in Georgia.
Director's Scholarship Award	276	$10,000	$1000	1–5	Engineering/Technology; Talent/Interest Area: leadership.
Doc Hurley Scholarship	751	$10,000	$2000	varies	Residence: Connecticut.
E. Wayne Kay Community College Scholarship Award	276	$10,000	$1000	1–20	Engineering/Technology, Trade/Technical Specialties.
Eagle Scout of the Year Scholarship	520	$10,000	$1000	1	Civic Affiliation: Boy Scouts; Residence: Nebraska.
Executive Women International Scholarship Program	862	$10,000	$1000	75–100	Must be in high school.
ExploraVision Science Competition	848	$10,000	$5000	varies	Talent/Interest Area: science.
Federation of American Consumers and Travelers Graduating High School Senior Scholarship	532	$10,000	$2500	varies	Civic Affiliation: Federation of American Consumers and Travelers.
Federation of American Consumers and Travelers In-School Scholarship	578	$10,000	$2500	varies	Corporate Affiliation.
Federation of American Consumers and Travelers Second Chance Scholarship	578	$10,000	$2500	varies	Corporate Affiliation.
Film and Fiction Scholarship	102	$10,000	$3000	2–6	Arts, Filmmaking/Video, Literature/English/Writing.
First Command Educational Foundation Scholarship	597	$10,000	$5000	varies	Employment/Volunteer Experience: community service.
Fisher Broadcasting Inc. Scholarship for Minorities	140	$10,000	$1000	5	Business/Consumer Services, Journalism, TV/Radio Broadcasting. Limited to ethnic minority students.
Girls Going Places Entrepreneurship Award Program	598	$10,000	$1000	15	Employment/Volunteer Experience: community service; Talent/Interest Area: entrepreneurship.
Governor's Scholars-Arkansas	733	$10,000	$4000	375	Residence: Arkansas; Studying in Arkansas.
Hellenic Times Scholarship Fund	683	$10,000	$ 500	30–40	Nationality: Greek.
Holocaust Remembrance Project Essay Contest	837	$10,000	$ 300	30	Talent/Interest Area: writing.
James R. Hoffa Memorial Scholarship Fund	536	$10,000	$1000	1–100	Civic Affiliation: International Brotherhood of Teamsters.
Janet L. Hoffmann Loan Assistance Repayment Program	234	$10,000	$1500	700	Education, Law/Legal Services, Nursing, Social Services, Therapy/Rehabilitation; Residence: Maryland; Studying in Maryland.
John Lennon Scholarship Program	411	$10,000	$5000	3	Music; Talent/Interest Area: music.
Junior Girls Scholarship Program	540	$10,000	$5000	2	Civic Affiliation: Veterans of Foreign Wars or Auxiliary; Talent/Interest Area: leadership.
Kappa Alpha Theta Foundation Merit Based Scholarship Program	539	$10,000	$1000	150–175	Civic Affiliation: Greek Organization.
Lee-Jackson Educational Foundation Scholarship Competition	769	$10,000	$1000	27	Residence: Virginia; Talent/Interest Area: writing.
Legislative Essay Scholarship	749	$10,000	$1000	62	Residence: Delaware.
Les Dames d'Escoffier Scholarship	205	$10,000	$2500	3	Culinary Arts, Food Science/Nutrition, Food Service/Hospitality.
Marine Corps Scholarship Foundation	663	$10,000	$1000	1000	Military Service: Marine Corps.
Medicus Student Exchange	701	$10,000	$2000	1–10	Nationality: Swiss; Talent/Interest Area: foreign language.
Miller Electric International World Skills Competition Scholarship	289	$10,000	$1000	1	Engineering-Related Technologies, Engineering/Technology, Materials Science, Engineering, and Metallurgy, Trade/Technical Specialties.
NAAS Awards	542	$10,000	$ 200	10–14	Civic Affiliation: National Academy of American Scholars.

Award Name	Page Number	Highest Dollar Amount	Lowest Dollar Amount	Number of Awards	Academic/Career Areas and Eligibility Requirements
National Aviation Explorer Scholarships	115	$10,000	$3000	5	Aviation/Aerospace; Talent/Interest Area: aviation, leadership.
National Honor Society Scholarships	544	$10,000	$1000	200	Civic Affiliation: National Honor Society.
National Italian American Foundation Category I Scholarship	693	$10,000	$2500	varies	Nationality: Italian.
National Italian American Foundation Category II Scholarship	97	$10,000	$2500	varies	Area/Ethnic Studies; Talent/Interest Area: Italian language.
National Peace Essay Contest	459	$10,000	$1000	50–53	Peace and Conflict Studies; Talent/Interest Area: writing.
National Society of Women Engineers Scholarships	196	$10,000	$1000	varies	Computer Science/Data Processing, Engineering/Technology.
NBFAA Youth Scholarship Program	604	$10,000	$ 500	varies	Employment/Volunteer Experience: police/firefighting; Residence: California, Connecticut, Georgia, Indiana, Kentucky, Louisiana, Maryland, Minnesota, New Jersey, New York, North Carolina, Pennsylvania, Tennessee, Virginia, Washington.
Needham and Company September 11th Scholarship Fund	867	$10,000	$7000	8–15	
Nightingale Awards of Pennsylvania Nursing Scholarship	448	$10,000	$6000	6	Nursing; Studying in Pennsylvania.
NRA Youth Educational Summit (YES) Scholarships	867	$10,000	$1000	1–6	Must be in high school.
Patriot's Pen	850	$10,000	$1000	44	Talent/Interest Area: writing.
Phelan Art Award in Filmmaking	308	$10,000	$5000	3	Filmmaking/Video.
Phelan Art Award in Video	308	$10,000	$5000	3	Filmmaking/Video.
Pride Foundation/Greater Seattle Business Association Scholarships	803	$10,000	$ 500	90–100	Residence: Alaska, Idaho, Montana, Oregon, Washington; Talent/Interest Area: LGBT issues.
R.O.S.E. Fund Scholarship Program	805	$10,000	$ 500	10	Studying in Connecticut, Maine, Massachusetts, New Hampshire, New Jersey, New York, Pennsylvania, Rhode Island, Vermont.
Ronald Reagan College Leaders Scholarship Program	844	$10,000	$1000	100	Talent/Interest Area: leadership.
San Diego Pathways to College Scholarship	611	$10,000	$1000	25	Employment/Volunteer Experience: community service; Residence: California; Studying in California.
Sir John M. Templeton Fellowships Essay Contest	864	$10,000	$1000	6	
Spencer Scholarship	365	$10,000	$5000	10–20	Insurance and Actuarial Science.
St. Anthony's Medical Center Norbert Siegfried Health Professions Scholarship	579	$10,000	$2000	varies	Corporate Affiliation; Studying in Illinois, Missouri.
Stephen Phillips Memorial Scholarship Fund	872	$10,000	$3000	150–200	
Tailhook Educational Foundation Scholarship	642	$10,000	$2000	50	Military Service: Coast Guard, Marine Corps, Navy.
Talbots Women's Scholarship Fund	873	$10,000	$1000	5–50	
Technical Minority Scholarship	165	$10,000	$1000	122	Chemical Engineering, Computer Science/Data Processing, Electrical Engineering/Electronics, Engineering-Related Technologies, Engineering/Technology, Materials Science, Engineering, and Metallurgy, Mechanical Engineering, Physical Sciences and Math. Limited to ethnic minority students.
Teletoon Animation Scholarship	106	$10,000	$5000	9	Arts, Filmmaking/Video; Residence: Alberta, British Columbia, Manitoba, New Brunswick, Newfoundland, North West Territories, Nova Scotia, Ontario, Prince Edward Island, Quebec, Saskatchewan.
Theodore R. and Vivian M. Johnson Scholarship Program for Children of UPS Employees or UPS Retirees	585	$10,000	$1000	1–50	Corporate Affiliation; Residence: Florida; Studying in Florida.
Toshiba/NSTA ExploraVision Awards Program	193	$10,000	$5000	16–32	Computer Science/Data Processing, Engineering/Technology, Nuclear Science, Physical Sciences and Math.

SCHOLARSHIPS, GRANTS & PRIZES AT-A-GLANCE

Award Name	Page Number	Highest Dollar Amount	Lowest Dollar Amount	Number of Awards	Academic/Career Areas and Eligibility Requirements
Tucson Osteopathic Medical Foundation Scholarship/Loan Program	343	$10,000	$6000	6–10	Health and Medical Sciences, Osteopathy; Residence: Arizona.
Washington State Achievers Program Scholarship	744	$10,000	$5000	600	Residence: Washington; Studying in Washington.
Worldfest Student Film Award	309	$10,000	$1000	10	Filmmaking/Video.
WRI College Scholarship Program	174	$10,000	$2500	varies	Civil Engineering.
Young American Creative Patriotic Art Awards Program	839	$10,000	$1500	4	Talent/Interest Area: art.
youngARTS	842	$10,000	$ 100	15	Talent/Interest Area: art, music/singing, photography/photogrammetry/filmmaking.
Belcourt Brosseau Metis Awards	681	$ 9000	$2000	140	Residence: Alberta; Studying in Alberta.
DeVry High School Community Scholars Award	750	$ 9000	$2000	varies	Studying in Ohio, Pennsylvania, Texas, Virginia, Washington.
DeVry University First Scholar Award	833	$ 9000	$2000	1	Talent/Interest Area: science.
Edward T. Conroy Memorial Scholarship Program	602	$ 9000	$7200	70	Employment/Volunteer Experience: police/firefighting; Military Service: General; Residence: Maryland; Studying in Maryland.
Delegate Scholarship Program-Maryland	774	$ 8650	$ 200	3500	Residence: Maryland; Studying in Maryland.
New Jersey Society of Certified Public Accountants High School Scholarship Program	60	$ 8500	$6500	15–20	Accounting; Residence: New Jersey.
North Carolina Student Loan Program for Health, Science, and Mathematics	213	$ 8500	$3000	1	Dental Health/Services, Health Administration, Health and Medical Sciences, Nursing, Physical Sciences and Math, Therapy/Rehabilitation; Residence: North Carolina.
Minnesota State Grant Program	780	$ 8372	$ 100	71,000–81,000	Residence: Minnesota; Studying in Minnesota.
AACE International Competitive Scholarship	89	$ 8000	$1000	15–25	Architecture, Aviation/Aerospace, Chemical Engineering, Civil Engineering, Construction Engineering/Management, Electrical Engineering/ Electronics, Engineering-Related Technologies, Engineering/Technology, Mechanical Engineering.
AIFS Diversity Scholarships	672	$ 8000	$2000	4	Talent/Interest Area: international exchange, leadership. Limited to ethnic minority students.
AIFS-HACU Scholarships	672	$ 8000	$6000	varies	Talent/Interest Area: international exchange. Limited to Hispanic students.
Kapadia Scholarships	283	$ 8000	$1500	varies	Engineering/Technology.
Liederkranz Foundation Scholarship Award for Voice	840	$ 8000	$1000	14–18	Talent/Interest Area: music/singing.
Nursing Education Loan/Scholarship-BSN	444	$ 8000	$4000	varies	Nursing; Residence: Mississippi; Studying in Mississippi.
Pat and Jim Host Scholarship	358	$ 8000	$2000	1	Hospitality Management, Travel/Tourism.
Vocational Nurse Scholarship Program	440	$ 8000	$4000	varies	Nursing; Residence: California.
YouthForce 2020 Scholarship Program	93	$ 8000	$2000	5	Architecture, Civil Engineering, Electrical Engineering/ Electronics, Mechanical Engineering; Residence: New York.
Vermont Part-time Student Grants	817	$ 7950	$ 250	varies	Residence: Vermont.
AGC Education and Research Foundation Undergraduate Scholarships	169	$ 7500	$2500	100	Civil Engineering, Construction Engineering/ Management, Engineering/Technology.
American Legion Department of Pennsylvania High School Oratorical Contest	729	$ 7500	$4000	3	Residence: Pennsylvania; Talent/Interest Area: public speaking.
Civil Air Patrol Academic Scholarships	528	$ 7500	$1000	40	Civic Affiliation: Civil Air Patrol.
E. Wayne Kay Scholarship	277	$ 7500	$2500	10–30	Engineering/Technology, Trade/Technical Specialties.
International Violoncello Competition	850	$ 7500	$2500	3	Talent/Interest Area: music.
Leveraged Incentive Grant Program	787	$ 7500	$ 250	varies	Residence: New Hampshire; Studying in New Hampshire.

Award Name	Page Number	Highest Dollar Amount	Lowest Dollar Amount	Number of Awards	Academic/Career Areas and Eligibility Requirements
National Association of Food Equipment Dealers Inc. Scholarship	527	$7500	$2500	2	Civic Affiliation: National Association of Food Equipment Dealers.
NJ Student Tuition Assistance Reward Scholarship	788	$7500	$2500	varies	Residence: New Jersey; Studying in New Jersey.
Outstanding Scholar Recruitment Program	789	$7500	$2500	varies	Residence: New Jersey; Studying in New Jersey.
Palmetto Fellows Scholarship Program	807	$7500	$6700	4846	Residence: South Carolina; Studying in South Carolina.
Paraprofessional Teacher Preparation Grant	234	$7500	$ 250	varies	Education; Residence: Massachusetts.
Society of Plastics Engineers Scholarship Program	163	$7500	$1000	25–30	Chemical Engineering, Electrical Engineering/Electronics, Industrial Design, Materials Science, Engineering, and Metallurgy, Trade/Technical Specialties.
Soozie Courter "Sharing a Brighter Tomorrow" Hemophilia Scholarship Program	629	$7500	$2500	20	Disability: physically disabled.
William Faulkner-William Wisdom Creative Writing Competition	844	$7500	$ 250	7	Talent/Interest Area: English language, writing.
Tuition Aid Grant	789	$7272	$ 868	varies	Residence: New Jersey; Studying in New Jersey.
Indiana National Guard Supplemental Grant	636	$7110	$ 20	503–925	Military Service: Air Force National Guard, Army National Guard; Residence: Indiana; Studying in Indiana.
Diversity Scholarships	673	$7000	$5000	2	Talent/Interest Area: leadership. Limited to ethnic minority students.
Freeman Awards for Study in Asia	862	$7000	$3000	varies	
GEAR UP Alaska Scholarship	718	$7000	$3500	varies	Residence: Alaska.
J. Wood Platt Caddie Scholarship Trust	601	$7000	$ 400	250–300	Employment/Volunteer Experience: private club/caddying.
Myrtle and Earl Walker Scholarship Fund	277	$7000	$1000	1–25	Engineering/Technology, Trade/Technical Specialties.
National Federation of the Blind Scholarships	605	$7000	$3000	17	Employment/Volunteer Experience: community service; Disability: visually impaired.
Senatorial Scholarships-Maryland	775	$7000	$ 400	7000	Residence: Maryland; Studying in Maryland.
Society of Hispanic Professional Engineers Foundation	162	$7000	$ 500	varies	Chemical Engineering, Civil Engineering, Electrical Engineering/Electronics, Engineering-Related Technologies, Engineering/Technology, Materials Science, Engineering, and Metallurgy, Mechanical Engineering, Natural Sciences, Physical Sciences and Math, Science, Technology, and Society. Limited to Hispanic students.
Twin Towers Orphan Fund	874	$7000	$5000	varies	
Passport to College Promise Scholarship	818	$6900	$ 1	1–150	Residence: Washington.
Competitive Cal Grant A	737	$6636	$2772	22,500	Residence: California; Studying in California.
Liquitex Excellence in Art Purchase Award Program	103	$6500	$5000	5	Arts.
Pennsylvania Burglar and Fire Alarm Association Youth Scholarship Program	608	$6500	$ 500	6–8	Employment/Volunteer Experience: police/firefighting; Residence: Pennsylvania.
Iowa National Guard Education Assistance Program	635	$6420	$1200	varies	Military Service: Air Force National Guard, Army National Guard; Residence: Iowa; Studying in Iowa.
Washington Scholars Program	819	$6290	$2676	147	Residence: Washington; Studying in Washington.
Adeline Rosenberg Memorial Prize	835	$6000	$4000	2	Talent/Interest Area: music.
Adult Vocational Training Competitive Scholarship	679	$6000	$3000	5	Limited to American Indian/Alaska Native students.
American Legion Department of New York High School Oratorical Contest	728	$6000	$2000	varies	Residence: New York; Talent/Interest Area: public speaking.
Archbold Scholarship Program	338	$6000	$ 600	50	Health and Medical Sciences, Nursing; Residence: Florida, Georgia.

SCHOLARSHIPS, GRANTS & PRIZES AT-A-GLANCE

Award Name	Page Number	Highest Dollar Amount	Lowest Dollar Amount	Number of Awards	Academic/Career Areas and Eligibility Requirements
Contemporary Record Society National Competition for Performing Artists	832	$6000	$2000	1	Talent/Interest Area: music/singing.
GCSAA Scholars Competition	353	$6000	$ 500	varies	Horticulture/Floriculture; Civic Affiliation: Golf Course Superintendents Association of America.
Georgia PROMISE Teacher Scholarship Program	229	$6000	$3000	700–1500	Education; Residence: Georgia; Studying in Georgia.
Golden Gate Restaurant Association Scholarship Foundation	315	$6000	$1000	9–15	Food Service/Hospitality, Hospitality Management; Residence: California.
Gulf Coast Hurricane Scholarship	163	$6000	$2000	1–3	Chemical Engineering, Engineering/Technology; Residence: Alabama, Florida, Louisiana, Mississippi, Texas.
Higher Education Scholarship Program	695	$6000	$ 50	72	Limited to American Indian/Alaska Native students.
Illinois Department of Public Health Center for Rural Health Nursing Education Scholarship Program	338	$6000	$1500	varies	Health and Medical Sciences, Nursing; Residence: Illinois; Studying in Illinois.
Marion Huber Learning Through Listening Awards	554	$6000	$2000	6	Civic Affiliation: Recording for the Blind and Dyslexic; Employment/Volunteer Experience: community service; Disability: learning disabled; Talent/Interest Area: leadership.
Mary P. Oenslager Scholastic Achievement Awards	554	$6000	$1000	9	Civic Affiliation: Recording for the Blind and Dyslexic; Employment/Volunteer Experience: community service; Disability: visually impaired; Talent/Interest Area: leadership.
Minnesota Indian Scholarship Program	692	$6000	$4000	6–700	Residence: Minnesota; Studying in Minnesota. Limited to American Indian/Alaska Native students.
Minority Scholarship Award for Academic Excellence in Physical Therapy	331	$6000	$5000	8–10	Health and Medical Sciences. Limited to ethnic minority students.
Mississippi Health Care Professions Loan/Scholarship Program	339	$6000	$1500	varies	Health and Medical Sciences, Psychology, Therapy/Rehabilitation; Residence: Mississippi; Studying in Mississippi.
National Competition for Composers' Recordings	832	$6000	$2000	1	Talent/Interest Area: music/singing.
Office and Professional Employees International Union Howard Coughlin memorial scholarship fund	549	$6000	$2400	18	Civic Affiliation: Office and Professional Employees International Union.
Optimist International Essay Contest	843	$6000	$ 650	50–56	Talent/Interest Area: writing.
Robert C. Byrd Honors Scholarship-Washington	818	$6000	$1500	varies	Residence: Washington.
TMS J. Keith Brimacombe Presidential Scholarship	294	$6000	$5000	1	Engineering-Related Technologies, Engineering/Technology, Materials Science, Engineering, and Metallurgy.
Undergraduate Competetive Scholarship	679	$6000	$3000	17	Limited to American Indian/Alaska Native students.
Future Teachers Conditional Scholarship and Loan Repayment Program	245	$5800	$2600	50	Education; Residence: Washington; Studying in Washington.
Academic Scholars Program	795	$5500	$1800	varies	Studying in Oklahoma.
Heartland Scholarship Fund	796	$5500	$3500	varies	Residence: Oklahoma.
Ohio Instructional Grant	795	$5466	$ 78	varies	Residence: Ohio; Studying in Ohio, Pennsylvania.
ASSE-United Parcel Service Scholarship	455	$5300	$4000	varies	Occupational Safety and Health; Civic Affiliation: American Society of Safety Engineers.
United Parcel Service Diversity Scholarship Program	456	$5250	$4000	varies	Occupational Safety and Health; Civic Affiliation: American Society of Safety Engineers. Limited to ethnic minority students.
BP/IET Faraday Lecture Scholarship	249	$5240	$3495	1	Electrical Engineering/Electronics, Engineering-Related Technologies.
"My Turn" Essay Competition	390	$5000	$1000	10	Literature/English/Writing; Talent/Interest Area: writing.

Award Name	Page Number	Highest Dollar Amount	Lowest Dollar Amount	Number of Awards	Academic/Career Areas and Eligibility Requirements
Academy of Motion Picture Arts and Sciences Student Academy Awards	306	$5000	$2000	3–12	Filmmaking/Video.
ACES/PRIMO Program	340	$5000	$3000	100	Health and Medical Sciences.
AHETEMS Scholarships	273	$5000	$1000	100	Engineering/Technology, Mathematics, Science, Technology, and Society.
Albert E. Wischmeyer Memorial Scholarship Award	273	$5000	$1000	1–10	Engineering/Technology; Residence: New York; Studying in New York.
All-Ink.com College Scholarship Program	853	$5000	$1000	5–10	
American Academy of Chefs Chair's Scholarship	202	$5000	$1000	5	Culinary Arts, Food Service/Hospitality.
American Chemical Society Scholars Program	153	$5000	$1000	100–200	Chemical Engineering, Materials Science, Engineering, and Metallurgy, Natural Sciences. Limited to American Indian/Alaska Native, Black (non-Hispanic), Hispanic students.
American Dental Hygienists' Association Institute Research Grant	208	$5000	$1000	1	Dental Health/Services; Civic Affiliation: American Dental Hygienist's Association.
American Occupational Therapy Foundation State Association Scholarships	330	$5000	$ 150	varies	Health and Medical Sciences, Therapy/Rehabilitation; Civic Affiliation: American Occupational Therapy Association.
Angus Foundation Scholarships	545	$5000	$1000	20	Civic Affiliation: American Angus Association.
Arthur and Gladys Cervenka Scholarship Award	273	$5000	$1000	1–10	Engineering/Technology.
Arthur J. Packard Memorial Scholarship	355	$5000	$2000	3	Hospitality Management.
Ashby B. Carter Memorial Scholarship Fund Founders Award	542	$5000	$2000	3	Civic Affiliation: National Alliance of Postal and Federal Employees.
Association of Peri-Operative Registered Nurses	433	$5000	$ 500	90–150	Nursing; Civic Affiliation: Association of Operating Room Nurses.
AXA Foundation Fund Achievement Scholarship	149	$5000	$2000	varies	Business/Consumer Services; Residence: New York; Talent/Interest Area: leadership. Limited to Black (non-Hispanic) students.
Battle of the Fans Prize	854	$5000	$ 100	2–54	
Best Buy Enterprise Employee Scholarship	64	$5000	$2500	2	Accounting, Business/Consumer Services, Communications, Journalism. Limited to Black (non-Hispanic) students.
BMI Student Composer Awards	100	$5000	$ 500	10	Arts, Music; Talent/Interest Area: music/singing.
Boys and Girls Clubs of Chicago Scholarships	525	$5000	$3000	varies	Civic Affiliation: Boys or Girls Club; Residence: Illinois.
Carpe Diem Foundation of Illinois Scholarship Competition	855	$5000	$2500	10–15	
Caterpillar Scholars Award Fund	273	$5000	$1000	1–15	Engineering/Technology.
Chapter 198-Downriver Detroit Scholarship	274	$5000	$1000	1–5	Engineering/Technology, Industrial Design, Mechanical Engineering, Trade/Technical Specialties; Studying in Michigan.
Chapter 23-Quad Cities Iowa/Illinois Scholarship	275	$5000	$1000	5	Engineering/Technology; Studying in Illinois, Iowa.
Chapter 31-Tri City Scholarship	275	$5000	$1000	5	Engineering/Technology; Studying in Michigan.
Chapter 3-Peoria Endowed Scholarship	275	$5000	$1000	5	Engineering/Technology; Residence: Illinois; Studying in Illinois.
Chapter 4-Lawrence A. Wacker Memorial Scholarship	273	$5000	$1000	1–10	Engineering/Technology, Mechanical Engineering; Studying in Wisconsin.
Chapter 63-Portland James E. Morrow Scholarship	274	$5000	$1000	5	Engineering/Technology; Residence: Oregon, Washington; Studying in Oregon, Washington.
Chapter 63-Portland Uncle Bud Smith Scholarship	275	$5000	$1000	5	Engineering/Technology; Residence: Oregon, Washington; Studying in Oregon, Washington.
Chapter 67-Phoenix Scholarship	274	$5000	$1000	1–5	Engineering/Technology, Industrial Design, Mechanical Engineering, Trade/Technical Specialties; Studying in Arizona.

Award Name	Page Number	Highest Dollar Amount	Lowest Dollar Amount	Number of Awards	Academic/Career Areas and Eligibility Requirements
Chapter 6-Fairfield County Scholarship	274	$5000	$1000	4	Engineering/Technology.
Chapter 93-Albuquerque Scholarship	274	$5000	$1000	1–5	Engineering/Technology; Studying in New Mexico.
Christa McAuliffe Teacher Scholarship Loan-Delaware	228	$5000	$1000	1–60	Education; Residence: Delaware; Studying in Delaware.
Clara Abbott Scholarship Program	577	$5000	$ 500	4000	Corporate Affiliation.
Clarence and Josephine Myers Scholarship	275	$5000	$1000	5	Engineering/Technology; Studying in Indiana.
Clinton J. Helton Manufacturing Scholarship Award Fund	275	$5000	$1000	1–5	Engineering/Technology, Trade/Technical Specialties; Studying in Colorado.
CMP Group Scholarship Fund	580	$5000	$1000	3	Corporate Affiliation; Residence: Maine.
College Scholarship Assistance Program	809	$5000	$ 400	varies	Residence: Virginia; Studying in Virginia.
College Scholarship Program	685	$5000	$2500	2900–3500	Nationality: Hispanic, Latin American/Caribbean, Mexican, Nicaraguan, Spanish. Limited to Hispanic students.
Colorado Student Grant	744	$5000	$1500	varies	Residence: Colorado; Studying in Colorado.
Congressional Hispanic Caucus Institute Scholarship Awards	595	$5000	$1000	111	Employment/Volunteer Experience: community service. Limited to Hispanic students.
Connie and Robert T. Gunter Scholarship	276	$5000	$1000	1–5	Engineering/Technology; Studying in Georgia.
Constant Memorial Scholarship for Aquidneck Island Residents	106	$5000	$2000	1–2	Arts, Music; Residence: Rhode Island; Talent/Interest Area: art, music.
Continental Society, Daughters of Indian Wars Scholarship	227	$5000	$2500	2	Education, Social Services. Limited to American Indian/Alaska Native students.
Culinary Trust Scholarship Program for Culinary Study and Research	203	$5000	$1000	21	Culinary Arts, Food Science/Nutrition, Food Service/Hospitality; Employment/Volunteer Experience: food service.
Daly Scholarship at Central Scholarship Bureau	592	$5000	$2500	2	Employment/Volunteer Experience: teaching; Residence: Maryland.
Delaware Nursing Incentive Scholarship Loan	435	$5000	$1000	1–40	Nursing; Residence: Delaware.
Delta Sigma Pi Undergraduate Scholarship	530	$5000	$ 500	15	Civic Affiliation: Greek Organization.
Denny's/Hispanic College Fund Scholarship	54	$5000	$ 500	80–100	Accounting, Architecture, Business/Consumer Services, Chemical Engineering, Communications, Computer Science/Data Processing, Electrical Engineering/Electronics, Engineering-Related Technologies. Limited to Hispanic students.
Department of Energy Scholarship Program	142	$5000	$ 500	15	Business/Consumer Services, Chemical Engineering, Electrical Engineering/Electronics, Energy and Power Engineering, Engineering-Related Technologies, Engineering/Technology, Environmental Science, Materials Science, Engineering, and Metallurgy, Mechanical Engineering, Natural Resources, Natural Sciences, Nuclear Science. Limited to Hispanic students.
Duke Energy Scholars Program	578	$5000	$1000	15	Corporate Affiliation.
E. Wayne Kay Co-op Scholarship	276	$5000	$1000	1–10	Engineering/Technology.
Education Exchange College Grant Program	835	$5000	$1000	34	Talent/Interest Area: leadership.
Edward M. Nagel Foundation Scholarship	65	$5000	$2000	varies	Accounting, Business/Consumer Services, Economics; Residence: California. Limited to Black (non-Hispanic) students.
Edward S. Roth Manufacturing Engineering Scholarship	276	$5000	$1000	1–10	Engineering/Technology; Studying in California, Florida, Illinois, Massachusetts, Minnesota, Ohio, Texas, Utah.
El Nuevo Constructor Scholarship Program	91	$5000	$ 500	varies	Architecture, Construction Engineering/Management. Limited to Hispanic students.
Electronic Document Systems Foundation Scholarship Awards	178	$5000	$ 250	40	Communications, Computer Science/Data Processing, Engineering/Technology, Graphics/Graphic Arts/Printing.

Award Name	Page Number	Highest Dollar Amount	Lowest Dollar Amount	Number of Awards	Academic/Career Areas and Eligibility Requirements
Elie Wiesel Prize in Ethics Essay Contest	834	$5000	$ 500	5	Talent/Interest Area: writing.
Elwood Grimes Literary Scholarship	830	$5000	$1000	3	Talent/Interest Area: writing.
Emerging Texas Artist Scholarship	107	$5000	$ 500	8–12	Arts; Studying in Texas; Talent/Interest Area: art.
Engineering Scholarship	154	$5000	$2500	1–5	Chemical Engineering, Civil Engineering, Electrical Engineering/Electronics, Engineering-Related Technologies, Engineering/Technology, Materials Science, Engineering, and Metallurgy, Mechanical Engineering; Residence: Pennsylvania.
Ernst and Young Scholarship Program	55	$5000	$ 500	varies	Accounting, Business/Consumer Services. Limited to Hispanic students.
Federated Garden Clubs of Connecticut Inc. Scholarships	131	$5000	$1000	2–5	Biology, Horticulture/Floriculture, Landscape Architecture; Residence: Connecticut; Studying in Connecticut.
Federation of American Consumers and Travelers Trade/Technical School Scholarship	532	$5000	$1000	varies	Civic Affiliation: Federation of American Consumers and Travelers.
First in My Family Scholarship Program	684	$5000	$ 500	100–200	Limited to Hispanic students.
Florida Association of Post-secondary Schools and Colleges Scholarship Program	753	$5000	$1000	225–600	Residence: Florida; Studying in Florida.
Florida Bankers Educational Foundation Scholarship/Loan	141	$5000	$ 750	10–15	Business/Consumer Services; Employment/Volunteer Experience: banking; Residence: Florida; Studying in Florida.
FORE Undergraduate Merit Scholarships	344	$5000	$1000	1	Health Information Management/Technology; Civic Affiliation: American Health Information Management Association.
Fort Wayne Chapter 56 Scholarship	277	$5000	$1000	1–10	Engineering/Technology, Industrial Design, Mechanical Engineering, Trade/Technical Specialties; Studying in Indiana.
Gene and John Athletic Scholarship	847	$5000	$2500	1–3	Talent/Interest Area: LGBT issues, athletics/sports.
George A. Nielsen Public Investor Scholarship	141	$5000	$2500	1–2	Business/Consumer Services, Public Policy and Administration.
Georgia Engineering Foundation Scholarship Program	264	$5000	$1000	45	Engineering/Technology; Employment/Volunteer Experience: community service; Residence: Georgia.
Geraldo Rivera Scholarship	374	$5000	$1000	varies	Journalism, TV/Radio Broadcasting.
Governors Scholarship Program	744	$5000	$1000	30	Residence: Washington; Studying in Washington.
Graco Inc. Scholarship Program	579	$5000	$3500	varies	Corporate Affiliation.
Graduate and Professional Scholarship Program-Maryland	212	$5000	$1000	40–200	Dental Health/Services, Health and Medical Sciences, Law/Legal Services, Nursing, Social Services; Residence: Maryland; Studying in Maryland.
Great Falls Broadcasters Association Scholarship	505	$5000	$2000	1	TV/Radio Broadcasting; Residence: Montana; Studying in Montana.
Greenhouse Scholars	759	$5000	$1000	30–50	Residence: Colorado; Talent/Interest Area: leadership.
Guiliano Mazzetti Scholarship Award	277	$5000	$1000	1–10	Engineering/Technology.
HANA Scholarship	682	$5000	$3000	varies	Religion: Methodist; Talent/Interest Area: leadership. Limited to American Indian/Alaska Native, Asian/Pacific Islander, Hispanic students.
Harry C. Jaecker Scholarship	343	$5000	$2000	varies	Health and Medical Sciences. Limited to Black (non-Hispanic) students.
HENAAC Scholars Program	194	$5000	$ 500	87	Computer Science/Data Processing, Engineering-Related Technologies, Materials Science, Engineering, and Metallurgy, Mathematics; Talent/Interest Area: leadership. Limited to Hispanic students.
Herbert Hoover Uncommon Student Award	760	$5000	$1000	15	Residence: Iowa.
Herschel C. Price Educational Foundation Scholarships	760	$5000	$ 500	200–300	Residence: West Virginia.
High School Journalism Workshops	370	$5000	$2500	27	Journalism.

Award Name	Page Number	Highest Dollar Amount	Lowest Dollar Amount	Number of Awards	Academic/Career Areas and Eligibility Requirements
Hispanic College Fund Scholarship Program	685	$5000	$ 500	600–750	Limited to Hispanic students.
Hispanic Engineer National Achievement Awards Corporation Scholarship Program	116	$5000	$ 500	12–20	Aviation/Aerospace, Biology, Chemical Engineering, Civil Engineering, Computer Science/Data Processing, Electrical Engineering/Electronics, Engineering/ Technology, Materials Science, Engineering, and Metallurgy, Mechanical Engineering, Nuclear Science. Limited to Hispanic students.
Hispanic Metropolitan Chamber Scholarships	685	$5000	$1000	55	Residence: Oregon, Washington. Limited to Hispanic students.
HOPE—Helping Outstanding Pupils Educationally	757	$5000	$ 300	200,000–210,000	Residence: Georgia; Studying in Georgia.
Houston Symphony Ima Hogg Young Artist Competition	413	$5000	$ 500	4	Music; Talent/Interest Area: music.
Howard Rock Foundation Scholarship Program	678	$5000	$2500	3	Limited to American Indian/Alaska Native students.
ICI Educational Foundation Scholarship Program	142	$5000	$ 500	varies	Business/Consumer Services, Computer Science/Data Processing, Engineering-Related Technologies, Engineering/Technology. Limited to Hispanic students.
IFMA Foundation Scholarships	292	$5000	$1500	20–25	Engineering-Related Technologies.
Indian American Scholarship Fund	687	$5000	$ 500	3	Nationality: Indian; Residence: Georgia. Limited to Asian/Pacific Islander students.
Indiana Nursing Scholarship Fund	452	$5000	$ 200	490–690	Nursing; Residence: Indiana; Studying in Indiana.
Instrumentation, Systems, and Automation Society (ISA) Scholarship Program	158	$5000	$ 500	5–15	Chemical Engineering, Electrical Engineering/ Electronics, Engineering-Related Technologies, Engineering/Technology, Heating, Air-Conditioning, and Refrigeration Mechanics, Mechanical Engineering.
Island Institute Scholarship Fund	772	$5000	$2500	2–30	Residence: Maine.
James L. and Genevieve H. Goodwin Memorial Scholarship	419	$5000	$1000	10	Natural Resources; Residence: Connecticut.
Jane M. Klausman Women in Business Scholarships	153	$5000	$4000	5	Business/Consumer Services.
Jerry McDowell Fund	293	$5000	$1000	1–3	Engineering-Related Technologies, Engineering/Technology.
Jesse Jones Jr. Scholarship	150	$5000	$2000	4	Business/Consumer Services. Limited to Black (non-Hispanic) students.
Jewish Vocational Service Scholarship Fund	715	$5000	$ 500	1	Residence: California; Religion: Jewish.
Jimi Hendrix Endowment Fund Scholarship	418	$5000	$2000	varies	Music. Limited to Black (non-Hispanic) students.
John Kimball, Jr. Memorial Trust Scholarship Program for the Study of History	348	$5000	$ 300	3–10	History; Residence: Massachusetts.
Joseph Shinoda Memorial Scholarship	353	$5000	$1000	10–20	Horticulture/Floriculture.
Judith McManus Price Scholarship	507	$5000	$2000	varies	Urban and Regional Planning. Limited to American Indian/Alaska Native, Black (non-Hispanic), Hispanic students.
Kansas City Initiative Scholarship	706	$5000	$2500	varies	Residence: Kansas, Missouri. Limited to Black (non-Hispanic) students.
Kappa Alpha Theta Foundation Named Endowment Grant Program	539	$5000	$ 100	50	Civic Affiliation: Greek Organization.
Keck Foundation Scholarship	875	$5000	$2000	varies	
Kentucky Minority Educator Recruitment and Retention (KMERR) Scholarship	232	$5000	$2500	400	Education; Residence: Kentucky; Studying in Kentucky. Limited to ethnic minority students.
Kentucky Teacher Scholarship Program	233	$5000	$ 325	600–700	Education; Residence: Kentucky; Studying in Kentucky.
Kosciuszko Foundation Chopin Piano Competition	413	$5000	$1500	3	Music, Performing Arts; Talent/Interest Area: music/singing.

Award Name	Page Number	Highest Dollar Amount	Lowest Dollar Amount	Number of Awards	Academic/Career Areas and Eligibility Requirements
L. Ron Hubbard's Illustrators of the Future Contest	829	$5000	$ 500	12	Talent/Interest Area: art.
L. Ron Hubbard's Writers of the Future Contest	829	$5000	$ 500	12	Talent/Interest Area: writing.
Leveraging Educational Assistance State Partnership Program (LEAP)	762	$5000	$ 400	varies	Residence: Idaho; Studying in Idaho.
Lilly Reintegration Scholarship	622	$5000	$2500	70–100	Disability: physically disabled.
LINC TELACU Scholarship Program	596	$5000	$ 500	600	Employment/Volunteer Experience: community service; Residence: California.
Lockheed Martin Scholarship Program	143	$5000	$ 500	varies	Business/Consumer Services, Chemical Engineering, Computer Science/Data Processing, Electrical Engineering/Electronics, Energy and Power Engineering, Engineering-Related Technologies, Engineering/Technology, Materials Science, Engineering, and Metallurgy, Physical Sciences and Math. Limited to Hispanic students.
Lucile B. Kaufman Women's Scholarship	277	$5000	$1000	1–5	Engineering/Technology.
M & T Bank/Hispanic College Fund Scholarship Program	55	$5000	$2500	5–10	Accounting, Business/Consumer Services, Economics; Residence: Maryland, New York, Pennsylvania, Virginia. Limited to Hispanic students.
Mae Maxey Memorial Scholarship	107	$5000	$1000	varies	Arts, Literature/English/Writing. Limited to Black (non-Hispanic) students.
Maine Community Foundation Scholarship Programs	773	$5000	$ 500	150–700	Residence: Maine.
Math, Engineering, Science, Business, Education, Computers Scholarships	139	$5000	$ 500	180	Business/Consumer Services, Computer Science/Data Processing, Education, Engineering/Technology, Humanities, Physical Sciences and Math, Science, Technology, and Society, Social Sciences. Limited to American Indian/Alaska Native students.
Minnesota Gay/Lesbian/Bisexual/Transgender Scholarship Fund	780	$5000	$1500	20–30	Residence: Minnesota; Studying in Minnesota; Talent/Interest Area: LGBT issues.
MOAA American Patriot Scholarship	657	$5000	$2500	60	Military Service: General.
Morris K. Udall Scholars	76	$5000	$ 350	130	Agriculture, Biology, Earth Science, Environmental Science, Geography, Natural Resources.
Morris K. Udall Scholars-Native American and Alaska Native	340	$5000	$ 350	130	Health Information Management/Technology, Health and Medical Sciences, Social Sciences, Social Services. Limited to American Indian/Alaska Native students.
National Asian-American Journalists Association Newhouse Scholarship	368	$5000	$1000	5	Journalism.
National High School Journalist of the Year/Sister Rita Jeanne Scholarships	180	$5000	$2000	1–6	Communications, Journalism.
Native American Journalists Association Scholarships	375	$5000	$ 500	10	Journalism; Civic Affiliation: Native American Journalists Association; Talent/Interest Area: writing. Limited to American Indian/Alaska Native students.
Native American Leadership in Education (NALE)	139	$5000	$ 500	30	Business/Consumer Services, Education, Humanities, Physical Sciences and Math, Science, Technology, and Society. Limited to American Indian/Alaska Native students.
Naval Reserve Association Scholarship Program	666	$5000	$1000	varies	Military Service: Navy.
New York State Tuition Assistance Program	791	$5000	$ 500	350,000–360,000	Residence: New York; Studying in New York.
North Central Region 9 Scholarship	278	$5000	$1000	1–10	Engineering/Technology, Industrial Design, Mechanical Engineering, Trade/Technical Specialties; Studying in Iowa, Michigan, Minnesota, Nebraska, North Dakota, South Dakota, Wisconsin.
NSCS Scholar Abroad Scholarship	546	$5000	$2500	2	Civic Affiliation: National Society of Collegiate Scholars.
Nurse Education Scholarship Loan Program (NESLP)	448	$5000	$ 400	varies	Nursing; Residence: North Carolina; Studying in North Carolina.
Nurse Scholars Program-Undergraduate (North Carolina)	449	$5000	$3000	450	Nursing; Residence: North Carolina; Studying in North Carolina.

SCHOLARSHIPS, GRANTS & PRIZES AT-A-GLANCE

Award Name	Page Number	Highest Dollar Amount	Lowest Dollar Amount	Number of Awards	Academic/Career Areas and Eligibility Requirements
Patrick Kerr Skateboard Scholarship	869	$5000	$1000	4	Must be in high school.
Pellegrini Scholarship Grants	701	$5000	$ 500	50	Nationality: Swiss; Residence: Connecticut, Delaware, New Jersey, New York, Pennsylvania.
Police Officers and Firefighters Survivors Education Assistance Program-Alabama	587	$5000	$2000	15–30	Employment/Volunteer Experience: police/firefighting; Residence: Alabama; Studying in Alabama.
Promise of Nursing Scholarship	438	$5000	$1000	varies	Nursing; Studying in California, Florida, Georgia, Illinois, Massachusetts, Michigan, New Jersey, Tennessee, Texas.
Raise the Nation Child of a Single Parent Scholarship	870	$5000	$ 100	1–50	
Raise the Nation Continuing Education Scholarship	870	$5000	$ 100	1–50	
Raise the Nation Student Loan Grant	610	$5000	$ 100	1–50	Employment/Volunteer Experience: community service.
Raymond W. Cannon Memorial Scholarship Program	386	$5000	$2000	varies	Law/Legal Services, Pharmacy. Limited to Black (non-Hispanic) students.
Regents Professional Opportunity Scholarships	791	$5000	$1000	220	Residence: New York; Studying in New York.
Regional and Restricted Scholarship Award Program	819	$5000	$ 250	200–250	Residence: Connecticut.
Sallie Mae Fund American Dream Scholarship	708	$5000	$ 500	varies	Limited to Black (non-Hispanic) students.
Scholarship for Minority Accounting Students	673	$5000	$1500	varies	Limited to ethnic minority students.
ScholarshipExperts.com Scholarship Program	871	$5000	$1000	21	
Scholarships for Minority Accounting Students	63	$5000	$1500	varies	Accounting; Civic Affiliation: American Institute of Certified Public Accountants. Limited to ethnic minority students.
Screen Actors Guild Foundation/John L. Dales Scholarship (Transitional)	556	$5000	$3000	12	Civic Affiliation: Screen Actors' Guild.
Sergeant Major Douglas R. Drum Memorial Scholarship Fund	650	$5000	$1000	1–24	Military Service: General.
Siemens Awards for Advanced Placement	871	$5000	$2000	102	Must be in high school.
Sigma Xi Grants-In-Aid of Research	78	$5000	$1000	400	Agriculture, Animal/Veterinary Sciences, Biology, Chemical Engineering, Earth Science, Engineering/ Technology, Health and Medical Sciences, Mechanical Engineering, Meteorology/Atmospheric Science, Physical Sciences and Math, Science, Technology, and Society, Social Sciences.
Sinfonia Educational Foundation Scholarship	846	$5000	$2500	2	Talent/Interest Area: music.
Society of Physics Students Scholarships	470	$5000	$2000	17–22	Physical Sciences and Math; Civic Affiliation: Society of Physics Students.
South Carolina Teacher Loan Program	241	$5000	$2500	1121	Education, Special Education; Residence: South Carolina; Studying in South Carolina.
SPENDonLIFE College Scholarship	871	$5000	$ 500	2–10	
Sun Student College Scholarship Program	609	$5000	$2000	1–16	Employment/Volunteer Experience: community service; Residence: Arizona.
Taylor Michaels Scholarship Fund	602	$5000	$1000	varies	Employment/Volunteer Experience: community service. Limited to ethnic minority students.
TCU Texas Youth Entrepreneur of the Year Awards	813	$5000	$1000	6	Residence: Texas; Talent/Interest Area: entrepreneurship.
Theta Delta Chi Educational Foundation Inc. Scholarship	874	$5000	$1000	15	
TMS/LMD Scholarship Program	294	$5000	$4000	2	Engineering-Related Technologies, Engineering/ Technology, Materials Science, Engineering, and Metallurgy.

Award Name	Page Number	Highest Dollar Amount	Lowest Dollar Amount	Number of Awards	Academic/Career Areas and Eligibility Requirements
Tribal Business Management Program (TBM)	49	$5000	$ 500	35	Accounting, Business/Consumer Services, Computer Science/Data Processing, Economics, Electrical Engineering/Electronics, Engineering-Related Technologies. Limited to American Indian/Alaska Native students.
Truckload Carriers Association Scholarship Fund	149	$5000	$1500	18	Business/Consumer Services, Transportation.
Undergraduate Research Program	120	$5000	$ 500	10	Aviation/Aerospace; Studying in South Carolina.
Underwood-Smith Teacher Scholarship Program	245	$5000	$1620	53	Education; Residence: West Virginia; Studying in West Virginia.
United Agribusiness League Scholarship Program	875	$5000	$1000	10–15	
United Agricultural Benefit Trust Scholarship	563	$5000	$1000	7	Civic Affiliation: United Agribusiness League.
Utah Centennial Opportunity Program for Education	816	$5000	$ 300	5183	Residence: Utah; Studying in Utah.
W. Price Jr. Memorial Scholarship	612	$5000	$2000	4	Employment/Volunteer Experience: food service.
Warner Norcross and Judd LLP Scholarship for Minority Students	384	$5000	$1000	3	Law/Legal Services; Residence: Michigan; Studying in Michigan. Limited to ethnic minority students.
Watson-Brown Foundation Scholarship	820	$5000	$3000	260–1000	Residence: Georgia, South Carolina.
William and Lucille Ash Scholarship	806	$5000	$1000	3	Residence: California; Studying in California.
William E. Weisel Scholarship Fund	251	$5000	$1000	1–10	Electrical Engineering/Electronics, Engineering/ Technology, Mechanical Engineering, Trade/Technical Specialties.
Willits Foundation Scholarship Program	587	$5000	$1000	10–15	Corporate Affiliation.
WJA Scholarship Program	108	$5000	$ 500	1	Arts, Trade/Technical Specialties; Talent/Interest Area: art.
Women's Independence Scholarship Program	872	$5000	$ 250	500–600	
Worldstudio AIGA Scholarships	108	$5000	$1000	20–25	Arts. Limited to ethnic minority students.
Worldstudio Foundation Scholarship Program	94	$5000	$1000	30–50	Architecture, Arts, Fashion Design, Filmmaking/Video, Graphics/Graphic Arts/Printing, Industrial Design, Interior Design, Landscape Architecture. Limited to ethnic minority students.
Xernona Clayton Scholarship Fund	177	$5000	$2000	varies	Communications, Journalism; Residence: Georgia; Studying in Georgia. Limited to Black (non-Hispanic) students.
Young Artist Competition	461	$5000	$ 500	8	Performing Arts; Residence: Illinois, Indiana, Iowa, Kansas, Manitoba, Michigan, Minnesota, Missouri, Nebraska, North Dakota, Ontario, South Dakota, Wisconsin; Talent/Interest Area: music.
Zinch.com "Student Government" Scholarship	852	$5000	$1000	1–8	Talent/Interest Area: leadership.
Zinch.com California Scholarship	822	$5000	$1000	1–8	Residence: California.
Zinch.com General Scholarship	877	$5000	$1000	1–8	Must be in high school.
Zinch.com New York Scholarship	822	$5000	$1000	1–8	Residence: New York.
Zinch.com Utah Scholarship	822	$5000	$1000	1–8	Residence: Utah.
Kentucky Transportation Cabinet Civil Engineering Scholarship Program	171	$4800	$4400	10–20	Civil Engineering; Residence: Kentucky; Studying in Kentucky.
Toward Excellence Access and Success (TEXAS Grant)	813	$4750	$1670	varies	Residence: Texas; Studying in Texas.
Hawaii Association of Broadcasters Scholarship	504	$4500	$ 500	20–30	TV/Radio Broadcasting.
North Carolina Veterans Scholarships	652	$4500	$1500	varies	Military Service: General; Residence: North Carolina.
Northeast Georgia Pilot Nurse Service Cancelable Loan	451	$4500	$2500	100	Nursing; Residence: Georgia; Studying in Georgia.
Pennsylvania State Grants	801	$4500	$3500	varies	Residence: Pennsylvania.

SCHOLARSHIPS, GRANTS & PRIZES AT-A-GLANCE

Award Name	Page Number	Highest Dollar Amount	Lowest Dollar Amount	Number of Awards	Academic/Career Areas and Eligibility Requirements
Registered Nurse Service Cancelable Loan Program	451	$4500	$ 100	15	Nursing; Residence: Georgia; Studying in Georgia.
Service-Cancelable Stafford Loan-Georgia	213	$4500	$2000	500–1200	Dental Health/Services, Health and Medical Sciences, Nursing, Therapy/Rehabilitation; Residence: Georgia; Studying in Georgia.
Tuition Opportunity Program for Students	772	$4434	$ 879	varies	Residence: Louisiana; Studying in Louisiana.
Federal Supplemental Educational Opportunity Grant Program	742	$4400	$ 100	varies	Residence: North Carolina.
John Edgar Thomson Foundation Grants	601	$4400	$ 500	144	Employment/Volunteer Experience: railroad industry.
New Jersey Educational Opportunity Fund Grants	214	$4350	$ 200	varies	Dental Health/Services, Health and Medical Sciences; Residence: New Jersey; Studying in New Jersey.
Charley Wootan Grant Program	873	$4245	$1000	varies	
American Legion Department of Indiana High School Oratorical Contest	726	$4200	$ 200	4–8	Residence: Indiana; Talent/Interest Area: public speaking.
Academy of Television Arts and Sciences College Television Awards	99	$4000	$ 500	25	Arts, Communications, Filmmaking/Video, Journalism, Performing Arts, Photojournalism/Photography, TV/Radio Broadcasting.
Alexander and Maude Hadden Scholarship	613	$4000	$2500	varies	Employment/Volunteer Experience: community service.
American Legion Department of New Jersey High School Oratorical Contest	825	$4000	$1000	5	Talent/Interest Area: public speaking.
American Legion Department of Tennessee High School Oratorical Contest	730	$4000	$1000	1–3	Residence: Tennessee; Talent/Interest Area: public speaking.
American Society for Enology and Viticulture Scholarships	72	$4000	$ 500	30	Agriculture, Chemical Engineering, Food Science/Nutrition, Horticulture/Floriculture.
Bridging Scholarship for Study Abroad in Japan	94	$4000	$2500	40–80	Area/Ethnic Studies, Asian Studies, Foreign Language.
C.A.R. Scholarship Foundation Award	475	$4000	$2000	varies	Real Estate; Residence: California; Studying in California.
California Wine Grape Growers Foundation Scholarship	592	$4000	$1000	1–6	Employment/Volunteer Experience: agriculture; Residence: California; Studying in California.
Canada Millennium Excellence Award Program	675	$4000	$2000	1–2300	
Carmel Music Society Competition	738	$4000	$ 500	3	Residence: California, Oregon, Washington; Talent/Interest Area: music.
Community Banker Association of Illinois Annual Scholarship Program	745	$4000	$1000	13	Residence: Illinois.
Community Banker Association of Illinois Children of Community Banking Scholarship William C. Harris Memorial Scholarship	528	$4000	$1000	1	Civic Affiliation: Community Banker Association of Illinois; Employment/Volunteer Experience: banking; Residence: Illinois.
Congressional Black Caucus Spouses Education Scholarship Fund	859	$4000	$ 500	200	
Congressional Black Caucus Spouses Health Initiatives	326	$4000	$ 500	200	Health Administration, Health Information Management/Technology, Health and Medical Sciences.
Elks Emergency Educational Grants	531	$4000	$1000	varies	Civic Affiliation: Elks Club.
Federal Junior Duck Stamp Conservation and Design Competition	108	$4000	$1000	3	Arts; Talent/Interest Area: art.
Glenn Miller Instrumental Scholarship	836	$4000	$1000	3	Talent/Interest Area: music/singing.
GMP Memorial Scholarship Program	534	$4000	$2000	10	Civic Affiliation: Glass, Molders, Pottery, Plastics and Allied Workers International Union.
International Foodservice Editorial Council Communications Scholarship	180	$4000	$1000	1–6	Communications, Food Science/Nutrition, Food Service/Hospitality, Graphics/Graphic Arts/Printing, Hospitality Management, Journalism, Literature/English/Writing, Photojournalism/Photography; Talent/Interest Area: photography/photogrammetry/filmmaking, writing.

Award Name	Page Number	Highest Dollar Amount	Lowest Dollar Amount	Number of Awards	Academic/Career Areas and Eligibility Requirements
Iowa Tuition Grant Program	765	$4000	$ 100	17,200	Residence: Iowa; Studying in Iowa.
John F. and Anna Lee Stacey Scholarship Fund	102	$4000	$1000	3–5	Arts; Talent/Interest Area: art.
Kaiser Permanente Allied Healthcare Scholarship	337	$4000	$3000	40	Health and Medical Sciences, Social Services, Therapy/ Rehabilitation; Residence: California; Studying in California.
Lieutenant General Clarence R. Huebner Scholarship Program	638	$4000	$1000	3–6	Military Service: Army.
Lois McMillen Memorial Scholarship Fund	108	$4000	$ 500	1	Arts; Residence: Connecticut.
Luterman Scholarship	520	$4000	$1000	7	Civic Affiliation: American Legion or Auxiliary; Military Service: Army.
Malcolm Baldrige Scholarship	152	$4000	$2000	1–2	Business/Consumer Services, International Studies; Residence: Connecticut; Studying in Connecticut.
Michael and Jane Sendzimir Fund Scholarship	418	$4000	$1000	2	Music; Talent/Interest Area: music, music/singing.
Mississippi Press Association Education Foundation Scholarship	373	$4000	$1000	1	Journalism; Residence: Mississippi.
National Leadership Development Grants	682	$4000	$1000	5–10	Religion: Methodist. Limited to ethnic minority students.
Nevada Student Incentive Grant	786	$4000	$ 200	400–800	Residence: Nevada; Studying in Nevada.
New Jersey State Golf Association Caddie Scholarship	606	$4000	$2000	241	Employment/Volunteer Experience: private club/ caddying; Residence: New Jersey.
New Mexico Vietnam Veteran Scholarship	659	$4000	$3500	115	Military Service: General; Residence: New Mexico; Studying in New Mexico.
Part-time Grant Program	811	$4000	$ 20	4680–6700	Residence: Indiana; Studying in Indiana.
Remington Club Scholarship	585	$4000	$1000	varies	Corporate Affiliation; Residence: California.
Samuel Robinson award	480	$4000	$ 250	60	Religion/Theology; Religion: Presbyterian.
Screen Actors Guild Foundation/John L. Dales Scholarship Fund (Standard)	556	$4000	$3000	100	Civic Affiliation: Screen Actors' Guild.
South Florida Fair College Scholarship	809	$4000	$1000	10	Residence: Florida.
Specialty Equipment Market Association Memorial Scholarship Fund	283	$4000	$1000	90	Engineering/Technology, Trade/Technical Specialties; Talent/Interest Area: automotive.
Tennessee Education Lottery Scholarship Program Tennessee HOPE Scholarship	812	$4000	$2000	varies	Residence: Tennessee; Studying in Tennessee.
Union Plus Credit Card Scholarship Program	510	$4000	$ 500	varies	Civic Affiliation: American Federation of State, County, and Municipal Employees.
Union Plus Scholarship Program	563	$4000	$ 500	100–120	Civic Affiliation: AFL-CIO.
Union Plus Scholarship Program	544	$4000	$ 500	3	Civic Affiliation: National Association of Letter Carriers.
University Film and Video Association Carole Fielding Student Grants	309	$4000	$1000	5	Filmmaking/Video.
Verizon Foundation Scholarship	710	$4000	$2000	1	Residence: Connecticut, Delaware, Maine, Maryland, Massachusetts, New Hampshire, New Jersey, New York, Pennsylvania, Rhode Island, Vermont. Limited to Black (non-Hispanic) students.
Vertical Flight Foundation Scholarship	126	$4000	$1000	10–14	Aviation/Aerospace, Electrical Engineering/Electronics, Mechanical Engineering.
Wenderoth Undergraduate Scholarship	552	$4000	$1750	1–4	Civic Affiliation: Phi Sigma Kappa.
Weyerhaeuser Company Foundation Scholarships	586	$4000	$1000	50	Corporate Affiliation.
Working Abroad Grant	864	$4000	$2000	5–8	
Sallie Mae Fund Unmet Need Scholarship Program	871	$3800	$1000	varies	
Kaiser Permanente Forgivable Student Loan Program	443	$3750	$2500	varies	Nursing, Corporate Affiliation; Residence: California; Studying in California.

Award Name	Page Number	Highest Dollar Amount	Lowest Dollar Amount	Number of Awards	Academic/Career Areas and Eligibility Requirements
Early Childhood Educators Scholarship Program	234	$3600	$ 150	varies	Education.
Teacher Assistant Scholarship Fund	237	$3600	$ 600	varies	Education; Employment/Volunteer Experience: teaching; Residence: North Carolina; Studying in North Carolina.
West Virginia Higher Education Grant Program	820	$3542	$ 375	10,755–11,000	Residence: West Virginia; Studying in Pennsylvania, West Virginia.
American Foreign Service Association (AFSA) Financial Aid Award Program	511	$3500	$1000	50–60	Civic Affiliation: American Foreign Service Association; Employment/Volunteer Experience: U.S. Foreign Service.
American Legion Department of Arkansas High School Oratorical Contest	725	$3500	$1250	4	Residence: Arkansas; Talent/Interest Area: public speaking.
American Society of Naval Engineers Scholarship	85	$3500	$2500	8–14	Applied Sciences, Aviation/Aerospace, Civil Engineering, Electrical Engineering/Electronics, Energy and Power Engineering, Engineering/Technology, Marine/Ocean Engineering, Materials Science, Engineering, and Metallurgy, Mechanical Engineering, Physical Sciences and Math.
Arkansas Academic Challenge Scholarship Program	732	$3500	$2500	7000–10,000	Residence: Arkansas; Studying in Arkansas.
Armenian Students Association of America Inc. Scholarships	674	$3500	$1000	30	Nationality: Armenian.
Charles and Lucille King Family Foundation Scholarships	177	$3500	$1250	10–20	Communications, Filmmaking/Video, TV/Radio Broadcasting.
National Federation of Paralegal Associates Inc. Thomson West Scholarship	385	$3500	$1500	2	Law/Legal Services.
Robert Guthrie PKU Scholarship and Awards	625	$3500	$ 500	6–12	Disability: physically disabled.
Virginia Tuition Assistance Grant Program (Private Institutions)	810	$3200	$1900	18,600	Residence: Virginia; Studying in Virginia.
Cal Grant C	737	$3168	$ 576	7761	Residence: California; Studying in California.
South Carolina Tuition Grants Program	808	$3100	$ 100	12,000	Residence: South Carolina; Studying in South Carolina.
Sussman-Miller Educational Assistance Fund	721	$3100	$ 500	29	Residence: New Mexico.
A.T. Cross Scholarship	585	$3000	$1000	varies	Corporate Affiliation; Residence: Rhode Island.
Actuarial Scholarships for Minority Students	364	$3000	$ 500	20–40	Insurance and Actuarial Science, Mathematics. Limited to American Indian/Alaska Native, Black (non-Hispanic), Hispanic students.
Air Force Sergeants Association Scholarship	631	$3000	$ 500	30	Military Service: Air Force, Air Force National Guard.
AKA Educational Advancement Foundation Youth Partners Accessing Capital Scholarship	509	$3000	$1000	varies	Civic Affiliation: Alpha Kappa Alpha.
Albert and Florence Newton Nurse Scholarship Newton Fund	448	$3000	$ 500	20	Nursing; Studying in Rhode Island.
AMBUCS Scholars-Scholarships for Therapists	109	$3000	$ 500	275	Audiology, Therapy/Rehabilitation.
American Dietetic Association Foundation Scholarship Program	311	$3000	$ 500	186	Food Science/Nutrition; Civic Affiliation: American Dietetic Association.
American Geological Institute Minority Scholarship	215	$3000	$ 250	20–30	Earth Science, Hydrology, Meteorology/Atmospheric Science, Oceanography. Limited to ethnic minority students.
American Hotel & Lodging Educational Foundation Pepsi Scholarship	355	$3000	$ 500	varies	Hospitality Management; Studying in District of Columbia.
American Nuclear Society Vogt Radiochemistry Scholarship	254	$3000	$2000	1	Engineering/Technology, Nuclear Science.

Award Name	Page Number	Highest Dollar Amount	Lowest Dollar Amount	Number of Awards	Academic/Career Areas and Eligibility Requirements
American Physical Society Corporate-Sponsored Scholarship for Minority Undergraduate Students Who Major in Physics	468	$3000	$2000	varies	Physical Sciences and Math. Limited to ethnic minority students.
American Physical Society Scholarship for Minority Undergraduate Physics Majors	466	$3000	$2000	20–25	Physical Sciences and Math. Limited to American Indian/Alaska Native, Black (non-Hispanic), Hispanic students.
American Savings Foundation Scholarships	731	$3000	$ 500	varies	Residence: Connecticut.
American Water Ski Educational Foundation Scholarship	524	$3000	$1500	5	Civic Affiliation: USA Water Ski; Talent/Interest Area: leadership.
Anchor Scholarship Foundation Program	665	$3000	$1000	25–40	Military Service: Navy.
Annual Scholarship Grant Program	314	$3000	$ 500	3	Food Service/Hospitality, Hospitality Management.
Appraisal Institute Education Trust Scholarship	475	$3000	$2000	20	Real Estate.
Arizona Nursery Association Foundation Scholarship	351	$3000	$ 500	12–15	Horticulture/Floriculture.
ASCPA University Scholarships	48	$3000	$1000	6	Accounting; Studying in Arizona.
Associated General Contractors of America-New York State Chapter Scholarship Program	169	$3000	$1500	10–15	Civil Engineering, Surveying; Surveying Technology, Cartography, or Geographic Information Science, Transportation; Residence: New York.
Astrid G. Cates and Myrtle Beinhauer Scholarship Funds	558	$3000	$1000	2–6	Civic Affiliation: Mutual Benefit Society; Nationality: Norwegian.
Canada Millennium Bursary	719	$3000	$2250	varies	Residence: Alberta.
Capitol Scholarship Program	747	$3000	$ 500	4500	Residence: Connecticut; Studying in Connecticut, District of Columbia, Maine, Massachusetts, New Hampshire, Pennsylvania, Rhode Island, Vermont.
Central Scholarship Bureau Grants	739	$3000	$1000	20–30	Residence: Maryland.
Chief Master Sergeants of the Air Force Scholarship Program	631	$3000	$ 500	30	Military Service: Air Force, Air Force National Guard.
College Tuition Assistance Program	691	$3000	$2000	25–30	Residence: New Jersey, New York. Limited to Hispanic students.
Daughters of the Cincinnati Scholarship	652	$3000	$1000	10	Military Service: General.
Deerfield Plastics/Barker Family Scholarship	577	$3000	$1500	1	Corporate Affiliation; Residence: Kentucky, Massachusetts.
Donaldson Company Inc. Scholarship Program	578	$3000	$1000	varies	Corporate Affiliation.
Don't Mess With Texas Scholarship Program	751	$3000	$1000	2–3	Residence: Texas; Studying in Texas.
Duck Brand Duct Tape "Stuck at Prom" Scholarship Contest	863	$3000	$1000	3	
DuPont Challenge Science Essay Awards Program	833	$3000	$ 100	100	Talent/Interest Area: writing.
Educators for Maine Forgivable Loan Program	228	$3000	$2000	500	Education; Residence: Maine.
EXceL Awards	764	$3000	$2000	18	Residence: Indiana.
Florida Society of Newspaper Editors Minority Scholarship Program	178	$3000	$1500	1	Communications, Journalism; Studying in Florida. Limited to ethnic minority students.
Florida Society of Newspaper Editors Multimedia Scholarship	178	$3000	$1500	varies	Communications, Journalism; Studying in Florida.
General Motors Foundation Undergraduate Scholarships	251	$3000	$1225	3	Electrical Engineering/Electronics, Engineering-Related Technologies, Engineering/Technology, Mechanical Engineering.
Hispanic Association of Colleges and Universities Scholarship Programs	684	$3000	$ 500	200	Limited to Hispanic students.

Award Name	Page Number	Highest Dollar Amount	Lowest Dollar Amount	Number of Awards	Academic/Career Areas and Eligibility Requirements
Hubertus W.V. Willems Scholarship for Male Students	161	$3000	$2000	1	Chemical Engineering, Engineering-Related Technologies, Engineering/Technology, Physical Sciences and Math; Civic Affiliation: National Association for the Advancement of Colored People. Limited to ethnic minority students.
Humana Foundation Scholarship Program	580	$3000	$1500	75	Corporate Affiliation.
International Airlines Travel Agent Network Foundation Scholarship	357	$3000	$ 500	10–15	Hospitality Management, Travel/Tourism.
James Duval Phelan Literary Award	845	$3000	$2000	3	Talent/Interest Area: writing.
Jo Anne J. Trow Scholarships	853	$3000	$1000	35	
Joseph H. Bearns Prize in Music	832	$3000	$2000	2	Talent/Interest Area: music.
Joseph Henry Jackson Literary Award	807	$3000	$2000	3	Residence: California, Nevada; Talent/Interest Area: writing.
Joseph S. Rumbaugh Historical Oration Contest	842	$3000	$1000	1–3	Talent/Interest Area: public speaking.
Kentucky Tuition Grant (KTG)	769	$3000	$ 200	10,000–12,000	Residence: Kentucky; Studying in Kentucky.
Kildee Scholarships	76	$3000	$2000	3	Agriculture, Animal/Veterinary Sciences.
Landscape Architecture Foundation/ California Landscape Architectural Student Fund Scholarships Program	354	$3000	$1000	15	Horticulture/Floriculture, Landscape Architecture; Studying in California.
Marion A. and Eva S. Peeples Scholarships	234	$3000	$1000	30–35	Education, Engineering/Technology, Food Science/ Nutrition, Nursing, Trade/Technical Specialties; Residence: Indiana; Studying in Indiana.
Maryland Artists Equity Foundation Visual Arts Annual Scholarship Competition	104	$3000	$ 500	25	Arts; Residence: Maryland; Talent/Interest Area: art.
Miss American Coed Pageant	841	$3000	$ 150	52	Talent/Interest Area: beauty pageant.
MRCA Foundation Scholarship Program	171	$3000	$ 500	2–12	Civil Engineering, Construction Engineering/ Management, Trade/Technical Specialties.
NAAS II National Awards	866	$3000	$ 500	1	
NASA Delaware Space Grant Undergraduate Tuition Scholarship	87	$3000	$2000	6–12	Applied Sciences, Aviation/Aerospace, Chemical Engineering, Civil Engineering, Earth Science, Electrical Engineering/Electronics, Engineering-Related Technologies, Engineering/Technology, Meteorology/ Atmospheric Science, Physical Sciences and Math; Studying in Delaware.
National Gay Pilots Association Scholarship	123	$3000	$2000	varies	Aviation/Aerospace, Engineering/Technology; Employment/Volunteer Experience: community service; Talent/Interest Area: LGBT issues, aviation.
National High School Essay Contest	848	$3000	$ 750	3	Talent/Interest Area: writing.
National Multiple Sclerosis Society Mid America Chapter Scholarship	624	$3000	$1000	100	Disability: physically disabled.
Native American Education Grant	698	$3000	$ 200	75	Limited to American Indian/Alaska Native students.
Navy-Marine Corps Relief Society-Surviving Children of Deceased Service Member Scholarship Program	664	$3000	$ 500	1	Military Service: Marine Corps, Navy.
New Jersey Society of Certified Public Accountants College Scholarship Program	60	$3000	$2500	40–50	Accounting; Residence: New Jersey; Studying in New Jersey.
Ohio American Legion Scholarships	520	$3000	$2000	15–18	Civic Affiliation: American Legion or Auxiliary; Military Service: General.
Oregon Collectors Association Bob Hasson Memorial Scholarship	799	$3000	$1500	varies	Residence: Oregon; Studying in Oregon.
Oregon Collectors Association Bob Hasson Memorial Scholarship Fund	796	$3000	$1500	3	Residence: Oregon; Studying in Oregon.
OSCPA Educational Foundation Scholarship Program	61	$3000	$ 500	50–100	Accounting; Residence: Oregon; Studying in Oregon.

Award Name	Page Number	Highest Dollar Amount	Lowest Dollar Amount	Number of Awards	Academic/Career Areas and Eligibility Requirements
Pennsylvania Institute of Certified Public Accountants Sophomore Scholarship	61	$3000	$1500	20	Accounting; Studying in Pennsylvania.
Pennsylvania Masonic Youth Foundation Educational Endowment Fund Scholarships	552	$3000	$1000	varies	Civic Affiliation: Freemasons.
PFLAG Scholarship Awards Program	801	$3000	$ 500	5–10	Residence: Georgia; Studying in Georgia; Talent/Interest Area: LGBT issues.
Plastics Pioneers Scholarships	162	$3000	$1500	30–40	Chemical Engineering, Engineering-Related Technologies, Engineering/Technology, Materials Science, Engineering, and Metallurgy, Trade/Technical Specialties.
Print and Graphics Scholarships	183	$3000	$ 500	200–300	Communications, Graphics/Graphic Arts/Printing.
Profile in Courage Essay Contest	390	$3000	$ 500	7	Literature/English/Writing; Talent/Interest Area: writing.
Rama Scholarship for the American Dream	356	$3000	$1000	1000–3000	Hospitality Management. Limited to ethnic minority students.
Roadway Worker Memorial Scholarship Program	590	$3000	$2000	2–5	Employment/Volunteer Experience: roadway workers.
Roothbert Fund Inc. Scholarship	805	$3000	$2000	20	Studying in Connecticut, Delaware, District of Columbia, Maryland, Massachusetts, New Hampshire, New Jersey, New York, Ohio, Pennsylvania, Rhode Island, Vermont, Virginia, West Virginia.
Scholarships for Education, Business and Religion	142	$3000	$ 500	varies	Business/Consumer Services, Education, Religion/ Theology; Residence: California.
Seaspace Scholarship Program	394	$3000	$ 500	10–15	Marine Biology, Oceanography.
Siemens Competition in Math, Science and Technology	481	$3000	$1000	varies	Science, Technology, and Society.
Society of Louisiana CPAs Scholarships	62	$3000	$ 500	varies	Accounting; Residence: Louisiana; Studying in Louisiana.
Sonne Scholarship	441	$3000	$1000	2–4	Nursing; Residence: Illinois; Studying in Illinois.
Sorantin Young Artist Award	416	$3000	$1000	5–12	Music, Performing Arts; Talent/Interest Area: music.
Student-View Scholarship program	872	$3000	$ 500	1–9	Must be in high school.
Texas History Essay Contest	81	$3000	$1000	3	American Studies, History; Talent/Interest Area: writing.
Two/Ten Footwear Foundation Scholarship	613	$3000	$ 210	200–250	Employment/Volunteer Experience: leather/footwear.
U.S. Marine Corps Historical Center Grants	349	$3000	$ 400	5	History, Military and Defense Studies.
USA Freestyle Martial Arts Scholarship	611	$3000	$1000	2	Employment/Volunteer Experience: community service; Residence: California; Talent/Interest Area: athletics/sports.
Video Contest for College Students	831	$3000	$ 100	8	Talent/Interest Area: art.
Vincent L. Hawkinson Scholarship for Peace and Justice	459	$3000	$1000	1–12	Peace and Conflict Studies; Residence: Iowa, Minnesota, North Dakota, South Dakota, Wisconsin; Studying in Iowa, Minnesota, North Dakota, South Dakota, Wisconsin; Talent/Interest Area: leadership.
William P. Willis Scholarship	796	$3000	$2000	32	Residence: Oklahoma; Studying in Oklahoma.
Wisconsin Higher Education Grants (WHEG)	821	$3000	$ 250	varies	Residence: Wisconsin; Studying in Wisconsin.
Writer's Digest Annual Writing Competition	851	$3000	$ 25	100	Talent/Interest Area: writing.
Writer's Digest Self-Published Book Awards	851	$3000	$1000	10	Talent/Interest Area: writing.
WSCPA Chapter Scholarships	68	$3000	$1000	1–24	Accounting; Studying in Washington.
WSCPA Scholarships for Accounting Majors	68	$3000	$1000	1–10	Accounting; Studying in Washington.
WSTLA American Justice Essay Scholarship Contest	386	$3000	$2000	3	Law/Legal Services; Studying in Washington.

Award Name	Page Number	Highest Dollar Amount	Lowest Dollar Amount	Number of Awards	Academic/Career Areas and Eligibility Requirements
California Farm Bureau Scholarship	68	$2750	$1800	30	Agribusiness, Agriculture; Residence: California; Studying in California.
Howard P. Rawlings Educational Excellence Awards Educational Assistance Grant	443	$2700	$ 400	15,000–30,000	Nursing; Residence: Maryland; Studying in Maryland.
Tennessee Education Lottery Scholarship Program Tennessee HOPE Access Grant	812	$2650	$1700	varies	Residence: Tennessee; Studying in Tennessee.
Postsecondary Child Care Grant Program-Minnesota	781	$2600	$ 100	varies	Residence: Minnesota; Studying in Minnesota.
ACES Copy Editing Scholarship	367	$2500	$1000	varies	Journalism; Talent/Interest Area: writing.
Agnes Jones Jackson Scholarship	542	$2500	$1500	1	Civic Affiliation: National Association for the Advancement of Colored People. Limited to ethnic minority students.
AIAA Undergraduate Scholarship	84	$2500	$2000	30	Applied Sciences, Aviation/Aerospace, Electrical Engineering/Electronics, Engineering/Technology, Materials Science, Engineering, and Metallurgy, Mechanical Engineering, Physical Sciences and Math, Science, Technology, and Society; Civic Affiliation: American Institute of Aeronautics and Astronautics.
Air Traffic Control Association Scholarship	112	$2500	$ 600	7–12	Aviation/Aerospace, Engineering/Technology; Employment/Volunteer Experience: air traffic controller field; Talent/Interest Area: aviation.
Alabama Student Assistance Program	718	$2500	$ 300	varies	Residence: Alabama; Studying in Alabama.
American Board of Funeral Service Education Scholarships	321	$2500	$ 500	50	Funeral Services/Mortuary Science.
American Council of the Blind Scholarships	615	$2500	$1000	16–20	Disability: visually impaired.
American Institute of Architects Minority/Disadvantaged Scholarship	90	$2500	$ 500	20	Architecture. Limited to ethnic minority students.
American Institute of Architects/ American Architectural Foundation Minority/Disadvantaged Scholarships	90	$2500	$ 500	20	Architecture. Limited to ethnic minority students.
American Legion Auxiliary Department of Florida National Presidents' Scholarship	643	$2500	$ 500	3–15	Military Service: General.
American Legion Auxiliary Department of Idaho National President's Scholarship	643	$2500	$2000	15	Military Service: General; Residence: Idaho.
American Legion Auxiliary Department of Maine National President's Scholarship	588	$2500	$1000	3	Employment/Volunteer Experience: community service; Military Service: General; Residence: Maine.
American Legion Auxiliary Department of Michigan National President's Scholarship	645	$2500	$1000	10–15	Military Service: General; Residence: Michigan.
American Legion Auxiliary Department of North Dakota National President's Scholarship	589	$2500	$1000	3	Employment/Volunteer Experience: community service; Military Service: General; Residence: North Dakota; Studying in North Dakota.
American Legion Auxiliary Department of Utah National President's Scholarship	515	$2500	$1000	15	Civic Affiliation: American Legion or Auxiliary; Military Service: General; Residence: Utah.
American Legion Auxiliary National President's Scholarships	648	$2500	$1000	15	Military Service: General.
American Legion Department of Washington Children and Youth Scholarships	521	$2500	$1500	2	Civic Affiliation: American Legion or Auxiliary; Military Service: General; Residence: Washington; Studying in Washington.
BIA Higher Education Grant	686	$2500	$ 50	1–130	Limited to American Indian/Alaska Native students.
Bildner Family Foundation Scholarship	703	$2500	$1000	varies	Residence: New Jersey. Limited to Black (non-Hispanic) students.
Breakthrough to Nursing Scholarships for Racial/Ethnic Minorities	438	$2500	$1000	varies	Nursing. Limited to ethnic minority students.

Award Name	Page Number	Highest Dollar Amount	Lowest Dollar Amount	Number of Awards	Academic/Career Areas and Eligibility Requirements
Bronislaw Kaper Awards for Young Artists	771	$2500	$ 500	4	Residence: California; Talent/Interest Area: music.
Buckingham Memorial Scholarship	587	$2500	$1000	2–4	Employment/Volunteer Experience: air traffic controller field.
California Council of the Blind Scholarships	616	$2500	$ 375	20	Disability: visually impaired; Residence: California; Studying in California.
Career Aid to Technology Students Program	787	$2500	$ 100	varies	Residence: New Hampshire.
Charter Fund Scholarship	802	$2500	$ 500	100	Residence: Colorado.
Clem Judd, Jr. Memorial Scholarship	356	$2500	$1000	2	Hospitality Management; Residence: Hawaii. Limited to Asian/Pacific Islander students.
Community Foundation Scholarship Program	746	$2500	$ 750	50	Residence: Florida.
Connecticut SPJ Bob Eddy Scholarship Program	370	$2500	$ 500	5	Journalism, Photojournalism/Photography; Residence: Connecticut; Studying in Connecticut; Talent/Interest Area: writing.
Deloras Jones RN Nursing as a Second Career Scholarship	442	$2500	$1000	varies	Nursing; Residence: California; Studying in California.
Deloras Jones RN Scholarship Program	442	$2500	$1000	varies	Nursing; Residence: California; Studying in California.
Deloras Jones RN Underrepresented Groups in Nursing Scholarship	442	$2500	$1000	varies	Nursing; Residence: California; Studying in California. Limited to ethnic minority students.
Donna Jamison Lago Memorial Scholarship	694	$2500	$ 500	9	Talent/Interest Area: writing. Limited to Black (non-Hispanic) students.
E. Wayne Kay High School Scholarship	277	$2500	$1000	1–20	Engineering/Technology.
Explosive Ordnance Disposal Memorial Scholarship	596	$2500	$1900	25–75	Employment/Volunteer Experience: explosive ordinance disposal; Military Service: General.
Foundation for Surgical Technology Scholarship Fund	336	$2500	$ 500	5–10	Health and Medical Sciences.
Foundation of the National Student Nurses' Association Career Mobility Scholarship	438	$2500	$1000	varies	Nursing.
Foundation of the National Student Nurses' Association General Scholarships	438	$2500	$1000	varies	Nursing.
Foundation of the National Student Nurses' Association Specialty Scholarship	438	$2500	$1000	varies	Nursing.
Fulfilling Our Dreams Scholarship Fund	699	$2500	$ 500	50–60	Nationality: Hispanic, Latin American/Caribbean; Residence: California; Studying in California. Limited to Hispanic students.
George M. Brooker Collegiate Scholarship for Minorities	476	$2500	$1000	3	Real Estate. Limited to ethnic minority students.
Harry and Rose Howell Scholarship	568	$2500	$2000	3	Civic Affiliation: Naval Sea Cadet Corps.
Hopi Education Award	686	$2500	$ 50	1–400	Limited to American Indian/Alaska Native students.
Institute of Food Technologists Food Engineering Division Junior/Senior Scholarship	312	$2500	$1000	21	Food Science/Nutrition.
Institute of Management Accountants Memorial Education Fund Scholarships	57	$2500	$1000	6–15	Accounting, Business/Consumer Services.
International Order Of The Golden Rule Award of Excellence	321	$2500	$ 500	1–3	Funeral Services/Mortuary Science.
Jennifer Curtis Byler Scholarship for the Study of Public Affairs	182	$2500	$1000	1	Communications, Public Policy and Administration.
Kentucky Society of Certified Public Accountants College Scholarship	57	$2500	$1000	23	Accounting; Residence: Kentucky; Studying in Kentucky.
Koniag Education Foundation Academic/Graduate Scholarship	689	$2500	$ 500	130–170	Limited to American Indian/Alaska Native students.

Award Name	Page Number	Highest Dollar Amount	Lowest Dollar Amount	Number of Awards	Academic/Career Areas and Eligibility Requirements
Korean-American Scholarship Foundation Northeastern Region Scholarships	689	$2500	$1000	60	Nationality: Korean; Studying in Connecticut, Maine, Massachusetts, New Hampshire, New Jersey, New York, Rhode Island, Vermont. Limited to Asian/Pacific Islander students.
Larry Fullerton Photojournalism Scholarship	464	$2500	$ 500	1–2	Photojournalism/Photography; Residence: Ohio; Studying in Ohio; Talent/Interest Area: photography/photogrammetry/filmmaking.
Law Enforcement Officers' Dependents Scholarship-Arkansas	590	$2500	$2000	27–32	Employment/Volunteer Experience: police/firefighting; Residence: Arkansas; Studying in Arkansas.
League Foundation Academic Scholarship	839	$2500	$1500	3–7	Talent/Interest Area: LGBT issues.
Legislative Endowment Scholarships	790	$2500	$1000	varies	Residence: New Mexico; Studying in New Mexico.
Leveraging Educational Assistance Partnership	732	$2500	$ 100	varies	Residence: Arizona; Studying in Arizona.
Library Research Grants	98	$2500	$ 500	varies	Art History, Arts; Studying in California; Talent/Interest Area: art.
Lilly Lorenzen Scholarship	731	$2500	$1500	1	Residence: Minnesota; Studying in Minnesota; Talent/Interest Area: Scandinavian language.
Literacy Initiative Grant Competition	535	$2500	$ 300	varies	Civic Affiliation: Phi Kappa Phi.
Lyndon Baines Johnson Foundation Grants-in-Aid Research	347	$2500	$ 500	10–20	History, Political Science; Studying in Texas.
Maine State Society Foundation Scholarship	774	$2500	$1000	5–10	Residence: Maine; Studying in Maine.
Marshall E. McCullough-National Dairy Shrine Scholarships	76	$2500	$1000	2	Agriculture, Animal/Veterinary Sciences.
Mary Rubin and Benjamin M. Rubin Scholarship Fund	739	$2500	$ 500	20–35	Residence: Maryland.
Massachusetts Gilbert Matching Student Grant Program	777	$2500	$ 200	varies	Residence: Massachusetts; Studying in Massachusetts.
Michelin North America Dependent Scholarship	575	$2500	$1000	15	Corporate Affiliation.
Michelin/TIA Scholarships	527	$2500	$1250	3	Civic Affiliation: Tire Industry Association.
Minority Scholarship Award for Academic Excellence-Physical Therapist Assistant	331	$2500	$2000	1	Health and Medical Sciences, Therapy/Rehabilitation. Limited to ethnic minority students.
Minority Undergraduate Retention Grant-Wisconsin	712	$2500	$ 250	varies	Residence: Wisconsin; Studying in Wisconsin. Limited to ethnic minority students.
Missouri Broadcasters Association Scholarship	505	$2500	$1000	3	TV/Radio Broadcasting; Residence: Missouri; Studying in Missouri.
Missouri Insurance Education Foundation Scholarship	364	$2500	$2000	6	Insurance and Actuarial Science; Residence: Missouri; Studying in Missouri.
National Asphalt Pavement Association Scholarship Program	172	$2500	$ 500	50–150	Civil Engineering, Construction Engineering/Management.
National Beef Ambassador Program	826	$2500	$ 500	1–3	Talent/Interest Area: public speaking.
New Jersey Association of Realtors Educational Foundation Scholarship Program	476	$2500	$1000	20–32	Real Estate; Civic Affiliation: New Jersey Association of Realtors; Residence: New Jersey.
New Mexico Student Incentive Grant	790	$2500	$ 200	varies	Residence: New Mexico; Studying in New Mexico.
North Carolina 4-H Development Fund Scholarships	743	$2500	$ 500	varies	Residence: North Carolina; Studying in North Carolina.
North Carolina Hispanic College Fund Scholarship	679	$2500	$ 500	varies	Residence: North Carolina. Limited to Hispanic students.
Ohio Environmental Science & Engineering Scholarships	305	$2500	$1250	18	Environmental Science; Studying in Ohio.
Parent Relocation Council Scholarship	869	$2500	$ 500	1	Must be in high school.
Prairie Baseball Academy Scholarships	721	$2500	$ 500	20–50	Residence: Alberta; Studying in Alberta; Talent/Interest Area: athletics/sports.
San Diego Fire Victims Scholarship-General Fund	806	$2500	$ 500	5	Residence: California.

Award Name	Page Number	Highest Dollar Amount	Lowest Dollar Amount	Number of Awards	Academic/Career Areas and Eligibility Requirements
San Diego Fire Victims Scholarship-Latino Fund	699	$2500	$ 500	5	Residence: California; Studying in California. Limited to Hispanic students.
Scotts Company Scholars Program	353	$2500	$ 500	7	Horticulture/Floriculture.
Seventeen Magazine Fiction Contest	846	$2500	$ 100	8	Talent/Interest Area: writing.
Sidney B. Meadows Scholarship	355	$2500	$1500	10–15	Horticulture/Floriculture; Residence: Arkansas, Florida, Georgia, Kentucky, Louisiana, Maryland, Mississippi, Missouri, North Carolina, Oklahoma, South Carolina, Tennessee, Texas, Virginia.
Simon Youth Foundation Community Scholarship Program	807	$2500	$1500	100–200	Residence: Arizona, California, Florida, Indiana, Kansas, Louisiana, Missouri, Ohio, Pennsylvania, Texas, Washington.
Simon Youth Foundation Educational Resource Centre Scholarship Program	807	$2500	$1500	varies	Residence: Arizona, California, Florida, Indiana, Kansas, Louisiana, Missouri, Ohio, Pennsylvania, Texas, Washington.
Society of Physics Students Outstanding Student in Research	470	$2500	$ 500	1–2	Physical Sciences and Math; Civic Affiliation: Society of Physics Students.
South Carolina Need-Based Grants Program	808	$2500	$1250	1–26,730	Residence: South Carolina; Studying in South Carolina.
Stockholm Scholarship Program	569	$2500	$2000	1	Civic Affiliation: Naval Sea Cadet Corps.
SuperCollege.com Scholarship	847	$2500	$ 500	1–5	Talent/Interest Area: leadership.
Swiss Benevolent Society of Chicago Scholarships	701	$2500	$ 750	30	Nationality: Swiss; Residence: Illinois, Wisconsin.
Tennessee Society of CPA Scholarship	64	$2500	$ 250	120–130	Accounting; Residence: Tennessee.
Undergraduate Marketing Education Merit Scholarships	138	$2500	$ 500	3	Business/Consumer Services, Music.
Utah Leveraging Educational Assistance Partnership	816	$2500	$ 300	3894	Residence: Utah; Studying in Utah.
WIFLE Scholarship Program	198	$2500	$ 500	varies	Computer Science/Data Processing, Law Enforcement/Police Administration, Physical Sciences and Math, Public Policy and Administration, Social Sciences; Employment/Volunteer Experience: community service.
Writer's Digest Popular Fiction Awards	851	$2500	$ 500	6	Talent/Interest Area: writing.
Y.C. Yang Civil Engineering Scholarship	168	$2500	$2000	2	Civil Engineering.
Datatel Scholars Foundation Scholarship	860	$2400	$1000	270	
Massachusetts Assistance for Student Success Program	776	$2400	$ 300	25,000–30,000	Residence: Massachusetts; Studying in Connecticut, District of Columbia, Maine, Massachusetts, New Hampshire, Pennsylvania, Rhode Island, Vermont.
Student Design Competition	363	$2400	$1200	5	Industrial Design.
Peter and Alice Koomruian Armenian Education Fund	697	$2250	$1000	5–20	Nationality: Armenian.
Student Research Scholarship	344	$2240	$ 640	15	Health and Medical Sciences; Talent/Interest Area: art.
Menominee Indian Tribe Adult Vocational Training Program	691	$2200	$ 100	50–70	Limited to American Indian/Alaska Native students.
Menominee Indian Tribe of Wisconsin Higher Education Grants	691	$2200	$ 100	136	Limited to American Indian/Alaska Native students.
Scholarship Incentive Program-Delaware	749	$2200	$ 700	1000–1300	Residence: Delaware; Studying in Delaware, Pennsylvania.
New Century Scholarship	816	$2166	$ 564	1	Residence: Utah; Studying in Utah.
Tennessee Student Assistance Award Program	812	$2130	$ 100	26,000	Residence: Tennessee; Studying in Tennessee.
Michigan Tuition Grant	778	$2100	$ 100	varies	Residence: Michigan; Studying in Michigan.
Osage Higher Education Scholarship	697	$2100	$1200	1000	Limited to American Indian/Alaska Native students.

Profiles of Scholarships, Grants & Prizes

Academic Fields/Career Goals

ACCOUNTING

ADELANTE! U.S. EDUCATION LEADERSHIP FUND http://www.adelantefund.org

ADELANTE FUND MILLER NATIONAL

Renewable award for college juniors or seniors. Award primarily created to enhance the leadership qualities of the recipients for transition into postgraduate education, business and/or corporate America. Financial need is a factor for this award. Minimum 3.0 GPA required. Awards available for colleges located in the states of California, New Mexico, Arizona, Texas, Florida, Illinois, and New York. Applicants should contact the scholarship aid office of their university.

Academic Fields/Career Goals: Accounting; Business/Consumer Services; Economics.

Award: Scholarship for use in junior or senior years; renewable. *Number:* 20–25. *Amount:* $3000.

Eligibility Requirements: Applicant must be enrolled or expecting to enroll full-time at a four-year institution or university; studying in Arizona, California, Florida, Illinois, New Mexico, New York, or Texas and must have an interest in leadership. Applicant must have 3.0 GPA or higher. Available to U.S. citizens.

Application Requirements: Application, essay, financial need analysis, references, transcript. *Deadline:* May 31.

Contact: Andrea Macias-Castillo, Executive Director
Adelante! U.S. Education Leadership Fund
8415 Datapoint Drive, Suite 400
San Antonio, TX 78229
Phone: 210-692-1971
Fax: 210-692-1951
E-mail: amacias-castillo@adelantefund.org

ALABAMA SOCIETY OF CERTIFIED PUBLIC ACCOUNTANTS http://www.ascpa.org

ASCPA EDUCATIONAL FOUNDATION SCHOLARSHIP

Scholarships available for students with a declared major in accounting. Must have completed intermediate accounting courses with a "B" average in all accounting courses, and a "B" average overall.

Academic Fields/Career Goals: Accounting.

Award: Scholarship for use in senior, graduate, or postgraduate years; not renewable. *Number:* up to 20. *Amount:* up to $1500.

Eligibility Requirements: Applicant must be enrolled or expecting to enroll full-time at a four-year institution or university. Applicant must have 3.0 GPA or higher. Available to U.S. citizens.

Application Requirements: Application, photo, transcript. *Deadline:* March 15.

Contact: Diane Christy, Communications Director
Alabama Society of Certified Public Accountants
1103 South Perry Street
PO Box 5000
Montgomery, AL 36104
Phone: 334-834-7650
Fax: 334-834-7310
E-mail: dchristy@ascpa.org

ALASKA SOCIETY OF CERTIFIED PUBLIC ACCOUNTANTS http://www.akcpa.org

PAUL HAGELBARGER MEMORIAL FUND SCHOLARSHIP

Scholarships open to all junior, senior, and graduate students who are majoring in accounting and attending institutions in Alaska.

Academic Fields/Career Goals: Accounting.

Award: Scholarship for use in junior, senior, or graduate years; not renewable. *Number:* 2–3. *Amount:* $2000.

Eligibility Requirements: Applicant must be enrolled or expecting to enroll full-time at a four-year institution or university and studying in Alaska. Available to U.S. citizens.

Application Requirements: Application, resume, references, transcript. *Deadline:* November 15.

Contact: Linda Plimpton, Executive Director
Alaska Society of Certified Public Accountants
341 West Tudor Road, Suite 105
Anchorage, AK 99503
Phone: 907-562-4334
Fax: 907-562-4025
E-mail: akcpa@ak.net

AMERICAN SOCIETY OF WOMEN ACCOUNTANTS http://www.aswa.org

AMERICAN SOCIETY OF WOMEN ACCOUNTANTS TWO-YEAR COLLEGE SCHOLARSHIP

Scholarship for students pursuing an accounting or finance degree in community, state, or two-year colleges. Must have a minimum cumulative college GPA of 3.0 and be a member of ASWA.

Academic Fields/Career Goals: Accounting.

Award: Scholarship for use in sophomore year; not renewable. *Number:* varies. *Amount:* varies.

Eligibility Requirements: Applicant must be enrolled or expecting to enroll full-time at a two-year institution. Applicant or parent of applicant must be member of American Society of Women Accountants. Applicant must have 3.0 GPA or higher. Available to U.S. citizens.

Application Requirements: Application, essay, financial need analysis, references, transcript. *Deadline:* varies.

Contact: Kristin Edwards, Administrator
American Society of Women Accountants
8405 Greensboro Drive, Suite 800
McLean, VA 22102
Phone: 703-506-3265
Fax: 703-506-3266
E-mail: kedwards@aswa.org

AMERICAN SOCIETY OF WOMEN ACCOUNTANTS UNDERGRADUATE SCHOLARSHIP

Scholarship awards are presented to students who have completed their sophomore year of college and are majoring in accounting or finance. Candidates will be reviewed on leadership, character, communication skills, scholastic average, and financial need.

Academic Fields/Career Goals: Accounting.

Award: Scholarship for use in junior, senior, or graduate years; not renewable. *Number:* varies. *Amount:* varies.

Eligibility Requirements: Applicant must be enrolled or expecting to enroll full- or part-time at a four-year institution or university and must have an interest in leadership. Available to U.S. and non-U.S. citizens.

Application Requirements: Application, essay, financial need analysis, references, transcript. *Deadline:* varies.

Contact: Kristin Edwards, Administrator
American Society of Women Accountants
8405 Greensboro Drive, Suite 800
McLean, VA 22102
Phone: 703-506-3265
Fax: 703-506-3266
E-mail: kedwards@aswa.org

ARIZONA SOCIETY OF CERTIFIED PUBLIC ACCOUNTANTS http://www.ascpa.com

ASCPA HIGH SCHOOL SCHOLARSHIPS

Scholarships awarded to eight high school seniors to study accounting. Applicants must enroll in an Arizona university or community college as a full-time student in the fall semester.

Academic Fields/Career Goals: Accounting.

Award: Scholarship for use in freshman year; not renewable. *Number:* 8. *Amount:* $1000.

Eligibility Requirements: Applicant must be high school student; planning to enroll or expecting to enroll full-time at a four-year or technical institution or university and studying in Arizona. Available to U.S. citizens.

Application Requirements: Application, references, transcript, personal statement of career goals and plans. *Deadline:* January 25.

Contact: Heidi Frei, Scholarship Committee
Arizona Society of Certified Public Accountants
2120 North Central Avenue, Suite 100
Phoenix, AZ 85004

ASCPA UNIVERSITY SCHOLARSHIPS

Scholarships for accounting majors in Arizona institutions who will begin their senior year and have a 3.5 minimum GPA. Application for scholarships is done through the accounting department of each of the universities.

Academic Fields/Career Goals: Accounting.

Award: Scholarship for use in senior year; not renewable. *Number:* 6. *Amount:* $1000–$3000.

Eligibility Requirements: Applicant must be enrolled or expecting to enroll full- or part-time at a four-year institution or university and studying in Arizona. Applicant must have 3.5 GPA or higher. Available to U.S. citizens.

Application Requirements: Application, interview, resume, statement of career goals and plans. *Deadline:* varies.

Contact: Heidi Frei, Director of Marketing and Membership
Arizona Society of Certified Public Accountants
4801 East Washington Street, Suite 225-B
Phoenix, AZ 85034
Phone: 602-252-4144 Ext. 206
Fax: 602-252-1511
E-mail: hfrei@ascpa.com

ASSOCIATION OF CERTIFIED FRAUD EXAMINERS http://www.acfe.com

RITCHIE-JENNINGS MEMORIAL SCHOLARSHIP

Applicant must be an undergraduate or graduate student, currently enrolled full-time (12 semester hours undergraduate; 9 semester hours graduate or equivalent) at an accredited four-year college or university (or equivalent) with a declared major or minor in accounting or criminal justice.

Academic Fields/Career Goals: Accounting; Criminal Justice/Criminology.

Award: Scholarship for use in freshman, sophomore, junior, senior, graduate, or postgraduate years; not renewable. *Number:* up to 30. *Amount:* $1000.

Eligibility Requirements: Applicant must be enrolled or expecting to enroll full-time at a four-year institution or university. Available to U.S. and non-U.S. citizens.

Application Requirements: Application, essay, interview, references, transcript. *Deadline:* April 18.

Contact: Scholarship Coordinator
Association of Certified Fraud Examiners
The Gregor Building, 716 West Avenue
Austin, TX 78701
Phone: 800-245-3321
Fax: 512-478-9297
E-mail: scholarships@acfe.com

ASSOCIATION OF LATINO PROFESSIONALS IN FINANCE AND ACCOUNTING http://www.alpfa.org

HSF-ALPFA SCHOLARSHIPS

One-time award to undergraduate and graduate Hispanic/Latino students pursuing degrees in accounting, finance, and related majors. Awarded based on financial need and academic performance. Must be enrolled full-time at a U.S. college or university. Minimum 3.0 GPA required. Must be U.S. citizens or legal permanent residents.

Academic Fields/Career Goals: Accounting; Business/Consumer Services.

Award: Scholarship for use in freshman, sophomore, junior, senior, or graduate years; not renewable. *Number:* varies. *Amount:* $1250–$1500.

Eligibility Requirements: Applicant must be of Hispanic heritage and enrolled or expecting to enroll full-time at a two-year or four-year institution or university. Applicant must have 3.0 GPA or higher. Available to U.S. citizens.

Application Requirements: Application, essay, financial need analysis, references, transcript. *Deadline:* March 15.

Contact: Geraldine Contreras, Scholarship Coordinator
Association of Latino Professionals in Finance and Accounting
801 South Grand Avenue, Suite 400
Los Angeles, CA 90017
Phone: 213-243-0004
Fax: 213-243-0006
E-mail: geraldine.contreras@national.alpfa.org

CALIFORNIA SOCIETY OF CERTIFIED PUBLIC ACCOUNTANTS http://www.aicpa.org

AICPA/ACCOUNTEMPS STUDENT SCHOLARSHIP

Financial assistance to two AICPA Student affiliate members pursuing studies in accounting, finance or information systems. Two awards, each worth $2500. Current CPAs are not eligible for this scholarship.

Academic Fields/Career Goals: Accounting; Business/Consumer Services.

Award: Scholarship for use in freshman, sophomore, junior, or senior years; not renewable. *Number:* 2–5. *Amount:* $2500.

Eligibility Requirements: Applicant must be enrolled or expecting to enroll full-time at a four-year institution or university. Applicant or parent of applicant must be member of American Institute of Certified Public Accountants. Applicant must have 3.0 GPA or higher. Available to U.S. citizens.

Application Requirements: Application, references, test scores, transcript. *Deadline:* April 1.

Contact: Danielle Grant, Education and Recruitment Coordinator
California Society of Certified Public Accountants
220 Leigh Farm Road
Durham, NC 27707-8110
Phone: 919-402-4014
Fax: 919-419-4705
E-mail: educat@aicpa.org

SCHOLARSHIPS FOR MINORITY ACCOUNTING STUDENTS

Non-renewable one-time award of $5000 to undergraduate students who have completed at least 30 semester hours or equivalent of college work, with at least six hours in accounting. All applicants must have a minimum overall and accounting GPA of 3.0. Must be a member of American Institute of Certified Public Accountants. Must be enrolled as a full-time student.

Academic Fields/Career Goals: Accounting.

Award: Scholarship for use in freshman, sophomore, junior, or senior years; not renewable. *Number:* up to 134. *Amount:* $5000.

Eligibility Requirements: Applicant must be American Indian/Alaska Native, Asian/Pacific Islander, Black (non-Hispanic), or Hispanic and enrolled or expecting to enroll full-time at a four-year institution or university. Applicant or parent of applicant must be member of American Institute of Certified Public Accountants. Applicant must have 3.0 GPA or higher. Available to U.S. citizens.

Application Requirements: Application, references, transcript. *Deadline:* June 1.

Contact: Danielle Grant, Education and Recruitment Coordinator
California Society of Certified Public Accountants
220 Leigh Farm Road
Durham, NC 27707-8110
Phone: 919-402-4014
Fax: 919-419-4705
E-mail: educat@aicpa.org

CATCHING THE DREAM http://www.catchingthedream.org

TRIBAL BUSINESS MANAGEMENT PROGRAM (TBM)

Renewable scholarships available for Native American and Alaska Native students to study business administration, economic development, and related subjects, with the goal to provide experts in business management to Native American tribes in the U.S. Must be at least one-quarter Native American from a federally recognized, state recognized, or terminated tribe. Must demonstrate high academic achievement, depth of character, leadership, seriousness of purpose, and service orientation.

Academic Fields/Career Goals: Accounting; Business/Consumer Services; Computer Science/Data Processing; Economics; Electrical Engineering/Electronics; Engineering-Related Technologies.

Award: Scholarship for use in freshman, sophomore, junior, senior, graduate, or postgraduate years; renewable. *Number:* up to 35. *Amount:* $500–$5000.

Eligibility Requirements: Applicant must be American Indian/Alaska Native and enrolled or expecting to enroll full-time at a four-year institution or university. Applicant must have 3.0 GPA or higher. Available to U.S. citizens.

Application Requirements: Application, essay, financial need analysis, photo, references, test scores, transcript, certificate of Indian blood. *Deadline:* varies.

Contact: Mary Frost, Recruiter
Catching the Dream
8200 Mountain Road, NE, Suite 203
Albuquerque, NM 87110
Phone: 505-262-2351
Fax: 505-262-0534
E-mail: nscholarsh@aol.com

CENTRAL INTELLIGENCE AGENCY http://www.cia.gov

CENTRAL INTELLIGENCE AGENCY UNDERGRADUATE SCHOLARSHIP PROGRAM

Need and merit-based award for students with minimum 3.0 GPA, who are interested in working for the Central Intelligence Agency upon graduation. Renewable for four years of undergraduate study. Must apply in senior year of high school or sophomore year in college. For further information refer to Web site: http://www.cia.gov.

Academic Fields/Career Goals: Accounting; Business/Consumer Services; Computer Science/Data Processing; Economics; Electrical Engineering/Electronics; Foreign Language; Geography; Graphics/Graphic Arts/Printing; International Studies; Political Science; Surveying; Surveying Technology, Cartography, or Geographic Information Science.

Award: Scholarship for use in freshman, sophomore, junior, or senior years; renewable. *Number:* varies. *Amount:* up to $18,000.

Eligibility Requirements: Applicant must be age 18 and over and enrolled or expecting to enroll full-time at a four-year institution or university. Applicant must have 3.0 GPA or higher. Available to U.S. citizens.

Application Requirements: Application, financial need analysis, resume, references, test scores, transcript. *Deadline:* November 1.

Contact: Van Patrick, Chief, College Relations
Central Intelligence Agency
Recruitment Center, L 100 LF7
Washington, DC 20505
Phone: 703-613-8388
Fax: 703-613-7676
E-mail: ivanilp0@ucia.gov

CIRI FOUNDATION (TCF) http://www.thecirifoundation.org

CARL H. MARRS SCHOLARSHIP FUND

Merit-based scholarship for exceptional academic and community service experience. Awards students seeking an undergraduate or graduate degree in business administration, economics, finance, organizational management, accounting, or similar field. Applicant must be Alaska Native original enrollee to CIRI or descendant. Minimum 3.7 cumulative GPA required.

Academic Fields/Career Goals: Accounting; Business/Consumer Services; Economics.

Award: Scholarship for use in freshman, sophomore, junior, senior, or graduate years; not renewable. *Number:* varies. *Amount:* $20,000.

Eligibility Requirements: Applicant must be American Indian/Alaska Native and enrolled or expecting to enroll full-time at a two-year or four-year institution or university. Available to U.S. and non-U.S. citizens.

Application Requirements: Application, essay, references, transcript, proof of eligibility, birth certificate or adoption decree. *Deadline:* June 1.

Contact: Susan Anderson, President and Chief Executive Officer
CIRI Foundation (TCF)
3600 San Jeronimo Drive, Suite 256
Anchorage, AK 99508-2870
Phone: 907-793-3575
Fax: 907-793-3585
E-mail: tcf@thecirifoundation.org

CLEVELAND SCHOLARSHIP PROGRAMS http://www.cspohio.org

CSP MANAGED FUNDS-CLEVELAND BROWNS MARION MOTLEY SCHOLARSHIP

Renewable scholarship of $2500 to students enrolled in a high school located in Northeast Ohio, on track to graduate from high school at the end of the current academic year and planning to enroll in college in the next academic year.

Academic Fields/Career Goals: Accounting; Business/Consumer Services; Engineering/Technology; Journalism; Public Policy and Administration.

Award: Scholarship for use in freshman year; renewable. *Number:* 2. *Amount:* $2500.

Eligibility Requirements: Applicant must be high school student; planning to enroll or expecting to enroll full- or part-time at a four-year institution or university; resident of Ohio and studying in Ohio. Applicant must have 2.5 GPA or higher. Available to U.S. citizens.

Application Requirements: Application, essay, resume, references, test scores, transcript, tax form, FAFSA. *Deadline:* October 26.

Contact: Scholarship Committee
Cleveland Scholarship Programs
200 Public Square, Suite 3820
Cleveland, OH 44114
Phone: 216-241-5587
Fax: 216-241-6184

COHEN & COMPANY CPAS http://www.cohencpa.com

COHEN AND COMPANY CPAS SCHOLARSHIP

Renewable scholarships for outstanding sophomores and juniors enrolled full-time at accredited Ohio colleges or universities. Must be majoring in accounting. Deadline varies.

Academic Fields/Career Goals: Accounting.

Award: Scholarship for use in sophomore or junior years; renewable. *Number:* varies. *Amount:* $500–$1000.

Eligibility Requirements: Applicant must be enrolled or expecting to enroll full-time at a four-year institution or university and studying in Ohio. Available to U.S. citizens.

Application Requirements: Application, essay, references. *Deadline:* varies.

Contact: Angela Ferenchka, Scholarship Coordinator
Cohen & Company CPAs
1350 Euclid Avenue, Suite 800
Cleveland, OH 44115
Phone: 216-579-1040
Fax: 216-579-0111

COLORADO SOCIETY OF CERTIFIED PUBLIC ACCOUNTANTS EDUCATIONAL FOUNDATION http://www.cocpa.org

COLORADO COLLEGE AND UNIVERSITY SCHOLARSHIPS

Award available to declared accounting majors at Colorado colleges and universities with accredited accounting programs. Must have completed at least 8 semester hours of accounting courses. Overall GPA and accounting GPA must be at least 3.0. Must be Colorado resident.

Academic Fields/Career Goals: Accounting.

Award: Scholarship for use in junior, senior, graduate, or postgraduate years; not renewable. *Number:* 15–20. *Amount:* $2500.

Eligibility Requirements: Applicant must be enrolled or expecting to enroll full- or part-time at a four-year institution or university; resident of Colorado and studying in Colorado. Applicant must have 3.0 GPA or higher. Available to U.S. citizens.

Application Requirements: Application, references, transcript. *Deadline:* varies.

Contact: Gena Mantz, Membership Coordinator
Colorado Society of Certified Public Accountants Educational Foundation
7979 East Tufts Avenue, Suite 1000
Denver, CO 80237-2845
Phone: 303-741-8613
Fax: 303-773-6344
E-mail: gmantz@cocpa.org

COLORADO HIGH SCHOOL SCHOLARSHIPS

Scholarships awarded in the spring of each year to outstanding high school seniors who plan to major in accounting.

Academic Fields/Career Goals: Accounting.

Award: Scholarship for use in freshman year; not renewable. *Number:* up to 10. *Amount:* $1000.

Eligibility Requirements: Applicant must be high school student; planning to enroll or expecting to enroll full- or part-time at a four-year institution or university; resident of Colorado and studying in Colorado. Applicant must have 3.0 GPA or higher. Available to U.S. citizens.

Application Requirements: Application, test scores, transcript. *Deadline:* March 1.

Contact: Gena Mantz, Membership Coordinator
Colorado Society of Certified Public Accountants Educational Foundation
7979 East Tufts Avenue, Suite 1000
Denver, CO 80237-2845
Phone: 303-741-8613
Fax: 303-773-6344
E-mail: gmantz@cocpa.org

COMMUNITY FOUNDATION OF WESTERN MASSACHUSETTS http://www.communityfoundation.org

GREATER SPRINGFIELD ACCOUNTANTS SCHOLARSHIP

Provided to undergraduates pursuing accounting or finance who have completed their sophomore year and are residents of Massachusetts or Hartford County, Connecticut.

Academic Fields/Career Goals: Accounting; Business/Consumer Services.

Award: Scholarship for use in junior or senior years; not renewable. *Number:* 1–5. *Amount:* $600.

Eligibility Requirements: Applicant must be enrolled or expecting to enroll full-time at a two-year or four-year institution and resident of Connecticut or Massachusetts. Available to U.S. citizens.

Application Requirements: Application, financial need analysis, transcript, Student Aid Report (SAR). *Deadline:* March 31.

Contact: Dorothy Theriaque, Education Associate
Community Foundation of Western Massachusetts
1500 Main Street, PO Box 15769
Springfield, MA 01115
Phone: 413-732-2858
Fax: 413-733-8565
E-mail: dtheriaque@communityfoundation.org

CONNECTICUT SOCIETY OF CERTIFIED PUBLIC ACCOUNTANTS http://www.cs-cpa.org

CSCPA CANDIDATE'S AWARD

Scholarship of $3000 that assists students in complying with the 150-hour requirement of the Connecticut State Board of Accountancy to sit for the Uniform Certified Public Accountant Examination. An overall GPA of 3.0.

Academic Fields/Career Goals: Accounting.

Award: Scholarship for use in senior or graduate years; not renewable. *Number:* 4. *Amount:* $3000.

Eligibility Requirements: Applicant must be enrolled or expecting to enroll full- or part-time at a four-year institution or university; resident of Connecticut and studying in Connecticut. Applicant must have 3.0 GPA or higher. Available to U.S. citizens.

Application Requirements: Application, essay, transcript. *Deadline:* August 31.

Contact: Ms. Jill A. Wise, Program Coordinator
Connecticut Society of Certified Public Accountants
845 Brook Street, Building Two
Rocky Hill, CT 06067

OUTSTANDING COMMUNITY COLLEGE ACCOUNTING STUDENT AWARD

Scholarship for Connecticut community college accounting students who plan to major in accounting at a four-year Connecticut college or university recognized by the Connecticut State Board of Accountancy. Students are recommended by their accounting department faculty.

Academic Fields/Career Goals: Accounting.

Award: Scholarship for use in freshman or sophomore years; not renewable. *Number:* varies. *Amount:* $500.

Eligibility Requirements: Applicant must be enrolled or expecting to enroll full- or part-time at a four-year institution or university; resident of Connecticut and studying in Connecticut. Available to U.S. citizens.

Application Requirements: Application, references, test scores, transcript. *Deadline:* varies.

Contact: Jill Wise, Academic and Student Relations Associate
Connecticut Society of Certified Public Accountants
845 Brook Street, Building Two
Rocky Hill, CT 06067-3405
Phone: 860-258-4800 Ext. 239
Fax: 860-258-4859
E-mail: jillw@cs-cpa.org

EDUCATIONAL FOUNDATION FOR WOMEN IN ACCOUNTING (EFWA) http://www.efwa.org

MICHELE L. MCDONALD SCHOLARSHIP

Individuals eligible for this award will be women who are returning to college from the workforce or after raising children. Scholarship recipients will be awarded $1000 to begin their studies in pursuit of a college degree in accounting.

Academic Fields/Career Goals: Accounting.

Award: Scholarship for use in freshman, sophomore, junior, or senior years; not renewable. *Number:* varies. *Amount:* $1000.

Eligibility Requirements: Applicant must be enrolled or expecting to enroll full- or part-time at a four-year institution or university and married female. Available to U.S. citizens.

Application Requirements: Application, financial need analysis, transcript. *Deadline:* April 15.

Contact: Cynthia Hires, Foundation Administrator
Educational Foundation for Women in Accounting (EFWA)
PO Box 1925
Southeastern, PA 19399-1925
Phone: 610-407-9229
Fax: 610-644-3713
E-mail: info@efwa.org

ROWLING, DOLD & ASSOCIATES LLP SCHOLARSHIP

One year $1000 scholarship award for minority women enrolled in an accounting program at an accredited college or university. Women returning to school with undergraduate status; incoming, current, or reentry juniors or seniors; or minority women are all eligible.

Academic Fields/Career Goals: Accounting.

Award: Scholarship for use in junior, senior, or graduate years; not renewable. *Number:* varies. *Amount:* $1000.

Eligibility Requirements: Applicant must be American Indian/Alaska Native, Asian/Pacific Islander, Black (non-Hispanic), or Hispanic; enrolled or expecting to enroll full- or part-time at a four-year institution or university and female. Available to U.S. citizens.

Application Requirements: Application, financial need analysis, transcript. *Deadline:* April 15.

Contact: Cynthia Hires, Foundation Administrator
Educational Foundation for Women in Accounting (EFWA)
PO Box 1925
Southeastern, PA 19399-1925
Phone: 610-407-9229
Fax: 610-644-3713
E-mail: info@efwa.org

SEATTLE AMERICAN SOCIETY OF WOMEN ACCOUNTANTS CHAPTER SCHOLARSHIP

Scholarship for an amount up to $2000 to be awarded to a women attending an accredited school within the State of Washington. The scholarship will be renewable for one additional year upon satisfactory completion of course requirements. Must pursue a degree in accounting.

Academic Fields/Career Goals: Accounting.

Award: Scholarship for use in freshman, sophomore, junior, or senior years; renewable. *Number:* varies. *Amount:* up to $2000.

Eligibility Requirements: Applicant must be enrolled or expecting to enroll full- or part-time at a four-year institution or university; female and studying in Washington. Available to U.S. citizens.

Application Requirements: Application, financial need analysis, transcript. *Deadline:* April 15.

Contact: Cynthia Hires, Foundation Administrator
Educational Foundation for Women in Accounting (EFWA)
PO Box 1925
Southeastern, PA 19399-1925
Phone: 610-407-9229
Fax: 610-644-3713
E-mail: info@efwa.org

WOMEN IN NEED SCHOLARSHIP

Scholarship provides financial assistance to female reentry students who wish to pursue a degree in accounting. Scholarship is available to incoming, current, or reentry juniors.

Academic Fields/Career Goals: Accounting.

Award: Scholarship for use in junior year; renewable. *Number:* 1. *Amount:* $2000.

Eligibility Requirements: Applicant must be enrolled or expecting to enroll full- or part-time at a four-year institution or university and female. Available to U.S. citizens.

Application Requirements: Application, financial need analysis, transcript. *Deadline:* April 15.

Contact: Cynthia Hires, Foundation Administrator
Educational Foundation for Women in Accounting (EFWA)
PO Box 1925
Southeastern, PA 19399-1925
Phone: 610-407-9229
Fax: 610-644-3713
E-mail: info@efwa.org

WOMEN IN TRANSITION SCHOLARSHIP

Renewable award available to incoming or current freshmen and women returning to school with a freshman status. Scholarship value may be up to $16,000 over four years.

Academic Fields/Career Goals: Accounting.

Award: Scholarship for use in freshman year; renewable. *Number:* 1. *Amount:* up to $4000.

Eligibility Requirements: Applicant must be enrolled or expecting to enroll full- or part-time at a four-year institution or university and female. Available to U.S. citizens.

Application Requirements: Application, financial need analysis, transcript. *Deadline:* April 15.

Contact: Cynthia Hires, Foundation Administrator
Educational Foundation for Women in Accounting (EFWA)
PO Box 1925
Southeastern, PA 19399-1925
Phone: 610-407-9229
Fax: 610-644-3713
E-mail: info@efwa.org

EDUCATIONAL FOUNDATION OF THE MASSACHUSETTS SOCIETY OF CERTIFIED PUBLIC ACCOUNTANTS http://www.CPATrack.com

F. GRANT WAITE, CPA, MEMORIAL SCHOLARSHIP

Scholarship available to undergraduate accounting major who has completed sophomore year. Must demonstrate financial need and superior academic standing. Preference given to married students with children. Information available on Web site at http://www.cpatrack.com.

Academic Fields/Career Goals: Accounting.

Award: Scholarship for use in junior or senior years; not renewable. *Number:* 1. *Amount:* $1000.

Eligibility Requirements: Applicant must be enrolled or expecting to enroll full-time at a four-year institution or university. Available to U.S. citizens.

Application Requirements: Application, financial need analysis, references, transcript. *Deadline:* March 17.

Contact: Barbara Iannoni, Academic Coordinator
Educational Foundation of the Massachusetts Society of Certified Public Accountants
105 Chauncy Street
Boston, MA 02111
Phone: 617-556-4000
Fax: 617-556-4126
E-mail: biannoni@mscpaonline.org

KATHLEEN M. PEABODY, CPA, MEMORIAL SCHOLARSHIP

Scholarship available for Massachusetts resident who has completed sophomore year. Must be accounting major with plans to seek an accounting career in Massachusetts. Must demonstrate academic excellence and financial need. Information on Web site at http://www.cpatrack.com.

Academic Fields/Career Goals: Accounting.

Award: Scholarship for use in junior or senior years; not renewable. *Number:* 1. *Amount:* $2500.

Eligibility Requirements: Applicant must be enrolled or expecting to enroll full-time at a four-year institution or university and resident of Massachusetts. Available to U.S. citizens.

Application Requirements: Application, financial need analysis, references, transcript. *Deadline:* March 17.

Contact: Barbara Iannoni, Academic Coordinator
Educational Foundation of the Massachusetts Society of Certified Public Accountants
105 Chauncy Street
Boston, MA 02111
Phone: 617-556-4000
Fax: 617-556-4126
E-mail: biannoni@mscpaonline.org

MSCPA FIRM SCHOLARSHIP

Scholarship to encourage individuals who have demonstrated academic excellence and financial need to pursue a career in public accounting in Massachusetts.

Academic Fields/Career Goals: Accounting.

Award: Scholarship for use in junior, senior, graduate, or postgraduate years; not renewable. *Number:* 12–16. *Amount:* $2500.

Eligibility Requirements: Applicant must be enrolled or expecting to enroll full-time at a four-year institution or university and resident of Massachusetts. Available to U.S. citizens.

Educational Foundation of the Massachusetts Society of Certified Public Accountants (continued)

Application Requirements: Application, essay, financial need analysis, references, transcript. *Deadline:* March 17.

Contact: Barbara Iannoni, Academic Coordinator
Educational Foundation of the Massachusetts Society of Certified Public Accountants
105 Chauncy Street
Boston, MA 02111
Phone: 617-556-4000
Fax: 617-556-4126
E-mail: biannoni@mscpaonline.org

PAYCHEX INC. ENTREPRENEUR SCHOLARSHIP

Scholarships available to students who are residents of Massachusetts and attending a Massachusetts college or university. Must be an accounting major entering their junior year, have a minimum 3.0 GPA, and demonstrate financial need. Application and information on Web site at http://www.cpatrack.com.

Academic Fields/Career Goals: Accounting.

Award: Scholarship for use in junior year; not renewable. *Number:* 1. *Amount:* $1000.

Eligibility Requirements: Applicant must be enrolled or expecting to enroll full-time at a four-year institution or university; resident of Massachusetts and studying in Massachusetts. Applicant must have 3.0 GPA or higher. Available to U.S. citizens.

Application Requirements: Application, financial need analysis, transcript. *Deadline:* March 17.

Contact: Barbara Iannoni, Academic Coordinator
Educational Foundation of the Massachusetts Society of Certified Public Accountants
105 Chauncy Street
Boston, MA 02111
Phone: 617-556-4000
Fax: 617-556-4126
E-mail: biannoni@mscpaonline.org

FLORIDA INSTITUTE OF CERTIFIED PUBLIC ACCOUNTANTS http://www.ficpa.org

FICPA EDUCATIONAL FOUNDATION SCHOLARSHIPS

Scholarship for full-time or part-time (minimum of six credit hours), 4th or 5th year accounting major at participating Florida colleges or universities. Must be a Florida resident and plan to practice accounting in Florida. See Web site for list of institutions: http://www1.ficpa.org/ficpa/Visitors/Careers/EdFoundation/Scholarships.

Academic Fields/Career Goals: Accounting.

Award: Scholarship for use in senior or graduate years; not renewable. *Number:* up to 100. *Amount:* $1000–$2000.

Eligibility Requirements: Applicant must be enrolled or expecting to enroll full- or part-time at a four-year institution or university; resident of Florida and studying in Florida. Applicant must have 3.0 GPA or higher. Available to U.S. citizens.

Application Requirements: Application, references, transcript. *Deadline:* March 15.

Contact: Mrs. Betsy Wilson, Educational Foundation Assistant
Florida Institute of Certified Public Accountants
325 West College Avenue
Tallahassee, FL 32301
Phone: 850-224-2727
Fax: 850-222-8190
E-mail: wilsonb@ficpa.org

1040K RACE SCHOLARSHIPS

Scholarship for African American permanent resident of Miami-Dade, Broward, Monroe or Palm Beach Counties. Applicants must be full-time, 4th- or 5th-year accounting majors at one of the following Florida institutions: Barry University, Florida Atlantic University, Florida International University, Florida Memorial College, Nova Southeastern University, St. Thomas University, or University of Miami. See Web site for details: http://www1.ficpa.org/ficpa/Visitors/Careers/EdFoundation/Scholar.ships/Availa.

Academic Fields/Career Goals: Accounting.

Award: Scholarship for use in senior or graduate years; not renewable. *Number:* up to 2. *Amount:* up to $3000.

Eligibility Requirements: Applicant must be Black (non-Hispanic); enrolled or expecting to enroll full-time at an institution or university; resident of Florida and studying in Florida. Applicant must have 3.0 GPA or higher. Available to U.S. citizens.

Application Requirements: Application, references, transcript, must be recommended by accounting faculty committee at college or university attended. *Deadline:* February 15.

Contact: Mrs. Betsy Wilson, Educational Foundation Assistant
Florida Institute of Certified Public Accountants
325 West College Avenue
Tallahassee, FL 32301
Phone: 850-224-2727 Ext. 224
Fax: 850-222-8190
E-mail: wilsonb@ficpa.org

GEORGIA GOVERNMENT FINANCE OFFICERS ASSOCIATION http://www.ggfoa.org

GGFOA SCHOLARSHIP

Scholarship will be awarded to undergraduate or graduate students who meet the eligibility requirements and are preparing for a career in public finance. Must maintain a GPA of 3.0 or higher.

Academic Fields/Career Goals: Accounting; Business/Consumer Services; Public Policy and Administration.

Award: Scholarship for use in freshman, sophomore, junior, senior, or graduate years; not renewable. *Number:* 1–2. *Amount:* $3000.

Eligibility Requirements: Applicant must be enrolled or expecting to enroll full-time at a four-year institution or university and studying in Georgia. Applicant must have 3.0 GPA or higher. Available to U.S. citizens.

Application Requirements: Application, essay, resume, references, test scores, transcript. *Deadline:* August 31.

Contact: Scholarship Selection Committee
Georgia Government Finance Officers Association
PO Box 6473
Athens, GA 30604-6473

GEORGIA SOCIETY OF CERTIFIED PUBLIC ACCOUNTANTS http://www.gscpa.org

BEN W. BRANNON MEMORIAL SCHOLARSHIP FUND

Scholarship for a rising junior or senior undergraduate accounting major or a graduate student enrolled in a master's level accounting or business administration program at a college or university accredited by the Southern Association of Colleges and Schools. Applicant must demonstrate a commitment to pursuing a career in accounting, be a resident of Georgia and maintain an overall GPA of 3.0.

Academic Fields/Career Goals: Accounting; Business/Consumer Services.

Award: Scholarship for use in junior, senior, or graduate years; not renewable. *Number:* 1. *Amount:* varies.

Eligibility Requirements: Applicant must be enrolled or expecting to enroll full- or part-time at a four-year institution or university and resident of Georgia. Applicant must have 3.0 GPA or higher. Available to U.S. citizens.

Application Requirements: Application, driver's license, essay, financial need analysis, resume, transcript, residence proof. *Deadline:* March 15.

Contact: Shelly Grunbaum, Educational Foundation Staff Liaison
Georgia Society of Certified Public Accountants
3353 Peachtree Road, NE, Suite 400
Atlanta, GA 30326-1414
Phone: 404-231-8676 Ext. 2956
E-mail: sgrunbaum@gscpa.org

CHAPTER AWARDED SCHOLARSHIPS

Scholarship for a rising junior or senior undergraduate accounting major or a graduate student enrolled in a master's level accounting or business administration program at a college or university accredited by the Southern Association of Colleges and Schools. Applicant must demonstrate a commitment to pursuing a career in accounting, be a resident of Georgia and maintain an overall GPA of 3.0. Must contact the local GSCPA chapter for more information.

Academic Fields/Career Goals: Accounting; Business/Consumer Services.

Award: Scholarship for use in junior, senior, or graduate years; not renewable. *Number:* 1. *Amount:* varies.

Eligibility Requirements: Applicant must be enrolled or expecting to enroll full- or part-time at a four-year institution or university and resident of Georgia. Applicant must have 3.0 GPA or higher. Available to U.S. citizens.

Application Requirements: Application, driver's license, essay, financial need analysis, resume, test scores, residence proof. *Deadline:* September 1.

Contact: Shelly Grunbaum, Educational Foundation Staff Liaison
Georgia Society of Certified Public Accountants
3353 Peachtree Road, NE, Suite 400
Atlanta, GA 30326-1414
Phone: 404-231-8676 Ext. 2956
Fax: 404-237-1291
E-mail: sgrunbaum@gscpa.org

CHERRY, BEKAERT AND HOLLAND LLP ACCOUNTING SCHOLARSHIP

Scholarship for a rising junior or senior undergraduate accounting major or a graduate student enrolled in a master's level accounting or business administration program at a college or university accredited by the Southern Association of Colleges and Schools. Applicant must demonstrate a commitment to pursuing a career in accounting, be a resident of Georgia and maintain an overall GPA of 3.0. Application URL: http://www.gscpa.org/Content/Files/Shelly/scholarship_application.pdf.

Academic Fields/Career Goals: Accounting; Business/Consumer Services.

Award: Scholarship for use in junior, senior, or graduate years; not renewable. *Number:* 1. *Amount:* varies.

Eligibility Requirements: Applicant must be enrolled or expecting to enroll full- or part-time at a four-year institution or university and resident of Georgia. Applicant must have 3.0 GPA or higher. Available to U.S. citizens.

Application Requirements: Application, driver's license, essay, financial need analysis, resume, transcript, residence proof. *Deadline:* March 15.

Contact: Shelly Grunbaum, Educational Foundation Staff Liaison
Georgia Society of Certified Public Accountants
3353 Peachtree Road, NE, Suite 400
Atlanta, GA 30326-1414
Phone: 404-231-8676 Ext. 2956
E-mail: sgrunbaum@gscpa.org

COLLINS/MOODY-COMPANY SCHOLARSHIP

Scholarship for a rising junior or senior undergraduate accounting major or a graduate student enrolled in a master's level accounting or business administration program at a college or university accredited by the Southern Association of Colleges and Schools. Applicant must demonstrate a commitment to pursuing a career in accounting, be a resident of Georgia and maintain an overall GPA of 3.0. Application URL: http://www.gscpa.org/Content/Files/Shelly/scholarship_application.pdf.

Academic Fields/Career Goals: Accounting; Business/Consumer Services.

Award: Scholarship for use in junior, senior, or graduate years; not renewable. *Number:* 1. *Amount:* varies.

Eligibility Requirements: Applicant must be enrolled or expecting to enroll full- or part-time at a four-year institution or university and resident of Georgia. Applicant must have 3.0 GPA or higher. Available to U.S. citizens.

Application Requirements: Application, driver's license, essay, financial need analysis, resume, transcript, residence proof. *Deadline:* March 15.

Contact: Shelly Grunbaum, Educational Foundation Staff Liaison
Georgia Society of Certified Public Accountants
3353 Peachtree Road, NE, Suite 400
Atlanta, GA 30326-1414
Phone: 404-231-8676 Ext. 2956
E-mail: sgrunbaum@gscpa.org

EDUCATIONAL FOUNDATION DIRECT SCHOLARSHIPS

Scholarship for a rising junior or senior undergraduate accounting major or a graduate student enrolled in a master's level accounting or business administration program at a college or university accredited by the Southern Association of Colleges and Schools. Applicant must demonstrate a commitment to pursuing a career in accounting, be a resident of Georgia and maintain an overall GPA of 3.0. Application URL: http://www.gscpa.org/Content/Files/Shelly/scholarship_application.pdf.

Academic Fields/Career Goals: Accounting; Business/Consumer Services.

Award: Scholarship for use in junior, senior, or graduate years; not renewable. *Number:* 1. *Amount:* varies.

Eligibility Requirements: Applicant must be enrolled or expecting to enroll full- or part-time at a four-year institution or university and resident of Georgia. Applicant must have 3.0 GPA or higher. Available to U.S. citizens.

Application Requirements: Application, driver's license, essay, financial need analysis, resume, transcript, residence proof. *Deadline:* March 15.

Contact: Shelly Grunbaum, Educational Foundation Staff Liaison
Georgia Society of Certified Public Accountants
3353 Peachtree Road, NE, Suite 400
Atlanta, GA 30326-1414
Phone: 404-231-8676 Ext. 2956
E-mail: sgrunbaum@gscpa.org

JULIUS M. JOHNSON MEMORIAL SCHOLARSHIP

Scholarship for a rising junior or senior undergraduate accounting major or a graduate student enrolled in a master's level accounting or business administration program at a college or university accredited by the Southern Association of Colleges and Schools. Applicant must demonstrate a commitment to pursuing a career in accounting, be a resident of Georgia and maintain an overall GPA of 3.0. Application URL: http://www.gscpa.org/Content/Files/Shelly/scholarship_application.pdf.

Academic Fields/Career Goals: Accounting; Business/Consumer Services.

Award: Scholarship for use in junior, senior, or graduate years; not renewable. *Number:* 1. *Amount:* varies.

Eligibility Requirements: Applicant must be enrolled or expecting to enroll full- or part-time at a four-year institution or university and resident of Georgia. Applicant must have 3.0 GPA or higher. Available to U.S. citizens.

Application Requirements: Application, driver's license, essay, financial need analysis, resume, transcript, residence proof. *Deadline:* March 15.

Contact: Shelly Grunbaum, Educational Foundation Staff Liaison
Georgia Society of Certified Public Accountants
3353 Peachtree Road, NE, Suite 400
Atlanta, GA 30326-1414
Phone: 404-231-8676 Ext. 2956
E-mail: sgrunbaum@gscpa.org

PAYCHEX ENTREPRENEUR SCHOLARSHIP

Scholarship for a rising junior or senior undergraduate accounting major or a graduate student enrolled in a master's level accounting or business administration program at a college or university accredited by the Southern Association of Colleges and Schools. Applicant must demonstrate a commitment to pursuing a career in accounting, be a resident of Georgia and maintain an overall GPA of 3.0. Application URL: http://www.gscpa.org/Content/Files/Shelly/scholarship_application.pdf.

Academic Fields/Career Goals: Accounting; Business/Consumer Services.

Award: Scholarship for use in junior, senior, or graduate years; not renewable. *Number:* 1. *Amount:* varies.

Eligibility Requirements: Applicant must be enrolled or expecting to enroll full- or part-time at a four-year institution or university and resident of Georgia. Applicant must have 3.0 GPA or higher. Available to U.S. citizens.

Georgia Society of Certified Public Accountants (continued)

Application Requirements: Application, driver's license, essay, financial need analysis, resume, transcript, residence proof. *Deadline:* March 15.

Contact: Shelly Grunbaum, Educational Foundation Staff Liaison
Georgia Society of Certified Public Accountants
3353 Peachtree Road, NE, Suite 400
Atlanta, GA 30326-1414
Phone: 404-231-8676 Ext. 2956
E-mail: sgrunbaum@gscpa.org

ROBERT H. LANGE MEMORIAL SCHOLARSHIP

Scholarship for a rising junior or senior undergraduate accounting major or a graduate student enrolled in a master's level accounting or business administration program at a college or university accredited by the Southern Association of Colleges and Schools. Applicant must demonstrate a commitment to pursuing a career in accounting, be a resident of Georgia and maintain an overall GPA of 3.0. Application URL: http://www.gscpa.org/Content/Files/scholarship_application.pdf.

Academic Fields/Career Goals: Accounting; Business/Consumer Services.

Award: Scholarship for use in junior, senior, or graduate years; not renewable. *Number:* 1. *Amount:* varies.

Eligibility Requirements: Applicant must be enrolled or expecting to enroll full- or part-time at a four-year institution or university and resident of Georgia. Applicant must have 3.0 GPA or higher. Available to U.S. citizens.

Application Requirements: Application, driver's license, essay, financial need analysis, resume, transcript, residence proof. *Deadline:* March 15.

Contact: Shelly Grunbaum, Educational Foundation Staff Liaison
Georgia Society of Certified Public Accountants
3353 Peachtree Road, NE, Suite 400
Atlanta, GA 30326-1414
Phone: 404-231-8676 Ext. 2956
E-mail: sgrunbaum@gscpa.org

GOVERNMENT FINANCE OFFICERS ASSOCIATION http://www.gfoa.org

MINORITIES IN GOVERNMENT FINANCE SCHOLARSHIP

Awards upper-division undergraduate or graduate students of public administration, governmental accounting, finance, political science, economics, or business administration to recognize outstanding performance by minority students preparing for a career in state and local government finance.

Academic Fields/Career Goals: Accounting; Business/Consumer Services; Economics; Political Science; Public Policy and Administration.

Award: Scholarship for use in freshman, sophomore, junior, senior, or graduate years; not renewable. *Number:* 1. *Amount:* $5000.

Eligibility Requirements: Applicant must be American Indian/Alaska Native, Asian/Pacific Islander, Black (non-Hispanic), or Hispanic and enrolled or expecting to enroll full- or part-time at a two-year or four-year institution or university. Available to U.S. and Canadian citizens.

Application Requirements: Application, essay, resume, references, transcript. *Deadline:* February 29.

Contact: Jake Lorentz, Assistant Director
Government Finance Officers Association
203 North LaSalle Street, Suite 2700
Chicago, IL 60601-1210
Phone: 312-977-9700 Ext. 267
Fax: 312-977-4806
E-mail: jlorentz@gfoa.org

GREATER WASHINGTON SOCIETY OF CERTIFIED PUBLIC ACCOUNTANTS http://www.gwscpa.org

GREATER WASHINGTON SOCIETY OF CPAS SCHOLARSHIP

Scholarship available to accounting students. School must offer an accounting degree that qualifies graduates to sit for the CPA exam (must meet the 150-hour rule). Minimum 3.0 GPA in major courses required.

Academic Fields/Career Goals: Accounting.

Award: Scholarship for use in junior, senior, or graduate years; not renewable. *Number:* up to 2. *Amount:* up to $5000.

Eligibility Requirements: Applicant must be enrolled or expecting to enroll full-time at a four-year institution or university; resident of District of Columbia and studying in District of Columbia. Applicant must have 3.0 GPA or higher. Available to U.S. citizens.

Application Requirements: Application, essay, resume, references, transcript. *Deadline:* varies.

Contact: Wayne Berson, President, Executive Committee
Greater Washington Society of Certified Public Accountants
1828 L Street, NW, Suite 900
Washington, DC 20036
Phone: 202-204-8014
Fax: 202-204-8015
E-mail: info@gwscpa.org

HAWAII SOCIETY OF CERTIFIED PUBLIC ACCOUNTANTS http://www.hscpa.org

HSCPA SCHOLARSHIP PROGRAM FOR ACCOUNTING STUDENTS

Scholarship for Hawaii resident currently attending an accredited Hawaii college or university. Minimum 3.0 GPA required. Must be majoring, or concentrating, in accounting with the intention to sit for the CPA exam, and have completed an intermediate accounting course. Number of awards vary from year to year.

Academic Fields/Career Goals: Accounting.

Award: Scholarship for use in freshman, sophomore, junior, or senior years; not renewable. *Number:* varies. *Amount:* $500–$1500.

Eligibility Requirements: Applicant must be enrolled or expecting to enroll full-time at a four-year institution or university; resident of Hawaii and studying in Hawaii. Applicant must have 3.0 GPA or higher. Available to U.S. citizens.

Application Requirements: Application, references, test scores, transcript. *Deadline:* January 31.

Contact: Kathy Castillo, Executive Director
Hawaii Society of Certified Public Accountants
900 Fort Street Mall, Suite 850
Honolulu, HI 96813
Phone: 808-537-9475
Fax: 808-537-3520
E-mail: info@hscpa.org

HISPANIC COLLEGE FUND INC. http://www.hispanicfund.org

ALPFA SCHOLARSHIP PROGRAM

Scholarships to full-time students pursuing studies in accounting, finance, IT or a related field. Must be U.S. citizen and of Hispanic descent, and maintain a cumulative GPA of at least 3.0.

Academic Fields/Career Goals: Accounting; Computer Science/Data Processing.

Award: Scholarship for use in freshman, sophomore, junior, or senior years; renewable. *Number:* varies. *Amount:* $1250.

Eligibility Requirements: Applicant must be Hispanic and enrolled or expecting to enroll full-time at a two-year or four-year institution or university. Applicant must have 3.0 GPA or higher. Available to U.S. citizens.

Application Requirements: Application, essay, financial need analysis, references, proof of family income, citizenship proof. *Deadline:* April 15.

Contact: Fernando Barrueta, Chief Executive Officer
Hispanic College Fund Inc.
1301 K Street, NW, Suite 450-A West
Washington, DC 20005
Phone: 202-296-5400
Fax: 202-296-3774
E-mail: hcf-info@hispanicfund.org

DENNY'S/HISPANIC COLLEGE FUND SCHOLARSHIP

One-time scholarship award open to full-time undergraduates of Hispanic descent pursuing a degree in business or a business-related major with a GPA of 3.0 or better. Eligible students who have applied to the Hispanic College Fund need not reapply.

Academic Fields/Career Goals: Accounting; Architecture; Business/Consumer Services; Chemical Engineering; Communications; Computer Science/Data Processing; Electrical Engineering/Electronics; Engineering-Related Technologies.

Award: Scholarship for use in freshman, sophomore, junior, or senior years; not renewable. *Number:* 80–100. *Amount:* $500–$5000.

Eligibility Requirements: Applicant must be Hispanic and enrolled or expecting to enroll full-time at a two-year or four-year institution or university. Applicant must have 3.0 GPA or higher. Available to U.S. citizens.

Application Requirements: Application, essay, financial need analysis, resume, references, test scores, transcript, college acceptance letter, copy of tax return, Student Aid Report (SAR). *Deadline:* March 15.

Contact: Fernando Barrueta, Chief Executive Officer
Hispanic College Fund Inc.
1301 K Street, NW, Suite 450-A West
Washington, DC 20005
Phone: 202-296-5400
Fax: 202-296-3774
E-mail: hcf-info@hispanicfund.org

ERNST AND YOUNG SCHOLARSHIP PROGRAM

Program intended for undergraduate student pursuing his or her bachelor's degree in accounting or related field. Applicant must be a U.S. citizen of Hispanic background; may reside in the United States or Puerto Rico. Must attend college or university in United States or Puerto Rico. Online application only: http://www.hispanicfund.org.

Academic Fields/Career Goals: Accounting; Business/Consumer Services.

Award: Scholarship for use in freshman, sophomore, junior, or senior years; not renewable. *Number:* varies. *Amount:* $500–$5000.

Eligibility Requirements: Applicant must be Hispanic and enrolled or expecting to enroll full-time at a two-year or four-year institution or university. Available to U.S. citizens.

Application Requirements: Application. *Deadline:* April 15.

Contact: Fernando Barrueta, Chief Executive Officer
Hispanic College Fund Inc.
1301 K Street, NW, Suite 450-A West
Washington, DC 20005
Phone: 202-296-5400
Fax: 202-296-3774
E-mail: hcf-info@hispanicfund.org

M & T BANK/HISPANIC COLLEGE FUND SCHOLARSHIP PROGRAM

One-time scholarship open to full-time undergraduates of Hispanic descent pursuing a degree in business, accounting, economics, or finance. Must be a U.S. citizen residing in Maryland, Pennsylvania, Virginia, or New York and have a minimum 3.0 GPA. Eligible students who have applied to the Hispanic College Fund need not reapply.

Academic Fields/Career Goals: Accounting; Business/Consumer Services; Economics.

Award: Scholarship for use in freshman, sophomore, junior, or senior years; not renewable. *Number:* 5–10. *Amount:* $2500–$5000.

Eligibility Requirements: Applicant must be Hispanic; enrolled or expecting to enroll full-time at a two-year or four-year institution or university and resident of Maryland, New York, Pennsylvania, or Virginia. Applicant must have 3.0 GPA or higher. Available to U.S. citizens.

Application Requirements: Application, essay, financial need analysis, resume, references, transcript, college acceptance letter, copy of taxes, Student Aid Report (SAR). *Deadline:* March 22.

Contact: Fernando Barrueta, Chief Executive Officer
Hispanic College Fund Inc.
1301 K Street, NW, Suite 450-A West
Washington, DC 20005
Phone: 202-296-5400
Fax: 202-296-3774
E-mail: hcf-info@hispanicfund.org

HISPANIC SCHOLARSHIP FUND http://www.hsf.net

HSF/CITIGROUP FELLOWS PROGRAM

Selected students of Hispanic heritage will receive $5000 for each of their junior and senior years provided the student maintains the standards of academic progress as defined by HSF. Fellows will also be paired with a Citigroup employee who will serve as a professional mentor. Minimum 3.0 GPA required. Must reside or attend college in one of the following locations: New York City metropolitan area, Miami, Ft. Lauderdale, or Tampa, Florida; Austin, Dallas, or San Antonio, Texas.

Academic Fields/Career Goals: Accounting; Business/Consumer Services; Economics.

Award: Scholarship for use in junior or senior years; renewable. *Number:* up to 10. *Amount:* up to $5000.

Eligibility Requirements: Applicant must be of Hispanic, Latin American/Caribbean, Mexican, Nicaraguan, or Spanish heritage; enrolled or expecting to enroll full-time at a four-year institution or university; resident of California, Florida, New York, or Texas and studying in California, Florida, New York, or Texas. Applicant must have 3.0 GPA or higher. Available to U.S. citizens.

Application Requirements: Application, essay, financial need analysis, references, transcript. *Deadline:* March 15.

Contact: John Schmucker, Scholarship Coordinator
Hispanic Scholarship Fund
55 Second Street, Suite 1500
San Francisco, CA 94105
Phone: 877-473-4636
E-mail: scholar1@hsf.net

HSF/MARATHON OIL CORPORATION COLLEGE SCHOLARSHIP

Selected minority students will receive up to $10,000 for two academic years for a possible total award of $20,000. In addition, scholars will be offered the opportunity to participate in a possible paid 8-10 week summer internship at various Marathon Oil Corporation locations and will be paired with a professional mentor. Minimum GPA of 3.0 required. See Web site for qualifying areas of study and additional details: http://www.hsf.net.

Academic Fields/Career Goals: Accounting; Chemical Engineering; Civil Engineering; Electrical Engineering/Electronics; Energy and Power Engineering; Engineering/Technology; Environmental Science; Materials Science, Engineering, and Metallurgy; Mechanical Engineering; Surveying; Surveying Technology, Cartography, or Geographic Information Science; Transportation.

Award: Scholarship for use in junior, senior, or graduate years; renewable. *Number:* 20. *Amount:* up to $10,000.

Eligibility Requirements: Applicant must be of Hispanic, Latin American/Caribbean, Mexican, Nicaraguan, or Spanish heritage; American Indian/Alaska Native, Asian/Pacific Islander, or Black (non-Hispanic) and enrolled or expecting to enroll full-time at a four-year institution or university. Applicant must have 3.0 GPA or higher. Available to U.S. citizens.

Application Requirements: Application, essay, financial need analysis, interview, references. *Deadline:* November 1.

Contact: Felix Flores, Jr., Program Officer, Scholarships and Internships
Hispanic Scholarship Fund
55 Second Street, Suite 1500
San Francisco, CA 94105
Phone: 415-808-2320
Fax: 415-808-2304
E-mail: fflores@hsf.net

HSF/WELLS FARGO SCHOLARSHIP PROGRAM

Provides scholarship support and career preparedness via internship opportunities for Hispanic college students interested in financial and banking careers. Applicants must be current sophomores enrolled full-time at a four-year accredited college or university in the U.S. and pursuing a degree in business, economics, finance, accounting or IT, including CIS, MIS and computer engineering. Minimum 3.0 GPA required. Priority given to students of selected schools and/or residing in selected states. See Web site for details: http://www.hsf.net.

Academic Fields/Career Goals: Accounting; Business/Consumer Services; Economics; Engineering/Technology; Engineering-Related Technologies.

Hispanic Scholarship Fund (continued)

Award: Scholarship for use in junior year; not renewable. *Number:* 1. *Amount:* $2000.

Eligibility Requirements: Applicant must be of Hispanic, Latin American/Caribbean, Mexican, Nicaraguan, or Spanish heritage; enrolled or expecting to enroll full-time at a four-year institution or university; resident of Alaska, Arizona, California, Colorado, Illinois, Indiana, Iowa, Louisiana, Michigan, Minnesota, Nebraska, Nevada, New Mexico, North Dakota, or Ohio and studying in Arizona, California, Iowa, Texas, or Washington. Applicant must have 3.0 GPA or higher. Available to U.S. citizens.

Application Requirements: Application, essay, financial need analysis, resume, references, transcript. *Deadline:* March 15.

Contact: John Schmucker, Scholarship Coordinator
Hispanic Scholarship Fund
55 Second Street, Suite 1500
San Francisco, CA 94105
Phone: 877-473-4636
E-mail: scholar1@hsf.net

ILLINOIS CPA SOCIETY http://www.icpas.org

HERMAN J. NEAL SCHOLARSHIP

Scholarships of $4000 available to African-American students who demonstrate strong academic performance in their goal to become a CPA and would benefit from scholarship support. College seniors as well as individuals that have graduated and wish to return to school to complete the coursework needed to become a CPA are encouraged to apply.

Academic Fields/Career Goals: Accounting.

Award: Scholarship for use in junior, senior, or graduate years; renewable. *Number:* 4. *Amount:* up to $4000.

Eligibility Requirements: Applicant must be Black (non-Hispanic); enrolled or expecting to enroll full-time at a four-year institution or university; resident of Illinois and studying in Illinois. Applicant must have 3.0 GPA or higher. Available to U.S. citizens.

Application Requirements: Application, transcript. *Deadline:* November 30.

Contact: Katie Miller, Scholarship Coordinator
Illinois CPA Society
550 West Jackson, Suite 900
Chicago, IL 60661-5716
Phone: 312-993-0407 Ext. 216
Fax: 312-993-9954
E-mail: millerk@icpas.org

ILLINOIS CPA SOCIETY ACCOUNTING SCHOLARSHIP

Awarded to high achieving Illinois college and university students who are completing their fifth year of education and planning to sit for the CPA Examination. The program is designed to help students who have CPA potential but need financial assistance for tuition and fees for their fifth year of education.

Academic Fields/Career Goals: Accounting.

Award: Scholarship for use in senior, graduate, or postgraduate years; not renewable. *Number:* 12. *Amount:* up to $4000.

Eligibility Requirements: Applicant must be enrolled or expecting to enroll full-time at a four-year institution or university; resident of Illinois and studying in Illinois. Applicant must have 3.0 GPA or higher. Available to U.S. citizens.

Application Requirements: Application, transcript. *Deadline:* November 30.

Contact: Katie Miller, Scholarship Coordinator
Illinois CPA Society
550 West Jackson, Suite 900
Chicago, IL 60661-5716
Phone: 312-993-0407 Ext. 216
Fax: 312-993-9954
E-mail: millerk@icpas.org

INDEPENDENT COLLEGE FUND OF MARYLAND (I-FUND) http://www.i-fundinfo.org

BRANCH BANKING & TRUST COMPANY SCHOLARSHIPS

Scholarship to a student pursuing a degree in a business-related major or have a demonstrated interest in a business career or should have six credit hours of accounting plus a demonstrated interest in financial accounting. Student must be a rising junior or senior in one of Maryland's independent colleges. Must have a minimum of 3.0 GPA.

Academic Fields/Career Goals: Accounting; Business/Consumer Services.

Award: Scholarship for use in junior or senior years; not renewable. *Number:* 1. *Amount:* $2500.

Eligibility Requirements: Applicant must be enrolled or expecting to enroll full-time at a four-year institution or university. Applicant must have 3.0 GPA or higher. Available to U.S. citizens.

Application Requirements: Application. *Deadline:* varies.

Contact: Lori Subotich, Director of Programs and Scholarships
Independent College Fund of Maryland (I-Fund)
3225 Ellerslie Avenue, Suite C160
Baltimore, MD 21218-3519
Phone: 443-997-5700
Fax: 443-997-2740
E-mail: lsubot@jhmi.edu

CHEVY CHASE BANK SCHOLARSHIP

Student must be majoring in or have a demonstrated interest in business management, finance, accounting, sales or marketing. Must be a rising sophomore, junior, or senior in one of Maryland's independent colleges. Must have a minimum at least 3.0 GPA.

Academic Fields/Career Goals: Accounting; Business/Consumer Services.

Award: Scholarship for use in sophomore, junior, or senior years; not renewable. *Number:* 1. *Amount:* $2500.

Eligibility Requirements: Applicant must be enrolled or expecting to enroll full-time at a four-year institution or university and studying in Maryland. Applicant must have 3.0 GPA or higher. Available to U.S. citizens.

Application Requirements: Application, thank you letters. *Deadline:* varies.

Contact: Lori Subotich, Director of Programs and Scholarships
Independent College Fund of Maryland (I-Fund)
3225 Ellerslie Avenue, Suite C160
Baltimore, MD 21218-3519
Phone: 443-997-5700
Fax: 443-997-2740
E-mail: lsubot@jhmi.edu

LEGG MASON SCHOLARSHIPS

Award to students majoring in business or have a demonstrated interested in financial services. Must be a rising junior or senior in one of Maryland's independent colleges.. Must have at least 3.0 GPA.

Academic Fields/Career Goals: Accounting; Business/Consumer Services.

Award: Scholarship for use in junior or senior years; not renewable. *Number:* 1. *Amount:* $2500.

Eligibility Requirements: Applicant must be enrolled or expecting to enroll full- or part-time at a four-year institution or university and studying in Maryland. Applicant must have 3.0 GPA or higher. Available to U.S. citizens.

Application Requirements: Application, thank you letters. *Deadline:* varies.

Contact: Lori Subotich, Director of Programs and Scholarships
Independent College Fund of Maryland (I-Fund)
3225 Ellerslie Avenue, Suite C160
Baltimore, MD 21218-3519
Phone: 443-997-5700
Fax: 443-997-2740
E-mail: lsubot@jhmi.edu

INSTITUTE OF INTERNAL AUDITORS RESEARCH FOUNDATION http://www.theiia.org

ESTHER R. SAWYER SCHOLARSHIP AWARD

Scholarship of $5000 awarded to a student entering or currently enrolled in internal auditing program at an IIA-endorsed school. Awarded based on submission of an original manuscript on a specific topic related to modern internal auditing.

Academic Fields/Career Goals: Accounting.

Award: Scholarship for use in freshman, sophomore, junior, senior, or graduate years; not renewable. *Number:* 1. *Amount:* $5000.

Eligibility Requirements: Applicant must be enrolled or expecting to enroll full-time at a four-year institution or university. Available to U.S. and non-U.S. citizens.

Application Requirements: Application, applicant must enter a contest, essay. *Deadline:* March 1.

Contact: Nicki Creatore, Manager, Operations
Institute of Internal Auditors Research Foundation
247 Maitland Avenue
Altamonte Springs, FL 32701-4201
Phone: 407-937-1356
Fax: 407-937-1101
E-mail: research@theiia.org

INSTITUTE OF MANAGEMENT ACCOUNTANTS http://www.imanet.org

INSTITUTE OF MANAGEMENT ACCOUNTANTS MEMORIAL EDUCATION FUND SCHOLARSHIPS

Scholarships for IMA undergraduate or graduate student members studying at accredited institutions in the U.S. and Puerto Rico. Must be pursuing a career in management accounting, financial management, or information technology, and have a minimum GPA of 3.0. Awards based on academic merit, IMA participation, strength of recommendations, and quality of written statements.

Academic Fields/Career Goals: Accounting; Business/Consumer Services.

Award: Scholarship for use in sophomore, junior, senior, or graduate years; not renewable. *Number:* 6–15. *Amount:* $1000–$2500.

Eligibility Requirements: Applicant must be enrolled or expecting to enroll full- or part-time at a two-year or four-year institution or university. Applicant must have 3.0 GPA or higher. Available to U.S. citizens.

Application Requirements: Application, essay, resume, references, transcript. *Deadline:* February 15.

Contact: Jodi Ryan, Manager of Student and Academic Relations
Institute of Management Accountants
10 Paragon Drive
Montvale, NJ 07645-1760
Phone: 800-638-4427 Ext. 1556
E-mail: jryan@imanet.org

STUART CAMERON AND MARGARET MCLEOD MEMORIAL SCHOLARSHIP

Scholarships for IMA undergraduate or graduate student members studying at accredited institutions in the U.S. and Puerto Rico, and carrying 12 credits per semester. Must be pursuing a career in management accounting, financial management, or information technology, and have a minimum GPA of 3.0. Awards based on academic merit, IMA participation, strength of recommendations, and quality of written statements.

Academic Fields/Career Goals: Accounting; Business/Consumer Services.

Award: Scholarship for use in junior, senior, or graduate years; not renewable. *Number:* 1. *Amount:* $5000.

Eligibility Requirements: Applicant must be enrolled or expecting to enroll full- or part-time at a four-year institution or university. Applicant must have 3.0 GPA or higher. Available to U.S. citizens.

Application Requirements: Application, essay, resume, transcript. *Deadline:* February 15.

Contact: Jodi Ryan, Manager of Student and Academic Relations
Institute of Management Accountants
10 Paragon Drive
Montvale, NJ 07645-1760
Phone: 800-638-4427 Ext. 1556
E-mail: jryan@imanet.org

KENTUCKY SOCIETY OF CERTIFIED PUBLIC ACCOUNTANTS http://www.kycpa.org

KENTUCKY SOCIETY OF CERTIFIED PUBLIC ACCOUNTANTS COLLEGE SCHOLARSHIP

Nonrenewable award for accounting majors at a Kentucky college or university. Must rank in upper third of class or have a minimum 3.0 GPA. Must be a Kentucky resident.

Academic Fields/Career Goals: Accounting.

Award: Scholarship for use in sophomore, junior, or senior years; not renewable. *Number:* up to 23. *Amount:* $1000–$2500.

Eligibility Requirements: Applicant must be enrolled or expecting to enroll full-time at a two-year or four-year institution or university; resident of Kentucky and studying in Kentucky. Applicant must have 3.0 GPA or higher. Available to U.S. and non-U.S. citizens.

Application Requirements: Application, essay, references, transcript. *Deadline:* January 31.

Contact: Becky Ackerman, Foundation Administrator
Kentucky Society of Certified Public Accountants
1735 Alliant Avenue
Louisville, KY 40299
Phone: 502-266-5272
Fax: 502-261-9512
E-mail: backerman@kycpa.org

LATINO BUSINESS PROFESSIONALS (LBP) OF NORTHERN CALIFORNIA http://www.lbpbayarea.org

LBP MONETARY SCHOLARSHIP

$500 to $1500 scholarships for minority students pursuing careers in accounting, finance, and business-related fields.

Academic Fields/Career Goals: Accounting.

Award: Scholarship for use in freshman, sophomore, junior, senior, graduate, or postgraduate years; not renewable. *Number:* 22. *Amount:* $500–$1500.

Eligibility Requirements: Applicant must be American Indian/Alaska Native, Asian/Pacific Islander, Black (non-Hispanic), or Hispanic and enrolled or expecting to enroll full- or part-time at a two-year or four-year institution or university. Available to U.S. and non-U.S. citizens.

Application Requirements: Application, transcript, tax return. *Deadline:* January 15.

Contact: Ms. Beatriz Quezada, Scholarship Coordinator
Latino Business Professionals (LBP) of Northern California
PO Box 193296
San Francisco, CA 94119-3296
Phone: 408-213-0350
Fax: 408-521-2009
E-mail: sf_president@lbpbayarea.org

LAWRENCE P. DOSS SCHOLARSHIP FOUNDATION http://www.lawrencepdossfnd.org

LAWRENCE P. DOSS SCHOLARSHIP FOUNDATION

Renewable scholarships are available to residents of Michigan who are seniors graduating from a high school in the greater Detroit area. Must be pursuing a degree in accounting, finance, management or business. Financial need considered.

Academic Fields/Career Goals: Accounting; Business/Consumer Services.

Award: Scholarship for use in freshman year; renewable. *Number:* 5. *Amount:* $20,000.

Eligibility Requirements: Applicant must be high school student; planning to enroll or expecting to enroll full-time at a four-year

Lawrence P. Doss Scholarship Foundation (continued)

institution or university; single and resident of Michigan. Applicant must have 2.5 GPA or higher. Available to U.S. citizens.

Application Requirements: Application, essay, financial need analysis, interview, references, test scores, transcript. *Deadline:* March 15.

Contact: Judith Doss, President and Chief Executive Officer
Lawrence P. Doss Scholarship Foundation
PO Box 351037
Detroit, MI 48235-9998
Phone: 313-891-5834
Fax: 313-891-4520
E-mail: lpdsfoundation@aol.com

MARYLAND ASSOCIATION OF CERTIFIED PUBLIC ACCOUNTANTS EDUCATIONAL FOUNDATION http://www.tomorrowscpa.org

STUDENT SCHOLARSHIP IN ACCOUNTING MD ASSOCIATION OF CPAS

Award for Maryland residents who will have completed at least 60 credit hours at a Maryland college or university by the time of the award. Must have 3.0 GPA, demonstrate commitment to 150 semester hours of education, and intend to pursue a career as a certified public accountant. Number of awards varies. Must submit accounting department chairman's signature on required statement. Must be a member of the Tomorrow's CPA program. U.S. citizenship required. See Web site at http://www.tomorrowscpa.org for further details.

Academic Fields/Career Goals: Accounting.

Award: Scholarship for use in junior, senior, or graduate years; renewable. *Number:* 10–20. *Amount:* $500–$1000.

Eligibility Requirements: Applicant must be enrolled or expecting to enroll full-time at a four-year institution or university; resident of Maryland and studying in Maryland. Applicant must have 3.0 GPA or higher. Available to U.S. citizens.

Application Requirements: Application, financial need analysis, references, transcript. *Deadline:* April 15.

Contact: Richard Rabicoff, Career Initiatives and Public Relations Manager
Maryland Association of Certified Public Accountants Educational Foundation
901 Dulaney Road, Suite 710
Towson, MD 21204
Phone: 443-632-2318
Fax: 443-632-2358
E-mail: richard@macpa.org

MICHIGAN ASSOCIATION OF CPAS http://www.michcpa.org

FIFTH/GRADUATE YEAR STUDENT SCHOLARSHIP

Scholarship for a full-time student in senior year, or a student with a combination of education and employment (defined as a minimum of two classes per term and 20 hours per week of employment). Must be majoring in accounting, and a U.S. citizen.

Academic Fields/Career Goals: Accounting.

Award: Scholarship for use in senior year; not renewable. *Number:* 16–25. *Amount:* up to $4000.

Eligibility Requirements: Applicant must be enrolled or expecting to enroll full-time at a four-year institution or university and studying in Michigan. Available to U.S. citizens.

Application Requirements: Application, essay, financial need analysis, references, transcript. *Deadline:* January 31.

Contact: MACPA Academic Services Specialist
Michigan Association of CPAs
5480 Corporate Drive, Suite 200
Troy, MI 48007-5068
Phone: 248-267-3700
Fax: 248-267-3737
E-mail: macpa@michcpa.org

MINNESOTA SOCIETY OF CERTIFIED PUBLIC ACCOUNTANTS http://www.mncpa.org

MNCPA SCHOLARSHIP PROGRAM

Scholarships given for graduate study in accounting to students from a Minnesota college or university who passed the CPA exam during the previous year. Must be a sophomore, junior or senior (going on to graduate school). At least a 3.0 GPA in accounting.

Academic Fields/Career Goals: Accounting.

Award: Scholarship for use in sophomore, junior, or senior years; not renewable. *Number:* up to 25. *Amount:* up to $1000.

Eligibility Requirements: Applicant must be enrolled or expecting to enroll full-time at a four-year institution or university and studying in Minnesota. Applicant must have 3.0 GPA or higher. Available to U.S. citizens.

Application Requirements: Application. *Deadline:* varies.

Contact: Membership Committee
Minnesota Society of Certified Public Accountants
1650 West 82nd Street, Suite 600
Bloomington, MN 55431
Phone: 952-885-5517
Fax: 952-831-7875

MONTANA SOCIETY OF CERTIFIED PUBLIC ACCOUNTANTS http://www.mscpa.org

MONTANA SOCIETY OF CERTIFIED PUBLIC ACCOUNTANTS SCHOLARSHIP

Scholarship available to one student in each of the following four schools: Montana State University Billings, MSU Bozeman, Carroll College, and University of Montana. Must be an accounting major, at least a junior with a minimum of one semester of coursework remaining, minimum GPA of 2.75 overall and 3.0 in business courses. Graduate students are also eligible. Preference will be given to student members of the MSCPA.

Academic Fields/Career Goals: Accounting.

Award: Scholarship for use in junior, senior, or graduate years; not renewable. *Number:* 1. *Amount:* $1000.

Eligibility Requirements: Applicant must be enrolled or expecting to enroll full-time at a four-year institution or university; resident of Montana and studying in Montana. Applicant must have 3.0 GPA or higher. Available to U.S. citizens.

Application Requirements: Application, resume, test scores, transcript. *Deadline:* varies.

Contact: Margaret Herriges, Communications Director
Montana Society of Certified Public Accountants
PO Box 138
Helena, MT 59624-0138
Phone: 406-442-7301
Fax: 406-443-7278
E-mail: margaret@mscpa.org

NATIONAL BLACK MBA ASSOCIATION-TWIN CITIES CHAPTER http://www.nbmbaatc.org

TWIN CITIES CHAPTER UNDERGRADUATE SCHOLARSHIP

Award for minority students in first, second, third or fourth year full-time in an accredited undergraduate business or management program during the fall semester working towards a bachelor's degree. Get application from Web site at http://www.nbmbaatc.org.

Academic Fields/Career Goals: Accounting; Business/Consumer Services.

Award: Scholarship for use in freshman, sophomore, junior, or senior years; not renewable. *Number:* 5. *Amount:* up to $3500.

Eligibility Requirements: Applicant must be Black (non-Hispanic); enrolled or expecting to enroll full-time at a four-year institution or university; resident of Minnesota and studying in Minnesota. Available to U.S. citizens.

Application Requirements: Application, essay, transcript. *Deadline:* April 7.

Contact: Victor Patterson, President
National Black MBA Association-Twin Cities Chapter
PO Box 2709
Minneapolis, MN 55402
Phone: 651-223-7373

NATIONAL SOCIETY OF ACCOUNTANTS http://www.nsacct.org

CHARLES EARP MEMORIAL SCHOLARSHIP

Annual award for the student designated as most outstanding of all National Society of Accountants scholarship recipients receive an additional stipend of approximately $200.

Academic Fields/Career Goals: Accounting.

Award: Scholarship for use in freshman, sophomore, junior, or senior years; not renewable. *Number:* 1. *Amount:* $200.

Eligibility Requirements: Applicant must be enrolled or expecting to enroll full- or part-time at a four-year institution or university. Available to U.S. and Canadian citizens.

Application Requirements: Application, financial need analysis, transcript, appraisal form. *Deadline:* March 10.

Contact: Sally Brasse, Director of Education Programs
National Society of Accountants
1010 North Fairfax Street
Alexandria, VA 22314-1574
Phone: 703-549-6400 Ext. 1307
E-mail: sbrasse@nsacct.org

NATIONAL SOCIETY OF ACCOUNTANTS SCHOLARSHIP

One-time award of $500 to $1000 available to undergraduate students. Applicants must maintain a 3.0 GPA and have declared a major in accounting. Must submit an appraisal form and transcripts in addition to application. Must be U.S. or Canadian citizen attending an accredited U.S. school.

Academic Fields/Career Goals: Accounting.

Award: Scholarship for use in freshman, sophomore, junior, or senior years; not renewable. *Number:* up to 40. *Amount:* $500–$1000.

Eligibility Requirements: Applicant must be enrolled or expecting to enroll full- or part-time at a two-year or four-year institution or university. Applicant must have 3.0 GPA or higher. Available to U.S. and Canadian citizens.

Application Requirements: Application, financial need analysis, transcript, appraisal form. *Deadline:* March 10.

Contact: Susan E. Noell, Director of Education Programs
National Society of Accountants
1010 North Fairfax Street
Alexandria, VA 22314-1574
Phone: 703-549-6400 Ext. 1312
Fax: 703-549-2984 Ext. 1312
E-mail: snoell@nsacct.org

NSA LOUIS AND FANNIE SAGER MEMORIAL SCHOLARSHIP AWARD

Up to $1000 will be awarded annually to a graduate of a Virginia public high school who is enrolled as an undergraduate at a Virginia college or university. Applicant must major in accounting. Must submit proof of graduation from a Virginia public school.

Academic Fields/Career Goals: Accounting.

Award: Scholarship for use in freshman, sophomore, junior, or senior years; not renewable. *Number:* 1. *Amount:* $500–$1000.

Eligibility Requirements: Applicant must be enrolled or expecting to enroll full- or part-time at a two-year or four-year institution or university; resident of Virginia and studying in Virginia. Applicant must have 3.0 GPA or higher. Available to U.S. and Canadian citizens.

Application Requirements: Application, financial need analysis, transcript, appraisal form. *Deadline:* March 10.

Contact: Sally Brasse, Director
National Society of Accountants
1010 North Fairfax Street
Alexandria, VA 22314-1574
Phone: 703-549-6400 Ext. 1307
E-mail: sbrasse@nsacct.org

STANLEY H. STEARMAN SCHOLARSHIP

One award for accounting major who is a relative of an active, retired, or deceased member of National Society of Accountants. Must be citizen of the United States or Canada and attend school in the United States. Minimum GPA of 3.0 required. Not available for freshman year. Submit application, appraisal form, and letter of intent.

Academic Fields/Career Goals: Accounting.

Award: Scholarship for use in freshman, sophomore, junior, senior, or graduate years; renewable. *Number:* 1. *Amount:* up to $2000.

Eligibility Requirements: Applicant must be enrolled or expecting to enroll full- or part-time at a two-year or four-year institution or university. Applicant or parent of applicant must be member of National Society of Accountants. Applicant must have 3.0 GPA or higher. Available to U.S. and Canadian citizens.

Application Requirements: Application, essay, financial need analysis, transcript, appraisal form. *Deadline:* March 10.

Contact: Sally Brasse, Director of Education Programs
National Society of Accountants
1010 North Fairfax Street
Alexandria, VA 22314-1574
Phone: 703-549-6400 Ext. 1307
Fax: 703-549-2984
E-mail: sbrasse@nsacct.org

NATIONAL SOCIETY OF COLLEGIATE SCHOLARS (NSCS) http://www.nscs.org

NSCS ERNST & YOUNG BOOK AWARD

Three $250 scholarship to all NSCS members working towards an undergraduate degree and two $500 scholarship to NSCS members working towards an undergraduate or MS degree in accounting or business.

Academic Fields/Career Goals: Accounting; Business/Consumer Services.

Award: Scholarship for use in freshman, sophomore, junior, senior, or graduate years; not renewable. *Number:* 5. *Amount:* $250–$500.

Eligibility Requirements: Applicant must be enrolled or expecting to enroll full- or part-time at a two-year or four-year or technical institution or university. Available to U.S. and non-U.S. citizens.

Application Requirements: Application. *Deadline:* January 31.

Contact: Stephen Loflin, Executive Director
National Society of Collegiate Scholars (NSCS)
11 Dupont Circle NW, Suite 650
Washington, DC 20036
Phone: 202-965-9000
Fax: 800-784-1015
E-mail: nscs@nscs.org

NEBRASKA SOCIETY OF CERTIFIED PUBLIC ACCOUNTANTS http://www.nescpa.com

NEBRASKA SOCIETY OF CPAS SCHOLARSHIP

Scholarship awards are presented to accounting students who have completed their junior year; accounting majors who plan to sit for the CPA exam; students who have the interest and capabilities of becoming a successful accountant and who are considering an accounting career in Nebraska are to be considered. Recipients need not necessarily have the highest scholastic average.

Academic Fields/Career Goals: Accounting.

Award: Scholarship for use in senior year; not renewable. *Number:* varies. *Amount:* varies.

Eligibility Requirements: Applicant must be enrolled or expecting to enroll full-time at a four-year institution or university. Available to U.S. citizens.

Nebraska Society of Certified Public Accountants (continued)

Application Requirements: Application, nomination letter. *Deadline:* August 1.

Contact: Sheila Burroughs, Vice President
Nebraska Society of Certified Public Accountants
635 South 14th Street, Suite 330
Lincoln, NE 68508
Phone: 402-476-8482
Fax: 402-476-8731
E-mail: society@nescpa.org

NEVADA SOCIETY OF CERTIFIED PUBLIC ACCOUNTANTS http://www.nevadacpa.org

NEVADA SOCIETY OF CPAS SCHOLARSHIP

Scholarships available for accounting students in one of Nevada's four community colleges, or for juniors or seniors attending either University of Nevada, Las Vegas, or University of Nevada, Reno. Must be planning a career in accounting.

Academic Fields/Career Goals: Accounting.

Award: Scholarship for use in freshman, sophomore, junior, or senior years; not renewable. *Number:* 6. *Amount:* up to $1500.

Eligibility Requirements: Applicant must be enrolled or expecting to enroll full-time at a two-year or four-year institution or university; resident of Nevada and studying in Nevada. Available to U.S. citizens.

Application Requirements: Application. *Deadline:* varies.

Contact: Sharon Uithoven, Executive Director
Nevada Society of Certified Public Accountants
5250 Neil Road, Suite 205
Reno, NV 89502
Phone: 775-826-6800 Ext. 104
Fax: 775-826-7942
E-mail: uithoven@nevadacpa.org

NEW HAMPSHIRE SOCIETY OF CERTIFIED PUBLIC ACCOUNTANTS http://www.nhscpa.org

NEW HAMPSHIRE SOCIETY OF CERTIFIED PUBLIC ACCOUNTANTS SCHOLARSHIP FUND

One-time award for New Hampshire resident majoring full-time in accounting. Must be entering junior or senior year at a four-year college or university or pursuing a master's degree. Maximum of four awards of up to $2000 are granted.

Academic Fields/Career Goals: Accounting.

Award: Scholarship for use in junior, senior, or graduate years; not renewable. *Number:* up to 4. *Amount:* up to $2000.

Eligibility Requirements: Applicant must be enrolled or expecting to enroll full-time at a four-year institution or university and resident of New Hampshire. Available to U.S. citizens.

Application Requirements: Application, references, transcript. *Deadline:* November 1.

Contact: Marlene Gazda, Executive Director
New Hampshire Society of Certified Public Accountants
1750 Elm Street, Suite 403
Manchester, NH 03104
Phone: 603-622-1999
Fax: 603-626-0204

NEW JERSEY SOCIETY OF CERTIFIED PUBLIC ACCOUNTANTS http://www.njscpa.org

NEW JERSEY SOCIETY OF CERTIFIED PUBLIC ACCOUNTANTS COLLEGE SCHOLARSHIP PROGRAM

Award for college juniors or those entering an accounting-related graduate program. Must be a New Jersey resident attending a four-year New Jersey institution. Must be nominated by accounting department chair or submit application directly. Minimum 3.0 GPA required. Award values from $2500 to $3000.

Academic Fields/Career Goals: Accounting.

Award: Scholarship for use in junior or senior years; not renewable. *Number:* 40–50. *Amount:* $2500–$3000.

Eligibility Requirements: Applicant must be enrolled or expecting to enroll full- or part-time at a four-year institution or university; resident of New Jersey and studying in New Jersey. Applicant must have 3.0 GPA or higher. Available to U.S. citizens.

Application Requirements: Application, interview, resume, references, transcript. *Deadline:* January 16.

Contact: Janice Amatucci, Student Programs Coordinator
New Jersey Society of Certified Public Accountants
425 Eagle Rock Avenue, Suite 100
Roseland, NJ 07068-1723
Phone: 973-226-4494
Fax: 973-226-7425
E-mail: jamatucci@njscpa.org

NEW JERSEY SOCIETY OF CERTIFIED PUBLIC ACCOUNTANTS HIGH SCHOOL SCHOLARSHIP PROGRAM

Renewable scholarship for New Jersey high school seniors who wish to pursue a degree in accounting. Must be resident of New Jersey. Scholarship value is from $6500 to $8500. Deadline varies.

Academic Fields/Career Goals: Accounting.

Award: Scholarship for use in freshman year; renewable. *Number:* 15–20. *Amount:* $6500–$8500.

Eligibility Requirements: Applicant must be high school student; planning to enroll or expecting to enroll full-time at a four-year institution or university and resident of New Jersey. Available to U.S. citizens.

Application Requirements: Application, interview, test scores. *Deadline:* varies.

Contact: Janice Amatucci, Student Programs Coordinator
New Jersey Society of Certified Public Accountants
425 Eagle Rock Avenue, Suite 100
Roseland, NJ 07068-1723
Phone: 973-226-4494
Fax: 973-226-7425
E-mail: jamatucci@njscpa.org

NEW YORK STATE EDUCATION DEPARTMENT http://www.highered.nysed.gov

REGENTS PROFESSIONAL OPPORTUNITY SCHOLARSHIP

Scholarship for New York residents beginning or already enrolled in an approved degree-granting program of study in New York that leads to licensure in a particular profession. See the Web site for the list of eligible professions. Must be U.S. citizen or permanent resident. Award recipients must agree to practice upon licensure in their profession in New York for 12 months for each annual payment received. Priority given to economically disadvantaged members of minority groups underrepresented in the professions.

Academic Fields/Career Goals: Accounting; Architecture; Dental Health/Services; Engineering/Technology; Health and Medical Sciences; Interior Design; Landscape Architecture; Law/Legal Services; Nursing; Pharmacy; Psychology; Social Services.

Award: Scholarship for use in freshman, sophomore, junior, senior, or graduate years; renewable. *Number:* 220. *Amount:* up to $5000.

Eligibility Requirements: Applicant must be enrolled or expecting to enroll full-time at a two-year or four-year institution or university; resident of New York and studying in New York. Available to U.S. citizens.

Application Requirements: Application. *Deadline:* May 31.

Contact: Lewis Hall, Supervisor
New York State Education Department
89 Washington Avenue, Room 1078 EBA
Albany, NY 12234
Phone: 518-486-1319
Fax: 518-486-5346
E-mail: scholar@mail.nysed.gov

NEW YORK STATE SOCIETY OF CERTIFIED PUBLIC ACCOUNTANTS FOUNDATION FOR ACCOUNTING EDUCATION http://www.nysscpa.org

FOUNDATION FOR ACCOUNTING EDUCATION SCHOLARSHIP

Awards up to $200 to $2500 scholarships to college students to encourage them to pursue a career in accounting. Must be a New York resident studying in New York and maintaining a 3.0 GPA.

Academic Fields/Career Goals: Accounting.

Award: Scholarship for use in junior, senior, or graduate years; not renewable. *Number:* 1–200. *Amount:* $2500.

Eligibility Requirements: Applicant must be enrolled or expecting to enroll full- or part-time at a four-year institution or university; resident of New York and studying in New York. Applicant must have 3.0 GPA or higher. Available to U.S. citizens.

Application Requirements: Application, financial need analysis, transcript. *Deadline:* April 15.

Contact: William Pape, Director Member Relations
New York State Society of Certified Public Accountants Foundation for Accounting Education
Three Park Avenue, 18th Floor
New York, NY 10016-5991
Phone: 212-719-8420
Fax: 212-719-3364
E-mail: wpape@nysscpa.org

OREGON ASSOCIATION OF PUBLIC ACCOUNTANTS SCHOLARSHIP FOUNDATION http://www.oaia.net

OAIA SCHOLARSHIP

Scholarships of $1000 to $2000 are awarded to full-time students. Must be a resident of the state of Oregon and major in accounting studies at an accredited school in the state of Oregon. The scholarship may be used for tuition, fees, books or other academic expenses incurred during the term.

Academic Fields/Career Goals: Accounting.

Award: Scholarship for use in freshman, sophomore, junior, or senior years; not renewable. *Number:* 5. *Amount:* $1000–$2000.

Eligibility Requirements: Applicant must be enrolled or expecting to enroll full-time at a two-year or four-year institution or university; resident of Oregon and studying in Oregon. Available to U.S. citizens.

Application Requirements: Application, financial need analysis, resume, references, test scores, transcript. *Deadline:* April 1.

Contact: Susan Robertson, Executive Director
Oregon Association of Public Accountants Scholarship Foundation
1804 43rd Avenue, NE
Portland, OR 97213
Phone: 503-282-7247
Fax: 503-282-7406
E-mail: srobertson4oaia@aol.com

OREGON STUDENT ASSISTANCE COMMISSION http://www.osac.state.or.us

HOMESTEAD CAPITAL HOUSING SCHOLARSHIP

Applicant must have graduated from an Oregon high school, be entering at least junior year, have a 2.75 minimum cumulative GPA, and be majoring in one of the following at a four-year Oregon or Washington college: accounting, architecture, community development, construction management, finance, real estate, or engineering (structural, civil, or environmental). Essay required. See Web site: http://www.osac.state.or.us for more information.

Academic Fields/Career Goals: Accounting; Architecture; Business/Consumer Services; Civil Engineering; Engineering/Technology; Real Estate.

Award: Scholarship for use in junior or senior years; renewable. *Number:* varies. *Amount:* varies.

Eligibility Requirements: Applicant must be enrolled or expecting to enroll full-time at a four-year institution or university; resident of Oregon and studying in Oregon or Washington. Available to U.S. and non-Canadian citizens.

Application Requirements: Application, essay, financial need analysis, transcript, activity chart. *Deadline:* March 1.

Contact: Director of Grant Programs
Oregon Student Assistance Commission
1500 Valley River Drive, Suite 100
Eugene, OR 97401-7020
Phone: 800-452-8807 Ext. 7395

OSCPA EDUCATIONAL FOUNDATION http://www.orcpa.org

OSCPA EDUCATIONAL FOUNDATION SCHOLARSHIP PROGRAM

One-time award for students majoring in accounting. Must attend an accredited Oregon college/university or community college on full-time basis. High school seniors must have a minimum 3.5 GPA. College students must have a minimum 3.2 GPA. Must be a U.S. citizen and Oregon resident.

Academic Fields/Career Goals: Accounting.

Award: Scholarship for use in freshman, sophomore, junior, senior, graduate, or postgraduate years; not renewable. *Number:* 50–100. *Amount:* $500–$3000.

Eligibility Requirements: Applicant must be enrolled or expecting to enroll full-time at a two-year or four-year or technical institution or university; resident of Oregon and studying in Oregon. Applicant must have 3.5 GPA or higher. Available to U.S. citizens.

Application Requirements: Application, resume, references, test scores, transcript. *Deadline:* February 12.

Contact: Tonna Hollis, Member Services and Manager
OSCPA Educational Foundation
PO Box 4555
Beaverton, OR 97076-4555
Phone: 503-641-7200 Ext. 29
Fax: 503-626-2942
E-mail: tonna@orcpa.org

PENNSYLVANIA INSTITUTE OF CERTIFIED PUBLIC ACCOUNTANTS http://www.cpazone.org

JOSEPH F. TARICANI MEMORIAL SCHOLARSHIP

The PICPA awards an one-time award up to $1000 to an eligible sophomore in the name of Joseph F. Taricani, in order to promote the accounting profession and CPA credential. Must be enrolled in a postsecondary institution in Pennsylvania.

Academic Fields/Career Goals: Accounting.

Award: Scholarship for use in sophomore year; not renewable. *Number:* 1. *Amount:* up to $1000.

Eligibility Requirements: Applicant must be enrolled or expecting to enroll full-time at a two-year or four-year or technical institution or university and studying in Pennsylvania. Applicant must have 3.0 GPA or higher. Available to U.S. and non-U.S. citizens.

Application Requirements: Application, essay, resume, references, test scores, transcript. *Deadline:* March 14.

Contact: Albert Trexler, Executive Director
Pennsylvania Institute of Certified Public Accountants
1650 Arch Street, 17th Floor
Philadelphia, PA 19103-2099
Phone: 215-972-6180
Fax: 215-496-9212
E-mail: atrexler@picpa.org

PENNSYLVANIA INSTITUTE OF CERTIFIED PUBLIC ACCOUNTANTS SOPHOMORE SCHOLARSHIP

To promote the accounting profession and CPA credential as an exciting and rewarding career path. Scholarship amounts range from $1000–$3000 and can be renewed annually until you graduate. Candidates must have completed a 36 credit hours and have a minimum 3.0 GPA.

Academic Fields/Career Goals: Accounting.

Award: Scholarship for use in junior or senior years; renewable. *Number:* 20. *Amount:* $1500–$3000.

Eligibility Requirements: Applicant must be enrolled or expecting to enroll full-time at a four-year institution or university and studying in Pennsylvania. Applicant must have 3.0 GPA or higher. Available to U.S. and non-U.S. citizens.

Pennsylvania Institute of Certified Public Accountants (continued)

Application Requirements: Application, essay, resume, references, transcript. *Deadline:* March 14.

Contact: Scholarship Committee
Pennsylvania Institute of Certified Public Accountants
1650 Arch Street, 17th Floor
Philadelphia, PA 19103
E-mail: schools@picpa.org

RHODE ISLAND FOUNDATION http://www.rifoundation.org

CARL W. CHRISTIANSEN SCHOLARSHIP

Award for Rhode Island residents pursuing full-time study in accounting or related fields. Must maintain a minimum 3.0 GPA, and for full-time study only.

Academic Fields/Career Goals: Accounting.

Award: Scholarship for use in freshman, sophomore, junior, senior, or graduate years; not renewable. *Number:* 1–9. *Amount:* $1000.

Eligibility Requirements: Applicant must be enrolled or expecting to enroll full-time at a two-year or four-year institution or university and resident of Rhode Island. Applicant must have 3.0 GPA or higher. Available to U.S. citizens.

Application Requirements: Application. *Deadline:* April 14.

Contact: Kris Moretti, RI Society of Public Accountants
Rhode Island Foundation
45 Royal Little Drive
Providence, RI 02904
Phone: 401-331-5720
E-mail: kmoretti@riscpa.org

RHODE ISLAND SOCIETY OF CERTIFIED PUBLIC ACCOUNTANTS http://www.riscpa.org

RHODE ISLAND SOCIETY OF CERTIFIED PUBLIC ACCOUNTANTS SCHOLARSHIP

Annual scholarship for graduates and undergraduates majoring in accounting, who are legal residents of Rhode Island and U.S. citizens. Must have interest in a career in public accounting, and submit one-page memo outlining that interest. Minimum GPA of 3.0 required. For more information, see Web site: http://www.riscpa.org.

Academic Fields/Career Goals: Accounting.

Award: Scholarship for use in freshman, sophomore, junior, senior, or graduate years; not renewable. *Number:* varies. *Amount:* varies.

Eligibility Requirements: Applicant must be enrolled or expecting to enroll full-time at a four-year institution or university and resident of Rhode Island. Applicant must have 3.0 GPA or higher. Available to U.S. citizens.

Application Requirements: Application, resume, references, test scores, transcript. *Deadline:* January 15.

Contact: Robert Mancini, Executive Director
Rhode Island Society of Certified Public Accountants
45 Royal Little Drive
Providence, RI 02904
Phone: 401-331-5720
Fax: 401-454-5780
E-mail: rmancini@riscpa.org

SAN DIEGO FOUNDATION http://www.sdfoundation.org

FRANK H. AULT SCHOLARSHIP

Scholarship to provide financial assistance for the next academic year to current students in their sophomore, junior, or senior year who have declared a major in finance or accounting. Applicants must have a demonstrated financial need and a minimum 3.0 GPA. Students must have participated in extracurricular or community service activities. Preference will be given to students who are active members of or have taken leadership in their school's accounting society.

Academic Fields/Career Goals: Accounting.

Award: Scholarship for use in sophomore, junior, or senior years; not renewable. *Number:* 6. *Amount:* $2500.

Eligibility Requirements: Applicant must be enrolled or expecting to enroll full-time at a four-year institution or university and resident of California. Applicant must have 3.0 GPA or higher. Available to U.S. citizens.

Application Requirements: Application, financial need analysis, references, transcript, personal statement, copy of tax return. *Deadline:* January 26.

Contact: Shryl Helvie, Scholarship Coordinator
San Diego Foundation
2508 Historic Decatur Road, Suite 200
San Diego, CA 92106
Phone: 619-814-1307
Fax: 619-239-1710
E-mail: shryl@sdfoundation.org

SOCIETY OF AUTOMOTIVE ANALYSTS http://www.cybersaa.org

SOCIETY OF AUTOMOTIVE ANALYSTS SCHOLARSHIP

A scholarship of $1500 awarded to students in economics, finance, business administration or marketing management. Minimum 3.0 GPA required. Must submit two letters of recommendation.

Academic Fields/Career Goals: Accounting; Business/Consumer Services; Economics.

Award: Scholarship for use in freshman, sophomore, junior, or senior years; not renewable. *Number:* 2. *Amount:* $1500.

Eligibility Requirements: Applicant must be enrolled or expecting to enroll full-time at a two-year or four-year or technical institution or university. Applicant must have 3.0 GPA or higher. Available to U.S. and non-U.S. citizens.

Application Requirements: Application, references, transcript. *Deadline:* June 1.

Contact: Lynne Hall, Awards and Scholarships
Society of Automotive Analysts
21400 Oakwood Boulevard
Dearborn, MI 48124
Phone: 313-240-4000
Fax: 313-240-8641

SOCIETY OF LOUISIANA CERTIFIED PUBLIC ACCOUNTANTS http://www.lcpa.org

SOCIETY OF LOUISIANA CPAS SCHOLARSHIPS

One-time award for accounting majors. Applicant must be a Louisiana resident attending a four-year college or university in Louisiana. For full-time undergraduates entering their junior or senior year, or full-time graduate students. Minimum 2.5 GPA required. Deadline varies. Must be U.S. citizen.

Academic Fields/Career Goals: Accounting.

Award: Scholarship for use in junior, senior, or graduate years; not renewable. *Number:* varies. *Amount:* $500–$3000.

Eligibility Requirements: Applicant must be enrolled or expecting to enroll full-time at a four-year institution or university; resident of Louisiana and studying in Louisiana. Applicant must have 2.5 GPA or higher. Available to U.S. citizens.

Application Requirements: Application, essay, references, transcript. *Deadline:* varies.

Contact: Lisa Richardson, Member Services Manager
Society of Louisiana Certified Public Accountants
2400 Veterans Boulevard, Suite 500
Kenner, LA 70062-4739
Phone: 504-904-1139
Fax: 504-469-7930
E-mail: lrichardson@lcpa.org

SOUTH CAROLINA ASSOCIATION OF CERTIFIED PUBLIC ACCOUNTANTS http://www.scacpa.org

ACCOUNTEMPS/AICPA SCHOLARSHIP

Scholarships available to full-time undergraduate and graduate students pursuing a degree in accounting, finance, or information systems. Must be AICPA student affiliate member with minimum overall and major GPA of 3.0. Selection based on demonstrated academic achievement, leadership activities, community service and future career interests.

Academic Fields/Career Goals: Accounting.

Award: Scholarship for use in freshman, sophomore, junior, senior, or graduate years; renewable. *Number:* 5. *Amount:* $2500.

Eligibility Requirements: Applicant must be enrolled or expecting to enroll full-time at a four-year institution or university. Applicant or parent of applicant must be member of American Institute of Certified Public Accountants. Applicant must have 3.0 GPA or higher. Available to U.S. and non-U.S. citizens.

Application Requirements: Application, references, test scores, transcript. *Deadline:* April 1.

Contact: Scholarship Committee
South Carolina Association of Certified Public Accountants
5001 East Commercenter Drive, Suite 220
Bakersfield, CA 93309-1655
Phone: 661-635-0332
Fax: 661-635-0344
E-mail: bakersfield@accountemps.com

AMERICAN SOCIETY OF WOMEN ACCOUNTANTS TWO-YEAR COLLEGE SCHOLARSHIP

Scholarship awards are presented to community college students entering their second year of an associate's degree program who have completed 15 semester hours or the equivalent by time of application deadline. Minimum cumulative GPA of 3.0 required. Must be majoring in accounting or finance. Candidates will be reviewed on leadership, character, communication skills, scholastic average and financial need.

Academic Fields/Career Goals: Accounting.

Award: Scholarship for use in sophomore year; renewable. *Number:* varies. *Amount:* varies.

Eligibility Requirements: Applicant must be enrolled or expecting to enroll full-time at a technical institution and must have an interest in leadership. Applicant must have 3.0 GPA or higher. Available to U.S. and non-U.S. citizens.

Application Requirements: Application, essay, financial need analysis, references, transcript. *Deadline:* March 1.

Contact: Glenna Minor, Peer Review and Member Services Manager
South Carolina Association of Certified Public Accountants
570 Chris Drive
West Columbia, SC 29169
Phone: 803-791-4181 Ext. 107
Fax: 803-791-4196
E-mail: gminor@scacpa.org

AMERICAN SOCIETY OF WOMEN ACCOUNTANTS UNDERGRADUATE SCHOLARSHIP

Scholarship awards are presented to students who have completed their sophomore year of college (60 semester hours or the equivalent by time of scholarship award) and are majoring in accounting or finance. Applicants will be reviewed on leadership, character, communication skills, scholastic average, and financial need.

Academic Fields/Career Goals: Accounting.

Award: Scholarship for use in junior or senior years; renewable. *Number:* varies. *Amount:* varies.

Eligibility Requirements: Applicant must be enrolled or expecting to enroll full-time at a four-year institution or university and must have an interest in leadership. Available to U.S. and non-U.S. citizens.

Application Requirements: Application, essay, references, transcript. *Deadline:* March 1.

Contact: Glenna Minor, Peer Review and Member Services Manager
South Carolina Association of Certified Public Accountants
570 Chris Drive
West Columbia, SC 29169
Phone: 803-791-4181 Ext. 107
Fax: 803-791-4196
E-mail: gminor@scacpa.org

AMERICAN WOMAN'S SOCIETY OF CPAS NATIONAL SCHOLARSHIP

Award to individuals aspiring to become a certified public accountant. Applicant must either be an entering senior, fifth year student, graduate student or a graduate, and must meet the minimum education requirements to sit for the CPA exam within one year of scholarship awarding. Minimum 3.0 GPA overall and in accounting required.

Academic Fields/Career Goals: Accounting.

Award: Scholarship for use in senior or graduate years; renewable. *Number:* varies. *Amount:* up to $2995.

Eligibility Requirements: Applicant must be enrolled or expecting to enroll full- or part-time at a four-year institution or university. Applicant must have 3.0 GPA or higher. Available to U.S. citizens.

Application Requirements: Application, essay, references, test scores, transcript. *Deadline:* June 1.

Contact: Glenna Minor, Peer Review and Member Services Manager
South Carolina Association of Certified Public Accountants
570 Chris Drive
West Columbia, SC 29169
Phone: 803-791-4181 Ext. 107
Fax: 803-791-4196
E-mail: gminor@scacpa.org

SCHOLARSHIPS FOR MINORITY ACCOUNTING STUDENTS

Scholarship program provides awards of up to $5000 to outstanding minority students with a declared accounting major and intention of pursing CPA credential. Must be enrolled as a full-time undergraduate or graduate student. All applicants must be an AICPA student affiliate member. Minimum cumulative and accounting GPA of 3.3 required.

Academic Fields/Career Goals: Accounting.

Award: Scholarship for use in freshman, sophomore, junior, senior, or graduate years; renewable. *Number:* varies. *Amount:* $1500–$5000.

Eligibility Requirements: Applicant must be American Indian/Alaska Native, Asian/Pacific Islander, Black (non-Hispanic), or Hispanic and enrolled or expecting to enroll full-time at a four-year institution or university. Applicant or parent of applicant must be member of American Institute of Certified Public Accountants. Available to U.S. citizens.

Application Requirements: Application, essay, financial need analysis, references, transcript. *Deadline:* June 2.

Contact: Glenna Minor, Peer Review and Member Services Manager
South Carolina Association of Certified Public Accountants
570 Chris Drive
West Columbia, SC 29169
Phone: 803-791-4181 Ext. 107
Fax: 803-791-4196
E-mail: gminor@scacpa.org

SOUTH DAKOTA CPA SOCIETY http://www.sdcpa.org

EXCELLENCE IN ACCOUNTING SCHOLARSHIP

Scholarships available for senior undergraduate and graduate students majoring in accounting. Must have completed 90 credit hours, demonstrated excellence in academics and leadership potential. Application available online at http://www.sdcpa.org.

Academic Fields/Career Goals: Accounting.

Award: Scholarship for use in senior or graduate years; renewable. *Number:* 4–10. *Amount:* $500–$1500.

Eligibility Requirements: Applicant must be enrolled or expecting to enroll full-time at a four-year institution or university. Available to U.S. citizens.

Application Requirements: Application, transcript. *Deadline:* December 1.

Contact: Laura Coome, Executive Director
South Dakota CPA Society
PO Box 1798
Sioux Falls, SD 57101
Phone: 605-334-3848

5TH YEAR FULL TUITION SCHOLARSHIP

Scholarship pays for the full tuition for a South Dakota student to attend an accredited South Dakota college or university. If awarded the scholarship, the student must become a member of the SD CPA Society, work for or be supervised by a member of the SD CPA Society for 2 years, and upon eligibility, must sit for a minimum of 4 parts of the CPA exam per year for two years or until completed.

Academic Fields/Career Goals: Accounting.

South Dakota CPA Society (continued)

Award: Scholarship for use in senior year; not renewable. *Number:* up to 2. *Amount:* $6800.

Eligibility Requirements: Applicant must be enrolled or expecting to enroll full-time at a four-year institution or university; resident of South Dakota and studying in South Dakota. Applicant must have 3.0 GPA or higher. Available to U.S. citizens.

Application Requirements: Application, essay, transcript. *Deadline:* December 1.

Contact: Laura Coome, Executive Director
South Dakota CPA Society
PO Box 1798
Sioux Falls, SD 57101-1798
Phone: 605-334-3848
E-mail: lcoome@iw.net

SOUTH DAKOTA RETAILERS ASSOCIATION http://www.sdra.org

SOUTH DAKOTA RETAILERS ASSOCIATION SCHOLARSHIP PROGRAM

One-time award to assist full-time students studying for a career in retailing. Applicants must have graduated from a South Dakota high school or be enrolled in postsecondary school in South Dakota. The award value and the number of awards granted varies annually.

Academic Fields/Career Goals: Accounting; Business/Consumer Services; Computer Science/Data Processing; Electrical Engineering/Electronics; Food Service/Hospitality; Graphics/Graphic Arts/Printing; Interior Design.

Award: Scholarship for use in freshman, sophomore, junior, senior, graduate, or postgraduate years; not renewable. *Number:* varies. *Amount:* $250–$1000.

Eligibility Requirements: Applicant must be enrolled or expecting to enroll full-time at a two-year or four-year or technical institution or university and studying in South Dakota. Available to U.S. and non-U.S. citizens.

Application Requirements: Application, essay, resume, references, transcript. *Deadline:* April 11.

Contact: Donna Leslie, Communications Director
South Dakota Retailers Association
PO Box 638
Pierre, SD 57501
Phone: 800-658-5545
Fax: 605-224-2059
E-mail: dleslie@sdra.org

TENNESSEE SOCIETY OF CPAS http://www.tncpa.org

TENNESSEE SOCIETY OF CPA SCHOLARSHIP

Scholarships are available only to full-time students who have completed introductory courses in accounting and/or students majoring in accounting. Applicants must be legal residents of Tennessee.

Academic Fields/Career Goals: Accounting.

Award: Scholarship for use in freshman, sophomore, junior, senior, or graduate years; not renewable. *Number:* 120–130. *Amount:* $250–$2500.

Eligibility Requirements: Applicant must be enrolled or expecting to enroll full-time at a four-year institution or university and resident of Tennessee. Available to U.S. citizens.

Application Requirements: Application, financial need analysis, references, transcript. *Deadline:* June 1.

Contact: Wendy Garvin, Member Services Manager
Tennessee Society of CPAs
201 Powell Place
Brentwood, TN 37027
Phone: 615-377-3825
Fax: 390-377-3904
E-mail: wgarvin@tscpa.com

TKE EDUCATIONAL FOUNDATION http://www.tke.org

HARRY J. DONNELLY MEMORIAL SCHOLARSHIP

One-time award of $900 given to a member of Tau Kappa Epsilon pursuing an undergraduate degree in accounting or a graduate degree in law. Applicant should have demonstrated leadership ability within his chapter, campus, or community.

Academic Fields/Career Goals: Accounting; Law/Legal Services.

Award: Scholarship for use in freshman, sophomore, junior, senior, or graduate years; not renewable. *Number:* 1. *Amount:* $900.

Eligibility Requirements: Applicant must be enrolled or expecting to enroll full-time at a four-year institution or university and must have an interest in leadership. Applicant or parent of applicant must be member of Tau Kappa Epsilon. Applicant must have 3.0 GPA or higher. Available to U.S. and non-U.S. citizens.

Application Requirements: Application, essay, photo, transcript, narrative summary of how TKE membership has benefited applicant. *Deadline:* February 29.

Contact: Gary A. Reed, President and Chief Executive Officer
TKE Educational Foundation
8645 Founders Road
Indianapolis, IN 46268-1393
Phone: 317-872-6533
Fax: 317-875-8353
E-mail: reedga@tke.org

W. ALLAN HERZOG SCHOLARSHIP

One $3000 award for an undergraduate member of TKE who is a full-time student pursuing a finance or accounting degree. Minimum 2.75 GPA required. Preference given to members of Nu Chapter. Applicant should have record of leadership within chapter and campus organizations.

Academic Fields/Career Goals: Accounting; Business/Consumer Services.

Award: Scholarship for use in freshman, sophomore, junior, or senior years; not renewable. *Number:* 1. *Amount:* $3000.

Eligibility Requirements: Applicant must be enrolled or expecting to enroll full-time at a four-year institution or university; male and must have an interest in leadership. Applicant or parent of applicant must be member of Tau Kappa Epsilon. Available to U.S. and non-U.S. citizens.

Application Requirements: Application, essay, photo, transcript, narrative summary of how TKE membership has benefited applicant. *Deadline:* February 29.

Contact: Gary A. Reed, President and Chief Executive Officer
TKE Educational Foundation
8645 Founders Road
Indianapolis, IN 46268-1393
Phone: 317-872-6533
Fax: 317-875-8353
E-mail: reedga@tke.org

UNITED NEGRO COLLEGE FUND http://www.uncf.org

BEST BUY ENTERPRISE EMPLOYEE SCHOLARSHIP

Offers two scholarship programs: for employee and non-employee. For the employee program, applicant must have worked for six consecutive months for Best Buy to be considered. For either program, applicants must attend a UNCF member colleges or universities and must demonstrate an unmet financial need. Minimum 3.0 GPA required. Prospective applicants should complete the student profile found at Web site: http://www.uncf.org.

Academic Fields/Career Goals: Accounting; Business/Consumer Services; Communications; Journalism.

Award: Scholarship for use in freshman, sophomore, junior, or senior years; not renewable. *Number:* 2. *Amount:* $2500–$5000.

Eligibility Requirements: Applicant must be Black (non-Hispanic) and enrolled or expecting to enroll full-time at a four-year institution or university. Applicant must have 3.0 GPA or higher. Available to U.S. and non-U.S. citizens.

Application Requirements: Application. *Deadline:* varies.

Contact: Director, Program Services
United Negro College Fund
8260 Willow Oaks Corporate Drive
PO Box 10444
Fairfax, VA 22031-8044
Phone: 800-331-2244
E-mail: rebecca.bennett@uncf.org

CARDINAL HEALTH SCHOLARSHIP

Open to all four-year accredited undergraduate colleges. Students must be a rising sophomore or junior, majoring in accounting/finance, IS, marketing purchasing/operations, engineering or chemistry, or in their first or second year of pursuing a degree in pharmacy. Applicants must demonstrate non-collegiate leadership experience. The scholarship value is $5000.

Academic Fields/Career Goals: Accounting; Business/Consumer Services; Chemical Engineering; Civil Engineering; Computer Science/Data Processing; Engineering/Technology; Mechanical Engineering; Pharmacy.

Award: Scholarship for use in freshman, sophomore, junior, or senior years; renewable. *Number:* varies. *Amount:* $5000.

Eligibility Requirements: Applicant must be Black (non-Hispanic); enrolled or expecting to enroll full-time at a four-year institution or university and must have an interest in leadership. Applicant must have 3.0 GPA or higher. Available to U.S. and non-U.S. citizens.

Application Requirements: Application, financial need analysis, FAFSA, Student Aid Report (SAR). *Deadline:* October 30.

Contact: Director, Program Services
United Negro College Fund
8260 Willow Oaks Corporate Drive
PO Box 10444
Fairfax, VA 22031-8044
Phone: 800-331-2244
E-mail: rebecca.bennett@uncf.org

CARGILL SCHOLARSHIP PROGRAM

Scholarship awarded to undergraduate freshman, sophomore, or junior enrolled in a UNCF member college or university or in one of the following institutions: Kansas State University, University of Illinois, University of Minnesota, Iowa State University, North Carolina A & T State University and University of Wisconsin-Madison. The students should have a minimum GPA of 3.0 and scholarship value is $5000.

Academic Fields/Career Goals: Accounting; Agriculture; Animal/Veterinary Sciences; Biology; Chemical Engineering; Computer Science/Data Processing; Food Science/Nutrition; Mechanical Engineering.

Award: Scholarship for use in freshman, sophomore, or junior years; renewable. *Number:* varies. *Amount:* $5000.

Eligibility Requirements: Applicant must be Black (non-Hispanic) and enrolled or expecting to enroll full-time at a four-year institution or university. Applicant must have 3.0 GPA or higher. Available to U.S. and non-U.S. citizens.

Application Requirements: Application, financial need analysis, FAFSA, Student Aid Report (SAR). *Deadline:* February 28.

Contact: Director, Program Services
United Negro College Fund
8260 Willow Oaks Corporate Drive
PO Box 10444
Fairfax, VA 22031-8044
Phone: 800-331-2244
E-mail: rebecca.bennett@uncf.org

EDWARD M. NAGEL FOUNDATION SCHOLARSHIP

Applicants must be residents of California within the top 25 percent of their high school graduating class to apply for this scholarship. Must be enrolled in a UNCF member college or university and pursue a degree in business, economics, or accounting. The scholarship value ranges from $2000 to $5000.

Academic Fields/Career Goals: Accounting; Business/Consumer Services; Economics.

Award: Scholarship for use in freshman, sophomore, junior, senior, or graduate years; not renewable. *Number:* varies. *Amount:* $2000–$5000.

Eligibility Requirements: Applicant must be Black (non-Hispanic); enrolled or expecting to enroll full-time at a four-year institution or university and resident of California. Applicant must have 3.0 GPA or higher. Available to U.S. citizens.

Application Requirements: Application, financial need analysis, FAFSA. *Deadline:* varies.

Contact: Director, Program Services
United Negro College Fund
8260 Willow Oaks Corporate Drive
PO Box 10444
Fairfax, VA 22031-8044
Phone: 800-331-2244
E-mail: rebecca.bennett@uncf.org

FORD/UNCF CORPORATE SCHOLARS PROGRAM

Annual scholarships to selected African-American college students with a unique educational opportunity. Must be undergraduate sophomores majoring in engineering, finance, accounting, information systems, marketing, computer science, operations management, or electrical engineering at a UNCF member college or university or at a selected historically black college or university. Minimum 3.0 GPA required.

Academic Fields/Career Goals: Accounting; Business/Consumer Services; Computer Science/Data Processing; Electrical Engineering/Electronics; Engineering/Technology.

Award: Scholarship for use in sophomore year; not renewable. *Number:* 1. *Amount:* up to $5000.

Eligibility Requirements: Applicant must be Black (non-Hispanic); enrolled or expecting to enroll full-time at a four-year institution and resident of Michigan. Applicant must have 3.0 GPA or higher. Available to U.S. citizens.

Application Requirements: Application, essay, financial need analysis, references, transcript. *Deadline:* June 1.

Contact: Director, Program Services
United Negro College Fund
8260 Willow Oaks Corporate Drive
PO Box 10444
Fairfax, VA 22031-8044
Phone: 800-331-2244
E-mail: rebecca.bennett@uncf.org

MASTERCARD WORLDWIDE SCHOLARS PROGRAM

Scholarship awarded covers the cost of tuition, fees, and room and board for students attending a UNCF member college or university. Students must major in business, finance, accounting, information systems, or marketing. Minimum 3.0 GPA required. Prospective applicants should complete the student profile found at Web site: http://www.uncf.org.

Academic Fields/Career Goals: Accounting; Business/Consumer Services.

Award: Scholarship for use in sophomore or junior years; not renewable. *Number:* 1. *Amount:* $4500.

Eligibility Requirements: Applicant must be Black (non-Hispanic); enrolled or expecting to enroll full-time at a four-year institution or university and resident of Connecticut, New Jersey, or New York. Applicant must have 3.0 GPA or higher. Available to U.S. and Canadian citizens.

Application Requirements: Application, financial need analysis. *Deadline:* varies.

Contact: Director, Program Services
United Negro College Fund
8260 Willow Oaks Corporate Drive
PO Box 10444
Fairfax, VA 22031-8044
Phone: 800-331-2244
E-mail: rebecca.bennett@uncf.org

MBIA/WILLIAM O. BAILEY SCHOLARS PROGRAM

Two full-tuition awards given to qualified juniors from New York, New Jersey, or Connecticut with at least a 3.0 GPA and majoring in business or finance. Must attend a UNCF member college or university. For more details visit Web site: http://www.uncf.org.

Academic Fields/Career Goals: Accounting; Business/Consumer Services.

United Negro College Fund (continued)

Award: Scholarship for use in junior year; not renewable. *Number:* 2. *Amount:* varies.

Eligibility Requirements: Applicant must be Black (non-Hispanic); enrolled or expecting to enroll full-time at a four-year institution or university and resident of Connecticut, New Jersey, or New York. Applicant must have 3.0 GPA or higher. Available to U.S. citizens.

Application Requirements: Application, financial need analysis. *Deadline:* continuous.

Contact: Director, Program Services
United Negro College Fund
8260 Willow Oaks Corporate Drive
PO Box 10444
Fairfax, VA 22031-8044
Phone: 800-331-2244
E-mail: rebecca.bennett@uncf.org

NASCAR/WENDELL SCOTT, SR. SCHOLARSHIP

Award for full-time junior or senior undergraduates or part-time graduate students. Undergraduates must have a 3.0 GPA and graduate students must have a 3.2 GPA. Undergraduates receive an award of $1500. Graduate recipients receive $2000. Please visit Web site for more information: http://www.uncf.org.

Academic Fields/Career Goals: Accounting; Business/Consumer Services; Communications; Computer Science/Data Processing; Engineering/Technology; Mechanical Engineering.

Award: Scholarship for use in junior, senior, or graduate years; renewable. *Number:* varies. *Amount:* $1500–$2000.

Eligibility Requirements: Applicant must be Black (non-Hispanic) and enrolled or expecting to enroll full- or part-time at a four-year institution or university. Available to U.S. citizens.

Application Requirements: Application, financial need analysis, photo, resume, references, transcript, FAFSA, Student Aid Report (SAR). *Deadline:* February 27.

Contact: Director, Program Services
United Negro College Fund
8260 Willow Oaks Corporate Drive
PO Box 10444
Fairfax, VA 22031-8044
Phone: 800-331-2244
E-mail: rebecca.bennett@uncf.org

PRINCIPAL FINANCIAL GROUP SCHOLARSHIPS

Scholarships available to students majoring in business, finance, information systems, or banking who are attending a UNCF member college or university. Minimum 3.0 GPA required. Prospective applicants should complete the Student Profile found at Web site: http://www.uncf.org.

Academic Fields/Career Goals: Accounting; Business/Consumer Services; Computer Science/Data Processing.

Award: Scholarship for use in freshman, sophomore, junior, or senior years; not renewable. *Number:* varies. *Amount:* up to $12,000.

Eligibility Requirements: Applicant must be Black (non-Hispanic) and enrolled or expecting to enroll full- or part-time at a four-year institution or university. Applicant must have 3.0 GPA or higher. Available to U.S. citizens.

Application Requirements: Application, financial need analysis. *Deadline:* March 1.

Contact: Director, Program Services
United Negro College Fund
8260 Willow Oaks Corporate Drive
PO Box 10444
Fairfax, VA 22031-8044
Phone: 800-331-2244
E-mail: rebecca.bennett@uncf.org

SPRINT NEXTEL SCHOLARSHIP/INTERNSHIP

Award includes a summer internship and a need-based scholarship to cover educational expenses for junior year. Must major in business, economics, accounting, math, statistics, engineering related or computer related studies. Must have 3.0 GPA. Visit Web site for more information: http://www.uncf.org.

Academic Fields/Career Goals: Accounting; Business/Consumer Services; Civil Engineering; Computer Science/Data Processing; Construction Engineering/Management; Economics; Electrical Engineering/Electronics; Engineering/Technology; Mechanical Engineering; Physical Sciences and Math.

Award: Scholarship for use in junior year; renewable. *Number:* varies. *Amount:* up to $5000.

Eligibility Requirements: Applicant must be American Indian/Alaska Native, Asian/Pacific Islander, Black (non-Hispanic), or Hispanic and enrolled or expecting to enroll full- or part-time at a four-year institution or university. Applicant must have 3.0 GPA or higher. Available to U.S. citizens.

Application Requirements: Application, financial need analysis, resume, references, transcript, FAFSA, Student Aid Report (SAR). *Deadline:* April 10.

Contact: Director, Program Services
United Negro College Fund
8260 Willow Oaks Corporate Drive
PO Box 10444
Fairfax, VA 22031-8044
Phone: 800-331-2244
E-mail: rebecca.bennett@uncf.org

TOYOTA SCHOLARSHIP

Scholarship to students with at least a 3.0 GPA majoring in engineering, business, finance, economics, accounting, information systems, marketing, communications, computer science, liberal arts, political science, english, history, psychology, electrical engineering, information technology, computer engineering, mechanical engineering, management information systems. Must attend one of the following UNCF member colleges or universities: Bethune-Cookman College, Clark Atlanta, Morehouse, Morris Brown, Spelman, Tuskegee, or Xavier.

Academic Fields/Career Goals: Accounting; Business/Consumer Services; Communications; Computer Science/Data Processing; Electrical Engineering/Electronics; History; Literature/English/Writing; Mechanical Engineering; Political Science; Psychology.

Award: Scholarship for use in freshman year; not renewable. *Number:* varies. *Amount:* $7500.

Eligibility Requirements: Applicant must be Black (non-Hispanic) and enrolled or expecting to enroll full-time at a four-year institution or university. Applicant must have 3.0 GPA or higher. Available to U.S. and non-U.S. citizens.

Application Requirements: Application, financial need analysis. *Deadline:* December 15.

Contact: Director, Program Services
United Negro College Fund
8260 Willow Oaks Corporate Drive
PO Box 10444
Fairfax, VA 22031-8044
Phone: 800-331-2244
E-mail: rebecca.bennett@uncf.org

UBS/PAINEWEBBER SCHOLARSHIPS

Applicant must be a sophomore or junior during the application at one of UNCF member institutions. Must have a GPA of 3.0 or above. Preferred majors include accounting, business administration, economics, finance, or any other business-related field. Have a documented unmet financial need verified by the financial aid director.

Academic Fields/Career Goals: Accounting; Business/Consumer Services.

Award: Scholarship for use in sophomore or junior years; not renewable. *Number:* 1. *Amount:* $8000.

Eligibility Requirements: Applicant must be Black (non-Hispanic) and enrolled or expecting to enroll full- or part-time at a four-year institution or university. Applicant must have 3.0 GPA or higher. Available to U.S. citizens.

Application Requirements: Application, essay, financial need analysis, photo, resume, references, transcript, letter of nomination. *Deadline:* November 27.

Contact: William Dunham, Scholarship Committee
United Negro College Fund
8260 Willow Oaks Corporate Drive, PO Box 10444
Fairfax, VA 22031
Phone: 800-331-2244

WELLS FARGO/UNCF SCHOLARSHIP FUND

Award for sophomores, juniors and graduate students. Must have 2.5 GPA. Must be a resident of California, Minnesota, Indiana, Arizona, Illinois, Ohio, Washington, Oregon, Wisconsin, Michigan, Alaska, Iowa, Texas, Nebraska, Colorado, Idaho, Montana, Nevada, New Mexico, North Dakota, South Dakota, Utah or Wyoming.

Academic Fields/Career Goals: Accounting; Architecture; Business/Consumer Services; Computer Science/Data Processing; Electrical Engineering/Electronics.

Award: Scholarship for use in freshman year; renewable. *Number:* varies. *Amount:* up to $2000.

Eligibility Requirements: Applicant must be American Indian/Alaska Native or Black (non-Hispanic) and enrolled or expecting to enroll full-time at a four-year institution or university. Applicant must have 2.5 GPA or higher. Available to U.S. citizens.

Application Requirements: Application, financial need analysis, FAFSA, Student Aid Report (SAR). *Deadline:* October 31.

Contact: Director, Program Services
United Negro College Fund
8260 Willow Oaks Corporate Drive
PO Box 10444
Fairfax, VA 22031-8044
Phone: 800-331-2244
E-mail: rebecca.bennett@uncf.org

VIRCHOW, KRAUSE & COMPANY, LLP http://www.virchowkrause.com

VIRCHOW, KRAUSE AND COMPANY SCHOLARSHIP

One-time scholarship for students enrolled either full-time or part-time in accredited colleges or universities of Wisconsin, majoring in accounting.

Academic Fields/Career Goals: Accounting.

Award: Scholarship for use in freshman, sophomore, junior, or senior years; not renewable. *Number:* up to 3. *Amount:* up to $1000.

Eligibility Requirements: Applicant must be enrolled or expecting to enroll full- or part-time at a two-year or four-year institution or university and studying in Wisconsin. Available to U.S. citizens.

Application Requirements: Application, transcript. *Deadline:* varies.

Contact: Darbie Miller, Human Resources Coordinator
Virchow, Krause & Company, LLP
4600 American Parkway, PO Box 7398
Madison, WI 53707-7398
Phone: 608-240-2474
Fax: 608-249-1411
E-mail: dmiller@virchowkrause.com

VIRGINIA SOCIETY OF CERTIFIED PUBLIC ACCOUNTANTS EDUCATION FOUNDATION http://www.cpastudentzone.com

H. BURTON BATES JR. ANNUAL SCHOLARSHIP

Award to a junior or senior accounting major currently enrolled in an accredited Virginia college or university, or to a student who has earned their undergraduate degree and is taking additional coursework in order to sit for the CPA exam. Must demonstrate academic excellence and financial need.

Academic Fields/Career Goals: Accounting.

Award: Scholarship for use in junior, senior, or graduate years; not renewable. *Number:* 1. *Amount:* $2500.

Eligibility Requirements: Applicant must be enrolled or expecting to enroll full-time at a four-year institution or university; resident of Virginia and studying in Virginia. Applicant must have 3.0 GPA or higher. Available to U.S. citizens.

Application Requirements: Application, essay, resume, references, transcript. *Deadline:* January 10.

Contact: Ms. Molly Wash, Career and Academic Relations Director
Virginia Society of Certified Public Accountants Education Foundation
4309 Cox Road
Glen Allen, VA 23060
E-mail: mwash@vscpa.com

THOMAS M. BERRY JR. ANNUAL SCHOLARSHIP

Awarded to a student who has demonstrated academic excellence, financial need, and exemplary leadership skills. Applicant must have completed three credit hours of accounting and be currently registered for at least three more accounting credit hours.

Academic Fields/Career Goals: Accounting.

Award: Scholarship for use in sophomore, junior, senior, or graduate years; not renewable. *Number:* 1. *Amount:* $2500.

Eligibility Requirements: Applicant must be enrolled or expecting to enroll full- or part-time at a two-year or four-year institution or university and studying in Virginia. Applicant must have 2.5 GPA or higher. Available to U.S. citizens.

Application Requirements: Application, essay, resume, references, transcript. *Deadline:* January 10.

Contact: Ms. Molly Wash, Career and Academic Relations Director
Virginia Society of Certified Public Accountants Education Foundation
4309 Cox Road
Glen Allen, VA 23060

VIRGINIA SOCIETY OF CPAS EDUCATIONAL FOUNDATION MINORITY SCHOLARSHIP

One-time award for a student currently enrolled in a Virginia college or university undergraduate program with the intent to pursue accounting or a business related field of study. Applicant must have at least six hours of accounting and be currently registered for at least 3 more accounting credit hours. Applicant must be a member of one of the VSCPA-defined minority groups (African-American, Hispanic-American, Native American or Asian Pacific American). Minimum overall and accounting GPA of 3.0 is required.

Academic Fields/Career Goals: Accounting; Business/Consumer Services.

Award: Scholarship for use in freshman, sophomore, junior, or senior years; not renewable. *Number:* 3–5. *Amount:* $1500.

Eligibility Requirements: Applicant must be American Indian/Alaska Native, Asian/Pacific Islander, Black (non-Hispanic), or Hispanic; enrolled or expecting to enroll full- or part-time at a four-year institution or university and studying in Virginia. Applicant must have 3.0 GPA or higher. Available to U.S. citizens.

Application Requirements: Application, essay, resume, references, transcript. *Deadline:* January 10.

Contact: Tracey Zink, Community Relations Coordinator
Virginia Society of Certified Public Accountants Education Foundation
PO Box 4620
Glen Allen, VA 23058-4620
Phone: 800-733-8272
Fax: 804-273-1741
E-mail: tzink@vscpa.com

VIRGINIA SOCIETY OF CPAS EDUCATIONAL FOUNDATION UNDERGRADUATE SCHOLARSHIP

One-time award for a student currently enrolled in a Virginia college or university undergraduate program with the intent to pursue accounting or a business related field of study. Applicant must have at least six hours of accounting and be currently registered for at least 3 more accounting credit hours. Minimum overall and accounting GPA of 3.0 is required.

Academic Fields/Career Goals: Accounting; Business/Consumer Services.

Award: Scholarship for use in freshman, sophomore, junior, or senior years; not renewable. *Number:* 8. *Amount:* $1500.

Virginia Society of Certified Public Accountants Education Foundation (continued)

Eligibility Requirements: Applicant must be enrolled or expecting to enroll full- or part-time at a four-year institution or university and studying in Virginia. Applicant must have 3.0 GPA or higher. Available to U.S. citizens.

Application Requirements: Application, essay, resume, references, transcript. *Deadline:* January 10.

Contact: Tracey Zink, Community Relations Coordinator
Virginia Society of Certified Public Accountants Education Foundation
PO Box 4620
Glen Allen, VA 23058-4620
Phone: 800-733-8272
Fax: 804-273-1741
E-mail: tzink@vscpa.com

WASHINGTON SOCIETY OF CERTIFIED PUBLIC ACCOUNTANTS http://www.wscpa.org

WSCPA CHAPTER SCHOLARSHIPS

Scholarships between $1000 and $3000 are available to a students who either reside in or graduated from a high school in specific WSCPA Chapter geographical areas. Students must be in at least their junior year and have declared accounting as their major. Minimum 3.0 GPA required.

Academic Fields/Career Goals: Accounting.

Award: Scholarship for use in junior, senior, or graduate years; not renewable. *Number:* 1–24. *Amount:* $1000–$3000.

Eligibility Requirements: Applicant must be enrolled or expecting to enroll full-time at a four-year institution or university and studying in Washington. Applicant must have 3.0 GPA or higher. Available to U.S. citizens.

Application Requirements: Application, essay, financial need analysis, resume, references, transcript. *Deadline:* March 1.

Contact: Mark Peterson, Academic and Student Relations Administrator
Washington Society of Certified Public Accountants
902 140th Avenue, NE
Bellevue, WA 98005-3480
Phone: 425-644-4800
Fax: 425-586-1119
E-mail: mpeterson@wscpa.org

WSCPA SCHOLARSHIPS FOR ACCOUNTING MAJORS

These $1000 merit-based and $3000 need-based scholarships are available to college juniors and seniors majoring in accounting. The one-time award is intended for those studying at a four-year college or university in the state of Washington and must be used for full-time study. Must maintain a 3.00 GPA.

Academic Fields/Career Goals: Accounting.

Award: Scholarship for use in junior, senior, graduate, or postgraduate years; not renewable. *Number:* 1–10. *Amount:* $1000–$3000.

Eligibility Requirements: Applicant must be enrolled or expecting to enroll full-time at a four-year institution or university and studying in Washington. Applicant must have 3.0 GPA or higher. Available to U.S. citizens.

Application Requirements: Application, essay, financial need analysis, resume, references, transcript. *Deadline:* March 1.

Contact: Mark Peterson, Academic and Student Relations Administrator
Washington Society of Certified Public Accountants
902 140th Avenue, NE
Bellevue, WA 98005-3480
Phone: 425-586-1118
Fax: 425-586-1119
E-mail: mpeterson@wscpa.org

WISS & COMPANY, CPA http://www.wiss.com

WISS EDWARD W. O'CONNELL MEMORIAL SCHOLARSHIP

Two to five annual awards to New Jersey high school seniors who will declare a major in accounting. Applicants must have already been accepted into an accredited New Jersey college or university as a matriculating student, full-time or part-time. Minimum 3.0 GPA required. Must be a New Jersey resident for a minimum of two years.

Academic Fields/Career Goals: Accounting.

Award: Scholarship for use in freshman, sophomore, junior, or senior years; not renewable. *Number:* 2–5. *Amount:* $1500–$2000.

Eligibility Requirements: Applicant must be enrolled or expecting to enroll full-time at a four-year institution or university; resident of New Jersey and studying in New Jersey. Applicant must have 3.0 GPA or higher. Available to U.S. citizens.

Application Requirements: Application, essay, references, transcript. *Deadline:* April 1.

Contact: Donna Merer, Scholarship Coordinator
Wiss & Company, CPA
354 Eisenhower Parkway
Livingston, NJ 07039
Phone: 973-994-9400
Fax: 973-992-6760

AFRICAN STUDIES

AMERICAN HISTORICAL ASSOCIATION http://www.historians.org

WESLEY-LOGAN PRIZE

Prize offered for book on some aspect of the history of dispersion, settlement, adjustment, and return of peoples originally from Africa. Only books of high scholarly and literary merit considered. Books published between May 1 and April 30 of the current year are eligible. Copies of book must be sent to each committee member.

Academic Fields/Career Goals: African Studies; Area/Ethnic Studies; History; International Migration.

Award: Prize for use in freshman, sophomore, junior, senior, graduate, or postgraduate years; not renewable. *Number:* 1. *Amount:* varies.

Eligibility Requirements: Applicant must be enrolled or expecting to enroll full- or part-time at a four-year institution or university and must have an interest in writing. Available to U.S. citizens.

Application Requirements: Applicant must enter a contest. *Deadline:* May 15.

Contact: Book Prize Administrator
American Historical Association
400 A Street, SE
Washington, DC 20003
E-mail: aha@theaha.org

AGRIBUSINESS

CALIFORNIA FARM BUREAU SCHOLARSHIP FOUNDATION http://www.cfbf.com

CALIFORNIA FARM BUREAU SCHOLARSHIP

Renewable award given to students attending a four-year college in California. Applicants must be California residents preparing for a career in the agricultural industry.

Academic Fields/Career Goals: Agribusiness; Agriculture.

Award: Scholarship for use in freshman, sophomore, junior, or senior years; renewable. *Number:* up to 30. *Amount:* $1800–$2750.

Eligibility Requirements: Applicant must be enrolled or expecting to enroll full-time at a four-year institution; resident of California and studying in California. Available to U.S. citizens.

Application Requirements: Application, essay, interview, references, transcript. *Deadline:* March 1.

Contact: Darlene Licciardo, Scholarship Coordinator
California Farm Bureau Scholarship Foundation
2300 River Plaza Drive
Sacramento, CA 95833
Phone: 916-561-5500
Fax: 916-561-5690
E-mail: dlicciardo@cfbf.com

CHS FOUNDATION http://www.chsfoundation.org

AGRICULTURE SCHOLARSHIPS

Merit-based awards for students enrolled in agricultural programs at participating vocational or technical and community colleges. Application must be submitted through the participating school, then the school submits ten applications to the foundation. Recipients are selected in the spring. One-time award of up to $750.

Academic Fields/Career Goals: Agribusiness; Agriculture.

Award: Scholarship for use in freshman or sophomore years; not renewable. *Number:* 50. *Amount:* up to $750.

Eligibility Requirements: Applicant must be enrolled or expecting to enroll full-time at a two-year or technical institution; resident of Colorado, Idaho, Iowa, Kansas, Minnesota, Montana, Nebraska, North Dakota, Oklahoma, Oregon, South Dakota, Utah, Washington, Wisconsin, or Wyoming and studying in Colorado, Idaho, Iowa, Kansas, Minnesota, Montana, Nebraska, North Dakota, Oklahoma, Oregon, South Dakota, or Utah. Available to U.S. and non-U.S. citizens.

Application Requirements: Application, resume, transcript. *Deadline:* continuous.

Contact: Scholarship Committee
CHS Foundation
5500 Cenex Drive
Inver Grove Heights, MN 55077
Phone: 651-355-5129
Fax: 651-355-5073

COOPERATIVE STUDIES SCHOLARSHIPS

Renewable awards for college juniors and seniors attending agricultural colleges of participating universities. Must be enrolled in courses on cooperative principles and business practices. Each university selects a recipient in the spring. If the award is given in the junior year, the student is eligible for an additional $750 in their senior year without reapplying provided the eligibility requirements are met. A maximum of $1500 will be awarded to any one student in the cooperative studies program.

Academic Fields/Career Goals: Agribusiness; Agriculture.

Award: Scholarship for use in junior or senior years; renewable. *Number:* 82. *Amount:* $750–$1500.

Eligibility Requirements: Applicant must be enrolled or expecting to enroll full-time at a four-year institution or university; resident of Colorado, Idaho, Iowa, Kansas, Minnesota, Montana, Nebraska, North Dakota, Oklahoma, Oregon, South Dakota, Utah, Washington, Wisconsin, or Wyoming and studying in Colorado, Idaho, Iowa, Kansas, Minnesota, Montana, Nebraska, North Dakota, Oklahoma, Oregon, South Dakota, or Utah. Available to U.S. and non-U.S. citizens.

Application Requirements: Application, resume, transcript. *Deadline:* varies.

Contact: Mary Kaste, Scholarship Director
CHS Foundation
5500 Cenex Drive
Inver Grove Heights, MN 55077
Phone: 651-355-6000
Fax: 651-355-5073
E-mail: mary.kaste@chsinc.com

GOLF COURSE SUPERINTENDENTS ASSOCIATION OF AMERICA http://www.gcsaa.org

GOLF COURSE SUPERINTENDENTS ASSOCIATION OF AMERICA STUDENT ESSAY CONTEST

Up to three awards for essays focusing on the golf course management profession. Undergraduates and graduate students pursuing turf grass science, agronomy, or any field related to golf course management may apply. Applicant must be a member of GCSAA. In addition to cash prizes, winning entries may be published or excerpted in News-line or Golf Course Management magazine.

Academic Fields/Career Goals: Agribusiness; Horticulture/Floriculture; Recreation, Parks, Leisure Studies.

Award: Prize for use in freshman, sophomore, junior, senior, or graduate years; not renewable. *Number:* up to 3. *Amount:* $1000–$2000.

Eligibility Requirements: Applicant must be enrolled or expecting to enroll full-time at a two-year or four-year institution or university. Applicant or parent of applicant must be member of Golf Course Superintendents Association of America. Available to U.S. and non-U.S. citizens.

Application Requirements: Application, applicant must enter a contest, essay. *Deadline:* March 31.

Contact: Mischia Wright, Senior Manager, Development
Golf Course Superintendents Association of America
1421 Research Park Drive
Lawrence, KS 66049-3859
Phone: 800-472-7878 Ext. 4424
Fax: 785-832-4449
E-mail: mwright@gcsaa.org

HOLSTEIN ASSOCIATION USA INC. http://www.holsteinusa.com

ROBERT H. RUMLER SCHOLARSHIP

Awards to encourage deserving and qualified persons with an established interest in the dairy field, who have demonstrated leadership qualities and managerial abilities to pursue a master's degree in business administration.

Academic Fields/Career Goals: Agribusiness; Business/Consumer Services.

Award: Scholarship for use in freshman, sophomore, junior, senior, or graduate years; not renewable. *Number:* 1. *Amount:* $3000.

Eligibility Requirements: Applicant must be enrolled or expecting to enroll full-time at an institution or university and must have an interest in leadership. Applicant must have 3.0 GPA or higher. Available to U.S. and non-U.S. citizens.

Application Requirements: Application, essay, photo, references, transcript. *Deadline:* April 15.

Contact: John Meyer, Chief Executive Officer
Holstein Association USA Inc.
One Holstein Place, PO Box 808
Brattleboro, VT 05302-0808
Phone: 802-254-4551
Fax: 802-254-8251
E-mail: jmeyer@holstein.com

INTERTRIBAL TIMBER COUNCIL http://www.itcnet.org

TRUMAN D. PICARD SCHOLARSHIP

The program is dedicated to assisting Native American/Native-Alaskan youth seeking careers in natural resources. Graduating senior high school students and those currently attending institutions of higher education are encouraged to apply. A valid tribal/Alaska native corporation's enrollment card is required.

Academic Fields/Career Goals: Agribusiness; Agriculture; Natural Resources.

Award: Scholarship for use in freshman, sophomore, junior, senior, or graduate years; not renewable. *Number:* 10–15. *Amount:* $1500–$2000.

Eligibility Requirements: Applicant must be American Indian/Alaska Native and enrolled or expecting to enroll full-time at a four-year institution or university. Available to U.S. citizens.

Application Requirements: Application, essay, resume, references, transcript, enrollment card. *Deadline:* March 31.

Contact: Joann Reynolds, Education Committee
Intertribal Timber Council
1112-21st Avenue, NE
Portland, OR 97232-2114
Phone: 503-282-4296
Fax: 503-282-1274
E-mail: itc1@teleport.com

MAINE DEPARTMENT OF AGRICULTURE, FOOD AND RURAL RESOURCES http://www.maine.gov/agriculture

MAINE RURAL REHABILITATION FUND SCHOLARSHIP PROGRAM

One-time scholarship open to Maine residents enrolled in or accepted by any school, college, or university. Must be full time and demonstrate financial need. Those opting for a Maine institution given preference. Major must lead to an agricultural career. Minimum 3.0 GPA required.

Academic Fields/Career Goals: Agribusiness; Agriculture; Animal/Veterinary Sciences.

Maine Department of Agriculture, Food and Rural Resources (continued)

Award: Scholarship for use in freshman, sophomore, junior, senior, graduate, or postgraduate years; not renewable. *Number:* 10–20. *Amount:* $800–$2000.

Eligibility Requirements: Applicant must be enrolled or expecting to enroll full-time at a two-year or four-year or technical institution or university and resident of Maine. Applicant must have 3.0 GPA or higher. Available to U.S. citizens.

Application Requirements: Application, autobiography, financial need analysis, transcript. *Deadline:* June 15.

Contact: Jane Aiudi, Director of Marketing
Maine Department of Agriculture, Food and Rural Resources
28 State House Station
Augusta, ME 04333-0028
Phone: 207-287-7628
Fax: 207-287-5576
E-mail: jane.aiudi@maine.gov

MINNESOTA SOYBEAN RESEARCH AND PROMOTION COUNCIL http://www.mnsoybean.org

MINNESOTA SOYBEAN RESEARCH AND PROMOTION COUNCIL YOUTH SOYBEAN SCHOLARSHIP

Eight $1000 awards available to high school seniors and two $2000 awards for juniors and seniors in college who are residents of Minnesota. Must demonstrate activity in agriculture with plans to study in an agricultural related program. For more details see Web site: http://www.mnsoybean.org.

Academic Fields/Career Goals: Agribusiness; Agriculture; Food Science/Nutrition.

Award: Scholarship for use in freshman, junior, or senior years; not renewable. *Number:* 10. *Amount:* $1000–$2000.

Eligibility Requirements: Applicant must be enrolled or expecting to enroll full-time at a two-year or four-year or technical institution or university and resident of Minnesota. Applicant or parent of applicant must have employment or volunteer experience in agriculture or farming. Available to U.S. citizens.

Application Requirements: Application, references, self-addressed stamped envelope, transcript. *Deadline:* February 26.

Contact: Vicki Trudeau, Scholarship Coordinator
Minnesota Soybean Research and Promotion Council
151 Saint Andrews Court, Suite 710
Mankato, MN 56001
Phone: 888-896-9678
Fax: 507-388-6751
E-mail: vicki@mnsoybean.com

MONSANTO AGRIBUSINESS SCHOLARSHIP http://www.monsanto.ca

MONSANTO CANADA OPPORTUNITY SCHOLARSHIP PROGRAM

Scholarship available to a first year postsecondary student who is a Canadian citizen. Must be majoring in the agriculture, forestry, business, or biotechnology at a Canadian institution.

Academic Fields/Career Goals: Agribusiness; Agriculture; Science, Technology, and Society.

Award: Scholarship for use in freshman year; not renewable. *Number:* 50–60. *Amount:* $1500.

Eligibility Requirements: Applicant must be of Canadian heritage; high school student and planning to enroll or expecting to enroll full-time at a four-year or technical institution or university. Available to Canadian citizens.

Application Requirements: Application, essay, references, transcript, university/college acceptance letter. *Deadline:* May 16.

Contact: Scholarship Coordinator
Monsanto Agribusiness Scholarship
900-One Research Road
Winnipeg, MB R3T 6E3
Canada
Phone: 204-985-1000
Fax: 888-667-4944

NATIONAL CATTLEMEN'S FOUNDATION http://www.nationalcattlemensfoundation.org

CME BEEF INDUSTRY SCHOLARSHIP

Ten $1500 scholarships will be awarded to students who intend to pursue a career in the beef industry, including areas such as agricultural education, communications, production, or research. Must be enrolled as an undergraduate student in a four-year institution.

Academic Fields/Career Goals: Agribusiness; Agriculture; Communications.

Award: Scholarship for use in freshman, sophomore, junior, or senior years; not renewable. *Number:* 10. *Amount:* $1500.

Eligibility Requirements: Applicant must be enrolled or expecting to enroll full-time at a four-year institution or university. Available to U.S. citizens.

Application Requirements: Application, essay, references, transcript. *Deadline:* varies.

Contact: RoxAnn Johnson, Executive Director
National Cattlemen's Foundation
9110 East Nichols Avenue, Suite 300
Centennial, CO 80112
Phone: 303-850-3388
Fax: 303-770-7745
E-mail: mcf@beef.org

NATIONAL DAIRY SHRINE http://www.dairyshrine.org

NDS STUDENT RECOGNITION CONTEST

Awards available to college seniors enrolled in dairy science courses. Applicants must be nominated by their college or university professor and must intend to continue in the dairy field. A college or university may nominate up to 2 applicants.

Academic Fields/Career Goals: Agribusiness; Agriculture; Animal/Veterinary Sciences; Food Science/Nutrition.

Award: Prize for use in senior year; not renewable. *Number:* varies. *Amount:* $500–$1500.

Eligibility Requirements: Applicant must be enrolled or expecting to enroll full-time at a four-year institution or university. Available to U.S. citizens.

Application Requirements: Application, applicant must enter a contest, references, transcript, nomination. *Deadline:* March 15.

Contact: Maurice E. Core, Executive Director
National Dairy Shrine
1224 Alton Darby Creek Road
Columbus, OH 43228-4792
Phone: 614-878-5333
Fax: 614-870-2622
E-mail: shrine@cobaselect.com

NATIONAL POTATO COUNCIL WOMEN'S AUXILIARY http://www.nationalpotatocouncil.org

POTATO INDUSTRY SCHOLARSHIP

The auxiliary scholarship is for full-time students studying in a potato-related field, who desire to work in the potato industry after graduation. Minimum 3.0 GPA required.

Academic Fields/Career Goals: Agribusiness; Agriculture; Food Science/Nutrition; Horticulture/Floriculture.

Award: Scholarship for use in senior, graduate, or postgraduate years; not renewable. *Number:* 1. *Amount:* $5000.

Eligibility Requirements: Applicant must be enrolled or expecting to enroll full-time at a four-year institution or university. Available to U.S. citizens.

Application Requirements: Application, essay, resume, references, transcript. *Deadline:* June 15.

Contact: John Keeling, Executive Vice President and Chief Executive Officer
National Potato Council Women's Auxiliary
1300 L Street, NW, Suite 910
Washington, DC 20005
Phone: 202-682-9456 Ext. 203
Fax: 202-682-0333
E-mail: johnkeeling@nationalpotatocouncil.org

NATIONAL POULTRY AND FOOD DISTRIBUTORS ASSOCIATION http://www.npfda.org

NATIONAL POULTRY AND FOOD DISTRIBUTORS ASSOCIATION SCHOLARSHIP FOUNDATION

The scholarships are awarded to full-time students in their junior or senior years at a U.S. college pursuing degrees in poultry science, food science, dietetics, or other related areas of study pertaining to the poultry and food industries.

Academic Fields/Career Goals: Agribusiness; Agriculture; Food Science/Nutrition; Food Service/Hospitality.

Award: Scholarship for use in junior or senior years; not renewable. *Number:* 4. *Amount:* $1500.

Eligibility Requirements: Applicant must be enrolled or expecting to enroll full-time at a four-year institution or university. Available to U.S. and non-U.S. citizens.

Application Requirements: Application, essay, references, transcript. *Deadline:* May 31.

Contact: Kristin McWhorter, Executive Director
National Poultry and Food Distributors Association
958 McEver Road, Suite B-8
Gainesville, GA 30504
Phone: 877-845-1545
Fax: 770-535-7385
E-mail: info@npfda.org

NEW YORK STATE ASSOCIATION OF AGRICULTURAL FAIRS http://www.nyfairs.org

NEW YORK STATE ASSOCIATION OF AGRICULTURAL FAIRS AND NEW YORK STATE SHOWPEOPLE'S ASSOCIATION ANNUAL SCHOLARSHIP

Scholarship of $1000 given to New York high school seniors and undergraduate students attending college and planning to pursue, or already pursuing a degree in an agricultural or fair management related field.

Academic Fields/Career Goals: Agribusiness; Agriculture.

Award: Scholarship for use in freshman, sophomore, junior, or senior years; not renewable. *Number:* 6. *Amount:* $1000.

Eligibility Requirements: Applicant must be enrolled or expecting to enroll full-time at a two-year or four-year institution or university and resident of New York. Available to U.S. citizens.

Application Requirements: Application, essay, transcript. *Deadline:* April 12.

Contact: Mark St. Jacques, President
New York State Association of Agricultural Fairs
392 Old Schuylerville Road
Greenwich, NY 12834
Phone: 518-692-2464
Fax: 518-692-1021
E-mail: markwashfair@aol.com

OHIO FARMERS UNION http://www.ohfarmersunion.org

VIRGIL THOMPSON MEMORIAL SCHOLARSHIP CONTEST

Award available to members of Ohio Farmers Union who are enrolled as full-time college sophomores, juniors or seniors. Awards of $1000 to winner and $500 each to two runners-up.

Academic Fields/Career Goals: Agribusiness; Agriculture.

Award: Scholarship for use in sophomore, junior, or senior years; not renewable. *Number:* 1–3. *Amount:* $500–$1000.

Eligibility Requirements: Applicant must be enrolled or expecting to enroll full-time at a four-year institution or university and resident of Ohio. Applicant or parent of applicant must be member of Ohio Farmers Union. Available to U.S. citizens.

Application Requirements: Application, applicant must enter a contest, essay. *Deadline:* December 31.

Contact: Maria Miller, Public Relations Director
Ohio Farmers Union
PO Box 363
Ottawa, OH 45875
Phone: 419-523-5300
Fax: 419-523-5913
E-mail: m-miller@ohfarmersunion.org

SOCIETY FOR RANGE MANAGEMENT http://www.rangelands.org

MASONIC RANGE SCIENCE SCHOLARSHIP

Renewable award for undergraduate students pursuing degree in agribusiness, agriculture, animal/veterinary sciences, earth science, natural resources and range science.

Academic Fields/Career Goals: Agribusiness; Agriculture; Animal/Veterinary Sciences; Earth Science; Natural Resources.

Award: Scholarship for use in freshman or sophomore years; renewable. *Number:* 1. *Amount:* $2000.

Eligibility Requirements: Applicant must be enrolled or expecting to enroll full-time at a four-year institution or university. Available to U.S. citizens.

Application Requirements: Application, autobiography, essay, references, test scores, transcript. *Deadline:* varies.

Contact: Vicky Skiff, Scholarship Office
Society for Range Management
445 Union Boulevard, Suite 230
Lakewood, CO 80228
Phone: 303-986-3309
Fax: 303-986-3892

SOIL AND WATER CONSERVATION SOCIETY-NEW JERSEY CHAPTER http://www.geocities.com/njswcs

EDWARD R. HALL SCHOLARSHIP

Two $500 scholarships awarded annually to students attending a New Jersey accredited college or New Jersey residents attending any out-of-state college. Undergraduate students, with the exception of freshmen, are eligible. Must be enrolled in a curriculum related to natural resources. Other areas related to conservation may qualify.

Academic Fields/Career Goals: Agribusiness; Agriculture; Animal/Veterinary Sciences; Biology; Earth Science; Environmental Science; Horticulture/Floriculture; Natural Resources; Natural Sciences.

Award: Scholarship for use in sophomore, junior, or senior years; not renewable. *Number:* 2. *Amount:* $500.

Eligibility Requirements: Applicant must be enrolled or expecting to enroll full-time at a two-year or four-year institution or university and resident of New Jersey. Available to U.S. and non-U.S. citizens.

Application Requirements: Application, essay, financial need analysis, references, transcript, list of clubs and organizations related to natural resources of which applicant is a member. *Deadline:* April 15.

Contact: Fireman E. Bear Chapter, c/o USDA-NRCS
Soil and Water Conservation Society-New Jersey Chapter
220 Davidson Avenue, Fourth Floor
Somerset, NJ 08873
Phone: 732-932-9295
E-mail: njswcs@yahoo.com

SOUTH DAKOTA BOARD OF REGENTS http://www.sdbor.edu

SOUTH DAKOTA BOARD OF REGENTS BJUGSTAD SCHOLARSHIP

Scholarship for graduating North or South Dakota high school senior who is a Native American. Must demonstrate academic achievement, character and leadership abilities. Must submit proof of tribal enrollment. One-time award of

South Dakota Board of Regents (continued)

$500. Must rank in upper half of class or have a minimum 2.5 GPA. Must be pursuing studies in agriculture, agribusiness, or natural resources.

Academic Fields/Career Goals: Agribusiness; Agriculture; Natural Resources.

Award: Scholarship for use in freshman year; not renewable. *Number:* 1. *Amount:* $500.

Eligibility Requirements: Applicant must be American Indian/Alaska Native; high school student; planning to enroll or expecting to enroll full-time at a four-year institution or university; resident of North Dakota or South Dakota and must have an interest in leadership. Applicant must have 2.5 GPA or higher. Available to U.S. citizens.

Application Requirements: Application, references, transcript, proof of tribal enrollment. *Deadline:* February 15.

Contact: Janelle Toman, Director of Institutional Research
South Dakota Board of Regents
306 East Capitol Avenue, Suite 200
Pierre, SD 57501-2545
Phone: 605-773-3455
Fax: 605-773-2422
E-mail: info@sdbor.edu

AGRICULTURE

AGRILIANCE, LAND O' LAKES, AND CROPLAN GENETICS http://www.agriliance.com

CAREERS IN AGRICULTURE SCHOLARSHIP PROGRAM

Awards $1000 to 20 high school seniors interested in agriculture-related studies. Must be planning to enroll in a two- or four-year agriculture-related curriculum.

Academic Fields/Career Goals: Agriculture.

Award: Scholarship for use in freshman year; not renewable. *Number:* 20. *Amount:* $1000.

Eligibility Requirements: Applicant must be high school student and planning to enroll or expecting to enroll full-time at a two-year or four-year institution or university. Available to U.S. citizens.

Application Requirements: Application, essay. *Deadline:* March 1.

Contact: Annette Degnan, Director, Advertising and Communications
Agriliance, Land O' Lakes, and Croplan Genetics
PO Box 64089
St. Paul, MN 55164-0089
Phone: 651-355-5126
E-mail: adegnan@mbrservices.com

ALABAMA GOLF COURSE SUPERINTENDENTS ASSOCIATION http://www.agcsa.org

ALABAMA GOLF COURSE SUPERINTENDENT'S ASSOCIATION'S DONNIE ARTHUR MEMORIAL SCHOLARSHIP

One-time award for students majoring in agriculture with an emphasis on turf-grass management. Must have a minimum 2.0 GPA. Applicant must be full-time student. High school students not considered. Award available to U.S. citizens.

Academic Fields/Career Goals: Agriculture; Horticulture/Floriculture.

Award: Scholarship for use in freshman, sophomore, junior, or senior years; not renewable. *Number:* 2. *Amount:* $1000.

Eligibility Requirements: Applicant must be enrolled or expecting to enroll full-time at a two-year or four-year institution or university. Available to U.S. citizens.

Application Requirements: Application, essay, references, transcript. *Deadline:* October 15.

Contact: Melanie Bonds, Secretary
Alabama Golf Course Superintendents Association
PO Box 661214
Birmingham, AL 35266-1214
Phone: 205-967-0397
Fax: 205-967-1466
E-mail: agcsa@charter.net

ALBERTA HERITAGE SCHOLARSHIP FUND/ ALBERTA SCHOLARSHIP PROGRAMS http://www.alis.gov.ab.ca

ALBERTA BARLEY COMMISSION-EUGENE BOYKO MEMORIAL SCHOLARSHIP

Award to recognize and encourage students entering the field of crop production and/or crop processing technology studies. Must be a Canadian citizen or landed immigrant attending an Alberta postsecondary institution. Students must be enrolled in the second or subsequent year of postsecondary study and taking courses that have an emphasis on crop production and/or crop processing technology.

Academic Fields/Career Goals: Agriculture.

Award: Scholarship for use in sophomore, junior, or senior years; not renewable. *Number:* 1. *Amount:* $500.

Eligibility Requirements: Applicant must be enrolled or expecting to enroll full-time at a four-year institution or university and resident of Alberta. Available to Canadian citizens.

Application Requirements: Application. *Deadline:* August 1.

Contact: Scholarship Committee
Alberta Heritage Scholarship Fund/Alberta Scholarship Programs
9940 106th Street, Fourth Floor, Sterling Place
PO Box 28000, Station Main
Edmonton, AB T5J 4R4
Canada
Phone: 780-427-8640
Fax: 780-427-1288
E-mail: scholarships@gov.ab.ca

AMERICAN SOCIETY FOR ENOLOGY AND VITICULTURE http://www.asev.org

AMERICAN SOCIETY FOR ENOLOGY AND VITICULTURE SCHOLARSHIPS

One-time award for college juniors, seniors, and graduate students residing in North America and enrolled in a program studying viticulture, enology, or any field related to the wine and grape industry. Minimum 3.0 GPA for undergraduates; minimum 3.2 GPA for graduate students. Must be a resident of the United States, Canada, or Mexico.

Academic Fields/Career Goals: Agriculture; Chemical Engineering; Food Science/Nutrition; Horticulture/Floriculture.

Award: Scholarship for use in junior, senior, or graduate years; not renewable. *Number:* up to 30. *Amount:* $500–$4000.

Eligibility Requirements: Applicant must be enrolled or expecting to enroll full-time at a four-year institution or university. Applicant must have 3.0 GPA or higher. Available to U.S. and non-U.S. citizens.

Application Requirements: Application, essay, financial need analysis, references, transcript. *Deadline:* March 1.

Contact: Laurie Radcliff, Office Coordinator
American Society for Enology and Viticulture
PO Box 1855
Davis, CA 95617-1855
Phone: 530-753-3142
Fax: 530-753-3318
E-mail: society@asev.org

AMERICAN SOCIETY OF AGRICULTURAL ENGINEERS http://www.asabe.org

AMERICAN SOCIETY OF AGRICULTURAL AND BIOLOGICAL ENGINEERS FOUNDATION SCHOLARSHIP

One scholarship will be awarded to an undergraduate student member of ASAE who has completed at least one year of undergraduate study. Must be majoring in agriculture or biological engineering. Must have a minimum of 2.5 GPA. For more details see Web site: http://www.asae.org.

Academic Fields/Career Goals: Agriculture.

Award: Scholarship for use in sophomore, junior, or senior years; not renewable. *Number:* 1. *Amount:* $1000.

Eligibility Requirements: Applicant must be enrolled or expecting to enroll full-time at a four-year institution or university. Applicant must have 2.5 GPA or higher. Available to U.S. and Canadian citizens.

Application Requirements: Application, essay, financial need analysis, resume, references. *Deadline:* March 17.

Contact: Carol Flautt, Scholarship Program
American Society of Agricultural Engineers
2950 Niles Road
St. Joseph, MI 49085
Phone: 269-428-6336
Fax: 269-429-3852
E-mail: flautt@asabe.org

WILLIAM J. AND MARIJANE E. ADAMS, JR. SCHOLARSHIP

One-time award for a full-time U.S. or Canadian undergraduate who is a student member of the American Society of Agricultural Engineers and a declared major in biological or agricultural engineering. Must be at least a sophomore and have minimum 2.5 GPA. Must be interested in agricultural machinery product design or development. Write for application procedures.

Academic Fields/Career Goals: Agriculture; Biology.

Award: Scholarship for use in sophomore, junior, or senior years; not renewable. *Number:* 1. *Amount:* $1000.

Eligibility Requirements: Applicant must be enrolled or expecting to enroll full-time at a four-year institution or university. Applicant must have 2.5 GPA or higher. Available to U.S. and Canadian citizens.

Application Requirements: Application, essay, financial need analysis, resume, references. *Deadline:* March 17.

Contact: Carol Flautt, Scholarship Program
American Society of Agricultural Engineers
2950 Niles Road
St. Joseph, MI 49085-9659
Phone: 269-428-6336
Fax: 269-429-3852
E-mail: flautt@asabe.org

AMERICAN SOCIETY OF AGRONOMY, CROP SCIENCE SOCIETY OF AMERICA, SOIL SCIENCE SOCIETY OF AMERICA http://www.asa-cssa-sssa.org

HANK BEACHELL FUTURE LEADER SCHOLARSHIP

Scholarship for undergraduate students for $3500 and negotiated travel expenses to the scholarship experience site. Must have completed the sophomore year, and must be majoring in agronomy, crop science, soil science, or other related disciplines. For more information on eligibility criteria and nominee qualifications visit Web site: https://www.agronomy.org/awards/award/detail/?a=5.

Academic Fields/Career Goals: Agriculture.

Award: Scholarship for use in junior or senior years; not renewable. *Number:* up to 4. *Amount:* up to $3500.

Eligibility Requirements: Applicant must be enrolled or expecting to enroll full-time at a two-year or four-year institution or university. Available to U.S. and non-U.S. citizens.

Application Requirements: Application, resume, references, letter of interest, nomination letter. *Deadline:* February 26.

Contact: Leann Malison, Program Manager
American Society of Agronomy, Crop Science Society of America, Soil Science Society of America
677 South Segoe Road
Madison, WI 53711
Phone: 608-268-4949
Fax: 608-273-2021
E-mail: lmalison@agronomy.org

J. FIELDING REED SCHOLARSHIP

Scholarship of $1000 to honor an outstanding undergraduate senior pursuing a career in soil or plant sciences. Must have GPA of 3.0, or above, and nominations should contain a history of community and campus leadership activities, specifically in agriculture. For more information on nomination and eligibility criteria, visit Web site: https://www.agronomy.org/awards/award/detail/?a=6.

Academic Fields/Career Goals: Agriculture.

Award: Scholarship for use in senior year; not renewable. *Number:* 1. *Amount:* up to $1000.

Eligibility Requirements: Applicant must be enrolled or expecting to enroll full-time at a four-year institution or university and must have an interest in leadership. Applicant or parent of applicant must have employment or volunteer experience in community service. Applicant must have 3.0 GPA or higher. Available to U.S. and non-U.S. citizens.

Application Requirements: Application, resume, references, letter of interest. *Deadline:* February 26.

Contact: Leann Malison, Program Manager
American Society of Agronomy, Crop Science Society of America, Soil Science Society of America
677 South Segoe Road
Madison, WI 53711
Phone: 608-268-4949
Fax: 608-273-2021
E-mail: lmalison@agronomy.org

CALCOT-SEITZ FOUNDATION http://www.calcot.com

CALCOT-SEITZ SCHOLARSHIP

Scholarship for young students from Arizona, New Mexico, Texas and California who plan to attend a college or are attending a college offering at least a four-year degree in agriculture.

Academic Fields/Career Goals: Agriculture.

Award: Scholarship for use in freshman, sophomore, junior, or senior years; not renewable. *Number:* 1–20. *Amount:* up to $3000.

Eligibility Requirements: Applicant must be enrolled or expecting to enroll full-time at a four-year institution and resident of Arizona, California, New Mexico, or Texas. Available to U.S. and non-U.S. citizens.

Application Requirements: Application, photo, references, test scores, transcript. *Deadline:* March 31.

Contact: Marci S. Cunningham, Scholarship Committee
Calcot-Seitz Foundation
PO Box 259
Bakersfield, CA 93302
Phone: 661-327-5961
Fax: 661-861-9870
E-mail: info@calcot.com

CALIFORNIA CATTLEMEN'S ASSOCIATION http://www.calcattlemen.org

CCA SCHOLARSHIP

Scholarship is available for YCC members pursuing careers within the industry. Applications are available on the Web site or through the CCA office. Applicant must be an U.S. citizen.

Academic Fields/Career Goals: Agriculture.

Award: Scholarship for use in freshman year; not renewable. *Number:* up to 5. *Amount:* varies.

Eligibility Requirements: Applicant must be high school student and planning to enroll or expecting to enroll full-time at a two-year or four-year or technical institution or university. Available to U.S. citizens.

Application Requirements: Application, essay, references, transcript. *Deadline:* July 20.

Contact: Megan Huber, Director of Finance
California Cattlemen's Association
1221 H Street
Sacramento, CA 95814-1910
Phone: 916-444-0845
Fax: 916-444-2194
E-mail: megan@calcattlemen.org

CALIFORNIA CITRUS MUTUAL SCHOLARSHIP FOUNDATION http://www.cacitrusmutual.com

CALIFORNIA CITRUS MUTUAL SCHOLARSHIP

Scholarship for college or university students from a family with membership in California Citrus Mutual. Must have a major or minor in agricultural-related field. Two awards of $1000 to $2000 granted. Must be resident of California.

Academic Fields/Career Goals: Agriculture.

Award: Scholarship for use in freshman, sophomore, junior, or senior years; not renewable. *Number:* 2. *Amount:* $1000–$2000.

Eligibility Requirements: Applicant must be enrolled or expecting to enroll full-time at a two-year or four-year or technical institution or

California Citrus Mutual Scholarship Foundation (continued)

university and resident of California. Applicant or parent of applicant must have employment or volunteer experience in agriculture. Available to U.S. citizens.

Application Requirements: Application, essay. *Deadline:* April 27.

Contact: Becky Carter, Administrative Assistant
California Citrus Mutual Scholarship Foundation
512 North Kaweah Avenue
Exeter, CA 93221
Phone: 559-592-3790
E-mail: beckyc@cacitrusmutual.com

CALIFORNIA FARM BUREAU SCHOLARSHIP FOUNDATION http://www.cfbf.com

CALIFORNIA FARM BUREAU SCHOLARSHIP

• *See page 68*

CALIFORNIA WATER AWARENESS CAMPAIGN http://www.wateraware.org

CALIFORNIA WATER AWARENESS CAMPAIGN WATER SCHOLAR

Provides economic support to graduating high school and/or junior college students who exhibit an interest or are actively pursuing a career in the water industry.

Academic Fields/Career Goals: Agriculture; Environmental Science; Hydrology; Landscape Architecture; Natural Resources.

Award: Scholarship for use in freshman, sophomore, or junior years; not renewable. *Number:* up to 2. *Amount:* $2500.

Eligibility Requirements: Applicant must be enrolled or expecting to enroll full-time at a four-year institution or university; resident of California and studying in California. Available to U.S. citizens.

Application Requirements: Application, essay, references, transcript. *Deadline:* March 16.

Contact: Lynne Wichmann, Executive Director
California Water Awareness Campaign
910 K Street, Suite 340
Sacramento, CA 95814
Phone: 916-325-2596
Fax: 916-325-4849
E-mail: cwac@acwa.com

CANADIAN RECREATIONAL CANOEING ASSOCIATION http://www.paddlingcanada.com

BILL MASON MEMORIAL SCHOLARSHIP FUND

One-time award for Canadian citizens attending a Canadian college or university. Applicant must at least be a sophomore majoring in an outdoor recreation or environmental studies program. An academic standing of B+ (75%) is required. Applicant must be planning a career in this field. Must also provide history of past involvement and leadership as it pertains to major and career goals. Background in canoeing and kayaking is considered an asset.

Academic Fields/Career Goals: Agriculture; Anthropology; Earth Science; Environmental Science; Geography; Marine Biology; Natural Resources; Natural Sciences; Oceanography; Recreation, Parks, Leisure Studies; Travel/Tourism.

Award: Scholarship for use in sophomore or senior years; renewable. *Number:* 1. *Amount:* $1000.

Eligibility Requirements: Applicant must be Canadian citizen; enrolled or expecting to enroll full-time at a two-year or four-year institution or university; resident of Alberta, British Columbia, Manitoba, New Brunswick, Newfoundland, North West Territories, Nova Scotia, Ontario, Prince Edward Island, Quebec, Saskatchewan, or Yukon and studying in Alberta, British Columbia, Manitoba, New Brunswick, Newfoundland, North West Territories, Nova Scotia, Ontario, Prince Edward Island, Quebec, Saskatchewan, or Yukon.

Application Requirements: Application, essay, financial need analysis, transcript, birth certificate, cover letter. *Deadline:* September 30.

Contact: Sue Hopson, Business Manager
Canadian Recreational Canoeing Association
PO Box 20069
RPO Taylor Kidd
Kingston, ON K7P 2T6
Canada
Phone: 613-547-3196
Fax: 613-547-4880
E-mail: info@paddlingcanada.com

CHS FOUNDATION http://www.chsfoundation.org

AGRICULTURE SCHOLARSHIPS

• *See page 69*

COOPERATIVE STUDIES SCHOLARSHIPS

• *See page 69*

DAIRY MANAGEMENT http://www.dairyinfo.com

JAMES H. LOPER JR. MEMORIAL SCHOLARSHIP

One-time scholarship of $1500 given to sophomores, juniors and seniors in college/university programs that emphasize dairy. Majors include communications/public relations, journalism, marketing, business, economics, nutrition, food science and agricultural education.

Academic Fields/Career Goals: Agriculture; Business/Consumer Services; Communications; Economics; Food Science/Nutrition; Journalism.

Award: Scholarship for use in sophomore, junior, or senior years; not renewable. *Number:* 1. *Amount:* $2500.

Eligibility Requirements: Applicant must be enrolled or expecting to enroll full-time at a two-year or four-year institution or university. Available to U.S. citizens.

Application Requirements: Application, references, transcript. *Deadline:* May 31.

Contact: Marykate Ginter, Scholarship Coordinator
Dairy Management
10255 West Higgins Road, Suite 900
Rosemont, IL 60018-5616
Phone: 847-627-3252
E-mail: marykateg@rosedmi.com

NATIONAL DAIRY PROMOTION AND RESEARCH BOARD SCHOLARSHIP

One-time scholarship of $1500 given to sophomores, juniors and seniors in college/university programs that emphasize dairy. Majors include communications/public relations, journalism, marketing, business, economics, nutrition, food science and agricultural education.

Academic Fields/Career Goals: Agriculture; Business/Consumer Services; Communications; Economics; Food Science/Nutrition; Journalism.

Award: Scholarship for use in sophomore, junior, or senior years; not renewable. *Number:* 19. *Amount:* $1500.

Eligibility Requirements: Applicant must be enrolled or expecting to enroll full-time at a two-year or four-year institution or university. Available to U.S. citizens.

Application Requirements: Application, references, transcript. *Deadline:* May 31.

Contact: Marykate Ginter, Scholarship Coordinator
Dairy Management
10255 West Higgins Road, Suite 900
Rosemont, IL 60018-5616
Phone: 847-627-3252
E-mail: marykateg@rosedmi.com

GARDEN CLUB OF AMERICA http://www.gcamerica.org

GARDEN CLUB OF AMERICA AWARDS FOR SUMMER ENVIRONMENTAL STUDIES

Award for college students who wish to pursue summer studies doing field work, research, or classroom work in the environmental field following their freshman, sophomore, or junior years. The scholarships encourage young men and women who are interested in furthering their studies and careers in the field of ecology and offer an opportunity to gain knowledge and experience beyond the regular course of study.

Academic Fields/Career Goals: Agriculture; Earth Science; Environmental Science; Natural Resources.

Award: Scholarship for use in freshman, sophomore, or junior years; not renewable. *Number:* 2. *Amount:* $2000.

Eligibility Requirements: Applicant must be enrolled or expecting to enroll full-time at a four-year institution or university. Available to U.S. and non-U.S. citizens.

Application Requirements: Application, essay, references, self-addressed stamped envelope, transcript. *Deadline:* February 10.

Contact: Judy Smith, Scholarship Committee Administrator
Garden Club of America
14 East 60th Street, Third Floor
New York, NY 10022-1002
Phone: 212-753-8287
Fax: 212-753-0134
E-mail: judy@gcamerica.org

GEORGE T. WELCH TRUST http://www.bakerboyer.com

BERNICE AND PAT MURPHY SCHOLARSHIP FUND

Grants for students majoring in agriculture. Must be enrolled full-time and maintain a minimum GPA of 2.0. Must reapply. The budget form must be completed and cover the entire school year.

Academic Fields/Career Goals: Agriculture.

Award: Scholarship for use in freshman, sophomore, junior, or senior years; not renewable. *Number:* varies. *Amount:* varies.

Eligibility Requirements: Applicant must be enrolled or expecting to enroll full-time at a four-year institution or university. Available to U.S. citizens.

Application Requirements: Application. *Deadline:* April 13.

Contact: Ted Cohan, Trust Portfolio Manager
George T. Welch Trust
Baker Boyer Bank, Investment Management & Trust Services
7 West Main, PO Box 1796
Walla Walla, WA 99362
Phone: 509-526-1204
Fax: 509-522-3136
E-mail: cohant@bakerboyer.com

G.B. PESCIALLO MEMORIAL SCHOLARSHIP FUND

Grants for students majoring in agriculture. Must be enrolled full-time and maintain a minimum GPA of 2.0. Must reapply. The budget form must be completed and cover the entire school year.

Academic Fields/Career Goals: Agriculture.

Award: Scholarship for use in freshman, sophomore, junior, or senior years; not renewable. *Number:* varies. *Amount:* varies.

Eligibility Requirements: Applicant must be enrolled or expecting to enroll full-time at a four-year institution or university. Available to U.S. citizens.

Application Requirements: Application, responsibility shown in one or more of the following areas: community, school, home, church. *Deadline:* April 13.

Contact: Ted Cohan, Trust Portfolio Manager
George T. Welch Trust
Baker Boyer Bank, Investment Management & Trust Services
7 West Main, PO Box 1796
Walla Walla, WA 99362
Phone: 509-526-1204
Fax: 509-522-3136
E-mail: cohant@bakerboyer.com

INTERTRIBAL TIMBER COUNCIL http://www.itcnet.org

TRUMAN D. PICARD SCHOLARSHIP

• *See page 69*

JAPANESE AMERICAN CITIZENS LEAGUE (JACL) http://www.jacl.org

NATIONAL JACL HEADQUARTERS SCHOLARSHIP

Scholarship offers over 30 awards to qualified students nationwide. Scholarships are provided to students at the entering freshman, undergraduate, graduate, law, financial need and creative & performing arts. All scholarships are one-time awards. Every applicant must be an active National JACL member at either an Individual or Student/Youth Level.

Academic Fields/Career Goals: Agriculture; Journalism; Law/Legal Services; Literature/English/Writing; Public Policy and Administration.

Award: Scholarship for use in freshman, sophomore, junior, senior, or graduate years; not renewable. *Number:* 30. *Amount:* varies.

Eligibility Requirements: Applicant must be of Japanese heritage; Asian/Pacific Islander and enrolled or expecting to enroll full-time at a two-year or four-year institution or university. Available to U.S. and non-U.S. citizens.

Application Requirements: Application, financial need analysis, references, transcript. *Deadline:* varies.

Contact: Scholarship Committee
Japanese American Citizens League (JACL)
1765 Sutter Street
San Francisco, CA 94115
Phone: 415-921-5225
E-mail: jacl@jacl.org

MAINE COMMUNITY FOUNDATION INC. http://www.mainecf.org

RONALD P. GUERRETTE FUTURE FARMERS OF AMERICA SCHOLARSHIP FUND

Scholarship assistance to a student from Maine. Applicants must be FFA members and have a demonstrated interest and motivation to pursue a career in farming and/or agriculture.

Academic Fields/Career Goals: Agriculture.

Award: Scholarship for use in freshman, sophomore, or junior years; not renewable. *Number:* up to 3. *Amount:* varies.

Eligibility Requirements: Applicant must be enrolled or expecting to enroll full-time at a four-year institution and resident of Maine. Applicant or parent of applicant must be member of Future Farmers of America. Available to U.S. citizens.

Application Requirements: Application, essay, financial need analysis, references, transcript. *Deadline:* March 1.

Contact: Doug Robertson, State FFA Adviser
Maine Community Foundation Inc.
Department of Education, 23 State House Station
Augusta, ME 04333-0023
Phone: 207-624-6744
Fax: 207-624-6731

MAINE DEPARTMENT OF AGRICULTURE, FOOD AND RURAL RESOURCES http://www.maine.gov/agriculture

MAINE RURAL REHABILITATION FUND SCHOLARSHIP PROGRAM

• *See page 69*

MINNESOTA SOYBEAN RESEARCH AND PROMOTION COUNCIL http://www.mnsoybean.org

MINNESOTA SOYBEAN RESEARCH AND PROMOTION COUNCIL YOUTH SOYBEAN SCHOLARSHIP

• *See page 70*

MONSANTO AGRIBUSINESS SCHOLARSHIP http://www.monsanto.ca

MONSANTO CANADA OPPORTUNITY SCHOLARSHIP PROGRAM

• *See page 70*

MORRIS K. UDALL FOUNDATION http://www.udall.gov

MORRIS K. UDALL SCHOLARS

One-time award to full-time college sophomores or juniors for study towards a career in environment-related fields. Must be nominated by college. Minimum GPA of 3.0 or the equivalent. Must be U.S. citizen, a permanent resident alien or U.S. national.

Academic Fields/Career Goals: Agriculture; Biology; Earth Science; Environmental Science; Geography; Natural Resources.

Award: Scholarship for use in sophomore or junior years; not renewable. *Number:* up to 130. *Amount:* $350–$5000.

Eligibility Requirements: Applicant must be enrolled or expecting to enroll full-time at a two-year or four-year institution. Applicant must have 3.0 GPA or higher. Available to U.S. citizens.

Application Requirements: Application, essay, references, transcript, nomination. *Deadline:* March 6.

Contact: Melissa Millage, Program Manager
Morris K. Udall Foundation
130 South Scott Avenue
Tucson, AZ 85701-1922
Phone: 520-901-8500
Fax: 520-901-8570
E-mail: millage@udall.gov

NATIONAL CATTLEMEN'S FOUNDATION http://www.nationalcattlemensfoundation.org

CME BEEF INDUSTRY SCHOLARSHIP

• *See page 70*

NATIONAL COUNCIL OF STATE GARDEN CLUBS INC. SCHOLARSHIP http://www.gardenclub.org

NATIONAL COUNCIL OF STATE GARDEN CLUBS INC. SCHOLARSHIP

Scholarship to students for study in agriculture education, horticulture, floriculture, landscape design, botany, biology, plant pathology/science, forestry, agronomy, environmental concerns.

Academic Fields/Career Goals: Agriculture; Biology; Environmental Science; Horticulture/Floriculture.

Award: Scholarship for use in sophomore, junior, senior, or graduate years; not renewable. *Number:* 34. *Amount:* $3500.

Eligibility Requirements: Applicant must be enrolled or expecting to enroll full-time at a two-year or four-year institution or university. Applicant must have 3.0 GPA or higher. Available to U.S. citizens.

Application Requirements: Application, financial need analysis, references, transcript. *Deadline:* March 1.

Contact: Kathy Romine, National Headquarters
National Council of State Garden Clubs Inc. Scholarship
4401 Magnolia Avenue
St. Louis, MO 63110-3492
Phone: 314-776-7574 Ext. 15
Fax: 314-776-5108
E-mail: headquarters@gardenclub.org

NATIONAL DAIRY SHRINE http://www.dairyshrine.org

KILDEE SCHOLARSHIPS

Top 25 contestants in the three most recent national intercollegiate dairy cattle judging contests are eligible to apply for two $3000 one-time scholarships for graduate study in the field related to dairy cattle production at the university of their choice. Also the top 25 contestants in the most recent National 4-H & National FFA Dairy Judging contests are eligible to apply for one $2000 scholarship for undergraduate study in the field related to dairy cattle production at the university of their choice.

Academic Fields/Career Goals: Agriculture; Animal/Veterinary Sciences.

Award: Scholarship for use in freshman, sophomore, junior, senior, graduate, or postgraduate years; not renewable. *Number:* 3. *Amount:* $2000–$3000.

Eligibility Requirements: Applicant must be enrolled or expecting to enroll full-time at a four-year institution or university. Available to U.S. and non-U.S. citizens.

Application Requirements: Application, applicant must enter a contest, references, transcript. *Deadline:* March 15.

Contact: Maurice E. Core, Executive Director
National Dairy Shrine
1224 Alton Darby Creek Road
Columbus, OH 43228-9792
Phone: 614-878-5333
Fax: 614-870-2622
E-mail: shrine@cobaselect.com

MARSHALL E. MCCULLOUGH-NATIONAL DAIRY SHRINE SCHOLARSHIPS

Scholarship for high school seniors planning to enter a four-year college or university with an intent to major in dairy/animal science with a communications emphasis, or agricultural journalism with a dairy/animal science emphasis.

Academic Fields/Career Goals: Agriculture; Animal/Veterinary Sciences.

Award: Scholarship for use in freshman year; not renewable. *Number:* 2. *Amount:* $1000–$2500.

Eligibility Requirements: Applicant must be high school student and planning to enroll or expecting to enroll full-time at a four-year institution or university. Available to U.S. and non-U.S. citizens.

Application Requirements: Application, references, transcript. *Deadline:* March 15.

Contact: Maurice E. Core, Executive Director
National Dairy Shrine
1224 Alton Darby Creek Road
Columbus, OH 43228-9792
E-mail: shrine@cobaselect.com

NATIONAL DAIRY SHRINE/DAIRY MARKETING INC. MILK MARKETING SCHOLARSHIPS

One-time awards for undergraduate students pursuing careers in marketing of dairy products. Major areas can include: dairy science, animal science, agricultural economics, agricultural communications, agricultural education, general education, food and nutrition, home economics and journalism.

Academic Fields/Career Goals: Agriculture; Animal/Veterinary Sciences; Food Science/Nutrition.

Award: Scholarship for use in sophomore, junior, or senior years; not renewable. *Number:* 7–10. *Amount:* $1000–$1500.

Eligibility Requirements: Applicant must be enrolled or expecting to enroll full-time at a four-year institution or university. Applicant must have 2.5 GPA or higher. Available to U.S. citizens.

Application Requirements: Application, photo, references, transcript. *Deadline:* March 15.

Contact: Maurice E. Core, Executive Director
National Dairy Shrine
1224 Alton Darby Creek Road
Columbus, OH 43228-9792
Phone: 614-878-5333
Fax: 614-870-2622
E-mail: shrine@cobaselect.com

NATIONAL DAIRY SHRINE/IAGER DAIRY SCHOLARSHIP

$1000 annual scholarship to encourage qualified second year dairy students in a two-year agricultural school to pursue careers in the dairy industry. Scholarships will be awarded based on academic standing, leadership ability, interest in the dairy industry, and plans for the future. Cumulative 2.5 GPA required.

Academic Fields/Career Goals: Agriculture.

Award: Scholarship for use in sophomore year; not renewable. *Number:* varies. *Amount:* up to $1000.

Eligibility Requirements: Applicant must be enrolled or expecting to enroll full-time at a two-year institution. Applicant must have 2.5 GPA or higher. Available to U.S. citizens.

Application Requirements: Application, references, transcript. *Deadline:* July 1.

Contact: Maurice Core, Executive Director
National Dairy Shrine
1224 Alton Darby Creek Road
Columbus, OH 43228-9792
Phone: 614-878-5333
Fax: 614-870-2622
E-mail: shrine@cobaselect.com

NATIONAL DAIRY SHRINE/KLUSSENDORF SCHOLARSHIP

The scholarship will be granted to a student successfully completing the first, second or third years at a two-year or four-year college or university. To be eligible, students must major in a dairy science (animal science) curriculum with plans to enter the dairy cattle field as a breeder, owner, herdsperson, or fitter.

Academic Fields/Career Goals: Agriculture; Animal/Veterinary Sciences.

Award: Scholarship for use in freshman, sophomore, or junior years; not renewable. *Number:* 1. *Amount:* $1000.

Eligibility Requirements: Applicant must be enrolled or expecting to enroll full-time at a two-year or four-year institution or university. Available to U.S. and non-U.S. citizens.

Application Requirements: Application, references, transcript. *Deadline:* March 15.

Contact: Maurice E. Core, Executive Director
National Dairy Shrine
1224 Alton Darby Creek Road
Columbus, OH 43228-9792
Phone: 614-878-5333
Fax: 614-870-2622
E-mail: shrine@cobaselect.com

NDS STUDENT RECOGNITION CONTEST

• *See page 70*

PROGRESSIVE DAIRY PRODUCER AWARD

The program grants two educational/travel awards for outstanding young dairy producers between 21 to 45 years of age. Open to an individual, couple, or family/multi-partner operation. Must be U.S. citizen.

Academic Fields/Career Goals: Agriculture; Animal/Veterinary Sciences.

Award: Prize for use in freshman year; not renewable. *Number:* 2. *Amount:* $2000.

Eligibility Requirements: Applicant must be age 21-45 and enrolled or expecting to enroll full- or part-time at a four-year institution or university. Available to U.S. citizens.

Application Requirements: Application, 6 copies of nomination and supporting information. *Deadline:* March 15.

Contact: Maurice E. Core, Executive Director
National Dairy Shrine
1224 Alton Darby Creek Road
Columbus, OH 43228-9792
Phone: 614-878-5333
Fax: 614-870-2622
E-mail: shrine@cobaselect.com

NATIONAL GARDEN CLUBS INC. http://www.gardenclub.org

NATIONAL GARDEN CLUBS INC. SCHOLARSHIP PROGRAM

One-time award for full-time students in plant sciences, agriculture and related or allied subjects. Applicants must have at least a 3.25 GPA.

Academic Fields/Career Goals: Agriculture; Biology; Earth Science; Environmental Science; Horticulture/Floriculture; Landscape Architecture.

Award: Scholarship for use in junior, senior, or graduate years; not renewable. *Number:* 34. *Amount:* $3500.

Eligibility Requirements: Applicant must be enrolled or expecting to enroll full-time at a four-year institution or university. Available to U.S. citizens.

Application Requirements: Application, financial need analysis, photo, resume, references, transcript. *Deadline:* March 1.

Contact: Sandra Robinson, Vice President for Scholarship
National Garden Clubs Inc.
4401 Magnolia Avenue
St. Louis, MO 63110
Phone: 606-878-7281
E-mail: sandyr@kayandkay.com

NATIONAL POTATO COUNCIL WOMEN'S AUXILIARY http://www.nationalpotatocouncil.org

POTATO INDUSTRY SCHOLARSHIP

• *See page 70*

NATIONAL POULTRY AND FOOD DISTRIBUTORS ASSOCIATION http://www.npfda.org

NATIONAL POULTRY AND FOOD DISTRIBUTORS ASSOCIATION SCHOLARSHIP FOUNDATION

• *See page 71*

NEW YORK STATE ASSOCIATION OF AGRICULTURAL FAIRS http://www.nyfairs.org

NEW YORK STATE ASSOCIATION OF AGRICULTURAL FAIRS AND NEW YORK STATE SHOWPEOPLE'S ASSOCIATION ANNUAL SCHOLARSHIP

• *See page 71*

NEW YORK STATE GRANGE http://www.nysgrange.com

HOWARD F. DENISE SCHOLARSHIP

Awards for undergraduates under 21 years old to pursue studies in agriculture. Must be a New York resident with a minimum 3.0 GPA. One-time award of $1000.

Academic Fields/Career Goals: Agriculture.

Award: Scholarship for use in freshman, sophomore, junior, or senior years; not renewable. *Number:* 1–6. *Amount:* $1000.

Eligibility Requirements: Applicant must be age 21 or under; enrolled or expecting to enroll full-time at a two-year or four-year institution and resident of New York. Applicant must have 3.0 GPA or higher. Available to U.S. citizens.

Application Requirements: Application, financial need analysis, references, transcript. *Deadline:* April 15.

Contact: Scholarship Committee
New York State Grange
100 Grange Place
Cortland, NY 13045
Phone: 607-756-7553
Fax: 607-756-7757
E-mail: nysgrange@nysgrange.com

OHIO FARMERS UNION http://www.ohfarmersunion.org

JOSEPH FITCHER SCHOLARSHIP CONTEST

Scholarship available to member of Ohio Farmers Union who is a high school junior or senior, or enrolled as a college freshman. Participants are to submit an application obtained from OFU and a typed essay on, "Agricultural Opportunities in the Future". Award of $1000 to winner and $250 to two runners-up.

Academic Fields/Career Goals: Agriculture.

Award: Scholarship for use in freshman year; not renewable. *Number:* 1–3. *Amount:* $250–$1000.

Eligibility Requirements: Applicant must be high school student; planning to enroll or expecting to enroll full-time at a four-year institution or university and resident of Ohio. Applicant or parent of applicant must be member of Ohio Farmers Union. Available to U.S. citizens.

Ohio Farmers Union (continued)

Application Requirements: Application, applicant must enter a contest, essay. *Deadline:* December 31.

Contact: Maria Miller, Public Relations Director
Ohio Farmers Union
PO Box 363
Ottawa, OH 45875
Phone: 419-523-5300
Fax: 419-523-5913
E-mail: m-miller@ohfarmersunion.org

VIRGIL THOMPSON MEMORIAL SCHOLARSHIP CONTEST
• *See page 71*

OHIO 4-H http://www.ohio4h.org

PAUL A. AND ETHEL I. SMITH 4-H SCHOLARSHIP

Scholarship of $2500 awarded to seniors in high school, and planning to enroll as a freshman in the fall at the Ohio State University, ATI or any of its regional campuses; in the College of Food, Agricultural, and Environmental Sciences, including the School of Natural Resources, to pursue an education in farming or agriculture. Must be 4-H member.

Academic Fields/Career Goals: Agriculture.

Award: Scholarship for use in freshman year; not renewable. *Number:* 7. *Amount:* $2500.

Eligibility Requirements: Applicant must be high school student; planning to enroll or expecting to enroll full- or part-time at a two-year or four-year institution or university and studying in Ohio. Applicant or parent of applicant must be member of National 4-H. Available to U.S. citizens.

Application Requirements: Application, essay, resume, references, transcript. *Deadline:* November 8.

Contact: Ryan Schmiesing, Interim Assistant Director
Ohio 4-H
4-H Centre, 2201 Fred Taylor Drive
Columbus, OH 43210
Phone: 614-292-4444
Fax: 614-292-5937
E-mail: schmiesing.3@cfaes.osu.edu

OREGON SHEEP GROWERS ASSOCIATION http://www.sheeporegon.com

OREGON SHEEP GROWERS ASSOCIATION MEMORIAL SCHOLARSHIP

One-time award for college students majoring in agricultural science or veterinary medicine pursuing careers in the sheep industry. Must be U.S. citizens and Oregon residents studying at a four-year institution or university. Freshmen are not eligible.

Academic Fields/Career Goals: Agriculture; Animal/Veterinary Sciences.

Award: Scholarship for use in sophomore, junior, senior, or graduate years; not renewable. *Number:* 1–2. *Amount:* $500–$1000.

Eligibility Requirements: Applicant must be enrolled or expecting to enroll full-time at a four-year institution or university and resident of Oregon. Available to U.S. citizens.

Application Requirements: Application, essay, references, transcript. *Deadline:* July 1.

Contact: Scholarship Committee
Oregon Sheep Growers Association
1270 Chemeketa Street, NE
Salem, OR 97301
Phone: 503-364-5462
Fax: 503-585-1921
E-mail: info@sheeporegon.com

OREGON STUDENT ASSISTANCE COMMISSION http://www.osac.state.or.us

AGRICULTURAL-WOMEN-IN-NETWORK SCHOLARSHIP

One scholarship for Oregon residents who are agricultural majors with junior or senior undergraduate standing. Must attend a four-year college in Washington, Oregon, or Idaho. Preference for female students.

Academic Fields/Career Goals: Agriculture.

Award: Scholarship for use in junior or senior years; renewable. *Number:* 1. *Amount:* varies.

Eligibility Requirements: Applicant must be enrolled or expecting to enroll full-time at a four-year institution or university; resident of Oregon and studying in Idaho, Oregon, or Washington. Available to U.S. citizens.

Application Requirements: Application, essay, financial need analysis, transcript, activity chart. *Deadline:* March 1.

Contact: Director of Grant Programs
Oregon Student Assistance Commission
1500 Valley River Drive, Suite 100
Eugene, OR 97401-7020
Phone: 800-452-8807 Ext. 7395

PENNSYLVANIA ASSOCIATION OF CONSERVATION DISTRICTS AUXILIARY http://www.pacd.org

PACD AUXILIARY SCHOLARSHIPS

Award for residents of Pennsylvania who are upperclassmen pursuing a degree program in agricultural and/or environmental science, and/or environmental education. Must be studying at a two- or four-year Pennsylvania institution. Must be U.S. citizens. Submit resume. One-time award of $500.

Academic Fields/Career Goals: Agriculture; Biology; Environmental Science; Horticulture/Floriculture.

Award: Scholarship for use in junior or senior years; not renewable. *Number:* 1. *Amount:* $500.

Eligibility Requirements: Applicant must be enrolled or expecting to enroll full- or part-time at a four-year institution or university; resident of Pennsylvania and studying in Pennsylvania. Available to U.S. citizens.

Application Requirements: Application, autobiography, essay, financial need analysis, resume, transcript, GPA verification. *Deadline:* June 15.

Contact: District Clerk
Pennsylvania Association of Conservation Districts Auxiliary
1407 Blair Street
Hollidaysburg, PA 16648-2468
Phone: 814-696-0877 Ext. 5
Fax: 814-696-9981
E-mail: bcd@blairconsevationdistrict.org

PROFESSIONAL GROUNDS MANAGEMENT SOCIETY http://www.pgms.org

ANNE SEAMAN PROFESSIONAL GROUNDS MANAGEMENT SOCIETY MEMORIAL SCHOLARSHIP

One-time award for citizens of the United States and Canada who are studying to enter the field of grounds management or a closely related field such as agronomy, horticulture, landscape contracting, and irrigation on a full-time basis. Write for further information. Must be sponsored by a PGMS member. The member must write a letter of recommendation for the applicant.

Academic Fields/Career Goals: Agriculture; Civil Engineering; Horticulture/Floriculture; Landscape Architecture.

Award: Scholarship for use in freshman, sophomore, junior, or senior years; not renewable. *Number:* 3. *Amount:* $250–$1500.

Eligibility Requirements: Applicant must be enrolled or expecting to enroll full-time at a two-year or four-year institution or university. Available to U.S. and Canadian citizens.

Application Requirements: Application, autobiography, financial need analysis, resume, references, self-addressed stamped envelope, transcript. *Deadline:* September 15.

Contact: Jenny Smith, Association Coordinator
Professional Grounds Management Society
720 Light Street
Baltimore, MD 21230-3816
Phone: 410-223-2861
Fax: 410-752-8295
E-mail: pgms@assnhqtrs.com

SIGMA XI, THE SCIENTIFIC RESEARCH SOCIETY http://www.sigmaxi.org

SIGMA XI GRANTS-IN-AID OF RESEARCH

Award to undergraduate and graduate students currently enrolled in degree seeking programs. Applications are accepted through an online form only.

Deadlines for all application material are March 15 and October 15 annually and are available online two months prior to the deadline (January 15 and August 14 respectively).

Academic Fields/Career Goals: Agriculture; Animal/Veterinary Sciences; Biology; Chemical Engineering; Earth Science; Engineering/Technology; Health and Medical Sciences; Mechanical Engineering; Meteorology/Atmospheric Science; Physical Sciences and Math; Science, Technology, and Society; Social Sciences.

Award: Grant for use in freshman, sophomore, junior, senior, or graduate years; renewable. *Number:* 400. *Amount:* $1000–$5000.

Eligibility Requirements: Applicant must be enrolled or expecting to enroll full-time at a four-year institution or university. Available to U.S. and non-U.S. citizens.

Application Requirements: Application, references. *Deadline:* varies.

Contact: Kevin Bowen, Grants Coordinator
Sigma Xi, The Scientific Research Society
99 Alexander Drive, PO Box 13975
Research Triangle Park, NC 27709
Phone: 800-243-6534
E-mail: giar@sigmaxi.org

SOCIETY FOR RANGE MANAGEMENT http://www.rangelands.org

MASONIC RANGE SCIENCE SCHOLARSHIP

• *See page 71*

SOCIETY OF WOMEN ENGINEERS http://www.swe.org

CATERPILLAR INC. SCHOLARSHIP

Three $2400 scholarships awarded to undergraduate and graduate students studying engineering. Must be U.S. citizen or authorized to work in the United States. Minimum 2.8 GPA is required.

Academic Fields/Career Goals: Agriculture; Chemical Engineering; Electrical Engineering/Electronics; Engineering/Technology; Materials Science, Engineering, and Metallurgy; Mechanical Engineering.

Award: Scholarship for use in junior, senior, or graduate years; not renewable. *Number:* 3. *Amount:* $2400.

Eligibility Requirements: Applicant must be enrolled or expecting to enroll full-time at a four-year institution or university and female. Available to U.S. citizens.

Application Requirements: Application, essay, references, transcript. *Deadline:* February 1.

Contact: Scholarship Committee
Society of Women Engineers
230 East Ohio Street, Suite 400
Chicago, IL 60611-3265
Phone: 312-596-5223
Fax: 312-596-5252
E-mail: scholarshipapplication@swe.org

SOIL AND WATER CONSERVATION SOCIETY-NEW JERSEY CHAPTER http://www.geocities.com/njswcs

EDWARD R. HALL SCHOLARSHIP

• *See page 71*

SOUTH DAKOTA BOARD OF REGENTS http://www.sdbor.edu

SOUTH DAKOTA BOARD OF REGENTS BJUGSTAD SCHOLARSHIP

• *See page 71*

SOUTH FLORIDA FAIR AND PALM BEACH COUNTY EXPOSITIONS INC. http://www.southfloridafair.com

SOUTH FLORIDA FAIR AGRICULTURAL COLLEGE SCHOLARSHIP

Renewable award of $2000 for students pursuing a degree in agriculture. Must be a permanent resident of Florida.

Academic Fields/Career Goals: Agriculture.

Award: Scholarship for use in freshman, sophomore, junior, or senior years; renewable. *Number:* 2. *Amount:* $2000.

Eligibility Requirements: Applicant must be enrolled or expecting to enroll full- or part-time at a four-year institution or university and resident of Florida. Available to U.S. and non-U.S. citizens.

Application Requirements: Application, essay, references, test scores, transcript. *Deadline:* October 15.

Contact: Agriculture Committee
South Florida Fair and Palm Beach County Expositions Inc.
PO Box 210367
West Palm Beach, FL 33421-0367
Phone: 561-790-5245

TURF AND ORNAMENTAL COMMUNICATION ASSOCIATION http://www.toca.org

TURF AND ORNAMENTAL COMMUNICATORS ASSOCIATION SCHOLARSHIP PROGRAM

One-time award for undergraduate students majoring or minoring in technical communications or in a green industry field such as horticulture, plant sciences, botany, or agronomy. The applicant must demonstrate an interest in using this course of study in the field of communications. An overall GPA of 3.0 is required in major area of study.

Academic Fields/Career Goals: Agriculture; Communications; Horticulture/Floriculture.

Award: Scholarship for use in freshman, sophomore, junior, or senior years; not renewable. *Number:* 1. *Amount:* $2500.

Eligibility Requirements: Applicant must be enrolled or expecting to enroll full-time at a two-year or four-year institution or university. Applicant must have 3.0 GPA or higher. Available to U.S. and non-U.S. citizens.

Application Requirements: Application, essay, portfolio, resume, references, transcript. *Deadline:* March 1.

Contact: Den Gardner, Executive Director
Turf and Ornamental Communication Association
120 West Main Street, Suite 200
PO Box 156
New Prague, MN 56071
Phone: 952-758-6340
Fax: 952-758-5813
E-mail: tocaassociation@aol.com

UNITED NEGRO COLLEGE FUND http://www.uncf.org

CARGILL SCHOLARSHIP PROGRAM

• *See page 65*

WASHINGTON ASSOCIATION OF WINE GRAPE GROWERS http://www.wawgg.org

WALTER J. CLORE SCHOLARSHIP

A scholarship of minimum $500 to a maximum $2000 is awarded to undergraduate and graduate students enrolled in areas of study pertaining to the wine industry. Scholarships will be given to students who are residents of the state of Washington. The number of awards vary each year.

Academic Fields/Career Goals: Agriculture; Food Science/Nutrition.

Award: Scholarship for use in freshman, sophomore, junior, senior, or graduate years; not renewable. *Number:* 6. *Amount:* $500–$2000.

Eligibility Requirements: Applicant must be enrolled or expecting to enroll full-time at a two-year or four-year institution or university and resident of Washington. Available to U.S. and non-U.S. citizens.

Application Requirements: Application, resume, references, transcript. *Deadline:* December 31.

Contact: Vicky Scharlau, Executive Director
Washington Association of Wine Grape Growers
PO Box 716
Cashmere, WA 98815
Phone: 509-782-8234
Fax: 509-782-1203
E-mail: vicky@501consultants.com

WOMEN GROCERS OF AMERICA http://www.nationalgrocers.org

MARY MACEY SCHOLARSHIP

Award for students intending to pursue a career in the independent sector of the grocery industry. One-time award for students who have completed freshman year. Submit statement and recommendation from sponsor in the grocery industry. Applicant should have a minimum 2.0 GPA.

Academic Fields/Career Goals: Agriculture; Business/Consumer Services; Food Service/Hospitality.

Award: Scholarship for use in sophomore, junior, senior, graduate, or postgraduate years; not renewable. *Number:* 2–7. *Amount:* $1000.

Eligibility Requirements: Applicant must be enrolled or expecting to enroll full-time at a two-year or four-year institution or university. Available to U.S. citizens.

Application Requirements: Application, references, transcript, personal statement. *Deadline:* May 15.

Contact: Kristen Comley, Director of Administration
Women Grocers of America
1005 North Glebe Road, Suite 250
Arlington, VA 22201-5758
Phone: 703-516-0700
Fax: 703-516-0115
E-mail: kcomley@nationalgrocers.org

AMERICAN STUDIES

AMERICAN FEDERATION OF STATE, COUNTY, AND MUNICIPAL EMPLOYEES http://www.afscme.org

AFSCME/UNCF UNION SCHOLARS PROGRAM

One-time award for a sophomore or junior majoring in ethnic studies, women's studies, labor studies, American studies, sociology, anthropology, history, political science, psychology, social work or economics. Must be African-American, Hispanic-American, Asian Pacific Islander, or American-Indian/Alaska Native. Minimum 2.5 GPA.

Academic Fields/Career Goals: American Studies; Anthropology; History; Political Science; Psychology; Social Sciences; Social Services; Women's Studies.

Award: Scholarship for use in sophomore or junior years; not renewable. *Number:* 10. *Amount:* up to $5000.

Eligibility Requirements: Applicant must be American Indian/Alaska Native, Asian/Pacific Islander, Black (non-Hispanic), or Hispanic and enrolled or expecting to enroll full-time at a four-year institution or university. Applicant must have 2.5 GPA or higher. Available to U.S. citizens.

Application Requirements: Application, essay, references, transcript. *Deadline:* February 28.

Contact: Philip Allen, Scholarship Coordinator
American Federation of State, County, and Municipal Employees
1625 L Street, NW
Washington, DC 20036-5687
Phone: 202-429-1250
Fax: 202-429-1272
E-mail: pallen@asscme.org

LINCOLN FORUM http://www.thelincolnforum.org

PLATT FAMILY SCHOLARSHIP PRIZE ESSAY CONTEST

Scholarship essay contest is designed for students who are full-time students in an American college or university. For details refer to Web site: http://www.thelincolnforum.org/essayContest.html.

Academic Fields/Career Goals: American Studies; History.

Award: Prize for use in freshman, sophomore, junior, senior, or graduate years; not renewable. *Number:* 3. *Amount:* $250–$1000.

Eligibility Requirements: Applicant must be enrolled or expecting to enroll full-time at a four-year institution or university and must have an interest in writing. Available to U.S. citizens.

Application Requirements: Applicant must enter a contest, essay. *Deadline:* July 31.

Contact: Don McCue, Curator
Lincoln Forum
125 West Vine Street
Redlands, CA 92373
Phone: 909-798-7632
E-mail: archives@akspl.org

ORGANIZATION OF AMERICAN HISTORIANS http://www.oah.org

BINKLEY-STEPHENSON AWARD

One-time award of $500 for the best scholarly article published in the Journal of American History during the preceding calendar year.

Academic Fields/Career Goals: American Studies; History.

Award: Prize for use in freshman, sophomore, junior, senior, graduate, or postgraduate years; not renewable. *Number:* 1. *Amount:* $500.

Eligibility Requirements: Applicant must be enrolled or expecting to enroll full- or part-time at a two-year or four-year or technical institution or university and must have an interest in writing. Available to U.S. and non-U.S. citizens.

Application Requirements: Application, applicant must enter a contest. *Deadline:* continuous.

Contact: Kara Hamm, Award and Prize Committee Coordinator
Organization of American Historians
112 North Bryan Avenue
PO Box 5457
Bloomington, IN 47407-5457
Phone: 812-855-9852
Fax: 812-855-0696
E-mail: awards@oah.org

SONS OF THE REPUBLIC OF TEXAS http://www.srttexas.org

PRESIDIO LA BAHIA AWARD

Award of $2000 is available annually for winning participants in the competition, with a minimum first place prize of $1200 for the best published book. Competition is open to any person interested in the Spanish Colonial influence on Texas culture. Refer to Web Site: http://www.srttexas.org/labahia.html for details.

Academic Fields/Career Goals: American Studies; History.

Award: Prize for use in freshman, sophomore, junior, senior, graduate, or postgraduate years; not renewable. *Number:* 1. *Amount:* $1200–$2000.

Eligibility Requirements: Applicant must be enrolled or expecting to enroll full- or part-time at a two-year or four-year or technical institution or university and must have an interest in writing. Available to U.S. and non-U.S. citizens.

Application Requirements: Application, applicant must enter a contest, four copies of published writings. *Deadline:* September 30.

Contact: Janet Hickl, Administrative Assistant
Sons of the Republic of Texas
1717 Eighth Street
Bay City, TX 77414
Phone: 979-245-6644
Fax: 979-244-3819
E-mail: srttexas@srttexas.org

SUMMERFIELD G. ROBERTS AWARD

Award of $2500 to the author of a work of creative writing on the Republic of Texas period (1836-1846). Manuscripts must be written or published during the calendar year for which the award is given. Refer to Web Site: http://www.srttexas.org/sumfield.html for details.

Academic Fields/Career Goals: American Studies; History.

Award: Prize for use in freshman, sophomore, junior, senior, graduate, or postgraduate years; not renewable. *Number:* 1. *Amount:* $2500.

Eligibility Requirements: Applicant must be enrolled or expecting to enroll full- or part-time at a two-year or four-year or technical institution or university and must have an interest in writing. Available to U.S. and non-U.S. citizens.

Application Requirements: Manuscript. *Deadline:* January 15.

Contact: Janet Hickl, Administrative Assistant
Sons of the Republic of Texas
1717 Eighth Street
Bay City, TX 77414
Phone: 979-245-6644
Fax: 979-244-3819
E-mail: srttexas@srttexas.org

TEXAS HISTORY ESSAY CONTEST

Contest for best essay on the history of Texas written by graduating seniors in any high school in the United States. History, government and English students are particularly encouraged to participate. Prizes will be scholarships to the college of each winner's choice or will be given to the student directly if he or she does not intend to attend a college or university. First prize $3000, second prize $2000, third prize $1000.

Academic Fields/Career Goals: American Studies; History.

Award: Prize for use in freshman year; not renewable. *Number:* 3. *Amount:* $1000–$3000.

Eligibility Requirements: Applicant must be high school student; planning to enroll or expecting to enroll full- or part-time at a two-year or four-year or technical institution or university and must have an interest in writing. Available to U.S. citizens.

Application Requirements: Applicant must enter a contest, essay. *Deadline:* January 31.

Contact: Janet Hickl, Administrative Assistant
Sons of the Republic of Texas
1717 Eighth Street
Bay City, TX 77414
Phone: 979-245-6644
E-mail: srttexas@srttexas.org

ANIMAL/VETERINARY SCIENCES

AMERICAN KENNEL CLUB http://www.akc.org

VETERINARY TECHNICIAN STUDENT SCHOLARSHIPS

Scholarship for full-time student at an American Veterinary Medical Association (AVMA) accredited veterinary technician school. Must be a NAVTA student member or a member of a NAVTA student chapter.

Academic Fields/Career Goals: Animal/Veterinary Sciences.

Award: Scholarship for use in freshman, sophomore, junior, senior, or graduate years; not renewable. *Number:* varies. *Amount:* varies.

Eligibility Requirements: Applicant must be enrolled or expecting to enroll full-time at a four-year institution or university. Applicant or parent of applicant must be member of National Association of Veterinary Technicians in America. Available to U.S. citizens.

Application Requirements: Application, essay, transcript, copy of NAVTA membership card. *Deadline:* May 1.

Contact: Debra Bonnefond, Director of Veterinary Services
American Kennel Club
5580 Centerview Drive
Raleigh, NC 27606
Phone: 919-816-3717
Fax: 919-816-3770
E-mail: info@akc.org

AMERICAN QUARTER HORSE FOUNDATION (AQHF) http://www.aqha.com/foundation

AQHF RACING SCHOLARSHIPS

Scholarships for members of AQHA/AQHYA who have experience within the racing industry or are seeking a career in the industry. Applicants seeking a career in the racing industry may specialize in veterinary medicine, racetrack management or other related fields. Members may apply during their senior year of high school or while enrolled at an accredited college, university or vocational school. Renewable up to four years. Minimum 2.5 GPA required.

Academic Fields/Career Goals: Animal/Veterinary Sciences.

Award: Scholarship for use in freshman, sophomore, junior, or senior years; renewable. *Number:* 5. *Amount:* $8000.

Eligibility Requirements: Applicant must be enrolled or expecting to enroll full-time at a two-year or four-year or technical institution or university and must have an interest in animal/agricultural competition. Applicant or parent of applicant must be member of American Quarter Horse Association. Applicant must have 2.5 GPA or higher. Available to U.S. and Canadian citizens.

Application Requirements: Application, essay, financial need analysis, photo, references, transcript. *Deadline:* January 2.

Contact: Laura Owens, Scholarship Office
American Quarter Horse Foundation (AQHF)
2601 East Interstate 40
Amarillo, TX 79104
Phone: 806-378-5029
Fax: 806-376-1005
E-mail: foundation@aqha.org

AQHF TELEPHONY EQUINE VETERINARY SCHOLARSHIP

Scholarship to an AQHA member in an equine veterinary medicine or surgery program who wishes to pursue an equine-focused veterinary practice. Applicants must be enrolled as a third year student when applying. Funding will be applied to students last year of the veterinary program. Minimum GPA 3.0 required.

Academic Fields/Career Goals: Animal/Veterinary Sciences.

Award: Scholarship for use in junior year; not renewable. *Number:* 1. *Amount:* $10,000.

Eligibility Requirements: Applicant must be enrolled or expecting to enroll full-time at a four-year institution or university. Applicant or parent of applicant must be member of American Quarter Horse Association. Applicant must have 3.0 GPA or higher. Available to U.S. and Canadian citizens.

Application Requirements: Application, financial need analysis, photo, references, transcript. *Deadline:* January 2.

Contact: Scholarship Office
American Quarter Horse Foundation (AQHF)
2601 East Interstate 40
Amarillo, TX 79104
Phone: 806-378-5029
Fax: 806-376-1005
E-mail: foundation@aqha.org

ARIZONA QUARTER HORSE YOUTH RACING SCHOLARSHIP

Scholarship to an AQHA/AQHYA member from Arizona who has experience within the racing industry or is seeking a career in the industry. Applicants seeking a career in the racing industry may specialize in veterinary medicine, racetrack management or other related fields. Members may apply during their senior year of high school or while enrolled at an accredited college, university or vocational school. Minimum GPA 2.5 required.

Academic Fields/Career Goals: Animal/Veterinary Sciences; Recreation, Parks, Leisure Studies.

Award: Scholarship for use in freshman, sophomore, junior, or senior years; not renewable. *Number:* 1. *Amount:* $500.

Eligibility Requirements: Applicant must be enrolled or expecting to enroll full-time at a two-year or four-year or technical institution or university and resident of Arizona. Applicant or parent of applicant must be member of American Quarter Horse Association. Applicant must have 2.5 GPA or higher. Available to U.S. and Canadian citizens.

Application Requirements: Application, driver's license, financial need analysis, photo, references, transcript, proof of residency. *Deadline:* January 2.

Contact: Scholarship Office
American Quarter Horse Foundation (AQHF)
2601 East Interstate 40
Amarillo, TX 79104
Phone: 806-378-5029
Fax: 806-376-1005
E-mail: foundation@aqha.org

APPALOOSA HORSE CLUB-APPALOOSA YOUTH PROGRAM http://www.appaloosa.com

LEW AND JOANN EKLUND EDUCATIONAL SCHOLARSHIP

One-time award for college juniors and seniors and graduate students studying a field related to the equine industry. Must be member or dependent of member of the Appaloosa Horse Club.

Academic Fields/Career Goals: Animal/Veterinary Sciences.

Award: Scholarship for use in junior, senior, or graduate years; not renewable. *Number:* 1. *Amount:* $2000.

Eligibility Requirements: Applicant must be enrolled or expecting to enroll full-time at a four-year institution or university. Applicant or parent of applicant must be member of Appaloosa Horse Club/Appaloosa Youth Association. Applicant must have 3.5 GPA or higher. Available to U.S. and non-U.S. citizens.

Application Requirements: Application, applicant must enter a contest, essay, photo, references, transcript. *Deadline:* June 10.

Contact: Anna Brown, AYF Coordinator
Appaloosa Horse Club-Appaloosa Youth Program
2720 West Pullman Road
Moscow, ID 83843
Phone: 208-882-5578 Ext. 264
Fax: 208-882-8150
E-mail: youth@appaloosa.com

ARKANSAS DEPARTMENT OF HIGHER EDUCATION http://www.adhe.edu

ARKANSAS HEALTH EDUCATION GRANT PROGRAM (ARHEG)

Award provides assistance to Arkansas residents pursuing professional degrees in dentistry, optometry, veterinary medicine, podiatry, chiropractic medicine, or osteopathic medicine at out-of-state, accredited institutions (programs that are unavailable in Arkansas).

Academic Fields/Career Goals: Animal/Veterinary Sciences; Dental Health/Services; Health and Medical Sciences; Osteopathy.

Award: Grant for use in freshman, sophomore, junior, senior, or graduate years; renewable. *Number:* 258–288. *Amount:* $5000–$14,600.

Eligibility Requirements: Applicant must be enrolled or expecting to enroll full-time at a four-year institution or university and resident of Arkansas. Available to U.S. citizens.

Application Requirements: Application, affidavit of Arkansas residency. *Deadline:* continuous.

Contact: Tara Smith, Director of Financial Aid
Arkansas Department of Higher Education
114 East Capitol Avenue
Little Rock, AR 72201-3818
Phone: 501-371-2000
Fax: 501-371-2002
E-mail: taras@adhe.edu

ASSOCIATION FOR WOMEN IN SCIENCE EDUCATIONAL FOUNDATION http://www.awis.org/careers/edfoundation.html

ASSOCIATION FOR WOMEN IN SCIENCE COLLEGE SCHOLARSHIP

Scholarship for women who plan a career in science as a researcher and/or teacher. Must maintain a GPA of 3.75 or higher and math plus verbal SAT scores. Open to U.S. citizens only.

Academic Fields/Career Goals: Animal/Veterinary Sciences; Biology; Chemical Engineering; Computer Science/Data Processing; Earth Science; Engineering/Technology; Materials Science, Engineering, and Metallurgy; Mechanical Engineering; Meteorology/Atmospheric Science; Natural Sciences; Nuclear Science; Physical Sciences and Math.

Award: Scholarship for use in freshman year; not renewable. *Number:* 2–10. *Amount:* $100–$1000.

Eligibility Requirements: Applicant must be high school student; planning to enroll or expecting to enroll full-time at a four-year institution or university and female. Available to U.S. citizens.

Application Requirements: Application, essay, references, test scores, transcript. *Deadline:* January 17.

Contact: Barbara Filner, President
Association for Women in Science Educational Foundation
7008 Richard Drive
Bethesda, MD 20817-4838
Phone: 301-229-9243
E-mail: awisedfd@awis.org

LOUISIANA OFFICE OF STUDENT FINANCIAL ASSISTANCE http://www.osfa.state.la.us

ROCKEFELLER STATE WILDLIFE SCHOLARSHIP

Awarded to high school graduates, college undergraduates and graduate students majoring in forestry, wildlife or marine science. Renewable up to five years as an undergraduate and two years as a graduate. Must have at least a 2.5 GPA and have taken the ACT or SAT.

Academic Fields/Career Goals: Animal/Veterinary Sciences; Marine Biology; Natural Resources; Natural Sciences.

Award: Scholarship for use in freshman, sophomore, junior, senior, or graduate years; renewable. *Number:* 60. *Amount:* $1000.

Eligibility Requirements: Applicant must be enrolled or expecting to enroll full-time at a four-year institution or university; resident of Louisiana and studying in Louisiana. Applicant must have 2.5 GPA or higher. Available to U.S. citizens.

Application Requirements: Application, test scores, transcript, FAFSA. *Deadline:* July 1.

Contact: Public Information
Louisiana Office of Student Financial Assistance
PO Box 91202
Baton Rouge, LA 70821-9202
Phone: 800-259-5626 Ext. 1012
Fax: 225-922-0790
E-mail: custserv@osfa.state.la.us

MAINE DEPARTMENT OF AGRICULTURE, FOOD AND RURAL RESOURCES http://www.maine.gov/agriculture

MAINE RURAL REHABILITATION FUND SCHOLARSHIP PROGRAM

• *See page 69*

NATIONAL DAIRY SHRINE http://www.dairyshrine.org

KILDEE SCHOLARSHIPS

• *See page 76*

MARSHALL E. MCCULLOUGH-NATIONAL DAIRY SHRINE SCHOLARSHIPS

• *See page 76*

NATIONAL DAIRY SHRINE/DAIRY MARKETING INC. MILK MARKETING SCHOLARSHIPS

• *See page 76*

NATIONAL DAIRY SHRINE/KLUSSENDORF SCHOLARSHIP

• *See page 77*

NDS STUDENT RECOGNITION CONTEST

• *See page 70*

PROGRESSIVE DAIRY PRODUCER AWARD

• *See page 77*

OREGON SHEEP GROWERS ASSOCIATION http://www.sheeporegon.com

OREGON SHEEP GROWERS ASSOCIATION MEMORIAL SCHOLARSHIP

• *See page 78*

OREGON STUDENT ASSISTANCE COMMISSION http://www.osac.state.or.us

ROYDEN M. BODLEY SCHOLARSHIP

One-time award open to high school graduates who earned their Eagle rank in Boy Scouts of America Cascade Pacific Council. Must major in forestry, wildlife, environment, or related field. Must attend an Oregon college.

Academic Fields/Career Goals: Animal/Veterinary Sciences; Environmental Science; Natural Resources; Natural Sciences.

Award: Scholarship for use in freshman year; renewable. *Number:* varies. *Amount:* varies.

Eligibility Requirements: Applicant must be enrolled or expecting to enroll full-time at a four-year institution; male; resident of Oregon and studying in Oregon. Applicant or parent of applicant must be member of Boy Scouts. Available to U.S. citizens.

Application Requirements: Application, essay, financial need analysis, transcript, activity chart. *Deadline:* March 1.

Contact: Director of Grant Programs
Oregon Student Assistance Commission
1500 Valley River Drive, Suite 100
Eugene, OR 97401-7020
Phone: 800-452-8807 Ext. 7395

RESOURCE CENTER

MARIE BLAHA MEDICAL GRANT

One-time award of up to $1000 given to students pursuing any medical related field (e.g. nursing, therapy, dental, psychiatry, veterinary science). In honor of Marie Blaha who lost her life in an auto accident. Deadlines: January 1 and July 1. Recipient selection will be based on a 250-word original essay and referral letters.

Academic Fields/Career Goals: Animal/Veterinary Sciences; Behavioral Science; Dental Health/Services; Health Administration; Health and Medical Sciences; Nursing; Pharmacy; Therapy/Rehabilitation.

Award: Grant for use in freshman, sophomore, junior, senior, graduate, or postgraduate years; not renewable. *Number:* 1–10. *Amount:* up to $1000.

Eligibility Requirements: Applicant must be enrolled or expecting to enroll full- or part-time at a two-year or four-year or technical institution or university. Available to U.S. and non-U.S. citizens.

Application Requirements: Application, essay, references, self-addressed stamped envelope, transcript. *Fee:* $5. *Deadline:* varies.

Contact: Dee Blaha, Owner
Resource Center
16362 Wilson Boulevard
Masaryktown, FL 34604-7335
Phone: 352-799-1381
E-mail: dblaha1@tampabay.rr.com

ROCKY MOUNTAIN ELK FOUNDATION http://www.elkfoundation.org

WILDLIFE LEADERSHIP AWARDS

Awards will be presented to up to 10 undergraduate wildlife students. Each award carries a $2000 scholarship, and a one-year membership to the RMEF.

Academic Fields/Career Goals: Animal/Veterinary Sciences; Natural Resources.

Award: Scholarship for use in junior, senior, or graduate years; not renewable. *Number:* up to 10. *Amount:* $2000.

Eligibility Requirements: Applicant must be enrolled or expecting to enroll full- or part-time at a two-year or four-year or technical institution or university and must have an interest in wildlife conservation/animal rescue. Available to U.S. and Canadian citizens.

Application Requirements: Application, applicant must enter a contest, autobiography. *Deadline:* March 1.

Contact: Sara Dexter, Scholarship Committee
Rocky Mountain Elk Foundation
PO Box 8249
Missoula, MT 59807-8249
Phone: 406-523-4548
E-mail: sdexter@rmef.org

SIGMA XI, THE SCIENTIFIC RESEARCH SOCIETY http://www.sigmaxi.org

SIGMA XI GRANTS-IN-AID OF RESEARCH

• *See page 78*

SOCIETY FOR RANGE MANAGEMENT http://www.rangelands.org

MASONIC RANGE SCIENCE SCHOLARSHIP

• *See page 71*

SOIL AND WATER CONSERVATION SOCIETY-NEW JERSEY CHAPTER http://www.geocities.com/njswcs

EDWARD R. HALL SCHOLARSHIP

• *See page 71*

UNITED NEGRO COLLEGE FUND http://www.uncf.org

CARGILL SCHOLARSHIP PROGRAM

• *See page 65*

WILSON ORNITHOLOGICAL SOCIETY http://www.wilsonsociety.org

GEORGE A. HALL/HAROLD F. MAYFIELD AWARD

One-time award for scientific research on birds. Available to independent researchers without access to funds or facilities at a college or university. Must be a nonprofessional to apply. Submit research proposal.

Academic Fields/Career Goals: Animal/Veterinary Sciences; Biology; Natural Resources.

Award: Grant for use in freshman, sophomore, junior, senior, graduate, or postgraduate years; not renewable. *Number:* 1. *Amount:* $1000.

Eligibility Requirements: Applicant must be enrolled or expecting to enroll full- or part-time at a four-year institution or university. Available to U.S. and non-U.S. citizens.

Application Requirements: Application, references, proposal. *Deadline:* February 1.

Contact: Dr. Robert Payne, Research Grants Coordinator
Wilson Ornithological Society
Museum of Zoology, University of Michigan
1109 Geddes Avenue
Ann Arbor, MI 48109-1079
Phone: 734-647-2208
Fax: 734-763-4080
E-mail: rbpayne@umich.edu

PAUL A. STEWART AWARDS

One-time award for studies of bird movements based on banding, analysis of recoveries, and returns of banded birds, or research with an emphasis on economic ornithology. Submit research proposal.

Academic Fields/Career Goals: Animal/Veterinary Sciences; Biology; Natural Resources.

Award: Grant for use in freshman, sophomore, junior, senior, graduate, or postgraduate years; not renewable. *Number:* 1–4. *Amount:* up to $500.

Eligibility Requirements: Applicant must be enrolled or expecting to enroll full- or part-time at a four-year institution or university. Available to U.S. and non-U.S. citizens.

Application Requirements: Application, references, proposal. *Deadline:* February 1.

Contact: Dr. Robert Payne, Research Grants Coordinator
Wilson Ornithological Society
Museum of Zoology, University of Michigan
1109 Geddes Avenue
Ann Arbor, MI 48109-1079
Phone: 734-647-2208
Fax: 734-763-4080
E-mail: rbpayne@umich.edu

ANTHROPOLOGY

AMERICAN FEDERATION OF STATE, COUNTY, AND MUNICIPAL EMPLOYEES http://www.afscme.org

AFSCME/UNCF UNION SCHOLARS PROGRAM

• *See page 80*

AMERICAN SCHOOL OF CLASSICAL STUDIES AT ATHENS http://www.ascsa.edu.gr

ASCSA SUMMER SESSIONS OPEN SCHOLARSHIPS

Award for undergraduate students, graduate students, middle school teachers, high school teachers, and college teachers. Six-week sessions are conducted to

American School of Classical Studies at Athens (continued)

help applicants become acquainted with Greece and its antiquities, and to improve their understanding of the relationship between the monuments, landscape, and climate of the country and its history, literature, and culture.

Academic Fields/Career Goals: Anthropology; Archaeology; Architecture; Art History; Arts; European Studies; Historic Preservation and Conservation; History; Humanities; Museum Studies; Philosophy; Religion/Theology.

Award: Scholarship for use in senior, graduate, or postgraduate years; not renewable. *Number:* 10. *Amount:* up to $3000.

Eligibility Requirements: Applicant must be enrolled or expecting to enroll full- or part-time at a four-year institution or university and must have an interest in international exchange. Available to U.S. and non-U.S. citizens.

Application Requirements: Application, references, transcript. *Deadline:* January 15.

Contact: Mary Darlington, Executive Assistant
American School of Classical Studies at Athens
6-8 Charlton Street
Princeton, NJ 08540-5232
Phone: 609-683-0800
Fax: 609-924-0578

CANADIAN RECREATIONAL CANOEING ASSOCIATION http://www.paddlingcanada.com

BILL MASON MEMORIAL SCHOLARSHIP FUND

• *See page 74*

POLISH HERITAGE ASSOCIATION OF MARYLAND http://www.pha-md.org

DR. JOSEPHINE WTULICH MEMORIAL SCHOLARSHIP

Scholarship will be awarded to a student whose major is in the humanities, sociology, or anthropology. Must be of Polish descent (at least two Polish grandparents), resident of Maryland, and a U.S. citizen. Scholarship value is $1500.

Academic Fields/Career Goals: Anthropology; Humanities; Social Sciences.

Award: Scholarship for use in freshman, sophomore, junior, or senior years; not renewable. *Number:* 1. *Amount:* up to $1500.

Eligibility Requirements: Applicant must be of Polish heritage; enrolled or expecting to enroll full-time at a two-year or four-year institution or university and resident of Maryland. Available to U.S. citizens.

Application Requirements: Application, essay, interview, photo, references, test scores, transcript. *Deadline:* March 31.

Contact: Thomas Hollowak, Scholarship Committee
Polish Heritage Association of Maryland
Seven Dendron Court
Baltimore, MD 21234
Phone: 410-837-4268
E-mail: thollowak@ubalt.edu

APPLIED SCIENCES

AMERICAN INDIAN SCIENCE AND ENGINEERING SOCIETY http://www.aises.org

A.T. ANDERSON MEMORIAL SCHOLARSHIP PROGRAM

Award for full-time students majoring in math, engineering, science, medicine, or natural resources. Must be at least one quarter American-Indian or Alaska Native or have tribal recognition, and be member of AISES. Must have minimum 3.0 GPA.

Academic Fields/Career Goals: Applied Sciences; Biology; Business/Consumer Services; Earth Science; Health and Medical Sciences; Meteorology/Atmospheric Science; Natural Resources; Natural Sciences; Nuclear Science; Physical Sciences and Math.

Award: Scholarship for use in freshman, sophomore, junior, senior, or graduate years; not renewable. *Number:* varies. *Amount:* $1000–$2000.

Eligibility Requirements: Applicant must be American Indian/Alaska Native and enrolled or expecting to enroll full-time at a two-year or four-year institution or university. Available to U.S. citizens.

Application Requirements: Application, essay, resume, references, transcript, tribal enrollment document. *Deadline:* June 15.

Contact: Scholarship Information
American Indian Science and Engineering Society
PO Box 9828
Albuquerque, NM 87119-9828
Phone: 505-765-1052
Fax: 505-765-5608
E-mail: info@aises.org

BURLINGTON NORTHERN SANTA FE FOUNDATION SCHOLARSHIP

Award for high school senior for study of science, business, education, and health administration. Must reside in Arizona, Colorado, Kansas, Minnesota, Montana, North Dakota, New Mexico, Oklahoma, Oregon, South Dakota, Washington, or California. Must be at least one quarter American-Indian or Alaska Native and/or member of federally recognized tribe. Minimum 2.0 GPA required.

Academic Fields/Career Goals: Applied Sciences; Biology; Business/Consumer Services; Health Administration; Meteorology/Atmospheric Science; Natural Sciences; Nuclear Science; Physical Sciences and Math.

Award: Scholarship for use in freshman, sophomore, junior, senior, graduate, or postgraduate years; renewable. *Number:* up to 5. *Amount:* up to $2500.

Eligibility Requirements: Applicant must be American Indian/Alaska Native; high school student; planning to enroll or expecting to enroll full-time at a two-year or four-year or technical institution or university and resident of Arizona, California, Colorado, Kansas, Minnesota, Montana, New Mexico, North Dakota, Oklahoma, Oregon, South Dakota, or Washington. Available to U.S. citizens.

Application Requirements: Application, essay, resume, references, transcript. *Deadline:* April 15.

Contact: Scholarship Information
American Indian Science and Engineering Society
PO Box 9828
Albuquerque, NM 87119-9828
Phone: 505-765-1052
Fax: 505-765-5608
E-mail: info@aises.org

AMERICAN INSTITUTE OF AERONAUTICS AND ASTRONAUTICS http://www.aiaa.org

AIAA UNDERGRADUATE SCHOLARSHIP

Renewable award available to college sophomores, juniors and seniors enrolled full-time in an accredited college/university. Must be AIAA student member or become one prior to receiving award. Course of study must provide entry into some field of science or engineering encompassed by AIAA. Minimum 3.3 GPA required.

Academic Fields/Career Goals: Applied Sciences; Aviation/Aerospace; Electrical Engineering/Electronics; Engineering/Technology; Materials Science, Engineering, and Metallurgy; Mechanical Engineering; Physical Sciences and Math; Science, Technology, and Society.

Award: Scholarship for use in freshman, sophomore, junior, or senior years; renewable. *Number:* 30. *Amount:* $2000–$2500.

Eligibility Requirements: Applicant must be enrolled or expecting to enroll full-time at a two-year or four-year or technical institution or university. Applicant or parent of applicant must be member of American Institute of Aeronautics and Astronautics. Available to U.S. and non-U.S. citizens.

Application Requirements: Application, essay, references, transcript. *Deadline:* January 31.

Contact: Jayesh Hirani, Student Programs Specialist
American Institute of Aeronautics and Astronautics
1801 Alexander Bell Drive, Suite 500
Reston, VA 20191
Phone: 703-264-7500
Fax: 703-264-7551
E-mail: jayeshh@aiaa.org

AMERICAN SOCIETY FOR ENGINEERING EDUCATION http://www.asee.org

SCIENCE, MATHEMATICS, AND RESEARCH FOR TRANSFORMATION DEFENSE SCHOLARSHIP FOR SERVICE PROGRAM

Award established by the Department of Defense to support the education, recruitment, and retention of undergraduate and graduate students in the fields of science, technology, engineering, and mathematics. Available only to full-time undergraduate or graduate students with 3.0 GPA or above.

Academic Fields/Career Goals: Applied Sciences; Engineering/Technology; Engineering-Related Technologies; Mathematics; Physical Sciences and Math.

Award: Scholarship for use in sophomore, junior, senior, or graduate years; renewable. *Number:* 200. *Amount:* $22,000–$39,000.

Eligibility Requirements: Applicant must be age 18 and over and enrolled or expecting to enroll full-time at a two-year or four-year institution or university. Applicant must have 3.0 GPA or higher. Available to U.S. citizens.

Application Requirements: Application, essay, references, transcript. *Deadline:* December 14.

Contact: Evan Gaines, Project Coordinator
American Society for Engineering Education
1818 N Street, NW, Suite 600
Washington, DC 20036
Phone: 202-331-3544
Fax: 202-265-8504
E-mail: smart@asee.org

AMERICAN SOCIETY OF HEATING, REFRIGERATING, AND AIR CONDITIONING ENGINEERS INC. http://www.ashrae.org

AMERICAN SOCIETY OF HEATING, REFRIGERATION, AND AIR CONDITIONING ENGINEERING TECHNOLOGY SCHOLARSHIP

Available to undergraduate engineering technology students enrolled full-time and pursuing a bachelor or associate degree in an engineering technology program that has been a preparatory curriculum for a career in HVAC&R. Applicants must have a GPA of at least 3.0. Two scholarships for associate degree students and one for a undergraduate degree student.

Academic Fields/Career Goals: Applied Sciences; Engineering/Technology; Heating, Air-Conditioning, and Refrigeration Mechanics; Trade/Technical Specialties.

Award: Scholarship for use in sophomore, junior, or senior years; not renewable. *Number:* 3. *Amount:* up to $3000.

Eligibility Requirements: Applicant must be enrolled or expecting to enroll full-time at a two-year or four-year institution and must have an interest in leadership. Applicant must have 3.0 GPA or higher. Available to U.S. and non-U.S. citizens.

Application Requirements: Application, financial need analysis, references, transcript. *Deadline:* May 1.

Contact: Lois Benedict, Scholarship Administrator
American Society of Heating, Refrigerating, and Air Conditioning Engineers Inc.
1791 Tullie Circle, NE
Atlanta, GA 30329
Phone: 404-636-8400
Fax: 404-321-5478
E-mail: lbenedict@ashrae.org

AMERICAN SOCIETY OF NAVAL ENGINEERS http://www.navalengineers.org

AMERICAN SOCIETY OF NAVAL ENGINEERS SCHOLARSHIP

Award for naval engineering students in the final year of an undergraduate program or after one year of graduate study at an accredited institution. Must be full-time student and a U.S. citizen. Minimum 2.5 GPA required. Award of $2500 for undergraduates and $3500 for graduate students. Graduate student applicants are required to be member of the American Society of Naval Engineers.

Academic Fields/Career Goals: Applied Sciences; Aviation/Aerospace; Civil Engineering; Electrical Engineering/Electronics; Energy and Power Engineering; Engineering/Technology; Marine/Ocean Engineering; Materials Science, Engineering, and Metallurgy; Mechanical Engineering; Physical Sciences and Math.

Award: Scholarship for use in senior or graduate years; renewable. *Number:* 8–14. *Amount:* $2500–$3500.

Eligibility Requirements: Applicant must be enrolled or expecting to enroll full-time at a four-year institution or university. Applicant must have 2.5 GPA or higher. Available to U.S. citizens.

Application Requirements: Application, photo, references, self-addressed stamped envelope, test scores, transcript. *Deadline:* February 15.

Contact: David Woodbury, Director, Business & Operations
American Society of Naval Engineers
1452 Duke Street
Alexandria, VA 22314
Phone: 703-836-6727
Fax: 703-836-7491
E-mail: dwoodbury@navalengineers.org

ARRL FOUNDATION INC. http://www.arrl.org

CHARLES N. FISHER MEMORIAL SCHOLARSHIP

One-time award available to amateur radio operators in any class. Applicant must be majoring in electronics, communications, or a related field. Preference is given to residents of Arizona and Los Angeles, Orange County, San Diego, or Santa Barbara, California. Must attend regionally accredited institution.

Academic Fields/Career Goals: Applied Sciences; Communications; Electrical Engineering/Electronics; Engineering/Technology.

Award: Scholarship for use in freshman, sophomore, junior, or senior years; not renewable. *Number:* 1. *Amount:* $1000.

Eligibility Requirements: Applicant must be enrolled or expecting to enroll full-time at a four-year institution or university; resident of Arizona or California and must have an interest in amateur radio. Available to U.S. citizens.

Application Requirements: Application, transcript. *Deadline:* February 1.

Contact: Mary M. Hobart, Secretary
ARRL Foundation Inc.
225 Main Street
Newington, CT 06111-1494
Phone: 860-594-0397
Fax: 860-594-0259
E-mail: k1mmh@arrl.org

MISSISSIPPI SCHOLARSHIP

Available to students pursuing a degree in electronics, communications, or related fields. Must be licensed in any class of amateur radio operators. Preference to Mississippi residents. Must attend a school in Mississippi, and be under 30 years of age.

Academic Fields/Career Goals: Applied Sciences; Communications; Electrical Engineering/Electronics; Engineering/Technology.

Award: Scholarship for use in freshman, sophomore, junior, or senior years; not renewable. *Number:* 1. *Amount:* $500.

Eligibility Requirements: Applicant must be age 30 or under; enrolled or expecting to enroll full-time at a four-year institution or university; resident of Mississippi; studying in Mississippi and must have an interest in amateur radio. Applicant or parent of applicant must be member of American Radio Relay League. Available to U.S. citizens.

Application Requirements: Application, transcript. *Deadline:* February 1.

Contact: Mary M. Hobart, Secretary
ARRL Foundation Inc.
225 Main Street
Newington, CT 06111-1494
Phone: 860-594-0397
Fax: 860-594-0259
E-mail: k1mmh@arrl.org

PAUL AND HELEN L. GRAUER SCHOLARSHIP

Available to students licensed as novice amateur radio operators. Applicant must be majoring in electronics, communications, or a related field. Preference given to residents of Iowa, Kansas, Missouri, and Nebraska. Pursuit of a baccalaureate or higher degree preferred at an institution in Iowa, Kansas, Missouri, or Nebraska.

ARRL Foundation Inc. (continued)

Academic Fields/Career Goals: Applied Sciences; Communications; Electrical Engineering/Electronics; Engineering/Technology.

Award: Scholarship for use in freshman, sophomore, junior, senior, or graduate years; not renewable. *Number:* 1. *Amount:* $1000.

Eligibility Requirements: Applicant must be enrolled or expecting to enroll full-time at a four-year institution or university; resident of Iowa, Kansas, Missouri, or Nebraska; studying in Iowa, Kansas, Missouri, or Nebraska and must have an interest in amateur radio. Available to U.S. citizens.

Application Requirements: Application, transcript. *Deadline:* February 1.

Contact: Mary M. Hobart, Secretary
ARRL Foundation Inc.
225 Main Street
Newington, CT 06111-1494
Phone: 860-594-0397
Fax: 860-594-0259
E-mail: k1mmh@arrl.org

ASSOCIATION OF CALIFORNIA WATER AGENCIES http://www.acwa.com

ASSOCIATION OF CALIFORNIA WATER AGENCIES SCHOLARSHIPS

Three $3000 awards available to juniors and seniors who are California residents attending California universities. Must be in a water-related field of study. Community college transfers are also eligible as long as they will hold junior class standing as of the fall.

Academic Fields/Career Goals: Applied Sciences; Biology; Civil Engineering; Environmental Science; Hydrology; Natural Resources; Natural Sciences; Surveying; Surveying Technology, Cartography, or Geographic Information Science.

Award: Scholarship for use in junior or senior years; not renewable. *Number:* 3. *Amount:* $3000.

Eligibility Requirements: Applicant must be enrolled or expecting to enroll full-time at a four-year institution or university; resident of California and studying in California. Available to U.S. citizens.

Application Requirements: Application, essay, references, transcript. *Deadline:* April 1.

Contact: Sheri Van Wert, Communications Coordinator
Association of California Water Agencies
901 K Street, Suite 100
Sacramento, CA 95814
Phone: 916-441-4545
Fax: 916-325-2316
E-mail: lavonnew@acwanet.com

CLAIR A. HILL SCHOLARSHIP

Scholarship is administered by a different member agency each year and guidelines vary based on the administrator. Contact ACWA for current information. Applicants must be in a water-related field of study and must be a resident of California enrolled in a California four-year college or university.

Academic Fields/Career Goals: Applied Sciences; Biology; Civil Engineering; Environmental Science; Hydrology; Natural Resources; Natural Sciences; Surveying; Surveying Technology, Cartography, or Geographic Information Science.

Award: Scholarship for use in junior or senior years; not renewable. *Number:* 1. *Amount:* $5000.

Eligibility Requirements: Applicant must be enrolled or expecting to enroll full-time at a four-year institution or university; resident of California and studying in California. Available to U.S. citizens.

Application Requirements: Application, essay, references, transcript. *Deadline:* February 1.

Contact: Sheri Van Wert, Communications Coordinator
Association of California Water Agencies
910 K Street, Suite 100
Sacramento, CA 95814
Phone: 916-441-4545
Fax: 916-325-2316
E-mail: sheriv@acwa.com

ASTRONAUT SCHOLARSHIP FOUNDATION http://www.astronautscholarship.org

ASTRONAUT SCHOLARSHIP FOUNDATION

Scholarship candidates must be nominated by the faculty members. Students may not apply directly for the scholarship. Must be U.S. citizens. Scholarship nominees must be engineering or natural or applied science students.

Academic Fields/Career Goals: Applied Sciences; Aviation/Aerospace; Biology; Chemical Engineering; Computer Science/Data Processing; Earth Science; Electrical Engineering/Electronics; Engineering-Related Technologies; Materials Science, Engineering, and Metallurgy; Mechanical Engineering; Meteorology/Atmospheric Science.

Award: Scholarship for use in sophomore, junior, senior, or graduate years; renewable. *Number:* 19. *Amount:* $10,000.

Eligibility Requirements: Applicant must be enrolled or expecting to enroll full-time at a four-year institution or university. Available to U.S. citizens.

Application Requirements: Financial need analysis, references, transcript. *Deadline:* varies.

Contact: Linn LeBlanc, Executive Director
Astronaut Scholarship Foundation
6225 Vectorspace Boulevard
Titusville, FL 32780
Phone: 321-269-6101 Ext. 6176
Fax: 321-264-9176
E-mail: linnleblanc@astronautscholarship.org

BARRY M. GOLDWATER SCHOLARSHIP AND EXCELLENCE IN EDUCATION FOUNDATION http://www.act.org/goldwater

BARRY M. GOLDWATER SCHOLARSHIP AND EXCELLENCE IN EDUCATION PROGRAM

One-time award to college juniors and seniors who will pursue advanced degrees in mathematics, natural sciences, or engineering. Students planning to study medicine are eligible if they plan a career in research. Candidates must be nominated by their college or university. Minimum 3.0 GPA required. Nomination deadline: February 1.

Academic Fields/Career Goals: Applied Sciences; Biology; Chemical Engineering; Civil Engineering; Computer Science/Data Processing; Earth Science; Engineering/Technology; Materials Science, Engineering, and Metallurgy; Mechanical Engineering; Natural Sciences; Nuclear Science; Physical Sciences and Math.

Award: Scholarship for use in junior or senior years; renewable. *Number:* up to 300. *Amount:* up to $7500.

Eligibility Requirements: Applicant must be enrolled or expecting to enroll full-time at a two-year or four-year institution or university. Applicant must have 3.0 GPA or higher. Available to U.S. and non-U.S. citizens.

Application Requirements: Application, autobiography, essay, references, transcript, school nomination. *Deadline:* February 1.

Contact: Lucy Decher, Administrative Officer
Barry M. Goldwater Scholarship and Excellence in Education Foundation
6225 Brandon Avenue, Suite 315
Springfield, VA 22150-2519
Phone: 703-756-6012
Fax: 703-756-6015
E-mail: goldh2o@vacoxmail.com

DESK AND DERRICK EDUCATIONAL TRUST http://www.addc.org

DESK AND DERRICK EDUCATIONAL TRUST

Scholarship for full-time or part-time junior and senior undergraduates enrolled in an energy related major such as oil, gas, allied industries, and alternative energy. Minimum 3.0 GPA required. The award value ranges from $750 to $1500.

Academic Fields/Career Goals: Applied Sciences; Chemical Engineering; Earth Science; Engineering-Related Technologies; Natural Resources; Natural Sciences; Nuclear Science.

Award: Scholarship for use in junior or senior years; not renewable. *Number:* up to 7. *Amount:* $750–$1500.

Eligibility Requirements: Applicant must be enrolled or expecting to enroll full- or part-time at a four-year institution or university. Applicant must have 3.0 GPA or higher. Available to U.S. and Canadian citizens.

Application Requirements: Application, financial need analysis, transcript. *Deadline:* April 1.

Contact: Cheryl Wootton, Chairman
Desk and Derrick Educational Trust
5153 East 51st Street, Suite 107
Tulsa, OK 74135
Phone: 918-622-1749
Fax: 918-622-1675
E-mail: cwootton@att.net

FOUNDATION FOR SCIENCE AND DISABILITY http://www.stemd.org

GRANTS FOR DISABLED STUDENTS IN THE SCIENCES

Available to graduate students who are disabled. Awards are given for an assistive device or as financial support for scientific research. Undergraduate seniors may apply. One-time award. Electronic application is available.

Academic Fields/Career Goals: Applied Sciences; Biology; Chemical Engineering; Civil Engineering; Computer Science/Data Processing; Electrical Engineering/Electronics; Engineering/Technology; Health and Medical Sciences; Mechanical Engineering; Physical Sciences and Math.

Award: Grant for use in senior or graduate years; not renewable. *Number:* 1–3. *Amount:* $1000.

Eligibility Requirements: Applicant must be enrolled or expecting to enroll full-time at an institution or university. Applicant must be hearing impaired, learning disabled, physically disabled, or visually impaired. Available to U.S. citizens.

Application Requirements: Application, essay, references, transcript. *Deadline:* December 1.

Contact: Richard Mankin, Grants Committee Chair
Foundation for Science and Disability
503 89th Street, NW
Gainesville, FL 32607
Phone: 352-374-5774
Fax: 352-374-5781
E-mail: rmankin@gainesville.usda.ufl.edu

INNOVATION AND SCIENCE COUNCIL OF BRITISH COLUMBIA http://www.bcinnovationcouncil.com

PAUL AND HELEN TRUSSEL SCIENCE AND TECHNOLOGY SCHOLARSHIP

CAN $5000 to $20,000 award to a new recipient each year over a 4 year period. Student must be enrolled in the sciences and have graduated high school in the Kootenay/Boundary region of British Columbia. Student must be entering 3rd year of studies at a BC or AB post secondary institution. Available to Canadian citizens and landed immigrants.

Academic Fields/Career Goals: Applied Sciences; Biology; Chemical Engineering; Computer Science/Data Processing; Earth Science; Geography; Meteorology/Atmospheric Science; Natural Resources; Natural Sciences; Nuclear Science; Physical Sciences and Math; Science, Technology, and Society.

Award: Scholarship for use in junior, senior, graduate, or postgraduate years; renewable. *Number:* 1.

Eligibility Requirements: Applicant must be Canadian citizen; enrolled or expecting to enroll full-time at a two-year or four-year institution or university; resident of British Columbia and studying in Alberta or British Columbia. Applicant must have 3.0 GPA or higher.

Application Requirements: Application, autobiography, references, transcript, proof of citizenship. *Deadline:* May 31.

Contact: BC Innovation Council
Innovation and Science Council of British Columbia
1188 West Georgia Street, Ninth Floor
Vancouver, BC V6E 4A2
Canada
Phone: 604-438-2752
Fax: 604-438-6564
E-mail: info@bcinnovationcouncil.com

INTERNATIONAL SOCIETY FOR OPTICAL ENGINEERING-SPIE http://www.spie.org

SPIE EDUCATIONAL SCHOLARSHIPS IN OPTICAL SCIENCE AND ENGINEERING

Scholarship for undergraduate/graduate students who are SPIE student member. High school students will receive a one-year complimentary student membership. Undergraduate and graduate students must be enrolled in an optics, photonics, imaging, optoelectronics program or related discipline for the full year beginning. Minimum 3.5 GPA required. More details on eligibility and application requirements/forms can be found at http://spie.org/scholarships.

Academic Fields/Career Goals: Applied Sciences; Chemical Engineering; Electrical Engineering/Electronics; Engineering/Technology; Engineering-Related Technologies; Materials Science, Engineering, and Metallurgy; Sports-Related/Exercise Science.

Award: Scholarship for use in freshman, sophomore, junior, senior, or graduate years; not renewable. *Number:* up to 150. *Amount:* $1000–$11,000.

Eligibility Requirements: Applicant must be enrolled or expecting to enroll full- or part-time at a two-year or four-year or technical institution or university. Applicant must have 3.5 GPA or higher. Available to U.S. and non-U.S. citizens.

Application Requirements: Application, essay, references. *Deadline:* January 15.

Contact: Pascale Barnett, Scholarship Coordinator
International Society for Optical Engineering-SPIE
1000 20th Street
PO Box 10
Bellingham, WA 98227-0010
Phone: 360-676-3290 Ext. 5452
Fax: 360-647-1445
E-mail: scholarships@spie.org

NASA DELAWARE SPACE GRANT CONSORTIUM http://www.delspace.org

NASA DELAWARE SPACE GRANT UNDERGRADUATE TUITION SCHOLARSHIP

The scholarships are awarded annually to encourage and recognize highly qualified undergraduate students interested in careers related to aerospace engineering and space science related fields. All must be enrolled in a DESGC affiliate member college or university. Must be a U.S. citizen.

Academic Fields/Career Goals: Applied Sciences; Aviation/Aerospace; Chemical Engineering; Civil Engineering; Earth Science; Electrical Engineering/Electronics; Engineering/Technology; Engineering-Related Technologies; Meteorology/Atmospheric Science; Physical Sciences and Math.

Award: Scholarship for use in freshman, sophomore, junior, or senior years; renewable. *Number:* 6–12. *Amount:* $2000–$3000.

Eligibility Requirements: Applicant must be enrolled or expecting to enroll full-time at a four-year institution or university and studying in Delaware. Available to U.S. citizens.

Application Requirements: Application, essay, references, transcript, proof of U.S. citizenship. *Deadline:* April 15.

Contact: Sherry L. Rowland-Perry, Program Coordinator
NASA Delaware Space Grant Consortium
217 Sharp Lab, University of Delaware
Newark, DE 19716-4793
Phone: 302-831-1094
Fax: 302-831-1843
E-mail: desgc@bartol.udel.edu

NASA IDAHO SPACE GRANT CONSORTIUM http://isgc.uidaho.edu

NASA IDAHO SPACE GRANT CONSORTIUM SCHOLARSHIP PROGRAM

Program awards $1000 scholarships ($500 for each semester) based on GPA (above 3.0), area of study (science/math/engineering or math/science education), full-time status, and attendance at an Idaho institution.

Academic Fields/Career Goals: Applied Sciences; Aviation/Aerospace; Biology; Chemical Engineering; Computer Science/Data Processing; Earth

NASA Idaho Space Grant Consortium (continued)

Science; Education; Electrical Engineering/Electronics; Engineering/Technology; Health and Medical Sciences; Physical Sciences and Math.

Award: Scholarship for use in freshman, sophomore, junior, or senior years; not renewable. *Number:* 1–40. *Amount:* $1000.

Eligibility Requirements: Applicant must be enrolled or expecting to enroll full-time at a four-year institution or university and studying in Idaho. Applicant must have 3.0 GPA or higher. Available to U.S. citizens.

Application Requirements: Application, essay, resume, references, test scores, transcript. *Deadline:* March 3.

Contact: Becky Highfill, Program Director
NASA Idaho Space Grant Consortium
University of Idaho, PO Box 441011
Moscow, ID 83844-1011
Phone: 208-885-4934
Fax: 208-885-1399
E-mail: isgc@uidaho.edu

NASA VERMONT SPACE GRANT CONSORTIUM http://www.cems.uvm.edu/VSGC

VERMONT SPACE GRANT CONSORTIUM SCHOLARSHIP PROGRAM

Applicants' career goals must be in areas related to NASA's interest. Must be resident of Vermont, U.S. citizen, and attend or plan to attend an institution within Vermont. Three scholarships are designated to Native-American recipients. Awards subject to availability of NASA funding.

Academic Fields/Career Goals: Applied Sciences; Aviation/Aerospace; Biology; Computer Science/Data Processing; Earth Science; Engineering/Technology; Engineering-Related Technologies; Materials Science, Engineering, and Metallurgy; Meteorology/Atmospheric Science; Physical Sciences and Math.

Award: Scholarship for use in freshman, sophomore, junior, or senior years; not renewable. *Number:* 10. *Amount:* up to $2000.

Eligibility Requirements: Applicant must be enrolled or expecting to enroll full-time at a two-year or four-year or technical institution or university; resident of Vermont and studying in Vermont. Applicant must have 3.0 GPA or higher. Available to U.S. citizens.

Application Requirements: Application, essay, references, test scores, transcript. *Deadline:* March 1.

Contact: Laurel Zeno, Grant Administrator and Program Coordinator
NASA Vermont Space Grant Consortium
University of Vermont, College of Engineering and Math, Votey Hall
Burlington, VT 05405-0156
Phone: 802-656-1429
Fax: 802-656-1102
E-mail: zeno@cems.uvm.edu

NATIONAL INVENTORS HALL OF FAME http://www.invent.org

COLLEGIATE INVENTORS COMPETITION FOR UNDERGRADUATE STUDENTS

National competition to encourage college students to be active in science, engineering, mathematics, technology, and creative invention, while stimulating their problem solving abilities. This prestigious challenge recognizes the working relationship between student and advisor who are involved in projects that can be patented. The prize winning undergraduate student or student-team receives a $10,000 cash prize.

Academic Fields/Career Goals: Applied Sciences; Biology; Chemical Engineering; Computer Science/Data Processing; Engineering/Technology; Engineering-Related Technologies; Environmental Science; Health and Medical Sciences; Materials Science, Engineering, and Metallurgy; Physical Sciences and Math.

Award: Prize for use in freshman, sophomore, junior, or senior years; not renewable. *Number:* up to 1. *Amount:* up to $10,000.

Eligibility Requirements: Applicant must be enrolled or expecting to enroll full-time at a four-year institution or university. Available to U.S. and non-U.S. citizens.

Application Requirements: Application, applicant must enter a contest. *Deadline:* May 16.

Contact: Program Coordinator
National Inventors Hall of Fame
221 South Broadway Street
Akron, OH 44308-1505
Phone: 703-706-0081

COLLEGIATE INVENTORS COMPETITION-GRAND PRIZE

The competition was designed to encourage college students to be active in science, engineering, mathematics, technology and creative invention, while stimulating their problem-solving abilities. This prestigious challenge recognizes the working relationship between a student and his or her advisor who are involved in projects leading to inventions that can be patented. The winning student or student team receives a $25,000 cash prize. The advisers of the winning entries will receive $3000.

Academic Fields/Career Goals: Applied Sciences; Biology; Chemical Engineering; Computer Science/Data Processing; Engineering/Technology; Engineering-Related Technologies; Environmental Science; Health and Medical Sciences; Materials Science, Engineering, and Metallurgy; Physical Sciences and Math.

Award: Prize for use in freshman, sophomore, junior, senior, graduate, or postgraduate years; not renewable. *Number:* up to 1. *Amount:* up to $25,000.

Eligibility Requirements: Applicant must be enrolled or expecting to enroll full-time at a two-year or four-year institution or university. Available to U.S. and non-U.S. citizens.

Application Requirements: Application, applicant must enter a contest. *Deadline:* May 16.

Contact: Program Coordinator
National Inventors Hall of Fame
221 South Broadway Street
Akron, OH 44308-1505
Phone: 703-706-0081

TKE EDUCATIONAL FOUNDATION http://www.tke.org

CARROL C. HALL MEMORIAL SCHOLARSHIP

One-time award of $700 given to a full-time undergraduate member of Tau Kappa Epsilon, who is earning a degree in education or science and has plans to become a teacher or pursue a profession in science. Applicant should have a demonstrated record of leadership within his chapter, on campus and the community.

Academic Fields/Career Goals: Applied Sciences; Biology; Earth Science; Education; Meteorology/Atmospheric Science; Physical Sciences and Math.

Award: Scholarship for use in freshman, sophomore, junior, or senior years; not renewable. *Number:* 1. *Amount:* $700.

Eligibility Requirements: Applicant must be enrolled or expecting to enroll full-time at a four-year institution or university and must have an interest in leadership. Applicant or parent of applicant must be member of Tau Kappa Epsilon. Applicant must have 3.0 GPA or higher. Available to U.S. and non-U.S. citizens.

Application Requirements: Application, essay, photo, transcript. *Deadline:* February 29.

Contact: Gary A. Reed, President and Chief Executive Officer
TKE Educational Foundation
8645 Founders Road
Indianapolis, IN 46268-1393
Phone: 317-872-6533
Fax: 317-875-8353
E-mail: reedga@tke.org

UNIVERSITIES SPACE RESEARCH ASSOCIATION http://www.usra.edu

UNIVERSITIES SPACE RESEARCH ASSOCIATION SCHOLARSHIP PROGRAM

Award for full-time undergraduate students who have completed at least two years of college credit by the time the award is received. Must be majoring in the physical sciences or engineering; which include, but are not limited to, aerospace engineering, astronomy, biophysics, chemistry, chemical engineering, computer science, electrical engineering, geophysics, geology, mathematics, mechanical engineering, physics, and space science education. Must be U.S. citizen. Minimum 3.5 GPA required.

Academic Fields/Career Goals: Applied Sciences; Aviation/Aerospace; Chemical Engineering; Civil Engineering; Earth Science; Electrical Engineering/Electronics; Engineering/Technology; Materials Science, Engineering, and Metallurgy; Mechanical Engineering; Nuclear Science; Physical Sciences and Math; Science, Technology, and Society.

Award: Scholarship for use in freshman, sophomore, junior, or senior years; not renewable. *Number:* 4. *Amount:* $1000.

Eligibility Requirements: Applicant must be enrolled or expecting to enroll full-time at a four-year institution or university. Applicant must have 3.5 GPA or higher. Available to U.S. citizens.

Application Requirements: Application, essay, references, transcript. *Deadline:* May 1.

Contact: Dr. Hussein Jirdeh, Scholarship Coordinator
Universities Space Research Association
10211 Wincopin Circle, Suite 500
Columbia, MD 21044-3432
Phone: 410-730-2656
Fax: 410-730-3496
E-mail: hjirdeh@usra.edu

ARCHAEOLOGY

AMERICAN PHILOLOGICAL ASSOCIATION http://www.apaclassics.org

MINORITY STUDENT SUMMER SCHOLARSHIP

Award to minority undergraduate students for a scholarship to further an undergraduate's preparation for graduate work in classics or archaeology. Eligible proposals might include (but are not limited to) participation in summer programs or field schools in Italy, Greece, Egypt, or language training at institutions in the U.S, Canada, or Europe. Amount of the award will be $3000. Application must be supported by a member of the APA or the AIA.

Academic Fields/Career Goals: Archaeology; Arts; Classics; Foreign Language; History.

Award: Scholarship for use in freshman, sophomore, junior, or senior years; not renewable. *Number:* 1. *Amount:* $3000.

Eligibility Requirements: Applicant must be American Indian/Alaska Native, Asian/Pacific Islander, Black (non-Hispanic), or Hispanic and enrolled or expecting to enroll full-time at a four-year institution or university. Available to U.S. and non-U.S. citizens.

Application Requirements: Application, essay, financial need analysis, references, transcript. *Deadline:* December 11.

Contact: Adam Blistein, Executive Director
American Philological Association
University of Pennsylvania, 249 South 36th Street, 292 Logan Hall
Philadelphia, PA 19104-6304
Phone: 215-898-4975
Fax: 210-573-7874
E-mail: apaclassics@sas.upenn.edu

AMERICAN SCHOOL OF CLASSICAL STUDIES AT ATHENS http://www.ascsa.edu.gr

ASCSA SUMMER SESSIONS OPEN SCHOLARSHIPS

• *See page 83*

HARVARD TRAVELLERS CLUB

HARVARD TRAVELLERS CLUB GRANTS

Approximately three grants made each year to persons with projects that involve intelligent travel and exploration. The travel must be intimately involved with research and/or exploration. Prefer applications from persons working on advanced degrees.

Academic Fields/Career Goals: Archaeology; Area/Ethnic Studies; Geography; History; Humanities; Natural Sciences.

Award: Grant for use in freshman, sophomore, junior, senior, graduate, or postgraduate years; not renewable. *Number:* 3–4. *Amount:* $500–$1000.

Eligibility Requirements: Applicant must be enrolled or expecting to enroll full- or part-time at a four-year institution or university. Available to U.S. and non-U.S. citizens.

Application Requirements: Application, financial need analysis, resume. *Deadline:* February 28.

Contact: George P. Bates, Trustee
Harvard Travellers Club
PO Box 162
Lincoln, MA 01773
Phone: 781-821-0400
Fax: 781-828-4254
E-mail: jessepage@comcast.net

ARCHITECTURE

AACE INTERNATIONAL http://www.aacei.org

AACE INTERNATIONAL COMPETITIVE SCHOLARSHIP

One-time awards to full-time students pursuing a degree in engineering, construction management, quantity surveying, and related fields. Applications accepted between January 1 and February 15.

Academic Fields/Career Goals: Architecture; Aviation/Aerospace; Chemical Engineering; Civil Engineering; Construction Engineering/Management; Electrical Engineering/Electronics; Engineering/Technology; Engineering-Related Technologies; Mechanical Engineering.

Award: Scholarship for use in freshman, sophomore, junior, senior, or graduate years; not renewable. *Number:* 15–25. *Amount:* $1000–$8000.

Eligibility Requirements: Applicant must be enrolled or expecting to enroll full-time at a two-year or four-year institution or university. Available to U.S. and non-U.S. citizens.

Application Requirements: Application, applicant must enter a contest, essay, transcript. *Deadline:* February 15.

Contact: Charla Miller, Staff Director, Education and Administration
AACE International
209 Prairie Avenue, Suite 100
Morgantown, WV 26501
Phone: 304-296-8444 Ext. 113
Fax: 304-291-5728
E-mail: cmiller@aacei.org

AIA NEW JERSEY/THE NEW JERSEY SOCIETY OF ARCHITECTS http://www.aia-nj.org

AIA NEW JERSEY SCHOLARSHIP PROGRAM

Scholarship available to New Jersey residents or residents from other states attending school in New Jersey. Must be full-time student in an accredited architectural program at a School of Architecture and have completed one full year of study toward a first professional degree. Applicant must indicate interest in and commitment to pursuing an architectural career in New Jersey after graduation. See Web site for more details: http://www.aia-nj.org/about/scholarship.shtml.

Academic Fields/Career Goals: Architecture.

Award: Scholarship for use in freshman, sophomore, junior, senior, or graduate years; renewable. *Number:* 4–6. *Amount:* up to $5000.

Eligibility Requirements: Applicant must be enrolled or expecting to enroll full-time at a four-year institution or university; resident of New Jersey and studying in New Jersey. Available to U.S. and non-U.S. citizens.

Application Requirements: Application, essay, financial need analysis, portfolio, references, transcript. *Fee:* $5. *Deadline:* June 6.

Contact: Robert Zaccone, President
AIA New Jersey/The New Jersey Society of Architects
414 River View Plaza
Trenton, NJ 08611-3420
Phone: 201-767-9575
Fax: 201-767-5541
E-mail: rzaarchitect@earthlink.net

AMERICAN ARCHITECTURAL FOUNDATION http://www.archfoundation.org

AMERICAN INSTITUTE OF ARCHITECTS MINORITY/DISADVANTAGED SCHOLARSHIP

$500 to $2500 renewable scholarship for minority and/or financially disadvantaged students who are high school seniors and college freshmen entering an architecture degree program. Must be nominated by an architecture firm, teacher, dean, or civic organization director. Must include drawing.

Academic Fields/Career Goals: Architecture.

Award: Scholarship for use in freshman year; renewable. *Number:* 20. *Amount:* $500–$2500.

Eligibility Requirements: Applicant must be American Indian/Alaska Native, Asian/Pacific Islander, Black (non-Hispanic), or Hispanic and enrolled or expecting to enroll full-time at a four-year institution or university. Available to U.S. citizens.

Application Requirements: Application, financial need analysis, references, test scores, transcript, drawing. *Deadline:* January 15.

Contact: Mary Felber, Director of Scholarship Programs
American Architectural Foundation
1735 New York Avenue, NW
Washington, DC 20006-5292
Phone: 202-626-7511
Fax: 202-626-7509
E-mail: mfelber@archfoundation.org

AMERICAN INSTITUTE OF ARCHITECTS http://www.aia.org

AMERICAN INSTITUTE OF ARCHITECTS/AMERICAN ARCHITECTURAL FOUNDATION MINORITY/DISADVANTAGED SCHOLARSHIPS

Award to aid high school seniors and college freshmen from minority or disadvantaged backgrounds who are planning to study architecture in an NAAB accredited program. Twenty awards per year, renewable for two additional years. Amounts based on financial need. Must be nominated by either a high school guidance counselor, AIA component, architect, or other individual who is aware of the student's interest and aptitude. Nomination deadline is early December; applications must be mailed to be eligible.

Academic Fields/Career Goals: Architecture.

Award: Scholarship for use in freshman year; renewable. *Number:* 20. *Amount:* $500–$2500.

Eligibility Requirements: Applicant must be American Indian/Alaska Native, Asian/Pacific Islander, Black (non-Hispanic), or Hispanic and enrolled or expecting to enroll full-time at a two-year or four-year or technical institution or university. Available to U.S. citizens.

Application Requirements: Application, essay, references, transcript, statement of disadvantaged circumstances, drawing. *Deadline:* varies.

Contact: Mary Felber, Scholarship Chair
American Institute of Architects
1735 New York Avenue, NW
Washington, DC 20006-5292
Phone: 202-626-7511
Fax: 202-626-7509
E-mail: mfelber@aia.org

AMERICAN INSTITUTE OF ARCHITECTS, NEW YORK CHAPTER http://www.aiany.org

DOUGLAS HASKELL AWARD FOR STUDENT JOURNALISM

One-time award for architectural students to encourage excellence in writing on architecture and related design fields. Submit ten copies of published article, essay, or journal with 100-word statement of purpose.

Academic Fields/Career Goals: Architecture; Art History; Engineering/Technology; Landscape Architecture.

Award: Prize for use in freshman, sophomore, junior, or senior years; not renewable. *Number:* 1–3. *Amount:* $5000.

Eligibility Requirements: Applicant must be enrolled or expecting to enroll full- or part-time at a two-year or four-year or technical institution or university and must have an interest in writing. Available to U.S. citizens.

Application Requirements: Application, essay. *Fee:* $15. *Deadline:* April 18.

Contact: Marcus Bleyer, Scholarship Committee
American Institute of Architects, New York Chapter
536 LaGuardia Place
New York, NY 10012
Phone: 212-358-6117
E-mail: mbleyer@aiany.org

WOMEN'S ARCHITECTURAL AUXILIARY ELEANOR ALLWORK SCHOLARSHIP GRANTS

Award available to students seeking first professional degree in architecture from an accredited New York school. Must demonstrate financial need. Must be a resident of New York metropolitan area. Must be nominated by Dean of architectural school.

Academic Fields/Career Goals: Architecture.

Award: Scholarship for use in freshman, sophomore, junior, senior, or graduate years; not renewable. *Number:* 3. *Amount:* $10,000.

Eligibility Requirements: Applicant must be enrolled or expecting to enroll full-time at a four-year institution or university; resident of New York and studying in New York. Available to U.S. citizens.

Application Requirements: Application, resume, references, self-addressed stamped envelope, student project in an 8.5 x 11 binder (flat artwork only), letter from an architect. *Deadline:* April 18.

Contact: Marcus Bleyer, Coordinator
American Institute of Architects, New York Chapter
536 LaGuardia Place
New York, NY 10012
Phone: 212-358-6117
E-mail: mbleyer@aiany.org

AMERICAN INSTITUTE OF ARCHITECTS, WEST VIRGINIA CHAPTER http://www.aiawv.org

AIA WEST VIRGINIA SCHOLARSHIP PROGRAM

Applicant must have completed junior year of an accredited undergraduate architectural program or enrolled in an accredited Masters of Architecture program. Applicant must present a portfolio of work to judging committee. The number of scholarships awarded varies based on the number of applicants. Refer to Web site for further details: http://www.aiawv.org.

Academic Fields/Career Goals: Architecture.

Award: Scholarship for use in senior or graduate years; not renewable. *Number:* varies. *Amount:* up to $11,000.

Eligibility Requirements: Applicant must be enrolled or expecting to enroll full-time at a four-year institution or university and resident of West Virginia. Available to U.S. citizens.

Application Requirements: Application, resume, references, transcript, personal letter. *Deadline:* May 30.

Contact: Roberta Guffey, Executive Director
American Institute of Architects, West Virginia Chapter
223 Hale Street
Charleston, WV 25301
Phone: 304-344-9872
Fax: 304-343-0205
E-mail: roberta.guffey@aiawv.org

AMERICAN SCHOOL OF CLASSICAL STUDIES AT ATHENS http://www.ascsa.edu.gr

ASCSA SUMMER SESSIONS OPEN SCHOLARSHIPS

• *See page 83*

AMERICAN SOCIETY OF HEATING, REFRIGERATING, AND AIR CONDITIONING ENGINEERS INC. http://www.ashrae.org

ASHRAE REGION IV BENNY BOOTLE SCHOLARSHIP

One-year $3000 scholarship available to an undergraduate engineering or architecture student enrolled full-time in a program accredited by ABET or NAAB and attending a school located within North and South Carolina, and Georgia. Minimum 3.0 GPA required.

Academic Fields/Career Goals: Architecture; Engineering/Technology.

Award: Scholarship for use in freshman, sophomore, junior, or senior years; not renewable. *Number:* 1. *Amount:* $3000.

Eligibility Requirements: Applicant must be enrolled or expecting to enroll full-time at a four-year institution or university and studying in Georgia, North Carolina, or South Carolina. Applicant must have 3.0 GPA or higher. Available to U.S. and non-U.S. citizens.

Application Requirements: Application, financial need analysis, references, transcript. *Deadline:* December 1.

Contact: Lois Benedict, Scholarship Administrator
American Society of Heating, Refrigerating, and Air Conditioning Engineers Inc.
1791 Tullie Circle, NE
Atlanta, GA 30329
Phone: 404-636-8400
Fax: 404-321-5478
E-mail: lbenedict@ashrae.org

ASSOCIATION FOR WOMEN IN ARCHITECTURE FOUNDATION http://www.awa-la.org

ASSOCIATION FOR WOMEN IN ARCHITECTURE SCHOLARSHIP

Must be a California resident or nonresident attending school in California. Must major in architecture or a related field and have completed one year (18 units) of schooling. Recipients may reapply. Open to women only. Interview in Los Angeles required. Applications available the beginning of February.

Academic Fields/Career Goals: Architecture; Interior Design; Landscape Architecture.

Award: Scholarship for use in sophomore, junior, senior, or graduate years; not renewable. *Number:* 5. *Amount:* $1000.

Eligibility Requirements: Applicant must be enrolled or expecting to enroll full-time at a two-year or four-year or technical institution or university; female and studying in California. Available to U.S. and non-U.S. citizens.

Application Requirements: Application, portfolio, references, self-addressed stamped envelope, transcript, personal statement. *Deadline:* April 15.

Contact: Mary Werk, Scholarship Chair
Association for Women in Architecture Foundation
22815 Frampton Avenue
Torrance, CA 90501-5034
Phone: 310-534-8466
Fax: 310-257-6885
E-mail: scholarship@awa-la.org

FLORIDA EDUCATIONAL FACILITIES PLANNERS' ASSOCIATION http://www.fefpa.org

FEFPA ASSISTANTSHIP

Renewable scholarship for full-time sophomores, juniors, seniors and graduate students enrolled in an accredited four-year Florida university or community college, majoring in facilities planning or a field related to facilities planning. Must be a resident of Florida with a 3.0 GPA.

Academic Fields/Career Goals: Architecture; Construction Engineering/Management.

Award: Scholarship for use in sophomore, junior, senior, or graduate years; renewable. *Number:* 2. *Amount:* $3000.

Eligibility Requirements: Applicant must be enrolled or expecting to enroll full-time at a four-year institution or university; resident of Florida and studying in Florida. Applicant must have 3.0 GPA or higher. Available to U.S. and non-U.S. citizens.

Application Requirements: Application, essay, financial need analysis, references, test scores, transcript. *Deadline:* June 1.

Contact: Robert Griffith, Selection Committee Chair
Florida Educational Facilities Planners' Association
Florida International University, University Park, CSC 142A
Miami, FL 33199
Phone: 305-348-4070 Ext. 4002
Fax: 305-348-4091
E-mail: griffith@fiu.edu

HELLENIC UNIVERSITY CLUB OF PHILADELPHIA http://www.hucphila.org

DIMITRI J. VERVERELLI MEMORIAL SCHOLARSHIP FOR ARCHITECTURE AND/OR ENGINEERING

$2000 award for full-time student enrolled in an architecture or engineering degree program at an accredited four-year college or university. High school seniors accepted for enrollment in such a degree program may also apply.Must be a U.S. citizen of Greek descent and a resident of particular counties in NJ or PA.

Academic Fields/Career Goals: Architecture; Engineering/Technology.

Award: Scholarship for use in freshman, sophomore, junior, or senior years; not renewable. *Number:* varies. *Amount:* up to $2000.

Eligibility Requirements: Applicant must be of Greek heritage; enrolled or expecting to enroll full-time at a four-year institution or university and resident of New Jersey or Pennsylvania. Available to U.S. citizens.

Application Requirements: Application, financial need analysis, transcript. *Deadline:* April 21.

Contact: Zoe Tripolitis, Scholarship Chairman
Hellenic University Club of Philadelphia
PO Box 42199
Philadelphia, PA 19101-2199
Phone: 215-483-7440
E-mail: hucphila@yahoo.com

HISPANIC COLLEGE FUND INC. http://www.hispanicfund.org

DENNY'S/HISPANIC COLLEGE FUND SCHOLARSHIP

• *See page 54*

EL NUEVO CONSTRUCTOR SCHOLARSHIP PROGRAM

Program intended for undergraduate student pursuing his or her associate's or bachelor's degree in a construction related field. Applicant must be a U.S. citizen with Hispanic background. Must attend college or university in United States or Puerto Rico. Online application only: http://www.hispanicfund.org.

Academic Fields/Career Goals: Architecture; Construction Engineering/Management.

Award: Scholarship for use in freshman, sophomore, junior, or senior years; not renewable. *Number:* varies. *Amount:* $500–$5000.

Eligibility Requirements: Applicant must be Hispanic and enrolled or expecting to enroll full-time at a two-year or four-year institution or university. Applicant must have 3.0 GPA or higher. Available to U.S. citizens.

Application Requirements: Application. *Deadline:* March 15.

Contact: Fernando Barrueta, Chief Executive Officer
Hispanic College Fund Inc.
1301 K Street, NW, Suite 450-A West
Washington, DC 20005
Phone: 202-296-5400
Fax: 202-296-3774
E-mail: hcf-info@hispanicfund.org

ILLUMINATING ENGINEERING SOCIETY OF NORTH AMERICA http://www.iesna.org

ROBERT W. THUNEN MEMORIAL SCHOLARSHIPS

One-time award for juniors, seniors, or graduate students enrolled at four-year colleges and universities in northern California, Nevada, Oregon, or Washington pursuing lighting career. Must submit statement describing proposed lighting course work or project and three recommendations, at least one from someone involved professionally or academically with lighting. Curriculum must be accredited by ABET, ACSA, or FIDER.

Academic Fields/Career Goals: Architecture; Engineering/Technology; Engineering-Related Technologies; Interior Design; Performing Arts; TV/Radio Broadcasting.

Award: Scholarship for use in junior, senior, or graduate years; not renewable. *Number:* 2. *Amount:* $2500.

Eligibility Requirements: Applicant must be enrolled or expecting to enroll full-time at a four-year institution or university and studying in California, Nevada, Oregon, or Washington. Available to U.S. and non-U.S. citizens.

Illuminating Engineering Society of North America (continued)

Application Requirements: Application, references, transcript. *Deadline:* April 1.

Contact: Phil Hall, Chairman
Illuminating Engineering Society of North America
120 Wall Street
New York, NY 10005-4001
Phone: 510-864-0204
Fax: 510-864-8511
E-mail: mrcatisbac@aol.com

ILLUMINATING ENGINEERING SOCIETY OF NORTH AMERICA–GOLDEN GATE SECTION http://www.iesgg.org

ALAN LUCAS MEMORIAL EDUCATIONAL SCHOLARSHIP

Scholarship available to full-time student for pursuit of lighting education or research as part of undergraduate, graduate, or doctoral studies. Scholarships may be made by those who will be a junior, senior, or graduate student in an accredited four-year college or university located in Northern California. The scholarships to be awarded will be at least $1500.

Academic Fields/Career Goals: Architecture; Electrical Engineering/ Electronics; Filmmaking/Video; Interior Design.

Award: Scholarship for use in junior, senior, or graduate years; not renewable. *Number:* 1. *Amount:* $1500.

Eligibility Requirements: Applicant must be enrolled or expecting to enroll full-time at a four-year institution or university and studying in California. Available to U.S. citizens.

Application Requirements: Application, references, transcript, statement of purpose, description of work in progress, scholar agreement form. *Deadline:* April 1.

Contact: Phil Hall, Scholarship Committee
Illuminating Engineering Society of North America–Golden Gate Section
1514 Gibbons Drive
Alameda, CA 94501
Phone: 510-864-0204
Fax: 510-864-8511
E-mail: iesggthunenfund@aol.com

NATIONAL ASSOCIATION OF WOMEN IN CONSTRUCTION http://www.nawic.org

NAWIC UNDERGRADUATE SCHOLARSHIPS

One-time award for any student having at least one year of study remaining in a construction-related program leading to an associate or higher degree. Awards range from $500 to $2000. Submit application and transcript of grades.

Academic Fields/Career Goals: Architecture; Civil Engineering; Drafting; Electrical Engineering/Electronics; Engineering/Technology; Engineering-Related Technologies; Interior Design; Landscape Architecture; Mechanical Engineering; Trade/Technical Specialties.

Award: Scholarship for use in sophomore or junior years; not renewable. *Number:* 40–50. *Amount:* $500–$2000.

Eligibility Requirements: Applicant must be enrolled or expecting to enroll full-time at a two-year or four-year or technical institution or university. Applicant must have 3.0 GPA or higher. Available to U.S. and Canadian citizens.

Application Requirements: Application, essay, financial need analysis, interview, transcript. *Deadline:* March 15.

Contact: Scholarship Committee
National Association of Women in Construction
327 South Adams Street
Fort Worth, TX 76104
Phone: 817-877-5551
Fax: 817-877-0324

NATIONAL FEDERATION OF THE BLIND http://www.nfb.org

HOWARD BROWN RICKARD SCHOLARSHIP

Award for legally blind students planning to study architecture, engineering, law, medicine, or natural science. Must submit a letter from NFB state officer with whom they have discussed their application. Award based on community service, financial need, and academic excellence. Minimum 3.5 GPA required.

Academic Fields/Career Goals: Architecture; Biology; Engineering/ Technology; Health and Medical Sciences; Law/Legal Services; Natural Resources; Physical Sciences and Math.

Award: Scholarship for use in freshman, sophomore, junior, senior, or graduate years; not renewable. *Number:* 1. *Amount:* $3000.

Eligibility Requirements: Applicant must be enrolled or expecting to enroll full-time at a two-year or four-year institution or university. Applicant or parent of applicant must have employment or volunteer experience in community service. Applicant must be visually impaired. Applicant must have 3.5 GPA or higher. Available to U.S. and non-U.S. citizens.

Application Requirements: Application, autobiography, essay, financial need analysis, references, transcript, letter from NFB state officer. *Deadline:* March 31.

Contact: Anil Lewis, Chairman, Scholarship Committee
National Federation of the Blind
315 West Ponce De Leon Avenue
Decatur, GA 30030
Phone: 404-371-1000
E-mail: alewis@nfbga.org

NEW YORK STATE EDUCATION DEPARTMENT http://www.highered.nysed.gov

REGENTS PROFESSIONAL OPPORTUNITY SCHOLARSHIP

• *See page 60*

OREGON STUDENT ASSISTANCE COMMISSION http://www.osac.state.or.us

HOMESTEAD CAPITAL HOUSING SCHOLARSHIP

• *See page 61*

PLUMBING-HEATING-COOLING CONTRACTORS ASSOCIATION EDUCATION FOUNDATION http://www.phccweb.org

BRADFORD WHITE CORPORATION SCHOLARSHIP

Scholarship for students enrolled in either an approved four-year PHCC apprenticeship program or at an accredited two-year community college, technical college, or trade school.

Academic Fields/Career Goals: Architecture; Business/Consumer Services; Civil Engineering; Engineering/Technology; Engineering-Related Technologies; Heating, Air-Conditioning, and Refrigeration Mechanics; Mechanical Engineering; Trade/Technical Specialties.

Award: Scholarship for use in freshman, sophomore, junior, or senior years; renewable. *Number:* 3. *Amount:* $2500.

Eligibility Requirements: Applicant must be enrolled or expecting to enroll full-time at a two-year or four-year or technical institution or university. Applicant must have 2.5 GPA or higher. Available to U.S. and Canadian citizens.

Application Requirements: Application, references, transcript. *Deadline:* June 1.

Contact: Iva Vest, Scholarship Coordinator
Plumbing-Heating-Cooling Contractors Association Education Foundation
PO Box 6808
Falls Church, VA 22046
Phone: 800-533-7694
Fax: 703-237-7442
E-mail: vest@naphcc.org

DELTA FAUCET COMPANY SCHOLARSHIP PROGRAM

Applicants must be sponsored by a member of the National Association of Plumbing-Heating-Cooling Contractors. Must pursue studies in a major related to the plumbing-heating-cooling industry. Visit Web site for additional information.

Academic Fields/Career Goals: Architecture; Business/Consumer Services; Civil Engineering; Engineering/Technology; Engineering-Related Technologies; Heating, Air-Conditioning, and Refrigeration Mechanics; Mechanical Engineering; Trade/Technical Specialties.

Award: Scholarship for use in freshman, sophomore, junior, or senior years; renewable. *Number:* 6. *Amount:* $2500.

Eligibility Requirements: Applicant must be enrolled or expecting to enroll full- or part-time at a two-year or four-year or technical institution or university. Applicant must have 2.5 GPA or higher. Available to U.S. and Canadian citizens.

Application Requirements: Application, interview, references, test scores, transcript. *Deadline:* June 1.

Contact: Iva Vest, Scholarship Coordinator
Plumbing-Heating-Cooling Contractors Association Education Foundation
PO Box 6808
Falls Church, VA 22046
Phone: 800-533-7694
Fax: 703-237-7442
E-mail: vest@naphcc.org

PHCC EDUCATIONAL FOUNDATION NEED-BASED SCHOLARSHIP

Need-based scholarship worth $2500 to a student enrolled in an approved four-year PHCC apprenticeship program, or at an accredited two-year technical college, community college, or an accredited four-year college or university.

Academic Fields/Career Goals: Architecture; Business/Consumer Services; Civil Engineering; Engineering/Technology; Engineering-Related Technologies; Heating, Air-Conditioning, and Refrigeration Mechanics; Mechanical Engineering; Trade/Technical Specialties.

Award: Scholarship for use in freshman, sophomore, junior, or senior years; renewable. *Number:* 1. *Amount:* $2500.

Eligibility Requirements: Applicant must be enrolled or expecting to enroll full-time at a two-year or four-year or technical institution or university. Applicant must have 2.5 GPA or higher. Available to U.S. and Canadian citizens.

Application Requirements: Application, references, transcript. *Deadline:* June 1.

Contact: Iva Vest, Scholarship Coordinator
Plumbing-Heating-Cooling Contractors Association Education Foundation
PO Box 6808
Falls Church, VA 22046
Phone: 800-533-7694
Fax: 703-237-7442
E-mail: vest@naphcc.org

TURNER CONSTRUCTION COMPANY http://www.turnerconstruction.com

YOUTHFORCE 2020 SCHOLARSHIP PROGRAM

Award for five graduating high school seniors from New York City schools of $2000 each year, a total of $8000 after completing four years of college. As a scholarship recipient, students must maintain a 2.80 GPA and complete a four-year summer internship at Turner that begins immediately following the first full year of college.

Academic Fields/Career Goals: Architecture; Civil Engineering; Electrical Engineering/Electronics; Mechanical Engineering.

Award: Scholarship for use in freshman year; not renewable. *Number:* 5. *Amount:* $2000–$8000.

Eligibility Requirements: Applicant must be high school student; planning to enroll or expecting to enroll full-time at a four-year institution or university and resident of New York. Available to U.S. citizens.

Application Requirements: Application, essay, financial need analysis, references, test scores, transcript. *Deadline:* May 8.

Contact: Stephanie V. Burns, Community Affairs Coordinator
Turner Construction Company
375 Hudson Street, Sixth Floor
New York, NY 10014
Phone: 212-229-6480
Fax: 212-229-6083
E-mail: sburns@tcco.com

UNICO NATIONAL INC. http://www.unico.org

THEODORE MAZZA SCHOLARSHIP

Scholarship available to a graduating high school senior. Must reside and attend high school within the corporate limits or adjoining suburbs of a city wherein an active chapter of UNICO National is located. Application must be signed by student's principal and properly certified by sponsoring chapter president and chapter secretary. Must have letter of endorsement from president or scholarship chairperson of sponsoring chapter.

Academic Fields/Career Goals: Architecture; Art History; Arts; Music.

Award: Scholarship for use in freshman year; not renewable. *Number:* up to 1. *Amount:* $1500.

Eligibility Requirements: Applicant must be high school student and planning to enroll or expecting to enroll full-time at a four-year institution or university. Available to U.S. citizens.

Application Requirements: Application, financial need analysis, references, transcript. *Deadline:* varies.

Contact: Ann Tichenor, Secretary
UNICO National Inc.
271 U.S. Highway 46 West, Suite A-108
Fairfield, NJ 07004
Phone: 973-808-0035
Fax: 973-808-0043

UNITED NEGRO COLLEGE FUND http://www.uncf.org

CDM SCHOLARSHIP/INTERNSHIP

Scholarship open to students attending a UNCF member college or university and majoring in computer science, chemical engineering, construction engineering/management, civil engineering, electrical engineering, environmental engineering, geography, hydrology/hydrogeology, mechanical engineering, structural, geographic information systems, information management systems or architectural engineering.

Academic Fields/Career Goals: Architecture; Chemical Engineering; Civil Engineering; Computer Science/Data Processing; Construction Engineering/Management; Electrical Engineering/Electronics; Engineering/Technology; Environmental Science; Geography; Hydrology; Mechanical Engineering.

Award: Scholarship for use in freshman, sophomore, junior, senior, or graduate years; not renewable. *Number:* varies. *Amount:* up to $6000.

Eligibility Requirements: Applicant must be Black (non-Hispanic) and enrolled or expecting to enroll full- or part-time at a four-year institution. Applicant must have 3.0 GPA or higher. Available to U.S. and non-U.S. citizens.

Application Requirements: Online application. *Deadline:* February 8.

Contact: Director, Program Services
United Negro College Fund
8260 Willow Oaks Corporate Drive
PO Box 10444
Fairfax, VA 22031-8044
Phone: 800-331-2244
E-mail: rebecca.bennett@uncf.org

GILBANE SCHOLARSHIP PROGRAM

Scholarship provides $6000 in financial assistance after students have completed a paid summer internship program. Applicants must major in engineering, mathematics or architecture at a UNCF member college or university. Mini-

United Negro College Fund (continued)

mum 2.5 GPA required. Prospective applicants should complete the student profile found at Web site: http://www.uncf.org.

Academic Fields/Career Goals: Architecture; Engineering/Technology; Mathematics.

Award: Scholarship for use in sophomore or junior years; not renewable. *Number:* 1. *Amount:* $6000.

Eligibility Requirements: Applicant must be Black (non-Hispanic); enrolled or expecting to enroll full-time at a four-year institution or university and resident of Delaware, New Jersey, or Pennsylvania. Applicant must have 2.5 GPA or higher. Available to U.S. citizens.

Application Requirements: Application. *Deadline:* October 30.

Contact: Director, Program Services
United Negro College Fund
8260 Willow Oaks Corporate Drive
PO Box 10444
Fairfax, VA 22031-8044
Phone: 800-331-2244
E-mail: rebecca.bennett@uncf.org

WELLS FARGO/UNCF SCHOLARSHIP FUND

• *See page 67*

WEST VIRGINIA SOCIETY OF ARCHITECTS/AIA http://www.aiawv.org

WEST VIRGINIA SOCIETY OF ARCHITECTS/AIA SCHOLARSHIP

Award for a West Virginia resident who has completed at least their sixth semester of an NAAB-accredited architectural program by application deadline. Must submit resume and letter stating need, qualifications, and desire.

Academic Fields/Career Goals: Architecture.

Award: Scholarship for use in junior, senior, graduate, or postgraduate years; not renewable. *Number:* varies. *Amount:* up to $11,000.

Eligibility Requirements: Applicant must be enrolled or expecting to enroll full-time at an institution or university and resident of West Virginia. Available to U.S. citizens.

Application Requirements: Application, resume, references, transcript. *Deadline:* May 30.

Contact: Ms. Roberta Guffey, Executive Director
West Virginia Society of Architects/AIA
223 Hale Street
Charleston, WV 25323
Phone: 304-344-9872
Fax: 304-343-0205
E-mail: roberta.guffey@aiawv.org

WORLDSTUDIO FOUNDATION http://www.aiga.org/

WORLDSTUDIO FOUNDATION SCHOLARSHIP PROGRAM

Scholarships to minority and economically disadvantaged students who are pursuing degrees in the design/arts disciplines in colleges and universities in the United States. Applicant should have a minimum GPA of 2.0.

Academic Fields/Career Goals: Architecture; Arts; Fashion Design; Filmmaking/Video; Graphics/Graphic Arts/Printing; Industrial Design; Interior Design; Landscape Architecture.

Award: Scholarship for use in freshman, sophomore, junior, senior, graduate, or postgraduate years; not renewable. *Number:* 30–50. *Amount:* $1000–$5000.

Eligibility Requirements: Applicant must be American Indian/Alaska Native, Asian/Pacific Islander, Black (non-Hispanic), or Hispanic and enrolled or expecting to enroll full-time at a two-year or four-year or technical institution or university. Available to U.S. citizens.

Application Requirements: Application, essay, financial need analysis, photo, portfolio, references, self-addressed stamped envelope, transcript. *Deadline:* April 13.

Contact: Maria Emmighausen, Scholarship Coordinator
Worldstudio Foundation
200 Varick Street, Suite 507
New York, NY 10014
Phone: 212-807-1990
Fax: 212-807-1799
E-mail: scholarship@aiga.org

AREA/ETHNIC STUDIES

AMERICAN COUNCIL FOR POLISH CULTURE http://www.polishcultureacpc.org

ACPC SUMMER STUDIES IN POLAND SCHOLARSHIP

Scholarship enables American students of Polish descent to participate in summer study offered by many of Poland's universities. Must be entering junior or senior year at a college or university.

Academic Fields/Career Goals: Area/Ethnic Studies; Foreign Language.

Award: Scholarship for use in junior, senior, or graduate years; renewable. *Number:* 1. *Amount:* $2000.

Eligibility Requirements: Applicant must be of Polish heritage and enrolled or expecting to enroll full-time at a four-year institution or university. Available to U.S. citizens.

Application Requirements: Application, resume, references, transcript. *Deadline:* February 1.

Contact: Ms. Camille Kopielski, Chairwoman
American Council for Polish Culture
1015 Cypress Drive
Arlington Heights, IL 60005
Phone: 847-394-2520

SKALNY SCHOLARSHIP FOR POLISH STUDIES

Scholarships are intended for students pursuing some Polish studies (major may be in other fields) at universities in the United States who have completed at least two years of college or university work at an accredited institution.

Academic Fields/Career Goals: Area/Ethnic Studies; Foreign Language.

Award: Scholarship for use in junior, senior, or graduate years; renewable. *Number:* 2. *Amount:* $1000.

Eligibility Requirements: Applicant must be enrolled or expecting to enroll full-time at a four-year institution or university. Available to U.S. citizens.

Application Requirements: Application, resume, references, transcript, copy of an academic project on a Polish topic in English. *Deadline:* May 3.

Contact: Ursula Brodowicz, Chair, Scholarships Committee
American Council for Polish Culture
11 Brinley Way
Newington, CT 06111
Phone: 860-521-0201
E-mail: ubrodowicz@earthlink.net

AMERICAN HISTORICAL ASSOCIATION http://www.historians.org

WESLEY-LOGAN PRIZE

• *See page 68*

ASSOCIATION OF TEACHERS OF JAPANESE BRIDGING CLEARINGHOUSE FOR STUDY ABROAD IN JAPAN

BRIDGING SCHOLARSHIP FOR STUDY ABROAD IN JAPAN

Scholarships for U.S. students studying in Japan on semester or year-long programs. Deadlines: April 7.

Academic Fields/Career Goals: Area/Ethnic Studies; Asian Studies; Foreign Language.

Award: Scholarship for use in junior or senior years; not renewable. *Number:* 40–80. *Amount:* $2500–$4000.

Eligibility Requirements: Applicant must be enrolled or expecting to enroll full-time at a four-year institution or university. Available to U.S. citizens.

Application Requirements: Application, essay, financial need analysis, references, transcript. *Deadline:* April 7.

Contact: Susan Schmidt, Executive Director
Association of Teachers of Japanese Bridging Clearinghouse for Study Abroad in Japan
University of Colorado, 240 Humanities Building
Campus Box 279
Boulder, CO 80309-0279
Phone: 303-492-5487
Fax: 303-492-5856
E-mail: atj@colorado.edu

CANADIAN INSTITUTE OF UKRAINIAN STUDIES http://www.cius.ca

CANADIAN INSTITUTE OF UKRAINIAN STUDIES RESEARCH GRANTS

Grants for students who pursue Ukrainian and Ukrainian-Canadian studies in history, literature, language, education, social sciences, women's studies, law, and library sciences.

Academic Fields/Career Goals: Area/Ethnic Studies; Canadian Studies; European Studies.

Award: Grant for use in freshman, sophomore, junior, or senior years; renewable. *Number:* 1. *Amount:* varies.

Eligibility Requirements: Applicant must be enrolled or expecting to enroll full-time at a four-year institution or university. Available to U.S. and non-U.S. citizens.

Application Requirements: Application. *Deadline:* March 1.

Contact: Iryna Pak, Administrator
Canadian Institute of Ukrainian Studies
University of Alberta, 450 Athabasca Hall
Edmonton, AB T6G 2E8
Canada
Phone: 780-492-2972
Fax: 780-492-4967
E-mail: cius@ualberta.ca

LEO J. KRYSA UNDERGRADUATE SCHOLARSHIP

One-time award for a Canadian citizen or a landed immigrant to enter their final year of undergraduate study in pursuit of a degree with emphasis on Ukrainian and/or Ukrainian-Canadian studies in the disciplines of education, history, humanities, or social sciences. To be used at any Canadian university for an eight-month period of study. Dollar amount CAN$3500.

Academic Fields/Career Goals: Area/Ethnic Studies; Education; History; Humanities; Social Sciences.

Award: Scholarship for use in senior year; not renewable. *Number:* 1.

Eligibility Requirements: Applicant must be Canadian citizen; enrolled or expecting to enroll full-time at a four-year institution or university; resident of Alberta, British Columbia, Manitoba, New Brunswick, Newfoundland, North West Territories, Nova Scotia, Ontario, Prince Edward Island, Quebec, Saskatchewan, or Yukon and studying in Alberta, British Columbia, Manitoba, New Brunswick, Newfoundland, Nova Scotia, Ontario, Prince Edward Island, Quebec, or Saskatchewan.

Application Requirements: Application, references, transcript. *Deadline:* March 1.

Contact: Iryna Pak, Administrator
Canadian Institute of Ukrainian Studies
University of Alberta, 450 Athabasca Hall
Edmonton, AB T6G 2E8
Canada
Phone: 780-492-2972
Fax: 780-492-4967
E-mail: cius@ualberta.ca

CLAN MACBEAN FOUNDATION http://www.clanmacbean.net

CLAN MACBEAN FOUNDATION GRANT PROGRAM

Award is open to men and women of any race, color, creed or nationality. Grant is for course of study or project which reflects direct involvement in the preservation or enhancement of Scottish culture, or an effort that would contribute directly to the improvement of the human family.

Academic Fields/Career Goals: Area/Ethnic Studies; Child and Family Studies.

Award: Grant for use in freshman, sophomore, junior, senior, or graduate years; not renewable. *Number:* 3–5. *Amount:* up to $5000.

Eligibility Requirements: Applicant must be enrolled or expecting to enroll full-time at a two-year or four-year institution or university. Available to U.S. and non-U.S. citizens.

Application Requirements: Application, references, transcript. *Deadline:* May 1.

Contact: Kenneth E. Bean, Chairman
Clan MacBean Foundation
441 Wadsworth Boulevard, Suite 213
Denver, CO 80226
Phone: 303-233-6002
Fax: 303-233-6002
E-mail: macbean@ecentral.com

COSTUME SOCIETY OF AMERICA http://www.costumesocietyamerica.com

ADELE FILENE TRAVEL AWARD

One-time award available to society members to assist with travel expenses to attend the Costume Society of America national symposium. Must be currently enrolled students. Recipient will present either a juried paper or a poster.

Academic Fields/Career Goals: Area/Ethnic Studies; Art History; Arts; Historic Preservation and Conservation; History; Home Economics; Museum Studies; Performing Arts.

Award: Prize for use in freshman, sophomore, junior, senior, or graduate years; not renewable. *Number:* 1. *Amount:* $150–$500.

Eligibility Requirements: Applicant must be enrolled or expecting to enroll full- or part-time at a two-year or four-year or technical institution or university. Applicant or parent of applicant must be member of Costume Society of America. Available to U.S. and non-U.S. citizens.

Application Requirements: Application, applicant must enter a contest, references. *Deadline:* March 1.

Contact: Noel Liccardi, Program Contact
Costume Society of America
203 Towne Center Drive
Hillsborough, NJ 08844
Phone: 800-272-9447
Fax: 908-450-1118
E-mail: national.office@costumesocietyamerica.com

STELLA BLUM RESEARCH GRANT

One-time award to support a CSA undergraduate or graduate student member in good standing working on a research project in the field of North American costume. Must be enrolled at an accredited institution. Must submit faculty recommendation. Merit-based award of $3000.

Academic Fields/Career Goals: Area/Ethnic Studies; Art History; Arts; Historic Preservation and Conservation; History; Home Economics; Museum Studies; Performing Arts.

Award: Grant for use in freshman, sophomore, junior, senior, or graduate years; not renewable. *Number:* 1. *Amount:* $3000.

Eligibility Requirements: Applicant must be enrolled or expecting to enroll full-time at a two-year or four-year or technical institution or university. Applicant or parent of applicant must be member of Costume Society of America. Available to U.S. and non-U.S. citizens.

Application Requirements: Application, essay, references, transcript, proposal of the research project (with budget analysis if necessary). *Deadline:* May 1.

Contact: Noel Liccardi, Program Contact
Costume Society of America
203 Towne Center Drive
Hillsborough, NJ 08844
Phone: 800-272-9447
Fax: 908-450-1118
E-mail: national.office@costumesocietyamerica.com

HARVARD TRAVELLERS CLUB

HARVARD TRAVELLERS CLUB GRANTS

• *See page 89*

HAWAIIAN LODGE, F & AM http://www.glhawaii.org/

HAWAIIAN LODGE SCHOLARSHIPS

Scholarship dedicated to worthy students in the areas of engineering, sciences, Hawaiian studies, and education, who would otherwise not be able to attend college.

Academic Fields/Career Goals: Area/Ethnic Studies; Biology; Chemical Engineering; Civil Engineering; Computer Science/Data Processing; Education; Electrical Engineering/Electronics; Energy and Power Engineering; Engineering/Technology; Engineering-Related Technologies; Health and Medical Sciences.

Award: Scholarship for use in freshman, sophomore, junior, or senior years; renewable. *Number:* 4–16. *Amount:* $1000.

Eligibility Requirements: Applicant must be enrolled or expecting to enroll full-time at a four-year institution or university; resident of Hawaii and must have an interest in Hawaiian language/culture. Applicant must have 3.0 GPA or higher. Available to U.S. citizens.

Application Requirements: Application, autobiography, essay, financial need analysis, interview, references, test scores, transcript. *Deadline:* June 1.

Contact: Chairman, Scholarship Committee
Hawaiian Lodge, F & AM
1227 Makiki Street
Honolulu, HI 96814
Phone: 808-979-7809
E-mail: secretary@hawaiianlodge.org

JAPANESE GOVERNMENT/THE MONBUSHO SCHOLARSHIP PROGRAM http://www.la.us.emb-japan.go.jp

JAPANESE STUDIES SCHOLARSHIP

One-time award of 134,000 yen (subject to change for budgetary reasons) per month will be given to each grantee which is open to undergraduate college/university students (university must be outside Japan). One-year course designed to develop Japanese language aptitude and knowledge of the country's culture, areas which the applicant must currently be studying. Scholarship comprises transportation, accommodations, medical expenses, and monthly and arrival allowances.

Academic Fields/Career Goals: Area/Ethnic Studies; Asian Studies; Foreign Language.

Award: Scholarship for use in freshman, sophomore, junior, or senior years; not renewable. *Number:* varies.

Eligibility Requirements: Applicant must be age 35 or under; enrolled or expecting to enroll full-time at a two-year or four-year institution or university and must have an interest in Japanese language. Available to U.S. citizens.

Application Requirements: Application, autobiography, interview, photo, references, test scores, transcript, medical certificate, certificate of enrollment. *Deadline:* March 4.

Contact: Jean Do, Scholarship Program Coordinator
Japanese Government/The Monbusho Scholarship Program
350 South Grand Avenue, Suite 1700
Los Angeles, CA 90071
Phone: 213-617-6700 Ext. 338
Fax: 213-617-6728
E-mail: info@la-cgjapan.org

JAPAN STUDIES SCHOLARSHIP FOUNDATION COMMITTEE

JAPAN STUDIES SCHOLARSHIP

Two $1500 awards for residents of Northern or Central California and Nevada who are currently enrolled sophomore, junior or senior students studying or researching Japanese culture, language, or Japan-U.S. relations. Must attend an award ceremony in August.

Academic Fields/Career Goals: Area/Ethnic Studies; Asian Studies; Foreign Language; International Studies.

Award: Scholarship for use in sophomore, junior, senior, or graduate years; not renewable. *Number:* 2. *Amount:* $1500.

Eligibility Requirements: Applicant must be enrolled or expecting to enroll full-time at a four-year institution or university and resident of California or Nevada. Available to U.S. citizens.

Application Requirements: Application, transcript. *Deadline:* May 5.

Contact: Hisako Takahashi, Senior Education Coordinator
Japan Studies Scholarship Foundation Committee
c/o Japan Information Center, 50 Fremont Street, Suite 2200
San Francisco, CA 94105
Phone: 415-346-2461
E-mail: education@cgjsf.org

KE ALI'I PAUAHI FOUNDATION http://www.pauahi.org

JOHNNY PINEAPPLE SCHOLARSHIP

Scholarship is for full-time students pursuing a degree in Hawaiian language or Hawaiian studies at an accredited institution of higher learning with minimum GPA of 3.5.

Academic Fields/Career Goals: Area/Ethnic Studies; Foreign Language.

Award: Scholarship for use in freshman, sophomore, junior, senior, or graduate years; not renewable. *Number:* 1. *Amount:* $1200.

Eligibility Requirements: Applicant must be enrolled or expecting to enroll full-time at a two-year or four-year institution or university and must have an interest in Hawaiian language/culture. Applicant must have 3.5 GPA or higher. Available to U.S. citizens.

Application Requirements: Essay, financial need analysis, references, transcript, signed online application confirmation page, completed SAR. *Deadline:* May 2.

Contact: Elizabeth Stevenson, Development Manager
Ke Ali'i Pauahi Foundation
567 South King Street, Suite 160
Honolulu, HI 96813
Phone: 808-534-3966
Fax: 808-534-3890
E-mail: scholarships@pauahi.org

KOSCIUSZKO FOUNDATION http://www.kosciuszkofoundation.org

YEAR ABROAD PROGRAM IN POLAND

Grants for upper division and graduate students who wish to study in Poland. Must be US citizen and permanent residents of Polish descent who are undergraduate sophomores, juniors, seniors and graduate students. Must have letters of recommendation, personal statement, and transcript. Covers tuition fees and provides stipend for housing. Application fee: $50. Minimum 3.0 GPA required. Restricted to U.S. citizens and permanent residents of Polish descent.

Academic Fields/Career Goals: Area/Ethnic Studies; Foreign Language.

Award: Scholarship for use in sophomore, junior, senior, or graduate years; not renewable. *Number:* varies. *Amount:* $675–$1350.

Eligibility Requirements: Applicant must be of Polish heritage; enrolled or expecting to enroll full-time at a four-year institution or university and must have an interest in Polish language. Applicant must have 3.0 GPA or higher. Available to U.S. and non-Canadian citizens.

Application Requirements: Application, interview, photo, references, transcript, personal statement. *Fee:* $50. *Deadline:* January 15.

Contact: Ms. Addy Tymczyszyn, Grants Department
Kosciuszko Foundation
15 East 65th Street
New York, NY 10021-6595
Phone: 212-734-2130 Ext. 210
Fax: 212-628-4552
E-mail: addy@thekf.org

MEMORIAL FOUNDATION FOR JEWISH CULTURE http://www.mfjc.org

MEMORIAL FOUNDATION FOR JEWISH CULTURE INTERNATIONAL SCHOLARSHIP PROGRAM FOR COMMUNITY SERVICE

Fellowship program is to assist well-qualified individuals in carrying out an independent scholarly, literary or art project, in a field of Jewish specialization, which makes a significant contribution to the understanding, preservation, enhancement or transmission of Jewish culture. Any qualified scholar, researcher or artist who possesses the knowledge and experience to formulate and implement a project in a field of Jewish specialization can apply for support.

Academic Fields/Career Goals: Area/Ethnic Studies; Religion/Theology; Social Services.

Award: Scholarship for use in freshman, sophomore, junior, or senior years; renewable. *Number:* varies. *Amount:* up to $3000.

Eligibility Requirements: Applicant must be enrolled or expecting to enroll full- or part-time at a two-year or four-year or technical institution or university and must have an interest in Jewish culture. Available to U.S. and non-U.S. citizens.

Application Requirements: Application, interview, references. *Deadline:* November 30.

Contact: Dr. Jerry Hochbaum, Executive Vice President
Memorial Foundation for Jewish Culture
50 Broadway, 34th Floor
New York, NY 10004
Phone: 212-425-6606
Fax: 212-425-6602
E-mail: office@mfjc.org

NATIONAL ITALIAN AMERICAN FOUNDATION http://www.niaf.org

NATIONAL ITALIAN AMERICAN FOUNDATION CATEGORY II SCHOLARSHIP

Award available to students majoring or minoring in Italian language, Italian Studies, Italian-American Studies or a related field who have outstanding potential and high academic achievements. Minimum 3.5 GPA required. Must be a U.S. citizen and be enrolled in an accredited institution of higher education. Application can only be submitted online. For further information, deadlines, and online application visit Web site: http://www.niaf.org/scholarships/index.asp.

Academic Fields/Career Goals: Area/Ethnic Studies.

Award: Scholarship for use in freshman, sophomore, junior, senior, graduate, or postgraduate years; not renewable. *Number:* varies. *Amount:* $2500–$10,000.

Eligibility Requirements: Applicant must be enrolled or expecting to enroll full- or part-time at a four-year institution or university and must have an interest in Italian language. Available to U.S. citizens.

Application Requirements: Application, essay, references, transcript. *Deadline:* March 7.

Contact: Miss. Molly Conti, Program Assistant, Education and Culture Programs
National Italian American Foundation
1860 19th Street, NW
Washington, DC 20009
Phone: 202-939-3119
Fax: 202-483-2618
E-mail: mconti@niaf.org

SONS OF NORWAY FOUNDATION http://www.sonsofnorway.com

KING OLAV V NORWEGIAN-AMERICAN HERITAGE FUND

Scholarship available to American students 18 or older interested in studying Norwegian heritage or modern Norway, or Norwegian students 18 or older interested in studying North American culture. Selection of applicants is based on a 500-word essay, educational and career goals, community service, work experience, and GPA. Must have minimum 3.0 GPA.

Academic Fields/Career Goals: Area/Ethnic Studies.

Award: Scholarship for use in freshman, sophomore, junior, or senior years; not renewable. *Number:* 12–15. *Amount:* $1000–$1500.

Eligibility Requirements: Applicant must be age 18 and over and enrolled or expecting to enroll full-time at a four-year institution or university. Applicant or parent of applicant must have employment or volunteer experience in community service. Applicant must have 3.0 GPA or higher. Available to U.S. and non-Canadian citizens.

Application Requirements: Application, essay, references, self-addressed stamped envelope, transcript. *Deadline:* March 1.

Contact: Scholarship Coordinator
Sons of Norway Foundation
1455 West Lake Street
Minneapolis, MN 55408-2666
Phone: 612-827-3611
Fax: 612-827-0658

WATERBURY FOUNDATION http://www.conncf.org

TADEUSZ SENDZIMIR SCHOLARSHIPS-ACADEMIC YEAR SCHOLARSHIPS

Scholarship of $5000 for graduate and undergraduate students of Polish descent, residing in Connecticut, who are studying Polish language, history or culture during the academic year at a college or university in the United States or Poland.

Academic Fields/Career Goals: Area/Ethnic Studies.

Award: Scholarship for use in freshman, sophomore, junior, senior, or graduate years; not renewable. *Number:* 1. *Amount:* up to $5000.

Eligibility Requirements: Applicant must be of Polish heritage; enrolled or expecting to enroll full- or part-time at a two-year or four-year institution or university and resident of Connecticut. Available to U.S. and non-Canadian citizens.

Application Requirements: Application, essay, references, transcript. *Deadline:* March 1.

Contact: Josh Carey, Program Officer
Waterbury Foundation
43 Field Street
Waterbury, CT 06702-1216
Phone: 203-753-1315
Fax: 203-756-3054
E-mail: jcarey@conncf.org

TADEUSZ SENDZIMIR SCHOLARSHIPS-SUMMER SCHOOL PROGRAMS

Scholarship of $3000 for graduate and undergraduate students of Polish descent, residing in Connecticut, who are studying Polish language, history or culture during the academic year at a college or university in the United States or Poland.

Academic Fields/Career Goals: Area/Ethnic Studies.

Award: Scholarship for use in freshman, sophomore, junior, senior, or graduate years; not renewable. *Number:* 1. *Amount:* up to $3000.

Eligibility Requirements: Applicant must be of Polish heritage; age 18 and over; enrolled or expecting to enroll full- or part-time at a two-year or four-year institution or university and resident of Connecticut. Available to U.S. and non-Canadian citizens.

Application Requirements: Application, financial need analysis, references, transcript, physician's certificate. *Deadline:* March 1.

Contact: Josh Carey, Program Officer
Waterbury Foundation
43 Field Street
Waterbury, CT 06702-1216
Phone: 203-753-1315
Fax: 203-756-3054
E-mail: jcarey@conncf.org

ART HISTORY

AMERICAN INSTITUTE OF ARCHITECTS, NEW YORK CHAPTER http://www.aiany.org

DOUGLAS HASKELL AWARD FOR STUDENT JOURNALISM

• *See page 90*

AMERICAN LEGION AUXILIARY DEPARTMENT OF WASHINGTON http://www.walegion-aux.org

AMERICAN LEGION AUXILIARY DEPARTMENT OF WASHINGTON FLORENCE LEMCKE MEMORIAL SCHOLARSHIP IN FINE ARTS

One-time award for the child of a deceased or living veteran. Must be senior in high school in Washington and planning to pursue an education in the fine arts. Must submit statement of veteran's military service. Must be a resident of Washington state.

American Legion Auxiliary Department of Washington (continued)

Academic Fields/Career Goals: Art History; Arts; Literature/English/Writing.

Award: Scholarship for use in freshman year; not renewable. *Number:* 1. *Amount:* $500.

Eligibility Requirements: Applicant must be high school student; age 20 or under; planning to enroll or expecting to enroll full-time at a two-year or four-year institution or university; resident of Washington; studying in Washington and must have an interest in art or writing. Available to U.S. citizens. Applicant or parent must meet one or more of the following requirements: general military experience; retired from active duty; disabled or killed as a result of military service; prisoner of war; or missing in action.

Application Requirements: Application, essay, references, transcript. *Deadline:* April 1.

Contact: Nicole Ross, News Department Secretary
American Legion Auxiliary Department of Washington
3600 Ruddell Road
Lacey, WA 98503
Phone: 360-456-5995
Fax: 360-491-7442
E-mail: alawash@qwest.net

AMERICAN SCHOOL OF CLASSICAL STUDIES AT ATHENS http://www.ascsa.edu.gr

ASCSA SUMMER SESSIONS OPEN SCHOLARSHIPS

• *See page 83*

CHARLES M. EDWARDS SCHOLARSHIP

Scholarship of $500 awarded to an exceptional undergraduate studying at the American School of Classical Studies. Must be U.S. citizen studying Greek language, history, philosophy, or other specific disciplines.

Academic Fields/Career Goals: Art History; Foreign Language; History; Philosophy.

Award: Scholarship for use in freshman, sophomore, junior, or senior years; not renewable. *Number:* 1. *Amount:* $500.

Eligibility Requirements: Applicant must be enrolled or expecting to enroll full- or part-time at a four-year institution or university. Available to U.S. citizens.

Application Requirements: Application. *Deadline:* January 15.

Contact: Mary Darlington, Executive Assistant
American School of Classical Studies at Athens
6-8 Charlton Street
Princeton, NJ 08540-5232
Phone: 609-683-0800
Fax: 609-924-0578

COSTUME SOCIETY OF AMERICA http://www.costumesocietyamerica.com

ADELE FILENE TRAVEL AWARD

• *See page 95*

STELLA BLUM RESEARCH GRANT

• *See page 95*

GETTY GRANT PROGRAM http://www.getty.edu/grants

LIBRARY RESEARCH GRANTS

Grant intended for scholars at any level who demonstrate compelling need to use materials in Getty Research Library. Applicant's place of residence must be at least 80 or more miles away from the center. Research period may last several days to a maximum of three months. Supports one research trip to the center. Grantee may reapply after two years; if project is different, grantee may reapply the next year.

Academic Fields/Career Goals: Art History; Arts.

Award: Grant for use in freshman, sophomore, junior, senior, graduate, or postgraduate years; renewable. *Number:* varies. *Amount:* $500–$2500.

Eligibility Requirements: Applicant must be enrolled or expecting to enroll full- or part-time at a four-year institution or university; studying in California and must have an interest in art. Available to U.S. and non-U.S. citizens.

Application Requirements: Application, financial need analysis, resume, references, project proposal. *Deadline:* November 1.

Contact: Kathleen Johnson, Program Associate
Getty Grant Program
1200 Getty Center Drive, Suite 800
Los Angeles, CA 90049-1685
Phone: 310-440-7320
Fax: 310-440-7703
E-mail: researchgrants@getty.edu

HISPANIC SCHOLARSHIP FUND http://www.hsf.net

HSF/MCNAMARA FAMILY CREATIVE ARTS PROJECT GRANT

In partnership with the McNamara Family Foundation, this program will provide financial resources to undergraduate and graduate students of Hispanic heritage enrolled full-time in a creative arts related field including media, film, performing arts, communications, writing, and others, to assist in completing an art project. Must have completed a minimum of 12 undergraduate credits. Minimum 3.0 GPA required.

Academic Fields/Career Goals: Art History; Arts; Communications; Fashion Design; Filmmaking/Video; Graphics/Graphic Arts/Printing; Literature/English/Writing; Music; Performing Arts; Photojournalism/Photography; TV/Radio Broadcasting.

Award: Grant for use in freshman, sophomore, junior, senior, or graduate years; not renewable. *Number:* 4–8. *Amount:* $5000–$20,000.

Eligibility Requirements: Applicant must be of Hispanic, Latin American/Caribbean, Mexican, Nicaraguan, or Spanish heritage and enrolled or expecting to enroll full-time at a two-year or four-year institution or university. Applicant must have 3.0 GPA or higher. Available to U.S. citizens.

Application Requirements: Application, essay, financial need analysis, references, transcript. *Deadline:* March 15.

Contact: John Schmucker, Scholarship Coordinator
Hispanic Scholarship Fund
55 Second Street, Suite 1500
San Francisco, CA 94105
Phone: 877-473-4636
E-mail: scholar1@hsf.net

ROBERT H. MOLLOHAN FAMILY CHARITABLE FOUNDATION INC. http://www.mollohanfoundation.org

MARY OLIVE EDDY JONES ART SCHOLARSHIP

Scholarship awarded to a rising sophomore or junior seriously interested in pursuing an art-related degree. Applicant must be a West Virginia resident attending a West Virginia college or university.

Academic Fields/Career Goals: Art History; Arts; Graphics/Graphic Arts/Printing.

Award: Scholarship for use in sophomore or junior years; not renewable. *Number:* 1–3. *Amount:* up to $1000.

Eligibility Requirements: Applicant must be enrolled or expecting to enroll full- or part-time at a four-year institution or university; resident of West Virginia; studying in West Virginia and must have an interest in art. Available to U.S. citizens.

Application Requirements: Application, essay, portfolio, resume, references, transcript. *Deadline:* February 11.

Contact: Beth Michalec, Program Manager
Robert H. Mollohan Family Charitable Foundation Inc.
1000 Technology Drive, Suite 2000
Fairmont, WV 26554
Phone: 304-333-2251
Fax: 304-333-3900
E-mail: bmichalec@wvhtf.org

STRAIGHTFORWARD MEDIA http://www.straightforwardmedia.com

STRAIGHTFORWARD MEDIA LIBERAL ARTS SCHOLARSHIP

Scholarship of $500 available exclusively to liberal arts students. Must be U.S. citizen. Awarded four times per year.

Academic Fields/Career Goals: Art History; Economics; Foreign Language; History; Humanities; Literature/English/Writing; Philosophy; Political Science; Psychology; Social Sciences.

Award: Scholarship for use in freshman, sophomore, junior, or senior years; not renewable. *Number:* 4. *Amount:* $500.

Eligibility Requirements: Applicant must be enrolled or expecting to enroll full-time at a four-year institution or university. Available to U.S. and non-U.S. citizens.

Application Requirements: Online application. *Deadline:* varies.

Contact: Scholarship Committee
StraightForward Media
2040 West Main Street, Suite 104
Rapid City, SD 57701
Phone: 605-348-3042
Fax: 605-348-3043

UNICO NATIONAL INC. http://www.unico.org

THEODORE MAZZA SCHOLARSHIP

• *See page 93*

ARTS

ACADEMY OF TELEVISION ARTS AND SCIENCES FOUNDATION http://www.emmysfoundation.org

ACADEMY OF TELEVISION ARTS AND SCIENCES COLLEGE TELEVISION AWARDS

Awards of up to $4000 for excellence in college student video, digital, and film productions. Open to those students who have produced their video while enrolled in a community college, college, or university the United States.

Academic Fields/Career Goals: Arts; Communications; Filmmaking/Video; Journalism; Performing Arts; Photojournalism/Photography; TV/Radio Broadcasting.

Award: Prize for use in freshman, sophomore, junior, senior, or graduate years; not renewable. *Number:* 25. *Amount:* $500–$4000.

Eligibility Requirements: Applicant must be enrolled or expecting to enroll full-time at a two-year or four-year or technical institution or university. Available to U.S. and non-U.S. citizens.

Application Requirements: Application, applicant must enter a contest. *Deadline:* December 15.

Contact: Nancy Robinson, Programs Coordinator
Academy of Television Arts and Sciences Foundation
5220 Lankershim Boulevard
North Hollywood, CA 91601
Phone: 818-754-2839
Fax: 818-761-8524
E-mail: collegeawards@emmys.org

ALLIANCE FOR YOUNG ARTISTS AND WRITERS INC. http://www.artandwriting.org

SCHOLASTIC ART AND WRITING AWARDS-ART SECTION

Awards only graduating students currently enrolled in grades 7 to 12 who attend a public, private, parochial, or home school in the United States, U.S. territories, or U.S. sponsored schools abroad. May submit an art and/or a photography portfolio.

Academic Fields/Career Goals: Arts; Literature/English/Writing.

Award: Scholarship for use in freshman year; not renewable. *Number:* varies. *Amount:* varies.

Eligibility Requirements: Applicant must be high school student; planning to enroll or expecting to enroll full- or part-time at a four-year institution or university and must have an interest in art or photography/photogrammetry/filmmaking. Available to U.S. and non-U.S. citizens.

Application Requirements: Application, applicant must enter a contest, essay, portfolio, references, original works, electronic files for regional judging. *Deadline:* varies.

Contact: Scholarship Committee
Alliance for Young Artists and Writers Inc.
557 Broadway
New York, NY 10012
Phone: 212-343-6493
E-mail: a&wgeneralinfo@scholastic.com

SCHOLASTIC ART AND WRITING AWARDS-WRITING SECTION SCHOLARSHIP

Students currently enrolled in grades 7 to 12 who attend a public, private, parochial, or home school in the United States, U.S. territories, or U.S. sponsored schools abroad may apply.

Academic Fields/Career Goals: Arts; Literature/English/Writing.

Award: Scholarship for use in freshman year; not renewable. *Number:* varies. *Amount:* varies.

Eligibility Requirements: Applicant must be high school student; planning to enroll or expecting to enroll full- or part-time at a four-year institution or university and must have an interest in writing. Available to U.S. and non-U.S. citizens.

Application Requirements: Application, applicant must enter a contest, essay, portfolio, references, manuscript. *Deadline:* varies.

Contact: General Information
Alliance for Young Artists and Writers Inc.
557 Broadway
New York, NY 10012-1396
Phone: 212-343-7791
Fax: 212-389-3939
E-mail: a&wgeneralinfo@scholastic.com

AMERICAN ART THERAPY ASSOCIATION http://www.arttherapy.org

MYRA LEVICK SCHOLARSHIP FUND

Scholarship available to students who can demonstrate financial need, acceptance into an AATA-approved art therapy program, and maintain minimum undergraduate GPA of 3.0. Applicants must be active student members of AATA.

Academic Fields/Career Goals: Arts; Therapy/Rehabilitation.

Award: Scholarship for use in freshman, sophomore, junior, or senior years; not renewable. *Number:* varies. *Amount:* varies.

Eligibility Requirements: Applicant must be enrolled or expecting to enroll full-time at a four-year institution or university. Applicant or parent of applicant must be member of American Art Therapy Association. Applicant must have 3.0 GPA or higher.

Application Requirements: Application, essay, references, transcript, proof of acceptance or enrollment in art therapy program. *Deadline:* June 15.

Contact: Doris Arrington, Scholarship Committee
American Art Therapy Association
1202 Allanson Road
Mundelein, IL 60060-9808
Phone: 888-290-0878
Fax: 708-566-4580
E-mail: daarrington@sbcglobal.net

AMERICAN INSTITUTE OF POLISH CULTURE INC. http://www.ampolinstitute.org

HARRIET IRSAY SCHOLARSHIP GRANT

Merit-based $1000 scholarships for students studying communications, public relations, and/or journalism. All U.S. citizens may apply, but preference will be given to U.S. citizens of Polish heritage. Must submit three letters of recommendation on appropriate letterhead with application mailed directly to AIPC. For study in the United States only. Non-refundable fee of $10 will be collected.

Academic Fields/Career Goals: Arts; Communications; Education; Foreign Language; Journalism; Public Policy and Administration.

Award: Scholarship for use in freshman, sophomore, junior, senior, or graduate years; not renewable. *Number:* 10–15. *Amount:* $1000.

American Institute of Polish Culture Inc. (continued)

Eligibility Requirements: Applicant must be enrolled or expecting to enroll full-time at a two-year or four-year institution or university. Available to U.S. citizens.

Application Requirements: Application, resume, references, self-addressed stamped envelope, transcript. *Fee:* $10. *Deadline:* April 20.

Contact: Scholarship Committee
American Institute of Polish Culture Inc.
1440 79th Street Causeway, Suite 117
Miami, FL 33141-3555
Phone: 305-864-2349
Fax: 305-865-5150
E-mail: info@ampolinstitute.org

AMERICAN LEGION AUXILIARY DEPARTMENT OF WASHINGTON http://www.walegion-aux.org

AMERICAN LEGION AUXILIARY DEPARTMENT OF WASHINGTON FLORENCE LEMCKE MEMORIAL SCHOLARSHIP IN FINE ARTS

• *See page 97*

AMERICAN PHILOLOGICAL ASSOCIATION http://www.apaclassics.org

MINORITY STUDENT SUMMER SCHOLARSHIP

• *See page 89*

AMERICAN SCHOOL OF CLASSICAL STUDIES AT ATHENS http://www.ascsa.edu.gr

ASCSA SUMMER SESSIONS OPEN SCHOLARSHIPS

• *See page 83*

ART DIRECTORS CLUB http://www.adcglobal.org

ART DIRECTORS CLUB NATIONAL SCHOLARSHIPS

Six $2500 scholarships for sophomores and juniors enrolled in accredited art schools and colleges around the country. Must have successfully completed the first year of an accredited undergraduate or portfolio program.

Academic Fields/Career Goals: Arts.

Award: Scholarship for use in sophomore or junior years; not renewable. *Number:* 6. *Amount:* $2500.

Eligibility Requirements: Applicant must be enrolled or expecting to enroll full-time at a four-year institution or university. Available to U.S. and non-U.S. citizens.

Application Requirements: Application, essay, portfolio, resume, references, transcript, 5 images of recent work on CD. *Deadline:* April 30.

Contact: Education Coordinator
Art Directors Club
106 West 29th Street
New York, NY 10009
Phone: 212-643-1440 Ext. 16
Fax: 212-643-4293
E-mail: isabel@adcglobal.org

BMI FOUNDATION INC. http://www.bmifoundation.org

BMI STUDENT COMPOSER AWARDS

One-time awards for original compositions in the classical genre for young student composers who are under age 26 and citizens of the Western Hemisphere. Must submit application and original musical score. Application available at Web site: http://www.bmifoundation.org.

Academic Fields/Career Goals: Arts; Music.

Award: Prize for use in freshman, sophomore, junior, senior, graduate, or postgraduate years; not renewable. *Number:* up to 10. *Amount:* $500–$5000.

Eligibility Requirements: Applicant must be age 26 or under; enrolled or expecting to enroll full-time at a two-year or four-year institution or university and must have an interest in music/singing. Available to U.S. and non-U.S. citizens.

Application Requirements: Application, self-addressed stamped envelope, original musical score. *Deadline:* February 1.

Contact: Mr. Ralph N. Jackson, Director
BMI Foundation Inc.
320 West 57th Street
New York, NY 10019
Phone: 212-586-2000
Fax: 212-245-8986
E-mail: classical@bmi.com

CHRISTOPHER PETTIET SCHOLARSHIP FUND http://www.theactorscircle.com/chris.html

CHRISTOPHER PETTIET MEMORIAL FUND

Provides scholarships for young actors to study. Total number of available awards and dollar value of each award varies. Award for both full-time and part-time study. Deadline varies.

Academic Fields/Career Goals: Arts.

Award: Scholarship for use in freshman, sophomore, junior, senior, or graduate years; not renewable. *Number:* varies. *Amount:* varies.

Eligibility Requirements: Applicant must be enrolled or expecting to enroll full- or part-time at a two-year or four-year or technical institution or university and must have an interest in theater. Available to U.S. and non-U.S. citizens.

Application Requirements: Application. *Deadline:* varies.

Contact: Scholarship Committee
Christopher Pettiet Scholarship Fund
The Actors Circle, 4475 Sepulveda Boulevard
Culver City, CA 90230
Phone: 310-837-4536
E-mail: workshops@theactorscircle.com

CIRI FOUNDATION (TCF) http://www.thecirifoundation.org

CIRI FOUNDATION SUSIE QIMMIQSAK BEVINS ENDOWMENT SCHOLARSHIP FUND

Award of $2000 maximum based on stated need is offered to Alaska Native original enrollee or descendants of Cook Inlet Region Inc., who are studying the literary, performing, or visual arts. Must be accepted or enrolled in a two- or four-year undergraduate degree or graduate degree program. Deadlines: June 1 and December 1.

Academic Fields/Career Goals: Arts; Literature/English/Writing; Performing Arts.

Award: Scholarship for use in freshman, sophomore, junior, senior, or graduate years; not renewable. *Number:* varies. *Amount:* up to $2000.

Eligibility Requirements: Applicant must be American Indian/Alaska Native and enrolled or expecting to enroll full-time at a two-year or four-year institution or university. Applicant must have 2.5 GPA or higher. Available to U.S. and non-U.S. citizens.

Application Requirements: Application, essay, references, transcript, proof of eligibility, birth certificate or adoption decree. *Deadline:* varies.

Contact: Susan Anderson, President and Chief Executive Officer
CIRI Foundation (TCF)
3600 San Jeronimo Drive, Suite 256
Anchorage, AK 99508-2870
Phone: 907-793-3575
Fax: 907-793-3585
E-mail: tcf@thecirifoundation.org

COLLEGEBOUND FOUNDATION http://www.collegeboundfoundation.org

JANET B. SONDHEIM SCHOLARSHIP

Award for Baltimore City public high school graduates. Must major in either fine arts, or any field of study with intent to teach. Minimum GPA of 3.0 is required. Must submit one-page essay on goals and accomplishments and the applicant's interest in the arts or teaching.

Academic Fields/Career Goals: Arts; Education; Music.

Award: Scholarship for use in freshman, sophomore, junior, or senior years; renewable. *Number:* 1. *Amount:* $500.

Eligibility Requirements: Applicant must be enrolled or expecting to enroll full-time at a two-year or four-year institution or university and resident of Maryland. Applicant must have 3.0 GPA or higher. Available to U.S. citizens.

Application Requirements: Application, essay, financial need analysis, references, transcript, financial aid award letters. *Deadline:* March 1.

Contact: Jamie Crouse, Scholarship Program Administrator
CollegeBound Foundation
300 Water Street, Suite 300
Baltimore, MD 21202
Phone: 410-783-2905 Ext. 207
Fax: 410-727-5786
E-mail: jcrouse@collegeboundfoundation.org

COMMUNITY FOUNDATION FOR GREATER ATLANTA INC. http://www.atlcf.org

JAMES M. AND VIRGINIA M. SMYTH SCHOLARSHIP

Scholarship of $2000 annually for up to four years to students enrolled at an accredited college pursuing an undergraduate degree. Applicant should pursue a degree in the arts and sciences, human services, music or ministry.

Academic Fields/Career Goals: Arts; Humanities; Music; Natural Sciences; Physical Sciences and Math; Religion/Theology.

Award: Scholarship for use in freshman, sophomore, junior, or senior years; renewable. *Number:* 12–15. *Amount:* $2000.

Eligibility Requirements: Applicant must be enrolled or expecting to enroll full-time at a four-year institution or university. Applicant must have 3.0 GPA or higher. Available to U.S. citizens.

Application Requirements: Application, financial need analysis. *Deadline:* March 26.

Contact: Kristina Morris, Program Associate
Community Foundation for Greater Atlanta Inc.
50 Hurt Plaza, Suite 449
Atlanta, GA 30303
Phone: 404-688-5525
Fax: 404-688-3060
E-mail: scholarships@atlcf.org

COSTUME SOCIETY OF AMERICA http://www.costumesocietyamerica.com

ADELE FILENE TRAVEL AWARD

• *See page 95*

STELLA BLUM RESEARCH GRANT

• *See page 95*

ELIZABETH GREENSHIELDS FOUNDATION

ELIZABETH GREENSHIELDS AWARD/GRANT

Award of $12,500 available to candidates working in painting, drawing, printmaking, or sculpture. Work must be representational or figurative. Must submit at least one color slide of each of six works. Must reapply to renew. Applications from self-taught individuals are also accepted.

Academic Fields/Career Goals: Arts.

Award: Grant for use in freshman, sophomore, junior, senior, or graduate years; not renewable. *Number:* 40–60. *Amount:* $12,500.

Eligibility Requirements: Applicant must be enrolled or expecting to enroll full- or part-time at a two-year or four-year or technical institution or university and must have an interest in art. Available to U.S. and non-U.S. citizens.

Application Requirements: Application, applicant must enter a contest. *Deadline:* continuous.

Contact: Diane Pitcher, Applications Coordinator
Elizabeth Greenshields Foundation
1814 Sherbrooke Street, W, Suite 1
Montreal, QC H3H IE4
Canada
Phone: 514-937-9225
Fax: 514-937-0141
E-mail: greenshields@bellnet.ca

FLORIDA PTA/PTSA http://www.floridapta.org

FLORIDA PTA/PTSA FINE ARTS SCHOLARSHIP

Renewable award of $1000 to a graduating Florida high school senior who plans to attend a fine arts program within the State of Florida. Must have a least a two-year attendance in a Florida PTA / PTSA high school. Minimum 3.0 GPA.

Academic Fields/Career Goals: Arts.

Award: Scholarship for use in freshman year; renewable. *Number:* 3. *Amount:* $1000.

Eligibility Requirements: Applicant must be high school student; planning to enroll or expecting to enroll full-time at a four-year institution or university; resident of Florida and studying in Florida. Applicant must have 3.0 GPA or higher. Available to U.S. citizens.

Application Requirements: Application, essay, references. *Deadline:* March 1.

Contact: Janice Bailey, Executive Director
Florida PTA/PTSA
1747 Orlando Central Parkway
Orlando, FL 32809
Phone: 407-855-7604
Fax: 407-240-9577
E-mail: janice@floridapta.org

GENERAL FEDERATION OF WOMEN'S CLUBS OF MASSACHUSETTS http://www.gfwcma.org

GENERAL FEDERATION OF WOMEN'S CLUBS OF MASSACHUSETTS PENNIES FOR ART SCHOLARSHIP

Scholarship in art for graduating high school seniors who are residents of Massachusetts. The award is for tuition only and will be sent directly to the recipient's college. Must submit letter of recommendation from high school art instructor.

Academic Fields/Career Goals: Arts.

Award: Scholarship for use in freshman year; not renewable. *Number:* varies. *Amount:* up to $800.

Eligibility Requirements: Applicant must be high school student; planning to enroll or expecting to enroll full-time at a four-year institution or university; resident of Massachusetts and must have an interest in art. Available to U.S. citizens.

Application Requirements: Application, autobiography, essay, portfolio, references, self-addressed stamped envelope. *Deadline:* March 1.

Contact: Joan Shanahan, Arts Chairman
General Federation of Women's Clubs of Massachusetts
PO Box 703
Upton, MA 01568-0703
E-mail: cmje@aol.com

GETTY GRANT PROGRAM http://www.getty.edu/grants

LIBRARY RESEARCH GRANTS

• *See page 98*

GOLDEN KEY INTERNATIONAL HONOUR SOCIETY http://www.goldenkey.org

VISUAL AND PERFORMING ARTS ACHIEVEMENT AWARDS

Award of $500 will be given to winners in each of the following nine categories: painting, drawing, photography, sculpture, computer-generated art/graphic design/illustration, mixed media, instrumental performance, vocal performance, and dance.

Academic Fields/Career Goals: Arts; Graphics/Graphic Arts/Printing.

Award: Prize for use in freshman, sophomore, junior, senior, graduate, or postgraduate years; not renewable. *Number:* 9. *Amount:* $500.

Eligibility Requirements: Applicant must be enrolled or expecting to enroll full- or part-time at a four-year institution or university and must have an interest in art. Available to U.S. and non-U.S. citizens.

Golden Key International Honour Society (continued)

Application Requirements: Application, applicant must enter a contest, artwork, cover letter. *Deadline:* April 1.

Contact: Scholarship Program Administrators
Golden Key International Honour Society
PO Box 23737
Nashville, TN 37202
Phone: 800-377-2401

GREAT FALLS ADVERTISING FEDERATION http://www.gfaf.com

COLLEGE SCHOLARSHIP

Scholarship of $2000 for college juniors who are residents of Montana. Must intend to pursue a career in communications, marketing, advertising, fine arts, or other related field. The number of awards vary. Must maintain a minimum 3.0 GPA.

Academic Fields/Career Goals: Arts; Business/Consumer Services; Communications.

Award: Scholarship for use in junior year; renewable. *Number:* varies. *Amount:* $2000.

Eligibility Requirements: Applicant must be enrolled or expecting to enroll full-time at a four-year institution or university and resident of Montana. Applicant must have 3.0 GPA or higher. Available to U.S. citizens.

Application Requirements: Application, essay, resume, references, transcript, work samples. *Deadline:* February 2.

Contact: Christine Depa, Administrative Assistant
Great Falls Advertising Federation
609 Tenth Avenue South, Suite B
Great Falls, MT 59405
Phone: 406-761-6453
Fax: 406-453-1128
E-mail: gfaf@gfaf.com

HIGH SCHOOL ART SCHOLARSHIP

Two scholarships of $2000 for high school seniors who are residents of Montana. Must intend to pursue a career in art or other related field.

Academic Fields/Career Goals: Arts.

Award: Scholarship for use in freshman year; not renewable. *Number:* 2. *Amount:* $2000.

Eligibility Requirements: Applicant must be high school student; planning to enroll or expecting to enroll full-time at a two-year or four-year institution or university and resident of Montana. Available to U.S. citizens.

Application Requirements: Application, essay, portfolio, resume, references, self-addressed stamped envelope, cover letter describing how the scholarship money will be used. *Deadline:* February 29.

Contact: Christine Depa, Administrative Assistant
Great Falls Advertising Federation
609 Tenth Avenue South, Suite B
Great Falls, MT 59405
Phone: 406-761-6453
Fax: 406-453-1128
E-mail: gfaf@gfaf.com

HISPANIC SCHOLARSHIP FUND http://www.hsf.net

HSF/MCNAMARA FAMILY CREATIVE ARTS PROJECT GRANT

• *See page 98*

INSTITUTE FOR HUMANE STUDIES http://www.theihs.org

FILM AND FICTION SCHOLARSHIP

Scholarship program to support students pursuing degrees in filmmaking or creative writing.

Academic Fields/Career Goals: Arts; Filmmaking/Video; Literature/English/Writing.

Award: Scholarship for use in senior or graduate years; renewable. *Number:* 2–6. *Amount:* $3000–$10,000.

Eligibility Requirements: Applicant must be enrolled or expecting to enroll full-time at a four-year institution or university. Available to U.S. and non-U.S. citizens.

Application Requirements: Application, essay. *Deadline:* January 15.

Contact: Keri Anderson, Program Coordinator
Institute for Humane Studies
3301 North Fairfax Drive, Suite 440
Arlington, VA 22201-4432
Phone: 703-993-4880
Fax: 703-993-4890
E-mail: ihs@gmu.edu

INTERNATIONAL FURNISHINGS AND DESIGN ASSOCIATION http://www.ifdaef.org

RUTH CLARK SCHOLARSHIP

Scholarship available to students studying design at an accredited college or design school with a focus on residential furniture design. Applicant must submit five examples of original designs, three of which must be residential furniture examples. May be CD-ROM (pdf format only), slides, photographs, or copies of drawings no larger than 8 1/2" x11". Include five sets of each design example with a short description of each illustration.

Academic Fields/Career Goals: Arts; Industrial Design.

Award: Scholarship for use in sophomore, junior, or senior years; not renewable. *Number:* 1. *Amount:* $2500.

Eligibility Requirements: Applicant must be enrolled or expecting to enroll full-time at a four-year institution or university. Available to U.S. and non-U.S. citizens.

Application Requirements: Application, essay, references, transcript, 2 digital copies of the design work done in class. *Deadline:* March 31.

Contact: Earline Feldman, Director
International Furnishings and Design Association
150 South Warner Road, Suite 156
King of Prussia, PA 19406
Phone: 610-535-6422
Fax: 610-535-6423
E-mail: tapis2@bellsouth.com

JACK J. ISGUR FOUNDATION

JACK J. ISGUR FOUNDATION SCHOLARSHIP

Awards scholarships to juniors, seniors, and graduate students with intentions of teaching the humanities in Missouri schools. Applicants interested in teaching in rural schools will take precedence.

Academic Fields/Career Goals: Arts; Education; Humanities; Literature/English/Writing; Music; Performing Arts.

Award: Scholarship for use in junior, senior, graduate, or postgraduate years; renewable. *Number:* up to 40. *Amount:* $500–$750.

Eligibility Requirements: Applicant must be enrolled or expecting to enroll full- or part-time at a four-year institution or university. Available to U.S. and non-U.S. citizens.

Application Requirements: Application, interview, references, transcript. *Deadline:* April 15.

Contact: Charles Jensen, Attorney at Law
Jack J. Isgur Foundation
c/o Charles F. Jensen, Stinson, Morrison, Hecker LLP
1201 Walnut Street, 28th Floor
Kansas City, MO 64106
Phone: 816-691-2760
Fax: 816-691-3495
E-mail: cjensen@stinson.com

JOHN F. AND ANNA LEE STACEY SCHOLARSHIP FUND http://www.nationalcowboymuseum.org

JOHN F. AND ANNA LEE STACEY SCHOLARSHIP FUND

Scholarships for artists who are high school graduates between the ages of 18 and 35, who are U.S. citizens, and whose work is devoted to the classical or conservative tradition of Western culture. Awards are for drawing or painting only. Must submit no more than ten 35mm color slides of work.

Academic Fields/Career Goals: Arts.

Award: Scholarship for use in freshman, sophomore, junior, senior, or graduate years; renewable. *Number:* 3–5. *Amount:* $1000–$4000.

Eligibility Requirements: Applicant must be age 18-35; enrolled or expecting to enroll full- or part-time at a four-year institution or university and must have an interest in art. Available to U.S. citizens.

Application Requirements: Application, photo, references, digital images. *Deadline:* February 1.

Contact: Ed Muno, Art Curator
John F. and Anna Lee Stacey Scholarship Fund
1700 Northeast 63rd Street
Oklahoma City, OK 73111
Phone: 405-478-2250
Fax: 405-478-4714
E-mail: emuno@nationalcowboymuseum.org

JUNIOR ACHIEVEMENT http://www.ja.org

WALT DISNEY COMPANY FOUNDATION SCHOLARSHIP

Applicant must be a high school senior who completed JA Company Program or JA Economics. Tuition-only scholarship, renewable annually for up to four years leading to a bachelor degree in either business administration or fine arts at an accredited college or university. Award of $200 cash accompanies the scholarship each year for incidental fees.

Academic Fields/Career Goals: Arts; Business/Consumer Services.

Award: Scholarship for use in freshman year; renewable. *Number:* 1. *Amount:* varies.

Eligibility Requirements: Applicant must be high school student and planning to enroll or expecting to enroll full-time at a four-year institution or university. Applicant or parent of applicant must be member of Junior Achievement. Available to U.S. and Canadian citizens.

Application Requirements: Application, references, test scores, transcript. *Deadline:* February 1.

Contact: Denise Terry, Scholarship Coordinator
Junior Achievement
One Education Way
Colorado Springs, CO 80906-4477
Phone: 719-540-6134
Fax: 719-540-6175
E-mail: dterry@ja.org

KE ALI'I PAUAHI FOUNDATION http://www.pauahi.org

BRUCE T. AND JACKIE MAHI ERICKSON GRANT

Grant to support an undergraduate or graduate student pursuing studies in the creation of crafts, art and photography, and/or independent research relating to historical Hawaiian crafts and arts. Must be in good academic standing, demonstrate financial need, and be pursuing a post-secondary degree.

Academic Fields/Career Goals: Arts; Photojournalism/Photography.

Award: Grant for use in freshman, sophomore, junior, senior, or graduate years; not renewable. *Number:* 1. *Amount:* up to $800.

Eligibility Requirements: Applicant must be enrolled or expecting to enroll full-time at a two-year or four-year institution or university and must have an interest in Hawaiian language/culture. Available to U.S. citizens.

Application Requirements: Application, financial need analysis, references, transcript, college acceptance letter, copy of SAR. *Deadline:* May 2.

Contact: Elizabeth Stevenson, Development Manager
Ke Ali'i Pauahi Foundation
567 South King Street, Suite 160
Honolulu, HI 96813
Phone: 808-534-3966
Fax: 808-534-3890
E-mail: scholarships@pauahi.org

NATIVE HAWAIIAN VISUAL ARTS SCHOLARSHIP

Scholarship open to Hawaii residents who are undergraduate or graduate students majoring in art, to encourage studies in the area of visual arts. This includes, but is not limited to, drawing, painting, printmaking, graphic design, fiber arts, sculpture, ceramics, digital art (computer), photography, and film-making or video production. Selection based on artistic merit as demonstrated by an artistic portfolio and academic achievements. Minimum GPA of 3.2 required.

Academic Fields/Career Goals: Arts.

Award: Scholarship for use in freshman, sophomore, junior, senior, or graduate years; not renewable. *Number:* 2. *Amount:* $1400.

Eligibility Requirements: Applicant must be enrolled or expecting to enroll full-time at an institution or university; resident of Hawaii; studying in Hawaii and must have an interest in art or photography/photogrammetry/filmmaking. Available to U.S. citizens.

Application Requirements: Application, financial need analysis, portfolio, transcript, Student Aid Report (SAR). *Deadline:* May 2.

Contact: Elizabeth Stevenson, Development Manager
Ke Ali'i Pauahi Foundation
567 South King Street, Suite 160
Honolulu, HI 96813
Phone: 808-534-3966
Fax: 808-534-3890
E-mail: scholarships@pauahi.org

LIBERTY GRAPHICS INC. http://www.lgtees.com

ANNUAL LIBERTY GRAPHICS ART CONTEST

One-time scholarship to the successful student who submits the winning design depicting appreciation of the natural environment of Maine. Applicants must be residents of Maine and be a high school senior. Original works in traditional flat media are the preferred format. Multiple submissions are allowed.

Academic Fields/Career Goals: Arts; Graphics/Graphic Arts/Printing.

Award: Prize for use in freshman year; not renewable. *Number:* 1. *Amount:* $1000.

Eligibility Requirements: Applicant must be high school student; planning to enroll or expecting to enroll full- or part-time at a two-year or four-year or technical institution or university and resident of Maine. Available to U.S. citizens.

Application Requirements: Application, applicant must enter a contest, self-addressed stamped envelope, artwork in keeping with the contest theme. *Deadline:* April 28.

Contact: Mr. Jay Sproul, Scholarship Coordinator
Liberty Graphics Inc.
3 Main Street, PO Box 5
Liberty, ME 04949
Phone: 207-589-4596
Fax: 207-589-4415
E-mail: jay@lgtees.com

LIQUITEX ARTIST MATERIALS PURCHASE AWARD PROGRAM http://www.liquitex.com

LIQUITEX EXCELLENCE IN ART PURCHASE AWARD PROGRAM

Prizes up to $5000 in cash plus $1500 in Liquitex products will be awarded to the best art submissions. Submission should be made on 35mm color slides. Void in Quebec or where prohibited by law. For more details see Web site: http://www.liquitex.com.

Academic Fields/Career Goals: Arts.

Award: Prize for use in freshman, sophomore, junior, senior, graduate, or postgraduate years; not renewable. *Number:* 5. *Amount:* $5000–$6500.

Eligibility Requirements: Applicant must be enrolled or expecting to enroll full- or part-time at a two-year or four-year or technical institution or university. Available to U.S. and Canadian citizens.

Application Requirements: Application, applicant must enter a contest, 35mm color slides of artwork. *Deadline:* January 15.

Contact: Mrs. Renee Hile, Vice President Marketing
Liquitex Artist Materials Purchase Award Program
11 Constitution Avenue
PO Box 1396
Piscataway, NJ 08855-1396
Phone: 732-562-0770
Fax: 732-562-0941

MARYLAND ARTISTS EQUITY FOUNDATION http://www.maef.org

MARYLAND ARTISTS EQUITY FOUNDATION VISUAL ARTS ANNUAL SCHOLARSHIP COMPETITION

Scholarships for senior high school students from Maryland public and private schools. Awarded for use at an accredited college or university for studies in the visual arts.

Academic Fields/Career Goals: Arts.

Award: Scholarship for use in freshman year; not renewable. *Number:* 25. *Amount:* $500–$3000.

Eligibility Requirements: Applicant must be high school student; planning to enroll or expecting to enroll full-time at a four-year institution or university; resident of Maryland and must have an interest in art. Available to U.S. citizens.

Application Requirements: Application, portfolio, five JPG images on CD. *Deadline:* December 21.

Contact: Mark Coates, Scholarship Chair
Maryland Artists Equity Foundation
PO Box 17050
Baltimore, MD 21297
Phone: 410-313-6634
Fax: 410-313-6634
E-mail: mark_coates@hcpss.org

MEDIA ACTION NETWORK FOR ASIAN AMERICANS http://www.manaa.org

MANAA MEDIA SCHOLARSHIPS FOR ASIAN AMERICAN STUDENTS

One-time award to students pursuing careers in film and television production as writers, directors, producers, and studio executives. Students must have a strong desire to advance a positive and enlightened understanding of the Asian-American experience in mainstream media. See Web site: http://www.manaa.org for application deadline and additional information.

Academic Fields/Career Goals: Arts; Filmmaking/Video; TV/Radio Broadcasting.

Award: Scholarship for use in freshman, sophomore, junior, senior, or graduate years; not renewable. *Number:* 1. *Amount:* $1000.

Eligibility Requirements: Applicant must be Asian/Pacific Islander and enrolled or expecting to enroll full-time at a two-year or four-year or technical institution or university. Available to U.S. citizens.

Application Requirements: Essay, financial need analysis, references, transcript, work sample. *Deadline:* varies.

Contact: Scholarship Coordinator
Media Action Network for Asian Americans
PO Box 11105
Burbank, CA 91510
E-mail: manaaletters@yahoo.com.

METAVUE CORPORATION http://www.metavue.com

FW RAUSCH ARTS AND HUMANITIES PAPER CONTEST

Eight awards given a year to undergraduate students enrolled at an accredited college or university in the U.S. Scholarships are granted for exemplary work in one of a variety of arts- and humanities-related areas the contestant may choose from. Work may focus on research, biography or critical essay. Additional information and rules are available at www.metavue.com.

Academic Fields/Career Goals: Arts; Humanities.

Award: Prize for use in freshman, sophomore, junior, or senior years; not renewable. *Number:* 6. *Amount:* $15–$500.

Eligibility Requirements: Applicant must be enrolled or expecting to enroll full-time at a two-year or four-year institution or university. Applicant must have 3.0 GPA or higher. Available to U.S. citizens.

Application Requirements: Applicant must enter a contest, essay. *Deadline:* May 1.

Contact: Michael Rufflo, Scholarship Committee
Metavue Corporation
1110 Surrey Drive
Sun Prairie, WI 53590
Phone: 608-577-0642
Fax: 512-685-4074
E-mail: rufflo@metavue.com

MINNESOTA COMMUNITY FOUNDATION http://www.mncommunityfoundation.org

FRANK CHANEY MEMORIAL SCHOLARSHIP

Scholarship to legal dependents of employees of the Andersen Corporation, who demonstrate artistic ability and wish to enroll in an art-related degree program in a postsecondary educational institution.

Academic Fields/Career Goals: Arts.

Award: Scholarship for use in freshman year; renewable. *Number:* varies. *Amount:* up to $3000.

Eligibility Requirements: Applicant must be high school student; planning to enroll or expecting to enroll full-time at a four-year institution or university and must have an interest in art. Applicant or parent of applicant must be affiliated with Andersen Corporation. Applicant must have 2.5 GPA or higher. Available to U.S. citizens.

Application Requirements: Application, portfolio, references. *Deadline:* April 4.

Contact: Donna Paulson, Administrative Assistant
Minnesota Community Foundation
55 Fifth Street East, Suite 600
St. Paul, MN 55101-1797
Phone: 651-325-4212
E-mail: dkp@mncommunityfoundation.org

NATIONAL ART MATERIALS TRADE ASSOCIATION http://www.namta.org

NATIONAL ART MATERIALS TRADE ASSOCIATION ART SCHOLARSHIP

Awards eight $1000 scholarships, payable to the recipient's college, technical institution or university. Candidates are judged on the basis of financial need, extracurricular activities and special interests. For details refer to Web site: http://www.namta.org/.

Academic Fields/Career Goals: Arts.

Award: Scholarship for use in freshman, sophomore, junior, senior, graduate, or postgraduate years; not renewable. *Number:* 8. *Amount:* $1000.

Eligibility Requirements: Applicant must be enrolled or expecting to enroll full- or part-time at a two-year or four-year or technical institution or university. Available to U.S. and non-U.S. citizens.

Application Requirements: Application, essay, test scores, transcript. *Deadline:* March 15.

Contact: Karen Brown, Administrative Assistant
National Art Materials Trade Association
15806 Brookway Drive, Suite 300
Huntersville, NC 28078
Phone: 704-892-6244
Fax: 704-892-6247
E-mail: kbrown@namta.org

NATIONAL FEDERATION OF THE BLIND http://www.nfb.org

NATIONAL FEDERATION OF THE BLIND HUMANITIES SCHOLARSHIP

One-time award for full-time postsecondary study in the humanities (art, English, foreign languages, history, philosophy, or religion). Must be legally blind. Minumum 3.5 GPA required. Award based on financial need, community service, and academic excellence.

Academic Fields/Career Goals: Arts; Foreign Language; History; Humanities; Literature/English/Writing.

Award: Scholarship for use in freshman, sophomore, junior, or senior years; not renewable. *Number:* 1. *Amount:* $3000.

Eligibility Requirements: Applicant must be enrolled or expecting to enroll full-time at a two-year or four-year institution or university. Applicant or parent of applicant must have employment or volunteer experience in community service. Applicant must be visually impaired. Applicant must have 3.5 GPA or higher. Available to U.S. and non-U.S. citizens.

Application Requirements: Application, autobiography, essay, financial need analysis, references, test scores, transcript. *Deadline:* March 31.

Contact: Peggy Elliot, Chairman, Scholarship Committee
National Federation of the Blind
805 Fifth Avenue
Grinnell, IA 50112-1653
Phone: 641-236-3369

NATIONAL OPERA ASSOCIATION http://www.noa.org

NOA VOCAL COMPETITION/LEGACY AWARD PROGRAM

Awards granted based on competitive audition to support study and career development. Singers compete in Scholarship and Artist Division. Legacy Awards are granted for study and career development in any opera-related career to those who further NOA's goal of increased minority participation in the profession.

Academic Fields/Career Goals: Arts; Performing Arts.

Award: Prize for use in freshman, sophomore, junior, senior, graduate, or postgraduate years; not renewable. *Number:* 3–8. *Amount:* $500–$2000.

Eligibility Requirements: Applicant must be age 18-24; enrolled or expecting to enroll full- or part-time at a two-year or four-year or technical institution or university and must have an interest in music or music/singing. Available to U.S. and non-U.S. citizens.

Application Requirements: Application, applicant must enter a contest, autobiography, photo, references, audition tape/proposal. *Fee:* $25. *Deadline:* October 15.

Contact: Robert Hansen, Executive Secretary
National Opera Association
2403 Russell Long Boulevard, PO Box 60869
Canyon, TX 79016-0001
Phone: 806-651-2857
Fax: 806-651-2958
E-mail: hansen@mail.wtamu.edu

NATIONAL SCULPTURE SOCIETY http://www.nationalsculpture.org

NATIONAL SCULPTURE SOCIETY ALEX J. ETTL GRANT

Grant awarded to a figurative or realist sculptor who has demonstrated a commitment to sculpting and an outstanding ability through his or her life's work. Must submit photos of work. Not available to NSS members.

Academic Fields/Career Goals: Arts.

Award: Grant for use in freshman, sophomore, junior, senior, graduate, or postgraduate years; not renewable. *Number:* 1. *Amount:* up to $4000.

Eligibility Requirements: Applicant must be enrolled or expecting to enroll full- or part-time at a two-year or four-year or technical institution or university and must have an interest in art. Available to U.S. citizens.

Application Requirements: Autobiography, self-addressed stamped envelope, photographs of work (CD). *Deadline:* January 7.

Contact: Gwen Pier, Executive Director
National Sculpture Society
237 Park Avenue
New York, NY 10017
Phone: 212-764-5645 Ext. 15
Fax: 212-764-5651
E-mail: gwen@nationalsculpture.org

NATIONAL SCULPTURE SOCIETY SCHOLARSHIPS

Scholarships available for students of figurative or representational sculpture. Scholarships are paid directly to the academic institution through which the student applies. Applicant must submit 8 to 10 photographs of at least three different works.

Academic Fields/Career Goals: Arts.

Award: Scholarship for use in freshman, sophomore, junior, senior, or graduate years; not renewable. *Number:* 1–6. *Amount:* $2000.

Eligibility Requirements: Applicant must be enrolled or expecting to enroll full- or part-time at a two-year or four-year or technical institution or university and must have an interest in art. Available to U.S. and non-U.S. citizens.

Application Requirements: Application, financial need analysis, references, self-addressed stamped envelope, transcript, photographs of work (CD). *Deadline:* May 30.

Contact: Gwen Pier, Executive Director
National Sculpture Society
237 Park Avenue
New York, NY 10017
Phone: 212-764-5645 Ext. 15
Fax: 212-764-5651
E-mail: gwen@nationalsculpture.org

P. BUCKLEY MOSS SOCIETY http://www.mosssociety.org

BUCKLEY MOSS ENDOWED SCHOLARSHIP

Scholarship of $1500 to one or more high school seniors with financial need, a certified language-related learning disability, and artistic talent who plan a career in visual arts.

Academic Fields/Career Goals: Arts.

Award: Scholarship for use in freshman year; not renewable. *Number:* 1. *Amount:* $1500.

Eligibility Requirements: Applicant must be high school student; planning to enroll or expecting to enroll part-time at a two-year or four-year institution or university and must have an interest in art. Applicant must be learning disabled. Available to U.S. citizens.

Application Requirements: Application, portfolio, transcript. *Deadline:* June 1.

Contact: Brenda Simmons, Administrative Assistant
P. Buckley Moss Society
20 Stoneridge Drive, Suite 102
Waynesboro, VA 22980
Phone: 540-943-5678
Fax: 540-949-8408
E-mail: brenda@mosssociety.org

PLAYWRIGHTS' CENTER http://www.pwcenter.org

MANY VOICES RESIDENCY PROGRAM

Program intended to enrich the American theater by offering playwriting residencies to artists of color. Must be a U.S. citizen.

Academic Fields/Career Goals: Arts; Literature/English/Writing.

Award: Grant for use in freshman, sophomore, junior, senior, graduate, or postgraduate years; not renewable. *Number:* 8. *Amount:* $1250–$2000.

Eligibility Requirements: Applicant must be American Indian/Alaska Native, Asian/Pacific Islander, Black (non-Hispanic), or Hispanic; enrolled or expecting to enroll full- or part-time at a two-year or four-year or technical institution or university; resident of Minnesota; studying in Minnesota and must have an interest in theater or writing. Available to U.S. citizens.

Application Requirements: Application, applicant must enter a contest, resume, writing sample. *Deadline:* July 25.

Contact: Kevin McLaughlin, Fellowships Technology and Space Manager
Playwrights' Center
2301 East Franklin Avenue
Minneapolis, MN 55406-1099
Phone: 612-332-7481 Ext. 15
Fax: 612-332-6037
E-mail: info@pwcenter.org

POLISH ARTS CLUB OF BUFFALO SCHOLARSHIP FOUNDATION http://www.pacb.bfn.org

POLISH ARTS CLUB OF BUFFALO SCHOLARSHIP FOUNDATION TRUST

Provides educational scholarships to students of Polish background who are legal residents of New York. Must be enrolled at the junior level or above in an accredited college or university in NY. Must be a U.S. citizen. Send SASE for more information.

Academic Fields/Career Goals: Arts; Filmmaking/Video; Humanities; Performing Arts.

Award: Scholarship for use in junior, senior, graduate, or postgraduate years; not renewable. *Number:* 1–3. *Amount:* $1000.

Polish Arts Club of Buffalo Scholarship Foundation (continued)

Eligibility Requirements: Applicant must be of Polish heritage and U.S. Colonial citizen; enrolled or expecting to enroll full- or part-time at a four-year institution or university and resident of New York. Available to U.S. citizens.

Application Requirements: Application, essay, interview, portfolio, resume, references, self-addressed stamped envelope. *Deadline:* May 15.

Contact: Anne Flansburg, Selection Chair
Polish Arts Club of Buffalo Scholarship Foundation
PO Box 1362
Williamsville, NY 14231-1362
Phone: 716-626-9083
E-mail: anneflanswz@aol.com

RHODE ISLAND FOUNDATION http://www.rifoundation.org

CONSTANT MEMORIAL SCHOLARSHIP FOR AQUIDNECK ISLAND RESIDENTS

Award to individuals who have been residents of Aquidneck Island for at least three years, are enrolled as a visual art or music major (sophomore, junior, or senior) in an accredited four-year post-secondary institution, and are able to demonstrate financial need.

Academic Fields/Career Goals: Arts; Music.

Award: Scholarship for use in sophomore, junior, or senior years; not renewable. *Number:* 1–2. *Amount:* $2000–$5000.

Eligibility Requirements: Applicant must be enrolled or expecting to enroll full-time at a four-year institution or university; resident of Rhode Island and must have an interest in art or music. Available to U.S. citizens.

Application Requirements: Application, essay, financial need analysis, references, transcript, samples of work done within the last 12 months. *Deadline:* June 9.

Contact: Libby Monahan, Funds Administrator
Rhode Island Foundation
One Union Station
Providence, RI 02903
Phone: 401-274-4564 Ext. 3117
Fax: 401-751-7983
E-mail: libbym@rifoundation.org

MJSA EDUCATION FOUNDATION JEWELRY SCHOLARSHIP

Scholarships ranging from $500 to $2000 are available for students enrolled in tool making, design, metals fabrication or other jewelry- related courses of study at colleges, universities or non-profit technical schools on the post-secondary level in the United States. Renewable up to four years if the student maintains good academic standing.

Academic Fields/Career Goals: Arts.

Award: Scholarship for use in freshman year; renewable. *Number:* varies. *Amount:* $500–$2000.

Eligibility Requirements: Applicant must be enrolled or expecting to enroll full-time at a two-year or four-year or technical institution or university and must have an interest in art. Available to U.S. citizens.

Application Requirements: Application, essay, financial need analysis, self-addressed stamped envelope, transcript. *Deadline:* May 14.

Contact: Libby Monahan, Funds Administrator
Rhode Island Foundation
One Union Station
Providence, RI 02903
Phone: 401-274-4564 Ext. 3117
Fax: 401-751-7983
E-mail: libbym@rifoundation.org

ROBERT H. MOLLOHAN FAMILY CHARITABLE FOUNDATION INC. http://www.mollohanfoundation.org

MARY OLIVE EDDY JONES ART SCHOLARSHIP

• *See page 98*

SERVICE EMPLOYEES INTERNATIONAL UNION (SEIU) http://www.seiu.org

SEIU MOE FONER SCHOLARSHIP PROGRAM FOR VISUAL AND PERFORMING ARTS

Scholarship for students pursuing a degree or training full time in the visual or performing arts. Scholarship funding must be applied to tuition at a two- or four-year college, university, or an accredited community college, technical or trade school in an arts-related field.

Academic Fields/Career Goals: Arts; Performing Arts.

Award: Scholarship for use in freshman, sophomore, junior, or senior years; not renewable. *Number:* 1. *Amount:* $5000.

Eligibility Requirements: Applicant must be enrolled or expecting to enroll full-time at a two-year or four-year or technical institution or university. Applicant or parent of applicant must be member of Service Employees International Union. Available to U.S. citizens.

Application Requirements: Application, essay, transcript, 6 copies of a single original creative work. *Deadline:* March 1.

Contact: c/o Scholarship Program Administrators, Inc.
Service Employees International Union (SEIU)
PO Box 23737
Nashville, TN 37202-3737
Phone: 615-320-3149
Fax: 615-320-3151
E-mail: info@spaprog.com

STRAIGHTFORWARD MEDIA http://www.straightforwardmedia.com

STRAIGHTFORWARD MEDIA ART SCHOOL SCHOLARSHIP

Award of $500 for students pursuing a degree in any art-related field. May be used for full- or part-time study. Scholarship is awarded four times per year. Deadlines: November 30, February 28, May 31, August 31.

Academic Fields/Career Goals: Arts.

Award: Scholarship for use in freshman, sophomore, junior, or senior years; not renewable. *Number:* 4. *Amount:* $500.

Eligibility Requirements: Applicant must be enrolled or expecting to enroll full- or part-time at a two-year or four-year institution or university. Available to U.S. and non-U.S. citizens.

Application Requirements: Online application. *Deadline:* varies.

Contact: Scholarship Committee
StraightForward Media
2040 West Main Street, Suite 104
Rapid City, SD 57701
Phone: 605-348-3042
Fax: 605-348-3043

TELETOON http://www.teletoon.com

TELETOON ANIMATION SCHOLARSHIP

Scholarship competition created by TELETOON to encourage creative, original, and imaginative animation by supporting Canadians studying in the animation field or intending to pursue studies in animation. One-time award. Must submit portfolio.

Academic Fields/Career Goals: Arts; Filmmaking/Video.

Award: Scholarship for use in freshman, sophomore, junior, senior, graduate, or postgraduate years; not renewable. *Number:* 9. *Amount:* $5000–$10,000.

Eligibility Requirements: Applicant must be enrolled or expecting to enroll full-time at a two-year or four-year or technical institution or university and resident of Alberta, British Columbia, Manitoba, New Brunswick, Newfoundland, North West Territories, Nova Scotia, Ontario, Prince Edward Island, Quebec, or Saskatchewan. Available to Canadian citizens.

Application Requirements: Application, autobiography, essay, portfolio, transcript, 5-minute film. *Deadline:* June 15.

Contact: Denise Vaughan, Senior Coordinator, Public Relations
Teletoon
BCE Place, 181 Bay Street
PO Box 787
Toronto, ON M5J 2T3
Canada
Phone: 416-956-2060
Fax: 416-956-2070
E-mail: denisev@teletoon.com

TEXAS ARTS AND CRAFTS EDUCATIONAL FOUNDATION http://www.tacef.org

EMERGING TEXAS ARTIST SCHOLARSHIP

Scholarships for art work offered to students attending colleges or universities in Texas either part-time or full-time. Scholarships are awarded as prizes in a juried art exhibit at the Texas State Arts and Crafts Fair. From 8 to 12 awards are granted annually.

Academic Fields/Career Goals: Arts.

Award: Scholarship for use in freshman, sophomore, junior, senior, graduate, or postgraduate years; not renewable. *Number:* 8–12. *Amount:* $500–$5000.

Eligibility Requirements: Applicant must be enrolled or expecting to enroll full- or part-time at a two-year or four-year or technical institution or university; studying in Texas and must have an interest in art. Available to U.S. citizens.

Application Requirements: Application, applicant must enter a contest, references, 4 color slides of work. *Deadline:* March 15.

Contact: Debbie Luce, Assistant Director
Texas Arts and Crafts Educational Foundation
4000 River Side Drive East
Kerrville, TX 78028
Phone: 830-896-5711
Fax: 830-896-5569
E-mail: info@tacef.org

UNICO NATIONAL INC. http://www.unico.org

THEODORE MAZZA SCHOLARSHIP

• *See page 93*

UNITARIAN UNIVERSALIST ASSOCIATION http://www.uua.org

MARION BARR STANFIELD ART SCHOLARSHIP

Scholarship for graduate or undergraduate Unitarian Universalist students preparing for a career in fine arts. Eligibility is limited to those in the study of painting, drawing, photography, and/or sculpture. Performing arts majors are not eligible.

Academic Fields/Career Goals: Arts; Photojournalism/Photography.

Award: Scholarship for use in freshman, sophomore, junior, or graduate years; not renewable. *Number:* varies. *Amount:* varies.

Eligibility Requirements: Applicant must be Unitarian Universalist and enrolled or expecting to enroll full-time at a four-year institution or university. Available to U.S. citizens.

Application Requirements: Application, essay, financial need analysis, portfolio, references, list of works, personal tax information. *Deadline:* varies.

Contact: Ms. Hillary Goodridge, Program Director
Unitarian Universalist Association
PO Box 301149
Boston, MA 02130
Phone: 617-971-9600
Fax: 617-971-0029
E-mail: uufp@aol.com

PAULY D'ORLANDO MEMORIAL ART SCHOLARSHIP

Scholarship for graduate or undergraduate students preparing for a career in fine arts. Student must be studying painting, drawing, photography, and/or sculpture. Performing arts majors are not eligible.

Academic Fields/Career Goals: Arts; Photojournalism/Photography.

Award: Scholarship for use in freshman, sophomore, junior, senior, or graduate years; not renewable. *Number:* varies. *Amount:* varies.

Eligibility Requirements: Applicant must be Unitarian Universalist and enrolled or expecting to enroll full-time at a four-year institution or university. Available to U.S. citizens.

Application Requirements: Application, essay, financial need analysis, references, list of works, personal tax information. *Deadline:* varies.

Contact: Ms. Hillary Goodridge, Program Director
Unitarian Universalist Association
PO Box 301149
Boston, MA 02130
Phone: 617-971-9600
Fax: 617-971-0029
E-mail: uufp@aol.com

STANFIELD AND D'ORLANDO ART SCHOLARSHIP

Scholarships for both master's and undergraduate Unitarian Universalist students studying the fields of art and law.

Academic Fields/Career Goals: Arts; Law/Legal Services.

Award: Scholarship for use in freshman, sophomore, junior, senior, or graduate years; not renewable. *Number:* varies. *Amount:* varies.

Eligibility Requirements: Applicant must be Unitarian Universalist and enrolled or expecting to enroll full- or part-time at a four-year institution or university. Available to U.S. citizens.

Application Requirements: Application. *Deadline:* February 15.

Contact: Ms. Hillary Goodridge, Program Director
Unitarian Universalist Association
PO Box 301149
Boston, MA 02130
Phone: 617-971-9600
Fax: 617-971-0029
E-mail: uufp@aol.com

UNITED NEGRO COLLEGE FUND http://www.uncf.org

HOUSTON SYMPHONY/TOP LADIES SCHOLARSHIP

Scholarship awarded to Iowa residents attending a UNCF member college or university and majoring in art. Minimum 2.5 GPA required. Prospective applicants should complete the Student Profile found at Web site: http://www.uncf.org.

Academic Fields/Career Goals: Arts.

Award: Scholarship for use in freshman, sophomore, junior, or senior years; not renewable. *Number:* 1. *Amount:* varies.

Eligibility Requirements: Applicant must be Black (non-Hispanic); enrolled or expecting to enroll full- or part-time at a four-year institution or university and resident of Iowa. Applicant must have 2.5 GPA or higher. Available to U.S. citizens.

Application Requirements: Application, financial need analysis. *Deadline:* continuous.

Contact: Director, Program Services
United Negro College Fund
8260 Willow Oaks Corporate Drive
PO Box 10444
Fairfax, VA 22031-8044
Phone: 800-331-2244
E-mail: rebecca.bennett@uncf.org

MAE MAXEY MEMORIAL SCHOLARSHIP

Award for students with an interest in poetry attending a UNCF member college or university. Minimum 2.5 GPA required. The scholarship value is ranges from $1000 to $5000.

Academic Fields/Career Goals: Arts; Literature/English/Writing.

Award: Scholarship for use in freshman, sophomore, junior, or senior years; not renewable. *Number:* varies. *Amount:* $1000–$5000.

Eligibility Requirements: Applicant must be Black (non-Hispanic) and enrolled or expecting to enroll full- or part-time at a four-year institution or university. Applicant must have 2.5 GPA or higher. Available to U.S. and non-U.S. citizens.

United Negro College Fund (continued)

Application Requirements: Application, financial need analysis. *Deadline:* continuous.

Contact: Director, Program Services
United Negro College Fund
8260 Willow Oaks Corporate Drive
PO Box 10444
Fairfax, VA 22031-8044
Phone: 800-331-2244
E-mail: rebecca.bennett@uncf.org

U.S. FISH AND WILDLIFE SERVICE http://www.fws.gov/duckstamps

FEDERAL JUNIOR DUCK STAMP CONSERVATION AND DESIGN COMPETITION

Any student in grades K-12, public, private, or home schooled, may enter this competition in all 50 states, the District of Columbia, and U.S. Territories. Teachers use the curriculum guide which is provided to teach conservation issues to students. Student then does an artistic rendering of one of the North American Migratory Waterfowl and enters it into their state's Junior Duck Stamp Contest. Each state picks one Best of Show to be sent to the National Office in Arlington, VA. Deadlines: South Carolina January 30, Florida February 21, all other states and territories March 15. Further information is available at http://duckstamps.fws.gov.

Academic Fields/Career Goals: Arts.

Award: Prize for use in freshman year; not renewable. *Number:* 3. *Amount:* $1000–$4000.

Eligibility Requirements: Applicant must be high school student; planning to enroll or expecting to enroll full- or part-time at a two-year or four-year institution and must have an interest in art. Available to U.S. citizens.

Application Requirements: Application, applicant must enter a contest. *Deadline:* varies.

Contact: Elizabeth Jackson, Program Coordinator
U.S. Fish and Wildlife Service
4401 North Fairfax Drive, Suite 4073
Arlington, VA 22203-1622
Phone: 703-358-2073
E-mail: elizabeth_jackson@fws.gov

VARIAZIONE MIXED MEDIA ARTISTS' COLLECTIVE http://www.zneart.com

LEARNING SCHOLARSHIP

Scholarship available to all high school seniors, undergraduate and graduate students, as well as artists who are not enrolled full-time, but enrolled in art classes in order to expand their skills.

Academic Fields/Career Goals: Arts.

Award: Scholarship for use in freshman, sophomore, junior, senior, or graduate years; not renewable. *Number:* varies. *Amount:* $100.

Eligibility Requirements: Applicant must be enrolled or expecting to enroll full- or part-time at a two-year or four-year or technical institution or university and must have an interest in art. Available to U.S. citizens.

Application Requirements: Application, applicant must enter a contest, autobiography, financial need analysis, collage work. *Deadline:* April 15.

Contact: Scholarship Coordinator
VariaZioNE Mixed Media Artists' Collective
1152 Crellin Road
Pleasanton, CA 94566

WATERBURY FOUNDATION http://www.conncf.org

LOIS MCMILLEN MEMORIAL SCHOLARSHIP FUND

One-time scholarship to a woman who is actively pursuing or who would like to pursue an artistic career. Must reside in Connecticut. Preference will be given to artists in the visual arts of painting and design.

Academic Fields/Career Goals: Arts.

Award: Scholarship for use in freshman, sophomore, junior, senior, or graduate years; not renewable. *Number:* 1. *Amount:* $500–$4000.

Eligibility Requirements: Applicant must be enrolled or expecting to enroll full- or part-time at a two-year or four-year institution or university; female and resident of Connecticut. Applicant or parent of applicant must have employment or volunteer experience in fine arts. Available to U.S. citizens.

Application Requirements: Application, essay, references. *Deadline:* March 1.

Contact: Josh Carey, Program Officer
Waterbury Foundation
43 Field Street
Waterbury, CT 06702-1216
Phone: 203-753-1315
Fax: 203-756-3054
E-mail: jcarey@conncf.org

WOMEN'S JEWELRY ASSOCIATION http://www.womensjewelry.org

WJA SCHOLARSHIP PROGRAM

Program is designed to encourage talented female students and help support their studies in the jewelry field. Applicants required to submit original drawings of their jewelry designs. Visit http://www.womensjewelry.org for current information.

Academic Fields/Career Goals: Arts; Trade/Technical Specialties.

Award: Scholarship for use in freshman, sophomore, junior, senior, graduate, or postgraduate years; not renewable. *Number:* 1. *Amount:* $500–$5000.

Eligibility Requirements: Applicant must be enrolled or expecting to enroll full- or part-time at a two-year or four-year or technical institution or university; female and must have an interest in art. Available to U.S. and non-U.S. citizens.

Application Requirements: Application, essay, portfolio. *Deadline:* May 1.

Contact: Scholarship Committee
Women's Jewelry Association
7000 West Southwest Highway, Suite 202
Chicago Ridge, IL 60415
Phone: 708-361-6266
Fax: 708-361-6166
E-mail: info@womensjewelry.org

WORLDSTUDIO FOUNDATION http://www.aiga.org/

SPECIAL ANIMATION AND ILLUSTRATION SCHOLARSHIP

Scholarships are for minority and economically disadvantaged students who are studying illustration, cartooning, and animation in American colleges and universities. Scholarship recipients are selected not only for their ability and their need, but also for their demonstrated commitment to giving back to the larger community through their work.

Academic Fields/Career Goals: Arts.

Award: Scholarship for use in freshman, sophomore, junior, senior, or graduate years; not renewable. *Number:* 25. *Amount:* $1500.

Eligibility Requirements: Applicant must be American Indian/Alaska Native, Asian/Pacific Islander, Black (non-Hispanic), or Hispanic and enrolled or expecting to enroll full-time at a two-year or four-year or technical institution or university. Applicant or parent of applicant must have employment or volunteer experience in community service. Applicant must have 2.5 GPA or higher. Available to U.S. citizens.

Application Requirements: Application, essay, financial need analysis, photo, portfolio, references, self-addressed stamped envelope, transcript. *Deadline:* April 13.

Contact: Maria Emmighausen, Scholarship Coordinator
Worldstudio Foundation
200 Varick Street, Suite 507
New York, NY 10014
Phone: 212-807-1990
Fax: 212-807-1799
E-mail: scholarship@aiga.org

WORLDSTUDIO AIGA SCHOLARSHIPS

Scholarships available for minority and economically disadvantaged students who are pursuing degrees in the design/arts disciplines in colleges and universities in the United States.

Academic Fields/Career Goals: Arts.

Award: Scholarship for use in freshman, sophomore, junior, senior, or graduate years; not renewable. *Number:* 20–25. *Amount:* $1000–$5000.

Eligibility Requirements: Applicant must be American Indian/Alaska Native, Asian/Pacific Islander, Black (non-Hispanic), or Hispanic and enrolled or expecting to enroll full-time at a two-year or four-year or technical institution or university. Available to U.S. citizens.

Application Requirements: Application, references, test scores, transcript. *Deadline:* April 11.

Contact: Leah Rico, Project Manager
Worldstudio Foundation
164 Fifth Avenue
New York, NY 10010
Phone: 212-807-1990
Fax: 212-807-1799
E-mail: scholarship@aiga.org

WORLDSTUDIO FOUNDATION SCHOLARSHIP PROGRAM

• *See page 94*

ASIAN STUDIES

ASSOCIATION OF TEACHERS OF JAPANESE BRIDGING CLEARINGHOUSE FOR STUDY ABROAD IN JAPAN

BRIDGING SCHOLARSHIP FOR STUDY ABROAD IN JAPAN

• *See page 94*

JAPANESE GOVERNMENT/THE MONBUSHO SCHOLARSHIP PROGRAM http://www.la.us.emb-japan.go.jp

JAPANESE STUDIES SCHOLARSHIP

• *See page 96*

JAPAN STUDIES SCHOLARSHIP FOUNDATION COMMITTEE

JAPAN STUDIES SCHOLARSHIP

• *See page 96*

AUDIOLOGY

AUDIOLOGY FOUNDATION OF AMERICA http://www.audfound.org

AUDIOLOGY FOUNDATION OF AMERICA'S OUTSTANDING AUD STUDENT SCHOLARSHIP

This award provides funds for students pursuing the Doctor of Audiology (AuD) degree and who are entering the second year of an AuD program. Students are recognized for their academic achievement and professional potential.

Academic Fields/Career Goals: Audiology.

Award: Scholarship for use in sophomore year; not renewable. *Number:* 2. *Amount:* $4500.

Eligibility Requirements: Applicant must be enrolled or expecting to enroll full-time at a four-year institution or university. Applicant must have 3.5 GPA or higher. Available to U.S. and Canadian citizens.

Application Requirements: Application, essay, photo, references, self-addressed stamped envelope, test scores, transcript, nomination by AuD program director, clinical evaluation forms. *Deadline:* July 15.

Contact: Becky White, Executive Assistant
Audiology Foundation of America
8 North Third Street, Suite 406
Lafayette, IN 47901-1247
Phone: 765-743-6283
Fax: 765-743-9283
E-mail: info-afa@audfound.com

NATIONAL AMBUCS INC. http://www.ambucs.org

AMBUCS SCHOLARS-SCHOLARSHIPS FOR THERAPISTS

Scholarships are open to students who are U.S. citizens at a junior level or above in college. Must be enrolled in an accredited program by the appropriate health therapy profession authority in physical therapy, occupational therapy, speech-language pathology, or audiology and must demonstrate a financial need. Application available on Web site at http://www.ambucs.com. Paper applications are not accepted.

Academic Fields/Career Goals: Audiology; Therapy/Rehabilitation.

Award: Scholarship for use in junior, senior, graduate, or postgraduate years; not renewable. *Number:* 275. *Amount:* $500–$3000.

Eligibility Requirements: Applicant must be enrolled or expecting to enroll full-time at a four-year institution or university. Available to U.S. citizens.

Application Requirements: Application, essay, financial need analysis, enrollment certification form. *Deadline:* April 15.

Contact: Janice Blankenship, Scholarship Coordinator
National AMBUCS Inc.
PO Box 5127
High Point, NC 27262
Phone: 336-852-0052
Fax: 336-887-8451
E-mail: janiceb@ambucs.org

AVIATION/AEROSPACE

AACE INTERNATIONAL http://www.aacei.org

AACE INTERNATIONAL COMPETITIVE SCHOLARSHIP

• *See page 89*

AIRCRAFT ELECTRONICS ASSOCIATION EDUCATIONAL FOUNDATION http://www.aea.net

BENDIX/KING AVIONICS SCHOLARSHIP

Scholarship of $1000 available to high school, college, vocational, or technical school students who plan to or are attending an avionics or aircraft repair program in an accredited school.

Academic Fields/Career Goals: Aviation/Aerospace.

Award: Scholarship for use in freshman, sophomore, junior, or senior years; not renewable. *Number:* 1. *Amount:* $1000.

Eligibility Requirements: Applicant must be enrolled or expecting to enroll full- or part-time at a two-year or four-year or technical institution or university. Applicant must have 2.5 GPA or higher. Available to U.S. citizens.

Application Requirements: Application, essay, transcript. *Deadline:* February 15.

Contact: Mike Adamson, Executive Director
Aircraft Electronics Association Educational Foundation
4217 South Hocker Drive
Independence, MO 64055-0963
Phone: 816-373-6565
Fax: 816-478-3100
E-mail: info@aea.net

BUD GLOVER MEMORIAL SCHOLARSHIP

Scholarship available to high school seniors and college students who plan to attend or are attending an avionics or aircraft repair program in an accredited school.

Academic Fields/Career Goals: Aviation/Aerospace; Trade/Technical Specialties.

Award: Scholarship for use in freshman, sophomore, junior, or senior years; not renewable. *Number:* 1. *Amount:* $1000.

Eligibility Requirements: Applicant must be enrolled or expecting to enroll full- or part-time at a two-year or four-year or technical institution or university. Applicant must have 2.5 GPA or higher. Available to U.S. citizens.

Aircraft Electronics Association Educational Foundation (continued)

Application Requirements: Application, essay, references, test scores, transcript. *Deadline:* February 15.

Contact: Mike Adamson, Executive Director
Aircraft Electronics Association Educational Foundation
4217 South Hocker Drive
Independence, MO 64055-0963
Phone: 816-373-6565
Fax: 816-478-3100
E-mail: info@aea.net

CHUCK PEACOCK MEMORIAL SCHOLARSHIP

Scholarship of $1000 for high school seniors or college students who plan to attend or are attending an aviation management program in an accredited school.

Academic Fields/Career Goals: Aviation/Aerospace.

Award: Scholarship for use in freshman, sophomore, junior, or senior years; not renewable. *Number:* 1. *Amount:* $1000.

Eligibility Requirements: Applicant must be enrolled or expecting to enroll full- or part-time at a two-year or four-year or technical institution or university. Applicant must have 2.5 GPA or higher. Available to U.S. citizens.

Application Requirements: Application, essay, transcript. *Deadline:* February 15.

Contact: Mike Adamson, Executive Director
Aircraft Electronics Association Educational Foundation
4217 South Hocker Drive
Independence, MO 64055-0963
Phone: 816-373-6565
Fax: 816-478-3100
E-mail: info@aea.net

DAVID ARVER MEMORIAL SCHOLARSHIP

Scholarship of $1000 available to high school seniors and college students who plan to or are attending an avionics or aircraft repair program in an accredited school. Restricted to use for study in the following states: Iowa, Illinois, Indiana, Kansas, Michigan, Minnesota, Mississippi, North Dakota, Nebraska, South Dakota, and Wisconsin. See Web site for details: www.aea.net/scholarship.

Academic Fields/Career Goals: Aviation/Aerospace.

Award: Scholarship for use in freshman, sophomore, junior, or senior years; not renewable. *Number:* 1. *Amount:* $1000.

Eligibility Requirements: Applicant must be enrolled or expecting to enroll full- or part-time at a two-year or four-year or technical institution or university. Applicant must have 2.5 GPA or higher. Available to U.S. citizens.

Application Requirements: Application, essay, references, test scores, transcript. *Deadline:* February 15.

Contact: Mike Adamson, Executive Director
Aircraft Electronics Association Educational Foundation
4217 South Hocker Drive
Independence, MO 64055-0963
Phone: 816-373-6565
Fax: 816-478-3100
E-mail: info@aea.net

DUTCH AND GINGER ARVER SCHOLARSHIP

Scholarship available to high school seniors or college students who plan to attend or are attending an avionics or aircraft repair program in an accredited school.

Academic Fields/Career Goals: Aviation/Aerospace; Trade/Technical Specialties.

Award: Scholarship for use in freshman, sophomore, junior, or senior years; not renewable. *Number:* 1. *Amount:* $1000.

Eligibility Requirements: Applicant must be enrolled or expecting to enroll full- or part-time at a two-year or four-year or technical institution or university. Applicant must have 2.5 GPA or higher. Available to U.S. citizens.

Application Requirements: Application, essay, references, test scores, transcript. *Deadline:* February 15.

Contact: Mike Adamson, Executive Director
Aircraft Electronics Association Educational Foundation
4217 South Hocker Drive
Independence, MO 64055-0963
Phone: 816-373-6565
Fax: 816-478-3100
E-mail: info@aea.net

FIELD AVIATION COMPANY INC. SCHOLARSHIP

Scholarship for high school seniors and college students who plan to or are attending an avionics or aircraft repair program in an accredited college/university. The educational institution must be located in Canada.

Academic Fields/Career Goals: Aviation/Aerospace.

Award: Scholarship for use in freshman, sophomore, junior, or senior years; not renewable. *Number:* 1. *Amount:* $1000.

Eligibility Requirements: Applicant must be enrolled or expecting to enroll full-time at a two-year or four-year or technical institution or university. Applicant must have 2.5 GPA or higher. Available to Canadian citizens.

Application Requirements: Application, essay, references, test scores, transcript. *Deadline:* February 15.

Contact: Mike Adamson, Executive Director
Aircraft Electronics Association Educational Foundation
4217 South Hocker Drive
Independence, MO 64055-0963
Phone: 816-373-6565
Fax: 816-478-3100
E-mail: info@aea.net

GARMIN SCHOLARSHIP

Scholarship available to high school seniors and college students who plan to attend or are attending an avionics or aircraft repair program in an accredited school.

Academic Fields/Career Goals: Aviation/Aerospace; Trade/Technical Specialties.

Award: Scholarship for use in freshman, sophomore, junior, or senior years; not renewable. *Number:* 1. *Amount:* $2000.

Eligibility Requirements: Applicant must be enrolled or expecting to enroll full- or part-time at a two-year or four-year or technical institution or university. Applicant must have 2.5 GPA or higher. Available to U.S. citizens.

Application Requirements: Application, essay, references, test scores, transcript. *Deadline:* February 15.

Contact: Mike Adamson, Executive Director
Aircraft Electronics Association Educational Foundation
4217 South Hocker Drive
Independence, MO 64055-0963
Phone: 816-373-6565
Fax: 816-478-3100
E-mail: info@aea.net

JOHNNY DAVIS MEMORIAL SCHOLARSHIP

Scholarship of $1000 available to high school seniors and college students who plan to or are attending an avionics or aircraft repair program in an accredited school.

Academic Fields/Career Goals: Aviation/Aerospace.

Award: Scholarship for use in freshman, sophomore, junior, or senior years; not renewable. *Number:* 1. *Amount:* $1000.

Eligibility Requirements: Applicant must be enrolled or expecting to enroll full- or part-time at a two-year or four-year or technical institution or university. Applicant must have 2.5 GPA or higher. Available to U.S. citizens.

Application Requirements: Application, essay, transcript. *Deadline:* February 15.

Contact: Mike Adamson, Executive Director
Aircraft Electronics Association Educational Foundation
4217 South Hocker Drive
Independence, MO 64055-0963
Phone: 816-373-6565
Fax: 816-478-3100
E-mail: info@aea.net

LEE TARBOX MEMORIAL SCHOLARSHIP

Scholarship available to high school seniors or college students who plan to attend or are attending an avionics or aircraft repair program in an accredited school.

Academic Fields/Career Goals: Aviation/Aerospace; Trade/Technical Specialties.

Award: Scholarship for use in freshman, sophomore, junior, or senior years; not renewable. *Number:* 1. *Amount:* $2500.

Eligibility Requirements: Applicant must be enrolled or expecting to enroll full- or part-time at a two-year or four-year or technical institution or university. Applicant must have 2.5 GPA or higher. Available to U.S. citizens.

Application Requirements: Application, essay, references, test scores, transcript. *Deadline:* February 15.

Contact: Mike Adamson, Executive Director
Aircraft Electronics Association Educational Foundation
4217 South Hocker Drive
Independence, MO 64055-0963
Phone: 816-373-6565
Fax: 816-478-3100
E-mail: info@aea.net

LOWELL GAYLOR MEMORIAL SCHOLARSHIP

Scholarship for high school seniors and college students who plan to attend or are attending an avionics or aircraft repair program in an accredited school. Minimum 2.5 GPA required.

Academic Fields/Career Goals: Aviation/Aerospace; Trade/Technical Specialties.

Award: Scholarship for use in freshman, sophomore, junior, or senior years; not renewable. *Number:* 1. *Amount:* $1000.

Eligibility Requirements: Applicant must be enrolled or expecting to enroll full- or part-time at a two-year or four-year or technical institution or university. Applicant must have 2.5 GPA or higher. Available to U.S. citizens.

Application Requirements: Application, essay, references, test scores, transcript. *Deadline:* February 15.

Contact: Mike Adamson, Executive Director
Aircraft Electronics Association Educational Foundation
4217 South Hocker Drive
Independence, MO 64055-0963
Phone: 816-373-6565
Fax: 816-478-3100
E-mail: info@aea.net

L-3 AVIONICS SYSTEMS SCHOLARSHIP

Scholarship of $2500 available to high school seniors and college students who plan to attend or are attending an avionics or aircraft repair program in an accredited school.

Academic Fields/Career Goals: Aviation/Aerospace.

Award: Scholarship for use in freshman, sophomore, junior, or senior years; not renewable. *Number:* 1. *Amount:* $2500.

Eligibility Requirements: Applicant must be enrolled or expecting to enroll full- or part-time at a two-year or four-year or technical institution or university. Applicant must have 2.5 GPA or higher. Available to U.S. citizens.

Application Requirements: Application, essay, transcript. *Deadline:* February 15.

Contact: Mike Adamson, Executive Director
Aircraft Electronics Association Educational Foundation
4217 South Hocker Drive
Independence, MO 64055-0963
Phone: 816-373-6565
Fax: 816-478-3100
E-mail: info@aea.net

MID-CONTINENT INSTRUMENT SCHOLARSHIP

Scholarship available to high school seniors or college students who plan to attend or are attending an avionics or aircraft repair program in an accredited school.

Academic Fields/Career Goals: Aviation/Aerospace; Trade/Technical Specialties.

Award: Scholarship for use in freshman, sophomore, junior, or senior years; not renewable. *Number:* 1. *Amount:* $1000.

Eligibility Requirements: Applicant must be enrolled or expecting to enroll full- or part-time at a two-year or four-year or technical institution or university. Applicant must have 2.5 GPA or higher. Available to U.S. citizens.

Application Requirements: Application, essay, references, test scores, transcript. *Deadline:* February 15.

Contact: Mike Adamson, Executive Director
Aircraft Electronics Association Educational Foundation
4217 South Hocker Drive
Independence, MO 64055-0963
Phone: 816-373-6565
Fax: 816-478-3100
E-mail: info@aea.net

MONTE R. MITCHELL GLOBAL SCHOLARSHIP

Scholarship of $1000 available to European students pursuing a degree in aviation maintenance technology, avionics, or aircraft repair at an accredited school located in Europe or the United States.

Academic Fields/Career Goals: Aviation/Aerospace.

Award: Scholarship for use in freshman, sophomore, junior, or senior years; not renewable. *Number:* 1. *Amount:* $1000.

Eligibility Requirements: Applicant must be enrolled or expecting to enroll full- or part-time at a two-year or four-year or technical institution or university. Applicant must have 2.5 GPA or higher. Available to citizens of countries other than the U.S. or Canada.

Application Requirements: Application, essay, references, transcript. *Deadline:* February 15.

Contact: Mike Adamson, Executive Director
Aircraft Electronics Association Educational Foundation
4217 South Hocker Drive
Independence, MO 64055-0963
Phone: 816-373-6565
Fax: 816-478-3100
E-mail: info@aea.net

PLANE AND PILOT MAGAZINE/GARMIN SCHOLARSHIP

Scholarship available for high school, college, or vocational or technical school students who plan to attend or are attending an avionics or aircraft repair program in an accredited vocational or technical school.

Academic Fields/Career Goals: Aviation/Aerospace; Trade/Technical Specialties.

Award: Scholarship for use in freshman, sophomore, junior, or senior years; not renewable. *Number:* 1. *Amount:* $2000.

Eligibility Requirements: Applicant must be enrolled or expecting to enroll full-time at a two-year or four-year or technical institution or university. Applicant must have 2.5 GPA or higher. Available to U.S. citizens.

Aircraft Electronics Association Educational Foundation (continued)

Application Requirements: Application, essay, references, test scores, transcript. *Deadline:* February 15.

Contact: Mike Adamson, Executive Director
Aircraft Electronics Association Educational Foundation
4217 South Hocker Drive
Independence, MO 64055-0963
Phone: 816-373-6565
Fax: 816-478-3100
E-mail: info@aea.net

SPORTY'S PILOT SHOP/CINCINNATI AVIONICS

Scholarship of $2000 available to high school seniors and college students who plan to attend or are attending an avionics or aircraft repair program in an accredited school.

Academic Fields/Career Goals: Aviation/Aerospace.

Award: Scholarship for use in freshman, sophomore, junior, or senior years; not renewable. *Number:* 1. *Amount:* $2000.

Eligibility Requirements: Applicant must be enrolled or expecting to enroll full- or part-time at a two-year or four-year or technical institution or university. Applicant must have 2.5 GPA or higher. Available to U.S. citizens.

Application Requirements: Application, essay, references, test scores, transcript. *Deadline:* February 15.

Contact: Mike Adamson, Executive Director
Aircraft Electronics Association Educational Foundation
4217 South Hocker Drive
Independence, MO 64055-0963
Phone: 816-373-6565
Fax: 816-478-3100
E-mail: info@aea.net

AIRPORTS COUNCIL INTERNATIONAL-NORTH AMERICA http://www.aci-na.org

ACI-NA AIRPORT COMMISSIONER'S SCHOLARSHIP

Up to 3 scholarships per fall and spring semesters may be awarded in amounts up to $2500 per recipient to an undergraduate or graduate student. Applicant must be majoring in airport management or airport administration. Deadlines: December 15 and April 15.

Academic Fields/Career Goals: Aviation/Aerospace.

Award: Scholarship for use in freshman, sophomore, junior, senior, or graduate years; not renewable. *Number:* up to 3. *Amount:* up to $2500.

Eligibility Requirements: Applicant must be enrolled or expecting to enroll full-time at a four-year institution or university. Applicant must have 3.0 GPA or higher. Available to U.S. and Canadian citizens.

Application Requirements: Application, essay, resume, references, transcript. *Deadline:* varies.

Contact: Scholarship Committee
Airports Council International-North America
1775 K Street NW, Suite 500
Washington, DC 20006
Phone: 202-293-8500
Fax: 202-331-1362

AIR TRAFFIC CONTROL ASSOCIATION INC. http://www.atca.org

AIR TRAFFIC CONTROL ASSOCIATION SCHOLARSHIP

Scholarships for students in programs leading to a bachelor's degree or higher in aviation-related courses of study, and for full-time employees engaged in advanced study to improve their skills in air traffic control or aviation. Visit Web site for additional information: http://www.atca.org.

Academic Fields/Career Goals: Aviation/Aerospace; Engineering/Technology.

Award: Scholarship for use in freshman, sophomore, junior, senior, or graduate years; not renewable. *Number:* 7–12. *Amount:* $600–$2500.

Eligibility Requirements: Applicant must be enrolled or expecting to enroll full- or part-time at a four-year institution or university and must have an interest in aviation. Applicant or parent of applicant must have employment or volunteer experience in air traffic controller field. Available to U.S. citizens.

Application Requirements: Application, autobiography, essay, financial need analysis, resume, references, transcript. *Deadline:* May 1.

Contact: Miguel Vazquez, Director
Air Traffic Control Association Inc.
1101 King Street, Suite 300
Alexandria, VA 22201-2302
Phone: 703-522-5717
Fax: 703-527-7251
E-mail: info@atca.org

ALASKAN AVIATION SAFETY FOUNDATION http://www.aasfonline.com

ALASKAN AVIATION SAFETY FOUNDATION MEMORIAL SCHOLARSHIP FUND

Scholarships for undergraduate or graduate study in aviation. Must be a resident of Alaska and a U.S. citizen. Write for deadlines and details.

Academic Fields/Career Goals: Aviation/Aerospace.

Award: Scholarship for use in freshman, sophomore, junior, senior, or graduate years; not renewable. *Number:* 1–3. *Amount:* $500–$750.

Eligibility Requirements: Applicant must be enrolled or expecting to enroll full- or part-time at a two-year or four-year or technical institution or university; resident of Alaska and must have an interest in aviation. Available to U.S. citizens.

Application Requirements: Application, autobiography, driver's license, financial need analysis, references, test scores, transcript. *Deadline:* May 30.

Contact: Scholarship Committee
Alaskan Aviation Safety Foundation
c/o Aviation Technology Division UAA, 2811 Merril Field Drive
Anchorage, AK 99501
Phone: 907-243-7237

AMERICAN ASSOCIATION OF AIRPORT EXECUTIVES http://www.aaae.org

AMERICAN ASSOCIATION OF AIRPORT EXECUTIVES FOUNDATION SCHOLARSHIP

Scholarships awarded each year to juniors or higher who are enrolled in aviation program and have a minimum 3.0 GPA. Awards based on academic records, financial need, school participation, community activities, work experience, and personal statement. Only one student from each school is eligible to participate. Multiple recommendations from the same institution will be returned.

Academic Fields/Career Goals: Aviation/Aerospace.

Award: Scholarship for use in junior or senior years; not renewable. *Number:* 1–10. *Amount:* $1000.

Eligibility Requirements: Applicant must be enrolled or expecting to enroll full-time at a four-year institution or university and must have an interest in aviation. Applicant must have 3.0 GPA or higher. Available to U.S. citizens.

Application Requirements: Application, financial need analysis, references, self-addressed stamped envelope, transcript. *Deadline:* May 31.

Contact: Scholarship Coordinator
American Association of Airport Executives
601 Madison Street, Suite 400
Alexandria, VA 22314
Phone: 703-824-0504
Fax: 703-820-1395
E-mail: member.services@airportnet.org

AMERICAN ASSOCIATION OF AIRPORT EXECUTIVES FOUNDATION SCHOLARSHIP-NATIVE AMERICAN

Scholarship of $1000 to a number of Native-American students who are juniors or higher and who are enrolled in an aviation program. Must have a minimum 3.0 GPA. Award based on academic records, financial need, school participation, community activities, work experience, race, and a personal statement. A recommendation from the school is also required.

Academic Fields/Career Goals: Aviation/Aerospace.

Award: Scholarship for use in junior or senior years; not renewable. *Number:* varies. *Amount:* $1000.

Eligibility Requirements: Applicant must be American Indian/Alaska Native and enrolled or expecting to enroll full-time at a four-year institution or university. Applicant must have 3.0 GPA or higher. Available to U.S. citizens.

Application Requirements: Application, financial need analysis, references, self-addressed stamped envelope, transcript. *Deadline:* March 31.

Contact: Cindy DeWitt, Membership Manager
American Association of Airport Executives
601 Madison Street, Suite 400
Alexandria, VA 22314
E-mail: cindy.dewitt@aaae.org

AMERICAN ASSOCIATION OF AIRPORT EXECUTIVES-SOUTHWEST CHAPTER http://www.swaaae.org

SWAAAE ACADEMIC SCHOLARSHIPS

A scholarship of $1500 for students pursuing an undergraduate or graduate degree in airport management may apply annually for an academic scholarship. Applicant must attend a college in Arizona, California, Nevada, Utah, or Hawaii.

Academic Fields/Career Goals: Aviation/Aerospace.

Award: Scholarship for use in sophomore, junior, senior, or graduate years; not renewable. *Number:* 5. *Amount:* $500–$1500.

Eligibility Requirements: Applicant must be enrolled or expecting to enroll full- or part-time at a four-year institution or university and studying in Arizona, California, Hawaii, Nevada, or Utah. Available to U.S. and non-U.S. citizens.

Application Requirements: Application. *Deadline:* September 29.

Contact: Charles Mangum, Scholarship Committee
American Association of Airport Executives-Southwest Chapter
8565 North Sand Dune Place
Tucson, AZ 85743
Phone: 520-682-9565
E-mail: cman2122@comcast.net

AMERICAN INSTITUTE OF AERONAUTICS AND ASTRONAUTICS http://www.aiaa.org

AIAA UNDERGRADUATE SCHOLARSHIP

• *See page 84*

AMERICAN SOCIETY OF NAVAL ENGINEERS http://www.navalengineers.org

AMERICAN SOCIETY OF NAVAL ENGINEERS SCHOLARSHIP

• *See page 85*

AOPA AIR SAFETY FOUNDATION http://www.asf.org

AOPA AIR SAFETY FOUNDATION/DONALD BURNSIDE MEMORIAL SCHOLARSHIP

Scholarship of $1000 given to a U.S. citizen who, without assistance, would find it difficult to obtain a college education. The recipient must be enrolled in and plan to continue a college curriculum leading to a degree in the field of aviation. Must maintain a 3.25 GPA.

Academic Fields/Career Goals: Aviation/Aerospace.

Award: Scholarship for use in junior or senior years; not renewable. *Number:* 1. *Amount:* $1000.

Eligibility Requirements: Applicant must be enrolled or expecting to enroll full- or part-time at a four-year institution or university. Available to U.S. citizens.

Application Requirements: Essay, transcript, original and 7 copies of entire application package. *Deadline:* March 31.

Contact: Dr. Mark Sherman, Scholarship Committee
AOPA Air Safety Foundation
Department of Aviation, 2000 University Avenue
Dubuque, IA 52001
Phone: 563-589-3823

AOPA AIR SAFETY FOUNDATION/MCALLISTER MEMORIAL SCHOLARSHIP

One-time scholarship of $1000 to U.S. citizens who would find it difficult to obtain a college education without assistance. The recipient must be enrolled in and plan to continue a college curriculum leading to a degree in the field of aviation. Must maintain a 3.25 GPA.

Academic Fields/Career Goals: Aviation/Aerospace.

Award: Scholarship for use in junior or senior years; not renewable. *Number:* 1. *Amount:* $1000.

Eligibility Requirements: Applicant must be enrolled or expecting to enroll full- or part-time at a four-year institution or university and must have an interest in aviation. Available to U.S. citizens.

Application Requirements: Essay, self-addressed stamped envelope, transcript, original and 7 copies of entire application packet. *Deadline:* March 31.

Contact: Dr. Mark Sherman, Scholarship Committee
AOPA Air Safety Foundation
Department of Aviation, 2000 University Avenue
Dubuque, IA 52001
Phone: 563-589-3823

ARMED FORCES COMMUNICATIONS AND ELECTRONICS ASSOCIATION, EDUCATIONAL FOUNDATION http://www.afcea.org

AFCEA/LOCKHEED MARTIN ORINCON IT SCHOLARSHIP

Scholarships of $3000 for U.S. citizens enrolled full-time in four-year, accredited colleges or universities in California majoring in electrical, computer, chemical, systems or aerospace engineering, computer science, physics or mathematics. Applicant must be a sophomore or junior with minimum GPA of 3.5.

Academic Fields/Career Goals: Aviation/Aerospace; Chemical Engineering; Computer Science/Data Processing; Electrical Engineering/Electronics; Engineering/Technology; Physical Sciences and Math.

Award: Scholarship for use in sophomore or junior years; not renewable. *Number:* 1. *Amount:* $3000.

Eligibility Requirements: Applicant must be enrolled or expecting to enroll full-time at a four-year institution or university and studying in California. Applicant must have 3.5 GPA or higher. Available to U.S. citizens.

Application Requirements: Application, references, transcript. *Deadline:* May 1.

Contact: Fred H. Rainbow, Vice President and Executive Director
Armed Forces Communications and Electronics Association, Educational Foundation
4400 Fair Lakes Court
Fairfax, VA 22033
Phone: 703-631-6149

AFCEA SCHOLARSHIP FOR WORKING PROFESSIONALS

Scholarship of $1500 to those part-time students pursuing an undergraduate or graduate degree while employed in the science or technology disciplines directly related to the mission of AFCEA. Undergraduate candidates must be at least second-year students attending a U.S. college or university. Graduate students must have completed at least two post graduate-level classes prior to the deadline date. Candidate must be a U.S. citizen. Minimum GPA of 3.4 is required.

Academic Fields/Career Goals: Aviation/Aerospace; Computer Science/Data Processing; Electrical Engineering/Electronics; Engineering/Technology; Physical Sciences and Math.

Award: Scholarship for use in sophomore, junior, senior, or graduate years; not renewable. *Number:* 1. *Amount:* $1500.

Eligibility Requirements: Applicant must be enrolled or expecting to enroll part-time at a two-year or four-year institution or university. Available to U.S. citizens.

Armed Forces Communications and Electronics Association, Educational Foundation (continued)

Application Requirements: Application, references, transcript. *Deadline:* September 1.

Contact: Norma Corrales, Scholarship Coordinator
Armed Forces Communications and Electronics Association, Educational Foundation
4400 Fair Lakes Court
Fairfax, VA 22033-3899
Phone: 703-631-6149
E-mail: scholarship@afcea.org

ARMED FORCES COMMUNICATIONS AND ELECTRONICS ASSOCIATION ROTC SCHOLARSHIP PROGRAM

Award for ROTC students in their sophomore or junior years enrolled in four-year accredited colleges or universities in the United States. Eligible fields of study are electronics or electrical, communications, or aerospace engineering; physics; mathematics; and computer science. Must exhibit academic excellence and potential to serve as an officer in the armed forces of the United States. Nominations are submitted by professors of military science, naval science, or aerospace studies.

Academic Fields/Career Goals: Aviation/Aerospace; Communications; Computer Science/Data Processing; Electrical Engineering/Electronics; Engineering/Technology; Mathematics; Physical Sciences and Math.

Award: Scholarship for use in sophomore or junior years; not renewable. *Number:* varies. *Amount:* $2000.

Eligibility Requirements: Applicant must be enrolled or expecting to enroll full-time at a four-year institution or university. Available to U.S. citizens. Applicant must have general military experience.

Application Requirements: Application, references, transcript. *Deadline:* April 1.

Contact: Norma Corrales, Director, Scholarships and Award Programs
Armed Forces Communications and Electronics Association, Educational Foundation
4400 Fair Lakes Court
Fairfax, VA 22033-3899
Phone: 703-631-6149
Fax: 703-631-4693
E-mail: scholarship@afcea.org

ASSOCIATION FOR FACILITIES ENGINEERING (AFE)

ASSOCIATION FOR FACILITIES ENGINEERING CEDAR VALLEY CHAPTER #132 SCHOLARSHIP

Awards a high school graduate who is a resident of Iowa, with 2.5 or higher GPA, enrolled in any engineering program leading to an AA, BA, or BS degree in an Iowa college or university. Awards are paid directly to the institution in the student's name.

Academic Fields/Career Goals: Aviation/Aerospace; Chemical Engineering; Civil Engineering; Electrical Engineering/Electronics; Engineering/Technology; Engineering-Related Technologies; Materials Science, Engineering, and Metallurgy; Mechanical Engineering; Trade/Technical Specialties.

Award: Scholarship for use in freshman year; renewable. *Number:* 1. *Amount:* $500.

Eligibility Requirements: Applicant must be high school student; planning to enroll or expecting to enroll full-time at a two-year or four-year or technical institution or university; resident of Iowa and studying in Iowa. Applicant must have 2.5 GPA or higher. Available to U.S. citizens.

Application Requirements: Application, autobiography, transcript, copy of birth certificate, high school diploma. *Deadline:* May 1.

Contact: Joe Zachar, Special Events Chair
Association for Facilities Engineering (AFE)
1203 Forest Glen Court, SE
Cedar Rapids, IA 52403
Phone: 319-364-4740
E-mail: zachar2@aol.com

ASTRONAUT SCHOLARSHIP FOUNDATION http://www.astronautscholarship.org

ASTRONAUT SCHOLARSHIP FOUNDATION

• *See page 86*

AVIATION COUNCIL OF PENNSYLVANIA http://www.acpfly.com

AVIATION COUNCIL OF PENNSYLVANIA SCHOLARSHIP PROGRAM

Awards for Pennsylvania residents to pursue studies at Pennsylvania institutions leading to career as professional pilot or in the fields of aviation technology or aviation management. Awards at discretion of Aviation Council of Pennsylvania. Three to four scholarships ranging from $500 to $1000. Applicants for the aviation management scholarship may attend institutions outside of Pennsylvania.

Academic Fields/Career Goals: Aviation/Aerospace.

Award: Scholarship for use in freshman, sophomore, junior, or senior years; not renewable. *Number:* 3–4. *Amount:* $500–$1000.

Eligibility Requirements: Applicant must be enrolled or expecting to enroll full- or part-time at a two-year or four-year or technical institution or university; resident of Pennsylvania; studying in Pennsylvania and must have an interest in aviation. Available to U.S. citizens.

Application Requirements: Application, financial need analysis, references, transcript. *Deadline:* varies.

Contact: Robert Rockmaker, Coordinator
Aviation Council of Pennsylvania
3111 Arcadia Avenue
Allentown, PA 18103-6903
Phone: 610-797-6911
Fax: 610-797-8238
E-mail: info@acpfly.com

AVIATION DISTRIBUTORS AND MANUFACTURERS ASSOCIATION INTERNATIONAL http://www.adma.org

ADMA SCHOLARSHIP

Scholarship to provide assistance to students pursuing careers in the aviation field. Those enrolled in an accredited Aviation program may be eligible.

Academic Fields/Career Goals: Aviation/Aerospace.

Award: Scholarship for use in junior or senior years; not renewable. *Number:* 1. *Amount:* up to $2000.

Eligibility Requirements: Applicant must be enrolled or expecting to enroll full-time at a two-year or four-year institution or university and must have an interest in aviation. Applicant must have 3.0 GPA or higher. Available to U.S. citizens.

Application Requirements: Application, essay, financial need analysis, references, transcript. *Deadline:* March 28.

Contact: Scholarship Committee
Aviation Distributors and Manufacturers Association International
100 North 20th Street, Fourth Floor
Philadelphia, PA 19103-1443
Phone: 215-564-3484
Fax: 215-963-9785
E-mail: adma@fernley.com

AVIATION INSURANCE ASSOCIATION http://www.aiaweb.org

AVIATION INSURANCE ASSOCIATION SCHOLARSHIP

A $5000 scholarship for a qualified aviation student currently enrolled in an undergraduate aviation degree program at a UAA member institution. Must maintain a GPA of 2.5 or higher.

Academic Fields/Career Goals: Aviation/Aerospace.

Award: Scholarship for use in freshman, sophomore, junior, or senior years; not renewable. *Number:* 1. *Amount:* $5000.

Eligibility Requirements: Applicant must be enrolled or expecting to enroll full-time at a two-year or four-year or technical institution or university. Applicant must have 2.5 GPA or higher. Available to U.S. and non-U.S. citizens.

Application Requirements: Application, references, transcript, letter describing activities, leadership qualities, goals and reason for applying, FAA certificates. *Deadline:* February 28.

Contact: Mandie Bannwarth, Executive Director
Aviation Insurance Association
14 West Third Street, Suite 200
Kansas City, MO 64105
Phone: 816-221-8488
Fax: 816-472-7765
E-mail: mandie@aiaweb.org

BOY SCOUTS OF AMERICA-MUSKINGUM VALLEY COUNCIL http://www.learning-for-life.org

NATIONAL AVIATION EXPLORER SCHOLARSHIPS

$3000–$10,000 scholarships for aviation Explorers pursuing a career in the aviation industry. The intent of these scholarships is to identify and reward those individuals who best exemplify the qualities that lead to success in the aviation industry. Must be participant of the Learning for Life Exploring program.

Academic Fields/Career Goals: Aviation/Aerospace.

Award: Scholarship for use in freshman, sophomore, junior, or senior years; not renewable. *Number:* 5. *Amount:* $3000–$10,000.

Eligibility Requirements: Applicant must be age 18 and over; enrolled or expecting to enroll full- or part-time at a technical institution and must have an interest in aviation or leadership. Available to U.S. and non-U.S. citizens.

Application Requirements: Application, essay, references. *Deadline:* March 31.

Contact: Bill Rogers, Associate Director
Boy Scouts of America-Muskingum Valley Council
1325 West Walnut Hill Lane
PO Box 152079
Irving, TX 75015-2079
Phone: 972-580-2433
Fax: 972-580-2137
E-mail: brogers@lflmail.org

CHARLIE WELLS MEMORIAL SCHOLARSHIP FUND http://www.wellsscholarship.com

CHARLIE WELLS MEMORIAL AVIATION GRANT

Applicant must be enrolled in and attending school regularly, or already have a high school diploma or GED. Must be a resident of the United States or one of its territories.

Academic Fields/Career Goals: Aviation/Aerospace.

Award: Grant for use in freshman, sophomore, junior, senior, or graduate years; not renewable. *Number:* varies. *Amount:* varies.

Eligibility Requirements: Applicant must be enrolled or expecting to enroll full- or part-time at a four-year institution or university. Available to U.S. citizens.

Application Requirements: Application, references, transcript. *Deadline:* April 30.

Contact: Roger Thompson, Manager
Charlie Wells Memorial Scholarship Fund
PO Box 262
Springfield, IL 62705-0262
Phone: 217-899-3263
E-mail: rog@wellsscholarship.com

CHARLIE WELLS MEMORIAL AVIATION SCHOLARSHIP

Scholarship(s) of varying amounts will be awarded each year when funds are available. The applicant must be a resident of the United States or one of its territories. Must be a full-time student majoring in an aviation-oriented curriculum.

Academic Fields/Career Goals: Aviation/Aerospace.

Award: Scholarship for use in freshman, sophomore, junior, senior, or graduate years; not renewable. *Number:* varies. *Amount:* varies.

Eligibility Requirements: Applicant must be enrolled or expecting to enroll full-time at a four-year institution or university. Available to U.S. citizens.

Application Requirements: Application, references, transcript. *Deadline:* April 30.

Contact: Roger Thompson, Manager
Charlie Wells Memorial Scholarship Fund
PO Box 262
Springfield, IL 62705-0262
Phone: 217-899-3263
E-mail: rog@wellsscholarship.com

CIVIL AIR PATROL, USAF AUXILIARY http://www.capnhq.gov

MAJOR GENERAL LUCAS V. BEAU FLIGHT SCHOLARSHIPS SPONSORED BY THE ORDER OF DAEDALIANS

One-time scholarships for active cadets of the Civil Air Patrol who desire a career in military aviation. Award is to be used toward flight training for a private pilot license. Must be 15 1/2 to 18 1/2 years of age on April 1st of the year for which applying. Must be an active CAP cadet officer. Not open to the general public.

Academic Fields/Career Goals: Aviation/Aerospace.

Award: Scholarship for use in freshman year; not renewable. *Number:* 5. *Amount:* $2100.

Eligibility Requirements: Applicant must be high school student; planning to enroll or expecting to enroll full- or part-time at a four-year institution or university; single and must have an interest in aviation. Applicant or parent of applicant must be member of Civil Air Patrol. Available to U.S. citizens.

Application Requirements: Application, essay, interview, photo, references, test scores, transcript. *Deadline:* March 1.

Contact: Kelly Easterly, Assistant Program Manager
Civil Air Patrol, USAF Auxiliary
105 South Hansell Street, Building 714
Maxwell Air Force Base, AL 36112-6332
Phone: 334-953-8640
Fax: 334-953-6699
E-mail: cpr@capnhq.gov

DAEDALIAN FOUNDATION http://www.daedalians.org

DAEDALIEAN FOUNDATION MATCHING SCHOLARSHIP PROGRAM

Scholarship program, wherein the foundation matches amounts given by flights, or chapters of the Order of Daedalians, to deserving college and university students who are pursuing a career as a military aviator.

Academic Fields/Career Goals: Aviation/Aerospace.

Award: Scholarship for use in freshman, sophomore, junior, senior, or graduate years; not renewable. *Number:* 75–80. *Amount:* up to $2000.

Eligibility Requirements: Applicant must be enrolled or expecting to enroll full-time at a four-year institution or university. Available to U.S. citizens.

Application Requirements: Application, photo, test scores, flight/ROTC/CAP recommendation. *Deadline:* December 31.

Contact: Carole Thomson, Program Executive Secretary
Daedalian Foundation
55 Main Circle, Building 676
Randolph AFB, TX 78148
Phone: 210-945-2113
Fax: 210-945-2112
E-mail: icarus@texas.net

EAA AVIATION FOUNDATION INC. http://www.eaa.org

HANSEN SCHOLARSHIP

Renewable scholarship of $1000 for a student enrolled in an accredited institution and pursuing a degree in aerospace engineering or aeronautical engineering. Student must be in good standing; financial need not a requirement. Must be an EAA member. Applications may be downloaded from the Web site http://www.youngeagles.org.

Academic Fields/Career Goals: Aviation/Aerospace.

Award: Scholarship for use in freshman, sophomore, junior, or senior years; not renewable. *Number:* up to 1. *Amount:* up to $1000.

Eligibility Requirements: Applicant must be enrolled or expecting to enroll full-time at a two-year or four-year or technical institution or

EAA Aviation Foundation Inc. (continued)

university. Applicant or parent of applicant must be member of Experimental Aircraft Association. Available to U.S. and non-U.S. citizens.

Application Requirements: Application. *Deadline:* February 29.

Contact: Jane Smith, Scholarship Coordinator
EAA Aviation Foundation Inc.
PO Box 3086
Oshkosh, WI 54903-3086
Phone: 920-426-6823
Fax: 920-426-6560
E-mail: jsmith@eaa.org

PAYZER SCHOLARSHIP

Scholarship for a student accepted or enrolled in an accredited college, university, or postsecondary school with an emphasis on technical information. Awarded to an individual who is seeking a major and declares an intention to pursue a professional career in engineering, mathematics, or the physical/biological sciences. Visit http://www.youngeagles.org for criteria and to download official application. Must be an EAA member.

Academic Fields/Career Goals: Aviation/Aerospace; Biology; Engineering/Technology; Physical Sciences and Math.

Award: Scholarship for use in freshman, sophomore, junior, or senior years; not renewable. *Number:* up to 1. *Amount:* up to $5000.

Eligibility Requirements: Applicant must be enrolled or expecting to enroll full-time at a two-year or four-year or technical institution or university. Applicant or parent of applicant must be member of Experimental Aircraft Association. Available to U.S. and non-U.S. citizens.

Application Requirements: Application. *Deadline:* February 29.

Contact: Jane Smith, Scholarship Coordinator
EAA Aviation Foundation Inc.
PO Box 3086
Oshkosh, WI 54903-3086
Phone: 920-426-6823
Fax: 920-426-6560
E-mail: jsmith@eaa.org

GENERAL AVIATION MANUFACTURERS ASSOCIATION

http://www.gama.aero

EDWARD W. STIMPSON "AVIATION EXCELLENCE" AWARD

One-time scholarship award for students who are graduating from high school and have been accepted to attend aviation college or university in the upcoming year. See Web site at http://www.gama.aero for more details.

Academic Fields/Career Goals: Aviation/Aerospace.

Award: Scholarship for use in freshman year; not renewable. *Number:* 1. *Amount:* $500.

Eligibility Requirements: Applicant must be high school student; planning to enroll or expecting to enroll full-time at a four-year institution or university and must have an interest in aviation. Applicant must have 3.0 GPA or higher. Available to U.S. citizens.

Application Requirements: Application, essay, references, transcript. *Deadline:* April 28.

Contact: Katie Pribyl, Director, Communications
General Aviation Manufacturers Association
1400 K Street, NW, Suite 801
Washington, DC 20005-2485
Phone: 202-393-1500
Fax: 202-842-4063
E-mail: kpribyl@gama.aero

HAROLD S. WOOD AWARD FOR EXCELLENCE

One-time scholarship award for an university student who is attending a National Intercollegiate Flying Association (NIFA) school. Must have completed at least one semester of coursework. See Web site at http://www.gama.aero for additional details.

Academic Fields/Career Goals: Aviation/Aerospace.

Award: Scholarship for use in freshman, sophomore, junior, or senior years; not renewable. *Number:* 1. *Amount:* $1000.

Eligibility Requirements: Applicant must be enrolled or expecting to enroll full-time at a four-year institution or university. Applicant must have 3.0 GPA or higher. Available to U.S. citizens.

Application Requirements: Application, references, transcript, nomination. *Deadline:* February 24.

Contact: Katie Pribyl, Director, Communications
General Aviation Manufacturers Association
1400 K Street, NW, Suite 801
Washington, DC 20005-2485
Phone: 202-393-1500
Fax: 202-842-4063
E-mail: kpribyl@gama.aero

GRAND RAPIDS COMMUNITY FOUNDATION

http://www.grfoundation.org

JOSHUA ESCH MITCHELL AVIATION SCHOLARSHIP

For students pursuing studies in the field of professional pilot with an emphasis on general aviation, flight engineer, or airway science. Applicant must be a U.S. citizens enrolled in a full- or part-time program at a college or university in the United States providing an accredited flight science curriculum. Applicant should have a minimum GPA of 2.75.

Academic Fields/Career Goals: Aviation/Aerospace.

Award: Scholarship for use in sophomore, junior, or senior years; not renewable. *Number:* 1. *Amount:* $1000.

Eligibility Requirements: Applicant must be enrolled or expecting to enroll full-time at a four-year institution and must have an interest in aviation. Applicant must have 2.5 GPA or higher. Available to U.S. citizens.

Application Requirements: Application, financial need analysis, references, transcript. *Deadline:* April 1.

Contact: Ruth Bishop, Education Program Officer
Grand Rapids Community Foundation
161 Ottawa Avenue, NW, 209 C
Grand Rapids, MI 49503-2757
Phone: 616-454-1751 Ext. 103
Fax: 616-454-6455
E-mail: rbishop@grfoundation.org

HISPANIC ENGINEER NATIONAL ACHIEVEMENT AWARDS CORPORATION (HENAAC)

http://www.henaac.org

HISPANIC ENGINEER NATIONAL ACHIEVEMENT AWARDS CORPORATION SCHOLARSHIP PROGRAM

Scholarships available to Hispanic students maintaining a 3.0 GPA. Must be studying an engineering or science-related field.

Academic Fields/Career Goals: Aviation/Aerospace; Biology; Chemical Engineering; Civil Engineering; Computer Science/Data Processing; Electrical Engineering/Electronics; Engineering/Technology; Materials Science, Engineering, and Metallurgy; Mechanical Engineering; Nuclear Science.

Award: Scholarship for use in freshman, sophomore, junior, senior, or graduate years; renewable. *Number:* 12–20. *Amount:* $500–$5000.

Eligibility Requirements: Applicant must be Hispanic and enrolled or expecting to enroll full-time at a four-year institution or university. Applicant must have 3.0 GPA or higher. Available to U.S. and non-U.S. citizens.

Application Requirements: Application, essay, resume, references, transcript. *Deadline:* April 30.

Contact: Kathy Barrera, Scholarship Selection Committee
Hispanic Engineer National Achievement Awards Corporation (HENAAC)
3900 Whiteside Street
Los Angeles, CA 90063
Phone: 323-262-0997
Fax: 323-262-0946
E-mail: kathy@henaac.org

ILLINOIS PILOTS ASSOCIATION

http://www.illinoispilots.com

ILLINOIS PILOTS ASSOCIATION MEMORIAL SCHOLARSHIP

Recipient must be a resident of Illinois established in an Illinois postsecondary institution in a full-time aviation-related program. Applicants will be judged by the scholarship committee, and the award (usually $500 annually) will be sent directly to the recipient's school. For further details visit Web site: http://www.illinoispilots.com.

Academic Fields/Career Goals: Aviation/Aerospace.

Award: Scholarship for use in sophomore, junior, or senior years; not renewable. *Number:* 1. *Amount:* $500.

Eligibility Requirements: Applicant must be enrolled or expecting to enroll full-time at a two-year or four-year or technical institution; resident of Illinois; studying in Illinois and must have an interest in aviation. Available to U.S. citizens.

Application Requirements: Application, essay, photo, references, transcript. *Deadline:* March 1.

Contact: Ruth Frantz, Scholarship Committee Chairman
Illinois Pilots Association
40W 297 Apache Lane
Huntley, IL 60142
Phone: 847-669-3821
Fax: 847-669-3822
E-mail: landings8e@aol.com

INTERNATIONAL SOCIETY OF WOMEN AIRLINE PILOTS (ISA+21) http://www.iswap.org

INTERNATIONAL SOCIETY OF WOMEN AIRLINE PILOTS AIRLINE SCHOLARSHIPS

Scholarships are available to women who are pursuing careers as airline pilots. Applicants must demonstrate financial need. Must have an U.S. FAA Commercial Pilot Certificate with an Instrument Rating and First Class Medical Certificate. Must have flight time in a fixed wing aircraft commensurate with the rating sought.

Academic Fields/Career Goals: Aviation/Aerospace.

Award: Scholarship for use in freshman, sophomore, junior, or senior years; not renewable. *Number:* up to 5. *Amount:* varies.

Eligibility Requirements: Applicant must be age 21 and over; enrolled or expecting to enroll full-time at a four-year institution or university and female. Available to U.S. and non-U.S. citizens.

Application Requirements: Application, autobiography, financial need analysis, interview, photo, resume, references, transcript, income tax forms, logbook pages, pilot licenses, medical certificates. *Deadline:* December 10.

Contact: Cheryl Konter, Scholarship Chairwoman
International Society of Women Airline Pilots (ISA+21)
2250 East Tropicana Avenue, Suite 19-395
Las Vegas, NV 89119-6594
Phone: 630-234-4199
E-mail: ckonter@yahoo.com

INTERNATIONAL SOCIETY OF WOMEN AIRLINE PILOTS FINANCIAL SCHOLARSHIP

Scholarships are available to women who are pursuing careers as airline pilots. Must have flight time in a fixed wing aircraft commensurate with the rating sought. Must have flight time in a fixed wing aircraft commensurate with the rating sought.

Academic Fields/Career Goals: Aviation/Aerospace.

Award: Scholarship for use in freshman, sophomore, junior, or senior years; not renewable. *Number:* 1. *Amount:* varies.

Eligibility Requirements: Applicant must be age 21 and over; enrolled or expecting to enroll full-time at a four-year institution or university and female. Available to U.S. and non-U.S. citizens.

Application Requirements: Application, autobiography, financial need analysis, interview, photo, resume, references, transcript, copies of income tax forms, logbook pages, pilot licenses, medical certificates. *Deadline:* December 10.

Contact: Cheryl Konter, Scholarship Chairwoman
International Society of Women Airline Pilots (ISA+21)
2250 East Tropicana Avenue, Suite 19-395
Las Vegas, NV 89119-6594
Phone: 630-234-4199
E-mail: ckonter@yahoo.com

INTERNATIONAL SOCIETY OF WOMEN AIRLINE PILOTS FIORENZA DE BERNARDI MERIT SCHOLARSHIP

Financial award will aid those pilots endeavoring to fill some of the basic squares, i.e. a CFI, CFII, MEI or any international equivalents. Must have flight time in a fixed wing aircraft commensurate with the rating sought. Must have flight time in a fixed wing aircraft commensurate with the rating sought.

Academic Fields/Career Goals: Aviation/Aerospace.

Award: Scholarship for use in freshman, sophomore, junior, or senior years; not renewable. *Number:* 1. *Amount:* varies.

Eligibility Requirements: Applicant must be age 21 and over; enrolled or expecting to enroll full- or part-time at a four-year institution or university and female. Available to U.S. and non-U.S. citizens.

Application Requirements: Application, autobiography, financial need analysis, interview, photo, resume, references, transcript, copies of income tax forms, logbook pages, pilot licenses, medical certificates. *Deadline:* December 10.

Contact: Cheryl Konter, Scholarship Chairwoman
International Society of Women Airline Pilots (ISA+21)
2250 East Tropicana Avenue, Suite 19-395
Las Vegas, NV 89119-6594
Phone: 630-234-4199
E-mail: ckonter@yahoo.com

INTERNATIONAL SOCIETY OF WOMEN AIRLINE PILOTS GRACE MCADAMS HARRIS SCHOLARSHIP

Scholarship may fund any ISA scholarship if the applicant has demonstrated an exceptionally spirited and ingenious attitude under difficult circumstances in the field of aviation. Applicants must have an U.S. FAA Commercial Pilot Certificate with an Instrument Rating and First Class Medical Certificate. Visit Web site: http://www.iswap.org for more details.

Academic Fields/Career Goals: Aviation/Aerospace.

Award: Scholarship for use in freshman, sophomore, junior, or senior years; not renewable. *Number:* 1. *Amount:* varies.

Eligibility Requirements: Applicant must be age 21 and over; enrolled or expecting to enroll full-time at a four-year institution or university; female and must have an interest in aviation. Available to U.S. and non-U.S. citizens.

Application Requirements: Application, autobiography, financial need analysis, interview, photo, references, transcript, copies of income tax forms, logbook pages, pilot licenses, medical certificates. *Deadline:* December 10.

Contact: Cheryl Konter, Scholarship Chairwoman
International Society of Women Airline Pilots (ISA+21)
2250 East Tropicana Avenue, Suite 19-395
Las Vegas, NV 89119-6594
Phone: 630-234-4199
E-mail: ckonter@yahoo.com

INTERNATIONAL SOCIETY OF WOMEN AIRLINE PILOTS HOLLY MULLENS MEMORIAL SCHOLARSHIP

Financial award is reserved for that applicant who is a single mother. Applicants must have an U.S. FAA Commercial Pilot Certificate with an Instrument Rating and First Class Medical Certificate. Visit Web site: http://www.iswap.org for more details.

Academic Fields/Career Goals: Aviation/Aerospace.

Award: Scholarship for use in freshman, sophomore, junior, or senior years; not renewable. *Number:* 1. *Amount:* varies.

Eligibility Requirements: Applicant must be age 21 and over; enrolled or expecting to enroll full-time at a four-year institution or university and single female. Available to U.S. and non-U.S. citizens.

Application Requirements: Application, autobiography, financial need analysis, interview, references, transcript, copies of income tax forms, logbook pages, pilot licenses, medical certificates. *Deadline:* December 10.

Contact: Cheryl Konter, Scholarship Chairwoman
International Society of Women Airline Pilots (ISA+21)
2250 East Tropicana Avenue, Suite 19-395
Las Vegas, NV 89119-6594
Phone: 630-234-4199
E-mail: ckonter@yahoo.com

INTERNATIONAL SOCIETY OF WOMEN AIRLINE PILOTS NORTH CAROLINA FINANCIAL SCHOLARSHIP

Scholarships for a woman pilot from North Carolina interested in a career in the airline world. Must have flight time in a fixed wing aircraft commensurate with the rating sought. Must have flight time in a fixed wing aircraft commensurate with the rating sought.

International Society of Women Airline Pilots (ISA+21) (continued)

Academic Fields/Career Goals: Aviation/Aerospace.

Award: Scholarship for use in freshman, sophomore, junior, or senior years; not renewable. *Number:* 1. *Amount:* varies.

Eligibility Requirements: Applicant must be age 21 and over; enrolled or expecting to enroll full-time at a four-year institution or university; female and resident of North Carolina. Available to U.S. and non-U.S. citizens.

Application Requirements: Application, autobiography, financial need analysis, interview, photo, resume, references, transcript, copies of income tax forms, logbook pages, pilot licenses, medical certificates. *Deadline:* December 10.

Contact: Cheryl Konter, Scholarship Chairwoman
International Society of Women Airline Pilots (ISA+21)
2250 East Tropicana Avenue, Suite 19-395
Las Vegas, NV 89119-6594
Phone: 630-234-4199
E-mail: ckonter@yahoo.com

LINCOLN COMMUNITY FOUNDATION http://www.lcf.org

LAWRENCE "LARRY" FRAZIER MEMORIAL SCHOLARSHIP

Scholarship for graduating seniors and former graduates of a high school in Nebraska who, upon graduation, intend to pursue a career in the fields of aviation, insurance, or law. Applicants must attend a two- or four-year college or university in Nebraska. Preferred applicants will have experience in debate and will have participated in Girl Scouts or Boy Scouts during her/his youth.

Academic Fields/Career Goals: Aviation/Aerospace; Business/Consumer Services; Law/Legal Services.

Award: Scholarship for use in freshman year; not renewable. *Number:* 1. *Amount:* $500–$1000.

Eligibility Requirements: Applicant must be high school student; planning to enroll or expecting to enroll full-time at a two-year or four-year institution or university; resident of Nebraska and studying in Nebraska. Applicant or parent of applicant must be member of Boy Scouts or Girl Scouts. Applicant must have 2.5 GPA or higher. Available to U.S. citizens.

Application Requirements: Application, essay, financial need analysis, test scores, transcript. *Deadline:* April 15.

Contact: Sonya Brakeman, Grants/Scholarships Coordinator
Lincoln Community Foundation
215 Centennial Mall South, Suite 100
Lincoln, NE 68508
Phone: 402-474-2345
Fax: 402-476-8532
E-mail: sonyab@lcf.org

NASA DELAWARE SPACE GRANT CONSORTIUM http://www.delspace.org

NASA DELAWARE SPACE GRANT UNDERGRADUATE TUITION SCHOLARSHIP

• *See page 87*

NASA IDAHO SPACE GRANT CONSORTIUM http://isgc.uidaho.edu

NASA IDAHO SPACE GRANT CONSORTIUM SCHOLARSHIP PROGRAM

• *See page 87*

NASA/MARYLAND SPACE GRANT CONSORTIUM http://www.mdspacegrant.org

NASA MARYLAND SPACE GRANT CONSORTIUM UNDERGRADUATE SCHOLARSHIPS

Scholarship for full-time student majoring in the biological and life sciences, chemistry, geological sciences, physics, astronomy, engineering, computer science, or other related fields. Must be a U.S. citizen and a Maryland resident. Enrollment in an affiliate institution of the Maryland Space Grant Consortium is necessary.

Academic Fields/Career Goals: Aviation/Aerospace; Biology; Chemical Engineering; Computer Science/Data Processing; Earth Science; Engineering/Technology; Environmental Science; Materials Science, Engineering, and Metallurgy; Mathematics; Physical Sciences and Math.

Award: Scholarship for use in freshman, sophomore, junior, or senior years; not renewable. *Number:* varies. *Amount:* up to $1000.

Eligibility Requirements: Applicant must be enrolled or expecting to enroll full-time at a four-year institution or university; resident of Maryland and studying in Maryland. Applicant must have 3.0 GPA or higher. Available to U.S. citizens.

Application Requirements: Application, essay, references. *Deadline:* May 15.

Contact: Richard Henry, Director
NASA/Maryland Space Grant Consortium
Johns Hopkins University, 203 Bloomberg Center for Physics and Astronomy, 3400 North Charles Street
Baltimore, MD 21218-2686
Phone: 410-516-7350
Fax: 410-516-4109
E-mail: henry@jhu.edu

NASA MINNESOTA SPACE GRANT CONSORTIUM http://www.aem.umn.edu/msgc

MINNESOTA SPACE GRANT CONSORTIUM

Between 30 and 80 scholarships, most ranging from $500 to $2000, are awarded to full-time students attending Minnesota colleges and universities that belong to the Minnesota Space Grant Consortium (see institution list on Web site). Preference is given to students studying aerospace engineering, space science, or related math, science, or engineering fields. Minimum 3.0 GPA required. Must be U.S. citizen. For more details see Web site: http://www.aem.umn.edu/msgc.

Academic Fields/Career Goals: Aviation/Aerospace; Earth Science; Engineering/Technology; Physical Sciences and Math.

Award: Scholarship for use in sophomore, junior, senior, graduate, or postgraduate years; renewable. *Number:* 30–80. *Amount:* $500–$2000.

Eligibility Requirements: Applicant must be enrolled or expecting to enroll full-time at a two-year or four-year institution or university and studying in Minnesota. Applicant must have 3.0 GPA or higher. Available to U.S. citizens.

Application Requirements: Application, references, transcript. *Deadline:* April 1.

Contact: Department of Aerospace Engineering
NASA Minnesota Space Grant Consortium
107 Akerman Hall, 110 Union Street, SE
Minneapolis, MN 55455
Phone: 612-626-9295
E-mail: mnsgc@aem.umn.edu

NASA MISSISSIPPI SPACE GRANT CONSORTIUM http://www.olemiss.edu/programs/nasa

MISSISSIPPI SPACE GRANT CONSORTIUM SCHOLARSHIP

Scholarship of $3000 awarded to undergraduate students in the fields of science, technology, engineering, and math. Must be U.S. citizens, community college graduates, and enrolled in a program of full-time study at one of the MSSGC universities. Minimum 3.0 GPA. Underrepresented minorities, females, and students with disabilities are encouraged to apply.

Academic Fields/Career Goals: Aviation/Aerospace; Engineering/Technology; Engineering-Related Technologies; Mathematics; Physical Sciences and Math.

Award: Scholarship for use in freshman, sophomore, junior, or senior years; not renewable. *Number:* 10. *Amount:* $3000.

Eligibility Requirements: Applicant must be enrolled or expecting to enroll full-time at a four-year institution or university. Applicant must have 3.0 GPA or higher. Available to U.S. citizens.

Application Requirements: Application, references, transcript, statement of goals and plan of study. *Deadline:* March 21.

Contact: Margaret Schaff, Project Coordinator
NASA Mississippi Space Grant Consortium
c/o University of Mississippi, 308 Vardaman Hall
PO Box 1848
University, MS 38677-1848
Phone: 662-915-1187
Fax: 662-915-3927
E-mail: mschaff@olemiss.edu

NASA MONTANA SPACE GRANT CONSORTIUM http://www.spacegrant.montana.edu

MONTANA SPACE GRANT SCHOLARSHIP PROGRAM

Awards are made on a competitive basis to students enrolled in fields of study relevant to the aerospace sciences and engineering. Must be U.S. citizen enrolled as full-time student at a Montana Consortium campus.

Academic Fields/Career Goals: Aviation/Aerospace; Biology; Chemical Engineering; Civil Engineering; Computer Science/Data Processing; Electrical Engineering/Electronics; Engineering/Technology; Mathematics; Mechanical Engineering.

Award: Scholarship for use in freshman, sophomore, junior, or senior years; not renewable. *Number:* 15–20. *Amount:* up to $1000.

Eligibility Requirements: Applicant must be enrolled or expecting to enroll full-time at a four-year institution or university and studying in Montana. Available to U.S. citizens.

Application Requirements: Application, essay, references, transcript. *Deadline:* April 2.

Contact: Glenda Winslow, Program Coordinator
NASA Montana Space Grant Consortium
416 Cobleigh Hall
Bozeman, MT 59717-3835
Phone: 406-994-4223
Fax: 406-994-4452
E-mail: winslow@spacegrant.montana.edu

NASA NEBRASKA SPACE GRANT CONSORTIUM http://nasa.unomaha.edu

NASA NEBRASKA SPACE GRANT

Undergraduate and graduate students attending any of the academic affiliates in Nebraska of the NASA Nebraska Space Grant are eligible for financial assistance in the form of scholarships. These funds assist students pursuing research with faculty or coursework in the aerospace and aeronautics fields. Must be U.S. citizen. Number of awards and amount varies.

Academic Fields/Career Goals: Aviation/Aerospace; Engineering/Technology.

Award: Scholarship for use in freshman, sophomore, junior, senior, or graduate years; not renewable. *Number:* varies. *Amount:* varies.

Eligibility Requirements: Applicant must be enrolled or expecting to enroll full- or part-time at a four-year institution or university and studying in Nebraska. Available to U.S. citizens.

Application Requirements: Application, transcript, proof of citizenship. *Deadline:* varies.

Contact: Melissa Wragge, Scholarship Coordinator
NASA Nebraska Space Grant Consortium
Allwine Hall 526, 6001 Dodge Street
Omaha, NE 68182-0589
Phone: 402-554-3772
Fax: 402-554-3781
E-mail: mwragge@mail.unomaha.edu

NASA NEVADA SPACE GRANT CONSORTIUM http://www.unr.edu/spacegrant

UNIVERSITY AND COMMUNITY COLLEGE SYSTEM OF NEVADA NASA SPACE GRANT AND FELLOWSHIP PROGRAM

The grant provides graduate fellowships and undergraduate scholarship to qualified student majoring in aerospace science, technology and related fields. Must be Nevada resident studying at a Nevada college/university. Minimum 2.5 GPA required.

Academic Fields/Career Goals: Aviation/Aerospace; Chemical Engineering; Computer Science/Data Processing; Engineering/Technology; Physical Sciences and Math.

Award: Scholarship for use in freshman, sophomore, junior, senior, or graduate years; not renewable. *Number:* 1–20. *Amount:* $2500–$30,000.

Eligibility Requirements: Applicant must be enrolled or expecting to enroll full-time at a two-year or four-year institution or university; resident of Nevada and studying in Nevada. Applicant must have 3.0 GPA or higher. Available to U.S. citizens.

Application Requirements: Application, autobiography, essay, resume, references, transcript, project proposal, budget. *Deadline:* April 13.

Contact: Cindy Routh, Program Coordinator
NASA Nevada Space Grant Consortium
2215 Raggio Parkway
Reno, NV 89512
Phone: 775-673-7674
Fax: 775-673-7485
E-mail: nvsg@dri.edu

NASA RHODE ISLAND SPACE GRANT CONSORTIUM http://www.planetary.brown.edu/RI_Space_Grant

NASA RHODE ISLAND SPACE GRANT CONSORTIUM UNDERGRADUATE RESEARCH SCHOLARSHIP

Scholarship for undergraduate students for study and/or outreach related to NASA and space sciences, engineering and/or technology. Must attend a Rhode Island Space Grant Consortium participating school. Recipients are expected to devote a maximum of 4 hours per week in science education for K-12 children and teachers. See Web site for additional information: http://www.spacegrant.brown.edu.

Academic Fields/Career Goals: Aviation/Aerospace; Engineering/Technology; Meteorology/Atmospheric Science.

Award: Scholarship for use in sophomore, junior, or senior years; not renewable. *Number:* up to 2. *Amount:* up to $4000.

Eligibility Requirements: Applicant must be enrolled or expecting to enroll full-time at a four-year institution or university and studying in Rhode Island. Applicant must have 3.0 GPA or higher. Available to U.S. citizens.

Application Requirements: Application, essay, resume, references, transcript. *Deadline:* varies.

Contact: Dorcas Metcalf, Program Manager
NASA Rhode Island Space Grant Consortium
Brown University
PO Box 1846
Providence, RI 02912
Phone: 401-863-1151
Fax: 401-863-3978
E-mail: dorcas_metcalf@brown.edu

NASA RISGC SCIENCE EN ESPANOL SCHOLARSHIP FOR UNDERGRADUATE STUDENTS

Award for undergraduate students attending a Rhode Island Space Grant Consortium participating school and studying in any space-related field of science, math, engineering, or other field with applications in space study. Recipients are expected to devote a maximum of 8 hours per week in outreach activities, supporting ESL teachers with science instruction.

Academic Fields/Career Goals: Aviation/Aerospace; Engineering/Technology; Mathematics.

Award: Scholarship for use in sophomore, junior, or senior years; not renewable. *Number:* 2. *Amount:* up to $4000.

Eligibility Requirements: Applicant must be enrolled or expecting to enroll full-time at a four-year institution or university and studying in Rhode Island. Applicant must have 3.0 GPA or higher. Available to U.S. citizens.

NASA Rhode Island Space Grant Consortium (continued)

Application Requirements: Application, essay, resume, transcript. *Deadline:* varies.

Contact: Dorcas Metcalf, Program Manager
NASA Rhode Island Space Grant Consortium
Brown University
PO Box 1846
Providence, RI 02912
Phone: 401-863-1151
Fax: 401-863-3978
E-mail: dorcas_metcalf@brown.edu

NASA RISGC SUMMER SCHOLARSHIP FOR UNDERGRADUATE STUDENTS

Scholarship for full-time summer study. Students are expected to devote 75 percent of their time to a research project with a faculty adviser and 25 percent to outreach activities in science education for K-12 students and teachers. Must attend a Rhode Island Space Grant Consortium participating school. See Web site for additional information: http://www.spacegrant.brown.edu.

Academic Fields/Career Goals: Aviation/Aerospace; Education.

Award: Scholarship for use in sophomore, junior, or senior years; not renewable. *Number:* up to 2. *Amount:* up to $4000.

Eligibility Requirements: Applicant must be enrolled or expecting to enroll full-time at a four-year institution or university and studying in Rhode Island. Applicant must have 3.0 GPA or higher. Available to U.S. citizens.

Application Requirements: Application, resume, references, letter of interest. *Deadline:* varies.

Contact: Dorcas Metcalf, Program Manager
NASA Rhode Island Space Grant Consortium
Brown University
PO Box 1846
Providence, RI 02912
Phone: 401-863-1151
Fax: 401-863-3978
E-mail: dorcas_metcalf@brown.edu

NASA SOUTH CAROLINA SPACE GRANT CONSORTIUM http://www.cofc.edu/~scsgrant

UNDERGRADUATE RESEARCH PROGRAM

Undergraduate research program is designed to increase the number of highly trained scientist and engineers and enable undergraduate students to conduct NASA-related research. Must be a citizen of U.S., attend a consortium member institution. Must be a rising junior or senior and have an interest in aerospace and space related studies. For details refer to Web Site: http://www.cofc.edu/

Academic Fields/Career Goals: Aviation/Aerospace.

Award: Grant for use in junior or senior years; renewable. *Number:* 10. *Amount:* $500–$5000.

Eligibility Requirements: Applicant must be enrolled or expecting to enroll full-time at a four-year institution or university and studying in South Carolina. Available to U.S. citizens.

Application Requirements: Application, essay, references, transcript, research proposal. *Deadline:* February 9.

Contact: Tara B. Scozzaro, Program Manager
NASA South Carolina Space Grant Consortium
College of Charleston, 66 George Street
Charleston, SC 29424
Phone: 843-953-5463
Fax: 843-953-5446
E-mail: scozzarot@cofc.edu

NASA SOUTH DAKOTA SPACE GRANT CONSORTIUM http://www.sdsmt.edu/space/

SOUTH DAKOTA SPACE GRANT CONSORTIUM UNDERGRADUATE SCHOLARSHIPS

Scholarship for undergraduate students pursuing studies in science, technology, engineering, math, aerospace, or related fields at South Dakota institutions. Women and minorities are encouraged to apply. For more information, see Web site: http://sdspacegrant.sdsmt.edu/.

Academic Fields/Career Goals: Aviation/Aerospace; Earth Science; Energy and Power Engineering; Engineering/Technology; Engineering-Related Technologies; Environmental Science; Materials Science, Engineering, and Metallurgy; Mathematics; Natural Sciences; Physical Sciences and Math; Science, Technology, and Society.

Award: Scholarship for use in freshman, sophomore, junior, or senior years; renewable. *Number:* varies. *Amount:* $1750.

Eligibility Requirements: Applicant must be enrolled or expecting to enroll full- or part-time at a four-year institution or university and studying in South Dakota. Applicant must have 3.0 GPA or higher. Available to U.S. citizens.

Application Requirements: Application, transcript. *Deadline:* varies.

Contact: Tom Durkin, Deputy Director and Coordinator
NASA South Dakota Space Grant Consortium
501 East Saint Joseph Street
Rapid City, SD 57701-3995
Phone: 605-394-1975
Fax: 605-394-5360
E-mail: thomas.durkin@sdsmt.edu

NASA VERMONT SPACE GRANT CONSORTIUM http://www.cems.uvm.edu/VSGC

VERMONT SPACE GRANT CONSORTIUM SCHOLARSHIP PROGRAM

• *See page 88*

NASA VIRGINIA SPACE GRANT CONSORTIUM http://www.vsgc.odu.edu

AEROSPACE UNDERGRADUATE RESEARCH SCHOLARSHIPS

Scholarships designated for undergraduate students pursuing any field of study with aerospace relevance. Must attend one of the five Virginia Space Grant colleges and universities. Must have minimum 3.0 GPA. Please refer to Web site for further details: http://www.vsgc.odu.edu.

Academic Fields/Career Goals: Aviation/Aerospace.

Award: Scholarship for use in junior or senior years; not renewable. *Number:* varies. *Amount:* $8500.

Eligibility Requirements: Applicant must be enrolled or expecting to enroll full-time at a four-year institution or university and studying in Virginia. Applicant must have 3.0 GPA or higher. Available to U.S. citizens.

Application Requirements: Application, essay, resume, references, transcript. *Deadline:* February 11.

Contact: Chris Carter, Educational Programs Manager
NASA Virginia Space Grant Consortium
Old Dominion University Peninsula Center, 600 Butler Farm Road
Hampton, VA 23666
Phone: 757-766-5210
Fax: 757-766-5205
E-mail: cxcarter@odu.edu

VIRGINIA SPACE GRANT CONSORTIUM COMMUNITY COLLEGE SCHOLARSHIPS

Scholarships designated for Virginia community college students studying technological fields involving aerospace. Applicant must be U.S. citizen with a minimum GPA of 3.0. Please refer to Web site for further details: http://www.vsgc.odu.edu.

Academic Fields/Career Goals: Aviation/Aerospace; Engineering/Technology.

Award: Scholarship for use in freshman or sophomore years; not renewable. *Number:* varies. *Amount:* $1500.

Eligibility Requirements: Applicant must be enrolled or expecting to enroll full-time at a two-year or technical institution and studying in Virginia. Applicant must have 3.0 GPA or higher. Available to U.S. citizens.

Application Requirements: Application, essay, resume, references, transcript. *Deadline:* February 29.

Contact: Chris Carter, Educational Programs Manager
NASA Virginia Space Grant Consortium
Old Dominion University Peninsula Center, 600 Butler Farm Road
Hampton, VA 23666
Phone: 757-766-5210
Fax: 757-766-5205
E-mail: cxcarter@odu.edu

VIRGINIA SPACE GRANT CONSORTIUM TEACHER EDUCATION SCHOLARSHIPS

Scholarships designated for students enrolled at a Virginia Space Grant college or university in a program that will lead to teacher certification in a pre-college setting. Students may apply as graduating high school seniors, sophomore community college students or any undergraduate year. Please refer to Web site for further details: http://www.vsgc.odu.edu.

Academic Fields/Career Goals: Aviation/Aerospace; Earth Science; Education; Engineering/Technology; Environmental Science; Physical Sciences and Math.

Award: Scholarship for use in freshman, sophomore, junior, or senior years; not renewable. *Number:* varies. *Amount:* $1000.

Eligibility Requirements: Applicant must be enrolled or expecting to enroll full-time at a two-year or four-year institution or university and studying in Virginia. Applicant must have 3.0 GPA or higher. Available to U.S. citizens.

Application Requirements: Application, essay, resume, references, transcript. *Deadline:* February 29.

Contact: Chris Carter, Educational Programs Manager
NASA Virginia Space Grant Consortium
Old Dominion University Peninsula Center, 600 Butler Farm Road
Hampton, VA 23666
Phone: 757-766-5210
Fax: 757-766-5205
E-mail: cxcarter@odu.edu

NASA WEST VIRGINIA SPACE GRANT CONSORTIUM http://www.nasa.wvu.edu

WEST VIRGINIA SPACE GRANT CONSORTIUM UNDERGRADUATE FELLOWSHIP PROGRAM

Scholarships intended to support undergraduate students pursuing a degree in science, technology, engineering, or math. Students are given opportunities to work with faculty members within their major department on research projects, or students may participate in the Consortium Challenge Program. Must be U.S. citizen. Refer to Web site for further details: http://www.nasa.wvu.edu.

Academic Fields/Career Goals: Aviation/Aerospace; Computer Science/Data Processing; Energy and Power Engineering; Engineering/Technology; Engineering-Related Technologies; Environmental Science; Meteorology/Atmospheric Science; Natural Sciences; Nuclear Science; Physical Sciences and Math.

Award: Scholarship for use in freshman, sophomore, junior, or senior years; not renewable. *Number:* varies. *Amount:* $1000–$2000.

Eligibility Requirements: Applicant must be enrolled or expecting to enroll full-time at a four-year institution or university. Available to U.S. citizens.

Application Requirements: Application. *Deadline:* March 7.

Contact: Candy Cordwell, Program Manager
NASA West Virginia Space Grant Consortium
West Virginia University, G-68 Engineering Sciences Building
PO Box 6070
Morgantown, WV 26506-6070
Phone: 304-293-4099 Ext. 3738
Fax: 304-293-4970
E-mail: cordwell@nasa.wvu.edu

NASA WISCONSIN SPACE GRANT CONSORTIUM http://www.uwgb.edu/WSGC

WISCONSIN SPACE GRANT CONSORTIUM UNDERGRADUATE RESEARCH PROGRAM

One-time award of up to $3500 for a U.S. citizen enrolled full-time, admitted to, or applying to any undergraduate program at a Wisconsin Space Grant Consortium college or university. Award goes to a student to create and implement their own small research study. Minimum 3.0 GPA required. Submit proposal with budget. Refer to Web site for more information: http://www.uwgb.edu/wsgc.

Academic Fields/Career Goals: Aviation/Aerospace.

Award: Grant for use in freshman, sophomore, junior, or senior years; not renewable. *Number:* 15. *Amount:* up to $3500.

Eligibility Requirements: Applicant must be enrolled or expecting to enroll full-time at a four-year institution or university; resident of Wisconsin and studying in Wisconsin. Applicant must have 3.0 GPA or higher. Available to U.S. citizens.

Application Requirements: Application, references, transcript, proposal with budget. *Deadline:* February 4.

Contact: Sue Weiler, Office Coordinator
NASA Wisconsin Space Grant Consortium
University of Wisconsin-Green Bay
Natural and Applied Sciences, 2420 Nicolet Drive
Green Bay, WI 54311-7001
Phone: 920-465-2108
Fax: 920-465-2376
E-mail: weilers@uwgb.edu

WISCONSIN SPACE GRANT CONSORTIUM UNDERGRADUATE SCHOLARSHIP PROGRAM

Scholarship of up to $1500 for a U.S. citizen enrolled full-time in, admitted to, or applying to any undergraduate program at a Wisconsin Space Grant Consortium college or university. Awards will be given to students with outstanding potential in programs of aerospace, space science, or other interdisciplinary space-related studies. Minimum 3.0 GPA required. Refer to Web site for more information: http://www.uwgb.edu/wsgc.

Academic Fields/Career Goals: Aviation/Aerospace.

Award: Scholarship for use in freshman, sophomore, junior, or senior years; not renewable. *Number:* 15–20. *Amount:* up to $1500.

Eligibility Requirements: Applicant must be enrolled or expecting to enroll full-time at a four-year institution or university; resident of Wisconsin and studying in Wisconsin. Applicant must have 3.0 GPA or higher. Available to U.S. citizens.

Application Requirements: Application, essay, references, transcript. *Deadline:* February 4.

Contact: Sue Weiler, Office Coordinator
NASA Wisconsin Space Grant Consortium
University of Wisconsin-Green Bay
Natural and Applied Sciences, 2420 Nicolet Drive
Green Bay, WI 54311-7001
Phone: 920-465-2108
Fax: 920-465-2376
E-mail: weilers@uwgb.edu

NATIONAL AIR TRANSPORTATION ASSOCIATION FOUNDATION http://www.nata.aero

DAN L. MEISINGER, SR. MEMORIAL LEARN TO FLY SCHOLARSHIP

A $2500 scholarship is available to students currently enrolled in an aviation program. Must be a high academic achiever. Application must be postmarked by the last Friday in November. For more details see Web site: http://www.nata-online.org.

Academic Fields/Career Goals: Aviation/Aerospace.

Award: Scholarship for use in freshman, sophomore, junior, or senior years; not renewable. *Number:* 1. *Amount:* $2500.

Eligibility Requirements: Applicant must be age 18 and over; enrolled or expecting to enroll full-time at a two-year or four-year institution or university and resident of Illinois, Kansas, or Missouri. Available to U.S. citizens.

National Air Transportation Association Foundation (continued)

Application Requirements: Application, interview, references, test scores, transcript. *Deadline:* November 28.

Contact: Adam Coulby, Manager, Education and Training
National Air Transportation Association Foundation
4226 King Street
Alexandria, VA 22302
Phone: 703-845-9000
Fax: 703-845-8176
E-mail: acoulby@nata.aero

NATA BUSINESS SCHOLARSHIP

Scholarship available for education or training to establish a career in the business aviation industry. Applicable education includes any aviation-related two-year, four-year or graduate degree program at an accredited college or university. Must be 18 years of age or older, be nominated and endorsed by a representative of a regular or associate member company of the NATA. Application packet postmarked no later than the last Friday in December.

Academic Fields/Career Goals: Aviation/Aerospace.

Award: Scholarship for use in freshman, sophomore, junior, senior, or graduate years; not renewable. *Number:* 1. *Amount:* up to $2500.

Eligibility Requirements: Applicant must be age 18 and over and enrolled or expecting to enroll full-time at a two-year or four-year institution or university. Available to U.S. citizens.

Application Requirements: Application, essay, resume, transcript. *Deadline:* December 1.

Contact: Adam Coulby, Manager, Education and Training
National Air Transportation Association Foundation
4226 King Street
Alexandria, VA 22302
Phone: 703-845-9000
Fax: 703-845-8176
E-mail: acoulby@nata.aero

PIONEERS OF FLIGHT SCHOLARSHIP PROGRAM

Two $1000 scholarships are available to college students currently enrolled in an aviation program. Must be a high academic achiever. Application must be postmarked by the last Friday in December. For more details see Web site: http://www.nata-online.org.

Academic Fields/Career Goals: Aviation/Aerospace.

Award: Scholarship for use in sophomore or junior years; not renewable. *Number:* 2. *Amount:* $1000.

Eligibility Requirements: Applicant must be age 18 and over and enrolled or expecting to enroll full-time at a four-year institution or university. Available to U.S. citizens.

Application Requirements: Application, interview, references, test scores, transcript. *Deadline:* December 26.

Contact: Adam Coulby, Manager, Education and Training
National Air Transportation Association Foundation
4226 King Street
Alexandria, VA 22302
Phone: 703-845-9000
Fax: 703-845-8176
E-mail: acoulby@nata.aero

NATIONAL BUSINESS AVIATION ASSOCIATION INC. http://www.nbaa.org

NBAA INTERNATIONAL OPERATORS SCHOLARSHIP

One-time $5000 scholarship offered to one or more recipients. Include with application: 500-word essay explaining how this scholarship will help the applicant achieve their international aviation career goals, statement of the funds required to achieve these goals, and at least one professional letter of recommendation, preferably from an NBAA member company employee.

Academic Fields/Career Goals: Aviation/Aerospace.

Award: Scholarship for use in freshman, sophomore, junior, or senior years; not renewable. *Number:* 1. *Amount:* $5000.

Eligibility Requirements: Applicant must be enrolled or expecting to enroll full- or part-time at a two-year or four-year or technical institution or university. Applicant must have 3.0 GPA or higher. Available to U.S. and non-U.S. citizens.

Application Requirements: Application, essay, references. *Deadline:* January 31.

Contact: Jay Evans, Director, Operations
National Business Aviation Association Inc.
1200 18th Street North West, Suite 400
Washington, DC 20036-2527
Phone: 202-783-9353
Fax: 202-331-8364
E-mail: jevans@nbaa.org

NBAA JANICE K. BARDEN SCHOLARSHIP

One-time $1000 scholarship for students officially enrolled in NBAA/UAA programs. Must be U.S. citizen, officially enrolled in an aviation-related program with 3.0 minimum GPA. Include with application: 250-word essay describing the applicant's interest and goals for a career in the business aviation industry; letter of recommendation from member of aviation department faculty at institution where applicant is enrolled.

Academic Fields/Career Goals: Aviation/Aerospace.

Award: Scholarship for use in sophomore, junior, senior, graduate, or postgraduate years; not renewable. *Number:* 5. *Amount:* $1000.

Eligibility Requirements: Applicant must be enrolled or expecting to enroll full-time at a two-year or four-year institution or university. Applicant must have 3.0 GPA or higher. Available to U.S. citizens.

Application Requirements: Application, essay, resume, references, transcript. *Deadline:* November 1.

Contact: Jay Evans, Director, Operations
National Business Aviation Association Inc.
1200 18th Street North West, Suite 400
Washington, DC 20036-2527
Phone: 202-783-9353
Fax: 202-331-8364
E-mail: jevans@nbaa.org

NBAA LAWRENCE GINOCCHIO AVIATION SCHOLARSHIP

One-time $5000 scholarship for students officially enrolled in NBAA/UAA programs. Must be officially enrolled in aviation-related program with 3.0 minimum GPA. Include with application: a 500- to 1000-word essay describing interest in and goals for a career in the business aviation industry while demonstrating strength of character. Must also have two letters of recommendation, including one from member of aviation department faculty at institution where applicant is enrolled.

Academic Fields/Career Goals: Aviation/Aerospace.

Award: Scholarship for use in sophomore, junior, senior, or graduate years; not renewable. *Number:* 5. *Amount:* $5000.

Eligibility Requirements: Applicant must be enrolled or expecting to enroll full-time at a four-year institution or university. Applicant must have 3.0 GPA or higher. Available to U.S. and Canadian citizens.

Application Requirements: Application, essay, resume, references, transcript, proof of enrollment. *Deadline:* August 1.

Contact: Jay Evans, Director, Operations
National Business Aviation Association Inc.
1200 18th Street North West, Suite 400
Washington, DC 20036-2527
Phone: 202-783-9353
Fax: 202-331-8364
E-mail: jevans@nbaa.org

NBAA WILLIAM M. FANNING MAINTENANCE SCHOLARSHIP

One-time award given to two students pursuing careers as maintenance technicians. One award will benefit a student who is currently enrolled in an accredited Airframe and Power-plant (A&P) program at an approved FAR Part 147 school. The second award will benefit an individual who is not currently enrolled but has been accepted into an A&P program. Include with application: a 250-word essay describing applicant's interest in and goals for a career in the aviation maintenance field. A letter of recommendation from an NBAA Member Company representative is encouraged.

Academic Fields/Career Goals: Aviation/Aerospace.

Award: Scholarship for use in freshman, sophomore, junior, senior, or graduate years; not renewable. *Number:* 2. *Amount:* $2500.

Eligibility Requirements: Applicant must be enrolled or expecting to enroll full-time at a two-year or four-year or technical institution or university. Available to U.S. citizens.

Application Requirements: Application, essay, resume, references, transcript. *Deadline:* August 1.

Contact: Jay Evans, Director, Operations
National Business Aviation Association Inc.
1200 18th Street North West, Suite 400
Washington, DC 20036-2527
Phone: 202-783-9353
Fax: 202-331-8364
E-mail: jevans@nbaa.org

U.S. AIRCRAFT INSURANCE GROUP PDP SCHOLARSHIP

One-time $1000 scholarship for applicants enrolled full-time in a college or university offering the NBAA (National Business Aviation Association) Professional Development Program (PDP). Must be U.S. citizen, officially enrolled in aviation-related program with 3.0 minimum GPA. Include with application: 250 word essay describing goals for a career in the business aviation flight department. A letter of recommendation from an NBAAA Member Company representative is encouraged.

Academic Fields/Career Goals: Aviation/Aerospace.

Award: Scholarship for use in sophomore, junior, senior, graduate, or postgraduate years; not renewable. *Number:* 1. *Amount:* $1000.

Eligibility Requirements: Applicant must be enrolled or expecting to enroll full-time at a two-year or four-year institution or university. Applicant must have 3.0 GPA or higher. Available to U.S. citizens.

Application Requirements: Application, essay, resume, references, transcript, proof of enrollment. *Deadline:* August 1.

Contact: Jay Evans, Director, Operations
National Business Aviation Association Inc.
1200 18th Street North West, Suite 400
Washington, DC 20036-2527
Phone: 202-783-9353
Fax: 202-331-8364
E-mail: jevans@nbaa.org

NATIONAL GAY PILOTS ASSOCIATION http://www.ngpa.org

NATIONAL GAY PILOTS ASSOCIATION SCHOLARSHIP

Scholarship for candidates pursuing a career as a professional pilot. Funds cannot be used to pay for the basic private certificate; they must be applied towards advanced fight training at a government certified flight school or to college tuition if enrolled in an accredited aviation degree program. Applicants must provide evidence of their contribution to the gay and lesbian community.

Academic Fields/Career Goals: Aviation/Aerospace; Engineering/Technology.

Award: Scholarship for use in freshman, sophomore, junior, senior, or graduate years; not renewable. *Number:* varies. *Amount:* $2000–$3000.

Eligibility Requirements: Applicant must be age 18 and over; enrolled or expecting to enroll full- or part-time at a two-year or four-year or technical institution or university and must have an interest in aviation or LGBT issues. Applicant or parent of applicant must have employment or volunteer experience in community service. Available to U.S. and non-U.S. citizens.

Application Requirements: Application, essay, references, transcript, SAT scores, copies of the applicant's pilot certificate, medical certificate. *Deadline:* March 1.

Contact: Scholarship Chairman
National Gay Pilots Association
PO Box 7271
Dallas, TX 75209-0271
Phone: 214-336-0873
Fax: 214-350-0447
E-mail: info@ngpa.org

PALWAUKEE AIRPORT PILOTS ASSOCIATION http://www.pwkpilots.org

PALWAUKEE AIRPORT PILOTS ASSOCIATION SCHOLARSHIP PROGRAM

Scholarship offered to Illinois residents who are attending accredited programs at Illinois institutions. Must be pursuing a course of study in an aviation-related program. Minimum GPA of 2.0. Applications available on Web site: http://www.pwkpilots.org.

Academic Fields/Career Goals: Aviation/Aerospace.

Award: Scholarship for use in freshman, sophomore, junior, or senior years; not renewable. *Number:* 2. *Amount:* $500–$1000.

Eligibility Requirements: Applicant must be age 18 and over; enrolled or expecting to enroll full-time at a two-year or four-year or technical institution or university; resident of Illinois; studying in Illinois and must have an interest in aviation. Available to U.S. citizens.

Application Requirements: Application, autobiography, references, transcript, copy of FAA medical certificate, pilot certificate. *Deadline:* May 1.

Contact: Raymond Chou, Chairman, Scholarship Committee
Palwaukee Airport Pilots Association
1020 South Plant Road
Wheeling, IL 60090
Phone: 847-537-2580
Fax: 847-537-8183
E-mail: scholarship@pwkpilots.org

PROFESSIONAL AVIATION MAINTENANCE FOUNDATION http://www.pama.org

PROFESSIONAL AVIATION MAINTENANCE FOUNDATION STUDENT SCHOLARSHIP PROGRAM

For students enrolled in an airframe and power plant licensing program. Must have a B average and have completed 25 percent of the program. Must reapply each year.

Academic Fields/Career Goals: Aviation/Aerospace; Trade/Technical Specialties.

Award: Scholarship for use in freshman, sophomore, junior, or senior years; not renewable. *Number:* 10–30. *Amount:* $1000.

Eligibility Requirements: Applicant must be enrolled or expecting to enroll full-time at a two-year or four-year or technical institution or university and must have an interest in aviation. Applicant must have 3.0 GPA or higher. Available to U.S. and non-U.S. citizens.

Application Requirements: Application, financial need analysis, references, self-addressed stamped envelope, transcript. *Deadline:* October 31.

Contact: Marge Milligan, Marketing Assistant
Professional Aviation Maintenance Foundation
717 Princess Street
Alexandria, VA 22314
Phone: 724-772-4092
Fax: 724-776-3049
E-mail: milligan@sae.org

RHODE ISLAND PILOTS ASSOCIATION http://www.ripilots.com

RHODE ISLAND PILOTS ASSOCIATION SCHOLARSHIP

A scholarship open to Rhode Island residents to begin or advance a career in aviation. Must be age 16 or above.

Academic Fields/Career Goals: Aviation/Aerospace.

Award: Scholarship for use in freshman, sophomore, junior, or senior years; not renewable. *Number:* 2–4. *Amount:* $500–$1000.

Eligibility Requirements: Applicant must be age 16 and over; enrolled or expecting to enroll full- or part-time at a two-year or four-year or technical institution; resident of Rhode Island and must have an interest in aviation. Available to U.S. citizens.

Application Requirements: Application, essay, financial need analysis, references, test scores, transcript. *Deadline:* February 28.

Contact: Marilyn Biagetti, Scholarship Chair
Rhode Island Pilots Association
Hangar One, 644 Airport Road
Warwick, RI 02886
Phone: 401-568-3497
Fax: 401-568-5392
E-mail: biagettim@cox.net

SOCIETY OF AUTOMOTIVE ENGINEERS http://www.sae.org

BMW/SAE ENGINEERING SCHOLARSHIP

Scholarship is provided by BMW AG in recognition of its commitment to excellence in engineering. This scholarship is in support of the SAE Foundation to ensure an adequate supply of well-trained engineers for the future. One scholarship will be awarded at $1500 per year, renewable for four years. Must have a 3.75 GPA, rank in the 90th percentile in both math and critical reading on SAT or composite ACT scores. A 3.0 GPA must be maintained to renew the scholarship.

Academic Fields/Career Goals: Aviation/Aerospace; Chemical Engineering; Electrical Engineering/Electronics; Engineering/Technology; Engineering-Related Technologies; Mechanical Engineering.

Award: Scholarship for use in freshman year; renewable. *Number:* 1. *Amount:* $1500.

Eligibility Requirements: Applicant must be high school student and planning to enroll or expecting to enroll full-time at a four-year institution or university. Available to U.S. citizens.

Application Requirements: Application, essay, test scores, transcript. *Deadline:* December 15.

Contact: Connie Harnish, SAE Educational Relations
Society of Automotive Engineers
400 Commonwealth Drive
Warrendale, PA 15096-0001
Phone: 724-772-4047
Fax: 724-776-0890
E-mail: connie@sae.org

EDWARD D. HENDRICKSON/SAE ENGINEERING SCHOLARSHIP

Scholarship of $4000 awarded at $1000 per year for four years. A 3.0 GPA and continued engineering enrollment must be maintained to renew the scholarship. Applicants must have a 3.75 GPA, rank in the 90th percentile in both math and critical reading on SAT or composite ACT scores, and pursue an engineering degree accredited by ABET.

Academic Fields/Career Goals: Aviation/Aerospace; Chemical Engineering; Electrical Engineering/Electronics; Engineering/Technology; Engineering-Related Technologies; Mechanical Engineering.

Award: Scholarship for use in freshman year; renewable. *Number:* 1. *Amount:* $1000.

Eligibility Requirements: Applicant must be high school student and planning to enroll or expecting to enroll full-time at a four-year institution or university. Available to U.S. citizens.

Application Requirements: Application, essay, test scores, transcript. *Deadline:* December 15.

Contact: Connie Harnish, SAE Educational Relations
Society of Automotive Engineers
400 Commonwealth Drive
Warrendale, PA 15096-0001
Phone: 724-772-4047
Fax: 724-776-0890
E-mail: connie@sae.org

TMC/SAE DONALD D. DAWSON TECHNICAL SCHOLARSHIP

One scholarship of $1500 a year for up to four years as long as a 3.0 GPA and continuing engineering enrollment is maintained. High school seniors must have a 3.25 or higher GPA, SAT math 600 or above and critical reading 550 or above and/or an ACT composite score 27 or above. Transfer students from accredited four-year colleges/universities must have a 3.0 GPA. Students from postsecondary technical/vocational schools must have a 3.5 GPA.

Academic Fields/Career Goals: Aviation/Aerospace; Chemical Engineering; Electrical Engineering/Electronics; Engineering/Technology; Engineering-Related Technologies; Materials Science, Engineering, and Metallurgy; Mechanical Engineering.

Award: Scholarship for use in freshman, sophomore, junior, or senior years; renewable. *Number:* 1. *Amount:* $1500.

Eligibility Requirements: Applicant must be enrolled or expecting to enroll full-time at a two-year or four-year or technical institution or university. Available to U.S. citizens.

Application Requirements: Application, essay, test scores, transcript. *Deadline:* December 15.

Contact: Connie Harnish, SAE Educational Relations
Society of Automotive Engineers
400 Commonwealth Drive
Warrendale, PA 15096-0001
Phone: 724-772-4047
Fax: 724-776-0890
E-mail: connie@sae.org

SOCIETY OF SATELLITE PROFESSIONALS INTERNATIONAL http://www.sspi.org

A.W. PERIGARD FUND SCHOLARSHIP

Scholarship of $2500 award open to students majoring or planning to major in fields related to satellite communications. Selection is based on academic and leadership achievement, commitment to pursue education and career opportunities in the satellite industry or a field making direct use of satellite technology. Available to members of SSPI.

Academic Fields/Career Goals: Aviation/Aerospace; Communications.

Award: Scholarship for use in freshman, sophomore, junior, or senior years; not renewable. *Number:* 1. *Amount:* $2500.

Eligibility Requirements: Applicant must be enrolled or expecting to enroll full-time at a two-year or four-year institution or university. Available to U.S. and non-U.S. citizens.

Application Requirements: Application, financial need analysis, transcript. *Deadline:* June 1.

Contact: Tamara Bond, Director of Membership Services
Society of Satellite Professionals International
The New York Information Technology Center, 55 Broad Street, 14th Floor
New York, NY 10004
Phone: 212-809-5199 Ext. 103
Fax: 212-825-0075
E-mail: tbond@sspi.org

PSSC LEGACY FUND

Scholarship of $2500 award open to students majoring or planning to major in fields related to international satellite applications and distance education. Available to members of SSPI.

Academic Fields/Career Goals: Aviation/Aerospace; Communications.

Award: Scholarship for use in freshman, sophomore, junior, senior, or graduate years; not renewable. *Number:* 1. *Amount:* $2500.

Eligibility Requirements: Applicant must be enrolled or expecting to enroll full-time at a four-year institution or university. Available to U.S. and non-U.S. citizens.

Application Requirements: Application, financial need analysis, transcript. *Deadline:* June 1.

Contact: Tamara Bond, Director of Membership Services
Society of Satellite Professionals International
The New York Information Technology Center, 55 Broad Street, 14th Floor
New York, NY 10004
Phone: 212-809-5199 Ext. 103
Fax: 212-825-0075
E-mail: tbond@sspi.org

SSPI NORTHEAST CHAPTER SCHOLARSHIP

Scholarship of $2500 to undergraduate students and graduate students attending schools in the Northeastern United States who are studying or intend to study satellite-related technologies, policies or applications. Available to members of SSPI.

Academic Fields/Career Goals: Aviation/Aerospace; Communications.

Award: Scholarship for use in freshman, sophomore, junior, senior, or graduate years; not renewable. *Number:* 1. *Amount:* $2500.

Eligibility Requirements: Applicant must be enrolled or expecting to enroll full-time at a two-year or four-year institution or university. Available to U.S. and non-U.S. citizens.

Application Requirements: Application, financial need analysis, transcript. *Deadline:* June 1.

Contact: Tamara Bond, Director of Membership Services
Society of Satellite Professionals International
The New York Information Technology Center, 55 Broad Street, 14th Floor
New York, NY 10004
Phone: 212-809-5199 Ext. 103
Fax: 212-825-0075
E-mail: tbond@sspi.org

SOCIETY OF WOMEN ENGINEERS http://www.swe.org

JUDITH RESNIK MEMORIAL SCHOLARSHIP

One-time award available to aerospace or astronautical engineering major at the sophomore, junior, or senior level. Must be a member of the Society of Women Engineers. Minimum 3.0 GPA required.

Academic Fields/Career Goals: Aviation/Aerospace; Engineering/Technology.

Award: Scholarship for use in sophomore, junior, or senior years; not renewable. *Number:* 1. *Amount:* $3000.

Eligibility Requirements: Applicant must be enrolled or expecting to enroll full-time at a four-year institution or university and female. Applicant or parent of applicant must be member of Society of Women Engineers. Applicant must have 3.0 GPA or higher. Available to U.S. citizens.

Application Requirements: Application, references, self-addressed stamped envelope, transcript. *Deadline:* February 1.

Contact: Scholarship Committee
Society of Women Engineers
230 East Ohio Street, Suite 400
Chicago, IL 60611-3265
Phone: 312-596-5223
Fax: 312-596-5252
E-mail: scholarshipapplication@swe.org

NORTHROP GRUMMAN FRESHMAN SCHOLARSHIP

Scholarships awarded to female undergraduate students majoring in computer engineering, computer science, aeronautical/aerospace engineering, electrical engineering, industrial engineering, mechanical engineering, or manufacturing engineering.

Academic Fields/Career Goals: Aviation/Aerospace; Computer Science/Data Processing; Electrical Engineering/Electronics; Engineering/Technology; Materials Science, Engineering, and Metallurgy; Mechanical Engineering.

Award: Scholarship for use in freshman year; not renewable. *Number:* 1. *Amount:* $5000.

Eligibility Requirements: Applicant must be enrolled or expecting to enroll full-time at a four-year institution or university and female. Applicant must have 3.5 GPA or higher. Available to U.S. citizens.

Application Requirements: Application, references, test scores, transcript, ABET acceptance letter. *Deadline:* May 15.

Contact: Scholarship Committee
Society of Women Engineers
230 East Ohio Street, Suite 400
Chicago, IL 60611-3265
Phone: 312-596-5223
Fax: 312-596-5252
E-mail: scholarshipapplication@swe.org

STUDENT PILOT NETWORK

STUDENT PILOT NETWORK-FLIGHT DREAM AWARD

Award is for General Aviation Pilot Flight Training. Open to all persons actively engaged in flight training at a registered SPN flight school. Must be a U.S. or Canadian citizen.

Academic Fields/Career Goals: Aviation/Aerospace.

Award: Grant for use in freshman, sophomore, junior, senior, graduate, or postgraduate years; renewable. *Number:* 1–3. *Amount:* $300–$750.

Eligibility Requirements: Applicant must be enrolled or expecting to enroll full- or part-time at a two-year or four-year or technical institution and must have an interest in aviation. Available to U.S. and Canadian citizens.

Application Requirements: Application, essay. *Deadline:* November 15.

Contact: William Terry, President
Student Pilot Network
1830 Wallace Avenue, Suite 208
St. Charles, IL 60174
Phone: 480-419-7927
E-mail: info@studentpilot.net

UNIVERSITIES SPACE RESEARCH ASSOCIATION http://www.usra.edu

UNIVERSITIES SPACE RESEARCH ASSOCIATION SCHOLARSHIP PROGRAM

• *See page 88*

UNIVERSITY AVIATION ASSOCIATION http://www.uaa.aero

CAE SIMUFLITE CITATION TYPE RATING SCHOLARSHIP

Scholarship open to undergraduate seniors and post-baccalaureate graduates of aviation degree programs up to two years after graduation. Must have a minimum 3.25 GPA.

Academic Fields/Career Goals: Aviation/Aerospace.

Award: Scholarship for use in senior year; not renewable. *Number:* 4. *Amount:* $10,500.

Eligibility Requirements: Applicant must be enrolled or expecting to enroll full-time at a four-year institution or university and must have an interest in aviation. Available to U.S. citizens.

Application Requirements: Application, essay, resume, references, transcript, FAA first class medical certificate. *Deadline:* March 31.

Contact: Dr. David NewMyer, Professor and Department Chair, Aviation Management and Flight
University Aviation Association
1365 Douglas Drive
Carbondale, IL 62901
Phone: 616-453-8898
Fax: 618-453-7286
E-mail: newmyer@siu.edu

JOSEPH FRASCA EXCELLENCE IN AVIATION SCHOLARSHIP

Established to encourage those who demonstrate the highest level of commitment to and achievement in aviation studies. Applicant must be a junior or senior currently enrolled in a UAA member institution. Must be FAA certified/qualified in either aviation maintenance or flight, have membership in at least one aviation organization, and be involved in aviation activities, projects, and events. Minimum 3.0 GPA required.

Academic Fields/Career Goals: Aviation/Aerospace.

Award: Scholarship for use in junior or senior years; not renewable. *Number:* 2. *Amount:* $2000.

Eligibility Requirements: Applicant must be enrolled or expecting to enroll full- or part-time at a four-year institution or university and must have an interest in aviation. Applicant must have 3.0 GPA or higher. Available to U.S. and non-U.S. citizens.

Application Requirements: Application, essay, financial need analysis, references, transcript, FAA certification. *Deadline:* April 10.

Contact: Dr. David A. NewMyer, Department Chair, Aviation Management and Flight
University Aviation Association
1365 Douglas Drive
Carbondale, IL 62901-6623
Phone: 618-453-8898
Fax: 618-453-4850
E-mail: newmyer@siu.edu

PAUL A. WHELAN AVIATION SCHOLARSHIP

One-time award of $2000 given to sophomore, junior, senior or graduate. Must be a U.S. citizen. Must be enrolled in University Aviation Association member institution. 2.5 GPA required. FAA certification, membership in aviation-related association preferred.

University Aviation Association (continued)

Academic Fields/Career Goals: Aviation/Aerospace.

Award: Scholarship for use in sophomore, junior, senior, or graduate years; not renewable. *Number:* 1. *Amount:* $2000.

Eligibility Requirements: Applicant must be enrolled or expecting to enroll full-time at a two-year or four-year institution or university and must have an interest in aviation. Applicant must have 2.5 GPA or higher. Available to U.S. citizens.

Application Requirements: Application, essay, references, transcript, FAA certification. *Deadline:* May 15.

Contact: David A. NewMyer, Department Chair, Aviation Management and Flight
University Aviation Association
Southern Illinois University at Carbondale, College of Applied Sciences and Arts, 1365 Douglas Drive
Carbondale, IL 62901-6623
Phone: 618-453-8898
Fax: 618-453-7268
E-mail: newmyer@siu.edu

VERTICAL FLIGHT FOUNDATION http://www.vtol.org

VERTICAL FLIGHT FOUNDATION SCHOLARSHIP

This award is available for undergraduate, graduate, or doctoral study in aerospace, electrical, or mechanical engineering. Applicants must have an interest in vertical flight technology.

Academic Fields/Career Goals: Aviation/Aerospace; Electrical Engineering/Electronics; Mechanical Engineering.

Award: Scholarship for use in freshman, sophomore, junior, senior, graduate, or postgraduate years; not renewable. *Number:* 10–14. *Amount:* $1000–$4000.

Eligibility Requirements: Applicant must be enrolled or expecting to enroll full-time at a four-year institution or university. Available to U.S. and non-U.S. citizens.

Application Requirements: Application, essay, references, transcript. *Deadline:* February 1.

Contact: Scholarship Coordinator
Vertical Flight Foundation
217 North Washington Street
Alexandria, VA 22314
Phone: 703-684-6777
Fax: 703-739-9279

VIRGINIA AVIATION AND SPACE EDUCATION FORUM http://www.doav.virginia.gov

JOHN R. LILLARD VIRGINIA AIRPORT OPERATORS COUNCIL SCHOLARSHIP PROGRAM

Scholarship of $3000 offered to high school seniors planning a career in the field of aviation. Must be enrolled or accepted into an aviation-related program at an accredited college. Minimum 3.75 unweighted GPA.

Academic Fields/Career Goals: Aviation/Aerospace.

Award: Scholarship for use in freshman year; not renewable. *Number:* 1. *Amount:* $3000.

Eligibility Requirements: Applicant must be high school student; planning to enroll or expecting to enroll full-time at a four-year institution or university and must have an interest in aviation. Available to U.S. and non-U.S. citizens.

Application Requirements: Application, essay, financial need analysis, references, transcript. *Deadline:* February 20.

Contact: Betty Wilson, Program Coordinator
Virginia Aviation and Space Education Forum
c/o Virginia Department of Aviation, 5702 Gulfstream
Richmond, VA 23250-2422
Phone: 804-236-3624
Fax: 804-236-3636
E-mail: betty.wilson@doav.virginia.gov

WILLARD G. PLENTL AVIATION SCHOLARSHIP PROGRAM

Scholarship of $1000 awarded to a high school senior who is planning an aviation career in a non-engineering area.

Academic Fields/Career Goals: Aviation/Aerospace.

Award: Scholarship for use in freshman year; not renewable. *Number:* 1. *Amount:* $1000.

Eligibility Requirements: Applicant must be high school student; planning to enroll or expecting to enroll full-time at a four-year institution or university and must have an interest in aviation. Applicant must have 3.5 GPA or higher. Available to U.S. and non-U.S. citizens.

Application Requirements: Application, essay, financial need analysis, references, transcript. *Deadline:* February 20.

Contact: Betty Wilson, Program Coordinator
Virginia Aviation and Space Education Forum
5702 Gulfstream Road
Richmond, VA 23250-2422
E-mail: betty.wilson@doav.virginia.gov

WOMEN IN AVIATION, INTERNATIONAL http://www.wai.org

AIRBUS LEADERSHIP GRANT

One scholarship to a college sophomore or higher level student who is pursuing a degree in an aviation-related field. Must have a minimum GPA of 3.0 and must exhibit leadership potential. Must be a WAI member.

Academic Fields/Career Goals: Aviation/Aerospace.

Award: Scholarship for use in sophomore, junior, or senior years; not renewable. *Number:* 1. *Amount:* $5000.

Eligibility Requirements: Applicant must be enrolled or expecting to enroll full- or part-time at a four-year institution or university and must have an interest in leadership. Applicant or parent of applicant must be member of Women in Aviation, International. Applicant must have 3.0 GPA or higher. Available to U.S. and non-U.S. citizens.

Application Requirements: Application, essay, resume, references. *Deadline:* December 1.

Contact: Scholarships Committee
Women in Aviation, International
Morningstar Airport, 3647 State Route 503 South
West Alexandria, OH 45381
Phone: 937-839-4647
Fax: 937-839-4645
E-mail: dklingenberger@wai.org

BOEING COMPANY CAREER ENHANCEMENT SCHOLARSHIP

Scholarship available for a woman who wishes to advance her career in aerospace technology or a related management field. Open to full-time or part-time employees currently in the aerospace industry or related field. Students pursuing aviation-related degrees that are at the junior level with a minimum GPA of 2.5 are also eligible.

Academic Fields/Career Goals: Aviation/Aerospace.

Award: Scholarship for use in junior or senior years; not renewable. *Number:* 1. *Amount:* $2500.

Eligibility Requirements: Applicant must be enrolled or expecting to enroll full- or part-time at a four-year institution or university and female. Applicant or parent of applicant must be member of Women in Aviation, International. Applicant must have 2.5 GPA or higher. Available to U.S. and non-U.S. citizens.

Application Requirements: Application, essay, resume, references. *Deadline:* December 1.

Contact: Scholarships Committee
Women in Aviation, International
Morningstar Airport, 3647 State Route 503 South
West Alexandria, OH 45381
Phone: 937-839-4647
Fax: 937-839-4645
E-mail: dklingenberger@wai.org

DASSAULT FALCON JET CORPORATION SCHOLARSHIP

Scholarship of $1000 available for a woman pursuing an undergraduate or graduate degree in an aviation-related field. Applicant must be a U.S. citizen with fluency in English. Must have minimum 3.0 GPA. Must be a member of WAI.

Academic Fields/Career Goals: Aviation/Aerospace.

Award: Scholarship for use in freshman, sophomore, junior, senior, or graduate years; not renewable. *Number:* 1. *Amount:* $1000.

Eligibility Requirements: Applicant must be enrolled or expecting to enroll full- or part-time at a four-year institution or university and female. Applicant or parent of applicant must be member of Women in Aviation, International. Applicant must have 3.0 GPA or higher. Available to U.S. citizens.

Application Requirements: Application, essay, resume, references. *Deadline:* December 1.

Contact: Scholarships Committee
Women in Aviation, International
Morningstar Airport, 3647 State Route 503 South
West Alexandria, OH 45381
Phone: 937-839-4647
Fax: 937-839-4645
E-mail: dklingenberger@wai.org

DELTA AIR LINES AIRCRAFT MAINTENANCE TECHNOLOGY SCHOLARSHIP

Scholarship of $5000 available to a student currently enrolled in an aviation maintenance technology program, or pursuing a degree in aviation maintenance technology. Applicant must be a full-time student with a minimum of two semesters left in the program or degree. Must have minimum GPA of 3.0. Must be a member of WAI. Must be an U.S. citizen or an eligible non-citizen.

Academic Fields/Career Goals: Aviation/Aerospace.

Award: Scholarship for use in freshman, sophomore, or junior years; not renewable. *Number:* 1. *Amount:* $5000.

Eligibility Requirements: Applicant must be enrolled or expecting to enroll full-time at a two-year or four-year or technical institution or university. Applicant or parent of applicant must be member of Women in Aviation, International. Applicant must have 3.0 GPA or higher. Available to U.S. and non-U.S. citizens.

Application Requirements: Application, essay, resume, references. *Deadline:* December 1.

Contact: Scholarships Committee
Women in Aviation, International
Morningstar Airport, 3647 State Route 503 South
West Alexandria, OH 45381
Phone: 937-839-4647
Fax: 937-839-4645
E-mail: dklingenberger@wai.org

DELTA AIR LINES ENGINEERING SCHOLARSHIP

Scholarship to a student currently enrolled in a baccalaureate degree in aerospace/ aeronautical, electrical, or mechanical engineering. Applicants must be full-time students at the junior or senior level with a minimum of two semesters left. Must have minimum GPA of 3.0. Must be a member of WAI. Must be U.S. citizens or eligible non-citizens.

Academic Fields/Career Goals: Aviation/Aerospace; Electrical Engineering/Electronics; Mechanical Engineering.

Award: Scholarship for use in junior or senior years; not renewable. *Number:* 1. *Amount:* $5000.

Eligibility Requirements: Applicant must be enrolled or expecting to enroll full-time at a four-year institution or university. Applicant or parent of applicant must be member of Women in Aviation, International. Applicant must have 3.0 GPA or higher. Available to U.S. and non-U.S. citizens.

Application Requirements: Application, essay, resume, references. *Deadline:* December 1.

Contact: Scholarships Committee
Women in Aviation, International
Morningstar Airport, 3647 State Route 503 South
West Alexandria, OH 45381
Phone: 937-839-4647
Fax: 937-839-4645
E-mail: dklingenberger@wai.org

DELTA AIR LINES MAINTENANCE MANAGEMENT/AVIATION BUSINESS MANAGEMENT SCHOLARSHIP

Scholarship to a student currently enrolled in an associate or baccalaureate degree in aviation maintenance management or aviation business management. Applicant must be a full-time college student, with a minimum of two semesters left. Must have a minimum GPA of 3.0. Must be a member of WAI and be a U.S. citizen or an eligible non-citizen.

Academic Fields/Career Goals: Aviation/Aerospace.

Award: Scholarship for use in freshman, sophomore, or junior years; not renewable. *Number:* 1. *Amount:* $5000.

Eligibility Requirements: Applicant must be enrolled or expecting to enroll full-time at a two-year or four-year institution or university. Applicant or parent of applicant must be member of Women in Aviation, International. Applicant must have 3.0 GPA or higher. Available to U.S. and non-U.S. citizens.

Application Requirements: Application, essay, resume, references. *Deadline:* December 1.

Contact: Scholarships Committee
Women in Aviation, International
Morningstar Airport, 3647 State Route 503 South
West Alexandria, OH 45381
Phone: 937-839-4647
Fax: 937-839-4645
E-mail: dklingenberger@wai.org

GAT WINGS TO THE FUTURE MANAGEMENT SCHOLARSHIP

Scholarship of $2500 to a female student in an aviation management or aviation business program at an accredited college or university. Applicant must be full-time student with a minimum 3.0 GPA. Must be a member of WAI. Refer to Web site for further details: http://www.wai.org.

Academic Fields/Career Goals: Aviation/Aerospace.

Award: Scholarship for use in freshman, sophomore, junior, or senior years; not renewable. *Number:* 1. *Amount:* $2500.

Eligibility Requirements: Applicant must be enrolled or expecting to enroll full-time at a two-year or four-year institution or university and female. Applicant or parent of applicant must be member of Women in Aviation, International. Applicant must have 3.0 GPA or higher. Available to U.S. and non-U.S. citizens.

Application Requirements: Application, essay, resume, references. *Deadline:* December 1.

Contact: Scholarships Committee
Women in Aviation, International
Morningstar Airport, 3647 State Route 503 South
West Alexandria, OH 45381
Phone: 937-839-4647
Fax: 937-839-4645
E-mail: dklingenberger@wai.org

KEEP FLYING SCHOLARSHIP

One scholarship of up to $3000 will be awarded to an individual working on an instrument or multi engine rating, commercial or initial flight instructor certificate. Flight training must be completed within one year. Minimum requirements: private pilot certificate, 100 hours of flight time, and a copy of a current written test (with passing grade) for the certificate/rating sought. Must be a member of WAI.

Academic Fields/Career Goals: Aviation/Aerospace.

Award: Scholarship for use in freshman year; not renewable. *Number:* 1. *Amount:* $3000.

Eligibility Requirements: Applicant must be enrolled or expecting to enroll full- or part-time at a technical institution. Applicant or parent of applicant must be member of Women in Aviation, International. Available to U.S. and non-U.S. citizens.

Application Requirements: Application, essay, resume, references. *Deadline:* December 1.

Contact: Scholarships Committee
Women in Aviation, International
Morningstar Airport, 3647 State Route 503 South
West Alexandria, OH 45381
Phone: 937-839-4647
Fax: 937-839-4645
E-mail: dklingenberger@wai.org

WOMEN IN AVIATION, INTERNATIONAL ACHIEVEMENT AWARDS

Two scholarships available at $750 each for full-time college or university student, and an individual, not necessarily a student, pursuing an aviation-related career goal. Must be a member of WAI.

Academic Fields/Career Goals: Aviation/Aerospace.

Award: Scholarship for use in freshman, sophomore, junior, senior, or graduate years; not renewable. *Number:* 2. *Amount:* $750.

Women in Aviation, International (continued)

Eligibility Requirements: Applicant must be enrolled or expecting to enroll full-time at a two-year or four-year institution or university. Applicant or parent of applicant must be member of Women in Aviation, International. Available to U.S. and non-U.S. citizens.

Application Requirements: Application. *Deadline:* December 1.

Contact: Scholarships Committee
Women in Aviation, International
Morningstar Airport, 3647 State Route 503 South
West Alexandria, OH 45381
Phone: 937-839-4647
Fax: 937-839-4645
E-mail: dklingenberger@wai.org

WOMEN IN AVIATION, INTERNATIONAL MANAGEMENT SCHOLARSHIPS

Scholarship available to a female in an aviation management field who has demonstrated traits of leadership, community spirit, and volunteerism. Must be a member of WAI. Scholarship to be used to attend a leadership-related course or seminar that raises the individual's level of management.

Academic Fields/Career Goals: Aviation/Aerospace.

Award: Scholarship for use in freshman, sophomore, junior, senior, or graduate years; not renewable. *Number:* 1. *Amount:* $1000.

Eligibility Requirements: Applicant must be enrolled or expecting to enroll full- or part-time at a two-year or four-year or technical institution or university; female and must have an interest in leadership. Applicant or parent of applicant must be member of Women in Aviation, International. Available to U.S. and non-U.S. citizens.

Application Requirements: Application. *Deadline:* December 1.

Contact: Scholarships Committee
Women in Aviation, International
Morningstar Airport, 3647 State Route 503 South
West Alexandria, OH 45381
Phone: 937-839-4647
Fax: 937-839-4645
E-mail: dklingenberger@wai.org

WOMEN IN CORPORATE AVIATION CAREER SCHOLARSHIPS

Scholarship to a person who is interested in continued pursuit of a career in any job classification in corporate/business aviation. Applicants should be actively working toward their goal and show financial need. Award can be used toward the NBAA professional development program courses, flight training, dispatcher training, or upgrades in aviation education, and so forth, but cannot include general business course work. Must be a member of WAI.

Academic Fields/Career Goals: Aviation/Aerospace.

Award: Scholarship for use in freshman, sophomore, junior, senior, or graduate years; not renewable. *Number:* 1. *Amount:* $2000.

Eligibility Requirements: Applicant must be enrolled or expecting to enroll full- or part-time at a two-year or four-year or technical institution or university and female. Applicant or parent of applicant must be member of Women in Aviation, International. Available to U.S. and non-U.S. citizens.

Application Requirements: Application, financial need analysis, resume, references. *Deadline:* December 1.

Contact: Scholarships Committee
Women in Aviation, International
Morningstar Airport, 3647 State Route 503 South
West Alexandria, OH 45381
Phone: 937-839-4647
Fax: 937-839-4645
E-mail: dklingenberger@wai.org

WOMEN MILITARY AVIATORS INC. DREAM OF FLIGHT SCHOLARSHIP

An annual $2500 scholarship for tuition or flight training for a FAA private pilot rating or advanced rating at an accredited institution or school. Applicant must be an academic student or a flight student. Must be able to complete training within one year of the award. Must be a member of WAI.

Academic Fields/Career Goals: Aviation/Aerospace.

Award: Scholarship for use in freshman, sophomore, junior, senior, or graduate years; not renewable. *Number:* 1. *Amount:* $2500.

Eligibility Requirements: Applicant must be enrolled or expecting to enroll full- or part-time at a two-year or four-year or technical institution or university. Applicant or parent of applicant must be member of Women in Aviation, International. Available to U.S. and non-U.S. citizens.

Application Requirements: Application, financial need analysis, resume, references. *Deadline:* December 1.

Contact: Scholarships Committee
Women in Aviation, International
Morningstar Airport, 3647 State Route 503 South
West Alexandria, OH 45381
Phone: 937-839-4647
Fax: 937-839-4645
E-mail: dklingenberger@wai.org

WRIGHT CHAPTER, WOMEN IN AVIATION, INTERNATIONAL, ELISHA HALL MEMORIAL SCHOLARSHIP

Scholarship offered to a woman seeking to further the aviation career in flight training, aircraft scheduling or dispatch, aviation management, aviation maintenance, or avionics. Preference will be given to applicants from Cincinnati area. Must be a member of WAI, but does not have to be member of Cincinnati Chapter.

Academic Fields/Career Goals: Aviation/Aerospace.

Award: Scholarship for use in freshman, sophomore, junior, senior, or graduate years; not renewable. *Number:* 1. *Amount:* $1000.

Eligibility Requirements: Applicant must be enrolled or expecting to enroll full- or part-time at a two-year or four-year or technical institution or university and female. Applicant or parent of applicant must be member of Women in Aviation, International. Available to U.S. and non-U.S. citizens.

Application Requirements: Application, essay, resume, references. *Deadline:* December 1.

Contact: Scholarships Committee
Women in Aviation, International
Morningstar Airport, 3647 State Route 503 South
West Alexandria, OH 45381
Phone: 937-839-4647
Fax: 937-839-4645
E-mail: dklingenberger@wai.org

BEHAVIORAL SCIENCE

MENTAL HEALTH ASSOCIATION IN NEW YORK STATE INC. http://www.mhanys.org

EDNA AIMES SCHOLARSHIP

One-time award for individuals studying the prevention and treatment of mental illness and the promotion of mental health. Must be a New York resident attending a New York four-year institution.

Academic Fields/Career Goals: Behavioral Science; Health and Medical Sciences; Neurobiology; Psychology; Public Health; Social Services; Therapy/Rehabilitation.

Award: Scholarship for use in junior, senior, or graduate years; not renewable. *Number:* 2. *Amount:* $2500.

Eligibility Requirements: Applicant must be enrolled or expecting to enroll full-time at a four-year institution or university; resident of New York and studying in New York. Available to U.S. citizens.

Application Requirements: Application, essay, financial need analysis, resume, references, transcript, work experience. *Deadline:* May 2.

Contact: Melissa Ramirez, Project Coordinator
Mental Health Association in New York State Inc.
194 Washington Avenue Suite 415
Albany, NY 12210
E-mail: scholarship@mhanys.org

RESOURCE CENTER

MARIE BLAHA MEDICAL GRANT

• *See page 83*

SOCIETY FOR APPLIED ANTHROPOLOGY http://www.sfaa.net

PETER KONG-MING NEW STUDENT PRIZE

Prize awarded for SFAA's annual student research competition in the applied social and behavioral sciences. The issue of research question should be in the domain of health care or human services (broadly construed). The winner of the competition will receive a cash prize of $1000, a crystal trophy, and travel funds to attend the annual meeting of the SFAA. For more details, see Web site at http://www.sfaa.net.

Academic Fields/Career Goals: Behavioral Science; Health and Medical Sciences; Social Sciences.

Award: Prize for use in freshman, sophomore, junior, senior, graduate, or postgraduate years; not renewable. *Number:* 1–3. *Amount:* up to $1000.

Eligibility Requirements: Applicant must be enrolled or expecting to enroll full- or part-time at a two-year or four-year or technical institution or university. Available to U.S. and non-U.S. citizens.

Application Requirements: Application, applicant must enter a contest, manuscript. *Deadline:* December 31.

Contact: J. May, Executive Director
Society for Applied Anthropology
PO Box 2436
Oklahoma City, OK 73101-2436
Phone: 405-843-5113
Fax: 405-843-8553
E-mail: tom@sfaa.net

SOCIETY FOR THE SCIENTIFIC STUDY OF SEXUALITY http://www.sexscience.org

SOCIETY FOR THE SCIENTIFIC STUDY OF SEXUALITY STUDENT RESEARCH GRANT

Award to support students doing scientific research related to sexuality. Purpose of research can be master's thesis or doctoral dissertation, but this is not a requirement. Must be enrolled in degree-granting program. Deadlines: February 1 and September 1. One-time award of $1000.

Academic Fields/Career Goals: Behavioral Science; Biology; Education; Health and Medical Sciences; Nursing; Psychology; Public Health; Religion/Theology; Social Sciences; Women's Studies.

Award: Grant for use in freshman, sophomore, junior, senior, or graduate years; not renewable. *Number:* 2. *Amount:* $1000.

Eligibility Requirements: Applicant must be enrolled or expecting to enroll full- or part-time at a four-year institution or university. Available to U.S. and non-U.S. citizens.

Application Requirements: Application, autobiography, resume. *Deadline:* varies.

Contact: David Fleming, Executive Director
Society for the Scientific Study of Sexuality
PO Box 416
Allentown, PA 18105
Phone: 610-530-2483
Fax: 610-530-2485
E-mail: thesociety@inetmail.att.net

BIOLOGY

ALBERTA HERITAGE SCHOLARSHIP FUND/ ALBERTA SCHOLARSHIP PROGRAMS http://www.alis.gov.ab.ca

ALBERTA HERITAGE SCHOLARSHIP FUND ABORIGINAL HEALTH CAREERS BURSARY

Award for aboriginal students in Alberta, entering their second or subsequent year of postsecondary education in a health field. Must be Indian, Inuit, or Metis students who have been living in Alberta for the last three years, and be enrolled or planning to enroll in a health field at the postsecondary level. Students are selected on the basis of financial need, previous academic record, program of study, involvement in the aboriginal community, and experience in the healthcare field.

Academic Fields/Career Goals: Biology; Dental Health/Services; Health Administration; Health and Medical Sciences; Nursing; Therapy/Rehabilitation.

Award: Scholarship for use in sophomore, junior, senior, or graduate years; not renewable. *Number:* 20–40.

Eligibility Requirements: Applicant must be Canadian citizen; American Indian/Alaska Native; enrolled or expecting to enroll full-time at a two-year or four-year or technical institution or university and resident of Alberta.

Application Requirements: Application, essay, financial need analysis, references, transcript, proof of Aboriginal status. *Deadline:* May 1.

Contact: Scholarship Committee
Alberta Heritage Scholarship Fund/Alberta Scholarship Programs
9940 106th Street, Fourth Floor, Sterling Place
PO Box 28000, Station Main
Edmonton, AB T5J 4R4
Canada
Phone: 780-427-8640
Fax: 780-427-1288
E-mail: scholarships@gov.ab.ca

AMERICAN INDIAN SCIENCE AND ENGINEERING SOCIETY http://www.aises.org

A.T. ANDERSON MEMORIAL SCHOLARSHIP PROGRAM

• *See page 84*

BURLINGTON NORTHERN SANTA FE FOUNDATION SCHOLARSHIP

• *See page 84*

AMERICAN SOCIETY OF AGRICULTURAL ENGINEERS http://www.asabe.org

WILLIAM J. AND MARIJANE E. ADAMS, JR. SCHOLARSHIP

• *See page 73*

AMERICAN SOCIETY OF ICHTHYOLOGISTS AND HERPETOLOGISTS http://www.asih.org

GAIGE FUND AWARD

Funds are used to provide support to young herpetologists for museum or laboratory study, travel, fieldwork, or any other activity that will effectively enhance their professional careers and their contributions to the science of herpetology. Applicants must be members of ASIH and be enrolled for an advanced degree. Visit Web site at http://www.asih.org for additional information.

Academic Fields/Career Goals: Biology.

Award: Grant for use in freshman, sophomore, junior, senior, or graduate years; not renewable. *Number:* 5–10. *Amount:* $400–$1000.

Eligibility Requirements: Applicant must be enrolled or expecting to enroll full-time at a four-year institution or university. Applicant or parent of applicant must be member of American Society of Ichthyologists and Herpetologists. Available to U.S. and non-U.S. citizens.

Application Requirements: Application, financial need analysis, references. *Deadline:* March 1.

Contact: Maureen Donnelly, Secretary
American Society of Ichthyologists and Herpetologists
11200 SW Eighth Street
Miami, FL 33199
Phone: 305-348-1235
Fax: 305-348-1986
E-mail: asih@fiu.edu

RANEY FUND AWARD

Applications are solicited for grants awarded from the Raney Fund for ichthyology. Funds are used to provide support for young ichthyologists for museums or laboratory study, travel, fieldwork, or any activity that will effectively enhance their professional careers and their contributions to the sciences of ichthyology. Must be a member of ASIH and be enrolled for an advanced degree. Visit Web site at http://www.asih.org for additional information.

Academic Fields/Career Goals: Biology.

American Society of Ichthyologists and Herpetologists (continued)

Award: Grant for use in freshman, sophomore, junior, senior, or graduate years; not renewable. *Number:* 5–10. *Amount:* $400–$1000.

Eligibility Requirements: Applicant must be enrolled or expecting to enroll full-time at a four-year institution or university. Applicant or parent of applicant must be member of American Society of Ichthyologists and Herpetologists. Available to U.S. and non-U.S. citizens.

Application Requirements: Application, financial need analysis, references. *Deadline:* March 1.

Contact: Maureen Donnelly, Secretary
American Society of Ichthyologists and Herpetologists
11200 SW Eighth Street
Miami, FL 33199
Phone: 305-348-1235
Fax: 305-348-1986
E-mail: asih@fiu.edu

ARNOLD AND MABEL BECKMAN FOUNDATION http://www.beckman-foundation.com

BECKMAN SCHOLARS PROGRAM

Scholarship for four-year college undergraduate students in chemistry, biochemistry, and the biological and medical sciences. Provides undergraduate research experiences and comprehensive faculty mentoring.

Academic Fields/Career Goals: Biology; Health and Medical Sciences; Neurobiology; Physical Sciences and Math.

Award: Scholarship for use in freshman, sophomore, junior, or senior years; not renewable. *Number:* varies. *Amount:* $19,300.

Eligibility Requirements: Applicant must be enrolled or expecting to enroll full-time at a four-year institution or university. Available to U.S. citizens.

Application Requirements: Application. *Deadline:* varies.

Contact: Program Administrator
Arnold and Mabel Beckman Foundation
100 Academy
PO Box 13219
Irvine, CA 92617
Phone: 949-721-2222
Fax: 949-721-2225
E-mail: beckmanscholars@beckman-foundation.com

ASSOCIATION FOR IRON AND STEEL TECHNOLOGY http://www.aist.org

ASSOCIATION FOR IRON AND STEEL TECHNOLOGY OHIO VALLEY CHAPTER SCHOLARSHIP

Scholarship of $1000 per year for up to four years provided that applicant continues to meet requirements and reapplies for scholarship. Applicant must be a dependent of Ohio Valley Chapter member, or student or Young Professional member. Must attend or plan to attend an accredited school full-time and pursue a degree in any technological field, including engineering, physics, computer sciences, chemistry or other fields approved by the scholarship committee.

Academic Fields/Career Goals: Biology; Computer Science/Data Processing; Electrical Engineering/Electronics; Engineering/Technology; Engineering-Related Technologies; Materials Science, Engineering, and Metallurgy; Physical Sciences and Math.

Award: Scholarship for use in freshman, sophomore, junior, or senior years; not renewable. *Number:* 1–2. *Amount:* $1000.

Eligibility Requirements: Applicant must be enrolled or expecting to enroll full-time at a four-year institution or university. Applicant or parent of applicant must be member of Association for Iron and Steel Technology. Applicant must have 3.0 GPA or higher. Available to U.S. and non-U.S. citizens.

Application Requirements: Application, essay, resume, references, test scores, transcript. *Deadline:* March 31.

Contact: Jeff McKain, Scholarship Chairman
Association for Iron and Steel Technology
11451 Reading Road
Cincinnati, OH 45241
Phone: 724-776-6040
E-mail: jeff.mckain@xtek.com

ASSOCIATION FOR WOMEN IN SCIENCE EDUCATIONAL FOUNDATION http://www.awis.org/careers/edfoundation.html

ASSOCIATION FOR WOMEN IN SCIENCE COLLEGE SCHOLARSHIP

• *See page 82*

ASSOCIATION OF CALIFORNIA WATER AGENCIES http://www.acwa.com

ASSOCIATION OF CALIFORNIA WATER AGENCIES SCHOLARSHIPS

• *See page 86*

CLAIR A. HILL SCHOLARSHIP

• *See page 86*

ASTRONAUT SCHOLARSHIP FOUNDATION http://www.astronautscholarship.org

ASTRONAUT SCHOLARSHIP FOUNDATION

• *See page 86*

BARRY M. GOLDWATER SCHOLARSHIP AND EXCELLENCE IN EDUCATION FOUNDATION http://www.act.org/goldwater

BARRY M. GOLDWATER SCHOLARSHIP AND EXCELLENCE IN EDUCATION PROGRAM

• *See page 86*

BUSINESS AND PROFESSIONAL WOMEN'S FOUNDATION http://www.bpwfoundation.org

BPW CAREER ADVANCEMENT SCHOLARSHIP PROGRAM FOR WOMEN

Applicants must be female, 25 years old or above, studying in one of the following fields: biological sciences, teacher education certification, engineering, social science, paralegal studies, humanities, business studies, mathematics, computer science, physical sciences. Must NOT be earning a doctoral-level or terminal degree, such as a PhD, MD, DDS, DVM, or JD. Critical financial need and clear career plans must be demonstrated. Send self-addressed double-stamped envelope between January 1 and April 1 for application.

Academic Fields/Career Goals: Biology; Computer Science/Data Processing; Dental Health/Services; Education; Engineering/Technology; Engineering-Related Technologies; Health and Medical Sciences; Humanities; Law/Legal Services; Physical Sciences and Math; Social Sciences.

Award: Scholarship for use in freshman, sophomore, junior, senior, or graduate years; not renewable. *Number:* varies. *Amount:* $1000–$2000.

Eligibility Requirements: Applicant must be age 25 and over; enrolled or expecting to enroll full- or part-time at a two-year or four-year or technical institution or university and female. Available to U.S. citizens.

Application Requirements: Application, essay, financial need analysis, references, self-addressed stamped envelope, transcript. *Deadline:* April 15.

Contact: Director of Programs
Business and Professional Women's Foundation
1900 M Street, NW, Suite 310
Washington, DC 20036
Phone: 202-777-8990
Fax: 202-861-0298
E-mail: sgans@bpwusa.org

CUSHMAN FOUNDATION FOR FORAMINIFERAL RESEARCH http://www.cushmanfoundation.org

LOEBLICH AND TAPPAN STUDENT RESEARCH AWARD

Research award given to both graduate and undergraduates interested in foraminiferal research. The maximum dollar value for the award is $2000.

Academic Fields/Career Goals: Biology; Marine Biology.

Award: Grant for use in freshman, sophomore, junior, senior, or graduate years; not renewable. *Number:* 1–57. *Amount:* up to $2000.

Eligibility Requirements: Applicant must be enrolled or expecting to enroll full- or part-time at a four-year institution or university. Available to U.S. and non-U.S. citizens.

Application Requirements: Resume, references, proposal for research. *Deadline:* September 15.

Contact: Jennifer Jett, Secretary and Treasurer
Cushman Foundation for Foraminiferal Research
MRC 121 Department Paleobiology, PO Box 37012
Washington, DC 20013-7012
E-mail: jettje@si.edu

EAA AVIATION FOUNDATION INC. http://www.eaa.org

PAYZER SCHOLARSHIP

• *See page 116*

ELECTROCHEMICAL SOCIETY INC. http://www.electrochem.org

H.H. DOW MEMORIAL STUDENT ACHIEVEMENT AWARD OF THE INDUSTRIAL ELECTROLYSIS AND ELECTROCHEMICAL ENGINEERING DIVISION OF THE ELECTROCHEMICAL SOCIETY INC.

Award to recognize promising young engineers and scientists in the field of electrochemical engineering and applied electrochemistry. Applicant must be enrolled or accepted for enrollment in a college or university as a graduate student. Must submit description of proposed research project and how it relates to the field of electrochemistry, a letter of recommendation from research supervisor, and biography or resume.

Academic Fields/Career Goals: Biology; Chemical Engineering; Construction Engineering/Management; Earth Science; Electrical Engineering/Electronics; Energy and Power Engineering; Engineering/Technology; Engineering-Related Technologies; Marine/Ocean Engineering; Materials Science, Engineering, and Metallurgy; Mechanical Engineering; Meteorology/Atmospheric Science.

Award: Scholarship for use in freshman, sophomore, junior, senior, or graduate years; not renewable. *Number:* 1. *Amount:* $1000.

Eligibility Requirements: Applicant must be enrolled or expecting to enroll full-time at a four-year institution or university. Available to U.S. and non-U.S. citizens.

Application Requirements: Application, resume, references, transcript, abstract of research project, statement of relationship of the project to the field of electrochemical engineering or applied electrochemistry. *Deadline:* September 15.

Contact: Amir Zaman, Director of Membership and Development
Electrochemical Society Inc.
65 South Main Street, Building D
Pennington, NJ 08534-2839
Phone: 609-737-1902 Ext. 126
Fax: 609-737-2743
E-mail: awards@electrochem.org

STUDENT ACHIEVEMENT AWARDS OF THE INDUSTRIAL ELECTROLYSIS AND ELECTROCHEMICAL ENGINEERING DIVISION OF THE ELECTROCHEMICAL SOCIETY INC.

Award to recognize promising young engineers and scientists in the field of electrochemical engineering. Applicant must be enrolled in a college or university or accepted for enrollment in a graduate program. Application must include outline of research project to be engaged in during the next year and how it relates to the field of electrochemical engineering and a letter of recommendation from research supervisor is required.

Academic Fields/Career Goals: Biology; Chemical Engineering; Construction Engineering/Management; Earth Science; Electrical Engineering/Electronics; Energy and Power Engineering; Engineering/Technology; Engineering-Related Technologies; Marine/Ocean Engineering; Materials Science, Engineering, and Metallurgy; Mechanical Engineering; Meteorology/Atmospheric Science.

Award: Scholarship for use in freshman, sophomore, junior, senior, or graduate years; not renewable. *Number:* 1. *Amount:* $1000.

Eligibility Requirements: Applicant must be enrolled or expecting to enroll full-time at a four-year institution or university. Available to U.S. and non-U.S. citizens.

Application Requirements: Application, resume, references, transcript, description of proposed research project. *Deadline:* September 15.

Contact: Amir Zaman, Director of Membership and Development
Electrochemical Society Inc.
65 South Main Street, Building D
Pennington, NJ 08534-2839
Phone: 609-737-1902 Ext. 126
Fax: 609-737-2743
E-mail: awards@electrochem.org

STUDENT RESEARCH AWARDS OF THE BATTERY DIVISION OF THE ELECTROCHEMICAL SOCIETY INC.

Award to recognize promising young engineers and scientists in the field of electrochemical power sources. Student must be enrolled or must have been accepted for enrollment at a college or university.

Academic Fields/Career Goals: Biology; Chemical Engineering; Construction Engineering/Management; Earth Science; Electrical Engineering/Electronics; Energy and Power Engineering; Engineering/Technology; Engineering-Related Technologies; Marine/Ocean Engineering; Materials Science, Engineering, and Metallurgy; Mechanical Engineering; Meteorology/Atmospheric Science.

Award: Prize for use in freshman, sophomore, junior, senior, or graduate years; not renewable. *Number:* 1. *Amount:* $1000.

Eligibility Requirements: Applicant must be enrolled or expecting to enroll full-time at a four-year institution or university. Available to U.S. and non-U.S. citizens.

Application Requirements: Application, resume, references, transcript, written summary of research accomplished. *Deadline:* March 15.

Contact: Amir Zaman, Director of Membership and Development
Electrochemical Society Inc.
65 South Main Street, Building D
Pennington, NJ 08534-2839
Phone: 609-737-1902 Ext. 126
Fax: 609-737-2743
E-mail: awards@electrochem.org

FEDERATED GARDEN CLUBS OF CONNECTICUT http://www.ctgardenclubs.org

FEDERATED GARDEN CLUBS OF CONNECTICUT INC. SCHOLARSHIPS

One-time award for Connecticut residents entering his or her junior, senior, or graduate year at a Connecticut college or university and pursuing studies in gardening, landscaping, or biology. Minimum 3.0 GPA. PhD candidates are not eligible.

Academic Fields/Career Goals: Biology; Horticulture/Floriculture; Landscape Architecture.

Award: Scholarship for use in junior, senior, or graduate years; not renewable. *Number:* 2–5. *Amount:* $1000–$5000.

Eligibility Requirements: Applicant must be enrolled or expecting to enroll full-time at a four-year institution or university; resident of Connecticut and studying in Connecticut. Applicant must have 3.0 GPA or higher. Available to U.S. citizens.

Application Requirements: Application, autobiography, financial need analysis, references, self-addressed stamped envelope, test scores, transcript. *Deadline:* July 1.

Contact: Barbara Bomblad, Office Manager
Federated Garden Clubs of Connecticut
14 Business Park Drive
PO Box 854
Branford, CT 06405-0854
Phone: 203-488-5528
Fax: 203-488-5528 Ext. 51
E-mail: fgcctoff@hotmail.com

FOUNDATION FOR SCIENCE AND DISABILITY http://www.stemd.org

GRANTS FOR DISABLED STUDENTS IN THE SCIENCES

• *See page 87*

GREATER KANAWHA VALLEY FOUNDATION http://www.tgkvf.org

MATH AND SCIENCE SCHOLARSHIP

Awarded to students pursuing a degree in math, science or engineering at any accredited college or university. For purposes of this Fund, science shall include chemistry, physics, biology and other scientific fields. Scholarships are awarded for one or more years. May apply for two Foundation scholarships but will only be chosen for one. Must be a resident of West Virginia.

Academic Fields/Career Goals: Biology; Engineering/Technology; Mathematics; Physical Sciences and Math.

Award: Scholarship for use in freshman, sophomore, junior, or senior years; renewable. *Number:* 1. *Amount:* $1000.

Eligibility Requirements: Applicant must be enrolled or expecting to enroll full-time at a four-year institution or university and resident of West Virginia. Applicant must have 2.5 GPA or higher. Available to U.S. citizens.

Application Requirements: Application, essay, references, transcript. *Deadline:* January 12.

Contact: Susan Hoover, Scholarship Coordinator
Greater Kanawha Valley Foundation
PO Box 3041
Charleston, WV 25331
Phone: 304-346-3620
Fax: 304-346-3640

HAWAIIAN LODGE, F & AM http://www.glhawaii.org/

HAWAIIAN LODGE SCHOLARSHIPS

• *See page 96*

HISPANIC ENGINEER NATIONAL ACHIEVEMENT AWARDS CORPORATION (HENAAC) http://www.henaac.org

HISPANIC ENGINEER NATIONAL ACHIEVEMENT AWARDS CORPORATION SCHOLARSHIP PROGRAM

• *See page 116*

INDEPENDENT COLLEGE FUND OF MARYLAND (I-FUND) http://www.i-fundinfo.org

HEALTH AND LIFE SCIENCES PROGRAM SCHOLARSHIPS

Program includes $5000 scholarships for students majoring in or demonstrating a career interest in the biological sciences, biochemistry, biophysics, microbiology and related scientific fields including chemistry, computer science, physics and environmental health. Must enroll at an independent college in Maryland.

Academic Fields/Career Goals: Biology; Chemical Engineering; Environmental Health; Health and Medical Sciences.

Award: Scholarship for use in sophomore, junior, or senior years; not renewable. *Number:* 1. *Amount:* $5000.

Eligibility Requirements: Applicant must be enrolled or expecting to enroll full-time at a four-year institution or university and studying in Maryland. Available to U.S. citizens.

Application Requirements: Application. *Deadline:* varies.

Contact: Lori Subotich, Director of Programs and Scholarships
Independent College Fund of Maryland (I-Fund)
3225 Ellerslie Avenue, Suite C160
Baltimore, MD 21218-3519
Phone: 443-997-5700
Fax: 443-997-2740
E-mail: lsubot@jhmi.edu

INDEPENDENT LABORATORIES INSTITUTE SCHOLARSHIP ALLIANCE http://www.acil.org

INDEPENDENT LABORATORIES INSTITUTE SCHOLARSHIP ALLIANCE

Scholarships are given to full-time undergraduate juniors or seniors, or graduate students majoring in the physical sciences: physics, chemistry, geology, engineering, biology or environmental science.

Academic Fields/Career Goals: Biology; Chemical Engineering; Civil Engineering; Earth Science; Electrical Engineering/Electronics; Engineering/Technology; Engineering-Related Technologies; Environmental Science; Fire Sciences; Materials Science, Engineering, and Metallurgy; Mechanical Engineering; Physical Sciences and Math.

Award: Scholarship for use in freshman, sophomore, junior, senior, or graduate years; not renewable. *Number:* 1–2. *Amount:* $1000–$2000.

Eligibility Requirements: Applicant must be enrolled or expecting to enroll full-time at a four-year institution or university. Available to U.S. citizens.

Application Requirements: Application, resume, references, transcript. *Deadline:* April 7.

Contact: Janet Allen, Senior Administrator
Independent Laboratories Institute Scholarship Alliance
1629 K Street, NW, Suite 400
Washington, DC 20006-1633
Phone: 202-887-5872 Ext. 204
Fax: 202-887-0021
E-mail: jallen@acil.org

INNOVATION AND SCIENCE COUNCIL OF BRITISH COLUMBIA http://www.bcinnovationcouncil.com

PAUL AND HELEN TRUSSEL SCIENCE AND TECHNOLOGY SCHOLARSHIP

• *See page 87*

INSTITUTE OF ENVIRONMENTAL SCIENCES AND TECHNOLOGY (IEST) http://www.iest.org

ROBERT N. HANCOCK MEMORIAL SCHOLARSHIP

Annual scholarship for the best original paper written by a student and published in the Journal of the IEST. Topics for papers must be in the fields of science or engineering. The Journal Editorial Board will determine the recipient of the award. For specific scholarship details please visit the Web site at http://www.iest.org.

Academic Fields/Career Goals: Biology; Chemical Engineering; Civil Engineering; Earth Science; Energy and Power Engineering; Engineering/Technology; Environmental Science; Materials Science, Engineering, and Metallurgy; Mechanical Engineering; Natural Sciences; Nuclear Science; Physical Sciences and Math.

Award: Scholarship for use in sophomore, junior, senior, or graduate years; not renewable. *Number:* 1. *Amount:* $500.

Eligibility Requirements: Applicant must be enrolled or expecting to enroll full-time at a two-year or four-year institution or university. Available to U.S. and non-U.S. citizens.

Application Requirements: Application, autobiography, original science or engineering technical paper submitted per procedures on IEST Web site, student ID, proof of full-time enrollment in accredited institution, address of school and contact where scholarship award should be sent. *Deadline:* January 15.

Contact: Kristin Thryselius, Staff Assistant
Institute of Environmental Sciences and Technology (IEST)
Arlington Place One, 2340 South Arlington Heights Road, Suite 100
Arlington Heights, IL 60005-4516
Phone: 847-981-0100 Ext. 21
Fax: 847-981-4130
E-mail: scholarship@iest.org

KENTUCKY NATURAL RESOURCES AND ENVIRONMENTAL PROTECTION CABINET http://www.uky.edu/waterresources

ENVIRONMENTAL PROTECTION SCHOLARSHIPS

Renewable awards for college juniors, seniors, and graduate students for tuition, fees, and room and board at a Kentucky state university. Minimum 3.0 GPA required. Must agree to work full-time for the Kentucky Natural Resources and Environmental Protection Cabinet upon graduation. Interview is required.

Academic Fields/Career Goals: Biology; Earth Science; Environmental Science; Natural Resources; Natural Sciences.

Award: Scholarship for use in junior, senior, or graduate years; renewable. *Number:* 1–4. *Amount:* $15,500–$22,700.

Eligibility Requirements: Applicant must be enrolled or expecting to enroll full-time at a four-year institution or university and studying in Kentucky. Applicant must have 3.0 GPA or higher. Available to U.S. and non-U.S. citizens.

Application Requirements: Application, essay, interview, references, transcript, proof of valid work permit. *Deadline:* February 15.

Contact: James Kipp, Scholarship Program Coordinator
Kentucky Natural Resources and Environmental Protection Cabinet
233 Mining/Mineral Resources Building
Lexington, KY 40506-0107
Phone: 859-257-1299
Fax: 859-323-1049
E-mail: kipp@uky.edu

MORRIS K. UDALL FOUNDATION http://www.udall.gov

MORRIS K. UDALL SCHOLARS

• *See page 76*

NASA IDAHO SPACE GRANT CONSORTIUM http://isgc.uidaho.edu

NASA IDAHO SPACE GRANT CONSORTIUM SCHOLARSHIP PROGRAM

• *See page 87*

NASA/MARYLAND SPACE GRANT CONSORTIUM http://www.mdspacegrant.org

NASA MARYLAND SPACE GRANT CONSORTIUM UNDERGRADUATE SCHOLARSHIPS

• *See page 118*

NASA MONTANA SPACE GRANT CONSORTIUM http://www.spacegrant.montana.edu

MONTANA SPACE GRANT SCHOLARSHIP PROGRAM

• *See page 119*

NASA VERMONT SPACE GRANT CONSORTIUM http://www.cems.uvm.edu/VSGC

VERMONT SPACE GRANT CONSORTIUM SCHOLARSHIP PROGRAM

• *See page 88*

NATIONAL ASSOCIATION FOR THE ADVANCEMENT OF COLORED PEOPLE http://www.naacp.org

LOUIS STOKES SCIENCE AND TECHNOLOGY AWARD

Scholarship for a freshman at a historically Black college or university and a major in one of the following: engineering, physics, chemistry, biology, computer science, or mathematical science. Must be full-time student and have 2.5 minimum GPA. Award requires financial need.

Academic Fields/Career Goals: Biology; Chemical Engineering; Computer Science/Data Processing; Engineering-Related Technologies; Physical Sciences and Math.

Award: Scholarship for use in freshman year; not renewable. *Number:* 1. *Amount:* $2000.

Eligibility Requirements: Applicant must be American Indian/Alaska Native, Asian/Pacific Islander, Black (non-Hispanic), or Hispanic; high school student and planning to enroll or expecting to enroll full-time at a four-year institution or university. Applicant or parent of applicant must be member of National Association for the Advancement of Colored People. Applicant must have 2.5 GPA or higher. Available to U.S. citizens.

Application Requirements: Application, financial need analysis, references, transcript. *Deadline:* April 30.

Contact: Victor Goode, Attorney
National Association for the Advancement of Colored People
4805 Mount Hope Drive
Baltimore, MD 21215-3297
Phone: 410-580-5760
Fax: 410-585-1329
E-mail: info@naacp.org

NATIONAL ASSOCIATION OF WATER COMPANIES-NEW JERSEY CHAPTER

NATIONAL ASSOCIATION OF WATER COMPANIES-NEW JERSEY CHAPTER SCHOLARSHIP

For college students interested in a career in the water utility industry or any related field. Must be U.S. citizen, five-year resident of New Jersey, high school senior or enrolled in a New Jersey college or university. Must maintain a 3.0 GPA.

Academic Fields/Career Goals: Biology; Business/Consumer Services; Communications; Computer Science/Data Processing; Earth Science; Economics; Engineering/Technology; Law/Legal Services; Natural Resources; Physical Sciences and Math; Trade/Technical Specialties.

Award: Scholarship for use in freshman, sophomore, junior, senior, or graduate years; not renewable. *Number:* 1–2. *Amount:* $2500.

Eligibility Requirements: Applicant must be enrolled or expecting to enroll full- or part-time at a two-year or four-year institution or university; resident of New Jersey and studying in New Jersey. Applicant must have 3.0 GPA or higher. Available to U.S. citizens.

Application Requirements: Application, essay, references, transcript. *Deadline:* April 1.

Contact: Gail Brady, Scholarship Committee Chairperson
National Association of Water Companies-New Jersey Chapter
49 Howell Drive
Verona, NJ 07044
Phone: 973-669-5807
Fax: 973-669-8327
E-mail: gbradygbconsult@comcast.net

NATIONAL COUNCIL OF STATE GARDEN CLUBS INC. SCHOLARSHIP http://www.gardenclub.org

NATIONAL COUNCIL OF STATE GARDEN CLUBS INC. SCHOLARSHIP

• *See page 76*

NATIONAL FEDERATION OF THE BLIND http://www.nfb.org

HOWARD BROWN RICKARD SCHOLARSHIP

• *See page 92*

NATIONAL FISH AND WILDLIFE FOUNDATION http://www.nfwf.org

BUDWEISER CONSERVATION SCHOLARSHIP PROGRAM

One-time award supports and promotes innovative research or study that seeks to respond to today's most pressing conservation issues. This competitive scholarship program is designed to respond to many of the most significant challenges in fish, wildlife, and plant conservation in the United States by providing scholarships to eligible graduate and undergraduate students who are poised to make a significant contribution to the field of conservation.

Academic Fields/Career Goals: Biology; Environmental Science; Geography; Natural Resources; Natural Sciences.

Award: Scholarship for use in freshman, sophomore, junior, senior, or graduate years; not renewable. *Number:* 10. *Amount:* up to $10,000.

Eligibility Requirements: Applicant must be age 21 and over; enrolled or expecting to enroll full-time at a four-year institution or university and must have an interest in wildlife conservation/animal rescue. Available to U.S. citizens.

National Fish and Wildlife Foundation (continued)

Application Requirements: Application, essay, references, transcript, title of proposed research, short abstract. *Deadline:* April 16.

Contact: Manager, Project Administration
National Fish and Wildlife Foundation
1120 Connecticut Avenue, NW, Suite 900
Washington, DC 20036
Phone: 202-857-0166
Fax: 202-857-0162

NATIONAL GARDEN CLUBS INC. http://www.gardenclub.org

NATIONAL GARDEN CLUBS INC. SCHOLARSHIP PROGRAM

• *See page 77*

NATIONAL INSTITUTES OF HEALTH http://www.ugsp.nih.gov

NIH UNDERGRADUATE SCHOLARSHIP PROGRAM FOR STUDENTS FROM DISADVANTAGED BACKGROUNDS

Award to student from a disadvantaged background is one who comes from a family with an annual income below a level based on low-income thresholds according to family size, as published by the U.S. Bureau of the Census. Must be enrolled full-time at a postsecondary institution. Visit Web Site: http://www.ugsp.nih.gov for more details.

Academic Fields/Career Goals: Biology; Health and Medical Sciences; Social Sciences.

Award: Scholarship for use in freshman, sophomore, junior, or senior years; renewable. *Number:* 7–10. *Amount:* $20,000.

Eligibility Requirements: Applicant must be enrolled or expecting to enroll full-time at a two-year or four-year institution or university. Applicant must have 3.5 GPA or higher. Available to U.S. citizens.

Application Requirements: Application, essay, financial need analysis, references, transcript. *Deadline:* February 29.

Contact: Executive Assistant
National Institutes of Health
Two Center Drive, Room 2E20, MSC 0230
Bethesda, MD 20892-0230
Phone: 888-352-3001
Fax: 301-480-3123
E-mail: wardron@mail.nih.gov

NATIONAL INVENTORS HALL OF FAME http://www.invent.org

COLLEGIATE INVENTORS COMPETITION FOR UNDERGRADUATE STUDENTS

• *See page 88*

COLLEGIATE INVENTORS COMPETITION-GRAND PRIZE

• *See page 88*

NEW JERSEY DIVISION OF FISH AND WILDLIFE/NJ CHAPTER OF THE WILDLIFE SOCIETY http://www.njfishandwildlife.com/cookhmschol.htm

RUSSELL A. COOKINGHAM SCHOLARSHIP

Scholarship to assist qualified students majoring in wildlife/fisheries or conservation education/communications. Conservation education/communications majors must have at least 15 credits in biological sciences. Applicants must have completed at least one-half of the degree requirements for their major. Must be a permanent resident of New Jersey, attending an institution in-state or out-of-state.

Academic Fields/Career Goals: Biology; Communications; Environmental Science; Natural Resources.

Award: Scholarship for use in junior or senior years; not renewable. *Number:* 1. *Amount:* $1000.

Eligibility Requirements: Applicant must be enrolled or expecting to enroll full-time at a four-year institution or university and resident of New Jersey. Available to U.S. citizens.

Application Requirements: Resume, references, transcript, cover letter. *Deadline:* April 1.

Contact: Jim Sciascia, Information and Education Bureau Chief
New Jersey Division of Fish and Wildlife/NJ Chapter of the Wildlife Society
605 Pequest Road
Oxford, NJ 07863
Phone: 609-984-6295
E-mail: jim.sciascia@dep.state.nj.us

OREGON STUDENT ASSISTANCE COMMISSION http://www.osac.state.or.us

OREGON FOUNDATION FOR BLACKTAIL DEER OUTDOOR AND WILDLIFE SCHOLARSHIP

Award for students majoring in forestry, biology, wildlife science or related fields indicating a serious commitment to careers in wildlife management. Must submit essay on, "Challenges of Wildlife Management in Coming Ten Years." Submit copy of previous year's hunting license. Must be an Oregon resident attending an Oregon institution.

Academic Fields/Career Goals: Biology; Natural Resources; Natural Sciences.

Award: Scholarship for use in freshman, sophomore, junior, or senior years; renewable. *Number:* varies. *Amount:* varies.

Eligibility Requirements: Applicant must be enrolled or expecting to enroll full-time at a four-year institution; resident of Oregon and studying in Oregon. Available to U.S. citizens.

Application Requirements: Application, essay, financial need analysis, references, transcript, hunting license, activities chart. *Deadline:* March 1.

Contact: Director of Grant Programs
Oregon Student Assistance Commission
1500 Valley River Drive, Suite 100
Eugene, OR 97401-7020
Phone: 800-452-8807 Ext. 7395

PEARSON BENJAMIN CUMMINGS http://www.aw-bc.com

BENJAMIN CUMMINGS ALLIED HEALTH STUDENT SCHOLARSHIP

Five scholarships of $1000 awarded to students currently enrolled in a course in anatomy & physiology or microbiology, or to any student who has successfully completed an anatomy & physiology or microbiology course in the past two years.

Academic Fields/Career Goals: Biology; Health and Medical Sciences.

Award: Scholarship for use in freshman, sophomore, junior, senior, or graduate years; not renewable. *Number:* 5. *Amount:* $1000.

Eligibility Requirements: Applicant must be enrolled or expecting to enroll full-time at a four-year institution or university. Available to U.S. citizens.

Application Requirements: Application, essay. *Deadline:* November 1.

Contact: Scholarship Committee
Pearson Benjamin Cummings
1301 Sansome Street
San Francisco, CA 94111
Phone: 415-402-2500
Fax: 415-402-2590

BENJAMIN CUMMINGS BIOLOGY PRIZE SCHOLARSHIP

Four scholarships of $1000 awarded to students enrolled in a full-time course of study and must have taken the general biology course.

Academic Fields/Career Goals: Biology.

Award: Scholarship for use in freshman, sophomore, junior, or senior years; not renewable. *Number:* 4. *Amount:* $1000.

Eligibility Requirements: Applicant must be enrolled or expecting to enroll full-time at a four-year institution or university. Available to U.S. citizens.

Application Requirements: Application. *Deadline:* November 1.

Contact: Scholarship Committee
Pearson Benjamin Cummings
1301 Sansome Street
San Francisco, CA 94111
Phone: 415-402-2500
Fax: 415-402-2590

PENNSYLVANIA ASSOCIATION OF CONSERVATION DISTRICTS AUXILIARY http://www.pacd.org

PACD AUXILIARY SCHOLARSHIPS

• *See page 78*

ROBERT H. MOLLOHAN FAMILY CHARITABLE FOUNDATION INC. http://www.mollohanfoundation.org

HIGH TECHNOLOGY SCHOLARS PROGRAM

Scholarship for West Virginia students pursuing a technology-related career and residing in one of the following counties: Barbour, Brooke, Calhoun, Doddridge, Gilmer, Grant, Hancock, Harrison, Marion, Marshall, Mineral, Monongalia, Ohio, Pleasants, Preston, Ritchie, Taylor, Tucker, Tyler, Wetzel, Wood. Scholarship recipients become eligible for a paid internship with a West Virginia business. Students may also apply for debt-forgiveness loans up to $2000 per year.

Academic Fields/Career Goals: Biology; Chemical Engineering; Computer Science/Data Processing; Electrical Engineering/Electronics; Energy and Power Engineering; Engineering/Technology; Engineering-Related Technologies; Mechanical Engineering; Physical Sciences and Math.

Award: Scholarship for use in freshman year; not renewable. *Number:* 1–60. *Amount:* $500–$2000.

Eligibility Requirements: Applicant must be high school student; planning to enroll or expecting to enroll full-time at a four-year institution or university and resident of West Virginia. Applicant must have 3.0 GPA or higher. Available to U.S. citizens.

Application Requirements: Application, essay, resume, references, test scores, transcript. *Deadline:* February 6.

Contact: Beth Michalec, Program Manager
Robert H. Mollohan Family Charitable Foundation Inc.
1000 Technology Drive, Suite 2000
Fairmont, WV 26554
Phone: 304-333-2251
Fax: 304-333-3900
E-mail: bmichalec@wvhtf.org

SAN DIEGO FOUNDATION http://www.sdfoundation.org

BIOCOM SCHOLARSHIP

Scholarship open to graduating high school seniors with a minimum 3.5 GPA, who plan to attend an accredited two-year college or four-year university in the United States. Applicants must demonstrate a likelihood of achieving academic success with primary emphasis in biology, chemistry, physical and computational bio-sciences or biomedical engineering. Scholarship may be renewable for four years provided the recipient maintains a positive academic and citizenship record.

Academic Fields/Career Goals: Biology; Physical Sciences and Math; Science, Technology, and Society.

Award: Scholarship for use in freshman year; renewable. *Number:* 5. *Amount:* $1500.

Eligibility Requirements: Applicant must be high school student; planning to enroll or expecting to enroll full-time at a two-year or four-year institution or university and resident of California. Applicant must have 3.5 GPA or higher. Available to U.S. citizens.

Application Requirements: Application, references, transcript, personal statement, copy of tax return. *Deadline:* January 26.

Contact: Shryl Helvie, Scholarship Coordinator
San Diego Foundation
2508 Historic Decatur Road, Suite 200
San Diego, CA 92106
Phone: 619-814-1307
Fax: 619-239-1710
E-mail: shryl@sdfoundation.org

SIGMA XI, THE SCIENTIFIC RESEARCH SOCIETY http://www.sigmaxi.org

SIGMA XI GRANTS-IN-AID OF RESEARCH

• *See page 78*

SOCIETY FOR MARINE MAMMALOGY http://www.marinemammalogy.org

FREDERIC FAIRFIELD MEMORIAL FUND AWARD

The purpose of the award is to recognize and support young scientists (students) who have developed or applied pioneering techniques or research tools for studying marine mammals. All students who indicate a wish to be considered for the award on the Biennial Conference abstract submission form will be considered. Award will be given to a student at each Biennial Conference on the Biology of Marine Mammals.

Academic Fields/Career Goals: Biology; Marine Biology.

Award: Scholarship for use in freshman, sophomore, junior, senior, or graduate years; not renewable. *Number:* varies. *Amount:* varies.

Eligibility Requirements: Applicant must be enrolled or expecting to enroll full-time at a four-year institution or university. Available to U.S. citizens.

Application Requirements: Application. *Deadline:* varies.

Contact: Carol Fairfield, Awards and Scholarship Chair
Society for Marine Mammalogy
49 Eastman Shore Drive, South
Laconia, NH 03246
Phone: 603-731-1333
Fax: 603-527-1868
E-mail: carol.fairfield@noaa.gov

SOCIETY FOR THE SCIENTIFIC STUDY OF SEXUALITY http://www.sexscience.org

SOCIETY FOR THE SCIENTIFIC STUDY OF SEXUALITY STUDENT RESEARCH GRANT

• *See page 129*

SOIL AND WATER CONSERVATION SOCIETY-NEW JERSEY CHAPTER http://www.geocities.com/njswcs

EDWARD R. HALL SCHOLARSHIP

• *See page 71*

TKE EDUCATIONAL FOUNDATION http://www.tke.org

CARROL C. HALL MEMORIAL SCHOLARSHIP

• *See page 88*

TIMOTHY L. TASCHWER SCHOLARSHIP

Scholarship available to an undergraduate member of Tau Kappa Epsilon. Must be a full-time student with at least sophomore year standing and a minimum GPA of 2.75. Applicant must be pursuing a degree in natural resources, earth sciences or related subjects and have a record of active TKE chapter leadership involvement. Preference shall be given to qualified graduates of the TKE Leadership Academy.

Academic Fields/Career Goals: Biology; Earth Science; Environmental Science; Natural Resources.

Award: Scholarship for use in sophomore, junior, or senior years; not renewable. *Number:* varies. *Amount:* $500.

Eligibility Requirements: Applicant must be enrolled or expecting to enroll full-time at a four-year institution or university; male and must have an interest in leadership. Applicant or parent of applicant must be member of Tau Kappa Epsilon. Available to U.S. and non-U.S. citizens.

Application Requirements: Application, photo, transcript, narrative summary of how TKE membership has benefited applicant. *Deadline:* February 29.

Contact: Scholarship Committee
TKE Educational Foundation
8645 Founders Road
Indianapolis, IN 46268-1336
Phone: 317-872-6533
Fax: 317-875-8353
E-mail: tef@tke.org

UNITED NEGRO COLLEGE FUND http://www.uncf.org

CARGILL SCHOLARSHIP PROGRAM

• *See page 65*

HEINZ ENVIRONMENTAL FELLOWS PROGRAM

Scholarships for UNCF institutions undergraduate sophomore from Pennsylvania majoring in science, biochemistry, biology, physics. A paid summer internship is included in this award. Minimum 2.5 GPA required. Prospective applicants should complete the Student Profile found at Web site: http://www.uncf.org.

Academic Fields/Career Goals: Biology; Physical Sciences and Math; Science, Technology, and Society.

Award: Scholarship for use in sophomore year; not renewable. *Number:* 1. *Amount:* $7500.

Eligibility Requirements: Applicant must be Black (non-Hispanic); enrolled or expecting to enroll full- or part-time at a four-year institution or university and resident of Pennsylvania. Applicant must have 2.5 GPA or higher. Available to U.S. citizens.

Application Requirements: Application, financial need analysis. *Deadline:* continuous.

Contact: Director, Program Services
United Negro College Fund
8260 Willow Oaks Corporate Drive
PO Box 10444
Fairfax, VA 22031-8044
Phone: 800-331-2244
E-mail: rebecca.bennett@uncf.org

MEDTRONIC FOUNDATION SCHOLARSHIP

Scholarship for undergraduate sophomores and juniors majoring in engineering or science related subjects and attending a UNCF member college or university. A paid summer internship is included in the award. Minimum 3.3 GPA required. Prospective applicants should complete the Student Profile found at Web site: http://www.uncf.org.

Academic Fields/Career Goals: Biology; Chemical Engineering; Civil Engineering; Electrical Engineering/Electronics; Engineering/Technology; Engineering-Related Technologies; Health and Medical Sciences; Mechanical Engineering; Physical Sciences and Math.

Award: Scholarship for use in sophomore or junior years; not renewable. *Number:* varies. *Amount:* $5000.

Eligibility Requirements: Applicant must be Black (non-Hispanic) and enrolled or expecting to enroll full- or part-time at a four-year institution or university. Available to U.S. citizens.

Application Requirements: Application, autobiography, financial need analysis, resume, references. *Deadline:* April 15.

Contact: Director, Program Services
United Negro College Fund
8260 Willow Oaks Corporate Drive
PO Box 10444
Fairfax, VA 22031-8044
Phone: 800-331-2244
E-mail: rebecca.bennett@uncf.org

VIRGINIA BUSINESS AND PROFESSIONAL WOMEN'S FOUNDATION http://www.vabpwfoundation.org

WOMEN IN SCIENCE AND TECHNOLOGY SCHOLARSHIP

One-time award offered to women completing a bachelor's, master's or doctoral degree within two years who are majoring in actuarial science, biology, bio-engineering, chemistry, computer science, dentistry, engineering, mathematics, medicine, physics or similar field. The award may be used for tuition, fees, books, transportation, living expenses, or dependent care. Must be a Virginia resident studying in Virginia.

Academic Fields/Career Goals: Biology; Computer Science/Data Processing; Dental Health/Services; Engineering/Technology; Health and Medical Sciences; Physical Sciences and Math; Science, Technology, and Society.

Award: Scholarship for use in junior, senior, graduate, or postgraduate years; not renewable. *Number:* 1–5. *Amount:* $100–$1000.

Eligibility Requirements: Applicant must be age 18 and over; enrolled or expecting to enroll full- or part-time at a four-year institution or university; female; resident of Virginia and studying in Virginia. Available to U.S. citizens.

Application Requirements: Application, essay, financial need analysis, references, transcript. *Deadline:* April 1.

Contact: Julia Kroos, Chair and Trustee
Virginia Business and Professional Women's Foundation
PO Box 4842
McLean, VA 22103-4842
Phone: 703-450-5108
E-mail: info@vabpwfoundation.org

WATER ENVIRONMENT FEDERATION http://www.wef.org

CANHAM GRADUATE STUDIES SCHOLARSHIPS

Applicants must be post-baccalaureate students in a water environment program who are members of Water Environment Federation. Recipients of scholarship are expected to make a commitment to work in the environmental field for two years following degree completion.

Academic Fields/Career Goals: Biology; Earth Science; Natural Resources; Nuclear Science; Science, Technology, and Society.

Award: Scholarship for use in freshman, sophomore, junior, or senior years; not renewable. *Number:* 1. *Amount:* up to $25,000.

Eligibility Requirements: Applicant must be enrolled or expecting to enroll full-time at a four-year institution or university. Applicant or parent of applicant must be member of Water Environment Federation. Available to U.S. and non-U.S. citizens.

Application Requirements: Application, essay, resume, references, transcript, statement of objectives. *Deadline:* April 1.

Contact: Program Manager
Water Environment Federation
601 Wythe Street
Alexandria, VA 22314

WILSON ORNITHOLOGICAL SOCIETY http://www.wilsonsociety.org

GEORGE A. HALL/HAROLD F. MAYFIELD AWARD

• *See page 83*

PAUL A. STEWART AWARDS

• *See page 83*

BUSINESS/CONSUMER SERVICES

ADELANTE! U.S. EDUCATION LEADERSHIP FUND http://www.adelantefund.org

ADELANTE FUND MILLER NATIONAL

• *See page 47*

ALL STUDENT LOAN CORPORATION http://www.allstudentloan.org

ALLSTUDENTLOAN.ORG COLLEGE SCHOLARSHIP PROGRAM

Scholarship for graduating high school seniors. Must be an active member of an eligible vocational student organization: Future Business Leaders of America-Phi Beta Lambda, Business Professionals of America or DECA.

Academic Fields/Career Goals: Business/Consumer Services.

Award: Scholarship for use in freshman year; not renewable. *Number:* 4. *Amount:* $500.

Eligibility Requirements: Applicant must be high school student and planning to enroll or expecting to enroll full-time at a two-year or four-year or technical institution or university. Available to U.S. citizens.

Application Requirements: Application, essay, financial need analysis, FAFSA. *Deadline:* June 1.

Contact: Amy Tien-Gordon, Vice President and Chief Student Lending Officer
ALL Student Loan Corporation
6701 Center Drive West, Suite 500
Los Angeles, CA 90045-1547
Phone: 888-271-9721 Ext. 8817
Fax: 310-979-4714
E-mail: atien@allstudentloan.org

AMERICAN CONGRESS ON SURVEYING AND MAPPING http://www.acsm.net

TRI-STATE SURVEYING AND PHOTOGRAMMETRY KRIS M. KUNZE MEMORIAL SCHOLARSHIP

One-time award of $1000 for students pursuing college-level courses in business administration or business management. Candidates, in order of priority, include professional land surveyors and certified photogrammetrists, land survey interns and students enrolled in a two- or four-year program in surveying and mapping. Must be ACSM member.

Academic Fields/Career Goals: Business/Consumer Services; Surveying; Surveying Technology, Cartography, or Geographic Information Science.

Award: Scholarship for use in freshman, sophomore, junior, or senior years; not renewable. *Number:* 1. *Amount:* $1000.

Eligibility Requirements: Applicant must be enrolled or expecting to enroll full- or part-time at a two-year or four-year institution or university. Applicant or parent of applicant must be member of American Congress on Surveying and Mapping. Available to U.S. citizens.

Application Requirements: Application, essay, references, transcript, membership proof. *Deadline:* October 1.

Contact: Dawn James, NSPS Executive Administrator
American Congress on Surveying and Mapping
6 Montgomery Village Avenue, Suite 403
Gaithersburg, MD 20879
Phone: 240-632-9716 Ext. 113
Fax: 240-632-1321
E-mail: dawn.james@acsm.net

AMERICAN INDIAN SCIENCE AND ENGINEERING SOCIETY http://www.aises.org

A.T. ANDERSON MEMORIAL SCHOLARSHIP PROGRAM

• *See page 84*

BURLINGTON NORTHERN SANTA FE FOUNDATION SCHOLARSHIP

• *See page 84*

AMERICAN PUBLIC TRANSPORTATION FOUNDATION http://www.apta.com

DAN REICHARD JR. SCHOLARSHIP

Scholarship for study towards a career in the business administration/ management area of the transit industry. Must be sponsored by APTA member organization and complete internship with APTA member organization. Minimum GPA of 3.0 required.

Academic Fields/Career Goals: Business/Consumer Services; Transportation.

Award: Scholarship for use in sophomore, junior, senior, or graduate years; renewable. *Number:* 1. *Amount:* $2500.

Eligibility Requirements: Applicant must be enrolled or expecting to enroll full-time at a two-year or four-year institution or university. Applicant must have 3.0 GPA or higher. Available to U.S. and Canadian citizens.

Application Requirements: Application, essay, financial need analysis, references, transcript, verification of enrollment for the current semester, copy of fee schedule from the college/university. *Deadline:* June 16.

Contact: Pamela Boswell, Vice President of Program Management
American Public Transportation Foundation
1666 K Street, NW
Washington, DC 20006-1215
Phone: 202-496-4803
Fax: 202-496-2323
E-mail: pboswell@apta.com

AMERICAN WELDING SOCIETY http://www.aws.org

JAMES A. TURNER, JR. MEMORIAL SCHOLARSHIP

Award for a full-time student pursuing minimum four-year bachelor's degree in business that will lead to a management career in welding store operations or a welding distributorship. Applicant must be working in this field at least 10 hours per week. Submit verification of employment, a copy of proposed curriculum, and acceptance letter.

Academic Fields/Career Goals: Business/Consumer Services.

Award: Scholarship for use in freshman, sophomore, junior, or senior years; renewable. *Number:* 1. *Amount:* $3500.

Eligibility Requirements: Applicant must be age 18 and over and enrolled or expecting to enroll full-time at a four-year institution or university. Available to U.S. citizens.

Application Requirements: Application, autobiography, financial need analysis, references, transcript. *Deadline:* January 15.

Contact: Vicki Pinsky, Manager, Foundation
American Welding Society
550 Le Jeune Road, NW
Miami, FL 33126
Phone: 800-443-9353 Ext. 212
Fax: 305-443-7559
E-mail: vpinsky@aws.org

AMERICAN WHOLESALE MARKETERS ASSOCIATION http://www.awmanet.org

RAY FOLEY MEMORIAL YOUTH EDUCATION FOUNDATION SCHOLARSHIP

Scholarship program annually offers two $5000 scholarships to deserving students. Awards are based on academic merit and a career interest in the candy/tobacco/ convenience-products wholesale industry. Must be employed by an AWMA wholesaler distributor member or be an immediate family member. Must be enrolled full-time in an undergraduate or graduate program. For details visit Web Site: http://www.awmanet.org/

Academic Fields/Career Goals: Business/Consumer Services.

Award: Scholarship for use in freshman, sophomore, junior, senior, or graduate years; not renewable. *Number:* 2. *Amount:* $5000.

Eligibility Requirements: Applicant must be enrolled or expecting to enroll full-time at a four-year institution or university. Available to U.S. citizens.

Application Requirements: Application, essay, references. *Deadline:* May 21.

Contact: Kathy Trost, Manager of Education
American Wholesale Marketers Association
2750 Prosperity Avenue, Suite 530
Fairfax, VA 22031
Phone: 800-482-2962 Ext. 648
Fax: 703-573-5738
E-mail: kathyt@awmanet.org

APICS EDUCATIONAL AND RESEARCH FOUNDATION INC. http://www.apics.org

DONALD W. FOGARTY INTERNATIONAL STUDENT PAPER COMPETITION

Annual competition on topics pertaining to resource management only. Must be original work of one or more authors. May submit one paper only. Must be in English. Open to full-time and part-time undergraduate. High school students are ineligible.

Academic Fields/Career Goals: Business/Consumer Services; Natural Resources.

APICS Educational and Research Foundation Inc. (continued)

Award: Prize for use in freshman, sophomore, junior, or senior years; not renewable. *Number:* 58. *Amount:* $100–$1000.

Eligibility Requirements: Applicant must be enrolled or expecting to enroll full- or part-time at a four-year institution or university. Available to U.S. and non-U.S. citizens.

Application Requirements: Application, applicant must enter a contest, essay, self-addressed stamped envelope. *Deadline:* May 15.

Contact: Bob Collins, Executive Director
APICS Educational and Research Foundation Inc.
5301 Shawnee Road
Alexandria, VA 22312-2317
E-mail: cjames938@aol.com

APOGEE SEARCH http://www.apogee-search.com

FIRST ANNUAL APOGEE SEARCH SCHOLARSHIP PROGRAM

One undergraduate or graduate student will be awarded a $1000 scholarship in recognition of his or her best social media campaign. This opportunity is open to all graduate and undergraduate students enrolled in either a two or four-year college or university in the United States.

Academic Fields/Career Goals: Business/Consumer Services; Communications.

Award: Scholarship for use in freshman, sophomore, junior, senior, or graduate years; not renewable. *Number:* 1. *Amount:* $1000.

Eligibility Requirements: Applicant must be age 18 and over and enrolled or expecting to enroll full-time at a two-year or four-year or technical institution or university. Available to U.S. citizens.

Application Requirements: Application, applicant must enter a contest, essay, resume, product outline. *Deadline:* June 1.

Contact: Mr. Chris Osborn, Copywriter
Apogee Search
9430 Research Boulevard, Echelon IV, Suite 200
Austin, TX 78759
Phone: 512-583-4200 Ext. 656
Fax: 512-583-4205
E-mail: scholarship@apogee-search.com

ARRL FOUNDATION INC. http://www.arrl.org

WILLIAM R. GOLDFARB MEMORIAL SCHOLARSHIP

Award for baccalaureate study in business, computers, medical or nursing, engineering, or sciences. Must be a licensed amateur radio operator. Must demonstrate financial need.

Academic Fields/Career Goals: Business/Consumer Services; Computer Science/Data Processing; Engineering/Technology; Health and Medical Sciences; Natural Sciences; Nursing; Physical Sciences and Math.

Award: Scholarship for use in freshman, sophomore, junior, or senior years; not renewable. *Number:* 1. *Amount:* $10,000.

Eligibility Requirements: Applicant must be enrolled or expecting to enroll full-time at a four-year institution or university and must have an interest in amateur radio. Available to U.S. citizens.

Application Requirements: Application, financial need analysis, transcript, FAFSA, SAR. *Deadline:* February 1.

Contact: Mary M. Hobart, Secretary
ARRL Foundation Inc.
225 Main Street
Newington, CT 06111-1494
Phone: 860-594-0397
Fax: 860-594-0259
E-mail: k1mmh@arrl.org

ASSOCIATION FOR FOOD AND DRUG OFFICIALS http://www.afdo.org

ASSOCIATION FOR FOOD AND DRUG OFFICIALS SCHOLARSHIP FUND

A $1500 scholarship for students in their third or fourth year of college/university who have demonstrated a desire for a career in research, regulatory work, quality control, or teaching in an area related to some aspect of food, drugs, or consumer products safety. Minimum 3.0 GPA required in first two years of undergraduate study. For further information visit Web site: http://www.afdo.org.

Academic Fields/Career Goals: Business/Consumer Services; Food Science/Nutrition.

Award: Scholarship for use in junior or senior years; not renewable. *Number:* 2. *Amount:* $1500.

Eligibility Requirements: Applicant must be enrolled or expecting to enroll full-time at a four-year institution or university. Applicant must have 3.0 GPA or higher. Available to U.S. and non-U.S. citizens.

Application Requirements: Application, essay, references, transcript. *Deadline:* February 1.

Contact: Leigh Stamdaugh, Administrative/Special Projects Assistant
Association for Food and Drug Officials
2550 Kingston Road, Suite 311
York, PA 17402
Phone: 717-757-2888
Fax: 717-755-8089
E-mail: afdo@afdo.org

ASSOCIATION OF LATINO PROFESSIONALS IN FINANCE AND ACCOUNTING http://www.alpfa.org

HSF-ALPFA SCHOLARSHIPS

• *See page 48*

BALTIMORE CHAPTER OF THE AMERICAN MARKETING ASSOCIATION http://www.amabaltimore.org

UNDERGRADUATE MARKETING EDUCATION MERIT SCHOLARSHIPS

Scholarship of $2500 awarded for first place and two $500 runner-up awards for full-time students in marketing. Must be attending a 4-year college or university in Maryland with credits equivalent to the status of a junior or senior as of September.

Academic Fields/Career Goals: Business/Consumer Services; Music.

Award: Scholarship for use in sophomore or junior years; not renewable. *Number:* 3. *Amount:* $500–$2500.

Eligibility Requirements: Applicant must be enrolled or expecting to enroll full-time at a four-year institution or university. Applicant must have 3.0 GPA or higher. Available to U.S. and non-U.S. citizens.

Application Requirements: Application, test scores. *Deadline:* February 16.

Contact: Marisa O'Brien, Scholarship Committee
Baltimore Chapter of the American Marketing Association
22 West Road, Suite 301
Towson, MD 21204
Phone: 410-467-2529
E-mail: scholarship@amabaltimore.org

BETA GAMMA SIGMA http://www.betagammasigma.org

BETA GAMMA SIGMA SCHOLARSHIP PROGRAM

Awards are available to junior or senior undergraduate and master's-level student members enrolled in a business administration program at a college or university accredited by AACSB International. Applicant should be a member of BGS.

Academic Fields/Career Goals: Business/Consumer Services.

Award: Scholarship for use in junior, senior, or graduate years; not renewable. *Number:* varies. *Amount:* $1000.

Eligibility Requirements: Applicant must be enrolled or expecting to enroll full- or part-time at a four-year institution or university. Available to U.S. citizens.

Application Requirements: Application. *Deadline:* varies.

Contact: Vicki Klutts, Associate Executive Director
Beta Gamma Sigma
125 Weldon Parkway
Maryland Heights, MO 63043
Phone: 314-432-5650
Fax: 314-432-7083
E-mail: vklutts@betagammasigma.org

CALIFORNIA SOCIETY OF CERTIFIED PUBLIC ACCOUNTANTS http://www.aicpa.org

AICPA/ACCOUNTEMPS STUDENT SCHOLARSHIP

• *See page 48*

CATCHING THE DREAM http://www.catchingthedream.org

MATH, ENGINEERING, SCIENCE, BUSINESS, EDUCATION, COMPUTERS SCHOLARSHIPS

Renewable scholarships for Native American students planning to study math, engineering, science, business, education, and computers, or presently studying in these fields. Study of social science, humanities and liberal arts also funded. Scholarships are awarded on merit and on the basis of likelihood of recipient improving the lives of Native American people. Scholarships are available nationwide.

Academic Fields/Career Goals: Business/Consumer Services; Computer Science/Data Processing; Education; Engineering/Technology; Humanities; Physical Sciences and Math; Science, Technology, and Society; Social Sciences.

Award: Scholarship for use in freshman, sophomore, junior, senior, graduate, or postgraduate years; renewable. *Number:* 180. *Amount:* $500–$5000.

Eligibility Requirements: Applicant must be American Indian/Alaska Native and enrolled or expecting to enroll full-time at a two-year or four-year institution or university. Applicant must have 3.0 GPA or higher. Available to U.S. citizens.

Application Requirements: Application, essay, financial need analysis, photo, references, test scores, transcript, certificate of Indian blood. *Deadline:* varies.

Contact: Mary Frost, Recruiter
Catching the Dream
8200 Mountain Road, NE, Suite 203
Albuquerque, NM 87110
Phone: 505-262-2351
Fax: 505-262-0534
E-mail: nscholarsh@aol.com

NATIVE AMERICAN LEADERSHIP IN EDUCATION (NALE)

Renewable scholarships available for Native American and Alaska Native students. Must be at least one-quarter Native American from a federally recognized, state recognized, or terminated tribe. Must be U.S. citizen. Must demonstrate high academic achievement, depth of character, leadership, seriousness of purpose, and service orientation.

Academic Fields/Career Goals: Business/Consumer Services; Education; Humanities; Physical Sciences and Math; Science, Technology, and Society.

Award: Scholarship for use in freshman, sophomore, junior, senior, graduate, or postgraduate years; renewable. *Number:* up to 30. *Amount:* $500–$5000.

Eligibility Requirements: Applicant must be American Indian/Alaska Native and enrolled or expecting to enroll full-time at a four-year institution or university. Applicant must have 3.0 GPA or higher. Available to U.S. citizens.

Application Requirements: Application, essay, financial need analysis, photo, references, test scores, transcript, certificate of Indian blood. *Deadline:* varies.

Contact: Mary Frost, Recruiter
Catching the Dream
8200 Mountain Road, NE, Suite 203
Albuquerque, NM 87110
Phone: 505-262-2351
Fax: 505-262-0534
E-mail: nscholarsh@aol.com

TRIBAL BUSINESS MANAGEMENT PROGRAM (TBM)

• *See page 49*

CENTRAL INTELLIGENCE AGENCY http://www.cia.gov

CENTRAL INTELLIGENCE AGENCY UNDERGRADUATE SCHOLARSHIP PROGRAM

• *See page 49*

CIRI FOUNDATION (TCF) http://www.thecirifoundation.org

CARL H. MARRS SCHOLARSHIP FUND

• *See page 49*

CLEVELAND SCHOLARSHIP PROGRAMS http://www.cspohio.org

CSP MANAGED FUNDS-CLEVELAND BROWNS MARION MOTLEY SCHOLARSHIP

• *See page 49*

COMMON KNOWLEDGE SCHOLARSHIP FOUNDATION http://www.cksf.org

NATIONAL BUSINESS SCHOOL SCHOLARSHIP

Scholarship competitions based on courses commonly associated with business school curricula.For more information about this scholarship, please visit: http://www.cksf.org/cksf.cfm?Page=Home&Subpage=NationalBusiness.

Academic Fields/Career Goals: Business/Consumer Services.

Award: Scholarship for use in freshman, sophomore, junior, senior, graduate, or postgraduate years; not renewable. *Number:* 1. *Amount:* up to $250.

Eligibility Requirements: Applicant must be enrolled or expecting to enroll full- or part-time at a two-year or four-year or technical institution or university. Available to U.S. citizens.

Application Requirements: Applicant must enter a contest. *Deadline:* varies.

Contact: Mr. Daryl Hulce, President
Common Knowledge Scholarship Foundation
PO Box 290361
Davie, FL 33329-0361
Phone: 954-262-8553
Fax: 954-262-2847
E-mail: hulce@cksf.org

COMMUNITY FOUNDATION OF WESTERN MASSACHUSETTS http://www.communityfoundation.org

GREATER SPRINGFIELD ACCOUNTANTS SCHOLARSHIP

• *See page 50*

CUBAN AMERICAN NATIONAL FOUNDATION http://www.masscholarships.org

MAS FAMILY SCHOLARSHIPS

Graduate and undergraduate scholarships in the fields of engineering, business, international relations, economics, communications, and journalism. Applicants must be Cuban-American and have graduated in the top 10 percent of high school class or have minimum 3.5 college GPA. Selection based on need, academic performance, leadership. Those who have already received awards and maintained high level of performance are given preference over new applicants.

Academic Fields/Career Goals: Business/Consumer Services; Chemical Engineering; Communications; Economics; Electrical Engineering/Electronics; Engineering/Technology; Engineering-Related Technologies; Journalism; Mechanical Engineering; Political Science.

Award: Scholarship for use in freshman, sophomore, junior, senior, or graduate years; renewable. *Number:* 10–15. *Amount:* up to $10,000.

Eligibility Requirements: Applicant must be of Latin American/Caribbean heritage; Hispanic; enrolled or expecting to enroll full-time at a two-year or four-year institution or university and must have an interest in leadership. Applicant must have 3.5 GPA or higher. Available to U.S. citizens.

Application Requirements: Application, autobiography, essay, financial need analysis, references, test scores, transcript, proof of Cuban descent, proof of admission. *Deadline:* March 31.

Contact: Melanie Martinez, Director of Community Relations
Cuban American National Foundation
PO Box 14-1898
Miami, FL 33114
Phone: 305-592-0075
Fax: 305-592-0085
E-mail: mmartinez@jmcffmasscholarships.org

DAIRY MANAGEMENT http://www.dairyinfo.com

JAMES H. LOPER JR. MEMORIAL SCHOLARSHIP

• *See page 74*

NATIONAL DAIRY PROMOTION AND RESEARCH BOARD SCHOLARSHIP

• *See page 74*

DECA (DISTRIBUTIVE EDUCATION CLUBS OF AMERICA) http://www.deca.org

HARRY A. APPLEGATE SCHOLARSHIP

Scholarship available to current DECA members for undergraduate study. Must major in marketing education, merchandising, and/or management. Nonrenewable award for high school students based on DECA activities, grades, and need.

Academic Fields/Career Goals: Business/Consumer Services; Education.

Award: Scholarship for use in freshman year; not renewable. *Number:* 20–25. *Amount:* $1000.

Eligibility Requirements: Applicant must be high school student; planning to enroll or expecting to enroll full-time at a two-year or four-year institution or university and must have an interest in leadership. Applicant or parent of applicant must be member of Distribution Ed Club or Future Business Leaders of America. Available to U.S. and non-U.S. citizens.

Application Requirements: Application, references, test scores, transcript. *Deadline:* February 15.

Contact: Kathy Onion, Marketing Specialist
DECA (Distributive Education Clubs of America)
1908 Association Drive
Reston, VA 20191-1594
Phone: 703-860-5000 Ext. 248
Fax: 703-860-4013
E-mail: kathy_onion@deca.org

FAMILY, CAREER AND COMMUNITY LEADERS OF AMERICA-TEXAS ASSOCIATION http://www.texasfccla.org

FCCLA HOUSTON LIVESTOCK SHOW AND RODEO SCHOLARSHIP

Renewable scholarship for graduating high school seniors enrolled in full-time program in family and consumer sciences. Must be Texas resident and should study in Texas. Must have minimum GPA of 3.5.

Academic Fields/Career Goals: Business/Consumer Services; Home Economics.

Award: Scholarship for use in freshman year; renewable. *Number:* up to 10. *Amount:* $12,000.

Eligibility Requirements: Applicant must be high school student; planning to enroll or expecting to enroll full-time at a four-year institution or university; single; resident of Texas and studying in Texas. Applicant or parent of applicant must be member of Family, Career and Community Leaders of America. Applicant must have 3.5 GPA or higher. Available to U.S. citizens.

Application Requirements: Application, essay, photo, references, test scores, transcript. *Deadline:* March 1.

Contact: Staff
Family, Career and Community Leaders of America-Texas Association
3530 Bee Caves Road, Suite 101
Austin, TX 78746-9616
Phone: 512-306-0099
Fax: 512-306-0041
E-mail: fccla@texasfccla.org

FCCLA REGIONAL SCHOLARSHIPS

One-time award for graduating high school seniors enrolled in full-time program in family and consumer sciences. Must be Texas resident and should study in Texas. Must have minimum GPA of 2.5.

Academic Fields/Career Goals: Business/Consumer Services; Home Economics.

Award: Scholarship for use in freshman year; not renewable. *Number:* up to 5. *Amount:* $1000.

Eligibility Requirements: Applicant must be high school student; planning to enroll or expecting to enroll full-time at a four-year institution or university; single; resident of Texas and studying in Texas. Applicant or parent of applicant must be member of Family, Career and Community Leaders of America. Applicant must have 2.5 GPA or higher. Available to U.S. citizens.

Application Requirements: Application, essay, references, test scores, transcript. *Deadline:* March 1.

Contact: Staff
Family, Career and Community Leaders of America-Texas Association
3530 Bee Caves Road, Suite 101
Austin, TX 78746-9616
Phone: 512-306-0099
Fax: 512-306-0041
E-mail: fccla@texasfccla.org

FCCLA TEXAS FARM BUREAU SCHOLARSHIP

One-time award for a graduating high school senior enrolled in full-time program in family and consumer sciences. Must be a Texas resident and must study in Texas. Must have minimum GPA of 2.5. The award value is $1000.

Academic Fields/Career Goals: Business/Consumer Services; Home Economics.

Award: Scholarship for use in freshman year; not renewable. *Number:* 1. *Amount:* $1000.

Eligibility Requirements: Applicant must be high school student; planning to enroll or expecting to enroll full-time at a four-year institution or university; single; resident of Texas and studying in Texas. Applicant or parent of applicant must be member of Family, Career and Community Leaders of America. Applicant must have 2.5 GPA or higher. Available to U.S. citizens.

Application Requirements: Application, autobiography, essay, references, test scores, transcript. *Deadline:* March 1.

Contact: Staff
Family, Career and Community Leaders of America-Texas Association
3530 Bee Caves Road, Suite 101
Austin, TX 78746-9616
Phone: 512-306-0099
Fax: 512-306-0041
E-mail: fccla@texasfccla.org

FISHER BROADCASTING COMPANY http://www.fsci.com

FISHER BROADCASTING INC. SCHOLARSHIP FOR MINORITIES

Applicant must be of non-white origin, must be at least a sophomore, must be a U.S. citizen and must be in broadcast, marketing or journalism courses. If the applicant is permanent resident of the states of Washington, Oregon, Idaho or Montana, tuition may be applied to an out-of-state school. If the applicant is not a permanent resident of the above-mentioned states, tuition must be applied to a school in Washington, Oregon, Idaho or Montana. Require a minimum of 2.5 GPA.

Academic Fields/Career Goals: Business/Consumer Services; Journalism; TV/Radio Broadcasting.

Award: Scholarship for use in sophomore, junior, or senior years; not renewable. *Number:* up to 5. *Amount:* $1000–$10,000.

Eligibility Requirements: Applicant must be American Indian/Alaska Native, Asian/Pacific Islander, Black (non-Hispanic), or Hispanic and enrolled or expecting to enroll full-time at a two-year or four-year or technical institution or university. Applicant must have 2.5 GPA or higher. Available to U.S. citizens.

Application Requirements: Application, essay, financial need analysis, interview, references, transcript, citizenship proof. *Deadline:* April 30.

Contact: Annnarie Hitchcock, Human Resources Administrator
Fisher Broadcasting Company
100 Fourth Avenue North, Suite 510
Seattle, WA 98109
Phone: 206-404-6050
Fax: 206-404-6760
E-mail: ahitchcock@fsci.com

FLORIDA BANKERS EDUCATIONAL FOUNDATION http://www.floridabankers.com

FLORIDA BANKERS EDUCATIONAL FOUNDATION SCHOLARSHIP/LOAN

Program designed to support the education of future and/or current Florida bankers. Minimum 2.5 GPA required. Must be a Florida resident enrolled for at least 12 credit hours per year at FBEF participating Florida university. Loan to be paid back if degree is not obtained. Must work for one year in a Florida bank upon graduation for loan to be forgiven.

Academic Fields/Career Goals: Business/Consumer Services.

Award: Forgivable loan for use in freshman, sophomore, junior, senior, or graduate years; renewable. *Number:* 10–15. *Amount:* $750–$5000.

Eligibility Requirements: Applicant must be enrolled or expecting to enroll full- or part-time at a four-year institution or university; resident of Florida and studying in Florida. Applicant or parent of applicant must have employment or volunteer experience in banking. Applicant must have 2.5 GPA or higher. Available to U.S. citizens.

Application Requirements: Application, driver's license, essay, interview, resume, references, transcript, credit check for loan. *Deadline:* varies.

Contact: Letty Newton, Director
Florida Bankers Educational Foundation
PO Box 1360
Tallahassee, FL 32302-1360
Phone: 850-224-2265
Fax: 850-222-6338
E-mail: lnewton@floridabankers.com

FUKUNAGA SCHOLARSHIP FOUNDATION

FUKUNAGA SCHOLARSHIP FOUNDATION

Renewable scholarships available only to Hawaii residents pursuing a business degree at the undergraduate level at an accredited institution. Minimum 3.0 GPA required.

Academic Fields/Career Goals: Business/Consumer Services.

Award: Scholarship for use in freshman, sophomore, junior, or senior years; renewable. *Number:* 15. *Amount:* $4000.

Eligibility Requirements: Applicant must be enrolled or expecting to enroll full-time at a four-year institution or university and resident of Hawaii. Applicant must have 3.0 GPA or higher. Available to U.S. and non-U.S. citizens.

Application Requirements: Application, financial need analysis, references, test scores, transcript, FAFSA, SAR. *Deadline:* March 1.

Contact: Sandy Wong, Administrator
Fukunaga Scholarship Foundation
PO Box 2788
Honolulu, HI 96803-2788
Phone: 808-564-1386
Fax: 808-523-3937
E-mail: sandyw@servco.com

GEORGIA GOVERNMENT FINANCE OFFICERS ASSOCIATION http://www.ggfoa.org

GGFOA SCHOLARSHIP
• *See page 52*

GEORGIA SOCIETY OF CERTIFIED PUBLIC ACCOUNTANTS http://www.gscpa.org

BEN W. BRANNON MEMORIAL SCHOLARSHIP FUND
• *See page 52*

CHAPTER AWARDED SCHOLARSHIPS
• *See page 52*

CHERRY, BEKAERT AND HOLLAND LLP ACCOUNTING SCHOLARSHIP
• *See page 53*

COLLINS/MOODY-COMPANY SCHOLARSHIP
• *See page 53*

EDUCATIONAL FOUNDATION DIRECT SCHOLARSHIPS
• *See page 53*

JULIUS M. JOHNSON MEMORIAL SCHOLARSHIP
• *See page 53*

PAYCHEX ENTREPRENEUR SCHOLARSHIP
• *See page 53*

ROBERT H. LANGE MEMORIAL SCHOLARSHIP
• *See page 54*

GOLDEN KEY INTERNATIONAL HONOUR SOCIETY http://www.goldenkey.org

BUSINESS ACHIEVEMENT AWARD

Award to members who excel in the study of business. Applicants will be asked to respond to a problem posed by an honorary member within the discipline. The response will be in the form of a professional business report. One winner will receive a $1000 award. The second place winner will receive $750 and the third place winner will receive $500.

Academic Fields/Career Goals: Business/Consumer Services.

Award: Prize for use in freshman, sophomore, junior, senior, graduate, or postgraduate years; not renewable. *Number:* 3. *Amount:* $500–$1000.

Eligibility Requirements: Applicant must be enrolled or expecting to enroll full- or part-time at a four-year institution or university. Available to U.S. and non-U.S. citizens.

Application Requirements: Application, applicant must enter a contest, essay, references, transcript, business-related report. *Deadline:* March 3.

Contact: Scholarship Program Administrators
Golden Key International Honour Society
PO Box 23737
Nashville, TN 37202-3737
Phone: 800-377-2401
E-mail: scholarships@goldenkey.org

GOVERNMENT FINANCE OFFICERS ASSOCIATION http://www.gfoa.org

FRANK L. GREATHOUSE GOVERNMENT ACCOUNTING SCHOLARSHIP

One to two scholarships awarded to undergraduate or graduate students enrolled full-time, preparing for a career in state or local government finance. Submit resume. One-time award of $3500.

Academic Fields/Career Goals: Business/Consumer Services; Public Policy and Administration.

Award: Scholarship for use in freshman, sophomore, junior, senior, or graduate years; not renewable. *Number:* 1–2. *Amount:* $3500.

Eligibility Requirements: Applicant must be enrolled or expecting to enroll full-time at a two-year or four-year or technical institution or university. Available to U.S. and Canadian citizens.

Application Requirements: Application, essay, resume, references, transcript. *Deadline:* February 29.

Contact: Jake Lorentz, Assistant Director
Government Finance Officers Association
203 North LaSalle Street, Suite 2700
Chicago, IL 60601-1210
Phone: 312-977-9700 Ext. 267
Fax: 312-977-4806
E-mail: jlorentz@gfoa.org

GEORGE A. NIELSEN PUBLIC INVESTOR SCHOLARSHIP

Award for an employee of local government or other public entity, who is enrolled or plans to enroll in an undergraduate or graduate program in public administration, finance, business administration, or a related field.

Academic Fields/Career Goals: Business/Consumer Services; Public Policy and Administration.

Award: Scholarship for use in freshman, sophomore, junior, senior, or graduate years; not renewable. *Number:* 1–2. *Amount:* $2500–$5000.

Eligibility Requirements: Applicant must be enrolled or expecting to enroll full- or part-time at a two-year or four-year institution or university. Applicant or parent of applicant must have employment or volunteer experience in government/politics. Available to U.S. and Canadian citizens.

Government Finance Officers Association (continued)

Application Requirements: Application, essay, resume, references, transcript. *Deadline:* February 29.

Contact: Jake Lorentz, Assistant Director
Government Finance Officers Association
203 North LaSalle Street, Suite 2700
Chicago, IL 60601-1210
Phone: 312-977-9700 Ext. 267
Fax: 312-977-4806
E-mail: jlorentz@gfoa.org

MINORITIES IN GOVERNMENT FINANCE SCHOLARSHIP

• *See page 54*

GRAND CHAPTER OF CALIFORNIA-ORDER OF THE EASTERN STAR

http://www.oescal.org

SCHOLARSHIPS FOR EDUCATION, BUSINESS AND RELIGION

Scholarship of $500 to $3000 awarded to students residing in California for post-secondary study. These scholarships are awarded for the study of business, education or religion.

Academic Fields/Career Goals: Business/Consumer Services; Education; Religion/Theology.

Award: Scholarship for use in freshman, sophomore, junior, senior, graduate, or postgraduate years; renewable. *Number:* varies. *Amount:* $500–$3000.

Eligibility Requirements: Applicant must be enrolled or expecting to enroll full-time at a two-year or four-year or technical institution or university and resident of California. Applicant must have 3.0 GPA or higher. Available to U.S. citizens.

Application Requirements: Application, financial need analysis, photo, references, self-addressed stamped envelope, transcript, proof of acceptance to college or university. *Deadline:* March 8.

Contact: Maryann Barrios, Grand Secretary
Grand Chapter of California-Order of the Eastern Star
16960 Bastanchury Road, Suite E
Yorba Linda, CA 92886-1711
Phone: 714-986-2380
Fax: 714-986-2385
E-mail: gsecretary@oescal.org

GREATER KANAWHA VALLEY FOUNDATION

http://www.tgkvf.org

WILLARD H. ERWIN JR. MEMORIAL SCHOLARSHIP FUND

Award of $1000 for West Virginia residents who are starting their junior or senior year of undergraduate or graduate studies in a business or health-care finance degree program. Must be enrolled at a college in West Virginia. May apply for two Foundation scholarships but will only be chosen for one. Scholarships are awarded on the basis of financial need and scholastic ability.

Academic Fields/Career Goals: Business/Consumer Services; Health Administration.

Award: Scholarship for use in junior, senior, or graduate years; renewable. *Number:* 1. *Amount:* $1000.

Eligibility Requirements: Applicant must be enrolled or expecting to enroll full- or part-time at a four-year institution or university; resident of West Virginia and studying in West Virginia. Applicant must have 2.5 GPA or higher. Available to U.S. citizens.

Application Requirements: Application, applicant must enter a contest, essay, financial need analysis, references, self-addressed stamped envelope, test scores, transcript. *Deadline:* January 12.

Contact: Susan Hoover, Scholarship Coordinator
Greater Kanawha Valley Foundation
PO Box 3041
Charleston, WV 25331
Phone: 304-346-3620
Fax: 304-346-3640

GREAT FALLS ADVERTISING FEDERATION

http://www.gfaf.com

COLLEGE SCHOLARSHIP

• *See page 102*

HIGH SCHOOL MARKETING/COMMUNICATIONS SCHOLARSHIP

Two scholarships of $2000 for high school seniors who are residents of Montana. Must intend to pursue a career in communications, marketing, advertising, or other related field.

Academic Fields/Career Goals: Business/Consumer Services; Communications.

Award: Scholarship for use in freshman year; not renewable. *Number:* 2. *Amount:* $2000.

Eligibility Requirements: Applicant must be high school student; planning to enroll or expecting to enroll full-time at a four-year institution or university and resident of Montana. Available to U.S. citizens.

Application Requirements: Application, essay, resume, references, self-addressed stamped envelope, cover letter describing how the scholarship money will be used. *Deadline:* February 29.

Contact: Christine Depa, Administrative Assistant
Great Falls Advertising Federation
609 Tenth Avenue South, Suite B
Great Falls, MT 59405
Phone: 406-761-6453
Fax: 406-453-1128
E-mail: gfaf@gfaf.com

HISPANIC COLLEGE FUND INC.

http://www.hispanicfund.org

DENNY'S/HISPANIC COLLEGE FUND SCHOLARSHIP

• *See page 54*

DEPARTMENT OF ENERGY SCHOLARSHIP PROGRAM

Scholarship available to full-time undergraduate students in their sophomore or junior year who are pursuing a degree in business science, engineering or DOE-related major. Must be U.S. citizen, have a minimum 3.0 GPA, and be available to participate in a paid summer internship.

Academic Fields/Career Goals: Business/Consumer Services; Chemical Engineering; Electrical Engineering/Electronics; Energy and Power Engineering; Engineering/Technology; Engineering-Related Technologies; Environmental Science; Materials Science, Engineering, and Metallurgy; Mechanical Engineering; Natural Resources; Natural Sciences; Nuclear Science.

Award: Scholarship for use in sophomore, junior, or senior years; not renewable. *Number:* 15. *Amount:* $500–$5000.

Eligibility Requirements: Applicant must be Hispanic and enrolled or expecting to enroll full-time at a four-year institution or university. Applicant must have 3.0 GPA or higher. Available to U.S. citizens.

Application Requirements: Application, essay, financial need analysis. *Deadline:* March 15.

Contact: Fernando Barrueta, Chief Executive Officer
Hispanic College Fund Inc.
1301 K Street, NW, Suite 450-A West
Washington, DC 20005
Phone: 202-296-5400
Fax: 202-296-3774
E-mail: hcf-info@hispanicfund.org

ERNST AND YOUNG SCHOLARSHIP PROGRAM

• *See page 55*

ICI EDUCATIONAL FOUNDATION SCHOLARSHIP PROGRAM

Program intended for undergraduate student pursuing his or her associates or bachelor's degree in business, computer science, or engineering. Applicant must be U.S. citizen of Hispanic background; May reside in United States or Puerto Rico. Must attend college in United States or Puerto Rico. Online application only: http://www.hispanicfund.org.

Academic Fields/Career Goals: Business/Consumer Services; Computer Science/Data Processing; Engineering/Technology; Engineering-Related Technologies.

Award: Scholarship for use in freshman, sophomore, junior, senior, or graduate years; not renewable. *Number:* varies. *Amount:* $500–$5000.

Eligibility Requirements: Applicant must be Hispanic and enrolled or expecting to enroll full-time at a two-year or four-year institution or university. Applicant must have 3.0 GPA or higher. Available to U.S. citizens.

Application Requirements: Application. *Deadline:* March 15.

Contact: Fernando Barrueta, Chief Executive Officer
Hispanic College Fund Inc.
1301 K Street, NW, Suite 450-A West
Washington, DC 20005
Phone: 202-296-5400
Fax: 202-296-3774
E-mail: hcf-info@hispanicfund.org

LOCKHEED MARTIN SCHOLARSHIP PROGRAM

Scholarship program for students studying full-time in the United States or Puerto Rico, pursuing degrees in business administration, science or engineering. Must be U.S. citizen residing in the United States. Must be Hispanic or of Hispanic descent. Must have a minimum GPA of a 3.0.

Academic Fields/Career Goals: Business/Consumer Services; Chemical Engineering; Computer Science/Data Processing; Electrical Engineering/Electronics; Energy and Power Engineering; Engineering/Technology; Engineering-Related Technologies; Materials Science, Engineering, and Metallurgy; Physical Sciences and Math.

Award: Scholarship for use in freshman, sophomore, junior, or senior years; not renewable. *Number:* varies. *Amount:* $500–$5000.

Eligibility Requirements: Applicant must be Hispanic and enrolled or expecting to enroll full-time at a four-year institution or university. Applicant must have 3.0 GPA or higher. Available to U.S. citizens.

Application Requirements: Application, essay, references, transcript, proof of family income, proof of citizenship status. *Deadline:* March 15.

Contact: Fernando Barrueta, Chief Executive Officer
Hispanic College Fund Inc.
1301 K Street, NW, Suite 450-A West
Washington, DC 20005
Phone: 202-296-5400
Fax: 202-296-3774
E-mail: hcf-info@hispanicfund.org

M & T BANK/HISPANIC COLLEGE FUND SCHOLARSHIP PROGRAM

• *See page 55*

HISPANIC SCHOLARSHIP FUND http://www.hsf.net

HSF/CITIGROUP FELLOWS PROGRAM

• *See page 55*

HSF/GENERAL MOTORS SCHOLARSHIP

Scholarships are available to Hispanic students pursuing a degree in business or engineering at an accredited U.S. four-year college. For more details and application see Web site: http://ww.hsf.net.

Academic Fields/Career Goals: Business/Consumer Services; Chemical Engineering; Civil Engineering; Electrical Engineering/Electronics; Engineering/Technology; Engineering-Related Technologies; Mechanical Engineering.

Award: Scholarship for use in freshman, sophomore, or junior years; not renewable. *Number:* varies. *Amount:* $2500.

Eligibility Requirements: Applicant must be of Hispanic, Latin American/Caribbean, Mexican, Nicaraguan, or Spanish heritage and enrolled or expecting to enroll full-time at a four-year institution or university. Applicant must have 3.0 GPA or higher. Available to U.S. citizens.

Application Requirements: Application, essay, financial need analysis, references, transcript. *Deadline:* June 30.

Contact: Program Officer
Hispanic Scholarship Fund
55 Second Street, Suite 1500
San Francisco, CA 94105
Phone: 877-473-4636
Fax: 415-808-2302
E-mail: highschool@hsf.net

HSF/NISSAN COMMUNITY COLLEGE TRANSFER SCHOLARSHIP PROGRAM

Scholarship available to community college students of Hispanic heritage who are transferring to a four-year institution in Dallas. TX, Los Angeles, CA, or Nashville, TN. Must be pursuing a degree in business, engineering, journalism/communications or public relations. Minimum 3.0 GPA required.

Academic Fields/Career Goals: Business/Consumer Services; Communications; Energy and Power Engineering; Engineering/Technology; Engineering-Related Technologies; Journalism; Materials Science, Engineering, and Metallurgy; Mechanical Engineering.

Award: Scholarship for use in sophomore or junior years; not renewable. *Number:* up to 50. *Amount:* $2500.

Eligibility Requirements: Applicant must be Hispanic; enrolled or expecting to enroll full-time at a four-year institution or university and studying in California, Tennessee, or Texas. Applicant must have 3.0 GPA or higher. Available to U.S. citizens.

Application Requirements: Application, essay, financial need analysis, references, transcript. *Deadline:* March 15.

Contact: John Schmucker, Scholarship Coordinator
Hispanic Scholarship Fund
55 Second Street, Suite 1500
San Francisco, CA 94105
Phone: 877-473-4636
E-mail: cctransfer@hsf.net

HSF/WELLS FARGO SCHOLARSHIP PROGRAM

• *See page 55*

HOLSTEIN ASSOCIATION USA INC. http://www.holsteinusa.com

ROBERT H. RUMLER SCHOLARSHIP

• *See page 69*

IDAHO STATE BROADCASTERS ASSOCIATION http://www.idahobroadcasters.org

WAYNE C. CORNILS MEMORIAL SCHOLARSHIP

Scholarship for students enrolled in an Idaho school on a full-time basis. Must be majoring in a broadcasting related field. Must have minimum GPA of 2.0 if in the first two years of school, or 2.5 in the last two years of school.

Academic Fields/Career Goals: Business/Consumer Services; Engineering/Technology; Journalism; TV/Radio Broadcasting.

Award: Scholarship for use in freshman, sophomore, junior, or senior years; not renewable. *Number:* 2. *Amount:* $1000.

Eligibility Requirements: Applicant must be enrolled or expecting to enroll full-time at a four-year institution or university and studying in Idaho. Available to U.S. citizens.

Application Requirements: Application, essay, references, transcript. *Deadline:* March 15.

Contact: Connie Searles, President
Idaho State Broadcasters Association
270 North 27th Street, Suite B
Boise, ID 83702-4741
Phone: 208-345-3072
Fax: 208-343-8046
E-mail: isba@idacomm.net

INDEPENDENT COLLEGE FUND OF MARYLAND (I-FUND) http://www.i-fundinfo.org

BRANCH BANKING & TRUST COMPANY SCHOLARSHIPS

• *See page 56*

Independent College Fund of Maryland (I-Fund) (continued)

CHEVY CHASE BANK SCHOLARSHIP

• *See page 56*

LEGG MASON SCHOLARSHIPS

• *See page 56*

INSTITUTE FOR OPERATIONS RESEARCH AND THE MANAGEMENT SCIENCES http://www.informs.org

GEORGE NICHOLSON STUDENT PAPER COMPETITION

Honors outstanding papers in the field of operations research and the management sciences. Entrant must be student on or after the year of application. Research papers present original results and be written by student. Electronic submission of paper required.

Academic Fields/Career Goals: Business/Consumer Services.

Award: Prize for use in junior, senior, graduate, or postgraduate years; not renewable. *Number:* up to 6. *Amount:* $100–$600.

Eligibility Requirements: Applicant must be enrolled or expecting to enroll full- or part-time at a four-year institution or university. Available to U.S. and non-U.S. citizens.

Application Requirements: Application, applicant must enter a contest, references. *Deadline:* June 30.

Contact: Mark Doherty, Executive Director
Institute for Operations Research and the Management Sciences
7240 Parkway Drive, Suite 310
Hanover, MD 21076-1310
Phone: 410-850-0300
Fax: 410-684-2963
E-mail: mark.doherty@informs.org

INSTITUTE OF INTERNATIONAL EDUCATION http://www.iie.org/nsep

NATIONAL SECURITY EDUCATION PROGRAM DAVID L. BOREN UNDERGRADUATE SCHOLARSHIPS

The National Security Education Program (NSEP) awards scholarships to American undergraduate students for study abroad in regions critical to U.S. national interests. Emphasized world areas include Africa, Asia, Central and Eastern Europe, the NIS, Latin America and the Caribbean, and the Middle East. NSEP scholarship recipients incur a service agreement. Must be a U.S. citizen.

Academic Fields/Career Goals: Business/Consumer Services; Economics; Engineering-Related Technologies; Environmental Science; Foreign Language; International Studies.

Award: Scholarship for use in freshman, sophomore, junior, or senior years; not renewable. *Number:* 150. *Amount:* up to $20,000.

Eligibility Requirements: Applicant must be enrolled or expecting to enroll full-time at a two-year or four-year institution or university. Available to U.S. citizens.

Application Requirements: Application, essay, financial need analysis, references, transcript, campus review. *Deadline:* February 12.

Contact: Susan Sharp, Specialist, Research and Education
Institute of International Education
1400 K Street, NW, Suite 650
Washington, DC 20005-2403
Phone: 800-618-6737
Fax: 202-326-7697
E-mail: nsep@iie.org

INSTITUTE OF MANAGEMENT ACCOUNTANTS http://www.imanet.org

INSTITUTE OF MANAGEMENT ACCOUNTANTS MEMORIAL EDUCATION FUND SCHOLARSHIPS

• *See page 57*

STUART CAMERON AND MARGARET MCLEOD MEMORIAL SCHOLARSHIP

• *See page 57*

JOHN M. AZARIAN MEMORIAL ARMENIAN YOUTH SCHOLARSHIP FUND http://www.azariangroup.com

JOHN M. AZARIAN MEMORIAL ARMENIAN YOUTH SCHOLARSHIP FUND

Grants awarded to undergraduate students of Armenian descent, attending full-time four-year college or university within the United States. Compelling financial need is the main criteria. Minimum 2.5 GPA required. Preference to business majors given. Applicant must be a member of Armenian Church.

Academic Fields/Career Goals: Business/Consumer Services.

Award: Grant for use in freshman, sophomore, junior, or senior years; renewable. *Number:* varies. *Amount:* varies.

Eligibility Requirements: Applicant must be a member of the specified denomination; of Armenian heritage and enrolled or expecting to enroll full-time at a four-year institution or university. Applicant must have 2.5 GPA or higher. Available to U.S. citizens.

Application Requirements: Application, autobiography, essay, financial need analysis, references, test scores, transcript. *Deadline:* May 31.

Contact: John Azarian, Jr., President
John M. Azarian Memorial Armenian Youth Scholarship Fund
The Azarian Group L.L.C.
6 Prospect Street, Suite 1B
Midland Park, NJ 07432
Phone: 201-444-7111 Ext. 27
Fax: 201-444-6655
E-mail: jazarian@azariangroup.com

JORGE MAS CANOSA FREEDOM FOUNDATION http://www.jorgemascanosa.org

MAS FAMILY SCHOLARSHIP AWARD

Scholarship for Cuban American student who is a direct descendant of those who left Cuba or was born in Cuba. Minimum 3.5 GPA in college. Scholarships available only in the fields of engineering, business, international relations, economics, communications and journalism.

Academic Fields/Career Goals: Business/Consumer Services; Chemical Engineering; Civil Engineering; Communications; Economics; Electrical Engineering/Electronics; Engineering-Related Technologies; International Studies; Journalism; Materials Science, Engineering, and Metallurgy; Mechanical Engineering.

Award: Scholarship for use in freshman, sophomore, junior, senior, or graduate years; renewable. *Number:* varies. *Amount:* varies.

Eligibility Requirements: Applicant must be of Latin American/Caribbean heritage; Hispanic and enrolled or expecting to enroll full-time at a two-year or four-year institution or university. Applicant must have 3.5 GPA or higher. Available to U.S. and non-U.S. citizens.

Application Requirements: Application, autobiography, essay, financial need analysis, references, test scores, transcript, proof of Cuban descent. *Deadline:* March 15.

Contact: Scholarship Coordinator
Jorge Mas Canosa Freedom Foundation
PO Box 14-1898
Miami, FL 33114-9925
Phone: 305-529-0075 Ext. 101
Fax: 305-592-7889
E-mail: ifalcone@masscholarships.org

JUNIOR ACHIEVEMENT http://www.ja.org

WALT DISNEY COMPANY FOUNDATION SCHOLARSHIP

• *See page 103*

KE ALI'I PAUAHI FOUNDATION http://www.pauahi.org

NATIVE HAWAIIAN CHAMBER OF COMMERCE SCHOLARSHIP

Scholarship for students enrolled in an undergraduate or graduate degree-seeking program from an accredited post-secondary educational institution majoring in business administration. Minimum 3.0 GPA of 3.0 required.

Academic Fields/Career Goals: Business/Consumer Services.

Award: Scholarship for use in freshman, sophomore, junior, senior, or graduate years; not renewable. *Number:* varies. *Amount:* varies.

Eligibility Requirements: Applicant must be enrolled or expecting to enroll full-time at a four-year institution or university. Applicant must have 3.0 GPA or higher. Available to U.S. citizens.

Application Requirements: Application, financial need analysis, transcript, SAR, college acceptance letter. *Deadline:* May 2.

Contact: Elizabeth Stevenson, Development Manager
Ke Ali'i Pauahi Foundation
567 South King Street, Suite 160
Honolulu, HI 96813
Phone: 808-534-3966
Fax: 808-534-3890
E-mail: scholarships@pauahi.org

LAGRANT FOUNDATION http://www.lagrantfoundation.org

LAGRANT FOUNDATION SCHOLARSHIP FOR GRADUATES

Awards are for undergraduate and graduate minority students who are attending accredited four-year institutions and are pursuing careers in the fields of advertising, marketing, and public relations. Minimum 3.2 GPA required.

Academic Fields/Career Goals: Business/Consumer Services; Communications.

Award: Scholarship for use in freshman, sophomore, junior, senior, graduate, or postgraduate years; renewable. *Number:* 12. *Amount:* up to $10,000.

Eligibility Requirements: Applicant must be American Indian/Alaska Native, Asian/Pacific Islander, Black (non-Hispanic), or Hispanic and enrolled or expecting to enroll full-time at a four-year institution or university. Available to U.S. citizens.

Application Requirements: Application, essay, resume, references, transcript. *Deadline:* February 28.

Contact: Program Manager
Lagrant Foundation
626 Wilshire Boulevard, Suite 700
Los Angeles, CA 90017-2920
Phone: 323-469-8680
Fax: 323-469-8683

LAGRANT FOUNDATION SCHOLARSHIP FOR UNDERGRADUATES

Awards are for undergraduate and graduate minority students who are attending accredited four-year institutions and are pursuing careers in the fields of advertising, marketing, and public relations. Minimum 2.75 GPA required.

Academic Fields/Career Goals: Business/Consumer Services; Communications.

Award: Scholarship for use in freshman, sophomore, junior, senior, or graduate years; renewable. *Number:* 22. *Amount:* up to $5000.

Eligibility Requirements: Applicant must be American Indian/Alaska Native, Asian/Pacific Islander, Black (non-Hispanic), or Hispanic and enrolled or expecting to enroll full-time at a four-year institution or university. Available to U.S. citizens.

Application Requirements: Application, essay, resume, references, transcript. *Deadline:* February 28.

Contact: Program Manager
Lagrant Foundation
626 Wilshire Boulevard, Suite 700
Los Angeles, CA 90017-2920
Phone: 323-469-8680
Fax: 323-469-8683

LAWRENCE P. DOSS SCHOLARSHIP FOUNDATION http://www.lawrencepdossfnd.org

LAWRENCE P. DOSS SCHOLARSHIP FOUNDATION

• *See page 57*

LEAGUE OF UNITED LATIN AMERICAN CITIZENS NATIONAL EDUCATIONAL SERVICE CENTERS INC. http://www.lnesc.org

GE/LULAC SCHOLARSHIP

The scholarship for business and engineering students offers outstanding minority or low-income students entering their sophomore year in pursuit of an undergraduate degree a renewable scholarship up to 3 years.

Academic Fields/Career Goals: Business/Consumer Services; Engineering/Technology.

Award: Scholarship for use in sophomore, junior, or senior years; renewable. *Number:* up to 9. *Amount:* up to $5000.

Eligibility Requirements: Applicant must be American Indian/Alaska Native, Asian/Pacific Islander, Black (non-Hispanic), or Hispanic and enrolled or expecting to enroll full-time at a four-year institution or university. Applicant must have 3.0 GPA or higher. Available to U.S. citizens.

Application Requirements: Application, references, transcript, personal statement with career goals. *Deadline:* July 15.

Contact: Scholarship Administrator
League of United Latin American Citizens National Educational Service Centers Inc.
2000 L Street NW, Suite 610
Washington, DC 20036
Phone: 202-835-9646 Ext. 10
Fax: 202-835-9685

LINCOLN COMMUNITY FOUNDATION http://www.lcf.org

LAWRENCE "LARRY" FRAZIER MEMORIAL SCHOLARSHIP

• *See page 118*

MAINE COMMUNITY COLLEGE SYSTEM http://www.mccs.me.edu

MAINE HIGHER EDUCATION ASSISTANCE SCHOLARSHIP

Award available each year to a second-year business or business related student. The $1000 scholarship rotates each year among the colleges.

Academic Fields/Career Goals: Business/Consumer Services.

Award: Scholarship for use in sophomore year; not renewable. *Number:* varies. *Amount:* $1000.

Eligibility Requirements: Applicant must be enrolled or expecting to enroll full-time at a two-year or technical institution; resident of Maine and studying in Maine. Available to U.S. citizens.

Application Requirements: Application. *Deadline:* varies.

Contact: Scholarship Committee
Maine Community College System
323 State Street
Augusta, ME 04330
Phone: 207-629-4000
Fax: 207-629-4048
E-mail: info@mccs.me.edu

MAINE EDUCATION SERVICES http://www.mesfoundation.com

MAINE STATE CHAMBER OF COMMERCE SCHOLARSHIP-HIGH SCHOOL SENIOR

Two scholarships available for graduating high school seniors, one who is planning to pursue an associate degree in a technical program, and one who is planning to pursue a bachelor's degree in a business-related area. Preference may be given to students attending Maine colleges. Awards are based on academic excellence, student activities, financial need, letters of recommendation, and a required essay.

Academic Fields/Career Goals: Business/Consumer Services; Engineering/Technology.

Award: Scholarship for use in freshman year; not renewable. *Number:* up to 2. *Amount:* up to $1500.

Eligibility Requirements: Applicant must be high school student; planning to enroll or expecting to enroll full-time at a two-year or four-year or technical institution or university and resident of Maine. Available to U.S. citizens.

Maine Education Services (continued)

Application Requirements: Application, essay, financial need analysis, references, transcript. *Deadline:* April 18.

Contact: Kim Benjamin, Vice President of Operations
Maine Education Services
131 Presumpscot Street
Portland, ME 04103
Phone: 207-791-3600
Fax: 207-791-3616

MARYLAND ASSOCIATION OF PRIVATE COLLEGES AND CAREER SCHOOLS http://www.mapccs.org

MARYLAND ASSOCIATION OF PRIVATE COLLEGES AND CAREER SCHOOLS SCHOLARSHIP

Awards for study at trade schools only. Must enter school same year high school is completed. For use only in Maryland and by Maryland residents.

Academic Fields/Career Goals: Business/Consumer Services; Computer Science/Data Processing; Dental Health/Services; Engineering/Technology; Food Science/Nutrition; Home Economics; Trade/Technical Specialties; TV/Radio Broadcasting.

Award: Scholarship for use in freshman year; not renewable. *Number:* 50. *Amount:* $500–$19,950.

Eligibility Requirements: Applicant must be high school student; planning to enroll or expecting to enroll full-time at a technical institution; resident of Maryland and studying in Maryland. Available to U.S. citizens.

Application Requirements: Application, references, transcript, letter of eligibility from the MAPCCS career school. *Deadline:* April 11.

Contact: Jeannie Schwartz, Director of Placements
Maryland Association of Private Colleges and Career Schools
1539 Merriet Boulevard, PO Box 206
Baltimore, MD 21222
Phone: 410-282-4012
Fax: 410-282-4133
E-mail: jeannie.schwartz@computertraining.com

NATIONAL ASSOCIATION FOR THE ADVANCEMENT OF COLORED PEOPLE http://www.naacp.org

EARL G. GRAVES NAACP SCHOLARSHIP

One-time award of $5000 to a full-time minority student. Must be an enrolled sophomore, junior or senior at an accredited college or university in the United States as a declared business major, or a graduate student enrolled or accepted in a master's or doctoral program within a business school at an accredited university. Must demonstrate financial need.

Academic Fields/Career Goals: Business/Consumer Services.

Award: Scholarship for use in sophomore, junior, senior, or graduate years; not renewable. *Number:* 1. *Amount:* $5000.

Eligibility Requirements: Applicant must be American Indian/Alaska Native, Asian/Pacific Islander, Black (non-Hispanic), or Hispanic and enrolled or expecting to enroll full-time at a four-year institution or university. Applicant must have 2.5 GPA or higher. Available to U.S. citizens.

Application Requirements: Application, financial need analysis, references, transcript. *Deadline:* April 30.

Contact: Victor Goode, Attorney
National Association for the Advancement of Colored People
4805 Mount Hope Drive
Baltimore, MD 21215-3297
Phone: 410-580-5760
Fax: 410-585-1329
E-mail: info@naacp.org

NATIONAL ASSOCIATION OF WATER COMPANIES-NEW JERSEY CHAPTER

NATIONAL ASSOCIATION OF WATER COMPANIES-NEW JERSEY CHAPTER SCHOLARSHIP

• *See page 133*

NATIONAL BLACK MBA ASSOCIATION http://www.nbmbaa.org

NATIONAL BLACK MBA ASSOCIATION UNDERGRADUATE SCHOLARSHIP PROGRAM

A $1000 scholarship is available to each of the NBMBAA's local chapters for disbursement to qualified minority students.

Academic Fields/Career Goals: Business/Consumer Services.

Award: Scholarship for use in freshman, sophomore, junior, or senior years; not renewable. *Number:* varies. *Amount:* $1000.

Eligibility Requirements: Applicant must be Black (non-Hispanic) and enrolled or expecting to enroll full- or part-time at a two-year or four-year or technical institution or university. Available to U.S. citizens.

Application Requirements: *Deadline:* varies.

Contact: Lori Johnson, Scholarship Committee
National Black MBA Association
180 North Michigan Avenue, Suite 1400
Chicago, IL 60601
Phone: 312-236-2622 Ext. 8086
Fax: 312-236-0390
E-mail: scholarship@nbmbaa.org

NATIONAL BLACK MBA ASSOCIATION-TWIN CITIES CHAPTER http://www.nbmbaatc.org

TWIN CITIES CHAPTER UNDERGRADUATE SCHOLARSHIP

• *See page 58*

NATIONAL SOCIETY OF COLLEGIATE SCHOLARS (NSCS) http://www.nscs.org

NSCS ERNST & YOUNG BOOK AWARD

• *See page 59*

NATIONAL URBAN LEAGUE http://www.nulbeep.org

BLACK EXECUTIVE EXCHANGE PROGRAM JERRY BARTOW SCHOLARSHIP FUND

Scholarships for undergraduate students at participating Historically Black Colleges and Universities. Must be sophomore, junior, or senior, majoring in business, management, technology, or education. Must be available to receive award at BEEP's annual conference.

Academic Fields/Career Goals: Business/Consumer Services; Education; Engineering/Technology.

Award: Scholarship for use in sophomore, junior, or senior years; not renewable. *Number:* 2. *Amount:* $5000.

Eligibility Requirements: Applicant must be Black (non-Hispanic) and enrolled or expecting to enroll full-time at a four-year institution or university. Applicant must have 2.5 GPA or higher. Available to U.S. citizens.

Application Requirements: Application. *Deadline:* February 1.

Contact: William Dawson, Scholarship Committee
National Urban League
120 Wall Street
New York, NY 10005
Phone: 212-558-5300
Fax: 212-344-5332
E-mail: beep2005@nul.org

NEBRASKA DECA http://www.nedeca.org

NEBRASKA DECA LEADERSHIP SCHOLARSHIP

Awards applicants who intend to pursue a full-time two- or four-year course of study in a marketing or business-related field. Applicant must be active in DECA and involved in community service activities.

Academic Fields/Career Goals: Business/Consumer Services.

Award: Scholarship for use in freshman year; not renewable. *Number:* 2–9. *Amount:* $250–$1000.

Eligibility Requirements: Applicant must be high school student; planning to enroll or expecting to enroll full-time at a two-year or four-year or technical institution or university and resident of Nebraska.

Applicant or parent of applicant must be member of Distribution Ed Club or Future Business Leaders of America. Applicant must have 2.5 GPA or higher. Available to U.S. citizens.

Application Requirements: Application, essay, resume, references, test scores, transcript, DECA participation and accomplishment documents. *Deadline:* February 1.

Contact: Scholarship Review Committee
Nebraska DECA
301 Centennial Mall South, PO Box 94987
Lincoln, NE 68509-4987
Phone: 402-471-4803
Fax: 402-471-0117
E-mail: nedeca@nedeca.org

NEW ENGLAND WATER WORKS ASSOCIATION http://www.newwa.org

FRANCIS X. CROWLEY SCHOLARSHIP

Scholarships are awarded to eligible civil engineering, environmental and business management students on the basis of merit, character, and need. Preference given to those students whose programs are considered by a committee as beneficial to water works practice in New England. NEWWA student membership is required to receive a scholarship award.

Academic Fields/Career Goals: Business/Consumer Services; Civil Engineering; Environmental Science.

Award: Scholarship for use in freshman, sophomore, junior, senior, or graduate years; not renewable. *Number:* 1. *Amount:* up to $3000.

Eligibility Requirements: Applicant must be enrolled or expecting to enroll full-time at a four-year institution or university. Applicant or parent of applicant must be member of New England Water Works Association. Available to U.S. citizens.

Application Requirements: Application, essay, references, transcript. *Fee:* $25. *Deadline:* July 1.

Contact: Thomas MacElhaney, Chair, Scholarship Committee
New England Water Works Association
c/o PRELOAD Inc., 60 Commerce Drive
Hauppauge, NY 11788
Phone: 631-231-8100
Fax: 978-418-9156
E-mail: tmacelhaney@preloadinc.com

OREGON STUDENT ASSISTANCE COMMISSION http://www.osac.state.or.us

HOMESTEAD CAPITAL HOUSING SCHOLARSHIP

• *See page 61*

PLUMBING-HEATING-COOLING CONTRACTORS ASSOCIATION EDUCATION FOUNDATION http://www.phccweb.org

BRADFORD WHITE CORPORATION SCHOLARSHIP

• *See page 92*

DELTA FAUCET COMPANY SCHOLARSHIP PROGRAM

• *See page 93*

PHCC EDUCATIONAL FOUNDATION NEED-BASED SCHOLARSHIP

• *See page 93*

PHCC EDUCATIONAL FOUNDATION SCHOLARSHIP PROGRAM

Applicants must be sponsored by a member of the National Association of Plumbing-Heating-Cooling Contractors. Must pursue studies in a major related to the plumbing-heating-cooling industry. Visit Web site for additional information.

Academic Fields/Career Goals: Business/Consumer Services; Civil Engineering; Engineering/Technology; Engineering-Related Technologies; Heating, Air-Conditioning, and Refrigeration Mechanics; Mechanical Engineering; Trade/Technical Specialties.

Award: Scholarship for use in freshman, sophomore, junior, or senior years; renewable. *Number:* 1. *Amount:* up to $12,000.

Eligibility Requirements: Applicant must be enrolled or expecting to enroll full-time at a two-year or four-year or technical institution or university. Applicant must have 2.5 GPA or higher. Available to U.S. and Canadian citizens.

Application Requirements: Application, interview, references, test scores, transcript. *Deadline:* June 1.

Contact: Iva Vest, Scholarship Coordinator
Plumbing-Heating-Cooling Contractors Association Education Foundation
PO Box 6808
Falls Church, VA 22046
Phone: 800-533-7694
Fax: 703-237-7442
E-mail: vest@naphcc.org

PROFESSIONAL INDEPENDENT INSURANCE AGENTS OF ILLINOIS http://www.piiai.org

G.A. MAVON MEMORIAL SCHOLARSHIP

Scholarship will be awarded at $1000 per semester to an Illinois resident who is a full-time junior or senior in college. Must be enrolled in a business degree program with an interest in insurance. It is not necessary for the applicant to be a member of PIIAI.

Academic Fields/Career Goals: Business/Consumer Services; Insurance and Actuarial Science.

Award: Scholarship for use in junior or senior years; not renewable. *Number:* 1. *Amount:* $2000.

Eligibility Requirements: Applicant must be enrolled or expecting to enroll full-time at a four-year institution or university and resident of Illinois. Available to U.S. citizens.

Application Requirements: Application, essay, interview, references, transcript. *Deadline:* July 1.

Contact: Shannon Churchill, Administrative Assistant
Professional Independent Insurance Agents of Illinois
4360 Wabash Avenue
Springfield, IL 62711
Phone: 217-793-6660
Fax: 217-793-6744
E-mail: schurchill@piiai.org

KEITH PAYNE MEMORIAL SCHOLARSHIP

Scholarship will be awarded at $500 per semester to an Illinois resident who is a full-time junior or senior in college. Must be enrolled in a business degree program with an interest in insurance. It is not necessary for the applicant to be a Member of PIIAI.

Academic Fields/Career Goals: Business/Consumer Services; Insurance and Actuarial Science.

Award: Scholarship for use in junior or senior years; not renewable. *Number:* 1. *Amount:* $1000.

Eligibility Requirements: Applicant must be enrolled or expecting to enroll full-time at a four-year institution or university and resident of Illinois. Available to U.S. citizens.

Application Requirements: Application, essay, interview, references, transcript. *Deadline:* July 1.

Contact: Shannon Churchill, Administrative Assistant
Professional Independent Insurance Agents of Illinois
4360 Wabash Avenue
Springfield, IL 62711
Phone: 217-793-6660
Fax: 217-793-6744
E-mail: schurchill@piiai.org

ROY AND HARRIET ROBINSON SCHOLARSHIP

Scholarship will be awarded at $500 per semester to an Illinois resident who is a full-time junior or senior in college. Must be enrolled in a business degree program with an interest in insurance. It is not necessary for the applicant to be a member of PIIAI.

Academic Fields/Career Goals: Business/Consumer Services; Insurance and Actuarial Science.

Award: Scholarship for use in junior or senior years; not renewable. *Number:* 1. *Amount:* $1000.

Professional Independent Insurance Agents of Illinois (continued)

Eligibility Requirements: Applicant must be enrolled or expecting to enroll full-time at a four-year institution or university and resident of Illinois. Available to U.S. citizens.

Application Requirements: Application, essay, interview, references, transcript. *Deadline:* July 1.

Contact: Shannon Churchill, Administrative Assistant
Professional Independent Insurance Agents of Illinois
4360 Wabash Avenue
Springfield, IL 62711
Phone: 217-793-6660
Fax: 217-793-6744
E-mail: schurchill@piiai.org

RHODE ISLAND FOUNDATION http://www.rifoundation.org

RAYMOND H. TROTT SCHOLARSHIP FOR BANKING

Scholarship for needy Rhode Island residents attending Rhode Island College whose studies are focused on banking and business. Must demonstrate financial need.

Academic Fields/Career Goals: Business/Consumer Services.

Award: Scholarship for use in senior year; not renewable. *Number:* 1. *Amount:* $1000.

Eligibility Requirements: Applicant must be American Indian/Alaska Native, Asian/Pacific Islander, Black (non-Hispanic), or Hispanic; enrolled or expecting to enroll full-time at a four-year institution or university and resident of Rhode Island. Available to U.S. citizens.

Application Requirements: Application, essay, financial need analysis, references, transcript. *Deadline:* June 10.

Contact: Libby Monahan, Funds Administrator
Rhode Island Foundation
One Union Station
Providence, RI 02903
Phone: 401-274-4564 Ext. 3117
Fax: 401-751-7983
E-mail: libbym@rifoundation.org

ROBERT H. MOLLOHAN FAMILY CHARITABLE FOUNDATION INC. http://www.mollohanfoundation.org

TEAMING TO WIN BUSINESS SCHOLARSHIP

Scholarship for a rising sophomore or junior pursuing a degree in business administration at a West Virginia college or university.

Academic Fields/Career Goals: Business/Consumer Services.

Award: Scholarship for use in sophomore or junior years; not renewable. *Number:* 2. *Amount:* up to $1000.

Eligibility Requirements: Applicant must be enrolled or expecting to enroll full- or part-time at a four-year institution or university; resident of West Virginia; studying in West Virginia and must have an interest in leadership. Applicant must have 3.0 GPA or higher. Available to U.S. citizens.

Application Requirements: Application, essay, interview, resume, references, test scores, transcript. *Deadline:* February 11.

Contact: Beth Michalec, Program Manager
Robert H. Mollohan Family Charitable Foundation Inc.
1000 Technology Drive, Suite 2000
Fairmont, WV 26554
Phone: 304-333-2251
Fax: 304-333-3900
E-mail: bmichalec@wvhtf.org

ROYAL BANK NATIVE STUDENTS AWARDS PROGRAM http://www.rbc.com

ROYAL BANK ABORIGINAL STUDENT AWARDS

Award for Canadian Aboriginal student who is status Indian, non-status Indian, Inuit or Metis, accepted or attending college or university in the directory of Canadian universities. Must be studying in a financial services discipline. Award covers maximum of four years at university or two years at college. Must be permanent resident/citizen of Canada.

Academic Fields/Career Goals: Business/Consumer Services; Computer Science/Data Processing; Economics.

Award: Scholarship for use in freshman, sophomore, junior, or senior years; renewable. *Number:* 5. *Amount:* up to $4000.

Eligibility Requirements: Applicant must be of Indian heritage and Canadian citizen; American Indian/Alaska Native and enrolled or expecting to enroll full-time at a two-year or four-year institution or university.

Application Requirements: Application, essay, financial need analysis, references, transcript. *Deadline:* January 31.

Contact: Awards Program Committee
Royal Bank Native Students Awards Program
20 King Street West, Tenth Floor
Toronto, ON M5H 1C4
Canada
E-mail: aboriginalstudentawards@rbc.com

SALES PROFESSIONALS-USA http://www.salesprofessionals-usa.com

SALES PROFESSIONALS-USA SCHOLARSHIP

Scholarships are awarded to students furthering their degree or obtaining a degree in business or marketing. The scholarships are initiated and awarded by the individual Sales Pros Clubs (located in Colorado, Kansas and Missouri) and are not nationally awarded. A listing of local clubs can be found at http://www.salesprofessionals-usa.com.

Academic Fields/Career Goals: Business/Consumer Services.

Award: Scholarship for use in freshman, sophomore, junior, or senior years; not renewable. *Number:* 3–5. *Amount:* $600–$1000.

Eligibility Requirements: Applicant must be enrolled or expecting to enroll full- or part-time at a two-year or four-year institution or university; resident of Colorado, Indiana, or Kansas and studying in Colorado, Kansas, or Missouri. Applicant must have 3.0 GPA or higher. Available to U.S. citizens.

Application Requirements: Application, essay. *Deadline:* varies.

Contact: Jay Berg, National President
Sales Professionals-USA
2870 North Speer Boulevard
Denver, CO 80001
Phone: 303-433-1051
E-mail: jberg@spacelogic.net

SAN DIEGO FOUNDATION http://www.sdfoundation.org

ENERGY OF ACHIEVEMENT SDG&E SCHOLARSHIP

Scholarship to provide financial assistance to graduating high school seniors who are attending an accredited two-year college or four-year university in the United States. Applicants must have a minimum 2.5 GPA and be majoring in business related areas, computer science, or engineering. Students must have a demonstrated financial need and be actively involved in extracurricular activities, community service, work experience, or athletics.

Academic Fields/Career Goals: Business/Consumer Services; Computer Science/Data Processing; Engineering/Technology.

Award: Scholarship for use in freshman year; not renewable. *Number:* 10. *Amount:* $2500.

Eligibility Requirements: Applicant must be high school student; planning to enroll or expecting to enroll full-time at a two-year or four-year institution or university and resident of California. Applicant or parent of applicant must have employment or volunteer experience in community service. Applicant must have 2.5 GPA or higher. Available to U.S. citizens.

Application Requirements: Application, references, transcript, personal statement, copy of tax return. *Deadline:* January 26.

Contact: Shryl Helvie, Scholarship Coordinator
San Diego Foundation
2508 Historic Decatur Road, Suite 200
San Diego, CA 92106
Phone: 619-814-1307
Fax: 619-239-1710
E-mail: shryl@sdfoundation.org

SOCIETY OF AUTOMOTIVE ANALYSTS http://www.cybersaa.org

SOCIETY OF AUTOMOTIVE ANALYSTS SCHOLARSHIP

• *See page 62*

SOUTH DAKOTA RETAILERS ASSOCIATION http://www.sdra.org

SOUTH DAKOTA RETAILERS ASSOCIATION SCHOLARSHIP PROGRAM

• *See page 64*

STRAIGHTFORWARD MEDIA http://www.straightforwardmedia.com

STRAIGHTFORWARD MEDIA BUSINESS SCHOOL SCHOLARSHIP

Scholarship of $500 for undergraduate and graduate students pursuing a business-related degree, including but not limited to economics, finance, marketing, and management. Students pursuing an online business degree are also eligible. Must be U.S. citizen enrolled in full-time study. Awarded four times per year. Deadlines: March 31, June 30, September 30, December 31.

Academic Fields/Career Goals: Business/Consumer Services; Economics.

Award: Scholarship for use in freshman, sophomore, junior, or senior years; not renewable. *Number:* 4. *Amount:* $500.

Eligibility Requirements: Applicant must be enrolled or expecting to enroll full-time at a four-year institution or university. Available to U.S. and non-U.S. citizens.

Application Requirements: Online application. *Deadline:* varies.

Contact: Scholarship Committee
StraightForward Media
2040 West Main Street, Suite 104
Rapid City, SD 57701
Phone: 605-348-3042
Fax: 605-348-3043

TEXAS FAMILY BUSINESS ASSOCIATION AND SCHOLARSHIP FOUNDATION http://www.texasfamilybusiness.org/

TEXAS FAMILY BUSINESS ASSOCIATION SCHOLARSHIP

Scholarships awarded to eligible Texas family business members to help them obtain an education in business. Applicants must be planning to return to or stay with their family business.

Academic Fields/Career Goals: Business/Consumer Services.

Award: Scholarship for use in freshman, sophomore, junior, or senior years; not renewable. *Number:* 1. *Amount:* varies.

Eligibility Requirements: Applicant must be enrolled or expecting to enroll full- or part-time at a four-year institution or university; resident of Texas; studying in Texas and must have an interest in entrepreneurship. Available to U.S. citizens.

Application Requirements: Application, essay, transcript. *Deadline:* varies.

Contact: William Kirshner, President
Texas Family Business Association and Scholarship Foundation
2301 Rodd Field Road
Corpus Christi, TX 78414
Phone: 361-882-1686
Fax: 361-888-6602
E-mail: info@texasfamilybusiness.org

TKE EDUCATIONAL FOUNDATION http://www.tke.org

W. ALLAN HERZOG SCHOLARSHIP

• *See page 64*

TRUCKLOAD CARRIERS ASSOCIATION http://www.truckload.org

TRUCKLOAD CARRIERS ASSOCIATION SCHOLARSHIP FUND

This scholarship fund is for persons affiliated with the trucking industry and their families to pursue higher education. Special consideration will be given to applicants pursuing transportation or business degrees. Minimum 3.3 GPA required. For junior and senior undergraduate students at four-year college or university. Further information and application deadlines available at Web site http://www.truckload.org.

Academic Fields/Career Goals: Business/Consumer Services; Transportation.

Award: Scholarship for use in junior or senior years; not renewable. *Number:* 18. *Amount:* $1500–$5000.

Eligibility Requirements: Applicant must be enrolled or expecting to enroll full-time at a four-year institution or university. Applicant or parent of applicant must have employment or volunteer experience in transportation industry. Available to U.S. and Canadian citizens.

Application Requirements: Application, essay, financial need analysis, transcript, course schedule including tuition and fees. *Deadline:* May 23.

Contact: Debbie Sparks, Vice President of Development
Truckload Carriers Association
555 East Braddock Road
Alexandria, VA 22314
Phone: 703-838-1950
Fax: 703-836-6610
E-mail: tca@truckload.org

UNITED DAUGHTERS OF THE CONFEDERACY http://www.hqudc.org

WALTER REED SMITH SCHOLARSHIP

Award for full-time female undergraduate students who are descendant of a Confederate soldier, studying nutrition, home economics, nursing, business administration, or computer science in accredited college or university. Minimum 3.0 GPA required. Submit letter of endorsement from sponsoring chapter of the United Daughters of the Confederacy.

Academic Fields/Career Goals: Business/Consumer Services; Computer Science/Data Processing; Food Science/Nutrition; Home Economics; Nursing.

Award: Scholarship for use in freshman, sophomore, junior, or senior years; renewable. *Number:* 1–2. *Amount:* $800–$1000.

Eligibility Requirements: Applicant must be enrolled or expecting to enroll full-time at a four-year institution or university and female. Applicant or parent of applicant must be member of United Daughters of the Confederacy. Applicant must have 3.0 GPA or higher. Available to U.S. citizens. Applicant or parent must meet one or more of the following requirements: Air Force, Army, or Navy experience; retired from active duty; disabled or killed as a result of military service; prisoner of war; or missing in action.

Application Requirements: Application, essay, financial need analysis, photo, references, self-addressed stamped envelope, transcript, copy of applicant's birth certificate, copy of confederate ancestor's proof of service. *Deadline:* March 15.

Contact: Deanna Bryant, Second Vice President General
United Daughters of the Confederacy
328 North Boulevard
Richmond, VA 23220-4009
Phone: 804-355-1636
Fax: 804-353-1396
E-mail: hqudc@rcn.com

UNITED NEGRO COLLEGE FUND http://www.uncf.org

AXA FOUNDATION FUND ACHIEVEMENT SCHOLARSHIP

Scholarship for New York residents attending a UNCF member college or university. Must declare business-related major. Minimum 3.0 GPA required. Applicants must exemplify high academic achievement, leadership ability, and community service. Prospective applicants should complete the Student Profile found at Web site: http://www.uncf.org.

Academic Fields/Career Goals: Business/Consumer Services.

Award: Scholarship for use in freshman, sophomore, junior, or senior years; not renewable. *Number:* varies. *Amount:* $2000–$5000.

Eligibility Requirements: Applicant must be Black (non-Hispanic); enrolled or expecting to enroll full- or part-time at a four-year institution or university; resident of New York and must have an interest in leadership. Applicant must have 3.0 GPA or higher. Available to U.S. citizens.

United Negro College Fund (continued)

Application Requirements: Application, financial need analysis. *Deadline:* January 30.

Contact: Director, Program Services
United Negro College Fund
8260 Willow Oaks Corporate Drive
PO Box 10444
Fairfax, VA 22031-8044
Phone: 800-331-2244
E-mail: rebecca.bennett@uncf.org

BEST BUY ENTERPRISE EMPLOYEE SCHOLARSHIP
• *See page 64*

BOOZ, ALLEN AND HAMILTON/WILLIAM F. STASIOR INTERNSHIP

Program available to college juniors majoring in engineering, business, finance, economics, math, science, information systems, or computer science at any of the following UNCF member colleges and universities. List of eligible schools available at Web site. Prospective applicants should complete the student profile found at Web site: http://www.uncf.org.

Academic Fields/Career Goals: Business/Consumer Services; Computer Science/Data Processing; Earth Science; Economics; Engineering/Technology; Physical Sciences and Math; Psychology.

Award: Scholarship for use in sophomore, junior, or senior years; not renewable. *Number:* varies. *Amount:* up to $10,000.

Eligibility Requirements: Applicant must be Black (non-Hispanic) and enrolled or expecting to enroll full-time at a four-year institution or university. Available to U.S. citizens.

Application Requirements: Application, financial need analysis. *Deadline:* March 31.

Contact: Director, Program Services
United Negro College Fund
8260 Willow Oaks Corporate Drive
PO Box 10444
Fairfax, VA 22031-8044
Phone: 800-331-2244
E-mail: rebecca.bennett@uncf.org

CARDINAL HEALTH SCHOLARSHIP
• *See page 65*

CASTLE ROCK FOUNDATION SCHOLARSHIP

Scholarship awarded to students majoring in business or engineering and who attend the following institutions: Bethune-Cookman College, LeMoyne-Owen College, More-house College, Shaw University, Spelman College, Tuskegee University, or Xavier University. Should have minimum GPA of 2.5 and the value of scholarship is $3600.

Academic Fields/Career Goals: Business/Consumer Services; Engineering/Technology.

Award: Scholarship for use in freshman, sophomore, junior, senior, or graduate years; renewable. *Number:* 10. *Amount:* $3600.

Eligibility Requirements: Applicant must be Black (non-Hispanic) and enrolled or expecting to enroll full-time at a four-year institution or university. Applicant must have 2.5 GPA or higher. Available to U.S. and non-U.S. citizens.

Application Requirements: Application, financial need analysis, FAFSA, Student Aid Report (SAR). *Deadline:* varies.

Contact: Director, Program Services
United Negro College Fund
8260 Willow Oaks Corporate Drive
PO Box 10444
Fairfax, VA 22031-8044
Phone: 800-331-2244
E-mail: rebecca.bennett@uncf.org

C.R. BARD SCHOLARSHIP AND INTERNSHIP PROGRAM

Scholarship awards $4000 to undergraduate sophomore majoring in business at a UNCF member college or university. Must have a minimum of 3.0 GPA. Program provides paid internship during summer at the C. R. Bard headquarters in Murray Hill, New Jersey. Please visit Web site for more information: http://www.uncf.org.

Academic Fields/Career Goals: Business/Consumer Services.

Award: Scholarship for use in sophomore year; not renewable. *Number:* varies. *Amount:* $4000.

Eligibility Requirements: Applicant must be Black (non-Hispanic); enrolled or expecting to enroll full- or part-time at a four-year institution or university and resident of New Jersey. Applicant must have 3.0 GPA or higher. Available to U.S. citizens.

Application Requirements: Application, financial need analysis, FAFSA, Student Aid Report (SAR). *Deadline:* varies.

Contact: William Dunham, Program Services
United Negro College Fund
8260 Willow Oaks Corporate Drive
Fairfax, VA 22031
Phone: 703-205-3486

EDWARD M. NAGEL FOUNDATION SCHOLARSHIP
• *See page 65*

FINANCIAL SERVICES INSTITUTION SCHOLARSHIP

Scholarship for students to learn about and be exposed directly to the financial services industry. Applicant must attend a UNCF member college or university. Must have a minimum GPA of 2.5 with finance as major. Scholarship value varies based on need.

Academic Fields/Career Goals: Business/Consumer Services.

Award: Scholarship for use in freshman, sophomore, junior, senior, or graduate years; renewable. *Number:* varies. *Amount:* varies.

Eligibility Requirements: Applicant must be Black (non-Hispanic) and enrolled or expecting to enroll full-time at a four-year institution or university. Applicant must have 2.5 GPA or higher. Available to U.S. and non-U.S. citizens.

Application Requirements: Application, financial need analysis, FAFSA. *Deadline:* varies.

Contact: Director, Program Services
United Negro College Fund
8260 Willow Oaks Corporate Drive
PO Box 10444
Fairfax, VA 22031-8044
Phone: 800-331-2244
E-mail: rebecca.bennett@uncf.org

FLOWERS INDUSTRIES SCHOLARSHIP

Awards given to students majoring in business, marketing, computer science, or food service at one of the following colleges or universities: Bethune-Cookman, Clark Atlanta, Stillman, Virginia Union. Minimum 2.5 GPA required. Prospective applicants should complete the student profile found at Web site: http://www.uncf.org.

Academic Fields/Career Goals: Business/Consumer Services; Computer Science/Data Processing; Food Service/Hospitality.

Award: Scholarship for use in freshman, sophomore, junior, or senior years; not renewable. *Number:* 1. *Amount:* $2500.

Eligibility Requirements: Applicant must be Black (non-Hispanic) and enrolled or expecting to enroll full-time at a four-year institution or university. Applicant must have 2.5 GPA or higher. Available to U.S. citizens.

Application Requirements: Application, financial need analysis. *Deadline:* continuous.

Contact: Director, Program Services
United Negro College Fund
8260 Willow Oaks Corporate Drive
PO Box 10444
Fairfax, VA 22031-8044
Phone: 800-331-2244
E-mail: rebecca.bennett@uncf.org

FORD/UNCF CORPORATE SCHOLARS PROGRAM
• *See page 65*

JESSE JONES JR. SCHOLARSHIP

Scholarship is funded through the Chrysler Minority Dealership Association for Business students attending a UNCF member college or university. Scholarship value ranges from $2000 to $5000.

Academic Fields/Career Goals: Business/Consumer Services.

Award: Scholarship for use in freshman, sophomore, junior, or senior years; not renewable. *Number:* 4. *Amount:* $2000–$5000.

Eligibility Requirements: Applicant must be Black (non-Hispanic) and enrolled or expecting to enroll full- or part-time at a four-year institution or university. Applicant must have 2.5 GPA or higher. Available to U.S. and non-U.S. citizens.

Application Requirements: Application, financial need analysis. *Deadline:* continuous.

Contact: Director, Program Services
United Negro College Fund
8260 Willow Oaks Corporate Drive
PO Box 10444
Fairfax, VA 22031-8044
Phone: 800-331-2244
E-mail: rebecca.bennett@uncf.org

MASTERCARD WORLDWIDE SCHOLARS PROGRAM

• *See page 65*

MAYTAG COMPANY SCHOLARSHIP

Scholarship for students majoring in engineering, business, computer science, or information technology at one of the following colleges or universities: Benedict, Claflin, Lane, LeMoyne-Owen, Morris, Paine, Voorhees, Wilberforce, or a historically black college or university. Minimum 2.5 GPA required. Prospective applicants should complete the Student Profile found at Web site: http://www.uncf.org.

Academic Fields/Career Goals: Business/Consumer Services; Computer Science/Data Processing; Engineering/Technology.

Award: Scholarship for use in freshman, sophomore, junior, or senior years; not renewable. *Number:* varies. *Amount:* $1250.

Eligibility Requirements: Applicant must be Black (non-Hispanic) and enrolled or expecting to enroll full- or part-time at a four-year institution or university. Applicant must have 2.5 GPA or higher. Available to U.S. citizens.

Application Requirements: Application, financial need analysis. *Deadline:* continuous.

Contact: Director, Program Services
United Negro College Fund
8260 Willow Oaks Corporate Drive
PO Box 10444
Fairfax, VA 22031-8044
Phone: 800-331-2244
E-mail: rebecca.bennett@uncf.org

MBIA/WILLIAM O. BAILEY SCHOLARS PROGRAM

• *See page 65*

NASCAR/WENDELL SCOTT, SR. SCHOLARSHIP

• *See page 66*

NORTHEAST UTILITIES SYSTEM SCHOLARSHIP PROGRAM

Scholarships available for African American students enrolled as a sophomore or junior at a participating UNCF college or university. Must be pursuing a degree in engineering, business, information systems, or computer science/MIS. Must complete an internship. Visit Web site for details. http://www.uncf.org.

Academic Fields/Career Goals: Business/Consumer Services; Computer Science/Data Processing; Energy and Power Engineering; Engineering/Technology; Engineering-Related Technologies.

Award: Scholarship for use in sophomore or junior years; not renewable. *Number:* varies. *Amount:* $10,000.

Eligibility Requirements: Applicant must be Black (non-Hispanic); enrolled or expecting to enroll full-time at a four-year institution or university and resident of Connecticut or Massachusetts. Applicant must have 3.0 GPA or higher. Available to U.S. citizens.

Application Requirements: Application. *Deadline:* varies.

Contact: Director, Program Services
United Negro College Fund
8260 Willow Oaks Corporate Drive
PO Box 10444
Fairfax, VA 22031-8044
Phone: 800-331-2244
E-mail: rebecca.bennett@uncf.org

PRINCIPAL FINANCIAL GROUP SCHOLARSHIPS

• *See page 66*

SPRINT NEXTEL SCHOLARSHIP/INTERNSHIP

• *See page 66*

THURMOND WOODARD/DELL/UNCF CORPORATE SCHOLARS PROGRAM

Program to provide MBA students, sophomores, juniors and seniors attending any four-year institution with an opportunity to gain invaluable internship experience and earn a $10,000 scholarship. Minimum 3.0 GPA required. Limited opportunities are available for students majoring in marketing, business administration, finance, human resources, engineering, logistics, or computer science.

Academic Fields/Career Goals: Business/Consumer Services; Computer Science/Data Processing; Electrical Engineering/Electronics; Engineering/Technology.

Award: Scholarship for use in sophomore, junior, senior, or graduate years; not renewable. *Number:* 1. *Amount:* up to $10,000.

Eligibility Requirements: Applicant must be Black (non-Hispanic); enrolled or expecting to enroll full-time at a four-year institution and resident of Texas. Applicant must have 3.0 GPA or higher. Available to U.S. citizens.

Application Requirements: Application, financial need analysis. *Deadline:* November 15.

Contact: Director, Program Services
United Negro College Fund
8260 Willow Oaks Corporate Drive
PO Box 10444
Fairfax, VA 22031-8044
Phone: 800-331-2244
E-mail: rebecca.bennett@uncf.org

TOYOTA SCHOLARSHIP

• *See page 66*

UBS/PAINEWEBBER SCHOLARSHIPS

• *See page 66*

UPS/UNCF CORPORATE SCHOLARS PROGRAM

Award consists of both a scholarship and internship. Applicant must be a sophomore or junior undergraduate majoring in civil engineering, computer science, electrical engineering, English, finance, human resources, industrial engineering, information technology, journalism, marketing, mechanical engineering or public relations. Must have 3.0 GPA.

Academic Fields/Career Goals: Business/Consumer Services; Civil Engineering; Computer Science/Data Processing; Electrical Engineering/Electronics; Journalism; Literature/English/Writing; Mechanical Engineering.

Award: Scholarship for use in sophomore or junior years; renewable. *Number:* varies. *Amount:* up to $10,000.

Eligibility Requirements: Applicant must be Black (non-Hispanic) and enrolled or expecting to enroll full- or part-time at a four-year institution or university. Applicant must have 3.0 GPA or higher. Available to U.S. citizens.

Application Requirements: Application, financial need analysis, FAFSA, Student Aid Report (SAR). *Deadline:* February 9.

Contact: Director, Program Services
United Negro College Fund
8260 Willow Oaks Corporate Drive
PO Box 10444
Fairfax, VA 22031-8044
Phone: 800-331-2244
E-mail: rebecca.bennett@uncf.org

WELLS FARGO/UNCF SCHOLARSHIP FUND

• *See page 67*

WEYERHAEUSER/UNCF CORPORATE SCHOLARS PROGRAM

Award for sophomores and juniors majoring in marketing, operations management, electrical engineering, industrial engineering, civil engineering, chemical engineering, mechanical engineering or forestry. Must have 3.0 GPA.

Academic Fields/Career Goals: Business/Consumer Services; Chemical Engineering; Electrical Engineering/Electronics; Engineering/Technology; Environmental Science; Mechanical Engineering; Natural Resources.

Award: Scholarship for use in sophomore or junior years; renewable. *Number:* varies. *Amount:* $10,000.

United Negro College Fund (continued)

Eligibility Requirements: Applicant must be Black (non-Hispanic) and enrolled or expecting to enroll full-time at a four-year institution or university. Applicant must have 3.0 GPA or higher. Available to U.S. citizens.

Application Requirements: Application, essay, financial need analysis, resume, references, transcript, FAFSA, Student Aid Report (SAR). *Deadline:* February 15.

Contact: Director, Program Services
United Negro College Fund
8260 Willow Oaks Corporate Drive
PO Box 10444
Fairfax, VA 22031-8044
Phone: 800-331-2244
E-mail: rebecca.bennett@uncf.org

WRIGLEY JR., WILLIAM SCHOLARSHIP/INTERNSHIP

Award for undergraduate sophomores and juniors at a UNCF member college. Need-based scholarships offered to business, engineering, and chemistry majors with at least a 3.0 GPA. Prospective applicants should complete the Student Profile found at Web site: http://www.uncf.org.

Academic Fields/Career Goals: Business/Consumer Services; Chemical Engineering; Engineering/Technology; Physical Sciences and Math.

Award: Scholarship for use in sophomore or junior years; not renewable. *Number:* varies. *Amount:* up to $3000.

Eligibility Requirements: Applicant must be Black (non-Hispanic) and enrolled or expecting to enroll full- or part-time at a four-year institution or university. Applicant must have 3.0 GPA or higher. Available to U.S. and non-U.S. citizens.

Application Requirements: Application, financial need analysis. *Deadline:* varies.

Contact: Director, Program Services
United Negro College Fund
8260 Willow Oaks Corporate Drive
PO Box 10444
Fairfax, VA 22031-8044
Phone: 800-331-2244
E-mail: rebecca.bennett@uncf.org

VIRGINIA SOCIETY OF CERTIFIED PUBLIC ACCOUNTANTS EDUCATION FOUNDATION http://www.cpastudentzone.com

VIRGINIA SOCIETY OF CPAS EDUCATIONAL FOUNDATION MINORITY SCHOLARSHIP

• *See page 67*

VIRGINIA SOCIETY OF CPAS EDUCATIONAL FOUNDATION UNDERGRADUATE SCHOLARSHIP

• *See page 67*

WATERBURY FOUNDATION http://www.conncf.org

MALCOLM BALDRIGE SCHOLARSHIP

One-time award for undergraduates studying in accredited colleges or universities of Connecticut majoring in international business or trade. Must be a Connecticut resident. The award value is in the range of $2000 to $4000 and up to two scholarships are granted annually.

Academic Fields/Career Goals: Business/Consumer Services; International Studies.

Award: Scholarship for use in freshman, sophomore, junior, or senior years; not renewable. *Number:* 1–2. *Amount:* $2000–$4000.

Eligibility Requirements: Applicant must be enrolled or expecting to enroll full- or part-time at a two-year or four-year institution or university; resident of Connecticut and studying in Connecticut. Available to U.S. citizens.

Application Requirements: Application, essay, financial need analysis, references, transcript. *Deadline:* March 1.

Contact: Josh Carey, Program Officer
Waterbury Foundation
43 Field Street
Waterbury, CT 06702-1216
Phone: 203-753-1315
Fax: 203-756-3054
E-mail: jcarey@conncf.org

WOMEN GROCERS OF AMERICA http://www.nationalgrocers.org

MARY MACEY SCHOLARSHIP

• *See page 80*

WOMEN IN LOGISTICS, NORTHERN CALIFORNIA http://www.womeninlogistics.org

WOMEN IN LOGISTICS SCHOLARSHIP

Award for students who plan to study and eventually pursue a career in logistics/supply chain management. Must be enrolled in a degree program at a San Francisco Bay Area institution. Deadline varies.

Academic Fields/Career Goals: Business/Consumer Services; Trade/Technical Specialties; Transportation.

Award: Scholarship for use in freshman, sophomore, junior, senior, or graduate years; not renewable. *Number:* 1–3. *Amount:* $2000.

Eligibility Requirements: Applicant must be enrolled or expecting to enroll full- or part-time at a two-year or four-year institution or university and studying in California. Applicant or parent of applicant must be member of Women in Logistics. Available to U.S. and non-U.S. citizens.

Application Requirements: Application, applicant must enter a contest, essay, resume, references. *Deadline:* varies.

Contact: Susan Cholette, Scholarship Director
Women in Logistics, Northern California
PO Box 194681
San Francisco, CA 94119-4681
Phone: 415-405-2173
Fax: 415-405-0364
E-mail: cholette@sfsu.edu

WYOMING TRUCKING ASSOCIATION

WYOMING TRUCKING ASSOCIATION TRUST FUND SCHOLARSHIP

One-time award for students enrolled at a Wyoming college. Must plan a career in the transportation industry in Wyoming. Course of study includes business and sales management, computer skills, accounting, office procedures and management, communications, mechanics, truck driver training and safety.

Academic Fields/Career Goals: Business/Consumer Services; Computer Science/Data Processing; Trade/Technical Specialties; Transportation.

Award: Scholarship for use in freshman, sophomore, junior, or senior years; renewable. *Number:* 1–10. *Amount:* $500–$1000.

Eligibility Requirements: Applicant must be enrolled or expecting to enroll full-time at a four-year institution or university; resident of Wyoming and studying in Wyoming. Available to U.S. citizens.

Application Requirements: Application, essay, financial need analysis, references, test scores, transcript. *Deadline:* March 3.

Contact: Kathy Cundall, Administrative Assistant
Wyoming Trucking Association
PO Box 1909
Casper, WY 82602-1909
Phone: 307-234-1579
Fax: 307-234-7082
E-mail: wytruck@aol.com

Y'S MEN INTERNATIONAL http://www.ysmenusa.com

ALEXANDER SCHOLARSHIP LOAN FUND

The purpose of the fund is to promote the training of staff of the YMCA and/or those seeking to become members or staff of the YMCA. Deadlines: May 30 for fall semester, and October 30 for spring semester.

Academic Fields/Career Goals: Business/Consumer Services; Child and Family Studies; Education; Human Resources; Social Sciences; Social Services; Sports-Related/Exercise Science.

Award: Scholarship for use in freshman, sophomore, junior, or senior years; renewable. *Number:* varies. *Amount:* varies.

Eligibility Requirements: Applicant must be enrolled or expecting to enroll full- or part-time at a two-year or four-year institution or university. Available to U.S. citizens.

Application Requirements: Application. *Fee:* $1. *Deadline:* varies.

Contact: Dean Currie, Area Service Director
Y's Men International
629 Lantana Lane
Imperial, CA 92251
Phone: 908-753-9493
Fax: 602-935-6322
E-mail: kidcurrie@adelphia.net

ZONTA INTERNATIONAL FOUNDATION http://www.zonta.org

JANE M. KLAUSMAN WOMEN IN BUSINESS SCHOLARSHIPS

Awards for female students entering their third or fourth year in an undergraduate business degree. Application available at Web site: http://www.zonta.org.

Academic Fields/Career Goals: Business/Consumer Services.

Award: Scholarship for use in junior or senior years; not renewable. *Number:* up to 5. *Amount:* $4000–$5000.

Eligibility Requirements: Applicant must be enrolled or expecting to enroll full-time at a four-year institution or university and female. Available to U.S. and non-U.S. citizens.

Application Requirements: Application, essay, references. *Deadline:* varies.

Contact: Ana Ubides, Program Coordinator
Zonta International Foundation
557 West Randolph Street
Chicago, IL 60661
Phone: 312-930-5848
Fax: 312-930-0951
E-mail: zontaintl@zonta.org

CAMPUS ACTIVITIES

NATIONAL ASSOCIATION FOR CAMPUS ACTIVITIES http://www.naca.org

MARKLEY SCHOLARSHIP

Scholarship available to students who are strongly involved in the field of student activities and/or student activities employment, and who have made significant contributions to NACA Central. Must be classified as a junior, senior or graduate student at a four-year school located in the former NACA South Central region, or a sophomore in the former NACA South Central region. Must have minimum 2.5 GPA.

Academic Fields/Career Goals: Campus Activities.

Award: Scholarship for use in junior, senior, or graduate years; not renewable. *Number:* up to 2. *Amount:* $250–$300.

Eligibility Requirements: Applicant must be enrolled or expecting to enroll full- or part-time at a four-year institution and studying in Arkansas, Louisiana, New Mexico, Oklahoma, or Texas. Applicant or parent of applicant must have employment or volunteer experience in community service. Applicant must have 2.5 GPA or higher. Available to U.S. citizens.

Application Requirements: Application, resume. *Deadline:* September 1.

Contact: Dionne Ellison, Administrative Assistant
National Association for Campus Activities
13 Harbison Way
Columbia, SC 29212-3401
Phone: 803-732-6222 Ext. 131
Fax: 803-749-1047
E-mail: dionnee@naca.org

CANADIAN STUDIES

CANADIAN INSTITUTE OF UKRAINIAN STUDIES http://www.cius.ca

CANADIAN INSTITUTE OF UKRAINIAN STUDIES RESEARCH GRANTS

• *See page 95*

CHEMICAL ENGINEERING

AACE INTERNATIONAL http://www.aacei.org

AACE INTERNATIONAL COMPETITIVE SCHOLARSHIP

• *See page 89*

AMERICAN CHEMICAL SOCIETY http://www.acs.org/scholars

AMERICAN CHEMICAL SOCIETY SCHOLARS PROGRAM

Renewable award for minority students pursuing studies in chemistry, biochemistry, chemical technology, chemical engineering, or any chemical sciences. Must be U.S. citizen or permanent resident and have minimum 3.0 GPA. Must be Native American, African-American, or Hispanic.

Academic Fields/Career Goals: Chemical Engineering; Materials Science, Engineering, and Metallurgy; Natural Sciences.

Award: Scholarship for use in freshman, sophomore, junior, or senior years; renewable. *Number:* 100–200. *Amount:* $1000–$5000.

Eligibility Requirements: Applicant must be American Indian/Alaska Native, Black (non-Hispanic), or Hispanic and enrolled or expecting to enroll full-time at a two-year or four-year or technical institution or university. Applicant must have 3.0 GPA or higher. Available to U.S. citizens.

Application Requirements: Application, financial need analysis, references, test scores, transcript. *Deadline:* March 1.

Contact: Robert Hughes, Manager
American Chemical Society
1155 16th Street, NW
Washington, DC 20036
Phone: 202-872-6048
Fax: 202-776-8003
E-mail: r_hughes@acs.org

AMERICAN CHEMICAL SOCIETY, RUBBER DIVISION http://www.rubber.org

AMERICAN CHEMICAL SOCIETY, RUBBER DIVISION UNDERGRADUATE SCHOLARSHIP

Candidate must be majoring in a technical discipline relevant to the rubber industry with a "B" or better overall academic average. Two scholarships are awarded to juniors and seniors enrolled in an accredited college or university in the United States, Canada, Mexico, India or Brazil.

Academic Fields/Career Goals: Chemical Engineering; Engineering/Technology; Materials Science, Engineering, and Metallurgy; Mechanical Engineering; Science, Technology, and Society.

Award: Scholarship for use in junior or senior years; not renewable. *Number:* 3. *Amount:* $5000.

Eligibility Requirements: Applicant must be enrolled or expecting to enroll full-time at a four-year institution or university. Applicant must have 3.0 GPA or higher. Available to U.S. and non-U.S. citizens.

Application Requirements: Application, essay, interview, references, test scores, transcript. *Deadline:* March 1.

Contact: Christie Robinson, Education and Publications Manager
American Chemical Society, Rubber Division
250 South Forge Road, PO Box 499
Akron, OH 44325
Phone: 330-972-7814
Fax: 330-972-5269
E-mail: education@rubber.org

AMERICAN COUNCIL OF ENGINEERING COMPANIES OF PENNSYLVANIA (ACEC/PA) http://www.acecpa.org

ENGINEERING SCHOLARSHIP

Scholarship for full-time engineering students enrolled in accredited colleges or universities. Must be U.S. citizen. Up to five awards are granted annually.

Academic Fields/Career Goals: Chemical Engineering; Civil Engineering; Electrical Engineering/Electronics; Engineering/Technology; Engineering-Related Technologies; Materials Science, Engineering, and Metallurgy; Mechanical Engineering.

Award: Scholarship for use in freshman, sophomore, junior, or senior years; not renewable. *Number:* 1–5. *Amount:* $2500–$5000.

Eligibility Requirements: Applicant must be enrolled or expecting to enroll full-time at a four-year institution or university and resident of Pennsylvania. Available to U.S. citizens.

Application Requirements: Application, essay, resume, references, transcript. *Deadline:* December 1.

Contact: Laurie Troutman, Administrative Assistant
American Council of Engineering Companies of Pennsylvania (ACEC/PA)
2040 Linglestown Road, Suite 200
Harrisburg, PA 17110
Phone: 717-540-6811
Fax: 717-540-6815
E-mail: laurie@acecpa.org

AMERICAN ELECTROPLATERS AND SURFACE FINISHERS SOCIETY http://www.nasf.org

AMERICAN ELECTROPLATERS AND SURFACE FINISHERS FOUNDATION SCHOLARSHIPS

One-time award to students majoring in materials science, chemical engineering, or environmental engineering. Applicant must be a junior or senior undergraduate studying full-time. Also open to graduate students.

Academic Fields/Career Goals: Chemical Engineering; Engineering/ Technology; Materials Science, Engineering, and Metallurgy.

Award: Scholarship for use in junior, senior, or graduate years; not renewable. *Number:* 5–10. *Amount:* $1500.

Eligibility Requirements: Applicant must be enrolled or expecting to enroll full-time at a four-year institution or university. Available to U.S. and non-U.S. citizens.

Application Requirements: Application, essay, resume, references, transcript. *Deadline:* April 15.

Contact: Scholarship Committee
American Electroplaters and Surface Finishers Society
1155 Fifteenth Street, NW, Suite 500
Washington, DC 20005
Phone: 202-457-8401
Fax: 202-530-0659

AMERICAN INSTITUTE OF CHEMICAL ENGINEERS http://www.aiche.org

CHEME-CAR NATIONAL LEVEL COMPETITION

Each student chapter region may send their first and second place winners to the design competition. Multiple entries from a single school may be permitted at the regional competitions, but only one entry per school is allowed at the national competition. Students majoring in chemical engineering can participate.

Academic Fields/Career Goals: Chemical Engineering.

Award: Prize for use in freshman, sophomore, junior, or senior years; not renewable. *Number:* up to 3. *Amount:* $200–$2000.

Eligibility Requirements: Applicant must be enrolled or expecting to enroll full-time at a four-year institution or university. Available to U.S. and non-U.S. citizens.

Application Requirements: Application, applicant must enter a contest, student chapter name, team contact, list of team members, title of entry, description of chemical reaction/drive system, list of chemicals to be used and estimated quantity needed. *Fee:* $100. *Deadline:* June 30.

Contact: Prof. David Dixon, Department of Chemistry and Chemical Engineering
American Institute of Chemical Engineers
South Dakota School of Mines and Technology, 501 East Saint Joseph Street
Rapid City, SD 57701
Phone: 605-394-1235
Fax: 605-394-1232
E-mail: david.dixon@sdsmt.edu

DONALD F. AND MILDRED TOPP OTHMER FOUNDATION-NATIONAL SCHOLARSHIP AWARDS

Awards for 15 national AICHE student members, a scholarship of $1000. Awards are presented on the basis of academic achievement and involvement in student chapter activities. The student chapter advisor must make nominations. Only one nomination will be accepted from each AICHE student chapter or chemical engineering club.

Academic Fields/Career Goals: Chemical Engineering.

Award: Scholarship for use in freshman, sophomore, junior, senior, or graduate years; not renewable. *Number:* 15. *Amount:* $1000.

Eligibility Requirements: Applicant must be enrolled or expecting to enroll full-time at a four-year institution or university. Available to U.S. and non-U.S. citizens.

Application Requirements: Application, essay, references, transcript, statement of long-range career plans. *Deadline:* May 11.

Contact: AIChE Awards Administrator
American Institute of Chemical Engineers
Three Park Avenue
New York, NY 10016-5901
Phone: 212-591-7107
Fax: 212-591-8882
E-mail: awards@aiche.org

ENVIRONMENTAL DIVISION UNDERGRADUATE STUDENT PAPER AWARD

Cash prizes awarded to full-time undergraduate students who prepare the best original papers based on the results of research or an investigation related to the environment. The work must be performed during the student's undergraduate enrollment, and the paper must be submitted prior to or within six months of graduation. Student must be the sole author of the paper, but faculty guidance is encouraged. Student must be a member of the American Institute of Chemical Engineers Student Chapter.

Academic Fields/Career Goals: Chemical Engineering; Environmental Science.

Award: Prize for use in freshman, sophomore, junior, or senior years; not renewable. *Number:* 3. *Amount:* $100–$300.

Eligibility Requirements: Applicant must be enrolled or expecting to enroll full-time at a four-year institution or university. Available to U.S. and non-U.S. citizens.

Application Requirements: Applicant must enter a contest, essay, references, 5 copies of the nomination package. *Deadline:* May 15.

Contact: Tapas Das, Environmental Division Awards Committee
American Institute of Chemical Engineers
125 Mandy Place, NE
Olympia, WA 98516
Phone: 360-456-0573
E-mail: shivaniki@comcast.net

JOHN J. MCKETTA UNDERGRADUATE SCHOLARSHIP

A $5000 scholarship will be awarded to a junior or senior student member of AICHE who is planning a career in the chemical engineering process industries. Must maintain a 3.0 GPA. Applicant should show leadership or activity in either the school's AICHE student chapter or other university sponsored campus activities. Must attend ABET-accredited school in the United States, Canada, or Mexico.

Academic Fields/Career Goals: Chemical Engineering.

Award: Scholarship for use in junior or senior years; not renewable. *Number:* 1. *Amount:* $5000.

Eligibility Requirements: Applicant must be enrolled or expecting to enroll full-time at a four-year institution or university and must have an interest in leadership. Applicant must have 3.0 GPA or higher. Available to U.S. and non-U.S. citizens.

Application Requirements: Application, essay, references. *Deadline:* May 25.

Contact: AIChE Awards Administrator
American Institute of Chemical Engineers
Three Park Avenue
New York, NY 10016
Phone: 212-591-7107
Fax: 212-591-8882
E-mail: awards@aiche.org

MINORITY AFFAIRS COMMITTEE AWARD FOR OUTSTANDING SCHOLASTIC ACHIEVEMENT

Award recognizing the outstanding achievements of a chemical engineering student who serves as a role model for minority students. Offers $1000 award and $500 travel allowance to attend AICHE meeting. Must be nominated.

Academic Fields/Career Goals: Chemical Engineering.

Award: Scholarship for use in freshman, sophomore, junior, senior, or graduate years; not renewable. *Number:* 1. *Amount:* $1500.

Eligibility Requirements: Applicant must be American Indian/Alaska Native, Asian/Pacific Islander, Black (non-Hispanic), or Hispanic and enrolled or expecting to enroll full-time at a four-year institution or university. Applicant must have 3.0 GPA or higher. Available to U.S. and non-U.S. citizens.

Application Requirements: Application. *Deadline:* May 15.

Contact: Dr. Emmanuel Dada, Scholarship Administrator
American Institute of Chemical Engineers
PO Box 8
Princeton, NJ 08543
Phone: 212-591-7107
E-mail: emmanuel_dada@fmc.com

MINORITY SCHOLARSHIP AWARDS FOR COLLEGE STUDENTS

Award for college undergraduates who are studying chemical engineering. Must be a member of a minority group that is underrepresented in chemical engineering. Must be an AICHE national student member at the time of application. Recipients of this scholarship are eligible to reapply.

Academic Fields/Career Goals: Chemical Engineering.

Award: Scholarship for use in freshman, sophomore, junior, or senior years; renewable. *Number:* up to 10. *Amount:* $1000.

Eligibility Requirements: Applicant must be American Indian/Alaska Native, Asian/Pacific Islander, Black (non-Hispanic), or Hispanic and enrolled or expecting to enroll full-time at a two-year or four-year institution or university. Applicant must have 3.0 GPA or higher. Available to U.S. and non-U.S. citizens.

Application Requirements: Application, essay, financial need analysis, references, transcript, career objective. *Deadline:* May 15.

Contact: Dr. Emmanuel Dada, FMC Corporation
American Institute of Chemical Engineers
PO Box 8
Princeton, NJ 08543
Phone: 212-591-7107
E-mail: emmanuel_dada@fmc.com

MINORITY SCHOLARSHIP AWARDS FOR INCOMING COLLEGE FRESHMEN

Up to ten awards of $1000 for high school graduates who are members of a minority group that is underrepresented in chemical engineering. Students must be high school seniors planning to enroll during the next academic year in a four-year college or university offering a science/engineering degree.

Academic Fields/Career Goals: Chemical Engineering.

Award: Scholarship for use in freshman year; not renewable. *Number:* up to 10. *Amount:* $1000.

Eligibility Requirements: Applicant must be American Indian/Alaska Native, Asian/Pacific Islander, Black (non-Hispanic), or Hispanic; high school student and planning to enroll or expecting to enroll full-time at a four-year institution or university. Applicant must have 3.0 GPA or higher. Available to U.S. and non-U.S. citizens.

Application Requirements: Application, essay, financial need analysis, references, transcript, confirmation of minority status. *Deadline:* May 15.

Contact: Dr. Emmanuel Dada, Minority Affairs Committee
American Institute of Chemical Engineers
PO Box 8
Princeton, NJ 08543
Phone: 212-591-7107
E-mail: emmanuel_dada@fmc.com

NATIONAL STUDENT DESIGN COMPETITION-INDIVIDUAL

Three cash prizes for student contest problem that typifies a real, working, chemical engineering design situation. Competition statements are distributed online to student chapter advisors and department heads.

Academic Fields/Career Goals: Chemical Engineering.

Award: Prize for use in freshman, sophomore, junior, senior, or graduate years; not renewable. *Number:* 3. *Amount:* $200–$500.

Eligibility Requirements: Applicant must be enrolled or expecting to enroll full-time at a four-year institution or university. Available to U.S. and non-U.S. citizens.

Application Requirements: Applicant must enter a contest, essay. *Deadline:* June 6.

Contact: AIChE Awards Administrator
American Institute of Chemical Engineers
Three Park Avenue
New York, NY 10016
Phone: 212-591-7107
Fax: 212-591-8882
E-mail: awards@aiche.org

NATIONAL STUDENT DESIGN COMPETITION-TEAM (WILLIAM CUNNINGHAM AWARD)

Design contest for chemical engineering students.

Academic Fields/Career Goals: Chemical Engineering.

Award: Prize for use in freshman, sophomore, junior, senior, or graduate years; not renewable. *Number:* 1. *Amount:* up to $600.

Eligibility Requirements: Applicant must be enrolled or expecting to enroll full-time at a four-year institution or university. Available to U.S. and non-U.S. citizens.

Application Requirements: Application, applicant must enter a contest, essay. *Deadline:* June 6.

Contact: AIChE Awards Administrator
American Institute of Chemical Engineers
Three Park Avenue
New York, NY 10016
Phone: 212-591-7107
Fax: 212-591-8882
E-mail: awards@aiche.org

NATIONAL STUDENT PAPER COMPETITION

First place winners from each of the nine regional student paper competitions present their prize-winning papers during the American Institute of Chemical Engineers meeting held in the current calendar year. First prize is $500, second prize is $300, and third prize is $200.

Academic Fields/Career Goals: Chemical Engineering.

Award: Prize for use in freshman, sophomore, junior, senior, or graduate years; not renewable. *Number:* 3. *Amount:* $200–$500.

Eligibility Requirements: Applicant must be enrolled or expecting to enroll full-time at a four-year institution or university. Available to U.S. and non-U.S. citizens.

American Institute of Chemical Engineers (continued)

Application Requirements: Applicant must enter a contest, student paper. *Deadline:* varies.

Contact: AIChE Awards Administrator
American Institute of Chemical Engineers
Three Park Avenue
New York, NY 10016-5901
Phone: 212-591-7107
Fax: 212-591-8882
E-mail: awards@aiche.org

NORTH AMERICAN MIXING FORUM (NAMF) STUDENT AWARD

Award to encourage, recognize, and reward students for quality research in the area of mixing. Any graduate or undergraduate student doing research in the field of fluid mixing at an accredited university in North America is eligible.

Academic Fields/Career Goals: Chemical Engineering.

Award: Prize for use in freshman, sophomore, junior, senior, or graduate years; not renewable. *Number:* 1. *Amount:* up to $500.

Eligibility Requirements: Applicant must be enrolled or expecting to enroll full-time at a four-year institution or university. Available to U.S. and non-U.S. citizens.

Application Requirements: Applicant must enter a contest, essay, references, cover letter including title of work, name and address of author, abstract, theory or model development, experimental setup/procedures, results and discussion. *Deadline:* March 15.

Contact: Dr. Ricahrd K. Grenville, Student Award Committee
American Institute of Chemical Engineers
1007 Market Street, B8214
Wilmington, DE 19898
Phone: 302-774-2256
Fax: 302-774-2457
E-mail: richard.k.grenville@usa.dupont.com

OUTSTANDING STUDENT CHAPTER ADVISOR AWARD

Award for service and leadership in guiding the activities of an AIChE student chapter in accordance with AIChE principles. Must be advisor of a chartered AIChE student chapter for at least the last three years. Award winners cannot be renominated.

Academic Fields/Career Goals: Chemical Engineering.

Award: Prize for use in freshman, sophomore, junior, or senior years; not renewable. *Number:* 1. *Amount:* up to $1000.

Eligibility Requirements: Applicant must be enrolled or expecting to enroll full-time at a four-year institution or university. Available to U.S. and non-U.S. citizens.

Application Requirements: Application, references, four copies of the nomination. *Deadline:* June 1.

Contact: Marvin Borgmeyer, Scholarship Committee
American Institute of Chemical Engineers
PO Box 1607
Baton Rouge, LA 70821-1607
Phone: 225-977-6206
Fax: 225-977-6396

PROCESS DEVELOPMENT DIVISION STUDENT PAPER AWARD

Award presented to a full-time graduate or undergraduate student who prepares the best technical paper to describe the results of process development related studies within chemical engineering. Must be carried out while the student is enrolled at a university with an accredited chemical engineering program. Student must be the primary author. Paper must be suitable for publication in a refereed journal. Must be a member of AIChE.

Academic Fields/Career Goals: Chemical Engineering.

Award: Prize for use in freshman, sophomore, junior, senior, or graduate years; not renewable. *Number:* 1. *Amount:* $200.

Eligibility Requirements: Applicant must be enrolled or expecting to enroll full-time at a four-year institution or university. Available to U.S. and non-U.S. citizens.

Application Requirements: References, original and five copies of the nomination form. *Deadline:* June 15.

Contact: A.R. Cartolano, Awards Committee Chair
American Institute of Chemical Engineers
7201 Hamilton Boulevard
Allentown, PA 18195-1501
Phone: 610-481-4262
E-mail: cartolar@airproducts.com

REGIONAL STUDENT PAPER COMPETITION

Students present technical papers at the student regional conferences which are held during spring. Deadlines for regional conferences vary. First prize is $200, second prize is $100, and third prize is $50. First place winner from each region present their paper at the regional competition.

Academic Fields/Career Goals: Chemical Engineering.

Award: Prize for use in freshman, sophomore, junior, or senior years; not renewable. *Number:* 3. *Amount:* $50–$200.

Eligibility Requirements: Applicant must be enrolled or expecting to enroll full-time at a four-year institution or university. Available to U.S. and non-U.S. citizens.

Application Requirements: Applicant must enter a contest, student paper. *Deadline:* varies.

Contact: AIChE Awards Administrator
American Institute of Chemical Engineers
Three Park Avenue
New York, NY 10016-5901
Phone: 212-591-7107
Fax: 212-591-8882
E-mail: awards@aiche.org

SAFETY AND CHEMICAL ENGINEERING EDUCATION (SACHE) STUDENT ESSAY AWARD FOR SAFETY

Awards individuals or a team submitting the best essays on the topic of chemical process safety. Essays may focus on process safety in education, relevance of safety in undergraduate education, or integrating safety principles into the undergraduate chemical engineering curriculum.

Academic Fields/Career Goals: Chemical Engineering.

Award: Prize for use in freshman, sophomore, junior, or senior years; not renewable. *Number:* up to 4. *Amount:* $500.

Eligibility Requirements: Applicant must be enrolled or expecting to enroll full-time at a four-year institution or university. Available to U.S. and non-U.S. citizens.

Application Requirements: Applicant must enter a contest, essay. *Deadline:* June 5.

Contact: AIChE Awards Administrator
American Institute of Chemical Engineers
Three Park Avenue
New York, NY 10016
Phone: 212-591-7107
Fax: 212-591-8880
E-mail: awards@aiche.org

SAFETY AND HEALTH NATIONAL STUDENT DESIGN COMPETITION AWARD FOR SAFETY

Four $600 awards available for each of the teams or individuals who apply one or more of the following concepts of inherent safety in their designs: design the plant for easier and effective maintainability; design the plant with less waste; design the plant with special features that demonstrate inherent safety; include design concepts regarding the entire life cycle. The school must have a student chapter of AIChE.

Academic Fields/Career Goals: Chemical Engineering; Industrial Design.

Award: Prize for use in freshman, sophomore, junior, senior, or graduate years; not renewable. *Number:* 4. *Amount:* $600.

Eligibility Requirements: Applicant must be enrolled or expecting to enroll full- or part-time at a four-year institution or university. Available to U.S. and non-U.S. citizens.

Application Requirements: Application, design. *Deadline:* June 6.

Contact: AIChE Awards Administrator
American Institute of Chemical Engineers
Three Park Avenue
New York, NY 10016
Phone: 212-591-7478
Fax: 212-591-8882
E-mail: awards@aiche.org

AMERICAN SOCIETY FOR ENOLOGY AND VITICULTURE http://www.asev.org

AMERICAN SOCIETY FOR ENOLOGY AND VITICULTURE SCHOLARSHIPS

• *See page 72*

ARMED FORCES COMMUNICATIONS AND ELECTRONICS ASSOCIATION, EDUCATIONAL FOUNDATION http://www.afcea.org

AFCEA/LOCKHEED MARTIN ORINCON IT SCHOLARSHIP

• *See page 113*

ASSOCIATION FOR FACILITIES ENGINEERING (AFE)

ASSOCIATION FOR FACILITIES ENGINEERING CEDAR VALLEY CHAPTER #132 SCHOLARSHIP

• *See page 114*

ASSOCIATION FOR IRON AND STEEL TECHNOLOGY http://www.aist.org

ASSOCIATION FOR IRON AND STEEL TECHNOLOGY DAVID H. SAMSON CANADIAN SCHOLARSHIP

Scholarship of $2000 available for children of AIST members who are Canadian citizens. Renewable for up to four years. Student must be studying engineering at a Canadian institution or, in the absence of engineering applicants, the award may be made to an eligible student studying chemistry, geology, mathematics, or physics.

Academic Fields/Career Goals: Chemical Engineering; Civil Engineering; Electrical Engineering/Electronics; Energy and Power Engineering; Engineering/Technology; Marine/Ocean Engineering; Materials Science, Engineering, and Metallurgy.

Award: Scholarship for use in freshman, sophomore, junior, or senior years; renewable. *Number:* 1. *Amount:* $2000.

Eligibility Requirements: Applicant must be Canadian citizen and enrolled or expecting to enroll full-time at a four-year institution or university. Applicant or parent of applicant must be member of Association for Iron and Steel Technology.

Application Requirements: Application, resume, references, test scores, transcript. *Deadline:* June 30.

Contact: Robert Kneale, AIST Northern Member Chapter Scholarship Chair
Association for Iron and Steel Technology
PO Box 1734
Cambridge, ON N1R 7G8
Canada

ASSOCIATION FOR WOMEN IN SCIENCE EDUCATIONAL FOUNDATION http://www.awis.org/careers/edfoundation.html

ASSOCIATION FOR WOMEN IN SCIENCE COLLEGE SCHOLARSHIP

• *See page 82*

ASTRONAUT SCHOLARSHIP FOUNDATION http://www.astronautscholarship.org

ASTRONAUT SCHOLARSHIP FOUNDATION

• *See page 86*

BARRY M. GOLDWATER SCHOLARSHIP AND EXCELLENCE IN EDUCATION FOUNDATION http://www.act.org/goldwater

BARRY M. GOLDWATER SCHOLARSHIP AND EXCELLENCE IN EDUCATION PROGRAM

• *See page 86*

CHEMICAL INSTITUTE OF CANADA http://www.cheminst.ca

CSCHE CHEMICAL ENGINEERING LOCAL SECTION SCHOLARSHIPS

Scholarships for undergraduate students in chemical engineering who are entering their final year of studies at a Canadian university. Applicants must be paid undergraduate student members of Canadian Society for Chemical Engineering. Leadership qualities, demonstrated contributions to the Society such as participation in student chapters, and academic performance will be considered.

Academic Fields/Career Goals: Chemical Engineering.

Award: Scholarship for use in senior year; not renewable. *Number:* 2. *Amount:* $2000.

Eligibility Requirements: Applicant must be enrolled or expecting to enroll full-time at an institution or university and studying in Alberta, British Columbia, Manitoba, New Brunswick, Newfoundland, Nova Scotia, Ontario, Prince Edward Island, Quebec, or Saskatchewan. Applicant or parent of applicant must be member of Canadian Society for Chemical Engineering. Available to U.S. and non-U.S. citizens.

Application Requirements: Resume, references, transcript. *Deadline:* April 30.

Contact: Student Affairs Manager
Chemical Institute of Canada
130 Slater Street, Suite 550
Ottawa, ON K1P 6E2
Canada
Phone: 613-232-6252 Ext. 223
Fax: 613-232-5862
E-mail: awards@cheminst.ca

CUBAN AMERICAN NATIONAL FOUNDATION http://www.masscholarships.org

MAS FAMILY SCHOLARSHIPS

• *See page 139*

DESK AND DERRICK EDUCATIONAL TRUST http://www.addc.org

DESK AND DERRICK EDUCATIONAL TRUST

• *See page 86*

ELECTROCHEMICAL SOCIETY INC. http://www.electrochem.org

H.H. DOW MEMORIAL STUDENT ACHIEVEMENT AWARD OF THE INDUSTRIAL ELECTROLYSIS AND ELECTROCHEMICAL ENGINEERING DIVISION OF THE ELECTROCHEMICAL SOCIETY INC.

• *See page 131*

STUDENT ACHIEVEMENT AWARDS OF THE INDUSTRIAL ELECTROLYSIS AND ELECTROCHEMICAL ENGINEERING DIVISION OF THE ELECTROCHEMICAL SOCIETY INC.

• *See page 131*

STUDENT RESEARCH AWARDS OF THE BATTERY DIVISION OF THE ELECTROCHEMICAL SOCIETY INC.

• *See page 131*

ENGINEERS' SOCIETY OF WESTERN PENNSYLVANIA http://www.eswp.com

JOSEPH A. LEVENDUSKY MEMORIAL SCHOLARSHIP

Scholarship of up to $7000 awarded to an undergraduate student in mechanical or chemical engineering. Must be accepted or enrolled in good standing as a student at an accredited institution.

Engineers' Society of Western Pennsylvania (continued)

Academic Fields/Career Goals: Chemical Engineering; Mechanical Engineering.

Award: Scholarship for use in freshman, sophomore, junior, or senior years; not renewable. *Number:* 1. *Amount:* $7000.

Eligibility Requirements: Applicant must be enrolled or expecting to enroll full-time at a two-year or four-year institution or university. Available to U.S. and non-U.S. citizens.

Application Requirements: Application, financial need analysis, references. *Deadline:* September 3.

Contact: Ryan Bock, International Bridge Conference Manager
Engineers' Society of Western Pennsylvania
337 Fourth Avenue, Pittsburgh Engineers' Building
Pittsburgh, PA 15222
Phone: 412-261-0710 Ext. 11
Fax: 412-261-1606
E-mail: r.bock@eswp.com

FOUNDATION FOR SCIENCE AND DISABILITY http://www.stemd.org

GRANTS FOR DISABLED STUDENTS IN THE SCIENCES

• *See page 87*

GREEN CHEMISTRY INSTITUTE-AMERICAN CHEMICAL SOCIETY http://www.acs.org/greenchemistry

JOSEPH BREEN MEMORIAL FELLOWSHIP IN GREEN CHEMISTRY

The award sponsors the participation of a young international Green Chemistry scholar in a Green Chemistry technical meeting, conference, or training program of their choice. International scholar is defined as undergraduate students and above, but below the level of assistant professor and within the first seven years of a professional career.

Academic Fields/Career Goals: Chemical Engineering; Environmental Science.

Award: Prize for use in freshman, sophomore, junior, senior, graduate, or postgraduate years; not renewable. *Number:* 1. *Amount:* varies.

Eligibility Requirements: Applicant must be enrolled or expecting to enroll full-time at a four-year institution or university. Available to U.S. and non-U.S. citizens.

Application Requirements: Applicant must enter a contest, essay, resume, references. *Deadline:* February 1.

Contact: Jennifer Young, Senior Program Manager
Green Chemistry Institute-American Chemical Society
1155 Sixteenth Street, NW
Washington, DC 20036
Phone: 202-872-6102
E-mail: gci@acs.org

HAWAIIAN LODGE, F & AM http://www.glhawaii.org/

HAWAIIAN LODGE SCHOLARSHIPS

• *See page 96*

HISPANIC COLLEGE FUND INC. http://www.hispanicfund.org

DENNY'S/HISPANIC COLLEGE FUND SCHOLARSHIP

• *See page 54*

DEPARTMENT OF ENERGY SCHOLARSHIP PROGRAM

• *See page 142*

LOCKHEED MARTIN SCHOLARSHIP PROGRAM

• *See page 143*

HISPANIC ENGINEER NATIONAL ACHIEVEMENT AWARDS CORPORATION (HENAAC) http://www.henaac.org

HISPANIC ENGINEER NATIONAL ACHIEVEMENT AWARDS CORPORATION SCHOLARSHIP PROGRAM

• *See page 116*

HISPANIC SCHOLARSHIP FUND http://www.hsf.net

HSF/GENERAL MOTORS SCHOLARSHIP

• *See page 143*

HSF/MARATHON OIL CORPORATION COLLEGE SCHOLARSHIP

• *See page 55*

INDEPENDENT COLLEGE FUND OF MARYLAND (I-FUND) http://www.i-fundinfo.org

HEALTH AND LIFE SCIENCES PROGRAM SCHOLARSHIPS

• *See page 132*

INDEPENDENT LABORATORIES INSTITUTE SCHOLARSHIP ALLIANCE http://www.acil.org

INDEPENDENT LABORATORIES INSTITUTE SCHOLARSHIP ALLIANCE

• *See page 132*

INNOVATION AND SCIENCE COUNCIL OF BRITISH COLUMBIA http://www.bcinnovationcouncil.com

PAUL AND HELEN TRUSSEL SCIENCE AND TECHNOLOGY SCHOLARSHIP

• *See page 87*

INSTITUTE OF ENVIRONMENTAL SCIENCES AND TECHNOLOGY (IEST) http://www.iest.org

ROBERT N. HANCOCK MEMORIAL SCHOLARSHIP

• *See page 132*

INSTRUMENTATION, SYSTEMS, AND AUTOMATION SOCIETY (ISA) http://www.isa.org

INSTRUMENTATION, SYSTEMS, AND AUTOMATION SOCIETY (ISA) SCHOLARSHIP PROGRAM

One-time scholarship for students enrolled full-time study majoring in one of the following: heating, air-conditioning, refrigeration mechanics, chemical engineering, mechanical engineering or electrical engineering/electronics. Must have a minimum GPA of 3.0. The scholarship value is $500 to $5000. Deadline February 15.

Academic Fields/Career Goals: Chemical Engineering; Electrical Engineering/Electronics; Engineering/Technology; Engineering-Related Technologies; Heating, Air-Conditioning, and Refrigeration Mechanics; Mechanical Engineering.

Award: Scholarship for use in sophomore, junior, senior, or graduate years; not renewable. *Number:* 5–15. *Amount:* $500–$5000.

Eligibility Requirements: Applicant must be enrolled or expecting to enroll full-time at a two-year or four-year or technical institution or university. Applicant must have 3.0 GPA or higher. Available to U.S. and non-U.S. citizens.

Application Requirements: Application, essay, references, self-addressed stamped envelope, transcript. *Deadline:* February 15.

Contact: Michaela Johnson-Tena, Scholarship Committee
Instrumentation, Systems, and Automation Society (ISA)
67 Alexander Drive
Research Triangle Park, NC 27709

INTERNATIONAL SOCIETY FOR OPTICAL ENGINEERING-SPIE http://www.spie.org

SPIE EDUCATIONAL SCHOLARSHIPS IN OPTICAL SCIENCE AND ENGINEERING

• *See page 87*

JORGE MAS CANOSA FREEDOM FOUNDATION http://www.jorgemascanosa.org

MAS FAMILY SCHOLARSHIP AWARD

• *See page 144*

LOS ANGELES COUNCIL OF BLACK PROFESSIONAL ENGINEERS http://www.lablackengineers.org

AL-BEN SCHOLARSHIP FOR ACADEMIC INCENTIVE

One-time scholarship for students enrolled full-time with scholastic achievements in the academic pursuits of engineering, math, computer or scientific studies. Must be from a minority group. Scholarship value is $500 to $1000. Two scholarships are granted annually. Preference given to residents of Southern California.

Academic Fields/Career Goals: Chemical Engineering; Civil Engineering; Computer Science/Data Processing; Electrical Engineering/Electronics; Engineering/Technology; Engineering-Related Technologies; Materials Science, Engineering, and Metallurgy; Mechanical Engineering; Physical Sciences and Math.

Award: Scholarship for use in freshman, sophomore, junior, or senior years; not renewable. *Number:* 2. *Amount:* $500–$1000.

Eligibility Requirements: Applicant must be American Indian/Alaska Native, Asian/Pacific Islander, Black (non-Hispanic), or Hispanic and enrolled or expecting to enroll full-time at a four-year institution or university. Available to U.S. citizens.

Application Requirements: Application, essay, references, transcript. *Deadline:* April 2.

Contact: Leroy Freelon, President
Los Angeles Council of Black Professional Engineers
PO Box 881029
Los Angeles, CA 90009
Phone: 310-635-7734
E-mail: lfreelonjr@aol.com

AL-BEN SCHOLARSHIP FOR PROFESSIONAL MERIT

One-time scholarship for students enrolled full-time with scholastic achievements in the academic pursuits of engineering, math, computer or scientific studies. Must be from a minority group. Scholarship value is $500 to $1000. Two scholarships are granted annually. Preference given to residents of Southern California.

Academic Fields/Career Goals: Chemical Engineering; Civil Engineering; Computer Science/Data Processing; Electrical Engineering/Electronics; Engineering/Technology; Engineering-Related Technologies; Materials Science, Engineering, and Metallurgy; Mechanical Engineering; Physical Sciences and Math.

Award: Scholarship for use in freshman, sophomore, junior, or senior years; not renewable. *Number:* 2. *Amount:* $500–$1000.

Eligibility Requirements: Applicant must be American Indian/Alaska Native, Asian/Pacific Islander, Black (non-Hispanic), or Hispanic and enrolled or expecting to enroll full-time at a four-year institution or university. Available to U.S. citizens.

Application Requirements: Application, essay, references, transcript. *Deadline:* April 2.

Contact: Leroy Freelon, President
Los Angeles Council of Black Professional Engineers
PO Box 881029
Los Angeles, CA 90009
Phone: 310-635-7734
E-mail: lfreelonjr@aol.com

AL-BEN SCHOLARSHIP FOR SCHOLASTIC ACHIEVEMENT

Scholarships for students enrolled full-time with scholastic achievements in the academic pursuits of engineering, math, computer or scientific studies. Must be from a minority group.

Academic Fields/Career Goals: Chemical Engineering; Civil Engineering; Computer Science/Data Processing; Electrical Engineering/Electronics; Engineering/Technology; Engineering-Related Technologies; Materials Science, Engineering, and Metallurgy; Mechanical Engineering; Physical Sciences and Math.

Award: Scholarship for use in freshman, sophomore, junior, or senior years; not renewable. *Number:* 2. *Amount:* $500–$1000.

Eligibility Requirements: Applicant must be American Indian/Alaska Native, Asian/Pacific Islander, Black (non-Hispanic), or Hispanic and enrolled or expecting to enroll full-time at a four-year institution or university. Available to U.S. citizens.

Application Requirements: Application, essay, references, transcript. *Deadline:* April 2.

Contact: Leroy Freelon, President
Los Angeles Council of Black Professional Engineers
PO Box 881029
Los Angeles, CA 90009
Phone: 310-635-7734
E-mail: lfreelonjr@aol.com

MICHIGAN SOCIETY OF PROFESSIONAL ENGINEERS http://www.michiganspe.org

ANTHONY C. FORTUNSKI, P.E. MEMORIAL GRANT

Grant of up to $1500 for an engineering student demonstrating an interest in the fields of manufacturing and industry. Preference given to a student attending Lawrence Technical University and majoring in manufacturing engineering. Must be a member of MSPE student chapter or a state member-at-large. Minimum 3.0 GPA required. Restricted to Michigan residents attending Michigan schools.

Academic Fields/Career Goals: Chemical Engineering; Civil Engineering; Engineering/Technology; Mechanical Engineering.

Award: Grant for use in freshman, sophomore, junior, or senior years; not renewable. *Number:* 1. *Amount:* $1000–$1500.

Eligibility Requirements: Applicant must be enrolled or expecting to enroll full-time at a four-year institution or university; resident of Michigan and studying in Michigan. Applicant or parent of applicant must be member of Michigan Society of Professional Engineers. Applicant must have 3.0 GPA or higher. Available to U.S. citizens.

Application Requirements: Application, essay, references, transcript. *Deadline:* varies.

Contact: Maura Nessan, Executive Director
Michigan Society of Professional Engineers
215 North Walnut Street
PO Box 15276
Lansing, MI 48901-5276
Phone: 517-487-9388
Fax: 517-487-0635
E-mail: mspe@voyager.net

MICHIGAN SOCIETY OF PROFESSIONAL ENGINEERS AUXILIARY GRANT

Two $1500 grants for top-ranking Michigan high school seniors interested in pursuing a career in engineering and planning to attend an ABET-accredited college or university in Michigan. Preference given to a son or daughter of a MSPE member. Minimum 3.0 GPA required in grades eleven and twelve.

Academic Fields/Career Goals: Chemical Engineering; Civil Engineering; Construction Engineering/Management; Electrical Engineering/Electronics; Engineering/Technology; Mechanical Engineering.

Award: Grant for use in freshman year; not renewable. *Number:* 2. *Amount:* $1500.

Eligibility Requirements: Applicant must be high school student; planning to enroll or expecting to enroll full-time at a four-year institution or university; resident of Michigan and studying in Michigan. Applicant or parent of applicant must be member of Michigan Society of Professional Engineers. Applicant must have 3.0 GPA or higher. Available to U.S. citizens.

Application Requirements: Application, test scores, transcript. *Deadline:* varies.

Contact: Maura Nessan, Executive Director
Michigan Society of Professional Engineers
215 North Walnut Street
PO Box 15276
Lansing, MI 48901-5276
Phone: 517-487-9388
Fax: 517-487-0635
E-mail: mspe@voyager.net

MICHIGAN SOCIETY OF PROFESSIONAL ENGINEERS HARRY R. BALL, P.E. GRANT

One $1000 grant for a Michigan high school student to study engineering at an ABET-accredited college or university in Michigan. Minimum 3.0 GPA required in grades eleven and twelve.

Michigan Society of Professional Engineers (continued)

Academic Fields/Career Goals: Chemical Engineering; Civil Engineering; Construction Engineering/Management; Electrical Engineering/Electronics; Engineering/Technology; Mechanical Engineering.

Award: Grant for use in freshman year; not renewable. *Number:* 1. *Amount:* $1000.

Eligibility Requirements: Applicant must be high school student; planning to enroll or expecting to enroll full-time at a four-year institution or university; resident of Michigan and studying in Michigan. Applicant must have 3.0 GPA or higher. Available to U.S. citizens.

Application Requirements: Application, test scores, transcript. *Deadline:* varies.

Contact: Maura Nessan, Executive Director
Michigan Society of Professional Engineers
215 North Walnut Street
PO Box 15276
Lansing, MI 48901-5276
Phone: 517-487-9388
Fax: 517-487-0635
E-mail: mspe@voyager.net

MICHIGAN SOCIETY OF PROFESSIONAL ENGINEERS KENNETH B. FISHBECK, P.E. MEMORIAL GRANT

One $1000 grant for a Michigan high school student to study engineering at an ABET-accredited college or university in Michigan. Submit application to local MSPE chapter chair. Applicants should demonstrate qualifications of high merit and professional ethics.

Academic Fields/Career Goals: Chemical Engineering; Civil Engineering; Construction Engineering/Management; Electrical Engineering/Electronics; Engineering/Technology; Mechanical Engineering.

Award: Grant for use in freshman year; not renewable. *Number:* 1. *Amount:* $1000.

Eligibility Requirements: Applicant must be high school student; planning to enroll or expecting to enroll full-time at a four-year institution or university; resident of Michigan and studying in Michigan. Applicant must have 3.0 GPA or higher. Available to U.S. citizens.

Application Requirements: Application, test scores, transcript. *Deadline:* varies.

Contact: Maura Nessan, Executive Director
Michigan Society of Professional Engineers
215 North Walnut Street
PO Box 15276
Lansing, MI 48901-5276
Phone: 517-487-9388
Fax: 517-487-0635
E-mail: mspe@voyager.net

MICHIGAN SOCIETY OF PROFESSIONAL ENGINEERS 1980 NATIONAL SOCIETY OF PROFESSIONAL ENGINEERS ANNUAL MEETING COMMITTEE GRANT

One $2000 grant for a Michigan high school senior to study engineering at an ABET-accredited college or university in Michigan. Minimum 3.0 GPA for the tenth and eleventh grades.

Academic Fields/Career Goals: Chemical Engineering; Civil Engineering; Construction Engineering/Management; Electrical Engineering/Electronics; Engineering/Technology; Mechanical Engineering.

Award: Grant for use in freshman year; not renewable. *Number:* 1. *Amount:* $2000.

Eligibility Requirements: Applicant must be high school student; planning to enroll or expecting to enroll full-time at a four-year institution or university; resident of Michigan and studying in Michigan. Applicant must have 3.0 GPA or higher. Available to U.S. citizens.

Application Requirements: Application, essay, interview, references, test scores, transcript. *Deadline:* varies.

Contact: Maura Nessan, Executive Director
Michigan Society of Professional Engineers
215 North Walnut Street
PO Box 15276
Lansing, MI 48901-5276
Phone: 517-487-9388
Fax: 517-487-0635
E-mail: mspe@voyager.net

MICHIGAN SOCIETY OF PROFESSIONAL ENGINEERS SCHOLARSHIP TRUST GRANT

One $2000 grant for a Michigan high school senior planning to pursue a career in engineering at a Michigan ABET-accredited college or university. Minimum 3.0 GPA for grades eleven and twelve required.

Academic Fields/Career Goals: Chemical Engineering; Civil Engineering; Construction Engineering/Management; Electrical Engineering/Electronics; Engineering/Technology; Mechanical Engineering.

Award: Grant for use in freshman year; not renewable. *Number:* 1. *Amount:* $2000.

Eligibility Requirements: Applicant must be high school student; planning to enroll or expecting to enroll full-time at a four-year institution or university; resident of Michigan and studying in Michigan. Applicant must have 3.0 GPA or higher. Available to U.S. citizens.

Application Requirements: Application, test scores, transcript. *Deadline:* varies.

Contact: Maura Nessan, Executive Director
Michigan Society of Professional Engineers
215 North Walnut Street
PO Box 15276
Lansing, MI 48901-5276
Phone: 517-487-9388
Fax: 517-487-0635
E-mail: mspe@voyager.net

MICHIGAN SOCIETY OF PROFESSIONAL ENGINEERS UNDESIGNATED GRANT

Grant of $2000 for a top-ranking student enrolled in an ABET-accredited engineering program at a Michigan college or university. Renewal based on academic performance and approval of both the MSPE scholarship trust and the dean of school. Must be a member of MSPE student chapter or a state member-at-large. Minimum 3.0 GPA required. Must be a Michigan resident.

Academic Fields/Career Goals: Chemical Engineering; Civil Engineering; Construction Engineering/Management; Electrical Engineering/Electronics; Engineering/Technology; Mechanical Engineering.

Award: Grant for use in freshman, sophomore, junior, or senior years; renewable. *Number:* 1. *Amount:* $2000.

Eligibility Requirements: Applicant must be enrolled or expecting to enroll full-time at a four-year institution or university; resident of Michigan and studying in Michigan. Applicant or parent of applicant must be member of Michigan Society of Professional Engineers. Applicant must have 3.0 GPA or higher. Available to U.S. citizens.

Application Requirements: Application, essay, references, test scores, transcript. *Deadline:* varies.

Contact: Maura Nessan, Executive Director
Michigan Society of Professional Engineers
215 North Walnut Street
PO Box 15276
Lansing, MI 48901-5276
Phone: 517-487-9388
Fax: 517-487-0635
E-mail: mspe@voyager.net

MICRON TECHNOLOGY FOUNDATION INC. http://www.micron.com/scholars

MICRON SCIENCE AND TECHNOLOGY SCHOLARS PROGRAM

Merit-based scholarship competition recognizing excellence in academics and leadership. Each year, the program awards a $25,000 college scholarship to six high school seniors. One male and one female student is selected from each of the following states: Idaho, Utah and Virginia. Awards will be paid out over 4 years. Must plan to major in computer science, physics, chemistry, material sciences, or electrical

Academic Fields/Career Goals: Chemical Engineering; Computer Science/Data Processing; Electrical Engineering/Electronics; Engineering/Technology; Engineering-Related Technologies; Materials Science, Engineering, and Metallurgy; Mechanical Engineering; Physical Sciences and Math.

Award: Scholarship for use in freshman year; renewable. *Number:* 6. *Amount:* $6250.

Eligibility Requirements: Applicant must be high school student; planning to enroll or expecting to enroll full-time at a four-year institution or university; resident of Idaho, Utah, or Virginia and must have an interest in leadership. Applicant must have 3.5 GPA or higher. Available to U.S. and non-U.S. citizens.

Application Requirements: Application, essay, interview, references, transcript, SAT or ACT scores. *Deadline:* January 19.

Contact: Lyn Dauffenbach, Scholarship America
Micron Technology Foundation Inc.
One Scholarship Way, PO Box 297
Saint Peter, MN 56082
Phone: 800-537-4180

NASA DELAWARE SPACE GRANT CONSORTIUM http://www.delspace.org

NASA DELAWARE SPACE GRANT UNDERGRADUATE TUITION SCHOLARSHIP

• *See page 87*

NASA IDAHO SPACE GRANT CONSORTIUM http://isgc.uidaho.edu

NASA IDAHO SPACE GRANT CONSORTIUM SCHOLARSHIP PROGRAM

• *See page 87*

NASA/MARYLAND SPACE GRANT CONSORTIUM http://www.mdspacegrant.org

NASA MARYLAND SPACE GRANT CONSORTIUM UNDERGRADUATE SCHOLARSHIPS

• *See page 118*

NASA MONTANA SPACE GRANT CONSORTIUM http://www.spacegrant.montana.edu

MONTANA SPACE GRANT SCHOLARSHIP PROGRAM

• *See page 119*

NASA NEVADA SPACE GRANT CONSORTIUM http://www.unr.edu/spacegrant

UNIVERSITY AND COMMUNITY COLLEGE SYSTEM OF NEVADA NASA SPACE GRANT AND FELLOWSHIP PROGRAM

• *See page 119*

NATIONAL ASSOCIATION FOR THE ADVANCEMENT OF COLORED PEOPLE http://www.naacp.org

HUBERTUS W.V. WILLEMS SCHOLARSHIP FOR MALE STUDENTS

Scholarship for a male, full-time student, majoring in one of the following: engineering, chemistry, physics, or mathematical sciences. Graduate student may be full- or part-time and have 2.5 minimum GPA. Graduating high school seniors and undergraduates must have 3.0 minimum GPA. Must demonstrate financial need. Undergraduate scholarship is $2000; and graduate scholarship is $3000.

Academic Fields/Career Goals: Chemical Engineering; Engineering/Technology; Engineering-Related Technologies; Physical Sciences and Math.

Award: Scholarship for use in freshman, sophomore, junior, senior, or graduate years; not renewable. *Number:* 1. *Amount:* $2000–$3000.

Eligibility Requirements: Applicant must be American Indian/Alaska Native, Asian/Pacific Islander, Black (non-Hispanic), or Hispanic; enrolled or expecting to enroll full- or part-time at a two-year or four-year institution or university and male. Applicant or parent of applicant must be member of National Association for the Advancement of Colored People. Applicant must have 3.0 GPA or higher. Available to U.S. citizens.

Application Requirements: Application, financial need analysis, references, transcript. *Deadline:* April 30.

Contact: Victor Goode, Attorney
National Association for the Advancement of Colored People
4805 Mount Hope Drive
Baltimore, MD 21215-3297
Phone: 410-580-5760
Fax: 410-585-1329
E-mail: info@naacp.org

LOUIS STOKES SCIENCE AND TECHNOLOGY AWARD

• *See page 133*

NATIONAL BOARD OF BOILER AND PRESSURE VESSEL INSPECTORS http://www.nationalboard.org

NATIONAL BOARD TECHNICAL SCHOLARSHIP

Two $6000 scholarships to selected students meeting eligibility standards, who are pursuing a bachelor's degree in certain engineering or related studies. Must be a child, step-child, grandchild, or great-grandchild of a past or present National Board member (living or deceased), or of a past or present Commissioned Inspector (living or deceased), employed by a member jurisdiction, or of a past or present National Board employee (living or deceased).

Academic Fields/Career Goals: Chemical Engineering; Electrical Engineering/Electronics; Mechanical Engineering.

Award: Scholarship for use in freshman, sophomore, junior, or senior years; not renewable. *Number:* 2. *Amount:* $6000.

Eligibility Requirements: Applicant must be enrolled or expecting to enroll full-time at a four-year or technical institution or university. Applicant or parent of applicant must be member of National Board of Boiler and Pressure Vessel Inspectors. Applicant must have 3.0 GPA or higher. Available to U.S. and Canadian citizens.

Application Requirements: Application, essay, references, transcript. *Deadline:* February 29.

Contact: Donald Tanner, Executive Director
National Board of Boiler and Pressure Vessel Inspectors
1055 Crupper Avenue
Columbus, OH 43229-1183
Phone: 614-888-8320
Fax: 614-888-0750
E-mail: dtanner@nationalboard.org

NATIONAL INVENTORS HALL OF FAME http://www.invent.org

COLLEGIATE INVENTORS COMPETITION FOR UNDERGRADUATE STUDENTS

• *See page 88*

COLLEGIATE INVENTORS COMPETITION-GRAND PRIZE

• *See page 88*

NATIONAL SOCIETY OF PROFESSIONAL ENGINEERS http://www.nspe.org

MAUREEN L. AND HOWARD N. BLITMAN, PE SCHOLARSHIP TO PROMOTE DIVERSITY IN ENGINEERING

Award of $5000 in two disbursements of $2,500 to a high school senior from an ethnic minority who has been accepted into an ABET-accredited engineering program at a four-year college or university.

Academic Fields/Career Goals: Chemical Engineering; Civil Engineering; Electrical Engineering/Electronics; Engineering/Technology; Engineering-Related Technologies; Materials Science, Engineering, and Metallurgy; Mechanical Engineering.

Award: Scholarship for use in freshman year; not renewable. *Number:* 1. *Amount:* $5000.

Eligibility Requirements: Applicant must be American Indian/Alaska Native, Black (non-Hispanic), or Hispanic; high school student and planning to enroll or expecting to enroll full-time at a four-year institution or university. Applicant must have 3.5 GPA or higher. Available to U.S. citizens.

National Society of Professional Engineers (continued)

Application Requirements: Application, essay, references, test scores, transcript. *Deadline:* March 1.

Contact: Mary Maul, Director of Education
National Society of Professional Engineers
1420 King Street
Alexandria, VA 22314-2794
Phone: 703-684-2833
Fax: 703-836-4875
E-mail: mmaul@nspe.org

PAUL H. ROBBINS HONORARY SCHOLARSHIP

Awarded annually to a current engineering undergraduate student entering the junior year in an ABET-accredited engineering program and attending a college/university that participates in the NSPE Professional Engineers in Higher Education (PEHE) Sustaining University Program(SUP).

Academic Fields/Career Goals: Chemical Engineering; Civil Engineering; Electrical Engineering/Electronics; Engineering/Technology; Engineering-Related Technologies; Materials Science, Engineering, and Metallurgy; Mechanical Engineering.

Award: Scholarship for use in junior year; renewable. *Number:* 1. *Amount:* $5000.

Eligibility Requirements: Applicant must be enrolled or expecting to enroll full-time at a four-year institution or university. Applicant or parent of applicant must be member of National Society of Professional Engineers. Available to U.S. citizens.

Application Requirements: Application, essay, references, test scores, transcript. *Deadline:* March 1.

Contact: Mary Maul, Director of Education
National Society of Professional Engineers
1420 King Street
Alexandria, VA 22314-2794
Phone: 703-684-2833
Fax: 703-836-4875
E-mail: mmaul@nspe.org

PROFESSIONAL ENGINEERS IN INDUSTRY SCHOLARSHIP

Applicants must be sponsored by an NSPE/PEI member. Students must have completed a minimum of two semesters or three quarters of undergraduate engineering studies (or be enrolled in graduate study) accredited by ABET.

Academic Fields/Career Goals: Chemical Engineering; Civil Engineering; Electrical Engineering/Electronics; Engineering/Technology; Engineering-Related Technologies; Materials Science, Engineering, and Metallurgy; Mechanical Engineering.

Award: Scholarship for use in sophomore, junior, senior, or graduate years; not renewable. *Number:* 1. *Amount:* $2500.

Eligibility Requirements: Applicant must be enrolled or expecting to enroll full-time at a four-year institution or university. Applicant must have 2.5 GPA or higher. Available to U.S. citizens.

Application Requirements: Application, essay, resume, references, transcript, work experience certificates. *Deadline:* April 1.

Contact: Erin Garcia Reyes, Practice Division Manager
National Society of Professional Engineers
1420 King Street
Alexandria, VA 22314
Phone: 703-684-2884
E-mail: egarcia@nspe.org

OREGON STUDENT ASSISTANCE COMMISSION http://www.osac.state.or.us

AMERICAN COUNCIL OF ENGINEERING COMPANIES OF OREGON SCHOLARSHIP

Award for graduating high school seniors or those who have had no previous college education. For use at any Oregon four-year college that offers accredited programs in chemical, civil, electrical, industrial, or mechanical engineering.

Academic Fields/Career Goals: Chemical Engineering; Civil Engineering; Electrical Engineering/Electronics; Engineering-Related Technologies; Mechanical Engineering.

Award: Scholarship for use in freshman, sophomore, junior, or senior years; renewable. *Number:* varies. *Amount:* varies.

Eligibility Requirements: Applicant must be enrolled or expecting to enroll full-time at a four-year institution; resident of Oregon and studying in Oregon. Available to U.S. citizens.

Application Requirements: Application, essay, transcript, activities chart. *Deadline:* March 1.

Contact: Director of Grant Programs
Oregon Student Assistance Commission
1500 Valley River Drive, Suite 100
Eugene, OR 97401-7020
Phone: 800-452-8807 Ext. 7395

PLASTICS INSTITUTE OF AMERICA http://www.plasticsinstitute.org

PLASTICS PIONEERS SCHOLARSHIPS

Financial grants awarded to undergraduate students needing help in their education expenses to enter into a full-time career in any and all segments of the plastics industry, with emphasis on "hands on" participation in the many fields where members of the Plastics Pioneers Association have spent their professional years. Applicants must be U.S. citizens.

Academic Fields/Career Goals: Chemical Engineering; Engineering/Technology; Engineering-Related Technologies; Materials Science, Engineering, and Metallurgy; Trade/Technical Specialties.

Award: Scholarship for use in freshman, sophomore, junior, or senior years; renewable. *Number:* 30–40. *Amount:* $1500–$3000.

Eligibility Requirements: Applicant must be enrolled or expecting to enroll full- or part-time at a two-year or four-year or technical institution. Available to U.S. citizens.

Application Requirements: Application, essay, resume, references, transcript. *Deadline:* April 1.

Contact: Aldo Crugnola, Executive Director
Plastics Institute of America
333 Aiken Street
Lowell, MA 01854
Phone: 978-934-2575
Fax: 978-459-9420
E-mail: pia@uml.edu

ROBERT H. MOLLOHAN FAMILY CHARITABLE FOUNDATION INC. http://www.mollohanfoundation.org

HIGH TECHNOLOGY SCHOLARS PROGRAM

• *See page 135*

SIGMA XI, THE SCIENTIFIC RESEARCH SOCIETY http://www.sigmaxi.org

SIGMA XI GRANTS-IN-AID OF RESEARCH

• *See page 78*

SOCIETY OF AUTOMOTIVE ENGINEERS http://www.sae.org

BMW/SAE ENGINEERING SCHOLARSHIP

• *See page 124*

EDWARD D. HENDRICKSON/SAE ENGINEERING SCHOLARSHIP

• *See page 124*

TMC/SAE DONALD D. DAWSON TECHNICAL SCHOLARSHIP

• *See page 124*

SOCIETY OF HISPANIC PROFESSIONAL ENGINEERS FOUNDATION http://www.henaac.org

SOCIETY OF HISPANIC PROFESSIONAL ENGINEERS FOUNDATION

Scholarships awarded to Hispanic engineering and science students throughout the United States. Scholarships are awarded at the beginning of every academic year based upon academic achievement, financial need, involvement in campus and community activities, career goals and counselor recommendations.

Academic Fields/Career Goals: Chemical Engineering; Civil Engineering; Electrical Engineering/Electronics; Engineering/Technology; Engineering-Related Technologies; Materials Science, Engineering, and Metallurgy; Mechanical Engineering; Natural Sciences; Physical Sciences and Math; Science, Technology, and Society.

Award: Scholarship for use in freshman, sophomore, junior, senior, or graduate years; not renewable. *Number:* varies. *Amount:* $500–$7000.

Eligibility Requirements: Applicant must be Hispanic and enrolled or expecting to enroll full-time at a four-year institution or university. Available to U.S. citizens.

Application Requirements: Application, financial need analysis, resume, references. *Deadline:* May 15.

Contact: Kathy Borunda Barrera, Manager, Scholars Program
Society of Hispanic Professional Engineers Foundation
3900 Whiteside Street
Los Angeles, CA 90063
Phone: 323-415-9600
Fax: 323-415-7038
E-mail: kathy@henaac.org

SOCIETY OF PLASTICS ENGINEERS (SPE) FOUNDATION http://www.4spe.org

FLEMING/BASZCAK SCHOLARSHIP

Award available for a full-time undergraduate student, with a demonstrated interest in the plastics industry. Must be a U.S. citizen and provide documentation of Mexican heritage.

Academic Fields/Career Goals: Chemical Engineering; Electrical Engineering/Electronics; Engineering/Technology; Industrial Design; Materials Science, Engineering, and Metallurgy; Trade/Technical Specialties.

Award: Scholarship for use in freshman, sophomore, junior, or senior years; not renewable. *Number:* 1. *Amount:* $2000.

Eligibility Requirements: Applicant must be of Mexican heritage; Hispanic and enrolled or expecting to enroll full-time at a two-year or four-year institution or university. Available to U.S. citizens.

Application Requirements: Application, essay, financial need analysis, references, transcript. *Deadline:* January 15.

Contact: Gail R. Bristol, Managing Director
Society of Plastics Engineers (SPE) Foundation
14 Fairfield Drive
Brookfield, CT 06804
Phone: 203-740-5447
Fax: 203-775-1157
E-mail: foundation@4spe.org

GULF COAST HURRICANE SCHOLARSHIP

Scholarship provides supplemental financial support to residents of the Gulf Coast who wish to attend a college, university or technical institute and pursue programs that support the plastics industry.

Academic Fields/Career Goals: Chemical Engineering; Engineering/Technology.

Award: Scholarship for use in freshman, sophomore, junior, or senior years; renewable. *Number:* 1–3. *Amount:* $2000–$6000.

Eligibility Requirements: Applicant must be enrolled or expecting to enroll full-time at a two-year or four-year institution or university and resident of Alabama, Florida, Louisiana, Mississippi, or Texas. Available to U.S. citizens.

Application Requirements: Application, essay, financial need analysis, references, transcript. *Deadline:* January 15.

Contact: Gail R. Bristol, Managing Director
Society of Plastics Engineers (SPE) Foundation
14 Fairfield Drive
Brookfield, CT 06804
Phone: 203-740-5447
Fax: 203-775-1157
E-mail: foundation@4spe.org

PLASTICS PIONEERS ASSOCIATION SCHOLARSHIPS

Scholarships available to undergraduate students who are committed to becoming "hands-on" workers in the plastics industry, such as plastics technicians or engineers.

Academic Fields/Career Goals: Chemical Engineering; Engineering/Technology.

Award: Scholarship for use in freshman, sophomore, junior, or senior years; renewable. *Number:* up to 10. *Amount:* $3000.

Eligibility Requirements: Applicant must be enrolled or expecting to enroll full-time at a two-year or four-year or technical institution or university. Available to U.S. and Canadian citizens.

Application Requirements: Application, essay, financial need analysis, resume, references, transcript. *Deadline:* January 15.

Contact: Ms. Gail Bristol, Managing Director
Society of Plastics Engineers (SPE) Foundation
14 Fairfield Drive
Brookfield, CT 06804
Phone: 203-740-5447
Fax: 203-775-1157
E-mail: foundation@4spe.org

SOCIETY OF PLASTICS ENGINEERS SCHOLARSHIP PROGRAM

Scholarships awarded to full-time students who have demonstrated or expressed an interest in the plastics industry. Major or course of study must be beneficial to a career in the plastics industry.

Academic Fields/Career Goals: Chemical Engineering; Electrical Engineering/Electronics; Industrial Design; Materials Science, Engineering, and Metallurgy; Trade/Technical Specialties.

Award: Scholarship for use in freshman, sophomore, junior, senior, or graduate years; not renewable. *Number:* 25–30. *Amount:* $1000–$7500.

Eligibility Requirements: Applicant must be enrolled or expecting to enroll full-time at a two-year or four-year or technical institution or university. Available to U.S. and non-U.S. citizens.

Application Requirements: Application, essay, financial need analysis, references, transcript. *Deadline:* January 15.

Contact: Gail R. Bristol, Managing Director
Society of Plastics Engineers (SPE) Foundation
14 Fairfield Drive
Brookfield, CT 06804
Phone: 203-740-5447
Fax: 203-775-1157
E-mail: foundation@4spe.org

SOCIETY OF WOMEN ENGINEERS http://www.swe.org

CATERPILLAR INC. SCHOLARSHIP

• *See page 79*

CHEVRON TEXACO CORPORATION SCHOLARSHIPS

Up to 8 one-time awards of $2000 open to women who are sophomores or juniors majoring in civil, chemical, mechanical, or petroleum engineering. Minimum 3.0 GPA required. Must be active SWE student member. Award includes a travel grant for SWE National Conference.

Academic Fields/Career Goals: Chemical Engineering; Civil Engineering; Engineering/Technology; Mechanical Engineering.

Award: Scholarship for use in sophomore or junior years; not renewable. *Number:* 7–8. *Amount:* $2000.

Eligibility Requirements: Applicant must be enrolled or expecting to enroll full-time at a four-year institution or university and female. Applicant or parent of applicant must be member of Society of Women Engineers. Applicant must have 3.0 GPA or higher. Available to U.S. and non-U.S. citizens.

Application Requirements: Application, essay, references, self-addressed stamped envelope, test scores, transcript. *Deadline:* February 1.

Contact: Scholarship Committee
Society of Women Engineers
230 East Ohio Street, Suite 400
Chicago, IL 60611-3265
Phone: 312-596-5223
Fax: 312-596-5252
E-mail: scholarshipapplication@swe.org

DOROTHY LEMKE HOWARTH SCHOLARSHIPS

One-time scholarship awarded to female students entering their sophomore year in an engineering program. Must be U.S. citizens attending a four-year institution. Minimum 3.0 GPA is required. Send self-addressed stamped envelope for more information.

Academic Fields/Career Goals: Chemical Engineering; Civil Engineering; Electrical Engineering/Electronics; Energy and Power Engineering; Engineering/Technology; Mechanical Engineering.

Society of Women Engineers (continued)

Award: Scholarship for use in sophomore year; not renewable. *Number:* 5. *Amount:* $2500.

Eligibility Requirements: Applicant must be enrolled or expecting to enroll full-time at a four-year institution or university and female. Applicant must have 3.0 GPA or higher. Available to U.S. citizens.

Application Requirements: Application, essay, references, self-addressed stamped envelope, test scores, transcript. *Deadline:* February 1.

Contact: Scholarship Committee
Society of Women Engineers
230 East Ohio Street, Suite 400
Chicago, IL 60611-3265
Phone: 312-596-5223
Fax: 312-596-5252
E-mail: scholarshipapplication@swe.org

DUPONT COMPANY SCHOLARSHIPS

Two awards of $1000 each for a sophomore, junior, or senior with a GPA of 3.0 or above in chemical engineering or mechanical engineering. Limited to schools in the Eastern U.S.

Academic Fields/Career Goals: Chemical Engineering; Mechanical Engineering.

Award: Scholarship for use in sophomore, junior, or senior years; not renewable. *Number:* 2. *Amount:* $1000.

Eligibility Requirements: Applicant must be enrolled or expecting to enroll full-time at a four-year institution or university and female. Applicant must have 3.0 GPA or higher. Available to U.S. citizens.

Application Requirements: Application, references, self-addressed stamped envelope, test scores, transcript. *Deadline:* varies.

Contact: Scholarship Committee
Society of Women Engineers
230 East Ohio Street, Suite 400
Chicago, IL 60611-3265
Phone: 312-596-5223
Fax: 312-596-5252
E-mail: scholarshipapplication@swe.org

GENERAL ELECTRIC FOUNDATION SCHOLARSHIP

Award for outstanding women engineering students. Renewable for three years with continued academic achievement. Minimum 3.0 GPA required. Must be a U.S. citizen. Includes a travel grant to SWE National Conference. Send self-addressed stamped envelope for more information.

Academic Fields/Career Goals: Chemical Engineering; Civil Engineering; Electrical Engineering/Electronics; Energy and Power Engineering; Engineering/Technology; Mechanical Engineering.

Award: Scholarship for use in freshman year; renewable. *Number:* 3. *Amount:* $1250.

Eligibility Requirements: Applicant must be enrolled or expecting to enroll full-time at a four-year institution or university and female. Applicant must have 3.0 GPA or higher. Available to U.S. citizens.

Application Requirements: Application, essay, references, self-addressed stamped envelope, test scores, transcript. *Deadline:* May 15.

Contact: Scholarship Committee
Society of Women Engineers
230 East Ohio Street, Suite 400
Chicago, IL 60611-3265
Phone: 312-596-5223
Fax: 312-596-5252
E-mail: scholarshipapplication@swe.org

LILLIAN MOLLER GILBRETH MEMORIAL SCHOLARSHIP

Renewable scholarship available for a female college junior or senior engineering student. Minimum GPA of 3.0 required. Must possess outstanding potential demonstrated by achievement.

Academic Fields/Career Goals: Chemical Engineering; Civil Engineering; Electrical Engineering/Electronics; Energy and Power Engineering; Engineering/Technology; Mechanical Engineering.

Award: Scholarship for use in junior or senior years; renewable; not renewable. *Number:* 1. *Amount:* $10,000.

Eligibility Requirements: Applicant must be enrolled or expecting to enroll full-time at a four-year institution or university and female. Applicant must have 3.0 GPA or higher. Available to U.S. citizens.

Application Requirements: Application, essay, references, self-addressed stamped envelope, test scores, transcript. *Deadline:* February 1.

Contact: Scholarship Committee
Society of Women Engineers
230 East Ohio Street, Suite 400
Chicago, IL 60611-3265
Phone: 312-596-5223
Fax: 312-596-5252
E-mail: scholarshipapplication@swe.org

MASWE MEMORIAL SCHOLARSHIP

Scholarship awarded to female college sophomore, junior or senior students in engineering who demonstrate outstanding scholarship and financial need. Minimum 3.0 GPA required.

Academic Fields/Career Goals: Chemical Engineering; Civil Engineering; Electrical Engineering/Electronics; Energy and Power Engineering; Engineering/Technology; Mechanical Engineering.

Award: Scholarship for use in sophomore, junior, or senior years; not renewable. *Number:* 4. *Amount:* $2000.

Eligibility Requirements: Applicant must be enrolled or expecting to enroll full-time at a four-year institution or university and female. Applicant must have 3.0 GPA or higher. Available to U.S. citizens.

Application Requirements: Application, essay, financial need analysis, references, self-addressed stamped envelope, test scores, transcript. *Deadline:* February 1.

Contact: Scholarship Committee
Society of Women Engineers
230 East Ohio Street, Suite 400
Chicago, IL 60611-3265
Phone: 312-596-5223
Fax: 312-596-5252
E-mail: scholarshipapplication@swe.org

SOCIETY OF WOMEN ENGINEERS-ROCKY MOUNTAIN SECTION http://www.swe-rms.org

SOCIETY OF WOMEN ENGINEERS-ROCKY MOUNTAIN SECTION SCHOLARSHIP PROGRAM

One-time award for female high school seniors in Colorado and Wyoming (except zip codes 80800 and 81599), who intend to enroll in engineering or computer science at an ABET-accredited college or university in those states. Female college students who have already enrolled in those programs may also apply. For more information visit Web site: http://www.swe-rms.org and look for local scholarships.

Academic Fields/Career Goals: Chemical Engineering; Computer Science/Data Processing; Engineering/Technology; Mechanical Engineering.

Award: Scholarship for use in freshman, sophomore, junior, senior, or graduate years; not renewable. *Number:* 3–5. *Amount:* $500–$1000.

Eligibility Requirements: Applicant must be enrolled or expecting to enroll full-time at a two-year or four-year or technical institution or university; female; resident of Colorado or Wyoming and studying in Colorado or Wyoming. Applicant must have 3.5 GPA or higher. Available to U.S. citizens.

Application Requirements: Application, essay, resume, references, test scores, transcript. *Deadline:* February 1.

Contact: Barbara Kontogiannis, Scholarship Chair
Society of Women Engineers-Rocky Mountain Section
PO Box 260692
Lakewood, CO 80226-0692
Phone: 303-971-5213
E-mail: barbekon@stanfordalumni.org

STRAIGHTFORWARD MEDIA http://www.straightforwardmedia.com

STRAIGHTFORWARD MEDIA ENGINEERING SCHOLARSHIP

Scholarship of $500 to students attending or planning to enroll in a postsecondary engineering program in the United States or abroad. Scholarship is awarded four times per year. Deadlines: March 31, June 30, September 30, December 31.

Academic Fields/Career Goals: Chemical Engineering; Civil Engineering; Engineering/Technology; Engineering-Related Technologies; Mechanical Engineering.

Award: Scholarship for use in freshman, sophomore, junior, or senior years; not renewable. *Number:* 4. *Amount:* $500.

Eligibility Requirements: Applicant must be enrolled or expecting to enroll full-time at a four-year institution or university. Available to U.S. and non-U.S. citizens.

Application Requirements: Online application. *Deadline:* varies.

Contact: Scholarship Committee
StraightForward Media
2040 West Main Street, Suite 104
Rapid City, SD 57701
Phone: 605-348-3042
Fax: 605-348-3043

UNITED NEGRO COLLEGE FUND http://www.uncf.org

CARDINAL HEALTH SCHOLARSHIP
• *See page 65*

CARGILL SCHOLARSHIP PROGRAM
• *See page 65*

CDM SCHOLARSHIP/INTERNSHIP
• *See page 93*

MEDTRONIC FOUNDATION SCHOLARSHIP
• *See page 136*

WEYERHAEUSER/UNCF CORPORATE SCHOLARS PROGRAM
• *See page 151*

WRIGLEY JR., WILLIAM SCHOLARSHIP/INTERNSHIP
• *See page 152*

UNIVERSITIES SPACE RESEARCH ASSOCIATION http://www.usra.edu

UNIVERSITIES SPACE RESEARCH ASSOCIATION SCHOLARSHIP PROGRAM
• *See page 88*

UTAH SOCIETY OF PROFESSIONAL ENGINEERS http://www.uspeonline.com

UTAH SOCIETY OF PROFESSIONAL ENGINEERS JOE RHOADS SCHOLARSHIP

One-time award for entering freshman pursuing studies in the field of engineering (civil, chemical, electrical, or engineering related technologies.) Minimum 3.5 GPA required. Must be a U.S. citizen and Utah resident attending school in Utah.

Academic Fields/Career Goals: Chemical Engineering; Civil Engineering; Electrical Engineering/Electronics; Energy and Power Engineering; Engineering/Technology; Mechanical Engineering.

Award: Scholarship for use in freshman year; not renewable. *Number:* 1. *Amount:* $1000.

Eligibility Requirements: Applicant must be high school student; planning to enroll or expecting to enroll full-time at a four-year institution or university; resident of Utah and studying in Utah. Applicant must have 3.5 GPA or higher. Available to U.S. citizens.

Application Requirements: Application, essay, resume, references, test scores, transcript. *Deadline:* March 23.

Contact: Dan Church, Joe Rhoads Scholarship Chair
Utah Society of Professional Engineers
488 East Winchester Street, Suite 400
Murray, UT 84107
E-mail: churchd@pbworld.com

XEROX http://www.xerox.com

TECHNICAL MINORITY SCHOLARSHIP

Scholarships are made available to minority students enrolled in technical degree programs at the bachelor's degree level or above. Eligible students must have a GPA of 3.0 or higher and show financial need. Refer to Web Site: http://www.xerox.com for details.

Academic Fields/Career Goals: Chemical Engineering; Computer Science/Data Processing; Electrical Engineering/Electronics; Engineering/Technology; Engineering-Related Technologies; Materials Science, Engineering, and Metallurgy; Mechanical Engineering; Physical Sciences and Math.

Award: Scholarship for use in freshman, sophomore, junior, senior, graduate, or postgraduate years; not renewable. *Number:* up to 122. *Amount:* $1000–$10,000.

Eligibility Requirements: Applicant must be American Indian/Alaska Native, Asian/Pacific Islander, Black (non-Hispanic), or Hispanic and enrolled or expecting to enroll full-time at a four-year institution or university. Applicant must have 3.0 GPA or higher. Available to U.S. citizens.

Application Requirements: Application, resume, transcript. *Deadline:* September 30.

Contact: Stephanie Michalowski, Supervisor Staffing Support Services
Xerox
150 State Street, Fourth Floor
Rochester, NY 14614
Phone: 585-244-1800 Ext. 4647
Fax: 585-482-3095
E-mail: xtmsp@rballiance.com

CHILD AND FAMILY STUDIES

CALIFORNIA STUDENT AID COMMISSION http://www.csac.ca.gov

CHILD DEVELOPMENT TEACHER AND SUPERVISOR GRANT PROGRAM

Award is for those students pursuing an approved course of study leading to a Child Development Permit issued by the California Commission on Teacher Credentialing. In exchange for each year funding is received, recipients agree to provide one year of service in a licensed childcare center.

Academic Fields/Career Goals: Child and Family Studies; Education.

Award: Grant for use in freshman, sophomore, junior, senior, or graduate years; renewable. *Number:* up to 300. *Amount:* $1000–$2000.

Eligibility Requirements: Applicant must be enrolled or expecting to enroll full- or part-time at a two-year or four-year institution or university; resident of California and studying in California. Applicant or parent of applicant must have employment or volunteer experience in teaching/education. Available to U.S. citizens.

Application Requirements: Application, financial need analysis, references, GPA verification. *Deadline:* April 16.

Contact: Catalina Mistler, Chief, Program Administration & Services Division
California Student Aid Commission
PO Box 419026
Rancho Cordova, CA 95741-9026
Phone: 916-526-7268
Fax: 916-526-8002
E-mail: studentsupport@csac.ca.gov

CLAN MACBEAN FOUNDATION http://www.clanmacbean.net

CLAN MACBEAN FOUNDATION GRANT PROGRAM
• *See page 95*

COLLEGEBOUND FOUNDATION http://www.collegeboundfoundation.org

JEANETTE R. WOLMAN SCHOLARSHIP

Renewable scholarship of $500 available for students specializing in pre-law, social work, or a field that focuses on child advocacy. Minimum cumulative GPA of 3.0 required.

Academic Fields/Career Goals: Child and Family Studies; Law/Legal Services; Social Services.

Award: Scholarship for use in freshman, sophomore, junior, or senior years; renewable. *Number:* 1. *Amount:* $500.

CollegeBound Foundation (continued)

Eligibility Requirements: Applicant must be enrolled or expecting to enroll full-time at a two-year or four-year institution or university. Applicant must have 3.0 GPA or higher. Available to U.S. citizens.

Application Requirements: Application, financial need analysis, transcript, financial aid award letters, SAR. *Deadline:* March 1.

Contact: Jamie Crouse, Scholarship Program Administrator
CollegeBound Foundation
300 Water Street, Suite 300
Baltimore, MD 21202
Phone: 410-783-2905 Ext. 207
Fax: 410-727-5786
E-mail: jcrouse@collegeboundfoundation.org

KE ALI'I PAUAHI FOUNDATION http://www.pauahi.org

MYRON & LAURA THOMPSON SCHOLARSHIP

Scholarships for students pursuing a degree in the field of early childhood education. Preference will be given to students who demonstrate an interest in working with Hawaiian children in Hawaii after completion of their education. Applicants must demonstrate financial need, an interest in the Hawaiian language, culture, history and values, and commitment to contribute to the greater community.

Academic Fields/Career Goals: Child and Family Studies; Education.

Award: Scholarship for use in freshman, sophomore, junior, senior, or graduate years; not renewable. *Number:* 2. *Amount:* $1200.

Eligibility Requirements: Applicant must be enrolled or expecting to enroll full-time at a four-year institution or university. Available to U.S. citizens.

Application Requirements: Application, financial need analysis, references, transcript, SAR, college acceptance letter. *Deadline:* May 2.

Contact: Elizabeth Stevenson, Development Manager
Ke Ali'i Pauahi Foundation
567 South King Street, Suite 160
Honolulu, HI 96813
Phone: 808-534-3966
Fax: 808-534-3890
E-mail: scholarships@pauahi.org

KENTUCKY HIGHER EDUCATION ASSISTANCE AUTHORITY (KHEAA) http://www.kheaa.com

EARLY CHILDHOOD DEVELOPMENT SCHOLARSHIP

Awards scholarship with conditional service commitment for part-time students currently employed by participating ECD facility or providing training in ECD for an approved organization.

Academic Fields/Career Goals: Child and Family Studies; Education.

Award: Scholarship for use in freshman, sophomore, junior, or senior years; not renewable. *Number:* 900–1000. *Amount:* up to $1800.

Eligibility Requirements: Applicant must be enrolled or expecting to enroll part-time at a four-year institution or university; resident of Kentucky and studying in Kentucky. Available to U.S. citizens.

Application Requirements: Application, resume. *Deadline:* continuous.

Contact: Early Childhood Development Authority
Kentucky Higher Education Assistance Authority (KHEAA)
275 East Main Street, 2W-E
Frankfort, KY 40621
Phone: 502-564-8099

MARGARET MCNAMARA MEMORIAL FUND http://www.wbfn.org

MARGARET MCNAMARA MEMORIAL FUND FELLOWSHIPS

One-time award for female students from developing countries enrolled in accredited graduate programs relating to women and children. Must be attending an accredited institution in the United States. Candidates must plan to return to their countries within two years. Must be over 25 years of age. U.S. citizens are not eligible.

Academic Fields/Career Goals: Child and Family Studies; Social Services; Women's Studies.

Award: Grant for use in freshman, sophomore, junior, senior, graduate, or postgraduate years; not renewable. *Number:* 5–6. *Amount:* up to $11,000.

Eligibility Requirements: Applicant must be age 25 and over; enrolled or expecting to enroll full-time at a four-year institution or university and female. Available to citizens of countries other than the U.S. or Canada.

Application Requirements: Application, essay, financial need analysis, photo, references, transcript, copy of visa, I20 and DS2019. *Deadline:* February 28.

Contact: Chairman, Selection Committee
Margaret McNamara Memorial Fund
MSN-H2-204, 1818 H Street, NW
Washington, DC 20433
Phone: 202-473-8751
Fax: 202-522-3142
E-mail: mmmf@worldbank.org

OHIO 4-H http://www.ohio4h.org

BEA CLEVELAND 4-H SCHOLARSHIP

One $1000 scholarship awarded to a 4-H member who is a senior in high school during the year of application. Applicant must be planning to enroll as a freshman in the College of Human Ecology at The Ohio State University or any of its regional campuses.

Academic Fields/Career Goals: Child and Family Studies; Food Science/Nutrition; Home Economics.

Award: Scholarship for use in freshman year; not renewable. *Number:* 1. *Amount:* $1000.

Eligibility Requirements: Applicant must be high school student; planning to enroll or expecting to enroll full- or part-time at a two-year or four-year institution or university and studying in Ohio. Applicant or parent of applicant must be member of National 4-H. Available to U.S. citizens.

Application Requirements: Application, essay, resume, references, transcript. *Deadline:* November 8.

Contact: Ryan Schmiesing, Interim Assistant Director
Ohio 4-H
4-H Centre, 2201 Fred Taylor Drive
Columbus, OH 43210
Phone: 614-292-4444
Fax: 614-292-5937
E-mail: schmiesing.3@cfaes.osu.edu

MABEL SARBAUGH 4-H SCHOLARSHIP

One $1000 scholarship is awarded. Applicant must be a 4-H member, senior in high school during the year of application, and planning to enroll in the College of Human Ecology as a freshman at The Ohio State University or any of its regional campuses.

Academic Fields/Career Goals: Child and Family Studies; Food Science/Nutrition; Home Economics.

Award: Scholarship for use in freshman year; not renewable. *Number:* 1. *Amount:* $1000.

Eligibility Requirements: Applicant must be high school student; planning to enroll or expecting to enroll full- or part-time at a two-year or four-year institution or university and studying in Ohio. Applicant or parent of applicant must be member of National 4-H. Available to U.S. citizens.

Application Requirements: Application, essay, resume, references, transcript. *Deadline:* November 8.

Contact: Ryan Schmiesing, Interim Assistant Director
Ohio 4-H
4-H Centre, 2201 Fred Taylor Drive
Columbus, OH 43210
Phone: 614-292-4444
Fax: 614-292-5937
E-mail: schmiesing.3@cfaes.osu.edu

SAN DIEGO FOUNDATION http://www.sdfoundation.org

CALIFORNIA ASSOCIATION OF FAMILY AND CONSUMER SCIENCES-SAN DIEGO CHAPTER

Scholarships to graduating high school seniors, current college students, or graduate students majoring in food sciences, dietetics, nutrition, food services, hospitality, human development or child and family development, apparel, fashion and textile services, housing and interiors, consumer economics, management and resources, or family and consumer science education. For more details visit: http://www.sdfoundation.org/scholarships/cafsc.shtml.

Academic Fields/Career Goals: Child and Family Studies; Fashion Design; Food Science/Nutrition; Food Service/Hospitality; Home Economics.

Award: Scholarship for use in freshman, sophomore, junior, senior, or graduate years; not renewable. *Number:* varies. *Amount:* varies.

Eligibility Requirements: Applicant must be enrolled or expecting to enroll full- or part-time at a two-year or four-year or technical institution or university and resident of California. Applicant must have 2.5 GPA or higher. Available to U.S. citizens.

Application Requirements: Application, references, transcript, personal statement, copy of tax return. *Deadline:* January 26.

Contact: Shryl Helvie, Scholarship Coordinator
San Diego Foundation
2508 Historic Decatur Road, Suite 200
San Diego, CA 92106
Phone: 619-814-1307
Fax: 619-239-1710
E-mail: shryl@sdfoundation.org

SOCIETY OF PEDIATRIC NURSES http://www.pedsnurses.org

SOCIETY OF PEDIATRIC NURSES EDUCATIONAL SCHOLARSHIP

Award to a member engaged in a BSN completion program or a graduate program that will advance the health of children. Nominee must be a current Society of Pediatric Nurses member.

Academic Fields/Career Goals: Child and Family Studies; Health and Medical Sciences; Nursing.

Award: Scholarship for use in freshman, sophomore, junior, senior, or graduate years; not renewable. *Number:* 1. *Amount:* $500.

Eligibility Requirements: Applicant must be enrolled or expecting to enroll full-time at a four-year institution or university. Applicant or parent of applicant must be member of Society of Pediatric Nurses. Applicant or parent of applicant must have employment or volunteer experience in nursing. Available to U.S. citizens.

Application Requirements: Application, essay, resume, references. *Deadline:* November 14.

Contact: Scholarship Committee
Society of Pediatric Nurses
7794 Grow Drive
Pensacola, FL 32514
Phone: 800-723-2902
Fax: 850-484-8762
E-mail: spn@puetzamc.com

SUNSHINE LADY FOUNDATION INC. http://www.sunshinelady.org

COUNSELOR, ADVOCATE, AND SUPPORT STAFF SCHOLARSHIP PROGRAM

Scholarship for workers in the field of domestic violence. Minimum one year working in the field of domestic violence and employer recommendation required. Scholarship value up to $3000.

Academic Fields/Career Goals: Child and Family Studies; Psychology; Social Sciences; Social Services; Therapy/Rehabilitation; Women's Studies.

Award: Scholarship for use in freshman, sophomore, junior, senior, or graduate years; renewable. *Number:* up to 50. *Amount:* up to $3000.

Eligibility Requirements: Applicant must be enrolled or expecting to enroll full- or part-time at a two-year or four-year or technical institution or university. Applicant or parent of applicant must have employment or volunteer experience in human services. Available to U.S. citizens.

Application Requirements: Application, essay, financial need analysis, references. *Deadline:* varies.

Contact: Nancy Soward, Program Director
Sunshine Lady Foundation Inc.
4900 Randall Parkway, Suite H
Wilmington, NC 28403
Phone: 910-397-7742 Ext. 101
Fax: 910-397-0023
E-mail: nancy@sunshinelady.org

Y'S MEN INTERNATIONAL http://www.ysmenusa.com

ALEXANDER SCHOLARSHIP LOAN FUND

• *See page 152*

ZETA PHI BETA SORORITY INC. NATIONAL EDUCATIONAL FOUNDATION http://www.zphib1920.org

LULLELIA W. HARRISON SCHOLARSHIP IN COUNSELING

Scholarships available for students enrolled in a graduate or undergraduate degree program in counseling. Awarded for full-time study for one academic year. See Web site for additional information and application: http://www.zphib1920.org.

Academic Fields/Career Goals: Child and Family Studies; Psychology; Social Sciences; Social Services.

Award: Scholarship for use in freshman, sophomore, junior, senior, or graduate years; not renewable. *Number:* 1. *Amount:* $500–$1000.

Eligibility Requirements: Applicant must be enrolled or expecting to enroll full-time at a four-year institution or university. Applicant or parent of applicant must be member of Zeta Phi Beta. Available to U.S. citizens.

Application Requirements: Application, essay, references, transcript, enrollment proof. *Deadline:* February 1.

Contact: Cheryl Williams, National Second Vice President
Zeta Phi Beta Sorority Inc. National Educational Foundation
1734 New Hampshire Avenue, NW
Washington, DC 20009-2595
Fax: 318-631-4028
E-mail: 2ndanti@zphib1920.org

CIVIL ENGINEERING

AACE INTERNATIONAL http://www.aacei.org

AACE INTERNATIONAL COMPETITIVE SCHOLARSHIP

• *See page 89*

AMERICAN COUNCIL OF ENGINEERING COMPANIES OF PENNSYLVANIA (ACEC/PA) http://www.acecpa.org

ENGINEERING SCHOLARSHIP

• *See page 154*

AMERICAN GROUND WATER TRUST http://www.agwt.org

AMERICAN GROUND WATER TRUST-THOMAS STETSON SCHOLARSHIP

For students entering their freshman year in a full-time program of study at a four-year accredited university or college located west of the Mississippi River and intending to pursue a career in ground water-related field. Must be U.S. citizen or legal resident with 3.0 GPA or higher. For more information see Web site: http://www.agwt.org.

Academic Fields/Career Goals: Civil Engineering; Hydrology; Natural Resources.

Award: Scholarship for use in freshman year; not renewable. *Number:* 1. *Amount:* up to $1500.

Eligibility Requirements: Applicant must be enrolled or expecting to enroll full-time at a four-year institution or university. Applicant must have 3.0 GPA or higher. Available to U.S. citizens.

American Ground Water Trust (continued)

Application Requirements: Application, essay, references, transcript. *Deadline:* June 1.

Contact: Andrew Stone, Executive Director
American Ground Water Trust
PO Box 1796
Concord, NH 03302-1796
Phone: 603-228-5444
Fax: 603-228-6557
E-mail: astone@agwt.org

AMERICAN PUBLIC TRANSPORTATION FOUNDATION http://www.apta.com

TRANSIT HALL OF FAME SCHOLARSHIP AWARD PROGRAM

Renewable award for sophomores, juniors, seniors or graduate students studying transportation or rail transit engineering. Must be sponsored by APTA member organization and complete an internship program with a member organization. Must have a minimum 3.0 GPA and be a U.S. or Canadian citizen.

Academic Fields/Career Goals: Civil Engineering; Electrical Engineering/Electronics; Engineering/Technology; Engineering-Related Technologies; Mechanical Engineering; Transportation.

Award: Scholarship for use in sophomore, junior, senior, or graduate years; renewable. *Number:* 1. *Amount:* $2500.

Eligibility Requirements: Applicant must be enrolled or expecting to enroll full-time at a two-year or four-year institution or university. Applicant must have 3.0 GPA or higher. Available to U.S. and Canadian citizens.

Application Requirements: Application, essay, financial need analysis, references, transcript, nomination by APTA member, verification of enrollment, copy of fee schedule from the college/university for the academic year. *Deadline:* June 16.

Contact: Pamela Boswell, Vice President of Program Management
American Public Transportation Foundation
1666 K Street, NW
Washington, DC 20006-1215
Phone: 202-496-4803
Fax: 202-496-4323

AMERICAN SOCIETY OF CIVIL ENGINEERS http://www.asce.org

EUGENE C. FIGG JR. CIVIL ENGINEERING SCHOLARSHIP

Applicant must be currently enrolled junior or senior civil engineering student at an ABET-accredited institution and an ASCE National Student Member in good standing.

Academic Fields/Career Goals: Civil Engineering.

Award: Scholarship for use in junior or senior years; not renewable. *Number:* 1. *Amount:* $3000.

Eligibility Requirements: Applicant must be enrolled or expecting to enroll full- or part-time at a four-year institution or university. Applicant or parent of applicant must be member of American Society of Civil Engineers. Available to U.S. citizens.

Application Requirements: Application, financial need analysis, resume, references, transcript, personal statement. *Deadline:* February 9.

Contact: Ting Wei, Scholarship Coordinator
American Society of Civil Engineers
1801 Alexander Bell Drive
Reston, VA 20191-4400
Phone: 703-295-6300 Ext. 6106
Fax: 703-295-6222

SAMUEL FLETCHER TAPMAN ASCE STUDENT CHAPTER/CLUB SCHOLARSHIP

Awards available to currently enrolled undergraduates. Must be a member of local ASCE Student Chapter/Club and an ASCE National Student Member in good standing. Selection is based on the applicant's justification of award, educational plan, academic performance and standing, potential for development, leadership capacity, ASCE activities, and financial need.

Academic Fields/Career Goals: Civil Engineering; Construction Engineering/Management.

Award: Scholarship for use in freshman, sophomore, junior, or senior years; not renewable. *Number:* 12. *Amount:* up to $2000.

Eligibility Requirements: Applicant must be enrolled or expecting to enroll full- or part-time at a four-year institution or university. Applicant or parent of applicant must be member of American Society of Civil Engineers. Available to U.S. citizens.

Application Requirements: Application, essay, financial need analysis, resume, references, transcript, annual budget. *Deadline:* February 9.

Contact: Ting Wei, Scholarship Coordinator
American Society of Civil Engineers
1801 Alexander Bell Drive
Reston, VA 20191-4400
Phone: 703-295-6300 Ext. 6106
Fax: 703-295-6222

Y.C. YANG CIVIL ENGINEERING SCHOLARSHIP

Applicants must be student members in good standing of the Society. Currently enrolled junior or senior civil engineering students at an institution with an ABET-accredited program and an interest in structural engineering may apply.

Academic Fields/Career Goals: Civil Engineering.

Award: Scholarship for use in junior or senior years; not renewable. *Number:* 2. *Amount:* $2000–$2500.

Eligibility Requirements: Applicant must be enrolled or expecting to enroll full- or part-time at a four-year institution or university. Available to U.S. and non-U.S. citizens.

Application Requirements: Application, financial need analysis, resume, references, test scores, transcript, personal statement. *Deadline:* February 9.

Contact: Ting Wei, Scholarship Coordinator
American Society of Civil Engineers
1801 Alexander Bell Drive
Reston, VA 20191-4400
Phone: 703-295-6300 Ext. 6106
Fax: 703-295-6222

AMERICAN SOCIETY OF CIVIL ENGINEERS-MAINE SECTION http://www.maineasce.org

AMERICAN SOCIETY OF CIVIL ENGINEERS-MAINE HIGH SCHOOL SCHOLARSHIP

One-time award available to high school student in senior year, pursuing a course of study in civil engineering. Must be resident of Maine. Essay, references and transcript required with application.

Academic Fields/Career Goals: Civil Engineering.

Award: Scholarship for use in freshman year; not renewable. *Number:* 2. *Amount:* $2000.

Eligibility Requirements: Applicant must be high school student; planning to enroll or expecting to enroll full-time at a four-year institution or university and resident of Maine. Available to U.S. and non-U.S. citizens.

Application Requirements: Application, essay, references, transcript. *Deadline:* January 31.

Contact: Leslie Corrow, Senior Project Engineer
American Society of Civil Engineers-Maine Section
141 Main Street
Pittsfield, ME 04967-0016
Phone: 207-487-3328 Ext. 243
Fax: 207-487-3124
E-mail: leslie.corrow@kleinschmidtusa.com

AMERICAN SOCIETY OF NAVAL ENGINEERS http://www.navalengineers.org

AMERICAN SOCIETY OF NAVAL ENGINEERS SCHOLARSHIP

• *See page 85*

AMERICAN WELDING SOCIETY http://www.aws.org

ARSHAM AMIRIKIAN ENGINEERING SCHOLARSHIP

Awarded to an undergraduate pursuing a minimum four-year degree in civil engineering or welding-related program at an accredited university. Applicant must be a minimum of 18 years of age, must have a minimum 3.0 GPA and must be a citizen of the United States.

Academic Fields/Career Goals: Civil Engineering; Materials Science, Engineering, and Metallurgy; Trade/Technical Specialties.

Award: Scholarship for use in freshman, sophomore, junior, or senior years; not renewable. *Number:* 1. *Amount:* $2500.

Eligibility Requirements: Applicant must be age 18 and over and enrolled or expecting to enroll full- or part-time at a four-year institution or university. Applicant must have 3.0 GPA or higher. Available to U.S. citizens.

Application Requirements: Application, autobiography, financial need analysis, references, transcript. *Deadline:* January 15.

Contact: Vicki Pinsky, Manager, Foundation
American Welding Society
550 Le Jeune Road, NW
Miami, FL 33126
Phone: 800-443-9353 Ext. 212
Fax: 305-443-7559
E-mail: vpinsky@aws.org

MATSUO BRIDGE COMPANY LTD. OF JAPAN SCHOLARSHIP

Awarded to a college junior or senior, or graduate student pursuing a minimum four-year degree in civil engineering, welding engineering, welding engineering technology, or related discipline. Applicant must have a minimum 3.0 overall GPA. Financial need is not required to apply. Must be U.S. citizen.

Academic Fields/Career Goals: Civil Engineering; Engineering/Technology; Engineering-Related Technologies; Materials Science, Engineering, and Metallurgy.

Award: Scholarship for use in junior, senior, or graduate years; not renewable. *Number:* 1. *Amount:* $2500.

Eligibility Requirements: Applicant must be age 18 and over and enrolled or expecting to enroll full- or part-time at a two-year or four-year institution or university. Applicant must have 3.0 GPA or higher. Available to U.S. citizens.

Application Requirements: Application, autobiography, financial need analysis, references, transcript. *Deadline:* January 15.

Contact: Vicki Pinsky, Manager, Foundation
American Welding Society
550 Le Jeune Road, NW
Miami, FL 33126
Phone: 800-443-9353 Ext. 212
Fax: 305-443-7559
E-mail: vpinsky@aws.org

ASSOCIATED GENERAL CONTRACTORS EDUCATION AND RESEARCH FOUNDATION http://www.agcfoundation.org

AGC EDUCATION AND RESEARCH FOUNDATION UNDERGRADUATE SCHOLARSHIPS

College sophomores and juniors enrolled or planning to enroll in a full-time, four or five-year ABET or ACCE-accredited construction management or construction-related engineering program are eligible to apply. High school seniors and college freshmen are not eligible.

Academic Fields/Career Goals: Civil Engineering; Construction Engineering/Management; Engineering/Technology.

Award: Scholarship for use in sophomore, junior, or senior years; renewable. *Number:* 100. *Amount:* $2500–$7500.

Eligibility Requirements: Applicant must be enrolled or expecting to enroll full-time at a four-year institution or university. Available to U.S. citizens.

Application Requirements: Application, essay, financial need analysis, references, transcript. *Deadline:* November 1.

Contact: Floretta Slade, Director of Programs
Associated General Contractors Education and Research Foundation
2300 Wilson Boulevard, Suite 400
Arlington, VA 22201
Phone: 703-837-5342
Fax: 703-837-5451
E-mail: sladef@agc.org

ASSOCIATED GENERAL CONTRACTORS OF AMERICA-NEW YORK STATE CHAPTER http://www.agcnys.org

ASSOCIATED GENERAL CONTRACTORS OF AMERICA-NEW YORK STATE CHAPTER SCHOLARSHIP PROGRAM

One-time scholarship for students enrolled full-time study in civil engineering, construction management and construction technology. Must have minimum GPA of 2.5. Scholarship value is from $1500 to $3000. Must be resident of New York.

Academic Fields/Career Goals: Civil Engineering; Surveying; Surveying Technology, Cartography, or Geographic Information Science; Transportation.

Award: Scholarship for use in sophomore, junior, or senior years; not renewable. *Number:* 10–15. *Amount:* $1500–$3000.

Eligibility Requirements: Applicant must be enrolled or expecting to enroll full-time at a four-year institution or university and resident of New York. Applicant must have 2.5 GPA or higher. Available to U.S. citizens.

Application Requirements: Application, references, transcript. *Deadline:* May 15.

Contact: Cathy Newell, Chief Operating Officer
Associated General Contractors of America-New York State Chapter
10 Airline Drive, Suite 203
Albany, NY 12205
Phone: 518-456-1134
Fax: 518-456-1198
E-mail: cnewell@agcnys.org

ASSOCIATION FOR FACILITIES ENGINEERING (AFE)

ASSOCIATION FOR FACILITIES ENGINEERING CEDAR VALLEY CHAPTER #132 SCHOLARSHIP

• *See page 114*

ASSOCIATION FOR IRON AND STEEL TECHNOLOGY http://www.aist.org

ASSOCIATION FOR IRON AND STEEL TECHNOLOGY DAVID H. SAMSON CANADIAN SCHOLARSHIP

• *See page 157*

ASSOCIATION OF CALIFORNIA WATER AGENCIES http://www.acwa.com

ASSOCIATION OF CALIFORNIA WATER AGENCIES SCHOLARSHIPS

• *See page 86*

CLAIR A. HILL SCHOLARSHIP

• *See page 86*

BARRY M. GOLDWATER SCHOLARSHIP AND EXCELLENCE IN EDUCATION FOUNDATION http://www.act.org/goldwater

BARRY M. GOLDWATER SCHOLARSHIP AND EXCELLENCE IN EDUCATION PROGRAM

• *See page 86*

CHI EPSILON http://www.chi-epsilon.org

"JAMES M. ROBBINS" EXCELLENCE IN TEACHING AWARD

Awards an undergraduate or a graduate pursuing civil engineering. Must have shown a dedication to teaching in the civil engineering profession. Nominations are due to District Councillor.

Academic Fields/Career Goals: Civil Engineering.

Award: Prize for use in freshman, sophomore, junior, senior, or graduate years; not renewable. *Number:* varies. *Amount:* varies.

Eligibility Requirements: Applicant must be enrolled or expecting to enroll full- or part-time at a four-year institution or university. Applicant or parent of applicant must have employment or volunteer experience in engineering/technology or teaching/education. Available to U.S. citizens.

Chi Epsilon (continued)

Application Requirements: Application, applicant must enter a contest, photo, resume, references. *Deadline:* November 15.

Contact: Thomas Petry, National Secretary and Treasurer
Chi Epsilon
University of Texas-Arlington
PO Box 19316
Arlington, TX 76019-0316
Phone: 866-554-0553
Fax: 817-272-2826
E-mail: tpetry@uta.edu

DALLAS ARCHITECTURAL FOUNDATION-HKS/ JOHN HUMPHRIES MINORITY SCHOLARSHIP http://www.dallasfoundation.org

JERE W. THOMPSON, JR., SCHOLARSHIP FUND

Renewable scholarships awarded to full-time undergraduate juniors or seniors with disadvantaged backgrounds, who are pursuing a degree in civil engineering and closely related disciplines at Texas colleges and universities. Up to $2000 awarded each semester, beginning with junior year. Must maintain 2.5 GPA. Special consideration given to students from Collin, Dallas, Denton, and Tarrant Counties, Texas.

Academic Fields/Career Goals: Civil Engineering.

Award: Scholarship for use in junior year; renewable. *Number:* 1–2. *Amount:* up to $4000.

Eligibility Requirements: Applicant must be enrolled or expecting to enroll full-time at a four-year institution or university; resident of Texas and studying in Texas. Applicant must have 2.5 GPA or higher. Available to U.S. citizens.

Application Requirements: Application, essay, financial need analysis, references, test scores, transcript. *Deadline:* April 1.

Contact: Mrs. Cathy McNally, Program Manager
Dallas Architectural Foundation-HKS/John Humphries Minority Scholarship
900 Jackson Street, Suite 150
Dallas, TX 75202
Phone: 214-741-9898
Fax: 214-741-9848
E-mail: cmcnally@dallasfoundation.org

ENGINEERS' SOCIETY OF WESTERN PENNSYLVANIA http://www.eswp.com

JAMES D. COOPER STUDENT PAPER COMPETITION

Prize of $1000 given to undergraduate and graduate students in civil engineering. The lead author of the winning paper in each category (undergraduate and graduate) will receive a $1000 IBC fellowship, complimentary conference registration, and hotel and travel allowances to attend the International Bridge Conference in Pittsburgh, Pennsylvania. Entry form is available at http://www.eswp.com/PDF/IBC Student Paper.pdf.

Academic Fields/Career Goals: Civil Engineering.

Award: Prize for use in freshman, sophomore, junior, senior, or graduate years; not renewable. *Number:* 2. *Amount:* up to $1000.

Eligibility Requirements: Applicant must be enrolled or expecting to enroll full- or part-time at a two-year or four-year institution or university. Available to U.S. and non-U.S. citizens.

Application Requirements: Application, applicant must enter a contest, self-addressed stamped envelope, 10-page manuscript. *Deadline:* March 1.

Contact: Ryan Bock, International Bridge Conference Manager
Engineers' Society of Western Pennsylvania
337 Fourth Avenue, Pittsburgh Engineers' Building
Pittsburgh, PA 15222
Phone: 412-261-0710 Ext. 11
Fax: 412-261-1606
E-mail: r.bock@eswp.com

FLORIDA ENGINEERING SOCIETY http://www.fleng.org

DAVID F. LUDOVICI SCHOLARSHIP

One-time scholarship of $1000 given to students in their junior or senior year in any Florida university engineering program, with at least 3.0 GPA. Applicants must be interested in civil, structural, or consulting engineering.

Academic Fields/Career Goals: Civil Engineering; Construction Engineering/Management; Engineering/Technology.

Award: Scholarship for use in junior or senior years; not renewable. *Number:* 1. *Amount:* $1000.

Eligibility Requirements: Applicant must be enrolled or expecting to enroll full-time at an institution or university; resident of Florida and studying in Florida. Applicant must have 3.0 GPA or higher. Available to U.S. citizens.

Application Requirements: Application, references, self-addressed stamped envelope, transcript. *Deadline:* February 1.

Contact: Scholarship Coordinator
Florida Engineering Society
125 South Gadsden Street
PO Box 750
Tallahassee, FL 32301
Phone: 850-224-7121
Fax: 850-222-4349
E-mail: fes@fleng.org

FECON SCHOLARSHIP

One-time scholarship of $1000 given to Florida citizens in their junior or senior year, who are enrolled or accepted into a Florida university engineering program. Minimum 3.0 GPA required. Applicant must be interested in pursuing a career in the field of construction.

Academic Fields/Career Goals: Civil Engineering; Construction Engineering/Management.

Award: Scholarship for use in junior or senior years; not renewable. *Number:* 1. *Amount:* $1000.

Eligibility Requirements: Applicant must be enrolled or expecting to enroll full-time at an institution or university; resident of Florida and studying in Florida. Applicant must have 3.0 GPA or higher. Available to U.S. citizens.

Application Requirements: Application, essay, references, self-addressed stamped envelope, transcript. *Deadline:* February 15.

Contact: Samantha Hobbs, FES Headquarters
Florida Engineering Society
PO Box 750
Tallahassee, FL 32302-0750
Phone: 850-224-7121

FOUNDATION FOR SCIENCE AND DISABILITY http://www.stemd.org

GRANTS FOR DISABLED STUDENTS IN THE SCIENCES

• *See page 87*

HAWAIIAN LODGE, F & AM http://www.glhawaii.org/

HAWAIIAN LODGE SCHOLARSHIPS

• *See page 96*

HISPANIC ENGINEER NATIONAL ACHIEVEMENT AWARDS CORPORATION (HENAAC) http://www.henaac.org

HISPANIC ENGINEER NATIONAL ACHIEVEMENT AWARDS CORPORATION SCHOLARSHIP PROGRAM

• *See page 116*

HISPANIC SCHOLARSHIP FUND http://www.hsf.net

HSF/GENERAL MOTORS SCHOLARSHIP

• *See page 143*

HSF/MARATHON OIL CORPORATION COLLEGE SCHOLARSHIP

• *See page 55*

INDEPENDENT LABORATORIES INSTITUTE SCHOLARSHIP ALLIANCE http://www.acil.org

INDEPENDENT LABORATORIES INSTITUTE SCHOLARSHIP ALLIANCE
• *See page 132*

INSTITUTE OF ENVIRONMENTAL SCIENCES AND TECHNOLOGY (IEST) http://www.iest.org

ROBERT N. HANCOCK MEMORIAL SCHOLARSHIP
• *See page 132*

JORGE MAS CANOSA FREEDOM FOUNDATION http://www.jorgemascanosa.org

MAS FAMILY SCHOLARSHIP AWARD
• *See page 144*

KENTUCKY TRANSPORTATION CABINET http://www.transportation.ky.gov/scholarship

KENTUCKY TRANSPORTATION CABINET CIVIL ENGINEERING SCHOLARSHIP PROGRAM

Cabinet awards scholarships to qualified Kentucky residents who wish to study civil engineering at Kentucky State University, Western Kentucky University, University of Louisville or University of Louisville. Applicant should be a graduate of an accredited Kentucky high school/high school graduates who are Kentucky residents.

Academic Fields/Career Goals: Civil Engineering.

Award: Scholarship for use in freshman, sophomore, junior, senior, or graduate years; renewable. *Number:* 10–20. *Amount:* $4400–$4800.

Eligibility Requirements: Applicant must be enrolled or expecting to enroll full-time at a four-year institution or university; resident of Kentucky and studying in Kentucky. Applicant must have 2.5 GPA or higher. Available to U.S. and non-U.S. citizens.

Application Requirements: Application, essay, interview, references, test scores, transcript. *Deadline:* March 1.

Contact: Jamie B. Byrd, Scholarship Program Administrator
Kentucky Transportation Cabinet
200 Mero Street
Frankfort, KY 40622
E-mail: jamie.bewleybyrd@ky.gov

LOS ANGELES COUNCIL OF BLACK PROFESSIONAL ENGINEERS http://www.lablackengineers.org

AL-BEN SCHOLARSHIP FOR ACADEMIC INCENTIVE
• *See page 159*

AL-BEN SCHOLARSHIP FOR PROFESSIONAL MERIT
• *See page 159*

AL-BEN SCHOLARSHIP FOR SCHOLASTIC ACHIEVEMENT
• *See page 159*

MICHIGAN SOCIETY OF PROFESSIONAL ENGINEERS http://www.michiganspe.org

ANTHONY C. FORTUNSKI, P.E. MEMORIAL GRANT
• *See page 159*

MICHIGAN SOCIETY OF PROFESSIONAL ENGINEERS ABRAMS GRANT

One $3000 grant for a top-ranking student interested in pursuing a career in civil or surveying engineering. Must be a Michigan resident enrolled in an ABET-accredited program at a Michigan college or university. Minimum 3.0 GPA required. Applicant must be a member of MSPE student chapter or a state member-at-large.

Academic Fields/Career Goals: Civil Engineering; Surveying; Surveying Technology, Cartography, or Geographic Information Science.

Award: Grant for use in freshman, sophomore, junior, or senior years; not renewable. *Number:* 1. *Amount:* $3000.

Eligibility Requirements: Applicant must be enrolled or expecting to enroll full-time at a four-year institution or university; resident of Michigan and studying in Michigan. Applicant or parent of applicant must be member of Michigan Society of Professional Engineers. Applicant must have 3.0 GPA or higher. Available to U.S. citizens.

Application Requirements: Application, essay, references, transcript. *Deadline:* varies.

Contact: Maura Nessan, Executive Director
Michigan Society of Professional Engineers
215 North Walnut Street
PO Box 15276
Lansing, MI 48901-5276
Phone: 517-487-9388
Fax: 517-487-0635
E-mail: mspe@voyager.net

MICHIGAN SOCIETY OF PROFESSIONAL ENGINEERS AUXILIARY GRANT
• *See page 159*

MICHIGAN SOCIETY OF PROFESSIONAL ENGINEERS HARRY R. BALL, P.E. GRANT
• *See page 159*

MICHIGAN SOCIETY OF PROFESSIONAL ENGINEERS KENNETH B. FISHBECK, P.E. MEMORIAL GRANT
• *See page 160*

MICHIGAN SOCIETY OF PROFESSIONAL ENGINEERS 1980 NATIONAL SOCIETY OF PROFESSIONAL ENGINEERS ANNUAL MEETING COMMITTEE GRANT
• *See page 160*

MICHIGAN SOCIETY OF PROFESSIONAL ENGINEERS SCHOLARSHIP TRUST GRANT
• *See page 160*

MICHIGAN SOCIETY OF PROFESSIONAL ENGINEERS UNDESIGNATED GRANT
• *See page 160*

MSPE AUXILIARY GRANT FOR UNDERGRADUATE STUDY

One grant of $1500 will be awarded to a student interested in pursuing a career in engineering. Preference is given to a son or daughter of a MSPE member.

Academic Fields/Career Goals: Civil Engineering; Construction Engineering/Management; Electrical Engineering/Electronics; Engineering/Technology; Mechanical Engineering.

Award: Grant for use in freshman, sophomore, junior, or senior years; not renewable. *Number:* 1. *Amount:* $1500.

Eligibility Requirements: Applicant must be enrolled or expecting to enroll full-time at a four-year institution or university; resident of Michigan and studying in Michigan. Applicant or parent of applicant must be member of Michigan Society of Professional Engineers. Applicant must have 3.0 GPA or higher. Available to U.S. citizens.

Application Requirements: Application, essay, references, transcript. *Deadline:* varies.

Contact: Maura Nessan, Executive Director
Michigan Society of Professional Engineers
215 North Walnut Street
PO Box 15276
Lansing, MI 48901-5276
Phone: 517-487-9388
Fax: 517-487-0635
E-mail: mspe@voyager.net

MIDWEST ROOFING CONTRACTORS ASSOCIATION http://www.mrca.org

MRCA FOUNDATION SCHOLARSHIP PROGRAM

Renewable scholarships for full-time students enrolled or intending to enroll in an accredited university, college, community college, or trade school. Applicant must be pursuing a curriculum leading to a career in the construction industry. Award amount ranges from $500 to $3000.

Academic Fields/Career Goals: Civil Engineering; Construction Engineering/Management; Trade/Technical Specialties.

Award: Scholarship for use in freshman, sophomore, junior, senior, or graduate years; renewable. *Number:* 2–12. *Amount:* $500–$3000.

Eligibility Requirements: Applicant must be enrolled or expecting to enroll full-time at a two-year or four-year or technical institution or university. Available to U.S. citizens.

Midwest Roofing Contractors Association (continued)

Application Requirements: Application, essay, financial need analysis, photo, references, test scores, transcript. *Deadline:* June 20.

Contact: Chrissy Neibarger, Membership Services Coordinator
Midwest Roofing Contractors Association
4840 Bob Billings Parkway, Suite 1000
Lawrence, KS 66049-3876
Phone: 800-497-6722
Fax: 785-843-7555
E-mail: membership@mrca.org

NASA DELAWARE SPACE GRANT CONSORTIUM http://www.delspace.org

NASA DELAWARE SPACE GRANT UNDERGRADUATE TUITION SCHOLARSHIP

• *See page 87*

NASA MONTANA SPACE GRANT CONSORTIUM http://www.spacegrant.montana.edu

MONTANA SPACE GRANT SCHOLARSHIP PROGRAM

• *See page 119*

NATIONAL ASPHALT PAVEMENT ASSOCIATION http://www.hotmix.org

NATIONAL ASPHALT PAVEMENT ASSOCIATION SCHOLARSHIP PROGRAM

Scholarship provides funding for full-time students majoring in civil engineering, construction management, or construction engineering. Applicant must take at least one course on HMA technology. Refer to Web site for more details: http://www.hotmix.org/main.htm. Some state restrictions.

Academic Fields/Career Goals: Civil Engineering; Construction Engineering/Management.

Award: Scholarship for use in freshman, sophomore, junior, senior, or graduate years; renewable. *Number:* 50–150. *Amount:* $500–$2500.

Eligibility Requirements: Applicant must be enrolled or expecting to enroll full-time at a two-year or four-year or technical institution or university. Applicant must have 2.5 GPA or higher. Available to U.S. citizens.

Application Requirements: Application. *Deadline:* varies.

Contact: Carolyn Wilson, Vice President, Finance and Operations
National Asphalt Pavement Association
NAPA Building
5100 Forbes Boulevard
Lanham, MD 20706-4413
Phone: 301-731-4748
Fax: 301-731-4621
E-mail: cwilson@hotmix.org

NATIONAL ASSOCIATION OF WOMEN IN CONSTRUCTION http://www.nawic.org

NAWIC UNDERGRADUATE SCHOLARSHIPS

• *See page 92*

NATIONAL SOCIETY OF PROFESSIONAL ENGINEERS http://www.nspe.org

MAUREEN L. AND HOWARD N. BLITMAN, PE SCHOLARSHIP TO PROMOTE DIVERSITY IN ENGINEERING

• *See page 161*

PAUL H. ROBBINS HONORARY SCHOLARSHIP

• *See page 162*

PROFESSIONAL ENGINEERS IN INDUSTRY SCHOLARSHIP

• *See page 162*

NEW ENGLAND WATER WORKS ASSOCIATION http://www.newwa.org

ELSON T. KILLAM MEMORIAL SCHOLARSHIP

Scholarships are awarded to eligible civil and environmental engineering students on the basis of merit, character, and need. Preference given to those students whose programs are considered by a committee as beneficial to water works practice in New England. NEWWA student membership is required to receive a scholarship award.

Academic Fields/Career Goals: Civil Engineering; Environmental Science.

Award: Scholarship for use in freshman, sophomore, junior, senior, or graduate years; not renewable. *Number:* 1. *Amount:* up to $1500.

Eligibility Requirements: Applicant must be enrolled or expecting to enroll full-time at a four-year institution or university. Applicant or parent of applicant must be member of New England Water Works Association. Available to U.S. citizens.

Application Requirements: Application, essay, references, transcript. *Fee:* $25. *Deadline:* July 1.

Contact: Thomas MacElhaney, Chair, Scholarship Committee
New England Water Works Association
c/o PRELOAD Inc., 60 Commerce Drive
Hauppauge, NY 11788
Phone: 631-231-8100
Fax: 978-418-9156
E-mail: tmacelhaney@preloadinc.com

FRANCIS X. CROWLEY SCHOLARSHIP

• *See page 147*

JOSEPH MURPHY SCHOLARSHIP

Scholarships are awarded to eligible civil or environmental engineering students on the basis of merit, character, and need. Preference given to those students whose programs are considered by a committee as beneficial to water works practice in New England. NEWWA student membership is required to receive a scholarship award.

Academic Fields/Career Goals: Civil Engineering; Environmental Science.

Award: Scholarship for use in freshman, sophomore, junior, senior, or graduate years; not renewable. *Number:* 1. *Amount:* up to $1500.

Eligibility Requirements: Applicant must be enrolled or expecting to enroll full-time at a four-year institution or university. Applicant or parent of applicant must be member of New England Water Works Association. Available to U.S. citizens.

Application Requirements: Application, essay, references, transcript. *Fee:* $25. *Deadline:* July 1.

Contact: Thomas MacElhaney, Chair, Scholarship Committee
New England Water Works Association
c/o PRELOAD Inc., 60 Commerce Drive
Hauppauge, NY 11788
Phone: 631-231-8100
Fax: 978-418-9156
E-mail: tmacelhaney@preloadinc.com

WORKS GEORGE E. WATTERS MEMORIAL SCHOLARSHIP.

Scholarships are awarded to eligible Civil Engineering students on the basis of merit, character, and need. Preference given to those students whose programs are considered by a committee as beneficial to water works practice in New England. NEWWA student membership is required to receive a scholarship award.

Academic Fields/Career Goals: Civil Engineering.

Award: Scholarship for use in freshman, sophomore, junior, or senior years; not renewable. *Number:* 1. *Amount:* up to $5000.

Eligibility Requirements: Applicant must be enrolled or expecting to enroll full-time at a four-year institution or university. Available to U.S. citizens.

Application Requirements: Application, essay, references, transcript. *Fee:* $25. *Deadline:* July 1.

Contact: Thomas MacElhaney, Chair, Scholarship Committee
New England Water Works Association
c/o PRELOAD Inc., 60 Commerce Drive
Hauppauge, NY 11788
Phone: 631-231-8100
Fax: 978-418-9156
E-mail: tmacelhaney@preloadinc.com

OREGON STUDENT ASSISTANCE COMMISSION http://www.osac.state.or.us

AMERICAN COUNCIL OF ENGINEERING COMPANIES OF OREGON SCHOLARSHIP
• *See page 162*

HOMESTEAD CAPITAL HOUSING SCHOLARSHIP
• *See page 61*

PLUMBING-HEATING-COOLING CONTRACTORS ASSOCIATION EDUCATION FOUNDATION http://www.phccweb.org

BRADFORD WHITE CORPORATION SCHOLARSHIP
• *See page 92*

DELTA FAUCET COMPANY SCHOLARSHIP PROGRAM
• *See page 93*

PHCC EDUCATIONAL FOUNDATION NEED-BASED SCHOLARSHIP
• *See page 93*

PHCC EDUCATIONAL FOUNDATION SCHOLARSHIP PROGRAM
• *See page 147*

PROFESSIONAL GROUNDS MANAGEMENT SOCIETY http://www.pgms.org

ANNE SEAMAN PROFESSIONAL GROUNDS MANAGEMENT SOCIETY MEMORIAL SCHOLARSHIP
• *See page 78*

SOCIETY OF HISPANIC PROFESSIONAL ENGINEERS FOUNDATION http://www.henaac.org

SOCIETY OF HISPANIC PROFESSIONAL ENGINEERS FOUNDATION
• *See page 162*

SOCIETY OF WOMEN ENGINEERS http://www.swe.org

ANNE MAUREEN WHITNEY BARROW MEMORIAL SCHOLARSHIP

Scholarship for a female undergraduate entering an engineering or engineering technology degree program. Minimum 3.5 GPA is required. Awarded only once per renewal.

Academic Fields/Career Goals: Civil Engineering; Electrical Engineering/Electronics; Energy and Power Engineering; Engineering/ Technology; Engineering-Related Technologies; Mechanical Engineering.

Award: Scholarship for use in freshman, sophomore, junior, or senior years; renewable. *Number:* 1. *Amount:* $6000.

Eligibility Requirements: Applicant must be enrolled or expecting to enroll full-time at a four-year institution or university and female. Applicant must have 3.5 GPA or higher. Available to U.S. citizens.

Application Requirements: Application, essay, references, self-addressed stamped envelope, test scores, transcript. *Deadline:* varies.

Contact: Scholarship Committee
Society of Women Engineers
230 East Ohio Street, Suite 400
Chicago, IL 60611-3265
Phone: 312-596-5223
Fax: 312-596-5252
E-mail: scholarshipapplication@swe.org

BECHTEL CORPORATION SCHOLARSHIP

Scholarship of $1400 available to female students in architectural, civil, electrical, environmental, or mechanical engineering. Must be a member of the Society of Women Engineers. Minimum 3.0 GPA required. Open to sophomores, juniors, and seniors.

Academic Fields/Career Goals: Civil Engineering; Electrical Engineering/Electronics; Engineering/Technology; Mechanical Engineering.

Award: Scholarship for use in sophomore, junior, or senior years; not renewable. *Number:* 2. *Amount:* $1400.

Eligibility Requirements: Applicant must be enrolled or expecting to enroll full-time at a four-year institution or university and female. Applicant or parent of applicant must be member of Society of Women Engineers. Applicant must have 3.0 GPA or higher. Available to U.S. citizens.

Application Requirements: Application, references, self-addressed stamped envelope, test scores, transcript. *Deadline:* February 1.

Contact: Scholarship Committee
Society of Women Engineers
230 East Ohio Street, Suite 400
Chicago, IL 60611-3265
Phone: 312-596-5223
Fax: 312-596-5252
E-mail: scholarshipapplication@swe.org

CHEVRON TEXACO CORPORATION SCHOLARSHIPS
• *See page 163*

DOROTHY LEMKE HOWARTH SCHOLARSHIPS
• *See page 163*

GENERAL ELECTRIC FOUNDATION SCHOLARSHIP
• *See page 164*

LILLIAN MOLLER GILBRETH MEMORIAL SCHOLARSHIP
• *See page 164*

MASWE MEMORIAL SCHOLARSHIP
• *See page 164*

STRAIGHTFORWARD MEDIA http://www.straightforwardmedia.com

STRAIGHTFORWARD MEDIA ENGINEERING SCHOLARSHIP
• *See page 164*

TEXAS DEPARTMENT OF TRANSPORTATION http://www.txdot.gov

CONDITIONAL GRANT PROGRAM

Renewable award to students who are considered economically disadvantaged based on federal guidelines. The maximum amount awarded per semester is $3,000 not to exceed $6000 per academic year. Students already enrolled in an undergraduate program should have minimum GPA 2.5 and students newly enrolling should have minimum GPA 3.0.

Academic Fields/Career Goals: Civil Engineering; Computer Science/ Data Processing; Occupational Safety and Health.

Award: Grant for use in freshman, sophomore, junior, or senior years; renewable. *Number:* varies. *Amount:* up to $6000.

Eligibility Requirements: Applicant must be enrolled or expecting to enroll full-time at a four-year institution or university; resident of Texas and studying in Texas. Available to U.S. citizens.

Texas Department of Transportation (continued)

Application Requirements: Application, essay, interview, references, test scores, transcript. *Deadline:* March 1.

Contact: Minnie Brown, Program Coordinator
Texas Department of Transportation
125 East 11th Street
Austin, TX 78701-2483
Phone: 512-416-4979
Fax: 512-416-4980
E-mail: mbrown2@dot.state.tx.us

TURNER CONSTRUCTION COMPANY http://www.turnerconstruction.com

YOUTHFORCE 2020 SCHOLARSHIP PROGRAM

• *See page 93*

UNITED NEGRO COLLEGE FUND http://www.uncf.org

CARDINAL HEALTH SCHOLARSHIP

• *See page 65*

CDM SCHOLARSHIP/INTERNSHIP

• *See page 93*

MEDTRONIC FOUNDATION SCHOLARSHIP

• *See page 136*

SPRINT NEXTEL SCHOLARSHIP/INTERNSHIP

• *See page 66*

UPS/UNCF CORPORATE SCHOLARS PROGRAM

• *See page 151*

UNIVERSITIES SPACE RESEARCH ASSOCIATION http://www.usra.edu

UNIVERSITIES SPACE RESEARCH ASSOCIATION SCHOLARSHIP PROGRAM

• *See page 88*

UTAH SOCIETY OF PROFESSIONAL ENGINEERS http://www.uspeonline.com

UTAH SOCIETY OF PROFESSIONAL ENGINEERS JOE RHOADS SCHOLARSHIP

• *See page 165*

WIRE REINFORCEMENT INSTITUTE EDUCATION FOUNDATION http://www.wirereinforcementinstitute.org

WRI COLLEGE SCHOLARSHIP PROGRAM

Academic scholarships for qualified high school seniors and current undergraduate and graduate level students intending to or presently pursuing four-year or graduate-level degrees in structural and/or civil engineering at accredited four-year universities or colleges.

Academic Fields/Career Goals: Civil Engineering.

Award: Scholarship for use in freshman, sophomore, junior, senior, or graduate years; not renewable. *Number:* varies. *Amount:* $2500–$10,000.

Eligibility Requirements: Applicant must be enrolled or expecting to enroll full-time at a four-year institution or university. Available to U.S. and Canadian citizens.

Application Requirements: Application, references, test scores, transcript. *Deadline:* April 15.

Contact: Scholarship Selection Committee
Wire Reinforcement Institute Education Foundation
942 Main Street, Suite 300
Hartford, CT 06103

CLASSICS

ACL/NJCL NATIONAL LATIN EXAM http://www.nle.org

NATIONAL LATIN EXAM SCHOLARSHIP

Scholarships to high school seniors who are gold medal winners in Latin III-IV Prose, III-IV Poetry, or Latin V-VI. Applicants must agree to take at least one year of Latin or classical Greek in college.

Academic Fields/Career Goals: Classics; Foreign Language.

Award: Scholarship for use in freshman year; renewable. *Number:* 21. *Amount:* $1000.

Eligibility Requirements: Applicant must be high school student; planning to enroll or expecting to enroll full-time at a four-year institution or university and must have an interest in Greek language or Latin language. Available to U.S. and non-U.S. citizens.

Application Requirements: Application, essay, test scores, transcript. *Deadline:* January 18.

Contact: Jane Hall, Co-Chair
ACL/NJCL National Latin Exam
University of Mary Washington, 1301 College Avenue
Fredericksburg, VA 22401
Phone: 888-378-7721
Fax: 540-654-1567
E-mail: nle@umw.edu

AMERICAN CLASSICAL LEAGUE/NATIONAL JUNIOR CLASSICAL LEAGUE http://www.aclclassics.org

NATIONAL JUNIOR CLASSICAL LEAGUE SCHOLARSHIP

A one-time award available to graduating high school seniors, who are members of the Junior Classical League. Preference is given to students who plan to major in the classics.

Academic Fields/Career Goals: Classics; Foreign Language; Humanities.

Award: Scholarship for use in freshman year; not renewable. *Number:* 7. *Amount:* $1000–$2000.

Eligibility Requirements: Applicant must be high school student; planning to enroll or expecting to enroll full-time at a two-year or four-year institution or university and must have an interest in foreign language. Applicant or parent of applicant must be member of Junior Classical League. Available to U.S. and non-U.S. citizens.

Application Requirements: Application, essay, references, transcript, list of 5 extra curricular activities and 5 community activities. *Deadline:* May 1.

Contact: Geri Dutra, Administrator
American Classical League/National Junior Classical League
Miami University, 422 Wells Mill Drive
Oxford, OH 45066
Phone: 513-529-7741
Fax: 513-529-7742
E-mail: info@aclclassics.org

AMERICAN PHILOLOGICAL ASSOCIATION http://www.apaclassics.org

MINORITY STUDENT SUMMER SCHOLARSHIP

• *See page 89*

COMMUNICATIONS

ACADEMY OF TELEVISION ARTS AND SCIENCES FOUNDATION http://www.emmysfoundation.org

ACADEMY OF TELEVISION ARTS AND SCIENCES COLLEGE TELEVISION AWARDS

• *See page 99*

ADC RESEARCH INSTITUTE http://www.adc.org

JACK SHAHEEN MASS COMMUNICATIONS SCHOLARSHIP AWARD

Awarded to Arab-American students who excel in the mass communications field (journalism, radio, television or film). Must be a junior or senior undergraduate or graduate student. Must be U.S. citizen. Minimum 3.0 GPA required.

Academic Fields/Career Goals: Communications; Filmmaking/Video; Journalism; TV/Radio Broadcasting.

Award: Scholarship for use in junior, senior, or graduate years; not renewable. *Number:* 1–6. *Amount:* $500–$1000.

Eligibility Requirements: Applicant must be of Arab heritage and enrolled or expecting to enroll full- or part-time at a four-year institution or university. Applicant must have 3.0 GPA or higher. Available to U.S. citizens.

Application Requirements: Application, essay, references, transcript, copies of original articles, videos, films. *Deadline:* April 12.

Contact: Mr. Nawar Shora, Director of Diversity and Law Enforcement Outreach
ADC Research Institute
1732 Wisconsin Avenue, NW
Washington, DC 20007
Phone: 202-244-2990
Fax: 202-244-3196
E-mail: nshora@adc.org

AMERICAN INSTITUTE OF POLISH CULTURE INC. http://www.ampolinstitute.org

HARRIET IRSAY SCHOLARSHIP GRANT

• *See page 99*

AMERICAN LEGION DEPARTMENT OF NEW YORK http://www.ny.legion.org

AMERICAN LEGION DEPARTMENT OF NEW YORK PRESS ASSOCIATION SCHOLARSHIP

A $1000 scholarship for children of NY American Legion or American Legion Auxiliary members, members of SAL or ALA Juniors or graduates of NY AL Boys State or Girls State. Must be entering or attending accredited four-year college pursuing communications degree.

Academic Fields/Career Goals: Communications.

Award: Scholarship for use in freshman, sophomore, junior, or senior years; not renewable. *Number:* 1. *Amount:* $1000.

Eligibility Requirements: Applicant must be enrolled or expecting to enroll full-time at a four-year institution or university and resident of New York. Applicant or parent of applicant must be member of American Legion or Auxiliary. Available to U.S. citizens. Applicant or parent must meet one or more of the following requirements: general military experience; retired from active duty; disabled or killed as a result of military service; prisoner of war; or missing in action.

Application Requirements: Application. *Deadline:* April 15.

Contact: Scholarship Chairman
American Legion Department of New York
PO Box 1239
Syracuse, NY 13201

AMERICAN LEGION PRESS CLUB OF NEW JERSEY

AMERICAN LEGION PRESS CLUB OF NEW JERSEY AND POST 170 ARTHUR DEHARDT MEMORIAL SCHOLARSHIP

Merit based scholarship awarded to two students (one male, one female) entering their freshman year. Eligible applicants will be the son, daughter, grandson, or granddaughter of a current card-holding member of the American Legion. Any student who has graduated from either American Legion Boys' State or Girls' State program shall be eligible.

Academic Fields/Career Goals: Communications; Journalism; Photojournalism/Photography; TV/Radio Broadcasting.

Award: Scholarship for use in freshman year; not renewable. *Number:* 2. *Amount:* $500.

Eligibility Requirements: Applicant must be high school student; planning to enroll or expecting to enroll full-time at a four-year institution or university; single and resident of New Jersey. Applicant or parent of applicant must be member of American Legion or Auxiliary. Available to U.S. citizens. Applicant or parent must meet one or more of the following requirements: general military experience; retired from active duty; disabled or killed as a result of military service; prisoner of war; or missing in action.

Application Requirements: Application, essay, transcript, copy of graduation certificates, DD-214. *Deadline:* July 1.

Contact: Dorothy Saunders, Scholarship Chairman
American Legion, Press Club of New Jersey
Three Lewis Street
Wayne, NJ 07470-4716

AMERICAN QUARTER HORSE FOUNDATION (AQHF) http://www.aqha.com/foundation

AQHF JOURNALISM OR COMMUNICATIONS SCHOLARSHIP

Scholarship of $8000 for AQHA/AQHYA members who hold the membership one year or more year, pursuing a degree in journalism or communications. Recipient must intend to pursue career in news, editorial or print journalism and/or photojournalism. Members may apply during their senior year of high school or while enrolled as a freshman at an accredited college, university or vocational school. Minimum 2.5 GPA required.

Academic Fields/Career Goals: Communications; Journalism.

Award: Scholarship for use in freshman, sophomore, junior, or senior years; renewable. *Number:* 1. *Amount:* $8000.

Eligibility Requirements: Applicant must be enrolled or expecting to enroll full-time at a two-year or four-year or technical institution or university and must have an interest in animal/agricultural competition. Applicant or parent of applicant must be member of American Quarter Horse Association. Applicant must have 2.5 GPA or higher. Available to U.S. and Canadian citizens.

Application Requirements: Application, essay, financial need analysis, photo, references, transcript. *Deadline:* January 2.

Contact: Laura Owens, Scholarship Office
American Quarter Horse Foundation (AQHF)
2601 East Interstate 40
Amarillo, TX 79104
Phone: 806-378-5029
Fax: 806-376-1005
E-mail: foundation@aqha.org

APOGEE SEARCH http://www.apogee-search.com

FIRST ANNUAL APOGEE SEARCH SCHOLARSHIP PROGRAM

• *See page 138*

ARAB AMERICAN SCHOLARSHIP FOUNDATION http://www.lahc.org

LEBANESE AMERICAN HERITAGE CLUB'S SCHOLARSHIP FUND

Scholarship for high school, undergraduate, or graduate students who are of Arab descent. Minimum 3.0 GPA required for high school and undergraduate applicants, 3.5 GPA for graduate student applicants. Must be U.S. citizens.

Academic Fields/Career Goals: Communications; Political Science.

Award: Scholarship for use in freshman, sophomore, junior, senior, or graduate years; not renewable. *Number:* 1. *Amount:* $1000.

Eligibility Requirements: Applicant must be of Arab heritage; enrolled or expecting to enroll full-time at a four-year institution or university and resident of Michigan. Applicant must have 3.0 GPA or higher. Available to U.S. citizens.

Application Requirements: Application, essay, financial need analysis, references, transcript, SAR. *Deadline:* April 6.

Contact: Suehalia Amen, Communications-Chair
Arab American Scholarship Foundation
The Lebanese American Heritage Club, 4337 Maple Road
Dearborn, MI 48126
Phone: 313-846-8480
Fax: 313-846-2710
E-mail: sueamen@lahc.org

ARMED FORCES COMMUNICATIONS AND ELECTRONICS ASSOCIATION, EDUCATIONAL FOUNDATION http://www.afcea.org

ARMED FORCES COMMUNICATIONS AND ELECTRONICS ASSOCIATION ROTC SCHOLARSHIP PROGRAM

• *See page 114*

ARRL FOUNDATION INC. http://www.arrl.org

CHARLES N. FISHER MEMORIAL SCHOLARSHIP

• *See page 85*

DR. JAMES L. LAWSON MEMORIAL SCHOLARSHIP

One-time award of $500 available to general amateur radio operators. Preference given to residents of Connecticut, Maine, New Hampshire, Rhode Island, Vermont, and New York state. For baccalaureate or higher course of study. Must be attending school in any of the above mentioned states. Preference given to communications or electronics majors.

Academic Fields/Career Goals: Communications; Electrical Engineering/Electronics.

Award: Scholarship for use in freshman, sophomore, junior, senior, or graduate years; not renewable. *Number:* 1. *Amount:* $500.

Eligibility Requirements: Applicant must be enrolled or expecting to enroll full-time at a four-year institution or university; resident of Connecticut, Maine, New Hampshire, New York, Rhode Island, or Vermont; studying in Connecticut, Maine, New Hampshire, New York, Rhode Island, or Vermont and must have an interest in amateur radio. Available to U.S. citizens.

Application Requirements: Application, transcript. *Deadline:* February 1.

Contact: Mary M. Hobart, Secretary
ARRL Foundation Inc.
225 Main Street
Newington, CT 06111-1494
Phone: 860-594-0397
Fax: 860-594-0259
E-mail: k1mmh@arrl.org

IRVINE W. COOK WA0CGS SCHOLARSHIP

One-time award of $1000 to students pursuing a baccalaureate or higher degree in communications, electronics, or related fields. Must be a amateur radio operator. Preference to Kansas resident but may attend school in any state.

Academic Fields/Career Goals: Communications; Electrical Engineering/Electronics.

Award: Scholarship for use in freshman, sophomore, junior, or senior years; not renewable. *Number:* 1. *Amount:* $1000.

Eligibility Requirements: Applicant must be enrolled or expecting to enroll full-time at a four-year institution or university; resident of Kansas and must have an interest in amateur radio. Available to U.S. citizens.

Application Requirements: Application, transcript. *Deadline:* February 1.

Contact: Mary M. Hobart, Secretary
ARRL Foundation Inc.
225 Main Street
Newington, CT 06111-1494
Phone: 860-594-0397
Fax: 860-594-0259
E-mail: k1mmh@arrl.org

L. PHIL WICKER SCHOLARSHIP

One-time award available to electronics or communications students pursuing a baccalaureate or higher degree. Must be a licensed general amateur radio operator. Preference given to those residing in North Carolina, South Carolina, Virginia or West Virginia. Must be attending a school in one of the four above mentioned states.

Academic Fields/Career Goals: Communications; Electrical Engineering/Electronics.

Award: Scholarship for use in freshman, sophomore, junior, senior, or graduate years; not renewable. *Number:* 1. *Amount:* $1000.

Eligibility Requirements: Applicant must be enrolled or expecting to enroll full-time at a four-year institution or university; studying in North Carolina, South Carolina, Virginia, or West Virginia and must have an interest in amateur radio. Available to U.S. citizens.

Application Requirements: Application, transcript. *Deadline:* February 1.

Contact: Mary M. Hobart, Secretary
ARRL Foundation Inc.
225 Main Street
Newington, CT 06111-1494
Phone: 860-594-0397
Fax: 860-594-0259
E-mail: k1mmh@arrl.org

MISSISSIPPI SCHOLARSHIP

• *See page 85*

PAUL AND HELEN L. GRAUER SCHOLARSHIP

• *See page 85*

ASIAN AMERICAN JOURNALISTS ASSOCIATION http://www.aaja.org

ASIAN-AMERICAN JOURNALISTS ASSOCIATION SCHOLARSHIP

Award of $5000 for high school seniors and college students pursuing careers in the news media. Asian heritage is not required. Minimum 2.5 GPA required. Based on scholarship, goals, journalistic ability, financial need, and commitment to the Asian-American community. Visit Web site http://www.aaja.org for application and details.

Academic Fields/Career Goals: Communications; Journalism; Photojournalism/Photography; TV/Radio Broadcasting.

Award: Scholarship for use in freshman, sophomore, junior, senior, or graduate years; renewable. *Number:* 10. *Amount:* $5000.

Eligibility Requirements: Applicant must be enrolled or expecting to enroll full-time at a two-year or four-year institution or university. Applicant or parent of applicant must have employment or volunteer experience in journalism/broadcasting. Applicant must have 2.5 GPA or higher. Available to U.S. and non-U.S. citizens.

Application Requirements: Application, essay, financial need analysis, resume, references, transcript. *Deadline:* March 28.

Contact: Kim Mizuhara, Programs Coordinator
Asian American Journalists Association
1182 Market Street, Suite 320
San Francisco, CA 94102
Phone: 415-346-2051 Ext. 102
Fax: 415-346-6343
E-mail: programs@aaja.org

ASSOCIATION FOR WOMEN IN SPORTS MEDIA http://www.awsmonline.org

WOMEN IN SPORTS MEDIA SCHOLARSHIP/INTERNSHIP PROGRAM

The top entrant is selected in four categories: writing, copy editing, broadcast, and public relations. Winners receive a $1000 scholarship, a $500 stipend for housing during their internship, and $300 for travel expenses. Runners-up receive an internship, $500 for housing, and $300 for travel. Entrants must be female and must submit a one-page essay of 750 words or less describing their most memorable experience in sports or sports media.

Academic Fields/Career Goals: Communications; Journalism; TV/Radio Broadcasting.

Award: Scholarship for use in freshman, sophomore, junior, senior, or graduate years; not renewable. *Number:* 5–10. *Amount:* $1000.

Eligibility Requirements: Applicant must be enrolled or expecting to enroll full-time at a four-year institution or university; female and must have an interest in athletics/sports or writing. Available to U.S. and non-U.S. citizens.

Application Requirements: Application, applicant must enter a contest, essay, interview, portfolio, resume, references. *Fee:* $15. *Deadline:* November 1.

Contact: Scholarship Committee
Association for Women in Sports Media
3899 North Front Street
Harrisburg, PA 17110
Phone: 717-703-3086

ATLANTA ASSOCIATION OF BLACK JOURNALISTS http://www.aabj.org

XERNONA CLAYTON SCHOLARSHIP FUND

Award for deserving full-time African-American students to pursue a journalism/mass communications degree at a Georgia college or university. Minimum 3.0 GPA required.

Academic Fields/Career Goals: Communications; Journalism.

Award: Scholarship for use in freshman, sophomore, junior, or senior years; not renewable. *Number:* varies. *Amount:* $2000–$5000.

Eligibility Requirements: Applicant must be Black (non-Hispanic); enrolled or expecting to enroll full-time at a four-year institution or university; resident of Georgia and studying in Georgia. Applicant must have 3.0 GPA or higher. Available to U.S. and non-U.S. citizens.

Application Requirements: Application, essay, references, transcript, two samples of published work, disclaimer for scholarship funds disbursement. *Deadline:* June 4.

Contact: BryAnn Chen, Scholarship Program Officer
Atlanta Association of Black Journalists
PO Box 54128
Atlanta, GA 30308
Phone: 404-688-5525
Fax: 408-688-3060
E-mail: bchen@atlcf.org

CALIFORNIA CHICANO NEWS MEDIA ASSOCIATION (CCNMA) http://www.ccnma.org

CCNMA SCHOLARSHIPS

Scholarships for Latinos interested in pursuing a career in journalism. Awards based on scholastic achievement, financial need, and community awareness. Submit sample of work. Award for California residents or those attending school in California.

Academic Fields/Career Goals: Communications; Journalism; Photojournalism/Photography; TV/Radio Broadcasting.

Award: Scholarship for use in freshman, sophomore, junior, senior, or graduate years; renewable. *Number:* 10–20. *Amount:* $500–$2000.

Eligibility Requirements: Applicant must be of Latin American/Caribbean heritage; Hispanic and enrolled or expecting to enroll full-time at a two-year or four-year or technical institution or university. Available to U.S. citizens.

Application Requirements: Application, applicant must enter a contest, essay, financial need analysis, interview, portfolio, references, transcript. *Deadline:* April 4.

Contact: Julio Moran, Executive Director
California Chicano News Media Association (CCNMA)
300 South Grand Avenue, Suite 3950
Los Angeles, CA 90071-8110
Phone: 213-437-4408
Fax: 213-437-4423
E-mail: ccnmainfo@ccnma.org

CANADIAN ASSOCIATION OF BROADCASTERS http://www.cab-acr.ca

ASTRAL MEDIA SCHOLARSHIP

Annual award is given to a French Canadian student with broadcasting experience or who is enrolled or wishes to begin or complete a program of studies in communications, at the university level in Canada.

Academic Fields/Career Goals: Communications; Journalism; TV/Radio Broadcasting.

Award: Scholarship for use in freshman, sophomore, junior, senior, graduate, or postgraduate years; renewable. *Number:* 1. *Amount:* $5000.

Eligibility Requirements: Applicant must be Canadian citizen; enrolled or expecting to enroll full-time at a four-year institution or university; studying in Alberta, British Columbia, Manitoba, New Brunswick, Newfoundland, North West Territories, Nova Scotia, Ontario, Prince Edward Island, Quebec, Saskatchewan, or Yukon and must have an interest in amateur radio or French language. Applicant or parent of applicant must have employment or volunteer experience in journalism/broadcasting.

Application Requirements: Application, essay, financial need analysis, references, transcript. *Deadline:* June 30.

Contact: Beth Mitchell, Manager, Member Relations and Special Events
Canadian Association of Broadcasters
PO Box 627, Station B
Ottawa, ON K1P 5S2
Canada
Phone: 613-233-4035 Ext. 329
Fax: 613-233-6961
E-mail: bmitchell@cab-acr.ca

RUTH HANCOCK MEMORIAL SCHOLARSHIP

This $1500 scholarship is awarded annually to 3 students enrolled in a communications course at a Canadian school, who possess strong leadership qualities, natural talent, and a willingness to assist others. Must be a Canadian citizen.

Academic Fields/Career Goals: Communications; TV/Radio Broadcasting.

Award: Scholarship for use in freshman, sophomore, junior, senior, graduate, or postgraduate years; renewable. *Number:* 3. *Amount:* $1500.

Eligibility Requirements: Applicant must be Canadian citizen; enrolled or expecting to enroll full-time at a four-year institution or university; studying in Alberta, British Columbia, Manitoba, New Brunswick, Newfoundland, North West Territories, Nova Scotia, Ontario, Prince Edward Island, Quebec, Saskatchewan, or Yukon and must have an interest in leadership.

Application Requirements: Application, essay, references. *Deadline:* June 30.

Contact: Beth Mitchell, Manager, Member Relations and Special Events
Canadian Association of Broadcasters
PO Box 627, Station B
Ottawa, ON K1P 5S2
Canada
Phone: 613-233-4035 Ext. 329
Fax: 613-233-6961
E-mail: bmitchell@cab-acr.ca

CHARLES & LUCILLE KING FAMILY FOUNDATION INC. http://www.kingfoundation.org

CHARLES AND LUCILLE KING FAMILY FOUNDATION SCHOLARSHIPS

Renewable award for college undergraduates at junior or senior level pursuing television, film, or communication studies to further their education. Must attend a four-year undergraduate institution. Minimum 3.0 GPA required to renew scholarship. Must have completed at least two years of study and be currently enrolled in a U.S. college or university.

Academic Fields/Career Goals: Communications; Filmmaking/Video; TV/Radio Broadcasting.

Award: Scholarship for use in sophomore, junior, or senior years; renewable. *Number:* 10–20. *Amount:* $1250–$3500.

Eligibility Requirements: Applicant must be enrolled or expecting to enroll full-time at a four-year institution or university. Applicant must have 3.0 GPA or higher. Available to U.S. and non-U.S. citizens.

Application Requirements: Application, essay, financial need analysis, references, transcript. *Deadline:* March 15.

Contact: Michael Donovan, Educational Director
Charles & Lucille King Family Foundation Inc.
366 Madison Avenue, Tenth Floor
New York, NY 10017
Phone: 212-682-2913
Fax: 212-949-0728
E-mail: info@kingfoundation.org

CINCINNATI LITHO CLUB http://www.cincylithoclub.org

BILL STAUDT/AL HARTNETT SCHOLARSHIP

Scholarship awarded to high school graduates who plan to attend, or are currently enrolled in, college or vocational school. Applicant must be pursuing a career in the areas of printing or publishing.

Academic Fields/Career Goals: Communications; Graphics/Graphic Arts/Printing.

Cincinnati Litho Club (continued)

Award: Scholarship for use in freshman year; not renewable. *Number:* varies. *Amount:* varies.

Eligibility Requirements: Applicant must be high school student and planning to enroll or expecting to enroll full-time at a two-year or four-year or technical institution or university. Available to U.S. citizens.

Application Requirements: Application, resume, transcript. *Deadline:* varies.

Contact: Scholarship Administrator
Cincinnati Litho Club
6550 Donjoy Drive
Cincinnati, OH 45242
Phone: 910-575-0399

DAY INTERNATIONAL SCHOLARSHIP

Scholarship awarded to high school graduates who plan to attend, or are currently enrolled in, college or vocational school. Applicant must be pursuing a career in the areas of printing or publishing.

Academic Fields/Career Goals: Communications; Graphics/Graphic Arts/Printing.

Award: Scholarship for use in freshman year; not renewable. *Number:* varies. *Amount:* varies.

Eligibility Requirements: Applicant must be high school student and planning to enroll or expecting to enroll full-time at a two-year or four-year or technical institution or university. Available to U.S. citizens.

Application Requirements: Application, resume, transcript. *Deadline:* varies.

Contact: Scholarship Administrator
Cincinnati Litho Club
6550 Donjoy Drive
Cincinnati, OH 45242
Phone: 910-575-0399

COMMON KNOWLEDGE SCHOLARSHIP FOUNDATION http://www.cksf.org

PR/COMMUNICATION SCHOLARSHIP

Scholarship competition that tests students' knowledge of core courses associated with the PR/communications curriculum. For more information about this scholarship, please visit:
http://www.cksf.org/CKSF.cfm?Page=CKSF_AvailableScholarships.

Academic Fields/Career Goals: Communications.

Award: Scholarship for use in freshman, sophomore, junior, senior, graduate, or postgraduate years; not renewable. *Number:* 1. *Amount:* up to $250.

Eligibility Requirements: Applicant must be enrolled or expecting to enroll full- or part-time at a two-year or four-year or technical institution or university. Available to U.S. citizens.

Application Requirements: Applicant must enter a contest. *Deadline:* varies.

Contact: Mr. Daryl Hulce, President
Common Knowledge Scholarship Foundation
PO Box 290361
Davie, FL 33329-0361
Phone: 954-262-8553
Fax: 954-262-2847
E-mail: hulce@cksf.org

CUBAN AMERICAN NATIONAL FOUNDATION http://www.masscholarships.org

MAS FAMILY SCHOLARSHIPS

• *See page 139*

DAIRY MANAGEMENT http://www.dairyinfo.com

JAMES H. LOPER JR. MEMORIAL SCHOLARSHIP

• *See page 74*

NATIONAL DAIRY PROMOTION AND RESEARCH BOARD SCHOLARSHIP

• *See page 74*

ELECTRONIC DOCUMENT SYSTEMS FOUNDATION http://www.edsf.org

ELECTRONIC DOCUMENT SYSTEMS FOUNDATION SCHOLARSHIP AWARDS

Scholarships are awarded to full-time students with a "B" minimum average who are preparing for careers in document preparation; production or distribution; one-to-one marketing; graphic arts and communication; e-commerce; imaging science; printing; web authoring; electronic publishing; computer science; telecommunications or related fields.

Academic Fields/Career Goals: Communications; Computer Science/Data Processing; Engineering/Technology; Graphics/Graphic Arts/Printing.

Award: Scholarship for use in freshman, sophomore, junior, senior, or graduate years; not renewable. *Number:* 40. *Amount:* $250–$5000.

Eligibility Requirements: Applicant must be enrolled or expecting to enroll full-time at a two-year or four-year or technical institution or university. Applicant must have 3.0 GPA or higher. Available to U.S. and non-U.S. citizens.

Application Requirements: Application, essay, references, transcript, description of activities and work experience. *Deadline:* May 15.

Contact: Ms. Brenda Kai, Executive Director
Electronic Document Systems Foundation
1845 Precinct Line Road, Suite 212
Hurst, TX 76054
Phone: 817-849-1145
Fax: 817-849-1185
E-mail: brenda.kai@edsf.org

FLORIDA SOCIETY OF NEWSPAPER EDITORS-SCHOLARSHIP COMMITTEE http://www.fsne.org/minorityscholar.html

FLORIDA SOCIETY OF NEWSPAPER EDITORS MINORITY SCHOLARSHIP PROGRAM

Awards full-time students in their junior year, majoring in journalism or mass communications at an accredited program in Florida. Must maintain a GPA of 3.0. Must be a member of an ethnic minority. In order to maintain eligibility, the applicant must successfully complete a paid summer internship at a Florida newspaper between the junior and senior year.

Academic Fields/Career Goals: Communications; Journalism.

Award: Scholarship for use in senior year; not renewable. *Number:* 1. *Amount:* $1500–$3000.

Eligibility Requirements: Applicant must be American Indian/Alaska Native, Asian/Pacific Islander, Black (non-Hispanic), or Hispanic; enrolled or expecting to enroll full-time at a four-year institution or university and studying in Florida. Applicant must have 3.0 GPA or higher. Available to U.S. citizens.

Application Requirements: Application, autobiography, resume. *Deadline:* March 15.

Contact: Rosemary Armao, Scholarship Committee
Florida Society of Newspaper Editors-Scholarship Committee
c/o Sarasota Herald Tribune, 801 South Tamiami Trial
Sarasota, FL 34230

FLORIDA SOCIETY OF NEWSPAPER EDITORS MULTIMEDIA SCHOLARSHIP

Scholarships for multicultural, full-time students, majoring in journalism or mass communications at an accredited program at a four-year college or university in Florida, and pursuing careers in the field of multimedia or multi-platform journalism. Must successfully complete a paid multimedia internship at a Florida newspaper. Must maintain a minimum GPA of 2.5.

Academic Fields/Career Goals: Communications; Journalism.

Award: Scholarship for use in freshman, sophomore, junior, or senior years; not renewable. *Number:* varies. *Amount:* $1500–$3000.

Eligibility Requirements: Applicant must be enrolled or expecting to enroll full-time at a four-year institution or university and studying in Florida. Applicant must have 2.5 GPA or higher. Available to U.S. citizens.

Application Requirements: Application, autobiography, resume, references, clips or examples of relevant classroom work. *Deadline:* May 1.

Contact: Pat Yack, Editor
Florida Society of Newspaper Editors-Scholarship Committee
The Florida Times-Union, One Riverside Avenue
Jacksonville, FL 32202
Phone: 904-359-4111
E-mail: pat.yack@jacksonville.com

GREATER KANAWHA VALLEY FOUNDATION http://www.tgkvf.org

WEST VIRGINIA BROADCASTERS ASSOCIATION FUND

Renewable award of $1000 for students seeking education at a college or university in the field of communications and related areas. Must be a West Virginia resident and maintain at least a 2.5 GPA. Open to employees and family members of station employees that are members of the West Virginia Broadcasters Association. May apply for two Foundation scholarships but will only be chosen for one.

Academic Fields/Career Goals: Communications; Foreign Language; Trade/Technical Specialties; TV/Radio Broadcasting.

Award: Scholarship for use in freshman, sophomore, junior, or senior years; renewable. *Number:* 4. *Amount:* $1000.

Eligibility Requirements: Applicant must be enrolled or expecting to enroll full-time at a four-year institution or university and resident of West Virginia. Applicant or parent of applicant must be member of West Virginia Broadcasters Association. Applicant or parent of applicant must have employment or volunteer experience in journalism/broadcasting. Applicant must have 2.5 GPA or higher. Available to U.S. citizens.

Application Requirements: Application, essay, financial need analysis, references, self-addressed stamped envelope, test scores, transcript. *Deadline:* January 12.

Contact: Susan Hoover, Scholarship Coordinator
Greater Kanawha Valley Foundation
PO Box 3041
Charleston, WV 25331
Phone: 304-346-3620
Fax: 304-346-3640

GREAT FALLS ADVERTISING FEDERATION http://www.gfaf.com

COLLEGE SCHOLARSHIP

• *See page 102*

HIGH SCHOOL MARKETING/COMMUNICATIONS SCHOLARSHIP

• *See page 142*

GREAT LAKES COMMISSION http://www.glc.org

CAROL A. RATZA MEMORIAL SCHOLARSHIP

One-time award to full-time students at a college or university in the Great Lake states (IL, IN, MI, MN, NY, OH, PA, WI) or Canadian provinces of Ontario or Quebec. Must have a demonstrated interest in the environmental or economic applications of electronic communications technology, exhibit academic excellence, and have a sincere appreciation for the Great Lakes and their protection.

Academic Fields/Career Goals: Communications; Computer Science/Data Processing; Environmental Science; Graphics/Graphic Arts/Printing; Journalism; Natural Resources; Natural Sciences; Science, Technology, and Society; TV/Radio Broadcasting.

Award: Scholarship for use in freshman, sophomore, junior, or senior years; not renewable. *Number:* 1. *Amount:* $1000.

Eligibility Requirements: Applicant must be enrolled or expecting to enroll full-time at a two-year or four-year or technical institution or university; resident of Illinois, Indiana, Michigan, Minnesota, New York, Ohio, Ontario, Pennsylvania, Quebec, or Wisconsin and studying in Illinois, Indiana, Michigan, Minnesota, New York, Ohio, Ontario, Pennsylvania, Quebec, or Wisconsin. Available to U.S. and Canadian citizens.

Application Requirements: Application, essay, resume, references, transcript, letter of intent explaining career goals. *Deadline:* March 31.

Contact: Christine Manninen, Program Manager
Great Lakes Commission
Eisenhower Corporate Park, 2805 South Industrial Highway, Suite 100
Ann Arbor, MI 48104-6791
Phone: 734-971-9135
Fax: 734-971-9150
E-mail: manninen@glc.org

HISPANIC COLLEGE FUND INC. http://www.hispanicfund.org

DENNY'S/HISPANIC COLLEGE FUND SCHOLARSHIP

• *See page 54*

HISPANIC SCHOLARSHIP FUND http://www.hsf.net

HSF/MCNAMARA FAMILY CREATIVE ARTS PROJECT GRANT

• *See page 98*

HSF/NISSAN COMMUNITY COLLEGE TRANSFER SCHOLARSHIP PROGRAM

• *See page 143*

INSTITUTE FOR HUMANE STUDIES http://www.theihs.org

HUMANE STUDIES FELLOWSHIPS

Renewable award for undergraduate and graduate students in selected disciplines. Applicants should have demonstrated interest in classical liberal or libertarian ideas and must intend to pursue a scholarly career. Minimum 3.5 GPA required. Application fee: $25.

Academic Fields/Career Goals: Communications; Economics; History; Humanities; Law/Legal Services; Literature/English/Writing; Political Science; Social Sciences.

Award: Scholarship for use in freshman, sophomore, junior, senior, or graduate years; renewable. *Number:* 120. *Amount:* $2000–$12,000.

Eligibility Requirements: Applicant must be enrolled or expecting to enroll full-time at a two-year or four-year institution or university. Applicant must have 3.5 GPA or higher. Available to U.S. and non-U.S. citizens.

Application Requirements: Application, autobiography, essay, resume, references, test scores, transcript. *Fee:* $25. *Deadline:* December 31.

Contact: Keri Anderson, Program Coordinator
Institute for Humane Studies
3301 North Fairfax Drive, Suite 440
Arlington, VA 22201-4432
Phone: 703-993-4880
Fax: 703-993-4890
E-mail: ihs@gmu.edu

INTERNATIONAL COMMUNICATIONS INDUSTRIES FOUNDATION http://www.infocomm.org/scholarships

ICIF SCHOLARSHIP FOR DEPENDENTS OF MEMBER ORGANIZATIONS

Scholarship for a spouse, child, stepchild or grandchild of an employee of an INFOCOMM member organization or for an employee of an INFOCOMM member organization. Must be majoring in audiovisual related fields, such as audio, video, audiovisual, electronics, telecommunications, technical theatre, data networking, software development, and information technology. Minimum of 2.75 GPA required.

Academic Fields/Career Goals: Communications; Computer Science/Data Processing; Electrical Engineering/Electronics; Filmmaking/Video.

Award: Scholarship for use in freshman, sophomore, junior, senior, or graduate years; renewable. *Number:* 1. *Amount:* $1500.

Eligibility Requirements: Applicant must be enrolled or expecting to enroll full-time at a two-year or four-year or technical institution or university. Available to U.S. and Canadian citizens.

International Communications Industries Foundation (continued)

Application Requirements: Application, essay, references, transcript. *Deadline:* April 16.

Contact: Shana Rieger, Social Media Program Manager
International Communications Industries Foundation
11242 Waples Mill Road, Suite 200
Fairfax, VA 22030
Phone: 703-273-7200 Ext. 3690
Fax: 703-278-8082
E-mail: membership@infocomm.org

INTERNATIONAL COMMUNICATIONS INDUSTRIES FOUNDATION AV SCHOLARSHIP

Scholarship for students majoring in audiovisual related fields such as audio, video, audiovisual, electronics, telecommunications, technical theatre, data networking, software development, information technology. Minimum 2.75 GPA required.

Academic Fields/Career Goals: Communications; Computer Science/ Data Processing; Electrical Engineering/Electronics; Filmmaking/Video.

Award: Scholarship for use in freshman, sophomore, junior, senior, or graduate years; renewable. *Number:* 1. *Amount:* up to $1200.

Eligibility Requirements: Applicant must be enrolled or expecting to enroll full-time at a two-year or four-year or technical institution or university. Available to U.S. and Canadian citizens.

Application Requirements: Application, essay, references, transcript. *Deadline:* April 16.

Contact: Shana Rieger, Social Media Program Manager
International Communications Industries Foundation
11242 Waples Mill Road, Suite 200
Fairfax, VA 22030
Phone: 703-273-7200 Ext. 3690
Fax: 703-278-8082
E-mail: membership@infocomm.org

INTERNATIONAL FOODSERVICE EDITORIAL COUNCIL http://www.ifeconline.com

INTERNATIONAL FOODSERVICE EDITORIAL COUNCIL COMMUNICATIONS SCHOLARSHIP

Applicant must be a full-time student enrolled in an accredited postsecondary educational institution working toward an associate's, bachelor's, or master's degree. Must rank in upper half of class or have a minimum 2.5 GPA. Must have background, education, and interests indicating preparedness for entering careers in editorial or public relations in the food-service industry.

Academic Fields/Career Goals: Communications; Food Science/ Nutrition; Food Service/Hospitality; Graphics/Graphic Arts/Printing; Hospitality Management; Journalism; Literature/English/Writing; Photojournalism/Photography.

Award: Scholarship for use in freshman, sophomore, junior, senior, graduate, or postgraduate years; not renewable. *Number:* 1–6. *Amount:* $1000–$4000.

Eligibility Requirements: Applicant must be enrolled or expecting to enroll full-time at a two-year or four-year or technical institution or university and must have an interest in photography/photogrammetry/ filmmaking or writing. Applicant must have 2.5 GPA or higher. Available to U.S. and non-U.S. citizens.

Application Requirements: Application, essay, resume, references, transcript. *Deadline:* March 15.

Contact: Carol Lally, Executive Director
International Foodservice Editorial Council
PO Box 491
Hyde Park, NY 12538-0491
Phone: 845-229-6973
Fax: 845-229-6993
E-mail: ifec@aol.com

JOHN BAYLISS BROADCAST FOUNDATION http://www.baylissfoundation.org

JOHN BAYLISS BROADCAST RADIO SCHOLARSHIP

One-time award for college juniors, seniors, or graduate students majoring in broadcast communications with a concentration in radio broadcasting. Must have history of radio-related activities and a GPA of at least 3.0.

Academic Fields/Career Goals: Communications; Journalism; TV/Radio Broadcasting.

Award: Scholarship for use in junior, senior, or graduate years; not renewable. *Number:* 14. *Amount:* $5000.

Eligibility Requirements: Applicant must be enrolled or expecting to enroll full-time at a four-year institution or university. Applicant or parent of applicant must have employment or volunteer experience in journalism/broadcasting. Applicant must have 3.0 GPA or higher. Available to U.S. and non-U.S. citizens.

Application Requirements: Application, essay, resume, references, self-addressed stamped envelope, transcript. *Deadline:* April 30.

Contact: Chairperson
John Bayliss Broadcast Foundation
171 17th Street
Pacific Grove, CA 93950
E-mail: info@baylissfoundation.org

JORGE MAS CANOSA FREEDOM FOUNDATION http://www.jorgemascanosa.org

MAS FAMILY SCHOLARSHIP AWARD

• *See page 144*

JOURNALISM EDUCATION ASSOCIATION http://www.jea.org

NATIONAL HIGH SCHOOL JOURNALIST OF THE YEAR/SISTER RITA JEANNE SCHOLARSHIPS

One-time award recognizes the nation's top high school journalists. Open to graduating high school seniors planning to study journalism and/or mass communications in college and pursue a career in the field. Applicants must have JEA member as adviser. Minimum 3.0 GPA required. Submit portfolio to state contest coordinator by February 15.

Academic Fields/Career Goals: Communications; Journalism.

Award: Scholarship for use in freshman year; not renewable. *Number:* 1–6. *Amount:* $2000–$5000.

Eligibility Requirements: Applicant must be high school student; age 17-19 and planning to enroll or expecting to enroll full-time at a four-year institution or university. Applicant must have 3.0 GPA or higher. Available to U.S. citizens.

Application Requirements: Application, applicant must enter a contest, essay, photo, portfolio, references, self-addressed stamped envelope, transcript, samples of work. *Deadline:* February 15.

Contact: Connie Fulkerson, Administrative Assistant
Journalism Education Association
103 Kedzie Hall
Manhattan, KS 66506-1505
Phone: 785-532-5532
Fax: 785-532-5563
E-mail: jea@spub.ksu.edu

KATU THOMAS R. DARGAN MINORITY SCHOLARSHIP http://www.katu.com

THOMAS R. DARGAN MINORITY SCHOLARSHIP

Up to four awards for minority students who are citizens of the United States pursuing broadcast or communications studies. Must be a resident of Oregon or Washington attending an out-of-state institution or be enrolled at a four-year college or university in Oregon or Washington. Minimum 3.0 GPA required.

Academic Fields/Career Goals: Communications; TV/Radio Broadcasting.

Award: Scholarship for use in freshman, sophomore, junior, or senior years; renewable. *Number:* 1–4. *Amount:* $4000.

Eligibility Requirements: Applicant must be American Indian/Alaska Native, Asian/Pacific Islander, Black (non-Hispanic), or Hispanic; enrolled or expecting to enroll full-time at a four-year institution or university and resident of Oregon or Washington. Applicant must have 3.0 GPA or higher. Available to U.S. citizens.

Application Requirements: Application, essay, financial need analysis, interview, references, transcript. *Deadline:* April 30.

Contact: Human Resources
KATU Thomas R. Dargan Minority Scholarship
PO Box 2
Portland, OR 97207-0002

KE ALI'I PAUAHI FOUNDATION http://www.pauahi.org

JOSEPH A. SOWA SCHOLARSHIP

Award for study in the field of communications. Requires a minimum GPA of 3.0 and intent to use knowledge to empower young people to maximize their potential. Must demonstrate financial need.

Academic Fields/Career Goals: Communications.

Award: Scholarship for use in freshman, sophomore, junior, senior, or graduate years; not renewable. *Number:* 1. *Amount:* $1400.

Eligibility Requirements: Applicant must be enrolled or expecting to enroll full-time at a four-year institution or university. Applicant must have 3.0 GPA or higher. Available to U.S. citizens.

Application Requirements: Application, essay, references, transcript, Student Aid Report (SAR), college acceptance letter. *Deadline:* May 2.

Contact: Elizabeth Stevenson, Development Manager
Ke Ali'i Pauahi Foundation
567 South King Street, Suite 160
Honolulu, HI 96813
Phone: 808-534-3966
Fax: 808-534-3890
E-mail: scholarships@pauahi.org

LAGRANT FOUNDATION http://www.lagrantfoundation.org

LAGRANT FOUNDATION SCHOLARSHIP FOR GRADUATES

• *See page 145*

LAGRANT FOUNDATION SCHOLARSHIP FOR UNDERGRADUATES

• *See page 145*

NATIONAL ACADEMY OF TELEVISION ARTS AND SCIENCES http://www.emmyonline.tv

NATIONAL ACADEMY OF TELEVISION ARTS AND SCIENCES JOHN CANNON MEMORIAL SCHOLARSHIP

Scholarships are distributed over a four-year period up to $40,000 awarded prior to the first year of study and three additional awards of $1000 granted in subsequent years if the recipient demonstrates satisfactory progress towards a degree in a communications-oriented program. Must submit SAT or ACT scores. Must be child or grandchild of NATAS member. Application available on the Web at: http://www.emmyonline.org/emmy/scholr.html.

Academic Fields/Career Goals: Communications; TV/Radio Broadcasting.

Award: Scholarship for use in freshman, sophomore, junior, or senior years; renewable. *Number:* 1–10. *Amount:* $1000–$40,000.

Eligibility Requirements: Applicant must be high school student and planning to enroll or expecting to enroll full-time at a four-year institution or university. Applicant must have 3.0 GPA or higher. Available to U.S. and non-U.S. citizens.

Application Requirements: Application, essay, references, test scores, transcript. *Deadline:* varies.

Contact: Ms. Pamela Kotch, Scholarship Manager
National Academy of Television Arts and Sciences
111 West 57th Street, Suite 600
New York, NY 10019
Phone: 212-586-8424
Fax: 212-246-8129
E-mail: pkotch@emmyonline.tv

NATIONAL ASSOCIATION OF BLACK JOURNALISTS http://www.nabj.org

NABJ SCHOLARSHIP

Scholarship for a student who is currently attending an accredited four-year college or university. Must be enrolled as an undergraduate or graduate student majoring in journalism (print, radio, online, or television). Minimum 2.5 GPA. Must be a member of NABJ. Scholarship value and the number of awards granted varies annually.

Academic Fields/Career Goals: Communications; Journalism; TV/Radio Broadcasting.

Award: Scholarship for use in freshman, sophomore, junior, senior, or graduate years; not renewable. *Number:* varies. *Amount:* varies.

Eligibility Requirements: Applicant must be enrolled or expecting to enroll full-time at a four-year institution or university. Applicant must have 2.5 GPA or higher. Available to U.S. and non-U.S. citizens.

Application Requirements: Application, autobiography, essay, interview, references, transcript. *Deadline:* March 17.

Contact: Irving Washington, Manager
National Association of Black Journalists
8701-A Adelphi Road
Adelphi, MD 20783-1716
Phone: 301-445-7100
Fax: 301-445-7101
E-mail: iwashington@nabj.org

NATIONAL ASSOCIATION OF BROADCASTERS http://www.nab.org

NATIONAL ASSOCIATION OF BROADCASTERS GRANTS FOR RESEARCH IN BROADCASTING

Award program is intended to fund research on economic, business, social, and policy issues important to station managers and other decision-makers in the United States commercial broadcast industry. Competition is open to all academic personnel. Graduate students and senior undergraduates are invited to submit proposals. For details refer to Web Site: http://www.nab.org.

Academic Fields/Career Goals: Communications; Journalism; TV/Radio Broadcasting.

Award: Grant for use in senior, graduate, or postgraduate years; not renewable. *Number:* 4–6. *Amount:* $5000.

Eligibility Requirements: Applicant must be enrolled or expecting to enroll full-time at a four-year institution or university. Available to U.S. and non-U.S. citizens.

Application Requirements: Application, references, research proposal, budget. *Deadline:* February 1.

Contact: Vice President
National Association of Broadcasters
1771 North Street, NW
Washington, DC 20036-2800
Phone: 202-429-5489
Fax: 202-429-4199

NATIONAL ASSOCIATION OF HISPANIC JOURNALISTS (NAHJ) http://www.nahj.org

NATIONAL ASSOCIATION OF HISPANIC JOURNALISTS SCHOLARSHIP

One-time award for high school seniors, college undergraduates, and first-year graduate students who are pursuing careers in English- or Spanish-language print, photo, broadcast, or online journalism. Students may major or plan to major in any subject, but must demonstrate a sincere desire to pursue a career in journalism. Must submit resume and work samples. Applications available only on Web site: http://www.nahj.org.

Academic Fields/Career Goals: Communications; Journalism; Photojournalism/Photography; TV/Radio Broadcasting.

Award: Scholarship for use in freshman, sophomore, junior, senior, or graduate years; not renewable. *Number:* varies. *Amount:* $1000–$2000.

Eligibility Requirements: Applicant must be enrolled or expecting to enroll full-time at a four-year institution or university and must have an interest in photography/photogrammetry/filmmaking or writing. Available to U.S. citizens.

National Association of Hispanic Journalists (NAHJ) (continued)

Application Requirements: Application, essay, financial need analysis, resume, references, transcript, work samples. *Deadline:* March 31.

Contact: Virginia Galindo, Program Assistant
National Association of Hispanic Journalists (NAHJ)
1000 National Press Building, 529 14th Street, NW, Suite 1000
Washington, DC 20045-2001
Phone: 202-662-7145
Fax: 202-662-7144
E-mail: vgalindo@nahj.org

NATIONAL ASSOCIATION OF WATER COMPANIES-NEW JERSEY CHAPTER

NATIONAL ASSOCIATION OF WATER COMPANIES-NEW JERSEY CHAPTER SCHOLARSHIP

• *See page 133*

NATIONAL CATTLEMEN'S FOUNDATION http://www.nationalcattlemensfoundation.org

CME BEEF INDUSTRY SCHOLARSHIP

• *See page 70*

NATIONAL INSTITUTE FOR LABOR RELATIONS RESEARCH http://www.nilrr.org

NATIONAL INSTITUTE FOR LABOR RELATIONS RESEARCH WILLIAM B. RUGGLES JOURNALISM SCHOLARSHIP

One-time award for undergraduate or graduate study in journalism or mass communications. Submit 500-word essay on the right-to-work principle. High school seniors accepted into certified journalism school may apply. Specify "Journalism" or "Ruggles" scholarship on any correspondence.

Academic Fields/Career Goals: Communications; Journalism.

Award: Scholarship for use in freshman, sophomore, junior, senior, or graduate years; not renewable. *Number:* 1. *Amount:* $2000.

Eligibility Requirements: Applicant must be enrolled or expecting to enroll full-time at a four-year institution or university and must have an interest in writing. Available to U.S. citizens.

Application Requirements: Application, essay, transcript. *Deadline:* December 31.

Contact: Cathy Jones, Scholarship Coordinator
National Institute for Labor Relations Research
5211 Port Royal Road, Suite 510
Springfield, VA 22151
Phone: 703-321-9606
Fax: 703-321-7143
E-mail: research@nilrr.org

NATIONAL SPEAKERS ASSOCIATION http://www.nsaspeaker.org

NATIONAL SPEAKERS ASSOCIATION SCHOLARSHIP

One-time award for junior, senior, or graduate student majoring or minoring in speech or a directly related field. Must be full-time student at accredited four-year institution with above average academic record. Submit 500 word essay on goals. Application available only on Web site: http://www.nsaspeaker.org.

Academic Fields/Career Goals: Communications.

Award: Scholarship for use in junior, senior, or graduate years; not renewable. *Number:* 4. *Amount:* $5000.

Eligibility Requirements: Applicant must be enrolled or expecting to enroll full-time at a four-year institution or university. Available to U.S. and non-U.S. citizens.

Application Requirements: Application, essay, references, transcript. *Deadline:* June 1.

Contact: Audrey O'Neal, Scholarship Coordinator
National Speakers Association
1500 South Priest Drive
Tempe, AZ 85281
Phone: 480-968-2552
Fax: 480-968-0911
E-mail: audrey@nsaspeaker.org

NATIONAL STONE, SAND AND GRAVEL ASSOCIATION (NSSGA) http://www.nssga.org

JENNIFER CURTIS BYLER SCHOLARSHIP FOR THE STUDY OF PUBLIC AFFAIRS

One-time award open to graduating high school seniors or students already enrolled in a public affairs major in college, who are sons or daughters of an aggregates company employee.

Academic Fields/Career Goals: Communications; Public Policy and Administration.

Award: Scholarship for use in freshman, sophomore, junior, or senior years; not renewable. *Number:* 1. *Amount:* $1000–$2500.

Eligibility Requirements: Applicant must be enrolled or expecting to enroll full-time at a four-year institution or university. Available to U.S. and non-U.S. citizens.

Application Requirements: Application, applicant must enter a contest, essay, references, transcript, 300- to 500-word statement of plans for career in public affairs. *Deadline:* May 31.

Contact: Scholarship Coordinator
National Stone, Sand and Gravel Association (NSSGA)
1605 King Street
Arlington, VA 22314
Phone: 703-525-8788
Fax: 703-525-7782
E-mail: info@nssga.org

NEW JERSEY BROADCASTERS ASSOCIATION http://www.njba.com

MICHAEL S. LIBRETTI SCHOLARSHIP

Scholarships for undergraduate students in broadcasting, communication and journalism. Must be a New Jersey resident.

Academic Fields/Career Goals: Communications; Journalism; TV/Radio Broadcasting.

Award: Scholarship for use in freshman, sophomore, junior, or senior years; not renewable. *Number:* 1. *Amount:* up to $5000.

Eligibility Requirements: Applicant must be enrolled or expecting to enroll full-time at a four-year institution or university and resident of New Jersey. Available to U.S. citizens.

Application Requirements: Application. *Deadline:* varies.

Contact: Phil Roberts, Scholarships Coordinator
New Jersey Broadcasters Association
Broadcast House, 348 Applegarth Road
Monroe Township, NJ 08831
Phone: 888-652-2366
Fax: 609-860-0110
E-mail: njba@njba.com

NEW JERSEY DIVISION OF FISH AND WILDLIFE/NJ CHAPTER OF THE WILDLIFE SOCIETY http://www.njfishandwildlife.com/cookhmschol.htm

RUSSELL A. COOKINGHAM SCHOLARSHIP

• *See page 134*

OREGON ASSOCIATION OF BROADCASTERS http://www.theoab.org

OAB FOUNDATION SCHOLARSHIP

Award for students to begin or continue their education in broadcast and related studies. Must have a minimum GPA of 3.25. Must be a resident of Oregon studying in Oregon. For more details, refer to Web site: http://www.theoab.org/eduopps_foundation.htm.

Academic Fields/Career Goals: Communications; Journalism; TV/Radio Broadcasting.

Award: Scholarship for use in freshman, sophomore, junior, or senior years; not renewable. *Number:* 6. *Amount:* $1000.

Eligibility Requirements: Applicant must be enrolled or expecting to enroll full-time at a two-year or four-year institution or university; resident of Oregon and studying in Oregon. Available to U.S. citizens.

Application Requirements: Application, autobiography, essay, financial need analysis, resume, references, transcript. *Deadline:* May 9.

Contact: Bill Johnstone, President and Chief Executive Officer
Oregon Association of Broadcasters
7150 Hampton Street, SW, Suite 240
Portland, OR 97223-8366
Phone: 503-443-2299
Fax: 503-443-2488
E-mail: theoab@theoab.org

OUTDOOR WRITERS ASSOCIATION OF AMERICA http://www.owaa.org

OUTDOOR WRITERS ASSOCIATION OF AMERICA BODIE MCDOWELL SCHOLARSHIP AWARD

One-time award for college juniors, seniors, and graduate level candidates who demonstrate outdoor communication talent and intend to make a career in this field. Applicants are nominated by their institution. One applicant per school in both graduate and undergraduate designations. Must submit examples of outdoor communications work.

Academic Fields/Career Goals: Communications; Filmmaking/Video; Journalism; Literature/English/Writing; Photojournalism/Photography; TV/Radio Broadcasting.

Award: Scholarship for use in junior, senior, or graduate years; not renewable. *Number:* 3–6. *Amount:* varies.

Eligibility Requirements: Applicant must be enrolled or expecting to enroll full- or part-time at a four-year institution or university and must have an interest in amateur radio, photography/photogrammetry/filmmaking, or writing. Available to U.S. and non-U.S. citizens.

Application Requirements: Application, essay, references, transcript. *Deadline:* March 1.

Contact: Kevin Rhoades, Executive Director
Outdoor Writers Association of America
121 Hickory Street, Suite 1
Missoula, MT 59801
Phone: 406-728-7434
Fax: 406-728-7445
E-mail: owaa@montana.com

PRINT AND GRAPHIC SCHOLARSHIP FOUNDATION http://www.pgsf.org

PRINT AND GRAPHICS SCHOLARSHIPS

Applicant must be interested in a career in graphic communications, printing technology or management, or publishing. Selection is based on academic record, class rank, recommendations, biographical information, and extracurricular activities. Deadlines are March 1 for high school students, April 1 for enrolled college students. Award available to applicants outside United States, as long as they are attending a U.S. institution.

Academic Fields/Career Goals: Communications; Graphics/Graphic Arts/Printing.

Award: Scholarship for use in freshman, sophomore, junior, senior, or graduate years; renewable. *Number:* 200–300. *Amount:* $500–$3000.

Eligibility Requirements: Applicant must be enrolled or expecting to enroll full-time at a two-year or four-year or technical institution or university. Applicant must have 3.0 GPA or higher. Available to U.S. and non-U.S. citizens.

Application Requirements: Application, essay, references, self-addressed stamped envelope, test scores, transcript. *Deadline:* varies.

Contact: Bernadine Eckert, Scholarship Administrator
Print and Graphic Scholarship Foundation
200 Deer Run Road
Sewickley, PA 15143-2600
Phone: 412-741-6860
Fax: 412-741-2311
E-mail: pgsf@gatf.org

PUBLIC RELATIONS STUDENT SOCIETY OF AMERICA http://www.prssa.org

PUBLIC RELATIONS SOCIETY OF AMERICA MULTICULTURAL AFFAIRS SCHOLARSHIP

Two, one-time $1500 awards for members of a principal minority group who are in their junior or senior year at an accredited four-year college or university. Must have at least a 3.0 GPA and be preparing for career in public relations or communications. Must be a full-time student and U.S. citizen.

Academic Fields/Career Goals: Communications.

Award: Scholarship for use in freshman, sophomore, junior, or senior years; not renewable. *Number:* 2. *Amount:* $1500.

Eligibility Requirements: Applicant must be American Indian/Alaska Native, Asian/Pacific Islander, Black (non-Hispanic), or Hispanic and enrolled or expecting to enroll full-time at a four-year institution or university. Applicant must have 3.0 GPA or higher. Available to U.S. citizens.

Application Requirements: Application, essay, financial need analysis, references, transcript. *Deadline:* April 18.

Contact: Dora Tovar, Chair, Multicultural Communications Section
Public Relations Student Society of America
33 Maiden Lane, 11th Floor
New York, NY 10038-5150
Phone: 212-460-1476
Fax: 212-995-0757
E-mail: jeneen.garcia@prsa.org

RADIO-TELEVISION NEWS DIRECTORS ASSOCIATION AND FOUNDATION http://www.rtndf.org

CAROLE SIMPSON SCHOLARSHIP

Award of $2000 for minority sophomore, junior, or senior undergraduate student enrolled in an electronic journalism program. Submit one to three examples of reporting or producing skills on audio cassette tape or videotape, totaling 15 minutes or less, with scripts.

Academic Fields/Career Goals: Communications; Journalism; TV/Radio Broadcasting.

Award: Scholarship for use in sophomore, junior, or senior years; not renewable. *Number:* 1. *Amount:* $2000.

Eligibility Requirements: Applicant must be American Indian/Alaska Native, Asian/Pacific Islander, Black (non-Hispanic), or Hispanic; enrolled or expecting to enroll full-time at a four-year institution or university and must have an interest in photography/photogrammetry/filmmaking or writing. Available to U.S. and non-U.S. citizens.

Application Requirements: Application, essay, resume, references, video or audio tape of work. *Deadline:* May 12.

Contact: Melanie Lo, Project Coordinator
Radio-Television News Directors Association and Foundation
1600 K Street, NW, Suite 700
Washington, DC 20006
Phone: 202-467-5218
Fax: 202-223-4007
E-mail: irvingw@rtndf.org

ED BRADLEY SCHOLARSHIP

One-time, $10,000 award for minority sophomore, junior, or senior undergraduate student enrolled in an electronic journalism program. Submit examples of reporting or producing skills on audio cassette tape or videotape, totaling 15 minutes or less, with scripts.

Academic Fields/Career Goals: Communications; Journalism; TV/Radio Broadcasting.

Radio-Television News Directors Association and Foundation (continued)

Award: Scholarship for use in sophomore, junior, or senior years; not renewable. *Number:* 1. *Amount:* $10,000.

Eligibility Requirements: Applicant must be American Indian/Alaska Native, Asian/Pacific Islander, Black (non-Hispanic), or Hispanic and enrolled or expecting to enroll full-time at a four-year institution or university. Available to U.S. and non-U.S. citizens.

Application Requirements: Application, essay, resume, references, video or audio tape of work. *Deadline:* May 12.

Contact: Stacey Staniak, Program Coordinator
Radio-Television News Directors Association and Foundation
4121 Plank Road 512
Fredericksburg, VA 22407-2838
Phone: 202-467-5218
Fax: 202-223-4007
E-mail: staceys@rtnda.org

KEN KASHIWAHARA SCHOLARSHIP

One-time award of $2500 for minority sophomore, junior, or senior whose career objective is electronic journalism. Submit examples showing reporting or producing skills on audio or video, with scripts.

Academic Fields/Career Goals: Communications; Journalism; TV/Radio Broadcasting.

Award: Scholarship for use in sophomore, junior, senior, or graduate years; not renewable. *Number:* 1. *Amount:* $2500.

Eligibility Requirements: Applicant must be American Indian/Alaska Native, Asian/Pacific Islander, Black (non-Hispanic), or Hispanic and enrolled or expecting to enroll full-time at a four-year institution or university. Available to U.S. and non-U.S. citizens.

Application Requirements: Application, essay, resume, references, video or audio tape of work, statement explaining career in electronic journalism. *Deadline:* May 12.

Contact: Melanie Lo, Program Coordinator
Radio-Television News Directors Association and Foundation
1600 K Street, NW, Suite 700
Washington, DC 20006
Phone: 202-467-5218
E-mail: melaniel@rtnda.org

LOU AND CAROLE PRATO SPORTS REPORTING SCHOLARSHIP

One-time tuition grant of $1000 is given to a deserving student with strong writing skills and planning a career as a sports reporter in television or radio.

Academic Fields/Career Goals: Communications; Journalism; TV/Radio Broadcasting.

Award: Grant for use in sophomore, junior, senior, or graduate years; not renewable. *Number:* 1. *Amount:* $1000.

Eligibility Requirements: Applicant must be enrolled or expecting to enroll full-time at a four-year institution or university and must have an interest in writing. Available to U.S. and non-U.S. citizens.

Application Requirements: Application, essay, resume, references, video or audio tape of work, cover letter with reasons for seeking scholarship. *Deadline:* May 12.

Contact: Stacey Staniak, Program Coordinator
Radio-Television News Directors Association and Foundation
4121 Plank Road 512
Fredericksburg, VA 22407-2838
Phone: 202-467-5218
Fax: 202-223-4007
E-mail: staceys@rtnda.org

MIKE REYNOLDS $1,000 SCHOLARSHIP

Scholarship for undergraduate students excluding freshman, pursuing careers in electronic journalism. Must be full-time college student.

Academic Fields/Career Goals: Communications; Journalism; TV/Radio Broadcasting.

Award: Scholarship for use in sophomore, junior, senior, or graduate years; not renewable. *Number:* 1. *Amount:* $1000.

Eligibility Requirements: Applicant must be enrolled or expecting to enroll full-time at a four-year institution or university. Available to U.S. and non-U.S. citizens.

Application Requirements: Application, essay, financial need analysis, resume, references, video or audio tape of work, cover letter with reasons for seeking scholarship, Student Aid Report (SAR). *Deadline:* May 12.

Contact: Stacey Staniak, Program Coordinator
Radio-Television News Directors Association and Foundation
4121 Plank Road 512
Fredericksburg, VA 22407-2838
Phone: 202-467-5218
Fax: 202-223-4007
E-mail: staceys@rtnda.org

PRESIDENT'S SCHOLARSHIP

Award available to full-time college student in sophomore, junior, or senior year whose career objective is electronic journalism. Must have at least one full year of college remaining.

Academic Fields/Career Goals: Communications; Journalism; TV/Radio Broadcasting.

Award: Scholarship for use in sophomore, junior, or senior years; not renewable. *Number:* 2. *Amount:* $2500.

Eligibility Requirements: Applicant must be enrolled or expecting to enroll full-time at a four-year institution or university. Available to U.S. and non-U.S. citizens.

Application Requirements: Application, essay, resume, references, video or audio tape of work. *Deadline:* May 12.

Contact: Stacey Staniak, Program Coordinator
Radio-Television News Directors Association and Foundation
4121 Plank Road 512
Fredericksburg, VA 22407-2838
Phone: 202-467-5218
Fax: 202-223-4007
E-mail: staceys@rtnda.org

RHODE ISLAND FOUNDATION

http://www.rifoundation.org

J. D. EDSAL ADVERTISING SCHOLARSHIP

Award to benefit Rhode Island residents studying advertising (ex: public relations, marketing, graphic design, film, video, television, or broadcast production) with the expectation of pursuing a career in one of more of these fields. Applicants must be college undergraduates, sophomore or above.

Academic Fields/Career Goals: Communications; Filmmaking/Video; Graphics/Graphic Arts/Printing; TV/Radio Broadcasting.

Award: Scholarship for use in sophomore, junior, or senior years; not renewable. *Number:* 1. *Amount:* $1500.

Eligibility Requirements: Applicant must be enrolled or expecting to enroll full-time at a four-year institution or university and resident of Rhode Island. Available to U.S. citizens.

Application Requirements: Application, essay, financial need analysis, references, self-addressed stamped envelope, transcript. *Deadline:* April 30.

Contact: Libby Monahan, Funds Administrator
Rhode Island Foundation
One Union Station
Providence, RI 02903
Phone: 401-274-4564 Ext. 3117
Fax: 401-751-7983
E-mail: libbym@rifoundation.org

RDW GROUP INC. MINORITY SCHOLARSHIP FOR COMMUNICATIONS

One-time award to provide support for minority students who wish to pursue a course of study in communications at the undergraduate or graduate level. Must be a Rhode Island resident and must demonstrate financial need.

Academic Fields/Career Goals: Communications.

Award: Scholarship for use in freshman, sophomore, junior, senior, or graduate years; not renewable. *Number:* 1. *Amount:* $2000.

Eligibility Requirements: Applicant must be American Indian/Alaska Native, Asian/Pacific Islander, Black (non-Hispanic), or Hispanic; enrolled or expecting to enroll full-time at a four-year institution or university and resident of Rhode Island. Available to U.S. citizens.

Application Requirements: Application, essay, self-addressed stamped envelope, transcript. *Deadline:* April 30.

Contact: Libby Monahan, Funds Administrator
Rhode Island Foundation
One Union Station
Providence, RI 02903
Phone: 401-274-4564 Ext. 3117
Fax: 401-751-7983
E-mail: libbym@rifoundation.org

SOCIETY FOR TECHNICAL COMMUNICATION http://www.stc.org

SOCIETY FOR TECHNICAL COMMUNICATION SCHOLARSHIP PROGRAM

Award for study relating to communication of information about technical subjects. Applicants must be full-time graduate students working toward a master's or doctoral degree, or undergraduate students working toward a bachelor's degree. Must have completed at least one year of postsecondary education and have at least one full year of academic work remaining. Two awards available for undergraduate students, two available for graduate students.

Academic Fields/Career Goals: Communications; Science, Technology, and Society.

Award: Scholarship for use in sophomore, junior, senior, or graduate years; not renewable. *Number:* up to 4. *Amount:* up to $1500.

Eligibility Requirements: Applicant must be enrolled or expecting to enroll full-time at a four-year institution or university. Available to U.S. and non-U.S. citizens.

Application Requirements: Application, essay, references, transcript. *Deadline:* February 15.

Contact: Scott DeLoach, Manager, ,Scholarship Selection Committee
Society for Technical Communication
834 C Dekalb Avenue, NE
Atlanta, GA 30307

SOCIETY FOR TECHNICAL COMMUNICATION–LONE STAR CHAPTER http://www.stc-dfw.org

LONE STAR COMMUNITY SCHOLARSHIPS

Scholarship for graduate or undergraduate student working toward a degree or certificate in the technical communication field. Must be a member of Society for Technical Communication or living or attending school in STC region five. For further information see Web site http://www.stc-dfw.org.

Academic Fields/Career Goals: Communications.

Award: Scholarship for use in freshman, sophomore, junior, senior, or graduate years; not renewable. *Number:* varies. *Amount:* varies.

Eligibility Requirements: Applicant must be enrolled or expecting to enroll full- or part-time at a four-year institution or university and resident of Texas. Available to U.S. and non-U.S. citizens.

Application Requirements: Application, references, transcript. *Deadline:* March 28.

Contact: Rob Harris, Scholarship Committee Manager
Society for Technical Communication–Lone Star Chapter
PO Box 515065
Dallas, TX 75251-5065
Phone: 940-391-0167
E-mail: scholarship@stc-dfw.org

SOCIETY OF PROFESSIONAL JOURNALISTS-SOUTH FLORIDA CHAPTER http://www.spjsofla.net/

GARTH REEVES, JR. MEMORIAL SCHOLARSHIPS

Scholarships for senior high school students, undergraduate, and graduate minority students preparing for a news career. Must be a South Florida resident. Amount is determined by need; minimum award is $500. One-time award, renewable upon application. Academic performance and quality of work for student or professional news media is considered.

Academic Fields/Career Goals: Communications; Journalism.

Award: Scholarship for use in freshman, sophomore, junior, senior, or graduate years; not renewable. *Number:* 1–12. *Amount:* $500–$1500.

Eligibility Requirements: Applicant must be American Indian/Alaska Native, Asian/Pacific Islander, Black (non-Hispanic), or Hispanic; enrolled or expecting to enroll full- or part-time at a two-year or four-year institution or university and resident of Florida. Applicant must have 3.0 GPA or higher. Available to U.S. citizens.

Application Requirements: Application, financial need analysis, resume, references, self-addressed stamped envelope, transcript, examples of applicant's journalism, three clips and photographs for print journalists, one tape for broadcast journalists. *Deadline:* April 15.

Contact: Oline Cogdill, Chair, Scholarship Committee
Society of Professional Journalists-South Florida Chapter
200 East Las Olas Boulevard
Fort Lauderdale, FL 33301
Phone: 954-356-4886
E-mail: ocogdill@sun-sentinel.com

SOCIETY OF SATELLITE PROFESSIONALS INTERNATIONAL http://www.sspi.org

A.W. PERIGARD FUND SCHOLARSHIP

• *See page 124*

PSSC LEGACY FUND

• *See page 124*

SSPI NORTHEAST CHAPTER SCHOLARSHIP

• *See page 124*

STRAIGHTFORWARD MEDIA http://www.straightforwardmedia.com

STRAIGHTFORWARD MEDIA MEDIA & COMMUNICATIONS SCHOLARSHIP

Scholarship of $500 available to students of media and communications. Must be majoring in programs such as journalism, broadcasting, advertising, speech, mass communications, or marketing. Awarded four times per year. Deadlines: March 31, June 30, September 30, December 31.

Academic Fields/Career Goals: Communications; Journalism; Photojournalism/Photography; TV/Radio Broadcasting.

Award: Scholarship for use in freshman, sophomore, junior, or senior years; not renewable. *Number:* 4. *Amount:* $500.

Eligibility Requirements: Applicant must be enrolled or expecting to enroll full-time at a four-year institution or university. Available to U.S. and non-U.S. citizens.

Application Requirements: Online application. *Deadline:* varies.

Contact: Scholarship Committee
StraightForward Media
2040 West Main Street, Suite 104
Rapid City, SD 57701
Phone: 605-348-3042
Fax: 605-348-3043

TEXAS ASSOCIATION OF BROADCASTERS http://www.tab.org

BELO TEXAS BROADCAST EDUCATION FOUNDATION SCHOLARSHIP

Scholarship of $2000 to undergraduate and graduate students enrolled in a fully accredited program of instruction that emphasizes radio or television broadcasting or communications at a four-year college or university in Texas. Student must be a member of the Texas Association of Broadcasters. Must have a GPA of 3.0 minimum.

Academic Fields/Career Goals: Communications; TV/Radio Broadcasting.

Award: Scholarship for use in freshman, sophomore, junior, senior, or graduate years; not renewable. *Number:* 1. *Amount:* $2000.

Eligibility Requirements: Applicant must be enrolled or expecting to enroll full-time at a four-year institution or university and studying in Texas. Applicant or parent of applicant must be member of Texas Association of Broadcasters. Applicant must have 3.0 GPA or higher. Available to U.S. and non-U.S. citizens.

Texas Association of Broadcasters (continued)

Application Requirements: Application, essay, financial need analysis, references. *Deadline:* May 4.

Contact: Craig Bean, Public Service Manager
Texas Association of Broadcasters
502 East 11th Street, Suite 200
Austin, TX 78701
Phone: 512-322-9944
Fax: 512-322-0522
E-mail: craig@tab.org

BONNER MCLANE TEXAS BROADCAST EDUCATION FOUNDATION SCHOLARSHIP

Scholarship of $2000 to a undergraduate and students enrolled in a fully accredited program of instruction that emphasizes radio or television broadcasting or communications at a four-year college or university in Texas. Student must be a member of the Texas Association of Broadcasters. Must have a GPA of 3.0 minimum.

Academic Fields/Career Goals: Communications; TV/Radio Broadcasting.

Award: Scholarship for use in freshman, sophomore, junior, senior, or graduate years; not renewable. *Number:* 1. *Amount:* $2000.

Eligibility Requirements: Applicant must be enrolled or expecting to enroll full-time at a four-year institution or university and studying in Texas. Applicant or parent of applicant must be member of Texas Association of Broadcasters. Applicant must have 3.0 GPA or higher. Available to U.S. and non-U.S. citizens.

Application Requirements: Application, essay, financial need analysis, references. *Deadline:* May 4.

Contact: Craig Bean, Public Service Manager
Texas Association of Broadcasters
502 East 11th Street, Suite 200
Austin, TX 78701
Phone: 512-322-9944
Fax: 512-322-0522
E-mail: craig@tab.org

STUDENT TEXAS BROADCAST EDUCATION FOUNDATION SCHOLARSHIP

Scholarship of $2000 to a undergraduate or a graduate student enrolled in a program of instruction that emphasizes radio or television broadcasting or communications at a two-year or technical school in Texas. Student must be a member of the Texas Association of Broadcasters. Must have a GPA of 3.0 minimum.

Academic Fields/Career Goals: Communications; TV/Radio Broadcasting.

Award: Scholarship for use in freshman, sophomore, junior, or senior years; not renewable. *Number:* 1. *Amount:* $2000.

Eligibility Requirements: Applicant must be enrolled or expecting to enroll full-time at a two-year or technical institution and studying in Texas. Applicant or parent of applicant must be member of Texas Association of Broadcasters. Applicant must have 3.0 GPA or higher. Available to U.S. and non-U.S. citizens.

Application Requirements: Application, essay, financial need analysis, references. *Deadline:* May 4.

Contact: Craig Bean, Public Service Manager
Texas Association of Broadcasters
502 East 11th Street, Suite 200
Austin, TX 78701
Phone: 512-322-9944
Fax: 512-322-0522
E-mail: craig@tab.org

TOM REIFF TEXAS BROADCAST EDUCATION FOUNDATION SCHOLARSHIP

Scholarship of $2000 to undergraduate and graduate students enrolled in a fully accredited program of instruction that emphasizes radio or television broadcasting or communications at a four-year college or university in Texas. Student must be a member of the Texas Association of Broadcasters. Must have a GPA of 3.0 minimum.

Academic Fields/Career Goals: Communications; TV/Radio Broadcasting.

Award: Scholarship for use in freshman, sophomore, junior, senior, or graduate years; not renewable. *Number:* 1. *Amount:* $2000.

Eligibility Requirements: Applicant must be enrolled or expecting to enroll full-time at a four-year institution or university and studying in Texas. Applicant or parent of applicant must be member of Texas Association of Broadcasters. Applicant must have 3.0 GPA or higher. Available to U.S. and non-U.S. citizens.

Application Requirements: Application, essay, financial need analysis, references. *Deadline:* May 4.

Contact: Craig Bean, Public Service Manager
Texas Association of Broadcasters
502 East 11th Street, Suite 200
Austin, TX 78701
Phone: 512-322-9944
Fax: 512-322-0522
E-mail: craig@tab.org

UNDERGRADUATE TEXAS BROADCAST EDUCATION FOUNDATION SCHOLARSHIP

Scholarship of $2000 to a undergraduate student enrolled in a fully accredited program of instruction that emphasizes radio or television broadcasting or communications at a four-year college or university in Texas. Student must be a member of the Texas Association of Broadcasters. Must have a GPA of 3.0 minimum.

Academic Fields/Career Goals: Communications; TV/Radio Broadcasting.

Award: Scholarship for use in freshman, sophomore, junior, or senior years; not renewable. *Number:* 1. *Amount:* $2000.

Eligibility Requirements: Applicant must be enrolled or expecting to enroll full-time at a four-year institution or university and studying in Texas. Applicant or parent of applicant must be member of Texas Association of Broadcasters. Applicant must have 3.0 GPA or higher. Available to U.S. and non-U.S. citizens.

Application Requirements: Application, essay, financial need analysis, references. *Deadline:* May 4.

Contact: Craig Bean, Public Service Manager
Texas Association of Broadcasters
502 East 11th Street, Suite 200
Austin, TX 78701
Phone: 512-322-9944
Fax: 512-322-0522
E-mail: craig@tab.org

VANN KENNEDY TEXAS BROADCAST EDUCATION FOUNDATION SCHOLARSHIP

Scholarship of $2000 to a undergraduate or graduate student enrolled in a fully accredited program of instruction that emphasizes radio or television broadcasting or communications at college or university in Texas. Student must be a member of the Texas Association of Broadcasters. Must have a GPA of 3.0 minimum.

Academic Fields/Career Goals: Communications; TV/Radio Broadcasting.

Award: Scholarship for use in freshman, sophomore, junior, or senior years; not renewable. *Number:* 1. *Amount:* $2000.

Eligibility Requirements: Applicant must be enrolled or expecting to enroll full-time at a two-year or four-year institution or university and studying in Texas. Applicant or parent of applicant must be member of Texas Association of Broadcasters. Applicant must have 3.0 GPA or higher. Available to U.S. and non-U.S. citizens.

Application Requirements: Application, essay, financial need analysis, references. *Deadline:* May 4.

Contact: Craig Bean, Public Service Manager
Texas Association of Broadcasters
502 East 11th Street, Suite 200
Austin, TX 78701
Phone: 512-322-9944
Fax: 512-322-0522
E-mail: craig@tab.org

TEXAS GRIDIRON CLUB INC. http://www.spjfw.org

TEXAS GRIDIRON CLUB SCHOLARSHIPS

$500 to $1000 scholarships for full-time or part-time college juniors, seniors, or graduate students majoring in newspaper, photojournalism, or broadcast fields. Must be Texas resident or going to school in Texas.

Academic Fields/Career Goals: Communications; Journalism; Photojournalism/Photography; TV/Radio Broadcasting.

Award: Scholarship for use in junior, senior, or graduate years; not renewable. *Number:* 10–15. *Amount:* $500–$1000.

Eligibility Requirements: Applicant must be enrolled or expecting to enroll full- or part-time at a four-year institution or university and resident of Texas. Available to U.S. citizens.

Application Requirements: Application, essay, financial need analysis, references, transcript, work samples. *Deadline:* March 3.

Contact: Angie Summers, Scholarships Coordinator
Texas Gridiron Club Inc.
709 Houston Street
Arlington, TX 76012
E-mail: asummers@star-telegram.com

TEXAS OUTDOOR WRITERS ASSOCIATION http://www.towa.org

TEXAS OUTDOOR WRITERS ASSOCIATION SCHOLARSHIP

Annual merit award available to students attending an accredited Texas college or university preparing for a career which would incorporate communications skills about the outdoors, environmental conservation, or resource management. Minimum 2.5 GPA required. Submit writing/photo samples.

Academic Fields/Career Goals: Communications; Environmental Science; Natural Resources.

Award: Scholarship for use in freshman, sophomore, junior, senior, graduate, or postgraduate years; not renewable. *Number:* 2. *Amount:* $1000–$1500.

Eligibility Requirements: Applicant must be enrolled or expecting to enroll full- or part-time at a four-year institution or university; resident of Texas; studying in Texas and must have an interest in writing. Applicant must have 2.5 GPA or higher. Available to U.S. citizens.

Application Requirements: Application, references, transcript, writing/photo samples. *Deadline:* February 15.

Contact: Chester Moore Jr., Scholarship Chair
Texas Outdoor Writers Association
101 Broad Street
Orange, TX 77630
Phone: 409-882-0945
Fax: 409-882-0945
E-mail: saltwater@fishgame.com

TKE EDUCATIONAL FOUNDATION http://www.tke.org

GEORGE W. WOOLERY MEMORIAL SCHOLARSHIP

Scholarship available to initiated undergraduate members of Tau Kappa Epsilon who are full-time students in good standing, and pursuing a degree in communications or marketing with a cumulative GPA of 2.5 or higher. Record of leadership within the TKE chapter and on campus should be submitted. Preference will be given to members of Beta-Sigma Chapter, but if no qualified candidate applies, the award will be open to any member of TKE.

Academic Fields/Career Goals: Communications.

Award: Scholarship for use in freshman, sophomore, junior, or senior years; not renewable. *Number:* 1. *Amount:* $600.

Eligibility Requirements: Applicant must be enrolled or expecting to enroll full-time at a four-year institution or university; male and must have an interest in leadership. Applicant or parent of applicant must be member of Tau Kappa Epsilon. Applicant must have 2.5 GPA or higher. Available to U.S. and non-U.S. citizens.

Application Requirements: Application, essay, photo, transcript, narrative summary of how TKE membership has benefited applicant. *Deadline:* February 29.

Contact: Scholarship Committee
TKE Educational Foundation
8645 Founders Road
Indianapolis, IN 46268-1336
Phone: 317-872-6533
Fax: 317-875-8353
E-mail: tef@tke.org

TURF AND ORNAMENTAL COMMUNICATION ASSOCIATION http://www.toca.org

TURF AND ORNAMENTAL COMMUNICATORS ASSOCIATION SCHOLARSHIP PROGRAM

• *See page 79*

UNITED METHODIST COMMUNICATIONS http://www.umcom.org

LEONARD M. PERRYMAN COMMUNICATIONS SCHOLARSHIP FOR ETHNIC MINORITY STUDENTS

One-time award to assist United Methodist ethnic minority students who are college students intending to pursue careers in religious communications.

Academic Fields/Career Goals: Communications; Journalism; Photojournalism/Photography; Religion/Theology; TV/Radio Broadcasting.

Award: Scholarship for use in junior or senior years; not renewable. *Number:* 1. *Amount:* $2500.

Eligibility Requirements: Applicant must be Methodist; American Indian/Alaska Native, Asian/Pacific Islander, Black (non-Hispanic), or Hispanic and enrolled or expecting to enroll full-time at a two-year or four-year institution or university. Available to U.S. citizens.

Application Requirements: Application, essay, photo, references, transcript. *Deadline:* March 15.

Contact: Communications Resourcing Team
United Methodist Communications
810 12th Avenue, South
PO Box 320
Nashville, TN 37202-0320
Phone: 888-278-4862
Fax: 615-742-5485
E-mail: scholarships@umcom.org

UNITED NEGRO COLLEGE FUND http://www.uncf.org

BEST BUY ENTERPRISE EMPLOYEE SCHOLARSHIP

• *See page 64*

C-SPAN SCHOLARSHIP PROGRAM

Scholarship for students majoring in communications, journalism, political science, English, history, or radio/TV/film. Applicant must be undergraduate sophomore or junior attending a UNCF member college or university. Must have a minimum of 3.0 GPA. Program offers a paid summer internship. Please visit Web site for more information: http://www.uncf.org.

Academic Fields/Career Goals: Communications; History; Journalism; Literature/English/Writing; Political Science; TV/Radio Broadcasting.

Award: Scholarship for use in sophomore or junior years; not renewable. *Number:* 1. *Amount:* $2000.

Eligibility Requirements: Applicant must be Black (non-Hispanic) and enrolled or expecting to enroll full- or part-time at a four-year institution or university. Applicant must have 3.0 GPA or higher. Available to U.S. citizens.

United Negro College Fund (continued)

Application Requirements: Application, financial need analysis, FAFSA, Student Aid Report (SAR). *Deadline:* varies.

Contact: William Dunham, Program Services
United Negro College Fund
8260 Willow Oaks Corporate Drive
Fairfax, VA 22031
Phone: 703-205-3486

JOHN LENNON ENDOWED SCHOLARSHIP

Scholarships for students at UNCF member institutes majoring in performing arts, music, mass communications and communications. Must have at least 3.0 GPA. Prospective applicants should complete the Student Profile found at Web site: http://www.uncf.org.

Academic Fields/Career Goals: Communications; Music; Performing Arts.

Award: Scholarship for use in freshman year; not renewable. *Number:* 1. *Amount:* up to $5000.

Eligibility Requirements: Applicant must be Black (non-Hispanic); high school student and planning to enroll or expecting to enroll full- or part-time at a four-year institution or university. Applicant must have 3.0 GPA or higher. Available to U.S. citizens.

Application Requirements: Application, essay, financial need analysis, photo, references, transcript. *Deadline:* April 20.

Contact: William Dunham, Program Services Department
United Negro College Fund
8260 Willow Oaks Corporate Drive, PO Box 10444
Fairfax, VA 22031
Phone: 703-205-3486

NASCAR/WENDELL SCOTT, SR. SCHOLARSHIP

• *See page 66*

READER'S DIGEST FOUNDATION SCHOLARSHIP

Scholarship for encouraging academically superior students, who write well, to enter the field of print journalism. Students attending UNCF member colleges and universities and majoring in communications, journalism or English are eligible to apply. Students must be in their junior or senior year and have a GPA of 3.0 or better. Applicants must submit a published writing sample with their application.

Academic Fields/Career Goals: Communications; Journalism; Literature/English/Writing.

Award: Scholarship for use in junior or senior years; not renewable. *Number:* 1. *Amount:* up to $5000.

Eligibility Requirements: Applicant must be Black (non-Hispanic) and enrolled or expecting to enroll full- or part-time at a four-year institution or university. Applicant must have 3.0 GPA or higher. Available to U.S. citizens.

Application Requirements: Application, financial need analysis, photo, resume, references, transcript, published writing sample. *Deadline:* February 15.

Contact: William Dunham, Program Services
United Negro College Fund
8260 Willow Oaks Corporate Drive
Fairfax, VA 22031
Phone: 703-205-3486

TOYOTA SCHOLARSHIP

• *See page 66*

VALLEY PRESS CLUB http://www.valleypressclub.com

VALLEY PRESS CLUB SCHOLARSHIPS, THE REPUBLICAN SCHOLARSHIP, CHANNEL 22 SCHOLARSHIP

Nonrenewable award for graduating high school seniors from Connecticut and Massachusetts, who are interested in television journalism, photojournalism, broadcast journalism, or print journalism.

Academic Fields/Career Goals: Communications; Journalism; Photojournalism/Photography; TV/Radio Broadcasting.

Award: Scholarship for use in freshman year; not renewable. *Number:* 5. *Amount:* $1000.

Eligibility Requirements: Applicant must be high school student; planning to enroll or expecting to enroll full-time at a four-year institution or university; resident of Connecticut or Massachusetts and must have an interest in writing. Available to U.S. citizens.

Application Requirements: Application, financial need analysis, interview, references, test scores, transcript. *Deadline:* April 1.

Contact: Robert McClellan, Scholarship Committee Chair
Valley Press Club
PO Box 5475
Springfield, MA 01101
Phone: 413-783-3355

VIRGINIA ASSOCIATION OF BROADCASTERS http://www.vabonline.com

VIRGINIA ASSOCIATION OF BROADCASTERS SCHOLARSHIP AWARD

Scholarships are available to entering juniors and seniors majoring in mass communications-related courses. Must either be a resident of Virginia or be enrolled at a Virginia college or university. Must be U.S. citizen and enrolled full-time.

Academic Fields/Career Goals: Communications.

Award: Scholarship for use in junior or senior years; renewable. *Number:* 4. *Amount:* $500–$1000.

Eligibility Requirements: Applicant must be enrolled or expecting to enroll full-time at a four-year institution or university; resident of Virginia and studying in Virginia. Available to U.S. and non-U.S. citizens.

Application Requirements: Application, essay, financial need analysis, transcript. *Deadline:* February 15.

Contact: Ruby Seal, Director of Administration
Virginia Association of Broadcasters
600 Peter Jefferson Parkway, Suite 300
Charlottesville, VA 22911
Phone: 434-977-3716
Fax: 434-979-2439
E-mail: ruby.seal@easterassociates.com

WASHINGTON NEWS COUNCIL http://www.wanewscouncil.org

DICK LARSEN SCHOLARSHIP PROGRAM

One-time award for a student at a Washington state four-year public or private college with a serious interest in a career in communications-journalism, public relations, politics, or a related field. Must be resident of Washington state and U.S. citizen. See web site for more information.

Academic Fields/Career Goals: Communications; Journalism; Political Science.

Award: Scholarship for use in freshman, sophomore, junior, senior, or graduate years; not renewable. *Number:* 1. *Amount:* $2000.

Eligibility Requirements: Applicant must be enrolled or expecting to enroll full-time at a four-year institution; resident of Washington and studying in Washington. Available to U.S. citizens.

Application Requirements: Application, essay, financial need analysis, references, transcript, 3 samples of work. *Deadline:* April 15.

Contact: Scholarship Committee
Washington News Council
PO Box 3672
Seattle, WA 98124-3672

HERB ROBINSON SCHOLARSHIP PROGRAM

One-time award to a graduating Washington state high school senior who is entering a four-year public or private college or university in Washington. Must have a serious interest in a career in communications-journalism, public relations, politics or a related field. Must be resident of Washington state and a U.S. citizen. See web site for more information.

Academic Fields/Career Goals: Communications; Journalism; Political Science.

Award: Scholarship for use in freshman year; not renewable. *Number:* 1. *Amount:* $2000.

Eligibility Requirements: Applicant must be high school student; planning to enroll or expecting to enroll full-time at a four-year institution or university; resident of Washington and studying in Washington. Available to U.S. citizens.

Application Requirements: Application, essay, financial need analysis, references, transcript. *Deadline:* April 15.

Contact: John Hamer, Executive Director
Washington News Council
PO Box 3672
Seattle, WA 98124-3672
Phone: 206-262-9793
Fax: 206-464-7902
E-mail: info@wanewscouncil.org

WISCONSIN BROADCASTERS ASSOCIATION FOUNDATION http://www.wi-broadcasters.org

WISCONSIN BROADCASTERS ASSOCIATION FOUNDATION SCHOLARSHIP

Four $2000 scholarships offered to assist students enrolled in broadcasting-related educational programs at four-year public or private institutions. Applicants must either have graduated from a Wisconsin high school, or be attending a Wisconsin college or university, must have completed at least 60 credits, and must be planning a career in radio or television broadcasting.

Academic Fields/Career Goals: Communications; TV/Radio Broadcasting.

Award: Scholarship for use in freshman, sophomore, junior, or senior years; not renewable. *Number:* 4. *Amount:* $2000.

Eligibility Requirements: Applicant must be enrolled or expecting to enroll full-time at a four-year institution or university and studying in Wisconsin. Available to U.S. citizens.

Application Requirements: Application, essay, references, transcript. *Deadline:* October 20.

Contact: John Laabs, President
Wisconsin Broadcasters Association Foundation
44 East Mifflin Street, Suite 900
Madison, WI 53703
Phone: 608-255-2600
Fax: 608-256-3986
E-mail: jlaabs@aol.com

WMTW-TV 8-AUBURN, MAINE http://www.wmtw.com

BOB ELLIOT-WMTW-TV 8 JOURNALISM SCHOLARSHIP

Awards $1500 to one graduating high school senior who plans to major in journalism, communications or a related area of study. This scholarship is one-time-only. Application available at http://www.wmtw.com.

Academic Fields/Career Goals: Communications; Journalism; TV/Radio Broadcasting.

Award: Scholarship for use in freshman year; not renewable. *Number:* 1. *Amount:* $1500.

Eligibility Requirements: Applicant must be high school student; planning to enroll or expecting to enroll full-time at a four-year institution or university and resident of Maine. Available to U.S. citizens.

Application Requirements: Application, essay, references, transcript. *Deadline:* March 24.

Contact: David Butta, Scholarship Coordinator
WMTW-TV 8-Auburn, Maine
PO Box 8
Auburn, ME 04211-0008
Phone: 207-514-1317
E-mail: wmtw@wmtw.com

WOMEN'S BASKETBALL COACHES ASSOCIATION http://www.wbca.org

ROBIN ROBERTS/WBCA SPORTS COMMUNICATIONS SCHOLARSHIP AWARD

One-time award for female student athletes who have completed their eligibility and plan to go to graduate school. Must major in communications. Must be nominated by the head coach of women's basketball who is a member of the WBCA.

Academic Fields/Career Goals: Communications; Journalism.

Award: Scholarship for use in senior, graduate, or postgraduate years; not renewable. *Number:* 1. *Amount:* $4000.

Eligibility Requirements: Applicant must be enrolled or expecting to enroll full- or part-time at a four-year institution or university; female and must have an interest in athletics/sports. Available to U.S. and non-U.S. citizens.

Application Requirements: Application, references, statistics. *Deadline:* February 15.

Contact: Betty Jaynes, Consultant
Women's Basketball Coaches Association
4646 Lawrenceville Highway
Lilburn, GA 30047-3620
Phone: 770-279-8027 Ext. 102
Fax: 770-279-6290
E-mail: bettyj@wbca.org

COMPUTER SCIENCE/DATA PROCESSING

ALICE L. HALTOM EDUCATIONAL FUND http://www.alhef.org

ALICE L. HALTOM EDUCATIONAL FUND SCHOLARSHIP

Award for students pursuing a career in information and records management. Up to $1000 for those in an associate degree program, and up to $2000 for students in a baccalaureate or advanced degree program.

Academic Fields/Career Goals: Computer Science/Data Processing; Library and Information Sciences.

Award: Scholarship for use in freshman, sophomore, junior, senior, or graduate years; not renewable. *Number:* varies. *Amount:* $1000–$2000.

Eligibility Requirements: Applicant must be enrolled or expecting to enroll full- or part-time at a two-year or four-year institution or university. Available to U.S. and non-U.S. citizens.

Application Requirements: Application, references, transcript. *Deadline:* May 1.

Contact: Teresa Matlock, Secretary
Alice L. Haltom Educational Fund
PO Box 70530
Houston, TX 77270
Phone: 281-372-5126
Fax: 281-372-5127
E-mail: contact@alhef.org

AMERICAN FOUNDATION FOR THE BLIND http://www.afb.org

PAUL W. RUCKES SCHOLARSHIP

Scholarship of $1000 to an undergraduate or graduate student studying in the field of engineering, or in computer, physical, or life sciences. For more information and application requirements, please visit http://www.afb.org/scholarships.asp.

Academic Fields/Career Goals: Computer Science/Data Processing; Electrical Engineering/Electronics; Engineering/Technology; Natural Sciences; Physical Sciences and Math.

Award: Scholarship for use in freshman, sophomore, junior, senior, or graduate years; not renewable. *Number:* 1. *Amount:* $1000.

Eligibility Requirements: Applicant must be enrolled or expecting to enroll full-time at a two-year or four-year institution or university. Applicant must be visually impaired. Available to U.S. citizens.

Application Requirements: Application, essay, references, transcript, proof of post-secondary acceptance and legal blindness, proof of citizenship, FAFSA. *Deadline:* March 31.

Contact: Dawn Bodrogi, Information Center
American Foundation for the Blind
11 Penn Plaza, Suite 300
New York, NY 10001
Phone: 212-502-7661
Fax: 212-502-7771
E-mail: afbinfo@afb.net

AMERICAN SOCIETY FOR INFORMATION SCIENCE AND TECHNOLOGY http://www.asis.org

JOHN WILEY & SONS BEST JASIST PAPER AWARD

Award of $1500 to recognize the best refereed paper published in the volume year of the JASIT preceding the ASIST annual meeting. John Wiley & Sons Inc., shall contribute $500 towards travel expenses to attend the ASIST annual meeting. No nomination procedure is used for this award. All eligible papers are considered.

Academic Fields/Career Goals: Computer Science/Data Processing; Library and Information Sciences.

Award: Prize for use in freshman, sophomore, junior, senior, graduate, or postgraduate years; not renewable. *Number:* 1. *Amount:* $2000.

Eligibility Requirements: Applicant must be enrolled or expecting to enroll full-time at a four-year institution or university. Available to U.S. and non-U.S. citizens.

Application Requirements: Application, essay. *Deadline:* varies.

Contact: Awards Coordinator
American Society for Information Science and Technology
1320 Fenwick Lane, Suite 510
Silver Spring, MD 20910-3602
Phone: 301-495-0900
Fax: 301-495-0810
E-mail: asis@asis.org

ARMED FORCES COMMUNICATIONS AND ELECTRONICS ASSOCIATION, EDUCATIONAL FOUNDATION http://www.afcea.org

AFCEA/LOCKHEED MARTIN ORINCON IT SCHOLARSHIP

• *See page 113*

AFCEA SCHOLARSHIP FOR WORKING PROFESSIONALS

• *See page 113*

AFCEA SGT. JEANNETTE L. WINTERS, USMC MEMORIAL SCHOLARSHIP

Applications are requested from men and women currently on active duty in the U.S. Marine Corps or U.S. Marine Corps men and women veterans who are honorably discharged and currently attending four-year colleges or universities in the United States. Applications will be accepted from qualified sophomore, junior, and senior undergraduate students enrolled either part-time or full-time in an eligible degree program. Minimum GPA requirement is 3.0.

Academic Fields/Career Goals: Computer Science/Data Processing; Electrical Engineering/Electronics; Engineering/Technology; Physical Sciences and Math.

Award: Scholarship for use in sophomore, junior, or senior years; not renewable. *Number:* 1. *Amount:* $2000.

Eligibility Requirements: Applicant must be enrolled or expecting to enroll full- or part-time at a four-year institution or university. Applicant must have 3.0 GPA or higher. Available to U.S. citizens. Applicant or parent must meet one or more of the following requirements: Marine Corps experience; retired from active duty; disabled or killed as a result of military service; prisoner of war; or missing in action.

Application Requirements: Application, references, transcript. *Deadline:* September 1.

Contact: Norma Corrales, Director of Scholarships and Awards
Armed Forces Communications and Electronics Association, Educational Foundation
4400 Fair Lakes Court
Fairfax, VA 22033
Phone: 703-631-6149
E-mail: scholarship@afcea.org

ARMED FORCES COMMUNICATIONS AND ELECTRONICS ASSOCIATION EDUCATIONAL FOUNDATION DISTANCE-LEARNING SCHOLARSHIP

Scholarships of $1500 will be awarded to full-time students pursuing either a bachelor of science or master of science degree by means of a distance-learning or on-line program. Candidate must be a U.S. citizen. Must be at least a second-year student. Graduate applicants must have completed at least one full semester of work.

Academic Fields/Career Goals: Computer Science/Data Processing; Electrical Engineering/Electronics; Engineering/Technology.

Award: Scholarship for use in sophomore, junior, senior, or graduate years; not renewable. *Number:* 1. *Amount:* $1500.

Eligibility Requirements: Applicant must be enrolled or expecting to enroll full-time at a four-year institution or university. Available to U.S. citizens.

Application Requirements: Application, references, transcript. *Deadline:* June 1.

Contact: Norma Corrales, Director of Scholarships and Awards
Armed Forces Communications and Electronics Association, Educational Foundation
4400 Fair Lakes Court
Fairfax, VA 22033
Phone: 703-631-6149
E-mail: scholarship@afcea.org

ARMED FORCES COMMUNICATIONS AND ELECTRONICS ASSOCIATION GENERAL EMMETT PAIGE SCHOLARSHIP

Scholarships of $2000 each will be awarded to persons on active duty in the uniformed military services, to veterans, and to their spouses or dependents, who are currently enrolled full-time in an eligible degree program at an accredited four-year college or university in the United States. Candidate must be a U.S. citizen, majoring in the C4I-related fields. Minimum GPA requirement is 3.4. Veterans attending college as freshmen are eligible to apply; all others must be at least sophomores.

Academic Fields/Career Goals: Computer Science/Data Processing; Electrical Engineering/Electronics; Engineering/Technology; Physical Sciences and Math.

Award: Scholarship for use in freshman, sophomore, junior, or senior years; not renewable. *Number:* 1. *Amount:* $2000.

Eligibility Requirements: Applicant must be enrolled or expecting to enroll full-time at a four-year institution or university. Available to U.S. citizens. Applicant or parent must meet one or more of the following requirements: general military experience; retired from active duty; disabled or killed as a result of military service; prisoner of war; or missing in action.

Application Requirements: Application, references, transcript. *Deadline:* March 1.

Contact: Norma Corrales, Director, Scholarships and Award Programs
Armed Forces Communications and Electronics Association, Educational Foundation
4400 Fair Lakes Court
Fairfax, VA 22033-3899
Phone: 703-631-6149
Fax: 703-631-4693
E-mail: scholarship@afcea.org

ARMED FORCES COMMUNICATIONS AND ELECTRONICS ASSOCIATION GENERAL JOHN A. WICKHAM SCHOLARSHIP

Scholarships of $2000 for U.S. citizens enrolled full-time in four-year, accredited colleges or universities in the United States and majoring in C4I-related fields. Applicant must be a sophomore or junior with minimum GPA of 3.5.

Academic Fields/Career Goals: Computer Science/Data Processing; Electrical Engineering/Electronics; Engineering/Technology; Physical Sciences and Math.

Award: Scholarship for use in sophomore or junior years; not renewable. *Number:* 1. *Amount:* $2000.

Eligibility Requirements: Applicant must be enrolled or expecting to enroll full-time at a four-year institution or university. Applicant must have 3.5 GPA or higher. Available to U.S. citizens.

Application Requirements: Application, references, transcript. *Deadline:* May 1.

Contact: Norma Corrales, Director, Scholarships and Award Programs
Armed Forces Communications and Electronics Association, Educational Foundation
4400 Fair Lakes Court
Fairfax, VA 22033-3899
Phone: 703-631-6149
Fax: 703-631-4693
E-mail: scholarship@afcea.org

ARMED FORCES COMMUNICATIONS AND ELECTRONICS ASSOCIATION ROTC SCHOLARSHIP PROGRAM

• *See page 114*

ARRL FOUNDATION INC. http://www.arrl.org

PHD ARA SCHOLARSHIP

Award for journalism, computer science, or electronic engineering students. Must be a amateur radio operator. Preference given to students residing in Iowa, Kansas, Missouri, or Nebraska and those who are children of deceased amateur radio operators. One award of $1000 per year.

Academic Fields/Career Goals: Computer Science/Data Processing; Electrical Engineering/Electronics; Journalism.

Award: Scholarship for use in freshman, sophomore, junior, or senior years; not renewable. *Number:* 1. *Amount:* $1000.

Eligibility Requirements: Applicant must be enrolled or expecting to enroll full-time at a four-year institution or university; resident of Iowa, Kansas, Missouri, or Nebraska and must have an interest in amateur radio. Available to U.S. citizens.

Application Requirements: Application, transcript. *Deadline:* February 1.

Contact: Mary M. Hobart, Secretary
ARRL Foundation Inc.
225 Main Street
Newington, CT 06111-1494
Phone: 860-594-0397
Fax: 860-594-0259
E-mail: k1mmh@arrl.org

WILLIAM R. GOLDFARB MEMORIAL SCHOLARSHIP

• *See page 138*

ASSOCIATION FOR IRON AND STEEL TECHNOLOGY http://www.aist.org

ASSOCIATION FOR IRON AND STEEL TECHNOLOGY OHIO VALLEY CHAPTER SCHOLARSHIP

• *See page 130*

ASSOCIATION FOR WOMEN IN SCIENCE EDUCATIONAL FOUNDATION http://www.awis.org/careers/edfoundation.html

ASSOCIATION FOR WOMEN IN SCIENCE COLLEGE SCHOLARSHIP

• *See page 82*

ASTRONAUT SCHOLARSHIP FOUNDATION http://www.astronautscholarship.org

ASTRONAUT SCHOLARSHIP FOUNDATION

• *See page 86*

BARRY M. GOLDWATER SCHOLARSHIP AND EXCELLENCE IN EDUCATION FOUNDATION http://www.act.org/goldwater

BARRY M. GOLDWATER SCHOLARSHIP AND EXCELLENCE IN EDUCATION PROGRAM

• *See page 86*

BUSINESS AND PROFESSIONAL WOMEN'S FOUNDATION http://www.bpwfoundation.org

BPW CAREER ADVANCEMENT SCHOLARSHIP PROGRAM FOR WOMEN

• *See page 130*

CATCHING THE DREAM http://www.catchingthedream.org

MATH, ENGINEERING, SCIENCE, BUSINESS, EDUCATION, COMPUTERS SCHOLARSHIPS

• *See page 139*

TRIBAL BUSINESS MANAGEMENT PROGRAM (TBM)

• *See page 49*

CENTRAL INTELLIGENCE AGENCY http://www.cia.gov

CENTRAL INTELLIGENCE AGENCY UNDERGRADUATE SCHOLARSHIP PROGRAM

• *See page 49*

DATATEL INC. http://www.datatel.com/dsf

NANCY GOODHUE LYNCH SCHOLARSHIP

For any undergraduate student in an Information Technology curriculum program. One-time award for students attending institutions which use Datatel administrative software. List can be found online at www.datatel.com/dsf. Available for students currently attending at least 6 credits. Completed on-line applications, including two letters of recommendation must be submitted electronically.

Academic Fields/Career Goals: Computer Science/Data Processing.

Award: Scholarship for use in freshman, sophomore, junior, or senior years; not renewable. *Number:* 2. *Amount:* $2500.

Eligibility Requirements: Applicant must be enrolled or expecting to enroll full- or part-time at a two-year or four-year or technical institution or university. Available to U.S. and non-U.S. citizens.

Application Requirements: Application, essay, references, transcript. *Deadline:* January 31.

Contact: Stacey Fessler, Project Leader
Datatel Inc.
4375 Fair Lakes Court
Fairfax, VA 22033
Phone: 800-486-4332
E-mail: scholars@datatel.com

DEVRY INC. http://www.devry.edu

CISCO NETWORKING ACADEMY SCHOLARSHIP

Award to high school graduates and GED recipients who successfully completed IT essentials I or CCNA semester prior to entering college. Amount of $1200 per semester, valued up to $10,800.

Academic Fields/Career Goals: Computer Science/Data Processing; Electrical Engineering/Electronics; Engineering/Technology; Engineering-Related Technologies.

Award: Scholarship for use in freshman year; renewable. *Number:* varies. *Amount:* up to $2400.

Eligibility Requirements: Applicant must be high school student and planning to enroll or expecting to enroll full-time at an institution or university. Available to U.S. and Canadian citizens.

Application Requirements: Application. *Deadline:* varies.

Contact: Thonie Simpson, National High School Program Manager
DeVry Inc.
One Tower Lane
Oak Brook Terrace, IL 60181-4624
Phone: 630-706-3122
Fax: 630-574-1696
E-mail: scholarships@devry.edu

ELECTRONIC DOCUMENT SYSTEMS FOUNDATION http://www.edsf.org

ELECTRONIC DOCUMENT SYSTEMS FOUNDATION SCHOLARSHIP AWARDS

• *See page 178*

FOUNDATION FOR SCIENCE AND DISABILITY http://www.stemd.org

GRANTS FOR DISABLED STUDENTS IN THE SCIENCES

• *See page 87*

GOLDEN KEY INTERNATIONAL HONOUR SOCIETY http://www.goldenkey.org

INFORMATION SYSTEMS ACHIEVEMENT AWARD

Award requires applicants to respond to a problem posed by an honorary member within the discipline. The response may be in the form of an essay or a design. One winner will receive a $1000 award. The second place applicant will receive a $750 award and the third place applicant will receive $500.

Academic Fields/Career Goals: Computer Science/Data Processing.

Award: Prize for use in junior, senior, graduate, or postgraduate years; not renewable. *Number:* 2. *Amount:* $500–$1000.

Golden Key International Honour Society (continued)

Eligibility Requirements: Applicant must be enrolled or expecting to enroll full- or part-time at a four-year institution or university. Available to U.S. and non-U.S. citizens.

Application Requirements: Application, applicant must enter a contest, essay, references, transcript. *Deadline:* March 1.

Contact: Tony Kearney, Director
Golden Key International Honour Society
621 North Avenue, NE, Suite C-100
Atlanta, GA 30308
Phone: 404-377-2400
Fax: 678-420-6757
E-mail: scholarships@goldenkey.org

GREAT LAKES COMMISSION http://www.glc.org

CAROL A. RATZA MEMORIAL SCHOLARSHIP
• *See page 179*

HAWAIIAN LODGE, F & AM http://www.glhawaii.org/

HAWAIIAN LODGE SCHOLARSHIPS
• *See page 96*

HEMOPHILIA HEALTH SERVICES http://www.hemophiliahealth.com

SCOTT TARBELL SCHOLARSHIP

Award to U.S. citizens with hemophilia A or B severe and related bleeding disorders. Students must be majoring or seeking a degree or certification in computer science and/or math. Applicants must be high school seniors, high school graduates (or equivalent/GED), college freshmen, sophomores, or juniors.

Academic Fields/Career Goals: Computer Science/Data Processing; Mathematics.

Award: Scholarship for use in freshman, sophomore, junior, or senior years; not renewable. *Number:* 1–2. *Amount:* $1500–$2000.

Eligibility Requirements: Applicant must be enrolled or expecting to enroll full-time at a four-year institution or university. Applicant must be physically disabled. Available to U.S. citizens.

Application Requirements: Application, essay, financial need analysis, references, test scores, transcript, doctor certification form. *Deadline:* May 1.

Contact: Sally Johnson, Manager Operations Support
Hemophilia Health Services
c/o Scholarship Program Administrators, Inc.
PO Box 23737
Nashville, TN 37202-3737
Phone: 615-850-5175
Fax: 615-352-2588
E-mail: scholarship@hemophiliahealth.com

HEWLETT-PACKARD COMPANY http://www.hp.com

HP SCHOLAR AWARD

Scholarship awards are $3000 per year for up to four years and are intended to help defray educational expenses. Applicants must be underrepresented minority (African American, Latino, or American Indian) students who will pursue a bachelor of science degree in computer science, computer engineering or electrical engineering at an HP Scholar partnership university.

Academic Fields/Career Goals: Computer Science/Data Processing; Electrical Engineering/Electronics.

Award: Scholarship for use in freshman, sophomore, junior, or senior years; renewable. *Number:* up to 30. *Amount:* up to $3000.

Eligibility Requirements: Applicant must be American Indian/Alaska Native, Black (non-Hispanic), or Hispanic and enrolled or expecting to enroll full-time at a four-year or technical institution or university. Available to U.S. citizens.

Application Requirements: Application, resume, references, transcript. *Deadline:* March 15.

Contact: Howard Templeton, Program Manager
Hewlett-Packard Company
3000 Hanover Street
Palo Alto, CA 94394-1185
Phone: 541-715-4181
E-mail: howard.templeton@hp.com

HISPANIC COLLEGE FUND INC. http://www.hispanicfund.org

ALPFA SCHOLARSHIP PROGRAM
• *See page 54*

DENNY'S/HISPANIC COLLEGE FUND SCHOLARSHIP
• *See page 54*

GOOGLE SCHOLARSHIP PROGRAM

Awards for college juniors and seniors pursing Masters or PhD degrees in computer science or computer engineering. Selected scholars will be invited to an all-expenses paid trip to the Google Headquarters in California. Must be Hispanic and have minimum 3.5 GPA.

Academic Fields/Career Goals: Computer Science/Data Processing.

Award: Scholarship for use in junior, senior, graduate, or postgraduate years; not renewable. *Number:* 10. *Amount:* up to $10,000.

Eligibility Requirements: Applicant must be Hispanic and enrolled or expecting to enroll full-time at a four-year institution or university. Applicant must have 3.5 GPA or higher. Available to U.S. citizens.

Application Requirements: Essay, references, proof of family income, citizenship proof. *Deadline:* March 29.

Contact: Fernando Barrueta, Chief Executive Officer
Hispanic College Fund Inc.
1301 K Street, NW, Suite 450-A West
Washington, DC 20005
Phone: 202-296-5400
Fax: 202-296-3774
E-mail: hcf-info@hispanicfund.org

ICI EDUCATIONAL FOUNDATION SCHOLARSHIP PROGRAM
• *See page 142*

LOCKHEED MARTIN SCHOLARSHIP PROGRAM
• *See page 143*

HISPANIC ENGINEER NATIONAL ACHIEVEMENT AWARDS CORPORATION (HENAAC) http://www.henaac.org

HISPANIC ENGINEER NATIONAL ACHIEVEMENT AWARDS CORPORATION SCHOLARSHIP PROGRAM
• *See page 116*

INNOVATION AND SCIENCE COUNCIL OF BRITISH COLUMBIA http://www.bcinnovationcouncil.com

PAUL AND HELEN TRUSSEL SCIENCE AND TECHNOLOGY SCHOLARSHIP
• *See page 87*

INTERNATIONAL COMMUNICATIONS INDUSTRIES FOUNDATION http://www.infocomm.org/scholarships

ICIF SCHOLARSHIP FOR DEPENDENTS OF MEMBER ORGANIZATIONS
• *See page 179*

INTERNATIONAL COMMUNICATIONS INDUSTRIES FOUNDATION AV SCHOLARSHIP
• *See page 180*

LOS ANGELES COUNCIL OF BLACK PROFESSIONAL ENGINEERS http://www.lablackengineers.org

AL-BEN SCHOLARSHIP FOR ACADEMIC INCENTIVE
• *See page 159*

AL-BEN SCHOLARSHIP FOR PROFESSIONAL MERIT
• *See page 159*

AL-BEN SCHOLARSHIP FOR SCHOLASTIC ACHIEVEMENT
• *See page 159*

MARYLAND ASSOCIATION OF PRIVATE COLLEGES AND CAREER SCHOOLS http://www.mapccs.org

MARYLAND ASSOCIATION OF PRIVATE COLLEGES AND CAREER SCHOOLS SCHOLARSHIP
• *See page 146*

MICRON TECHNOLOGY FOUNDATION INC. http://www.micron.com/scholars

MICRON SCIENCE AND TECHNOLOGY SCHOLARS PROGRAM
• *See page 160*

MICROSOFT CORPORATION http://www.microsoft.com

YOU CAN MAKE A DIFFERENCE SCHOLARSHIP

Scholarship for high school students who want make an impact with technology. All students who submit proposals will receive a free copy of Microsoft Visual Studio NET Academic Edition.

Academic Fields/Career Goals: Computer Science/Data Processing.

Award: Scholarship for use in freshman year; not renewable. *Number:* 10. *Amount:* $5000.

Eligibility Requirements: Applicant must be high school student and planning to enroll or expecting to enroll full- or part-time at a four-year institution or university. Available to U.S. citizens.

Application Requirements: Application, transcript. *Deadline:* April 30.

Contact: Scholarship Committee
Microsoft Corporation
One Microsoft Way
Redmond, WA 98052-6399
Phone: 800-642-7676
Fax: 425-936-7329
E-mail: award-info@microsoft.com

NASA IDAHO SPACE GRANT CONSORTIUM http://isgc.uidaho.edu

NASA IDAHO SPACE GRANT CONSORTIUM SCHOLARSHIP PROGRAM
• *See page 87*

NASA/MARYLAND SPACE GRANT CONSORTIUM http://www.mdspacegrant.org

NASA MARYLAND SPACE GRANT CONSORTIUM UNDERGRADUATE SCHOLARSHIPS
• *See page 118*

NASA MONTANA SPACE GRANT CONSORTIUM http://www.spacegrant.montana.edu

MONTANA SPACE GRANT SCHOLARSHIP PROGRAM
• *See page 119*

NASA NEVADA SPACE GRANT CONSORTIUM http://www.unr.edu/spacegrant

UNIVERSITY AND COMMUNITY COLLEGE SYSTEM OF NEVADA NASA SPACE GRANT AND FELLOWSHIP PROGRAM
• *See page 119*

NASA VERMONT SPACE GRANT CONSORTIUM http://www.cems.uvm.edu/VSGC

VERMONT SPACE GRANT CONSORTIUM SCHOLARSHIP PROGRAM
• *See page 88*

NASA WEST VIRGINIA SPACE GRANT CONSORTIUM http://www.nasa.wvu.edu

WEST VIRGINIA SPACE GRANT CONSORTIUM UNDERGRADUATE FELLOWSHIP PROGRAM
• *See page 121*

NATIONAL ASSOCIATION FOR THE ADVANCEMENT OF COLORED PEOPLE http://www.naacp.org

LOUIS STOKES SCIENCE AND TECHNOLOGY AWARD
• *See page 133*

NATIONAL ASSOCIATION OF WATER COMPANIES-NEW JERSEY CHAPTER

NATIONAL ASSOCIATION OF WATER COMPANIES-NEW JERSEY CHAPTER SCHOLARSHIP
• *See page 133*

NATIONAL FEDERATION OF THE BLIND http://www.nfb.org

NATIONAL FEDERATION OF THE BLIND COMPUTER SCIENCE SCHOLARSHIP

One-time award for students who are legally blind and studying computer science. Must submit recommendation from state officer of NFB. Awards based on financial need, and community service. Must attend school in United States.

Academic Fields/Career Goals: Computer Science/Data Processing.

Award: Scholarship for use in freshman, sophomore, junior, or senior years; not renewable. *Number:* 1. *Amount:* $3000.

Eligibility Requirements: Applicant must be enrolled or expecting to enroll full-time at a four-year institution or university. Applicant or parent of applicant must have employment or volunteer experience in community service. Applicant must be visually impaired. Applicant must have 3.5 GPA or higher. Available to U.S. and non-U.S. citizens.

Application Requirements: Application, autobiography, essay, financial need analysis, references, transcript, letter from state officer of NFB. *Deadline:* March 31.

Contact: Anil Lewis, Chairman, Scholarship Committee
National Federation of the Blind
315 West Ponce De Leon Avenue
Decatur, GA 30030
Phone: 404-371-1000
E-mail: alewis@nfbga.org

NATIONAL INVENTORS HALL OF FAME http://www.invent.org

COLLEGIATE INVENTORS COMPETITION FOR UNDERGRADUATE STUDENTS
• *See page 88*

COLLEGIATE INVENTORS COMPETITION-GRAND PRIZE
• *See page 88*

NATIONAL SCIENCE TEACHERS ASSOCIATION http://www.nsta.org

TOSHIBA/NSTA EXPLORAVISION AWARDS PROGRAM

A competition for all students in grades K-12 attending a public, private or home school in the United States, Canada, or U.S. Territories. It is designed to encourage students to combine their imagination with their knowledge of science and technology to explore visions of the future.

Academic Fields/Career Goals: Computer Science/Data Processing; Engineering/Technology; Nuclear Science; Physical Sciences and Math.

Award: Prize for use in freshman year; not renewable. *Number:* 16–32. *Amount:* $5000–$10,000.

Eligibility Requirements: Applicant must be high school student; age 21 or under and planning to enroll or expecting to enroll full-time at a two-year or four-year or technical institution or university. Available to U.S. and Canadian citizens.

National Science Teachers Association (continued)

Application Requirements: Application, applicant must enter a contest, essay, project description, bibliography, 5 Web page graphics, abstract. *Deadline:* January 29.

Contact: Award Program Coordinator
National Science Teachers Association
1840 Wilson Boulevard
Arlington, VA 22201
Phone: 800-397-5679
Fax: 703-243-7177
E-mail: exploravision@nsta.org

NATIONAL SECURITY AGENCY http://www.nsa.gov

NATIONAL SECURITY AGENCY STOKES EDUCATIONAL SCHOLARSHIP PROGRAM

Renewable awards for high school students planning to attend a four-year undergraduate institution to study foreign languages, computer science, math, electrical engineering, or computer engineering. Must be at least 16 to apply. Must be a U.S. citizen. Minimum 3.0 GPA required, and minimum SAT score of 1100. For application visit Web site: http://www.nsa.gov/programs/employ/index.html.

Academic Fields/Career Goals: Computer Science/Data Processing; Electrical Engineering/Electronics; Foreign Language; Mathematics.

Award: Scholarship for use in freshman year; renewable. *Number:* 10–30. *Amount:* varies.

Eligibility Requirements: Applicant must be high school student; age 16 and over and planning to enroll or expecting to enroll full-time at a four-year institution or university. Applicant must have 3.0 GPA or higher. Available to U.S. citizens.

Application Requirements: Application, essay, interview, resume, references, test scores, transcript. *Deadline:* November 30.

Contact: Ceil O'Connor, Program Manager
National Security Agency
9800 Savage Road, Suite 6779
Fort Meade, MD 20755-6779
Phone: 866-672-4473
Fax: 410-854-3002
E-mail: cmoconn@nsa.gov

OREGON STUDENT ASSISTANCE COMMISSION http://www.osac.state.or.us

MENTOR GRAPHICS SCHOLARSHIP

One-time award for computer science, computer engineering, or electrical engineering majors entering junior or senior year at a four-year institution. Preference for one award to female, African-American, Native American, or Hispanic applicant.

Academic Fields/Career Goals: Computer Science/Data Processing; Electrical Engineering/Electronics.

Award: Scholarship for use in junior or senior years; not renewable. *Number:* varies. *Amount:* varies.

Eligibility Requirements: Applicant must be enrolled or expecting to enroll full-time at a four-year institution and resident of Oregon. Available to U.S. citizens.

Application Requirements: Application, essay, financial need analysis, references, transcript, activity chart. *Deadline:* March 1.

Contact: Director of Grant Programs
Oregon Student Assistance Commission
1500 Valley River Drive, Suite 100
Eugene, OR 97401-7020
Phone: 800-452-8807 Ext. 7395

ROBERT H. MOLLOHAN FAMILY CHARITABLE FOUNDATION INC. http://www.mollohanfoundation.org

HIGH TECHNOLOGY SCHOLARS PROGRAM

• *See page 135*

ROYAL BANK NATIVE STUDENTS AWARDS PROGRAM http://www.rbc.com

ROYAL BANK ABORIGINAL STUDENT AWARDS

• *See page 148*

SAN DIEGO FOUNDATION http://www.sdfoundation.org

ENERGY OF ACHIEVEMENT SDG&E SCHOLARSHIP

• *See page 148*

SOCIETY OF FLIGHT TEST ENGINEERS http://www.sfte.org

SOCIETY OF FLIGHT TEST ENGINEERS SCHOLARSHIP

Scholarship for son or daughter of member of Society of Flight Test Engineers in good standing or a student member in good standing. Applicant shall be pursuing his or her first undergraduate degree majoring in engineering, computer sciences, mathematics, physics or other technical discipline. Scholarship value varies.

Academic Fields/Career Goals: Computer Science/Data Processing; Engineering/Technology; Mathematics; Physical Sciences and Math.

Award: Scholarship for use in freshman, sophomore, junior, or senior years; not renewable. *Amount:* varies.

Eligibility Requirements: Applicant must be enrolled or expecting to enroll full-time at a four-year institution or university. Applicant or parent of applicant must be member of Society of Flight Test Engineers. Available to U.S. and non-U.S. citizens.

Application Requirements: Application, references, transcript. *Deadline:* July 1.

Contact: Margaret Drury, Executive Director
Society of Flight Test Engineers
44814 North Elm Avenue
Lancaster, CA 93534
Phone: 661-949-2095
Fax: 661-949-2096
E-mail: sfte@sfte.org

SOCIETY OF HISPANIC PROFESSIONAL ENGINEERS FOUNDATION http://www.henaac.org

HENAAC SCHOLARS PROGRAM

Applicants must be student leaders majoring in engineering, math, computer science, or material science. Must be of Hispanic origin and/or significantly participate in and promote organizations and activates in the Hispanic Community.

Academic Fields/Career Goals: Computer Science/Data Processing; Engineering-Related Technologies; Materials Science, Engineering, and Metallurgy; Mathematics.

Award: Scholarship for use in freshman, sophomore, junior, senior, or graduate years; renewable. *Number:* up to 87. *Amount:* $500–$5000.

Eligibility Requirements: Applicant must be Hispanic; enrolled or expecting to enroll full-time at a four-year institution or university and must have an interest in leadership. Applicant must have 3.0 GPA or higher. Available to U.S. and non-U.S. citizens.

Application Requirements: Application, essay, resume, references, transcript. *Deadline:* April 30.

Contact: Kathy Borunda Barrera, Manager, Scholars Program
Society of Hispanic Professional Engineers Foundation
3900 Whiteside Street
Los Angeles, CA 90063
Phone: 323-262-0997
Fax: 323-262-0947
E-mail: kathy@henaac.org

SOCIETY OF WOMEN ENGINEERS http://www.swe.org

AGILENT MENTORING SCHOLARSHIP

One $1000 scholarship for undergraduate sophomore or junior studying biological engineering, computer engineering, computer science, electrical engineering, or mechanical engineering.

Academic Fields/Career Goals: Computer Science/Data Processing; Electrical Engineering/Electronics; Engineering/Technology; Mechanical Engineering.

Award: Scholarship for use in sophomore or junior years; not renewable. *Number:* 1. *Amount:* $1000.

Eligibility Requirements: Applicant must be enrolled or expecting to enroll full-time at a four-year institution or university and female. Applicant must have 3.0 GPA or higher. Available to U.S. citizens.

Application Requirements: Application. *Deadline:* February 1.

Contact: Scholarship Committee
Society of Women Engineers
230 East Ohio Street, Suite 400
Chicago, IL 60611-3265
Phone: 312-596-5223
Fax: 312-596-5252
E-mail: scholarshipapplication@swe.org

DELL COMPUTER CORPORATION SCHOLARSHIPS

Awarded to entering female juniors and seniors majoring in computer science, computer engineering, electrical engineering, or mechanical engineering who demonstrate financial need and maintain a minimum 3.0 GPA.

Academic Fields/Career Goals: Computer Science/Data Processing; Electrical Engineering/Electronics; Engineering/Technology; Mechanical Engineering.

Award: Scholarship for use in junior or senior years; not renewable. *Number:* 2. *Amount:* $2250.

Eligibility Requirements: Applicant must be enrolled or expecting to enroll full-time at a four-year institution or university and female. Applicant must have 3.0 GPA or higher. Available to U.S. citizens.

Application Requirements: Application, essay, financial need analysis, references, self-addressed stamped envelope, test scores, transcript. *Deadline:* February 1.

Contact: Scholarship Committee
Society of Women Engineers
230 East Ohio Street, Suite 400
Chicago, IL 60611-3265
Phone: 312-596-5223
Fax: 312-596-5252
E-mail: scholarshipapplication@swe.org

GUIDANT CORPORATION SCHOLARSHIP

Two $5000 scholarships available to undergraduate seniors majoring in chemical engineering, computer engineering, computer science, electrical engineering, industrial engineering, mechanical engineering, manufacturing engineering, or materials science and engineering.

Academic Fields/Career Goals: Computer Science/Data Processing; Electrical Engineering/Electronics; Engineering/Technology; Engineering-Related Technologies; Materials Science, Engineering, and Metallurgy; Mechanical Engineering.

Award: Scholarship for use in senior year; not renewable. *Number:* 2. *Amount:* $5000.

Eligibility Requirements: Applicant must be enrolled or expecting to enroll full-time at a four-year institution or university and female. Applicant must have 3.0 GPA or higher. Available to U.S. citizens.

Application Requirements: Application, references, transcript. *Deadline:* February 1.

Contact: Scholarship Committee
Society of Women Engineers
230 East Ohio Street, Suite 400
Chicago, IL 60611-3265
Phone: 312-596-5223
Fax: 312-596-5252
E-mail: scholarshipapplication@swe.org

LYDIA I. PICKUP MEMORIAL SCHOLARSHIP

Available to female sophomore, junior, or senior undergraduate student or graduate student. For advance career in engineering or computer science. Minimum 3.0 GPA required.

Academic Fields/Career Goals: Computer Science/Data Processing; Engineering/Technology.

Award: Scholarship for use in sophomore, junior, senior, or graduate years; not renewable. *Number:* 1. *Amount:* $4000.

Eligibility Requirements: Applicant must be enrolled or expecting to enroll full- or part-time at a four-year institution or university and female. Applicant must have 3.0 GPA or higher. Available to U.S. citizens.

Application Requirements: Application, references, self-addressed stamped envelope, transcript. *Deadline:* February 1.

Contact: Scholarship Committee
Society of Women Engineers
230 East Ohio Street, Suite 400
Chicago, IL 60611-3265
Phone: 312-596-5223
Fax: 312-596-5252
E-mail: scholarshipapplication@swe.org

MICROSOFT CORPORATION SCHOLARSHIPS

Scholarships of $2500 for female computer engineering or computer science students in sophomore, junior, or senior year; or first year master's degree students. GPA of 3.5 or above required.

Academic Fields/Career Goals: Computer Science/Data Processing.

Award: Scholarship for use in sophomore, junior, senior, or graduate years; renewable. *Number:* 2. *Amount:* $2500.

Eligibility Requirements: Applicant must be enrolled or expecting to enroll full-time at a four-year institution or university and female. Applicant must have 3.5 GPA or higher. Available to U.S. citizens.

Application Requirements: Application, essay, references, test scores, transcript. *Deadline:* February 1.

Contact: Scholarship Committee
Society of Women Engineers
230 East Ohio Street, Suite 400
Chicago, IL 60611-3265
Phone: 312-596-5223
Fax: 312-596-5252
E-mail: scholarshipapplication@swe.org

NORTHROP GRUMMAN FRESHMAN SCHOLARSHIP

• *See page 125*

ROCKWELL AUTOMATION SCHOLARSHIP

Two awards of $2500 for a junior or senior with a GPA of 3.0 in computer engineering, electrical engineering, industrial engineering, mechanical engineering or software engineering. Must have demonstrated leadership potential. Underrepresented groups preferred.

Academic Fields/Career Goals: Computer Science/Data Processing; Electrical Engineering/Electronics; Engineering/Technology; Mechanical Engineering.

Award: Scholarship for use in junior or senior years; not renewable. *Number:* 2. *Amount:* $2500.

Eligibility Requirements: Applicant must be enrolled or expecting to enroll full-time at a four-year institution or university; female and must have an interest in leadership. Applicant must have 3.0 GPA or higher. Available to U.S. citizens.

Application Requirements: Application, references, self-addressed stamped envelope, transcript. *Deadline:* February 1.

Contact: Scholarship Committee
Society of Women Engineers
230 East Ohio Street, Suite 400
Chicago, IL 60611-3265
Phone: 312-596-5223
Fax: 312-596-5252
E-mail: scholarshipapplication@swe.org

SWE BATON ROUGE SECTION SCHOLARSHIPS

Scholarship of $1000 available to female applicants who plan to attend the college in fall semester engineering or computer science. Only for full-time study.

Academic Fields/Career Goals: Computer Science/Data Processing; Engineering/Technology.

Award: Scholarship for use in freshman year; not renewable. *Number:* 6–7. *Amount:* $1000.

Eligibility Requirements: Applicant must be enrolled or expecting to enroll full-time at a four-year institution or university; female and resident of Louisiana. Available to U.S. citizens.

Society of Women Engineers (continued)

Application Requirements: Application, test scores, transcript. *Deadline:* April 21.

Contact: Scholarship Committee
Society of Women Engineers
230 East Ohio Street, Suite 400
Chicago, IL 60611-3265
Phone: 312-596-5223
Fax: 312-596-5252
E-mail: scholarshipapplication@swe.org

SWE CALIFORNIA GOLDEN GATE SECTION SCHOLARSHIPS

Scholarships awarded to female entering freshmen pursuing degrees in engineering, computer science, physical science, or mathematics. Applicants must be attending high school, or living within the boundaries of the Golden Gate Section.

Academic Fields/Career Goals: Computer Science/Data Processing; Engineering/Technology; Physical Sciences and Math.

Award: Scholarship for use in freshman year; not renewable. *Number:* 10–15. *Amount:* $1000.

Eligibility Requirements: Applicant must be enrolled or expecting to enroll full-time at a four-year institution or university; female and resident of California. Available to U.S. citizens.

Application Requirements: Application, essay, references, transcript. *Deadline:* April 13.

Contact: Lisa M. Duncan, Scholarship Chair
Society of Women Engineers
2625 Alcatraz Avenue, PO Box 356
Berkeley, CA 94705
Phone: 510-242-2554

SWE CONNECTICUT SECTION JEAN R. BEERS SCHOLARSHIP

Tuition-based annual scholarship program for qualified female students attending school in Oregon living within the boundaries of the Connecticut Section. Amount of $1500 for entering sophomore, junior, or senior student. The number of scholarships offered depends upon the amount of donations received and the number of qualified applicants.

Academic Fields/Career Goals: Computer Science/Data Processing; Engineering/Technology; Physical Sciences and Math.

Award: Scholarship for use in sophomore, junior, or senior years; not renewable. *Number:* varies. *Amount:* $1500.

Eligibility Requirements: Applicant must be enrolled or expecting to enroll full- or part-time at a four-year institution or university; female and resident of Connecticut. Available to U.S. citizens.

Application Requirements: Application, essay, financial need analysis. *Deadline:* January 31.

Contact: Scholarship Committee
Society of Women Engineers
230 East Ohio Street, Suite 400
Chicago, IL 60611-3265
Phone: 312-596-5223
Fax: 312-596-5252
E-mail: scholarshipapplication@swe.org

SWE GREATER NEW ORLEANS SECTION SCHOLARSHIP

Scholarships available to women pursuing baccalaureate or graduate degree in an ABET-accredited or SWE-approved schools for engineering, or CSAB/ABET accredited schools, or SWE approved schools for computer science. Available to students from the following parishes: Jefferson, Lafourche, Orleans, Plaquemines, St. Bernard, St. Charles, St. James, St. John, St. Tammany, Tangipahoa, or Terrebonne.

Academic Fields/Career Goals: Computer Science/Data Processing; Engineering/Technology.

Award: Scholarship for use in freshman, sophomore, junior, senior, or graduate years; not renewable. *Number:* 1. *Amount:* varies.

Eligibility Requirements: Applicant must be enrolled or expecting to enroll full-time at a four-year institution or university; female and resident of Louisiana. Available to U.S. citizens.

Application Requirements: Application. *Deadline:* March 31.

Contact: Scholarship Committee
Society of Women Engineers
230 East Ohio Street, Suite 400
Chicago, IL 60611-3265
Phone: 312-596-5223
Fax: 312-596-5252
E-mail: scholarshipapplication@swe.org

SOCIETY OF WOMEN ENGINEERS-DALLAS SECTION http://www.dallaswe.org

NATIONAL SOCIETY OF WOMEN ENGINEERS SCHOLARSHIPS

Provides financial assistance to women admitted to accredited baccalaureate or graduate programs, in preparation for careers in engineering, engineering technology, and computer science. Minimum GPA of 3.5 for freshman applicants and 3.0 for sophomore, junior, senior, and graduate applicants.

Academic Fields/Career Goals: Computer Science/Data Processing; Engineering/Technology.

Award: Scholarship for use in freshman, sophomore, junior, senior, or graduate years; not renewable. *Number:* varies. *Amount:* $1000–$10,000.

Eligibility Requirements: Applicant must be enrolled or expecting to enroll full-time at a four-year institution or university and female. Applicant must have 3.5 GPA or higher. Available to U.S. and non-U.S. citizens.

Application Requirements: Application, essay, references, transcript, letter of acceptance from the accredited college or university. *Deadline:* May 15.

Contact: Scholarship Selection Committee
Society of Women Engineers-Dallas Section
230 East Ohio Street, Suite 400
Chicago, IL 60611-3265
Phone: 312-596-5223
E-mail: scholarshipapplication@swe.org

SOCIETY OF WOMEN ENGINEERS-ROCKY MOUNTAIN SECTION http://www.swe-rms.org

SOCIETY OF WOMEN ENGINEERS-ROCKY MOUNTAIN SECTION SCHOLARSHIP PROGRAM

• *See page 164*

SOCIETY OF WOMEN ENGINEERS-TWIN TIERS SECTION http://www.swetwintiers.org

SOCIETY OF WOMEN ENGINEERS-TWIN TIERS SECTION SCHOLARSHIP

Scholarship available to female students who reside or attend school in the Twin Tiers SWE section of New York. This is limited to zip codes that begin with 148, 149, 169 and residents of Bradford County, Pennsylvania. Applicant must be accepted or enrolled in an undergraduate degree program in engineering or computer science at an ABET-, CSAB- or SWE-accredited school.

Academic Fields/Career Goals: Computer Science/Data Processing; Engineering/Technology.

Award: Scholarship for use in freshman year; not renewable. *Number:* 6. *Amount:* $1500.

Eligibility Requirements: Applicant must be high school student; planning to enroll or expecting to enroll full-time at a four-year institution or university; female and resident of New York or Pennsylvania. Available to U.S. citizens.

Application Requirements: Application, essay, resume, references, self-addressed stamped envelope, transcript, letter of acceptance, personal information, and achievements. *Deadline:* March 30.

Contact: Amy Litwiler, Scholarship Chair
Society of Women Engineers-Twin Tiers Section
PO Box 798
Corning, NY 14830
Phone: 607-974-6261
E-mail: litwilerak@corning.com

SOUTH DAKOTA RETAILERS ASSOCIATION http://www.sdra.org

SOUTH DAKOTA RETAILERS ASSOCIATION SCHOLARSHIP PROGRAM

• See page 64

TEXAS DEPARTMENT OF TRANSPORTATION http://www.txdot.gov

CONDITIONAL GRANT PROGRAM

• See page 173

UNITED DAUGHTERS OF THE CONFEDERACY http://www.hqudc.org

WALTER REED SMITH SCHOLARSHIP

• See page 149

UNITED NEGRO COLLEGE FUND http://www.uncf.org

ACCENTURE SCHOLARSHIP

Scholarship of $2000 to undergraduate sophomore and junior with the GPA of 3.0 or higher. Applicant must be majoring in engineering or computer science, enrolled at one of the following schools: Morehouse College, Spelman College. Please visit Web site for more information: http://www.uncf.org.

Academic Fields/Career Goals: Computer Science/Data Processing; Engineering/Technology.

Award: Scholarship for use in sophomore or junior years; not renewable. *Number:* 5. *Amount:* $2000.

Eligibility Requirements: Applicant must be Black (non-Hispanic); enrolled or expecting to enroll full-time at a four-year institution or university and studying in Georgia. Applicant must have 3.0 GPA or higher. Available to U.S. citizens.

Application Requirements: Application, financial need analysis, FAFSA, Student Aid Report (SAR). *Deadline:* varies.

Contact: William Dunham, Program Services
United Negro College Fund
8260 Willow Oaks Corporate Drive
Fairfax, VA 22031
Phone: 703-205-3486

BOOZ, ALLEN AND HAMILTON/WILLIAM F. STASIOR INTERNSHIP

• See page 150

CARDINAL HEALTH SCHOLARSHIP

• See page 65

CARGILL SCHOLARSHIP PROGRAM

• See page 65

CDM SCHOLARSHIP/INTERNSHIP

• See page 93

CISCO/UNCF SCHOLARS PROGRAM

Scholarship provides financial support for African-American electrical engineering or computer science majors, attending specific UNCF member college or university with a special focus on women and students who demonstrate community service. Minimum 3.2 GPA required. Prospective applicants should complete the Student Profile found at Web site: http://www.uncf.org.

Academic Fields/Career Goals: Computer Science/Data Processing; Electrical Engineering/Electronics.

Award: Scholarship for use in sophomore year; not renewable. *Number:* 1. *Amount:* $4000.

Eligibility Requirements: Applicant must be Black (non-Hispanic) and enrolled or expecting to enroll full-time at a four-year institution or university. Available to U.S. and non-U.S. citizens.

Application Requirements: Application, financial need analysis. *Deadline:* April 15.

Contact: Director, Program Services
United Negro College Fund
8260 Willow Oaks Corporate Drive
PO Box 10444
Fairfax, VA 22031-8044
Phone: 800-331-2244
E-mail: rebecca.bennett@uncf.org

FLOWERS INDUSTRIES SCHOLARSHIP

• See page 150

FORD/UNCF CORPORATE SCHOLARS PROGRAM

• See page 65

KODAK ENGINEERING EXCELLENCE PROGRAM SCHOLARSHIP

Scholarship of $9000 for engineering or computer science majors attending a UNCF member college or university. For both full-time and part-time study. Minimum 3.0 GPA required.

Academic Fields/Career Goals: Computer Science/Data Processing; Engineering/Technology.

Award: Scholarship for use in junior year; not renewable. *Number:* varies. *Amount:* $9000.

Eligibility Requirements: Applicant must be Black (non-Hispanic) and enrolled or expecting to enroll full- or part-time at a four-year institution or university. Applicant must have 3.0 GPA or higher. Available to U.S. and non-U.S. citizens.

Application Requirements: Application, financial need analysis, photo, resume, references, transcript. *Deadline:* November 15.

Contact: Director, Program Services
United Negro College Fund
8260 Willow Oaks Corporate Drive
PO Box 10444
Fairfax, VA 22031-8044
Phone: 800-331-2244
E-mail: rebecca.bennett@uncf.org

MAYTAG COMPANY SCHOLARSHIP

• See page 151

NASCAR/WENDELL SCOTT, SR. SCHOLARSHIP

• See page 66

NORTHEAST UTILITIES SYSTEM SCHOLARSHIP PROGRAM

• See page 151

PRINCIPAL FINANCIAL GROUP SCHOLARSHIPS

• See page 66

SPRINT NEXTEL SCHOLARSHIP/INTERNSHIP

• See page 66

THURMOND WOODARD/DELL/UNCF CORPORATE SCHOLARS PROGRAM

• See page 151

TOYOTA SCHOLARSHIP

• See page 66

TRW INFORMATION TECHNOLOGY MINORITY SCHOLARSHIP

Award for sophomore and junior minority college students majoring in engineering, computer science, and other information sciences at Howard University, George Mason University, Morgan State, Virginia Polytechnic Institute, or Pennsylvania State. Must have 3.0 GPA. Please visit Web site for more information: http://www.uncf.org.

Academic Fields/Career Goals: Computer Science/Data Processing; Engineering/Technology.

Award: Scholarship for use in sophomore or junior years; renewable. *Number:* varies. *Amount:* $3000.

Eligibility Requirements: Applicant must be Black (non-Hispanic) and enrolled or expecting to enroll full- or part-time at a four-year institution or university. Applicant must have 3.0 GPA or higher. Available to U.S. and non-U.S. citizens.

Application Requirements: Application, financial need analysis, FAFSA, Student Aid Report (SAR). *Deadline:* varies.

Contact: Director, Program Services
United Negro College Fund
8260 Willow Oaks Corporate Drive
PO Box 10444
Fairfax, VA 22031-8044
Phone: 800-331-2244
E-mail: rebecca.bennett@uncf.org

United Negro College Fund (continued)

UPS/UNCF CORPORATE SCHOLARS PROGRAM

• *See page 151*

USENIX ASSOCIATION SCHOLARSHIP

Applicants should be majors in computer science, or information systems. Must have 3.5 GPA to qualify. Funds may be used for tuition, room/board, books, or to repay federal student loans. For use in UNCF member colleges and universities only.

Academic Fields/Career Goals: Computer Science/Data Processing.

Award: Scholarship for use in freshman, sophomore, junior, senior, or graduate years; not renewable. *Number:* varies. *Amount:* up to $10,000.

Eligibility Requirements: Applicant must be Black (non-Hispanic) and enrolled or expecting to enroll full- or part-time at a four-year institution or university. Applicant must have 3.5 GPA or higher. Available to U.S. and non-U.S. citizens.

Application Requirements: Application, financial need analysis. *Deadline:* continuous.

Contact: Director, Program Services
United Negro College Fund
8260 Willow Oaks Corporate Drive
PO Box 10444
Fairfax, VA 22031-8044
Phone: 800-331-2244
E-mail: rebecca.bennett@uncf.org

WELLS FARGO/UNCF SCHOLARSHIP FUND

• *See page 67*

VIRGINIA BUSINESS AND PROFESSIONAL WOMEN'S FOUNDATION http://www.vabpwfoundation.org

WOMEN IN SCIENCE AND TECHNOLOGY SCHOLARSHIP

• *See page 136*

WOMEN IN FEDERAL LAW ENFORCEMENT http://www.wifle.org

WIFLE SCHOLARSHIP PROGRAM

Scholarship to encourage women to pursue a career in federal law enforcement. Applicant must be enrolled in, or be transferring to, a four-year program in criminal justice, social sciences, public administration, chemistry, physics, computer science, and have a GPA of 3.0. May also be in a graduate program. Must demonstrate commitment to the community through volunteer community service or an internship in a law enforcement agency. Must be a United States citizen.

Academic Fields/Career Goals: Computer Science/Data Processing; Law Enforcement/Police Administration; Physical Sciences and Math; Public Policy and Administration; Social Sciences.

Award: Scholarship for use in sophomore, junior, senior, graduate, or postgraduate years; renewable. *Number:* varies. *Amount:* $500–$2500.

Eligibility Requirements: Applicant must be enrolled or expecting to enroll full-time at a four-year institution or university and female. Applicant or parent of applicant must have employment or volunteer experience in community service. Applicant must have 3.0 GPA or higher. Available to U.S. citizens.

Application Requirements: Application, essay, references, transcript. *Deadline:* May 1.

Contact: Ms. Monica Blodgett Rocchio, Deputy Executive Director
Women in Federal Law Enforcement
2200 Wilson Boulevard, Suite 102, PMB-204
Arlington, VA 22201-3324
Phone: 703-548-9211
Fax: 410-451-7373
E-mail: wifle@comcast.net

WYOMING TRUCKING ASSOCIATION

WYOMING TRUCKING ASSOCIATION TRUST FUND SCHOLARSHIP

• *See page 152*

XEROX http://www.xerox.com

TECHNICAL MINORITY SCHOLARSHIP

• *See page 165*

CONSTRUCTION ENGINEERING/ MANAGEMENT

AACE INTERNATIONAL http://www.aacei.org

AACE INTERNATIONAL COMPETITIVE SCHOLARSHIP

• *See page 89*

AMERICAN SOCIETY OF CIVIL ENGINEERS http://www.asce.org

CONSTRUCTION ENGINEERING SCHOLARSHIP

Scholarship for freshman, sophomore, junior, or first-year senior who is a Construction Institute (CI) student member and/or ASCE National Student Member in good standing at the time of application and award.

Academic Fields/Career Goals: Construction Engineering/Management.

Award: Scholarship for use in freshman, sophomore, junior, or senior years; renewable. *Number:* varies. *Amount:* varies.

Eligibility Requirements: Applicant must be enrolled or expecting to enroll full- or part-time at a four-year institution or university. Applicant or parent of applicant must be member of American Society of Civil Engineers. Available to U.S. citizens.

Application Requirements: Application, financial need analysis, resume, references, transcript, annual budget. *Deadline:* April 1.

Contact: Construction Scholarship
American Society of Civil Engineers
1801 Alexander Bell Drive
Reston, VA 20191-4400

SAMUEL FLETCHER TAPMAN ASCE STUDENT CHAPTER/CLUB SCHOLARSHIP

• *See page 168*

ASSOCIATED BUILDERS AND CONTRACTORS SCHOLARSHIP PROGRAM http://www.abc.org

TRIMMER EDUCATION FOUNDATION SCHOLARSHIPS FOR CONSTRUCTION MANAGEMENT

Scholarships are available to students in a major related to the construction industry. Applicants must be enrolled at an educational institution with an ABC student chapter. Architecture and most engineering programs are excluded, as there are other funds available for these areas. Applicants must have a minimum overall GPA of 2.85. Visit Web site: http://www.abc.org.

Academic Fields/Career Goals: Construction Engineering/Management.

Award: Scholarship for use in sophomore, junior, or senior years; not renewable. *Number:* 10–15. *Amount:* up to $5000.

Eligibility Requirements: Applicant must be enrolled or expecting to enroll full-time at a two-year or four-year institution or university. Available to U.S. citizens.

Application Requirements: Application, essay, financial need analysis, references, transcript. *Deadline:* May 23.

Contact: John Strock, Director, Career and Constructions
Associated Builders and Contractors Scholarship Program
4250 North Fairfax Drive, Ninth Floor
Arlington, VA 22203-1607
Phone: 703-812-2008
Fax: 703-812-8234
E-mail: strock@abc.org

ASSOCIATED GENERAL CONTRACTORS EDUCATION AND RESEARCH FOUNDATION http://www.agcfoundation.org

AGC EDUCATION AND RESEARCH FOUNDATION GRADUATE SCHOLARSHIPS

College seniors enrolled in, or others possessing a degree in, an undergraduate construction management or construction-related engineering program, are eligible to apply. Applicant must be enrolled or planning to enroll in a graduate level construction management or construction-related engineering degree program as a full-time student.

Academic Fields/Career Goals: Construction Engineering/Management.

Award: Scholarship for use in senior or graduate years; not renewable. *Number:* 2. *Amount:* $7500.

Eligibility Requirements: Applicant must be enrolled or expecting to enroll full-time at a four-year institution or university. Available to U.S. citizens.

Application Requirements: Application, essay, financial need analysis, transcript. *Deadline:* November 1.

Contact: Floretta Slade, Director of Programs
Associated General Contractors Education and Research Foundation
2300 Wilson Boulevard, Suite 400
Arlington, VA 22201
Phone: 703-837-5342
Fax: 703-837-5451
E-mail: sladef@agc.org

AGC EDUCATION AND RESEARCH FOUNDATION UNDERGRADUATE SCHOLARSHIPS

• *See page 169*

COLORADO CONTRACTORS ASSOCIATION INC. http://www.coloradocontractors.org

CCA SCHOLARSHIP PROGRAM

Scholarships of $2500 for junior and senior students who are interested in pursuing a career in heavy-highway-municipal-utility construction. Scholarships are only awarded to students who attend the following institutions: Colorado School of Mines, Colorado State University–Fort Collins, Colorado State University–Pueblo.

Academic Fields/Career Goals: Construction Engineering/Management.

Award: Scholarship for use in junior or senior years; not renewable. *Number:* varies. *Amount:* $2500.

Eligibility Requirements: Applicant must be enrolled or expecting to enroll full- or part-time at a four-year institution or university. Available to U.S. citizens.

Application Requirements: Application. *Deadline:* varies.

Contact: Scholarship Program Coordinator
Colorado Contractors Association Inc.
6880 South Yosemite Court, Suite 200
Centennial, CO 80112-1421
Phone: 290-290-6611
Fax: 290-290-9141
E-mail: info@coloradocontractors.org

ELECTROCHEMICAL SOCIETY INC. http://www.electrochem.org

H.H. DOW MEMORIAL STUDENT ACHIEVEMENT AWARD OF THE INDUSTRIAL ELECTROLYSIS AND ELECTROCHEMICAL ENGINEERING DIVISION OF THE ELECTROCHEMICAL SOCIETY INC.

• *See page 131*

STUDENT ACHIEVEMENT AWARDS OF THE INDUSTRIAL ELECTROLYSIS AND ELECTROCHEMICAL ENGINEERING DIVISION OF THE ELECTROCHEMICAL SOCIETY INC.

• *See page 131*

STUDENT RESEARCH AWARDS OF THE BATTERY DIVISION OF THE ELECTROCHEMICAL SOCIETY INC.

• *See page 131*

FLORIDA EDUCATIONAL FACILITIES PLANNERS' ASSOCIATION http://www.fefpa.org

FEFPA ASSISTANTSHIP

• *See page 91*

FLORIDA ENGINEERING SOCIETY http://www.fleng.org

DAVID F. LUDOVICI SCHOLARSHIP

• *See page 170*

FECON SCHOLARSHIP

• *See page 170*

HISPANIC COLLEGE FUND INC. http://www.hispanicfund.org

EL NUEVO CONSTRUCTOR SCHOLARSHIP PROGRAM

• *See page 91*

MICHIGAN SOCIETY OF PROFESSIONAL ENGINEERS http://www.michiganspe.org

MICHIGAN SOCIETY OF PROFESSIONAL ENGINEERS AUXILIARY GRANT

• *See page 159*

MICHIGAN SOCIETY OF PROFESSIONAL ENGINEERS HARRY R. BALL, P.E. GRANT

• *See page 159*

MICHIGAN SOCIETY OF PROFESSIONAL ENGINEERS KENNETH B. FISHBECK, P.E. MEMORIAL GRANT

• *See page 160*

MICHIGAN SOCIETY OF PROFESSIONAL ENGINEERS 1980 NATIONAL SOCIETY OF PROFESSIONAL ENGINEERS ANNUAL MEETING COMMITTEE GRANT

• *See page 160*

MICHIGAN SOCIETY OF PROFESSIONAL ENGINEERS SCHOLARSHIP TRUST GRANT

• *See page 160*

MICHIGAN SOCIETY OF PROFESSIONAL ENGINEERS UNDESIGNATED GRANT

• *See page 160*

MSPE AUXILIARY GRANT FOR UNDERGRADUATE STUDY

• *See page 171*

ROBERT E. FOLMSBEE, P.E. MEMORIAL GRANT

Grant for a top-ranking student interested in pursuing a career in construction engineering. Preference given to a construction engineering student interested in general fields of construction engineering. Restricted to Michigan students attending Michigan postsecondary institutions. Must be a member of MSPE student chapter or a state member-at-large. Minimum 3.0 GPA required.

Academic Fields/Career Goals: Construction Engineering/Management.

Award: Grant for use in freshman, sophomore, junior, or senior years; not renewable. *Number:* 1. *Amount:* $1000–$1500.

Eligibility Requirements: Applicant must be enrolled or expecting to enroll full-time at a four-year institution or university; resident of Michigan and studying in Michigan. Applicant or parent of applicant must be member of Michigan Society of Professional Engineers. Applicant must have 3.0 GPA or higher. Available to U.S. citizens.

Application Requirements: Application, essay, references, test scores, transcript. *Deadline:* varies.

Contact: Maura Nessan, Executive Director
Michigan Society of Professional Engineers
215 North Walnut Street
PO Box 15276
Lansing, MI 48901-5276
Phone: 517-487-9388
Fax: 517-487-0635
E-mail: mspe@voyager.net

MIDWEST ROOFING CONTRACTORS ASSOCIATION http://www.mrca.org

MRCA FOUNDATION SCHOLARSHIP PROGRAM

• See page 171

NATIONAL ASPHALT PAVEMENT ASSOCIATION http://www.hotmix.org

NATIONAL ASPHALT PAVEMENT ASSOCIATION SCHOLARSHIP PROGRAM

• See page 172

UNITED NEGRO COLLEGE FUND http://www.uncf.org

CDM SCHOLARSHIP/INTERNSHIP

• See page 93

SPRINT NEXTEL SCHOLARSHIP/INTERNSHIP

• See page 66

COSMETOLOGY

AMERICAN ASSOCIATION OF COSMETOLOGY SCHOOLS http://www.beautyschools.org

NATIONAL COALITION OF ESTHETICIANS MANUFACTURES/ DISTRIBUTORS ASSOCIATION FIRST ESTHETICIAN SCHOLARSHIP

Scholarship of $1000 is available to students following an esthetician course of study. Applicants must be studying in a member school of American Association of Cosmetology Schools.

Academic Fields/Career Goals: Cosmetology.

Award: Scholarship for use in freshman or sophomore years; not renewable. *Number:* 4. *Amount:* $1000.

Eligibility Requirements: Applicant must be enrolled or expecting to enroll full-time at a two-year or four-year institution or university. Applicant must have 3.0 GPA or higher. Available to U.S. and non-U.S. citizens.

Application Requirements: Application, financial need analysis. *Deadline:* varies.

Contact: Chris Cox, Member Services Manager
American Association of Cosmetology Schools
15825 North 71st Street, Suite 100
Scottsdale, AZ 85254-1521
Phone: 800-831-1086 Ext. 116
Fax: 480-905-0993
E-mail: chris@beautyschools.org

AMERICAN HEALTH AND BEAUTY AIDS INSTITUTE http://www.ahbai.org

FRED LUSTER, SR. EDUCATION FOUNDATION SCHOLARSHIP FUND

Scholarship of $250 awarded to cosmetology students currently enrolled in, or accepted by, a state-approved cosmetic art training facility prior to applying for scholarship. Student must have completed initial 300 hours before funds are approved or disbursed to the facility.

Academic Fields/Career Goals: Cosmetology.

Award: Scholarship for use in senior year; not renewable. *Number:* varies. *Amount:* $250.

Eligibility Requirements: Applicant must be enrolled or expecting to enroll full-time at a four-year institution or university. Available to U.S. and non-U.S. citizens.

Application Requirements: Application, photo, references, transcript. *Deadline:* April 15.

Contact: Geri Jones, Executive Director
American Health and Beauty Aids Institute
PO Box 19510
Chicago, IL 60619-0510
Phone: 708-633-6328
Fax: 708-633-6329
E-mail: ahbai1@sbcglobal.net

JOE FRANCIS HAIRCARE SCHOLARSHIP FOUNDATION http://www.joefrancis.com

JOE FRANCIS HAIRCARE SCHOLARSHIP PROGRAM

Scholarships are awarded for $1000 each, with a minimum of seventeen scholarships awarded annually. Applicants are evaluated for their potential to successfully complete school, their financial need, and their commitment to a long-term career in cosmetology. Must be enrolled in school by fall of award year.

Academic Fields/Career Goals: Cosmetology.

Award: Scholarship for use in freshman or sophomore years; not renewable. *Number:* 18. *Amount:* $1000.

Eligibility Requirements: Applicant must be enrolled or expecting to enroll full- or part-time at a four-year institution. Available to U.S. and non-U.S. citizens.

Application Requirements: Application, essay, financial need analysis, references. *Deadline:* June 1.

Contact: Ms. Kim Larson, Secretary
Joe Francis Haircare Scholarship Foundation
PO Box 50625
Minneapolis, MN 55405
Phone: 651-769-1757
Fax: 651-459-8371
E-mail: mklarson@qwest.net

CRIMINAL JUSTICE/CRIMINOLOGY

ALBERTA HERITAGE SCHOLARSHIP FUND/ ALBERTA SCHOLARSHIP PROGRAMS http://www.alis.gov.ab.ca

ROBERT C. CARSON MEMORIAL BURSARY

Award of CAN$500 to provide financial assistance to aboriginal students who are Alberta residents and full-time students enrolled in the second year of law enforcement or criminal justice program. Must be attending and nomiated by one of the following qualifying Alberta institutions: Lethbridge Community College, Mount Royal College, Grant MacEwan College, the University of Calgary, or the University of Alberta.

Academic Fields/Career Goals: Criminal Justice/Criminology; Law Enforcement/Police Administration; Law/Legal Services.

Award: Scholarship for use in sophomore year; not renewable. *Number:* 5.

Eligibility Requirements: Applicant must be Canadian citizen; American Indian/Alaska Native; enrolled or expecting to enroll full-time at a two-year or four-year institution or university; resident of Alberta and studying in Alberta.

Application Requirements: Application, transcript. *Deadline:* October 1.

Contact: Scholarship Committee
Alberta Heritage Scholarship Fund/Alberta Scholarship Programs
9940 106th Street, Fourth Floor, Sterling Place
PO Box 28000, Station Main
Edmonton, AB T5J 4R4
Canada
Phone: 780-427-8640
Fax: 780-427-1288
E-mail: scholarships@gov.ab.ca

AMERICAN CRIMINAL JUSTICE ASSOCIATION-LAMBDA ALPHA EPSILON http://www.acjalae.org

AMERICAN CRIMINAL JUSTICE ASSOCIATION-LAMBDA ALPHA EPSILON NATIONAL SCHOLARSHIP

Awarded only to members of the American Criminal Justice Association. One-time award of $100 to $400. Members may reapply each year. Must have minimum 3.0 GPA. Must pursue studies in law/legal services, criminal justice/law, or the social sciences.

Academic Fields/Career Goals: Criminal Justice/Criminology; Law/Legal Services; Social Sciences.

Award: Scholarship for use in freshman, sophomore, junior, senior, or graduate years; not renewable. *Number:* 9. *Amount:* $100–$400.

Eligibility Requirements: Applicant must be enrolled or expecting to enroll full- or part-time at a two-year or four-year institution or university. Applicant or parent of applicant must be member of American Criminal Justice Association. Applicant must have 3.0 GPA or higher. Available to U.S. citizens.

Application Requirements: Application, references, transcript. *Deadline:* December 31.

Contact: Karen Campbell, Executive Secretary
American Criminal Justice Association-Lambda Alpha Epsilon
PO Box 601047
Sacramento, CA 95860-1047
Phone: 916-484-6553
Fax: 916-488-2227
E-mail: acjalae@aol.com

AMERICAN SOCIETY OF CRIMINOLOGY http://www.asc41.com

AMERICAN SOCIETY OF CRIMINOLOGY GENE CARTE STUDENT PAPER COMPETITION

Award for full-time undergraduate or graduate students. Must submit a conceptual or empirical paper on a subject directly relating to criminology. Papers must be 7500 words or less.

Academic Fields/Career Goals: Criminal Justice/Criminology; Law Enforcement/Police Administration; Law/Legal Services; Social Sciences.

Award: Prize for use in freshman, sophomore, junior, senior, or graduate years; not renewable. *Number:* 3. *Amount:* $200–$500.

Eligibility Requirements: Applicant must be enrolled or expecting to enroll full-time at a four-year institution or university and must have an interest in writing. Available to U.S. and non-U.S. citizens.

Application Requirements: Applicant must enter a contest, conceptual or empirical paper on a subject directly relating to criminology. *Deadline:* April 15.

Contact: Andrew Hochstetlet, Scholarship Committee
American Society of Criminology
Iowa State University, 203D East Hall
Ames, IA 50011-4504
Phone: 515-294-2841
E-mail: hochstet@iastate.edu

ASSOCIATION OF CERTIFIED FRAUD EXAMINERS http://www.acfe.com

RITCHIE-JENNINGS MEMORIAL SCHOLARSHIP

• *See page 48*

CONNECTICUT ASSOCIATION OF WOMEN POLICE http://www.cawp.net

CONNECTICUT ASSOCIATION OF WOMEN POLICE SCHOLARSHIP

Available to Connecticut residents graduating from an accredited high school, and entering a college or university in Connecticut as a criminal justice major.

Academic Fields/Career Goals: Criminal Justice/Criminology; Law Enforcement/Police Administration.

Award: Scholarship for use in freshman year; not renewable. *Number:* 1–3. *Amount:* $200–$500.

Eligibility Requirements: Applicant must be high school student; planning to enroll or expecting to enroll full-time at a two-year or four-year institution or university; resident of Connecticut and studying in Connecticut. Available to U.S. citizens.

Application Requirements: Application, essay, financial need analysis, references, transcript. *Deadline:* April 30.

Contact: Gail McDonnell, Scholarship Committee
Connecticut Association of Women Police
PO Box 1653
Hartford, CT 06144
Phone: 860-527-7300

INDIANA SHERIFFS' ASSOCIATION http://www.indianasheriffs.org

INDIANA SHERIFFS' ASSOCIATION SCHOLARSHIP PROGRAM

Applicant must be an Indiana resident majoring in a criminal justice/law enforcement field at an Indiana college or university. Must be a member or dependent child or grandchild of a member of the association. Must be a full-time student with at least 12 credit hours.

Academic Fields/Career Goals: Criminal Justice/Criminology; Law Enforcement/Police Administration.

Award: Scholarship for use in freshman, sophomore, junior, or senior years; not renewable. *Number:* up to 40. *Amount:* up to $500.

Eligibility Requirements: Applicant must be enrolled or expecting to enroll full-time at a two-year or four-year institution or university; resident of Indiana and studying in Indiana. Applicant or parent of applicant must be member of Indiana Sheriffs' Association. Available to U.S. and non-U.S. citizens.

Application Requirements: Application, essay, transcript, SAT scores. *Deadline:* April 1.

Contact: Laura Vest, Administrative Assistant
Indiana Sheriffs' Association
PO Box 19127
Indianapolis, IN 46219
Phone: 317-356-3633
Fax: 317-356-3996
E-mail: laura_vest@hotmail.com

MISSOURI SHERIFFS' ASSOCIATION http://www.mosheriffs.com

JOHN DENNIS SCHOLARSHIP

Awards for Missouri high school seniors planning to attend a Missouri college or university and pursing a career in criminal justice. Award is based on financial need. Students must be in upper one-third of their graduating class and participate in extracurricular activities. Minimum 2.0 GPA required.

Academic Fields/Career Goals: Criminal Justice/Criminology.

Award: Scholarship for use in freshman year; not renewable. *Number:* 16. *Amount:* $1000.

Eligibility Requirements: Applicant must be high school student; planning to enroll or expecting to enroll full-time at a four-year institution or university; resident of Missouri and studying in Missouri. Available to U.S. citizens.

Application Requirements: Application, essay, financial need analysis, test scores. *Deadline:* January 31.

Contact: Karen Logan, Administrative Assistant
Missouri Sheriffs' Association
6605 Business Highway 50 West
Jefferson City, MO 65109-6307
Phone: 573-635-5925 Ext. 10
Fax: 573-635-2128
E-mail: karen@mosheriffs.com

NATIONAL BLACK POLICE ASSOCIATION http://www.blackpolice.org

ALPHONSO DEAL SCHOLARSHIP AWARD

$500 scholarship for high school senior and U.S. citizen to attend a two-year college or university. Must study law enforcement or other related criminal justice field. Minimum 2.5 GPA required.

Academic Fields/Career Goals: Criminal Justice/Criminology; Law Enforcement/Police Administration; Law/Legal Services; Social Sciences; Social Services.

Award: Scholarship for use in freshman year; not renewable. *Number:* 2. *Amount:* $500.

Eligibility Requirements: Applicant must be high school student and planning to enroll or expecting to enroll full-time at a two-year or four-year institution or university. Applicant must have 2.5 GPA or higher. Available to U.S. citizens.

National Black Police Association (continued)

Application Requirements: Application, autobiography, photo, references, transcript, letter of acceptance. *Deadline:* June 1.

Contact: Ronald Hampton, Executive Director
National Black Police Association
3251 Mount Pleasant Street, NW
Washington, DC 20010-2103
Phone: 202-986-2070
Fax: 202-986-0410
E-mail: nbpanatofc@worldnet.att.net

NORTH CAROLINA STATE EDUCATION ASSISTANCE AUTHORITY http://www.ncseaa.edu

NORTH CAROLINA SHERIFFS' ASSOCIATION UNDERGRADUATE CRIMINAL JUSTICE SCHOLARSHIPS

One-time award for full-time North Carolina resident undergraduate students majoring in criminal justice at a University of North Carolina school. Priority given to child of any North Carolina law enforcement officer. Letter of recommendation from county sheriff required.

Academic Fields/Career Goals: Criminal Justice/Criminology; Law Enforcement/Police Administration.

Award: Scholarship for use in freshman, sophomore, junior, or senior years; not renewable. *Number:* up to 10. *Amount:* $1000–$2000.

Eligibility Requirements: Applicant must be enrolled or expecting to enroll full-time at a four-year institution or university; resident of North Carolina and studying in North Carolina. Applicant or parent of applicant must have employment or volunteer experience in police/firefighting. Available to U.S. citizens.

Application Requirements: Application, financial need analysis, references, transcript, statement of career goals. *Deadline:* continuous.

Contact: Nolita Goldston, Assistant, Scholarship and Grant Division
North Carolina State Education Assistance Authority
PO Box 13663
Research Triangle Park, NC 27709
Phone: 919-549-8614
Fax: 919-248-4687
E-mail: ngoldston@ncseaa.edu

CULINARY ARTS

AMERICAN ACADEMY OF CHEFS http://www.acfchefs.org

CHAINE DES ROTISSEURS SCHOLARSHIPS

Applicant must be an exemplary student, or be currently enrolled in an accredited, postsecondary school of culinary arts, or other postsecondary culinary training program, or should have completed a grading or marking period (trimester, semester or quarter). Must submit two letters of recommendation from industry and/or culinary professionals; financial aid release form; official transcript showing current GPA.

Academic Fields/Career Goals: Culinary Arts.

Award: Scholarship for use in freshman, sophomore, junior, or senior years; not renewable. *Number:* varies. *Amount:* up to $1000.

Eligibility Requirements: Applicant must be enrolled or expecting to enroll full-time at a two-year or four-year institution or university. Available to U.S. citizens.

Application Requirements: Application, financial need analysis, references, transcript. *Deadline:* December 1.

Contact: Jennifer DiMayo, Executive Coordinator
American Academy of Chefs
180 Center Place Way
St. Augustine, FL 32095
Phone: 800-624-9458
Fax: 904-825-4758
E-mail: jdimayo@acfchefs.net

AMERICAN CULINARY FEDERATION http://www.acfchefs.org

AMERICAN ACADEMY OF CHEFS CHAINE DES ROTISSEURS SCHOLARSHIP

One-time award to exemplary students currently enrolled in a full-time two-year culinary program. Must have completed a grading or marking period.

Academic Fields/Career Goals: Culinary Arts; Food Service/Hospitality.

Award: Scholarship for use in freshman year; not renewable. *Number:* 10. *Amount:* $1000–$21,000.

Eligibility Requirements: Applicant must be enrolled or expecting to enroll full- or part-time at a two-year institution. Available to U.S. and non-U.S. citizens.

Application Requirements: Application, references, transcript. *Deadline:* December 1.

Contact: Debra Moore, Academic Administrator
American Culinary Federation
180 Center Place Way
St. Augustine, FL 32095
Phone: 800-624-9458
Fax: 904-825-4758
E-mail: academy@acfchefs.net

AMERICAN ACADEMY OF CHEFS CHAIR'S SCHOLARSHIP

One-time award to exemplary students currently enrolled in a full-time two- or four-year culinary program. Must have a career goal of becoming a chef or pastry chef.

Academic Fields/Career Goals: Culinary Arts; Food Service/Hospitality.

Award: Scholarship for use in freshman, sophomore, junior, or senior years; not renewable. *Number:* 5. *Amount:* $1000–$5000.

Eligibility Requirements: Applicant must be enrolled or expecting to enroll full- or part-time at a two-year or four-year or technical institution or university. Available to U.S. and non-U.S. citizens.

Application Requirements: Application, references, transcript. *Deadline:* July 1.

Contact: Scholarship Committee
American Culinary Federation
180 Center Place Way
St. Augustine, FL 32095

AMERICAN HOTEL AND LODGING EDUCATIONAL FOUNDATION http://www.ahlef.org

INCOMING FRESHMAN SCHOLARSHIPS

This program is exclusively for incoming freshman interested in pursing hospitality-related undergraduate programs. Preference will be given to any applicant who is a graduate of the Educational Institute's Lodging Management Program (LMP, which is a two-year high school program.) Must have a minimum 2.0 GPA.

Academic Fields/Career Goals: Culinary Arts; Hospitality Management; Travel/Tourism.

Award: Scholarship for use in freshman year; not renewable. *Number:* 1. *Amount:* $1000–$2000.

Eligibility Requirements: Applicant must be high school student and planning to enroll or expecting to enroll full-time at a four-year institution or university. Available to U.S. and non-U.S. citizens.

Application Requirements: Application, references, transcript. *Deadline:* May 1.

Contact: Crystal Hammond, Director of Foundation Programs
American Hotel and Lodging Educational Foundation
1201 New York Avenue NW, Suite 600
Washington, DC 20005-3197
Phone: 202-289-3188
Fax: 202-289-3199
E-mail: chammond@ahlef.org

CALIFORNIA ADOLESCENT NUTRITION AND FITNESS (CANFIT) PROGRAM http://www.canfit.org

CALIFORNIA ADOLESCENT NUTRITION AND FITNESS (CANFIT) PROGRAM SCHOLARSHIP

Awards undergraduate and graduate African-American, American-Indian/Alaska Native, Asian/Pacific Islander or Latino/Hispanic students who express financial need and are studying nutrition, physical fitness, or culinary arts in California. GPA of minimum 2.5 for undergraduates and 3.0 for graduates. See Web site for essay topic: http://www.canfit.org.

Academic Fields/Career Goals: Culinary Arts; Food Science/Nutrition; Food Service/Hospitality; Health and Medical Sciences; Sports-Related/Exercise Science.

Award: Scholarship for use in junior, senior, graduate, or postgraduate years; not renewable. *Number:* 5–10. *Amount:* $500–$1500.

Eligibility Requirements: Applicant must be American Indian/Alaska Native, Asian/Pacific Islander, Black (non-Hispanic), or Hispanic; enrolled or expecting to enroll full-time at a four-year or technical institution or university; resident of California and studying in California. Available to U.S. citizens.

Application Requirements: Application, autobiography, essay, financial need analysis, photo, references, transcript. *Deadline:* March 31.

Contact: Mrs. Betty A. Geishirt Cantrell, Program Administrator
California Adolescent Nutrition and Fitness (CANFit) Program
2140 Shattuck Avenue, Suite 610
Berkeley, CA 94704
Phone: 510-644-1533
Fax: 510-644-1535
E-mail: info@canfit.org

CAREERS THROUGH CULINARY ARTS PROGRAM INC. http://www.ccapinc.org

CAREERS THROUGH CULINARY ARTS PROGRAM COOKING COMPETITION FOR SCHOLARSHIPS

Cooking competition with finalists receiving a scholarship. Must be a senior in a C-CAP designated partner high school in Arizona, Tidewater Virginia, or the cities of Boston, Chicago, Los Angeles, New York, Philadelphia or Washington, DC. Must demonstrate mastery of select culinary skills.

Academic Fields/Career Goals: Culinary Arts.

Award: Scholarship for use in freshman, sophomore, junior, or senior years; not renewable. *Number:* 88–95. *Amount:* $1000–$78,000.

Eligibility Requirements: Applicant must be age 21 or under; enrolled or expecting to enroll full- or part-time at a two-year or four-year or technical institution and resident of Arizona, California, District of Columbia, Illinois, Massachusetts, New York, Pennsylvania, or Virginia. Available to U.S. and non-U.S. citizens.

Application Requirements: Application, applicant must enter a contest, essay, interview, references, test scores, transcript. *Deadline:* varies.

Contact: Mei Campanella, College Adviser
Careers Through Culinary Arts Program Inc.
250 West 57th Street, Suite 2015
New York, NY 10107
Phone: 212-974-7111
Fax: 212-974-7117
E-mail: mcampanella@ccapinc.org

CHEF2CHEF SCHOLARSHIP FUND http://www.chefs4students.org

CHEF4STUDENTS CULINARY GRANT PROGRAM

Awards to students attending an accredited culinary school or institute. Based on demonstrated financial need, participation in online culinary forum, essay. Deadline varies.

Academic Fields/Career Goals: Culinary Arts.

Award: Grant for use in freshman, sophomore, junior, or senior years; renewable. *Number:* up to 30. *Amount:* up to $1000.

Eligibility Requirements: Applicant must be enrolled or expecting to enroll full- or part-time at a four-year institution or university. Available to U.S. and non-U.S. citizens.

Application Requirements: Application, essay, financial need analysis, references, transcript. *Deadline:* varies.

Contact: David Nelson, Program Manager
Chef2Chef Scholarship Fund
1360 Indian Trail Number 13
Steamboat Springs, CO 80487
Phone: 970-846-0059
Fax: 970-871-6115
E-mail: dnelson@chefs4students.org

CULINARY TRUST http://www.theculinarytrust.com

CULINARY TRUST SCHOLARSHIP PROGRAM FOR CULINARY STUDY AND RESEARCH

Scholarships provides funds to qualified applicants for beginning, continuing, and specialty education courses at accredited culinary schools worldwide, as well as, independent study for research projects. Applicants must have at least two years of food service experience (paid, volunteer, or combination of both), a minimum 3.0 GPA and must write an essay. Application fee: $25.

Academic Fields/Career Goals: Culinary Arts; Food Science/Nutrition; Food Service/Hospitality.

Award: Scholarship for use in freshman, sophomore, junior, senior, graduate, or postgraduate years; not renewable. *Number:* 21. *Amount:* $1000–$5000.

Eligibility Requirements: Applicant must be age 18 and over and enrolled or expecting to enroll full- or part-time at a two-year or four-year or technical institution or university. Applicant or parent of applicant must have employment or volunteer experience in food service. Applicant must have 3.0 GPA or higher. Available to U.S. and non-U.S. citizens.

Application Requirements: Application, essay, interview, references, transcript. *Fee:* $25. *Deadline:* December 15.

Contact: Trina Gribbins, Director of Administration
Culinary Trust
304 West Liberty Street, Suite 201
Louisville, KY 40202-3068
Phone: 502-581-9786 Ext. 264
Fax: 502-589-3602
E-mail: tgribbins@hqtrs.com

ILLINOIS RESTAURANT ASSOCIATION EDUCATIONAL FOUNDATION http://www.illinoisrestaurants.org

ILLINOIS RESTAURANT ASSOCIATION EDUCATIONAL FOUNDATION SCHOLARSHIPS

Scholarship available to Illinois residents enrolled in a food service management, culinary arts, or hospitality management concentration in an accredited program of a two- or four-year college or university. Must be a U.S. citizen.

Academic Fields/Career Goals: Culinary Arts; Food Science/Nutrition; Food Service/Hospitality; Hospitality Management.

Award: Scholarship for use in freshman, sophomore, junior, senior, graduate, or postgraduate years; not renewable. *Number:* 50–70. *Amount:* $750–$24,000.

Eligibility Requirements: Applicant must be enrolled or expecting to enroll full- or part-time at a two-year or four-year or technical institution or university and resident of Illinois. Applicant or parent of applicant must have employment or volunteer experience in food service or hospitality/hotel administration/operations. Available to U.S. citizens.

Application Requirements: Application, essay, photo, references, transcript. *Deadline:* May 15.

Contact: Blue Ribbon Scholarship Committee
Illinois Restaurant Association Educational Foundation
200 North LaSalle, Suite 880
Chicago, IL 60601-1014
Phone: 312-787-4000
Fax: 312-787-4792

JAMES BEARD FOUNDATION INC.

http://www.jamesbeard.org

AMERICAN RESTAURANT SCHOLARSHIP

Scholarships available for students who plan to enroll or are already enrolled at a licensed or accredited culinary school, and are residents of Florida, Kansas, Missouri, or Pennsylvania.

Academic Fields/Career Goals: Culinary Arts.

Award: Scholarship for use in freshman, sophomore, junior, senior, or graduate years; not renewable. *Number:* up to 2. *Amount:* up to $4500.

Eligibility Requirements: Applicant must be enrolled or expecting to enroll full-time at a four-year institution or university and resident of Florida, Kansas, Missouri, or Pennsylvania. Available to U.S. and non-U.S. citizens.

Application Requirements: Application, essay, financial need analysis, references, transcript. *Deadline:* May 15.

Contact: Caroline Stuart, Scholarship Director
James Beard Foundation Inc.
54 Comstock Hill Road
New Canaan, CT 06840
Phone: 212-675-4984 Ext. 311
Fax: 212-645-1438
E-mail: jamesbeardfound@hotmail.com

BRYAN CLOSE POLO GRILL SCHOLARSHIP

One $1000 scholarship towards tuition at an accredited culinary school of student's choice. For $1000 scholarship, applicant must be a resident of Oklahoma, Texas, Kansas, Arkansas, Mississippi or Louisiana. For $500 scholarship, applicant must be a resident of Oklahoma. Applicant must have had at least one year of culinary experience either as a student or as an employee. Applicant must demonstrate a strong commitment to the culinary arts.

Academic Fields/Career Goals: Culinary Arts.

Award: Scholarship for use in freshman, sophomore, junior, senior, or graduate years; not renewable. *Number:* 1. *Amount:* $500–$1000.

Eligibility Requirements: Applicant must be enrolled or expecting to enroll full- or part-time at a four-year institution or university and resident of Arkansas, Kansas, Louisiana, Mississippi, Oklahoma, or Texas. Available to U.S. and non-U.S. citizens.

Application Requirements: Application, essay, financial need analysis, references, transcript. *Deadline:* May 15.

Contact: Caroline Stuart, Scholarship Director
James Beard Foundation Inc.
167 West 12th Street
New York, NY 10011
Phone: 212-675-4984 Ext. 311
Fax: 212-645-1438
E-mail: jamesbeardfound@hotmail.com

CLAY TRIPLETTE SCHOLARSHIP

Scholarship for deserving students who want to pursue a baking and pastry degree. Up to two awards of $5000. Applicants must plan to enroll or already be enrolled in an accredited baking or pastry studies program at a licensed or accredited culinary school.

Academic Fields/Career Goals: Culinary Arts.

Award: Scholarship for use in freshman, sophomore, junior, or senior years; not renewable. *Number:* up to 4. *Amount:* up to $4000.

Eligibility Requirements: Applicant must be enrolled or expecting to enroll full-time at a four-year institution or university. Available to U.S. citizens.

Application Requirements: Application, essay, financial need analysis, references, transcript. *Deadline:* May 15.

Contact: Caroline Stuart, Scholarship Director
James Beard Foundation Inc.
167 West 12th Street
New York, NY 10011
Phone: 212-675-4984 Ext. 311
Fax: 212-645-1438
E-mail: jamesbeardfound@hotmail.com

DESEO AT THE WESTIN SCHOLARSHIP

Scholarship for residents of Arizona who can substantiate residency, who have participated in the Arizona Careers Through Culinary Arts (C-CAP) program, and have been recommended by Arizona C-CAP.

Academic Fields/Career Goals: Culinary Arts.

Award: Scholarship for use in freshman, sophomore, junior, or senior years; not renewable. *Number:* up to 2. *Amount:* up to $3125.

Eligibility Requirements: Applicant must be enrolled or expecting to enroll full-time at a four-year institution or university and resident of Arizona. Available to U.S. citizens.

Application Requirements: Application, essay, financial need analysis, references, transcript. *Deadline:* May 18.

Contact: Caroline Stuart, Scholarship Director
James Beard Foundation Inc.
167 West 12th Street
New York, NY 10011
Phone: 212-675-4984 Ext. 311
Fax: 212-645-1438
E-mail: jamesbeardfound@hotmail.com

GENE HOVIS MEMORIAL SCHOLARSHIP

Scholarship available for African-American female student who is planning to enroll or currently enrolled at a licensed or accredited culinary school. Must submit a 500-word essay on culinary goals and how this scholarship will help to attain them.

Academic Fields/Career Goals: Culinary Arts.

Award: Scholarship for use in freshman, sophomore, junior, or senior years; not renewable. *Number:* 1. *Amount:* up to $4000.

Eligibility Requirements: Applicant must be Black (non-Hispanic); enrolled or expecting to enroll full-time at a four-year institution or university and female. Available to U.S. citizens.

Application Requirements: Application, essay, financial need analysis, references, transcript. *Deadline:* May 18.

Contact: Caroline Stuart, Scholarship Director
James Beard Foundation Inc.
167 West 12th Street
New York, NY 10011
Phone: 212-675-4984 Ext. 311
Fax: 212-645-1438
E-mail: jamesbeardfound@hotmail.com

JAMES BEARD FOUNDATION GENERAL SCHOLARSHIPS

Awards up to fifty one-time scholarships valued $2000 towards tuition at an accredited culinary school of student's choice. The amount of each scholarship will be at the discretion of the James Beard Foundation scholarship committee. Candidates must demonstrate a strong commitment to the culinary arts, an exceptional academic or work record, and financial need.

Academic Fields/Career Goals: Culinary Arts.

Award: Scholarship for use in freshman, sophomore, junior, senior, or graduate years; not renewable. *Number:* up to 50. *Amount:* $2000.

Eligibility Requirements: Applicant must be enrolled or expecting to enroll full- or part-time at a four-year institution or university. Available to U.S. and non-U.S. citizens.

Application Requirements: Application, essay, financial need analysis, references, transcript. *Deadline:* April 15.

Contact: Caroline Stuart, Scholarship Director
James Beard Foundation Inc.
167 West 12th Street
New York, NY 10011
Phone: 212-675-4984 Ext. 311
Fax: 212-645-1438
E-mail: jamesbeardfound@hotmail.com

LA TOQUE SCHOLARSHIP IN WINE STUDIES

Scholarship for $3000 toward tuition at an accredited culinary school of the student's choice. For both full-time and part-time study. See Web site at http://www.jamesbeard.org for further details.

Academic Fields/Career Goals: Culinary Arts.

Award: Scholarship for use in freshman, sophomore, junior, senior, or graduate years; not renewable. *Number:* 2. *Amount:* $3000.

Eligibility Requirements: Applicant must be enrolled or expecting to enroll full- or part-time at a four-year institution or university. Available to U.S. and non-U.S. citizens.

Application Requirements: Application, essay, financial need analysis, references, transcript. *Deadline:* May 15.

Contact: Caroline Stuart, Scholarship Director
James Beard Foundation Inc.
167 West 12th Street
New York, NY 10011
Phone: 212-675-4984 Ext. 311
Fax: 212-645-1438
E-mail: jamesbeardfound@hotmail.com

PETER CAMERON SCHOLARSHIP

Nonrenewable scholarships for high school seniors planning to enroll at a licensed or accredited culinary school who have a minimum GPA of 3.0.

Academic Fields/Career Goals: Culinary Arts.

Award: Scholarship for use in freshman year; not renewable. *Number:* 1. *Amount:* up to $5000.

Eligibility Requirements: Applicant must be high school student and planning to enroll or expecting to enroll full-time at a four-year institution or university. Applicant must have 3.0 GPA or higher. Available to U.S. and non-U.S. citizens.

Application Requirements: Application, essay, financial need analysis, references, transcript. *Deadline:* May 15.

Contact: Caroline Stuart, Scholarship Director
James Beard Foundation Inc.
167 West 12th Street
New York, NY 10011
Phone: 212-675-4984 Ext. 311
Fax: 212-645-1438
E-mail: jamesbeardfound@hotmail.com

PETER KUMP MEMORIAL SCHOLARSHIP

One-time award towards tuition at an accredited or licensed culinary school of student's choice. Applicant must submit a 500 word essay on culinary goals and how this scholarship can help attain them. Candidates must demonstrate a strong commitment to the culinary arts, an exceptional academic or work record, and financial need.

Academic Fields/Career Goals: Culinary Arts.

Award: Scholarship for use in freshman year; not renewable. *Number:* 4. *Amount:* $5000.

Eligibility Requirements: Applicant must be high school student and planning to enroll or expecting to enroll full- or part-time at a four-year institution or university. Applicant must have 3.5 GPA or higher. Available to U.S. and non-U.S. citizens.

Application Requirements: Application, essay, financial need analysis, references, transcript. *Deadline:* May 15.

Contact: Caroline Stuart, Scholarship Director
James Beard Foundation Inc.
167 West 12th Street
New York, NY 10011
Phone: 212-675-4984 Ext. 311
Fax: 212-645-1438
E-mail: jamesbeardfound@hotmail.com

ST. REGIS HOUSTON SCHOLARSHIP

Scholarship available for students who plan to enroll or are already enrolled at a licensed or accredited culinary school, and reside in the greater Houston, TX area and substantiate residency.

Academic Fields/Career Goals: Culinary Arts.

Award: Scholarship for use in freshman year; not renewable. *Number:* 1. *Amount:* up to $3500.

Eligibility Requirements: Applicant must be enrolled or expecting to enroll full-time at a four-year institution or university and resident of Texas. Available to U.S. citizens.

Application Requirements: Application, essay, financial need analysis, references, transcript. *Deadline:* May 15.

Contact: Caroline Stuart, Scholarship Director
James Beard Foundation Inc.
167 West 12th Street
New York, NY 10011
Phone: 212-675-4984 Ext. 311
Fax: 212-645-1438
E-mail: jamesbeardfound@hotmail.com

WALLY JOE SCHOLARSHIP

One-time award of $2000 towards tuition at an accredited culinary school for applicants who are residents of Mississippi, Tennessee, Arkansas, or Louisiana. Candidates must demonstrate a strong commitment to the culinary arts, an exceptional academic or work record, and financial need. See Web site at http://www.jamesbeard.org for further details.

Academic Fields/Career Goals: Culinary Arts.

Award: Scholarship for use in freshman, sophomore, junior, senior, or graduate years; not renewable. *Number:* 1. *Amount:* $2000.

Eligibility Requirements: Applicant must be enrolled or expecting to enroll full- or part-time at a four-year institution or university and resident of Alaska, Louisiana, Mississippi, or Tennessee. Available to U.S. and non-U.S. citizens.

Application Requirements: Application, essay, financial need analysis, references, transcript. *Deadline:* May 15.

Contact: Caroline Stuart, Scholarship Director
James Beard Foundation Inc.
167 West 12th Street
New York, NY 10011
Phone: 212-675-4984 Ext. 311
Fax: 212-645-1438
E-mail: jamesbeardfound@hotmail.com

LES DAMES D'ESCOFFIER http://www.ldei.org

LES DAMES D'ESCOFFIER SCHOLARSHIP

One-time scholarship for women of all ages seeking training in the areas of food, wine, hospitality, nutrition, food technology, the arts of the table, and other fields. Scholarship valued at $2500 to $10,000. Deadline varies.

Academic Fields/Career Goals: Culinary Arts; Food Science/Nutrition; Food Service/Hospitality.

Award: Scholarship for use in freshman, sophomore, junior, senior, graduate, or postgraduate years; not renewable. *Number:* 3. *Amount:* $2500–$10,000.

Eligibility Requirements: Applicant must be enrolled or expecting to enroll full- or part-time at a two-year or four-year or technical institution or university and female. Available to U.S. and Canadian citizens.

Application Requirements: Application, essay, references, self-addressed stamped envelope, transcript. *Deadline:* varies.

Contact: Greg Jewell, Executive Director
Les Dames d'Escoffier
KBC MPI Headquarters, PO Box 4961
Louisville, KY 40204
Phone: 502-456-1851
Fax: 502-456-1821
E-mail: gjewell@aecmanagement.com

MAINE RESTAURANT ASSOCIATION http://www.mainerestaurant.com

RUSS CASEY/MAINE RESTAURANT ASSOCIATES SCHOLARSHIP FUND

Scholarship available to students who wish to pursue higher education in culinary arts, restaurant, and hotel or hospitality management. Preference will be given to those in Maine-based institutions and those who intend to pursue a career in food service.

Academic Fields/Career Goals: Culinary Arts; Hospitality Management.

Award: Scholarship for use in freshman, sophomore, junior, or senior years; renewable. *Number:* 1–5. *Amount:* $1000.

Eligibility Requirements: Applicant must be enrolled or expecting to enroll full- or part-time at a two-year or four-year or technical institution or university. Available to U.S. citizens.

Maine Restaurant Association (continued)

Application Requirements: Application, essay, financial need analysis, transcript. *Deadline:* May 1.

Contact: Becky Jacobson, Business Manager
Maine Restaurant Association
Five Wade Street
PO Box 5060
Augusta, ME 04332-5060
Phone: 207-623-2178
Fax: 207-623-8377
E-mail: info@mainerestaurant.com

MAINE SCHOOL FOOD SERVICE ASSOCIATION (MSFSA) http://www.mainesfsa.org

MAINE SCHOOL FOOD SERVICE ASSOCIATION CONTINUING EDUCATION SCHOLARSHIP

Awarded to students from Maine enrolling in nutrition or culinary arts. It is also available to employees of school nutrition programs wishing to continue their education. Applicant can be a high school senior, college student, or member of MSFSA. Applicant must be attending an institution in Maine.

Academic Fields/Career Goals: Culinary Arts; Food Science/Nutrition; Food Service/Hospitality; Home Economics.

Award: Scholarship for use in freshman, sophomore, junior, or senior years; not renewable. *Number:* 1–4. *Amount:* $300–$1200.

Eligibility Requirements: Applicant must be enrolled or expecting to enroll full- or part-time at a two-year or four-year or technical institution or university; resident of Maine and studying in Maine. Available to U.S. citizens.

Application Requirements: Application, essay, resume, references, transcript, acceptance letter. *Deadline:* April 15.

Contact: Judith Campbell, Education Committee Chair
Maine School Food Service Association (MSFSA)
9 Wentworth Drive
Scarborough, ME 04074

OREGON STUDENT ASSISTANCE COMMISSION http://www.osac.state.or.us

OREGON WINE BROTHERHOOD SCHOLARSHIP

Award for students majoring in enology, viticulture, or culinary arts with an emphasis on wine. Must attend Chemeketa Community College, Mt. Hood Community College, Oregon State University, or University of California, Davis. May reapply each year for up to three years.

Academic Fields/Career Goals: Culinary Arts; Food Science/Nutrition.

Award: Scholarship for use in freshman, sophomore, junior, or senior years; renewable. *Number:* varies. *Amount:* varies.

Eligibility Requirements: Applicant must be enrolled or expecting to enroll full-time at a two-year or four-year institution or university and resident of Oregon. Applicant must have 3.0 GPA or higher. Available to U.S. citizens.

Application Requirements: Application, essay, financial need analysis, transcript, activities chart. *Deadline:* March 1.

Contact: Director of Grant Programs
Oregon Student Assistance Commission
1500 Valley River Drive, Suite 100
Eugene, OR 97401-7020
Phone: 800-452-8807 Ext. 7395

WISCONSIN BAKERS ASSOCIATION (WBA) http://www.umwba.org

ROBERT W. HILLER SCHOLARSHIP FUND

Scholarship of $1000 awarded for students at all levels in a baking/pastry arts-related program that prepares candidates for a retail baking profession. Minimum 2.85 GPA required.

Academic Fields/Career Goals: Culinary Arts.

Award: Scholarship for use in freshman, sophomore, junior, senior, graduate, or postgraduate years; not renewable. *Number:* varies. *Amount:* $1000.

Eligibility Requirements: Applicant must be enrolled or expecting to enroll full-time at a four-year institution or university. Available to U.S. citizens.

Application Requirements: Application, essay, resume, references. *Deadline:* June 2.

Contact: Rebeca Borrero-Hoover, Scholarship Committee
Wisconsin Bakers Association (WBA)
8112 West Bluemound Road, Suite 71
Milwaukee, WI 53213
Phone: 414-258-5552
Fax: 414-258-5582
E-mail: information@umwba.org

WOMEN CHEFS AND RESTAURATEURS http://www.womenchefs.org

FRENCH CULINARY INSTITUTE/ITALIAN CULINARY EXPERIENCE SCHOLARSHIP

Scholarship intended for a culinary student wishing to specialize in Italian cuisine. Recipient must be a new enrollment and satisfy all entrance requirements of the FCI. Scholarship award is applied to total program fee.

Academic Fields/Career Goals: Culinary Arts; Food Service/Hospitality.

Award: Scholarship for use in freshman, sophomore, junior, senior, graduate, or postgraduate years; not renewable. *Number:* 1. *Amount:* $5000.

Eligibility Requirements: Applicant must be enrolled or expecting to enroll full-time at a four-year institution or university. Available to U.S. and non-U.S. citizens.

Application Requirements: Application, essay. *Fee:* $25. *Deadline:* March 31.

Contact: Dori Sacksteder, Director of Programs
Women Chefs and Restaurateurs
455 South Fourth Street, Suite 650
Louisville, KY 40202
Phone: 502-581-0300 Ext. 219
Fax: 502-589-3602
E-mail: dsacksteder@hqtrs.com

DENTAL HEALTH/SERVICES

ALBERTA HERITAGE SCHOLARSHIP FUND/ ALBERTA SCHOLARSHIP PROGRAMS http://www.alis.gov.ab.ca

ALBERTA HERITAGE SCHOLARSHIP FUND ABORIGINAL HEALTH CAREERS BURSARY

• *See page 129*

JASON LANG SCHOLARSHIP

Award to reward the outstanding academic achievement of Alberta postsecondary students who are continuing full-time in an undergraduate program in Alberta. Must be a Canadian citizen or permanent resident and Alberta resident. Must be enrolled full-time in an undergraduate or professional program, such as law, medicine, pharmacy, or dentistry at an eligible Alberta postsecondary institution. Nominated on the basis of achieving a minimum GPA of 3.2 in the previous academic year.

Academic Fields/Career Goals: Dental Health/Services; Health and Medical Sciences; Law/Legal Services; Pharmacy.

Award: Scholarship for use in sophomore, junior, senior, or graduate years; not renewable. *Number:* 8500. *Amount:* $1000.

Eligibility Requirements: Applicant must be enrolled or expecting to enroll full-time at a two-year or four-year or technical institution or university; resident of Alberta and studying in Alberta. Available to Canadian citizens.

Application Requirements: Application, test scores, transcript. *Deadline:* varies.

Contact: Scholarship Committee
Alberta Heritage Scholarship Fund/Alberta Scholarship Programs
9940 106th Street, Fourth Floor, Sterling Place
PO Box 28000, Station Main
Edmonton, AB T5J 4R4
Canada
Phone: 780-427-8640
Fax: 780-427-1288
E-mail: scholarships@gov.ab.ca

AMERICAN ACADEMY OF ORAL AND MAXILLOFACIAL RADIOLOGY http://www.aaomr.org

CHARLES R. MORRIS STUDENT RESEARCH AWARD

Award to applicants from accredited programs performing research in oral and maxillofacial radiology. Applicant must be a full-time undergraduate or predoctoral student at the time of research, be nominated by the institution where research was carried out, and submit a manuscript detailing the research project.

Academic Fields/Career Goals: Dental Health/Services.

Award: Grant for use in junior, senior, or graduate years; not renewable. *Number:* 1. *Amount:* $1000.

Eligibility Requirements: Applicant must be enrolled or expecting to enroll full-time at a four-year institution or university. Available to U.S. and non-U.S. citizens.

Application Requirements: Application, references, manuscript. *Deadline:* June 16.

Contact: J. Sean Hubar, Program Coordinator
American Academy of Oral and Maxillofacial Radiology
LSU School of Dentistry, 1100 Florida Avenue
New Orleans, LA 70119
Phone: 504-619-8623
Fax: 504-619-8741
E-mail: jhubar@lsumc.edu

AMERICAN DENTAL ASSISTANTS ASSOCIATION http://www.dentalassistant.org

JULIETTE A. SOUTHARD/ORAL B LABORATORIES SCHOLARSHIP

Leadership-based award available to students enrolled in an ADAA dental assistant's program. Proof of acceptance into ADAA program and two letters of reference are required.

Academic Fields/Career Goals: Dental Health/Services.

Award: Scholarship for use in freshman, sophomore, junior, senior, graduate, or postgraduate years; not renewable. *Number:* up to 10. *Amount:* varies.

Eligibility Requirements: Applicant must be enrolled or expecting to enroll full- or part-time at a two-year or four-year institution or university and must have an interest in leadership. Applicant or parent of applicant must be member of American Dental Assistants Association. Available to U.S. citizens.

Application Requirements: Application, essay, financial need analysis, references, transcript. *Deadline:* March 1.

Contact: Erek Armentrout, Membership Development Manager
American Dental Assistants Association
35 East Wacker Drive, Suite 1730
Chicago, IL 60601-2211
Phone: 312-541-1550
Fax: 312-541-1496
E-mail: earmentrout@adaa1.com

AMERICAN DENTAL ASSOCIATION (ADA) FOUNDATION http://www.adafoundation.org

AMERICAN DENTAL ASSOCIATION FOUNDATION DENTAL ASSISTING SCHOLARSHIP PROGRAM

One-time award of $1000. Applicant must be enrolled full-time with a minimum of 12 hours in an accredited dental assistant program. Must submit autobiographical sketch. Must be a U.S. citizen and have at least a 3.0 GPA . Application materials can be obtained from the financial aid officer of the school where the applicant is enrolled currently. Applicants must demonstrate a minimum financial need of $1000.

Academic Fields/Career Goals: Dental Health/Services.

Award: Scholarship for use in freshman year; not renewable. *Number:* up to 10. *Amount:* up to $1000.

Eligibility Requirements: Applicant must be enrolled or expecting to enroll full-time at a two-year or four-year institution. Applicant must have 3.0 GPA or higher. Available to U.S. citizens.

Application Requirements: Application, autobiography, essay, financial need analysis, references. *Deadline:* October 16.

Contact: Rose Famularo, Manager
American Dental Association (ADA) Foundation
211 East Chicago Avenue, 12th Floor
Chicago, IL 60611
Phone: 312-440-2547
Fax: 312-440-3526
E-mail: adaf@ada.org

AMERICAN DENTAL ASSOCIATION FOUNDATION DENTAL HYGIENE SCHOLARSHIP PROGRAM

Applicant must be enrolled full-time with a minimum of 12 hours as a student in an accredited dental hygiene program. Must be U.S. citizen with minimum 3.0 GPA. Must submit autobiographical statement. Applicants may obtain application materials from financial aid officer of the school where they are enrolled currently. Applicants must demonstrate a minimum financial need of $1000.

Academic Fields/Career Goals: Dental Health/Services.

Award: Scholarship for use in senior year; not renewable. *Number:* up to 15. *Amount:* up to $1000.

Eligibility Requirements: Applicant must be enrolled or expecting to enroll full-time at a four-year institution or university. Applicant must have 3.0 GPA or higher. Available to U.S. citizens.

Application Requirements: Application, autobiography, essay, financial need analysis, references. *Deadline:* October 16.

Contact: Rose Famularo, Manager
American Dental Association (ADA) Foundation
211 East Chicago Avenue, 12th Floor
Chicago, IL 60611
Phone: 312-440-2547
Fax: 312-440-3526
E-mail: adaf@ada.org

AMERICAN DENTAL ASSOCIATION FOUNDATION DENTAL LAB TECHNOLOGY SCHOLARSHIP

Applicant must be enrolled full-time with a minimum of 12 hours as a last-year student in an accredited dental laboratory technology program. Must be U.S. citizen with a minimum 3.0 GPA. Must submit autobiographical statement. Application materials can be obtained from financial aid officer of the school where the applicant is currently enrolled. Applicants must demonstrate a minimum financial need of $1000.

Academic Fields/Career Goals: Dental Health/Services.

Award: Scholarship for use in senior year; not renewable. *Number:* up to 5. *Amount:* up to $1000.

Eligibility Requirements: Applicant must be enrolled or expecting to enroll full-time at a four-year institution or university. Applicant must have 3.0 GPA or higher. Available to U.S. citizens.

Application Requirements: Application, autobiography, essay, financial need analysis, references. *Deadline:* October 16.

Contact: Rose Famularo, Manager
American Dental Association (ADA) Foundation
211 East Chicago Avenue, 12th Floor
Chicago, IL 60611
Phone: 312-440-2547
Fax: 312-440-3526
E-mail: adaf@ada.org

AMERICAN DENTAL ASSOCIATION FOUNDATION DENTAL STUDENT SCHOLARSHIP PROGRAM

One-time award for second-year students at an accredited dental school. Must have 3.0 GPA, and be enrolled full-time (minimum of 12 hours). Must show

American Dental Association (ADA) Foundation (continued)

financial need and be a U.S. citizen. Applicants may obtain application materials from financial aid officer of the school where they are currently enrolled.

Academic Fields/Career Goals: Dental Health/Services.

Award: Scholarship for use in sophomore year; not renewable. *Number:* up to 25. *Amount:* up to $2500.

Eligibility Requirements: Applicant must be enrolled or expecting to enroll full-time at a four-year institution or university. Applicant must have 3.0 GPA or higher. Available to U.S. citizens.

Application Requirements: Application, autobiography, essay, financial need analysis, references, school's letter of acceptance. *Deadline:* October 16.

Contact: Rose Famularo, Manager
American Dental Association (ADA) Foundation
211 East Chicago Avenue, 12th Floor
Chicago, IL 60611
Phone: 312-440-2547
Fax: 312-440-3526
E-mail: adaf@ada.org

AMERICAN DENTAL ASSOCIATION FOUNDATION MINORITY DENTAL STUDENT SCHOLARSHIP PROGRAM

Scholarship for second-year students of a minority group that is underrepresented in dental school enrollment. Based on financial need and academic achievement. Must be U.S. citizen and full-time students (minimum 12 hours). Must have minimum 3.0 GPA. Applicant must be enrolled in a dental school accredited by the Commission on Dental Accreditation. Applicants may obtain application materials from financial aid officer of the school where they are currently enrolled. Applicants must demonstrate a minimum financial need of $2500.

Academic Fields/Career Goals: Dental Health/Services.

Award: Scholarship for use in sophomore year; not renewable. *Number:* up to 25. *Amount:* up to $2500.

Eligibility Requirements: Applicant must be American Indian/Alaska Native, Asian/Pacific Islander, Black (non-Hispanic), or Hispanic and enrolled or expecting to enroll full-time at a four-year institution or university. Applicant must have 3.0 GPA or higher. Available to U.S. citizens.

Application Requirements: Application, autobiography, essay, financial need analysis, references. *Deadline:* October 16.

Contact: Rose Famularo, Manager
American Dental Association (ADA) Foundation
211 East Chicago Avenue, 12th Floor
Chicago, IL 60611
Phone: 312-440-2547
Fax: 312-440-3526
E-mail: adaf@ada.org

AMERICAN DENTAL HYGIENISTS' ASSOCIATION (ADHA) INSTITUTE http://www.adha.org

ADHA INSTITUTE GENERAL SCHOLARSHIPS

One-time award to students enrolled in an accredited dental hygiene program in the United States. Must be a full-time student with a minimum 3.0 GPA and completed one year in a dental hygiene curriculum. Must be a SADHA or ADHA member.

Academic Fields/Career Goals: Dental Health/Services.

Award: Scholarship for use in sophomore, junior, senior, or graduate years; not renewable. *Number:* varies. *Amount:* $1500.

Eligibility Requirements: Applicant must be enrolled or expecting to enroll full-time at a two-year or four-year or technical institution or university. Applicant or parent of applicant must be member of American Dental Hygienist's Association. Applicant must have 3.0 GPA or higher. Available to U.S. citizens.

Application Requirements: Application, financial need analysis, references. *Deadline:* May 1.

Contact: Star Abernathy, Administrator
American Dental Hygienists' Association (ADHA) Institute
444 North Michigan Avenue, Suite 3400
Chicago, IL 60611
Phone: 312-440-8944
Fax: 312-467-1806
E-mail: stara@adha.org

AMERICAN DENTAL HYGIENISTS' ASSOCIATION INSTITUTE MINORITY SCHOLARSHIP

Nonrenewable awards for members of minority groups currently underrepresented in dental hygiene, including males. Must have minimum 3.0 GPA. Must have completed one year of a dental hygiene curriculum, and show financial need of at least $1500. ADHA of SADHA membership required. Refer to Web site: http://www.adha.org for more details.

Academic Fields/Career Goals: Dental Health/Services.

Award: Scholarship for use in sophomore, junior, senior, or graduate years; not renewable. *Number:* 2. *Amount:* $1500–$2000.

Eligibility Requirements: Applicant must be American Indian/Alaska Native, Asian/Pacific Islander, Black (non-Hispanic), or Hispanic and enrolled or expecting to enroll full-time at a two-year or four-year institution or university. Applicant or parent of applicant must be member of American Dental Hygienist's Association. Applicant must have 3.0 GPA or higher. Available to U.S. citizens.

Application Requirements: Application, financial need analysis, references. *Deadline:* May 1.

Contact: Star Abernathy, Administrator
American Dental Hygienists' Association (ADHA) Institute
444 North Michigan Avenue, Suite 3400
Chicago, IL 60611
Phone: 312-440-8944
Fax: 312-467-1806
E-mail: stara@adha.org

AMERICAN DENTAL HYGIENISTS' ASSOCIATION INSTITUTE RESEARCH GRANT

Award for a licensed dental hygienist or a student pursuing a dental hygiene degree to promote the oral health of the public by improving dental hygiene education and practice. Must submit research proposal. ADHA membership required. Must be a U.S. citizen. Refer to Web site for further details http://www.adha.org.

Academic Fields/Career Goals: Dental Health/Services.

Award: Grant for use in freshman, sophomore, junior, senior, or graduate years; renewable. *Number:* 1. *Amount:* $1000–$5000.

Eligibility Requirements: Applicant must be enrolled or expecting to enroll full-time at a four-year institution or university. Applicant or parent of applicant must be member of American Dental Hygienist's Association. Available to U.S. citizens.

Application Requirements: Application, proposal. *Deadline:* February 28.

Contact: Star Abernathy, Administrator
American Dental Hygienists' Association (ADHA) Institute
444 North Michigan Avenue, Suite 3400
Chicago, IL 60611
Phone: 312-440-8944
Fax: 312-467-1806
E-mail: stara@adha.org

AMERICAN DENTAL HYGIENISTS' ASSOCIATION PART-TIME SCHOLARSHIP

Awarded to a dental student pursuing a certificate, associate, baccalaureate, or graduate degree on a part-time basis. Must be an active SADHA or ADHA member. Must have completed one year of dental hygiene curricula at an accredited dental hygiene program in United States. Must demonstrate GPA of at least 3.0, and financial need of $1500 or more.

Academic Fields/Career Goals: Dental Health/Services.

Award: Scholarship for use in sophomore, junior, senior, or graduate years; not renewable. *Number:* 1. *Amount:* $1500.

Eligibility Requirements: Applicant must be enrolled or expecting to enroll part-time at a two-year or four-year institution or university.

Applicant or parent of applicant must be member of American Dental Hygienist's Association. Applicant must have 3.0 GPA or higher. Available to U.S. citizens.

Application Requirements: Application, financial need analysis, references. *Deadline:* May 1.

Contact: Scholarship Information
American Dental Hygienists' Association (ADHA) Institute
444 North Michigan Avenue, Suite 3400
Chicago, IL 60611
Phone: 800-735-4916

COLGATE "BRIGHT SMILES, BRIGHT FUTURES" MINORITY SCHOLARSHIP

Scholarships are awarded to members of minority groups currently underrepresented in dental hygiene programs at the certificate educational level. Must be an active SADHA or ADHA member. Applicant must have completed one year of dental hygiene curricula at an accredited dental hygiene program in United States. Applicant must demonstrate GPA of at least 3.0, and financial need of $1500 or more.

Academic Fields/Career Goals: Dental Health/Services.

Award: Scholarship for use in sophomore year; not renewable. *Number:* 2. *Amount:* $1250.

Eligibility Requirements: Applicant must be American Indian/Alaska Native, Asian/Pacific Islander, Black (non-Hispanic), or Hispanic and enrolled or expecting to enroll full-time at a technical institution. Applicant or parent of applicant must be member of American Dental Hygienist's Association. Applicant must have 3.0 GPA or higher. Available to U.S. citizens.

Application Requirements: Application, financial need analysis, references. *Deadline:* May 1.

Contact: Scholarship Committee
American Dental Hygienists' Association (ADHA) Institute
444 North Michigan Avenue, Suite 3400
Chicago, IL 60611
Phone: 800-735-4916

DR. ALFRED C. FONES SCHOLARSHIP

One-time award to an applicant in the baccalaureate or graduate degree categories who intends to become a dental hygiene teacher/educator. Must have a minimum 3.0 GPA. Must have completed one year of dental hygiene curriculum at an accredited dental hygiene program in United States. Must demonstrate a financial need of $1500 or more. Must be an active SADHA or ADHA member.

Academic Fields/Career Goals: Dental Health/Services.

Award: Scholarship for use in sophomore, junior, senior, or graduate years; not renewable. *Number:* 1. *Amount:* $1500.

Eligibility Requirements: Applicant must be enrolled or expecting to enroll full-time at a four-year institution or university. Applicant or parent of applicant must be member of American Dental Hygienist's Association. Applicant must have 3.0 GPA or higher. Available to U.S. citizens.

Application Requirements: Application, financial need analysis, references. *Deadline:* May 1.

Contact: Scholarship Committee
American Dental Hygienists' Association (ADHA) Institute
444 North Michigan Avenue, Suite 3400
Chicago, IL 60611
Phone: 800-735-4916

DR. HAROLD HILLENBRAND SCHOLARSHIP

Scholarship to an applicant who demonstrates specific academic excellence and outstanding clinical performance. Must have completed one year of dental hygiene curricula at an accredited dental hygiene program in United States. Must demonstrate a financial need of $1500 or more. Must be an active SADHA or ADHA member. Must demonstrate GPA of at least 3.5.

Academic Fields/Career Goals: Dental Health/Services.

Award: Scholarship for use in sophomore, junior, senior, or graduate years; not renewable. *Number:* 1. *Amount:* $1500.

Eligibility Requirements: Applicant must be enrolled or expecting to enroll full-time at a two-year or four-year institution or university. Applicant or parent of applicant must be member of American Dental Hygienist's Association. Applicant must have 3.5 GPA or higher. Available to U.S. citizens.

Application Requirements: Application, financial need analysis, references. *Deadline:* May 1.

Contact: Scholarship Committee
American Dental Hygienists' Association (ADHA) Institute
444 North Michigan Avenue, Suite 3400
Chicago, IL 60611
Phone: 800-735-4916

IRENE E. NEWMAN SCHOLARSHIP

Scholarship to an applicant at the baccalaureate or graduate degree level who demonstrates strong potential in public health or community dental health. Must be an active SADHA or ADHA member. Must have completed one year of dental hygiene curricula at an accredited dental hygiene program in United States. Applicant must demonstrate GPA of at least 3.0. Must demonstrate a financial need of $1500 or more.

Academic Fields/Career Goals: Dental Health/Services; Public Health.

Award: Scholarship for use in sophomore, junior, senior, or graduate years; not renewable. *Number:* 1. *Amount:* $1500.

Eligibility Requirements: Applicant must be enrolled or expecting to enroll full-time at a four-year institution or university. Applicant or parent of applicant must be member of American Dental Hygienist's Association. Applicant must have 3.0 GPA or higher. Available to U.S. citizens.

Application Requirements: Application, financial need analysis, references. *Deadline:* May 1.

Contact: Scholarship Committee
American Dental Hygienists' Association (ADHA) Institute
444 North Michigan Avenue, Suite 3400
Chicago, IL 60611
Phone: 800-735-4916

MARGARET E. SWANSON SCHOLARSHIP

Scholarship is awarded to certificate/associate-level applicant who demonstrates exceptional organizational leadership potential. Must be an active SADHA or ADHA member. Must have completed one year of dental hygiene curricula at an accredited dental hygiene program in United States. Must demonstrate GPA of at least 3.0, and financial need of $1500 or more.

Academic Fields/Career Goals: Dental Health/Services.

Award: Scholarship for use in sophomore year; not renewable. *Number:* 1. *Amount:* $1500.

Eligibility Requirements: Applicant must be enrolled or expecting to enroll full-time at a two-year or technical institution and must have an interest in leadership. Applicant or parent of applicant must be member of American Dental Hygienist's Association. Applicant must have 3.0 GPA or higher. Available to U.S. citizens.

Application Requirements: Application, financial need analysis, references. *Deadline:* May 1.

Contact: Scholarship Committee
American Dental Hygienists' Association (ADHA) Institute
444 North Michigan Avenue, Suite 3400
Chicago, IL 60611
Phone: 800-735-4916

MARSH AFFINITY GROUP SERVICES SCHOLARSHIP

Scholarships to applicants pursuing baccalaureate degrees in dental hygiene. Must be an active SADHA or ADHA member. Must have completed one year of dental hygiene curricula at an accredited dental hygiene program in United States. Must demonstrate GPA between 3.0 and 3.5, and financial need of $1500 or more.

Academic Fields/Career Goals: Dental Health/Services.

Award: Scholarship for use in sophomore, junior, or senior years; not renewable. *Number:* 1. *Amount:* $1000.

Eligibility Requirements: Applicant must be enrolled or expecting to enroll full-time at a four-year institution or university. Applicant or parent of applicant must be member of American Dental Hygienist's Association. Available to U.S. citizens.

American Dental Hygienists' Association (ADHA) Institute (continued)

Application Requirements: Application, essay, financial need analysis, references. *Deadline:* May 1.

Contact: Star Abernathy, Administrator
American Dental Hygienists' Association (ADHA) Institute
444 North Michigan Avenue, Suite 3400
Chicago, IL 60611
Phone: 312-440-8944
Fax: 312-467-1806
E-mail: stara@adha.org

ORAL-B LABORATORIES DENTAL HYGIENE SCHOLARSHIP

Scholarships to baccalaureate degree students who demonstrate intent to encourage professional excellence, promote quality research, and support dental hygiene through public and private education. Must be an active SADHA or ADHA member. Must have completed one year of dental hygiene curricula at an accredited dental hygiene program in United States. Must demonstrate GPA of at least 3.5, and financial need of $1500 or more.

Academic Fields/Career Goals: Dental Health/Services.

Award: Scholarship for use in sophomore, junior, or senior years; not renewable. *Number:* 2. *Amount:* $1000.

Eligibility Requirements: Applicant must be enrolled or expecting to enroll full-time at a four-year institution or university. Applicant or parent of applicant must be member of American Dental Hygienist's Association. Applicant must have 3.5 GPA or higher. Available to U.S. citizens.

Application Requirements: Application, essay, financial need analysis, references. *Deadline:* May 1.

Contact: Star Abernathy, Administrator
American Dental Hygienists' Association (ADHA) Institute
444 North Michigan Avenue, Suite 3400
Chicago, IL 60611
Phone: 312-440-8944
Fax: 312-467-1806
E-mail: stara@adha.org

SIGMA PHI ALPHA UNDERGRADUATE SCHOLARSHIP

Awarded to an outstanding Sigma Phi Alpha member pursuing a certificate/associate or baccalaureate degree at a school with an active chapter of the Sigma Phi Alpha Dental Hygiene Honor Society. Applicant must demonstrate GPA of at least 3.5. Must have completed one year of dental hygiene curricula at an accredited dental hygiene program in United States. Must demonstrate a financial need of $1500 or more. Must be an active SADHA or ADHA member.

Academic Fields/Career Goals: Dental Health/Services.

Award: Scholarship for use in sophomore, junior, or senior years; not renewable. *Number:* 1. *Amount:* $1000.

Eligibility Requirements: Applicant must be enrolled or expecting to enroll full-time at a two-year or four-year or technical institution or university. Applicant or parent of applicant must be member of American Dental Hygienist's Association. Applicant must have 3.5 GPA or higher. Available to U.S. citizens.

Application Requirements: Application, financial need analysis, references, transcript. *Deadline:* May 1.

Contact: Scholarship Committee
American Dental Hygienists' Association (ADHA) Institute
444 North Michigan Avenue, Suite 3400
Chicago, IL 60611
Phone: 800-735-4916
E-mail: institute@adha.net

WILMA MOTLEY CALIFORNIA MERIT SCHOLARSHIP

One-time merit based award to full-time students pursuing an associate/certificate or baccalaureate degree in an accredited dental hygiene program within the state of California. Must demonstrate leadership experience. Minimum 3.5 GPA required. Must submit a copy of SADHA or ADHA membership card with application. Please refer to Web site for further details http://www.adha.org.

Academic Fields/Career Goals: Dental Health/Services.

Award: Scholarship for use in freshman, sophomore, junior, or senior years; not renewable. *Number:* 1. *Amount:* up to $1000.

Eligibility Requirements: Applicant must be enrolled or expecting to enroll full-time at a two-year or four-year institution or university and studying in California. Applicant or parent of applicant must be member of American Dental Hygienist's Association. Applicant must have 3.5 GPA or higher. Available to U.S. citizens.

Application Requirements: Application, references, copy of SADHA or ADHA membership card. *Deadline:* May 1.

Contact: Star Abernathy, Administrator
American Dental Hygienists' Association (ADHA) Institute
444 North Michigan Avenue, Suite 3400
Chicago, IL 60611
Phone: 312-440-8944
Fax: 312-467-1806
E-mail: stara@adha.org

AMERICAN LEGION AUXILIARY DEPARTMENT OF WYOMING

AMERICAN LEGION AUXILIARY DEPARTMENT OF WYOMING PAST PRESIDENTS' PARLEY HEALTH CARE SCHOLARSHIP

Scholarship of $300 is available for a student in the human healthcare field. Must be a resident of Wyoming, a U.S. citizen, and attend a school in Wyoming. Minimum 3.5 GPA required.

Academic Fields/Career Goals: Dental Health/Services; Health and Medical Sciences; Nursing; Therapy/Rehabilitation.

Award: Scholarship for use in sophomore year; not renewable. *Number:* up to 2. *Amount:* $300.

Eligibility Requirements: Applicant must be enrolled or expecting to enroll full-time at a two-year or four-year or technical institution or university; resident of Wyoming and studying in Wyoming. Applicant must have 3.5 GPA or higher. Available to U.S. citizens.

Application Requirements: Application, financial need analysis, transcript. *Deadline:* June 1.

Contact: Sonja Wright, Department Secretary
American Legion Auxiliary Department of Wyoming
PO Box 2198
Gillette, WY 82717
Phone: 307-686-7137
Fax: 307-686-7137
E-mail: deptwy@collinscom.net

AMERICAN MEDICAL TECHNOLOGISTS http://www.amt1.com

AMERICAN MEDICAL TECHNOLOGISTS STUDENT SCHOLARSHIP

One-time award for the undergraduate study of medical technology, medical laboratory technician, office laboratory technician, phlebotomy, or medical, dental assisting. Include SASE.

Academic Fields/Career Goals: Dental Health/Services; Health and Medical Sciences.

Award: Scholarship for use in freshman, sophomore, junior, or senior years; not renewable. *Number:* 5. *Amount:* $500.

Eligibility Requirements: Applicant must be enrolled or expecting to enroll full- or part-time at a two-year or four-year institution or university. Available to U.S. citizens.

Application Requirements: Application, essay, financial need analysis, references, self-addressed stamped envelope, transcript. *Deadline:* April 1.

Contact: Linda Kujbida, Scholarship Coordinator
American Medical Technologists
10700 West Higgins Road, Suite 150
Rosemont, IL 60018-5765
Phone: 847-823-5169
Fax: 847-823-0458
E-mail: amtmail@aol.com

ARKANSAS DEPARTMENT OF HIGHER EDUCATION http://www.adhe.edu

ARKANSAS HEALTH EDUCATION GRANT PROGRAM (ARHEG)

• *See page 82*

BETHESDA LUTHERAN HOMES AND SERVICES, INC. http://www.blhs.org

DEVELOPMENTAL DISABILITIES SCHOLASTIC ACHIEVEMENT SCHOLARSHIP FOR LUTHERAN COLLEGE STUDENTS

One-time award for Lutheran college students who have completed sophomore year in studies related to developmental disabilities. Awards of up to $1500. 3.0 GPA required.

Academic Fields/Career Goals: Dental Health/Services; Education; Health Administration; Health and Medical Sciences; Health Information Management/Technology; Humanities; Social Services; Special Education; Therapy/Rehabilitation.

Award: Scholarship for use in junior or senior years; not renewable. *Number:* 1–3. *Amount:* up to $1500.

Eligibility Requirements: Applicant must be Lutheran and enrolled or expecting to enroll full-time at a four-year institution or university. Applicant must have 3.0 GPA or higher. Available to U.S. and Canadian citizens.

Application Requirements: Application, autobiography, essay, references, transcript. *Deadline:* April 15.

Contact: Thomas Heuer, Coordinator, Outreach Programs and Services
Bethesda Lutheran Homes and Services, Inc.
600 Hoffmann Drive
Watertown, WI 53094-6294
Phone: 920-261-3050 Ext. 4449
Fax: 920-262-6513
E-mail: theuer@blhs.org

BUSINESS AND PROFESSIONAL WOMEN'S FOUNDATION http://www.bpwfoundation.org

BPW CAREER ADVANCEMENT SCHOLARSHIP PROGRAM FOR WOMEN

• *See page 130*

DELAWARE STATE DENTAL SOCIETY http://www.delawarestatedentalsociety.org

G. LAYTON GRIER SCHOLARSHIP

One-time award for Delaware residents to study dentistry. Freshmen are not eligible. Must be a U.S. citizen. Student must have financial need and good academic standing.

Academic Fields/Career Goals: Dental Health/Services.

Award: Scholarship for use in sophomore or graduate years; not renewable. *Number:* 3. *Amount:* $1000.

Eligibility Requirements: Applicant must be enrolled or expecting to enroll full-time at a four-year institution or university and resident of Delaware. Available to U.S. citizens.

Application Requirements: Application, autobiography, driver's license, financial need analysis, interview, references, transcript, proof of residency, biographical sketch. *Deadline:* March 1.

Contact: Scholarship Coordinator
Delaware State Dental Society
1925 Layering Avenue
Wilmington, DE 19806
Phone: 302-654-4335

FLORIDA DENTAL HEALTH FOUNDATION http://www.floridadental.org

DENTAL ASSISTING SCHOLARSHIPS

One-time award for dental assistant study. Must be resident of Florida for at least two years. Must have minimum 2.5 GPA and references from an accredited dental assistant's school. Application available on Web site.

Academic Fields/Career Goals: Dental Health/Services.

Award: Scholarship for use in freshman, sophomore, junior, or senior years; not renewable. *Number:* 20–25. *Amount:* $200–$500.

Eligibility Requirements: Applicant must be enrolled or expecting to enroll full- or part-time at a four-year institution or university; resident of Florida and studying in Florida. Applicant must have 2.5 GPA or higher. Available to U.S. and non-U.S. citizens.

Application Requirements: Application, references, transcript. *Deadline:* varies.

Contact: Cheri Sutherland, Secretary
Florida Dental Health Foundation
1111 East Tennessee Street
Tallahassee, FL 32308-6914
Phone: 850-681-3629 Ext. 119
Fax: 850-681-0116
E-mail: csutherland@floridadental.org

HELLENIC UNIVERSITY CLUB OF PHILADELPHIA http://www.hucphila.org

NICHOLAS S. HETOS, DDS MEMORIAL GRADUATE SCHOLARSHIP

$2000 scholarships for a senior undergraduate or graduate student with financial need pursuing studies leading to a Doctor of Dental Medicine or Doctor of Dental Surgery degree. Must be a U.S. citizen of Greek descent and a resident of particular counties in NJ or PA.

Academic Fields/Career Goals: Dental Health/Services.

Award: Scholarship for use in senior or graduate years; not renewable. *Number:* up to 1. *Amount:* $2000.

Eligibility Requirements: Applicant must be of Greek heritage; enrolled or expecting to enroll full-time at a four-year institution or university and resident of New Jersey or Pennsylvania. Available to U.S. citizens.

Application Requirements: Application, financial need analysis, transcript. *Deadline:* April 21.

Contact: Zoe Tripolitis, Scholarship Chairman
Hellenic University Club of Philadelphia
PO Box 42199
Philadelphia, PA 19101-2199
Phone: 215-483-7440
E-mail: hucphila@yahoo.com

HISPANIC DENTAL ASSOCIATION http://www.hdassoc.org

DR. JUAN D. VILLARREAL/HISPANIC DENTAL ASSOCIATION FOUNDATION

Scholarship offered to Hispanic U.S. students who have been accepted into or are currently enrolled in an accredited dental or dental hygiene program in the state of Texas. Scholarship will obligate the grantees to complete the current year of their dental or dental hygiene program. Scholastic achievement, leadership skills, community service and commitment to improving the health of the Hispanic community will all be considered.

Academic Fields/Career Goals: Dental Health/Services.

Award: Scholarship for use in freshman, sophomore, junior, or senior years; not renewable. *Number:* up to 3. *Amount:* $500–$1000.

Eligibility Requirements: Applicant must be of Hispanic heritage; enrolled or expecting to enroll full-time at a two-year or four-year institution or university; resident of Texas and studying in Texas. Available to U.S. citizens.

Application Requirements: Application, transcript. *Deadline:* varies.

Contact: Scholarship Committee
Hispanic Dental Association
3085 Stevenson Drive, Suite 200
Springfield, IL 62703
Phone: 217-529-9120
Fax: 217-529-9120

PROCTOR AND GAMBLE ORAL CARE AND HDA FOUNDATION SCHOLARSHIP

Scholarships available to Hispanic students entering into their first year of an accredited dental, dental hygiene, dental assisting, or dental technician program. Scholastic achievement, community service, leadership, and commitment to improving health of the Hispanic community will all be considered.

Academic Fields/Career Goals: Dental Health/Services.

Award: Scholarship for use in freshman year; not renewable. *Number:* up to 15. *Amount:* $500–$1000.

Eligibility Requirements: Applicant must be Hispanic; high school student and planning to enroll or expecting to enroll full-time at a two-year or technical institution. Available to U.S. citizens.

Hispanic Dental Association (continued)

Application Requirements: Application, transcript. *Deadline:* varies.

Contact: Rita Brummett, Member Services Director
Hispanic Dental Association
3085 Stevenson Drive, Suite 200
Springfield, IL 62703
Phone: 217-529-6517
Fax: 217-529-9120
E-mail: rbrummett@hdassoc.org

INDIAN HEALTH SERVICES, UNITED STATES DEPARTMENT OF HEALTH AND HUMAN SERVICES http://www.ihs.gov

INDIAN HEALTH SERVICE HEALTH PROFESSIONS PRE-GRADUATE SCHOLARSHIPS

Renewable scholarship for Native American students who are enrolled either part- or full-time in courses leading to a bachelor degree in the areas of pre-medicine or pre-dentistry. Must intend to serve Indian people upon completion of professional healthcare education. Minimum 2.0 GPA required.

Academic Fields/Career Goals: Dental Health/Services; Health and Medical Sciences.

Award: Scholarship for use in freshman, sophomore, junior, or senior years; renewable. *Number:* varies. *Amount:* varies.

Eligibility Requirements: Applicant must be American Indian/Alaska Native and enrolled or expecting to enroll full- or part-time at a two-year or four-year or technical institution or university. Available to U.S. citizens.

Application Requirements: Application, applicant must enter a contest, essay, references, transcript, proof of descent. *Deadline:* February 28.

Contact: Dawn Kelly, Branch Chief
Indian Health Services, United States Department of Health and Human Services
801 Thompson Avenue, Suite 120
Rockville, MD 20852
Phone: 301-443-6197
Fax: 301-443-6048
E-mail: dawn.kelly@ihs.gov

INTERNATIONAL ORDER OF THE KING'S DAUGHTERS AND SONS http://www.iokds.org

HEALTH CAREERS SCHOLARSHIP

Award for students preparing for careers in medicine, dentistry, pharmacy, physical or occupational therapy, and medical technologies. Must be a U.S. or Canadian citizen, enrolled full-time in a school accredited in the field involved and located in the U.S. or Canada. For all students, except those preparing for an RN degree, application must be for at least the third year of college. RN students must have completed the first year of schooling. Pre-medicine students are not eligible to apply. For those students seeking degrees of MD or DDS application must be for at least the second year of medical or dental school. Each applicant must supply proof of acceptance in the school involved.

Academic Fields/Career Goals: Dental Health/Services; Health and Medical Sciences; Nursing; Therapy/Rehabilitation.

Award: Scholarship for use in sophomore, junior, senior, or graduate years; not renewable. *Number:* 40–50. *Amount:* $500–$1000.

Eligibility Requirements: Applicant must be enrolled or expecting to enroll full-time at a four-year institution or university. Available to U.S. and Canadian citizens.

Application Requirements: Application, photo, resume, references, self-addressed stamped envelope, transcript, itemized budget. *Deadline:* varies.

Contact: Director, Health Careers Department
International Order of the King's Daughters and Sons
PO Box 1017
Chautauqua, NY 14722-1017
Phone: 716-357-4951

JEWISH FOUNDATION FOR EDUCATION OF WOMEN http://www.jfew.org

JFEW SCHOLARSHIPS FOR EMIGRES IN THE HEALTH SCIENCES

Scholarships for emigres from the former Soviet Union to train in medicine, dentistry, dental hygiene, nursing, pharmacy, occupational and physical therapy, physician assistant programs, sonography, and cardiovascular technology programs. Students must already be enrolled or about to be enrolled in one of these programs to be eligible. Scholarships will be awarded for a maximum of $5000.

Academic Fields/Career Goals: Dental Health/Services; Health and Medical Sciences; Nursing; Pharmacy; Therapy/Rehabilitation.

Award: Scholarship for use in freshman, sophomore, junior, senior, or graduate years; renewable. *Number:* varies. *Amount:* up to $5000.

Eligibility Requirements: Applicant must be of former Soviet Union heritage; enrolled or expecting to enroll full-time at a two-year or four-year institution or university; female and studying in New York. Available to U.S. citizens.

Application Requirements: Application, financial need analysis. *Deadline:* June 16.

Contact: Leonard Petlakh, Assistant Executive Director
Jewish Foundation for Education of Women
135 East 64th Street
New York, NY 10065
Phone: 212-288-3931
Fax: 212-288-5798
E-mail: info@jfew.org

MARYLAND ASSOCIATION OF PRIVATE COLLEGES AND CAREER SCHOOLS http://www.mapccs.org

MARYLAND ASSOCIATION OF PRIVATE COLLEGES AND CAREER SCHOOLS SCHOLARSHIP

• *See page 146*

MARYLAND HIGHER EDUCATION COMMISSION http://www.mhec.state.md.us

GRADUATE AND PROFESSIONAL SCHOLARSHIP PROGRAM-MARYLAND

Graduate and professional scholarships provide need-based financial assistance to students attending a Maryland school of medicine, dentistry, law, pharmacy, social work, or nursing. Funds are provided to specific Maryland colleges and universities. Students must demonstrate financial need and be Maryland residents. Contact institution financial aid office for more information.

Academic Fields/Career Goals: Dental Health/Services; Health and Medical Sciences; Law/Legal Services; Nursing; Social Services.

Award: Scholarship for use in freshman, sophomore, junior, senior, graduate, or postgraduate years; renewable. *Number:* 40–200. *Amount:* $1000–$5000.

Eligibility Requirements: Applicant must be enrolled or expecting to enroll full- or part-time at a four-year institution or university; resident of Maryland and studying in Maryland. Available to U.S. citizens.

Application Requirements: Application, financial need analysis, contact institution financial aid office. *Deadline:* March 1.

Contact: Elizabeth Urbanski, Associate Director
Maryland Higher Education Commission
839 Bestgate Road, Suite 400
Annapolis, MD 21401-3013
Phone: 410-260-4561
Fax: 410-260-3202
E-mail: eurbansk@mhec.state.md.us

MISSOURI DEPARTMENT OF HEALTH AND SENIOR SERVICES http://www.dhss.mo.gov

PRIMARY CARE RESOURCE INITIATIVE FOR MISSOURI LOAN PROGRAM

Forgivable loans for Missouri residents attending Missouri institutions pursuing a degree as a primary care physician or dentist, studying for a bachelors degree as a dental hygienist, or a master of science degree in nursing leading to certification as an Advanced Practice Nurse. To be forgiven participant must work in a Missouri health professional shortage area.

Academic Fields/Career Goals: Dental Health/Services; Health and Medical Sciences; Nursing.

Award: Forgivable loan for use in freshman, sophomore, junior, senior, graduate, or postgraduate years; not renewable. *Number:* 100. *Amount:* $5000–$20,000.

Eligibility Requirements: Applicant must be enrolled or expecting to enroll full- or part-time at a four-year institution or university; resident of Missouri and studying in Missouri. Applicant must have 2.5 GPA or higher. Available to U.S. and non-U.S. citizens.

Application Requirements: Application, driver's license, proof of Missouri residency. *Deadline:* June 30.

Contact: Kristie Frank, Health Program Representative
Missouri Department of Health and Senior Services
PO Box 570
Jefferson City, MO 65102-0570
Phone: 800-891-7415
Fax: 573-522-8146
E-mail: frank@dhss.mo.gov

NATIONAL ARAB AMERICAN MEDICAL ASSOCIATION http://www.naama.com

FOUNDATION SCHOLARSHIP

Scholarship of $1000 each to qualified students of Arabic extraction enrolled in a U.S. or Canadian medical, osteopathic, or dental school.

Academic Fields/Career Goals: Dental Health/Services; Health and Medical Sciences; Osteopathy.

Award: Scholarship for use in freshman, sophomore, junior, senior, or graduate years; not renewable. *Number:* 2. *Amount:* $1000.

Eligibility Requirements: Applicant must be of Arab heritage and enrolled or expecting to enroll full-time at a four-year institution or university. Applicant must have 3.0 GPA or higher. Available to U.S. and Canadian citizens.

Application Requirements: Application, essay, financial need analysis, transcript. *Deadline:* July 1.

Contact: Mouhanad Hammami, Executive Director
National Arab American Medical Association
801 South Adams Road, Suite 208
Birmingham, MI 48009
Phone: 248-646-3661
Fax: 248-646-0617
E-mail: naama@naama.com

NATIONAL DENTAL ASSOCIATION FOUNDATION http://www.ndaonline.org

NATIONAL DENTAL ASSOCIATION FOUNDATION COLGATE-PALMOLIVE SCHOLARSHIP PROGRAM (UNDERGRADUATES)

A scholarship of up to $1000 is given to sophomores through juniors in a dental school who are under-represented minority students. Applicants should be a member of NDA. Number of scholarships granted varies.

Academic Fields/Career Goals: Dental Health/Services.

Award: Scholarship for use in sophomore, junior, or senior years; not renewable. *Number:* up to 100. *Amount:* $700–$1000.

Eligibility Requirements: Applicant must be American Indian/Alaska Native, Asian/Pacific Islander, Black (non-Hispanic), or Hispanic and enrolled or expecting to enroll full-time at a four-year institution or university. Available to U.S. citizens.

Application Requirements: Application, financial need analysis, resume, references, transcript, letter of request. *Deadline:* May 15.

Contact: Roosevelt Brown, President
National Dental Association Foundation
3517 16th Street, NW
Washington, DC 20010
Phone: 501-681-6110
Fax: 541-376-4008
E-mail: rbndaf1@comcast.net

NEW MEXICO COMMISSION ON HIGHER EDUCATION http://www.hed.state.nm.us

ALLIED HEALTH STUDENT LOAN PROGRAM-NEW MEXICO

Award to New Mexico residents studying in New Mexico to increase the number of physician assistants in areas of the state which have experienced shortages of health practitioners. Provides educational loans to students seeking certification/licensers in an eligible health field. As a condition of each loan, the student must declare intent to practice as a health professional in a designated shortage area. For every year of service, a portion of the loan will be forgiven.

Academic Fields/Career Goals: Dental Health/Services; Health and Medical Sciences; Nursing; Therapy/Rehabilitation.

Award: Forgivable loan for use in freshman, sophomore, junior, senior, or graduate years; renewable. *Number:* 1–40. *Amount:* up to $12,000.

Eligibility Requirements: Applicant must be enrolled or expecting to enroll full- or part-time at a four-year institution or university; resident of New Mexico and studying in New Mexico. Available to U.S. citizens.

Application Requirements: Application, financial need analysis, transcript, FAFSA. *Deadline:* July 1.

Contact: Tashina Banks-Moore, Interim Director of Financial Aid
New Mexico Commission on Higher Education
1068 Cerrillos Road
Santa Fe, NM 87505-1650
Phone: 505-476-6549
Fax: 505-476-6511
E-mail: tashina.banks-moore@state.nm.us

NEW YORK STATE EDUCATION DEPARTMENT http://www.highered.nysed.gov

REGENTS PROFESSIONAL OPPORTUNITY SCHOLARSHIP

• *See page 60*

NORTH CAROLINA STATE EDUCATION ASSISTANCE AUTHORITY http://www.ncseaa.edu

NORTH CAROLINA STUDENT LOAN PROGRAM FOR HEALTH, SCIENCE, AND MATHEMATICS

Renewable award for North Carolina residents studying health-related fields, or science or math education. Based on merit, need, and promise of service as a health professional or educator in an under-served area of North Carolina. Need two co-signers. Submit surety statement.

Academic Fields/Career Goals: Dental Health/Services; Health Administration; Health and Medical Sciences; Nursing; Physical Sciences and Math; Therapy/Rehabilitation.

Award: Forgivable loan for use in freshman, sophomore, junior, senior, or graduate years; renewable. *Number:* 1. *Amount:* $3000–$8500.

Eligibility Requirements: Applicant must be enrolled or expecting to enroll full-time at a two-year or four-year institution or university and resident of North Carolina. Available to U.S. citizens.

Application Requirements: Application, financial need analysis, transcript. *Deadline:* June 1.

Contact: Edna Williams, Manager, Selection and Origination
North Carolina State Education Assistance Authority
PO Box 14223
Research Triangle Park, NC 27709
Phone: 800-700-1775 Ext. 4658
E-mail: eew@ncseaa.edu

RESOURCE CENTER

MARIE BLAHA MEDICAL GRANT

• *See page 83*

STATE OF GEORGIA http://www.gsfc.org

SERVICE-CANCELABLE STAFFORD LOAN-GEORGIA

Scholarship assists Georgia students enrolled in critical fields of study in allied health. For use at GSFA-approved schools. Awards $4500 forgivable loan for dentistry students only. Contact school financial aid officer for more details.

Academic Fields/Career Goals: Dental Health/Services; Health and Medical Sciences; Nursing; Therapy/Rehabilitation.

Award: Forgivable loan for use in freshman, sophomore, junior, senior, or graduate years; not renewable. *Number:* 500–1200. *Amount:* $2000–$4500.

Eligibility Requirements: Applicant must be enrolled or expecting to enroll full- or part-time at a two-year or four-year or technical institution or university; resident of Georgia and studying in Georgia. Available to U.S. citizens.

State of Georgia (continued)

Application Requirements: Application, financial need analysis. *Deadline:* continuous.

Contact: Peggy Matthews, Manager, GSFA Origination
State of Georgia
2082 East Exchange Place, Suite 230
Tucker, GA 30084
Phone: 770-724-9230
Fax: 770-724-9225
E-mail: peggy@gsfc.org

SUPREME GUARDIAN COUNCIL, INTERNATIONAL ORDER OF JOB'S DAUGHTERS http://www.iojd.org

GROTTO SCHOLARSHIP

Scholarships of $1500 to aid Job's Daughters students of outstanding ability whom have a sincerity of purpose. High school seniors, or graduates, junior college, technical school, or college students who are in early graduation programs, and pursuing an education in dentistry, preferably with some training in the handicapped field are eligible to apply.

Academic Fields/Career Goals: Dental Health/Services.

Award: Scholarship for use in freshman, sophomore, junior, senior, graduate, or postgraduate years; not renewable. *Number:* 1. *Amount:* $1500.

Eligibility Requirements: Applicant must be enrolled or expecting to enroll full- or part-time at a two-year or four-year or technical institution or university and female. Applicant or parent of applicant must be member of Jobs Daughters. Applicant or parent of applicant must have employment or volunteer experience in helping handicapped. Available to U.S. and non-U.S. citizens.

Application Requirements: Application, essay, references, transcript. *Deadline:* April 30.

Contact: Barbara Hill, Scholarship Committee Chairman
Supreme Guardian Council, International Order of Job's Daughters
337 Illinois Street
Pekin, IL 61554-2270
Phone: 309-346-5564
E-mail: dubahill@grics.net

UNITED STATES PUBLIC HEALTH SERVICE-HEALTH RESOURCES AND SERVICES ADMINISTRATION, BUREAU OF HEALTH PROFESSIONS http://bhpr.hrsa.gov/dsa

HEALTH RESOURCES AND SERVICES ADMINISTRATION-BUREAU OF HEALTH PROFESSIONS SCHOLARSHIPS FOR DISADVANTAGED STUDENTS

One-time award for full-time students from disadvantaged backgrounds enrolled in health professions and nursing programs. Institution must apply for funding and must be eligible to receive SDS funds. Students must contact financial aid office to apply.

Academic Fields/Career Goals: Dental Health/Services; Health and Medical Sciences; Nursing; Therapy/Rehabilitation.

Award: Scholarship for use in freshman, sophomore, junior, senior, or graduate years; not renewable. *Number:* up to 400. *Amount:* varies.

Eligibility Requirements: Applicant must be enrolled or expecting to enroll full-time at a two-year or four-year institution or university. Available to U.S. citizens.

Application Requirements: Application, financial need analysis. *Deadline:* varies.

Contact: Andrea Stampone, Scholarship Coordinator
United States Public Health Service-Health Resources and Services Administration, Bureau of Health Professions
Division of Health Careers Diversity Development, 5600 Fishers Lane, Parklawn Building, Room 8-34
Rockville, MD 20857
Phone: 301-443-4776
Fax: 301-446-0846
E-mail: callcenter@hrsa.gov

UNIVERSITY OF MEDICINE AND DENTISTRY OF NJ SCHOOL OF OSTEOPATHIC MEDICINE http://www.umdnj.edu

NEW JERSEY EDUCATIONAL OPPORTUNITY FUND GRANTS

Grants up to $4350 per year. Must be a New Jersey resident for at least twelve consecutive months and attend a New Jersey institution. Must be from a disadvantaged background as defined by EOF guidelines. EOF grant applicants must also apply for financial aid. EOF recipients may qualify for the Martin Luther King Physician/Dentistry Scholarships for graduate study at a professional institution.

Academic Fields/Career Goals: Dental Health/Services; Health and Medical Sciences.

Award: Grant for use in freshman, sophomore, junior, senior, or graduate years; renewable. *Number:* varies. *Amount:* $200–$4350.

Eligibility Requirements: Applicant must be enrolled or expecting to enroll full-time at a four-year institution or university; resident of New Jersey and studying in New Jersey. Available to U.S. citizens.

Application Requirements: Application, financial need analysis. *Deadline:* continuous.

Contact: Glenn Lang, EOF Executive Director
University of Medicine and Dentistry of NJ School of Osteopathic Medicine
40 East Laurel Road, Primary Care Center 119
Trenton, NJ 08625-0542
Phone: 609-984-2709
Fax: 609-292-7225
E-mail: glang@che.state.nj.us

VIRGINIA BUSINESS AND PROFESSIONAL WOMEN'S FOUNDATION http://www.vabpwfoundation.org

WOMEN IN SCIENCE AND TECHNOLOGY SCHOLARSHIP

• *See page 136*

DRAFTING

NATIONAL ASSOCIATION OF WOMEN IN CONSTRUCTION http://www.nawic.org

NAWIC UNDERGRADUATE SCHOLARSHIPS

• *See page 92*

PROFESSIONAL CONSTRUCTION ESTIMATORS ASSOCIATION http://www.pcea.org

TED WILSON MEMORIAL SCHOLARSHIP FOUNDATION

Amount up to $1500 to a deserving student (high school senior, college freshman, sophomore, or junior) based on their academic ability, need, and desire to enter the construction industry.

Academic Fields/Career Goals: Drafting; Electrical Engineering/Electronics; Engineering/Technology; Heating, Air-Conditioning, and Refrigeration Mechanics; Landscape Architecture; Mechanical Engineering; Surveying; Surveying Technology, Cartography, or Geographic Information Science.

Award: Scholarship for use in freshman, sophomore, or junior years; not renewable. *Number:* 5. *Amount:* up to $1500.

Eligibility Requirements: Applicant must be enrolled or expecting to enroll full-time at a two-year or four-year or technical institution and studying in Florida, Georgia, North Carolina, South Carolina, or Virginia. Available to U.S. and non-U.S. citizens.

Application Requirements: Application, financial need analysis, interview, references, transcript. *Deadline:* March 15.

Contact: Kim Lybrand, National Office Manager
Professional Construction Estimators Association
PO Box 680336
Charlotte, NC 28216-0336
Phone: 704-987-9978
Fax: 704-987-9979
E-mail: pcea@pcea.org

EARTH SCIENCE

ALASKA GEOLOGICAL SOCIETY INC. http://www.alaskageology.org

ALASKA GEOLOGICAL SOCIETY SCHOLARSHIP

Scholarship available for full-time junior and senior undergraduate or graduate student enrolled at any Alaska university, with academic emphasis in earth sciences.

Academic Fields/Career Goals: Earth Science.

Award: Scholarship for use in junior, senior, or graduate years; not renewable. *Number:* 3–6. *Amount:* $500–$1500.

Eligibility Requirements: Applicant must be enrolled or expecting to enroll full-time at a four-year institution or university and studying in Alaska. Available to U.S. and non-U.S. citizens.

Application Requirements: Financial need analysis, references, transcript, cover letter, thesis proposal (for graduate students). *Deadline:* March 20.

Contact: Micaela Weeks, Scholarship Committee Chair
Alaska Geological Society Inc.
PO Box 101288
Anchorage, AK 99510-1288
Phone: 907-564-5635
E-mail: micaela.weeks@bp.com

AMERICAN GEOLOGICAL INSTITUTE http://www.agiweb.org

AMERICAN GEOLOGICAL INSTITUTE MINORITY SCHOLARSHIP

Scholarship available only to students currently enrolled in an accredited institution as an undergraduate or graduate student majoring in geoscience, including the geoscience sub-disciplines of geology, geophysics, geochemistry, hydrology, meteorology, physical oceanography, planetary geology, or earth-science education. Verifiable ethnic minority status as Black, Hispanic, or Native American is required.

Academic Fields/Career Goals: Earth Science; Hydrology; Meteorology/Atmospheric Science; Oceanography.

Award: Scholarship for use in sophomore, junior, senior, or graduate years; renewable. *Number:* 20–30. *Amount:* $250–$3000.

Eligibility Requirements: Applicant must be American Indian/Alaska Native, Asian/Pacific Islander, Black (non-Hispanic), or Hispanic and enrolled or expecting to enroll full-time at a two-year or four-year institution or university. Available to U.S. citizens.

Application Requirements: Application, references, test scores, transcript. *Deadline:* March 1.

Contact: Cindy Martinez, Geo-Science Workforce Specialist
American Geological Institute
4220 King Street
Alexandria, VA 22302-1507
Phone: 703-379-2480 Ext. 244
Fax: 703-379-7563
E-mail: cmm@agiweb.org

AMERICAN INDIAN SCIENCE AND ENGINEERING SOCIETY http://www.aises.org

A.T. ANDERSON MEMORIAL SCHOLARSHIP PROGRAM

• *See page 84*

ARIZONA HYDROLOGICAL SOCIETY http://www.azhydrosoc.org

ARIZONA HYDROLOGICAL SOCIETY SCHOLARSHIP

One-time award to outstanding undergraduate or graduate students who have demonstrated academic excellence in water resources related fields as a means of encouraging them to continue to develop as water resources professionals. Must be a resident of Arizona and be enrolled in a postsecondary Arizona institution.

Academic Fields/Career Goals: Earth Science; Hydrology; Natural Resources; Nuclear Science; Science, Technology, and Society.

Award: Scholarship for use in sophomore, junior, senior, or graduate years; not renewable. *Number:* 3. *Amount:* $3000.

Eligibility Requirements: Applicant must be enrolled or expecting to enroll full-time at a two-year or four-year or technical institution or university; resident of Arizona and studying in Arizona. Available to U.S. citizens.

Application Requirements: Application, essay, financial need analysis, references, transcript. *Deadline:* April 30.

Contact: Aregai Tecle, Professor
Arizona Hydrological Society
PO Box 15018
Flagstaff, AZ 86011
Phone: 928-523-6642
Fax: 928-556-7112
E-mail: aregai.tecle@nau.edu

ASSOCIATION FOR WOMEN GEOSCIENTISTS, PUGET SOUND CHAPTER http://www.awg.org

AWG CRAWFORD FIELD CAMP SCHOLARSHIP

Two $500 scholarships will be awarded to promising undergraduate women students who will be attending field camp during the summer.

Academic Fields/Career Goals: Earth Science.

Award: Scholarship for use in freshman, sophomore, junior, or senior years; not renewable. *Number:* 2. *Amount:* $500.

Eligibility Requirements: Applicant must be enrolled or expecting to enroll full-time at a four-year institution or university and female. Applicant must have 3.0 GPA or higher. Available to U.S. citizens.

Application Requirements: Application, essay, references, transcript. *Deadline:* February 16.

Contact: Richard Yuretich, Department of Geosciences, University of Massachusetts-Amherst
Association for Women Geoscientists, Puget Sound Chapter
611 North Pleasant Street, 233 Morrill Science Center
Amherst, MA 01003-9297

AWG MINORITY SCHOLARSHIP

Scholarship available for an African American, Hispanic, or Native American full-time student who is pursuing an undergraduate degree in the geosciences at an accredited college or university.

Academic Fields/Career Goals: Earth Science.

Award: Scholarship for use in freshman, sophomore, junior, or senior years; not renewable. *Number:* 1. *Amount:* up to $5000.

Eligibility Requirements: Applicant must be American Indian/Alaska Native, Black (non-Hispanic), or Hispanic; enrolled or expecting to enroll full-time at a four-year institution or university and female. Available to U.S. citizens.

Application Requirements: Application, references, transcript, SAT or ACT scores. *Deadline:* June 30.

Contact: Kim Begay Jackson, Minority Scholarship Coordinator
Association for Women Geoscientists, Puget Sound Chapter
PO Box 30645
Lincoln, NE 68503-0645
E-mail: awgscholarship@yahoo.com

OSAGE CHAPTER SCHOLARSHIP

Scholarship for undergraduate women pursuing independent research in geosciences. Amount varies based on merit up to $500.

Academic Fields/Career Goals: Earth Science.

Award: Scholarship for use in freshman, sophomore, junior, or senior years; not renewable. *Number:* 1. *Amount:* up to $500.

Eligibility Requirements: Applicant must be enrolled or expecting to enroll full-time at a four-year institution or university and female. Available to U.S. citizens.

Association for Women Geoscientists, Puget Sound Chapter (continued)

Application Requirements: Application, transcript, one-page description of research project, budget, letter of support from research supervisor. *Deadline:* April 1.

Contact: Jessica Finnearty, AWG Osage Chapter President
Association for Women Geoscientists, Puget Sound Chapter
University of Kansas, 1475 Jayhawk Boulevard, Room 120
Lawrence, KS 66045
E-mail: jfinne@ku.edu

PENELOPE HANSHAW SCHOLARSHIP

Scholarship available for women who are currently enrolled as full-time, graduate or undergraduate geoscience majors in an accredited, degree-granting college or university in Delaware, the District of Columbia, Maryland, Virginia, or West Virginia. The candidate must demonstrate academic excellence by a GPA not lower than 3.0 and awareness of the importance of community outreach by participation in geoscience or Earth science education activities.

Academic Fields/Career Goals: Earth Science; Education.

Award: Scholarship for use in freshman, sophomore, junior, senior, or graduate years; not renewable. *Number:* 1. *Amount:* $500.

Eligibility Requirements: Applicant must be enrolled or expecting to enroll full-time at a four-year institution or university; female and studying in Delaware, District of Columbia, Maryland, Virginia, or West Virginia. Applicant or parent of applicant must have employment or volunteer experience in teaching/education. Applicant must have 3.0 GPA or higher. Available to U.S. citizens.

Application Requirements: Application, references, transcript. *Deadline:* April 30.

Contact: Laurel M. Bybell, U.S. Geological Survey
Association for Women Geoscientists, Puget Sound Chapter
926 National Center
Reston, VA 20192

PUGET SOUND CHAPTER SCHOLARSHIP

Scholarship for undergraduate women committed to completing a bachelor's degree and pursuing a career or graduate work in the geosciences, including geology, environmental/engineering geology, geochemistry, geophysics, and hydrology. Must be sophomore, junior, or senior woman enrolled in a university or two-year college in western Washington State, west of the Columbia and Okanogan Rivers. Must have minimum 3.2 GPA. Must be a U.S. citizen or permanent resident.

Academic Fields/Career Goals: Earth Science; Environmental Science; Hydrology; Physical Sciences and Math.

Award: Scholarship for use in freshman, sophomore, junior, or senior years; not renewable. *Number:* 1. *Amount:* $1000.

Eligibility Requirements: Applicant must be enrolled or expecting to enroll full-time at a two-year or four-year institution or university; female and studying in Washington. Available to U.S. citizens.

Application Requirements: Essay, financial need analysis, references, transcript. *Deadline:* November 3.

Contact: Anne Udaloy, Scholarship Committee Chair
Association for Women Geoscientists, Puget Sound Chapter
1910 East Fourth Avenue, PO Box 65
Olympia, WA 98506
Phone: 206-543-9024
E-mail: scholarship@awg-ps.org

SUSAN EKDALE MEMORIAL SCHOLARSHIP

A single $1500 scholarship will be awarded to a female student in the geosciences to help defray field camp expenses. Applicant must be attending a Utah institution of higher learning, or be a Utah resident attending college elsewhere.

Academic Fields/Career Goals: Earth Science.

Award: Scholarship for use in freshman, sophomore, junior, senior, or graduate years; not renewable. *Number:* 1. *Amount:* $1500.

Eligibility Requirements: Applicant must be enrolled or expecting to enroll full-time at a four-year institution or university; female and resident of Utah. Available to U.S. citizens.

Application Requirements: Application, essay, references, self-addressed stamped envelope, letter of eligibility from the department verifying field of study. *Deadline:* March 28.

Contact: Janae Wallace, Scholarship Committee
Association for Women Geoscientists, Puget Sound Chapter
PO Box 146100
Salt Lake City, UT 84114

WILLIAM RUCKER GREENWOOD SCHOLARSHIP

Scholarship available for minority women who are currently enrolled as full-time, graduate or undergraduate geoscience majors in an accredited, degree-granting college or university in Delaware, the District of Columbia, Maryland, Virginia, or West Virginia. The candidate must demonstrate awareness of the importance of community outreach by participation in geoscience or Earth science education activities that reflect AWG's goals and potential for leadership as a future geoscience professional.

Academic Fields/Career Goals: Earth Science; Education.

Award: Scholarship for use in freshman, sophomore, junior, senior, or graduate years; not renewable. *Number:* 1. *Amount:* $1000.

Eligibility Requirements: Applicant must be American Indian/Alaska Native, Asian/Pacific Islander, Black (non-Hispanic), or Hispanic; enrolled or expecting to enroll full-time at a four-year institution or university; female and studying in Delaware, District of Columbia, Maryland, Virginia, or West Virginia. Applicant or parent of applicant must have employment or volunteer experience in teaching/education. Available to U.S. citizens.

Application Requirements: Application, references. *Deadline:* April 30.

Contact: Laurel M. Bybell, U.S. Geological Survey
Association for Women Geoscientists, Puget Sound Chapter
926 National Center
Reston, VA 20192

ASSOCIATION FOR WOMEN IN SCIENCE EDUCATIONAL FOUNDATION http://www.awis.org/careers/edfoundation.html

ASSOCIATION FOR WOMEN IN SCIENCE COLLEGE SCHOLARSHIP

• *See page 82*

AWIS KIRSTEN R. LORENTZEN AWARD IN PHYSICS

Award for female undergraduate students, to be used in their junior or senior year of study. Must be studying toward a degree in physics or geoscience, and excel in both academic and non-academic pursuits. Must be U.S. citizens.

Academic Fields/Career Goals: Earth Science; Physical Sciences and Math.

Award: Scholarship for use in junior or senior years; not renewable. *Number:* 1. *Amount:* $1000.

Eligibility Requirements: Applicant must be enrolled or expecting to enroll full-time at a four-year institution or university and female. Available to U.S. citizens.

Application Requirements: Application, essay, references, transcript. *Deadline:* January 31.

Contact: Barbara Filner, President
Association for Women in Science Educational Foundation
7008 Richard Drive
Bethesda, MD 20817-4838
Phone: 301-229-9243
E-mail: awisedfd@awis.org

ASSOCIATION OF ENGINEERING GEOLOGISTS http://www.aegfoundation.org

MARLIAVE FUND

One-time award to support undergraduate and graduate students studying engineering geology and geological engineering.

Academic Fields/Career Goals: Earth Science; Engineering/Technology; Engineering-Related Technologies.

Award: Scholarship for use in senior or graduate years; not renewable. *Number:* 1. *Amount:* $1000.

Eligibility Requirements: Applicant must be enrolled or expecting to enroll full-time at a four-year institution or university. Available to U.S. citizens.

Application Requirements: Application, essay, resume, references, transcript. *Deadline:* April 15.

Contact: Paul M. Santi, Scholarship Committee
Association of Engineering Geologists
Department of Geology and Geological Engineering, Berthoud Hall
Golden, CO 80401
Phone: 303-757-2926

TILFORD FUND

Scholarship of $1000 for student members of AEG. Three to four awards are granted annually. For undergraduate students, the scholarship goes toward the cost of a geology field camp course or senior thesis field research. For graduate students, the scholarship would apply to field research.

Academic Fields/Career Goals: Earth Science.

Award: Scholarship for use in freshman, sophomore, junior, senior, or graduate years; not renewable. *Number:* 3–4. *Amount:* $1000.

Eligibility Requirements: Applicant must be enrolled or expecting to enroll full-time at a four-year institution or university. Applicant or parent of applicant must be member of Association of Engineering Geologists. Available to U.S. citizens.

Application Requirements: Application, essay, resume, references, transcript. *Deadline:* February 1.

Contact: Deb Green Tilford, Chairman, Scholarship Committee
Association of Engineering Geologists
79 Forest Lane
Placitas, NM 87043
E-mail: tilgreen@aol.com

ASTRONAUT SCHOLARSHIP FOUNDATION http://www.astronautscholarship.org

ASTRONAUT SCHOLARSHIP FOUNDATION

• *See page 86*

BARRY M. GOLDWATER SCHOLARSHIP AND EXCELLENCE IN EDUCATION FOUNDATION http://www.act.org/goldwater

BARRY M. GOLDWATER SCHOLARSHIP AND EXCELLENCE IN EDUCATION PROGRAM

• *See page 86*

CANADIAN RECREATIONAL CANOEING ASSOCIATION http://www.paddlingcanada.com

BILL MASON MEMORIAL SCHOLARSHIP FUND

• *See page 74*

DESK AND DERRICK EDUCATIONAL TRUST http://www.addc.org

DESK AND DERRICK EDUCATIONAL TRUST

• *See page 86*

ELECTROCHEMICAL SOCIETY INC. http://www.electrochem.org

H.H. DOW MEMORIAL STUDENT ACHIEVEMENT AWARD OF THE INDUSTRIAL ELECTROLYSIS AND ELECTROCHEMICAL ENGINEERING DIVISION OF THE ELECTROCHEMICAL SOCIETY INC.

• *See page 131*

STUDENT ACHIEVEMENT AWARDS OF THE INDUSTRIAL ELECTROLYSIS AND ELECTROCHEMICAL ENGINEERING DIVISION OF THE ELECTROCHEMICAL SOCIETY INC.

• *See page 131*

STUDENT RESEARCH AWARDS OF THE BATTERY DIVISION OF THE ELECTROCHEMICAL SOCIETY INC.

• *See page 131*

GAMMA THETA UPSILON-INTERNATIONAL GEOGRAPHIC HONOR SOCIETY http://gtuhonors.org

CHRISTOPHERSON GEOSYSTEMS SCHOLARSHIP

Scholarship for undergraduate or graduate study in geosystems. Applicant must be a member of Gamma Theta Upsilon prior to submitting the application form. Must submit publishable term paper on geosystems. Must maintain a minimum GPA of 3.0.

Academic Fields/Career Goals: Earth Science; Geography.

Award: Scholarship for use in freshman, sophomore, junior, senior, or graduate years; not renewable. *Number:* 2. *Amount:* $1000.

Eligibility Requirements: Applicant must be enrolled or expecting to enroll full-time at a four-year institution or university. Applicant or parent of applicant must be member of Gamma Theta Upsilon. Applicant must have 3.0 GPA or higher. Available to U.S. and non-U.S. citizens.

Application Requirements: Application, references, transcript, term papers. *Deadline:* May 31.

Contact: Dr. Donald Zeigler, Scholarship Committee
Gamma Theta Upsilon-International Geographic Honor Society
Old Dominion University, 1881 University Drive
Virginia Beach, VA 23453

GARDEN CLUB OF AMERICA http://www.gcamerica.org

GARDEN CLUB OF AMERICA AWARDS FOR SUMMER ENVIRONMENTAL STUDIES

• *See page 74*

INDEPENDENT LABORATORIES INSTITUTE SCHOLARSHIP ALLIANCE http://www.acil.org

INDEPENDENT LABORATORIES INSTITUTE SCHOLARSHIP ALLIANCE

• *See page 132*

INNOVATION AND SCIENCE COUNCIL OF BRITISH COLUMBIA http://www.bcinnovationcouncil.com

PAUL AND HELEN TRUSSEL SCIENCE AND TECHNOLOGY SCHOLARSHIP

• *See page 87*

INSTITUTE OF ENVIRONMENTAL SCIENCES AND TECHNOLOGY (IEST) http://www.iest.org

ROBERT N. HANCOCK MEMORIAL SCHOLARSHIP

• *See page 132*

INTERNATIONAL ASSOCIATION OF GREAT LAKES RESEARCH http://www.iaglr.org

PAUL W. RODGERS SCHOLARSHIP

Award given to any senior undergraduate, master's or doctoral student who wishes to pursue a future in research, conservation, education, communication, management, or other knowledge-based activity pertaining to the Great Lakes.

Academic Fields/Career Goals: Earth Science; Education; Environmental Science; Hydrology; Marine Biology; Natural Resources; Natural Sciences.

Award: Scholarship for use in senior or graduate years; not renewable. *Number:* 1. *Amount:* $2000.

Eligibility Requirements: Applicant must be enrolled or expecting to enroll full-time at a four-year institution or university. Available to U.S. citizens.

Application Requirements: Application, essay, references, transcript. *Deadline:* March 1.

Contact: Wendy Foster, Business Manager
International Association of Great Lakes Research
Business Office, 2205 Commonwealth Boulevard
Ann Arbor, MI 48105
Phone: 734-665-5303
Fax: 734-741-2055
E-mail: office@iaglr.org

KENTUCKY NATURAL RESOURCES AND ENVIRONMENTAL PROTECTION CABINET http://www.uky.edu/waterresources

ENVIRONMENTAL PROTECTION SCHOLARSHIPS

• *See page 132*

MINERALOGICAL SOCIETY OF AMERICA http://www.minsocam.org

MINERALOGICAL SOCIETY OF AMERICA-GRANT FOR STUDENT RESEARCH IN MINERALOGY AND PETROLOGY

A $5000 grant for research in mineralogy and petrology. Selection based on qualifications of applicant; quality, innovativeness, and scientific significance of the research; and likelihood of project success. Application available on Web site at http://www.minsocam.org.

Academic Fields/Career Goals: Earth Science; Gemology; Natural Resources; Natural Sciences; Physical Sciences and Math.

Award: Grant for use in freshman, sophomore, junior, senior, or graduate years; not renewable. *Number:* 2. *Amount:* $5000.

Eligibility Requirements: Applicant must be enrolled or expecting to enroll full-time at a four-year institution or university. Available to U.S. and non-U.S. citizens.

Application Requirements: Application. *Deadline:* June 1.

Contact: J. Alexander Speer, Executive Director
Mineralogical Society of America
3635 Concorde Parkway, Suite 500
Chantilly, VA 20151-1125
Phone: 703-652-9950
Fax: 703-652-9951
E-mail: j_a_speer@minsocam.org

MINERALOGY SOCIETY OF AMERICA-GRANT FOR RESEARCH IN CRYSTALLOGRAPHY

A $5000 grant for research in crystallography. Award selection based on qualifications of applicant; quality, innovativeness, and scientific significance of proposed research; and likelihood of project success. Application available on Web site at http://www.minsocam.org. Applicable only for applicants between the ages of 25 and 35.

Academic Fields/Career Goals: Earth Science; Gemology; Materials Science, Engineering, and Metallurgy; Natural Resources; Natural Sciences; Physical Sciences and Math.

Award: Grant for use in junior, senior, or graduate years; not renewable. *Number:* 1. *Amount:* $5000.

Eligibility Requirements: Applicant must be age 25-35 and enrolled or expecting to enroll full-time at a four-year institution or university. Available to U.S. and non-U.S. citizens.

Application Requirements: Application. *Deadline:* June 1.

Contact: J. Alexander Speer, Executive Director
Mineralogical Society of America
3635 Concorde Parkway, Suite 500
Chantilly, VA 20151-1125
Phone: 703-652-9950
Fax: 703-652-9951
E-mail: j_a_speer@minsocam.org

MONTANA FEDERATION OF GARDEN CLUBS http://www.mtfgc.org

LIFE MEMBER MONTANA FEDERATION OF GARDEN CLUBS SCHOLARSHIP

Applicant must be at least a sophomore, majoring in conservation, horticulture, park or forestry, floriculture, greenhouse management, land management, or related subjects. Must be in need of assistance. Must have a potential for a successful future. Must be ranked in upper half of class or have a minimum 2.7 GPA. Must be a Montana resident and all study must be done in Montana.

Academic Fields/Career Goals: Earth Science; Horticulture/Floriculture; Landscape Architecture; Natural Resources.

Award: Scholarship for use in sophomore, junior, or senior years; not renewable. *Number:* 1. *Amount:* $1000.

Eligibility Requirements: Applicant must be enrolled or expecting to enroll full-time at a four-year institution or university; resident of Montana and studying in Montana. Applicant must have 2.5 GPA or higher. Available to U.S. citizens.

Application Requirements: Autobiography, references, transcript. *Deadline:* May 1.

Contact: Joyce Backa, Life Members Scholarship Chairman
Montana Federation of Garden Clubs
513 Skyline Drive
Craig, MT 59404-8712
Phone: 406-235-4229
E-mail: rjback@bresnan.net

MORRIS K. UDALL FOUNDATION http://www.udall.gov

MORRIS K. UDALL SCHOLARS

• *See page 76*

NASA DELAWARE SPACE GRANT CONSORTIUM http://www.delspace.org

NASA DELAWARE SPACE GRANT UNDERGRADUATE TUITION SCHOLARSHIP

• *See page 87*

NASA IDAHO SPACE GRANT CONSORTIUM http://isgc.uidaho.edu

NASA IDAHO SPACE GRANT CONSORTIUM SCHOLARSHIP PROGRAM

• *See page 87*

NASA/MARYLAND SPACE GRANT CONSORTIUM http://www.mdspacegrant.org

NASA MARYLAND SPACE GRANT CONSORTIUM UNDERGRADUATE SCHOLARSHIPS

• *See page 118*

NASA MINNESOTA SPACE GRANT CONSORTIUM http://www.aem.umn.edu/msgc

MINNESOTA SPACE GRANT CONSORTIUM

• *See page 118*

NASA SOUTH DAKOTA SPACE GRANT CONSORTIUM http://www.sdsmt.edu/space/

SOUTH DAKOTA SPACE GRANT CONSORTIUM UNDERGRADUATE SCHOLARSHIPS

• *See page 120*

NASA VERMONT SPACE GRANT CONSORTIUM http://www.cems.uvm.edu/VSGC

VERMONT SPACE GRANT CONSORTIUM SCHOLARSHIP PROGRAM

• *See page 88*

NASA VIRGINIA SPACE GRANT CONSORTIUM http://www.vsgc.odu.edu

VIRGINIA SPACE GRANT CONSORTIUM TEACHER EDUCATION SCHOLARSHIPS

• *See page 121*

NATIONAL ASSOCIATION OF GEOSCIENCE TEACHERS & FAR WESTERN SECTION http://www.mlkwolves.org

NATIONAL ASSOCIATION OF GEOSCIENCE TEACHERS-FAR WESTERN SECTION SCHOLARSHIP

Academically superior students currently enrolled in school in Hawaii, Nevada, or California are eligible to apply for one of three $500 scholarships to the school of their choice. High school senior or community college students enrolling full-time (12 quarter units) in a bachelor's degree program in geology at a four year institution. Undergraduate geology majors enrolling in an upper division field geology course of approximately 30 field mapping days.

Academic Fields/Career Goals: Earth Science.

Award: Scholarship for use in freshman, sophomore, junior, senior, or graduate years; not renewable. *Number:* 1. *Amount:* $500.

Eligibility Requirements: Applicant must be enrolled or expecting to enroll full- or part-time at a four-year institution or university and studying in California, Hawaii, or Nevada. Available to U.S. citizens.

Application Requirements: Application, references, transcript, endorsement signature of a regular member of NAGT-FWS in the reference letter. *Deadline:* March 1.

Contact: Mike Martin, Geology Scholarship Coordinator
National Association of Geoscience Teachers & Far Western Section
c/o Martin Luther King High School, 9301 Wood Road
Riverside, CA 92508
Phone: 951-789-5690
Fax: 951-788-5680
E-mail: mmartin@rusd.k12.ca.us

NATIONAL ASSOCIATION OF WATER COMPANIES-NEW JERSEY CHAPTER

NATIONAL ASSOCIATION OF WATER COMPANIES-NEW JERSEY CHAPTER SCHOLARSHIP

• *See page 133*

NATIONAL GARDEN CLUBS INC. http://www.gardenclub.org

NATIONAL GARDEN CLUBS INC. SCHOLARSHIP PROGRAM

• *See page 77*

OZARKA NATURAL SPRING WATER http://www.ozarkawater.com

EARTH SCIENCE SCHOLARSHIP

Scholarships offered to qualified students who are currently enrolled or planning to enroll in an earth/environmental sciences program at a public or private, not-for-profit, four-year college or university. Must be Texas resident with a minimum 3.0 GPA.

Academic Fields/Career Goals: Earth Science; Environmental Science.

Award: Scholarship for use in freshman, sophomore, junior, or senior years; not renewable. *Number:* 2. *Amount:* $10,000.

Eligibility Requirements: Applicant must be enrolled or expecting to enroll full-time at a four-year institution or university and resident of Texas. Applicant must have 3.0 GPA or higher. Available to U.S. citizens.

Application Requirements: Application, essay, transcript. *Deadline:* March 31.

Contact: David Feckley, Scholarship Committee
Ozarka Natural Spring Water
3265 FM 2869
Hawkins, TX 75765
Phone: 800-678-4448
E-mail: edcfund@texas.net

ROCKY MOUNTAIN COAL MINING INSTITUTE http://www.rmcmi.org

ROCKY MOUNTAIN COAL MINING INSTITUTE SCHOLARSHIP

Must be full-time college sophomore or junior at time of application, pursuing a degree in mining-related fields or engineering disciplines such as mining, geology, mineral processing, or metallurgy. For residents of Arizona, Colorado, Montana, New Mexico, North Dakota, Texas, Utah, and Wyoming. Scholarship value is $2000.

Academic Fields/Career Goals: Earth Science; Engineering/Technology; Materials Science, Engineering, and Metallurgy.

Award: Scholarship for use in junior or senior years; renewable. *Number:* 16. *Amount:* $2000.

Eligibility Requirements: Applicant must be enrolled or expecting to enroll full-time at a four-year institution or university and resident of Arizona, Colorado, Montana, New Mexico, North Dakota, Texas, Utah, or Wyoming. Available to U.S. citizens.

Application Requirements: Application, interview, references. *Deadline:* February 1.

Contact: Karen Inzano, Executive Director
Rocky Mountain Coal Mining Institute
8057 South Yukon Way
Littleton, CO 80128-5510
Phone: 303-948-3300
Fax: 303-948-1132
E-mail: mail@rmcmi.org

SIGMA XI, THE SCIENTIFIC RESEARCH SOCIETY http://www.sigmaxi.org

SIGMA XI GRANTS-IN-AID OF RESEARCH

• *See page 78*

SOCIETY FOR RANGE MANAGEMENT http://www.rangelands.org

MASONIC RANGE SCIENCE SCHOLARSHIP

• *See page 71*

SOIL AND WATER CONSERVATION SOCIETY http://www.swcs.org

DONALD A. WILLIAMS SCHOLARSHIP SOIL CONSERVATION SCHOLARSHIP

Scholarship provides financial assistance to members of SWCS, who are currently employed but who wish to improve their technical or administrative competence in a conservation-related field through course work at an accredited college or through a program of special study. Download the application form from the SWCS homepage at http://www.swcs.org.

Academic Fields/Career Goals: Earth Science; Natural Resources; Natural Sciences.

Award: Scholarship for use in freshman, sophomore, junior, or senior years; renewable. *Number:* up to 3. *Amount:* $1500.

Eligibility Requirements: Applicant must be enrolled or expecting to enroll full- or part-time at a four-year institution or university. Applicant or parent of applicant must be affiliated with Swanson Brothers Lumber Company. Applicant or parent of applicant must be member of Soil and Water Conservation Society. Applicant or parent of applicant must have employment or volunteer experience in environmental-related field. Available to U.S. and non-U.S. citizens.

Application Requirements: Application, financial need analysis, budget. *Deadline:* February 13.

Contact: Sue Lynes, Executive Assistant
Soil and Water Conservation Society
945 Ankeny Road, SW
Ankeny, IA 50023-9723
Phone: 515-289-2331 Ext. 112
Fax: 515-289-1227
E-mail: sueann.lynes@swcs.org

SOIL AND WATER CONSERVATION SOCIETY-NEW JERSEY CHAPTER http://www.geocities.com/njswcs

EDWARD R. HALL SCHOLARSHIP

• *See page 71*

TKE EDUCATIONAL FOUNDATION http://www.tke.org

CARROL C. HALL MEMORIAL SCHOLARSHIP

• *See page 88*

TIMOTHY L. TASCHWER SCHOLARSHIP

• *See page 135*

UNITED NEGRO COLLEGE FUND http://www.uncf.org

BOOZ, ALLEN AND HAMILTON/WILLIAM F. STASIOR INTERNSHIP

• *See page 150*

UNIVERSITIES SPACE RESEARCH ASSOCIATION http://www.usra.edu

UNIVERSITIES SPACE RESEARCH ASSOCIATION SCHOLARSHIP PROGRAM
• *See page 88*

WATER ENVIRONMENT FEDERATION http://www.wef.org

CANHAM GRADUATE STUDIES SCHOLARSHIPS
• *See page 136*

ECONOMICS

ADELANTE! U.S. EDUCATION LEADERSHIP FUND http://www.adelantefund.org

ADELANTE FUND MILLER NATIONAL
• *See page 47*

CATCHING THE DREAM http://www.catchingthedream.org

TRIBAL BUSINESS MANAGEMENT PROGRAM (TBM)
• *See page 49*

CENTRAL INTELLIGENCE AGENCY http://www.cia.gov

CENTRAL INTELLIGENCE AGENCY UNDERGRADUATE SCHOLARSHIP PROGRAM
• *See page 49*

CIRI FOUNDATION (TCF) http://www.thecirifoundation.org

CARL H. MARRS SCHOLARSHIP FUND
• *See page 49*

CUBAN AMERICAN NATIONAL FOUNDATION http://www.masscholarships.org

MAS FAMILY SCHOLARSHIPS
• *See page 139*

DAIRY MANAGEMENT http://www.dairyinfo.com

JAMES H. LOPER JR. MEMORIAL SCHOLARSHIP
• *See page 74*

NATIONAL DAIRY PROMOTION AND RESEARCH BOARD SCHOLARSHIP
• *See page 74*

GOVERNMENT FINANCE OFFICERS ASSOCIATION http://www.gfoa.org

MINORITIES IN GOVERNMENT FINANCE SCHOLARSHIP
• *See page 54*

HISPANIC COLLEGE FUND INC. http://www.hispanicfund.org

M & T BANK/HISPANIC COLLEGE FUND SCHOLARSHIP PROGRAM
• *See page 55*

HISPANIC SCHOLARSHIP FUND http://www.hsf.net

HSF/CITIGROUP FELLOWS PROGRAM
• *See page 55*

HSF/WELLS FARGO SCHOLARSHIP PROGRAM
• *See page 55*

INSTITUTE FOR HUMANE STUDIES http://www.theihs.org

HUMANE STUDIES FELLOWSHIPS
• *See page 179*

INSTITUTE OF INTERNATIONAL EDUCATION http://www.iie.org/nsep

NATIONAL SECURITY EDUCATION PROGRAM DAVID L. BOREN UNDERGRADUATE SCHOLARSHIPS
• *See page 144*

JORGE MAS CANOSA FREEDOM FOUNDATION http://www.jorgemascanosa.org

MAS FAMILY SCHOLARSHIP AWARD
• *See page 144*

NATIONAL ASSOCIATION OF NEGRO BUSINESS AND PROFESSIONAL WOMEN'S CLUBS INC. http://www.nanbpwc.org

JULIANNE MALVEAUX SCHOLARSHIP

Scholarship for African-American women who are college sophomores or juniors enrolled in an accredited college or university. Applicants must be majoring in journalism, economics, or a related field. Minimum 3.0 GPA required. Must be a U.S. citizen.

Academic Fields/Career Goals: Economics; Journalism.

Award: Scholarship for use in sophomore or junior years; not renewable. *Number:* 1. *Amount:* $1000.

Eligibility Requirements: Applicant must be Black (non-Hispanic); enrolled or expecting to enroll full-time at a four-year institution or university and female. Applicant must have 3.0 GPA or higher. Available to U.S. citizens.

Application Requirements: Application, essay, references, transcript. *Deadline:* April 30.

Contact: Scholarship Program Director
National Association of Negro Business and Professional Women's Clubs Inc.
1806 New Hampshire Avenue, NW
Washington, DC 20009-3298
Phone: 202-483-4206
E-mail: info@nanbpwc.org

NATIONAL ASSOCIATION OF WATER COMPANIES-NEW JERSEY CHAPTER

NATIONAL ASSOCIATION OF WATER COMPANIES-NEW JERSEY CHAPTER SCHOLARSHIP
• *See page 133*

NATIONAL SOCIETY DAUGHTERS OF THE AMERICAN REVOLUTION http://www.dar.org

NATIONAL SOCIETY DAUGHTERS OF THE AMERICAN REVOLUTION ENID HALL GRISWOLD MEMORIAL SCHOLARSHIP

Scholarship of $1000 awarded to a deserving junior or senior enrolled in an accredited college or university in the United States who is majoring in political science, history, government, or economics.

Academic Fields/Career Goals: Economics; History; Political Science.

Award: Scholarship for use in junior or senior years; not renewable. *Number:* 1. *Amount:* $1000.

Eligibility Requirements: Applicant must be enrolled or expecting to enroll full-time at a four-year institution or university. Available to U.S. citizens.

Application Requirements: Application, financial need analysis, references, self-addressed stamped envelope, transcript, letter of sponsorship. *Deadline:* February 15.

Contact: Eric Weisz, Manager, Office of the Reporter General
National Society Daughters of the American Revolution
1776 D Street, NW
Washington, DC 20006-5303
Phone: 202-628-1776
Fax: 202-879-3348
E-mail: nsdarscholarships@dar.org

OFFICE AND PROFESSIONAL EMPLOYEES INTERNATIONAL UNION http://www.opeiu.org

JOHN KELLY LABOR STUDIES SCHOLARSHIP FUND

Scholarship of up to $3000 given to graduate or undergraduate students who have labor studies, social sciences, industrial relation as their major. Ten scholarships are granted. Applicants should be a member or associate member of the union.

Academic Fields/Career Goals: Economics; Social Sciences.

Award: Scholarship for use in freshman, sophomore, junior, senior, or graduate years; not renewable. *Number:* 10. *Amount:* up to $3000.

Eligibility Requirements: Applicant must be enrolled or expecting to enroll full-time at a four-year institution or university. Available to U.S. citizens.

Application Requirements: Application, essay, transcript. *Deadline:* March 31.

Contact: Nancy Wohlforth, Secretary and Treasurer
Office and Professional Employees International Union
1660 L Street, NW, Suite 801
Washington, DC 20036
Phone: 202-393-4464
Fax: 202-347-0649
E-mail: opeiu@opeiudc.org

ROYAL BANK NATIVE STUDENTS AWARDS PROGRAM http://www.rbc.com

ROYAL BANK ABORIGINAL STUDENT AWARDS

• *See page 148*

SOCIETY OF AUTOMOTIVE ANALYSTS http://www.cybersaa.org

SOCIETY OF AUTOMOTIVE ANALYSTS SCHOLARSHIP

• *See page 62*

STRAIGHTFORWARD MEDIA http://www.straightforwardmedia.com

STRAIGHTFORWARD MEDIA BUSINESS SCHOOL SCHOLARSHIP

• *See page 149*

STRAIGHTFORWARD MEDIA LIBERAL ARTS SCHOLARSHIP

• *See page 99*

UNITED NEGRO COLLEGE FUND http://www.uncf.org

BOOZ, ALLEN AND HAMILTON/WILLIAM F. STASIOR INTERNSHIP

• *See page 150*

EDWARD M. NAGEL FOUNDATION SCHOLARSHIP

• *See page 65*

SPRINT NEXTEL SCHOLARSHIP/INTERNSHIP

• *See page 66*

EDUCATION

ALBERTA HERITAGE SCHOLARSHIP FUND/ ALBERTA SCHOLARSHIP PROGRAMS http://www.alis.gov.ab.ca

ANNA AND JOHN KOLESAR MEMORIAL SCHOLARSHIPS

Award to recognize and reward the academic excellence of a high school student entering a faculty of education. Must be resident of Alberta and plan to enroll full-time in the first year of a program in a faculty of education. Must be from a family where neither parents have obtained an university degree. Selection based on the highest average obtained on three grade 12 subjects. Must be a Canadian citizen or permanent resident.

Academic Fields/Career Goals: Education; Special Education.

Award: Scholarship for use in freshman year; not renewable. *Number:* 1. *Amount:* $1200.

Eligibility Requirements: Applicant must be Canadian citizen; high school student; planning to enroll or expecting to enroll full-time at a two-year or four-year institution or university and resident of Alberta. Applicant must have 3.0 GPA or higher.

Application Requirements: Application, test scores, transcript. *Deadline:* July 1.

Contact: Scholarship Committee
Alberta Heritage Scholarship Fund/Alberta Scholarship Programs
9940 106th Street, Fourth Floor, Sterling Place
PO Box 28000, Station Main
Edmonton, AB T5J 4R4
Canada
Phone: 780-427-8640
Fax: 780-427-1288
E-mail: scholarships@gov.ab.ca

LANGUAGES IN TEACHER EDUCATION SCHOLARSHIPS

Award to Alberta students enrolled in a recognized teacher preparation program and taking courses that will allow them to teach languages other than English in Alberta schools. Must be Canadian citizens or individuals lawfully admitted to Canada for permanent residence. Visa students are not eligible for this award. Must be registered full-time in their final two years of a recognized teacher preparation program at an Alberta faculty of education.

Academic Fields/Career Goals: Education; Foreign Language.

Award: Scholarship for use in freshman, sophomore, junior, or senior years; not renewable. *Number:* 13. *Amount:* $2500.

Eligibility Requirements: Applicant must be enrolled or expecting to enroll full-time at a two-year or four-year or technical institution or university; resident of Alberta and studying in Alberta. Available to Canadian citizens.

Application Requirements: Nomination by institution. *Deadline:* varies.

Contact: Scholarship Committee
Alberta Heritage Scholarship Fund/Alberta Scholarship Programs
9940 106th Street, Fourth Floor, Sterling Place
PO Box 28000, Station Main
Edmonton, AB T5J 4R4
Canada
Phone: 780-427-8640
Fax: 780-427-1288
E-mail: scholarships@gov.ab.ca

ALPHA DELTA KAPPA FOUNDATION http://www.alphadeltakappa.org

INTERNATIONAL TEACHER EDUCATION SCHOLARSHIP

The scholarship enables women from foreign countries to study for their master's degree in the United States. Applicants must be single with no dependants, aged between 20 and 35, non-U.S. citizens residing outside the United States, have at least one year of college completed, and plan to enter the teaching profession.

Academic Fields/Career Goals: Education.

Award: Scholarship for use in sophomore, junior, senior, or graduate years; renewable. *Number:* up to 7. *Amount:* $10,000.

Eligibility Requirements: Applicant must be age 20-35; enrolled or expecting to enroll full-time at a four-year institution or university and single female. Applicant must have 3.5 GPA or higher. Available to Canadian and non-U.S. citizens.

Application Requirements: Application, autobiography, financial need analysis, photo, references, test scores, transcript, certificates of health from physician and dentist, TOEFL scores, college acceptance. *Deadline:* January 1.

Contact: Dee Frost, Scholarships and Grants Coordinator
Alpha Delta Kappa Foundation
1615 West 92nd Street
Kansas City, MO 64114-3296
Phone: 816-363-5525
Fax: 816-363-4010
E-mail: headquarters@alphadeltakappa.org

ALPHA KAPPA ALPHA http://www.akaeaf.org

AKA EDUCATIONAL ADVANCEMENT FOUNDATION MERIT SCHOLARSHIP

Scholarships for students demonstrating exceptional academic achievements. Applicant must have completed a minimum of one year in a degree-granting institution and be continuing their program in that institution. Must have GPA of 3.0 or higher and show evidence of leadership by participating in community or campus activities.

Academic Fields/Career Goals: Education.

Award: Scholarship for use in sophomore, junior, senior, or graduate years; not renewable. *Number:* varies. *Amount:* $1000–$2000.

Eligibility Requirements: Applicant must be enrolled or expecting to enroll full-time at a four-year institution or university and must have an interest in leadership. Applicant or parent of applicant must have employment or volunteer experience in community service. Applicant must have 3.0 GPA or higher. Available to U.S. and non-U.S. citizens.

Application Requirements: Application, references. *Deadline:* varies.

Contact: Andrea Kerr, Program Coordinator
Alpha Kappa Alpha
5656 South Stony Island Avenue
Chicago, IL 60637
Phone: 773-947-0026 Ext. 8
E-mail: akaeaf@akaeaf.net

AMERICAN ASSOCIATION FOR HEALTH EDUCATION http://www.aahperd.org/aahe

BILL KANE SCHOLARSHIP

Scholarship available to any undergraduate student officially enrolled as a health education major at an accredited college or university in the United States or a U.S. territory.

Academic Fields/Career Goals: Education.

Award: Scholarship for use in freshman, sophomore, junior, or senior years; not renewable. *Number:* 1. *Amount:* $1000.

Eligibility Requirements: Applicant must be enrolled or expecting to enroll full-time at a four-year institution or university. Applicant must have 3.0 GPA or higher. Available to U.S. and non-U.S. citizens.

Application Requirements: Application, essay, resume, references, transcript. *Deadline:* November 15.

Contact: Ms. Linda Moore, Program Manager
American Association for Health Education
1900 Association Drive
Reston, VA 20191-1599
Phone: 703-476-3837
Fax: 703-476-6638
E-mail: aahe@aahperd.org

AMERICAN FEDERATION OF TEACHERS http://www.aft.org

ROBERT G. PORTER SCHOLARS PROGRAM-AFT MEMBERS

Nonrenewable grant provides continuing education for school teachers, paraprofessionals and school-related personnel, higher education faculty and professionals, employees of state and local governments, nurses and other health professionals. Must be member of the American Federation of Teachers for at least one year.

Academic Fields/Career Goals: Education.

Award: Grant for use in freshman, sophomore, junior, senior, graduate, or postgraduate years; not renewable. *Number:* up to 10. *Amount:* $1000.

Eligibility Requirements: Applicant must be enrolled or expecting to enroll full- or part-time at a four-year institution or university. Applicant or parent of applicant must have employment or volunteer experience in nursing or teaching/education. Available to U.S. citizens.

Application Requirements: Application, essay, references, statement of need. *Deadline:* March 31.

Contact: Bernadette Bailey, Scholarship Coordinator
American Federation of Teachers
555 New Jersey Avenue, NW
Washington, DC 20001
Phone: 202-879-4481
Fax: 202-879-4406
E-mail: bbailey@aft.org

AMERICAN FOUNDATION FOR THE BLIND http://www.afb.org

DELTA GAMMA FOUNDATION FLORENCE MARGARET HARVEY MEMORIAL SCHOLARSHIP

The scholarship provides one scholarship of $1000 to an undergraduate or graduate student who has exhibited academic excellence, and is studying in the field of rehabilitation and/or education of persons who are blind or visually impaired. Must submit proof of legal blindness. For additional information and application requirements, refer to Web site: www.afb.org/scholarships.asp.

Academic Fields/Career Goals: Education; Therapy/Rehabilitation.

Award: Scholarship for use in freshman, sophomore, junior, senior, or graduate years; not renewable. *Number:* 1. *Amount:* $1000.

Eligibility Requirements: Applicant must be enrolled or expecting to enroll full- or part-time at a two-year or four-year institution or university. Applicant must be visually impaired. Available to U.S. citizens.

Application Requirements: Application, essay, references, transcript, proof of post-secondary acceptance and legal blindness. *Deadline:* March 31.

Contact: Dawn Bodrogi, Information Center and Library Coordinator
American Foundation for the Blind
11 Penn Plaza, Suite 300
New York, NY 10001
Phone: 212-502-7661
Fax: 212-502-7771
E-mail: afbinfo@afb.net

RUDOLPH DILLMAN MEMORIAL SCHOLARSHIP

One-time award not open to previous recipients. Four scholarships of $2500 each to undergraduate or graduate students who are studying in the field of rehabilitation and/or education of persons who are blind or visually impaired. One of these grants is specifically for a student who meets all requirements and submits evidence of economic need. Must submit proof of legal blindness. For additional information and application requirements, visit Web site: www.afb.org/scholarships.asp.

Academic Fields/Career Goals: Education; Therapy/Rehabilitation.

Award: Scholarship for use in freshman, sophomore, junior, senior, or graduate years; not renewable. *Number:* up to 4. *Amount:* $2500.

Eligibility Requirements: Applicant must be enrolled or expecting to enroll full- or part-time at a two-year or four-year institution or university. Applicant must be visually impaired. Available to U.S. citizens.

Application Requirements: Application, essay, financial need analysis, references, transcript, proof of legal blindness, acceptance letter. *Deadline:* March 31.

Contact: Dawn Bodrogi, Information Center and Library Coordinator
American Foundation for the Blind
11 Penn Plaza, Suite 300
New York, NY 10001
Phone: 212-502-7661
Fax: 212-502-7771
E-mail: afbinfo@afb.net

AMERICAN INSTITUTE OF POLISH CULTURE INC. http://www.ampolinstitute.org

HARRIET IRSAY SCHOLARSHIP GRANT

• *See page 99*

AMERICAN LEGION AUXILIARY DEPARTMENT OF IOWA http://www.ialegion.org

AMERICAN LEGION AUXILIARY DEPARTMENT OF IOWA HARRIET HOFFMAN MEMORIAL SCHOLARSHIP FOR TEACHER TRAINING

One-time award for Iowa residents attending Iowa institutions who are the children, grandchildren, or great-grandchildren of veterans. Preference given to descendants of deceased veterans.

Academic Fields/Career Goals: Education.

Award: Scholarship for use in freshman, sophomore, junior, or senior years; not renewable. *Number:* 1. *Amount:* $400.

Eligibility Requirements: Applicant must be enrolled or expecting to enroll full-time at a four-year institution or university; resident of Iowa and studying in Iowa. Available to U.S. citizens. Applicant or parent must meet one or more of the following requirements: general military experience; retired from active duty; disabled or killed as a result of military service; prisoner of war; or missing in action.

Application Requirements: Application, autobiography, essay, financial need analysis, photo, references, self-addressed stamped envelope, test scores, transcript. *Deadline:* June 1.

Contact: Marlene Valentine, Secretary and Treasurer
American Legion Auxiliary Department of Iowa
720 Lyon Street
Des Moines, IA 50309
Phone: 515-282-7987
Fax: 515-282-7583
E-mail: alasectreas@ialegion.org

AMERICAN LEGION DEPARTMENT OF MISSOURI http://www.missourilegion.org

ERMAN W. TAYLOR MEMORIAL SCHOLARSHIP

Two $500 awards are given annually to a student planning on obtaining a degree in education. Applicants must be unmarried Missouri resident below age 21, and must use the scholarship as a full-time student in an accredited college or university. Must be an unmarried descendant of a veteran having served 90 days on active duty in the Army, Air Force, Navy, Marine Corps or Coast Guard of the United States, and having an honorable discharge.

Academic Fields/Career Goals: Education.

Award: Scholarship for use in freshman year; not renewable. *Number:* 2. *Amount:* $500.

Eligibility Requirements: Applicant must be high school student; age 21 or under; planning to enroll or expecting to enroll full-time at a two-year or four-year institution or university; single and resident of Missouri. Available to U.S. citizens. Applicant or parent must meet one or more of the following requirements: general military experience; retired from active duty; disabled or killed as a result of military service; prisoner of war; or missing in action.

Application Requirements: Application, essay, test scores, discharge certificate. *Deadline:* April 20.

Contact: John Doane, Chairman
American Legion, Department of Missouri
PO Box 179
Jefferson City, MO 65102
Phone: 417-924-8596
Fax: 573-893-2980
E-mail: info@missourilegion.org

AMERICAN SOCIETY OF RADIOLOGIC TECHNOLOGISTS EDUCATION AND RESEARCH FOUNDATION http://www.asrt.org/foundation

ELEKTA RADIATION THERAPY EDUCATORS SCHOLARSHIP

Open to ASRT members only who are therapist-educators and completing a bachelor's, master's, or doctoral degree to enhance their position as a program director, faculty member, clinical coordinator or clinical instructor. Must have ARRT registration or unrestricted state license and have worked in radiologic sciences for at least one of the last five years.

Academic Fields/Career Goals: Education; Health and Medical Sciences; Oncology.

Award: Scholarship for use in freshman, sophomore, junior, senior, or graduate years; not renewable. *Number:* up to 4. *Amount:* up to $5000.

Eligibility Requirements: Applicant must be enrolled or expecting to enroll full- or part-time at a four-year institution or university. Applicant or parent of applicant must be member of American Society of Radiologic Technologists. Applicant or parent of applicant must have employment or volunteer experience in physical therapy/rehabilitation. Available to U.S. and non-U.S. citizens.

Application Requirements: Application, essay, financial need analysis, resume, references, copy of unrestricted state license, current ARRT card or equivalent, letter on official letterhead verifying employment in the radiologic sciences for at least one of the past five years. *Deadline:* February 1.

Contact: Phelosha Collaros, Program Manager/Associate Development Officer
American Society of Radiologic Technologists Education and Research Foundation
15000 Central Avenue, SE
Albuquerque, NM 87123-3909
Phone: 505-298-4500 Ext. 2541
Fax: 505-298-5063
E-mail: foundation@asrt.org

MONSTER MEDICAL IMAGING EDUCATORS SCHOLARSHIP

Open to ASRT members only who are completing a bachelor's, master's, or doctoral degree to enhance their position as a program director, faculty member, clinical coordinator or clinical instructor. Must have ARRT registration or unrestricted state license and have worked in radiologic sciences for at least one of the last five years.

Academic Fields/Career Goals: Education; Health and Medical Sciences; Radiology.

Award: Scholarship for use in freshman, sophomore, junior, senior, or graduate years; not renewable. *Number:* up to 4. *Amount:* up to $5000.

Eligibility Requirements: Applicant must be enrolled or expecting to enroll full- or part-time at a four-year institution or university. Applicant or parent of applicant must be member of American Society of Radiologic Technologists. Available to U.S. and non-U.S. citizens.

Application Requirements: Application, essay, financial need analysis, resume, references, copy of unrestricted state license, current ARRT card or equivalent, letter on official letterhead verifying employment in the radiologic sciences for at least one of the past five years. *Deadline:* February 1.

Contact: Phelosha Collaros, Program Manager/Associate Development Officer
American Society of Radiologic Technologists Education and Research Foundation
15000 Central Avenue, SE
Albuquerque, NM 87123-3909
Phone: 505-298-4500 Ext. 2541
Fax: 505-298-5063
E-mail: foundation@asrt.org

ARCTIC INSTITUTE OF NORTH AMERICA http://www.arctic.ucalgary.ca

JIM BOURQUE SCHOLARSHIP

One-time award of CAN$1000 to Canadian aboriginal student enrolled in postsecondary training in education, environmental studies, traditional knowledge or telecommunications. Must submit, in 500 words or less, a description of their intended program of study and reasons for their choice of program.

Academic Fields/Career Goals: Education; Natural Resources; Natural Sciences.

Award: Scholarship for use in freshman, sophomore, junior, or senior years; not renewable. *Number:* 1.

Eligibility Requirements: Applicant must be of Canadian heritage and Canadian citizen; American Indian/Alaska Native and enrolled or expecting to enroll full-time at a four-year institution or university.

Arctic Institute of North America (continued)

Application Requirements: Essay, financial need analysis, references, transcript, proof of enrollment in or application to a post-secondary institution. *Deadline:* July 18.

Contact: Benoit Beauchamp, Executive Director
Arctic Institute of North America
University of Calgary, 2500 University Drive, NW
Calgary, AB T2N 1N4
Canada
Phone: 403-220-7515
Fax: 403-282-4609

ARIZONA BUSINESS EDUCATION ASSOCIATION http://www.azbea.org

ABEA STUDENT TEACHER SCHOLARSHIPS

Scholarships awarded to future business education teachers. Must be member of ABEA. Must be a student in last semester or two of an undergraduate Arizona business education teacher program at an accredited university or four-year college or in a post-baccalaureate Arizona business education teacher certification program at an accredited university or four-year college.

Academic Fields/Career Goals: Education.

Award: Scholarship for use in junior or senior years; not renewable. *Number:* up to 3. *Amount:* $500.

Eligibility Requirements: Applicant must be enrolled or expecting to enroll full-time at a four-year institution or university and resident of Arizona. Applicant or parent of applicant must be member of Arizona Business Education Association. Available to U.S. citizens.

Application Requirements: Application, resume, references, transcript. *Deadline:* April 1.

Contact: Shirley Eittreim, Scholarships Committee Chair
Arizona Business Education Association
Northland Pioneer College, PO Box 610
Holbrook, AZ 86025
Phone: 928-532-6151
E-mail: sjeittreim@cybertrails.com

ARIZONA HIGHER EDUCATION LOAN AUTHORITY http://www.ahela.org

AHELA EDUCATORS SCHOLARSHIP

This scholarship is to address Arizona's teacher shortage by supporting education students. Students will be selected based on academic achievement, financial need, and involvement in organizations and community activities related to education.

Academic Fields/Career Goals: Education.

Award: Scholarship for use in freshman, sophomore, junior, or senior years; not renewable. *Number:* 4. *Amount:* $1000.

Eligibility Requirements: Applicant must be enrolled or expecting to enroll full-time at a two-year or four-year institution or university and studying in Arizona. Applicant must have 2.5 GPA or higher. Available to U.S. citizens.

Application Requirements: Application, driver's license, resume. *Deadline:* March 5.

Contact: Dana Macke-Redford, Manager, Marketing, Scholarship and Outreach
Arizona Higher Education Loan Authority
2141 East Broadway Road, Suite 202
Tempe, AZ 85282
Phone: 480-383-8707 Ext. 207
E-mail: dredford@ahela.org

ASSOCIATION FOR WOMEN GEOSCIENTISTS, PUGET SOUND CHAPTER http://www.awg.org

PENELOPE HANSHAW SCHOLARSHIP

• *See page 216*

WILLIAM RUCKER GREENWOOD SCHOLARSHIP

• *See page 216*

ASSOCIATION OF RETIRED TEACHERS OF CONNECTICUT http://www.ctretiredteachers.org

ARTC GLEN MOON SCHOLARSHIP

Renewable scholarship to Connecticut high school seniors, who intend to pursue a career in teaching. Must demonstrate a positive financial need.

Academic Fields/Career Goals: Education.

Award: Scholarship for use in freshman year; renewable. *Number:* 2–3. *Amount:* $1500–$2000.

Eligibility Requirements: Applicant must be high school student; planning to enroll or expecting to enroll full- or part-time at a four-year institution or university and resident of Connecticut. Available to U.S. citizens.

Application Requirements: Application, autobiography, financial need analysis, references, test scores, transcript. *Deadline:* March 31.

Contact: Teresa Barton, Scholarship Committee
Association of Retired Teachers of Connecticut
111 South Road
Farmington, CT 06032
Phone: 866-343-2782
E-mail: info@ctretiredteachers.org

ASSOCIATION ON AMERICAN INDIAN AFFAIRS (AAIA) http://www.indian-affairs.org

EMILIE HESEMEYER MEMORIAL SCHOLARSHIP

Scholarship is open to undergraduates. A preference is given, but not limited to students in the education curriculum. Students in a 2 year college must be on track to transfer to a 4 year. See our Web site at www.indian-affairs.org for details.

Academic Fields/Career Goals: Education.

Award: Scholarship for use in freshman, sophomore, junior, or senior years; renewable. *Number:* varies. *Amount:* up to $1500.

Eligibility Requirements: Applicant must be American Indian/Alaska Native and enrolled or expecting to enroll full-time at a four-year institution or university. Available to U.S. citizens.

Application Requirements: Application, essay, financial need analysis, references, transcript. *Deadline:* July 1.

Contact: Lisa Wyzlic, Director of Scholarship Programs
Association on American Indian Affairs (AAIA)
966 Hungerford Drive, Suite 12-B
Rockville, MD 20850
Phone: 240-314-7155
Fax: 240-314-7159
E-mail: lw.aaia@verizon.net

BETHESDA LUTHERAN HOMES AND SERVICES, INC. http://www.blhs.org

DEVELOPMENTAL DISABILITIES SCHOLASTIC ACHIEVEMENT SCHOLARSHIP FOR LUTHERAN COLLEGE STUDENTS

• *See page 211*

BUSINESS AND PROFESSIONAL WOMEN'S FOUNDATION http://www.bpwfoundation.org

BPW CAREER ADVANCEMENT SCHOLARSHIP PROGRAM FOR WOMEN

• *See page 130*

CALIFORNIA STUDENT AID COMMISSION http://www.csac.ca.gov

CHILD DEVELOPMENT TEACHER AND SUPERVISOR GRANT PROGRAM

• *See page 165*

CALIFORNIA TEACHERS ASSOCIATION (CTA) http://www.cta.org

L. GORDON BITTLE MEMORIAL SCHOLARSHIP

Awards scholarships annually to active SCTA members for study in a teacher preparatory program. Students may reapply each year. Not available to those who are currently working in public schools as members of CTA. Minimum 3.5 GPA.

Academic Fields/Career Goals: Education.

Award: Scholarship for use in freshman, sophomore, junior, senior, or graduate years; not renewable. *Number:* up to 3. *Amount:* $2500.

Eligibility Requirements: Applicant must be enrolled or expecting to enroll full-time at a two-year or four-year institution or university and resident of California. Applicant or parent of applicant must be member of California Teachers Association. Applicant must have 3.5 GPA or higher. Available to U.S. citizens.

Application Requirements: Application, essay, references, transcript. *Deadline:* February 8.

Contact: Janeya Collins, Scholarship Coordinator
California Teachers Association (CTA)
PO Box 921
Burlingame, CA 94011-0921
Phone: 650-552-5468
Fax: 650-552-5001
E-mail: scholarships@cta.org

MARTIN LUTHER KING, JR. MEMORIAL SCHOLARSHIP

Awards for ethnic minority members of the California Teachers Association, their dependent children, and ethnic minority members of Student California Teachers Association who want to pursue degrees or credentials in public education. Minimum 3.5 GPA.

Academic Fields/Career Goals: Education.

Award: Scholarship for use in freshman, sophomore, junior, senior, or graduate years; not renewable. *Number:* varies. *Amount:* $1000–$2000.

Eligibility Requirements: Applicant must be American Indian/Alaska Native, Asian/Pacific Islander, Black (non-Hispanic), or Hispanic; enrolled or expecting to enroll full-time at a two-year or four-year institution or university and resident of California. Applicant or parent of applicant must be member of California Teachers Association. Applicant must have 3.5 GPA or higher. Available to U.S. citizens.

Application Requirements: Application, essay, financial need analysis, references. *Deadline:* March 14.

Contact: Janeya Collins, Scholarship Coordinator
California Teachers Association (CTA)
PO Box 921
Burlingame, CA 94011-0921
Phone: 650-552-5468
Fax: 650-552-5001
E-mail: scholarships@cta.org

CANADIAN INSTITUTE OF UKRAINIAN STUDIES http://www.cius.ca

LEO J. KRYSA UNDERGRADUATE SCHOLARSHIP

• *See page 95*

CATCHING THE DREAM http://www.catchingthedream.org

MATH, ENGINEERING, SCIENCE, BUSINESS, EDUCATION, COMPUTERS SCHOLARSHIPS

• *See page 139*

NATIVE AMERICAN LEADERSHIP IN EDUCATION (NALE)

• *See page 139*

COLLEGEBOUND FOUNDATION http://www.collegeboundfoundation.org

ALICE G. PINDERHUGHES SCHOLARSHIP

Scholarship to students majoring in education and planning to teach in grades K-12. Must have a cumulative high school GPA of at least 3.0 and demonstrate financial need. Must submit a one-page typed essay describing "a teacher who has made an impact on you and the reasons why you want to become a teacher".

Academic Fields/Career Goals: Education.

Award: Scholarship for use in freshman, sophomore, junior, or senior years; renewable. *Number:* 1. *Amount:* $500.

Eligibility Requirements: Applicant must be enrolled or expecting to enroll full-time at a two-year or four-year institution or university and resident of Maryland. Applicant must have 3.0 GPA or higher. Available to U.S. citizens.

Application Requirements: Application, essay, financial need analysis, references, transcript, financial aid award letters. *Deadline:* March 1.

Contact: Jamie Crouse, Scholarship Program Administrator
CollegeBound Foundation
300 Water Street, Suite 300
Baltimore, MD 21202
Phone: 410-783-2905 Ext. 207
Fax: 410-727-5786
E-mail: jcrouse@collegeboundfoundation.org

JANET B. SONDHEIM SCHOLARSHIP

• *See page 100*

SHEILA Z. KOLMAN MEMORIAL SCHOLARSHIP

One-time scholarship award of $1000 for a high school graduate who is an aspiring teacher. Minimum GPA of 2.5 required. Must demonstrate financial need and submit an essay (500-1000 words) describing how a teacher affected your life in a positive way.

Academic Fields/Career Goals: Education.

Award: Scholarship for use in freshman year; renewable. *Number:* 1. *Amount:* $1000.

Eligibility Requirements: Applicant must be high school student; planning to enroll or expecting to enroll full-time at a four-year institution or university and resident of Maryland. Applicant must have 2.5 GPA or higher. Available to U.S. citizens.

Application Requirements: Application, essay, financial need analysis, references, transcript, financial aid award letters, SAR. *Deadline:* March 1.

Contact: Jamie Crouse, Scholarship Program Administrator
CollegeBound Foundation
300 Water Street, Suite 300
Baltimore, MD 21202
Phone: 410-783-2905 Ext. 207
Fax: 410-727-5786
E-mail: jcrouse@collegeboundfoundation.org

COLLEGE FOUNDATION OF NORTH CAROLINA INC. http://www.cfnc.org

DOTTIE MARTIN TEACHERS SCHOLARSHIP

Awards annual scholarship of $500. Must be currently enrolled in an education program with an established career plan for teaching in North Carolina. Recent high school graduates are not eligible to apply. Applications may be downloaded from http://www.ncfrw.com/programs/dmtsf.html.

Academic Fields/Career Goals: Education.

Award: Scholarship for use in freshman, sophomore, junior, or senior years; not renewable. *Number:* 2–3. *Amount:* $500.

Eligibility Requirements: Applicant must be enrolled or expecting to enroll full-time at a two-year or four-year institution or university. Available to U.S. citizens.

Application Requirements: Application, transcript. *Deadline:* June 1.

Contact: Joyce Glass, Scholarship Committee
College Foundation of North Carolina Inc.
4413 Driftwood Drive
Clemmons, NC 27012
Phone: 336-766-0067
E-mail: fwglass@earthlink.net

COMMON KNOWLEDGE SCHOLARSHIP FOUNDATION http://www.cksf.org

FUTURE TEACHERS OF AMERICA SCHOLARSHIP

Scholarship contest available for college students quizzed on their knowledge of core curriculum education courses. For more information about this scholarship, please visit:
http://www.cksf.org/CKSF.cfm?Page=CKSF_AvailableScholarships.

Academic Fields/Career Goals: Education.

Award: Scholarship for use in freshman, sophomore, junior, senior, graduate, or postgraduate years; not renewable. *Number:* 1. *Amount:* up to $250.

Eligibility Requirements: Applicant must be enrolled or expecting to enroll full- or part-time at a two-year or four-year or technical institution or university. Available to U.S. citizens.

Common Knowledge Scholarship Foundation (continued)

Application Requirements: Applicant must enter a contest. *Deadline:* varies.

Contact: Mr. Daryl Hulce, President
Common Knowledge Scholarship Foundation
PO Box 290361
Davie, FL 33329-0361
Phone: 954-262-8553
Fax: 954-262-2847
E-mail: hulce@cksf.org

COMMUNITY FOUNDATION OF WESTERN MASSACHUSETTS http://www.communityfoundation.org

MARGARET E. AND AGNES K. O'DONNELL SCHOLARSHIP FUND

For graduating seniors of Northampton High School and Smith Vocational High School, and for students of the College of Our Lady of the Elms and Fitchburg State College majoring in education.

Academic Fields/Career Goals: Education.

Award: Scholarship for use in freshman year; renewable. *Number:* up to 18. *Amount:* $1000–$1950.

Eligibility Requirements: Applicant must be enrolled or expecting to enroll full-time at a four-year institution or university and resident of Massachusetts. Available to U.S. citizens.

Application Requirements: Application, financial need analysis, transcript, Student Aid Report (SAR). *Deadline:* March 31.

Contact: Dorothy Theriaque, Education Associate
Community Foundation of Western Massachusetts
1500 Main Street, PO Box 15769
Springfield, MA 01115
Phone: 413-732-2858
Fax: 413-733-8565
E-mail: dtheriaque@communityfoundation.org

CONFEDERATED TRIBES OF GRAND RONDE http://www.grandronde.org

EULA PETITE MEMORIAL COMPETITIVE SCHOLARSHIP

Available to any enrolled member of the Confederated Tribes of Grand Ronde. Available to education majors only. Renewable for six terms/four semesters of continuous study. Intended for last two years of undergraduate study, or any two years of graduate study.

Academic Fields/Career Goals: Education.

Award: Scholarship for use in junior, senior, or graduate years; renewable. *Number:* 1. *Amount:* $7000.

Eligibility Requirements: Applicant must be American Indian/Alaska Native and enrolled or expecting to enroll full- or part-time at a four-year institution or university. Available to U.S. and non-U.S. citizens.

Application Requirements: Application, essay, references, transcript, verification of tribal enrollment. *Deadline:* April 30.

Contact: Luhui Whitebear, Tribal Scholarship Coordinator
Confederated Tribes of Grand Ronde
9615 Grand Ronde Road
Grand Ronde, OR 97347
Phone: 800-422-0232 Ext. 2275
Fax: 503-879-2286
E-mail: education@grandronde.org

CONNECTICUT ASSOCIATION FOR HEALTH, PHYSICAL EDUCATION, RECREATION AND DANCE http://www.ctahperd.org

GIBSON-LAEMEL CTAHPERD SCHOLARSHIP

Awarded to a college junior or senior accepted into a program of professional studies of health, physical education, recreation or dance. Must be a Connecticut resident and attend a university or four-year college in Connecticut. Minimum 2.5 GPA required.

Academic Fields/Career Goals: Education; Sports-Related/Exercise Science.

Award: Scholarship for use in junior or senior years; not renewable. *Number:* 1–2. *Amount:* $1000.

Eligibility Requirements: Applicant must be enrolled or expecting to enroll full-time at a four-year institution or university; resident of Connecticut and studying in Connecticut. Applicant must have 2.5 GPA or higher. Available to U.S. citizens.

Application Requirements: Application, essay, references, transcript. *Deadline:* May 1.

Contact: Ms. Janice Skene, Scholarship Chair
Connecticut Association for Health, Physical Education, Recreation and Dance
Eastbury School, Neipsic Road
Glastonbury, CT 06033
Phone: 860-652-7858
E-mail: skenej@glastonburyus.org

MARY BENEVENTO CTAHPERD SCHOLARSHIP

Scholarship awarded to a graduating high school senior who plans to engage in professional studies in the fields of health education, physical education, recreation, or dance. Must be resident of Connecticut and plan to attend a university or four-year college in Connecticut.

Academic Fields/Career Goals: Education; Sports-Related/Exercise Science.

Award: Scholarship for use in freshman year; not renewable. *Number:* 1–2. *Amount:* $1000.

Eligibility Requirements: Applicant must be high school student; planning to enroll or expecting to enroll full-time at a four-year institution or university; resident of Connecticut and studying in Connecticut. Available to U.S. citizens.

Application Requirements: Application, essay, references, test scores, transcript. *Deadline:* April 1.

Contact: Janice Skene, Scholarship Chair
Connecticut Association for Health, Physical Education, Recreation and Dance
Eastbury School, Neipsic Road
Glastonbury, CT 06033
Phone: 860-652-7858
E-mail: skenej@glastonburyus.org

CONNECTICUT ASSOCIATION OF LATIN AMERICANS IN HIGHER EDUCATION (CALAHE) http://www.calahe.org

CONNECTICUT ASSOCIATION OF LATIN AMERICANS IN HIGHER EDUCATION SCHOLARSHIPS

Must demonstrate involvement with, and commitment to, activities that promote Latino pursuit of education. Must have a 3.0 GPA, be a U.S. citizen or permanent resident, be a resident of Connecticut, and attend a Connecticut higher education institution.

Academic Fields/Career Goals: Education.

Award: Scholarship for use in freshman, sophomore, junior, or senior years; not renewable. *Number:* 5–9. *Amount:* $1000.

Eligibility Requirements: Applicant must be enrolled or expecting to enroll full-time at a two-year or four-year or technical institution; resident of Connecticut and studying in Connecticut. Applicant must have 3.0 GPA or higher. Available to U.S. citizens.

Application Requirements: Application, essay, financial need analysis, transcript, Student Aid Report (SAR). *Deadline:* March 17.

Contact: Dr. Wilson Luna, Gateway Community-Technical College
Connecticut Association of Latin Americans in Higher Education (CALAHE)
60 Sargent Drive
New Haven, CT 06511
Phone: 203-285-2210
Fax: 203-285-2211
E-mail: wluna@gwcc.commnet.edu

CONNECTICUT DEPARTMENT OF HIGHER EDUCATION http://www.ctdhe.org

MINORITY TEACHER INCENTIVE GRANT PROGRAM

Program provides up to $5,000 a year for two years of full-time study in a teacher preparation program, for the junior or senior year at a Connecticut college or university. Applicant must be African-American, Hispanic/Latino, Asian American or Native American heritage, and be nominated by the Education Dean. Program graduates who teach in Connecticut public schools may be eligible for loan reimbursement stipends up to $2,500 per year for up to four years.

Academic Fields/Career Goals: Education.

Award: Grant for use in junior or senior years; renewable. *Number:* 1. *Amount:* up to $5000.

Eligibility Requirements: Applicant must be American Indian/Alaska Native, Asian/Pacific Islander, Black (non-Hispanic), or Hispanic; enrolled or expecting to enroll full-time at a four-year institution or university and studying in Connecticut. Available to U.S. citizens.

Application Requirements: Application. *Deadline:* October 1.

Contact: Associate Director
Connecticut Department of Higher Education
61 Woodland Street
Hartford, CT 06105-2326
Phone: 860-947-1855
Fax: 860-947-1311
E-mail: mfrench@ctdhe.org

CONNECTICUT EDUCATION FOUNDATION INC. http://www.cea.org

SCHOLARSHIP FOR MINORITY COLLEGE STUDENTS

An award for qualified minority candidates who have been accepted into a teacher preparation program at an accredited Connecticut college or university. Must have a 2.75 GPA.

Academic Fields/Career Goals: Education.

Award: Scholarship for use in freshman, sophomore, junior, or senior years; not renewable. *Number:* 1. *Amount:* up to $750.

Eligibility Requirements: Applicant must be American Indian/Alaska Native, Asian/Pacific Islander, Black (non-Hispanic), or Hispanic; enrolled or expecting to enroll full-time at a two-year or four-year institution or university and studying in Connecticut. Available to U.S. citizens.

Application Requirements: Application, essay, references, transcript, income verification, letter of acceptance, copy of SAR. *Deadline:* May 1.

Contact: President
Connecticut Education Foundation Inc.
21 Oak Street, Suite 500
Hartford, CT 06106
Phone: 860-525-5641

SCHOLARSHIP FOR MINORITY HIGH SCHOOL STUDENTS

Award for qualified minority candidates who have been accepted into an accredited two or four-year Connecticut college or university and intend to enter the teaching profession. Must have 2.75 GPA.

Academic Fields/Career Goals: Education.

Award: Scholarship for use in freshman year; not renewable. *Number:* 1. *Amount:* up to $500.

Eligibility Requirements: Applicant must be American Indian/Alaska Native, Asian/Pacific Islander, Black (non-Hispanic), or Hispanic; high school student; planning to enroll or expecting to enroll full-time at a four-year institution or university and studying in Connecticut. Available to U.S. citizens.

Application Requirements: Application, essay, references, transcript, letter of acceptance, income verification, copy of SAR. *Deadline:* May 1.

Contact: President
Connecticut Education Foundation Inc.
21 Oak Street, Suite 500
Hartford, CT 06106
Phone: 860-525-5641

CONTINENTAL SOCIETY, DAUGHTERS OF INDIAN WARS

CONTINENTAL SOCIETY, DAUGHTERS OF INDIAN WARS SCHOLARSHIP

Award for a certified Indian tribal member enrolled in an undergraduate degree program in education or social service. Must maintain minimum 3.0 GPA and work with a Native American after college; work must be on a reservation. Preference given to those in or entering junior year.

Academic Fields/Career Goals: Education; Social Services.

Award: Scholarship for use in freshman, sophomore, junior, or senior years; not renewable. *Number:* 2. *Amount:* $2500–$5000.

Eligibility Requirements: Applicant must be American Indian/Alaska Native and enrolled or expecting to enroll full-time at a two-year or four-year institution or university. Applicant must have 3.0 GPA or higher. Available to U.S. citizens.

Application Requirements: Application, autobiography, essay, financial need analysis, references, transcript. *Deadline:* June 15.

Contact: Jean Brown, Scholarship Chairperson
Continental Society, Daughters of Indian Wars
61300 East 10010 Road
Miami, OK 74357-4726
Phone: 770-382-6676
Fax: 918-540-0664
E-mail: ottawahillpt@neok.com

COUNCIL FOR INTERNATIONAL EDUCATIONAL EXCHANGE http://www.ciee.org

DEPARTMENT OF EDUCATION SCHOLARSHIP FOR PROGRAMS IN CHINA

Scholarships offered to students who are pursuing Chinese language programs in China. Must be a U.S. citizen enrolled in a CIEE program. Students must have the equivalent of two years study in Chinese language documented. Deadlines: April 1 and November 1.

Academic Fields/Career Goals: Education.

Award: Scholarship for use in junior, senior, or graduate years; not renewable. *Number:* 8–15. *Amount:* $2000–$12,000.

Eligibility Requirements: Applicant must be enrolled or expecting to enroll full-time at a four-year institution or university and must have an interest in foreign language. Applicant must have 3.0 GPA or higher. Available to U.S. citizens.

Application Requirements: Application, essay, financial need analysis, references, transcript. *Deadline:* varies.

Contact: Chris Wilson, Grant Programs Manager
Council for International Educational Exchange
300 Fore Street
Portland, ME 04101
Phone: 800-448-9944 Ext. 4117
Fax: 207-553-4299
E-mail: scholarships@ciee.org

CULTURAL SERVICES OF THE FRENCH EMBASSY http://www.frenchculture.org

TEACHING ASSISTANTSHIP IN FRANCE

Grants support American students as they teach English in the French school system. Must be U.S. citizen or a permanent resident. Must have working knowledge of French and may not have received a similar grant from the French government for the last three years.

Academic Fields/Career Goals: Education.

Award: Grant for use in junior, senior, graduate, or postgraduate years; not renewable. *Number:* up to 1500. *Amount:* varies.

Eligibility Requirements: Applicant must be age 20-30; enrolled or expecting to enroll full- or part-time at a four-year institution or university; single and must have an interest in French language. Available to U.S. citizens.

Application Requirements: Application, photo, references, self-addressed stamped envelope, transcript. *Fee:* $35. *Deadline:* February 8.

Contact: Marjorie Nelson, Assistantship Coordinator
Cultural Services of the French Embassy
4101 Reservoir Road, NW
Washington, DC 20007
Phone: 202-944-6294
Fax: 202-944-6268
E-mail: assistant.washington-amba@diplomatie.gouv.fr

DECA (DISTRIBUTIVE EDUCATION CLUBS OF AMERICA) http://www.deca.org

HARRY A. APPLEGATE SCHOLARSHIP

• *See page 140*

DELAWARE HIGHER EDUCATION COMMISSION http://www.doe.k12.de.us

CHRISTA MCAULIFFE TEACHER SCHOLARSHIP LOAN-DELAWARE

Award for legal residents of Delaware who are U.S. citizens or eligible non-citizens. Must be full-time student enrolled at a Delaware college in an undergraduate program leading to teacher certification. High school seniors must rank in upper half of class and have a combined score of 1570 on the SAT. Undergraduates must have at least a 2.75 cumulative GPA. For details visit Web site: http://www.doe.k12.de.us.

Academic Fields/Career Goals: Education.

Award: Forgivable loan for use in freshman, sophomore, junior, or senior years; renewable. *Number:* 1–60. *Amount:* $1000–$5000.

Eligibility Requirements: Applicant must be enrolled or expecting to enroll full-time at a four-year institution or university; resident of Delaware and studying in Delaware. Available to U.S. citizens.

Application Requirements: Application, essay, test scores, transcript. *Deadline:* March 28.

Contact: Carylin Brinkley, Program Administrator
Delaware Higher Education Commission
Carvel State Office Building, 820 North French Street, Fifth Floor
Wilmington, DE 19801-3509
Phone: 302-577-5240
Fax: 302-577-6765
E-mail: cbrinkley@doe.k12.de.us

EDUCATION PARTNERSHIP http://www.edpartnership.org

LOUIS FEINSTEIN MEMORIAL SCHOLARSHIPS

Scholarship for students who are interested in a teaching career and best exemplify the qualities of brotherhood, compassion, integrity, leadership, and a determination to make a positive difference in the lives of others. Students will receive benefits including an $8000 scholarship for those attending Rhode Island colleges and universities, and $2000 to all scholars upon graduation.

Academic Fields/Career Goals: Education.

Award: Scholarship for use in freshman year; renewable. *Number:* 10–20. *Amount:* up to $10,000.

Eligibility Requirements: Applicant must be high school student; age 16-17; planning to enroll or expecting to enroll full-time at a four-year institution or university; studying in Rhode Island and must have an interest in leadership. Applicant must have 2.5 GPA or higher. Available to U.S. citizens.

Application Requirements: Application, essay, interview, references, test scores, transcript. *Deadline:* June 30.

Contact: Keturah Johnson, Scholarships and Communications Coordinator
Education Partnership
345 South Main Street
Providence, RI 02903
Phone: 401-331-5222 Ext. 112
Fax: 401-331-1659
E-mail: kjohnson@edpartnership.org

FINANCE AUTHORITY OF MAINE http://www.famemaine.com

EDUCATORS FOR MAINE FORGIVABLE LOAN PROGRAM

Forgivable loan for residents of Maine who are high school seniors, college students, or college graduates with a minimum 3.0 GPA, studying or preparing to study teacher education. Must teach in Maine upon graduation. Award based on merit. For application information see Web site: http://www.famemaine.com.

Academic Fields/Career Goals: Education.

Award: Forgivable loan for use in freshman, sophomore, junior, senior, or graduate years; renewable. *Number:* up to 500. *Amount:* $2000–$3000.

Eligibility Requirements: Applicant must be enrolled or expecting to enroll full-time at a two-year or four-year institution or university and resident of Maine. Applicant must have 3.0 GPA or higher. Available to U.S. citizens.

Application Requirements: Application, essay, test scores, transcript. *Deadline:* May 15.

Contact: Lisa Bongiovanni, Manager, Operations
Finance Authority of Maine
Five Community Drive
PO Box 949
Augusta, ME 04332-0949
Phone: 207-623-3263
Fax: 207-623-0095
E-mail: education@famemaine.com

QUALITY CHILD CARE EDUCATION SCHOLARSHIP PROGRAM

Open to residents of Maine who are taking a minimum of one childhood education course or are pursuing a child development associate certificate, associate degree, baccalaureate degree, or post-baccalaureate teacher certification in child-care related fields. Scholarships of up to $500 per course or $2000 per year available. See Web site for information: http://www.famemaine.com.

Academic Fields/Career Goals: Education.

Award: Scholarship for use in freshman, sophomore, junior, senior, or graduate years; not renewable. *Number:* 70–150. *Amount:* $500–$2000.

Eligibility Requirements: Applicant must be enrolled or expecting to enroll full- or part-time at a two-year or four-year institution and resident of Maine. Available to U.S. citizens.

Application Requirements: Application, financial need analysis, tax return. *Deadline:* continuous.

Contact: Lisa Bongiovanni, Manager, Operations
Finance Authority of Maine
Five Community Drive
PO Box 949
Augusta, ME 04332-0949
Phone: 207-623-3263
Fax: 207-623-0095
E-mail: education@famemaine.com

FLORIDA DEPARTMENT OF EDUCATION http://www.floridastudentfinancialaid.org

CRITICAL TEACHER SHORTAGE STUDENT LOAN FORGIVENESS PROGRAM-FLORIDA

Award program provides financial assistance to eligible Florida teachers who hold a valid Florida teachers certificate or Florida department of health license, by assisting them in the repayment of undergraduate and graduate educational loans that led to certification in a critical teacher shortage subject area. Must teach full-time at a publicly-funded school.

Academic Fields/Career Goals: Education.

Award: Forgivable loan for use in freshman, sophomore, junior, senior, or graduate years; renewable. *Number:* varies. *Amount:* up to $5000.

Eligibility Requirements: Applicant must be enrolled or expecting to enroll full- or part-time at a two-year or four-year institution or university and resident of Florida. Applicant or parent of applicant must have employment or volunteer experience in teaching/education. Available to U.S. citizens.

Application Requirements: Application, transcript. *Deadline:* July 15.

Contact: Theresa Antworth, Director State Scholarships and Grants
Florida Department of Education
Office of Student Financial Assistance, 1940 North Monroe Street, Suite 70
Tallahassee, FL 32303-4759
Phone: 850-410-5185
Fax: 850-487-6244
E-mail: theresa.antworth@fldoe.org

GENERAL BOARD OF HIGHER EDUCATION AND MINISTRY http://www.gbhem.org

EDITH M. ALLEN SCHOLARSHIP

Scholarship for outstanding African-American graduate or undergraduate students pursuing a degree in education, social work, medicine, and/or other health professions.Must be enrolled at a United Methodist college or university and be an active, full member of the United Methodist Church for at least three years.

Academic Fields/Career Goals: Education; Health and Medical Sciences; Social Services.

Award: Scholarship for use in freshman, sophomore, junior, senior, or graduate years; not renewable. *Number:* varies. *Amount:* varies.

Eligibility Requirements: Applicant must be Methodist; Black (non-Hispanic) and enrolled or expecting to enroll full-time at a four-year institution or university. Available to U.S. citizens.

Application Requirements: Application, essay, references, transcript. *Deadline:* May 1.

Contact: Scholarship Committee
General Board of Higher Education and Ministry
The United Methodist Church, 1001 Nineteenth Avenue South
PO Box 340007
Nashville, TN 37202
Phone: 615-340-7344
Fax: 615-340-7367
E-mail: sddm@gbhem.org

GENERAL FEDERATION OF WOMEN'S CLUBS OF MASSACHUSETTS http://www.gfwcma.org

NEWTONVILLE WOMAN'S CLUB SCHOLARSHIPS

Applicant must be a senior in a Massachusetts high school in who will enroll in a four-year accredited college or university in a teacher-training program that leads to certification to teach.

Academic Fields/Career Goals: Education.

Award: Scholarship for use in freshman year; not renewable. *Number:* 1. *Amount:* $600.

Eligibility Requirements: Applicant must be high school student; planning to enroll or expecting to enroll full-time at a four-year institution or university and resident of Massachusetts. Available to U.S. citizens.

Application Requirements: Application, autobiography, essay, interview, references, self-addressed stamped envelope, transcript. *Deadline:* March 1.

Contact: Marta DiBenedetto, Scholarship Chairman
General Federation of Women's Clubs of Massachusetts
245 Dutton Road, PO Box 679
Sudbury, MA 01776-0679
Phone: 978-444-9105
E-mail: marta_dibenedetto@nylim.com

GEORGE T. WELCH TRUST http://www.bakerboyer.com

SARA CARLSON MEMORIAL FUND

Grants for students majoring in education. Must be enrolled full-time and maintain a minimum GPA of 2.0. Must reapply. The budget form must be completed and cover the entire school year.

Academic Fields/Career Goals: Education.

Award: Scholarship for use in freshman, sophomore, junior, or senior years; not renewable. *Number:* varies. *Amount:* up to $300.

Eligibility Requirements: Applicant must be enrolled or expecting to enroll full-time at a four-year institution or university. Available to U.S. citizens.

Application Requirements: Application. *Deadline:* April 13.

Contact: Ted Cohan, Trust Portfolio Manager
George T. Welch Trust
Baker Boyer Bank, Investment Management & Trust Services
7 West Main, PO Box 1796
Walla Walla, WA 99362
Phone: 509-526-1204
Fax: 509-522-3136
E-mail: cohant@bakerboyer.com

GEORGIA ASSOCIATION OF EDUCATORS http://www.gae.org

GAE GFIE SCHOLARSHIP FOR ASPIRING TEACHERS

Scholarships will be awarded to graduating seniors who currently attend a fully accredited public Georgia high school and will attend a fully accredited Georgia college or university within the next twelve months. Must have a 3.0 GPA. Must submit three letters of recommendation. Must have plans to enter the teaching profession.

Academic Fields/Career Goals: Education.

Award: Scholarship for use in freshman year; not renewable. *Number:* up to 20. *Amount:* $1000.

Eligibility Requirements: Applicant must be enrolled or expecting to enroll full-time at a two-year or four-year institution or university; resident of Georgia and studying in Georgia. Applicant must have 3.0 GPA or higher. Available to U.S. citizens.

Application Requirements: Application, references, transcript. *Deadline:* February 1.

Contact: Sharon Henderson, Staff Associate
Georgia Association of Educators
100 Crescent Centre Parkway, Suite 500
Tucker, GA 30084-7049
Phone: 678-837-1114
Fax: 678-837-1150
E-mail: sharon.henderson@gae.org

GEORGIA STUDENT FINANCE COMMISSION http://www.gsfc.org

GEORGIA PROMISE TEACHER SCHOLARSHIP PROGRAM

Renewable, forgivable loans for junior undergraduates at Georgia colleges who have been accepted for enrollment into a teacher education program leading to initial certification. Minimum cumulative 3.0 GPA required. Recipient must teach at a Georgia public school for one year for each $1500 awarded. Available to seniors for renewal only. Write for deadlines.

Academic Fields/Career Goals: Education.

Award: Forgivable loan for use in junior or senior years; renewable. *Number:* 700–1500. *Amount:* $3000–$6000.

Eligibility Requirements: Applicant must be enrolled or expecting to enroll full- or part-time at a four-year institution or university; resident of Georgia and studying in Georgia. Applicant must have 3.0 GPA or higher. Available to U.S. citizens.

Application Requirements: Application, transcript, selective service registration, official certification of admittance into an approved teacher education program in Georgia. *Deadline:* continuous.

Contact: Stan DeWitt, Manager of Teacher Scholarships
Georgia Student Finance Commission
2082 East Exchange Place, Suite 100
Tucker, GA 30084
Phone: 770-724-9060
Fax: 770-724-9031
E-mail: stand@gsfc.org

GOLDEN APPLE FOUNDATION http://www.goldenapple.org

GOLDEN APPLE SCHOLARS OF ILLINOIS

Applicants must be between the ages of 16 and 21 and maintain a GPA of 2.5. Eligible applicants must be residents of Illinois studying in Illinois. Recipients must agree to teach in high-need Illinois schools.

Academic Fields/Career Goals: Education.

Award: Scholarship for use in freshman, sophomore, junior, or senior years; renewable. *Number:* 125. *Amount:* $4500.

Eligibility Requirements: Applicant must be age 16-21; enrolled or expecting to enroll full-time at a four-year institution or university; resident of Illinois and studying in Illinois. Applicant must have 2.5 GPA or higher. Available to U.S. citizens.

Application Requirements: Application, autobiography, essay, interview, photo, references, test scores, transcript. *Deadline:* December 1.

Contact: Ms. Patricia Kilduff, Director of Recruitment and Placement
Golden Apple Foundation
8 South Michigan Avenue, Suite 700
Chicago, IL 60603-3318
Phone: 312-407-0006 Ext. 105
Fax: 312-407-0344
E-mail: kilduff@goldenapple.org

GOLDEN KEY INTERNATIONAL HONOUR SOCIETY http://www.goldenkey.org

EDUCATION ACHIEVEMENT AWARDS

Awards members who excel in the study of education. Eligible applicants are undergraduate, graduate and postgraduate members who are currently enrolled in classes at a degree-granting program. One winner will receive a $1000 award. The second place winner will receive $750 and the third place winner will receive $500.

Academic Fields/Career Goals: Education.

Award: Prize for use in freshman, sophomore, junior, senior, graduate, or postgraduate years; not renewable. *Number:* 3. *Amount:* $500–$1000.

Eligibility Requirements: Applicant must be enrolled or expecting to enroll full- or part-time at a four-year institution or university. Available to U.S. and non-U.S. citizens.

Application Requirements: Application, applicant must enter a contest, essay, references, transcript, education related paper or report. *Deadline:* March 3.

Contact: Scholarship Program Administrators
Golden Key International Honour Society
PO Box 23737
Nashville, TN 37202-3737
Phone: 800-377-2401
E-mail: scholarships@goldenkey.org

GRAND CHAPTER OF CALIFORNIA-ORDER OF THE EASTERN STAR http://www.oescal.org

SCHOLARSHIPS FOR EDUCATION, BUSINESS AND RELIGION

• *See page 142*

GREATER KANAWHA VALLEY FOUNDATION http://www.tgkvf.org

JOSEPH C. BASILE, II MEMORIAL SCHOLARSHIP FUND

Award for residents of West Virginia who are majoring in education. Must be an undergraduate at a college or university in West Virginia. Award based on financial need. May apply for only two Foundation scholarships but will only be chosen for one.

Academic Fields/Career Goals: Education.

Award: Scholarship for use in freshman, sophomore, junior, or senior years; not renewable. *Number:* 1. *Amount:* $1000.

Eligibility Requirements: Applicant must be enrolled or expecting to enroll full-time at a four-year institution or university; resident of West Virginia and studying in West Virginia. Applicant must have 2.5 GPA or higher. Available to U.S. citizens.

Application Requirements: Application, essay, financial need analysis, references, self-addressed stamped envelope, test scores, transcript. *Deadline:* January 12.

Contact: Susan Hoover, Scholarship Coordinator
Greater Kanawha Valley Foundation
PO Box 3041
Charleston, WV 25331
Phone: 304-346-3620
Fax: 304-346-3640

HAWAIIAN LODGE, F & AM http://www.glhawaii.org/

HAWAIIAN LODGE SCHOLARSHIPS

• *See page 96*

HAWAII EDUCATION ASSOCIATION http://www.heaed.com

FAITH C. AI LAI HEA STUDENT TEACHER SCHOLARSHIP

Scholarship of $5000 established for student teachers who are enrolled in a full-time undergraduate or post-baccalaureate program in accredited institution of higher learning. Minimum 3.6 GPA required.

Academic Fields/Career Goals: Education.

Award: Scholarship for use in senior, graduate, or postgraduate years; not renewable. *Number:* 4. *Amount:* $5000.

Eligibility Requirements: Applicant must be enrolled or expecting to enroll full-time at a four-year institution or university and resident of Hawaii. Applicant must have 3.5 GPA or higher. Available to U.S. citizens.

Application Requirements: Application, autobiography, essay, financial need analysis, photo, references, transcript. *Deadline:* April 1.

Contact: Scholarship Committee
Hawaii Education Association
1953 South Beretania Street, Suite 3C
Honolulu, HI 96826-1340
Phone: 808-949-6657
Fax: 808-944-2032
E-mail: hea.office@heaed.com

HAWAII EDUCATION ASSOCIATION STUDENT TEACHER SCHOLARSHIP

Scholarship available to children or grandchildren of HEA members. Intent is to minimize the need for employment during student teaching semester. Must be enrolled full-time in an undergraduate or post-baccalaureate program in accredited institution of higher learning.

Academic Fields/Career Goals: Education.

Award: Scholarship for use in senior, graduate, or postgraduate years; not renewable. *Number:* up to 2. *Amount:* up to $3000.

Eligibility Requirements: Applicant must be enrolled or expecting to enroll full-time at a four-year institution or university. Applicant or parent of applicant must be member of Hawaii Education Association. Available to U.S. citizens.

Application Requirements: Application, autobiography, financial need analysis, photo, references, transcript. *Deadline:* April 1.

Contact: Scholarship Committee
Hawaii Education Association
1953 South Beretania Street, Suite 3C
Honolulu, HI 96826-1304
Phone: 808-949-6657
Fax: 808-944-2032
E-mail: hea.office@heaed.com

HIROSHI BARBARA KIM YAMASHITA HEA SCHOLARSHIP

Two $2000 scholarships awarded to full-time undergraduate education majors currently attending an accredited institution of higher learning and intending to teach in a Hawaii public school. Minimum 3.2 GPA required.

Academic Fields/Career Goals: Education.

Award: Scholarship for use in freshman, sophomore, junior, or senior years; not renewable. *Number:* 2. *Amount:* $2000.

Eligibility Requirements: Applicant must be enrolled or expecting to enroll full-time at a two-year or four-year or technical institution or university. Available to U.S. citizens.

Application Requirements: Application, financial need analysis, references, test scores. *Deadline:* April 1.

Contact: Carol Yoneshige, Executive Director
Hawaii Education Association
1953 South Beretania Street, Suite 3C
Honolulu, HI 96826-1340
Phone: 808-949-6657
Fax: 808-944-2032
E-mail: hea.office@heaed.com

MAY AND HUBERT EVERLY HEA SCHOLARSHIP

Scholarship for education majors who intend to teach in state of Hawaii at K-12 level. Undergraduate student in two- or four-year college/university. $1000 scholarship paid beginning of each semester.

Academic Fields/Career Goals: Education.

Award: Scholarship for use in junior or senior years; not renewable. *Number:* 1. *Amount:* $2000.

Eligibility Requirements: Applicant must be enrolled or expecting to enroll full-time at a two-year or four-year institution or university; resident of Hawaii and studying in Hawaii. Applicant must have 3.0 GPA or higher. Available to U.S. citizens.

Application Requirements: Application, autobiography, financial need analysis, photo, references, transcript. *Deadline:* April 1.

Contact: Scholarship Committee
Hawaii Education Association
1953 South Beretania Street, Suite 3C
Honolulu, HI 96826-1304
Phone: 808-949-6657
Fax: 808-944-2032
E-mail: hea.office@heaed.com

ILLINOIS PTA http://www.illinoispta.org

ILLINOIS PTA LILLIAN E. GLOVER SCHOLARSHIP

Scholarship has evolved to encourage Illinois college-bound high school seniors entering the field of education or an education-related field at the college/university of their choice.

Academic Fields/Career Goals: Education.

Award: Scholarship for use in freshman year; not renewable. *Amount:* $500–$1000.

Eligibility Requirements: Applicant must be high school student; planning to enroll or expecting to enroll full-time at a four-year institution or university and resident of Illinois. Available to U.S. citizens.

Application Requirements: Application, essay, resume, references, test scores, transcript. *Deadline:* March 5.

Contact: Toni Bugay, Scholarship Chairman
Illinois PTA
901 South Spring Street
Springfield, IL 62704
Phone: 217-528-9617
Fax: 217-528-9490
E-mail: il_office@pta.org

ILLINOIS STUDENT ASSISTANCE COMMISSION (ISAC) http://www.collegezone.org

ILLINOIS FUTURE TEACHERS CORPS PROGRAM

Scholarships are available for students planning to become teachers in Illinois. Students must be Illinois residents, enrolled or accepted as a junior or above in a Teacher Education Program at an Illinois college or university. By receiving the award, students agree to teach for five years at either a public, private, or parochial Illinois preschool, or at a public elementary or secondary school.

Academic Fields/Career Goals: Education.

Award: Forgivable loan for use in junior, senior, or graduate years; renewable. *Number:* 1150. *Amount:* $5000–$15,000.

Eligibility Requirements: Applicant must be enrolled or expecting to enroll full- or part-time at a four-year institution or university; resident of Illinois and studying in Illinois. Applicant must have 2.5 GPA or higher. Available to U.S. citizens.

Application Requirements: Application, financial need analysis, FAFSA. *Deadline:* March 1.

Contact: College Zone Counselor
Illinois Student Assistance Commission (ISAC)
1755 Lake Cook Road
Deerfield, IL 60015-5209
Phone: 800-899-4722
E-mail: collegezone@isac.org

MINORITY TEACHERS OF ILLINOIS SCHOLARSHIP PROGRAM

Award for minority students intending to become school teachers. Number of scholarships and the individual dollar amount awarded vary.

Academic Fields/Career Goals: Education; Special Education.

Award: Scholarship for use in freshman, sophomore, junior, senior, graduate, or postgraduate years; renewable. *Number:* 450–550. *Amount:* up to $5000.

Eligibility Requirements: Applicant must be American Indian/Alaska Native, Asian/Pacific Islander, Black (non-Hispanic), or Hispanic; enrolled or expecting to enroll full- or part-time at a two-year or four-year institution or university; resident of Illinois and studying in Illinois. Applicant must have 2.5 GPA or higher. Available to U.S. citizens.

Application Requirements: Application, transcript. *Deadline:* March 1.

Contact: College Zone Counselor
Illinois Student Assistance Commission (ISAC)
1755 Lake Cook Road
Deerfield, IL 60015-5209
Phone: 800-899-4722
E-mail: collegezone@isac.org

PAUL DOUGLAS TEACHER SCHOLARSHIP (PDTS) PROGRAM

Program enables and encourages outstanding high school graduates to pursue teaching careers at the preschool, elementary or secondary school level by providing financial assistance.

Academic Fields/Career Goals: Education.

Award: Scholarship for use in freshman year; not renewable. *Number:* varies. *Amount:* up to $5000.

Eligibility Requirements: Applicant must be high school student; planning to enroll or expecting to enroll full-time at a four-year institution or university; resident of Illinois and studying in Illinois. Available to U.S. citizens.

Application Requirements: Application, financial need analysis. *Deadline:* August 1.

Contact: College Zone Counselor
Illinois Student Assistance Commission (ISAC)
1755 Lake Cook Road
Deerfield, IL 60015-5209
Phone: 800-899-4722
E-mail: collegezone@isac.org

INDIANA RETIRED TEACHER'S ASSOCIATION (IRTA) http://www.retiredteachers.org

INDIANA RETIRED TEACHERS ASSOCIATION FOUNDATION SCHOLARSHIP

Scholarship available to college sophomores or juniors who are enrolled full-time in an education program at an Indiana college or university for a baccalaureate degree. The applicant must be the child, grandchild, legal dependant or spouse of an active, retired or deceased member of the Indiana State Teachers Retirement Fund.

Academic Fields/Career Goals: Education.

Award: Scholarship for use in sophomore or junior years; not renewable. *Number:* 8. *Amount:* $1500.

Eligibility Requirements: Applicant must be enrolled or expecting to enroll full-time at a four-year institution or university; resident of Indiana and studying in Indiana. Applicant or parent of applicant must have employment or volunteer experience in teaching/education. Available to U.S. and non-U.S. citizens.

Application Requirements: Application, essay, financial need analysis, references, transcript. *Deadline:* February 22.

Contact: Executive Director
Indiana Retired Teacher's Association (IRTA)
150 West Market Street, Suite 610
Indianapolis, IN 46204-2812
Phone: 888-454-9333
Fax: 317-637-9671

INTERNATIONAL ASSOCIATION OF GREAT LAKES RESEARCH http://www.iaglr.org

PAUL W. RODGERS SCHOLARSHIP

• *See page 217*

INTERNATIONAL TECHNOLOGY EDUCATION ASSOCIATION http://www.iteaconnect.org

INTERNATIONAL TECHNOLOGY EDUCATION ASSOCIATION UNDERGRADUATE SCHOLARSHIP IN TECHNOLOGY EDUCATION

A scholarship for undergraduate students pursuing a degree in technology education and technological studies. Applicants must be members of the association.

Academic Fields/Career Goals: Education; Engineering/Technology; Science, Technology, and Society.

Award: Scholarship for use in freshman, sophomore, junior, or senior years; not renewable. *Number:* 3. *Amount:* $1000.

International Technology Education Association (continued)

Eligibility Requirements: Applicant must be enrolled or expecting to enroll full-time at a four-year institution or university. Applicant or parent of applicant must be member of International Technology Education Association. Applicant must have 2.5 GPA or higher. Available to U.S. and non-U.S. citizens.

Application Requirements: Application, resume, references, transcript. *Deadline:* December 1.

Contact: Scholarship Committee
International Technology Education Association
1914 Association Drive, Suite 201
Reston, VA 20191
Phone: 703-860-2100
Fax: 703-860-0353
E-mail: iteaordr@iris.org

JACK J. ISGUR FOUNDATION

JACK J. ISGUR FOUNDATION SCHOLARSHIP

• *See page 102*

KANSAS BOARD OF REGENTS http://www.kansasregents.org

KANSAS TEACHER SERVICE SCHOLARSHIP

Scholarship to encourage talented students to enter the teaching profession and teach in Kansas in specific curriculum areas or in underserved areas of Kansas. For more details, refer to Web site: http://www.kansasregents.org/financial_aid/teacher.html.

Academic Fields/Career Goals: Education.

Award: Scholarship for use in junior, senior, or graduate years; renewable. *Number:* varies. *Amount:* $5000.

Eligibility Requirements: Applicant must be enrolled or expecting to enroll full- or part-time at a four-year institution or university. Applicant must have 3.0 GPA or higher. Available to U.S. citizens.

Application Requirements: Application, financial need analysis, resume, references, test scores, transcript. *Fee:* $10. *Deadline:* May 1.

Contact: Diane Lindeman, Director of Student Financial Assistance
Kansas Board of Regents
1000 Jackson, SW, Suite 520
Topeka, KS 66612-1368
Phone: 785-296-3517
Fax: 785-296-0983
E-mail: dlindeman@ksbor.org

KAPPA DELTA PI http://www.kdp.org

HAROLD D. DRUMMOND SCHOLARSHIP

One-time scholarship of $500 for undergraduate and graduate students enrolled full-time in elementary education. Must be U.S. citizen.

Academic Fields/Career Goals: Education.

Award: Scholarship for use in freshman, sophomore, junior, senior, or graduate years; not renewable. *Number:* 4. *Amount:* $500.

Eligibility Requirements: Applicant must be enrolled or expecting to enroll full-time at a four-year institution or university. Available to U.S. and non-U.S. citizens.

Application Requirements: Application, essay, financial need analysis, references, transcript. *Deadline:* April 25.

Contact: Rachel Thompson, Development Associate
Kappa Delta Pi
3707 Woodview Trace
Indianapolis, IN 46268-1158
Phone: 317-829-1543 Ext. 1543
Fax: 317-704-2323
E-mail: rachel@kdp.org

KE ALI'I PAUAHI FOUNDATION http://www.pauahi.org

DAN AND RACHEL MAHI EDUCATIONAL SCHOLARSHIP

Scholarship provides support to undergraduate or graduate students. Must demonstrate financial need. Minimum GPA of 2.0 required.

Academic Fields/Career Goals: Education.

Award: Scholarship for use in freshman, sophomore, junior, senior, or graduate years; not renewable. *Number:* up to 1. *Amount:* up to $1200.

Eligibility Requirements: Applicant must be enrolled or expecting to enroll full-time at a two-year or four-year institution or university. Available to U.S. citizens.

Application Requirements: Application, financial need analysis, references, transcript, college acceptance letter, copy of SAR. *Deadline:* May 2.

Contact: Elizabeth Stevenson, Development Manager
Ke Ali'i Pauahi Foundation
567 South King Street, Suite 160
Honolulu, HI 96813
Phone: 808-534-3966
Fax: 808-534-3890
E-mail: scholarships@pauahi.org

GLADYS KAMAKAKUOKALANI AINOA BRANDT SCHOLARSHIP

Provides scholarships for full-time junior, senior or graduate students at an accredited university aspiring to enter the educational profession. Applicants must demonstrate financial need, a GPA of 2.5 or higher is required, and priority will be given to current or former residents of Kauai.

Academic Fields/Career Goals: Education.

Award: Scholarship for use in junior, senior, or graduate years; not renewable. *Number:* 4. *Amount:* $2600.

Eligibility Requirements: Applicant must be enrolled or expecting to enroll full-time at a four-year institution or university. Applicant must have 2.5 GPA or higher. Available to U.S. citizens.

Application Requirements: Financial need analysis, references, transcript, signed application confirmation page, copy of completed SAR. *Deadline:* May 2.

Contact: Elizabeth Stevenson, Development Manager
Ke Ali'i Pauahi Foundation
567 South King Street, Suite 160
Honolulu, HI 96813
Phone: 808-534-3966
Fax: 808-534-3890
E-mail: scholarships@pauahi.org

INSPIRATIONAL EDUCATOR SCHOLARSHIP

In recognition of inspirational educators who have made a difference in the lives of students, this endowment provides educational scholarships for full- or part-time college students pursuing a career in the field of education.

Academic Fields/Career Goals: Education.

Award: Scholarship for use in freshman, sophomore, junior, senior, or graduate years; not renewable. *Number:* 1. *Amount:* $2000.

Eligibility Requirements: Applicant must be enrolled or expecting to enroll full- or part-time at a two-year or four-year institution or university. Available to U.S. citizens.

Application Requirements: Essay, financial need analysis, references, transcript, college acceptance letter, copy of signed online application confirmation page, copy of completed SAR. *Deadline:* May 2.

Contact: Elizabeth Stevenson, Development Manager
Ke Ali'i Pauahi Foundation
567 South King Street, Suite 160
Honolulu, HI 96813
Phone: 808-534-3966
Fax: 808-534-3890
E-mail: scholarships@pauahi.org

MYRON & LAURA THOMPSON SCHOLARSHIP

• *See page 166*

KENTUCKY DEPARTMENT OF EDUCATION http://www.education.ky.gov

KENTUCKY MINORITY EDUCATOR RECRUITMENT AND RETENTION (KMERR) SCHOLARSHIP

Scholarship for minority teacher candidates who rank in the upper half of their class or have a minimum 2.5 GPA. Must be a U.S. citizen and Kentucky resident enrolled in one of Kentucky's eight public institutions. Must teach one semester in Kentucky for each semester the scholarship is received.

Academic Fields/Career Goals: Education.

Award: Forgivable loan for use in freshman, sophomore, junior, senior, or graduate years; renewable. *Number:* 400. *Amount:* $2500–$5000.

Eligibility Requirements: Applicant must be American Indian/Alaska Native, Asian/Pacific Islander, Black (non-Hispanic), or Hispanic; enrolled or expecting to enroll full-time at a two-year or four-year institution or university; resident of Kentucky and studying in Kentucky. Applicant must have 2.5 GPA or higher. Available to U.S. citizens.

Application Requirements: Application, references, test scores, transcript. *Deadline:* continuous.

Contact: Michael Dailey, Division Director
Kentucky Department of Education
500 Mero Street, 17th Floor
Frankfort, KY 40601
Phone: 502-564-1479
Fax: 502-564-6952
E-mail: michael.dailey@education.ky.gov

KENTUCKY HIGHER EDUCATION ASSISTANCE AUTHORITY (KHEAA) http://www.kheaa.com

EARLY CHILDHOOD DEVELOPMENT SCHOLARSHIP

• *See page 166*

KENTUCKY TEACHER SCHOLARSHIP PROGRAM

Awards Kentucky residents attending Kentucky institutions and pursuing initial teacher certification programs. Must teach one semester for each semester of award received. In critical shortage areas, must teach one semester for every two semesters of award received.

Academic Fields/Career Goals: Education.

Award: Scholarship for use in freshman, sophomore, junior, senior, or graduate years; renewable. *Number:* 600–700. *Amount:* $325–$5000.

Eligibility Requirements: Applicant must be enrolled or expecting to enroll full-time at a two-year or four-year institution or university; resident of Kentucky and studying in Kentucky. Available to U.S. citizens.

Application Requirements: Application, financial need analysis. *Deadline:* May 1.

Contact: Tim Phelps, Student Aid Branch Manager
Kentucky Higher Education Assistance Authority (KHEAA)
PO Box 798
Frankfort, KY 40602
Phone: 502-696-7393
Fax: 502-696-7496
E-mail: tphelps@kheaa.com

MINORITY EDUCATOR RECRUITMENT AND RETENTION SCHOLARSHIP

Conversion loan or scholarship for Kentucky residents. Provides up to $5000 per academic year to minority students majoring in teacher education and pursuing initial teacher certification. Must be repaid with interest if scholarship requirements are not met.

Academic Fields/Career Goals: Education; Special Education.

Award: Forgivable loan for use in freshman, sophomore, junior, senior, or graduate years; not renewable. *Number:* 200–300. *Amount:* up to $5000.

Eligibility Requirements: Applicant must be American Indian/Alaska Native, Asian/Pacific Islander, Black (non-Hispanic), or Hispanic; enrolled or expecting to enroll full-time at a two-year or four-year institution or university; resident of Kentucky and studying in Kentucky. Applicant must have 2.5 GPA or higher. Available to U.S. citizens.

Application Requirements: Application. *Deadline:* continuous.

Contact: Natasha Murray, Program Director
Kentucky Higher Education Assistance Authority (KHEAA)
500 Metro Street
Frankfort, KY 40601
Phone: 502-564-1479
E-mail: natasha.murray@education.ky.gov

LINCOLN COMMUNITY FOUNDATION http://www.lcf.org

DALE E. SIEFKES MEMORIAL SCHOLARSHIP

One scholarship available to a college student currently pursuing a career in education. Applicant should be a junior or senior level Nebraska college or university student with a GPA of 3.8 or higher. See Web site for application: http://www.lcf.org.

Academic Fields/Career Goals: Education.

Award: Scholarship for use in junior or senior years; not renewable. *Number:* 1. *Amount:* $500–$1000.

Eligibility Requirements: Applicant must be enrolled or expecting to enroll full-time at a four-year institution or university and studying in Nebraska. Applicant must have 3.5 GPA or higher. Available to U.S. citizens.

Application Requirements: Application, essay, financial need analysis, test scores, transcript. *Deadline:* April 15.

Contact: Sonya Brakeman, Grants/Scholarships Coordinator
Lincoln Community Foundation
215 Centennial Mall South, Suite 100
Lincoln, NE 68508
Phone: 402-474-2345
Fax: 402-476-8532
E-mail: sonyab@lcf.org

FLORENCE TURNER KARLIN SCHOLARSHIP FOR UNDERGRADUATES

Scholarship for former graduate of any high school in Nebraska who is pursuing a degree in education in a college or university in Nebraska. Applicants must have completed at least their sophomore year in college and have a GPA of 3.0 or better.

Academic Fields/Career Goals: Education.

Award: Scholarship for use in junior or senior years; not renewable. *Number:* 1–10. *Amount:* $500–$1000.

Eligibility Requirements: Applicant must be enrolled or expecting to enroll full-time at a two-year or four-year institution or university; resident of Nebraska and studying in Nebraska. Applicant must have 3.0 GPA or higher. Available to U.S. citizens.

Application Requirements: Application, essay, references, test scores, transcript. *Deadline:* March 15.

Contact: Sonya Brakeman, Grants/Scholarships Coordinator
Lincoln Community Foundation
215 Centennial Mall South, Suite 100
Lincoln, NE 68508
Phone: 402-474-2345
Fax: 402-476-8532
E-mail: sonyab@lcf.org

GEORGE AND LYNNA GENE COOK SCHOLARSHIP

Applicants must be a current graduating senior or a former graduate of any high school in Nebraska with a GPA of 3.0 or better. Must be members of First Church of God congregations that are affiliated with the church body located in Anderson, Indiana. Must be pursuing a degree in ministry or education and demonstrate financial need.

Academic Fields/Career Goals: Education; Religion/Theology.

Award: Scholarship for use in freshman, sophomore, junior, or senior years; renewable. *Number:* 1. *Amount:* $500.

Eligibility Requirements: Applicant must be enrolled or expecting to enroll full-time at a two-year or four-year institution or university. Applicant must have 3.0 GPA or higher. Available to U.S. citizens.

Application Requirements: Application, financial need analysis, test scores, transcript, letter of recommendation from the pastor or other current congregation leader. *Deadline:* March 15.

Contact: Sonya Brakeman, Grants/Scholarships Coordinator
Lincoln Community Foundation
215 Centennial Mall South, Suite 100
Lincoln, NE 68508
Phone: 402-474-2345
Fax: 402-476-8532
E-mail: sonyab@lcf.org

NEBRASKA RURAL COMMUNITY SCHOOLS ASSOCIATION SCHOLARSHIP

Scholarships for students attending schools in Nebraska and holding current memberships in NRCSA. Must major in education and demonstrate financial need. Applicants should also demonstrate academic achievement, leadership, character, and initiative. Preferred students will be involved in extracurricular activities. Minimum GPA of 3.5 is required.

Academic Fields/Career Goals: Education.

Award: Scholarship for use in freshman year; not renewable. *Number:* 6. *Amount:* $500–$1000.

Lincoln Community Foundation (continued)

Eligibility Requirements: Applicant must be high school student; planning to enroll or expecting to enroll full-time at a four-year institution or university; resident of Nebraska and studying in Nebraska. Applicant must have 3.5 GPA or higher. Available to U.S. citizens.

Application Requirements: Application, essay, financial need analysis, references. *Deadline:* February 9.

Contact: Sonya Brakeman, Grants/Scholarships Coordinator
Lincoln Community Foundation
215 Centennial Mall South, Suite 100
Lincoln, NE 68508
Phone: 402-474-2345
Fax: 402-476-8532
E-mail: sonyab@lcf.org

MARION D. AND EVA S. PEEPLES FOUNDATION TRUST SCHOLARSHIP PROGRAM http://www.jccf.org

MARION A. AND EVA S. PEEPLES SCHOLARSHIPS

Award for undergraduate study in nursing, dietetics, and teaching in industrial arts. Applicant must reapply each year for renewal. Recipient must maintain 2.5 GPA. Must be Indiana resident and attending an Indiana school.

Academic Fields/Career Goals: Education; Engineering/Technology; Food Science/Nutrition; Nursing; Trade/Technical Specialties.

Award: Scholarship for use in freshman, sophomore, junior, or senior years; not renewable. *Number:* 30–35. *Amount:* $1000–$3000.

Eligibility Requirements: Applicant must be enrolled or expecting to enroll full-time at a two-year or four-year or technical institution or university; resident of Indiana and studying in Indiana. Applicant must have 2.5 GPA or higher. Available to U.S. citizens.

Application Requirements: Application, autobiography, financial need analysis, interview, references, self-addressed stamped envelope, test scores, transcript. *Deadline:* March 1.

Contact: Kim Kastings, Scholarship Director
Marion D. and Eva S. Peeples Foundation Trust Scholarship Program
PO Box 217
Franklin, IN 46131-2311
Phone: 317-738-2213
Fax: 317-738-9113
E-mail: kimk@jccf.org

MARYLAND HIGHER EDUCATION COMMISSION http://www.mhec.state.md.us

JANET L. HOFFMANN LOAN ASSISTANCE REPAYMENT PROGRAM

Provides assistance for repayment of loan debt to Maryland residents working full-time in nonprofit organizations and state or local governments. Must submit Employment Verification Form and Lender Verification Form.

Academic Fields/Career Goals: Education; Law/Legal Services; Nursing; Social Services; Therapy/Rehabilitation.

Award: Grant for use in freshman, sophomore, junior, senior, or graduate years; not renewable. *Number:* up to 700. *Amount:* $1500–$10,000.

Eligibility Requirements: Applicant must be enrolled or expecting to enroll full-time at a four-year institution or university; resident of Maryland and studying in Maryland. Applicant or parent of applicant must have employment or volunteer experience in government/politics. Available to U.S. citizens.

Application Requirements: Application, transcript, IRS 1040 form. *Deadline:* September 30.

Contact: Tamika McKelvin, Office of Student Financial Assistance
Maryland Higher Education Commission
839 Bestgate Road, Suite 400
Annapolis, MD 21401
Phone: 410-260-4546
Fax: 410-260-3203
E-mail: tmckelvil@mhec.state.md.us

MASSACHUSETTS OFFICE OF STUDENT FINANCIAL ASSISTANCE http://www.osfa.mass.edu

EARLY CHILDHOOD EDUCATORS SCHOLARSHIP PROGRAM

Scholarship to provide financial assistance for currently employed early childhood educators and providers who enroll in an associate or bachelor degree program in Early Childhood Education or related programs. Awards are not based on financial need. Individuals taking their first college-level ECE course are eligible for 100 percent tuition, while subsequent ECE courses are awarded at 50 percent tuition. Can be used for one class each semester.

Academic Fields/Career Goals: Education.

Award: Scholarship for use in freshman, sophomore, junior, or senior years; not renewable. *Number:* varies. *Amount:* $150–$3600.

Eligibility Requirements: Applicant must be enrolled or expecting to enroll full- or part-time at a four-year institution or university. Available to U.S. citizens.

Application Requirements: Application. *Deadline:* July 1.

Contact: Robert Brun, Director of Scholarships and Grants
Massachusetts Office of Student Financial Assistance
454 Broadway, Suite 200
Revere, MA 02151
Phone: 617-727-9420
Fax: 617-727-0667
E-mail: osfa@osfa.mass.edu

PARAPROFESSIONAL TEACHER PREPARATION GRANT

Grant providing financial aid assistance to Massachusetts residents, who are currently employed as paraprofessionals in Massachusetts public schools and wish to obtain higher education and become certified as full-time teachers.

Academic Fields/Career Goals: Education.

Award: Grant for use in freshman, sophomore, junior, or senior years; not renewable. *Number:* varies. *Amount:* $250–$7500.

Eligibility Requirements: Applicant must be enrolled or expecting to enroll full- or part-time at a two-year or four-year institution or university and resident of Massachusetts. Available to U.S. citizens.

Application Requirements: Application, FAFSA. *Deadline:* August 1.

Contact: Robert Brun, Director of Scholarships and Grants
Massachusetts Office of Student Financial Assistance
454 Broadway, Suite 200
Revere, MA 02151
Phone: 617-727-9420
Fax: 617-727-0667
E-mail: osfa@osfa.mass.edu

MELLON NEW ENGLAND http://www.mellon.com

JOHN L. BATES SCHOLARSHIP

Scholarship only for students who are pursuing a career in education. Not for graduate study programs. Must be resident of Massachusetts. Eligible applicant must be recommended by educational institution.

Academic Fields/Career Goals: Education.

Award: Scholarship for use in freshman, sophomore, junior, or senior years; not renewable. *Number:* varies. *Amount:* $300–$2000.

Eligibility Requirements: Applicant must be enrolled or expecting to enroll full-time at a four-year institution or university and resident of Massachusetts. Available to U.S. citizens.

Application Requirements: Application, essay, transcript. *Deadline:* April 15.

Contact: Sandra Brown-McMullen, Vice President
Mellon New England
1 Boston Place, 024-0084
Boston, MA 02108
Phone: 617-722-3891
E-mail: brown-mcmullen.s@mellon.com

MEMORIAL FOUNDATION FOR JEWISH CULTURE http://www.mfjc.org

MEMORIAL FOUNDATION FOR JEWISH CULTURE SCHOLARSHIPS FOR POST-RABBINICAL STUDENTS

Scholarship program is to assist well-qualified individuals to train for careers in the rabbinate, Jewish education, social work, and as religious functionaries in

Diaspora Jewish communities in need of such personnel. Open to any individual, regardless of country of origin, who is presently receiving, or plans to undertake, training in a recognized yeshiva, teacher training seminary, school of social work, university or other educational institution.

Academic Fields/Career Goals: Education; Religion/Theology; Social Services.

Award: Scholarship for use in freshman, sophomore, junior, or senior years; renewable. *Number:* varies. *Amount:* varies.

Eligibility Requirements: Applicant must be Jewish; enrolled or expecting to enroll full- or part-time at a two-year or four-year or technical institution or university and must have an interest in Jewish culture. Available to U.S. and non-U.S. citizens.

Application Requirements: Application, photo, references. *Deadline:* November 30.

Contact: Dr. Jerry Hochbaum, Executive Vice President
Memorial Foundation for Jewish Culture
50 Broadway, 34th Floor
New York, NY 10004
Phone: 212-425-6606
Fax: 212-425-6602
E-mail: office@mfjc.org

MISSISSIPPI STATE STUDENT FINANCIAL AID http://www.ihl.state.ms.us

CRITICAL NEEDS TEACHER LOAN/SCHOLARSHIP

Eligible applicants will agree to employment immediately upon degree completion as a full-time classroom teacher in a public school located in a critical teacher shortage area in the state of Mississippi. Must verify the intention to pursue a first bachelor's degree in teacher education. Award covers tuition and required fees, average cost of room and meals plus allowance for books. Must be enrolled at a Mississippi college or university.

Academic Fields/Career Goals: Education; Psychology; Therapy/Rehabilitation.

Award: Forgivable loan for use in junior or senior years; not renewable. *Number:* varies. *Amount:* varies.

Eligibility Requirements: Applicant must be enrolled or expecting to enroll full- or part-time at a four-year institution or university; resident of Mississippi and studying in Mississippi. Applicant must have 2.5 GPA or higher. Available to U.S. and non-U.S. citizens.

Application Requirements: Application, test scores, transcript. *Deadline:* March 31.

Contact: Mary Covington, Assistant Director, State Student Financial Aid
Mississippi State Student Financial Aid
3825 Ridgewood Road
Jackson, MS 39211-6453
Phone: 800-327-2980
E-mail: sfa@ihl.state.ms.us

WILLIAM WINTER TEACHER SCHOLAR LOAN

Scholarship available to a junior or senior student at a four-year Mississippi college or university. Applicants must enroll in a program of study leading to a Class "A" teacher educator license.

Academic Fields/Career Goals: Education.

Award: Scholarship for use in junior or senior years; renewable. *Number:* varies. *Amount:* up to $4000.

Eligibility Requirements: Applicant must be enrolled or expecting to enroll full-time at a four-year institution or university; resident of Mississippi and studying in Mississippi. Applicant must have 2.5 GPA or higher. Available to U.S. citizens.

Application Requirements: Application. *Deadline:* March 31.

Contact: Mary Covington, Assistant Director, State Student Financial Aid
Mississippi State Student Financial Aid
3825 Ridgewood Road
Jackson, MS 39211-6453
Phone: 800-327-2980
E-mail: sfa@ihl.state.ms.us

MISSOURI DEPARTMENT OF ELEMENTARY AND SECONDARY EDUCATION http://www.dese.mo.gov

MISSOURI MINORITY TEACHING SCHOLARSHIP

Scholarship is competitive and is a renewable award of $3000 for up to four years. Must be a Missouri resident of African-American, Asian American, Hispanic American, or Native American heritage. High school seniors, college students, or returning adults are eligible.

Academic Fields/Career Goals: Education.

Award: Scholarship for use in freshman, sophomore, junior, or senior years; renewable. *Number:* varies. *Amount:* $3000.

Eligibility Requirements: Applicant must be American Indian/Alaska Native, Asian/Pacific Islander, Black (non-Hispanic), or Hispanic; enrolled or expecting to enroll full-time at a four-year institution or university; resident of Missouri and studying in Missouri. Applicant must have 3.0 GPA or higher. Available to U.S. citizens.

Application Requirements: Application, essay, financial need analysis, resume, references, test scores, transcript. *Deadline:* February 15.

Contact: Laura Harrison, Administrative Assistant
Missouri Department of Elementary and Secondary Education
PO Box 480
Jefferson City, MO 65102-0480
Phone: 573-751-1668
Fax: 573-526-3580
E-mail: laura.harrison@dese.mo.gov

MISSOURI TEACHER EDUCATION SCHOLARSHIP (GENERAL)

Nonrenewable award for Missouri high school seniors or Missouri resident college students. Must attend approved teacher training program at a participating Missouri institution and rank in top 15 percent of high school class on ACT/SAT. Merit-based award. Recipients must commit to teach in Missouri for five years at a public elementary or secondary school or award must be repaid.

Academic Fields/Career Goals: Education.

Award: Scholarship for use in freshman, sophomore, junior, or senior years; not renewable. *Number:* 200–240. *Amount:* up to $2000.

Eligibility Requirements: Applicant must be enrolled or expecting to enroll full-time at a two-year or four-year institution or university; resident of Missouri and studying in Missouri. Available to U.S. citizens.

Application Requirements: Application, essay, resume, references, test scores, transcript. *Deadline:* February 15.

Contact: Laura Harrison, Administrative Assistant II
Missouri Department of Elementary and Secondary Education
PO Box 480
Jefferson City, MO 65102-0480
Phone: 573-751-1668
Fax: 573-526-3580
E-mail: laura.harrison@dese.mo.gov

NASA IDAHO SPACE GRANT CONSORTIUM http://isgc.uidaho.edu

NASA IDAHO SPACE GRANT CONSORTIUM SCHOLARSHIP PROGRAM

• *See page 87*

NASA RHODE ISLAND SPACE GRANT CONSORTIUM http://www.planetary.brown.edu/RI_Space_Grant

NASA RISGC SUMMER SCHOLARSHIP FOR UNDERGRADUATE STUDENTS

• *See page 120*

NASA VIRGINIA SPACE GRANT CONSORTIUM http://www.vsgc.odu.edu

VIRGINIA SPACE GRANT CONSORTIUM TEACHER EDUCATION SCHOLARSHIPS

• *See page 121*

NATIONAL ASSOCIATION FOR THE ADVANCEMENT OF COLORED PEOPLE http://www.naacp.org

NAACP LILLIAN AND SAMUEL SUTTON EDUCATION SCHOLARSHIP

Scholarship for a full-time student who is enrolled in an accredited college in the United States. Graduating high school seniors and undergraduate students must have 2.5 minimum GPA. Graduate students must have 3.0 minimum GPA. Undergraduate scholarship is for $1000; and graduate scholarship is $2000.

Academic Fields/Career Goals: Education.

Award: Scholarship for use in freshman, sophomore, junior, senior, or graduate years; not renewable. *Number:* 1. *Amount:* $1000–$2000.

Eligibility Requirements: Applicant must be American Indian/Alaska Native, Asian/Pacific Islander, Black (non-Hispanic), or Hispanic and enrolled or expecting to enroll full- or part-time at a four-year institution or university. Applicant or parent of applicant must be member of National Association for the Advancement of Colored People. Available to U.S. citizens.

Application Requirements: Application, financial need analysis, references, transcript. *Deadline:* April 30.

Contact: Victor Goode, Attorney
National Association for the Advancement of Colored People
4805 Mount Hope Drive
Baltimore, MD 21215-3297
Phone: 410-580-5760
Fax: 410-585-1329
E-mail: info@naacp.org

THURGOOD MARSHALL COLLEGE FUND

Scholarship for full-time students in historically Black public colleges or universities. Must have minimum high school GPA of 3.0.

Academic Fields/Career Goals: Education.

Award: Scholarship for use in freshman, sophomore, junior, senior, or graduate years; renewable. *Number:* 22. *Amount:* $2200.

Eligibility Requirements: Applicant must be American Indian/Alaska Native, Asian/Pacific Islander, Black (non-Hispanic), or Hispanic and enrolled or expecting to enroll full-time at a four-year institution or university. Applicant must have 3.0 GPA or higher. Available to U.S. citizens.

Application Requirements: Application, essay, financial need analysis, photo, resume, references, transcript. *Deadline:* May 1.

Contact: Beverly Colbert, Office Manager
National Association for the Advancement of Colored People
80 Maiden Lane, Suite 2204
New York, NY 10038
Phone: 212-573-8888
Fax: 212-573-8497
E-mail: bcolbert@tmcfund.org

NATIONAL COUNCIL OF TEACHERS OF MATHEMATICS http://www.nctm.org

PROSPECTIVE SECONDARY TEACHER COURSE WORK SCHOLARSHIPS

Grant provides financial support to college students preparing for teaching secondary school mathematics. Award of $10,000 will be granted in two phases, with $5000 for the recipient's third year of full-time study, and $5000 for fourth year. Must be student members of NCTM and cannot reapply. Must submit proposal, essay, letters of recommendation, and transcripts.

Academic Fields/Career Goals: Education; Mathematics.

Award: Scholarship for use in junior or senior years; not renewable. *Number:* 2. *Amount:* up to $5000.

Eligibility Requirements: Applicant must be enrolled or expecting to enroll full-time at a four-year institution or university. Available to U.S. and non-U.S. citizens.

Application Requirements: Application, essay, references, transcript, written proposal. *Deadline:* May 9.

Contact: Mathematics Education Trust
National Council of Teachers of Mathematics
1906 Association Drive
Reston, VA 20191-1502
Phone: 703-620-9840 Ext. 2112
Fax: 703-476-2970
E-mail: exec@nctm.org

NATIONAL FEDERATION OF THE BLIND http://www.nfb.org

NATIONAL FEDERATION OF THE BLIND EDUCATOR OF TOMORROW AWARD

Award for students who are legally blind and pursuing teaching careers. Selection based on academic excellence, service to the community, and financial need. Must be planning a career in elementary, secondary, or postsecondary teaching. Minimum 3.5 GPA required.

Academic Fields/Career Goals: Education.

Award: Scholarship for use in freshman, sophomore, junior, or senior years; not renewable. *Number:* 1. *Amount:* $3000.

Eligibility Requirements: Applicant must be enrolled or expecting to enroll full- or part-time at a two-year or four-year institution or university. Applicant or parent of applicant must have employment or volunteer experience in community service. Applicant must be visually impaired. Applicant must have 3.5 GPA or higher. Available to U.S. and non-U.S. citizens.

Application Requirements: Application, autobiography, essay, financial need analysis, references, transcript, recommendation letter from state officer of NFB. *Deadline:* March 31.

Contact: Anil Lewis, Chairman, Scholarship Committee
National Federation of the Blind
315 West Ponce de Leon Avenue, Suite 603
Decatur, GA 30030
Phone: 404-371-1000
E-mail: alewis@nfbga.org

NATIONAL FEDERATION OF THE BLIND OF CONNECTICUT http://www.nfbct.org

BRIAN CUMMINS MEMORIAL SCHOLARSHIP

Scholarship of $5000 awarded to college or graduate student enrolled in a full-time program to teach blind and visually impaired students in Connecticut.

Academic Fields/Career Goals: Education; Special Education.

Award: Scholarship for use in freshman, sophomore, junior, senior, or graduate years; not renewable. *Number:* 1. *Amount:* $5000.

Eligibility Requirements: Applicant must be enrolled or expecting to enroll full-time at a four-year institution or university and resident of Connecticut. Available to U.S. citizens.

Application Requirements: Application, references, transcript. *Deadline:* October 15.

Contact: Scholarship Committee
National Federation of the Blind of Connecticut
477 Connecticut Boulevard, Suite 217
East Hartford, CT 06108
Phone: 860-289-1971
Fax: 860-291-2795
E-mail: info@nfbct.org

NATIONAL INSTITUTE FOR LABOR RELATIONS RESEARCH http://www.nilrr.org

APPLEGATE/JACKSON/PARKS FUTURE TEACHER SCHOLARSHIP

Scholarship available to all education majors currently attending school. High school seniors accepted into a teacher education program may also apply. Award is based on an essay demonstrating knowledge of and interest in compulsory unionism in education. Specify "Education" or "Future Teacher Scholarship" on any correspondence.

Academic Fields/Career Goals: Education; Special Education.

Award: Scholarship for use in freshman, sophomore, junior, senior, or graduate years; not renewable. *Number:* 1. *Amount:* $1000.

Eligibility Requirements: Applicant must be enrolled or expecting to enroll full-time at a four-year institution or university. Available to U.S. citizens.

Application Requirements: Application, essay, transcript. *Deadline:* December 31.

Contact: Cathy Jones, Scholarship Coordinator
National Institute for Labor Relations Research
5211 Port Royal Road
Springfield, VA 22151
Phone: 703-321-9606
Fax: 703-321-7143
E-mail: research@nilrr.org

NATIONAL URBAN LEAGUE http://www.nulbeep.org

BLACK EXECUTIVE EXCHANGE PROGRAM JERRY BARTOW SCHOLARSHIP FUND

• *See page 146*

NEW HAMPSHIRE POSTSECONDARY EDUCATION COMMISSION http://www.nh.gov/postsecondary

WORKFORCE INCENTIVE PROGRAM

The program provides incentive for students to pursue careers in critical workforce shortage areas at appropriate New Hampshire institutions and to encourage students to then seek employment in New Hampshire after completion of their career program. May be a part- or full-time student in an approved program, and should demonstrate financial need as determined by the institution.

Academic Fields/Career Goals: Education; Foreign Language; Nursing; Special Education.

Award: Forgivable loan for use in freshman, sophomore, junior, senior, graduate, or postgraduate years; not renewable. *Number:* varies. *Amount:* varies.

Eligibility Requirements: Applicant must be enrolled or expecting to enroll full- or part-time at a four-year institution or university; resident of New Hampshire and studying in New Hampshire. Available to U.S. citizens.

Application Requirements: Application. *Deadline:* varies.

Contact: Judith Knapp, Coordinator of Financial Aid Programs
New Hampshire Postsecondary Education Commission
Three Barrell Court, Suite 300
Concord, NH 03301-8543
Phone: 603-271-2555 Ext. 352
Fax: 603-271-2696
E-mail: jknapp@pec.state.nh.us

NEW MEXICO COMMISSION ON HIGHER EDUCATION http://www.hed.state.nm.us

TEACHER LOAN-FOR-SERVICE

The purpose of the Teacher Loan-for-Service is to proactively address New Mexico's teacher shortage by providing students with the financial resources to complete or enhance their post-secondary teacher preparation education.

Academic Fields/Career Goals: Education.

Award: Forgivable loan for use in freshman, sophomore, junior, senior, or graduate years; renewable. *Number:* 1. *Amount:* up to $4000.

Eligibility Requirements: Applicant must be enrolled or expecting to enroll full- or part-time at a four-year institution or university; resident of New Mexico and studying in New Mexico. Available to U.S. citizens.

Application Requirements: Application, financial need analysis, FAFSA. *Deadline:* July 1.

Contact: Tashina Banks-Moore, Interim Director of Financial Aid
New Mexico Commission on Higher Education
1068 Cerrillos Road
Santa Fe, NM 87505-1650
Phone: 505-476-6549
Fax: 505-476-6511
E-mail: tashin.banks-moore@state.nm.us

NORTH CAROLINA ASSOCIATION OF EDUCATORS http://www.ncae.org

MARY MORROW-EDNA RICHARDS SCHOLARSHIP

One-time award for junior year of study in four-year education degree program. Preference given to members of the student branch of the North Carolina Association of Educators. Must be North Carolina resident attending a North Carolina institution. Must agree to teach in North Carolina for two years after graduation. Must be a junior in college when application is filed.

Academic Fields/Career Goals: Education.

Award: Scholarship for use in junior or senior years; not renewable. *Number:* 3. *Amount:* up to $1000.

Eligibility Requirements: Applicant must be enrolled or expecting to enroll full-time at a four-year institution or university; resident of North Carolina and studying in North Carolina. Available to U.S. citizens.

Application Requirements: Application, essay, financial need analysis, references, transcript. *Deadline:* January 14.

Contact: Annette Montgomery, Communications Secretary
North Carolina Association of Educators
PO Box 27347
Raleigh, NC 27611
Phone: 800-662-7924
Fax: 919-839-8229
E-mail: annette.montgomery@ncae.org

NORTH CAROLINA STATE EDUCATION ASSISTANCE AUTHORITY http://www.ncseaa.edu

TEACHER ASSISTANT SCHOLARSHIP FUND

Funding to attend a public or private four-year college or university in North Carolina with an approved teacher education program. Applicant must be employed full-time as a teacher assistant in an instructional area while pursuing licensure and maintain employment to remain eligible. Must have at least 3.0 cumulative GPA. Refer to Web site for further details: http://www.ncseaa.edu/tas.htm.

Academic Fields/Career Goals: Education.

Award: Scholarship for use in freshman, sophomore, junior, or senior years; renewable. *Number:* varies. *Amount:* $600–$3600.

Eligibility Requirements: Applicant must be enrolled or expecting to enroll full- or part-time at a four-year institution or university; resident of North Carolina and studying in North Carolina. Applicant or parent of applicant must have employment or volunteer experience in teaching/education. Applicant must have 3.0 GPA or higher. Available to U.S. citizens.

Application Requirements: Application, financial need analysis, transcript, FAFSA. *Deadline:* March 31.

Contact: Rashonn Albritton, Processing Assistant
North Carolina State Education Assistance Authority
PO Box 13663
Research Triangle Park, NC 27709
Phone: 919-549-8614
Fax: 919-248-4687
E-mail: ralbritton@ncseaa.edu

NORTH CAROLINA TEACHING FELLOWS COMMISSION http://www.teachingfellows.org

NORTH CAROLINA TEACHING FELLOWS SCHOLARSHIP PROGRAM

Award for North Carolina high school seniors planning to pursue teacher training studies. Must agree to teach in a North Carolina public or government school for four years or repay award. For more details visit Web site: http://www.teachingfellows.org.

Academic Fields/Career Goals: Education.

Award: Forgivable loan for use in freshman year; renewable. *Number:* 500. *Amount:* $6500.

Eligibility Requirements: Applicant must be high school student; planning to enroll or expecting to enroll full-time at a four-year institution or university; resident of North Carolina and studying in North Carolina. Applicant must have 3.5 GPA or higher. Available to U.S. citizens.

North Carolina Teaching Fellows Commission (continued)

Application Requirements: Application, essay, interview, references, test scores, transcript. *Deadline:* varies.

Contact: Lynne Stewart, Program Officer
North Carolina Teaching Fellows Commission
3739 National Drive, Suite 100
Raleigh, NC 27612
Phone: 919-781-6833 Ext. 103
Fax: 919-781-6527
E-mail: tfellows@ncforum.org

OKLAHOMA STATE REGENTS FOR HIGHER EDUCATION http://www.okhighered.org

FUTURE TEACHER SCHOLARSHIP-OKLAHOMA

Open to outstanding Oklahoma high school graduates who agree to teach in shortage areas. Must rank in top 15 percent of graduating class or score above 85th percentile on ACT or similar test, or be accepted in an educational program. Students nominated by institution. Reapply to renew. Must attend college/university in Oklahoma.

Academic Fields/Career Goals: Education.

Award: Scholarship for use in freshman, sophomore, junior, senior, or graduate years; renewable. *Number:* 85. *Amount:* $500–$1500.

Eligibility Requirements: Applicant must be enrolled or expecting to enroll full- or part-time at a two-year or four-year institution or university; resident of Oklahoma and studying in Oklahoma. Available to U.S. citizens.

Application Requirements: Application, essay, test scores, transcript. *Deadline:* varies.

Contact: Scholarship Programs Coordinator
Oklahoma State Regents for Higher Education
PO Box 108850
Oklahoma City, OK 73101-8850
Phone: 800-858-1840
Fax: 405-225-9230
E-mail: studentinfo@osrhe.edu

OREGON PTA http://www.oregonpta.org

TEACHER EDUCATION SCHOLARSHIP

Nonrenewable scholarships to high school seniors or college students who are Oregon residents who want to teach in Oregon at an elementary or secondary school. The scholarship may be used at any Oregon public college or university that trains teachers or that transfers credits in education.

Academic Fields/Career Goals: Education.

Award: Scholarship for use in freshman, sophomore, junior, or senior years; not renewable. *Number:* varies. *Amount:* $500.

Eligibility Requirements: Applicant must be enrolled or expecting to enroll full-time at a two-year or four-year institution or university; resident of Oregon and studying in Oregon. Available to U.S. citizens.

Application Requirements: Application, autobiography, essay, references, self-addressed stamped envelope, test scores, transcript. *Deadline:* March 21.

Contact: Scholarship Committee
Oregon PTA
4506 SE Belmont Street, Suite 108-B
Portland, OR 97215
Fax: 503-234-6024
E-mail: or_office@pta.org

OREGON STUDENT ASSISTANCE COMMISSION http://www.osac.state.or.us

ALPHA DELTA KAPPA/HARRIET SIMMONS SCHOLARSHIP

One-time award for elementary and secondary education majors entering their senior year, or graduate students enrolled in a fifth-year program leading to a teaching certificate. Visit Web site http://www.osac.state.or.us for more information.

Academic Fields/Career Goals: Education.

Award: Scholarship for use in senior or graduate years; not renewable. *Number:* varies. *Amount:* varies.

Eligibility Requirements: Applicant must be enrolled or expecting to enroll full-time at a four-year institution or university and resident of Oregon. Available to U.S. citizens.

Application Requirements: Application, essay, financial need analysis, transcript, activity chart. *Deadline:* March 1.

Contact: Director of Grant Programs
Oregon Student Assistance Commission
1500 Valley River Drive, Suite 100
Eugene, OR 97401-7020
Phone: 800-452-8807 Ext. 7395

FRIENDS OF OREGON STUDENTS SCHOLARSHIP

Award to students pursuing careers in teaching or nursing with cumulative GPA of 2.5 in last three quarters of solid coursework. Must be Oregon resident. Only prior recipients are eligible to apply for this scholarship. Preference to non-traditional students (older, returning, single parent) who are working and will continue to work more than 20 hours per week while attending college at least three-quarters time.

Academic Fields/Career Goals: Education; Nursing.

Award: Scholarship for use in freshman, sophomore, junior, senior, or graduate years; renewable. *Number:* varies. *Amount:* varies.

Eligibility Requirements: Applicant must be enrolled or expecting to enroll full-time at a four-year institution or university and resident of Oregon. Applicant must have 2.5 GPA or higher. Available to U.S. citizens.

Application Requirements: Application, essay, financial need analysis, interview, references, transcript, activity chart. *Deadline:* March 1.

Contact: Director of Grant Programs
Oregon Student Assistance Commission
1500 Valley River Drive, Suite 100
Eugene, OR 97401-7020
Phone: 800-452-8807 Ext. 7395

HARRIET A. SIMMONS SCHOLARSHIP

One-time award available for elementary, secondary education majors entering senior or fifth-year or graduate students in fifth year for elementary or secondary certificate. Must be a resident of Oregon.

Academic Fields/Career Goals: Education.

Award: Scholarship for use in senior or graduate years; not renewable. *Number:* 1. *Amount:* varies.

Eligibility Requirements: Applicant must be enrolled or expecting to enroll full-time at a four-year institution or university and resident of Oregon. Available to U.S. citizens.

Application Requirements: Application, essay, financial need analysis, transcript, activities chart. *Deadline:* March 1.

Contact: Director of Grant Programs
Oregon Student Assistance Commission
1500 Valley River Drive, Suite 100
Eugene, OR 97401-7020
Phone: 800-452-8807 Ext. 7395

JAMES CARLSON MEMORIAL SCHOLARSHIP

One-time award for elementary or secondary education majors entering senior or fifth year, or graduate students in fifth year for elementary or secondary certificate. Priority given to African-American, Asian, Hispanic, Native American ethnic groups, dependents of Oregon Education Association members, and others committed to teaching autistic children.

Academic Fields/Career Goals: Education; Special Education.

Award: Scholarship for use in senior or graduate years; not renewable. *Number:* 3. *Amount:* varies.

Eligibility Requirements: Applicant must be American Indian/Alaska Native, Asian/Pacific Islander, Black (non-Hispanic), or Hispanic; enrolled or expecting to enroll full-time at a four-year institution and resident of Oregon. Applicant or parent of applicant must be member of Oregon Education Association. Available to U.S. citizens.

Application Requirements: Application, essay, financial need analysis, transcript, activity chart. *Deadline:* March 1.

Contact: Director of Grant Programs
Oregon Student Assistance Commission
1500 Valley River Drive, Suite 100
Eugene, OR 97401-7020
Phone: 800-452-8807 Ext. 7395

NETTIE HANSELMAN JAYNES SCHOLARSHIP

One-time award for elementary and secondary education majors entering their senior or fifth year. Graduate students in their fifth year for elementary or secondary certificate also may apply.

Academic Fields/Career Goals: Education.

Award: Scholarship for use in senior or graduate years; not renewable. *Number:* varies. *Amount:* varies.

Eligibility Requirements: Applicant must be enrolled or expecting to enroll full-time at a four-year institution or university and resident of Oregon. Available to U.S. citizens.

Application Requirements: Application, essay, financial need analysis, transcript, activities chart. *Deadline:* March 1.

Contact: Director of Grant Programs
Oregon Student Assistance Commission
1500 Valley River Drive, Suite 100
Eugene, OR 97401-7020
Phone: 800-452-8807 Ext. 7395

OREGON EDUCATION ASSOCIATION SCHOLARSHIP

Renewable scholarship open to graduating seniors of any Oregon public high school, who plan to become teachers. Must be planning to complete baccalaureate degree and teaching certificate requirements. Oregon colleges only.

Academic Fields/Career Goals: Education.

Award: Scholarship for use in freshman, sophomore, junior, or senior years; renewable. *Number:* varies. *Amount:* varies.

Eligibility Requirements: Applicant must be high school student; planning to enroll or expecting to enroll full-time at a four-year institution; resident of Oregon and studying in Oregon. Available to U.S. citizens.

Application Requirements: Application, essay, transcript, activity chart. *Deadline:* March 1.

Contact: Director of Grant Programs
Oregon Student Assistance Commission
1500 Valley River Drive, Suite 100
Eugene, OR 97401-7020
Phone: 800-452-8807 Ext. 7935

PI LAMBDA THETA INC. http://www.pilambda.org

DISTINGUISHED STUDENT SCHOLAR AWARD

The award is presented in recognition of an education major who has displayed leadership potential and a strong dedication to education. Award given out in odd years. Minimum 3.5 GPA required.

Academic Fields/Career Goals: Education.

Award: Prize for use in freshman, sophomore, junior, or senior years; not renewable. *Number:* 1. *Amount:* $500.

Eligibility Requirements: Applicant must be enrolled or expecting to enroll full- or part-time at a four-year institution or university and must have an interest in leadership. Applicant or parent of applicant must have employment or volunteer experience in community service. Applicant must have 3.5 GPA or higher. Available to U.S. and non-U.S. citizens.

Application Requirements: Application, resume, references, transcript, 2 letters of support from faculty members other than the nominator, letter of endorsement from the nominee's chapter. *Deadline:* February 10.

Contact: Pam Todd, Manager, Member Services
Pi Lambda Theta Inc.
4101 East Third Street, PO Box 6626
Bloomington, IN 47407-6626
Phone: 812-339-3411
Fax: 812-339-3462
E-mail: office@pilambda.org

GRADUATE STUDENT SCHOLAR AWARD

The award is presented in recognition of an outstanding graduate student who is an education major. Award given out in odd years. Minimum 3.5 GPA required.

Academic Fields/Career Goals: Education.

Award: Prize for use in senior or graduate years; not renewable. *Number:* 1. *Amount:* $1000.

Eligibility Requirements: Applicant must be enrolled or expecting to enroll full- or part-time at a four-year institution or university and must have an interest in leadership. Applicant or parent of applicant must have employment or volunteer experience in community service. Applicant must have 3.5 GPA or higher. Available to U.S. and non-U.S. citizens.

Application Requirements: Application, essay, resume, references, transcript, letter of endorsement from nominee's chapter. *Deadline:* February 10.

Contact: Pam Todd, Manager, Member Services
Pi Lambda Theta Inc.
4101 East Third Street, PO Box 6626
Bloomington, IN 47407-6626
Phone: 812-339-3411
Fax: 812-339-3462
E-mail: office@pilambda.org

NADEEN BURKEHOLDER WILLIAMS MUSIC SCHOLARSHIP

The scholarship provides $1000 to an outstanding K-12 teacher who is pursuing a graduate degree at an accredited college or university and who is either a music education teacher or applies music systematically in teaching another subject. Minimum 3.5 GPA required.

Academic Fields/Career Goals: Education; Music.

Award: Scholarship for use in freshman, sophomore, junior, senior, or graduate years; not renewable. *Number:* 1–5. *Amount:* $1000.

Eligibility Requirements: Applicant must be enrolled or expecting to enroll full- or part-time at a four-year institution or university and must have an interest in music. Applicant or parent of applicant must have employment or volunteer experience in teaching/education. Applicant must have 3.5 GPA or higher. Available to U.S. and non-U.S. citizens.

Application Requirements: Application, essay, portfolio, resume, references. *Deadline:* February 10.

Contact: Pam Todd, Manager, Member Services
Pi Lambda Theta Inc.
4101 East Third Street, PO Box 6626
Bloomington, IN 47407-6626
Phone: 812-339-3411
Fax: 812-339-3462
E-mail: office@pilambda.org

STUDENT SUPPORT SCHOLARSHIP

The scholarship is available to current members of Pi Lambda Theta who will be a full-time or part-time student enrolled in a minimum of three semester hours at a regionally accredited institution during the year following the award. Minimum 3.5 GPA required.

Academic Fields/Career Goals: Education.

Award: Scholarship for use in sophomore, junior, senior, graduate, or postgraduate years; not renewable. *Number:* 1–6. *Amount:* $750.

Eligibility Requirements: Applicant must be enrolled or expecting to enroll full- or part-time at a two-year or four-year or technical institution or university. Applicant must have 3.5 GPA or higher. Available to U.S. and non-U.S. citizens.

Pi Lambda Theta Inc. (continued)

Application Requirements: Application, essay, transcript. *Deadline:* February 10.

Contact: Pam Todd, Manager, Member Services
Pi Lambda Theta Inc.
4101 East Third Street, PO Box 6626
Bloomington, IN 47407-6626
Phone: 812-339-3411
Fax: 812-339-3462
E-mail: office@pilambda.org

TOBIN SORENSON PHYSICAL EDUCATION SCHOLARSHIP

The scholarship provides $1000 for tuition to an outstanding student who intends to pursue a career at the K-12 level as a physical education teacher, adaptive physical education teacher, coach, recreational therapist, dance therapist, or similar professional focusing on teaching the knowledge and use of the human body. Awarded in odd years only. Minimum 3.5 GPA required.

Academic Fields/Career Goals: Education; Sports-Related/Exercise Science; Therapy/Rehabilitation.

Award: Scholarship for use in sophomore, junior, senior, or graduate years; not renewable. *Number:* 1. *Amount:* $1000.

Eligibility Requirements: Applicant must be enrolled or expecting to enroll full- or part-time at a two-year or four-year institution or university. Applicant must have 3.5 GPA or higher. Available to U.S. and non-U.S. citizens.

Application Requirements: Application, resume, references, transcript. *Deadline:* February 10.

Contact: Pam Todd, Controller
Pi Lambda Theta Inc.
4101 East Third Street, PO Box 6626
Bloomington, IN 47407-6626
Phone: 812-339-3411
Fax: 812-339-3462
E-mail: office@pilambda.org

SARAH KLENKE MEMORIAL TEACHING SCHOLARSHIP http://www.sarahklenkescholarship.org

SARAH ELIZABETH KLENKE MEMORIAL TEACHING SCHOLARSHIP

Scholarship for graduating senior or high school graduate enrolling in secondary schooling. Should have a desire to major in education. Minimum 2.0 GPA required. Participation in JROTC or team sport is required.

Academic Fields/Career Goals: Education.

Award: Scholarship for use in freshman or senior years; not renewable. *Number:* 1. *Amount:* $1000.

Eligibility Requirements: Applicant must be enrolled or expecting to enroll full-time at a two-year or four-year institution or university. Available to U.S. and non-U.S. citizens.

Application Requirements: Application, essay, references, letter from coach or teacher confirming participation in ROTC or team sport. *Deadline:* April 15.

Contact: Aaron Klenke, Scholarship Committee
Sarah Klenke Memorial Teaching Scholarship
3131 Glade Springs
Kingwood, TX 77339
Phone: 281-358-7933
E-mail: aaron.klenke@gmail.com

SIEMENS FOUNDATION/SIEMENS-WESTINGHOUSE SCHOLARSHIP http://www.siemens-foundation.org

SIEMENS TEACHER SCHOLARSHIP

Scholarships for undergraduate and graduate students majoring in education, and enrolled at historically black colleges and universities that are members of the Thurgood Marshall Scholarship Fund and the United Negro College Fund. The scholarship value and the number of scholarships granted varies annually.

Academic Fields/Career Goals: Education.

Award: Scholarship for use in freshman, sophomore, junior, senior, or graduate years; not renewable. *Number:* varies. *Amount:* varies.

Eligibility Requirements: Applicant must be Black (non-Hispanic) and enrolled or expecting to enroll full- or part-time at a four-year institution or university. Available to U.S. and non-U.S. citizens.

Application Requirements: Application. *Deadline:* varies.

Contact: Scholarship Committee
Siemens Foundation/Siemens-Westinghouse Scholarship
170 Wood Avenue South
Iselin, NJ 08830
Phone: 877-822-5233
Fax: 732-603-5890
E-mail: foundation.us@siemens.com

SIGMA ALPHA IOTA PHILANTHROPIES INC. http://www.sigmaalphaiota.org

SIGMA ALPHA IOTA MUSICIANS WITH SPECIAL NEEDS SCHOLARSHIP

One-time award of $1000 offered yearly for female member of SAI who is visually impaired, and a member of a college or alumnae chapter. Submit fifteen-minute tape or evidence of work in composition, musicology, or research. Application fee: $25.

Academic Fields/Career Goals: Education; Music; Performing Arts.

Award: Scholarship for use in freshman, sophomore, junior, senior, or graduate years; not renewable. *Number:* 1. *Amount:* $1000.

Eligibility Requirements: Applicant must be enrolled or expecting to enroll full- or part-time at a four-year institution or university; female and must have an interest in music/singing. Applicant or parent of applicant must be member of Sigma Alpha Iota. Applicant must be visually impaired. Available to U.S. and non-U.S. citizens.

Application Requirements: Application, essay, resume, references, transcript, videotape or DVD. *Fee:* $25. *Deadline:* March 15.

Contact: Karen Louise Gearreald, Director
Sigma Alpha Iota Philanthropies Inc.
One Tunnel Road
Asheville, NC 28805
Phone: 828-251-0606
Fax: 828-251-0644
E-mail: hadley@exis.net

SIGMA ALPHA IOTA UNDERGRADUATE SCHOLARSHIPS

One-time awards of $1500 to $2000 to female undergraduate members of SAI who are freshman, sophomores or juniors. For use in sophomore, junior, or senior year. Must be over 18 years of age and studying performing arts or performing arts education. Contact local chapter for further details.

Academic Fields/Career Goals: Education; Performing Arts.

Award: Scholarship for use in freshman, sophomore, junior, or senior years; not renewable. *Number:* 15. *Amount:* $1500–$2000.

Eligibility Requirements: Applicant must be age 18 and over; enrolled or expecting to enroll full-time at a four-year institution or university; female and must have an interest in music/singing. Applicant or parent of applicant must be member of Sigma Alpha Iota. Available to U.S. and non-U.S. citizens.

Application Requirements: Application, essay, financial need analysis, references, transcript. *Deadline:* March 15.

Contact: Eleanor B. Tapscott, Project Director
Sigma Alpha Iota Philanthropies Inc.
One Tunnel Road
Asheville, NC 28805
Phone: 828-251-0606
Fax: 828-251-0644
E-mail: saiphxalum@joetapscott.com

SOCIETY FOR THE SCIENTIFIC STUDY OF SEXUALITY http://www.sexscience.org

SOCIETY FOR THE SCIENTIFIC STUDY OF SEXUALITY STUDENT RESEARCH GRANT

• *See page 129*

SOUTH CAROLINA STUDENT LOAN CORPORATION http://www.scstudentloan.org

SOUTH CAROLINA TEACHER LOAN PROGRAM

One-time awards for South Carolina residents attending four-year postsecondary institutions in South Carolina. Recipients must teach in the South Carolina public school system in a critical-need area after graduation. Twenty percent of loan forgiven for each year of service. Write for additional requirements.

Academic Fields/Career Goals: Education; Special Education.

Award: Forgivable loan for use in freshman, sophomore, junior, senior, or graduate years; not renewable. *Number:* up to 1121. *Amount:* $2500–$5000.

Eligibility Requirements: Applicant must be enrolled or expecting to enroll full- or part-time at a four-year institution or university; resident of South Carolina and studying in South Carolina. Applicant must have 3.0 GPA or higher. Available to U.S. citizens.

Application Requirements: Application, references, test scores, promissory note. *Deadline:* June 1.

Contact: Jennifer Jones-Gaddy, Vice President
South Carolina Student Loan Corporation
PO Box 21487
Columbia, SC 29221
Phone: 803-798-0916
Fax: 803-772-9410
E-mail: jgaddy@slc.sc.edu

SOUTH DAKOTA BOARD OF REGENTS http://www.sdbor.edu

HAINES MEMORIAL SCHOLARSHIP

One-time scholarship for South Dakota public university students who are sophomores, juniors, or seniors having at least a 2.5 GPA and majoring in a teacher education program. Must include resume with application. Must be South Dakota resident.

Academic Fields/Career Goals: Education.

Award: Scholarship for use in sophomore, junior, or senior years; not renewable. *Number:* 1. *Amount:* $2150.

Eligibility Requirements: Applicant must be enrolled or expecting to enroll full-time at an institution or university; resident of South Dakota and studying in South Dakota. Applicant must have 2.5 GPA or higher. Available to U.S. citizens.

Application Requirements: Application, autobiography, essay, resume, typed statement describing personal philosophy and philosophy of education. *Deadline:* February 8.

Contact: Janelle Toman, Director of Institutional Research
South Dakota Board of Regents
306 East Capitol Avenue, Suite 200
Pierre, SD 57501-2545
Phone: 605-773-3455
Fax: 605-773-2422
E-mail: info@sdbor.edu

SOUTH DAKOTA BOARD OF REGENTS ANNIS I. FOWLER/KADEN SCHOLARSHIP

Scholarship for graduating South Dakota high school seniors to pursue a career in elementary education at a South Dakota public university. University must be one of the following: BHSU, BSU, NSU or USD. Applicants must have a cumulative GPA of 3.0 after three years of high school. One-time award.

Academic Fields/Career Goals: Education.

Award: Scholarship for use in freshman year; not renewable. *Number:* 2. *Amount:* $1000.

Eligibility Requirements: Applicant must be high school student; planning to enroll or expecting to enroll full-time at a four-year institution or university; resident of South Dakota and studying in South Dakota. Applicant must have 3.0 GPA or higher. Available to U.S. citizens.

Application Requirements: Application, essay, references, test scores, transcript, ACT scores. *Deadline:* February 15.

Contact: Janelle Toman, Director of Institutional Research
South Dakota Board of Regents
306 East Capitol Avenue, Suite 200
Pierre, SD 57501-2545
Phone: 605-773-3455
Fax: 605-773-2422
E-mail: info@sdbor.edu

STATE COUNCIL OF HIGHER EDUCATION FOR VIRGINIA http://www.schev.edu

HIGHER EDUCATION TEACHER ASSISTANCE PROGRAM

Need-based scholarship for Virginia residents enrolled in a K-12 teacher preparation program in a participating Virginia college or university. Must be nominated by a faculty member in the Education Department at the institution. Applications must be obtained from and returned to the financial aid office at the participating institution.

Academic Fields/Career Goals: Education; Special Education.

Award: Scholarship for use in freshman, sophomore, junior, or senior years; renewable. *Number:* varies. *Amount:* $1000–$2000.

Eligibility Requirements: Applicant must be enrolled or expecting to enroll full-time at a two-year or four-year institution or university; resident of Virginia and studying in Virginia. Applicant must have 2.5 GPA or higher. Available to U.S. citizens.

Application Requirements: Application, financial need analysis, references, FAFSA. *Deadline:* continuous.

Contact: Lee Andes, Assistant Director for Financial Aid
State Council of Higher Education for Virginia
James Monroe Building, 101 North 14th Street, 10th Floor
Richmond, VA 23219
Phone: 804-225-2614
E-mail: leeandes@schev.edu

SOUTHSIDE VIRGINIA TOBACCO TEACHER SCHOLARSHIP/LOAN

Need-based scholarship for Southside Virginia natives to pursue a degree in K-12 teacher education in any four-year U.S. institution and then return to the Southside region to live and work. Must teach in Southside Virginia public school for scholarship/loan forgiveness.

Academic Fields/Career Goals: Education.

Award: Forgivable loan for use in freshman, sophomore, junior, or senior years; renewable. *Number:* varies. *Amount:* up to $4000.

Eligibility Requirements: Applicant must be enrolled or expecting to enroll full- or part-time at a two-year or four-year institution or university; resident of Virginia and studying in Virginia. Available to U.S. citizens.

Application Requirements: Application, financial need analysis, FAFSA. *Deadline:* varies.

Contact: Christine Fields, Scholarship Committee
State Council of Higher Education for Virginia
PO Box 1987
Abingdon, VA 24212
Phone: 276-619-4376 Ext. 4002

VIRGINIA TEACHING SCHOLARSHIP LOAN PROGRAM

Forgivable loan for Virginia resident students enrolled full- or part-time in a Virginia institution pursuing a teaching degree. The loan is forgiven if the student teaches for specified period of time. Must maintain a minimum GPA of 2.7. Must be nominated by the education department of the eligible institution.

Academic Fields/Career Goals: Education.

Award: Forgivable loan for use in sophomore, junior, senior, or graduate years; not renewable. *Number:* varies. *Amount:* up to $3720.

Eligibility Requirements: Applicant must be enrolled or expecting to enroll full- or part-time at a four-year institution or university; resident of Virginia and studying in Virginia. Available to U.S. citizens.

State Council of Higher Education for Virginia (continued)

Application Requirements: Application, references. *Deadline:* varies.

Contact: Lee Andes, Assistant Director for Financial Aid
State Council of Higher Education for Virginia
James Monroe Building, 101 North 14th Street, 10th Floor
Richmond, VA 23219
Phone: 804-225-2614
E-mail: leeandes@schev.edu

STATE OF GEORGIA http://www.gsfc.org

TEACHER PREPARATION RECRUITMENT INITIATIVE

One-time award of up to $5000 targeted at preparing second career candidates to become teachers in high-need schools. Within six months of completion of the program, the individual will become a teacher and repay the scholarship by working in a school district and school that faces a serious teacher shortage.

Academic Fields/Career Goals: Education.

Award: Forgivable loan for use in freshman, sophomore, junior, or senior years; not renewable. *Number:* varies. *Amount:* up to $5000.

Eligibility Requirements: Applicant must be enrolled or expecting to enroll full- or part-time at a four-year institution or university; resident of Georgia and studying in Georgia. Available to U.S. citizens.

Application Requirements: Application. *Deadline:* June 3.

Contact: Peggy Matthews, Manager, GSFA Origination
State of Georgia
2082 East Exchange Place, Suite 230
Tucker, GA 30084
Phone: 770-724-9230
Fax: 770-724-9225
E-mail: peggy@gsfc.org

STATE OF WYOMING, ADMINISTERED BY UNIVERSITY OF WYOMING http://www.uwyo.edu/scholarships

SUPERIOR STUDENT IN EDUCATION SCHOLARSHIP-WYOMING

Scholarship available each year to sixteen new Wyoming high school graduates who plan to teach in Wyoming. The award covers costs of undergraduate tuition at the University of Wyoming or any Wyoming community college.

Academic Fields/Career Goals: Education.

Award: Scholarship for use in freshman year; renewable. *Number:* 16. *Amount:* varies.

Eligibility Requirements: Applicant must be high school student; planning to enroll or expecting to enroll full-time at a four-year institution or university; resident of Wyoming and studying in Wyoming. Applicant must have 3.0 GPA or higher. Available to U.S. citizens.

Application Requirements: Application, references, test scores, transcript. *Deadline:* October 31.

Contact: Tammy Mack, Assistant Director, Scholarships
State of Wyoming, Administered by University of Wyoming
Student Financial Aid Department 3335, 1000 East University Avenue
Laramie, WY 82071-3335
Phone: 307-766-2117
Fax: 307-766-3800
E-mail: finaid@uwyo.edu

STRAIGHTFORWARD MEDIA http://www.straightforwardmedia.com

STRAIGHTFORWARD MEDIA TEACHER SCHOLARSHIP

Scholarship of $500 for students planning to be teachers of any kind and at any level. Must be U.S. citizen. Awarded four times per year. Deadlines: January 14, April 14, July 14, October 14.

Academic Fields/Career Goals: Education; Special Education.

Award: Scholarship for use in freshman, sophomore, junior, senior, or graduate years; not renewable. *Number:* 4. *Amount:* $500.

Eligibility Requirements: Applicant must be enrolled or expecting to enroll full-time at a two-year or four-year institution or university. Available to U.S. citizens.

Application Requirements: Online application. *Deadline:* varies.

Contact: Scholarship Committee
StraightForward Media
2040 West Main Street, Suite 104
Rapid City, SD 57701
Phone: 605-348-3042
Fax: 605-348-3043

SUZUKI ASSOCIATION OF THE AMERICAS http://www.suzukiassociation.org

SUZUKI ASSOCIATION OF THE AMERICAS TEACHER DEVELOPMENT SCHOLARSHIPS

Scholarship provides tuition assistance for pedagogy study at approved summer institutes, workshops, apprenticeships, or in SAA-approved long-term teacher development programs. The scholarship has two sub-divisions: short-term range from $350 to $475, long-term range from $300 to $700.

Academic Fields/Career Goals: Education; Music.

Award: Scholarship for use in freshman, sophomore, junior, senior, graduate, or postgraduate years; renewable. *Number:* up to 30. *Amount:* $300–$700.

Eligibility Requirements: Applicant must be enrolled or expecting to enroll full- or part-time at a four-year institution or university. Available to U.S. and non-U.S. citizens.

Application Requirements: Application, applicant must enter a contest, financial need analysis, resume, references. *Deadline:* February 15.

Contact: Pam Brasch, Director
Suzuki Association of the Americas
PO Box 17310
Boulder, CO 80308
Phone: 303-444-0948
E-mail: info@suzukiassociation.org

TENNESSEE EDUCATION ASSOCIATION http://www.teateachers.org

TEA DON SAHLI-KATHY WOODALL FUTURE TEACHERS OF AMERICA SCHOLARSHIP

Scholarship is available to a high school senior planning to major in education, attending a high school which has an FTA Chapter affiliated with TEA, and planning to enroll in a Tennessee college.

Academic Fields/Career Goals: Education.

Award: Scholarship for use in freshman year; not renewable. *Number:* 1. *Amount:* $1000.

Eligibility Requirements: Applicant must be high school student; planning to enroll or expecting to enroll full-time at a four-year institution or university; resident of Tennessee and studying in Tennessee. Applicant must have 3.0 GPA or higher. Available to U.S. citizens.

Application Requirements: Application, applicant must enter a contest, essay, financial need analysis, references, transcript, statement of income. *Deadline:* March 1.

Contact: Stephanie Faulkner, Manager of Business Affairs
Tennessee Education Association
801 Second Avenue North
Nashville, TN 37201-1099
Phone: 615-242-8392
Fax: 615-259-4581
E-mail: sfaulkner@tea.nea.org

TEA DON SAHLI-KATHY WOODALL MINORITY SCHOLARSHIP

Scholarship is available to a minority high school senior planning to major in education and planning to enroll in a Tennessee college. Application must be made by an FTA Chapter, or by the student with the recommendation of an active TEA member.

Academic Fields/Career Goals: Education.

Award: Scholarship for use in freshman year; not renewable. *Number:* 1. *Amount:* $1000.

Eligibility Requirements: Applicant must be American Indian/Alaska Native, Asian/Pacific Islander, Black (non-Hispanic), or Hispanic; high school student; planning to enroll or expecting to enroll full-time at a four-year institution or university; resident of Tennessee and studying in Tennessee. Applicant must have 3.0 GPA or higher. Available to U.S. citizens.

Application Requirements: Application, applicant must enter a contest, essay, financial need analysis, references, transcript, statement of income. *Deadline:* March 1.

Contact: Stephanie Faulkner, Manager of Business Affairs
Tennessee Education Association
801 Second Avenue North
Nashville, TN 37201-1099
Phone: 615-242-8392
Fax: 615-259-4581
E-mail: sfaulkner@tea.nea.org

TEA DON SAHLI-KATHY WOODALL UNDERGRADUATE SCHOLARSHIP

Scholarship is available to undergraduate students who are student TEA members. Application must be made through the local STEA Chapter. Amount varies form $500 to $1000.

Academic Fields/Career Goals: Education.

Award: Scholarship for use in freshman, sophomore, junior, or senior years; not renewable. *Number:* 4. *Amount:* $500–$1000.

Eligibility Requirements: Applicant must be enrolled or expecting to enroll full- or part-time at a four-year institution or university; resident of Tennessee and studying in Tennessee. Applicant or parent of applicant must be member of Tennessee Education Association. Applicant must have 3.0 GPA or higher. Available to U.S. citizens.

Application Requirements: Application, essay, financial need analysis, references, transcript, statement of income. *Deadline:* March 1.

Contact: Stephanie Faulkner, Manager of Business Affairs
Tennessee Education Association
801 Second Avenue North
Nashville, TN 37201-1099
Phone: 615-242-8392
Fax: 615-259-4581
E-mail: sfaulkner@tea.nea.org

TENNESSEE STUDENT ASSISTANCE CORPORATION http://www.collegepaystn.com

CHRISTA MCAULIFFE SCHOLARSHIP PROGRAM

Scholarship to assist and support Tennessee students who have demonstrated a commitment to a career in educating the youth of Tennessee. Offered to college seniors for a period of one academic year. Must have a high school GPA of minimum 3.5. Must have attained scores on either the ACT or SAT which meet or exceed the national norms.

Academic Fields/Career Goals: Education.

Award: Scholarship for use in senior year; renewable. *Number:* up to 1. *Amount:* up to $500.

Eligibility Requirements: Applicant must be enrolled or expecting to enroll full-time at a four-year institution or university; resident of Tennessee and studying in Tennessee. Applicant must have 3.5 GPA or higher. Available to U.S. citizens.

Application Requirements: Application. *Deadline:* April 1.

Contact: Scholarship Committee
Tennessee Student Assistance Corporation
404 James Robertson Parkway, Suite 1510, Parkway Towers
Nashville, TN 37243-0820
Phone: 615-741-1346
Fax: 615-741-6101

MINORITY TEACHING FELLOWS PROGRAM/TENNESSEE

Forgivable loan for minority Tennessee residents pursuing teaching careers. Minimum 2.75 GPA required for high school applicant, minimum 2.5 GPA required for college applicant. Must be in the top quarter of the class or score an 18 on ACT. Must teach one year for each year the award is received, or repay loan.

Academic Fields/Career Goals: Education; Special Education.

Award: Forgivable loan for use in freshman, sophomore, junior, or senior years; renewable. *Number:* 19–29. *Amount:* up to $5000.

Eligibility Requirements: Applicant must be American Indian/Alaska Native, Asian/Pacific Islander, Black (non-Hispanic), or Hispanic; enrolled or expecting to enroll full-time at a two-year or four-year institution or university; resident of Tennessee and studying in Tennessee. Available to U.S. citizens.

Application Requirements: Application, essay, references, test scores, transcript, statement of intent. *Deadline:* April 15.

Contact: Mike McCormack, Scholarship Coordinator
Tennessee Student Assistance Corporation
Parkway Towers, 404 James Robertson Parkway, Suite 1950
Nashville, TN 37243-0820
Phone: 615-741-1346
Fax: 615-741-6101
E-mail: mike.mccormack@state.tn.us

TENNESSEE TEACHING SCHOLARS PROGRAM

Forgivable loan for college juniors, seniors, and college graduates admitted to an education program in Tennessee with a minimum GPA of 2.75. Students must commit to teach in a Tennessee public school one year for each year of the award. Must be a U.S. citizen and resident of Tennessee.

Academic Fields/Career Goals: Education.

Award: Forgivable loan for use in junior, senior, or graduate years; renewable. *Number:* varies. *Amount:* up to $4500.

Eligibility Requirements: Applicant must be enrolled or expecting to enroll full- or part-time at a four-year institution or university; resident of Tennessee and studying in Tennessee. Available to U.S. citizens.

Application Requirements: Application, references, test scores, transcript. *Deadline:* April 15.

Contact: Mike McCormack, Scholarship Administrator
Tennessee Student Assistance Corporation
404 James Robertson Parkway, Suite 1510, Parkway Towers
Nashville, TN 37243-0820
Phone: 615-741-1346
Fax: 615-741-6101
E-mail: mike.mccormack@state.tn.us

TKE EDUCATIONAL FOUNDATION http://www.tke.org

CARROL C. HALL MEMORIAL SCHOLARSHIP

• *See page 88*

FRANCIS J. FLYNN MEMORIAL SCHOLARSHIP

Award of $1300 for an undergraduate member of TKE who is a full-time student pursuing a degree in mathematics or education. Minimum 2.75 GPA required. Leadership within chapter or campus organizations recognized. Preference will be given to members of Theta-Sigma Chapter.

Academic Fields/Career Goals: Education; Mathematics.

Award: Scholarship for use in freshman, sophomore, junior, or senior years; not renewable. *Number:* 1. *Amount:* $1300.

Eligibility Requirements: Applicant must be enrolled or expecting to enroll full-time at a four-year institution or university; male and must have an interest in leadership. Applicant or parent of applicant must be member of Tau Kappa Epsilon. Available to U.S. and non-U.S. citizens.

Application Requirements: Application, essay, photo, transcript, narrative summary of how TKE membership has benefited applicant. *Deadline:* February 29.

Contact: Gary A. Reed, President and Chief Executive Officer
TKE Educational Foundation
8645 Founders Road
Indianapolis, IN 46268-1393
Phone: 317-872-6533
Fax: 317-875-8353
E-mail: reedga@tke.org

UNITED NEGRO COLLEGE FUND http://www.uncf.org

EARL C. SAMS FOUNDATION SCHOLARSHIP

Award for elementary or secondary education majors attending Jarvis Christian College, Paul Quinn College, or Wiley College. Must have a minimum GPA of 2.5 and the scholarship value is up to $3000.

Academic Fields/Career Goals: Education.

Award: Scholarship for use in freshman, sophomore, junior, or senior years; not renewable. *Number:* varies. *Amount:* up to $3000.

Eligibility Requirements: Applicant must be Black (non-Hispanic); enrolled or expecting to enroll full-time at a two-year or four-year

United Negro College Fund (continued)

institution or university and resident of Texas. Applicant must have 2.5 GPA or higher. Available to U.S. citizens.

Application Requirements: Application, financial need analysis, FAFSA, Student Aid Report (SAR). *Deadline:* varies.

Contact: Director, Program Services
United Negro College Fund
8260 Willow Oaks Corporate Drive
PO Box 10444
Fairfax, VA 22031-8044
Phone: 800-331-2244
E-mail: rebecca.bennett@uncf.org

UTAH STATE BOARD OF REGENTS http://www.utahsbr.edu

TERRILL H. BELL TEACHING INCENTIVE LOAN

Designed to provide financial assistance to outstanding Utah students pursuing a degree in education. The incentive loan funds full-time tuition and general fees for eight semesters. After graduation/certification the loan may be forgiven if the recipient teaches in a Utah public school or accredited private school (K-12). Dollar value varies. Loan forgiveness is done on a year-for-year basis. For more details see Web site: http://www.utahsbr.edu.

Academic Fields/Career Goals: Education.

Award: Forgivable loan for use in freshman, sophomore, junior, senior, or graduate years; renewable. *Number:* 365. *Amount:* varies.

Eligibility Requirements: Applicant must be enrolled or expecting to enroll full-time at a two-year or four-year institution or university; resident of Utah and studying in Utah. Available to U.S. citizens.

Application Requirements: Application, essay, references, test scores, transcript. *Deadline:* varies.

Contact: Charles Downer, Compliance Officer
Utah State Board of Regents
Board of Regents Building, The Gateway, 60 South 400 West
Salt Lake City, UT 84101-1284
Phone: 801-321-7221
Fax: 801-366-8470
E-mail: cdowner@utahsbr.edu

UTAH STATE OFFICE OF EDUCATION http://www.schools.utah.gov/cert

T.H. BELL TEACHING INCENTIVE LOAN-UTAH

Renewable awards for Utah residents who are high school seniors wishing to pursue teaching careers. The award value varies depending upon tuition and fees at a Utah institution. Must agree to teach in a Utah public school or pay back loan through monthly installments. Must be a U.S. citizen.

Academic Fields/Career Goals: Education; Special Education.

Award: Forgivable loan for use in freshman year; renewable. *Number:* 25–50. *Amount:* varies.

Eligibility Requirements: Applicant must be high school student; planning to enroll or expecting to enroll full-time at a four-year institution or university; resident of Utah and studying in Utah. Available to U.S. citizens.

Application Requirements: Application, essay, test scores, transcript. *Deadline:* March 31.

Contact: Diane DeMan, Executive Secretary
Utah State Office of Education
250 East 500 South, PO Box 144200
Salt Lake City, UT 84111
Phone: 801-538-7741
Fax: 801-538-7973

VERMONT-NEA http://www.vtnea.org

VERMONT-NEA/MAIDA F. TOWNSEND SCHOLARSHIP

Scholarship of $1000 to sons and daughters of Vermont-NEA members in their last year of high school, undergraduates, and graduate students. Students majoring in any discipline are eligible to apply, but preference may be given to those majoring in education, or having that intention.

Academic Fields/Career Goals: Education.

Award: Scholarship for use in freshman, sophomore, junior, senior, or graduate years; not renewable. *Number:* 5. *Amount:* $1000.

Eligibility Requirements: Applicant must be enrolled or expecting to enroll full- or part-time at a two-year or four-year or technical institution or university. Applicant or parent of applicant must be member of Vermont-NEA. Available to U.S. and non-U.S. citizens.

Application Requirements: Application, essay, references, test scores, transcript, cover letter. *Deadline:* February 1.

Contact: Sandy Perkins, Administrative Assistant
Vermont-NEA
10 Wheelock Street
Montpelier, VT 05602-3737
Phone: 802-223-6375
E-mail: sperkins@vtnea.org

VERMONT TEACHER DIVERSITY SCHOLARSHIP PROGRAM http://www.vsc.edu/teacherdiversity/

VERMONT TEACHER DIVERSITY SCHOLARSHIP PROGRAM

Loan forgiveness program for students from diverse racial and ethnic backgrounds who attend college in Vermont with a goal of becoming public school teachers. Preference will be given to residents of Vermont.

Academic Fields/Career Goals: Education.

Award: Forgivable loan for use in freshman, sophomore, junior, senior, or graduate years; not renewable. *Number:* 4. *Amount:* $4000.

Eligibility Requirements: Applicant must be American Indian/Alaska Native, Asian/Pacific Islander, Black (non-Hispanic), or Hispanic; enrolled or expecting to enroll full- or part-time at a four-year institution or university; resident of Vermont and studying in Vermont. Available to U.S. citizens.

Application Requirements: Application, resume, references, transcript. *Deadline:* April 5.

Contact: Ms. Phyl Newbeck, Director
Vermont Teacher Diversity Scholarship Program
PO Box 359
Waterbury, VT 05676-0359
Phone: 802-241-3379
Fax: 802-241-3369

VIRGINIA CONGRESS OF PARENTS AND TEACHERS http://www.vapta.org

FRIEDA L. KOONTZ SCHOLARSHIP

Scholarship of $1200 to graduating high school students planning to enter teaching or other youth-serving professions in Virginia. Must be Virginia residents graduating from a Virginia public high school and attending a Virginia college or university. Minimum 2.5 GPA required.

Academic Fields/Career Goals: Education.

Award: Scholarship for use in freshman year; not renewable. *Number:* 1. *Amount:* $1200.

Eligibility Requirements: Applicant must be high school student; planning to enroll or expecting to enroll full-time at a four-year institution or university; resident of Virginia and studying in Virginia. Applicant must have 2.5 GPA or higher. Available to U.S. citizens.

Application Requirements: Application, essay. *Deadline:* March 1.

Contact: Scholarship Chair
Virginia Congress of Parents and Teachers
1027 Wilmer Avenue
Richmond, VA 23227-2419
Phone: 434-264-1234
E-mail: info@vapta.org

S. JOHN DAVIS SCHOLARSHIP

Scholarship of $1200 to Virginia residents graduating from a Virginia public school. Must be planning attend a Virginia college or university and pursuing a career in teaching or qualifying for service with a youth-serving agency in Virginia. Minimum 2.5 GPA required.

Academic Fields/Career Goals: Education.

Award: Scholarship for use in freshman year; not renewable. *Number:* 1. *Amount:* $1200.

Eligibility Requirements: Applicant must be high school student; planning to enroll or expecting to enroll full-time at a four-year institution or university; resident of Virginia and studying in Virginia. Applicant must have 2.5 GPA or higher. Available to U.S. citizens.

Application Requirements: Application, essay. *Deadline:* March 1.

Contact: Scholarship Chair
Virginia Congress of Parents and Teachers
1027 Wilmer Avenue
Richmond, VA 23227-2419
Phone: 434-264-1234
E-mail: info@vapta.org

WASHINGTON HIGHER EDUCATION COORDINATING BOARD http://www.hecb.wa.gov

FUTURE TEACHERS CONDITIONAL SCHOLARSHIP AND LOAN REPAYMENT PROGRAM

Participants must agree to teach in Washington K-12 schools in return for conditional scholarships or loan repayments. Additional consideration is given to individuals seeking certification or additional endorsements in teacher subject shortage areas, as well as to individuals with demonstrated bilingual ability. Must be residents of Washington and attend an institution in Washington.

Academic Fields/Career Goals: Education.

Award: Forgivable loan for use in freshman, sophomore, junior, or senior years; renewable. *Number:* 50. *Amount:* $2600–$5800.

Eligibility Requirements: Applicant must be enrolled or expecting to enroll full- or part-time at a two-year or four-year institution or university; resident of Washington and studying in Washington. Available to U.S. citizens.

Application Requirements: Application, essay, references, transcript, bilingual verification (if applicable). *Deadline:* October 15.

Contact: Mary Knutson, Program Coordinator
Washington Higher Education Coordinating Board
917 Lakeridge Way, PO Box 43430
Olympia, WA 98504-3430
Phone: 360-753-7845
Fax: 360-753-7808
E-mail: futureteachers@hecb.wa.gov

WEST VIRGINIA HIGHER EDUCATION POLICY COMMISSION-OFFICE OF FINANCIAL AID AND OUTREACH SERVICES http://wvhepcnew.wvnet.edu/

UNDERWOOD-SMITH TEACHER SCHOLARSHIP PROGRAM

Award for West Virginia residents at West Virginia institutions pursuing teaching careers. Must have a 3.5 GPA after completion of two years of course work. Must teach two years in West Virginia public schools for each year the award is received. Recipients will be required to sign an agreement acknowledging an understanding of the program's requirements and their willingness to repay the award if appropriate teaching service is not rendered.

Academic Fields/Career Goals: Education.

Award: Scholarship for use in junior, senior, or graduate years; renewable. *Number:* 53. *Amount:* $1620–$5000.

Eligibility Requirements: Applicant must be enrolled or expecting to enroll full-time at a four-year institution or university; resident of West Virginia and studying in West Virginia. Applicant must have 3.5 GPA or higher. Available to U.S. citizens.

Application Requirements: Application, essay, references. *Deadline:* March 1.

Contact: Darlene Elmore, Scholarship Coordinator
West Virginia Higher Education Policy Commission-Office of Financial Aid and Outreach Services
1018 Kanawha Boulevard, East, Suite 700
Charleston, WV 25301
E-mail: elmore@hepc.wvnet.edu

WISCONSIN CONGRESS OF PARENTS AND TEACHERS INC. http://www.wisconsinpta.org

BROOKMIRE-HASTINGS SCHOLARSHIPS

One-time award to graduating high school seniors from Wisconsin public schools. Must pursue a degree in education. High school must have an active PTA in good standing of the Wisconsin PTA.

Academic Fields/Career Goals: Education; Special Education.

Award: Scholarship for use in freshman year; not renewable. *Number:* up to 2. *Amount:* $1000.

Eligibility Requirements: Applicant must be high school student; planning to enroll or expecting to enroll full-time at a four-year institution or university and resident of Wisconsin. Available to U.S. citizens.

Application Requirements: Application, essay, interview, references, transcript. *Deadline:* March 1.

Contact: Kim Schwantes, Executive Administrator
Wisconsin Congress of Parents and Teachers Inc.
4797 Hayes Road, Suite 2
Madison, WI 53704-3256
Phone: 608-244-1455

WISCONSIN MATHEMATICS COUNCIL INC. http://www.wismath.org

ARNE ENGEBRETSEN WISCONSIN MATHEMATICS COUNCIL SCHOLARSHIP

Scholarship for Wisconsin high school senior who is planning to study mathematics education and teach mathematics at K-12 level.

Academic Fields/Career Goals: Education; Mathematics.

Award: Scholarship for use in freshman year; not renewable. *Number:* 1. *Amount:* $2000.

Eligibility Requirements: Applicant must be high school student; planning to enroll or expecting to enroll full-time at a four-year institution or university and resident of Wisconsin. Available to U.S. citizens.

Application Requirements: Application, essay, resume, references, transcript. *Deadline:* March 1.

Contact: Jane Wucherer, Scholarship Committee
Wisconsin Mathematics Council Inc.
W175 N11117 Stonewood Drive, Suite 204
Germantown, WI 53022
Phone: 262-437-0174
Fax: 262-532-2430
E-mail: wmc@wismath.org

ETHEL A. NEIJAHR WISCONSIN MATHEMATICS COUNCIL SCHOLARSHIP

Scholarship for a Wisconsin resident who is currently enrolled in teacher education programs in a Wisconsin institution studying mathematics education. Minimum GPA of 3.0 required.

Academic Fields/Career Goals: Education; Mathematics.

Award: Scholarship for use in junior, senior, or graduate years; not renewable. *Number:* 1. *Amount:* $2000.

Eligibility Requirements: Applicant must be enrolled or expecting to enroll full-time at a four-year institution or university; resident of Wisconsin and studying in Wisconsin. Applicant must have 3.0 GPA or higher. Available to U.S. citizens.

Application Requirements: Application, essay, resume, references, transcript. *Deadline:* March 1.

Contact: Jane Wucherer, Scholarship Committee
Wisconsin Mathematics Council Inc.
W175 N11117 Stonewood Drive, Suite 204
Germantown, WI 53022
Phone: 262-437-0174
Fax: 262-532-2430
E-mail: wmc@wismath.org

SISTER MARY PETRONIA VAN STRATEN WISCONSIN MATHEMATICS COUNCIL SCHOLARSHIP

Scholarship for a Wisconsin resident who is currently enrolled in teacher education programs in Wisconsin institution studying mathematics education. Minimum GPA of 3.0 required.

Academic Fields/Career Goals: Education; Mathematics.

Award: Scholarship for use in junior, senior, or graduate years; not renewable. *Number:* 1. *Amount:* $2000.

Eligibility Requirements: Applicant must be enrolled or expecting to enroll full-time at a four-year institution or university; resident of Wisconsin and studying in Wisconsin. Applicant must have 3.0 GPA or higher. Available to U.S. citizens.

Wisconsin Mathematics Council Inc. (continued)

Application Requirements: Application, essay, resume, references, transcript. *Deadline:* March 1.

Contact: Jane Wucherer, Scholarship Committee
Wisconsin Mathematics Council Inc.
W175 N11117 Stonewood Drive, Suite 204
Germantown, WI 53022
Phone: 262-437-0174
Fax: 262-532-2430
E-mail: wmc@wismath.org

WOMEN BAND DIRECTORS INTERNATIONAL http://www.womenbanddirectors.org

CHARLOTTE PLUMMER OWEN MEMORIAL SCHOLARSHIP

One-time award for women instrumental music majors enrolled in a four-year institution. Applicants must be working toward a degree in music education with the intention of becoming a band director. See Web site for application: http://www.womenbanddirectors.org/.

Academic Fields/Career Goals: Education; Music; Performing Arts.

Award: Scholarship for use in freshman, sophomore, junior, or senior years; not renewable. *Number:* 4. *Amount:* $300.

Eligibility Requirements: Applicant must be enrolled or expecting to enroll full-time at a four-year institution or university; female and must have an interest in music/singing. Available to U.S. and non-U.S. citizens.

Application Requirements: Application, essay, photo, references, transcript. *Deadline:* December 1.

Contact: Nicole Aakre-Rubis, Scholarship Chair
Women Band Directors International
16085 Excel Way
Rosemount, MN 55068

HELEN MAY BUTLER MEMORIAL SCHOLARSHIP

One-time award for women instrumental music majors enrolled in a four-year institution. Applicants must be working toward a degree in music education with the intention of becoming a band director. Three of the scholarships are designated for college upperclassmen, and one is open to all levels. See Web site for application: http://www.womenbanddirectors.org/.

Academic Fields/Career Goals: Education; Music; Performing Arts.

Award: Scholarship for use in freshman, sophomore, junior, senior, or graduate years; not renewable. *Number:* 4. *Amount:* $300.

Eligibility Requirements: Applicant must be enrolled or expecting to enroll full-time at a four-year institution or university; female and must have an interest in music/singing. Available to U.S. and non-U.S. citizens.

Application Requirements: Application, essay, photo, references, transcript. *Deadline:* December 1.

Contact: Nicole Aakre-Rubis, Scholarship Chair
Women Band Directors International
16085 Excel Way
Rosemount, MN 55068

MARTHA ANN STARK MEMORIAL SCHOLARSHIP

One-time award for women instrumental music majors enrolled in a four-year institution. Applicants must be working toward a degree in music education with the intention of becoming a band director. Three of the scholarships are designated for college upperclassmen, and one is open to all levels. See Web site for application: http://www.womenbanddirectors.org/.

Academic Fields/Career Goals: Education; Music; Performing Arts.

Award: Scholarship for use in freshman, sophomore, junior, or senior years; not renewable. *Number:* 4. *Amount:* $300.

Eligibility Requirements: Applicant must be enrolled or expecting to enroll full-time at a four-year institution or university; female and must have an interest in music/singing. Available to U.S. and non-U.S. citizens.

Application Requirements: Application, essay, photo, references, transcript. *Deadline:* December 1.

Contact: Nicole Aakre-Rubis, Scholarship Chair
Women Band Directors International
16085 Excel Way
Rosemount, MN 55068

VOLKWEIN MEMORIAL SCHOLARSHIP

One-time award for female instrumental music majors enrolled in a four-year institution. Applicants must be working toward a degree in music education with the intention of becoming a band director. Three of the scholarships are designated for college upperclassmen, and one is open to all levels. See Web site for application: http://www.womenbanddirectors.org/.

Academic Fields/Career Goals: Education; Music; Performing Arts.

Award: Scholarship for use in freshman, sophomore, junior, senior, or graduate years; not renewable. *Number:* 4. *Amount:* $300.

Eligibility Requirements: Applicant must be enrolled or expecting to enroll full-time at a four-year institution or university; female and must have an interest in music/singing. Available to U.S. and non-U.S. citizens.

Application Requirements: Application, essay, photo, references, self-addressed stamped envelope, transcript. *Deadline:* December 1.

Contact: Nicole Aakre-Rubis, Scholarship Chair
Women Band Directors International
16085 Excel Way
Rosemount, MN 55068

Y'S MEN INTERNATIONAL http://www.ysmenusa.com

ALEXANDER SCHOLARSHIP LOAN FUND

• *See page 152*

ZETA PHI BETA SORORITY INC. NATIONAL EDUCATIONAL FOUNDATION http://www.zphib1920.org

ISABEL M. HERSON SCHOLARSHIP IN EDUCATION

Scholarships available for graduate or undergraduate students enrolled in a degree program in either elementary or secondary education. Award for full-time study for one academic year. See Web site for additional information and application: http://www.zphib1920.org.

Academic Fields/Career Goals: Education.

Award: Scholarship for use in freshman, sophomore, junior, senior, or graduate years; not renewable. *Number:* 1. *Amount:* $500–$1000.

Eligibility Requirements: Applicant must be enrolled or expecting to enroll full-time at a four-year institution or university. Available to U.S. citizens.

Application Requirements: Application, essay, references, transcript, enrollment proof. *Deadline:* February 1.

Contact: Cheryl Williams, National Second Vice President
Zeta Phi Beta Sorority Inc. National Educational Foundation
1734 New Hampshire Avenue, NW
Washington, DC 20009-2595
Fax: 318-631-4028
E-mail: 2ndanti@zphib1920.org

ELECTRICAL ENGINEERING/ ELECTRONICS

AACE INTERNATIONAL http://www.aacei.org

AACE INTERNATIONAL COMPETITIVE SCHOLARSHIP

• *See page 89*

AMERICAN COUNCIL OF ENGINEERING COMPANIES OF PENNSYLVANIA (ACEC/PA) http://www.acecpa.org

ENGINEERING SCHOLARSHIP

• *See page 154*

AMERICAN FOUNDATION FOR THE BLIND http://www.afb.org

PAUL W. RUCKES SCHOLARSHIP

• *See page 189*

AMERICAN INSTITUTE OF AERONAUTICS AND ASTRONAUTICS http://www.aiaa.org

AIAA UNDERGRADUATE SCHOLARSHIP

• *See page 84*

AMERICAN PUBLIC TRANSPORTATION FOUNDATION http://www.apta.com

LOUIS T. KLAUDER SCHOLARSHIP

Scholarships for study towards a career in the rail transit industry as an electrical or mechanical engineer. Must be sponsored by APTA member organization and complete internship with APTA member organization. Minimum GPA of 3.0 required.

Academic Fields/Career Goals: Electrical Engineering/Electronics; Mechanical Engineering.

Award: Scholarship for use in sophomore, junior, senior, or graduate years; renewable. *Number:* 1. *Amount:* $2500.

Eligibility Requirements: Applicant must be enrolled or expecting to enroll full-time at a two-year or four-year institution or university. Applicant must have 3.0 GPA or higher. Available to U.S. and Canadian citizens.

Application Requirements: Application, essay, financial need analysis, references, transcript, verification of enrollment for the current semester, copy of fee schedule from the college/university. *Deadline:* June 16.

Contact: Pamela Boswell, Vice President of Program Management
American Public Transportation Foundation
1666 K Street, NW
Washington, DC 20006-1215
Phone: 202-496-4803
Fax: 202-496-2323
E-mail: pboswell@apta.com

TRANSIT HALL OF FAME SCHOLARSHIP AWARD PROGRAM

• *See page 168*

AMERICAN SOCIETY OF HEATING, REFRIGERATING, AND AIR CONDITIONING ENGINEERS INC. http://www.ashrae.org

ALWIN B. NEWTON SCHOLARSHIP FUND

Available to undergraduate students pursuing a bachelor of science or engineering degree, who are enrolled full-time in a program accredited by the Accreditation Board for Engineering and Technology. Minimum 3.0 GPA required.

Academic Fields/Career Goals: Electrical Engineering/Electronics; Engineering/Technology; Heating, Air-Conditioning, and Refrigeration Mechanics; Mechanical Engineering; Trade/Technical Specialties.

Award: Scholarship for use in sophomore, junior, or senior years; not renewable. *Number:* 1. *Amount:* $3000.

Eligibility Requirements: Applicant must be enrolled or expecting to enroll full-time at a four-year institution or university and must have an interest in leadership. Applicant must have 3.0 GPA or higher. Available to U.S. and non-U.S. citizens.

Application Requirements: Application, financial need analysis, references, transcript. *Deadline:* December 1.

Contact: Lois Benedict, Scholarship Administrator
American Society of Heating, Refrigerating, and Air Conditioning Engineers Inc.
1791 Tullie Circle, NE
Atlanta, GA 30329
Phone: 404-636-8400
Fax: 404-321-5478
E-mail: lbenedict@ashrae.org

REUBEN TRANE SCHOLARSHIP

Two-year $10,000 undergraduate engineering scholarships awarded in two disbursements of $5000 each at the beginning of the students junior and senior year. Must be a full-time student enrolled in a bachelor of science or engineering degree accredited by the Accreditation Board for Engineering and Technology. Minimum 3.0 GPA required.

Academic Fields/Career Goals: Electrical Engineering/Electronics; Heating, Air-Conditioning, and Refrigeration Mechanics; Mechanical Engineering; Trade/Technical Specialties.

Award: Scholarship for use in junior or senior years; renewable. *Number:* 4. *Amount:* $5000.

Eligibility Requirements: Applicant must be enrolled or expecting to enroll full-time at a four-year institution or university. Applicant must have 3.0 GPA or higher. Available to U.S. and non-U.S. citizens.

Application Requirements: Application, financial need analysis, references, transcript. *Deadline:* December 1.

Contact: Lois Benedict, Scholarship Administrator
American Society of Heating, Refrigerating, and Air Conditioning Engineers Inc.
1791 Tullie Circle, NE
Atlanta, GA 30329
Phone: 404-636-8400
Fax: 404-321-5478
E-mail: lbenedict@ashrae.org

AMERICAN SOCIETY OF NAVAL ENGINEERS http://www.navalengineers.org

AMERICAN SOCIETY OF NAVAL ENGINEERS SCHOLARSHIP

• *See page 85*

ARMED FORCES COMMUNICATIONS AND ELECTRONICS ASSOCIATION, EDUCATIONAL FOUNDATION http://www.afcea.org

AFCEA/LOCKHEED MARTIN ORINCON IT SCHOLARSHIP

• *See page 113*

AFCEA SCHOLARSHIP FOR WORKING PROFESSIONALS

• *See page 113*

AFCEA SGT. JEANNETTE L. WINTERS, USMC MEMORIAL SCHOLARSHIP

• *See page 190*

ARMED FORCES COMMUNICATIONS AND ELECTRONICS ASSOCIATION EDUCATIONAL FOUNDATION DISTANCE-LEARNING SCHOLARSHIP

• *See page 190*

ARMED FORCES COMMUNICATIONS AND ELECTRONICS ASSOCIATION GENERAL EMMETT PAIGE SCHOLARSHIP

• *See page 190*

ARMED FORCES COMMUNICATIONS AND ELECTRONICS ASSOCIATION GENERAL JOHN A. WICKHAM SCHOLARSHIP

• *See page 190*

ARMED FORCES COMMUNICATIONS AND ELECTRONICS ASSOCIATION ROTC SCHOLARSHIP PROGRAM

• *See page 114*

ARRL FOUNDATION INC. http://www.arrl.org

CHARLES N. FISHER MEMORIAL SCHOLARSHIP

• *See page 85*

ARRL Foundation Inc. (continued)

DR. JAMES L. LAWSON MEMORIAL SCHOLARSHIP
• *See page 176*

EARL I. ANDERSON SCHOLARSHIP

Award for students in electronic engineering or related technical field. Student must be an amateur radio operator and member of the American Radio Relay League. Preference given to students who reside and attend classes in Illinois, Indiana, Michigan, or Florida.

Academic Fields/Career Goals: Electrical Engineering/Electronics.

Award: Scholarship for use in freshman, sophomore, junior, or senior years; not renewable. *Number:* 3. *Amount:* $1250.

Eligibility Requirements: Applicant must be enrolled or expecting to enroll full-time at a four-year institution or university; resident of Florida, Illinois, Indiana, or Michigan; studying in Florida, Illinois, Indiana, or Michigan and must have an interest in amateur radio. Applicant or parent of applicant must be member of American Radio Relay League. Available to U.S. citizens.

Application Requirements: Application, transcript. *Deadline:* February 1.

Contact: Mary M. Hobart, Secretary
ARRL Foundation Inc.
225 Main Street
Newington, CT 06111-1494
Phone: 860-594-0397
Fax: 860-594-0259
E-mail: k1mmh@arrl.org

EDMOND A. METZGER SCHOLARSHIP

Scholarship for licensed amateur radio operators, novice minimum. Applicants must be undergraduate or graduate electrical engineering students and members of the Amateur Radio Relay League. Must reside in Illinois, Indiana, or Wisconsin and attend a school in those states.

Academic Fields/Career Goals: Electrical Engineering/Electronics.

Award: Scholarship for use in freshman, sophomore, junior, senior, or graduate years; not renewable. *Number:* 1. *Amount:* $500.

Eligibility Requirements: Applicant must be enrolled or expecting to enroll full-time at a four-year institution or university; resident of Illinois, Indiana, or Wisconsin; studying in Illinois, Indiana, or Wisconsin and must have an interest in amateur radio. Applicant or parent of applicant must be member of American Radio Relay League. Available to U.S. citizens.

Application Requirements: Application, transcript. *Deadline:* February 1.

Contact: Mary M. Hobbart, Secretary
ARRL Foundation Inc.
225 Main Street
Newington, CT 06111-1494
Phone: 860-594-0397
Fax: 860-594-0259
E-mail: k1mmh@arrl.org

IRVINE W. COOK WA0CGS SCHOLARSHIP
• *See page 176*

L. PHIL WICKER SCHOLARSHIP
• *See page 176*

MISSISSIPPI SCHOLARSHIP
• *See page 85*

PAUL AND HELEN L. GRAUER SCHOLARSHIP
• *See page 85*

PERRY F. HADLOCK MEMORIAL SCHOLARSHIP

For students licensed as technicians. Preference given to students attending Clarkson University, Potsdam, New York. If no Clarkson applicants, open to all Atlantic and Hudson Divisions. Applicants must pursue a bachelor's or higher degree. Preference to electrical and electronics engineering majors.

Academic Fields/Career Goals: Electrical Engineering/Electronics.

Award: Scholarship for use in freshman, sophomore, junior, senior, or graduate years; not renewable. *Number:* 1. *Amount:* $2000.

Eligibility Requirements: Applicant must be enrolled or expecting to enroll full-time at a four-year institution or university and must have an interest in amateur radio. Available to U.S. citizens.

Application Requirements: Application, transcript. *Deadline:* February 1.

Contact: Mary M. Hobart, Secretary
ARRL Foundation Inc.
225 Main Street
Newington, CT 06111-1494
Phone: 860-594-0397
Fax: 860-594-0259
E-mail: k1mmh@arrl.org

PHD ARA SCHOLARSHIP
• *See page 191*

ASSOCIATION FOR FACILITIES ENGINEERING (AFE)

ASSOCIATION FOR FACILITIES ENGINEERING CEDAR VALLEY CHAPTER #132 SCHOLARSHIP
• *See page 114*

ASSOCIATION FOR IRON AND STEEL TECHNOLOGY http://www.aist.org

ASSOCIATION FOR IRON AND STEEL TECHNOLOGY DAVID H. SAMSON CANADIAN SCHOLARSHIP
• *See page 157*

ASSOCIATION FOR IRON AND STEEL TECHNOLOGY OHIO VALLEY CHAPTER SCHOLARSHIP
• *See page 130*

ASTRONAUT SCHOLARSHIP FOUNDATION http://www.astronautscholarship.org

ASTRONAUT SCHOLARSHIP FOUNDATION
• *See page 86*

CATCHING THE DREAM http://www.catchingthedream.org

TRIBAL BUSINESS MANAGEMENT PROGRAM (TBM)
• *See page 49*

CENTRAL INTELLIGENCE AGENCY http://www.cia.gov

CENTRAL INTELLIGENCE AGENCY UNDERGRADUATE SCHOLARSHIP PROGRAM
• *See page 49*

CUBAN AMERICAN NATIONAL FOUNDATION http://www.masscholarships.org

MAS FAMILY SCHOLARSHIPS
• *See page 139*

DEVRY INC. http://www.devry.edu

CISCO NETWORKING ACADEMY SCHOLARSHIP
• *See page 191*

ELECTROCHEMICAL SOCIETY INC. http://www.electrochem.org

H.H. DOW MEMORIAL STUDENT ACHIEVEMENT AWARD OF THE INDUSTRIAL ELECTROLYSIS AND ELECTROCHEMICAL ENGINEERING DIVISION OF THE ELECTROCHEMICAL SOCIETY INC.
• *See page 131*

STUDENT ACHIEVEMENT AWARDS OF THE INDUSTRIAL ELECTROLYSIS AND ELECTROCHEMICAL ENGINEERING DIVISION OF THE ELECTROCHEMICAL SOCIETY INC.
• *See page 131*

STUDENT RESEARCH AWARDS OF THE BATTERY DIVISION OF THE ELECTROCHEMICAL SOCIETY INC.
• *See page 131*

FOUNDATION FOR SCIENCE AND DISABILITY http://www.stemd.org

GRANTS FOR DISABLED STUDENTS IN THE SCIENCES
• *See page 87*

HAWAIIAN LODGE, F & AM http://www.glhawaii.org/

HAWAIIAN LODGE SCHOLARSHIPS

• See page 96

HEWLETT-PACKARD COMPANY http://www.hp.com

HP SCHOLAR AWARD

• See page 192

HISPANIC COLLEGE FUND INC. http://www.hispanicfund.org

DENNY'S/HISPANIC COLLEGE FUND SCHOLARSHIP

• See page 54

DEPARTMENT OF ENERGY SCHOLARSHIP PROGRAM

• See page 142

LOCKHEED MARTIN SCHOLARSHIP PROGRAM

• See page 143

HISPANIC ENGINEER NATIONAL ACHIEVEMENT AWARDS CORPORATION (HENAAC) http://www.henaac.org

HISPANIC ENGINEER NATIONAL ACHIEVEMENT AWARDS CORPORATION SCHOLARSHIP PROGRAM

• See page 116

HISPANIC SCHOLARSHIP FUND http://www.hsf.net

HSF/GENERAL MOTORS SCHOLARSHIP

• See page 143

HSF/MARATHON OIL CORPORATION COLLEGE SCHOLARSHIP

• See page 55

ILLUMINATING ENGINEERING SOCIETY OF NORTH AMERICA–GOLDEN GATE SECTION http://www.iesgg.org

ALAN LUCAS MEMORIAL EDUCATIONAL SCHOLARSHIP

• See page 92

INDEPENDENT LABORATORIES INSTITUTE SCHOLARSHIP ALLIANCE http://www.acil.org

INDEPENDENT LABORATORIES INSTITUTE SCHOLARSHIP ALLIANCE

• See page 132

INSTITUTION OF ELECTRICAL ENGINEERS http://www.theiet.org

BP/IET FARADAY LECTURE SCHOLARSHIP

Award to assist outstanding students, embarking on an IET-accredited MEg degree course, to obtain professional qualifications in electrical, electronic, IT, manufacturing or related engineering, in the U.K. or Ireland.

Academic Fields/Career Goals: Electrical Engineering/Electronics; Engineering-Related Technologies.

Award: Scholarship for use in freshman year; renewable. *Number:* 1. *Amount:* $3495–$5240.

Eligibility Requirements: Applicant must be high school student and planning to enroll or expecting to enroll full-time at an institution or university. Available to U.S. and non-U.S. citizens.

Application Requirements: Application, interview, photo, references, test scores. *Deadline:* June 30.

Contact: Scholarships and Prizes
Institution of Electrical Engineers
Michael Faraday House
Six Hills Way, Stevenage
Hertfordshire SG1 2AY
United Kingdom
E-mail: awards@theiet.org

IET JUBILEE SCHOLARSHIP

Award to assist outstanding students, embarking on an IET-accredited MEng degree course, to obtain professional qualifications in electrical, electronic, IT, manufacturing or related engineering, in the UK or Ireland. Jubilee Scholarships are worth GBP1000 per annum.

Academic Fields/Career Goals: Electrical Engineering/Electronics; Engineering/Technology.

Award: Scholarship for use in freshman year; renewable. *Number:* 11.

Eligibility Requirements: Applicant must be high school student and planning to enroll or expecting to enroll full-time at an institution or university. Available to U.S. and non-U.S. citizens.

Application Requirements: Application, interview, photo, references, test scores. *Deadline:* June 30.

Contact: Scholarships and Prizes
Institution of Electrical Engineers
Michael Faraday House
Six Hills Way, Stevenage
Hertfordshire SG1 2AY
United Kingdom
E-mail: awards@theiet.org

INSTRUMENTATION, SYSTEMS, AND AUTOMATION SOCIETY (ISA) http://www.isa.org

INSTRUMENTATION, SYSTEMS, AND AUTOMATION SOCIETY (ISA) SCHOLARSHIP PROGRAM

• See page 158

INTERNATIONAL COMMUNICATIONS INDUSTRIES FOUNDATION http://www.infocomm.org/scholarships

ICIF SCHOLARSHIP FOR DEPENDENTS OF MEMBER ORGANIZATIONS

• See page 179

INTERNATIONAL COMMUNICATIONS INDUSTRIES FOUNDATION AV SCHOLARSHIP

• See page 180

INTERNATIONAL SOCIETY FOR OPTICAL ENGINEERING-SPIE http://www.spie.org

SPIE EDUCATIONAL SCHOLARSHIPS IN OPTICAL SCIENCE AND ENGINEERING

• See page 87

JORGE MAS CANOSA FREEDOM FOUNDATION http://www.jorgemascanosa.org

MAS FAMILY SCHOLARSHIP AWARD

• See page 144

KOREAN-AMERICAN SCIENTISTS AND ENGINEERS ASSOCIATION http://www.ksea.org

KSEA SCHOLARSHIPS

Scholarship for undergraduate or graduate students in the United States with Korean heritage. Applicant should major in science, engineering, or related fields and should be a KSEA member.

Academic Fields/Career Goals: Electrical Engineering/Electronics; Engineering/Technology; Engineering-Related Technologies; Science, Technology, and Society.

Award: Scholarship for use in freshman, sophomore, junior, senior, or graduate years; not renewable. *Number:* 1. *Amount:* $1000.

Eligibility Requirements: Applicant must be of Korean heritage; Asian/Pacific Islander and enrolled or expecting to enroll full-time at a

Korean-American Scientists and Engineers Association (continued)

two-year or four-year institution or university. Applicant or parent of applicant must be member of Korean-American Scientists and Engineers Association. Available to U.S. citizens.

Application Requirements: Application, essay, resume, references, transcript. *Deadline:* February 15.

Contact: Scholarships Coordinator
Korean-American Scientists and Engineers Association
1952 Gallows Road, Suite 300
Vienna, VA 22182
Phone: 703-748-1221
Fax: 703-748-1331
E-mail: sejong@ksea.org

LOS ANGELES COUNCIL OF BLACK PROFESSIONAL ENGINEERS http://www.lablackengineers.org

AL-BEN SCHOLARSHIP FOR ACADEMIC INCENTIVE
• *See page 159*

AL-BEN SCHOLARSHIP FOR PROFESSIONAL MERIT
• *See page 159*

AL-BEN SCHOLARSHIP FOR SCHOLASTIC ACHIEVEMENT
• *See page 159*

MICHIGAN SOCIETY OF PROFESSIONAL ENGINEERS http://www.michiganspe.org

MICHIGAN SOCIETY OF PROFESSIONAL ENGINEERS AUXILIARY GRANT
• *See page 159*

MICHIGAN SOCIETY OF PROFESSIONAL ENGINEERS HARRY R. BALL, P.E. GRANT
• *See page 159*

MICHIGAN SOCIETY OF PROFESSIONAL ENGINEERS KENNETH B. FISHBECK, P.E. MEMORIAL GRANT
• *See page 160*

MICHIGAN SOCIETY OF PROFESSIONAL ENGINEERS 1980 NATIONAL SOCIETY OF PROFESSIONAL ENGINEERS ANNUAL MEETING COMMITTEE GRANT
• *See page 160*

MICHIGAN SOCIETY OF PROFESSIONAL ENGINEERS SCHOLARSHIP TRUST GRANT
• *See page 160*

MICHIGAN SOCIETY OF PROFESSIONAL ENGINEERS UNDESIGNATED GRANT
• *See page 160*

MSPE AUXILIARY GRANT FOR UNDERGRADUATE STUDY
• *See page 171*

MICRON TECHNOLOGY FOUNDATION INC. http://www.micron.com/scholars

MICRON SCIENCE AND TECHNOLOGY SCHOLARS PROGRAM
• *See page 160*

NASA DELAWARE SPACE GRANT CONSORTIUM http://www.delspace.org

NASA DELAWARE SPACE GRANT UNDERGRADUATE TUITION SCHOLARSHIP
• *See page 87*

NASA IDAHO SPACE GRANT CONSORTIUM http://isgc.uidaho.edu

NASA IDAHO SPACE GRANT CONSORTIUM SCHOLARSHIP PROGRAM
• *See page 87*

NASA MONTANA SPACE GRANT CONSORTIUM http://www.spacegrant.montana.edu

MONTANA SPACE GRANT SCHOLARSHIP PROGRAM
• *See page 119*

NATIONAL ASSOCIATION OF WOMEN IN CONSTRUCTION http://www.nawic.org

NAWIC UNDERGRADUATE SCHOLARSHIPS
• *See page 92*

NATIONAL BOARD OF BOILER AND PRESSURE VESSEL INSPECTORS http://www.nationalboard.org

NATIONAL BOARD TECHNICAL SCHOLARSHIP
• *See page 161*

NATIONAL SECURITY AGENCY http://www.nsa.gov

NATIONAL SECURITY AGENCY STOKES EDUCATIONAL SCHOLARSHIP PROGRAM
• *See page 194*

NATIONAL SOCIETY OF PROFESSIONAL ENGINEERS http://www.nspe.org

MAUREEN L. AND HOWARD N. BLITMAN, PE SCHOLARSHIP TO PROMOTE DIVERSITY IN ENGINEERING
• *See page 161*

PAUL H. ROBBINS HONORARY SCHOLARSHIP
• *See page 162*

PROFESSIONAL ENGINEERS IN INDUSTRY SCHOLARSHIP
• *See page 162*

OREGON STUDENT ASSISTANCE COMMISSION http://www.osac.state.or.us

AMERICAN COUNCIL OF ENGINEERING COMPANIES OF OREGON SCHOLARSHIP
• *See page 162*

MENTOR GRAPHICS SCHOLARSHIP
• *See page 194*

PROFESSIONAL CONSTRUCTION ESTIMATORS ASSOCIATION http://www.pcea.org

TED WILSON MEMORIAL SCHOLARSHIP FOUNDATION
• *See page 214*

ROBERT H. MOLLOHAN FAMILY CHARITABLE FOUNDATION INC. http://www.mollohanfoundation.org

HIGH TECHNOLOGY SCHOLARS PROGRAM
• *See page 135*

SOCIETY OF AUTOMOTIVE ENGINEERS http://www.sae.org

BMW/SAE ENGINEERING SCHOLARSHIP
• *See page 124*

EDWARD D. HENDRICKSON/SAE ENGINEERING SCHOLARSHIP
• *See page 124*

TMC/SAE DONALD D. DAWSON TECHNICAL SCHOLARSHIP
• *See page 124*

SOCIETY OF BROADCAST ENGINEERS INC. http://www.sbe.org

ROBERT GREENBERG/HAROLD E. ENNES SCHOLARSHIP FUND AND ENNES EDUCATIONAL FOUNDATION BROADCAST TECHNOLOGY SCHOLARSHIP

Merit-based awards for undergraduate students to study the technical aspects of broadcast engineering. Students should apply as high school senior or college freshman and may use the award for a two- or four-year college or university program. One-time award of $1000.

Academic Fields/Career Goals: Electrical Engineering/Electronics; Engineering-Related Technologies; TV/Radio Broadcasting.

Award: Scholarship for use in freshman, sophomore, junior, or senior years; renewable. *Number:* 3. *Amount:* $1000.

Eligibility Requirements: Applicant must be enrolled or expecting to enroll full-time at a two-year or four-year institution or university. Applicant must have 3.0 GPA or higher. Available to U.S. citizens.

Application Requirements: Application, autobiography, essay, references, self-addressed stamped envelope, transcript. *Deadline:* July 1.

Contact: Executive Secretary
Society of Broadcast Engineers Inc.
9102 North Meridian Street, Suite 150
Indianapolis, IN 46260
Phone: 317-846-9000
Fax: 317-846-9120

SOCIETY OF HISPANIC PROFESSIONAL ENGINEERS FOUNDATION http://www.henaac.org

SOCIETY OF HISPANIC PROFESSIONAL ENGINEERS FOUNDATION

• See page 162

SOCIETY OF MANUFACTURING ENGINEERS EDUCATION FOUNDATION http://www.sme.org/foundation

WILLIAM E. WEISEL SCHOLARSHIP FUND

Scholarship will be given to a full-time undergraduate student enrolled in an engineering or technology degree program in the U.S. or Canada, seeking a career in manufacturing. Consideration will be given to students who intend to apply their knowledge in the sub-specialty of medical robotics. Minimum of 3.0 GPA is required. Scholarships will be limited to United States and Canadian citizens.

Academic Fields/Career Goals: Electrical Engineering/Electronics; Engineering/Technology; Mechanical Engineering; Trade/Technical Specialties.

Award: Scholarship for use in freshman, sophomore, junior, or senior years; not renewable. *Number:* 1–10. *Amount:* $1000–$5000.

Eligibility Requirements: Applicant must be enrolled or expecting to enroll full-time at a four-year institution or university. Applicant must have 3.0 GPA or higher. Available to U.S. and Canadian citizens.

Application Requirements: Application, essay, resume, references, transcript. *Deadline:* February 1.

Contact: Chris Milantoni, Program Coordinator
Society of Manufacturing Engineers Education Foundation
One SME Drive
PO Box 930
Dearborn, MI 48121-0930
Phone: 313-425-3300
Fax: 313-425-3411
E-mail: foundation@sme.org

SOCIETY OF PLASTICS ENGINEERS (SPE) FOUNDATION http://www.4spe.org

FLEMING/BASZCAK SCHOLARSHIP

• See page 163

SOCIETY OF PLASTICS ENGINEERS SCHOLARSHIP PROGRAM

• See page 163

SOCIETY OF WOMEN ENGINEERS http://www.swe.org

AGILENT MENTORING SCHOLARSHIP

• See page 194

ANNE MAUREEN WHITNEY BARROW MEMORIAL SCHOLARSHIP

• See page 173

BECHTEL CORPORATION SCHOLARSHIP

• See page 173

BERTHA LAMME MEMORIAL SCHOLARSHIP

Scholarship of $1200 is awarded to one freshman electrical engineering student, who is a U.S. citizen. Must have a minimum GPA of 3.5. For full-time study only.

Academic Fields/Career Goals: Electrical Engineering/Electronics.

Award: Scholarship for use in freshman year; renewable. *Number:* 1. *Amount:* $1200.

Eligibility Requirements: Applicant must be high school student; planning to enroll or expecting to enroll full-time at a four-year institution or university and female. Applicant must have 3.5 GPA or higher. Available to U.S. citizens.

Application Requirements: Application, essay, references, transcript. *Deadline:* May 15.

Contact: Scholarship Committee
Society of Women Engineers
230 East Ohio Street, Suite 400
Chicago, IL 60611-3265
Phone: 312-596-5223
Fax: 312-596-5252
E-mail: scholarshipapplication@swe.org

CATERPILLAR INC. SCHOLARSHIP

• See page 79

DAIMLER CHRYSLER CORPORATION SCHOLARSHIP

Renewable award for entering female sophomore majoring in mechanical or electrical engineering at an accredited school. Must have GPA of 3.0.

Academic Fields/Career Goals: Electrical Engineering/Electronics; Mechanical Engineering.

Award: Scholarship for use in sophomore or junior years; renewable. *Number:* 1. *Amount:* $2000.

Eligibility Requirements: Applicant must be enrolled or expecting to enroll full-time at a four-year institution or university and female. Applicant must have 3.0 GPA or higher. Available to U.S. citizens.

Application Requirements: Application, essay, references, self-addressed stamped envelope, test scores, transcript. *Deadline:* February 1.

Contact: Scholarship Committee
Society of Women Engineers
230 East Ohio Street, Suite 400
Chicago, IL 60611-3265
Phone: 312-596-5223
Fax: 312-596-5252
E-mail: scholarshipapplication@swe.org

DELL COMPUTER CORPORATION SCHOLARSHIPS

• See page 195

DOROTHY LEMKE HOWARTH SCHOLARSHIPS

• See page 163

GENERAL ELECTRIC FOUNDATION SCHOLARSHIP

• See page 164

GENERAL MOTORS FOUNDATION UNDERGRADUATE SCHOLARSHIPS

Awards for female engineering students entering sophomore or junior year with interest in pursuing an automotive/manufacturing career. Minimum of 3.5 GPA is required.

Academic Fields/Career Goals: Electrical Engineering/Electronics; Engineering/Technology; Engineering-Related Technologies; Mechanical Engineering.

Award: Scholarship for use in sophomore or junior years; not renewable. *Number:* 3. *Amount:* $1225–$3000.

Eligibility Requirements: Applicant must be enrolled or expecting to enroll full-time at a four-year institution or university and female. Applicant must have 3.5 GPA or higher. Available to U.S. citizens.

Society of Women Engineers (continued)

Application Requirements: Application, essay, references, self-addressed stamped envelope, test scores, transcript. *Deadline:* February 1.

Contact: Scholarship Committee
Society of Women Engineers
230 East Ohio Street, Suite 400
Chicago, IL 60611-3265
Phone: 312-596-5223
Fax: 312-596-5252
E-mail: scholarshipapplication@swe.org

GUIDANT CORPORATION SCHOLARSHIP
• *See page 195*

LILLIAN MOLLER GILBRETH MEMORIAL SCHOLARSHIP
• *See page 164*

LOCKHEED MARTIN AERONAUTICS COMPANY SCHOLARSHIPS

Two $1500 scholarships for entering female juniors majoring in electrical or mechanical engineering. One scholarship for each major. Minimum 3.5 GPA required.

Academic Fields/Career Goals: Electrical Engineering/Electronics; Mechanical Engineering.

Award: Scholarship for use in junior year; not renewable. *Number:* 2. *Amount:* $1500.

Eligibility Requirements: Applicant must be enrolled or expecting to enroll full-time at a four-year institution or university and female. Applicant must have 3.5 GPA or higher. Available to U.S. citizens.

Application Requirements: Application, essay, references, self-addressed stamped envelope, test scores, transcript. *Deadline:* February 1.

Contact: Scholarship Committee
Society of Women Engineers
230 East Ohio Street, Suite 400
Chicago, IL 60611-3265
Phone: 312-596-5223
Fax: 312-596-5252
E-mail: scholarshipapplication@swe.org

MASWE MEMORIAL SCHOLARSHIP
• *See page 164*

NORTHROP GRUMMAN FRESHMAN SCHOLARSHIP
• *See page 125*

ROCKWELL AUTOMATION SCHOLARSHIP
• *See page 195*

SOUTH DAKOTA RETAILERS ASSOCIATION http://www.sdra.org

SOUTH DAKOTA RETAILERS ASSOCIATION SCHOLARSHIP PROGRAM
• *See page 64*

TURNER CONSTRUCTION COMPANY http://www.turnerconstruction.com

YOUTHFORCE 2020 SCHOLARSHIP PROGRAM
• *See page 93*

UNITED NEGRO COLLEGE FUND http://www.uncf.org

CDM SCHOLARSHIP/INTERNSHIP
• *See page 93*

CISCO/UNCF SCHOLARS PROGRAM
• *See page 197*

FORD/UNCF CORPORATE SCHOLARS PROGRAM
• *See page 65*

MEDTRONIC FOUNDATION SCHOLARSHIP
• *See page 136*

SPRINT NEXTEL SCHOLARSHIP/INTERNSHIP
• *See page 66*

THURMOND WOODARD/DELL/UNCF CORPORATE SCHOLARS PROGRAM
• *See page 151*

TOYOTA SCHOLARSHIP
• *See page 66*

UPS/UNCF CORPORATE SCHOLARS PROGRAM
• *See page 151*

WELLS FARGO/UNCF SCHOLARSHIP FUND
• *See page 67*

WEYERHAEUSER/UNCF CORPORATE SCHOLARS PROGRAM
• *See page 151*

UNIVERSITIES SPACE RESEARCH ASSOCIATION http://www.usra.edu

UNIVERSITIES SPACE RESEARCH ASSOCIATION SCHOLARSHIP PROGRAM
• *See page 88*

UTAH SOCIETY OF PROFESSIONAL ENGINEERS http://www.uspeonline.com

UTAH SOCIETY OF PROFESSIONAL ENGINEERS JOE RHOADS SCHOLARSHIP
• *See page 165*

VERTICAL FLIGHT FOUNDATION http://www.vtol.org

VERTICAL FLIGHT FOUNDATION SCHOLARSHIP
• *See page 126*

WEST VIRGINIA HIGHER EDUCATION POLICY COMMISSION-OFFICE OF FINANCIAL AID AND OUTREACH SERVICES http://wvhepcnew.wvnet.edu/

WEST VIRGINIA ENGINEERING, SCIENCE AND TECHNOLOGY SCHOLARSHIP PROGRAM

Award for full-time students attending West Virginia institutions, pursuing a degree in engineering, science, or technology. Must be a resident of West Virginia. Must have a 3.0 GPA, and after graduation, must work in the fields of engineering, science, or technology in West Virginia one year for each year the award was received.

Academic Fields/Career Goals: Electrical Engineering/Electronics; Engineering/Technology; Engineering-Related Technologies; Science, Technology, and Society.

Award: Scholarship for use in freshman, sophomore, junior, or senior years; renewable. *Number:* 200. *Amount:* up to $3000.

Eligibility Requirements: Applicant must be enrolled or expecting to enroll full-time at a two-year or four-year or technical institution or university; resident of West Virginia and studying in West Virginia. Applicant must have 3.0 GPA or higher. Available to U.S. citizens.

Application Requirements: Application, essay, test scores, transcript. *Deadline:* March 1.

Contact: Darlene Elmore, Scholarship Coordinator
West Virginia Higher Education Policy Commission-Office of Financial Aid and Outreach Services
1018 Kanawha Boulevard East, Suite 700
Charleston, WV 25301
Phone: 304-558-4618
Fax: 304-558-4622
E-mail: elmore@hepc.wvnet.edu

WOMEN IN AVIATION, INTERNATIONAL http://www.wai.org

DELTA AIR LINES ENGINEERING SCHOLARSHIP
• *See page 127*

XEROX http://www.xerox.com

TECHNICAL MINORITY SCHOLARSHIP
• *See page 165*

ENERGY AND POWER ENGINEERING

AMERICAN NUCLEAR SOCIETY http://www.ans.org

DECOMMISSIONING, DECONTAMINATION, AND REUTILIZATION SCHOLARSHIP

Undergraduate scholarship for students who have completed two or more years in a course of study leading to a degree in nuclear science, nuclear engineering, or a nuclear-related field.

Academic Fields/Career Goals: Energy and Power Engineering; Nuclear Science.

Award: Scholarship for use in junior or senior years; not renewable. *Number:* 1–21. *Amount:* $2000.

Eligibility Requirements: Applicant must be enrolled or expecting to enroll full-time at a four-year institution or university. Available to U.S. citizens.

Application Requirements: Application, essay, references, transcript. *Deadline:* February 1.

Contact: Scholarship Coordinator
American Nuclear Society
555 North Kensington Avenue
La Grange Park, IL 60526
Phone: 708-352-6611
Fax: 708-352-0499
E-mail: outreach@ans.org

AMERICAN SOCIETY OF NAVAL ENGINEERS http://www.navalengineers.org

AMERICAN SOCIETY OF NAVAL ENGINEERS SCHOLARSHIP
• See page 85

ASSOCIATION FOR IRON AND STEEL TECHNOLOGY http://www.aist.org

ASSOCIATION FOR IRON AND STEEL TECHNOLOGY DAVID H. SAMSON CANADIAN SCHOLARSHIP
• See page 157

ELECTROCHEMICAL SOCIETY INC. http://www.electrochem.org

H.H. DOW MEMORIAL STUDENT ACHIEVEMENT AWARD OF THE INDUSTRIAL ELECTROLYSIS AND ELECTROCHEMICAL ENGINEERING DIVISION OF THE ELECTROCHEMICAL SOCIETY INC.
• See page 131

STUDENT ACHIEVEMENT AWARDS OF THE INDUSTRIAL ELECTROLYSIS AND ELECTROCHEMICAL ENGINEERING DIVISION OF THE ELECTROCHEMICAL SOCIETY INC.
• See page 131

STUDENT RESEARCH AWARDS OF THE BATTERY DIVISION OF THE ELECTROCHEMICAL SOCIETY INC.
• See page 131

HAWAIIAN LODGE, F & AM http://www.glhawaii.org/

HAWAIIAN LODGE SCHOLARSHIPS
• See page 96

HISPANIC COLLEGE FUND INC. http://www.hispanicfund.org

DEPARTMENT OF ENERGY SCHOLARSHIP PROGRAM
• See page 142

LOCKHEED MARTIN SCHOLARSHIP PROGRAM
• See page 143

HISPANIC SCHOLARSHIP FUND http://www.hsf.net

HSF/MARATHON OIL CORPORATION COLLEGE SCHOLARSHIP
• See page 55

HSF/NISSAN COMMUNITY COLLEGE TRANSFER SCHOLARSHIP PROGRAM
• See page 143

INSTITUTE OF ENVIRONMENTAL SCIENCES AND TECHNOLOGY (IEST) http://www.iest.org

ROBERT N. HANCOCK MEMORIAL SCHOLARSHIP
• See page 132

NASA SOUTH DAKOTA SPACE GRANT CONSORTIUM http://www.sdsmt.edu/space/

SOUTH DAKOTA SPACE GRANT CONSORTIUM UNDERGRADUATE SCHOLARSHIPS
• See page 120

NASA WEST VIRGINIA SPACE GRANT CONSORTIUM http://www.nasa.wvu.edu

WEST VIRGINIA SPACE GRANT CONSORTIUM UNDERGRADUATE FELLOWSHIP PROGRAM
• See page 121

ROBERT H. MOLLOHAN FAMILY CHARITABLE FOUNDATION INC. http://www.mollohanfoundation.org

HIGH TECHNOLOGY SCHOLARS PROGRAM
• See page 135

SOCIETY OF WOMEN ENGINEERS http://www.swe.org

ANNE MAUREEN WHITNEY BARROW MEMORIAL SCHOLARSHIP
• See page 173

DOROTHY LEMKE HOWARTH SCHOLARSHIPS
• See page 163

GENERAL ELECTRIC FOUNDATION SCHOLARSHIP
• See page 164

LILLIAN MOLLER GILBRETH MEMORIAL SCHOLARSHIP
• See page 164

MASWE MEMORIAL SCHOLARSHIP
• See page 164

UNITED NEGRO COLLEGE FUND http://www.uncf.org

NORTHEAST UTILITIES SYSTEM SCHOLARSHIP PROGRAM
• See page 151

UTAH SOCIETY OF PROFESSIONAL ENGINEERS http://www.uspeonline.com

UTAH SOCIETY OF PROFESSIONAL ENGINEERS JOE RHOADS SCHOLARSHIP
• See page 165

WOMEN'S INTERNATIONAL NETWORK OF UTILITY PROFESSIONALS http://www.winup.org

WINUP MEMBERSHIP SCHOLARSHIP

Scholarship of $500 annually given to a member of WiNUP who desires to further education in any field that is applicable to the energy industry.

Academic Fields/Career Goals: Energy and Power Engineering.

Award: Scholarship for use in freshman, sophomore, junior, senior, or graduate years; not renewable. *Number:* 1. *Amount:* $500.

Eligibility Requirements: Applicant must be enrolled or expecting to enroll full- or part-time at a two-year or four-year or technical institution or university. Applicant or parent of applicant must be member of Women's International Network of Utility Professionals. Available to U.S. and non-U.S. citizens.

Women's International Network of Utility Professionals (continued)

Application Requirements: Application, references, transcript. *Deadline:* March 1.

Contact: Theresa Drexler, Executive Director
Women's International Network of Utility Professionals
PO Box 817
Fergus Falls, MN 56538-0817
Phone: 218-731-1659
Fax: 320-284-2299
E-mail: tdrexler@otpco.com

ENGINEERING/TECHNOLOGY

AACE INTERNATIONAL http://www.aacei.org

AACE INTERNATIONAL COMPETITIVE SCHOLARSHIP

• *See page 89*

AIR TRAFFIC CONTROL ASSOCIATION INC. http://www.atca.org

AIR TRAFFIC CONTROL ASSOCIATION SCHOLARSHIP

• *See page 112*

AMERICAN CHEMICAL SOCIETY, RUBBER DIVISION http://www.rubber.org

AMERICAN CHEMICAL SOCIETY, RUBBER DIVISION UNDERGRADUATE SCHOLARSHIP

• *See page 153*

AMERICAN COUNCIL OF ENGINEERING COMPANIES OF PENNSYLVANIA (ACEC/PA) http://www.acecpa.org

ENGINEERING SCHOLARSHIP

• *See page 154*

AMERICAN ELECTROPLATERS AND SURFACE FINISHERS SOCIETY http://www.nasf.org

AMERICAN ELECTROPLATERS AND SURFACE FINISHERS FOUNDATION SCHOLARSHIPS

• *See page 154*

AMERICAN FOUNDATION FOR THE BLIND http://www.afb.org

PAUL W. RUCKES SCHOLARSHIP

• *See page 189*

AMERICAN INSTITUTE OF AERONAUTICS AND ASTRONAUTICS http://www.aiaa.org

AIAA UNDERGRADUATE SCHOLARSHIP

• *See page 84*

AMERICAN INSTITUTE OF ARCHITECTS, NEW YORK CHAPTER http://www.aiany.org

DOUGLAS HASKELL AWARD FOR STUDENT JOURNALISM

• *See page 90*

AMERICAN NUCLEAR SOCIETY http://www.ans.org

AMERICAN NUCLEAR SOCIETY VOGT RADIOCHEMISTRY SCHOLARSHIP

One-time award for juniors, seniors, and first-year graduate students enrolled or proposing research in radio-analytical or analytical application of nuclear science. Must be U.S. citizen or permanent resident.

Academic Fields/Career Goals: Engineering/Technology; Nuclear Science.

Award: Scholarship for use in junior, senior, or graduate years; not renewable. *Number:* 1. *Amount:* $2000–$3000.

Eligibility Requirements: Applicant must be enrolled or expecting to enroll full-time at a four-year institution or university. Available to U.S. citizens.

Application Requirements: Application, references, transcript, sponsorship letter from ANS organization. *Deadline:* February 1.

Contact: Scholarship Coordinator
American Nuclear Society
555 North Kensington Avenue
La Grange Park, IL 60526
Phone: 708-352-6611
Fax: 708-352-0499
E-mail: outreach@ans.org

AMERICAN PUBLIC TRANSPORTATION FOUNDATION http://www.apta.com

JACK GILSTRAP SCHOLARSHIP

Awarded the APTF scholarship to the applicant with the highest score. Must be in public transportation industry-related fields of study. Must be sponsored by AFTA member organization and complete an internship program with a member organization. Minimum 3.0 GPA required.

Academic Fields/Career Goals: Engineering/Technology; Transportation.

Award: Scholarship for use in sophomore, junior, senior, or graduate years; renewable. *Number:* 1. *Amount:* $2500.

Eligibility Requirements: Applicant must be enrolled or expecting to enroll full-time at a two-year or four-year institution or university. Applicant must have 3.0 GPA or higher. Available to U.S. and Canadian citizens.

Application Requirements: Application, essay, financial need analysis, references, transcript, verification of enrollment for the current semester and copy of fee schedule from the college/university. *Deadline:* June 16.

Contact: Pamela Boswell, Vice President of Program Management
American Public Transportation Foundation
1666 K Street, NW
Washington, DC 20006-1215
Phone: 202-496-4803
Fax: 202-496-2323
E-mail: pboswell@apta.com

TRANSIT HALL OF FAME SCHOLARSHIP AWARD PROGRAM

• *See page 168*

AMERICAN RAILWAY ENGINEERING AND MAINTENANCE OF WAY ASSOCIATION http://www.arema.org

AREMA MICHAEL R. GARCIA SCHOLARSHIP

Award for students enrolled in a four or five year program leading to a bachelor's degree in engineering or engineering technology. This scholarship is for students who are married and/or are supporting a family while enrolled as a student.

Academic Fields/Career Goals: Engineering/Technology.

Award: Scholarship for use in freshman, sophomore, junior, or senior years; not renewable. *Number:* 1. *Amount:* $2000.

Eligibility Requirements: Applicant must be enrolled or expecting to enroll full-time at a four-year institution or university. Available to U.S. citizens.

Application Requirements: Application, resume, references, transcript, cover letter. *Deadline:* March 14.

Contact: Stacy Elder, Director of Committees and Technical Services
American Railway Engineering and Maintenance of Way Association
10003 Derekwood Lane, Suite 210
Lanham, MD 20706
Phone: 301-459-3200 Ext. 706
Fax: 301-459-8077
E-mail: selder@arema.org

AREMA PRESIDENTIAL SPOUSE SCHOLARSHIP

• *See page 285*

AREMA UNDERGRADUATE SCHOLARSHIPS

Scholarships are awarded to engineering students who have a potential interest in railway engineering careers. Minimum 2.0 GPA required.

Academic Fields/Career Goals: Engineering/Technology.

Award: Scholarship for use in freshman, sophomore, junior, or senior years; not renewable. *Number:* 17. *Amount:* $1000.

Eligibility Requirements: Applicant must be enrolled or expecting to enroll full-time at a four-year institution or university. Available to U.S. citizens.

Application Requirements: Application, resume, references, transcript, cover letter. *Deadline:* March 14.

Contact: Scholarship Committee
American Railway Engineering and Maintenance of Way Association
10003 Derekwood Lane, Suite 210
Lanham, MD 20706

COMMITTEE 12-RAIL TRANSIT UNDERGRADUATE SCHOLARSHIP

• *See page 286*

CSX SCHOLARSHIP

• *See page 286*

JOHN J. CUNNINGHAM MEMORIAL SCHOLARSHIP

Scholarship awarded to a junior or senior college student pursuing an undergraduate degree in a professional field that has direct applications in the passenger rail sector. Minimum 2.00 GPA required.

Academic Fields/Career Goals: Engineering/Technology; Transportation.

Award: Scholarship for use in junior or senior years; not renewable. *Number:* varies. *Amount:* $1000.

Eligibility Requirements: Applicant must be enrolled or expecting to enroll full-time at a four-year institution or university. Available to U.S. citizens.

Application Requirements: Application, resume, references, transcript, cover letter. *Deadline:* March 14.

Contact: Scholarship Committee
American Railway Engineering and Maintenance of Way Association
10003 Derekwood Lane, Suite 210
Lanham, MD 20706

NORFOLK SOUTHERN FOUNDATION SCHOLARSHIP

• *See page 286*

PB RAIL ENGINEERING SCHOLARSHIP

• *See page 286*

REMSA SCHOLARSHIP

• *See page 286*

AMERICAN SOCIETY FOR ENGINEERING EDUCATION http://www.asee.org

SCIENCE, MATHEMATICS, AND RESEARCH FOR TRANSFORMATION DEFENSE SCHOLARSHIP FOR SERVICE PROGRAM

• *See page 85*

AMERICAN SOCIETY OF AGRICULTURAL ENGINEERS http://www.asabe.org

AMERICAN SOCIETY OF AGRICULTURAL AND BIOLOGICAL ENGINEERS STUDENT ENGINEER OF THE YEAR SCHOLARSHIP

Award for full-time engineering undergraduate student in the U.S. or Canada. Must be active student member of the American Society of Agricultural Engineers. Must have a minimum of 3.0 GPA. Write for more information and special application procedures. One-time award of $1000. Must have completed one year of school, and must submit paper titled "My Goals in the Engineering Profession."

Academic Fields/Career Goals: Engineering/Technology.

Award: Scholarship for use in sophomore, junior, or senior years; not renewable. *Number:* 1. *Amount:* $1000.

Eligibility Requirements: Applicant must be enrolled or expecting to enroll full-time at a four-year institution or university. Applicant must have 3.0 GPA or higher. Available to U.S. and Canadian citizens.

Application Requirements: Application, essay, financial need analysis, resume, references. *Deadline:* March 17.

Contact: Carol Flautt, Scholarship Program
American Society of Agricultural Engineers
2950 Niles Road
St. Joseph, MI 49085
Phone: 269-428-6336
Fax: 269-429-3852
E-mail: flautt@asabe.org

AMERICAN SOCIETY OF CERTIFIED ENGINEERING TECHNICIANS http://www.ascet.org

JOSEPH C. JOHNSON MEMORIAL GRANT

Grant for $750 given to qualified applicants in order to offset the cost of tuition, books and lab fees. Applicant must be a U.S. citizen or a legal resident of the country in which the applicant is currently living, as well as be either a student, certified, regular, registered or associate member of ASCET. Student must be enrolled in an engineering technology program. For further information, visit http://www.ascet.org.

Academic Fields/Career Goals: Engineering/Technology.

Award: Grant for use in freshman, sophomore, junior, or senior years; not renewable. *Number:* 1. *Amount:* $750.

Eligibility Requirements: Applicant must be enrolled or expecting to enroll full- or part-time at a two-year or four-year or technical institution or university. Applicant must have 3.0 GPA or higher. Available to U.S. citizens.

Application Requirements: Application, financial need analysis, photo, references, transcript. *Deadline:* April 1.

Contact: Mr. Tim Latham, General Manager
American Society of Certified Engineering Technicians
PO Box 1536
Brandon, MS 39043
Phone: 601-824-8991
E-mail: tim-latham@ascet.org

JOSEPH M. PARISH MEMORIAL GRANT

Grant of $500 will be awarded to a student to be used to offset the cost of tuition, books and lab fees. Applicant must be a student member of ASCET and be a U.S. citizen or a legal resident of the country in which the applicant is currently living. The award will be given to full time students enrolled in an engineering technology program; students pursuing a BS degree in engineering are not eligible for this grant. For more information, visit http://www.ascet.org.

Academic Fields/Career Goals: Engineering/Technology.

Award: Grant for use in sophomore or senior years; not renewable. *Number:* 1. *Amount:* $500.

Eligibility Requirements: Applicant must be enrolled or expecting to enroll full-time at a two-year or four-year institution. Applicant must have 3.0 GPA or higher. Available to U.S. citizens.

Application Requirements: Application, financial need analysis, photo. *Deadline:* April 1.

Contact: Mr. Tim Latham, General Manager
American Society of Certified Engineering Technicians
PO Box 1536
Brandon, MS 39043
Phone: 601-824-8991
E-mail: tim-latham@ascet.org

AMERICAN SOCIETY OF HEATING, REFRIGERATING, AND AIR CONDITIONING ENGINEERS INC. http://www.ashrae.org

ALWIN B. NEWTON SCHOLARSHIP FUND

• *See page 247*

AMERICAN SOCIETY OF HEATING, REFRIGERATION, AND AIR CONDITIONING ENGINEERING TECHNOLOGY SCHOLARSHIP

• *See page 85*

American Society of Heating, Refrigerating, and Air Conditioning Engineers Inc. (continued)

ASHRAE MEMORIAL SCHOLARSHIP
• *See page 286*

ASHRAE REGION IV BENNY BOOTLE SCHOLARSHIP
• *See page 90*

ASHRAE REGION VIII SCHOLARSHIP

One-year $3000 scholarship available to an undergraduate engineering student enrolled full-time in an ABET-accredited program at a school located within the geographic boundaries of ASHRAE'S Region VIII comprising Arkansas, Louisiana, Texas, Oklahoma, and Mexico. Must have a minimum GPA of 3.0.

Academic Fields/Career Goals: Engineering/Technology.

Award: Scholarship for use in freshman, sophomore, junior, or senior years; not renewable. *Number:* 1. *Amount:* $3000.

Eligibility Requirements: Applicant must be enrolled or expecting to enroll full-time at a four-year institution or university and studying in Arkansas, Louisiana, Oklahoma, or Texas. Applicant must have 3.0 GPA or higher. Available to U.S. and non-U.S. citizens.

Application Requirements: Application, financial need analysis, references, transcript. *Deadline:* December 1.

Contact: Lois Benedict, Scholarship Administrator
American Society of Heating, Refrigerating, and Air Conditioning Engineers Inc.
1791 Tullie Circle, NE
Atlanta, GA 30329
Phone: 404-636-8400
Fax: 404-321-5478
E-mail: lbenedict@ashrae.org

ASHRAE SCHOLARSHIPS
• *See page 287*

HENRY ADAMS SCHOLARSHIP
• *See page 287*

AMERICAN SOCIETY OF MECHANICAL ENGINEERS (ASME INTERNATIONAL) http://www.asme.org

AMERICAN SOCIETY OF MECHANICAL ENGINEERS STEPHEN T. KUGLE SCHOLARSHIP

Scholarship for an ASME student member attending a public college or university in one of the states in District E (Arizona, Arkansas, Colorado, Louisiana, New Mexico, Oklahoma, Texas, Utah, and Wyoming). Must be a junior or senior, a U.S. citizen by birth, and have a 3.0 minimum GPA. Students from University of Texas at Arlington are not eligible.

Academic Fields/Career Goals: Engineering/Technology.

Award: Scholarship for use in junior or senior years; not renewable. *Number:* 1. *Amount:* $2000.

Eligibility Requirements: Applicant must be enrolled or expecting to enroll full-time at a four-year institution or university and studying in Arizona, Arkansas, Colorado, Louisiana, New Mexico, Oklahoma, Texas, Utah, or Wyoming. Applicant or parent of applicant must be member of American Society of Mechanical Engineers. Applicant must have 3.0 GPA or higher. Available to U.S. citizens.

Application Requirements: Application, transcript. *Deadline:* March 15.

Contact: Maisha Phillips, Coordinator, Student Development ASME
American Society of Mechanical Engineers (ASME International)
Three Park Avenue
New York, NY 10016-5990
Phone: 212-591-8131
Fax: 212-591-7143
E-mail: phillipsm@asme.org

AMERICAN SOCIETY OF NAVAL ENGINEERS http://www.navalengineers.org

AMERICAN SOCIETY OF NAVAL ENGINEERS SCHOLARSHIP
• *See page 85*

AMERICAN SOCIETY OF PLUMBING ENGINEERS http://www.aspe.org

ALFRED STEELE ENGINEERING SCHOLARSHIP

Scholarships of $1000 are awarded for the members of American society of plumbing engineers towards education and professional development on plumbing engineering and designing.

Academic Fields/Career Goals: Engineering/Technology; Industrial Design.

Award: Scholarship for use in freshman, sophomore, junior, or senior years; not renewable. *Number:* 5. *Amount:* $1000.

Eligibility Requirements: Applicant must be enrolled or expecting to enroll full-time at a two-year or four-year or technical institution or university. Applicant must have 3.0 GPA or higher. Available to U.S. and non-U.S. citizens.

Application Requirements: Application, essay, references, transcript, statement of personal achievement. *Deadline:* September 1.

Contact: Stacey Kidd, Membership Director
American Society of Plumbing Engineers
8614 Catalpa Avenue, Suite 1007
Chicago, IL 60656-1116
Phone: 773-693-2773
Fax: 773-695-9007
E-mail: skidd@aspe.org

AMERICAN WELDING SOCIETY http://www.aws.org

AIRGAS-TERRY JARVIS MEMORIAL SCHOLARSHIP
• *See page 287*

AMERICAN WELDING SOCIETY INTERNATIONAL SCHOLARSHIP
• *See page 288*

DONALD AND SHIRLEY HASTINGS SCHOLARSHIP

Award for U.S. citizen at least 18 years of age pursuing a four-year undergraduate degree in welding engineering or welding engineering technology. Priority given to welding engineering students. Preference is given to students residing or attending school in California or Ohio. Submit copy of proposed curriculum. Minimum GPA of 2.5 required.

Academic Fields/Career Goals: Engineering/Technology; Materials Science, Engineering, and Metallurgy.

Award: Scholarship for use in freshman, sophomore, junior, or senior years; not renewable. *Number:* 1. *Amount:* $2500.

Eligibility Requirements: Applicant must be age 18 and over and enrolled or expecting to enroll full- or part-time at a four-year institution or university. Applicant must have 2.5 GPA or higher. Available to U.S. citizens.

Application Requirements: Application, autobiography, financial need analysis, references, transcript, FAFSA form. *Deadline:* January 15.

Contact: Vicki Pinsky, Manager, Foundation
American Welding Society
550 Le Jeune Road, NW
Miami, FL 33126
Phone: 800-443-9353 Ext. 212
Fax: 305-443-7559
E-mail: vpinsky@aws.org

DONALD F. HASTINGS SCHOLARSHIP
• *See page 288*

EDWARD J. BRADY MEMORIAL SCHOLARSHIP
• *See page 288*

HOWARD E. AND WILMA J. ADKINS MEMORIAL SCHOLARSHIP
• *See page 288*

ILLINOIS TOOL WORKS WELDING COMPANIES SCHOLARSHIP
• *See page 288*

JOHN C. LINCOLN MEMORIAL SCHOLARSHIP
• *See page 289*

MATSUO BRIDGE COMPANY LTD. OF JAPAN SCHOLARSHIP
• *See page 169*

MILLER ELECTRIC INTERNATIONAL WORLD SKILLS COMPETITION SCHOLARSHIP

• *See page 289*

PAST PRESIDENTS' SCHOLARSHIP

Scholarship available to students pursuing a bachelor's degree in welding engineering, welding engineering technology, or an engineering program with emphasis on welding. Also open to graduate students pursuing a master's or doctorate in engineering or management.

Academic Fields/Career Goals: Engineering/Technology; Mechanical Engineering.

Award: Scholarship for use in junior, senior, graduate, or postgraduate years; not renewable. *Number:* 1. *Amount:* $2500.

Eligibility Requirements: Applicant must be enrolled or expecting to enroll full- or part-time at a four-year institution. Available to U.S. citizens.

Application Requirements: Application, autobiography, financial need analysis, references, transcript. *Deadline:* January 15.

Contact: Ms. Vicki Pinsky, Manager
American Welding Society
550 NW LeJeune Road
Miami, FL 33126

PRAXAIR INTERNATIONAL SCHOLARSHIP

• *See page 289*

RESISTANCE WELDER MANUFACTURERS' ASSOCIATION SCHOLARSHIP

$2500 award to students who express an interest in the resistance welding process while pursuing a career in welding engineering. Available to U.S. and Canadian citizens. Must be a junior in a four-year program only and maintain a minimum 3.0 GPA.

Academic Fields/Career Goals: Engineering/Technology; Materials Science, Engineering, and Metallurgy.

Award: Scholarship for use in junior year; not renewable. *Number:* 1. *Amount:* $2500.

Eligibility Requirements: Applicant must be enrolled or expecting to enroll full- or part-time at a four-year institution or university. Applicant must have 3.0 GPA or higher. Available to U.S. and Canadian citizens.

Application Requirements: Application, essay, resume, transcript. *Deadline:* January 15.

Contact: Vicki Pinsky, Manager, Foundation
American Welding Society
550 Le Jeune Road, NW
Miami, FL 33126
Phone: 800-443-9353 Ext. 212
Fax: 305-443-7559
E-mail: vpinsky@aws.org

ROBERT L. PEASLEE DETROIT BRAZING AND SOLDERING DIVISION SCHOLARSHIP

$2500 award for students pursuing a minimum four-year bachelors degree in welding engineering or welding engineering technology with an emphasis on brazing and soldering applications.Must be minimum 18 years of age and at least a college junior. 3.0 GPA required.

Academic Fields/Career Goals: Engineering/Technology; Materials Science, Engineering, and Metallurgy.

Award: Scholarship for use in junior or senior years; not renewable. *Number:* 1. *Amount:* $2500.

Eligibility Requirements: Applicant must be age 18 and over and enrolled or expecting to enroll full- or part-time at a four-year institution or university. Applicant must have 3.0 GPA or higher. Available to U.S. and Canadian citizens.

Application Requirements: Application, financial need analysis, resume, references, transcript, statement of unmet financial need. *Deadline:* January 15.

Contact: Vicki Pinsky, Manager, Foundation
American Welding Society
550 Le Jeune Road, NW
Miami, FL 33126
Phone: 800-443-9353 Ext. 212
Fax: 305-443-7559
E-mail: vpinsky@aws.org

RWMA SCHOLARSHIP

Scholarship to junior college student in welding engineering or welding engineering technology. Must demonstrate interest in the resistance welding process. Must submit essay of 500 words or less about why the student wishes to become involved in the resistance welding industry. Minimum cumulative GPA of 3.0 required.

Academic Fields/Career Goals: Engineering/Technology; Mechanical Engineering.

Award: Scholarship for use in junior year; not renewable. *Number:* 1. *Amount:* $2500.

Eligibility Requirements: Applicant must be enrolled or expecting to enroll full- or part-time at a four-year institution. Applicant must have 3.0 GPA or higher. Available to U.S. and Canadian citizens.

Application Requirements: Application, autobiography, essay, financial need analysis, transcript. *Deadline:* January 15.

Contact: Ms. Vicki Pinsky, Manager
American Welding Society
550 NW LeJeune Road
Miami, FL 33126

WILLIAM B. HOWELL MEMORIAL SCHOLARSHIP

• *See page 289*

ARIZONA PROFESSIONAL CHAPTER OF AISES http://www.azpcofaises.org

ARIZONA PROFESSIONAL CHAPTER OF AISES SCHOLARSHIP

Scholarship awarded to American Indian/Alaska Natives attending Arizona schools of higher education pursuing degrees in the sciences, engineering, medicine, natural resources, math, and technology. Student must be a full-time undergraduate student (at least 12 hours per semester) at an accredited two-year or four-year college or university.

Academic Fields/Career Goals: Engineering/Technology; Health and Medical Sciences; Natural Resources; Physical Sciences and Math.

Award: Scholarship for use in freshman, sophomore, junior, or senior years; not renewable. *Number:* varies. *Amount:* varies.

Eligibility Requirements: Applicant must be American Indian/Alaska Native; enrolled or expecting to enroll full-time at a two-year or four-year institution or university and studying in Arizona. Applicant must have 2.5 GPA or higher. Available to U.S. citizens.

Application Requirements: Application, essay, portfolio, resume, references, transcript, proof of tribal enrollment, copy of AISES membership card. *Deadline:* August 17.

Contact: Jaime Ashike, Scholarship Committee
Arizona Professional Chapter of AISES
PO Box 2528
Phoenix, AZ 85002
Phone: 480-326-0958
E-mail: amazing_butterfly@hotmail.com

ARMED FORCES COMMUNICATIONS AND ELECTRONICS ASSOCIATION, EDUCATIONAL FOUNDATION http://www.afcea.org

AFCEA/LOCKHEED MARTIN ORINCON IT SCHOLARSHIP

• *See page 113*

AFCEA SCHOLARSHIP FOR WORKING PROFESSIONALS

• *See page 113*

AFCEA SGT. JEANNETTE L. WINTERS, USMC MEMORIAL SCHOLARSHIP

• *See page 190*

Armed Forces Communications and Electronics Association, Educational Foundation (continued)

ARMED FORCES COMMUNICATIONS AND ELECTRONICS ASSOCIATION EDUCATIONAL FOUNDATION DISTANCE-LEARNING SCHOLARSHIP

• *See page 190*

ARMED FORCES COMMUNICATIONS AND ELECTRONICS ASSOCIATION GENERAL EMMETT PAIGE SCHOLARSHIP

• *See page 190*

ARMED FORCES COMMUNICATIONS AND ELECTRONICS ASSOCIATION GENERAL JOHN A. WICKHAM SCHOLARSHIP

• *See page 190*

ARMED FORCES COMMUNICATIONS AND ELECTRONICS ASSOCIATION ROTC SCHOLARSHIP PROGRAM

• *See page 114*

VICE ADMIRAL JERRY O. TUTTLE, USN (RET.) AND MRS. BARBARA A. TUTTLE SCIENCE AND TECHNOLOGY SCHOLARSHIP

• *See page 289*

ARRL FOUNDATION INC. http://www.arrl.org

CHARLES N. FISHER MEMORIAL SCHOLARSHIP

• *See page 85*

MISSISSIPPI SCHOLARSHIP

• *See page 85*

PAUL AND HELEN L. GRAUER SCHOLARSHIP

• *See page 85*

WILLIAM R. GOLDFARB MEMORIAL SCHOLARSHIP

• *See page 138*

ASM MATERIALS EDUCATION FOUNDATION http://www.asminternational.org/foundation

ASM OUTSTANDING SCHOLARS AWARDS

Awards for student members of ASM International studying metallurgy or materials science and engineering. Must have completed at least one year of college to apply. Awards are merit-based; financial need is not considered.

Academic Fields/Career Goals: Engineering/Technology; Materials Science, Engineering, and Metallurgy.

Award: Scholarship for use in sophomore, junior, or senior years; not renewable. *Number:* 3. *Amount:* $2000.

Eligibility Requirements: Applicant must be enrolled or expecting to enroll full-time at a four-year institution or university. Applicant or parent of applicant must be member of ASM International. Available to U.S. and non-U.S. citizens.

Application Requirements: Application, essay, photo, references, transcript. *Deadline:* May 1.

Contact: Pergentina Deatherage, Administrator, Foundation Programs
ASM Materials Education Foundation
9639 Kinsman Road
Materials Park, OH 44073-0002
Phone: 440-338-5151
Fax: 440-338-4634

EDWARD J. DULIS SCHOLARSHIP

Award of $1500 for student members of ASM International studying metallurgy or materials science and engineering. Award is merit based; financial need is not considered.

Academic Fields/Career Goals: Engineering/Technology; Materials Science, Engineering, and Metallurgy.

Award: Scholarship for use in freshman, sophomore, junior, or senior years; not renewable. *Number:* 1. *Amount:* $1500.

Eligibility Requirements: Applicant must be enrolled or expecting to enroll full-time at a four-year institution or university. Applicant or parent of applicant must be member of ASM International. Available to U.S. and Canadian citizens.

Application Requirements: Application, photo, references, transcript. *Deadline:* May 1.

Contact: Pergentina Deatherage, Administrator, Foundation Programs
ASM Materials Education Foundation
9639 Kinsman Road
Materials Park, OH 44073-0002
Phone: 440-338-5151
Fax: 440-338-4634

GEORGE A. ROBERTS SCHOLARSHIP

Awards for college juniors or seniors studying metallurgy or materials engineering in North America. Applicants must be student members of ASM International. Awards based on need, interest in field, academics, and character.

Academic Fields/Career Goals: Engineering/Technology; Materials Science, Engineering, and Metallurgy.

Award: Scholarship for use in junior or senior years; not renewable. *Number:* 7. *Amount:* $6000.

Eligibility Requirements: Applicant must be enrolled or expecting to enroll full-time at an institution or university. Applicant or parent of applicant must be member of ASM International. Available to U.S. and Canadian citizens.

Application Requirements: Application, essay, financial need analysis, photo, references, transcript. *Deadline:* May 1.

Contact: Pergentina Deatherage, Administrator, Foundation Programs
ASM Materials Education Foundation
9639 Kinsman Road
Materials Park, OH 44073-0002
Phone: 440-338-5151
Fax: 440-338-4634

JOHN M. HANIAK SCHOLARSHIP

Award for student members of ASM International studying metallurgy or materials science and engineering. Must have completed at least one year of college to apply. Award is merit based; financial need is not considered.

Academic Fields/Career Goals: Engineering/Technology; Materials Science, Engineering, and Metallurgy.

Award: Scholarship for use in freshman, sophomore, junior, or senior years; not renewable. *Number:* 1. *Amount:* $1500.

Eligibility Requirements: Applicant must be enrolled or expecting to enroll full-time at a four-year institution or university. Applicant or parent of applicant must be member of ASM International. Available to U.S. and Canadian citizens.

Application Requirements: Application, essay, references, self-addressed stamped envelope, transcript. *Deadline:* May 1.

Contact: Pergentina Deatherage, Administrator, Foundation Programs
ASM Materials Education Foundation
9639 Kinsman Road
Materials Park, OH 44073-0002
Phone: 440-338-5151
Fax: 440-338-4634

NICHOLAS J. GRANT SCHOLARSHIP

Full tuition for student member of ASM International studying metallurgy or materials science and engineering. Must provide proof of financial status.

Academic Fields/Career Goals: Engineering/Technology; Materials Science, Engineering, and Metallurgy.

Award: Scholarship for use in junior or senior years; not renewable. *Number:* 1. *Amount:* varies.

Eligibility Requirements: Applicant must be enrolled or expecting to enroll full-time at an institution or university. Applicant or parent of applicant must be member of ASM International. Available to U.S. and Canadian citizens.

Application Requirements: Application, essay, financial need analysis, photo, references, transcript. *Deadline:* May 1.

Contact: Pergentina Deatherage, Administrator, Foundation Programs
ASM Materials Education Foundation
9639 Kinsman Road
Materials Park, OH 44073-0002

WILLIAM P. WOODSIDE FOUNDER'S SCHOLARSHIP

$10,000 scholarship for college junior or senior studying metallurgy or materials engineering in North America. Must be a student member of ASM International. Award based on need, interest in field, academics, and character.

Academic Fields/Career Goals: Engineering/Technology; Materials Science, Engineering, and Metallurgy.

Award: Scholarship for use in junior or senior years; not renewable. *Number:* 1. *Amount:* up to $10,000.

Eligibility Requirements: Applicant must be enrolled or expecting to enroll full-time at an institution or university. Applicant or parent of applicant must be member of ASM International. Available to U.S. and Canadian citizens.

Application Requirements: Application, essay, financial need analysis, photo, references, transcript. *Deadline:* May 1.

Contact: Pergentina Deatherage, Administrator, Foundation Programs
ASM Materials Education Foundation
9639 Kinsman Road
Materials Park, OH 44073-0002
Phone: 440-338-5151
Fax: 440-338-4634

ASPRS, THE IMAGING AND GEOSPATIAL INFORMATION SOCIETY http://www.asprs.org

ROBERT E. ALTENHOFEN MEMORIAL SCHOLARSHIP

One-time award of $2000 available for undergraduate or graduate study in theoretical photogrammetry. Applicant must supply a sample of work in photogrammetry and a statement of plans for future study in the field. Must be a member of ASPRS.

Academic Fields/Career Goals: Engineering/Technology; Surveying; Surveying Technology, Cartography, or Geographic Information Science.

Award: Scholarship for use in freshman, sophomore, junior, senior, or graduate years; not renewable. *Number:* 1. *Amount:* $2000.

Eligibility Requirements: Applicant must be enrolled or expecting to enroll full-time at a two-year or four-year institution or university and must have an interest in photography/photogrammetry/filmmaking. Applicant or parent of applicant must be member of American Society for Photogrammetry and Remote Sensing. Available to U.S. and non-U.S. citizens.

Application Requirements: Application, essay, references, transcript, work sample. *Deadline:* December 3.

Contact: Jesse Winch, Program Manager
ASPRS, The Imaging and Geospatial Information Society
5410 Grosvenor Lane, Suite 210
Bethesda, MD 20814-2160
Phone: 301-493-0290 Ext. 101
Fax: 301-493-0208
E-mail: scholarships@asprs.org

ASSOCIATED GENERAL CONTRACTORS EDUCATION AND RESEARCH FOUNDATION http://www.agcfoundation.org

AGC EDUCATION AND RESEARCH FOUNDATION UNDERGRADUATE SCHOLARSHIPS

• *See page 169*

ASSOCIATION FOR FACILITIES ENGINEERING (AFE)

ASSOCIATION FOR FACILITIES ENGINEERING CEDAR VALLEY CHAPTER #132 SCHOLARSHIP

• *See page 114*

ASSOCIATION FOR IRON AND STEEL TECHNOLOGY http://www.aist.org

AIST ALFRED B. GLOSSBRENNER AND JOHN KLUSCH SCHOLARSHIPS

Scholarship intended to award high school senior who plans on pursuing a degree in metallurgy or engineering. Student must have previous academic excellence in science courses. Applicant must be a dependent of a AIST Northeastern Ohio chapter member.

Academic Fields/Career Goals: Engineering/Technology; Materials Science, Engineering, and Metallurgy.

Award: Scholarship for use in freshman year; not renewable. *Number:* 2. *Amount:* $1000.

Eligibility Requirements: Applicant must be high school student and planning to enroll or expecting to enroll full-time at a four-year institution or university. Applicant or parent of applicant must be member of Association for Iron and Steel Technology. Available to U.S. and non-U.S. citizens.

Application Requirements: Application, essay, resume, references, test scores, transcript. *Deadline:* April 30.

Contact: Richard J. Kurz, Chapter Secretary
Association for Iron and Steel Technology
22831 East State Street, Route 62
Alliance, OH 44601

AIST WILLIAM E. SCHWABE MEMORIAL SCHOLARSHIP

One-time $3000 scholarship awarded to a full-time undergraduate student in engineering, metallurgy, or materials science program at an accredited North American university.

Academic Fields/Career Goals: Engineering/Technology; Materials Science, Engineering, and Metallurgy.

Award: Scholarship for use in freshman, sophomore, junior, or senior years; not renewable. *Number:* 1. *Amount:* $3000.

Eligibility Requirements: Applicant must be enrolled or expecting to enroll full-time at a four-year institution or university. Applicant must have 3.0 GPA or higher. Available to U.S. and non-U.S. citizens.

Application Requirements: Application, essay, resume, references, transcript. *Deadline:* March 2.

Contact: Lori Wharrey, Board Administrator
Association for Iron and Steel Technology
186 Thorn Hill Road
Warrendale, PA 15086-7528
Phone: 724-776-6040 Ext. 621
Fax: 724-776-1880
E-mail: lwharrey@aist.org

ASSOCIATION FOR IRON AND STEEL TECHNOLOGY BALTIMORE CHAPTER SCHOLARSHIP

• *See page 290*

ASSOCIATION FOR IRON AND STEEL TECHNOLOGY DAVID H. SAMSON CANADIAN SCHOLARSHIP

• *See page 157*

ASSOCIATION FOR IRON AND STEEL TECHNOLOGY MIDWEST CHAPTER BETTY MCKERN SCHOLARSHIP

Scholarship awarded to a graduating female high school senior, or to an undergraduate freshman, sophomore, or junior enrolled in a fully AIST-accredited college or university. Applicant must be in good academic standing. Must be a dependant of an AIST Midwest chapter member.

Academic Fields/Career Goals: Engineering/Technology.

Award: Scholarship for use in freshman, sophomore, junior, or senior years; not renewable. *Number:* 1. *Amount:* $3000.

Eligibility Requirements: Applicant must be enrolled or expecting to enroll full-time at a four-year institution or university and female. Applicant or parent of applicant must be member of Association for Iron and Steel Technology. Available to U.S. and non-U.S. citizens.

Association for Iron and Steel Technology (continued)

Application Requirements: Application, essay, resume, references, test scores, transcript. *Deadline:* March 15.

Contact: AIST Midwest Member Chapter Scholarships Chair
Association for Iron and Steel Technology
c/o Barry Felton, 250 West US Highway 12
Burns Harbor, IN 46304

ASSOCIATION FOR IRON AND STEEL TECHNOLOGY MIDWEST CHAPTER DON NELSON SCHOLARSHIP

One scholarship for a graduating high school senior, or undergraduate freshman, sophomore or junior enrolled in a fully AIST-accredited college or university. Applicant must be in good academic standing. Must be a dependent of an AIST Midwest chapter member. May reapply each year for the duration of college education.

Academic Fields/Career Goals: Engineering/Technology.

Award: Scholarship for use in freshman, sophomore, junior, or senior years; not renewable. *Number:* 1. *Amount:* up to $1000.

Eligibility Requirements: Applicant must be enrolled or expecting to enroll full-time at a four-year institution or university. Applicant or parent of applicant must be member of Association for Iron and Steel Technology. Available to U.S. and non-U.S. citizens.

Application Requirements: Application, essay, resume, references, test scores, transcript. *Deadline:* March 15.

Contact: AIST Midwest Member Chapter Scholarships Chair
Association for Iron and Steel Technology
c/o Barry Felton, 250 West US Highway 12
Burns Harbor, IN 46304

ASSOCIATION FOR IRON AND STEEL TECHNOLOGY MIDWEST CHAPTER ENGINEERING SCHOLARSHIP

Two four-year scholarships awarded to graduating high school senior or undergraduate freshman, sophomore or junior enrolled in a fully AIST-accredited college or university majoring engineering. Applicant must be in good academic standing. Must be a dependent of an AIST Midwest chapter member. May reapply each year for the duration of college education.

Academic Fields/Career Goals: Engineering/Technology.

Award: Scholarship for use in freshman, sophomore, or junior years; renewable. *Number:* 2. *Amount:* $1500.

Eligibility Requirements: Applicant must be enrolled or expecting to enroll full-time at a four-year institution or university. Applicant or parent of applicant must be member of Association for Iron and Steel Technology. Available to U.S. and non-U.S. citizens.

Application Requirements: Application, essay, resume, references, test scores, transcript. *Deadline:* March 15.

Contact: AIST Midwest Member Chapter Scholarships Chair
Association for Iron and Steel Technology
c/o Barry Felton, 250 West US Highway 12
Burns Harbor, IN 46304

ASSOCIATION FOR IRON AND STEEL TECHNOLOGY MIDWEST CHAPTER JACK GILL SCHOLARSHIP

Scholarship for a graduating high school senior, or undergraduate freshman, sophomore, or junior enrolled in a fully AIST-accredited college or university majoring engineering. Applicant must be in good academic standing. Must be a dependent of an AIST Midwest chapter member. May reapply each year for the duration of college education.

Academic Fields/Career Goals: Engineering/Technology.

Award: Scholarship for use in freshman, sophomore, junior, or senior years; not renewable. *Number:* 1. *Amount:* $3000.

Eligibility Requirements: Applicant must be enrolled or expecting to enroll full-time at a four-year institution or university. Applicant or parent of applicant must be member of Association for Iron and Steel Technology. Available to U.S. and non-U.S. citizens.

Application Requirements: Application, essay, resume, references, test scores, transcript. *Deadline:* March 15.

Contact: AIST Midwest Member Chapter Scholarships Chair
Association for Iron and Steel Technology
c/o Barry Felton, 250 West US Highway 12
Burns Harbor, IN 46304

ASSOCIATION FOR IRON AND STEEL TECHNOLOGY MIDWEST CHAPTER MEL NICKEL SCHOLARSHIP

Scholarship awarded to a graduating high school senior, or undergraduate freshman, sophomore or junior enrolled in a fully AIST-accredited college or university majoring engineering. Applicant must be in good academic standing. Must be a dependent of an AIST Midwest chapter member. May reapply each year for the term of their college education.

Academic Fields/Career Goals: Engineering/Technology.

Award: Scholarship for use in freshman, sophomore, junior, or senior years; not renewable. *Number:* 1. *Amount:* $3000.

Eligibility Requirements: Applicant must be enrolled or expecting to enroll full-time at a four-year institution or university. Applicant or parent of applicant must be member of Association for Iron and Steel Technology. Available to U.S. and non-U.S. citizens.

Application Requirements: Application, essay, resume, references, test scores, transcript. *Deadline:* March 15.

Contact: AIST Midwest Member Chapter Scholarships Chair
Association for Iron and Steel Technology
c/o Barry Felton, 250 West US Highway 12
Burns Harbor, IN 46304

ASSOCIATION FOR IRON AND STEEL TECHNOLOGY MIDWEST CHAPTER NON-ENGINEERING SCHOLARSHIP

Scholarship for graduating high school senior, or undergraduate freshman, sophomore, or junior enrolled in a fully AIST-accredited college or university. Applicant must be in good academic standing and dependent of an AIST Midwest chapter member. Recipients may reapply each year for the term of their college education.

Academic Fields/Career Goals: Engineering/Technology.

Award: Scholarship for use in freshman, sophomore, junior, or senior years; not renewable. *Number:* 3. *Amount:* $1500.

Eligibility Requirements: Applicant must be enrolled or expecting to enroll full-time at a four-year institution or university. Applicant or parent of applicant must be member of Association for Iron and Steel Technology. Available to U.S. and non-U.S. citizens.

Application Requirements: Application, essay, resume, references, test scores, transcript. *Deadline:* March 15.

Contact: AIST Midwest Member Chapter Scholarships Chair
Association for Iron and Steel Technology
c/o Barry Felton, 250 West US Highway 12
Burns Harbor, IN 46304

ASSOCIATION FOR IRON AND STEEL TECHNOLOGY MIDWEST CHAPTER WESTERN STATES SCHOLARSHIP

Scholarship of $3000 awarded to a graduating high school senior, or undergraduate freshman, sophomore, junior, or senior enrolled in a fully AIST-accredited college or university. Applicant must be in good academic standing and a dependant of an AIST Midwest chapter member. Recipients may reapply each year for the term of their college education.

Academic Fields/Career Goals: Engineering/Technology.

Award: Scholarship for use in freshman, sophomore, junior, or senior years; not renewable. *Number:* 1. *Amount:* $3000.

Eligibility Requirements: Applicant must be enrolled or expecting to enroll full-time at a four-year institution or university. Applicant or parent of applicant must be member of Association for Iron and Steel Technology. Available to U.S. and non-U.S. citizens.

Application Requirements: Application, essay, resume, references, test scores, transcript. *Deadline:* March 15.

Contact: AIST Midwest Member Chapter Scholarships Chair
Association for Iron and Steel Technology
c/o Barry Felton, 250 West US Highway 12
Burns Harbor, IN 46304

ASSOCIATION FOR IRON AND STEEL TECHNOLOGY NORTHWEST MEMBER CHAPTER SCHOLARSHIP

Scholarships of $1000 available to encourage a Pacific Northwest area student to prepare for a career in engineering. Must be the child, grandchild, spouse, or niece/nephew of a member in good standing of the AIST Northwest Chapter. Award based on academic achievements in chemistry, mathematics, and physics.

Academic Fields/Career Goals: Engineering/Technology; Materials Science, Engineering, and Metallurgy.

Award: Scholarship for use in freshman, sophomore, junior, or senior years; not renewable. *Number:* 2. *Amount:* $1000.

Eligibility Requirements: Applicant must be enrolled or expecting to enroll full- or part-time at a four-year institution or university. Applicant or parent of applicant must be member of Association for Iron and Steel Technology. Available to U.S. citizens.

Application Requirements: Application, essay, resume, references, test scores, transcript. *Deadline:* April 30.

Contact: Gerardo L. Giraldo, AIST Northwest Chapter Secretary
Association for Iron and Steel Technology
2434 Eyres Place West
Seattle, WA 98199
Phone: 206-285-7897
E-mail: acero9938@comcast.net

ASSOCIATION FOR IRON AND STEEL TECHNOLOGY OHIO VALLEY CHAPTER SCHOLARSHIP

• *See page 130*

ASSOCIATION FOR IRON AND STEEL TECHNOLOGY PITTSBURGH CHAPTER SCHOLARSHIP

Scholarships of $2500 for children, stepchildren, grandchildren, or spouse of a member in good standing of the Pittsburgh Chapter. Applicant must be a high school senior or currently enrolled undergraduate preparing for a career in engineering or metallurgy.

Academic Fields/Career Goals: Engineering/Technology; Materials Science, Engineering, and Metallurgy.

Award: Scholarship for use in freshman, sophomore, junior, or senior years; not renewable. *Number:* 2–3. *Amount:* $2500.

Eligibility Requirements: Applicant must be enrolled or expecting to enroll full-time at a four-year institution or university. Applicant or parent of applicant must be member of Association for Iron and Steel Technology. Available to U.S. citizens.

Application Requirements: Application, essay, resume, references, test scores, transcript. *Deadline:* April 30.

Contact: Daniel J. Kos, Program Coordinator
Association for Iron and Steel Technology
375 Saxonburg Boulevard
Saxonburg, PA 16056
E-mail: dkos@ii-vi.com

ASSOCIATION FOR IRON AND STEEL TECHNOLOGY SOUTHEAST MEMBER CHAPTER SCHOLARSHIP

Scholarship of $3000 for children, stepchildren, grandchildren, or spouse of active Southeast Chapter members who are pursuing a career in engineering, the sciences, or other majors relating to iron and steel production. Students may reapply for the scholarship each year for their term of college.

Academic Fields/Career Goals: Engineering/Technology; Materials Science, Engineering, and Metallurgy.

Award: Scholarship for use in freshman, sophomore, junior, or senior years; renewable. *Number:* 1. *Amount:* $3000.

Eligibility Requirements: Applicant must be enrolled or expecting to enroll full- or part-time at a four-year institution or university. Applicant or parent of applicant must be member of Association for Iron and Steel Technology. Available to U.S. citizens.

Application Requirements: Application, essay, resume, references, test scores, transcript. *Deadline:* April 30.

Contact: Mike Hutson, AIST Southeast Chapter Secretary
Association for Iron and Steel Technology
803 Floyd Street
Kings Mountain, NC 29086
Phone: 704-730-8320
Fax: 704-730-8321
E-mail: mike@johnhutsoncompany.com

ASSOCIATION FOR WOMEN IN SCIENCE EDUCATIONAL FOUNDATION http://www.awis.org/careers/edfoundation.html

ASSOCIATION FOR WOMEN IN SCIENCE COLLEGE SCHOLARSHIP

• *See page 82*

ASSOCIATION OF ENGINEERING GEOLOGISTS http://www.aegfoundation.org

MARLIAVE FUND

• *See page 216*

ASSOCIATION OF IRON AND STEEL ENGINEERS http://www.aist.org

AIST DAVID H. SAMSON CANADIAN SCHOLARSHIP

Scholarship for children of AIST members who are Canadian citizens. The student must be accepted in an eligible full-time course studying engineering at an accredited Canadian university or college.

Academic Fields/Career Goals: Engineering/Technology.

Award: Scholarship for use in freshman, sophomore, junior, or senior years; renewable. *Number:* 1. *Amount:* $2000.

Eligibility Requirements: Applicant must be of Canadian heritage and enrolled or expecting to enroll full-time at a four-year institution or university. Applicant must have 3.0 GPA or higher. Available to Canadian citizens.

Application Requirements: Application, essay, resume, references, transcript. *Deadline:* June 30.

Contact: Ms. Lori Wharrey, Board Administrator
Association of Iron and Steel Engineers
186 Thorn Hill Road
Warrendale, PA 15086-7528
Phone: 724-776-6040 Ext. 621
Fax: 724-776-1880
E-mail: lwharrey@aist.org

AIST WILLY KORF MEMORIAL FUND

Scholarships granted to full-time undergraduate students with a genuine demonstrated interest in a career in the iron and steel industry and majoring in the field of engineering, metallurgy or materials science at an accredited U.S. college or university.

Academic Fields/Career Goals: Engineering/Technology; Materials Science, Engineering, and Metallurgy.

Award: Scholarship for use in sophomore, junior, or senior years; renewable. *Number:* 3. *Amount:* $3000.

Eligibility Requirements: Applicant must be enrolled or expecting to enroll full-time at a four-year institution or university. Applicant must have 3.0 GPA or higher. Available to U.S. and Canadian citizens.

Application Requirements: Application, essay, resume, references, transcript. *Deadline:* March 2.

Contact: Ms. Lori Wharrey, Board Administrator
Association of Iron and Steel Engineers
186 Thorn Hill Road
Warrendale, PA 15086-7528
Phone: 724-776-6040 Ext. 621
Fax: 724-776-1880
E-mail: lwharrey@aist.org

AUTOMOTIVE HALL OF FAME http://www.automotivehalloffame.org

AUTOMOTIVE HALL OF FAME EDUCATIONAL FUNDS

• *See page 290*

BARRY M. GOLDWATER SCHOLARSHIP AND EXCELLENCE IN EDUCATION FOUNDATION http://www.act.org/goldwater

BARRY M. GOLDWATER SCHOLARSHIP AND EXCELLENCE IN EDUCATION PROGRAM

• *See page 86*

BOYS AND GIRLS CLUBS OF GREATER SAN DIEGO http://www.sdyouth.org

SPENCE REESE SCHOLARSHIP FUND

Renewable scholarship for graduating male high school seniors in the United States for study of law, medicine, engineering, and political science. Minimum 2.5 GPA required. Awarded based on academic ability, financial need, and character. Required to attend a personal interview in San Diego, California. Travel expenses for the interview will be reimbursed by the scholarship foundation. Application fee: $10.

Academic Fields/Career Goals: Engineering/Technology; Health and Medical Sciences; Law/Legal Services; Political Science.

Award: Scholarship for use in freshman year; renewable. *Number:* up to 4. *Amount:* up to $2000.

Eligibility Requirements: Applicant must be high school student; planning to enroll or expecting to enroll full-time at a four-year institution or university and male. Applicant must have 2.5 GPA or higher. Available to U.S. citizens.

Application Requirements: Application, financial need analysis, interview, self-addressed stamped envelope, test scores, transcript. *Fee:* $10. *Deadline:* April 15.

Contact: Jean Pilley, Scholarship Coordinator
Boys and Girls Clubs of Greater San Diego
4635 Clairemont Mesa Boulevard
San Diego, CA 92117
Phone: 619-298-3520
Fax: 619-298-3615
E-mail: bgcsandiego@yahoo.com

BUSINESS AND PROFESSIONAL WOMEN'S FOUNDATION http://www.bpwfoundation.org

BPW CAREER ADVANCEMENT SCHOLARSHIP PROGRAM FOR WOMEN

• *See page 130*

CATCHING THE DREAM http://www.catchingthedream.org

MATH, ENGINEERING, SCIENCE, BUSINESS, EDUCATION, COMPUTERS SCHOLARSHIPS

• *See page 139*

CLEVELAND SCHOLARSHIP PROGRAMS http://www.cspohio.org

CSP MANAGED FUNDS-CLEVELAND BROWNS MARION MOTLEY SCHOLARSHIP

• *See page 49*

COLLEGEBOUND FOUNDATION http://www.collegeboundfoundation.org

DR. FREEMAN A. HRABOWSKI, III SCHOLARSHIP

Scholarship for students who major in the field of mathematics and/or science/technology. Must have a GPA of at least 3.0 and a competitive SAT (critical reading and math) score. Preference will be given to students who will attend a Maryland university.

Academic Fields/Career Goals: Engineering/Technology; Mathematics.

Award: Scholarship for use in freshman, sophomore, junior, or senior years; renewable. *Number:* 1. *Amount:* $1500.

Eligibility Requirements: Applicant must be high school student; planning to enroll or expecting to enroll full-time at a four-year institution or university and resident of Maryland. Applicant must have 3.0 GPA or higher. Available to U.S. citizens.

Application Requirements: Application, financial need analysis, resume, references, test scores, transcript. *Deadline:* March 1.

Contact: Jamie Crouse, Scholarship Program Administrator
CollegeBound Foundation
300 Water Street, Suite 300
Baltimore, MD 21202
Phone: 410-783-2905 Ext. 207
Fax: 410-727-5786
E-mail: jcrouse@collegeboundfoundation.org

GEORGE V. MCGOWAN SCHOLARSHIP

Scholarship for students majoring in engineering at Bowie State University, Coppin State University, Frostburg State University, Morgan State University, St. Mary's College of Maryland, Towson University, University of Maryland College Park, University of Maryland Eastern Shore, or Villa Julie College. Must have a GPA of 3.0 or better, and an SAT (critical reading and math) score of 1000.

Academic Fields/Career Goals: Engineering/Technology.

Award: Scholarship for use in freshman year; renewable. *Number:* 1. *Amount:* $1500.

Eligibility Requirements: Applicant must be high school student; planning to enroll or expecting to enroll full-time at a two-year or four-year institution or university; resident of Maryland and studying in Maryland. Applicant must have 3.0 GPA or higher. Available to U.S. citizens.

Application Requirements: Application, financial need analysis, references, test scores, transcript. *Deadline:* March 1.

Contact: Jamie Crouse, Scholarship Program Administrator
CollegeBound Foundation
300 Water Street, Suite 300
Baltimore, MD 21202
Phone: 410-783-2905 Ext. 207
Fax: 410-727-5786
E-mail: jcrouse@collegeboundfoundation.org

COMMUNITY FOUNDATION FOR GREATER ATLANTA INC. http://www.atlcf.org

TECH HIGH SCHOOL ALUMNI ASSOCIATION/W.O. CHENEY MERIT SCHOLARSHIP FUND

Scholarship for students pursuing degrees in Mathematics, Engineering, or one of the Physical Sciences. Cumulative high school GPA of 3.7 or higher or in upper 10 percent of graduating class. SAT (math and critical reading) of at least 1300. For complete eligibility requirements and application, visit www.atlcf.org

Academic Fields/Career Goals: Engineering/Technology; Mathematics; Physical Sciences and Math.

Award: Scholarship for use in freshman, sophomore, junior, or senior years; renewable. *Number:* 1–4. *Amount:* up to $5000.

Eligibility Requirements: Applicant must be high school student; planning to enroll or expecting to enroll full-time at a four-year institution or university and resident of Georgia. Available to U.S. citizens.

Application Requirements: Application, essay, financial need analysis, references. *Deadline:* March 26.

Contact: Kristina Morris, Program Associate
Community Foundation for Greater Atlanta Inc.
50 Hurt Plaza, Suite 449
Atlanta, GA 30303
Phone: 404-688-5525
Fax: 404-688-3060
E-mail: scholarships@atlcf.org

COMMUNITY FOUNDATION OF WESTERN MASSACHUSETTS http://www.communityfoundation.org

JAMES L. SHRIVER SCHOLARSHIP

• *See page 290*

CUBAN AMERICAN NATIONAL FOUNDATION http://www.masscholarships.org

MAS FAMILY SCHOLARSHIPS

• *See page 139*

DAYTON FOUNDATION http://www.daytonfoundation.org

R.C. APPENZELLER FAMILY ENDOWMENT FUND

Renewable scholarships to students pursuing a career in engineering at an accredited college or university.

Academic Fields/Career Goals: Engineering/Technology.

Award: Scholarship for use in freshman, sophomore, junior, or senior years; renewable. *Number:* 10–12. *Amount:* up to $1000.

Eligibility Requirements: Applicant must be enrolled or expecting to enroll full-time at a two-year or four-year institution or university. Available to U.S. citizens.

Application Requirements: Application, financial need analysis, references, transcript. *Deadline:* March 28.

Contact: Diane Timmons, Vice President, Grants and Programs
Dayton Foundation
2300 Kettering Tower
Dayton, OH 45423
Phone: 937-225-9966
E-mail: dtimmons@daytonfoundation.org

DENVER FOUNDATION http://www.denverfoundation.org

RBC DAIN RAUSCHER COLORADO SCHOLARSHIP FUND

Scholarships for undergraduate education to outstanding Colorado high school seniors. Five $5000 scholarships will be awarded to students intending to pursue a degree in science or engineering. Must have at least a 3.75 cumulative GPA. Students who have a parent, step-parent, grandparent, aunt, or uncle who is employed by RBC Dain Rauscher are not eligible to apply.

Academic Fields/Career Goals: Engineering/Technology; Science, Technology, and Society.

Award: Scholarship for use in freshman year; not renewable. *Number:* 5. *Amount:* $5000.

Eligibility Requirements: Applicant must be high school student; planning to enroll or expecting to enroll full-time at a four-year institution or university and studying in Colorado. Available to U.S. citizens.

Application Requirements: Application, test scores, transcript. *Deadline:* April 4.

Contact: Karla Bieniulis, Scholarship Committee
Denver Foundation
55 Madison Street, Eighth Floor
Denver, CO 80206
Phone: 303-300-1790 Ext. 103
Fax: 303-300-6547
E-mail: info@denverfoundation.org

DEVRY INC. http://www.devry.edu

CISCO NETWORKING ACADEMY SCHOLARSHIP

• *See page 191*

EAA AVIATION FOUNDATION INC. http://www.eaa.org

PAYZER SCHOLARSHIP

• *See page 116*

ELECTROCHEMICAL SOCIETY INC. http://www.electrochem.org

H.H. DOW MEMORIAL STUDENT ACHIEVEMENT AWARD OF THE INDUSTRIAL ELECTROLYSIS AND ELECTROCHEMICAL ENGINEERING DIVISION OF THE ELECTROCHEMICAL SOCIETY INC.

• *See page 131*

STUDENT ACHIEVEMENT AWARDS OF THE INDUSTRIAL ELECTROLYSIS AND ELECTROCHEMICAL ENGINEERING DIVISION OF THE ELECTROCHEMICAL SOCIETY INC.

• *See page 131*

STUDENT RESEARCH AWARDS OF THE BATTERY DIVISION OF THE ELECTROCHEMICAL SOCIETY INC.

• *See page 131*

ELECTRONIC DOCUMENT SYSTEMS FOUNDATION http://www.edsf.org

ELECTRONIC DOCUMENT SYSTEMS FOUNDATION SCHOLARSHIP AWARDS

• *See page 178*

ENGINEERS FOUNDATION OF OHIO http://www.ohioengineer.com

ENGINEERS FOUNDATION OF OHIO GENERAL FUND SCHOLARSHIP

Applicant must be a college junior or senior at the end of the academic year in which the application is submitted. Must be enrolled full-time at an Ohio college or university in a curriculum leading to a BS degree in engineering or its equivalent. Minimum GPA of 3.0 required. Must be a U.S. citizen and permanent resident of Ohio.

Academic Fields/Career Goals: Engineering/Technology.

Award: Scholarship for use in junior or senior years; not renewable. *Number:* 1. *Amount:* $1000.

Eligibility Requirements: Applicant must be enrolled or expecting to enroll full-time at a four-year institution or university; resident of Ohio and studying in Ohio. Applicant must have 3.0 GPA or higher. Available to U.S. citizens.

Application Requirements: Application, test scores. *Deadline:* varies.

Contact: Pam McClure, Manager of Administration
Engineers Foundation of Ohio
400 South Fifth Street, Suite 300
Columbus, OH 43215
Phone: 614-223-1177
Fax: 614-223-1131
E-mail: efo@ohioengineer.com

LLOYD A. CHACEY, PE-OHIO SOCIETY OF PROFESSIONAL ENGINEERS MEMORIAL SCHOLARSHIP

Scholarship available for a son, daughter, brother, sister, niece, nephew, spouse or grandchild of a current member of the Ohio Society of Professional Engineers, or of a deceased member who was in good standing at the time of his or her death. Must be enrolled full-time at an Ohio college or university in a curriculum leading to a degree in engineering or its equivalent. Must have a minimum of 3.0 GPA. Must be a U.S. citizen and permanent resident of Ohio.

Academic Fields/Career Goals: Engineering/Technology.

Award: Scholarship for use in junior or senior years; renewable. *Number:* 1. *Amount:* $2000.

Eligibility Requirements: Applicant must be enrolled or expecting to enroll full-time at a four-year institution or university and resident of Ohio. Applicant must have 3.0 GPA or higher. Available to U.S. citizens.

Application Requirements: Application, financial need analysis, test scores, transcript. *Deadline:* varies.

Contact: Pam McClure, Manager of Administration
Engineers Foundation of Ohio
400 South Fifth Street, Suite 300
Columbus, OH 43215
Phone: 614-223-1177
Fax: 614-223-1131
E-mail: efo@ohioengineer.com

RAYMOND H. FULLER, PE MEMORIAL SCHOLARSHIP

Scholarship of $1000 to graduating high school seniors. Recipients must be accepted for enrollment in an engineering program at an Ohio college or university. Must have a minimum of 3.0 GPA. Must be a U.S. citizen and permanent resident of Ohio. Consideration will be given to the prospective recipient's academic achievement, interest in a career in engineering and financial need as determined by interviews and from references.

Academic Fields/Career Goals: Engineering/Technology.

Award: Scholarship for use in freshman year; not renewable. *Number:* 1. *Amount:* $1000.

Eligibility Requirements: Applicant must be high school student; planning to enroll or expecting to enroll full-time at a four-year institution or university; resident of Ohio and studying in Ohio. Applicant must have 3.0 GPA or higher. Available to U.S. citizens.

Engineers Foundation of Ohio (continued)

Application Requirements: Application, financial need analysis, interview, references, test scores. *Deadline:* varies.

Contact: Pam McClure, Manager of Administration
Engineers Foundation of Ohio
400 South Fifth Street, Suite 300
Columbus, OH 43215
Phone: 614-223-1177
Fax: 614-223-1131
E-mail: efo@ohioengineer.com

FLORIDA ENGINEERING SOCIETY http://www.fleng.org

ACEC/FLORIDA SCHOLARSHIP

One-time scholarship of $1000 given to Florida citizen pursuing a bachelor's degree in an ABET-approved engineering program or in an accredited land surveying program. Students must be entering their junior, senior, or fifth year of college.

Academic Fields/Career Goals: Engineering/Technology; Surveying; Surveying Technology, Cartography, or Geographic Information Science.

Award: Scholarship for use in junior, senior, or graduate years; not renewable. *Number:* 1. *Amount:* $1000.

Eligibility Requirements: Applicant must be enrolled or expecting to enroll full-time at a four-year institution or university; resident of Florida and studying in Florida. Available to U.S. citizens.

Application Requirements: Application, essay, test scores, transcript. *Deadline:* October 13.

Contact: Scholarship Coordinator
Florida Engineering Society
125 South Gadsden Street
PO Box 750
Tallahassee, FL 32301
Phone: 850-224-7121
Fax: 850-222-4349
E-mail: fes@fleng.org

DAVID F. LUDOVICI SCHOLARSHIP

• *See page 170*

ERIC PRIMAVERA MEMORIAL SCHOLARSHIP

One-time scholarship of $1000 given to students in their junior or senior year in a Florida university engineering program. Minimum 3.0 GPA required.

Academic Fields/Career Goals: Engineering/Technology.

Award: Scholarship for use in junior or senior years; not renewable. *Number:* 1. *Amount:* $1000.

Eligibility Requirements: Applicant must be enrolled or expecting to enroll full-time at an institution or university; resident of Florida and studying in Florida. Applicant must have 3.0 GPA or higher. Available to U.S. citizens.

Application Requirements: Application, references, self-addressed stamped envelope, transcript. *Deadline:* February 1.

Contact: Scholarship Coordinator
Florida Engineering Society
125 South Gadsden Street
PO Box 750
Tallahassee, FL 32301
Phone: 850-224-7121
Fax: 850-222-4349
E-mail: fes@fleng.org

HIGH SCHOOL SCHOLARSHIP

One-time scholarship of $2000 given to high school seniors who are residents of Florida. Minimum 3.5 GPA required. Applicant must have genuine interest in engineering.

Academic Fields/Career Goals: Engineering/Technology.

Award: Scholarship for use in freshman year; not renewable. *Number:* 6. *Amount:* $2000.

Eligibility Requirements: Applicant must be high school student; planning to enroll or expecting to enroll full-time at a four-year institution or university and resident of Florida. Applicant must have 3.5 GPA or higher. Available to U.S. citizens.

Application Requirements: Application, test scores, transcript, IB and AP exam results. *Deadline:* February 1.

Contact: Scholarship Coordinator
Florida Engineering Society
125 South Gadsden Street
PO Box 750
Tallahassee, FL 32301
Phone: 850-224-7121
Fax: 850-222-4349
E-mail: fes@fleng.org

RAYMOND W. MILLER, PE SCHOLARSHIP

One-time scholarship of $2000 given to students in their junior or senior year in a Florida university engineering program. Minimum 3.0 GPA required.

Academic Fields/Career Goals: Engineering/Technology.

Award: Scholarship for use in junior or senior years; not renewable. *Number:* 1. *Amount:* $2000.

Eligibility Requirements: Applicant must be enrolled or expecting to enroll full-time at an institution or university; resident of Florida and studying in Florida. Applicant must have 3.0 GPA or higher. Available to U.S. citizens.

Application Requirements: Application, references, self-addressed stamped envelope, transcript. *Deadline:* February 1.

Contact: Scholarship Coordinator
Florida Engineering Society
125 South Gadsden Street
PO Box 750
Tallahassee, FL 32301
Phone: 850-224-7121
Fax: 850-222-4349
E-mail: fes@fleng.org

RICHARD B. GASSETT, PE SCHOLARSHIP

One-time scholarship of $2000 given to students in their junior or senior year in a Florida university engineering program. Minimum 3.0 GPA required.

Academic Fields/Career Goals: Engineering/Technology.

Award: Scholarship for use in junior or senior years; not renewable. *Number:* 1. *Amount:* $2000.

Eligibility Requirements: Applicant must be enrolled or expecting to enroll full-time at an institution or university; resident of Florida and studying in Florida. Applicant must have 3.0 GPA or higher. Available to U.S. citizens.

Application Requirements: Application, references, self-addressed stamped envelope, transcript. *Deadline:* February 1.

Contact: Scholarship Coordinator
Florida Engineering Society
125 South Gadsden Street
PO Box 750
Tallahassee, FL 32301
Phone: 850-224-7121
Fax: 850-222-4349
E-mail: fes@fleng.org

FOUNDATION FOR SCIENCE AND DISABILITY http://www.stemd.org

GRANTS FOR DISABLED STUDENTS IN THE SCIENCES

• *See page 87*

GEORGIA ENGINEERING FOUNDATION/GEORGIA SOCIETY OF PROFESSIONAL ENGINEERS http://www.gefinc.org

GEORGIA ENGINEERING FOUNDATION SCHOLARSHIP PROGRAM

Awards scholarships to students who are preparing for a career in engineering or engineering technology. Must be U.S. citizens and legal residents of Georgia. Must be attending or accepted in an ABET-accredited program. Separate applications are available: one for use by high school seniors and new college freshman; and one for use by college upperclassman.

Academic Fields/Career Goals: Engineering/Technology.

Award: Scholarship for use in freshman year; not renewable. *Number:* 45. *Amount:* $1000–$5000.

Eligibility Requirements: Applicant must be enrolled or expecting to enroll full-time at a four-year institution or university and resident of Georgia. Applicant or parent of applicant must have employment or volunteer experience in community service. Available to U.S. citizens.

Application Requirements: Application, photo, references, transcript. *Deadline:* August 31.

Contact: Roseana Richards, Scholarship Committee
Georgia Engineering Foundation/Georgia Society of Professional Engineers
233 Peachtree Street, Suite 700, Harris Tower
Atlanta, GA 30303
Phone: 404-521-2324
E-mail: richardsr@pondco.com

GOLDEN KEY INTERNATIONAL HONOUR SOCIETY http://www.goldenkey.org

ENGINEERING/TECHNOLOGY ACHIEVEMENT AWARD

Award to members who excel in the study of engineering or technology. Applicants will be asked to respond to a problem posed by an honorary member within the discipline. One winner will receive a $1000 award. The second place winner will receive $750 and the third place winner will receive $500.

Academic Fields/Career Goals: Engineering/Technology.

Award: Prize for use in freshman, sophomore, junior, senior, graduate, or postgraduate years; not renewable. *Number:* 3. *Amount:* $500–$1000.

Eligibility Requirements: Applicant must be enrolled or expecting to enroll full- or part-time at a four-year institution or university. Available to U.S. and non-U.S. citizens.

Application Requirements: Application, applicant must enter a contest, essay, references, transcript, engineering-related report, cover page from the online registration. *Deadline:* March 3.

Contact: Scholarship Program Administrators
Golden Key International Honour Society
PO Box 23737
Nashville, TN 37202-3737
Phone: 800-377-2401
E-mail: scholarships@goldenkey.org

FORD MOTOR COMPANY ENGINEERING AND LEADERSHIP SCHOLARSHIP

The scholarship provides opportunities for engineering majors and helps to further the interests of one of the society's key partners, Ford Motor Company. One award of $10,000 provided each year.

Academic Fields/Career Goals: Engineering/Technology.

Award: Scholarship for use in freshman, sophomore, junior, or senior years; not renewable. *Number:* 1. *Amount:* $10,000.

Eligibility Requirements: Applicant must be enrolled or expecting to enroll full-time at a four-year institution or university. Applicant or parent of applicant must be member of Golden Key National Honor Society. Applicant must have 3.5 GPA or higher. Available to U.S. and non-U.S. citizens.

Application Requirements: Application, essay, resume, transcript. *Deadline:* March 1.

Contact: Scholarship Program Administrators
Golden Key International Honour Society
PO Box 23737
Nashville, TN 37202
Phone: 800-377-2401

GREATER KANAWHA VALLEY FOUNDATION http://www.tgkvf.org

MATH AND SCIENCE SCHOLARSHIP

• *See page 132*

HAWAIIAN LODGE, F & AM http://www.glhawaii.org/

HAWAIIAN LODGE SCHOLARSHIPS

• *See page 96*

HELLENIC UNIVERSITY CLUB OF PHILADELPHIA http://www.hucphila.org

DIMITRI J. VERVERELLI MEMORIAL SCHOLARSHIP FOR ARCHITECTURE AND/OR ENGINEERING

• *See page 91*

HISPANIC COLLEGE FUND INC. http://www.hispanicfund.org

DEPARTMENT OF ENERGY SCHOLARSHIP PROGRAM

• *See page 142*

ICI EDUCATIONAL FOUNDATION SCHOLARSHIP PROGRAM

• *See page 142*

LOCKHEED MARTIN SCHOLARSHIP PROGRAM

• *See page 143*

HISPANIC ENGINEER NATIONAL ACHIEVEMENT AWARDS CORPORATION (HENAAC) http://www.henaac.org

HISPANIC ENGINEER NATIONAL ACHIEVEMENT AWARDS CORPORATION SCHOLARSHIP PROGRAM

• *See page 116*

HISPANIC SCHOLARSHIP FUND http://www.hsf.net

HSF/GENERAL MOTORS SCHOLARSHIP

• *See page 143*

HSF/MARATHON OIL CORPORATION COLLEGE SCHOLARSHIP

• *See page 55*

HSF/NISSAN COMMUNITY COLLEGE TRANSFER SCHOLARSHIP PROGRAM

• *See page 143*

HSF/WELLS FARGO SCHOLARSHIP PROGRAM

• *See page 55*

IDAHO STATE BROADCASTERS ASSOCIATION http://www.idahobroadcasters.org

WAYNE C. CORNILS MEMORIAL SCHOLARSHIP

• *See page 143*

ILLINOIS SOCIETY OF PROFESSIONAL ENGINEERS http://www.illinoisengineer.com

ILLINOIS SOCIETY OF PROFESSIONAL ENGINEERS ADVANTAGE AWARD/FOUNDATION SCHOLARSHIP

Applicant must be son or daughter of ISPE member in good standing and attend an Illinois university approved by the Accreditation Board of Engineering. Applicant must be at least a junior at the approved university. Required essay must address why applicant wishes to become a professional engineer. Must have a "B" average.

Academic Fields/Career Goals: Engineering/Technology.

Award: Scholarship for use in junior or senior years; not renewable. *Number:* 1. *Amount:* $1200.

Eligibility Requirements: Applicant must be enrolled or expecting to enroll full-time at a four-year institution and studying in Illinois. Available to U.S. and non-U.S. citizens.

Illinois Society of Professional Engineers (continued)

Application Requirements: Application, essay, references, transcript. *Deadline:* January 31.

Contact: Chris Baker, Member Services Coordinator
Illinois Society of Professional Engineers
600 South Second Street, Suite 403
Springfield, IL 62704
Phone: 217-544-7424
Fax: 217-528-6545
E-mail: chrisbaker@illinoisengineer.com

ILLINOIS SOCIETY OF PROFESSIONAL ENGINEERS/MELVIN E. AMSTUTZ MEMORIAL AWARD

Applicant must attend an Illinois university approved by the Accreditation Board of Engineering. Applicant must be at least a junior in university he or she attends, and must prove financial need. Essay must address why applicant wishes to become a professional engineer. Must have a "B" average.

Academic Fields/Career Goals: Engineering/Technology.

Award: Scholarship for use in junior or senior years; not renewable. *Number:* 1. *Amount:* $1500.

Eligibility Requirements: Applicant must be enrolled or expecting to enroll full-time at a four-year institution and studying in Illinois. Available to U.S. and non-U.S. citizens.

Application Requirements: Application, essay, financial need analysis, references. *Deadline:* January 31.

Contact: Chris Baker, Member Services Coordinator
Illinois Society of Professional Engineers
600 South Second Street, Suite 403
Springfield, IL 62704
Phone: 217-544-7424
Fax: 217-528-6545
E-mail: chrisbaker@illinoisengineer.com

ILLUMINATING ENGINEERING SOCIETY OF NORTH AMERICA http://www.iesna.org

ROBERT W. THUNEN MEMORIAL SCHOLARSHIPS

• *See page 91*

INDEPENDENT LABORATORIES INSTITUTE SCHOLARSHIP ALLIANCE http://www.acil.org

INDEPENDENT LABORATORIES INSTITUTE SCHOLARSHIP ALLIANCE

• *See page 132*

INDIANA SOCIETY OF PROFESSIONAL ENGINEERS http://www.indspe.org

INDIANA ENGINEERING SCHOLARSHIP

Award for Indiana resident who attends an Indiana educational institution, or commutes daily to a school outside Indiana. Applicant must have accrued the minimum of one-half the credits required for an undergraduate ABET-accredited engineering degree. For details and an application visit Web site: http://indspe.org.

Academic Fields/Career Goals: Engineering/Technology.

Award: Scholarship for use in freshman, sophomore, junior, or senior years; not renewable. *Number:* 3. *Amount:* $750.

Eligibility Requirements: Applicant must be enrolled or expecting to enroll full-time at an institution or university; resident of Indiana and studying in Indiana. Available to U.S. citizens.

Application Requirements: Application, interview, references, transcript. *Deadline:* May 1.

Contact: Scholarship Coordinator
Indiana Society of Professional Engineers
PO Box 20806
Indianapolis, IN 46220
Phone: 317-255-2267
Fax: 317-255-2530
E-mail: lhowe@indy.net

INSTITUTE OF ENVIRONMENTAL SCIENCES AND TECHNOLOGY (IEST) http://www.iest.org

EUGENE BORSON SCHOLARSHIP

• *See page 291*

ROBERT N. HANCOCK MEMORIAL SCHOLARSHIP

• *See page 132*

INSTITUTE OF INDUSTRIAL ENGINEERS http://www.iienet.org

A.O. PUTNAM MEMORIAL SCHOLARSHIP

One-time award for industrial engineering undergraduates at four-year accredited institutions. Applicants must be members of the Institute of Industrial Engineers, have a 3.4 GPA, and be nominated by a department head. Priority given to students who have demonstrated an interest in management consulting.

Academic Fields/Career Goals: Engineering/Technology.

Award: Scholarship for use in freshman, sophomore, junior, or senior years; not renewable. *Number:* 1. *Amount:* up to $600.

Eligibility Requirements: Applicant must be enrolled or expecting to enroll full-time at a four-year institution or university. Applicant or parent of applicant must be member of Institute of Industrial Engineers. Available to U.S. and non-U.S. citizens.

Application Requirements: Application, references, transcript, nomination. *Deadline:* November 15.

Contact: Bonnie Cameron, Operations Administrator
Institute of Industrial Engineers
3577 Parkway Lane, Suite 200
Norcross, GA 30092-2988
Phone: 770-449-0461 Ext. 105
Fax: 770-263-8532
E-mail: bcameron@iienet.org

C.B. GAMBRELL UNDERGRADUATE SCHOLARSHIP

One-time award of $600 for undergraduate industrial engineering students who are U.S. citizens graduated from a U.S. high school with a class standing above freshman level in an ABET-accredited IE program. Must be a member of Industrial Engineers, have a minimum GPA of 3.4, and be nominated by a department head.

Academic Fields/Career Goals: Engineering/Technology.

Award: Scholarship for use in sophomore, junior, or senior years; not renewable. *Number:* up to 1. *Amount:* $600.

Eligibility Requirements: Applicant must be enrolled or expecting to enroll full-time at a four-year institution or university. Applicant or parent of applicant must be member of Institute of Industrial Engineers. Available to U.S. citizens.

Application Requirements: Application, references, nomination. *Deadline:* November 15.

Contact: Bonnie Cameron, Operations Administrator
Institute of Industrial Engineers
3577 Parkway Lane, Suite 200
Norcross, GA 30092-2988
Phone: 770-449-0461 Ext. 105
Fax: 770-263-8532
E-mail: bcameron@iienet.org

DWIGHT D. GARDNER SCHOLARSHIP

Scholarship available to undergraduate students enrolled in an industrial engineering program in any school in the United States and its territories, Canada, and Mexico, provided the school's engineering program or equivalent is accredited by an agency recognized by IIE. Must be an IIE member. Minimum 3.4 GPA required. Must be nominated by department head.

Academic Fields/Career Goals: Engineering/Technology.

Award: Scholarship for use in freshman, sophomore, junior, or senior years; not renewable. *Number:* up to 2. *Amount:* up to $1000.

Eligibility Requirements: Applicant must be enrolled or expecting to enroll full-time at a four-year institution or university. Applicant or parent of applicant must be member of Institute of Industrial Engineers. Available to U.S. and non-U.S. citizens.

Application Requirements: Application, essay, financial need analysis, references, transcript, nomination. *Deadline:* November 15.

Contact: Bonnie Cameron, Operations Administrator
Institute of Industrial Engineers
3577 Parkway Lane, Suite 200
Norcross, GA 30092-2988
Phone: 770-449-0461 Ext. 105
Fax: 770-263-8532
E-mail: bcameron@iienet.org

IIE COUNCIL OF FELLOWS UNDERGRADUATE SCHOLARSHIP

Awards to undergraduate students enrolled in any school in the United States and its territories, Canada and Mexico, provided the school's engineering program or equivalent is accredited by an agency recognized by IIE and the student is pursuing a course of study in industrial engineering. Must be IIE member and have minimum 3.4 GPA. Write to IIE Headquarters to obtain application form.

Academic Fields/Career Goals: Engineering/Technology.

Award: Scholarship for use in freshman, sophomore, junior, or senior years; not renewable. *Number:* varies. *Amount:* up to $1000.

Eligibility Requirements: Applicant must be enrolled or expecting to enroll full-time at a four-year institution or university. Applicant or parent of applicant must be member of Institute of Industrial Engineers. Available to U.S. and non-U.S. citizens.

Application Requirements: Application. *Deadline:* November 15.

Contact: Bonnie Cameron, Operations Administrator
Institute of Industrial Engineers
3577 Parkway Lane, Suite 200
Norcross, GA 30092-2988
Phone: 770-449-0461 Ext. 105
Fax: 770-263-8532
E-mail: bcameron@iienet.org

LISA ZAKEN AWARD FOR EXCELLENCE

Award of $600 for undergraduate and graduate students enrolled in any school, and pursuing a course of study in industrial engineering. Award is intended to recognize excellence in scholarly activities and leadership related to the industrial engineering profession on campus.

Academic Fields/Career Goals: Engineering/Technology.

Award: Prize for use in freshman, sophomore, junior, senior, or graduate years; not renewable. *Number:* up to 1. *Amount:* $600.

Eligibility Requirements: Applicant must be enrolled or expecting to enroll full-time at a four-year institution or university. Applicant or parent of applicant must be member of Institute of Industrial Engineers. Applicant must have 3.0 GPA or higher. Available to U.S. and non-U.S. citizens.

Application Requirements: Application, essay, references, nomination form. *Deadline:* November 15.

Contact: Bonnie Cameron, Operations Administrator
Institute of Industrial Engineers
3577 Parkway Lane, Suite 200
Norcross, GA 30092-2988
Phone: 770-449-0461 Ext. 105
Fax: 770-263-8532
E-mail: bcameron@iienet.org

MARVIN MUNDEL MEMORIAL SCHOLARSHIP

Scholarship of $600 awarded to undergraduate students enrolled in any school in the United States, Canada, or Mexico with an accredited industrial engineering program. Priority given to students who have demonstrated an interest in work measurement and methods engineering. Must be active Institute members with 3.4 GPA or above. Must be nominated by department head or faculty adviser.

Academic Fields/Career Goals: Engineering/Technology.

Award: Scholarship for use in freshman, sophomore, junior, or senior years; not renewable. *Number:* up to 1. *Amount:* $600.

Eligibility Requirements: Applicant must be enrolled or expecting to enroll full-time at a four-year institution or university. Applicant or parent of applicant must be member of Institute of Industrial Engineers. Available to U.S. and non-U.S. citizens.

Application Requirements: Application, nomination. *Deadline:* November 15.

Contact: Bonnie Cameron, Operations Administrator
Institute of Industrial Engineers
3577 Parkway Lane, Suite 200
Norcross, GA 30092-2988
Phone: 770-449-0461 Ext. 105
Fax: 770-263-8532
E-mail: bcameron@iienet.org

UNITED PARCEL SERVICE SCHOLARSHIP FOR FEMALE STUDENTS

One-time award for female undergraduate students enrolled at any school in the United States, Canada, or Mexico in an industrial engineering program. Must be a member of Institute of Industrial Engineers, have a minimum GPA of 3.4, and be nominated by a department head.

Academic Fields/Career Goals: Engineering/Technology.

Award: Scholarship for use in freshman, sophomore, junior, or senior years; not renewable. *Number:* 1. *Amount:* up to $4000.

Eligibility Requirements: Applicant must be enrolled or expecting to enroll full-time at a four-year or technical institution or university and female. Applicant or parent of applicant must be member of Institute of Industrial Engineers. Available to U.S. and non-U.S. citizens.

Application Requirements: Application, references, transcript, nomination. *Deadline:* November 15.

Contact: Bonnie Cameron, Operations Administrator
Institute of Industrial Engineers
3577 Parkway Lane, Suite 200
Norcross, GA 30092-2988
Phone: 770-449-0461 Ext. 105
Fax: 770-263-8532
E-mail: bcameron@iienet.org

UPS SCHOLARSHIP FOR MINORITY STUDENTS

One-time award for minority undergraduate students enrolled at any school in the United States, Canada, or Mexico in an industrial engineering program. Must be a member of Institute of Industrial Engineers. Nominated students by IE department heads will be sent an application package to complete and return before November 15.

Academic Fields/Career Goals: Engineering/Technology.

Award: Scholarship for use in freshman, sophomore, junior, or senior years; not renewable. *Number:* 1. *Amount:* up to $4000.

Eligibility Requirements: Applicant must be American Indian/Alaska Native, Asian/Pacific Islander, Black (non-Hispanic), or Hispanic and enrolled or expecting to enroll full-time at a four-year or technical institution or university. Applicant or parent of applicant must be member of Institute of Industrial Engineers. Applicant must have 3.0 GPA or higher. Available to U.S. and non-U.S. citizens.

Application Requirements: Application, references, transcript, nomination. *Deadline:* November 15.

Contact: Bonnie Cameron, Operations Administrator
Institute of Industrial Engineers
3577 Parkway Lane, Suite 200
Norcross, GA 30092-2988
Phone: 770-449-0461 Ext. 105
Fax: 770-263-8532
E-mail: bcameron@iienet.org

INSTITUTION OF ELECTRICAL ENGINEERS

http://www.theiet.org

IET ENGINEERING DEGREE SCHOLARSHIPS FOR WOMEN

• *See page 292*

IET FUNDING UNDERGRADUATES TO STUDY ENGINEERING (FUSE) SCHOLARSHIP

• *See page 292*

IET JUBILEE SCHOLARSHIP

• *See page 249*

INSTRUMENTATION, SYSTEMS, AND AUTOMATION SOCIETY (ISA) http://www.isa.org

INSTRUMENTATION, SYSTEMS, AND AUTOMATION SOCIETY (ISA) SCHOLARSHIP PROGRAM

• *See page 158*

INTERNATIONAL SOCIETY FOR OPTICAL ENGINEERING-SPIE http://www.spie.org

D.J. LOVELL SCHOLARSHIP

Scholarship for full-time student in the optical engineering field who is not also a full-time employee in industry, government or academia. Applicants must be presenting an accepted paper at an SPIE-sponsored meeting.

Academic Fields/Career Goals: Engineering/Technology.

Award: Scholarship for use in freshman, sophomore, junior, senior, or graduate years; not renewable. *Number:* varies. *Amount:* $11,000.

Eligibility Requirements: Applicant must be enrolled or expecting to enroll full-time at a four-year institution or university. Available to U.S. citizens.

Application Requirements: Application, references. *Deadline:* varies.

Contact: Scholarship Committee
International Society for Optical Engineering-SPIE
PO Box 10
Bellingham, WA 98227-0010
Phone: 360-685-5452
Fax: 360-647-1445
E-mail: scholarships@spie.org

MICHAEL KIDGER MEMORIAL SCHOLARSHIP IN OPTICAL DESIGN

Awarded to a student engaged in optical design of either imaging or non-imaging systems. Must have at least one year after the award to complete his or her chosen course of study, must submit a summary (five pages maximum) of his or her academic background and interest in pursuing training or research in optical design.

Academic Fields/Career Goals: Engineering/Technology.

Award: Scholarship for use in freshman, sophomore, junior, graduate, or postgraduate years; not renewable. *Number:* varies. *Amount:* $5000.

Eligibility Requirements: Applicant must be enrolled or expecting to enroll full- or part-time at a four-year institution or university. Available to U.S. citizens.

Application Requirements: Application, references, letter of summary. *Deadline:* March 31.

Contact: Scholarship Committee
International Society for Optical Engineering-SPIE
PO Box 10
Bellingham, WA 98227-0010
E-mail: education@spie.org

SPIE EDUCATIONAL SCHOLARSHIPS IN OPTICAL SCIENCE AND ENGINEERING

• *See page 87*

INTERNATIONAL SOCIETY OF EXPLOSIVES ENGINEERS http://www.isee.org

JERRY MCDOWELL FUND

• *See page 293*

INTERNATIONAL TECHNOLOGY EDUCATION ASSOCIATION http://www.iteaconnect.org

INTERNATIONAL TECHNOLOGY EDUCATION ASSOCIATION UNDERGRADUATE SCHOLARSHIP IN TECHNOLOGY EDUCATION

• *See page 231*

INTERNATIONAL UNION OF ELECTRONIC, ELECTRICAL, SALARIED, MACHINE, AND FURNITURE WORKERS-CWA http://www.iue-cwa.org

DAVID J. FITZMAURICE ENGINEERING SCHOLARSHIP

One-time award of $2000 for a student whose parent or grandparent is a member of the IUE-CWA. Applicant must be pursuing undergraduate engineering degree. Submit family financial status form with application.

Academic Fields/Career Goals: Engineering/Technology.

Award: Scholarship for use in freshman, sophomore, junior, or senior years; not renewable. *Number:* 1. *Amount:* $2000.

Eligibility Requirements: Applicant must be enrolled or expecting to enroll full-time at a four-year institution or university. Applicant or parent of applicant must be member of International Union of Electronic, Electrical, Salaries, Machine and Furniture Workers. Available to U.S. and Canadian citizens.

Application Requirements: Application, essay, financial need analysis, references, test scores, transcript. *Deadline:* March 31.

Contact: Sue McElroy, Scholarship Committee
International Union of Electronic, Electrical, Salaried, Machine, and Furniture Workers-CWA
501 Third Street, NW
Washington, DC 20001
Phone: 202-434-0676
Fax: 202-434-1250

KOREAN-AMERICAN SCIENTISTS AND ENGINEERS ASSOCIATION http://www.ksea.org/index.asp

INYONG HAM SCHOLARSHIP

Scholarship of $1000 awarded to undergraduate and graduate students of Korean heritage majoring in science, engineering or related fields. Must be KSEA members or apply for membership at the time of scholarship application.

Academic Fields/Career Goals: Engineering/Technology.

Award: Scholarship for use in freshman, sophomore, junior, senior, or graduate years; not renewable. *Number:* 1. *Amount:* $1000.

Eligibility Requirements: Applicant must be of Korean heritage; Asian/Pacific Islander and enrolled or expecting to enroll full-time at a two-year or four-year institution or university. Applicant or parent of applicant must be member of Korean-American Scientists and Engineers Association. Available to U.S. citizens.

Application Requirements: Application, essay, resume, references, test scores, transcript. *Deadline:* February 15.

Contact: Scholarship Committee
Korean-American Scientists and Engineers Association
1952 Gallows Road, Suite 300
Vienna, VA 22182
Phone: 703-748-1221

KSEA SCHOLARSHIPS

• *See page 249*

LEAGUE OF UNITED LATIN AMERICAN CITIZENS NATIONAL EDUCATIONAL SERVICE CENTERS INC. http://www.lnesc.org

GE/LULAC SCHOLARSHIP

• *See page 145*

GM/LULAC SCHOLARSHIP

Renewable award for minority students who are pursuing an undergraduate degree in engineering at an accredited college or university. Must maintain a minimum 3.0 GPA. Selection is based in part on the likelihood of pursuing a successful career in engineering.

Academic Fields/Career Goals: Engineering/Technology.

Award: Scholarship for use in freshman, sophomore, junior, or senior years; renewable. *Number:* up to 20. *Amount:* up to $2000.

Eligibility Requirements: Applicant must be American Indian/Alaska Native, Asian/Pacific Islander, Black (non-Hispanic), or Hispanic and enrolled or expecting to enroll full-time at a four-year institution or university. Applicant must have 3.0 GPA or higher. Available to U.S. citizens.

Application Requirements: Application, essay, references, transcript. *Deadline:* July 15.

Contact: Scholarship Administrator
League of United Latin American Citizens National Educational Service Centers Inc.
2000 L Street NW, Suite 610
Washington, DC 20036
Phone: 202-835-9646 Ext. 10
Fax: 202-835-9685

LOS ANGELES COUNCIL OF BLACK PROFESSIONAL ENGINEERS http://www.lablackengineers.org

AL-BEN SCHOLARSHIP FOR ACADEMIC INCENTIVE
• See page 159

AL-BEN SCHOLARSHIP FOR PROFESSIONAL MERIT
• See page 159

AL-BEN SCHOLARSHIP FOR SCHOLASTIC ACHIEVEMENT
• See page 159

MAINE EDUCATION SERVICES http://www.mesfoundation.com

MAINE STATE CHAMBER OF COMMERCE SCHOLARSHIP-HIGH SCHOOL SENIOR
• See page 145

MAINE SOCIETY OF PROFESSIONAL ENGINEERS http://www.mespe.org

MAINE SOCIETY OF PROFESSIONAL ENGINEERS VERNON T. SWAINE-ROBERT E. CHUTE SCHOLARSHIP
• See page 293

MARINE TECHNOLOGY SOCIETY http://www.mtsociety.org

MTS STUDENT SCHOLARSHIP FOR GRADUATING HIGH SCHOOL SENIORS

Scholarship of $2000 available to high school seniors who have been accepted into a full-time undergraduate program and have an interest in marine technology.

Academic Fields/Career Goals: Engineering/Technology; Marine/Ocean Engineering.

Award: Scholarship for use in freshman year; not renewable. *Number:* varies. *Amount:* $2000.

Eligibility Requirements: Applicant must be high school student and planning to enroll or expecting to enroll full-time at a four-year institution or university. Available to U.S. and non-U.S. citizens.

Application Requirements: Application, essay, references, transcript, college acceptance letter. *Deadline:* April 15.

Contact: Suzanne Voelker, Operations Administrator
Marine Technology Society
5565 Sterrett Place, Suite 108
Columbia, MD 21044
Phone: 410-884-5330
E-mail: suzanne.voelker@mtsociety.org

MARION D. AND EVA S. PEEPLES FOUNDATION TRUST SCHOLARSHIP PROGRAM http://www.jccf.org

MARION A. AND EVA S. PEEPLES SCHOLARSHIPS
• See page 234

MARYLAND ASSOCIATION OF PRIVATE COLLEGES AND CAREER SCHOOLS http://www.mapccs.org

MARYLAND ASSOCIATION OF PRIVATE COLLEGES AND CAREER SCHOOLS SCHOLARSHIP
• See page 146

MICHIGAN SOCIETY OF PROFESSIONAL ENGINEERS http://www.michiganspe.org

ANTHONY C. FORTUNSKI, P.E. MEMORIAL GRANT
• See page 159

MICHIGAN SOCIETY OF PROFESSIONAL ENGINEERS AUXILIARY GRANT
• See page 159

MICHIGAN SOCIETY OF PROFESSIONAL ENGINEERS HARRY R. BALL, P.E. GRANT
• See page 159

MICHIGAN SOCIETY OF PROFESSIONAL ENGINEERS KENNETH B. FISHBECK, P.E. MEMORIAL GRANT
• See page 160

MICHIGAN SOCIETY OF PROFESSIONAL ENGINEERS 1980 NATIONAL SOCIETY OF PROFESSIONAL ENGINEERS ANNUAL MEETING COMMITTEE GRANT
• See page 160

MICHIGAN SOCIETY OF PROFESSIONAL ENGINEERS SCHOLARSHIP TRUST GRANT
• See page 160

MICHIGAN SOCIETY OF PROFESSIONAL ENGINEERS UNDESIGNATED GRANT
• See page 160

MSPE AUXILIARY GRANT FOR UNDERGRADUATE STUDY
• See page 171

MICRON TECHNOLOGY FOUNDATION INC. http://www.micron.com/scholars

MICRON SCIENCE AND TECHNOLOGY SCHOLARS PROGRAM
• See page 160

MINERALS, METALS, AND MATERIALS SOCIETY (TMS) http://www.tms.org

TMS/EMPMD GILBERT CHIN SCHOLARSHIP
• See page 293

TMS/EPD SCHOLARSHIP
• See page 294

TMS/INTERNATIONAL SYMPOSIUM ON SUPERALLOYS SCHOLARSHIP PROGRAM
• See page 294

TMS J. KEITH BRIMACOMBE PRESIDENTIAL SCHOLARSHIP
• See page 294

TMS/LMD SCHOLARSHIP PROGRAM
• See page 294

TMS OUTSTANDING STUDENT PAPER CONTEST-UNDERGRADUATE
• See page 294

TMS/STRUCTURAL MATERIALS DIVISION SCHOLARSHIP
• See page 294

MINNESOTA COMMUNITY FOUNDATION http://www.mncommunityfoundation.org

HANS O. NYMAN ENGINEERING SCHOLARSHIP

One renewable scholarship of $1500 to students with at least two years of undergraduate study, currently participating in Co-Op Learning Internship at District Energy.

Academic Fields/Career Goals: Engineering/Technology.

Award: Scholarship for use in junior or senior years; renewable. *Number:* 1. *Amount:* $1500.

Eligibility Requirements: Applicant must be enrolled or expecting to enroll full- or part-time at a four-year institution or university. Available to U.S. citizens.

Application Requirements: Application, transcript. *Deadline:* varies.

Contact: Donna Paulson, Administrative Assistant
Minnesota Community Foundation
55 Fifth Street East, Suite 600
St. Paul, MN 55101-1797
Phone: 651-325-4212
E-mail: dkp@mncommunityfoundation.org

MISSOURI SOCIETY OF PROFESSIONAL ENGINEERS EDUCATIONAL FOUNDATION http://www.mspe.org

MSPE EDUCATIONAL FOUNDATION SCHOLARSHIP PROGRAM

Scholarship of $2000 given to high school seniors who have at least 3.0 GPA for the tenth and eleventh grades and an ACT test score of 29 in math and 25 in

Missouri Society of Professional Engineers Educational Foundation (continued)

English. Must enroll in an engineering program that has been accredited by the Engineering Accreditation Commission of the Accreditation Board for Engineering and Technology (ABET-EAC).

Academic Fields/Career Goals: Engineering/Technology.

Award: Scholarship for use in sophomore or junior years; not renewable. *Number:* 1. *Amount:* $2000.

Eligibility Requirements: Applicant must be enrolled or expecting to enroll full-time at a four-year institution or university. Applicant must have 3.0 GPA or higher. Available to U.S. citizens.

Application Requirements: Application, photo, references, test scores, transcript. *Deadline:* January 1.

Contact: Bruce Wylie, Executive Director and Secretary
Missouri Society of Professional Engineers Educational Foundation
200 East McCarty Street, Suite 200
Jefferson City, MO 65101-3133
Phone: 573-636-4861
Fax: 573-636-5475
E-mail: brucewylie@mspe.org

NASA DELAWARE SPACE GRANT CONSORTIUM http://www.delspace.org

NASA DELAWARE SPACE GRANT UNDERGRADUATE TUITION SCHOLARSHIP

• *See page 87*

NASA IDAHO SPACE GRANT CONSORTIUM http://isgc.uidaho.edu

NASA IDAHO SPACE GRANT CONSORTIUM SCHOLARSHIP PROGRAM

• *See page 87*

NASA/MARYLAND SPACE GRANT CONSORTIUM http://www.mdspacegrant.org

NASA MARYLAND SPACE GRANT CONSORTIUM UNDERGRADUATE SCHOLARSHIPS

• *See page 118*

NASA MINNESOTA SPACE GRANT CONSORTIUM http://www.aem.umn.edu/msgc

MINNESOTA SPACE GRANT CONSORTIUM

• *See page 118*

NASA MISSISSIPPI SPACE GRANT CONSORTIUM http://www.olemiss.edu/programs/nasa

MISSISSIPPI SPACE GRANT CONSORTIUM SCHOLARSHIP

• *See page 118*

NASA MONTANA SPACE GRANT CONSORTIUM http://www.spacegrant.montana.edu

MONTANA SPACE GRANT SCHOLARSHIP PROGRAM

• *See page 119*

NASA NEBRASKA SPACE GRANT CONSORTIUM http://nasa.unomaha.edu

NASA NEBRASKA SPACE GRANT

• *See page 119*

NASA NEVADA SPACE GRANT CONSORTIUM http://www.unr.edu/spacegrant

UNIVERSITY AND COMMUNITY COLLEGE SYSTEM OF NEVADA NASA SPACE GRANT AND FELLOWSHIP PROGRAM

• *See page 119*

NASA RHODE ISLAND SPACE GRANT CONSORTIUM http://www.planetary.brown.edu/RI_Space_Grant

NASA RHODE ISLAND SPACE GRANT CONSORTIUM UNDERGRADUATE RESEARCH SCHOLARSHIP

• *See page 119*

NASA RISGC SCIENCE EN ESPANOL SCHOLARSHIP FOR UNDERGRADUATE STUDENTS

• *See page 119*

NASA SOUTH DAKOTA SPACE GRANT CONSORTIUM http://www.sdsmt.edu/space/

SOUTH DAKOTA SPACE GRANT CONSORTIUM UNDERGRADUATE SCHOLARSHIPS

• *See page 120*

NASA VERMONT SPACE GRANT CONSORTIUM http://www.cems.uvm.edu/VSGC

VERMONT SPACE GRANT CONSORTIUM SCHOLARSHIP PROGRAM

• *See page 88*

NASA VIRGINIA SPACE GRANT CONSORTIUM http://www.vsgc.odu.edu

VIRGINIA SPACE GRANT CONSORTIUM COMMUNITY COLLEGE SCHOLARSHIPS

• *See page 120*

VIRGINIA SPACE GRANT CONSORTIUM TEACHER EDUCATION SCHOLARSHIPS

• *See page 121*

NASA WEST VIRGINIA SPACE GRANT CONSORTIUM http://www.nasa.wvu.edu

WEST VIRGINIA SPACE GRANT CONSORTIUM UNDERGRADUATE FELLOWSHIP PROGRAM

• *See page 121*

NATIONAL ACTION COUNCIL FOR MINORITIES IN ENGINEERING-NACME INC. http://www.nacme.org

NACME SCHOLARS PROGRAM

Renewable award for African-American, American-Indian, or Latino student enrolled in a baccalaureate engineering program. Must attend an ABET-accredited institution full-time and complete one semester with a minimum 2.7 GPA. Must be a U.S. citizen. Award money is given to participating institutions who select applicants and disperse funds. Check Web site for details: http://www.nacme.org.

Academic Fields/Career Goals: Engineering/Technology.

Award: Scholarship for use in freshman, sophomore, junior, or senior years; renewable. *Number:* varies. *Amount:* up to $5000.

Eligibility Requirements: Applicant must be American Indian/Alaska Native, Black (non-Hispanic), or Hispanic and enrolled or expecting to enroll full-time at a four-year institution or university. Available to U.S. citizens.

Application Requirements: Application, financial need analysis, references. *Deadline:* continuous.

Contact: Aileen M. Walter, Director, Scholar Management
National Action Council for Minorities in Engineering-NACME Inc.
440 Hamilton Avenue, Suite 302
White Plains, NY 10601
Phone: 914-539-4010

NATIONAL ASSOCIATION FOR THE ADVANCEMENT OF COLORED PEOPLE http://www.naacp.org

HUBERTUS W.V. WILLEMS SCHOLARSHIP FOR MALE STUDENTS

• *See page 161*

NATIONAL ASSOCIATION OF WATER COMPANIES-NEW JERSEY CHAPTER

NATIONAL ASSOCIATION OF WATER COMPANIES-NEW JERSEY CHAPTER SCHOLARSHIP
• See page 133

NATIONAL ASSOCIATION OF WOMEN IN CONSTRUCTION http://www.nawic.org

NAWIC UNDERGRADUATE SCHOLARSHIPS
• See page 92

NATIONAL FEDERATION OF THE BLIND http://www.nfb.org

HOWARD BROWN RICKARD SCHOLARSHIP
• See page 92

NATIONAL GAY PILOTS ASSOCIATION http://www.ngpa.org

NATIONAL GAY PILOTS ASSOCIATION SCHOLARSHIP
• See page 123

NATIONAL INVENTORS HALL OF FAME http://www.invent.org

COLLEGIATE INVENTORS COMPETITION FOR UNDERGRADUATE STUDENTS
• See page 88

COLLEGIATE INVENTORS COMPETITION-GRAND PRIZE
• See page 88

NATIONAL SCIENCE TEACHERS ASSOCIATION http://www.nsta.org

TOSHIBA/NSTA EXPLORAVISION AWARDS PROGRAM
• See page 193

NATIONAL SOCIETY OF PROFESSIONAL ENGINEERS http://www.nspe.org

MAUREEN L. AND HOWARD N. BLITMAN, PE SCHOLARSHIP TO PROMOTE DIVERSITY IN ENGINEERING
• See page 161

PAUL H. ROBBINS HONORARY SCHOLARSHIP
• See page 162

PROFESSIONAL ENGINEERS IN INDUSTRY SCHOLARSHIP
• See page 162

NATIONAL URBAN LEAGUE http://www.nulbeep.org

BLACK EXECUTIVE EXCHANGE PROGRAM JERRY BARTOW SCHOLARSHIP FUND
• See page 146

NEW YORK STATE EDUCATION DEPARTMENT http://www.highered.nysed.gov

REGENTS PROFESSIONAL OPPORTUNITY SCHOLARSHIP
• See page 60

OREGON STUDENT ASSISTANCE COMMISSION http://www.osac.state.or.us

HOMESTEAD CAPITAL HOUSING SCHOLARSHIP
• See page 61

PENNSYLVANIA HIGHER EDUCATION ASSISTANCE AGENCY http://www.pheaa.org

NEW ECONOMY TECHNOLOGY AND SCITECH SCHOLARSHIPS
• See page 295

PLASTICS INSTITUTE OF AMERICA http://www.plasticsinstitute.org

PLASTICS PIONEERS SCHOLARSHIPS
• See page 162

PLUMBING-HEATING-COOLING CONTRACTORS ASSOCIATION EDUCATION FOUNDATION http://www.phccweb.org

BRADFORD WHITE CORPORATION SCHOLARSHIP
• See page 92

DELTA FAUCET COMPANY SCHOLARSHIP PROGRAM
• See page 93

PHCC EDUCATIONAL FOUNDATION NEED-BASED SCHOLARSHIP
• See page 93

PHCC EDUCATIONAL FOUNDATION SCHOLARSHIP PROGRAM
• See page 147

PROFESSIONAL CONSTRUCTION ESTIMATORS ASSOCIATION http://www.pcea.org

TED WILSON MEMORIAL SCHOLARSHIP FOUNDATION
• See page 214

ROBERT H. MOLLOHAN FAMILY CHARITABLE FOUNDATION INC. http://www.mollohanfoundation.org

HIGH TECHNOLOGY SCHOLARS PROGRAM
• See page 135

ROCKY MOUNTAIN COAL MINING INSTITUTE http://www.rmcmi.org

ROCKY MOUNTAIN COAL MINING INSTITUTE SCHOLARSHIP
• See page 219

SAN DIEGO FOUNDATION http://www.sdfoundation.org

ENERGY OF ACHIEVEMENT SDG&E SCHOLARSHIP
• See page 148

QUALCOMM SAN DIEGO SCIENCE, TECHNOLOGY, ENGINEERING, AND MATHEMATICS SCHOLARSHIP

Scholarship to provide financial assistance to students majoring in science, technology, engineering, or mathematics, and attending the University of California, San Diego, San Diego State University or California State University, San Marcos. Consideration will be given to students who have participated in extracurricular activities, community service or work experience. Scholarship may be renewable for up to four years provided students adhere to the terms and conditions.

Academic Fields/Career Goals: Engineering/Technology; Mathematics; Science, Technology, and Society.

Award: Scholarship for use in freshman, sophomore, junior, or senior years; renewable. *Number:* 5. *Amount:* $2500.

Eligibility Requirements: Applicant must be enrolled or expecting to enroll full-time at an institution or university; resident of California and studying in California. Applicant or parent of applicant must have employment or volunteer experience in community service. Applicant must have 3.5 GPA or higher. Available to U.S. citizens.

Application Requirements: Application, financial need analysis, references, transcript, personal statement, copy of tax return. *Deadline:* January 26.

Contact: Shryl Helvie, Scholarship Coordinator
San Diego Foundation
2508 Historic Decatur Road, Suite 200
San Diego, CA 92106
Phone: 619-814-1307
Fax: 619-239-1710
E-mail: shryl@sdfoundation.org

SIGMA XI, THE SCIENTIFIC RESEARCH SOCIETY http://www.sigmaxi.org

SIGMA XI GRANTS-IN-AID OF RESEARCH

• See page 78

SIMPLEHUMAN http://www.simplehuman.com

SIMPLE SOLUTIONS DESIGN COMPETITION

• See page 296

SOCIETY FOR IMAGING SCIENCE AND TECHNOLOGY http://www.imaging.org

RAYMOND DAVIS SCHOLARSHIP

Award available to an undergraduate junior or senior or graduate student enrolled full-time in an accredited program of photographic, imaging science or engineering. Minimum award is $1000. Applications processed between October 15 and December 15 only.

Academic Fields/Career Goals: Engineering/Technology; Physical Sciences and Math.

Award: Scholarship for use in junior, senior, or graduate years; renewable. *Number:* 1–2. *Amount:* $1000.

Eligibility Requirements: Applicant must be enrolled or expecting to enroll full-time at a four-year institution or university. Available to U.S. and non-U.S. citizens.

Application Requirements: Application, autobiography, references, transcript. *Deadline:* December 15.

Contact: Donna Smith, Production Manager
Society for Imaging Science and Technology
7003 Kilworth Lane
Springfield, VA 22151
Phone: 703-642-9090 Ext. 17
Fax: 703-642-9094
E-mail: info@imaging.org

SOCIETY OF AUTOMOTIVE ENGINEERS http://www.sae.org

BMW/SAE ENGINEERING SCHOLARSHIP

• See page 124

DETROIT SECTION SAE TECHNICAL SCHOLARSHIP

• See page 296

EDWARD D. HENDRICKSON/SAE ENGINEERING SCHOLARSHIP

• See page 124

FRED M. YOUNG SR./SAE ENGINEERING SCHOLARSHIP

Scholarship of $4000 awarded at $1000 per year for four years. Applicants must have a 3.75 GPA, rank in the 90th percentile in both math and critical reading on SAT or composite ACT scores, and pursue an engineering degree accredited by ABET. A 3.0 GPA and continued engineering enrollment must be maintained to renew the scholarship.

Academic Fields/Career Goals: Engineering/Technology.

Award: Scholarship for use in freshman year; renewable. *Number:* 1. *Amount:* $1000.

Eligibility Requirements: Applicant must be high school student and planning to enroll or expecting to enroll full-time at a four-year institution or university. Available to U.S. citizens.

Application Requirements: Application, essay, test scores, transcript. *Deadline:* December 15.

Contact: Connie Harnish, SAE Educational Relations
Society of Automotive Engineers
400 Commonwealth Drive
Warrendale, PA 15096
Phone: 724-772-4047
E-mail: connie@sae.org

RALPH K. HILLQUIST HONORARY SAE SCHOLARSHIP

• See page 296

SAE BALTIMORE SECTION BILL BRUBAKER SCHOLARSHIP

Nonrenewable scholarship for any family member of a Baltimore SAE member, or any high school senior accepted to an engineering program at a Maryland university.

Academic Fields/Career Goals: Engineering/Technology.

Award: Scholarship for use in freshman year; not renewable. *Number:* 1. *Amount:* up to $1000.

Eligibility Requirements: Applicant must be high school student; planning to enroll or expecting to enroll full-time at an institution or university and studying in Maryland. Applicant or parent of applicant must be member of Society of Automotive Engineers. Available to U.S. citizens.

Application Requirements: Application, essay, resume, transcript. *Deadline:* May 10.

Contact: Marguerite Milligan, Marketing Assistant
Society of Automotive Engineers
400 Commonwealth Drive
Warrendale, PA 15096-0001
Phone: 724-772-7158
Fax: 724-776-3049
E-mail: customerservice@sae.org

SAE LONG TERM MEMBER SPONSORED SCHOLARSHIP

The scholarship recognizes outstanding SAE student members who actively support SAE and its activities. Applications may be submitted by the student or by the SAE faculty advisor, an SAE Section officer or a community leader. The student must be a junior who will be entering the senior year of undergraduate engineering studies. Number of award varies.

Academic Fields/Career Goals: Engineering/Technology.

Award: Scholarship for use in senior year; not renewable. *Number:* varies. *Amount:* $1000.

Eligibility Requirements: Applicant must be enrolled or expecting to enroll full-time at a four-year institution or university. Applicant or parent of applicant must be member of Society of Automotive Engineers. Available to U.S. citizens.

Application Requirements: Application, references. *Deadline:* April 1.

Contact: Connie Harnish, SAE Educational Relations
Society of Automotive Engineers
400 Commonwealth Drive
Warrendale, PA 15096
Phone: 724-772-4047
E-mail: connie@sae.org

SAE WILLIAM G. BELFREY MEMORIAL GRANT

• See page 296

TAU BETA PI/SAE ENGINEERING SCHOLARSHIP

Six scholarships valued at $1000 each will be awarded for the freshman year only. Applicants must have a 3.75 GPA, rank in the 90th percentile in both math and critical reading for SAT scores or for composite ACT scores, and pursue an engineering program accredited by the engineering accreditation commission of the Accreditation Board for Engineering and Technology.

Academic Fields/Career Goals: Engineering/Technology.

Award: Scholarship for use in freshman year; not renewable. *Number:* 6. *Amount:* $1000.

Eligibility Requirements: Applicant must be high school student and planning to enroll or expecting to enroll full- or part-time at a four-year institution or university. Available to U.S. citizens.

Application Requirements: Application, essay, test scores, transcript. *Deadline:* December 15.

Contact: Connie Harnish, SAE Educational Relations
Society of Automotive Engineers
400 Commonwealth Drive
Warrendale, PA 15096
Phone: 724-772-4047
E-mail: connie@sae.org

TMC/SAE DONALD D. DAWSON TECHNICAL SCHOLARSHIP

• See page 124

YANMAR/SAE SCHOLARSHIP
• *See page 297*

SOCIETY OF FLIGHT TEST ENGINEERS http://www.sfte.org

SOCIETY OF FLIGHT TEST ENGINEERS SCHOLARSHIP
• *See page 194*

SOCIETY OF HISPANIC PROFESSIONAL ENGINEERS http://www.shpe.org

AHETEMS SCHOLARSHIPS

Merit-based and need-based scholarships are awarded, in the amount of $1000 to $5000 to high school graduating seniors, undergraduate students, and graduate students who demonstrate both significant motivation and aptitude for a career in science, technology, engineering or mathematics. Must have a minimum GPA of 3.0 (for high school seniors and undergraduates) and 3.25 for graduate students.

Academic Fields/Career Goals: Engineering/Technology; Mathematics; Science, Technology, and Society.

Award: Scholarship for use in freshman, sophomore, junior, senior, or graduate years; not renewable. *Number:* up to 100. *Amount:* $1000–$5000.

Eligibility Requirements: Applicant must be enrolled or expecting to enroll full-time at a two-year or four-year or technical institution or university. Applicant must have 3.0 GPA or higher. Available to U.S. and non-U.S. citizens.

Application Requirements: Application, references, transcript, personal statement. *Deadline:* April 1.

Contact: Rafaela Schwan, AHETEMS Office
Society of Hispanic Professional Engineers
The University of Texas at Arlington, College of Engineering, PO Box 19019
Arlington, TX 76019-0019
Phone: 817-272-0776
Fax: 817-272-2548
E-mail: rschwan@shpe.org

SOCIETY OF HISPANIC PROFESSIONAL ENGINEERS FOUNDATION http://www.henaac.org

SOCIETY OF HISPANIC PROFESSIONAL ENGINEERS FOUNDATION
• *See page 162*

SOCIETY OF MANUFACTURING ENGINEERS EDUCATION FOUNDATION http://www.sme.org/foundation

ALBERT E. WISCHMEYER MEMORIAL SCHOLARSHIP AWARD

Applicants must be residents of Western New York State, graduating high school seniors or current undergraduate students enrolled in an accredited degree program in manufacturing engineering, manufacturing engineering technology or mechanical technology in New York. Must have an GPA of 3.0.

Academic Fields/Career Goals: Engineering/Technology.

Award: Scholarship for use in freshman, sophomore, junior, or senior years; not renewable. *Number:* 1–10. *Amount:* $1000–$5000.

Eligibility Requirements: Applicant must be enrolled or expecting to enroll full-time at a four-year institution or university; resident of New York and studying in New York. Applicant must have 3.0 GPA or higher. Available to U.S. citizens.

Application Requirements: Application, essay, resume, references, transcript. *Deadline:* February 1.

Contact: Chris Milantoni, Program Coordinator
Society of Manufacturing Engineers Education Foundation
One SME Drive
PO Box 930
Dearborn, MI 48121-0930
Phone: 313-425-3300
Fax: 313-425-3411
E-mail: foundation@sme.org

ARTHUR AND GLADYS CERVENKA SCHOLARSHIP AWARD

One-time award to full-time students enrolled in a degree program in manufacturing engineering or technology. Preference given to students attending a Florida institution. Minimum 3.0 GPA required.

Academic Fields/Career Goals: Engineering/Technology.

Award: Scholarship for use in freshman, sophomore, junior, or senior years; not renewable. *Number:* 1–10. *Amount:* $1000–$5000.

Eligibility Requirements: Applicant must be enrolled or expecting to enroll full-time at a four-year institution or university. Applicant must have 3.0 GPA or higher. Available to U.S. citizens.

Application Requirements: Application, essay, resume, references, transcript. *Deadline:* February 1.

Contact: Chris Milantoni, Program Coordinator
Society of Manufacturing Engineers Education Foundation
One SME Drive
PO Box 930
Dearborn, MI 48121-0930
Phone: 313-425-3300
Fax: 313-425-3411
E-mail: foundation@sme.org

CATERPILLAR SCHOLARS AWARD FUND

Supports five one-time scholarships for full-time students enrolled in a manufacturing engineering program. Minority applicants may apply as incoming freshmen. Applicants must have an overall minimum GPA of 3.0.

Academic Fields/Career Goals: Engineering/Technology.

Award: Scholarship for use in freshman, sophomore, junior, or senior years; not renewable. *Number:* 1–15. *Amount:* $1000–$5000.

Eligibility Requirements: Applicant must be enrolled or expecting to enroll full-time at a four-year institution or university. Applicant must have 3.0 GPA or higher. Available to U.S. and Canadian citizens.

Application Requirements: Application, essay, resume, references, transcript. *Deadline:* February 1.

Contact: Chris Milantoni, Program Coordinator
Society of Manufacturing Engineers Education Foundation
One SME Drive
PO Box 930
Dearborn, MI 48121-0930
Phone: 313-425-3300
Fax: 313-425-3411
E-mail: foundation@sme.org

CHAPTER 4-LAWRENCE A. WACKER MEMORIAL SCHOLARSHIP

Awards available to full-time students enrolled in or accepted to a degree program in manufacturing, mechanical or industrial engineering at a college or university in the state of Wisconsin. One scholarship will be granted to a graduating high school senior and the other will be granted to a current undergraduate student. Minimum GPA of 3.0 required.

Academic Fields/Career Goals: Engineering/Technology; Mechanical Engineering.

Award: Scholarship for use in freshman, sophomore, junior, or senior years; not renewable. *Number:* 1–10. *Amount:* $1000–$5000.

Eligibility Requirements: Applicant must be enrolled or expecting to enroll full-time at a four-year institution or university and studying in Wisconsin. Applicant must have 3.0 GPA or higher. Available to U.S. citizens.

Society of Manufacturing Engineers Education Foundation (continued)

Application Requirements: Application, essay, resume, references, transcript. *Deadline:* February 1.

Contact: Chris Milantoni, Program Coordinator
Society of Manufacturing Engineers Education Foundation
One SME Drive
PO Box 930
Dearborn, MI 48121-0930
Phone: 313-425-3300
Fax: 313-425-3411
E-mail: foundation@sme.org

CHAPTER 93-ALBUQUERQUE SCHOLARSHIP

Scholarship to students entering freshmen or current undergraduate students pursuing a bachelor's degree in manufacturing engineering or a related field who plan to or are attending an accredited college or university in New Mexico.

Academic Fields/Career Goals: Engineering/Technology.

Award: Scholarship for use in freshman, sophomore, junior, or senior years; not renewable. *Number:* 1–5. *Amount:* $1000–$5000.

Eligibility Requirements: Applicant must be enrolled or expecting to enroll full-time at a four-year institution or university and studying in New Mexico. Applicant must have 2.5 GPA or higher. Available to U.S. citizens.

Application Requirements: Application, essay, resume, references, test scores, transcript. *Deadline:* February 1.

Contact: Chris Milantoni, Program Coordinator
Society of Manufacturing Engineers Education Foundation
One SME Drive
PO Box 930
Dearborn, MI 48121-0930
Phone: 313-425-3300
Fax: 313-425-3411
E-mail: foundation@sme.org

CHAPTER 198-DOWNRIVER DETROIT SCHOLARSHIP

One-time award for an individual seeking an associates degree, bachelor's degree, or graduate degree in manufacturing, mechanical or industrial engineering, engineering technology, or industrial technology at an accredited public or private college or university in Michigan. Must have a minimum GPA of 2.5. Preference is given to applicants who are a child or grandchild of a current SME Downriver Chapter No. 198 member, a member of its student chapter, or a Michigan resident.

Academic Fields/Career Goals: Engineering/Technology; Industrial Design; Mechanical Engineering; Trade/Technical Specialties.

Award: Scholarship for use in freshman, sophomore, junior, senior, or graduate years; not renewable. *Number:* 1–5. *Amount:* $1000–$5000.

Eligibility Requirements: Applicant must be enrolled or expecting to enroll full-time at a two-year or four-year institution or university and studying in Michigan. Applicant must have 2.5 GPA or higher. Available to U.S. citizens.

Application Requirements: Application, essay, resume, references, test scores, transcript, student statement letter. *Deadline:* February 1.

Contact: Chris Milantoni, Program Coordinator
Society of Manufacturing Engineers Education Foundation
One SME Drive
PO Box 930
Dearborn, MI 48121-0930
Phone: 313-425-3300
Fax: 313-425-3411
E-mail: foundation@sme.org

CHAPTER 17-ST. LOUIS SCHOLARSHIP

Scholarship will be given to full-time or part-time students enrolled in a manufacturing engineering, industrial technology, or other related program. Must study in Missouri or Illinois. Minimum of 2.5 GPA is required.

Academic Fields/Career Goals: Engineering/Technology.

Award: Scholarship for use in freshman, sophomore, junior, or senior years; not renewable. *Number:* varies. *Amount:* varies.

Eligibility Requirements: Applicant must be enrolled or expecting to enroll full-time at a four-year institution or university and studying in Illinois or Missouri. Available to U.S. and Canadian citizens.

Application Requirements: Application, essay, resume, references, transcript. *Deadline:* February 1.

Contact: Chris Milantoni, Program Coordinator
Society of Manufacturing Engineers Education Foundation
One SME Drive
PO Box 930
Dearborn, MI 48121-0930
Phone: 313-425-3300
Fax: 313-425-3411
E-mail: foundation@sme.org

CHAPTER 6-FAIRFIELD COUNTY SCHOLARSHIP

Scholarship applicants must be full-time undergraduate students enrolled in a degree program in manufacturing engineering, technology, or a closely related field in the United States or Canada. Preference is given to residents of, or students studying in, the eastern part of the United States.

Academic Fields/Career Goals: Engineering/Technology.

Award: Scholarship for use in freshman, sophomore, or junior years; not renewable. *Number:* up to 4. *Amount:* $1000–$5000.

Eligibility Requirements: Applicant must be enrolled or expecting to enroll full-time at a two-year or four-year or technical institution. Applicant must have 3.0 GPA or higher. Available to U.S. and Canadian citizens.

Application Requirements: Application, essay, resume, references, test scores, transcript. *Deadline:* February 1.

Contact: Chris Milantoni, Program Coordinator
Society of Manufacturing Engineers Education Foundation
One SME Drive
PO Box 930
Dearborn, MI 48121-0930
Phone: 313-425-3300
Fax: 313-425-3411
E-mail: foundation@sme.org

CHAPTER 67-PHOENIX SCHOLARSHIP

Award for a high school senior who plans on enrolling in a manufacturing program technology or manufacturing technology program or an undergraduate student enrolled in a manufacturing engineering technology, manufacturing technology, industrial technology, or closely related program at an accredited college or university in Arizona. Applicants must have an overall GPA of 2.5. Scholarship ranges from $1000 to $5000.

Academic Fields/Career Goals: Engineering/Technology; Industrial Design; Mechanical Engineering; Trade/Technical Specialties.

Award: Scholarship for use in freshman, sophomore, junior, or senior years; not renewable. *Number:* 1–5. *Amount:* $1000–$5000.

Eligibility Requirements: Applicant must be enrolled or expecting to enroll full-time at a two-year or four-year institution or university and studying in Arizona. Applicant must have 2.5 GPA or higher. Available to U.S. citizens.

Application Requirements: Application, essay, resume, references, test scores, transcript. *Deadline:* February 1.

Contact: Chris Milantoni, Program Coordinator
Society of Manufacturing Engineers Education Foundation
One SME Drive
PO Box 930
Dearborn, MI 48121-0930
Phone: 313-425-3300
Fax: 313-425-3411
E-mail: foundation@sme.org

CHAPTER 63-PORTLAND JAMES E. MORROW SCHOLARSHIP

Applicants must be pursuing a career in manufacturing or a related field. Preference will be given to students planning to attend Oregon or southwest Washington schools. Preference will also be given to applicants who reside within the states of Oregon or southwest Washington.

Academic Fields/Career Goals: Engineering/Technology.

Award: Scholarship for use in freshman, sophomore, or junior years; not renewable. *Number:* up to 5. *Amount:* $1000–$5000.

Eligibility Requirements: Applicant must be enrolled or expecting to enroll full-time at a two-year or four-year or technical institution or university; resident of Oregon or Washington and studying in Oregon or Washington. Available to U.S. and Canadian citizens.

Application Requirements: Application, essay, resume, references, test scores, transcript. *Deadline:* February 1.

Contact: Chris Milantoni, Program Coordinator
Society of Manufacturing Engineers Education Foundation
One SME Drive
PO Box 930
Dearborn, MI 48121-0930
Phone: 313-425-3300
Fax: 313-425-3411
E-mail: foundation@sme.org

CHAPTER 63-PORTLAND UNCLE BUD SMITH SCHOLARSHIP

Applicants must be pursuing a career in manufacturing or a related field. Preference will be given to students planning to attend Oregon or southwest Washington schools. Preference will also be given to applicants who reside within the states of Oregon or southwest Washington.

Academic Fields/Career Goals: Engineering/Technology.

Award: Scholarship for use in freshman, sophomore, or junior years; not renewable. *Number:* up to 5. *Amount:* $1000–$5000.

Eligibility Requirements: Applicant must be enrolled or expecting to enroll full-time at a two-year or four-year or technical institution or university; resident of Oregon or Washington and studying in Oregon or Washington. Applicant must have 2.5 GPA or higher. Available to U.S. and Canadian citizens.

Application Requirements: Application, essay, resume, references, test scores, transcript. *Deadline:* February 1.

Contact: Chris Milantoni, Program Coordinator
Society of Manufacturing Engineers Education Foundation
One SME Drive
PO Box 930
Dearborn, MI 48121-0930
Phone: 313-425-3300
Fax: 313-425-3411
E-mail: foundation@sme.org

CHAPTER 31-TRI CITY SCHOLARSHIP

Applicants must be seeking a bachelor's degree in manufacturing, mechanical, or industrial engineering, engineering technology, industrial technology or closely related field of study. Must be enrolled in or plan to attend an accredited college or university in the state of Michigan.

Academic Fields/Career Goals: Engineering/Technology.

Award: Scholarship for use in freshman, sophomore, junior, or senior years; not renewable. *Number:* up to 5. *Amount:* $1000–$5000.

Eligibility Requirements: Applicant must be enrolled or expecting to enroll full-time at a two-year or four-year or technical institution or university and studying in Michigan. Applicant must have 3.0 GPA or higher. Available to U.S. and Canadian citizens.

Application Requirements: Application, essay, resume, test scores, transcript. *Deadline:* February 1.

Contact: Chris Milantoni, Program Coordinator
Society of Manufacturing Engineers Education Foundation
One SME Drive
PO Box 930
Dearborn, MI 48121-0930
Phone: 313-425-3300
Fax: 313-425-3411
E-mail: foundation@sme.org

CHAPTER 3-PEORIA ENDOWED SCHOLARSHIP

Applicants must be seeking a bachelor's degree in manufacturing engineering, industrial engineering, manufacturing technology, or a manufacturing-related degree program at either Bradley University (Peoria, Illinois) or Illinois State University (Normal, Illinois).

Academic Fields/Career Goals: Engineering/Technology.

Award: Scholarship for use in freshman, sophomore, or junior years; not renewable. *Number:* up to 5. *Amount:* $1000–$5000.

Eligibility Requirements: Applicant must be enrolled or expecting to enroll full-time at a two-year or four-year or technical institution or university; resident of Illinois and studying in Illinois. Applicant must have 3.0 GPA or higher. Available to U.S. and Canadian citizens.

Application Requirements: Application, essay, resume, references, test scores, transcript. *Deadline:* February 1.

Contact: Chris Milantoni, Program Coordinator
Society of Manufacturing Engineers Education Foundation
One SME Drive
PO Box 930
Dearborn, MI 48121-0930
Phone: 313-425-3300
Fax: 313-425-3411
E-mail: foundation@sme.org

CHAPTER 23-QUAD CITIES IOWA/ILLINOIS SCHOLARSHIP

Scholarship applicant must be entering freshman or current undergraduate student pursuing a bachelor's degree in manufacturing engineering or a related field at an accredited college or university in Iowa or Illinois.

Academic Fields/Career Goals: Engineering/Technology.

Award: Scholarship for use in freshman, sophomore, or junior years; not renewable. *Number:* up to 5. *Amount:* $1000–$5000.

Eligibility Requirements: Applicant must be enrolled or expecting to enroll full-time at a four-year institution or university and studying in Illinois or Iowa. Applicant must have 2.5 GPA or higher. Available to U.S. and Canadian citizens.

Application Requirements: Application, essay, resume, references, test scores, transcript. *Deadline:* February 1.

Contact: Chris Milantoni, Program Coordinator
Society of Manufacturing Engineers Education Foundation
One SME Drive
PO Box 930
Dearborn, MI 48121-0930
Phone: 313-425-3300
Fax: 313-425-3411
E-mail: foundation@sme.org

CLARENCE AND JOSEPHINE MYERS SCHOLARSHIP

Applicants must be an undergraduate or graduate student pursing a degree in engineering or a manufacturing-related field at a college within the state of Indiana.

Academic Fields/Career Goals: Engineering/Technology.

Award: Scholarship for use in freshman, sophomore, junior, or senior years; not renewable. *Number:* up to 5. *Amount:* $1000–$5000.

Eligibility Requirements: Applicant must be enrolled or expecting to enroll full-time at a two-year or four-year or technical institution or university and studying in Indiana. Available to U.S. and Canadian citizens.

Application Requirements: Application, essay, references, test scores, transcript. *Deadline:* February 1.

Contact: Chris Milantoni, Program Coordinator
Society of Manufacturing Engineers Education Foundation
One SME Drive
PO Box 930
Dearborn, MI 48121-0930
Phone: 313-425-3300
Fax: 313-425-3411
E-mail: foundation@sme.org

CLINTON J. HELTON MANUFACTURING SCHOLARSHIP AWARD FUND

One-time award to full-time students enrolled in a degree program in manufacturing engineering or technology at one of the following institutions: Colorado State University, University of Colorado—all campuses. Applicants must possess an overall minimum GPA of 3.3.

Academic Fields/Career Goals: Engineering/Technology; Trade/Technical Specialties.

Award: Scholarship for use in freshman, sophomore, junior, or senior years; not renewable. *Number:* 1–5. *Amount:* $1000–$5000.

Eligibility Requirements: Applicant must be enrolled or expecting to enroll full-time at a four-year institution or university and studying in Colorado. Available to U.S. citizens.

Society of Manufacturing Engineers Education Foundation (continued)

Application Requirements: Application, essay, references, test scores, transcript. *Deadline:* February 1.

Contact: Chris Milantoni, Program Coordinator
Society of Manufacturing Engineers Education Foundation
One SME Drive
PO Box 930
Dearborn, MI 48121-0930
Phone: 313-425-3300
Fax: 313-425-3411
E-mail: foundation@sme.org

CONNIE AND ROBERT T. GUNTER SCHOLARSHIP

One-time award will be given for full-time undergraduate students enrolled in a degree program in manufacturing engineering or technology. Minimum 3.5 GPA is required. Must study in Georgia.

Academic Fields/Career Goals: Engineering/Technology.

Award: Scholarship for use in freshman, sophomore, junior, or senior years; not renewable. *Number:* 1–5. *Amount:* $1000–$5000.

Eligibility Requirements: Applicant must be enrolled or expecting to enroll full-time at a four-year institution or university and studying in Georgia. Applicant must have 3.5 GPA or higher. Available to U.S. citizens.

Application Requirements: Application, essay, resume, references, transcript. *Deadline:* February 1.

Contact: Chris Milantoni, Program Coordinator
Society of Manufacturing Engineers Education Foundation
One SME Drive
PO Box 930
Dearborn, MI 48121-0930
Phone: 313-425-3300
Fax: 313-425-3411
E-mail: foundation@sme.org

DETROIT CHAPTER ONE-FOUNDING CHAPTER SCHOLARSHIP

Several awards will be available in each of the following: associate degree and equivalent, baccalaureate degree and graduate degree programs. Minimum GPA of 3.5 is required. Preference given to undergraduate or graduate student enrolled in a manufacturing engineering or technology program at one of the sponsored institutions.

Academic Fields/Career Goals: Engineering/Technology.

Award: Scholarship for use in freshman, sophomore, junior, senior, or graduate years; not renewable. *Number:* 3. *Amount:* $1000.

Eligibility Requirements: Applicant must be enrolled or expecting to enroll full- or part-time at a two-year or four-year institution or university and studying in Michigan. Applicant must have 3.5 GPA or higher. Available to U.S. citizens.

Application Requirements: Application, references. *Deadline:* February 1.

Contact: Chris Milantoni, Program Coordinator
Society of Manufacturing Engineers Education Foundation
One SME Drive
PO Box 930
Dearborn, MI 48121-0930
Phone: 313-425-3300
Fax: 313-425-3411
E-mail: foundation@sme.org

DIRECTOR'S SCHOLARSHIP AWARD

Scholarship award for full-time undergraduate students enrolled in a manufacturing or related degree program in the United States or Canada. Preference will be given to students who demonstrate leadership skills in a community, academic, or professional environment. Average GPA of 3.5 required.

Academic Fields/Career Goals: Engineering/Technology.

Award: Scholarship for use in freshman, sophomore, junior, or senior years; not renewable. *Number:* 1–5. *Amount:* $1000–$10,000.

Eligibility Requirements: Applicant must be enrolled or expecting to enroll full-time at a four-year institution or university and must have an interest in leadership. Applicant must have 3.5 GPA or higher. Available to U.S. and Canadian citizens.

Application Requirements: Application, essay, resume, references, transcript. *Deadline:* February 1.

Contact: Chris Milantoni, Program Coordinator
Society of Manufacturing Engineers Education Foundation
One SME Drive
PO Box 930
Dearborn, MI 48121-0930
Phone: 313-425-3300
Fax: 313-425-3411
E-mail: foundation@sme.org

EDWARD S. ROTH MANUFACTURING ENGINEERING SCHOLARSHIP

Award to a graduating high school senior, a current full-time undergraduate or graduate student enrolled in an accredited four-year degree program in manufacturing engineering at a sponsored ABET-accredited school. Minimum GPA of 3.0 and be a U.S. citizen.

Academic Fields/Career Goals: Engineering/Technology.

Award: Scholarship for use in freshman, sophomore, junior, senior, or graduate years; not renewable. *Number:* 1–10. *Amount:* $1000–$5000.

Eligibility Requirements: Applicant must be enrolled or expecting to enroll full-time at a four-year institution or university and studying in California, Florida, Illinois, Massachusetts, Minnesota, Ohio, Texas, or Utah. Applicant must have 3.0 GPA or higher. Available to U.S. citizens.

Application Requirements: Application, interview, resume, references, transcript. *Deadline:* February 1.

Contact: Chris Milantoni, Program Coordinator
Society of Manufacturing Engineers Education Foundation
One SME Drive
PO Box 930
Dearborn, MI 48121-0930
Phone: 313-425-3300
Fax: 313-425-3411
E-mail: foundation@sme.org

E. WAYNE KAY COMMUNITY COLLEGE SCHOLARSHIP AWARD

One-time award to full-time students enrolled at an accredited community college or trade school which offers programs in manufacturing or closely related field in the United States or Canada. Minimum GPA of 3.0 required. Scholarship applicants may be entering freshmen or sophomore students with less than 60 college credit hours completed and be seeking a career in manufacturing engineering or technology.

Academic Fields/Career Goals: Engineering/Technology; Trade/Technical Specialties.

Award: Scholarship for use in freshman or sophomore years; not renewable. *Number:* 1–20. *Amount:* $1000–$10,000.

Eligibility Requirements: Applicant must be enrolled or expecting to enroll full-time at a two-year or four-year or technical institution or university. Applicant must have 3.0 GPA or higher. Available to U.S. and Canadian citizens.

Application Requirements: Application, essay, resume, references, transcript. *Deadline:* February 1.

Contact: Chris Milantoni, Program Coordinator
Society of Manufacturing Engineers Education Foundation
One SME Drive
PO Box 930
Dearborn, MI 48121-0930
Phone: 313-425-3300
Fax: 313-425-3411
E-mail: foundation@sme.org

E. WAYNE KAY CO-OP SCHOLARSHIP

Scholarship will be awarded for graduating high school senior or full-time undergraduate student enrolled in a degree program in manufacturing or a closely related field at a two year Community College or trade school in the United States or Canada. Average of 3.0 GPA is required.

Academic Fields/Career Goals: Engineering/Technology.

Award: Scholarship for use in freshman, sophomore, junior, or senior years; not renewable. *Number:* 1–10. *Amount:* $1000–$5000.

Eligibility Requirements: Applicant must be enrolled or expecting to enroll full-time at a two-year or four-year or technical institution or university. Applicant must have 3.0 GPA or higher. Available to U.S. and non-U.S. citizens.

Application Requirements: Application, essay, resume, references, transcript. *Deadline:* February 1.

Contact: Chris Milantoni, Program Coordinator
Society of Manufacturing Engineers Education Foundation
One SME Drive
PO Box 930
Dearborn, MI 48121-0930
Phone: 313-425-3300
Fax: 313-425-3411
E-mail: foundation@sme.org

E. WAYNE KAY HIGH SCHOOL SCHOLARSHIP

Scholarship available for student enrolled full-time in manufacturing engineering or technology program at an accredited college or university. Minimum 3.0 GPA required.

Academic Fields/Career Goals: Engineering/Technology.

Award: Scholarship for use in freshman, sophomore, junior, or senior years; renewable. *Number:* 1–20. *Amount:* $1000–$2500.

Eligibility Requirements: Applicant must be enrolled or expecting to enroll full-time at a four-year institution or university. Applicant must have 3.0 GPA or higher. Available to U.S. and Canadian citizens.

Application Requirements: Application, essay, references, test scores, transcript. *Deadline:* February 1.

Contact: Chris Milantoni, Program Coordinator
Society of Manufacturing Engineers Education Foundation
One SME Drive
PO Box 930
Dearborn, MI 48121-0930
Phone: 313-425-3300
Fax: 313-425-3411
E-mail: foundation@sme.org

E. WAYNE KAY SCHOLARSHIP

Scholarship for full-time undergraduate students enrolled in a degree program in manufacturing engineering, technology, or a closely related field in the United States or Canada. Minimum of 3.0 GPA is required.

Academic Fields/Career Goals: Engineering/Technology; Trade/Technical Specialties.

Award: Scholarship for use in freshman, sophomore, junior, or senior years; not renewable. *Number:* 10–30. *Amount:* $2500–$7500.

Eligibility Requirements: Applicant must be enrolled or expecting to enroll full-time at a four-year institution or university. Applicant must have 3.0 GPA or higher. Available to U.S. and Canadian citizens.

Application Requirements: Application, essay, resume, references, test scores, transcript. *Deadline:* February 1.

Contact: Chris Milantoni, Program Coordinator
Society of Manufacturing Engineers Education Foundation
One SME Drive
PO Box 930
Dearborn, MI 48121-0930
Phone: 313-425-3300
Fax: 313-425-3411
E-mail: foundation@sme.org

FORT WAYNE CHAPTER 56 SCHOLARSHIP

One-time award for an individual seeking an associates degree, bachelor's degree, or graduate degree in manufacturing, mechanical or industrial engineering, engineering technology, or industrial technology at an accredited public or private college or university in Indiana. Must have a minimum GPA of 2.5. Preference given to applicants who are a child or grandchild of a current SME Fort Wayne Chapter No. 56 member, a member of its student chapter, or an Indiana resident.

Academic Fields/Career Goals: Engineering/Technology; Industrial Design; Mechanical Engineering; Trade/Technical Specialties.

Award: Scholarship for use in freshman, sophomore, junior, senior, or graduate years; not renewable. *Number:* 1–10. *Amount:* $1000–$5000.

Eligibility Requirements: Applicant must be enrolled or expecting to enroll full-time at a two-year or four-year institution or university and studying in Indiana. Applicant must have 2.5 GPA or higher. Available to U.S. citizens.

Application Requirements: Application, essay, resume, references, transcript. *Deadline:* February 1.

Contact: Chris Milantoni, Program Coordinator
Society of Manufacturing Engineers Education Foundation
One SME Drive
PO Box 930
Dearborn, MI 48121-0930
Phone: 313-425-3300
Fax: 313-425-3411
E-mail: foundation@sme.org

GUILIANO MAZZETTI SCHOLARSHIP AWARD

One-time award available to full-time students enrolled in a degree program in manufacturing engineering or technology in the United States or Canada. Minimum GPA of 3.0 required.

Academic Fields/Career Goals: Engineering/Technology.

Award: Scholarship for use in freshman, sophomore, junior, or senior years; not renewable. *Number:* 1–10. *Amount:* $1000–$5000.

Eligibility Requirements: Applicant must be enrolled or expecting to enroll full-time at a four-year institution or university. Applicant must have 3.0 GPA or higher. Available to U.S. and Canadian citizens.

Application Requirements: Application, essay, resume, references, transcript. *Deadline:* February 1.

Contact: Chris Milantoni, Program Coordinator
Society of Manufacturing Engineers Education Foundation
One SME Drive
PO Box 930
Dearborn, MI 48121-0930
Phone: 313-425-3300
Fax: 313-425-3411
E-mail: foundation@sme.org

LUCILE B. KAUFMAN WOMEN'S SCHOLARSHIP

Scholarships available for female full-time undergraduate students enrolled in a degree program in manufacturing engineering, technology or a closely related field in the United States or Canada. Minimum of 3.0 GPA is required. Scholarship value and the number of awards granted varies.

Academic Fields/Career Goals: Engineering/Technology.

Award: Scholarship for use in freshman, sophomore, junior, or senior years; not renewable. *Number:* 1–5. *Amount:* $1000–$5000.

Eligibility Requirements: Applicant must be enrolled or expecting to enroll full-time at a four-year institution or university and female. Applicant must have 3.0 GPA or higher. Available to U.S. and Canadian citizens.

Application Requirements: Application, essay, resume, references, transcript. *Deadline:* February 1.

Contact: Chris Milantoni, Program Coordinator
Society of Manufacturing Engineers Education Foundation
One SME Drive
PO Box 930
Dearborn, MI 48121-0930
Phone: 313-425-3300
Fax: 313-425-3411
E-mail: foundation@sme.org

MYRTLE AND EARL WALKER SCHOLARSHIP FUND

Scholarship available to full-time undergraduate students enrolled in a degree program in manufacturing engineering or technology in the United States or Canada. Minimum GPA of 3.0. Scholarship value and number of awards granted varies.

Academic Fields/Career Goals: Engineering/Technology; Trade/Technical Specialties.

Award: Scholarship for use in freshman, sophomore, junior, or senior years; not renewable. *Number:* 1–25. *Amount:* $1000–$7000.

Eligibility Requirements: Applicant must be enrolled or expecting to enroll full-time at a two-year or four-year or technical institution or university. Applicant must have 3.0 GPA or higher. Available to U.S. and Canadian citizens.

Society of Manufacturing Engineers Education Foundation (continued)

Application Requirements: Application, essay, resume, references, test scores, transcript. *Deadline:* February 1.

Contact: Chris Milantoni, Program Coordinator
Society of Manufacturing Engineers Education Foundation
One SME Drive
PO Box 930
Dearborn, MI 48121-0930
Phone: 313-425-3300
Fax: 313-425-3411
E-mail: foundation@sme.org

NORTH CENTRAL REGION 9 SCHOLARSHIP

Award to a full-time student enrolled in a manufacturing, mechanical, or industrial engineering degree program in North Central Region 9 (Iowa, Minnesota, Nebraska, North Dakota, South Dakota, Wisconsin, and the upper peninsula of Michigan). Applicants must have a 3.0 GPA.

Academic Fields/Career Goals: Engineering/Technology; Industrial Design; Mechanical Engineering; Trade/Technical Specialties.

Award: Scholarship for use in freshman, sophomore, junior, or senior years; not renewable. *Number:* 1–10. *Amount:* $1000–$5000.

Eligibility Requirements: Applicant must be enrolled or expecting to enroll full-time at a four-year institution or university and studying in Iowa, Michigan, Minnesota, Nebraska, North Dakota, South Dakota, or Wisconsin. Applicant must have 3.0 GPA or higher. Available to U.S. citizens.

Application Requirements: Application, essay, resume, references, transcript. *Deadline:* February 1.

Contact: Chris Milantoni, Program Coordinator
Society of Manufacturing Engineers Education Foundation
One SME Drive
PO Box 930
Dearborn, MI 48121-0930
Phone: 313-425-3300
Fax: 313-425-3411
E-mail: foundation@sme.org

SME FAMILY SCHOLARSHIP

Scholarships awarded to children or grandchildren of Society of Manufacturing Engineers members. Must be graduating high school senior planning to pursue full-time studies for an undergraduate degree in manufacturing engineering, manufacturing engineering technology, or a closely related engineering study at an accredited college or university. Minimum GPA of 3.0 required. Scholarship value and the number of awards granted varies annually.

Academic Fields/Career Goals: Engineering/Technology.

Award: Scholarship for use in freshman, sophomore, junior, or senior years; renewable. *Number:* 1–10. *Amount:* $5000–$80,000.

Eligibility Requirements: Applicant must be enrolled or expecting to enroll full-time at a four-year institution or university. Applicant must have 3.0 GPA or higher. Available to U.S. and non-U.S. citizens.

Application Requirements: Application, autobiography, essay, interview, photo, resume, references, test scores, transcript. *Deadline:* February 1.

Contact: Chris Milantoni, Program Coordinator
Society of Manufacturing Engineers Education Foundation
One SME Drive
PO Box 930
Dearborn, MI 48121-0930
Phone: 313-425-3300
Fax: 313-425-3411
E-mail: foundation@sme.org

WALT BARTRAM MEMORIAL EDUCATION AWARD

Scholarship available for graduating high school seniors who commit to enroll in, or full-time college or university students pursuing a degree in, manufacturing engineering or a closely related field within the areas of New Mexico, Arizona or Southern California.

Academic Fields/Career Goals: Engineering/Technology.

Award: Scholarship for use in freshman, sophomore, junior, or senior years; not renewable. *Number:* 1. *Amount:* $1500.

Eligibility Requirements: Applicant must be enrolled or expecting to enroll full-time at a four-year institution or university; resident of Arizona, California, or New Mexico and studying in Arizona, California, or New Mexico. Applicant or parent of applicant must be member of Soil and Water Conservation Society. Applicant must have 3.5 GPA or higher. Available to U.S. and Canadian citizens.

Application Requirements: Application, resume, references, transcript, 2 copies of student statement letter. *Deadline:* February 1.

Contact: Chris Milantoni, Program Coordinator
Society of Manufacturing Engineers Education Foundation
One SME Drive
PO Box 930
Dearborn, MI 48121-0930
Phone: 313-425-3300
Fax: 313-425-3411
E-mail: foundation@sme.org

WICHITA CHAPTER 52 SCHOLARSHIP

Award for an individual seeking an associates degree, bachelor's degree, or graduate degree in manufacturing, mechanical or industrial engineering, engineering technology, or industrial technology at an accredited public or private college or university in Kansas, Oklahoma or Missouri. Applicants must have a minimum GPA of 2.5. Preference given to applicants who are a relative of a current SME Wichita Chapter No. 52 member or a Kansas resident.

Academic Fields/Career Goals: Engineering/Technology; Industrial Design; Mechanical Engineering; Trade/Technical Specialties.

Award: Scholarship for use in freshman, sophomore, junior, senior, or graduate years; not renewable. *Number:* 1. *Amount:* up to $1500.

Eligibility Requirements: Applicant must be enrolled or expecting to enroll full-time at a two-year or four-year institution or university and studying in Kansas, Missouri, or Oklahoma. Applicant must have 2.5 GPA or higher. Available to U.S. citizens.

Application Requirements: Application, resume, references, transcript, student statement letter. *Deadline:* February 1.

Contact: Chris Milantoni, Program Coordinator
Society of Manufacturing Engineers Education Foundation
One SME Drive
PO Box 930
Dearborn, MI 48121-0930
Phone: 313-425-3300
Fax: 313-425-3411
E-mail: foundation@sme.org

WILLIAM E. WEISEL SCHOLARSHIP FUND

• *See page 251*

SOCIETY OF PETROLEUM ENGINEERS http://www.spe.org

GUS ARCHIE MEMORIAL SCHOLARSHIPS

Renewable award for students who have not attended college or university before and are planning to enroll in a petroleum engineering degree program at a four-year institution. Must have minimum 3.0 GPA.

Academic Fields/Career Goals: Engineering/Technology.

Award: Scholarship for use in freshman, sophomore, junior, or senior years; renewable. *Number:* 1–2. *Amount:* $6000.

Eligibility Requirements: Applicant must be enrolled or expecting to enroll full-time at a four-year institution or university. Applicant must have 3.0 GPA or higher. Available to U.S. and non-U.S. citizens.

Application Requirements: Application, autobiography, financial need analysis, photo, references, test scores, transcript. *Deadline:* April 30.

Contact: Professional Development Manager
Society of Petroleum Engineers
PO Box 833836
Richardson, TX 75083
Phone: 972-952-9452
Fax: 972-952-9435
E-mail: twhipple@spe.org

SOCIETY OF PLASTICS ENGINEERS (SPE) FOUNDATION http://www.4spe.org

FLEMING/BASZCAK SCHOLARSHIP

• *See page 163*

GULF COAST HURRICANE SCHOLARSHIP
• See page 163

PLASTICS PIONEERS ASSOCIATION SCHOLARSHIPS
• See page 163

SOCIETY OF WOMEN ENGINEERS http://www.swe.org

ADMIRAL GRACE MURRAY HOPPER MEMORIAL SCHOLARSHIP

Scholarships for female freshmen entering the study of engineering in a four-year program. Must attend an ABET-accredited or SWE-approved school and have minimum GPA of 3.5. Preference is given to student in computer-related engineering majors.

Academic Fields/Career Goals: Engineering/Technology.

Award: Scholarship for use in freshman year; not renewable. *Number:* 5. *Amount:* $1500.

Eligibility Requirements: Applicant must be high school student; planning to enroll or expecting to enroll full-time at a four-year institution or university and female. Applicant must have 3.5 GPA or higher. Available to U.S. citizens.

Application Requirements: Application, essay, self-addressed stamped envelope, test scores, transcript. *Deadline:* May 15.

Contact: Scholarship Committee
Society of Women Engineers
230 East Ohio Street, Suite 400
Chicago, IL 60611-3265
Phone: 312-596-5223
Fax: 312-596-5252
E-mail: scholarshipapplication@swe.org

ADOBE SYSTEMS COMPUTER SCIENCE SCHOLARSHIP

Two scholarships available to female engineering students in junior or senior year with 3.0 GPA or above. Preference given to students attending selected schools in the San Francisco Bay area.

Academic Fields/Career Goals: Engineering/Technology.

Award: Scholarship for use in junior or senior years; renewable. *Number:* 2. *Amount:* $1500–$2000.

Eligibility Requirements: Applicant must be enrolled or expecting to enroll full- or part-time at a four-year institution or university and female. Applicant must have 3.0 GPA or higher. Available to U.S. citizens.

Application Requirements: Application, references, self-addressed stamped envelope, transcript. *Deadline:* February 1.

Contact: Scholarship Committee
Society of Women Engineers
230 East Ohio Street, Suite 400
Chicago, IL 60611-3265
Phone: 312-596-5223
Fax: 312-596-5252
E-mail: scholarshipapplication@swe.org

AGILENT MENTORING SCHOLARSHIP
• See page 194

ANNE MAUREEN WHITNEY BARROW MEMORIAL SCHOLARSHIP
• See page 173

ARIZONA SECTION SCHOLARSHIP
• See page 297

BECHTEL CORPORATION SCHOLARSHIP
• See page 173

B.J. HARROD SCHOLARSHIP

Two $2000 awards made to an incoming female freshman majoring in engineering. The minimum GPA is 3.5 for freshman applicants. US citizens are eligible to apply.

Academic Fields/Career Goals: Engineering/Technology.

Award: Scholarship for use in freshman year; not renewable. *Number:* 2. *Amount:* $2000.

Eligibility Requirements: Applicant must be high school student; planning to enroll or expecting to enroll full-time at a two-year or four-year institution or university and female. Applicant must have 3.5 GPA or higher. Available to U.S. citizens.

Application Requirements: Application, essay, references, self-addressed stamped envelope, test scores, transcript. *Deadline:* May 15.

Contact: Scholarship Committee
Society of Women Engineers
230 East Ohio Street, Suite 400
Chicago, IL 60611-3265
Phone: 312-596-5223
Fax: 312-596-5252
E-mail: scholarshipapplication@swe.org

B.K. KRENZER MEMORIAL REENTRY SCHOLARSHIP

Preference is given female engineers with degrees who desire to return to the workforce following a period of temporary retirement. Recipients may be entering any year of an engineering program, undergraduate or graduate, as full-time or part-time students. Applicants must have been out of the engineering job market as well as out of school for a minimum of two years.

Academic Fields/Career Goals: Engineering/Technology.

Award: Scholarship for use in freshman, sophomore, junior, senior, or graduate years; not renewable. *Number:* 1. *Amount:* $2000.

Eligibility Requirements: Applicant must be enrolled or expecting to enroll full- or part-time at a two-year or four-year or technical institution or university and female. Applicant must have 3.0 GPA or higher. Available to U.S. citizens.

Application Requirements: Application, essay, references, self-addressed stamped envelope, test scores, transcript. *Deadline:* May 15.

Contact: Scholarship Committee
Society of Women Engineers
230 East Ohio Street, Suite 400
Chicago, IL 60611-3265
Phone: 312-596-5223
Fax: 312-596-5252
E-mail: scholarshipapplication@swe.org

CATERPILLAR INC. SCHOLARSHIP
• See page 79

CHEVRON TEXACO CORPORATION SCHOLARSHIPS
• See page 163

COLUMBIA RIVER SECTION SCHOLARSHIPS

Scholarships available to students attending University of Portland, Portland State University, or Oregon Institute of Technology or a transfer student from an Oregon or Southwest Washington Community College planning or pursuing an engineering degree at one of those schools.

Academic Fields/Career Goals: Engineering/Technology.

Award: Scholarship for use in freshman, sophomore, junior, or senior years; not renewable. *Number:* 2. *Amount:* $300–$750.

Eligibility Requirements: Applicant must be enrolled or expecting to enroll full-time at a four-year institution or university; female and studying in Oregon or Washington. Applicant must have 2.5 GPA or higher. Available to U.S. citizens.

Application Requirements: Application, essay, references, transcript. *Deadline:* March 1.

Contact: Scholarship Committee
Society of Women Engineers
230 East Ohio Street, Suite 400
Chicago, IL 60611-3265
Phone: 312-596-5223
Fax: 312-596-5252
E-mail: scholarshipapplication@swe.org

DELL COMPUTER CORPORATION SCHOLARSHIPS
• See page 195

DOROTHY LEMKE HOWARTH SCHOLARSHIPS
• See page 163

DOROTHY M. AND EARL S. HOFFMAN SCHOLARSHIP

Renewable three-year scholarship for female freshman engineering students. Minimum of 3.5 GPA is required. Preference given to students at Bucknell University and Rensselaer Polytechnic University.

Academic Fields/Career Goals: Engineering/Technology.

Award: Scholarship for use in freshman year; renewable. *Number:* 5. *Amount:* $3000.

Society of Women Engineers (continued)

Eligibility Requirements: Applicant must be enrolled or expecting to enroll full-time at a four-year institution or university and female. Applicant must have 3.5 GPA or higher. Available to U.S. citizens.

Application Requirements: Application, references, self-addressed stamped envelope, transcript. *Deadline:* May 15.

Contact: Scholarship Committee
Society of Women Engineers
230 East Ohio Street, Suite 400
Chicago, IL 60611-3265
Phone: 312-596-5223
Fax: 312-596-5252
E-mail: scholarshipapplication@swe.org

DOROTHY P. MORRIS SCHOLARSHIP

One award of $1000 will be given to a sophomore, junior, or senior with a minimum 3.0 GPA in any engineering fields. For full-time study only.

Academic Fields/Career Goals: Engineering/Technology.

Award: Scholarship for use in sophomore, junior, or senior years; not renewable. *Number:* 1. *Amount:* $1000.

Eligibility Requirements: Applicant must be enrolled or expecting to enroll full-time at a four-year institution or university and female. Applicant must have 3.0 GPA or higher. Available to U.S. citizens.

Application Requirements: Application, essay, references, transcript. *Deadline:* February 1.

Contact: Scholarship Committee
Society of Women Engineers
230 East Ohio Street, Suite 400
Chicago, IL 60611-3265
Phone: 312-596-5223
Fax: 312-596-5252
E-mail: scholarshipapplication@swe.org

ELECTRONICS FOR IMAGING (EFI) SCHOLARSHIPS

Four scholarships available to female engineering students in sophomore, junior, senior year, or graduate study. Preference given to students attending selected schools in the San Francisco Bay area.

Academic Fields/Career Goals: Engineering/Technology.

Award: Scholarship for use in sophomore, junior, senior, or graduate years; not renewable. *Number:* 4. *Amount:* $4000.

Eligibility Requirements: Applicant must be enrolled or expecting to enroll full-time at a four-year institution or university and female. Applicant must have 3.0 GPA or higher. Available to U.S. citizens.

Application Requirements: Application, references, self-addressed stamped envelope, transcript. *Deadline:* February 1.

Contact: Scholarship Committee
Society of Women Engineers
230 East Ohio Street, Suite 400
Chicago, IL 60611-3265
Phone: 312-596-5223
Fax: 312-596-5252
E-mail: scholarshipapplication@swe.org

EXELON CORPORATION SCHOLARSHIPS

Scholarships of $1000 are awarded for up to five freshman students studying engineering. Must maintain a minimum GPA of 3.5. For full-time study only.

Academic Fields/Career Goals: Engineering/Technology.

Award: Scholarship for use in freshman year; not renewable. *Number:* 5. *Amount:* $1000.

Eligibility Requirements: Applicant must be enrolled or expecting to enroll full-time at a four-year institution or university and female. Applicant must have 3.5 GPA or higher. Available to U.S. citizens.

Application Requirements: Application, references, transcript. *Deadline:* May 15.

Contact: Scholarship Committee
Society of Women Engineers
230 East Ohio Street, Suite 400
Chicago, IL 60611-3265
Phone: 312-596-5223
Fax: 312-596-5252
E-mail: scholarshipapplication@swe.org

GENERAL ELECTRIC FOUNDATION SCHOLARSHIP

• *See page 164*

GENERAL ELECTRIC WOMEN'S NETWORK SCHOLARSHIP

Awards of $2425 for a sophomore, junior, or senior with a GPA of 3.0 or above in any engineering major. There is a preferred list of schools and U.S. citizenship is required.

Academic Fields/Career Goals: Engineering/Technology.

Award: Scholarship for use in sophomore, junior, or senior years; not renewable. *Number:* 12. *Amount:* $2425.

Eligibility Requirements: Applicant must be enrolled or expecting to enroll full-time at a four-year institution or university and female. Applicant must have 3.0 GPA or higher. Available to U.S. citizens.

Application Requirements: Application, references, transcript. *Deadline:* February 1.

Contact: Scholarship Committee
Society of Women Engineers
230 East Ohio Street, Suite 400
Chicago, IL 60611-3265
Phone: 312-596-5223
Fax: 312-596-5252
E-mail: scholarshipapplication@swe.org

GENERAL MOTORS FOUNDATION UNDERGRADUATE SCHOLARSHIPS

• *See page 251*

GUIDANT CORPORATION SCHOLARSHIP

• *See page 195*

IVY M. PARKER MEMORIAL SCHOLARSHIP

One-time award for female engineering major. Must be in junior or senior year and have a minimum 3.0 GPA. Selection also based on financial need.

Academic Fields/Career Goals: Engineering/Technology.

Award: Scholarship for use in junior or senior years; not renewable. *Number:* 1. *Amount:* $2500.

Eligibility Requirements: Applicant must be enrolled or expecting to enroll full-time at a four-year institution or university and female. Applicant must have 3.0 GPA or higher. Available to U.S. citizens.

Application Requirements: Application, financial need analysis, references, self-addressed stamped envelope, transcript. *Deadline:* February 1.

Contact: Scholarship Committee
Society of Women Engineers
230 East Ohio Street, Suite 400
Chicago, IL 60611-3265
Phone: 312-596-5223
Fax: 312-596-5252
E-mail: scholarshipapplication@swe.org

JUDITH RESNIK MEMORIAL SCHOLARSHIP

• *See page 125*

LILLIAN MOLLER GILBRETH MEMORIAL SCHOLARSHIP

• *See page 164*

LOCKHEED MARTIN FRESHMAN SCHOLARSHIPS

Two scholarships of $3000 awarded to female incoming freshmen majoring in engineering. Minimum 3.5 GPA is required. For full-time study only. Includes travel grant for the SWE National Conference.

Academic Fields/Career Goals: Engineering/Technology.

Award: Scholarship for use in freshman year; not renewable. *Number:* 2. *Amount:* $3000.

Eligibility Requirements: Applicant must be enrolled or expecting to enroll full-time at a four-year institution or university and female. Applicant must have 3.5 GPA or higher. Available to U.S. citizens.

Application Requirements: Application, essay, references, self-addressed stamped envelope, test scores, transcript. *Deadline:* May 15.

Contact: Scholarship Committee
Society of Women Engineers
230 East Ohio Street, Suite 400
Chicago, IL 60611-3265
Phone: 312-596-5223
Fax: 312-596-5252
E-mail: scholarshipapplication@swe.org

LYDIA I. PICKUP MEMORIAL SCHOLARSHIP

• *See page 195*

MASWE MEMORIAL SCHOLARSHIP

• *See page 164*

MERIDITH THOMS MEMORIAL SCHOLARSHIP

Renewable award available to female engineering majors. Minimum 3.0 GPA required. Must be in ABET-accredited engineering program at SWE-approved colleges and universities.

Academic Fields/Career Goals: Engineering/Technology.

Award: Scholarship for use in sophomore, junior, or senior years; renewable. *Number:* 6. *Amount:* $2000.

Eligibility Requirements: Applicant must be enrolled or expecting to enroll full- or part-time at a four-year institution or university and female. Applicant must have 3.0 GPA or higher. Available to U.S. citizens.

Application Requirements: Application, references, self-addressed stamped envelope, test scores, transcript. *Deadline:* February 1.

Contact: Scholarship Committee
Society of Women Engineers
230 East Ohio Street, Suite 400
Chicago, IL 60611-3265
Phone: 312-596-5223
Fax: 312-596-5252
E-mail: scholarshipapplication@swe.org

MINNESOTA SWE SECTION SCHOLARSHIP

Scholarship of $1000 for qualified women students with junior or senior standing in an accredited engineering program at schools in Minnesota, North Dakota and South Dakota. Applicants are judged on the basis of potential to succeed as an engineers, communication skills, extracurricular or community involvement and leadership skills, demonstration of work experience and successes and academic success.

Academic Fields/Career Goals: Engineering/Technology.

Award: Scholarship for use in junior or senior years; not renewable. *Number:* 1. *Amount:* $1000.

Eligibility Requirements: Applicant must be enrolled or expecting to enroll full-time at a four-year institution or university; female and studying in Minnesota, North Dakota, or South Dakota. Available to U.S. citizens.

Application Requirements: Application, references, transcript. *Deadline:* March 15.

Contact: Scholarship Committee
Society of Women Engineers
230 East Ohio Street, Suite 400
Chicago, IL 60611-3265
Phone: 312-596-5223
Fax: 312-596-5252
E-mail: scholarshipapplication@swe.org

NEW JERSEY SCHOLARSHIP

Scholarship granted to female New Jersey resident majoring in engineering. Available to incoming freshman. Minimum 3.5 GPA required.

Academic Fields/Career Goals: Engineering/Technology.

Award: Scholarship for use in freshman year; not renewable. *Number:* 1. *Amount:* $1500.

Eligibility Requirements: Applicant must be enrolled or expecting to enroll full-time at a four-year institution or university; female and resident of New Jersey. Applicant must have 3.5 GPA or higher. Available to U.S. citizens.

Application Requirements: Application, essay, references, self-addressed stamped envelope, test scores, transcript. *Deadline:* May 15.

Contact: Scholarship Committee
Society of Women Engineers
230 East Ohio Street, Suite 400
Chicago, IL 60611-3265
Phone: 312-596-5223
Fax: 312-596-5252
E-mail: scholarshipapplication@swe.org

NORTHROP GRUMMAN FRESHMAN SCHOLARSHIP

• *See page 125*

OLIVE LYNN SALEMBIER MEMORIAL REENTRY SCHOLARSHIP

Scholarship of $2000 for female students entering any undergraduate or graduate year as full- or part-time students. Applicants must have been out of the engineering job market as well as out of school for a minimum of two years.

Academic Fields/Career Goals: Engineering/Technology.

Award: Scholarship for use in freshman, sophomore, junior, senior, or graduate years; not renewable. *Number:* 1. *Amount:* $2000.

Eligibility Requirements: Applicant must be enrolled or expecting to enroll full- or part-time at a four-year institution or university and female. Available to U.S. citizens.

Application Requirements: Application, essay, references, self-addressed stamped envelope, test scores, transcript. *Deadline:* May 15.

Contact: Scholarship Committee
Society of Women Engineers
230 East Ohio Street, Suite 400
Chicago, IL 60611-3265
Phone: 312-596-5223
Fax: 312-596-5252
E-mail: scholarshipapplication@swe.org

PAST PRESIDENTS SCHOLARSHIPS

Scholarship of $2000 will be offered to two female undergraduate or graduate students majoring in engineering. Minimum 3.0 GPA required.

Academic Fields/Career Goals: Engineering/Technology.

Award: Scholarship for use in sophomore, junior, senior, or graduate years; renewable. *Number:* 2. *Amount:* $2000.

Eligibility Requirements: Applicant must be enrolled or expecting to enroll full-time at a four-year institution or university and female. Applicant must have 3.0 GPA or higher. Available to U.S. citizens.

Application Requirements: Application, essay, references, self-addressed stamped envelope, test scores, transcript. *Deadline:* February 1.

Contact: Scholarship Committee
Society of Women Engineers
230 East Ohio Street, Suite 400
Chicago, IL 60611-3265
Phone: 312-596-5223
Fax: 312-596-5252
E-mail: scholarshipapplication@swe.org

ROCKWELL AUTOMATION SCHOLARSHIP

• *See page 195*

SUSAN MISZKOWITZ MEMORIAL SCHOLARSHIP

Scholarship of $1500 is open to sophomores, juniors, or seniors studying engineering. For full-time study only. Must maintain a minimum GPA of 3.0.

Academic Fields/Career Goals: Engineering/Technology.

Award: Scholarship for use in sophomore, junior, or senior years; not renewable. *Number:* 1. *Amount:* $1500.

Eligibility Requirements: Applicant must be enrolled or expecting to enroll full-time at a four-year institution or university and female. Applicant must have 3.0 GPA or higher. Available to U.S. citizens.

Application Requirements: Application, references, transcript. *Deadline:* February 1.

Contact: Scholarship Committee
Society of Women Engineers
230 East Ohio Street, Suite 400
Chicago, IL 60611-3265
Phone: 312-596-5223
Fax: 312-596-5252
E-mail: scholarshipapplication@swe.org

Society of Women Engineers (continued)

SWE BATON ROUGE SECTION SCHOLARSHIPS
• *See page 195*

SWE CALIFORNIA GOLDEN GATE SECTION SCHOLARSHIPS
• *See page 196*

SWE CALIFORNIA SANTA CLARA VALLEY SECTION SCHOLARSHIP

Scholarship of $1000 for entering freshman, sophomore, junior, senior, graduate students. Applicants meeting the following requirements are eligible to apply, plan to attend school full-time in the fall next year in and ABET-accredited engineering program, permanent residents or attend school in the South San Francisco Bay area.

Academic Fields/Career Goals: Engineering/Technology.

Award: Scholarship for use in freshman, sophomore, junior, senior, or graduate years; not renewable. *Number:* 15. *Amount:* $1000.

Eligibility Requirements: Applicant must be enrolled or expecting to enroll full-time at a four-year institution or university; female; resident of California and studying in California. Available to U.S. citizens.

Application Requirements: Application, references, transcript. *Deadline:* March 31.

Contact: Scholarship Committee
Society of Women Engineers
230 East Ohio Street, Suite 400
Chicago, IL 60611-3265
Phone: 312-596-5223
Fax: 312-596-5252
E-mail: scholarshipapplication@swe.org

SWE CHICAGO REGIONAL SECTION SCHOLARSHIPS

Scholarships are available for female high school seniors, continuing college students, transfer college students, graduate students and re-entry students who will be attending an ABET-accredited engineering school to pursue a BS or higher degree full-time or studying an ABET-accredited program.

Academic Fields/Career Goals: Engineering/Technology.

Award: Scholarship for use in freshman, sophomore, junior, or senior years; not renewable. *Number:* 1. *Amount:* $1000.

Eligibility Requirements: Applicant must be enrolled or expecting to enroll full-time at a four-year institution or university; female and resident of Illinois. Available to U.S. citizens.

Application Requirements: Application, essay, transcript, acceptance letter. *Deadline:* April 15.

Contact: Scholarship Committee
Society of Women Engineers
230 East Ohio Street, Suite 400
Chicago, IL 60611-3265
Phone: 312-596-5223
Fax: 312-596-5252
E-mail: scholarshipapplication@swe.org

SWE CONNECTICUT SECTION JEAN R. BEERS SCHOLARSHIP
• *See page 196*

SWE GREATER NEW ORLEANS SECTION SCHOLARSHIP
• *See page 196*

SWE LEHIGH VALLEY SECTION SCHOLARSHIP

Applicants must be female graduating high school seniors, within the Lehigh Valley Section, planning on attending an ABET-accredited college or university in the following fall semester.

Academic Fields/Career Goals: Engineering/Technology.

Award: Scholarship for use in freshman year; not renewable. *Number:* 6–10. *Amount:* $1000.

Eligibility Requirements: Applicant must be high school student; planning to enroll or expecting to enroll full-time at a four-year institution or university; female; resident of Pennsylvania and must have an interest in leadership. Available to U.S. citizens.

Application Requirements: Application, acceptance letter, survey form and supplemental form. *Deadline:* April 15.

Contact: Scholarship Committee
Society of Women Engineers
230 East Ohio Street, Suite 400
Chicago, IL 60611-3265
Phone: 312-596-5223
Fax: 312-596-5252
E-mail: scholarshipapplication@swe.org

SWE ST. LOUIS SCHOLARSHIP

One $500 scholarship will be awarded to an entering sophomore, junior, or senior undergraduate student, or a graduate student attending one of the following colleges or universities: Southern Illinois University, Parks College of Engineering and Aviation, St. Louis University, University of Missouri, or Washington University.

Academic Fields/Career Goals: Engineering/Technology.

Award: Scholarship for use in sophomore, junior, senior, or graduate years; not renewable. *Number:* 1. *Amount:* $500.

Eligibility Requirements: Applicant must be enrolled or expecting to enroll full-time at a four-year institution or university; female and studying in Illinois or Missouri. Applicant or parent of applicant must be member of Society of Women Engineers. Available to U.S. citizens.

Application Requirements: Application, references, test scores, transcript. *Deadline:* varies.

Contact: Scholarship Committee
Society of Women Engineers
230 East Ohio Street, Suite 400
Chicago, IL 60611-3265
Phone: 312-596-5223
Fax: 312-596-5252
E-mail: scholarshipapplication@swe.org

SWE SOUTH OHIO SCIENCE FAIR SCHOLARSHIP
• *See page 297*

SOCIETY OF WOMEN ENGINEERS-DALLAS SECTION **http://www.dallaswe.org**

FRESHMAN ENGINEERING SCHOLARSHIP FOR DALLAS WOMEN

Scholarship for freshman women pursuing a degree in engineering. Applicant must be a Texas resident. Please refer to Web site for further details: http://www.dallaswe.org.

Academic Fields/Career Goals: Engineering/Technology.

Award: Scholarship for use in freshman year; not renewable. *Number:* 2. *Amount:* $500.

Eligibility Requirements: Applicant must be high school student; planning to enroll or expecting to enroll full-time at a four-year institution or university; female and resident of Texas. Available to U.S. citizens.

Application Requirements: Application, financial need analysis, references, transcript, confirmation of enrollment. *Deadline:* May 15.

Contact: Luanne Beckley, Scholarship Coordinator
Society of Women Engineers-Dallas Section
PO Box 852022
Richardson, TX 75085-2022
Phone: 214-670-9273

NATIONAL SOCIETY OF WOMEN ENGINEERS SCHOLARSHIPS
• *See page 196*

SOCIETY OF WOMEN ENGINEERS-ROCKY MOUNTAIN SECTION **http://www.swe-rms.org**

SOCIETY OF WOMEN ENGINEERS-ROCKY MOUNTAIN SECTION SCHOLARSHIP PROGRAM
• *See page 164*

SOCIETY OF WOMEN ENGINEERS-TWIN TIERS SECTION **http://www.swetwintiers.org**

SOCIETY OF WOMEN ENGINEERS-TWIN TIERS SECTION SCHOLARSHIP
• *See page 196*

SPECIALTY EQUIPMENT MARKET ASSOCIATION http://www.sema.org

SPECIALTY EQUIPMENT MARKET ASSOCIATION MEMORIAL SCHOLARSHIP FUND

Scholarship for higher education in the automotive field. All applicants must be attending a U.S. institution. For further details visit Web site: http://www.sema.org.

Academic Fields/Career Goals: Engineering/Technology; Trade/Technical Specialties.

Award: Scholarship for use in freshman, sophomore, junior, senior, or graduate years; not renewable. *Number:* up to 90. *Amount:* $1000–$4000.

Eligibility Requirements: Applicant must be enrolled or expecting to enroll full-time at a two-year or four-year or technical institution or university and must have an interest in automotive. Applicant must have 2.5 GPA or higher. Available to U.S. and non-U.S. citizens.

Application Requirements: Application, essay, photo, references, self-addressed stamped envelope, transcript. *Deadline:* April 20.

Contact: Pat Talaska-Benson, Director, Educational Services
Specialty Equipment Market Association
1575 South Valley Vista Drive
PO Box 4910
Diamond Bar, CA 91765
Phone: 909-396-0289 Ext. 137
Fax: 909-860-0184
E-mail: patt@sema.org

STRAIGHTFORWARD MEDIA http://www.straightforwardmedia.com

STRAIGHTFORWARD MEDIA ENGINEERING SCHOLARSHIP

• *See page 164*

TAU BETA PI ASSOCIATION http://www.tbp.org

TAU BETA PI SCHOLARSHIP PROGRAM

One-time award for initiated members of Tau Beta Pi in their senior year of full-time undergraduate engineering study. Must submit application and two letters of recommendation. Contact for complete details or visit http://www.tbp.org.

Academic Fields/Career Goals: Engineering/Technology.

Award: Scholarship for use in senior year; not renewable. *Number:* up to 150. *Amount:* $2000.

Eligibility Requirements: Applicant must be enrolled or expecting to enroll full-time at a four-year institution or university. Applicant or parent of applicant must be member of Tau Beta Pi Association. Applicant must have 3.5 GPA or higher. Available to U.S. and non-U.S. citizens.

Application Requirements: Application, essay, references. *Deadline:* March 1.

Contact: D. Stephen Pierre, Jr., Director of Fellowships
Tau Beta Pi Association
PO Box 2697
Knoxville, TN 37901-2697
Fax: 334-694-2310
E-mail: dspierre@southernco.com

TECHNICAL ASSOCIATION OF THE PULP & PAPER INDUSTRY (TAPPI) http://www.tappi.org

NONWOVENS DIVISION SCHOLARSHIP

Award to applicants enrolled as a full-time student in a state accredited undergraduate program. Must be in a program preparatory to a career in the nonwovens industry or demonstrate an interest in the areas, be recommended and endorsed by an instructor or faculty member and must maintain 3.0 GPA.

Academic Fields/Career Goals: Engineering/Technology; Paper and Pulp Engineering.

Award: Scholarship for use in freshman, sophomore, junior, or senior years; not renewable. *Number:* 1. *Amount:* $1000.

Eligibility Requirements: Applicant must be enrolled or expecting to enroll full-time at a four-year institution or university. Applicant must have 3.0 GPA or higher. Available to U.S. and non U.S. citizens.

Application Requirements: Application, references, transcript. *Deadline:* February 15.

Contact: Veranda Edmondson, TAPPI-Member Group Specialist
Technical Association of the Pulp & Paper Industry (TAPPI)
15 Technology Parkway, South
Norcross, GA 30092
E-mail: vedmondson@tappi.org

PAPER AND BOARD DIVISION SCHOLARSHIPS

Award to TAPPI student member or an undergraduate member of a TAPPI Student Chapter, enrolled as a college or university undergraduate in an engineering or science program, must be sophomore, junior, or senior and able to show a significant interest in the paper industry. Refer to Web Site: http://www.tappi.org/content/pdf/member_groups/CurrentScholar.pdf for more details.

Academic Fields/Career Goals: Engineering/Technology; Paper and Pulp Engineering.

Award: Scholarship for use in sophomore, junior, or senior years; not renewable. *Number:* varies. *Amount:* $1000.

Eligibility Requirements: Applicant must be enrolled or expecting to enroll full-time at a four-year institution or university. Available to U.S. and non-U.S. citizens.

Application Requirements: Application, references, transcript. *Deadline:* February 15.

Contact: Veranda Edmondson, TAPPI-Member Group Specialist
Technical Association of the Pulp & Paper Industry (TAPPI)
15 Technology Parkway, South
Norcross, GA 30092
E-mail: vedmondson@tappi.org

TRIANGLE EDUCATION FOUNDATION http://www.triangle.org

KAPADIA SCHOLARSHIPS

Award ranges from $1500 to $8000 to an undergraduate or graduate Triangle members in good standing, with preference to engineering majors, non-US citizens, members of the Zoroastrian religion and Michigan State student.

Academic Fields/Career Goals: Engineering/Technology.

Award: Scholarship for use in freshman, sophomore, junior, senior, or graduate years; not renewable. *Number:* varies. *Amount:* $1500–$8000.

Eligibility Requirements: Applicant must be enrolled or expecting to enroll full-time at a four-year institution or university and male. Applicant must have 3.0 GPA or higher. Available to U.S. and non-U.S. citizens.

Application Requirements: Application, essay, financial need analysis, references, self-addressed stamped envelope, transcript. *Deadline:* February 15.

Contact: Scott Bova, President
Triangle Education Foundation
120 South Center Street
Plainfield, IN 46168-1214
Phone: 317-705-9803
Fax: 317-837-9642
E-mail: sbova@triangle.org

RUST SCHOLARSHIP

Awards $5500 annually based on a combination of need, grades and participation in campus and Triangle Activities. All other things being equal, preference is given to applicants in the core engineering disciplines or hard sciences.

Academic Fields/Career Goals: Engineering/Technology.

Award: Scholarship for use in freshman, sophomore, junior, or senior years; not renewable. *Number:* 1. *Amount:* up to $5500.

Eligibility Requirements: Applicant must be enrolled or expecting to enroll full-time at a four-year institution or university and male. Applicant must have 3.0 GPA or higher. Available to U.S. and non-U.S. citizens.

Triangle Education Foundation (continued)

Application Requirements: Application, essay, financial need analysis, references, self-addressed stamped envelope, transcript. *Deadline:* February 15.

Contact: Scott Bova, President
Triangle Education Foundation
120 South Center Street
Plainfield, IN 46168-1214
Phone: 317-705-9803
Fax: 317-837-9642
E-mail: sbova@triangle.org

SEVCIK SCHOLARSHIP

One-time award up to $1000 annually for active member of the Triangle Fraternity based on need, preference to an Ohio State student, preference to an Engineering student. Refer to Web Site: http://www.triangle.org/programs/scholarshipsloans/ for details.

Academic Fields/Career Goals: Engineering/Technology.

Award: Scholarship for use in freshman, sophomore, junior, or senior years; not renewable. *Number:* 1. *Amount:* up to $1000.

Eligibility Requirements: Applicant must be American Indian/Alaska Native, Asian/Pacific Islander, Black (non-Hispanic), or Hispanic; enrolled or expecting to enroll full-time at a four-year institution or university and male. Applicant must have 3.0 GPA or higher. Available to U.S. and non-U.S. citizens.

Application Requirements: Application, essay, financial need analysis, references, self-addressed stamped envelope, transcript. *Deadline:* February 15.

Contact: Scott Bova, President
Triangle Education Foundation
120 South Center Street
Plainfield, IN 46168-1214
Phone: 317-705-9803
Fax: 317-837-9642
E-mail: sbova@triangle.org

UNITED NEGRO COLLEGE FUND http://www.uncf.org

ACCENTURE SCHOLARSHIP

• *See page 197*

BATTELLE SCHOLARS PROGRAM

Scholarship of $10,000 for undergraduate juniors majoring in engineering attending a UNCF member college or university or Ohio State University. Applicant must have a minimum of 3.0 GPA. Please visit Web site for more information: http://www.uncf.org.

Academic Fields/Career Goals: Engineering/Technology.

Award: Scholarship for use in junior year; not renewable. *Number:* varies. *Amount:* $10,000.

Eligibility Requirements: Applicant must be Black (non-Hispanic) and enrolled or expecting to enroll full- or part-time at a four-year institution or university. Applicant must have 3.0 GPA or higher. Available to U.S. citizens.

Application Requirements: Application, financial need analysis, FAFSA, Student Aid Report (SAR). *Deadline:* varies.

Contact: William Dunham, Program Services
United Negro College Fund
8260 Willow Oaks Corporate Drive
Fairfax, VA 22031
Phone: 703-205-3486

BOOZ, ALLEN AND HAMILTON/WILLIAM F. STASIOR INTERNSHIP

• *See page 150*

CARDINAL HEALTH SCHOLARSHIP

• *See page 65*

CARTER AND BURGESS SCHOLARSHIP

The scholarship is for students from Ft. Worth, TX. If there aren't enough civil engineering students in Ft. Worth, the scholarship pool may extend to the entire state of Texas. Students studying engineering with minimum GPA of 2.5 are eligible. The scholarship value varies.

Academic Fields/Career Goals: Engineering/Technology.

Award: Scholarship for use in freshman, sophomore, junior, senior, or graduate years; renewable. *Number:* 1. *Amount:* varies.

Eligibility Requirements: Applicant must be Black (non-Hispanic); enrolled or expecting to enroll full-time at a four-year institution or university and resident of Texas. Applicant must have 2.5 GPA or higher. Available to U.S. citizens.

Application Requirements: Application, financial need analysis, FAFSA, Student Aid Report (SAR). *Deadline:* varies.

Contact: Director, Program Services
United Negro College Fund
8260 Willow Oaks Corporate Drive
PO Box 10444
Fairfax, VA 22031-8044
Phone: 800-331-2244
E-mail: rebecca.bennett@uncf.org

CASTLE ROCK FOUNDATION SCHOLARSHIP

• *See page 150*

CDM SCHOLARSHIP/INTERNSHIP

• *See page 93*

CHEVRONTEXACO SCHOLARS PROGRAM

Scholarships for college sophomores or juniors. Must be enrolled full-time in one of the following schools: Clark Atlanta, Morehouse, Spelman or Tuskegee. Minimum 2.5 GPA required. It is preferred that students are permanent residents of Texas, Florida or California, however students from other states are eligible to apply.

Academic Fields/Career Goals: Engineering/Technology.

Award: Scholarship for use in sophomore or junior years; not renewable. *Number:* 1. *Amount:* up to $3000.

Eligibility Requirements: Applicant must be Black (non-Hispanic) and enrolled or expecting to enroll full-time at a four-year institution or university. Applicant must have 2.5 GPA or higher. Available to U.S. citizens.

Application Requirements: Application, financial need analysis. *Deadline:* February 18.

Contact: Director, Program Services
United Negro College Fund
8260 Willow Oaks Corporate Drive
PO Box 10444
Fairfax, VA 22031-8044
Phone: 800-331-2244
E-mail: rebecca.bennett@uncf.org

FORD/UNCF CORPORATE SCHOLARS PROGRAM

• *See page 65*

GILBANE SCHOLARSHIP PROGRAM

• *See page 93*

KODAK ENGINEERING EXCELLENCE PROGRAM SCHOLARSHIP

• *See page 197*

MAYTAG COMPANY SCHOLARSHIP

• *See page 151*

MEDTRONIC FOUNDATION SCHOLARSHIP

• *See page 136*

NASCAR/WENDELL SCOTT, SR. SCHOLARSHIP

• *See page 66*

NORTHEAST UTILITIES SYSTEM SCHOLARSHIP PROGRAM

• *See page 151*

SPRINT NEXTEL SCHOLARSHIP/INTERNSHIP

• *See page 66*

THURMOND WOODARD/DELL/UNCF CORPORATE SCHOLARS PROGRAM

• *See page 151*

TRW INFORMATION TECHNOLOGY MINORITY SCHOLARSHIP

• *See page 197*

WEYERHAEUSER/UNCF CORPORATE SCHOLARS PROGRAM

• *See page 151*

WRIGLEY JR., WILLIAM SCHOLARSHIP/INTERNSHIP
• *See page 152*

UNIVERSITIES SPACE RESEARCH ASSOCIATION http://www.usra.edu

UNIVERSITIES SPACE RESEARCH ASSOCIATION SCHOLARSHIP PROGRAM
• *See page 88*

UTAH SOCIETY OF PROFESSIONAL ENGINEERS http://www.uspeonline.com

UTAH SOCIETY OF PROFESSIONAL ENGINEERS JOE RHOADS SCHOLARSHIP
• *See page 165*

VIRGINIA BUSINESS AND PROFESSIONAL WOMEN'S FOUNDATION http://www.vabpwfoundation.org

WOMEN IN SCIENCE AND TECHNOLOGY SCHOLARSHIP
• *See page 136*

WEST VIRGINIA HIGHER EDUCATION POLICY COMMISSION-OFFICE OF FINANCIAL AID AND OUTREACH SERVICES http://wvhepcnew.wvnet.edu/

WEST VIRGINIA ENGINEERING, SCIENCE AND TECHNOLOGY SCHOLARSHIP PROGRAM
• *See page 252*

WISCONSIN SOCIETY OF PROFESSIONAL ENGINEERS http://www.wspe.org

WISCONSIN SOCIETY OF PROFESSIONAL ENGINEERS SCHOLARSHIPS

Scholarships are awarded each year to high school seniors having qualifications for success in engineering education. Must be a U.S. citizen and Wisconsin resident and have a minimum GPA of 3.0.

Academic Fields/Career Goals: Engineering/Technology.

Award: Scholarship for use in freshman year; not renewable. *Number:* 3. *Amount:* $1000.

Eligibility Requirements: Applicant must be high school student; planning to enroll or expecting to enroll full-time at a four-year institution or university and resident of Wisconsin. Applicant must have 3.0 GPA or higher. Available to U.S. citizens.

Application Requirements: Application, essay, interview, references, self-addressed stamped envelope, test scores, transcript. *Deadline:* December 17.

Contact: Nancy Short, Executive Director
Wisconsin Society of Professional Engineers
7044 South 13th Street
Oak Creek, WI 53154
Phone: 414-908-4950 Ext. 135
Fax: 414-768-8001
E-mail: n.short@wspe.org

XEROX http://www.xerox.com

TECHNICAL MINORITY SCHOLARSHIP
• *See page 165*

ENGINEERING-RELATED TECHNOLOGIES

AACE INTERNATIONAL http://www.aacei.org

AACE INTERNATIONAL COMPETITIVE SCHOLARSHIP
• *See page 89*

AMERICAN COUNCIL OF ENGINEERING COMPANIES OF PENNSYLVANIA (ACEC/PA) http://www.acecpa.org

ENGINEERING SCHOLARSHIP
• *See page 154*

AMERICAN INDIAN SCIENCE AND ENGINEERING SOCIETY http://www.aises.org

GENERAL MOTORS ENGINEERING SCHOLARSHIP

A $3000 scholarship will be given to a current AISES member. Must be a member of an American-Indian tribe or otherwise be considered to be an American-Indian by the tribe with which affiliation is claimed. Must maintain a 3.0 GPA.

Academic Fields/Career Goals: Engineering-Related Technologies.

Award: Scholarship for use in freshman, sophomore, junior, senior, or graduate years; not renewable. *Number:* varies. *Amount:* up to $3000.

Eligibility Requirements: Applicant must be American Indian/Alaska Native and enrolled or expecting to enroll full-time at a four-year institution or university. Applicant must have 3.0 GPA or higher. Available to U.S. citizens.

Application Requirements: Application, essay, resume, references, transcript. *Deadline:* June 15.

Contact: Shirley Lacourse, Deputy Director
American Indian Science and Engineering Society
2305 Renard, SE, Suite 200
PO Box 9828
Albuquerque, NM 87119-9828
Phone: 505-765-1052
Fax: 505-765-5608
E-mail: shirley@aises.org

HENRY RODRIGUEZ RECLAMATION COLLEGE SCHOLARSHIP AND INTERNSHIP

A $5000 scholarship will be given to a current AISES member. Must be enrolled full-time in an accredited college or university. Must maintain a 2.5 GPA. Must be seeking a BA in engineering or science, relating to water resources or an environmentally-related field. Must be a member of a Federally recognized Indian tribe.

Academic Fields/Career Goals: Engineering-Related Technologies; Environmental Science; Hydrology; Natural Resources.

Award: Scholarship for use in freshman, sophomore, junior, or senior years; renewable. *Number:* varies. *Amount:* up to $5000.

Eligibility Requirements: Applicant must be American Indian/Alaska Native and enrolled or expecting to enroll full-time at a four-year institution or university. Applicant must have 2.5 GPA or higher. Available to U.S. citizens.

Application Requirements: Application, essay, resume, references, transcript. *Deadline:* June 15.

Contact: Shirley Lacourse, Deputy Director
American Indian Science and Engineering Society
2305 Renard, SE, Suite 200
PO Box 9828
Albuquerque, NM 87119-9828
Phone: 505-765-1052
Fax: 505-765-5608
E-mail: shirley@aises.org

AMERICAN PUBLIC TRANSPORTATION FOUNDATION http://www.apta.com

TRANSIT HALL OF FAME SCHOLARSHIP AWARD PROGRAM
• *See page 168*

AMERICAN RAILWAY ENGINEERING AND MAINTENANCE OF WAY ASSOCIATION http://www.arema.org

AREMA PRESIDENTIAL SPOUSE SCHOLARSHIP

Scholarship is awarded to an enrolled female student who has completed at least one quarter or semester in an accredited four- or five-year engineering or engineering technology undergraduate degree program.

American Railway Engineering and Maintenance of Way Association (continued)

Academic Fields/Career Goals: Engineering/Technology; Engineering-Related Technologies.

Award: Scholarship for use in freshman, sophomore, junior, or senior years; not renewable. *Number:* varies. *Amount:* $1000.

Eligibility Requirements: Applicant must be enrolled or expecting to enroll full-time at a four-year institution or university and female. Available to U.S. citizens.

Application Requirements: Application, references, transcript, cover letter. *Deadline:* March 14.

Contact: Stacy Spaulding, Scholarship Committee
American Railway Engineering and Maintenance of Way Association
10003 Derekwood Lane, Suite 210
Lanham, MD 20706

COMMITTEE 12-RAIL TRANSIT UNDERGRADUATE SCHOLARSHIP

Applicants must be enrolled as full-time students, or as a part-time students working full-time in the railway industry, in an accredited four- or five-year program leading to a bachelor's degree in engineering or engineering technology. Must have completed at least one quarter or semester in college prior to submitting an application, and have a minimum 2.00 GPA.

Academic Fields/Career Goals: Engineering/Technology; Engineering-Related Technologies.

Award: Scholarship for use in freshman, sophomore, junior, or senior years; not renewable. *Number:* varies. *Amount:* $1000.

Eligibility Requirements: Applicant must be enrolled or expecting to enroll full- or part-time at a four-year institution or university. Applicant or parent of applicant must have employment or volunteer experience in railroad industry. Available to U.S. citizens.

Application Requirements: Application, resume, references, transcript, cover letter. *Deadline:* March 14.

Contact: Scholarship Committee
American Railway Engineering and Maintenance of Way Association
10003 Derekwood Lane, Suite 210
Lanham, MD 20706

CSX SCHOLARSHIP

Applicants must be enrolled as full-time students in a four- or five-year program leading to a bachelor's degree in engineering or engineering technology in a curriculum which has been accredited by the Accreditation Board of Engineering and Technology (or comparable accreditation in Canada and Mexico). Must have completed at least one quarter or semester in college prior to submitting an application, and have a minimum 2.00 GPA.

Academic Fields/Career Goals: Engineering/Technology; Engineering-Related Technologies.

Award: Scholarship for use in freshman, sophomore, junior, or senior years; not renewable. *Number:* varies. *Amount:* $2500.

Eligibility Requirements: Applicant must be enrolled or expecting to enroll full-time at a four-year institution or university. Available to U.S. citizens.

Application Requirements: Application, resume, references, self-addressed stamped envelope, transcript, cover letter. *Deadline:* March 14.

Contact: Scholarship Committee
American Railway Engineering and Maintenance of Way Association
10003 Derekwood Lane, Suite 210
Lanham, MD 20706

NORFOLK SOUTHERN FOUNDATION SCHOLARSHIP

Applicants must be enrolled as full-time students in a four- or five-year undergraduate program in engineering or engineering technology. Institution must be located in Norfolk Southern's service area (22 states, the District of Columbia, and Ontario, Canada). Must have completed at least one quarter or semester in college prior to submitting an application, and have a minimum 2.00 GPA.

Academic Fields/Career Goals: Engineering/Technology; Engineering-Related Technologies.

Award: Scholarship for use in freshman, sophomore, junior, or senior years; not renewable. *Number:* varies. *Amount:* $1000.

Eligibility Requirements: Applicant must be enrolled or expecting to enroll full-time at a four-year institution or university. Available to U.S. citizens.

Application Requirements: Application, resume, references, transcript, cover letter. *Deadline:* March 14.

Contact: Scholarship Committee
American Railway Engineering and Maintenance of Way Association
10003 Derekwood Lane, Suite 210
Lanham, MD 20706

PB RAIL ENGINEERING SCHOLARSHIP

Applicants must be enrolled as full-time students in a four- or five-year program leading to a bachelor's degree in engineering or engineering technology in a curriculum which has been accredited by the Accreditation Board of Engineering and Technology (or comparable accreditation in Canada and Mexico). Must have completed at least one quarter or semester in college prior to submitting an application, and have a minimum 2.00 GPA.

Academic Fields/Career Goals: Engineering/Technology; Engineering-Related Technologies.

Award: Scholarship for use in freshman, sophomore, junior, or senior years; not renewable. *Number:* varies. *Amount:* $2000.

Eligibility Requirements: Applicant must be enrolled or expecting to enroll full-time at a four-year institution or university. Available to U.S. citizens.

Application Requirements: Application, resume, references, self-addressed stamped envelope, transcript, cover letter. *Deadline:* March 14.

Contact: Scholarship Committee
American Railway Engineering and Maintenance of Way Association
10003 Derekwood Lane, Suite 210
Lanham, MD 20706

REMSA SCHOLARSHIP

Applicants must be enrolled as full-time students in a four- or five-year program leading to a bachelor's degree in engineering or engineering technology in a curriculum which has been accredited by the Accreditation Board of Engineering and Technology (or comparable accreditation in Canada and Mexico). Must have completed at least one quarter or semester in college prior to submitting an application, and have a minimum 2.0 GPA.

Academic Fields/Career Goals: Engineering/Technology; Engineering-Related Technologies.

Award: Scholarship for use in freshman, sophomore, junior, or senior years; not renewable. *Number:* varies. *Amount:* $1000.

Eligibility Requirements: Applicant must be enrolled or expecting to enroll full-time at a four-year institution or university. Available to U.S. citizens.

Application Requirements: Application, resume, references, self-addressed stamped envelope, transcript, cover letter. *Deadline:* March 14.

Contact: Scholarship Committee
American Railway Engineering and Maintenance of Way Association
10003 Derekwood Lane, Suite 210
Lanham, MD 20706

AMERICAN SOCIETY FOR ENGINEERING EDUCATION http://www.asee.org

SCIENCE, MATHEMATICS, AND RESEARCH FOR TRANSFORMATION DEFENSE SCHOLARSHIP FOR SERVICE PROGRAM

• *See page 85*

AMERICAN SOCIETY OF HEATING, REFRIGERATING, AND AIR CONDITIONING ENGINEERS INC. http://www.ashrae.org

ASHRAE MEMORIAL SCHOLARSHIP

One-time $3000 award for full-time study in heating, ventilating, refrigeration, and air conditioning in an ABET-accredited program at an accredited school. Applicant must be pursuing a bachelor of science or engineering degree with a minimum GPA of 3.0.

Academic Fields/Career Goals: Engineering/Technology; Engineering-Related Technologies; Heating, Air-Conditioning, and Refrigeration Mechanics; Trade/Technical Specialties.

Award: Scholarship for use in freshman, sophomore, junior, or senior years; not renewable. *Number:* 1. *Amount:* $3000.

Eligibility Requirements: Applicant must be enrolled or expecting to enroll full-time at a four-year institution or university. Applicant must have 3.0 GPA or higher. Available to U.S. and non-U.S. citizens.

Application Requirements: Application, financial need analysis, references, transcript. *Deadline:* December 1.

Contact: Lois Benedict, Scholarship Administrator
American Society of Heating, Refrigerating, and Air Conditioning Engineers Inc.
1791 Tullie Circle, NE
Atlanta, GA 30329
Phone: 404-636-8400
Fax: 404-321-5478
E-mail: lbenedict@ashrae.org

ASHRAE SCHOLARSHIPS

One-time award of $3000 for full-time study in heating, ventilating, refrigeration, and air conditioning in an ABET-accredited program at an accredited school. Must be pursuing a bachelor of science or engineering degree with a GPA of minimum 3.0.

Academic Fields/Career Goals: Engineering/Technology; Engineering-Related Technologies; Heating, Air-Conditioning, and Refrigeration Mechanics; Trade/Technical Specialties.

Award: Scholarship for use in freshman, sophomore, junior, or senior years; not renewable. *Number:* 2. *Amount:* $3000.

Eligibility Requirements: Applicant must be enrolled or expecting to enroll full-time at a four-year institution or university and must have an interest in leadership. Applicant must have 3.0 GPA or higher. Available to U.S. and non-U.S. citizens.

Application Requirements: Application, financial need analysis, references, transcript. *Deadline:* December 1.

Contact: Lois Benedict, Scholarship Administrator
American Society of Heating, Refrigerating, and Air Conditioning Engineers Inc.
1791 Tullie Circle, NE
Atlanta, GA 30329
Phone: 404-636-8400
Fax: 404-321-5478
E-mail: lbenedict@ashrae.org

DUANE HANSON SCHOLARSHIP

Available to undergraduate students pursuing a bachelor of science or engineering degree, who are enrolled full-time in a program. One-time $3000 award for study in heating, ventilating, refrigeration, and air conditioning in an ABET-accredited program at an accredited school.

Academic Fields/Career Goals: Engineering-Related Technologies; Heating, Air-Conditioning, and Refrigeration Mechanics; Trade/Technical Specialties.

Award: Scholarship for use in freshman, sophomore, junior, or senior years; not renewable. *Number:* 1. *Amount:* $3000.

Eligibility Requirements: Applicant must be enrolled or expecting to enroll full-time at a four-year institution or university. Applicant must have 3.0 GPA or higher. Available to U.S. and non-U.S. citizens.

Application Requirements: Application, financial need analysis, references, transcript. *Deadline:* December 1.

Contact: Lois Benedict, Scholarship Administrator
American Society of Heating, Refrigerating, and Air Conditioning Engineers Inc.
1791 Tullie Circle, NE
Atlanta, GA 30329
Phone: 404-636-8400
Fax: 404-321-5478
E-mail: lbenedict@ashrae.org

HENRY ADAMS SCHOLARSHIP

One-time $3000 award for full-time study in heating, ventilating, refrigeration, and air conditioning in an ABET-accredited program at an accredited school. Must have a minimum GPA of 3.0. Must be pursuing a bachelor of science or engineering degree.

Academic Fields/Career Goals: Engineering/Technology; Engineering-Related Technologies; Heating, Air-Conditioning, and Refrigeration Mechanics; Trade/Technical Specialties.

Award: Scholarship for use in freshman, sophomore, junior, or senior years; not renewable. *Number:* 1. *Amount:* $3000.

Eligibility Requirements: Applicant must be enrolled or expecting to enroll full-time at a four-year institution or university and must have an interest in leadership. Applicant must have 3.0 GPA or higher. Available to U.S. and non-U.S. citizens.

Application Requirements: Application, financial need analysis, references, transcript. *Deadline:* December 1.

Contact: Lois Benedict, Scholarship Administrator
American Society of Heating, Refrigerating, and Air Conditioning Engineers Inc.
1791 Tullie Circle, NE
Atlanta, GA 30329
Phone: 404-636-8400
Fax: 404-321-5478
E-mail: benedict@ashrae.org

AMERICAN WELDING SOCIETY http://www.aws.org

AIRGAS-JERRY BAKER SCHOLARSHIP

Awarded to full-time undergraduate pursuing a minimum four-year degree in welding engineering or welding engineering technology. Applicant must be a minimum of eighteen years of age, must have 3.0 GPA. Priority will be given to those individuals residing or attending school in the states of Alabama, Georgia or Florida.

Academic Fields/Career Goals: Engineering-Related Technologies; Materials Science, Engineering, and Metallurgy.

Award: Scholarship for use in freshman, sophomore, junior, or senior years; not renewable. *Number:* 1. *Amount:* $2500.

Eligibility Requirements: Applicant must be age 18 and over and enrolled or expecting to enroll full-time at a four-year institution or university. Applicant must have 3.0 GPA or higher. Available to U.S. and Canadian citizens.

Application Requirements: Application, autobiography, essay, financial need analysis, references, transcript. *Deadline:* January 15.

Contact: Vicki Pinsky, Manager, Foundation
American Welding Society
550 Le Jeune Road, NW
Miami, FL 33126
Phone: 800-443-9353 Ext. 212
Fax: 305-443-7559
E-mail: vpinsky@aws.org

AIRGAS-TERRY JARVIS MEMORIAL SCHOLARSHIP

Award for a full-time undergraduate pursuing a minimum four-year degree in welding engineering or welding engineering technology. Must have a minimum 2.8 overall GPA with a 3.0 GPA in engineering courses. Priority given to applicants residing or attending school in Florida, Georgia, or Alabama.

Academic Fields/Career Goals: Engineering/Technology; Engineering-Related Technologies; Materials Science, Engineering, and Metallurgy.

Award: Scholarship for use in freshman, sophomore, junior, or senior years; not renewable. *Number:* 1. *Amount:* $2500.

Eligibility Requirements: Applicant must be age 18 and over and enrolled or expecting to enroll full-time at a four-year institution or university. Applicant must have 3.0 GPA or higher. Available to U.S. and Canadian citizens.

Application Requirements: Application, autobiography, essay, financial need analysis, references, transcript. *Deadline:* January 15.

Contact: Vicki Pinsky, Manager, Foundation
American Welding Society
550 Le Jeune Road, NW
Miami, FL 33126
Phone: 800-443-9353 Ext. 212
Fax: 305-443-7559
E-mail: vpinsky@aws.org

AMERICAN WELDING SOCIETY DISTRICT SCHOLARSHIP PROGRAM

Award for students in vocational training, community college, or a degree program in welding or a related field of study. Applicants must be high school

American Welding Society (continued)

graduates or equivalent. Must reside in the United States and attend a U.S. institution. Recipients may reapply. Must include personal statement of career goals.

Academic Fields/Career Goals: Engineering-Related Technologies; Trade/Technical Specialties.

Award: Scholarship for use in freshman, sophomore, junior, or senior years; not renewable. *Number:* 66–150. *Amount:* $500–$1000.

Eligibility Requirements: Applicant must be age 18 and over and enrolled or expecting to enroll full- or part-time at a two-year or four-year or technical institution or university. Available to U.S. citizens.

Application Requirements: Application, autobiography, financial need analysis, transcript. *Deadline:* March 1.

Contact: Nazdhia Prado-Pulido, Assistant, Foundation
American Welding Society
550 Le Jeune Road, NW
Miami, FL 33126
Phone: 800-443-9353 Ext. 250
Fax: 305-443-7559
E-mail: nprado-pulido@aws.org

AMERICAN WELDING SOCIETY INTERNATIONAL SCHOLARSHIP

Award for full-time international students pursuing a bachelor's or graduate degree in joining technologies. Scholarship not available to students residing in North America. Applicants must have completed at least one year of welding or related field of study at a baccalaureate degree-granting institution and be in the top 20 percent of that institution's grading system. For more information see Web site: http://www.aws.org/foundation/intl_scholarships.html.

Academic Fields/Career Goals: Engineering/Technology; Engineering-Related Technologies; Materials Science, Engineering, and Metallurgy; Trade/Technical Specialties.

Award: Scholarship for use in freshman, sophomore, junior, senior, or graduate years; not renewable. *Number:* 1. *Amount:* up to $2500.

Eligibility Requirements: Applicant must be enrolled or expecting to enroll full-time at a four-year institution or university. Available to citizens of countries other than the U.S. or Canada.

Application Requirements: Application, autobiography, essay, financial need analysis, resume, references, transcript, proof of citizenship, proof of acceptance. *Deadline:* April 1.

Contact: Vicki Pinsky, Manager, Foundation
American Welding Society
550 Le Jeune Road, NW
Miami, FL 33126
Phone: 800-443-9353 Ext. 212
Fax: 305-443-7559
E-mail: vpinsky@aws.org

DONALD F. HASTINGS SCHOLARSHIP

Award for undergraduate pursuing a four-year degree either full-time or part-time in welding engineering or welding engineering technology. Preference given to students residing or attending school in California or Ohio. Submit copy of proposed curriculum. Must rank in upper half of class or have a minimum GPA of 2.5. Must also include acceptance letter.

Academic Fields/Career Goals: Engineering/Technology; Engineering-Related Technologies; Trade/Technical Specialties.

Award: Scholarship for use in freshman, sophomore, junior, or senior years; renewable. *Number:* 1. *Amount:* $2500.

Eligibility Requirements: Applicant must be age 18 and over and enrolled or expecting to enroll full- or part-time at a four-year institution or university. Applicant must have 2.5 GPA or higher. Available to U.S. citizens.

Application Requirements: Application, autobiography, financial need analysis, references, transcript. *Deadline:* January 15.

Contact: Vicki Pinsky, Manager, Foundation
American Welding Society
550 Le Jeune Road, NW
Miami, FL 33126
Phone: 800-443-9353 Ext. 212
Fax: 305-443-7559
E-mail: vpinsky@aws.org

EDWARD J. BRADY MEMORIAL SCHOLARSHIP

Award for an undergraduate student pursuing a four-year degree either full- or part-time in welding engineering or welding engineering technology.

Academic Fields/Career Goals: Engineering/Technology; Engineering-Related Technologies; Trade/Technical Specialties.

Award: Scholarship for use in freshman, sophomore, junior, or senior years; not renewable. *Number:* 1. *Amount:* $2500.

Eligibility Requirements: Applicant must be age 18 and over and enrolled or expecting to enroll full- or part-time at a four-year institution or university. Applicant must have 2.5 GPA or higher. Available to U.S. citizens.

Application Requirements: Application, autobiography, essay, financial need analysis, references, transcript, copy of proposed curriculum, acceptance letter. *Deadline:* January 15.

Contact: Vicki Pinsky, Manager, Foundation
American Welding Society
550 LeJeune Road, NW
Miami, FL 33126
Phone: 800-443-9353 Ext. 212
Fax: 305-443-7559
E-mail: vpinsky@aws.org

HOWARD E. AND WILMA J. ADKINS MEMORIAL SCHOLARSHIP

Award for a full-time junior or senior in welding engineering or welding engineering technology. Preference to welding engineering students and those residing or attending school in Wisconsin or Kentucky. Must have at least 3.2 GPA in engineering, scientific, and technical subjects and a 2.8 GPA overall. No financial need is required to apply. Award may be granted a maximum of two years. Reapply each year. Submit copy of proposed curriculum and an acceptance letter.

Academic Fields/Career Goals: Engineering/Technology; Engineering-Related Technologies; Trade/Technical Specialties.

Award: Scholarship for use in junior or senior years; not renewable. *Number:* 1. *Amount:* $2500.

Eligibility Requirements: Applicant must be age 18 and over and enrolled or expecting to enroll full-time at a four-year institution. Applicant must have 3.5 GPA or higher. Available to U.S. citizens.

Application Requirements: Application, autobiography, essay, references, transcript. *Deadline:* January 15.

Contact: Vicki Pinsky, Manager, Foundation
American Welding Society
550 Le Jeune Road, NW
Miami, FL 33126
Phone: 800-443-9353 Ext. 212
Fax: 305-443-7559
E-mail: vpinsky@aws.org

ILLINOIS TOOL WORKS WELDING COMPANIES SCHOLARSHIP

Two awards of $3000 each are available for undergraduate students who will be seniors in a four-year bachelors degree in welding engineering technology or welding engineering. Applicant must be U.S. citizen planning to attend a U.S. institution and have a minimum 3.0 GPA. Priority given to students attending Ferris State University. Must exhibit a strong interest in welding equipment and have prior work experience in the welding equipment field.

Academic Fields/Career Goals: Engineering/Technology; Engineering-Related Technologies; Materials Science, Engineering, and Metallurgy; Trade/Technical Specialties.

Award: Scholarship for use in senior year; not renewable. *Number:* 2. *Amount:* $3000.

Eligibility Requirements: Applicant must be age 18 and over and enrolled or expecting to enroll full- or part-time at a four-year institution or university. Applicant must have 3.0 GPA or higher. Available to U.S. citizens.

Application Requirements: Application, transcript. *Deadline:* January 15.

Contact: Vicki Pinsky, Manager, Foundation
American Welding Society
550 Le Jeune Road, NW
Miami, FL 33126
Phone: 800-443-9353 Ext. 212
Fax: 305-443-7559
E-mail: vpinsky@aws.org

JOHN C. LINCOLN MEMORIAL SCHOLARSHIP

Award for an undergraduate pursuing a four-year degree either full time or part time in engineering or welding engineering technology. Priority given to welding engineering students residing or attending school in the states of Ohio or Arizona. Applicant must have a minimum 2.5 overall GPA. Proof of financial need is required to qualify.

Academic Fields/Career Goals: Engineering/Technology; Engineering-Related Technologies; Materials Science, Engineering, and Metallurgy.

Award: Scholarship for use in freshman, sophomore, junior, or senior years; not renewable. *Number:* 1. *Amount:* $3500.

Eligibility Requirements: Applicant must be age 18 and over and enrolled or expecting to enroll full- or part-time at a four-year institution. Applicant must have 2.5 GPA or higher. Available to U.S. citizens.

Application Requirements: Application, autobiography, financial need analysis, references, transcript. *Deadline:* January 15.

Contact: Vicki Pinsky, Manager, Foundation
American Welding Society
550 Le Jeune Road, NW
Miami, FL 33126
Phone: 800-443-9353 Ext. 212
Fax: 305-443-7559
E-mail: vpinsky@aws.org

MATSUO BRIDGE COMPANY LTD. OF JAPAN SCHOLARSHIP

• *See page 169*

MILLER ELECTRIC INTERNATIONAL WORLD SKILLS COMPETITION SCHOLARSHIP

Applicant must compete in the National Skills USA-VICA Competition for Welding, and advance to the AWS Weld Trials at the AWS International Welding and Fabricating Exposition and Convention, which is held on a bi-annual basis. The winner of the U.S. Weld Trial Competition will receive the scholarship for $10,000 and runner up will receive $1000. For additional information, see Web site: http://www.aws.org/foundation/national_scholarships.html.

Academic Fields/Career Goals: Engineering/Technology; Engineering-Related Technologies; Materials Science, Engineering, and Metallurgy; Trade/Technical Specialties.

Award: Scholarship for use in freshman, sophomore, junior, senior, graduate, or postgraduate years; renewable. *Number:* 1. *Amount:* $1000–$10,000.

Eligibility Requirements: Applicant must be enrolled or expecting to enroll full- or part-time at a four-year institution or university. Available to U.S. citizens.

Application Requirements: Applicant must enter a contest. *Deadline:* varies.

Contact: Vicki Pinsky, Manager, Foundation
American Welding Society
550 Le Jeune Road, NW
Miami, FL 33126
Phone: 800-443-9353 Ext. 212
Fax: 305-443-7559
E-mail: vpinsky@aws.org

PRAXAIR INTERNATIONAL SCHOLARSHIP

Award for a full-time student demonstrating leadership and pursuing a four-year degree in welding engineering or welding engineering technology. Priority given to welding engineering students. Must be a U.S. or Canadian citizen. Financial need is not required. Must have minimum 2.5 GPA.

Academic Fields/Career Goals: Engineering/Technology; Engineering-Related Technologies; Materials Science, Engineering, and Metallurgy.

Award: Scholarship for use in freshman, sophomore, junior, or senior years; not renewable. *Number:* 1. *Amount:* $2500.

Eligibility Requirements: Applicant must be age 18 and over and enrolled or expecting to enroll full-time at a four-year institution or university. Applicant must have 2.5 GPA or higher. Available to U.S. and Canadian citizens.

Application Requirements: Application, autobiography, financial need analysis, references, transcript. *Deadline:* January 15.

Contact: Vicki Pinsky, Manager, Foundation
American Welding Society
550 Le Jeune Road, NW
Miami, FL 33126
Phone: 800-443-9353 Ext. 212
Fax: 305-443-7559
E-mail: vpinsky@aws.org

WILLIAM A. AND ANN M. BROTHERS SCHOLARSHIP

Awarded to a full-time undergraduate pursuing a bachelor's degree in welding or welding-related program at an accredited university. Applicant must have a minimum 2.5 overall GPA. Proof of financial need is required.

Academic Fields/Career Goals: Engineering-Related Technologies; Materials Science, Engineering, and Metallurgy.

Award: Scholarship for use in freshman, sophomore, junior, or senior years; not renewable. *Number:* 1. *Amount:* $2500.

Eligibility Requirements: Applicant must be age 18 and over and enrolled or expecting to enroll full-time at a four-year institution or university. Applicant must have 2.5 GPA or higher. Available to U.S. citizens.

Application Requirements: Application, autobiography, financial need analysis, references, transcript. *Deadline:* January 15.

Contact: Vicki Pinsky, Manager, Foundation
American Welding Society
550 Le Jeune Road, NW
Miami, FL 33126
Phone: 800-443-9353 Ext. 212
Fax: 305-443-7559
E-mail: vpinsky@aws.org

WILLIAM B. HOWELL MEMORIAL SCHOLARSHIP

Awarded to a full-time undergraduate student pursuing a minimum four-year degree in a welding program at an accredited university. Priority will be given to those individuals residing or attending schools in the state of Florida, Michigan, and Ohio. Minimum 2.5 GPA required.

Academic Fields/Career Goals: Engineering/Technology; Engineering-Related Technologies; Materials Science, Engineering, and Metallurgy.

Award: Scholarship for use in freshman, sophomore, junior, or senior years; not renewable. *Number:* 1. *Amount:* $2500.

Eligibility Requirements: Applicant must be age 18 and over; enrolled or expecting to enroll full-time at a four-year institution; resident of Florida, Michigan, or Ohio and studying in Florida, Michigan, or Ohio. Applicant must have 2.5 GPA or higher. Available to U.S. citizens.

Application Requirements: Application, autobiography, essay, financial need analysis, references, transcript. *Deadline:* January 15.

Contact: Vicki Pinsky, Manager, Foundation
American Welding Society
550 Le Jeune Road, NW
Miami, FL 33126
Phone: 305-443-9353 Ext. 212
Fax: 305-443-7559
E-mail: vpinsky@aws.org

ARMED FORCES COMMUNICATIONS AND ELECTRONICS ASSOCIATION, EDUCATIONAL FOUNDATION

http://www.afcea.org

VICE ADMIRAL JERRY O. TUTTLE, USN (RET.) AND MRS. BARBARA A. TUTTLE SCIENCE AND TECHNOLOGY SCHOLARSHIP

Scholarships of $2000 for students working full-time toward an undergraduate bachelor of science technology degree. Candidate must be a U.S. citizen enrolled in a technology-related field and be a sophomore or junior at the time of application. Primary consideration will be given to military enlisted candidates.

Armed Forces Communications and Electronics Association, Educational Foundation (continued)

Academic Fields/Career Goals: Engineering/Technology; Engineering-Related Technologies; Science, Technology, and Society.

Award: Scholarship for use in sophomore or junior years; not renewable. *Number:* 1. *Amount:* $2000.

Eligibility Requirements: Applicant must be enrolled or expecting to enroll full-time at a four-year institution or university. Available to U.S. citizens. Applicant must have general military experience.

Application Requirements: Application, references, transcript. *Deadline:* November 1.

Contact: Norma Corrales, Director of Scholarships and Awards
Armed Forces Communications and Electronics Association, Educational Foundation
4400 Fair Lakes Court
Fairfax, VA 22033
Phone: 703-631-6149
E-mail: scholarship@afcea.org

ASSOCIATION FOR FACILITIES ENGINEERING (AFE)

ASSOCIATION FOR FACILITIES ENGINEERING CEDAR VALLEY CHAPTER #132 SCHOLARSHIP

• *See page 114*

ASSOCIATION FOR IRON AND STEEL TECHNOLOGY http://www.aist.org

ASSOCIATION FOR IRON AND STEEL TECHNOLOGY BALTIMORE CHAPTER SCHOLARSHIP

Scholarship for child, grandchild, or spouse of a member of the Baltimore Chapter of AIST. Must be high school seniors who are currently enrolled undergraduate students pursuing a career in engineering or metallurgy. Student may reapply each year for the term of their college education.

Academic Fields/Career Goals: Engineering/Technology; Engineering-Related Technologies; Materials Science, Engineering, and Metallurgy.

Award: Scholarship for use in freshman, sophomore, junior, or senior years; not renewable. *Number:* 1. *Amount:* $1500.

Eligibility Requirements: Applicant must be enrolled or expecting to enroll full-time at a four-year institution or university. Applicant or parent of applicant must be member of Association for Iron and Steel Technology. Available to U.S. citizens.

Application Requirements: Application, essay, test scores, transcript. *Deadline:* April 30.

Contact: Thomas J. Russo, Program Coordinator
Association for Iron and Steel Technology
1430 Sparrows Point Boulevard
Sparrows Point, MD 21219-1014

ASSOCIATION FOR IRON AND STEEL TECHNOLOGY OHIO VALLEY CHAPTER SCHOLARSHIP

• *See page 130*

ASSOCIATION OF ENGINEERING GEOLOGISTS http://www.aegfoundation.org

MARLIAVE FUND

• *See page 216*

ASSOCIATION OF IRON AND STEEL ENGINEERS http://www.aist.org

AISI/AIST FOUNDATION PREMIER SCHOLARSHIP

Two year renewable scholarships for full-time undergraduate engineering student enrolled at an accredited North American university. Must have a demonstrated interest in the steel industry, a minimum 3.0 GPA, and commit to a paid summer internship at a North American steel company.

Academic Fields/Career Goals: Engineering-Related Technologies.

Award: Scholarship for use in junior or senior years; renewable. *Number:* 1. *Amount:* $10,000.

Eligibility Requirements: Applicant must be enrolled or expecting to enroll full-time at a four-year institution or university. Applicant must have 3.0 GPA or higher. Available to U.S. and Canadian citizens.

Application Requirements: Application, essay, resume, references, transcript. *Deadline:* May 2.

Contact: Ms. Lori Wharrey, Board Administrator
Association of Iron and Steel Engineers
186 Thorn Hill Road
Warrendale, PA 15086-7528
Phone: 724-776-6040 Ext. 621
Fax: 724-776-1880
E-mail: lwharrey@aist.org

ASTRONAUT SCHOLARSHIP FOUNDATION http://www.astronautscholarship.org

ASTRONAUT SCHOLARSHIP FOUNDATION

• *See page 86*

AUTOMOTIVE HALL OF FAME http://www.automotivehalloffame.org

AUTOMOTIVE HALL OF FAME EDUCATIONAL FUNDS

Award for full-time undergraduate and graduate students pursuing studies in automotive engineering and related technologies. Must submit two letters of recommendation. Minimum 3.0 GPA required.

Academic Fields/Career Goals: Engineering/Technology; Engineering-Related Technologies.

Award: Scholarship for use in freshman, sophomore, junior, senior, or graduate years; renewable. *Number:* 20. *Amount:* $500–$2000.

Eligibility Requirements: Applicant must be enrolled or expecting to enroll full-time at a two-year or four-year or technical institution or university and must have an interest in automotive. Applicant must have 3.0 GPA or higher. Available to U.S. and non-U.S. citizens.

Application Requirements: Application, financial need analysis, references, self-addressed stamped envelope, transcript. *Deadline:* June 1.

Contact: Lynne Hall, Scholarship Coordinator
Automotive Hall of Fame
21400 Oakwood Boulevard
Dearborn, MI 48124-4078
Phone: 313-240-4000
Fax: 313-240-8641

BUSINESS AND PROFESSIONAL WOMEN'S FOUNDATION http://www.bpwfoundation.org

BPW CAREER ADVANCEMENT SCHOLARSHIP PROGRAM FOR WOMEN

• *See page 130*

CATCHING THE DREAM http://www.catchingthedream.org

TRIBAL BUSINESS MANAGEMENT PROGRAM (TBM)

• *See page 49*

COMMUNITY FOUNDATION OF WESTERN MASSACHUSETTS http://www.communityfoundation.org

JAMES L. SHRIVER SCHOLARSHIP

For Western Massachusetts residents pursuing technical careers through college, trade, or technical school. Visit http://www.communityfoundation.org for more information.

Academic Fields/Career Goals: Engineering/Technology; Engineering-Related Technologies; Trade/Technical Specialties.

Award: Scholarship for use in freshman or sophomore years; renewable. *Number:* 1. *Amount:* up to $500.

Eligibility Requirements: Applicant must be enrolled or expecting to enroll full- or part-time at a two-year or technical institution and resident of Massachusetts. Available to U.S. citizens.

Application Requirements: Application, financial need analysis, transcript, Student Aid Report (SAR). *Deadline:* March 31.

Contact: Dorothy Theriaque, Education Associate
Community Foundation of Western Massachusetts
1500 Main Street, PO Box 15769
Springfield, MA 01115
Phone: 413-732-2858
Fax: 413-733-8565
E-mail: dtheriaque@communityfoundation.org

CUBAN AMERICAN NATIONAL FOUNDATION http://www.masscholarships.org

MAS FAMILY SCHOLARSHIPS

• *See page 139*

DELAWARE HIGHER EDUCATION COMMISSION http://www.doe.k12.de.us

DELAWARE SOLID WASTE AUTHORITY JOHN P. "PAT" HEALY SCHOLARSHIP

Award for legal residents of Delaware who are U.S. citizens or eligible non-citizens. Must be high school seniors or full-time college students in their freshman or sophomore years. Must major in either environmental engineering or environmental sciences at a Delaware college. Selection based on financial need, academic performance, community and school involvement, and leadership ability.

Academic Fields/Career Goals: Engineering-Related Technologies; Environmental Science.

Award: Scholarship for use in freshman or sophomore years; renewable. *Number:* 1. *Amount:* $2000.

Eligibility Requirements: Applicant must be enrolled or expecting to enroll full-time at a two-year or four-year institution or university; resident of Delaware; studying in Delaware and must have an interest in leadership. Applicant or parent of applicant must have employment or volunteer experience in community service. Applicant must have 3.0 GPA or higher. Available to U.S. citizens.

Application Requirements: Application, financial need analysis, FAFSA, Student Aid Report (SAR). *Deadline:* March 14.

Contact: Carylin Brinkley, Program Administrator
Delaware Higher Education Commission
Carvel State Office Building, 820 North French Street, Fifth Floor
Wilmington, DE 19801-3509
Phone: 302-577-5240
Fax: 302-577-6765
E-mail: cbrinkley@doe.k12.de.us

DESK AND DERRICK EDUCATIONAL TRUST http://www.addc.org

DESK AND DERRICK EDUCATIONAL TRUST

• *See page 86*

DEVRY INC. http://www.devry.edu

CISCO NETWORKING ACADEMY SCHOLARSHIP

• *See page 191*

ELECTROCHEMICAL SOCIETY INC. http://www.electrochem.org

H.H. DOW MEMORIAL STUDENT ACHIEVEMENT AWARD OF THE INDUSTRIAL ELECTROLYSIS AND ELECTROCHEMICAL ENGINEERING DIVISION OF THE ELECTROCHEMICAL SOCIETY INC.

• *See page 131*

STUDENT ACHIEVEMENT AWARDS OF THE INDUSTRIAL ELECTROLYSIS AND ELECTROCHEMICAL ENGINEERING DIVISION OF THE ELECTROCHEMICAL SOCIETY INC.

• *See page 131*

STUDENT RESEARCH AWARDS OF THE BATTERY DIVISION OF THE ELECTROCHEMICAL SOCIETY INC.

• *See page 131*

GLOBAL AUTOMOTIVE AFTERMARKET SYMPOSIUM http://www.automotivescholarships.com

GAAS SCHOLARSHIP

Qualified applicants must either be a graduating high school senior or have graduated from high school within the past two years. To receive a scholarship, applicants must be enrolled in a college-level program or an ASE/NATEF certified postsecondary automotive technical program.

Academic Fields/Career Goals: Engineering-Related Technologies; Trade/Technical Specialties.

Award: Scholarship for use in freshman year; not renewable. *Number:* up to 150. *Amount:* $1000.

Eligibility Requirements: Applicant must be enrolled or expecting to enroll full-time at a four-year institution or university. Available to U.S. and Canadian citizens.

Application Requirements: Application, references, transcript. *Deadline:* March 31.

Contact: Annette Wofford, Scholarship Committee
Global Automotive Aftermarket Symposium
Research Triangle Park
PO Box 13966, NC 27709-3966
Phone: 919-406-8802
E-mail: awofford@mema.org

HAWAIIAN LODGE, F & AM http://www.glhawaii.org/

HAWAIIAN LODGE SCHOLARSHIPS

• *See page 96*

HISPANIC COLLEGE FUND INC. http://www.hispanicfund.org

DENNY'S/HISPANIC COLLEGE FUND SCHOLARSHIP

• *See page 54*

DEPARTMENT OF ENERGY SCHOLARSHIP PROGRAM

• *See page 142*

ICI EDUCATIONAL FOUNDATION SCHOLARSHIP PROGRAM

• *See page 142*

LOCKHEED MARTIN SCHOLARSHIP PROGRAM

• *See page 143*

HISPANIC SCHOLARSHIP FUND http://www.hsf.net

HSF/GENERAL MOTORS SCHOLARSHIP

• *See page 143*

HSF/NISSAN COMMUNITY COLLEGE TRANSFER SCHOLARSHIP PROGRAM

• *See page 143*

HSF/WELLS FARGO SCHOLARSHIP PROGRAM

• *See page 55*

ILLUMINATING ENGINEERING SOCIETY OF NORTH AMERICA http://www.iesna.org

ROBERT W. THUNEN MEMORIAL SCHOLARSHIPS

• *See page 91*

INDEPENDENT LABORATORIES INSTITUTE SCHOLARSHIP ALLIANCE http://www.acil.org

INDEPENDENT LABORATORIES INSTITUTE SCHOLARSHIP ALLIANCE

• *See page 132*

INSTITUTE OF ENVIRONMENTAL SCIENCES AND TECHNOLOGY (IEST) http://www.iest.org

EUGENE BORSON SCHOLARSHIP

One-time award for undergraduate college or university students enrolled full-time in an accredited institution and majoring in science or engineering. Must have minimum 3.0 GPA. For specific scholarship details visit the Web site: http://www.iest.org.

Institute of Environmental Sciences and Technology (IEST) (continued)

Academic Fields/Career Goals: Engineering/Technology; Engineering-Related Technologies.

Award: Scholarship for use in freshman, sophomore, junior, or senior years; not renewable. *Number:* 1. *Amount:* $500.

Eligibility Requirements: Applicant must be enrolled or expecting to enroll full-time at a two-year or four-year institution or university. Applicant must have 3.0 GPA or higher. Available to U.S. and non-U.S. citizens.

Application Requirements: Application, essay, references, transcript, student ID, proof of full-time enrollment in accredited institution, any verified relevant experience as described on application form, address of school and contact where scholarship award should be sent. *Deadline:* January 15.

Contact: Kristin Thryselius, Staff Assistant
Institute of Environmental Sciences and Technology (IEST)
Arlington Place One, 2340 South Arlington Heights Road, Suite 100
Arlington Heights, IL 60005-4516
Phone: 847-981-0100 Ext. 21
Fax: 847-981-4130
E-mail: scholarship@iest.org

INSTITUTE OF INTERNATIONAL EDUCATION http://www.iie.org/nsep

NATIONAL SECURITY EDUCATION PROGRAM DAVID L. BOREN UNDERGRADUATE SCHOLARSHIPS

• *See page 144*

INSTITUTION OF ELECTRICAL ENGINEERS http://www.theiet.org

BP/IET FARADAY LECTURE SCHOLARSHIP

• *See page 249*

IET ENGINEERING DEGREE SCHOLARSHIPS FOR WOMEN

Award to encourage women students in their final year of college or sixth form to enter the engineering profession. Scholarship is worth GBP1000 per annum and is tenable for the duration of an accredited degree course.

Academic Fields/Career Goals: Engineering/Technology; Engineering-Related Technologies.

Award: Scholarship for use in freshman year; renewable. *Number:* 10.

Eligibility Requirements: Applicant must be high school student; planning to enroll or expecting to enroll full-time at an institution or university and female. Available to U.S. and non-U.S. citizens.

Application Requirements: Application, photo, references, test scores. *Deadline:* June 30.

Contact: Scholarships and Prizes
Institution of Electrical Engineers
Michael Faraday House
Six Hills Way, Stevenage
Hertfordshire SG1 2AY
United Kingdom
E-mail: awards@theiet.org

IET FUNDING UNDERGRADUATES TO STUDY ENGINEERING (FUSE) SCHOLARSHIP

Award to assist students of high ability in need of financial support, who are in their penultimate year of college, or are about to commence an IET-accredited degree course in the UK or Ireland. Applicants must be receiving a DFES loan or grant. Scholarship worth GBP1000 a year.

Academic Fields/Career Goals: Engineering/Technology; Engineering-Related Technologies.

Award: Scholarship for use in freshman year; renewable. *Number:* 50.

Eligibility Requirements: Applicant must be high school student and planning to enroll or expecting to enroll full-time at an institution or university. Available to U.S. and non-U.S. citizens.

Application Requirements: Application, financial need analysis, photo, references, test scores. *Deadline:* June 30.

Contact: Scholarships and Prizes
Institution of Electrical Engineers
Michael Faraday House
Six Hills Way, Stevenage
Hertfordshire SG1 2AY
United Kingdom
E-mail: awards@theiet.org

INSTRUMENTATION, SYSTEMS, AND AUTOMATION SOCIETY (ISA) http://www.isa.org

INSTRUMENTATION, SYSTEMS, AND AUTOMATION SOCIETY (ISA) SCHOLARSHIP PROGRAM

• *See page 158*

INTERNATIONAL FACILITY MANAGEMENT ASSOCIATION FOUNDATION http://www.ifmafoundation.org

IFMA FOUNDATION SCHOLARSHIPS

One-time scholarships of up to $5000 awarded to students currently enrolled in full-time facility management programs or related programs. Minimum 3.2 GPA required for undergraduates and 3.5 for graduate students.

Academic Fields/Career Goals: Engineering-Related Technologies.

Award: Scholarship for use in junior, senior, graduate, or postgraduate years; not renewable. *Number:* 20–25. *Amount:* $1500–$5000.

Eligibility Requirements: Applicant must be enrolled or expecting to enroll full-time at a four-year institution or university. Available to U.S. and non-U.S. citizens.

Application Requirements: Application, resume, references, transcript, letter of professional intent. *Deadline:* May 31.

Contact: William Rub, Executive Director
International Facility Management Association Foundation
One East Greenway Plaza, Suite 1100
Houston, TX 77046
Phone: 713-623-4362 Ext. 158
E-mail: william.rub@ifma.org

INTERNATIONAL SOCIETY FOR MEASUREMENT AND CONTROL-DOWNEAST MAINE SECTION http://www.isa.org

ISA EDUCATIONAL FOUNDATION SCHOLARSHIPS

Scholarships to graduate and undergraduate students who demonstrate outstanding potential for long-range contribution to the fields of automation and control.

Academic Fields/Career Goals: Engineering-Related Technologies.

Award: Scholarship for use in freshman, sophomore, junior, senior, or graduate years; renewable. *Number:* up to 10. *Amount:* up to $5000.

Eligibility Requirements: Applicant must be enrolled or expecting to enroll full-time at a two-year or four-year institution or university. Applicant must have 3.0 GPA or higher. Available to U.S. and non-U.S. citizens.

Application Requirements: Application, essay, references, transcript. *Deadline:* February 15.

Contact: Scholarship Committee
International Society for Measurement and Control-Downeast Maine Section
67 Alexander Drive
Research Triangle Park, NC

INTERNATIONAL SOCIETY FOR OPTICAL ENGINEERING-SPIE http://www.spie.org

BACUS SCHOLARSHIP

Scholarship is available to a full-time undergraduate or graduate student in the field of microlithography with an emphasis on optical tooling and/or semiconductor manufacturing technologies. Applicants must not be full-time employees in industry, government, or academia, and must be presenting an accepted paper at an SPIE-sponsored meeting.

Academic Fields/Career Goals: Engineering-Related Technologies.

Award: Scholarship for use in freshman, sophomore, junior, senior, or graduate years; not renewable. *Number:* varies. *Amount:* $4000.

Eligibility Requirements: Applicant must be enrolled or expecting to enroll full-time at a four-year institution or university. Available to U.S. citizens.

Application Requirements: Application, references, written support from chair. *Deadline:* varies.

Contact: Pascale Barnett, Scholarship Coordinator
International Society for Optical Engineering-SPIE
1000 20th Street
PO Box 10
Bellingham, WA 98227-0010
Phone: 360-676-3290 Ext. 5452
Fax: 360-647-1445
E-mail: scholarships@spie.org

SPIE EDUCATIONAL SCHOLARSHIPS IN OPTICAL SCIENCE AND ENGINEERING

• *See page 87*

WILLIAM H. PRICE SCHOLARSHIP

Scholarship awarded to a full-time graduate or undergraduate student in the field of optical design and engineering. Must not be full-time employees in industry, government, or academia. Applicants must be presenting an accepted paper at an SPIE-sponsored meeting.

Academic Fields/Career Goals: Engineering-Related Technologies.

Award: Scholarship for use in freshman, sophomore, junior, senior, or graduate years; not renewable. *Number:* varies. *Amount:* $3000.

Eligibility Requirements: Applicant must be enrolled or expecting to enroll full-time at a four-year institution or university. Available to U.S. citizens.

Application Requirements: Application, references. *Deadline:* varies.

Contact: Scholarship Committee
International Society for Optical Engineering-SPIE
PO Box 10
Bellingham, WA 98227-0010
Phone: 360-685-5452
Fax: 360-647-1445
E-mail: scholarships@spie.org

INTERNATIONAL SOCIETY OF EXPLOSIVES ENGINEERS http://www.isee.org

JERRY MCDOWELL FUND

Scholarship of $1000 to $5000 to students whose field of education is related to the commercial explosives industry.

Academic Fields/Career Goals: Engineering/Technology; Engineering-Related Technologies.

Award: Scholarship for use in freshman, sophomore, junior, or senior years; not renewable. *Number:* 1–3. *Amount:* $1000–$5000.

Eligibility Requirements: Applicant must be enrolled or expecting to enroll full-time at a two-year or four-year institution or university. Available to U.S. and non-U.S. citizens.

Application Requirements: Application, financial need analysis, references, transcript, statement of goal. *Deadline:* May 1.

Contact: Arlene Chafe, Assistant to the Executive Director
International Society of Explosives Engineers
30325 Bainbridge Road
Cleveland, OH 44139
Phone: 440-349-4400
Fax: 440-349-3788
E-mail: foundation@isee.org

JORGE MAS CANOSA FREEDOM FOUNDATION http://www.jorgemascanosa.org

MAS FAMILY SCHOLARSHIP AWARD

• *See page 144*

KOREAN-AMERICAN SCIENTISTS AND ENGINEERS ASSOCIATION http://www.ksea.org

KSEA SCHOLARSHIPS

• *See page 249*

LOS ANGELES COUNCIL OF BLACK PROFESSIONAL ENGINEERS http://www.lablackengineers.org

AL-BEN SCHOLARSHIP FOR ACADEMIC INCENTIVE

• *See page 159*

AL-BEN SCHOLARSHIP FOR PROFESSIONAL MERIT

• *See page 159*

AL-BEN SCHOLARSHIP FOR SCHOLASTIC ACHIEVEMENT

• *See page 159*

MAINE SOCIETY OF PROFESSIONAL ENGINEERS http://www.mespe.org

MAINE SOCIETY OF PROFESSIONAL ENGINEERS VERNON T. SWAINE-ROBERT E. CHUTE SCHOLARSHIP

Nonrenewable scholarship for full-time study for freshmen only. Must be a Maine resident. Application can also be obtained by sending e-mail to rgmglads@twi.net

Academic Fields/Career Goals: Engineering/Technology; Engineering-Related Technologies.

Award: Scholarship for use in freshman year; not renewable. *Number:* 1–2. *Amount:* $1500.

Eligibility Requirements: Applicant must be high school student; planning to enroll or expecting to enroll full-time at a four-year institution or university; resident of Maine and studying in Maine. Applicant must have 2.5 GPA or higher. Available to U.S. citizens.

Application Requirements: Application, essay, interview, references, self-addressed stamped envelope, test scores, transcript. *Deadline:* March 1.

Contact: Robert G. Martin, Scholarship Committee Chairman
Maine Society of Professional Engineers
1387 Augusta Road
Belgrade, ME 04917
Phone: 207-495-2244
E-mail: rgmglads@twi.net

MICRON TECHNOLOGY FOUNDATION INC. http://www.micron.com/scholars

MICRON SCIENCE AND TECHNOLOGY SCHOLARS PROGRAM

• *See page 160*

MINERALS, METALS, AND MATERIALS SOCIETY (TMS) http://www.tms.org

TMS/EMPMD GILBERT CHIN SCHOLARSHIP

Award for TMS student members who are college undergraduates studying subjects in relation to electronic, magnetic, and/or photonic materials. Only to sophomore and junior undergraduate applicants enrolled full-time in a program that includes the study of electronic materials.

Academic Fields/Career Goals: Engineering/Technology; Engineering-Related Technologies; Materials Science, Engineering, and Metallurgy.

Award: Scholarship for use in sophomore or junior years; not renewable. *Number:* 1. *Amount:* $2000.

Eligibility Requirements: Applicant must be enrolled or expecting to enroll full-time at a four-year institution or university. Available to U.S. and non-U.S. citizens.

Minerals, Metals, and Materials Society (TMS) (continued)

Application Requirements: Application, essay, references, transcript. *Deadline:* March 15.

Contact: TMS Student Awards Program
Minerals, Metals, and Materials Society (TMS)
184 Thorn Hill Road
Warrendale, PA 15086
Phone: 724-776-9000 Ext. 259
Fax: 724-776-3770
E-mail: students@tms.org

TMS/EPD SCHOLARSHIP

Four awards ranging from $2000 to $2500 for TMS student members majoring in the extraction and processing of materials. It is given to college sophomore and juniors enrolled full-time in a program relating to the extraction and processing of minerals, metals, and materials. Recipients are given the opportunity to select up to five Extraction and Processing Division-sponsored conference proceedings or textbooks to be donated to the recipient's college/university in his/her name.

Academic Fields/Career Goals: Engineering/Technology; Engineering-Related Technologies; Materials Science, Engineering, and Metallurgy.

Award: Scholarship for use in sophomore or junior years; not renewable. *Number:* 4. *Amount:* $2000.

Eligibility Requirements: Applicant must be enrolled or expecting to enroll full-time at a four-year institution or university. Available to U.S. and non-U.S. citizens.

Application Requirements: Application, essay, references, transcript. *Deadline:* March 15.

Contact: TMS Student Awards Program
Minerals, Metals, and Materials Society (TMS)
184 Thorn Hill Road
Warrendale, PA 15086
Phone: 724-776-9000 Ext. 259
Fax: 724-776-3770

TMS/INTERNATIONAL SYMPOSIUM ON SUPERALLOYS SCHOLARSHIP PROGRAM

Two awards of $2000 for undergraduate (sophomore and junior) and graduate student member of TMS majoring in metallurgy, materials science and engineering, or materials processing/extraction programs. Preference given to students pursuing a curriculum/career in super alloys.

Academic Fields/Career Goals: Engineering/Technology; Engineering-Related Technologies; Materials Science, Engineering, and Metallurgy.

Award: Scholarship for use in sophomore, junior, or graduate years; not renewable. *Number:* 2. *Amount:* $2000.

Eligibility Requirements: Applicant must be enrolled or expecting to enroll full-time at a four-year institution or university. Available to U.S. and non-U.S. citizens.

Application Requirements: Application, essay, references, transcript. *Deadline:* March 15.

Contact: TMS Student Awards Program
Minerals, Metals, and Materials Society (TMS)
184 Thorn Hill Road
Warrendale, PA 15086
Phone: 724-776-9000 Ext. 259
Fax: 724-776-3770

TMS J. KEITH BRIMACOMBE PRESIDENTIAL SCHOLARSHIP

One award for a Minerals, Metals, and Materials Society student member who is an undergraduate student (sophomore and junior) majoring in metallurgical engineering, materials science and engineering, or minerals processing/extraction programs.

Academic Fields/Career Goals: Engineering/Technology; Engineering-Related Technologies; Materials Science, Engineering, and Metallurgy.

Award: Scholarship for use in sophomore or junior years; not renewable. *Number:* 1. *Amount:* $5000–$6000.

Eligibility Requirements: Applicant must be enrolled or expecting to enroll full-time at a four-year institution or university. Applicant must have 2.5 GPA or higher. Available to U.S. and non-U.S. citizens.

Application Requirements: Application, essay, references, transcript. *Deadline:* March 15.

Contact: TMS Student Awards Program
Minerals, Metals, and Materials Society (TMS)
184 Thorn Hill Road
Warrendale, PA 15086
Phone: 724-776-9000 Ext. 259
Fax: 724-776-3770

TMS/LMD SCHOLARSHIP PROGRAM

At least two awards for undergraduate (sophomore and junior) TMS student members majoring in the study of non-ferrous metallurgy. Preference given to juniors and seniors enrolled full-time in a non-ferrous metallurgy program, and to individuals who have participated in a relevant industrial co-op program.

Academic Fields/Career Goals: Engineering/Technology; Engineering-Related Technologies; Materials Science, Engineering, and Metallurgy.

Award: Scholarship for use in sophomore or junior years; not renewable. *Number:* 2. *Amount:* $4000–$5000.

Eligibility Requirements: Applicant must be enrolled or expecting to enroll full-time at a four-year institution or university. Available to U.S. and non-U.S. citizens.

Application Requirements: Application, essay, references, transcript. *Deadline:* March 15.

Contact: TMS Student Awards Program
Minerals, Metals, and Materials Society (TMS)
184 Thorn Hill Road
Warrendale, PA 15086
Phone: 724-776-9000 Ext. 259
Fax: 724-776-3770

TMS OUTSTANDING STUDENT PAPER CONTEST-UNDERGRADUATE

Two prizes for essays on global or national issues, as well as technical research papers. Metallurgy or materials science papers will be considered. Applicants must be TMS student members or include completed membership application with dues payment and essay to become eligible. Submit one entry per student. Prize includes cash and travel expenses.

Academic Fields/Career Goals: Engineering/Technology; Engineering-Related Technologies; Materials Science, Engineering, and Metallurgy.

Award: Prize for use in freshman, sophomore, junior, or senior years; not renewable. *Number:* 1. *Amount:* $500–$1000.

Eligibility Requirements: Applicant must be enrolled or expecting to enroll full-time at a four-year institution or university. Available to U.S. and non-U.S. citizens.

Application Requirements: Application, applicant must enter a contest, essay, transcript. *Deadline:* March 15.

Contact: TMS Student Awards Program
Minerals, Metals, and Materials Society (TMS)
184 Thorn Hill Road
Warrendale, PA 15086
Phone: 724-776-9000 Ext. 259
Fax: 724-776-3770

TMS/STRUCTURAL MATERIALS DIVISION SCHOLARSHIP

Two awards for TMS student members who are undergraduates (sophomore and junior) majoring in materials science and engineering or physical metallurgy. Recipient will be given $500 in travel expenses to the TMS Annual Meeting to accept his/her award. Preference given to seniors enrolled full-time in an engineering program relating to the structure, property, and processing of materials. The award value is $2000.

Academic Fields/Career Goals: Engineering/Technology; Engineering-Related Technologies; Materials Science, Engineering, and Metallurgy.

Award: Scholarship for use in sophomore or junior years; not renewable. *Number:* 1. *Amount:* $2000.

Eligibility Requirements: Applicant must be enrolled or expecting to enroll full-time at a four-year institution or university. Available to U.S. and non-U.S. citizens.

Application Requirements: Application, essay, references, transcript. *Deadline:* March 15.

Contact: TMS Student Awards Program
Minerals, Metals, and Materials Society (TMS)
184 Thorn Hill Road
Warrendale, PA 15086
Phone: 724-776-9000 Ext. 259
Fax: 724-776-3770

NASA DELAWARE SPACE GRANT CONSORTIUM http://www.delspace.org

NASA DELAWARE SPACE GRANT UNDERGRADUATE TUITION SCHOLARSHIP
• *See page 87*

NASA MISSISSIPPI SPACE GRANT CONSORTIUM http://www.olemiss.edu/programs/nasa

MISSISSIPPI SPACE GRANT CONSORTIUM SCHOLARSHIP
• *See page 118*

NASA RHODE ISLAND SPACE GRANT CONSORTIUM http://www.planetary.brown.edu/RI_Space_Grant

NASA RHODE ISLAND SPACE GRANT CONSORTIUM OUTREACH SCHOLARSHIP FOR UNDERGRADUATE STUDENTS

Scholarship for undergraduate students attending a Rhode Island Space Grant Consortium participating institution and studying in any space-related field of science, math, engineering, or other field with applications in space study. Recipients are expected to devote a maximum of 8 hours per week to outreach activities in science education for K-12 children and teachers.

Academic Fields/Career Goals: Engineering-Related Technologies; Mathematics; Science, Technology, and Society.

Award: Scholarship for use in sophomore, junior, or senior years; not renewable. *Number:* up to 2. *Amount:* up to $4000.

Eligibility Requirements: Applicant must be enrolled or expecting to enroll full-time at a four-year institution or university and studying in Rhode Island. Applicant must have 3.0 GPA or higher. Available to U.S. citizens.

Application Requirements: Application, essay, resume, references, transcript, letter of interest. *Deadline:* varies.

Contact: Dorcas Metcalf, Program Manager
NASA Rhode Island Space Grant Consortium
Brown University
PO Box 1846
Providence, RI 02912
Phone: 401-863-1151
Fax: 401-863-3978
E-mail: dorcas_metcalf@brown.edu

NASA SOUTH DAKOTA SPACE GRANT CONSORTIUM http://www.sdsmt.edu/space/

SOUTH DAKOTA SPACE GRANT CONSORTIUM UNDERGRADUATE SCHOLARSHIPS
• *See page 120*

NASA VERMONT SPACE GRANT CONSORTIUM http://www.cems.uvm.edu/VSGC

VERMONT SPACE GRANT CONSORTIUM SCHOLARSHIP PROGRAM
• *See page 88*

NASA WEST VIRGINIA SPACE GRANT CONSORTIUM http://www.nasa.wvu.edu

WEST VIRGINIA SPACE GRANT CONSORTIUM UNDERGRADUATE FELLOWSHIP PROGRAM
• *See page 121*

NATIONAL ASSOCIATION FOR THE ADVANCEMENT OF COLORED PEOPLE http://www.naacp.org

HUBERTUS W.V. WILLEMS SCHOLARSHIP FOR MALE STUDENTS
• *See page 161*

LOUIS STOKES SCIENCE AND TECHNOLOGY AWARD
• *See page 133*

NATIONAL ASSOCIATION OF WOMEN IN CONSTRUCTION http://www.nawic.org

NAWIC UNDERGRADUATE SCHOLARSHIPS
• *See page 92*

NATIONAL INVENTORS HALL OF FAME http://www.invent.org

COLLEGIATE INVENTORS COMPETITION FOR UNDERGRADUATE STUDENTS
• *See page 88*

COLLEGIATE INVENTORS COMPETITION-GRAND PRIZE
• *See page 88*

NATIONAL SOCIETY OF PROFESSIONAL ENGINEERS http://www.nspe.org

MAUREEN L. AND HOWARD N. BLITMAN, PE SCHOLARSHIP TO PROMOTE DIVERSITY IN ENGINEERING
• *See page 161*

PAUL H. ROBBINS HONORARY SCHOLARSHIP
• *See page 162*

PROFESSIONAL ENGINEERS IN INDUSTRY SCHOLARSHIP
• *See page 162*

NATIONAL STONE, SAND AND GRAVEL ASSOCIATION (NSSGA) http://www.nssga.org

BARRY K. WENDT MEMORIAL SCHOLARSHIP

Scholarship is restricted to a student in an engineering school who plans to pursue a career in the aggregates industry. One-time award for full-time students attending a four-year college or university.

Academic Fields/Career Goals: Engineering-Related Technologies; Materials Science, Engineering, and Metallurgy.

Award: Scholarship for use in freshman, sophomore, junior, or senior years; not renewable. *Number:* 1. *Amount:* up to $2500.

Eligibility Requirements: Applicant must be enrolled or expecting to enroll full-time at a four-year institution or university. Available to U.S. and non-U.S. citizens.

Application Requirements: Application, essay, references, transcript, 300- to 500-word statement of plans for career in the aggregates industry. *Deadline:* June 2.

Contact: Scholarship Committee
National Stone, Sand and Gravel Association (NSSGA)
1605 King Street
Arlington, VA 22314
Phone: 703-525-8788
Fax: 703-525-7782
E-mail: info@nssga.org

OREGON STUDENT ASSISTANCE COMMISSION http://www.osac.state.or.us

AMERICAN COUNCIL OF ENGINEERING COMPANIES OF OREGON SCHOLARSHIP
• *See page 162*

PENNSYLVANIA HIGHER EDUCATION ASSISTANCE AGENCY http://www.pheaa.org

NEW ECONOMY TECHNOLOGY AND SCITECH SCHOLARSHIPS

Renewable award for Pennsylvania residents pursuing a degree in science or technology at a PHEAA-approved two- or four-year Pennsylvania college or

Pennsylvania Higher Education Assistance Agency (continued)

university. Must maintain minimum GPA of 3.0. Must commence employment in Pennsylvania in a field related to degree within one year after graduation, and work one year for each year the scholarship was awarded.

Academic Fields/Career Goals: Engineering/Technology; Engineering-Related Technologies; Natural Sciences; Physical Sciences and Math.

Award: Scholarship for use in freshman, sophomore, junior, or senior years; renewable. *Number:* varies. *Amount:* varies.

Eligibility Requirements: Applicant must be age 18 and over; enrolled or expecting to enroll full-time at a two-year or four-year or technical institution or university; resident of Pennsylvania and studying in Pennsylvania. Applicant must have 3.0 GPA or higher. Available to U.S. citizens.

Application Requirements: Application, FAFSA. *Deadline:* December 31.

Contact: State Grant and Special Programs Division
Pennsylvania Higher Education Assistance Agency
1200 North Seventh Street
Harrisburg, PA 17102-1444
Phone: 800-692-7392

PLASTICS INSTITUTE OF AMERICA http://www.plasticsinstitute.org

PLASTICS PIONEERS SCHOLARSHIPS

• *See page 162*

PLUMBING-HEATING-COOLING CONTRACTORS ASSOCIATION EDUCATION FOUNDATION http://www.phccweb.org

BRADFORD WHITE CORPORATION SCHOLARSHIP

• *See page 92*

DELTA FAUCET COMPANY SCHOLARSHIP PROGRAM

• *See page 93*

PHCC EDUCATIONAL FOUNDATION NEED-BASED SCHOLARSHIP

• *See page 93*

PHCC EDUCATIONAL FOUNDATION SCHOLARSHIP PROGRAM

• *See page 147*

ROBERT H. MOLLOHAN FAMILY CHARITABLE FOUNDATION INC. http://www.mollohanfoundation.org

HIGH TECHNOLOGY SCHOLARS PROGRAM

• *See page 135*

SIMPLEHUMAN http://www.simplehuman.com

SIMPLE SOLUTIONS DESIGN COMPETITION

IDSA-endorsed competition to promote creative problem-solving through product design and increase public awareness of industrial design. Applicants must be enrolled at a NASAD-accredited design school and must design a new, innovative product/technology/concept for making household chores easier. Entries evaluated on utility, efficiency, innovation, research, and aesthetics. See Web site for details: http://www.simplehuman.com/design

Academic Fields/Career Goals: Engineering/Technology; Engineering-Related Technologies; Industrial Design.

Award: Prize for use in freshman, sophomore, junior, senior, graduate, or postgraduate years; not renewable. *Number:* 1. *Amount:* $5000.

Eligibility Requirements: Applicant must be enrolled or expecting to enroll full- or part-time at a two-year or four-year or technical institution or university. Available to U.S. citizens.

Application Requirements: Application, applicant must enter a contest, design, specs, materials, explanation. *Deadline:* February 29.

Contact: Sarah Beachler, Marketing and Communications Associate
simplehuman
19801 South Vermont Avenue
Torrance, CA 90502
Phone: 310-436-2278
Fax: 310-538-9196
E-mail: sbeachler@simplehuman.com

SOCIETY OF AUTOMOTIVE ENGINEERS http://www.sae.org

BMW/SAE ENGINEERING SCHOLARSHIP

• *See page 124*

DETROIT SECTION SAE TECHNICAL SCHOLARSHIP

Two $3500 renewable freshman scholarships will be awarded. Applicants must be a child or grandchild of a current SAE Detroit Section member. Student must maintain a 2.5 GPA and remain in good standing at the college or university in order to qualify for scholarship renewal. A student having completed a two-year program may continue for an additional consecutive two years at a second school offering a complete engineering or science baccalaureate degree program.

Academic Fields/Career Goals: Engineering/Technology; Engineering-Related Technologies; Mechanical Engineering.

Award: Scholarship for use in freshman or junior years; renewable. *Number:* 2. *Amount:* $3500.

Eligibility Requirements: Applicant must be enrolled or expecting to enroll full-time at a two-year or four-year institution or university. Applicant or parent of applicant must be member of Society of Automotive Engineers. Applicant must have 2.5 GPA or higher. Available to U.S. citizens.

Application Requirements: Application, financial need analysis, test scores, transcript, FAFSA forms. *Deadline:* December 1.

Contact: Connie Harnish, SAE Educational Relations
Society of Automotive Engineers
400 Commonwealth Drive
Warrendale, PA 15096-0001
Phone: 724-772-4047
E-mail: connie@sae.org

EDWARD D. HENDRICKSON/SAE ENGINEERING SCHOLARSHIP

• *See page 124*

RALPH K. HILLQUIST HONORARY SAE SCHOLARSHIP

A $1000 nonrenewable scholarship awarded every other year at the SAE Noise and Vibration Conference. Applicants must be U.S. citizens enrolled full-time as a junior in a U.S. university. A minimum 3.0 GPA with significant academic and leadership achievements is required. The student must also have a declared major in mechanical engineering or an automotive-related engineering discipline, with preference given to those with studies in the areas of expertise related to noise and vibration.

Academic Fields/Career Goals: Engineering/Technology; Engineering-Related Technologies; Mechanical Engineering.

Award: Scholarship for use in junior year; not renewable. *Number:* 1. *Amount:* $1000.

Eligibility Requirements: Applicant must be enrolled or expecting to enroll full-time at a four-year institution or university. Applicant or parent of applicant must be member of Society of Automotive Engineers. Applicant must have 3.0 GPA or higher. Available to U.S. citizens.

Application Requirements: Application, essay, transcript. *Deadline:* February 1.

Contact: Connie Harnish, SAE Educational Relations
Society of Automotive Engineers
400 Commonwealth Drive
Warrendale, PA 15096-0001
Phone: 724-772-4047
E-mail: connie@sae.org

SAE WILLIAM G. BELFREY MEMORIAL GRANT

Two $1000 grants awarded annually. One grant will be awarded to a Canadian citizen enrolled at any Canadian university, and one grant will be specific to the University of Toronto. Applicants must be citizens of Canada.

Academic Fields/Career Goals: Engineering/Technology; Engineering-Related Technologies.

Award: Grant for use in junior year; not renewable. *Number:* 2. *Amount:* $1000.

Eligibility Requirements: Applicant must be Canadian citizen and enrolled or expecting to enroll full-time at a four-year institution or university.

Application Requirements: Application, essay, resume, references, transcript. *Deadline:* April 1.

Contact: Connie Harnish, SAE Educational Relations
Society of Automotive Engineers
400 Commonwealth Drive
Warrendale, PA 15096-0001
Phone: 724-772-4047
E-mail: connie@sae.org

TMC/SAE DONALD D. DAWSON TECHNICAL SCHOLARSHIP
• *See page 124*

YANMAR/SAE SCHOLARSHIP

Eligible applicants will be citizens of North America (U.S., Canada, Mexico) and will be entering their junior year of undergraduate engineering or enrolled in a postgraduate engineering or related science program. Applicants must be pursuing a course of study or research related to the conservation of energy in transportation, agriculture, construction, and power generation. Emphasis will be placed on research or study related to the internal combustion engine.

Academic Fields/Career Goals: Engineering/Technology; Engineering-Related Technologies; Materials Science, Engineering, and Metallurgy; Mechanical Engineering.

Award: Scholarship for use in junior, senior, or graduate years; renewable. *Number:* 1. *Amount:* $1000.

Eligibility Requirements: Applicant must be enrolled or expecting to enroll full-time at a four-year institution or university. Available to U.S. and non-U.S. citizens.

Application Requirements: Application, essay, self-addressed stamped envelope, test scores, transcript. *Deadline:* April 1.

Contact: Connie Harnish, SAE Educational Relations
Society of Automotive Engineers
400 Commonwealth Drive
Warrendale, PA 15096
Phone: 724-772-4047
E-mail: connie@sae.org

SOCIETY OF BROADCAST ENGINEERS INC. http://www.sbe.org

ROBERT GREENBERG/HAROLD E. ENNES SCHOLARSHIP FUND AND ENNES EDUCATIONAL FOUNDATION BROADCAST TECHNOLOGY SCHOLARSHIP
• *See page 251*

SOCIETY OF HISPANIC PROFESSIONAL ENGINEERS FOUNDATION http://www.henaac.org

HENAAC SCHOLARS PROGRAM
• *See page 194*

SOCIETY OF HISPANIC PROFESSIONAL ENGINEERS FOUNDATION
• *See page 162*

SOCIETY OF WOMEN ENGINEERS http://www.swe.org

ANNE MAUREEN WHITNEY BARROW MEMORIAL SCHOLARSHIP
• *See page 173*

ARIZONA SECTION SCHOLARSHIP

Two to three scholarships for female students use in freshman year. Must be either residents of Arizona or attending a school in that state. Must be studying an engineering related field. Minimum 3.5 GPA required.

Academic Fields/Career Goals: Engineering/Technology; Engineering-Related Technologies.

Award: Scholarship for use in freshman year; not renewable. *Number:* 2–3. *Amount:* $1000.

Eligibility Requirements: Applicant must be high school student; planning to enroll or expecting to enroll full-time at a four-year institution or university; female; resident of Arizona and studying in Arizona. Applicant must have 3.5 GPA or higher. Available to U.S. citizens.

Application Requirements: Application, essay, resume, references, self-addressed stamped envelope, test scores, transcript. *Deadline:* May 15.

Contact: Scholarship Committee
Society of Women Engineers
230 East Ohio Street, Suite 400
Chicago, IL 60611-3265
Phone: 312-596-5223
Fax: 312-596-5252
E-mail: scholarshipapplication@swe.org

GENERAL MOTORS FOUNDATION UNDERGRADUATE SCHOLARSHIPS
• *See page 251*

GUIDANT CORPORATION SCHOLARSHIP
• *See page 195*

SWE SOUTH OHIO SCIENCE FAIR SCHOLARSHIP

Two $300 scholarships awarded to graduating high school senior females for outstanding achievement in engineering or the related sciences.

Academic Fields/Career Goals: Engineering/Technology; Engineering-Related Technologies.

Award: Scholarship for use in freshman year; not renewable. *Number:* 2. *Amount:* $300.

Eligibility Requirements: Applicant must be high school student; planning to enroll or expecting to enroll full-time at a four-year institution or university; female; resident of Ohio and must have an interest in science. Available to U.S. citizens.

Application Requirements: Application, references, test scores, transcript. *Deadline:* varies.

Contact: Scholarship Committee
Society of Women Engineers
230 East Ohio Street, Suite 400
Chicago, IL 60611-3265
Phone: 312-596-5223
Fax: 312-596-5252
E-mail: scholarshipapplication@swe.org

SOLE-THE INTERNATIONAL LOGISTICS SOCIETY http://www.sole.org

LOGISTICS EDUCATION FOUNDATION SCHOLARSHIP

One-time award for students enrolled in a program of study in logistics. Must have a minimum 3.0 GPA. Must submit transcript and references with application.

Academic Fields/Career Goals: Engineering-Related Technologies.

Award: Scholarship for use in freshman, sophomore, junior, senior, or graduate years; not renewable. *Number:* 5–10. *Amount:* up to $1000.

Eligibility Requirements: Applicant must be enrolled or expecting to enroll full-time at a four-year institution or university. Applicant must have 3.0 GPA or higher. Available to U.S. and non-U.S. citizens.

Application Requirements: Application, references, transcript. *Deadline:* May 15.

Contact: Sarah James, Executive Director
SOLE-The International Logistics Society
8100 Professional Place, Suite 111
Hyattsville, MD 20785
Phone: 301-459-8446
Fax: 301-459-1522
E-mail: solehq@erols.com

STRAIGHTFORWARD MEDIA http://www.straightforwardmedia.com

STRAIGHTFORWARD MEDIA ENGINEERING SCHOLARSHIP
• *See page 164*

TAG AND LABEL MANUFACTURERS INSTITUTE INC. http://www.tlmi.com

TLMI FOUR-YEAR COLLEGES/FULL-TIME STUDENTS SCHOLARSHIP

A $5000 scholarship awarded to a sophomore or junior attending a four-year accredited college or university on a full-time basis. Must demonstrate interest in entering the tag and label industry during their junior or senior year.

Tag and Label Manufacturers Institute Inc. (continued)

Academic Fields/Career Goals: Engineering-Related Technologies; Flexography; Graphics/Graphic Arts/Printing.

Award: Scholarship for use in sophomore, junior, or senior years; renewable. *Number:* 6. *Amount:* $5000.

Eligibility Requirements: Applicant must be enrolled or expecting to enroll full-time at a four-year institution or university. Applicant must have 3.0 GPA or higher. Available to U.S. and Canadian citizens.

Application Requirements: Application, autobiography, interview, portfolio, resume, references, transcript. *Deadline:* March 31.

Contact: Karen Planz, Office Manager
Tag and Label Manufacturers Institute Inc.
40 Shuman Boulevard, Suite 295
Naperville, IL 60563-8465
Phone: 630-357-9222 Ext. 11
Fax: 630-357-0192
E-mail: office@tlmi.com

TECHNICAL ASSOCIATION OF THE PULP & PAPER INDUSTRY (TAPPI) http://www.tappi.org

CORRUGATED PACKAGING DIVISION SCHOLARSHIPS

Award to applicants working full-time or part-time in the box business and attending day/night school for a Graduate or Undergraduate degree or full-time student in a two- or a four-year college, university or technical school.

Academic Fields/Career Goals: Engineering-Related Technologies; Paper and Pulp Engineering.

Award: Scholarship for use in freshman, sophomore, junior, senior, or graduate years; not renewable. *Number:* 8. *Amount:* $1000–$2000.

Eligibility Requirements: Applicant must be enrolled or expecting to enroll full- or part-time at a four-year or technical institution or university. Applicant must have 3.0 GPA or higher. Available to U.S. and non-U.S. citizens.

Application Requirements: Application, references, transcript. *Deadline:* varies.

Contact: Veranda Edmondson, TAPPI-Member Group Specialist
Technical Association of the Pulp & Paper Industry (TAPPI)
15 Technology Parkway, South
Norcross, GA 30092
Phone: 770-209-7536

TRANSPORTATION CLUBS INTERNATIONAL http://www.transportationclubsinternational.com

TRANSPORTATION CLUBS INTERNATIONAL FRED A. HOOPER MEMORIAL SCHOLARSHIP

Merit-based award available to currently enrolled college students majoring in traffic management, transportation, physical distribution, logistics, or a related field. Must have completed at least one year of post-high school education. One-time award of $1500. Must submit three references. Available to citizens of the United States, Canada, and Mexico.

Academic Fields/Career Goals: Engineering-Related Technologies; Transportation.

Award: Scholarship for use in freshman, sophomore, junior, senior, graduate, or postgraduate years; not renewable. *Number:* 1. *Amount:* $1500.

Eligibility Requirements: Applicant must be enrolled or expecting to enroll full- or part-time at a two-year or four-year or technical institution or university. Available to U.S. and non-U.S. citizens.

Application Requirements: Application, essay, photo, references, transcript. *Deadline:* April 30.

Contact: Bill Blair, Scholarships Trustee
Transportation Clubs International
15710 JFK Boulevard
Houston, TX 77032
Phone: 832-300-5905
E-mail: bblair@zimmerworldwide.com

UNITED NEGRO COLLEGE FUND http://www.uncf.org

MEDTRONIC FOUNDATION SCHOLARSHIP

• *See page 136*

NORTHEAST UTILITIES SYSTEM SCHOLARSHIP PROGRAM

• *See page 151*

WEST VIRGINIA HIGHER EDUCATION POLICY COMMISSION-OFFICE OF FINANCIAL AID AND OUTREACH SERVICES http://wvhepcnew.wvnet.edu/

WEST VIRGINIA ENGINEERING, SCIENCE AND TECHNOLOGY SCHOLARSHIP PROGRAM

• *See page 252*

XEROX http://www.xerox.com

TECHNICAL MINORITY SCHOLARSHIP

• *See page 165*

ENTOMOLOGY

ENTOMOLOGICAL FOUNDATION http://www.entfdn.org

BIOQUIP UNDERGRADUATE SCHOLARSHIP

Award to assist students in obtaining a degree in entomology or pursuing a career as an entomologist. Must have minimum of 90 college credit hours by September 1 following the application deadline, and either completed two junior-level entomology courses or a research project in entomology. Preference will be given to students with demonstrated financial need.

Academic Fields/Career Goals: Entomology.

Award: Scholarship for use in sophomore, junior, or senior years; renewable. *Number:* up to 1. *Amount:* up to $2000.

Eligibility Requirements: Applicant must be enrolled or expecting to enroll full- or part-time at a four-year institution or university. Available to U.S. and non-U.S. citizens.

Application Requirements: Application, resume, references, transcript. *Deadline:* July 1.

Contact: Melodie Dziduch, Awards Coordinator
Entomological Foundation
9332 Annapolis Road, Suite 210
Lanham, MD 20706-4876
Phone: 301-459-9082
Fax: 301-459-9084
E-mail: melodie@entfdn.org

ENTOMOLOGICAL SOCIETY OF AMERICA http://www.entsoc.org

INTERNATIONAL CONGRESS ON INSECT NEUROCHEMISTRY AND NEUROPHYSIOLOGY (ICINN) STUDENT RECOGNITION AWARD IN INSECT PHYSIOLOGY, BIOCHEMISTRY, TOXICOLOGY, AND MOLECULAR BIOLOGY

Award for innovative research in the areas of insect physiology, biochemistry, toxicology, and molecular biology. Must be a student and an active ESA member. Nomination or application packages should be submitted electronically. For details visit Web site: http://www.entsoc.org/awards/student/icinn.htm.

Academic Fields/Career Goals: Entomology.

Award: Prize for use in freshman, sophomore, junior, senior, graduate, or postgraduate years; not renewable. *Number:* varies. *Amount:* varies.

Eligibility Requirements: Applicant must be enrolled or expecting to enroll full-time at a four-year institution or university. Applicant or parent of applicant must be member of Entomological Society of America. Available to U.S. and Canadian citizens.

Application Requirements: Application, essay, references, transcript. *Deadline:* July 1.

Contact: Melodie Dziduch, Foundation Awards Administrator
Entomological Society of America
10001 Derekwood Lane, Suite 100
Lanham, MD 20706-4876
Phone: 301-459-9082
E-mail: melodie@entfdn.org

ENVIRONMENTAL HEALTH

COLLEGE BOARD/ROBERT WOOD JOHNSON FOUNDATION YES PROGRAM http://www.collegeboard.com

YOUNG EPIDEMIOLOGY SCHOLARS COMPETITION

Two $50,000 scholarships awarded to students who present outstanding research projects in the field of epidemiology. A select number of national finalists receive $15,000, $20,000, and $35,000 scholarships. YES Competition is open to high school juniors and seniors who are U.S. citizens or permanent residents.

Academic Fields/Career Goals: Environmental Health; Health and Medical Sciences; Public Health.

Award: Prize for use in freshman year; not renewable. *Number:* up to 120. *Amount:* $1000–$50,000.

Eligibility Requirements: Applicant must be high school student and planning to enroll or expecting to enroll full- or part-time at a four-year institution or university. Available to U.S. citizens.

Application Requirements: Application, applicant must enter a contest, research project report. *Deadline:* February 2.

Contact: The College Board
College Board/Robert Wood Johnson Foundation YES Program
11911 Freedom Drive, Suite 300
Reston, VA 20190
Phone: 800-626-9795 Ext. 5849
Fax: 703-707-5599
E-mail: yes@collegeboard.org

FLORIDA ENVIRONMENTAL HEALTH ASSOCIATION http://www.feha.org

FLORIDA ENVIRONMENTAL HEALTH ASSOCIATION EDUCATIONAL SCHOLARSHIP

Scholarships offered to students interested in pursuing a career in the field of environmental health, or to enhance an existing career in environmental health. Applicant must be a member of FEHA in good standing.

Academic Fields/Career Goals: Environmental Health.

Award: Scholarship for use in junior, senior, graduate, or postgraduate years; renewable. *Number:* 4–6. *Amount:* $500.

Eligibility Requirements: Applicant must be enrolled or expecting to enroll full- or part-time at a four-year institution or university. Applicant or parent of applicant must be member of Florida Environmental Health Association. Applicant must have 2.5 GPA or higher. Available to U.S. citizens.

Application Requirements: Application, references, transcript. *Deadline:* varies.

Contact: Michelle Kearney, Scholarship Committee Chair
Florida Environmental Health Association
5101 Ortega Boulevard
Jacksonville, FL 32210-8305
Phone: 850-245-4444 Ext. 2716
E-mail: michelle_kearney@doh.state.fl.us

INDEPENDENT COLLEGE FUND OF MARYLAND (I-FUND) http://www.i-fundinfo.org

HEALTH AND LIFE SCIENCES PROGRAM SCHOLARSHIPS

• *See page 132*

NATIONAL ENVIRONMENTAL HEALTH ASSOCIATION/AMERICAN ACADEMY OF SANITARIANS http://www.neha.org

NATIONAL ENVIRONMENTAL HEALTH ASSOCIATION/AMERICAN ACADEMY OF SANITARIANS SCHOLARSHIP

One-time award for college juniors, seniors, and graduate students pursuing studies in environmental health sciences or public health. Undergraduates must be enrolled full-time in an approved program that is accredited by the Environmental Health Accreditation Council (EHAC) or a NEHA institutional/educational or sustaining member school.

Academic Fields/Career Goals: Environmental Health; Public Health.

Award: Scholarship for use in junior, senior, or graduate years; renewable. *Number:* 3–4. *Amount:* $1000–$2000.

Eligibility Requirements: Applicant must be enrolled or expecting to enroll full-time at a two-year or four-year institution or university. Available to U.S. citizens.

Application Requirements: Application, references, transcript. *Deadline:* February 1.

Contact: Cindy Dimmitt, Scholarship Coordinator
National Environmental Health Association/American Academy of Sanitarians
720 South Colorado Boulevard, Suite 1000-N
Denver, CO 80246-1926
Phone: 303-756-9090
Fax: 303-691-9490
E-mail: cdimmitt@neha.org

SAEMS-SOUTHERN ARIZONA ENVIRONMENTAL MANAGEMENT SOCIETY http://www.saems.org

ENVIRONMENTAL SCHOLARSHIPS

Applicant must be a student in any accredited Southern Arizona college or university. Student must have a minimum GPA of 2.5 or be a full- or part-time student and plan on pursuing a career in the environmental arena.

Academic Fields/Career Goals: Environmental Health; Environmental Science; Natural Resources.

Award: Scholarship for use in freshman, sophomore, junior, senior, or graduate years; not renewable. *Number:* 2. *Amount:* $3000.

Eligibility Requirements: Applicant must be enrolled or expecting to enroll full- or part-time at a two-year or four-year institution or university and studying in Arizona. Applicant must have 2.5 GPA or higher. Available to U.S. and non-U.S. citizens.

Application Requirements: Application, essay, interview. *Deadline:* March 15.

Contact: Dan Uthe, Scholarship Committee Chair
SAEMS-Southern Arizona Environmental Management Society
PO Box 41433
Tucson, AZ 85717
Phone: 520-791-5630
Fax: 520-791-5346
E-mail: dan.uthe@tucsonaz.com

WINDSTAR FOUNDATION http://www.wstar.org

WINDSTAR ENVIRONMENTAL STUDIES SCHOLARSHIPS

Two $500 scholarships for qualified undergraduates entering their junior or senior year of college, and one $1000 scholarship for graduate students entering their second year of graduate school.

Academic Fields/Career Goals: Environmental Health; Environmental Science.

Award: Scholarship for use in junior, senior, or graduate years; renewable. *Number:* up to 3. *Amount:* $500–$1000.

Eligibility Requirements: Applicant must be enrolled or expecting to enroll full-time at a four-year institution or university. Applicant must have 3.0 GPA or higher. Available to U.S. citizens.

Application Requirements: Application, essay, transcript. *Deadline:* June 1.

Contact: Executive Director
Windstar Foundation
PO Box 656
Snowmass, CO 81654
E-mail: windstarco@wstar.org

WISCONSIN ASSOCIATION FOR FOOD PROTECTION http://www.wafp-wi.org

E.H. MARTH FOOD AND ENVIRONMENTAL SCHOLARSHIP

Scholarship awarded to promote and sustain interest in the fields of study that may lead to a career in dairy, food, or environmental sanitation. One scholarship is awarded per year and previous applicants and recipients may reapply.

Academic Fields/Career Goals: Environmental Health.

Award: Scholarship for use in freshman, sophomore, junior, or senior years; not renewable. *Number:* 1. *Amount:* $1500.

Wisconsin Association for Food Protection (continued)

Eligibility Requirements: Applicant must be enrolled or expecting to enroll full-time at a four-year institution or university; resident of Wisconsin and studying in Wisconsin. Available to U.S. and non-U.S. citizens.

Application Requirements: Application, references, transcript. *Deadline:* July 1.

Contact: George Nelson, Chair, Scholarship Committee
Wisconsin Association for Food Protection
PO Box 329
Sun Prairie, WI 53590
Phone: 715-235-4114
E-mail: nelsong@uwstout.edu

ENVIRONMENTAL SCIENCE

AIR & WASTE MANAGEMENT ASSOCIATION–ALLEGHENY MOUNTAIN SECTION http://www.ams-awma.org

ALLEGHENY MOUNTAIN SECTION AIR & WASTE MANAGEMENT ASSOCIATION SCHOLARSHIP

Scholarships for qualified students enrolled in an undergraduate program leading to a career in a field related directly to the environment. Open to current undergraduate students or high school students accepted full-time in a four-year college or university program in Western Pennsylvania or West Virginia. Applicants must have a minimum B average or a 3.0 GPA.

Academic Fields/Career Goals: Environmental Science.

Award: Scholarship for use in freshman, sophomore, junior, or senior years; not renewable. *Number:* up to 2. *Amount:* up to $1500.

Eligibility Requirements: Applicant must be enrolled or expecting to enroll full-time at a four-year institution or university; resident of Pennsylvania or West Virginia and studying in Pennsylvania or West Virginia. Applicant must have 3.0 GPA or higher. Available to U.S. citizens.

Application Requirements: Application, essay, resume, references, transcript, plan of study. *Deadline:* March 31.

Contact: David Testa, Scholarship Chair
Air & Waste Management Association–Allegheny Mountain Section
c/o Equitable Resources Inc., 225 North Shore Drive
Pittsburgh, PA 15212
Phone: 412-787-6803
Fax: 412-787-6717
E-mail: dtesta@calgoncarbon-us.com

AIR & WASTE MANAGEMENT ASSOCIATION–COASTAL PLAINS CHAPTER http://www.awmacoastalplains.org

COASTAL PLAINS CHAPTER OF THE AIR AND WASTE MANAGEMENT ASSOCIATION ENVIRONMENTAL STEWARD SCHOLARSHIP

Scholarships awarded to first- or second-year students pursuing a career in environmental science or physical science. Minimum high school and college GPA of 2.5 required. A 500-word paper on personal and professional goals must be submitted.

Academic Fields/Career Goals: Environmental Science; Physical Sciences and Math.

Award: Scholarship for use in freshman or sophomore years; not renewable. *Number:* 5. *Amount:* $800.

Eligibility Requirements: Applicant must be enrolled or expecting to enroll full-time at a two-year or four-year institution or university. Applicant must have 2.5 GPA or higher. Available to U.S. citizens.

Application Requirements: Application, references, test scores, 500-word paper on personal and professional goals. *Deadline:* varies.

Contact: Dwain G. Waters, Treasurer
Air & Waste Management Association–Coastal Plains Chapter
One Energy Place
Pensacola, FL 32520-0328
Phone: 850-444-6527
Fax: 850-444-6217
E-mail: gdwaters@southernco.com

AMERICAN INDIAN SCIENCE AND ENGINEERING SOCIETY http://www.aises.org

HENRY RODRIGUEZ RECLAMATION COLLEGE SCHOLARSHIP AND INTERNSHIP

• *See page 285*

AMERICAN INSTITUTE OF CHEMICAL ENGINEERS http://www.aiche.org

ENVIRONMENTAL DIVISION UNDERGRADUATE STUDENT PAPER AWARD

• *See page 154*

AMERICAN METEOROLOGICAL SOCIETY http://www.ametsoc.org

AMS FRESHMAN UNDERGRADUATE SCHOLARSHIP

Scholarships will be awarded, based on academic excellence, to high school seniors entering their freshman year of study in the atmospheric, oceanic, or hydrologic sciences. For use in freshman and sophomore years, with second-year funding dependent on successful completion of first year.

Academic Fields/Career Goals: Environmental Science; Hydrology; Marine/Ocean Engineering; Meteorology/Atmospheric Science.

Award: Scholarship for use in freshman year; not renewable. *Number:* 14. *Amount:* $5000.

Eligibility Requirements: Applicant must be high school student and planning to enroll or expecting to enroll full-time at a two-year or four-year or technical institution or university. Applicant must have 3.0 GPA or higher. Available to U.S. and non-U.S. citizens.

Application Requirements: Application, essay, references, test scores, transcript. *Deadline:* February 22.

Contact: Mrs. Donna Sampson, Development and Student Program Manager
American Meteorological Society
45 Beacon Street
Boston, MA 02108
Phone: 617-227-2426 Ext. 246
Fax: 617-742-8718
E-mail: dfernand@ametsoc.org

ASSOCIATION FOR WOMEN GEOSCIENTISTS, PUGET SOUND CHAPTER http://www.awg.org

PUGET SOUND CHAPTER SCHOLARSHIP

• *See page 216*

ASSOCIATION OF CALIFORNIA WATER AGENCIES http://www.acwa.com

ASSOCIATION OF CALIFORNIA WATER AGENCIES SCHOLARSHIPS

• *See page 86*

CLAIR A. HILL SCHOLARSHIP

• *See page 86*

ASSOCIATION OF NEW JERSEY ENVIRONMENTAL COMMISSIONS http://www.anjec.org

LECHNER SCHOLARSHIP

Award of $1000 scholarship for a student entering his/her junior or senior year at an accredited New Jersey college or university. Must be a New Jersey resident and have a minimum GPA of 3.0.

Academic Fields/Career Goals: Environmental Science.

Award: Scholarship for use in junior or senior years; not renewable. *Number:* 1. *Amount:* $1000.

Eligibility Requirements: Applicant must be enrolled or expecting to enroll full-time at a four-year institution or university; resident of New Jersey and studying in New Jersey. Applicant must have 3.0 GPA or higher. Available to U.S. citizens.

Application Requirements: Application, essay, references, transcript. *Deadline:* April 14.

Contact: Abigail Fair, Water Resources Director
Association of New Jersey Environmental Commissions
PO Box 157
Mendham, NJ 07945
Phone: 973-539-7547
Fax: 973-539-7713
E-mail: afair@anjec.org

AUDUBON SOCIETY OF WESTERN PENNSYLVANIA http://www.aswp.org

BEULAH FREY ENVIRONMENTAL SCHOLARSHIP

Scholarship available to high school seniors pursuing studies in the environmental and natural sciences. Students who are applying to a two- or four-year college to further their studies in an environmentally-related field are eligible to apply. Scholarship is restricted to the residents of the seven counties around Pittsburgh.

Academic Fields/Career Goals: Environmental Science; Natural Sciences.

Award: Scholarship for use in freshman year; not renewable. *Number:* 1–2. *Amount:* $1000.

Eligibility Requirements: Applicant must be high school student; planning to enroll or expecting to enroll full-time at a two-year or four-year institution or university and resident of Pennsylvania. Available to U.S. citizens.

Application Requirements: Application, essay, references, test scores, transcript. *Deadline:* March 31.

Contact: Patricia O'Neill, Director of Education
Audubon Society of Western Pennsylvania
614 Dorseyville Road
Pittsburgh, PA 15238
Phone: 412-963-6100
Fax: 412-963-6761
E-mail: toneill@aswp.org

CALIFORNIA WATER AWARENESS CAMPAIGN http://www.wateraware.org

CALIFORNIA WATER AWARENESS CAMPAIGN WATER SCHOLAR

• *See page 74*

CANADIAN RECREATIONAL CANOEING ASSOCIATION http://www.paddlingcanada.com

BILL MASON MEMORIAL SCHOLARSHIP FUND

• *See page 74*

CONFEDERATED TRIBES OF GRAND RONDE http://www.grandronde.org

RAY MCKNIGHT MEMORIAL COMPETITIVE SCHOLARSHIP

Scholarship available to any enrolled member of the Confederated Tribes of Grand Ronde. Intended for junior and senior years of a natural resource-related full-time bachelor degree program. Award is renewable for up to six terms/four semesters of continuous study.

Academic Fields/Career Goals: Environmental Science; Natural Resources.

Award: Scholarship for use in junior or senior years; renewable. *Number:* 1. *Amount:* $6000.

Eligibility Requirements: Applicant must be American Indian/Alaska Native and enrolled or expecting to enroll full-time at a four-year institution or university. Available to U.S. and non-U.S. citizens.

Application Requirements: Application, essay, references, transcript, verification of tribal enrollment. *Deadline:* April 30.

Contact: Luhui Whitebear, Tribal Scholarship Coordinator
Confederated Tribes of Grand Ronde
9615 Grand Ronde Road
Grand Ronde, OR 97347
Phone: 800-422-0232 Ext. 2275
Fax: 503-879-2286
E-mail: education@grandronde.org

CONSERVATION FEDERATION OF MISSOURI http://www.confedmo.org

CHARLES P. BELL CONSERVATION SCHOLARSHIP

Eight scholarships of $250 to $600 for Missouri students and/or teachers whose studies or projects are related to natural science, resource conservation, earth resources, or environmental protection. Must be used for study in Missouri. See application for eligibility details.

Academic Fields/Career Goals: Environmental Science; Natural Resources; Natural Sciences.

Award: Scholarship for use in freshman, sophomore, junior, senior, or graduate years; not renewable. *Number:* 8. *Amount:* $250–$600.

Eligibility Requirements: Applicant must be enrolled or expecting to enroll full- or part-time at a four-year institution or university; resident of Missouri and studying in Missouri. Available to U.S. citizens.

Application Requirements: Application, financial need analysis, references, transcript, work experience certificate. *Deadline:* January 15.

Contact: Administrative Associate
Conservation Federation of Missouri
728 West Main Street
Jefferson City, MO 65101-1559
Phone: 573-634-2322
Fax: 573-634-8205
E-mail: confedmo@sockets.net

DELAWARE HIGHER EDUCATION COMMISSION http://www.doe.k12.de.us

DELAWARE SOLID WASTE AUTHORITY JOHN P. "PAT" HEALY SCHOLARSHIP

• *See page 291*

EARTH ISLAND INSTITUTE http://www.earthisland.org

BROWER YOUTH AWARDS

An annual national award that recognizes 6 young people for their outstanding activism and achievements in the fields of environmental and social justice advocacy. The winners of the award receive $3000 in cash, a trip to California for the award ceremony and Yosemite camping trip, and ongoing access to resources and opportunities to further their work at Earth Island Institute. Applicant's age must be between 13 to 22.

Academic Fields/Career Goals: Environmental Science; Peace and Conflict Studies.

Award: Prize for use in freshman, sophomore, junior, or senior years; not renewable. *Number:* 6. *Amount:* $3000.

Eligibility Requirements: Applicant must be age 13-22 and enrolled or expecting to enroll full- or part-time at a two-year or four-year or technical institution or university. Available to U.S. and non-U.S. citizens.

Application Requirements: Application, essay, photo, references. *Deadline:* May 15.

Contact: Ms. Sharon Smith, Program Director
Earth Island Institute
300 Broadway, Suite 28
San Francisco, CA 94133
Phone: 415-788-3666 Ext. 144
E-mail: bya@earthisland.org

ENVIRONMENTAL PROFESSIONALS' ORGANIZATION OF CONNECTICUT http://www.epoc.org

EPOC ENVIRONMENTAL SCHOLARSHIP FUND

Scholarships awarded annually to junior, senior, and graduate level students (full- or part-time) enrolled in accepted programs of study leading the student to become an environmental professional in Connecticut.

Academic Fields/Career Goals: Environmental Science.

Award: Scholarship for use in junior, senior, or graduate years; not renewable. *Number:* 2–3. *Amount:* varies.

Eligibility Requirements: Applicant must be enrolled or expecting to enroll full- or part-time at a four-year institution or university. Available to U.S. citizens.

Application Requirements: Application, essay, financial need analysis, references, transcript. *Deadline:* May 7.

Contact: John Figurelli, Scholarship Fund Coordinator
Environmental Professionals' Organization of Connecticut
PO Box 176
Amston, CT 06231-0176
Phone: 860-513-1473
Fax: 860-228-4902
E-mail: figurelj@wseinc.com

FRIENDS OF THE FRELINGHUYSEN ARBORETUM http://www.arboretumfriends.org

BENJAMIN C. BLACKBURN SCHOLARSHIP

One-time award for undergraduate and graduate students who are pursuing degrees in horticulture, landscape architecture, or environmental studies. Must be a New Jersey resident. Minimum 3.0 GPA required.

Academic Fields/Career Goals: Environmental Science; Horticulture/Floriculture; Landscape Architecture; Natural Resources.

Award: Scholarship for use in sophomore, junior, senior, or graduate years; not renewable. *Number:* 1. *Amount:* $5000.

Eligibility Requirements: Applicant must be enrolled or expecting to enroll full- or part-time at a four-year institution or university and resident of New Jersey. Applicant must have 3.0 GPA or higher. Available to U.S. citizens.

Application Requirements: Application, essay, references, transcript. *Deadline:* April 14.

Contact: Ann Abrams, Scholarship Committee
Friends of the Frelinghuysen Arboretum
53 East Hanover Avenue, PO Box 1295
Morristown, NJ 07962-1295
Phone: 973-326-7603
E-mail: aabrams@morrisparks.net

GARDEN CLUB OF AMERICA http://www.gcamerica.org

CAROLINE THORN KISSEL SUMMER ENVIRONMENTAL STUDIES SCHOLARSHIP

Award of $2000 for college students, graduate students, or non-degree-seeking applicants above the high school level. Scholarship promotes environmental studies by students who are either residents of the state of New Jersey, or non-residents pursuing study in New Jersey or its surrounding waters.

Academic Fields/Career Goals: Environmental Science.

Award: Scholarship for use in freshman, sophomore, junior, senior, graduate, or postgraduate years; not renewable. *Number:* 1. *Amount:* $2000.

Eligibility Requirements: Applicant must be enrolled or expecting to enroll full- or part-time at a two-year or four-year or technical institution or university; resident of New Jersey and studying in New Jersey. Available to U.S. citizens.

Application Requirements: Application, essay, references. *Deadline:* February 10.

Contact: Judy Smith, Scholarship Committee Administrator
Garden Club of America
14 East 60th Street, Third Floor
New York, NY 10022-1002
Phone: 212-753-8287
Fax: 212-753-0134
E-mail: judy@gcamerica.org

GARDEN CLUB OF AMERICA AWARDS FOR SUMMER ENVIRONMENTAL STUDIES

• *See page 74*

GREAT LAKES COMMISSION http://www.glc.org

CAROL A. RATZA MEMORIAL SCHOLARSHIP

• *See page 179*

GREEN CHEMISTRY INSTITUTE-AMERICAN CHEMICAL SOCIETY http://www.acs.org/greenchemistry

JOSEPH BREEN MEMORIAL FELLOWSHIP IN GREEN CHEMISTRY

• *See page 158*

HISPANIC COLLEGE FUND INC. http://www.hispanicfund.org

DEPARTMENT OF ENERGY SCHOLARSHIP PROGRAM

• *See page 142*

HISPANIC SCHOLARSHIP FUND http://www.hsf.net

HSF/MARATHON OIL CORPORATION COLLEGE SCHOLARSHIP

• *See page 55*

INDEPENDENT LABORATORIES INSTITUTE SCHOLARSHIP ALLIANCE http://www.acil.org

INDEPENDENT LABORATORIES INSTITUTE SCHOLARSHIP ALLIANCE

• *See page 132*

INDIANA WILDLIFE FEDERATION ENDOWMENT http://www.indianawildlife.org

CHARLES A. HOLT INDIANA WILDLIFE FEDERATION ENDOWMENT SCHOLARSHIP

A $1000 scholarship will be awarded to an Indiana resident enrolled in or planning to enroll in a course of study related to resource conservation or environmental education at the undergraduate level.

Academic Fields/Career Goals: Environmental Science; Natural Resources.

Award: Scholarship for use in sophomore, junior, or senior years; not renewable. *Number:* 1. *Amount:* $1000.

Eligibility Requirements: Applicant must be enrolled or expecting to enroll full-time at a four-year institution or university; resident of Indiana and studying in Indiana. Available to U.S. citizens.

Application Requirements: Application, essay, references. *Deadline:* May 1.

Contact: Debbie Twardy, Office Manager
Indiana Wildlife Federation Endowment
4715 West 106th Street
Zionsville, IN 46077
Phone: 317-875-9453
Fax: 317-875-9442
E-mail: info@indianawildlife.org

INSTITUTE OF ENVIRONMENTAL SCIENCES AND TECHNOLOGY (IEST) http://www.iest.org

PARK ESPENSCHADE MEMORIAL SCHOLARSHIP

Annual award of $500 for the best, original technical paper written by a student on a topic related to the environmental sciences. Must have minimum GPA of 3.0. For specific scholarship details visit Web site: http://www.iest.org.

Academic Fields/Career Goals: Environmental Science.

Award: Scholarship for use in freshman, sophomore, junior, or senior years; not renewable. *Number:* 1. *Amount:* $500.

Eligibility Requirements: Applicant must be enrolled or expecting to enroll full-time at a two-year or four-year institution or university. Applicant must have 3.0 GPA or higher. Available to U.S. and non-U.S. citizens.

Application Requirements: Application, essay, references, transcript, student ID, proof of full-time enrollment in accredited institution, any verified relevant experience as described on application form, address of school and contact where scholarship award should be sent. *Deadline:* January 15.

Contact: Kristin Thryselius, Staff Assistant
Institute of Environmental Sciences and Technology (IEST)
Arlington Place One, 2340 South Arlington Heights Road, Suite 100
Arlington Heights, IL 60005-4516
Phone: 847-981-0100 Ext. 21
Fax: 847-981-4130
E-mail: scholarship@iest.org

ROBERT N. HANCOCK MEMORIAL SCHOLARSHIP

• *See page 132*

INSTITUTE OF INTERNATIONAL EDUCATION http://www.iie.org/nsep

NATIONAL SECURITY EDUCATION PROGRAM DAVID L. BOREN UNDERGRADUATE SCHOLARSHIPS

• *See page 144*

INTERNATIONAL ASSOCIATION OF GREAT LAKES RESEARCH http://www.iaglr.org

PAUL W. RODGERS SCHOLARSHIP

• *See page 217*

JUST WITHIN REACH FOUNDATION

ENVIRONMENTAL SCIENCES AND MARINE STUDIES SCHOLARSHIP

Three scholarships of $2000 are given to environmental science scholars and three of $2000 are given to marine studies scholars. Must be U.S. citizens and must be either undergraduate students currently enrolled in a postsecondary institution or high school seniors accepted as full-time students of an accredited, public or private four-year college or university in the United States. Minimum 3.0 GPA required.

Academic Fields/Career Goals: Environmental Science; Marine Biology.

Award: Scholarship for use in freshman, sophomore, junior, or senior years; not renewable. *Number:* 6. *Amount:* $2000.

Eligibility Requirements: Applicant must be enrolled or expecting to enroll full-time at a four-year institution or university. Applicant must have 3.0 GPA or higher. Available to U.S. citizens.

Application Requirements: Application, essay, financial need analysis, resume, references, transcript. *Deadline:* March 12.

Contact: Scholarship Committee
Just Within Reach Foundation
3940 Laurel Canyon Boulevard, PO Box 256
Studio City, CA 91604

KENTUCKY NATURAL RESOURCES AND ENVIRONMENTAL PROTECTION CABINET http://www.uky.edu/waterresources

ENVIRONMENTAL PROTECTION SCHOLARSHIPS

• *See page 132*

MAINE COMMUNITY FOUNDATION INC. http://www.mainecf.org

R.V. "GADABOUT" GADDIS CHARITABLE FUND

Award available to Maine high school graduates who are college juniors or seniors majoring in outdoor writing or a related environmental field.

Academic Fields/Career Goals: Environmental Science; Literature/English/Writing.

Award: Scholarship for use in junior or senior years; not renewable. *Number:* varies. *Amount:* varies.

Eligibility Requirements: Applicant must be enrolled or expecting to enroll full- or part-time at a four-year institution or university and resident of Maine. Available to U.S. citizens.

Application Requirements: Application, essay, financial need analysis, copy of college financial aid offer. *Deadline:* April 1.

Contact: Jean Warren, Scholarship Coordinator
Maine Community Foundation Inc.
245 Main Street
Ellsworth, ME 04605
Phone: 207-667-9735
Fax: 207-667-0447
E-mail: info@mainecf.org

MANITOBA FORESTRY ASSOCIATION http://www.mbforestryassoc.ca

DR. ALAN BEAVEN FORESTRY SCHOLARSHIP

Awarded annually to a Manitoba resident selected by a committee of association members. Must be a recent high school graduate entering first year forestry program at a Canadian university or technical school. Scholarship of $500 will be paid in the student's name to the university or school as part of the tuition.

Academic Fields/Career Goals: Environmental Science; Natural Resources.

Award: Scholarship for use in freshman year; not renewable. *Number:* 1. *Amount:* $500.

Eligibility Requirements: Applicant must be Canadian citizen; high school student; planning to enroll or expecting to enroll full-time at a four-year institution or university and resident of Manitoba.

Application Requirements: Application, references, transcript. *Deadline:* July 31.

Contact: Petricia Pohrebniuk, Executive Director
Manitoba Forestry Association
900 Corydon Avenue
Winnipeg, MB R3M 0Y4
Canada
Phone: 204-453-3182
Fax: 204-477-5765
E-mail: mfainc@mts.net

MISSOURI DEPARTMENT OF NATURAL RESOURCES http://www.dnr.mo.gov

ENVIRONMENTAL EDUCATION SCHOLARSHIP PROGRAM (EESP)

Scholarship to minority and other underrepresented students pursuing a bachelor's or master's degree in an environmental course of study. Must be a Missouri resident having a cumulative high school GPA of 3.0 or if enrolled in college, must have cumulative GPA of 2.5.

Academic Fields/Career Goals: Environmental Science.

Award: Scholarship for use in freshman, sophomore, junior, senior, or graduate years; renewable. *Number:* 16. *Amount:* $2000.

Eligibility Requirements: Applicant must be American Indian/Alaska Native, Asian/Pacific Islander, Black (non-Hispanic), or Hispanic; enrolled or expecting to enroll full-time at a four-year institution or university and resident of Missouri. Applicant must have 3.0 GPA or higher. Available to U.S. citizens.

Application Requirements: Application, essay, references, transcript. *Deadline:* June 1.

Contact: Dana Muessig, Executive
Missouri Department of Natural Resources
PO Box 176
Jefferson City, MO 65102
Phone: 800-361-4827
Fax: 573-526-3878
E-mail: danamuessig@dnr.mo.gov

MORRIS K. UDALL FOUNDATION http://www.udall.gov

MORRIS K. UDALL SCHOLARS

• *See page 76*

MORRIS LAND CONSERVANCY http://www.morrislandconservancy.org

ROGERS FAMILY SCHOLARSHIP

Scholarship to deserving individuals who plan careers in environmental science, natural resource management, conservation, horticulture, park administration, or a related field. Must be a resident of New Jersey and considering a career in New Jersey. Payment is made directly to the institution that the successful candidate attends.

Academic Fields/Career Goals: Environmental Science; Horticulture/Floriculture; Natural Resources; Recreation, Parks, Leisure Studies.

Award: Scholarship for use in freshman, sophomore, junior, or senior years; not renewable. *Number:* varies. *Amount:* varies.

Eligibility Requirements: Applicant must be enrolled or expecting to enroll full- or part-time at a four-year institution or university and resident of New Jersey. Applicant must have 3.0 GPA or higher. Available to U.S. citizens.

Application Requirements: Application, essay, resume, references, transcript. *Deadline:* April 1.

Contact: Scholarship Committee
Morris Land Conservancy
19 Boonton Avenue
Boonton, NJ 07005
Phone: 973-541-1010
Fax: 973-541-1131
E-mail: info@morrislandconservancy.org

RUSSELL W. MYERS SCHOLARSHIP

Scholarship to deserving individuals who plan careers in environmental science, natural resource management, conservation, horticulture, park administration, or a related field. Must be a resident of New Jersey and considering a career in New Jersey. Payment is made directly to the institution that the successful candidate attends.

Academic Fields/Career Goals: Environmental Science; Horticulture/Floriculture; Natural Resources; Recreation, Parks, Leisure Studies.

Award: Scholarship for use in freshman, sophomore, junior, or senior years; not renewable. *Number:* varies. *Amount:* varies.

Eligibility Requirements: Applicant must be enrolled or expecting to enroll full-time at a four-year institution or university and resident of New Jersey. Applicant must have 3.0 GPA or higher. Available to U.S. citizens.

Application Requirements: Application, essay, references, transcript. *Deadline:* April 1.

Contact: Scholarship Committee
Morris Land Conservancy
19 Boonton Avenue
Boonton, NJ 07005
Phone: 973-541-1010
Fax: 973-541-1131
E-mail: info@morrislandconservancy.org

NASA/MARYLAND SPACE GRANT CONSORTIUM http://www.mdspacegrant.org

NASA MARYLAND SPACE GRANT CONSORTIUM UNDERGRADUATE SCHOLARSHIPS

• *See page 118*

NASA SOUTH DAKOTA SPACE GRANT CONSORTIUM http://www.sdsmt.edu/space/

SOUTH DAKOTA SPACE GRANT CONSORTIUM UNDERGRADUATE SCHOLARSHIPS

• *See page 120*

NASA VIRGINIA SPACE GRANT CONSORTIUM http://www.vsgc.odu.edu

VIRGINIA SPACE GRANT CONSORTIUM TEACHER EDUCATION SCHOLARSHIPS

• *See page 121*

NASA WEST VIRGINIA SPACE GRANT CONSORTIUM http://www.nasa.wvu.edu

WEST VIRGINIA SPACE GRANT CONSORTIUM UNDERGRADUATE FELLOWSHIP PROGRAM

• *See page 121*

NATIONAL COUNCIL OF STATE GARDEN CLUBS INC. SCHOLARSHIP http://www.gardenclub.org

NATIONAL COUNCIL OF STATE GARDEN CLUBS INC. SCHOLARSHIP

• *See page 76*

NATIONAL FISH AND WILDLIFE FOUNDATION http://www.nfwf.org

BUDWEISER CONSERVATION SCHOLARSHIP PROGRAM

• *See page 133*

NATIONAL GARDEN CLUBS INC. http://www.gardenclub.org

NATIONAL GARDEN CLUBS INC. SCHOLARSHIP PROGRAM

• *See page 77*

NATIONAL INVENTORS HALL OF FAME http://www.invent.org

COLLEGIATE INVENTORS COMPETITION FOR UNDERGRADUATE STUDENTS

• *See page 88*

COLLEGIATE INVENTORS COMPETITION-GRAND PRIZE

• *See page 88*

NATIONAL SAFETY COUNCIL http://www.cshema.org

CAMPUS SAFETY, HEALTH AND ENVIRONMENTAL MANAGEMENT ASSOCIATION SCHOLARSHIP AWARD PROGRAM

One $2000 scholarship available to full-time undergraduate or graduate students in all majors to encourage the study of safety and environmental management.

Academic Fields/Career Goals: Environmental Science; Occupational Safety and Health.

Award: Scholarship for use in freshman, sophomore, junior, senior, or graduate years; not renewable. *Number:* 1. *Amount:* $2000.

Eligibility Requirements: Applicant must be enrolled or expecting to enroll full-time at a four-year institution or university. Available to U.S. and Canadian citizens.

Application Requirements: Application, essay, transcript. *Deadline:* March 31.

Contact: Scholarship Committee
National Safety Council
12100 Sunset Hills Road, Suite 130
Reston, VA 20190-3221
Phone: 703-234-4141
Fax: 703-435-4390

NEW ENGLAND WATER WORKS ASSOCIATION http://www.newwa.org

ELSON T. KILLAM MEMORIAL SCHOLARSHIP

• *See page 172*

FRANCIS X. CROWLEY SCHOLARSHIP

• *See page 147*

JOSEPH MURPHY SCHOLARSHIP

• *See page 172*

NEW JERSEY DIVISION OF FISH AND WILDLIFE/NJ CHAPTER OF THE WILDLIFE SOCIETY http://www.njfishandwildlife.com/cookhmschol.htm

RUSSELL A. COOKINGHAM SCHOLARSHIP

• *See page 134*

OHIO ACADEMY OF SCIENCE/OHIO ENVIRONMENTAL EDUCATION FUND http://www.ohiosci.org

OHIO ENVIRONMENTAL SCIENCE & ENGINEERING SCHOLARSHIPS

Merit-based, non-renewable, tuition-only scholarships awarded to undergraduate students admitted to Ohio state or private colleges and universities. Must be able to demonstrate knowledge of, and commitment to, careers in environmental sciences or environmental engineering.

Academic Fields/Career Goals: Environmental Science.

Award: Scholarship for use in senior year; not renewable. *Number:* 18. *Amount:* $1250–$2500.

Eligibility Requirements: Applicant must be enrolled or expecting to enroll full- or part-time at a two-year or four-year institution or university and studying in Ohio. Applicant must have 3.0 GPA or higher. Available to U.S. citizens.

Application Requirements: Application, essay, resume, references, self-addressed stamped envelope, transcript. *Deadline:* June 1.

Contact: Mr. Lynn E. Elfner, Chief Executive Officer
Ohio Academy of Science/Ohio Environmental Education Fund
1500 West Third Avenue, Suite 228
Columbus, OH 43212-2817
Phone: 614-488-2228
Fax: 614-488-7629
E-mail: oas@iwaynet.net

OREGON STUDENT ASSISTANCE COMMISSION http://www.osac.state.or.us

ROYDEN M. BODLEY SCHOLARSHIP

• *See page 82*

OZARKA NATURAL SPRING WATER http://www.ozarkawater.com

EARTH SCIENCE SCHOLARSHIP

• *See page 219*

PENNSYLVANIA ASSOCIATION OF CONSERVATION DISTRICTS AUXILIARY http://www.pacd.org

PACD AUXILIARY SCHOLARSHIPS

• *See page 78*

SAEMS-SOUTHERN ARIZONA ENVIRONMENTAL MANAGEMENT SOCIETY http://www.saems.org

ENVIRONMENTAL SCHOLARSHIPS

• *See page 299*

SOIL AND WATER CONSERVATION SOCIETY-NEW JERSEY CHAPTER http://www.geocities.com/njswcs

EDWARD R. HALL SCHOLARSHIP

• *See page 71*

TECHNICAL ASSOCIATION OF THE PULP & PAPER INDUSTRY (TAPPI) http://www.tappi.org

ENVIRONMENTAL DIVISION SCHOLARSHIP

Annual awards for SME student members, who are undergraduate students at or above the level of a sophomore, enrolled at ABET-accredited or equivalent college. Minimum of one $2500 Scholarship.

Academic Fields/Career Goals: Environmental Science; Paper and Pulp Engineering.

Award: Scholarship for use in sophomore, junior, or senior years; not renewable. *Number:* 1. *Amount:* $2500.

Eligibility Requirements: Applicant must be enrolled or expecting to enroll full-time at a four-year institution or university. Applicant must have 3.0 GPA or higher. Available to U.S. and non-U.S. citizens.

Application Requirements: Application, essay, interview, references, transcript. *Deadline:* February 15.

Contact: Karen Roman, Member Group Specialist
Technical Association of the Pulp & Paper Industry (TAPPI)
15 Technology Parkway, South
Norcross, GA 30092
Phone: 770-209-7416
Fax: 770-446-6947
E-mail: kroman@tappi.org

TEXAS OUTDOOR WRITERS ASSOCIATION http://www.towa.org

TEXAS OUTDOOR WRITERS ASSOCIATION SCHOLARSHIP

• *See page 187*

TKE EDUCATIONAL FOUNDATION http://www.tke.org

TIMOTHY L. TASCHWER SCHOLARSHIP

• *See page 135*

UNITED NEGRO COLLEGE FUND http://www.uncf.org

CDM SCHOLARSHIP/INTERNSHIP

• *See page 93*

MELLON ECOLOGY PROGRAM (S.E.E.D.S)

Program gives minority students exposure to research in ecology and ecology-related careers. Must attend a UNCF member college or university. Prospective applicants should complete the Student Profile found at Web site: http://www.uncf.org.

Academic Fields/Career Goals: Environmental Science; Natural Resources.

Award: Scholarship for use in freshman, sophomore, junior, or senior years; not renewable. *Number:* 1. *Amount:* varies.

Eligibility Requirements: Applicant must be Black (non-Hispanic) and enrolled or expecting to enroll full- or part-time at a four-year institution or university. Available to U.S. citizens.

Application Requirements: Application, financial need analysis. *Deadline:* continuous.

Contact: Director, Program Services
United Negro College Fund
8260 Willow Oaks Corporate Drive
PO Box 10444
Fairfax, VA 22031-8044
Phone: 800-331-2244
E-mail: rebecca.bennett@uncf.org

WEYERHAEUSER/UNCF CORPORATE SCHOLARS PROGRAM

• *See page 151*

UNITED STATES ENVIRONMENTAL PROTECTION AGENCY http://www.epa.gov/enviroed

NATIONAL NETWORK FOR ENVIRONMENTAL MANAGEMENT STUDIES FELLOWSHIP

Fellowship program designed to provide undergraduate and graduate students with research opportunities at one of EPA's facilities nationwide. EPA awards approximately 40 NNEMS fellowships per year. Selected students receive a stipend for performing their research project. EPA develops an annual catalog of research projects available for student application. Submit a complete application package as described in the annual catalog. Minimum 3.0 GPA required.

Academic Fields/Career Goals: Environmental Science; Natural Resources.

Award: Grant for use in freshman, sophomore, junior, senior, graduate, or postgraduate years; not renewable. *Number:* 20–25. *Amount:* varies.

Eligibility Requirements: Applicant must be enrolled or expecting to enroll full- or part-time at a two-year or four-year institution or university. Applicant must have 3.0 GPA or higher. Available to U.S. citizens.

United States Environmental Protection Agency (continued)

Application Requirements: Application, resume, references, transcript. *Deadline:* January 22.

Contact: Michael Baker, Acting Director
United States Environmental Protection Agency
Environmental Education Division, 1200 Pennsylvania Avenue, NW, MC 1704A
Washington, DC 20460
Phone: 202-564-0446
Fax: 202-564-2754
E-mail: baker.michael@epa.gov

VIRGINIA ASSOCIATION OF SOIL AND WATER CONSERVATION DISTRICTS EDUCATIONAL FOUNDATION INC. http://www.vaswcd.org

VASWCD EDUCATIONAL FOUNDATION INC. SCHOLARSHIP AWARDS PROGRAM

Scholarship to provide financial support to Virginia residents majoring in, or showing a strong desire to major in, a course curriculum related to natural resource conservation and/or environmental studies. Applicants must be full-time students who have applied to an undergraduate freshman-level curriculum. Must rank in the top 20 percent of graduating class or have a 3.0 or greater GPA, and demonstrate an active interest in conservation. Recipients may reapply to their individual SWCD for scholarship consideration in ensuing years.

Academic Fields/Career Goals: Environmental Science; Natural Resources.

Award: Scholarship for use in freshman year; not renewable. *Number:* 4. *Amount:* $1000.

Eligibility Requirements: Applicant must be high school student; planning to enroll or expecting to enroll full-time at a four-year institution or university and resident of Virginia. Applicant must have 3.0 GPA or higher. Available to U.S. citizens.

Application Requirements: Application, essay, financial need analysis, references, transcript. *Deadline:* March 1.

Contact: Jennifer Krick, District Manager
Virginia Association of Soil and Water Conservation Districts Educational Foundation Inc.
John Marshall Soil and Water
98 Alexandria Pike, Suite 31
Warrenton, VA 20186
Phone: 540-347-3120 Ext. 116
Fax: 540-349-0878
E-mail: jennifer.krick@va.nacdnet.net

WINDSTAR FOUNDATION http://www.wstar.org

WINDSTAR ENVIRONMENTAL STUDIES SCHOLARSHIPS

• *See page 299*

EUROPEAN STUDIES

AMERICAN SCHOOL OF CLASSICAL STUDIES AT ATHENS http://www.ascsa.edu.gr

ASCSA SUMMER SESSIONS OPEN SCHOLARSHIPS

• *See page 83*

CANADIAN INSTITUTE OF UKRAINIAN STUDIES http://www.cius.ca

CANADIAN INSTITUTE OF UKRAINIAN STUDIES RESEARCH GRANTS

• *See page 95*

GERMAN ACADEMIC EXCHANGE SERVICE (DAAD) http://www.daad.org

GERMAN ACADEMIC EXCHANGE INFORMATION VISITS

Grants are available for an information visit of seven to twelve days to groups of 10 to 15 students, accompanied by a faculty member. The purpose of this program is to increase the knowledge of specific German subjects and institutions within the framework of an academic study tour. Preference will be given to groups with a homogeneous academic background. Application should reach DAAD, New York at least six months before the beginning date of the planned visit.

Academic Fields/Career Goals: European Studies; German Studies.

Award: Grant for use in junior, senior, or graduate years; not renewable. *Number:* varies. *Amount:* varies.

Eligibility Requirements: Applicant must be enrolled or expecting to enroll full-time at a four-year institution or university. Available to U.S. and non-U.S. citizens.

Application Requirements: Application, applicant must enter a contest. *Deadline:* varies.

Contact: Jane Fu, Information Officer
German Academic Exchange Service (DAAD)
871 United Nations Plaza
New York, NY 10017
Phone: 212-758-3223 Ext. 201
Fax: 212-755-5780
E-mail: daadny@daad.org

FASHION DESIGN

HISPANIC SCHOLARSHIP FUND http://www.hsf.net

HSF/MCNAMARA FAMILY CREATIVE ARTS PROJECT GRANT

• *See page 98*

OREGON STUDENT ASSISTANCE COMMISSION http://www.osac.state.or.us

FASHION GROUP INTERNATIONAL OF PORTLAND SCHOLARSHIP

Award for Oregon residents planning to pursue a career in a fashion-related field. Must be enrolled at least half-time at the sophomore or higher level. Minimum GPA of 3.0 required. Semifinalists will be interviewed by donor group in Portland. Must attend college in Oregon, Washington, California, or Idaho.

Academic Fields/Career Goals: Fashion Design.

Award: Scholarship for use in sophomore, junior, or senior years; renewable. *Number:* varies. *Amount:* varies.

Eligibility Requirements: Applicant must be enrolled or expecting to enroll full-time at a four-year institution or university; resident of Oregon and studying in California, Idaho, Oregon, or Washington. Applicant must have 3.0 GPA or higher. Available to U.S. citizens.

Application Requirements: Application, essay, financial need analysis, interview, references, transcript, activity chart. *Deadline:* March 1.

Contact: Director of Grant Programs
Oregon Student Assistance Commission
1500 Valley River Drive, Suite 100
Eugene, OR 97401-7020
Phone: 800-452-8807 Ext. 7395

SAN DIEGO FOUNDATION http://www.sdfoundation.org

CALIFORNIA ASSOCIATION OF FAMILY AND CONSUMER SCIENCES-SAN DIEGO CHAPTER

• *See page 166*

WORLDSTUDIO FOUNDATION http://www.aiga.org/

WORLDSTUDIO FOUNDATION SCHOLARSHIP PROGRAM

• *See page 94*

FILMMAKING/VIDEO

ACADEMY FOUNDATION OF THE ACADEMY OF MOTION PICTURE ARTS AND SCIENCES http://www.oscars.org/saa

ACADEMY OF MOTION PICTURE ARTS AND SCIENCES STUDENT ACADEMY AWARDS

Award available to students who have made a narrative, documentary, alternative, or animated film of up to 60 minutes within the curricular structure of an accredited college or university. Initial entry must be on 1/2 inch VHS tape. 16mm or larger format print or digital beta-cam tape required for further rounds. Prizes awarded in four categories. Each category awards gold ($5000), silver ($3000), and bronze ($2000). Visit Web site for details and application: http://www.oscars.org/saa.

Academic Fields/Career Goals: Filmmaking/Video.

Award: Prize for use in freshman, sophomore, junior, senior, or graduate years; not renewable. *Number:* 3–12. *Amount:* $2000–$5000.

Eligibility Requirements: Applicant must be enrolled or expecting to enroll full-time at a two-year or four-year institution or university. Available to U.S. and non-U.S. citizens.

Application Requirements: Application, applicant must enter a contest, 16mm or larger format film print or NTSC digital betacam version of the entry (BetaSP format is not acceptable), DVD. *Deadline:* April 2.

Contact: Richard Miller, Awards Administration Director
Academy Foundation of the Academy of Motion Picture Arts and Sciences
8949 Wilshire Boulevard
Beverly Hills, CA 90211-1972
Phone: 310-247-3000 Ext. 129
Fax: 310-859-9619
E-mail: rmiller@oscars.org

ACADEMY OF MOTION PICTURE STUDENT ACADEMY AWARD-HONORARY FOREIGN FILM

One award is given to an applicant from an institution outside the U.S. and a member of CILECT. Visit Web site for applications: http://www.oscars.org/saa.

Academic Fields/Career Goals: Filmmaking/Video.

Award: Prize for use in freshman, sophomore, junior, senior, or graduate years; not renewable. *Number:* 1. *Amount:* $1000.

Eligibility Requirements: Applicant must be enrolled or expecting to enroll full-time at a four-year institution or university. Available to Canadian and non-U.S. citizens.

Application Requirements: Application, applicant must enter a contest, self-addressed stamped envelope, 16mm, 35mm, 70mm, or digital betacam version. *Deadline:* March 23.

Contact: Richard Miller, Awards Administration Director
Academy Foundation of the Academy of Motion Picture Arts and Sciences
8949 Wilshire Boulevard
Beverly Hills, CA 90211-1972
Phone: 310-247-3000
Fax: 310-859-9619
E-mail: rmiller@oscars.org

ACADEMY OF TELEVISION ARTS AND SCIENCES FOUNDATION http://www.emmysfoundation.org

ACADEMY OF TELEVISION ARTS AND SCIENCES COLLEGE TELEVISION AWARDS

• *See page 99*

ADC RESEARCH INSTITUTE http://www.adc.org

JACK SHAHEEN MASS COMMUNICATIONS SCHOLARSHIP AWARD

• *See page 175*

CASUALTY ACTUARIES OF THE SOUTHEAST http://www.casact.org

CASUALTY ACTUARIES OF THE SOUTHEAST SCHOLARSHIP PROGRAM

Scholarships available for undergraduate students in the southeastern states for the study of actuarial science. Must be studying in: Alabama, Arkansas, Florida, Georgia, Kentucky, Louisiana, Mississippi, North Carolina, South Carolina, Tennessee, or Virginia. Incoming freshmen/first-year students are not eligible for the scholarship.

Award: Scholarship for use in sophomore, junior, or senior years; not renewable. *Number:* 2. *Amount:* $1500.

Eligibility Requirements: Applicant must be enrolled or expecting to enroll full-time at a four-year institution or university and studying in Alabama, Arkansas, Florida, Georgia, Kentucky, Louisiana, Mississippi, North Carolina, South Carolina, Tennessee, or Virginia. Available to U.S. and Canadian citizens.

Application Requirements: Application, references. *Deadline:* May 1.

Contact: Vice President of College Relations
Casualty Actuaries of the Southeast
3500 Lenox Road, Suite 900
Atlanta, GA 30326-4238
Phone: 404-365-1549
Fax: 404-365-1663
E-mail: michael.miller@towersperrin.com

CHARLES & LUCILLE KING FAMILY FOUNDATION INC. http://www.kingfoundation.org

CHARLES AND LUCILLE KING FAMILY FOUNDATION SCHOLARSHIPS

• *See page 177*

HISPANIC SCHOLARSHIP FUND http://www.hsf.net

HSF/MCNAMARA FAMILY CREATIVE ARTS PROJECT GRANT

• *See page 98*

ILLUMINATING ENGINEERING SOCIETY OF NORTH AMERICA–GOLDEN GATE SECTION http://www.iesgg.org

ALAN LUCAS MEMORIAL EDUCATIONAL SCHOLARSHIP

• *See page 92*

INSTITUTE FOR HUMANE STUDIES http://www.theihs.org

FILM AND FICTION SCHOLARSHIP

• *See page 102*

INTERNATIONAL COMMUNICATIONS INDUSTRIES FOUNDATION http://www.infocomm.org/scholarships

ICIF SCHOLARSHIP FOR DEPENDENTS OF MEMBER ORGANIZATIONS

• *See page 179*

INTERNATIONAL COMMUNICATIONS INDUSTRIES FOUNDATION AV SCHOLARSHIP

• *See page 180*

MEDIA ACTION NETWORK FOR ASIAN AMERICANS http://www.manaa.org

MANAA MEDIA SCHOLARSHIPS FOR ASIAN AMERICAN STUDENTS

• *See page 104*

OUTDOOR WRITERS ASSOCIATION OF AMERICA http://www.owaa.org

OUTDOOR WRITERS ASSOCIATION OF AMERICA BODIE MCDOWELL SCHOLARSHIP AWARD

• *See page 183*

PHI DELTA THETA EDUCATIONAL FOUNDATION http://www.phideltatheta.org

FRANCIS D. LYON SCHOLARSHIPS

Award to honor Francis D. Lyon, who had a distinguished motion picture and television career as a film editor, director, and producer. Both undergraduate and graduate students are invited to apply. Applicants must be pursuing a filmmaking career and must attend school in the U.S. or Canada.

Academic Fields/Career Goals: Filmmaking/Video.

Award: Scholarship for use in junior, senior, graduate, or postgraduate years; not renewable. *Number:* 2. *Amount:* up to $3000.

Eligibility Requirements: Applicant must be enrolled or expecting to enroll full-time at a four-year institution or university. Available to U.S. and non-U.S. citizens.

Phi Delta Theta Educational Foundation (continued)

Application Requirements: Application, essay, photo, references, transcript. *Deadline:* March 10.

Contact: Mrs. Carmalieta Jenkins, Assistant to the President
Phi Delta Theta Educational Foundation
Two South Campus Avenue
Oxford, OH 45056-1801
Phone: 513-523-6966
Fax: 513-523-9200
E-mail: carmalieta@phideltatheta.org

POLISH ARTS CLUB OF BUFFALO SCHOLARSHIP FOUNDATION http://www.pacb.bfn.org

POLISH ARTS CLUB OF BUFFALO SCHOLARSHIP FOUNDATION TRUST

• *See page 105*

PRINCESS GRACE FOUNDATION-USA http://www.pgfusa.org

PRINCESS GRACE SCHOLARSHIPS IN DANCE, THEATER, AND FILM

One-time scholarship for students enrolled either part-time or full-time in film or video, dance, or theater program. For dance,applicant must have completed at least one year of undergraduate study; for theater, final year of study in either undergraduate or graduate level; and for film, must be in thesis program. The number of scholarships varies from fifteen to twenty annually.

Academic Fields/Career Goals: Filmmaking/Video; Performing Arts.

Award: Scholarship for use in sophomore, junior, senior, or graduate years; not renewable. *Number:* 15–20. *Amount:* $5000–$25,000.

Eligibility Requirements: Applicant must be enrolled or expecting to enroll full- or part-time at a four-year institution or university. Available to U.S. citizens.

Application Requirements: Application, applicant must enter a contest, essay, photo, portfolio, resume, references, self-addressed stamped envelope, nomination. *Deadline:* varies.

Contact: Kathleen Richards, Program Manager
Princess Grace Foundation-USA
150 East 58th Street, 25th Floor
New York, NY 10155
Phone: 212-317-1470
Fax: 212-317-1473
E-mail: grants@pgfusa.org

RHODE ISLAND FOUNDATION http://www.rifoundation.org

J. D. EDSAL ADVERTISING SCHOLARSHIP

• *See page 184*

SAN FRANCISCO FOUNDATION http://www.sff.org

PHELAN ART AWARD IN FILMMAKING

Award presented in every even-numbered year to recognize achievement in film making. Must have been born in California, but need not be a current resident. Applicants must provide a copy of their birth certificate with their application. Scholarship values from $5000 to $10,000. Deadline varies.

Academic Fields/Career Goals: Filmmaking/Video.

Award: Prize for use in freshman, sophomore, junior, senior, graduate, or postgraduate years; not renewable. *Number:* 3. *Amount:* $5000–$10,000.

Eligibility Requirements: Applicant must be enrolled or expecting to enroll full- or part-time at a two-year or four-year institution or university. Available to U.S. citizens.

Application Requirements: Application, applicant must enter a contest, self-addressed stamped envelope. *Deadline:* varies.

Contact: Art Awards Coordinator
San Francisco Foundation
225 Bush Street, Suite 500
San Francisco, CA 94104
Phone: 415-733-8500

PHELAN ART AWARD IN VIDEO

Award presented in every even-numbered year to recognize achievement in video. Must have been born in California, but need not be a current resident. Applicants must provide a copy of their birth certificates with their application. Scholarship value is $5000 to $10,000. Deadline varies.

Academic Fields/Career Goals: Filmmaking/Video.

Award: Prize for use in freshman, sophomore, junior, senior, graduate, or postgraduate years; not renewable. *Number:* 3. *Amount:* $5000–$10,000.

Eligibility Requirements: Applicant must be enrolled or expecting to enroll full- or part-time at a two-year or four-year institution or university. Available to U.S. citizens.

Application Requirements: Application, applicant must enter a contest, self-addressed stamped envelope. *Deadline:* varies.

Contact: Art Awards Coordinator
San Francisco Foundation
225 Bush Street, Suite 500
San Francisco, CA 94104
Phone: 415-733-8500

SOCIETY OF MOTION PICTURE AND TELEVISION ENGINEERS http://www.smpte.org

LOU WOLF MEMORIAL SCHOLARSHIP

Award for students enrolled in an accredited high school, two-year or four-year college or university. Must be members of Society of Motion Picture and Television Engineers.

Academic Fields/Career Goals: Filmmaking/Video.

Award: Scholarship for use in freshman, sophomore, junior, senior, graduate, or postgraduate years; not renewable. *Number:* varies. *Amount:* up to $2000.

Eligibility Requirements: Applicant must be enrolled or expecting to enroll full- or part-time at a two-year or four-year institution or university. Applicant or parent of applicant must be member of Society of Motion Picture and Television Engineers. Available to U.S. and non-U.S. citizens.

Application Requirements: Application, essay, references, transcript. *Deadline:* June 1.

Contact: Sally-Ann D'Amato, Director of Operations
Society of Motion Picture and Television Engineers
Third Barker Avenue
White Plains, NY 10601
Phone: 914-761-1100 Ext. 4965
Fax: 914-761-3115
E-mail: sdamato@smpte.org

STUDENT PAPER AWARD

Contest for best paper by a current Student Member of SMPTE. Paper must deal with some technical phase of motion pictures, television, photographic instrumentation, or their closely allied arts and sciences. For more information see Web site: http://www.smpte.org.

Academic Fields/Career Goals: Filmmaking/Video.

Award: Prize for use in freshman, sophomore, junior, senior, graduate, or postgraduate years; not renewable. *Number:* 1. *Amount:* varies.

Eligibility Requirements: Applicant must be enrolled or expecting to enroll full- or part-time at a four-year institution or university. Applicant or parent of applicant must be member of Society of Motion Picture and Television Engineers. Available to U.S. and non-U.S. citizens.

Application Requirements: Application, applicant must enter a contest, essay, student ID card. *Deadline:* July 1.

Contact: Sally-Ann D'Amato, Director of Operations
Society of Motion Picture and Television Engineers
Third Barker Avenue
White Plains, NY 10601
Phone: 914-761-1100 Ext. 4965
Fax: 914-761-3115
E-mail: sdamato@smpte.org

TELETOON http://www.teletoon.com

TELETOON ANIMATION SCHOLARSHIP

• *See page 106*

UNIVERSITY FILM AND VIDEO ASSOCIATION http://www.ufva.org

UNIVERSITY FILM AND VIDEO ASSOCIATION CAROLE FIELDING STUDENT GRANTS

Up to $4000 is available for production grants in narrative, documentary, experimental, new-media/installation, or animation. Up to $1000 is available for grants in research. Applicant must be sponsored by a faculty person who is an active member of the University Film and Video Association. Fifty percent of award distributed upon completion of project.

Academic Fields/Career Goals: Filmmaking/Video.

Award: Grant for use in freshman, sophomore, junior, senior, or graduate years; not renewable. *Number:* up to 5. *Amount:* $1000–$4000.

Eligibility Requirements: Applicant must be enrolled or expecting to enroll full- or part-time at a two-year or four-year institution or university. Available to U.S. and non-U.S. citizens.

Application Requirements: Application, essay, resume, references, project description, budget. *Deadline:* December 15.

Contact: Prof. Robert Johnson, Jr., Chair
University Film and Video Association
Framingham State College, 100 State Street
Framingham, MA 01701-9101
Phone: 508-626-4684
Fax: 508-626-4847
E-mail: rjohnso@frc.mass.edu

WOMEN IN FILM AND TELEVISION (WIFT) http://www.wif.org

WIF FOUNDATION SCHOLARSHIP

Scholarships for female students based on their academic standing, artistic talents and commitment to a film-based curriculum with special consideration for financial need, regardless of age, ethnicity or religious affiliation. Scholarships to such schools as University of California, Los Angles, University of Southern California, Chapman University and AFI are available to female students who are already enrolled and have been nominated by instructors and faculty at respective schools.

Academic Fields/Career Goals: Filmmaking/Video.

Award: Scholarship for use in freshman, sophomore, junior, or senior years; not renewable. *Number:* up to 3. *Amount:* up to $1000.

Eligibility Requirements: Applicant must be enrolled or expecting to enroll part-time at a two-year or four-year or technical institution or university and female. Available to U.S. citizens.

Application Requirements: Application, essay, financial need analysis, references, transcript. *Deadline:* varies.

Contact: Gayle Nachlis, Executive Director
Women in Film and Television (WIFT)
8857 West Olympic Boulevard, Suite 201
Beverly Hills, CA 90211
Phone: 310-657-5144 Ext. 28
Fax: 310-657-5154
E-mail: gnachlis@wif.org

WORLDFEST INTERNATIONAL FILM AND VIDEO FESTIVAL http://www.worldfest.org

WORLDFEST STUDENT FILM AWARD

Award for students enrolled full-time or part-time in accredited colleges or universities majoring filmmaking.

Academic Fields/Career Goals: Filmmaking/Video.

Award: Prize for use in freshman, sophomore, junior, senior, or graduate years; not renewable. *Number:* 10. *Amount:* $1000–$10,000.

Eligibility Requirements: Applicant must be enrolled or expecting to enroll full- or part-time at a two-year or four-year or technical institution or university. Available to U.S. and non-U.S. citizens.

Application Requirements: Application, applicant must enter a contest, references, film/tape entry, student ID. *Fee:* $45. *Deadline:* December 15.

Contact: Hunter Todd, Executive Director
Worldfest International Film and Video Festival
9898 BIssonnet Street, Suite 650
PO Box 56566
Houston, TX 77256-6566
Phone: 713-965-9955
Fax: 713-965-9960
E-mail: hunter@worldfest.org

WORLDSTUDIO FOUNDATION http://www.aiga.org/

WORLDSTUDIO FOUNDATION SCHOLARSHIP PROGRAM

• *See page 94*

FIRE SCIENCES

BOY SCOUTS OF AMERICA-MUSKINGUM VALLEY COUNCIL http://www.learning-for-life.org

INTERNATIONAL ASSOCIATION OF FIRE CHIEFS FOUNDATION SCHOLARSHIP

Two $500 scholarships for Explorers who are pursuing a full-time career in the fire sciences. Must be high school senior and participant of the Learning for Life Exploring program.

Academic Fields/Career Goals: Fire Sciences.

Award: Scholarship for use in freshman year; not renewable. *Number:* 2. *Amount:* $500.

Eligibility Requirements: Applicant must be high school student and planning to enroll or expecting to enroll full-time at a four-year institution or university. Available to U.S. and non-U.S. citizens.

Application Requirements: Application, essay, photo, references, test scores, transcript. *Deadline:* July 1.

Contact: Scholarship Committee
Boy Scouts of America-Muskingum Valley Council
S210, PO Box 152079
Irving, TX

INDEPENDENT LABORATORIES INSTITUTE SCHOLARSHIP ALLIANCE http://www.acil.org

INDEPENDENT LABORATORIES INSTITUTE SCHOLARSHIP ALLIANCE

• *See page 132*

INTERNATIONAL ASSOCIATION OF ARSON INVESTIGATORS EDUCATIONAL FOUNDATION INC. http://www.fire-investigators.org/

JOHN CHARLES WILSON SCHOLARSHIP

One-time award to members in good standing of IAAI or the immediate family of a member or must be sponsored by an IAAI member. Must enroll or plan to enroll full-time in an accredited college or university that offers courses in police, fire sciences, or any arson investigation-related field. Application available at Web site.

Academic Fields/Career Goals: Fire Sciences; Law Enforcement/Police Administration.

Award: Scholarship for use in freshman, sophomore, junior, senior, or graduate years; not renewable. *Number:* up to 5. *Amount:* up to $1000.

International Association of Arson Investigators Educational Foundation Inc. (continued)

Eligibility Requirements: Applicant must be enrolled or expecting to enroll full-time at a two-year or four-year institution or university. Available to U.S. and non-U.S. citizens.

Application Requirements: Application, autobiography, driver's license, essay, resume, references, test scores, transcript. *Deadline:* February 15.

Contact: Marsha Sipes, Office Manager
International Association of Arson Investigators Educational Foundation Inc.
12770 Boenker Road
Bridgeton, MO 63044
Phone: 314-739-4224
Fax: 314-739-4219
E-mail: iaai@firearson.com

LEARNING FOR LIFE http://www.learning-for-life.org

INTERNATIONAL ASSOCIATIONS OF FIRE CHIEFS FOUNDATION SCHOLARSHIP

Applicant must be a graduating high school senior in May or June of the year the application is issued and a Fire Service Explorer. The school selected by the applicant must be an accredited public or proprietary institution.

Academic Fields/Career Goals: Fire Sciences.

Award: Scholarship for use in freshman year; not renewable. *Number:* 2. *Amount:* $500.

Eligibility Requirements: Applicant must be high school student and planning to enroll or expecting to enroll full- or part-time at a two-year or four-year institution or university. Applicant or parent of applicant must be member of Explorer Program/Learning for Life. Available to U.S. citizens.

Application Requirements: Application, essay, photo, references, transcript. *Deadline:* July 1.

Contact: Scholarship Committee
Learning for Life
1325 West Walnut Hill Lane
PO Box 152079
Irving, TX 75015-2079
Phone: 972-580-2433

MARYLAND HIGHER EDUCATION COMMISSION http://www.mhec.state.md.us

CHARLES W. RILEY FIRE AND EMERGENCY MEDICAL SERVICES TUITION REIMBURSEMENT PROGRAM

Award intended to reimburse members of rescue organizations serving Maryland communities for tuition costs of course work towards a degree or certificate in fire service or medical technology. Must attend a two- or four-year school in Maryland. Minimum 2.0 GPA. The scholarship is worth up to $6500.

Academic Fields/Career Goals: Fire Sciences; Health and Medical Sciences; Trade/Technical Specialties.

Award: Scholarship for use in freshman, sophomore, junior, or senior years; not renewable. *Number:* up to 150. *Amount:* up to $6500.

Eligibility Requirements: Applicant must be enrolled or expecting to enroll full- or part-time at a two-year or four-year institution or university; resident of Maryland and studying in Maryland. Applicant or parent of applicant must have employment or volunteer experience in police/firefighting. Available to U.S. citizens.

Application Requirements: Application, transcript, tuition receipt, proof of enrollment. *Deadline:* July 1.

Contact: Gerrie Rogers, Office of Student Financial Assistance
Maryland Higher Education Commission
839 Bestgate Road, Suite 400
Annapolis, MD 21401-3013
Phone: 410-260-4574
Fax: 410-260-3203
E-mail: grogers@mhec.state.md.us

FLEXOGRAPHY

FOUNDATION OF FLEXOGRAPHIC TECHNICAL ASSOCIATION http://www.flexography.org

FOUNDATION OF FLEXOGRAPHIC TECHNICAL ASSOCIATION SCHOLARSHIP COMPETITION

Awards students enrolled in a FFTA Flexo in Education Program with plans to attend a postsecondary institution, or be currently enrolled in a postsecondary institution offering a course of study in flexography. Must demonstrate an interest in a career in flexography, and maintain an overall GPA of at least 3.0. Must reapply.

Academic Fields/Career Goals: Flexography.

Award: Scholarship for use in freshman, sophomore, junior, or senior years; not renewable. *Number:* 10–15. *Amount:* up to $2000.

Eligibility Requirements: Applicant must be enrolled or expecting to enroll full-time at a four-year or technical institution or university. Applicant must have 3.0 GPA or higher. Available to U.S. citizens.

Application Requirements: Application, essay, references, transcript. *Deadline:* March 14.

Contact: Shelley Rubin, Educational Program Coordinator
Foundation of Flexographic Technical Association
900 Marconi Avenue
Ronkonkoma, NY 11779-7212
Phone: 631-737-6020 Ext. 36
Fax: 631-737-6813
E-mail: srubin@flexography.org

TAG AND LABEL MANUFACTURERS INSTITUTE INC. http://www.tlmi.com

TLMI FOUR-YEAR COLLEGES/FULL-TIME STUDENTS SCHOLARSHIP

• *See page 297*

TLMI SCHOLARSHIP GRANT FOR STUDENTS OF TWO-YEAR COLLEGES

Scholarship program for students enrolled in a flexography printing program at a two-year college or in a technical program where degrees are granted. Must submit statements including personal information, financial circumstances, career and/or educational goals, employment experience, and reasons applicant should be selected for this award.

Academic Fields/Career Goals: Flexography.

Award: Scholarship for use in freshman or sophomore years; renewable. *Number:* 4. *Amount:* $1000.

Eligibility Requirements: Applicant must be enrolled or expecting to enroll full- or part-time at a two-year institution. Applicant must have 3.0 GPA or higher. Available to U.S. citizens.

Application Requirements: Application, autobiography, financial need analysis, transcript. *Deadline:* March 31.

Contact: Karen Planz, Office Manager
Tag and Label Manufacturers Institute Inc.
40 Shuman Boulevard, Suite 295
Naperville, IL 60563-8465
Phone: 630-357-9222 Ext. 11
Fax: 630-357-0192
E-mail: office@tlmi.com

FOOD SCIENCE/NUTRITION

AMERICAN ASSOCIATION OF CEREAL CHEMISTS http://www.aaccnet.org

UNDERGRADUATE SCHOLARSHIP AWARD

One-time award to encourage scholastically outstanding undergraduate students in academic preparation for a career in grain-based food science and technology, and to attract and encourage outstanding students to enter this field. Must be a current AACC Intl. student member. Minimum 3.0 GPA required. Application must be submitted to the association by March 1.

Academic Fields/Career Goals: Food Science/Nutrition.

Award: Scholarship for use in junior or senior years; not renewable. *Number:* 3–5. *Amount:* $1000–$2000.

Eligibility Requirements: Applicant must be enrolled or expecting to enroll full-time at a four-year institution or university. Applicant must have 3.0 GPA or higher. Available to U.S. and non-U.S. citizens.

Application Requirements: Application, essay, references, transcript. *Deadline:* March 1.

Contact: Linda Schmitt, Scholarship Coordinator
American Association of Cereal Chemists
3340 Pilot Knob Road
St. Paul, MN 55121-2097
Phone: 651-994-3828
Fax: 651-454-0766
E-mail: lschmitt@scisoc.org

AMERICAN DIETETIC ASSOCIATION http://www.eatright.org

AMERICAN DIETETIC ASSOCIATION FOUNDATION SCHOLARSHIP PROGRAM

ADAF scholarships are available for undergraduate and graduate students enrolled in programs, including dietetic internships, preparing for entry to dietetics practice as well as dietetics professionals engaged in continuing education at the graduate level. Scholarship funds are provided by many state dietetic associations, dietetic practice groups, past ADA leaders and corporate donors. All scholarships require ADA membership. Details available on Web site http://www.eatright.org.

Academic Fields/Career Goals: Food Science/Nutrition.

Award: Scholarship for use in sophomore, junior, senior, graduate, or postgraduate years; not renewable. *Number:* 186. *Amount:* $500–$3000.

Eligibility Requirements: Applicant must be enrolled or expecting to enroll full- or part-time at a two-year or four-year institution. Applicant or parent of applicant must be member of American Dietetic Association. Available to U.S. citizens.

Application Requirements: Application, essay, financial need analysis, references, transcript. *Deadline:* February 15.

Contact: Eva Donovan, Education Coordinator
American Dietetic Association
120 South Riverside Plaza, Suite 2000
Chicago, IL 60606-6695
Phone: 312-899-0040 Ext. 4876
Fax: 312-899-4817
E-mail: education@eatright.org

AMERICAN INSTITUTE OF WINE AND FOOD-PACIFIC NORTHWEST CHAPTER http://www.aiwf.org

CULINARY, VINIFERA, AND HOSPITALITY SCHOLARSHIP

One-time award available to residents of Washington State. Must be enrolled full-time in an accredited culinary, vinifera, or hospitality program in Washington State. Must have completed two years. Minimum 3.0 GPA required. Deadline: continuous.

Academic Fields/Career Goals: Food Science/Nutrition; Food Service/Hospitality; Hospitality Management.

Award: Scholarship for use in junior or senior years; not renewable. *Number:* 4. *Amount:* $1500.

Eligibility Requirements: Applicant must be enrolled or expecting to enroll full-time at a two-year or four-year or technical institution or university; resident of Washington and studying in Washington. Applicant must have 3.0 GPA or higher. Available to U.S. and non-U.S. citizens.

Application Requirements: Application, resume, references. *Deadline:* continuous.

Contact: Brad Sturman, Scholarship Coordinator
American Institute of Wine and Food-Pacific Northwest Chapter
224 18th Avenue
Kirkland, WA 98033
Phone: 206-679-6228

AMERICAN SOCIETY FOR ENOLOGY AND VITICULTURE http://www.asev.org

AMERICAN SOCIETY FOR ENOLOGY AND VITICULTURE SCHOLARSHIPS

• *See page 72*

ASSOCIATION FOR FOOD AND DRUG OFFICIALS http://www.afdo.org

ASSOCIATION FOR FOOD AND DRUG OFFICIALS SCHOLARSHIP FUND

• *See page 138*

CALIFORNIA ADOLESCENT NUTRITION AND FITNESS (CANFIT) PROGRAM http://www.canfit.org

CALIFORNIA ADOLESCENT NUTRITION AND FITNESS (CANFIT) PROGRAM SCHOLARSHIP

• *See page 203*

CHILD NUTRITION FOUNDATION http://www.schoolnutrition.org

NANCY CURRY SCHOLARSHIP

Scholarship assists members of the American School Food Service Association and their dependents to pursue educational and career advancement in school food-service or child nutrition.

Academic Fields/Career Goals: Food Science/Nutrition; Food Service/Hospitality.

Award: Scholarship for use in freshman, sophomore, junior, senior, graduate, or postgraduate years; not renewable. *Number:* varies. *Amount:* varies.

Eligibility Requirements: Applicant must be enrolled or expecting to enroll full- or part-time at a two-year or four-year or technical institution or university. Applicant or parent of applicant must have employment or volunteer experience in food service. Applicant must have 3.0 GPA or higher. Available to U.S. citizens.

Application Requirements: Application, essay, resume, references, test scores, transcript, proof of enrollment. *Deadline:* April 15.

Contact: Ruth O'Brien, Scholarship Manager
Child Nutrition Foundation
700 South Washington Street, Suite 300
Alexandria, VA 22314
Phone: 703-739-3900 Ext. 150
E-mail: robrien@asfsa.org

PROFESSIONAL GROWTH SCHOLARSHIP

Scholarships for child nutrition professionals who are pursuing graduate education in a food science management or nutrition-related field of study.

Academic Fields/Career Goals: Food Science/Nutrition; Food Service/Hospitality.

Award: Scholarship for use in freshman, sophomore, junior, senior, graduate, or postgraduate years; not renewable. *Number:* varies. *Amount:* varies.

Eligibility Requirements: Applicant must be enrolled or expecting to enroll full- or part-time at a two-year or four-year or technical institution or university. Applicant or parent of applicant must have employment or volunteer experience in food service. Applicant must have 3.5 GPA or higher. Available to U.S. citizens.

Application Requirements: Application, essay, resume, references, transcript, proof of enrollment, official program requirement. *Deadline:* April 15.

Contact: Scholarship Manager
Child Nutrition Foundation
700 South Washington Street, Suite 300
Alexandria, VA 22314
Phone: 703-739-3900 Ext. 150
Fax: 703-739-3915
E-mail: robrien@asfsa.org

SCHWAN'S FOOD SERVICE SCHOLARSHIP

Program is designed to assist members of the American School Food Service Association and their dependents as they pursue educational advancement in the field of child nutrition.

Academic Fields/Career Goals: Food Science/Nutrition; Food Service/Hospitality.

Award: Scholarship for use in freshman, sophomore, junior, senior, graduate, or postgraduate years; not renewable. *Number:* varies. *Amount:* varies.

Child Nutrition Foundation (continued)

Eligibility Requirements: Applicant must be enrolled or expecting to enroll full- or part-time at a two-year or four-year or technical institution or university. Applicant or parent of applicant must have employment or volunteer experience in food service. Applicant must have 2.5 GPA or higher. Available to U.S. citizens.

Application Requirements: Application, essay, resume, references, transcript, proof of enrollment, official program requirements. *Deadline:* April 15.

Contact: Ruth O'Brien, Scholarship Manager
Child Nutrition Foundation
700 South Washington Street, Suite 300
Alexandria, VA 22314
Phone: 703-739-3900 Ext. 150
E-mail: robrien@asfsa.org

CULINARY TRUST http://www.theculinarytrust.com

CULINARY TRUST SCHOLARSHIP PROGRAM FOR CULINARY STUDY AND RESEARCH

• *See page 203*

DAIRY MANAGEMENT http://www.dairyinfo.com

JAMES H. LOPER JR. MEMORIAL SCHOLARSHIP

• *See page 74*

NATIONAL DAIRY PROMOTION AND RESEARCH BOARD SCHOLARSHIP

• *See page 74*

ILLINOIS RESTAURANT ASSOCIATION EDUCATIONAL FOUNDATION http://www.illinoisrestaurants.org

ILLINOIS RESTAURANT ASSOCIATION EDUCATIONAL FOUNDATION SCHOLARSHIPS

• *See page 203*

INSTITUTE OF FOOD TECHNOLOGISTS http://www.ift.org

INSTITUTE OF FOOD TECHNOLOGISTS FOOD ENGINEERING DIVISION JUNIOR/SENIOR SCHOLARSHIP

One-time award for junior or senior level students in an Institute of Food Technologists-approved program, with demonstrated intent to pursue professional activities in food science or food technology.

Academic Fields/Career Goals: Food Science/Nutrition.

Award: Scholarship for use in junior or senior years; not renewable. *Number:* 21. *Amount:* $1000–$2500.

Eligibility Requirements: Applicant must be enrolled or expecting to enroll full-time at a four-year institution or university. Available to U.S. and non-U.S. citizens.

Application Requirements: Application, references, transcript. *Deadline:* February 1.

Contact: Elizabeth Plummer, Manager of Foundation Development
Institute of Food Technologists
525 West Van Buren Street, Suite 1000
Chicago, IL 60607
Phone: 312-782-8424 Ext. 226
Fax: 312-416-7919
E-mail: ejplummer@ift.org

INSTITUTE OF FOOD TECHNOLOGISTS FRESHMAN SCHOLARSHIPS

Awards for scholastically outstanding high school graduates or seniors entering college in an approved four-year program in food sciences or technology. Program must be approved by the Institute of Food Technologists Education Committee.

Academic Fields/Career Goals: Food Science/Nutrition.

Award: Scholarship for use in freshman year; not renewable. *Number:* 8. *Amount:* $1000.

Eligibility Requirements: Applicant must be enrolled or expecting to enroll full-time at a four-year institution or university. Applicant must have 3.0 GPA or higher. Available to U.S. and non-U.S. citizens.

Application Requirements: Application, references, transcript. *Deadline:* February 15.

Contact: Elizabeth Plummer, Manager of Foundation Development
Institute of Food Technologists
525 West Van Buren Street, Suite 1000
Chicago, IL 60607
Phone: 312-782-8424 Ext. 226
Fax: 312-416-7919
E-mail: ejplummer@ift.org

INSTITUTE OF FOOD TECHNOLOGISTS QUALITY ASSURANCE DIVISION JUNIOR/SENIOR SCHOLARSHIPS

One-time award for college juniors and seniors who are taking or have taken a course in quality assurance and have demonstrated an interest in the quality assurance area.

Academic Fields/Career Goals: Food Science/Nutrition.

Award: Scholarship for use in junior or senior years; not renewable. *Number:* 2. *Amount:* $2000.

Eligibility Requirements: Applicant must be enrolled or expecting to enroll full-time at a four-year institution. Available to U.S. and non-U.S. citizens.

Application Requirements: Application, references, transcript. *Deadline:* February 1.

Contact: Elizabeth Plummer, Manager of Foundation Development
Institute of Food Technologists
525 West Van Buren Street, Suite 1000
Chicago, IL 60607
Phone: 312-782-8424 Ext. 226
Fax: 312-416-7919
E-mail: ejplummer@ift.org

INSTITUTE OF FOOD TECHNOLOGISTS SOPHOMORE SCHOLARSHIPS

Awards available to college freshmen for use in sophomore year. Applicants must major in food science or food technology in a four-year Institute of Food Technologists Education Committee-approved program and must have a 2.5 GPA.

Academic Fields/Career Goals: Food Science/Nutrition.

Award: Scholarship for use in sophomore year; not renewable. *Number:* 8. *Amount:* $1000.

Eligibility Requirements: Applicant must be enrolled or expecting to enroll full-time at a four-year institution or university. Applicant must have 2.5 GPA or higher. Available to U.S. and non-U.S. citizens.

Application Requirements: Application, references, transcript. *Deadline:* March 1.

Contact: Elizabeth Plummer, Manager of Foundation Development
Institute of Food Technologists
525 West Van Buren Street, Suite 1000
Chicago, IL 60607
Phone: 312-782-8424 Ext. 226
Fax: 312-416-7919
E-mail: ejplummer@ift.org

INTERNATIONAL FOODSERVICE EDITORIAL COUNCIL http://www.ifeconline.com

INTERNATIONAL FOODSERVICE EDITORIAL COUNCIL COMMUNICATIONS SCHOLARSHIP

• *See page 180*

JAMES BEARD FOUNDATION INC. http://www.jamesbeard.org

BERN LAXER MEMORIAL SCHOLARSHIP

Scholarships of $2500 toward tuition for students seeking careers in food service and hospitality management. One scholarship given in each of three programs: culinary, hospitality management, and viticulture/oenology. Program and school must be accredited in accordance with the James Beard Foundation scholarship criteria. Applicants must be residents of Florida and substantiate; have a high school diploma or the equivalent; have a minimum of one-year culinary experience either as a student or employee, and submit a minimum 500-word essay. See Web site at http://www.jamesbeard.org for further details.

Academic Fields/Career Goals: Food Science/Nutrition.

Award: Scholarship for use in freshman, sophomore, junior, senior, or graduate years; not renewable. *Number:* 3. *Amount:* $2500.

Eligibility Requirements: Applicant must be enrolled or expecting to enroll full- or part-time at a four-year institution or university. Available to U.S. and non-U.S. citizens.

Application Requirements: Application, essay, financial need analysis, references, transcript. *Deadline:* May 15.

Contact: Diane Brown, Director, Educational and Community Programming
James Beard Foundation Inc.
6 West 18th Street, 10th Floor
New York, NY 10011
Phone: 212-627-1128
Fax: 212-627-1064
E-mail: dhbrown@jamesbeard.org

DANA CAMPBELL MEMORIAL SCHOLARSHIP

Scholarship for $3000 awarded to an applicant with career interests in food journalism who is in his/her second or third year in an accredited bachelor degree program in journalism or a food-related curriculum. Must be resident of a "Southern" state within the Southern Living readership area (Alabama, Florida, Georgia, North Carolina, South Carolina, Louisiana, Virginia, Arkansas, Texas, Mississippi, Kentucky, Maryland, Missouri, Oklahoma, West Virginia, or Delaware) and substantiate residency. The scholarship recipient will also be considered for an internship at Southern Living. See Web site at http://www.jamesbeard.org for further details.

Academic Fields/Career Goals: Food Science/Nutrition.

Award: Scholarship for use in sophomore or junior years; not renewable. *Number:* 1. *Amount:* $3000.

Eligibility Requirements: Applicant must be enrolled or expecting to enroll full- or part-time at a four-year institution or university and resident of Alabama, Arkansas, Delaware, Florida, Georgia, Kentucky, Louisiana, Maryland, Mississippi, Missouri, North Carolina, Oklahoma, South Carolina, Texas, or Virginia. Available to U.S. and non-U.S. citizens.

Application Requirements: Application, essay, financial need analysis, references, transcript. *Deadline:* May 15.

Contact: Caroline Stuart, Scholarship Director
James Beard Foundation Inc.
167 West 12th Street
New York, NY 10011
Phone: 212-675-4984 Ext. 311
Fax: 212-645-1438
E-mail: jamesbeardfound@hotmail.com

LES DAMES D'ESCOFFIER — http://www.ldei.org

LES DAMES D'ESCOFFIER SCHOLARSHIP
• *See page 205*

MAINE SCHOOL FOOD SERVICE ASSOCIATION (MSFSA) — http://www.mainesfsa.org

MAINE SCHOOL FOOD SERVICE ASSOCIATION CONTINUING EDUCATION SCHOLARSHIP
• *See page 206*

MARION D. AND EVA S. PEEPLES FOUNDATION TRUST SCHOLARSHIP PROGRAM — http://www.jccf.org

MARION A. AND EVA S. PEEPLES SCHOLARSHIPS
• *See page 234*

MARYLAND ASSOCIATION OF PRIVATE COLLEGES AND CAREER SCHOOLS — http://www.mapccs.org

MARYLAND ASSOCIATION OF PRIVATE COLLEGES AND CAREER SCHOOLS SCHOLARSHIP
• *See page 146*

MINNESOTA SOYBEAN RESEARCH AND PROMOTION COUNCIL — http://www.mnsoybean.org

MINNESOTA SOYBEAN RESEARCH AND PROMOTION COUNCIL YOUTH SOYBEAN SCHOLARSHIP
• *See page 70*

NATIONAL DAIRY SHRINE — http://www.dairyshrine.org

NATIONAL DAIRY SHRINE/DAIRY MARKETING INC. MILK MARKETING SCHOLARSHIPS
• *See page 76*

NDS STUDENT RECOGNITION CONTEST
• *See page 70*

NATIONAL POTATO COUNCIL WOMEN'S AUXILIARY — http://www.nationalpotatocouncil.org

POTATO INDUSTRY SCHOLARSHIP
• *See page 70*

NATIONAL POULTRY AND FOOD DISTRIBUTORS ASSOCIATION — http://www.npfda.org

NATIONAL POULTRY AND FOOD DISTRIBUTORS ASSOCIATION SCHOLARSHIP FOUNDATION
• *See page 71*

OHIO 4-H — http://www.ohio4h.org

BEA CLEVELAND 4-H SCHOLARSHIP
• *See page 166*

MABEL SARBAUGH 4-H SCHOLARSHIP
• *See page 166*

OREGON STUDENT ASSISTANCE COMMISSION — http://www.osac.state.or.us

OREGON WINE BROTHERHOOD SCHOLARSHIP
• *See page 206*

SAN DIEGO FOUNDATION — http://www.sdfoundation.org

CALIFORNIA ASSOCIATION OF FAMILY AND CONSUMER SCIENCES-SAN DIEGO CHAPTER
• *See page 166*

UNITED DAUGHTERS OF THE CONFEDERACY — http://www.hqudc.org

WALTER REED SMITH SCHOLARSHIP
• *See page 149*

UNITED NEGRO COLLEGE FUND — http://www.uncf.org

CARGILL SCHOLARSHIP PROGRAM
• *See page 65*

WASHINGTON ASSOCIATION OF WINE GRAPE GROWERS — http://www.wawgg.org

WALTER J. CLORE SCHOLARSHIP
• *See page 79*

FOOD SERVICE/HOSPITALITY

AMERICAN CULINARY FEDERATION — http://www.acfchefs.org

AMERICAN ACADEMY OF CHEFS CHAINE DES ROTISSEURS SCHOLARSHIP
• *See page 202*

AMERICAN ACADEMY OF CHEFS CHAIR'S SCHOLARSHIP
• *See page 202*

AMERICAN HOTEL AND LODGING EDUCATIONAL FOUNDATION http://www.ahlef.org

ANNUAL SCHOLARSHIP GRANT PROGRAM

Students are selected for this award by their school. Available to full-time students who have completed at least one or two years of a hospitality-related degree, are U.S. citizens or have permanent U.S. resident status. Minimum GPA of 3.0.

Academic Fields/Career Goals: Food Service/Hospitality; Hospitality Management.

Award: Scholarship for use in sophomore, junior, or senior years; renewable. *Number:* 3. *Amount:* $500–$3000.

Eligibility Requirements: Applicant must be enrolled or expecting to enroll full-time at a two-year or four-year institution. Applicant must have 3.0 GPA or higher. Available to U.S. citizens.

Application Requirements: Application, essay, financial need analysis, transcript, nomination from school. *Deadline:* June 1.

Contact: Crystal Hammond, Director of Foundation Programs
American Hotel and Lodging Educational Foundation
1201 New York Avenue, NW, Suite 600
Washington, DC 20005-3931
Phone: 202-289-3188
Fax: 202-289-3199
E-mail: chammond@ahlef.org

AMERICAN INSTITUTE OF WINE AND FOOD-PACIFIC NORTHWEST CHAPTER http://www.aiwf.org

CULINARY, VINIFERA, AND HOSPITALITY SCHOLARSHIP

• *See page 311*

CALIFORNIA ADOLESCENT NUTRITION AND FITNESS (CANFIT) PROGRAM http://www.canfit.org

CALIFORNIA ADOLESCENT NUTRITION AND FITNESS (CANFIT) PROGRAM SCHOLARSHIP

• *See page 203*

CALIFORNIA RESTAURANT ASSOCIATION EDUCATIONAL FOUNDATION http://www.calrest.org

ACADEMIC SCHOLARSHIP FOR HIGH SCHOOL SENIORS

One-time scholarship awarded to high school seniors to support their education in the restaurant and/or food service industry. Applicants must be citizens of the United States or its territories (American Samoa, Guam, Puerto Rico, and U.S. Virgin Islands).

Academic Fields/Career Goals: Food Service/Hospitality.

Award: Scholarship for use in freshman year; not renewable. *Number:* varies. *Amount:* up to $2000.

Eligibility Requirements: Applicant must be high school student; planning to enroll or expecting to enroll full-time at a two-year or four-year or technical institution or university and resident of California. Available to U.S. and non-U.S. citizens.

Application Requirements: Application, essay, interview, resume, references, transcript. *Deadline:* April 14.

Contact: Amy Wulfestieg, Scholarships and Mentoring Program Coordinator
California Restaurant Association Educational Foundation
175 West Jackson Boulevard, Suite 1500
Chicago, IL 60604-2814
Phone: 916-431-2749
E-mail: awulfestieg@calrest.org

ACADEMIC SCHOLARSHIP FOR UNDERGRADUATE STUDENTS

Scholarships awarded to college students to support their education in the restaurant and food service industry. Minimum 2.75 GPA required. Individuals must be citizens of the United States or its territories (American Samoa, Guam, Puerto Rico, and U.S. Virgin Islands).

Academic Fields/Career Goals: Food Service/Hospitality.

Award: Scholarship for use in freshman, sophomore, junior, or senior years; not renewable. *Number:* varies. *Amount:* varies.

Eligibility Requirements: Applicant must be enrolled or expecting to enroll full-time at a four-year institution or university and resident of California. Available to U.S. and non-U.S. citizens.

Application Requirements: Application, essay, interview, references, transcript. *Deadline:* March 31.

Contact: Ms. Amy Wulfestieg, Scholarship and Grant Coordinator
California Restaurant Association Educational Foundation
621 Capitol Mall, Suite 2000
Sacramento, CA 95814
Phone: 800-765-4842 Ext. 2749
Fax: 916-431-2762
E-mail: awulfestieg@calrest.org

CHILD NUTRITION FOUNDATION http://www.schoolnutrition.org

NANCY CURRY SCHOLARSHIP

• *See page 311*

PROFESSIONAL GROWTH SCHOLARSHIP

• *See page 311*

SCHWAN'S FOOD SERVICE SCHOLARSHIP

• *See page 311*

COLORADO RESTAURANT ASSOCIATION http://www.coloradorestaurant.com

CRA UNDERGRADUATE SCHOLARSHIPS

Scholarship of $1000 to $2000 for applicants intending to pursue education in the undergraduate level in the field of food service or hospitality and have a GPA of at least 2.75.

Academic Fields/Career Goals: Food Service/Hospitality.

Award: Scholarship for use in freshman, sophomore, junior, or senior years; not renewable. *Number:* 15. *Amount:* $1000–$2000.

Eligibility Requirements: Applicant must be enrolled or expecting to enroll full- or part-time at a four-year institution or university. Available to U.S. and non-U.S. citizens.

Application Requirements: Application, resume, references, transcript. *Deadline:* April 6.

Contact: Mary Mino, President
Colorado Restaurant Association
730 East Seventh Avenue
Denver, CO 80203
Phone: 800-522-2972
Fax: 303-830-2973
E-mail: info@coloradorestaurant.com

PROSTART SCHOLARSHIPS

Scholarship of $500 to $1000 for applicants currently in high school and intending to pursue education in the field of food service or hospitality and have a GPA of at least 3.0.

Academic Fields/Career Goals: Food Service/Hospitality.

Award: Scholarship for use in freshman year; not renewable. *Number:* 15. *Amount:* $500–$1000.

Eligibility Requirements: Applicant must be high school student and planning to enroll or expecting to enroll full- or part-time at a four-year institution or university. Applicant must have 3.0 GPA or higher. Available to U.S. and non-U.S. citizens.

Application Requirements: Application, resume, references, transcript. *Deadline:* April 6.

Contact: Mary Mino, President
Colorado Restaurant Association
730 East Seventh Avenue
Denver, CO 80203
Phone: 800-522-2972
Fax: 303-830-2973
E-mail: info@coloradorestaurant.com

CULINARY TRUST http://www.theculinarytrust.com

CULINARY TRUST SCHOLARSHIP PROGRAM FOR CULINARY STUDY AND RESEARCH

• *See page 203*

GOLDEN GATE RESTAURANT ASSOCIATION http://www.ggra.org

GOLDEN GATE RESTAURANT ASSOCIATION SCHOLARSHIP FOUNDATION

One-time award for any student pursuing a food service degree at a 501(c)(3) institution, or institutions approved by the Board of Trustees. California residency and personal interview in San Francisco is required. Minimum GPA of 2.75 required. Write for further information.

Academic Fields/Career Goals: Food Service/Hospitality; Hospitality Management.

Award: Scholarship for use in freshman, sophomore, junior, or senior years; not renewable. *Number:* 9–15. *Amount:* $1000–$6000.

Eligibility Requirements: Applicant must be enrolled or expecting to enroll full- or part-time at a two-year or four-year or technical institution or university and resident of California. Available to U.S. citizens.

Application Requirements: Application, essay, financial need analysis, interview, references, transcript. *Deadline:* April 30.

Contact: Donnalyn Murphy, Trustee and Secretary
Golden Gate Restaurant Association
120 Montgomery Street, Suite 1280
San Francisco, CA 94104
Phone: 415-781-5348 Ext. 812
Fax: 415-781-3925
E-mail: education@ggra.org

ILLINOIS RESTAURANT ASSOCIATION EDUCATIONAL FOUNDATION http://www.illinoisrestaurants.org

ILLINOIS RESTAURANT ASSOCIATION EDUCATIONAL FOUNDATION SCHOLARSHIPS

• *See page 203*

INTERNATIONAL EXECUTIVE HOUSEKEEPERS ASSOCIATION http://www.ieha.org

INTERNATIONAL EXECUTIVE HOUSEKEEPERS EDUCATIONAL FOUNDATION

One-time award of up to $800 for students planning careers in the area of facilities management. Must be enrolled in IEHA-approved courses at a participating college or university. Must be a member of IEHA.

Academic Fields/Career Goals: Food Service/Hospitality; Home Economics; Trade/Technical Specialties.

Award: Scholarship for use in freshman, sophomore, junior, or senior years; not renewable. *Number:* 10. *Amount:* up to $800.

Eligibility Requirements: Applicant must be enrolled or expecting to enroll full- or part-time at a two-year or four-year or technical institution or university. Applicant or parent of applicant must be member of International Executive Housekeepers Association. Available to U.S. and non-U.S. citizens.

Application Requirements: Application, essay, transcript. *Deadline:* January 10.

Contact: Beth Risinger, Chief Executive Officer and Executive Director
International Executive Housekeepers Association
Education Department, 1001 Eastwind Drive, Suite 301
Westerville, OH 43081-3361
Phone: 800-200-6342
Fax: 614-895-7166
E-mail: excel@ieha.org

INTERNATIONAL FOODSERVICE EDITORIAL COUNCIL http://www.ifeconline.com

INTERNATIONAL FOODSERVICE EDITORIAL COUNCIL COMMUNICATIONS SCHOLARSHIP

• *See page 180*

INTERNATIONAL FOOD SERVICE EXECUTIVES ASSOCIATION http://www.ifsea.com

WORTHY GOAL SCHOLARSHIP FUND

Scholarships to assist individuals in receiving food service management or vocational training beyond high school. Applicant must be enrolled or accepted as full-time student in a food service related major for the fall term following the award.

Academic Fields/Career Goals: Food Service/Hospitality.

Award: Scholarship for use in freshman, sophomore, junior, senior, or graduate years; not renewable. *Number:* 15. *Amount:* $1000–$1500.

Eligibility Requirements: Applicant must be enrolled or expecting to enroll full-time at a two-year or four-year or technical institution or university. Available to U.S. citizens.

Application Requirements: Essay, financial need analysis, references, transcript, financial statement summary, work experience documentation. *Deadline:* March 1.

Contact: Ed H. Manley, Scholarship Chairperson
International Food Service Executives Association
2609 Surfwood Drive
Las Vegas, NV 89128
Phone: 702-430-9217
Fax: 702-430-9223
E-mail: ed@ehmanley.com

KENTUCKY RESTAURANT ASSOCIATION EDUCATIONAL FOUNDATION http://www.kyra.org

KENTUCKY RESTAURANT ASSOCIATION EDUCATIONAL FOUNDATION SCHOLARSHIP

Scholarship available for high school graduate or equivalent accepted to an associate or bachelor's degree program in food service, or student already enrolled in an associate, bachelor's, or master's degree food service program. Applicant must be a resident of Kentucky or within 25 miles of Kentucky's borders for previous 18 months.

Academic Fields/Career Goals: Food Service/Hospitality.

Award: Scholarship for use in freshman, sophomore, junior, or senior years; renewable. *Number:* varies. *Amount:* varies.

Eligibility Requirements: Applicant must be enrolled or expecting to enroll full-time at a four-year institution or university and resident of Kentucky. Available to U.S. citizens.

Application Requirements: Application, references, transcript, proof of acceptance. *Deadline:* varies.

Contact: Scholarship Committee
Kentucky Restaurant Association Educational Foundation
133 Evergreen Road, Suite 201
Louisville, KY 40243
Phone: 800-896-0414
Fax: 502-896-0465
E-mail: info@kyra.org

LES DAMES D'ESCOFFIER http://www.ldei.org

LES DAMES D'ESCOFFIER SCHOLARSHIP

• *See page 205*

MAINE SCHOOL FOOD SERVICE ASSOCIATION (MSFSA) http://www.mainesfsa.org

MAINE SCHOOL FOOD SERVICE ASSOCIATION CONTINUING EDUCATION SCHOLARSHIP

• *See page 206*

MISSOURI TRAVEL COUNCIL http://www.missouritravel.com

MISSOURI TRAVEL COUNCIL TOURISM SCHOLARSHIP

One-time award for Missouri resident pursuing hospitality-related major such as hotel/restaurant management or parks and recreation. Applicant must be currently enrolled in an accredited college or university in the state of Missouri. Selection is based on essay, GPA, community involvement, academic activities, and hospitality-related experience.

Academic Fields/Career Goals: Food Service/Hospitality; Hospitality Management; Travel/Tourism.

Award: Scholarship for use in sophomore, junior, or senior years; not renewable. *Number:* 2. *Amount:* $1000.

Eligibility Requirements: Applicant must be enrolled or expecting to enroll full-time at a four-year institution or university; resident of Missouri and studying in Missouri. Applicant must have 3.0 GPA or higher. Available to U.S. citizens.

Application Requirements: Application, essay, references, transcript. *Deadline:* March 1.

Contact: Pat Amick, Executive Director
Missouri Travel Council
204 East High Street
Jefferson City, MO 65101-3287
Phone: 573-636-2814
Fax: 573-636-5783
E-mail: pamick@sockets.net

NATIONAL POULTRY AND FOOD DISTRIBUTORS ASSOCIATION http://www.npfda.org

NATIONAL POULTRY AND FOOD DISTRIBUTORS ASSOCIATION SCHOLARSHIP FOUNDATION

• *See page 71*

NATIONAL RESTAURANT ASSOCIATION EDUCATIONAL FOUNDATION http://www.nraef.org

COCA-COLA SALUTE TO EXCELLENCE SCHOLARSHIP AWARD

Scholarship for a student currently enrolled in college who has completed at least one semester in a restaurant and/or foodservice-related program.

Academic Fields/Career Goals: Food Service/Hospitality.

Award: Scholarship for use in sophomore, junior, senior, graduate, or postgraduate years; not renewable. *Number:* 2. *Amount:* $5000.

Eligibility Requirements: Applicant must be enrolled or expecting to enroll full-time at a two-year or four-year or technical institution or university. Applicant or parent of applicant must have employment or volunteer experience in food service. Available to U.S. citizens.

Application Requirements: Application, essay, transcript, proof of total hours worked. *Deadline:* March 21.

Contact: Shanna Young, Manager
National Restaurant Association Educational Foundation
175 West Jackson Boulevard, Suite 1500
Chicago, IL 60604-2702
Phone: 800-765-2122 Ext. 744
Fax: 312-566-9733
E-mail: syoung@nraef.org

NATIONAL RESTAURANT ASSOCIATION EDUCATIONAL FOUNDATION UNDERGRADUATE SCHOLARSHIPS FOR COLLEGE STUDENTS

Awarded to college students who have demonstrated a commitment to both postsecondary hospitality education and to a career in the industry with 750 hours of industry work experience. Minimum 2.75 GPA required. Application deadlines: March 31, July 31 and October 31.

Academic Fields/Career Goals: Food Service/Hospitality; Hospitality Management.

Award: Scholarship for use in sophomore, junior, or senior years; not renewable. *Number:* varies. *Amount:* $2000.

Eligibility Requirements: Applicant must be enrolled or expecting to enroll full- or part-time at a four-year institution or university. Applicant or parent of applicant must have employment or volunteer experience in food service. Available to U.S. citizens.

Application Requirements: Application, essay, resume, references, transcript, copies of paycheck stubs or a letter from employers verifying total work hours. *Deadline:* varies.

Contact: Shanna Young, Manager
National Restaurant Association Educational Foundation
175 West Jackson Boulevard, Suite 1500
Chicago, IL 60604-2702
Phone: 800-765-2122 Ext. 744
Fax: 312-566-9733
E-mail: syoung@nraef.org

NATIONAL RESTAURANT ASSOCIATION EDUCATIONAL FOUNDATION UNDERGRADUATE SCHOLARSHIPS FOR HIGH SCHOOL SENIORS AND GENERAL EDUCATION DIPLOMA (GED) GRADUATES

Scholarship awarded to high school students who have demonstrated a commitment to both postsecondary hospitality education and to a career in the industry. Must have 250 hours of industry experience, be between ages of 17 and 19, and have minimum 2.75 GPA.

Academic Fields/Career Goals: Food Service/Hospitality; Hospitality Management.

Award: Scholarship for use in freshman year; not renewable. *Number:* varies. *Amount:* $2000.

Eligibility Requirements: Applicant must be age 17-19 and enrolled or expecting to enroll full-time at a four-year institution or university. Applicant or parent of applicant must have employment or volunteer experience in food service. Available to U.S. citizens.

Application Requirements: Application, essay, references, transcript, letter of acceptance, industrial experience letter. *Deadline:* May 16.

Contact: Shanna Young, Manager
National Restaurant Association Educational Foundation
175 West Jackson Boulevard, Suite 1500
Chicago, IL 60604-2702
Phone: 800-765-2122 Ext. 744
Fax: 312-566-9733
E-mail: syoung@nraef.org

PROSTART® NATIONAL CERTIFICATE OF ACHIEVEMENT SCHOLARSHIP

For high school junior and senior students who have earned Pro Start National Certificate of Achievement and are continuing their education in a restaurant or foodservice program. For application and details visit Web site: http://nraef.org

Academic Fields/Career Goals: Food Service/Hospitality.

Award: Scholarship for use in freshman year; not renewable. *Number:* varies. *Amount:* $2000.

Eligibility Requirements: Applicant must be high school student and planning to enroll or expecting to enroll full- or part-time at a four-year institution or university. Available to U.S. citizens.

Application Requirements: Application. *Deadline:* August 15.

Contact: Shanna Young, Manager
National Restaurant Association Educational Foundation
175 West Jackson Boulevard, Suite 1500
Chicago, IL 60604-2702
Phone: 800-765-2122 Ext. 744
Fax: 312-566-9733
E-mail: syoung@nraef.org

NATIONAL TOURISM FOUNDATION http://www.ntfonline.com

CLEVELAND LEGACY I AND II SCHOLARSHIP AWARDS

Award for Ohio residents pursuing travel and tourism studies. Must be enrolled full-time in two- or four-year institution and a resident of Ohio. Minimum 3.0 GPA required. Submit resume.

Academic Fields/Career Goals: Food Service/Hospitality; Hospitality Management; Travel/Tourism.

Award: Scholarship for use in freshman, sophomore, junior, or senior years; not renewable. *Number:* 1. *Amount:* $1000.

Eligibility Requirements: Applicant must be enrolled or expecting to enroll full-time at a two-year or four-year institution or university and resident of Ohio. Applicant must have 3.0 GPA or higher. Available to U.S. citizens.

Application Requirements: Application, essay, resume, references, transcript. *Deadline:* May 10.

Contact: Michelle Gorin, Projects Coordinator
National Tourism Foundation
546 East Main Street
Lexington, KY 40508-3071
Phone: 800-682-8886
Fax: 859-226-4437

NEW HORIZONS KATHY LETARTE SCHOLARSHIP

One $1000 scholarship awarded to an undergraduate student entering his or her junior year of study. Applicant must be enrolled in a tourism-related program at an accredited four-year college or university. Must have minimum 3.0 GPA. Applicant must be Michigan resident. Refer to Web site for further details: http://www.ntfonline.com/scholarships/index.php

Academic Fields/Career Goals: Food Service/Hospitality; Hospitality Management; Travel/Tourism.

Award: Scholarship for use in freshman, sophomore, junior, or senior years; not renewable. *Number:* 1. *Amount:* $1000.

Eligibility Requirements: Applicant must be enrolled or expecting to enroll full-time at a two-year or four-year institution or university and resident of Michigan. Applicant must have 3.0 GPA or higher. Available to U.S. citizens.

Application Requirements: Application, essay, resume, references, transcript. *Deadline:* May 10.

Contact: Michelle Gorin, Projects Coordinator
National Tourism Foundation
546 East Main Street
Lexington, KY 40508-3071
Phone: 800-682-8886
Fax: 859-226-4437

SOCIETIE DES CASINOS DU QUEBEC SCHOLARSHIP

Award for resident of Quebec who is pursuing travel and tourism studies. May attend a four-year college or university. Minimum 3.0 GPA required.

Academic Fields/Career Goals: Food Service/Hospitality; Hospitality Management; Travel/Tourism.

Award: Scholarship for use in freshman, sophomore, junior, or senior years; not renewable. *Number:* 1. *Amount:* $1000.

Eligibility Requirements: Applicant must be enrolled or expecting to enroll full-time at a two-year or four-year institution and resident of Quebec. Applicant must have 3.0 GPA or higher. Available to Canadian citizens.

Application Requirements: Application, essay, resume, references, transcript. *Deadline:* May 10.

Contact: Michelle Gorin, Projects Coordinator
National Tourism Foundation
546 East Main Street
Lexington, KY 40508-3071
Phone: 800-682-8886
Fax: 859-226-4437

TAMPA, HILLSBOROUGH LEGACY SCHOLARSHIP

One-time award for Florida resident who is pursuing studies in travel and tourism. Must attend a Florida college or university. Minimum 3.0 GPA required.

Academic Fields/Career Goals: Food Service/Hospitality; Hospitality Management; Travel/Tourism.

Award: Scholarship for use in freshman, sophomore, junior, or senior years; not renewable. *Number:* 1. *Amount:* $1000.

Eligibility Requirements: Applicant must be enrolled or expecting to enroll full-time at a two-year or four-year institution or university; resident of Florida and studying in Florida. Applicant must have 3.0 GPA or higher. Available to U.S. citizens.

Application Requirements: Application, essay, resume, references, transcript. *Deadline:* May 10.

Contact: Michelle Gorin, Projects Coordinator
National Tourism Foundation
546 East Main Street
Lexington, KY 40508-3071
Phone: 800-682-8886
Fax: 859-226-4437

TAUCK SCHOLARS SCHOLARSHIPS

Four undergraduate scholarships awarded to students entering their sophomore or junior years of study in travel and tourism-related degrees. Applicants will receive $3000 over two years; $1500 awarded first year and $1500 awarded the following year. Must have minimum 3.0 GPA. Please refer to Web site for further details: http://www.ntfonline.org.

Academic Fields/Career Goals: Food Service/Hospitality; Hospitality Management; Travel/Tourism.

Award: Scholarship for use in sophomore or junior years; renewable. *Number:* 4. *Amount:* $1500.

Eligibility Requirements: Applicant must be enrolled or expecting to enroll full-time at a two-year or four-year institution or university. Applicant must have 3.0 GPA or higher. Available to U.S. citizens.

Application Requirements: Application, essay, resume, references, transcript. *Deadline:* May 10.

Contact: Michelle Gorin, Projects Coordinator
National Tourism Foundation
546 East Main Street
Lexington, KY 40508-3071
Phone: 800-682-8886
Fax: 859-226-4437

TULSA SCHOLARSHIP AWARDS

Scholarship available for Oklahoma residents pursuing travel and tourism studies. Must be enrolled in an Oklahoma four-year institution. Minimum 3.0 GPA required. Submit resume.

Academic Fields/Career Goals: Food Service/Hospitality; Hospitality Management; Travel/Tourism.

Award: Scholarship for use in freshman, sophomore, junior, or senior years; not renewable. *Number:* 1. *Amount:* $500.

Eligibility Requirements: Applicant must be enrolled or expecting to enroll full-time at a four-year institution or university; resident of Oklahoma and studying in Oklahoma. Applicant must have 3.0 GPA or higher. Available to U.S. citizens.

Application Requirements: Application, essay, resume, references, transcript. *Deadline:* May 10.

Contact: Michelle Gorin, Projects Coordinator
National Tourism Foundation
546 East Main Street
Lexington, KY 40508-3071
Phone: 800-682-8886
Fax: 859-226-4437

YELLOW RIBBON SCHOLARSHIP

One-time scholarship for residents of North America with physical or sensory disabilities who are pursuing travel and tourism studies at a North American institution. Must be entering postsecondary education with a minimum 3.0 GPA or must be maintaining at least a 2.5 GPA at college level. Must submit resume and essay explaining plans to utilize his or her education in travel and tourism career.

Academic Fields/Career Goals: Food Service/Hospitality; Hospitality Management; Travel/Tourism.

Award: Scholarship for use in freshman, sophomore, junior, or senior years; not renewable. *Number:* 1. *Amount:* $2500.

Eligibility Requirements: Applicant must be enrolled or expecting to enroll full-time at a two-year or four-year institution or university. Applicant must be hearing impaired, physically disabled, or visually impaired. Available to U.S. and Canadian citizens.

National Tourism Foundation (continued)

Application Requirements: Application, essay, resume, references, transcript. *Deadline:* May 10.

Contact: Michelle Gorin, Projects Coordinator
National Tourism Foundation
546 East Main Street
Lexington, KY 40508-3071
Phone: 800-682-8886
Fax: 859-226-4437

SAN DIEGO FOUNDATION http://www.sdfoundation.org

CALIFORNIA ASSOCIATION OF FAMILY AND CONSUMER SCIENCES-SAN DIEGO CHAPTER
• *See page 166*

SOUTH DAKOTA RETAILERS ASSOCIATION http://www.sdra.org

SOUTH DAKOTA RETAILERS ASSOCIATION SCHOLARSHIP PROGRAM
• *See page 64*

UNITED NEGRO COLLEGE FUND http://www.uncf.org

FLOWERS INDUSTRIES SCHOLARSHIP
• *See page 150*

WOMEN CHEFS AND RESTAURATEURS http://www.womenchefs.org

FRENCH CULINARY INSTITUTE/ITALIAN CULINARY EXPERIENCE SCHOLARSHIP
• *See page 206*

WOMEN GROCERS OF AMERICA http://www.nationalgrocers.org

MARY MACEY SCHOLARSHIP
• *See page 80*

FOREIGN LANGUAGE

ACL/NJCL NATIONAL LATIN EXAM http://www.nle.org

NATIONAL LATIN EXAM SCHOLARSHIP
• *See page 174*

ALBERTA HERITAGE SCHOLARSHIP FUND/ ALBERTA SCHOLARSHIP PROGRAMS http://www.alis.gov.ab.ca

FELLOWSHIPS FOR FULL-TIME STUDIES IN FRENCH

Award assists Albertans in pursuing postsecondary studies taught in French. Must be Alberta residents, Canadian citizens, or landed immigrants, and plan to register full-time in a postsecondary program of at least one semester in length. Must be enrolled in a minimum of three courses per semester which have French as the language of instruction.

Academic Fields/Career Goals: Foreign Language.

Award: Scholarship for use in freshman, sophomore, junior, or senior years; not renewable. *Number:* varies. *Amount:* $500–$1000.

Eligibility Requirements: Applicant must be Canadian citizen; enrolled or expecting to enroll full-time at a two-year or four-year or technical institution or university; resident of Alberta and must have an interest in French language.

Application Requirements: Application, transcript. *Deadline:* November 15.

Contact: Scholarship Committee
Alberta Heritage Scholarship Fund/Alberta Scholarship Programs
9940 106th Street, Fourth Floor, Sterling Place
PO Box 28000, Station Main
Edmonton, AB T5J 4R4
Canada
Phone: 780-427-8640
Fax: 780-427-1288
E-mail: scholarships@gov.ab.ca

LANGUAGES IN TEACHER EDUCATION SCHOLARSHIPS
• *See page 221*

ALPHA MU GAMMA, THE NATIONAL COLLEGIATE FOREIGN LANGUAGE SOCIETY http://www.lacitycollege.edu

NATIONAL ALPHA MU GAMMA SCHOLARSHIPS

One-time award to student members of Alpha Mu Gamma with a minimum 3.5 GPA, who plan to continue study of a foreign language. Must participate in a national scholarship competition. Apply through local chapter advisers. Freshmen are not eligible. Must submit a copy of Alpha Mu Gamma membership certificate. Can study overseas if part of his/her school program.

Academic Fields/Career Goals: Foreign Language.

Award: Scholarship for use in sophomore, junior, senior, graduate, or postgraduate years; not renewable. *Number:* 3. *Amount:* up to $750.

Eligibility Requirements: Applicant must be enrolled or expecting to enroll full- or part-time at a two-year or four-year institution or university. Applicant or parent of applicant must be member of Alpha Mu Gamma. Applicant must have 3.5 GPA or higher. Available to U.S. and non-U.S. citizens.

Application Requirements: Application, applicant must enter a contest, essay, references, transcript, photocopy of Alpha Mud Gamma membership. *Deadline:* February 1.

Contact: Hisham Malek, Scholarship Coordinator
Alpha Mu Gamma, The National Collegiate Foreign Language Society
855 North Vermont Avenue
Los Angeles, CA 90029
Phone: 323-644-9752
Fax: 323-644-9752
E-mail: amgnat@lacitycollege.edu

AMERICAN CLASSICAL LEAGUE/NATIONAL JUNIOR CLASSICAL LEAGUE http://www.aclclassics.org

NATIONAL JUNIOR CLASSICAL LEAGUE SCHOLARSHIP
• *See page 174*

AMERICAN COUNCIL FOR POLISH CULTURE http://www.polishcultureacpc.org

ACPC SUMMER STUDIES IN POLAND SCHOLARSHIP
• *See page 94*

POLISH HERITAGE SOCIETY OF PHILADELPHIA SCHOLARSHIP

Scholarship for high school seniors or students accepted to or already enrolled at a college or university. These applicants must be either of Polish descent or students pursuing courses in Polish or Slavic language, history or culture in college. The high school applicant must be college-bound in the subsequent autumn after graduation.

Academic Fields/Career Goals: Foreign Language.

Award: Scholarship for use in freshman, sophomore, junior, senior, or graduate years; not renewable. *Number:* 3. *Amount:* $500–$1000.

Eligibility Requirements: Applicant must be of Polish heritage and enrolled or expecting to enroll full-time at a four-year institution or university. Applicant must have 3.0 GPA or higher. Available to U.S. citizens.

Application Requirements: Application, essay, photo, resume, references, transcript. *Deadline:* January 30.

Contact: Deborah Majka, Scholarship Coordinator
American Council for Polish Culture
812 Lombard Street, Number 12
Philadelphia, PA 19147
Phone: 215-627-1391
E-mail: dziecko2@comcast.net

SKALNY SCHOLARSHIP FOR POLISH STUDIES
• *See page 94*

AMERICAN FOUNDATION FOR TRANSLATION AND INTERPRETATION http://www.afti.org

AFTI SCHOLARSHIPS IN SCIENTIFIC AND TECHNICAL TRANSLATION, LITERARY TRANSLATION, AND INTERPRETATION

Scholarships for full-time students enrolled or planning to enroll in a degree program in scientific and technical translation, literary translation, or interpreter training. Must have a 3.0 GPA.

Academic Fields/Career Goals: Foreign Language.

Award: Scholarship for use in sophomore, junior, senior, or graduate years; not renewable. *Number:* 1–2. *Amount:* $2500.

Eligibility Requirements: Applicant must be enrolled or expecting to enroll full-time at a four-year institution or university. Applicant must have 3.0 GPA or higher. Available to U.S. citizens.

Application Requirements: Application, essay, references, transcript, proof of admission to T/I program. *Deadline:* June 1.

Contact: Eleanor Krawutschke, Executive Director, AFTI
American Foundation for Translation and Interpretation
350 East Michigan Avenue, Columbia Plaza, Suite 101
Kalamazoo, MI 49007
Phone: 269-383-6893
E-mail: aftiorg@aol.com

AMERICAN INSTITUTE OF POLISH CULTURE INC. http://www.ampolinstitute.org

HARRIET IRSAY SCHOLARSHIP GRANT
• *See page 99*

AMERICAN PHILOLOGICAL ASSOCIATION http://www.apaclassics.org

MINORITY STUDENT SUMMER SCHOLARSHIP
• *See page 89*

AMERICAN SCHOOL OF CLASSICAL STUDIES AT ATHENS http://www.ascsa.edu.gr

CHARLES M. EDWARDS SCHOLARSHIP
• *See page 98*

ASSOCIATION OF TEACHERS OF JAPANESE BRIDGING CLEARINGHOUSE FOR STUDY ABROAD IN JAPAN

BRIDGING SCHOLARSHIP FOR STUDY ABROAD IN JAPAN
• *See page 94*

CENTRAL INTELLIGENCE AGENCY http://www.cia.gov

CENTRAL INTELLIGENCE AGENCY UNDERGRADUATE SCHOLARSHIP PROGRAM
• *See page 49*

DONALD KEENE CENTER OF JAPANESE CULTURE http://www.donaldkeenecenter.org

JAPAN-U.S. FRIENDSHIP COMMISSION PRIZE FOR THE TRANSLATION OF JAPANESE LITERATURE

The Donald Keene Center of Japanese Culture offers an annual prize for the best translation into English of a modern work of literature or for the best classical literary translation, or the prize is divided between a classical and a modern work. To qualify, works must be book-length translations of Japanese literary works: novels, collections of short stories, literary essays, memoirs, drama or poetry.

Academic Fields/Career Goals: Foreign Language.

Award: Prize for use in freshman, sophomore, junior, senior, graduate, or postgraduate years; not renewable. *Number:* 2. *Amount:* $3000.

Eligibility Requirements: Applicant must be enrolled or expecting to enroll full- or part-time at a two-year or four-year or technical institution or university. Available to U.S. citizens.

Application Requirements: Application, applicant must enter a contest, resume, unpublished manuscripts. *Deadline:* February 29.

Contact: Miho Walsh, Associate Director
Donald Keene Center of Japanese Culture
Columbia University
507 Kent Hall
New York, NY 10027
Phone: 212-854-5036
Fax: 212-854-4019
E-mail: donald-keene-center@columbia.edu

GERMAN ACADEMIC EXCHANGE SERVICE (DAAD) http://www.daad.org

DAAD UNIVERSITY SUMMER COURSE GRANT

Scholarship for summer language study at Germany's universities. Intermediate level classes; open to students of all fields.

Academic Fields/Career Goals: Foreign Language.

Award: Grant for use in sophomore, junior, senior, or graduate years; not renewable. *Number:* varies. *Amount:* varies.

Eligibility Requirements: Applicant must be enrolled or expecting to enroll full-time at a four-year institution or university and must have an interest in German language/culture. Available to U.S. and non-U.S. citizens.

Application Requirements: Application, applicant must enter a contest, essay, resume, references, transcript. *Deadline:* January 31.

Contact: Jane Fu, Information Officer
German Academic Exchange Service (DAAD)
871 United Nations Plaza
New York, NY 10017
Phone: 212-758-3223
Fax: 212-755-5780
E-mail: daadny@daad.org

GREATER KANAWHA VALLEY FOUNDATION http://www.tgkvf.org

WEST VIRGINIA BROADCASTERS ASSOCIATION FUND
• *See page 179*

INSTITUTE OF INTERNATIONAL EDUCATION http://www.iie.org/nsep

NATIONAL SECURITY EDUCATION PROGRAM DAVID L. BOREN UNDERGRADUATE SCHOLARSHIPS
• *See page 144*

JAPANESE GOVERNMENT/THE MONBUSHO SCHOLARSHIP PROGRAM http://www.la.us.emb-japan.go.jp

JAPANESE STUDIES SCHOLARSHIP
• *See page 96*

JAPAN STUDIES SCHOLARSHIP FOUNDATION COMMITTEE

JAPAN STUDIES SCHOLARSHIP
• *See page 96*

KE ALI'I PAUAHI FOUNDATION http://www.pauahi.org

JOHNNY PINEAPPLE SCHOLARSHIP

• See page 96

SARAH KELI'ILOLENA LUM KONIA NAKOA SCHOLARSHIP

Award to recognize the academic achievements of students pursuing the study and perpetuation of the Hawaiian language, including Hawaiian culture and history. Must be a full-time student, Hawaii resident, and demonstrate a financial need.

Academic Fields/Career Goals: Foreign Language; History.

Award: Scholarship for use in freshman, sophomore, junior, senior, or graduate years; not renewable. *Number:* 1. *Amount:* $600.

Eligibility Requirements: Applicant must be enrolled or expecting to enroll full-time at a four-year institution or university; resident of Hawaii; studying in Hawaii and must have an interest in Hawaiian language/culture. Available to U.S. citizens.

Application Requirements: Application, essay, financial need analysis, transcript, SAR, college acceptance letter. *Deadline:* May 2.

Contact: Elizabeth Stevenson, Development Manager
Ke Ali'i Pauahi Foundation
567 South King Street, Suite 160
Honolulu, HI 96813
Phone: 808-534-3966
Fax: 808-534-3890
E-mail: scholarships@pauahi.org

KLINGON LANGUAGE INSTITUTE http://www.kli.org

KOR MEMORIAL SCHOLARSHIP

Scholarship for undergraduate or graduate student in a program leading to a degree in a field related to language studies. Must send application materials by mail.

Academic Fields/Career Goals: Foreign Language.

Award: Scholarship for use in freshman, sophomore, junior, senior, or graduate years; not renewable. *Number:* 1. *Amount:* $500.

Eligibility Requirements: Applicant must be enrolled or expecting to enroll full-time at a four-year institution or university and must have an interest in foreign language. Available to U.S. citizens.

Application Requirements: Application, resume, references, nominating letter from chair, head, or dean, a brief statement of goals. *Deadline:* June 1.

Contact: Dr. Lawrence Schoen, Director
Klingon Language Institute
PO Box 634
Flourtown, PA 19031
E-mail: lawrence@kli.org

KOSCIUSZKO FOUNDATION http://www.kosciuszkofoundation.org

YEAR ABROAD PROGRAM IN POLAND

• See page 96

NATIONAL ASSOCIATION OF HISPANIC JOURNALISTS (NAHJ) http://www.nahj.org

MARIA ELENA SALINAS SCHOLARSHIP

One-time scholarship for high school seniors, college undergraduates, and first-year graduate students who are pursuing careers in Spanish-language broadcast (radio or TV) journalism. Students may major or plan to major in any subject, but must demonstrate a sincere desire to pursue a career in this field. Must submit essays and demo tapes (audio or video) in Spanish. Scholarship includes the opportunity to serve an internship with Univision Spanish-language television news network.

Academic Fields/Career Goals: Foreign Language; Journalism; TV/Radio Broadcasting.

Award: Scholarship for use in freshman, sophomore, junior, senior, or graduate years; not renewable. *Number:* 2. *Amount:* $5000.

Eligibility Requirements: Applicant must be enrolled or expecting to enroll full-time at a four-year institution or university and must have an interest in Spanish language. Available to U.S. citizens.

Application Requirements: Application, autobiography, essay, financial need analysis, resume, references, transcript. *Deadline:* March 31.

Contact: Virginia Galindo, Program Assistant
National Association of Hispanic Journalists (NAHJ)
1000 National Press Building, 529 14th Street, NW, Suite 1000
Washington, DC 20045-2001
Phone: 202-662-7145
Fax: 202-662-7144
E-mail: vgalindo@nahj.org

NATIONAL FEDERATION OF THE BLIND http://www.nfb.org

MICHAEL AND MARIE MARUCCI SCHOLARSHIP

One-time award for legally blind students pursuing full-time studies in the United States. Must be studying a foreign language or comparative literature; pursuing a degree in history, geography, or political science with a concentration in international studies; or majoring in any other discipline that includes study abroad. Must also show competency in a foreign language.

Academic Fields/Career Goals: Foreign Language; History; International Studies; Literature/English/Writing; Political Science.

Award: Scholarship for use in freshman, sophomore, junior, or senior years; not renewable. *Number:* 1. *Amount:* $5000.

Eligibility Requirements: Applicant must be enrolled or expecting to enroll full-time at a two-year or four-year institution or university. Applicant must be visually impaired. Available to U.S. and non-U.S. citizens.

Application Requirements: Application, essay, financial need analysis, references, test scores, transcript. *Deadline:* March 31.

Contact: Anil Lewis, Chairman, Scholarship Committee
National Federation of the Blind
315 West Ponce De Leon Avenue
Decatur, GA 30030
Phone: 404-371-1000
E-mail: alewis@nfbga.org

NATIONAL FEDERATION OF THE BLIND HUMANITIES SCHOLARSHIP

• See page 104

NATIONAL SECURITY AGENCY http://www.nsa.gov

NATIONAL SECURITY AGENCY STOKES EDUCATIONAL SCHOLARSHIP PROGRAM

• See page 194

NEW HAMPSHIRE POSTSECONDARY EDUCATION COMMISSION http://www.nh.gov/postsecondary

WORKFORCE INCENTIVE PROGRAM

• See page 237

NORWICH JUBILEE ESPERANTO FOUNDATION http://www.esperanto-gb.org

NOJEF TRAVEL GRANTS

Grants to help young Esperanto-speakers to use and improve their knowledge of the language, by traveling to congresses, and summer courses. Applicant must already speak Esperanto sufficiently well enough to take part in planned activity, and should be under 26 years old. For more information, refer to Web site: http://www.esperanto-gb.org/nojef/nojef-en.htm.

Academic Fields/Career Goals: Foreign Language.

Award: Grant for use in freshman, sophomore, junior, senior, or graduate years; not renewable. *Number:* 1–20. *Amount:* $64–$1600.

Eligibility Requirements: Applicant must be age 26 or under; enrolled or expecting to enroll full- or part-time at a two-year or four-year or technical institution or university and must have an interest in Spanish language. Available to U.S. and non-U.S. citizens.

Application Requirements: Application, essay, references. *Deadline:* continuous.

Contact: Dr. Kathleen M. Hall, Scholarship Committee
Norwich Jubilee Esperanto Foundation
37 Granville Court, Cheney Lane
Oxford OX3 0HS
United Kingdom
Phone: 44-1865-245-509

SONS OF ITALY FOUNDATION http://www.osia.org

SONS OF ITALY NATIONAL LEADERSHIP GRANTS COMPETITION LANGUAGE SCHOLARSHIP

Scholarships for undergraduate students in their junior or senior year of study who are majoring in Italian language studies. Must be a U.S. citizen of Italian descent. For more details see Web site: http://www.osia.org.

Academic Fields/Career Goals: Foreign Language.

Award: Scholarship for use in junior or senior years; not renewable. *Number:* up to 1. *Amount:* up to $10,000.

Eligibility Requirements: Applicant must be of Italian heritage and enrolled or expecting to enroll full-time at a four-year institution or university. Available to U.S. citizens.

Application Requirements: Application, autobiography, essay, resume, references, self-addressed stamped envelope, test scores, transcript. *Fee:* $30. *Deadline:* February 28.

Contact: Margaret O'Rourke, Scholarship Coordinator
Sons of Italy Foundation
219 E Street, NE
Washington, DC 20002
Phone: 202-547-2900
Fax: 202-546-8168
E-mail: scholarships@osia.org

STRAIGHTFORWARD MEDIA http://www.straightforwardmedia.com

STRAIGHTFORWARD MEDIA LIBERAL ARTS SCHOLARSHIP

• *See page 99*

FUNERAL SERVICES/MORTUARY SCIENCE

ALABAMA FUNERAL DIRECTORS ASSOCIATION INC. http://www.alabamafda.org

ALABAMA FUNERAL DIRECTORS ASSOCIATION SCHOLARSHIP

Two $1000 scholarships available to Alabama residents. Applicant must have been accepted by an accredited mortuary science school and be sponsored by a member of the AFDA. Must maintain a minimum 2.5 GPA. Deadline: no later than 30 days prior to the AFDA mid winter meeting and annual convention.

Academic Fields/Career Goals: Funeral Services/Mortuary Science.

Award: Scholarship for use in freshman, sophomore, junior, or senior years; not renewable. *Number:* 2. *Amount:* $1000.

Eligibility Requirements: Applicant must be enrolled or expecting to enroll full- or part-time at a four-year institution or university and resident of Alabama. Applicant must have 2.5 GPA or higher. Available to U.S. citizens.

Application Requirements: Application, driver's license, essay, photo, references, transcript, two proofs of residency (such as voter registration, drivers license, or tax returns). *Deadline:* varies.

Contact: Denise Edmisten, Executive Director
Alabama Funeral Directors Association Inc.
7956 Vaughn Road, PO Box 380
Montgomery, AL 36116
Phone: 334-956-8000
Fax: 334-956-8001

AMERICAN BOARD OF FUNERAL SERVICE EDUCATION http://www.abfse.org

AMERICAN BOARD OF FUNERAL SERVICE EDUCATION SCHOLARSHIPS

One-time award for students who are enrolled in an accredited funeral science education program. Deadlines: March 1 and September 1. For more details see Web site: http//www.abfse.org.

Academic Fields/Career Goals: Funeral Services/Mortuary Science.

Award: Scholarship for use in freshman, sophomore, junior, or senior years; not renewable. *Number:* 50. *Amount:* $500–$2500.

Eligibility Requirements: Applicant must be enrolled or expecting to enroll full-time at a two-year or four-year institution or university. Available to U.S. and non-U.S. citizens.

Application Requirements: Application, essay, financial need analysis, references, transcript. *Deadline:* varies.

Contact: Michael Smith, Executive Director
American Board of Funeral Service Education
3432 Ashland Avenue, Suite U
St. Joseph, MO 64506
Phone: 816-233-3747
Fax: 816-233-3793
E-mail: exdir@abfse.org

INTERNATIONAL ORDER OF THE GOLDEN RULE http://www.ogr.org

INTERNATIONAL ORDER OF THE GOLDEN RULE AWARD OF EXCELLENCE

One-time scholarship for mortuary science students to prepare for a career in funeral service. Must be enrolled in a mortuary science degree program at an accredited mortuary school. Minimum 3.0 GPA required.

Academic Fields/Career Goals: Funeral Services/Mortuary Science.

Award: Scholarship for use in freshman, sophomore, junior, or senior years; not renewable. *Number:* 1–3. *Amount:* $500–$2500.

Eligibility Requirements: Applicant must be enrolled or expecting to enroll full- or part-time at a two-year or four-year or technical institution or university. Applicant must have 3.0 GPA or higher. Available to U.S. and non-U.S. citizens.

Application Requirements: Application, essay, financial need analysis, transcript. *Deadline:* October 1.

Contact: Jenny Gabbert, Education and Meetings Coordinator
International Order of the Golden Rule
13523 Lakefront Drive
Earth City, MO 63045-1189
Phone: 800-637-8030
Fax: 314-209-1289
E-mail: jgabbert@ogr.org

MISSOURI FUNERAL DIRECTOR'S ASSOCIATION http://www.mofuneral.org

MISSOURI FUNERAL DIRECTORS ASSOCIATION SCHOLARSHIPS

Scholarship to Missouri residents pursuing a career in funeral services or mortuary science. Minimum 3.0 GPA required.

Academic Fields/Career Goals: Funeral Services/Mortuary Science.

Award: Scholarship for use in freshman, sophomore, junior, or senior years; not renewable. *Number:* up to 4. *Amount:* $750.

Eligibility Requirements: Applicant must be enrolled or expecting to enroll full-time at a four-year institution or university and resident of Missouri. Applicant must have 3.0 GPA or higher. Available to U.S. citizens.

Application Requirements: Application, essay, financial need analysis, references, test scores, transcript. *Deadline:* October 15.

Contact: Don Otto, Jr., Executive Director
Missouri Funeral Director's Association
PO Box 104688
Jefferson City, MO 65110-4688
Phone: 573-635-1661
Fax: 573-635-9494
E-mail: info@mofuneral.org

NATIONAL FUNERAL DIRECTORS AND MORTICIANS ASSOCIATION http://www.nfdma.com

NATIONAL FUNERAL DIRECTORS AND MORTICIANS ASSOCIATION SCHOLARSHIP

Awards for high school graduates who have preferably worked in or had one year of apprenticeship in the funeral home business.

Academic Fields/Career Goals: Funeral Services/Mortuary Science.

Award: Scholarship for use in freshman year; not renewable. *Number:* 1. *Amount:* $1500.

Eligibility Requirements: Applicant must be high school student and planning to enroll or expecting to enroll full- or part-time at a four-year institution or university. Available to U.S. citizens.

Application Requirements: Application, resume, references, test scores. *Deadline:* April 15.

Contact: Eva Cranford, Scholarship Coordinator
National Funeral Directors and Morticians Association
Omega World Center, 3951 Snapfinger Parkway, Suite 570
Decatur, GA 30035
Phone: 718-625-4656
E-mail: lladyc23@aol.com

WALLACE S. AND WILMA K. LAUGHLIN FOUNDATION TRUST http://www.nefda.org

WALLACE S. AND WILMA K. LAUGHLIN SCHOLARSHIP

Scholarships for Nebraska students entering mortuary science programs in order to become a licensed funeral director. Must be U.S. citizen. Must be high school graduate. Scholarship value and the number of awards granted varies annually.

Academic Fields/Career Goals: Funeral Services/Mortuary Science.

Award: Scholarship for use in junior or senior years; not renewable. *Number:* varies. *Amount:* varies.

Eligibility Requirements: Applicant must be enrolled or expecting to enroll full-time at a four-year institution or university and resident of Nebraska. Available to U.S. citizens.

Application Requirements: Application, financial need analysis, interview, references, transcript. *Deadline:* June 30.

Contact: Leo Seger, President
Wallace S. and Wilma K. Laughlin Foundation Trust
6000 South 58th Street, Suite B
Lincoln, NE 68516
Phone: 402-423-8900
Fax: 402-420-9716
E-mail: segerfh@morcomm.net

GEMOLOGY

MINERALOGICAL SOCIETY OF AMERICA http://www.minsocam.org

MINERALOGICAL SOCIETY OF AMERICA-GRANT FOR STUDENT RESEARCH IN MINERALOGY AND PETROLOGY

• *See page 218*

MINERALOGY SOCIETY OF AMERICA-GRANT FOR RESEARCH IN CRYSTALLOGRAPHY

• *See page 218*

GEOGRAPHY

CANADIAN RECREATIONAL CANOEING ASSOCIATION http://www.paddlingcanada.com

BILL MASON MEMORIAL SCHOLARSHIP FUND

• *See page 74*

CENTRAL INTELLIGENCE AGENCY http://www.cia.gov

CENTRAL INTELLIGENCE AGENCY UNDERGRADUATE SCHOLARSHIP PROGRAM

• *See page 49*

GAMMA THETA UPSILON-INTERNATIONAL GEOGRAPHIC HONOR SOCIETY http://gtuhonors.org

BUZZARD-MAXFIELD-RICHASON AND RECHLIN SCHOLARSHIP

Award is granted to a student who is a Gamma Theta Upsilon member, majoring in geography, will be a senior undergraduate and who has been accepted into a graduate program in geography.

Academic Fields/Career Goals: Geography.

Award: Scholarship for use in senior or graduate years; not renewable. *Number:* 5. *Amount:* $1000.

Eligibility Requirements: Applicant must be enrolled or expecting to enroll full-time at a four-year institution or university. Applicant or parent of applicant must be member of Gamma Theta Upsilon. Applicant must have 3.0 GPA or higher. Available to U.S. and non-U.S. citizens.

Application Requirements: Application, references, transcript. *Deadline:* May 31.

Contact: Dr. Donald Zeigler, Scholarship Committee
Gamma Theta Upsilon-International Geographic Honor Society
Old Dominion University, 1881 University Drive
Virginia Beach, VA 23453
E-mail: dzeigler@odu.edu

CHRISTOPHERSON GEOSYSTEMS SCHOLARSHIP

• *See page 217*

GTU JOHN WILEY-STRAHLER PHYSICAL GEOGRAPHY SCHOLARSHIP

Scholarship for undergraduate or graduate study in physical geography. Applicant must be a member of Gamma Theta Upsilon prior to submitting the application form. Must submit publishable term paper on physical geography.

Academic Fields/Career Goals: Geography.

Award: Scholarship for use in freshman, sophomore, junior, senior, or graduate years; not renewable. *Number:* 2. *Amount:* $1000.

Eligibility Requirements: Applicant must be enrolled or expecting to enroll full-time at a four-year institution or university. Applicant or parent of applicant must be member of Gamma Theta Upsilon. Applicant must have 3.0 GPA or higher. Available to U.S. and non-U.S. citizens.

Application Requirements: Application, references, transcript, term papers. *Deadline:* May 31.

Contact: Dr. Donald Zeigler, Scholarship Committee
Gamma Theta Upsilon-International Geographic Honor Society
Old Dominion University, 1881 University Drive
Virginia Beach, VA 23453
E-mail: dzeigler@odu.edu

ROWNTREE LEWIS PRICE AND WYCOFF SCHOLARSHIP

Scholarship for undergraduate or graduate study in regional geography. Applicant must be a member of Gamma Theta Upsilon prior to submitting the application form. Must submit publishable term paper on regional geography. Must have a minimum GPA of 3.0.

Academic Fields/Career Goals: Geography.

Award: Scholarship for use in freshman, sophomore, junior, senior, or graduate years; not renewable. *Number:* 2. *Amount:* $500.

Eligibility Requirements: Applicant must be enrolled or expecting to enroll full-time at a four-year institution or university. Applicant or parent of applicant must be member of Gamma Theta Upsilon. Applicant must have 3.0 GPA or higher. Available to U.S. and non-U.S. citizens.

Application Requirements: Application, references, transcript, term papers. *Deadline:* June 1.

Contact: Dr. Howard G. Johnson, Scholarship Committee
Gamma Theta Upsilon-International Geographic Honor Society
206 Martin Hall, Jacksonville State University
Jacksonville, AL 36265

HARVARD TRAVELLERS CLUB

HARVARD TRAVELLERS CLUB GRANTS
• *See page 89*

INNOVATION AND SCIENCE COUNCIL OF BRITISH COLUMBIA http://www.bcinnovationcouncil.com

PAUL AND HELEN TRUSSEL SCIENCE AND TECHNOLOGY SCHOLARSHIP
• *See page 87*

MORRIS K. UDALL FOUNDATION http://www.udall.gov

MORRIS K. UDALL SCHOLARS
• *See page 76*

NATIONAL FISH AND WILDLIFE FOUNDATION http://www.nfwf.org

BUDWEISER CONSERVATION SCHOLARSHIP PROGRAM
• *See page 133*

UNITED NEGRO COLLEGE FUND http://www.uncf.org

CDM SCHOLARSHIP/INTERNSHIP
• *See page 93*

GERMAN STUDIES

GERMAN ACADEMIC EXCHANGE SERVICE (DAAD) http://www.daad.org

GERMAN ACADEMIC EXCHANGE INFORMATION VISITS
• *See page 306*

GRAPHICS/GRAPHIC ARTS/ PRINTING

CENTRAL INTELLIGENCE AGENCY http://www.cia.gov

CENTRAL INTELLIGENCE AGENCY UNDERGRADUATE SCHOLARSHIP PROGRAM
• *See page 49*

CINCINNATI LITHO CLUB http://www.cincylithoclub.org

BILL STAUDT/AL HARTNETT SCHOLARSHIP
• *See page 177*

DAY INTERNATIONAL SCHOLARSHIP
• *See page 178*

ELECTRONIC DOCUMENT SYSTEMS FOUNDATION http://www.edsf.org

ELECTRONIC DOCUMENT SYSTEMS FOUNDATION SCHOLARSHIP AWARDS
• *See page 178*

GOLDEN KEY INTERNATIONAL HONOUR SOCIETY http://www.goldenkey.org

VISUAL AND PERFORMING ARTS ACHIEVEMENT AWARDS
• *See page 101*

GRAVURE EDUCATION FOUNDATION http://www.gaa.org

GEF RESOURCE CENTER SCHOLARSHIPS

Scholarships are awarded annually to students enrolled full-time at one of the designated GEF gravure printing resource centers: Arizona State University, California Polytechnic State University, Clemson University, Murray State University, Rochester Institute of Technology, University of Wisconsin-Stout, and Western Michigan University.

Academic Fields/Career Goals: Graphics/Graphic Arts/Printing.

Award: Scholarship for use in sophomore, junior, senior, or graduate years; not renewable. *Number:* varies. *Amount:* varies.

Eligibility Requirements: Applicant must be enrolled or expecting to enroll full-time at a four-year institution or university. Applicant must have 3.0 GPA or higher. Available to U.S. citizens.

Application Requirements: Application. *Deadline:* May 31.

Contact: Robert Sheridan, Director of Development
Gravure Education Foundation
1200 A Scottsville Road
Rochester, NY 14624
Phone: 518-589-5153
Fax: 585-436-7689
E-mail: rbsheridan@gaa.org

GRAVURE CATALOG AND INSERT COUNCIL SCHOLARSHIP

Scholarship of up to $1000 for a student enrolled full-time at a college or university designated by GEF as a gravure printing resource center. Must be at least a junior and have a minimum GPA of 3.0.

Academic Fields/Career Goals: Graphics/Graphic Arts/Printing.

Award: Scholarship for use in junior or senior years; not renewable. *Number:* 1. *Amount:* up to $1000.

Eligibility Requirements: Applicant must be enrolled or expecting to enroll full-time at a four-year institution or university. Applicant must have 3.0 GPA or higher. Available to U.S. and non-U.S. citizens.

Application Requirements: Application, essay, transcript. *Deadline:* May 31.

Contact: Robert Sheridan, Director of Development
Gravure Education Foundation
1200 A Scottsville Road
Rochester, NY 14624
Phone: 518-589-5153
Fax: 585-436-7689
E-mail: rbsheridan@gaa.org

GRAVURE EDUCATION FOUNDATION CORPORATE LEADERSHIP SCHOLARSHIPS

Scholarships for full-time sophomore, junior, senior, or graduate students enrolled at any of the GEF-funded colleges or universities. Must demonstrate a declared major in printing, graphic arts, or graphic communications. Minimum 3.0 GPA required.

Academic Fields/Career Goals: Graphics/Graphic Arts/Printing.

Award: Scholarship for use in sophomore, junior, senior, or graduate years; not renewable. *Number:* 3–6. *Amount:* up to $2000.

Eligibility Requirements: Applicant must be enrolled or expecting to enroll full-time at a four-year institution or university. Applicant must have 3.0 GPA or higher. Available to U.S. and non-U.S. citizens.

Application Requirements: Application, essay, transcript. *Deadline:* May 31.

Contact: Robert Sheridan, Director of Development
Gravure Education Foundation
GEF, 1200-A Scottsville Road
Rochester, NY 14624
E-mail: rbsheridan@gaa.org

HALLMARK GRAPHIC ARTS SCHOLARSHIP

One scholarship award of up to $1500 for a student enrolled full-time at a college or university designated by GEF as a gravure resource center. Must be at least a junior and maintain a minimum GPA of 3.0. Must demonstrate interest in gravure printing and graphic arts.

Academic Fields/Career Goals: Graphics/Graphic Arts/Printing.

Award: Scholarship for use in junior or senior years; not renewable. *Number:* 1. *Amount:* up to $1500.

Eligibility Requirements: Applicant must be enrolled or expecting to enroll full-time at a four-year institution or university and must have an interest in leadership. Applicant must have 3.0 GPA or higher. Available to U.S. citizens.

Gravure Education Foundation (continued)

Application Requirements: Application, essay, transcript. *Deadline:* March 31.

Contact: Robert Sheridan, Director of Development
Gravure Education Foundation
1200 A Scottsville Road
Rochester, NY 14624
Phone: 518-589-5153
Fax: 585-436-7689
E-mail: rbsheridan@gaa.org

LEON C. HART MEMORIAL SCHOLARSHIP

One scholarship of up to $1000 awarded to a student enrolled full-time at a college or university designated by GEF as a gravure printing resource center. Must maintain a minimum GPA of 3.0. Preference given to students who show an interest in printing education as a career path.

Academic Fields/Career Goals: Graphics/Graphic Arts/Printing.

Award: Scholarship for use in freshman, sophomore, junior, senior, graduate, or postgraduate years; not renewable. *Number:* 1. *Amount:* up to $1000.

Eligibility Requirements: Applicant must be enrolled or expecting to enroll full-time at a two-year or four-year or technical institution or university. Applicant or parent of applicant must have employment or volunteer experience in community service. Applicant must have 3.0 GPA or higher. Available to U.S. citizens.

Application Requirements: Application, essay, financial need analysis, transcript. *Deadline:* May 31.

Contact: Robert Sheridan, Director of Development
Gravure Education Foundation
1200 A Scottsville Road
Rochester, NY 14624
Phone: 518-589-5153
Fax: 585-436-7689
E-mail: rbsheridan@gaa.org

WERNER B. THIELE MEMORIAL SCHOLARSHIP

Two scholarships of up to $1250 each are awarded to students enrolled full-time at a college or university designated by GEF as a gravure printing resource center: Arizona State University, California Polytechnic State University, Clemson University, Murray State University, Rochester Institute of Technology, University of Wisconsin-Stout, and Western Michigan University. Minimum GPA of 3.0 required.

Academic Fields/Career Goals: Graphics/Graphic Arts/Printing.

Award: Scholarship for use in junior or senior years; not renewable. *Number:* up to 2. *Amount:* up to $1250.

Eligibility Requirements: Applicant must be enrolled or expecting to enroll full-time at a four-year institution or university. Applicant must have 3.0 GPA or higher. Available to U.S. citizens.

Application Requirements: Application, essay, transcript. *Deadline:* May 31.

Contact: Robert Sheridan, Director of Development
Gravure Education Foundation
1200 A Scottsville Road
Rochester, NY 14624
Phone: 518-589-5153
Fax: 585-436-7689
E-mail: rbsheridan@gaa.org

GREAT LAKES COMMISSION http://www.glc.org

CAROL A. RATZA MEMORIAL SCHOLARSHIP

• *See page 179*

HISPANIC SCHOLARSHIP FUND http://www.hsf.net

HSF/MCNAMARA FAMILY CREATIVE ARTS PROJECT GRANT

• *See page 98*

INTERNATIONAL FOODSERVICE EDITORIAL COUNCIL http://www.ifeconline.com

INTERNATIONAL FOODSERVICE EDITORIAL COUNCIL COMMUNICATIONS SCHOLARSHIP

• *See page 180*

LIBERTY GRAPHICS INC. http://www.lgtees.com

ANNUAL LIBERTY GRAPHICS ART CONTEST

• *See page 103*

MAINE GRAPHICS ARTS ASSOCIATION http://www.megaa.org

MAINE GRAPHICS ART ASSOCIATION

One-time award for Maine high school students majoring in graphic arts at any university. Must submit transcript and references with application.

Academic Fields/Career Goals: Graphics/Graphic Arts/Printing.

Award: Scholarship for use in freshman year; not renewable. *Number:* up to 20. *Amount:* $100–$500.

Eligibility Requirements: Applicant must be high school student; planning to enroll or expecting to enroll full- or part-time at a four-year institution or university and resident of Maine. Available to U.S. citizens.

Application Requirements: Application, references, transcript. *Deadline:* May 15.

Contact: Angie Dougherty, Director
Maine Graphics Arts Association
PO Box 874
Auburn, ME 04212-0874
Phone: 207-883-9525
Fax: 207-883-3158
E-mail: edpougher@maine.rr.com

NATIONAL ASSOCIATION OF HISPANIC JOURNALISTS (NAHJ) http://www.nahj.org

NEWHOUSE SCHOLARSHIP PROGRAM

Two-year $5000 annually award for students who are pursuing careers in the newspaper industry as reporters, editors, graphic artists, or photojournalists. Recipient is expected to participate in summer internship at a Newhouse newspaper following their junior year. Students must submit resume and writing samples.

Academic Fields/Career Goals: Graphics/Graphic Arts/Printing; Journalism; Photojournalism/Photography.

Award: Scholarship for use in junior or senior years; not renewable. *Number:* varies. *Amount:* $5000.

Eligibility Requirements: Applicant must be enrolled or expecting to enroll full-time at a four-year institution or university. Available to U.S. citizens.

Application Requirements: Application, essay, financial need analysis, resume, references, transcript, work samples. *Deadline:* March 31.

Contact: Virginia Galindo, Program Assistant
National Association of Hispanic Journalists (NAHJ)
1000 National Press Building, 529 14th Street, NW, Suite 1000
Washington, DC 20045-2001
Phone: 202-662-7145
Fax: 202-662-7144
E-mail: vgalindo@nahj.org

NEW ENGLAND PRINTING AND PUBLISHING COUNCIL http://www.ppcne.org

NEW ENGLAND GRAPHIC ARTS SCHOLARSHIP

Applicants must be residents of New England who have admission to an accredited two-year vocational or technical college or a four-year college or university that offers a degree program related to printing or graphic arts. Renewable for up to four years if student maintains 2.5 GPA.

Academic Fields/Career Goals: Graphics/Graphic Arts/Printing.

Award: Scholarship for use in freshman, sophomore, junior, or senior years; renewable. *Number:* varies. *Amount:* up to $2500.

Eligibility Requirements: Applicant must be enrolled or expecting to enroll full-time at a two-year or four-year or technical institution or

university and resident of Connecticut, Maine, Massachusetts, New Hampshire, Rhode Island, or Vermont. Applicant must have 2.5 GPA or higher. Available to U.S. citizens.

Application Requirements: Application, financial need analysis, test scores, transcript. *Deadline:* May 15.

Contact: Jay Smith, Scholarship Chair
New England Printing and Publishing Council
166 New Boston Street
Woburn, MA 01801
Phone: 781-944-1116
Fax: 781-944-3905
E-mail: jay@mhcp.com

PRINT AND GRAPHIC SCHOLARSHIP FOUNDATION http://www.pgsf.org

PRINT AND GRAPHICS SCHOLARSHIPS
• *See page 183*

PRINTING INDUSTRY OF MINNESOTA EDUCATION FOUNDATION http://www.pimn.org

PRINTING INDUSTRY OF MINNESOTA EDUCATION FOUNDATION SCHOLARSHIP FUND

The fund offers $1000 renewable scholarships to full-time students enrolled in two- or four-year institutions and technical colleges offering degrees in the print communications discipline. Applicant must be a Minnesota resident and be committed to a career in the print communications industry. Minimum 3.0 GPA required. Priority given to children of PIM member company employees.

Academic Fields/Career Goals: Graphics/Graphic Arts/Printing; Journalism.

Award: Scholarship for use in freshman, sophomore, junior, or senior years; renewable. *Number:* 10–15. *Amount:* $1000.

Eligibility Requirements: Applicant must be enrolled or expecting to enroll full-time at a two-year or four-year or technical institution or university; resident of Minnesota and studying in Minnesota, New York, or Wisconsin. Applicant must have 3.0 GPA or higher. Available to U.S. citizens.

Application Requirements: Application, autobiography, essay, references, test scores, transcript, copy of college admission form, proof of admission. *Deadline:* April 1.

Contact: Kristin Davis, Director of Education Services
Printing Industry of Minnesota Education Foundation
2829 University Avenue, SE, Suite 750
Minneapolis, MN 55414-3248
Phone: 651-789-5508
E-mail: kristinp@pimn.org

RHODE ISLAND FOUNDATION http://www.rifoundation.org

J. D. EDSAL ADVERTISING SCHOLARSHIP
• *See page 184*

ROBERT H. MOLLOHAN FAMILY CHARITABLE FOUNDATION INC. http://www.mollohanfoundation.org

MARY OLIVE EDDY JONES ART SCHOLARSHIP
• *See page 98*

SAN FRANCISCO FOUNDATION http://www.sff.org

PHELAN AWARD IN PRINTMAKING

Award presented in every odd-numbered year to recognize achievement in printmaking for students. Must have been born in California, but need not be a current resident. Applicants must provide a copy of their birth certificate with their application. This award is not a scholarship.

Academic Fields/Career Goals: Graphics/Graphic Arts/Printing.

Award: Prize for use in freshman, sophomore, junior, senior, graduate, or postgraduate years; not renewable. *Number:* 2. *Amount:* up to $4000.

Eligibility Requirements: Applicant must be enrolled or expecting to enroll full- or part-time at a two-year or four-year institution or university. Available to U.S. citizens.

Application Requirements: Application, applicant must enter a contest, self-addressed stamped envelope. *Deadline:* May 4.

Contact: Art Awards Coordinator
San Francisco Foundation
225 Bush Street, Suite 500
San Francisco, CA 94104
Phone: 415-733-8500

SOUTH DAKOTA RETAILERS ASSOCIATION http://www.sdra.org

SOUTH DAKOTA RETAILERS ASSOCIATION SCHOLARSHIP PROGRAM
• *See page 64*

TAG AND LABEL MANUFACTURERS INSTITUTE INC. http://www.tlmi.com

TLMI FOUR-YEAR COLLEGES/FULL-TIME STUDENTS SCHOLARSHIP
• *See page 297*

TECHNICAL ASSOCIATION OF THE PULP & PAPER INDUSTRY (TAPPI) http://www.tappi.org

COATING AND GRAPHIC ARTS DIVISION SCHOLARSHIP

Scholarship program is to encourage talented science and engineering students to pursue careers in the paper industry and to utilize their capabilities in advancing the science and technology of coated paper and paperboard manufacturing and the graphic arts industry. The division may award up to four $1000 awards annually.

Academic Fields/Career Goals: Graphics/Graphic Arts/Printing; Paper and Pulp Engineering.

Award: Scholarship for use in freshman, sophomore, junior, or senior years; not renewable. *Number:* 1–4. *Amount:* $1000.

Eligibility Requirements: Applicant must be enrolled or expecting to enroll full-time at a four-year institution or university. Applicant must have 3.0 GPA or higher. Available to U.S. and non-U.S. citizens.

Application Requirements: Application, references, transcript. *Deadline:* February 15.

Contact: Veranda Edmondson, Member Group Specialist
Technical Association of the Pulp & Paper Industry (TAPPI)
15 Technology Parkway, South
Norcross, GA 30092
Phone: 770-209-7536
Fax: 770-446-6947
E-mail: vedmondson@tappi.org

WORLDSTUDIO FOUNDATION http://www.aiga.org/

WORLDSTUDIO FOUNDATION SCHOLARSHIP PROGRAM
• *See page 94*

HEALTH ADMINISTRATION

ALBERTA HERITAGE SCHOLARSHIP FUND/ ALBERTA SCHOLARSHIP PROGRAMS http://www.alis.gov.ab.ca

ALBERTA HERITAGE SCHOLARSHIP FUND ABORIGINAL HEALTH CAREERS BURSARY
• *See page 129*

AMERICAN INDIAN SCIENCE AND ENGINEERING SOCIETY http://www.aises.org

BURLINGTON NORTHERN SANTA FE FOUNDATION SCHOLARSHIP
• *See page 84*

BETHESDA LUTHERAN HOMES AND SERVICES, INC. http://www.blhs.org

DEVELOPMENTAL DISABILITIES SCHOLASTIC ACHIEVEMENT SCHOLARSHIP FOR LUTHERAN COLLEGE STUDENTS
• *See page 211*

CANADIAN SOCIETY FOR MEDICAL LABORATORY SCIENCE http://www.csmls.org

E.V. BOOTH SCHOLARSHIP AWARD

The fund was established to assist CSMLS members in fulfilling their vision of achieving university level education in the medical laboratory sciences. One-time award of CAN$500. Must be a Canadian citizen.

Academic Fields/Career Goals: Health Administration; Health and Medical Sciences; Health Information Management/Technology.

Award: Scholarship for use in freshman, sophomore, junior, senior, or graduate years; not renewable. *Number:* 2.

Eligibility Requirements: Applicant must be Canadian citizen and enrolled or expecting to enroll full- or part-time at a four-year institution or university. Applicant or parent of applicant must be member of Canadian Society for Medical Laboratory Science.

Application Requirements: Application, financial need analysis, self-addressed stamped envelope, transcript. *Deadline:* April 1.

Contact: Lisa Low, Executive Assistant
Canadian Society for Medical Laboratory Science
LCD One, PO Box 2830
Hamilton, ON L8N 3N8
Canada
Phone: 905-528-8642 Ext. 12
Fax: 905-528-4968
E-mail: lisal@csmls.org

CONGRESSIONAL BLACK CAUCUS SPOUSES PROGRAM http://www.cbcfinc.org

CONGRESSIONAL BLACK CAUCUS SPOUSES HEALTH INITIATIVES

Award made to students who reside or attend school in a congressional district represented by an African-American member of Congress. Awards scholarships to academically talented and highly motivated students who intend to pursue full-time undergraduate, graduate or doctoral degrees in health related areas. Minimum 2.5 GPA required. Contact the congressional office in the appropriate district for information and applications.

Academic Fields/Career Goals: Health Administration; Health and Medical Sciences; Health Information Management/Technology.

Award: Scholarship for use in freshman, sophomore, junior, senior, or graduate years; renewable. *Number:* 200. *Amount:* $500–$4000.

Eligibility Requirements: Applicant must be enrolled or expecting to enroll full-time at a two-year or four-year institution or university. Applicant must have 2.5 GPA or higher. Available to U.S. citizens.

Application Requirements: Application, essay, financial need analysis, photo, references, transcript. *Deadline:* May 1.

Contact: Janet Carter, Scholarship Coordinator
Congressional Black Caucus Spouses Program
1720 Massachusetts Avenue, NW
Washington, DC 20036
Phone: 202-263-2840
Fax: 202-263-0844
E-mail: jcarter@cbcfinc.org

GREATER KANAWHA VALLEY FOUNDATION http://www.tgkvf.org

WILLARD H. ERWIN JR. MEMORIAL SCHOLARSHIP FUND

• *See page 142*

HEALTHCARE INFORMATION AND MANAGEMENT SYSTEMS SOCIETY FOUNDATION http://www.himss.org

HIMSS FOUNDATION SCHOLARSHIP PROGRAM

One-time award available to undergraduate (junior level or higher), Management Engineering student (junior level or higher), graduate, or PhD candidate. Given for academic excellence and the potential for future leadership in the health care information and management systems industry. Must be full-time student and a member of HIMSS.

Academic Fields/Career Goals: Health Administration; Health and Medical Sciences; Health Information Management/Technology; Science, Technology, and Society.

Award: Scholarship for use in junior, senior, graduate, or postgraduate years; renewable. *Number:* 3–5. *Amount:* $5000.

Eligibility Requirements: Applicant must be enrolled or expecting to enroll full-time at a two-year or four-year institution or university. Applicant or parent of applicant must be member of Healthcare Information and Management Systems Society. Available to U.S. and non-U.S. citizens.

Application Requirements: Application, autobiography, essay, photo, resume, references, transcript. *Deadline:* October 1.

Contact: Betty Sanders, Member Relations Coordinator
Healthcare Information and Management Systems Society Foundation
230 East Ohio, Suite 500
Chicago, IL 60611
Phone: 312-915-9269
Fax: 312-664-6143
E-mail: bsanders@himss.org

HEALTH RESEARCH COUNCIL OF NEW ZEALAND http://www.hrc.govt.nz

PACIFIC HEALTH WORKFORCE AWARD

Intended to support students studying towards a health or health-related qualification. The eligible courses of study are: health, health administration, or a recognized qualification aligned with the Pacific Island. Priority given to management training, medical, and nursing students. Applicants should be New Zealand citizens or hold residency in New Zealand at the time of application and be of Pacific Island descent. The value of the awards and dollar value will vary and for one year of study.

Academic Fields/Career Goals: Health Administration; Health and Medical Sciences; Health Information Management/Technology; Nursing.

Award: Scholarship for use in freshman, sophomore, junior, senior, graduate, or postgraduate years; not renewable. *Number:* varies. *Amount:* varies.

Eligibility Requirements: Applicant must be New Zealander citizen; Asian/Pacific Islander and enrolled or expecting to enroll full-time at a two-year or four-year institution or university. Available to citizens of countries other than the U.S. or Canada.

Application Requirements: Application, autobiography, essay, financial need analysis, references, transcript. *Deadline:* October 10.

Contact: Ngamau Wichman Tou, Manger, Pacific Health Research
Health Research Council of New Zealand
Wellesley Street
PO Box 5541
Auckland 1036
New Zealand
Phone: 64 9 3035255
Fax: 64 9 377 9988
E-mail: nwichmantou@hrc.govt.nz

PACIFIC MENTAL HEALTH WORK FORCE AWARD

Intended to provide one year of support for students studying towards a mental health or mental health-related qualification. Eligible courses of study include: nursing, psychology, health, health administration or a recognized qualification aligned with the Pacific Island mental health priority areas. Applicants should be New Zealand citizens or hold residency in New Zealand at the time of application and be of Pacific Island descent.

Academic Fields/Career Goals: Health Administration; Health and Medical Sciences; Health Information Management/Technology; Nursing; Psychology.

Award: Scholarship for use in freshman, sophomore, junior, senior, graduate, or postgraduate years; not renewable. *Number:* varies. *Amount:* varies.

Eligibility Requirements: Applicant must be New Zealander citizen; Asian/Pacific Islander and enrolled or expecting to enroll full-time at a two-year or four-year institution or university. Available to citizens of countries other than the U.S. or Canada.

Application Requirements: Application, essay, financial need analysis, resume, references, transcript. *Deadline:* October 10.

Contact: Ngamau Wichman Tou, Manger, Pacific Health Research
Health Research Council of New Zealand
Wellesley Street
PO Box 5541
Auckland 1036
New Zealand
Phone: 64 9 3035255
Fax: 64 9 377 9988
E-mail: nwichmantou@hrc.govt.nz

INDIANA HEALTH CARE FOUNDATION http://www.ihca.org

WILLIAM SENTENEY MEMORIAL SCHOLARSHIP FOR HEALTH FACILITY ADMINISTRATORS

Scholarships available for health facility administrators who are registered for the IHCA Health Facility Administrators course.

Academic Fields/Career Goals: Health Administration.

Award: Scholarship for use in freshman or sophomore years; not renewable. *Number:* 1. *Amount:* $750–$1000.

Eligibility Requirements: Applicant must be enrolled or expecting to enroll full- or part-time at a two-year or four-year or technical institution or university and resident of Indiana. Available to U.S. citizens.

Application Requirements: Application, essay, interview, references, transcript. *Deadline:* March 3.

Contact: Dorothy Henry, Executive Director
Indiana Health Care Foundation
One North Capitol, Suite 1115
Indianapolis, IN 46204
Phone: 317-636-6406
Fax: 877-561-3757
E-mail: dhenry@ihca.org

INDIAN HEALTH SERVICES, UNITED STATES DEPARTMENT OF HEALTH AND HUMAN SERVICES http://www.ihs.gov

HEALTH PROFESSIONS PREPARATORY SCHOLARSHIP PROGRAM

Renewable scholarship for undergraduate, graduate, or doctoral study in programs related to health professions and allied health professions. Minimum 2.0 GPA required. The dollar amount and number of awards varies annually.

Academic Fields/Career Goals: Health Administration; Health and Medical Sciences; Nursing; Pharmacy; Public Health.

Award: Scholarship for use in sophomore, junior, senior, or graduate years; renewable. *Number:* varies. *Amount:* varies.

Eligibility Requirements: Applicant must be American Indian/Alaska Native and enrolled or expecting to enroll full- or part-time at a two-year or four-year or technical institution or university. Available to U.S. citizens.

Application Requirements: Application, applicant must enter a contest, essay, references, transcript, proof of descent. *Deadline:* February 28.

Contact: Dawn Kelly, Branch Chief
Indian Health Services, United States Department of Health and Human Services
801 Thompson Avenue, Suite 120
Rockville, MD 20852
Phone: 301-443-6197
Fax: 301-443-6048
E-mail: dawn.kelly@ihs.gov

INDIAN HEALTH SERVICE HEALTH PROFESSIONS SCHOLARSHIP PROGRAM

Renewable scholarship for Native American students who are enrolled either part- or full-time in undergraduate programs relating to health professions or allied health professions. Minimum 2.0 GPA required. Service obligations are incurred upon acceptance of scholarship funding. Number of awards and the dollar value varies.

Academic Fields/Career Goals: Health Administration; Health and Medical Sciences; Nursing; Therapy/Rehabilitation.

Award: Scholarship for use in freshman, sophomore, junior, or senior years; renewable. *Number:* varies. *Amount:* varies.

Eligibility Requirements: Applicant must be American Indian/Alaska Native and enrolled or expecting to enroll full- or part-time at a two-year or four-year or technical institution or university. Available to U.S. citizens.

Application Requirements: Application, applicant must enter a contest, essay, references, transcript, proof of descent. *Deadline:* February 28.

Contact: Dawn Kelly, Branch Chief
Indian Health Services, United States Department of Health and Human Services
801 Thompson Avenue, Suite 120
Rockville, MD 20852
Phone: 301-443-6197
Fax: 301-443-6048
E-mail: dawn.kelly@ihs.gov

MINNESOTA COMMUNITY FOUNDATION http://www.mncommunityfoundation.org

TWO FEATHERS ENDOWMENT HEALTH INITIATIVE SCHOLARSHIP

Scholarship for students enrolled in a health-related field of study and intend to practice in Minnesota. Must be a Minnesota resident or have significant ties to a Minnesota Tribe.

Academic Fields/Career Goals: Health Administration.

Award: Scholarship for use in freshman, sophomore, junior, or senior years; not renewable. *Number:* varies. *Amount:* up to $5000.

Eligibility Requirements: Applicant must be enrolled or expecting to enroll full- or part-time at a four-year institution or university and resident of Minnesota. Available to U.S. citizens.

Application Requirements: Application, essay, resume, references. *Deadline:* July 1.

Contact: Dayonna Knutson, Program Assistant
Phone: 651-325-4252
E-mail: dlk@mncommunityfoundation.org

NATIONAL SOCIETY OF THE COLONIAL DAMES OF AMERICA http://www.nscda.org

AMERICAN INDIAN NURSE SCHOLARSHIP AWARDS

Renewable award of $500 to $1000. Currently able to fund between 10 and 15 students. Intended originally to benefit females only, the program has expanded to include males and the career goals now include not only nursing careers, but jobs in health care and health education, as well.

Academic Fields/Career Goals: Health Administration; Nursing.

Award: Scholarship for use in freshman, sophomore, junior, senior, graduate, or postgraduate years; renewable. *Number:* 10–15. *Amount:* $500–$1000.

Eligibility Requirements: Applicant must be American Indian/Alaska Native and enrolled or expecting to enroll full-time at a two-year or four-year or technical institution or university. Applicant must have 2.5 GPA or higher. Available to U.S. citizens.

Application Requirements: Application, autobiography, financial need analysis, photo, references, transcript. *Deadline:* continuous.

Contact: Mrs. Joe Calvin, Scholarship Awards Consultant
National Society of The Colonial Dames of America
Nine Cross Creek Drive
Birmingham, AL 35213
Phone: 205-871-4072
E-mail: info@nscda.org

NORTH CAROLINA STATE EDUCATION ASSISTANCE AUTHORITY http://www.ncseaa.edu

NORTH CAROLINA STUDENT LOAN PROGRAM FOR HEALTH, SCIENCE, AND MATHEMATICS

• *See page 213*

RESOURCE CENTER

MARIE BLAHA MEDICAL GRANT

• *See page 83*

HEALTH AND MEDICAL SCIENCES

ALBERTA HERITAGE SCHOLARSHIP FUND/ ALBERTA SCHOLARSHIP PROGRAMS http://www.alis.gov.ab.ca

ALBERTA HERITAGE SCHOLARSHIP FUND ABORIGINAL HEALTH CAREERS BURSARY

• *See page 129*

JASON LANG SCHOLARSHIP

• *See page 206*

NORTHERN ALBERTA DEVELOPMENT COUNCIL BURSARY FOR MEDICAL STUDENTS

Award to increase the number of trained professionals in Northern Alberta and to encourage students from Northern Alberta to obtain a postsecondary education. Must be residents of Alberta and enrolled in a medical program. Applicants must not be in default of a provincial student loan. Bursaries are valued at $5000 and available for four years of medical school. Students must live and work for one year in Northern Alberta. For details visit Web site: http://www.alis.gov.ab.ca.

Academic Fields/Career Goals: Health and Medical Sciences.

Award: Grant for use in freshman, sophomore, junior, or senior years; not renewable. *Number:* 1. *Amount:* $5000.

Eligibility Requirements: Applicant must be enrolled or expecting to enroll full-time at a two-year or four-year or technical institution or university; resident of Alberta and studying in Alberta. Available to Canadian citizens.

Application Requirements: Application, essay. *Deadline:* June 1.

Contact: Scholarship Committee
Alberta Heritage Scholarship Fund/Alberta Scholarship Programs
9940 106th Street, Fourth Floor, Sterling Place
PO Box 28000, Station Main
Edmonton, AB T5J 4R4
Canada
Phone: 780-427-8640
Fax: 780-427-1288
E-mail: scholarships@gov.ab.ca

ALPENA REGIONAL MEDICAL CENTER http://www.alpenaregionalmedicalcenter.org

THELMA ORR MEMORIAL SCHOLARSHIP

Two $1500 scholarships for students pursuing a course of study related to human medicine at any state accredited Michigan college or university.

Academic Fields/Career Goals: Health and Medical Sciences.

Award: Scholarship for use in freshman, sophomore, junior, or senior years; not renewable. *Number:* 2. *Amount:* $1500.

Eligibility Requirements: Applicant must be enrolled or expecting to enroll full-time at a four-year institution or university; resident of Michigan and studying in Michigan. Available to U.S. citizens.

Application Requirements: Application. *Deadline:* April 15.

Contact: Marlene Pear, Director, Voluntary Services
Alpena Regional Medical Center
1501 West Chisholm Street
Alpena, MI 49707
Phone: 989-356-7351
E-mail: info@agh.org

ALPHA OMEGA ALPHA http://www.alphaomegaalpha.org

HELEN H. GLASER STUDENT ESSAY AWARDS

Award of $2000 first, $750 second, $500 third, and up to three honorable mention awards of $250 each. Authors must be enrolled at medical schools with active Alpha Omega Alpha chapters.

Academic Fields/Career Goals: Health and Medical Sciences.

Award: Prize for use in freshman, sophomore, junior, or senior years; not renewable. *Number:* varies. *Amount:* $250–$2000.

Eligibility Requirements: Applicant must be enrolled or expecting to enroll full-time at a two-year or four-year or technical institution or university. Available to U.S. and non-U.S. citizens.

Application Requirements: Application, applicant must enter a contest, essay. *Deadline:* January 31.

Contact: Debbie Lancaster, Managing Editor
Alpha Omega Alpha
525 Middlefield Road, Suite 130
Menlo Park, CA 94025
Phone: 650-329-0291
Fax: 650-329-1618
E-mail: d.lancaster@alphaomegaalpha.org

PHAROS POETRY COMPETITION

Awards of $100 to $500 to encourage medical students to write poetry on medical subjects and to recognize and reward excellent and thoughtful compositions. Students must be enrolled at medical schools with active Alpha Omega Alpha chapters, but need not be members.

Academic Fields/Career Goals: Health and Medical Sciences.

Award: Prize for use in freshman, sophomore, junior, or senior years; not renewable. *Number:* 3. *Amount:* $100–$500.

Eligibility Requirements: Applicant must be enrolled or expecting to enroll full- or part-time at a two-year or four-year or technical institution or university and must have an interest in writing. Available to U.S. and non-U.S. citizens.

Application Requirements: Application, applicant must enter a contest, essay. *Deadline:* January 31.

Contact: Debbie Lancaster, Managing Editor
Alpha Omega Alpha
525 Middlefield Road, Suite 130
Menlo Park, CA 94025
Phone: 650-329-0291
E-mail: d.lancaster@alphaomegaalpha.org

AMERICAN INDIAN SCIENCE AND ENGINEERING SOCIETY http://www.aises.org

A.T. ANDERSON MEMORIAL SCHOLARSHIP PROGRAM

• *See page 84*

AMERICAN LEGION AUXILIARY DEPARTMENT OF ARIZONA http://www.azlegion.org/majorp~2.htm

AMERICAN LEGION AUXILIARY DEPARTMENT OF ARIZONA HEALTH CARE OCCUPATION SCHOLARSHIPS

Award for Arizona residents enrolled at an institution in Arizona that awards degree or certificate in health occupations. Preference given to an immediate family member of a veteran. Must be a U.S. citizen and Arizona resident for at least one year.

Academic Fields/Career Goals: Health and Medical Sciences.

Award: Scholarship for use in freshman, sophomore, junior, or senior years; not renewable. *Number:* up to 4. *Amount:* $400.

Eligibility Requirements: Applicant must be enrolled or expecting to enroll full- or part-time at a two-year or four-year institution or university; resident of Arizona and studying in Arizona. Available to U.S. citizens.

Application Requirements: Application, autobiography, essay, financial need analysis, photo, references, test scores, transcript. *Deadline:* May 15.

Contact: Department Secretary and Treasurer
American Legion Auxiliary Department of Arizona
4701 North 19th Avenue, Suite 100
Phoenix, AZ 85015-3727
Phone: 602-241-1080
Fax: 602-604-9640
E-mail: amlegauxaz@mcleodusa.net

AMERICAN LEGION AUXILIARY DEPARTMENT OF MAINE http://www.mainelegion.org

AMERICAN LEGION AUXILIARY DEPARTMENT OF MAINE PAST PRESIDENTS' PARLEY NURSES SCHOLARSHIP

One-time award for child, grandchild, sister, or brother of veteran. Must be resident of Maine and wishing to continue education at accredited school in medical field. Must submit photo, doctor's statement, and evidence of civic activity. Minimum 3.5 GPA required.

Academic Fields/Career Goals: Health and Medical Sciences; Nursing.

Award: Scholarship for use in freshman, sophomore, junior, or senior years; not renewable. *Number:* 1. *Amount:* $300.

Eligibility Requirements: Applicant must be age 18 and over; enrolled or expecting to enroll full-time at a two-year or four-year or technical institution or university and resident of Maine. Applicant or parent of applicant must have employment or volunteer experience in community service. Applicant must have 3.5 GPA or higher. Available to U.S. citizens. Applicant or parent must meet one or more of the following requirements: general military experience; retired from active duty; disabled or killed as a result of military service; prisoner of war; or missing in action.

Application Requirements: Application, photo, references, transcript, doctor's statement. *Deadline:* March 31.

Contact: Mary Wells, Education Chairman
American Legion Auxiliary Department of Maine
21 Limerock Street
PO Box 434
Rockland, ME 04841
Phone: 207-532-6007
E-mail: aladeptsecme@verizon.net

AMERICAN LEGION AUXILIARY DEPARTMENT OF MICHIGAN http://www.michalaux.org

AMERICAN LEGION AUXILIARY DEPARTMENT OF MICHIGAN MEDICAL CAREER SCHOLARSHIP

Award for training in Michigan as registered nurse, licensed practical nurse, physical therapist, respiratory therapist, or in any medical career. Must be child, grandchild, great-grandchild, wife, or widow of honorably discharged or deceased veteran who has served during the eligibility dates for American Legion membership. Must be Michigan resident attending a Michigan school.

Academic Fields/Career Goals: Health and Medical Sciences; Nursing; Therapy/Rehabilitation.

Award: Scholarship for use in freshman year; not renewable. *Number:* 5–20. *Amount:* up to $500.

Eligibility Requirements: Applicant must be high school student; planning to enroll or expecting to enroll full-time at a two-year or four-year or technical institution or university; resident of Michigan and studying in Michigan. Applicant must have 3.5 GPA or higher. Available to U.S. citizens. Applicant or parent must meet one or more of the following requirements: general military experience; retired from active duty; disabled or killed as a result of military service; prisoner of war; or missing in action.

Application Requirements: Application, financial need analysis, references, test scores, transcript, veteran's discharge papers, copy of pages 1 and 2 of federal income tax return. *Deadline:* April 1.

Contact: Ms. Priscilla Kelsey, Chairman
American Legion Auxiliary Department of Michigan
212 North Verlinden Avenue
Lansing, MI 48915
Phone: 517-371-4720 Ext. 19
Fax: 517-371-2401
E-mail: michalaux@voyager.net

AMERICAN LEGION AUXILIARY DEPARTMENT OF MINNESOTA http://www.mnlegion.org

AMERICAN LEGION AUXILIARY DEPARTMENT OF MINNESOTA PAST PRESIDENTS' PARLEY HEALTH CARE SCHOLARSHIP

One-time $1000 award for American Legion Auxiliary Department of Minnesota member for at least three years who is needy and deserving, to begin or continue education in any phase of the health care field. Must be a Minnesota resident, attend a vocational or postsecondary institution and maintain at least a C average in school.

Academic Fields/Career Goals: Health and Medical Sciences.

Award: Scholarship for use in freshman, sophomore, junior, or senior years; not renewable. *Number:* 1–10. *Amount:* $1000.

Eligibility Requirements: Applicant must be enrolled or expecting to enroll full-time at a two-year or four-year or technical institution or university; resident of Minnesota and studying in Minnesota. Applicant or parent of applicant must be member of American Legion or Auxiliary. Available to U.S. citizens.

Application Requirements: Application, financial need analysis. *Deadline:* March 15.

Contact: Eleanor Johnson, Executive Secretary
American Legion Auxiliary Department of Minnesota
State Veterans Service Building, 20 West 12th Street, Room 314
St. Paul, MN 55155
Phone: 651-224-7634
Fax: 651-224-5243

AMERICAN LEGION AUXILIARY DEPARTMENT OF TEXAS http://www.alatexas.org

AMERICAN LEGION AUXILIARY DEPARTMENT OF TEXAS PAST PRESIDENTS' PARLEY MEDICAL SCHOLARSHIP

Scholarships available for full-time students pursuing studies in human health care. Must be a resident of Texas. Must be a veteran or child, grandchild, great grandchild of a veteran who served in the Armed Forces during period of eligibility.

Academic Fields/Career Goals: Health and Medical Sciences.

Award: Scholarship for use in freshman, sophomore, junior, senior, graduate, or postgraduate years; not renewable. *Number:* varies. *Amount:* $500.

Eligibility Requirements: Applicant must be enrolled or expecting to enroll full-time at a two-year or four-year or technical institution or university and resident of Texas. Available to U.S. citizens. Applicant or parent must meet one or more of the following requirements: general military experience; retired from active duty; disabled or killed as a result of military service; prisoner of war; or missing in action.

Application Requirements: Application, financial need analysis, photo, references, self-addressed stamped envelope, transcript, letter stating qualifications and intentions. *Deadline:* May 1.

Contact: Paula Raney, Department Secretary
American Legion Auxiliary Department of Texas
PO Box 140407
Austin, TX 78714-0407
Phone: 512-476-7278
Fax: 512-482-8391
E-mail: alatexas@txlegion.org

AMERICAN LEGION AUXILIARY DEPARTMENT OF WYOMING

AMERICAN LEGION AUXILIARY DEPARTMENT OF WYOMING PAST PRESIDENTS' PARLEY HEALTH CARE SCHOLARSHIP

• *See page 210*

AMERICAN MEDICAL ASSOCIATION FOUNDATION http://www.amafoundation.org

AMA FOUNDATION PHYSICIANS OF TOMORROW SCHOLARSHIP

An annual scholarship of $10,000 will be awarded to current third-year medical students who are entering their fourth year of study. Based on academic excellence and/or financial need. Awards four scholarships. Each medical school may submit one nomination for each of these scholarship opportunities.

Academic Fields/Career Goals: Health and Medical Sciences.

Award: Scholarship for use in senior or graduate years; not renewable. *Number:* 1–7. *Amount:* $10,000.

Eligibility Requirements: Applicant must be enrolled or expecting to enroll full-time at an institution or university. Available to U.S. citizens.

American Medical Association Foundation (continued)

Application Requirements: Application, financial need analysis, references. *Deadline:* May 30.

Contact: Dina Lindenberg, Scholarship Coordinator
American Medical Association Foundation
515 North State Street
Chicago, IL 60610
Phone: 312-464-4193
Fax: 312-464-4142
E-mail: dina.lindenberg@ama-assn.org

JOHNSON F. HAMMOND, MD MEMORIAL SCHOLARSHIP

An annual scholarship of $10,000 will be awarded to a medical student of high moral character and outstanding achievement with demonstrated interest and involvement in medical journalism. Must submit letter of nomination from the office of the dean.

Academic Fields/Career Goals: Health and Medical Sciences; Journalism.

Award: Scholarship for use in junior, senior, graduate, or postgraduate years; not renewable. *Number:* 1. *Amount:* $10,000.

Eligibility Requirements: Applicant must be enrolled or expecting to enroll full-time at an institution or university. Available to U.S. citizens.

Application Requirements: Autobiography, financial need analysis, portfolio, resume, references, letter of nomination from dean. *Deadline:* May 31.

Contact: Kathleen MacArthur, Executive Director
American Medical Association Foundation
515 North State Street
Chicago, IL 60610
Phone: 312-464-5852
Fax: 312-464-4142
E-mail: scholarships@ama-assn.org

ROCK SLEYSTER MEMORIAL SCHOLARSHIP

Award available to school-nominated college seniors studying medicine, who aspire to specialize in psychiatry. Must be enrolled at an accredited U.S. or Canadian school that grants the MD. Minimum 3.0 GPA required. Must be U.S. citizen.

Academic Fields/Career Goals: Health and Medical Sciences.

Award: Scholarship for use in senior or graduate years; not renewable. *Number:* 1. *Amount:* $10,000.

Eligibility Requirements: Applicant must be enrolled or expecting to enroll full-time at an institution or university. Applicant must have 3.0 GPA or higher. Available to U.S. citizens.

Application Requirements: Application, autobiography, essay, financial need analysis, references, transcript. *Deadline:* May 31.

Contact: Director of Financial Aid
American Medical Association Foundation
515 North State Street
Chicago, IL 60610
Phone: 312-464-4200
Fax: 312-464-4142
E-mail: financialaid@siumed.edu

AMERICAN MEDICAL TECHNOLOGISTS http://www.amt1.com

AMERICAN MEDICAL TECHNOLOGISTS STUDENT SCHOLARSHIP

• *See page 210*

AMERICAN OCCUPATIONAL THERAPY FOUNDATION INC. http://www.aotf.org

AMERICAN OCCUPATIONAL THERAPY FOUNDATION STATE ASSOCIATION SCHOLARSHIPS

Awards offered at the state association level by the foundation, for study leading to associate, baccalaureate and graduate degrees in occupational therapy. Must be an association member. Requirements vary by state. See Web site at http://www.aotf.org for further details.

Academic Fields/Career Goals: Health and Medical Sciences; Therapy/Rehabilitation.

Award: Scholarship for use in freshman, sophomore, junior, senior, or graduate years; not renewable. *Number:* varies. *Amount:* $150–$5000.

Eligibility Requirements: Applicant must be enrolled or expecting to enroll full-time at a two-year or four-year institution or university. Applicant or parent of applicant must be member of American Occupational Therapy Association. Available to U.S. citizens.

Application Requirements: Application, essay, financial need analysis, references, transcript, curriculum director's statement. *Deadline:* March 1.

Contact: Charles Christiansen, Executive Director
American Occupational Therapy Foundation Inc.
4720 Montgomery Lane
PO Box 31220
Bethesda, MD 20824-1220
Phone: 301-652-6611 Ext. 2551
Fax: 301-656-3620
E-mail: aotf@aotf.org

CARLOTTA WELLES SCHOLARSHIP

Award for study leading to an occupational therapy associate degree at an accredited institution. Must be a member of the association.

Academic Fields/Career Goals: Health and Medical Sciences; Therapy/Rehabilitation.

Award: Scholarship for use in sophomore year; not renewable. *Number:* varies. *Amount:* $500.

Eligibility Requirements: Applicant must be enrolled or expecting to enroll full-time at a two-year institution. Applicant or parent of applicant must be member of American Occupational Therapy Association. Available to U.S. citizens.

Application Requirements: Application, essay, financial need analysis, references, transcript, curriculum director's statement. *Deadline:* March 1.

Contact: Charles Christiansen, Executive Director
American Occupational Therapy Foundation Inc.
4720 Montgomery Lane
PO Box 31220
Bethesda, MD 20824-1220
Phone: 301-652-6611 Ext. 2551
Fax: 301-656-3620
E-mail: aotf@aotf.org

FLORENCE WOOD/ARKANSAS OCCUPATIONAL THERAPY ASSOCIATION SCHOLARSHIP

One scholarship of $500 awarded to an Arkansas resident enrolled in an accredited occupational therapy educational program in Arkansas.

Academic Fields/Career Goals: Health and Medical Sciences; Therapy/Rehabilitation.

Award: Scholarship for use in junior, senior, or graduate years; not renewable. *Number:* 1. *Amount:* $500.

Eligibility Requirements: Applicant must be enrolled or expecting to enroll full-time at a four-year institution or university; resident of Arkansas and studying in Arkansas. Available to U.S. citizens.

Application Requirements: Application, essay, financial need analysis, references, transcript, curriculum director's statement. *Deadline:* March 1.

Contact: Charles Christiansen, Executive Director
American Occupational Therapy Foundation Inc.
4720 Montgomery Lane
PO Box 31220
Bethesda, MD 20824-1220
Phone: 301-652-6611 Ext. 2551
Fax: 301-656-3620
E-mail: aotf@aotf.org

KAPPA DELTA PHI SCHOLARSHIP FOR OCCUPATIONAL THERAPY ASSISTANT

Award for study leading to an occupational therapy assistant degree at an accredited institution. Must be a member of the association.

Academic Fields/Career Goals: Health and Medical Sciences; Therapy/Rehabilitation.

Award: Scholarship for use in sophomore year; not renewable. *Number:* 2. *Amount:* $2000.

Eligibility Requirements: Applicant must be enrolled or expecting to enroll full-time at a two-year institution. Applicant or parent of applicant must be member of American Occupational Therapy Association. Available to U.S. citizens.

Application Requirements: Application, essay, financial need analysis, references, transcript, curriculum director's statement. *Deadline:* February 8.

Contact: Charles Christiansen, Executive Director
American Occupational Therapy Foundation Inc.
4720 Montgomery Lane
PO Box 31220
Bethesda, MD 20824-1220
Phone: 301-652-6611 Ext. 2551
Fax: 301-656-3620
E-mail: aotf@aotf.org

AMERICAN PHYSICAL THERAPY ASSOCIATION http://www.apta.org

MINORITY SCHOLARSHIP AWARD FOR ACADEMIC EXCELLENCE IN PHYSICAL THERAPY

Scholarships available to minority students enrolled in the final year of an accredited physical therapy program. Information is available on Web site: http://www.apta.org.

Academic Fields/Career Goals: Health and Medical Sciences.

Award: Scholarship for use in senior year; not renewable. *Number:* 8–10. *Amount:* $5000–$6000.

Eligibility Requirements: Applicant must be American Indian/Alaska Native, Asian/Pacific Islander, Black (non-Hispanic), or Hispanic and enrolled or expecting to enroll full-time at a four-year institution or university. Available to U.S. citizens.

Application Requirements: Application, essay, resume, references, transcript. *Deadline:* December 1.

Contact: Eva Jones, Assistant to the Director
American Physical Therapy Association
1111 North Fairfax Street
Alexandria, VA 22314-1488
Phone: 800-999-2782 Ext. 3144
Fax: 703-684-7343
E-mail: evajones@apta.org

MINORITY SCHOLARSHIP AWARD FOR ACADEMIC EXCELLENCE-PHYSICAL THERAPIST ASSISTANT

Scholarships available for minority students enrolled in the final year of an accredited physical therapist assistant program. Information and application is available on Web site: http://www.apta.org.

Academic Fields/Career Goals: Health and Medical Sciences; Therapy/Rehabilitation.

Award: Scholarship for use in senior year; not renewable. *Number:* 1. *Amount:* $2000–$2500.

Eligibility Requirements: Applicant must be American Indian/Alaska Native, Asian/Pacific Islander, Black (non-Hispanic), or Hispanic and enrolled or expecting to enroll full-time at a four-year institution or university. Available to U.S. citizens.

Application Requirements: Application, essay, resume, references, transcript. *Deadline:* December 1.

Contact: Eva Jones, Assistant to the Director
American Physical Therapy Association
1111 North Fairfax Street
Alexandria, VA 22314-1488
Phone: 800-999-2782 Ext. 3144
Fax: 703-684-7343
E-mail: evajones@apta.org

AMERICAN PHYSIOLOGICAL SOCIETY http://www.the-aps.org

DAVID S. BRUCE AWARDS FOR EXCELLENCE IN UNDERGRADUATE RESEARCH

Award available for research in physiology. The student must be enrolled as an undergraduate student at the time of the application and at the time of the EB meeting. The applicant must be the first author on a submitted abstract for the EB meeting and must be working with an APS member who attests that the student is deserving of the first authorship.

Academic Fields/Career Goals: Health and Medical Sciences.

Award: Prize for use in freshman, sophomore, junior, or senior years; not renewable. *Number:* 6–10. *Amount:* up to $500.

Eligibility Requirements: Applicant must be enrolled or expecting to enroll full-time at a four-year institution or university. Available to U.S. and non-U.S. citizens.

Application Requirements: Application, essay, references, first author abstract. *Deadline:* January 12.

Contact: Melinda Lowy, Education Office
American Physiological Society
9650 Rockville Pike
Bethesda, MD 20814
Phone: 301-634-7098
E-mail: mlowy@the-aps.org

AMERICAN RESPIRATORY CARE FOUNDATION http://www.arcfoundation.org

JIMMY A. YOUNG MEMORIAL EDUCATION RECOGNITION AWARD

Award available to students studying respiratory care at an American Medical Association-approved institution. Preference given to minority students. Must submit letters of recommendation and a paper on a respiratory care topic. Must have a minimum 3.0 GPA.

Academic Fields/Career Goals: Health and Medical Sciences; Therapy/Rehabilitation.

Award: Prize for use in freshman, sophomore, junior, or senior years; not renewable. *Number:* 1. *Amount:* up to $1000.

Eligibility Requirements: Applicant must be enrolled or expecting to enroll full- or part-time at a two-year or four-year institution or university. Applicant must have 3.0 GPA or higher. Available to U.S. citizens.

Application Requirements: Application, references, transcript, paper on respiratory care topic. *Deadline:* June 16.

Contact: Jill Nelson, Administrative Coordinator
American Respiratory Care Foundation
9425 North MacArthur Boulevard, Suite 100
Irving, TX 75063-4706
Phone: 972-243-2272
Fax: 972-484-2720
E-mail: info@arcfoundation.org

MORTON B. DUGGAN, JR. MEMORIAL EDUCATION RECOGNITION AWARD

Awards students with a minimum 3.0 GPA, enrolled in an American Medical Association-approved respiratory care program. Must be U.S. citizen or permanent resident. Need proof of college enrollment. Must submit an original referenced paper on respiratory care. Preference given to Georgia and South Carolina residents. One-time merit-based award of up to $1000, and includes airfare, registration to AARC Congress, and one night's lodging.

Academic Fields/Career Goals: Health and Medical Sciences; Therapy/Rehabilitation.

Award: Scholarship for use in freshman, sophomore, junior, or senior years; not renewable. *Number:* 1. *Amount:* up to $1000.

Eligibility Requirements: Applicant must be enrolled or expecting to enroll full- or part-time at a two-year or four-year institution or university. Applicant must have 3.0 GPA or higher. Available to U.S. citizens.

Application Requirements: Application, references, transcript, paper on respiratory care. *Deadline:* June 16.

Contact: Jill Nelson, Administrative Coordinator
American Respiratory Care Foundation
9425 North MacArthur Boulevard, Suite 100
Irving, TX 75063-4706
Phone: 972-243-2272
Fax: 972-484-2720
E-mail: info@arcfoundation.org

NBRC/AMP ROBERT M. LAWRENCE, MD EDUCATION RECOGNITION AWARD

Merit-based award to a third- or fourth-year student with a minimum 3.0 GPA, enrolled in an accredited undergraduate respiratory therapy program leading to a baccalaureate degree.

American Respiratory Care Foundation (continued)

Academic Fields/Career Goals: Health and Medical Sciences; Therapy/Rehabilitation.

Award: Scholarship for use in junior or senior years; not renewable. *Number:* 1. *Amount:* up to $2500.

Eligibility Requirements: Applicant must be enrolled or expecting to enroll full- or part-time at a four-year institution or university. Applicant must have 3.0 GPA or higher. Available to U.S. and non-U.S. citizens.

Application Requirements: Application, references, transcript, paper on respiratory care. *Deadline:* June 16.

Contact: Jill Nelson, Administrative Coordinator
American Respiratory Care Foundation
9425 North MacArthur Boulevard, Suite 100
Irving, TX 75063-4706
Phone: 972-243-2272
Fax: 972-484-2720
E-mail: info@arcfoundation.org

NBRC/AMP WILLIAM W. BURGIN, MD EDUCATION RECOGNITION AWARD

Merit-based award for second-year students enrolled in an accredited respiratory therapy program leading to an associate degree. Minimum GPA of 3.0 required. For more information visit Web site: http://www.arcfoundation.org/awards/undergraduate/burgin.cfm.

Academic Fields/Career Goals: Health and Medical Sciences; Therapy/Rehabilitation.

Award: Prize for use in sophomore year; not renewable. *Number:* 1. *Amount:* up to $2500.

Eligibility Requirements: Applicant must be enrolled or expecting to enroll full- or part-time at a two-year institution. Applicant must have 3.0 GPA or higher. Available to U.S. and non-U.S. citizens.

Application Requirements: Application, references, transcript, paper on respiratory care. *Deadline:* June 16.

Contact: Jill Nelson, Administrative Coordinator
American Respiratory Care Foundation
9425 North MacArthur Boulevard, Suite 100
Irving, TX 75063-4706
Phone: 972-243-2272
Fax: 972-484-2720
E-mail: info@arcfoundation.org

SEPRACOR ACHIEVEMENT AWARD FOR EXCELLENCE IN PULMONARY DISEASE STATE MANAGEMENT

Nominations may be made by anyone by submitting a paper of not more than 1000 words describing why a nominee should be considered for the award. Must be a member of the American Association for Respiratory Care. Must be a respiratory therapist or other healthcare professional, including physician. Nominees must have demonstrated the attainment of positive healthcare outcomes as a direct result of their disease-oriented practice of respiratory care, regardless of care setting.

Academic Fields/Career Goals: Health and Medical Sciences; Therapy/Rehabilitation.

Award: Prize for use in freshman, sophomore, junior, senior, graduate, or postgraduate years; not renewable. *Number:* 1. *Amount:* up to $2500.

Eligibility Requirements: Applicant must be enrolled or expecting to enroll full- or part-time at a four-year institution or university. Applicant or parent of applicant must have employment or volunteer experience in physical therapy/rehabilitation. Available to U.S. and non-U.S. citizens.

Application Requirements: Resume, references, paper describing why a nominee should be considered for the award. *Deadline:* June 1.

Contact: Jill Nelson, Administrative Coordinator
American Respiratory Care Foundation
9425 North MacArthur Boulevard, Suite 100
Irving, TX 75063-4706
Phone: 972-243-2272
Fax: 972-484-2720
E-mail: info@arcfoundation.org

AMERICAN SOCIETY FOR CLINICAL LABORATORY SCIENCE http://www.ascls.org

ASCLS FORUM FOR CONCERNS OF MINORITIES SCHOLARSHIP

Two scholarships awarded to a CLS/MT and a CLS/MLT student, if eligible applicants from both groups apply. Applicant must be a minority student accepted in an NAACLS accredited clinical laboratory science/medical technology or medical laboratory technician program. Must demonstrate financial need.

Academic Fields/Career Goals: Health and Medical Sciences.

Award: Scholarship for use in freshman, sophomore, junior, or senior years; not renewable. *Number:* 2. *Amount:* varies.

Eligibility Requirements: Applicant must be American Indian/Alaska Native, Asian/Pacific Islander, Black (non-Hispanic), or Hispanic and enrolled or expecting to enroll full- or part-time at a two-year or four-year or technical institution or university. Available to U.S. and non-U.S. citizens.

Application Requirements: Application, financial need analysis, references. *Deadline:* April 1.

Contact: Mildred K. Fuller, Chair, Allied Health Department
American Society for Clinical Laboratory Science
Norfolk State University, 700 Park Avenue
Norfolk, VA 23504
Phone: 757-823-2366
E-mail: mkfuller@nsu.edu

ASCLS REGION II VIRGINIA SOCIETY FOR CLINICAL LABORATORY SCIENCE SCHOLARSHIPS

One $1000 scholarship available to a clinical laboratory student. Applicant must be in their final clinical year in an accredited cytology or histology program. Must attend program within the Commonwealth of Virginia, have a minimum of 2.0 GPA and demonstrate financial need.

Academic Fields/Career Goals: Health and Medical Sciences.

Award: Scholarship for use in senior year; not renewable. *Number:* 1. *Amount:* $1000.

Eligibility Requirements: Applicant must be enrolled or expecting to enroll full- or part-time at a two-year or four-year or technical institution or university; resident of Virginia and studying in Virginia. Available to U.S. citizens.

Application Requirements: Application, financial need analysis, references, transcript. *Deadline:* December 15.

Contact: Shirley Jenkins, Scholarship Committee Chairperson
American Society for Clinical Laboratory Science
PO Box 135
Hood, VA 22723
E-mail: shirley.jenkins@mjh.org

ASCLS REGION IV OHIO SOCIETY FOR CLINICAL LABORATORY SCIENCE GERALDINE DIEBLER/STELLA GRIFFIN AWARD

One $1000 scholarship for a student enrolled either full-time or part-time in a clinical laboratory science curriculum in the Akron/Canton/Steubenville area in Ohio. Applicant must be a permanent resident of Ohio. Must have minimum 2.5 GPA.

Academic Fields/Career Goals: Health and Medical Sciences.

Award: Scholarship for use in freshman, sophomore, junior, or senior years; not renewable. *Number:* 1. *Amount:* $1000.

Eligibility Requirements: Applicant must be enrolled or expecting to enroll full- or part-time at a two-year or four-year or technical institution or university; resident of Ohio and studying in Ohio. Applicant must have 2.5 GPA or higher. Available to U.S. citizens.

Application Requirements: Application, financial need analysis, references, transcript, personal statement. *Deadline:* March 15.

Contact: Sondra Sutherland, CLT and PBT Program Director
American Society for Clinical Laboratory Science
Jefferson Community College
4000 Sunset Boulevard
Steubenville, OH 43952
Phone: 740-264-5591 Ext. 165
Fax: 740-264-9504
E-mail: ssutherlan@jcc.edu

ASCLS REGION IV OHIO SOCIETY FOR CLINICAL LABORATORY SCIENCE STELLA GRIFFIN MEMORIAL SCHOLARSHIP

One scholarship for a student enrolled either full-time or part-time in a clinical laboratory science program in Ohio. Applicant must be a permanent resident of Ohio with a minimum 2.5 GPA.

Academic Fields/Career Goals: Health and Medical Sciences.

Award: Scholarship for use in freshman, sophomore, junior, or senior years; not renewable. *Number:* 1. *Amount:* $1000.

Eligibility Requirements: Applicant must be enrolled or expecting to enroll full- or part-time at a two-year or four-year or technical institution or university; resident of Ohio and studying in Ohio. Applicant must have 2.5 GPA or higher. Available to U.S. citizens.

Application Requirements: Application, financial need analysis, references, transcript, personal statement. *Deadline:* March 15.

Contact: Sondra Sutherland, CLT and PBT Program Director
American Society for Clinical Laboratory Science
Jefferson Community College, 4000 Sunset Boulevard
Steubenville, OH 43952
Phone: 740-264-5591 Ext. 165
Fax: 740-264-6504
E-mail: ssutherlan@jcc.edu

ASCLS REGION VI MISSOURI ORGANIZATION FOR CLINICAL LABORATORY SCIENCE EDUCATION SCHOLARSHIP

Scholarship provides financial assistance for formal education, research, or continuing education which directly relates to laboratory science. For receiving formal education assistance, applicant must be enrolled in a degree program directly related to laboratory science and have a minimum of one year MoCLS membership if an undergraduate student, and two years MoCLS membership for advanced degree student. Scholarship value varies. Deadline varies.

Academic Fields/Career Goals: Health and Medical Sciences.

Award: Scholarship for use in senior or graduate years; not renewable. *Number:* 1. *Amount:* varies.

Eligibility Requirements: Applicant must be enrolled or expecting to enroll full- or part-time at a two-year or four-year or technical institution or university. Applicant or parent of applicant must be member of American Society for Clinical Laboratory Science. Available to U.S. and non-U.S. citizens.

Application Requirements: Application, financial need analysis, references, transcript, proof of enrollment, personal letter, membership proof, research proposal. *Deadline:* varies.

Contact: Tom Reddig, Missouri Scholarship Fund Chair
American Society for Clinical Laboratory Science
31 West 59th Street
Kansas City, MO 64113
Phone: 816-931-8080
E-mail: treddig@hotmail.com

ASCLS REGION VI MISSOURI ORGANIZATION FOR CLINICAL LABORATORY SCIENCE STUDENT SCHOLARSHIP

Scholarship for clinical laboratory science or medical laboratory technology students, beginning or continuing their formal education, or conducting research that directly relates to laboratory science. Must be resident of Missouri. Scholarship value is $200.

Academic Fields/Career Goals: Health and Medical Sciences.

Award: Scholarship for use in senior or graduate years; not renewable. *Number:* 1. *Amount:* $200.

Eligibility Requirements: Applicant must be enrolled or expecting to enroll full- or part-time at a two-year or four-year or technical institution or university and resident of Missouri. Available to U.S. and non-U.S. citizens.

Application Requirements: Application, references, personal letter, proof of acceptance. *Deadline:* varies.

Contact: Tom Reddig, Missouri Scholarship Fund Chair
American Society for Clinical Laboratory Science
31 West 59th Street
Kansas City, MO 64113
Phone: 816-931-8080
E-mail: treddig@hotmail.com

AMERICAN SOCIETY OF RADIOLOGIC TECHNOLOGISTS EDUCATION AND RESEARCH FOUNDATION

http://www.asrt.org/foundation

ELEKTA RADIATION THERAPY EDUCATORS SCHOLARSHIP

• *See page 223*

HOWARD S. STERN SCHOLARSHIP

Open to ASRT members only who are certificate, undergraduate or graduate students. Must have ARRT registration or unrestricted state license and have worked in radiologic sciences for at least one of the last five years.

Academic Fields/Career Goals: Health and Medical Sciences; Oncology; Radiology.

Award: Scholarship for use in freshman, sophomore, junior, senior, or graduate years; not renewable. *Number:* up to 10. *Amount:* up to $1000.

Eligibility Requirements: Applicant must be enrolled or expecting to enroll full- or part-time at a two-year or four-year or technical institution or university. Applicant or parent of applicant must be member of American Society of Radiologic Technologists. Available to U.S. and non-U.S. citizens.

Application Requirements: Application, essay, financial need analysis, resume, references, copy of unrestricted state license, current ARRT card or equivalent, letter on official letterhead verifying employment in the radiologic sciences for at least one of the past five years. *Deadline:* February 1.

Contact: Phelosha Collaros, Program Manager/Associate Development Officer
American Society of Radiologic Technologists Education and Research Foundation
15000 Central Avenue, SE
Albuquerque, NM 87123-3909
Phone: 505-298-4500 Ext. 2541
Fax: 505-298-5063
E-mail: foundation@asrt.org

JERMAN-CAHOON STUDENT SCHOLARSHIP

Merit scholarship for certificate or undergraduate students. Must have completed at least one semester in the radiological sciences to apply. Financial need is a factor. Requirements include 3.0 GPA, recommendation and 450 to 500-word essay.

Academic Fields/Career Goals: Health and Medical Sciences; Radiology.

Award: Scholarship for use in freshman, sophomore, junior, or senior years; not renewable. *Number:* up to 7. *Amount:* up to $2500.

Eligibility Requirements: Applicant must be enrolled or expecting to enroll full- or part-time at a two-year or four-year or technical institution or university. Applicant must have 3.0 GPA or higher. Available to U.S. citizens.

Application Requirements: Application, essay, financial need analysis, references, transcript. *Deadline:* February 1.

Contact: Phelosha Collaros, Program Manager/Associate Development Officer
American Society of Radiologic Technologists Education and Research Foundation
15000 Central Avenue, SE
Albuquerque, NM 87123-3909
Phone: 505-298-4500 Ext. 2541
Fax: 505-298-5063
E-mail: foundation@asrt.org

MONSTER MEDICAL IMAGING EDUCATORS SCHOLARSHIP

• *See page 223*

ROYCE OSBORN MINORITY STUDENT SCHOLARSHIP

Minority scholarship for certificate or undergraduate students. Must have completed at least one semester in the radiological sciences to apply. Financial need is a factor. Requirements include 3.0 GPA, recommendation, and 450- to 500-word essay.

Academic Fields/Career Goals: Health and Medical Sciences; Radiology.

Award: Scholarship for use in freshman, sophomore, or junior years; not renewable. *Number:* up to 7. *Amount:* up to $4000.

Eligibility Requirements: Applicant must be American Indian/Alaska Native, Asian/Pacific Islander, Black (non-Hispanic), or Hispanic and

American Society of Radiologic Technologists Education and Research Foundation (continued)

enrolled or expecting to enroll full- or part-time at a two-year or four-year or technical institution or university. Applicant must have 3.0 GPA or higher. Available to U.S. citizens.

Application Requirements: Application, essay, financial need analysis, references, transcript. *Deadline:* February 1.

Contact: Phelosha Collaros, Program Manager/Associate Development Officer
American Society of Radiologic Technologists Education and Research Foundation
15000 Central Avenue, SE
Albuquerque, NM 87123-3909
Phone: 505-298-4500 Ext. 2541
Fax: 505-298-5063
E-mail: foundation@asrt.org

SIEMENS CLINICAL ADVANCEMENT SCHOLARSHIP

Open to ASRT members only who are undergraduate or graduate students. Must have ARRT registration or unrestricted state license, and must have worked in the radiological sciences profession for at least one year in the past five years.

Academic Fields/Career Goals: Health and Medical Sciences; Oncology; Radiology.

Award: Scholarship for use in freshman, sophomore, junior, senior, or graduate years; not renewable. *Number:* 6. *Amount:* $3000.

Eligibility Requirements: Applicant must be enrolled or expecting to enroll full- or part-time at a two-year or four-year or technical institution or university. Applicant or parent of applicant must be member of American Society of Radiologic Technologists. Available to U.S. and Canadian citizens.

Application Requirements: Application, essay, financial need analysis, resume, references, copy of unrestricted state license, current ARRT card or equivalent, letter on official letterhead verifying employment in the radiologic sciences for at least one of the past five years. *Deadline:* February 1.

Contact: Phelosha Collaros, Program Manager/Associate Development Officer
American Society of Radiologic Technologists Education and Research Foundation
15000 Central Avenue, SE
Albuquerque, NM 87123-3909
Phone: 505-298-4500 Ext. 2541
Fax: 505-298-5063
E-mail: foundation@asrt.org

VARIAN RADIATION THERAPY STUDENT SCHOLARSHIP

Merit scholarship for undergraduate or certificate students accepted or enrolled in a radiation therapy program. Financial need is a factor. Requirements include 3.0 GPA, recommendation and 450 to 500-word essay.

Academic Fields/Career Goals: Health and Medical Sciences; Oncology; Radiology.

Award: Scholarship for use in freshman, sophomore, junior, or senior years; not renewable. *Number:* up to 19. *Amount:* up to $5000.

Eligibility Requirements: Applicant must be enrolled or expecting to enroll full- or part-time at a two-year or four-year or technical institution or university. Applicant must have 3.0 GPA or higher. Available to U.S. citizens.

Application Requirements: Application, essay, financial need analysis, references, transcript. *Deadline:* February 1.

Contact: Phelosha Collaros, Program Manager/Associate Development Officer
American Society of Radiologic Technologists Education and Research Foundation
15000 Central Avenue, SE
Albuquerque, NM 87123-3909
Phone: 505-298-4500 Ext. 2541
Fax: 505-298-5063
E-mail: foundation@asrt.org

ARIZONA PROFESSIONAL CHAPTER OF AISES http://www.azpcofaises.org

ARIZONA PROFESSIONAL CHAPTER OF AISES SCHOLARSHIP

• *See page 257*

ARKANSAS DEPARTMENT OF HIGHER EDUCATION http://www.adhe.edu

ARKANSAS HEALTH EDUCATION GRANT PROGRAM (ARHEG)

• *See page 82*

ARNOLD AND MABEL BECKMAN FOUNDATION http://www.beckman-foundation.com

BECKMAN SCHOLARS PROGRAM

• *See page 130*

ARRL FOUNDATION INC. http://www.arrl.org

WILLIAM R. GOLDFARB MEMORIAL SCHOLARSHIP

• *See page 138*

ASSOCIATION OF SURGICAL TECHNOLOGISTS http://www.ast.org

DELMAR CENGAGE LEARNING SURGICAL TECHNOLOGY SCHOLARSHIP

Scholarship offers students in CAAHEP-accredited surgical technology programs the opportunity to apply for financial assistance. Must have a 2.5 GPA.

Academic Fields/Career Goals: Health and Medical Sciences.

Award: Scholarship for use in freshman, sophomore, junior, or senior years; not renewable. *Number:* 1. *Amount:* $1000.

Eligibility Requirements: Applicant must be enrolled or expecting to enroll full-time at a two-year or four-year institution or university. Applicant must have 2.5 GPA or higher. Available to U.S. citizens.

Application Requirements: Application, essay, references, self-addressed stamped envelope, transcript, course fee schedule. *Deadline:* April 1.

Contact: Karen Ludwig, Director of Publishing
Association of Surgical Technologists
Six West Dry Creek Circle, Suite 200
Littleton, CO 80120
Phone: 800-637-7433
Fax: 303-694-9169
E-mail: kludwig@ast.org

FOUNDATION STUDENT SCHOLARSHIP

Scholarship to encourage and reward educational excellence as well as to respond to the financial need demonstrated by the surgical technology student and offer assistance to those who seek a career in surgical technology. High school students also eligible to apply. Minimum GPA 3.2 is required.

Academic Fields/Career Goals: Health and Medical Sciences.

Award: Scholarship for use in freshman, sophomore, junior, or senior years; not renewable. *Number:* up to 12. *Amount:* $500–$2000.

Eligibility Requirements: Applicant must be enrolled or expecting to enroll full-time at a two-year or four-year institution or university. Available to U.S. citizens.

Application Requirements: Application, essay, financial need analysis, references, self-addressed stamped envelope, transcript. *Deadline:* April 1.

Contact: Karen Ludwig, Director of Publishing
Association of Surgical Technologists
Six West Dry Creek Circle, Suite 200
Littleton, CO 80120
Phone: 800-637-7433
Fax: 303-694-9169
E-mail: kludwig@ast.org

ASSOCIATION ON AMERICAN INDIAN AFFAIRS (AAIA) http://www.indian-affairs.org

ELIZABETH AND SHERMAN ASCHE MEMORIAL SCHOLARSHIP FUND

Scholarship of up to $1500 available for undergraduate and graduate students seeking a bachelor's or master's degree in science or public health. Must be a Native American. See Web site for details: http://www.indian-affairs.org.

Academic Fields/Career Goals: Health and Medical Sciences; Public Health.

Award: Scholarship for use in freshman, sophomore, junior, senior, or graduate years; not renewable. *Number:* varies. *Amount:* up to $1500.

Eligibility Requirements: Applicant must be American Indian/Alaska Native and enrolled or expecting to enroll full-time at a two-year or four-year institution or university. Available to U.S. citizens.

Application Requirements: Application, essay, financial need analysis, references, transcript. *Deadline:* July 1.

Contact: Lisa Wyzlic, Director of Scholarship Programs
Association on American Indian Affairs (AAIA)
966 Hungerford Drive, Suite 12-B
Rockville, MD 20850
Phone: 240-314-7155
Fax: 240-314-7159
E-mail: lw.aaia@verizon.net

ATLANTIC HEALTH SYSTEM OVERLOOK HOSPITAL FOUNDATION http://www.overlookhospitalfoundation.com

OVERLOOK HOSPITAL FOUNDATION PROFESSIONAL DEVELOPMENT PROGRAM

Nursing and other allied health students who live in New Jersey are eligible to apply. Pays for one to two years of tuition in exchange for a commitment to work at Overlook Hospital upon graduation.

Academic Fields/Career Goals: Health and Medical Sciences; Nursing.

Award: Scholarship for use in freshman, sophomore, junior, or senior years; not renewable. *Number:* varies. *Amount:* varies.

Eligibility Requirements: Applicant must be enrolled or expecting to enroll full- or part-time at a two-year or four-year institution and resident of New Jersey. Available to U.S. citizens.

Application Requirements: Application. *Deadline:* varies.

Contact: Betsy Koehler, Scholarship Coordinator
Atlantic Health System Overlook Hospital Foundation
99 Beauvoir Avenue
Summit, NJ 07902
Phone: 908-522-2835
E-mail: betsy.koehler@ahsys.org

BETHESDA LUTHERAN HOMES AND SERVICES, INC. http://www.blhs.org

DEVELOPMENTAL DISABILITIES AWARENESS AWARDS FOR LUTHERAN HIGH SCHOOL STUDENTS

Award available to students interested in the developmental disabilities field. Students must complete two activities from a suggested list, which, together with the application process, are designed to promote the student's knowledge of careers in the field of developmental disabilities services. Up to three awards are given—$250, $150, $100. For more information visit Web site at : http://www.blhs.org.

Academic Fields/Career Goals: Health and Medical Sciences; Social Services; Special Education; Therapy/Rehabilitation.

Award: Scholarship for use in freshman year; not renewable. *Number:* 1–3. *Amount:* $100–$250.

Eligibility Requirements: Applicant must be Lutheran; high school student and planning to enroll or expecting to enroll full-time at a two-year or four-year or technical institution or university. Applicant must have 3.0 GPA or higher. Available to U.S. and Canadian citizens.

Application Requirements: Application, autobiography, essay, references, transcript. *Deadline:* April 15.

Contact: Thomas Heuer, Coordinator, Outreach Programs and Services
Bethesda Lutheran Homes and Services, Inc.
600 Hoffmann Drive
Watertown, WI 53094
Phone: 920-206-4449
Fax: 920-262-6513
E-mail: theuer@blhs.org

DEVELOPMENTAL DISABILITIES SCHOLASTIC ACHIEVEMENT SCHOLARSHIP FOR LUTHERAN COLLEGE STUDENTS

• *See page 211*

BOYS AND GIRLS CLUBS OF GREATER SAN DIEGO http://www.sdyouth.org

SPENCE REESE SCHOLARSHIP FUND

• *See page 262*

BUSINESS AND PROFESSIONAL WOMEN'S FOUNDATION http://www.bpwfoundation.org

BPW CAREER ADVANCEMENT SCHOLARSHIP PROGRAM FOR WOMEN

• *See page 130*

CALIFORNIA ADOLESCENT NUTRITION AND FITNESS (CANFIT) PROGRAM http://www.canfit.org

CALIFORNIA ADOLESCENT NUTRITION AND FITNESS (CANFIT) PROGRAM SCHOLARSHIP

• *See page 203*

CANADIAN SOCIETY FOR MEDICAL LABORATORY SCIENCE http://www.csmls.org

CANADIAN SOCIETY OF LABORATORY TECHNOLOGISTS STUDENT SCHOLARSHIP PROGRAM

Six one-time awards of CAN$500 available to students enrolled in their final year of general medical laboratory technology, cytotechnology, or clinical genetic studies. Must be student member of Canadian Society for Medical Laboratory Science, and Canadian citizen or permanent resident of Canada.

Academic Fields/Career Goals: Health and Medical Sciences.

Award: Scholarship for use in senior or graduate years; not renewable. *Number:* 6.

Eligibility Requirements: Applicant must be Canadian citizen and enrolled or expecting to enroll full-time at an institution or university. Applicant or parent of applicant must be member of Canadian Society for Medical Laboratory Science.

Application Requirements: Application, financial need analysis, references, self-addressed stamped envelope, transcript. *Deadline:* October 1.

Contact: Lisa Low, Executive Assistant
Canadian Society for Medical Laboratory Science
LCD One, PO Box 2830
Hamilton, ON L8N 3N8
Canada
Phone: 905-528-8642 Ext. 12
Fax: 905-528-4968
E-mail: lisal@csmls.org

E.V. BOOTH SCHOLARSHIP AWARD

• *See page 326*

CENTRAL SCHOLARSHIP BUREAU http://www.centralsb.org

CHESAPEAKE UROLOGY ASSOCIATES SCHOLARSHIP

Scholarship provides assistance to Maryland residents who are full-time undergraduate students pursuing a degree in pre-medicine, pre-nursing, and ancillary health fields. Recipients will be selected based on demonstrated commitment to the medical field, financial need, and academic achievement.

Academic Fields/Career Goals: Health and Medical Sciences; Nursing.

Award: Scholarship for use in sophomore, junior, senior, or graduate years; renewable. *Number:* 3. *Amount:* up to $5000.

Eligibility Requirements: Applicant must be enrolled or expecting to enroll full-time at a two-year or four-year institution or university and resident of Maryland. Applicant must have 3.0 GPA or higher. Available to U.S. citizens.

Application Requirements: Application, essay, financial need analysis, interview, transcript. *Deadline:* May 31.

Contact: Roberta Goldman, Program Director
Central Scholarship Bureau
1700 Reisterstown Road, Suite 220
Baltimore, MD 21208-2903
Phone: 410-415-5558
Fax: 410-415-5501
E-mail: rgoldman@centralsb.org

CHRISTIANA CARE HEALTH SYSTEMS http://www.christianacare.org

RUTH SHAW JUNIOR BOARD SCHOLARSHIP

Offers financial assistance to students currently enrolled in nursing and selected allied health programs. Applicants are selected based on academic achievement and a proven commitment to quality patient care. Students receiving assistance are required to commit to a minimum of one year of employment with Christiana Care.

Academic Fields/Career Goals: Health and Medical Sciences; Nursing.

Award: Scholarship for use in freshman, sophomore, junior, or senior years; not renewable. *Number:* varies. *Amount:* varies.

Eligibility Requirements: Applicant must be enrolled or expecting to enroll full- or part-time at a four-year institution or university. Applicant or parent of applicant must have employment or volunteer experience in nursing. Available to U.S. citizens.

Application Requirements: Application, autobiography, resume, references, transcript. *Deadline:* April 30.

Contact: Wendy Gable, Scholarship Committee
Christiana Care Health Systems
200 Hygeia Drive, PO Box 6001
Newark, DE 19713
Phone: 302-428-5710
E-mail: wgable@christianacare.org

COLLEGE BOARD/ROBERT WOOD JOHNSON FOUNDATION YES PROGRAM http://www.collegeboard.com

YOUNG EPIDEMIOLOGY SCHOLARS COMPETITION

• *See page 299*

COLLEGE IN COLORADO http://www.collegeincolorado.org

9HEALTH FAIR KNOWLEDGE AWARD

Student must be a high school senior, with commitment to health care. Nine $1000 scholarships have been awarded. Minimum GPA 3.0 required.

Academic Fields/Career Goals: Health and Medical Sciences.

Award: Scholarship for use in freshman year; not renewable. *Number:* 9. *Amount:* $1000.

Eligibility Requirements: Applicant must be enrolled or expecting to enroll full- or part-time at a four-year institution or university. Applicant must have 3.0 GPA or higher. Available to U.S. citizens.

Application Requirements: Application, financial need analysis, transcript. *Deadline:* March 31.

Contact: Shelby Burnette, Outreach Coordinator
College in Colorado
1801 Broadway, Suite 360
Denver, CO 80202
Phone: 720-264-8570
E-mail: shelby.burnette@cic.state.co.us

COMMUNITY FOUNDATION FOR GREATER ATLANTA INC. http://www.atlcf.org

STEVE DEARDUFF SCHOLARSHIP

Scholarship for undergraduate and graduate students pursuing degrees in medicine or social work. Legal resident of Georgia. Minimum 2.0 GPA. Previous recipients are encouraged to reapply, but are not guaranteed additional awards. For complete eligibility requirements or to download an application, visit www.atlcf.org.

Academic Fields/Career Goals: Health and Medical Sciences; Social Sciences.

Award: Scholarship for use in freshman, sophomore, junior, senior, or graduate years; not renewable. *Number:* 1–3. *Amount:* up to $2500.

Eligibility Requirements: Applicant must be enrolled or expecting to enroll full- or part-time at a four-year institution or university and resident of Georgia. Available to U.S. citizens.

Application Requirements: Application, essay, references, transcript. *Deadline:* March 26.

Contact: Kristina Morris, Program Associate
Community Foundation for Greater Atlanta Inc.
50 Hurt Plaza, Suite 449
Atlanta, GA 30303
Phone: 404-688-5525
Fax: 404-688-3060
E-mail: scholarships@atlcf.org

CONGRESSIONAL BLACK CAUCUS SPOUSES PROGRAM http://www.cbcfinc.org

CONGRESSIONAL BLACK CAUCUS SPOUSES HEALTH INITIATIVES

• *See page 326*

CYNTHIA E. MORGAN SCHOLARSHIP FUND (CEMS) http://www.cemsfund.com

CYNTHIA E. MORGAN MEMORIAL SCHOLARSHIP

Award for a high school junior or senior, or a current undergraduate, who is a Maryland resident and first generation college student. No previous generation (parents or grandparents) may have attended any college/university. Scholarship for use at a Maryland post-secondary school. Must be majoring in, or plan to enter, a medical-related field (including doctor, nurse, radiologist).

Academic Fields/Career Goals: Health and Medical Sciences; Nursing; Occupational Safety and Health; Oncology; Osteopathy; Pharmacy; Psychology; Radiology; Therapy/Rehabilitation.

Award: Scholarship for use in freshman, sophomore, junior, senior, graduate, or postgraduate years; not renewable. *Number:* 1. *Amount:* $1000.

Eligibility Requirements: Applicant must be enrolled or expecting to enroll full- or part-time at a two-year or four-year or technical institution or university; resident of Maryland and studying in Maryland. Available to U.S. citizens.

Application Requirements: Application, essay. *Deadline:* February 25.

Contact: Mr. John Kantorski, Founder and President
Cynthia E. Morgan Scholarship Fund (CEMS)
5516 Maudes Way
White Marsh, MD 21162-3417
Phone: 410-458-6312
E-mail: johnk@cemsfund.com

FOUNDATION FOR SCIENCE AND DISABILITY http://www.stemd.org

GRANTS FOR DISABLED STUDENTS IN THE SCIENCES

• *See page 87*

FOUNDATION FOR SURGICAL TECHNOLOGY http://www.ffst.org

FOUNDATION FOR SURGICAL TECHNOLOGY SCHOLARSHIP FUND

Scholarships available for students who are currently enrolled in a CAAHEP-accredited surgical technology program. Must be preparing for a career as a surgical technologist. Minimum 3.0 GPA is required. One-time award. Amount varies from year to year. Applicant must be selected by sponsoring institution. Visit Web site for more information.

Academic Fields/Career Goals: Health and Medical Sciences.

Award: Scholarship for use in freshman, sophomore, junior, or senior years; not renewable. *Number:* 5–10. *Amount:* $500–$2500.

Eligibility Requirements: Applicant must be enrolled or expecting to enroll full-time at a two-year or four-year or technical institution or university. Applicant must have 3.0 GPA or higher. Available to U.S. citizens.

Application Requirements: Application, financial need analysis, references, transcript. *Deadline:* April 1.

Contact: Karen Ludwig, Director of Publishing
Foundation for Surgical Technology
6 West Dry Creek Circle
Littleton, CO 80120
Phone: 303-694-9130
Fax: 303-694-9169

FOUNDATION OF THE PENNSYLVANIA MEDICAL SOCIETY (THE) http://www.foundationpamedsoc.org

ENDOWMENT FOR SOUTH ASIAN STUDENTS OF INDIAN DESCENT SCHOLARSHIP

Scholarship for South Asian Indian immigrants to the U.S., or applicants of South Asian Indian descent, attending (full-time) an accredited Pennsylvania medical school. Applicant must be a Pennsylvania resident for at least 12 months prior to registering as a medical student. Proof of citizenship and birth descent may be required if selected. More information on http://www.foundationpamedsoc.org.

Academic Fields/Career Goals: Health and Medical Sciences.

Award: Scholarship for use in sophomore, junior, or senior years; not renewable. *Number:* 1. *Amount:* $2000.

Eligibility Requirements: Applicant must be of Indian heritage; American Indian/Alaska Native; enrolled or expecting to enroll full-time at an institution or university; resident of Pennsylvania and studying in Pennsylvania. Available to U.S. citizens.

Application Requirements: Application, essay, references, enrollment verification from medical school. *Deadline:* September 30.

Contact: Jennifer Dunn, Student Loan and Scholarship Assistant
Foundation of the Pennsylvania Medical Society (The)
777 East Park Drive, PO Box 8820
Harrisburg, PA 17105-8820
Phone: 717-558-7852
Fax: 717-558-7818
E-mail: studentservices-foundation@pamedsoc.org

GARDEN CLUB OF AMERICA http://www.gcamerica.org

ZELLER SUMMER SCHOLARSHIP IN MEDICINAL BOTANY

Scholarship of $1500 to students who show interest in medicinal botany, as evidenced by course work and/or professor recommendations. Established to encourage summer studies of medicinal botany at the undergraduate level for students enrolled in accredited U.S. colleges and universities.

Academic Fields/Career Goals: Health and Medical Sciences; Horticulture/Floriculture; Natural Sciences.

Award: Scholarship for use in freshman, sophomore, junior, or senior years; not renewable. *Number:* 1. *Amount:* $1500.

Eligibility Requirements: Applicant must be enrolled or expecting to enroll full-time at a four-year institution or university. Available to U.S. citizens.

Application Requirements: Application, essay, references, transcript. *Deadline:* February 1.

Contact: Judy Smith, Scholarship Committee Administrator
Garden Club of America
14 East 60th Street, Third Floor
New York, NY 10022-1002
Phone: 212-753-8287
Fax: 212-753-0134
E-mail: judy@gcamerica.org

GENERAL BOARD OF HIGHER EDUCATION AND MINISTRY http://www.gbhem.org

EDITH M. ALLEN SCHOLARSHIP

• *See page 228*

GENESIS HEALTH SERVICES FOUNDATION http://www.genesishealth.com

GENESIS HEALTH GROUP SCHOLARSHIPS

Eight scholarship of $1500 to encourage local students to remain in the bi-state region and pursue careers as physicians, nurses, medical assistants, radiology technicians and other health professionals.

Academic Fields/Career Goals: Health and Medical Sciences; Health Information Management/Technology; Nursing.

Award: Scholarship for use in freshman, sophomore, junior, senior, or graduate years; not renewable. *Number:* 8. *Amount:* $1500.

Eligibility Requirements: Applicant must be enrolled or expecting to enroll full- or part-time at a four-year institution or university; resident of Illinois or Iowa and studying in Illinois or Iowa. Available to U.S. citizens.

Application Requirements: Application. *Deadline:* March 21.

Contact: Melinda Gowey, Executive Director
Genesis Health Services Foundation
1227 East Rusholme Street
Davenport, IA 52803
Phone: 563-421-6865
Fax: 563-421-6869
E-mail: goweym@genesishealth.com

GREATER KANAWHA VALLEY FOUNDATION http://www.tgkvf.org

NICHOLAS AND MARY AGNES TRIVILLIAN MEMORIAL SCHOLARSHIP FUND

Renewable award for West Virginia residents pursuing medical or pharmacy programs. Must show financial need and academic merit. May apply for two Foundation scholarships but will only be chosen for one.

Academic Fields/Career Goals: Health and Medical Sciences; Pharmacy.

Award: Scholarship for use in freshman, sophomore, junior, senior, or graduate years; renewable. *Number:* 28. *Amount:* $1000.

Eligibility Requirements: Applicant must be enrolled or expecting to enroll full-time at a four-year institution or university and resident of West Virginia. Applicant must have 2.5 GPA or higher. Available to U.S. citizens.

Application Requirements: Application, essay, financial need analysis, references, self-addressed stamped envelope, test scores, transcript. *Deadline:* January 12.

Contact: Susan Hoover, Scholarship Coordinator
Greater Kanawha Valley Foundation
PO Box 3041
Charleston, WV 25331
Phone: 304-346-3620
Fax: 304-346-3640

HAWAIIAN LODGE, F & AM http://www.glhawaii.org/

HAWAIIAN LODGE SCHOLARSHIPS

• *See page 96*

HEALTHCARE INFORMATION AND MANAGEMENT SYSTEMS SOCIETY FOUNDATION http://www.himss.org

HIMSS FOUNDATION SCHOLARSHIP PROGRAM

• *See page 326*

HEALTH PROFESSIONS EDUCATION FOUNDATION http://www.healthprofessions.ca.gov

KAISER PERMANENTE ALLIED HEALTHCARE SCHOLARSHIP

One-time award available to students enrolled in, or accepted to California accredited allied health education programs. Scholarship worth up to $4500. Deadlines: March 24 and September 11.

Academic Fields/Career Goals: Health and Medical Sciences; Social Services; Therapy/Rehabilitation.

Award: Scholarship for use in freshman, sophomore, junior, senior, graduate, or postgraduate years; not renewable. *Number:* up to 40. *Amount:* $3000–$4000.

Eligibility Requirements: Applicant must be enrolled or expecting to enroll full- or part-time at a two-year or four-year or technical institution or university; resident of California and studying in California. Available to U.S. citizens.

Application Requirements: Application, autobiography, financial need analysis, resume, references, transcript, SAR or tax return with W2. *Deadline:* varies.

Contact: Margarita Miranda, Program Administrator
Health Professions Education Foundation
818 K Street, Suite 210
Sacramento, CA 95814
Phone: 916-326-3640
Fax: 916-324-6585

HEALTH RESEARCH COUNCIL OF NEW ZEALAND http://www.hrc.govt.nz

PACIFIC HEALTH WORKFORCE AWARD

• *See page 326*

PACIFIC MENTAL HEALTH WORK FORCE AWARD

• *See page 326*

HELLENIC UNIVERSITY CLUB OF PHILADELPHIA http://www.hucphila.org

DR. PETER A. THEODOS MEMORIAL GRADUATE SCHOLARSHIP

$2500 scholarship awarded to a senior undergraduate or graduate student with financial need pursuing studies leading to a Doctor of Medicine degree. Must be a U.S. citizen of Greek descent and a resident of particular counties in NJ or PA.

Academic Fields/Career Goals: Health and Medical Sciences.

Award: Scholarship for use in senior or graduate years; not renewable. *Number:* up to 1. *Amount:* up to $2500.

Eligibility Requirements: Applicant must be of Greek heritage; enrolled or expecting to enroll full-time at a four-year institution or university and resident of New Jersey or Pennsylvania. Available to U.S. citizens.

Application Requirements: Application, financial need analysis, transcript. *Deadline:* April 21.

Contact: Zoe Tripolitis, Scholarship Chairman
Hellenic University Club of Philadelphia
PO Box 42199
Philadelphia, PA 19101-2199
Phone: 215-483-7440
E-mail: hucphila@yahoo.com

ILLINOIS STUDENT ASSISTANCE COMMISSION (ISAC) http://www.collegezone.org

ILLINOIS DEPARTMENT OF PUBLIC HEALTH CENTER FOR RURAL HEALTH ALLIED HEALTH CARE PROFESSIONAL SCHOLARSHIP PROGRAM

Scholarship for Illinois student who wants to be a nurse practitioner, physician assistant, or certified nurse midwife. Funding available for up to two years. Must fulfill an obligation to practice full-time in a designated shortage area as an allied healthcare professional in Illinois for one year for each year of scholarship funding.

Academic Fields/Career Goals: Health and Medical Sciences; Nursing.

Award: Scholarship for use in freshman, sophomore, junior, or senior years; renewable. *Number:* varies. *Amount:* up to $7500.

Eligibility Requirements: Applicant must be enrolled or expecting to enroll full- or part-time at a two-year or four-year institution or university; resident of Illinois and studying in Illinois. Available to U.S. citizens.

Application Requirements: Application, financial need analysis. *Deadline:* June 30.

Contact: Marcia Franklin, Department of Public Health
Illinois Student Assistance Commission (ISAC)
535 West Jefferson Street
Springfield, IL 62761-0001
Phone: 217-782-1624

ILLINOIS DEPARTMENT OF PUBLIC HEALTH CENTER FOR RURAL HEALTH NURSING EDUCATION SCHOLARSHIP PROGRAM

Scholarship for Illinois students pursuing a certificate, diploma, or degree in nursing. Must demonstrate financial need. Provides up to four years of financial aid in return for full- or part-time employment as a licensed practical or registered nurse in Illinois upon graduation. Must remain employed in Illinois for a period equivalent to the educational time that was supported by the scholarship.

Academic Fields/Career Goals: Health and Medical Sciences; Nursing.

Award: Scholarship for use in freshman, sophomore, junior, or senior years; renewable. *Number:* varies. *Amount:* $1500–$6000.

Eligibility Requirements: Applicant must be enrolled or expecting to enroll full- or part-time at a two-year or four-year institution or university; resident of Illinois and studying in Illinois. Available to U.S. citizens.

Application Requirements: Application, financial need analysis, transcript, Student Aid Report (SAR). *Deadline:* May 31.

Contact: Illinois Department of Public Health
Illinois Student Assistance Commission (ISAC)
535 West Jefferson Street
Springfield, IL 62761-0001
Phone: 212-782-1624

INDEPENDENT COLLEGE FUND OF MARYLAND (I-FUND) http://www.i-fundinfo.org

HEALTH AND LIFE SCIENCES PROGRAM SCHOLARSHIPS

• *See page 132*

INDIAN HEALTH SERVICES, UNITED STATES DEPARTMENT OF HEALTH AND HUMAN SERVICES http://www.ihs.gov

HEALTH PROFESSIONS PREPARATORY SCHOLARSHIP PROGRAM

• *See page 327*

INDIAN HEALTH SERVICE HEALTH PROFESSIONS PRE-GRADUATE SCHOLARSHIPS

• *See page 212*

INDIAN HEALTH SERVICE HEALTH PROFESSIONS SCHOLARSHIP PROGRAM

• *See page 327*

INTERNATIONAL ORDER OF THE KING'S DAUGHTERS AND SONS http://www.iokds.org

HEALTH CAREERS SCHOLARSHIP

• *See page 212*

J.D. ARCHBOLD MEMORIAL HOSPITAL http://www.archbold.org

ARCHBOLD SCHOLARSHIP PROGRAM

Service cancelable loan awarded for a clinical degree. Awarded to residents of Southwest Georgia and North Florida. Specific clinical degree may vary, depending on need in area. Must agree to full-time employment for one to three years upon graduation.

Academic Fields/Career Goals: Health and Medical Sciences; Nursing.

Award: Forgivable loan for use in freshman, sophomore, junior, or senior years; not renewable. *Number:* 50. *Amount:* $600–$6000.

Eligibility Requirements: Applicant must be enrolled or expecting to enroll full- or part-time at a four-year institution or university and resident of Florida or Georgia. Available to U.S. citizens.

Application Requirements: Application, interview, references, transcript. *Deadline:* continuous.

Contact: Donna McMillan, Education Coordinator
J.D. Archbold Memorial Hospital
PO Box 1018
Thomasville, GA 31799
Phone: 229-228-2795
Fax: 229-228-8584

JEWISH FOUNDATION FOR EDUCATION OF WOMEN http://www.jfew.org

JFEW SCHOLARSHIPS FOR EMIGRES IN THE HEALTH SCIENCES

• *See page 212*

LADIES AUXILIARY TO THE VETERANS OF FOREIGN WARS, DEPARTMENT OF MAINE

FRANCIS L. BOOTH MEDICAL SCHOLARSHIP SPONSORED BY LAVFW DEPARTMENT OF MAINE

Award for an undergraduate student majoring in the field of medicine who has a parent or grandparent who is a member of the Maine VFW or VFW auxiliary.

Academic Fields/Career Goals: Health and Medical Sciences; Humanities; Nursing; Therapy/Rehabilitation.

Award: Scholarship for use in freshman, sophomore, junior, or senior years; renewable. *Number:* 2. *Amount:* $500–$1000.

Eligibility Requirements: Applicant must be enrolled or expecting to enroll full-time at a two-year or four-year institution or university and resident of Maine. Applicant or parent of applicant must be member of Veterans of Foreign Wars or Auxiliary. Applicant must have 3.0 GPA or higher. Available to U.S. citizens.

Application Requirements: Application, essay, financial need analysis, resume, references, transcript, personal letter. *Deadline:* March 31.

Contact: Sheila Webber, Secretary
Ladies Auxiliary to the Veterans of Foreign Wars, Department of Maine
PO Box 493
Old Orchard Beach, ME 04064
Phone: 207-934-2405
E-mail: swebber2@maine.rr.com

LINCOLN COMMUNITY FOUNDATION http://www.lcf.org

MEDICAL RESEARCH SCHOLARSHIP

Scholarship available to students who have completed appropriate undergraduate education and are currently pursuing an advanced degree in a medical related field with the exception of nurses who may apply as undergraduates. Preference will be given to females pursuing careers as physicians and nurses who demonstrate financial need.

Academic Fields/Career Goals: Health and Medical Sciences; Nursing.

Award: Scholarship for use in freshman, sophomore, junior, senior, graduate, or postgraduate years; renewable. *Number:* 1–5. *Amount:* $500–$1000.

Eligibility Requirements: Applicant must be enrolled or expecting to enroll full- or part-time at a two-year or four-year institution or university. Available to U.S. citizens.

Application Requirements: Application, essay, financial need analysis, test scores, transcript. *Deadline:* May 30.

Contact: Sonya Brakeman, Grants/Scholarships Coordinator
Lincoln Community Foundation
215 Centennial Mall South, Suite 100
Lincoln, NE 68508
Phone: 402-474-2345
Fax: 402-476-8532
E-mail: sonyab@lcf.org

MAINE OSTEOPATHIC ASSOCIATION MEMORIAL SCHOLARSHIP/MAINE OSTEOPATHIC ASSOCIATION http://www.mainedo.org

BEALE FAMILY MEMORIAL SCHOLARSHIP

One award of $1000 is made to a well qualified student in their second, third or fourth year of study at an osteopathic college, who has evidence of interest in returning to Maine to practice or in teaching in an osteopathic college in New England.

Academic Fields/Career Goals: Health and Medical Sciences; Osteopathy.

Award: Scholarship for use in sophomore, junior, or senior years; not renewable. *Number:* 1. *Amount:* $1000.

Eligibility Requirements: Applicant must be enrolled or expecting to enroll full- or part-time at a four-year institution or university. Available to U.S. citizens.

Application Requirements: Application, proof of residence. *Deadline:* May 1.

Contact: Dianne Jackson, Office Manager and Convention Coordinator
Maine Osteopathic Association Memorial Scholarship/Maine Osteopathic Association
693 Western Avenue, Suite 1
Manchester, ME 04351
Phone: 207-623-1101
Fax: 207-623-4228
E-mail: djackson@mainedo.org

MAINE OSTEOPATHIC ASSOCIATION MEMORIAL SCHOLARSHIP

One award of $1000 to a second, third, or fourth year student who is a resident of Maine. Must present proof of enrollment at an approved osteopathic college.

Academic Fields/Career Goals: Health and Medical Sciences; Osteopathy.

Award: Scholarship for use in sophomore, junior, or senior years; not renewable. *Number:* 1. *Amount:* $1000.

Eligibility Requirements: Applicant must be enrolled or expecting to enroll full- or part-time at a four-year institution or university and resident of Maine. Available to U.S. citizens.

Application Requirements: Application, proof of residence, proof of enrollment at an approved osteopathic college. *Deadline:* May 1.

Contact: Dianne Jackson, Office Manager and Convention Coordinator
Maine Osteopathic Association Memorial Scholarship/Maine Osteopathic Association
693 Western Avenue, Suite 1
Manchester, ME 04351
Phone: 207-623-1101
Fax: 207-623-4228
E-mail: djackson@mainedo.org

MAINE OSTEOPATHIC ASSOCIATION SCHOLARSHIP

One award of $1000 to a student who is a resident of Maine and able to present proof of enrollment at an approved osteopathic college.

Academic Fields/Career Goals: Health and Medical Sciences; Osteopathy.

Award: Scholarship for use in freshman year; not renewable. *Number:* 1. *Amount:* $1000.

Eligibility Requirements: Applicant must be high school student; planning to enroll or expecting to enroll full- or part-time at a two-year or four-year or technical institution or university and resident of Maine. Available to U.S. citizens.

Application Requirements: Application, transcript, proof of Maine residence. *Deadline:* May 1.

Contact: Dianne Jackson, Office Manager and Convention Coordinator
Maine Osteopathic Association Memorial Scholarship/Maine Osteopathic Association
693 Western Avenue, Suite 1
Manchester, ME 04351
Phone: 207-623-1101
Fax: 207-623-4228
E-mail: djackson@mainedo.org

MARYLAND HIGHER EDUCATION COMMISSION http://www.mhec.state.md.us

CHARLES W. RILEY FIRE AND EMERGENCY MEDICAL SERVICES TUITION REIMBURSEMENT PROGRAM

• *See page 310*

GRADUATE AND PROFESSIONAL SCHOLARSHIP PROGRAM-MARYLAND

• *See page 212*

MENTAL HEALTH ASSOCIATION IN NEW YORK STATE INC. http://www.mhanys.org

EDNA AIMES SCHOLARSHIP

• *See page 128*

MISSISSIPPI STATE STUDENT FINANCIAL AID http://www.ihl.state.ms.us

MISSISSIPPI HEALTH CARE PROFESSIONS LOAN/SCHOLARSHIP PROGRAM

Renewable award for junior and senior undergraduates studying psychology or speech pathology, and graduate students studying physical therapy or occupational therapy. Must be Mississippi residents attending four-year colleges or universities in Mississippi. Must fulfill work obligation in Mississippi on the basis of one year's service for one year's loan received, or pay back as loan.

Academic Fields/Career Goals: Health and Medical Sciences; Psychology; Therapy/Rehabilitation.

Award: Forgivable loan for use in junior, senior, or graduate years; renewable. *Number:* varies. *Amount:* $1500–$6000.

Eligibility Requirements: Applicant must be enrolled or expecting to enroll full-time at a four-year institution or university; resident of Mississippi and studying in Mississippi. Available to U.S. citizens.

Mississippi State Student Financial Aid (continued)

Application Requirements: Application, driver's license, references, transcript. *Deadline:* March 31.

Contact: Susan Eckels, Program Administrator
Mississippi State Student Financial Aid
3825 Ridgewood Road
Jackson, MS 39211-6453
Phone: 601-432-6997
E-mail: sme@ihl.state.ms.us

MISSOURI DEPARTMENT OF HEALTH AND SENIOR SERVICES http://www.dhss.mo.gov

ACES/PRIMO PROGRAM

Program of the Missouri Area Health Education Centers (MAHEC) And the Primary Care Resource Initiative for Missouri students interested in Primary Care. Applicant should have a minimum GPA of 3.0.

Academic Fields/Career Goals: Health and Medical Sciences.

Award: Forgivable loan for use in freshman, sophomore, junior, senior, graduate, or postgraduate years; not renewable. *Number:* 100. *Amount:* $3000–$5000.

Eligibility Requirements: Applicant must be enrolled or expecting to enroll full- or part-time at a four-year institution or university. Applicant must have 3.0 GPA or higher. Available to U.S. and non-U.S. citizens.

Application Requirements: Application, driver's license, proof of Missouri residency. *Deadline:* June 30.

Contact: Kristie Frank, Health Program Representative
Missouri Department of Health and Senior Services
PO Box 570
Jefferson City, MO 65401-0570
Phone: 800-891-7415
Fax: 573-522-8146
E-mail: kris.frank@dhss.mo.gov

PRIMARY CARE RESOURCE INITIATIVE FOR MISSOURI LOAN PROGRAM

• *See page 212*

MORRIS K. UDALL FOUNDATION http://www.udall.gov

MORRIS K. UDALL SCHOLARS-NATIVE AMERICAN AND ALASKA NATIVE

One-time award to Native American or Alaska Native enrolled full-time at a two year or four year college. Must be studying fields related to health care or tribal public policy. Must be nominated by college. Must be a matriculated sophomore or junior pursing a degree. Tribal documentation must be submitted.

Academic Fields/Career Goals: Health and Medical Sciences; Health Information Management/Technology; Social Sciences; Social Services.

Award: Scholarship for use in sophomore or junior years; not renewable. *Number:* up to 130. *Amount:* $350–$5000.

Eligibility Requirements: Applicant must be American Indian/Alaska Native and enrolled or expecting to enroll full-time at a two-year or four-year institution. Applicant must have 3.0 GPA or higher. Available to U.S. citizens.

Application Requirements: Application, essay, references, transcript, nomination. *Deadline:* March 6.

Contact: Melissa Millage, Program Manager
Morris K. Udall Foundation
130 South Scott Avenue
Tucson, AZ 85701-1922
Phone: 520-901-8500
Fax: 520-901-8570
E-mail: millage@udall.gov

NASA IDAHO SPACE GRANT CONSORTIUM http://isgc.uidaho.edu

NASA IDAHO SPACE GRANT CONSORTIUM SCHOLARSHIP PROGRAM

• *See page 87*

NATIONAL ARAB AMERICAN MEDICAL ASSOCIATION http://www.naama.com

FOUNDATION SCHOLARSHIP

• *See page 213*

NATIONAL ATHLETIC TRAINERS' ASSOCIATION RESEARCH AND EDUCATION FOUNDATION http://www.natafoundation.org

NATIONAL ATHLETIC TRAINERS' ASSOCIATION RESEARCH AND EDUCATION FOUNDATION SCHOLARSHIP PROGRAM

One-time award available to full-time students who are members of NATA. Minimum 3.2 GPA required. Open to undergraduate upperclassmen and graduate/postgraduate students.

Academic Fields/Career Goals: Health and Medical Sciences; Health Information Management/Technology; Sports-Related/Exercise Science; Therapy/Rehabilitation.

Award: Scholarship for use in junior, senior, graduate, or postgraduate years; not renewable. *Number:* 70. *Amount:* $2000.

Eligibility Requirements: Applicant must be enrolled or expecting to enroll full-time at a four-year institution or university. Applicant or parent of applicant must be member of National Athletic Trainers Association. Available to U.S. and non-U.S. citizens.

Application Requirements: Application, essay, references, transcript. *Deadline:* February 10.

Contact: Patsy Brown, Scholarship Coordinator
National Athletic Trainers' Association Research and Education Foundation
2952 Stemmons Freeway, Suite 200
Dallas, TX 75247
Phone: 214-637-6282 Ext. 151
Fax: 214-637-2206
E-mail: patsyb@nata.org

NATIONAL FEDERATION OF THE BLIND http://www.nfb.org

HOWARD BROWN RICKARD SCHOLARSHIP

• *See page 92*

NATIONAL HEALTHCARE SCHOLARS FOUNDATION http://www.nhsfonline.org

NHSF MEDICAL SCHOLARSHIP

Scholarships of $5000 are awarded to qualified African-American, Asian, Hispanic and Native American students in the field of medicine. Medical students must be classified as a sophomore.

Academic Fields/Career Goals: Health and Medical Sciences.

Award: Scholarship for use in sophomore year; renewable. *Number:* 1–5. *Amount:* $5000.

Eligibility Requirements: Applicant must be American Indian/Alaska Native, Asian/Pacific Islander, Black (non-Hispanic), or Hispanic and enrolled or expecting to enroll full-time at a four-year or technical institution or university. Available to U.S. citizens.

Application Requirements: Application, references, test scores, transcript. *Deadline:* varies.

Contact: Scholarship Committee
National Healthcare Scholars Foundation
300 River Place, Suite 4950
Detroit, MI 48207
Phone: 313-393-4549
Fax: 313-393-3394
E-mail: information@nhsfonline.org

NATIONAL INSTITUTES OF HEALTH http://www.ugsp.nih.gov

NIH UNDERGRADUATE SCHOLARSHIP PROGRAM FOR STUDENTS FROM DISADVANTAGED BACKGROUNDS

• *See page 134*

NATIONAL INVENTORS HALL OF FAME http://www.invent.org

COLLEGIATE INVENTORS COMPETITION FOR UNDERGRADUATE STUDENTS

• *See page 88*

COLLEGIATE INVENTORS COMPETITION-GRAND PRIZE

• *See page 88*

NEW MEXICO COMMISSION ON HIGHER EDUCATION http://www.hed.state.nm.us

ALLIED HEALTH STUDENT LOAN PROGRAM-NEW MEXICO

• *See page 213*

NEW YORK STATE EDUCATION DEPARTMENT http://www.highered.nysed.gov

REGENTS PROFESSIONAL OPPORTUNITY SCHOLARSHIP

• *See page 60*

NORTH CAROLINA STATE EDUCATION ASSISTANCE AUTHORITY http://www.ncseaa.edu

NORTH CAROLINA STUDENT LOAN PROGRAM FOR HEALTH, SCIENCE, AND MATHEMATICS

• *See page 213*

OREGON COMMUNITY FOUNDATION http://www.ocf1.org

DR. FRANZ AND KATHRYN STENZEL FUND

Scholarships for Oregon residents, with a focus on three types of students: (a) those pursuing any type of undergraduate degree, (b) those pursing a nursing education through a two-year, four-year, or graduate program, and (3) medical students.

Academic Fields/Career Goals: Health and Medical Sciences; Nursing.

Award: Scholarship for use in freshman, sophomore, junior, senior, or graduate years; not renewable. *Number:* up to 40. *Amount:* $2000.

Eligibility Requirements: Applicant must be enrolled or expecting to enroll full-time at a two-year or four-year institution or university and resident of Oregon. Available to U.S. citizens.

Application Requirements: Application, references. *Deadline:* March 1.

Contact: Dianne Causey, Program Associate for Scholarships and Grants
Oregon Community Foundation
1221 Yamhill, SW, Suite 100
Portland, OR 97205
Phone: 503-227-6846
Fax: 503-274-7771
E-mail: diannec@ocf1.org

OREGON STUDENT ASSISTANCE COMMISSION http://www.osac.state.or.us

MARION A. LINDEMAN SCHOLARSHIP

Award for Willamette View employees who have completed one or more years of service. Must be pursuing degree or certificate in nursing, speech, physical or occupational therapy, or other health-related fields. Must enroll at least half time.

Academic Fields/Career Goals: Health and Medical Sciences; Nursing; Therapy/Rehabilitation.

Award: Scholarship for use in freshman, sophomore, junior, or senior years; renewable. *Number:* varies. *Amount:* varies.

Eligibility Requirements: Applicant must be enrolled or expecting to enroll full- or part-time at a two-year or four-year institution and resident of Oregon. Applicant or parent of applicant must be affiliated with Willamette View. Available to U.S. citizens.

Application Requirements: Application, essay, financial need analysis, references, transcript, activity chart. *Deadline:* March 1.

Contact: Director of Grant Programs
Oregon Student Assistance Commission
1500 Valley River Drive, Suite 100
Eugene, OR 97401-7020
Phone: 800-452-8807 Ext. 7395

OUM CHIROPRACTOR PROGRAM http://www.oumchiropractor.com

WELLNESS WORKS SCHOLARSHIP

Scholarships for part-time students currently enrolled in U.S. colleges of chiropractic. Applicants must submit their best idea in the form of an essay, marketing campaign, or storyboard for marketing chiropractic care nationally as proactive health maintenance. Award valued up to $1000. Deadline varies.

Academic Fields/Career Goals: Health and Medical Sciences.

Award: Scholarship for use in junior, senior, or graduate years; not renewable. *Number:* 1–3. *Amount:* up to $1000.

Eligibility Requirements: Applicant must be enrolled or expecting to enroll full-time at a four-year institution or university. Available to U.S. citizens.

Application Requirements: Application, essay, photo, transcript. *Deadline:* varies.

Contact: Karen Edwards, Marketing Specialist
OUM Chiropractor Program
110 Westwood Place
Brentwood, TN 37027
Phone: 800-423-1504 Ext. 7
Fax: 800-453-2776
E-mail: info@oumchiropractor.com

PACERS FOUNDATION INC. http://www.pacersfoundation.org

LINDA CRAIG MEMORIAL SCHOLARSHIP PRESENTED BY ST. VINCENT SPORTS MEDICINE

Scholarship presented by St. Vincent Sports Medicine is for currently-enrolled juniors and seniors with declared majors of medicine, sports medicine, and/or physical therapy. Students must have completed at least 4 semesters and attend a school in Indiana. Minimum 3.0 GPA required.

Academic Fields/Career Goals: Health and Medical Sciences; Sports-Related/Exercise Science; Therapy/Rehabilitation.

Award: Scholarship for use in junior, senior, graduate, or postgraduate years; renewable. *Number:* 1–2. *Amount:* $2000.

Eligibility Requirements: Applicant must be enrolled or expecting to enroll full-time at a two-year or four-year institution or university and studying in Indiana. Applicant must have 3.0 GPA or higher. Available to U.S. citizens.

Application Requirements: Application, essay, references, transcript. *Deadline:* March 1.

Contact: Jami Marsh, Executive Director
Pacers Foundation Inc.
125 South Pennsylvania Street
Indianapolis, IN 46204
Phone: 317-917-2856
E-mail: foundation@pacers.com

PEARSON BENJAMIN CUMMINGS http://www.aw-bc.com

BENJAMIN CUMMINGS ALLIED HEALTH STUDENT SCHOLARSHIP

• *See page 134*

PHYSICIAN ASSISTANT FOUNDATION http://www.aapa.org/paf

PHYSICIAN ASSISTANT FOUNDATION ANNUAL SCHOLARSHIP

One-time award for student members of the American Academy of Physician Assistants enrolled in an ARC PA-accredited physician assistant program. Award based on financial need, academic achievement, and goals.

Academic Fields/Career Goals: Health and Medical Sciences.

Award: Scholarship for use in junior or senior years; not renewable. *Number:* up to 75. *Amount:* $2000.

Physician Assistant Foundation (continued)

Eligibility Requirements: Applicant must be enrolled or expecting to enroll full- or part-time at a four-year institution or university. Applicant or parent of applicant must be member of American Academy of Physicians Assistants. Available to U.S. and non-U.S. citizens.

Application Requirements: Application, essay, financial need analysis, photo, test scores, transcript. *Deadline:* January 15.

Contact: Tara Burnett, Scholarship Committee
Physician Assistant Foundation
950 North Washington Street
Alexandria, VA 22314-1552
Phone: 703-519-5686
Fax: 703-684-1924
E-mail: tburnett@aapa.org

PILOT INTERNATIONAL FOUNDATION http://www.pilotinternational.org

PILOT INTERNATIONAL FOUNDATION RUBY NEWHALL MEMORIAL SCHOLARSHIP

Scholarship available to international students for full-time study in the United States or Canada. Applicants must have visa or green card and must be majoring in a field related to human health and welfare. Minimum of one full academic semester in an accredited college in the United States or Canada must be completed before applying for the scholarship. Applicants must be sponsored by Pilot Club in their home town, or in the city in which their college or university is located.

Academic Fields/Career Goals: Health and Medical Sciences; Nursing; Psychology; Public Health; Social Services; Special Education; Therapy/Rehabilitation.

Award: Scholarship for use in freshman, sophomore, junior, or senior years; not renewable. *Number:* 8–10. *Amount:* up to $1500.

Eligibility Requirements: Applicant must be enrolled or expecting to enroll full- or part-time at a two-year or four-year or technical institution. Applicant must have 3.0 GPA or higher. Available to Canadian and non-U.S. citizens.

Application Requirements: Application, essay, financial need analysis, references, self-addressed stamped envelope, transcript, visa or F1 status. *Deadline:* March 1.

Contact: Jennifer Overbay, Foundation Services Director
Pilot International Foundation
PO Box 4844
Macon, GA 31208-5600
Phone: 478-743-7403
Fax: 478-474-7229
E-mail: pifinfo@pilothq.org

PILOT INTERNATIONAL FOUNDATION SCHOLARSHIP PROGRAM

Scholarship program for undergraduate students preparing for a career helping those with brain related disorders or disabilities. Applicant must have visa or green card. Minimum GPA Score to be 3.25.

Academic Fields/Career Goals: Health and Medical Sciences; Nursing; Psychology; Special Education; Therapy/Rehabilitation.

Award: Scholarship for use in freshman, sophomore, or junior years; not renewable. *Number:* 8–10. *Amount:* up to $2000.

Eligibility Requirements: Applicant must be enrolled or expecting to enroll full- or part-time at a two-year or four-year or technical institution. Available to U.S. and non-U.S. citizens.

Application Requirements: Application, essay, financial need analysis, references, self-addressed stamped envelope, transcript, visa or F1 status. *Deadline:* March 1.

Contact: Jennifer Overbay, Foundation Services Director
Pilot International Foundation
PO Box 4844
Macon, GA 31208-5600
Phone: 478-743-7403
Fax: 478-474-7229
E-mail: pifinfo@pilothq.org

RESOURCE CENTER

MARIE BLAHA MEDICAL GRANT

• *See page 83*

SIGMA XI, THE SCIENTIFIC RESEARCH SOCIETY http://www.sigmaxi.org

SIGMA XI GRANTS-IN-AID OF RESEARCH

• *See page 78*

SOCIETY FOR APPLIED ANTHROPOLOGY http://www.sfaa.net

PETER KONG-MING NEW STUDENT PRIZE

• *See page 129*

SOCIETY FOR THE SCIENTIFIC STUDY OF SEXUALITY http://www.sexscience.org

SOCIETY FOR THE SCIENTIFIC STUDY OF SEXUALITY STUDENT RESEARCH GRANT

• *See page 129*

SOCIETY OF NUCLEAR MEDICINE http://www.snm.org

PAUL COLE SCHOLARSHIP

Scholarship for students who are enrolled in or accepted for enrollment in associate, baccalaureate or certificate programs in nuclear medicine technology. Academic merit considered. Minimum 2.5 GPA required.

Academic Fields/Career Goals: Health and Medical Sciences; Nuclear Science; Radiology.

Award: Scholarship for use in freshman, sophomore, junior, or senior years; not renewable. *Number:* varies. *Amount:* $1000.

Eligibility Requirements: Applicant must be enrolled or expecting to enroll full- or part-time at a two-year or four-year institution or university. Applicant must have 2.5 GPA or higher. Available to U.S. citizens.

Application Requirements: Application, essay, references, transcript, acceptance letter. *Deadline:* October 15.

Contact: Development Office
Society of Nuclear Medicine
1850 Samuel Morse Drive
Reston, VA 20190
Phone: 703-708-9000 Ext. 1255
E-mail: grantinfo@snm.org

SOCIETY OF PEDIATRIC NURSES http://www.pedsnurses.org

SOCIETY OF PEDIATRIC NURSES EDUCATIONAL SCHOLARSHIP

• *See page 167*

STATE OF GEORGIA http://www.gsfc.org

SERVICE-CANCELABLE STAFFORD LOAN-GEORGIA

• *See page 213*

TEXAS HIGHER EDUCATION COORDINATING BOARD http://www.collegefortexans.com

OUTSTANDING RURAL SCHOLAR PROGRAM

Award enables rural communities to sponsor a student going into health professions. The students must agree to work in that community once they receive their degree. Must be Texas resident entering a Texas institution on a full-time basis. Must demonstrate financial need. Deadline varies.

Academic Fields/Career Goals: Health and Medical Sciences; Nursing.

Award: Scholarship for use in freshman, sophomore, junior, or senior years; renewable. *Number:* varies. *Amount:* varies.

Eligibility Requirements: Applicant must be enrolled or expecting to enroll full-time at a four-year institution or university; resident of Texas and studying in Texas. Applicant must have 3.0 GPA or higher. Available to U.S. citizens.

Application Requirements: Application, financial need analysis, transcript, nomination. *Deadline:* varies.

Contact: Office of Rural Community Affairs
Texas Higher Education Coordinating Board
PO Box 1708
Austin, TX 78767
Phone: 512-479-8891
E-mail: grantinfo@thecb.state.tx.us

TRIANGLE COMMUNITY FOUNDATION http://www.trianglecf.org

GERTRUDE B. ELION MENTORED MEDICAL STUDENT RESEARCH AWARDS

An annual award of $10,000 to women, enrolled as full-time students, and should have completed at least one year of medical school prior to the start of the award. Applicants must be from the Duke University Medical Center and University of North Carolina.

Academic Fields/Career Goals: Health and Medical Sciences.

Award: Prize for use in sophomore, junior, or senior years; not renewable. *Number:* varies. *Amount:* $10,000.

Eligibility Requirements: Applicant must be enrolled or expecting to enroll full-time at a four-year institution or university and female. Available to U.S. and Canadian citizens.

Application Requirements: Application, resume, references, sponsor's statement of nomination, research plan. *Deadline:* September 20.

Contact: Libby Long, Scholarships and Special Projects Coordinator
Triangle Community Foundation
324 BlackWell Street, Suite 1220
Durham, NC 27701
Phone: 919-474-8370 Ext. 134
Fax: 919-949-9208
E-mail: libby@trianglecf.org

TUCSON OSTEOPATHIC MEDICAL FOUNDATION http://www.tomf.org

TUCSON OSTEOPATHIC MEDICAL FOUNDATION SCHOLARSHIP/LOAN PROGRAM

Award for Arizona residents enrolled in osteopathic medical college. Applicant any year of the academic predoctoral program. Preference given to residents of southeastern counties of Arizona. Must file Graduate and Professional Student Financial Aid application. Write for deadline and further information. One-time award of $6000 to $10,000. A percentage per year is forgiven for students who practice in Southern Arizona upon graduation.

Academic Fields/Career Goals: Health and Medical Sciences; Osteopathy.

Award: Scholarship for use in freshman, sophomore, junior, or senior years; not renewable. *Number:* 6–10. *Amount:* $6000–$10,000.

Eligibility Requirements: Applicant must be enrolled or expecting to enroll full-time at a four-year institution or university and resident of Arizona. Available to U.S. citizens.

Application Requirements: Application, interview, photo, resume, references, transcript, goal statement. *Deadline:* December 1.

Contact: Cece Pappas, Medical Education Manager
Tucson Osteopathic Medical Foundation
3182 North Swan Road
Tucson, AZ 85712
Phone: 520-299-4545
Fax: 520-299-4609
E-mail: cece@tomf.org

UNITED NEGRO COLLEGE FUND http://www.uncf.org

ALTON AND DOROTHY HIGGINS, MD SCHOLARSHIP

Scholarship available for junior, senior or pre-medicine graduate students attending a UNCF member college or university or Morehouse School of Medicine. Minimum 3.0 GPA is required. Undergraduates will receive $5000 per year and medical school students will receive up to $10,000 per year.

Academic Fields/Career Goals: Health and Medical Sciences.

Award: Scholarship for use in junior, senior, or graduate years; not renewable. *Number:* varies. *Amount:* $5000–$10,000.

Eligibility Requirements: Applicant must be Black (non-Hispanic) and enrolled or expecting to enroll full-time at a four-year institution or university. Applicant must have 3.0 GPA or higher. Available to U.S. and non-U.S. citizens.

Application Requirements: Application, essay, financial need analysis, references, transcript. *Deadline:* varies.

Contact: Director, Program Services
United Negro College Fund
8260 Willow Oaks Corporate Drive
PO Box 10444
Fairfax, VA 22031-8044
Phone: 800-331-2244
E-mail: rebecca.bennett@uncf.org

HARRY C. JAECKER SCHOLARSHIP

Award for pre-medical students attending a UNCF member college or university. Minimum 2.5 GPA required. The Scholarship value ranges from $2000 to $5000.

Academic Fields/Career Goals: Health and Medical Sciences.

Award: Scholarship for use in freshman, sophomore, junior, or senior years; not renewable. *Number:* varies. *Amount:* $2000–$5000.

Eligibility Requirements: Applicant must be Black (non-Hispanic) and enrolled or expecting to enroll full- or part-time at a four-year institution or university. Applicant must have 2.5 GPA or higher. Available to U.S. and non-U.S. citizens.

Application Requirements: Application, financial need analysis. *Deadline:* varies.

Contact: Director, Program Services
United Negro College Fund
8260 Willow Oaks Corporate Drive
PO Box 10444
Fairfax, VA 22031-8044
Phone: 800-331-2244
E-mail: rebecca.bennett@uncf.org

MEDTRONIC FOUNDATION SCHOLARSHIP

• *See page 136*

SODEXHO SCHOLARSHIP

Award available to incoming freshmen attending UNCF member colleges or universities or historically black colleges and universities. Must demonstrate leadership abilities. Minimum GPA of 3.0 required. Visit Web site for more information: http://www.uncf.org.

Academic Fields/Career Goals: Health and Medical Sciences; Nursing; Political Science; Social Services.

Award: Scholarship for use in freshman year; renewable. *Number:* varies. *Amount:* up to $3500.

Eligibility Requirements: Applicant must be Black (non-Hispanic); high school student and planning to enroll or expecting to enroll full- or part-time at a four-year institution or university. Applicant must have 3.0 GPA or higher. Available to U.S. citizens.

Application Requirements: Application, financial need analysis, references, transcript, FAFSA, Student Aid Report (SAR). *Deadline:* August 22.

Contact: Annette Singletary, Senior Program Manager
United Negro College Fund
8260 Willow Oaks Corporate Drive
Fairfax, VA 22031
Phone: 800-331-2244

UNITED STATES PUBLIC HEALTH SERVICE-HEALTH RESOURCES AND SERVICES ADMINISTRATION, BUREAU OF HEALTH PROFESSIONS http://bhpr.hrsa.gov/dsa

HEALTH RESOURCES AND SERVICES ADMINISTRATION-BUREAU OF HEALTH PROFESSIONS SCHOLARSHIPS FOR DISADVANTAGED STUDENTS

• *See page 214*

UNIVERSITY OF MEDICINE AND DENTISTRY OF NJ SCHOOL OF OSTEOPATHIC MEDICINE http://www.umdnj.edu

NEW JERSEY EDUCATIONAL OPPORTUNITY FUND GRANTS

• *See page 214*

VESALIUS TRUST FOR VISUAL COMMUNICATION IN THE HEALTH SCIENCES http://www.vesaliustrust.org

STUDENT RESEARCH SCHOLARSHIP

Scholarships available to students currently enrolled in an undergraduate or graduate school program of bio-communications (medical illustration) who have completed one full year of the curriculum.

Academic Fields/Career Goals: Health and Medical Sciences.

Award: Scholarship for use in sophomore, junior, senior, or graduate years; not renewable. *Number:* 15. *Amount:* $640–$2240.

Eligibility Requirements: Applicant must be enrolled or expecting to enroll full- or part-time at a four-year institution or university and must have an interest in art. Available to U.S. and non-U.S. citizens.

Application Requirements: Application, autobiography, portfolio, references, transcript. *Deadline:* November 9.

Contact: Wendy Hiller Gee, Student Grants and Scholarships
Vesalius Trust for Visual Communication in the Health Sciences
1100 Grundy Lane
San Bruno, CA 94066
Phone: 650-244-4320
E-mail: wendy.hillergee@krames.com

VIRGINIA BUSINESS AND PROFESSIONAL WOMEN'S FOUNDATION http://www.vabpwfoundation.org

WOMEN IN SCIENCE AND TECHNOLOGY SCHOLARSHIP

• *See page 136*

WASHINGTON HIGHER EDUCATION COORDINATING BOARD http://www.hecb.wa.gov

HEALTH PROFESSIONAL SCHOLARSHIP PROGRAM

The program was created to attract and retain health professionals, to serve in critical shortage areas in Washington state. Must sign a promissory note agreeing to serve for a minimum of three years in a designated shortage area in Washington state or pay back funds at double penalty with the interest.

Academic Fields/Career Goals: Health and Medical Sciences.

Award: Forgivable loan for use in junior, senior, or graduate years; renewable. *Number:* varies. *Amount:* varies.

Eligibility Requirements: Applicant must be enrolled or expecting to enroll full- or part-time at a four-year institution or university. Available to U.S. citizens.

Application Requirements: Application, references, transcript. *Deadline:* April 30.

Contact: Kathy McVay, Program Administrator
Washington Higher Education Coordinating Board
PO Box 47834
Olympia, WA 98504-7834
Phone: 360-236-2816
E-mail: kathy.mcvay@doh.wa.gov

WASHINGTON STATE ENVIRONMENTAL HEALTH ASSOCIATION http://www.wseha.org

CIND M. TRESER MEMORIAL SCHOLARSHIP PROGRAM

Scholarships are available for undergraduate students pursuing a major in environmental health or related science and intending to practice environmental health. Must be a resident of Washington. For more details see Web site: http://www.wseha.org.

Academic Fields/Career Goals: Health and Medical Sciences.

Award: Scholarship for use in freshman, sophomore, junior, or senior years; not renewable. *Number:* up to 2. *Amount:* up to $1000.

Eligibility Requirements: Applicant must be enrolled or expecting to enroll full-time at a two-year or four-year institution or university and resident of Washington. Available to U.S. citizens.

Application Requirements: Application, references, transcript. *Deadline:* March 15.

Contact: Charles Treser, Scholarships Committee Chair
Washington State Environmental Health Association
3045 57th Street, NW
Seattle, WA 98107
Phone: 206-616-2097
Fax: 206-543-8123
E-mail: ctreser@u.washington.edu

ZETA PHI BETA SORORITY INC. NATIONAL EDUCATIONAL FOUNDATION http://www.zphib1920.org

S. EVELYN LEWIS MEMORIAL SCHOLARSHIP IN MEDICAL HEALTH SCIENCES

Scholarships available for graduate or undergraduate women enrolled in a program leading to a degree in medicine or health sciences. Must be a full-time student. See Web site for information and application: http://www.zphib1920.org.

Academic Fields/Career Goals: Health and Medical Sciences.

Award: Scholarship for use in freshman, sophomore, junior, senior, or graduate years; not renewable. *Number:* 1. *Amount:* $500–$1000.

Eligibility Requirements: Applicant must be enrolled or expecting to enroll full-time at a four-year institution or university and female. Available to U.S. citizens.

Application Requirements: Application, essay, references, transcript, enrollment proof. *Deadline:* February 1.

Contact: Cheryl Williams, National Second Vice President
Zeta Phi Beta Sorority Inc. National Educational Foundation
1734 New Hampshire Avenue, NW
Washington, DC 20009-2595
Fax: 318-631-4028
E-mail: 2ndanti@zphib1920.org

HEALTH INFORMATION MANAGEMENT/TECHNOLOGY

AMERICAN HEALTH INFORMATION MANAGEMENT ASSOCIATION/FOUNDATION OF RESEARCH AND EDUCATION http://www.ahima.org/fore

FORE UNDERGRADUATE MERIT SCHOLARSHIPS

Renewable merit scholarships for undergraduate health information management students. Must be a member of AHIMA. One standard application for all available scholarships. Applicant must have a minimum cumulative GPA of 3.0 (out of 4.0) or 4.0 (out of 5.0). Applications can be downloaded at http://www.ahima.org.

Academic Fields/Career Goals: Health Information Management/Technology.

Award: Scholarship for use in freshman, sophomore, junior, or senior years; renewable. *Number:* 1. *Amount:* $1000–$5000.

Eligibility Requirements: Applicant must be enrolled or expecting to enroll full- or part-time at a two-year or four-year institution or university. Applicant or parent of applicant must be member of American Health Information Management Association. Applicant must have 3.0 GPA or higher. Available to U.S. and non-U.S. citizens.

Application Requirements: Application, essay, references, transcript, program director verification. *Deadline:* April 1.

Contact: Development Assistant
American Health Information Management Association/ Foundation of Research and Education
233 North Michigan Avenue, 21st Floor
Chicago, IL 60601-5800
Phone: 312-233-1100
E-mail: fore@ahima.org

BETHESDA LUTHERAN HOMES AND SERVICES, INC. http://www.blhs.org

DEVELOPMENTAL DISABILITIES SCHOLASTIC ACHIEVEMENT SCHOLARSHIP FOR LUTHERAN COLLEGE STUDENTS

• *See page 211*

CANADIAN SOCIETY FOR MEDICAL LABORATORY SCIENCE http://www.csmls.org

E.V. BOOTH SCHOLARSHIP AWARD

• *See page 326*

CONGRESSIONAL BLACK CAUCUS SPOUSES PROGRAM http://www.cbcfinc.org

CONGRESSIONAL BLACK CAUCUS SPOUSES HEALTH INITIATIVES

• *See page 326*

GENESIS HEALTH SERVICES FOUNDATION http://www.genesishealth.com

GENESIS HEALTH GROUP SCHOLARSHIPS

• *See page 337*

HEALTHCARE INFORMATION AND MANAGEMENT SYSTEMS SOCIETY FOUNDATION http://www.himss.org

HIMSS FOUNDATION SCHOLARSHIP PROGRAM

• *See page 326*

HEALTH RESEARCH COUNCIL OF NEW ZEALAND http://www.hrc.govt.nz

PACIFIC HEALTH WORKFORCE AWARD

• *See page 326*

PACIFIC MENTAL HEALTH WORK FORCE AWARD

• *See page 326*

MORRIS K. UDALL FOUNDATION http://www.udall.gov

MORRIS K. UDALL SCHOLARS-NATIVE AMERICAN AND ALASKA NATIVE

• *See page 340*

NATIONAL ATHLETIC TRAINERS' ASSOCIATION RESEARCH AND EDUCATION FOUNDATION http://www.natafoundation.org

NATIONAL ATHLETIC TRAINERS' ASSOCIATION RESEARCH AND EDUCATION FOUNDATION SCHOLARSHIP PROGRAM

• *See page 340*

NATIONAL STRENGTH AND CONDITIONING ASSOCIATION http://www.nsca-lift.org

GNC NUTRITION RESEARCH GRANT

Grant to undergraduate and graduate students for nutrition based research. The purpose of the project must fall within the mission of the NSCA. Applicant must submit: cover letter, abstract, proposal, itemized budget, and proof of institutional review board approval, and abbreviated vitae of faculty co-investigator.

Academic Fields/Career Goals: Health Information Management/Technology; Sports-Related/Exercise Science; Therapy/Rehabilitation.

Award: Grant for use in junior, senior, or graduate years; not renewable. *Number:* 1. *Amount:* up to $2500.

Eligibility Requirements: Applicant must be enrolled or expecting to enroll full-time at a four-year institution or university. Applicant or parent of applicant must be member of National Strength and Conditioning Association. Available to U.S. and non-U.S. citizens.

Application Requirements: Application, references, transcript, abstract, itemized budget, time schedule, consent form, vitae of faculty co-investigator in one copy. *Deadline:* March 15.

Contact: Line Saole, Membership Specialist
National Strength and Conditioning Association
1885 Bob Johnson Drive
Colorado Springs, CO 80906-4000
Phone: 719-632-6722 Ext. 120
Fax: 719-632-6367
E-mail: foundation@nsca-lift.org

NSCA MINORITY SCHOLARSHIP

Scholarship to encourage minority students who are age 17 and older to enter into the field of strength and conditioning. Award is for full-time study.

Academic Fields/Career Goals: Health Information Management/Technology; Sports-Related/Exercise Science; Therapy/Rehabilitation.

Award: Scholarship for use in freshman, sophomore, junior, senior, or graduate years; not renewable. *Number:* 1–2. *Amount:* $1000.

Eligibility Requirements: Applicant must be American Indian/Alaska Native, Asian/Pacific Islander, Black (non-Hispanic), or Hispanic; age 17 and over and enrolled or expecting to enroll full-time at a two-year or four-year institution or university. Applicant or parent of applicant must be member of National Strength and Conditioning Association. Available to U.S. and non-U.S. citizens.

Application Requirements: Application, essay, resume, references, transcript. *Deadline:* March 15.

Contact: Line Saole, Membership Specialist
National Strength and Conditioning Association
1885 Bob Johnson Drive
Colorado Springs, CO 80906-4000
Phone: 719-632-6722 Ext. 120
Fax: 719-632-6367
E-mail: foundation@nsca-lift.org

POWER SYSTEMS PROFESSIONAL SCHOLARSHIP

One-time scholarship for students in pursuit of a career as a strength and conditioning coach. Must be a member of National Strength and Conditioning Association.

Academic Fields/Career Goals: Health Information Management/Technology; Sports-Related/Exercise Science; Therapy/Rehabilitation.

Award: Scholarship for use in freshman, sophomore, junior, senior, or graduate years; not renewable. *Number:* 1. *Amount:* $1000.

Eligibility Requirements: Applicant must be enrolled or expecting to enroll full-time at a two-year or four-year institution or university. Applicant or parent of applicant must be member of National Strength and Conditioning Association. Available to U.S. and non-U.S. citizens.

Application Requirements: Application, essay, photo, resume, references, transcript. *Deadline:* March 15.

Contact: Line Saole, Membership Specialist
National Strength and Conditioning Association
1885 Bob Johnson Drive
Colorado Springs, CO 80906-4000
Phone: 719-632-6722 Ext. 120
Fax: 719-632-6367
E-mail: foundation@nsca-lift.org

HEATING, AIR-CONDITIONING, AND REFRIGERATION MECHANICS

AMERICAN SOCIETY OF HEATING, REFRIGERATING, AND AIR CONDITIONING ENGINEERS INC. http://www.ashrae.org

ALWIN B. NEWTON SCHOLARSHIP FUND

• *See page 247*

AMERICAN SOCIETY OF HEATING, REFRIGERATION, AND AIR CONDITIONING ENGINEERING TECHNOLOGY SCHOLARSHIP

• *See page 85*

American Society of Heating, Refrigerating, and Air Conditioning Engineers Inc. (continued)

ASHRAE MEMORIAL SCHOLARSHIP
• See page 286

ASHRAE SCHOLARSHIPS
• See page 287

DUANE HANSON SCHOLARSHIP
• See page 287

HENRY ADAMS SCHOLARSHIP
• See page 287

REUBEN TRANE SCHOLARSHIP
• See page 247

INSTRUMENTATION, SYSTEMS, AND AUTOMATION SOCIETY (ISA) http://www.isa.org

INSTRUMENTATION, SYSTEMS, AND AUTOMATION SOCIETY (ISA) SCHOLARSHIP PROGRAM
• See page 158

PLUMBING-HEATING-COOLING CONTRACTORS ASSOCIATION EDUCATION FOUNDATION http://www.phccweb.org

BRADFORD WHITE CORPORATION SCHOLARSHIP
• See page 92

DELTA FAUCET COMPANY SCHOLARSHIP PROGRAM
• See page 93

PHCC EDUCATIONAL FOUNDATION NEED-BASED SCHOLARSHIP
• See page 93

PHCC EDUCATIONAL FOUNDATION SCHOLARSHIP PROGRAM
• See page 147

PROFESSIONAL CONSTRUCTION ESTIMATORS ASSOCIATION http://www.pcea.org

TED WILSON MEMORIAL SCHOLARSHIP FOUNDATION
• See page 214

SOUTH CAROLINA ASSOCIATION OF HEATING AND AIR CONDITIONING CONTRACTORS http://www.schvac.org

SOUTH CAROLINA ASSOCIATION OF HEATING AND AIR CONDITIONING CONTRACTORS SCHOLARSHIP

Scholarship of $500 to pursue a career in the heating and air conditioning industry. Participating students must maintain an overall GPA of 2.5 and a GPA of 3.0 in all major topics. Deadline varies.

Academic Fields/Career Goals: Heating, Air-Conditioning, and Refrigeration Mechanics.

Award: Scholarship for use in freshman year; renewable. *Number:* varies. *Amount:* $500.

Eligibility Requirements: Applicant must be high school student and planning to enroll or expecting to enroll full- or part-time at a technical institution. Applicant must have 2.5 GPA or higher. Available to U.S. and non-U.S. citizens.

Application Requirements: Application, references. *Deadline:* varies.

Contact: Leigh Faircloth, Scholarship Committee
South Carolina Association of Heating and Air Conditioning Contractors
PO Box 11035
Columbia, SC 29211
Phone: 800-395-9276
Fax: 803-252-7799
E-mail: staff@schvac.org

HISTORIC PRESERVATION AND CONSERVATION

AMERICAN SCHOOL OF CLASSICAL STUDIES AT ATHENS http://www.ascsa.edu.gr

ASCSA SUMMER SESSIONS OPEN SCHOLARSHIPS
• See page 83

COSTUME SOCIETY OF AMERICA http://www.costumesocietyamerica.com

ADELE FILENE TRAVEL AWARD
• See page 95

STELLA BLUM RESEARCH GRANT
• See page 95

GEORGIA TRUST FOR HISTORIC PRESERVATION http://www.georgiatrust.org

GEORGIA TRUST FOR HISTORIC PRESERVATION SCHOLARSHIP

Each year, the Trust awards two $1000 scholarships to encourage the study of historic preservation and related fields. Recipients are chosen on the basis of leadership and academic achievement. Applicants must be residents of Georgia enrolled in an accredited Georgia institution. A GPA of 3.0 is required.

Academic Fields/Career Goals: Historic Preservation and Conservation.

Award: Scholarship for use in freshman, sophomore, junior, senior, or graduate years; not renewable. *Number:* 2. *Amount:* $1000.

Eligibility Requirements: Applicant must be enrolled or expecting to enroll full-time at a four-year institution or university; resident of Georgia and studying in Georgia. Applicant must have 3.0 GPA or higher. Available to U.S. citizens.

Application Requirements: Application, essay, resume, references, transcript. *Deadline:* February 15.

Contact: Scholarship Coordinator
Georgia Trust for Historic Preservation
1516 Peachtree Street, NW
Atlanta, GA 30309
Phone: 404-885-7819
Fax: 404-875-2205
E-mail: scholarship@georgiatrust.org

HISTORY

AMERICAN FEDERATION OF STATE, COUNTY, AND MUNICIPAL EMPLOYEES http://www.afscme.org

AFSCME/UNCF UNION SCHOLARS PROGRAM
• See page 80

AMERICAN HISTORICAL ASSOCIATION http://www.historians.org

WESLEY-LOGAN PRIZE
• See page 68

AMERICAN PHILOLOGICAL ASSOCIATION http://www.apaclassics.org

MINORITY STUDENT SUMMER SCHOLARSHIP
• See page 89

AMERICAN SCHOOL OF CLASSICAL STUDIES AT ATHENS http://www.ascsa.edu.gr

ASCSA SUMMER SESSIONS OPEN SCHOLARSHIPS
• See page 83

CHARLES M. EDWARDS SCHOLARSHIP
• See page 98

CANADIAN INSTITUTE OF UKRAINIAN STUDIES http://www.cius.ca

LEO J. KRYSA UNDERGRADUATE SCHOLARSHIP

• *See page 95*

COLLEGEBOUND FOUNDATION http://www.collegeboundfoundation.org

DECATUR H. MILLER SCHOLARSHIP

Scholarship for students majoring in the fields of political science, history, or pre-law. Must have a 3.0 GPA, an SAT (critical reading and math) score of 1100, and must attend Bowie State University, Coppin State University, Frostburg State University, Morgan State University, St. Mary's College of Maryland, Towson University, University of Maryland College Park, University of Maryland Eastern Shore, or Villa Julie College. Preference will be given to students who plan to attend law school after graduating from college.

Academic Fields/Career Goals: History; Law/Legal Services; Political Science.

Award: Scholarship for use in freshman, sophomore, junior, or senior years; renewable. *Number:* 1. *Amount:* $1500.

Eligibility Requirements: Applicant must be high school student; planning to enroll or expecting to enroll full-time at a four-year institution or university; resident of Maryland and studying in Maryland. Applicant must have 3.0 GPA or higher. Available to U.S. citizens.

Application Requirements: Application, financial need analysis, references, test scores, transcript. *Deadline:* March 1.

Contact: Jamie Crouse, Scholarship Program Administrator
CollegeBound Foundation
300 Water Street, Suite 300
Baltimore, MD 21202
Phone: 410-783-2905 Ext. 207
Fax: 410-727-5786
E-mail: jcrouse@collegeboundfoundation.org

COSTUME SOCIETY OF AMERICA http://www.costumesocietyamerica.com

ADELE FILENE TRAVEL AWARD

• *See page 95*

STELLA BLUM RESEARCH GRANT

• *See page 95*

GREATER SALINA COMMUNITY FOUNDATION http://www.gscf.org

KANSAS FEDERATION OF REPUBLICAN WOMEN SCHOLARSHIP

Awards female students currently attending a Kansas college or university with declared major of political science, history, or public administration. Must be entering junior or senior year of undergraduate study, or attending graduate school. Must be Kansas residents and maintain cumulative GPA of 3.0 or better. Applicants must be registered members of the Republican Party. Must be involved in extracurricular activities.

Academic Fields/Career Goals: History; Political Science; Public Policy and Administration.

Award: Scholarship for use in junior, senior, or graduate years; renewable. *Number:* 1. *Amount:* up to $1000.

Eligibility Requirements: Applicant must be enrolled or expecting to enroll full-time at a two-year or four-year institution or university; female; resident of Kansas and studying in Kansas. Applicant must have 3.0 GPA or higher. Available to U.S. citizens.

Application Requirements: Application, essay. *Deadline:* March 31.

Contact: Michelle Griffin, Scholarship and Affiliate Coordinator
Greater Salina Community Foundation
PO Box 2876
Salina, KS 67402-2876
Phone: 785-823-1800
E-mail: michellegriffin@gscf.org

HARVARD TRAVELLERS CLUB

HARVARD TRAVELLERS CLUB GRANTS

• *See page 89*

INSTITUTE FOR HUMANE STUDIES http://www.theihs.org

HUMANE STUDIES FELLOWSHIPS

• *See page 179*

KE ALI'I PAUAHI FOUNDATION http://www.pauahi.org

SARAH KELI'ILOLENA LUM KONIA NAKOA SCHOLARSHIP

• *See page 320*

LINCOLN FORUM http://www.thelincolnforum.org

PLATT FAMILY SCHOLARSHIP PRIZE ESSAY CONTEST

• *See page 80*

LYNDON BAINES JOHNSON FOUNDATION http://www.lbjlib.utexas.edu

LYNDON BAINES JOHNSON FOUNDATION GRANTS-IN-AID RESEARCH

Awards a limited number of grants in aid of research, for the periods October 1 through March 31 and April 1 through September 30. October through March deadline is August 31. April through September deadline is February 28. Funds are to help defray cost while doing research at the LBJ library. Must contact the archives division of the library prior to submitting proposal concerning material availability for the proposed topic. Candidates for assistance should have thoughtful and well-written proposals that state clearly and precisely how the holdings of the library will contribute to historical research.

Academic Fields/Career Goals: History; Political Science.

Award: Grant for use in freshman, sophomore, junior, senior, graduate, or postgraduate years; not renewable. *Number:* 10–20. *Amount:* $500–$2500.

Eligibility Requirements: Applicant must be enrolled or expecting to enroll full- or part-time at a two-year or four-year or technical institution or university and studying in Texas. Available to U.S. and non-U.S. citizens.

Application Requirements: Application, references, research proposal. *Deadline:* varies.

Contact: Executive Director
Lyndon Baines Johnson Foundation
2313 Red River Street
Austin, TX 78705-5702
Phone: 512-478-7829
E-mail: library@johnson.nara.gov

NATIONAL FEDERATION OF THE BLIND http://www.nfb.org

MICHAEL AND MARIE MARUCCI SCHOLARSHIP

• *See page 320*

NATIONAL FEDERATION OF THE BLIND HUMANITIES SCHOLARSHIP

• *See page 104*

NATIONAL SOCIETY DAUGHTERS OF THE AMERICAN REVOLUTION http://www.dar.org

NATIONAL SOCIETY DAUGHTERS OF THE AMERICAN REVOLUTION DR. AURA-LEE A. PITTENGER AND JAMES HOBBS PITTENGER AMERICAN HISTORY SCHOLARSHIP

Scholarship of $2000 each year for up to four consecutive years to a graduating high school senior who will have a concentrated study of a minimum of 24 credit hours in American history or American government while in college. United States citizens residing abroad may apply through a Units Overseas chapter.

Academic Fields/Career Goals: History; Political Science.

Award: Scholarship for use in freshman year; renewable. *Number:* 1. *Amount:* $2000.

Eligibility Requirements: Applicant must be high school student and planning to enroll or expecting to enroll full-time at a four-year institution or university. Available to U.S. citizens.

National Society Daughters of the American Revolution (continued)

Application Requirements: Application, references, self-addressed stamped envelope, transcript, letter of sponsorship. *Deadline:* February 15.

Contact: Eric Weisz, Manager, Office of the Reporter General
National Society Daughters of the American Revolution
1776 D Street, NW
Washington, DC 20006-5303
Phone: 202-628-1776
Fax: 202-879-3348
E-mail: nsdarscholarships@dar.org

NATIONAL SOCIETY DAUGHTERS OF THE AMERICAN REVOLUTION ENID HALL GRISWOLD MEMORIAL SCHOLARSHIP
• *See page 220*

ORGANIZATION OF AMERICAN HISTORIANS http://www.oah.org

BINKLEY-STEPHENSON AWARD
• *See page 80*

PHI ALPHA THETA HISTORY HONOR SOCIETY INC. http://www.phialphatheta.org

PHI ALPHA THETA PAPER PRIZES

Award for best graduate and undergraduate student papers. Grants $500 prize for best graduate student paper, $500 prize for best undergraduate paper, and four $350 prizes for either graduate or undergraduate papers. All applicants must be members of the association.

Academic Fields/Career Goals: History.

Award: Prize for use in freshman, sophomore, junior, senior, or graduate years; not renewable. *Number:* 6. *Amount:* $350–$500.

Eligibility Requirements: Applicant must be enrolled or expecting to enroll full-time at a four-year institution or university. Applicant must have 3.0 GPA or higher. Available to U.S. and non-U.S. citizens.

Application Requirements: Applicant must enter a contest, essay, references. *Deadline:* June 30.

Contact: Dr. Clayton Drees, Department of History
Phi Alpha Theta History Honor Society Inc.
Virginia Wesleyan College, 1584 Wesleyan Drive
Norfolk, VA 23502-5599
E-mail: cdrees@vwc.edu

PHI ALPHA THETA UNDERGRADUATE STUDENT SCHOLARSHIP

Awards of $1000 available to exceptional juniors entering the senior year and majoring in modern European history (1815 to present). Must be Phi Alpha Theta members. Based on both financial need and merit.

Academic Fields/Career Goals: History.

Award: Scholarship for use in junior year; not renewable. *Number:* 1. *Amount:* $1000.

Eligibility Requirements: Applicant must be enrolled or expecting to enroll full-time at a four-year institution or university. Applicant or parent of applicant must be member of Phi Alpha Theta. Available to U.S. and non-U.S. citizens.

Application Requirements: Application, resume, references, transcript. *Deadline:* March 1.

Contact: Dr. Graydon Tunstall, Executive Director
Phi Alpha Theta History Honor Society Inc.
SOC 107, 4202 East Fowler Avenue
Tampa, FL 33620-8100
Phone: 800-394-8195
Fax: 813-974-8215
E-mail: phialpha@phialphatheta.org

PHI ALPHA THETA/WESTERN FRONT ASSOCIATION PAPER PRIZE

Essay competition open to full-time undergraduate members of the association. The paper must be from 12 to 15 typed pages and must address the American experience in World War I, must be dealing with virtually any aspect of American involvement during the period from 1912 (second Moroccan crisis) to 1924 (Dawes plan). Primary source material must be used. For further details visit Web site: http://www.phialphatheta.org/awards2.htm.

Academic Fields/Career Goals: History.

Award: Prize for use in freshman, sophomore, junior, or senior years; not renewable. *Number:* 1. *Amount:* $1000.

Eligibility Requirements: Applicant must be enrolled or expecting to enroll full-time at a four-year institution or university and must have an interest in writing. Applicant must have 3.0 GPA or higher. Available to U.S. and non-U.S. citizens.

Application Requirements: Application, applicant must enter a contest, essay, 5 copies of the paper, CD-ROM containing a file of the paper and cover letter. *Deadline:* January 31.

Contact: Prof. Graydon A. Tunstall, Executive Director
Phi Alpha Theta History Honor Society Inc.
University of South Florida, 4202 East Fowler Avenue, SOC107
Tampa, FL 33620-8100
Phone: 813-974-8212
Fax: 813-974-8215
E-mail: info@phialphatheta.org

PHI ALPHA THETA WORLD HISTORY ASSOCIATION PAPER PRIZE

Awards one undergraduate and one graduate-level prize for papers examining any historical issue with global implications such as: exchange or interchange of cultures, comparison of civilizations or cultures. This is a joint award with the World History Association. Must be a member of the association or Phi Alpha Theta. Paper must have been composed while enrolled at an accredited college or university. Must send in two copies of paper along with professor's letter.

Academic Fields/Career Goals: History; Humanities; International Studies; Social Sciences.

Award: Prize for use in freshman, sophomore, junior, senior, or graduate years; not renewable. *Number:* 2. *Amount:* $400.

Eligibility Requirements: Applicant must be enrolled or expecting to enroll full-time at a four-year institution or university. Applicant or parent of applicant must be member of Phi Alpha Theta. Applicant must have 3.0 GPA or higher. Available to U.S. and non-U.S. citizens.

Application Requirements: References, 2 copies of paper, abstract, letter from faculty member or professor. *Deadline:* June 30.

Contact: Prof. Joel E. Tishken, Professor of History
Phi Alpha Theta History Honor Society Inc.
Columbus State University, 4225 University Avenue
Columbus, GA 31907

SONS OF THE REPUBLIC OF TEXAS http://www.srttexas.org

PRESIDIO LA BAHIA AWARD
• *See page 80*

SUMMERFIELD G. ROBERTS AWARD
• *See page 80*

TEXAS HISTORY ESSAY CONTEST
• *See page 81*

STRAIGHTFORWARD MEDIA http://www.straightforwardmedia.com

STRAIGHTFORWARD MEDIA LIBERAL ARTS SCHOLARSHIP
• *See page 99*

TOPSFIELD HISTORICAL SOCIETY http://www.topsfieldhistory.org

JOHN KIMBALL, JR. MEMORIAL TRUST SCHOLARSHIP PROGRAM FOR THE STUDY OF HISTORY

Scholarship grants funds for tuition, books, and other educational and research expenses to undergraduate and graduate students; as well as college, university, and graduate school instructors and professors who have excelled in, and/or have a passion for the study of history and related disciplines; and who reside in, or have a substantial connection to Topsfield, Massachusetts.

Academic Fields/Career Goals: History.

Award: Grant for use in freshman, sophomore, junior, senior, graduate, or postgraduate years; renewable. *Number:* 3–10. *Amount:* $300–$5000.

Eligibility Requirements: Applicant must be enrolled or expecting to enroll full- or part-time at a two-year or four-year institution or university and resident of Massachusetts. Available to U.S. and non-U.S. citizens.

Application Requirements: Application. *Deadline:* April 15.

Contact: Mr. Norman J. Isler, Trustee
Topsfield Historical Society
PO Box 323
Topsfield, MA 01983

UNITED DAUGHTERS OF THE CONFEDERACY http://www.hqudc.org

HELEN JAMES BREWER SCHOLARSHIP

Award for full-time undergraduate student who is a descendant of a Confederate soldier, sailor or marine. Must be from Alabama, Florida, Georgia, South Carolina, Tennessee or Virginia. Recipient must be enrolled in an accredited college or university and studying history and literature. Must be a member or former member of the Children of the Confederacy. Minimum 3.0 GPA required.

Academic Fields/Career Goals: History; Literature/English/Writing.

Award: Scholarship for use in freshman, sophomore, junior, or senior years; renewable. *Number:* 1–2. *Amount:* $800–$1000.

Eligibility Requirements: Applicant must be enrolled or expecting to enroll full-time at a four-year institution or university and resident of Alabama, Florida, Georgia, South Carolina, Tennessee, or Virginia. Applicant or parent of applicant must be member of United Daughters of the Confederacy. Applicant must have 3.0 GPA or higher. Available to U.S. citizens. Applicant or parent must meet one or more of the following requirements: Air Force, Army, or Navy experience; retired from active duty; disabled or killed as a result of military service; prisoner of war; or missing in action.

Application Requirements: Application, essay, financial need analysis, photo, references, self-addressed stamped envelope, transcript, copy of applicant's birth certificate, copy of confederate ancestor's proof of service. *Deadline:* March 15.

Contact: Deanna Bryant, Second Vice President General
United Daughters of the Confederacy
328 North Boulevard
Richmond, VA 23220-4009
Phone: 804-355-1636
Fax: 804-353-1396
E-mail: hqudc@rcn.com

UNITED NEGRO COLLEGE FUND http://www.uncf.org

C-SPAN SCHOLARSHIP PROGRAM

• *See page 187*

TOYOTA SCHOLARSHIP

• *See page 66*

UNITED STATES MARINE CORPS HISTORICAL CENTER http://www.history.usmc.mil

U.S. MARINE CORPS HISTORICAL CENTER GRANTS

Research grants for graduate-level and advanced study in Marine Corps history and related fields. Must submit preliminary letter outlining qualifications and a topic or request for a topic. Pending approval, applicants must submit a writing sample, transcripts, and a formal application. Program gives preference to pre-1975 period topics. A portion of the research may be done in Washington, DC. Applications considered year-round.

Academic Fields/Career Goals: History; Military and Defense Studies.

Award: Grant for use in freshman, sophomore, junior, senior, graduate, or postgraduate years; not renewable. *Number:* 5. *Amount:* $400–$3000.

Eligibility Requirements: Applicant must be enrolled or expecting to enroll full-time at a four-year institution or university. Available to U.S. and non-U.S. citizens.

Application Requirements: Application, resume, references, transcript, writing sample. *Deadline:* continuous.

Contact: Coordinator, Grants and Fellowships
United States Marine Corps Historical Center
3079 Moreell Avenue
Quantico, VA 22134
Phone: 703-432-4877

HOME ECONOMICS

COSTUME SOCIETY OF AMERICA http://www.costumesocietyamerica.com

ADELE FILENE TRAVEL AWARD

• *See page 95*

STELLA BLUM RESEARCH GRANT

• *See page 95*

FAMILY, CAREER AND COMMUNITY LEADERS OF AMERICA-TEXAS ASSOCIATION http://www.texasfccla.org

C.J. DAVIDSON SCHOLARSHIP FOR FCCLA

Renewable award for graduating high school seniors enrolled in full-time program in family and consumer sciences. Must be Texas resident and should study in Texas. Must have minimum GPA of 2.5.

Academic Fields/Career Goals: Home Economics.

Award: Scholarship for use in freshman year; renewable. *Number:* up to 10. *Amount:* up to $16,000.

Eligibility Requirements: Applicant must be high school student; planning to enroll or expecting to enroll full-time at a four-year institution or university; single; resident of Texas and studying in Texas. Applicant or parent of applicant must be member of Family, Career and Community Leaders of America. Applicant must have 2.5 GPA or higher. Available to U.S. citizens.

Application Requirements: Application, essay, references, test scores, transcript. *Deadline:* March 1.

Contact: Staff
Family, Career and Community Leaders of America-Texas Association
3530 Bee Caves Road, Suite 101
Austin, TX 78746-9616
Phone: 512-306-0099
Fax: 512-306-0041
E-mail: fccla@texasfccla.org

FCCLA HOUSTON LIVESTOCK SHOW AND RODEO SCHOLARSHIP

• *See page 140*

FCCLA REGIONAL SCHOLARSHIPS

• *See page 140*

FCCLA TEXAS FARM BUREAU SCHOLARSHIP

• *See page 140*

INTERNATIONAL EXECUTIVE HOUSEKEEPERS ASSOCIATION http://www.ieha.org

INTERNATIONAL EXECUTIVE HOUSEKEEPERS EDUCATIONAL FOUNDATION

• *See page 315*

MAINE SCHOOL FOOD SERVICE ASSOCIATION (MSFSA) http://www.mainesfsa.org

MAINE SCHOOL FOOD SERVICE ASSOCIATION CONTINUING EDUCATION SCHOLARSHIP

• *See page 206*

MARYLAND ASSOCIATION OF PRIVATE COLLEGES AND CAREER SCHOOLS http://www.mapccs.org

MARYLAND ASSOCIATION OF PRIVATE COLLEGES AND CAREER SCHOOLS SCHOLARSHIP

• *See page 146*

OHIO 4-H http://www.ohio4h.org

BEA CLEVELAND 4-H SCHOLARSHIP

• *See page 166*

MABEL SARBAUGH 4-H SCHOLARSHIP

• *See page 166*

SAN DIEGO FOUNDATION http://www.sdfoundation.org

CALIFORNIA ASSOCIATION OF FAMILY AND CONSUMER SCIENCES-SAN DIEGO CHAPTER
• *See page 166*

UNITED DAUGHTERS OF THE CONFEDERACY http://www.hqudc.org

WALTER REED SMITH SCHOLARSHIP
• *See page 149*

HORTICULTURE/FLORICULTURE

ALABAMA GOLF COURSE SUPERINTENDENTS ASSOCIATION http://www.agcsa.org

ALABAMA GOLF COURSE SUPERINTENDENT'S ASSOCIATION'S DONNIE ARTHUR MEMORIAL SCHOLARSHIP
• *See page 72*

AMERICAN NURSERY AND LANDSCAPE ASSOCIATION http://www.anla.org/research

CARVILLE M. AKEHURST MEMORIAL SCHOLARSHIP

Scholarship is available to resident of Maryland, Virginia, or West Virginia. Applicant must be enrolled in an accredited undergraduate or graduate landscape/ horticulture program or related discipline at a two- or four-year institution and must have minimum 3.0 GPA.

Academic Fields/Career Goals: Horticulture/Floriculture; Landscape Architecture.

Award: Scholarship for use in junior, senior, or graduate years; renewable. *Number:* 1. *Amount:* $4000.

Eligibility Requirements: Applicant must be enrolled or expecting to enroll full-time at a two-year or four-year or technical institution or university and resident of Maryland, Virginia, or West Virginia. Applicant must have 3.0 GPA or higher. Available to U.S. citizens.

Application Requirements: Application, essay, financial need analysis, resume, references, transcript. *Deadline:* April 1.

Contact: Ms. Teresa Jodon, Endowment Program Administrator
American Nursery and Landscape Association
1000 Vermont Avenue, NW, Suite 300
Washington, DC 20005
Phone: 202-789-5980 Ext. 3014
Fax: 202-789-1893
E-mail: hriresearch@anla.org

HORTICULTURE RESEARCH INSTITUTE TIMOTHY BIGELOW AND PALMER W. BIGELOW, JR. SCHOLARSHIP

Award for students who are enrolled in accredited undergraduate or graduate landscape/horticulture program. Must be resident of Connecticut, Maine, Massachusetts, New Hampshire, Rhode Island, or Vermont. Undergraduates must have a GPA of 2.25. Financial need, desire to work in nursery industry are factors.

Academic Fields/Career Goals: Horticulture/Floriculture; Landscape Architecture.

Award: Scholarship for use in junior, senior, or graduate years; not renewable. *Number:* 1. *Amount:* $3500.

Eligibility Requirements: Applicant must be enrolled or expecting to enroll full-time at a four-year institution or university and resident of Connecticut, Maine, Massachusetts, New Hampshire, Rhode Island, or Vermont. Available to U.S. citizens.

Application Requirements: Application, essay, financial need analysis, references, transcript. *Deadline:* April 1.

Contact: Ms. Teresa Jodon, Endowment Program Administrator
American Nursery and Landscape Association
1000 Vermont Street, NW, Suite 300
Washington, DC 20005
Phone: 202-789-5980 Ext. 3014
Fax: 202-789-1893
E-mail: hriresearch@anla.org

MUGGETS SCHOLARSHIP

Annual scholarship available to students enrolled in an accredited undergraduate or graduate horticulture, landscape, or related discipline at a two- or four-year institution. Students in vocational agriculture programs will also be considered. High school seniors may apply for this scholarship. Minimum 2.5 GPA required.

Academic Fields/Career Goals: Horticulture/Floriculture; Landscape Architecture.

Award: Scholarship for use in freshman, sophomore, junior, senior, or graduate years; not renewable. *Number:* 1. *Amount:* $1500.

Eligibility Requirements: Applicant must be enrolled or expecting to enroll full-time at a two-year or four-year or technical institution or university. Applicant must have 2.5 GPA or higher. Available to U.S. and non-U.S. citizens.

Application Requirements: Application, essay, financial need analysis, references, transcript. *Deadline:* April 1.

Contact: Ms. Teresa Jodon, Endowment Program Administrator
American Nursery and Landscape Association
1000 Vermont Avenue NW, Suite 300
Washington, DC 20005-4914
Phone: 202-789-5980 Ext. 3014
Fax: 202-478-7288
E-mail: hriresearch@anla.org

SPRING MEADOW NURSERY SCHOLARSHIP

Scholarship for the full-time study of horticulture or landscape architecture students in undergraduate or graduate landscape horticulture program or related discipline at a two- or four-year institution. Applicant must have minimum 2.5 GPA.

Academic Fields/Career Goals: Horticulture/Floriculture; Landscape Architecture.

Award: Scholarship for use in freshman, sophomore, junior, senior, or graduate years; renewable. *Number:* 1. *Amount:* $2500.

Eligibility Requirements: Applicant must be enrolled or expecting to enroll full-time at a two-year or four-year or technical institution or university. Applicant must have 2.5 GPA or higher. Available to U.S. and Canadian citizens.

Application Requirements: Application, essay, financial need analysis, resume, references, transcript. *Deadline:* April 1.

Contact: Ms. Teresa Jodon, Endowment Program Administrator
American Nursery and Landscape Association
1000 Vermont Avenue, NW, Suite 300
Washington, DC 20005-4914
Phone: 202-789-5980 Ext. 3014
Fax: 202-789-1893
E-mail: hriresearch@anla.org

USREY FAMILY SCHOLARSHIP

Award for students accredited in undergraduate or graduate landscape horticulture program or related discipline at a two- or four-year institution. Preference given to applicants who plan to work within the industry. Must have a minimum 2.5 GPA.

Academic Fields/Career Goals: Horticulture/Floriculture; Landscape Architecture.

Award: Scholarship for use in sophomore, junior, senior, graduate, or postgraduate years; renewable. *Number:* 1. *Amount:* $1500.

Eligibility Requirements: Applicant must be enrolled or expecting to enroll full-time at a two-year or four-year or technical institution or university and studying in California. Applicant must have 2.5 GPA or higher. Available to U.S. and non-U.S. citizens.

Application Requirements: Application, essay, financial need analysis, references, transcript. *Deadline:* April 1.

Contact: Teresa Jodon, Endowment Program Administrator
American Nursery and Landscape Association
1000 Vermont Avenue, NW, Suite 300
Washington, DC 20005
Phone: 202-789-2900 Ext. 3014
Fax: 202-789-1893
E-mail: hriresearch@anla.org

AMERICAN SOCIETY FOR ENOLOGY AND VITICULTURE http://www.asev.org

AMERICAN SOCIETY FOR ENOLOGY AND VITICULTURE SCHOLARSHIPS

• *See page 72*

AMERICAN SOCIETY FOR HORTICULTURAL SCIENCE http://www.ashs.org

ASHS SCHOLARS AWARD

Two annual scholarships of $1500 given to undergraduate students majoring in horticulture at a four-year institution. Applicants must be nominated by the chair/head of the department in which they are majoring, but only one applicant per department may be nominated.

Academic Fields/Career Goals: Horticulture/Floriculture.

Award: Scholarship for use in freshman, sophomore, junior, or senior years; not renewable. *Number:* 2. *Amount:* $1500.

Eligibility Requirements: Applicant must be enrolled or expecting to enroll full-time at a four-year institution or university and must have an interest in leadership. Applicant or parent of applicant must have employment or volunteer experience in community service. Available to U.S. and non-U.S. citizens.

Application Requirements: Application, essay, resume, references, transcript. *Deadline:* February 4.

Contact: Michael Neff, Executive Director
American Society for Horticultural Science
113 Southwest Street, Suite 200
Alexandria, VA 22314
Phone: 703-836-4606 Ext. 325
Fax: 703-836-2024
E-mail: mwneff@ashs.org

E. TED SIMS JR. MEMORIAL SCHOLARSHIP

A scholarship of $1000 for a full-time junior or senior class student standing beginning fall of award year and must show commitment to the horticulture profession. Applicants must be nominated by the chair/head of the department in which they are majoring, but only one applicant may be nominated per department.

Academic Fields/Career Goals: Horticulture/Floriculture.

Award: Scholarship for use in junior or senior years; not renewable. *Number:* 1. *Amount:* $1000.

Eligibility Requirements: Applicant must be enrolled or expecting to enroll full-time at a four-year institution or university. Available to U.S. citizens.

Application Requirements: Application, essay, resume, references, transcript. *Deadline:* February 4.

Contact: Michael Neff, Executive Director
American Society for Horticultural Science
113 Southwest Street, Suite 200
Alexandria, VA 22314
Phone: 703-836-4606 Ext. 325
Fax: 703-836-2024
E-mail: mwneff@ashs.org

ARIZONA NURSERY ASSOCIATION http://www.azna.org

ARIZONA NURSERY ASSOCIATION FOUNDATION SCHOLARSHIP

Provides research grants and scholarships for the green industry. Applicant must be an Arizona resident currently or planning to be enrolled in a horticultural related curriculum at an Arizona university, community college, or continuing education program. See Web site for further details: http://www.azna.org.

Academic Fields/Career Goals: Horticulture/Floriculture.

Award: Scholarship for use in freshman, sophomore, junior, senior, or postgraduate years; renewable. *Number:* 12–15. *Amount:* $500–$3000.

Eligibility Requirements: Applicant must be enrolled or expecting to enroll full- or part-time at a two-year or four-year or technical institution or university. Available to U.S. citizens.

Application Requirements: Application, references, transcript. *Deadline:* April 15.

Contact: Cheryl Goar, Executive Director
Arizona Nursery Association
1430 West Broadway Road, Suite 110
Tempe, AZ 85282
Phone: 480-966-1610
Fax: 480-966-0923
E-mail: cgoar@azna.org

CALIFORNIA ASSOCIATION OF NURSERYMEN ENDOWMENT FOR RESEARCH AND SCHOLARSHIPS http://www.cangc.org

CANERS FOUNDATION ENDOWMENT SCHOLARSHIP

Applicants must be college students who are currently enrolled in no fewer than six units within a program related to the nursery industry and who are entering or returning to college in a horticulture-related field in the fall.

Academic Fields/Career Goals: Horticulture/Floriculture.

Award: Scholarship for use in freshman, sophomore, junior, or senior years; not renewable. *Number:* varies. *Amount:* varies.

Eligibility Requirements: Applicant must be enrolled or expecting to enroll full-time at a four-year institution or university. Available to U.S. citizens.

Application Requirements: Application, transcript. *Deadline:* varies.

Contact: Darrelyn Adams, Membership Director
California Association of Nurserymen Endowment for Research and Scholarships
3947 Lennane Drive, Suite 150
Sacramento, CA 95834
Phone: 916-928-3900 Ext. 13
Fax: 916-567-0505
E-mail: dadams@cangc.org

CONNECTICUT NURSERYMEN'S FOUNDATION INC. http://www.flowersplantsinct.com/cnla_cnf.htm

CONNECTICUT NURSERYMEN'S FOUNDATION SCHOLARSHIP

Award to graduating high school seniors who will enter college in the fall semester, majoring in horticulture. This award is renewable for up to four years. Must be a resident of Connecticut and a U.S. citizen.

Academic Fields/Career Goals: Horticulture/Floriculture.

Award: Scholarship for use in freshman year; renewable. *Number:* 1. *Amount:* $5000.

Eligibility Requirements: Applicant must be high school student; planning to enroll or expecting to enroll full-time at a two-year or four-year institution or university and resident of Connecticut. Applicant must have 3.0 GPA or higher. Available to U.S. citizens.

Application Requirements: Application, financial need analysis, interview, references, test scores, transcript. *Deadline:* March 17.

Contact: Judy Mattson, Scholarship Committee Chairman
Connecticut Nurserymen's Foundation Inc.
131 Hollister Street
Manchester, CT 06042
Phone: 860-643-8363
Fax: 860-643-2778
E-mail: jmattson.negs@sbcglobal.net

FEDERATED GARDEN CLUBS OF CONNECTICUT http://www.ctgardenclubs.org

FEDERATED GARDEN CLUBS OF CONNECTICUT INC. SCHOLARSHIPS

• *See page 131*

FEDERATED GARDEN CLUBS OF MARYLAND http://hometown.aol.com/fgcofmd

ROBERT LEWIS BAKER SCHOLARSHIP

Scholarship awards of up to $5000 to encourage the study of ornamental horticulture, and landscape design. Applicants must be high school graduates, current college and/or graduate students, and Maryland residents. Can attend any accredited college/university in the United States.

Academic Fields/Career Goals: Horticulture/Floriculture; Landscape Architecture.

Award: Scholarship for use in freshman, sophomore, junior, senior, or graduate years; not renewable. *Number:* 1. *Amount:* $5000.

Eligibility Requirements: Applicant must be enrolled or expecting to enroll full-time at a four-year institution or university and resident of Maryland. Available to U.S. citizens.

Application Requirements: Application. *Deadline:* June 30.

Contact: Marjorie Schiebel, Scholarship Chairman
Federated Garden Clubs of Maryland
1105 A Providence Road
Baltimore, MD 21286
Phone: 410-296-6961
E-mail: fgcofmd@aol.com

VIRGINIA P. HENRY SCHOLARSHIP

Scholarship of up to $1000 available to qualified undergraduate students enrolled in horticultural studies. For full-time study. Must be legal residents of Maryland.

Academic Fields/Career Goals: Horticulture/Floriculture.

Award: Scholarship for use in freshman, sophomore, junior, or senior years; not renewable. *Number:* 1. *Amount:* $1000.

Eligibility Requirements: Applicant must be enrolled or expecting to enroll full-time at a four-year institution or university and resident of Maryland. Available to U.S. citizens.

Application Requirements: Application. *Deadline:* May 1.

Contact: Marjorie Schiebel, Scholarship Chairman
Federated Garden Clubs of Maryland
1105 A Providence Road
Baltimore, MD 21286
Phone: 410-296-6961
E-mail: fgcofmd@aol.com

FRIENDS OF THE FRELINGHUYSEN ARBORETUM http://www.arboretumfriends.org

BENJAMIN C. BLACKBURN SCHOLARSHIP

• *See page 302*

GARDEN CLUB OF AMERICA http://www.gcamerica.org

GARDEN CLUB OF AMERICA SUMMER SCHOLARSHIP IN FIELD BOTANY

Scholarship of $1500 to undergraduate or graduate students up to master's level wishing to pursue summer field work in botany. All candidates must be enrolled in a U.S. college or university.

Academic Fields/Career Goals: Horticulture/Floriculture; Natural Sciences.

Award: Scholarship for use in freshman, sophomore, junior, senior, or graduate years; not renewable. *Number:* 1. *Amount:* $1500.

Eligibility Requirements: Applicant must be enrolled or expecting to enroll full-time at a four-year institution or university. Available to U.S. citizens.

Application Requirements: Application, essay, references, transcript. *Deadline:* February 1.

Contact: Judy Smith, Scholarship Committee Administrator
Garden Club of America
14 East 60th Street, Third Floor
New York, NY 10022-1002
Phone: 212-753-8287
Fax: 212-753-0134
E-mail: judy@gcamerica.org

JOAN K. HUNT AND RACHEL M. HUNT SUMMER SCHOLARSHIP IN FIELD BOTANY

Scholarship of up to $1500 towards summer study in field botany. Purpose is to promote the awareness of the importance of botany to horticulture. For study within the U.S. only. Undergraduates and graduate students up to master's level may apply.

Academic Fields/Career Goals: Horticulture/Floriculture; Natural Sciences.

Award: Scholarship for use in freshman, sophomore, junior, senior, or graduate years; not renewable. *Number:* 1. *Amount:* up to $1500.

Eligibility Requirements: Applicant must be enrolled or expecting to enroll full-time at a four-year institution or university. Available to U.S. citizens.

Application Requirements: Application, essay, references, transcript. *Deadline:* February 1.

Contact: Judy Smith, Scholarship Committee Administrator
Garden Club of America
14 East 60th Street, Third Floor
New York, NY 10022-1002
Phone: 212-753-8287
Fax: 212-753-0134
E-mail: judy@gcamerica.org

KATHARINE M. GROSSCUP SCHOLARSHIP

Scholarships to encourage the study of horticulture and related fields by providing financial assistance to students who wish to pursue these academic endeavors. Preference is given to young men and women who are college juniors, seniors, or graduate students from Ohio, Pennsylvania, West Virginia, Michigan, Indiana, and Kentucky.

Academic Fields/Career Goals: Horticulture/Floriculture; Landscape Architecture.

Award: Scholarship for use in sophomore, junior, senior, or graduate years; not renewable. *Number:* varies. *Amount:* up to $3000.

Eligibility Requirements: Applicant must be enrolled or expecting to enroll full-time at a four-year institution or university and resident of Indiana, Kentucky, Michigan, Ohio, Pennsylvania, or West Virginia. Available to U.S. citizens.

Application Requirements: Application, interview, references, self-addressed stamped envelope, transcript. *Deadline:* January 25.

Contact: Nancy Stevenson, Grosscup Scholarship Committee
Garden Club of America
Cleveland Botanical Garden, 11030 East Boulevard
Cleveland, OH 44106
Fax: 216-721-2056

LOY MCCANDLESS MARKS SCHOLARSHIP IN TROPICAL ORNAMENTAL HORTICULTURE

Award of $2000 to graduate or advanced undergraduate student. Provides an opportunity to study at a leading foreign institution that specializes in the field of tropical plants.

Academic Fields/Career Goals: Horticulture/Floriculture.

Award: Scholarship for use in sophomore, junior, senior, or graduate years; not renewable. *Number:* 1. *Amount:* $2000.

Eligibility Requirements: Applicant must be enrolled or expecting to enroll full-time at a four-year institution or university. Available to U.S. citizens.

Application Requirements: Application, interview, references, self-addressed stamped envelope, transcript, budget. *Deadline:* January 15.

Contact: Judy Smith, Scholarship Committee Administrator
Garden Club of America
14 East 60th Street, Third Floor
New York, NY 10022-1002
Phone: 212-753-8287
Fax: 212-753-0134
E-mail: judy@gcamerica.org

ZELLER SUMMER SCHOLARSHIP IN MEDICINAL BOTANY

• *See page 337*

GOLDEN STATE BONSAI FEDERATION http://www.gsbf-bonsai.org

HORTICULTURE SCHOLARSHIPS

Scholarship for study towards a certificate in ornamental horticulture from an accredited school. Applicant must be a current member of a GSBF member club and have a letter of recommendation from club president, or a responsible spokesperson from GSBF. Deadline varies.

Academic Fields/Career Goals: Horticulture/Floriculture.

Award: Scholarship for use in freshman, sophomore, junior, senior, graduate, or postgraduate years; not renewable. *Number:* 1–5. *Amount:* up to $400.

Eligibility Requirements: Applicant must be enrolled or expecting to enroll full-time at a two-year or four-year or technical institution or university. Applicant or parent of applicant must be member of Golden State Bonsai Federation. Available to U.S. citizens.

Application Requirements: Application, references. *Deadline:* varies.

Contact: Abe Far, Grants and Scholarship Committee
Golden State Bonsai Federation
2451 Galahad Road
San Diego, CA 92123
Phone: 619-234-3434
E-mail: abefar@cox.net

GOLF COURSE SUPERINTENDENTS ASSOCIATION OF AMERICA http://www.gcsaa.org

GCSAA SCHOLARS COMPETITION

Competition for outstanding students planning careers in golf course management. Must be full-time college undergraduates currently enrolled in a two-year or more accredited program related to golf course management and have completed one year of program. Must be member of GCSAA.

Academic Fields/Career Goals: Horticulture/Floriculture.

Award: Scholarship for use in sophomore, junior, or senior years; not renewable. *Number:* varies. *Amount:* $500–$6000.

Eligibility Requirements: Applicant must be enrolled or expecting to enroll full-time at a two-year or four-year institution or university. Applicant or parent of applicant must be member of Golf Course Superintendents Association of America. Available to U.S. and non-U.S. citizens.

Application Requirements: Application, applicant must enter a contest, essay, references, transcript, adviser's report, superintendent's report. *Deadline:* June 1.

Contact: Mischia Wright, Senior Manager, Development
Golf Course Superintendents Association of America
1421 Research Park Drive
Lawrence, KS 66049-3859
Phone: 800-472-7878 Ext. 4424
Fax: 785-832-4449
E-mail: mwright@gcsaa.org

GOLF COURSE SUPERINTENDENTS ASSOCIATION OF AMERICA STUDENT ESSAY CONTEST

• *See page 69*

SCOTTS COMPANY SCHOLARS PROGRAM

Applicant must be a graduating high school senior or freshman, sophomore, or junior in college. Applicants must be pursuing a career in the green industry.

Academic Fields/Career Goals: Horticulture/Floriculture.

Award: Scholarship for use in freshman, sophomore, or junior years; not renewable. *Number:* up to 7. *Amount:* $500–$2500.

Eligibility Requirements: Applicant must be enrolled or expecting to enroll full-time at a two-year or four-year institution or university. Available to U.S. and non-U.S. citizens.

Application Requirements: Application, essay, references, transcript. *Deadline:* March 1.

Contact: Mischia Wright, Senior Manager, Development
Golf Course Superintendents Association of America
1421 Research Park Drive
Lawrence, KS 66049-3859
Phone: 800-472-7878 Ext. 4424
Fax: 785-832-4449
E-mail: mwright@gcsaa.org

HERB SOCIETY OF AMERICA, WESTERN RESERVE UNIT

FRANCIS SYLVIA ZVERINA SCHOLARSHIP

Awards are given to needy students who plan a career in horticulture or related field. Preference will be given to applicants whose horticultural career goals involve teaching, research, or work in the public or nonprofit sector, such as public gardens, botanical gardens, parks, arboreta, city planning, public education, and awareness.

Academic Fields/Career Goals: Horticulture/Floriculture; Landscape Architecture.

Award: Scholarship for use in sophomore, junior, or senior years; not renewable. *Number:* 1. *Amount:* $5000.

Eligibility Requirements: Applicant must be enrolled or expecting to enroll full-time at a four-year institution or university. Available to U.S. citizens.

Application Requirements: Application, essay, references, transcript. *Deadline:* April 1.

Contact: Jewelann Stefanar, Committee Chair
Herb Society of America, Western Reserve Unit
4706 Bentwood Drive
Brooklyn, OH 44144
Phone: 216-741-0985
E-mail: jewelann1@roadrunner.com

WESTERN RESERVE HERB SOCIETY SCHOLARSHIP

Awards are given to needy students who plan a career in horticulture or related field. Preference will be given to applicants whose horticultural career goals involve teaching, research, or work in the public or nonprofit sector, such as public gardens, botanical gardens, parks, arboreta, city planning, public education and awareness.

Academic Fields/Career Goals: Horticulture/Floriculture; Landscape Architecture.

Award: Scholarship for use in sophomore, junior, senior, or graduate years; not renewable. *Number:* 1. *Amount:* $4000.

Eligibility Requirements: Applicant must be enrolled or expecting to enroll full-time at a four-year institution or university and resident of Ohio. Available to U.S. citizens.

Application Requirements: Application, essay, references, transcript. *Deadline:* April 1.

Contact: Jewelann Stefanar, Committee Chair
Herb Society of America, Western Reserve Unit
4706 Bentwood Drive
Brooklyn, OH 44144
Phone: 216-741-0985
E-mail: jewelann1@roadrunner.com

JOSEPH SHINODA MEMORIAL SCHOLARSHIP FOUNDATION http://www.shinodascholarship.org

JOSEPH SHINODA MEMORIAL SCHOLARSHIP

One-time award for undergraduates in accredited colleges and universities. Must be furthering their education in the field of floriculture (production, distribution, research, or retail).

Academic Fields/Career Goals: Horticulture/Floriculture.

Award: Scholarship for use in sophomore, junior, or senior years; not renewable. *Number:* 10–20. *Amount:* $1000–$5000.

Joseph Shinoda Memorial Scholarship Foundation (continued)

Eligibility Requirements: Applicant must be enrolled or expecting to enroll full-time at a four-year institution or university. Available to U.S. citizens.

Application Requirements: Application, essay, financial need analysis, photo, references, transcript. *Deadline:* March 30.

Contact: Barbara A. McCaleb, Executive Secretary
Joseph Shinoda Memorial Scholarship Foundation
234 Via La Paz
San Luis Obispo, CA 93401
Phone: 805-756-2897

LANDSCAPE ARCHITECTURE FOUNDATION http://www.lafoundation.org

CLASS FUND ORNAMENTAL HORTICULTURE PROGRAM

Awards up to three $1000 scholarships to juniors and/or seniors enrolled in an ornamental horticulture curriculum.

Academic Fields/Career Goals: Horticulture/Floriculture.

Award: Grant for use in junior or senior years; not renewable. *Number:* up to 3. *Amount:* up to $1000.

Eligibility Requirements: Applicant must be enrolled or expecting to enroll full- or part-time at a four-year institution or university and studying in California. Available to U.S. citizens.

Application Requirements: Application, essay, references. *Deadline:* February 15.

Contact: Ron Figura, Development Director
Landscape Architecture Foundation
818 18 Street, NW, Suite 810
Washington, DC 20006
Phone: 202-331-7070 Ext. 10
Fax: 202-331-7079
E-mail: rfigura@lafoundation.org

LANDSCAPE ARCHITECTURE FOUNDATION/CALIFORNIA LANDSCAPE ARCHITECTURAL STUDENT FUND SCHOLARSHIPS PROGRAM

Nonrenewable scholarships designed to assist undergraduate or graduate students enrolled in landscape architecture and ornamental horticulture programs at eligible institutions in California. Based on financial need and commitment to profession.

Academic Fields/Career Goals: Horticulture/Floriculture; Landscape Architecture.

Award: Scholarship for use in freshman, sophomore, junior, or senior years; not renewable. *Number:* up to 15. *Amount:* $1000–$3000.

Eligibility Requirements: Applicant must be enrolled or expecting to enroll full-time at a four-year institution or university and studying in California. Available to U.S. and non-U.S. citizens.

Application Requirements: Application, financial need analysis, references, 300 word statement on profession. *Deadline:* February 15.

Contact: Ron Figura, Development Director
Landscape Architecture Foundation
818 18 Street, NW, Suite 810
Washington, DC 20006
Phone: 202-331-7070 Ext. 10
Fax: 202-331-7079
E-mail: rfigura@lafoundation.org

LANDSCAPE ARCHITECTURE FOUNDATION/CALIFORNIA LANDSCAPE ARCHITECTURE STUDENT FUND UNIVERSITY SCHOLARSHIP PROGRAM

Nonrenewable scholarships for juniors and/or seniors enrolled in landscape architecture curriculum in California. Based on financial need and commitment to profession.

Academic Fields/Career Goals: Horticulture/Floriculture; Landscape Architecture.

Award: Scholarship for use in junior or senior years; not renewable. *Number:* up to 6. *Amount:* up to $2000.

Eligibility Requirements: Applicant must be enrolled or expecting to enroll full- or part-time at a four-year institution or university and studying in California. Available to U.S. and non-U.S. citizens.

Application Requirements: Application, financial need analysis, references, 300-word statement on profession, 100-word statement on intended use of funds. *Deadline:* February 15.

Contact: Ron Figura, Development Director
Landscape Architecture Foundation
818 18 Street, NW, Suite 810
Washington, DC 20006
Phone: 202-331-7070 Ext. 10
Fax: 202-331-7079
E-mail: rfigura@lafoundation.org

MONTANA FEDERATION OF GARDEN CLUBS http://www.mtfgc.org

LIFE MEMBER MONTANA FEDERATION OF GARDEN CLUBS SCHOLARSHIP

• *See page 218*

NATIONAL GARDEN CLUBS SCHOLARSHIP

Scholarship for a college student majoring in some branch of horticulture. Applicants must have sophomore or higher standing and be a legal resident of Montana.

Academic Fields/Career Goals: Horticulture/Floriculture.

Award: Scholarship for use in sophomore, junior, or senior years; not renewable. *Number:* 1. *Amount:* up to $3500.

Eligibility Requirements: Applicant must be enrolled or expecting to enroll full-time at a four-year institution or university and resident of Montana. Available to U.S. citizens.

Application Requirements: Application, financial need analysis. *Deadline:* February 28.

Contact: Margaret Yaw, Scholarship Committee, State Chairman
Montana Federation of Garden Clubs
2603 Spring Creek Drive
Bozeman, MT 59715-3621
Phone: 406-587-3621

MORRIS LAND CONSERVANCY http://www.morrislandconservancy.org

ROGERS FAMILY SCHOLARSHIP

• *See page 304*

RUSSELL W. MYERS SCHOLARSHIP

• *See page 304*

NATIONAL COUNCIL OF STATE GARDEN CLUBS INC. SCHOLARSHIP http://www.gardenclub.org

NATIONAL COUNCIL OF STATE GARDEN CLUBS INC. SCHOLARSHIP

• *See page 76*

NATIONAL GARDEN CLUBS INC. http://www.gardenclub.org

NATIONAL GARDEN CLUBS INC. SCHOLARSHIP PROGRAM

• *See page 77*

NATIONAL POTATO COUNCIL WOMEN'S AUXILIARY http://www.nationalpotatocouncil.org

POTATO INDUSTRY SCHOLARSHIP

• *See page 70*

PENNSYLVANIA ASSOCIATION OF CONSERVATION DISTRICTS AUXILIARY http://www.pacd.org

PACD AUXILIARY SCHOLARSHIPS

• *See page 78*

PROFESSIONAL GROUNDS MANAGEMENT SOCIETY http://www.pgms.org

ANNE SEAMAN PROFESSIONAL GROUNDS MANAGEMENT SOCIETY MEMORIAL SCHOLARSHIP

• *See page 78*

SOIL AND WATER CONSERVATION SOCIETY-NEW JERSEY CHAPTER http://www.geocities.com/njswcs

EDWARD R. HALL SCHOLARSHIP
• *See page 71*

SOUTHERN NURSERY ASSOCIATION http://www.sna.org

SIDNEY B. MEADOWS SCHOLARSHIP

Scholarship up to $2500 to students enrolled in an accredited undergraduate or graduate ornamental horticulture program or related discipline at a four-year institution. Student must be in a junior or senior standing at time of application. For undergraduate students minimum grade point average of 2.25 or 3.0 on a scale of 4.0 for graduate students

Academic Fields/Career Goals: Horticulture/Floriculture.

Award: Scholarship for use in junior, senior, or graduate years; not renewable. *Number:* 10–15. *Amount:* $1500–$2500.

Eligibility Requirements: Applicant must be enrolled or expecting to enroll full-time at a four-year institution or university and resident of Arkansas, Florida, Georgia, Kentucky, Louisiana, Maryland, Mississippi, Missouri, North Carolina, Oklahoma, South Carolina, Tennessee, Texas, or Virginia. Available to U.S. and non-U.S. citizens.

Application Requirements: Application, resume, references, self-addressed stamped envelope, transcript. *Deadline:* May 31.

Contact: Program Director
Southern Nursery Association
1827 Powers Ferry Road, Building Four, Suite 100
Atlanta, GA 30339-8422
Phone: 770-953-3311
Fax: 770-953-4411
E-mail: mail@sna.org

TURF AND ORNAMENTAL COMMUNICATION ASSOCIATION http://www.toca.org

TURF AND ORNAMENTAL COMMUNICATORS ASSOCIATION SCHOLARSHIP PROGRAM
• *See page 79*

WOMAN'S NATIONAL FARM AND GARDEN ASSOCIATION http://www.wnfga.org

WOMAN'S NATIONAL FARM AND GARDEN ASSOCIATION, INC. BURLINGAME/GERRITY HORTICULTURAL THERAPY SCHOLARSHIP

$500 scholarship for a student enrolled in a bachelor's degree program in horticultural therapy. The recipient is chosen by their college.

Academic Fields/Career Goals: Horticulture/Floriculture.

Award: Scholarship for use in freshman, sophomore, junior, or senior years; not renewable. *Number:* 1. *Amount:* $500.

Eligibility Requirements: Applicant must be enrolled or expecting to enroll full- or part-time at a four-year institution or university and female. Available to U.S. citizens.

Application Requirements: Application. *Deadline:* varies.

Contact: Scholarship Coordinator
Woman's National Farm and Garden Association
Ninth Jenness Road
PO Box 1175
Midland, MI 48641-1175
Phone: 734-662-8661
E-mail: cscioly@hotmail.com

HOSPITALITY MANAGEMENT

AMERICAN HOTEL AND LODGING EDUCATIONAL FOUNDATION http://www.ahlef.org

AAA FIVE DIAMOND HOSPITALITY SCHOLARSHIP

Scholarship of $5000 is awarded to full-time student at the sophomore, junior, or senior level studying hospitality management.. Minimum 3.0 GPA required. Must be a U.S. resident.

Academic Fields/Career Goals: Hospitality Management.

Award: Scholarship for use in sophomore, junior, or senior years; not renewable. *Number:* varies. *Amount:* $5000.

Eligibility Requirements: Applicant must be enrolled or expecting to enroll full-time at a four-year institution or university. Applicant must have 3.0 GPA or higher. Available to U.S. citizens.

Application Requirements: Application, financial need analysis, references, transcript, nomination from school. *Deadline:* May 1.

Contact: Ms. Crystal Hammond, Director of Foundation Programs
American Hotel and Lodging Educational Foundation
1201 New York Avenue NW, Suite 600
Washington, DC 20005-3931
Phone: 202-289-3188
Fax: 202-289-3199
E-mail: chammond@ahlef.org

AMERICAN EXPRESS SCHOLARSHIP PROGRAM

Award for hotel employees of American Hotel and Lodging Association member properties and their dependents. For full- and part-time students in undergraduate program leading to degree in hospitality management. Must be employed at hotel which is a property of AH&LA. Application available at Web site: http://www.ahlef.org.

Academic Fields/Career Goals: Hospitality Management.

Award: Scholarship for use in freshman, sophomore, junior, or senior years; not renewable. *Number:* varies. *Amount:* $500–$2000.

Eligibility Requirements: Applicant must be enrolled or expecting to enroll full- or part-time at a two-year or four-year institution or university. Applicant or parent of applicant must have employment or volunteer experience in hospitality/hotel administration/operations. Available to U.S. and non-U.S. citizens.

Application Requirements: Application, essay, financial need analysis, transcript. *Deadline:* May 1.

Contact: Crystal Hammond, Director of Foundation Programs
American Hotel and Lodging Educational Foundation
1201 New York Avenue NW, Suite 600
Washington, DC 20005-3931
Phone: 202-289-3188
Fax: 202-289-3199
E-mail: chammond@ahlef.org

AMERICAN HOTEL & LODGING EDUCATIONAL FOUNDATION PEPSI SCHOLARSHIP

Scholarships of $500 to $3000 awarded to hospitality high school seniors and undergraduates. Minimum 2.5 GPA required.

Academic Fields/Career Goals: Hospitality Management.

Award: Scholarship for use in freshman, sophomore, junior, or senior years; not renewable. *Number:* varies. *Amount:* $500–$3000.

Eligibility Requirements: Applicant must be enrolled or expecting to enroll full- or part-time at a four-year institution or university and studying in District of Columbia. Applicant must have 2.5 GPA or higher. Available to U.S. and non-U.S. citizens.

Application Requirements: Application, financial need analysis, transcript, nomination from school. *Deadline:* May 1.

Contact: Ms. Crystal Hammond, Director of Foundation Programs
American Hotel and Lodging Educational Foundation
1201 New York Avenue NW, Suite 600
Washington, DC 20005-3931
Phone: 202-289-3188
Fax: 202-289-3199
E-mail: chammond@ahlef.org

ANNUAL SCHOLARSHIP GRANT PROGRAM
• *See page 314*

ARTHUR J. PACKARD MEMORIAL SCHOLARSHIP

Each university nominates its best qualified student to compete in the national competition. First place winner receives a $5000 scholarship, second-place receives $3000 and third-place receives $2000.

Academic Fields/Career Goals: Hospitality Management.

Award: Scholarship for use in junior or senior years; not renewable. *Number:* 3. *Amount:* $2000–$5000.

American Hotel and Lodging Educational Foundation (continued)

Eligibility Requirements: Applicant must be enrolled or expecting to enroll full-time at a four-year institution. Applicant must have 3.5 GPA or higher. Available to U.S. citizens.

Application Requirements: Application, financial need analysis, references, transcript, nomination from school. *Deadline:* May 1.

Contact: Ms. Crystal Hammond, Director of Foundation Programs
American Hotel and Lodging Educational Foundation
1201 New York Avenue NW, Suite 600
Washington, DC 20005-3931
Phone: 202-289-3188
Fax: 202-289-3199
E-mail: chammond@ahlef.org

ECOLAB SCHOLARSHIP PROGRAM

Award for students enrolled full-time in United States baccalaureate or associate program leading to degree in hospitality management. Must complete appropriate application and submit copy of college curriculum and IRS 1040 form. Application available at Web site: http://www.ahlef.org.

Academic Fields/Career Goals: Hospitality Management.

Award: Scholarship for use in freshman, sophomore, junior, or senior years; not renewable. *Number:* varies. *Amount:* $1000–$2000.

Eligibility Requirements: Applicant must be enrolled or expecting to enroll full-time at a four-year institution or university. Available to U.S. and non-U.S. citizens.

Application Requirements: Application, essay, financial need analysis, transcript, IRS 1040 form. *Deadline:* May 1.

Contact: Ms. Crystal Hammond, Manager of Foundation Programs
American Hotel and Lodging Educational Foundation
1201 New York Avenue SW, Suite 600
Washington, DC 20005-3931
Phone: 202-289-3188
Fax: 202-289-3199
E-mail: chammond@ahlef.org

HYATT HOTELS FUND FOR MINORITY LODGING MANAGEMENT

Scholarship available for African-American, Hispanic, American Indian, Alaskan Native, Asian, or Pacific Islander in a baccalaureate hospitality management program. Must be at least a sophomore in a four-year program.

Academic Fields/Career Goals: Hospitality Management.

Award: Scholarship for use in sophomore, junior, or senior years; not renewable. *Number:* varies. *Amount:* $2000.

Eligibility Requirements: Applicant must be American Indian/Alaska Native, Asian/Pacific Islander, Black (non-Hispanic), or Hispanic and enrolled or expecting to enroll full-time at a four-year institution. Available to U.S. citizens.

Application Requirements: Application, applicant must enter a contest, financial need analysis, transcript. *Deadline:* May 1.

Contact: Ms. Crystal Hammond, Director
American Hotel and Lodging Educational Foundation
1201 New York Avenue, Suite 600
Washington, DC 20005
Phone: 202-289-3188
Fax: 202-289-3199
E-mail: chammond@ahlef.org

INCOMING FRESHMAN SCHOLARSHIPS

• *See page 202*

RAMA SCHOLARSHIP FOR THE AMERICAN DREAM

Scholarship for students in an undergraduate or graduate program in hospitality management. School must give preference to students of Asian-Indian descent or other minority groups, as well as JHM employees and their dependents.

Academic Fields/Career Goals: Hospitality Management.

Award: Scholarship for use in sophomore, junior, or senior years; not renewable. *Number:* 1000–3000. *Amount:* $1000–$3000.

Eligibility Requirements: Applicant must be American Indian/Alaska Native, Asian/Pacific Islander, Black (non-Hispanic), or Hispanic and enrolled or expecting to enroll full- or part-time at a four-year institution. Applicant must have 2.5 GPA or higher. Available to U.S. citizens.

Application Requirements: Application, financial need analysis, references, transcript, nomination from school. *Deadline:* May 1.

Contact: Ms. Crystal Hammond, Director
American Hotel and Lodging Educational Foundation
1201 New York Avenue, NW, Suite 600
Washington, DC 20005
Phone: 202-289-3188
Fax: 202-289-3199
E-mail: chammond@ahlef.org

STEVEN HYMANS EXTENDED STAY SCHOLARSHIP

This program is for applicants with some experience either working or interning (paid or unpaid) at a lodging property. Preference will be given to those applicants with experience at an extended stay property. Must have a 3.0 GPA.

Academic Fields/Career Goals: Hospitality Management.

Award: Scholarship for use in freshman, sophomore, junior, or senior years; renewable. *Number:* 500–2000. *Amount:* $500–$2000.

Eligibility Requirements: Applicant must be enrolled or expecting to enroll full- or part-time at a two-year or four-year institution. Applicant must have 3.0 GPA or higher. Available to U.S. citizens.

Application Requirements: Application, financial need analysis, references, transcript. *Deadline:* May 1.

Contact: Ms. Crystal Hammond, Director
American Hotel and Lodging Educational Foundation
1201 New York Avenue NW, Suite 600
Washington, DC 20005
Phone: 202-289-3188
Fax: 202-289-3199
E-mail: chammond@ahlef.org

AMERICAN INSTITUTE OF WINE AND FOOD-PACIFIC NORTHWEST CHAPTER http://www.aiwf.org

CULINARY, VINIFERA, AND HOSPITALITY SCHOLARSHIP

• *See page 311*

CLUB FOUNDATION http://www.clubfoundation.org

JOE PERDUE SCHOLARSHIP PROGRAM

Awards for candidates seeking a managerial career in the private club industry and currently attending an accredited four year college or university. Must have completed freshman year and be enrolled full-time. Must have achieved and continue to maintain a GPA of at least 2.5. Minimum two awards of $2500 granted annually.

Academic Fields/Career Goals: Hospitality Management.

Award: Scholarship for use in sophomore, junior, or senior years; not renewable. *Number:* 2. *Amount:* $2500.

Eligibility Requirements: Applicant must be enrolled or expecting to enroll full-time at a four-year institution or university. Applicant must have 2.5 GPA or higher. Available to U.S. citizens.

Application Requirements: Application, essay, resume, references, self-addressed stamped envelope, transcript. *Deadline:* May 1.

Contact: Ashleigh Hill, Program Specialist
Club Foundation
1733 King Street
Alexandria, VA 22314
Phone: 703-299-4268 Ext. 268
Fax: 703-739-0124
E-mail: ashleigh.hill@cmaa.org

GOLDEN GATE RESTAURANT ASSOCIATION http://www.ggra.org

GOLDEN GATE RESTAURANT ASSOCIATION SCHOLARSHIP FOUNDATION

• *See page 315*

HAWAII HOTEL AND LODGING ASSOCIATION http://www.hawaiihotels.org

CLEM JUDD, JR. MEMORIAL SCHOLARSHIP

Scholarship for a Hawaii resident who must be able to prove Hawaiian ancestry. Applicant must be enrolled full-time at a U.S. accredited university/college majoring in hotel management. Must have a minimum 3.0 GPA.

Academic Fields/Career Goals: Hospitality Management.

Award: Scholarship for use in freshman, sophomore, junior, or senior years; not renewable. *Number:* 2. *Amount:* $1000–$2500.

Eligibility Requirements: Applicant must be Asian/Pacific Islander; enrolled or expecting to enroll full-time at a four-year institution and resident of Hawaii. Applicant must have 3.0 GPA or higher. Available to U.S. citizens.

Application Requirements: Application, autobiography, driver's license, essay, references. *Deadline:* July 1.

Contact: Scholarship Committee
Hawaii Hotel and Lodging Association
2270 Kalakaua Avenue, Suite 1506
Honolulu, HI 96815
Phone: 808-923-0407
Fax: 808-924-3843
E-mail: hhla@hawaiihotels.org

R.W. BOB HOLDEN SCHOLARSHIP

One $1000 award for a student attending or planning to attend an accredited university or college in Hawaii, majoring in hotel management. Must be a Hawaii resident and a US citizen. Must have a minimum 3.0 GPA.

Academic Fields/Career Goals: Hospitality Management; Travel/Tourism.

Award: Scholarship for use in junior, senior, or graduate years; not renewable. *Number:* 1–5. *Amount:* $1000.

Eligibility Requirements: Applicant must be enrolled or expecting to enroll full-time at a two-year or four-year institution or university; resident of Hawaii and studying in Hawaii. Applicant must have 3.0 GPA or higher. Available to U.S. citizens.

Application Requirements: Application, autobiography, driver's license, essay, photo, references, transcript. *Deadline:* July 1.

Contact: Naomi Kanna, Director of Membership Services
Hawaii Hotel and Lodging Association
2270 Kalakaua Avenue, Suite 1506
Honolulu, HI 96815-2564
Phone: 808-923-0407
Fax: 808-924-3843
E-mail: hhla@hawaiihotels.org

HISPANIC COLLEGE FUND INC. http://www.hispanicfund.org

MARRIOTT SCHOLARS PROGRAM

$9000 scholarship for Hispanic students pursing studies in hospitality management, hotel management, culinary or food and beverage field. Must be U.S. citizen and have minimum 3.0 GPA.

Academic Fields/Career Goals: Hospitality Management.

Award: Scholarship for use in freshman, sophomore, junior, or senior years; renewable. *Number:* varies. *Amount:* up to $9000.

Eligibility Requirements: Applicant must be Hispanic and enrolled or expecting to enroll full-time at a two-year or four-year institution or university. Applicant must have 3.0 GPA or higher. Available to U.S. citizens.

Application Requirements: Application, essay, references, proof of family income, citizenship proof. *Deadline:* April 15.

Contact: Fernando Barrueta, Chief Executive Officer
Hispanic College Fund Inc.
1301 K Street, NW, Suite 450-A West
Washington, DC 20005
Phone: 202-296-5400
Fax: 202-296-3774
E-mail: hcf-info@hispanicfund.org

ILLINOIS RESTAURANT ASSOCIATION EDUCATIONAL FOUNDATION http://www.illinoisrestaurants.org

ILLINOIS RESTAURANT ASSOCIATION EDUCATIONAL FOUNDATION SCHOLARSHIPS

• *See page 203*

INTERNATIONAL AIRLINES TRAVEL AGENT NETWORK http://www.iatan.org

INTERNATIONAL AIRLINES TRAVEL AGENT NETWORK FOUNDATION SCHOLARSHIP

Scholarships available annually to individuals who are interested in pursuing or enhancing their careers in travel. Must be U.S. citizens or permanent legal residents of the United States and not less than 17 years of age. Must have been employed for at least six months by an IATAN accredited travel agency or who are registered students at a recognized postsecondary educational/vocational institution having direct links with the travel industry.

Academic Fields/Career Goals: Hospitality Management; Travel/Tourism.

Award: Scholarship for use in freshman, sophomore, junior, senior, graduate, or postgraduate years; not renewable. *Number:* 10–15. *Amount:* $500–$3000.

Eligibility Requirements: Applicant must be age 17 and over and enrolled or expecting to enroll full- or part-time at a two-year or four-year or technical institution or university. Applicant or parent of applicant must have employment or volunteer experience in travel and tourism industry. Available to U.S. citizens.

Application Requirements: Application, essay, resume, references, transcript. *Deadline:* April 25.

Contact: Neil Scotten, Customer Service Representative
International Airlines Travel Agent Network
800 Place Victoria, Suite 800, PO Box 113
Montreal, QC H4Z 1M1
Canada
Phone: 514-868-8800 Ext. 4407
Fax: 514-868-8850
E-mail: scottenn@iata.org

INTERNATIONAL FOODSERVICE EDITORIAL COUNCIL http://www.ifeconline.com

INTERNATIONAL FOODSERVICE EDITORIAL COUNCIL COMMUNICATIONS SCHOLARSHIP

• *See page 180*

MAINE RESTAURANT ASSOCIATION http://www.mainerestaurant.com

RUSS CASEY/MAINE RESTAURANT ASSOCIATES SCHOLARSHIP FUND

• *See page 205*

MISSOURI TRAVEL COUNCIL http://www.missouritravel.com

MISSOURI TRAVEL COUNCIL TOURISM SCHOLARSHIP

• *See page 316*

NATIONAL RESTAURANT ASSOCIATION EDUCATIONAL FOUNDATION http://www.nraef.org

NATIONAL RESTAURANT ASSOCIATION EDUCATIONAL FOUNDATION UNDERGRADUATE SCHOLARSHIPS FOR COLLEGE STUDENTS

• *See page 316*

NATIONAL RESTAURANT ASSOCIATION EDUCATIONAL FOUNDATION UNDERGRADUATE SCHOLARSHIPS FOR HIGH SCHOOL SENIORS AND GENERAL EDUCATION DIPLOMA (GED) GRADUATES

• *See page 316*

NATIONAL TOURISM FOUNDATION http://www.ntfonline.com

ACADEMY OF TRAVEL AND TOURISM SCHOLARSHIPS

One $500 scholarship available for a graduating high school senior planning to attend accredited postsecondary education tourism-related program. Applicant must be completing senior year of high school at Academy of Travel and Tourism location. Each academy may submit most qualified student.

Academic Fields/Career Goals: Hospitality Management; Political Science; Travel/Tourism.

Award: Scholarship for use in freshman year; not renewable. *Number:* 1. *Amount:* $500.

National Tourism Foundation (continued)

Eligibility Requirements: Applicant must be high school student and planning to enroll or expecting to enroll full-time at a two-year or four-year institution or university. Applicant must have 3.0 GPA or higher. Available to U.S. citizens.

Application Requirements: Application, essay, resume, references. *Deadline:* May 10.

Contact: Michelle Gorin, Projects Coordinator
National Tourism Foundation
546 East Main Street
Lexington, KY 40508-3071
Phone: 800-682-8886
Fax: 859-226-4437

CLEVELAND LEGACY I AND II SCHOLARSHIP AWARDS

• *See page 316*

NEW HORIZONS KATHY LETARTE SCHOLARSHIP

• *See page 317*

PAT AND JIM HOST SCHOLARSHIP

Award for students who have a degree emphasis in a travel and tourism related field. Must maintain a 3.0 GPA for renewal.

Academic Fields/Career Goals: Hospitality Management; Travel/Tourism.

Award: Scholarship for use in freshman, sophomore, junior, or senior years; renewable. *Number:* 1. *Amount:* $2000–$8000.

Eligibility Requirements: Applicant must be enrolled or expecting to enroll full-time at a four-year institution or university. Applicant must have 3.0 GPA or higher. Available to U.S. citizens.

Application Requirements: Application, essay, resume, references, transcript. *Deadline:* May 10.

Contact: Michelle Gorin, Projects Coordinator
National Tourism Foundation
546 East Main Street
Lexington, KY 40508-3071
Phone: 800-682-8886
Fax: 859-226-4437

SOCIETIE DES CASINOS DU QUEBEC SCHOLARSHIP

• *See page 317*

TAMPA, HILLSBOROUGH LEGACY SCHOLARSHIP

• *See page 317*

TAUCK SCHOLARS SCHOLARSHIPS

• *See page 317*

TULSA SCHOLARSHIP AWARDS

• *See page 317*

YELLOW RIBBON SCHOLARSHIP

• *See page 317*

UNITED NEGRO COLLEGE FUND http://www.uncf.org

AMERICAN HOTEL FOUNDATION SCHOLARSHIP

Scholarship available to hotel management majors attending UNCF member colleges and universities. Minimum 2.5 GPA required. Prospective applicants should complete the Student Profile found at Web site: http://www.uncf.org.

Academic Fields/Career Goals: Hospitality Management.

Award: Scholarship for use in freshman, sophomore, junior, or senior years; not renewable. *Number:* varies. *Amount:* $1500.

Eligibility Requirements: Applicant must be Black (non-Hispanic) and enrolled or expecting to enroll full-time at a four-year institution or university. Applicant must have 2.5 GPA or higher. Available to U.S. and non-U.S. citizens.

Application Requirements: Application. *Deadline:* continuous.

Contact: Director, Program Services
United Negro College Fund
8260 Willow Oaks Corporate Drive
PO Box 10444
Fairfax, VA 22031-8044
Phone: 800-331-2244
E-mail: rebecca.bennett@uncf.org

HUMAN RESOURCES

NEW ENGLAND EMPLOYEE BENEFITS COUNCIL http://www.neebc.org

NEW ENGLAND EMPLOYEE BENEFITS COUNCIL SCHOLARSHIP PROGRAM

Renewable award designed to encourage undergraduate or graduate students to pursue a course of study leading to a bachelor's degree or higher in the employee benefits field. Must be a resident of/or studying in Maine, Massachusetts, New Hampshire, Rhode Island, Connecticut or Vermont. Must have demonstrated interest in the fields of employee benefits, human resources, business law.

Academic Fields/Career Goals: Human Resources.

Award: Scholarship for use in freshman, sophomore, junior, senior, or graduate years; renewable. *Number:* 1–3. *Amount:* up to $5000.

Eligibility Requirements: Applicant must be enrolled or expecting to enroll full- or part-time at a four-year institution or university; resident of Connecticut, Maine, Massachusetts, New Hampshire, Rhode Island, or Vermont and studying in Connecticut, Maine, Massachusetts, New Hampshire, Rhode Island, or Vermont. Available to U.S. citizens.

Application Requirements: Application, essay, references, transcript. *Deadline:* April 1.

Contact: Linda Viens, Office Manager
New England Employee Benefits Council
440 Totten Pond Road
Waltham, MA 02451
Phone: 781-684-8700
Fax: 781-684-9200
E-mail: linda@neebc.org

SHRM FOUNDATION-SOCIETY FOR HUMAN RESOURCE MANAGEMENT http://www.shrm.org

BARBARA SANCHEZ SCHOLARSHIP

One-time award for national SHRM members, (professional, general, or associate) who are working full-time in human resources in the media field (print, publishing, cable and satellite, broadcasting, motion picture, Internet or communications). Applicants must be pursuing a college degree in human resources or a related field and must begin study within six months of award receipt. Primarily merit-based.

Academic Fields/Career Goals: Human Resources.

Award: Scholarship for use in freshman, sophomore, junior, senior, or graduate years; not renewable. *Number:* 5. *Amount:* $1500.

Eligibility Requirements: Applicant must be enrolled or expecting to enroll full- or part-time at a four-year institution or university. Applicant or parent of applicant must be member of Society for Human Resource Management. Applicant or parent of applicant must have employment or volunteer experience in human services. Available to U.S. and non-U.S. citizens.

Application Requirements: Application, essay, financial need analysis, resume, references, college notice of certification or letter of acceptance. *Deadline:* July 15.

Contact: Beth McFarland, Manager, Special Projects
SHRM Foundation-Society for Human Resource Management
1800 Duke Street
Alexandria, VA 22314
Phone: 703-535-7476
Fax: 703-535-6474
E-mail: bmcfarland@shrm.org

Y'S MEN INTERNATIONAL http://www.ysmenusa.com

ALEXANDER SCHOLARSHIP LOAN FUND
• *See page 152*

HUMANITIES

ALBERTA HERITAGE SCHOLARSHIP FUND/ ALBERTA SCHOLARSHIP PROGRAMS http://www.alis.gov.ab.ca

LOIS HOLE HUMANITIES AND SOCIAL SCIENCES SCHOLARSHIP

Awards students enrolled full-time in the second or subsequent year of postsecondary study in the faculty of humanities or the faculty of social sciences, at University of Alberta, University of Calgary, University of Lethbridge, or at Athabasca University. Awarded on the basis of academic merit, demonstrated leadership, and community service. For further information, contact the Student Awards Office.

Academic Fields/Career Goals: Humanities; Social Sciences.

Award: Scholarship for use in sophomore, junior, or senior years; not renewable. *Number:* 4. *Amount:* $5000.

Eligibility Requirements: Applicant must be enrolled or expecting to enroll full-time at a four-year institution or university; resident of Alberta; studying in Alberta and must have an interest in leadership. Available to Canadian citizens.

Application Requirements: Application. *Deadline:* varies.

Contact: Scholarship Committee
Alberta Heritage Scholarship Fund/Alberta Scholarship Programs
9940 106th Street, Fourth Floor, Sterling Place
PO Box 28000, Station Main
Edmonton, AB T5J 4R4
Canada
Phone: 780-427-8640
Fax: 780-427-1288
E-mail: scholarships@gov.ab.ca

AMERICAN CLASSICAL LEAGUE/NATIONAL JUNIOR CLASSICAL LEAGUE http://www.aclclassics.org

NATIONAL JUNIOR CLASSICAL LEAGUE SCHOLARSHIP
• *See page 174*

AMERICAN SCHOOL OF CLASSICAL STUDIES AT ATHENS http://www.ascsa.edu.gr

ASCSA SUMMER SESSIONS OPEN SCHOLARSHIPS
• *See page 83*

BETHESDA LUTHERAN HOMES AND SERVICES, INC. http://www.blhs.org

DEVELOPMENTAL DISABILITIES SCHOLASTIC ACHIEVEMENT SCHOLARSHIP FOR LUTHERAN COLLEGE STUDENTS
• *See page 211*

BUSINESS AND PROFESSIONAL WOMEN'S FOUNDATION http://www.bpwfoundation.org

BPW CAREER ADVANCEMENT SCHOLARSHIP PROGRAM FOR WOMEN
• *See page 130*

CANADIAN INSTITUTE OF UKRAINIAN STUDIES http://www.cius.ca

LEO J. KRYSA UNDERGRADUATE SCHOLARSHIP
• *See page 95*

CATCHING THE DREAM http://www.catchingthedream.org

MATH, ENGINEERING, SCIENCE, BUSINESS, EDUCATION, COMPUTERS SCHOLARSHIPS
• *See page 139*

NATIVE AMERICAN LEADERSHIP IN EDUCATION (NALE)
• *See page 139*

COMMUNITY FOUNDATION FOR GREATER ATLANTA INC. http://www.atlcf.org

JAMES M. AND VIRGINIA M. SMYTH SCHOLARSHIP
• *See page 101*

HARVARD TRAVELLERS CLUB

HARVARD TRAVELLERS CLUB GRANTS
• *See page 89*

INSTITUTE FOR HUMANE STUDIES http://www.theihs.org

HUMANE STUDIES FELLOWSHIPS
• *See page 179*

JACK J. ISGUR FOUNDATION

JACK J. ISGUR FOUNDATION SCHOLARSHIP
• *See page 102*

KE ALI'I PAUAHI FOUNDATION http://www.pauahi.org

DENIS WONG & ASSOCIATES SCHOLARSHIP

Scholarship to recognize an outstanding student pursuing an undergraduate degree in liberal arts or science, or a graduate degree in a professional field from an accredited university. Recipient must have a well-rounded and balanced record of achievement in preparation for career objectives, demonstrate a commitment to contribute to the greater community. Minimum GPA of 3.5 required.

Academic Fields/Career Goals: Humanities; Science, Technology, and Society.

Award: Scholarship for use in freshman, sophomore, junior, senior, or graduate years; not renewable. *Number:* up to 3. *Amount:* up to $1100.

Eligibility Requirements: Applicant must be enrolled or expecting to enroll full-time at a four-year institution or university. Applicant must have 3.5 GPA or higher. Available to U.S. citizens.

Application Requirements: Application, financial need analysis, references, transcript, college acceptance letter, printed signature confirmation page, copy of SAR. *Deadline:* May 2.

Contact: Elizabeth Stevenson, Development Manager
Ke Ali'i Pauahi Foundation
567 South King Street, Suite 160
Honolulu, HI 96813
Phone: 808-534-3966
Fax: 808-534-3890
E-mail: scholarships@pauahi.org

LADIES AUXILIARY TO THE VETERANS OF FOREIGN WARS, DEPARTMENT OF MAINE

FRANCIS L. BOOTH MEDICAL SCHOLARSHIP SPONSORED BY LAVFW DEPARTMENT OF MAINE
• *See page 338*

METAVUE CORPORATION http://www.metavue.com

FW RAUSCH ARTS AND HUMANITIES PAPER CONTEST
• *See page 104*

NATIONAL FEDERATION OF THE BLIND http://www.nfb.org

NATIONAL FEDERATION OF THE BLIND HUMANITIES SCHOLARSHIP
• *See page 104*

PHI ALPHA THETA HISTORY HONOR SOCIETY INC. http://www.phialphatheta.org

PHI ALPHA THETA WORLD HISTORY ASSOCIATION PAPER PRIZE
• *See page 348*

POLISH ARTS CLUB OF BUFFALO SCHOLARSHIP FOUNDATION http://www.pacb.bfn.org

POLISH ARTS CLUB OF BUFFALO SCHOLARSHIP FOUNDATION TRUST

• *See page 105*

POLISH HERITAGE ASSOCIATION OF MARYLAND http://www.pha-md.org

DR. JOSEPHINE WTULICH MEMORIAL SCHOLARSHIP

• *See page 84*

ROBERT P. PULA MEMORIAL SCHOLARSHIP

Scholarship will be awarded to a student whose major is in the humanities, social sciences, literature, or Polish studies. Must be of Polish descent (at least two Polish grandparents), a U.S. citizen, and a resident of Maryland. Scholarship value is $1500.

Academic Fields/Career Goals: Humanities; Literature/English/Writing; Social Sciences.

Award: Scholarship for use in freshman, sophomore, junior, or senior years; not renewable. *Number:* 1. *Amount:* up to $1500.

Eligibility Requirements: Applicant must be of Polish heritage; enrolled or expecting to enroll full-time at a four-year institution or university and resident of Maryland. Available to U.S. citizens.

Application Requirements: Application, essay, financial need analysis, interview, transcript. *Deadline:* March 31.

Contact: Thomas Hollowak, Scholarship Chair
Polish Heritage Association of Maryland
Seven Dendron Court
Baltimore, MD 21234
Phone: 410-837-4268
Fax: 410-668-2513
E-mail: thollowalk@ubmail.ubalt.edu

SOCIAL SCIENCES AND HUMANITIES RESEARCH COUNCIL OF CANADA http://www.sshrc.ca

RESEARCH DEVELOPMENT INITIATIVE

The program supports research in its initial stages by supporting the development of new ways of analyzing, structuring, integrating, and transferring knowledge in the field of humanities and the social sciences. For more details and an application see Web site: http://www.sshrc.ca.

Academic Fields/Career Goals: Humanities; Social Sciences.

Award: Grant for use in freshman, sophomore, junior, senior, graduate, or postgraduate years; not renewable. *Number:* varies. *Amount:* $40,000.

Eligibility Requirements: Applicant must be Canadian citizen and enrolled or expecting to enroll full-time at a four-year institution or university.

Application Requirements: Application. *Deadline:* varies.

Contact: Garry Pinard, Program Officer
Social Sciences and Humanities Research Council of Canada
350 Albert Street, PO Box 1610
Ottawa, ON K1P 6G4
Canada
Phone: 613-992-5129
Fax: 613-947-0223
E-mail: garry.pinard@sshrc.ca

STRAIGHTFORWARD MEDIA http://www.straightforwardmedia.com

STRAIGHTFORWARD MEDIA LIBERAL ARTS SCHOLARSHIP

• *See page 99*

UNITED NEGRO COLLEGE FUND http://www.uncf.org

MCCLARE FAMILY TRUST SCHOLARSHIP

Scholarship for college freshmen majoring in the humanities with an interest in English literature. Must attend UNCF member institution.

Academic Fields/Career Goals: Humanities; Literature/English/Writing.

Award: Scholarship for use in freshman year; not renewable. *Number:* varies. *Amount:* varies.

Eligibility Requirements: Applicant must be Black (non-Hispanic); enrolled or expecting to enroll full- or part-time at a four-year institution or university and must have an interest in English language. Applicant must have 3.0 GPA or higher. Available to U.S. citizens.

Application Requirements: Application, financial need analysis, FAFSA. *Deadline:* varies.

Contact: Director, Program Services
United Negro College Fund
8260 Willow Oaks Corporate Drive
PO Box 10444
Fairfax, VA 22031-8044
Phone: 800-331-2244
E-mail: rebecca.bennett@uncf.org

HYDROLOGY

AMERICAN GEOLOGICAL INSTITUTE http://www.agiweb.org

AMERICAN GEOLOGICAL INSTITUTE MINORITY SCHOLARSHIP

• *See page 215*

AMERICAN GROUND WATER TRUST http://www.agwt.org

AMERICAN GROUND WATER TRUST-AMTROL INC. SCHOLARSHIP

Award for college/university entry-level students intending to pursue a career in ground water-related field. Must either have completed a science/environmental project involving ground water resources or have had vacation work experience related to the environment and natural resources. Must be U.S. citizen or legal resident with minimum 3.0 GPA. Submit two letters of recommendation and transcript.

Academic Fields/Career Goals: Hydrology; Natural Resources.

Award: Scholarship for use in freshman year; not renewable. *Number:* 1. *Amount:* up to $1000.

Eligibility Requirements: Applicant must be enrolled or expecting to enroll full-time at a four-year institution or university. Applicant or parent of applicant must have employment or volunteer experience in environmental-related field. Applicant must have 3.0 GPA or higher. Available to U.S. citizens.

Application Requirements: Application, essay, references, transcript. *Deadline:* June 1.

Contact: Garret Grasskamp, Ground Water Specialist
American Ground Water Trust
PO Box 1796
Concord, NH 03302-1796
Phone: 603-228-5444
Fax: 603-228-6557
E-mail: ggraaskamp@agwt.org

AMERICAN GROUND WATER TRUST-THOMAS STETSON SCHOLARSHIP

• *See page 167*

AMERICAN INDIAN SCIENCE AND ENGINEERING SOCIETY http://www.aises.org

HENRY RODRIGUEZ RECLAMATION COLLEGE SCHOLARSHIP AND INTERNSHIP

• *See page 285*

AMERICAN METEOROLOGICAL SOCIETY http://www.ametsoc.org

AMERICAN METEOROLOGICAL SOCIETY DR. PEDRO GRAU UNDERGRADUATE SCHOLARSHIP

Award for full-time undergraduate students majoring in atmospheric or related oceanic and hydrologic sciences. Must be enrolled at a U.S. institution. Minimum GPA of 3.25 required. Must be U.S. citizen or permanent resident to apply. Award of $2500 annually for four years.

Academic Fields/Career Goals: Hydrology; Meteorology/Atmospheric Science; Oceanography.

Award: Scholarship for use in freshman, sophomore, junior, or senior years; not renewable. *Number:* 1. *Amount:* $2500.

Eligibility Requirements: Applicant must be enrolled or expecting to enroll full-time at a four-year institution or university. Available to U.S. citizens.

Application Requirements: Application, essay, references, transcript. *Deadline:* February 20.

Contact: Donna Fernandez, Development Program Coordinator
American Meteorological Society
45 Beacon Street
Boston, MA 02108-3693
Phone: 617-227-2426 Ext. 246
Fax: 617-742-8718
E-mail: dfernand@ametsoc.org

AMERICAN METEOROLOGICAL SOCIETY/INDUSTRY MINORITY SCHOLARSHIPS

Two-year scholarship of $3,000 per year for minority students entering their freshman year of college. Must plan to pursue careers in the atmospheric and related oceanic and hydrologic sciences. Must be U.S. citizen or permanent resident to apply.

Academic Fields/Career Goals: Hydrology; Meteorology/Atmospheric Science; Oceanography.

Award: Scholarship for use in freshman year; not renewable. *Number:* 6–13. *Amount:* $3000.

Eligibility Requirements: Applicant must be American Indian/Alaska Native, Asian/Pacific Islander, Black (non-Hispanic), or Hispanic; high school student and planning to enroll or expecting to enroll full-time at a four-year institution or university. Applicant must have 3.0 GPA or higher. Available to U.S. citizens.

Application Requirements: Application, references, test scores, transcript. *Deadline:* February 22.

Contact: Donna Sampson, Development and Student Program Manager
American Meteorological Society
45 Beacon Street
Boston, MA 02108-3693
Phone: 617-227-2426 Ext. 246
Fax: 617-742-8718
E-mail: dfernand@ametsoc.org

AMERICAN METEOROLOGICAL SOCIETY MARK J. SCHROEDER SCHOLARSHIP IN METEOROLOGY

Award for full-time students entering their final year of undergraduate study majoring in atmospheric or related oceanic and hydrologic sciences. Must be enrolled at a U.S. institution. Minimum GPA of 3.25 is required. Must be U.S. citizen or permanent resident to apply.

Academic Fields/Career Goals: Hydrology; Meteorology/Atmospheric Science; Oceanography.

Award: Scholarship for use in senior year; not renewable. *Number:* varies. *Amount:* varies.

Eligibility Requirements: Applicant must be enrolled or expecting to enroll full-time at a four-year institution or university. Available to U.S. citizens.

Application Requirements: Application, essay, financial need analysis, references, transcript. *Deadline:* February 20.

Contact: Donna Fernandez, Development Program Coordinator
American Meteorological Society
45 Beacon Street
Boston, MA 02108-3693
Phone: 617-227-2426 Ext. 246
Fax: 617-742-8718
E-mail: dfernand@ametsoc.org

AMERICAN METEOROLOGICAL SOCIETY RICHARD AND HELEN HAGEMEYER SCHOLARSHIP

Award for full-time students entering their final year of undergraduate study majoring in atmospheric or related oceanic and hydrologic sciences. Must be enrolled at a U.S. institution. Minimum GPA of 3.25 is required. One-time award of $3000. Must be U.S. citizen or permanent resident to apply.

Academic Fields/Career Goals: Hydrology; Meteorology/Atmospheric Science; Oceanography.

Award: Scholarship for use in junior or senior years; not renewable. *Number:* varies. *Amount:* $3000.

Eligibility Requirements: Applicant must be enrolled or expecting to enroll full-time at a two-year or four-year institution or university. Available to U.S. citizens.

Application Requirements: Application, essay, references, transcript. *Deadline:* February 20.

Contact: Donna Fernandez, Development Program Coordinator
American Meteorological Society
45 Beacon Street
Boston, MA 02108-3693
Phone: 617-227-2426 Ext. 246
Fax: 617-742-8718
E-mail: dfernand@ametsoc.org

AMERICAN METEOROLOGICAL SOCIETY 75TH ANNIVERSARY SCHOLARSHIP

Award for full-time students entering their final year of undergraduate study majoring in atmospheric or related oceanic and hydrologic sciences. Must show clear intent to make the atmospheric or related sciences their career. Must be enrolled at a U.S. institution. Minimum GPA of 3.25 required. One-time award of $2000. Must be U.S. citizen or permanent resident to apply.

Academic Fields/Career Goals: Hydrology; Meteorology/Atmospheric Science; Oceanography.

Award: Scholarship for use in senior year; not renewable. *Number:* 7–10. *Amount:* $2000.

Eligibility Requirements: Applicant must be enrolled or expecting to enroll full-time at a four-year institution or university. Available to U.S. citizens.

Application Requirements: Application, essay, references, transcript. *Deadline:* February 20.

Contact: Donna Fernandez, Development Program Coordinator
American Meteorological Society
45 Beacon Street
Boston, MA 02108-3693
Phone: 617-227-2426 Ext. 246
Fax: 617-742-8718
E-mail: dfernand@ametsoc.org

AMERICAN METEOROLOGICAL SOCIETY WERNER A. BAUM UNDERGRADUATE SCHOLARSHIP

Award for full-time students entering final year of undergraduate study majoring in atmospheric or related oceanic or hydrologic science, and/or must show clear intent to make the atmospheric or related sciences their career. Must be enrolled at a U.S. institution. Minimum GPA of 3.25 is required. Must be U.S. citizen or permanent resident.

Academic Fields/Career Goals: Hydrology; Meteorology/Atmospheric Science; Oceanography.

Award: Scholarship for use in senior year; not renewable. *Number:* varies. *Amount:* $5000.

Eligibility Requirements: Applicant must be enrolled or expecting to enroll full-time at a four-year institution or university. Applicant must have 3.5 GPA or higher. Available to U.S. citizens.

Application Requirements: Application, essay, financial need analysis, references, transcript. *Deadline:* February 20.

Contact: Donna Fernandez, Development Program Coordinator
American Meteorological Society
45 Beacon Street
Boston, MA 02108-3693
Phone: 617-227-2426 Ext. 246
Fax: 617-742-8718
E-mail: dfernand@ametsoc.org

AMS FRESHMAN UNDERGRADUATE SCHOLARSHIP

• *See page 300*

CARL W. KREITZBERG ENDOWED SCHOLARSHIP

Scholarships of $2000 for full-time students entering their final year of undergraduate study, majoring in atmospheric or related oceanic/hydrologic science programs at accredited U.S. institutions. Minimum 3.25 GPA required. Must be U.S. citizen.

Academic Fields/Career Goals: Hydrology; Meteorology/Atmospheric Science; Oceanography.

American Meteorological Society (continued)

Award: Scholarship for use in senior year; not renewable. *Number:* 1. *Amount:* up to $2000.

Eligibility Requirements: Applicant must be enrolled or expecting to enroll full-time at a four-year institution or university. Available to U.S. citizens.

Application Requirements: Application, essay, references, transcript. *Deadline:* February 20.

Contact: Donna Fernandez, Development Program Coordinator
American Meteorological Society
45 Beacon Street
Boston, MA 02108-3693
Phone: 617-227-2426 Ext. 246
Fax: 617-742-8718
E-mail: dfernand@ametsoc.org

ETHAN AND ALLAN MURPHY MEMORIAL SCHOLARSHIP

Award for entering their final year of undergraduate study majoring in atmospheric or related oceanic and hydrologic science. Must show clear intent to make the atmospheric or related sciences a career. Must be enrolled in an accredited U.S. institution. Minimum 3.25 GPA required. Must be a U.S. citizen.

Academic Fields/Career Goals: Hydrology; Meteorology/Atmospheric Science; Oceanography.

Award: Scholarship for use in senior year; not renewable. *Number:* varies. *Amount:* $2000.

Eligibility Requirements: Applicant must be enrolled or expecting to enroll full-time at a four-year institution or university. Available to U.S. citizens.

Application Requirements: Application, essay, references, transcript. *Deadline:* February 20.

Contact: Donna Fernandez, Development Program Coordinator
American Meteorological Society
45 Beacon Street
Boston, MA 02108-3693
Phone: 617-227-2426 Ext. 246
Fax: 617-742-8718
E-mail: dfernand@ametsoc.org

GEORGE S. BENTON SCHOLARSHIP

Scholarships are awarded to full-time students entering their final year of undergraduate study at accredited U.S. institutions for study in atmospheric sciences or related oceanic or hydrologic science. Minimum 3.25 GPA required. Must be U.S. citizen or permanent resident.

Academic Fields/Career Goals: Hydrology; Meteorology/Atmospheric Science; Oceanography.

Award: Scholarship for use in senior year; not renewable. *Number:* 1. *Amount:* up to $3500.

Eligibility Requirements: Applicant must be enrolled or expecting to enroll full-time at a four-year institution or university. Available to U.S. citizens.

Application Requirements: Application, financial need analysis, resume, transcript. *Deadline:* February 20.

Contact: Donna Fernandez, Development Program Coordinator
American Meteorological Society
45 Beacon Street
Boston, MA 02108-3693
Phone: 617-227-2426 Ext. 246
Fax: 617-742-8718
E-mail: dfernand@ametsoc.org

GUILLERMO SALAZAR RODRIGUES SCHOLARSHIP

Award for full-time undergraduate students majoring in atmospheric or related oceanic and hydrologic science. Must show clear intent to make the atmospheric or related sciences a career. Must be enrolled in an accredited U.S. institution. Minimum 3.25 GPA required. Must be a U.S. citizen. Award of $2,500 annually for four years.

Academic Fields/Career Goals: Hydrology; Meteorology/Atmospheric Science; Oceanography.

Award: Scholarship for use in freshman, sophomore, junior, or senior years; not renewable. *Number:* varies. *Amount:* $2500.

Eligibility Requirements: Applicant must be enrolled or expecting to enroll full-time at a four-year institution or university. Available to U.S. citizens.

Application Requirements: Application, essay, references, transcript. *Deadline:* February 20.

Contact: Donna Fernandez, Development Program Coordinator
American Meteorological Society
45 Beacon Street
Boston, MA 02108-3693
Phone: 617-227-2426 Ext. 246
Fax: 617-742-8718
E-mail: dfernand@ametsoc.org

JOHN R. HOPE SCHOLARSHIP

Award for students entering their final year of undergraduate study majoring in atmospheric or related oceanic and hydrological science. Must show clear intent to make the atmospheric or related science a career. Minimum 3.25 GPA required. Must be enrolled in an accredited U.S. institution. Must be a U.S. citizen to apply.

Academic Fields/Career Goals: Hydrology; Meteorology/Atmospheric Science; Oceanography.

Award: Scholarship for use in senior year; not renewable. *Number:* 1. *Amount:* up to $2500.

Eligibility Requirements: Applicant must be enrolled or expecting to enroll full-time at a four-year institution or university. Available to U.S. citizens.

Application Requirements: Application, essay, references, transcript. *Deadline:* February 20.

Contact: Donna Fernandez, Development Program Coordinator
American Meteorological Society
45 Beacon Street
Boston, MA 02108-3693
Phone: 617-227-2426 Ext. 246
Fax: 617-742-8718
E-mail: dfernand@ametsoc.org

LOREN W. CROW SCHOLARSHIP

One-time award for full-time students entering their final year of undergraduate study majoring in atmospheric or related oceanic and hydrologic sciences. Must be enrolled full-time at a U.S. institution with a 3.25 GPA. Must be U.S. citizen or permanent resident to apply.

Academic Fields/Career Goals: Hydrology; Meteorology/Atmospheric Science; Oceanography.

Award: Scholarship for use in senior year; not renewable. *Number:* varies. *Amount:* up to $2000.

Eligibility Requirements: Applicant must be enrolled or expecting to enroll full-time at a four-year institution or university. Available to U.S. citizens.

Application Requirements: Application, essay, references, transcript. *Deadline:* February 20.

Contact: Donna Fernandez, Development Program Coordinator
American Meteorological Society
45 Beacon Street
Boston, MA 02108-3693
Phone: 617-227-2426 Ext. 246
Fax: 617-742-8718
E-mail: dfernand@ametsoc.org

ARIZONA HYDROLOGICAL SOCIETY

http://www.azhydrosoc.org

ARIZONA HYDROLOGICAL SOCIETY SCHOLARSHIP

• *See page 215*

ASSOCIATION FOR WOMEN GEOSCIENTISTS, PUGET SOUND CHAPTER

http://www.awg.org

PUGET SOUND CHAPTER SCHOLARSHIP

• *See page 216*

ASSOCIATION OF CALIFORNIA WATER AGENCIES http://www.acwa.com

ASSOCIATION OF CALIFORNIA WATER AGENCIES SCHOLARSHIPS

• *See page 86*

CLAIR A. HILL SCHOLARSHIP

• *See page 86*

CALIFORNIA GROUNDWATER ASSOCIATION http://www.groundh2o.org

CALIFORNIA GROUNDWATER ASSOCIATION SCHOLARSHIP

Award for California residents who demonstrate an interest in some facet of groundwater technology. One to two $1000 awards. Must use for study in California. Submit letter of recommendation.

Academic Fields/Career Goals: Hydrology; Natural Resources.

Award: Scholarship for use in freshman, sophomore, junior, or senior years; not renewable. *Number:* 1–2. *Amount:* $1000.

Eligibility Requirements: Applicant must be enrolled or expecting to enroll full-time at a two-year or four-year or technical institution or university; resident of California and studying in California. Available to U.S. citizens.

Application Requirements: Application, essay, references, transcript. *Deadline:* April 1.

Contact: Mike Mortensson, Executive Director
California Groundwater Association
PO Box 14369
Santa Rosa, CA 95402
Phone: 707-578-4408
Fax: 707-546-4906
E-mail: wellguy@groundh2o.org

CALIFORNIA WATER AWARENESS CAMPAIGN http://www.wateraware.org

CALIFORNIA WATER AWARENESS CAMPAIGN WATER SCHOLAR

• *See page 74*

INTERNATIONAL ASSOCIATION OF GREAT LAKES RESEARCH http://www.iaglr.org

PAUL W. RODGERS SCHOLARSHIP

• *See page 217*

NATIONAL GROUND WATER ASSOCIATION http://www.ngwa.org

NATIONAL GROUND WATER EDUCATION FOUNDATION LEN ASSANTE SCHOLARSHIP FUND

Scholarships granted to full-time students only, including high school graduates and currently enrolled undergradutes (four-year programs or well-drilling two-year associate degree programs). Applicant must be entering a field of study that serves, supports, or promotes the ground water industry. Minimum 2.5 GPA required. Previous recipients are ineligible.

Academic Fields/Career Goals: Hydrology.

Award: Scholarship for use in freshman, sophomore, junior, or senior years; not renewable. *Number:* varies. *Amount:* $1000–$2000.

Eligibility Requirements: Applicant must be enrolled or expecting to enroll full-time at a two-year or four-year institution or university. Applicant must have 2.5 GPA or higher. Available to U.S. and non-U.S. citizens.

Application Requirements: Application, autobiography, essay, transcript. *Deadline:* April 1.

Contact: Barbette Howell, Special Projects Coordinator
National Ground Water Association
601 Dempsey Road
Westerville, OH 43081
Phone: 614-898-7791 Ext. 568
Fax: 614-898-7786
E-mail: bhowell@ngwa.org

UNITED NEGRO COLLEGE FUND http://www.uncf.org

CDM SCHOLARSHIP/INTERNSHIP

• *See page 93*

INDUSTRIAL DESIGN

AMERICAN INSTITUTE OF CHEMICAL ENGINEERS http://www.aiche.org

SAFETY AND HEALTH NATIONAL STUDENT DESIGN COMPETITION AWARD FOR SAFETY

• *See page 156*

AMERICAN SOCIETY OF PLUMBING ENGINEERS http://www.aspe.org

ALFRED STEELE ENGINEERING SCHOLARSHIP

• *See page 256*

INDUSTRIAL DESIGNERS SOCIETY OF AMERICA http://www.idsa.org

INDUSTRIAL DESIGNERS SOCIETY OF AMERICA UNDERGRADUATE SCHOLARSHIP

One-time award to a U.S. citizen or permanent U.S. resident currently enrolled in an industrial design program. Must submit twenty visual examples of work and study full-time.

Academic Fields/Career Goals: Industrial Design.

Award: Scholarship for use in junior year; not renewable. *Number:* 2. *Amount:* $2500.

Eligibility Requirements: Applicant must be enrolled or expecting to enroll full-time at an institution or university. Applicant must have 3.0 GPA or higher. Available to U.S. citizens.

Application Requirements: Application, references, transcript, twenty visual examples of work. *Deadline:* May 18.

Contact: Max Taylor, Executive Assistant
Industrial Designers Society of America
45195 Business Court, Suite 250
Dulles, VA 20166
Phone: 703-707-6000
Fax: 703-787-8501
E-mail: maxt@idsa.org

INTERNATIONAL FURNISHINGS AND DESIGN ASSOCIATION http://www.ifdaef.org

RUTH CLARK SCHOLARSHIP

• *See page 102*

INTERNATIONAL HOUSEWARES ASSOCIATION http://www.housewares.org

STUDENT DESIGN COMPETITION

Prizes awarded to full-time students enrolled in a degree program for industrial design at a U.S. college. Must design a housewares project according to specified guidelines. Must call to obtain entry form. Details on Web site: http://www.ifpte.org.

Academic Fields/Career Goals: Industrial Design.

Award: Prize for use in freshman, sophomore, junior, or senior years; not renewable. *Number:* 5. *Amount:* $1200–$2400.

Eligibility Requirements: Applicant must be enrolled or expecting to enroll full-time at a four-year institution or university. Available to U.S. and non-U.S. citizens.

International Housewares Association (continued)

Application Requirements: Application, applicant must enter a contest, entry form, drawings, slides, new product and document. *Deadline:* December 28.

Contact: Victoria Matranga, Design Programs Coordinator
International Housewares Association
6400 Shafer Court, Suite 650
Rosemont, IL 60018
Phone: 847-692-0136
Fax: 847-292-4211
E-mail: vmatranga@housewares.org

RHODE ISLAND FOUNDATION http://www.rifoundation.org

JAMES J. BURNS AND C. A. HAYNES SCHOLARSHIP

Award of $1000 for students enrolled in a textile program at an educational institution offering this program, such as University of Massachusetts Dartmouth, Rhode Island School of Design, Philadelphia University, North Carolina State University, Clemson University, Georgia Tech and Auburn University. Preference given to children of members of National Association of Textile Supervisors. Must demonstrate financial need.

Academic Fields/Career Goals: Industrial Design.

Award: Scholarship for use in freshman, sophomore, junior, or senior years; not renewable. *Number:* 1–2. *Amount:* $1000.

Eligibility Requirements: Applicant must be enrolled or expecting to enroll full-time at a two-year or four-year institution or university. Available to U.S. citizens.

Application Requirements: Application, essay, financial need analysis, references, transcript. *Deadline:* April 30.

Contact: Libby Monahan, Funds Administrator
Rhode Island Foundation
One Union Station
Providence, RI 02903
Phone: 401-274-4564 Ext. 3117
Fax: 401-751-7983
E-mail: libbym@rifoundation.org

SIMPLEHUMAN http://www.simplehuman.com

SIMPLE SOLUTIONS DESIGN COMPETITION

• *See page 296*

SOCIETY OF MANUFACTURING ENGINEERS EDUCATION FOUNDATION http://www.sme.org/foundation

CHAPTER 198-DOWNRIVER DETROIT SCHOLARSHIP

• *See page 274*

CHAPTER 67-PHOENIX SCHOLARSHIP

• *See page 274*

FORT WAYNE CHAPTER 56 SCHOLARSHIP

• *See page 277*

NORTH CENTRAL REGION 9 SCHOLARSHIP

• *See page 278*

WICHITA CHAPTER 52 SCHOLARSHIP

• *See page 278*

SOCIETY OF PLASTICS ENGINEERS (SPE) FOUNDATION http://www.4spe.org

FLEMING/BASZCAK SCHOLARSHIP

• *See page 163*

SOCIETY OF PLASTICS ENGINEERS SCHOLARSHIP PROGRAM

• *See page 163*

WORLDSTUDIO FOUNDATION http://www.aiga.org/

WORLDSTUDIO FOUNDATION SCHOLARSHIP PROGRAM

• *See page 94*

INSURANCE AND ACTUARIAL SCIENCE

CASUALTY ACTUARIAL SOCIETY/SOCIETY OF ACTUARIES JOINT COMMITTEE ON MINORITY RECRUITING http://www.BeAnActuary.org/minority

ACTUARIAL SCHOLARSHIPS FOR MINORITY STUDENTS

Award for underrepresented minority students planning careers in actuarial science or mathematics. Applicants should have taken the ACT Assessment or the SAT. Must be a U.S. citizen or permanent resident. All scholarship information including application is available online: http://www.BeAnActuary.org/minority. Do not send award inquiries by mail.

Academic Fields/Career Goals: Insurance and Actuarial Science; Mathematics.

Award: Scholarship for use in freshman, sophomore, junior, senior, or graduate years; renewable. *Number:* 20–40. *Amount:* $500–$3000.

Eligibility Requirements: Applicant must be American Indian/Alaska Native, Black (non-Hispanic), or Hispanic and enrolled or expecting to enroll full-time at a two-year or four-year institution or university. Applicant must have 3.0 GPA or higher. Available to U.S. and Canadian citizens.

Application Requirements: Application, financial need analysis, references, test scores, transcript, nomination form. *Deadline:* January 17.

Contact: Kathryn Wiener, Communications Assistant
Casualty Actuarial Society/Society of Actuaries Joint Committee on Minority Recruiting
Society of Actuaries
475 North Martingale Road, Suite 600
Schaumburg, IL 60173-2226
Phone: 847-706-3500 Ext. 3501
Fax: 847-706-3599
E-mail: kwiener@soa.org

D.W. SIMPSON & COMPANY http://www.dwsimpson.com

D.W. SIMPSON ACTUARIAL SCIENCE SCHOLARSHIP

One-time award for full-time actuarial science students. Must be entering senior year of undergraduate study in actuarial science. GPA of 3.2 or better in actuarial science and an overall GPA of 3.0 or better required. Must have passed at least one actuarial exam and be eligible to work in the U.S. Deadlines: April 30 for fall and October 31 for spring.

Academic Fields/Career Goals: Insurance and Actuarial Science.

Award: Scholarship for use in senior year; not renewable. *Number:* up to 2. *Amount:* up to $1000.

Eligibility Requirements: Applicant must be enrolled or expecting to enroll full-time at a four-year institution or university. Applicant must have 3.0 GPA or higher. Available to U.S. citizens.

Application Requirements: Application, essay, resume, test scores. *Deadline:* varies.

Contact: Bethany Rave, Partner-Operations
D.W. Simpson & Company
1800 West Larchmont Avenue
Chicago, IL 60613
Phone: 312-867-2300
Fax: 312-951-8386
E-mail: scholarship@dwsimpson.com

MISSOURI INSURANCE EDUCATION FOUNDATION http://www.mief.org

MISSOURI INSURANCE EDUCATION FOUNDATION SCHOLARSHIP

One $2500 scholarship and five $2000 scholarships available to college and university students in their junior or senior year. Must be Missouri resident.

Academic Fields/Career Goals: Insurance and Actuarial Science.

Award: Scholarship for use in junior or senior years; renewable. *Number:* 6. *Amount:* $2000–$2500.

Eligibility Requirements: Applicant must be enrolled or expecting to enroll full-time at a four-year institution or university; resident of Missouri and studying in Missouri. Applicant must have 2.5 GPA or higher. Available to U.S. citizens.

Application Requirements: Application, financial need analysis, references, transcript. *Deadline:* March 31.

Contact: Amy Hamacher, Scholarship Chairman
Missouri Insurance Education Foundation
PO Box 1654
Jefferson City, MO 65102
Phone: 573-893-4234
Fax: 573-893-4996
E-mail: miis@midamerica.net

PROFESSIONAL INDEPENDENT INSURANCE AGENTS OF ILLINOIS http://www.piiai.org

G.A. MAVON MEMORIAL SCHOLARSHIP

• *See page 147*

KEITH PAYNE MEMORIAL SCHOLARSHIP

• *See page 147*

ROY AND HARRIET ROBINSON SCHOLARSHIP

• *See page 147*

SPENCER EDUCATIONAL FOUNDATION INC. http://www.spencered.org

SPENCER SCHOLARSHIP

Scholarship is available to outstanding applicants who are focused on a career in risk management, insurance, and related disciplines.

Academic Fields/Career Goals: Insurance and Actuarial Science.

Award: Scholarship for use in junior, senior, graduate, or postgraduate years; renewable. *Number:* 10–20. *Amount:* $5000–$10,000.

Eligibility Requirements: Applicant must be enrolled or expecting to enroll full-time at a two-year or four-year institution or university. Applicant must have 3.0 GPA or higher. Available to U.S. and non-U.S. citizens.

Application Requirements: Application, resume, references, transcript. *Deadline:* January 31.

Contact: Angela Sabatino, Secretary and Foundation Administrator
Spencer Educational Foundation Inc.
1065 Avenue of the Americas, 13th Floor
New York, NY 10018
Phone: 212-655-6223
Fax: 212-655-6044
E-mail: asabatino@rims.org

INTERIOR DESIGN

AMERICAN SOCIETY OF INTERIOR DESIGNERS (ASID) EDUCATION FOUNDATION INC. http://www.asid.org

ASID EDUCATIONAL FOUNDATION/YALE R. BURGE COMPETITION

Open to all students in their final years of undergraduate study enrolled in at least a three-year program of interior design. The competition is designed to encourage students to seriously plan their portfolios. Scholarship value is $750.

Academic Fields/Career Goals: Interior Design.

Award: Prize for use in senior year; not renewable. *Number:* 1. *Amount:* $750.

Eligibility Requirements: Applicant must be enrolled or expecting to enroll full-time at a four-year institution or university. Available to U.S. citizens.

Application Requirements: Application, applicant must enter a contest, portfolio. *Fee:* $10. *Deadline:* April 30.

Contact: Lisa Armstrong, Education Department
American Society of Interior Designers (ASID) Education Foundation Inc.
608 Massachusetts Avenue, NE
Washington, DC 20002-6006
Phone: 202-546-3480
Fax: 202-546-3240
E-mail: education@asid.org

ASSOCIATION FOR WOMEN IN ARCHITECTURE FOUNDATION http://www.awa-la.org

ASSOCIATION FOR WOMEN IN ARCHITECTURE SCHOLARSHIP

• *See page 91*

ILLUMINATING ENGINEERING SOCIETY OF NORTH AMERICA http://www.iesna.org

ROBERT W. THUNEN MEMORIAL SCHOLARSHIPS

• *See page 91*

ILLUMINATING ENGINEERING SOCIETY OF NORTH AMERICA–GOLDEN GATE SECTION http://www.iesgg.org

ALAN LUCAS MEMORIAL EDUCATIONAL SCHOLARSHIP

• *See page 92*

INTERNATIONAL FURNISHINGS AND DESIGN ASSOCIATION http://www.ifdaef.org

CHARLES D. MAYO SCHOLARSHIP

Scholarship available to students who have completed four courses related to the field of interior design. Award of $1000 to full-time student. Applicant does not have to be IFDA student member. Applicant must submit 300 to 500 word essay explaining future plans and goals, indicating why they believe that they are deserving of this award. Decision based upon student's academic achievement, awards and accomplishments, future plans and goals, and letter of recommendation. Documents sent along with the application should be sent individually to the four judges (4 copies).

Academic Fields/Career Goals: Interior Design; Trade/Technical Specialties.

Award: Scholarship for use in sophomore, junior, or senior years; not renewable. *Number:* 1. *Amount:* $1000.

Eligibility Requirements: Applicant must be enrolled or expecting to enroll full-time at a four-year institution or university. Available to U.S. and non-U.S. citizens.

Application Requirements: Application, essay, references, transcript, 2 digital pictures of design work done in class. *Deadline:* March 31.

Contact: Earline Feldman, Director
International Furnishings and Design Association
150 South Warner Road, Suite 156
King of Prussia, PA 19406
Phone: 610-535-6422
Fax: 610-535-6423
E-mail: tapis2@bellsouth.com

IFDA STUDENT SCHOLARSHIP

Scholarship available to students who have completed four courses related to the field of interior design. Award of $2000 to full-time student. Applicant must be IFDA student member. Applicant must submit 300 to 500 word essay explaining why they joined IFDA, discuss future plans and goals, and indicate why they are deserving of this award. Decision based upon student's academic achievement, awards and accomplishments, future plans and goals, and letter of recommendation. Documents sent along with the application should be sent individually to the four judges (4 copies).

Academic Fields/Career Goals: Interior Design; Trade/Technical Specialties.

Award: Scholarship for use in sophomore, junior, or senior years; not renewable. *Number:* 1. *Amount:* $2000.

Eligibility Requirements: Applicant must be enrolled or expecting to enroll full-time at a four-year institution or university. Available to U.S. and non-U.S. citizens.

Application Requirements: Application, essay, references, transcript, 2 digital copies of the design work done in class. *Deadline:* March 31.

Contact: Earline Feldman, Director
International Furnishings and Design Association
150 South Warner Road, Suite 156
King of Prussia, PA 19406
Phone: 610-535-6422
Fax: 610-535-6423
E-mail: tapis2@bellsouth.com

INTERNATIONAL INTERIOR DESIGN ASSOCIATION (IIDA) FOUNDATION http://www.iida.org

KIMBALL OFFICE SCHOLARSHIP FUND

Three-year program that will award $5000 to a senior year student pursuing a degree in interior design. Deadline varies.

Academic Fields/Career Goals: Interior Design.

Award: Scholarship for use in senior year; not renewable. *Number:* 1. *Amount:* $5000.

Eligibility Requirements: Applicant must be enrolled or expecting to enroll full- or part-time at a four-year institution or university. Available to U.S. citizens.

Application Requirements: Application, resume. *Deadline:* varies.

Contact: Jocelyn Pysarchuk, Senior Director, Communications and Marketing
International Interior Design Association (IIDA) Foundation
222 Merchandise Mart Plaza
Chicago, IL 60654-1104
Phone: 312-467-1950
Fax: 312-467-0779
E-mail: jpysarchuk@iida.org

MINNESOTA COMMUNITY FOUNDATION http://www.mncommunityfoundation.org

ASID MINNESOTA CHAPTER SCHOLARSHIP FUND

Scholarship to students enrolled full-time or part-time in the upper division (junior or senior year) of a four year Interior Design program at: University of Minnesota, South Dakota State University, North Dakota State University or University of Wisconsin during the upcoming academic year.

Academic Fields/Career Goals: Interior Design.

Award: Scholarship for use in junior or senior years; renewable. *Number:* 1. *Amount:* $2000.

Eligibility Requirements: Applicant must be enrolled or expecting to enroll full- or part-time at a four-year institution or university and studying in Minnesota, North Dakota, South Dakota, or Wisconsin. Applicant must have 3.0 GPA or higher. Available to U.S. citizens.

Application Requirements: Application, portfolio, references, transcript. *Deadline:* April 18.

Contact: Donna Paulson, Administrative Assistant
Minnesota Community Foundation
55 Fifth Street East, Suite 600
St. Paul, MN 55101-1797
Phone: 651-325-4212
E-mail: dkp@mncommunityfoundation.org

NATIONAL ASSOCIATION OF WOMEN IN CONSTRUCTION http://www.nawic.org

NAWIC UNDERGRADUATE SCHOLARSHIPS
• *See page 92*

NEW YORK STATE EDUCATION DEPARTMENT http://www.highered.nysed.gov

REGENTS PROFESSIONAL OPPORTUNITY SCHOLARSHIP
• *See page 60*

SOUTH DAKOTA RETAILERS ASSOCIATION http://www.sdra.org

SOUTH DAKOTA RETAILERS ASSOCIATION SCHOLARSHIP PROGRAM
• *See page 64*

WORLDSTUDIO FOUNDATION http://www.aiga.org/

WORLDSTUDIO FOUNDATION SCHOLARSHIP PROGRAM
• *See page 94*

INTERNATIONAL MIGRATION

AMERICAN HISTORICAL ASSOCIATION http://www.historians.org

WESLEY-LOGAN PRIZE
• *See page 68*

INTERNATIONAL STUDIES

ARRL FOUNDATION INC. http://www.arrl.org

DONALD RIEBHOFF MEMORIAL SCHOLARSHIP

One $1000 award available to students with a technician class license for radio operation. Must be pursuing a baccalaureate or higher degree in international studies at any accredited institution above the high school level. Must be an ARRL member.

Academic Fields/Career Goals: International Studies.

Award: Scholarship for use in freshman, sophomore, junior, senior, or graduate years; not renewable. *Number:* 1. *Amount:* $1000.

Eligibility Requirements: Applicant must be enrolled or expecting to enroll full-time at a four-year institution or university and must have an interest in amateur radio. Applicant or parent of applicant must be member of American Radio Relay League. Available to U.S. citizens.

Application Requirements: Application, transcript. *Deadline:* February 1.

Contact: Mary M. Hobart, Secretary
ARRL Foundation Inc.
225 Main Street
Newington, CT 06111-1494
Phone: 860-594-0397
Fax: 860-594-0259
E-mail: k1mmh@arrl.org

CENTRAL INTELLIGENCE AGENCY http://www.cia.gov

CENTRAL INTELLIGENCE AGENCY UNDERGRADUATE SCHOLARSHIP PROGRAM
• *See page 49*

INSTITUTE OF INTERNATIONAL EDUCATION http://www.iie.org/nsep

NATIONAL SECURITY EDUCATION PROGRAM DAVID L. BOREN UNDERGRADUATE SCHOLARSHIPS
• *See page 144*

JAPAN STUDIES SCHOLARSHIP FOUNDATION COMMITTEE

JAPAN STUDIES SCHOLARSHIP
• *See page 96*

JORGE MAS CANOSA FREEDOM FOUNDATION http://www.jorgemascanosa.org

MAS FAMILY SCHOLARSHIP AWARD
• *See page 144*

NATIONAL FEDERATION OF THE BLIND http://www.nfb.org

MICHAEL AND MARIE MARUCCI SCHOLARSHIP
• *See page 320*

PACIFIC AND ASIAN AFFAIRS COUNCIL http://www.paachawaii.org

PAAC SCHOLARSHIP

Scholarships available for college, study abroad, and other educational opportunities. Must be a student in Hawaii public or private high school involved in PAAC activities.

Academic Fields/Career Goals: International Studies.

Award: Scholarship for use in freshman year; not renewable. *Number:* 7. *Amount:* $100–$1000.

Eligibility Requirements: Applicant must be high school student; planning to enroll or expecting to enroll full- or part-time at a two-year or four-year or technical institution or university and resident of Hawaii. Available to U.S. and non-U.S. citizens.

Application Requirements: Application. *Deadline:* April 18.

Contact: Natasha Chappel, High School Program Director
Pacific and Asian Affairs Council
1601 East-West Road, Fourth Floor
Honolulu, HI 96848-1601
Phone: 808-944-7759
Fax: 808-944-7785
E-mail: hs@paachawaii.org

PHI ALPHA THETA HISTORY HONOR SOCIETY INC. http://www.phialphatheta.org

PHI ALPHA THETA WORLD HISTORY ASSOCIATION PAPER PRIZE

• *See page 348*

WATERBURY FOUNDATION http://www.conncf.org

MALCOLM BALDRIGE SCHOLARSHIP

• *See page 152*

JOURNALISM

ACADEMY OF TELEVISION ARTS AND SCIENCES FOUNDATION http://www.emmysfoundation.org

ACADEMY OF TELEVISION ARTS AND SCIENCES COLLEGE TELEVISION AWARDS

• *See page 99*

ADC RESEARCH INSTITUTE http://www.adc.org

JACK SHAHEEN MASS COMMUNICATIONS SCHOLARSHIP AWARD

• *See page 175*

AMERICAN COPY EDITORS SOCIETY http://www.copydesk.org

ACES COPY EDITING SCHOLARSHIP

Several $2500 scholarships awarded each year. Students not chosen as an Aubespin scholar are automatically eligible for ACES' other awards of $1000 each. Open to undergraduate students entering their junior or senior year, graduate students, and graduating students who will take full-time copy editing jobs or internships.

Academic Fields/Career Goals: Journalism.

Award: Scholarship for use in junior, senior, or graduate years; not renewable. *Number:* varies. *Amount:* $1000–$2500.

Eligibility Requirements: Applicant must be enrolled or expecting to enroll full-time at a four-year institution or university and must have an interest in writing. Applicant must have 2.5 GPA or higher. Available to U.S. citizens.

Application Requirements: Application, applicant must enter a contest, essay, references, list of course work relevant to copy editing, copy of a story edited by the applicant, copies of five to ten headlines. *Deadline:* November 15.

Contact: Kathy Schenck, Assistant Managing Editor
American Copy Editors Society
Milwaukee Journal Sentinel, 333 West State Street
Milwaukee, WI 53203
Phone: 414-224-2237

AMERICAN INSTITUTE OF POLISH CULTURE INC. http://www.ampolinstitute.org

HARRIET IRSAY SCHOLARSHIP GRANT

• *See page 99*

AMERICAN LEGION, PRESS CLUB OF NEW JERSEY

AMERICAN LEGION PRESS CLUB OF NEW JERSEY AND POST 170 ARTHUR DEHARDT MEMORIAL SCHOLARSHIP

• *See page 175*

AMERICAN MEDICAL ASSOCIATION FOUNDATION http://www.amafoundation.org

JOHNSON F. HAMMOND, MD MEMORIAL SCHOLARSHIP

• *See page 330*

AMERICAN QUARTER HORSE FOUNDATION (AQHF) http://www.aqha.com/foundation

AQHF JOURNALISM OR COMMUNICATIONS SCHOLARSHIP

• *See page 175*

ARAB AMERICAN INSTITUTE FOUNDATION http://www.aaiusa.org

AL-MUAMMAR SCHOLARSHIP FOR JOURNALISM

Four scholarship grants of $5000 each to eligible Arab American college students who are majoring in journalism, as well as college seniors who have been accepted to a graduate journalism school.

Academic Fields/Career Goals: Journalism.

Award: Scholarship for use in sophomore, junior, senior, graduate, or postgraduate years; not renewable. *Number:* 1–4. *Amount:* $5000.

Eligibility Requirements: Applicant must be of Arab heritage and enrolled or expecting to enroll full- or part-time at a two-year or four-year institution or university. Available to U.S. citizens.

Application Requirements: Application, essay, portfolio, resume, transcript. *Deadline:* March 14.

Contact: Sabeen Altaf, Program Manager
Arab American Institute Foundation
1600 K Street NW, Suite 601
Washington, DC 20006
Phone: 202-429-9210
Fax: 202-429-9214
E-mail: saltaf@aaiusa.org

ARRL FOUNDATION INC. http://www.arrl.org

PHD ARA SCHOLARSHIP

• *See page 191*

ASIAN AMERICAN JOURNALISTS ASSOCIATION http://www.aaja.org

AAJA/COX FOUNDATION SCHOLARSHIP

Award of up to $1250 to full-time students pursuing careers in print, broadcast, or photo journalism. Must maintain an minimum GPA of 2.5.

Academic Fields/Career Goals: Journalism; TV/Radio Broadcasting.

Award: Scholarship for use in freshman, sophomore, junior, senior, or graduate years; not renewable. *Number:* varies. *Amount:* $1250.

Eligibility Requirements: Applicant must be Asian/Pacific Islander and enrolled or expecting to enroll full-time at a two-year or four-year or technical institution or university. Applicant must have 2.5 GPA or higher. Available to U.S. and non-U.S. citizens.

Application Requirements: Application, essay, financial need analysis, resume, references, transcript. *Deadline:* March 28.

Contact: Kim Mizuhara, Program Coordinator
Asian American Journalists Association
1182 Market Street, Suite 320
San Francisco, CA 94102
Phone: 415-346-2051 Ext. 102
Fax: 415-346-6343
E-mail: programs@aaja.org

Asian American Journalists Association (continued)

ASIAN-AMERICAN JOURNALISTS ASSOCIATION SCHOLARSHIP

• *See page 176*

MARY MOY QUAN ING MEMORIAL SCHOLARSHIP AWARD

One-time award of up to $2000 for a deserving high school senior for undergraduate study. Must intend to pursue a journalism career and must show a commitment to the Asian-American community. Visit Web site http://www.aaja.org for application and details.

Academic Fields/Career Goals: Journalism.

Award: Scholarship for use in freshman year; not renewable. *Number:* 1. *Amount:* up to $2000.

Eligibility Requirements: Applicant must be Asian/Pacific Islander; high school student and planning to enroll or expecting to enroll full-time at a two-year or four-year institution. Available to U.S. and non-U.S. citizens.

Application Requirements: Application, essay, financial need analysis, resume, references, transcript. *Deadline:* March 28.

Contact: Kim Mizuhara, Programs Coordinator
Asian American Journalists Association
1182 Market Street, Suite 320
San Francisco, CA 94102
Phone: 415-346-2051 Ext. 102
Fax: 415-346-6343
E-mail: programs@aaja.org

MINORU YASUI MEMORIAL SCHOLARSHIP AWARD

One-time award of $2000 for a promising Asian undergraduate male who will pursue a broadcasting career. For use at an accredited two- or four-year institution. Visit Web site http://www.aaja.org for application and details.

Academic Fields/Career Goals: Journalism; TV/Radio Broadcasting.

Award: Scholarship for use in freshman, sophomore, junior, or senior years; not renewable. *Number:* 1. *Amount:* $2000.

Eligibility Requirements: Applicant must be Asian/Pacific Islander; enrolled or expecting to enroll full-time at a two-year or four-year institution or university and male. Available to U.S. and non-U.S. citizens.

Application Requirements: Application, essay, financial need analysis, resume, references, transcript. *Deadline:* March 28.

Contact: Kim Mizuhara, Programs Coordinator
Asian American Journalists Association
1182 Market Street, Suite 320
San Francisco, CA 94102
Phone: 415-346-2051 Ext. 102
Fax: 415-346-6343
E-mail: programs@aaja.org

NATIONAL ASIAN-AMERICAN JOURNALISTS ASSOCIATION NEWHOUSE SCHOLARSHIP

Awards up to $5000 for high school seniors and college students who plan to or are currently enrolled in a journalism program at any two- or four-year postsecondary institution. Scholarship awardees will be eligible for summer internships with a Newhouse publication. Applicants from underrepresented Asian Pacific American groups including Vietnamese, Hmong, Cambodians, and other Southeast Asians, South Asians, and Pacific Islanders are especially encouraged. Visit Web site: http://www.aaja.org for application and details.

Academic Fields/Career Goals: Journalism.

Award: Scholarship for use in freshman, sophomore, junior, or senior years; not renewable. *Number:* 5. *Amount:* $1000–$5000.

Eligibility Requirements: Applicant must be enrolled or expecting to enroll full-time at a two-year or four-year institution or university. Applicant must have 2.5 GPA or higher. Available to U.S. and non-U.S. citizens.

Application Requirements: Application, essay, financial need analysis, resume, references, transcript. *Deadline:* March 28.

Contact: Kim Mizuhara, Programs Coordinator
Asian American Journalists Association
1182 Market Street, Suite 320
San Francisco, CA 94102
Phone: 415-346-2051 Ext. 102
Fax: 415-346-6343
E-mail: programs@aaja.org

VINCENT CHIN MEMORIAL SCHOLARSHIP

$5000 award to a journalism student committed to keeping Vincent Chin's memory alive. Minimum GPA of 2.5.

Academic Fields/Career Goals: Journalism.

Award: Scholarship for use in freshman, sophomore, junior, senior, or graduate years; not renewable. *Number:* 1. *Amount:* up to $5000.

Eligibility Requirements: Applicant must be Asian/Pacific Islander and enrolled or expecting to enroll full-time at a two-year or four-year or technical institution or university. Applicant must have 2.5 GPA or higher. Available to U.S. and non-U.S. citizens.

Application Requirements: Application, essay, financial need analysis, resume, references, transcript, work samples. *Deadline:* March 28.

Contact: Kim Mizuhara, Program Coordinator
Asian American Journalists Association
1182 Market Street, Suite 320
San Francisco, CA 94102
Phone: 415-346-2051 Ext. 102
Fax: 415-346-6343
E-mail: programs@aaja.org

ASSOCIATED PRESS http://www.aptra.org

ASSOCIATED PRESS TELEVISION/RADIO ASSOCIATION-CLETE ROBERTS JOURNALISM SCHOLARSHIP AWARDS

Award for college undergraduates and graduate students studying in California, Nevada or Hawaii and pursuing careers in broadcast journalism. Submit application, references, and examples of broadcast-related work.

Academic Fields/Career Goals: Journalism; TV/Radio Broadcasting.

Award: Scholarship for use in freshman, sophomore, junior, senior, or graduate years; not renewable. *Number:* 3. *Amount:* $1500.

Eligibility Requirements: Applicant must be enrolled or expecting to enroll full-time at a two-year or four-year institution or university and studying in California, Hawaii, or Nevada. Available to U.S. citizens.

Application Requirements: Application, references. *Deadline:* December 14.

Contact: Roberta Gonzales, Scholarship Committee
Associated Press
CBS 5 TV, 855 Battery Street
San Francisco, CA 94111

KATHRYN DETTMAN MEMORIAL JOURNALISM SCHOLARSHIP

One-time award of $1500 for broadcast journalism students, enrolled at a California, Hawaii or Nevada college or university. Must submit entry form and examples of broadcast-related work.

Academic Fields/Career Goals: Journalism; TV/Radio Broadcasting.

Award: Scholarship for use in freshman, sophomore, junior, or senior years; renewable. *Number:* 1–4. *Amount:* $1500.

Eligibility Requirements: Applicant must be enrolled or expecting to enroll full-time at a two-year or four-year institution or university and studying in California, Hawaii, or Nevada. Available to U.S. citizens.

Application Requirements: Application, examples of broadcast-related work. *Deadline:* December 14.

Contact: Roberta Gonzales, Scholarship Committee
Associated Press
CBS 5 TV, 855 Battery Street
San Francisco, CA 94111

ASSOCIATION FOR WOMEN IN COMMUNICATIONS-SEATTLE PROFESSIONAL CHAPTER http://www.seattleawc.org

SEATTLE PROFESSIONAL CHAPTER OF THE ASSOCIATION FOR WOMEN IN COMMUNICATIONS

Scholarship of $3000 for women pursuing journalism in the state of Washington. For more details on eligibility criteria or selection procedure, refer to Web site: http://www.seattleawc.org/scholarships.html.

Academic Fields/Career Goals: Journalism.

Award: Scholarship for use in sophomore, junior, or senior years; not renewable. *Number:* 2. *Amount:* $3000.

Eligibility Requirements: Applicant must be enrolled or expecting to enroll full-time at a two-year or four-year or technical institution or university; female; resident of Washington and studying in Washington. Available to U.S. citizens.

Application Requirements: Application, resume, transcript, sample of work, cover letter. *Deadline:* March 16.

Contact: Jaron Snow, Office Administrator
Association for Women in Communications-Seattle Professional Chapter
PO Box 472
Mountlake Terrace, WA 98043
Phone: 425-771-4189
E-mail: awcseattle@verizon.net

ASSOCIATION FOR WOMEN IN SPORTS MEDIA http://www.awsmonline.org

WOMEN IN SPORTS MEDIA SCHOLARSHIP/INTERNSHIP PROGRAM

• *See page 176*

ATLANTA ASSOCIATION OF BLACK JOURNALISTS http://www.aabj.org

XERNONA CLAYTON SCHOLARSHIP FUND

• *See page 177*

ATLANTA PRESS CLUB INC. http://www.atlantapressclub.org

ATLANTA PRESS CLUB JOURNALISM SCHOLARSHIP PROGRAM

Awards outstanding Georgia college or university sophomores, juniors, and seniors who are pursuing careers in journalism. Must attend an interview with the selection committee. Must be a U.S. citizen.

Academic Fields/Career Goals: Journalism; TV/Radio Broadcasting.

Award: Scholarship for use in sophomore, junior, or senior years; not renewable. *Number:* 4. *Amount:* $1500.

Eligibility Requirements: Applicant must be enrolled or expecting to enroll full- or part-time at a four-year institution or university; resident of Georgia; studying in Georgia and must have an interest in writing. Available to U.S. citizens.

Application Requirements: Application, essay, interview, portfolio, transcript, clips/tapes/CD. *Deadline:* February 15.

Contact: Elaine Hudson, Assistant Director, Scholarship Committee
Atlanta Press Club Inc.
34 Broad Street, 18th Floor
Atlanta, GA 30303
Phone: 404-577-7377
Fax: 404-223-3706
E-mail: ehudson@atlpressclub.org

BAY AREA BLACK JOURNALISTS ASSOCIATION SCHOLARSHIP CONTEST http://www.babja.org

YOUNG JOURNALISTS SCHOLARSHIP

Nonrenewable scholarship of $2500 open to photojournalism students. Applicant must be enrolled in any college or university nationwide. Must be studying journalism (television, radio, print, online).

Academic Fields/Career Goals: Journalism; Photojournalism/Photography.

Award: Scholarship for use in freshman, sophomore, junior, senior, or graduate years; not renewable. *Number:* varies. *Amount:* $2500.

Eligibility Requirements: Applicant must be enrolled or expecting to enroll full- or part-time at a four-year institution or university. Available to U.S. citizens.

Application Requirements: Application, essay, resume, references, transcript, work samples. *Deadline:* October 2.

Contact: Scholarship Committee
Bay Area Black Journalists Association Scholarship Contest
1714 Franklin Street, Suite 100-260
Oakland, CA 94612
Phone: 510-986-9390
Fax: 510-382-1980
E-mail: info@babja.org

CALIFORNIA CHICANO NEWS MEDIA ASSOCIATION (CCNMA) http://www.ccnma.org

CCNMA SCHOLARSHIPS

• *See page 177*

CANADIAN ASSOCIATION OF BROADCASTERS http://www.cab-acr.ca

ASTRAL MEDIA SCHOLARSHIP

• *See page 177*

JIM ALLARD BROADCAST JOURNALISM SCHOLARSHIP

This CAN$2500 scholarship is awarded annually to aspiring broadcasters enrolled in broadcast journalism courses at a Canadian college or university. The award is given to the student who best combines academic achievement with natural talent. Must be a Canadian citizen.

Academic Fields/Career Goals: Journalism; TV/Radio Broadcasting.

Award: Scholarship for use in freshman, sophomore, junior, senior, graduate, or postgraduate years; renewable. *Number:* 1.

Eligibility Requirements: Applicant must be Canadian citizen; enrolled or expecting to enroll full-time at a four-year institution or university; studying in Alberta, British Columbia, Manitoba, New Brunswick, Newfoundland, North West Territories, Nova Scotia, Ontario, Prince Edward Island, Quebec, Saskatchewan, or Yukon and must have an interest in leadership.

Application Requirements: Application, essay, references. *Deadline:* June 30.

Contact: Beth Mitchell, Manager, Member Relations and Special Events
Canadian Association of Broadcasters
PO Box 627, Station B
Ottawa, ON K1P 5S2
Canada
Phone: 613-233-4035 Ext. 329
Fax: 613-233-6961
E-mail: bmitchell@cab-acr.ca

CANADIAN PRESS http://www.thecanadianpress.com

GIL PURCELL MEMORIAL JOURNALISM SCHOLARSHIP FOR NATIVE CANADIANS

Scholarship is designed to encourage native Canadian students to enter the field of journalism in Canada. Awards aboriginal Canadians (status or non-status Indian, Metis, or Inuit) who are pursuing postsecondary studies and intend to work in the field of journalism.

Academic Fields/Career Goals: Journalism.

Award: Scholarship for use in freshman, sophomore, junior, senior, graduate, or postgraduate years; not renewable. *Number:* 1. *Amount:* $4000.

Eligibility Requirements: Applicant must be of Canadian heritage and Canadian citizen; American Indian/Alaska Native and enrolled or expecting to enroll full- or part-time at a four-year institution or university.

Canadian Press (continued)

Application Requirements: Application, resume. *Deadline:* November 15.

Contact: Paul Woods, Director of Human Resources
Canadian Press
36 King Street, East
Toronto, ON M5C 2L9
Canada
Phone: 416-507-2133
Fax: 416-507-2033
E-mail: paul.woods@thecanadianpress.com

CHRONICLE OF HIGHER EDUCATION http://chronicle.com

DAVID W. MILLER AWARD FOR STUDENT JOURNALISTS

Award for undergraduate students studying journalism. Applicants may be students in any country. The award consists of a $2500 prize and a certificate, and is presented annually. For further information see Web site: http://chronicle.com.

Academic Fields/Career Goals: Journalism.

Award: Prize for use in freshman, sophomore, junior, or senior years; not renewable. *Number:* 1. *Amount:* $2500.

Eligibility Requirements: Applicant must be enrolled or expecting to enroll full- or part-time at a four-year institution or university. Available to U.S. and non-U.S. citizens.

Application Requirements: Application, applicant must enter a contest, essay, three samples of published work, a one-page letter describing the articles and why they were chosen for submission. *Deadline:* June 2.

Contact: Philip Semas, Editor in Chief
Chronicle of Higher Education
1255 23rd Street, NW
Washington, DC 20037
Phone: 202-466-1032
E-mail: milleraward@chronicle.com

CLEVELAND SCHOLARSHIP PROGRAMS http://www.cspohio.org

CSP MANAGED FUNDS-CLEVELAND BROWNS MARION MOTLEY SCHOLARSHIP

• *See page 49*

CONNECTICUT CHAPTER OF SOCIETY OF PROFESSIONAL JOURNALISTS http://www.ctspj.org

CONNECTICUT SPJ BOB EDDY SCHOLARSHIP PROGRAM

Five one-time awards of $500 to $2500 for college juniors or seniors planning a career in journalism. Must be a Connecticut resident attending a four year college or any student attending a four year college in Connecticut.

Academic Fields/Career Goals: Journalism; Photojournalism/Photography.

Award: Scholarship for use in junior or senior years; not renewable. *Number:* 5. *Amount:* $500–$2500.

Eligibility Requirements: Applicant must be enrolled or expecting to enroll full-time at a four-year institution or university; resident of Connecticut; studying in Connecticut and must have an interest in writing. Available to U.S. and non-U.S. citizens.

Application Requirements: Application, essay, financial need analysis, transcript. *Deadline:* March 14.

Contact: Debra Estock, Scholarship Committee Chairman
Connecticut Chapter of Society of Professional Journalists
71 Kenwood Avenue
Fairfield, CT 06430
Phone: 203-255-2127
E-mail: destock963@aol.com

CUBAN AMERICAN NATIONAL FOUNDATION http://www.masscholarships.org

MAS FAMILY SCHOLARSHIPS

• *See page 139*

DAIRY MANAGEMENT http://www.dairyinfo.com

JAMES H. LOPER JR. MEMORIAL SCHOLARSHIP

• *See page 74*

NATIONAL DAIRY PROMOTION AND RESEARCH BOARD SCHOLARSHIP

• *See page 74*

DOW JONES NEWSPAPER FUND http://djnewspaperfund.dowjones.com

DOW JONES-SPORTS EDITING PROGRAM

Award to encourage students to consider sports copy editing as a career in by providing training, paid summer internships and scholarship grants. Must pursue their career in newspaper journalism.

Academic Fields/Career Goals: Journalism.

Award: Scholarship for use in junior, senior, or graduate years; not renewable. *Number:* 12. *Amount:* $1000.

Eligibility Requirements: Applicant must be enrolled or expecting to enroll full-time at a four-year institution or university. Available to U.S. and non-U.S. citizens.

Application Requirements: Application, essay, resume, references, transcript. *Deadline:* November 1.

Contact: Linda Waller Shockley, Deputy Director
Dow Jones Newspaper Fund
PO Box 300
Princeton, NJ 08543-0300
Phone: 609-452-2820
Fax: 609-520-5804
E-mail: newsfund@wsj.dowjones.com

HIGH SCHOOL JOURNALISM WORKSHOPS

Award to encourage high school students to consider careers in journalism by providing an opportunity to work with professional journalists and instructors on reporting, writing and editing a student newspaper.

Academic Fields/Career Goals: Journalism.

Award: Grant for use in freshman year; not renewable. *Number:* 27. *Amount:* $2500–$5000.

Eligibility Requirements: Applicant must be high school student and planning to enroll or expecting to enroll full-time at a four-year institution or university. Available to U.S. and Canadian citizens.

Application Requirements: Application, essay, portfolio, resume, references, transcript. *Deadline:* October 1.

Contact: Linda Waller Shockley, Deputy Director
Dow Jones Newspaper Fund
PO Box 300
Princeton, NJ 08543-0300
Phone: 609-452-2820
Fax: 609-520-5804
E-mail: newsfund@wsj.dowjones.com

ELLEN MASIN PERSINA/NATIONAL PRESS CLUB SCHOLARSHIP FOR MINORITIES IN JOURNALISM http://npc.press.org

PERSINA SCHOLARSHIP FOR MINORITIES IN JOURNALISM

Scholarship of $5000 per year awarded to a talented minority student planning to pursue a career in journalism. Applicant must be a high school senior. Must have a 3.0 or better GPA. Must have applied to or been accepted by a college or university for the upcoming year.

Academic Fields/Career Goals: Journalism.

Award: Scholarship for use in freshman year; not renewable. *Number:* 1. *Amount:* up to $5000.

Eligibility Requirements: Applicant must be American Indian/Alaska Native, Asian/Pacific Islander, Black (non-Hispanic), or Hispanic; high school student and planning to enroll or expecting to enroll full- or part-time at a four-year institution or university. Applicant must have 3.0 GPA or higher. Available to U.S. and non-U.S. citizens.

Application Requirements: Application, essay, financial need analysis, references, transcript, work samples demonstrating an ongoing interest in journalism. *Deadline:* March 1.

Contact: Joann Booze, Scholarship Coordinator
Ellen Masin Persina/National Press Club Scholarship for Minorities in Journalism
529 14th Street, NW
Washington, DC 20045
Phone: 202-662-7500
Fax: 202-662-7512
E-mail: jbooze@press.org

FISHER BROADCASTING COMPANY http://www.fsci.com

FISHER BROADCASTING INC. SCHOLARSHIP FOR MINORITIES

• *See page 140*

FLORIDA SOCIETY OF NEWSPAPER EDITORS-SCHOLARSHIP COMMITTEE http://www.fsne.org/minorityscholar.html

FLORIDA SOCIETY OF NEWSPAPER EDITORS MINORITY SCHOLARSHIP PROGRAM

• *See page 178*

FLORIDA SOCIETY OF NEWSPAPER EDITORS MULTIMEDIA SCHOLARSHIP

• *See page 178*

FREEDOM FORUM http://www.freedomforum.org

AL NEUHARTH FREE SPIRIT SCHOLARSHIP

One-time award for high school seniors interested in pursuing a career in journalism. Must be actively involved in high school journalism and demonstrate qualities such as being a visionary, an innovative leader, an entrepreneur or a courageous achiever. See Web site at http://www.freedomforum.org for further information.

Academic Fields/Career Goals: Journalism.

Award: Scholarship for use in freshman year; not renewable. *Number:* up to 102. *Amount:* $1000.

Eligibility Requirements: Applicant must be high school student; planning to enroll or expecting to enroll full-time at a four-year institution and must have an interest in entrepreneurship, leadership, or writing. Available to U.S. citizens.

Application Requirements: Application, essay, photo, references, transcript, sample of journalistic work. *Deadline:* October 15.

Contact: Diana Leckie, Administrator
Freedom Forum
555 Pennsylvania Avenue, NW
Washington, DC 20001
Phone: 202-292-6100
E-mail: freespirit@freedomforum.org

CHIPS QUINN SCHOLARS PROGRAM

One-time award for college juniors, seniors or recent graduates. Open to students with a definite interest in print journalism as a career. Award requires paid internship. Applicants may be nominated by their schools, by newspaper editors or by direct application with supporting letters of endorsement. See Web site at http://www.freedomforum.org or http://www.chipsquinn.org for further information.

Academic Fields/Career Goals: Journalism.

Award: Scholarship for use in junior or senior years; not renewable. *Number:* 60. *Amount:* $1000.

Eligibility Requirements: Applicant must be American Indian/Alaska Native, Asian/Pacific Islander, Black (non-Hispanic), or Hispanic and enrolled or expecting to enroll full-time at a four-year institution. Available to U.S. citizens.

Application Requirements: Application, driver's license, essay, photo, portfolio, resume, references, transcript. *Deadline:* October 15.

Contact: Karen Catone, Director
Freedom Forum
555 Pennsylvania Avenue, NW
Washington, DC 20001
Phone: 202-292-6271
Fax: 202-292-6275
E-mail: kcatone@freedomforum.org

GEORGIA PRESS EDUCATIONAL FOUNDATION INC. http://www.gapress.org

DURWOOD MCALISTER SCHOLARSHIP

Scholarship awarded annually to an outstanding student majoring in print journalism at a Georgia college or university.

Academic Fields/Career Goals: Journalism.

Award: Scholarship for use in freshman, sophomore, junior, senior, graduate, or postgraduate years; not renewable. *Number:* 1. *Amount:* $500–$1500.

Eligibility Requirements: Applicant must be enrolled or expecting to enroll full-time at a two-year or four-year or technical institution or university; resident of Georgia and must have an interest in writing. Available to U.S. citizens.

Application Requirements: Application, essay, photo, references, transcript. *Deadline:* February 1.

Contact: Jenifer Farmer, Manager
Georgia Press Educational Foundation Inc.
3066 Mercer University Drive, Suite 200
Atlanta, GA 30341-4137
Phone: 770-454-6776
Fax: 770-454-6778

GEORGIA PRESS EDUCATIONAL FOUNDATION SCHOLARSHIPS

One-time awards to Georgia high school seniors and college undergraduates. Based on prior interest in newspaper journalism. Must be recommended by high school counselor, professor, and/or Georgia Press Educational Foundation member. Must reside and attend school in Georgia.

Academic Fields/Career Goals: Journalism.

Award: Scholarship for use in freshman, sophomore, junior, or senior years; not renewable. *Number:* 16. *Amount:* $500–$1500.

Eligibility Requirements: Applicant must be enrolled or expecting to enroll full-time at a two-year or four-year institution or university; resident of Georgia; studying in Georgia and must have an interest in writing. Available to U.S. citizens.

Application Requirements: Application, financial need analysis, photo, references, test scores, transcript. *Deadline:* February 1.

Contact: Jenifer Farmer, Manager
Georgia Press Educational Foundation Inc.
3066 Mercer University Drive, Suite 200
Atlanta, GA 30341-4137
Phone: 770-454-6776
Fax: 770-454-6778

KIRK SUTLIVE SCHOLARSHIP

Scholarship awarded annually to a junior or senior majoring in either the news-editorial or public relations sequence.

Academic Fields/Career Goals: Journalism.

Award: Scholarship for use in junior or senior years; not renewable. *Number:* 1. *Amount:* $500–$1500.

Eligibility Requirements: Applicant must be enrolled or expecting to enroll full-time at a four-year institution or university. Available to U.S. citizens.

Georgia Press Educational Foundation Inc. (continued)

Application Requirements: Application, essay, financial need analysis, photo, transcript. *Deadline:* February 1.

Contact: Jenifer Farmer, Manager
Georgia Press Educational Foundation Inc.
3066 Mercer University Drive, Suite 200
Atlanta, GA 30341-4137
Phone: 770-454-6776
Fax: 770-454-6778

MORRIS NEWSPAPER CORPORATION SCHOLARSHIP

Scholarship awarded annually to an outstanding print journalism student. Applications are submitted through newspapers in the Morris Newspaper Corporation chain and recipients are named by the Foundation.

Academic Fields/Career Goals: Journalism.

Award: Scholarship for use in freshman, sophomore, junior, or senior years; not renewable. *Number:* 1. *Amount:* $500–$1500.

Eligibility Requirements: Applicant must be enrolled or expecting to enroll full-time at a four-year or technical institution or university; resident of Georgia and must have an interest in writing. Available to U.S. citizens.

Application Requirements: Application, essay, photo, references, transcript. *Deadline:* February 1.

Contact: Jenifer Farmer, Manager
Georgia Press Educational Foundation Inc.
3066 Mercer University Drive, Suite 200
Atlanta, GA 30341-4137
Phone: 770-454-6776
Fax: 770-454-6778

WILLIAM C. ROGERS SCHOLARSHIP

Scholarship awarded to a junior or senior majoring in the news-editorial sequence. For full-time study only. Must be a resident of Georgia.

Academic Fields/Career Goals: Journalism.

Award: Scholarship for use in junior or senior years; not renewable. *Number:* 1. *Amount:* $500–$1500.

Eligibility Requirements: Applicant must be enrolled or expecting to enroll full-time at a four-year institution or university; resident of Georgia and must have an interest in writing. Available to U.S. citizens.

Application Requirements: Application, essay, photo, references, transcript. *Deadline:* February 1.

Contact: Jenifer Farmer, Manager
Georgia Press Educational Foundation Inc.
3066 Mercer University Drive, Suite 200
Atlanta, GA 30341-4137
Phone: 770-454-6776
Fax: 770-454-6778

GREAT LAKES COMMISSION http://www.glc.org

CAROL A. RATZA MEMORIAL SCHOLARSHIP

• *See page 179*

HISPANIC SCHOLARSHIP FUND http://www.hsf.net

HSF/NISSAN COMMUNITY COLLEGE TRANSFER SCHOLARSHIP PROGRAM

• *See page 143*

IDAHO STATE BROADCASTERS ASSOCIATION http://www.idahobroadcasters.org

WAYNE C. CORNILS MEMORIAL SCHOLARSHIP

• *See page 143*

INDIANA BROADCASTERS ASSOCIATION http://www.indianabroadcasters.org

INDIANA BROADCASTERS FOUNDATION SCHOLARSHIP

Awards a student majoring in broadcasting, electronic media, or journalism. Must maintain a 3.0 GPA and be a resident of Indiana. One-time award for full-time undergraduate study in Indiana.

Academic Fields/Career Goals: Journalism; TV/Radio Broadcasting.

Award: Scholarship for use in freshman, sophomore, junior, or senior years; not renewable. *Number:* up to 10. *Amount:* $500–$2000.

Eligibility Requirements: Applicant must be enrolled or expecting to enroll full-time at a two-year or four-year or technical institution or university; resident of Indiana and studying in Indiana. Applicant must have 3.0 GPA or higher. Available to U.S. citizens.

Application Requirements: Application, essay, references, transcript. *Deadline:* March 3.

Contact: Gwen C. Piening, Scholarship Administrator
Indiana Broadcasters Association
3003 East 98th Street, Suite 161
Indianapolis, IN 46280
Phone: 317-573-0119
Fax: 317-573-0895
E-mail: indba@aol.com

INTERNATIONAL FOODSERVICE EDITORIAL COUNCIL http://www.ifeconline.com

INTERNATIONAL FOODSERVICE EDITORIAL COUNCIL COMMUNICATIONS SCHOLARSHIP

• *See page 180*

JAPANESE AMERICAN CITIZENS LEAGUE (JACL) http://www.jacl.org

NATIONAL JACL HEADQUARTERS SCHOLARSHIP

• *See page 75*

JOHN BAYLISS BROADCAST FOUNDATION http://www.baylissfoundation.org

JOHN BAYLISS BROADCAST RADIO SCHOLARSHIP

• *See page 180*

JORGE MAS CANOSA FREEDOM FOUNDATION http://www.jorgemascanosa.org

MAS FAMILY SCHOLARSHIP AWARD

• *See page 144*

JOURNALISM EDUCATION ASSOCIATION http://www.jea.org

NATIONAL HIGH SCHOOL JOURNALIST OF THE YEAR/SISTER RITA JEANNE SCHOLARSHIPS

• *See page 180*

LIN TELEVISION CORPORATION http://www.lintv.com

LINTV MINORITY SCHOLARSHIP

Scholarship to help educate and train outstanding minority candidates who seek to enter the television broadcast field. Minimum 3.0 cumulative GPA required. Must have declared major in journalism or related broadcast field at an accredited university or college. Must be a sophomore or have completed sufficient semester hours or similar educational units to be within two years of receiving a bachelor's degree.

Academic Fields/Career Goals: Journalism; TV/Radio Broadcasting.

Award: Scholarship for use in sophomore year; not renewable. *Number:* 1. *Amount:* varies.

Eligibility Requirements: Applicant must be American Indian/Alaska Native, Asian/Pacific Islander, Black (non-Hispanic), or Hispanic and enrolled or expecting to enroll full-time at a two-year or four-year institution or university. Applicant must have 3.0 GPA or higher. Available to U.S. citizens.

Application Requirements: Application, transcript. *Deadline:* March 15.

Contact: Don Donohue, Director, Human Resources
Lin Television Corporation
One Richmond Square, Suite 230E
Providence, RI 02906
Phone: 401-457-9402
E-mail: dan.donohue@lintv.com

MAINE COMMUNITY FOUNDATION INC. http://www.mainecf.org

GUY P. GANNETT SCHOLARSHIP FUND

Renewable awards available to graduates of Maine high schools or home-school programs pursuing a major in journalism or a related media field.

Academic Fields/Career Goals: Journalism.

Award: Scholarship for use in freshman, sophomore, junior, senior, or graduate years; renewable. *Number:* 10–20. *Amount:* varies.

Eligibility Requirements: Applicant must be enrolled or expecting to enroll full-time at a four-year institution or university and resident of Maine. Available to U.S. citizens.

Application Requirements: Application, essay, financial need analysis, references, transcript, work samples. *Deadline:* May 1.

Contact: Amy Pollien, Program Administrator
Maine Community Foundation Inc.
245 Main Street
Ellsworth, ME 04605
Phone: 877-700-6800
E-mail: info@mainecf.org

MARYLAND/DELAWARE/DISTRICT OF COLUMBIA PRESS FOUNDATION http://www.mddcpress.com

MICHAEL J. POWELL HIGH SCHOOL JOURNALIST OF THE YEAR

Scholarship of $1500 to an outstanding high school student. Applicant must submit five samples of work, mounted on unlined paper, a letter of recommendation from the nominee's advisor, an autobiography geared to the publication activities in which the nominee participated, and the nominee should write a paragraph or two on the most important aspect of scholastic journalism.

Academic Fields/Career Goals: Journalism.

Award: Scholarship for use in freshman year; not renewable. *Number:* 1. *Amount:* $1500.

Eligibility Requirements: Applicant must be high school student; planning to enroll or expecting to enroll full- or part-time at a four-year institution or university and must have an interest in writing. Available to U.S. citizens.

Application Requirements: Application, applicant must enter a contest, autobiography, references, five sample articles. *Deadline:* January 31.

Contact: Jennifer Thornberry, Administration Associate Coordinator
Maryland/Delaware/District of Columbia Press Foundation
2191 Defense Highway, Suite 300
Crofton, MD 21114-2487
Phone: 410-721-4000 Ext. 20
Fax: 410-721-4557
E-mail: info@mddcpress.com

MISSISSIPPI ASSOCIATION OF BROADCASTERS http://www.msbroadcasters.org

MISSISSIPPI ASSOCIATION OF BROADCASTERS SCHOLARSHIP

Scholarship available to a student enrolled in a fully accredited broadcast curriculum at a Mississippi two- or four-year college.

Academic Fields/Career Goals: Journalism; TV/Radio Broadcasting.

Award: Scholarship for use in freshman, sophomore, junior, or senior years; not renewable. *Number:* up to 8. *Amount:* $2000.

Eligibility Requirements: Applicant must be enrolled or expecting to enroll full-time at a two-year or four-year institution or university; resident of Mississippi and studying in Mississippi. Available to U.S. citizens.

Application Requirements: Application, financial need analysis, references, extracurricular activities and community involvement also considered. *Deadline:* May 1.

Contact: Jackie Lett, Scholarship Coordinator
Mississippi Association of Broadcasters
855 South Pear Orchard Road, Suite 403
Ridgeland, MS 39157
Phone: 601-957-9121
Fax: 601-957-9175
E-mail: jackie@msbroadcasters.org

MISSISSIPPI PRESS ASSOCIATION EDUCATION FOUNDATION http://www.mspress.org/foundation/

MISSISSIPPI PRESS ASSOCIATION EDUCATION FOUNDATION SCHOLARSHIP

The foundation annually offers $1000 ($500 per semester) scholarships to qualified students enrolled in print journalism, and who are residents of Mississippi. The recipient who maintains a 3.0 GPA. Total value of the scholarship can be as much as $4000 when awarded to an incoming freshman who remains qualified throughout their four years of print journalism education.

Academic Fields/Career Goals: Journalism.

Award: Scholarship for use in freshman, sophomore, junior, or senior years; renewable. *Number:* 1. *Amount:* $1000–$4000.

Eligibility Requirements: Applicant must be enrolled or expecting to enroll full-time at a two-year or four-year institution or university and resident of Mississippi. Applicant must have 3.0 GPA or higher. Available to U.S. citizens.

Application Requirements: Application, resume, references, sample of work. *Deadline:* April 1.

Contact: Beth Boone, Scholarship Coordinator
Mississippi Press Association Education Foundation
371 Edgewood Terrace
Jackson, MS 39206
Phone: 601-981-3060
Fax: 601-981-3676
E-mail: bboone@mspress.org

NATIONAL ACADEMY OF TELEVISION ARTS AND SCIENCES-NATIONAL CAPITAL/CHESAPEAKE BAY CHAPTER http://www.natasdc.org

BETTY ENDICOTT/NTA-NCCB STUDENT SCHOLARSHIP

Scholarship for a full-time sophomore, junior or non-graduating senior student pursuing a career in communication, television or broadcast journalism. Must be enrolled in an accredited four-year college or university in Maryland, Virginia or Washington, D.C. Minimum GPA of 3.0 required. Must demonstrate an aptitude or interest in communication, television or broadcast journalism. Application URL: http://capitalemmys.tv/betty_endicott.htm.

Academic Fields/Career Goals: Journalism; TV/Radio Broadcasting.

Award: Scholarship for use in sophomore, junior, or senior years; not renewable. *Number:* 1. *Amount:* $5000.

Eligibility Requirements: Applicant must be enrolled or expecting to enroll full-time at a four-year institution or university and studying in District of Columbia, Maryland, or Virginia. Applicant must have 3.0 GPA or higher. Available to U.S. citizens.

Application Requirements: Application, essay, resume, references, transcript, work samples (resume tape in VHS format and radio or television broadcast scripts). *Deadline:* April 22.

Contact: Diane Bruno, Student Affairs Committee
National Academy of Television Arts and Sciences-National Capital/Chesapeake Bay Chapter
9405 Russell Road
Silver Spring, MD 20910
Phone: 301-587-3993
E-mail: capitalemmys@aol.com

NATIONAL ASSOCIATION OF BLACK JOURNALISTS http://www.nabj.org

ALLISON FISHER SCHOLARSHIP

Scholarship for students currently attending an accredited college or university. Must be majoring in print journalism and maintain a 3.0 GPA. Recipient will attend NABJ convention and participate in the mentor program. Scholarship value and the number of awards granted varies.

Academic Fields/Career Goals: Journalism.

Award: Scholarship for use in freshman, sophomore, junior, senior, or graduate years; not renewable. *Number:* varies. *Amount:* varies.

Eligibility Requirements: Applicant must be enrolled or expecting to enroll full-time at a four-year institution or university. Applicant must have 3.0 GPA or higher. Available to U.S. and non-U.S. citizens.

National Association of Black Journalists (continued)

Application Requirements: Autobiography, references, proof of enrollment. *Deadline:* March 17.

Contact: Irving Washington, Manager
National Association of Black Journalists
8701-A Adelphi Road
Adelphi, MD 20783-1716
Phone: 301-445-7100
Fax: 301-445-7101
E-mail: iwashington@nabj.org

GERALD BOYD/ROBIN STONE NON-SUSTAINING SCHOLARSHIP

One-time scholarship for students enrolled in an accredited four-year institution. Must be enrolled as an undergraduate or graduate student and maintain a 3.0 GPA. Must major in print journalism. Must be a member of NABJ. Scholarship value and the number of awards granted annually varies.

Academic Fields/Career Goals: Journalism.

Award: Scholarship for use in freshman, sophomore, junior, senior, or graduate years; not renewable. *Number:* varies. *Amount:* varies.

Eligibility Requirements: Applicant must be enrolled or expecting to enroll full-time at a four-year institution or university. Applicant must have 3.0 GPA or higher. Available to U.S. and non-U.S. citizens.

Application Requirements: Application, essay, photo, references, transcript, 6 samples of work. *Deadline:* March 17.

Contact: Irving Washington, Manager
National Association of Black Journalists
8701-A Adelphi Road
Adelphi, MD 20783-1716
Phone: 301-445-7100
Fax: 301-445-7101
E-mail: iwashington@nabj.org

NABJ SCHOLARSHIP

• *See page 181*

NATIONAL ASSOCIATION OF BLACK JOURNALISTS AND NEWHOUSE FOUNDATION SCHOLARSHIP

Award for high school seniors planning to attend an accredited four-year college or university and major in journalism. Minimum 3.0 GPA required. Must be a member of NABJ. The scholarship value and the number of awards granted varies.

Academic Fields/Career Goals: Journalism.

Award: Scholarship for use in freshman, sophomore, junior, or senior years; not renewable. *Number:* varies. *Amount:* varies.

Eligibility Requirements: Applicant must be enrolled or expecting to enroll full-time at a four-year institution or university and must have an interest in writing. Applicant must have 3.0 GPA or higher. Available to U.S. and non-U.S. citizens.

Application Requirements: Application, autobiography, essay, interview, references, transcript. *Deadline:* March 17.

Contact: Irving Washington, Manager
National Association of Black Journalists
8701-A Adelphi Road
Adelphi, MD 20783-1716
Phone: 301-445-7100
Fax: 301-445-7101
E-mail: iwashington@nabj.org

NATIONAL ASSOCIATION OF BLACK JOURNALISTS NON-SUSTAINING SCHOLARSHIP AWARDS

One-time award for college students attending a four-year institution and majoring in journalism. Minimum 2.5 GPA required. Must be a member of NABJ. Scholarship value and the number of awards varies annually.

Academic Fields/Career Goals: Journalism; Photojournalism/Photography; TV/Radio Broadcasting.

Award: Scholarship for use in freshman, sophomore, junior, or senior years; not renewable. *Number:* varies. *Amount:* varies.

Eligibility Requirements: Applicant must be enrolled or expecting to enroll full-time at a four-year institution or university and must have an interest in writing. Applicant must have 2.5 GPA or higher. Available to U.S. and non-U.S. citizens.

Application Requirements: Application, autobiography, photo, references, transcript, proof of enrollment. *Deadline:* March 17.

Contact: Irving Washington, Manager
National Association of Black Journalists
8701-A Adelphi Road
Adelphi, MD 20783-1716
Phone: 301-445-7100
Fax: 301-445-7101
E-mail: iwashington@nabj.org

NATIONAL ASSOCIATION OF BROADCASTERS http://www.nab.org

NATIONAL ASSOCIATION OF BROADCASTERS GRANTS FOR RESEARCH IN BROADCASTING

• *See page 181*

NATIONAL ASSOCIATION OF HISPANIC JOURNALISTS (NAHJ) http://www.nahj.org

GERALDO RIVERA SCHOLARSHIP

Awards available to college undergraduates and graduate students pursuing careers in English- or Spanish-language TV broadcast journalism. Applications available on Web site: http://www.nahj.org.

Academic Fields/Career Goals: Journalism; TV/Radio Broadcasting.

Award: Scholarship for use in senior or graduate years; not renewable. *Number:* varies. *Amount:* $1000–$5000.

Eligibility Requirements: Applicant must be enrolled or expecting to enroll full-time at a four-year institution or university. Available to U.S. citizens.

Application Requirements: Application, financial need analysis, resume, references, transcript. *Deadline:* March 31.

Contact: Virginia Galindo, Program Assistant
National Association of Hispanic Journalists (NAHJ)
1000 National Press Building, 529 14th Street, NW, Suite 1000
Washington, DC 20045-2001
Phone: 202-662-7145
Fax: 202-662-7144
E-mail: vgalindo@nahj.org

MARIA ELENA SALINAS SCHOLARSHIP

• *See page 320*

NATIONAL ASSOCIATION OF HISPANIC JOURNALISTS SCHOLARSHIP

• *See page 181*

NEWHOUSE SCHOLARSHIP PROGRAM

• *See page 324*

WASHINGTON POST YOUNG JOURNALISTS SCHOLARSHIP

Four-year award of $10,000 for high school seniors in D.C. metropolitan area. Contact educational programs manager for application and information.

Academic Fields/Career Goals: Journalism.

Award: Scholarship for use in freshman year; not renewable. *Number:* varies. *Amount:* $10,000.

Eligibility Requirements: Applicant must be high school student; planning to enroll or expecting to enroll full-time at a four-year institution or university and resident of District of Columbia, Maryland, or Virginia. Available to U.S. citizens.

Application Requirements: Application, references, transcript. *Deadline:* March 31.

Contact: Virginia Galindo, Program Assistant
National Association of Hispanic Journalists (NAHJ)
1000 National Press Building, 529 14th Street, NW, Suite 1000
Washington, DC 20045-2001
Phone: 202-662-7145
Fax: 202-662-7144
E-mail: vgalindo@nahj.org

NATIONAL ASSOCIATION OF NEGRO BUSINESS AND PROFESSIONAL WOMEN'S CLUBS INC. http://www.nanbpwc.org

JULIANNE MALVEAUX SCHOLARSHIP

• *See page 220*

NATIONAL INSTITUTE FOR LABOR RELATIONS RESEARCH http://www.nilrr.org

NATIONAL INSTITUTE FOR LABOR RELATIONS RESEARCH WILLIAM B. RUGGLES JOURNALISM SCHOLARSHIP

• *See page 182*

NATIONAL PRESS FOUNDATION http://www.nationalpress.org

EVERT CLARK/SETH PAYNE AWARD

Award to recognize outstanding reporting and writing in any field of science. Limited to non-technical, print journalism only. Articles published in newspapers (including college newspapers), magazines, and newsletters are eligible. Both freelancers and staff writers are eligible.

Academic Fields/Career Goals: Journalism; Literature/English/Writing.

Award: Prize for use in freshman, sophomore, junior, senior, graduate, or postgraduate years; not renewable. *Number:* 1000. *Amount:* varies.

Eligibility Requirements: Applicant must be age 30 or under; enrolled or expecting to enroll full- or part-time at a two-year or four-year or technical institution or university and must have an interest in writing. Available to U.S. citizens.

Application Requirements: Application, applicant must enter a contest, five photocopies of each article. *Deadline:* June 30.

Contact: John Carey, Scholarship Committee
National Press Foundation
1211 Connecticut Avenue, Suite 310
Washington, DC 20036
Phone: 202-383-2100

NATIONAL SCHOLASTIC PRESS ASSOCIATION http://www.studentpress.org

NSPA JOURNALISM HONOR ROLL SCHOLARSHIP

Scholarship to student journalists who have achieved a 3.75 or higher GPA and have worked in student media for two or more years.

Academic Fields/Career Goals: Journalism.

Award: Scholarship for use in freshman year; not renewable. *Number:* 1–3. *Amount:* $1000.

Eligibility Requirements: Applicant must be high school student and planning to enroll or expecting to enroll full-time at a four-year institution or university. Applicant or parent of applicant must have employment or volunteer experience in journalism/broadcasting. Available to U.S. and non-U.S. citizens.

Application Requirements: Application, essay, resume, references, transcript, proof of NSPA membership required. *Deadline:* February 15.

Contact: Marisa Dobson, Sponsorship Contest Coordinator
National Scholastic Press Association
2221 University Avenue, SE, Suite 121
Minneapolis, MN 55414
Phone: 612-625-6519
Fax: 612-626-0720
E-mail: marisa@studentpress.org

NATIONAL WRITERS ASSOCIATION FOUNDATION http://www.nationalwriters.com

NATIONAL WRITERS ASSOCIATION FOUNDATION SCHOLARSHIPS

Scholarships available to talented young writers with serious interest in any writing field.

Academic Fields/Career Goals: Journalism; Literature/English/Writing.

Award: Scholarship for use in freshman, sophomore, junior, senior, graduate, or postgraduate years; not renewable. *Number:* up to 4. *Amount:* $1000.

Eligibility Requirements: Applicant must be enrolled or expecting to enroll full- or part-time at a two-year or four-year or technical institution or university and must have an interest in writing. Available to U.S. and non-U.S. citizens.

Application Requirements: Application, transcript, writing samples. *Deadline:* January 15.

Contact: Sandy Welchel, Executive Director
National Writers Association Foundation
10940 South Parker Road, Suite 508
Parker, CO 80134
Phone: 303-841-0246
Fax: 303-841-2607
E-mail: natlwritersassn@hotmail.com

NATIVE AMERICAN JOURNALISTS ASSOCIATION http://www.naja.com

NATIVE AMERICAN JOURNALISTS ASSOCIATION SCHOLARSHIPS

One-time award for undergraduate study leading to journalism career at accredited colleges and universities. Applicants must be current members of Native-American Journalists Association or may join at time of application. Applicants must have proof of tribal association. Send cover letter, letters of reference, and work samples with application. Financial need considered.

Academic Fields/Career Goals: Journalism.

Award: Scholarship for use in freshman, sophomore, junior, or senior years; not renewable. *Number:* 10. *Amount:* $500–$5000.

Eligibility Requirements: Applicant must be American Indian/Alaska Native; enrolled or expecting to enroll full-time at a two-year or four-year institution or university and must have an interest in writing. Applicant or parent of applicant must be member of Native American Journalists Association. Applicant must have 2.5 GPA or higher. Available to U.S. and Canadian citizens.

Application Requirements: Application, driver's license, essay, financial need analysis, interview, photo, portfolio, resume, references, test scores, transcript. *Deadline:* April 1.

Contact: Jeffrey Palmer, Education Director
Native American Journalists Association
University of Oklahoma, Gaylord School of Journalism
395 West Linsey Street
Norman, OK 73019
Phone: 405-325-9008
Fax: 866-694-4264
E-mail: jeffrey.p.palmer@ou.edu

NEBRASKA PRESS ASSOCIATION http://www.nebpress.com

NEBRASKA PRESS ASSOCIATION FOUNDATION INC. SCHOLARSHIP

Award for graduates of Nebraska high schools who have a minimum GPA of 2.5 and are enrolled or planning to enroll in programs in Nebraska colleges or universities leading to careers in print journalism.

Academic Fields/Career Goals: Journalism; Photojournalism/Photography.

Award: Scholarship for use in freshman, sophomore, or junior years; not renewable. *Number:* 2–4. *Amount:* $2000.

Eligibility Requirements: Applicant must be enrolled or expecting to enroll full-time at a four-year institution or university; resident of Nebraska and studying in Nebraska. Applicant must have 2.5 GPA or higher. Available to U.S. citizens.

Application Requirements: Application, references. *Deadline:* March 1.

Contact: Allen Beermann, Executive Director
Nebraska Press Association
845 South Street
Lincoln, NE 68508-1226
Phone: 402-476-2851
Fax: 402-476-2942
E-mail: abeermann@nebpress.com

NEW JERSEY BROADCASTERS ASSOCIATION http://www.njba.com

MICHAEL S. LIBRETTI SCHOLARSHIP

• *See page 182*

NEW JERSEY PRESS FOUNDATION http://www.njnf.org

BERNARD KILGORE MEMORIAL SCHOLARSHIP FOR THE NJ HIGH SCHOOL JOURNALIST OF THE YEAR

Program co-sponsored with the Garden State Scholastic Press Association. Winning student is nominated to the Journalism Education Association for the National High School Journalist of the Year Competition. Must be in high school with plans of entering a four-year college or university on a full-time basis. Minimum 3.0 GPA required.

Academic Fields/Career Goals: Journalism.

Award: Scholarship for use in freshman year; not renewable. *Number:* 1. *Amount:* $5000.

Eligibility Requirements: Applicant must be high school student; planning to enroll or expecting to enroll full-time at a four-year institution or university; resident of New Jersey and must have an interest in writing. Applicant must have 3.0 GPA or higher. Available to U.S. citizens.

Application Requirements: Application, essay, portfolio, resume, references, transcript. *Deadline:* February 15.

Contact: Thomas Engleman, Program Director
New Jersey Press Foundation
840 Bear Tavern Road, Suite 305
West Trenton, NJ 08628-1019
Phone: 609-406-0600 Ext. 19
Fax: 609-406-0300
E-mail: programs@njnf.org

INTERNSHIP/SCHOLARSHIP PROGRAM

For New Jersey residents. Students selected will be assigned paid internships at New Jersey newspapers (minimum $300/week for eight weeks). Scholarship awarded after successful completion of internship. Recipients must have at least one term of college left following the internship.

Academic Fields/Career Goals: Journalism.

Award: Scholarship for use in freshman, sophomore, or junior years; not renewable. *Number:* up to 8. *Amount:* $1500.

Eligibility Requirements: Applicant must be enrolled or expecting to enroll full-time at a two-year or four-year institution or university and resident of New Jersey. Available to U.S. citizens.

Application Requirements: Application, essay, resume, references, transcript, portfolio including a maximum of 3 clippings or photocopies of articles, photos, graphics, or other published journalistic work. *Deadline:* November 15.

Contact: Thomas Engleman, Program Director
New Jersey Press Foundation
840 Bear Tavern Road, Suite 305
West Trenton, NJ 08628-1019
Phone: 609-406-0600 Ext. 19
Fax: 609-406-0300
E-mail: programs@njnf.org

NEWSPAPER GUILD-CWA http://www.newsguild.org

DAVID S. BARR AWARD

Award for high school seniors and college students for their journalistic achievements and to encourage young journalists to focus on issues of social justice. One $500 award will be given to a graduating high school senior and one $1500 award will be given to a college student.

Academic Fields/Career Goals: Journalism.

Award: Scholarship for use in freshman, sophomore, junior, or senior years; not renewable. *Number:* up to 2. *Amount:* $500–$1500.

Eligibility Requirements: Applicant must be enrolled or expecting to enroll full- or part-time at a four-year institution or university. Available to U.S. and Canadian citizens.

Application Requirements: Application, applicant must enter a contest. *Deadline:* January 25.

Contact: Collective Bargaining Secretary
Newspaper Guild-CWA
501 Third Street, NW, Sixth Floor
Washington, DC 20001
Phone: 202-434-0675
Fax: 202-434-1472
E-mail: kdeneau@cwa-union.org

NORTHWEST JOURNALISTS OF COLOR http://www.aajaseattle.org

NORTHWEST JOURNALISTS OF COLOR SCHOLARSHIP

One-time award for Washington state high school and college students seeking careers in journalism. Must be an undergraduate enrolled in an accredited college or university or a senior in high school. Must be Asian-American, African-American, Native-American, or Latino.

Academic Fields/Career Goals: Journalism.

Award: Scholarship for use in freshman, sophomore, junior, senior, or graduate years; not renewable. *Number:* 1–6. *Amount:* $250–$1000.

Eligibility Requirements: Applicant must be American Indian/Alaska Native, Asian/Pacific Islander, Black (non-Hispanic), or Hispanic; enrolled or expecting to enroll full-time at a two-year or four-year or technical institution or university and resident of Washington. Applicant must have 2.5 GPA or higher. Available to U.S. citizens.

Application Requirements: Application, essay, financial need analysis, references, transcript, work samples. *Deadline:* May 2.

Contact: Lori Matsukawa, Scholarship Coordinator
Northwest Journalists of Color
333 Dexter Avenue North
Seattle, WA 98109
Phone: 206-448-3853
Fax: 206-448-4525
E-mail: lmatsukawa@king5.com

OHIO NEWSPAPERS FOUNDATION http://www.ohionews.org/foundation.html

OHIO NEWSPAPERS FOUNDATION MINORITY SCHOLARSHIP

Three scholarships for minority high school seniors who plan to pursue a newspaper journalism career. Applicants must be enrolled in an accredited Ohio college or university. Must be African-American, Hispanic, Asian-American or American-Indian. A minimum high school GPA of 2.5 required.

Academic Fields/Career Goals: Journalism.

Award: Scholarship for use in freshman year; not renewable. *Number:* 3. *Amount:* $1000.

Eligibility Requirements: Applicant must be American Indian/Alaska Native, Asian/Pacific Islander, Black (non-Hispanic), or Hispanic; high school student; planning to enroll or expecting to enroll full-time at a four-year institution or university; resident of Ohio and studying in Ohio. Applicant must have 2.5 GPA or higher. Available to U.S. citizens.

Application Requirements: Application, autobiography, essay, transcript. *Deadline:* March 31.

Contact: Kathleen Pouliot, Secretary
Ohio Newspapers Foundation
1335 Dublin Road, Suite 216-B
Columbus, OH 43215-7038
Phone: 614-486-6677
Fax: 614-486-4940
E-mail: kpouliot@ohionews.org

OHIO NEWSPAPERS FOUNDATION UNIVERSITY JOURNALISM SCHOLARSHIP

One-time $1500 scholarship for a student who is enrolled in an Ohio college or university, majoring in journalism or equivalent degree program. Preference will be given to students demonstrating a career commitment to newspaper journalism. A minimum GPA of 2.5 required.

Academic Fields/Career Goals: Journalism.

Award: Scholarship for use in freshman, sophomore, junior, or senior years; not renewable. *Number:* 1. *Amount:* $1500.

Eligibility Requirements: Applicant must be enrolled or expecting to enroll full-time at a four-year institution or university; resident of Ohio and studying in Ohio. Applicant must have 2.5 GPA or higher. Available to U.S. citizens.

Application Requirements: Application, autobiography, essay, references, transcript. *Deadline:* March 31.

Contact: Kathleen Pouliot, Secretary
Ohio Newspapers Foundation
1335 Dublin Road, Suite 216-B
Columbus, OH 43215-7038
Phone: 614-486-6677
Fax: 614-486-4940
E-mail: kpouliot@ohionews.org

OHIO NEWSPAPER WOMEN'S SCHOLARSHIP

One-time scholarship for female student who is enrolled as a junior or senior in an Ohio college or university, majoring in journalism or an equivalent degree program. Must be U.S. citizen.

Academic Fields/Career Goals: Journalism.

Award: Scholarship for use in junior or senior years; not renewable. *Number:* 1. *Amount:* $1000.

Eligibility Requirements: Applicant must be enrolled or expecting to enroll full-time at a four-year institution or university; female and studying in Ohio. Available to U.S. citizens.

Application Requirements: Application, references, test scores, transcript. *Deadline:* March 31.

Contact: Kathleen Pouliot, Secretary
Ohio Newspapers Foundation
1335 Dublin Road, Suite 216-B
Columbus, OH 43215-7038
Phone: 614-486-6677
Fax: 614-486-4940
E-mail: kpouliot@ohionews.org

OREGON ASSOCIATION OF BROADCASTERS http://www.theoab.org

OAB FOUNDATION SCHOLARSHIP

• *See page 182*

OREGON COMMUNITY FOUNDATION http://www.ocf1.org

JACKSON FOUNDATION JOURNALISM SCHOLARSHIP FUND

Scholarship for students attending an Oregon college or university and majoring in, or with emphasis on, journalism. For both full-time and part-time. Must be a resident of Oregon.

Academic Fields/Career Goals: Journalism.

Award: Scholarship for use in freshman, sophomore, junior, or senior years; not renewable. *Number:* 1. *Amount:* $1500–$2000.

Eligibility Requirements: Applicant must be enrolled or expecting to enroll full-time at a four-year institution or university; resident of Oregon and studying in Oregon. Available to U.S. citizens.

Application Requirements: Application, references. *Deadline:* March 1.

Contact: Dianne Causey, Program Associate for Scholarships and Grants
Oregon Community Foundation
1221 Yamhill, SW, Suite 100
Portland, OR 97205
Phone: 503-227-6846
Fax: 503-274-7771
E-mail: diannec@ocf1.org

OREGON STUDENT ASSISTANCE COMMISSION http://www.osac.state.or.us

JACKSON FOUNDATION JOURNALISM SCHOLARSHIP

Award for graduates of Oregon high schools pursuing a major in journalism. Must be enrolled in an Oregon college.

Academic Fields/Career Goals: Journalism.

Award: Scholarship for use in freshman, sophomore, junior, or senior years; renewable. *Number:* varies. *Amount:* varies.

Eligibility Requirements: Applicant must be enrolled or expecting to enroll full-time at a two-year or four-year institution; resident of Oregon and studying in Oregon. Available to U.S. citizens.

Application Requirements: Application, essay, financial need analysis, references, transcript, activity chart. *Deadline:* March 1.

Contact: Director of Grant Programs
Oregon Student Assistance Commission
1500 Valley River Drive, Suite 100
Eugene, OR 97401-7020
Phone: 800-452-8807 Ext. 7395

MARK HASS JOURNALISM AWARD

One-time award for journalism majors who are graduating Oregon high school seniors and college undergraduates. Visit Web site http://www.osac.state.or.us for application procedures, requirements and deadlines.

Academic Fields/Career Goals: Journalism.

Award: Scholarship for use in freshman, sophomore, junior, or senior years; not renewable. *Number:* varies. *Amount:* varies.

Eligibility Requirements: Applicant must be enrolled or expecting to enroll full-time at a four-year institution or university and resident of Oregon. Available to U.S. citizens.

Application Requirements: Application, essay, financial need analysis, references, transcript, activity chart. *Deadline:* March 1.

Contact: Director of Grant Programs
Oregon Student Assistance Commission
1500 Valley River Drive, Suite 100
Eugene, OR 97401-7020
Phone: 800-452-8807 Ext. 7395

OUTDOOR WRITERS ASSOCIATION OF AMERICA http://www.owaa.org

OUTDOOR WRITERS ASSOCIATION OF AMERICA BODIE MCDOWELL SCHOLARSHIP AWARD

• *See page 183*

OVERSEAS PRESS CLUB FOUNDATION http://www.overseaspressclubfoundation.org

OVERSEAS PRESS CLUB FOUNDATION SCHOLARSHIPS

Students aspiring to become foreign correspondents can apply. Must write an essay of no more than 500 words concentrating on an area of the world or an international issue that is in keeping with the applicant's interest. Must be studying at an American college or university.

Academic Fields/Career Goals: Journalism.

Award: Scholarship for use in freshman, sophomore, junior, senior, or graduate years; not renewable. *Number:* 12. *Amount:* $2000.

Eligibility Requirements: Applicant must be enrolled or expecting to enroll full- or part-time at a two-year or four-year institution or university and must have an interest in writing. Available to U.S. and non-U.S. citizens.

Application Requirements: Application, essay, resume, cover letter. *Deadline:* December 1.

Contact: William J. Holstein, President
Overseas Press Club Foundation
40 West 45th Street
New York, NY 10036
Phone: 212-626-9220
Fax: 212-626-9210
E-mail: foundation@opcofamerica.org

PALM BEACH ASSOCIATION OF BLACK JOURNALISTS http://www.pbabj.org

PALM BEACH ASSOCIATION OF BLACK JOURNALISTS SCHOLARSHIP

Scholarship of $1000 are awarded to African-American graduating high school seniors plan to pursue a degree in journalism-print, television, radio broadcasting or photography industries. Have a GPA of 2.7 or better.

Academic Fields/Career Goals: Journalism; Photojournalism/Photography; TV/Radio Broadcasting.

Award: Scholarship for use in freshman year; not renewable. *Number:* 1. *Amount:* $1000.

Palm Beach Association of Black Journalists (continued)

Eligibility Requirements: Applicant must be Black (non-Hispanic); high school student and planning to enroll or expecting to enroll full- or part-time at a four-year institution or university. Available to U.S. and non-U.S. citizens.

Application Requirements: Application, autobiography, transcript, college acceptance proof. *Deadline:* March 30.

Contact: Christopher Smith, Scholarship Chair
Palm Beach Association of Black Journalists
PO Box 19533
West Palm Beach, FL 33416

PHILADELPHIA ASSOCIATION OF BLACK JOURNALISTS http://www.pabj.org

PHILADELPHIA ASSOCIATION OF BLACK JOURNALISTS SCHOLARSHIP

One-time award available to deserving high school students in the Delaware Valley who are interested in becoming journalists. Must have a 2.5 GPA. All applicants must state their intention to pursue journalism careers.

Academic Fields/Career Goals: Journalism.

Award: Scholarship for use in freshman, sophomore, junior, or senior years; not renewable. *Number:* 2. *Amount:* up to $1000.

Eligibility Requirements: Applicant must be Black (non-Hispanic); enrolled or expecting to enroll full-time at a four-year institution or university; resident of Pennsylvania and must have an interest in writing. Applicant must have 2.5 GPA or higher. Available to U.S. citizens.

Application Requirements: Application, autobiography, essay, references, transcript. *Deadline:* May 1.

Contact: Manny Smith, Scholarship Committee
Philadelphia Association of Black Journalists
PO Box 8232
Philadelphia, PA 19101
E-mail: manuelsmith@gmail.com

PRINTING INDUSTRY OF MINNESOTA EDUCATION FOUNDATION http://www.pimn.org

PRINTING INDUSTRY OF MINNESOTA EDUCATION FOUNDATION SCHOLARSHIP FUND

• *See page 325*

QUILL AND SCROLL FOUNDATION http://www.uiowa.edu/~quill-sc

EDWARD J. NELL MEMORIAL SCHOLARSHIP IN JOURNALISM

Merit-based award for high school seniors planning to major in journalism. Must have won a National Quill and Scroll Writing Award or a Photography or Yearbook Excellence contest. Entry forms available from journalism adviser or Quill and Scroll. Must rank in upper third of class or have a minimum 3.0 GPA.

Academic Fields/Career Goals: Journalism.

Award: Scholarship for use in freshman year; not renewable. *Number:* 6–8. *Amount:* $500–$1500.

Eligibility Requirements: Applicant must be high school student; planning to enroll or expecting to enroll full-time at a four-year institution or university and must have an interest in photography/photogrammetry/filmmaking or writing. Applicant must have 3.0 GPA or higher. Available to U.S. citizens.

Application Requirements: Application, essay, photo, references, self-addressed stamped envelope, test scores, transcript. *Deadline:* May 10.

Contact: Vanessa Shelton, Executive Director
Quill and Scroll Foundation
School of Journalism, E346AJB
Iowa City, IA 52242-1528
Phone: 319-335-3457
Fax: 319-335-3989
E-mail: quill-scroll@uiowa.edu

RADIO-TELEVISION NEWS DIRECTORS ASSOCIATION AND FOUNDATION http://www.rtndf.org

CAROLE SIMPSON SCHOLARSHIP

• *See page 183*

ED BRADLEY SCHOLARSHIP

• *See page 183*

KEN KASHIWAHARA SCHOLARSHIP

• *See page 184*

LOU AND CAROLE PRATO SPORTS REPORTING SCHOLARSHIP

• *See page 184*

MIKE REYNOLDS $1,000 SCHOLARSHIP

• *See page 184*

PRESIDENT'S SCHOLARSHIP

• *See page 184*

ST. PETERSBURG TIMES FUND INC. http://sptimes.com

ST. PETERSBURG TIMES JOURNALISM SCHOLARSHIPS

Scholarship to high school seniors in the Times' circulation area who have a demonstrated interest in pursuing journalism major in college and career after graduation.

Academic Fields/Career Goals: Journalism.

Award: Scholarship for use in freshman year; renewable. *Number:* 1. *Amount:* $2500.

Eligibility Requirements: Applicant must be high school student; planning to enroll or expecting to enroll full-time at a four-year institution or university and resident of Florida. Available to U.S. citizens.

Application Requirements: Application, essay, portfolio, resume, references. *Deadline:* January 5.

Contact: Nancy Waclawek, Director
St. Petersburg Times Fund Inc.
PO Box 1121
St. Petersburg, FL 33731
Phone: 727-893-8780
Fax: 727-892-2257
E-mail: waclawek@sptimes.com

SEATTLE POST-INTELLIGENCER http://www.seattlepi.com

BOBBI MCCALLUM MEMORIAL SCHOLARSHIP

Scholarship for female college juniors and seniors who are Washington residents studying in Washington and have an interest in print journalism. Minimum 3.0 GPA required. Must submit clips of published stories with transcripts, financial need analysis, application, and two letters of recommendation.

Academic Fields/Career Goals: Journalism.

Award: Scholarship for use in junior or senior years; not renewable. *Number:* 1. *Amount:* $1000.

Eligibility Requirements: Applicant must be enrolled or expecting to enroll full- or part-time at a four-year institution or university; female; resident of Washington and studying in Washington. Applicant must have 3.0 GPA or higher. Available to U.S. citizens.

Application Requirements: Application, financial need analysis, portfolio, resume, references, transcript. *Deadline:* April 1.

Contact: Janet Grimley, Assistant Managing Editor
Seattle Post-Intelligencer
101 Elliot Avenue West
Seattle, WA 98119
Phone: 206-448-8316
Fax: 206-448-8305
E-mail: janetgrimley@seattlep-i.com

SIGMA DELTA CHI FOUNDATION OF WASHINGTON D.C. http://www.spj.org/washdcpro

SIGMA DELTA CHI SCHOLARSHIPS

One-time award to help pay tuition for full-time students in their junior or senior year demonstrating a clear intention to become journalists. Must demonstrate financial need. Grades and skills are also considered. Must be enrolled in a college or university in the Washington, D.C., metropolitan area. Sponsored by the Society of Professional Journalists.

Academic Fields/Career Goals: Journalism.

Award: Scholarship for use in sophomore or junior years; not renewable. *Number:* 5. *Amount:* $4000.

Eligibility Requirements: Applicant must be enrolled or expecting to enroll full-time at a four-year institution or university and studying in District of Columbia, Maryland, or Virginia. Applicant must have 3.0 GPA or higher. Available to U.S. and non-U.S. citizens.

Application Requirements: Application, essay, financial need analysis, interview, portfolio, references, transcript. *Deadline:* March 1.

Contact: Scholarship Committee
Sigma Delta Chi Foundation of Washington D.C.
PO Box 19555
Washington, DC 20036-0555
Phone: 301-405-5292
Fax: 301-314-9166

SOCIETY OF PROFESSIONAL JOURNALISTS, LOS ANGELES CHAPTER http://www.spj.org/losangeles

BILL FARR SCHOLARSHIP

Award available to a student who is either a resident of Los Angeles, Ventura or Orange counties or is enrolled at a university in one of those counties. Must have completed sophomore year and be enrolled in or accepted to a journalism program.

Academic Fields/Career Goals: Journalism.

Award: Scholarship for use in junior, senior, or graduate years; not renewable. *Number:* 1. *Amount:* $500–$1000.

Eligibility Requirements: Applicant must be enrolled or expecting to enroll full-time at a four-year institution or university; resident of California and studying in California. Available to U.S. citizens.

Application Requirements: Application, essay, financial need analysis, resume, references, work samples. *Deadline:* April 15.

Contact: Daniel Garvey, Scholarship Chairman
Society of Professional Journalists, Los Angeles Chapter
1250 Bellflower
Long Beach, CA 90840
Phone: 562-985-5779

CARL GREENBERG SCHOLARSHIP

Award for a student who is either a resident of Los Angeles, Ventura or Orange counties or is enrolled at a university in one of those three California counties. Must have completed sophomore year and be enrolled in or accepted to an investigative or political journalism program.

Academic Fields/Career Goals: Journalism.

Award: Scholarship for use in junior, senior, or graduate years; not renewable. *Number:* 1. *Amount:* $1000.

Eligibility Requirements: Applicant must be enrolled or expecting to enroll full-time at a four-year institution or university; resident of California and studying in California. Available to U.S. citizens.

Application Requirements: Application, essay, financial need analysis, resume, references, work samples. *Deadline:* April 15.

Contact: Daniel Garvey, Scholarship Chairman
Society of Professional Journalists, Los Angeles Chapter
1250 Bellflower
Long Beach, CA 90840
Phone: 562-985-5779

HELEN JOHNSON SCHOLARSHIP

Awards are available to a student who is a resident of Los Angeles, Ventura or Orange counties or is enrolled at a university in one of those three California counties. Must have completed sophomore year and be enrolled in or accepted to a broadcast journalism program.

Academic Fields/Career Goals: Journalism; TV/Radio Broadcasting.

Award: Scholarship for use in junior, senior, or graduate years; not renewable. *Number:* 1. *Amount:* $500–$1000.

Eligibility Requirements: Applicant must be enrolled or expecting to enroll full-time at a four-year institution or university; resident of California and studying in California. Available to U.S. citizens.

Application Requirements: Application, essay, financial need analysis, resume, references, work samples. *Deadline:* April 15.

Contact: Daniel Garvey, Scholarship Chairman
Society of Professional Journalists, Los Angeles Chapter
1250 Bellflower
Long Beach, CA 90840
Phone: 562-985-5779

KEN INOUYE SCHOLARSHIP

Awards are available to a minority student who is either a resident of Los Angeles, Ventura or Orange counties or is enrolled at a university in one of those three California counties. Must have completed sophomore year and be enrolled in or accepted to a journalism program.

Academic Fields/Career Goals: Journalism.

Award: Scholarship for use in junior, senior, or graduate years; renewable. *Number:* 1. *Amount:* $500–$1000.

Eligibility Requirements: Applicant must be American Indian/Alaska Native, Asian/Pacific Islander, Black (non-Hispanic), or Hispanic; enrolled or expecting to enroll full-time at a four-year institution or university; resident of California and studying in California. Available to U.S. citizens.

Application Requirements: Application, essay, financial need analysis, resume, references, work samples. *Deadline:* April 15.

Contact: Daniel Garvey, Scholarship Chairman
Society of Professional Journalists, Los Angeles Chapter
1250 Bellflower
Long Beach, CA 90840
Phone: 562-985-5779

SOCIETY OF PROFESSIONAL JOURNALISTS MARYLAND PRO CHAPTER http://www.spj.org/mdpro

MARYLAND SPJ PRO CHAPTER COLLEGE SCHOLARSHIP

Scholarships for journalism students whose regular home residence is in Maryland. May attend colleges or universities in Virginia, Washington D.C., or Pennsylvania.

Academic Fields/Career Goals: Journalism.

Award: Scholarship for use in freshman, sophomore, junior, or senior years; not renewable. *Number:* varies. *Amount:* varies.

Eligibility Requirements: Applicant must be enrolled or expecting to enroll full- or part-time at a four-year institution or university; resident of Maryland and studying in District of Columbia, Maryland, Pennsylvania, or Virginia. Available to U.S. citizens.

Application Requirements: Application, essay, financial need analysis, references, transcript, awards or honors received. *Deadline:* May 9.

Contact: Sue Kopen Katcef, Scholarship Chair
Society of Professional Journalists Maryland Pro Chapter
402 Fox Hollow Lane
Annapolis, MD 21403
Phone: 301-405-7526
E-mail: susiekk@aol.com

SOCIETY OF PROFESSIONAL JOURNALISTS-SOUTH FLORIDA CHAPTER http://www.spjsofla.net/

GARTH REEVES, JR. MEMORIAL SCHOLARSHIPS

• *See page 185*

SOUTH ASIAN JOURNALISTS ASSOCIATION (SAJA) http://www.saja.org

SAJA JOURNALISM SCHOLARSHIP

Scholarships for students in North America who are of South Asian descent (includes Bangladesh, Bhutan, India, Maldives, Nepal, Pakistan and Sri Lanka, Indo-Caribbean) or those with a demonstrated interest in South Asia or South Asian issues. Must be interested in pursuing journalism. Applicant must be a high school senior, undergraduate student or graduate-level student.

Academic Fields/Career Goals: Journalism.

Award: Scholarship for use in freshman, sophomore, junior, senior, graduate, or postgraduate years; not renewable. *Number:* 1–4. *Amount:* $1000–$2000.

South Asian Journalists Association (SAJA) (continued)

Eligibility Requirements: Applicant must be Asian/Pacific Islander and enrolled or expecting to enroll full-time at a two-year or four-year institution or university. Available to U.S. and non-U.S. citizens.

Application Requirements: Application, essay, financial need analysis, portfolio, resume, references, journalism clips or work samples. *Deadline:* February 15.

Contact: Sudeep Reddy, Student Committee and Scholarships
South Asian Journalists Association (SAJA)
Columbia Graduate School of Journalism
2950 Broadway
New York, NY 10027
Phone: 212-854-0191
E-mail: sudeepreddysaja@gmail.com

SOUTH CAROLINA PRESS ASSOCIATION FOUNDATION http://www.scpress.org

SOUTH CAROLINA PRESS ASSOCIATION FOUNDATION NEWSPAPER SCHOLARSHIPS

Renewable award for students entering junior year at a South Carolina institution. Based on grades, journalistic activities in college, and recommendations. Must agree to work in the newspaper field for two years after graduation or repay as loan.

Academic Fields/Career Goals: Journalism.

Award: Scholarship for use in junior year; renewable. *Number:* up to 3. *Amount:* $500–$1375.

Eligibility Requirements: Applicant must be enrolled or expecting to enroll full-time at a four-year institution or university and studying in South Carolina. Available to U.S. and non-U.S. citizens.

Application Requirements: Application, essay, financial need analysis, portfolio, resume, references, transcript. *Deadline:* January 20.

Contact: William C. Rogers, Secretary
South Carolina Press Association Foundation
PO Box 11429
Columbia, SC 29211-1429
Phone: 803-750-9561
Fax: 803-551-0903
E-mail: brogers@scpress.org

STRAIGHTFORWARD MEDIA http://www.straightforwardmedia.com

STRAIGHTFORWARD MEDIA MEDIA & COMMUNICATIONS SCHOLARSHIP

• *See page 185*

TEXAS GRIDIRON CLUB INC. http://www.spjfw.org

TEXAS GRIDIRON CLUB SCHOLARSHIPS

• *See page 187*

UNITED METHODIST COMMUNICATIONS http://www.umcom.org

LEONARD M. PERRYMAN COMMUNICATIONS SCHOLARSHIP FOR ETHNIC MINORITY STUDENTS

• *See page 187*

UNITED NEGRO COLLEGE FUND http://www.uncf.org

BEST BUY ENTERPRISE EMPLOYEE SCHOLARSHIP

• *See page 64*

C-SPAN SCHOLARSHIP PROGRAM

• *See page 187*

READER'S DIGEST FOUNDATION SCHOLARSHIP

• *See page 188*

UPS/UNCF CORPORATE SCHOLARS PROGRAM

• *See page 151*

VALLEY PRESS CLUB http://www.valleypressclub.com

VALLEY PRESS CLUB SCHOLARSHIPS, THE REPUBLICAN SCHOLARSHIP, CHANNEL 22 SCHOLARSHIP

• *See page 188*

WASHINGTON NEWS COUNCIL http://www.wanewscouncil.org

DICK LARSEN SCHOLARSHIP PROGRAM

• *See page 188*

HERB ROBINSON SCHOLARSHIP PROGRAM

• *See page 188*

WMTW-TV 8-AUBURN, MAINE http://www.wmtw.com

BOB ELLIOT-WMTW-TV 8 JOURNALISM SCHOLARSHIP

• *See page 189*

WOMEN'S BASKETBALL COACHES ASSOCIATION http://www.wbca.org

ROBIN ROBERTS/WBCA SPORTS COMMUNICATIONS SCHOLARSHIP AWARD

• *See page 189*

LANDSCAPE ARCHITECTURE

AMERICAN INSTITUTE OF ARCHITECTS, NEW YORK CHAPTER http://www.aiany.org

DOUGLAS HASKELL AWARD FOR STUDENT JOURNALISM

• *See page 90*

AMERICAN NURSERY AND LANDSCAPE ASSOCIATION http://www.anla.org/research

CARVILLE M. AKEHURST MEMORIAL SCHOLARSHIP

• *See page 350*

HORTICULTURE RESEARCH INSTITUTE TIMOTHY BIGELOW AND PALMER W. BIGELOW, JR. SCHOLARSHIP

• *See page 350*

MUGGETS SCHOLARSHIP

• *See page 350*

SPRING MEADOW NURSERY SCHOLARSHIP

• *See page 350*

USREY FAMILY SCHOLARSHIP

• *See page 350*

ASSOCIATION FOR WOMEN IN ARCHITECTURE FOUNDATION http://www.awa-la.org

ASSOCIATION FOR WOMEN IN ARCHITECTURE SCHOLARSHIP

• *See page 91*

CALIFORNIA WATER AWARENESS CAMPAIGN http://www.wateraware.org

CALIFORNIA WATER AWARENESS CAMPAIGN WATER SCHOLAR

• *See page 74*

FEDERATED GARDEN CLUBS OF CONNECTICUT http://www.ctgardenclubs.org

FEDERATED GARDEN CLUBS OF CONNECTICUT INC. SCHOLARSHIPS

• *See page 131*

FEDERATED GARDEN CLUBS OF MARYLAND http://hometown.aol.com/fgcofmd

ROBERT LEWIS BAKER SCHOLARSHIP

• *See page 352*

FRIENDS OF THE FRELINGHUYSEN ARBORETUM http://www.arboretumfriends.org

BENJAMIN C. BLACKBURN SCHOLARSHIP
• See page 302

GARDEN CLUB OF AMERICA http://www.gcamerica.org

KATHARINE M. GROSSCUP SCHOLARSHIP
• See page 352

HERB SOCIETY OF AMERICA, WESTERN RESERVE UNIT

FRANCIS SYLVIA ZVERINA SCHOLARSHIP
• See page 353

WESTERN RESERVE HERB SOCIETY SCHOLARSHIP
• See page 353

LANDSCAPE ARCHITECTURE FOUNDATION http://www.lafoundation.org

ASLA COUNCIL OF FELLOWS SCHOLARSHIP

Scholarship to aid promising students with unmet financial need. Eligible applicants must be permanent U.S. citizens or permanent resident aliens who are third-, fourth-, or fifth-year undergraduates at landscape architecture accreditation board accredited programs.

Academic Fields/Career Goals: Landscape Architecture.

Award: Scholarship for use in junior or senior years; renewable. *Number:* up to 2. *Amount:* up to $4000.

Eligibility Requirements: Applicant must be enrolled or expecting to enroll full- or part-time at a four-year institution or university. Available to U.S. citizens.

Application Requirements: Application, essay, financial need analysis, references. *Deadline:* February 15.

Contact: Ron Figura, Development Director
Landscape Architecture Foundation
818 18 Street, NW, Suite 810
Washington, DC 20006
Phone: 202-331-7070 Ext. 10
Fax: 202-331-7079
E-mail: rfigura@lafoundation.org

COURTLAND PAUL SCHOLARSHIP

Scholarship for undergraduate students in the final two years of study in landscape architecture accreditation board accredited schools. Applicants must demonstrate financial need, be a U.S. citizen, and have a minimum GPA of C.

Academic Fields/Career Goals: Landscape Architecture.

Award: Scholarship for use in junior or senior years; renewable. *Number:* 1. *Amount:* up to $5000.

Eligibility Requirements: Applicant must be enrolled or expecting to enroll full- or part-time at a four-year institution or university. Applicant must have 3.0 GPA or higher. Available to U.S. citizens.

Application Requirements: Application, essay, financial need analysis, references. *Deadline:* February 15.

Contact: Ron Figura, Development Director
Landscape Architecture Foundation
818 18 Street, NW, Suite 810
Washington, DC 20006
Phone: 202-331-7070 Ext. 10
Fax: 202-331-7079
E-mail: rfigura@lafoundation.org

EDSA MINORITY SCHOLARSHIP

Scholarship established to help African-American, Hispanic, Native American and minority students of other cultural and ethnic backgrounds to continue their landscape architecture education as they enter into their final two years of undergraduate study.

Academic Fields/Career Goals: Landscape Architecture.

Award: Scholarship for use in junior or senior years; renewable. *Number:* up to 1. *Amount:* up to $5000.

Eligibility Requirements: Applicant must be American Indian/Alaska Native, Asian/Pacific Islander, Black (non-Hispanic), or Hispanic and enrolled or expecting to enroll full- or part-time at a four-year institution or university. Available to U.S. and non-U.S. citizens.

Application Requirements: Application, essay, references, photos of work samples. *Deadline:* February 15.

Contact: Ron Figura, Development Director
Landscape Architecture Foundation
818 18 Street, NW, Suite 810
Washington, DC 20006
Phone: 202-331-7070 Ext. 10
Fax: 202-331-7079
E-mail: rfigura@lafoundation.org

HAWAII CHAPTER/DAVID T. WOOLSEY SCHOLARSHIP

One-time award for a third-, fourth-, or fifth-year undergraduate, or graduate student of landscape architecture. Must be permanent resident of Hawaii.

Academic Fields/Career Goals: Landscape Architecture.

Award: Scholarship for use in junior, senior, or graduate years; not renewable. *Number:* 1. *Amount:* up to $2000.

Eligibility Requirements: Applicant must be enrolled or expecting to enroll full- or part-time at a four-year institution and resident of Hawaii. Available to U.S. citizens.

Application Requirements: Application, autobiography, essay, financial need analysis, references, photos of work, proof of Hawaii residency. *Deadline:* February 15.

Contact: Ron Figura, Development Director
Landscape Architecture Foundation
818 18 Street, NW, Suite 810
Washington, DC 20006
Phone: 202-331-7070 Ext. 10
Fax: 202-331-7079
E-mail: rfigura@lafoundation.org

LANDSCAPE ARCHITECTURE FOUNDATION/CALIFORNIA LANDSCAPE ARCHITECTURAL STUDENT FUND SCHOLARSHIPS PROGRAM
• See page 354

LANDSCAPE ARCHITECTURE FOUNDATION/CALIFORNIA LANDSCAPE ARCHITECTURE STUDENT FUND UNIVERSITY SCHOLARSHIP PROGRAM
• See page 354

RAIN BIRD INTELLIGENT USE OF WATER SCHOLARSHIP

One-time need-based award for students in the final two years of undergraduate study in landscape architecture.

Academic Fields/Career Goals: Landscape Architecture.

Award: Scholarship for use in junior or senior years; not renewable. *Number:* 1. *Amount:* $2500.

Eligibility Requirements: Applicant must be enrolled or expecting to enroll full- or part-time at a four-year institution or university. Available to U.S. and non-U.S. citizens.

Application Requirements: Application, essay, references, cover letter. *Deadline:* February 15.

Contact: Ron Figura, Development Director
Landscape Architecture Foundation
818 18 Street, NW, Suite 810
Washington, DC 20006
Phone: 202-331-7070 Ext. 10
Fax: 202-331-7079
E-mail: rfigura@lafoundation.org

MONTANA FEDERATION OF GARDEN CLUBS http://www.mtfgc.org

LIFE MEMBER MONTANA FEDERATION OF GARDEN CLUBS SCHOLARSHIP
• See page 218

NATIONAL ASSOCIATION OF WOMEN IN CONSTRUCTION http://www.nawic.org

NAWIC UNDERGRADUATE SCHOLARSHIPS
• See page 92

NATIONAL GARDEN CLUBS INC. http://www.gardenclub.org

NATIONAL GARDEN CLUBS INC. SCHOLARSHIP PROGRAM
• See page 77

NEW YORK STATE EDUCATION DEPARTMENT http://www.highered.nysed.gov

REGENTS PROFESSIONAL OPPORTUNITY SCHOLARSHIP
• See page 60

PROFESSIONAL CONSTRUCTION ESTIMATORS ASSOCIATION http://www.pcea.org

TED WILSON MEMORIAL SCHOLARSHIP FOUNDATION
• See page 214

PROFESSIONAL GROUNDS MANAGEMENT SOCIETY http://www.pgms.org

ANNE SEAMAN PROFESSIONAL GROUNDS MANAGEMENT SOCIETY MEMORIAL SCHOLARSHIP
• See page 78

WORLDSTUDIO FOUNDATION http://www.aiga.org/

WORLDSTUDIO FOUNDATION SCHOLARSHIP PROGRAM
• See page 94

LAW ENFORCEMENT/POLICE ADMINISTRATION

ALBERTA HERITAGE SCHOLARSHIP FUND/ ALBERTA SCHOLARSHIP PROGRAMS http://www.alis.gov.ab.ca

ROBERT C. CARSON MEMORIAL BURSARY
• See page 200

AMERICAN SOCIETY OF CRIMINOLOGY http://www.asc41.com

AMERICAN SOCIETY OF CRIMINOLOGY GENE CARTE STUDENT PAPER COMPETITION
• See page 201

BOY SCOUTS OF AMERICA-MUSKINGUM VALLEY COUNCIL http://www.learning-for-life.org

SHERYL A. HORAK MEMORIAL SCHOLARSHIP

$1000 one-time scholarship for students enrolled either for full- or part-time study in a law enforcement field. Must be participant of the Learning for Life Exploring program.

Academic Fields/Career Goals: Law Enforcement/Police Administration.

Award: Scholarship for use in freshman, sophomore, junior, or senior years; not renewable. *Number:* 1. *Amount:* $1000.

Eligibility Requirements: Applicant must be enrolled or expecting to enroll full- or part-time at a two-year or four-year or technical institution or university. Available to U.S. and non-U.S. citizens.

Application Requirements: Application, essay, photo, references, transcript. *Deadline:* March 31.

Contact: Scholarship Committee
Boy Scouts of America-Muskingum Valley Council
1325 West Walnut Hill Lane, PO Box 152079
Irving, TX 75015-2079

CONNECTICUT ASSOCIATION OF WOMEN POLICE http://www.cawp.net

CONNECTICUT ASSOCIATION OF WOMEN POLICE SCHOLARSHIP
• See page 201

INDIANA SHERIFFS' ASSOCIATION http://www.indianasheriffs.org

INDIANA SHERIFFS' ASSOCIATION SCHOLARSHIP PROGRAM
• See page 201

INTERNATIONAL ASSOCIATION OF ARSON INVESTIGATORS EDUCATIONAL FOUNDATION INC. http://www.fire-investigators.org/

JOHN CHARLES WILSON SCHOLARSHIP
• See page 309

LEARNING FOR LIFE http://www.learning-for-life.org

BUREAU OF ALCOHOL, TOBACCO, FIREARMS AND EXPLOSIVES SCHOLARSHIP-LAW ENFORCEMENT

Scholarship for Law Enforcement Explorers whose achievements reflect the high degree of motivation, commitment, and community concern that epitomizes the law enforcement profession. Scholarships are awarded in the amount of $1000.

Academic Fields/Career Goals: Law Enforcement/Police Administration.

Award: Scholarship for use in freshman, sophomore, junior, or senior years; not renewable. *Number:* 2. *Amount:* $1000.

Eligibility Requirements: Applicant must be enrolled or expecting to enroll full-time at a two-year or four-year institution or university. Applicant or parent of applicant must be member of Explorer Program/ Learning for Life. Available to U.S. citizens.

Application Requirements: Application, essay, references, transcript. *Deadline:* March 15.

Contact: Scholarship Committee
Learning for Life
1325 West Walnut Hill Lane
PO Box 152079
Irving, TX 75015-2079
Phone: 972-580-2433

CAPTAIN JAMES J. REGAN SCHOLARSHIP

Two one-time $500 scholarships are presented annually to Law Enforcement Explorers graduating from high school or from an accredited college program. Evaluation will be based on academic record.

Academic Fields/Career Goals: Law Enforcement/Police Administration.

Award: Scholarship for use in freshman, sophomore, junior, senior, or graduate years; not renewable. *Number:* 2. *Amount:* $500.

Eligibility Requirements: Applicant must be age 20 or under and enrolled or expecting to enroll full-time at a two-year or four-year or technical institution or university. Applicant or parent of applicant must be member of Explorer Program/Learning for Life. Available to U.S. citizens.

Application Requirements: Application, essay, photo, references, transcript. *Deadline:* March 31.

Contact: Jim Kaminski, Scholarships and Awards Coordinator
Learning for Life
1325 West Walnut Hill Lane, PO Box 152079
Irving, TX 75015-2079
Phone: 972-580-2241
E-mail: jkaminsk@lflmail.org

DEA DRUG ABUSE PREVENTION SERVICE AWARDS

The award recognizes a Law Enforcement Explorer for outstanding service in drug abuse prevention.

Academic Fields/Career Goals: Law Enforcement/Police Administration.

Award: Prize for use in freshman, sophomore, junior, or senior years; not renewable. *Number:* 1. *Amount:* $1000.

Eligibility Requirements: Applicant must be enrolled or expecting to enroll full-time at a two-year or four-year institution or university. Applicant or parent of applicant must be member of Explorer Program/ Learning for Life. Applicant or parent of applicant must have employment or volunteer experience in alcohol or drug abuse counseling/treatment/prevention. Available to U.S. citizens.

Application Requirements: Application, photo. *Deadline:* March 31.

Contact: Scholarship Committee
Learning for Life
1325 West Walnut Hill Lane
PO Box 152079
Irving, TX 75015-2079
Phone: 972-580-2433

FEDERAL CRIMINAL INVESTIGATORS SERVICE AWARD

The award recognizes Law Enforcement Explorers who render outstanding service to law enforcement agencies.

Academic Fields/Career Goals: Law Enforcement/Police Administration.

Award: Prize for use in freshman, sophomore, junior, or senior years; not renewable. *Number:* 1. *Amount:* $500.

Eligibility Requirements: Applicant must be enrolled or expecting to enroll full- or part-time at a two-year or four-year institution or university. Applicant or parent of applicant must be member of Explorer Program/Learning for Life. Available to U.S. citizens.

Application Requirements: Application, essay, photo, references. *Deadline:* March 31.

Contact: Scholarship Committee
Learning for Life
1325 West Walnut Hill Lane
PO Box 152079
Irving, TX 75015-2079
Phone: 972-580-2433

SHERYL A. HORAK MEMORIAL SCHOLARSHIP

Award for graduating high school students who are Law Enforcement Explorers joining a program in law enforcement in accredited college or university. Provides a one-time scholarship of $1000.

Academic Fields/Career Goals: Law Enforcement/Police Administration.

Award: Scholarship for use in freshman year; not renewable. *Number:* 1. *Amount:* $1000.

Eligibility Requirements: Applicant must be enrolled or expecting to enroll full-time at a two-year or four-year institution or university. Applicant or parent of applicant must be member of Explorer Program/ Learning for Life. Available to U.S. citizens.

Application Requirements: Application, essay, photo, references, transcript. *Deadline:* March 31.

Contact: Scholarship Committee
Learning for Life
1325 West Walnut Hill Lane
PO Box 152079
Irving, TX 75015-2079
Phone: 972-580-2433

NATIONAL BLACK POLICE ASSOCIATION http://www.blackpolice.org

ALPHONSO DEAL SCHOLARSHIP AWARD

• *See page 201*

NORTH CAROLINA STATE EDUCATION ASSISTANCE AUTHORITY http://www.ncseaa.edu

NORTH CAROLINA SHERIFFS' ASSOCIATION UNDERGRADUATE CRIMINAL JUSTICE SCHOLARSHIPS

• *See page 202*

SOUTH CAROLINA POLICE CORPS http://www.citadel.edu

SOUTH CAROLINA POLICE CORPS SCHOLARSHIP

Tuition reimbursement scholarship available to a full-time student of an U.S. accredited college. Must agree to serve for four years on community patrol with a participating South Carolina police or sheriff's department. Up to $7500 per academic year with a limit of $30,000 per student.

Academic Fields/Career Goals: Law Enforcement/Police Administration.

Award: Scholarship for use in freshman, sophomore, junior, senior, or graduate years; renewable. *Number:* 20. *Amount:* $7500–$30,000.

Eligibility Requirements: Applicant must be enrolled or expecting to enroll full-time at a four-year institution or university. Available to U.S. citizens.

Application Requirements: Application, autobiography, driver's license, essay, interview, references, test scores, transcript. *Deadline:* varies.

Contact: Bryan C. Jones, Community Action Team
South Carolina Police Corps
5623 Two Notch Road
Columbia, SC 29223
Phone: 803-865-4486
E-mail: bryan.jones@hcahealthcare.com

WOMEN IN FEDERAL LAW ENFORCEMENT http://www.wifle.org

WIFLE SCHOLARSHIP PROGRAM

• *See page 198*

LAW/LEGAL SERVICES

ALBERTA HERITAGE SCHOLARSHIP FUND/ ALBERTA SCHOLARSHIP PROGRAMS http://www.alis.gov.ab.ca

JASON LANG SCHOLARSHIP

• *See page 206*

ROBERT C. CARSON MEMORIAL BURSARY

• *See page 200*

AMERICAN ASSOCIATION OF LAW LIBRARIES http://www.aallnet.org

AALL LIBRARY SCHOOL SCHOLARSHIPS FOR NON-LAW SCHOOL GRADUATES

One-time award for college graduate with meaningful law library experience who is a degree candidate in an accredited library school with the intention of having a career as a law librarian. Preference given to AALL members. Scholarship amount and the number granted varies. Must submit evidence of financial need.

Academic Fields/Career Goals: Law/Legal Services.

Award: Scholarship for use in freshman, sophomore, junior, senior, or graduate years; not renewable. *Number:* varies. *Amount:* varies.

Eligibility Requirements: Applicant must be enrolled or expecting to enroll full- or part-time at a four-year institution or university. Applicant or parent of applicant must be member of American Association of Law Librarians. Applicant or parent of applicant must have employment or volunteer experience in library work. Available to U.S. and non-U.S. citizens.

Application Requirements: Application, essay, financial need analysis, references, self-addressed stamped envelope, transcript. *Deadline:* April 1.

Contact: Chair, Scholarships Committee
American Association of Law Libraries
53 West Jackson Boulevard, Suite 940
Chicago, IL 60604-3695
Phone: 312-939-4764
Fax: 312-431-1097
E-mail: scholarships@aall.org

AMERICAN CRIMINAL JUSTICE ASSOCIATION-LAMBDA ALPHA EPSILON http://www.acjalae.org

AMERICAN CRIMINAL JUSTICE ASSOCIATION-LAMBDA ALPHA EPSILON NATIONAL SCHOLARSHIP

• *See page 200*

AMERICAN SOCIETY OF CRIMINOLOGY http://www.asc41.com

AMERICAN SOCIETY OF CRIMINOLOGY GENE CARTE STUDENT PAPER COMPETITION

• *See page 201*

BLACK ENTERTAINMENT AND SPORTS LAWYERS ASSOCIATION INC. http://www.besla.org

BESLA SCHOLARSHIP LEGAL WRITING COMPETITION

$1500 award for the best 1000-word, or two-page essay on a compelling legal issue facing the entertainment or sports industry. Essay must be written by law school student who has completed at least one full year at an accredited law school. Minimum GPA of 2.8 required.

Academic Fields/Career Goals: Law/Legal Services.

Award: Scholarship for use in freshman, sophomore, junior, senior, or graduate years; not renewable. *Number:* 2. *Amount:* $1500.

Eligibility Requirements: Applicant must be enrolled or expecting to enroll full-time at a four-year institution or university. Available to U.S. and non-U.S. citizens.

Application Requirements: Application, essay, resume, transcript. *Deadline:* varies.

Contact: Rev. Phyllicia Hatton, Executive Administrator
Black Entertainment and Sports Lawyers Association Inc.
PO Box 441485
Fort Washington, MD 20749-1485
Phone: 301-248-1818
Fax: 301-248-0700
E-mail: beslamailbox@aol.com

BOYS AND GIRLS CLUBS OF GREATER SAN DIEGO http://www.sdyouth.org

SPENCE REESE SCHOLARSHIP FUND

• *See page 262*

BUSINESS AND PROFESSIONAL WOMEN'S FOUNDATION http://www.bpwfoundation.org

BPW CAREER ADVANCEMENT SCHOLARSHIP PROGRAM FOR WOMEN

• *See page 130*

COLLEGEBOUND FOUNDATION http://www.collegeboundfoundation.org

DECATUR H. MILLER SCHOLARSHIP

• *See page 347*

JEANETTE R. WOLMAN SCHOLARSHIP

• *See page 165*

GRAND RAPIDS COMMUNITY FOUNDATION http://www.grfoundation.org

WARNER NORCROSS AND JUDD LLP SCHOLARSHIP FOR MINORITY STUDENTS

Financial assistance to students who are residents of Michigan, or attend a college/university/vocational school in Michigan, and are of racial and ethnic minority heritage pursuing a career in law, paralegal, or a legal secretarial program. Law school scholarship ($5000), paralegal scholarship ($2000), legal secretary scholarship ($1000).

Academic Fields/Career Goals: Law/Legal Services.

Award: Scholarship for use in freshman, sophomore, junior, senior, or graduate years; not renewable. *Number:* up to 3. *Amount:* $1000–$5000.

Eligibility Requirements: Applicant must be American Indian/Alaska Native, Asian/Pacific Islander, Black (non-Hispanic), or Hispanic; enrolled or expecting to enroll full-time at a two-year or four-year institution or university; resident of Michigan and studying in Michigan. Applicant must have 2.5 GPA or higher. Available to U.S. citizens.

Application Requirements: Application, essay, financial need analysis, references, transcript. *Deadline:* April 15.

Contact: Ruth Bishop, Education Program Officer
Grand Rapids Community Foundation
161 Ottawa Avenue, NW, 209 C
Grand Rapids, MI 49503-2757
Phone: 616-454-1751 Ext. 103
Fax: 616-454-6455
E-mail: rbishop@grfoundation.org

GREATER KANAWHA VALLEY FOUNDATION http://www.tgkvf.org

BERNICE PICKINS PARSONS FUND

Renewable award of $1000 open to students pursuing education or training in the fields of library science, nursing and paraprofessional training in the legal field. May apply for two foundation scholarships, but will only be chosen for one. Grant based on financial need. Must be a resident of West Virginia.

Academic Fields/Career Goals: Law/Legal Services; Library and Information Sciences; Nursing.

Award: Grant for use in freshman, sophomore, junior, or senior years; renewable. *Number:* 8. *Amount:* $1000.

Eligibility Requirements: Applicant must be enrolled or expecting to enroll full-time at a two-year or four-year institution or university and resident of West Virginia. Applicant must have 2.5 GPA or higher. Available to U.S. citizens.

Application Requirements: Application, essay, financial need analysis, references, self-addressed stamped envelope, test scores, transcript. *Deadline:* January 12.

Contact: Susan Hoover, Scholarship Coordinator
Greater Kanawha Valley Foundation
1600 Huntington Square, 900 Lee Street, East
PO Box 3041
Charleston, WV 25301
Phone: 304-346-3620
Fax: 304-346-3640
E-mail: shoover@tgkvf.org

INSTITUTE FOR HUMANE STUDIES http://www.theihs.org

HUMANE STUDIES FELLOWSHIPS

• *See page 179*

JAPANESE AMERICAN CITIZENS LEAGUE (JACL) http://www.jacl.org

NATIONAL JACL HEADQUARTERS SCHOLARSHIP

• *See page 75*

LINCOLN COMMUNITY FOUNDATION http://www.lcf.org

LAWRENCE "LARRY" FRAZIER MEMORIAL SCHOLARSHIP

• *See page 118*

MARYLAND HIGHER EDUCATION COMMISSION http://www.mhec.state.md.us

GRADUATE AND PROFESSIONAL SCHOLARSHIP PROGRAM-MARYLAND

• *See page 212*

JANET L. HOFFMANN LOAN ASSISTANCE REPAYMENT PROGRAM

• *See page 234*

NATIONAL ASSOCIATION OF WATER COMPANIES-NEW JERSEY CHAPTER

NATIONAL ASSOCIATION OF WATER COMPANIES-NEW JERSEY CHAPTER SCHOLARSHIP

• *See page 133*

NATIONAL BLACK POLICE ASSOCIATION http://www.blackpolice.org

ALPHONSO DEAL SCHOLARSHIP AWARD

• *See page 201*

NATIONAL COURT REPORTERS ASSOCIATION http://www.ncraonline.org

COUNCIL ON APPROVED STUDENT EDUCATION'S SCHOLARSHIP FUND

Applicant must have a writing speed of 140 to 180 words/min, and must be in an NCRA-approved court reporting program. Must write a two-page essay on topic chosen for the year and is also required to enter the competition.

Academic Fields/Career Goals: Law/Legal Services.

Award: Scholarship for use in sophomore year; not renewable. *Number:* 3. *Amount:* $500–$1500.

Eligibility Requirements: Applicant must be enrolled or expecting to enroll full- or part-time at a two-year or four-year or technical institution. Applicant must have 3.0 GPA or higher. Available to U.S. and Canadian citizens.

Application Requirements: Application, applicant must enter a contest, essay, references, transcript. *Deadline:* April 1.

Contact: Donna M. Gaede, Approval Program Manager
National Court Reporters Association
8224 Old Courthouse Road
Vienna, VA 22182
Phone: 703-556-6272 Ext. 171
Fax: 703-556-6291
E-mail: dgaede@ncrahq.org

FRANK SARLI MEMORIAL SCHOLARSHIP

One-time award to a student who is nearing graduation from a trade/technical school or four-year college. Must be enrolled in a court reporting program. Minimum 3.5 GPA required.

Academic Fields/Career Goals: Law/Legal Services.

Award: Scholarship for use in senior year; not renewable. *Number:* 1. *Amount:* $2000.

Eligibility Requirements: Applicant must be enrolled or expecting to enroll full- or part-time at a four-year or technical institution or university. Applicant or parent of applicant must be member of National Federation of Press Women. Applicant must have 3.5 GPA or higher. Available to U.S. and non-U.S. citizens.

Application Requirements: Application. *Deadline:* February 28.

Contact: B.J. Shorak, Deputy Executive Director
National Court Reporters Association
8224 Old Courthouse Road
Vienna, VA 22182-3808
Phone: 703-556-6272 Ext. 126
Fax: 703-556-6291
E-mail: bjshorak@ncrahq.org

STUDENT MEMBER TUITION GRANT

Four $500 awards for students in good academic standing in a court reporting program. Students are required to write 120 to 200 words/min.

Academic Fields/Career Goals: Law/Legal Services.

Award: Grant for use in freshman, sophomore, junior, or senior years; not renewable. *Number:* 4. *Amount:* $500.

Eligibility Requirements: Applicant must be enrolled or expecting to enroll full- or part-time at a four-year or technical institution or university. Available to U.S. and non-U.S. citizens.

Application Requirements: Application. *Deadline:* May 31.

Contact: Amy Davidson, Assistant Director of Membership
National Court Reporters Association
8224 Old Courthouse Road
Vienna, VA 22182
Phone: 703-556-6272 Ext. 123
E-mail: adavidson@ncrahq.org

NATIONAL FEDERATION OF PARALEGAL ASSOCIATIONS INC. (NFPA) http://www.paralegals.org

NATIONAL FEDERATION OF PARALEGAL ASSOCIATES INC. THOMSON WEST SCHOLARSHIP

Applicants must be full- or part-time students enrolled in an accredited paralegal education program or college-level program with emphasis in paralegal studies. Minimum GPA of 3.0 required. NFPA membership is not required. Travel stipend to annual convention in Arkansas, where recipients will receive awards, also provided.

Academic Fields/Career Goals: Law/Legal Services.

Award: Scholarship for use in freshman, sophomore, junior, senior, graduate, or postgraduate years; not renewable. *Number:* 2. *Amount:* $1500–$3500.

Eligibility Requirements: Applicant must be enrolled or expecting to enroll full- or part-time at a two-year or four-year or technical institution or university. Applicant must have 3.0 GPA or higher. Available to U.S. and non-U.S. citizens.

Application Requirements: Application, essay, references, transcript. *Deadline:* August 4.

Contact: Cindy Byfield, Managing Director
National Federation of Paralegal Associations Inc. (NFPA)
PO Box 2016
Edmonds, WA 98020
Phone: 425-967-0045
Fax: 425-771-9588
E-mail: info@paralegals.org

NATIONAL FEDERATION OF THE BLIND http://www.nfb.org

HOWARD BROWN RICKARD SCHOLARSHIP

• *See page 92*

NEW YORK STATE EDUCATION DEPARTMENT http://www.highered.nysed.gov

REGENTS PROFESSIONAL OPPORTUNITY SCHOLARSHIP

• *See page 60*

OKLAHOMA PARALEGAL ASSOCIATION http://www.okparalegal.org

JAMIE BOWIE MEMORIAL SCHOLARSHIP

Applicant must be currently enrolled in a legal assistant program at an ABA-approved institution and have successfully completed at least six credit hours. The director of the legal assistant program must provide verification of current enrollment. Recipient must be present at the presentation of the scholarship on the date to be announced.

Academic Fields/Career Goals: Law/Legal Services.

Award: Scholarship for use in freshman, sophomore, junior, or senior years; not renewable. *Number:* 1. *Amount:* $250.

Eligibility Requirements: Applicant must be enrolled or expecting to enroll full- or part-time at a four-year institution or university. Available to U.S. citizens.

Application Requirements: Application, financial need analysis, transcript. *Deadline:* April 15.

Contact: Emily Buckmaster, Student Director
Oklahoma Paralegal Association
714 Maple Drive
Weatherford, OK 73096
Phone: 405-235-7000
E-mail: ebuckmaster@hartzoglaw.com

RICHARD V. CRUZ MEMORIAL FOUNDATION http://www.rvcruzfoundation.2givenow.org

RICHARD V. CRUZ MEMORIAL FOUNDATION SCHOLARSHIP

$2000 scholarships to students from underserved populations enrolled in a California ABA-accredited law school. Applicants must have begun or completed their first year of law school and must be in good academic standing.

Academic Fields/Career Goals: Law/Legal Services.

Award: Scholarship for use in sophomore, junior, senior, or graduate years; not renewable. *Number:* varies. *Amount:* $2000.

Eligibility Requirements: Applicant must be Hispanic; enrolled or expecting to enroll full-time at a four-year institution or university and studying in California. Available to U.S. citizens.

Application Requirements: Application, financial need analysis, interview, resume, references, personal statement. *Deadline:* April 17.

Contact: Scholarship Committee
Richard V. Cruz Memorial Foundation
1605 Hope Street, Suite 210
South Pasadena, CA 91030
Phone: 626-799-7880
Fax: 626-799-0449

TKE EDUCATIONAL FOUNDATION http://www.tke.org

HARRY J. DONNELLY MEMORIAL SCHOLARSHIP

• *See page 64*

UNITARIAN UNIVERSALIST ASSOCIATION http://www.uua.org

STANFIELD AND D'ORLANDO ART SCHOLARSHIP

• *See page 107*

UNITED NEGRO COLLEGE FUND http://www.uncf.org

RAYMOND W. CANNON MEMORIAL SCHOLARSHIP PROGRAM

Annual scholarship awarded to students majoring in pharmacy or pre-law, and who have demonstrated leadership in high school and college. Awards undergraduate juniors with 2.5 GPA.

Academic Fields/Career Goals: Law/Legal Services; Pharmacy.

Award: Scholarship for use in junior year; not renewable. *Number:* varies. *Amount:* $2000–$5000.

Eligibility Requirements: Applicant must be Black (non-Hispanic) and enrolled or expecting to enroll full- or part-time at a four-year institution or university. Applicant must have 2.5 GPA or higher. Available to U.S. and non-U.S. citizens.

Application Requirements: Application, financial need analysis. *Deadline:* continuous.

Contact: Director, Program Services
United Negro College Fund
8260 Willow Oaks Corporate Drive
PO Box 10444
Fairfax, VA 22031-8044
Phone: 800-331-2244
E-mail: rebecca.bennett@uncf.org

VIRGINIA STATE BAR http://www.vsb.org

LAW IN SOCIETY AWARD COMPETITION

Participants write an essay in response to a hypothetical situation dealing with legal issues. Awards are based on superior understanding of the value of law in everyday life. The top thirty essays are awarded prizes of a plaque and dictionary/thesaurus set. First place receives $2000 U.S. Savings Bond or $1000 cash; second place, $1,500 bond or $750 cash; third place, $1,000 bond or $500 cash; honorable mentions, $200 bond or $100 cash.

Academic Fields/Career Goals: Law/Legal Services.

Award: Prize for use in freshman year; not renewable. *Number:* up to 10. *Amount:* $100–$1000.

Eligibility Requirements: Applicant must be high school student; age 19 or under; planning to enroll or expecting to enroll full- or part-time at a four-year institution or university; resident of Virginia and must have an interest in writing. Available to U.S. citizens.

Application Requirements: Application, applicant must enter a contest, essay. *Deadline:* February 1.

Contact: Sandy Adkins, Public Relations Assistant
Virginia State Bar
707 East Main Street, Suite 1500
Richmond, VA 23219-2800
Phone: 804-775-0594
Fax: 804-775-0582
E-mail: adkins@vsb.org

WASHINGTON STATE TRIAL LAWYERS ASSOCIATION http://www.wstla.org

WSTLA AMERICAN JUSTICE ESSAY SCHOLARSHIP CONTEST

The purpose of the scholarship is to foster an awareness and understanding of the American justice system. The essay contest deals with advocacy in the American justice system and related topics. Three scholarships are available to students who are attending high school in Washington state.

Academic Fields/Career Goals: Law/Legal Services.

Award: Scholarship for use in freshman year; not renewable. *Number:* 3. *Amount:* $2000–$3000.

Eligibility Requirements: Applicant must be high school student; planning to enroll or expecting to enroll full- or part-time at a two-year or four-year institution or university and studying in Washington. Available to U.S. and non-U.S. citizens.

Application Requirements: Application, applicant must enter a contest, essay. *Deadline:* March 21.

Contact: Adrianne Williams, Scholarship Coordinator
Washington State Trial Lawyers Association
1511 State Avenue NW
Olympia, WA 98506

LIBRARY AND INFORMATION SCIENCES

ALICE L. HALTOM EDUCATIONAL FUND http://www.alhef.org

ALICE L. HALTOM EDUCATIONAL FUND SCHOLARSHIP

• *See page 189*

AMERICAN SOCIETY FOR INFORMATION SCIENCE AND TECHNOLOGY http://www.asis.org

JOHN WILEY & SONS BEST JASIST PAPER AWARD

• *See page 190*

BIBLIOGRAPHICAL SOCIETY OF AMERICA http://www.bibsocamer.org

JUSTIN G. SCHILLER PRIZE FOR BIBLIOGRAPHICAL WORK IN PRE-20TH-CENTURY CHILDREN'S BOOKS

Award for bibliographic work in the field of pre-20th century children's books. Winner will receive a cash award of $2000 and a year's membership in the Society.

Academic Fields/Career Goals: Library and Information Sciences; Literature/English/Writing.

Award: Prize for use in freshman, sophomore, junior, or senior years; not renewable. *Number:* 1. *Amount:* $2000.

Eligibility Requirements: Applicant must be enrolled or expecting to enroll full- or part-time at a four-year institution or university. Available to U.S. and non-U.S. citizens.

Application Requirements: Application, applicant must enter a contest, resume, documentation regarding the approval of a thesis or dissertation or confirming the date of publication. *Deadline:* September 1.

Contact: Michele Randall, Executive Secretary
Bibliographical Society of America
PO Box 1537, Lenox Hill Station
New York, NY 10021
Phone: 212-452-2710
Fax: 212-452-2710
E-mail: bsa@bibsocamer.org

CALIFORNIA SCHOOL LIBRARY ASSOCIATION http://www.schoolibrary.org

JOHN BLANCHARD MEMORIAL FUND SCHOLARSHIP

Provides assistance to school library paraprofessional in obtaining preparation needed to qualify and serve as a school library media teacher in California. Applicant must be a member of the California School Library Association.

Academic Fields/Career Goals: Library and Information Sciences.

Award: Scholarship for use in freshman, sophomore, junior, senior, or graduate years; not renewable. *Number:* 1. *Amount:* $1000.

Eligibility Requirements: Applicant must be enrolled or expecting to enroll full- or part-time at an institution or university; resident of California and studying in California. Applicant or parent of applicant must have employment or volunteer experience in library work. Available to U.S. citizens.

Application Requirements: Application, references. *Deadline:* April 30.

Contact: Penny Kastanis, Executive Director
California School Library Association
1001 26th Street
Sacramento, CA 95816
Phone: 916-447-2684
Fax: 916-447-2695
E-mail: csla@pacbell.net

DANIEL KOVACH SCHOLARSHIP FOUNDATION http://www.collegescholarships.org

LIBRARY AND INFORMATION SCIENCES SCHOLARSHIP

Scholarship of $1000 to a college student enrolled in full time study. Applicant must have major in the field of library and information science. Minimum 3.0 GPA required. Must be a U.S. citizen.

Academic Fields/Career Goals: Library and Information Sciences.

Award: Scholarship for use in freshman, sophomore, junior, senior, or graduate years; not renewable. *Number:* 1. *Amount:* $1000.

Eligibility Requirements: Applicant must be enrolled or expecting to enroll full-time at a four-year institution or university. Applicant must have 3.0 GPA or higher. Available to U.S. citizens.

Application Requirements: Application, essay. *Deadline:* December 24.

Contact: Daniel Kovach, Scholarship Committee
Daniel Kovach Scholarship Foundation
5506 Red Robin Road
Raleigh, NC 27613
Phone: 919-630-4895
E-mail: danielkovach@gmail.com

FLORIDA ASSOCIATION FOR MEDIA IN EDUCATION http://www.floridamedia.org

FAME/SANDY ULM SCHOLARSHIP

Scholarship for students studying to be school library media specialists. The scholarship awards at least $1000 to one or more students each year. Deadlines: September 15 and February 15.

Academic Fields/Career Goals: Library and Information Sciences.

Award: Scholarship for use in freshman year; not renewable. *Number:* varies. *Amount:* $1000.

Eligibility Requirements: Applicant must be high school student; planning to enroll or expecting to enroll full-time at a two-year or four-year or technical institution or university and studying in Florida. Available to U.S. citizens.

Application Requirements: Application. *Deadline:* varies.

Contact: Larry Bodkin, Executive Director
Florida Association for Media in Education
2563 Capital Medical Boulevard
Tallahassee, FL 32308
Phone: 850-531-8350
Fax: 850-531-8344
E-mail: lbodkin@floridamedia.org

GREATER KANAWHA VALLEY FOUNDATION http://www.tgkvf.org

BERNICE PICKINS PARSONS FUND

• *See page 384*

IDAHO LIBRARY ASSOCIATION http://www.idaholibraries.org

IDAHO LIBRARY ASSOCIATION GARDNER HANKS SCHOLARSHIP

Scholarship for students who are beginning or continuing formal library education, pursuing a Master's of Library Science degree or Media Generalist certification. Must be an ILA member.

Academic Fields/Career Goals: Library and Information Sciences.

Award: Scholarship for use in freshman, sophomore, junior, or senior years; not renewable. *Number:* 1. *Amount:* $100–$500.

Eligibility Requirements: Applicant must be enrolled or expecting to enroll full-time at a four-year institution or university. Applicant or parent of applicant must be member of Idaho Library Association. Available to U.S. citizens.

Application Requirements: Application, financial need analysis, references. *Deadline:* September 1.

Contact: Karen Tate-pettinger, Chairperson
Idaho Library Association
5210 Stuart Avenue
Chubbuck, ID 83202
Phone: 208-237-2192
Fax: 208-237-2194

IDAHO LIBRARY ASSOCIATION LIBRARY SCIENCE SCHOLARSHIPS

One-time award for students studying library science. Must be a member of the Idaho Library Association. Must be a resident of Idaho.

Academic Fields/Career Goals: Library and Information Sciences.

Award: Scholarship for use in freshman, sophomore, junior, senior, or graduate years; not renewable. *Number:* 2–6. *Amount:* $100–$500.

Eligibility Requirements: Applicant must be enrolled or expecting to enroll full- or part-time at a two-year or four-year institution or university and resident of Idaho. Applicant or parent of applicant must be member of Idaho Library Association. Available to U.S. and non-U.S. citizens.

Application Requirements: Application, essay, resume, references. *Deadline:* September 1.

Contact: Suzy Ricks, Scholarship Committee
Idaho Library Association
Eastern Idaho Technical College Library
1600 South 2500 East
Idaho Falls, ID 83404
Phone: 208-524-3000 Ext. 3312
E-mail: sricks@eitc.edu

INDIANA LIBRARY FEDERATION http://www.ilfonline.org

AIME SCHOLARSHIP FUND

Scholarships are provided for undergraduate or graduate students entering or currently enrolled in a program to receive educational certification in the field of school library media services. For more details see Web site: http://www.ilfonline.org.

Academic Fields/Career Goals: Library and Information Sciences.

Award: Scholarship for use in freshman, sophomore, junior, senior, or graduate years; not renewable. *Number:* varies. *Amount:* varies.

Eligibility Requirements: Applicant must be enrolled or expecting to enroll full-time at a four-year institution or university and resident of Indiana. Available to U.S. citizens.

Application Requirements: Application, references, transcript. *Deadline:* June 30.

Contact: Crissy Gallion, Publications Manager
Indiana Library Federation
941 East 86th Street, Suite 260
Indianapolis, IN 46240
Phone: 317-257-2040
Fax: 317-257-1389
E-mail: cgallion@ilfonline.org

PENNSYLVANIA LIBRARY ASSOCIATION http://www.palibraries.org

BRODART/PENNSYLVANIA LIBRARY ASSOCIATION UNDERGRADUATE SCHOLARSHIP GRANT

Applicant must be enrolled in a state certified institution and must complete a minimum of three credits in library science courses leading to state certification. Credits must be completed during the summer session or academic year which begins the year of the scholarship award.

Academic Fields/Career Goals: Library and Information Sciences.

Award: Scholarship for use in freshman, sophomore, junior, or senior years; not renewable. *Number:* 2. *Amount:* $1000.

Eligibility Requirements: Applicant must be enrolled or expecting to enroll full-time at a two-year or four-year institution or university; resident of Pennsylvania and studying in Pennsylvania. Available to U.S. citizens.

Pennsylvania Library Association (continued)

Application Requirements: Application, references. *Deadline:* May 15.

Contact: Ellen Wharton, Administrative Assistant
Pennsylvania Library Association
220 Cumberland Parkway, Suite 10
Mechanicsburg, PA 17055-5683
Phone: 717-766-7663
Fax: 717-766-5440
E-mail: ellen@palibraries.org

SPECIAL LIBRARIES ASSOCIATION http://www.sla.org

SPECIAL LIBRARIES ASSOCIATION AFFIRMATIVE ACTION SCHOLARSHIP

One $6000 scholarship for graduate study in librarianship leading to a master's degree. Must be U.S. citizen either by birth or naturalization or permanent resident alien and a member of a minority group. Must have an interest in special librarianship and submit evidence of financial need.

Academic Fields/Career Goals: Library and Information Sciences.

Award: Scholarship for use in senior or graduate years; not renewable. *Number:* 1. *Amount:* $6000.

Eligibility Requirements: Applicant must be American Indian/Alaska Native, Asian/Pacific Islander, Black (non-Hispanic), or Hispanic and enrolled or expecting to enroll full-time at a four-year institution or university. Available to U.S. citizens.

Application Requirements: Application, essay, financial need analysis, interview, references, test scores, transcript, statement of provisional acceptance. *Deadline:* September 30.

Contact: Teniakka Greene, Membership Services Associate
Special Libraries Association
331 South Patrick Street
Alexandria, VA 22314-3501
Phone: 703-647-4900
Fax: 703-647-4901
E-mail: tgreene@sla.org

SPECIAL LIBRARIES ASSOCIATION SCHOLARSHIP

Up to three $6000 awards for graduate study in librarianship leading to a master's degree at a recognized school of library or information science. Must be college graduate or college senior with an interest in special librarianship.

Academic Fields/Career Goals: Library and Information Sciences.

Award: Scholarship for use in senior or graduate years; not renewable. *Number:* up to 3. *Amount:* $6000.

Eligibility Requirements: Applicant must be enrolled or expecting to enroll full-time at a four-year institution or university. Available to U.S. citizens.

Application Requirements: Application, essay, financial need analysis, interview, references, test scores, transcript, statement of provisional acceptance. *Deadline:* September 30.

Contact: Teniakka Greene, Membership Services Associate
Special Libraries Association
331 South Patrick Street
Alexandria, VA 22314-3501
Phone: 703-647-4900
Fax: 703-647-4901
E-mail: tgreene@sla.org

WISCONSIN LIBRARY ASSOCIATION http://www.wla.lib.wi.us

SCHOLARSHIP FOR THE EDUCATION OF RURAL LIBRARIANS GLORIA HOEGH MEMORIAL FUND

Scholarship awarded to librarians planning to attend a workshop, conference, and/or a continuing education program within or outside Wisconsin. Applicant must be a library employee working in a Wisconsin community with a current population of 5000 or less or who works with library employees in those communities.

Academic Fields/Career Goals: Library and Information Sciences.

Award: Scholarship for use in freshman, sophomore, junior, senior, or graduate years; not renewable. *Number:* varies. *Amount:* $1000.

Eligibility Requirements: Applicant must be enrolled or expecting to enroll full- or part-time at a four-year institution or university and resident of Wisconsin. Applicant or parent of applicant must have employment or volunteer experience in library work. Available to U.S. citizens.

Application Requirements: Application, essay, financial need analysis. *Deadline:* August 1.

Contact: Brigitte Rupp Vacha, Member Service Coordinator
Wisconsin Library Association
5250 East Terrace Drive, Suite A1
Madison, WI 53718-8345
Phone: 608-245-3640
Fax: 608-245-3646
E-mail: ruppvacha@scls.lib.wi.us

WAAL SCHOLARSHIP

Scholarship available to currently enrolled library and information science undergraduate and graduate student who is a member of Wisconsin Library Association.

Academic Fields/Career Goals: Library and Information Sciences.

Award: Scholarship for use in freshman, sophomore, junior, senior, or graduate years; not renewable. *Number:* varies. *Amount:* varies.

Eligibility Requirements: Applicant must be enrolled or expecting to enroll full- or part-time at a four-year institution or university and resident of Wisconsin. Applicant or parent of applicant must be member of Wisconsin Library Association. Available to U.S. citizens.

Application Requirements: Application, essay. *Deadline:* February 21.

Contact: Dexter Library
Wisconsin Library Association
1411 Ellis Avenue
Ashland, WI 54806
Phone: 715-682-1302
Fax: 715-682-1693
E-mail: jtrojan@northland.edu

WLA CONTINUING EDUCATION SCHOLARSHIP

Scholarship awarded to employee who is planning to attend a continuing education program within or outside of Wisconsin. Applicant must be able to communicate the knowledge gained from the continuing education program to fellow librarians and information professionals in Wisconsin, employed in a library and information agency in Wisconsin.

Academic Fields/Career Goals: Library and Information Sciences.

Award: Scholarship for use in freshman, sophomore, junior, senior, graduate, or postgraduate years; not renewable. *Number:* varies. *Amount:* varies.

Eligibility Requirements: Applicant must be enrolled or expecting to enroll full- or part-time at a four-year institution or university and resident of Wisconsin. Available to U.S. citizens.

Application Requirements: Application, copy of the continuing education program. *Deadline:* March 1.

Contact: Brigitte Rupp Vacha, Member Service Coordinator
Wisconsin Library Association
5250 East Terrace Drive, Suite A1
Madison, WI 53718-8345
Phone: 608-245-3640
Fax: 608-245-3646
E-mail: ruppvacha@scls.lib.wi.us

LITERATURE/ENGLISH/WRITING

AIM MAGAZINE SHORT STORY CONTEST http://www.aimmagazine.org

AMERICA'S INTERCULTURAL MAGAZINE (AIM) SHORT STORY CONTEST

Short fiction award for a previously unpublished story that embodies the magazine's goal of furthering the brotherhood of man through the written word. Must provide proof that people from different racial/ethnic backgrounds are more alike than they are different. Maximum length 4000 words. Story should not moralize.

Academic Fields/Career Goals: Literature/English/Writing.

Award: Prize for use in freshman, sophomore, junior, senior, or graduate years; not renewable. *Number:* 1–2. *Amount:* $75–$100.

Eligibility Requirements: Applicant must be enrolled or expecting to enroll full- or part-time at a two-year or four-year or technical institution or university and must have an interest in writing. Available to U.S. and Canadian citizens.

Application Requirements: Application, applicant must enter a contest, essay. *Deadline:* August 15.

Contact: Mark Boone, Fiction Editor
Aim Magazine Short Story Contest
PO Box 1174
Maywood, IL 60153
Phone: 708-344-4414
E-mail: apiladoone@aol.com

ALLIANCE FOR YOUNG ARTISTS AND WRITERS INC. http://www.artandwriting.org

SCHOLASTIC ART AND WRITING AWARDS-ART SECTION

• *See page 99*

SCHOLASTIC ART AND WRITING AWARDS-WRITING SECTION SCHOLARSHIP

• *See page 99*

AMERICAN FOUNDATION FOR THE BLIND http://www.afb.org

R.L. GILLETTE SCHOLARSHIP

Two scholarships of $1000 each to women who are enrolled in a four-year undergraduate degree program in literature or music. In addition to the general requirements, applicants must submit a performance tape not to exceed 30 minutes, or a creative writing sample. Must submit proof of legal blindness. For additional information and application requirements, refer to Web site: www.afb.org/scholarships.asp.

Academic Fields/Career Goals: Literature/English/Writing; Music.

Award: Scholarship for use in freshman, sophomore, junior, or senior years; not renewable. *Number:* up to 2. *Amount:* $1000.

Eligibility Requirements: Applicant must be enrolled or expecting to enroll full-time at a four-year institution or university and female. Applicant must be visually impaired. Available to U.S. citizens.

Application Requirements: Application, essay, financial need analysis, references, transcript, performance tape (not to exceed 30 minutes) or creative writing sample, proof of legal blindness, acceptance letter. *Deadline:* March 31.

Contact: Dawn Bodrogi, Information Center and Library Coordinator
American Foundation for the Blind
11 Penn Plaza, Suite 300
New York, NY 10001
Phone: 212-502-7661
Fax: 212-502-7771
E-mail: afbinfo@afb.net

AMERICAN LEGION AUXILIARY DEPARTMENT OF WASHINGTON http://www.walegion-aux.org

AMERICAN LEGION AUXILIARY DEPARTMENT OF WASHINGTON FLORENCE LEMCKE MEMORIAL SCHOLARSHIP IN FINE ARTS

• *See page 97*

AMERICAN-SCANDINAVIAN FOUNDATION http://www.amscan.org

AMERICAN-SCANDINAVIAN FOUNDATION TRANSLATION PRIZE

Two prizes are awarded for outstanding English translations of poetry, fiction, drama or literary prose originally written in Danish, Finnish, Icelandic, Norwegian or Swedish. One-time award of $2000.

Academic Fields/Career Goals: Literature/English/Writing.

Award: Prize for use in freshman, sophomore, junior, senior, graduate, or postgraduate years; not renewable. *Number:* 2. *Amount:* $2000.

Eligibility Requirements: Applicant must be enrolled or expecting to enroll full- or part-time at a two-year or four-year or technical institution or university and must have an interest in Scandinavian language. Available to U.S. and non-U.S. citizens.

Application Requirements: Application, applicant must enter a contest, resume. *Deadline:* June 1.

Contact: Director of Fellowships and Grants
American-Scandinavian Foundation
58 Park Avenue
New York, NY 10016
Phone: 212-879-9779
Fax: 212-686-2115
E-mail: info@amscan.org

AMY LOWELL POETRY TRAVELING SCHOLARSHIP TRUST http://www.amylowell.org

AMY LOWELL POETRY TRAVELING SCHOLARSHIP

Scholarship to a poet of American birth. Upon acceptance, the recipient agrees to spend one year outside the continent of North America in a place deemed by the recipient suitable to advance the art of poetry. At the end of the year, the recipient shall submit at least three poems for consideration by the trust's committee. For additional information visit Web site: http://www.amylowell.org.

Academic Fields/Career Goals: Literature/English/Writing.

Award: Scholarship for use in freshman, sophomore, junior, senior, graduate, or postgraduate years; not renewable. *Number:* 1. *Amount:* up to $50,000.

Eligibility Requirements: Applicant must be enrolled or expecting to enroll full- or part-time at a two-year or four-year or technical institution or university and must have an interest in writing. Available to U.S. citizens.

Application Requirements: Application, applicant must enter a contest, resume, poetry sample. *Deadline:* October 15.

Contact: Cathleen Croft, Trustee
Amy Lowell Poetry Traveling Scholarship Trust
Two International Place
Boston, MA 02110
Phone: 617-248-4855
Fax: 617-248-4000
E-mail: amylowell@choate.com

BIBLIOGRAPHICAL SOCIETY OF AMERICA http://www.bibsocamer.org

JUSTIN G. SCHILLER PRIZE FOR BIBLIOGRAPHICAL WORK IN PRE-20TH-CENTURY CHILDREN'S BOOKS

• *See page 386*

BREAD LOAF WRITERS' CONFERENCE http://www.middlebury.edu/~blwc

BREAD LOAF WRITERS' CONFERENCE SCHOLARSHIP

Scholarship of $2164 is given to both graduate and undergraduate students enrolled either full-time or part-time study who are 18 years of age and above.

Academic Fields/Career Goals: Literature/English/Writing.

Award: Scholarship for use in freshman, sophomore, junior, senior, or graduate years; not renewable. *Number:* varies. *Amount:* $2164.

Eligibility Requirements: Applicant must be age 18 and over; enrolled or expecting to enroll full- or part-time at a two-year or four-year or technical institution or university and must have an interest in writing. Available to U.S. and non-U.S. citizens.

Application Requirements: Application, essay. *Deadline:* March 1.

Contact: Noreen Cargill, Administrative Manager
Bread Loaf Writers' Conference
Middlebury College
Middlebury, VT 05753
Phone: 802-443-5286
Fax: 802-443-2087
E-mail: ncargill@middlebury.edu

CENTER FOR LESBIAN AND GAY STUDIES (C.L.A.G.S.) http://www.clags.org

CENTER FOR GAY AND LESBIAN STUDIES UNDERGRADUATE PAPER AWARDS

A cash prize of $250 awarded to the best paper written in a California University of New York or State University of New York undergraduate class on a topic related to gay, lesbian, bisexual, queer, or transgender experiences. Essays should be between 12 and 30 pages.

Academic Fields/Career Goals: Literature/English/Writing.

Award: Prize for use in freshman, sophomore, junior, or senior years; not renewable. *Number:* 1. *Amount:* $250.

Eligibility Requirements: Applicant must be enrolled or expecting to enroll full- or part-time at a four-year institution or university and must have an interest in LGBT issues. Available to U.S. and non-U.S. citizens.

Application Requirements: Applicant must enter a contest, essay. *Deadline:* June 1.

Contact: Naz Qazi, Fellowship Membership Coordinator
Center for Lesbian and Gay Studies (C.L.A.G.S.)
365 Fifth Avenue, Room 7115
New York, NY 10016
Phone: 212-817-1955
Fax: 212-817-1567
E-mail: clags@gc.cuny.edu

CIRI FOUNDATION (TCF) http://www.thecirifoundation.org

CIRI FOUNDATION SUSIE QIMMIQSAK BEVINS ENDOWMENT SCHOLARSHIP FUND

• *See page 100*

DAVIDSON INSTITUTE FOR TALENT DEVELOPMENT http://www.davidsoninstitute.org

DAVIDSON FELLOWS

One-time award to recognize outstanding achievements of young people. Must be under the age of 18. Must have completed a significant piece of work in one of the following areas: science, technology, mathematics, humanities (music, literature or philosophy). Must be a U.S. citizen or a permanent resident.

Academic Fields/Career Goals: Literature/English/Writing; Mathematics; Music; Philosophy; Science, Technology, and Society.

Award: Scholarship for use in freshman, sophomore, junior, senior, graduate, or postgraduate years; not renewable. *Number:* 15–20. *Amount:* $10,000–$50,000.

Eligibility Requirements: Applicant must be age 18 or under and enrolled or expecting to enroll full- or part-time at a two-year or four-year or technical institution or university. Available to U.S. citizens.

Application Requirements: Application, essay, portfolio, references. *Deadline:* March 25.

Contact: Tacie Moessner, Davidson Fellows Program Manager
Davidson Institute for Talent Development
9665 Gateway Drive, Suite B
Reno, NV 89521
Phone: 775-852-3483 Ext. 423
Fax: 775-852-2184
E-mail: davidsonfellows@ditd.org

GOLDEN KEY INTERNATIONAL HONOUR SOCIETY http://www.goldenkey.org

LITERARY ACHIEVEMENT AWARDS

Award of $1000 will be given to winners in each of the following four categories: fiction, non-fiction, poetry, and feature writing. Eligible applicants are undergraduate, graduate and postgraduate members who are currently enrolled in classes at a degree-granting program.

Academic Fields/Career Goals: Literature/English/Writing.

Award: Prize for use in freshman, sophomore, junior, senior, graduate, or postgraduate years; not renewable. *Number:* 4. *Amount:* $1000.

Eligibility Requirements: Applicant must be enrolled or expecting to enroll full- or part-time at a four-year institution or university and must have an interest in writing. Available to U.S. and non-U.S. citizens.

Application Requirements: Application, applicant must enter a contest, essay, original composition. *Deadline:* April 1.

Contact: Scholarship Program Administrators
Golden Key International Honour Society
PO Box 23737
Nashville, TN 37202-3737
Phone: 800-377-2401
E-mail: scholarships@goldenkey.org

HISPANIC SCHOLARSHIP FUND http://www.hsf.net

HSF/MCNAMARA FAMILY CREATIVE ARTS PROJECT GRANT

• *See page 98*

INSTITUTE FOR HUMANE STUDIES http://www.theihs.org

FILM AND FICTION SCHOLARSHIP

• *See page 102*

HUMANE STUDIES FELLOWSHIPS

• *See page 179*

INTERNATIONAL FOODSERVICE EDITORIAL COUNCIL http://www.ifeconline.com

INTERNATIONAL FOODSERVICE EDITORIAL COUNCIL COMMUNICATIONS SCHOLARSHIP

• *See page 180*

JACK J. ISGUR FOUNDATION

JACK J. ISGUR FOUNDATION SCHOLARSHIP

• *See page 102*

JAPANESE AMERICAN CITIZENS LEAGUE (JACL) http://www.jacl.org

NATIONAL JACL HEADQUARTERS SCHOLARSHIP

• *See page 75*

JOHN F. KENNEDY LIBRARY FOUNDATION http://www.jfklibrary.org

PROFILE IN COURAGE ESSAY CONTEST

Essay contest open to all high school students, grades nine to twelve. Students in U.S. territories and U.S. citizens attending schools overseas may also apply. All essays will be judged on the overall originality of topic and the clear communication of ideas through language. Winner and their nominating teacher are invited to Kennedy Library to accept award. Winner receives $3000, nomination teacher receives grant of $500; second place receives $1000 and five finalists receive $500.

Academic Fields/Career Goals: Literature/English/Writing.

Award: Prize for use in freshman year; not renewable. *Number:* 7. *Amount:* $500–$3000.

Eligibility Requirements: Applicant must be high school student; age 19 or under; planning to enroll or expecting to enroll full-time at a four-year institution and must have an interest in writing. Available to U.S. citizens.

Application Requirements: Application, applicant must enter a contest, essay, bibliography. *Deadline:* January 7.

Contact: Esther Kohn, Essay Contest Coordinator
John F. Kennedy Library Foundation
Columbia Point
Boston, MA 02125
Phone: 617-514-1649
Fax: 617-514-1641
E-mail: profiles@nara.gov

KAPLAN/NEWSWEEK http://www.kaptest.com

"MY TURN" ESSAY COMPETITION

Essay contest open to high school students entering college or university. Contestants can win up to $5000. Must be U.S. citizen. To enter, a student must submit 500- to 1000-word essay expressing their opinion, experience, or personal feelings on a topic of their own choice. First prize: $5000; second prize: $2000; and 8 finalists are awarded $1000.

Academic Fields/Career Goals: Literature/English/Writing.

Award: Scholarship for use in freshman year; not renewable. *Number:* up to 10. *Amount:* $1000–$5000.

Eligibility Requirements: Applicant must be high school student; planning to enroll or expecting to enroll full- or part-time at a two-year or four-year institution or university and must have an interest in writing. Available to U.S. and non-U.S. citizens.

Application Requirements: Application, applicant must enter a contest, essay. *Deadline:* March 1.

Contact: Scholarship Committee
Kaplan/Newsweek
1440 Broadway, Ninth Floor
New York, NY 10018
Phone: 212-997-5886

LAMBDA IOTA TAU, COLLEGE LITERATURE HONOR SOCIETY http://www.bsu.edu/english/undergraduate/lit/

LAMBDA IOTA TAU LITERATURE SCHOLARSHIP

Scholarships for members of Lambda Iota Tau who are pursuing the study of literature. Must be nominated by chapter sponsor and have 3.5 GPA.

Academic Fields/Career Goals: Literature/English/Writing.

Award: Scholarship for use in freshman, sophomore, junior, senior, graduate, or postgraduate years; not renewable. *Number:* 2–4. *Amount:* $1000.

Eligibility Requirements: Applicant must be enrolled or expecting to enroll full-time at a two-year or four-year institution or university. Applicant or parent of applicant must be member of Lambda Iota Tau Literature Honor Society. Applicant must have 3.5 GPA or higher. Available to U.S. citizens.

Application Requirements: Application, essay, references, transcript, nomination letter. *Deadline:* May 31.

Contact: Prof. Bruce Hozeski, Executive Secretary and Treasurer
Lambda Iota Tau, College Literature Honor Society
Ball State University, Department of English
2000 West University Avenue
Muncie, IN 47306-0460
Phone: 765-285-8456
Fax: 765-285-3765
E-mail: bhozeski@bsu.edu

MAINE COMMUNITY FOUNDATION INC. http://www.mainecf.org

R.V. "GADABOUT" GADDIS CHARITABLE FUND

• *See page 303*

METAVUE CORPORATION http://www.metavue.com

FAMOUS PEOPLE AND THEIR WORK

The scholarship contest is looking for good biographies dealing with a famous person who has made a contribution to our lives and society. From Madam Curie and the discovery of radium to B.F. Skinner expanding our understanding of behavior, there are many possibilities. This scholarship contest is most appropriate for upper high schools levels, and undergraduate students pursuing a liberal arts education. Visit http://www.metavue.com for additional details.

Academic Fields/Career Goals: Literature/English/Writing.

Award: Prize for use in freshman, sophomore, junior, or senior years; not renewable. *Number:* 1–5. *Amount:* $15–$500.

Eligibility Requirements: Applicant must be enrolled or expecting to enroll full-time at a four-year institution or university and must have an interest in writing. Applicant must have 3.0 GPA or higher. Available to U.S. citizens.

Application Requirements: Application, applicant must enter a contest, essay. *Deadline:* February 1.

Contact: Michael Rufflo, Scholarship Committee
Metavue Corporation
1110 Surrey Drive
Sun Prairie, WI 53590
Phone: 608-577-0642
Fax: 512-685-4074
E-mail: rufflo@metavue.com

NATIONAL FEDERATION OF THE BLIND http://www.nfb.org

MICHAEL AND MARIE MARUCCI SCHOLARSHIP

• *See page 320*

NATIONAL FEDERATION OF THE BLIND HUMANITIES SCHOLARSHIP

• *See page 104*

NATIONAL PRESS FOUNDATION http://www.nationalpress.org

EVERT CLARK/SETH PAYNE AWARD

• *See page 375*

NATIONAL WRITERS ASSOCIATION FOUNDATION http://www.nationalwriters.com

NATIONAL WRITERS ASSOCIATION FOUNDATION SCHOLARSHIPS

• *See page 375*

OREGON STUDENT ASSISTANCE COMMISSION http://www.osac.state.or.us

SEHAR SALEHA AHMAD AND ABRAHIM EKRAMULLAH ZAFAR FOUNDATION SCHOLARSHIP

Scholarship to graduating seniors of Oregon high schools. Must major in English with minimum 3.5 GPA. Preference given to females.

Academic Fields/Career Goals: Literature/English/Writing.

Award: Scholarship for use in freshman year; renewable. *Number:* varies. *Amount:* varies.

Eligibility Requirements: Applicant must be high school student; planning to enroll or expecting to enroll full-time at a four-year institution and resident of Oregon. Applicant must have 3.5 GPA or higher. Available to U.S. citizens.

Application Requirements: Application, essay, financial need analysis, references, transcript, activity chart. *Deadline:* March 1.

Contact: Director of Grant Programs
Oregon Student Assistance Commission
1500 Valley River Drive, Suite 100
Eugene, OR 97401-7020
Phone: 800-452-8807 Ext. 7395

OUTDOOR WRITERS ASSOCIATION OF AMERICA http://www.owaa.org

OUTDOOR WRITERS ASSOCIATION OF AMERICA BODIE MCDOWELL SCHOLARSHIP AWARD

• *See page 183*

PLAYWRIGHTS' CENTER http://www.pwcenter.org

MANY VOICES RESIDENCY PROGRAM

• *See page 105*

POLISH HERITAGE ASSOCIATION OF MARYLAND http://www.pha-md.org

ROBERT P. PULA MEMORIAL SCHOLARSHIP

• *See page 360*

SIGMA TAU DELTA http://www.english.org

HENRY REGNERY ENDOWED SCHOLARSHIP

One-time award of up to $2500 given to sophomore, junior, senior or graduates who has registered as full-time students in an English degree program or as

Sigma Tau Delta (continued)

full-time students with coursework in one or more English-related fields. Applicant should be a member of Sigma Tau Delta.

Academic Fields/Career Goals: Literature/English/Writing.

Award: Scholarship for use in sophomore, junior, senior, or graduate years; not renewable. *Number:* varies. *Amount:* up to $2500.

Eligibility Requirements: Applicant must be enrolled or expecting to enroll full-time at a four-year institution or university. Applicant or parent of applicant must be member of Supreme Council of Sociedade Do Espirito Santo. Applicant must have 3.0 GPA or higher. Available to U.S. and non-U.S. citizens.

Application Requirements: Application, essay, references, transcript, sample paper, professional goals. *Deadline:* October 30.

Contact: Sidney Watson, Scholarship Committee Chair
Sigma Tau Delta
Department of English, Northern Illinois University
DeKalb, IL 60115
Phone: 405-878-2201
E-mail: sidney.watson@okbu.edu

SIGMA TAU DELTA JUNIOR SCHOLARSHIP

One-time scholarship of up to $3000 given to juniors in college level who have registered as full-time students in an English degree program or as full-time students with coursework in one or more English-related fields. Applicant should be a member of Sigma Tau Delta.

Academic Fields/Career Goals: Literature/English/Writing.

Award: Scholarship for use in junior year; not renewable. *Number:* varies. *Amount:* up to $3000.

Eligibility Requirements: Applicant must be enrolled or expecting to enroll full-time at a four-year institution or university. Applicant or parent of applicant must be member of Supreme Council of Sociedade Do Espirito Santo. Applicant must have 3.0 GPA or higher. Available to U.S. and non-U.S. citizens.

Application Requirements: Application, essay, references, transcript, professional goals. *Deadline:* October 30.

Contact: Sidney Watson, Scholarship Committee Chair
Sigma Tau Delta
Oklahoma Baptist University
500 West University
Shawnee, OK 74804-2558
Phone: 405-878-2210
E-mail: sidney.watson@okbu.edu

SIGMA TAU DELTA SCHOLARSHIP

One-time scholarship of up to $4000 given to sophomore, junior, senior, or graduates who have registered as full-time students in an English degree program or as full-time students with coursework in one or more English related fields. Applicant should be a member of Sigma Tau Delta.

Academic Fields/Career Goals: Literature/English/Writing.

Award: Scholarship for use in sophomore, junior, senior, or graduate years; not renewable. *Number:* varies. *Amount:* up to $4000.

Eligibility Requirements: Applicant must be enrolled or expecting to enroll full-time at a four-year institution or university. Applicant or parent of applicant must be member of Supreme Council of Sociedade Do Espirito Santo. Applicant must have 3.0 GPA or higher. Available to U.S. and non-U.S. citizens.

Application Requirements: Application, essay, references, transcript, sample paper, professional goals. *Deadline:* October 30.

Contact: Sidney Watson, Scholarship Committee Chair
Sigma Tau Delta
Department of English, Northern Illinois University
DeKalb, IL 60115
Phone: 405-878-2201
E-mail: sidney.watson@okbu.edu

SIGMA TAU DELTA SENIOR SCHOLARSHIP

One-time scholarship of up to $3000 given to seniors in college level who have registered as full-time students in an English degree program or as full-time students with coursework in one or more English related fields. Applicant should be a member of Sigma Tau Delta.

Academic Fields/Career Goals: Literature/English/Writing.

Award: Scholarship for use in senior year; not renewable. *Number:* varies. *Amount:* up to $3000.

Eligibility Requirements: Applicant must be enrolled or expecting to enroll full-time at a four-year institution or university. Applicant or parent of applicant must be member of Supreme Council of Sociedade Do Espirito Santo. Applicant must have 3.0 GPA or higher. Available to U.S. and non-U.S. citizens.

Application Requirements: Application, essay, references, transcript, summary of professional goals. *Deadline:* October 30.

Contact: Sidney Watson, Scholarship Committee Chair
Sigma Tau Delta
Oklahoma Baptist University
500 West University
Shawnee, OK 74804-2558
Phone: 405-878-2210
E-mail: sidney.watson@okbu.edu

SIGMA TAU DELTA STUDY ABROAD SCHOLARSHIP

One-time scholarship of up to $3000 given to sophomore, junior, senior, or graduates who have registered as full-time students in an English degree program or as full-time students with coursework in one or more English related fields. Applicant should be a member of Sigma Tau Delta. Deadlines: March 30 and October 30.

Academic Fields/Career Goals: Literature/English/Writing.

Award: Scholarship for use in sophomore, junior, or senior years; not renewable. *Number:* varies. *Amount:* up to $3000.

Eligibility Requirements: Applicant must be enrolled or expecting to enroll full-time at a four-year institution or university. Applicant or parent of applicant must be member of Supreme Council of Sociedade Do Espirito Santo. Applicant must have 3.0 GPA or higher. Available to U.S. and non-U.S. citizens.

Application Requirements: Application, essay, references, transcript, sample paper, professional goals. *Deadline:* varies.

Contact: Sidney Watson, Scholarship Committee Chair
Sigma Tau Delta
Department of English, Northern Illinois University
DeKalb, IL 60115
Phone: 405-878-2201
E-mail: sidney.watson@okbu.edu

STRAIGHTFORWARD MEDIA http://www.straightforwardmedia.com

STRAIGHTFORWARD MEDIA LIBERAL ARTS SCHOLARSHIP

• *See page 99*

UNITED DAUGHTERS OF THE CONFEDERACY http://www.hqudc.org

HELEN JAMES BREWER SCHOLARSHIP

• *See page 349*

UNITED NEGRO COLLEGE FUND http://www.uncf.org

C-SPAN SCHOLARSHIP PROGRAM

• *See page 187*

MAE MAXEY MEMORIAL SCHOLARSHIP

• *See page 107*

MCCLARE FAMILY TRUST SCHOLARSHIP

• *See page 360*

READER'S DIGEST FOUNDATION SCHOLARSHIP

• *See page 188*

TOYOTA SCHOLARSHIP

• *See page 66*

UPS/UNCF CORPORATE SCHOLARS PROGRAM

• *See page 151*

WILLA CATHER FOUNDATION http://www.willacather.org

NORMA ROSS WALTER SCHOLARSHIP

Award to provide financial assistance to female graduates of Nebraska high schools who are or will be planning to enroll as English majors in accredited colleges or universities. Must be prospective first-year college women students who have been or plan to be graduated from Nebraska high schools and who plan to continue their education as English majors in accredited colleges or universities.

Academic Fields/Career Goals: Literature/English/Writing.

Award: Scholarship for use in freshman year; not renewable. *Number:* 1. *Amount:* $1000.

Eligibility Requirements: Applicant must be high school student; planning to enroll or expecting to enroll full-time at a four-year institution or university; female and resident of Nebraska. Applicant must have 3.0 GPA or higher. Available to U.S. citizens.

Application Requirements: Application, essay, portfolio, references, test scores, transcript. *Deadline:* January 31.

Contact: Betty Kort, Executive Director
Willa Cather Foundation
413 North Webster Street
Red Cloud, NE 68970
Phone: 402-746-2653
Fax: 402-746-2652
E-mail: wcpmt@gpcom.net

MARINE BIOLOGY

CANADIAN RECREATIONAL CANOEING ASSOCIATION http://www.paddlingcanada.com

BILL MASON MEMORIAL SCHOLARSHIP FUND

• *See page 74*

CUSHMAN FOUNDATION FOR FORAMINIFERAL RESEARCH http://www.cushmanfoundation.org

LOEBLICH AND TAPPAN STUDENT RESEARCH AWARD

• *See page 131*

INTERNATIONAL ASSOCIATION OF GREAT LAKES RESEARCH http://www.iaglr.org

PAUL W. RODGERS SCHOLARSHIP

• *See page 217*

JUST WITHIN REACH FOUNDATION

ENVIRONMENTAL SCIENCES AND MARINE STUDIES SCHOLARSHIP

• *See page 303*

LOUISIANA OFFICE OF STUDENT FINANCIAL ASSISTANCE http://www.osfa.state.la.us

ROCKEFELLER STATE WILDLIFE SCHOLARSHIP

• *See page 82*

MARINE TECHNOLOGY SOCIETY http://www.mtsociety.org

CHARLES H. BUSSMAN UNDERGRADUATE SCHOLARSHIP

Scholarship for undergraduate students enrolled full-time in a marine-related field. Must be a member of Marine Technology Society.

Academic Fields/Career Goals: Marine Biology; Marine/Ocean Engineering; Oceanography.

Award: Scholarship for use in freshman, sophomore, junior, or senior years; not renewable. *Number:* varies. *Amount:* up to $2500.

Eligibility Requirements: Applicant must be enrolled or expecting to enroll full-time at a four-year institution or university. Applicant or parent of applicant must be member of Marine Technology Society. Available to U.S. and non-U.S. citizens.

Application Requirements: Application, autobiography, references, transcript, proof of acceptance for an undergraduate course. *Deadline:* April 15.

Contact: Suzanne Voelker, Operations Administrator
Marine Technology Society
5565 Sterrett Place, Suite 108
Columbia, MD 21044
Phone: 410-884-5330
Fax: 410-884-9060
E-mail: suzanne.voelker@mtsociety.org

JOHN C. BAJUS SCHOLARSHIP

Scholarship available to undergraduate and graduate students enrolled full-time in a marine-related field. Must be a MTS student member with demonstrated commitment to community service/volunteer activities.

Academic Fields/Career Goals: Marine Biology; Marine/Ocean Engineering; Oceanography.

Award: Scholarship for use in freshman, sophomore, junior, senior, or graduate years; not renewable. *Number:* varies. *Amount:* up to $1000.

Eligibility Requirements: Applicant must be enrolled or expecting to enroll full-time at a four-year institution or university. Applicant or parent of applicant must be member of Marine Technology Society. Available to U.S. and non-U.S. citizens.

Application Requirements: Application, autobiography, references, transcript. *Deadline:* April 15.

Contact: Suzanne Voelker, Operations Administrator
Marine Technology Society
5565 Sterrett Place, Suite 108
Columbia, MD 21044
Phone: 410-884-5330
Fax: 410-884-9060
E-mail: suzanne.voelker@mtsociety.org

MTS STUDENT SCHOLARSHIP

Scholarships available to both Marine Technology Society members and non-members, undergraduates and graduate students, enrolled full-time in a marine-related field.

Academic Fields/Career Goals: Marine Biology; Marine/Ocean Engineering; Oceanography.

Award: Scholarship for use in freshman, sophomore, junior, senior, or graduate years; not renewable. *Number:* varies. *Amount:* up to $2000.

Eligibility Requirements: Applicant must be enrolled or expecting to enroll full-time at a four-year institution or university. Available to U.S. and non-U.S. citizens.

Application Requirements: Application, autobiography, references, transcript. *Deadline:* April 15.

Contact: Suzanne Voelker, Operations Administrator
Marine Technology Society
5565 Sterrett Place, Suite 108
Columbia, MD 21044
Phone: 410-884-5330
Fax: 410-884-9060
E-mail: suzanne.voelker@mtsociety.org

MTS STUDENT SCHOLARSHIP FOR GRADUATE AND UNDERGRADUATE STUDENTS

Scholarship of $2000 available to undergraduate students who are enrolled full-time in a marine-related field.

Academic Fields/Career Goals: Marine Biology; Marine/Ocean Engineering.

Award: Scholarship for use in freshman, sophomore, junior, senior, or graduate years; not renewable. *Number:* varies. *Amount:* $2000.

Eligibility Requirements: Applicant must be enrolled or expecting to enroll full-time at a four-year institution or university. Available to U.S. and non-U.S. citizens.

Marine Technology Society (continued)

Application Requirements: Application, essay, references, transcript. *Deadline:* April 15.

Contact: Suzanne Voelker, Operations Administrator
Marine Technology Society
5565 Sterrett Place, Suite 108
Columbia, MD 21044
Phone: 410-884-5330
E-mail: suzanne.voelker@mtsociety.org

MTS STUDENT SCHOLARSHIP FOR TWO-YEAR TECHNICAL, ENGINEERING AND COMMUNITY COLLEGE STUDENTS

Scholarship of $2000 available to students enrolled in a two-year technical, engineering, or community college in a marine-related field.

Academic Fields/Career Goals: Marine Biology; Marine/Ocean Engineering.

Award: Scholarship for use in freshman or sophomore years; not renewable. *Number:* varies. *Amount:* $2000.

Eligibility Requirements: Applicant must be enrolled or expecting to enroll full-time at a two-year institution. Available to U.S. and non-U.S. citizens.

Application Requirements: Application, essay, references, transcript. *Deadline:* April 15.

Contact: Suzanne Voelker, Operations Administrator
Marine Technology Society
5565 Sterrett Place, Suite 108
Columbia, MD 21044
Phone: 410-884-5330
E-mail: suzanne.voelker@mtsociety.org

PAROS-DIGIQUARTZ SCHOLARSHIP

Scholarships available to both MTS members and non-members, undergraduates and graduate students, enrolled full-time in a marine-related field with an interest in marine instrumentation. High school seniors who have been accepted into a full-time undergraduate program in a marine-related field are also eligible to apply.

Academic Fields/Career Goals: Marine Biology; Marine/Ocean Engineering; Oceanography.

Award: Scholarship for use in freshman, sophomore, junior, senior, or graduate years; not renewable. *Number:* varies. *Amount:* up to $2000.

Eligibility Requirements: Applicant must be enrolled or expecting to enroll full-time at a four-year institution or university. Available to U.S. and non-U.S. citizens.

Application Requirements: Application, autobiography, references, transcript. *Deadline:* April 15.

Contact: Suzanne Voelker, Operations Administrator
Marine Technology Society
5565 Sterrett Place, Suite 108
Columbia, MD 21044
Phone: 410-884-5330
Fax: 410-884-9060
E-mail: suzanne.voelker@mtsociety.org

ROV SCHOLARSHIP

Scholarships for undergraduate and graduate students interested in remotely operated vehicles or underwater work that furthers the use of ROVs. Open to MTS student members and non-MTS members.

Academic Fields/Career Goals: Marine Biology; Marine/Ocean Engineering; Oceanography.

Award: Scholarship for use in freshman, sophomore, junior, senior, or graduate years; not renewable. *Number:* varies. *Amount:* up to $10,000.

Eligibility Requirements: Applicant must be enrolled or expecting to enroll full-time at a four-year institution or university. Available to U.S. and non-U.S. citizens.

Application Requirements: Application, autobiography, essay, references, transcript. *Deadline:* April 15.

Contact: Chuck Richards, Chair, Scholarship Committee
Marine Technology Society
c/o C.A. Richards and Associates Inc.
777 North Eldridge Parkway, Suite 280
Houston, TX 77079

SEASPACE INC. http://www.seaspace.org

SEASPACE SCHOLARSHIP PROGRAM

One-time award open to college junior/senior or graduate students pursuing degrees in the marine/aquatic sciences. Must be enrolled full-time with a minimum overall GPA of 3.3. Must be enrolled in an accredited U.S. institution. Must demonstrate financial need.

Academic Fields/Career Goals: Marine Biology; Oceanography.

Award: Scholarship for use in junior, senior, or graduate years; not renewable. *Number:* 10–15. *Amount:* $500–$3000.

Eligibility Requirements: Applicant must be enrolled or expecting to enroll full-time at a four-year institution or university. Available to U.S. and non-U.S. citizens.

Application Requirements: Application, financial need analysis, self-addressed stamped envelope, transcript. *Deadline:* December 1.

Contact: Jesse Cancelmo, Scholarship Committee Chairman
Seaspace Inc.
PO Box 3753
Houston, TX 77253-3753
Phone: 713-302-7920
E-mail: jesse@cancelmophoto.com

SOCIETY FOR MARINE MAMMALOGY http://www.marinemammalogy.org

FREDERIC FAIRFIELD MEMORIAL FUND AWARD

• *See page 135*

WOMAN'S SEAMEN'S FRIEND SOCIETY OF CONNECTICUT INC.

FINANCIAL SUPPORT FOR MARINE OR MARITIME STUDIES

Applicant must be full-time student. High school students not considered. Award available to U.S. citizens. Must be majoring in marine sciences at any college or university.

Academic Fields/Career Goals: Marine Biology; Oceanography.

Award: Scholarship for use in freshman, sophomore, junior, or senior years; not renewable. *Number:* varies. *Amount:* varies.

Eligibility Requirements: Applicant must be enrolled or expecting to enroll full-time at a four-year institution or university. Available to U.S. citizens.

Application Requirements: Application, financial need analysis, resume, references, test scores, transcript. *Deadline:* varies.

Contact: Marshall Davidson, Executive Director
Woman's Seamen's Friend Society of Connecticut Inc.
291 Whitney Avenue Suite 403
New Haven, CT 06511
Phone: 203-777-2165
Fax: 203-777-5774
E-mail: wsfsofct@earthlink.net

MARINE/OCEAN ENGINEERING

AMERICAN METEOROLOGICAL SOCIETY http://www.ametsoc.org

AMS FRESHMAN UNDERGRADUATE SCHOLARSHIP

• *See page 300*

AMERICAN SOCIETY OF NAVAL ENGINEERS http://www.navalengineers.org

AMERICAN SOCIETY OF NAVAL ENGINEERS SCHOLARSHIP

• *See page 85*

ASSOCIATION FOR IRON AND STEEL TECHNOLOGY http://www.aist.org

ASSOCIATION FOR IRON AND STEEL TECHNOLOGY DAVID H. SAMSON CANADIAN SCHOLARSHIP

• *See page 157*

ELECTROCHEMICAL SOCIETY INC. http://www.electrochem.org

H.H. DOW MEMORIAL STUDENT ACHIEVEMENT AWARD OF THE INDUSTRIAL ELECTROLYSIS AND ELECTROCHEMICAL ENGINEERING DIVISION OF THE ELECTROCHEMICAL SOCIETY INC.

• *See page 131*

STUDENT ACHIEVEMENT AWARDS OF THE INDUSTRIAL ELECTROLYSIS AND ELECTROCHEMICAL ENGINEERING DIVISION OF THE ELECTROCHEMICAL SOCIETY INC.

• *See page 131*

STUDENT RESEARCH AWARDS OF THE BATTERY DIVISION OF THE ELECTROCHEMICAL SOCIETY INC.

• *See page 131*

MARINE TECHNOLOGY SOCIETY http://www.mtsociety.org

CHARLES H. BUSSMAN UNDERGRADUATE SCHOLARSHIP

• *See page 393*

JOHN C. BAJUS SCHOLARSHIP

• *See page 393*

MTS STUDENT SCHOLARSHIP

• *See page 393*

MTS STUDENT SCHOLARSHIP FOR GRADUATE AND UNDERGRADUATE STUDENTS

• *See page 393*

MTS STUDENT SCHOLARSHIP FOR GRADUATING HIGH SCHOOL SENIORS

• *See page 269*

MTS STUDENT SCHOLARSHIP FOR TWO-YEAR TECHNICAL, ENGINEERING AND COMMUNITY COLLEGE STUDENTS

• *See page 394*

PAROS-DIGIQUARTZ SCHOLARSHIP

• *See page 394*

ROV SCHOLARSHIP

• *See page 394*

MATERIALS SCIENCE, ENGINEERING, AND METALLURGY

AMERICAN CHEMICAL SOCIETY http://www.acs.org/scholars

AMERICAN CHEMICAL SOCIETY SCHOLARS PROGRAM

• *See page 153*

AMERICAN CHEMICAL SOCIETY, RUBBER DIVISION http://www.rubber.org

AMERICAN CHEMICAL SOCIETY, RUBBER DIVISION UNDERGRADUATE SCHOLARSHIP

• *See page 153*

AMERICAN COUNCIL OF ENGINEERING COMPANIES OF PENNSYLVANIA (ACEC/PA) http://www.acecpa.org

ENGINEERING SCHOLARSHIP

• *See page 154*

AMERICAN ELECTROPLATERS AND SURFACE FINISHERS SOCIETY http://www.nasf.org

AMERICAN ELECTROPLATERS AND SURFACE FINISHERS FOUNDATION SCHOLARSHIPS

• *See page 154*

AMERICAN INSTITUTE OF AERONAUTICS AND ASTRONAUTICS http://www.aiaa.org

AIAA UNDERGRADUATE SCHOLARSHIP

• *See page 84*

AMERICAN SOCIETY OF MECHANICAL ENGINEERS (ASME INTERNATIONAL) http://www.asme.org

AMERICAN SOCIETY OF MECHANICAL ENGINEERS PETROLEUM DIVISION STUDENT SCHOLARSHIP PROGRAM

Scholarships available to ASME student members interested in any phase of the petroleum industry, including drilling completions, facilities, pipelines, rigs, operations, materials, equipment manufacturing, plant design and operation, maintenance, environmental protection, and innovations. For further details visit Web site at http://www.asme-petroleumdiv.org/students/scholarshipsbody.htm.

Academic Fields/Career Goals: Materials Science, Engineering, and Metallurgy; Mechanical Engineering.

Award: Prize for use in junior or senior years; not renewable. *Number:* 5. *Amount:* $2000.

Eligibility Requirements: Applicant must be enrolled or expecting to enroll full- or part-time at a four-year institution or university. Applicant or parent of applicant must be member of American Society of Mechanical Engineers. Applicant must have 2.5 GPA or higher. Available to U.S. and non-U.S. citizens.

Application Requirements: Application, essay, references, transcript. *Deadline:* March 15.

Contact: Manny Mones, Student Scholarship Program
American Society of Mechanical Engineers (ASME International)
11757 Katy Freeway, Suite 865
Houston, TX 77079
Phone: 281-493-3491
Fax: 281-493-3493

AMERICAN SOCIETY OF NAVAL ENGINEERS http://www.navalengineers.org

AMERICAN SOCIETY OF NAVAL ENGINEERS SCHOLARSHIP

• *See page 85*

AMERICAN WELDING SOCIETY http://www.aws.org

AIRGAS-JERRY BAKER SCHOLARSHIP

• *See page 287*

AIRGAS-TERRY JARVIS MEMORIAL SCHOLARSHIP

• *See page 287*

AMERICAN WELDING SOCIETY INTERNATIONAL SCHOLARSHIP

• *See page 288*

ARSHAM AMIRIKIAN ENGINEERING SCHOLARSHIP

• *See page 168*

DONALD AND SHIRLEY HASTINGS SCHOLARSHIP

• *See page 256*

ILLINOIS TOOL WORKS WELDING COMPANIES SCHOLARSHIP

• *See page 288*

JERRY ROBINSON-INWELD CORPORATION SCHOLARSHIP

Awarded to a student with significant financial need interested in pursuing a career in welding. Applicant must have a 2.5 overall GPA. Applicant must be 18 years of age by October 1 of the year the scholarship is awarded. Must be U.S. citizen.

Academic Fields/Career Goals: Materials Science, Engineering, and Metallurgy; Trade/Technical Specialties.

Award: Scholarship for use in freshman, sophomore, junior, or senior years; renewable. *Number:* 1. *Amount:* $2500.

Eligibility Requirements: Applicant must be age 18 and over and enrolled or expecting to enroll full-time at a four-year institution or university. Applicant must have 2.5 GPA or higher. Available to U.S. citizens.

American Welding Society (continued)

Application Requirements: Application, autobiography, essay, financial need analysis, photo, references, transcript, copies of student's and parent or guardian's previous year's tax returns. *Deadline:* January 15.

Contact: Vicki Pinsky, Manager, Foundation
American Welding Society
550 Le Jeune Road, NW
Miami, FL 33126
Phone: 800-443-9353 Ext. 212
Fax: 305-443-7559
E-mail: vpinsky@aws.org

JOHN C. LINCOLN MEMORIAL SCHOLARSHIP
• *See page 289*

MATSUO BRIDGE COMPANY LTD. OF JAPAN SCHOLARSHIP
• *See page 169*

MILLER ELECTRIC INTERNATIONAL WORLD SKILLS COMPETITION SCHOLARSHIP
• *See page 289*

PRAXAIR INTERNATIONAL SCHOLARSHIP
• *See page 289*

RESISTANCE WELDER MANUFACTURERS' ASSOCIATION SCHOLARSHIP
• *See page 257*

ROBERT L. PEASLEE DETROIT BRAZING AND SOLDERING DIVISION SCHOLARSHIP
• *See page 257*

WILLIAM A. AND ANN M. BROTHERS SCHOLARSHIP
• *See page 289*

WILLIAM B. HOWELL MEMORIAL SCHOLARSHIP
• *See page 289*

ASM MATERIALS EDUCATION FOUNDATION http://www.asminternational.org/foundation

ASM OUTSTANDING SCHOLARS AWARDS
• *See page 258*

EDWARD J. DULIS SCHOLARSHIP
• *See page 258*

GEORGE A. ROBERTS SCHOLARSHIP
• *See page 258*

JOHN M. HANIAK SCHOLARSHIP
• *See page 258*

NICHOLAS J. GRANT SCHOLARSHIP
• *See page 258*

WILLIAM P. WOODSIDE FOUNDER'S SCHOLARSHIP
• *See page 259*

ASSOCIATION FOR FACILITIES ENGINEERING (AFE)

ASSOCIATION FOR FACILITIES ENGINEERING CEDAR VALLEY CHAPTER #132 SCHOLARSHIP
• *See page 114*

ASSOCIATION FOR IRON AND STEEL TECHNOLOGY http://www.aist.org

AIST ALFRED B. GLOSSBRENNER AND JOHN KLUSCH SCHOLARSHIPS
• *See page 259*

AIST WILLIAM E. SCHWABE MEMORIAL SCHOLARSHIP
• *See page 259*

ASSOCIATION FOR IRON AND STEEL TECHNOLOGY BALTIMORE CHAPTER SCHOLARSHIP
• *See page 290*

ASSOCIATION FOR IRON AND STEEL TECHNOLOGY BENJAMIN F. FAIRLESS SCHOLARSHIP

Scholarships for students of metallurgy, metallurgical engineering, or materials science, interested in a career in ferrous related industries as demonstrated by an internship or related experience, or who have plans to pursue such experiences during college. Student may apply after first term of freshman year of college and must join the AIST at the student rate.

Academic Fields/Career Goals: Materials Science, Engineering, and Metallurgy.

Award: Scholarship for use in freshman, sophomore, junior, or senior years; not renewable. *Number:* 3. *Amount:* $2000.

Eligibility Requirements: Applicant must be enrolled or expecting to enroll full-time at a four-year institution or university. Applicant must have 3.0 GPA or higher. Available to U.S. and non-U.S. citizens.

Application Requirements: Application, essay, resume, references, transcript. *Deadline:* March 2.

Contact: Lori Wharrey, Board Administrator
Association for Iron and Steel Technology
186 Thorn Hill Road
Warrendale, PA 15086-7528
Phone: 724-776-6040 Ext. 621
Fax: 724-776-1880
E-mail: lwharrey@aist.org

ASSOCIATION FOR IRON AND STEEL TECHNOLOGY DAVID H. SAMSON CANADIAN SCHOLARSHIP
• *See page 157*

ASSOCIATION FOR IRON AND STEEL TECHNOLOGY FERROUS METALLURGY EDUCATION TODAY (FEMET)

Scholarship of $5000 to provide tuition for senior year of study. Award includes a paid summer internship with a North American steel company between junior and senior year. Must be enrolled full-time in metallurgy or materials science program at an accredited North American university.

Academic Fields/Career Goals: Materials Science, Engineering, and Metallurgy.

Award: Scholarship for use in junior or senior years; renewable. *Number:* 10. *Amount:* $5000.

Eligibility Requirements: Applicant must be enrolled or expecting to enroll full-time at a four-year institution or university. Applicant or parent of applicant must be member of Association for Iron and Steel Technology. Applicant must have 3.0 GPA or higher. Available to U.S. and non-U.S. citizens.

Application Requirements: Application, essay, resume, references, transcript, list of source and amount of any other grants and scholarships being applied. *Deadline:* March 2.

Contact: Lori Wharrey, Board Administrator
Association for Iron and Steel Technology
186 Thorn Hill Road
Warrendale, PA 15086-7528
Phone: 724-776-6040 Ext. 621
Fax: 724-776-1880
E-mail: lwharrey@aist.org

ASSOCIATION FOR IRON AND STEEL TECHNOLOGY NORTHWEST MEMBER CHAPTER SCHOLARSHIP
• *See page 261*

ASSOCIATION FOR IRON AND STEEL TECHNOLOGY OHIO VALLEY CHAPTER SCHOLARSHIP
• *See page 130*

ASSOCIATION FOR IRON AND STEEL TECHNOLOGY PITTSBURGH CHAPTER SCHOLARSHIP
• *See page 261*

ASSOCIATION FOR IRON AND STEEL TECHNOLOGY RONALD E. LINCOLN SCHOLARSHIP

Scholarship for students of metallurgy, metallurgical engineering, or materials science, interested in a career in ferrous related industries as demonstrated by an internship or related experience, or who have plans to pursue such experiences during college. Student may apply after first term of freshman year of college and must join the AIST at the student rate.

Academic Fields/Career Goals: Materials Science, Engineering, and Metallurgy.

Award: Scholarship for use in freshman, sophomore, junior, or senior years; not renewable. *Number:* 2. *Amount:* $3000.

Eligibility Requirements: Applicant must be enrolled or expecting to enroll full-time at a four-year institution or university. Applicant must have 3.0 GPA or higher. Available to U.S. and non-U.S. citizens.

Application Requirements: Application, essay, resume, references, transcript. *Deadline:* March 2.

Contact: Lori Wharrey, Board Administrator
Association for Iron and Steel Technology
186 Thorn Hill Road
Warrendale, PA 15086-7528
Phone: 724-776-6040 Ext. 621
Fax: 724-776-1880
E-mail: lwharrey@aist.org

ASSOCIATION FOR IRON AND STEEL TECHNOLOGY SOUTHEAST MEMBER CHAPTER SCHOLARSHIP

• *See page 261*

ASSOCIATION FOR IRON AND STEEL TECHNOLOGY WILLY KORF MEMORIAL SCHOLARSHIP

Scholarships for students of metallurgy, metallurgical engineering, or materials science, who have a genuine interest in a career in ferrous related industries as demonstrated by an internship or related experience, or who have plans to pursue such experiences during college. Student may apply at first term of freshman year of college and must join the AIST at the student rate.

Academic Fields/Career Goals: Materials Science, Engineering, and Metallurgy.

Award: Scholarship for use in freshman, sophomore, junior, or senior years; not renewable. *Number:* 3. *Amount:* $3000.

Eligibility Requirements: Applicant must be enrolled or expecting to enroll full-time at a four-year institution or university. Applicant must have 3.0 GPA or higher. Available to U.S. and non-U.S. citizens.

Application Requirements: Application, essay, resume, references, transcript. *Deadline:* March 2.

Contact: Lori Wharrey, AIST Board Administrator
Association for Iron and Steel Technology
186 Thorn Hill Road
Warrendale, PA 15086
Phone: 724-776-6040 Ext. 621
E-mail: lwharrey@aist.org

ASSOCIATION FOR WOMEN IN SCIENCE EDUCATIONAL FOUNDATION http://www.awis.org/careers/edfoundation.html

ASSOCIATION FOR WOMEN IN SCIENCE COLLEGE SCHOLARSHIP

• *See page 82*

ASSOCIATION OF IRON AND STEEL ENGINEERS http://www.aist.org

AIST BENJAMIN F. FAIRLESS SCHOLARSHIP

Scholarships will be granted to full-time undergraduate students with a genuine demonstrated interest in a career in the iron and steel industry and majoring in the field of engineering, metallurgy or materials science field at an accredited North American college or university.

Academic Fields/Career Goals: Materials Science, Engineering, and Metallurgy.

Award: Scholarship for use in freshman, sophomore, junior, or senior years; not renewable. *Number:* 2. *Amount:* $2000.

Eligibility Requirements: Applicant must be enrolled or expecting to enroll full-time at a four-year institution or university. Applicant must have 3.0 GPA or higher. Available to U.S. and non-U.S. citizens.

Application Requirements: Application, essay, resume, references, transcript. *Deadline:* March 2.

Contact: Ms. Lori Wharrey, Board Administrator
Association of Iron and Steel Engineers
186 Thorn Hill Road
Warrendale, PA 15086-7528
Phone: 724-776-6040 Ext. 621
Fax: 724-776-1880
E-mail: lwharrey@aist.org

AIST DON NELSON SCHOLARSHIP

Scholarships will be granted to full-time undergraduate students with a genuine demonstrated interest in a career in the iron and steel industry and majoring in the field of engineering, metallurgy or materials science field at Midwest chapters of North America.

Academic Fields/Career Goals: Materials Science, Engineering, and Metallurgy.

Award: Scholarship for use in freshman, sophomore, junior, or senior years; not renewable. *Number:* 1. *Amount:* $1000.

Eligibility Requirements: Applicant must be enrolled or expecting to enroll full-time at a four-year institution or university. Applicant must have 3.0 GPA or higher. Available to U.S. and non-U.S. citizens.

Application Requirements: Application, essay, resume, references, transcript. *Deadline:* March 15.

Contact: Ms. Lori Wharrey, Board Administrator
Association of Iron and Steel Engineers
186 Thorn Hill Road
Warrendale, PA 15086-7528
Phone: 724-776-6040 Ext. 621
Fax: 724-776-1880
E-mail: lwharrey@aist.org

AIST RONALD E. LINCOLN MEMORIAL SCHOLARSHIP

Scholarships granted to full-time undergraduate students with a genuine demonstrated interest in a career in the iron and steel industry and majoring in the field of engineering, metallurgy or materials science field at an accredited U.S. college or university.

Academic Fields/Career Goals: Materials Science, Engineering, and Metallurgy.

Award: Scholarship for use in freshman, sophomore, junior, or senior years; not renewable. *Number:* 2. *Amount:* $2000.

Eligibility Requirements: Applicant must be enrolled or expecting to enroll full-time at a four-year institution or university. Applicant must have 3.0 GPA or higher. Available to U.S. citizens.

Application Requirements: Application, essay, resume, references, transcript. *Deadline:* March 2.

Contact: Ms. Lori Wharrey, Board Administrator
Association of Iron and Steel Engineers
186 Thorn Hill Road
Warrendale, PA 15086-7528
Phone: 724-776-6040 Ext. 621
Fax: 724-776-1880
E-mail: lwharrey@aist.org

AIST WILLIAM E. SCHWABE MEMORIAL SCHOLARSHIP

Scholarships granted to an undergraduate student enrolled full-time and majoring in the field of engineering, metallurgy or materials science program at an accredited North American university. The applicant should have a demonstrated interest in a career, or plans to pursue a career, in the iron and steel industry.

Academic Fields/Career Goals: Materials Science, Engineering, and Metallurgy.

Award: Scholarship for use in freshman, sophomore, junior, or senior years; not renewable. *Number:* 1. *Amount:* $1500.

Eligibility Requirements: Applicant must be enrolled or expecting to enroll full-time at a four-year institution or university. Applicant must have 3.0 GPA or higher. Available to U.S. and non-U.S. citizens.

Association of Iron and Steel Engineers (continued)

Application Requirements: Application, essay, resume, references, transcript. *Deadline:* March 2.

Contact: Ms. Lori Wharrey, Board Administrator
Association of Iron and Steel Engineers
186 Thorn Hill Road
Warrendale, PA 15086-7528
Phone: 724-776-6040 Ext. 621
Fax: 724-776-1880
E-mail: lwharrey@aist.org

AIST WILLY KORF MEMORIAL FUND

• *See page 261*

FEMET DESIGN GRANT PROGRAM

Program to increase the number of students studying metallurgy and materials science in North America, and to increase the number of such students electing to pursue careers in the iron and steel industry upon graduation. The number and value of the awards depend on the availability of the fund.

Academic Fields/Career Goals: Materials Science, Engineering, and Metallurgy.

Award: Grant for use in freshman, sophomore, junior, or senior years; renewable. *Number:* varies. *Amount:* varies.

Eligibility Requirements: Applicant must be enrolled or expecting to enroll full-time at a four-year institution or university. Applicant must have 3.0 GPA or higher. Available to U.S. and non-U.S. citizens.

Application Requirements: Application. *Deadline:* June 1.

Contact: B.V. Lakshminarayana, Grant Foundation
Association of Iron and Steel Engineers
186 Thorn Hill Road
Warrendale, PA 15086-7528
Phone: 202-452-7143
E-mail: blakshmi@steel.org

FEMET SCHOLARSHIP

Scholarship to increase the number of students studying metallurgy and materials science in North America, and to increase the number of such students electing to pursue careers in the iron and steel industry upon graduation. For more details, refer to Web site: http://www.aist.org/femet/femet_scholarship.htm.

Academic Fields/Career Goals: Materials Science, Engineering, and Metallurgy.

Award: Scholarship for use in junior or senior years; not renewable. *Number:* 10. *Amount:* $5000.

Eligibility Requirements: Applicant must be enrolled or expecting to enroll full-time at a four-year institution or university. Applicant must have 3.0 GPA or higher. Available to U.S. and non-U.S. citizens.

Application Requirements: Application, essay, resume, references, transcript. *Deadline:* March 2.

Contact: Ms. Lori Wharrey, Board Administrator
Association of Iron and Steel Engineers
186 Thorn Hill Road
Warrendale, PA 15086-7528
Phone: 724-776-6040 Ext. 621
Fax: 724-776-1880
E-mail: lwharrey@aist.org

LEWIS E. AND ELIZABETH W. YOUNG SCHOLARSHIPS

Scholarship to high school seniors or undergraduate students studying mining, metallurgical, materials science or petroleum engineering.

Academic Fields/Career Goals: Materials Science, Engineering, and Metallurgy.

Award: Scholarship for use in freshman year; renewable. *Number:* varies. *Amount:* varies.

Eligibility Requirements: Applicant must be high school student and planning to enroll or expecting to enroll full- or part-time at a four-year institution or university. Applicant must have 3.0 GPA or higher. Available to U.S. and non-U.S. citizens.

Application Requirements: Application, essay, resume, references, transcript. *Deadline:* varies.

Contact: Ms. Lori Wharrey, Board Administrator
Association of Iron and Steel Engineers
186 Thorn Hill Road
Warrendale, PA 15086-7528
Phone: 724-776-6040 Ext. 621
Fax: 724-776-1880
E-mail: lwharrey@aist.org

ASTRONAUT SCHOLARSHIP FOUNDATION http://www.astronautscholarship.org

ASTRONAUT SCHOLARSHIP FOUNDATION

• *See page 86*

BARRY M. GOLDWATER SCHOLARSHIP AND EXCELLENCE IN EDUCATION FOUNDATION http://www.act.org/goldwater

BARRY M. GOLDWATER SCHOLARSHIP AND EXCELLENCE IN EDUCATION PROGRAM

• *See page 86*

ELECTROCHEMICAL SOCIETY INC. http://www.electrochem.org

H.H. DOW MEMORIAL STUDENT ACHIEVEMENT AWARD OF THE INDUSTRIAL ELECTROLYSIS AND ELECTROCHEMICAL ENGINEERING DIVISION OF THE ELECTROCHEMICAL SOCIETY INC.

• *See page 131*

STUDENT ACHIEVEMENT AWARDS OF THE INDUSTRIAL ELECTROLYSIS AND ELECTROCHEMICAL ENGINEERING DIVISION OF THE ELECTROCHEMICAL SOCIETY INC.

• *See page 131*

STUDENT RESEARCH AWARDS OF THE BATTERY DIVISION OF THE ELECTROCHEMICAL SOCIETY INC.

• *See page 131*

H.H. HARRIS FOUNDATION http://www.afsinc.org

H.H. HARRIS FOUNDATION ANNUAL SCHOLARSHIP

Scholarships averaging $1000 will be awarded to students and professionals in the metallurgical and casting of metals field who are U.S. citizens. Total number of available awards varies. For more details see Web site: http://www.afsinc.org.

Academic Fields/Career Goals: Materials Science, Engineering, and Metallurgy.

Award: Scholarship for use in freshman, sophomore, junior, senior, graduate, or postgraduate years; not renewable. *Number:* varies. *Amount:* $500–$1000.

Eligibility Requirements: Applicant must be enrolled or expecting to enroll full- or part-time at a four-year institution or university. Available to U.S. citizens.

Application Requirements: Application, references. *Deadline:* June 30.

Contact: John Hough, Trustee
H.H. Harris Foundation
30 South Wacker Drive, Suite 2300
Chicago, IL 60606
Fax: 312-346-0904
E-mail: johnhh@aol.com

HISPANIC COLLEGE FUND INC. http://www.hispanicfund.org

DEPARTMENT OF ENERGY SCHOLARSHIP PROGRAM

• *See page 142*

LOCKHEED MARTIN SCHOLARSHIP PROGRAM

• *See page 143*

HISPANIC ENGINEER NATIONAL ACHIEVEMENT AWARDS CORPORATION (HENAAC) http://www.henaac.org

HISPANIC ENGINEER NATIONAL ACHIEVEMENT AWARDS CORPORATION SCHOLARSHIP PROGRAM
• *See page 116*

HISPANIC SCHOLARSHIP FUND http://www.hsf.net

HSF/MARATHON OIL CORPORATION COLLEGE SCHOLARSHIP
• *See page 55*

HSF/NISSAN COMMUNITY COLLEGE TRANSFER SCHOLARSHIP PROGRAM
• *See page 143*

INDEPENDENT LABORATORIES INSTITUTE SCHOLARSHIP ALLIANCE http://www.acil.org

INDEPENDENT LABORATORIES INSTITUTE SCHOLARSHIP ALLIANCE
• *See page 132*

INSTITUTE OF ENVIRONMENTAL SCIENCES AND TECHNOLOGY (IEST) http://www.iest.org

ROBERT N. HANCOCK MEMORIAL SCHOLARSHIP
• *See page 132*

INTERNATIONAL SOCIETY FOR OPTICAL ENGINEERING-SPIE http://www.spie.org

SPIE EDUCATIONAL SCHOLARSHIPS IN OPTICAL SCIENCE AND ENGINEERING
• *See page 87*

JORGE MAS CANOSA FREEDOM FOUNDATION http://www.jorgemascanosa.org

MAS FAMILY SCHOLARSHIP AWARD
• *See page 144*

LOS ANGELES COUNCIL OF BLACK PROFESSIONAL ENGINEERS http://www.lablackengineers.org

AL-BEN SCHOLARSHIP FOR ACADEMIC INCENTIVE
• *See page 159*

AL-BEN SCHOLARSHIP FOR PROFESSIONAL MERIT
• *See page 159*

AL-BEN SCHOLARSHIP FOR SCHOLASTIC ACHIEVEMENT
• *See page 159*

MAINE METAL PRODUCTS ASSOCIATION http://www.mainemfg.com

MAINE METAL PRODUCTS ASSOCIATION SCHOLARSHIP PROGRAM

MMPA offers scholarship awards to individuals seeking education in the metal trades/precision manufacturing field of study. Any Maine student or worker can apply for tuition assistance at any Maine institute of higher learning. All applicants must be full-time students and maintain a minimum of a C average.

Academic Fields/Career Goals: Materials Science, Engineering, and Metallurgy; Mechanical Engineering; Trade/Technical Specialties.

Award: Scholarship for use in freshman, sophomore, junior, senior, graduate, or postgraduate years; renewable. *Number:* 15–25. *Amount:* $250–$1000.

Eligibility Requirements: Applicant must be enrolled or expecting to enroll full-time at a two-year or four-year or technical institution or university; resident of Maine and studying in Maine. Applicant must have 2.5 GPA or higher. Available to U.S. citizens.

Application Requirements: Application, essay, references, transcript. *Deadline:* May 1.

Contact: Lisa G. Martin, Executive Director
Maine Metal Products Association
28 Stroudwater Street, Suite 4
Westbrook, ME 04092
Phone: 207-854-2153
Fax: 207-854-3865
E-mail: info@mainemfg.com

MICRON TECHNOLOGY FOUNDATION INC. http://www.micron.com/scholars

MICRON SCIENCE AND TECHNOLOGY SCHOLARS PROGRAM
• *See page 160*

MINERALOGICAL SOCIETY OF AMERICA http://www.minsocam.org

MINERALOGY SOCIETY OF AMERICA-GRANT FOR RESEARCH IN CRYSTALLOGRAPHY
• *See page 218*

MINERALS, METALS, AND MATERIALS SOCIETY (TMS) http://www.tms.org

TMS/EMPMD GILBERT CHIN SCHOLARSHIP
• *See page 293*

TMS/EPD SCHOLARSHIP
• *See page 294*

TMS/INTERNATIONAL SYMPOSIUM ON SUPERALLOYS SCHOLARSHIP PROGRAM
• *See page 294*

TMS J. KEITH BRIMACOMBE PRESIDENTIAL SCHOLARSHIP
• *See page 294*

TMS/LMD SCHOLARSHIP PROGRAM
• *See page 294*

TMS OUTSTANDING STUDENT PAPER CONTEST-UNDERGRADUATE
• *See page 294*

TMS/STRUCTURAL MATERIALS DIVISION SCHOLARSHIP
• *See page 294*

NASA/MARYLAND SPACE GRANT CONSORTIUM http://www.mdspacegrant.org

NASA MARYLAND SPACE GRANT CONSORTIUM UNDERGRADUATE SCHOLARSHIPS
• *See page 118*

NASA SOUTH DAKOTA SPACE GRANT CONSORTIUM http://www.sdsmt.edu/space/

SOUTH DAKOTA SPACE GRANT CONSORTIUM UNDERGRADUATE SCHOLARSHIPS
• *See page 120*

NASA VERMONT SPACE GRANT CONSORTIUM http://www.cems.uvm.edu/VSGC

VERMONT SPACE GRANT CONSORTIUM SCHOLARSHIP PROGRAM
• *See page 88*

NATIONAL INVENTORS HALL OF FAME http://www.invent.org

COLLEGIATE INVENTORS COMPETITION FOR UNDERGRADUATE STUDENTS
• *See page 88*

COLLEGIATE INVENTORS COMPETITION-GRAND PRIZE
• *See page 88*

NATIONAL SOCIETY OF PROFESSIONAL ENGINEERS http://www.nspe.org

MAUREEN L. AND HOWARD N. BLITMAN, PE SCHOLARSHIP TO PROMOTE DIVERSITY IN ENGINEERING
• See page 161

PAUL H. ROBBINS HONORARY SCHOLARSHIP
• See page 162

PROFESSIONAL ENGINEERS IN INDUSTRY SCHOLARSHIP
• See page 162

NATIONAL STONE, SAND AND GRAVEL ASSOCIATION (NSSGA) http://www.nssga.org

BARRY K. WENDT MEMORIAL SCHOLARSHIP
• See page 295

PLASTICS INSTITUTE OF AMERICA http://www.plasticsinstitute.org

PLASTICS PIONEERS SCHOLARSHIPS
• See page 162

ROCKY MOUNTAIN COAL MINING INSTITUTE http://www.rmcmi.org

ROCKY MOUNTAIN COAL MINING INSTITUTE SCHOLARSHIP
• See page 219

SOCIETY OF AUTOMOTIVE ENGINEERS http://www.sae.org

TMC/SAE DONALD D. DAWSON TECHNICAL SCHOLARSHIP
• See page 124

YANMAR/SAE SCHOLARSHIP
• See page 297

SOCIETY OF HISPANIC PROFESSIONAL ENGINEERS FOUNDATION http://www.henaac.org

HENAAC SCHOLARS PROGRAM
• See page 194

SOCIETY OF HISPANIC PROFESSIONAL ENGINEERS FOUNDATION
• See page 162

SOCIETY OF PLASTICS ENGINEERS (SPE) FOUNDATION http://www.4spe.org

FLEMING/BASZCAK SCHOLARSHIP
• See page 163

SOCIETY OF PLASTICS ENGINEERS SCHOLARSHIP PROGRAM
• See page 163

SOCIETY OF WOMEN ENGINEERS http://www.swe.org

CATERPILLAR INC. SCHOLARSHIP
• See page 79

GUIDANT CORPORATION SCHOLARSHIP
• See page 195

NORTHROP GRUMMAN FRESHMAN SCHOLARSHIP
• See page 125

UNIVERSITIES SPACE RESEARCH ASSOCIATION http://www.usra.edu

UNIVERSITIES SPACE RESEARCH ASSOCIATION SCHOLARSHIP PROGRAM
• See page 88

XEROX http://www.xerox.com

TECHNICAL MINORITY SCHOLARSHIP
• See page 165

MATHEMATICS

AMERICAN MATHEMATICAL ASSOCIATION OF TWO YEAR COLLEGES http://www.amatyc.org

CHARLES MILLER SCHOLARSHIP

A grand prize of $3000 for the qualified individual with the highest total score of the student mathematics league exam. Funds to continue education at an accredited four-year institution. In the case of a tie for the grand prize, the scholarship will be evenly divided.

Academic Fields/Career Goals: Mathematics.

Award: Scholarship for use in freshman or sophomore years; not renewable. *Number:* 1. *Amount:* $3000.

Eligibility Requirements: Applicant must be enrolled or expecting to enroll full-time at a two-year institution. Available to U.S. citizens.

Application Requirements: Applicant must enter a contest, test scores. *Deadline:* September 30.

Contact: Cheryl Cleaves, Executive Director of Office Operations
American Mathematical Association of Two Year Colleges
c/o Southwest Tennessee Community College
5983 Macon Cove
Memphis, TN 38134
Phone: 901-333-4643
Fax: 901-333-4651
E-mail: amatyc@amatyc.org

AMERICAN SOCIETY FOR ENGINEERING EDUCATION http://www.asee.org

SCIENCE, MATHEMATICS, AND RESEARCH FOR TRANSFORMATION DEFENSE SCHOLARSHIP FOR SERVICE PROGRAM
• See page 85

ARMED FORCES COMMUNICATIONS AND ELECTRONICS ASSOCIATION, EDUCATIONAL FOUNDATION http://www.afcea.org

ARMED FORCES COMMUNICATIONS AND ELECTRONICS ASSOCIATION ROTC SCHOLARSHIP PROGRAM
• See page 114

ASSOCIATION FOR WOMEN IN MATHEMATICS http://www.awm-math.org

ALICE T. SCHAFER MATHEMATICS PRIZE FOR EXCELLENCE IN MATHEMATICS BY AN UNDERGRADUATE WOMAN

One-time merit award for women undergraduates in the math field. Based on quality of performance in math courses and special programs, ability to work independently, interest in math, and performance in competitions. Must be nominated by a professor or an adviser.

Academic Fields/Career Goals: Mathematics.

Award: Prize for use in freshman, sophomore, junior, or senior years; not renewable. *Number:* 1. *Amount:* $250–$1000.

Eligibility Requirements: Applicant must be enrolled or expecting to enroll full-time at a four-year institution or university and female. Available to U.S. citizens.

Application Requirements: Application, applicant must enter a contest, references, transcript, 5 complete copies of nominations. *Deadline:* October 1.

Contact: Jennifer Lewis, Managing Director
Association for Women in Mathematics
11240 Waples Mill Road, Suite 200
Fairfax, VA 22030-2461
Phone: 703-934-0163 Ext. 213
Fax: 703-359-7562
E-mail: jennifer@awm-math.org

CASUALTY ACTUARIAL SOCIETY/SOCIETY OF ACTUARIES JOINT COMMITTEE ON MINORITY RECRUITING http://www.BeAnActuary.org/minority

ACTUARIAL SCHOLARSHIPS FOR MINORITY STUDENTS

• *See page 364*

COLLEGEBOUND FOUNDATION http://www.collegeboundfoundation.org

DR. FREEMAN A. HRABOWSKI, III SCHOLARSHIP

• *See page 262*

COMMUNITY FOUNDATION FOR GREATER ATLANTA INC. http://www.atlcf.org

TECH HIGH SCHOOL ALUMNI ASSOCIATION/W.O. CHENEY MERIT SCHOLARSHIP FUND

• *See page 262*

DAVIDSON INSTITUTE FOR TALENT DEVELOPMENT http://www.davidsoninstitute.org

DAVIDSON FELLOWS

• *See page 390*

GREATER KANAWHA VALLEY FOUNDATION http://www.tgkvf.org

MATH AND SCIENCE SCHOLARSHIP

• *See page 132*

HEMOPHILIA HEALTH SERVICES http://www.hemophiliahealth.com

SCOTT TARBELL SCHOLARSHIP

• *See page 192*

MICHIGAN COUNCIL OF TEACHERS OF MATHEMATICS http://www.mictm.org

MIRIAM SCHAEFER SCHOLARSHIP

A scholarship of $1500 is given to a senior or a junior enrolled full-time in undergraduate degree with mathematics specialty. Applicants should be a resident of Michigan but citizenship does not matter.

Academic Fields/Career Goals: Mathematics.

Award: Scholarship for use in junior or senior years; not renewable. *Number:* 5. *Amount:* $1500.

Eligibility Requirements: Applicant must be enrolled or expecting to enroll full-time at a four-year institution or university and resident of Michigan. Applicant must have 3.0 GPA or higher. Available to U.S. and non-U.S. citizens.

Application Requirements: Application, essay, references, transcript. *Deadline:* April 1.

Contact: Alecia Powell, Business Manager
Michigan Council of Teachers of Mathematics
3300 Washtenaw Avenue, Suite 220
Ann Arbor, MI 48104
Phone: 734-477-0421
Fax: 734-677-2407
E-mail: alecia@ucia2.com

NASA/MARYLAND SPACE GRANT CONSORTIUM http://www.mdspacegrant.org

NASA MARYLAND SPACE GRANT CONSORTIUM UNDERGRADUATE SCHOLARSHIPS

• *See page 118*

NASA MISSISSIPPI SPACE GRANT CONSORTIUM http://www.olemiss.edu/programs/nasa

MISSISSIPPI SPACE GRANT CONSORTIUM SCHOLARSHIP

• *See page 118*

NASA MONTANA SPACE GRANT CONSORTIUM http://www.spacegrant.montana.edu

MONTANA SPACE GRANT SCHOLARSHIP PROGRAM

• *See page 119*

NASA RHODE ISLAND SPACE GRANT CONSORTIUM http://www.planetary.brown.edu/RI_Space_Grant

NASA RHODE ISLAND SPACE GRANT CONSORTIUM OUTREACH SCHOLARSHIP FOR UNDERGRADUATE STUDENTS

• *See page 295*

NASA RISGC SCIENCE EN ESPANOL SCHOLARSHIP FOR UNDERGRADUATE STUDENTS

• *See page 119*

NASA SOUTH DAKOTA SPACE GRANT CONSORTIUM http://www.sdsmt.edu/space/

SOUTH DAKOTA SPACE GRANT CONSORTIUM UNDERGRADUATE SCHOLARSHIPS

• *See page 120*

NATIONAL COUNCIL OF TEACHERS OF MATHEMATICS http://www.nctm.org

PROSPECTIVE SECONDARY TEACHER COURSE WORK SCHOLARSHIPS

• *See page 236*

NATIONAL SECURITY AGENCY http://www.nsa.gov

NATIONAL SECURITY AGENCY STOKES EDUCATIONAL SCHOLARSHIP PROGRAM

• *See page 194*

SAN DIEGO FOUNDATION http://www.sdfoundation.org

QUALCOMM SAN DIEGO SCIENCE, TECHNOLOGY, ENGINEERING, AND MATHEMATICS SCHOLARSHIP

• *See page 271*

SOCIETY OF FLIGHT TEST ENGINEERS http://www.sfte.org

SOCIETY OF FLIGHT TEST ENGINEERS SCHOLARSHIP

• *See page 194*

SOCIETY OF HISPANIC PROFESSIONAL ENGINEERS http://www.shpe.org

AHETEMS SCHOLARSHIPS

• *See page 273*

SOCIETY OF HISPANIC PROFESSIONAL ENGINEERS FOUNDATION http://www.henaac.org

HENAAC SCHOLARS PROGRAM

• *See page 194*

TKE EDUCATIONAL FOUNDATION http://www.tke.org

FRANCIS J. FLYNN MEMORIAL SCHOLARSHIP

• *See page 243*

UNITED NEGRO COLLEGE FUND http://www.uncf.org

GILBANE SCHOLARSHIP PROGRAM

• *See page 93*

WISCONSIN MATHEMATICS COUNCIL INC. http://www.wismath.org

ARNE ENGEBRETSEN WISCONSIN MATHEMATICS COUNCIL SCHOLARSHIP

• *See page 245*

ETHEL A. NEIJAHR WISCONSIN MATHEMATICS COUNCIL SCHOLARSHIP

• *See page 245*

Wisconsin Mathematics Council Inc. (continued)

SISTER MARY PETRONIA VAN STRATEN WISCONSIN MATHEMATICS COUNCIL SCHOLARSHIP
• *See page 245*

MECHANICAL ENGINEERING

AACE INTERNATIONAL http://www.aacei.org

AACE INTERNATIONAL COMPETITIVE SCHOLARSHIP
• *See page 89*

AMERICAN CHEMICAL SOCIETY, RUBBER DIVISION http://www.rubber.org

AMERICAN CHEMICAL SOCIETY, RUBBER DIVISION UNDERGRADUATE SCHOLARSHIP
• *See page 153*

AMERICAN COUNCIL OF ENGINEERING COMPANIES OF PENNSYLVANIA (ACEC/PA) http://www.acecpa.org

ENGINEERING SCHOLARSHIP
• *See page 154*

AMERICAN INSTITUTE OF AERONAUTICS AND ASTRONAUTICS http://www.aiaa.org

AIAA UNDERGRADUATE SCHOLARSHIP
• *See page 84*

AMERICAN PUBLIC TRANSPORTATION FOUNDATION http://www.apta.com

LOUIS T. KLAUDER SCHOLARSHIP
• *See page 247*

TRANSIT HALL OF FAME SCHOLARSHIP AWARD PROGRAM
• *See page 168*

AMERICAN SOCIETY OF HEATING, REFRIGERATING, AND AIR CONDITIONING ENGINEERS INC. http://www.ashrae.org

ALWIN B. NEWTON SCHOLARSHIP FUND
• *See page 247*

REUBEN TRANE SCHOLARSHIP
• *See page 247*

AMERICAN SOCIETY OF MECHANICAL ENGINEERS (ASME INTERNATIONAL) http://www.asme.org

AMERICAN SOCIETY OF MECHANICAL ENGINEERS FOUNDATION ASME AUXILIARY FIRST CLARK SCHOLARSHIP

Scholarships to graduating high school seniors who are members of a FIRST Robotics Competition team. Must be planning to enroll no later than the fall semester following high school graduation in an ABET-accredited or substantially equivalent mechanical engineering or mechanical engineering technology program. The society does not accept applications directly from students for this program. Must be nominated by ASME members, Auxiliary members, or student members who are also active with FIRST.

Academic Fields/Career Goals: Mechanical Engineering.

Award: Scholarship for use in freshman year; not renewable. *Number:* 9. *Amount:* $5000.

Eligibility Requirements: Applicant must be high school student and planning to enroll or expecting to enroll full-time at a four-year institution or university. Applicant or parent of applicant must be member of American Society of Mechanical Engineers. Available to U.S. and non-U.S. citizens.

Application Requirements: Applicant must enter a contest, financial need analysis, transcript, nomination letter from ASME member. *Deadline:* March 20.

Contact: Mel Torre, Director of Communication
American Society of Mechanical Engineers (ASME International)
Three Park Avenue
New York, NY 10016-5990
Phone: 212-591-8157
Fax: 212-591-7143
E-mail: torrec@asme.org

AMERICAN SOCIETY OF MECHANICAL ENGINEERS FOUNDATION SCHOLARSHIP

Award for college sophomores, juniors, and seniors who are student members of the American Society of Mechanical Engineers. Must be enrolled in an ABET-accredited or substantially equivalent mechanical engineering, mechanical engineering technology or related baccalaureate program. There are no citizenship or geographic requirements.

Academic Fields/Career Goals: Mechanical Engineering.

Award: Scholarship for use in sophomore, junior, or senior years; not renewable. *Number:* 16. *Amount:* $1500.

Eligibility Requirements: Applicant must be enrolled or expecting to enroll full-time at a two-year or four-year institution or university. Applicant or parent of applicant must be member of American Society of Mechanical Engineers. Available to U.S. and non-U.S. citizens.

Application Requirements: Application, essay, financial need analysis, references, self-addressed stamped envelope, transcript. *Deadline:* March 15.

Contact: Maisha Phillips, Coordinator, Student Development ASME
American Society of Mechanical Engineers (ASME International)
Three Park Avenue
New York, NY 10016-5990
Phone: 212-591-8131
Fax: 212-591-7143
E-mail: phillipsm@asme.org

AMERICAN SOCIETY OF MECHANICAL ENGINEERS PETROLEUM DIVISION STUDENT SCHOLARSHIP PROGRAM
• *See page 395*

AMERICAN SOCIETY OF MECHANICAL ENGINEERS SOLID WASTE PROCESSING DIVISION UNDERGRADUATE SCHOLARSHIP

One undergraduate scholarship available for study of established programs in solid waste management at North American colleges and universities. Full-time undergraduate students who plan to continue their undergraduate studies or high school seniors who plan to graduate in the upcoming academic year are eligible to apply. Enrollment must include solid waste management related courses. Must be a member of ASME, with solid waste processing division as a chosen field.

Academic Fields/Career Goals: Mechanical Engineering.

Award: Scholarship for use in freshman, sophomore, junior, or senior years; not renewable. *Number:* 1. *Amount:* $2000.

Eligibility Requirements: Applicant must be enrolled or expecting to enroll full-time at a four-year institution or university. Applicant or parent of applicant must be member of American Society of Mechanical Engineers. Available to U.S. and non-U.S. citizens.

Application Requirements: Application, essay, references, transcript. *Deadline:* June 5.

Contact: Elio Manes, Senior Manager
American Society of Mechanical Engineers (ASME International)
Three Park Avenue
New York, NY 10016-5990
Phone: 212-591-7797
Fax: 212-591-7671
E-mail: manese@asme.org

FRANK WILLIAM AND DOROTHY GIVEN MILLER SCHOLARSHIP

Award for college juniors and seniors who are student members of the American Society of Mechanical Engineers. Must be attending a four-year institution in

North America and pursuing studies in mechanical engineering or mechanical engineering technology. Must be U.S. citizens and North American residents.

Academic Fields/Career Goals: Mechanical Engineering.

Award: Scholarship for use in sophomore, junior, or senior years; not renewable. *Number:* 2. *Amount:* $1500.

Eligibility Requirements: Applicant must be enrolled or expecting to enroll full-time at a four-year institution or university. Applicant or parent of applicant must be member of American Society of Mechanical Engineers. Available to U.S. citizens.

Application Requirements: Application, essay, financial need analysis, references, self-addressed stamped envelope, transcript. *Deadline:* March 15.

Contact: Maisha Phillips, Coordinator, Student Development ASME
American Society of Mechanical Engineers (ASME International)
Three Park Avenue
New York, NY 10016-5990
Phone: 212-591-8131
Fax: 212-591-7143
E-mail: phillipsm@asme.org

F.W. "BEICH" BEICHLEY SCHOLARSHIP

One-time award for college juniors and seniors who are student members of the American Society of Mechanical Engineers. Must be enrolled in an ABET-accredited or substantially equivalent mechanical engineering, mechanical engineering technology or related baccalaureate program in the United States.

Academic Fields/Career Goals: Mechanical Engineering.

Award: Scholarship for use in junior or senior years; not renewable. *Number:* 1. *Amount:* $2500.

Eligibility Requirements: Applicant must be enrolled or expecting to enroll full-time at a four-year institution or university. Available to U.S. and non-U.S. citizens.

Application Requirements: Application, essay, financial need analysis, references, self-addressed stamped envelope, transcript. *Deadline:* March 15.

Contact: Maisha Phillips, Coordinator, Student Development ASME
American Society of Mechanical Engineers (ASME International)
Three Park Avenue
New York, NY 10016-5990
Phone: 212-591-8131
Fax: 212-591-7143
E-mail: phillipsm@asme.org

GARLAND DUNCAN SCHOLARSHIP

Award for college juniors and seniors who are student members of the American Society of Mechanical Engineers. Must be enrolled in an ABET-accredited or substantially equivalent mechanical engineering, mechanical engineering technology or related baccalaureate program.

Academic Fields/Career Goals: Mechanical Engineering.

Award: Scholarship for use in junior or senior years; not renewable. *Number:* 2. *Amount:* $4500.

Eligibility Requirements: Applicant must be enrolled or expecting to enroll full-time at a four-year institution or university. Applicant or parent of applicant must be member of American Society of Mechanical Engineers. Available to U.S. and non-U.S. citizens.

Application Requirements: Application, essay, financial need analysis, references, self-addressed stamped envelope, transcript. *Deadline:* March 15.

Contact: Maisha Phillips, Coordinator, Student Development ASME
American Society of Mechanical Engineers (ASME International)
Three Park Avenue
New York, NY 10016-5990
Phone: 212-591-8131
Fax: 212-591-7143
E-mail: phillipsm@asme.org

JOHN AND ELSA GRACIK SCHOLARSHIPS

Scholarships available to undergraduate ASME student members enrolled in an ABET-accredited mechanical engineering, mechanical engineering technology or related program, who are U.S. citizens with excellent academic records and demonstrated financial need. Must be enrolled in a school or university in United States only.

Academic Fields/Career Goals: Mechanical Engineering.

Award: Scholarship for use in sophomore, junior, or senior years; not renewable. *Number:* 18. *Amount:* $1500.

Eligibility Requirements: Applicant must be enrolled or expecting to enroll full-time at a four-year institution or university. Applicant or parent of applicant must be member of American Society of Mechanical Engineers. Available to U.S. citizens.

Application Requirements: Application, essay, financial need analysis, references, self-addressed stamped envelope, transcript. *Deadline:* March 15.

Contact: Maisha Phillips, Coordinator, Student Development ASME
American Society of Mechanical Engineers (ASME International)
Three Park Avenue
New York, NY 10016-5990
Phone: 212-591-8131
Fax: 212-591-7143
E-mail: phillipsm@asme.org

KENNETH ANDREW ROE SCHOLARSHIP

Award of $10,000 for college juniors and seniors who are student members of ASME. Must be U.S. citizens and North American residents. Must be enrolled in an ABET-accredited, or substantially equivalent, mechanical engineering baccalaureate program in the United States.

Academic Fields/Career Goals: Mechanical Engineering.

Award: Scholarship for use in junior or senior years; not renewable. *Number:* 1. *Amount:* $10,000.

Eligibility Requirements: Applicant must be enrolled or expecting to enroll full-time at a four-year institution or university. Available to U.S. citizens.

Application Requirements: Application, essay, financial need analysis, references, self-addressed stamped envelope, transcript. *Deadline:* March 15.

Contact: Maisha Phillips, Coordinator, Student Development ASME
American Society of Mechanical Engineers (ASME International)
Three Park Avenue
New York, NY 10016-5990
Phone: 212-591-8131
Fax: 212-591-7143
E-mail: phillipsm@asme.org

MELVIN R. GREEN SCHOLARSHIP

Award for college juniors and seniors who are student members of the American Society of Mechanical Engineers, enrolled in an ABET-accredited or substantially equivalent mechanical engineering, mechanical engineering technology or related baccalaureate program.

Academic Fields/Career Goals: Mechanical Engineering.

Award: Scholarship for use in junior or senior years; not renewable. *Number:* 2. *Amount:* $3500.

Eligibility Requirements: Applicant must be enrolled or expecting to enroll full-time at a four-year institution or university. Applicant or parent of applicant must be member of American Society of Mechanical Engineers. Available to U.S. and non-U.S. citizens.

Application Requirements: Application, essay, financial need analysis, references, self-addressed stamped envelope, transcript. *Deadline:* March 15.

Contact: Maisha Phillips, Coordinator, Student Development ASME
American Society of Mechanical Engineers (ASME International)
Three Park Avenue
New York, NY 10016-5990
Phone: 212-591-8131
Fax: 212-591-7143
E-mail: phillipsm@asme.org

WILLIAM J. & MARIJANE E. ADAMS, JR. SCHOLARSHIP

Applicants must be ASME student members attending a college or university in California, Hawaii or Nevada and demonstrates a special interest in product

American Society of Mechanical Engineers (ASME International) (continued)

development and design. Awarded to sophomores, juniors and seniors. Applicants must be enrolled in an ABET-accredited, or substantially equivalent mechanical engineering baccalaureate program. Minimum GPA 2.5 required. Must demonstrate financial need.

Academic Fields/Career Goals: Mechanical Engineering.

Award: Scholarship for use in sophomore, junior, or senior years; not renewable. *Number:* 1. *Amount:* $3000.

Eligibility Requirements: Applicant must be enrolled or expecting to enroll full-time at a four-year institution or university and studying in California, Hawaii, or Nevada. Applicant or parent of applicant must be member of American Society of Mechanical Engineers. Applicant must have 2.5 GPA or higher. Available to U.S. and non-U.S. citizens.

Application Requirements: Application, essay, financial need analysis, references, self-addressed stamped envelope, transcript. *Deadline:* March 15.

Contact: Maisha Phillips, Coordinator, Student Development ASME
American Society of Mechanical Engineers (ASME International)
Three Park Avenue
New York, NY 10016-5990
Phone: 212-591-8131
Fax: 212-591-7143
E-mail: phillipsm@asme.org

AMERICAN SOCIETY OF MECHANICAL ENGINEERS AUXILIARY INC. http://www.asme.org

AGNES MALAKATE KEZIOS SCHOLARSHIP

Scholarship to college juniors for use in final year at a four year college. Must be majoring in mechanical engineering, be member of ASME (if available), and exhibit leadership values. Must be U.S. citizen enrolled in a college/university in the United States that has ABET accreditation. Scholarship value is $2000 and the number of awards granted varies.

Academic Fields/Career Goals: Mechanical Engineering.

Award: Scholarship for use in junior or senior years; not renewable. *Number:* varies. *Amount:* $2000.

Eligibility Requirements: Applicant must be enrolled or expecting to enroll full-time at a four-year institution or university. Available to U.S. citizens.

Application Requirements: Application, autobiography, references, self-addressed stamped envelope, transcript. *Deadline:* March 15.

Contact: Alverta Cover, Undergraduate Scholarships
American Society of Mechanical Engineers Auxiliary Inc.
5425 Caldwell Mill Road
Birmingham, AL 35242
Phone: 205-991-6109
E-mail: covera@asme.org

ALLEN J. BALDWIN SCHOLARSHIP

Scholarship available to college juniors for use in final year at a four year college. Must be majoring in mechanical engineering, be member of ASME (if available), and exhibit leadership values. Must be U.S. citizen enrolled in a college/university in the United States that has ABET accreditation. Scholarship value is $2000 and the number of awards granted varies.

Academic Fields/Career Goals: Mechanical Engineering.

Award: Scholarship for use in junior or senior years; not renewable. *Number:* varies. *Amount:* $2000.

Eligibility Requirements: Applicant must be enrolled or expecting to enroll full-time at a four-year institution or university. Available to U.S. citizens.

Application Requirements: Application, autobiography, financial need analysis, references, self-addressed stamped envelope, transcript. *Deadline:* March 15.

Contact: Alverta Cover, Undergraduate Scholarships
American Society of Mechanical Engineers Auxiliary Inc.
5425 Caldwell Mill Road
Birmingham, AL 35242
Phone: 205-991-6109
E-mail: covera@asme.org

AMERICAN SOCIETY OF MECHANICAL ENGINEERS-AMERICAN SOCIETY OF MECHANICAL ENGINEERS AUXILIARY FIRST CLARKE SCHOLARSHIP

Scholarships available for high school seniors only, who are active on FIRST teams. Applicant must be a member or nominated by a member of ASME or ASME Auxiliary. Must enrolled full-time in an ABET-accredited mechanical engineering or mechanical engineering technology program.

Academic Fields/Career Goals: Mechanical Engineering.

Award: Scholarship for use in freshman year; not renewable. *Number:* up to 10. *Amount:* up to $5000.

Eligibility Requirements: Applicant must be high school student and planning to enroll or expecting to enroll full-time at a two-year or four-year or technical institution or university. Available to U.S. citizens.

Application Requirements: Application, financial need analysis, resume, transcript, nomination letter from an ASME member/auxiliary member/student member. *Deadline:* March 15.

Contact: Maisha Phillips, Program Coordinator
American Society of Mechanical Engineers Auxiliary Inc.
Three Park Avenue
New York, NY 10016-5990
Phone: 800-843-2763
E-mail: phillipsm@asme.org

ASME AUXILIARY UNDERGRADUATE SCHOLARSHIP CHARLES B. SHARP

Award of $2000 available only to ASME student members to be used in final year of undergraduate study in mechanical engineering. Must be a U.S. citizen.

Academic Fields/Career Goals: Mechanical Engineering.

Award: Scholarship for use in senior year; not renewable. *Number:* up to 4. *Amount:* $2000.

Eligibility Requirements: Applicant must be enrolled or expecting to enroll full-time at a four-year institution or university. Applicant or parent of applicant must be member of American Society of Mechanical Engineers. Available to U.S. citizens.

Application Requirements: Application, financial need analysis, references, transcript. *Deadline:* March 15.

Contact: Alverta Cover, Undergraduate Scholarship Chairman
American Society of Mechanical Engineers Auxiliary Inc.
5425 Caldwell Mill Road
Birmingham, AL 35242
Phone: 205-991-6109
E-mail: covera@asme.org

BERNA LOU CARTWRIGHT SCHOLARSHIP

Scholarship for college juniors for use in final year at a four year college. Must be majoring in mechanical engineering. Must be a U.S. citizen, enrolled in a college/university in the United States that has ABET accreditation. Number of awards varies.

Academic Fields/Career Goals: Mechanical Engineering.

Award: Scholarship for use in junior or senior years; not renewable. *Number:* varies. *Amount:* $2000.

Eligibility Requirements: Applicant must be enrolled or expecting to enroll full-time at a four-year institution or university and must have an interest in leadership. Available to U.S. citizens.

Application Requirements: Application, autobiography, references, self-addressed stamped envelope, transcript. *Deadline:* March 15.

Contact: Alverta Cover, Undergraduate Scholarships
American Society of Mechanical Engineers Auxiliary Inc.
5425 Caldwell Mill Road
Birmingham, AL 35242
Phone: 205-991-6109
E-mail: covera@asme.org

SYLVIA W. FARNY SCHOLARSHIP

One-time awards of $2000 to ASME student members for the final year of undergraduate study in mechanical engineering. Must be a U.S. citizen, enrolled in a college/university in the United States that has ABET accreditation. Number of scholarships granted varies.

Academic Fields/Career Goals: Mechanical Engineering.

Award: Scholarship for use in junior or senior years; not renewable. *Number:* varies. *Amount:* $2000.

Eligibility Requirements: Applicant must be enrolled or expecting to enroll full-time at a four-year institution or university. Available to U.S. citizens.

Application Requirements: Application, references, transcript. *Deadline:* March 15.

Contact: Alverta Cover, Undergraduate Scholarships
American Society of Mechanical Engineers Auxiliary Inc.
5425 Caldwell Mill Road
Birmingham, AL 35242
Phone: 205-991-6109
E-mail: covera@asme.org

AMERICAN SOCIETY OF NAVAL ENGINEERS http://www.navalengineers.org

AMERICAN SOCIETY OF NAVAL ENGINEERS SCHOLARSHIP
• See page 85

AMERICAN WELDING SOCIETY http://www.aws.org

PAST PRESIDENTS' SCHOLARSHIP
• See page 257

RWMA SCHOLARSHIP
• See page 257

ASSOCIATION FOR FACILITIES ENGINEERING (AFE)

ASSOCIATION FOR FACILITIES ENGINEERING CEDAR VALLEY CHAPTER #132 SCHOLARSHIP
• See page 114

ASSOCIATION FOR WOMEN IN SCIENCE EDUCATIONAL FOUNDATION http://www.awis.org/careers/edfoundation.html

ASSOCIATION FOR WOMEN IN SCIENCE COLLEGE SCHOLARSHIP
• See page 82

ASTRONAUT SCHOLARSHIP FOUNDATION http://www.astronautscholarship.org

ASTRONAUT SCHOLARSHIP FOUNDATION
• See page 86

BARRY M. GOLDWATER SCHOLARSHIP AND EXCELLENCE IN EDUCATION FOUNDATION http://www.act.org/goldwater

BARRY M. GOLDWATER SCHOLARSHIP AND EXCELLENCE IN EDUCATION PROGRAM
• See page 86

CUBAN AMERICAN NATIONAL FOUNDATION http://www.masscholarships.org

MAS FAMILY SCHOLARSHIPS
• See page 139

ELECTROCHEMICAL SOCIETY INC. http://www.electrochem.org

H.H. DOW MEMORIAL STUDENT ACHIEVEMENT AWARD OF THE INDUSTRIAL ELECTROLYSIS AND ELECTROCHEMICAL ENGINEERING DIVISION OF THE ELECTROCHEMICAL SOCIETY INC.
• See page 131

STUDENT ACHIEVEMENT AWARDS OF THE INDUSTRIAL ELECTROLYSIS AND ELECTROCHEMICAL ENGINEERING DIVISION OF THE ELECTROCHEMICAL SOCIETY INC.
• See page 131

STUDENT RESEARCH AWARDS OF THE BATTERY DIVISION OF THE ELECTROCHEMICAL SOCIETY INC.
• See page 131

ENGINEERS' SOCIETY OF WESTERN PENNSYLVANIA http://www.eswp.com

JOSEPH A. LEVENDUSKY MEMORIAL SCHOLARSHIP
• See page 157

FOUNDATION FOR SCIENCE AND DISABILITY http://www.stemd.org

GRANTS FOR DISABLED STUDENTS IN THE SCIENCES
• See page 87

HISPANIC COLLEGE FUND INC. http://www.hispanicfund.org

DEPARTMENT OF ENERGY SCHOLARSHIP PROGRAM
• See page 142

HISPANIC ENGINEER NATIONAL ACHIEVEMENT AWARDS CORPORATION (HENAAC) http://www.henaac.org

HISPANIC ENGINEER NATIONAL ACHIEVEMENT AWARDS CORPORATION SCHOLARSHIP PROGRAM
• See page 116

HISPANIC SCHOLARSHIP FUND http://www.hsf.net

HSF/GENERAL MOTORS SCHOLARSHIP
• See page 143

HSF/MARATHON OIL CORPORATION COLLEGE SCHOLARSHIP
• See page 55

HSF/NISSAN COMMUNITY COLLEGE TRANSFER SCHOLARSHIP PROGRAM
• See page 143

INDEPENDENT LABORATORIES INSTITUTE SCHOLARSHIP ALLIANCE http://www.acil.org

INDEPENDENT LABORATORIES INSTITUTE SCHOLARSHIP ALLIANCE
• See page 132

INSTITUTE OF ENVIRONMENTAL SCIENCES AND TECHNOLOGY (IEST) http://www.iest.org

ROBERT N. HANCOCK MEMORIAL SCHOLARSHIP
• See page 132

INSTRUMENTATION, SYSTEMS, AND AUTOMATION SOCIETY (ISA) http://www.isa.org

INSTRUMENTATION, SYSTEMS, AND AUTOMATION SOCIETY (ISA) SCHOLARSHIP PROGRAM
• See page 158

JORGE MAS CANOSA FREEDOM FOUNDATION http://www.jorgemascanosa.org

MAS FAMILY SCHOLARSHIP AWARD
• See page 144

LOS ANGELES COUNCIL OF BLACK PROFESSIONAL ENGINEERS http://www.lablackengineers.org

AL-BEN SCHOLARSHIP FOR ACADEMIC INCENTIVE
• *See page 159*

AL-BEN SCHOLARSHIP FOR PROFESSIONAL MERIT
• *See page 159*

AL-BEN SCHOLARSHIP FOR SCHOLASTIC ACHIEVEMENT
• *See page 159*

MAINE EDUCATION SERVICES http://www.mesfoundation.com

MAINE METAL PRODUCTS ASSOCIATION SCHOLARSHIP

Awards available for individuals demonstrating an outstanding record and overall potential to attend an institution of higher learning majoring in: mechanical engineering, machine tool technician, sheet metal fabrication, welding, CAD/CAM for metals industry. Restricted to the study of metal working trades. The award value and the number of awards granted varies annually.

Academic Fields/Career Goals: Mechanical Engineering; Trade/Technical Specialties.

Award: Scholarship for use in freshman, sophomore, junior, or senior years; not renewable. *Number:* varies. *Amount:* varies.

Eligibility Requirements: Applicant must be enrolled or expecting to enroll full- or part-time at a two-year or four-year or technical institution or university; resident of Maine and studying in Maine. Available to U.S. citizens.

Application Requirements: Application, references, transcript. *Deadline:* April 18.

Contact: Kim Benjamin, Vice President of Operations
Maine Education Services
131 Presumpscot Street
Portland, ME 04103
Phone: 207-791-3600
Fax: 207-791-3616

MAINE METAL PRODUCTS ASSOCIATION http://www.mainemfg.com

MAINE METAL PRODUCTS ASSOCIATION SCHOLARSHIP PROGRAM
• *See page 399*

MICHIGAN SOCIETY OF PROFESSIONAL ENGINEERS http://www.michiganspe.org

ANTHONY C. FORTUNSKI, P.E. MEMORIAL GRANT
• *See page 159*

MICHIGAN SOCIETY OF PROFESSIONAL ENGINEERS AUXILIARY GRANT
• *See page 159*

MICHIGAN SOCIETY OF PROFESSIONAL ENGINEERS HARRY R. BALL, P.E. GRANT
• *See page 159*

MICHIGAN SOCIETY OF PROFESSIONAL ENGINEERS KENNETH B. FISHBECK, P.E. MEMORIAL GRANT
• *See page 160*

MICHIGAN SOCIETY OF PROFESSIONAL ENGINEERS 1980 NATIONAL SOCIETY OF PROFESSIONAL ENGINEERS ANNUAL MEETING COMMITTEE GRANT
• *See page 160*

MICHIGAN SOCIETY OF PROFESSIONAL ENGINEERS SCHOLARSHIP TRUST GRANT
• *See page 160*

MICHIGAN SOCIETY OF PROFESSIONAL ENGINEERS UNDESIGNATED GRANT
• *See page 160*

MSPE AUXILIARY GRANT FOR UNDERGRADUATE STUDY
• *See page 171*

MICRON TECHNOLOGY FOUNDATION INC. http://www.micron.com/scholars

MICRON SCIENCE AND TECHNOLOGY SCHOLARS PROGRAM
• *See page 160*

NASA MONTANA SPACE GRANT CONSORTIUM http://www.spacegrant.montana.edu

MONTANA SPACE GRANT SCHOLARSHIP PROGRAM
• *See page 119*

NATIONAL ASSOCIATION OF WOMEN IN CONSTRUCTION http://www.nawic.org

NAWIC UNDERGRADUATE SCHOLARSHIPS
• *See page 92*

NATIONAL BOARD OF BOILER AND PRESSURE VESSEL INSPECTORS http://www.nationalboard.org

NATIONAL BOARD TECHNICAL SCHOLARSHIP
• *See page 161*

NATIONAL SOCIETY OF PROFESSIONAL ENGINEERS http://www.nspe.org

MAUREEN L. AND HOWARD N. BLITMAN, PE SCHOLARSHIP TO PROMOTE DIVERSITY IN ENGINEERING
• *See page 161*

PAUL H. ROBBINS HONORARY SCHOLARSHIP
• *See page 162*

PROFESSIONAL ENGINEERS IN INDUSTRY SCHOLARSHIP
• *See page 162*

OREGON STUDENT ASSISTANCE COMMISSION http://www.osac.state.or.us

AMERICAN COUNCIL OF ENGINEERING COMPANIES OF OREGON SCHOLARSHIP
• *See page 162*

PLUMBING-HEATING-COOLING CONTRACTORS ASSOCIATION EDUCATION FOUNDATION http://www.phccweb.org

BRADFORD WHITE CORPORATION SCHOLARSHIP
• *See page 92*

DELTA FAUCET COMPANY SCHOLARSHIP PROGRAM
• *See page 93*

PHCC EDUCATIONAL FOUNDATION NEED-BASED SCHOLARSHIP
• *See page 93*

PHCC EDUCATIONAL FOUNDATION SCHOLARSHIP PROGRAM
• *See page 147*

PROFESSIONAL CONSTRUCTION ESTIMATORS ASSOCIATION http://www.pcea.org

TED WILSON MEMORIAL SCHOLARSHIP FOUNDATION
• *See page 214*

ROBERT H. MOLLOHAN FAMILY CHARITABLE FOUNDATION INC. http://www.mollohanfoundation.org

HIGH TECHNOLOGY SCHOLARS PROGRAM
• *See page 135*

SIGMA XI, THE SCIENTIFIC RESEARCH SOCIETY http://www.sigmaxi.org

SIGMA XI GRANTS-IN-AID OF RESEARCH
• *See page 78*

SOCIETY OF AUTOMOTIVE ENGINEERS http://www.sae.org

BMW/SAE ENGINEERING SCHOLARSHIP
• See page 124

DETROIT SECTION SAE TECHNICAL SCHOLARSHIP
• See page 296

EDWARD D. HENDRICKSON/SAE ENGINEERING SCHOLARSHIP
• See page 124

RALPH K. HILLQUIST HONORARY SAE SCHOLARSHIP
• See page 296

TMC/SAE DONALD D. DAWSON TECHNICAL SCHOLARSHIP
• See page 124

YANMAR/SAE SCHOLARSHIP
• See page 297

SOCIETY OF HISPANIC PROFESSIONAL ENGINEERS FOUNDATION http://www.henaac.org

SOCIETY OF HISPANIC PROFESSIONAL ENGINEERS FOUNDATION
• See page 162

SOCIETY OF MANUFACTURING ENGINEERS EDUCATION FOUNDATION http://www.sme.org/foundation

CHAPTER 4-LAWRENCE A. WACKER MEMORIAL SCHOLARSHIP
• See page 273

CHAPTER 198-DOWNRIVER DETROIT SCHOLARSHIP
• See page 274

CHAPTER 67-PHOENIX SCHOLARSHIP
• See page 274

FORT WAYNE CHAPTER 56 SCHOLARSHIP
• See page 277

NORTH CENTRAL REGION 9 SCHOLARSHIP
• See page 278

WICHITA CHAPTER 52 SCHOLARSHIP
• See page 278

WILLIAM E. WEISEL SCHOLARSHIP FUND
• See page 251

SOCIETY OF WOMEN ENGINEERS http://www.swe.org

AGILENT MENTORING SCHOLARSHIP
• See page 194

ANNE MAUREEN WHITNEY BARROW MEMORIAL SCHOLARSHIP
• See page 173

BECHTEL CORPORATION SCHOLARSHIP
• See page 173

CATERPILLAR INC. SCHOLARSHIP
• See page 79

CHEVRON TEXACO CORPORATION SCHOLARSHIPS
• See page 163

DAIMLER CHRYSLER CORPORATION SCHOLARSHIP
• See page 251

DELL COMPUTER CORPORATION SCHOLARSHIPS
• See page 195

DOROTHY LEMKE HOWARTH SCHOLARSHIPS
• See page 163

DUPONT COMPANY SCHOLARSHIPS
• See page 164

GENERAL ELECTRIC FOUNDATION SCHOLARSHIP
• See page 164

GENERAL MOTORS FOUNDATION UNDERGRADUATE SCHOLARSHIPS
• See page 251

GUIDANT CORPORATION SCHOLARSHIP
• See page 195

LILLIAN MOLLER GILBRETH MEMORIAL SCHOLARSHIP
• See page 164

LOCKHEED MARTIN AERONAUTICS COMPANY SCHOLARSHIPS
• See page 252

MASWE MEMORIAL SCHOLARSHIP
• See page 164

NORTHROP GRUMMAN FRESHMAN SCHOLARSHIP
• See page 125

ROCKWELL AUTOMATION SCHOLARSHIP
• See page 195

SOCIETY OF WOMEN ENGINEERS-ROCKY MOUNTAIN SECTION http://www.swe-rms.org

SOCIETY OF WOMEN ENGINEERS-ROCKY MOUNTAIN SECTION SCHOLARSHIP PROGRAM
• See page 164

STRAIGHTFORWARD MEDIA http://www.straightforwardmedia.com

STRAIGHTFORWARD MEDIA ENGINEERING SCHOLARSHIP
• See page 164

TURNER CONSTRUCTION COMPANY http://www.turnerconstruction.com

YOUTHFORCE 2020 SCHOLARSHIP PROGRAM
• See page 93

UNITED NEGRO COLLEGE FUND http://www.uncf.org

CARDINAL HEALTH SCHOLARSHIP
• See page 65

CARGILL SCHOLARSHIP PROGRAM
• See page 65

CDM SCHOLARSHIP/INTERNSHIP
• See page 93

MEDTRONIC FOUNDATION SCHOLARSHIP
• See page 136

NASCAR/WENDELL SCOTT, SR. SCHOLARSHIP
• See page 66

SPRINT NEXTEL SCHOLARSHIP/INTERNSHIP
• See page 66

TOYOTA SCHOLARSHIP
• See page 66

UPS/UNCF CORPORATE SCHOLARS PROGRAM
• See page 151

WEYERHAEUSER/UNCF CORPORATE SCHOLARS PROGRAM
• See page 151

UNIVERSITIES SPACE RESEARCH ASSOCIATION http://www.usra.edu

UNIVERSITIES SPACE RESEARCH ASSOCIATION SCHOLARSHIP PROGRAM
• See page 88

UTAH SOCIETY OF PROFESSIONAL ENGINEERS http://www.uspeonline.com

UTAH SOCIETY OF PROFESSIONAL ENGINEERS JOE RHOADS SCHOLARSHIP
• See page 165

VERTICAL FLIGHT FOUNDATION http://www.vtol.org

VERTICAL FLIGHT FOUNDATION SCHOLARSHIP
• *See page 126*

WOMEN IN AVIATION, INTERNATIONAL http://www.wai.org

DELTA AIR LINES ENGINEERING SCHOLARSHIP
• *See page 127*

XEROX http://www.xerox.com

TECHNICAL MINORITY SCHOLARSHIP
• *See page 165*

METEOROLOGY/ATMOSPHERIC SCIENCE

AMERICAN GEOLOGICAL INSTITUTE http://www.agiweb.org

AMERICAN GEOLOGICAL INSTITUTE MINORITY SCHOLARSHIP
• *See page 215*

AMERICAN INDIAN SCIENCE AND ENGINEERING SOCIETY http://www.aises.org

A.T. ANDERSON MEMORIAL SCHOLARSHIP PROGRAM
• *See page 84*

BURLINGTON NORTHERN SANTA FE FOUNDATION SCHOLARSHIP
• *See page 84*

AMERICAN METEOROLOGICAL SOCIETY http://www.ametsoc.org

AMERICAN METEOROLOGICAL SOCIETY DR. PEDRO GRAU UNDERGRADUATE SCHOLARSHIP
• *See page 360*

AMERICAN METEOROLOGICAL SOCIETY HOWARD H. HANKS, JR. METEOROLOGICAL SCHOLARSHIP

Scholarship of $700 available for college or university student entering final year in undergraduate study. Applicant must be a major in a meteorology department or other department actively engaged in work on some aspect of the atmospheric sciences, and must intend to make atmospheric science his or her career. Must be enrolled full-time at a U.S. institution with a 3.25 minimum GPA. U.S. citizenship required.

Academic Fields/Career Goals: Meteorology/Atmospheric Science.

Award: Scholarship for use in senior year; not renewable. *Number:* 1. *Amount:* $700.

Eligibility Requirements: Applicant must be enrolled or expecting to enroll full-time at a four-year institution or university. Available to U.S. citizens.

Application Requirements: Application, essay, references, transcript. *Deadline:* varies.

Contact: Donna Fernandez, Development Program Coordinator
American Meteorological Society
45 Beacon Street
Boston, MA 02108-3693
Phone: 617-227-2426 Ext. 246
Fax: 617-742-8718
E-mail: dfernand@ametsoc.org

AMERICAN METEOROLOGICAL SOCIETY HOWARD T. ORVILLE METEOROLOGY SCHOLARSHIP

One-time award for full-time students entering their final year of undergraduate study. Must major in a meteorology department or other department actively engaged in work on some aspect of the atmospheric sciences, and must intend to make atmospheric science his or her career. Must be enrolled full-time at a U.S. institution with a minimum of 3.25 GPA. Must be U.S. citizen or permanent resident to apply.

Academic Fields/Career Goals: Meteorology/Atmospheric Science.

Award: Scholarship for use in senior year; not renewable. *Number:* varies. *Amount:* up to $5000.

Eligibility Requirements: Applicant must be enrolled or expecting to enroll full-time at a four-year institution or university. Applicant must have 3.5 GPA or higher. Available to U.S. citizens.

Application Requirements: Application, essay, references, transcript. *Deadline:* February 20.

Contact: Donna Fernandez, Development Program Coordinator
American Meteorological Society
45 Beacon Street
Boston, MA 02108-3693
Phone: 617-227-2426 Ext. 246
Fax: 617-742-8718
E-mail: dfernand@ametsoc.org

AMERICAN METEOROLOGICAL SOCIETY/INDUSTRY MINORITY SCHOLARSHIPS
• *See page 361*

AMERICAN METEOROLOGICAL SOCIETY MARK J. SCHROEDER SCHOLARSHIP IN METEOROLOGY
• *See page 361*

AMERICAN METEOROLOGICAL SOCIETY RICHARD AND HELEN HAGEMEYER SCHOLARSHIP
• *See page 361*

AMERICAN METEOROLOGICAL SOCIETY 75TH ANNIVERSARY SCHOLARSHIP
• *See page 361*

AMERICAN METEOROLOGICAL SOCIETY WERNER A. BAUM UNDERGRADUATE SCHOLARSHIP
• *See page 361*

AMS FRESHMAN UNDERGRADUATE SCHOLARSHIP
• *See page 300*

CARL W. KREITZBERG ENDOWED SCHOLARSHIP
• *See page 361*

ETHAN AND ALLAN MURPHY MEMORIAL SCHOLARSHIP
• *See page 362*

FATHER JAMES B. MACELWANE ANNUAL AWARDS

Available to enrolled undergraduates who submit a paper on a phase of atmospheric sciences with a statement from a supervisor on the student's original contribution to the work. Minimum 3.0 GPA required. No more than two students from any one institution may enter papers in one contest. Must submit letter from department head or faculty member confirming applicant's undergraduate status and paper's originality. Must be a U.S. citizen.

Academic Fields/Career Goals: Meteorology/Atmospheric Science.

Award: Prize for use in sophomore, junior, or senior years; not renewable. *Number:* 1. *Amount:* $1000.

Eligibility Requirements: Applicant must be enrolled or expecting to enroll full-time at a four-year institution or university. Applicant must have 3.0 GPA or higher. Available to U.S. citizens.

Application Requirements: Applicant must enter a contest, references, original copy of paper, letter of application from the author, letter from the department head, abstract of no more than 250 words. *Deadline:* June 13.

Contact: Donna Sampson, Development and Student Program Manager
American Meteorological Society
45 Beacon Street
Boston, MA 02108-3693
Phone: 617-227-2426 Ext. 246
Fax: 617-742-8718
E-mail: dfernand@ametsoc.org

GEORGE S. BENTON SCHOLARSHIP
• *See page 362*

GUILLERMO SALAZAR RODRIGUES SCHOLARSHIP
• *See page 362*

JOHN R. HOPE SCHOLARSHIP
• *See page 362*

LOREN W. CROW SCHOLARSHIP

• *See page 362*

OM AND SARASWATI BAHETHI SCHOLARSHIP

Assists full-time students pursuing degrees in the atmospheric and related sciences. Minimum GPA of 3.25 required.

Academic Fields/Career Goals: Meteorology/Atmospheric Science.

Award: Scholarship for use in junior or senior years; not renewable. *Number:* 1. *Amount:* up to $2000.

Eligibility Requirements: Applicant must be enrolled or expecting to enroll full-time at a two-year or four-year institution or university. Available to U.S. citizens.

Application Requirements: Application, essay, references, transcript. *Deadline:* February 10.

Contact: Donna Fernandez, Development Program Coordinator
American Meteorological Society
45 Beacon Street
Boston, MA 02108-3693
Phone: 617-227-2426 Ext. 246
Fax: 617-742-8718
E-mail: dfernand@ametsoc.org

ASSOCIATION FOR WOMEN IN SCIENCE EDUCATIONAL FOUNDATION http://www.awis.org/careers/edfoundation.html

ASSOCIATION FOR WOMEN IN SCIENCE COLLEGE SCHOLARSHIP

• *See page 82*

ASTRONAUT SCHOLARSHIP FOUNDATION http://www.astronautscholarship.org

ASTRONAUT SCHOLARSHIP FOUNDATION

• *See page 86*

ELECTROCHEMICAL SOCIETY INC. http://www.electrochem.org

H.H. DOW MEMORIAL STUDENT ACHIEVEMENT AWARD OF THE INDUSTRIAL ELECTROLYSIS AND ELECTROCHEMICAL ENGINEERING DIVISION OF THE ELECTROCHEMICAL SOCIETY INC.

• *See page 131*

STUDENT ACHIEVEMENT AWARDS OF THE INDUSTRIAL ELECTROLYSIS AND ELECTROCHEMICAL ENGINEERING DIVISION OF THE ELECTROCHEMICAL SOCIETY INC.

• *See page 131*

STUDENT RESEARCH AWARDS OF THE BATTERY DIVISION OF THE ELECTROCHEMICAL SOCIETY INC.

• *See page 131*

INNOVATION AND SCIENCE COUNCIL OF BRITISH COLUMBIA http://www.bcinnovationcouncil.com

PAUL AND HELEN TRUSSEL SCIENCE AND TECHNOLOGY SCHOLARSHIP

• *See page 87*

NASA DELAWARE SPACE GRANT CONSORTIUM http://www.delspace.org

NASA DELAWARE SPACE GRANT UNDERGRADUATE TUITION SCHOLARSHIP

• *See page 87*

NASA RHODE ISLAND SPACE GRANT CONSORTIUM http://www.planetary.brown.edu/RI_Space_Grant

NASA RHODE ISLAND SPACE GRANT CONSORTIUM UNDERGRADUATE RESEARCH SCHOLARSHIP

• *See page 119*

NASA VERMONT SPACE GRANT CONSORTIUM http://www.cems.uvm.edu/VSGC

VERMONT SPACE GRANT CONSORTIUM SCHOLARSHIP PROGRAM

• *See page 88*

NASA WEST VIRGINIA SPACE GRANT CONSORTIUM http://www.nasa.wvu.edu

WEST VIRGINIA SPACE GRANT CONSORTIUM UNDERGRADUATE FELLOWSHIP PROGRAM

• *See page 121*

SIGMA XI, THE SCIENTIFIC RESEARCH SOCIETY http://www.sigmaxi.org

SIGMA XI GRANTS-IN-AID OF RESEARCH

• *See page 78*

TKE EDUCATIONAL FOUNDATION http://www.tke.org

CARROL C. HALL MEMORIAL SCHOLARSHIP

• *See page 88*

MILITARY AND DEFENSE STUDIES

INDEPENDENT COLLEGE FUND OF MARYLAND (I-FUND) http://www.i-fundinfo.org

NATIONAL SECURITY SCHOLARS PROGRAM

Program offers $15,000, assistance with national security clearance processing, paid summer internships with government and private industry plus the opportunity for job placement following graduation. Program is open to students with outstanding academic records.

Academic Fields/Career Goals: Military and Defense Studies.

Award: Scholarship for use in freshman, sophomore, junior, or senior years; not renewable. *Number:* 1. *Amount:* $15,000.

Eligibility Requirements: Applicant must be enrolled or expecting to enroll full-time at a four-year institution or university. Available to U.S. citizens.

Application Requirements: Application, test scores, transcript. *Deadline:* October 1.

Contact: Lori Subotich, Director of Programs and Scholarships
Independent College Fund of Maryland (I-Fund)
3225 Ellerslie Avenue, Suite C160
Baltimore, MD 21218-3519
Phone: 443-997-5700
Fax: 443-997-2740
E-mail: lsubot@jhmi.edu

NATIONAL MILITARY INTELLIGENCE ASSOCIATION http://www.nmia.org

NATIONAL MILITARY INTELLIGENCE ASSOCIATION SCHOLARSHIP

Scholarships to support the growth of professional studies in the field of military intelligence and to recognize and reward excellence in the development and transfer of knowledge about military and associated intelligence disciplines.

Academic Fields/Career Goals: Military and Defense Studies.

Award: Scholarship for use in freshman, sophomore, junior, or senior years; not renewable. *Number:* 3. *Amount:* $1000.

Eligibility Requirements: Applicant must be enrolled or expecting to enroll full-time at a four-year institution or university. Applicant or parent of applicant must be member of National Military Intelligence Association. Applicant must have 3.0 GPA or higher. Available to U.S. citizens.

Application Requirements: Application, test scores. *Deadline:* August 1.

Contact: Debra Davis, Director of Business development
National Military Intelligence Association
PO Box 479
Hamilton, VA 20159
Phone: 540-338-1143
Fax: 703-738-7487
E-mail: nmiassoc@comcast.net

UNITED STATES MARINE CORPS HISTORICAL CENTER http://www.history.usmc.mil

U.S. MARINE CORPS HISTORICAL CENTER GRANTS
• See page 349

WOMEN IN DEFENSE (WID), A NATIONAL SECURITY ORGANIZATION http://wid.ndia.org

HORIZONS FOUNDATION SCHOLARSHIP

Scholarships awarded to provide financial assistance to further educational objectives of women either currently employed in, or planning careers in, defense or national security arenas (not law enforcement or criminal justice). Must be U.S. citizen. Minimum 3.5 GPA required.

Academic Fields/Career Goals: Military and Defense Studies.

Award: Scholarship for use in junior, senior, graduate, or postgraduate years; renewable. *Number:* 5–10. *Amount:* $500–$1000.

Eligibility Requirements: Applicant must be enrolled or expecting to enroll full-time at a four-year institution or university and female. Applicant must have 3.5 GPA or higher. Available to U.S. citizens.

Application Requirements: Application, essay, financial need analysis, references, self-addressed stamped envelope, transcript. *Deadline:* July 1.

Contact: Jane Patrick Casey, Director
Women in Defense (WID), A National Security Organization
2111 Wilson Boulevard, Suite 400
Arlington, VA 22201-3061
Phone: 703-247-2564
Fax: 703-522-1885
E-mail: wid@ndia.org

MUSEUM STUDIES

AMERICAN SCHOOL OF CLASSICAL STUDIES AT ATHENS http://www.ascsa.edu.gr

ASCSA SUMMER SESSIONS OPEN SCHOLARSHIPS
• See page 83

COSTUME SOCIETY OF AMERICA http://www.costumesocietyamerica.com

ADELE FILENE TRAVEL AWARD
• See page 95

STELLA BLUM RESEARCH GRANT
• See page 95

MUSIC

AMERICAN COLLEGE OF MUSICIANS/NATIONAL GUILD OF PIANO TEACHERS http://www.pianoguild.com

AMERICAN COLLEGE OF MUSICIANS/NATIONAL GUILD OF PIANO TEACHERS $200 SCHOLARSHIPS

Award available only to student affiliate members who have participated in National Guild of Piano Teachers auditions over a ten-year period. Must be Paderewski Medal winner and be sponsored by Guild member. Contact American College of Musicians for more information.

Academic Fields/Career Goals: Music.

Award: Scholarship for use in freshman, sophomore, junior, or senior years; not renewable. *Number:* up to 150. *Amount:* $200.

Eligibility Requirements: Applicant must be enrolled or expecting to enroll full-time at a two-year or four-year or technical institution or university and must have an interest in music. Applicant or parent of applicant must be member of American College of Musicians. Available to U.S. and non-U.S. citizens.

Application Requirements: Application, test scores. *Deadline:* September 15.

Contact: Scholarship Committee
American College of Musicians/National Guild of Piano Teachers
PO Box 1807
Austin, TX 78767-1807

AMERICAN COUNCIL FOR POLISH CULTURE http://www.polishcultureacpc.org

MARCELLA KOCHANSKA SEMBRICH VOCAL COMPETITION

Prize of $1500 given to high school graduates, male or female up to the age of 35 years who have pursued or are currently pursuing higher education study in voice or in the early stage of their vocal career. Contestant must be a U.S. citizen of Polish descent.

Academic Fields/Career Goals: Music.

Award: Prize for use in freshman, sophomore, junior, senior, or graduate years; renewable. *Number:* 1. *Amount:* $1500.

Eligibility Requirements: Applicant must be of Polish heritage; age 35 or under; enrolled or expecting to enroll full- or part-time at a two-year or four-year institution or university and must have an interest in music/singing. Available to U.S. citizens.

Application Requirements: Application, applicant must enter a contest, 3 copies of a cassette or CD containing applicant's operatic vocal performance. *Deadline:* April 1.

Contact: Mr. Jaroslaw Golembiowski, ACPC Music Committee Chair
American Council for Polish Culture
1532 N. Artesian
Chicago, IL 60622-1750
Phone: 773-862-4686
E-mail: yaromusic@dsl.polel.us

AMERICAN FOUNDATION FOR THE BLIND http://www.afb.org

R.L. GILLETTE SCHOLARSHIP
• See page 389

AMERICAN LEGION DEPARTMENT OF KANSAS http://www.ksamlegion.org

MUSIC COMMITTEE SCHOLARSHIP

One-time award open to a high school senior or college freshman or sophomore. Must be a Kansas resident. Must have distinguished background in the field of music at an approved Kansas junior college, college or university. Award of $1000, with the disbursement as $500 award for each of the two semesters.

Academic Fields/Career Goals: Music; Performing Arts.

Award: Scholarship for use in freshman or sophomore years; not renewable. *Number:* 1. *Amount:* $1000.

Eligibility Requirements: Applicant must be enrolled or expecting to enroll full-time at a two-year or four-year or technical institution or university; resident of Kansas; studying in Kansas and must have an interest in music/singing. Available to U.S. citizens.

Application Requirements: Application, financial need analysis, photo, references, transcript, latest 1040 income statement of supporting parents. *Deadline:* February 15.

Contact: Jim Gravenstein, Chairman, Scholarship Committee
American Legion Department of Kansas
1314 Topeka Boulevard, SW
Topeka, KS 66612
Phone: 785-232-9315
Fax: 782-232-1399

BALTIMORE CHAPTER OF THE AMERICAN MARKETING ASSOCIATION http://www.amabaltimore.org

UNDERGRADUATE MARKETING EDUCATION MERIT SCHOLARSHIPS
• See page 138

BMI FOUNDATION INC. http://www.bmifoundation.org

BMI STUDENT COMPOSER AWARDS

• *See page 100*

JOHN LENNON SCHOLARSHIP PROGRAM

Scholarships available to songwriters and composers from music schools, universities, and youth orchestras. Also submissions from the Music Educators National Conference are solicited. The submitted work must be an original song with lyrics accompanied by whatever instrumentation is chosen by the applicant.

Academic Fields/Career Goals: Music.

Award: Scholarship for use in freshman, sophomore, junior, senior, graduate, or postgraduate years; not renewable. *Number:* up to 3. *Amount:* $5000–$10,000.

Eligibility Requirements: Applicant must be age 15-24; enrolled or expecting to enroll full- or part-time at a two-year or four-year or technical institution or university and must have an interest in music. Available to U.S. citizens.

Application Requirements: Application, applicant must enter a contest, CD or audio tape of a song written by the applicant with original words and music, three typed copies of the lyric. *Deadline:* January 26.

Contact: Mr. Ralph N. Jackson, President
BMI Foundation Inc.
320 West 57th Street
New York, NY 10019
Phone: 212-586-2000
Fax: 212-245-8986
E-mail: info@bmifoundation.org

PEERMUSIC LATIN SCHOLARSHIP

Award for the best song or instrumental work in any Latin genre. The competition is open to songwriters and composers betweent the ages of 16 and 24 who are current students at colleges and universities. Must submit an original work. Applicants must not have had any musical work commercially recorded or distributed.

Academic Fields/Career Goals: Music.

Award: Scholarship for use in freshman, sophomore, junior, senior, graduate, or postgraduate years; not renewable. *Number:* 1. *Amount:* up to $5000.

Eligibility Requirements: Applicant must be age 16-24; enrolled or expecting to enroll full-time at a two-year or four-year or technical institution or university and must have an interest in music. Available to U.S. citizens.

Application Requirements: Application, applicant must enter a contest, CD of original song or instrumental work, three typed lyric sheets. *Deadline:* varies.

Contact: Mr. Ralph N. Jackson, President
BMI Foundation Inc.
320 West 57th Street
New York, NY 10019
Phone: 212-586-2000
Fax: 212-245-8986
E-mail: rjackson@bmi.com

CHOPIN FOUNDATION OF THE UNITED STATES http://www.chopin.org

CHOPIN FOUNDATION OF THE UNITED STATES SCHOLARSHIP

Program aimed to help young American pianists to continue their piano education. Award(s) are available to students between ages 14 and 17 whose field of study is music and whose major is piano. Renewable for up to four years. Students will be assisted in preparing to qualify for the American National Chopin Piano Competition. Must be U.S. citizen or legal resident.

Academic Fields/Career Goals: Music; Performing Arts.

Award: Scholarship for use in freshman, sophomore, junior, or senior years; renewable. *Number:* 10. *Amount:* $1000.

Eligibility Requirements: Applicant must be age 14-17; enrolled or expecting to enroll full- or part-time at a four-year institution or university and must have an interest in music. Available to U.S. citizens.

Application Requirements: Application, applicant must enter a contest, references, 20- to 30-minute DVD of Chopin work. *Fee:* $25. *Deadline:* February 15.

Contact: Jadwiga Gewert, Executive Director
Chopin Foundation of the United States
1440 79th Street Causeway, Suite 117
Miami, FL 33141
Phone: 305-868-0624
Fax: 305-865-5150
E-mail: info@chopin.org

COLLEGEBOUND FOUNDATION http://www.collegeboundfoundation.org

JANET B. SONDHEIM SCHOLARSHIP

• *See page 100*

COMMUNITY FOUNDATION FOR GREATER ATLANTA INC. http://www.atlcf.org

JAMES M. AND VIRGINIA M. SMYTH SCHOLARSHIP

• *See page 101*

DAVIDSON INSTITUTE FOR TALENT DEVELOPMENT http://www.davidsoninstitute.org

DAVIDSON FELLOWS

• *See page 390*

DAYTON FOUNDATION http://www.daytonfoundation.org

MU PHI EPSILON SCHOLARSHIP FUND

Scholarship to assist individuals in furthering their music studies. Should be enrolled full-time at Wright State University, University of Dayton, Central State University, Sinclair Community College, Wilberforce University or Cedarville University.

Academic Fields/Career Goals: Music.

Award: Scholarship for use in sophomore or junior years; not renewable. *Number:* 1. *Amount:* up to $1000.

Eligibility Requirements: Applicant must be enrolled or expecting to enroll full-time at a two-year or four-year institution or university and studying in Ohio. Applicant must have 3.0 GPA or higher. Available to U.S. citizens.

Application Requirements: Application, essay, references, transcript. *Deadline:* March 3.

Contact: Diane Timmons, Director Grants and Programs
Dayton Foundation
2300 Kettering Tower
Dayton, OH 45423
Phone: 937-225-9966
E-mail: dtimmons@daytonfoundation.org

DELTA OMICRON INTERNATIONAL MUSIC FRATERNITY/DELTA OMICRON FOUNDATION INC. http://www.delta-omicron.org

DELTA OMICRON FROUNDATION EDUCATIONAL GRANTS IN MUSIC

Grants available to those studying music at a four-year college or university. Must have a minimum 2.5 GPA. Must be a member of Delta Omicron International Music Fraternity.

Academic Fields/Career Goals: Music.

Award: Grant for use in freshman, sophomore, junior, senior, or graduate years; not renewable. *Number:* 10–20. *Amount:* $500.

Eligibility Requirements: Applicant must be enrolled or expecting to enroll full- or part-time at a four-year institution or university and must have an interest in music. Applicant must have 2.5 GPA or higher. Available to U.S. and non-U.S. citizens.

Delta Omicron International Music Fraternity/Delta Omicron Foundation Inc. (continued)

Application Requirements: Application, resume, references. *Deadline:* April 30.

Contact: Kay C. Wideman, President
Delta Omicron International Music Fraternity/Delta Omicron Foundation Inc.
503 Greystone Lane
Douglasville, GA 30134
Phone: 770-920-2417
Fax: 770-577-5863
E-mail: widemans@bellsouth.net

DELTA OMICRON SUMMER SCHOLARSHIPS

Scholarships awarded to assist with summer study in the area of music for summer workshops, seminars, study abroad. Award cannot be used for college tuition.

Academic Fields/Career Goals: Music.

Award: Scholarship for use in freshman, sophomore, junior, senior, graduate, or postgraduate years; not renewable. *Number:* 8. *Amount:* $400–$500.

Eligibility Requirements: Applicant must be enrolled or expecting to enroll part-time at a four-year institution or university and must have an interest in music. Available to U.S. and non-U.S. citizens.

Application Requirements: Application. *Deadline:* April 2.

Contact: Ms. Michelle A. May, Chair, Summer Scholarships
Delta Omicron International Music Fraternity/Delta Omicron Foundation Inc.
1635 West Boston Boulevard
Detroit, MI 48206
Phone: 313-865-1149
E-mail: maybiz@aol.com

DOMENIC TROIANO GUITAR SCHOLARSHIP http://www.domenictroiano.com

DOMENIC TROIANO GUITAR SCHOLARSHIP

Scholarship of $3000 is presented annually to a Canadian guitarist who will be pursuing postsecondary guitar education in Canada or elsewhere. Any university, college or private institution guitar program will be funded. Funds will be forwarded directly to the chosen institution of the winner. Must submit a one-page letter outlining background and reasons why applicant should be considered for the scholarship.

Academic Fields/Career Goals: Music.

Award: Scholarship for use in freshman, sophomore, junior, senior, graduate, or postgraduate years; not renewable. *Number:* up to 2. *Amount:* $3000.

Eligibility Requirements: Applicant must be Canadian citizen; enrolled or expecting to enroll full-time at a four-year institution or university and must have an interest in music.

Application Requirements: References, two-song demo of the applicant playing guitar. *Deadline:* October 31.

Contact: Clinton Somerton, Administrator
Domenic Troiano Guitar Scholarship
18 Sherbourne Street
Toronto, ON M5A 2R2
Canada
Phone: 416-367-0178
Fax: 416-367-0178
E-mail: clinton@domenictroiano.com

GENERAL FEDERATION OF WOMEN'S CLUBS OF MASSACHUSETTS http://www.gfwcma.org

DORCHESTER WOMEN'S CLUB MUSIC SCHOLARSHIP

Scholarship for undergraduate major in voice. Applicant must be a Massachusetts resident and an undergraduate currently enrolled in a four-year accredited college, university or school of music, majoring in voice.

Academic Fields/Career Goals: Music; Performing Arts.

Award: Scholarship for use in freshman, sophomore, junior, or senior years; not renewable. *Number:* 1. *Amount:* $500.

Eligibility Requirements: Applicant must be enrolled or expecting to enroll full-time at a four-year institution or university; resident of Massachusetts and must have an interest in music/singing. Available to U.S. and Canadian citizens.

Application Requirements: Application, applicant must enter a contest, autobiography, interview, references, self-addressed stamped envelope, transcript. *Deadline:* March 1.

Contact: Joan Korslund, Music Chairman
General Federation of Women's Clubs of Massachusetts
25 Apple Lane
Wrentham, MA 02093
E-mail: nonnalda@aol.com

GENERAL FEDERATION OF WOMEN'S CLUBS OF MASSACHUSETTS NICKEL FOR NOTES MUSIC SCHOLARSHIP

Scholarship for high school seniors majoring in piano, instrument, music education, music therapy or voice. Applicant must be a senior in a Massachusetts High School.

Academic Fields/Career Goals: Music; Performing Arts.

Award: Scholarship for use in freshman year; not renewable. *Number:* varies. *Amount:* up to $800.

Eligibility Requirements: Applicant must be high school student; planning to enroll or expecting to enroll full-time at a four-year institution or university; resident of Massachusetts and must have an interest in music/singing. Available to U.S. citizens.

Application Requirements: Application, essay, interview, references, self-addressed stamped envelope, transcript. *Deadline:* March 1.

Contact: Joan Korslund, Music Chairman
General Federation of Women's Clubs of Massachusetts
25 Apple Lane
Wrentham, MA 02093
E-mail: nonnalda@aol.com

GRAND RAPIDS COMMUNITY FOUNDATION http://www.grfoundation.org

LLEWELLYN L. CAYVAN STRING INSTRUMENT SCHOLARSHIP

Scholarship for undergraduate students studying the violin, the viola, the violoncello, and/or the bass viol. High school students not considered. To apply, submit required application form, transcript, essay, and reference.

Academic Fields/Career Goals: Music.

Award: Scholarship for use in freshman, sophomore, junior, or senior years; not renewable. *Number:* 6. *Amount:* $1000.

Eligibility Requirements: Applicant must be enrolled or expecting to enroll full-time at a four-year institution or university and must have an interest in music. Available to U.S. citizens.

Application Requirements: Application, references, transcript. *Deadline:* April 1.

Contact: Ruth Bishop, Education Program Officer
Grand Rapids Community Foundation
161 Ottawa Avenue, NW, 209 C
Grand Rapids, MI 49503-2757
Phone: 616-454-1751 Ext. 103
Fax: 616-454-6455
E-mail: rbishop@grfoundation.org

HAPCO MUSIC FOUNDATION INC. http://www.hapcopromo.org

TRADITIONAL MARCHING BAND EXTRAVAGANZA SCHOLARSHIP AWARD

Scholarship is offered to deserving students who will continue their participation in any college music program. Minimum 3.0 GPA required. Applicant should have best composite score of 970 SAT or 20 ACT.

Academic Fields/Career Goals: Music.

Award: Scholarship for use in freshman year; not renewable. *Number:* varies. *Amount:* $250–$1000.

Eligibility Requirements: Applicant must be enrolled or expecting to enroll full-time at a two-year or four-year institution or university and must have an interest in music. Applicant must have 3.0 GPA or higher. Available to U.S. citizens.

Application Requirements: Application, essay, photo, references, test scores, transcript. *Deadline:* varies.

Contact: Joseph McMullen, President
HapCo Music Foundation Inc.
PO Box 784581
Winter Garden, FL 34778-4581
Phone: 407-877-2262
Fax: 407-654-0308
E-mail: hapcopromo@aol.com

HARTFORD JAZZ SOCIETY INC. http://www.hartfordjazzsociety.com

HARTFORD JAZZ SOCIETY SCHOLARSHIPS

Scholarship of up to $3000 is awarded to graduating high school senior attending a four-year college or university. Must be a Connecticut resident. Music major with interest in jazz required.

Academic Fields/Career Goals: Music.

Award: Scholarship for use in freshman year; not renewable. *Number:* 2–3. *Amount:* up to $3000.

Eligibility Requirements: Applicant must be high school student; planning to enroll or expecting to enroll full- or part-time at a four-year institution or university; resident of Connecticut and must have an interest in music. Available to U.S. and Canadian citizens.

Application Requirements: Application, references, cassette tape or CD. *Deadline:* May 1.

Contact: Scholarship Committee Chair
Hartford Jazz Society Inc.
116 Cottage Grove Road
Bloomfield, CT 06002
Phone: 860-242-6688
Fax: 860-243-8871
E-mail: hartjazzsocinc@aol.com

HISPANIC SCHOLARSHIP FUND http://www.hsf.net

HSF/MCNAMARA FAMILY CREATIVE ARTS PROJECT GRANT

• *See page 98*

HOUSTON SYMPHONY http://www.houstonsymphony.org

HOUSTON SYMPHONY IMA HOGG YOUNG ARTIST COMPETITION

Competition for musicians ages 16 to 29 who play standard instruments of the symphony orchestra. Goal is to offer a review by panel of music professionals and further career of an advanced student or a professional musician. Participants must be U.S. citizens or studying in the United States. Application fee is $30.

Academic Fields/Career Goals: Music.

Award: Prize for use in freshman, sophomore, junior, senior, graduate, or postgraduate years; not renewable. *Number:* 4. *Amount:* $500–$5000.

Eligibility Requirements: Applicant must be age 16-29; enrolled or expecting to enroll full-time at a two-year or four-year or technical institution or university and must have an interest in music. Available to U.S. and non-U.S. citizens.

Application Requirements: Application, applicant must enter a contest, CD with required repertoire. *Fee:* $30. *Deadline:* February 9.

Contact: Carol Wilson, Education Coordinator
Houston Symphony
615 Louisiana Street, Suite 102
Houston, TX 77002
Phone: 713-238-1447
Fax: 713-224-0453
E-mail: e&o@houstonsymphony.org

HOUSTON SYMPHONY LEAGUE CONCERTO COMPETITION

Competition is open to student musicians 18 years of age or younger, who have not yet graduated from high school, and who play any standard orchestral instrument or piano. Must live within a 150-mile radius of Houston and submit a screening CD or tape of one movement of their concerto.

Academic Fields/Career Goals: Music.

Award: Prize for use in freshman year; not renewable. *Number:* up to 3. *Amount:* $250–$1000.

Eligibility Requirements: Applicant must be high school student; age 18 or under; planning to enroll or expecting to enroll full- or part-time at a four-year institution or university; resident of Texas and must have an interest in music. Available to U.S. citizens.

Application Requirements: Application, applicant must enter a contest, references, CD. *Fee:* $25. *Deadline:* November 18.

Contact: Carol Wilson, Education Coordinator
Houston Symphony
615 Louisiana Street, Suite 102
Houston, TX 77002
Phone: 713-238-1449
Fax: 713-224-0453
E-mail: e&o@houstonsymphony.org

JACK J. ISGUR FOUNDATION

JACK J. ISGUR FOUNDATION SCHOLARSHIP

• *See page 102*

KE ALI'I PAUAHI FOUNDATION http://www.pauahi.org

EDWIN MAHIAI COPP BEAMER SCHOLARSHIP

Award supports a post-secondary student pursuing a career in music, specifically piano and/or voice, with emphasis on Hawaiian music, opera or musical theatre. Must demonstrate a serious commitment to music training, a career in music and dedication to artistic excellence, and demonstrate financial need.

Academic Fields/Career Goals: Music; Performing Arts.

Award: Scholarship for use in freshman, sophomore, junior, senior, graduate, or postgraduate years; not renewable. *Number:* 1. *Amount:* $1000.

Eligibility Requirements: Applicant must be enrolled or expecting to enroll full-time at a two-year or four-year or technical institution or university and must have an interest in Hawaiian language/culture, music, or music/singing. Available to U.S. citizens.

Application Requirements: Application, essay, financial need analysis, transcript, college acceptance letter, printed signature confirmation page, copy of completed SAR. *Deadline:* May 2.

Contact: Elizabeth Stevenson, Development Manager
Ke Ali'i Pauahi Foundation
567 South King Street, Suite 160
Honolulu, HI 96813
Phone: 808-534-3966
Fax: 808-534-3890
E-mail: scholarships@pauahi.org

KOSCIUSZKO FOUNDATION http://www.kosciuszkofoundation.org

KOSCIUSZKO FOUNDATION CHOPIN PIANO COMPETITION

Three awards for students majoring or planning to major in piano studies, who are between the ages of 16 and 22. Application fee: $50. Must be U.S. citizen or full-time international student in the United States with valid visa.

Academic Fields/Career Goals: Music; Performing Arts.

Award: Prize for use in freshman, sophomore, junior, or senior years; not renewable. *Number:* 3. *Amount:* $1500–$5000.

Eligibility Requirements: Applicant must be age 16-22; enrolled or expecting to enroll full- or part-time at a four-year institution or university and must have an interest in music/singing. Available to U.S. and non-U.S. citizens.

Application Requirements: Application, applicant must enter a contest, photo, resume, references, proof of age. *Fee:* $50. *Deadline:* March 7.

Contact: Tom Pniewski, Director of Cultural Programs
Kosciuszko Foundation
15 East 65th Street
New York, NY 10021-6595
Phone: 212-734-2130
Fax: 212-628-4552
E-mail: tompkf@aol.com

MELLON NEW ENGLAND http://www.mellon.com

SUSAN GLOVER HITCHCOCK SCHOLARSHIP

Award for women who are majoring in music. Must be a Massachusetts resident. Eligible applicant must be recommended by educational institution. Not for graduate study programs.

Academic Fields/Career Goals: Music.

Award: Scholarship for use in freshman, sophomore, junior, or senior years; not renewable. *Number:* varies. *Amount:* up to $2000.

Eligibility Requirements: Applicant must be enrolled or expecting to enroll full-time at a two-year or four-year or technical institution or university; female and resident of Massachusetts. Available to U.S. citizens.

Application Requirements: Application, essay, transcript. *Deadline:* April 15.

Contact: Sandra Brown-McMullen, Vice President
Mellon New England
1 Boston Place, 024-0084
Boston, MA 02108
Phone: 617-722-3891
E-mail: brown-mcmullen.s@mellon.com

NATIONAL ASSOCIATION OF PASTORAL MUSICIANS http://www.npm.org

DAN SCHUTTE SCHOLARSHIP

Scholarship for NPM members enrolled full-or part-time in an undergraduate or graduate pastoral music program. Applicant must intend to work at least two years in the field of pastoral music following graduation/program completion.

Academic Fields/Career Goals: Music.

Award: Scholarship for use in freshman, sophomore, junior, senior, or graduate years; not renewable. *Number:* varies. *Amount:* $1000.

Eligibility Requirements: Applicant must be enrolled or expecting to enroll full- or part-time at a two-year or four-year institution or university and must have an interest in music/singing. Applicant or parent of applicant must be member of National Association of Pastoral Musicians. Available to U.S. and non-U.S. citizens.

Application Requirements: Application, essay, financial need analysis, resume, references, tape of performance. *Deadline:* March 7.

Contact: Kathleen Haley, Director of Membership Services
National Association of Pastoral Musicians
962 Wayne Avenue, Suite 210
Silver Spring, MD 20910-4461
Phone: 240-247-3000
Fax: 240-247-3001
E-mail: haley@npm.org

ELAINE RENDLER-RENE DOSOGNE-GEORGETOWN CHORALE SCHOLARSHIP

Awards NPM members enrolled full-time or part-time in a graduate or undergraduate degree program of studies related to the field of pastoral music. Applicant must intend to work at least two years in the field of pastoral music following graduation or program completion.

Academic Fields/Career Goals: Music; Religion/Theology.

Award: Scholarship for use in freshman, sophomore, junior, senior, or graduate years; not renewable. *Number:* 1. *Amount:* $1000.

Eligibility Requirements: Applicant must be enrolled or expecting to enroll full- or part-time at a two-year or four-year institution or university and must have an interest in music/singing. Applicant or parent of applicant must be member of National Association of Pastoral Musicians. Available to U.S. and non-U.S. citizens.

Application Requirements: Application, essay, financial need analysis, resume, references, tape of performance. *Deadline:* March 7.

Contact: J. Michael McMahon, President
National Association of Pastoral Musicians
962 Wayne Avenue, Suite 210
Silver Spring, MD 20910
Phone: 240-247-3000
Fax: 240-247-3001
E-mail: npmsing@npm.org

FUNK FAMILY MEMORIAL SCHOLARSHIP

Awards NPM members enrolled full-time or part-time in a graduate or undergraduate degree program of studies related to the field of pastoral music. Applicant must intend to work at least two years in the field of pastoral music following graduation or program completion.

Academic Fields/Career Goals: Music; Religion/Theology.

Award: Scholarship for use in freshman, sophomore, junior, senior, or graduate years; not renewable. *Number:* 1. *Amount:* $1000.

Eligibility Requirements: Applicant must be enrolled or expecting to enroll full- or part-time at a two-year or four-year or technical institution or university and must have an interest in music/singing. Applicant or parent of applicant must be member of National Association of Pastoral Musicians. Available to U.S. and non-U.S. citizens.

Application Requirements: Application, essay, financial need analysis, resume, references, tape of performance. *Deadline:* March 7.

Contact: Kathleen Haley, Director of Membership Services
National Association of Pastoral Musicians
962 Wayne Avenue, Suite 210
Silver Spring, MD 20910-4461
Phone: 240-247-3000
Fax: 240-247-3001
E-mail: haley@npm.org

GIA PUBLICATION PASTORAL MUSICIAN SCHOLARSHIP

Awards NPM members enrolled full-time or part-time in a graduate or undergraduate degree program of studies related to the field of pastoral music. Applicant must intend to work at least two years in the field of pastoral music following graduation or program completion.

Academic Fields/Career Goals: Music; Religion/Theology.

Award: Scholarship for use in freshman, sophomore, junior, senior, or graduate years; not renewable. *Number:* 1. *Amount:* $2000.

Eligibility Requirements: Applicant must be enrolled or expecting to enroll full- or part-time at a two-year or four-year institution or university and must have an interest in music/singing. Applicant or parent of applicant must be member of National Association of Pastoral Musicians. Available to U.S. and non-U.S. citizens.

Application Requirements: Application, essay, financial need analysis, resume, references, tape of performance. *Deadline:* March 7.

Contact: Kathleen Haley, Director of Membership Services
National Association of Pastoral Musicians
962 Wayne Avenue, Suite 210
Silver Spring, MD 20910-4461
Phone: 240-247-3000
Fax: 240-247-3001
E-mail: haley@npm.org

MUSONICS SCHOLARSHIP

Awards NPM members enrolled full-time or part-time in a graduate or undergraduate degree program of studies related to the field of pastoral music. Applicant must intend to work at least two years in the field of pastoral music following graduation or program completion.

Academic Fields/Career Goals: Music; Religion/Theology.

Award: Scholarship for use in freshman, sophomore, junior, senior, or graduate years; not renewable. *Number:* 1. *Amount:* up to $3000.

Eligibility Requirements: Applicant must be enrolled or expecting to enroll full- or part-time at a two-year or four-year institution or university and must have an interest in music/singing. Applicant or parent of applicant must be member of National Association of Pastoral Musicians. Available to U.S. and non-U.S. citizens.

Application Requirements: Application, essay, financial need analysis, resume, references, tape of performance. *Deadline:* March 7.

Contact: Kathleen Haley, Director of Membership Services
National Association of Pastoral Musicians
962 Wayne Avenue, Suite 210
Silver Spring, MD 20910-4461
Phone: 240-247-3000
Fax: 240-247-3001
E-mail: haley@npm.org

NATIONAL ASSOCIATION OF PASTORAL MUSICIANS MEMBERS' SCHOLARSHIP

Awards NPM members enrolled full-time or part-time in a graduate or undergraduate degree program of studies related to the field of pastoral music. Applicant must intend to work at least two years in the field of pastoral music following graduation or program completion.

Academic Fields/Career Goals: Music; Religion/Theology.

Award: Scholarship for use in freshman, sophomore, junior, senior, or graduate years; not renewable. *Number:* 1. *Amount:* $3500.

Eligibility Requirements: Applicant must be enrolled or expecting to enroll full- or part-time at a two-year or four-year or technical institution or university and must have an interest in music/singing. Applicant or parent of applicant must be member of National Association of Pastoral Musicians. Available to U.S. and non-U.S. citizens.

Application Requirements: Application, essay, financial need analysis, resume, references, tape of performance. *Deadline:* March 7.

Contact: Kathleen Haley, Director of Membership Services
National Association of Pastoral Musicians
962 Wayne Avenue, Suite 210
Silver Spring, MD 20910-4461
Phone: 240-247-3000
Fax: 240-247-3001
E-mail: haley@npm.org

NPM BOARD OF DIRECTORS SCHOLARSHIP

Scholarship for NPM members enrolled full- or part-time in an undergraduate or graduate pastoral music program. Must intend to work at least two years in the field of pastoral music following graduation/ program completion.

Academic Fields/Career Goals: Music.

Award: Scholarship for use in freshman, sophomore, junior, senior, or graduate years; not renewable. *Number:* varies. *Amount:* $2000.

Eligibility Requirements: Applicant must be enrolled or expecting to enroll full- or part-time at a two-year or four-year institution or university and must have an interest in music/singing. Applicant or parent of applicant must be member of National Association of Pastoral Musicians. Available to U.S. and non-U.S. citizens.

Application Requirements: Application, essay, financial need analysis, resume, references, tape of performance. *Deadline:* March 7.

Contact: Kathleen Haley, Director of Membership Services
National Association of Pastoral Musicians
962 Wayne Avenue, Suite 210
Silver Spring, MD 20910-4461
Phone: 240-247-3000
Fax: 240-247-3001
E-mail: haley@npm.org

NPM COMPOSERS AND AUTHORS SCHOLARSHIP

Scholarship for NPM members pursuing studies related to the field of pastoral music. Must intend to work at least two years in the field of pastoral music following graduation or program completion. Applicant must submit a definition of "pastoral music," description of talents and previous experience, and a 5 minute performance cassette of the choir/ensemble.

Academic Fields/Career Goals: Music.

Award: Scholarship for use in freshman, sophomore, junior, senior, or graduate years; not renewable. *Number:* varies. *Amount:* $1750.

Eligibility Requirements: Applicant must be enrolled or expecting to enroll full- or part-time at a two-year or four-year institution or university and must have an interest in music/singing. Applicant or parent of applicant must be member of National Association of Pastoral Musicians. Available to U.S. and non-U.S. citizens.

Application Requirements: Application, essay, financial need analysis, resume, references, tape of performance. *Deadline:* March 3.

Contact: Kathleen Haley, Director of Membership Services
National Association of Pastoral Musicians
962 Wayne Avenue, Suite 210
Silver Spring, MD 20910-4461
Phone: 240-247-3000
Fax: 240-247-3001
E-mail: haley@npm.org

NPM KOINONIA/BOARD OF DIRECTORS SCHOLARSHIP

Awards NPM members enrolled full-time or part-time in a graduate or undergraduate degree program of studies related to the field of pastoral music. Applicant must intend to work at least two years in the field of pastoral music following graduation or program completion.

Academic Fields/Career Goals: Music; Religion/Theology.

Award: Scholarship for use in freshman, sophomore, junior, senior, or graduate years; not renewable. *Number:* 1. *Amount:* $2000.

Eligibility Requirements: Applicant must be enrolled or expecting to enroll full- or part-time at a two-year or four-year institution or university and must have an interest in music/singing. Applicant or parent of applicant must be member of National Association of Pastoral Musicians. Available to U.S. and non-U.S. citizens.

Application Requirements: Application, essay, financial need analysis, resume, references, tape of performance. *Deadline:* March 7.

Contact: Kathleen Haley, Director of Membership Services
National Association of Pastoral Musicians
962 Wayne Avenue, Suite 210
Silver Spring, MD 20910-4461
Phone: 240-247-3000
Fax: 240-247-3001
E-mail: haley@npm.org

NPM MIAMI VALLEY CATHOLIC CHURCH MUSICIANS SCHOLARSHIP

Scholarship for NPM members pursuing studies related to the field of pastoral music. Must intend to work at least two years in the field of pastoral music following graduation or program completion. Applicant must submit a definition of "pastoral music," description of talents and previous experience, and a 5 minute performance cassette of the choir/ensemble.

Academic Fields/Career Goals: Music.

Award: Scholarship for use in freshman, sophomore, junior, senior, or graduate years; not renewable. *Number:* varies. *Amount:* $1250.

Eligibility Requirements: Applicant must be enrolled or expecting to enroll full- or part-time at a two-year or four-year institution or university and must have an interest in music/singing. Applicant or parent of applicant must be member of National Association of Pastoral Musicians. Available to U.S. and non-U.S. citizens.

Application Requirements: Application, essay, financial need analysis, resume, references, tape of performance. *Deadline:* March 3.

Contact: Kathleen Haley, Director of Membership Services
National Association of Pastoral Musicians
962 Wayne Avenue, Suite 210
Silver Spring, MD 20910-4461
Phone: 240-247-3000
Fax: 240-247-3001
E-mail: haley@npm.org

NPM PERROT SCHOLARSHIP

Awards NPM members enrolled full-time or part-time in a graduate or undergraduate degree program of studies related to the field of pastoral music. Applicant must intend to work at least two years in the field of pastoral music following graduation or program completion.

Academic Fields/Career Goals: Music.

Award: Scholarship for use in freshman, sophomore, junior, senior, or graduate years; not renewable. *Number:* 1. *Amount:* $3500.

Eligibility Requirements: Applicant must be enrolled or expecting to enroll full- or part-time at a two-year or four-year institution or university. Applicant or parent of applicant must be member of National Association of Pastoral Musicians. Available to U.S. and non-U.S. citizens.

Application Requirements: Application, essay, financial need analysis, resume, references, tape of performance. *Deadline:* March 7.

Contact: Kathleen Haley, Director of Membership Services
National Association of Pastoral Musicians
962 Wayne Avenue, Suite 210
Silver Spring, MD 20910-4461
Phone: 240-247-3000
Fax: 240-247-3001
E-mail: haley@npm.org

OREGON CATHOLIC PRESS SCHOLARSHIP

Awards NPM members enrolled full-time or part-time in a graduate or undergraduate degree program of studies related to the field of pastoral music. Applicant must intend to work at least two years in the field of pastoral music following graduation or program completion.

Academic Fields/Career Goals: Music; Religion/Theology.

Award: Scholarship for use in freshman, sophomore, junior, senior, or graduate years; not renewable. *Number:* 1. *Amount:* up to $2500.

National Association of Pastoral Musicians (continued)

Eligibility Requirements: Applicant must be enrolled or expecting to enroll full- or part-time at a two-year or four-year institution or university and must have an interest in music/singing. Available to U.S. and non-U.S. citizens.

Application Requirements: Application, essay, financial need analysis, resume, references, tape of performance. *Deadline:* March 7.

Contact: Kathleen Haley, Director of Membership Services
National Association of Pastoral Musicians
962 Wayne Avenue, Suite 210
Silver Spring, MD 20910-4461
Phone: 240-247-3000
Fax: 240-247-3001
E-mail: haley@npm.org

PALUCH FAMILY FOUNDATION/WORLD LIBRARY PUBLICATIONS SCHOLARSHIP

Awards NPM members enrolled full-time or part-time in a graduate or undergraduate degree program of studies related to the field of pastoral music. Applicant must intend to work at least two years in the field of pastoral music following graduation or program completion.

Academic Fields/Career Goals: Music; Religion/Theology.

Award: Scholarship for use in freshman, sophomore, junior, senior, or graduate years; not renewable. *Number:* 1. *Amount:* up to $2500.

Eligibility Requirements: Applicant must be enrolled or expecting to enroll full- or part-time at a two-year or four-year institution or university and must have an interest in music/singing. Available to U.S. and non-U.S. citizens.

Application Requirements: Application, essay, financial need analysis, resume, references, tape of performance. *Deadline:* March 7.

Contact: Kathleen Haley, Director of Membership Services
National Association of Pastoral Musicians
962 Wayne Avenue, Suite 210
Silver Spring, MD 20910-4461
Phone: 240-247-3000
Fax: 240-247-3001
E-mail: haley@npm.org

STEVEN C. WARNER SCHOLARSHIP

Scholarship for NPM members enrolled full-or part-time in an undergraduate or graduate pastoral music program. Applicant must intend to work at least two years in the field of pastoral music following graduation/program completion.

Academic Fields/Career Goals: Music.

Award: Scholarship for use in freshman, sophomore, junior, senior, or graduate years; not renewable. *Number:* varies. *Amount:* $750.

Eligibility Requirements: Applicant must be enrolled or expecting to enroll full- or part-time at a two-year or four-year institution or university and must have an interest in music/singing. Applicant or parent of applicant must be member of National Association of Pastoral Musicians. Available to U.S. and non-U.S. citizens.

Application Requirements: Application, essay, financial need analysis, resume, references, tape of performance. *Deadline:* March 7.

Contact: Kathleen Haley, Director of Membership Services
National Association of Pastoral Musicians
962 Wayne Avenue, Suite 210
Silver Spring, MD 20910-4461
Phone: 240-247-3000
Fax: 240-247-3001
E-mail: haley@npm.org

PI LAMBDA THETA INC. http://www.pilambda.org

NADEEN BURKEHOLDER WILLIAMS MUSIC SCHOLARSHIP

• *See page 239*

QUEEN ELISABETH INTERNATIONAL MUSIC COMPETITION OF BELGIUM http://www.qeimc.be

QUEEN ELISABETH COMPETITION

Competition is open to musicians who have already completed their training and who are ready to launch their international careers. The competition covers the following musical disciplines: piano, voice, violin and composition.

Academic Fields/Career Goals: Music.

Award: Prize for use in freshman, sophomore, junior, senior, or graduate years; not renewable. *Number:* varies. *Amount:* $1337–$26,749.

Eligibility Requirements: Applicant must be age 17-27; enrolled or expecting to enroll full- or part-time at a two-year or four-year or technical institution or university and must have an interest in music or music/singing. Available to U.S. and non-U.S. citizens.

Application Requirements: Application, applicant must enter a contest, photo, CD/DVD recording. *Deadline:* January 15.

Contact: Michel-Etienne Van Neste, Secretary General
Queen Elisabeth International Music Competition of Belgium
Rue Aux Laines 20
Brussels 1000
Belgium
Phone: 32 2 213 40 50
Fax: 32 2 514 32 97
E-mail: info@qeimc.be

RHODE ISLAND FOUNDATION http://www.rifoundation.org

BACH ORGAN AND KEYBOARD MUSIC SCHOLARSHIP

Scholarship for Rhode Island residents attending college as a music major or a church organist who is a Rhode Island resident and an ABO member. Applicants must demonstrate good grades and financial need. Must include music tape.

Academic Fields/Career Goals: Music.

Award: Scholarship for use in freshman, sophomore, junior, or senior years; not renewable. *Number:* up to 3. *Amount:* up to $1000.

Eligibility Requirements: Applicant must be enrolled or expecting to enroll full-time at a two-year or four-year institution or university; resident of Rhode Island and must have an interest in music/singing. Available to U.S. citizens.

Application Requirements: Application, financial need analysis, references, self-addressed stamped envelope, transcript. *Deadline:* June 9.

Contact: Libby Monahan, Funds Administrator
Rhode Island Foundation
One Union Station
Providence, RI 02903
Phone: 401-274-4564 Ext. 3117
Fax: 401-751-7983
E-mail: libbym@rifoundation.org

CONSTANT MEMORIAL SCHOLARSHIP FOR AQUIDNECK ISLAND RESIDENTS

• *See page 106*

SAN ANGELO SYMPHONY SOCIETY http://www.sanangelosymphony.org

SORANTIN YOUNG ARTIST AWARD

Prizes awarded to full-time or part-time students in the field of music (pianists and string instrumentalists), who are under 28 years of age. Award amount ranges from $1000 to $3000. Overall winner will appear with the San Angelo Symphony Orchestra. Application fee of $50 is required. Deadline varies.

Academic Fields/Career Goals: Music; Performing Arts.

Award: Prize for use in freshman, sophomore, junior, senior, graduate, or postgraduate years; not renewable. *Number:* 5–12. *Amount:* $1000–$3000.

Eligibility Requirements: Applicant must be age 28 or under; enrolled or expecting to enroll full- or part-time at a two-year or four-year institution or university and must have an interest in music. Available to U.S. and non-U.S. citizens.

Application Requirements: Application, applicant must enter a contest, autobiography, photo, photocopy of a birth certificate. *Fee:* $50. *Deadline:* varies.

Contact: Jennifer Odom, Executive Director
San Angelo Symphony Society
PO Box 5922
San Angelo, TX 76902-5922
Phone: 325-658-5877
Fax: 325-653-1045
E-mail: assistant@sanangelosymphony.org

SAN DIEGO FOUNDATION http://www.sdfoundation.org

DR. BARTA-LEHMAN MUSICAL SCHOLARSHIP

Scholarship to graduating high school seniors, or current undergraduate or graduate students. Applicants must be serious and talented musicians who are planning to pursue a career in music and/or play professionally (string instruments preferred). Applicants must have a minimum 3.0 GPA and plan to attend an accredited four-year university or music academy in the U.S. Scholarship may be used for tuition, books and fees.

Academic Fields/Career Goals: Music.

Award: Scholarship for use in freshman, sophomore, junior, senior, or graduate years; not renewable. *Number:* 4. *Amount:* $2000.

Eligibility Requirements: Applicant must be enrolled or expecting to enroll full-time at a four-year institution or university; resident of California and must have an interest in music. Applicant must have 3.0 GPA or higher. Available to U.S. citizens.

Application Requirements: Application, references, transcript, personal statement, CD or video of applicant's music, copy of tax return. *Deadline:* January 26.

Contact: Shryl Helvie, Scholarship Coordinator
San Diego Foundation
2508 Historic Decatur Road, Suite 200
San Diego, CA 92106
Phone: 619-814-1307
Fax: 619-239-1710
E-mail: shryl@sdfoundation.org

SIGMA ALPHA IOTA PHILANTHROPIES INC. http://www.sigmaalphaiota.org

SIGMA ALPHA IOTA JAZZ PERFORMANCE AWARDS

Award for a college-initiated member of Sigma Alpha Iota who is enrolled in an undergraduate or graduate program in jazz studies or jazz performance at the time of application. Applicant must be no older than age 32.

Academic Fields/Career Goals: Music.

Award: Prize for use in freshman, sophomore, junior, senior, or graduate years; not renewable. *Number:* 2. *Amount:* $1500–$2000.

Eligibility Requirements: Applicant must be age 32 or under; enrolled or expecting to enroll full- or part-time at a four-year institution or university; female and must have an interest in music/singing. Applicant or parent of applicant must be member of Sigma Alpha Iota. Available to U.S. and non-U.S. citizens.

Application Requirements: Application, essay. *Fee:* $25. *Deadline:* March 15.

Contact: Jaide Fried Massin, Project Director
Sigma Alpha Iota Philanthropies Inc.
One Tunnel Road
Asheville, NC 28805
Phone: 828-251-0606
Fax: 828-251-0644
E-mail: toffuti@hotmail.com

SIGMA ALPHA IOTA JAZZ STUDIES SCHOLARSHIP

Award for an initiated member of Sigma Alpha Iota in good financial standing with the Fraternity. Scholarship must be applied toward study leading to a music degree with an emphasis in jazz studies.

Academic Fields/Career Goals: Music.

Award: Scholarship for use in freshman, sophomore, junior, or senior years; not renewable. *Number:* varies. *Amount:* $1500.

Eligibility Requirements: Applicant must be enrolled or expecting to enroll full- or part-time at a four-year institution or university; female and must have an interest in music/singing. Applicant or parent of applicant must be member of Sigma Alpha Iota. Available to U.S. and non-U.S. citizens.

Application Requirements: Application, financial need analysis, references, transcript. *Fee:* $25. *Deadline:* March 15.

Contact: Jaide Fried Massen, Project Director
Sigma Alpha Iota Philanthropies Inc.
One Tunnel Road
Asheville, NC 28805
Phone: 828-251-0606
Fax: 828-251-0644
E-mail: toffuti@hotmail.com

SIGMA ALPHA IOTA MUSIC BUSINESS/TECHNOLOGY SCHOLARSHIP

Tuition scholarship for an initiated member of Sigma Alpha Iota in good financial standing with the Fraternity. Must be enrolled full-time in a bachelor's degree program and entering the junior or senior year of study in fall semester. Minimum GPA of 3.0 required.

Academic Fields/Career Goals: Music.

Award: Scholarship for use in junior or senior years; not renewable. *Number:* varies. *Amount:* $2000.

Eligibility Requirements: Applicant must be enrolled or expecting to enroll full-time at a four-year institution or university; female and must have an interest in music/singing. Applicant or parent of applicant must be member of Sigma Alpha Iota. Applicant must have 3.0 GPA or higher. Available to U.S. and non-U.S. citizens.

Application Requirements: Application, references, transcript, statement of purpose, including career goals. *Fee:* $25. *Deadline:* March 15.

Contact: Kim L. Wangler, Director
Sigma Alpha Iota Philanthropies Inc.
One Tunnel Road
Asheville, NC 28805
Phone: 828-251-0606
Fax: 828-251-0644
E-mail: wanglerkl@appstate.edu

SIGMA ALPHA IOTA MUSICIANS WITH SPECIAL NEEDS SCHOLARSHIP

• *See page 240*

SIGMA ALPHA IOTA MUSIC THERAPY SCHOLARSHIP

One-time award offered yearly for female undergraduate and graduate members of SAI who have completed two years in music therapy training at a university approved by the American Music Therapy Association. Contact local chapter for further information. Application fee: $25.

Academic Fields/Career Goals: Music; Therapy/Rehabilitation.

Award: Scholarship for use in freshman, sophomore, junior, senior, or graduate years; not renewable. *Number:* 1. *Amount:* $1000.

Eligibility Requirements: Applicant must be enrolled or expecting to enroll full-time at a four-year institution or university; female and must have an interest in music/singing. Applicant or parent of applicant must be member of Sigma Alpha Iota. Available to U.S. and non-U.S. citizens.

Application Requirements: Application, essay, financial need analysis, references, transcript. *Fee:* $25. *Deadline:* March 15.

Contact: Michelle Gaddis Kennemer, Director
Sigma Alpha Iota Philanthropies Inc.
One Tunnel Road
Asheville, NC 28805
Phone: 828-251-0606
Fax: 828-251-0644
E-mail: jmichelle17@hotmail.com

SIGMA ALPHA IOTA SUMMER MUSIC SCHOLARSHIPS IN THE U.S. OR ABROAD

One-time award for use at summer music programs in the United States or abroad. Must be a female member of SAI and accepted by the summer music program. Contact local chapter for details. Application fee: $25.

Academic Fields/Career Goals: Music; Performing Arts.

Award: Scholarship for use in freshman, sophomore, junior, senior, or graduate years; not renewable. *Number:* 10. *Amount:* up to $1000.

Eligibility Requirements: Applicant must be enrolled or expecting to enroll full-time at a four-year institution or university; female and must have an interest in music/singing. Applicant or parent of applicant must be member of Sigma Alpha Iota. Available to U.S. and non-U.S. citizens.

Sigma Alpha Iota Philanthropies Inc. (continued)

Application Requirements: Application, essay, resume, references, transcript, acceptance letter. *Fee:* $25. *Deadline:* March 15.

Contact: Mary Jennings, Director
Sigma Alpha Iota Philanthropies Inc.
One Tunnel Road
Asheville, NC 28805
Phone: 828-251-0606
Fax: 828-251-0644
E-mail: maryj10101@aol.com

SIGMA ALPHA IOTA UNDERGRADUATE PERFORMANCE SCHOLARSHIPS

$1500 awards offered triennially for female SAI members in freshman, sophomore or junior year studying voice; keyboard and percussion; strings; or winds and brass. Must be younger than 25 years of age. Winners perform at national convention. Must submit tape with required repertoire. Consult local chapter for details. Application fee: $25.

Academic Fields/Career Goals: Music; Performing Arts.

Award: Scholarship for use in freshman, sophomore, junior, or senior years; not renewable. *Number:* 4. *Amount:* $1500.

Eligibility Requirements: Applicant must be age 25 or under; enrolled or expecting to enroll full-time at a four-year institution or university; female and must have an interest in music/singing. Applicant or parent of applicant must be member of Sigma Alpha Iota. Available to U.S. and non-U.S. citizens.

Application Requirements: Application, applicant must enter a contest, essay, references, self-addressed stamped envelope, transcript, CD recording. *Fee:* $25. *Deadline:* March 15.

Contact: Dr. Emily White, Director
Sigma Alpha Iota Philanthropies Inc.
One Tunnel Road
Asheville, NC 28805
Phone: 828-251-0606
Fax: 828-251-0644
E-mail: hornstein1@aol.com

SINFONIA FOUNDATION http://www.sinfonia.org

DELTA IOTA ALUMNI SCHOLARSHIP

Scholarship for the collegiate members and chapters of Sinfonia. Must have been a collegiate member in good standing for at least two semesters, and maintain good standing status during the academic year of scholarship awarded. Should submit an essay on "How alumni support is essential for the advancement of the Sinfonia".

Academic Fields/Career Goals: Music.

Award: Scholarship for use in sophomore, junior, senior, or graduate years; not renewable. *Number:* 1. *Amount:* $500.

Eligibility Requirements: Applicant must be enrolled or expecting to enroll full- or part-time at a four-year institution or university and must have an interest in music. Applicant or parent of applicant must be member of Sinfonia. Available to U.S. citizens.

Application Requirements: Application, essay, photo, references, transcript, name and address of hometown newspaper. *Deadline:* May 1.

Contact: Matthew Garber, Director of Development
Sinfonia Foundation
10600 Old State Road
Evansville, IN 47711
Phone: 812-867-2433 Ext. 110
Fax: 812-867-0633
E-mail: garber@sinfonia.org

SUZUKI ASSOCIATION OF THE AMERICAS http://www.suzukiassociation.org

SUZUKI ASSOCIATION OF THE AMERICAS TEACHER DEVELOPMENT SCHOLARSHIPS

• *See page 242*

UNICO NATIONAL INC. http://www.unico.org

THEODORE MAZZA SCHOLARSHIP

• *See page 93*

UNITED NEGRO COLLEGE FUND http://www.uncf.org

JIMI HENDRIX ENDOWMENT FUND SCHOLARSHIP

Scholarship supports students majoring in music and attending a UNCF member college or university. Minimum 2.5 GPA required. The scholarship value ranges from $2000 to $5000.

Academic Fields/Career Goals: Music.

Award: Scholarship for use in freshman, sophomore, junior, or senior years; not renewable. *Number:* varies. *Amount:* $2000–$5000.

Eligibility Requirements: Applicant must be Black (non-Hispanic) and enrolled or expecting to enroll full- or part-time at a four-year institution or university. Applicant must have 2.5 GPA or higher. Available to U.S. and non-U.S. citizens.

Application Requirements: Application, financial need analysis. *Deadline:* varies.

Contact: Director, Program Services
United Negro College Fund
8260 Willow Oaks Corporate Drive
PO Box 10444
Fairfax, VA 22031-8044
Phone: 800-331-2244
E-mail: rebecca.bennett@uncf.org

JOHN LENNON ENDOWED SCHOLARSHIP

• *See page 188*

WATERBURY FOUNDATION http://www.conncf.org

MICHAEL AND JANE SENDZIMIR FUND SCHOLARSHIP

One-time scholarships for women artists who are actively pursuing a career in classical music either as a vocalist or instrumentalist. The award is from $1000 to $4000. Maximum two grants are awarded.

Academic Fields/Career Goals: Music.

Award: Scholarship for use in freshman, sophomore, junior, senior, or graduate years; not renewable. *Number:* up to 2. *Amount:* $1000–$4000.

Eligibility Requirements: Applicant must be enrolled or expecting to enroll full- or part-time at a two-year or four-year institution or university; female and must have an interest in music or music/singing. Available to U.S. and non-U.S. citizens.

Application Requirements: Application, essay, references. *Deadline:* March 1.

Contact: Josh Carey, Program Officer
Waterbury Foundation
43 Field Street
Waterbury, CT 06702-1216
Phone: 203-753-1315
Fax: 203-756-3054
E-mail: jcarey@conncf.org

WOMEN BAND DIRECTORS INTERNATIONAL http://www.womenbanddirectors.org

CHARLOTTE PLUMMER OWEN MEMORIAL SCHOLARSHIP

• *See page 246*

HELEN MAY BUTLER MEMORIAL SCHOLARSHIP

• *See page 246*

MARTHA ANN STARK MEMORIAL SCHOLARSHIP

• *See page 246*

VOLKWEIN MEMORIAL SCHOLARSHIP

• *See page 246*

NATURAL RESOURCES

AMERICAN GROUND WATER TRUST http://www.agwt.org

AMERICAN GROUND WATER TRUST-AMTROL INC. SCHOLARSHIP

• *See page 360*

AMERICAN GROUND WATER TRUST-BAROID SCHOLARSHIP

Award for entry-level students intending to pursue a career in ground water-related field. Must either have completed a science/environmental project involving ground water resources or have had vacation work experience related to the environment and natural resources. Must be U.S. citizen or legal resident with minimum 3.0 GPA. Submit two letters of recommendation and transcript.

Academic Fields/Career Goals: Natural Resources.

Award: Scholarship for use in freshman year; not renewable. *Number:* 1. *Amount:* up to $2000.

Eligibility Requirements: Applicant must be enrolled or expecting to enroll full-time at a four-year institution or university. Applicant must have 3.0 GPA or higher. Available to U.S. citizens.

Application Requirements: Application, essay, references, transcript. *Deadline:* June 1.

Contact: Garret Grasskamp, Ground Water Specialist
American Ground Water Trust
PO Box 1796
Concord, NH 03302-1796
Phone: 603-228-5444
Fax: 603-228-6557
E-mail: ggraaskamp@agwt.org

AMERICAN GROUND WATER TRUST-THOMAS STETSON SCHOLARSHIP

• *See page 167*

AMERICAN INDIAN SCIENCE AND ENGINEERING SOCIETY http://www.aises.org

A.T. ANDERSON MEMORIAL SCHOLARSHIP PROGRAM

• *See page 84*

HENRY RODRIGUEZ RECLAMATION COLLEGE SCHOLARSHIP AND INTERNSHIP

• *See page 285*

AMERICAN WATER RESOURCES ASSOCIATION http://www.awra.org

AWRA RICHARD A. HERBERT MEMORIAL SCHOLARSHIP

Two scholarships are available: one for full-time undergraduate student and one for a full-time graduate student, each working toward a degree in water resources. All applicants must be national AWRA members.

Academic Fields/Career Goals: Natural Resources.

Award: Scholarship for use in freshman, sophomore, junior, senior, or graduate years; not renewable. *Number:* 2. *Amount:* $2000.

Eligibility Requirements: Applicant must be enrolled or expecting to enroll full-time at a four-year institution or university. Available to U.S. and non-U.S. citizens.

Application Requirements: Application, essay, references, transcript. *Deadline:* April 23.

Contact: Terry Meyer, Marketing Director
American Water Resources Association
4 West Federal Street, PO Box 1626
Middleburg, VA 20118-1626
Phone: 540-687-8390
Fax: 540-687-8395
E-mail: info@awra.org

APICS EDUCATIONAL AND RESEARCH FOUNDATION INC. http://www.apics.org

DONALD W. FOGARTY INTERNATIONAL STUDENT PAPER COMPETITION

• *See page 137*

ARCTIC INSTITUTE OF NORTH AMERICA http://www.arctic.ucalgary.ca

JIM BOURQUE SCHOLARSHIP

• *See page 223*

ARIZONA HYDROLOGICAL SOCIETY http://www.azhydrosoc.org

ARIZONA HYDROLOGICAL SOCIETY SCHOLARSHIP

• *See page 215*

ARIZONA PROFESSIONAL CHAPTER OF AISES http://www.azpcofaises.org

ARIZONA PROFESSIONAL CHAPTER OF AISES SCHOLARSHIP

• *See page 257*

ASSOCIATION OF CALIFORNIA WATER AGENCIES http://www.acwa.com

ASSOCIATION OF CALIFORNIA WATER AGENCIES SCHOLARSHIPS

• *See page 86*

CLAIR A. HILL SCHOLARSHIP

• *See page 86*

CALIFORNIA GROUNDWATER ASSOCIATION http://www.groundh2o.org

CALIFORNIA GROUNDWATER ASSOCIATION SCHOLARSHIP

• *See page 363*

CALIFORNIA WATER AWARENESS CAMPAIGN http://www.wateraware.org

CALIFORNIA WATER AWARENESS CAMPAIGN WATER SCHOLAR

• *See page 74*

CANADIAN RECREATIONAL CANOEING ASSOCIATION http://www.paddlingcanada.com

BILL MASON MEMORIAL SCHOLARSHIP FUND

• *See page 74*

CONFEDERATED TRIBES OF GRAND RONDE http://www.grandronde.org

RAY MCKNIGHT MEMORIAL COMPETITIVE SCHOLARSHIP

• *See page 301*

CONNECTICUT FOREST AND PARK ASSOCIATION http://www.ctwoodlands.org

JAMES L. AND GENEVIEVE H. GOODWIN MEMORIAL SCHOLARSHIP

To support Connecticut residents enrolled in a curriculum of silviculture or forest resource management. The scholarship value ranges from $1000 to $5000.

Academic Fields/Career Goals: Natural Resources.

Award: Scholarship for use in freshman, sophomore, junior, senior, or graduate years; renewable. *Number:* up to 10. *Amount:* $1000–$5000.

Eligibility Requirements: Applicant must be enrolled or expecting to enroll full-time at a two-year or four-year institution or university and resident of Connecticut. Available to U.S. citizens.

Application Requirements: Application, essay, financial need analysis, transcript. *Deadline:* March 15.

Contact: Adam R. Moore, Executive Director
Connecticut Forest and Park Association
16 Meriden Road
Rockfall, CT 06481-2961
Phone: 860-346-2372
Fax: 860-347-7463
E-mail: info@ctwoodlands.org

CONSERVATION FEDERATION OF MISSOURI http://www.confedmo.org

CHARLES P. BELL CONSERVATION SCHOLARSHIP
• See page 301

DESK AND DERRICK EDUCATIONAL TRUST http://www.addc.org

DESK AND DERRICK EDUCATIONAL TRUST
• See page 86

FRIENDS OF THE FRELINGHUYSEN ARBORETUM http://www.arboretumfriends.org

BENJAMIN C. BLACKBURN SCHOLARSHIP
• See page 302

GARDEN CLUB OF AMERICA http://www.gcamerica.org

GARDEN CLUB OF AMERICA AWARDS FOR SUMMER ENVIRONMENTAL STUDIES
• See page 74

GREAT LAKES COMMISSION http://www.glc.org

CAROL A. RATZA MEMORIAL SCHOLARSHIP
• See page 179

HISPANIC COLLEGE FUND INC. http://www.hispanicfund.org

DEPARTMENT OF ENERGY SCHOLARSHIP PROGRAM
• See page 142

INDIANA WILDLIFE FEDERATION ENDOWMENT http://www.indianawildlife.org

CHARLES A. HOLT INDIANA WILDLIFE FEDERATION ENDOWMENT SCHOLARSHIP
• See page 302

INNOVATION AND SCIENCE COUNCIL OF BRITISH COLUMBIA http://www.bcinnovationcouncil.com

PAUL AND HELEN TRUSSEL SCIENCE AND TECHNOLOGY SCHOLARSHIP
• See page 87

INTERNATIONAL ASSOCIATION OF GREAT LAKES RESEARCH http://www.iaglr.org

PAUL W. RODGERS SCHOLARSHIP
• See page 217

INTERTRIBAL TIMBER COUNCIL http://www.itcnet.org

TRUMAN D. PICARD SCHOLARSHIP
• See page 69

KENTUCKY NATURAL RESOURCES AND ENVIRONMENTAL PROTECTION CABINET http://www.uky.edu/waterresources

ENVIRONMENTAL PROTECTION SCHOLARSHIPS
• See page 132

LOUISIANA OFFICE OF STUDENT FINANCIAL ASSISTANCE http://www.osfa.state.la.us

ROCKEFELLER STATE WILDLIFE SCHOLARSHIP
• See page 82

MANITOBA FORESTRY ASSOCIATION http://www.mbforestryassoc.ca

DR. ALAN BEAVEN FORESTRY SCHOLARSHIP
• See page 303

MINERALOGICAL SOCIETY OF AMERICA http://www.minsocam.org

MINERALOGICAL SOCIETY OF AMERICA-GRANT FOR STUDENT RESEARCH IN MINERALOGY AND PETROLOGY
• See page 218

MINERALOGY SOCIETY OF AMERICA-GRANT FOR RESEARCH IN CRYSTALLOGRAPHY
• See page 218

MONTANA FEDERATION OF GARDEN CLUBS http://www.mtfgc.org

LIFE MEMBER MONTANA FEDERATION OF GARDEN CLUBS SCHOLARSHIP
• See page 218

MORRIS K. UDALL FOUNDATION http://www.udall.gov

MORRIS K. UDALL SCHOLARS
• See page 76

MORRIS LAND CONSERVANCY http://www.morrislandconservancy.org

ROGERS FAMILY SCHOLARSHIP
• See page 304

RUSSELL W. MYERS SCHOLARSHIP
• See page 304

NATIONAL ASSOCIATION OF WATER COMPANIES-NEW JERSEY CHAPTER

NATIONAL ASSOCIATION OF WATER COMPANIES-NEW JERSEY CHAPTER SCHOLARSHIP
• See page 133

NATIONAL FEDERATION OF THE BLIND http://www.nfb.org

HOWARD BROWN RICKARD SCHOLARSHIP
• See page 92

NATIONAL FISH AND WILDLIFE FOUNDATION http://www.nfwf.org

BUDWEISER CONSERVATION SCHOLARSHIP PROGRAM
• See page 133

NEW JERSEY DIVISION OF FISH AND WILDLIFE/NJ CHAPTER OF THE WILDLIFE SOCIETY http://www.njfishandwildlife.com/cookhmschol.htm

RUSSELL A. COOKINGHAM SCHOLARSHIP
• See page 134

OHIO FORESTRY ASSOCIATION http://www.ohioforest.org

OHIO FORESTRY ASSOCIATION MEMORIAL SCHOLARSHIP

Minimum of one scholarship will be awarded to provide assistance toward forest resource education to quality college students. Preference given to students attending Ohio colleges and universities.

Academic Fields/Career Goals: Natural Resources.

Award: Scholarship for use in freshman, sophomore, junior, or senior years; not renewable. *Number:* 1. *Amount:* $1000.

Eligibility Requirements: Applicant must be enrolled or expecting to enroll full-time at a two-year or four-year or technical institution or university and resident of Ohio. Available to U.S. citizens.

Application Requirements: Application, essay, test scores. *Deadline:* April 15.

Contact: John Dorka, Executive Director
Ohio Forestry Association
4080 South High Street
PO Box 970
Columbus, OH 43207
Phone: 614-497-9580
Fax: 614-497-9581
E-mail: johnd@ohioforest.org

OREGON STUDENT ASSISTANCE COMMISSION http://www.osac.state.or.us

OREGON FOUNDATION FOR BLACKTAIL DEER OUTDOOR AND WILDLIFE SCHOLARSHIP

• *See page 134*

ROYDEN M. BODLEY SCHOLARSHIP

• *See page 82*

RAILWAY TIE ASSOCIATION http://www.rta.org

JOHN MABRY FORESTRY SCHOLARSHIP

One-time award to potential forestry industry leaders. Open to junior and senior undergraduates who will be enrolled in accredited forestry schools. One scholarship is also available to second-year students in a two-year college. Applications reviewed with emphasis on leadership qualities, career objectives, scholastic achievement, and financial need.

Academic Fields/Career Goals: Natural Resources.

Award: Scholarship for use in sophomore, junior, or senior years; not renewable. *Number:* 2. *Amount:* $1500.

Eligibility Requirements: Applicant must be enrolled or expecting to enroll full-time at a two-year or four-year institution or university. Available to U.S. and Canadian citizens.

Application Requirements: Application, autobiography, essay, references, transcript. *Deadline:* June 30.

Contact: Debbie Corallo, Administrator
Railway Tie Association
115 Commerce Drive, Suite C
Fayetteville, GA 30214
Phone: 770-460-5553
Fax: 770-460-5573
E-mail: ties@rta.org

ROCKY MOUNTAIN ELK FOUNDATION http://www.elkfoundation.org

WILDLIFE LEADERSHIP AWARDS

• *See page 83*

SAEMS-SOUTHERN ARIZONA ENVIRONMENTAL MANAGEMENT SOCIETY http://www.saems.org

ENVIRONMENTAL SCHOLARSHIPS

• *See page 299*

SOCIETY FOR RANGE MANAGEMENT http://www.rangelands.org

MASONIC RANGE SCIENCE SCHOLARSHIP

• *See page 71*

SOIL AND WATER CONSERVATION SOCIETY http://www.swcs.org

DONALD A. WILLIAMS SCHOLARSHIP SOIL CONSERVATION SCHOLARSHIP

• *See page 219*

SOIL AND WATER CONSERVATION SOCIETY-MISSOURI SHOW-ME CHAPTER http://www.swcs.missouri.edu

MO SHOW-ME CHAPTER SWCS SCHOLARSHIP

Scholarships for students wishing to pursue studies in a natural resources conservation career. Must be high school seniors or have graduated from a Missouri high school and are pursuing an undergraduate degree. Need not be an SWCS member.

Academic Fields/Career Goals: Natural Resources.

Award: Scholarship for use in freshman, sophomore, junior, or senior years; not renewable. *Number:* 1–2. *Amount:* $1000–$2000.

Eligibility Requirements: Applicant must be enrolled or expecting to enroll full-time at a four-year institution or university; resident of Missouri and studying in Missouri. Available to U.S. citizens.

Application Requirements: Application, essay, references, transcript, list of activities and leadership positions. *Deadline:* November 26.

Contact: Beverly Maltsberger, Scholarship Committee
Soil and Water Conservation Society-Missouri Show-Me Chapter
4125 Mitchell Avenue
St. Joseph, MO 64507
Phone: 816-279-1691
Fax: 816-279-3982
E-mail: maltsbergerb@missouri.edu

SOIL AND WATER CONSERVATION SOCIETY-NEW JERSEY CHAPTER http://www.geocities.com/njswcs

EDWARD R. HALL SCHOLARSHIP

• *See page 71*

SOUTH DAKOTA BOARD OF REGENTS http://www.sdbor.edu

SOUTH DAKOTA BOARD OF REGENTS BJUGSTAD SCHOLARSHIP

• *See page 71*

TECHNICAL ASSOCIATION OF THE PULP & PAPER INDUSTRY (TAPPI) http://www.tappi.org

PULP MANUFACTURE DIVISION SCHOLARSHIPS

Scholarship of $1000 to $2000 for a rising sophomore in a southern school of forest resources. For more details refer http://www.tappi.org/content/pdf/member_groups/CurrentScholar.pdf.

Academic Fields/Career Goals: Natural Resources; Paper and Pulp Engineering.

Award: Scholarship for use in sophomore, junior, or senior years; not renewable. *Number:* up to 5. *Amount:* $1000–$2000.

Eligibility Requirements: Applicant must be enrolled or expecting to enroll full-time at a four-year institution or university. Available to U.S. and non-U.S. citizens.

Application Requirements: Application, essay, references, transcript. *Deadline:* May 15.

Contact: Veranda Edmondson, TAPPI-Member Group Specialist
Technical Association of the Pulp & Paper Industry (TAPPI)
15 Technology Parkway, South
Norcross, GA 30092
Phone: 770-209-7536

WILLIAM L. CULLISON SCHOLARSHIP

Scholarship provides incentive for students to pursue an academic path related to the pulp and paper industry. Eligible students must meet all criteria, and will have completed two years of undergraduate school, with two years (or three years in a five-year program) remaining. For details refer to Web Site: http://www.tappi.org/content/pdf/member_groups/CullisonSchApp.pdf.

Academic Fields/Career Goals: Natural Resources; Paper and Pulp Engineering.

Award: Scholarship for use in junior or senior years; renewable. *Number:* 1. *Amount:* $4000.

Technical Association of the Pulp & Paper Industry (TAPPI) (continued)

Eligibility Requirements: Applicant must be enrolled or expecting to enroll full-time at a four-year institution or university. Applicant must have 3.5 GPA or higher. Available to U.S. and non-U.S. citizens.

Application Requirements: Application, essay, references, transcript. *Deadline:* May 1.

Contact: Veranda Edmondson, TAPPI-Member Group Specialist
Technical Association of the Pulp & Paper Industry (TAPPI)
15 Technology Parkway, South
Norcross, GA 30092
Phone: 770-209-7536
Fax: 770-446-6947
E-mail: vedmondson@tappi.org

TEXAS OUTDOOR WRITERS ASSOCIATION http://www.towa.org

TEXAS OUTDOOR WRITERS ASSOCIATION SCHOLARSHIP
- *See page 187*

TKE EDUCATIONAL FOUNDATION http://www.tke.org

TIMOTHY L. TASCHWER SCHOLARSHIP
- *See page 135*

UNITED NEGRO COLLEGE FUND http://www.uncf.org

MELLON ECOLOGY PROGRAM (S.E.E.D.S)
- *See page 305*

WEYERHAEUSER/UNCF CORPORATE SCHOLARS PROGRAM
- *See page 151*

UNITED STATES ENVIRONMENTAL PROTECTION AGENCY http://www.epa.gov/enviroed

NATIONAL NETWORK FOR ENVIRONMENTAL MANAGEMENT STUDIES FELLOWSHIP
- *See page 305*

VIRGINIA ASSOCIATION OF SOIL AND WATER CONSERVATION DISTRICTS EDUCATIONAL FOUNDATION INC. http://www.vaswcd.org

VASWCD EDUCATIONAL FOUNDATION INC. SCHOLARSHIP AWARDS PROGRAM
- *See page 306*

WATER ENVIRONMENT FEDERATION http://www.wef.org

CANHAM GRADUATE STUDIES SCHOLARSHIPS
- *See page 136*

WILSON ORNITHOLOGICAL SOCIETY http://www.wilsonsociety.org

GEORGE A. HALL/HAROLD F. MAYFIELD AWARD
- *See page 83*

PAUL A. STEWART AWARDS
- *See page 83*

NATURAL SCIENCES

AMERICAN CHEMICAL SOCIETY http://www.acs.org/scholars

AMERICAN CHEMICAL SOCIETY SCHOLARS PROGRAM
- *See page 153*

AMERICAN FOUNDATION FOR THE BLIND http://www.afb.org

PAUL W. RUCKES SCHOLARSHIP
- *See page 189*

AMERICAN INDIAN SCIENCE AND ENGINEERING SOCIETY http://www.aises.org

A.T. ANDERSON MEMORIAL SCHOLARSHIP PROGRAM
- *See page 84*

BURLINGTON NORTHERN SANTA FE FOUNDATION SCHOLARSHIP
- *See page 84*

ARCTIC INSTITUTE OF NORTH AMERICA http://www.arctic.ucalgary.ca

JIM BOURQUE SCHOLARSHIP
- *See page 223*

ARRL FOUNDATION INC. http://www.arrl.org

WILLIAM R. GOLDFARB MEMORIAL SCHOLARSHIP
- *See page 138*

ASSOCIATION FOR WOMEN IN SCIENCE EDUCATIONAL FOUNDATION http://www.awis.org/careers/edfoundation.html

ASSOCIATION FOR WOMEN IN SCIENCE COLLEGE SCHOLARSHIP
- *See page 82*

ASSOCIATION OF CALIFORNIA WATER AGENCIES http://www.acwa.com

ASSOCIATION OF CALIFORNIA WATER AGENCIES SCHOLARSHIPS
- *See page 86*

CLAIR A. HILL SCHOLARSHIP
- *See page 86*

AUDUBON SOCIETY OF WESTERN PENNSYLVANIA http://www.aswp.org

BEULAH FREY ENVIRONMENTAL SCHOLARSHIP
- *See page 301*

BARRY M. GOLDWATER SCHOLARSHIP AND EXCELLENCE IN EDUCATION FOUNDATION http://www.act.org/goldwater

BARRY M. GOLDWATER SCHOLARSHIP AND EXCELLENCE IN EDUCATION PROGRAM
- *See page 86*

CANADIAN RECREATIONAL CANOEING ASSOCIATION http://www.paddlingcanada.com

BILL MASON MEMORIAL SCHOLARSHIP FUND
- *See page 74*

COMMUNITY FOUNDATION FOR GREATER ATLANTA INC. http://www.atlcf.org

JAMES M. AND VIRGINIA M. SMYTH SCHOLARSHIP
- *See page 101*

CONSERVATION FEDERATION OF MISSOURI http://www.confedmo.org

CHARLES P. BELL CONSERVATION SCHOLARSHIP
- *See page 301*

DESK AND DERRICK EDUCATIONAL TRUST http://www.addc.org

DESK AND DERRICK EDUCATIONAL TRUST
- *See page 86*

EXPLORERS CLUB http://www.explorers.org/

YOUTH ACTIVITY FUND

Award given to college students or high school students pursuing a research project in the field of science. Applicants must have two letters of recommendation, one-page description of project, and a budget or plan.

Academic Fields/Career Goals: Natural Sciences; Science, Technology, and Society.

Award: Grant for use in freshman, sophomore, junior, or senior years; not renewable. *Number:* 10–15. *Amount:* $500–$1500.

Eligibility Requirements: Applicant must be enrolled or expecting to enroll full-time at a four-year institution or university. Available to U.S. and non-U.S. citizens.

Application Requirements: Application, essay, financial need analysis, references. *Deadline:* March 1.

Contact: Matt Williams, Member Services Director
Explorers Club
46 East 70th Street
New York, NY 10021
Phone: 212-628-8383
Fax: 212-327-1548
E-mail: mwilliams@explorers.org

GARDEN CLUB OF AMERICA http://www.gcamerica.org

FRANCES M. PEACOCK SCHOLARSHIP FOR NATIVE BIRD HABITAT

Scholarship of $4000 offers scholars the opportunity to pursue habitat-related issues that will benefit bird species and lend useful information for land management decisions. Provides financial aid to advanced students to study areas in the United States that provide winter or summer habitat for threatened and endangered native birds.

Academic Fields/Career Goals: Natural Sciences.

Award: Scholarship for use in senior or graduate years; not renewable. *Number:* 1. *Amount:* $4000.

Eligibility Requirements: Applicant must be enrolled or expecting to enroll full- or part-time at a four-year institution or university. Available to U.S. citizens.

Application Requirements: Application, essay, references, self-addressed stamped envelope, budget. *Deadline:* January 15.

Contact: Scott Sutcliffe, Scholarship Committee
Garden Club of America
Cornell Lab of Ornithology
159 Sapsucker Woods Road
Ithaca, NY 14850
Fax: 607-254-2415
E-mail: lh17@cornell.edu

GARDEN CLUB OF AMERICA SUMMER SCHOLARSHIP IN FIELD BOTANY

• *See page 352*

JOAN K. HUNT AND RACHEL M. HUNT SUMMER SCHOLARSHIP IN FIELD BOTANY

• *See page 352*

ZELLER SUMMER SCHOLARSHIP IN MEDICINAL BOTANY

• *See page 337*

GREAT LAKES COMMISSION http://www.glc.org

CAROL A. RATZA MEMORIAL SCHOLARSHIP

• *See page 179*

HARVARD TRAVELLERS CLUB

HARVARD TRAVELLERS CLUB GRANTS

• *See page 89*

HISPANIC COLLEGE FUND INC. http://www.hispanicfund.org

DEPARTMENT OF ENERGY SCHOLARSHIP PROGRAM

• *See page 142*

INNOVATION AND SCIENCE COUNCIL OF BRITISH COLUMBIA http://www.bcinnovationcouncil.com

PAUL AND HELEN TRUSSEL SCIENCE AND TECHNOLOGY SCHOLARSHIP

• *See page 87*

INSTITUTE OF ENVIRONMENTAL SCIENCES AND TECHNOLOGY (IEST) http://www.iest.org

ROBERT N. HANCOCK MEMORIAL SCHOLARSHIP

• *See page 132*

INTERNATIONAL ASSOCIATION OF GREAT LAKES RESEARCH http://www.iaglr.org

PAUL W. RODGERS SCHOLARSHIP

• *See page 217*

KENTUCKY NATURAL RESOURCES AND ENVIRONMENTAL PROTECTION CABINET http://www.uky.edu/waterresources

ENVIRONMENTAL PROTECTION SCHOLARSHIPS

• *See page 132*

LOUISIANA OFFICE OF STUDENT FINANCIAL ASSISTANCE http://www.osfa.state.la.us

ROCKEFELLER STATE WILDLIFE SCHOLARSHIP

• *See page 82*

MINERALOGICAL SOCIETY OF AMERICA http://www.minsocam.org

MINERALOGICAL SOCIETY OF AMERICA-GRANT FOR STUDENT RESEARCH IN MINERALOGY AND PETROLOGY

• *See page 218*

MINERALOGY SOCIETY OF AMERICA-GRANT FOR RESEARCH IN CRYSTALLOGRAPHY

• *See page 218*

NASA SOUTH DAKOTA SPACE GRANT CONSORTIUM http://www.sdsmt.edu/space/

SOUTH DAKOTA SPACE GRANT CONSORTIUM UNDERGRADUATE SCHOLARSHIPS

• *See page 120*

NASA WEST VIRGINIA SPACE GRANT CONSORTIUM http://www.nasa.wvu.edu

WEST VIRGINIA SPACE GRANT CONSORTIUM UNDERGRADUATE FELLOWSHIP PROGRAM

• *See page 121*

NATIONAL FISH AND WILDLIFE FOUNDATION http://www.nfwf.org

BUDWEISER CONSERVATION SCHOLARSHIP PROGRAM

• *See page 133*

OREGON STUDENT ASSISTANCE COMMISSION http://www.osac.state.or.us

OREGON FOUNDATION FOR BLACKTAIL DEER OUTDOOR AND WILDLIFE SCHOLARSHIP

• *See page 134*

ROYDEN M. BODLEY SCHOLARSHIP

• *See page 82*

PENNSYLVANIA HIGHER EDUCATION ASSISTANCE AGENCY http://www.pheaa.org

NEW ECONOMY TECHNOLOGY AND SCITECH SCHOLARSHIPS

• *See page 295*

SOCIETY OF HISPANIC PROFESSIONAL ENGINEERS FOUNDATION http://www.henaac.org

SOCIETY OF HISPANIC PROFESSIONAL ENGINEERS FOUNDATION
• *See page 162*

SOIL AND WATER CONSERVATION SOCIETY http://www.swcs.org

DONALD A. WILLIAMS SCHOLARSHIP SOIL CONSERVATION SCHOLARSHIP
• *See page 219*

SOIL AND WATER CONSERVATION SOCIETY-NEW JERSEY CHAPTER http://www.geocities.com/njswcs

EDWARD R. HALL SCHOLARSHIP
• *See page 71*

NEUROBIOLOGY

ARNOLD AND MABEL BECKMAN FOUNDATION http://www.beckman-foundation.com

BECKMAN SCHOLARS PROGRAM
• *See page 130*

MENTAL HEALTH ASSOCIATION IN NEW YORK STATE INC. http://www.mhanys.org

EDNA AIMES SCHOLARSHIP
• *See page 128*

NUCLEAR SCIENCE

AMERICAN INDIAN SCIENCE AND ENGINEERING SOCIETY http://www.aises.org

A.T. ANDERSON MEMORIAL SCHOLARSHIP PROGRAM
• *See page 84*

BURLINGTON NORTHERN SANTA FE FOUNDATION SCHOLARSHIP
• *See page 84*

AMERICAN NUCLEAR SOCIETY http://www.ans.org

AMERICAN NUCLEAR SOCIETY OPERATIONS AND POWER SCHOLARSHIP

Undergraduate scholarship for students who have completed two or more years in a course of study leading to a degree in nuclear science, nuclear engineering, or a nuclear-related field.

Academic Fields/Career Goals: Nuclear Science.

Award: Scholarship for use in junior or senior years; not renewable. *Number:* 1–21. *Amount:* $2500.

Eligibility Requirements: Applicant must be enrolled or expecting to enroll full- or part-time at a four-year institution or university. Available to U.S. citizens.

Application Requirements: Application, references, transcript. *Deadline:* February 1.

Contact: Scholarship Coordinator
American Nuclear Society
555 North Kensington Avenue
La Grange Park, IL 60526
Phone: 708-352-6611
Fax: 708-352-0499
E-mail: outreach@ans.org

AMERICAN NUCLEAR SOCIETY UNDERGRADUATE SCHOLARSHIPS

Maximum of four scholarships for students who have completed one year in a course of study leading to a degree in nuclear science, nuclear engineering, or a nuclear-related field and who will be sophomores in the upcoming academic year; and a maximum of twenty one scholarships for students who have completed two or more years and will be entering as juniors or seniors. Must be sponsored by ANS member or branch. Must be U.S. citizen or permanent resident.

Academic Fields/Career Goals: Nuclear Science.

Award: Scholarship for use in junior or senior years; not renewable. *Number:* 4–21. *Amount:* $2000.

Eligibility Requirements: Applicant must be enrolled or expecting to enroll full-time at a four-year institution or university. Available to U.S. citizens.

Application Requirements: Application, references, transcript. *Deadline:* February 1.

Contact: Scholarship Coordinator
American Nuclear Society
555 North Kensington Avenue
La Grange Park, IL 60526
Phone: 708-352-6611
Fax: 708-352-0499
E-mail: outreach@ans.org

AMERICAN NUCLEAR SOCIETY VOGT RADIOCHEMISTRY SCHOLARSHIP
• *See page 254*

ANS INCOMING FRESHMAN SCHOLARSHIP

Scholarship for graduating high school seniors who have enrolled or plan to enroll full-time in a nuclear engineering degree program. Scholarships will be awarded based on an applicant's high school academic achievement and course of undergraduate study.

Academic Fields/Career Goals: Nuclear Science.

Award: Scholarship for use in freshman year; not renewable. *Number:* 1–4. *Amount:* $1000.

Eligibility Requirements: Applicant must be high school student and planning to enroll or expecting to enroll full-time at a four-year institution or university. Available to U.S. and non-U.S. citizens.

Application Requirements: Application, essay, references, transcript. *Deadline:* April 1.

Contact: Scholarship Committee
American Nuclear Society
555 North Kensington Avenue
La Grange Park, IL 60526
Phone: 708-352-6611
Fax: 708-352-0499

CHARLES (TOMMY) THOMAS MEMORIAL SCHOLARSHIP DIVISION SCHOLARSHIP

Undergraduate scholarship for students who have completed two or more years in a course of study leading to a degree in nuclear science, nuclear engineering, or a nuclear-related field.

Academic Fields/Career Goals: Nuclear Science.

Award: Scholarship for use in junior or senior years; not renewable. *Number:* 1–21. *Amount:* $2000.

Eligibility Requirements: Applicant must be enrolled or expecting to enroll full-time at a four-year institution or university. Available to U.S. citizens.

Application Requirements: Application, references, transcript. *Deadline:* February 1.

Contact: Scholarship Coordinator
American Nuclear Society
555 North Kensington Avenue
La Grange Park, IL 60526
Phone: 708-352-6611
Fax: 708-352-0499
E-mail: outreach@ans.org

DECOMMISSIONING, DECONTAMINATION, AND REUTILIZATION SCHOLARSHIP
• *See page 253*

DELAYED EDUCATION FOR WOMEN SCHOLARSHIPS

One-time award given to enable mature women whose formal studies in nuclear science, nuclear engineering, or related fields have been delayed or interrupted at least one year. Must be U.S. citizen or permanent resident. Minimum GPA of 2.5 required.

Academic Fields/Career Goals: Nuclear Science.

Award: Scholarship for use in freshman, sophomore, junior, or senior years; not renewable. *Number:* 1. *Amount:* $3500.

Eligibility Requirements: Applicant must be enrolled or expecting to enroll full-time at a four-year institution or university and female. Applicant must have 2.5 GPA or higher. Available to U.S. citizens.

Application Requirements: Application, financial need analysis, references, transcript. *Deadline:* February 1.

Contact: Scholarship Coordinator
American Nuclear Society
555 North Kensington Avenue
La Grange Park, IL 60526
Phone: 708-352-6611
Fax: 708-352-0499
E-mail: outreach@ans.org

JOHN AND MURIEL LANDIS SCHOLARSHIP AWARDS

Maximum of eight scholarships are awarded to undergraduate and graduate students who have greater than average financial need. Applicants should be planning a career in nuclear science, nuclear engineering, or a nuclear related field and be enrolled or planning to enroll in a college or university located in the United States, but need not be U.S. citizens.

Academic Fields/Career Goals: Nuclear Science.

Award: Scholarship for use in freshman, sophomore, junior, senior, or graduate years; not renewable. *Number:* 1–8. *Amount:* $3500.

Eligibility Requirements: Applicant must be enrolled or expecting to enroll full-time at a four-year institution or university. Available to U.S. and non-U.S. citizens.

Application Requirements: Application, financial need analysis, references, transcript. *Deadline:* February 1.

Contact: Scholarship Coordinator
American Nuclear Society
555 North Kensington Avenue
La Grange Park, IL 60526
Phone: 708-352-6611
Fax: 708-352-0469
E-mail: outreach@ans.org

JOHN R. LAMARSH SCHOLARSHIP

Undergraduate scholarship for students who have completed two or more years in a course of study leading to a degree in nuclear science, nuclear engineering, or a nuclear-related field.

Academic Fields/Career Goals: Nuclear Science.

Award: Scholarship for use in junior or senior years; not renewable. *Number:* 1–21. *Amount:* $2000.

Eligibility Requirements: Applicant must be enrolled or expecting to enroll full- or part-time at a four-year institution or university. Available to U.S. citizens.

Application Requirements: Application, references, transcript. *Deadline:* February 1.

Contact: Scholarship Coordinator
American Nuclear Society
555 North Kensington Avenue
La Grange Park, IL 60526
Phone: 708-352-6611
Fax: 708-352-0499
E-mail: outreach@ans.org

JOSEPH R. DIETRICH SCHOLARSHIP

Undergraduate scholarship for students who have completed two or more years in a course of study leading to a degree in nuclear science, nuclear engineering, or a nuclear-related field.

Academic Fields/Career Goals: Nuclear Science.

Award: Scholarship for use in junior or senior years; not renewable. *Number:* 1–21. *Amount:* $2000.

Eligibility Requirements: Applicant must be enrolled or expecting to enroll full- or part-time at a four-year institution or university. Available to U.S. citizens.

Application Requirements: Application, references, transcript. *Deadline:* February 1.

Contact: Scholarship Coordinator
American Nuclear Society
555 North Kensington Avenue
La Grange Park, IL 60526
Phone: 708-352-6611
Fax: 708-352-0499
E-mail: outreach@ans.org

RAYMOND DISALVO SCHOLARSHIP

Undergraduate scholarship for students who have completed two or more years in a course of study leading to a degree in nuclear science, nuclear engineering, or a nuclear-related field.

Academic Fields/Career Goals: Nuclear Science.

Award: Scholarship for use in junior or senior years; not renewable. *Number:* 1–21. *Amount:* $2000.

Eligibility Requirements: Applicant must be enrolled or expecting to enroll full-time at a four-year institution or university. Available to U.S. and non-U.S. citizens.

Application Requirements: Application, references, transcript, sponsorship letter from ANS organization. *Deadline:* February 1.

Contact: Scholarship Coordinator
American Nuclear Society
555 North Kensington Avenue
La Grange Park, IL 60526
Phone: 708-352-6611
Fax: 708-352-0499
E-mail: outreach@ans.org

ROBERT G. LACY SCHOLARSHIP

Undergraduate scholarship for students who have completed two or more years in a course of study leading to a degree in nuclear science, nuclear engineering, or a nuclear-related field.

Academic Fields/Career Goals: Nuclear Science.

Award: Scholarship for use in junior or senior years; not renewable. *Number:* 1–21. *Amount:* $2000.

Eligibility Requirements: Applicant must be enrolled or expecting to enroll full-time at a four-year institution or university. Available to U.S. and non-U.S. citizens.

Application Requirements: Application, references, transcript, sponsorship letter from ANS organization. *Deadline:* February 1.

Contact: Scholarship Coordinator
American Nuclear Society
555 North Kensington Avenue
La Grange Park, IL 60526
Phone: 708-352-6611
Fax: 708-352-0499
E-mail: outreach@ans.org

ROBERT T. "BOB" LINER SCHOLARSHIP

Undergraduate scholarship for students who have completed two or more years in a course of study leading to a degree in nuclear science, nuclear engineering, or a nuclear-related field.

Academic Fields/Career Goals: Nuclear Science.

Award: Scholarship for use in junior or senior years; not renewable. *Number:* 1–21. *Amount:* $2000.

Eligibility Requirements: Applicant must be enrolled or expecting to enroll full-time at a four-year institution or university. Available to U.S. and non-U.S. citizens.

Application Requirements: Application, references, transcript, sponsorship letter from ANS organization. *Deadline:* February 1.

Contact: Scholarship Coordinator
American Nuclear Society
555 North Kensington Avenue
La Grange Park, IL 60526
Phone: 708-352-6611
Fax: 708-352-0499
E-mail: outreach@ans.org

ARIZONA HYDROLOGICAL SOCIETY http://www.azhydrosoc.org

ARIZONA HYDROLOGICAL SOCIETY SCHOLARSHIP

• *See page 215*

ASSOCIATION FOR WOMEN IN SCIENCE EDUCATIONAL FOUNDATION http://www.awis.org/careers/edfoundation.html

ASSOCIATION FOR WOMEN IN SCIENCE COLLEGE SCHOLARSHIP

• *See page 82*

BARRY M. GOLDWATER SCHOLARSHIP AND EXCELLENCE IN EDUCATION FOUNDATION http://www.act.org/goldwater

BARRY M. GOLDWATER SCHOLARSHIP AND EXCELLENCE IN EDUCATION PROGRAM

• *See page 86*

DESK AND DERRICK EDUCATIONAL TRUST http://www.addc.org

DESK AND DERRICK EDUCATIONAL TRUST

• *See page 86*

HISPANIC COLLEGE FUND INC. http://www.hispanicfund.org

DEPARTMENT OF ENERGY SCHOLARSHIP PROGRAM

• *See page 142*

HISPANIC ENGINEER NATIONAL ACHIEVEMENT AWARDS CORPORATION (HENAAC) http://www.henaac.org

HISPANIC ENGINEER NATIONAL ACHIEVEMENT AWARDS CORPORATION SCHOLARSHIP PROGRAM

• *See page 116*

INNOVATION AND SCIENCE COUNCIL OF BRITISH COLUMBIA http://www.bcinnovationcouncil.com

PAUL AND HELEN TRUSSEL SCIENCE AND TECHNOLOGY SCHOLARSHIP

• *See page 87*

INSTITUTE OF ENVIRONMENTAL SCIENCES AND TECHNOLOGY (IEST) http://www.iest.org

ROBERT N. HANCOCK MEMORIAL SCHOLARSHIP

• *See page 132*

NASA WEST VIRGINIA SPACE GRANT CONSORTIUM http://www.nasa.wvu.edu

WEST VIRGINIA SPACE GRANT CONSORTIUM UNDERGRADUATE FELLOWSHIP PROGRAM

• *See page 121*

NATIONAL SCIENCE TEACHERS ASSOCIATION http://www.nsta.org

TOSHIBA/NSTA EXPLORAVISION AWARDS PROGRAM

• *See page 193*

SOCIETY OF NUCLEAR MEDICINE http://www.snm.org

PAUL COLE SCHOLARSHIP

• *See page 342*

UNIVERSITIES SPACE RESEARCH ASSOCIATION http://www.usra.edu

UNIVERSITIES SPACE RESEARCH ASSOCIATION SCHOLARSHIP PROGRAM

• *See page 88*

WATER ENVIRONMENT FEDERATION http://www.wef.org

CANHAM GRADUATE STUDIES SCHOLARSHIPS

• *See page 136*

NURSING

AIR FORCE RESERVE OFFICER TRAINING CORPS http://www.afrotc.com

AIR FORCE ROTC FOUR-YEAR NURSING SCHOLARSHIP

Scholarship offers qualified individuals the chance to compete for scholarships of up to $15,000 per academic year. Nursing students can compete for scholarships through the In-College Scholarship Program, or may qualify for a nursing scholarship.

Academic Fields/Career Goals: Nursing.

Award: Scholarship for use in sophomore, junior, or senior years; not renewable. *Number:* varies. *Amount:* up to $15,000.

Eligibility Requirements: Applicant must be enrolled or expecting to enroll full-time at a four-year institution or university. Available to U.S. citizens.

Application Requirements: Application. *Deadline:* varies.

Contact: Capt. Elmarko Magee, Chief of Advertising
Air Force Reserve Officer Training Corps
551 East Maxwell Boulevard
Maxwell AFB, AL 36112-6106
Phone: 866-423-7682

ALBERTA HERITAGE SCHOLARSHIP FUND/ ALBERTA SCHOLARSHIP PROGRAMS http://www.alis.gov.ab.ca

ALBERTA HERITAGE SCHOLARSHIP FUND ABORIGINAL HEALTH CAREERS BURSARY

• *See page 129*

AMARILLO AREA FOUNDATION http://www.aaf-hf.org

E. EUGENE WAIDE, MD MEMORIAL SCHOLARSHIP

Scholarship for graduating senior from Ochiltree, Hansford, Lipscomb, Hutchinson, Roberts or Hemphill counties. Applicant must pursue a career as LVN, BSN (junior or senior), MSN.

Academic Fields/Career Goals: Nursing.

Award: Scholarship for use in freshman, sophomore, junior, senior, or graduate years; not renewable. *Number:* varies. *Amount:* varies.

Eligibility Requirements: Applicant must be enrolled or expecting to enroll full- or part-time at a two-year or four-year or technical institution or university and resident of Texas. Available to U.S. citizens.

Application Requirements: Application, photo. *Deadline:* February 1.

Contact: Scholarship Screening Committee
Amarillo Area Foundation
801 South Fillmore Street, Suite 700
Amarillo, TX 79101
Phone: 806-376-4521

NANCY GERALD MEMORIAL NURSING SCHOLARSHIP

Scholarship of $500 for graduating senior from one of the 26 counties in Texas. Applicant must be majoring in the field of nursing at Amarillo College or West Texas A & M University pursuing AAS, BSN or MSN degree.

Academic Fields/Career Goals: Nursing.

Award: Scholarship for use in freshman, sophomore, junior, senior, or graduate years; not renewable. *Number:* varies. *Amount:* $500.

Eligibility Requirements: Applicant must be enrolled or expecting to enroll full- or part-time at a two-year or four-year institution or university; resident of Texas and studying in Texas. Applicant must have 2.5 GPA or higher. Available to U.S. citizens.

Application Requirements: Application, photo. *Deadline:* February 1.

Contact: Scholarship Screening Committee
Amarillo Area Foundation
801 South Fillmore Street, Suite 700
Amarillo, TX 79101
Phone: 806-376-4521

AMERICAN ASSOCIATION OF CRITICAL-CARE NURSES (AACN) http://www.aacn.org

AACN EDUCATIONAL ADVANCEMENT SCHOLARSHIPS-BSN COMPLETION

Award for juniors and seniors currently enrolled in a baccalaureate degree program in nursing accredited by State Board of Nursing. Must be AACN member with active RN license who is currently or has recently worked in critical care. Minimum 3.0 GPA. Student may receive award a maximum of two times.

Academic Fields/Career Goals: Nursing.

Award: Scholarship for use in junior or senior years; not renewable. *Number:* 50–100. *Amount:* $1500.

Eligibility Requirements: Applicant must be enrolled or expecting to enroll full- or part-time at a four-year institution or university. Applicant or parent of applicant must be member of American Association of Critical Care Nurses. Applicant or parent of applicant must have employment or volunteer experience in nursing. Applicant must have 3.0 GPA or higher. Available to U.S. and Canadian citizens.

Application Requirements: Application, essay, references, transcript, verification of critical care experience. *Deadline:* April 1.

Contact: Mary Fran Tracy, President
American Association of Critical-Care Nurses (AACN)
101 Columbia
Aliso Viejo, CA 92656-4109
Phone: 949-362-2000
Fax: 949-362-2020
E-mail: research@aacn.org

AMERICAN ASSOCIATION OF NEUROSCIENCE NURSES http://www.aann.org

NEUROSCIENCE NURSING FOUNDATION SCHOLARSHIP

Scholarship available for registered nurse to attend an NLN accredited school. Submit letter of school acceptance along with application, transcript, and copy of current RN license. Applicants should have diploma or AD.

Academic Fields/Career Goals: Nursing.

Award: Scholarship for use in freshman, sophomore, junior, senior, or graduate years; not renewable. *Number:* varies. *Amount:* $1500.

Eligibility Requirements: Applicant must be enrolled or expecting to enroll full- or part-time at a two-year or four-year institution or university. Applicant must have 3.0 GPA or higher. Available to U.S. citizens.

Application Requirements: Application, transcript, letter of acceptance. *Deadline:* January 15.

Contact: Scholarship Programs Coordinator
American Association of Neuroscience Nurses
4700 West Lake Avenue
Glenview, IL 60025-1485
Phone: 888-557-2266
E-mail: info@aann.org

AMERICAN HOLISTIC NURSES ASSOCIATION (AHNA) http://www.ahna.org

AHNA CHARLOTTE MCGUIRE SCHOLRSHIP

Scholarship for students pursuing holistic nursing education. Applicants should maintain a GPA of 3.0 and should be a member of AHNA.

Academic Fields/Career Goals: Nursing.

Award: Scholarship for use in freshman, sophomore, junior, senior, or graduate years; not renewable. *Number:* varies. *Amount:* varies.

Eligibility Requirements: Applicant must be enrolled or expecting to enroll full- or part-time at a four-year institution or university. Applicant or parent of applicant must be member of American Holistic Nurses Association. Applicant must have 3.0 GPA or higher. Available to U.S. citizens.

Application Requirements: Application, essay, financial need analysis, transcript. *Deadline:* March 15.

Contact: Scholarship Committee
American Holistic Nurses Association (AHNA)
323 North San Francisco Street, Suite 201
Flagstaff, AZ 86001
Phone: 800-278-2462 Ext. 10
Fax: 928-526-2752
E-mail: info@ahna.org

AMERICAN LEGION AUXILIARY DEPARTMENT OF ARIZONA http://www.azlegion.org/majorp~2.htm

AMERICAN LEGION AUXILIARY DEPARTMENT OF ARIZONA NURSES' SCHOLARSHIPS

Award for Arizona residents enrolled in their second year at an institution in Arizona awarding degree as a registered nurse. Preference given to immediate family member of a veteran. Must be a U.S. citizen and resident of Arizona for one year.

Academic Fields/Career Goals: Nursing.

Award: Scholarship for use in sophomore, junior, or senior years; not renewable. *Number:* 4. *Amount:* $500.

Eligibility Requirements: Applicant must be enrolled or expecting to enroll full-time at a two-year or four-year institution or university; resident of Arizona and studying in Arizona. Available to U.S. citizens.

Application Requirements: Application, autobiography, essay, financial need analysis, photo, references, test scores, transcript. *Deadline:* May 15.

Contact: Department Secretary and Treasurer
American Legion Auxiliary Department of Arizona
4701 North 19th Avenue, Suite 100
Phoenix, AZ 85015-3727
Phone: 602-241-1080
Fax: 602-604-9640
E-mail: amlegauxaz@mcleodusa.net

AMERICAN LEGION AUXILIARY DEPARTMENT OF ARKANSAS http://www.arlegion.org

AMERICAN LEGION AUXILIARY DEPARTMENT OF ARKANSAS NURSE SCHOLARSHIP

One-time award of $250 for Arkansas residents who are the children of veterans who served during eligibility dates for membership. Must attend nursing program in Arkansas. Open to high school seniors. Selection is based on character, Americanism, leadership, financial need, and scholarship.

Academic Fields/Career Goals: Nursing.

Award: Scholarship for use in freshman year; not renewable. *Number:* 1. *Amount:* $250.

Eligibility Requirements: Applicant must be high school student; planning to enroll or expecting to enroll full-time at a four-year institution or university; resident of Arkansas; studying in Arkansas and must have an interest in leadership. Available to U.S. citizens. Applicant or parent must meet one or more of the following requirements: general military experience; retired from active duty; disabled or killed as a result of military service; prisoner of war; or missing in action.

Application Requirements: Application, essay, financial need analysis, references, self-addressed stamped envelope, test scores, transcript, copy of veteran discharge papers, branch of service, dates of service, DD Form 214. *Deadline:* March 1.

Contact: Department Secretary
American Legion Auxiliary Department of Arkansas
1415 West Seventh Street
Little Rock, AR 72201
Phone: 501-374-5836
Fax: 501-372-0855
E-mail: arkaux@juno.com

AMERICAN LEGION AUXILIARY DEPARTMENT OF CALIFORNIA http://www.calegionaux.org

AMERICAN LEGION AUXILIARY DEPARTMENT OF CALIFORNIA PAST PRESIDENTS' PARLEY NURSING SCHOLARSHIPS

Award for student entering into or continuing studies in a nursing program.

Academic Fields/Career Goals: Nursing.

Award: Scholarship for use in freshman, sophomore, junior, or senior years; not renewable. *Number:* varies. *Amount:* $500–$1000.

Eligibility Requirements: Applicant must be enrolled or expecting to enroll full- or part-time at a four-year institution or university. Available to U.S. citizens. Applicant or parent must meet one or more of the following requirements: Army experience; retired from active duty; disabled or killed as a result of military service; prisoner of war; or missing in action.

Application Requirements: Application, references, transcript. *Deadline:* April 4.

Contact: Theresa Jacob, Secretary/Treasurer
American Legion Auxiliary Department of California
401 Van Ness Avenue, Room 113
San Francisco, CA 94102
Phone: 415-862-5092
Fax: 415-861-8365
E-mail: calegionaux@calegionaux.org

AMERICAN LEGION AUXILIARY DEPARTMENT OF COLORADO http://www.coloradolegion.org

AMERICAN LEGION AUXILIARY DEPARTMENT OF COLORADO PAST PRESIDENTS' PARLEY NURSES SCHOLARSHIP

Open to children, spouses, grandchildren, and great-grandchildren of American Legion veterans, and veterans who served in the armed forces during eligibility dates for membership in the American Legion. Must be Colorado residents who have been accepted by an accredited school of nursing in Colorado.

Academic Fields/Career Goals: Nursing.

Award: Scholarship for use in freshman, sophomore, junior, senior, or graduate years; not renewable. *Number:* 3–5. *Amount:* up to $500.

Eligibility Requirements: Applicant must be enrolled or expecting to enroll full- or part-time at a four-year institution or university; resident of Colorado and studying in Colorado. Applicant or parent of applicant must be member of American Legion or Auxiliary. Available to U.S. citizens. Applicant or parent must meet one or more of the following requirements: general military experience; retired from active duty; disabled or killed as a result of military service; prisoner of war; or missing in action.

Application Requirements: Application, essay, financial need analysis, references. *Deadline:* April 1.

Contact: Department of Colorado
American Legion Auxiliary Department of Colorado
7465 East First Avenue, Suite D
Denver, CO 80230
Phone: 303-367-5388
E-mail: ala@coloradolegion.org

AMERICAN LEGION AUXILIARY DEPARTMENT OF IDAHO

AMERICAN LEGION AUXILIARY DEPARTMENT OF IDAHO NURSING SCHOLARSHIP

Scholarship available to veterans or the children of veterans who are majoring in nursing. Applicants must be 17 to 35 years of age and residents of Idaho for five years prior to applying. One-time award of $1000.

Academic Fields/Career Goals: Nursing.

Award: Scholarship for use in freshman, sophomore, junior, or senior years; not renewable. *Number:* 1. *Amount:* $1000.

Eligibility Requirements: Applicant must be age 17-35; enrolled or expecting to enroll full-time at a four-year institution or university and resident of Idaho. Available to U.S. citizens. Applicant or parent must meet one or more of the following requirements: general military experience; retired from active duty; disabled or killed as a result of military service; prisoner of war; or missing in action.

Application Requirements: Application, financial need analysis, photo, references, self-addressed stamped envelope, transcript. *Deadline:* May 15.

Contact: Mary Chase, Secretary
American Legion Auxiliary Department of Idaho
905 South Warren Street
Boise, ID 83706-3825
Phone: 208-342-7066
Fax: 208-342-7066
E-mail: idalegionaux@msn.com

AMERICAN LEGION AUXILIARY DEPARTMENT OF IOWA http://www.ialegion.org

AMERICAN LEGION AUXILIARY DEPARTMENT OF IOWA M.V. MCCRAE MEMORIAL NURSES SCHOLARSHIP

One-time award available to the child of an Iowa American Legion Post member or Iowa American Legion Auxiliary Unit member. Award is for full-time study in an accredited nursing program. Must be U.S. citizen and Iowa resident. Must attend an Iowa institution.

Academic Fields/Career Goals: Nursing.

Award: Scholarship for use in freshman, sophomore, junior, or senior years; not renewable. *Number:* 1. *Amount:* $400.

Eligibility Requirements: Applicant must be enrolled or expecting to enroll full-time at a two-year or four-year institution or university; resident of Iowa and studying in Iowa. Applicant or parent of applicant must be member of American Legion or Auxiliary. Available to U.S. citizens. Applicant or parent must meet one or more of the following requirements: general military experience; retired from active duty; disabled or killed as a result of military service; prisoner of war; or missing in action.

Application Requirements: Application, autobiography, essay, financial need analysis, photo, references, self-addressed stamped envelope, test scores, transcript. *Deadline:* June 1.

Contact: Marlene Valentine, Secretary and Treasurer
American Legion Auxiliary Department of Iowa
720 Lyon Street
Des Moines, IA 50309
Phone: 515-282-7987
Fax: 515-282-7583
E-mail: alasectreas@ialegion.org

AMERICAN LEGION AUXILIARY DEPARTMENT OF MAINE http://www.mainelegion.org

AMERICAN LEGION AUXILIARY DEPARTMENT OF MAINE PAST PRESIDENTS' PARLEY NURSES SCHOLARSHIP

• *See page 329*

AMERICAN LEGION AUXILIARY DEPARTMENT OF MARYLAND http://www.alamd.org

AMERICAN LEGION AUXILIARY DEPARTMENT OF MARYLAND PAST PRESIDENTS' PARLEY NURSES SCHOLARSHIP

One scholarship of $2000 for undergraduate students enrolled full-time in nursing study at accredited colleges or universities. Must be U.S. citizen and a descendant of an ex-service woman or ex-service veteran.

Academic Fields/Career Goals: Nursing.

Award: Scholarship for use in freshman, sophomore, junior, or senior years; renewable. *Number:* 1. *Amount:* $2000.

Eligibility Requirements: Applicant must be enrolled or expecting to enroll full-time at a four-year institution or university. Available to U.S. and non-U.S. citizens. Applicant or parent must meet one or more of the following requirements: general military experience; retired from active duty; disabled or killed as a result of military service; prisoner of war; or missing in action.

Application Requirements: Application, financial need analysis, references, transcript. *Deadline:* May 1.

Contact: Meredith Beeg, Vice President
American Legion Auxiliary Department of Maryland
1589 Sulphur Spring Road, Suite 105
Baltimore, MD 21227
Phone: 410-242-9519
Fax: 410-242-9553
E-mail: hq@alamd.org

AMERICAN LEGION AUXILIARY DEPARTMENT OF MICHIGAN http://www.michalaux.org

AMERICAN LEGION AUXILIARY DEPARTMENT OF MICHIGAN MEDICAL CAREER SCHOLARSHIP

• *See page 329*

AMERICAN LEGION AUXILIARY DEPARTMENT OF MISSOURI

AMERICAN LEGION AUXILIARY DEPARTMENT OF MISSOURI PAST PRESIDENTS' PARLEY SCHOLARSHIP

Scholarship of $500 is awarded to high school graduate who has chosen to study nursing. $250 will be awarded each semester upon receipt of verification from the college that student is enrolled. The applicant must be a resident of Missouri and a member of a veteran's family. The applicant must be validated by the sponsoring unit. Check with sponsoring unit for details on required recommendation letters.

Academic Fields/Career Goals: Nursing.

Award: Scholarship for use in freshman year; not renewable. *Number:* 1. *Amount:* $500.

Eligibility Requirements: Applicant must be high school student; planning to enroll or expecting to enroll full-time at a two-year or four-year or technical institution or university and resident of Missouri. Applicant or parent of applicant must be member of American Legion or Auxiliary. Available to U.S. citizens. Applicant or parent must meet one or more of the following requirements: general military experience; retired from active duty; disabled or killed as a result of military service; prisoner of war; or missing in action.

Application Requirements: Application, photo, resume. *Deadline:* March 1.

Contact: Mary Doerhoff, Department Secretary/Treasurer
American Legion Auxiliary Department of Missouri
600 Ellis Boulevard
Jefferson City, MO 65101-1615
Phone: 573-636-9133
Fax: 573-635-3467

AMERICAN LEGION AUXILIARY DEPARTMENT OF NEBRASKA http://www.nebraskalegionaux.net

AMERICAN LEGION AUXILIARY DEPARTMENT OF NEBRASKA NURSE'S GIFT TUITION SCHOLARSHIP

One-time scholarship for a Nebraska resident who is a veteran or a child of a veteran who served in the armed forces during the dates of eligibility for American Legion membership. Proof of enrollment in nursing program at eligible institution required. Must rank in upper third of class or have a minimum 3.0 GPA.

Academic Fields/Career Goals: Nursing.

Award: Scholarship for use in freshman, sophomore, junior, or senior years; not renewable. *Number:* 1–20. *Amount:* $200–$400.

Eligibility Requirements: Applicant must be enrolled or expecting to enroll full-time at a two-year or four-year institution or university and resident of Nebraska. Applicant must have 3.0 GPA or higher. Available to U.S. citizens. Applicant or parent must meet one or more of the following requirements: general military experience; retired from active duty; disabled or killed as a result of military service; prisoner of war; or missing in action.

Application Requirements: Application, essay, financial need analysis, references, test scores, transcript, letter of acceptance, proof of enrollment. *Deadline:* March 15.

Contact: Jackie O'Neill, Department Secretary
American Legion Auxiliary Department of Nebraska
PO Box 5227
Lincoln, NE 68505-0227
Phone: 402-466-1808
Fax: 402-466-0182
E-mail: neaux@alltel.net

AMERICAN LEGION AUXILIARY DEPARTMENT OF NEBRASKA PRACTICAL NURSE SCHOLARSHIP

Nonrenewable scholarship for a veteran or a child of a veteran who served in the armed forces during the dates of eligibility for American Legion membership. For full-time undergraduate study toward nursing degree at eligible institution. Must be a Nebraska resident. Must rank in upper third of class or have a minimum 3.0 GPA.

Academic Fields/Career Goals: Nursing.

Award: Scholarship for use in freshman, sophomore, junior, or senior years; not renewable. *Number:* 1–3. *Amount:* $200–$400.

Eligibility Requirements: Applicant must be enrolled or expecting to enroll full-time at a two-year or four-year institution or university and resident of Nebraska. Applicant must have 3.0 GPA or higher. Available to U.S. citizens. Applicant or parent must meet one or more of the following requirements: general military experience; retired from active duty; disabled or killed as a result of military service; prisoner of war; or missing in action.

Application Requirements: Application, essay, financial need analysis, references, test scores, transcript, letter of acceptance, proof of enrollment. *Deadline:* March 15.

Contact: Jackie O'Neill, Department Secretary
American Legion Auxiliary Department of Nebraska
PO Box 5227
Lincoln, NE 68505-0227
Phone: 402-466-1808
Fax: 402-466-0182
E-mail: neaux@alltel.net

AMERICAN LEGION AUXILIARY DEPARTMENT OF NEW MEXICO

AMERICAN LEGION AUXILIARY DEPARTMENT OF NEW MEXICO PAST PRESIDENTS' PARLEY NURSES SCHOLARSHIP

One-time award of $250 available to children of veterans who served in the Armed Forces during the eligibility dates for American Legion membership. Must be New Mexico resident, high school senior, and in pursuit of a nursing degree full-time at an accredited institution.

Academic Fields/Career Goals: Nursing.

Award: Scholarship for use in freshman year; not renewable. *Number:* 1. *Amount:* $250.

Eligibility Requirements: Applicant must be high school student; planning to enroll or expecting to enroll full-time at a two-year or four-year institution or university and resident of New Mexico. Available to U.S. citizens. Applicant or parent must meet one or more of the following requirements: general military experience; retired from active duty; disabled or killed as a result of military service; prisoner of war; or missing in action.

Application Requirements: Application, essay, references, self-addressed stamped envelope, transcript. *Deadline:* April 4.

Contact: Loreen Jorgensen, Treasurer
American Legion Auxiliary Department of New Mexico
1215 Mountain Road, NE
Albuquerque, NM 87102
Phone: 505-242-9918
Fax: 505-247-0478

AMERICAN LEGION AUXILIARY DEPARTMENT OF NORTH DAKOTA http://www.ndlegion.org

AMERICAN LEGION AUXILIARY DEPARTMENT OF NORTH DAKOTA PAST PRESIDENTS' PARLEY NURSES SCHOLARSHIP

One-time award for North Dakota resident who is the child, grandchild, or great-grandchild of a member of the American Legion or Auxiliary. Must be a graduate of a North Dakota high school and attending a nursing program in North Dakota. A minimum 2.5 GPA is required.

Academic Fields/Career Goals: Nursing.

Award: Scholarship for use in freshman year; not renewable. *Number:* 5. *Amount:* $500.

Eligibility Requirements: Applicant must be enrolled or expecting to enroll full- or part-time at a four-year institution or university; resident of North Dakota and studying in North Dakota. Applicant or parent of applicant must be member of American Legion or Auxiliary. Applicant must have 2.5 GPA or higher. Available to U.S. citizens. Applicant or parent must meet one or more of the following requirements: general military experience; retired from active duty; disabled or killed as a result of military service; prisoner of war; or missing in action.

Application Requirements: Application, autobiography, essay, financial need analysis, self-addressed stamped envelope, test scores, transcript. *Deadline:* May 15.

Contact: Myrna Ronholm, Department Secretary
American Legion Auxiliary Department of North Dakota
PO Box 1060
Jamestown, ND 58402-1060
Phone: 701-253-5992
E-mail: ala-hq@ndlegion.org

AMERICAN LEGION AUXILIARY DEPARTMENT OF OHIO

AMERICAN LEGION AUXILIARY DEPARTMENT OF OHIO PAST PRESIDENTS' PARLEY NURSES SCHOLARSHIP

One-time award worth $300 to $500 for Ohio residents who are the children or grandchildren of a veteran, living or deceased. Must enroll or be enrolled in a nursing program. Application requests must be received by May 1.

Academic Fields/Career Goals: Nursing.

Award: Scholarship for use in freshman, sophomore, junior, or senior years; not renewable. *Number:* 15–20. *Amount:* $300–$500.

Eligibility Requirements: Applicant must be enrolled or expecting to enroll full-time at a two-year or four-year institution or university and resident of Ohio. Available to U.S. citizens. Applicant or parent must meet one or more of the following requirements: general military experience; retired from active duty; disabled or killed as a result of military service; prisoner of war; or missing in action.

Application Requirements: Application, references. *Deadline:* May 1.

Contact: Heather Amspaugh, Scholarship Coordinator
American Legion Auxiliary Department of Ohio
PO Box 2760
Zanesville, OH 43702-2760
Phone: 740-452-8245
Fax: 740-452-2620
E-mail: hamspaugh@rrohio.com

AMERICAN LEGION AUXILIARY DEPARTMENT OF OREGON

AMERICAN LEGION AUXILIARY DEPARTMENT OF OREGON NURSES SCHOLARSHIP

One-time award for Oregon residents entering their freshman year who are the children of veterans who served during eligibility dates for American Legion membership. Must enroll in a nursing program. Contact local units for application.

Academic Fields/Career Goals: Nursing.

Award: Scholarship for use in freshman year; not renewable. *Number:* 1. *Amount:* $1500.

Eligibility Requirements: Applicant must be high school student; planning to enroll or expecting to enroll full- or part-time at a four-year institution or university and resident of Oregon. Available to U.S. citizens. Applicant or parent must meet one or more of the following requirements: general military experience; retired from active duty; disabled or killed as a result of military service; prisoner of war; or missing in action.

Application Requirements: Application, essay, financial need analysis, interview, transcript. *Deadline:* May 15.

Contact: Pat Calhoun-Floren, Secretary
American Legion Auxiliary Department of Oregon
PO Box 1730
Wilsonville, OR 97070
Phone: 503-682-3162
Fax: 503-685-5008
E-mail: pcalhoun@pcez.com

AMERICAN LEGION AUXILIARY DEPARTMENT OF SOUTH DAKOTA

AMERICAN LEGION AUXILIARY DEPARTMENT OF SOUTH DAKOTA LOIS HALLBERG NURSE'S SCHOLARSHIP

Award of $500 for residents of South Dakota who are graduates of an accredited high school and interested in a career in nursing. Must be a veteran's or auxiliary member's child or grandchild.

Academic Fields/Career Goals: Nursing.

Award: Scholarship for use in freshman year; not renewable. *Number:* 2. *Amount:* $500.

Eligibility Requirements: Applicant must be high school student; planning to enroll or expecting to enroll full-time at a four-year institution or university and resident of South Dakota. Applicant or parent of applicant must be member of American Legion or Auxiliary. Available to U.S. and non-U.S. citizens. Applicant or parent must meet one or more of the following requirements: general military experience; retired from active duty; disabled or killed as a result of military service; prisoner of war; or missing in action.

Application Requirements: Application, essay, financial need analysis, references. *Deadline:* March 1.

Contact: Patricia Coyle, Executive Secretary
American Legion Auxiliary Department of South Dakota
PO Box 117
Huron, SD 57350
Phone: 605-353-1793
Fax: 605-352-0336
E-mail: sdlegionaux@msn.com

AMERICAN LEGION AUXILIARY DEPARTMENT OF WASHINGTON http://www.walegion-aux.org

AMERICAN LEGION AUXILIARY DEPARTMENT OF WASHINGTON MARGARITE MCALPIN NURSE'S SCHOLARSHIP

One award for a child or grandchild of a veteran pursuing an education in nursing or have served in the Armed Forces. May be a high school senior or an enrolled nursing student. Submit a brief statement of military service of veteran parent or grandparent. Must be Washington residents.

Academic Fields/Career Goals: Nursing.

Award: Scholarship for use in freshman, sophomore, junior, senior, or graduate years; not renewable. *Number:* 1. *Amount:* $300.

Eligibility Requirements: Applicant must be enrolled or expecting to enroll full-time at a two-year or four-year institution or university and resident of Washington. Available to U.S. citizens. Applicant or parent must meet one or more of the following requirements: general military experience; retired from active duty; disabled or killed as a result of military service; prisoner of war; or missing in action.

Application Requirements: Application, autobiography, essay, financial need analysis, references, transcript. *Deadline:* April 1.

Contact: Nicole Ross, News Department Secretary
American Legion Auxiliary Department of Washington
3600 Ruddell Road
Lacey, WA 98503
Phone: 360-456-5995
Fax: 360-491-7442
E-mail: alawash@qwest.net

AMERICAN LEGION AUXILIARY DEPARTMENT OF WISCONSIN http://www.amlegionauxwi.org

AMERICAN LEGION AUXILIARY DEPARTMENT OF WISCONSIN PAST PRESIDENTS' PARLEY REGISTERED NURSE SCHOLARSHIP

One-time award of $1000. Applicant must be in nursing school or have positive acceptance to an accredited hospital or university registered nursing program. Applicant must be a daughter, son, wife, or widow of a veteran. Granddaughters and great-granddaughters of veterans who are auxiliary members may also apply. Must submit certification of an American Legion Auxiliary unit president, copy of proof that veteran was in service (i.e. discharge papers), letters of recommendation, transcripts, and essay. Must have minimum 3.5 GPA, show financial need, and be a resident of Wisconsin. Applications available on Web site: http://www.legion-aux.org.

Academic Fields/Career Goals: Nursing.

Award: Scholarship for use in freshman, sophomore, junior, or senior years; not renewable. *Number:* 3. *Amount:* $1000.

Eligibility Requirements: Applicant must be enrolled or expecting to enroll full- or part-time at an institution or university and resident of Wisconsin. Applicant or parent of applicant must be member of American Legion or Auxiliary. Applicant must have 3.5 GPA or higher. Available to U.S. citizens. Applicant or parent must meet one or more of the following requirements: general military experience; retired from active duty; disabled or killed as a result of military service; prisoner of war; or missing in action.

Application Requirements: Application, essay, financial need analysis, references, transcript. *Deadline:* March 15.

Contact: Kim Henderson, Scholarship Information
American Legion Auxiliary Department of Wisconsin
PO Box 140
Portage, WI 53901-0140
Phone: 608-745-0124
Fax: 608-745-1947

AMERICAN LEGION AUXILIARY DEPARTMENT OF WYOMING

AMERICAN LEGION AUXILIARY DEPARTMENT OF WYOMING PAST PRESIDENTS' PARLEY HEALTH CARE SCHOLARSHIP

• *See page 210*

AMERICAN LEGION DEPARTMENT OF KANSAS http://www.ksamlegion.org

HOBBLE (LPN) NURSING SCHOLARSHIP

Award of $300, payable one-time at the start of the first semester. Awarded only upon acceptance and verification of enrollment by the scholarship winner in an accredited Kansas school which awards a diploma for Licensed Practical Nursing (LPN). Must pursue this profession in a health related institution such as a nursing home or hospital in Kansas. Must have attained the age of 18 prior to taking the Kansas state board examination. Must be a Kansas resident.

Academic Fields/Career Goals: Nursing.

Award: Scholarship for use in freshman year; not renewable. *Number:* 1. *Amount:* $300.

Eligibility Requirements: Applicant must be age 18 and over; enrolled or expecting to enroll full-time at a two-year institution; resident of Kansas and studying in Kansas. Available to U.S. citizens.

Application Requirements: Application, financial need analysis. *Deadline:* February 15.

Contact: Jim Gravenstein, Chairman, Scholarship Committee
American Legion Department of Kansas
1314 SW Topeka Boulevard
Topeka, MD 66612
Phone: 785-232-9513
Fax: 785-232-1399

AMERICAN LEGION DEPARTMENT OF MISSOURI http://www.missourilegion.org

M.D. "JACK" MURPHY MEMORIAL SCHOLARSHIP

One $750 award for two successive semesters will be given to a Missouri resident who is a RN and under the age of 21. Applicant must be unmarried and a descendant of a veteran with at least ninety days active service in the U.S. Army, Navy, Air Force, Marines or Coast Guard receiving a Honorable Discharge for service. Applicant must have graduated in the top forty percent of their high school class or have a "C" or equivalent.

Academic Fields/Career Goals: Nursing.

Award: Scholarship for use in freshman year; not renewable. *Number:* 1. *Amount:* $750.

Eligibility Requirements: Applicant must be high school student; age 21 or under; planning to enroll or expecting to enroll full-time at a two-year or four-year institution or university; single female and resident of Missouri. Available to U.S. citizens. Applicant or parent must meet one or more of the following requirements: general military experience; retired from active duty; disabled or killed as a result of military service; prisoner of war; or missing in action.

Application Requirements: Application, financial need analysis, test scores, copy of the veteran's discharge or separation notice. *Deadline:* April 20.

Contact: John Doane, Chairman
American Legion, Department of Missouri
PO Box 179
Jefferson City, MO 65102-0179
Phone: 417-924-8186
Fax: 573-893-2980

AMERICAN MOBILE HEALTHCARE http://www.americanmobile.com

AMERICAN MOBILE HEALTHCARE ANNUAL SCHOLARSHIP

Scholarship of $2000 awarded to students enrolled in a bachelor's degree in nursing or master's degree in nursing program. Applicant must be enrolled in full time study.

Academic Fields/Career Goals: Nursing.

Award: Scholarship for use in freshman, sophomore, junior, senior, or graduate years; not renewable. *Number:* 1. *Amount:* up to $2000.

Eligibility Requirements: Applicant must be enrolled or expecting to enroll full-time at a four-year institution or university. Available to U.S. citizens.

Application Requirements: Application. *Deadline:* June 1.

Contact: Scholarship Committee
American Mobile Healthcare
12400 High Bluff Drive
San Diego, CA 92130
Phone: 800-282-0300
Fax: 800-282-0328
E-mail: contact@americanmobile.com

AMERICAN NEPHROLOGY NURSES' ASSOCIATION http://www.annanurse.org

ABBOTT/PAMELA BALZER CAREER MOBILITY SCHOLARSHIP

Scholarships available to support qualified ANNA members, who have been members for a minimum of two years, in the pursuit of either a BSN or advanced degree in nursing that will enhance their nephrology nursing practice. Details on Web site http://www.annanurse.org.

Academic Fields/Career Goals: Nursing.

Award: Scholarship for use in freshman, sophomore, junior, senior, graduate, or postgraduate years; not renewable. *Number:* 1. *Amount:* $2500.

Eligibility Requirements: Applicant must be enrolled or expecting to enroll full- or part-time at a four-year institution or university. Applicant or parent of applicant must be member of American Nephrology Nurses' Association. Applicant or parent of applicant must have employment or volunteer experience in nursing. Available to U.S. citizens.

American Nephrology Nurses' Association (continued)

Application Requirements: Application, essay, references, transcript. *Deadline:* October 15.

Contact: Sharon Longton, Awards, Scholarships, and Grants Chairperson
American Nephrology Nurses' Association
200 East Holly Avenue, PO Box 56
Pitman, NJ 08071-0056
Phone: 313-966-2674
E-mail: slongton@dmc.org

AMERICAN NEPHROLOGY NURSES' ASSOCIATION CAREER MOBILITY SCHOLARSHIP

Scholarships available to support qualified ANNA members, who have been a member for a minimum two years, in the pursuit of either BSN or advanced degrees in nursing that will enhance their nephrology nursing practice. Must be accepted or enrolled in baccalaureate or higher degree program in nursing. Must be actively involved in nephrology nursing related health care services. Details on Web site http://www.annanurse.org.

Academic Fields/Career Goals: Nursing.

Award: Scholarship for use in freshman, sophomore, junior, senior, graduate, or postgraduate years; not renewable. *Number:* 5. *Amount:* $2000.

Eligibility Requirements: Applicant must be enrolled or expecting to enroll full- or part-time at a four-year institution or university. Applicant or parent of applicant must be member of American Nephrology Nurses' Association. Applicant or parent of applicant must have employment or volunteer experience in nursing. Available to U.S. citizens.

Application Requirements: Application, essay, references, transcript, acceptance letter. *Deadline:* October 15.

Contact: Sharon Longton, Awards, Scholarships and Grants Chairperson
American Nephrology Nurses' Association
200 East Holly Avenue, PO Box 56
Pitman, NJ 08071-0056
Phone: 313-966-2674
E-mail: slongton@dmc.org

AMERICAN NEPHROLOGY NURSES' ASSOCIATION NNCC CAREER MOBILITY SCHOLARSHIP

Applicants must be current full member of ANNA, having been a member for a minimum of two years. Must have been accepted or enrolled in a baccalaureate or higher degree program in nursing. Must be actively involved in nephrology nursing related health care services. The applicant must hold a current credential as a certified nephrology nurse (CNN) or certified dialysis nurse (CDN) administered by the Nephrology Nursing Certification Commission (NNCC).

Academic Fields/Career Goals: Nursing.

Award: Scholarship for use in freshman, sophomore, junior, senior, graduate, or postgraduate years; not renewable. *Number:* 3. *Amount:* $2000.

Eligibility Requirements: Applicant must be enrolled or expecting to enroll full- or part-time at a four-year institution or university. Applicant or parent of applicant must be member of American Nephrology Nurses' Association. Applicant or parent of applicant must have employment or volunteer experience in nursing. Available to U.S. citizens.

Application Requirements: Application, essay, references, transcript. *Deadline:* October 15.

Contact: Sharon Longton, Awards, Scholarships and Grants Chairperson
American Nephrology Nurses' Association
200 East Holly Avenue, PO Box 56
Pitman, NJ 08071-0056
Phone: 313-966-2674
E-mail: slongton@dmc.org

AMERICAN NEPHROLOGY NURSES' ASSOCIATION WATSON PHARMA INC. CAREER MOBILITY SCHOLARSHIP

Applicants must be current full member of ANNA, having been a member for a minimum of two years. Must have been accepted or enrolled in a baccalaureate or higher degree program in nursing. Must be actively involved in nephrology nursing related health care services. For details visit the Web site http://www.annanurse.org.

Academic Fields/Career Goals: Nursing.

Award: Scholarship for use in freshman, sophomore, junior, senior, graduate, or postgraduate years; not renewable. *Number:* 1. *Amount:* $2500.

Eligibility Requirements: Applicant must be enrolled or expecting to enroll full- or part-time at a four-year institution or university. Applicant or parent of applicant must be member of American Nephrology Nurses' Association. Applicant or parent of applicant must have employment or volunteer experience in nursing. Available to U.S. citizens.

Application Requirements: Application, essay, references, transcript. *Deadline:* October 15.

Contact: Sharon Longton, Awards, Scholarships and Grants Chairperson
American Nephrology Nurses' Association
200 East Holly Avenue, PO Box 56
Pitman, NJ 08071-0056
Phone: 313-966-2674
E-mail: slongton@dmc.org

ANNA ALCAVIS INTERNATIONAL, INC. CAREER MOBILITY SCHOLARSHIP

Scholarship to students accepted or enrolled in a baccalaureate or higher degree program in nursing. Applicant must hold a current credential as a Certified Nephrology Nurse (CNN) or Certified Dialysis Nurse (CDN) administered by the Nephrology Nursing Certification Commission (NNCC).

Academic Fields/Career Goals: Nursing.

Award: Forgivable loan for use in freshman, sophomore, junior, senior, or graduate years; renewable. *Number:* 5. *Amount:* $2000.

Eligibility Requirements: Applicant must be enrolled or expecting to enroll full-time at a four-year institution or university. Applicant or parent of applicant must be member of American Nephrology Nurses' Association. Applicant or parent of applicant must have employment or volunteer experience in nursing. Available to U.S. and non-Canadian citizens.

Application Requirements: Application, essay, financial need analysis, transcript. *Deadline:* October 15.

Contact: Sharon Longton, Awards, Scholarships, and Grants Chairperson
American Nephrology Nurses' Association
East Holly Avenue
PO Box 56
Pitman, NJ 08071-0056
Phone: 313-966-2674
E-mail: slongton@dmc.org

JANEL PARKER CAREER MOBILTY SCHOLARSHIP CAREER MOBILITY SCHOLARSHIP

Applicants must be current full member of ANNA, having been a member for a minimum of two years. Must have been accepted or enrolled in a baccalaureate or higher degree program in nursing. Must be actively involved in nephrology nursing related health care services. For details visit the Web site http://www.annanurse.org.

Academic Fields/Career Goals: Nursing.

Award: Scholarship for use in freshman, sophomore, junior, senior, graduate, or postgraduate years; not renewable. *Number:* 1. *Amount:* up to $2500.

Eligibility Requirements: Applicant must be enrolled or expecting to enroll full- or part-time at a two-year or four-year institution or university. Applicant or parent of applicant must be member of American Nephrology Nurses' Association. Applicant or parent of applicant must have employment or volunteer experience in nursing. Available to U.S. citizens.

Application Requirements: Application, essay, references, transcript. *Deadline:* October 15.

Contact: Sharon Longton, Awards, Scholarships, and Grants Chairperson
American Nephrology Nurses' Association
200 East Holly Avenue, PO Box 56
Pitman, NJ 08071-0056
Phone: 313-966-2674
E-mail: slongton@dmc.org

AMVETS DEPARTMENT OF ILLINOIS http://www.ilamvets.org

ILLINOIS AMVETS SAD SACKS NURSING SCHOLARSHIPS

Applicant must be a resident of Illinois and accepted for training at an approved school of nursing in Illinois. Preference given to child of deceased veteran and/or student nurse in training in the order: third, second, first-year student. Must submit IRS 1040 form.

Academic Fields/Career Goals: Nursing.

Award: Scholarship for use in freshman, sophomore, or junior years; not renewable. *Number:* 2–3. *Amount:* $500–$750.

Eligibility Requirements: Applicant must be age 18 and over; enrolled or expecting to enroll full-time at a two-year or four-year or technical institution or university; resident of Illinois and studying in Illinois. Available to U.S. citizens.

Application Requirements: Application, financial need analysis, references, test scores, transcript, IRS 1040 form, acceptance letter. *Deadline:* March 1.

Contact: Sara Van Dyke, Scholarship Director
AMVETS Department of Illinois
2200 South Sixth Street
Springfield, IL 62703-3496
Phone: 217-528-4713
Fax: 217-528-9896
E-mail: scholarship@amvetsillinois.com

ARIZONA HIGHER EDUCATION LOAN AUTHORITY http://www.ahela.org

AHELA NURSES SCHOLARSHIP

Scholarship to address Arizona's nurse shortage by supporting nursing education students. Nursing students will be selected based on academic achievement, financial need, and involvement in nursing organizations and community activities related to health care.

Academic Fields/Career Goals: Nursing.

Award: Scholarship for use in freshman, sophomore, junior, or senior years; not renewable. *Number:* 4. *Amount:* $1000.

Eligibility Requirements: Applicant must be enrolled or expecting to enroll full-time at a four-year institution or university and studying in Arizona. Applicant must have 2.5 GPA or higher. Available to U.S. citizens.

Application Requirements: Application, driver's license, resume. *Deadline:* March 5.

Contact: Dana Macke-Redford, Manager, Marketing, Scholarship and Outreach
Arizona Higher Education Loan Authority
2141 East Broadway Road, Suite 202
Tempe, AZ 85282
Phone: 480-383-8707 Ext. 207
E-mail: dredford@ahela.org

ARRL FOUNDATION INC. http://www.arrl.org

WILLIAM R. GOLDFARB MEMORIAL SCHOLARSHIP

• *See page 138*

ASSOCIATION OF PERI-OPERATIVE REGISTERED NURSES http://www.aorn.org/foundation

ASSOCIATION OF PERI-OPERATIVE REGISTERED NURSES

Applicant must be an RN and a member of AORN for twelve consecutive months to apply for a scholarship for an advanced degree. Recipients may reapply. Amount and number of one-time awards vary. Must be pursuing studies in nursing. Students working toward their RN need not be members of AORN. See Web site: http://www.aorn.org for application and further details.

Academic Fields/Career Goals: Nursing.

Award: Scholarship for use in freshman, sophomore, junior, senior, or graduate years; not renewable. *Number:* 90–150. *Amount:* $500–$5000.

Eligibility Requirements: Applicant must be enrolled or expecting to enroll full- or part-time at a two-year or four-year institution or university. Applicant or parent of applicant must be member of Association of Operating Room Nurses. Applicant must have 3.0 GPA or higher. Available to U.S. citizens.

Application Requirements: Application, essay, transcript. *Deadline:* June 15.

Contact: Ingrid Bendzsa, Scholarship Coordinator
Association of Peri-Operative Registered Nurses
2170 South Parker Road, Suite 300
Denver, CO 80231
Phone: 800-755-2676 Ext. 328
Fax: 303-755-4219
E-mail: ibendzsa@aorn.org

ATLANTIC HEALTH SYSTEM OVERLOOK HOSPITAL FOUNDATION http://www.overlookhospitalfoundation.com

OVERLOOK HOSPITAL FOUNDATION PROFESSIONAL DEVELOPMENT PROGRAM

• *See page 335*

BETHESDA LUTHERAN HOMES AND SERVICES, INC. http://www.blhs.org

NURSING SCHOLASTIC ACHIEVEMENT SCHOLARSHIP FOR LUTHERAN COLLEGE STUDENTS

One-time award for college nursing students with minimum 3.0 GPA who are Lutheran and have completed the sophomore year of a four-year nursing program or one year of a two-year nursing program. Must be interested in working with people with developmental disabilities. Awards of up to $1500.

Academic Fields/Career Goals: Nursing.

Award: Scholarship for use in junior or senior years; not renewable. *Number:* 1–2. *Amount:* up to $1500.

Eligibility Requirements: Applicant must be Lutheran and enrolled or expecting to enroll full-time at a two-year or four-year institution or university. Applicant must have 3.0 GPA or higher. Available to U.S. and Canadian citizens.

Application Requirements: Application, autobiography, essay, references, transcript. *Deadline:* April 15.

Contact: Thomas Heuer, Coordinator, Outreach Programs and Services
Bethesda Lutheran Homes and Services, Inc.
600 Hoffmann Drive
Watertown, WI 53094
Phone: 920-261-3050 Ext. 4449
Fax: 920-262-6513
E-mail: theuer@blhs.org

CAMBRIDGE HOME HEALTH CARE http://www.cambridgehomehealth.com

CAMBRIDGE HOME HEALTH CARE NURSING EXCELLENCE SCHOLARSHIPS

Scholarships available for study towards LPN or RN degree. Must be a home health aide/nurse's aide or LPN who has worked for two of the past three years in that position. Two scholarships awarded to Cambridge employees, and two scholarships awarded to residents of the counties where Cambridge Home Health Care offices are located.

Academic Fields/Career Goals: Nursing.

Award: Scholarship for use in freshman, sophomore, junior, or senior years; not renewable. *Number:* up to 4. *Amount:* up to $1000.

Eligibility Requirements: Applicant must be enrolled or expecting to enroll full-time at a four-year institution or university. Applicant or parent of applicant must have employment or volunteer experience in nursing. Available to U.S. citizens.

Application Requirements: Application, essay, references. *Deadline:* May 15.

Contact: Elizabeth Bever, Director of Community Relations
Cambridge Home Health Care
4085 Embassy Parkway
Akron, OH 44333
Phone: 330-668-1922 Ext. 105
Fax: 330-668-1311
E-mail: lbever@cambridgehomehealth.com

CANADIAN NURSES FOUNDATION http://www.cnf-fiic.ca

CANADIAN NURSES FOUNDATION SCHOLARSHIPS

Study awards are granted annually to Canadian nurses wishing to pursue education and research. Must be a Canadian citizen or permanent resident and provide proof of citizenship. Current CNF membership required. Must be studying in Canada. Baccalaureate students must be full-time, masters and doctoral students may be full- or part-time (enrolled in a minimum of 2 courses per semester). Additional restrictions vary by specific scholarship.

Academic Fields/Career Goals: Nursing.

Award: Scholarship for use in sophomore, junior, senior, graduate, or postgraduate years; not renewable. *Number:* up to 30. *Amount:* varies.

Eligibility Requirements: Applicant must be Canadian citizen and enrolled or expecting to enroll full- or part-time at a four-year institution or university. Applicant or parent of applicant must be member of Canadian Nurses Foundation. Applicant or parent of applicant must have employment or volunteer experience in nursing.

Application Requirements: Application, references, transcript. *Fee:* $35. *Deadline:* March 31.

Contact: Jacqueline SolÝs, Foundation Coordinator
Canadian Nurses Foundation
50 Driveway
Ottawa, ON K2P IE2
Canada
Phone: 613-237-2159 Ext. 242
Fax: 613-237-3520
E-mail: jsolis@cna-aiic.ca

CENTRAL SCHOLARSHIP BUREAU http://www.centralsb.org

CHESAPEAKE UROLOGY ASSOCIATES SCHOLARSHIP

• *See page 335*

CHILDREN'S HEALTHCARE OF ATLANTA http://www.choa.org

CHANCES-CHILDREN'S HEALTHCARE OF ATLANTA NURSING COMMITMENT TO EMPLOYMENT AND STUDY PROGRAM (CHANCES)

Applicants will receive tuition equivalent assistance up to $16,000. Must be accepted into a nursing program. Minimum 3.0 GPA required.

Academic Fields/Career Goals: Nursing.

Award: Scholarship for use in freshman, sophomore, junior, senior, graduate, or postgraduate years; renewable. *Number:* varies. *Amount:* up to $16,000.

Eligibility Requirements: Applicant must be enrolled or expecting to enroll full-time at a four-year institution or university. Applicant must have 3.0 GPA or higher. Available to U.S. citizens.

Application Requirements: Essay, resume, references, online application. *Deadline:* May 1.

Contact: Shannon Dunlap, Program Coordinator
Children's Healthcare of Atlanta
1600 Tullie Circle NE
Atlanta, GA 30329-2321
Phone: 404-785-7211
E-mail: shannon.dunlap@choa.org

OPPORTUNITIES-CHILDREN'S HEALTHCARE OF ATLANTA BILINGUAL SCHOLARSHIP

Nursing scholarship to bilingual students interested in a pediatric nursing career. Open to students or individuals looking for a career change. Minimum 3.0 GPA required.

Academic Fields/Career Goals: Nursing.

Award: Scholarship for use in freshman, sophomore, junior, senior, graduate, or postgraduate years; renewable. *Number:* varies. *Amount:* $10,000.

Eligibility Requirements: Applicant must be enrolled or expecting to enroll full-time at a four-year institution or university. Applicant must have 3.0 GPA or higher. Available to U.S. citizens.

Application Requirements: Essay, interview, resume, references, online application. *Deadline:* May 1.

Contact: Shannon Dunlap, Program Coordinator
Children's Healthcare of Atlanta
1600 Tullie Circle NE
Atlanta, GA 30329-2321
Phone: 404-785-7211
E-mail: shannon.dunlap@choa.org

CHRISTIANA CARE HEALTH SYSTEMS http://www.christianacare.org

RUTH SHAW JUNIOR BOARD SCHOLARSHIP

• *See page 336*

CLINIQUE LABORATORIES LLC http://www.clinique.com

CLINIQUE NURSING SCHOLARSHIP PROGRAM

Awarded to prospective or current students who are working toward a bachelors degree in nursing. Award amount will not exceed $6000. Minimum 3.0 GPA required.

Academic Fields/Career Goals: Nursing.

Award: Scholarship for use in freshman, sophomore, junior, or senior years; renewable. *Number:* varies. *Amount:* up to $6000.

Eligibility Requirements: Applicant must be enrolled or expecting to enroll full- or part-time at a four-year institution or university. Applicant must have 3.0 GPA or higher. Available to U.S. citizens.

Application Requirements: Application, autobiography, essay, resume, references, transcript, FAFSA, Student Aid Report (SAR). *Deadline:* May 5.

Contact: Scholarship Committee
Clinique Laboratories LLC
767 Fifth Avenue, 37th Floor
New York, NY 10153

COMMON KNOWLEDGE SCHOLARSHIP FOUNDATION http://www.cksf.org

NATIONAL NURSING SCHOLARSHIP

$400-$600 award testing students' knowledge of core college courses associated with the nursing curriculum.For more information about this scholarship, please refer to the following Web site: http://www.cksf.org/cksf.cfm?Page=Home&Subpage=NationalNursing.

Academic Fields/Career Goals: Nursing.

Award: Scholarship for use in freshman, sophomore, junior, senior, graduate, or postgraduate years; not renewable. *Number:* 1. *Amount:* $400–$600.

Eligibility Requirements: Applicant must be enrolled or expecting to enroll full- or part-time at a two-year or four-year or technical institution or university. Available to U.S. citizens.

Application Requirements: Applicant must enter a contest. *Deadline:* varies.

Contact: Mr. Daryl Hulce, President
Common Knowledge Scholarship Foundation
PO Box 290361
Davie, FL 33329-0361
Phone: 954-262-8553
Fax: 954-262-2847
E-mail: hulce@cksf.org

CONNECTICUT LEAGUE FOR NURSING http://www.ctleaguefornursing.org/scholarships.html

CONNECTICUT LEAGUE FOR NURSING SCHOLARSHIP

Award is open to nursing students. Must be a resident of Connecticut. Scholarship amount and number of awards varies.

Academic Fields/Career Goals: Nursing.

Award: Scholarship for use in freshman, sophomore, junior, senior, or graduate years; not renewable. *Number:* varies. *Amount:* varies.

Eligibility Requirements: Applicant must be enrolled or expecting to enroll full- or part-time at a two-year or four-year institution or university and resident of Connecticut. Available to U.S. citizens.

Application Requirements: Application, financial need analysis, references, transcript. *Deadline:* October 14.

Contact: Executive Director
Connecticut League for Nursing
51 North Main Street, Suite 3D
PO Box 365
Southington, CT 06489
Phone: 860-265-9621
Fax: 860-276-8798
E-mail: education@ctleaguefornursing.org

CYNTHIA E. MORGAN SCHOLARSHIP FUND (CEMS) http://www.cemsfund.com

CYNTHIA E. MORGAN MEMORIAL SCHOLARSHIP

• *See page 336*

DANISH SISTERHOOD OF AMERICA http://www.danishsisterhood.org

ELIZABETH GARDE NURSING SCHOLARSHIP

One-time award for student seeking to be in the medical profession. Must be a member of the Danish Sisterhood of America or be a son or daughter of a member. Minimum GPA of 3.0. Write for further details.

Academic Fields/Career Goals: Nursing.

Award: Scholarship for use in freshman, sophomore, junior, senior, graduate, or postgraduate years; not renewable. *Number:* 1. *Amount:* $850.

Eligibility Requirements: Applicant must be enrolled or expecting to enroll full- or part-time at a two-year or four-year or technical institution or university. Applicant or parent of applicant must be member of Danish Sisterhood of America. Applicant must have 3.0 GPA or higher. Available to U.S. and non-U.S. citizens.

Application Requirements: Application, essay, references, transcript. *Deadline:* February 28.

Contact: Donna Hansen, Scholarship Chairman
Danish Sisterhood of America
1605 South 58th street
Lincoln, NE 68506
Phone: 402-488-5820

DELAWARE HIGHER EDUCATION COMMISSION http://www.doe.k12.de.us

DELAWARE NURSING INCENTIVE SCHOLARSHIP LOAN

Award for legal residents of Delaware who are U.S. citizens or eligible non-citizens. Must be full-time student enrolled in an accredited program leading to certification as an RN or LPN. High school seniors must rank in upper half of class with at least a 2.5 cumulative GPA.

Academic Fields/Career Goals: Nursing.

Award: Forgivable loan for use in freshman, sophomore, junior, or senior years; renewable. *Number:* 1–40. *Amount:* $1000–$5000.

Eligibility Requirements: Applicant must be enrolled or expecting to enroll full- or part-time at a two-year or four-year institution and resident of Delaware. Applicant must have 2.5 GPA or higher. Available to U.S. citizens.

Application Requirements: Application, essay, test scores, transcript. *Deadline:* March 28.

Contact: Carylin Brinkley, Program Administrator
Delaware Higher Education Commission
Carvel State Office Building
820 North French Street, Fifth Floor
Wilmington, DE 19801-3509
Phone: 302-577-5240
Fax: 302-577-6765
E-mail: cbrinkley@doe.k12.de.us

DEPARTMENT OF THE ARMY http://www.goarmy.com/rotc

U.S. ARMY ROTC FOUR-YEAR NURSING SCHOLARSHIP

One-time award for freshman interested in nursing and accepted into an accredited nursing program. Must join ROTC program at the institution, pass physical evaluation, and have minimum GPA of 2.5. Applicant must be a U.S. citizen, have a qualifying SAT or ACT score, and be at least 17 years of age by college enrollment and under 31 years of age at time of graduation. Online application available.

Academic Fields/Career Goals: Nursing.

Award: Scholarship for use in freshman year; not renewable. *Number:* 250. *Amount:* up to $10,000.

Eligibility Requirements: Applicant must be age 17-31 and enrolled or expecting to enroll full-time at a four-year institution or university. Applicant must have 2.5 GPA or higher. Available to U.S. citizens. Applicant must have served in the Army or Army National Guard.

Application Requirements: Application, essay, interview, references, test scores, transcript. *Deadline:* January 10.

Contact: Sarah Williams, Scholarship Management Branch
Department of the Army
U.S. Army Cadet Command
55 Patch Road, Building 56
Fort Monroe, VA 23651-1052
Phone: 757-788-5772
Fax: 757-788-4643
E-mail: sarah.williams@usacc.army.mil

DERMATOLOGY NURSES' ASSOCIATION http://www.dnanurse.org

DERMIK LABORATORIES CAREER MOBILITY SCHOLARSHIP

Provides financial assistance to members of the Dermatology Nurses' Association (DNA) who are pursuing an undergraduate or graduate degree. The candidate must be a DNA member for two years, and be employed in the specialty of dermatology.

Academic Fields/Career Goals: Nursing.

Award: Scholarship for use in freshman, sophomore, junior, senior, or graduate years; not renewable. *Number:* 2. *Amount:* $2500.

Eligibility Requirements: Applicant must be enrolled or expecting to enroll full- or part-time at a four-year or technical institution or university. Applicant or parent of applicant must be member of Dermatology Nurses' Association. Applicant or parent of applicant must have employment or volunteer experience in nursing. Available to U.S. and non-U.S. citizens.

Application Requirements: Application, essay, financial need analysis, references, transcript. *Deadline:* October 1.

Contact: Program Coordinator
Dermatology Nurses' Association
East Holly Avenue, PO Box 56
Pitman, NJ 08071
Phone: 800-454-4362
Fax: 856-589-7463
E-mail: dna@mail.ajj.com

GALDERMA LABORATORIES CAREER MOBILITY SCHOLARSHIP

Applicants must be Dermatology Nurses' Association (DNA) members for at least two years, be employed in the specialty of dermatology, and be pursuing a degree in nursing or advanced degree in nursing.

Academic Fields/Career Goals: Nursing.

Award: Scholarship for use in freshman, sophomore, junior, senior, or graduate years; not renewable. *Number:* varies. *Amount:* varies.

Eligibility Requirements: Applicant must be enrolled or expecting to enroll full- or part-time at a four-year or technical institution or university. Applicant or parent of applicant must be member of Dermatology Nurses' Association. Applicant or parent of applicant must have employment or volunteer experience in nursing. Available to U.S. and non-U.S. citizens.

Application Requirements: Application, financial need analysis, references, transcript. *Deadline:* October 1.

Contact: Program Coordinator
Dermatology Nurses' Association
East Holly Avenue, PO Box 56
Pitman, NJ 08071
Phone: 800-454-4362
Fax: 856-589-7463
E-mail: dna@mail.ajj.com

EMERGENCY NURSES ASSOCIATION (ENA) FOUNDATION

http://www.ena.org/foundation

ADDITIONAL ENA FOUNDATION UNDERGRADUATE SCHOLARSHIPS

Scholarships available to nurses (RN, LPN, LVN) who are pursuing baccalaureate degrees in nursing. Applicants must be ENA members for a minimum of twelve months prior to applying.

Academic Fields/Career Goals: Nursing.

Award: Scholarship for use in freshman, sophomore, junior, or senior years; not renewable. *Number:* 3. *Amount:* $3000.

Eligibility Requirements: Applicant must be enrolled or expecting to enroll full- or part-time at a four-year institution or university. Applicant or parent of applicant must be member of Emergency Nurses Association. Available to U.S. and non-U.S. citizens.

Application Requirements: Application, references, transcript, proof of acceptance. *Deadline:* June 1.

Contact: Scholarship Committee
Emergency Nurses Association (ENA) Foundation
915 Lee Street
Des Plaines, IL 60016-6569
Phone: 847-460-4100
E-mail: foundation@ena.org

CHARLES KUNZ MEMORIAL UNDERGRADUATE SCHOLARSHIP

Scholarship awarded to a nurse (RN, LPN or LVN) who is pursuing a baccalaureate degree in nursing. Applicants must be ENA members for a minimum of twelve months prior to applying. Must be attending a NLN or AACN accredited school.

Academic Fields/Career Goals: Nursing.

Award: Scholarship for use in freshman, sophomore, junior, or senior years; not renewable. *Number:* 1. *Amount:* $3000.

Eligibility Requirements: Applicant must be enrolled or expecting to enroll full- or part-time at a four-year institution or university. Applicant or parent of applicant must be member of Emergency Nurses Association. Available to U.S. and non-U.S. citizens.

Application Requirements: Application, references, transcript. *Deadline:* June 1.

Contact: Scholarship Committee
Emergency Nurses Association (ENA) Foundation
915 Lee Street
Des Plaines, IL 60016-6569
Phone: 847-460-4100
E-mail: foundation@ena.org

ENA FOUNDATION CEN UNDERGRADUATE SCHOLARSHIP

Scholarship awarded to a nurse (RN, LPN, LVN) who is pursuing a baccalaureate degree in nursing. Applicants must be attending a NLN or AACN accredited school. Must be ENA members for a minimum of twelve months prior to applying.

Academic Fields/Career Goals: Nursing.

Award: Scholarship for use in freshman, sophomore, junior, or senior years; not renewable. *Number:* 1. *Amount:* $2000.

Eligibility Requirements: Applicant must be enrolled or expecting to enroll full- or part-time at a four-year institution or university. Applicant or parent of applicant must be member of Emergency Nurses Association. Available to U.S. and non-U.S. citizens.

Application Requirements: Application, references, transcript. *Deadline:* June 1.

Contact: Scholarship Committee
Emergency Nurses Association (ENA) Foundation
915 Lee Street
Des Plaines, IL 60016-6569
Phone: 847-460-4100
E-mail: foundation@ena.org

MARGARET MILLER MEMORIAL UNDERGRADUATE SCHOLARSHIP

Scholarship toward tuition costs for a nurse (RN, LPN, or LVN) in pursuit of a baccalaureate degree in nursing. Applicants must be attending a NLN or AACN accredited school. Applicants must be ENA members for a minimum of twelve months immediately prior to applying.

Academic Fields/Career Goals: Nursing.

Award: Scholarship for use in freshman, sophomore, junior, or senior years; not renewable. *Number:* 1. *Amount:* $3000.

Eligibility Requirements: Applicant must be enrolled or expecting to enroll full- or part-time at a four-year institution or university. Applicant or parent of applicant must be member of Emergency Nurses Association. Available to U.S. and non-U.S. citizens.

Application Requirements: Application, references, transcript. *Deadline:* June 1.

Contact: Scholarship Committee
Emergency Nurses Association (ENA) Foundation
915 Lee Street
Des Plaines, IL 60016-6569
Phone: 847-460-4100
E-mail: foundation@ena.org

MONSTER NON-RN UNDERGRADUATE SCHOLARSHIP

Scholarship available to a nursing student who is currently a non-RN nurse studying to obtain an undergraduate degree in nursing. Applicants need not be ENA members to apply, however, applicants must be members of the National Student Nurses Association.

Academic Fields/Career Goals: Nursing.

Award: Scholarship for use in freshman, sophomore, junior, or senior years; not renewable. *Number:* 1. *Amount:* $2500.

Eligibility Requirements: Applicant must be enrolled or expecting to enroll full- or part-time at a four-year institution or university. Applicant or parent of applicant must be member of National Student Nurses Association. Available to U.S. and non-U.S. citizens.

Application Requirements: Application, references, transcript, statement of professional/educational goals, proof of acceptance. *Deadline:* June 1.

Contact: Scholarship Committee
Emergency Nurses Association (ENA) Foundation
915 Lee Street
Des Plaines, IL 60016-6569
Phone: 847-460-4100
E-mail: foundation@ena.org

EXCEPTIONALNURSE.COM

http://www.exceptionalnurse.com

ANNA MAY ROLANDO SCHOLARSHIP AWARD

Scholarship of $500 awarded to a nursing student with a disability. Preference will be given to a graduate student who has demonstrated a commitment to working with people with disabilities.

Academic Fields/Career Goals: Nursing.

Award: Scholarship for use in freshman, sophomore, junior, senior, graduate, or postgraduate years; not renewable. *Number:* 1. *Amount:* $500.

Eligibility Requirements: Applicant must be enrolled or expecting to enroll full-time at a four-year institution or university. Applicant must be hearing impaired, learning disabled, physically disabled, or visually impaired. Available to U.S. citizens.

Application Requirements: Application, essay, references, transcript, medical verification of disability form. *Deadline:* June 1.

Contact: Donna Maheady, Founder
ExceptionalNurse.com
13019 Coastal Circle
Palm Beach Gardens, FL 33410
Phone: 561-627-9872
Fax: 561-776-9254
E-mail: exceptionalnurse@aol.com

BRUNO ROLANDO SCHOLARSHIP AWARD

Scholarship of $250 awarded to a nursing student with a disability. Preference will be given to a nursing student who is employed at a Veteran's Hospital.

Academic Fields/Career Goals: Nursing.

Award: Scholarship for use in freshman, sophomore, junior, senior, graduate, or postgraduate years; not renewable. *Number:* 1. *Amount:* $250.

Eligibility Requirements: Applicant must be enrolled or expecting to enroll full-time at a four-year institution or university. Applicant or parent of applicant must have employment or volunteer experience in nursing. Applicant must be hearing impaired, learning disabled, physically disabled, or visually impaired. Available to U.S. citizens.

Application Requirements: Application, essay, references, transcript, medical verification of disability form. *Deadline:* June 1.

Contact: Donna Maheady, Founder
ExceptionalNurse.com
13019 Coastal Circle
Palm Beach Gardens, FL 33410
Phone: 561-627-9872
Fax: 561-776-9254
E-mail: exceptionalnurse@aol.com

CAROLINE SIMPSON MAHEADY SCHOLARSHIP AWARD

Scholarship of $250 awarded to a nursing student with a disability. Preference will be given to an undergraduate student, of Scottish descent, who has demonstrated a commitment to working with people with disabilities.

Academic Fields/Career Goals: Nursing.

Award: Scholarship for use in freshman, sophomore, junior, senior, graduate, or postgraduate years; not renewable. *Number:* 1. *Amount:* $250.

Eligibility Requirements: Applicant must be enrolled or expecting to enroll full-time at a four-year institution or university. Applicant must be hearing impaired, learning disabled, physically disabled, or visually impaired. Available to U.S. citizens.

Application Requirements: Application, essay, references, transcript, medical verification of disability form. *Deadline:* June 1.

Contact: Donna Maheady, Founder
ExceptionalNurse.com
13019 Coastal Circle
Palm Beach Gardens, FL 33410
Phone: 561-627-9872
Fax: 561-776-9254
E-mail: exceptionalnurse@aol.com

GENEVIEVE SARAN RICHMOND AWARD

Scholarship of $500 awarded to a nursing student with a disability.

Academic Fields/Career Goals: Nursing.

Award: Scholarship for use in freshman, sophomore, junior, senior, graduate, or postgraduate years; not renewable. *Number:* 1. *Amount:* $500.

Eligibility Requirements: Applicant must be enrolled or expecting to enroll full-time at a four-year institution or university. Applicant must be hearing impaired, learning disabled, physically disabled, or visually impaired. Available to U.S. citizens.

Application Requirements: Application, essay, references, transcript, medical verification of disability form. *Deadline:* June 1.

Contact: Donna Maheady, Founder
ExceptionalNurse.com
13019 Coastal Circle
Palm Beach Gardens, FL 33410
Phone: 561-627-9872
Fax: 561-776-9254
E-mail: exceptionalnurse@aol.com

JILL LAURA CREEDON SCHOLARSHIP AWARD

Scholarship of $500 awarded to a nursing student with a disability or medical challenge.

Academic Fields/Career Goals: Nursing.

Award: Scholarship for use in freshman, sophomore, junior, senior, graduate, or postgraduate years; not renewable. *Number:* 1. *Amount:* $500.

Eligibility Requirements: Applicant must be enrolled or expecting to enroll full-time at a four-year institution or university. Applicant must be hearing impaired, learning disabled, physically disabled, or visually impaired. Available to U.S. citizens.

Application Requirements: Application, essay, references, transcript, medical verification of disability form. *Deadline:* June 1.

Contact: Donna Maheady, Founder
ExceptionalNurse.com
13019 Coastal Circle
Palm Beach Gardens, FL 33410
Phone: 561-627-9872
Fax: 561-776-9254
E-mail: exceptionalnurse@aol.com

MARY SERRA GILI SCHOLARSHIP AWARD

Scholarship of $250 awarded to a nursing student with a disability.

Academic Fields/Career Goals: Nursing.

Award: Scholarship for use in freshman, sophomore, junior, senior, graduate, or postgraduate years; not renewable. *Number:* 1. *Amount:* $250.

Eligibility Requirements: Applicant must be enrolled or expecting to enroll full-time at a four-year institution or university. Applicant must be hearing impaired, learning disabled, physically disabled, or visually impaired. Available to U.S. citizens.

Application Requirements: Application, essay, references, transcript, medical verification of disability form. *Deadline:* June 1.

Contact: Donna Maheady, Founder
ExceptionalNurse.com
13019 Coastal Circle
Palm Beach Gardens, FL 33410
Phone: 561-627-9872
Fax: 561-776-9254
E-mail: exceptionalnurse@aol.com

PETER GILI SCHOLARSHIP AWARD

Scholarship of $500 awarded to a nursing student with a disability.

Academic Fields/Career Goals: Nursing.

Award: Scholarship for use in freshman, sophomore, junior, senior, graduate, or postgraduate years; not renewable. *Number:* 1. *Amount:* $500.

Eligibility Requirements: Applicant must be enrolled or expecting to enroll full-time at a four-year institution or university. Applicant must be hearing impaired, learning disabled, physically disabled, or visually impaired. Available to U.S. citizens.

Application Requirements: Application, essay, references, transcript, medical verification of disability form. *Deadline:* June 1.

Contact: Donna Maheady, Founder
ExceptionalNurse.com
13019 Coastal Circle
Palm Beach Gardens, FL 33410
Phone: 561-627-9872
Fax: 561-776-9254
E-mail: exceptionalnurse@aol.com

FLORIDA NURSES ASSOCIATION

http://www.floridanurse.org

EDNA HICKS FUND SCHOLARSHIP

Applicant should be enrolled in a nationally accredited nursing program. Must be in associate, baccalaureate, or master's degree nursing programs or doctoral programs. Preference given to nurse researcher from South Florida.

Academic Fields/Career Goals: Nursing.

Award: Scholarship for use in freshman, sophomore, junior, senior, or graduate years; not renewable. *Number:* varies. *Amount:* varies.

Eligibility Requirements: Applicant must be enrolled or expecting to enroll full- or part-time at a four-year institution or university. Available to U.S. citizens.

Application Requirements: Application, references, transcript. *Deadline:* June 2.

Contact: Jaclyn Spencer, Scholarship Committee
Florida Nurses Association
1235 East Concord Street
PO Box 536985
Orlando, FL 32853-6985
Phone: 407-896-3261
Fax: 407-896-9042
E-mail: foundation@floridanurse.org

FOUNDATION FOR NEONATAL RESEARCH AND EDUCATION (FN) http://www.inurse.com/fnre/

FNRE BSN SCHOLARSHIP

Scholarship for students admitted into a bachelor's degree program in nursing. Applicant should have a minimum GPA of 3.0. Candidate must be a professionally active neonatal nurse. Application deadline May 1.

Academic Fields/Career Goals: Nursing.

Award: Scholarship for use in freshman, sophomore, junior, or senior years; not renewable. *Number:* varies. *Amount:* varies.

Eligibility Requirements: Applicant must be enrolled or expecting to enroll full- or part-time at a four-year institution or university. Applicant or parent of applicant must have employment or volunteer experience in nursing. Applicant must have 3.0 GPA or higher. Available to U.S. citizens.

Application Requirements: Application, resume, acceptance letter. *Deadline:* May 1.

Contact: Coordinator
Foundation for Neonatal Research and Education (FN)
c/o Anthony J. Jannetti, Inc.
East Holly Avenue, PO Box 56
Pitman, NJ 08071-0056
Phone: 856-256-2343
E-mail: fnre@ajj.com

FOUNDATION OF THE NATIONAL STUDENT NURSES' ASSOCIATION http://www.nsna.org

BREAKTHROUGH TO NURSING SCHOLARSHIPS FOR RACIAL/ETHNIC MINORITIES

Available to minority students enrolled in nursing or pre-nursing programs. Awards based on need, scholarship, and health-related activities. Application fee of $10. Send self-addressed stamped envelope with two stamps along with application request. Number of awards varies based on donors.

Academic Fields/Career Goals: Nursing.

Award: Scholarship for use in freshman, sophomore, junior, or senior years; not renewable. *Number:* varies. *Amount:* $1000–$2500.

Eligibility Requirements: Applicant must be American Indian/Alaska Native, Asian/Pacific Islander, Black (non-Hispanic), or Hispanic and enrolled or expecting to enroll full- or part-time at a two-year or four-year institution or university. Available to U.S. citizens.

Application Requirements: Application, financial need analysis, self-addressed stamped envelope, transcript. *Fee:* $10. *Deadline:* January 11.

Contact: Lauren Sperle, Scholarship Chairperson
Foundation of the National Student Nurses' Association
45 Main Street, Suite 606
Brooklyn, NY 11201
Phone: 718-210-0705
Fax: 718-210-0710
E-mail: lauren@nsna.org

FOUNDATION OF THE NATIONAL STUDENT NURSES' ASSOCIATION CAREER MOBILITY SCHOLARSHIP

One-time award open to registered nurses enrolled in nursing or licensed practical or vocational nurses enrolled in a program leading to licensure as a registered nurse. The award value is $1000 to $2500 and the number of awards varies. Submit copy of license. Application fee: $10. Send self-addressed stamped envelope.

Academic Fields/Career Goals: Nursing.

Award: Scholarship for use in freshman, sophomore, junior, or senior years; not renewable. *Number:* varies. *Amount:* $1000–$2500.

Eligibility Requirements: Applicant must be enrolled or expecting to enroll full- or part-time at a two-year or four-year institution or university. Available to U.S. citizens.

Application Requirements: Application, financial need analysis, self-addressed stamped envelope, transcript. *Fee:* $10. *Deadline:* January 11.

Contact: Lauren Sperle, Scholarship Chairperson
Foundation of the National Student Nurses' Association
45 Main Street, Suite 606
Brooklyn, NY 11201
Phone: 718-210-0705
Fax: 718-210-0710
E-mail: lauren@nsna.org

FOUNDATION OF THE NATIONAL STUDENT NURSES' ASSOCIATION GENERAL SCHOLARSHIPS

One-time award for National Student Nurses' Association members and nonmembers enrolled in nursing programs. Graduating high school seniors are not eligible. Send self-addressed stamped envelope with two stamps for application.

Academic Fields/Career Goals: Nursing.

Award: Scholarship for use in freshman, sophomore, junior, or senior years; not renewable. *Number:* varies. *Amount:* $1000–$2500.

Eligibility Requirements: Applicant must be enrolled or expecting to enroll full- or part-time at a two-year or four-year institution or university. Available to U.S. citizens.

Application Requirements: Application, financial need analysis, self-addressed stamped envelope, transcript. *Fee:* $10. *Deadline:* January 11.

Contact: Lauren Sperle, Scholarship Chairperson
Foundation of the National Student Nurses' Association
45 Main Street, Suite 606
Brooklyn, NY 11201
Phone: 718-210-0705
Fax: 718-210-0710
E-mail: lauren@nsna.org

FOUNDATION OF THE NATIONAL STUDENT NURSES' ASSOCIATION SPECIALTY SCHOLARSHIP

One-time award available to students currently enrolled in a state-approved school of nursing or pre-nursing. Must have interest in a specialty area of nursing. The award value is $1000 to $2500 and the number of awards granted varies.

Academic Fields/Career Goals: Nursing.

Award: Scholarship for use in freshman, sophomore, junior, or senior years; not renewable. *Number:* varies. *Amount:* $1000–$2500.

Eligibility Requirements: Applicant must be enrolled or expecting to enroll full- or part-time at a two-year or four-year institution or university. Available to U.S. citizens.

Application Requirements: Application, financial need analysis, self-addressed stamped envelope, transcript. *Fee:* $10. *Deadline:* January 11.

Contact: Lauren Sperle, Scholarship Chairperson
Foundation of the National Student Nurses' Association
45 Main Street, Suite 606
Brooklyn, NY 11201
Phone: 718-210-0705
Fax: 718-210-0710
E-mail: lauren@nsna.org

PROMISE OF NURSING SCHOLARSHIP

Applicants attending nursing school in California, South Florida, Georgia, Illinois, Massachusetts, Michigan, New Jersey, Tennessee, or Dallas/Fort Worth, Texas are eligible. Number of awards granted varies.

Academic Fields/Career Goals: Nursing.

Award: Scholarship for use in freshman, sophomore, junior, or senior years; renewable. *Number:* varies. *Amount:* $1000–$5000.

Eligibility Requirements: Applicant must be enrolled or expecting to enroll full- or part-time at a two-year or four-year institution or university and studying in California, Florida, Georgia, Illinois, Massachusetts, Michigan, New Jersey, Tennessee, or Texas. Available to U.S. citizens.

Application Requirements: Application, financial need analysis, self-addressed stamped envelope, transcript. *Fee:* $10. *Deadline:* January 11.

Contact: Lauren Sperle, Scholarship Chairperson
Foundation of the National Student Nurses' Association
45 Main Street, Suite 606
Brooklyn, NY 11201
Phone: 718-210-0705
Fax: 718-210-0710
E-mail: lauren@nsna.org

FREEMAN FOUNDATION http://www.freemannurse.org

FREEMAN NURSE SCHOLARS PROGRAM

Applicants must be accepted at one of Vermont's five schools of nursing: Castleton State College, Norwich University, Southern Vermont College, University of Vermont, or Vermont Technical College. Must agree to practice in Vermont for a minimum of two years. Minimum GPA of 3.0 for undergraduate students or 3.5 for graduate students required.

Academic Fields/Career Goals: Nursing.

Award: Scholarship for use in freshman, sophomore, junior, senior, or graduate years; renewable. *Number:* 49. *Amount:* $7500–$34,000.

Eligibility Requirements: Applicant must be enrolled or expecting to enroll full- or part-time at a four-year institution or university and studying in Vermont. Available to U.S. citizens.

Application Requirements: Application, evidence of academic excellence/promise. *Deadline:* April 1.

Contact: Toni Kaeding, Program Coordinator
Freeman Foundation
University of Vermont
106 Carrigan Drive, Rowell 216
Burlington, VT 05405
Phone: 802-656-5496
Fax: 802-656-2191
E-mail: toni.kaeding@uvm.edu

GENESIS HEALTH SERVICES FOUNDATION http://www.genesishealth.com

GALA NURSING SCHOLARSHIPS

Scholarships of $6000 for up to five recipients who are seeking admission to, or have been accepted into, an undergraduate baccalaureate program in nursing.

Academic Fields/Career Goals: Nursing.

Award: Scholarship for use in freshman, sophomore, junior, or senior years; not renewable. *Number:* up to 5. *Amount:* $6000.

Eligibility Requirements: Applicant must be enrolled or expecting to enroll full-time at a four-year institution or university; resident of Illinois or Iowa and studying in Illinois or Iowa. Available to U.S. citizens.

Application Requirements: Application, transcript. *Deadline:* March 8.

Contact: Melinda Gowey, Executive Director
Genesis Health Services Foundation
1227 East Rusholme Street
Davenport, IA 52803
Phone: 563-421-6865
Fax: 563-421-6869
E-mail: goweym@genesishealth.com

GENESIS HEALTH GROUP SCHOLARSHIPS

• *See page 337*

GOOD SAMARITAN FOUNDATION http://www.gsftx.org

GOOD SAMARITAN FOUNDATION SCHOLARSHIP

Scholarship for nursing students in their clinical level of education. Must be a resident of Texas and plan to work in a U.S. health-care system.

Academic Fields/Career Goals: Nursing.

Award: Scholarship for use in freshman, sophomore, junior, senior, graduate, or postgraduate years; renewable. *Number:* varies. *Amount:* $1000.

Eligibility Requirements: Applicant must be enrolled or expecting to enroll full-time at a four-year institution or university and resident of Texas. Available to U.S. and non-U.S. citizens.

Application Requirements: Application. *Deadline:* varies.

Contact: Kay Crawford, Scholarship Director
Good Samaritan Foundation
5615 Kirby Drive, Suite 610
Houston, TX 77005
Phone: 713-529-4646
Fax: 713-521-1169
E-mail: kcrawford@gsftx.org

GREATER KANAWHA VALLEY FOUNDATION http://www.tgkvf.org

BERNICE PICKINS PARSONS FUND

• *See page 384*

ELEANORA G. WYLIE SCHOLARSHIP FUND FOR NURSING

Award of $350 awarded to persons to attend any accredited college or university, with preference given to applicants pursuing a nursing education, either at the undergraduate or graduate level, in the field of gerontology. May apply for two Foundation scholarships but will only be chosen for one. Must be a resident of West Virginia.

Academic Fields/Career Goals: Nursing.

Award: Scholarship for use in freshman, sophomore, junior, senior, or graduate years; renewable. *Number:* 1. *Amount:* $350.

Eligibility Requirements: Applicant must be enrolled or expecting to enroll full-time at a four-year institution or university and resident of West Virginia. Applicant must have 2.5 GPA or higher. Available to U.S. citizens.

Application Requirements: Application, essay, financial need analysis, references, transcript. *Deadline:* January 12.

Contact: Susan Hoover, Scholarship Coordinator
Greater Kanawha Valley Foundation
PO Box 3041
Charleston, WV 25331
Phone: 304-346-3620
Fax: 304-346-3640

GUSTAVUS B. CAPITO FUND

Scholarships awarded to students who show financial need and are seeking education in nursing at any accredited college or university with a nursing program in West Virginia. Scholarships are awarded for one or more years. May apply for two Foundation scholarships but will only be chosen for one. Must be a resident of West Virginia.

Academic Fields/Career Goals: Nursing.

Award: Scholarship for use in freshman, sophomore, junior, or senior years; renewable. *Number:* 7. *Amount:* $1000.

Eligibility Requirements: Applicant must be enrolled or expecting to enroll full-time at a four-year institution or university; resident of West Virginia and studying in West Virginia. Applicant must have 2.5 GPA or higher. Available to U.S. citizens.

Application Requirements: Application, essay, financial need analysis, references, transcript. *Deadline:* January 12.

Contact: Susan Hoover, Scholarship Coordinator
Greater Kanawha Valley Foundation
PO Box 3041
Charleston, WV 25331
Phone: 304-346-3620
Fax: 304-346-3640

HAVANA NATIONAL BANK, TRUSTEE http://www.havanabank.com

MCFARLAND CHARITABLE NURSING SCHOLARSHIP

Scholarship for registered nursing students only. Must sign contract obliging to work in Havana, Illinois for two years for each year of funding or repay award with interest and liquidated damages. Must submit test scores, essay, transcripts, references, financial need analysis, and autobiography with application. Preference given to local residents. GPA is an important consideration in selection.

Academic Fields/Career Goals: Nursing.

Award: Forgivable loan for use in freshman, sophomore, junior, senior, graduate, or postgraduate years; renewable. *Number:* 3–5. *Amount:* $1000–$15,000.

Havana National Bank, Trustee (continued)

Eligibility Requirements: Applicant must be enrolled or expecting to enroll full-time at a two-year or four-year institution or university. Available to U.S. and non-U.S. citizens.

Application Requirements: Application, autobiography, essay, financial need analysis, interview, photo, references, test scores, transcript. *Deadline:* April 1.

Contact: Trust Officer
Havana National Bank, Trustee
PO Box 200
Havana, IL 62644
Phone: 309-543-3361
Fax: 309-543-3441
E-mail: info@havanabank.com

HCR MANOR CARE INC. http://www.hcr-manorcare.com

HCR MANOR CARE NURSING SCHOLARSHIP PROGRAM

Scholarship program to help applicants pursue a career in nursing. Must be U.S. citizens.

Academic Fields/Career Goals: Nursing.

Award: Scholarship for use in freshman, sophomore, junior, or senior years; renewable. *Number:* 1. *Amount:* $2500.

Eligibility Requirements: Applicant must be enrolled or expecting to enroll full- or part-time at a two-year or four-year institution or university. Available to U.S. citizens.

Application Requirements: Application, transcript. *Deadline:* continuous.

Contact: Jamie Trabbic, Scholarship Administrator
HCR Manor Care Inc.
333 North Summit Street
PO Box 10086
Toledo, OH 43604
Phone: 419-254-7780
Fax: 419-422-2098
E-mail: jtrabbic@hcr-manorcare.com

HEALTH PROFESSIONS EDUCATION FOUNDATION http://www.healthprofessions.ca.gov

ASSOCIATE DEGREE NURSING SCHOLARSHIP PROGRAM

One-time award to nursing students accepted to or enrolled in associate degree nursing programs. Eligible applicants may receive up to $8000 per year in financial assistance. Deadlines: March 24 and September 11. Must be a resident of California. Minimum 2.0 GPA.

Academic Fields/Career Goals: Nursing.

Award: Scholarship for use in freshman, sophomore, junior, senior, graduate, or postgraduate years; not renewable. *Number:* up to 30. *Amount:* up to $8000.

Eligibility Requirements: Applicant must be enrolled or expecting to enroll full- or part-time at a two-year or four-year institution or university; resident of California and studying in California. Available to U.S. citizens.

Application Requirements: Application, essay, financial need analysis, references, transcript, graduation date verification form, verification of language fluency. *Deadline:* varies.

Contact: James Hall, Program Administrator
Health Professions Education Foundation
400 R street
Sacramento, CA 95811
Phone: 916-326-3640
Fax: 916-324-6585

HEALTH PROFESSIONS EDUCATION FOUNDATION BACHELOR OF SCIENCE NURSING SCHOLARSHIP PROGRAM

Scholarship of up to $10,000 for students pursuing bachelor's degree in nursing. Available for both full- and part-time students. Must be U.S. citizen.

Academic Fields/Career Goals: Nursing.

Award: Scholarship for use in freshman, sophomore, junior, senior, graduate, or postgraduate years; not renewable. *Number:* up to 40. *Amount:* up to $10,000.

Eligibility Requirements: Applicant must be enrolled or expecting to enroll full- or part-time at a two-year or four-year institution or university. Available to U.S. citizens.

Application Requirements: Application, references, transcript, personal statement, Student Aid Report (SAR) or tax return with W2, certification of enrollment. *Deadline:* varies.

Contact: Margarita Miranda, Program Administrator
Health Professions Education Foundation
400 R street
Sacramento, CA 95811
Phone: 916-326-3640

REGISTERED NURSE EDUCATION LOAN REPAYMENT PROGRAM

Repays governmental and commercial loans that were obtained for tuition expenses, books, equipment, and reasonable living expenses associated with attending college. In return for the repayment of educational debt, loan repayment recipients are required to practice full-time in direct patient care in a medically underserved area or county health facility. Deadlines: March 24 and September 11. Must be resident of California.

Academic Fields/Career Goals: Nursing.

Award: Grant for use in senior, graduate, or postgraduate years; not renewable. *Number:* 50–70. *Amount:* up to $10,000.

Eligibility Requirements: Applicant must be enrolled or expecting to enroll full- or part-time at a four-year institution or university; resident of California and studying in California. Available to U.S. citizens.

Application Requirements: Application, driver's license, financial need analysis, references, transcript. *Deadline:* varies.

Contact: Monique Scott, Program Director
Health Professions Education Foundation
818 K Street, Suite 210
Sacramento, CA 95814
Phone: 916-324-6500
Fax: 916-324-6585
E-mail: mvoss@oshpd.state.ca.us

RN EDUCATION SCHOLARSHIP PROGRAM

One-time award to nursing students accepted to or enrolled in baccalaureate degree nursing programs in California. Eligible applicants may receive up to $10,000 per year in financial assistance. Deadlines: March 24 and September 11. Must be resident of California and a U.S. citizen. Minimum 2.0 GPA.

Academic Fields/Career Goals: Nursing.

Award: Scholarship for use in freshman, sophomore, junior, or senior years; not renewable. *Number:* 50–70. *Amount:* up to $10,000.

Eligibility Requirements: Applicant must be enrolled or expecting to enroll full- or part-time at a two-year or four-year institution or university; resident of California and studying in California. Available to U.S. citizens.

Application Requirements: Application, essay, financial need analysis, references, transcript, employment verification form, proof of RN license, verification of language fluency. *Deadline:* varies.

Contact: Monique Scott, Program Director
Health Professions Education Foundation
818 K Street, Suite 210
Sacramento, CA 95814
Phone: 916-324-6500
Fax: 916-324-6585
E-mail: mvoss@oshpd.state.ca.us

VOCATIONAL NURSE SCHOLARSHIP PROGRAM

Scholarships are available to students who are enrolled or accepted in an accredited Vocational Nurse program. Awardees must sign a contract with the Office of Statewide Health Planning and Development. Minimum 2.0 GPA required. Deadlines: March 24 and September 11.

Academic Fields/Career Goals: Nursing.

Award: Scholarship for use in freshman or sophomore years; not renewable. *Number:* varies. *Amount:* $4000–$8000.

Eligibility Requirements: Applicant must be enrolled or expecting to enroll full- or part-time at a two-year or technical institution and resident of California. Available to U.S. citizens.

Application Requirements: Application, references, transcript, Student Aid Report (SAR), personal statement, educational debt reporting form. *Deadline:* varies.

Contact: Scholarship Committee
Health Professions Education Foundation
400 R Street
Sacramento, CA 95811
Phone: 916-326-3640

HEALTH RESEARCH COUNCIL OF NEW ZEALAND http://www.hrc.govt.nz

PACIFIC HEALTH WORKFORCE AWARD

• *See page 326*

PACIFIC MENTAL HEALTH WORK FORCE AWARD

• *See page 326*

HISPANIC COLLEGE FUND INC. http://www.hispanicfund.org

KAISER PERMANENTE COLLEGE TO CARING PROGRAM

Program offers funds to students who are juniors or seniors in college pursuing a bachelors degree in nursing. Students who are selected will receive a scholarship of $8000 each year they attend nursing school. Must be Hispanic and have minimum 3.0 GPA.

Academic Fields/Career Goals: Nursing.

Award: Scholarship for use in junior or senior years; not renewable. *Number:* varies. *Amount:* $8000.

Eligibility Requirements: Applicant must be Hispanic and enrolled or expecting to enroll full-time at a four-year institution or university. Applicant must have 3.0 GPA or higher. Available to U.S. citizens.

Application Requirements: Application, essay, references, proof of family income, citizenship proof. *Deadline:* March 29.

Contact: Fernando Barrueta, Chief Executive Officer
Hispanic College Fund Inc.
1301 K Street, NW, Suite 450-A West
Washington, DC 20005
Phone: 202-296-5400
Fax: 202-296-3774
E-mail: hcf-info@hispanicfund.org

ILLINOIS NURSES ASSOCIATION http://www.illinoisnurses.com

SONNE SCHOLARSHIP

One-time award of up to $3000 available to nursing students. Funds may be used to cover tuition, fees, or any other cost encountered by students enrolled in Illinois state-approved nursing program. Award limited to U.S. citizens who are residents of Illinois. Recipients will receive a year's free membership in INA upon graduation.

Academic Fields/Career Goals: Nursing.

Award: Scholarship for use in freshman, sophomore, junior, or senior years; not renewable. *Number:* 2–4. *Amount:* $1000–$3000.

Eligibility Requirements: Applicant must be enrolled or expecting to enroll full-time at a four-year institution or university; resident of Illinois and studying in Illinois. Applicant must have 2.5 GPA or higher. Available to U.S. citizens.

Application Requirements: Application, essay, financial need analysis, references, transcript. *Deadline:* May 1.

Contact: Sonne Scholarship Committee
Illinois Nurses Association
105 West Adams Street, Suite 2101
Chicago, IL 60603

ILLINOIS STUDENT ASSISTANCE COMMISSION (ISAC) http://www.collegezone.org

ILLINOIS DEPARTMENT OF PUBLIC HEALTH CENTER FOR RURAL HEALTH ALLIED HEALTH CARE PROFESSIONAL SCHOLARSHIP PROGRAM

• *See page 338*

ILLINOIS DEPARTMENT OF PUBLIC HEALTH CENTER FOR RURAL HEALTH NURSING EDUCATION SCHOLARSHIP PROGRAM

• *See page 338*

INDEPENDENT COLLEGE FUND OF NEW JERSEY http://www.njcolleges.org

C.R. BARD FOUNDATION, INC. NURSING SCHOLARSHIP

Applicant must be entering at least the second semester of their sophomore year, or the second semester of the second year of their nursing program, and be enrolled full time at an ICFNJ member college or university. Must maintain a minimum GPA of 3.0.

Academic Fields/Career Goals: Nursing.

Award: Scholarship for use in sophomore, junior, or senior years; not renewable. *Number:* 7. *Amount:* $2500.

Eligibility Requirements: Applicant must be enrolled or expecting to enroll full-time at a four-year institution or university and studying in New Jersey. Applicant must have 3.0 GPA or higher. Available to U.S. citizens.

Application Requirements: Application, essay, financial need analysis, resume, references, transcript. *Deadline:* March 31.

Contact: John Wilson, President
Independent College Fund of New Jersey
797 Springfield Avenue
Summit, NJ 07901-1107
Phone: 908-277-3424
Fax: 908-277-0851
E-mail: jbwilson@njcolleges.org

INDIANA HEALTH CARE FOUNDATION http://www.ihca.org

INDIANA HEALTH CARE FOUNDATION NURSING SCHOLARSHIP

One-time award of up to $1500 for Indiana residents studying nursing at an institution in Indiana, Ohio, Kentucky, Illinois or Michigan. Minimum 2.5 GPA. Total number of awards varies.

Academic Fields/Career Goals: Nursing.

Award: Scholarship for use in freshman, sophomore, junior, senior, graduate, or postgraduate years; not renewable. *Number:* varies. *Amount:* $750–$1500.

Eligibility Requirements: Applicant must be enrolled or expecting to enroll full- or part-time at a two-year or four-year or technical institution or university; resident of Indiana and studying in Illinois, Indiana, Kentucky, Michigan, or Ohio. Applicant must have 2.5 GPA or higher. Available to U.S. citizens.

Application Requirements: Application, essay, interview, references, transcript. *Deadline:* May 16.

Contact: Dorothy Henry, Executive Director
Indiana Health Care Foundation
One North Capitol, Suite 1115
Indianapolis, IN 46204
Phone: 317-636-6406
Fax: 877-561-3757
E-mail: dhenry@ihca.org

INDIAN HEALTH SERVICES, UNITED STATES DEPARTMENT OF HEALTH AND HUMAN SERVICES http://www.ihs.gov

HEALTH PROFESSIONS PREPARATORY SCHOLARSHIP PROGRAM

• *See page 327*

INDIAN HEALTH SERVICE HEALTH PROFESSIONS SCHOLARSHIP PROGRAM

• *See page 327*

INOVA HEALTH SYSTEM, EDELMAN NURSING CAREER DEVELOPMENT http://www.inova.org

INOVA SPECIAL NURSING CAREER SCHOLARSHIP PROGRAM

Scholarships will be awarded to high potential Inova employees, academically recognized college seniors, students enrolled in specially designated nursing

Inova Health System, Edelman Nursing Career Development (continued)

programs, and Inova nurses working on an advanced degree. Must be entering senior year or final semester at an accredited nursing program. Must maintain a minimum of a 3.0 GPA.

Academic Fields/Career Goals: Nursing.

Award: Scholarship for use in senior or graduate years; not renewable. *Number:* varies. *Amount:* varies.

Eligibility Requirements: Applicant must be enrolled or expecting to enroll full-time at a four-year institution or university. Applicant or parent of applicant must be affiliated with Inova Health System. Applicant must have 3.0 GPA or higher. Available to U.S. citizens.

Application Requirements: Application, references, transcript. *Deadline:* May 31.

Contact: Scholarship Coordinator
Inova Health System, Edelman Nursing Career Development
2990 Telestar Court, Fourth Floor
Falls Church, VA 22042
E-mail: edelmancareercenter@inova.org

INTERNATIONAL ORDER OF THE KING'S DAUGHTERS AND SONS http://www.iokds.org

HEALTH CAREERS SCHOLARSHIP

• *See page 212*

INTERNATIONAL UNION OF ELECTRONIC, ELECTRICAL, SALARIED, MACHINE, AND FURNITURE WORKERS-CWA http://www.iue-cwa.org

JAMES B. CAREY SCHOLARSHIP AWARD

Awards for students who are children or grandchildren of IUE-CWA members who are undergraduate students at accredited two-year, four-year, nursing, and technical schools.

Academic Fields/Career Goals: Nursing; Trade/Technical Specialties.

Award: Scholarship for use in freshman, sophomore, junior, or senior years; not renewable. *Number:* 1–9. *Amount:* $1000.

Eligibility Requirements: Applicant must be enrolled or expecting to enroll full-time at a two-year or four-year or technical institution or university. Applicant or parent of applicant must be member of International Union of Electronic, Electrical, Salaries, Machine and Furniture Workers. Available to U.S. and Canadian citizens.

Application Requirements: Application, essay, financial need analysis, references, test scores, transcript. *Deadline:* March 31.

Contact: Sue McElroy, Scholarship Committee
International Union of Electronic, Electrical, Salaried, Machine, and Furniture Workers-CWA
501 Third Street, NW
Washington, DC 20001
Phone: 202-434-0676
Fax: 202-434-1250

J.D. ARCHBOLD MEMORIAL HOSPITAL http://www.archbold.org

ARCHBOLD SCHOLARSHIP PROGRAM

• *See page 338*

JEWISH FOUNDATION FOR EDUCATION OF WOMEN http://www.jfew.org

JFEW SCHOLARSHIPS FOR EMIGRES IN THE HEALTH SCIENCES

• *See page 212*

KAISER PERMANENTE http://xnet.kp.org/hr/ca/kpapan

DELORAS JONES RN EXCELLENCE IN BACHELOR'S DEGREE NURSING SCHOLARSHIP

Merit-based scholarships of $5000 are awarded to Kaiser Permanente employees who are pursuing a bachelor's degree in nursing. Minimum 3.0 GPA required.

Academic Fields/Career Goals: Nursing.

Award: Scholarship for use in freshman, sophomore, junior, or senior years; not renewable. *Number:* varies. *Amount:* $5000.

Eligibility Requirements: Applicant must be enrolled or expecting to enroll full-time at a four-year institution or university and resident of California. Applicant or parent of applicant must be affiliated with Kaiser Permanente. Applicant must have 3.0 GPA or higher. Available to U.S. citizens.

Application Requirements: Application, transcript. *Deadline:* varies.

Contact: Pauline Tsai, Scholarship Committee
Kaiser Permanente
PO Box 950
Pasadena, CA 91102-0950
Phone: 909-427-3966
E-mail: pauline.b.tsai@kp.org

DELORAS JONES RN NURSING AS A SECOND CAREER SCHOLARSHIP

Need-based scholarships of $1000 to $2500 are offered to students enrolled in approved nursing degree programs in California. Applicants must be pursuing nursing as a second career. Minimum 2.5 GPA required.

Academic Fields/Career Goals: Nursing.

Award: Scholarship for use in freshman, sophomore, junior, senior, or graduate years; not renewable. *Number:* varies. *Amount:* $1000–$2500.

Eligibility Requirements: Applicant must be enrolled or expecting to enroll full-time at a four-year institution or university; resident of California and studying in California. Applicant must have 2.5 GPA or higher. Available to U.S. citizens.

Application Requirements: Application, transcript. *Deadline:* varies.

Contact: Pauline Tsai, Scholarship Committee
Kaiser Permanente
PO Box 950
Pasadena, CA 91102-0950
Phone: 909-427-3966
E-mail: pauline.b.tsai@kp.org

DELORAS JONES RN SCHOLARSHIP PROGRAM

Scholarship of up to $2500 awarded to nursing students in California having completed at least one academic term with minimum GPA of 2.5.

Academic Fields/Career Goals: Nursing.

Award: Scholarship for use in sophomore, junior, or senior years; not renewable. *Number:* varies. *Amount:* $1000–$2500.

Eligibility Requirements: Applicant must be enrolled or expecting to enroll full-time at a four-year institution or university; resident of California and studying in California. Applicant must have 2.5 GPA or higher. Available to U.S. citizens.

Application Requirements: Application, financial need analysis, references, transcript, copy of federal income tax return. *Deadline:* March 15.

Contact: Pauline Tsai, Scholarship Committee
Kaiser Permanente
PO Box 950
Pasadena, CA 91102-0950
Phone: 909-427-3966
E-mail: pauline.b.tsai@kp.org

DELORAS JONES RN UNDERREPRESENTED GROUPS IN NURSING SCHOLARSHIP

Need-based scholarships of $1000 to $2500 are offered to minority and male students enrolled in approved nursing degree programs in California.

Academic Fields/Career Goals: Nursing.

Award: Scholarship for use in freshman, sophomore, junior, senior, or graduate years; not renewable. *Number:* varies. *Amount:* $1000–$2500.

Eligibility Requirements: Applicant must be American Indian/Alaska Native, Asian/Pacific Islander, Black (non-Hispanic), or Hispanic; enrolled or expecting to enroll full- or part-time at a four-year institution or university; resident of California and studying in California. Available to U.S. citizens.

Application Requirements: Application. *Deadline:* varies.

Contact: Pauline Tsai, Scholarship Committee
Kaiser Permanente
PO Box 950
Pasadena, CA 91102-0950
Phone: 909-427-3966
E-mail: pauline.b.tsai@kp.org

KAISER PERMANENTE FORGIVABLE STUDENT LOAN PROGRAM

Forgivable loan of $2500 to $3750 available to students in their final one to three years of study. Graduate students may also apply. Following graduation, loans may be forgiven through qualifying employment with a Kaiser Permanente facility in Northern or Southern California. Minimum 3.0 GPA required.

Academic Fields/Career Goals: Nursing.

Award: Forgivable loan for use in sophomore, junior, senior, or graduate years; not renewable. *Number:* varies. *Amount:* $2500–$3750.

Eligibility Requirements: Applicant must be enrolled or expecting to enroll full-time at a four-year institution or university; resident of California and studying in California. Applicant or parent of applicant must be affiliated with Kaiser Permanente. Applicant must have 3.0 GPA or higher. Available to U.S. citizens.

Application Requirements: Application, applicant must enter a contest, references. *Deadline:* varies.

Contact: Pauline Tsai, Scholarship Committee
Kaiser Permanente
PO Box 950
Pasadena, CA 91102-0950
Phone: 909-427-3966
E-mail: pauline.b.tsai@kp.org

KANSAS BOARD OF REGENTS http://www.kansasregents.org

KANSAS NURSE SERVICE SCHOLARSHIP PROGRAM

This is a service scholarship loan program available to students attending two year or four year public and private postsecondary institutions, as well as vocational technical schools with nursing education programs. Students can be pursuing either LPN or RN licensure.

Academic Fields/Career Goals: Nursing.

Award: Scholarship for use in freshman, sophomore, junior, or senior years; renewable. *Number:* varies. *Amount:* $3500.

Eligibility Requirements: Applicant must be enrolled or expecting to enroll full-time at a two-year or four-year or technical institution or university. Available to U.S. citizens.

Application Requirements: Application, financial need analysis, test scores, transcript. *Fee:* $10. *Deadline:* May 1.

Contact: Diane Lindeman, Director of Student Financial Assistance
Kansas Board of Regents
1000 Jackson, SW, Suite 520
Topeka, KS 66612-1368
Phone: 785-296-3517
Fax: 785-296-0983
E-mail: dlindeman@ksbor.org

LADIES AUXILIARY TO THE VETERANS OF FOREIGN WARS, DEPARTMENT OF MAINE

FRANCIS L. BOOTH MEDICAL SCHOLARSHIP SPONSORED BY LAVFW DEPARTMENT OF MAINE

• *See page 338*

LINCOLN COMMUNITY FOUNDATION http://www.lcf.org

MEDICAL RESEARCH SCHOLARSHIP

• *See page 339*

MARION D. AND EVA S. PEEPLES FOUNDATION TRUST SCHOLARSHIP PROGRAM http://www.jccf.org

MARION A. AND EVA S. PEEPLES SCHOLARSHIPS

• *See page 234*

MARSHA'S ANGELS SCHOLARSHIP FUND http://www.marshasangels.org

MARSHA'S ANGELS SCHOLARSHIP

Scholarship for students who have completed all prerequisites to enter their first year of an accredited nursing program. Applicants living in Sedgwick County, Kansas or one of the surrounding counties may attend an accredited nursing program anywhere in the U.S.; applicants from any other state in the U.S. may use the scholarship to attend a program in Sedgwick County, Kansas, one of the surrounding counties, or St. Luke's College in Missouri.

Academic Fields/Career Goals: Nursing.

Award: Scholarship for use in freshman year; not renewable. *Number:* varies. *Amount:* $1600–$1800.

Eligibility Requirements: Applicant must be high school student and planning to enroll or expecting to enroll full- or part-time at a four-year institution or university. Available to U.S. citizens.

Application Requirements: Application, transcript. *Deadline:* June 30.

Contact: Scholarship Committee
Marsha's Angels Scholarship Fund
PO Box 401
Valley Center, KS 67147-0401
E-mail: marshasangels@gmail.com

MARYLAND HIGHER EDUCATION COMMISSION http://www.mhec.state.md.us

GRADUATE AND PROFESSIONAL SCHOLARSHIP PROGRAM-MARYLAND

• *See page 212*

HOWARD P. RAWLINGS EDUCATIONAL EXCELLENCE AWARDS EDUCATIONAL ASSISTANCE GRANT

Award for Maryland residents accepted or enrolled in a full-time undergraduate degree or certificate program at a Maryland institution or hospital nursing school. Must submit financial aid form by March 1. Must earn 2.0 GPA in college to maintain award.

Academic Fields/Career Goals: Nursing.

Award: Grant for use in freshman, sophomore, junior, or senior years; renewable. *Number:* 15,000–30,000. *Amount:* $400–$2700.

Eligibility Requirements: Applicant must be enrolled or expecting to enroll full-time at a two-year or four-year institution or university; resident of Maryland and studying in Maryland. Available to U.S. citizens.

Application Requirements: Application, financial need analysis. *Deadline:* March 1.

Contact: Office of Student Financial Assistance
Maryland Higher Education Commission
839 Bestgate Road, Suite 400
Annapolis, MD 21401-3013
Phone: 800-974-1024
Fax: 410-260-3200
E-mail: osfamail@mhec.state.md.us

JANET L. HOFFMANN LOAN ASSISTANCE REPAYMENT PROGRAM

• *See page 234*

TUITION REDUCTION FOR NON-RESIDENT NURSING STUDENTS

Available to nonresidents of Maryland who attend a two-year or four-year public institution in Maryland. It is renewable provided student maintains academic requirements designated by institution attended. Recipient must agree to serve as a full-time nurse in a hospital or related institution for two to four years.

Academic Fields/Career Goals: Nursing.

Award: Scholarship for use in freshman, sophomore, junior, or senior years; renewable. *Number:* varies. *Amount:* varies.

Eligibility Requirements: Applicant must be enrolled or expecting to enroll full- or part-time at a two-year or four-year institution and studying in Maryland. Available to U.S. citizens.

Maryland Higher Education Commission (continued)

Application Requirements: Application. *Deadline:* varies.

Contact: Elizabeth Urbanski, Associate Director
Maryland Higher Education Commission
839 Bestgate Road, Suite 400
Annapolis, MD 21401-3013
Phone: 410-260-4561
Fax: 410-260-3202
E-mail: eurbansk@mhec.state.md.us

MICHIGAN BUREAU OF STUDENT FINANCIAL ASSISTANCE http://www.michigan.gov/studentaid

MICHIGAN NURSING SCHOLARSHIP

Scholarship for students enrolled in an LPN, associate degree in nursing, bachelor of science in nursing, or master of science in nursing programs. Colleges determine application procedure and select recipients. Recipients must fulfill in-state work commitment or repay scholarship.

Academic Fields/Career Goals: Nursing.

Award: Scholarship for use in freshman, sophomore, junior, senior, or graduate years; renewable. *Number:* varies. *Amount:* up to $4000.

Eligibility Requirements: Applicant must be enrolled or expecting to enroll full- or part-time at a two-year or four-year institution or university; resident of Michigan and studying in Michigan. Available to U.S. citizens.

Application Requirements: Recipients are selected by their college. *Deadline:* varies.

Contact: Scholarship and Grant Director
Michigan Bureau of Student Financial Assistance
PO Box 30462
Lansing, MI 48909-7962
Phone: 888-447-2687
E-mail: osg@michigan.gov

MICHIGAN LEAGUE FOR NURSING http://www.michleaguenursing.org

NURSING STUDENT SCHOLARSHIP

Four $500 scholarships will be awarded to students currently enrolled in a licensed practical nurse, associate degree, or bachelors degree nursing education program. Must have successfully completed at least one nursing course with a clinical component. For Michigan residents to use at colleges and universities within the state of Michigan.

Academic Fields/Career Goals: Nursing.

Award: Scholarship for use in sophomore, junior, or senior years; not renewable. *Number:* 4. *Amount:* $500.

Eligibility Requirements: Applicant must be enrolled or expecting to enroll full-time at a two-year or four-year institution; resident of Michigan and studying in Michigan. Available to U.S. and non-U.S. citizens.

Application Requirements: Application, essay, references, transcript, letters of endorsement. *Deadline:* January 1.

Contact: Carole Stacy, Director
Michigan League for Nursing
2410 Woodlake Drive
Okemos, MI 48864
Phone: 517-347-8091
Fax: 517-347-4096
E-mail: cstacy@mhc.org

MINORITY NURSE MAGAZINE http://www.minoritynurse.com

MINORITY NURSE MAGAZINE SCHOLARSHIP PROGRAM

Scholarships to help academically excellent, financially needy racial and ethnic minority nursing students, complete a BSN degree.

Academic Fields/Career Goals: Nursing.

Award: Scholarship for use in junior, senior, or graduate years; not renewable. *Number:* 4. *Amount:* $500–$1000.

Eligibility Requirements: Applicant must be American Indian/Alaska Native, Asian/Pacific Islander, Black (non-Hispanic), or Hispanic and enrolled or expecting to enroll full- or part-time at a four-year institution or university. Applicant must have 3.0 GPA or higher. Available to U.S. citizens.

Application Requirements: Application, essay, financial need analysis, references, transcript. *Deadline:* June 15.

Contact: Pam Chwedyk, Senior Editor and Editorial Manager
Minority Nurse Magazine
211 West Wacker Drive, Suite 900
Chicago, IL 60606
Phone: 312-525-3095
Fax: 312-429-3336
E-mail: pchwedyk@alloyeducation.com

MISSISSIPPI NURSES' ASSOCIATION (MNA) http://www.msnurses.org

MISSISSIPPI NURSES' ASSOCIATION FOUNDATION SCHOLARSHIP

Scholarship of $1000 to a Mississippi resident. Applicant should major in nursing and be a member of MASN.

Academic Fields/Career Goals: Nursing.

Award: Scholarship for use in freshman, sophomore, junior, or senior years; not renewable. *Number:* 1. *Amount:* $1000.

Eligibility Requirements: Applicant must be enrolled or expecting to enroll full- or part-time at a four-year institution or university and resident of Mississippi. Available to U.S. citizens.

Application Requirements: Application, essay, references, transcript. *Deadline:* October 1.

Contact: Scholarship Committee
Mississippi Nurses' Association (MNA)
31 Woodgreen Place
Madison, MS 39110
Phone: 601-898-0850
E-mail: foundation@msnurses.org

MISSISSIPPI STATE STUDENT FINANCIAL AID http://www.ihl.state.ms.us

NURSING EDUCATION LOAN/SCHOLARSHIP-BSN

Award available to junior and senior students pursuing a baccalaureate degree in nursing as well as to the licensed registered nurse who wishes to continue education to the baccalaureate degree. Include transcript and references with application. Minimum 2.5 GPA required. Must be a Mississippi resident and agree to employment in professional nursing (patient care) in Mississippi.

Academic Fields/Career Goals: Nursing.

Award: Forgivable loan for use in junior or senior years; renewable. *Number:* varies. *Amount:* $4000–$8000.

Eligibility Requirements: Applicant must be enrolled or expecting to enroll full- or part-time at a four-year institution or university; resident of Mississippi and studying in Mississippi. Applicant must have 2.5 GPA or higher. Available to U.S. citizens.

Application Requirements: Application, driver's license, financial need analysis, references, transcript. *Deadline:* March 31.

Contact: Mary Covington, Assistant Director, State Student Financial Aid
Mississippi State Student Financial Aid
3825 Ridgewood Road
Jackson, MS 39211-6453
Phone: 800-327-2980
E-mail: sfa@ihl.state.ms.us

MISSOURI DEPARTMENT OF HEALTH AND SENIOR SERVICES http://www.dhss.mo.gov

MISSOURI PROFESSIONAL AND PRACTICAL NURSING STUDENT LOAN PROGRAM

Scholarship for Missouri residents attending institutions in Missouri. Forgivable loan for nursing student. Upon graduation, the student must work as a facility in a Health professional shortage area in Missouri or any Hospital in Missouri. Minimum 2.5 GPA required for applicants.

Academic Fields/Career Goals: Nursing.

Award: Forgivable loan for use in freshman, sophomore, junior, senior, graduate, or postgraduate years; not renewable. *Number:* up to 70. *Amount:* up to $5000.

Eligibility Requirements: Applicant must be enrolled or expecting to enroll full-time at a two-year or four-year institution or university; resident of Missouri and studying in Missouri. Applicant must have 3.0 GPA or higher. Available to U.S. and non-U.S. citizens.

Application Requirements: Application, driver's license, proof of Missouri residency. *Deadline:* June 30.

Contact: Kristie Frank, Help Program Representative
Missouri Department of Health and Senior Services
PO Box 570
Jefferson City, MO 65102-0570
Phone: 573-751-6219
Fax: 573-522-8146
E-mail: kris.frank@dhss.mo.gov

PRIMARY CARE RESOURCE INITIATIVE FOR MISSOURI LOAN PROGRAM
• *See page 212*

MOUNT SINAI HOSPITAL DEPARTMENT OF NURSING http://www.mountsinai.org

BSN STUDENT SCHOLARSHIP/WORK REPAYMENT PROGRAM

Award for senior nursing student or in the last semester/year of the program. Minimum GPA is 3.25. Award value is $3000.

Academic Fields/Career Goals: Nursing.

Award: Scholarship for use in senior year; not renewable. *Number:* varies. *Amount:* $3000.

Eligibility Requirements: Applicant must be enrolled or expecting to enroll full-time at a four-year institution or university. Available to U.S. citizens.

Application Requirements: Application, resume, references, transcript. *Deadline:* October 1.

Contact: Maria L. Vezina, Director, Nursing Education and Recruitment
Mount Sinai Hospital Department of Nursing
One Gustave Levy Place, PO Box 1144
New York, NY 10029

NATIONAL ASSOCIATION DIRECTORS OF NURSING ADMINISTRATION http://www.nadona.org

NADONA/LTC STEPHANIE CARROLL MEMORIAL SCHOLARSHIP

Scholarship is for nursing student enrolled in an accredited nursing program or nursing students in an undergraduate or graduate program.

Academic Fields/Career Goals: Nursing.

Award: Scholarship for use in freshman, sophomore, junior, senior, or graduate years; not renewable. *Number:* varies. *Amount:* varies.

Eligibility Requirements: Applicant must be enrolled or expecting to enroll full- or part-time at a two-year or four-year institution or university. Available to U.S. citizens.

Application Requirements: Application. *Deadline:* April 1.

Contact: Barbara Smith, Director of Operations and Marketing
National Association Directors of Nursing Administration
Reed Hartman Tower,11353 Reed Hartman Highway, Suite 210
Cincinnati, OH 45241
Phone: 513-791-3679
Fax: 513-791-3699
E-mail: info@nadona.org

NATIONAL ASSOCIATION OF HISPANIC NURSES http://www.thehispanicnurses.org

KAISER PERMANENTE AND NAHN SCHOLARSHIPS

Awards are presented to NAHN members enrolled in associate, diploma, baccalaureate, graduate or practical/vocational nursing programs. Selection based on current academic standing. Scholarship award recipients are a select group of Hispanic students who demonstrate promise of future professional contributions to the nursing profession and who have the potential to act as role models for other aspiring nursing students.

Academic Fields/Career Goals: Nursing.

Award: Scholarship for use in freshman, sophomore, junior, senior, or graduate years; not renewable. *Number:* up to 10. *Amount:* up to $1000.

Eligibility Requirements: Applicant must be Hispanic and enrolled or expecting to enroll full-time at a four-year or technical institution or university. Available to U.S. citizens.

Application Requirements: Application, essay, references, transcript. *Deadline:* varies.

Contact: Carmen Ramirez, Awards and Scholarships Committee Chair
National Association of Hispanic Nurses
1501 16th Street, NW
Washington, DC 20036
Phone: 202-387-2477
Fax: 202-483-7183
E-mail: info@thehispanicnurses.org

NATIONAL BLACK NURSES ASSOCIATION INC. http://www.nbna.org

DR. HILDA RICHARDS SCHOLARSHIP

Scholarship for nurses currently enrolled in a nursing program who are members of NBNA. Applicant must have at least one full year of school remaining.

Academic Fields/Career Goals: Nursing.

Award: Scholarship for use in freshman, sophomore, junior, senior, graduate, or postgraduate years; not renewable. *Number:* 1. *Amount:* $1000–$2000.

Eligibility Requirements: Applicant must be enrolled or expecting to enroll full-time at a two-year or four-year institution or university. Applicant or parent of applicant must be member of National Black Nurses' Association. Applicant or parent of applicant must have employment or volunteer experience in community service. Available to U.S. and non-U.S. citizens.

Application Requirements: Application, essay, photo, references, self-addressed stamped envelope, transcript. *Deadline:* April 15.

Contact: Scholarship Committee
National Black Nurses Association Inc.
8630 Fenton Street, Suite 330
Silver Spring, MD 20910-3803
Phone: 301-589-3200
Fax: 301-589-3223
E-mail: nbna@erols.com

DR. LAURANNE SAMS SCHOLARSHIP

Award available for NBNA member who is currently enrolled full-time in a nursing program. Applicant must have at least one full year of school remaining. Scholarships will range from $1000 to $2000.

Academic Fields/Career Goals: Nursing.

Award: Scholarship for use in freshman, sophomore, junior, senior, graduate, or postgraduate years; not renewable. *Number:* up to 5. *Amount:* $1000–$2000.

Eligibility Requirements: Applicant must be enrolled or expecting to enroll full-time at a two-year or four-year institution or university. Applicant or parent of applicant must be member of National Black Nurses' Association. Available to U.S. and non-U.S. citizens.

Application Requirements: Application, essay, references, self-addressed stamped envelope, transcript. *Deadline:* April 15.

Contact: Scholarship Committee
National Black Nurses Association Inc.
8630 Fenton Street, Suite 330
Silver Spring, MD 20910-3803
Phone: 301-589-3200
Fax: 301-589-3223
E-mail: nbna@erols.com

KAISER PERMANENTE SCHOOL OF ANESTHESIA SCHOLARSHIP

Scholarship for nurses currently enrolled in a nursing program who are active members of NBNA. Must have at least one full year of school remaining.

Academic Fields/Career Goals: Nursing.

Award: Scholarship for use in freshman, sophomore, junior, senior, graduate, or postgraduate years; not renewable. *Number:* 1. *Amount:* $1000–$2000.

Eligibility Requirements: Applicant must be enrolled or expecting to enroll full-time at a two-year or four-year institution or university.

National Black Nurses Association Inc. (continued)

Applicant or parent of applicant must be member of National Black Nurses' Association. Available to U.S. and non-U.S. citizens.

Application Requirements: Application, essay, references, self-addressed stamped envelope, transcript. *Deadline:* April 15.

Contact: Scholarship Committee
National Black Nurses Association Inc.
8630 Fenton Street, Suite 330
Silver Spring, MD 20910-3803
Phone: 301-589-3200
Fax: 301-589-3223
E-mail: nbna@erols.com

MARTHA R. DUDLEY LVN/LPN SCHOLARSHIP

Scholarship available for nurses currently enrolled full-time in a nursing program and must be a member of NBNA. Applicant must have at least one full year of school remaining. Scholarships will range from $1000 to $2000.

Academic Fields/Career Goals: Nursing.

Award: Scholarship for use in freshman, sophomore, junior, senior, graduate, or postgraduate years; not renewable. *Number:* 1. *Amount:* $1000–$2000.

Eligibility Requirements: Applicant must be Black (non-Hispanic) and enrolled or expecting to enroll full-time at a two-year or four-year institution or university. Applicant or parent of applicant must be member of National Black Nurses' Association. Applicant or parent of applicant must have employment or volunteer experience in community service. Available to U.S. and non-U.S. citizens.

Application Requirements: Application, essay, photo, references, self-addressed stamped envelope, transcript. *Deadline:* April 15.

Contact: Scholarship Committee
National Black Nurses Association Inc.
8630 Fenton Street, Suite 330
Silver Spring, MD 20910-3803
Phone: 301-589-3200
Fax: 301-589-3223
E-mail: nbna@erols.com

MAYO FOUNDATIONS SCHOLARSHIP

Scholarship for nurses currently enrolled full-time in a nursing program who are members of NBNA. Applicant must have at least one full year of school remaining.

Academic Fields/Career Goals: Nursing.

Award: Scholarship for use in freshman, sophomore, junior, senior, graduate, or postgraduate years; not renewable. *Number:* 1. *Amount:* $1000–$2000.

Eligibility Requirements: Applicant must be enrolled or expecting to enroll full-time at a two-year or four-year institution or university. Applicant or parent of applicant must be member of National Black Nurses' Association. Available to U.S. and non-U.S. citizens.

Application Requirements: Application, essay, photo, references, self-addressed stamped envelope, transcript. *Deadline:* April 15.

Contact: Scholarship Committee
National Black Nurses Association Inc.
8630 Fenton Street, Suite 330
Silver Spring, MD 20910-3803
Phone: 301-589-3200
Fax: 301-589-3223
E-mail: nbna@erols.com

NBNA BOARD OF DIRECTORS SCHOLARSHIP

The scholarship enables nurses to grow and better contribute their talents to the health and healthcare of communities. Candidate must be currently enrolled in a nursing program with at least one full year of school remaining and must be a member of NBNA.

Academic Fields/Career Goals: Nursing.

Award: Scholarship for use in freshman, sophomore, junior, senior, graduate, or postgraduate years; not renewable. *Number:* up to 2. *Amount:* $1000–$2000.

Eligibility Requirements: Applicant must be enrolled or expecting to enroll full-time at a two-year or four-year institution or university. Applicant or parent of applicant must be member of National Black Nurses' Association. Applicant or parent of applicant must have employment or volunteer experience in community service. Available to U.S. and non-U.S. citizens.

Application Requirements: Application, essay, photo, references, self-addressed stamped envelope, transcript. *Deadline:* April 15.

Contact: Scholarship Committee
National Black Nurses Association Inc.
8630 Fenton Street, Suite 330
Silver Spring, MD 20910-3803
Phone: 301-589-3200
Fax: 301-589-3223
E-mail: nbna@erols.com

NURSING SPECTRUM SCHOLARSHIP

Scholarship enables nurses to grow and better contribute their talents to the health and healthcare of communities. Candidate must be currently enrolled in a nursing program and be a member of NBNA. Applicant must have at least one full year of school remaining.

Academic Fields/Career Goals: Nursing.

Award: Scholarship for use in freshman, sophomore, junior, senior, graduate, or postgraduate years; not renewable. *Number:* 1. *Amount:* $1000–$2000.

Eligibility Requirements: Applicant must be enrolled or expecting to enroll full-time at a two-year or four-year institution or university. Applicant or parent of applicant must be member of National Black Nurses' Association. Available to U.S. and non-U.S. citizens.

Application Requirements: Application, essay, references, self-addressed stamped envelope, transcript. *Deadline:* April 15.

Contact: Scholarship Committee
National Black Nurses Association Inc.
8630 Fenton Street, Suite 330
Silver Spring, MD 20910-3803
Phone: 301-589-3200
Fax: 301-589-3223
E-mail: nbna@erols.com

NATIONAL HEALTHCARE SCHOLARS FOUNDATION http://www.nhsfonline.org

NHSF UNDERGRADUATE NURSING SCHOLARSHIP

Scholarships of $1500 to qualified African-American, Asian, Hispanic and Native American undergraduate students in the field of nursing.

Academic Fields/Career Goals: Nursing.

Award: Scholarship for use in freshman, sophomore, junior, or senior years; renewable. *Number:* varies. *Amount:* $1500.

Eligibility Requirements: Applicant must be American Indian/Alaska Native, Asian/Pacific Islander, Black (non-Hispanic), or Hispanic and enrolled or expecting to enroll full-time at a four-year or technical institution or university. Available to U.S. citizens.

Application Requirements: Application, essay, references, test scores, transcript. *Deadline:* varies.

Contact: Scholarship Committee
National Healthcare Scholars Foundation
300 River Place, Suite 4950
Detroit, MI 48207
Phone: 313-393-4549
Fax: 313-393-3394
E-mail: information@nhsfonline.org

NATIONAL SOCIETY DAUGHTERS OF THE AMERICAN REVOLUTION http://www.dar.org

NATIONAL SOCIETY DAUGHTERS OF THE AMERICAN REVOLUTION CAROLINE E. HOLT NURSING SCHOLARSHIPS

One-time award of $1000 for students who are in financial need and have been accepted or are enrolled in an accredited school of nursing. A letter of acceptance into the nursing program or the transcript stating that the applicant is enrolled in the nursing program must be included with the application.

Academic Fields/Career Goals: Nursing.

Award: Scholarship for use in freshman, sophomore, junior, or senior years; not renewable. *Number:* varies. *Amount:* $1000.

Eligibility Requirements: Applicant must be enrolled or expecting to enroll full-time at a two-year or four-year institution or university. Available to U.S. citizens.

Application Requirements: Application, financial need analysis, self-addressed stamped envelope, transcript, letter of sponsorship. *Deadline:* February 15.

Contact: Eric Weisz, Manager, Office of the Reporter General
National Society Daughters of the American Revolution
1776 D Street, NW
Washington, DC 20006-5303
Phone: 202-628-1776
Fax: 202-879-3348
E-mail: nsdarscholarships@dar.org

NATIONAL SOCIETY DAUGHTERS OF THE AMERICAN REVOLUTION MADELINE PICKETT (HALBERT) COGSWELL NURSING SCHOLARSHIP

Scholarship available to students who have been accepted or are currently enrolled in an accredited school of nursing, who are members of NSDAR, descendants of members of NSDAR, or are eligible to be members of NSDAR. A letter of acceptance into the nursing program or transcript showing enrollment in nursing program must be included with the application. DAR member number must be on the application.

Academic Fields/Career Goals: Nursing.

Award: Scholarship for use in freshman, sophomore, junior, or senior years; not renewable. *Number:* varies. *Amount:* $1000.

Eligibility Requirements: Applicant must be enrolled or expecting to enroll full-time at a two-year or four-year institution or university. Applicant or parent of applicant must be member of Daughters of the American Revolution. Available to U.S. and non-U.S. citizens.

Application Requirements: Application, references, self-addressed stamped envelope, letter of sponsorship. *Deadline:* February 15.

Contact: Eric Weisz, Manager, Office of the Reporter General
National Society Daughters of the American Revolution
1776 D Street, NW
Washington, DC 20006-5303
Phone: 202-628-1776
Fax: 202-879-3348
E-mail: nsdarscholarships@dar.org

NATIONAL SOCIETY DAUGHTERS OF THE AMERICAN REVOLUTION MILDRED NUTTING NURSING SCHOLARSHIP

A one-time $1000 scholarship for students who are in financial need and who have been accepted or are currently enrolled in an accredited school of nursing. A letter of acceptance into the nursing program or the transcript stating that the applicant is in the nursing program must be enclosed with the application. Preference will be given to candidates from the Lowell, Massachusetts area.

Academic Fields/Career Goals: Nursing.

Award: Scholarship for use in freshman, sophomore, junior, or senior years; not renewable. *Number:* varies. *Amount:* $1000.

Eligibility Requirements: Applicant must be enrolled or expecting to enroll full-time at a two-year or four-year institution or university. Available to U.S. citizens.

Application Requirements: Application, essay, financial need analysis, references, self-addressed stamped envelope, test scores, transcript, letter of sponsorship. *Deadline:* February 15.

Contact: Eric Weisz, Manager, Office of the Reporter General
National Society Daughters of the American Revolution
1776 D Street, NW
Washington, DC 20006-5303
Phone: 202-628-1776
Fax: 202-879-3348
E-mail: nsdarscholarships@dar.org

NATIONAL SOCIETY OF THE COLONIAL DAMES OF AMERICA http://www.nscda.org

AMERICAN INDIAN NURSE SCHOLARSHIP AWARDS

• *See page 327*

NEW HAMPSHIRE POSTSECONDARY EDUCATION COMMISSION http://www.nh.gov/postsecondary

WORKFORCE INCENTIVE PROGRAM

• *See page 237*

NEW JERSEY STATE NURSES ASSOCIATION http://www.njsna.org

INSTITUTE FOR NURSING SCHOLARSHIP

Applicants must be New Jersey residents currently enrolled in a diploma, associate, baccalaureate, master's, or doctoral program in nursing or a related field. The amount awarded in each scholarship will be $1000 per recipient.

Academic Fields/Career Goals: Nursing.

Award: Scholarship for use in freshman, sophomore, junior, senior, or graduate years; not renewable. *Number:* 14. *Amount:* $1000.

Eligibility Requirements: Applicant must be enrolled or expecting to enroll full-time at a two-year or four-year institution or university and resident of New Jersey. Available to U.S. citizens.

Application Requirements: Application, references, transcript, tax form. *Deadline:* varies.

Contact: Sandy Kerr, Executive Assistant
New Jersey State Nurses Association
1479 Pennington Road
Trenton, NJ 08618-2661
Phone: 609-883-5335
Fax: 609-883-5343
E-mail: sandy@njsna.org

NEW MEXICO COMMISSION ON HIGHER EDUCATION http://www.hed.state.nm.us

ALLIED HEALTH STUDENT LOAN PROGRAM-NEW MEXICO

• *See page 213*

NURSE EDUCATOR LOAN-FOR-SERVICE

Forgivable loan of up to $5000 for New Mexico nursing majors to obtain undergraduate, graduate, or post graduate degree in the state of New Mexico. Each loan has a service agreement wherein the student declares his/her intent to serve in a nurse faculty position in a New Mexico public, post-secondary institution. For every academic year of service, a portion of the loan is forgiven and if the entire service agreement is fulfilled, the entire loan is eligible for forgiveness. Must be a U.S. citizen.

Academic Fields/Career Goals: Nursing.

Award: Forgivable loan for use in senior or graduate years; renewable. *Number:* varies. *Amount:* up to $5000.

Eligibility Requirements: Applicant must be enrolled or expecting to enroll full- or part-time at a four-year institution or university; resident of New Mexico and studying in New Mexico. Available to U.S. citizens.

Application Requirements: Application, essay, transcript. *Deadline:* July 1.

Contact: Tashina Banks-Moore, Interim Director of Financial Aid
New Mexico Commission on Higher Education
1068 Cerrillos Road
Santa Fe, NM 85705-1650
Phone: 505-476-6549
Fax: 505-476-6511
E-mail: tashina.banks-moore@state.nm.us

NURSING STUDENT LOAN-FOR-SERVICE PROGRAM

Award to increase the number of nurses in areas of the state which have experienced shortages by making educational loans to students entering nursing programs. As a condition of each loan, the student shall declare his/her intent to practice as a health professional in a designated shortage area. For every year of service, a portion of the loan will be forgiven.

Academic Fields/Career Goals: Nursing.

Award: Forgivable loan for use in freshman, sophomore, junior, or senior years; renewable. *Number:* varies. *Amount:* up to $12,000.

Eligibility Requirements: Applicant must be enrolled or expecting to enroll full- or part-time at a four-year institution or university; resident of New Mexico and studying in New Mexico. Available to U.S. citizens.

New Mexico Commission on Higher Education (continued)

Application Requirements: Application, financial need analysis, transcript, FAFSA. *Deadline:* July 1.

Contact: Tashina Banks Moore, Interim Director of Financial Aid
New Mexico Commission on Higher Education
1068 Cerrillos Road
Santa Fe, NM 87505
Phone: 505-476-6549
Fax: 505-476-6511
E-mail: tashina.banks-moore@state.nm.us

NEWTON NURSE SCHOLARS RHODE ISLAND FOUNDATION http://www.rifoundation.org

ALBERT AND FLORENCE NEWTON NURSE SCHOLARSHIP NEWTON FUND

Funds schools in Rhode Island only. Ascribes funds to: registered nurses seeking BS degree in nursing; senior nursing students in final year of education to become a registered nurse; registered nurses with BS degree seeking graduate degree; programs selected which are targeted to increase the availability of new registered nurses.

Academic Fields/Career Goals: Nursing.

Award: Scholarship for use in freshman, sophomore, junior, or senior years; renewable. *Number:* up to 20. *Amount:* $500–$3000.

Eligibility Requirements: Applicant must be enrolled or expecting to enroll full- or part-time at a two-year or four-year institution or university and studying in Rhode Island. Available to U.S. citizens.

Application Requirements: Application, essay, financial need analysis. *Deadline:* April 18.

Contact: Libby Monahan, Funds Administrator
Newton Nurse Scholars Rhode Island Foundation
One Union Station
Providence, RI 02903
Phone: 401-274-4564
E-mail: libbym@rifoundation.org

NEW YORK STATE EDUCATION DEPARTMENT http://www.highered.nysed.gov

REGENTS PROFESSIONAL OPPORTUNITY SCHOLARSHIP

• *See page 60*

NEW YORK STATE EMERGENCY NURSES ASSOCIATION (ENA) http://www.ena.org

NEW YORK STATE ENA SEPTEMBER 11 SCHOLARSHIP FUND

Scholarships to rescue workers who are going to school to obtain their undergraduate nursing degree. Eligible rescue workers include prehospital care providers, fire fighters, and police officers. The scholarship is not limited geographically. The scholarship winner will also be awarded a complimentary one year ENA membership.

Academic Fields/Career Goals: Nursing.

Award: Scholarship for use in freshman, sophomore, junior, senior, graduate, or postgraduate years; not renewable. *Number:* 1. *Amount:* $2000.

Eligibility Requirements: Applicant must be enrolled or expecting to enroll full- or part-time at a four-year institution or university. Available to U.S. citizens.

Application Requirements: Application. *Deadline:* varies.

Contact: Educational Services
New York State Emergency Nurses Association (ENA)
915 Lee Street
Des Plaines, IL 60016-6569
Phone: 847-460-4123
Fax: 847-460-4005
E-mail: education@ena.org

NEW YORK STATE GRANGE http://www.nysgrange.com

JUNE GILL NURSING SCHOLARSHIP

One annual scholarship award to verified NYS Grange member pursuing a career in nursing. Selection based on verification of NYS Grange membership and enrollment in a nursing program, as well as applicant's career statement, academic records, and financial need. Payment made after successful completion of one term.

Academic Fields/Career Goals: Nursing.

Award: Scholarship for use in freshman, sophomore, junior, or senior years; not renewable. *Number:* 1. *Amount:* varies.

Eligibility Requirements: Applicant must be enrolled or expecting to enroll full-time at a two-year or four-year institution and resident of New York. Applicant or parent of applicant must be member of Grange Association. Available to U.S. citizens.

Application Requirements: Application, financial need analysis, transcript, nursing program enrollment letter, career statement. *Deadline:* April 15.

Contact: Scholarship Committee
New York State Grange
100 Grange Place
Cortland, NY 13045
Phone: 607-756-7553
Fax: 607-756-7757
E-mail: nysgrange@nysgrange.com

NIGHTINGALE AWARDS OF PENNSYLVANIA http://www.nightingaleawards.org

NIGHTINGALE AWARDS OF PENNSYLVANIA NURSING SCHOLARSHIP

Scholarships for students who are studying nursing at the basic or advanced level and intend to practice in Pennsylvania. Regardless of the type of nursing program, all candidates accepted into or presently enrolled in accredited nursing programs in Pennsylvania may apply. Scholarships are awarded to students who enter professional nursing programs, practical nursing programs, and advanced degree programs.

Academic Fields/Career Goals: Nursing.

Award: Scholarship for use in freshman, sophomore, junior, senior, or graduate years; not renewable. *Number:* up to 6. *Amount:* $6000–$10,000.

Eligibility Requirements: Applicant must be enrolled or expecting to enroll full-time at a four-year institution or university and studying in Pennsylvania. Available to U.S. citizens.

Application Requirements: Application, references, test scores, transcript. *Deadline:* January 31.

Contact: Christine Filipovich, President
Nightingale Awards of Pennsylvania
2090 Linglestown Road, Suite 107
Harrisburg, PA 17110
Phone: 717-909-0350
Fax: 717-234-6798
E-mail: nightingale@pronursingresources.com

NORTH CAROLINA STATE EDUCATION ASSISTANCE AUTHORITY http://www.ncseaa.edu

NORTH CAROLINA STUDENT LOAN PROGRAM FOR HEALTH, SCIENCE, AND MATHEMATICS

• *See page 213*

NURSE EDUCATION SCHOLARSHIP LOAN PROGRAM (NESLP)

Must be U.S. citizen and North Carolina resident. Award available through financial aid offices of North Carolina colleges and universities that offer programs to prepare students for licensure in the state as LPN or RN. Recipients enter contract with the State of North Carolina to work full time as a licensed nurse. Loans not repaid through service must be repaid in cash. Award based upon financial need. Maximum award for students enrolled in Associate Degree Nursing and Practical Nurse Education programs is $5000. Maximum award for students enrolled in a baccalaureate program is $400.

Academic Fields/Career Goals: Nursing.

Award: Forgivable loan for use in freshman, sophomore, junior, or senior years; renewable. *Number:* varies. *Amount:* $400–$5000.

Eligibility Requirements: Applicant must be enrolled or expecting to enroll full- or part-time at a four-year institution or university; resident of North Carolina and studying in North Carolina. Available to U.S. citizens.

Application Requirements: Application, financial need analysis. *Deadline:* continuous.

Contact: Bill Carswell, Manager of Scholarship and Grant Division
North Carolina State Education Assistance Authority
PO Box 14103
Research Triangle Park, NC 27709
Phone: 919-549-8614
Fax: 919-248-4687
E-mail: carswellb@ncseaa.edu

NURSE SCHOLARS PROGRAM-UNDERGRADUATE (NORTH CAROLINA)

Forgivable loans to residents of North Carolina who have been accepted to a North Carolina institution of higher education that offers a nursing program. Must apply to the North Carolina State Education and Welfare division. Must serve as a registered nurse in North Carolina for one year for each year of funding. Minimum 3.0 GPA required. Amount of award is based upon type of nursing education sought. Deadline varies.

Academic Fields/Career Goals: Nursing.

Award: Forgivable loan for use in freshman, sophomore, junior, or senior years; renewable. *Number:* up to 450. *Amount:* $3000–$5000.

Eligibility Requirements: Applicant must be enrolled or expecting to enroll full-time at a two-year or four-year institution or university; resident of North Carolina and studying in North Carolina. Applicant must have 3.0 GPA or higher. Available to U.S. citizens.

Application Requirements: Application, essay, references, test scores, transcript. *Deadline:* varies.

Contact: Terrence Scarborough, Manager, Merit-Based Scholarship Loan Programs
North Carolina State Education Assistance Authority
PO Box 13663
Research Triangle Park, NC 27709
Phone: 919-549-8614
Fax: 919-248-4687
E-mail: terrence@ncseaa.edu

ODD FELLOWS AND REBEKAHS http://www.ioofme.org

ODD FELLOWS AND REBEKAHS ELLEN F. WASHBURN NURSES TRAINING AWARD

Award for high school seniors and college undergraduates to attend an accredited Maine institution and pursue a registered nursing degree. Must have a minimum 2.5 GPA. Can reapply for award for up to four years.

Academic Fields/Career Goals: Nursing.

Award: Scholarship for use in freshman, sophomore, junior, or senior years; renewable. *Number:* up to 30. *Amount:* $150–$400.

Eligibility Requirements: Applicant must be enrolled or expecting to enroll full- or part-time at a two-year or four-year institution or university and studying in Maine. Applicant must have 2.5 GPA or higher. Available to U.S. citizens.

Application Requirements: Application, financial need analysis, photo, references. *Deadline:* April 15.

Contact: Joyce Young, Chairman
Odd Fellows and Rebekahs
131 Queen Street Extension
Gorham, ME 04038
Phone: 207-839-4723

ONS FOUNDATION http://www.ons.org

ONS FOUNDATION ETHNIC MINORITY BACHELOR'S SCHOLARSHIP

Three one-time scholarships of $2000 available to registered nurses with a demonstrated interest in oncology nursing. Must be currently enrolled in an undergraduate program at an NLN-accredited school, and must currently hold a license to practice as a registered nurse. Must be minority student who has not received any BA grants previously from ONF.

Academic Fields/Career Goals: Nursing.

Award: Scholarship for use in freshman, sophomore, junior, or senior years; not renewable. *Number:* 3. *Amount:* $2000.

Eligibility Requirements: Applicant must be American Indian/Alaska Native, Asian/Pacific Islander, Black (non-Hispanic), or Hispanic and enrolled or expecting to enroll full- or part-time at a four-year institution or university. Applicant or parent of applicant must have employment or volunteer experience in nursing. Available to U.S. citizens.

Application Requirements: Application, transcript. *Fee:* $5. *Deadline:* February 1.

Contact: Bonny Revo, Executive Assistant
ONS Foundation
125 Enterprise Drive
Pittsburgh, PA 15275
Phone: 412-859-6100
Fax: 412-859-6162
E-mail: brevo@ons.org

ONS FOUNDATION/ONCOLOGY NURSING CERTIFICATION CORPORATION BACHELOR'S SCHOLARSHIPS

One-time awards to improve oncology nursing by assisting registered nurses in furthering their education. Applicants must hold a current license to practice and be enrolled in an undergraduate nursing degree program at an NLN-accredited school.

Academic Fields/Career Goals: Nursing; Oncology.

Award: Scholarship for use in freshman, sophomore, junior, or senior years; not renewable. *Number:* 3. *Amount:* $2000.

Eligibility Requirements: Applicant must be enrolled or expecting to enroll full- or part-time at a four-year institution or university. Applicant or parent of applicant must have employment or volunteer experience in nursing. Available to U.S. and non-U.S. citizens.

Application Requirements: Application, transcript. *Fee:* $5. *Deadline:* February 1.

Contact: Bonny Revo, Executive Assistant
ONS Foundation
125 Enterprise Drive
Pittsburgh, PA 15275
Phone: 412-859-6100
Fax: 412-859-6162
E-mail: brevo@ons.org

ONS FOUNDATION/PEARL MOORE CAREER DEVELOPMENT AWARDS

Awards to practicing staff nurses who possess or are pursuing a BSN and have two years oncology practice experience.

Academic Fields/Career Goals: Nursing; Oncology.

Award: Prize for use in freshman, sophomore, junior, or senior years; not renewable. *Number:* 3. *Amount:* $3000.

Eligibility Requirements: Applicant must be enrolled or expecting to enroll full- or part-time at a four-year institution or university. Applicant or parent of applicant must have employment or volunteer experience in nursing. Available to U.S. citizens.

Application Requirements: Application, autobiography, references. *Deadline:* December 1.

Contact: Bonny Revo, Executive Assistant
ONS Foundation
125 Enterprise Drive
Pittsburgh, PA 15275
Phone: 412-859-6100
Fax: 412-859-6162
E-mail: brevo@ons.org

ONS FOUNDATION ROBERTA PIERCE SCOFIELD BACHELOR'S SCHOLARSHIPS

One-time awards to improve oncology nursing by assisting registered nurses in furthering their education. Applicants must hold a current license to practice and be enrolled in an undergraduate nursing degree program at an NLN-accredited school.

Academic Fields/Career Goals: Nursing; Oncology.

Award: Scholarship for use in freshman, sophomore, junior, or senior years; not renewable. *Number:* 1. *Amount:* $2000.

Eligibility Requirements: Applicant must be enrolled or expecting to enroll full- or part-time at a four-year institution or university. Applicant or parent of applicant must have employment or volunteer experience in nursing. Available to U.S. and non-U.S. citizens.

ONS Foundation (continued)

Application Requirements: Application, transcript. *Fee:* $5. *Deadline:* February 1.

Contact: Bonny Revo, Executive Assistant
ONS Foundation
125 Enterprise Drive
Pittsburgh, PA 15275
Phone: 412-859-6100
Fax: 412-859-6162
E-mail: brevo@ons.org

OREGON COMMUNITY FOUNDATION http://www.ocf1.org

DR. FRANZ AND KATHRYN STENZEL FUND

• *See page 341*

NLN ELLA MCKINNEY SCHOLARSHIP FUND

Award for Oregon high school graduates (or the equivalent) for use in the pursuit of an undergraduate or graduate nursing education. Must attend a nonprofit college or university in Oregon accredited by the NLN Accrediting Commission.

Academic Fields/Career Goals: Nursing.

Award: Scholarship for use in freshman, sophomore, junior, senior, or graduate years; not renewable. *Number:* up to 5. *Amount:* $1000–$1500.

Eligibility Requirements: Applicant must be enrolled or expecting to enroll full-time at a four-year institution or university; resident of Oregon and studying in Oregon. Available to U.S. citizens.

Application Requirements: Application, references. *Deadline:* March 1.

Contact: Dianne Causey, Program Associate for Scholarships and Grants
Oregon Community Foundation
1221 Yamhill, SW, Suite 100
Portland, OR 97205
Phone: 503-227-6846
Fax: 503-274-7771
E-mail: diannec@ocf1.org

OREGON NURSES ASSOCIATION http://www.oregonrn.org

ONF CENTENNIAL EDUCATION SCHOLARSHIPS

Scholarship available to Oregon residents accepted into or enrolled in an accredited nursing program in Oregon. Minimum 3.0 GPA required.

Academic Fields/Career Goals: Nursing.

Award: Scholarship for use in freshman year; not renewable. *Number:* 1. *Amount:* $1000.

Eligibility Requirements: Applicant must be enrolled or expecting to enroll full-time at a two-year or four-year institution or university; resident of Oregon and studying in Oregon. Applicant must have 3.0 GPA or higher. Available to U.S. citizens.

Application Requirements: Application, transcript, letter of acceptance from the nursing program. *Deadline:* varies.

Contact: Melissa Tangedal, Program Assistant
Oregon Nurses Association
18765 SW Boones Ferry Road, Suite 200
Tualatin, OR 97062
Phone: 503-293-0011
Fax: 503-293-0013
E-mail: tangedal@oregonrn.org

ONF-SMITH EDUCATION SCHOLARSHIP

Award for nursing students enrolled in an undergraduate or graduate program in Oregon. RN recipients must be current ONA members. Non-RN recipients of the baccalaureate scholarship must join the nurses association in their state of residence upon graduation.

Academic Fields/Career Goals: Nursing.

Award: Scholarship for use in freshman, sophomore, junior, senior, or graduate years; not renewable. *Number:* 3. *Amount:* $1000.

Eligibility Requirements: Applicant must be enrolled or expecting to enroll full-time at a two-year or four-year institution or university and studying in Oregon. Applicant must have 3.0 GPA or higher. Available to U.S. citizens.

Application Requirements: Application, references, letter of acceptance from nursing program. *Deadline:* February 1.

Contact: Melissa Tangedal, Program Assistant
Oregon Nurses Association
18765 SW Boones Ferry Road, Suite 200
Tualatin, OR 97062
Phone: 503-293-0011
Fax: 503-293-0013
E-mail: tangedal@oregonrn.org

OREGON STUDENT ASSISTANCE COMMISSION http://www.osac.state.or.us

BERTHA P. SINGER NURSES SCHOLARSHIP

One-time award for Oregon residents pursuing a nursing career. Must attend a college or university in Oregon. Must have completed one year of undergraduate study. Proof of enrollment in third year of four-year nursing degree program or second year of a two-year associate degree nursing program is required. Transcripts alone are not sufficient proof, must obtain a form or letter from department. U.S. Bancorp employees, their children, or close relatives are not eligible.

Academic Fields/Career Goals: Nursing.

Award: Scholarship for use in sophomore, junior, senior, or graduate years; renewable. *Number:* 23. *Amount:* varies.

Eligibility Requirements: Applicant must be enrolled or expecting to enroll full-time at a two-year or four-year institution or university; resident of Oregon and studying in Oregon. Applicant must have 3.0 GPA or higher. Available to U.S. citizens.

Application Requirements: Application, essay, financial need analysis, test scores, transcript, form or letter from department. *Deadline:* March 1.

Contact: Director of Grant Programs
Oregon Student Assistance Commission
1500 Valley River Drive, Suite 100
Eugene, OR 97401-7020
Phone: 800-452-8807 Ext. 7395

FRIENDS OF OREGON STUDENTS SCHOLARSHIP

• *See page 238*

MARION A. LINDEMAN SCHOLARSHIP

• *See page 341*

WALTER AND MARIE SCHMIDT SCHOLARSHIP

Scholarship available to students enrolling in programs to become registered nurses and intending to pursue careers in geriatric health care. Applicants must submit an additional essay describing their desire to pursue a nursing career in geriatrics. U.S. Bancorp employees, their children, or near relatives are not eligible. Preference to students from Lane County.

Academic Fields/Career Goals: Nursing.

Award: Scholarship for use in freshman or sophomore years; renewable. *Number:* varies. *Amount:* varies.

Eligibility Requirements: Applicant must be enrolled or expecting to enroll full- or part-time at a two-year or four-year institution and resident of Oregon. Available to U.S. citizens.

Application Requirements: Application, essay, financial need analysis, references, transcript, activity chart. *Deadline:* March 1.

Contact: Director of Grant Programs
Oregon Student Assistance Commission
1500 Valley River Drive, Suite 100
Eugene, OR 97401-7020
Phone: 800-452-8807 Ext. 7395

PILOT INTERNATIONAL FOUNDATION http://www.pilotinternational.org

PILOT INTERNATIONAL FOUNDATION RUBY NEWHALL MEMORIAL SCHOLARSHIP

• *See page 342*

PILOT INTERNATIONAL FOUNDATION SCHOLARSHIP PROGRAM

• *See page 342*

RESOURCE CENTER

MARIE BLAHA MEDICAL GRANT

• *See page 83*

RHODE ISLAND FOUNDATION http://www.rifoundation.org

ALBERT E. AND FLORENCE W. NEWTON NURSE SCHOLARSHIP

Applicant must be studying nursing on a full- or part-time basis. Preference will be given to Rhode Island residents committed to practicing in Rhode Island. Must be able to demonstrate financial need. Must be in one of the following categories: A registered nurse enrolled in a nursing baccalaureate degree program; student enrolled in a baccalaureate nursing program; student in a diploma nursing program; student in a two-year associate degree nursing program.

Academic Fields/Career Goals: Nursing.

Award: Scholarship for use in freshman, sophomore, junior, or senior years; renewable. *Number:* varies. *Amount:* varies.

Eligibility Requirements: Applicant must be enrolled or expecting to enroll full- or part-time at a two-year or four-year institution or university. Available to U.S. citizens.

Application Requirements: Application, essay, financial need analysis, self-addressed stamped envelope, transcript, copy of college acceptance letter, copy of most recent income tax return. *Deadline:* October 1.

Contact: Libby Monahan, Funds Administrator
Rhode Island Foundation
One Union Station
Providence, RI 02903
Phone: 401-274-4564 Ext. 3117
Fax: 401-751-7983
E-mail: libbym@rifoundation.org

SOCIETY FOR THE SCIENTIFIC STUDY OF SEXUALITY http://www.sexscience.org

SOCIETY FOR THE SCIENTIFIC STUDY OF SEXUALITY STUDENT RESEARCH GRANT

• *See page 129*

SOCIETY OF PEDIATRIC NURSES http://www.pedsnurses.org

SOCIETY OF PEDIATRIC NURSES EDUCATIONAL SCHOLARSHIP

• *See page 167*

STATE OF GEORGIA http://www.gsfc.org

DEPARTMENT OF HUMAN RESOURCES FEDERAL STAFFORD LOAN WITH THE SERVICE CANCELABLE LOAN OPTION

Forgivable loan of $4000 to $10,000 awarded to current Department of Human Resources employee who will be enrolled in a baccalaureate or advanced nursing degree program at an eligible participating school in Georgia. Loans are cancelled upon two calendar years of service as a registered nurse for the Georgia DHR or any Georgia county board of health.

Academic Fields/Career Goals: Nursing.

Award: Forgivable loan for use in freshman, sophomore, junior, senior, or graduate years; not renewable. *Number:* 1. *Amount:* $4000–$10,000.

Eligibility Requirements: Applicant must be enrolled or expecting to enroll full- or part-time at a four-year institution or university; resident of Georgia and studying in Georgia. Applicant or parent of applicant must have employment or volunteer experience in human services. Available to U.S. citizens.

Application Requirements: Application, financial need analysis. *Deadline:* June 4.

Contact: Peggy Matthews, Manager, GSFA Origination
State of Georgia
2082 East Exchange Place, Suite 230
Tucker, GA 30084
Phone: 770-724-9230
Fax: 770-724-9225
E-mail: peggy@gsfc.org

LADDERS IN NURSING CAREER SERVICE CANCELABLE LOAN PROGRAM

Forgivable loans of $3000 are awarded to students who agree to serve for one calendar year at an approved site within the state of Georgia. Eligible applicants will be residents of Georgia who are studying nursing at a Georgia institution.

Academic Fields/Career Goals: Nursing.

Award: Forgivable loan for use in freshman, sophomore, junior, senior, or graduate years; not renewable. *Number:* 5. *Amount:* $3000.

Eligibility Requirements: Applicant must be enrolled or expecting to enroll full- or part-time at a two-year or four-year or technical institution or university; resident of Georgia and studying in Georgia. Available to U.S. citizens.

Application Requirements: Application, financial need analysis. *Deadline:* June 3.

Contact: Peggy Matthews, Manager, GSFA Origination
State of Georgia
2082 East Exchange Place, Suite 230
Tucker, GA 30084
Phone: 770-724-9230
Fax: 770-724-9225
E-mail: peggy@gsfc.org

NORTHEAST GEORGIA PILOT NURSE SERVICE CANCELABLE LOAN

Awards up to 100 forgivable loans between $2500 and $4500 to undergraduate students who are residents of Georgia studying nursing in Georgia. Loans can be repaid by working as a nurse in northeast Georgia.

Academic Fields/Career Goals: Nursing.

Award: Forgivable loan for use in freshman, sophomore, junior, or senior years; not renewable. *Number:* up to 100. *Amount:* $2500–$4500.

Eligibility Requirements: Applicant must be enrolled or expecting to enroll full-time at a four-year institution or university; resident of Georgia and studying in Georgia. Available to U.S. citizens.

Application Requirements: Application, financial need analysis. *Deadline:* June 3.

Contact: Peggy Matthews, Manager, GSFA Origination
State of Georgia
2082 East Exchange Place, Suite 230
Tucker, GA 30084
Phone: 770-724-9230
Fax: 770-724-9225
E-mail: peggy@gsfc.org

REGISTERED NURSE SERVICE CANCELABLE LOAN PROGRAM

Forgivable loans awarded to undergraduate students who are residents of Georgia studying nursing in a two- or four-year school in Georgia. Loans can be repaid by working as a registered nurse in the state of Georgia.

Academic Fields/Career Goals: Nursing.

Award: Forgivable loan for use in freshman, sophomore, junior, or senior years; not renewable. *Number:* 15. *Amount:* $100–$4500.

Eligibility Requirements: Applicant must be enrolled or expecting to enroll full- or part-time at a two-year or four-year institution or university; resident of Georgia and studying in Georgia. Available to U.S. citizens.

Application Requirements: Application, financial need analysis. *Deadline:* June 3.

Contact: Peggy Matthews, Manager, GSFA Origination
State of Georgia
2082 East Exchange Place, Suite 230
Tucker, GA 30084
Phone: 770-724-9230
Fax: 770-724-9225
E-mail: peggy@gsfc.org

State of Georgia (continued)

SERVICE-CANCELABLE STAFFORD LOAN-GEORGIA

• *See page 213*

STATE STUDENT ASSISTANCE COMMISSION OF INDIANA (SSACI) http://www.in.gov/ssaci

INDIANA NURSING SCHOLARSHIP FUND

Need-based tuition funding for nursing students enrolled full- or part-time at an eligible Indiana institution. Must be a U.S. citizen and an Indiana resident and have a minimum 2.0 GPA or meet the minimum requirements for the nursing program. Upon graduation, recipients must practice as a nurse in an Indiana health care setting for two years.

Academic Fields/Career Goals: Nursing.

Award: Scholarship for use in freshman, sophomore, junior, or senior years; not renewable. *Number:* 490–690. *Amount:* $200–$5000.

Eligibility Requirements: Applicant must be enrolled or expecting to enroll full- or part-time at a two-year or four-year institution or university; resident of Indiana and studying in Indiana. Available to U.S. citizens.

Application Requirements: Application, financial need analysis, FAFSA. *Deadline:* continuous.

Contact: Yvonne Heflin, Director, Special Programs
State Student Assistance Commission of Indiana (SSACI)
150 West Market Street, Suite 500
Indianapolis, IN 46204-2805
Phone: 317-232-2350
Fax: 317-232-3260

STRAIGHTFORWARD MEDIA http://www.straightforwardmedia.com

STRAIGHTFORWARD MEDIA NURSING SCHOOL SCHOLARSHIP

Scholarship of $500 available to students majoring in nursing. Must be U.S. citizen. Awarded four times per year. Deadlines: April 14, July 14, October 14, January 14.

Academic Fields/Career Goals: Nursing.

Award: Scholarship for use in freshman, sophomore, junior, or senior years; not renewable. *Number:* 4. *Amount:* $500.

Eligibility Requirements: Applicant must be enrolled or expecting to enroll full-time at a two-year or four-year institution or university. Available to U.S. and non-U.S. citizens.

Application Requirements: Online application. *Deadline:* varies.

Contact: Scholarship Committee
StraightForward Media
2040 West Main Street, Suite 104
Rapid City, SD 57701
Phone: 605-348-3042
Fax: 605-348-3043

TAFFORD UNIFORMS http://www.tafford.com

TAFFORD UNIFORMS NURSING SCHOLARSHIP PROGRAM

Two scholarships of $1000 each awarded to nursing students enrolled in undergraduate and graduate study. Minimum 2.5 GPA required.

Academic Fields/Career Goals: Nursing.

Award: Scholarship for use in freshman, sophomore, junior, senior, or graduate years; not renewable. *Number:* 2. *Amount:* $1000.

Eligibility Requirements: Applicant must be enrolled or expecting to enroll full-time at a two-year or four-year institution or university. Applicant must have 2.5 GPA or higher. Available to U.S. citizens.

Application Requirements: Application. *Deadline:* May 15.

Contact: David Kaplan, Vice President of Marketing
Tafford Uniforms
1370 Welsh Road
North Wales, PA 19454
Phone: 215-643-9666
Fax: 215-643-4922
E-mail: dkaplan@tafford.com

TEXAS HIGHER EDUCATION COORDINATING BOARD http://www.collegefortexans.com

OUTSTANDING RURAL SCHOLAR PROGRAM

• *See page 342*

TOUCHMARK FOUNDATION http://www.touchmarkfoundation.org

TOUCHMARK FOUNDATION NURSING SCHOLARSHIP

Students pursuing nursing degrees at any level are encouraged to apply, including nurses interested pursuing advanced degrees in order to teach. Scholarship application deadlines are June 30 and December 30 of each year.

Academic Fields/Career Goals: Nursing.

Award: Scholarship for use in freshman, sophomore, junior, senior, or graduate years; not renewable. *Number:* varies. *Amount:* varies.

Eligibility Requirements: Applicant must be enrolled or expecting to enroll full-time at a four-year institution or university. Available to U.S. citizens.

Application Requirements: Application, essay, references, transcript, FAFSA, copy of acceptance letter. *Deadline:* varies.

Contact: Brett Cope, President
Touchmark Foundation
5150 SW Griffith Drive
Beaverton, OR 97005
Phone: 800-796-8744
Fax: 503-644-3568
E-mail: bjc@touchmark.com

ULMAN CANCER FUND FOR YOUNG ADULTS http://www.ulmanfund.org

BARBARA PALO FOSTER MEMORIAL SCHOLARSHIP

Scholarship for people who have lost a parent to cancer or have a parent with cancer and are seeking or receiving postsecondary education in the field of nursing. Currently attending, or planning to attend, a two- or four-year college or university or training program and seeking a degree in the field of nursing (including graduate and professional schools).

Academic Fields/Career Goals: Nursing.

Award: Scholarship for use in freshman, sophomore, junior, or senior years; not renewable. *Number:* varies. *Amount:* up to $1000.

Eligibility Requirements: Applicant must be age 16-35 and enrolled or expecting to enroll full- or part-time at a two-year or four-year institution or university. Available to U.S. citizens.

Application Requirements: Application, financial need analysis, references, physician verification form, deceased parent/guardian verification form. *Deadline:* May 10.

Contact: Fay Baker, Scholarship Coordinator
Ulman Cancer Fund for Young Adults
4725 Dorsey Hall Drive, Suite A
PO Box 505
Ellicott City, MD 21042
Phone: 410-964-0202
Fax: 410-964-0402
E-mail: scholarship@ulmanfund.org

UNITED DAUGHTERS OF THE CONFEDERACY http://www.hqudc.org

PHOEBE PEMBER MEMORIAL SCHOLARSHIP

Award for full-time undergraduate students who are descendants of a Confederate soldier, enrolled in a school of nursing. Must be enrolled in an accredited college or university and have a minimum 3.0 GPA. Submit letter of endorsement from sponsoring Chapter of the United Daughters of the Confederacy.

Academic Fields/Career Goals: Nursing.

Award: Scholarship for use in freshman, sophomore, junior, or senior years; renewable. *Number:* 1–2. *Amount:* $800–$1000.

Eligibility Requirements: Applicant must be enrolled or expecting to enroll full-time at a four-year institution or university. Applicant or parent of applicant must be member of United Daughters of the Confederacy. Applicant must have 3.0 GPA or higher. Available to U.S. citizens. Applicant or parent must meet one or more of the following requirements: Air Force, Army, or Navy experience; retired from active duty; disabled or killed as a result of military service; prisoner of war; or missing in action.

Application Requirements: Application, essay, financial need analysis, photo, references, self-addressed stamped envelope, transcript, copy of applicant's birth certificate, copy of confederate ancestor's proof of service. *Deadline:* March 15.

Contact: Deanna Bryant, Second Vice President General
United Daughters of the Confederacy
328 North Boulevard
Richmond, VA 23220-4009
Phone: 804-355-1636
Fax: 804-353-1396
E-mail: hqudc@rcn.com

WALTER REED SMITH SCHOLARSHIP

• *See page 149*

UNITED NEGRO COLLEGE FUND http://www.uncf.org

SODEXHO SCHOLARSHIP

• *See page 343*

UNITED STATES PUBLIC HEALTH SERVICE-HEALTH RESOURCES AND SERVICES ADMINISTRATION, BUREAU OF HEALTH PROFESSIONS http://bhpr.hrsa.gov/dsa

HEALTH RESOURCES AND SERVICES ADMINISTRATION-BUREAU OF HEALTH PROFESSIONS SCHOLARSHIPS FOR DISADVANTAGED STUDENTS

• *See page 214*

VIRGINIA DEPARTMENT OF HEALTH, OFFICE OF HEALTH POLICY AND PLANNING http://www.vdh.virginia.gov

MARY MARSHALL PRACTICAL NURSING SCHOLARSHIPS

Award for practical nursing students who are Virginia residents. Must attend a nursing program in Virginia. Recipient must agree to work in Virginia after graduation. Minimum 3.0 GPA required. Scholarship value and the number of scholarships granted varies annually.

Academic Fields/Career Goals: Nursing.

Award: Scholarship for use in freshman, sophomore, junior, or senior years; not renewable. *Number:* varies. *Amount:* varies.

Eligibility Requirements: Applicant must be enrolled or expecting to enroll full- or part-time at a four-year institution or university; resident of Virginia and studying in Virginia. Applicant must have 3.0 GPA or higher. Available to U.S. citizens.

Application Requirements: Application, financial need analysis, references, transcript. *Deadline:* June 30.

Contact: Business Manager and Policy Analyst
Virginia Department of Health, Office of Health Policy and Planning
PO Box 2448
Richmond, VA 23218-2448
Phone: 804-864-7433
Fax: 804-864-7440

MARY MARSHALL REGISTERED NURSING PROGRAM SCHOLARSHIPS

Award for registered nursing students who are Virginia residents. Must attend a nursing program in Virginia. Recipient must agree to work in Virginia after graduation. Minimum 3.0 GPA required. The amount of each scholarship award is dependent upon the amount of money appropriated by the Virginia General Assembly and the number of qualified applicants.

Academic Fields/Career Goals: Nursing.

Award: Scholarship for use in freshman, sophomore, junior, or senior years; not renewable. *Number:* 60–100. *Amount:* varies.

Eligibility Requirements: Applicant must be enrolled or expecting to enroll full- or part-time at a four-year institution or university; resident of Virginia and studying in Virginia. Applicant must have 3.0 GPA or higher. Available to U.S. citizens.

Application Requirements: Application, financial need analysis, references, transcript. *Deadline:* June 30.

Contact: Business Manager and Policy Analyst
Virginia Department of Health, Office of Health Policy and Planning
PO Box 2448
Richmond, VA 23218-2448
Phone: 804-864-7433
Fax: 804-864-7440

NURSE PRACTITIONERS/NURSE MIDWIFE PROGRAM SCHOLARSHIPS

One-time award for nurse practitioner/nurse midwife students who have been residents of Virginia for at least one year. Must attend a nursing program in Virginia. Recipient must agree to work in an under-served community in Virginia following graduation. The amount of each scholarship award is dependent upon the amount of funds appropriated by the Virginia General Assembly. Minimum 3.0 GPA required.

Academic Fields/Career Goals: Nursing.

Award: Scholarship for use in freshman, sophomore, junior, or senior years; not renewable. *Number:* 5. *Amount:* $5000.

Eligibility Requirements: Applicant must be enrolled or expecting to enroll full- or part-time at a four-year institution or university; resident of Virginia and studying in Virginia. Applicant must have 3.0 GPA or higher. Available to U.S. citizens.

Application Requirements: Application, financial need analysis, references, transcript. *Deadline:* June 30.

Contact: Business Manager and Policy Analyst
Virginia Department of Health, Office of Health Policy and Planning
PO Box 2448
Richmond, VA 23218-2448
Phone: 804-864-7433
Fax: 804-864-7440

WEST VIRGINIA NURSES ASSOCIATION http://www.wvnurses.org

BERNICE L. VANCE SCHOLARSHIP

Scholarship for native West Virginian students enrolled in an accredited full-time or part-time nursing program

Academic Fields/Career Goals: Nursing.

Award: Scholarship for use in freshman, sophomore, junior, senior, graduate, or postgraduate years; not renewable. *Number:* 2. *Amount:* varies.

Eligibility Requirements: Applicant must be enrolled or expecting to enroll full- or part-time at a four-year institution or university and resident of West Virginia. Available to U.S. citizens.

Application Requirements: Application, financial need analysis, references, transcript. *Deadline:* July 1.

Contact: Monique Fortson, Scholarship Committee
West Virginia Nurses Association
PO Box 1946
Charleston, WV 25327
Phone: 304-342-1169
Fax: 304-414-3369
E-mail: centraloffice@wvnurses.org

WISCONSIN LEAGUE FOR NURSING INC. http://www.wisconsinwln.org

NURSING SCHOLARSHIP FOR HIGH SCHOOL SENIORS

One scholarship for a Wisconsin high school senior who will be pursing a professional nursing career. The senior must have been accepted by a Wisconsin NLN accredited school of nursing, have financial need, demonstrate scholastic excellence and leadership potential. Contact the WLN office by mail to request an application.

Academic Fields/Career Goals: Nursing.

Award: Scholarship for use in freshman year; not renewable. *Number:* 1. *Amount:* $500.

Wisconsin League for Nursing Inc. (continued)

Eligibility Requirements: Applicant must be high school student; planning to enroll or expecting to enroll full-time at a two-year or four-year institution or university; resident of Wisconsin and studying in Wisconsin. Available to U.S. citizens.

Application Requirements: Application, financial need analysis. *Deadline:* March 1.

Contact: Mary Ann Tanner, Administrative Secretary
Wisconsin League for Nursing Inc.
2121 East Newport Avenue
Milwaukee, WI 53211-2952
Phone: 888-755-3329
Fax: 888-755-3329
E-mail: wln@wisconsinwln.org

WISCONSIN LEAGUE FOR NURSING INC., SCHOLARSHIP

One-time award for Wisconsin residents who have completed half of an accredited Wisconsin school of nursing program. Financial need of student must be demonstrated. For further information visit Web site: http://www.wisconsinwln.org/Scholarships.htm.

Academic Fields/Career Goals: Nursing.

Award: Scholarship for use in junior, senior, or graduate years; not renewable. *Number:* 12. *Amount:* $500–$1000.

Eligibility Requirements: Applicant must be enrolled or expecting to enroll full-time at a two-year or four-year institution or university; resident of Wisconsin and studying in Wisconsin. Available to U.S. citizens.

Application Requirements: Application, financial need analysis. *Deadline:* March 1.

Contact: Mary Ann Tanner, Administrative Secretary
Wisconsin League for Nursing Inc.
2121 East Newport Avenue
Milwaukee, WI 53211-2952
Phone: 888-755-3329
Fax: 888-755-3329
E-mail: wln@wisconsinwln.org

WOUND, OSTOMY AND CONTINENCE NURSES SOCIETY http://www.wocn.org

WOCN ACCREDITED NURSING EDUCATION PROGRAM SCHOLARSHIP

Scholarships are awarded to deserving individuals committed to working within the wound, ostomy and continence nursing specialty. Applicants must agree to support the WOCN Society philosophy and scope of practice. Number of scholarships and the dollar value varies annually. Deadlines: May 1 or November 1.

Academic Fields/Career Goals: Nursing.

Award: Scholarship for use in freshman, sophomore, junior, or senior years; not renewable. *Number:* varies. *Amount:* varies.

Eligibility Requirements: Applicant must be enrolled or expecting to enroll full-time at a two-year or four-year or technical institution or university. Available to U.S. and non-U.S. citizens.

Application Requirements: Application, references, acceptance letter, proof of current enrollment or certificate of completion from a WOCN accredited education program. *Deadline:* varies.

Contact: Scholarship Committee
Wound, Ostomy and Continence Nurses Society
15000 Commerce Parkway, Suite C
Mt. Laurel, NJ 08054
Phone: 888-224-9626
Fax: 856-439-0525

OCCUPATIONAL SAFETY AND HEALTH

AMERICAN SOCIETY OF SAFETY ENGINEERS (ASSE) FOUNDATION http://www.asse.org

AMERICA RESPONDS MEMORIAL SCHOLARSHIP

Scholarship of $1000 will be awarded to a student pursuing an undergraduate degree in occupational safety and health or a closely related field. Must have completed 60 semester hours and maintain at least a 3.0 GPA. Applicant must be a member of ASSE. Must be a U.S. citizen.

Academic Fields/Career Goals: Occupational Safety and Health.

Award: Scholarship for use in sophomore, junior, or senior years; not renewable. *Number:* 1. *Amount:* up to $1000.

Eligibility Requirements: Applicant must be enrolled or expecting to enroll full-time at a four-year institution or university. Applicant or parent of applicant must be member of American Society of Safety Engineers. Applicant must have 3.0 GPA or higher. Available to U.S. citizens.

Application Requirements: Application, essay, financial need analysis, references, transcript. *Deadline:* December 1.

Contact: Mary Goranson, Scholarship Coordinator
American Society of Safety Engineers (ASSE) Foundation
1800 East Oakton Street
Des Plaines, IL 60018
Phone: 847-768-3412
E-mail: mgoranson@asse.org

ASSE-EDWIN P. GRANBERRY JR. DISTINGUISHED SERVICE AWARD SCHOLARSHIP

Scholarships for students pursuing an undergraduate degree in occupational safety and health. Completion of at least 60 current semester hours and minimum GPA of 3.0 required. ASSE student membership is required.

Academic Fields/Career Goals: Occupational Safety and Health.

Award: Scholarship for use in sophomore, junior, or senior years; not renewable. *Number:* 1. *Amount:* up to $1000.

Eligibility Requirements: Applicant must be enrolled or expecting to enroll full-time at a four-year institution or university. Applicant or parent of applicant must be member of American Society of Safety Engineers. Applicant must have 3.0 GPA or higher. Available to U.S. citizens.

Application Requirements: Application, essay, references, transcript. *Deadline:* December 1.

Contact: Mary Goranson, Scholarship Coordinator
American Society of Safety Engineers (ASSE) Foundation
1800 East Oakton Street
Des Plaines, IL 60018
Phone: 847-768-3435
E-mail: mgoranson@asse.org

ASSE-GULF COAST PAST PRESIDENTS SCHOLARSHIP

Scholarship of $1000 will be awarded to a part- or full-time student pursuing an undergraduate degree in occupational safety and health or a closely related field. Must have completed 60 semester hours and maintain at least a 3.0 GPA. ASSE general or professional membership required if applicant is a part-time student. If applicant is a full-time student, must be student member of ASSE.

Academic Fields/Career Goals: Occupational Safety and Health.

Award: Scholarship for use in sophomore, junior, or senior years; not renewable. *Number:* 2. *Amount:* $1000.

Eligibility Requirements: Applicant must be enrolled or expecting to enroll full- or part-time at a four-year institution or university. Applicant or parent of applicant must be member of American Society of Safety Engineers. Applicant must have 3.0 GPA or higher. Available to U.S. citizens.

Application Requirements: Application, essay, financial need analysis, references, transcript. *Deadline:* December 1.

Contact: Mary Goranson, Scholarship Coordinator
American Society of Safety Engineers (ASSE) Foundation
1800 East Oakton Street
Des Plaines, IL 60018
Phone: 847-768-3412
E-mail: mgoranson@asse.org

ASSE-MARSH RISK CONSULTING SCHOLARSHIP

Scholarship for students pursuing an undergraduate degree in occupational safety. Completion of at least 60 credit hours and minimum GPA of 3.0 required. Must be a student member of ASSE.

Academic Fields/Career Goals: Occupational Safety and Health.

Award: Scholarship for use in sophomore, junior, or senior years; not renewable. *Number:* 1. *Amount:* up to $5000.

Eligibility Requirements: Applicant must be enrolled or expecting to enroll full-time at a four-year institution or university. Applicant or parent of applicant must be member of American Society of Safety Engineers. Applicant must have 3.0 GPA or higher. Available to U.S. and non-U.S. citizens.

Application Requirements: Application, essay, references, transcript. *Deadline:* December 1.

Contact: Mary Goranson, Scholarship Coordinator
American Society of Safety Engineers (ASSE) Foundation
1800 East Oakton Street
Des Plaines, IL 60018
Phone: 847-768-3435
E-mail: mgoranson@asse.org

ASSE-REGION IV/EDWIN P. GRANBERRY SCHOLARSHIP

Scholarship of $1000 will be awarded to a student pursuing an undergraduate degree in occupational safety and health or a closely related field. Must reside in the ASSE Region IV area (Louisiana, Alabama, Mississippi, Georgia, Florida, Puerto Rico or United States Virgin Islands). Natives of Region IV attending school elsewhere are also eligible. Must have completed 60 semester hours and maintain at least a 3.2 GPA. Eligible applicants will be members of American Society of Safety Engineers.

Academic Fields/Career Goals: Occupational Safety and Health.

Award: Scholarship for use in freshman, sophomore, junior, or senior years; not renewable. *Number:* 1. *Amount:* up to $1000.

Eligibility Requirements: Applicant must be enrolled or expecting to enroll full-time at a two-year or four-year institution or university and resident of Alabama, Florida, Georgia, Louisiana, Mississippi, or Puerto Rico. Applicant or parent of applicant must be member of American Society of Safety Engineers. Available to U.S. citizens.

Application Requirements: Application, essay, financial need analysis, references, transcript. *Deadline:* December 1.

Contact: Mary Goranson, Scholarship Coordinator
American Society of Safety Engineers (ASSE) Foundation
1800 East Oakton Street
Des Plaines, IL 60018
Phone: 847-768-3412

ASSE-UNITED PARCEL SERVICE SCHOLARSHIP

Scholarships for students pursuing a four-year BS or BA degree in occupational safety and health or related area. Completion of at least 60 current semester hours and a minimum 3.0 GPA is required. Must be a student member of ASSE.

Academic Fields/Career Goals: Occupational Safety and Health.

Award: Scholarship for use in sophomore, junior, or senior years; not renewable. *Number:* varies. *Amount:* $4000–$5300.

Eligibility Requirements: Applicant must be enrolled or expecting to enroll full-time at a four-year institution or university. Applicant or parent of applicant must be member of American Society of Safety Engineers. Applicant must have 3.0 GPA or higher. Available to U.S. and non-U.S. citizens.

Application Requirements: Application, essay, references, transcript. *Deadline:* December 1.

Contact: Mary Goranson, Scholarship Coordinator
American Society of Safety Engineers (ASSE) Foundation
1800 East Oakton Street
Des Plaines, IL 60018
Phone: 847-768-3412
E-mail: mgoranson@asse.org

BECHTEL FOUNDATION SCHOLARSHIP PROGRAM FOR SAFETY AND HEALTH

Scholarship of $5000 for students pursuing an undergraduate degree in occupational safety and health, with an emphasis on construction safety. ASSE student membership required. Must have a minimum GPA of 3.0. Must have completed at least 60 semester hours in the undergraduate study program.

Academic Fields/Career Goals: Occupational Safety and Health.

Award: Scholarship for use in sophomore, junior, or senior years; not renewable. *Number:* 1. *Amount:* $5000.

Eligibility Requirements: Applicant must be enrolled or expecting to enroll full-time at a four-year institution or university. Applicant or parent of applicant must be member of American Society of Safety Engineers. Applicant must have 3.0 GPA or higher. Available to U.S. and non-U.S. citizens.

Application Requirements: Application, essay, references, transcript. *Deadline:* December 1.

Contact: Mary Goranson, Scholarship Coordinator
American Society of Safety Engineers (ASSE) Foundation
1800 East Oakton Street
Des Plaines, IL 60018
Phone: 847-768-3435
Fax: 847-296 Ext. 9220
E-mail: agabanski@asse.org

FORD MOTOR COMPANY SCHOLARSHIP-UNDERGRADUATE

Scholarship for women pursuing an undergraduate degree in occupational safety. Completion of at least 60 current semester hours and minimum GPA of 3.0 required. Applicant must be a member of ASSE.

Academic Fields/Career Goals: Occupational Safety and Health.

Award: Scholarship for use in sophomore, junior, or senior years; not renewable. *Number:* 2. *Amount:* up to $3450.

Eligibility Requirements: Applicant must be enrolled or expecting to enroll full-time at a four-year institution or university and female. Applicant or parent of applicant must be member of American Society of Safety Engineers. Applicant must have 3.0 GPA or higher. Available to U.S. and non-U.S. citizens.

Application Requirements: Application, essay, references, transcript. *Deadline:* December 1.

Contact: Mary Goranson, Scholarship Coordinator
American Society of Safety Engineers (ASSE) Foundation
1800 East Oakton Street
Des Plaines, IL 60018
Phone: 847-768-3435
E-mail: mgoranson@asse.org

GEORGIA CHAPTER OF ASSE ANNUAL SCHOLARSHIP

Scholarship of $1000 will be awarded to a student pursuing an undergraduate degree in occupational safety and health or a closely related field. Applicant must be a Georgia resident. Must have completed 60 semester hours and maintain at least a 3.0 GPA. Must be a member of American Society of Safety Engineers.

Academic Fields/Career Goals: Occupational Safety and Health.

Award: Scholarship for use in sophomore, junior, or senior years; not renewable. *Number:* 1. *Amount:* $1000.

Eligibility Requirements: Applicant must be enrolled or expecting to enroll full-time at a four-year institution or university; resident of Georgia and studying in Georgia. Applicant or parent of applicant must be member of American Society of Safety Engineers. Applicant must have 3.0 GPA or higher. Available to U.S. and non-U.S. citizens.

Application Requirements: Application, essay, financial need analysis, references, transcript. *Deadline:* December 1.

Contact: Mary Goranson, Scholarship Coordinator
American Society of Safety Engineers (ASSE) Foundation
1800 East Oakton Street
Des Plaines, IL 60018
Phone: 847-768-3412
E-mail: mgoranson@asse.org

GOLD COUNTRY SECTION AND REGION II SCHOLARSHIP

Scholarship of $1000 for students pursuing an undergraduate or graduate degree in occupational safety and health or a closely related field. Student residing within region II (MT, ID, WY, CO, UT, NV, AZ, NM) area will have priority on this award. ASSE student membership required. Must have completed at least 60 semester hours in the study program for undergraduate students. Minimum GPA is 3.0 for undergraduates and 3.5 for graduates.

Academic Fields/Career Goals: Occupational Safety and Health.

Award: Scholarship for use in sophomore, junior, senior, or graduate years; not renewable. *Number:* 1. *Amount:* up to $1000.

Eligibility Requirements: Applicant must be enrolled or expecting to enroll full-time at a four-year institution or university and resident of Arizona, Colorado, Idaho, Montana, Nevada, New Mexico, Utah, or Wyoming. Applicant or parent of applicant must be member of American Society of Safety Engineers. Available to U.S. and non-U.S. citizens.

American Society of Safety Engineers (ASSE) Foundation (continued)

Application Requirements: Application, financial need analysis, transcript. *Deadline:* December 1.

Contact: Mary Goranson, Scholarship Coordinator
American Society of Safety Engineers (ASSE) Foundation
1800 East Oakton Street
Des Plaines, IL 60018
Phone: 847-768-3412
E-mail: mgoranson@asse.org

HAROLD F. POLSTON SCHOLARSHIP

Scholarship of $2000 for students pursuing undergraduate or graduate degree in occupational safety and health or a closely related field. Priority will be given to students that belong to the Middle Tennessee Chapter, attending Middle Tennessee State University in Murfreesboro, TN, Murray State University in Murray, KY and those that live in the Region VII. Must have a minimum GPA of 3.0 for undergraduate study and 3.5 for graduate study. Must be a student member of ASSE.

Academic Fields/Career Goals: Occupational Safety and Health.

Award: Scholarship for use in sophomore, junior, senior, or graduate years; not renewable. *Number:* 1. *Amount:* $2000.

Eligibility Requirements: Applicant must be enrolled or expecting to enroll full-time at a four-year institution or university. Applicant or parent of applicant must be member of American Society of Safety Engineers. Available to U.S. and non-U.S. citizens.

Application Requirements: Application, essay, financial need analysis, references, transcript. *Deadline:* December 1.

Contact: Mary Goranson, Scholarship Coordinator
American Society of Safety Engineers (ASSE) Foundation
1800 East Oakton Street
Des Plaines, IL 60018
Phone: 847-768-3412
E-mail: mgoranson@asse.org

HARRY TABACK 9/11 MEMORIAL SCHOLARSHIP

Scholarship for students pursuing an undergraduate or graduate degree in occupational safety and health or a closely related field. Student must be a natural born United States citizen. Minimum GPA is 3.0 for undergraduates and 3.5 for graduates. Must be a student member of ASSE.

Academic Fields/Career Goals: Occupational Safety and Health.

Award: Scholarship for use in sophomore, junior, senior, or graduate years; not renewable. *Number:* 1. *Amount:* $1000.

Eligibility Requirements: Applicant must be enrolled or expecting to enroll full-time at a four-year institution or university. Applicant or parent of applicant must be member of American Society of Safety Engineers. Available to U.S. citizens.

Application Requirements: Application, financial need analysis, references, transcript. *Deadline:* December 1.

Contact: Mary Goranson, Scholarship Coordinator
American Society of Safety Engineers (ASSE) Foundation
1800 East Oakton Street
Des Plaines, IL 60018
Phone: 847-768-3412
E-mail: mgoranson@asse.org

LIBERTY MUTUAL SCHOLARSHIP

Scholarship of $3000 for students pursuing an undergraduate degree in occupational safety and health or a closely related field. ASSE student membership required. Minimum 3.0 GPA required. Must have completed 60 semester hours in the study program.

Academic Fields/Career Goals: Occupational Safety and Health.

Award: Scholarship for use in sophomore, junior, or senior years; not renewable. *Number:* 1. *Amount:* up to $3000.

Eligibility Requirements: Applicant must be enrolled or expecting to enroll full-time at a four-year institution or university. Applicant or parent of applicant must be member of American Society of Safety Engineers. Applicant must have 3.0 GPA or higher. Available to U.S. and non-U.S. citizens.

Application Requirements: Application, financial need analysis, transcript. *Deadline:* December 1.

Contact: Mary Goranson, Scholarship Coordinator
American Society of Safety Engineers (ASSE) Foundation
1800 East Oakton Street
Des Plaines, IL 60018
Phone: 847-768-3412
E-mail: mgoranson@asse.org

NORTHEASTERN ILLINOIS CHAPTER SCHOLARSHIP

Scholarship of $2500 for students pursuing an undergraduate or graduate degree in occupational safety and health or a closely related field. Students attending school in the Northeastern Illinois region, including Illinois and Wisconsin have priority on this award. ASSE student membership required. Undergraduate students must have completed at least 60 semester hours. Minimum GPA is 3.0 for undergraduates and 3.5 for graduates.

Academic Fields/Career Goals: Occupational Safety and Health.

Award: Scholarship for use in sophomore, junior, senior, graduate, or postgraduate years; not renewable. *Number:* 1. *Amount:* up to $2500.

Eligibility Requirements: Applicant must be enrolled or expecting to enroll full-time at a four-year institution or university and resident of Illinois or Wisconsin. Applicant or parent of applicant must be member of American Society of Safety Engineers. Available to U.S. citizens.

Application Requirements: Application, financial need analysis, transcript. *Deadline:* December 1.

Contact: Mary Goranson, Scholarship Coordinator
American Society of Safety Engineers (ASSE) Foundation
1800 East Oakton Street
Des Plaines, IL 60018
Phone: 847-768-3412
E-mail: mgoranson@asse.org

SCOTT DOMINGUEZ-CRATERS OF THE MOON SCHOLARSHIP

Scholarship for part-or full-time students pursuing an undergraduate or graduate degree in occupational safety and health or a closely related field. Students residing within the Craters of the Moon Chapter, Idaho, and Region II (MT, ID, WY, CO, UT, NV, AZ, NM) will have priority. ASSE student membership required for full-time student. ASSE general or professional membership required for part-time students. Minimum GPA is 3.0 for undergraduates and 3.5 for graduates.

Academic Fields/Career Goals: Occupational Safety and Health.

Award: Scholarship for use in sophomore, junior, senior, or graduate years; not renewable. *Number:* 1. *Amount:* up to $1000.

Eligibility Requirements: Applicant must be enrolled or expecting to enroll full- or part-time at a four-year institution or university and resident of Arizona, Colorado, Idaho, Montana, Nevada, New Mexico, Utah, or Wyoming. Applicant or parent of applicant must be member of American Society of Safety Engineers. Available to U.S. citizens.

Application Requirements: Application, financial need analysis, transcript. *Deadline:* December 1.

Contact: Mary Goranson, Scholarship Coordinator
American Society of Safety Engineers (ASSE) Foundation
1800 East Oakton Street
Des Plaines, IL 60018
Phone: 847-768-3412
E-mail: mgoranson@asse.org

UNITED PARCEL SERVICE DIVERSITY SCHOLARSHIP PROGRAM

Scholarship for students pursuing an undergraduate degree in occupational safety and health or a closely related field. Student must be of a minority ethnic or racial group and must be a United States citizen. Must be an ASSE member, and have a minimum 3.0 GPA.

Academic Fields/Career Goals: Occupational Safety and Health.

Award: Scholarship for use in sophomore, junior, or senior years; not renewable. *Number:* varies. *Amount:* $4000–$5250.

Eligibility Requirements: Applicant must be American Indian/Alaska Native, Asian/Pacific Islander, Black (non-Hispanic), or Hispanic and enrolled or expecting to enroll full-time at a four-year institution or university. Applicant or parent of applicant must be member of American Society of Safety Engineers. Applicant must have 3.0 GPA or higher. Available to U.S. citizens.

Application Requirements: Application, essay, financial need analysis, references, transcript. *Deadline:* December 1.

Contact: Mary Goranson, Scholarship Coordinator
American Society of Safety Engineers (ASSE) Foundation
1800 East Oakton Street
Des Plaines, IL 60018
Phone: 847-768-3412

CYNTHIA E. MORGAN SCHOLARSHIP FUND (CEMS) http://www.cemsfund.com

CYNTHIA E. MORGAN MEMORIAL SCHOLARSHIP
• *See page 336*

NATIONAL SAFETY COUNCIL http://www.cshema.org

CAMPUS SAFETY, HEALTH AND ENVIRONMENTAL MANAGEMENT ASSOCIATION SCHOLARSHIP AWARD PROGRAM
• *See page 304*

TEXAS DEPARTMENT OF TRANSPORTATION http://www.txdot.gov

CONDITIONAL GRANT PROGRAM
• *See page 173*

OCEANOGRAPHY

AMERICAN GEOLOGICAL INSTITUTE http://www.agiweb.org

AMERICAN GEOLOGICAL INSTITUTE MINORITY SCHOLARSHIP
• *See page 215*

AMERICAN METEOROLOGICAL SOCIETY http://www.ametsoc.org

AMERICAN METEOROLOGICAL SOCIETY DR. PEDRO GRAU UNDERGRADUATE SCHOLARSHIP
• *See page 360*

AMERICAN METEOROLOGICAL SOCIETY/INDUSTRY MINORITY SCHOLARSHIPS
• *See page 361*

AMERICAN METEOROLOGICAL SOCIETY MARK J. SCHROEDER SCHOLARSHIP IN METEOROLOGY
• *See page 361*

AMERICAN METEOROLOGICAL SOCIETY RICHARD AND HELEN HAGEMEYER SCHOLARSHIP
• *See page 361*

AMERICAN METEOROLOGICAL SOCIETY 75TH ANNIVERSARY SCHOLARSHIP
• *See page 361*

AMERICAN METEOROLOGICAL SOCIETY WERNER A. BAUM UNDERGRADUATE SCHOLARSHIP
• *See page 361*

CARL W. KREITZBERG ENDOWED SCHOLARSHIP
• *See page 361*

ETHAN AND ALLAN MURPHY MEMORIAL SCHOLARSHIP
• *See page 362*

GEORGE S. BENTON SCHOLARSHIP
• *See page 362*

GUILLERMO SALAZAR RODRIGUES SCHOLARSHIP
• *See page 362*

JOHN R. HOPE SCHOLARSHIP
• *See page 362*

LOREN W. CROW SCHOLARSHIP
• *See page 362*

CANADIAN RECREATIONAL CANOEING ASSOCIATION http://www.paddlingcanada.com

BILL MASON MEMORIAL SCHOLARSHIP FUND
• *See page 74*

MARINE TECHNOLOGY SOCIETY http://www.mtsociety.org

CHARLES H. BUSSMAN UNDERGRADUATE SCHOLARSHIP
• *See page 393*

JOHN C. BAJUS SCHOLARSHIP
• *See page 393*

MTS STUDENT SCHOLARSHIP
• *See page 393*

PAROS-DIGIQUARTZ SCHOLARSHIP
• *See page 394*

ROV SCHOLARSHIP
• *See page 394*

SEASPACE INC. http://www.seaspace.org

SEASPACE SCHOLARSHIP PROGRAM
• *See page 394*

WOMAN'S NATIONAL FARM AND GARDEN ASSOCIATION http://www.wnfga.org

WARREN, SANDERS, MCNAUGHTON OCEANOGRAPHIC SCHOLARSHIP

Upon receiving this award the student agrees to follow and complete the program of study or research as outlined in the application, and to communicate with the Scholarship Chair any changes in the program, as well as periodic progress reports. For further information visit Web site: http://www.wnfga.org/code/scholarships.htm.

Academic Fields/Career Goals: Oceanography.

Award: Scholarship for use in freshman, sophomore, junior, senior, graduate, or postgraduate years; not renewable. *Number:* 1. *Amount:* $1500.

Eligibility Requirements: Applicant must be enrolled or expecting to enroll full- or part-time at a four-year institution or university. Available to U.S. citizens.

Application Requirements: Resume, references, transcript. *Deadline:* May 25.

Contact: Scholarship Coordinator
Woman's National Farm and Garden Association
Ninth Jenness Road
PO Box 1175
Midland, MI 48641-1175
Phone: 734-662-8661
E-mail: cscioly@hotmail.com

WOMAN'S SEAMEN'S FRIEND SOCIETY OF CONNECTICUT INC.

FINANCIAL SUPPORT FOR MARINE OR MARITIME STUDIES
• *See page 394*

ONCOLOGY

AMERICAN SOCIETY OF RADIOLOGIC TECHNOLOGISTS EDUCATION AND RESEARCH FOUNDATION http://www.asrt.org/foundation

ELEKTA RADIATION THERAPY EDUCATORS SCHOLARSHIP
• *See page 223*

HOWARD S. STERN SCHOLARSHIP
• *See page 333*

SIEMENS CLINICAL ADVANCEMENT SCHOLARSHIP
• *See page 334*

American Society of Radiologic Technologists Education and Research Foundation (continued)

VARIAN RADIATION THERAPY STUDENT SCHOLARSHIP
• *See page 334*

CYNTHIA E. MORGAN SCHOLARSHIP FUND (CEMS) http://www.cemsfund.com

CYNTHIA E. MORGAN MEMORIAL SCHOLARSHIP
• *See page 336*

ONS FOUNDATION http://www.ons.org

ONS FOUNDATION/ONCOLOGY NURSING CERTIFICATION CORPORATION BACHELOR'S SCHOLARSHIPS
• *See page 449*

ONS FOUNDATION/PEARL MOORE CAREER DEVELOPMENT AWARDS
• *See page 449*

ONS FOUNDATION ROBERTA PIERCE SCOFIELD BACHELOR'S SCHOLARSHIPS
• *See page 449*

OPTOMETRY

AMERICAN OPTOMETRIC FOUNDATION http://www.aaopt.org

VISTAKON AWARD OF EXCELLENCE IN CONTACT LENS PATIENT CARE

Open to any fourth-year student attending any school or college of optometry. Must have 3.0 GPA. Student's knowledge of subject matter and skillful, professional clinical contact lens patient care are considered. School makes selection and sends application to AOF.

Academic Fields/Career Goals: Optometry.

Award: Scholarship for use in senior or graduate years; not renewable. *Number:* 19. *Amount:* $1000.

Eligibility Requirements: Applicant must be enrolled or expecting to enroll full-time at a four-year institution or university. Applicant must have 3.0 GPA or higher. Available to U.S. and non-U.S. citizens.

Application Requirements: Application, references. *Deadline:* September 1.

Contact: Alisa Moore, Program Administrator
American Optometric Foundation
6110 Executive Boulevard, Suite 506
Rockville, MD 20852
Phone: 240-880-3084
Fax: 301-984-4737
E-mail: alisam@aaopt.org

WASHINGTON HIGHER EDUCATION COORDINATING BOARD http://www.hecb.wa.gov

WICHE PROFESSIONAL STUDENT EXCHANGE PROGRAM

Students who are Washington residents may receive conditional loans to study optometry or osteopathy, two professional degree programs not offered in Washington. Participants must agree to provide care in a Washington state shortage area. The state will forgive one year of the loan for every one year of service with a minimum service commitment of three years. Awards are available for up to four years.

Academic Fields/Career Goals: Optometry; Osteopathy.

Award: Forgivable loan for use in senior, graduate, or postgraduate years; renewable. *Number:* 14. *Amount:* $13,300–$17,000.

Eligibility Requirements: Applicant must be enrolled or expecting to enroll full-time at an institution or university; resident of Washington and studying in Washington. Available to U.S. citizens.

Application Requirements: Application, financial need analysis, transcript. *Deadline:* October 15.

Contact: Student Exchange Program Coordinator
Washington Higher Education Coordinating Board
917 Lakeridge Way, PO Box 43430
Olympia, WA 98504
Phone: 360-541-0214
E-mail: info-sep@wiche.edu

OSTEOPATHY

ARKANSAS DEPARTMENT OF HIGHER EDUCATION http://www.adhe.edu

ARKANSAS HEALTH EDUCATION GRANT PROGRAM (ARHEG)
• *See page 82*

CYNTHIA E. MORGAN SCHOLARSHIP FUND (CEMS) http://www.cemsfund.com

CYNTHIA E. MORGAN MEMORIAL SCHOLARSHIP
• *See page 336*

MAINE OSTEOPATHIC ASSOCIATION MEMORIAL SCHOLARSHIP/MAINE OSTEOPATHIC ASSOCIATION http://www.mainedo.org

BEALE FAMILY MEMORIAL SCHOLARSHIP
• *See page 339*

MAINE OSTEOPATHIC ASSOCIATION MEMORIAL SCHOLARSHIP
• *See page 339*

MAINE OSTEOPATHIC ASSOCIATION SCHOLARSHIP
• *See page 339*

NATIONAL ARAB AMERICAN MEDICAL ASSOCIATION http://www.naama.com

FOUNDATION SCHOLARSHIP
• *See page 213*

TUCSON OSTEOPATHIC MEDICAL FOUNDATION http://www.tomf.org

TUCSON OSTEOPATHIC MEDICAL FOUNDATION SCHOLARSHIP/LOAN PROGRAM
• *See page 343*

WASHINGTON HIGHER EDUCATION COORDINATING BOARD http://www.hecb.wa.gov

WICHE PROFESSIONAL STUDENT EXCHANGE PROGRAM
• *See page 458*

PAPER AND PULP ENGINEERING

TECHNICAL ASSOCIATION OF THE PULP & PAPER INDUSTRY (TAPPI) http://www.tappi.org

COATING AND GRAPHIC ARTS DIVISION SCHOLARSHIP
• *See page 325*

CORRUGATED PACKAGING DIVISION SCHOLARSHIPS
• *See page 298*

ENGINEERING DIVISION SCHOLARSHIP

Up to two $1500 scholarships will be offered. One may be awarded to a student who will be in his or her junior year, and the other will be offered to a student who will be in his or her senior year, at the beginning of the next academic year. Refer to Web Site for details: http://www.tappi.org/content/pdf/member_groups/CurrentScholar.pdf.

Academic Fields/Career Goals: Paper and Pulp Engineering.

Award: Scholarship for use in junior or senior years; not renewable. *Number:* 1–2. *Amount:* up to $1500.

Eligibility Requirements: Applicant must be enrolled or expecting to enroll full-time at a four-year institution or university. Applicant must have 3.0 GPA or higher. Available to U.S. and non-U.S. citizens.

Application Requirements: Application, essay, references, transcript. *Deadline:* February 15.

Contact: Veranda Edmondson, TAPPI-Member Group Specialist
Technical Association of the Pulp & Paper Industry (TAPPI)
15 Technology Parkway, South
Norcross, GA 30092
Phone: 770-209-7536
E-mail: vedmondson@tappi.org

ENVIRONMENTAL DIVISION SCHOLARSHIP
• *See page 305*

NONWOVENS DIVISION SCHOLARSHIP
• *See page 283*

PAPER AND BOARD DIVISION SCHOLARSHIPS
• *See page 283*

PULP MANUFACTURE DIVISION SCHOLARSHIPS
• *See page 421*

RALPH A. KLUCKEN SCHOLARSHIP AWARD

Award to high school senior, college undergraduate or graduate students attending college full-time, part-time students working full-time and attending night school are eligible to apply. Refer to Web Site: http://www.tappi.org/content/pdf/member_groups/CurrentScholar.pdf for more details.

Academic Fields/Career Goals: Paper and Pulp Engineering.

Award: Scholarship for use in freshman, sophomore, junior, senior, or graduate years; not renewable. *Number:* 1. *Amount:* $1000.

Eligibility Requirements: Applicant must be enrolled or expecting to enroll full- or part-time at a four-year institution or university. Available to U.S. and non-U.S. citizens.

Application Requirements: Application, references, transcript. *Deadline:* May 31.

Contact: Veranda Edmondson, TAPPI-Member Group Specialist
Technical Association of the Pulp & Paper Industry (TAPPI)
15 Technology Parkway, South
Norcross, GA 30092
E-mail: vedmondson@tappi.org

WILLIAM L. CULLISON SCHOLARSHIP
• *See page 421*

PEACE AND CONFLICT STUDIES

EARTH ISLAND INSTITUTE http://www.earthisland.org

BROWER YOUTH AWARDS
• *See page 301*

GRANDMOTHERS FOR PEACE INTERNATIONAL http://www.grandmothersforpeace.org

BARBARA WIEDNER AND DOROTHY VANDERCOOK MEMORIAL PEACE SCHOLARSHIP

Scholarship given to a high school senior involved in peace and social justice, nuclear disarmament issues, or conflict resolution. There are no GPA or age requirements, and students from any country may apply.

Academic Fields/Career Goals: Peace and Conflict Studies.

Award: Scholarship for use in freshman year; not renewable. *Number:* 1–4. *Amount:* $250–$500.

Eligibility Requirements: Applicant must be high school student and planning to enroll or expecting to enroll full- or part-time at a two-year or four-year institution. Available to U.S. and non-U.S. citizens.

Application Requirements: Application, autobiography, references, self-addressed stamped envelope, transcript. *Deadline:* March 1.

Contact: Leal Portis, President
Grandmothers for Peace International
301 Redbud Way
Nevada City, CA 95959
Phone: 530-265-3887
E-mail: portis.leal@gmail.com

UNITED STATES INSTITUTE OF PEACE http://www.usip.org

NATIONAL PEACE ESSAY CONTEST

Essay contest designed to have students research and write about international peace and conflict resolution. Topic changes yearly. State winners are invited to Washington, D.C. for the awards program. Must be enrolled in a U.S. high school.

Academic Fields/Career Goals: Peace and Conflict Studies.

Award: Scholarship for use in freshman year; not renewable. *Number:* 50–53. *Amount:* $1000–$10,000.

Eligibility Requirements: Applicant must be high school student; planning to enroll or expecting to enroll full-time at a two-year or four-year institution or university and must have an interest in writing. Available to U.S. and non-U.S. citizens.

Application Requirements: Application, applicant must enter a contest, essay, bibliography. *Deadline:* February 1.

Contact: Contest Coordinator, Education Program
United States Institute of Peace
1200 17th Street, NW, Second Floor
Washington, DC 20036-3011
Phone: 202-457-3854
Fax: 202-429-6063
E-mail: essay_contest@usip.org

VINCENT L. HAWKINSON FOUNDATION FOR PEACE AND JUSTICE http://www.graceattheu.org

VINCENT L. HAWKINSON SCHOLARSHIP FOR PEACE AND JUSTICE

Scholarship awarded to students who have demonstrated a commitment to peace and justice through participation in a peace and justice project, leadership and participation in a peace organization, or serving as a role model. Candidates are screened based on submitted essays and reference letters, and recipients are selected based a personal interview which takes place in Minneapolis. Applicants must either reside or study in Iowa, Minnesota, North Dakota, South Dakota, or Wisconsin.

Academic Fields/Career Goals: Peace and Conflict Studies.

Award: Scholarship for use in freshman, sophomore, junior, senior, or graduate years; not renewable. *Number:* 1–12. *Amount:* $1000–$3000.

Eligibility Requirements: Applicant must be enrolled or expecting to enroll full- or part-time at a two-year or four-year institution or university; resident of Iowa, Minnesota, North Dakota, South Dakota, or Wisconsin; studying in Iowa, Minnesota, North Dakota, South Dakota, or Wisconsin and must have an interest in leadership. Available to U.S. and non-U.S. citizens.

Application Requirements: Application, essay, interview, references, transcript. *Deadline:* March 15.

Contact: Scholarship Committee
Vincent L. Hawkinson Foundation for Peace and Justice
Grace University Lutheran Church
324 Harvard Street SE
Minneapolis, MN 55414
Phone: 612-331-8125
E-mail: info@graceattheu.org

PERFORMING ARTS

ACADEMY OF TELEVISION ARTS AND SCIENCES FOUNDATION http://www.emmysfoundation.org

ACADEMY OF TELEVISION ARTS AND SCIENCES COLLEGE TELEVISION AWARDS

• *See page 99*

AMERICAN LEGION DEPARTMENT OF KANSAS http://www.ksamlegion.org

MUSIC COMMITTEE SCHOLARSHIP

• *See page 410*

CHOPIN FOUNDATION OF THE UNITED STATES http://www.chopin.org

CHOPIN FOUNDATION OF THE UNITED STATES SCHOLARSHIP

• *See page 411*

CIRI FOUNDATION (TCF) http://www.thecirifoundation.org

CIRI FOUNDATION SUSIE QIMMIQSAK BEVINS ENDOWMENT SCHOLARSHIP FUND

• *See page 100*

CONGRESSIONAL BLACK CAUCUS SPOUSES PROGRAM http://www.cbcfinc.org

CONGRESSIONAL BLACK CAUCUS SPOUSES PERFORMING ARTS SCHOLARSHIP

Award made to students who reside or attend school in a congressional district represented by an African-American member of Congress. Must be full-time student enrolled in a performing arts program. Minimum 2.5 GPA required. Contact the congressional office in the appropriate district for information and applications. See http://www.cbcfinc.org for a list of district offices.

Academic Fields/Career Goals: Performing Arts.

Award: Scholarship for use in freshman, sophomore, junior, or senior years; not renewable. *Number:* 10. *Amount:* $3000.

Eligibility Requirements: Applicant must be enrolled or expecting to enroll full-time at a two-year or four-year or technical institution or university. Applicant must have 2.5 GPA or higher. Available to U.S. citizens.

Application Requirements: Application, essay, financial need analysis, interview, photo, references, transcript, video of performance. *Deadline:* May 1.

Contact: Janet Carter, Scholarship Coordinator
Congressional Black Caucus Spouses Program
1720 Massachusetts Avenue, NW
Washington, DC 20036
Phone: 202-263-2840
Fax: 202-263-0844
E-mail: jcarter@cbcfinc.org

COSTUME SOCIETY OF AMERICA http://www.costumesocietyamerica.com

ADELE FILENE TRAVEL AWARD

• *See page 95*

STELLA BLUM RESEARCH GRANT

• *See page 95*

DONNA REED FOUNDATION FOR THE PERFORMING ARTS http://www.donnareed.org

DONNA REED PERFORMING ARTS SCHOLARSHIPS

Three scholarships awarded to division finalists in acting and musical theatre. Three awards are given to second level winners. Must be a graduating high school senior. To remain eligible, applicant must be attending an accredited postsecondary or approved program of study. Finalists will compete at the Donna Reed Festival in Iowa during the third week of June.

Academic Fields/Career Goals: Performing Arts.

Award: Scholarship for use in freshman year; not renewable. *Number:* 6. *Amount:* $250–$1000.

Eligibility Requirements: Applicant must be high school student; planning to enroll or expecting to enroll full-time at a two-year or four-year or technical institution and must have an interest in music, music/singing, or theater. Available to U.S. and non-U.S. citizens.

Application Requirements: Application, applicant must enter a contest, video/audio tape, CD or 3-minute DVD. *Deadline:* June 1.

Contact: Kenny Kahl, Festival Coordinator
Donna Reed Foundation for the Performing Arts
1305 Broadway
Denison, IA 51442
Phone: 712-263-3334
Fax: 712-263-8026
E-mail: info@donnareed.org

GENERAL FEDERATION OF WOMEN'S CLUBS OF MASSACHUSETTS http://www.gfwcma.org

DORCHESTER WOMEN'S CLUB MUSIC SCHOLARSHIP

• *See page 412*

GENERAL FEDERATION OF WOMEN'S CLUBS OF MASSACHUSETTS NICKEL FOR NOTES MUSIC SCHOLARSHIP

• *See page 412*

HISPANIC SCHOLARSHIP FUND http://www.hsf.net

HSF/MCNAMARA FAMILY CREATIVE ARTS PROJECT GRANT

• *See page 98*

HOSTESS COMMITTEE SCHOLARSHIPS/MISS AMERICA PAGEANT http://www.missamerica.org

EUGENIA VELLNER FISCHER AWARD FOR PERFORMING ARTS

Scholarship for Miss America contestants pursuing degree in performing arts. Award available to women who have competed within the Miss America system on the local, state, or national level from 1993 to the present, regardless of whether title was won. One or more scholarships are awarded annually, depending on qualifications of applicants. Applications must be received by June 30. Late or incomplete applications are not accepted.

Academic Fields/Career Goals: Performing Arts.

Award: Scholarship for use in freshman, sophomore, junior, senior, or graduate years; not renewable. *Number:* varies. *Amount:* varies.

Eligibility Requirements: Applicant must be enrolled or expecting to enroll full- or part-time at a four-year institution or university; female and must have an interest in beauty pageant. Available to U.S. citizens.

Application Requirements: Application, essay, financial need analysis, references, transcript. *Deadline:* June 30.

Contact: Doreen Lindell Gordon, Controller and Scholarship Administrator
Hostess Committee Scholarships/Miss America Pageant
Two Miss America Way, Suite 1000
Atlantic City, NJ 08401
Phone: 609-345-7571 Ext. 27
Fax: 609-653-8740
E-mail: doreen@missamerica.org

ILLUMINATING ENGINEERING SOCIETY OF NORTH AMERICA http://www.iesna.org

ROBERT W. THUNEN MEMORIAL SCHOLARSHIPS

• *See page 91*

JACK J. ISGUR FOUNDATION

JACK J. ISGUR FOUNDATION SCHOLARSHIP

• *See page 102*

KE ALI'I PAUAHI FOUNDATION http://www.pauahi.org

EDWIN MAHIAI COPP BEAMER SCHOLARSHIP

• *See page 413*

KOSCIUSZKO FOUNDATION http://www.kosciuszkofoundation.org

KOSCIUSZKO FOUNDATION CHOPIN PIANO COMPETITION

• *See page 413*

NATIONAL OPERA ASSOCIATION http://www.noa.org

NOA VOCAL COMPETITION/LEGACY AWARD PROGRAM

• *See page 105*

POLISH ARTS CLUB OF BUFFALO SCHOLARSHIP FOUNDATION http://www.pacb.bfn.org

POLISH ARTS CLUB OF BUFFALO SCHOLARSHIP FOUNDATION TRUST

• *See page 105*

PRINCESS GRACE FOUNDATION-USA http://www.pgfusa.org

PRINCESS GRACE SCHOLARSHIPS IN DANCE, THEATER, AND FILM

• *See page 308*

SAN ANGELO SYMPHONY SOCIETY http://www.sanangelosymphony.org

SORANTIN YOUNG ARTIST AWARD

• *See page 416*

SERVICE EMPLOYEES INTERNATIONAL UNION (SEIU) http://www.seiu.org

SEIU MOE FONER SCHOLARSHIP PROGRAM FOR VISUAL AND PERFORMING ARTS

• *See page 106*

SIGMA ALPHA IOTA PHILANTHROPIES INC. http://www.sigmaalphaiota.org

SIGMA ALPHA IOTA MUSICIANS WITH SPECIAL NEEDS SCHOLARSHIP

• *See page 240*

SIGMA ALPHA IOTA SUMMER MUSIC SCHOLARSHIPS IN THE U.S. OR ABROAD

• *See page 417*

SIGMA ALPHA IOTA UNDERGRADUATE PERFORMANCE SCHOLARSHIPS

• *See page 418*

SIGMA ALPHA IOTA UNDERGRADUATE SCHOLARSHIPS

• *See page 240*

UNITED NEGRO COLLEGE FUND http://www.uncf.org

JOHN LENNON ENDOWED SCHOLARSHIP

• *See page 188*

VSA ARTS http://www.vsarts.org

VSA ARTS-INTERNATIONAL YOUNG SOLOIST AWARD

Musical performance competition for persons with disabilities. Age limit for U.S residents is 25 or below and for international applicants is 35 or below. One-time award of $5000. Submit audio or videotape of performance. Contact VSA arts for information and application materials.

Academic Fields/Career Goals: Performing Arts.

Award: Scholarship for use in freshman, sophomore, junior, or senior years; not renewable. *Number:* 4. *Amount:* $5000.

Eligibility Requirements: Applicant must be age 35 or under; enrolled or expecting to enroll full- or part-time at a four-year institution or university and must have an interest in music/singing. Applicant must be hearing impaired, learning disabled, physically disabled, or visually impaired. Available to U.S. citizens.

Application Requirements: Application, applicant must enter a contest, autobiography, audition tape. *Deadline:* November 15.

Contact: Liz McCloskey, Performing Arts Manager
VSA arts
818 Connecticut Avenue, NW, Suite 600
Washington, DC 20006
Phone: 800-933-8721
Fax: 202-429-0868
E-mail: info@vsarts.org

WAMSO-MINNESOTA ORCHESTRA VOLUNTEER ASSOCIATION http://www.wamso.org

YOUNG ARTIST COMPETITION

Scholarship of $500 to $5000 for graduates and undergraduates. Applicant should be Canadian/ U.S citizens.

Academic Fields/Career Goals: Performing Arts.

Award: Prize for use in freshman, sophomore, junior, senior, graduate, or postgraduate years; not renewable. *Number:* 8. *Amount:* $500–$5000.

Eligibility Requirements: Applicant must be age 15-26; enrolled or expecting to enroll full- or part-time at a two-year or four-year or technical institution or university; resident of Illinois, Indiana, Iowa, Kansas, Manitoba, Michigan, Minnesota, Missouri, Nebraska, North Dakota, Ontario, South Dakota, or Wisconsin and must have an interest in music. Available to U.S. and Canadian citizens.

Application Requirements: Application, applicant must enter a contest, taped performance of specific repertoire. *Fee:* $75. *Deadline:* varies.

Contact: Eloise Breikjern, Executive Director
WAMSO-Minnesota Orchestra Volunteer Association
1111 Nicollet Mall, Orchestra Hall
Minneapolis, MN 55403-2477
Phone: 612-371-5654
Fax: 612-371-7176
E-mail: wamso@mnorch.org

WOMEN BAND DIRECTORS INTERNATIONAL http://www.womenbanddirectors.org

CHARLOTTE PLUMMER OWEN MEMORIAL SCHOLARSHIP

• *See page 246*

HELEN MAY BUTLER MEMORIAL SCHOLARSHIP

• *See page 246*

MARTHA ANN STARK MEMORIAL SCHOLARSHIP

• *See page 246*

VOLKWEIN MEMORIAL SCHOLARSHIP

• *See page 246*

PHARMACY

ALBERTA HERITAGE SCHOLARSHIP FUND/ ALBERTA SCHOLARSHIP PROGRAMS http://www.alis.gov.ab.ca

JASON LANG SCHOLARSHIP

• *See page 206*

NORTHERN ALBERTA DEVELOPMENT COUNCIL BURSARY FOR PHARMACY STUDENTS

Award to increase the number of trained professionals in Northern Alberta and to encourage students from Northern Alberta to obtain a postsecondary education. Must be a resident of Alberta based on student's finance regulations, must be enrolled in a four-year pharmacy degree program (years one to four) leading to a BSc in pharmacy, must plan to live and work in Northern Alberta upon completion of studies, and must not be in default of a provincial student loan. For further information visit Web site: http://www.nadc.gov.ab.ca.

Academic Fields/Career Goals: Pharmacy.

Award: Scholarship for use in freshman, sophomore, junior, or senior years; not renewable. *Number:* 125. *Amount:* up to $3500.

Alberta Heritage Scholarship Fund/Alberta Scholarship Programs (continued)

Eligibility Requirements: Applicant must be enrolled or expecting to enroll full-time at a four-year institution or university; resident of Alberta and studying in Alberta. Available to Canadian citizens.

Application Requirements: Application, essay. *Deadline:* May 15.

Contact: Scholarship Committee
Alberta Heritage Scholarship Fund/Alberta Scholarship Programs
9940 106th Street, Fourth Floor, Sterling Place
PO Box 28000, Station Main
Edmonton, AB T5J 4R4
Canada
Phone: 780-427-8640
Fax: 780-427-1288
E-mail: scholarships@gov.ab.ca

AMERICAN FOUNDATION FOR PHARMACEUTICAL EDUCATION http://www.afpenet.org

AFPE GATEWAY TO RESEARCH SCHOLARSHIP PROGRAM

Scholarship for baccalaureate degree science students at any college and professional degree pharmacy students to undertake a faculty-mentored research program. Student applicants must be nominated by a faculty member.

Academic Fields/Career Goals: Pharmacy.

Award: Scholarship for use in sophomore, junior, senior, or graduate years; not renewable. *Number:* 10–15. *Amount:* up to $5000.

Eligibility Requirements: Applicant must be enrolled or expecting to enroll full-time at a four-year institution or university. Available to U.S. and non-U.S. citizens.

Application Requirements: Application, essay, references, transcript, faculty sponsor's curriculum vitae. *Deadline:* January 26.

Contact: Asinia Crawford, Grants Manager
American Foundation for Pharmaceutical Education
One Church Street, Suite 202
Rockville, MD 20850
Phone: 301-738-2160
Fax: 301-738-2161
E-mail: asinia.crawford@afpenet.org

KAPPA EPSILON-NELLIE WAKEMAN-AFPE FIRST YEAR GRADUATE SCHOOL SCHOLARSHIP

Applicant must be in final year of a pharmacy college BS or PharmD program or have completed a pharmacy degree. At time of application, the Kappa Epsilon member must be in good financial standing with the Fraternity and planning to pursue a PhD, master's degree, or combined Residency/master's degree program at an accredited U.S. College or School of Pharmacy.

Academic Fields/Career Goals: Pharmacy.

Award: Scholarship for use in senior year; not renewable. *Number:* 1. *Amount:* $7500.

Eligibility Requirements: Applicant must be enrolled or expecting to enroll full-time at a four-year institution or university. Available to U.S. citizens.

Application Requirements: Application, resume, references, transcript, student statement of interest in graduate school. *Deadline:* February 1.

Contact: Ms. Nancy Stankiewicz, Executive Director, Kappa Epsilon
American Foundation for Pharmaceutical Education
7700 Shawnee Mission Parkway
Overland Park, KS 66202
Phone: 913-262-2749
Fax: 913-432-9040
E-mail: kefrat@aol.com

PHI LAMBDA SIGMA-GLAXOSMITHKLINE-AFPE FIRST YEAR GRADUATE SCHOOL SCHOLARSHIP

Applicant must be in final year of pharmacy college BS or PharmD program and be a member of Phi Lambda Sigma.

Academic Fields/Career Goals: Pharmacy.

Award: Scholarship for use in senior year; not renewable. *Number:* 1. *Amount:* $7500.

Eligibility Requirements: Applicant must be enrolled or expecting to enroll full-time at an institution or university. Available to U.S. citizens.

Application Requirements: Application, essay, resume, references, test scores, transcript, statement of interest in graduate school. *Deadline:* February 1.

Contact: Mary Euler, Executive Director, Phi Lambda Sigma
American Foundation for Pharmaceutical Education
5005 Rockhill Road
Kansas City, MO 64110
Phone: 816-235-1738
Fax: 816-235-5190
E-mail: eulerm@umkc.edu

COMMON KNOWLEDGE SCHOLARSHIP FOUNDATION http://www.cksf.org

PHARMACY SCHOLARSHIP

Scholarship contest that tests students' knowledge of the core courses associated with the pharmacy curriculum. For more information about this scholarship, please visit:
http://www.cksf.org/cksf.cfm?Page=Home&Subpage=PharmacyScholarship

Academic Fields/Career Goals: Pharmacy.

Award: Scholarship for use in freshman, sophomore, junior, senior, graduate, or postgraduate years; not renewable. *Number:* 1. *Amount:* up to $250.

Eligibility Requirements: Applicant must be enrolled or expecting to enroll full- or part-time at a two-year or four-year or technical institution or university. Available to U.S. citizens.

Application Requirements: Applicant must enter a contest. *Deadline:* varies.

Contact: Mr. Daryl Hulce, President
Common Knowledge Scholarship Foundation
PO Box 290361
Davie, FL 33329-0361
Phone: 954-262-8553
Fax: 954-262-2847
E-mail: hulce@cksf.org

CYNTHIA E. MORGAN SCHOLARSHIP FUND (CEMS) http://www.cemsfund.com

CYNTHIA E. MORGAN MEMORIAL SCHOLARSHIP

• *See page 336*

GREATER KANAWHA VALLEY FOUNDATION http://www.tgkvf.org

NICHOLAS AND MARY AGNES TRIVILLIAN MEMORIAL SCHOLARSHIP FUND

• *See page 337*

INDIAN HEALTH SERVICES, UNITED STATES DEPARTMENT OF HEALTH AND HUMAN SERVICES http://www.ihs.gov

HEALTH PROFESSIONS PREPARATORY SCHOLARSHIP PROGRAM

• *See page 327*

JEWISH FOUNDATION FOR EDUCATION OF WOMEN http://www.jfew.org

JFEW SCHOLARSHIPS FOR EMIGRES IN THE HEALTH SCIENCES

• *See page 212*

NATIONAL COMMUNITY PHARMACIST ASSOCIATION (NCPA) FOUNDATION http://www.ncpanet.org

NATIONAL COMMUNITY PHARMACIST ASSOCIATION FOUNDATION PRESIDENTIAL SCHOLARSHIP

One-time award to student members of NCPA. Must be enrolled in an accredited U.S. school or college of pharmacy on a full-time basis. Award based on leadership qualities and accomplishments with a demonstrated interest in independent pharmacy, as well as involvement in extracurricular activities.

Academic Fields/Career Goals: Pharmacy.

Award: Scholarship for use in freshman, sophomore, junior, or senior years; not renewable. *Number:* up to 15. *Amount:* up to $2000.

Eligibility Requirements: Applicant must be enrolled or expecting to enroll full-time at a four-year institution or university and must have an interest in leadership. Applicant must have 2.5 GPA or higher. Available to U.S. citizens.

Application Requirements: Application, essay, resume, references, transcript. *Deadline:* March 15.

Contact: Jackie Lopez, Administrative Assistant
National Community Pharmacist Association (NCPA) Foundation
100 Daingerfield Road
Alexandria, VA 22314
Phone: 703-683-8200
Fax: 703-683-3619
E-mail: jackie.lopez@ncpanet.org

NEW YORK STATE EDUCATION DEPARTMENT http://www.highered.nysed.gov

REGENTS PROFESSIONAL OPPORTUNITY SCHOLARSHIP

• *See page 60*

RESOURCE CENTER

MARIE BLAHA MEDICAL GRANT

• *See page 83*

UNITED NEGRO COLLEGE FUND http://www.uncf.org

CARDINAL HEALTH SCHOLARSHIP

• *See page 65*

CVS/PHARMACY SCHOLARSHIP

Scholarship is awarded to third and fourth year Pharmacy majors from the Washington, D.C. Area or Detroit, Michigan. Must have minimum 2.8 GPA and the scholarship value is $2000.

Academic Fields/Career Goals: Pharmacy.

Award: Scholarship for use in junior or senior years; not renewable. *Number:* varies. *Amount:* $2000.

Eligibility Requirements: Applicant must be Black (non-Hispanic); enrolled or expecting to enroll full-time at a four-year institution or university and resident of District of Columbia or Michigan. Available to U.S. citizens.

Application Requirements: Application, financial need analysis, FAFSA, Student Aid Report (SAR). *Deadline:* varies.

Contact: Director, Program Services
United Negro College Fund
8260 Willow Oaks Corporate Drive
PO Box 10444
Fairfax, VA 22031-8044
Phone: 800-331-2244
E-mail: rebecca.bennett@uncf.org

RAYMOND W. CANNON MEMORIAL SCHOLARSHIP PROGRAM

• *See page 386*

PHILOSOPHY

AMERICAN SCHOOL OF CLASSICAL STUDIES AT ATHENS http://www.ascsa.edu.gr

ASCSA SUMMER SESSIONS OPEN SCHOLARSHIPS

• *See page 83*

CHARLES M. EDWARDS SCHOLARSHIP

• *See page 98*

DAVIDSON INSTITUTE FOR TALENT DEVELOPMENT http://www.davidsoninstitute.org

DAVIDSON FELLOWS

• *See page 390*

STRAIGHTFORWARD MEDIA http://www.straightforwardmedia.com

STRAIGHTFORWARD MEDIA LIBERAL ARTS SCHOLARSHIP

• *See page 99*

PHOTOJOURNALISM/ PHOTOGRAPHY

ACADEMY OF TELEVISION ARTS AND SCIENCES FOUNDATION http://www.emmysfoundation.org

ACADEMY OF TELEVISION ARTS AND SCIENCES COLLEGE TELEVISION AWARDS

• *See page 99*

AMERICAN LEGION, PRESS CLUB OF NEW JERSEY

AMERICAN LEGION PRESS CLUB OF NEW JERSEY AND POST 170 ARTHUR DEHARDT MEMORIAL SCHOLARSHIP

• *See page 175*

ASIAN AMERICAN JOURNALISTS ASSOCIATION http://www.aaja.org

ASIAN-AMERICAN JOURNALISTS ASSOCIATION SCHOLARSHIP

• *See page 176*

BAY AREA BLACK JOURNALISTS ASSOCIATION SCHOLARSHIP CONTEST http://www.babja.org

LUCI S. WILLIAMS HOUSTON MEMORIAL SCHOLARSHIP

Nonrenewable scholarship of $2500 to photojournalism students. Applicant must be enrolled in any college or university nationwide. Must be studying photojournalism (including print, television, and online).

Academic Fields/Career Goals: Photojournalism/Photography.

Award: Scholarship for use in freshman, sophomore, junior, senior, or graduate years; not renewable. *Number:* varies. *Amount:* $2500.

Eligibility Requirements: Applicant must be enrolled or expecting to enroll full- or part-time at a four-year institution or university. Available to U.S. citizens.

Application Requirements: Application, essay, resume, references, transcript, work samples. *Deadline:* October 2.

Contact: Scholarship Committee
Bay Area Black Journalists Association Scholarship Contest
1714 Franklin Street, Suite 100-260
Oakland, CA 94612
Phone: 510-986-9390
Fax: 510-382-1980
E-mail: info@babja.org

YOUNG JOURNALISTS SCHOLARSHIP

• *See page 369*

CALIFORNIA CHICANO NEWS MEDIA ASSOCIATION (CCNMA) http://www.ccnma.org

CCNMA SCHOLARSHIPS

• *See page 177*

COLLEGE PHOTOGRAPHER OF THE YEAR http://www.cpoy.org

COLLEGE PHOTOGRAPHER OF THE YEAR COMPETITION

Awards undergraduate and graduate students for juried contest of individual photographs, picture stories and photographic essay and multimedia presentations. Two awards in the dollar value of $500 and $1000 are granted. Deadline varies.

Academic Fields/Career Goals: Photojournalism/Photography.

Award: Prize for use in freshman, sophomore, junior, senior, or graduate years; not renewable. *Number:* up to 2. *Amount:* $500–$1000.

College Photographer of the Year (continued)

Eligibility Requirements: Applicant must be enrolled or expecting to enroll full- or part-time at a four-year institution or university. Available to U.S. and non-U.S. citizens.

Application Requirements: Application, applicant must enter a contest, essay, photo, portfolio. *Deadline:* varies.

Contact: Rita Ann Reed, Program Director
College Photographer of the Year
University of Missouri, School of Journalism
107 Lee Hills Hall
Columbia, MO 65211
Phone: 573-882-2198
Fax: 573-884-4999
E-mail: info@cpoy.org

CONNECTICUT CHAPTER OF SOCIETY OF PROFESSIONAL JOURNALISTS http://www.ctspj.org

CONNECTICUT SPJ BOB EDDY SCHOLARSHIP PROGRAM

• *See page 370*

DAYTON FOUNDATION http://www.daytonfoundation.org

LARRY FULLERTON PHOTOJOURNALISM SCHOLARSHIP

One-time scholarship for Ohio residents pursuing careers in photojournalism. Must have experience and submit examples of work. Award for use in sophomore, junior or senior year at an Ohio two- or four-year college or university. High school students are ineligible. Minimum 2.5 GPA required. Must be U.S. citizen.

Academic Fields/Career Goals: Photojournalism/Photography.

Award: Scholarship for use in sophomore, junior, or senior years; not renewable. *Number:* 1–2. *Amount:* $500–$2500.

Eligibility Requirements: Applicant must be enrolled or expecting to enroll full-time at a two-year or four-year institution or university; resident of Ohio; studying in Ohio and must have an interest in photography/photogrammetry/filmmaking. Applicant must have 2.5 GPA or higher. Available to U.S. citizens.

Application Requirements: Application, financial need analysis, portfolio, transcript, slide portfolio. *Deadline:* January 31.

Contact: Diane Timmons, Vice President, Grants and Programs
Dayton Foundation
2300 Kettering Tower
Dayton, OH 45423
Phone: 937-222-0410
Fax: 937-222-0636
E-mail: dtimmons@daytonfoundation.org

HISPANIC SCHOLARSHIP FUND http://www.hsf.net

HSF/MCNAMARA FAMILY CREATIVE ARTS PROJECT GRANT

• *See page 98*

INTERNATIONAL FOODSERVICE EDITORIAL COUNCIL http://www.ifeconline.com

INTERNATIONAL FOODSERVICE EDITORIAL COUNCIL COMMUNICATIONS SCHOLARSHIP

• *See page 180*

KE ALI'I PAUAHI FOUNDATION http://www.pauahi.org

BRUCE T. AND JACKIE MAHI ERICKSON GRANT

• *See page 103*

NATIONAL ASSOCIATION OF BLACK JOURNALISTS http://www.nabj.org

NATIONAL ASSOCIATION OF BLACK JOURNALISTS NON-SUSTAINING SCHOLARSHIP AWARDS

• *See page 374*

VISUAL TASK FORCE SCHOLARSHIP

Scholarship for students attending an accredited four-year college or university and majoring in visual journalism. Minimum 3.0 GPA required. Must be a member of NABJ. Scholarship value and the number of scholarships granted varies annually.

Academic Fields/Career Goals: Photojournalism/Photography.

Award: Scholarship for use in freshman, sophomore, junior, senior, or graduate years; not renewable. *Number:* varies. *Amount:* varies.

Eligibility Requirements: Applicant must be enrolled or expecting to enroll full-time at a four-year institution or university. Applicant must have 3.0 GPA or higher. Available to U.S. and non-U.S. citizens.

Application Requirements: Application, autobiography, essay, interview, references, transcript. *Deadline:* March 17.

Contact: Irving Washington, Manager
National Association of Black Journalists
8701-A Adelphi Road
Adelphi, MD 20783-1716
Phone: 301-445-7100
Fax: 301-445-7101
E-mail: iwashington@nabj.org

NATIONAL ASSOCIATION OF HISPANIC JOURNALISTS (NAHJ) http://www.nahj.org

NATIONAL ASSOCIATION OF HISPANIC JOURNALISTS SCHOLARSHIP

• *See page 181*

NEWHOUSE SCHOLARSHIP PROGRAM

• *See page 324*

NATIONAL PRESS PHOTOGRAPHERS FOUNDATION INC. http://www.nppa.org

BOB EAST SCHOLARSHIP

Award of $2000 for applicant who is either an undergraduate in the first three and one-half years of college or is planning to pursue postgraduate work and offers indication of acceptance in such a program. Award is chosen primarily on portfolio quality.

Academic Fields/Career Goals: Photojournalism/Photography.

Award: Scholarship for use in freshman, sophomore, junior, senior, graduate, or postgraduate years; not renewable. *Number:* 1. *Amount:* $2000.

Eligibility Requirements: Applicant must be enrolled or expecting to enroll full-time at a four-year institution or university. Available to U.S. citizens.

Application Requirements: Application, applicant must enter a contest, essay, financial need analysis, portfolio, self-addressed stamped envelope, transcript. *Deadline:* March 1.

Contact: Chuck Fadely, Scholarship Committee
National Press Photographers Foundation Inc.
The Miami Herald
One Herald Plaza
Miami, FL 33132
Phone: 305-376-2015

NATIONAL PRESS PHOTOGRAPHERS FOUNDATION STILL PHOTOGRAPHER SCHOLARSHIP

Award of $2000 for students who have completed one year at a four-year college or university having photojournalism courses. Applicant must be pursuing a bachelor's degree and must have at least one-half year of undergraduate schooling remaining at the time of award.

Academic Fields/Career Goals: Photojournalism/Photography.

Award: Scholarship for use in sophomore, junior, or senior years; not renewable. *Number:* 1. *Amount:* $2000.

Eligibility Requirements: Applicant must be enrolled or expecting to enroll full-time at a four-year institution or university. Available to U.S. citizens.

Application Requirements: Application, applicant must enter a contest, financial need analysis, portfolio, self-addressed stamped envelope, transcript. *Deadline:* March 1.

Contact: Bill Sanders, Photo Editor
National Press Photographers Foundation Inc.
Asheville Citizen-Times, PO Box 2090
Asheville, NC 28802
E-mail: wsanders@citizen-times.com

NATIONAL PRESS PHOTOGRAPHERS FOUNDATION TELEVISION NEWS SCHOLARSHIP

Award of $1000 for student enrolled in a four-year college or university having courses in TV news photojournalism. Applicant must be pursuing a bachelor's degree and be in his/her junior or senior year at the time of award.

Academic Fields/Career Goals: Photojournalism/Photography; TV/Radio Broadcasting.

Award: Scholarship for use in junior or senior years; not renewable. *Number:* 1. *Amount:* $1000.

Eligibility Requirements: Applicant must be enrolled or expecting to enroll full-time at a four-year institution or university. Available to U.S. citizens.

Application Requirements: Application, applicant must enter a contest, autobiography, essay, financial need analysis, portfolio, references, self-addressed stamped envelope, transcript. *Deadline:* March 1.

Contact: Ed Dooks, Scholarship Committee
National Press Photographers Foundation Inc.
Five Mohawk Drive
Lexington, MA 02421-6217
Phone: 781-861-6062
E-mail: dooks@verizon.net

REID BLACKBURN SCHOLARSHIP

Award of $2000 for a student who has completed one year of a photojournalism program at a four-year college or university in preparation for a bachelor's degree. Must have at least one-half year of undergraduate schooling remaining at time of award. The philosophy and goals statement is particularly important in this selection.

Academic Fields/Career Goals: Photojournalism/Photography.

Award: Scholarship for use in sophomore, junior, or senior years; not renewable. *Number:* 1. *Amount:* $2000.

Eligibility Requirements: Applicant must be enrolled or expecting to enroll full-time at a four-year institution or university. Available to U.S. citizens.

Application Requirements: Application, applicant must enter a contest, essay, financial need analysis, portfolio, self-addressed stamped envelope, transcript. *Deadline:* March 1.

Contact: Fay Blackburn, Manager
National Press Photographers Foundation Inc.
The Columbian, PO Box 180
Vancouver, WA 98666
Phone: 360-759-8027
E-mail: fay.blackburn@columbian.com

NEBRASKA PRESS ASSOCIATION — http://www.nebpress.com

NEBRASKA PRESS ASSOCIATION FOUNDATION INC. SCHOLARSHIP

• *See page 375*

OUTDOOR WRITERS ASSOCIATION OF AMERICA — http://www.owaa.org

OUTDOOR WRITERS ASSOCIATION OF AMERICA BODIE MCDOWELL SCHOLARSHIP AWARD

• *See page 183*

PALM BEACH ASSOCIATION OF BLACK JOURNALISTS — http://www.pbabj.org

PALM BEACH ASSOCIATION OF BLACK JOURNALISTS SCHOLARSHIP

• *See page 377*

SAN FRANCISCO FOUNDATION — http://www.sff.org

PHELAN AWARD IN PHOTOGRAPHY

Award presented in every odd-numbered year to recognize achievement in photography. Applicants must provide a copy of their birth certificate with their application.

Academic Fields/Career Goals: Photojournalism/Photography.

Award: Prize for use in freshman, sophomore, junior, senior, graduate, or postgraduate years; not renewable. *Number:* 3. *Amount:* $2500.

Eligibility Requirements: Applicant must be enrolled or expecting to enroll full- or part-time at a two-year or four-year institution or university. Available to U.S. citizens.

Application Requirements: Application, applicant must enter a contest, self-addressed stamped envelope. *Deadline:* May 4.

Contact: Art Awards Coordinator
San Francisco Foundation
225 Bush Street, Suite 500
San Francisco, CA 94104
Phone: 415-733-8500

STRAIGHTFORWARD MEDIA — http://www.straightforwardmedia.com

STRAIGHTFORWARD MEDIA MEDIA & COMMUNICATIONS SCHOLARSHIP

• *See page 185*

TEXAS GRIDIRON CLUB INC. — http://www.spjfw.org

TEXAS GRIDIRON CLUB SCHOLARSHIPS

• *See page 187*

UNITARIAN UNIVERSALIST ASSOCIATION — http://www.uua.org

MARION BARR STANFIELD ART SCHOLARSHIP

• *See page 107*

PAULY D'ORLANDO MEMORIAL ART SCHOLARSHIP

• *See page 107*

UNITED METHODIST COMMUNICATIONS — http://www.umcom.org

LEONARD M. PERRYMAN COMMUNICATIONS SCHOLARSHIP FOR ETHNIC MINORITY STUDENTS

• *See page 187*

VALLEY PRESS CLUB — http://www.valleypressclub.com

VALLEY PRESS CLUB SCHOLARSHIPS, THE REPUBLICAN SCHOLARSHIP, CHANNEL 22 SCHOLARSHIP

• *See page 188*

PHYSICAL SCIENCES AND MATH

AIR & WASTE MANAGEMENT ASSOCIATION–COASTAL PLAINS CHAPTER — http://www.awmacoastalplains.org

COASTAL PLAINS CHAPTER OF THE AIR AND WASTE MANAGEMENT ASSOCIATION ENVIRONMENTAL STEWARD SCHOLARSHIP

• *See page 300*

AMERICAN FOUNDATION FOR THE BLIND — http://www.afb.org

PAUL W. RUCKES SCHOLARSHIP

• *See page 189*

AMERICAN INDIAN SCIENCE AND ENGINEERING SOCIETY — http://www.aises.org

A.T. ANDERSON MEMORIAL SCHOLARSHIP PROGRAM

• *See page 84*

American Indian Science and Engineering Society (continued)

BURLINGTON NORTHERN SANTA FE FOUNDATION SCHOLARSHIP
• *See page 84*

AMERICAN INSTITUTE OF AERONAUTICS AND ASTRONAUTICS http://www.aiaa.org

AIAA UNDERGRADUATE SCHOLARSHIP
• *See page 84*

AMERICAN LEGION DEPARTMENT OF MARYLAND http://www.mdlegion.org

AMERICAN LEGION DEPARTMENT OF MARYLAND MATH-SCIENCE SCHOLARSHIP

Scholarship for study in math or the sciences. Must be a Maryland resident and the dependent child of a veteran. Must submit essay, financial need analysis, and transcript with application. Nonrenewable award for freshman. Application available on Web site: http://mdlegion.org.

Academic Fields/Career Goals: Physical Sciences and Math.

Award: Scholarship for use in freshman year; not renewable. *Number:* up to 3. *Amount:* up to $500.

Eligibility Requirements: Applicant must be high school student; planning to enroll or expecting to enroll full-time at a two-year or four-year institution or university and resident of Maryland. Available to U.S. citizens. Applicant or parent must meet one or more of the following requirements: general military experience; retired from active duty; disabled or killed as a result of military service; prisoner of war; or missing in action.

Application Requirements: Application, essay, financial need analysis, transcript. *Deadline:* April 1.

Contact: Thomas Davis, Department Adjutant
American Legion, Department of Maryland
101 North Gay, Room E
Baltimore, MD 21202
Phone: 410-752-1405
Fax: 410-752-3822
E-mail: tom@mdlegion.org

AMERICAN PHYSICAL SOCIETY http://www.aps.org/programs/minorities

AMERICAN PHYSICAL SOCIETY SCHOLARSHIP FOR MINORITY UNDERGRADUATE PHYSICS MAJORS

One-time renewable award for high school seniors, college freshmen and sophomores planning to major in physics. Must be African-American, Hispanic, or Native American. Must be a U.S. citizen or a legal resident. For legal residents, a copy of alien registration card is required.

Academic Fields/Career Goals: Physical Sciences and Math.

Award: Scholarship for use in freshman or sophomore years; renewable. *Number:* 20–25. *Amount:* $2000–$3000.

Eligibility Requirements: Applicant must be American Indian/Alaska Native, Black (non-Hispanic), or Hispanic and enrolled or expecting to enroll full-time at a four-year institution or university. Available to U.S. citizens.

Application Requirements: Application, essay, references, test scores, transcript, copy of alien registration card. *Deadline:* February 1.

Contact: Arlene Modeste Knowles, Scholarship Administrator
American Physical Society
One Physics Ellipse
College Park, MD 20740
Phone: 301-209-3232
Fax: 301-209-0865
E-mail: knowles@aps.org

AMERICAN SOCIETY FOR ENGINEERING EDUCATION http://www.asee.org

SCIENCE, MATHEMATICS, AND RESEARCH FOR TRANSFORMATION DEFENSE SCHOLARSHIP FOR SERVICE PROGRAM
• *See page 85*

AMERICAN SOCIETY OF NAVAL ENGINEERS http://www.navalengineers.org

AMERICAN SOCIETY OF NAVAL ENGINEERS SCHOLARSHIP
• *See page 85*

ARIZONA PROFESSIONAL CHAPTER OF AISES http://www.azpcofaises.org

ARIZONA PROFESSIONAL CHAPTER OF AISES SCHOLARSHIP
• *See page 257*

ARMED FORCES COMMUNICATIONS AND ELECTRONICS ASSOCIATION, EDUCATIONAL FOUNDATION http://www.afcea.org

AFCEA/LOCKHEED MARTIN ORINCON IT SCHOLARSHIP
• *See page 113*

AFCEA SCHOLARSHIP FOR WORKING PROFESSIONALS
• *See page 113*

AFCEA SGT. JEANNETTE L. WINTERS, USMC MEMORIAL SCHOLARSHIP
• *See page 190*

ARMED FORCES COMMUNICATIONS AND ELECTRONICS ASSOCIATION GENERAL EMMETT PAIGE SCHOLARSHIP
• *See page 190*

ARMED FORCES COMMUNICATIONS AND ELECTRONICS ASSOCIATION GENERAL JOHN A. WICKHAM SCHOLARSHIP
• *See page 190*

ARMED FORCES COMMUNICATIONS AND ELECTRONICS ASSOCIATION ROTC SCHOLARSHIP PROGRAM
• *See page 114*

ARNOLD AND MABEL BECKMAN FOUNDATION http://www.beckman-foundation.com

BECKMAN SCHOLARS PROGRAM
• *See page 130*

ARRL FOUNDATION INC. http://www.arrl.org

WILLIAM R. GOLDFARB MEMORIAL SCHOLARSHIP
• *See page 138*

ASSOCIATION FOR IRON AND STEEL TECHNOLOGY http://www.aist.org

ASSOCIATION FOR IRON AND STEEL TECHNOLOGY OHIO VALLEY CHAPTER SCHOLARSHIP
• *See page 130*

ASSOCIATION FOR WOMEN GEOSCIENTISTS, PUGET SOUND CHAPTER http://www.awg.org

PUGET SOUND CHAPTER SCHOLARSHIP
• *See page 216*

ASSOCIATION FOR WOMEN IN SCIENCE EDUCATIONAL FOUNDATION http://www.awis.org/careers/edfoundation.html

ASSOCIATION FOR WOMEN IN SCIENCE COLLEGE SCHOLARSHIP
• *See page 82*

AWIS KIRSTEN R. LORENTZEN AWARD IN PHYSICS
• *See page 216*

BARRY M. GOLDWATER SCHOLARSHIP AND EXCELLENCE IN EDUCATION FOUNDATION http://www.act.org/goldwater

BARRY M. GOLDWATER SCHOLARSHIP AND EXCELLENCE IN EDUCATION PROGRAM
• *See page 86*

BUSINESS AND PROFESSIONAL WOMEN'S FOUNDATION http://www.bpwfoundation.org

BPW CAREER ADVANCEMENT SCHOLARSHIP PROGRAM FOR WOMEN

• See page 130

CATCHING THE DREAM http://www.catchingthedream.org

MATH, ENGINEERING, SCIENCE, BUSINESS, EDUCATION, COMPUTERS SCHOLARSHIPS

• See page 139

NATIVE AMERICAN LEADERSHIP IN EDUCATION (NALE)

• See page 139

CHEMICAL INSTITUTE OF CANADA http://www.cheminst.ca

ALFRED BADER SCHOLARSHIP

Scholarships available to undergraduate seniors who are members of the Canadian Society for Chemistry and who have achieved excellence in organic chemistry or biochemistry. Students must be nominated and submit a project report. U.S. citizens must be enrolled in a Canadian university.

Academic Fields/Career Goals: Physical Sciences and Math.

Award: Scholarship for use in senior year; not renewable. *Number:* 1–3. *Amount:* $1000.

Eligibility Requirements: Applicant must be enrolled or expecting to enroll full-time at an institution or university. Applicant or parent of applicant must be member of Canadian Society for Chemistry. Available to U.S. and Canadian citizens.

Application Requirements: Application, references, transcript. *Deadline:* May 30.

Contact: Student Affairs Manager
Chemical Institute of Canada
130 Slater Street, Suite 550
Ottawa, ON K1P 6E2
Canada
Phone: 613-232-6252 Ext. 223
Fax: 613-232-5862
E-mail: gwilbee@cheminst.ca

COMMUNITY FOUNDATION FOR GREATER ATLANTA INC. http://www.atlcf.org

JAMES M. AND VIRGINIA M. SMYTH SCHOLARSHIP

• See page 101

TECH HIGH SCHOOL ALUMNI ASSOCIATION/W.O. CHENEY MERIT SCHOLARSHIP FUND

• See page 262

DAYTON FOUNDATION http://www.daytonfoundation.org

THRYSA FRAZIER SVAGER SCHOLARSHIP

Scholarship for African-American female students majoring in mathematics and attending Central State University, Wilberforce University, Wright State University, University of Dayton, Howard University or Spelman College. Must maintain average grade of "B" or better.

Academic Fields/Career Goals: Physical Sciences and Math.

Award: Scholarship for use in sophomore, junior, or senior years; renewable. *Number:* up to 2. *Amount:* $2000.

Eligibility Requirements: Applicant must be Black (non-Hispanic); enrolled or expecting to enroll full-time at a four-year institution or university; female and studying in District of Columbia, Georgia, or Ohio. Applicant must have 3.0 GPA or higher. Available to U.S. citizens.

Application Requirements: Application, essay, transcript. *Deadline:* March 28.

Contact: Diane K. Timmons, Director of Grants and Programs
Dayton Foundation
2300 Kettering Tower
Dayton, OH 45423
Phone: 937-222-0410
Fax: 937-222-0636
E-mail: dtimmons@daytonfoundation.org

EAA AVIATION FOUNDATION INC. http://www.eaa.org

PAYZER SCHOLARSHIP

• See page 116

FOUNDATION FOR SCIENCE AND DISABILITY http://www.stemd.org

GRANTS FOR DISABLED STUDENTS IN THE SCIENCES

• See page 87

GREATER KANAWHA VALLEY FOUNDATION http://www.tgkvf.org

MATH AND SCIENCE SCHOLARSHIP

• See page 132

GREEN CHEMISTRY INSTITUTE-AMERICAN CHEMICAL SOCIETY http://www.acs.org/greenchemistry

KENNETH G. HANCOCK MEMORIAL AWARD IN GREEN CHEMISTRY

Award of $1000 for the students who have completed their education or research in green chemistry. The scholarship provides national recognition for outstanding student contributions to furthering the goals of green chemistry through research or education.

Academic Fields/Career Goals: Physical Sciences and Math.

Award: Prize for use in freshman, sophomore, junior, senior, or graduate years; not renewable. *Number:* 2. *Amount:* $1000.

Eligibility Requirements: Applicant must be enrolled or expecting to enroll full-time at a four-year institution or university. Available to U.S. and non-U.S. citizens.

Application Requirements: Application, applicant must enter a contest, essay. *Deadline:* February 1.

Contact: Jennifer Young, Senior Program Manager
Green Chemistry Institute-American Chemical Society
1155 16th Street, NW
Washington, DC 20036
Phone: 202-872-6102
Fax: 202-872-6206
E-mail: gci@acs.org

HISPANIC COLLEGE FUND INC. http://www.hispanicfund.org

LOCKHEED MARTIN SCHOLARSHIP PROGRAM

• See page 143

INDEPENDENT LABORATORIES INSTITUTE SCHOLARSHIP ALLIANCE http://www.acil.org

INDEPENDENT LABORATORIES INSTITUTE SCHOLARSHIP ALLIANCE

• See page 132

INNOVATION AND SCIENCE COUNCIL OF BRITISH COLUMBIA http://www.bcinnovationcouncil.com

PAUL AND HELEN TRUSSEL SCIENCE AND TECHNOLOGY SCHOLARSHIP

• See page 87

INSTITUTE OF ENVIRONMENTAL SCIENCES AND TECHNOLOGY (IEST) http://www.iest.org

ROBERT N. HANCOCK MEMORIAL SCHOLARSHIP

• See page 132

LOS ANGELES COUNCIL OF BLACK PROFESSIONAL ENGINEERS http://www.lablackengineers.org

AL-BEN SCHOLARSHIP FOR ACADEMIC INCENTIVE

• See page 159

AL-BEN SCHOLARSHIP FOR PROFESSIONAL MERIT

• See page 159

AL-BEN SCHOLARSHIP FOR SCHOLASTIC ACHIEVEMENT

• See page 159

MICRON TECHNOLOGY FOUNDATION INC. http://www.micron.com/scholars

MICRON SCIENCE AND TECHNOLOGY SCHOLARS PROGRAM
• See page 160

MINERALOGICAL SOCIETY OF AMERICA http://www.minsocam.org

MINERALOGICAL SOCIETY OF AMERICA-GRANT FOR STUDENT RESEARCH IN MINERALOGY AND PETROLOGY
• See page 218

MINERALOGY SOCIETY OF AMERICA-GRANT FOR RESEARCH IN CRYSTALLOGRAPHY
• See page 218

NASA DELAWARE SPACE GRANT CONSORTIUM http://www.delspace.org

NASA DELAWARE SPACE GRANT UNDERGRADUATE TUITION SCHOLARSHIP
• See page 87

NASA IDAHO SPACE GRANT CONSORTIUM http://isgc.uidaho.edu

NASA IDAHO SPACE GRANT CONSORTIUM SCHOLARSHIP PROGRAM
• See page 87

NASA/MARYLAND SPACE GRANT CONSORTIUM http://www.mdspacegrant.org

NASA MARYLAND SPACE GRANT CONSORTIUM UNDERGRADUATE SCHOLARSHIPS
• See page 118

NASA MINNESOTA SPACE GRANT CONSORTIUM http://www.aem.umn.edu/msgc

MINNESOTA SPACE GRANT CONSORTIUM
• See page 118

NASA MISSISSIPPI SPACE GRANT CONSORTIUM http://www.olemiss.edu/programs/nasa

MISSISSIPPI SPACE GRANT CONSORTIUM SCHOLARSHIP
• See page 118

NASA NEVADA SPACE GRANT CONSORTIUM http://www.unr.edu/spacegrant

UNIVERSITY AND COMMUNITY COLLEGE SYSTEM OF NEVADA NASA SPACE GRANT AND FELLOWSHIP PROGRAM
• See page 119

NASA SOUTH DAKOTA SPACE GRANT CONSORTIUM http://www.sdsmt.edu/space/

SOUTH DAKOTA SPACE GRANT CONSORTIUM UNDERGRADUATE SCHOLARSHIPS
• See page 120

NASA VERMONT SPACE GRANT CONSORTIUM http://www.cems.uvm.edu/VSGC

VERMONT SPACE GRANT CONSORTIUM SCHOLARSHIP PROGRAM
• See page 88

NASA VIRGINIA SPACE GRANT CONSORTIUM http://www.vsgc.odu.edu

VIRGINIA SPACE GRANT CONSORTIUM TEACHER EDUCATION SCHOLARSHIPS
• See page 121

NASA WEST VIRGINIA SPACE GRANT CONSORTIUM http://www.nasa.wvu.edu

WEST VIRGINIA SPACE GRANT CONSORTIUM UNDERGRADUATE FELLOWSHIP PROGRAM
• See page 121

NATIONAL ASSOCIATION FOR THE ADVANCEMENT OF COLORED PEOPLE http://www.naacp.org

HUBERTUS W.V. WILLEMS SCHOLARSHIP FOR MALE STUDENTS
• See page 161

LOUIS STOKES SCIENCE AND TECHNOLOGY AWARD
• See page 133

NATIONAL ASSOCIATION OF WATER COMPANIES-NEW JERSEY CHAPTER

NATIONAL ASSOCIATION OF WATER COMPANIES-NEW JERSEY CHAPTER SCHOLARSHIP
• See page 133

NATIONAL FEDERATION OF THE BLIND http://www.nfb.org

HOWARD BROWN RICKARD SCHOLARSHIP
• See page 92

NATIONAL INVENTORS HALL OF FAME http://www.invent.org

COLLEGIATE INVENTORS COMPETITION FOR UNDERGRADUATE STUDENTS
• See page 88

COLLEGIATE INVENTORS COMPETITION-GRAND PRIZE
• See page 88

NATIONAL SCIENCE TEACHERS ASSOCIATION http://www.nsta.org

TOSHIBA/NSTA EXPLORAVISION AWARDS PROGRAM
• See page 193

NATIONAL SOCIETY OF BLACK PHYSICISTS http://www.nsbp.org

AMERICAN PHYSICAL SOCIETY CORPORATE-SPONSORED SCHOLARSHIP FOR MINORITY UNDERGRADUATE STUDENTS WHO MAJOR IN PHYSICS

Scholarship available for minority undergraduate students majoring in physics. Award of $2000 per year for new corporate scholars, and $3000 per year for renewal students. In addition, each physics department that hosts one or more APS minority undergraduate scholars and assigns a mentor for their students will receive a $500 award for programs to encourage minority students.

Academic Fields/Career Goals: Physical Sciences and Math.

Award: Scholarship for use in freshman, sophomore, junior, or senior years; not renewable. *Number:* varies. *Amount:* $2000–$3000.

Eligibility Requirements: Applicant must be American Indian/Alaska Native, Asian/Pacific Islander, Black (non-Hispanic), or Hispanic and enrolled or expecting to enroll full- or part-time at a two-year or four-year institution or university. Available to U.S. citizens.

Application Requirements: Application, references, transcript. *Deadline:* December 1.

Contact: Dr. Kennedy Reed, Scholarship Chairman
National Society of Black Physicists
6704G Lee Highway
Arlington, VA 22205
Phone: 703-536-4207
Fax: 703-536-4203
E-mail: scholarships@nsbp.org

CHARLES S. BROWN SCHOLARSHIP IN PHYSICS

Scholarship providing and African-American student with financial assistance while enrolled in a physics degree program. Number of awards and dollar value varies.

Academic Fields/Career Goals: Physical Sciences and Math.

Award: Scholarship for use in freshman, sophomore, junior, senior, or graduate years; not renewable. *Number:* varies. *Amount:* varies.

Eligibility Requirements: Applicant must be Black (non-Hispanic) and enrolled or expecting to enroll full- or part-time at a four-year institution or university. Available to U.S. and non-U.S. citizens.

Application Requirements: Application, financial need analysis, self-addressed stamped envelope. *Deadline:* January 12.

Contact: Scholarship Committee Chair
National Society of Black Physicists
6704G Lee Highway
Arlington, VA 22205
Phone: 703-536-4207
Fax: 703-536-4203
E-mail: scholarship@nsbp.org

ELMER S. IMES SCHOLARSHIP IN PHYSICS

Graduating high school seniors and undergraduate students already enrolled in college as physics majors may apply for the scholarship. U.S citizenship is required.

Academic Fields/Career Goals: Physical Sciences and Math.

Award: Scholarship for use in freshman, sophomore, junior, or senior years; not renewable. *Number:* 1. *Amount:* $1000.

Eligibility Requirements: Applicant must be enrolled or expecting to enroll full-time at a two-year or four-year institution or university. Available to U.S. citizens.

Application Requirements: Application, autobiography, essay, resume, references, transcript. *Deadline:* January 12.

Contact: Scholarship Committee Chair
National Society of Black Physicists
6704G Lee Highway
Arlington, VA 22205
Phone: 703-536-4207
Fax: 703-536-4203
E-mail: scholarship@nsbp.org

HARVEY WASHINGTON BANKS SCHOLARSHIP IN ASTRONOMY

One-time award for an African American student pursuing an undergraduate degree in astronomy/physics.

Academic Fields/Career Goals: Physical Sciences and Math.

Award: Scholarship for use in freshman, sophomore, junior, or senior years; not renewable. *Number:* 1. *Amount:* $1000.

Eligibility Requirements: Applicant must be Black (non-Hispanic) and enrolled or expecting to enroll full-time at a two-year or four-year institution or university. Available to U.S. citizens.

Application Requirements: Application, essay, references, transcript. *Deadline:* January 12.

Contact: Dr. Kennedy Reed, Scholarship Chairman
National Society of Black Physicists
6704G Lee Highway
Arlington, VA 22205
Phone: 703-536-4207
Fax: 703-536-4203
E-mail: scholarships@nsbp.org

MICHAEL P. ANDERSON SCHOLARSHIP IN SPACE SCIENCE

One-time award for an African American undergraduate student majoring in space science/physics.

Academic Fields/Career Goals: Physical Sciences and Math.

Award: Scholarship for use in freshman, sophomore, junior, or senior years; not renewable. *Number:* 1. *Amount:* $1000.

Eligibility Requirements: Applicant must be Black (non-Hispanic) and enrolled or expecting to enroll full-time at a two-year or four-year institution or university. Available to U.S. citizens.

Application Requirements: Application, essay, references, transcript. *Deadline:* January 12.

Contact: Dr. Kennedy Reed, Scholarship Chairman
National Society of Black Physicists
6704G Lee Highway
Arlington, VA 22205
Phone: 703-536-4207
Fax: 703-536-4203
E-mail: scholarships@nsbp.org

NATIONAL SOCIETY OF BLACK PHYSICISTS AND LAWRENCE LIVERMORE NATIONAL LIBRARY UNDERGRADUATE SCHOLARSHIP

Scholarship for a graduating high school senior or undergraduate student enrolled in a physics major. Scholarship renewable up to four years if student maintains a 3.0 GPA and remains a physics major.

Academic Fields/Career Goals: Physical Sciences and Math.

Award: Scholarship for use in freshman, sophomore, junior, or senior years; renewable. *Number:* 1. *Amount:* $5000.

Eligibility Requirements: Applicant must be Black (non-Hispanic) and enrolled or expecting to enroll full-time at a two-year or four-year institution or university. Applicant must have 3.0 GPA or higher. Available to U.S. citizens.

Application Requirements: Application, essay, references, transcript. *Deadline:* December 1.

Contact: Dr. Kennedy Reed, Scholarship Chairman
National Society of Black Physicists
6704G Lee Highway
Arlington, VA 22205
Phone: 703-536-4207
Fax: 703-536-4203
E-mail: scholarships@nsbp.org

RONALD E. MCNAIR SCHOLARSHIP IN SPACE AND OPTICAL PHYSICS

One-time award for African American undergraduate student majoring in physics. Must be U.S. citizen.

Academic Fields/Career Goals: Physical Sciences and Math.

Award: Scholarship for use in freshman, sophomore, junior, or senior years; not renewable. *Number:* 1. *Amount:* $1000.

Eligibility Requirements: Applicant must be Black (non-Hispanic) and enrolled or expecting to enroll full-time at a two-year or four-year institution or university. Available to U.S. citizens.

Application Requirements: Application, essay, references, transcript. *Deadline:* January 12.

Contact: Dr. Kennedy Reed, Scholarship Chairman
National Society of Black Physicists
6704G Lee Highway
Arlington, VA 22205
Phone: 703-536-4207
Fax: 703-536-4203
E-mail: scholarships@nsbp.org

WALTER SAMUEL MCAFEE SCHOLARSHIP IN SPACE PHYSICS

One-time scholarship for African American full-time undergraduate student majoring in physics. Must be U.S. citizen.

Academic Fields/Career Goals: Physical Sciences and Math.

Award: Scholarship for use in freshman, sophomore, junior, or senior years; not renewable. *Number:* 1. *Amount:* $1000.

Eligibility Requirements: Applicant must be Black (non-Hispanic) and enrolled or expecting to enroll full-time at a two-year or four-year institution or university. Available to U.S. citizens.

National Society of Black Physicists (continued)

Application Requirements: Application, essay, references, transcript. *Deadline:* January 12.

Contact: Dr. Kennedy Reed, Scholarship Chairman
National Society of Black Physicists
6704G Lee Highway
Arlington, VA 22205
Phone: 703-536-4207
Fax: 703-536-4203
E-mail: scholarships@nsbp.org

WILLIE HOBBS MOORE, HARRY L. MORRISON, AND ARTHUR B.C. WALKER PHYSICS SCHOLARSHIPS

Scholarships are intended for African American undergraduate physics majors. Applicants should be either sophomores or juniors. Award for use in junior or senior year of study.

Academic Fields/Career Goals: Physical Sciences and Math.

Award: Scholarship for use in sophomore, junior, or senior years; not renewable. *Number:* 3. *Amount:* $1000.

Eligibility Requirements: Applicant must be Black (non-Hispanic) and enrolled or expecting to enroll full-time at a two-year or four-year institution or university. Available to U.S. citizens.

Application Requirements: Application, essay, references, transcript. *Deadline:* January 12.

Contact: Dr. Kennedy Reed, Scholarship Chairman
National Society of Black Physicists
6704G Lee Highway
Arlington, VA 22205
Phone: 703-536-4207
Fax: 703-536-4203
E-mail: scholarships@nsbp.org

NORTH CAROLINA STATE EDUCATION ASSISTANCE AUTHORITY http://www.ncseaa.edu

NORTH CAROLINA STUDENT LOAN PROGRAM FOR HEALTH, SCIENCE, AND MATHEMATICS

• *See page 213*

PENNSYLVANIA HIGHER EDUCATION ASSISTANCE AGENCY http://www.pheaa.org

NEW ECONOMY TECHNOLOGY AND SCITECH SCHOLARSHIPS

• *See page 295*

ROBERT H. MOLLOHAN FAMILY CHARITABLE FOUNDATION INC. http://www.mollohanfoundation.org

HIGH TECHNOLOGY SCHOLARS PROGRAM

• *See page 135*

SAN DIEGO FOUNDATION http://www.sdfoundation.org

BIOCOM SCHOLARSHIP

• *See page 135*

SIGMA XI, THE SCIENTIFIC RESEARCH SOCIETY http://www.sigmaxi.org

SIGMA XI GRANTS-IN-AID OF RESEARCH

• *See page 78*

SOCIETY FOR IMAGING SCIENCE AND TECHNOLOGY http://www.imaging.org

RAYMOND DAVIS SCHOLARSHIP

• *See page 272*

SOCIETY OF FLIGHT TEST ENGINEERS http://www.sfte.org

SOCIETY OF FLIGHT TEST ENGINEERS SCHOLARSHIP

• *See page 194*

SOCIETY OF HISPANIC PROFESSIONAL ENGINEERS FOUNDATION http://www.henaac.org

SOCIETY OF HISPANIC PROFESSIONAL ENGINEERS FOUNDATION

• *See page 162*

SOCIETY OF PHYSICS STUDENTS http://www.spsnational.org

SOCIETY OF PHYSICS STUDENTS OUTSTANDING STUDENT IN RESEARCH

Available to members of the Society of Physics Students. Winners will receive a $500 honorarium and a $500 award for their SPS Chapter. In addition, expenses for transportation, room, board, and registration for the ICPS will by paid by SPS.

Academic Fields/Career Goals: Physical Sciences and Math.

Award: Prize for use in freshman, sophomore, junior, or senior years; not renewable. *Number:* 1–2. *Amount:* $500–$2500.

Eligibility Requirements: Applicant must be enrolled or expecting to enroll full-time at a two-year or four-year institution or university. Applicant or parent of applicant must be member of Society of Physics Students. Available to U.S. and non-U.S. citizens.

Application Requirements: Application, references, abstract. *Deadline:* April 15.

Contact: Secretary
Society of Physics Students
One Physics Ellipse
College Park, MD 20740
Phone: 301-209-3007
Fax: 301-209-0839
E-mail: sps@aip.org

SOCIETY OF PHYSICS STUDENTS PEGGY DIXON TWO-YEAR COLLEGE SCHOLARSHIP

Scholarship available to Society of Physics Students (SPS) members. Award based on performance both in physics and overall studies, and SPS participation. Must have completed at least one semester or quarter of the introductory physics sequence, and be currently registered in the appropriate subsequent physics courses.

Academic Fields/Career Goals: Physical Sciences and Math.

Award: Scholarship for use in freshman or sophomore years; not renewable. *Number:* 1. *Amount:* $2000.

Eligibility Requirements: Applicant must be enrolled or expecting to enroll full-time at a two-year or four-year institution or university. Applicant or parent of applicant must be member of Society of Physics Students. Available to U.S. and non-U.S. citizens.

Application Requirements: Application, financial need analysis, transcript, letters from at least two faculty members. *Deadline:* February 15.

Contact: Kendra Rand, Project Administrator
Society of Physics Students
One Physics Ellipse
College Park, MD 20740-3843
Phone: 301-209-3007
Fax: 301-209-0839
E-mail: sps@aip.org

SOCIETY OF PHYSICS STUDENTS SCHOLARSHIPS

Scholarships of $2000 to $5000 are awarded to members of Society of Physics Students (SPS) for undergraduate study. The number of awards granted ranges from 17 to 22.

Academic Fields/Career Goals: Physical Sciences and Math.

Award: Scholarship for use in sophomore, junior, or senior years; not renewable. *Number:* 17–22. *Amount:* $2000–$5000.

Eligibility Requirements: Applicant must be enrolled or expecting to enroll full-time at a two-year or four-year institution or university. Applicant or parent of applicant must be member of Society of Physics Students. Available to U.S. and non-U.S. citizens.

Application Requirements: Application, references, transcript. *Deadline:* February 15.

Contact: Scholarship Committee
Society of Physics Students
One Physics Ellipse
College Park, MD 20740
Phone: 301-209-3007
Fax: 301-209-0839
E-mail: sps@aip.org

SOCIETY OF WOMEN ENGINEERS http://www.swe.org

SWE CALIFORNIA GOLDEN GATE SECTION SCHOLARSHIPS
• *See page 196*

SWE CONNECTICUT SECTION JEAN R. BEERS SCHOLARSHIP
• *See page 196*

TKE EDUCATIONAL FOUNDATION http://www.tke.org

CARROL C. HALL MEMORIAL SCHOLARSHIP
• *See page 88*

UNITED NEGRO COLLEGE FUND http://www.uncf.org

BOOZ, ALLEN AND HAMILTON/WILLIAM F. STASIOR INTERNSHIP
• *See page 150*

HEINZ ENVIRONMENTAL FELLOWS PROGRAM
• *See page 136*

MEDTRONIC FOUNDATION SCHOLARSHIP
• *See page 136*

SPRINT NEXTEL SCHOLARSHIP/INTERNSHIP
• *See page 66*

WRIGLEY JR., WILLIAM SCHOLARSHIP/INTERNSHIP
• *See page 152*

UNIVERSITIES SPACE RESEARCH ASSOCIATION http://www.usra.edu

UNIVERSITIES SPACE RESEARCH ASSOCIATION SCHOLARSHIP PROGRAM
• *See page 88*

VIRGINIA BUSINESS AND PROFESSIONAL WOMEN'S FOUNDATION http://www.vabpwfoundation.org

WOMEN IN SCIENCE AND TECHNOLOGY SCHOLARSHIP
• *See page 136*

WOMEN IN FEDERAL LAW ENFORCEMENT http://www.wifle.org

WIFLE SCHOLARSHIP PROGRAM
• *See page 198*

XEROX http://www.xerox.com

TECHNICAL MINORITY SCHOLARSHIP
• *See page 165*

POLITICAL SCIENCE

AMERICAN FEDERATION OF STATE, COUNTY, AND MUNICIPAL EMPLOYEES http://www.afscme.org

AFSCME/UNCF UNION SCHOLARS PROGRAM
• *See page 80*

JERRY CLARK MEMORIAL SCHOLARSHIP

Renewable award for a student majoring in political science for his or her junior and senior years of study. Must be a child of an AFSCME member. Minimum 2.5 GPA required. Once awarded, the scholarship will be renewed for the senior year provided the student remains enrolled full-time as a political science major.

Academic Fields/Career Goals: Political Science.

Award: Scholarship for use in junior or senior years; renewable. *Number:* 2. *Amount:* $5000.

Eligibility Requirements: Applicant must be enrolled or expecting to enroll full-time at a four-year institution or university. Applicant or parent of applicant must be member of American Federation of State, County, and Municipal Employees. Applicant must have 2.5 GPA or higher. Available to U.S. citizens.

Application Requirements: Application, transcript, proof of parent. *Deadline:* July 1.

Contact: Philip Allen, Scholarship Coordinator
American Federation of State, County, and Municipal Employees
1625 L Street, NW
Washington, DC 20036-5687
Phone: 202-429-1250
Fax: 202-429-1272
E-mail: pallen@asscme.org

AMERICAN LEGION AUXILIARY DEPARTMENT OF ARIZONA http://www.azlegion.org/majorp~2.htm

AMERICAN LEGION AUXILIARY DEPARTMENT OF ARIZONA WILMA HOYAL-MAXINE CHILTON MEMORIAL SCHOLARSHIP

Annual scholarship to a student in second year or higher in one of the three state universities in Arizona. Must be enrolled in a program of study in political science, public programs, or special education. Must be a citizen of United States and of Arizona for at least one year. Honorably discharged veterans or immediate family members are given preference.

Academic Fields/Career Goals: Political Science; Public Policy and Administration; Social Services; Special Education.

Award: Scholarship for use in sophomore, junior, senior, graduate, or postgraduate years; not renewable. *Number:* 3. *Amount:* $1000.

Eligibility Requirements: Applicant must be enrolled or expecting to enroll full-time at a two-year or four-year institution or university; resident of Arizona and studying in Arizona. Available to U.S. citizens.

Application Requirements: Application, autobiography, essay, financial need analysis, photo, references, test scores, transcript. *Deadline:* May 15.

Contact: Department Secretary and Treasurer
American Legion Auxiliary Department of Arizona
4701 North 19th Avenue, Suite 100
Phoenix, AZ 85015-3727
Phone: 602-241-1080
Fax: 602-604-9640
E-mail: amlegauxaz@mcleodusa.net

ARAB AMERICAN SCHOLARSHIP FOUNDATION http://www.lahc.org

LEBANESE AMERICAN HERITAGE CLUB'S SCHOLARSHIP FUND
• *See page 175*

BOYS AND GIRLS CLUBS OF GREATER SAN DIEGO http://www.sdyouth.org

SPENCE REESE SCHOLARSHIP FUND
• *See page 262*

CENTRAL INTELLIGENCE AGENCY http://www.cia.gov

CENTRAL INTELLIGENCE AGENCY UNDERGRADUATE SCHOLARSHIP PROGRAM
• *See page 49*

COLLEGEBOUND FOUNDATION http://www.collegeboundfoundation.org

DECATUR H. MILLER SCHOLARSHIP
• *See page 347*

CUBAN AMERICAN NATIONAL FOUNDATION http://www.masscholarships.org

MAS FAMILY SCHOLARSHIPS
• *See page 139*

GOVERNMENT FINANCE OFFICERS ASSOCIATION http://www.gfoa.org

MINORITIES IN GOVERNMENT FINANCE SCHOLARSHIP
• See page 54

GREATER SALINA COMMUNITY FOUNDATION http://www.gscf.org

KANSAS FEDERATION OF REPUBLICAN WOMEN SCHOLARSHIP
• See page 347

HARRY S. TRUMAN SCHOLARSHIP FOUNDATION http://www.truman.gov

HARRY S. TRUMAN SCHOLARSHIP

Scholarships for U.S. citizens or U.S. nationals who are college or university students with junior-level academic standing and who wish to attend professional or graduate school to prepare for careers in government or the nonprofit and advocacy sectors. Candidates must be nominated by their institution. Public service and leadership record considered. Visit Web site: http://www.truman.gov for further information and application.

Academic Fields/Career Goals: Political Science; Public Policy and Administration.

Award: Scholarship for use in junior year; renewable. *Number:* 65. *Amount:* $30,000.

Eligibility Requirements: Applicant must be enrolled or expecting to enroll full-time at a four-year institution or university and must have an interest in leadership. Available to U.S. citizens.

Application Requirements: Application, interview, references, policy proposal. *Deadline:* February 5.

Contact: Tonji Wade, Program Officer
Harry S. Truman Scholarship Foundation
712 Jackson Place, NW
Washington, DC 20006
Phone: 202-395-4831
Fax: 202-395-6995
E-mail: office@truman.gov

INSTITUTE FOR HUMANE STUDIES http://www.theihs.org

HUMANE STUDIES FELLOWSHIPS
• See page 179

LYNDON BAINES JOHNSON FOUNDATION http://www.lbjlib.utexas.edu

LYNDON BAINES JOHNSON FOUNDATION GRANTS-IN-AID RESEARCH
• See page 347

NATIONAL FEDERATION OF THE BLIND http://www.nfb.org

MICHAEL AND MARIE MARUCCI SCHOLARSHIP
• See page 320

NATIONAL SOCIETY DAUGHTERS OF THE AMERICAN REVOLUTION http://www.dar.org

NATIONAL SOCIETY DAUGHTERS OF THE AMERICAN REVOLUTION DR. AURA-LEE A. PITTENGER AND JAMES HOBBS PITTENGER AMERICAN HISTORY SCHOLARSHIP
• See page 347

NATIONAL SOCIETY DAUGHTERS OF THE AMERICAN REVOLUTION ENID HALL GRISWOLD MEMORIAL SCHOLARSHIP
• See page 220

NATIONAL TOURISM FOUNDATION http://www.ntfonline.com

ACADEMY OF TRAVEL AND TOURISM SCHOLARSHIPS
• See page 357

STRAIGHTFORWARD MEDIA http://www.straightforwardmedia.com

STRAIGHTFORWARD MEDIA LIBERAL ARTS SCHOLARSHIP
• See page 99

TKE EDUCATIONAL FOUNDATION http://www.tke.org

BRUCE B. MELCHERT SCHOLARSHIP

One-time award of $500 given to an undergraduate member of Tau Kappa Epsilon with sophomore, junior, or senior standing. Must be pursuing a degree in political science or government and have a record of leadership within his fraternity and other campus organizations. Should have as a goal to serve in a political or government position. Recent head and shoulders photograph must be submitted with application. Minimum 3.0 GPA required.

Academic Fields/Career Goals: Political Science.

Award: Scholarship for use in sophomore, junior, or senior years; not renewable. *Number:* 1. *Amount:* $500.

Eligibility Requirements: Applicant must be enrolled or expecting to enroll full-time at a four-year institution or university and must have an interest in leadership. Applicant or parent of applicant must be member of Tau Kappa Epsilon. Applicant must have 3.0 GPA or higher. Available to U.S. and non-U.S. citizens.

Application Requirements: Application, essay, photo, transcript, narrative summary of how TKE membership has benefited applicant. *Deadline:* February 29.

Contact: Gary A. Reed, President and Chief Executive Officer
TKE Educational Foundation
8645 Founders Road
Indianapolis, IN 46268-1393
Phone: 317-872-6533
Fax: 317-875-8353
E-mail: reedga@tke.org

UNITED NEGRO COLLEGE FUND http://www.uncf.org

C-SPAN SCHOLARSHIP PROGRAM
• See page 187

SODEXHO SCHOLARSHIP
• See page 343

TOYOTA SCHOLARSHIP
• See page 66

WASHINGTON CROSSING FOUNDATION http://www.gwcf.org

WASHINGTON CROSSING FOUNDATION SCHOLARSHIP

Renewable, merit-based awards available to high school seniors who are planning a career in government service. Must write an essay stating reason for deciding on a career in public service. Minimum 3.0 GPA required.

Academic Fields/Career Goals: Political Science; Public Policy and Administration.

Award: Scholarship for use in freshman year; renewable. *Number:* 5–10. *Amount:* $1000–$20,000.

Eligibility Requirements: Applicant must be high school student and planning to enroll or expecting to enroll full-time at a four-year institution or university. Applicant must have 3.0 GPA or higher. Available to U.S. citizens.

Application Requirements: Application, essay, interview, photo, references, test scores, transcript. *Deadline:* January 15.

Contact: Eugene C. Fish, Vice Chairman
Washington Crossing Foundation
PO Box 503
Levittown, PA 19058-0503
Phone: 215-949-8841
Fax: 215-949-8843
E-mail: info@gwcf.org

WASHINGTON NEWS COUNCIL http://www.wanewscouncil.org

DICK LARSEN SCHOLARSHIP PROGRAM
• See page 188

HERB ROBINSON SCHOLARSHIP PROGRAM
• *See page 188*

PSYCHOLOGY

AMERICAN FEDERATION OF STATE, COUNTY, AND MUNICIPAL EMPLOYEES http://www.afscme.org

AFSCME/UNCF UNION SCHOLARS PROGRAM
• *See page 80*

AMERICAN PSYCHOLOGICAL ASSOCIATION http://www.apa.org

AMERICAN PSYCHOLOGICAL ASSOCIATION TEACHERS OF PSYCHOLOGY IN SECONDARY SCHOOLS SCHOLARS ESSAY COMPETITION

Three prizes of $500 each for essays of 3000 words with an abstract of 120 words. Applicants must have completed or be presently enrolled in a psychology course.

Academic Fields/Career Goals: Psychology.

Award: Prize for use in freshman year; not renewable. *Number:* 3. *Amount:* $500.

Eligibility Requirements: Applicant must be high school student; planning to enroll or expecting to enroll full- or part-time at a two-year or four-year institution or university and must have an interest in writing. Available to U.S. and non-U.S. citizens.

Application Requirements: Applicant must enter a contest, essay, cover letter. *Deadline:* March 3.

Contact: Jewel Beamon, Special Projects Associate
American Psychological Association
750 First Street, NE
Washington, DC 20002-4242
Phone: 202-336-6076
Fax: 202-336-5962
E-mail: jbeamon@apa.org

CYNTHIA E. MORGAN SCHOLARSHIP FUND (CEMS) http://www.cemsfund.com

CYNTHIA E. MORGAN MEMORIAL SCHOLARSHIP
• *See page 336*

HEALTH RESEARCH COUNCIL OF NEW ZEALAND http://www.hrc.govt.nz

PACIFIC MENTAL HEALTH WORK FORCE AWARD
• *See page 326*

MENTAL HEALTH ASSOCIATION IN NEW YORK STATE INC. http://www.mhanys.org

EDNA AIMES SCHOLARSHIP
• *See page 128*

MISSISSIPPI STATE STUDENT FINANCIAL AID http://www.ihl.state.ms.us

CRITICAL NEEDS TEACHER LOAN/SCHOLARSHIP
• *See page 235*

MISSISSIPPI HEALTH CARE PROFESSIONS LOAN/SCHOLARSHIP PROGRAM
• *See page 339*

NEW YORK STATE EDUCATION DEPARTMENT http://www.highered.nysed.gov

REGENTS PROFESSIONAL OPPORTUNITY SCHOLARSHIP
• *See page 60*

PI LAMBDA THETA INC. http://www.pilambda.org

JANET ISHIKAWA-DANIEL FULLMER SCHOLARSHIP IN COUNSELING

Scholarship provides $1000 to outstanding students pursuing graduate degrees in counseling or counseling psychology. Applicant should display leadership potential and be involved in extracurricular activities. Must have a cumulative GPA of at least 3.5 during the junior or senior years of the undergraduate degree program and, if applicable, in all courses taken while enrolled in a graduate program.

Academic Fields/Career Goals: Psychology.

Award: Scholarship for use in freshman, sophomore, junior, senior, or graduate years; not renewable. *Number:* 1. *Amount:* $1000.

Eligibility Requirements: Applicant must be enrolled or expecting to enroll full- or part-time at an institution or university. Applicant must have 3.5 GPA or higher. Available to U.S. and non-U.S. citizens.

Application Requirements: Application, resume, references, transcript. *Deadline:* February 10.

Contact: Pam Todd, Controller
Pi Lambda Theta Inc.
PO Box 6626
Bloomington, IN 47407-6626
Phone: 812-339-3411
Fax: 812-339-3462
E-mail: ellen@pilambda.org

PILOT INTERNATIONAL FOUNDATION http://www.pilotinternational.org

PILOT INTERNATIONAL FOUNDATION RUBY NEWHALL MEMORIAL SCHOLARSHIP
• *See page 342*

PILOT INTERNATIONAL FOUNDATION SCHOLARSHIP PROGRAM
• *See page 342*

SOCIETY FOR THE SCIENTIFIC STUDY OF SEXUALITY http://www.sexscience.org

SOCIETY FOR THE SCIENTIFIC STUDY OF SEXUALITY STUDENT RESEARCH GRANT
• *See page 129*

STRAIGHTFORWARD MEDIA http://www.straightforwardmedia.com

STRAIGHTFORWARD MEDIA LIBERAL ARTS SCHOLARSHIP
• *See page 99*

SUNSHINE LADY FOUNDATION INC. http://www.sunshinelady.org

COUNSELOR, ADVOCATE, AND SUPPORT STAFF SCHOLARSHIP PROGRAM
• *See page 167*

UNITED NEGRO COLLEGE FUND http://www.uncf.org

BOOZ, ALLEN AND HAMILTON/WILLIAM F. STASIOR INTERNSHIP
• *See page 150*

TOYOTA SCHOLARSHIP
• *See page 66*

ZETA PHI BETA SORORITY INC. NATIONAL EDUCATIONAL FOUNDATION http://www.zphib1920.org

LULLELIA W. HARRISON SCHOLARSHIP IN COUNSELING
• *See page 167*

PUBLIC HEALTH

AMERICAN DENTAL HYGIENISTS' ASSOCIATION (ADHA) INSTITUTE http://www.adha.org

IRENE E. NEWMAN SCHOLARSHIP
• *See page 209*

ASSOCIATION ON AMERICAN INDIAN AFFAIRS (AAIA) http://www.indian-affairs.org

ELIZABETH AND SHERMAN ASCHE MEMORIAL SCHOLARSHIP FUND
• See page 334

COLLEGE BOARD/ROBERT WOOD JOHNSON FOUNDATION YES PROGRAM http://www.collegeboard.com

YOUNG EPIDEMIOLOGY SCHOLARS COMPETITION
• See page 299

GENERAL FEDERATION OF WOMEN'S CLUBS OF MASSACHUSETTS http://www.gfwcma.org

CATHERINE E. PHILBIN SCHOLARSHIP

One scholarship of $500 will be awarded to a graduate or undergraduate student studying public health. Eligible applicants will be residents of Massachusetts. Along with the application, students must send a personal statement of no more than 500 words addressing professional goals and financial need.

Academic Fields/Career Goals: Public Health.

Award: Scholarship for use in freshman, sophomore, junior, senior, or graduate years; not renewable. *Number:* 1. *Amount:* $500.

Eligibility Requirements: Applicant must be enrolled or expecting to enroll full-time at a four-year institution or university and resident of Massachusetts. Available to U.S. citizens.

Application Requirements: Application, essay, references, transcript. *Deadline:* March 1.

Contact: Jane Howard, Scholarship Chairman
General Federation of Women's Clubs of Massachusetts
PO Box 679
Sudbury, MA 01776-0679
E-mail: jhoward@mountida.edu

INDIAN HEALTH SERVICES, UNITED STATES DEPARTMENT OF HEALTH AND HUMAN SERVICES http://www.ihs.gov

HEALTH PROFESSIONS PREPARATORY SCHOLARSHIP PROGRAM
• See page 327

MENTAL HEALTH ASSOCIATION IN NEW YORK STATE INC. http://www.mhanys.org

EDNA AIMES SCHOLARSHIP
• See page 128

NATIONAL ENVIRONMENTAL HEALTH ASSOCIATION/AMERICAN ACADEMY OF SANITARIANS http://www.neha.org

NATIONAL ENVIRONMENTAL HEALTH ASSOCIATION/AMERICAN ACADEMY OF SANITARIANS SCHOLARSHIP
• See page 299

OREGON STUDENT ASSISTANCE COMMISSION http://www.osac.state.or.us

LAURENCE R. FOSTER MEMORIAL SCHOLARSHIP

One-time award to students enrolled or planning to enroll in a public health degree program. First preference given to those working in the public health field and those pursuing a graduate degree in public health. Undergraduates entering junior or senior year health programs may apply if seeking a public health career, and not private practice. Prefer applicants from diverse cultures. Must provide three references. Additional essay required. Must be resident of Oregon.

Academic Fields/Career Goals: Public Health.

Award: Scholarship for use in junior, senior, graduate, or postgraduate years; renewable. *Number:* varies. *Amount:* varies.

Eligibility Requirements: Applicant must be enrolled or expecting to enroll full- or part-time at a four-year institution and resident of Oregon. Available to U.S. citizens.

Application Requirements: Application, essay, financial need analysis, references, transcript, activity chart. *Deadline:* March 1.

Contact: Director of Grant Programs
Oregon Student Assistance Commission
1500 Valley River Drive, Suite 100
Eugene, OR 97401-7020
Phone: 800-452-8807 Ext. 7395

PILOT INTERNATIONAL FOUNDATION http://www.pilotinternational.org

PILOT INTERNATIONAL FOUNDATION RUBY NEWHALL MEMORIAL SCHOLARSHIP
• See page 342

SOCIETY FOR THE SCIENTIFIC STUDY OF SEXUALITY http://www.sexscience.org

SOCIETY FOR THE SCIENTIFIC STUDY OF SEXUALITY STUDENT RESEARCH GRANT
• See page 129

PUBLIC POLICY AND ADMINISTRATION

AMERICAN INSTITUTE OF POLISH CULTURE INC. http://www.ampolinstitute.org

HARRIET IRSAY SCHOLARSHIP GRANT
• See page 99

AMERICAN LEGION AUXILIARY DEPARTMENT OF ARIZONA http://www.azlegion.org/majorp~2.htm

AMERICAN LEGION AUXILIARY DEPARTMENT OF ARIZONA WILMA HOYAL-MAXINE CHILTON MEMORIAL SCHOLARSHIP
• See page 471

CLEVELAND SCHOLARSHIP PROGRAMS http://www.cspohio.org

CSP MANAGED FUNDS-CLEVELAND BROWNS MARION MOTLEY SCHOLARSHIP
• See page 49

GEORGIA GOVERNMENT FINANCE OFFICERS ASSOCIATION http://www.ggfoa.org

GGFOA SCHOLARSHIP
• See page 52

GOVERNMENT FINANCE OFFICERS ASSOCIATION http://www.gfoa.org

FRANK L. GREATHOUSE GOVERNMENT ACCOUNTING SCHOLARSHIP
• See page 141

GEORGE A. NIELSEN PUBLIC INVESTOR SCHOLARSHIP
• See page 141

MINORITIES IN GOVERNMENT FINANCE SCHOLARSHIP
• See page 54

GREATER SALINA COMMUNITY FOUNDATION http://www.gscf.org

KANSAS FEDERATION OF REPUBLICAN WOMEN SCHOLARSHIP
• See page 347

HARRY S. TRUMAN SCHOLARSHIP FOUNDATION http://www.truman.gov

HARRY S. TRUMAN SCHOLARSHIP
• See page 472

JAPANESE AMERICAN CITIZENS LEAGUE (JACL) http://www.jacl.org

NATIONAL JACL HEADQUARTERS SCHOLARSHIP

• *See page 75*

NATIONAL STONE, SAND AND GRAVEL ASSOCIATION (NSSGA) http://www.nssga.org

JENNIFER CURTIS BYLER SCHOLARSHIP FOR THE STUDY OF PUBLIC AFFAIRS

• *See page 182*

WASHINGTON CROSSING FOUNDATION http://www.gwcf.org

WASHINGTON CROSSING FOUNDATION SCHOLARSHIP

• *See page 472*

WOMEN IN FEDERAL LAW ENFORCEMENT http://www.wifle.org

WIFLE SCHOLARSHIP PROGRAM

• *See page 198*

RADIOLOGY

AMERICAN SOCIETY OF RADIOLOGIC TECHNOLOGISTS EDUCATION AND RESEARCH FOUNDATION http://www.asrt.org/foundation

HOWARD S. STERN SCHOLARSHIP

• *See page 333*

JERMAN-CAHOON STUDENT SCHOLARSHIP

• *See page 333*

MONSTER MEDICAL IMAGING EDUCATORS SCHOLARSHIP

• *See page 223*

ROYCE OSBORN MINORITY STUDENT SCHOLARSHIP

• *See page 333*

SIEMENS CLINICAL ADVANCEMENT SCHOLARSHIP

• *See page 334*

VARIAN RADIATION THERAPY STUDENT SCHOLARSHIP

• *See page 334*

CYNTHIA E. MORGAN SCHOLARSHIP FUND (CEMS) http://www.cemsfund.com

CYNTHIA E. MORGAN MEMORIAL SCHOLARSHIP

• *See page 336*

SOCIETY OF NUCLEAR MEDICINE http://www.snm.org

PAUL COLE SCHOLARSHIP

• *See page 342*

REAL ESTATE

APPRAISAL INSTITUTE http://www.appraisalinstitute.org

APPRAISAL INSTITUTE EDUCATION TRUST SCHOLARSHIP

Scholarships for undergraduate and graduate students majoring in real estate appraisal, land economics, real estate, or allied fields. Must be a U.S. citizen attending a university or community college in the United States. Selection is based on academic excellence.

Academic Fields/Career Goals: Real Estate.

Award: Scholarship for use in sophomore, junior, senior, or graduate years; not renewable. *Number:* up to 20. *Amount:* $2000–$3000.

Eligibility Requirements: Applicant must be enrolled or expecting to enroll full-time at a four-year institution or university. Applicant must have 2.5 GPA or higher. Available to U.S. citizens.

Application Requirements: Application, essay, references, transcript, copy of study program. *Deadline:* March 15.

Contact: Olivia Carreon, Project Coordinator
Appraisal Institute
550 West Van Buren Street, Suite 1000
Chicago, IL 60607
Phone: 312-335-4100 Ext. 4148
E-mail: sdavila@appraisalinstitute.org

MINORITIES AND WOMEN EDUCATIONAL SCHOLARSHIP PROGRAM

Applicants must be enrolled full- or part-time in real estate courses within a degree granting college, university, or junior college. Scholarships are available only to women and minorities including American Indians or Alaska Natives, Asians, Black or African-Americans, Hispanics or Latinos, and Native Hawaiians or other Pacific Islanders. Cumulative GPA of no less than 2.5 and demonstration of financial need are required.

Academic Fields/Career Goals: Real Estate.

Award: Scholarship for use in freshman, sophomore, junior, or senior years; not renewable. *Number:* varies. *Amount:* $1000.

Eligibility Requirements: Applicant must be American Indian/Alaska Native, Asian/Pacific Islander, Black (non-Hispanic), or Hispanic; enrolled or expecting to enroll full- or part-time at a four-year institution or university and female. Applicant must have 2.5 GPA or higher. Available to U.S. citizens.

Application Requirements: Application, essay, financial need analysis, photo, resume, references, transcript. *Deadline:* April 15.

Contact: Olivia Carreon, Project Coordinator
Appraisal Institute
550 West Van Buren Street, Suite 1000
Chicago, IL 60607
Phone: 312-335-4278
Fax: 312-335-4279
E-mail: hrichmond@appraisalinstitute.org

CALIFORNIA ASSOCIATION OF REALTORS http://www.car.org

C.A.R. SCHOLARSHIP FOUNDATION AWARD

Scholarships to students enrolled at a California College or University for professions which are centered on, or support a career in real estate transactional activity. Must have maintained a cumulative GPA of 2.6 or higher.

Academic Fields/Career Goals: Real Estate.

Award: Scholarship for use in sophomore, junior, or senior years; not renewable. *Number:* varies. *Amount:* $2000–$4000.

Eligibility Requirements: Applicant must be enrolled or expecting to enroll full-time at a two-year or four-year institution or university; resident of California and studying in California. Available to U.S. citizens.

Application Requirements: Application, driver's license, essay, references, transcript. *Deadline:* May 11.

Contact: Mary Martinez, Scholarship Coordinator
California Association of Realtors
525 South Virgil Avenue
Los Angeles, CA 90020
Phone: 213-739-8200
Fax: 213-480-7724
E-mail: scholarship@car.org

ILLINOIS REAL ESTATE EDUCATIONAL FOUNDATION http://www.ilreef.org

ILLINOIS REAL ESTATE EDUCATIONAL FOUNDATION ACADEMIC SCHOLARSHIPS

Awards for Illinois residents attending an accredited two-or four-year junior college, college or university in Illinois. Must have completed 30 college credit hours and be pursuing a degree with an emphasis in real estate. Must be a U.S. citizen.

Academic Fields/Career Goals: Real Estate.

Award: Scholarship for use in freshman, sophomore, junior, or senior years; renewable. *Number:* varies. *Amount:* $1000.

Eligibility Requirements: Applicant must be enrolled or expecting to enroll full-time at a two-year or four-year institution or university; resident of Illinois and studying in Illinois. Available to U.S. citizens.

Illinois Real Estate Educational Foundation (continued)

Application Requirements: Application, essay, interview, references, transcript. *Deadline:* April 1.

Contact: Stephen Sundquist, General Manager
Illinois Real Estate Educational Foundation
3180 Adloff Lane
Springfield, IL 62703-9451
Phone: 217-529-2600
Fax: 217-529-3904
E-mail: ssundquist@ilreef.org

THOMAS F. SEAY SCHOLARSHIP

Award of $2000 to students pursuing a degree with an emphasis in real estate. Must be a U.S. citizen and attending any accredited U.S. college or university full-time. Must have completed at least 30 college credit hours. Minimum 3.5 GPA required.

Academic Fields/Career Goals: Real Estate.

Award: Scholarship for use in freshman, sophomore, junior, or senior years; renewable. *Number:* varies. *Amount:* $2000.

Eligibility Requirements: Applicant must be enrolled or expecting to enroll full-time at a two-year or four-year institution or university and resident of Illinois. Applicant must have 3.5 GPA or higher. Available to U.S. citizens.

Application Requirements: Application, essay, interview, references, transcript. *Deadline:* April 1.

Contact: Stephen Sundquist, General Manager
Illinois Real Estate Educational Foundation
3180 Adloff Lane
Springfield, IL 62703
Phone: 217-529-2600
Fax: 217-529-3904
E-mail: ssundquist@ilreef.org

INSTITUTE OF REAL ESTATE MANAGEMENT FOUNDATION http://www.iremfoundation.org

GEORGE M. BROOKER COLLEGIATE SCHOLARSHIP FOR MINORITIES

One-time award for minority college juniors, seniors, and graduate students who are U.S. citizens and are committed to a career in real estate, specifically real estate management. Must have a minimum GPA of 3.0.

Academic Fields/Career Goals: Real Estate.

Award: Scholarship for use in junior, senior, or graduate years; not renewable. *Number:* up to 3. *Amount:* $1000–$2500.

Eligibility Requirements: Applicant must be American Indian/Alaska Native, Asian/Pacific Islander, Black (non-Hispanic), or Hispanic and enrolled or expecting to enroll full-time at a four-year institution or university. Applicant must have 3.0 GPA or higher. Available to U.S. citizens.

Application Requirements: Application, essay, interview, resume, references, transcript. *Deadline:* March 31.

Contact: Kimberly Holmes, Foundation Administrator
Institute of Real Estate Management Foundation
430 North Michigan Avenue, Seventh Floor
Chicago, IL 60611-4090
Phone: 312-329-6008
Fax: 312-410-7908
E-mail: foundatn@irem.org

INTERNATIONAL COUNCIL OF SHOPPING CENTERS EDUCATIONAL FOUNDATION http://www.icscfoundation.org

ICSC JOHN. T RIORDAN PROFESSIONAL EDUCATION SCHOLARSHIP

Award for higher education for shopping center professionals. Must be a official ICSC member in good standing, actively employed in the shopping center industry for a minimum of one year, or recent graduate of college/university with coursework emphasis in real estate; or a graduate of REAP or Inroads programs within the past eighteen months prior to year end when the application is submitted.

Academic Fields/Career Goals: Real Estate.

Award: Scholarship for use in freshman or sophomore years; not renewable. *Number:* up to 10. *Amount:* up to $3000.

Eligibility Requirements: Applicant must be enrolled or expecting to enroll full-time at a four-year institution or university. Available to U.S. and non-U.S. citizens.

Application Requirements: Application, essay, resume, references. *Deadline:* March 14.

Contact: Valerie Cammiso, Executive Director
International Council of Shopping Centers Educational Foundation
1221 Avenue of the Americas, 41st Floor
New York, NY 10020-5370
Phone: 646-728-3559
Fax: 732-694-1676
E-mail: vcammiso@icsc.org

NEW JERSEY ASSOCIATION OF REALTORS http://www.njar.com

NEW JERSEY ASSOCIATION OF REALTORS EDUCATIONAL FOUNDATION SCHOLARSHIP PROGRAM

One-time awards for New Jersey residents who are high school seniors pursuing studies in real estate or allied fields. Preference to students considering a career in real estate. Must be member of NJAR or relative of a member. Selected candidates are interviewed in June. Must be a U.S. citizen.

Academic Fields/Career Goals: Real Estate.

Award: Scholarship for use in freshman year; not renewable. *Number:* 20–32. *Amount:* $1000–$2500.

Eligibility Requirements: Applicant must be high school student; planning to enroll or expecting to enroll full-time at a four-year institution or university and resident of New Jersey. Applicant or parent of applicant must be member of New Jersey Association of Realtors. Available to U.S. citizens.

Application Requirements: Application, essay, financial need analysis, interview, transcript, letter of verification of realtor/realtor associate/association staff. *Deadline:* April 9.

Contact: Diane Hatley, Educational Foundation
New Jersey Association of Realtors
PO Box 2098
Edison, NJ 08818
Phone: 732-494-5616
Fax: 732-494-4723

OREGON STUDENT ASSISTANCE COMMISSION http://www.osac.state.or.us

HOMESTEAD CAPITAL HOUSING SCHOLARSHIP

• *See page 61*

RECREATION, PARKS, LEISURE STUDIES

AMERICAN ALLIANCE FOR HEALTH, PHYSICAL EDUCATION, RECREATION AND DANCE http://www.aahperd.org

ROBERT W. CRAWFORD STUDENT LITERARY AWARD

Annual award recognizing writing excellence among graduate and undergraduate students. Any student enrolled in an HPERD professional track (health, physical education, recreation or dance) is eligible to submit. Applicants must submit manuscripts with a focus on leisure and recreation. Students must have a faculty sponsor to submit a paper for this award.

Academic Fields/Career Goals: Recreation, Parks, Leisure Studies.

Award: Scholarship for use in freshman, sophomore, junior, senior, or graduate years; not renewable. *Number:* 2. *Amount:* $500.

Eligibility Requirements: Applicant must be enrolled or expecting to enroll full- or part-time at a four-year institution or university. Available to U.S. and non-U.S. citizens.

Application Requirements: Application, applicant must enter a contest, essay, resume, faculty sponsor, sample evaluation sheets. *Deadline:* January 1.

Contact: Chris Neumann, Senior Program Manager
American Alliance for Health, Physical Education, Recreation and Dance
1900 Association Drive
Reston, VA 20191
Phone: 703-476-3432
Fax: 703-476-9527
E-mail: aapar@aahperd.org

RUTH ABERNATHY PRESIDENTIAL SCHOLARSHIP

Three award for undergraduate students and two for graduate students in January of each year. Must be majoring in the field of health, physical education, recreation or dance. Undergraduate awards are in the amount of $1000 each and graduate awards are in the amount of $1500 each. Recipients also receive a complimentary three-year AAHPERD membership. Applicant must be current member of AAHPERD.

Academic Fields/Career Goals: Recreation, Parks, Leisure Studies; Sports-Related/Exercise Science.

Award: Scholarship for use in freshman, sophomore, junior, senior, or graduate years; not renewable. *Number:* 5. *Amount:* $1000–$1500.

Eligibility Requirements: Applicant must be enrolled or expecting to enroll full-time at a four-year institution or university and must have an interest in leadership. Applicant must have 3.5 GPA or higher. Available to U.S. and non-U.S. citizens.

Application Requirements: Application, transcript, photocopy of AAHPERD membership card or completed AAHPERD membership application form, letter from the school's dean indicating full-time status, 3 letters of recommendation. *Deadline:* varies.

Contact: Deb Callis, Secretary to Chief Executive Officer
American Alliance for Health, Physical Education, Recreation and Dance
1900 Association Drive
Reston, VA 20191
Phone: 703-476-3405
Fax: 703-476-9537
E-mail: dcallis@aahperd.org

AMERICAN QUARTER HORSE FOUNDATION (AQHF) http://www.aqha.com/foundation

ARIZONA QUARTER HORSE YOUTH RACING SCHOLARSHIP

• *See page 81*

CANADIAN RECREATIONAL CANOEING ASSOCIATION http://www.paddlingcanada.com

BILL MASON MEMORIAL SCHOLARSHIP FUND

• *See page 74*

GOLF COURSE SUPERINTENDENTS ASSOCIATION OF AMERICA http://www.gcsaa.org

GOLF COURSE SUPERINTENDENTS ASSOCIATION OF AMERICA STUDENT ESSAY CONTEST

• *See page 69*

MAINE CAMPGROUND OWNERS ASSOCIATION http://www.campmaine.com/home.php

MAINE CAMPGROUND OWNERS ASSOCIATION SCHOLARSHIP

One-time award of $500 to a Maine resident pursuing a career in outdoor recreation. Must have completed one year of study and have a minimum GPA of 2.5.

Academic Fields/Career Goals: Recreation, Parks, Leisure Studies.

Award: Scholarship for use in sophomore, junior, senior, graduate, or postgraduate years; not renewable. *Number:* 1. *Amount:* $500.

Eligibility Requirements: Applicant must be enrolled or expecting to enroll full-time at a two-year or four-year or technical institution or university and resident of Maine. Applicant must have 2.5 GPA or higher. Available to U.S. and non-U.S. citizens.

Application Requirements: Application, essay, financial need analysis, transcript. *Deadline:* March 31.

Contact: Richard Abare, Executive Director
Maine Campground Owners Association
10 Falcon Road, Suite 1
Lewiston, ME 04240
Phone: 207-782-5874
Fax: 207-782-4497
E-mail: info@campmaine.com

MAINE RECREATION AND PARKS ASSOCIATION SCHOLARSHIP http://www.merpa.org

MAINE RECREATION AND PARK ASSOCIATION HIGH SCHOOL SCHOLARSHIP

Scholarship of $500 available to graduating Maine high school seniors expecting to enroll in a four-year recreation, parks, or leisure services curriculum in the fall semester immediately following high school graduation.

Academic Fields/Career Goals: Recreation, Parks, Leisure Studies.

Award: Scholarship for use in freshman year; not renewable. *Number:* 1. *Amount:* $500.

Eligibility Requirements: Applicant must be high school student; planning to enroll or expecting to enroll full-time at a four-year institution or university and studying in Maine. Available to U.S. citizens.

Application Requirements: Application, essay, resume, references, transcript. *Deadline:* April 1.

Contact: Kathy Mazzuchelli, Scholarship Committee Chair
Maine Recreation and Parks Association Scholarship
55 Bennett Drive
Caribou, ME 04736
Phone: 207-493-4224
E-mail: kathy@cariboumaine.org

MAINE RECREATION AND PARKS ASSOCIATION SCHOLARSHIP

Scholarship of $750 available to currently enrolled college sophomore, junior and senior candidates enrolled in a four-year recreation, parks, or leisure services curriculum or to nontraditional students seeking to continue their education in this field.

Academic Fields/Career Goals: Recreation, Parks, Leisure Studies.

Award: Scholarship for use in sophomore, junior, or senior years; not renewable. *Number:* 2. *Amount:* $750.

Eligibility Requirements: Applicant must be enrolled or expecting to enroll full-time at a four-year institution or university and studying in Maine. Available to U.S. citizens.

Application Requirements: Application, essay, resume, references, transcript. *Deadline:* April 1.

Contact: Kathy Mazzuchelli, Scholarship Committee Chair
Maine Recreation and Parks Association Scholarship
55 Bennett Drive
Caribou, ME 04736
Phone: 207-493-4224
E-mail: kathy@cariboumaine.org

MORRIS LAND CONSERVANCY http://www.morrislandconservancy.org

ROGERS FAMILY SCHOLARSHIP

• *See page 304*

RUSSELL W. MYERS SCHOLARSHIP

• *See page 304*

NATIONAL RECREATION AND PARK ASSOCIATION http://www.nrpa.org

AFRS STUDENT SCHOLARSHIP

Applicant must be currently enrolled in a NRPA accredited recreation/parks curriculum or related field. Number of awards varies.

Academic Fields/Career Goals: Recreation, Parks, Leisure Studies.

Award: Scholarship for use in freshman or sophomore years; not renewable. *Number:* varies. *Amount:* $500.

National Recreation and Park Association (continued)

Eligibility Requirements: Applicant must be enrolled or expecting to enroll full- or part-time at a four-year institution or university. Applicant must have 3.0 GPA or higher. Available to U.S. citizens.

Application Requirements: Application, essay, references, test scores, transcript. *Deadline:* June 1.

Contact: Jessica Lytle, Senior Manager
National Recreation and Park Association
Director of Professional Services, 22377 Belmont Ridge Road
Ashburn, VA 20148
Phone: 703-858-2150
Fax: 703-858-0974
E-mail: jlytle@nrpa.org

RELIGION/THEOLOGY

AMERICAN SCHOOL OF CLASSICAL STUDIES AT ATHENS http://www.ascsa.edu.gr

ASCSA SUMMER SESSIONS OPEN SCHOLARSHIPS

• *See page 83*

BANK OF AMERICA

WILLIAM HEATH EDUCATION SCHOLARSHIP FOR MINISTERS, PRIESTS AND MISSIONARIES

One-time award available to male students who are graduates from a high school in Alabama, Florida, Georgia, Kentucky, Louisiana, Maryland, Mississippi, North Carolina, South Carolina, Tennessee, Virginia, or West Virginia. Students must be under the age of 35 and pursuing an undergraduate or graduate degree in order to serve in the ministry, as a missionary or as a social worker. Primary consideration is given to those candidates who are of the Methodist or Episcopalian denominations.

Academic Fields/Career Goals: Religion/Theology; Social Services.

Award: Scholarship for use in freshman, sophomore, junior, senior, or graduate years; not renewable. *Number:* 15. *Amount:* $100–$350.

Eligibility Requirements: Applicant must be Episcopalian or Methodist; age 35 or under; enrolled or expecting to enroll full- or part-time at a two-year or four-year institution or university; male and resident of Alabama, Florida, Georgia, Kentucky, Louisiana, Maryland, Mississippi, North Carolina, South Carolina, Tennessee, Virginia, or West Virginia. Available to U.S. citizens.

Application Requirements: Application, essay, references, transcript, copy of high school diploma, birth certificate. *Deadline:* June 30.

Contact: Ms. Lori Nichols, Relationship Trust Officer
Bank of America
PO Box 479
Clearwater, FL 33757-0479
Phone: 727-298-5928
Fax: 727-298-5940
E-mail: lori.j.nichols@ustrust.com

COMMUNITY FOUNDATION FOR GREATER ATLANTA INC. http://www.atlcf.org

JAMES M. AND VIRGINIA M. SMYTH SCHOLARSHIP

• *See page 101*

DISCIPLES OF CHRIST HOMELAND MINISTRIES http://www.discipleshomemissions.org

DAVID TAMOTSU KAGIWADA MEMORIAL SCHOLARSHIP

Scholarship of $2000 is available to Asian-American ministerial students. Must be a member of the Christian Church (Disciples of Christ), demonstrate financial need, have a C+ average, be a full-time student, and be under care of a regional Commission on the Ministry. Application may be submitted electronically.

Academic Fields/Career Goals: Religion/Theology.

Award: Scholarship for use in freshman, sophomore, junior, or senior years; not renewable. *Number:* varies. *Amount:* $2000.

Eligibility Requirements: Applicant must be Disciple of Christ; Asian/Pacific Islander and enrolled or expecting to enroll full-time at a two-year or four-year institution or university. Applicant must have 2.5 GPA or higher. Available to U.S. and Canadian citizens.

Application Requirements: Application, financial need analysis, references, transcript. *Deadline:* March 15.

Contact: Anne Moyars, Administrative Assistant
Disciples of Christ Homeland Ministries
PO Box 1986
Indianapolis, IN 46204-1986
Phone: 317-713-2666
Fax: 317-635-4426
E-mail: amoyars@dhm.disciples.org

DISCIPLE CHAPLAINS SCHOLARSHIP

Scholarship of $2000 is available to first year seminarians. Must be a member of the Christian Church (Disciples of Christ), demonstrate financial need, have a C+ average, be a full-time student, and be under the care of a regional Commission on the Ministry. Application may be submitted electronically.

Academic Fields/Career Goals: Religion/Theology.

Award: Scholarship for use in freshman year; not renewable. *Number:* varies. *Amount:* $2000.

Eligibility Requirements: Applicant must be Disciple of Christ; high school student and planning to enroll or expecting to enroll full-time at a four-year institution or university. Applicant must have 2.5 GPA or higher. Available to U.S. citizens.

Application Requirements: Application, financial need analysis, references, transcript. *Deadline:* March 15.

Contact: Anne Moyars, Administrative Assistant
Disciples of Christ Homeland Ministries
PO Box 1986
Indianapolis, IN 46204-1986
Phone: 317-713-2666
Fax: 317-635-4426
E-mail: amoyars@dhm.disciples.org

EDWIN G. AND LAURETTA M. MICHAEL SCHOLARSHIP

Scholarship of $2000 available to ministers wives. Must be a member of the Christian Church (Disciples of Christ), demonstrate financial need, have a C+ average, be a full-time student, and be under the care of a regional Commission on the Ministry. Application may be submitted electronically.

Academic Fields/Career Goals: Religion/Theology.

Award: Scholarship for use in freshman, sophomore, junior, or senior years; not renewable. *Number:* varies. *Amount:* $2000.

Eligibility Requirements: Applicant must be Disciple of Christ; enrolled or expecting to enroll full-time at a two-year or four-year institution or university and married female. Applicant must have 2.5 GPA or higher. Available to U.S. and non-U.S. citizens.

Application Requirements: Application, financial need analysis, references, transcript. *Deadline:* March 15.

Contact: Anne Moyars, Administrative Assistant
Disciples of Christ Homeland Ministries
PO Box 1986
Indianapolis, IN 46204-1986
Phone: 317-713-2666
Fax: 317-635-4426
E-mail: amoyars@dhm.disciples.org

KATHERINE J. SHUTZE MEMORIAL SCHOLARSHIP

Scholarship of $2000 is available to female seminary students. Must be a member of the Christian Church (Disciples of Christ), demonstrate financial need, have a C+ average, be a full-time student, and be under the care of a regional Commission on the Ministry. Application may be submitted electronically.

Academic Fields/Career Goals: Religion/Theology.

Award: Scholarship for use in freshman, sophomore, junior, or senior years; not renewable. *Number:* varies. *Amount:* $2000.

Eligibility Requirements: Applicant must be Disciple of Christ; enrolled or expecting to enroll full-time at a four-year institution or university and female. Applicant must have 2.5 GPA or higher. Available to U.S. and non-U.S. citizens.

Application Requirements: Application, financial need analysis, references, transcript. *Deadline:* March 15.

Contact: Anne Moyars, Administrative Assistant
Disciples of Christ Homeland Ministries
PO Box 1986
Indianapolis, IN 46204-1986
Phone: 317-713-2666
Fax: 317-635-4426
E-mail: amoyars@dhm.disciples.org

ROWLEY/MINISTERIAL EDUCATION SCHOLARSHIP

Scholarship of $2000 is available to seminary students preparing for the ministry. Must be a member of the Christian Church (Disciples of Christ), demonstrate financial need, have a C+ average, be a full-time student and be under the care of a regional Commission on the Ministry. Application may be submitted electronically.

Academic Fields/Career Goals: Religion/Theology.

Award: Scholarship for use in freshman, sophomore, junior, senior, or graduate years; not renewable. *Number:* varies. *Amount:* $2000.

Eligibility Requirements: Applicant must be Disciple of Christ and enrolled or expecting to enroll full-time at a two-year or four-year institution or university. Applicant must have 2.5 GPA or higher. Available to U.S. and non-U.S. citizens.

Application Requirements: Application, financial need analysis, references, transcript. *Deadline:* March 15.

Contact: Anne Moyars, Administrative Assistant
Disciples of Christ Homeland Ministries
PO Box 1986
Indianapolis, IN 46204-1986
Phone: 317-713-2666
Fax: 317-635-4426
E-mail: amoyars@dhm.disciples.org

STAR SUPPORTER SCHOLARSHIP/LOAN

Scholarships in the form of forgivable loans are available to Black/African-Americans preparing for ministry. One year of full-time professional ministry reduces loan by one third. Three years of service repays loan. Must be member of the Christian Church (Disciples of Christ), have a C+ average, demonstrate financial need, be a full-time student in an accredited school or seminary and be under the care of a regional Commission on the Ministry. Application may be submitted electronically.

Academic Fields/Career Goals: Religion/Theology.

Award: Forgivable loan for use in freshman, sophomore, junior, or senior years; not renewable. *Number:* varies. *Amount:* $2000.

Eligibility Requirements: Applicant must be Disciple of Christ; Black (non-Hispanic) and enrolled or expecting to enroll full-time at a two-year or four-year institution or university. Applicant must have 2.5 GPA or higher. Available to U.S. citizens.

Application Requirements: Application, financial need analysis, references, transcript. *Deadline:* March 15.

Contact: Anne Moyars, Administrative Assistant
Disciples of Christ Homeland Ministries
PO Box 1986
Indianapolis, IN 46204-1986
Phone: 317-713-2666
Fax: 317-635-4426
E-mail: amoyars@dhm.disciples.org

ED E. AND GLADYS HURLEY FOUNDATION

ED E. AND GLADYS HURLEY FOUNDATION SCHOLARSHIP

Provides scholarships up to $1000 per year per student. Applicant must be Protestant enrolled or expecting to enroll full or part-time at a two-year or four-year institution or university and studying in Texas. Available to U.S. citizens.

Academic Fields/Career Goals: Religion/Theology.

Award: Scholarship for use in freshman, sophomore, junior, senior, graduate, or postgraduate years; not renewable. *Number:* 100–150. *Amount:* up to $1000.

Eligibility Requirements: Applicant must be Protestant; enrolled or expecting to enroll full- or part-time at a two-year or four-year institution or university; resident of Arkansas, Louisiana, or Texas and studying in Texas. Available to U.S. citizens.

Application Requirements: Application, financial need analysis, references. *Deadline:* April 30.

Contact: Rose Davis, Financial Aid Coordinator
Ed E. and Gladys Hurley Foundation
Houston Graduate School-Theology, 2501 Central Parkway, Suite A19
Houston, TX 77092
Phone: 713-942-9505
E-mail: rdavis@hgst.edu

FIRST PRESBYTERIAN CHURCH http://www.firstchurchtulsa.org

ELSA EVERETT MEMORIAL TRUST FUND

Scholarships for students from First Presbyterian Church who are studying for the ministry or Christian education work.

Academic Fields/Career Goals: Religion/Theology.

Award: Scholarship for use in freshman, sophomore, junior, senior, graduate, or postgraduate years; not renewable. *Number:* varies. *Amount:* $500–$2000.

Eligibility Requirements: Applicant must be Presbyterian and enrolled or expecting to enroll full-time at a two-year or four-year or technical institution or university. Available to U.S. and non-U.S. citizens.

Application Requirements: Application, financial need analysis, interview, references, transcript. *Deadline:* April 15.

Contact: Tonye Briscoe, Facilities and Benefits Coordinator
First Presbyterian Church
706 South Boston Avenue
Tulsa, OK 74119-1629
Phone: 918-584-4701
Fax: 918-584-5233
E-mail: tbriscoe@firstchurchtulsa.org

FIRST PRESBYTERIAN CHURCH SCHOLARSHIP PROGRAM

Awards to students pursuing full-time study at an accredited college, university or seminary. Preference given to church members in Tulsa, East Oklahoma, Synod of Sun, and at-large. Minimum 2.0 GPA. Must be a communicant member of the Presbyterian Church (U.S.A.).

Academic Fields/Career Goals: Religion/Theology.

Award: Scholarship for use in freshman, sophomore, junior, senior, or graduate years; not renewable. *Number:* 3–5. *Amount:* $500–$2000.

Eligibility Requirements: Applicant must be Presbyterian and enrolled or expecting to enroll full-time at a four-year institution or university. Available to U.S. citizens.

Application Requirements: Application, financial need analysis, interview, references, transcript. *Deadline:* April 15.

Contact: Tonye Briscoe, Administrative Assistant
First Presbyterian Church
709 South Boston Avenue
Tulsa, OK 74119-1629
Phone: 918-584-4701 Ext. 240
Fax: 918-584-5233
E-mail: tbriscoe@firstchurchtulsa.org

ULLERY CHARITABLE TRUST FUND

Awards to assist students pursuing full-time Christian work with the Presbyterian Church. Must be a member of the Presbyterian Church, preference given to members of the First Presbyterian Church, Tulsa, OK.

Academic Fields/Career Goals: Religion/Theology.

Award: Scholarship for use in freshman year; not renewable. *Number:* 5–7. *Amount:* $500–$2000.

Eligibility Requirements: Applicant must be Presbyterian; high school student and planning to enroll or expecting to enroll full-time at a four-year institution or university. Available to U.S. and non-U.S. citizens.

First Presbyterian Church (continued)

Application Requirements: Application, financial need analysis, interview, references, transcript. *Deadline:* April 15.

Contact: Tonye Briscoe, Facilities and Benefits Coordinator
First Presbyterian Church
706 South Boston Avenue
Tulsa, OK 74119-1629
Phone: 918-584-4701
Fax: 918-584-5233
E-mail: tbriscoe@firstchurchtulsa.org

GRAND CHAPTER OF CALIFORNIA-ORDER OF THE EASTERN STAR http://www.oescal.org

SCHOLARSHIPS FOR EDUCATION, BUSINESS AND RELIGION
• *See page 142*

LINCOLN COMMUNITY FOUNDATION http://www.lcf.org

GEORGE AND LYNNA GENE COOK SCHOLARSHIP
• *See page 233*

MEMORIAL FOUNDATION FOR JEWISH CULTURE http://www.mfjc.org

MEMORIAL FOUNDATION FOR JEWISH CULTURE INTERNATIONAL SCHOLARSHIP PROGRAM FOR COMMUNITY SERVICE
• *See page 96*

MEMORIAL FOUNDATION FOR JEWISH CULTURE SCHOLARSHIPS FOR POST-RABBINICAL STUDENTS
• *See page 234*

NATIONAL ASSOCIATION OF PASTORAL MUSICIANS http://www.npm.org

ELAINE RENDLER-RENE DOSOGNE-GEORGETOWN CHORALE SCHOLARSHIP
• *See page 414*

FUNK FAMILY MEMORIAL SCHOLARSHIP
• *See page 414*

GIA PUBLICATION PASTORAL MUSICIAN SCHOLARSHIP
• *See page 414*

MUSONICS SCHOLARSHIP
• *See page 414*

NATIONAL ASSOCIATION OF PASTORAL MUSICIANS MEMBERS' SCHOLARSHIP
• *See page 414*

NPM KOINONIA/BOARD OF DIRECTORS SCHOLARSHIP
• *See page 415*

OREGON CATHOLIC PRESS SCHOLARSHIP
• *See page 415*

PALUCH FAMILY FOUNDATION/WORLD LIBRARY PUBLICATIONS SCHOLARSHIP
• *See page 416*

PRESBYTERIAN CHURCH (USA) http://www.pcusa.org/financialaid

SAMUEL ROBINSON AWARD

Prize granted to full-time junior and senior students attending a Presbyterian related college or university who successfully recite answers to the Westminster Shorter Catechism and write an essay on an assigned topic.

Academic Fields/Career Goals: Religion/Theology.

Award: Prize for use in junior or senior years; not renewable. *Number:* 60. *Amount:* $250–$4000.

Eligibility Requirements: Applicant must be Presbyterian and enrolled or expecting to enroll full-time at a four-year institution or university. Available to U.S. citizens.

Application Requirements: Applicant must enter a contest, essay, references. *Deadline:* April 1.

Contact: Mrs. Frances Cook, Associate
Presbyterian Church (USA)
100 Witherspoon Street
Louisville, KY 40202-1396
Phone: 888-728-7228 Ext. 5776
Fax: 502-569-8766
E-mail: frances.cook@pcusa.org

SOCIETY FOR THE SCIENTIFIC STUDY OF SEXUALITY http://www.sexscience.org

SOCIETY FOR THE SCIENTIFIC STUDY OF SEXUALITY STUDENT RESEARCH GRANT
• *See page 129*

UNITARIAN UNIVERSALIST ASSOCIATION http://www.uua.org

ROY H. POLLACK SCHOLARSHIP

Scholarship given to a junior or senior student with academic excellence and good character, studying for ordained ministry who actively participates in extracurricular activities at their theological school. Applicant must be pursuing in Divinity degree.

Academic Fields/Career Goals: Religion/Theology.

Award: Scholarship for use in junior or senior years; not renewable. *Number:* varies. *Amount:* varies.

Eligibility Requirements: Applicant must be Unitarian Universalist and enrolled or expecting to enroll full- or part-time at a four-year institution or university. Available to U.S. citizens.

Application Requirements: Application, financial need analysis. *Deadline:* April 15.

Contact: Ms. Hillary Goodridge, Program Director
Unitarian Universalist Association
PO Box 301149
Boston, MA 02130
Phone: 617-971-9600
Fax: 617-971-0029
E-mail: uufp@aol.com

UNITED METHODIST COMMUNICATIONS http://www.umcom.org

LEONARD M. PERRYMAN COMMUNICATIONS SCHOLARSHIP FOR ETHNIC MINORITY STUDENTS
• *See page 187*

SCIENCE, TECHNOLOGY, AND SOCIETY

AMERICAN CHEMICAL SOCIETY, RUBBER DIVISION http://www.rubber.org

AMERICAN CHEMICAL SOCIETY, RUBBER DIVISION UNDERGRADUATE SCHOLARSHIP
• *See page 153*

AMERICAN INSTITUTE OF AERONAUTICS AND ASTRONAUTICS http://www.aiaa.org

AIAA UNDERGRADUATE SCHOLARSHIP
• *See page 84*

ARIZONA HYDROLOGICAL SOCIETY http://www.azhydrosoc.org

ARIZONA HYDROLOGICAL SOCIETY SCHOLARSHIP
• *See page 215*

ARMED FORCES COMMUNICATIONS AND ELECTRONICS ASSOCIATION, EDUCATIONAL FOUNDATION http://www.afcea.org

VICE ADMIRAL JERRY O. TUTTLE, USN (RET.) AND MRS. BARBARA A. TUTTLE SCIENCE AND TECHNOLOGY SCHOLARSHIP
• *See page 289*

CATCHING THE DREAM http://www.catchingthedream.org

MATH, ENGINEERING, SCIENCE, BUSINESS, EDUCATION, COMPUTERS SCHOLARSHIPS
• *See page 139*

NATIVE AMERICAN LEADERSHIP IN EDUCATION (NALE)
• *See page 139*

DAVIDSON INSTITUTE FOR TALENT DEVELOPMENT http://www.davidsoninstitute.org

DAVIDSON FELLOWS
• *See page 390*

DENVER FOUNDATION http://www.denverfoundation.org

RBC DAIN RAUSCHER COLORADO SCHOLARSHIP FUND
• *See page 263*

EXPLORERS CLUB http://www.explorers.org/

YOUTH ACTIVITY FUND
• *See page 423*

GREAT LAKES COMMISSION http://www.glc.org

CAROL A. RATZA MEMORIAL SCHOLARSHIP
• *See page 179*

HEALTHCARE INFORMATION AND MANAGEMENT SYSTEMS SOCIETY FOUNDATION http://www.himss.org

HIMSS FOUNDATION SCHOLARSHIP PROGRAM
• *See page 326*

INNOVATION AND SCIENCE COUNCIL OF BRITISH COLUMBIA http://www.bcinnovationcouncil.com

PAUL AND HELEN TRUSSEL SCIENCE AND TECHNOLOGY SCHOLARSHIP
• *See page 87*

INTERNATIONAL TECHNOLOGY EDUCATION ASSOCIATION http://www.iteaconnect.org

INTERNATIONAL TECHNOLOGY EDUCATION ASSOCIATION UNDERGRADUATE SCHOLARSHIP IN TECHNOLOGY EDUCATION
• *See page 231*

KE ALI'I PAUAHI FOUNDATION http://www.pauahi.org

DENIS WONG & ASSOCIATES SCHOLARSHIP
• *See page 359*

KOREAN-AMERICAN SCIENTISTS AND ENGINEERS ASSOCIATION http://www.ksea.org

KSEA SCHOLARSHIPS
• *See page 249*

MONSANTO AGRIBUSINESS SCHOLARSHIP http://www.monsanto.ca

MONSANTO CANADA OPPORTUNITY SCHOLARSHIP PROGRAM
• *See page 70*

NASA RHODE ISLAND SPACE GRANT CONSORTIUM http://www.planetary.brown.edu/RI_Space_Grant

NASA RHODE ISLAND SPACE GRANT CONSORTIUM OUTREACH SCHOLARSHIP FOR UNDERGRADUATE STUDENTS
• *See page 295*

NASA SOUTH DAKOTA SPACE GRANT CONSORTIUM http://www.sdsmt.edu/space/

SOUTH DAKOTA SPACE GRANT CONSORTIUM UNDERGRADUATE SCHOLARSHIPS
• *See page 120*

SAN DIEGO FOUNDATION http://www.sdfoundation.org

BIOCOM SCHOLARSHIP
• *See page 135*

QUALCOMM SAN DIEGO SCIENCE, TECHNOLOGY, ENGINEERING, AND MATHEMATICS SCHOLARSHIP
• *See page 271*

SIEMENS FOUNDATION/SIEMENS-WESTINGHOUSE SCHOLARSHIP http://www.siemens-foundation.org

SIEMENS COMPETITION IN MATH, SCIENCE AND TECHNOLOGY

$1000 to $3000 scholarships for high school students willing to challenge themselves through science research. Students may enter as individuals or as part of a team.

Academic Fields/Career Goals: Science, Technology, and Society.

Award: Scholarship for use in freshman year; not renewable. *Number:* varies. *Amount:* $1000–$3000.

Eligibility Requirements: Applicant must be high school student and planning to enroll or expecting to enroll full-time at a four-year institution or university. Available to U.S. citizens.

Application Requirements: Application, applicant must enter a contest. *Deadline:* October 2.

Contact: Scholarship Committee
Siemens Foundation/Siemens-Westinghouse Scholarship
170 Wood Avenue South
Iselin, NJ 08830
Phone: 877-822-5233
Fax: 732-603-5890
E-mail: foundation.us@siemens.com

SIGMA XI, THE SCIENTIFIC RESEARCH SOCIETY http://www.sigmaxi.org

SIGMA XI GRANTS-IN-AID OF RESEARCH
• *See page 78*

SOCIETY FOR TECHNICAL COMMUNICATION http://www.stc.org

SOCIETY FOR TECHNICAL COMMUNICATION SCHOLARSHIP PROGRAM
• *See page 185*

SOCIETY OF HISPANIC PROFESSIONAL ENGINEERS http://www.shpe.org

AHETEMS SCHOLARSHIPS
• *See page 273*

SOCIETY OF HISPANIC PROFESSIONAL ENGINEERS FOUNDATION http://www.henaac.org

SOCIETY OF HISPANIC PROFESSIONAL ENGINEERS FOUNDATION
• *See page 162*

UNITED NEGRO COLLEGE FUND http://www.uncf.org

CHARLES E. CULPEPPER SCHOLARSHIP

Scholarship of $1000 for students attending UNCF member colleges and universities who are completing the Fisk Pre-Medicine program. Should have minimum GPA of 3.0 with majors in Science.

Academic Fields/Career Goals: Science, Technology, and Society.

Award: Scholarship for use in freshman, sophomore, junior, senior, or graduate years; not renewable. *Number:* varies. *Amount:* $1000.

Eligibility Requirements: Applicant must be Black (non-Hispanic) and enrolled or expecting to enroll full- or part-time at a four-year institution or university. Applicant must have 3.0 GPA or higher. Available to U.S. and non-U.S. citizens.

United Negro College Fund (continued)

Application Requirements: Application, financial need analysis, FAFSA, Student Aid Report (SAR). *Deadline:* varies.

Contact: Director, Program Services
United Negro College Fund
8260 Willow Oaks Corporate Drive
PO Box 10444
Fairfax, VA 22031-8044
Phone: 800-331-2244
E-mail: rebecca.bennett@uncf.org

HEINZ ENVIRONMENTAL FELLOWS PROGRAM
• *See page 136*

UNIVERSITIES SPACE RESEARCH ASSOCIATION http://www.usra.edu

UNIVERSITIES SPACE RESEARCH ASSOCIATION SCHOLARSHIP PROGRAM
• *See page 88*

VIRGINIA BUSINESS AND PROFESSIONAL WOMEN'S FOUNDATION http://www.vabpwfoundation.org

WOMEN IN SCIENCE AND TECHNOLOGY SCHOLARSHIP
• *See page 136*

WATER ENVIRONMENT FEDERATION http://www.wef.org

CANHAM GRADUATE STUDIES SCHOLARSHIPS
• *See page 136*

WEST VIRGINIA HIGHER EDUCATION POLICY COMMISSION-OFFICE OF FINANCIAL AID AND OUTREACH SERVICES http://wvhepcnew.wvnet.edu/

WEST VIRGINIA ENGINEERING, SCIENCE AND TECHNOLOGY SCHOLARSHIP PROGRAM
• *See page 252*

SOCIAL SCIENCES

ALBERTA HERITAGE SCHOLARSHIP FUND/ ALBERTA SCHOLARSHIP PROGRAMS http://www.alis.gov.ab.ca

LOIS HOLE HUMANITIES AND SOCIAL SCIENCES SCHOLARSHIP
• *See page 359*

AMERICAN CRIMINAL JUSTICE ASSOCIATION-LAMBDA ALPHA EPSILON http://www.acjalae.org

AMERICAN CRIMINAL JUSTICE ASSOCIATION-LAMBDA ALPHA EPSILON NATIONAL SCHOLARSHIP
• *See page 200*

AMERICAN FEDERATION OF STATE, COUNTY, AND MUNICIPAL EMPLOYEES http://www.afscme.org

AFSCME/UNCF UNION SCHOLARS PROGRAM
• *See page 80*

AMERICAN SOCIETY OF CRIMINOLOGY http://www.asc41.com

AMERICAN SOCIETY OF CRIMINOLOGY GENE CARTE STUDENT PAPER COMPETITION
• *See page 201*

BUSINESS AND PROFESSIONAL WOMEN'S FOUNDATION http://www.bpwfoundation.org

BPW CAREER ADVANCEMENT SCHOLARSHIP PROGRAM FOR WOMEN
• *See page 130*

CANADIAN INSTITUTE OF UKRAINIAN STUDIES http://www.cius.ca

LEO J. KRYSA UNDERGRADUATE SCHOLARSHIP
• *See page 95*

CATCHING THE DREAM http://www.catchingthedream.org

MATH, ENGINEERING, SCIENCE, BUSINESS, EDUCATION, COMPUTERS SCHOLARSHIPS
• *See page 139*

COMMUNITY FOUNDATION FOR GREATER ATLANTA INC. http://www.atlcf.org

STEVE DEARDUFF SCHOLARSHIP
• *See page 336*

INSTITUTE FOR HUMANE STUDIES http://www.theihs.org

HUMANE STUDIES FELLOWSHIPS
• *See page 179*

MORRIS K. UDALL FOUNDATION http://www.udall.gov

MORRIS K. UDALL SCHOLARS-NATIVE AMERICAN AND ALASKA NATIVE
• *See page 340*

NATIONAL BLACK POLICE ASSOCIATION http://www.blackpolice.org

ALPHONSO DEAL SCHOLARSHIP AWARD
• *See page 201*

NATIONAL INSTITUTES OF HEALTH http://www.ugsp.nih.gov

NIH UNDERGRADUATE SCHOLARSHIP PROGRAM FOR STUDENTS FROM DISADVANTAGED BACKGROUNDS
• *See page 134*

OFFICE AND PROFESSIONAL EMPLOYEES INTERNATIONAL UNION http://www.opeiu.org

JOHN KELLY LABOR STUDIES SCHOLARSHIP FUND
• *See page 221*

ORGONE BIOPHYSICAL RESEARCH LABORATORY http://www.orgonelab.org

LOU HOCHBERG-HIGH SCHOOL ESSAY AWARDS

One-time award of up to $500 will be given for the best high school student essay paper addressing Wilhlem Reich's sociological discoveries. Maximum length of 25 pages.

Academic Fields/Career Goals: Social Sciences.

Award: Prize for use in freshman year; not renewable. *Number:* 1. *Amount:* up to $500.

Eligibility Requirements: Applicant must be high school student and planning to enroll or expecting to enroll full- or part-time at a four-year institution or university. Available to U.S. and non-U.S. citizens.

Application Requirements: Applicant must enter a contest, essay, transcript, photocopy of student ID. *Deadline:* continuous.

Contact: Director
Orgone Biophysical Research Laboratory
PO Box 1148
Ashland, OR 97520
Phone: 541-552-0118
Fax: 541-552-0118
E-mail: info@orgonelab.org

PARAPSYCHOLOGY FOUNDATION http://www.parapsychology.org

CHARLES T. AND JUDITH A. TART STUDENT INCENTIVE

An annual incentive is awarded to promote the research of an undergraduate or graduate student, who shows dedication to work within parapsychology. For more details see Web site: http://www.parapsychology.org.

Academic Fields/Career Goals: Social Sciences.

Award: Scholarship for use in freshman, sophomore, junior, senior, graduate, or postgraduate years; not renewable. *Number:* 1. *Amount:* $500.

Eligibility Requirements: Applicant must be enrolled or expecting to enroll full-time at a two-year or four-year institution or university. Available to U.S. citizens.

Application Requirements: Application, essay, references, transcript. *Deadline:* October 15.

Contact: Lisette Coly, Vice President
Parapsychology Foundation
PO Box 1562
New York, NY 10021-0043
Phone: 212-628-1550
Fax: 212-628-1559
E-mail: office@parapsychology.org

EILEEN J. GARRETT SCHOLARSHIP FOR PARAPSYCHOLOGICAL RESEARCH

Scholarship requires applicants to demonstrate academic interest in the science of parapsychology through completed research, term papers, and courses for which credit was received. Those with only a general interest will not be considered. Visit Web site for additional information.

Academic Fields/Career Goals: Social Sciences.

Award: Scholarship for use in freshman, sophomore, junior, senior, graduate, or postgraduate years; not renewable. *Number:* 1. *Amount:* $3000.

Eligibility Requirements: Applicant must be enrolled or expecting to enroll full-time at a two-year or four-year institution or university. Available to U.S. citizens.

Application Requirements: Application, essay, references, transcript. *Deadline:* July 15.

Contact: Lisette Coly, Vice President
Parapsychology Foundation
PO Box 1562
New York, NY 10021-0043
Phone: 212-628-1550
Fax: 212-628-1559
E-mail: office@parapsychology.org

PHI ALPHA THETA HISTORY HONOR SOCIETY INC. http://www.phialphatheta.org

PHI ALPHA THETA WORLD HISTORY ASSOCIATION PAPER PRIZE

• *See page 348*

POLISH HERITAGE ASSOCIATION OF MARYLAND http://www.pha-md.org

DR. JOSEPHINE WTULICH MEMORIAL SCHOLARSHIP

• *See page 84*

ROBERT P. PULA MEMORIAL SCHOLARSHIP

• *See page 360*

SIGMA XI, THE SCIENTIFIC RESEARCH SOCIETY http://www.sigmaxi.org

SIGMA XI GRANTS-IN-AID OF RESEARCH

• *See page 78*

SOCIAL SCIENCES AND HUMANITIES RESEARCH COUNCIL OF CANADA http://www.sshrc.ca

RESEARCH DEVELOPMENT INITIATIVE

• *See page 360*

SOCIETY FOR APPLIED ANTHROPOLOGY http://www.sfaa.net

PETER KONG-MING NEW STUDENT PRIZE

• *See page 129*

SOCIETY FOR THE SCIENTIFIC STUDY OF SEXUALITY http://www.sexscience.org

SOCIETY FOR THE SCIENTIFIC STUDY OF SEXUALITY STUDENT RESEARCH GRANT

• *See page 129*

STRAIGHTFORWARD MEDIA http://www.straightforwardmedia.com

STRAIGHTFORWARD MEDIA LIBERAL ARTS SCHOLARSHIP

• *See page 99*

SUNSHINE LADY FOUNDATION INC. http://www.sunshinelady.org

COUNSELOR, ADVOCATE, AND SUPPORT STAFF SCHOLARSHIP PROGRAM

• *See page 167*

WOMEN IN FEDERAL LAW ENFORCEMENT http://www.wifle.org

WIFLE SCHOLARSHIP PROGRAM

• *See page 198*

Y'S MEN INTERNATIONAL http://www.ysmenusa.com

ALEXANDER SCHOLARSHIP LOAN FUND

• *See page 152*

ZETA PHI BETA SORORITY INC. NATIONAL EDUCATIONAL FOUNDATION http://www.zphib1920.org

LULLELIA W. HARRISON SCHOLARSHIP IN COUNSELING

• *See page 167*

SOCIAL SERVICES

AMERICAN FEDERATION OF STATE, COUNTY, AND MUNICIPAL EMPLOYEES http://www.afscme.org

AFSCME/UNCF UNION SCHOLARS PROGRAM

• *See page 80*

AMERICAN LEGION AUXILIARY DEPARTMENT OF ARIZONA http://www.azlegion.org/majorp~2.htm

AMERICAN LEGION AUXILIARY DEPARTMENT OF ARIZONA WILMA HOYAL-MAXINE CHILTON MEMORIAL SCHOLARSHIP

• *See page 471*

BANK OF AMERICA

WILLIAM HEATH EDUCATION SCHOLARSHIP FOR MINISTERS, PRIESTS AND MISSIONARIES

• *See page 478*

BETHESDA LUTHERAN HOMES AND SERVICES, INC. http://www.blhs.org

DEVELOPMENTAL DISABILITIES AWARENESS AWARDS FOR LUTHERAN HIGH SCHOOL STUDENTS

• *See page 335*

DEVELOPMENTAL DISABILITIES SCHOLASTIC ACHIEVEMENT SCHOLARSHIP FOR LUTHERAN COLLEGE STUDENTS

• *See page 211*

COLLEGEBOUND FOUNDATION http://www.collegeboundfoundation.org

JEANETTE R. WOLMAN SCHOLARSHIP
• See page 165

CONTINENTAL SOCIETY, DAUGHTERS OF INDIAN WARS

CONTINENTAL SOCIETY, DAUGHTERS OF INDIAN WARS SCHOLARSHIP
• See page 227

GENERAL BOARD OF HIGHER EDUCATION AND MINISTRY http://www.gbhem.org

EDITH M. ALLEN SCHOLARSHIP
• See page 228

HEALTH PROFESSIONS EDUCATION FOUNDATION http://www.healthprofessions.ca.gov

KAISER PERMANENTE ALLIED HEALTHCARE SCHOLARSHIP
• See page 337

JEWISH VOCATIONAL SERVICE–CHICAGO http://www.jvschicago.org

JEWISH FEDERATION ACADEMIC SCHOLARSHIP PROGRAM

Scholarship for Jewish students who are born or raised in Chicago metropolitan area or Northwest Indiana or one continuous year of full-time employment in Chicago metropolitan area prior to starting professional education. Must intend to remain in the Chicago metropolitan area after completing school. For more details visit Web site: http://www.jvschicago.org/scholarship.

Academic Fields/Career Goals: Social Services.

Award: Scholarship for use in junior, senior, or graduate years; renewable. *Number:* up to 100. *Amount:* varies.

Eligibility Requirements: Applicant must be of Jewish heritage; enrolled or expecting to enroll full-time at a four-year institution or university and resident of Illinois or Indiana. Available to U.S. citizens.

Application Requirements: Application, financial need analysis, references. *Deadline:* February 15.

Contact: Scholarship Secretary
Jewish Vocational Service–Chicago
216 West Jackson Boulevard, Suite 700
Chicago, IL 60606
Phone: 312-673-3457
Fax: 312-553-5544
E-mail: jvsscholarship@jvschicago.org

MARGARET MCNAMARA MEMORIAL FUND http://www.wbfn.org

MARGARET MCNAMARA MEMORIAL FUND FELLOWSHIPS
• See page 166

MARYLAND HIGHER EDUCATION COMMISSION http://www.mhec.state.md.us

GRADUATE AND PROFESSIONAL SCHOLARSHIP PROGRAM-MARYLAND
• See page 212

JANET L. HOFFMANN LOAN ASSISTANCE REPAYMENT PROGRAM
• See page 234

MEMORIAL FOUNDATION FOR JEWISH CULTURE http://www.mfjc.org

MEMORIAL FOUNDATION FOR JEWISH CULTURE INTERNATIONAL SCHOLARSHIP PROGRAM FOR COMMUNITY SERVICE
• See page 96

MEMORIAL FOUNDATION FOR JEWISH CULTURE SCHOLARSHIPS FOR POST-RABBINICAL STUDENTS
• See page 234

MENTAL HEALTH ASSOCIATION IN NEW YORK STATE INC. http://www.mhanys.org

EDNA AIMES SCHOLARSHIP
• See page 128

MORRIS K. UDALL FOUNDATION http://www.udall.gov

MORRIS K. UDALL SCHOLARS-NATIVE AMERICAN AND ALASKA NATIVE
• See page 340

NATIONAL BLACK POLICE ASSOCIATION http://www.blackpolice.org

ALPHONSO DEAL SCHOLARSHIP AWARD
• See page 201

NEW YORK STATE EDUCATION DEPARTMENT http://www.highered.nysed.gov

REGENTS PROFESSIONAL OPPORTUNITY SCHOLARSHIP
• See page 60

PILOT INTERNATIONAL FOUNDATION http://www.pilotinternational.org

PILOT INTERNATIONAL FOUNDATION RUBY NEWHALL MEMORIAL SCHOLARSHIP
• See page 342

SUNSHINE LADY FOUNDATION INC. http://www.sunshinelady.org

COUNSELOR, ADVOCATE, AND SUPPORT STAFF SCHOLARSHIP PROGRAM
• See page 167

UNITED COMMUNITY SERVICES FOR WORKING FAMILIES

TED BRICKER SCHOLARSHIP

One-time award available to child of a union member who is a parent or guardian. Must be a resident of Pennsylvania. Must submit essay that is clear, concise, persuasive, and shows a commitment to the community.

Academic Fields/Career Goals: Social Services.

Award: Scholarship for use in freshman year; not renewable. *Number:* 1. *Amount:* up to $500.

Eligibility Requirements: Applicant must be high school student; planning to enroll or expecting to enroll full-time at a four-year institution or university and resident of Pennsylvania. Applicant or parent of applicant must be member of AFL-CIO. Applicant or parent of applicant must have employment or volunteer experience in community service. Available to U.S. citizens.

Application Requirements: Application, essay, financial need analysis, transcript. *Deadline:* June 27.

Contact: Ruth Mathews, Executive Director
United Community Services for Working Families
116 North Fifth Street
Reading, PA 19601
Phone: 610-374-3319
Fax: 610-374-6521
E-mail: ruth.mathews@comcast.net

UNITED NEGRO COLLEGE FUND http://www.uncf.org

FANNIE MAE FOUNDATION SCHOLARSHIP

Scholarship benefits students attending one of the following schools: Benedict College, Bethune-Cookman College, Johnson C. Smith University, LeMoyne-Owen College or UNCF member colleges and universities. Minimum 3.0 GPA required. Prospective applicants should complete the Student Profile found at Web site: http://www.uncf.org.

Academic Fields/Career Goals: Social Services.

Award: Scholarship for use in junior year; not renewable. *Number:* 12. *Amount:* varies.

Eligibility Requirements: Applicant must be Black (non-Hispanic) and enrolled or expecting to enroll full- or part-time at a four-year institution or university. Applicant must have 3.0 GPA or higher. Available to U.S. citizens.

Application Requirements: Application, financial need analysis. *Deadline:* November 5.

Contact: Director, Program Services
United Negro College Fund
8260 Willow Oaks Corporate Drive
PO Box 10444
Fairfax, VA 22031-8044
Phone: 800-331-2244
E-mail: rebecca.bennett@uncf.org

SODEXHO SCHOLARSHIP
• *See page 343*

WHOMENTORS.COM INC. http://www.WHOmentors.com

GENERATION "E" GRANTS AND SCHOLARSHIPS

Awards to encourage both full-time and part-time students of at least 21 years of age to obtain formal mentor education and competency certification and to seek designation as an appointed mentor. Applicants should have a specific interest in mentoring. The dollar value of the award varies annually. Minimum 2.0 GPA required.

Academic Fields/Career Goals: Social Services.

Award: Grant for use in freshman, sophomore, junior, senior, or graduate years; not renewable. *Number:* 10,000. *Amount:* varies.

Eligibility Requirements: Applicant must be age 17-21 and enrolled or expecting to enroll full- or part-time at a four-year institution or university. Applicant or parent of applicant must have employment or volunteer experience in mentoring/advising. Available to U.S. and non-U.S. citizens.

Application Requirements: Application, autobiography, essay, financial need analysis, interview, photo, references, self-addressed stamped envelope, test scores, transcript. *Deadline:* May 15.

Contact: Rauhmel Fox Robinson, President
WHOmentors.com Inc.
110 Pacific Avenue, Suite 250
San Francisco, CA 94111
Phone: 888-946-6368
E-mail: rauhmel@whomentors.com

Y'S MEN INTERNATIONAL http://www.ysmenusa.com

ALEXANDER SCHOLARSHIP LOAN FUND
• *See page 152*

ZETA PHI BETA SORORITY INC. NATIONAL EDUCATIONAL FOUNDATION http://www.zphib1920.org

LULLELIA W. HARRISON SCHOLARSHIP IN COUNSELING
• *See page 167*

SPECIAL EDUCATION

ALBERTA HERITAGE SCHOLARSHIP FUND/ ALBERTA SCHOLARSHIP PROGRAMS http://www.alis.gov.ab.ca

ANNA AND JOHN KOLESAR MEMORIAL SCHOLARSHIPS
• *See page 221*

AMERICAN LEGION AUXILIARY DEPARTMENT OF ARIZONA http://www.azlegion.org/majorp~2.htm

AMERICAN LEGION AUXILIARY DEPARTMENT OF ARIZONA WILMA HOYAL-MAXINE CHILTON MEMORIAL SCHOLARSHIP
• *See page 471*

ARC OF WASHINGTON TRUST FUND http://www.arcwa.org

ARC OF WASHINGTON TRUST FUND STIPEND PROGRAM

Stipends of up to $5000 will be awarded to upper division or graduate students in schools in the states of Washington, Alaska, Oregon or Idaho. Applicants must have a demonstrated interest in the field of mental retardation. The application can be downloaded from the Web site: http://www.arcwa.org.

Academic Fields/Career Goals: Special Education.

Award: Scholarship for use in junior, senior, graduate, or postgraduate years; not renewable. *Number:* 1–8. *Amount:* up to $5000.

Eligibility Requirements: Applicant must be enrolled or expecting to enroll full- or part-time at a four-year institution or university and studying in Alaska, Idaho, Oregon, or Washington. Available to U.S. citizens.

Application Requirements: Application, autobiography, essay, references, transcript. *Deadline:* February 29.

Contact: Neal Lessenger, Secretary
ARC of Washington Trust Fund
PO Box 27028
Seattle, WA 98165-1428
Phone: 206-363-2206
E-mail: arcwatrust@charter.net

BETHESDA LUTHERAN HOMES AND SERVICES, INC. http://www.blhs.org

DEVELOPMENTAL DISABILITIES AWARENESS AWARDS FOR LUTHERAN HIGH SCHOOL STUDENTS
• *See page 335*

DEVELOPMENTAL DISABILITIES SCHOLASTIC ACHIEVEMENT SCHOLARSHIP FOR LUTHERAN COLLEGE STUDENTS
• *See page 211*

ILLINOIS STUDENT ASSISTANCE COMMISSION (ISAC) http://www.collegezone.org

ILLINOIS SPECIAL EDUCATION TEACHER TUITION WAIVER

Teachers or students who are pursuing a career in special education as public, private or parochial preschool, elementary or secondary school teachers in Illinois may be eligible for this program. This program will exempt such individuals from paying tuition and mandatory fees at an eligible institution, for up to four years. The individual dollar amount awarded are subject to sufficient annual appropriations by the Illinois General Assembly.

Academic Fields/Career Goals: Special Education.

Award: Forgivable loan for use in freshman, sophomore, junior, senior, or graduate years; renewable. *Number:* up to 250. *Amount:* varies.

Eligibility Requirements: Applicant must be enrolled or expecting to enroll full- or part-time at a four-year institution or university; resident of Illinois and studying in Illinois. Available to U.S. citizens.

Application Requirements: Application. *Deadline:* March 1.

Contact: College Zone Counselor
Illinois Student Assistance Commission (ISAC)
1755 Lake Cook Road
Deerfield, IL 60015-5209
Phone: 800-899-4722
E-mail: collegezone@isac.org

MINORITY TEACHERS OF ILLINOIS SCHOLARSHIP PROGRAM
• *See page 231*

KENTUCKY HIGHER EDUCATION ASSISTANCE AUTHORITY (KHEAA) http://www.kheaa.com

MINORITY EDUCATOR RECRUITMENT AND RETENTION SCHOLARSHIP
• *See page 233*

NATIONAL FEDERATION OF THE BLIND OF CONNECTICUT http://www.nfbct.org

BRIAN CUMMINS MEMORIAL SCHOLARSHIP
• *See page 236*

NATIONAL INSTITUTE FOR LABOR RELATIONS RESEARCH http://www.nilrr.org

APPLEGATE/JACKSON/PARKS FUTURE TEACHER SCHOLARSHIP
• See page 236

NEW HAMPSHIRE POSTSECONDARY EDUCATION COMMISSION http://www.nh.gov/postsecondary

WORKFORCE INCENTIVE PROGRAM
• See page 237

OREGON STUDENT ASSISTANCE COMMISSION http://www.osac.state.or.us

JAMES CARLSON MEMORIAL SCHOLARSHIP
• See page 238

P. BUCKLEY MOSS SOCIETY http://www.mosssociety.org

JUDITH CARY MEMORIAL SCHOLARSHIP

Scholarship of $1000 award to one student who is pursuing either a bachelor's or a master's degree in special education.

Academic Fields/Career Goals: Special Education.

Award: Scholarship for use in freshman, sophomore, junior, senior, or graduate years; not renewable. *Number:* 1. *Amount:* $1000.

Eligibility Requirements: Applicant must be enrolled or expecting to enroll full- or part-time at a four-year institution or university. Available to U.S. and non-U.S. citizens.

Application Requirements: Application, essay, references. *Deadline:* March 31.

Contact: Brenda Simmons, Administrative Assistant
P. Buckley Moss Society
20 Stoneridge Drive, Suite 102
Waynesboro, VA 22980
Phone: 540-943-5678
Fax: 540-949-8408
E-mail: brenda@mosssociety.org

PILOT INTERNATIONAL FOUNDATION http://www.pilotinternational.org

PILOT INTERNATIONAL FOUNDATION RUBY NEWHALL MEMORIAL SCHOLARSHIP
• See page 342

PILOT INTERNATIONAL FOUNDATION SCHOLARSHIP PROGRAM
• See page 342

SOUTH CAROLINA STUDENT LOAN CORPORATION http://www.scstudentloan.org

SOUTH CAROLINA TEACHER LOAN PROGRAM
• See page 241

STATE COUNCIL OF HIGHER EDUCATION FOR VIRGINIA http://www.schev.edu

HIGHER EDUCATION TEACHER ASSISTANCE PROGRAM
• See page 241

STRAIGHTFORWARD MEDIA http://www.straightforwardmedia.com

STRAIGHTFORWARD MEDIA TEACHER SCHOLARSHIP
• See page 242

TEACHERS-TEACHERS.COM http://www.teachers-teachers.com

ASPIRING EDUCATOR SCHOLARSHIP

Award available to students attending a postsecondary school in the U.S. who are majoring in a state approved special education or related service program (including Speech Language Pathology/Therapy, Occupational Therapy, Physical Therapy, or Emotional Behavior Disorders).

Academic Fields/Career Goals: Special Education; Therapy/Rehabilitation.

Award: Scholarship for use in junior, senior, or graduate years; not renewable. *Number:* 5. *Amount:* $1000.

Eligibility Requirements: Applicant must be enrolled or expecting to enroll full- or part-time at a four-year institution or university. Available to U.S. and non-U.S. citizens.

Application Requirements: Application, essay, transcript. *Deadline:* June 30.

Contact: Allison Layton, Marketing Coordinator
Teachers-Teachers.com
PO Box 2519
Columbia, MD 21045
Phone: 877-812-4071
Fax: 713-583-9925
E-mail: alayton@teachers-teachers.com

TENNESSEE STUDENT ASSISTANCE CORPORATION http://www.collegepaystn.com

MINORITY TEACHING FELLOWS PROGRAM/TENNESSEE
• See page 243

UTAH STATE OFFICE OF EDUCATION http://www.schools.utah.gov/cert

T.H. BELL TEACHING INCENTIVE LOAN-UTAH
• See page 244

WISCONSIN CONGRESS OF PARENTS AND TEACHERS INC. http://www.wisconsinpta.org

BROOKMIRE-HASTINGS SCHOLARSHIPS
• See page 245

SPORTS-RELATED/EXERCISE SCIENCE

AMERICAN ALLIANCE FOR HEALTH, PHYSICAL EDUCATION, RECREATION AND DANCE http://www.aahperd.org

RUTH ABERNATHY PRESIDENTIAL SCHOLARSHIP
• See page 477

CALIFORNIA ADOLESCENT NUTRITION AND FITNESS (CANFIT) PROGRAM http://www.canfit.org

CALIFORNIA ADOLESCENT NUTRITION AND FITNESS (CANFIT) PROGRAM SCHOLARSHIP
• See page 203

CONNECTICUT ASSOCIATION FOR HEALTH, PHYSICAL EDUCATION, RECREATION AND DANCE http://www.ctahperd.org

GIBSON-LAEMEL CTAHPERD SCHOLARSHIP
• See page 226

MARY BENEVENTO CTAHPERD SCHOLARSHIP
• See page 226

INTERNATIONAL SOCIETY FOR OPTICAL ENGINEERING-SPIE http://www.spie.org

SPIE EDUCATIONAL SCHOLARSHIPS IN OPTICAL SCIENCE AND ENGINEERING
• See page 87

NATIONAL ATHLETIC TRAINERS' ASSOCIATION RESEARCH AND EDUCATION FOUNDATION http://www.natafoundation.org

NATIONAL ATHLETIC TRAINERS' ASSOCIATION RESEARCH AND EDUCATION FOUNDATION SCHOLARSHIP PROGRAM

• *See page 340*

NATIONAL STRENGTH AND CONDITIONING ASSOCIATION http://www.nsca-lift.org

GNC NUTRITION RESEARCH GRANT

• *See page 345*

NATIONAL STRENGTH AND CONDITIONING ASSOCIATION HIGH SCHOOL SCHOLARSHIP

One-time award to high school seniors preparing to enter college. Must demonstrate acceptance into an accredited institution and intention to graduate with a degree in a strength and conditioning field. Minimum 3.0 GPA required. Must be a member of NCSA.

Academic Fields/Career Goals: Sports-Related/Exercise Science; Therapy/Rehabilitation.

Award: Scholarship for use in freshman year; not renewable. *Number:* 1–2. *Amount:* $1000.

Eligibility Requirements: Applicant must be high school student and planning to enroll or expecting to enroll full-time at a four-year institution or university. Applicant or parent of applicant must be member of National Strength and Conditioning Association. Applicant must have 3.0 GPA or higher. Available to U.S. and non-U.S. citizens.

Application Requirements: Application, essay, references, transcript, letter of acceptance, cover letter. *Deadline:* March 15.

Contact: Line Saole, Membership Specialist
National Strength and Conditioning Association
1885 Bob Johnson Drive
Colorado Springs, CO 80906-4000
Phone: 719-632-6722 Ext. 120
Fax: 719-632-6367
E-mail: foundation@nsca-lift.org

NATIONAL STRENGTH AND CONDITIONING ASSOCIATION WOMEN'S SCHOLARSHIP

Scholarship to encourage women of ages 17 and older, to enter into the field of strength and conditioning. Scholarship value is $1000. Up to two awards are granted.

Academic Fields/Career Goals: Sports-Related/Exercise Science; Therapy/Rehabilitation.

Award: Scholarship for use in freshman, sophomore, junior, senior, or graduate years; not renewable. *Number:* 1–2. *Amount:* $1000.

Eligibility Requirements: Applicant must be age 17 and over; enrolled or expecting to enroll full-time at a two-year or four-year institution or university and female. Applicant or parent of applicant must be member of National Strength and Conditioning Association. Available to U.S. and non-U.S. citizens.

Application Requirements: Application, essay, resume, references, self-addressed stamped envelope, transcript, cover letter. *Deadline:* March 15.

Contact: Line Saole, Membership Specialist
National Strength and Conditioning Association
1885 Bob Johnson Drive
Colorado Springs, CO 80906-4000
Phone: 719-632-6722 Ext. 120
Fax: 719-632-6367
E-mail: foundation@nsca-lift.org

NSCA MINORITY SCHOLARSHIP

• *See page 345*

POWER SYSTEMS PROFESSIONAL SCHOLARSHIP

• *See page 345*

VELOCITY SPORTS PERFORMANCE CHALLENGE SCHOLARSHIP

One-time scholarship for undergraduate or graduate students in strength and conditioning-related fields. Must be NSCA member. Scholarship value is $1000 and up to twelve awards are granted annually.

Academic Fields/Career Goals: Sports-Related/Exercise Science; Therapy/Rehabilitation.

Award: Scholarship for use in freshman, sophomore, junior, senior, or graduate years; not renewable. *Number:* 1–12. *Amount:* $1000.

Eligibility Requirements: Applicant must be enrolled or expecting to enroll full-time at a two-year or four-year institution or university. Applicant or parent of applicant must be member of National Strength and Conditioning Association. Available to U.S. and non-U.S. citizens.

Application Requirements: Application, essay, financial need analysis, photo, resume, references, transcript, cover letter. *Deadline:* March 15.

Contact: Line Saole, Membership Specialist
National Strength and Conditioning Association
1885 Bob Johnson Drive
Colorado Springs, CO 80906-4000
Phone: 719-632-6722 Ext. 120
Fax: 719-632-6367
E-mail: foundation@nsca-lift.org

PACERS FOUNDATION INC. http://www.pacersfoundation.org

LINDA CRAIG MEMORIAL SCHOLARSHIP PRESENTED BY ST. VINCENT SPORTS MEDICINE

• *See page 341*

PI LAMBDA THETA INC. http://www.pilambda.org

TOBIN SORENSON PHYSICAL EDUCATION SCHOLARSHIP

• *See page 240*

Y'S MEN INTERNATIONAL http://www.ysmenusa.com

ALEXANDER SCHOLARSHIP LOAN FUND

• *See page 152*

SURVEYING; SURVEYING TECHNOLOGY, CARTOGRAPHY, OR GEOGRAPHIC INFORMATION SCIENCE

AMERICAN CONGRESS ON SURVEYING AND MAPPING http://www.acsm.net

ACSM FELLOWS SCHOLARSHIP

One-time award available to a student with a junior or higher standing in any ACSM discipline. Must be ACSM member.

Academic Fields/Career Goals: Surveying; Surveying Technology, Cartography, or Geographic Information Science.

Award: Scholarship for use in freshman, sophomore, junior, or senior years; not renewable. *Number:* 1. *Amount:* $2000.

Eligibility Requirements: Applicant must be enrolled or expecting to enroll full- or part-time at a four-year institution or university. Applicant or parent of applicant must be member of American Congress on Surveying and Mapping. Available to U.S. citizens.

Application Requirements: Application, essay, references, transcript, membership proof. *Deadline:* October 1.

Contact: Dawn James, NSPS Executive Administrator
American Congress on Surveying and Mapping
6 Montgomery Village Avenue, Suite 403
Gaithersburg, MD 20879
Phone: 240-632-9716 Ext. 113
Fax: 240-632-1321
E-mail: dawn.james@acsm.net

AMERICAN ASSOCIATION FOR GEODETIC SURVEYING JOSEPH F. DRACUP SCHOLARSHIP AWARD

Award for students enrolled in four-year degree program in surveying (or in closely-related degree programs such as geomatics or surveying engineering). Preference given to applicants from programs with significant focus on geodetic surveying. Must be ACSM member.

American Congress on Surveying and Mapping (continued)

Academic Fields/Career Goals: Surveying; Surveying Technology, Cartography, or Geographic Information Science.

Award: Scholarship for use in freshman, sophomore, junior, or senior years; not renewable. *Number:* 1. *Amount:* $2000.

Eligibility Requirements: Applicant must be enrolled or expecting to enroll full- or part-time at a four-year institution or university. Applicant or parent of applicant must be member of American Congress on Surveying and Mapping. Available to U.S. citizens.

Application Requirements: Application, essay, references, transcript. *Deadline:* October 1.

Contact: Dawn James, NSPS Executive Administrator
American Congress on Surveying and Mapping
6 Montgomery Village Avenue, Suite 403
Gaithersburg, MD 20879
Phone: 240-632-9716 Ext. 113
Fax: 240-632-1321
E-mail: dawn.james@acsm.net

BERNTSEN INTERNATIONAL SCHOLARSHIP IN SURVEYING

Award of $1500 for full-time students enrolled in four-year degree program in surveying, or in closely-related degree program, such as geomatics or surveying engineering. Must be ACSM member.

Academic Fields/Career Goals: Surveying; Surveying Technology, Cartography, or Geographic Information Science.

Award: Scholarship for use in freshman, sophomore, junior, or senior years; not renewable. *Number:* 1. *Amount:* $1500.

Eligibility Requirements: Applicant must be enrolled or expecting to enroll full-time at a four-year institution or university. Applicant or parent of applicant must be member of American Congress on Surveying and Mapping. Available to U.S. citizens.

Application Requirements: Application, essay, references, transcript. *Deadline:* October 1.

Contact: Dawn James, NSPS Executive Administrator
American Congress on Surveying and Mapping
6 Montgomery Village Avenue, Suite 403
Gaithersburg, MD 20879
Phone: 240-632-9716 Ext. 113
Fax: 240-632-1321
E-mail: dawn.james@acsm.net

BERNTSEN INTERNATIONAL SCHOLARSHIP IN SURVEYING TECHNOLOGY

Award for full-time undergraduate students enrolled in a two-year degree program in surveying technology. For U.S. study only. Must be a member of the American Congress on Surveying and Mapping. See Web site for application and more details: http://www.acsm.net/scholar.html.

Academic Fields/Career Goals: Surveying; Surveying Technology, Cartography, or Geographic Information Science.

Award: Scholarship for use in freshman or sophomore years; not renewable. *Number:* 1. *Amount:* $500.

Eligibility Requirements: Applicant must be enrolled or expecting to enroll full-time at a two-year institution. Applicant or parent of applicant must be member of American Congress on Surveying and Mapping. Available to U.S. citizens.

Application Requirements: Application, essay, references, transcript, proof of membership in ACSM. *Deadline:* October 1.

Contact: Dawn James, NSPS Executive Administrator
American Congress on Surveying and Mapping
6 Montgomery Village Avenue, Suite 403
Gaithersburg, MD 20879
Phone: 240-632-9716 Ext. 113
Fax: 240-632-1321
E-mail: dawn.james@acsm.net

CADY MCDONNELL MEMORIAL SCHOLARSHIP

Award of $1000 for female surveying student. Must be a resident of one of the following western states: Alaska, Arizona, California, Colorado, Hawaii, Idaho, Montana, Nevada, New Mexico, Oregon, Utah, Washington, and Wyoming. Must provide proof of legal home residence and be a member of the American Congress on Surveying and Mapping.

Academic Fields/Career Goals: Surveying; Surveying Technology, Cartography, or Geographic Information Science.

Award: Scholarship for use in freshman, sophomore, junior, or senior years; not renewable. *Number:* 1. *Amount:* $1000.

Eligibility Requirements: Applicant must be enrolled or expecting to enroll full- or part-time at a two-year or four-year institution or university; female and resident of Alaska, Arizona, California, Colorado, Hawaii, Idaho, Montana, Nevada, New Mexico, Oregon, Utah, Washington, or Wyoming. Applicant or parent of applicant must be member of American Congress on Surveying and Mapping. Available to U.S. citizens.

Application Requirements: Application, essay, financial need analysis, references, transcript, proof of residence, membership proof, personal statement. *Deadline:* October 1.

Contact: Dawn James, NSPS Executive Administrator
American Congress on Surveying and Mapping
6 Montgomery Village Avenue, Suite 403
Gaithersburg, MD 20879
Phone: 240-632-9716 Ext. 113
Fax: 240-632-1321
E-mail: dawn.james@acsm.net

NATIONAL SOCIETY OF PROFESSIONAL SURVEYORS BOARD OF GOVERNORS SCHOLARSHIP

Award available to students enrolled in surveying program entering junior year of study at four-year institution. Minimum 3.0 GPA required. Must be ACSM member.

Academic Fields/Career Goals: Surveying; Surveying Technology, Cartography, or Geographic Information Science.

Award: Scholarship for use in junior year; not renewable. *Number:* 1. *Amount:* up to $1000.

Eligibility Requirements: Applicant must be enrolled or expecting to enroll full- or part-time at a four-year institution or university. Applicant or parent of applicant must be member of American Congress on Surveying and Mapping. Applicant must have 3.0 GPA or higher. Available to U.S. citizens.

Application Requirements: Application, essay, financial need analysis, references, transcript, membership proof. *Deadline:* October 1.

Contact: Dawn James, NSPS Executive Administrator
American Congress on Surveying and Mapping
6 Montgomery Village Avenue, Suite 403
Gaithersburg, MD 20879
Phone: 240-632-9716 Ext. 113
Fax: 240-632-1321
E-mail: dawn.james@acsm.net

NATIONAL SOCIETY OF PROFESSIONAL SURVEYORS SCHOLARSHIPS

Two awards of $1000 each to students enrolled full-time in a four-year undergraduate surveying program. Must be ACSM member.

Academic Fields/Career Goals: Surveying; Surveying Technology, Cartography, or Geographic Information Science.

Award: Scholarship for use in freshman, sophomore, junior, or senior years; not renewable. *Number:* 2. *Amount:* $1000.

Eligibility Requirements: Applicant must be enrolled or expecting to enroll full-time at a four-year institution or university. Applicant or parent of applicant must be member of American Congress on Surveying and Mapping. Available to U.S. citizens.

Application Requirements: Application, essay, references, transcript. *Deadline:* October 1.

Contact: Dawn James, NSPS Executive Administrator
American Congress on Surveying and Mapping
6 Montgomery Village Avenue, Suite 403
Gaithersburg, MD 20879
Phone: 240-632-9716 Ext. 113
Fax: 240-632-1321
E-mail: dawn.james@acsm.net

NETTIE DRACUP MEMORIAL SCHOLARSHIP

Award for undergraduate student enrolled in four-year geodetic surveying program at an accredited college or university. Must be U.S. citizen. Must be ACSM member.

Academic Fields/Career Goals: Surveying; Surveying Technology, Cartography, or Geographic Information Science.

Award: Scholarship for use in freshman, sophomore, junior, or senior years; not renewable. *Number:* 1. *Amount:* $2000.

Eligibility Requirements: Applicant must be enrolled or expecting to enroll full-time at a four-year institution or university. Applicant or parent of applicant must be member of American Congress on Surveying and Mapping. Available to U.S. citizens.

Application Requirements: Application, essay, financial need analysis, references, transcript. *Deadline:* October 1.

Contact: Dawn James, NSPS Executive Administrator
American Congress on Surveying and Mapping
6 Montgomery Village Avenue, Suite 403
Gaithersburg, MD 20879
Phone: 240-632-9716 Ext. 113
Fax: 240-632-1321
E-mail: dawn.james@acsm.net

SCHONSTEDT SCHOLARSHIP IN SURVEYING

Award preference given to applicants with junior or senior standing in a four-year program in surveying. Schonstedt donates magnetic locator to surveying program at each recipient's school. Must be ACSM member.

Academic Fields/Career Goals: Surveying; Surveying Technology, Cartography, or Geographic Information Science.

Award: Scholarship for use in junior or senior years; not renewable. *Number:* 2. *Amount:* $1500.

Eligibility Requirements: Applicant must be enrolled or expecting to enroll full-time at a four-year institution or university. Applicant or parent of applicant must be member of American Congress on Surveying and Mapping. Available to U.S. citizens.

Application Requirements: Application, essay, references, transcript. *Deadline:* October 1.

Contact: Dawn James, NSPS Executive Administrator
American Congress on Surveying and Mapping
6 Montgomery Village Avenue, Suite 403
Gaithersburg, MD 20879
Phone: 240-632-9716 Ext. 113
Fax: 240-632-1321
E-mail: dawn.james@acsm.net

TRI-STATE SURVEYING AND PHOTOGRAMMETRY KRIS M. KUNZE MEMORIAL SCHOLARSHIP

• *See page 137*

ASPRS, THE IMAGING AND GEOSPATIAL INFORMATION SOCIETY http://www.asprs.org

ROBERT E. ALTENHOFEN MEMORIAL SCHOLARSHIP

• *See page 259*

ASSOCIATED GENERAL CONTRACTORS OF AMERICA-NEW YORK STATE CHAPTER http://www.agcnys.org

ASSOCIATED GENERAL CONTRACTORS OF AMERICA-NEW YORK STATE CHAPTER SCHOLARSHIP PROGRAM

• *See page 169*

ASSOCIATION OF CALIFORNIA WATER AGENCIES http://www.acwa.com

ASSOCIATION OF CALIFORNIA WATER AGENCIES SCHOLARSHIPS

• *See page 86*

CLAIR A. HILL SCHOLARSHIP

• *See page 86*

CENTRAL INTELLIGENCE AGENCY http://www.cia.gov

CENTRAL INTELLIGENCE AGENCY UNDERGRADUATE SCHOLARSHIP PROGRAM

• *See page 49*

FLORIDA ENGINEERING SOCIETY http://www.fleng.org

ACEC/FLORIDA SCHOLARSHIP

• *See page 264*

HISPANIC SCHOLARSHIP FUND http://www.hsf.net

HSF/MARATHON OIL CORPORATION COLLEGE SCHOLARSHIP

• *See page 55*

MICHIGAN SOCIETY OF PROFESSIONAL ENGINEERS http://www.michiganspe.org

MICHIGAN SOCIETY OF PROFESSIONAL ENGINEERS ABRAMS GRANT

• *See page 171*

OREGON STUDENT ASSISTANCE COMMISSION http://www.osac.state.or.us

PROFESSIONAL LAND SURVEYORS OF OREGON SCHOLARSHIPS

Award for sophomores or above enrolled in a course of study leading to land-surveying career. Community college applicants must intend to transfer to four-year college. Oregon colleges or out-of-state residents enrolled at Oregon colleges may apply. Must intend to take Fundamentals of Land Surveying exam. Additional essay stating education/career goals and their relation to land surveying is required.

Academic Fields/Career Goals: Surveying; Surveying Technology, Cartography, or Geographic Information Science.

Award: Scholarship for use in sophomore, junior, or senior years; renewable. *Number:* 1. *Amount:* $500.

Eligibility Requirements: Applicant must be enrolled or expecting to enroll full-time at a four-year institution or university and studying in Oregon. Available to U.S. citizens.

Application Requirements: Application, essay, financial need analysis, references, transcript, activity chart. *Deadline:* March 1.

Contact: Director of Grant Programs
Oregon Student Assistance Commission
1500 Valley River Drive, Suite 100
Eugene, OR 97401-7020
Phone: 800-452-8807 Ext. 7395

PROFESSIONAL CONSTRUCTION ESTIMATORS ASSOCIATION http://www.pcea.org

TED WILSON MEMORIAL SCHOLARSHIP FOUNDATION

• *See page 214*

RHODE ISLAND SOCIETY OF PROFESSIONAL LAND SURVEYORS http://www.rispls.org

PIERRE H. GUILLEMETTE SCHOLARSHIP

Scholarship available to any Rhode Island resident enrolled in a certificate or degree program in land surveying at a qualified institution of higher learning.

Academic Fields/Career Goals: Surveying; Surveying Technology, Cartography, or Geographic Information Science.

Award: Scholarship for use in freshman, sophomore, junior, or senior years; not renewable. *Number:* varies. *Amount:* varies.

Eligibility Requirements: Applicant must be enrolled or expecting to enroll full- or part-time at a four-year institution or university and resident of Rhode Island. Available to U.S. citizens.

Application Requirements: Application, resume, transcript. *Deadline:* October 30.

Contact: Scholarship Coordinator
Rhode Island Society of Professional Land Surveyors
PO Box 544
East Greenwich, RI 02818
Phone: 401-294-1262
E-mail: info@rispls.org

SOUTH CAROLINA DIVISION OF VETERANS AFFAIRS http://www.govoepp.state.sc.us/vetaff.htm

EDUCATIONAL ASSISTANCE FOR CERTAIN WAR VETERANS DEPENDENTS SCHOLARSHIP-SOUTH CAROLINA

Scholarship for South Carolina residents who meet or whose parents meet the following criteria: general military experience; retired from active duty; disabled or killed as a result of military service; prisoner of war; or missing in action. Must be age 18-25 and enrolled or expecting to enroll full or part-time at a two-year or four-year technical institution or university in South Carolina.

Academic Fields/Career Goals: Surveying; Surveying Technology, Cartography, or Geographic Information Science.

Award: Scholarship for use in freshman, sophomore, junior, senior, graduate, or postgraduate years; not renewable. *Number:* varies. *Amount:* varies.

Eligibility Requirements: Applicant must be age 18-26; enrolled or expecting to enroll full- or part-time at a two-year or four-year or technical institution or university and studying in South Carolina. Available to U.S. citizens. Applicant or parent must meet one or more of the following requirements: general military experience; retired from active duty; disabled or killed as a result of military service; prisoner of war; or missing in action.

Application Requirements: Application, transcript. *Deadline:* continuous.

Contact: Dianne Coley, Free Tuition Assistant
South Carolina Division of Veterans Affairs
South Carolina Governor's Office
1205 Pendleton Street, Suite 369
Columbia, SC 29201
Phone: 803-255-4317
Fax: 803-255-4257
E-mail: va@oepp.sc.gov

THERAPY/REHABILITATION

ALBERTA HERITAGE SCHOLARSHIP FUND/ ALBERTA SCHOLARSHIP PROGRAMS http://www.alis.gov.ab.ca

ALBERTA HERITAGE SCHOLARSHIP FUND ABORIGINAL HEALTH CAREERS BURSARY
• *See page 129*

AMERICAN ART THERAPY ASSOCIATION http://www.arttherapy.org

MYRA LEVICK SCHOLARSHIP FUND
• *See page 99*

AMERICAN FOUNDATION FOR THE BLIND http://www.afb.org

DELTA GAMMA FOUNDATION FLORENCE MARGARET HARVEY MEMORIAL SCHOLARSHIP
• *See page 222*

RUDOLPH DILLMAN MEMORIAL SCHOLARSHIP
• *See page 222*

AMERICAN LEGION AUXILIARY DEPARTMENT OF MICHIGAN http://www.michalaux.org

AMERICAN LEGION AUXILIARY DEPARTMENT OF MICHIGAN MEDICAL CAREER SCHOLARSHIP
• *See page 329*

AMERICAN LEGION AUXILIARY DEPARTMENT OF WYOMING

AMERICAN LEGION AUXILIARY DEPARTMENT OF WYOMING PAST PRESIDENTS' PARLEY HEALTH CARE SCHOLARSHIP
• *See page 210*

AMERICAN OCCUPATIONAL THERAPY FOUNDATION INC. http://www.aotf.org

AMERICAN OCCUPATIONAL THERAPY FOUNDATION STATE ASSOCIATION SCHOLARSHIPS
• *See page 330*

CARLOTTA WELLES SCHOLARSHIP
• *See page 330*

FLORENCE WOOD/ARKANSAS OCCUPATIONAL THERAPY ASSOCIATION SCHOLARSHIP
• *See page 330*

KAPPA DELTA PHI SCHOLARSHIP FOR OCCUPATIONAL THERAPY ASSISTANT
• *See page 330*

AMERICAN PHYSICAL THERAPY ASSOCIATION http://www.apta.org

MINORITY SCHOLARSHIP AWARD FOR ACADEMIC EXCELLENCE-PHYSICAL THERAPIST ASSISTANT
• *See page 331*

AMERICAN RESPIRATORY CARE FOUNDATION http://www.arcfoundation.org

JIMMY A. YOUNG MEMORIAL EDUCATION RECOGNITION AWARD
• *See page 331*

MORTON B. DUGGAN, JR. MEMORIAL EDUCATION RECOGNITION AWARD
• *See page 331*

NBRC/AMP ROBERT M. LAWRENCE, MD EDUCATION RECOGNITION AWARD
• *See page 331*

NBRC/AMP WILLIAM W. BURGIN, MD EDUCATION RECOGNITION AWARD
• *See page 332*

SEPRACOR ACHIEVEMENT AWARD FOR EXCELLENCE IN PULMONARY DISEASE STATE MANAGEMENT
• *See page 332*

BETHESDA LUTHERAN HOMES AND SERVICES, INC. http://www.blhs.org

DEVELOPMENTAL DISABILITIES AWARENESS AWARDS FOR LUTHERAN HIGH SCHOOL STUDENTS
• *See page 335*

DEVELOPMENTAL DISABILITIES SCHOLASTIC ACHIEVEMENT SCHOLARSHIP FOR LUTHERAN COLLEGE STUDENTS
• *See page 211*

CYNTHIA E. MORGAN SCHOLARSHIP FUND (CEMS) http://www.cemsfund.com

CYNTHIA E. MORGAN MEMORIAL SCHOLARSHIP
• *See page 336*

HEALTH PROFESSIONS EDUCATION FOUNDATION http://www.healthprofessions.ca.gov

KAISER PERMANENTE ALLIED HEALTHCARE SCHOLARSHIP
• *See page 337*

INDIAN HEALTH SERVICES, UNITED STATES DEPARTMENT OF HEALTH AND HUMAN SERVICES http://www.ihs.gov

INDIAN HEALTH SERVICE HEALTH PROFESSIONS SCHOLARSHIP PROGRAM
• *See page 327*

INTERNATIONAL ORDER OF THE KING'S DAUGHTERS AND SONS http://www.iokds.org

HEALTH CAREERS SCHOLARSHIP

• *See page 212*

JEWISH FOUNDATION FOR EDUCATION OF WOMEN http://www.jfew.org

JFEW SCHOLARSHIPS FOR EMIGRES IN THE HEALTH SCIENCES

• *See page 212*

LADIES AUXILIARY TO THE VETERANS OF FOREIGN WARS, DEPARTMENT OF MAINE

FRANCIS L. BOOTH MEDICAL SCHOLARSHIP SPONSORED BY LAVFW DEPARTMENT OF MAINE

• *See page 338*

MARYLAND HIGHER EDUCATION COMMISSION http://www.mhec.state.md.us

JANET L. HOFFMANN LOAN ASSISTANCE REPAYMENT PROGRAM

• *See page 234*

MENTAL HEALTH ASSOCIATION IN NEW YORK STATE INC. http://www.mhanys.org

EDNA AIMES SCHOLARSHIP

• *See page 128*

MISSISSIPPI STATE STUDENT FINANCIAL AID http://www.ihl.state.ms.us

CRITICAL NEEDS TEACHER LOAN/SCHOLARSHIP

• *See page 235*

MISSISSIPPI HEALTH CARE PROFESSIONS LOAN/SCHOLARSHIP PROGRAM

• *See page 339*

NATIONAL AMBUCS INC. http://www.ambucs.org

AMBUCS SCHOLARS-SCHOLARSHIPS FOR THERAPISTS

• *See page 109*

NATIONAL ATHLETIC TRAINERS' ASSOCIATION RESEARCH AND EDUCATION FOUNDATION http://www.natafoundation.org

NATIONAL ATHLETIC TRAINERS' ASSOCIATION RESEARCH AND EDUCATION FOUNDATION SCHOLARSHIP PROGRAM

• *See page 340*

NATIONAL SOCIETY DAUGHTERS OF THE AMERICAN REVOLUTION http://www.dar.org

NATIONAL SOCIETY DAUGHTERS OF THE AMERICAN REVOLUTION OCCUPATIONAL THERAPY SCHOLARSHIP

Scholarship of $1000 for students who are in financial need and have been accepted or are attending an accredited school of occupational therapy including art, music or physical therapy. A letter of acceptance into the occupational therapy program or the transcript stating the applicant is in the occupational therapy program must be included with the application.

Academic Fields/Career Goals: Therapy/Rehabilitation.

Award: Scholarship for use in freshman, sophomore, junior, senior, or graduate years; not renewable. *Number:* varies. *Amount:* $1000.

Eligibility Requirements: Applicant must be enrolled or expecting to enroll full- or part-time at a two-year or four-year institution or university. Available to U.S. citizens.

Application Requirements: Application, essay, financial need analysis, references, self-addressed stamped envelope, transcript, letter of sponsorship. *Deadline:* February 15.

Contact: Eric Weisz, Manager, Office of the Reporter General
National Society Daughters of the American Revolution
1776 D Street, NW
Washington, DC 20006-5303
Phone: 202-628-1776
Fax: 202-879-3348
E-mail: nsdarscholarships@dar.org

NATIONAL STRENGTH AND CONDITIONING ASSOCIATION http://www.nsca-lift.org

GNC NUTRITION RESEARCH GRANT

• *See page 345*

NATIONAL STRENGTH AND CONDITIONING ASSOCIATION HIGH SCHOOL SCHOLARSHIP

• *See page 487*

NATIONAL STRENGTH AND CONDITIONING ASSOCIATION WOMEN'S SCHOLARSHIP

• *See page 487*

NSCA MINORITY SCHOLARSHIP

• *See page 345*

POWER SYSTEMS PROFESSIONAL SCHOLARSHIP

• *See page 345*

VELOCITY SPORTS PERFORMANCE CHALLENGE SCHOLARSHIP

• *See page 487*

NEW MEXICO COMMISSION ON HIGHER EDUCATION http://www.hed.state.nm.us

ALLIED HEALTH STUDENT LOAN PROGRAM-NEW MEXICO

• *See page 213*

NORTH CAROLINA STATE EDUCATION ASSISTANCE AUTHORITY http://www.ncseaa.edu

NORTH CAROLINA STUDENT LOAN PROGRAM FOR HEALTH, SCIENCE, AND MATHEMATICS

• *See page 213*

OREGON STUDENT ASSISTANCE COMMISSION http://www.osac.state.or.us

MARION A. LINDEMAN SCHOLARSHIP

• *See page 341*

PACERS FOUNDATION INC. http://www.pacersfoundation.org

LINDA CRAIG MEMORIAL SCHOLARSHIP PRESENTED BY ST. VINCENT SPORTS MEDICINE

• *See page 341*

PI LAMBDA THETA INC. http://www.pilambda.org

TOBIN SORENSON PHYSICAL EDUCATION SCHOLARSHIP

• *See page 240*

PILOT INTERNATIONAL FOUNDATION http://www.pilotinternational.org

PILOT INTERNATIONAL FOUNDATION RUBY NEWHALL MEMORIAL SCHOLARSHIP

• *See page 342*

PILOT INTERNATIONAL FOUNDATION SCHOLARSHIP PROGRAM

• *See page 342*

RESOURCE CENTER

MARIE BLAHA MEDICAL GRANT

• *See page 83*

SIGMA ALPHA IOTA PHILANTHROPIES INC. http://www.sigmaalphaiota.org

SIGMA ALPHA IOTA MUSIC THERAPY SCHOLARSHIP
• *See page 417*

STATE OF GEORGIA http://www.gsfc.org

SERVICE-CANCELABLE STAFFORD LOAN-GEORGIA
• *See page 213*

SUNSHINE LADY FOUNDATION INC. http://www.sunshinelady.org

COUNSELOR, ADVOCATE, AND SUPPORT STAFF SCHOLARSHIP PROGRAM
• *See page 167*

TEACHERS-TEACHERS.COM http://www.teachers-teachers.com

ASPIRING EDUCATOR SCHOLARSHIP
• *See page 486*

UNITED STATES PUBLIC HEALTH SERVICE-HEALTH RESOURCES AND SERVICES ADMINISTRATION, BUREAU OF HEALTH PROFESSIONS http://bhpr.hrsa.gov/dsa

HEALTH RESOURCES AND SERVICES ADMINISTRATION-BUREAU OF HEALTH PROFESSIONS SCHOLARSHIPS FOR DISADVANTAGED STUDENTS
• *See page 214*

TRADE/TECHNICAL SPECIALTIES

AIRCRAFT ELECTRONICS ASSOCIATION EDUCATIONAL FOUNDATION http://www.aea.net

BUD GLOVER MEMORIAL SCHOLARSHIP
• *See page 109*

DUTCH AND GINGER ARVER SCHOLARSHIP
• *See page 110*

GARMIN SCHOLARSHIP
• *See page 110*

LEE TARBOX MEMORIAL SCHOLARSHIP
• *See page 111*

LOWELL GAYLOR MEMORIAL SCHOLARSHIP
• *See page 111*

MID-CONTINENT INSTRUMENT SCHOLARSHIP
• *See page 111*

PLANE AND PILOT MAGAZINE/GARMIN SCHOLARSHIP
• *See page 111*

ALBERTA HERITAGE SCHOLARSHIP FUND/ ALBERTA SCHOLARSHIP PROGRAMS http://www.alis.gov.ab.ca

ALBERTA APPRENTICESHIP AND INDUSTRY TRAINING SCHOLARSHIPS

Award to recognize the excellence of Alberta apprentices in a trade, and trainees in a designated occupation; and to encourage recipients to complete their apprenticeship or occupational training programs. Must be registered as an Alberta apprentice in a trade, have passed their first or subsequent period apprenticeship and industry training exam, have at least one more period of technical training remaining in their program. For further details visit Web site: http://www.tradesecrets.gov.ab.ca.

Academic Fields/Career Goals: Trade/Technical Specialties.

Award: Scholarship for use in freshman year; not renewable. *Number:* 165. *Amount:* $1000.

Eligibility Requirements: Applicant must be enrolled or expecting to enroll full-time at a technical institution. Available to Canadian citizens.

Application Requirements: Application, essay, financial need analysis, references, employer recommendation form. *Deadline:* July 31.

Contact: Scholarship Committee
Alberta Heritage Scholarship Fund/Alberta Scholarship Programs
9940 106th Street, Fourth Floor, Sterling Place
PO Box 28000, Station Main
Edmonton, AB T5J 4R4
Canada
Phone: 780-427-8640
Fax: 780-427-1288
E-mail: scholarships@gov.ab.ca

MICHAEL LUCHKOVICH SCHOLARSHIPS FOR CAREER DEVELOPMENT

Award to provide an incentive and means to members of Alberta's labor force to upgrade their education or training. Must be residents of Alberta and have been working full-time in Alberta for a minimum of three years. Program of study may be up to six months of full-time study or up to one year of part-time study.

Academic Fields/Career Goals: Trade/Technical Specialties.

Award: Scholarship for use in freshman year; not renewable. *Number:* varies. *Amount:* up to $2000.

Eligibility Requirements: Applicant must be enrolled or expecting to enroll full- or part-time at a two-year or four-year or technical institution or university and resident of Alberta. Available to Canadian citizens.

Application Requirements: Application. *Deadline:* varies.

Contact: Scholarship Committee
Alberta Heritage Scholarship Fund/Alberta Scholarship Programs
9940 106th Street, Fourth Floor, Sterling Place
PO Box 28000, Station Main
Edmonton, AB T5J 4R4
Canada
Phone: 780-427-8640
Fax: 780-427-1288
E-mail: scholarships@gov.ab.ca

AMERICAN LEGION DEPARTMENT OF PENNSYLVANIA http://www.pa-legion.com

ROBERT W. VALIMONT ENDOWMENT FUND SCHOLARSHIP (PART II)

Scholarships for any Pennsylvania high school senior seeking admission to a two-year college, post-high school trade/technical school, or training program. Must attend school in Pennsylvania. Continuation of award is based on grades. Renewable award of $600. Number of awards varies from year to year. Membership in an American Legion post in Pennsylvania is not required, but it must be documented if it does apply.

Academic Fields/Career Goals: Trade/Technical Specialties.

Award: Scholarship for use in freshman year; renewable. *Number:* varies. *Amount:* $600.

Eligibility Requirements: Applicant must be high school student; planning to enroll or expecting to enroll full-time at a two-year or technical institution; resident of Pennsylvania and studying in Pennsylvania. Applicant must have 2.5 GPA or higher. Available to U.S. citizens.

Application Requirements: Application, financial need analysis, test scores, transcript. *Deadline:* May 30.

Contact: Debbie Watson, Emblem Sales Supervisor
American Legion Department of Pennsylvania
PO Box 2324
Harrisburg, PA 17105-2324
Phone: 717-730-9100
Fax: 717-975-2836
E-mail: hq@pa-legion.com

AMERICAN SOCIETY OF HEATING, REFRIGERATING, AND AIR CONDITIONING ENGINEERS INC. http://www.ashrae.org

ALWIN B. NEWTON SCHOLARSHIP FUND
• *See page 247*

AMERICAN SOCIETY OF HEATING, REFRIGERATION, AND AIR CONDITIONING ENGINEERING TECHNOLOGY SCHOLARSHIP
• *See page 85*

ASHRAE MEMORIAL SCHOLARSHIP
• *See page 286*

ASHRAE SCHOLARSHIPS
• *See page 287*

DUANE HANSON SCHOLARSHIP
• *See page 287*

HENRY ADAMS SCHOLARSHIP
• *See page 287*

REUBEN TRANE SCHOLARSHIP
• *See page 247*

AMERICAN WELDING SOCIETY http://www.aws.org

AMERICAN WELDING SOCIETY DISTRICT SCHOLARSHIP PROGRAM
• *See page 287*

AMERICAN WELDING SOCIETY INTERNATIONAL SCHOLARSHIP
• *See page 288*

ARSHAM AMIRIKIAN ENGINEERING SCHOLARSHIP
• *See page 168*

DONALD F. HASTINGS SCHOLARSHIP
• *See page 288*

EDWARD J. BRADY MEMORIAL SCHOLARSHIP
• *See page 288*

HOWARD E. AND WILMA J. ADKINS MEMORIAL SCHOLARSHIP
• *See page 288*

ILLINOIS TOOL WORKS WELDING COMPANIES SCHOLARSHIP
• *See page 288*

JERRY ROBINSON-INWELD CORPORATION SCHOLARSHIP
• *See page 395*

MILLER ELECTRIC INTERNATIONAL WORLD SKILLS COMPETITION SCHOLARSHIP
• *See page 289*

ASSOCIATION FOR FACILITIES ENGINEERING (AFE)

ASSOCIATION FOR FACILITIES ENGINEERING CEDAR VALLEY CHAPTER #132 SCHOLARSHIP
• *See page 114*

BOY SCOUTS OF AMERICA-MUSKINGUM VALLEY COUNCIL http://www.learning-for-life.org

AFL-CIO SKILL TRADES SCHOLARSHIP

Two $1000 scholarships awarded annually to skilled trade explorers to help them support their education. Must be a graduating high school senior in May or June of the year the application is made. School selected by the applicant must be an accredited public or proprietary institution or union apprentice program.

Academic Fields/Career Goals: Trade/Technical Specialties.

Award: Scholarship for use in freshman year; not renewable. *Number:* 2. *Amount:* $1000.

Eligibility Requirements: Applicant must be high school student and planning to enroll or expecting to enroll full- or part-time at a technical institution. Available to U.S. and non-U.S. citizens.

Application Requirements: Application, driver's license, essay, photo, references, transcript. *Deadline:* April 30.

Contact: Bill Rogers, Associate Director
Boy Scouts of America-Muskingum Valley Council
1325 West Walnut Hill Lane
PO Box 152079
Irving, TX 75015-2079
Phone: 972-580-2433
Fax: 972-580-2137
E-mail: brogers@lflmail.org

COLLEGE FOUNDATION OF NORTH CAROLINA INC. http://www.cfnc.org

PROGRESS ENERGY SCHOLARSHIP PROGRAM

Scholarship for a North Carolina resident enrolled, or planning to enroll as a full-time student in a course of study leading to a two-year technical degree at Cape Fear Community College, Fayetteville Technical Community College, or Wake Technical Community College in an approved major. Scholarship may be renewed provided the requirements are met. Individual awards are determined be each college.

Academic Fields/Career Goals: Trade/Technical Specialties.

Award: Scholarship for use in freshman or sophomore years; renewable. *Number:* 3.

Eligibility Requirements: Applicant must be enrolled or expecting to enroll full-time at a two-year or technical institution; resident of North Carolina and studying in North Carolina. Available to U.S. citizens.

Application Requirements: Application, transcript. *Deadline:* continuous.

Contact: Scholarship Committee
College Foundation of North Carolina Inc.
PO Box 41966
Raleigh, NC 27629-1966
Phone: 888-234-6400
E-mail: programinformation@cfnc.org

WACHOVIA TECHNICAL SCHOLARSHIP PROGRAM

Scholarships are offered to students enrolled in two-year technical programs. Recipient must be enrolled full-time in the second year of a two-year technical program at a North Carolina community college. There is no special application form for the scholarship. Each institution selects its own recipients from applicants meeting the criteria. Contact the financial aid office of the college to get more information.

Academic Fields/Career Goals: Trade/Technical Specialties.

Award: Scholarship for use in freshman or sophomore years; not renewable. *Number:* up to 113. *Amount:* $500.

Eligibility Requirements: Applicant must be enrolled or expecting to enroll full-time at a two-year or technical institution and studying in North Carolina. Available to U.S. citizens.

Application Requirements: *Deadline:* continuous.

Contact: Scholarship Committee
College Foundation of North Carolina Inc.
PO Box 41966
Raleigh, NC 27629-1966
Phone: 888-234-6400
E-mail: programinformation@cfnc.org

COMMUNITY FOUNDATION OF WESTERN MASSACHUSETTS http://www.communityfoundation.org

JAMES L. SHRIVER SCHOLARSHIP
• *See page 290*

GLOBAL AUTOMOTIVE AFTERMARKET SYMPOSIUM http://www.automotivescholarships.com

GAAS SCHOLARSHIP
• *See page 291*

GREATER KANAWHA VALLEY FOUNDATION http://www.tgkvf.org

WEST VIRGINIA BROADCASTERS ASSOCIATION FUND
• *See page 179*

INTERNATIONAL EXECUTIVE HOUSEKEEPERS ASSOCIATION http://www.ieha.org

INTERNATIONAL EXECUTIVE HOUSEKEEPERS EDUCATIONAL FOUNDATION
• *See page 315*

INTERNATIONAL FURNISHINGS AND DESIGN ASSOCIATION http://www.ifdaef.org

CHARLES D. MAYO SCHOLARSHIP

• *See page 365*

IFDA STUDENT SCHOLARSHIP

• *See page 365*

INTERNATIONAL UNION OF ELECTRONIC, ELECTRICAL, SALARIED, MACHINE, AND FURNITURE WORKERS-CWA http://www.iue-cwa.org

JAMES B. CAREY SCHOLARSHIP AWARD

• *See page 442*

LEARNING FOR LIFE http://www.learning-for-life.org

AFL-CIO SKILLED TRADES EXPLORING SCHOLARSHIPS

Two $1000 scholarships awarded annually to Explorers to help them support their education toward a career in skilled trades. Applicant must be a graduating high school senior in May or June of the year the application is issued. The school selected by the applicant must be an accredited public or proprietary institution or a union apprentice program.

Academic Fields/Career Goals: Trade/Technical Specialties.

Award: Scholarship for use in freshman year; not renewable. *Number:* up to 2. *Amount:* $1000.

Eligibility Requirements: Applicant must be high school student and planning to enroll or expecting to enroll full- or part-time at a technical institution. Applicant or parent of applicant must be member of Explorer Program/Learning for Life. Available to U.S. citizens.

Application Requirements: Application, essay, photo, references, transcript. *Deadline:* April 30.

Contact: Marty Walsh, National Office S210
Learning for Life
PO Box 152079
Irving, TX 75015-2079
Phone: 972-580-2483
E-mail: mwalsh@lflmail.org

MAINE COMMUNITY COLLEGE SYSTEM http://www.mccs.me.edu

MAINE ANTIQUE POWER SCHOLARSHIP

Scholarship of $400 is available each year to second-year students enrolled in an automotive technology program.

Academic Fields/Career Goals: Trade/Technical Specialties.

Award: Scholarship for use in sophomore year; not renewable. *Number:* varies. *Amount:* $400.

Eligibility Requirements: Applicant must be enrolled or expecting to enroll full-time at a two-year or technical institution; resident of Maine; studying in Maine and must have an interest in automotive. Available to U.S. citizens.

Application Requirements: Application. *Deadline:* varies.

Contact: Scholarship Committee
Maine Community College System
323 State Street
Augusta, ME 04330
Phone: 207-629-4000
Fax: 207-629-4048
E-mail: info@mccs.me.edu

MAINE AUTOMOTIVE TRADE SHOW ASSOCIATION SCHOLARSHIP

Award of $500 to a second-year student enrolled in an automotive technology program at one of the community colleges.

Academic Fields/Career Goals: Trade/Technical Specialties.

Award: Scholarship for use in sophomore year; not renewable. *Number:* varies. *Amount:* $500.

Eligibility Requirements: Applicant must be enrolled or expecting to enroll full-time at a two-year or technical institution; resident of Maine; studying in Maine and must have an interest in automotive. Available to U.S. citizens.

Application Requirements: Application. *Deadline:* varies.

Contact: Scholarship Committee
Maine Community College System
323 State Street
Augusta, ME 04330
Phone: 207-629-4000
Fax: 207-629-4048
E-mail: info@mccs.me.edu

MAINE EDUCATION SERVICES http://www.mesfoundation.com

MAINE METAL PRODUCTS ASSOCIATION SCHOLARSHIP

• *See page 406*

MAINE METAL PRODUCTS ASSOCIATION http://www.mainemfg.com

MAINE METAL PRODUCTS ASSOCIATION SCHOLARSHIP PROGRAM

• *See page 399*

MARION D. AND EVA S. PEEPLES FOUNDATION TRUST SCHOLARSHIP PROGRAM http://www.jccf.org

MARION A. AND EVA S. PEEPLES SCHOLARSHIPS

• *See page 234*

MARYLAND ASSOCIATION OF PRIVATE COLLEGES AND CAREER SCHOOLS http://www.mapccs.org

MARYLAND ASSOCIATION OF PRIVATE COLLEGES AND CAREER SCHOOLS SCHOLARSHIP

• *See page 146*

MARYLAND HIGHER EDUCATION COMMISSION http://www.mhec.state.md.us

CHARLES W. RILEY FIRE AND EMERGENCY MEDICAL SERVICES TUITION REIMBURSEMENT PROGRAM

• *See page 310*

MIDWEST ROOFING CONTRACTORS ASSOCIATION http://www.mrca.org

MRCA FOUNDATION SCHOLARSHIP PROGRAM

• *See page 171*

NATIONAL ASSOCIATION OF WATER COMPANIES-NEW JERSEY CHAPTER

NATIONAL ASSOCIATION OF WATER COMPANIES-NEW JERSEY CHAPTER SCHOLARSHIP

• *See page 133*

NATIONAL ASSOCIATION OF WOMEN IN CONSTRUCTION http://www.nawic.org

NAWIC CONSTRUCTION TRADES SCHOLARSHIP

Scholarship for women pursuing a trade apprenticeship program. Only for students attending school in the United States or Canada.

Academic Fields/Career Goals: Trade/Technical Specialties.

Award: Scholarship for use in sophomore or junior years; not renewable. *Number:* 1. *Amount:* $1000–$2000.

Eligibility Requirements: Applicant must be enrolled or expecting to enroll full-time at a technical institution. Available to U.S. and Canadian citizens.

Application Requirements: Application, essay, transcript. *Deadline:* March 15.

Contact: Scholarship Committee
National Association of Women in Construction
327 South Adams Street
Fort Worth, TX 76104
Phone: 817-877-5551
Fax: 817-877-0324

NAWIC UNDERGRADUATE SCHOLARSHIPS
• *See page 92*

PLASTICS INSTITUTE OF AMERICA http://www.plasticsinstitute.org

PLASTICS PIONEERS SCHOLARSHIPS
• *See page 162*

PLUMBING-HEATING-COOLING CONTRACTORS ASSOCIATION EDUCATION FOUNDATION http://www.phccweb.org

BRADFORD WHITE CORPORATION SCHOLARSHIP
• *See page 92*

DELTA FAUCET COMPANY SCHOLARSHIP PROGRAM
• *See page 93*

PHCC EDUCATIONAL FOUNDATION NEED-BASED SCHOLARSHIP
• *See page 93*

PHCC EDUCATIONAL FOUNDATION SCHOLARSHIP PROGRAM
• *See page 147*

PROFESSIONAL AVIATION MAINTENANCE FOUNDATION http://www.pama.org

PROFESSIONAL AVIATION MAINTENANCE FOUNDATION STUDENT SCHOLARSHIP PROGRAM
• *See page 123*

SOCIETY OF MANUFACTURING ENGINEERS EDUCATION FOUNDATION http://www.sme.org/foundation

CHAPTER 198-DOWNRIVER DETROIT SCHOLARSHIP
• *See page 274*

CHAPTER 67-PHOENIX SCHOLARSHIP
• *See page 274*

CLINTON J. HELTON MANUFACTURING SCHOLARSHIP AWARD FUND
• *See page 275*

E. WAYNE KAY COMMUNITY COLLEGE SCHOLARSHIP AWARD
• *See page 276*

E. WAYNE KAY SCHOLARSHIP
• *See page 277*

FORT WAYNE CHAPTER 56 SCHOLARSHIP
• *See page 277*

MYRTLE AND EARL WALKER SCHOLARSHIP FUND
• *See page 277*

NORTH CENTRAL REGION 9 SCHOLARSHIP
• *See page 278*

WICHITA CHAPTER 52 SCHOLARSHIP
• *See page 278*

WILLIAM E. WEISEL SCHOLARSHIP FUND
• *See page 251*

SOCIETY OF PLASTICS ENGINEERS (SPE) FOUNDATION http://www.4spe.org

FLEMING/BASZCAK SCHOLARSHIP
• *See page 163*

SOCIETY OF PLASTICS ENGINEERS SCHOLARSHIP PROGRAM
• *See page 163*

SPECIALTY EQUIPMENT MARKET ASSOCIATION http://www.sema.org

SPECIALTY EQUIPMENT MARKET ASSOCIATION MEMORIAL SCHOLARSHIP FUND
• *See page 283*

STATE OF GEORGIA http://www.gsfc.org

INTELLECTUAL CAPITAL PARTNERSHIP PROGRAM, ICAPP

Forgivable loans will be awarded to undergraduate students who are residents of Georgia studying high-tech related fields at a Georgia institution. Repayment for every $2500 that is awarded is one-year service in a high-tech field in Georgia. Can be enrolled in a certificate or degree program.

Academic Fields/Career Goals: Trade/Technical Specialties.

Award: Forgivable loan for use in freshman, sophomore, junior, or senior years; not renewable. *Number:* up to 328. *Amount:* up to $7500.

Eligibility Requirements: Applicant must be enrolled or expecting to enroll full- or part-time at a two-year or four-year institution or university; resident of Georgia and studying in Georgia. Available to U.S. citizens.

Application Requirements: Application, financial need analysis. *Deadline:* June 3.

Contact: Peggy Matthews, Manager, GSFA Origination
State of Georgia
2082 East Exchange Place, Suite 230
Tucker, GA 30084
Phone: 770-724-9230
Fax: 770-724-9225
E-mail: peggy@gsfc.org

STRAIGHTFORWARD MEDIA http://www.straightforwardmedia.com

STRAIGHTFORWARD MEDIA VOCATIONAL-TECHNICAL SCHOOL SCHOLARSHIP

Scholarship of $500 available to students enrolled in vocational and technical education programs. Awarded four times per year. Deadlines: November 30, February 28, May 31, August 31.

Academic Fields/Career Goals: Trade/Technical Specialties.

Award: Scholarship for use in freshman or sophomore years; not renewable. *Number:* 4. *Amount:* $500.

Eligibility Requirements: Applicant must be enrolled or expecting to enroll full-time at a two-year or technical institution. Available to U.S. and non-U.S. citizens.

Application Requirements: Online application. *Deadline:* varies.

Contact: Scholarship Committee
StraightForward Media
2040 West Main Street, Suite 104
Rapid City, SD 57701
Phone: 605-348-3042
Fax: 605-348-3043

VIRGINIA BUSINESS AND PROFESSIONAL WOMEN'S FOUNDATION http://www.vabpwfoundation.org

KAREN B. LEWIS CAREER EDUCATION SCHOLARSHIP

The scholarship is offered to women pursuing postsecondary job-oriented career education, offering training in business, trade and industrial occupations (not to be used for education leading to a bachelor's or higher degree). This award may be used for tuition, fees, books, transportation, living expenses, or dependent care. Must be a Virginia resident studying in Virginia.

Academic Fields/Career Goals: Trade/Technical Specialties.

Award: Scholarship for use in freshman or sophomore years; not renewable. *Number:* 1–10. *Amount:* $100–$1000.

Eligibility Requirements: Applicant must be enrolled or expecting to enroll full- or part-time at a two-year or technical institution; female; resident of Virginia and studying in Virginia. Available to U.S. citizens.

Application Requirements: Application, essay, financial need analysis, references, transcript. *Deadline:* April 1.

Contact: Julia Kroos, Chair and Trustee
Virginia Business and Professional Women's Foundation
PO Box 4842
McLean, VA 22103-4842
Phone: 703-450-5108
E-mail: info@vabpwfoundation.org

WOMEN IN LOGISTICS, NORTHERN CALIFORNIA http://www.womeninlogistics.org

WOMEN IN LOGISTICS SCHOLARSHIP

• See page 152

WOMEN'S JEWELRY ASSOCIATION http://www.womensjewelry.org

WJA SCHOLARSHIP PROGRAM

• See page 108

WYOMING TRUCKING ASSOCIATION

WYOMING TRUCKING ASSOCIATION TRUST FUND SCHOLARSHIP

• See page 152

TRANSPORTATION

AMERICAN PUBLIC TRANSPORTATION FOUNDATION http://www.apta.com

DAN REICHARD JR. SCHOLARSHIP

• See page 137

DONALD C. HYDE ESSAY PROGRAM

Award of $500 for the best response to the required essay component of the program.

Academic Fields/Career Goals: Transportation.

Award: Prize for use in sophomore, junior, senior, or graduate years; not renewable. *Number:* 1. *Amount:* $500.

Eligibility Requirements: Applicant must be enrolled or expecting to enroll full-time at a two-year or four-year institution or university. Applicant must have 3.0 GPA or higher. Available to U.S. and Canadian citizens.

Application Requirements: Application, applicant must enter a contest, essay, financial need analysis, references, transcript. *Deadline:* June 16.

Contact: Pamela Boswell, Vice President of Program Management
American Public Transportation Foundation
1666 K Street, NW
Washington, DC 20006-1215
Phone: 202-496-4803
Fax: 202-496-2323
E-mail: pboswell@apta.com

DR. GEORGE M. SMERK SCHOLARSHIP

Scholarship for study towards a career in career in public transit management. Must be sponsored by APTA member organization. Minimum GPA of 3.0 required. College sophomores (30 hours or more satisfactorily completed), juniors, seniors, or those seeking advanced degrees may apply.

Academic Fields/Career Goals: Transportation.

Award: Scholarship for use in sophomore, junior, senior, or graduate years; not renewable. *Number:* 1. *Amount:* $2500.

Eligibility Requirements: Applicant must be enrolled or expecting to enroll full-time at a two-year or four-year institution or university. Applicant must have 3.0 GPA or higher. Available to U.S. citizens.

Application Requirements: Application, essay, financial need analysis, references, test scores, transcript, verification of enrollment for the fall semester, copy of fee schedule from the college/university. *Deadline:* June 16.

Contact: Pamela Boswell, Vice President of Program Management
American Public Transportation Foundation
1666 K Street, NW
Washington, DC 20006-1215
Phone: 202-496-4803
Fax: 202-496-2323
E-mail: pboswell@apta.com

JACK GILSTRAP SCHOLARSHIP

• See page 254

PARSONS BRINCKERHOFF-JIM LAMMIE SCHOLARSHIP

Scholarship for study in public transportation engineering field. Must be sponsored by APTA member organization and complete internship with APTA member organization. Minimum GPA of 3.0 required.

Academic Fields/Career Goals: Transportation.

Award: Scholarship for use in sophomore, junior, senior, or graduate years; renewable. *Number:* 1. *Amount:* $2500.

Eligibility Requirements: Applicant must be enrolled or expecting to enroll full-time at a two-year or four-year institution or university. Applicant must have 3.0 GPA or higher. Available to U.S. and Canadian citizens.

Application Requirements: Application, essay, financial need analysis, references, transcript, verification of enrollment for the current year and copy of fee schedule from the college/university. *Deadline:* June 16.

Contact: Pamela Boswell, Vice President of Program Management
American Public Transportation Foundation
1666 K Street, NW
Washington, DC 20006-1215
Phone: 202-496-4803
Fax: 202-496-2323
E-mail: pboswell@apta.com

TRANSIT HALL OF FAME SCHOLARSHIP AWARD PROGRAM

• See page 168

AMERICAN RAILWAY ENGINEERING AND MAINTENANCE OF WAY ASSOCIATION http://www.arema.org

JOHN J. CUNNINGHAM MEMORIAL SCHOLARSHIP

• See page 255

ASSOCIATED GENERAL CONTRACTORS OF AMERICA-NEW YORK STATE CHAPTER http://www.agcnys.org

ASSOCIATED GENERAL CONTRACTORS OF AMERICA-NEW YORK STATE CHAPTER SCHOLARSHIP PROGRAM

• See page 169

COMMERCIAL DRIVER TRAINING FOUNDATION http://www.cdtfi.org

MILITARY SCHOLARSHIP ASSISTANCE PROGRAM

More than 2200 scholarships in the amount of $500 for retired honorably discharged veterans of the U.S. armed services to defray a portion of the cost of attending truck driver training programs. Applicants must meet the requirements for commercial drivers that have been established by the Federal Motor Carrier Safety Administration, as well as enrollment criteria of the particular institution. Scholarships are only valid and available for new admissions.

Academic Fields/Career Goals: Transportation.

Award: Scholarship for use in freshman year; not renewable. *Number:* 2200. *Amount:* $500.

Eligibility Requirements: Applicant must be enrolled or expecting to enroll full-time at a technical institution. Available to U.S. citizens. Applicant or parent must meet one or more of the following requirements: general military experience; retired from active duty; disabled or killed as a result of military service; prisoner of war; or missing in action.

Application Requirements: Application, copy of discharge order (form DD214). *Deadline:* varies.

Contact: Michael O'Connell, Executive Director
Commercial Driver Training Foundation
PO Box 5310
Springfield, VA 22150
Phone: 703-642-9444
Fax: 703-642-3334

HISPANIC SCHOLARSHIP FUND http://www.hsf.net

HSF/MARATHON OIL CORPORATION COLLEGE SCHOLARSHIP

• *See page 55*

NATIONAL CUSTOMS BROKERS AND FORWARDERS ASSOCIATION OF AMERICA http://www.ncbfaa.org

NATIONAL CUSTOMS BROKERS AND FORWARDERS ASSOCIATION OF AMERICA SCHOLARSHIP AWARD

One-time award for employees of NCBFAA member organizations and their children. Must be studying transportation logistics or international trade full time. Require minimum 2 GPA.

Academic Fields/Career Goals: Transportation.

Award: Scholarship for use in freshman, sophomore, junior, senior, or graduate years; not renewable. *Number:* 1. *Amount:* $5000.

Eligibility Requirements: Applicant must be enrolled or expecting to enroll full-time at a four-year institution or university. Applicant or parent of applicant must have employment or volunteer experience in customs brokering. Available to U.S. citizens.

Application Requirements: Essay, employment verification letter from NCBFAA regular member firm, proof of acceptance to or current enrollment in an accredited college or university. *Deadline:* February 1.

Contact: Tom Mathers, Director Communications
National Customs Brokers and Forwarders Association of America
1200 18th Street, NW, Suite 901
Washington, DC 20036
Phone: 202-466-0222
Fax: 202-466-0226
E-mail: tom@ncbfaa.org

TRANSPORTATION ASSOCIATION OF CANADA http://www.tac-atc.ca

TRANSPORTATION ASSOCIATION OF CANADA/CEMENT ASSOCIATION OF CANADA SCHOLARSHIP

Scholarship for full-time undergraduate and postgraduate students enrolled in transportation-related disciplines. Must be Canadian citizen.

Academic Fields/Career Goals: Transportation.

Award: Scholarship for use in junior, senior, graduate, or postgraduate years; not renewable. *Number:* varies. *Amount:* $5000.

Eligibility Requirements: Applicant must be enrolled or expecting to enroll full-time at a four-year institution or university. Available to Canadian citizens.

Application Requirements: Application, references, transcript. *Deadline:* March 3.

Contact: Gilbert Morier, Manager, Member Services and Public Affairs
Transportation Association of Canada
2323 Street Laurent Boulevard
Ottawa, ON K1G 4J8
Canada
Phone: 613-736-1350
Fax: 613-736-1395
E-mail: gmorier@tac-atc.ca

TRANSPORTATION ASSOCIATION OF CANADA FOUNDATION/BA GROUP SCHOLARSHIP

Scholarship for full-time undergraduate and postgraduate study in transportation planning or transportation engineering. Must be Canadian citizens.

Academic Fields/Career Goals: Transportation.

Award: Scholarship for use in junior, senior, graduate, or postgraduate years; not renewable. *Number:* varies. *Amount:* $5000.

Eligibility Requirements: Applicant must be enrolled or expecting to enroll full-time at a four-year institution or university. Available to Canadian citizens.

Application Requirements: Application, references, transcript. *Deadline:* March 3.

Contact: Gilbert Morier, Manager, Member Services and Public Affairs
Transportation Association of Canada
2323 Street Laurent Boulevard
Ottawa, ON K1G 4J8
Canada
Phone: 613-736-1350
Fax: 613-736-1395
E-mail: gmorier@tac-atc.ca

TRANSPORTATION ASSOCIATION OF CANADA FOUNDATION/DELCAN CORPORATION SCHOLARSHIP

Scholarship for full-time undergraduate and postgraduate students enrolled in transportation-related disciplines. Must be Canadian citizen.

Academic Fields/Career Goals: Transportation.

Award: Scholarship for use in junior, senior, graduate, or postgraduate years; not renewable. *Number:* varies. *Amount:* $5000.

Eligibility Requirements: Applicant must be enrolled or expecting to enroll full-time at a four-year institution or university. Available to Canadian citizens.

Application Requirements: Application, references, transcript. *Deadline:* March 3.

Contact: Gilbert Morier, Manager, Member Services and Public Affairs
Transportation Association of Canada
2323 Street Laurent Boulevard
Ottawa, ON K1G 4J8
Canada
Phone: 613-736-1350
Fax: 613-736-1395
E-mail: gmorier@tac-atc.ca

TRANSPORTATION ASSOCIATION OF CANADA FOUNDATION/EBA ENGINEERING CONSULTANTS LTD SCHOLARSHIP

Scholarship provided for graduate and postgraduate research in transportation infrastructure and systems. Preference is given for research in the areas of design, construction, maintenance and operation of roadway transportation systems in rural and urban environments. Must be Canadian citizen.

Academic Fields/Career Goals: Transportation.

Award: Scholarship for use in junior, senior, graduate, or postgraduate years; not renewable. *Number:* varies. *Amount:* $5000.

Eligibility Requirements: Applicant must be enrolled or expecting to enroll full-time at a four-year institution or university. Available to Canadian citizens.

Application Requirements: Application, references, transcript. *Deadline:* March 3.

Contact: Gilbert Morier, Manager, Member Services and Public Affairs
Transportation Association of Canada
2323 Street Laurent Boulevard
Ottawa, ON K1G 4J8
Canada
Phone: 613-736-1350
Fax: 613-736-1395
E-mail: gmorier@tac-atc.ca

TRANSPORTATION ASSOCIATION OF CANADA FOUNDATION/IBI GROUP SCHOLARSHIP

Scholarship for full-time undergraduate and postgraduate students enrolled in transportation-related disciplines. Must be Canadian citizen.

Academic Fields/Career Goals: Transportation.

Award: Scholarship for use in junior, senior, graduate, or postgraduate years; not renewable. *Number:* varies. *Amount:* $5000.

Eligibility Requirements: Applicant must be enrolled or expecting to enroll full-time at a four-year institution or university. Available to Canadian citizens.

Transportation Association of Canada (continued)

Application Requirements: Application, references, transcript. *Deadline:* March 3.

Contact: Gilbert Morier, Manager, Member Services and Public Affairs
Transportation Association of Canada
2323 Street Laurent Boulevard
Ottawa, ON K1G 4J8
Canada
Phone: 613-736-1350
Fax: 613-736-1395
E-mail: gmorier@tac-atc.ca

TRANSPORTATION ASSOCIATION OF CANADA FOUNDATION/3M CANADA COMPANY SCHOLARSHIP

Scholarship for undergraduate and postgraduate students enrolled full-time in the transportation field. Must be Canadian citizen enrolled in a Canadian University.

Academic Fields/Career Goals: Transportation.

Award: Scholarship for use in junior, senior, graduate, or postgraduate years; not renewable. *Number:* varies. *Amount:* $5000.

Eligibility Requirements: Applicant must be enrolled or expecting to enroll full-time at a four-year institution or university. Available to Canadian citizens.

Application Requirements: Application, references, transcript. *Deadline:* March 3.

Contact: Gilbert Morier, Manager, Member Services and Public Affairs
Transportation Association of Canada
2323 Street Laurent Boulevard
Ottawa, ON K1G 4J8
Canada
Phone: 613-736-1350
Fax: 613-736-1395
E-mail: gmorier@tac-atc.ca

TRANSPORTATION CLUBS INTERNATIONAL http://www.transportationclubsinternational.com

ALICE GLAISYER WARFIELD MEMORIAL SCHOLARSHIP

Award is available to currently enrolled students majoring in transportation, logistics, traffic management, or related fields. Available to citizens of the United States, Canada, and Mexico. See Web site for application: http://www.transportationclubsinternational.com/

Academic Fields/Career Goals: Transportation.

Award: Scholarship for use in freshman, sophomore, junior, senior, graduate, or postgraduate years; not renewable. *Number:* 1. *Amount:* $1000.

Eligibility Requirements: Applicant must be enrolled or expecting to enroll full- or part-time at a two-year or four-year or technical institution or university. Applicant or parent of applicant must be member of Transportation Club International. Available to U.S. and non-U.S. citizens.

Application Requirements: Application, essay, photo, references, transcript. *Deadline:* April 30.

Contact: Bill Blair, Scholarships Trustee
Transportation Clubs International
15710 JFK Boulevard
Houston, TX 77032
Phone: 832-300-5905
E-mail: bblair@zimmerworldwide.com

DENNY LYDIC SCHOLARSHIP

Award is available to currently enrolled college students majoring in transportation, logistics, traffic management, or related fields. Available to citizens of the United States, Canada, and Mexico. See Web site for application: http://www.transportationclubsinternational.com/

Academic Fields/Career Goals: Transportation.

Award: Scholarship for use in freshman, sophomore, junior, senior, graduate, or postgraduate years; not renewable. *Number:* 1. *Amount:* $500.

Eligibility Requirements: Applicant must be enrolled or expecting to enroll full- or part-time at a two-year or four-year or technical institution or university. Applicant or parent of applicant must be member of Transportation Club International. Available to U.S. and non-U.S. citizens.

Application Requirements: Application, essay, photo, references, transcript. *Deadline:* April 30.

Contact: Bill Blair, Scholarships Trustee
Transportation Clubs International
15710 JFK Boulevard
Houston, TX 77032
Phone: 832-300-5905
E-mail: bblair@zimmerworldwide.com

TEXAS TRANSPORTATION SCHOLARSHIP

Merit-based award for a student who is at least a sophomore studying transportation, traffic management, and related fields. Must have been enrolled in a school in Texas during some phase of education (elementary, secondary, high school). Must include photo and submit three references. One-time scholarship of $1000. See Web site for application: http://www.transportationclubsinternational.com/

Academic Fields/Career Goals: Transportation.

Award: Scholarship for use in sophomore, junior, senior, graduate, or postgraduate years; not renewable. *Number:* 1. *Amount:* $1000.

Eligibility Requirements: Applicant must be enrolled or expecting to enroll full- or part-time at a two-year or four-year or technical institution or university. Applicant or parent of applicant must be member of Transportation Club International. Available to U.S. citizens.

Application Requirements: Application, essay, photo, references, transcript. *Deadline:* April 30.

Contact: Bill Blair, Scholarships Trustee
Transportation Clubs International
15710 JFK Boulevard
Houston, TX 77032
Phone: 832-300-5905
E-mail: bblair@zimmerworldwide.com

TRANSPORTATION CLUBS INTERNATIONAL CHARLOTTE WOODS SCHOLARSHIP

Award available to an enrolled college student majoring in transportation or traffic management. Must be a member or a dependant of a member of Transportation Clubs International. Must have completed at least one year of post-high school education. One-time award of $1000. See Web site for application: http://www.transportationclubsinternational.com/

Academic Fields/Career Goals: Transportation.

Award: Scholarship for use in freshman, sophomore, junior, senior, graduate, or postgraduate years; not renewable. *Number:* 1. *Amount:* $1000.

Eligibility Requirements: Applicant must be enrolled or expecting to enroll full- or part-time at a two-year or four-year or technical institution or university. Applicant or parent of applicant must be member of Transportation Club International. Available to U.S. and non-U.S. citizens.

Application Requirements: Application, essay, photo, references, transcript. *Deadline:* April 30.

Contact: Bill Blair, Scholarship Trustee
Transportation Clubs International
15710 JFK Boulevard
Houston, TX 77032
Phone: 832-300-5905
E-mail: bblair@zimmerworldwide.com

TRANSPORTATION CLUBS INTERNATIONAL FRED A. HOOPER MEMORIAL SCHOLARSHIP

• *See page 298*

TRANSPORTATION CLUBS INTERNATIONAL GINGER AND FRED DEINES CANADA SCHOLARSHIP

One-time award for a student of Canadian heritage, who is attending college or university in Canada or the United States and majoring in transportation, traffic management, logistics, or a related field. Academic merit is considered. See Web site for application: http://www.transportationclubsinternational.com/

Academic Fields/Career Goals: Transportation.

Award: Scholarship for use in freshman, sophomore, junior, senior, graduate, or postgraduate years; not renewable. *Number:* 1. *Amount:* $1500.

Eligibility Requirements: Applicant must be of Canadian heritage and Canadian citizen and enrolled or expecting to enroll full- or part-time at a two-year or four-year or technical institution or university. Applicant or parent of applicant must be member of Transportation Club International.

Application Requirements: Application, essay, photo, references, transcript. *Deadline:* April 30.

Contact: Bill Blair, Scholarships Trustee
Transportation Clubs International
15710 JFK Boulevard
Houston, TX 77032
Phone: 832-300-5905
E-mail: bblair@zimmerworldwide.com

TRANSPORTATION CLUBS INTERNATIONAL GINGER AND FRED DEINES MEXICO SCHOLARSHIP

Scholarship of $1500 for a student who is enrolled in an accredited institution of higher learning in a vocational or degree program in the fields of transportation, logistics or traffic management, or related fields. See Web site for application: http://www.transportationclubsinternational.com/

Academic Fields/Career Goals: Transportation.

Award: Scholarship for use in freshman, sophomore, junior, senior, graduate, or postgraduate years; not renewable. *Number:* 1. *Amount:* $1500.

Eligibility Requirements: Applicant must be Mexican citizen and enrolled or expecting to enroll full- or part-time at a two-year or four-year or technical institution or university. Applicant or parent of applicant must be member of Transportation Club International. Available to citizens of countries other than the U.S. or Canada.

Application Requirements: Application, essay, photo, references, transcript. *Deadline:* April 30.

Contact: Bill Blair, Scholarships Trustee
Transportation Clubs International
15710 JFK Boulevard
Houston, TX 77032
Phone: 832-300-5905
E-mail: bblair@zimmerworldwide.com

TRUCKLOAD CARRIERS ASSOCIATION http://www.truckload.org

TRUCKLOAD CARRIERS ASSOCIATION SCHOLARSHIP FUND
• *See page 149*

WOMEN IN LOGISTICS, NORTHERN CALIFORNIA http://www.womeninlogistics.org

WOMEN IN LOGISTICS SCHOLARSHIP
• *See page 152*

WYOMING TRUCKING ASSOCIATION

WYOMING TRUCKING ASSOCIATION TRUST FUND SCHOLARSHIP
• *See page 152*

TRAVEL/TOURISM

AMERICAN HOTEL AND LODGING EDUCATIONAL FOUNDATION http://www.ahlef.org

INCOMING FRESHMAN SCHOLARSHIPS
• *See page 202*

AMERICAN SOCIETY OF TRAVEL AGENTS (ASTA) FOUNDATION http://www.astanet.com

AMERICAN EXPRESS TRAVEL SCHOLARSHIP

Candidate must be enrolled in a travel or tourism program in either a two- or four-year college or university or proprietary travel school. Must write 500-word essay on student's view of travel industry's future. Minimum 2.5 GPA required.

Academic Fields/Career Goals: Travel/Tourism.

Award: Scholarship for use in freshman, sophomore, junior, or senior years; not renewable. *Number:* varies. *Amount:* varies.

Eligibility Requirements: Applicant must be enrolled or expecting to enroll full- or part-time at a two-year or four-year institution or university. Applicant must have 2.5 GPA or higher. Available to U.S. and Canadian citizens.

Application Requirements: Application, driver's license, resume, references, transcript, 500-word paper detailing the student's plans in travel. *Deadline:* July 31.

Contact: Verlette Mitchell, Manager
American Society of Travel Agents (ASTA) Foundation
1101 King Street
Alexandria, VA 22314-2187
Phone: 703-739-8721
Fax: 703-684-8319
E-mail: scholarship@astahq.com

ARIZONA CHAPTER DEPENDENT/EMPLOYEE MEMBERSHIP SCHOLARSHIP

Candidate must be a dependent of an ASTA Arizona Chapter Active, Active Associate or Travel Professional member, or an employee of an Arizona ASTA member agency for a minimum of six months whose ASTA membership dues are current. One award of $1500 will be given. Must attend Arizona institution. Must be enrolled in their final year in a two year college, or as a junior or senior in a four-year college/university. Minimum 2.5 GPA required.

Academic Fields/Career Goals: Travel/Tourism.

Award: Scholarship for use in sophomore, junior, or senior years; not renewable. *Number:* 1. *Amount:* $1500.

Eligibility Requirements: Applicant must be enrolled or expecting to enroll full- or part-time at a two-year or four-year institution or university; resident of Arizona and studying in Arizona. Applicant or parent of applicant must be member of American Society of Travel Agents. Applicant must have 2.5 GPA or higher. Available to U.S. and Canadian citizens.

Application Requirements: Application, driver's license, references, transcript, 500-word paper entitled "My Career Goals". *Deadline:* July 31.

Contact: Verlette Mitchell, Manager
American Society of Travel Agents (ASTA) Foundation
1101 King Street
Alexandria, VA 22314-2187
Phone: 703-739-8721
Fax: 703-684-8319
E-mail: scholarship@astahq.com

ARIZONA CHAPTER GOLD SCHOLARSHIP

One-time award for college undergraduates who are Arizona residents pursuing a travel or tourism degree at a four-year Arizona institution. Freshmen are not eligible. Must submit essay on career plans and interests. Minimum 2.5 GPA required. Must be a U.S. citizen or Canadian citizen.

Academic Fields/Career Goals: Travel/Tourism.

Award: Scholarship for use in sophomore, junior, or senior years; not renewable. *Number:* 1. *Amount:* $3000.

Eligibility Requirements: Applicant must be enrolled or expecting to enroll full- or part-time at a four-year institution or university; resident of Arizona and studying in Arizona. Applicant must have 2.5 GPA or higher. Available to U.S. and Canadian citizens.

Application Requirements: Application, driver's license, references, transcript. *Deadline:* July 31.

Contact: Verlette Mitchell, Manager
American Society of Travel Agents (ASTA) Foundation
1101 King Street
Alexandria, VA 22314-2187
Phone: 703-739-8721
Fax: 703-684-8319
E-mail: scholarship@astahq.com

AVIS SCHOLARSHIP

Scholarship of $2000 for individuals who have already gained experience and/or training in the travel industry. Candidate must have a minimum of two years of full-time travel industry experience or an undergraduate degree in travel/tourism and must currently be employed in the travel industry. Must be enrolled in a minimum of two courses per semester in an accredited undergraduate or graduate level degree program in business, or equivalent degree program. Minimum GPA of 3.0 required.

Academic Fields/Career Goals: Travel/Tourism.

American Society of Travel Agents (ASTA) Foundation (continued)

Award: Scholarship for use in freshman, sophomore, junior, senior, or graduate years; renewable. *Number:* 1. *Amount:* $2000.

Eligibility Requirements: Applicant must be enrolled or expecting to enroll full- or part-time at a four-year institution or university. Applicant must have 3.0 GPA or higher. Available to U.S. and Canadian citizens.

Application Requirements: Application, driver's license, references, transcript, proof of current employment in the travel industry. *Deadline:* July 31.

Contact: Verlette Mitchell, Manager
American Society of Travel Agents (ASTA) Foundation
1101 King Street
Alexandria, VA 22314-2187
Phone: 703-739-8721
Fax: 703-684-8319
E-mail: scholarship@astahq.com

DONALD ESTEY SCHOLARSHIP FUND-ROCKY MOUNTAIN CHAPTER

Applicants must be enrolled in a licensed preparatory travel program or must be participating in either an ASTA sponsored training program, The Travel Institute Destination Specialist, or other industry training programs. Must have letter of recommendation from ASTA Rocky Mountain Chapter. Must be Colorado, Utah, or Wyoming resident. Must have a minimum of 2.5 GPA. Must be a U.S. citizen or Canadian citizen.

Academic Fields/Career Goals: Travel/Tourism.

Award: Scholarship for use in freshman or sophomore years; not renewable. *Number:* 3. *Amount:* $1000.

Eligibility Requirements: Applicant must be enrolled or expecting to enroll full- or part-time at a two-year or technical institution; resident of Colorado, Utah, or Wyoming and studying in Colorado, Utah, or Wyoming. Applicant or parent of applicant must be member of American Society of Travel Agents. Applicant or parent of applicant must have employment or volunteer experience in travel and tourism industry. Applicant must have 2.5 GPA or higher. Available to U.S. and Canadian citizens.

Application Requirements: Application, driver's license, financial need analysis, references, test scores, transcript, statement indicating the program's expected benefit. *Deadline:* varies.

Contact: Verlette Mitchell, Manager
American Society of Travel Agents (ASTA) Foundation
1101 King Street
Alexandria, VA 22314-2187
Phone: 703-739-8721
Fax: 703-684-8319
E-mail: scholarship@astahq.com

GEORGE REINKE SCHOLARSHIPS

Applicant must write a 500-word essay on career goals in the travel or tourism industry. Must be a U.S. citizen living and studying in the United States and enrolled in a travel agent studies program in a junior college or travel school. Must have a minimum GPA of 2.5.

Academic Fields/Career Goals: Travel/Tourism.

Award: Scholarship for use in freshman or sophomore years; not renewable. *Number:* up to 6. *Amount:* $2000.

Eligibility Requirements: Applicant must be enrolled or expecting to enroll full- or part-time at a two-year institution. Applicant must have 2.5 GPA or higher. Available to U.S. citizens.

Application Requirements: Application, driver's license, references, transcript, 500-word paper entitled "My Objectives in the Travel Agency Industry". *Deadline:* July 31.

Contact: Verlette Mitchell, Manager
American Society of Travel Agents (ASTA) Foundation
1101 King Street
Alexandria, VA 22314-2187
Phone: 703-739-8721
Fax: 703-684-8319
E-mail: scholarship@astahq.com

HEALY SCHOLARSHIP

One-time award of $2000 for a college undergraduate pursuing a travel or tourism degree. Must submit essay suggesting improvements for the travel industry. Must be a citizen of United States or Canada. Minimum 2.5 GPA required.

Academic Fields/Career Goals: Travel/Tourism.

Award: Scholarship for use in freshman, sophomore, junior, or senior years; not renewable. *Number:* 1. *Amount:* $2000.

Eligibility Requirements: Applicant must be enrolled or expecting to enroll full- or part-time at a four-year institution or university. Applicant must have 2.5 GPA or higher. Available to U.S. and Canadian citizens.

Application Requirements: Application, driver's license, references, self-addressed stamped envelope, transcript, 500-word paper suggesting improvements in the travel industry. *Deadline:* July 31.

Contact: Verlette Mitchell, Manager
American Society of Travel Agents (ASTA) Foundation
1101 King Street
Alexandria, VA 22314-2187
Phone: 703-739-8721
Fax: 703-684-8319
E-mail: scholarship@astahq.com

HOLLAND-AMERICA LINE WESTOURS SCHOLARSHIPS

Students must write 500-word essay on the future of the cruise industry and must be enrolled in travel or tourism program at a two- or four-year college or proprietary travel school. Minimum 2.5 GPA required. Must be a U.S. or Canadian citizen.

Academic Fields/Career Goals: Travel/Tourism.

Award: Scholarship for use in freshman, sophomore, junior, or senior years; not renewable. *Number:* 2. *Amount:* $3000.

Eligibility Requirements: Applicant must be enrolled or expecting to enroll full- or part-time at a two-year or four-year institution or university. Applicant must have 2.5 GPA or higher. Available to U.S. and Canadian citizens.

Application Requirements: Application, driver's license, financial need analysis, resume, references, transcript, 500-word paper on the future of the cruise industry. *Deadline:* July 31.

Contact: Verlette Mitchell, Manager
American Society of Travel Agents (ASTA) Foundation
1101 King Street
Alexandria, VA 22314-2187
Phone: 703-739-8721
Fax: 703-684-8319
E-mail: scholarship@astahq.com

JOHN HJORTH SCHOLARSHIP FUND-SAN DIEGO CHAPTER

Any employee of a San Diego ASTA Chapter member pursuing one of the Travel Institute certification programs, The Travel Institute Destination Specialists programs, or any ASTA Educational program is eligible to apply. Must have a minimum of two years travel industry experience. Must be a U.S. citizen or Canadian citizen.

Academic Fields/Career Goals: Travel/Tourism.

Award: Scholarship for use in freshman or sophomore years; not renewable. *Number:* 3. *Amount:* up to $250.

Eligibility Requirements: Applicant must be enrolled or expecting to enroll full- or part-time at a technical institution and resident of California. Applicant or parent of applicant must be member of American Society of Travel Agents. Applicant or parent of applicant must have employment or volunteer experience in travel and tourism industry. Applicant must have 2.5 GPA or higher. Available to U.S. and Canadian citizens.

Application Requirements: Application, essay, references, letter of interest and/or need. *Deadline:* July 31.

Contact: Verlette Mitchell, Manager
American Society of Travel Agents (ASTA) Foundation
1101 King Street
Alexandria, VA 22314-2187
Phone: 703-739-8721
Fax: 703-684-8319
E-mail: scholarship@astahq.com

JOSEPH R. STONE SCHOLARSHIPS

One-time award for high school senior or college undergraduate pursuing a travel or tourism degree. Must have a parent in the industry and proof of employment. Must submit a 500-word essay explaining career goals. Minimum 2.5 GPA required. Must be a citizen of United States or Canada.

Academic Fields/Career Goals: Travel/Tourism.

Award: Scholarship for use in freshman, sophomore, junior, or senior years; not renewable. *Number:* 3. *Amount:* $2400.

Eligibility Requirements: Applicant must be enrolled or expecting to enroll full- or part-time at a four-year institution or university. Applicant must have 2.5 GPA or higher. Available to U.S. and Canadian citizens.

Application Requirements: Application, references, transcript, 500-word paper on applicant's goals. *Deadline:* July 31.

Contact: Verlette Mitchell, Manager
American Society of Travel Agents (ASTA) Foundation
1101 King Street
Alexandria, VA 22314-2187
Phone: 703-739-8721
Fax: 703-684-8319
E-mail: scholarship@astahq.com

NANCY STEWART SCHOLARSHIP FUND-ALLEGHENY CHAPTER

One-time award for travel professionals working for an agency that is a member of American Society of Travel Agents' Allegheny Chapter. Must be pursuing one of The Travel Institute's four certification programs: CTC accreditation, Destination Specialist, Travel Career Development, Professional Management; or an ASTA educational program. Must be Pennsylvania resident. Must also have at least three years of travel industry experience. Must have a minimum of 2.5 GPA.

Academic Fields/Career Goals: Travel/Tourism.

Award: Scholarship for use in freshman or sophomore years; not renewable. *Number:* 3. *Amount:* $400.

Eligibility Requirements: Applicant must be enrolled or expecting to enroll part-time at a technical institution and resident of Pennsylvania. Applicant or parent of applicant must be member of American Society of Travel Agents. Applicant or parent of applicant must have employment or volunteer experience in travel and tourism industry. Applicant must have 2.5 GPA or higher. Available to U.S. and Canadian citizens.

Application Requirements: Application, essay, references, letter of intent. *Deadline:* July 31.

Contact: Verlette Mitchell, Manager
American Society of Travel Agents (ASTA) Foundation
1101 King Street
Alexandria, VA 22314-2187
Phone: 703-739-8721
Fax: 703-684-8319
E-mail: scholarship@astahq.com

NORTHERN CALIFORNIA CHAPTER RICHARD EPPING SCHOLARSHIP

Scholarship of $2000. Applicant must be currently enrolled in a travel and tourism curriculum at a college, university, or proprietary travel and tourism school in Northern California or Northern Nevada. Minimum 2.5 GPA required. Must be a U.S. or Canadian citizen.

Academic Fields/Career Goals: Travel/Tourism.

Award: Scholarship for use in freshman, sophomore, junior, or senior years; not renewable. *Number:* 1. *Amount:* $2000.

Eligibility Requirements: Applicant must be enrolled or expecting to enroll full- or part-time at a two-year or four-year institution or university and studying in California or Nevada. Applicant must have 2.5 GPA or higher. Available to U.S. and Canadian citizens.

Application Requirements: Application, essay, references, transcript. *Deadline:* July 31.

Contact: Verlette Mitchell, Manager
American Society of Travel Agents (ASTA) Foundation
1101 King Street
Alexandria, VA 22314-2187
Phone: 703-739-8721
Fax: 703-684-8319
E-mail: scholarship@astahq.com

ORANGE COUNTY CHAPTER/HARRY JACKSON SCHOLARSHIP FUND

Awards are available to any Active or Associate member of the Orange County ASTA office pursuing one of the following programs: ASTA Educational Programs, The Travel Institute certification programs, CTC, Destination Specialist, The Travel Institute Educational Programs, and The Travel Institute forums. The applicant must also have at least two years of travel industry experience. Must have a minimum of 2.5 GPA.

Academic Fields/Career Goals: Travel/Tourism.

Award: Scholarship for use in freshman or sophomore years; not renewable. *Number:* varies. *Amount:* $250.

Eligibility Requirements: Applicant must be enrolled or expecting to enroll full- or part-time at a technical institution and resident of California. Applicant or parent of applicant must be member of American Society of Travel Agents. Applicant must have 2.5 GPA or higher. Available to U.S. and Canadian citizens.

Application Requirements: Application, financial need analysis, resume, references, transcript, letter of interest. *Deadline:* July 31.

Contact: Verlette Mitchell, Manager
American Society of Travel Agents (ASTA) Foundation
1101 King Street
Alexandria, VA 22314-2187
Phone: 703-739-8721
Fax: 703-684-8319
E-mail: scholarship@astahq.com

PACIFIC NORTHWEST CHAPTER-WILLIAM HUNT SCHOLARSHIP FUND

One-time award for travel professionals. Applicant must be employed in the travel industry in an ASTA office or enrolled in a travel and tourism program in either a two- or four-year college, university or proprietary travel school. Must be a resident of and studying in one of the following states: Alaska, Idaho, Montana, Oregon, or Washington. Must be a U.S. or Canadian citizen. Must have a minimum of 2.5 GPA.

Academic Fields/Career Goals: Travel/Tourism.

Award: Scholarship for use in freshman, sophomore, junior, or senior years; not renewable. *Number:* up to 3. *Amount:* up to $1000.

Eligibility Requirements: Applicant must be enrolled or expecting to enroll full- or part-time at a two-year or four-year or technical institution or university; resident of Alaska, Idaho, Montana, Oregon, or Washington and studying in Alaska, Idaho, Montana, Oregon, or Washington. Applicant or parent of applicant must be member of American Society of Travel Agents. Applicant must have 2.5 GPA or higher. Available to U.S. and Canadian citizens.

Application Requirements: Application, essay, references, transcript, 300-word letter explaining reasons for interest in further training in travel. *Deadline:* July 31.

Contact: Verlette Mitchell, Manager
American Society of Travel Agents (ASTA) Foundation
1101 King Street
Alexandria, VA 22314-2187
Phone: 703-739-8721
Fax: 703-684-8319
E-mail: scholarship@astahq.com

PRINCESS CRUISES AND PRINCESS TOURS SCHOLARSHIP

Merit-based award for student accepted or enrolled as an undergraduate in a travel or tourism program. Submit 300-word essay on two features cruise ships will need to offer passengers in the next ten years. Minimum 2.5 GPA required. Must be a U.S. citizen or Canadian citizen.

Academic Fields/Career Goals: Travel/Tourism.

Award: Scholarship for use in freshman, sophomore, junior, or senior years; not renewable. *Number:* 2. *Amount:* $2000.

Eligibility Requirements: Applicant must be enrolled or expecting to enroll full- or part-time at a two-year or four-year institution or university. Applicant must have 2.5 GPA or higher. Available to U.S. and Canadian citizens.

Application Requirements: Application, references, transcript, 300-word paper on the two features cruise ships will need to offer passengers in the next ten years. *Deadline:* July 31.

Contact: Verlette Mitchell, Manager
American Society of Travel Agents (ASTA) Foundation
1101 King Street
Alexandria, VA 22314-2187
Phone: 703-739-8721
Fax: 703-684-8319
E-mail: scholarship@astahq.com

SOUTHEAST AMERICAN SOCIETY OF TRAVEL AGENTS CHAPTER SCHOLARSHIP

Applicants must be Active Associate members in good standing of the SEASTA chapter, and have at least two years of travel industry experience. Applicants must be pursuing any of the ASTA Specialist certification programs, ASTA

American Society of Travel Agents (ASTA) Foundation (continued)

educational conferences, The Travel Institute CTA, The Travel Institute CTC, or The Travel Institute Destination certification programs. Applicant must apply for scholarship within one year of receiving certification.

Academic Fields/Career Goals: Travel/Tourism.

Award: Scholarship for use in freshman year; not renewable. *Number:* up to 6. *Amount:* $350.

Eligibility Requirements: Applicant must be enrolled or expecting to enroll part-time at a technical institution; resident of Alabama, Georgia, Kentucky, Louisiana, Mississippi, North Carolina, South Carolina, or Tennessee and studying in Alabama, Georgia, Kentucky, Louisiana, Mississippi, North Carolina, South Carolina, or Tennessee. Applicant or parent of applicant must be member of American Society of Travel Agents. Applicant or parent of applicant must have employment or volunteer experience in travel and tourism industry. Applicant must have 2.5 GPA or higher. Available to U.S. and Canadian citizens.

Application Requirements: Application, references, letter of interest or need, proof of course certification. *Deadline:* July 31.

Contact: Verlette Mitchell, Manager
American Society of Travel Agents (ASTA) Foundation
1101 King Street
Alexandria, VA 22314-2187
Phone: 703-739-8721
Fax: 703-684-8319
E-mail: scholarship@astahq.com

SOUTHERN CALIFORNIA CHAPTER/PLEASANT HAWAIIAN HOLIDAYS SCHOLARSHIP

Two awards for students pursuing travel or tourism degrees. One award given to student attending college in southern California, and one award given to a student attending school anywhere in the United States. Applicant must be U.S. citizens. Minimum 2.5 GPA required.

Academic Fields/Career Goals: Travel/Tourism.

Award: Scholarship for use in freshman, sophomore, junior, or senior years; not renewable. *Number:* 2. *Amount:* $2500.

Eligibility Requirements: Applicant must be enrolled or expecting to enroll full- or part-time at a four-year institution or university. Applicant must have 2.5 GPA or higher. Available to U.S. citizens.

Application Requirements: Application, references, transcript, 500-word paper entitled "My Goals in the Travel Industry". *Deadline:* July 31.

Contact: Verlette Mitchell, Manager
American Society of Travel Agents (ASTA) Foundation
1101 King Street
Alexandria, VA 22314-2187
Phone: 703-739-8721
Fax: 703-684-8319
E-mail: scholarship@astahq.com

STAN AND LEONE POLLARD SCHOLARSHIPS

Candidate must be re-entering the job market by being enrolled in a travel and tourism curriculum in either a recognized proprietary travel school or a two-year junior college. Two awards of $2000 each will be given. Must have a minimum GPA of 2.5 and be a U.S. or Canadian citizen.

Academic Fields/Career Goals: Travel/Tourism.

Award: Scholarship for use in freshman or sophomore years; not renewable. *Number:* 2. *Amount:* $2000.

Eligibility Requirements: Applicant must be enrolled or expecting to enroll full- or part-time at a two-year or technical institution. Applicant must have 2.5 GPA or higher. Available to U.S. and Canadian citizens.

Application Requirements: Application, references, transcript, 500-word paper on the student's objectives in the travel and tourism industry. *Deadline:* July 31.

Contact: Verlette Mitchell, Manager
American Society of Travel Agents (ASTA) Foundation
1101 King Street
Alexandria, VA 22314-2187
Phone: 703-739-8721
Fax: 703-684-8319
E-mail: scholarship@astahq.com

CANADIAN RECREATIONAL CANOEING ASSOCIATION http://www.paddlingcanada.com

BILL MASON MEMORIAL SCHOLARSHIP FUND
• *See page 74*

HAWAII HOTEL AND LODGING ASSOCIATION http://www.hawaiihotels.org

R.W. BOB HOLDEN SCHOLARSHIP
• *See page 357*

INTERNATIONAL AIRLINES TRAVEL AGENT NETWORK http://www.iatan.org

INTERNATIONAL AIRLINES TRAVEL AGENT NETWORK FOUNDATION SCHOLARSHIP
• *See page 357*

MISSOURI TRAVEL COUNCIL http://www.missouritravel.com

MISSOURI TRAVEL COUNCIL TOURISM SCHOLARSHIP
• *See page 316*

NATIONAL TOURISM FOUNDATION http://www.ntfonline.com

ACADEMY OF TRAVEL AND TOURISM SCHOLARSHIPS
• *See page 357*

CLEVELAND LEGACY I AND II SCHOLARSHIP AWARDS
• *See page 316*

NEW HORIZONS KATHY LETARTE SCHOLARSHIP
• *See page 317*

PAT AND JIM HOST SCHOLARSHIP
• *See page 358*

SOCIETIE DES CASINOS DU QUEBEC SCHOLARSHIP
• *See page 317*

TAMPA, HILLSBOROUGH LEGACY SCHOLARSHIP
• *See page 317*

TAUCK SCHOLARS SCHOLARSHIPS
• *See page 317*

TULSA SCHOLARSHIP AWARDS
• *See page 317*

YELLOW RIBBON SCHOLARSHIP
• *See page 317*

TV/RADIO BROADCASTING

ACADEMY OF TELEVISION ARTS AND SCIENCES FOUNDATION http://www.emmysfoundation.org

ACADEMY OF TELEVISION ARTS AND SCIENCES COLLEGE TELEVISION AWARDS
• *See page 99*

ADC RESEARCH INSTITUTE http://www.adc.org

JACK SHAHEEN MASS COMMUNICATIONS SCHOLARSHIP AWARD
• *See page 175*

ALABAMA BROADCASTERS ASSOCIATION http://www.al-ba.com

ALABAMA BROADCASTERS ASSOCIATION SCHOLARSHIP

Scholarship available to Alabama residents studying broadcasting at any accredited Alabama technical school, 2- or 4-year college, or university.

Academic Fields/Career Goals: TV/Radio Broadcasting.

Award: Scholarship for use in junior or senior years; not renewable. *Number:* up to 4. *Amount:* up to $2500.

Eligibility Requirements: Applicant must be enrolled or expecting to enroll full-time at a two-year or four-year or technical institution or university; resident of Alabama and studying in Alabama. Available to U.S. citizens.

Application Requirements: Application, references. *Deadline:* April 30.

Contact: Sharon Tinsley, President
Alabama Broadcasters Association
2180 Parkway Lake Drive
Hoover, AL 35244
Phone: 205-982-5001
Fax: 205-982-0015
E-mail: stinsley@al-ba.com

AMERICAN LEGION, PRESS CLUB OF NEW JERSEY

AMERICAN LEGION PRESS CLUB OF NEW JERSEY AND POST 170 ARTHUR DEHARDT MEMORIAL SCHOLARSHIP
• *See page 175*

ASIAN AMERICAN JOURNALISTS ASSOCIATION http://www.aaja.org

AAJA/COX FOUNDATION SCHOLARSHIP
• *See page 367*

ASIAN-AMERICAN JOURNALISTS ASSOCIATION SCHOLARSHIP
• *See page 176*

MINORU YASUI MEMORIAL SCHOLARSHIP AWARD
• *See page 368*

ASSOCIATED PRESS http://www.aptra.org

ASSOCIATED PRESS TELEVISION/RADIO ASSOCIATION-CLETE ROBERTS JOURNALISM SCHOLARSHIP AWARDS
• *See page 368*

KATHRYN DETTMAN MEMORIAL JOURNALISM SCHOLARSHIP
• *See page 368*

ASSOCIATION FOR WOMEN IN SPORTS MEDIA http://www.awsmonline.org

WOMEN IN SPORTS MEDIA SCHOLARSHIP/INTERNSHIP PROGRAM
• *See page 176*

ATLANTA PRESS CLUB INC. http://www.atlantapressclub.org

ATLANTA PRESS CLUB JOURNALISM SCHOLARSHIP PROGRAM
• *See page 369*

CALIFORNIA BROADCASTERS FOUNDATION http://www.cabroadcasters.org

CALIFORNIA BROADCASTERS FOUNDATION INTERN SCHOLARSHIP

Two $500 scholarships awarded to radio interns and two $500 scholarships awarded to television interns each semester. Any enrolled college student working as an intern at any California Broadcasters Foundation or Association member radio or television station is eligible. No minimum number of hours per week required. Immediate family of current Foundation Board Members are not eligible. Deadlines: June 18 for fall and December 10 for spring.

Academic Fields/Career Goals: TV/Radio Broadcasting.

Award: Scholarship for use in freshman, sophomore, junior, senior, graduate, or postgraduate years; not renewable. *Number:* up to 4. *Amount:* $500.

Eligibility Requirements: Applicant must be enrolled or expecting to enroll full- or part-time at a two-year or four-year or technical institution or university and resident of California. Available to U.S. citizens.

Application Requirements: Application, essay, references. *Deadline:* varies.

Contact: Mark Powers, Government Affairs
California Broadcasters Foundation
915 L Street, Suite 1150
Sacramento, CA 95814
Phone: 916-444-2237
E-mail: cbapowers@cabroadcasters.org

CALIFORNIA CHICANO NEWS MEDIA ASSOCIATION (CCNMA) http://www.ccnma.org

CCNMA SCHOLARSHIPS
• *See page 177*

CANADIAN ASSOCIATION OF BROADCASTERS http://www.cab-acr.ca

ASTRAL MEDIA SCHOLARSHIP
• *See page 177*

JIM ALLARD BROADCAST JOURNALISM SCHOLARSHIP
• *See page 369*

RUTH HANCOCK MEMORIAL SCHOLARSHIP
• *See page 177*

CHARLES & LUCILLE KING FAMILY FOUNDATION INC. http://www.kingfoundation.org

CHARLES AND LUCILLE KING FAMILY FOUNDATION SCHOLARSHIPS
• *See page 177*

CIRI FOUNDATION (TCF) http://www.thecirifoundation.org

CAP LATHROP SCHOLARSHIP PROGRAM

Award for an Alaska Native enrollee or descendant of original enrollee to an ANCSA regional or village corporation. Must be enrolled or accepted into an accredited or authorized college or university as a full-time student and have a minimum 3.0 GPA. Applicants should plan to work in the broadcast or telecommunications industry in Alaska upon completion of the academic degree.

Academic Fields/Career Goals: TV/Radio Broadcasting.

Award: Scholarship for use in freshman, sophomore, junior, senior, or graduate years; not renewable. *Number:* varies. *Amount:* up to $4000.

Eligibility Requirements: Applicant must be American Indian/Alaska Native and enrolled or expecting to enroll full-time at a two-year or four-year institution or university. Applicant must have 3.0 GPA or higher. Available to U.S. and Canadian citizens.

Application Requirements: Application, essay, financial need analysis, photo, references, transcript, proof of eligibility, statement of purpose. *Deadline:* June 1.

Contact: Susan Anderson, President and Chief Executive Officer
CIRI Foundation (TCF)
3600 San Jeronimo Drive, Suite 256
Anchorage, AK 99508-2870
Phone: 907-793-3575
Fax: 907-793-3585
E-mail: tcf@thecirifoundation.org

COLORADO BROADCASTERS ASSOCIATION http://www.coloradobroadcasters.org

CONTINUING EDUCATION SCHOLARSHIP PROGRAM

Program is for regular, full-time broadcast employees who are seeking to improve their education while continuing to work.

Academic Fields/Career Goals: TV/Radio Broadcasting.

Award: Scholarship for use in freshman, sophomore, junior, or senior years; renewable. *Number:* up to 6. *Amount:* $500.

Eligibility Requirements: Applicant must be enrolled or expecting to enroll full-time at a two-year or four-year or technical institution or university and resident of Colorado. Available to U.S. citizens.

Colorado Broadcasters Association (continued)

Application Requirements: Application. *Deadline:* varies.

Contact: Marilyn Hogan, President
Colorado Broadcasters Association
2042 Boreas Pass Road
PO Box 2369
Breckenridge, CO 80424
Phone: 970-547-1388
Fax: 970-547-1384
E-mail: cobroadcasters@earthlink.net

VOCATIONAL SCHOOL SCHOLARSHIP PROGRAM

Scholarship open to students at any accredited professional training school offering programs in broadcasting or some other aspect of professional media education that explicitly prepares students for careers in broadcasting. Applicants must be residents of Colorado.

Academic Fields/Career Goals: TV/Radio Broadcasting.

Award: Scholarship for use in freshman or sophomore years; not renewable. *Number:* 1. *Amount:* up to $1000.

Eligibility Requirements: Applicant must be enrolled or expecting to enroll full-time at a two-year or technical institution and resident of Colorado. Available to U.S. citizens.

Application Requirements: Application, references. *Deadline:* February 10.

Contact: Marilyn Hogan, President
Colorado Broadcasters Association
2042 Boreas Pass Road
PO Box 2369
Breckenridge, CO 80424
Phone: 970-547-1388
Fax: 970-547-1384
E-mail: cobroadcasters@earthlink.net

FISHER BROADCASTING COMPANY http://www.fsci.com

FISHER BROADCASTING INC. SCHOLARSHIP FOR MINORITIES

• *See page 140*

GREATER KANAWHA VALLEY FOUNDATION http://www.tgkvf.org

WEST VIRGINIA BROADCASTERS ASSOCIATION FUND

• *See page 179*

GREAT LAKES COMMISSION http://www.glc.org

CAROL A. RATZA MEMORIAL SCHOLARSHIP

• *See page 179*

HAWAII ASSOCIATION OF BROADCASTERS INC. http://www.hawaiibroadcasters.com

HAWAII ASSOCIATION OF BROADCASTERS SCHOLARSHIP

Renewable scholarship for full-time college students with the career goal of working in the broadcast industry in Hawaii upon graduation. Minimum GPA of 2.75 required. Number of awards granted ranges between twenty and thirty.

Academic Fields/Career Goals: TV/Radio Broadcasting.

Award: Scholarship for use in freshman year; renewable. *Number:* 20–30. *Amount:* $500–$4500.

Eligibility Requirements: Applicant must be enrolled or expecting to enroll full-time at a two-year or four-year institution or university. Available to U.S. and non-U.S. citizens.

Application Requirements: Application, references, transcript. *Deadline:* April 30.

Contact: Scholarship Committee
Hawaii Association of Broadcasters Inc.
PO Box 22112
Honolulu, HI 96823-2112
Phone: 808-599-1455
Fax: 808-599-7784

HISPANIC SCHOLARSHIP FUND http://www.hsf.net

HSF/MCNAMARA FAMILY CREATIVE ARTS PROJECT GRANT

• *See page 98*

IDAHO STATE BROADCASTERS ASSOCIATION http://www.idahobroadcasters.org

WAYNE C. CORNILS MEMORIAL SCHOLARSHIP

• *See page 143*

ILLUMINATING ENGINEERING SOCIETY OF NORTH AMERICA http://www.iesna.org

ROBERT W. THUNEN MEMORIAL SCHOLARSHIPS

• *See page 91*

INDIANA BROADCASTERS ASSOCIATION http://www.indianabroadcasters.org

INDIANA BROADCASTERS FOUNDATION SCHOLARSHIP

• *See page 372*

JOHN BAYLISS BROADCAST FOUNDATION http://www.baylissfoundation.org

JOHN BAYLISS BROADCAST RADIO SCHOLARSHIP

• *See page 180*

KATU THOMAS R. DARGAN MINORITY SCHOLARSHIP http://www.katu.com

THOMAS R. DARGAN MINORITY SCHOLARSHIP

• *See page 180*

LIN TELEVISION CORPORATION http://www.lintv.com

LINTV MINORITY SCHOLARSHIP

• *See page 372*

LOUISIANA ASSOCIATION OF BROADCASTERS http://www.broadcasters.org

BROADCAST SCHOLARSHIP PROGRAM

Scholarship to students enrolled and attending classes, full-time, in a fully accredited broadcast curriculum at a Louisiana four-year college. Must be a Louisiana resident and maintain a minimum 2.5 GPA. Previous LAB Scholarship Award winners are eligible.

Academic Fields/Career Goals: TV/Radio Broadcasting.

Award: Scholarship for use in junior or senior years; not renewable. *Number:* 2. *Amount:* $2000.

Eligibility Requirements: Applicant must be enrolled or expecting to enroll full-time at a four-year institution or university; resident of Louisiana and studying in Louisiana. Applicant must have 2.5 GPA or higher. Available to U.S. citizens.

Application Requirements: Application, essay, references, transcript. *Deadline:* February 1.

Contact: Louise L. Munson, Scholarship Coordinator
Louisiana Association of Broadcasters
660 Florida Boulevard
Baton Rouge, LA 70801
Phone: 225-267-4522
Fax: 225-267-4329
E-mail: lmunson@broadcasters.org

MARYLAND ASSOCIATION OF PRIVATE COLLEGES AND CAREER SCHOOLS http://www.mapccs.org

MARYLAND ASSOCIATION OF PRIVATE COLLEGES AND CAREER SCHOOLS SCHOLARSHIP

• *See page 146*

MASSACHUSETTS BROADCASTERS ASSOCIATION http://www.massbroadcasters.org

MBA STUDENT BROADCASTER SCHOLARSHIP

Scholarship available to permanent residents of Massachusetts who will be enrolling or are currently enrolled at an accredited vocational school, two- or four-year college or university in the United States. Must be full-time students pursuing studies in radio and television broadcasting.

Academic Fields/Career Goals: TV/Radio Broadcasting.

Award: Scholarship for use in freshman, sophomore, junior, or senior years; not renewable. *Number:* varies. *Amount:* $2000.

Eligibility Requirements: Applicant must be enrolled or expecting to enroll full-time at a two-year or four-year or technical institution or university and resident of Massachusetts. Available to U.S. citizens.

Application Requirements: Application, financial need analysis, references, transcript. *Deadline:* April 4.

Contact: B. Sprague, President
Massachusetts Broadcasters Association
43 Riverside Avenue
PO Box 401
Medford, MA 02155
Phone: 800-471-1875
Fax: 800-471-1876
E-mail: als@massbroadcasters.org

MEDIA ACTION NETWORK FOR ASIAN AMERICANS http://www.manaa.org

MANAA MEDIA SCHOLARSHIPS FOR ASIAN AMERICAN STUDENTS

• *See page 104*

MICHIGAN ASSOCIATION OF BROADCASTERS FOUNDATION http://www.michmab.com

WXYZ-TV BROADCASTING SCHOLARSHIP

One-time $1000 scholarship to assist students who are actively pursuing a career in a broadcast-related field. No limit on the number of awards within the program. Interested applicants should send a cover letter, resume, letters of recommendation, and an essay (200 to 300 words). The scholarship is open to Michigan residents currently attending college in Michigan.

Academic Fields/Career Goals: TV/Radio Broadcasting.

Award: Scholarship for use in freshman year; not renewable. *Number:* 1. *Amount:* $1000.

Eligibility Requirements: Applicant must be high school student; planning to enroll or expecting to enroll full-time at a two-year or four-year institution or university; resident of Michigan and studying in Michigan. Available to U.S. citizens.

Application Requirements: Application, autobiography, essay, references. *Deadline:* January 15.

Contact: Julie Sochay, Executive Vice President
Michigan Association of Broadcasters Foundation
819 North Washington Avenue
Lansing, MI 48906
Phone: 517-484-7444
Fax: 517-484-5810
E-mail: mabf@michmab.com

MINNESOTA BROADCASTERS ASSOCIATION http://www.minnesotabroadcasters.com

JAMES J. WYCHOR SCHOLARSHIP

One-time scholarships to Minnesota residents interested in broadcasting who are planning to enter the broadcasting field or other electronic media. Minimum 3.0 GPA is required. Submit proof of enrollment at an accredited postsecondary institution.

Academic Fields/Career Goals: TV/Radio Broadcasting.

Award: Scholarship for use in freshman, sophomore, junior, senior, or graduate years; not renewable. *Number:* 10. *Amount:* $1500.

Eligibility Requirements: Applicant must be enrolled or expecting to enroll full-time at a four-year institution or university and resident of Minnesota. Applicant must have 3.0 GPA or higher. Available to U.S. citizens.

Application Requirements: Application, essay, references, transcript. *Deadline:* May 31.

Contact: Linda Lasere, Member Services Director
Minnesota Broadcasters Association
3033 Excelsior Boulevard, Suite 440
Minneapolis, MN 55416-4675
Phone: 612-926-8123
Fax: 612-926-9761
E-mail: llasere@minnesotabroadcasters.com

MISSISSIPPI ASSOCIATION OF BROADCASTERS http://www.msbroadcasters.org

MISSISSIPPI ASSOCIATION OF BROADCASTERS SCHOLARSHIP

• *See page 373*

MISSOURI BROADCASTERS ASSOCIATION SCHOLARSHIP PROGRAM http://www.mbaweb.org

MISSOURI BROADCASTERS ASSOCIATION SCHOLARSHIP

Scholarship for a Missouri resident enrolled or planning to enroll in a broadcast or related curriculum which provides training and expertise applicable to a broadcast operation. Must maintain a GPA of at least 3.0 or equivalent. Multiple awards may be assigned each year and the amount of the scholarship will vary.

Academic Fields/Career Goals: TV/Radio Broadcasting.

Award: Scholarship for use in freshman, sophomore, junior, or senior years; not renewable. *Number:* 3. *Amount:* $1000–$2500.

Eligibility Requirements: Applicant must be enrolled or expecting to enroll full-time at a two-year or four-year institution or university; resident of Missouri and studying in Missouri. Applicant must have 3.0 GPA or higher. Available to U.S. citizens.

Application Requirements: Application, financial need analysis, references. *Deadline:* March 31.

Contact: Conny Heiland, Executive Assistant
Missouri Broadcasters Association Scholarship Program
PO Box 104445
Jefferson City, MO 65110-4445
Phone: 573-636-6692
Fax: 573-634-8258
E-mail: cheiland@mbaweb.org

MONTANA BROADCASTERS ASSOCIATION http://www.mtbroadcasters.org

GREAT FALLS BROADCASTERS ASSOCIATION SCHOLARSHIP

Scholarship available to a student who has graduated from a north-central Montana high school (Cascade, Meagher, Judith Basin, Fergus, Choteau, Teton, Pondera, Glacier, Toole, Liberty, Hill, Blaine, Phillips, and Valley counties) and is enrolled as at least a second year student in radio-TV at any public or private Montana college or university.

Academic Fields/Career Goals: TV/Radio Broadcasting.

Award: Scholarship for use in sophomore year; not renewable. *Number:* 1. *Amount:* $2000–$5000.

Eligibility Requirements: Applicant must be enrolled or expecting to enroll full-time at a two-year or four-year institution or university; resident of Montana and studying in Montana. Available to U.S. citizens.

Application Requirements: Application, essay, references, transcript. *Deadline:* March 15.

Contact: Gregory McDonald, Scholarship Coordinator
Montana Broadcasters Association
HC 70 PO Box 98
Bonner, MT 59823
Phone: 406-244-4622
Fax: 406-244-5518
E-mail: mba@mtbroadcasters.org

NATIONAL ACADEMY OF TELEVISION ARTS AND SCIENCES http://www.emmyonline.tv

NATIONAL ACADEMY OF TELEVISION ARTS AND SCIENCES JOHN CANNON MEMORIAL SCHOLARSHIP

• *See page 181*

NATIONAL ACADEMY OF TELEVISION ARTS AND SCIENCES-NATIONAL CAPITAL/CHESAPEAKE BAY CHAPTER http://www.natasdc.org

BETTY ENDICOTT/NTA-NCCB STUDENT SCHOLARSHIP
• See page 373

NATIONAL ASSOCIATION OF BLACK JOURNALISTS http://www.nabj.org

NABJ SCHOLARSHIP
• See page 181

NATIONAL ASSOCIATION OF BLACK JOURNALISTS NON-SUSTAINING SCHOLARSHIP AWARDS
• See page 374

NATIONAL ASSOCIATION OF BROADCASTERS http://www.nab.org

NATIONAL ASSOCIATION OF BROADCASTERS GRANTS FOR RESEARCH IN BROADCASTING
• See page 181

NATIONAL ASSOCIATION OF HISPANIC JOURNALISTS (NAHJ) http://www.nahj.org

GERALDO RIVERA SCHOLARSHIP
• See page 374

MARIA ELENA SALINAS SCHOLARSHIP
• See page 320

NATIONAL ASSOCIATION OF HISPANIC JOURNALISTS SCHOLARSHIP
• See page 181

NATIONAL PRESS PHOTOGRAPHERS FOUNDATION INC. http://www.nppa.org

NATIONAL PRESS PHOTOGRAPHERS FOUNDATION TELEVISION NEWS SCHOLARSHIP
• See page 465

NEW JERSEY BROADCASTERS ASSOCIATION http://www.njba.com

MICHAEL S. LIBRETTI SCHOLARSHIP
• See page 182

NORTH CAROLINA ASSOCIATION OF BROADCASTERS http://www.ncbroadcast.com

NCAB SCHOLARSHIP

One-time scholarship for high school seniors enrolled as full-time students in a North Carolina college or university with an interest in broadcasting. Must be between ages 17 and 20.

Academic Fields/Career Goals: TV/Radio Broadcasting.

Award: Scholarship for use in freshman year; not renewable. *Number:* 2. *Amount:* $10,000.

Eligibility Requirements: Applicant must be high school student; age 17-20; planning to enroll or expecting to enroll full-time at a two-year or four-year institution or university and studying in North Carolina. Available to U.S. citizens.

Application Requirements: Application, essay, references, transcript. *Deadline:* April 15.

Contact: Lisa Reynolds, Executive Manager
North Carolina Association of Broadcasters
PO Box 627
Raleigh, NC 27602
Phone: 919-821-7300
Fax: 919-839-0304

OREGON ASSOCIATION OF BROADCASTERS http://www.theoab.org

OAB FOUNDATION SCHOLARSHIP
• See page 182

OUTDOOR WRITERS ASSOCIATION OF AMERICA http://www.owaa.org

OUTDOOR WRITERS ASSOCIATION OF AMERICA BODIE MCDOWELL SCHOLARSHIP AWARD
• See page 183

PALM BEACH ASSOCIATION OF BLACK JOURNALISTS http://www.pbabj.org

PALM BEACH ASSOCIATION OF BLACK JOURNALISTS SCHOLARSHIP
• See page 377

RADIO-TELEVISION NEWS DIRECTORS ASSOCIATION AND FOUNDATION http://www.rtndf.org

CAROLE SIMPSON SCHOLARSHIP
• See page 183

ED BRADLEY SCHOLARSHIP
• See page 183

KEN KASHIWAHARA SCHOLARSHIP
• See page 184

LOU AND CAROLE PRATO SPORTS REPORTING SCHOLARSHIP
• See page 184

MIKE REYNOLDS $1,000 SCHOLARSHIP
• See page 184

PRESIDENT'S SCHOLARSHIP
• See page 184

RHODE ISLAND FOUNDATION http://www.rifoundation.org

J. D. EDSAL ADVERTISING SCHOLARSHIP
• See page 184

SOCIETY OF BROADCAST ENGINEERS INC. http://www.sbe.org

ROBERT GREENBERG/HAROLD E. ENNES SCHOLARSHIP FUND AND ENNES EDUCATIONAL FOUNDATION BROADCAST TECHNOLOGY SCHOLARSHIP
• See page 251

YOUTH SCHOLARSHIP

Award available to senior in high school with a serious interest in pursuing studies leading to a career in broadcast engineering or closely related field.

Academic Fields/Career Goals: TV/Radio Broadcasting.

Award: Scholarship for use in freshman year; renewable. *Number:* 1. *Amount:* $1000.

Eligibility Requirements: Applicant must be high school student and planning to enroll or expecting to enroll full-time at a four-year institution. Available to U.S. citizens.

Application Requirements: Application, autobiography, transcript, written statement of education plans after high school. *Deadline:* July 1.

Contact: Debbie Hennessey, Executive Secretary
Society of Broadcast Engineers Inc.
9102 North Meridian Street, Suite 150
Indianapolis, IN 46260
Phone: 317-846-9000
Fax: 317-846-9120
E-mail: dhennessey@sbe.org

SOCIETY OF PROFESSIONAL JOURNALISTS, LOS ANGELES CHAPTER http://www.spj.org/losangeles

HELEN JOHNSON SCHOLARSHIP
• See page 379

STRAIGHTFORWARD MEDIA http://www.straightforwardmedia.com

STRAIGHTFORWARD MEDIA MEDIA & COMMUNICATIONS SCHOLARSHIP

• See page 185

TEXAS ASSOCIATION OF BROADCASTERS http://www.tab.org

BELO TEXAS BROADCAST EDUCATION FOUNDATION SCHOLARSHIP

• See page 185

BONNER MCLANE TEXAS BROADCAST EDUCATION FOUNDATION SCHOLARSHIP

• See page 186

STUDENT TEXAS BROADCAST EDUCATION FOUNDATION SCHOLARSHIP

• See page 186

TOM REIFF TEXAS BROADCAST EDUCATION FOUNDATION SCHOLARSHIP

• See page 186

UNDERGRADUATE TEXAS BROADCAST EDUCATION FOUNDATION SCHOLARSHIP

• See page 186

VANN KENNEDY TEXAS BROADCAST EDUCATION FOUNDATION SCHOLARSHIP

• See page 186

TEXAS GRIDIRON CLUB INC. http://www.spjfw.org

TEXAS GRIDIRON CLUB SCHOLARSHIPS

• See page 187

UNITED METHODIST COMMUNICATIONS http://www.umcom.org

LEONARD M. PERRYMAN COMMUNICATIONS SCHOLARSHIP FOR ETHNIC MINORITY STUDENTS

• See page 187

UNITED NEGRO COLLEGE FUND http://www.uncf.org

C-SPAN SCHOLARSHIP PROGRAM

• See page 187

VALLEY PRESS CLUB http://www.valleypressclub.com

VALLEY PRESS CLUB SCHOLARSHIPS, THE REPUBLICAN SCHOLARSHIP, CHANNEL 22 SCHOLARSHIP

• See page 188

WISCONSIN BROADCASTERS ASSOCIATION FOUNDATION http://www.wi-broadcasters.org

WISCONSIN BROADCASTERS ASSOCIATION FOUNDATION SCHOLARSHIP

• See page 189

WMTW-TV 8-AUBURN, MAINE http://www.wmtw.com

BOB ELLIOT-WMTW-TV 8 JOURNALISM SCHOLARSHIP

• See page 189

WOWT-TV-OMAHA, NEBRASKA http://www.wowt.com

WOWT-TV BROADCASTING SCHOLARSHIP PROGRAM

Two annual scholarships of $1000 for high school graduates in the Channel 6 viewing area of Nebraska. Must be pursuing a full-time career in broadcasting and have a minimum GPA of 3.0.

Academic Fields/Career Goals: TV/Radio Broadcasting.

Award: Scholarship for use in freshman year; not renewable. *Number:* up to 2. *Amount:* up to $1000.

Eligibility Requirements: Applicant must be high school student; planning to enroll or expecting to enroll full-time at a two-year or four-year institution or university and resident of Nebraska. Applicant must have 3.0 GPA or higher. Available to U.S. citizens.

Application Requirements: Application, essay, interview, references, test scores, transcript. *Deadline:* March 16.

Contact: Gail Backer, Scholarship Committee
WOWT-TV-Omaha, Nebraska
3501 Farnam Street
Omaha, NE 68131
Phone: 402-346-6666
Fax: 402-233-7880

YOUNG AMERICAN BROADCASTERS SCHOLARSHIP http://www.youngamericanbroadcasters.org

YOUNG AMERICAN BROADCASTERS SCHOLARSHIP

Scholarship for ethnically diverse college population to encourage pursuit of studies in radio and Internet broadcasting. One-time scholarship for part-time students who have completed at least one year of study.

Academic Fields/Career Goals: TV/Radio Broadcasting.

Award: Scholarship for use in sophomore, junior, or senior years; not renewable. *Number:* varies. *Amount:* up to $5000.

Eligibility Requirements: Applicant must be enrolled or expecting to enroll part-time at a four-year institution or university. Available to U.S. and non-U.S. citizens.

Application Requirements: Application, applicant must enter a contest, transcript. *Deadline:* varies.

Contact: Scholarship Committee
Young American Broadcasters Scholarship
1030 15th Street, NW, Suite 1028
Washington, DC 20005
Phone: 202-408-8255
Fax: 202-408-5188

URBAN AND REGIONAL PLANNING

AMERICAN PLANNING ASSOCIATION http://www.planning.org

JUDITH MCMANUS PRICE SCHOLARSHIP

Scholarship available to women and underrepresented minority students enrolled in an approved Planning Accreditation Board (PAB) planning program who are U.S. citizens and intend to pursue careers as practicing planners in the public sector. Must demonstrate financial need. For further information visit http://www.planning.org/institutions/scholarship.htm.

Academic Fields/Career Goals: Urban and Regional Planning.

Award: Scholarship for use in freshman, sophomore, junior, senior, or graduate years; not renewable. *Number:* varies. *Amount:* $2000–$5000.

Eligibility Requirements: Applicant must be American Indian/Alaska Native, Black (non-Hispanic), or Hispanic and enrolled or expecting to enroll full-time at a four-year institution or university. Available to U.S. citizens.

Application Requirements: Application, financial need analysis, resume, transcript, 2- to 5-page personal and background statement written by the school, 2 letters of recommendation, acceptance letter. *Deadline:* April 30.

Contact: Kriss Blank, Leadership Affairs Associate
American Planning Association
122 South Michigan Avenue, Suite 1600
Chicago, IL 60603
Phone: 312-786-6722
Fax: 312-786-6727
E-mail: kblank@planning.org

CONNECTICUT CHAPTER OF THE AMERICAN PLANNING ASSOCIATION http://www.ccapa.org

DIANA DONALD SCHOLARSHIP

One-time award of $1000 for full-time students enrolled in a graduate or undergraduate program in city planning or a closely related field. Must be resident of Connecticut and study in Connecticut. Deadline varies.

Connecticut Chapter of the American Planning Association (continued)

Academic Fields/Career Goals: Urban and Regional Planning.

Award: Scholarship for use in freshman, sophomore, junior, senior, or graduate years; not renewable. *Number:* up to 1. *Amount:* up to $1000.

Eligibility Requirements: Applicant must be enrolled or expecting to enroll full-time at a four-year institution or university; resident of Connecticut and studying in Connecticut. Available to U.S. and non-U.S. citizens.

Application Requirements: Application, essay, financial need analysis, references, transcript. *Deadline:* varies.

Contact: Laurie Whitten, Program Coordinator
Connecticut Chapter of the American Planning Association
Town of East Windsor
11 Rye Street
Broad Brook, CT 06016
Phone: 860-292-8256
E-mail: lwhitten@eastwindsorct.com

WOMEN'S STUDIES

AMERICAN FEDERATION OF STATE, COUNTY, AND MUNICIPAL EMPLOYEES http://www.afscme.org

AFSCME/UNCF UNION SCHOLARS PROGRAM

• *See page 80*

MARGARET MCNAMARA MEMORIAL FUND http://www.wbfn.org

MARGARET MCNAMARA MEMORIAL FUND FELLOWSHIPS

• *See page 166*

SOCIETY FOR THE SCIENTIFIC STUDY OF SEXUALITY http://www.sexscience.org

SOCIETY FOR THE SCIENTIFIC STUDY OF SEXUALITY STUDENT RESEARCH GRANT

• *See page 129*

SUNSHINE LADY FOUNDATION INC. http://www.sunshinelady.org

COUNSELOR, ADVOCATE, AND SUPPORT STAFF SCHOLARSHIP PROGRAM

• *See page 167*

Nonacademic/Noncareer Criteria

CIVIC, PROFESSIONAL, SOCIAL, OR UNION AFFILIATION

AIR LINE PILOTS ASSOCIATION, INTERNATIONAL http://www.alpa.org

AIRLINE PILOTS ASSOCIATION SCHOLARSHIP PROGRAM

Scholarship for children of medically retired, long-term disabled, or deceased pilot members of the association. The total monetary value is $12,000 with $3000 disbursed annually to the recipient for four consecutive years, provided that a GPA of 3.0 is maintained.

Award: Scholarship for use in freshman, sophomore, junior, or senior years; not renewable. *Number:* 1. *Amount:* up to $3000.

Eligibility Requirements: Applicant must be enrolled or expecting to enroll full-time at a four-year institution or university. Applicant or parent of applicant must be member of Airline Pilots Association. Applicant must have 3.0 GPA or higher. Available to U.S. and Canadian citizens.

Application Requirements: Application, financial need analysis, references, test scores, transcript. *Deadline:* April 1.

Contact: Maggie Erzen, Coordinator
Air Line Pilots Association, International
1625 Massachusetts Avenue, NW
Washington, DC 20036
Phone: 202-797-4059
Fax: 202-797-4007
E-mail: maggie.erzen@alpa.org

ALBERTA AGRICULTURE FOOD AND RURAL DEVELOPMENT 4-H BRANCH http://www.4h.ab.ca

ALBERTA AGRICULTURE FOOD AND RURAL DEVELOPMENT 4-H SCHOLARSHIP PROGRAM

Awards will be given to current and incoming students attending any institute of higher learning. Must have been a member of the Alberta 4-H Program and be a Canadian citizen. Must be a resident of Alberta.

Award: Scholarship for use in freshman, sophomore, junior, senior, or graduate years; not renewable. *Number:* 115–120. *Amount:* $200–$1500.

Eligibility Requirements: Applicant must be enrolled or expecting to enroll full-time at a two-year or four-year or technical institution or university and resident of Alberta. Applicant or parent of applicant must be member of National 4-H. Available to Canadian citizens.

Application Requirements: Application, essay, references, transcript. *Deadline:* May 5.

Contact: Susann Stone, Scholarship Coordinator
Alberta Agriculture Food and Rural Development 4-H Branch
RR1 West Rose
Edmonton, AB T0C 2V0
Canada
Phone: 780-682-2153
Fax: 780-682-3784
E-mail: foundation@4hab.com

ALBERTA HERITAGE SCHOLARSHIP FUND/ ALBERTA SCHOLARSHIP PROGRAMS http://www.alis.gov.ab.ca

BOYS AND GIRLS CLUB OF ALBERTA SCHOLARSHIPS

Award to assist members of the Boys and Girls Clubs pursue higher education. Must be Canadian citizens or landed immigrants and residents of Alberta. Candidates must be 24 years of age or younger, be current or former members of a Boys and Girls Club in Alberta, and enrolled or planning to enroll full-time in a postsecondary program. Selection is based on level of club and community involvement, letter of sponsorship, and essay written outlining goals and aspirations.

Award: Scholarship for use in freshman, sophomore, junior, or senior years; not renewable. *Number:* 1. *Amount:* $500.

Eligibility Requirements: Applicant must be age 24 or under; enrolled or expecting to enroll full-time at a two-year or four-year or technical institution or university and resident of Alberta. Applicant or parent of applicant must be member of Boys or Girls Club. Available to Canadian citizens.

Application Requirements: Application, essay, references, transcript. *Deadline:* July 1.

Contact: Scholarship Committee
Alberta Heritage Scholarship Fund/Alberta Scholarship Programs
9940 106th Street, Fourth Floor, Sterling Place
PO Box 28000, Station Main
Edmonton, AB T5J 4R4
Canada
Phone: 780-427-8640
Fax: 780-427-1288
E-mail: scholarships@gov.ab.ca

ALPHA KAPPA ALPHA http://www.akaeaf.org

AKA EDUCATIONAL ADVANCEMENT FOUNDATION YOUTH PARTNERS ACCESSING CAPITAL SCHOLARSHIP

Scholarship for a member of the society. Must be an undergraduate of at least sophomore status. Must have a minimum GPA of 3.0 and participate in leadership, volunteer, civic, or campus activities. Must demonstrate academic achievement or financial need.

Award: Scholarship for use in sophomore, junior, or senior years; not renewable. *Number:* varies. *Amount:* $1000–$3000.

Eligibility Requirements: Applicant must be enrolled or expecting to enroll full-time at a four-year institution or university. Applicant or parent of applicant must be member of Alpha Kappa Alpha. Applicant must have 3.0 GPA or higher. Available to U.S. and non-U.S. citizens.

Application Requirements: Application, references, transcript. *Deadline:* April 15.

Contact: Andrea Kerr, Program Coordinator
Alpha Kappa Alpha
5656 South Stony Island Avenue
Chicago, IL 60637
Phone: 773-947-0026 Ext. 8
E-mail: akaeaf@akaeaf.net

AMERICAN ASSOCIATION OF BIOANALYSTS http://www.aab.org

DAVID BIRENBAUM SCHOLARSHIP FUND

One-time award based on merit for regular or current or associate members or dependents of the members of the American Association of Bioanalysts for study in any discipline for any academic year.

Award: Scholarship for use in freshman, sophomore, junior, senior, graduate, or postgraduate years; not renewable. *Number:* 1–10. *Amount:* $500.

Eligibility Requirements: Applicant must be enrolled or expecting to enroll full- or part-time at a two-year or four-year or technical institution or university. Applicant or parent of applicant must be member of American Association of Bioanalysts. Available to U.S. and non-U.S. citizens.

Application Requirements: Application, essay, financial need analysis, photo, references, transcript. *Deadline:* April 15.

Contact: Leann Hampton, Administrator
American Association of Bioanalysts
906 Locust Street, Suite 1100
St. Louis, MO 63101-1419
Phone: 314-241-1445
Fax: 314-241-1449

AMERICAN BOWLING CONGRESS http://www.bowl.com

CHUCK HALL STAR OF TOMORROW SCHOLARSHIP

$1500 scholarship, renewable for up to three years, available to male high school seniors or college students who hold an average bowling score of 175 or greater. Minimum 2.5 GPA required. Must be a current USBC Youth or USBC member in good standing and currently compete in certified events.

Award: Scholarship for use in freshman, sophomore, junior, or senior years; renewable. *Number:* 1. *Amount:* $1500.

Eligibility Requirements: Applicant must be age 22 or under; enrolled or expecting to enroll full- or part-time at a two-year or four-year or technical institution or university; male and must have an interest in bowling. Applicant or parent of applicant must be member of Young American Bowling Alliance. Applicant must have 2.5 GPA or higher. Available to U.S. and Canadian citizens.

Application Requirements: Application, essay, references, self-addressed stamped envelope, transcript. *Deadline:* October 1.

Contact: Ed Gocha, Scholarship Administrator
American Bowling Congress
5301 South 76th Street
Greendale, WI 53129-1192
Phone: 800-514-2695 Ext. 3343
Fax: 414-421-3014
E-mail: smart@bowl.com

AMERICAN FEDERATION OF SCHOOL ADMINISTRATORS http://www.admin.org

AMERICAN FEDERATION OF SCHOOL ADMINISTRATORS SCHOLARSHIP PROGRAM

Scholarship for children of American Federation of School Administrators members who will be entering college for the first time. The dollar amount and number of awards vary.

Award: Scholarship for use in freshman year; not renewable. *Number:* varies. *Amount:* varies.

Eligibility Requirements: Applicant must be high school student and planning to enroll or expecting to enroll full-time at a four-year institution or university. Applicant or parent of applicant must be member of American Federation of School Administrators. Available to U.S. and non-U.S. citizens.

Application Requirements: Application, essay, photo, references, test scores, transcript. *Deadline:* March 1.

Contact: Joseph Stankavage, Assistant to President
American Federation of School Administrators
1101 17th Street NW, Suite 408
Washington, DC 20036
Phone: 202-986-4209
Fax: 202-986-4211
E-mail: afsa@admin.org

AMERICAN FEDERATION OF STATE, COUNTY, AND MUNICIPAL EMPLOYEES http://www.afscme.org

AMERICAN FEDERATION OF STATE, COUNTY, AND MUNICIPAL EMPLOYEES SCHOLARSHIP PROGRAM

Scholarship for family dependents of American Federation of State, County, and Municipal Employees members. Must be a graduating high school senior planning to pursue postsecondary education at a four-year institution. Submit proof of parent's membership. Renewable award of $2000.

Award: Scholarship for use in freshman, sophomore, junior, or senior years; renewable. *Number:* 13. *Amount:* $2000.

Eligibility Requirements: Applicant must be high school student and planning to enroll or expecting to enroll full-time at a four-year institution or university. Applicant or parent of applicant must be member of American Federation of State, County, and Municipal Employees. Available to U.S. citizens.

Application Requirements: Application, essay, references, test scores, transcript. *Deadline:* December 31.

Contact: Philip Allen, Scholarship Coordinator
American Federation of State, County, and Municipal Employees
1625 L Street, NW
Washington, DC 20036-5687
Phone: 202-429-1250
Fax: 202-429-1272
E-mail: pallen@asscme.org

UNION PLUS CREDIT CARD SCHOLARSHIP PROGRAM

One-time award for AFSCME members, their spouses and dependent children. Graduate students and grandchildren are not eligible.

Award: Scholarship for use in freshman, sophomore, junior, or senior years; not renewable. *Number:* varies. *Amount:* $500–$4000.

Eligibility Requirements: Applicant must be enrolled or expecting to enroll full-time at a two-year or four-year or technical institution or university. Applicant or parent of applicant must be member of American Federation of State, County, and Municipal Employees. Available to U.S. citizens.

Application Requirements: Application, autobiography, essay, references, transcript. *Deadline:* January 31.

Contact: Philip Allen, Scholarship Coordinator
American Federation of State, County, and Municipal Employees
1625 L Street, NW
Washington, DC 20036-5687
Phone: 202-429-1250
Fax: 202-429-1272
E-mail: pallen@asscme.org

AMERICAN FEDERATION OF TEACHERS http://www.aft.org

ROBERT G. PORTER SCHOLARS PROGRAM-AMERICAN FEDERATION OF TEACHERS DEPENDENTS

Scholarship of up to $8000 for high school seniors who are dependents of AFT members. Must submit transcript, test scores, essay, and recommendations with application. Must be U.S. citizen.

Award: Scholarship for use in freshman year; renewable. *Number:* 4. *Amount:* $8000.

Eligibility Requirements: Applicant must be high school student and planning to enroll or expecting to enroll full-time at a four-year institution or university. Applicant or parent of applicant must be member of American Federation of Teachers. Available to U.S. citizens.

Application Requirements: Application, essay, references, test scores, transcript. *Deadline:* March 31.

Contact: Bernadette Bailey, Scholarship Coordinator
American Federation of Teachers
555 New Jersey Avenue, NW
Washington, DC 20001-2079
Phone: 202-879-4481
Fax: 202-879-4406
E-mail: bbailey@aft.org

AMERICAN FOREIGN SERVICE ASSOCIATION http://www.afsa.org

AMERICAN FOREIGN SERVICE ASSOCIATION (AFSA)/AAFSW MERIT AWARD PROGRAM

One-time award for a high school senior whose parent is a U.S. Government Foreign Service employee. Must maintain a satisfactory academic record of 2.0 GPA. Parent must be a member of AFSA or AAFSW. Children of military parents or international students are not eligible. Award based upon academic and artistic achievements of the applicant.

Award: Prize for use in freshman year; not renewable. *Number:* 6–15. *Amount:* $1500.

Eligibility Requirements: Applicant must be high school student; planning to enroll or expecting to enroll full-time at a four-year institution or university; single and must have an interest in art. Applicant or parent of applicant must be member of American Foreign Service Association. Applicant or parent of applicant must have employment or volunteer experience in U.S. government foreign service. Available to U.S. citizens.

Application Requirements: Application, essay, references, self-addressed stamped envelope, test scores, transcript. *Deadline:* February 6.

Contact: Lori Dec, Scholarship Director
American Foreign Service Association
2101 East Street NW
Washington, DC 20037
Phone: 202-944-5504
Fax: 202-338-6820
E-mail: dec@afsa.org

AMERICAN FOREIGN SERVICE ASSOCIATION (AFSA) FINANCIAL AID AWARD PROGRAM

Need-based financial aid scholarship program open to students whose parents are in the U.S. Government Foreign Service. Must attend or will be attending full-time as an undergraduate at a two- or four-year accredited college, university, community college, art school, or conservatory. Must maintain a 2.0 GPA, and demonstrate financial need.

Award: Scholarship for use in freshman, sophomore, junior, or senior years; not renewable. *Number:* 50–60. *Amount:* $1000–$3500.

Eligibility Requirements: Applicant must be enrolled or expecting to enroll full-time at a two-year or four-year institution or university and single. Applicant or parent of applicant must be member of American Foreign Service Association. Applicant or parent of applicant must have employment or volunteer experience in U.S. government foreign service. Available to U.S. citizens.

Application Requirements: Application, financial need analysis, transcript, CSS profile. *Deadline:* February 6.

Contact: Lori Dec, Scholarship Director
American Foreign Service Association
2101 East Street, NW
Washington, DC 20037
Phone: 202-944-5504
Fax: 202-338-6820
E-mail: dec@afsa.org

AMERICAN LEGION AUXILIARY DEPARTMENT OF CALIFORNIA http://www.calegionaux.org

AMERICAN LEGION AUXILIARY DEPARTMENT OF CALIFORNIA JUNIOR SCHOLARSHIP

Award for undergraduate students. Must be a California resident. Must have consecutive membership as a Junior for three years and be current with membership in the American Legion Auxiliary.

Award: Scholarship for use in freshman year; not renewable. *Number:* 1. *Amount:* $300–$1000.

Eligibility Requirements: Applicant must be high school student; age 17 and over; planning to enroll or expecting to enroll full- or part-time at a four-year institution or university and resident of California. Applicant or parent of applicant must be member of American Legion or Auxiliary. Available to U.S. citizens. Applicant or parent must meet one or more of the following requirements: Army experience; retired from active duty; disabled or killed as a result of military service; prisoner of war; or missing in action.

Application Requirements: Application. *Deadline:* April 13.

Contact: Theresa Jacob, Secretary/Treasurer
American Legion Auxiliary Department of California
401 Van Ness Avenue, Room 113
San Francisco, CA 94102
Phone: 415-862-5092
Fax: 415-861-8365
E-mail: calegionaux@calegionaux.org

AMERICAN LEGION AUXILIARY DEPARTMENT OF CONNECTICUT http://www.ct.legion.org

AMERICAN LEGION AUXILIARY DEPARTMENT OF CONNECTICUT MEMORIAL EDUCATIONAL GRANT

Half the number of available grants are awarded to children of veterans who are also residents of CT. Remaining grants awarded to child or grandchild of a member (or member at time of death) of the CT Departments of the American Legion/American Legion Auxiliary, regardless of residency; or are members of the CT Departments of the American Legion Auxiliary/Sons of the American Legion, regardless of residency. Contact local unit President. Must include list of community service activities.

Award: Grant for use in freshman, sophomore, junior, or senior years; not renewable. *Number:* 4. *Amount:* $500.

Eligibility Requirements: Applicant must be age 16-23 and enrolled or expecting to enroll full-time at a two-year or four-year or technical institution or university. Applicant or parent of applicant must be member of American Legion or Auxiliary. Applicant or parent of applicant must have employment or volunteer experience in community service. Available to U.S. citizens. Applicant or parent must meet one or more of the following requirements: general military experience; retired from active duty; disabled or killed as a result of military service; prisoner of war; or missing in action.

Application Requirements: Application, financial need analysis, references, self-addressed stamped envelope, transcript. *Deadline:* March 10.

Contact: Rita Barylski, State Secretary
American Legion Auxiliary Department of Connecticut
287 West Street
PO Box 266
Rocky Hill, CT 06067
Phone: 860-721-5945
Fax: 860-721-5828
E-mail: ctalahq@juno.com

AMERICAN LEGION AUXILIARY DEPARTMENT OF CONNECTICUT PAST PRESIDENTS' PARLEY MEMORIAL EDUCATION GRANT

The program gives preference a child or grandchild of an ex-service woman, who was or is a member of the CT departments of the American Legion/American Legion Auxiliary. In the event of a deficiency of preferred applicants, award may be granted to child or grandchild of a member of the CT Departments of the American Legion/American Legion Auxiliary or Sons of the American Legion. Minimum five-year membership required, or five years prior to death. Contact local unit President. Must include list of community service activities.

Award: Grant for use in freshman, sophomore, junior, or senior years; not renewable. *Number:* 4. *Amount:* up to $500.

Eligibility Requirements: Applicant must be age 16-23; enrolled or expecting to enroll full-time at a two-year or four-year or technical institution or university and resident of Connecticut. Applicant or parent of applicant must be member of American Legion or Auxiliary. Available to U.S. citizens. Applicant or parent must meet one or more of the

American Legion Auxiliary Department of Connecticut (continued)

following requirements: general military experience; retired from active duty; disabled or killed as a result of military service; prisoner of war; or missing in action.

Application Requirements: Application, financial need analysis, references, test scores, transcript, list of school and community activities. *Deadline:* March 5.

Contact: Rita Barylski, State Secretary
American Legion Auxiliary Department of Connecticut
287 West Street
PO Box 266
Rocky Hill, CT 06067
Phone: 860-721-5945
Fax: 860-721-5828
E-mail: ctalahq@juno.com

AMERICAN LEGION AUXILIARY DEPARTMENT OF FLORIDA http://www.alafl.org

AMERICAN LEGION AUXILIARY DEPARTMENT OF FLORIDA MEMORIAL SCHOLARSHIP

Scholarship for a member, daughter, or granddaughter of a member of Florida American Legion Auxiliary with a minimum three-year membership. Award for Florida resident for undergraduate study in Florida school. Minimum 2.5 GPA required.

Award: Scholarship for use in freshman, sophomore, junior, or senior years; renewable. *Number:* 1–6. *Amount:* $500–$1000.

Eligibility Requirements: Applicant must be enrolled or expecting to enroll full-time at a two-year or four-year or technical institution or university; female; resident of Florida and studying in Florida. Applicant or parent of applicant must be member of American Legion or Auxiliary. Applicant must have 2.5 GPA or higher. Available to U.S. citizens. Applicant or parent must meet one or more of the following requirements: general military experience; retired from active duty; disabled or killed as a result of military service; prisoner of war; or missing in action.

Application Requirements: Application, financial need analysis, references, transcript. *Deadline:* March 1.

Contact: Robin Briere, Department Secretary and Treasurer
American Legion Auxiliary Department of Florida
PO Box 547917
Orlando, FL 32854-7917
Phone: 407-293-7411
Fax: 407-299-6522
E-mail: contact@alafl.org

AMERICAN LEGION AUXILIARY DEPARTMENT OF MARYLAND http://www.alamd.org

AMERICAN LEGION AUXILIARY DEPARTMENT OF MARYLAND GIRL SCOUT ACHIEVEMENT AWARD

Scholarship available to Girl Scout who has received the Girl Scout Gold Award. Must be senior in high school, an active member of her religious institution, and must have received the appropriate religious emblem, Cadette or Senior Scout level. Number of awards and the deadline varies annually.

Award: Scholarship for use in freshman year; not renewable. *Number:* varies. *Amount:* $1000.

Eligibility Requirements: Applicant must be high school student; planning to enroll or expecting to enroll full-time at a four-year institution or university and female. Applicant or parent of applicant must be member of Girl Scouts. Available to U.S. citizens.

Application Requirements: Application, references, transcript. *Deadline:* varies.

Contact: Meredith Beeg, Vice President
American Legion Auxiliary Department of Maryland
1589 Sulphur Spring Road, Suite 105
Baltimore, MD 21227
Phone: 410-242-9519
Fax: 410-242-9553
E-mail: hq@alamd.org

AMERICAN LEGION AUXILIARY DEPARTMENT OF MARYLAND NATIONAL PRESIDENT'S SCHOLARSHIP

Daughters, step-daughters, sons or step-sons of veterans who served in the Armed Forces during eligibility dates for membership in the American Legion are eligible. Previous National President's Scholarship recipients are not eligible. Scholarship value and the number of awards granted varies annually.

Award: Scholarship for use in freshman, sophomore, junior, senior, or graduate years; not renewable. *Number:* varies. *Amount:* varies.

Eligibility Requirements: Applicant must be enrolled or expecting to enroll full-time at a four-year institution or university. Applicant or parent of applicant must be member of American Legion or Auxiliary. Available to U.S. citizens. Applicant or parent must meet one or more of the following requirements: general military experience; retired from active duty; disabled or killed as a result of military service; prisoner of war; or missing in action.

Application Requirements: Application, financial need analysis, references, test scores, transcript. *Deadline:* May 1.

Contact: Meredith Beeg, Vice President
American Legion Auxiliary Department of Maryland
1589 Sulphur Spring Road, Suite 105
Baltimore, MD 21227
Phone: 410-242-9519
Fax: 410-242-9553
E-mail: hq@alamd.org

AMERICAN LEGION AUXILIARY DEPARTMENT OF MARYLAND SCHOLARSHIP FOR NON-TRADITIONAL STUDENTS

Scholarship available for a student who has at least one year of college and is in need of financial assistance to pursue an undergraduate degree. Must be a member of the American Legion Auxiliary or Sons of the American Legion. The scholarship value and the number of scholarships granted varies annually.

Award: Scholarship for use in sophomore, junior, senior, graduate, or postgraduate years; not renewable. *Number:* varies. *Amount:* $1000.

Eligibility Requirements: Applicant must be enrolled or expecting to enroll full-time at a two-year or four-year or technical institution or university. Applicant or parent of applicant must be member of American Legion or Auxiliary. Available to U.S. citizens. Applicant or parent must meet one or more of the following requirements: general military experience; retired from active duty; disabled or killed as a result of military service; prisoner of war; or missing in action.

Application Requirements: Application, financial need analysis, references, transcript. *Deadline:* March 1.

Contact: Meredith Beeg, Vice President
American Legion Auxiliary Department of Maryland
1589 Sulphur Spring Road, Suite 105
Baltimore, MD 21227
Phone: 410-242-9519
Fax: 410-242-9553
E-mail: hq@alamd.org

AMERICAN LEGION AUXILIARY DEPARTMENT OF MARYLAND SPIRIT OF YOUTH SCHOLARSHIP FOR JUNIOR MEMBERS

Scholarship for undergraduate students enrolled full-time in accredited colleges or universities. The applicant must have held membership in the American Legion Auxiliary for the past three years, hold a current membership card, and continue to maintain membership throughout the four-year scholarship period.

Award: Scholarship for use in freshman, sophomore, junior, or senior years; not renewable. *Number:* varies. *Amount:* varies.

Eligibility Requirements: Applicant must be enrolled or expecting to enroll full-time at a four-year institution or university. Applicant or parent of applicant must be member of American Legion or Auxiliary. Applicant must have 3.0 GPA or higher. Available to U.S. citizens. Applicant or parent must meet one or more of the following requirements: general military experience; retired from active duty; disabled or killed as a result of military service; prisoner of war; or missing in action.

Application Requirements: Application, financial need analysis, references, test scores, transcript. *Deadline:* May 1.

Contact: Meredith Beeg, Vice President
American Legion Auxiliary Department of Maryland
1589 Sulphur Spring Road, Suite 105
Baltimore, MD 21227
Phone: 410-242-9519
Fax: 410-242-9553
E-mail: hq@alamd.org

AMERICAN LEGION AUXILIARY DEPARTMENT OF MICHIGAN http://www.michalaux.org

AMERICAN LEGION AUXILIARY DEPARTMENT OF MICHIGAN GIRL SCOUT ACHIEVEMENT AWARD

Award consists of $1000 scholarship, and a trip to the national convention to receive the award after graduation from high school. Must have received the Girl Scout Gold award, be an active member of the religious institution, and must have received the appropriate religious emblem at the Cadette or senior scout level.

Award: Scholarship for use in freshman year; not renewable. *Number:* varies. *Amount:* $1000.

Eligibility Requirements: Applicant must be high school student; planning to enroll or expecting to enroll full-time at a four-year institution or university and female. Applicant or parent of applicant must be member of Girl Scouts. Available to U.S. citizens.

Application Requirements: References, nomination application. *Deadline:* February 10.

Contact: LeAnn Knott, Scholarship Staff Assistant
American Legion Auxiliary Department of Michigan
212 North Verlinden Avenue
Lansing, MI 48915
Phone: 517-371-4720 Ext. 22
Fax: 517-371-2401
E-mail: info@michalaux.org

AMERICAN LEGION AUXILIARY DEPARTMENT OF MICHIGAN SPIRIT OF YOUTH SCHOLARSHIP

Scholarship valued at $1000 per year for four years is available to one junior member in each division. The applicant must have held membership in the American Legion Auxiliary for the past three years, must hold a current membership card, and must continue to maintain their membership throughout the four-year scholarship period.

Award: Scholarship for use in freshman, sophomore, junior, or senior years; not renewable. *Number:* varies. *Amount:* up to $1000.

Eligibility Requirements: Applicant must be enrolled or expecting to enroll full-time at a four-year institution or university. Applicant or parent of applicant must be member of American Academy of Allergy, Asthma, and Immunology. Applicant must have 3.0 GPA or higher. Available to U.S. citizens.

Application Requirements: Application, references, original article (1000-word maximum, typed and double-spaced). *Deadline:* March 1.

Contact: LeAnn Knott, Scholarship Staff Assistant
American Legion Auxiliary Department of Michigan
212 North Verlinden Avenue
Lansing, MI 48915
Phone: 517-371-4720 Ext. 22
Fax: 517-371-2401
E-mail: info@michalaux.org

AMERICAN LEGION AUXILIARY DEPARTMENT OF MISSOURI

AMERICAN LEGION AUXILIARY DEPARTMENT OF MISSOURI LELA MURPHY SCHOLARSHIP

Scholarship of $500 for high school graduate. $250 will be awarded each semester. Applicant must be Missouri resident and the granddaughter or great-granddaughter of a living or deceased Auxiliary member. Sponsoring unit and department must validate application.

Award: Scholarship for use in freshman year; not renewable. *Number:* 1. *Amount:* $500.

Eligibility Requirements: Applicant must be high school student; planning to enroll or expecting to enroll full-time at a two-year or four-year or technical institution or university; female and resident of Missouri. Applicant or parent of applicant must be member of American Legion or Auxiliary. Available to U.S. citizens. Applicant or parent must meet one or more of the following requirements: general military experience; retired from active duty; disabled or killed as a result of military service; prisoner of war; or missing in action.

Application Requirements: Application. *Deadline:* March 1.

Contact: Mary Doerhoff, Department Secretary/Treasurer
American Legion Auxiliary Department of Missouri
600 Ellis Boulevard
Jefferson City, MO 65101-1615
Phone: 573-636-9133
Fax: 573-635-3467

AMERICAN LEGION AUXILIARY DEPARTMENT OF MISSOURI NATIONAL PRESIDENT'S SCHOLARSHIP

State-level award. Offers two $500 scholarships. Applicant must complete 50 hours of community service during their high school years. Sponsoring unit and department must validate application. Applicant must be Missouri resident.

Award: Scholarship for use in freshman year; not renewable. *Number:* 2. *Amount:* $500.

Eligibility Requirements: Applicant must be high school student; planning to enroll or expecting to enroll full-time at a two-year or four-year or technical institution or university and resident of Missouri. Applicant or parent of applicant must be member of American Legion or Auxiliary. Applicant or parent of applicant must have employment or volunteer experience in community service. Available to U.S. citizens. Applicant or parent must meet one or more of the following requirements: general military experience; retired from active duty; disabled or killed as a result of military service; prisoner of war; or missing in action.

Application Requirements: Application, resume. *Deadline:* March 1.

Contact: Mary Doerhoff, Department Secretary/Treasurer
American Legion Auxiliary Department of Missouri
600 Ellis Boulevard
Jefferson City, MO 65101-1615
Phone: 573-636-9133
Fax: 573-635-3467
E-mail: dptmoala@embarqmail.com

AMERICAN LEGION AUXILIARY DEPARTMENT OF NEBRASKA http://www.nebraskalegionaux.net

AMERICAN LEGION AUXILIARY DEPARTMENT OF NEBRASKA PRESIDENT'S SCHOLARSHIP FOR JUNIOR MEMBERS

One-time prize for female resident of Nebraska, who has entered into the National President's Scholarship for Junior Members contest and has not won at the national level. Must be in grades nine to twelve. Must rank in upper third of class or have a minimum 3.0 GPA.

Award: Prize for use in freshman year; not renewable. *Number:* 1. *Amount:* $200.

Eligibility Requirements: Applicant must be high school student; planning to enroll or expecting to enroll full-time at a four-year institution or university; female and resident of Nebraska. Applicant or parent of applicant must be member of American Legion or Auxiliary. Applicant must have 3.0 GPA or higher. Available to U.S. citizens. Applicant or parent must meet one or more of the following requirements: general military experience; retired from active duty; disabled or killed as a result of military service; prisoner of war; or missing in action.

Application Requirements: Application, essay, financial need analysis, references, test scores, transcript, letter of acceptance, proof of enrollment. *Deadline:* March 15.

Contact: Jackie O'Neill, Department Secretary
American Legion Auxiliary Department of Nebraska
PO Box 5227
Lincoln, NE 68505-0227
Phone: 402-466-1808
Fax: 402-466-0182
E-mail: neaux@alltel.net

AMERICAN LEGION AUXILIARY DEPARTMENT OF NEBRASKA RUBY PAUL CAMPAIGN FUND SCHOLARSHIP

One-time award for Nebraska residents who are children, grandchildren, or great-grandchildren of an American Legion Auxiliary member, or who have

American Legion Auxiliary Department of Nebraska (continued)

been members of the American Legion, American Legion Auxiliary, or Sons of the American Legion or Auxiliary for two years prior to issuing the application. Must rank in upper third of class or have minimum 3.0 GPA.

Award: Scholarship for use in freshman year; not renewable. *Number:* 1–3. *Amount:* $100–$300.

Eligibility Requirements: Applicant must be high school student; planning to enroll or expecting to enroll full-time at a four-year institution or university and resident of Nebraska. Applicant or parent of applicant must be member of American Legion or Auxiliary. Applicant must have 3.0 GPA or higher. Available to U.S. citizens. Applicant or parent must meet one or more of the following requirements: general military experience; retired from active duty; disabled or killed as a result of military service; prisoner of war; or missing in action.

Application Requirements: Application, essay, financial need analysis, references, test scores, transcript, letter of acceptance, proof of enrollment. *Deadline:* March 15.

Contact: Jackie O'Neill, Department Secretary
American Legion Auxiliary Department of Nebraska
PO Box 5227
Lincoln, NE 68505-0227
Phone: 402-466-1808
Fax: 402-466-0182
E-mail: neaux@alltel.net

AMERICAN LEGION AUXILIARY DEPARTMENT OF OREGON

AMERICAN LEGION AUXILIARY DEPARTMENT OF OREGON SPIRIT OF YOUTH SCHOLARSHIP

One-time award available to Oregon high school seniors. Must be a current female junior member of the American Legion Auxiliary with a three-year membership history. Apply through local units.

Award: Scholarship for use in freshman year; not renewable. *Number:* 1. *Amount:* $1000.

Eligibility Requirements: Applicant must be high school student; planning to enroll or expecting to enroll full- or part-time at a four-year institution or university; female and resident of Oregon. Applicant or parent of applicant must be member of American Legion or Auxiliary. Applicant must have 3.0 GPA or higher. Available to U.S. citizens. Applicant or parent must meet one or more of the following requirements: general military experience; retired from active duty; disabled or killed as a result of military service; prisoner of war; or missing in action.

Application Requirements: Application, essay, financial need analysis, interview, references, transcript. *Deadline:* March 1.

Contact: Pat Calhoun-Floren, Secretary
American Legion Auxiliary Department of Oregon
PO Box 1730
Wilsonville, OR 97070
Phone: 503-682-3162
Fax: 503-685-5008
E-mail: pcalhoun@pcez.com

AMERICAN LEGION AUXILIARY DEPARTMENT OF SOUTH DAKOTA

AMERICAN LEGION AUXILIARY DEPARTMENT OF SOUTH DAKOTA COLLEGE SCHOLARSHIPS

One-time award of $500 to assist veterans children or auxiliary members' children from South Dakota ages 16 to 22 to secure an education at a four-year school. Write for more information.

Award: Scholarship for use in freshman, sophomore, junior, or senior years; not renewable. *Number:* 2. *Amount:* $500.

Eligibility Requirements: Applicant must be age 16-22; enrolled or expecting to enroll full-time at a four-year institution or university and resident of South Dakota. Applicant or parent of applicant must be member of American Legion or Auxiliary. Available to U.S. and non-U.S. citizens. Applicant or parent must meet one or more of the following requirements: general military experience; retired from active duty; disabled or killed as a result of military service; prisoner of war; or missing in action.

Application Requirements: Application, essay, financial need analysis, references. *Deadline:* March 1.

Contact: Patricia Coyle, Executive Secretary
American Legion Auxiliary Department of South Dakota
PO Box 117
Huron, SD 57350
Phone: 605-353-1793
Fax: 605-352-0336
E-mail: sdlegionaux@msn.com

AMERICAN LEGION AUXILIARY DEPARTMENT OF SOUTH DAKOTA SENIOR SCHOLARSHIP

Award of $400 for current senior member of South Dakota American Legion Auxiliary who has been a member for three years. Based on financial need.

Award: Scholarship for use in freshman year; not renewable. *Number:* 1. *Amount:* $400.

Eligibility Requirements: Applicant must be high school student; planning to enroll or expecting to enroll full-time at a two-year or four-year or technical institution; female and resident of South Dakota. Applicant or parent of applicant must be member of American Legion or Auxiliary. Available to U.S. and non-U.S. citizens. Applicant or parent must meet one or more of the following requirements: general military experience; retired from active duty; disabled or killed as a result of military service; prisoner of war; or missing in action.

Application Requirements: Application, essay, financial need analysis, references, transcript. *Deadline:* March 1.

Contact: Patricia Coyle, Executive Secretary
American Legion Auxiliary Department of South Dakota
PO Box 117
Huron, SD 57350
Phone: 605-353-1793
Fax: 605-352-0336
E-mail: sdlegionaux@msn.com

AMERICAN LEGION AUXILIARY DEPARTMENT OF SOUTH DAKOTA THELMA FOSTER SCHOLARSHIP FOR SENIOR AUXILIARY MEMBERS

One-time award of $300 must be used within twelve months for a current senior member of the South Dakota American Legion Auxiliary who has been a member for three years. Applicant may be a high school senior or older and must be female.

Award: Scholarship for use in freshman year; not renewable. *Number:* 1. *Amount:* $300.

Eligibility Requirements: Applicant must be high school student; planning to enroll or expecting to enroll full-time at a four-year institution or university and female. Applicant or parent of applicant must be member of American Legion or Auxiliary. Available to U.S. and non-U.S. citizens. Applicant or parent must meet one or more of the following requirements: general military experience; retired from active duty; disabled or killed as a result of military service; prisoner of war; or missing in action.

Application Requirements: Application, essay, financial need analysis, references. *Deadline:* March 1.

Contact: Patricia Coyle, Executive Secretary
American Legion Auxiliary Department of South Dakota
PO Box 117
Huron, SD 57350
Phone: 605-353-1793
Fax: 605-352-0336
E-mail: sdlegionaux@msn.com

AMERICAN LEGION AUXILIARY DEPARTMENT OF SOUTH DAKOTA THELMA FOSTER SCHOLARSHIPS FOR JUNIOR AUXILIARY MEMBERS

One-time award of $300 for junior member of the South Dakota American Legion Auxiliary who has held membership for the past three years and holds a membership card for the current year. Must be a senior in high school.

Award: Scholarship for use in freshman year; not renewable. *Number:* 1. *Amount:* $300.

Eligibility Requirements: Applicant must be high school student; planning to enroll or expecting to enroll full-time at a four-year institution or university and female. Applicant or parent of applicant must be member of American Legion or Auxiliary. Available to U.S. and non-U.S. citizens. Applicant or parent must meet one or more of the following requirements: general military experience; retired from active duty; disabled or killed as a result of military service; prisoner of war; or missing in action.

Application Requirements: Application, essay, financial need analysis, references, transcript. *Deadline:* March 1.

Contact: Patricia Coyle, Executive Secretary
American Legion Auxiliary Department of South Dakota
PO Box 117
Huron, SD 57350
Phone: 605-353-1793
Fax: 605-352-0336
E-mail: sdlegionaux@msn.com

AMERICAN LEGION AUXILIARY DEPARTMENT OF SOUTH DAKOTA VOCATIONAL SCHOLARSHIP

One-time award of $500 to assist veterans children or auxiliary members children from South Dakota ages 16 to 22, secure a vocational education beyond the high school level. Write for more information.

Award: Scholarship for use in freshman or sophomore years; not renewable. *Number:* 2. *Amount:* $500.

Eligibility Requirements: Applicant must be age 16-22; enrolled or expecting to enroll full-time at a technical institution; resident of South Dakota and studying in South Dakota. Applicant or parent of applicant must be member of American Legion or Auxiliary. Available to U.S. and non-U.S. citizens. Applicant or parent must meet one or more of the following requirements: general military experience; retired from active duty; disabled or killed as a result of military service; prisoner of war; or missing in action.

Application Requirements: Application, essay, financial need analysis, references. *Deadline:* March 1.

Contact: Patricia Coyle, Executive Secretary
American Legion Auxiliary Department of South Dakota
PO Box 117
Huron, SD 57350
Phone: 605-353-1793
Fax: 605-352-0336
E-mail: sdlegionaux@msn.com

AMERICAN LEGION AUXILIARY DEPARTMENT OF UTAH http://www.legion-aux.org

AMERICAN LEGION AUXILIARY DEPARTMENT OF UTAH NATIONAL PRESIDENT'S SCHOLARSHIP

Scholarships available for graduating high school seniors. Must be a resident of Utah, a U.S. citizen, and the direct descendant of a veteran.

Award: Scholarship for use in freshman year; not renewable. *Number:* 15. *Amount:* $1000–$2500.

Eligibility Requirements: Applicant must be high school student; planning to enroll or expecting to enroll full-time at a two-year or four-year or technical institution or university; single and resident of Utah. Applicant or parent of applicant must be member of American Legion or Auxiliary. Available to U.S. citizens. Applicant or parent must meet one or more of the following requirements: general military experience; retired from active duty; disabled or killed as a result of military service; prisoner of war; or missing in action.

Application Requirements: Application, essay, references, test scores, transcript, statement of parent's military service. *Deadline:* March 1.

Contact: Lucia Anderson, Public Relations Manager and Associate Editor
American Legion Auxiliary Department of Utah
455 East 400 South, Suite 50
Salt Lake City, UT 84111
Phone: 801-539-1015
Fax: 801-521-9191
E-mail: landerson@legion-aux.org

AMERICAN LEGION AUXILIARY DEPARTMENT OF WISCONSIN http://www.amlegionauxwi.org

AMERICAN LEGION AUXILIARY DEPARTMENT OF WISCONSIN DELLA VAN DEUREN MEMORIAL SCHOLARSHIP

One-time award of $1000 for Wisconsin residents. Applicant or mother of applicant must be a member of an Auxiliary unit. Must submit certification of an American Legion Auxiliary unit president, copy of proof that veteran was in service (i.e. discharge papers), letters of recommendation, transcripts, and essay. Minimum 3.5 GPA required. Must demonstrate financial need. Applications available on Web site: http://www.legion-aux.org.

Award: Scholarship for use in freshman, sophomore, junior, or senior years; not renewable. *Number:* 2. *Amount:* $1000.

Eligibility Requirements: Applicant must be enrolled or expecting to enroll full- or part-time at a four-year institution or university and resident of Wisconsin. Applicant or parent of applicant must be member of American Legion or Auxiliary. Applicant must have 3.5 GPA or higher. Available to U.S. citizens. Applicant or parent must meet one or more of the following requirements: general military experience; retired from active duty; disabled or killed as a result of military service; prisoner of war; or missing in action.

Application Requirements: Application, essay, financial need analysis, references, transcript. *Deadline:* March 15.

Contact: Kim Henderson, Scholarship Information
American Legion Auxiliary Department of Wisconsin
PO Box 140
Portage, WI 53901-0140
Phone: 608-745-0124
Fax: 608-745-1947

AMERICAN LEGION AUXILIARY DEPARTMENT OF WISCONSIN H.S. AND ANGELINE LEWIS SCHOLARSHIPS

One-time award of $1000. Applicant must be a daughter, son, wife, or widow of a veteran. Granddaughters and great-granddaughters of veterans who are auxiliary members may also apply. Must submit certification of an American Legion Auxiliary unit president, copy of proof that veteran was in service (i.e. discharge papers), letters of recommendation, transcripts and essay. Must have minimum 3.5 GPA, show financial need, and be a resident of Wisconsin. Applications available on Web site: http://www.legion-aux.org.

Award: Scholarship for use in freshman, sophomore, junior, senior, or graduate years; not renewable. *Number:* 6. *Amount:* $1000.

Eligibility Requirements: Applicant must be enrolled or expecting to enroll full- or part-time at a two-year or four-year institution or university and resident of Wisconsin. Applicant or parent of applicant must be member of American Legion or Auxiliary. Applicant must have 3.5 GPA or higher. Available to U.S. citizens. Applicant or parent must meet one or more of the following requirements: general military experience; retired from active duty; disabled or killed as a result of military service; prisoner of war; or missing in action.

Application Requirements: Application, essay, financial need analysis, references, transcript. *Deadline:* March 15.

Contact: Katherine Ardnt, Education Chairman
American Legion Auxiliary Department of Wisconsin
2930 American Legion Drive
PO Box 140
Portage, WI 53901-0140
Phone: 715-453-1613
Fax: 608-745-1947
E-mail: katyann@newnorth.net

AMERICAN LEGION AUXILIARY DEPARTMENT OF WISCONSIN MERIT AND MEMORIAL SCHOLARSHIPS

One-time award of $1000. Applicant must be a daughter, son, wife, or widow of a veteran. Granddaughters and great-granddaughters of veterans who are auxiliary members may also apply. Must submit certification of an American Legion Auxiliary unit president, copy of proof that veteran was in service (i.e. discharge papers), letters of recommendation, transcripts, and essay. Must have minimum 3.5 GPA, show financial need, and be a resident of Wisconsin. Applications available on Web site: http://www.legion-aux.org.

Award: Scholarship for use in freshman, sophomore, junior, or senior years; not renewable. *Number:* 6. *Amount:* $1000.

Eligibility Requirements: Applicant must be enrolled or expecting to enroll full- or part-time at a four-year institution or university and resident of Wisconsin. Applicant or parent of applicant must be member of American Legion or Auxiliary. Applicant must have 3.5 GPA or higher. Available to U.S. citizens. Applicant or parent must meet one or more of the following requirements: general military experience; retired from active duty; disabled or killed as a result of military service; prisoner of war; or missing in action.

American Legion Auxiliary Department of Wisconsin (continued)

Application Requirements: Application, essay, financial need analysis, references, transcript. *Deadline:* March 15.

Contact: Kim Henderson, Scholarship Information
American Legion Auxiliary Department of Wisconsin
PO Box 140
Portage, WI 53901-0140
Phone: 608-745-0124
Fax: 608-745-1947

AMERICAN LEGION AUXILIARY DEPARTMENT OF WISCONSIN PAST PRESIDENTS' PARLEY HEALTH CAREER SCHOLARSHIPS

One-time award of $1000. Course of study need not be a four-year program. A hospital, university, or technical school program is also acceptable. Applicant must be a daughter, son, wife, or widow of a veteran. Granddaughters and great-granddaughters of veterans who are auxiliary members may also apply. Must submit certification of an American Legion Auxiliary unit president, copy of proof that veteran was in service (i.e. discharge papers), letters of recommendation, transcripts, and essay. Must have minimum 3.5 GPA, show financial need, and be a resident of Wisconsin. Applications available on Web site: http://www.legion-aux.org.

Award: Scholarship for use in freshman, sophomore, junior, or senior years; not renewable. *Number:* 2. *Amount:* $1000.

Eligibility Requirements: Applicant must be enrolled or expecting to enroll full- or part-time at a two-year or four-year or technical institution or university and resident of Wisconsin. Applicant or parent of applicant must be member of American Legion or Auxiliary. Applicant must have 3.5 GPA or higher. Available to U.S. citizens. Applicant or parent must meet one or more of the following requirements: general military experience; retired from active duty; disabled or killed as a result of military service; prisoner of war; or missing in action.

Application Requirements: Application, essay, financial need analysis, references, transcript. *Deadline:* March 15.

Contact: Kim Henderson, Scholarship Information
American Legion Auxiliary Department of Wisconsin
PO Box 140
Portage, WI 53901-0140
Phone: 608-745-0124
Fax: 608-745-1947

AMERICAN LEGION AUXILIARY DEPARTMENT OF WISCONSIN PRESIDENT'S SCHOLARSHIPS

One-time award of $1000. The mother of the applicant or the applicant must be a member of an Auxiliary unit. Must submit certification of an American Legion Auxiliary unit president, copy of proof that veteran was in service (i.e. discharge papers), letters of recommendation, transcripts, and essay. Must have minimum 3.5 GPA, show financial need, and be a resident of Wisconsin. Applications available on Web site: http://www.legion-aux.org.

Award: Scholarship for use in freshman, sophomore, junior, or senior years; not renewable. *Number:* 3. *Amount:* $1000.

Eligibility Requirements: Applicant must be enrolled or expecting to enroll full- or part-time at a four-year institution or university and resident of Wisconsin. Applicant or parent of applicant must be member of American Legion or Auxiliary. Applicant must have 3.5 GPA or higher. Available to U.S. citizens. Applicant or parent must meet one or more of the following requirements: general military experience; retired from active duty; disabled or killed as a result of military service; prisoner of war; or missing in action.

Application Requirements: Application, essay, financial need analysis, references, transcript. *Deadline:* March 15.

Contact: Kim Henderson, Scholarship Information
American Legion Auxiliary Department of Wisconsin
PO Box 140
Portage, WI 53901-0140
Phone: 608-745-0124
Fax: 608-745-1947

AMERICAN LEGION AUXILIARY NATIONAL HEADQUARTERS http://www.legion-aux.org

AMERICAN LEGION AUXILIARY GIRL SCOUT ACHIEVEMENT AWARD

One scholarship available to recipients of Girl Scout Gold Award. Must be active in religious institution and have received appropriate religious emblem, Cadet or Senior Scout level. Must show practical citizenship in religious institution, community, and school.

Award: Scholarship for use in freshman year; not renewable. *Number:* 1. *Amount:* $1000.

Eligibility Requirements: Applicant must be high school student; planning to enroll or expecting to enroll full-time at a four-year institution or university and female. Applicant or parent of applicant must be member of Girl Scouts. Applicant or parent of applicant must have employment or volunteer experience in community service. Available to U.S. citizens.

Application Requirements: Application, applicant must enter a contest, essay, references, self-addressed stamped envelope, test scores, transcript. *Deadline:* February 10.

Contact: Maria Potts, Program Coordinator
American Legion Auxiliary National Headquarters
777 North Meridian Street, Third Floor
Indianapolis, IN 46204
Phone: 317-955-3845
Fax: 317-955-3884
E-mail: mpotts@legion-aux.org

AMERICAN LEGION AUXILIARY NON-TRADITIONAL STUDENTS SCHOLARSHIPS

One-time award for students returning to the classroom after some period of time in which his/her formal schooling was interrupted or a student who has had at least one year of college and is in need of financial assistance to pursue an undergraduate degree. Must be a member of the American Legion, American Legion Auxiliary or Sons of the American Legion.

Award: Scholarship for use in freshman, sophomore, junior, or senior years; not renewable. *Number:* 5. *Amount:* $1000.

Eligibility Requirements: Applicant must be enrolled or expecting to enroll full-time at a two-year or four-year or technical institution or university. Applicant or parent of applicant must be member of American Legion or Auxiliary. Available to U.S. citizens. Applicant or parent must meet one or more of the following requirements: general military experience; retired from active duty; disabled or killed as a result of military service; prisoner of war; or missing in action.

Application Requirements: Application, essay, financial need analysis, references, test scores, transcript, statement of the military service of parents. *Deadline:* March 1.

Contact: Maria Potts, Program Coordinator
American Legion Auxiliary National Headquarters
777 North Meridian Street, Third Floor
Indianapolis, IN 46204
Phone: 317-955-3845
Fax: 317-955-3884
E-mail: mpotts@legion-aux.org

AMERICAN LEGION AUXILIARY SPIRIT OF YOUTH SCHOLARSHIPS FOR JUNIOR MEMBERS

Renewable scholarship for graduating high school seniors. Must be women and current junior members of the American Legion Auxiliary, with a three-year membership history.

Award: Scholarship for use in freshman, sophomore, junior, or senior years; renewable. *Number:* 5. *Amount:* $1000.

Eligibility Requirements: Applicant must be high school student; planning to enroll or expecting to enroll full-time at a four-year institution or university and female. Applicant or parent of applicant must be member of American Legion or Auxiliary. Available to U.S. citizens.

Application Requirements: Application, essay, references, self-addressed stamped envelope, test scores, transcript. *Deadline:* March 1.

Contact: Maria Potts, Program Coordinator
American Legion Auxiliary National Headquarters
777 North Meridian Street, Third Floor
Indianapolis, IN 46204
Phone: 317-955-3845
Fax: 317-955-3884
E-mail: mpotts@legion-aux.org

AMERICAN LEGION DEPARTMENT OF ARKANSAS http://www.arklegion.homestead.com

AMERICAN LEGION DEPARTMENT OF ARKANSAS COUDRET SCHOLARSHIP AWARD

Awards child, grandchild, or great-grandchild of American Legionnaire in good standing for two years. Two-year requirement is waived for Desert Storm and deceased veterans. One-time award for graduating Arkansas high school seniors.

Award: Scholarship for use in freshman year; not renewable. *Number:* 4. *Amount:* $1000.

Eligibility Requirements: Applicant must be high school student; age 16-24; planning to enroll or expecting to enroll full-time at a two-year or four-year or technical institution or university and resident of Arkansas. Applicant or parent of applicant must be member of American Legion or Auxiliary. Applicant must have 2.5 GPA or higher. Available to U.S. citizens. Applicant or parent must meet one or more of the following requirements: general military experience; retired from active duty; disabled or killed as a result of military service; prisoner of war; or missing in action.

Application Requirements: Application, autobiography, essay, financial need analysis, photo, references, transcript. *Deadline:* April 15.

Contact: William Winchell, Department Adjutant
American Legion Department of Arkansas
PO Box 3280
Little Rock, AR 72203-3280
Phone: 501-375-1104
Fax: 501-375-4236
E-mail: alegion@swbell.net

AMERICAN LEGION DEPARTMENT OF IDAHO http://idlegion.home.mindspring.com

AMERICAN LEGION DEPARTMENT OF IDAHO SCHOLARSHIP

One-time award of $500 to $750 for residents of Idaho studying at an Idaho institution. Minimum 2.5 GPA.

Award: Scholarship for use in freshman year; not renewable. *Number:* 1–7. *Amount:* $500–$750.

Eligibility Requirements: Applicant must be high school student; planning to enroll or expecting to enroll full-time at a four-year institution or university; resident of Idaho and studying in Idaho. Applicant or parent of applicant must be member of American Legion or Auxiliary. Applicant must have 2.5 GPA or higher. Available to U.S. citizens. Applicant or parent must meet one or more of the following requirements: general military experience; retired from active duty; disabled or killed as a result of military service; prisoner of war; or missing in action.

Application Requirements: Application, autobiography, financial need analysis, resume, references, self-addressed stamped envelope, test scores, transcript. *Deadline:* June 1.

Contact: Rickey Helsley, Department Adjunct
American Legion, Department of Idaho
901 Warren Street
Boise, ID 83706-3825
Phone: 208-342-7061
Fax: 208-342-1964
E-mail: idlegion@mindspring.com

AMERICAN LEGION DEPARTMENT OF ILLINOIS http://www.illegion.org

AMERICAN ESSAY CONTEST SCHOLARSHIP

Scholarship for students in seventh to twelfth grades of any accredited Illinois high school. Must write a 500-word essay on selected topic.

Award: Scholarship for use in freshman year; not renewable. *Number:* up to 60. *Amount:* $50–$75.

Eligibility Requirements: Applicant must be high school student; planning to enroll or expecting to enroll full-time at a four-year institution or university; resident of Illinois and must have an interest in writing. Applicant or parent of applicant must be member of American Legion or Auxiliary. Available to U.S. citizens.

Application Requirements: Application, applicant must enter a contest, essay. *Deadline:* February 3.

Contact: Bill Bechtel, Assistant Adjutant
American Legion Department of Illinois
PO Box 2910
Bloomington, IL 61702
Phone: 309-663-0361
Fax: 309-663-5783

AMERICAN LEGION DEPARTMENT OF ILLINOIS BOY SCOUT/EXPLORER SCHOLARSHIP

Scholarship for a graduating high school senior who is a qualified Boy Scout or Explorer and a resident of Illinois. Must write a 500-word essay on Legion's Americanism and Boy Scout programs.

Award: Scholarship for use in freshman year; not renewable. *Number:* up to 5. *Amount:* $200–$1000.

Eligibility Requirements: Applicant must be high school student; planning to enroll or expecting to enroll full- or part-time at a four-year institution or university and resident of Illinois. Applicant or parent of applicant must be member of Boy Scouts. Available to U.S. citizens.

Application Requirements: Application, applicant must enter a contest, essay. *Deadline:* April 30.

Contact: Bill Bechtel, Assistant Adjutant
American Legion Department of Illinois
PO Box 2910
Bloomington, IL 61702
Phone: 309-663-0361
Fax: 309-663-5783

AMERICAN LEGION DEPARTMENT OF ILLINOIS SCHOLARSHIPS

Awards twenty $1000 scholarships for graduating students of Illinois high schools. May be used at any accredited college, university, trade or technical school. Applicant must be a child or grandchild of members of the American Legion-Illinois. Awards will be based on academic merit and financial need.

Award: Scholarship for use in freshman year; not renewable. *Number:* up to 20. *Amount:* $1000.

Eligibility Requirements: Applicant must be high school student; planning to enroll or expecting to enroll full- or part-time at a two-year or four-year or technical institution or university and resident of Illinois. Applicant or parent of applicant must be member of American Legion or Auxiliary. Available to U.S. citizens.

Application Requirements: Application, financial need analysis, photo, test scores, transcript. *Deadline:* March 15.

Contact: Bill Bechtel, Assistant Adjutant
American Legion Department of Illinois
PO Box 2910
Bloomington, IL 61702
Phone: 309-663-0361
Fax: 309-663-5783

AMERICAN LEGION DEPARTMENT OF INDIANA http://www.indlegion.org

AMERICAN LEGION FAMILY SCHOLARSHIP

Scholarship open to children and grandchildren of current members of The American Legion, American Legion Auxiliary, and The Sons of the American Legion. Also open to the children and grandchildren of deceased members who were current paid members of the above organizations at the time of their death.

Award: Scholarship for use in freshman or sophomore years; not renewable. *Number:* up to 3. *Amount:* $700–$1000.

Eligibility Requirements: Applicant must be enrolled or expecting to enroll full-time at a two-year or four-year or technical institution or university. Applicant or parent of applicant must be member of American Legion or Auxiliary. Applicant must have 3.5 GPA or higher. Available to U.S. citizens.

American Legion Department of Indiana (continued)

Application Requirements: Application, essay, transcript. *Deadline:* April 1.

Contact: Susan Long, Program Coordinator
American Legion Department of Indiana
777 North Meridan Street, Room 104
Indianapolis, IN 46204
Phone: 317-630-1264
Fax: 317-237-9891
E-mail: slong@indlegion.org

AMERICAN LEGION DEPARTMENT OF IOWA http://www.ialegion.org

AMERICAN LEGION DEPARTMENT OF IOWA EAGLE SCOUT OF THE YEAR SCHOLARSHIP

Three one-time award for Eagle Scouts who are residents of Iowa. For full-time study only.

Award: Scholarship for use in freshman year; not renewable. *Number:* up to 3. *Amount:* $250–$1000.

Eligibility Requirements: Applicant must be high school student; planning to enroll or expecting to enroll full-time at a two-year or four-year institution or university; male and resident of Iowa. Applicant or parent of applicant must be member of Boy Scouts. Available to U.S. citizens.

Application Requirements: Application, applicant must enter a contest, references. *Deadline:* March 1.

Contact: Program Director
American Legion Department of Iowa
720 Lyon Street
Des Moines, IA 50309
Phone: 515-282-5068

AMERICAN LEGION DEPARTMENT OF KANSAS http://www.ksamlegion.org

ALBERT M. LAPPIN SCHOLARSHIP

Scholarship for children of the members of Kansas American Legion or its auxiliary. Membership must have been active for the past three years. The children of deceased members are also eligible if parents' dues were paid at the time of death. Applicant must be a son/daughter of a veteran. Must be high school senior or college freshman or sophomore. Must use award at a Kansas college, university, or trade school.

Award: Scholarship for use in freshman or sophomore years; not renewable. *Number:* 1. *Amount:* $1000.

Eligibility Requirements: Applicant must be enrolled or expecting to enroll full-time at a two-year or four-year or technical institution or university and studying in Kansas. Applicant or parent of applicant must be member of American Legion or Auxiliary. Available to U.S. citizens. Applicant or parent must meet one or more of the following requirements: general military experience; retired from active duty; disabled or killed as a result of military service; prisoner of war; or missing in action.

Application Requirements: Application, essay, financial need analysis, photo, transcript. *Deadline:* February 15.

Contact: Jim Gravenstein, Chairman, Scholarship Committee
American Legion Department of Kansas
1314 Topeka Boulevard, SW
Topeka, KS 66612
Phone: 785-232-9513
Fax: 785-232-1399

CHARLES W. AND ANNETTE HILL SCHOLARSHIP

Scholarship of $1000 to the descendants of veterans who are American Legion members or American Legion Auxiliary members holding membership for the past three consecutive years. Descendants of deceased members can also apply. Must be high school seniors or college freshmen or sophomores in a Kansas institution. Scholarship for use at an approved college, university, or trade school in Kansas. Must maintain a 3.0 GPA. Disbursement: $500 at beginning each semester for one year.

Award: Scholarship for use in freshman or sophomore years; not renewable. *Number:* 1. *Amount:* $1000.

Eligibility Requirements: Applicant must be enrolled or expecting to enroll full-time at a two-year or four-year or technical institution or university; resident of Kansas and studying in Kansas. Applicant or parent of applicant must be member of American Legion or Auxiliary. Applicant must have 3.0 GPA or higher. Available to U.S. citizens. Applicant or parent must meet one or more of the following requirements: general military experience; retired from active duty; disabled or killed as a result of military service; prisoner of war; or missing in action.

Application Requirements: Application, essay, references, transcript, latest 1040 income statement of supporting parents. *Deadline:* February 15.

Contact: Jim Gravenstein, Chairman, Scholarship Committee
American Legion Department of Kansas
1314 Topeka Boulevard, SW
Topeka, KS 66612
Phone: 785-232-9513
Fax: 785-232-1399

HUGH A. SMITH SCHOLARSHIP FUND

One-year scholarship of $500 to the children of American Legion/Auxiliary members holding membership for the past three consecutive years. Children of a deceased member can also apply. Parent of the applicant must be a veteran. Must be high school seniors or college freshmen or sophomores in a Kansas institution. Scholarship for use at an approved college, university, or trade school in Kansas. Must maintain a C average in college.

Award: Scholarship for use in freshman or sophomore years; not renewable. *Number:* 1. *Amount:* $500.

Eligibility Requirements: Applicant must be enrolled or expecting to enroll full-time at a two-year or four-year or technical institution or university; resident of Kansas and studying in Kansas. Applicant or parent of applicant must be member of American Legion or Auxiliary. Available to U.S. citizens. Applicant or parent must meet one or more of the following requirements: general military experience; retired from active duty; disabled or killed as a result of military service; prisoner of war; or missing in action.

Application Requirements: Application, financial need analysis, photo, references, transcript, latest 1040 income statement of supporting parents. *Deadline:* February 15.

Contact: Jim Gravenstein, Chairman, Scholarship Committee
American Legion Department of Kansas
1314 Topeka Boulevard, SW
Topeka, KS 66612
Phone: 785-232-9513
Fax: 785-232-1399

ROSEDALE POST 346 SCHOLARSHIP

Two scholarships of $1500 each awarded to the children of American Legion members or of American Legion Auxiliary members holding membership for the past three consecutive years. Children of a deceased member can also apply. Parent of the applicant must be a veteran. Must be high school seniors or college freshmen or sophomores in a Kansas institution. Scholarship for use at an approved college, university, or trade school in Kansas. Must maintain a C average in college.

Award: Scholarship for use in freshman or sophomore years; not renewable. *Number:* 2. *Amount:* $1500.

Eligibility Requirements: Applicant must be enrolled or expecting to enroll full-time at a two-year or four-year or technical institution or university; resident of Kansas and studying in Kansas. Applicant or parent of applicant must be member of American Legion or Auxiliary. Available to U.S. citizens. Applicant or parent must meet one or more of the following requirements: general military experience; retired from active duty; disabled or killed as a result of military service; prisoner of war; or missing in action.

Application Requirements: Application, essay, financial need analysis, photo, references, transcript, latest 1040 income statement of supporting parents). *Deadline:* February 15.

Contact: Jim Gravenstein, Chairman, Scholarship Committee
American Legion Department of Kansas
1314 Topeka Boulevard, SW
Topeka, KS 66612
Phone: 785-232-9513
Fax: 785-232-1399

TED AND NORA ANDERSON SCHOLARSHIPS

Scholarship of $250 for each semester (one year only) given to the children of American Legion members or Auxiliary members who are holding membership for the past three consecutive years. Children of a deceased member can also apply. Parent of the applicant must be a veteran. Must be high school seniors or college freshmen or sophomores in a Kansas institution. Scholarship for use at an approved college, university, or trade school in Kansas. Must maintain a C average in college.

Award: Scholarship for use in freshman or sophomore years; not renewable. *Number:* 4. *Amount:* $250–$500.

Eligibility Requirements: Applicant must be enrolled or expecting to enroll full-time at a two-year or four-year or technical institution or university; resident of Kansas and studying in Kansas. Applicant or parent of applicant must be member of American Legion or Auxiliary. Available to U.S. citizens. Applicant or parent must meet one or more of the following requirements: general military experience; retired from active duty; disabled or killed as a result of military service; prisoner of war; or missing in action.

Application Requirements: Application, essay, financial need analysis, photo, references, transcript. *Deadline:* February 15.

Contact: Jim Gravenstein, Chairman, Scholarship Committee
American Legion Department of Kansas
1314 Topeka Boulevard, SW
Topeka, KS 66612
Phone: 785-232-9315
Fax: 785-232-1399

AMERICAN LEGION DEPARTMENT OF MAINE http://www.mainelegion.org

JAMES V. DAY SCHOLARSHIP

One-time $500 award for a Maine resident whose parent is a member of the American Legion in Maine. Must be a U.S. citizen. Based on character and financial need.

Award: Scholarship for use in freshman, sophomore, junior, senior, or graduate years; not renewable. *Number:* 1–2. *Amount:* up to $500.

Eligibility Requirements: Applicant must be enrolled or expecting to enroll full-time at a two-year or four-year or technical institution or university and resident of Maine. Applicant or parent of applicant must be member of American Legion or Auxiliary. Available to U.S. citizens. Applicant or parent must meet one or more of the following requirements: general military experience; retired from active duty; disabled or killed as a result of military service; prisoner of war; or missing in action.

Application Requirements: Application, references, transcript. *Deadline:* May 1.

Contact: Department Adjutant
American Legion, Department of Maine
21 College Avenue
PO Box 900
Waterville, ME 04903-0900
Phone: 207-873-3229
Fax: 207-872-0501
E-mail: legionme@me.acadia.net

AMERICAN LEGION DEPARTMENT OF MINNESOTA http://www.mnlegion.org

AMERICAN LEGION DEPARTMENT OF MINNESOTA MEMORIAL SCHOLARSHIP

Scholarship available to Minnesota residents who are dependents of members of the Minnesota American Legion or auxiliary. One-time award of $500 for study at a Minnesota institution or neighboring state with reciprocating agreement.

Award: Scholarship for use in freshman, sophomore, junior, or senior years; not renewable. *Number:* 6. *Amount:* $500.

Eligibility Requirements: Applicant must be enrolled or expecting to enroll full- or part-time at a two-year or four-year or technical institution or university; resident of Minnesota and studying in Iowa, Minnesota, North Dakota, South Dakota, or Wisconsin. Applicant or parent of applicant must be member of American Legion or Auxiliary. Applicant must have 2.5 GPA or higher. Available to U.S. citizens. Applicant or parent must meet one or more of the following requirements: general military experience; retired from active duty; disabled or killed as a result of military service; prisoner of war; or missing in action.

Application Requirements: Application, essay, financial need analysis, references, transcript. *Deadline:* April 1.

Contact: Jennifer Kelley, Program Coordinator
American Legion Department of Minnesota
20 West 12th Street, Room 300-A
St. Paul, MN 55155
Phone: 651-291-1800
Fax: 651-291-1057
E-mail: department@mnlegion.org

MINNESOTA LEGIONNAIRES INSURANCE TRUST SCHOLARSHIP

Scholarship for Minnesota residents who are veterans or dependents of veterans. One-time award of $500 for study at a Minnesota institution or neighboring state with reciprocating agreement. All applications must be approved and recommended by a post of the American Legion.

Award: Scholarship for use in freshman, sophomore, junior, senior, graduate, or postgraduate years; not renewable. *Number:* 3. *Amount:* $500.

Eligibility Requirements: Applicant must be enrolled or expecting to enroll full- or part-time at a two-year or four-year institution or university; resident of Minnesota and studying in Iowa, Minnesota, North Dakota, South Dakota, or Wisconsin. Applicant or parent of applicant must be member of American Legion or Auxiliary. Applicant must have 2.5 GPA or higher. Available to U.S. citizens. Applicant or parent must meet one or more of the following requirements: general military experience; retired from active duty; disabled or killed as a result of military service; prisoner of war; or missing in action.

Application Requirements: Application, essay, financial need analysis, references, transcript. *Deadline:* April 1.

Contact: Jennifer Kelley, Program Coordinator
American Legion Department of Minnesota
20 West 12th Street, Room 300-A
St. Paul, MN 55155
Phone: 651-291-1800
Fax: 651-291-1057
E-mail: department@mnlegion.org

AMERICAN LEGION DEPARTMENT OF MISSOURI http://www.missourilegion.org

CHARLES L. BACON MEMORIAL SCHOLARSHIP

Two awards of $500 are given. Applicant must be a member of The American Legion, the American Legion Auxiliary, or the Sons of The American Legion, or a descendant of a member of any thereof. Applicants must be unmarried Missouri resident below age 21, and must use the scholarship as a full-time student in an accredited college or university in Missouri. Must submit proof of American Legion membership.

Award: Scholarship for use in freshman year; not renewable. *Number:* 2. *Amount:* $500.

Eligibility Requirements: Applicant must be high school student; age 21 or under; planning to enroll or expecting to enroll full-time at a two-year or four-year institution or university; single and resident of Missouri. Applicant or parent of applicant must be member of American Legion or Auxiliary. Available to U.S. citizens. Applicant or parent must meet one or more of the following requirements: general military experience; retired from active duty; disabled or killed as a result of military service; prisoner of war; or missing in action.

American Legion, Department of Missouri (continued)

Application Requirements: Application, financial need analysis, test scores, discharge certificate. *Deadline:* April 20.

Contact: John Doane, Chairman
American Legion, Department of Missouri
PO Box 179
Jefferson City, MO 65102
Phone: 417-924-8596
Fax: 573-893-2980
E-mail: info@missourilegion.org

AMERICAN LEGION DEPARTMENT OF NEBRASKA http://www.nebraskalegion.net

EAGLE SCOUT OF THE YEAR SCHOLARSHIP

Scholarship of $1000 is awarded to one recipient each year by The American Legion, Department of Nebraska. The Department recipient is then entered into The American Legion National Eagle Scout of the Year and is eligible to receive a $10,000 scholarship, or one of three second place scholarships of $2500.

Award: Scholarship for use in freshman, sophomore, junior, or senior years; not renewable. *Number:* 1. *Amount:* $1000–$10,000.

Eligibility Requirements: Applicant must be age 18 or under; enrolled or expecting to enroll full- or part-time at a two-year or four-year or technical institution or university; male and resident of Nebraska. Applicant or parent of applicant must be member of Boy Scouts. Available to U.S. citizens.

Application Requirements: Application, photo, references, transcript. *Deadline:* March 1.

Contact: Mr. Jody Moeller, Activities Director
American Legion Department of Nebraska
PO Box 5205
Lincoln, NE 68505-0205
Phone: 402-464-6338
Fax: 402-464-6330
E-mail: actdirlegion@alltel.net

MAYNARD JENSEN AMERICAN LEGION MEMORIAL SCHOLARSHIP

Scholarship for dependents or grandchildren of members, prisoner-of-war, missing-in-action veterans, killed-in-action veterans, or any deceased veterans of the American Legion. One-time award is based on academic achievement and financial need for Nebraska residents attending Nebraska institutions. Several scholarships of $500 each. Must have minimum 2.5 GPA and must submit school certification of GPA.

Award: Scholarship for use in freshman, sophomore, junior, or senior years; not renewable. *Number:* 1–10. *Amount:* $500.

Eligibility Requirements: Applicant must be enrolled or expecting to enroll full-time at a two-year or four-year or technical institution or university; resident of Nebraska and studying in Nebraska. Applicant or parent of applicant must be member of American Legion or Auxiliary. Applicant must have 2.5 GPA or higher. Available to U.S. citizens. Applicant or parent must meet one or more of the following requirements: general military experience; retired from active duty; disabled or killed as a result of military service; prisoner of war; or missing in action.

Application Requirements: Application, financial need analysis, test scores. *Deadline:* March 1.

Contact: Burdette Burkhart, Adjutant
American Legion Department of Nebraska
PO Box 5205
Lincoln, NE 68505-0205
Phone: 402-464-6338
Fax: 402-464-6330
E-mail: nebraska@legion.org

AMERICAN LEGION DEPARTMENT OF NEW JERSEY http://www.njamericanlegion.org

LUTERMAN SCHOLARSHIP

Applicant must be a natural or adopted descendant of a member of American Legion, Department of New Jersey. Applicant must be a member of the graduating class of high school including Vo-tech.

Award: Scholarship for use in freshman year; not renewable. *Number:* 7. *Amount:* $1000–$4000.

Eligibility Requirements: Applicant must be high school student and planning to enroll or expecting to enroll full-time at a two-year or four-year or technical institution or university. Applicant or parent of applicant must be member of American Legion or Auxiliary. Available to U.S. citizens. Applicant or parent must meet one or more of the following requirements: Army experience; retired from active duty; disabled or killed as a result of military service; prisoner of war; or missing in action.

Application Requirements: Application. *Deadline:* February 15.

Contact: Raymond Zawacki, Department Adjutant
American Legion Department of New Jersey
135 West Hanover Street
Trenton, NJ 08618
Phone: 609-695-5418
Fax: 609-394-1532
E-mail: ray@njamericanlegion.org

STUTZ SCHOLARSHIP

Award to natural or adopted son or daughter of a member of The American Legion, Department of New Jersey. Applicant must be a member of the graduating class of high school including Vo-tech.

Award: Scholarship for use in freshman year; not renewable. *Number:* 1. *Amount:* $4000.

Eligibility Requirements: Applicant must be high school student and planning to enroll or expecting to enroll full-time at a two-year or four-year or technical institution or university. Applicant or parent of applicant must be member of American Legion or Auxiliary. Available to U.S. citizens. Applicant or parent must meet one or more of the following requirements: Army experience; retired from active duty; disabled or killed as a result of military service; prisoner of war; or missing in action.

Application Requirements: Application. *Deadline:* February 15.

Contact: Raymond Zawacki, Department Adjutant
American Legion Department of New Jersey
135 West Hanover Street
Trenton, NJ 08618
Phone: 609-695-5418
Fax: 609-394-1532
E-mail: ray@njamericanlegion.org

AMERICAN LEGION DEPARTMENT OF OHIO http://www.ohiolegion.com

OHIO AMERICAN LEGION SCHOLARSHIPS

One-time award for full-time students attending an accredited institution. Open to students of any postsecondary academic year. Must have minimum 3.0 GPA. Must be a member of the American Legion, a direct descendent of a Legionnaire (living or deceased), or surviving spouse or child of a deceased U.S. military person who died on active duty or of injuries received on active duty.

Award: Scholarship for use in freshman, sophomore, junior, or senior years; not renewable. *Number:* 15–18. *Amount:* $2000–$3000.

Eligibility Requirements: Applicant must be enrolled or expecting to enroll full-time at a two-year or four-year or technical institution or university. Applicant or parent of applicant must be member of American Legion or Auxiliary. Applicant must have 3.0 GPA or higher. Available to U.S. and non-U.S. citizens. Applicant or parent must meet one or more of the following requirements: general military experience; retired from active duty; disabled or killed as a result of military service; prisoner of war; or missing in action.

Application Requirements: Application, resume, transcript. *Deadline:* April 15.

Contact: Donald Lanthorn, Service Director
American Legion, Department of Ohio
60 Big Run Road, PO Box 8007
Delaware, OH 43015
Phone: 740-362-7478
Fax: 740-362-1429
E-mail: dlanthorn@iwaynet.net

AMERICAN LEGION DEPARTMENT OF PENNSYLVANIA http://www.pa-legion.com

JOSEPH P. GAVENONIS COLLEGE SCHOLARSHIP (PLAN I)

Scholarships for Pennsylvania residents seeking a four-year degree from a Pennsylvania college or university. Must be the child of a member of a Pennsylvania American Legion post. Must be a graduating high school senior. Award amount and number of awards determined annually. Renewable award. Must maintain 2.5 GPA in college. Total number of awards varies.

Award: Scholarship for use in freshman year; renewable. *Number:* varies. *Amount:* $500–$1000.

Eligibility Requirements: Applicant must be high school student; planning to enroll or expecting to enroll full-time at a four-year institution or university; resident of Pennsylvania and studying in Pennsylvania. Applicant or parent of applicant must be member of American Legion or Auxiliary. Applicant must have 2.5 GPA or higher. Available to U.S. citizens.

Application Requirements: Application, financial need analysis, test scores, transcript. *Deadline:* May 30.

Contact: Debbie Watson, Emblem Sales Supervisor
American Legion Department of Pennsylvania
PO Box 2324
Harrisburg, PA 17105-2324
Phone: 717-730-9100
Fax: 717-975-2836
E-mail: hq@pa-legion.com

AMERICAN LEGION DEPARTMENT OF TENNESSEE http://www.tennesseelegion.org

AMERICAN LEGION DEPARTMENT OF TENNESSEE EAGLE SCOUT OF THE YEAR

Scholarship for graduating high school seniors who are Eagle Scouts, enrolled either part-time or full-time for study in accredited colleges or universities. Scholarship value is $1500. Deadline varies.

Award: Scholarship for use in freshman year; renewable. *Number:* 1. *Amount:* $1500.

Eligibility Requirements: Applicant must be high school student; planning to enroll or expecting to enroll full- or part-time at a four-year institution or university and resident of Tennessee. Applicant or parent of applicant must be member of Boy Scouts. Available to U.S. citizens.

Application Requirements: Application, financial need analysis, transcript. *Deadline:* varies.

Contact: Darlene Burgess, Executive Assistant
American Legion Department of Tennessee
215 Eighth Avenue, North
Nashville, TN 37203
Phone: 615-254-0568
Fax: 615-255-1551
E-mail: tnleg1@bellsouth.net

AMERICAN LEGION DEPARTMENT OF VERMONT http://www.legionvthq.com

AMERICAN LEGION EAGLE SCOUT OF THE YEAR

Awarded to the Boy Scout chosen for outstanding service to his religious institution, school, and community. Must receive the award and reside in Vermont.

Award: Scholarship for use in freshman year; not renewable. *Number:* 1. *Amount:* $1000.

Eligibility Requirements: Applicant must be high school student; age 18 or under; planning to enroll or expecting to enroll full-time at a four-year institution or university and resident of Vermont. Applicant or parent of applicant must be member of Boy Scouts. Applicant or parent of applicant must have employment or volunteer experience in community service. Available to U.S. citizens.

Application Requirements: Application, photo. *Deadline:* March 1.

Contact: Frank Killay, Chairman
American Legion Department of Vermont
PO Box 396
Montpelier, VT 05601-0396
Phone: 802-223-7131
Fax: 802-223-0318
E-mail: alvthq@verizon.net

AMERICAN LEGION DEPARTMENT OF WASHINGTON http://www.walegion.org

AMERICAN LEGION DEPARTMENT OF WASHINGTON CHILDREN AND YOUTH SCHOLARSHIPS

One-time award for the son or daughter of a Washington American Legion or Auxiliary member, living or deceased. Must be high school senior and Washington resident planning to attend an accredited institution of higher education in Washington. Award based on need.

Award: Scholarship for use in freshman year; not renewable. *Number:* 2. *Amount:* $1500–$2500.

Eligibility Requirements: Applicant must be high school student; planning to enroll or expecting to enroll full- or part-time at a four-year institution or university; resident of Washington and studying in Washington. Applicant or parent of applicant must be member of American Legion or Auxiliary. Available to U.S. citizens. Applicant or parent must meet one or more of the following requirements: general military experience; retired from active duty; disabled or killed as a result of military service; prisoner of war; or missing in action.

Application Requirements: Application, financial need analysis, transcript. *Deadline:* April 1.

Contact: Marc O'Connor, Chairman, Children and Youth Commission
American Legion, Department of Washington
3600 Ruddell Road, SE
PO Box 3917
Lacey, WA 98509-3917
Phone: 360-423-9542
E-mail: oconnorred@comcast.net

AMERICAN LEGION DEPARTMENT OF WEST VIRGINIA http://www.wvlegion.org

SONS OF THE AMERICAN LEGION WILLIAM F. "BILL" JOHNSON MEMORIAL SCHOLARSHIP

Applicant is required to write an essay based on a different question each year. Award is given during the second semester of college provided the winner has passing grades in the first semester. Must submit a copy of passing GPA of their first semester of college. Must be a resident of West Virginia and the child or grandchild of a member of The American Legion.

Award: Scholarship for use in freshman year; not renewable. *Number:* up to 2. *Amount:* up to $1500.

Eligibility Requirements: Applicant must be high school student; planning to enroll or expecting to enroll full-time at a two-year or four-year institution or university and resident of West Virginia. Applicant or parent of applicant must be member of American Legion or Auxiliary. Available to U.S. citizens. Applicant or parent must meet one or more of the following requirements: general military experience; retired from active duty; disabled or killed as a result of military service; prisoner of war; or missing in action.

Application Requirements: Application, essay, transcript. *Deadline:* May 15.

Contact: Miles Epling, State Adjutant
American Legion Department of West Virginia
2016 Kanawha Boulevard East, PO Box 3191
Charleston, WV 25332-3191
Phone: 304-343-7591
Fax: 304-343-7592
E-mail: wvlegion@suddenlinkmail.com

AMERICAN LEGION NATIONAL HEADQUARTERS

http://www.legion.org

AMERICAN LEGION NATIONAL HEADQUARTERS EAGLE SCOUT OF THE YEAR

The winner of the competition receives a $10,000 scholarship and 3 runners-up are each awarded $2500 scholarships. May be used to attend any state accredited postsecondary institution in the U.S.

Award: Scholarship for use in freshman year; not renewable. *Number:* 4. *Amount:* $2500–$10,000.

Eligibility Requirements: Applicant must be high school student; age 15-18; planning to enroll or expecting to enroll full-time at a two-year or four-year institution or university and male. Applicant or parent of applicant must be member of American Legion or Auxiliary or Boy Scouts. Applicant or parent of applicant must have employment or volunteer experience in community service. Available to U.S. citizens.

Application Requirements: Application, essay, references, transcript. *Deadline:* March 1.

Contact: Robert Caudell, Assistant Director
American Legion National Headquarters
PO Box 1055
Indianapolis, IN 46206-1055
Phone: 317-630-1212
Fax: 317-630-1369
E-mail: rcaudell@legion.org

AMERICAN POSTAL WORKERS UNION

http://www.apwu.org

E.C. HALLBECK SCHOLARSHIP FUND

Scholarship for children of American Postal Workers Union members. Applicant must be a child, grandchild, stepchild, or legally adopted child of an active member, Retirees Department member, or deceased member of American Postal Workers Union. Must be a senior attending high school or other corresponding secondary school. Must be 18 years or older. Recipient must attend accredited community college or university as a full-time student. Scholarship will be $1000 for each year of four consecutive years of college. Scholarship will provide five area winners. For additional information and to download applications go to Web site: http://www.apwu.org.

Award: Scholarship for use in freshman year; renewable. *Number:* 5. *Amount:* $1000.

Eligibility Requirements: Applicant must be high school student; age 18 and over and planning to enroll or expecting to enroll full-time at a two-year or four-year or technical institution or university. Applicant or parent of applicant must be member of American Postal Workers Union. Applicant or parent of applicant must have employment or volunteer experience in federal/postal service. Available to U.S. citizens.

Application Requirements: Application, essay, references, test scores, transcript. *Deadline:* March 15.

Contact: Terry Stapleton, Secretary and Treasurer
American Postal Workers Union
1300 L Street, NW
Washington, DC 20005
Phone: 202-842-4215
Fax: 202-842-8530

VOCATIONAL SCHOLARSHIP PROGRAM

A scholarship for a child, grandchild, stepchild, or legally adopted child of an active member, Retiree's Department member, or deceased member of the American Postal Workers Union. Applicant must be a senior attending high school who plans on attending an accredited vocational school or community college vocational program as a full-time student. The award is $1000 per year consecutively or until completion of the course. For additional information see Web site: http://www.apwu.org.

Award: Scholarship for use in freshman year; renewable. *Number:* 5. *Amount:* $1000.

Eligibility Requirements: Applicant must be high school student and planning to enroll or expecting to enroll full-time at a four-year institution or university. Applicant or parent of applicant must be member of American Postal Workers Union. Applicant or parent of applicant must have employment or volunteer experience in federal/postal service. Available to U.S. citizens.

Application Requirements: Application, essay, references, test scores, transcript. *Deadline:* March 15.

Contact: Terry Stapleton, Secretary and Treasurer
American Postal Workers Union
1300 L Street, NW
Washington, DC 20005
Phone: 202-842-4215
Fax: 202-842-8530

AMERICAN QUARTER HORSE FOUNDATION (AQHF)

http://www.aqha.com/foundation

AMERICAN QUARTER HORSE FOUNDATION YOUTH SCHOLARSHIPS

Scholarship to the members of AQHA/AQHYA who have completed a minimum of three years cumulative membership. Members must apply during their senior year of high school or home school equivalency. Students currently enrolled as a first-year college freshman are not eligible for consideration. Minimum 2.5 GPA required.

Award: Scholarship for use in sophomore, junior, or senior years; renewable. *Number:* 27. *Amount:* $8000.

Eligibility Requirements: Applicant must be enrolled or expecting to enroll full-time at a two-year or four-year or technical institution or university. Applicant or parent of applicant must be member of American Quarter Horse Association. Applicant must have 3.5 GPA or higher. Available to U.S. and Canadian citizens.

Application Requirements: Application, financial need analysis, references, transcript. *Deadline:* January 2.

Contact: Scholarship Office
American Quarter Horse Foundation (AQHF)
2601 East Interstate 40
Amarillo, TX 79104
Phone: 806-378-5029
Fax: 806-376-1005
E-mail: foundation@aqha.org

DR. GERALD O'CONNOR MICHIGAN SCHOLARSHIP

Scholarships for AQHA/AQHYA members from Michigan. Members may apply during their senior year of high school or while enrolled at an accredited college, university or vocational school. Minimum 2.5 GPA required. Renewable up to four years.

Award: Scholarship for use in freshman, sophomore, junior, or senior years; renewable. *Number:* 1. *Amount:* $2000.

Eligibility Requirements: Applicant must be enrolled or expecting to enroll full-time at a two-year or four-year or technical institution or university; resident of Michigan and must have an interest in animal/agricultural competition. Applicant or parent of applicant must be member of American Quarter Horse Association. Applicant must have 2.5 GPA or higher. Available to U.S. and Canadian citizens.

Application Requirements: Application, driver's license, essay, financial need analysis, photo, references, transcript. *Deadline:* January 2.

Contact: Laura Owens, Scholarship Office
American Quarter Horse Foundation (AQHF)
2601 East Interstate 40
Amarillo, TX 79104
Phone: 806-378-5029
Fax: 806-376-1005
E-mail: foundation@aqha.org

EXCELLENCE IN EQUINE/AGRICULTURAL INVOLVEMENT SCHOLARSHIP

Scholarship to an AQHA/AQHYA member who exemplifies the characteristics of leadership and excellence acquired through participation in equine and or agriculture activities. Members may apply during their senior year of high school or while enrolled at an accredited college, university or vocational school. Renewable up to four years. Minimum GPA 3.5 required.

Award: Scholarship for use in freshman, sophomore, junior, or senior years; renewable. *Number:* 1. *Amount:* $25,000.

Eligibility Requirements: Applicant must be enrolled or expecting to enroll full-time at a two-year or four-year or technical institution or university. Applicant or parent of applicant must be member of American Quarter Horse Association. Applicant or parent of applicant must have employment or volunteer experience in agriculture. Applicant must have 3.5 GPA or higher. Available to U.S. and Canadian citizens.

Application Requirements: Application, financial need analysis, photo, references, transcript, telephone interview. *Deadline:* January 2.

Contact: Scholarship Office
American Quarter Horse Foundation (AQHF)
2601 East Interstate 40
Amarillo, TX 79104
Phone: 806-378-5029
Fax: 806-376-1005
E-mail: foundation@aqha.org

FARM AND RANCH HERITAGE SCHOLARSHIP

Scholarships to AQHA/AQHYA members from farming and or ranching backgrounds. Members may apply during their senior year of high school or while enrolled at an accredited college, university or vocational school. Minimum GPA 3.0 required.

Award: Scholarship for use in freshman, sophomore, junior, or senior years; renewable. *Number:* 4. *Amount:* $12,500.

Eligibility Requirements: Applicant must be enrolled or expecting to enroll full-time at a two-year or four-year or technical institution or university. Applicant or parent of applicant must be member of American Quarter Horse Association. Applicant or parent of applicant must have employment or volunteer experience in farming. Applicant must have 3.0 GPA or higher. Available to U.S. and Canadian citizens.

Application Requirements: Application, essay, financial need analysis, photo, references, transcript. *Deadline:* January 2.

Contact: Scholarship Office
American Quarter Horse Foundation (AQHF)
2601 East Interstate 40
Amarillo, TX 79104
Phone: 806-378-5029
Fax: 806-376-1005
E-mail: foundation@aqha.org

GUY STOOPS MEMORIAL PROFESSIONAL HORSEMEN'S FAMILY SCHOLARSHIP

Two scholarships of $500 to AQHA members whose parent is an AQHA Professional Horseman in good standing for three or more years. Members may apply during their senior year of high school or while enrolled at an accredited college, university or vocational school. Minimum GPA 2.5 required.

Award: Scholarship for use in freshman, sophomore, junior, or senior years; not renewable. *Number:* 2. *Amount:* $500.

Eligibility Requirements: Applicant must be enrolled or expecting to enroll full-time at a two-year or four-year or technical institution or university. Applicant or parent of applicant must be member of American Quarter Horse Association or Professional Horsemen Association. Applicant must have 2.5 GPA or higher. Available to U.S. and Canadian citizens.

Application Requirements: Application, financial need analysis, photo, references, transcript. *Deadline:* January 2.

Contact: Scholarship Office
American Quarter Horse Foundation (AQHF)
2601 East Interstate 40
Amarillo, TX 79104
Phone: 806-378-5029
Fax: 806-376-1005
E-mail: foundation@aqha.org

INDIANA QUARTER HORSE YOUTH SCHOLARSHIP

Scholarships of $1000 for AQHA/AQHYA members from Indiana. Applicants must also be a current member of the Indiana Quarter Horse Association and must have maintained two or more years of membership. Members may apply during their senior year of high school or while enrolled at an accredited college, university or vocational school. Minimum 2.5 GPA required.

Award: Scholarship for use in freshman, sophomore, junior, or senior years; not renewable. *Number:* 1. *Amount:* $1000.

Eligibility Requirements: Applicant must be enrolled or expecting to enroll full-time at a two-year or four-year or technical institution or university and resident of Indiana. Applicant or parent of applicant must be member of American Quarter Horse Association. Applicant must have 2.5 GPA or higher. Available to U.S. and Canadian citizens.

Application Requirements: Application, driver's license, essay, financial need analysis, photo, references, transcript. *Deadline:* January 2.

Contact: Scholarship Office
American Quarter Horse Foundation (AQHF)
2601 East Interstate 40
Amarillo, TX 79104
Phone: 806-378-5029
Fax: 806-376-1005
E-mail: foundation@aqha.org

JOAN CAIN FLORIDA QUARTER HORSE YOUTH SCHOLARSHIP

Scholarship to an AQHA/AQHYA member from Florida. Applicants must also be a current member of the Florida Quarter Horse Youth Association and maintained two or more years of membership. Members may apply during their senior year of high school or while enrolled at an accredited college, university or vocational school. Minimum GPA 2.5 required.

Award: Scholarship for use in freshman, sophomore, junior, or senior years; not renewable. *Number:* 1. *Amount:* $1000.

Eligibility Requirements: Applicant must be enrolled or expecting to enroll full-time at a two-year or four-year or technical institution or university and resident of Florida. Applicant or parent of applicant must be member of American Quarter Horse Association. Applicant must have 2.5 GPA or higher. Available to U.S. and Canadian citizens.

Application Requirements: Application, driver's license, photo, references, transcript, proof of residency. *Deadline:* January 2.

Contact: Scholarship Office
American Quarter Horse Foundation (AQHF)
2601 East Interstate 40
Amarillo, TX 79104
Phone: 806-378-5029
Fax: 806-376-1005
E-mail: foundation@aqha.org

NEBRASKA QUARTER HORSE YOUTH SCHOLARSHIP

Scholarship to an AQHA/AQHYA member from Nebraska. Members may apply during their senior year of high school or while enrolled at an accredited college, university or vocational school. Renewable up to four years. Minimum GPA 2.5 required.

Award: Scholarship for use in freshman, sophomore, junior, or senior years; renewable. *Number:* 1. *Amount:* $2000.

Eligibility Requirements: Applicant must be enrolled or expecting to enroll full-time at a two-year or four-year or technical institution or university and resident of Nebraska. Applicant or parent of applicant must be member of American Quarter Horse Association. Applicant or parent of applicant must have employment or volunteer experience in agriculture. Applicant must have 2.5 GPA or higher. Available to U.S. and Canadian citizens.

Application Requirements: Application, driver's license, financial need analysis, photo, references, transcript, proof of residency. *Deadline:* January 2.

Contact: Scholarship Office
American Quarter Horse Foundation (AQHF)
2601 East Interstate 40
Amarillo, TX 79104
Phone: 806-378-5029
Fax: 806-376-1005
E-mail: foundation@aqha.org

RAY MELTON MEMORIAL VIRGINIA QUARTER HORSE YOUTH SCHOLARSHIP

Scholarship to an AQHA/AQHYA member from Virginia. Members may apply during their senior year of high school or while enrolled at an accredited college, university or vocational school. Minimum GPA 2.5 required.

Award: Scholarship for use in freshman, sophomore, junior, or senior years; not renewable. *Number:* 1. *Amount:* $500.

Eligibility Requirements: Applicant must be enrolled or expecting to enroll full-time at a two-year or four-year or technical institution or university and resident of Virginia. Applicant or parent of applicant must be member of American Quarter Horse Association. Applicant must have 2.5 GPA or higher. Available to U.S. and Canadian citizens.

American Quarter Horse Foundation (AQHF) (continued)

Application Requirements: Application, driver's license, financial need analysis, photo, references, transcript, proof of residency. *Deadline:* January 2.

Contact: Scholarship Office
American Quarter Horse Foundation (AQHF)
2601 East Interstate 40
Amarillo, TX 79104
Phone: 806-378-5029
Fax: 806-376-1005
E-mail: foundation@aqha.org

SWAYZE WOODRUFF MEMORIAL MID-SOUTH SCHOLARSHIP

Scholarships for AQHA/AQHYA members from Alabama, Arkansas, Louisiana, Mississippi or Tennessee. Applicants must compete in AQHA or AQHYA-approved shows. Members may apply during their senior year of high school or while enrolled at an accredited college, university or vocational school. Minimum 2.5 GPA required. Recipient receives $2000 per year for four-year degree plan. Must be renewed annually.

Award: Scholarship for use in freshman, sophomore, junior, or senior years; renewable. *Number:* 1. *Amount:* $2000.

Eligibility Requirements: Applicant must be enrolled or expecting to enroll full-time at a two-year or four-year or technical institution or university; resident of Alabama, Arkansas, Louisiana, Mississippi, or Tennessee and must have an interest in animal/agricultural competition. Applicant or parent of applicant must be member of American Quarter Horse Association. Applicant must have 2.5 GPA or higher. Available to U.S. and Canadian citizens.

Application Requirements: Application, driver's license, essay, financial need analysis, photo, references, transcript. *Deadline:* January 2.

Contact: Laura Owens, Scholarship Office
American Quarter Horse Foundation (AQHF)
2601 East Interstate 40
Amarillo, TX 79104
Phone: 806-378-5029
Fax: 806-376-1005
E-mail: foundation@aqha.org

AMERICAN WATER SKI EDUCATIONAL FOUNDATION http://www.waterskihalloffame.com

AMERICAN WATER SKI EDUCATIONAL FOUNDATION SCHOLARSHIP

Awards for incoming college sophomores through incoming seniors who are members of U.S.A. Water Ski. Awards are based upon academics, leadership, extracurricular activities, recommendations, and financial need.

Award: Scholarship for use in sophomore, junior, or senior years; renewable. *Number:* 5. *Amount:* $1500–$3000.

Eligibility Requirements: Applicant must be enrolled or expecting to enroll full-time at a two-year or four-year institution or university and must have an interest in leadership. Applicant or parent of applicant must be member of USA Water Ski. Available to U.S. citizens.

Application Requirements: Application, essay, financial need analysis, references, self-addressed stamped envelope, transcript. *Deadline:* April 1.

Contact: Carole Lowe, Scholarship Director
American Water Ski Educational Foundation
1251 Holy Cow Road
Polk City, FL 33868-8200
Phone: 863-324-2472
Fax: 863-324-3996
E-mail: info@waterskihalloffame.com

AMVETS AUXILIARY http://www.amvetsaux.org

AMVETS NATIONAL LADIES AUXILIARY SCHOLARSHIP

One-time award of up to $1000 for a member of AMVETS or the Auxiliary. Applicant may also be the family member of a member. Award for full-time study at any accredited U.S. institution. Minimum 2.5 GPA required.

Award: Scholarship for use in sophomore, junior, or senior years; not renewable. *Number:* up to 7. *Amount:* $750–$1000.

Eligibility Requirements: Applicant must be enrolled or expecting to enroll full-time at a two-year or four-year or technical institution. Applicant or parent of applicant must be member of AMVETS Auxiliary. Applicant must have 2.5 GPA or higher. Available to U.S. citizens. Applicant or parent must meet one or more of the following requirements: general military experience; retired from active duty; disabled or killed as a result of military service; prisoner of war; or missing in action.

Application Requirements: Application, essay, references, transcript. *Deadline:* June 1.

Contact: Kellie Haggerty, Executive Administrator
AMVETS Auxiliary
4647 Forbes Boulevard
Lanham, MD 20706-4380
Phone: 301-459-6255
Fax: 301-459-5403
E-mail: auxhdqs@amvets.org

ANCIENT ACCEPTED SCOTTISH RITE OF FREEMASONRY, NORTHERN JURISDICTION SUPREME COUNCIL, 33 http://www.supremecouncil.org

LEON M. ABBOTT SCHOLARSHIPS

Scholarships for the continuing education of young men and women from Scottish Rite families and Masonic-related youth groups. May be the child or grandchild of a Scottish Rite Mason in the Northern Masonic Jurisdiction, or a graduate of one of the thirty second degree Masonic Learning Centers for Children in the Northern Masonic Jurisdiction.

Award: Scholarship for use in sophomore, junior, or senior years; not renewable. *Number:* varies. *Amount:* varies.

Eligibility Requirements: Applicant must be enrolled or expecting to enroll full-time at a two-year or four-year institution or university. Applicant or parent of applicant must be member of Freemasons. Applicant must have 2.5 GPA or higher. Available to U.S. citizens.

Application Requirements: Application, financial need analysis, transcript, FAFSA. *Deadline:* April 1.

Contact: David Olmstead, Public Relations
Ancient Accepted Scottish Rite of Freemasonry, Northern Jurisdiction Supreme Council, 33
PO Box 519
Lexington, MA 02420-0519
Phone: 781-862-4410
Fax: 781-862-1833
E-mail: dolmstead@supremecouncil.org

APPALOOSA HORSE CLUB-APPALOOSA YOUTH PROGRAM http://www.appaloosa.com

APPALOOSA YOUTH EDUCATIONAL SCHOLARSHIPS

Scholarship of $1000 available for members or dependents of members of the Appaloosa Youth Association or Appaloosa Horse Club. Based on academics, leadership, sportsmanship, and horsemanship.

Award: Scholarship for use in freshman, sophomore, junior, senior, or graduate years; not renewable. *Number:* 6–8. *Amount:* $1000.

Eligibility Requirements: Applicant must be enrolled or expecting to enroll full-time at a two-year or four-year institution or university and must have an interest in animal/agricultural competition or leadership. Applicant or parent of applicant must be member of Appaloosa Horse Club/Appaloosa Youth Association. Applicant must have 2.5 GPA or higher. Available to U.S. citizens.

Application Requirements: Application, applicant must enter a contest, essay, photo, references, test scores, transcript. *Deadline:* June 10.

Contact: Anna Brown, AYF Coordinator
Appaloosa Horse Club-Appaloosa Youth Program
2720 West Pullman Road
Moscow, ID 83843
Phone: 208-882-5578 Ext. 264
Fax: 208-882-8150
E-mail: youth@appaloosa.com

ARRL FOUNDATION INC. http://www.arrl.org

IRARC MEMORIAL JOSEPH P. RUBINO WA4MMD SCHOLARSHIP

Need-based award available to licensed amateur radio operators. Preference is given to Brevard County residents or, secondarily, to Florida residents. Must maintain 2.5 GPA and pursue undergraduate degree or electronic technician certification.

Award: Scholarship for use in freshman, sophomore, junior, or senior years; not renewable. *Number:* varies. *Amount:* $750.

Eligibility Requirements: Applicant must be enrolled or expecting to enroll full-time at a four-year or technical institution or university; resident of Florida and must have an interest in amateur radio. Applicant or parent of applicant must be member of American Radio Relay League. Applicant must have 2.5 GPA or higher. Available to U.S. citizens.

Application Requirements: Application, financial need analysis, transcript. *Deadline:* February 1.

Contact: Mary M. Hobart, Secretary
ARRL Foundation Inc.
225 Main Street
Newington, CT 06111-1494
Phone: 860-594-0397
Fax: 860-594-0259
E-mail: k1mmh@arrl.org

YOU'VE GOT A FRIEND IN PENNSYLVANIA SCHOLARSHIP

One-time award available to licensed general amateur radio operators. Must be a member of American Radio Relay League. Residents of Pennsylvania preferred.

Award: Scholarship for use in freshman, sophomore, junior, senior, graduate, or postgraduate years; not renewable. *Number:* 1. *Amount:* $2000.

Eligibility Requirements: Applicant must be enrolled or expecting to enroll full-time at a two-year or four-year or technical institution or university; resident of Pennsylvania and must have an interest in amateur radio. Applicant or parent of applicant must be member of American Radio Relay League. Available to U.S. citizens.

Application Requirements: Application, transcript. *Deadline:* February 1.

Contact: Mary M. Hobart, Secretary
ARRL Foundation Inc.
225 Main Street
Newington, CT 06111-1494
Phone: 860-594-0397
Fax: 860-594-0259
E-mail: k1mmh@arrl.org

ARTIST-BLACKSMITH'S ASSOCIATION OF NORTH AMERICA INC. http://www.abana.org

ARTIST'S-BLACKSMITH'S ASSOCIATION OF NORTH AMERICA INC. SCHOLARSHIP PROGRAM

The award is designed to provide financial assistance to ABANA members at all skill levels to assist with the development of their blacksmithing skills and abilities. Award money may be used for blacksmith workshops, demonstrations, or lectures. Deadlines: June 1 or December 1.

Award: Scholarship for use in freshman, sophomore, junior, senior, graduate, or postgraduate years; not renewable. *Number:* 8–10. *Amount:* $200–$1500.

Eligibility Requirements: Applicant must be enrolled or expecting to enroll part-time at a two-year or four-year or technical institution or university. Applicant or parent of applicant must be member of Artist's-Blacksmith's Association of North America. Available to U.S. and non-U.S. citizens.

Application Requirements: Application, financial need analysis, photo, resume, references, self-addressed stamped envelope. *Deadline:* varies.

Contact: Heather Hutton, Central Office Administrator
Artist-Blacksmith's Association of North America Inc.
PO Box 3425
Knoxville, TN 37927-3425
Phone: 865-546-7733
Fax: 865-546-9964
E-mail: abana@abana.org

AUTOMOTIVE RECYCLERS ASSOCIATION SCHOLARSHIP FOUNDATION http://www.a-r-a.org

AUTOMOTIVE RECYCLERS ASSOCIATION SCHOLARSHIP FOUNDATION SCHOLARSHIP

Scholarships are available for the post-high school educational pursuits of the children of employees of direct ARA member companies.

Award: Scholarship for use in freshman, sophomore, junior, or senior years; not renewable. *Number:* varies. *Amount:* varies.

Eligibility Requirements: Applicant must be enrolled or expecting to enroll full-time at a two-year or four-year institution or university. Applicant or parent of applicant must be member of Automotive Recyclers Association. Applicant must have 3.0 GPA or higher. Available to U.S. and non-U.S. citizens.

Application Requirements: Application, photo, transcript, letter verifying parents' employment. *Deadline:* March 15.

Contact: Kelly Badillo, Director Member Services
Automotive Recyclers Association Scholarship Foundation
3975 Fair Ridge Drive, Suite 20-North
Fairfax, VA 22033
Phone: 703-385-1001 Ext. 26
Fax: 703-385-1494
E-mail: kelly@a-r-a.org

BOYS AND GIRLS CLUBS OF AMERICA http://www.bgca.org

BOYS AND GIRLS CLUBS OF AMERICA NATIONAL YOUTH OF THE YEAR AWARD

Nonrenewable award available to youths 14 to 18 years old who have been active members of their Boys Club or Girls Club for at least one year. Contact local club for nomination form. Minimum 3.0 GPA required. Must be nominated by local club.

Award: Scholarship for use in freshman, sophomore, junior, or senior years; not renewable. *Number:* 5. *Amount:* up to $10,000.

Eligibility Requirements: Applicant must be age 14-18; enrolled or expecting to enroll full- or part-time at a two-year or four-year or technical institution; single and must have an interest in leadership. Applicant or parent of applicant must be member of Boys or Girls Club. Applicant must have 3.0 GPA or higher. Available to U.S. citizens.

Application Requirements: Application, essay, interview, resume, references. *Deadline:* varies.

Contact: Kelvin Davis, Program Services Director
Boys and Girls Clubs of America
1230 West Peachtree Street, NW
Atlanta, GA 30309
Phone: 404-815-5700
Fax: 404-815-5789

BOYS AND GIRLS CLUBS OF CHICAGO http://www.bgcc.org

BOYS AND GIRLS CLUBS OF CHICAGO SCHOLARSHIPS

Scholarships are awarded to graduating high school seniors who are local Club members. Scholarships are based upon academic achievement, club involvement, financial need, and personal interviews. Students are asked to maintain their grades, seek internships and job opportunities, and lend guidance to younger children.

Award: Scholarship for use in freshman year; renewable. *Number:* varies. *Amount:* $3000–$5000.

Eligibility Requirements: Applicant must be high school student; planning to enroll or expecting to enroll full- or part-time at a two-year or four-year or technical institution or university and resident of Illinois. Applicant or parent of applicant must be member of Boys or Girls Club. Applicant must have 2.5 GPA or higher. Available to U.S. citizens.

Boys and Girls Clubs of Chicago (continued)

Application Requirements: Application, transcript. *Deadline:* varies.

Contact: Katie Huckaby, Project Director
Boys and Girls Clubs of Chicago
550 West Van Buren Street, Suite 350
Chicago, IL 60607
Phone: 312-235-8000 Ext. 8008
Fax: 312-427-4110
E-mail: khuckaby@bgcc.org

BOYS AND GIRLS CLUBS OF GREATER SAN DIEGO http://www.sdyouth.org

BOYS AND GIRLS CLUBS FOUNDATION SCHOLARSHIP

Renewable scholarship for graduating high school seniors from a qualified high school within the Club's service area. Must have been a member of the Boys and Girls Clubs of Greater San Diego for one or more years.

Award: Scholarship for use in freshman year; renewable. *Number:* up to 20. *Amount:* up to $1000.

Eligibility Requirements: Applicant must be high school student; planning to enroll or expecting to enroll full-time at a four-year institution or university and resident of California. Applicant or parent of applicant must be member of Boys or Girls Club. Applicant must have 3.0 GPA or higher. Available to U.S. and non-U.S. citizens.

Application Requirements: Application, financial need analysis. *Deadline:* April 15.

Contact: Jean Pilley, Scholarship Coordinator
Boys and Girls Clubs of Greater San Diego
4635 Clairemont Mesa Boulevard
San Diego, CA 92117
Phone: 858-273-1645
E-mail: bgcsandiego@yahoo.com

BUFFALO AFL-CIO COUNCIL http://www.wnyalf.org

AFL-CIO COUNCIL OF BUFFALO SCHOLARSHIP WNY ALF SCHOLARSHIP

One-time award of up to $1000 for a high school senior who is a son or daughter of a member of a local union affiliated with the Buffalo AFL-CIO Council. Must be a New York resident and use the award for study in New York.

Award: Scholarship for use in freshman year; not renewable. *Number:* up to 3. *Amount:* up to $1000.

Eligibility Requirements: Applicant must be high school student; planning to enroll or expecting to enroll full-time at a two-year or four-year institution or university; resident of New York and studying in New York. Applicant or parent of applicant must be member of AFL-CIO. Available to U.S. and Canadian citizens.

Application Requirements: Application, essay, references, transcript. *Deadline:* March 31.

Contact: Mike Hoffert, President
Buffalo AFL-CIO Council
2495 Main Street, Suite 440
Buffalo, NY 14214
Phone: 716-852-0375
Fax: 716-855-1802
E-mail: mhoffert@wnyalf.org

CALIFORNIA GRANGE FOUNDATION http://www.californiagrange.org

CALIFORNIA GRANGE FOUNDATION SCHOLARSHIP

Scholarship program available for Grange members residing in California who wish to attend a higher institution of learning of their choice.

Award: Scholarship for use in freshman, sophomore, junior, or senior years; renewable. *Number:* 5–8. *Amount:* $500–$1000.

Eligibility Requirements: Applicant must be enrolled or expecting to enroll full- or part-time at a two-year or four-year or technical institution or university and resident of California. Applicant or parent of applicant must be member of Grange Association. Available to U.S. citizens.

Application Requirements: Application, financial need analysis, references, transcript. *Deadline:* April 1.

Contact: Jay Hardz, Property Manager
California Grange Foundation
3830 U Street
Sacramento, CA 95817-1336
Phone: 916-454-5805
Fax: 916-739-8189
E-mail: info@californiagrange.org

CALIFORNIA STATE PARENT-TEACHER ASSOCIATION http://www.capta.org

CONTINUING EDUCATION-PTA VOLUNTEERS SCHOLARSHIP

Scholarships are available annually from the California State PTA to be used for continuing education at accredited colleges, universities, trade or technical schools. These scholarships recognize volunteer service in PTA and enable PTA volunteers to continue their education.

Award: Scholarship for use in freshman, sophomore, junior, senior, or graduate years; not renewable. *Number:* varies. *Amount:* $500.

Eligibility Requirements: Applicant must be enrolled or expecting to enroll full- or part-time at a two-year or four-year or technical institution or university and resident of California. Applicant or parent of applicant must be member of Parent-Teacher Association/Organization. Applicant or parent of applicant must have employment or volunteer experience in community service. Available to U.S. citizens.

Application Requirements: Application, essay, references, transcript, copy of membership card. *Deadline:* November 15.

Contact: Becky Reece, Scholarship and Award Chairman
California State Parent-Teacher Association
930 Georgia Street
Los Angeles, CA 90015-1322
Phone: 213-620-1100
Fax: 213-620-1141

CALIFORNIA TEACHERS ASSOCIATION (CTA) http://www.cta.org

CALIFORNIA TEACHERS ASSOCIATION SCHOLARSHIP FOR DEPENDENT CHILDREN

Awards scholarships annually for dependant children of active, retired, or deceased members of California Teachers Association. Minimum 3.5 GPA required.

Award: Scholarship for use in freshman, sophomore, junior, senior, or graduate years; not renewable. *Number:* up to 25. *Amount:* $2500.

Eligibility Requirements: Applicant must be enrolled or expecting to enroll full-time at a two-year or four-year or technical institution or university. Applicant or parent of applicant must be member of California Teachers Association. Applicant must have 3.5 GPA or higher. Available to U.S. citizens.

Application Requirements: Application, essay, references, transcript. *Deadline:* February 8.

Contact: Janeya Collins, Scholarship Coordinator
California Teachers Association (CTA)
PO Box 921
Burlingame, CA 94011-0921
Phone: 650-552-5468
Fax: 650-552-5001
E-mail: scholarships@cta.org

CALIFORNIA TEACHERS ASSOCIATION SCHOLARSHIP FOR MEMBERS

Must be an active member of California Teachers Association (including members working on an emergency credential). Available for study in a degree, credential, or graduate program.

Award: Scholarship for use in freshman, sophomore, junior, senior, or graduate years; not renewable. *Number:* 5. *Amount:* $2500.

Eligibility Requirements: Applicant must be enrolled or expecting to enroll full-time at a two-year or four-year institution or university and resident of California. Applicant or parent of applicant must be member of California Teachers Association. Applicant or parent of applicant must have employment or volunteer experience in teaching/education. Applicant must have 3.0 GPA or higher. Available to U.S. citizens.

Application Requirements: Application, essay, references, transcript. *Deadline:* February 8.

Contact: Janeya Collins, Scholarship Coordinator
California Teachers Association (CTA)
PO Box 921
Burlingame, CA 94011-0921
Phone: 650-552-5468
E-mail: scholarships@cta.org

CATHOLIC KOLPING SOCIETY OF AMERICA http://www.kolping.org

FATHER KREWITT SCHOLARSHIP

Scholarship based on an essay of 500 words on a specific topic selected by the board of the Kolping Society. Must be a member of the Kolping Society, or a child or grandchild of a member.

Award: Scholarship for use in freshman, sophomore, junior, senior, or graduate years; not renewable. *Number:* 1. *Amount:* $1000.

Eligibility Requirements: Applicant must be enrolled or expecting to enroll full-time at a two-year or four-year or technical institution or university. Applicant or parent of applicant must be member of Catholic Kolping Society of America. Available to U.S. and non-U.S. citizens.

Application Requirements: Application, applicant must enter a contest, essay. *Deadline:* February 28.

Contact: Patricia Farkas, National Administrator
Catholic Kolping Society of America
c/o Edward Farkas
1223 Van Houton Avenue
Clifton, NJ 07013
Phone: 877-659-7237
Fax: 201-666-5262
E-mail: patfarkas@aol.com

CATHOLIC WORKMAN http://www.fcsla.com

FIRST CATHOLIC SLOVAK LADIES ASSOCIATION COLLEGE SCHOLARSHIP

$1250 scholarship for young member of FCSLA. Must be a member in good standing for at least three years prior to date of application.

Award: Scholarship for use in freshman, sophomore, junior, or senior years; not renewable. *Number:* 15–55. *Amount:* $1250.

Eligibility Requirements: Applicant must be enrolled or expecting to enroll full-time at a two-year or four-year institution or university. Applicant or parent of applicant must be member of First Catholic Slovak Ladies Association. Available to U.S. and non-U.S. citizens.

Application Requirements: Application, autobiography, transcript, letter of acceptance. *Deadline:* March 1.

Contact: Lenore Krava, Executive Secretary
Catholic Workman
24950 Chagrin Boulevard
Beachwood, OH 44122-5634
Phone: 216-464-8015
Fax: 216-464-9260
E-mail: info@fcsla.com

THERESA SAJAN SCHOLARSHIP FOR GRADUATE STUDENTS

Scholarship for graduate study available to a member in good standing of the First Catholic Slovak Ladies Association. Must be member of the association for at least three years prior to date of application. For more information check the Web site: http://www.fcsla.com/scholarship.shtml.

Award: Scholarship for use in freshman, sophomore, junior, or senior years; renewable. *Number:* 15–55. *Amount:* $1250–$1750.

Eligibility Requirements: Applicant must be enrolled or expecting to enroll full-time at a four-year institution. Applicant or parent of applicant must be member of First Catholic Slovak Ladies Association. Available to U.S. and non-U.S. citizens.

Application Requirements: Application, autobiography, test scores, transcript, document of acceptance. *Deadline:* varies.

Contact: Lenore Krava, Executive Secretary
Catholic Workman
24950 Chagrin Boulevard
Beachwood, OH 44122-5634
Phone: 216-464-8015
Fax: 216-464-9260
E-mail: info@fcsla.com

CENTER FOR SCHOLARSHIP ADMINISTRATION http://www.scholarshipprograms.org

GREENVILLE AREA PERSONNEL ASSOCIATION WALTER L. MARTIN MEMORIAL SCHOLARSHIP PROGRAM

One-time, nonrenewable award for dependent children of GAPA members. Applicant must be a high school senior or an undergraduate college student already enrolled. Must have a cumulative GPA of 2.5. The recipient's school of choice must be exempt from federal income tax under Section 501(c)(3) of the Internal Revenue Code.

Award: Scholarship for use in freshman, sophomore, junior, or senior years; not renewable. *Number:* varies. *Amount:* $1500.

Eligibility Requirements: Applicant must be high school student and planning to enroll or expecting to enroll full-time at a two-year or four-year or technical institution or university. Applicant or parent of applicant must be member of Greenville Area Personnel Association. Applicant or parent of applicant must have employment or volunteer experience in community service. Applicant must have 2.5 GPA or higher. Available to U.S. citizens.

Application Requirements: Application, essay, references, transcript. *Deadline:* February 28.

Contact: Scholarship Committee
Center for Scholarship Administration
PO Box 1465
Taylors, SC 29687-0031
Phone: 864-268-3363
Fax: 864-268-7160
E-mail: cfsainc@bellsouth.net

MICHELIN/TIA SCHOLARSHIPS

Renewable scholarships available to qualified employees and dependent children of qualified employees of tire dealers who are members of the Tire Industry Association. Applicants must be seniors in high school, and must be planning to pursue a postsecondary education at an accredited two- or four-year college, university or vocational technical school. Must have a cumulative GPA of 3.0.

Award: Scholarship for use in freshman year; renewable. *Number:* 3. *Amount:* $1250–$2500.

Eligibility Requirements: Applicant must be high school student and planning to enroll or expecting to enroll full-time at a two-year or four-year or technical institution or university. Applicant or parent of applicant must be member of Tire Industry Association. Applicant must have 3.0 GPA or higher. Available to U.S. citizens.

Application Requirements: Application, essay, references, transcript. *Deadline:* March 31.

Contact: Scholarship Committee
Center for Scholarship Administration
PO Box 1465
Taylors, SC 29687-0031
Phone: 864-268-3363
Fax: 864-268-7160
E-mail: cfsainc@bellsouth.net

NATIONAL ASSOCIATION OF FOOD EQUIPMENT DEALERS INC. SCHOLARSHIP

Nonrenewable scholarships available to the dependent children of qualified employees of NAFED dealers. Contact NAFED owner for more detailed information on additional criteria.

Award: Scholarship for use in freshman, sophomore, junior, or senior years; not renewable. *Number:* 2. *Amount:* $2500–$7500.

Eligibility Requirements: Applicant must be high school student and planning to enroll or expecting to enroll full-time at a two-year or four-year or technical institution or university. Applicant or parent of

Center for Scholarship Administration (continued)

applicant must be member of National Association of Food Equipment Dealers. Applicant must have 3.0 GPA or higher. Available to U.S. citizens.

Application Requirements: Application, essay, references, transcript. *Deadline:* January 31.

Contact: Scholarship Committee
Center for Scholarship Administration
PO Box 1465
Taylors, SC 29687-0031
Phone: 864-268-3363
Fax: 864-268-7160
E-mail: cfsainc@bellsouth.net

CIVIL AIR PATROL, USAF AUXILIARY http://www.capnhq.gov

CIVIL AIR PATROL ACADEMIC SCHOLARSHIPS

One-time award for active members of the Civil Air Patrol to pursue undergraduate, graduate, or trade or technical education. Must be a current CAP member. Significant restrictions apply. Not open to the general public.

Award: Scholarship for use in freshman, sophomore, junior, senior, or graduate years; not renewable. *Number:* up to 40. *Amount:* $1000–$7500.

Eligibility Requirements: Applicant must be enrolled or expecting to enroll full-time at a two-year or four-year or technical institution or university. Applicant or parent of applicant must be member of Civil Air Patrol. Available to U.S. citizens.

Application Requirements: Application, essay, photo, resume, references, test scores, transcript. *Deadline:* January 31.

Contact: Kelly Easterly, Assistant Program Manager
Civil Air Patrol, USAF Auxiliary
105 South Hansell Street, Building 714
Maxwell Air Force Base, AL 36112-6332
Phone: 334-953-8640
Fax: 334-953-6699
E-mail: cpr@capnhq.gov

CLEVELAND SCHOLARSHIP PROGRAMS http://www.cspohio.org

CSP MANAGED FUNDS-LABORERS' INTERNATIONAL UNION OF NORTH AMERICA, AFL_CIO LOCAL NO. 84 SCHOLARSHIP

Scholarship to assist graduating high school seniors and current college students, who are sons or daughters of members of LIUNA Local 894 and who meet specific criteria. Minimum 3.0 GPA required. Students selected for this scholarship should follow a full-time college course of study or major in a four-year college.

Award: Scholarship for use in freshman, sophomore, junior, or senior years; not renewable. *Number:* 1–10. *Amount:* $1500.

Eligibility Requirements: Applicant must be enrolled or expecting to enroll full-time at a four-year institution or university. Applicant or parent of applicant must be member of AFL-CIO. Applicant must have 3.0 GPA or higher. Available to U.S. citizens.

Application Requirements: Application, references, transcript. *Deadline:* varies.

Contact: Latasha Williams, Senior Manager of Programs
Cleveland Scholarship Programs
200 Public Square, Suite 3820
Cleveland, OH 44114
Phone: 216-241-5587
Fax: 216-241-6184
E-mail: lwilliams@cspohio.org

COLORADO STATE GRANGE LEADERSHIP AND SCHOLARSHIP FOUNDATION http://www.coloradogrange.org

COLORADO STATE GRANGE SCHOLARSHIPS

A scholarship of $750 is awarded to up to twelve undergraduate students who are members of Colorado State Grange. Must be high school seniors or currently-enrolled college students.

Award: Scholarship for use in freshman, sophomore, junior, or senior years; not renewable. *Number:* 10–12. *Amount:* $750.

Eligibility Requirements: Applicant must be enrolled or expecting to enroll full-time at a two-year or four-year institution or university; studying in Colorado and must have an interest in leadership. Applicant or parent of applicant must be member of Colorado State Grange. Available to U.S. citizens.

Application Requirements: Application, resume, references, transcript. *Deadline:* April 15.

Contact: Marge Sassman, Secretary
Colorado State Grange Leadership and Scholarship Foundation
7275 South Lima Street
Centennial, CO 80112-3850
Phone: 303-708-0606
Fax: 303-708-0411
E-mail: cogrange@na800.net

COMMUNITY BANKER ASSOCIATION OF ILLINOIS http://www.cbai.com

COMMUNITY BANKER ASSOCIATION OF ILLINOIS CHILDREN OF COMMUNITY BANKING SCHOLARSHIP WILLIAM C. HARRIS MEMORIAL SCHOLARSHIP

Eligible Illinois community banks can submit one name for each $1000 they have donated to the CBAI Foundation. Children of eligible community bankers and part-time bank employees entering freshman year of higher education are eligible. Winner determined by drawing. Must be Illinois resident.

Award: Scholarship for use in freshman year; not renewable. *Number:* 1. *Amount:* $1000–$4000.

Eligibility Requirements: Applicant must be high school student; planning to enroll or expecting to enroll full-time at a four-year institution or university and resident of Illinois. Applicant or parent of applicant must be member of Community Banker Association of Illinois. Applicant or parent of applicant must have employment or volunteer experience in banking. Available to U.S. citizens.

Application Requirements: Application. *Deadline:* August 15.

Contact: Andrea Cusick, Senior Vice President of Communications
Community Banker Association of Illinois
901 Community Drive
Springfield, IL 62703-5184
Phone: 217-529-2265
Fax: 217-585-8738
E-mail: cbaicom@cbai.com

COMMUNITY FOUNDATION OF WESTERN MASSACHUSETTS http://www.communityfoundation.org

HORACE HILL SCHOLARSHIP

Scholarships are given to children or grandchildren of a member of the Springfield Newspapers 25-Year Club. For more information or application visit http://www.communityfoundation.org.

Award: Scholarship for use in freshman, sophomore, junior, senior, or graduate years; renewable. *Number:* 4. *Amount:* up to $500.

Eligibility Requirements: Applicant must be enrolled or expecting to enroll full- or part-time at a two-year or four-year institution or university. Applicant or parent of applicant must be member of Springfield Newspaper 25-Year Club. Applicant or parent of applicant must have employment or volunteer experience in journalism/broadcasting. Available to U.S. citizens.

Application Requirements: Application, financial need analysis, transcript, Student Aid Report (SAR). *Deadline:* March 31.

Contact: Dorothy Theriaque, Education Associate
Community Foundation of Western Massachusetts
1500 Main Street, PO Box 15769
Springfield, MA 01115
Phone: 413-732-2858
Fax: 413-733-8565
E-mail: dtheriaque@communityfoundation.org

DANISH SISTERHOOD OF AMERICA

http://www.danishsisterhood.org

BETTY HANSEN CONTINUING EDUCATION GRANT

Grant is available to part-time students for use at any level, including community education classes. Must be a member of the Danish Sisterhood of America.

Award: Grant for use in freshman, sophomore, junior, or senior years; not renewable. *Number:* up to 10. *Amount:* up to $500.

Eligibility Requirements: Applicant must be enrolled or expecting to enroll full- or part-time at a two-year or four-year institution or university. Applicant or parent of applicant must be member of Danish Sisterhood of America. Available to U.S. and non-U.S. citizens.

Application Requirements: Application, references, transcript. *Deadline:* February 28.

Contact: Donna Hansen, Scholarship Chairman
Danish Sisterhood of America
1605 South 58th street
Lincoln, NE 68506
Phone: 402-488-5820

NATIONAL SCHOLARSHIP, MILDRED SORENSEN, OLGA CHRISTENSEN AND BETTY HANSEN SCHOLARSHIPS

One-time awards for full-time, postsecondary students who are members, or a son or daughter of member of the Danish Sisterhood of America. Candidates must have a minimum 2.5 GPA. Write for further details.

Award: Scholarship for use in freshman, sophomore, junior, or senior years; not renewable. *Number:* up to 12. *Amount:* $750.

Eligibility Requirements: Applicant must be enrolled or expecting to enroll full-time at a two-year or four-year or technical institution or university. Applicant or parent of applicant must be member of Danish Sisterhood of America. Applicant must have 2.5 GPA or higher. Available to U.S. and Canadian citizens.

Application Requirements: Application, references, test scores, transcript. *Deadline:* February 28.

Contact: Donna Hansen, Scholarship Chairman
Danish Sisterhood of America
1605 South 58th street
Lincoln, NE 68506
Phone: 402-488-5820

DAUGHTERS OF PENELOPE FOUNDATION

ALEXANDRA APOSTOLIDES SONENFELD SCHOLARSHIP

Annual award for female graduating high school seniors or undergraduate students who are members of the Daughters of Penelope or the Maids of Athena, or have a member of the immediate family in the Daughters of Penelope, or the Order of AHEPA. Membership must be for a minimum of two years in good standing.

Award: Scholarship for use in freshman, sophomore, junior, or senior years; not renewable. *Number:* 1. *Amount:* up to $1500.

Eligibility Requirements: Applicant must be of Greek heritage; enrolled or expecting to enroll full-time at a two-year or four-year or technical institution or university and female. Applicant or parent of applicant must be member of Daughters of Penelope/Maids of Athena/Order of Ahepa. Available to U.S. citizens.

Application Requirements: Application, essay, references, test scores, transcript, IRS forms. *Deadline:* June 1.

Contact: Helen Santire, National Scholarship Chairman
Daughters of Penelope Foundation
PO Box 19709
Houston, TX 77024
Phone: 713-468-6531
E-mail: helen.santire@duchesne.org

JOANNE V. HOLOGGITAS, PHD SCHOLARSHIP

Annual award for female graduating high school seniors or undergraduate students who are related to an AHEPAN or a Daughter of Penelope, or must be members of the Maids of Athens. Membership must be for a minimum of two years in good standing.

Award: Scholarship for use in freshman, sophomore, junior, or senior years; not renewable. *Number:* 1. *Amount:* up to $1500.

Eligibility Requirements: Applicant must be of Greek heritage; enrolled or expecting to enroll full-time at a two-year or four-year or technical institution or university and female. Applicant or parent of applicant must be member of Daughters of Penelope/Maids of Athena/Order of Ahepa. Available to U.S. and Canadian citizens.

Application Requirements: Application, essay, references, test scores, transcript, IRS forms. *Deadline:* June 1.

Contact: Helen Santire, National Scholarship Chairman
Daughters of Penelope Foundation
PO Box 19709
Houston, TX 77024
Phone: 713-468-6531
E-mail: helen.santire@duchesne.org

KOTTIS FAMILY SCHOLARSHIP

Annual award for female graduating high school seniors or undergraduate students who are related to an AHEPAN or a Daughter of Penelope, or a member of the Maids of Athens. Membership must be for a minimum of two years in good standing.

Award: Scholarship for use in freshman, sophomore, junior, or senior years; not renewable. *Number:* 1. *Amount:* up to $1500.

Eligibility Requirements: Applicant must be of Greek heritage; enrolled or expecting to enroll full-time at a two-year or four-year or technical institution or university and female. Applicant or parent of applicant must be member of Daughters of Penelope/Maids of Athena/Order of Ahepa. Available to U.S. and Canadian citizens.

Application Requirements: Application, essay, references, test scores, transcript, IRS forms. *Deadline:* June 1.

Contact: Helen Santire, National Scholarship Chairman
Daughters of Penelope Foundation
PO Box 19709
Houston, TX 77024
Phone: 713-468-6531
E-mail: helen.santire@duchesne.org

MARY M. VERGES SCHOLARSHIP

Annual award for female graduating high school seniors or undergraduate students who are members of the Daughters of Penelope or the Maids of Athena, or have a member of the immediate family in the Daughters of Penelope, or the Order of AHEPA. Membership must be for a minimum of two years in good standing.

Award: Scholarship for use in freshman, sophomore, junior, or senior years; not renewable. *Number:* 1. *Amount:* up to $1500.

Eligibility Requirements: Applicant must be of Greek heritage; enrolled or expecting to enroll full-time at a two-year or four-year or technical institution or university and female. Applicant or parent of applicant must be member of Daughters of Penelope/Maids of Athena/Order of Ahepa. Available to U.S. and Canadian citizens.

Application Requirements: Application, essay, references, test scores, transcript, IRS forms. *Deadline:* June 1.

Contact: Helen Santire, National Scholarship Chairman
Daughters of Penelope Foundation
PO Box 19709
Houston, TX 77024
Phone: 713-468-6531
E-mail: helen.santire@duchesne.org

PAST GRAND PRESIDENTS SCHOLARSHIP

Scholarship for female students of Greek descent. Must be a graduating high school senior or an undergraduate student who is related to an AHEPAN or a Daughter of Penelope, or must be a member of the Maids of Athens. Must be a citizen of the United States, Canada, Greece, or any country in which there is an established Daughters of Penelope chapter.

Award: Scholarship for use in freshman, sophomore, junior, or senior years; not renewable. *Number:* 1. *Amount:* up to $1500.

Eligibility Requirements: Applicant must be of Greek heritage; enrolled or expecting to enroll full-time at a two-year or four-year or technical institution or university and female. Applicant or parent of applicant must be member of Daughters of Penelope/Maids of Athena/Order of Ahepa. Available to U.S. and Canadian citizens.

Daughters of Penelope Foundation (continued)

Application Requirements: Application, essay, references, test scores, transcript, IRS forms. *Deadline:* June 1.

Contact: Helen Santire, National Scholarship Chairman
Daughters of Penelope Foundation
PO Box 19709
Houston, TX 77024
Phone: 713-468-6531
E-mail: helen.santire@duchesne.org

DAVIS-ROBERTS SCHOLARSHIP FUND INC.

DAVIS-ROBERTS SCHOLARSHIPS

Renewable award to assist DeMolays and Jobs Daughters in the state of Wyoming with their education, providing they are attending or planning to attend school full-time. Scholarship value is from $350 to $1000.

Award: Scholarship for use in freshman, sophomore, junior, senior, or graduate years; renewable. *Number:* 3–5. *Amount:* $350–$1000.

Eligibility Requirements: Applicant must be enrolled or expecting to enroll full-time at a two-year or four-year or technical institution or university and resident of Wyoming. Applicant or parent of applicant must be member of Demolay or Jobs Daughters. Applicant must have 2.5 GPA or higher. Available to U.S. citizens.

Application Requirements: Application, essay, financial need analysis, photo, references, transcript. *Deadline:* June 15.

Contact: Gary Skillern, Secretary
Davis-Roberts Scholarship Fund Inc.
PO Box 20645
Cheyenne, WY 82003
Phone: 307-632-0491

DELTA DELTA DELTA FOUNDATION http://www.tridelta.org

DELTA DELTA DELTA UNDERGRADUATE SCHOLARSHIP

One-time award to any initiated sophomore or junior member in good-standing of Delta Delta Delta based on academic achievement, campus, chapter, and community involvement. Application and information available at Web site: http://www.tridelta.org.

Award: Scholarship for use in sophomore or junior years; not renewable. *Number:* 48–50. *Amount:* $500–$1500.

Eligibility Requirements: Applicant must be enrolled or expecting to enroll full-time at a four-year institution or university and single female. Applicant or parent of applicant must have employment or volunteer experience in community service. Available to U.S. and Canadian citizens.

Application Requirements: Application, references, transcript, alumna adviser check-off, personal statement. *Deadline:* March 15.

Contact: Laura Allen, Foundation Manager of Scholarships and Financial Services
Delta Delta Delta Foundation
PO Box 5987
Arlington, TX 76005
Phone: 817-633-8001
Fax: 817-652-0212
E-mail: lallen@trideltaeo.org

DELTA GAMMA FOUNDATION http://www.deltagamma.org

DELTA GAMMA FOUNDATION SCHOLARSHIPS

Award for initiated members of the Delta Gamma Fraternity. Must be female. Applicants must have completed three semesters or five quarters of college with a minimum 3.0 GPA. Must be active in campus, community, and chapter activities.

Award: Scholarship for use in sophomore or junior years; not renewable. *Number:* 150–175. *Amount:* $1000.

Eligibility Requirements: Applicant must be enrolled or expecting to enroll full-time at a four-year institution or university and female. Applicant must have 3.0 GPA or higher. Available to U.S. and Canadian citizens.

Application Requirements: Application, autobiography, essay, photo, references, self-addressed stamped envelope, transcript. *Deadline:* February 15.

Contact: Kathleen Williams, Assistant Development Director
Delta Gamma Foundation
3250 Riverside Drive, PO Box 21397
Columbus, OH 43221-0397
Phone: 614-481-8169 Ext. 324
E-mail: kathleen@deltagamma.org

DELTA PHI EPSILON EDUCATIONAL FOUNDATION http://www.dphie.org

DELTA PHI EPSILON EDUCATIONAL FOUNDATION GRANT

Scholarships are awarded based on three criteria: service and involvement, academics, and need. Applications may be submitted for undergraduate only. Applicants must be members of Delta Phi Epsilon or the sons/daughters of members. Refer to Web Site: http://www.dphie.org/foundation/apply.shtml for details.

Award: Grant for use in freshman, sophomore, junior, or senior years; not renewable. *Number:* 6–8. *Amount:* $1000.

Eligibility Requirements: Applicant must be enrolled or expecting to enroll full-time at a four-year institution or university. Available to U.S. and non-U.S. citizens.

Application Requirements: Application, autobiography, essay, financial need analysis, photo, references, transcript. *Deadline:* April 15.

Contact: Nicole DeFeo, Executive Director
Delta Phi Epsilon Educational Foundation
251 South Camac Street
Philadelphia, PA 19107
Phone: 215-732-5901
Fax: 215-732-5906
E-mail: info@dphie.org

DELTA SIGMA PI http://www.dspnet.org

DELTA SIGMA PI UNDERGRADUATE SCHOLARSHIP

Applicant must be a member of Delta Sigma Pi in good standing with at least one full semester or quarter of college remaining. Awarded in the fall.

Award: Scholarship for use in sophomore, junior, or senior years; not renewable. *Number:* up to 15. *Amount:* $500–$5000.

Eligibility Requirements: Applicant must be enrolled or expecting to enroll full-time at a four-year institution or university. Available to U.S. citizens.

Application Requirements: Application, financial need analysis, references, transcript, description of fraternity, campus, community involvement. *Deadline:* June 30.

Contact: Bill Schilling, Executive Director
Delta Sigma Pi
330 South Campus Avenue, PO Box 230
Oxford, OH 45056-0230
Phone: 513-523-1907
Fax: 513-523-7292
E-mail: bill@dspnet.org

DELTA TAU DELTA EDUCATIONAL FUND http://www.deltfoundation.org

FILE SCHOLARSHIP AND AWARD FOR UNDERGRADUATE EXCELLENCE

Scholarship to recognize individual efforts of excellence as well as superior academic achievement in undergraduate program. Scholarship value is $1500. Number of scholarships granted varies.

Award: Scholarship for use in sophomore, junior, or senior years; not renewable. *Number:* 1. *Amount:* $1500.

Eligibility Requirements: Applicant must be enrolled or expecting to enroll full- or part-time at a four-year institution or university. Applicant or parent of applicant must be member of Delta Tau Delta Educational Foundation. Available to U.S. citizens.

Application Requirements: Application, essay, references, transcript. *Deadline:* December 1.

Contact: Carla Bullman, Administrative Assistant
Delta Tau Delta Educational Fund
10000 Allisonville Road
Fishers, IN 46038
Phone: 317-284-0210 Ext. 1322
Fax: 317-284-0215
E-mail: carla.bullman@delts.net

NED H. GUSTAFSON/KEVIN R. JOHNS SCHOLARSHIP

Two scholarships of $1500 awarded to sophomores, juniors, or seniors who have displayed outstanding leadership, campus, and civic involvement. GPA of at least 2.5 required. Applicant must be a member of the Delta Tau Delta Educational Foundation.

Award: Scholarship for use in sophomore, junior, or senior years; not renewable. *Number:* 2. *Amount:* $1500.

Eligibility Requirements: Applicant must be enrolled or expecting to enroll full- or part-time at a four-year institution or university and must have an interest in leadership. Applicant or parent of applicant must be member of Delta Tau Delta Educational Foundation. Applicant must have 2.5 GPA or higher. Available to U.S. citizens.

Application Requirements: Application, essay, transcript. *Deadline:* December 1.

Contact: Carla Bullman, Administrative Assistant
Delta Tau Delta Educational Fund
10000 Allisonville Road
Fishers, IN 46038
Phone: 317-284-0210 Ext. 1322
Fax: 317-284-0215
E-mail: carla.bullman@delts.net

DEVRY INC. http://www.devry.edu

GIRL SCOUT GOLD AWARD SCHOLARSHIP-HIGH SCHOOL GRADUATE

Award of $1000 per semester, valued up to $9000 for high school graduates or GED recipients. Must have earned a Girl Scout Gold Award.

Award: Scholarship for use in freshman year; renewable. *Number:* varies. *Amount:* up to $2000.

Eligibility Requirements: Applicant must be high school student; planning to enroll or expecting to enroll full-time at an institution or university and female. Applicant or parent of applicant must be member of Girl Scouts. Applicant or parent of applicant must have employment or volunteer experience in community service. Available to U.S. and Canadian citizens.

Application Requirements: Application. *Deadline:* varies.

Contact: Thonie Simpson, National High School Program Manager
DeVry Inc.
One Tower Lane
Oak Brook Terrace, IL 60181-4624
Phone: 630-706-3122
Fax: 630-574-1696
E-mail: scholarships@devry.edu

EASTERN ORTHODOX COMMITTEE ON SCOUTING http://www.eocs.org

EASTERN ORTHODOX COMMITTEE ON SCOUTING SCHOLARSHIPS

One-time award for high school seniors planning to attend a four-year institution. Must be a registered member of a Boy or Girl Scout unit, an Eagle Scout or Gold Award recipient, active member of an Eastern Orthodox Church, and recipient of the Alpha Omega religious award.

Award: Scholarship for use in freshman year; not renewable. *Number:* 2. *Amount:* $500–$1000.

Eligibility Requirements: Applicant must be Eastern Orthodox; high school student; planning to enroll or expecting to enroll full-time at a four-year institution or university and single. Applicant or parent of applicant must be member of Boy Scouts or Girl Scouts. Available to U.S. citizens.

Application Requirements: Application, autobiography, references, self-addressed stamped envelope, test scores, transcript. *Deadline:* May 1.

Contact: George Boulukos, Scholarship Chairman
Eastern Orthodox Committee on Scouting
862 Guy Lombardo Avenue
Freeport, NY 11520
Phone: 516-868-4050
Fax: 516-868-4052
E-mail: geobou03@aol.com

EASTERN SURFING ASSOCIATION (ESA) http://www.surfesa.org

ESA MARSH SCHOLARSHIP PROGRAM

Grants are awarded to ESA current members in good standing on the basis of academics and U.S. citizenship rather than athletic ability.

Award: Scholarship for use in freshman, sophomore, junior, or senior years; not renewable. *Number:* 2. *Amount:* up to $8000.

Eligibility Requirements: Applicant must be enrolled or expecting to enroll full-time at a four-year institution or university. Applicant or parent of applicant must be member of Eastern Surfing Association. Available to U.S. citizens.

Application Requirements: Application, essay, references, transcript. *Deadline:* May 15.

Contact: Debbie Hodges, Scholarship Committee
Eastern Surfing Association (ESA)
PO Box 625
Virginia Beach, VA 23451
Phone: 757-233-1790
Fax: 757-233-1396
E-mail: centralhq@surfesa.org

ELKS NATIONAL FOUNDATION http://www.elks.org/enf

ELKS EMERGENCY EDUCATIONAL GRANTS

Grant available to children of Elks who are deceased or totally incapacitated. Applicants for the one-year renewable awards must be unmarried, under the age of 23, be a full-time undergraduate student, and demonstrate financial need.

Award: Grant for use in freshman, sophomore, junior, or senior years; renewable. *Number:* varies. *Amount:* $1000–$4000.

Eligibility Requirements: Applicant must be age 23 or under; enrolled or expecting to enroll full-time at a two-year or four-year or technical institution or university and single. Applicant or parent of applicant must be member of Elks Club. Applicant must have 2.5 GPA or higher. Available to U.S. citizens.

Application Requirements: Application, applicant must enter a contest, essay, financial need analysis, references, self-addressed stamped envelope, transcript. *Deadline:* varies.

Contact: Jeannine Kunz, Program Coordinator
Elks National Foundation
2750 North Lakeview Avenue
Chicago, IL 60614-2256
Phone: 773-755-4732
Fax: 773-755-4733
E-mail: scholarship@elks.org

ELKS NATIONAL FOUNDATION LEGACY AWARDS

Awards up to five hundred $1000 one-year scholarships for children and grandchildren of Elks in good standing. Parent or grandparent must have been an Elk for two years.

Award: Scholarship for use in freshman year; not renewable. *Number:* up to 500. *Amount:* up to $1000.

Eligibility Requirements: Applicant must be high school student and planning to enroll or expecting to enroll full-time at a two-year or four-year institution or university. Applicant or parent of applicant must be member of Elks Club. Applicant must have 2.5 GPA or higher. Available to U.S. citizens.

Elks National Foundation (continued)

Application Requirements: Application, applicant must enter a contest, essay, references, self-addressed stamped envelope, test scores, transcript. *Deadline:* varies.

Contact: Jeannine Kunz, Program Coordinator
Elks National Foundation
2750 North Lakeview Avenue
Chicago, IL 60614-2256
Phone: 773-755-4732
Fax: 773-755-4733
E-mail: scholarship@elks.org

FEDERAL EMPLOYEE EDUCATION AND ASSISTANCE FUND http://www.feea.org

FEEA/NARFE SCHOLARSHIP

Award available to children and grandchildren of National Association of Retired Federal Employees members. Must be a high school senior planning to enroll in an accredited two- or four-year postsecondary school. Minimum 3.0 GPA required.

Award: Scholarship for use in freshman year; not renewable. *Number:* 60. *Amount:* $1000.

Eligibility Requirements: Applicant must be high school student and planning to enroll or expecting to enroll full-time at a two-year or four-year institution or university. Applicant or parent of applicant must be member of National Association for the Advancement of Colored People. Applicant or parent of applicant must have employment or volunteer experience in federal/postal service. Applicant must have 3.0 GPA or higher. Available to U.S. citizens.

Application Requirements: Application, essay, references, test scores, transcript. *Deadline:* April 30.

Contact: Scholarship Committee
Federal Employee Education and Assistance Fund
8441 West Bowles Avenue, Suite 200
Littleton, CO 80123-9501
Phone: 303-933-7580
Fax: 303-933-7587

FEDERATION OF AMERICAN CONSUMERS AND TRAVELERS http://www.usafact.org

FEDERATION OF AMERICAN CONSUMERS AND TRAVELERS GRADUATING HIGH SCHOOL SENIOR SCHOLARSHIP

A minimum of one $10,000 scholarship and one $2500 scholarship are given to graduating high school seniors. Eligible applicants will be a member or the child or grandchild of a member of FACT. Awards are designed for the so-called "average" student: the young man or woman who may never have made the honor roll or who did not excel on the athletic field and wants to obtain a higher education, but is all too often overlooked by other scholarship sources.

Award: Scholarship for use in freshman year; not renewable. *Number:* varies. *Amount:* $2500–$10,000.

Eligibility Requirements: Applicant must be high school student and planning to enroll or expecting to enroll full-time at a two-year or four-year institution or university. Applicant or parent of applicant must be member of Federation of American Consumers and Travelers. Available to U.S. citizens.

Application Requirements: Application, autobiography, essay, references, test scores, transcript. *Deadline:* January 15.

Contact: Vicki Rolens, Managing Director
Federation of American Consumers and Travelers
PO Box 104
Edwardsville, IL 62025
Phone: 800-872-3228
Fax: 618-656-5369
E-mail: vrolens@usafact.org

FEDERATION OF AMERICAN CONSUMERS AND TRAVELERS TRADE/ TECHNICAL SCHOOL SCHOLARSHIP

Scholarships are offered in four categories, for current high school seniors, for persons who graduated from high school four or more years ago and now plan to go to a university or college, for students currently enrolled in a college or university, and for trade or technical school aspirants. Members of FACT, their children and grandchildren are eligible to apply.

Award: Scholarship for use in freshman, sophomore, junior, or senior years; not renewable. *Number:* varies. *Amount:* $1000–$5000.

Eligibility Requirements: Applicant must be enrolled or expecting to enroll full- or part-time at a four-year or technical institution or university. Applicant or parent of applicant must be member of Federation of American Consumers and Travelers. Available to U.S. citizens.

Application Requirements: Application, essay, resume, references, test scores, transcript. *Deadline:* January 15.

Contact: Vicki Rolens, Scholarship Coordinator and Managing Director
Federation of American Consumers and Travelers
PO Box 104
Edwardsville, IL 62025
Phone: 800-872-3228
Fax: 618-656-5369
E-mail: vrolens@usafact.org

FIRST CATHOLIC SLOVAK LADIES ASSOCIATION http://www.fcsla.org

FIRST CATHOLIC SLOVAK LADIES ASSOCIATION HIGH SCHOOL SCHOLARSHIPS

Scholarship for high school students. A written report of approximately 250 words on "What This High School Scholarship Will Do for Me" must be submitted with application. Candidate must have been a beneficial member of the Association for at least three years prior to date of application.

Award: Scholarship for use in freshman year; renewable. *Number:* up to 32. *Amount:* $1000.

Eligibility Requirements: Applicant must be high school student and planning to enroll or expecting to enroll full-time at a four-year institution or university. Applicant or parent of applicant must be member of First Catholic Slovak Ladies Association. Available to U.S. and Canadian citizens.

Application Requirements: Application, essay, photo, transcript. *Deadline:* March 1.

Contact: Director of Fraternal Scholarships
First Catholic Slovak Ladies Association
24950 Chagrin Boulevard
Beachwood, OH 44122
Phone: 800-464-4642
E-mail: info@fcsla.com

FLEET RESERVE ASSOCIATION http://www.fra.org

FLEET RESERVE ASSOCIATION SCHOLARSHIP

Dependent children/grandchildren and spouses of members in good standing of the Fleet Reserve Association or deceased while in aforementioned status, and member of the FRA may be eligible for up to $5000. Selection is based on financial need, academic standing, character, and leadership qualities. FRA members may access applications on Web site: http://www.fra.org/.

Award: Scholarship for use in freshman, sophomore, junior, or senior years; not renewable. *Number:* 1. *Amount:* $5000.

Eligibility Requirements: Applicant must be enrolled or expecting to enroll full-time at a four-year institution or university and must have an interest in leadership. Applicant or parent of applicant must be member of Fleet Reserve Association/Auxiliary. Applicant must have 3.0 GPA or higher. Available to U.S. citizens. Applicant or parent must meet one or more of the following requirements: Coast Guard, Marine Corps, or Navy experience; retired from active duty; disabled or killed as a result of military service; prisoner of war; or missing in action.

Application Requirements: Application, essay, financial need analysis, references, test scores, transcript. *Deadline:* April 15.

Contact: Vince Cuthie Sr., Scholarship Administrator
Fleet Reserve Association
125 North West Street
Alexandria, VA 22314-2754
Phone: 800-372-1924
E-mail: fra@fra.org

OLIVER AND ESTHER R. HOWARD SCHOLARSHIP

Scholarship for children of members in good standing of the Fleet Reserve Association or the Ladies Auxiliary of the Fleet Reserve Association or a member in good standing at time of death. Must pursue an undergraduate degree at a postsecondary institution. Minimum 3.0 GPA required. Awards are alternated annually between female dependents (in even numbered years) and male dependents (in odd numbered years).

Award: Scholarship for use in freshman, sophomore, junior, or senior years; not renewable. *Number:* 1. *Amount:* varies.

Eligibility Requirements: Applicant must be enrolled or expecting to enroll full-time at a two-year or four-year institution or university. Applicant or parent of applicant must be member of Fleet Reserve Association/Auxiliary. Applicant must have 3.0 GPA or higher. Available to U.S. citizens. Applicant or parent must meet one or more of the following requirements: Coast Guard, Marine Corps, or Navy experience; retired from active duty; disabled or killed as a result of military service; prisoner of war; or missing in action.

Application Requirements: Application, essay, financial need analysis, references, test scores, transcript, proof of citizenship, proof of college attendance. *Deadline:* April 15.

Contact: Mr. Vince Cuthie, Scholarship Administrator
Fleet Reserve Association
125 North West Street
Alexandria, VA 22314-2754
Phone: 800-372-1924
E-mail: fra@fra.org

SCHUYLER S. PYLE AWARD

Dependent children/grandchildren and spouses of members in good standing of the Fleet Reserve Association or a member in good standing at time of death, and members of FRA may be eligible for up to $5000. Selection is based on financial need, academic standing, character, and leadership qualities.

Award: Scholarship for use in freshman, sophomore, junior, or senior years; not renewable. *Number:* 1. *Amount:* up to $5000.

Eligibility Requirements: Applicant must be enrolled or expecting to enroll full-time at a four-year institution or university and must have an interest in leadership. Applicant or parent of applicant must be member of Fleet Reserve Association/Auxiliary. Applicant must have 3.0 GPA or higher. Available to U.S. citizens. Applicant or parent must meet one or more of the following requirements: Coast Guard, Marine Corps, or Navy experience; retired from active duty; disabled or killed as a result of military service; prisoner of war; or missing in action.

Application Requirements: Application, essay, financial need analysis, references, test scores, transcript. *Deadline:* April 15.

Contact: Vince Cuthie Sr., Scholarship Administrator
Fleet Reserve Association
125 North West Street
Alexandria, VA 22314-2754
Phone: 703-683-1400

FLORIDA LAND TITLE ASSOCIATION — http://www.flta.org

JOHN STARR THORNTON JR. MEMORIAL SCHOLARSHIPS

Award for a member or the child, grandchild, spouse, brother, niece/nephew of a principal or employee of FLTA member. Must be a resident of Florida.

Award: Scholarship for use in freshman, sophomore, junior, senior, or graduate years; not renewable. *Number:* 1. *Amount:* $1500.

Eligibility Requirements: Applicant must be enrolled or expecting to enroll full-time at a two-year or four-year institution or university and resident of Florida. Applicant or parent of applicant must be member of Florida Land Title Association. Available to U.S. citizens.

Application Requirements: Application, essay. *Deadline:* August 31.

Contact: Lee Huszagh, Secretary and Treasurer
Florida Land Title Association
249 East Virginia Street
Tallahassee, FL 32302
Phone: 850-681-6422
Fax: 850-681-6271
E-mail: flta@flta.org

MARJORIE S. SCHWARTZ MEMORIAL SCHOLARSHIPS

Award for a member or the child, grandchild, spouse, brother, niece/nephew of a principal or employee of FLTA member. Must be a resident of Florida.

Award: Scholarship for use in freshman, sophomore, junior, senior, or graduate years; not renewable. *Number:* 1. *Amount:* $1500.

Eligibility Requirements: Applicant must be enrolled or expecting to enroll full-time at a two-year or four-year institution or university and resident of Florida. Applicant or parent of applicant must be member of Florida Land Title Association. Available to U.S. citizens.

Application Requirements: Application, essay. *Deadline:* August 31.

Contact: Lee Huszagh, Secretary and Treasurer
Florida Land Title Association
249 East Virginia Street
Tallahassee, FL 32302
Phone: 850-681-6422
Fax: 850-681-6271
E-mail: flta@flta.org

SAM D. MANSFIELD MEMORIAL SCHOLARSHIPS

Award for a member or the child, grandchild, spouse, brother, niece/nephew of a principal or employee of FLTA member. Must be a resident of Florida.

Award: Scholarship for use in freshman, sophomore, junior, senior, or graduate years; not renewable. *Number:* 1. *Amount:* $1500.

Eligibility Requirements: Applicant must be enrolled or expecting to enroll full-time at a two-year or four-year institution or university and resident of Florida. Applicant or parent of applicant must be member of Florida Land Title Association. Available to U.S. citizens.

Application Requirements: Application, essay. *Deadline:* August 31.

Contact: Scholarship Committee
Florida Land Title Association
249 East Virginia Street
Tallahassee, FL 32301
Phone: 850-681-6422
E-mail: leeh@flta.org

GEOLOGICAL SOCIETY OF AMERICA — http://www.geosociety.org

NORTHEASTERN SECTION UNDERGRADUATE STUDENT RESEARCH GRANTS

Grants to support individual research by sophomore or junior undergraduates attending universities within geographic boundaries of the Northeastern Section. Must be a student associate or a member of GSA.

Award: Grant for use in sophomore or junior years; not renewable. *Number:* varies. *Amount:* varies.

Eligibility Requirements: Applicant must be enrolled or expecting to enroll full- or part-time at a four-year institution or university. Applicant or parent of applicant must be member of Geological Society of America. Available to U.S. citizens.

Application Requirements: Application, financial need analysis, proposal text, endorsement form. *Deadline:* February 28.

Contact: Stephen Pollock, Secretary
Geological Society of America
37 College Avenue
Gorham, ME 04038
Phone: 207-780-5353
Fax: 207-228-8361
E-mail: pollock@usm.maine.edu

GIRL SCOUTS OF CONNECTICUT — http://www.gsofct.org

EMILY CHAISON GOLD AWARD SCHOLARSHIP

An annual scholarship of $750 is awarded each year to one Gold Award recipient from the state of Connecticut during her senior year.

Award: Scholarship for use in freshman year; not renewable. *Number:* 1. *Amount:* $750.

Eligibility Requirements: Applicant must be high school student; planning to enroll or expecting to enroll full- or part-time at a four-year institution or university; female and resident of Connecticut. Applicant or parent of applicant must be member of Girl Scouts. Available to U.S. citizens.

Girl Scouts of Connecticut (continued)

Application Requirements: Application, essay, references. *Deadline:* April 1.

Contact: Nancy Bussman, Scholarship Committee
Girl Scouts of Connecticut
340 Washington Street
Hartford, CT 06106
Phone: 203-239-2922
E-mail: nbussman@gsofct.org

GLASS, MOLDERS, POTTERY, PLASTICS AND ALLIED WORKERS INTERNATIONAL UNION http://www.gmpiu.org

GMP MEMORIAL SCHOLARSHIP PROGRAM

Scholarship of $4000 per year, renewable each year for a full four-year college program if adequate academic standards are maintained, to the sons and daughters of members of the union.

Award: Scholarship for use in freshman year; renewable. *Number:* 10. *Amount:* $2000–$4000.

Eligibility Requirements: Applicant must be high school student and planning to enroll or expecting to enroll full-time at a four-year institution or university. Applicant or parent of applicant must be member of Glass, Molders, Pottery, Plastics and Allied Workers International Union. Available to U.S. and Canadian citizens.

Application Requirements: Application, autobiography, test scores. *Deadline:* November 1.

Contact: Bruce R. Smith, International Secretary and Treasurer
Glass, Molders, Pottery, Plastics and Allied Workers International Union
608 East Baltimore Pike, PO Box 607
Media, PA 19063
Phone: 610-892-0143
Fax: 610-892-9657

GOLDEN KEY INTERNATIONAL HONOUR SOCIETY http://www.goldenkey.org

GEICO LIFE SCHOLARSHIP

Ten $1000 awards will be given to outstanding students while balancing additional responsibilities. Must have completed at least 12 undergraduate credit hours in the previous year. Must be enrolled at the time of application and must be working toward a baccalaureate degree.

Award: Scholarship for use in freshman, sophomore, junior, or senior years; not renewable. *Number:* 10. *Amount:* $1000.

Eligibility Requirements: Applicant must be enrolled or expecting to enroll full- or part-time at a four-year institution or university. Applicant or parent of applicant must be member of Golden Key National Honor Society. Available to U.S. and non-U.S. citizens.

Application Requirements: Application, essay, references, transcript. *Deadline:* April 1.

Contact: Scholarship Program Administrators
Golden Key International Honour Society
PO Box 23737
Nashville, TN 37202
Phone: 800-377-2401

GOLDEN KEY STUDY ABROAD SCHOLARSHIPS

Ten $1000 scholarships will be awarded each year to assist students in the pursuit of a study abroad program. Eligible members are undergraduate members who are currently enrolled in a study abroad program or will be enrolled in the academic year immediately following the granting of the award. Deadlines: April 15 and October 20.

Award: Scholarship for use in freshman, sophomore, junior, or senior years; not renewable. *Number:* 10. *Amount:* $1000.

Eligibility Requirements: Applicant must be enrolled or expecting to enroll full-time at a four-year institution or university. Applicant or parent of applicant must be member of Golden Key National Honor Society. Available to U.S. and non-U.S. citizens.

Application Requirements: Application, essay, transcript, description of the planned academic program. *Deadline:* varies.

Contact: Scholarship Program Administrators
Golden Key International Honour Society
PO Box 23737
Nashville, TN 37202-3737
Phone: 800-377-2401
E-mail: scholarships@goldenkey.org

INTERNATIONAL STUDENT LEADERS AWARD

The award is designed to recognize one talented Golden Key member for outstanding commitment to the society, as well as for campus and community leadership and academic achievement. The recipient of the award will receive $1000. Winners for the regional student leader awards will then be considered as candidates for this award. Deadline varies.

Award: Scholarship for use in freshman, sophomore, junior, senior, graduate, or postgraduate years; not renewable. *Number:* 1. *Amount:* $1000.

Eligibility Requirements: Applicant must be enrolled or expecting to enroll full- or part-time at a four-year institution or university and must have an interest in leadership. Applicant or parent of applicant must be member of Golden Key National Honor Society. Available to U.S. and non-U.S. citizens.

Application Requirements: Application, applicant must enter a contest, essay, resume, references. *Deadline:* varies.

Contact: Scholarship Program Administrators
Golden Key International Honour Society
PO Box 23737
Nashville, TN 37202-3737
Phone: 800-377-2401
E-mail: scholarships@goldenkey.org

GOLF COURSE SUPERINTENDENTS ASSOCIATION OF AMERICA http://www.gcsaa.org

GOLF COURSE SUPERINTENDENTS ASSOCIATION OF AMERICA LEGACY AWARD

Awards of $1500 for the children or grandchildren of Golf Course Superintendents Association of America members. Applicants must be enrolled full-time at an accredited institution of higher learning, or for high school seniors, they must have been accepted at such an institution for the next academic year.

Award: Scholarship for use in freshman, sophomore, junior, senior, or graduate years; not renewable. *Number:* 20. *Amount:* $1500.

Eligibility Requirements: Applicant must be enrolled or expecting to enroll full-time at a two-year or four-year or technical institution or university. Applicant or parent of applicant must be member of Golf Course Superintendents Association of America. Available to U.S. and non-U.S. citizens.

Application Requirements: Application, essay, references, transcript. *Deadline:* April 15.

Contact: Mischia Wright, Senior Manager, Development
Golf Course Superintendents Association of America
1421 Research Park Drive
Lawrence, KS 66049-3859
Phone: 800-472-7878 Ext. 4424
Fax: 785-832-4449
E-mail: mwright@gcsaa.org

JOSEPH S. GARSHE COLLEGIATE GRANT PROGRAM

Renewable award of $2500 available to children/step children of GCSAA members who have been an active member for five or more consecutive years, for use at an accredited college or trade school. Applicant must be a graduating high school senior and be accepted at an institution of higher learning for the upcoming year.

Award: Scholarship for use in freshman year; renewable. *Number:* 1–2. *Amount:* $2500.

Eligibility Requirements: Applicant must be high school student and planning to enroll or expecting to enroll full-time at a two-year or four-year or technical institution or university. Applicant or parent of applicant must be member of Golf Course Superintendents Association of America. Available to U.S. and non-U.S. citizens.

Application Requirements: Application, essay, transcript, letter of acceptance. *Deadline:* March 15.

Contact: Mischia Wright, Senior Manager, Development
Golf Course Superintendents Association of America
1421 Research Park Drive
Lawrence, KS 66049-3859
Phone: 800-472-7878 Ext. 4424
Fax: 785-832-4449
E-mail: mwright@gcsaa.org

HANSCOM FEDERAL CREDIT UNION http://hfcu.org

JOHN F. CONDON MEMORIAL SCHOLARSHIP

Scholarship of $1500 given graduating high school seniors. All applicants must be members in good standing, in their own right (have a prime share account in their own name), before submitting an application.

Award: Scholarship for use in freshman year; not renewable. *Number:* 5. *Amount:* $1500.

Eligibility Requirements: Applicant must be high school student and planning to enroll or expecting to enroll full-time at a four-year institution or university. Applicant or parent of applicant must be member of Healthcare Information and Management Systems Society. Available to U.S. and non-U.S. citizens.

Application Requirements: Application, essay, resume, test scores, transcript. *Deadline:* March 10.

Contact: Arlene Bellacini, Executive Administrative Assistant
Hanscom Federal Credit Union
1610 Eglin Street
Hanscom AFB, MA 01731
Phone: 800-656-4328 Ext. 2203
E-mail: abellacini@hfcu.org

HAWAII EDUCATION ASSOCIATION http://www.heaed.com

HAWAII EDUCATION ASSOCIATION HIGH SCHOOL STUDENT SCHOLARSHIP

Scholarship available to high school seniors planning on attending four-year college/university. Must be children or grandchildren of HEA members. Membership must be for at least one year.

Award: Scholarship for use in freshman year; not renewable. *Number:* up to 5. *Amount:* up to $1000.

Eligibility Requirements: Applicant must be high school student; planning to enroll or expecting to enroll full-time at a four-year institution or university and resident of Hawaii. Applicant or parent of applicant must be member of Hawaii Education Association. Available to U.S. citizens.

Application Requirements: Application, autobiography, financial need analysis, photo, references, transcript. *Deadline:* April 1.

Contact: Scholarship Committee
Hawaii Education Association
1953 South Beretania Street, Suite 3C
Honolulu, HI 96826-1304
Phone: 808-949-6657
Fax: 808-944-2032
E-mail: hea.office@heaed.com

HAWAII EDUCATION ASSOCIATION UNDERGRADUATE COLLEGE STUDENT SCHOLARSHIP

Scholarships to children and grandchildren of HEA members. To qualify the HEA member should have at least one year membership in HEA. Four scholarships of $1000 each is offered to deserving continuing, full-time undergraduate college students in any two- or four-year accredited institution of higher learning.

Award: Scholarship for use in freshman, sophomore, junior, or senior years; not renewable. *Number:* up to 4. *Amount:* up to $1000.

Eligibility Requirements: Applicant must be enrolled or expecting to enroll full-time at a two-year or four-year institution or university. Applicant or parent of applicant must be member of Hawaii Education Association. Available to U.S. citizens.

Application Requirements: Application, financial need analysis, references, transcript, personal statement. *Deadline:* April 1.

Contact: Carol Yoneshige, Executive Director
Hawaii Education Association
1953 South Beretania Street, Suite 3C
Honolulu, HI 96826-1304
Phone: 808-949-6657
Fax: 808-944-2032

HEBREW IMMIGRANT AID SOCIETY http://www.hias.org

HEBREW IMMIGRANT AID SOCIETY SCHOLARSHIP AWARDS COMPETITION

Contestants must be Hebrew Immigrant Aid Society-assisted refugee who came to the United States after January 1, 1992. Must have completed two semesters at a U.S. high school, college, or graduate school. Application and information are available at Web site http://www.hias.org. Applications will be accepted only if submitted online.

Award: Scholarship for use in freshman, sophomore, junior, senior, or graduate years; not renewable. *Number:* 150. *Amount:* $2000.

Eligibility Requirements: Applicant must be of Jewish heritage and enrolled or expecting to enroll full-time at a two-year or four-year or technical institution or university. Applicant or parent of applicant must be member of Hebrew Immigrant Aid Society. Available to U.S. citizens.

Application Requirements: Application, applicant must enter a contest, essay, financial need analysis, test scores, transcript. *Deadline:* February 19.

Contact: Lisa Polakov, Scholarship Committee
Hebrew Immigrant Aid Society
333 Seventh Avenue, 16th Floor
New York, NY 10001-5004
Phone: 212-613-1358
Fax: 212-967-4356
E-mail: scholarship@hias.org

HELLENIC UNIVERSITY CLUB OF PHILADELPHIA http://www.hucphila.org

PAIDEIA SCHOLARSHIP

$3000 merit scholarship awarded to the child of a Hellenic University Club of Philadelphia member. Must be a U.S. citizen of Greek descent and a resident of particular counties in NJ or PA.

Award: Scholarship for use in freshman, sophomore, junior, or senior years; not renewable. *Number:* 1. *Amount:* up to $3000.

Eligibility Requirements: Applicant must be of Greek heritage; enrolled or expecting to enroll full-time at a four-year institution or university and resident of New Jersey or Pennsylvania. Applicant or parent of applicant must be member of Hellenic University Club of Pennsylvania. Available to U.S. citizens.

Application Requirements: Application, financial need analysis, transcript. *Deadline:* April 21.

Contact: Zoe Tripolitis, Scholarship Chairman
Hellenic University Club of Philadelphia
PO Box 42199
Philadelphia, PA 19101-2199
Phone: 215-483-7440
E-mail: hucphila@yahoo.com

HONOR SOCIETY OF PHI KAPPA PHI http://www.phikappaphi.org

LITERACY INITIATIVE GRANT COMPETITION

Grants up to $2500 are awarded to Phi Kappa Phi members for projects relating to literacy. These projects should fulfill the spirit of volunteerism and community. The total number of awards varies for each year.

Award: Grant for use in freshman, sophomore, junior, senior, graduate, or postgraduate years; not renewable. *Number:* varies. *Amount:* $300–$2500.

Eligibility Requirements: Applicant must be enrolled or expecting to enroll full- or part-time at a two-year or four-year or technical institution or university. Applicant or parent of applicant must be member of Phi Kappa Phi. Available to U.S. and non-U.S. citizens.

Honor Society of Phi Kappa Phi (continued)

Application Requirements: Application, financial need analysis. *Deadline:* February 4.

Contact: Theresa Bard, Fellowships Coordinator
Honor Society of Phi Kappa Phi
7576 Goodwood Boulevard
Baton Rouge, LA 70806
Phone: 225-388-4917 Ext. 13
Fax: 225-388-4900
E-mail: fellows@phikappaphi.org

STUDY ABROAD GRANT COMPETITION

Grants up to $1000 are awarded to undergraduate as support for seeking knowledge and experience by studying abroad.

Award: Grant for use in freshman, sophomore, junior, or senior years; not renewable. *Number:* 38. *Amount:* $1000.

Eligibility Requirements: Applicant must be enrolled or expecting to enroll full-time at a four-year institution or university. Applicant or parent of applicant must be member of Phi Kappa Phi. Applicant must have 3.5 GPA or higher. Available to U.S. and non-U.S. citizens.

Application Requirements: Application, references, transcript, letter of acceptance into a study abroad program. *Deadline:* February 18.

Contact: Maria Davis, Marketing Development Manager
Honor Society of Phi Kappa Phi
7576 Goodwood Boulevard
Baton Rouge, LA 70893-6000
Phone: 225-388-4917 Ext. 35
Fax: 225-388-4900
E-mail: mariad@phikappaphi.org

INDEPENDENT OFFICE PRODUCTS AND FURNITURE DEALERS ASSOCIATION http://www.iopfda.org

NOPA AND OFDA SCHOLARSHIP AWARD

Candidates must have graduated from high school or its equivalent before July 1 of the year in which they would use the scholarship. Must have an academic record sufficient to be accepted by an accredited college, junior college or technical institute. Must be a relative of a member of NOPA or OFDA.

Award: Scholarship for use in freshman, sophomore, junior, or senior years; renewable. *Number:* up to 20. *Amount:* $2000.

Eligibility Requirements: Applicant must be enrolled or expecting to enroll full-time at a two-year or four-year or technical institution or university. Applicant or parent of applicant must be member of Independent Office Products and Furniture Dealers Association. Available to U.S. and non-U.S. citizens.

Application Requirements: Application, references, transcript. *Deadline:* March 14.

Contact: Billie Zidek, Scholarship Administrator
Independent Office Products and Furniture Dealers Association
301 North Fairfax Street, Suite 200
Alexandria, VA 22314-2696
Phone: 703-549-9040 Ext. 121
Fax: 703-683-7552
E-mail: bzidek@iopfda.org

INTERNATIONAL BROTHERHOOD OF TEAMSTERS SCHOLARSHIP FUND http://www.teamster.org

JAMES R. HOFFA MEMORIAL SCHOLARSHIP FUND

Scholarships available to the children and dependents of members of the International Brotherhood of Teamsters. Scholarships will be renewed on an annual basis. The recipients must maintain 3.0 GPA.

Award: Scholarship for use in freshman, sophomore, junior, senior, graduate, or postgraduate years; renewable. *Number:* 1–100. *Amount:* $1000–$10,000.

Eligibility Requirements: Applicant must be enrolled or expecting to enroll full-time at a two-year or four-year or technical institution or university. Applicant or parent of applicant must be member of International Brotherhood of Teamsters. Applicant must have 3.0 GPA or higher. Available to U.S. and Canadian citizens.

Application Requirements: Application, references, transcript, ACT or SAT scores. *Deadline:* March 31.

Contact: Traci Jacobs, Manager
International Brotherhood of Teamsters Scholarship Fund
25 Louisiana Avenue, NW
Washington, DC 20001
Phone: 202-624-8988
Fax: 202-624-7457
E-mail: scholarship@teamster.org

INTERNATIONAL CHEMICAL WORKERS UNION http://www.icwuc.org

WALTER L. MITCHELL MEMORIAL AWARDS

Award available to children of International Chemical Workers Union members. Applicants must be starting their freshman year of college.

Award: Grant for use in freshman year; not renewable. *Number:* 13. *Amount:* $1500.

Eligibility Requirements: Applicant must be high school student and planning to enroll or expecting to enroll full-time at a two-year or four-year or technical institution or university. Applicant or parent of applicant must be member of International Chemical Workers Union. Available to U.S. citizens.

Application Requirements: Application, autobiography, test scores, transcript. *Deadline:* April 25.

Contact: Sue Everhart, Secretary for Research and Education
International Chemical Workers Union
1799 Akron-Peninsula Road
Akron, OH 44313
E-mail: severhart@icwuc.org

INTERNATIONAL EXECUTIVE HOUSEKEEPERS ASSOCIATION http://www.ieha.org

INTERNATIONAL EXECUTIVE HOUSEKEEPERS ASSOCIATION EDUCATIONAL FOUNDATION AWARD

One-time award of $500 given for any year of full- or part-time undergraduate study. Must be a current member of IEHA.

Award: Scholarship for use in freshman, sophomore, junior, or senior years; not renewable. *Number:* 10. *Amount:* up to $500.

Eligibility Requirements: Applicant must be enrolled or expecting to enroll full- or part-time at a two-year or four-year or technical institution or university. Applicant or parent of applicant must be member of International Executive Housekeepers Association. Available to U.S. and non-U.S. citizens.

Application Requirements: Application, essay, transcript. *Deadline:* January 10.

Contact: Beth Risinger, Chief Executive Officer and Executive Director
International Executive Housekeepers Association
Education Department, 1001 Eastwind Drive, Suite 301
Westerville, OH 43081-3361
Phone: 800-200-6342
Fax: 614-895-1248
E-mail: excel@ieha.org

INTERNATIONAL EXECUTIVE HOUSEKEEPERS ASSOCIATION EDUCATIONAL FOUNDATION SPARTAN SCHOLARSHIP

Award available to IEHA members and their immediate families. Scholarship will be awarded to the best qualified candidate as determined by IEHA's education committee.

Award: Scholarship for use in freshman, sophomore, junior, or senior years; not renewable. *Number:* 1. *Amount:* $1500.

Eligibility Requirements: Applicant must be enrolled or expecting to enroll full- or part-time at a four-year institution or university. Applicant or parent of applicant must be member of International Executive Housekeepers Association. Available to U.S. and non-U.S. citizens.

Application Requirements: Application, financial need analysis. *Deadline:* September 10.

Contact: Scholarship Selection Committee
International Executive Housekeepers Association
1001 Eastwind Drive, Suite 301
Westerville, OH 43081-3361
Phone: 800-200-6342
Fax: 614-895-1248

INTERNATIONAL FEDERATION OF PROFESSIONAL AND TECHNICAL ENGINEERS http://www.ifpte.org

INTERNATIONAL FEDERATION OF PROFESSIONAL AND TECHNICAL ENGINEERS ANNUAL SCHOLARSHIP

Scholarship for high school seniors who have demonstrated academic achievement and service to their school and community. Only children or grandchildren of IFPTE members are eligible. Must be a U.S. or Canadian citizen. Three scholarships of $1500 are granted.

Award: Scholarship for use in freshman year; not renewable. *Number:* 3. *Amount:* $1500.

Eligibility Requirements: Applicant must be high school student and planning to enroll or expecting to enroll full-time at a four-year institution or university. Applicant or parent of applicant must be member of International Federation of Professional and Technical Engineers. Applicant or parent of applicant must have employment or volunteer experience in community service. Available to U.S. and Canadian citizens.

Application Requirements: Application, essay, references, transcript. *Deadline:* March 15.

Contact: Candace M. Rhett, Communications Representative
International Federation of Professional and Technical Engineers
8630 Fenton Street, Suite 400
Silver Spring, MD 20910
Phone: 301-565-9016
Fax: 301-565-0018
E-mail: crhett@ifpte.org

INTERNATIONAL UNION OF BRICKLAYERS AND ALLIED CRAFTWORKERS http://www.bacweb.org

CANADIAN BATES SCHOLARSHIP PROGRAM

Renewable scholarship for high school seniors for their undergraduate study. Two scholarships are granted annually and the award value is CAN$1200 or CAN$1500. Must be the son or daughter of a Canadian BAC member in good standing of a Canadian BAC local, and a high school senior planning to attend college in the fall.

Award: Scholarship for use in freshman year; renewable. *Number:* 2.

Eligibility Requirements: Applicant must be Canadian citizen; high school student and planning to enroll or expecting to enroll full- or part-time at a four-year institution or university. Applicant or parent of applicant must be member of International Union of Bricklayers and Allied Craftworkers.

Application Requirements: Application. *Deadline:* March 1.

Contact: Constance Lambert, Director of Education
International Union of Bricklayers and Allied Craftworkers
620 F Street, NW
Washington, DC 20004
Phone: 202-383-3110
Fax: 202-772-3800
E-mail: mmccarthy@bacweb.org

U.S. BATES SCHOLARSHIP PROGRAM

Scholarship awards a stipend of $2000 per year for up to four years to two students annually. The program is open to sons and daughters of U.S. BAC members in good standing of U.S. BAC locals who will be juniors in high school, and who either have taken or plan to take the standardized PSAT exam.

Award: Scholarship for use in freshman year; renewable. *Number:* 2. *Amount:* $2000.

Eligibility Requirements: Applicant must be high school student and planning to enroll or expecting to enroll full- or part-time at a four-year institution or university. Applicant or parent of applicant must be member of International Union of Bricklayers and Allied Craftworkers. Available to U.S. citizens.

Application Requirements: Application. *Deadline:* March 1.

Contact: Constance Lambert, Director of Education
International Union of Bricklayers and Allied Craftworkers
620 F Street, NW
Washington, DC 20004
Phone: 202-383-3110
Fax: 202-772-3800
E-mail: mmccarthy@bacweb.org

INTERNATIONAL UNION OF ELECTRONIC, ELECTRICAL, SALARIED, MACHINE, AND FURNITURE WORKERS-CWA http://www.iue-cwa.org

CWA JOE BEIRNE FOUNDATION SCHOLARSHIP PROGRAM

Scholarships of $3000 annually to Communication Workers of America members, their spouses, children, and grandchildren (including dependents of laid-off, retired or deceased CWA members). A second-year award is contingent on academic accomplishment of the first year. No specific studies are required. Scholarship winners may pursue whatever courses they wish. Winner chosen by lottery drawing.

Award: Scholarship for use in freshman, sophomore, junior, senior, or graduate years; not renewable. *Number:* up to 30. *Amount:* $3000.

Eligibility Requirements: Applicant must be enrolled or expecting to enroll full-time at a two-year or four-year institution or university. Applicant or parent of applicant must be member of AFL-CIO. Available to U.S. and Canadian citizens.

Application Requirements: Application, essay. *Deadline:* April 30.

Contact: Sue McElroy, Scholarship Committee
International Union of Electronic, Electrical, Salaried, Machine, and Furniture Workers-CWA
501 Third Street, NW
Washington, DC 20001
Phone: 202-434-0676
Fax: 202-434-1250

IUE-CWA INTERNATIONAL BRUCE VAN ESS SCHOLARSHIP

Scholarship of $2500 to all IUE-CWA members and employees and their children and grandchildren. Applicant must be accepted for admission or already enrolled as a full-time student at an accredited college or university, nursing, or technical school offering college credit courses. All study must be completed at the undergraduate level.

Award: Scholarship for use in freshman, sophomore, junior, or senior years; not renewable. *Number:* 1. *Amount:* $2500.

Eligibility Requirements: Applicant must be enrolled or expecting to enroll full-time at a four-year institution or university. Applicant or parent of applicant must be member of International Union of Electronic, Electrical, Salaries, Machine and Furniture Workers. Available to U.S. and Canadian citizens.

Application Requirements: Application, essay, financial need analysis, references, test scores, transcript. *Deadline:* March 31.

Contact: Sue McElroy, Scholarship Committee
International Union of Electronic, Electrical, Salaried, Machine, and Furniture Workers-CWA
501 Third Street, NW
Washington, DC 20001
Phone: 202-434-0676
Fax: 202-434-1250

IUE-CWA ROBERT L. LIVINGSTON SCHOLARSHIPS

Scholarships of $1500 to a child of an IUE-CWA Automotive Conference Board member (or the child of a deceased or retired IUE-CWA Conference Board member). Applicant must be accepted for admission or already enrolled as a full-time student at an accredited college or university, nursing or technical school offering college credit courses. All study must be completed at the undergraduate level.

Award: Scholarship for use in freshman, sophomore, junior, or senior years; not renewable. *Number:* 2. *Amount:* $1500.

Eligibility Requirements: Applicant must be enrolled or expecting to enroll full-time at a four-year institution or university. Applicant or parent

International Union of Electronic, Electrical, Salaried, Machine, and Furniture Workers-CWA (continued)

of applicant must be member of International Union of Electronic, Electrical, Salaries, Machine and Furniture Workers. Available to U.S. and Canadian citizens.

Application Requirements: Application, essay, financial need analysis, references, transcript, career objectives, documentation of civic commitment and extracurricular activities. *Deadline:* March 31.

Contact: Sue McElroy, Scholarship Committee
International Union of Electronic, Electrical, Salaried, Machine, and Furniture Workers-CWA
501 Third Street, NW
Washington, DC 20001
Phone: 202-434-0676
Fax: 202-434-1250

PAUL JENNINGS SCHOLARSHIP AWARD

One award for a student whose parent or grandparent is or has been a local union elected official. Families of full-time international union officers are not eligible. Submit family financial status form with application.

Award: Scholarship for use in freshman, sophomore, junior, senior, or graduate years; not renewable. *Number:* 1. *Amount:* $3000.

Eligibility Requirements: Applicant must be enrolled or expecting to enroll full-time at a two-year or four-year or technical institution or university. Applicant or parent of applicant must be member of International Union of Electronic, Electrical, Salaries, Machine and Furniture Workers. Available to U.S. and Canadian citizens.

Application Requirements: Application, essay, financial need analysis, references, test scores, transcript. *Deadline:* March 31.

Contact: Sue McElroy, Scholarship Committee
International Union of Electronic, Electrical, Salaried, Machine, and Furniture Workers-CWA
501 Third Street, NW
Washington, DC 20001
Phone: 202-434-0676
Fax: 202-434-1250

WILLIE RUDD SCHOLARSHIP

One-time award available to all IUE-CWA members and employees and their children and grandchildren. Applicant must be accepted for admission or already enrolled as a full-time student at an accredited college or university, nursing, or technical school offering college credit courses. All study must be completed at the undergraduate level.

Award: Scholarship for use in freshman, sophomore, junior, or senior years; not renewable. *Number:* 1. *Amount:* $1000.

Eligibility Requirements: Applicant must be enrolled or expecting to enroll full-time at a four-year or technical institution or university. Applicant or parent of applicant must be member of International Union of Electronic, Electrical, Salaries, Machine and Furniture Workers. Available to U.S. and Canadian citizens.

Application Requirements: Application, essay, financial need analysis, references, test scores, transcript. *Deadline:* March 31.

Contact: Sue McElroy, Scholarship Committee
International Union of Electronic, Electrical, Salaried, Machine, and Furniture Workers-CWA
501 Third Street, NW
Washington, DC 20001
Phone: 202-434-0676
Fax: 202-434-1250

ITALIAN CATHOLIC FEDERATION INC. http://www.icf.org

ITALIAN CATHOLIC FEDERATION FIRST YEAR SCHOLARSHIP

Scholarship for undergraduate students of the Catholic faith and of Italian heritage (or children or grand children of non-Italian ICF members). Must have minimum 3.2 GPA.

Award: Scholarship for use in freshman year; not renewable. *Number:* 180–200. *Amount:* varies.

Eligibility Requirements: Applicant must be Roman Catholic; high school student; planning to enroll or expecting to enroll full-time at a four-year institution or university and resident of Arizona, California, Illinois, or Nevada. Applicant or parent of applicant must be member of Italian Catholic Federation. Available to U.S. citizens.

Application Requirements: Application, essay, financial need analysis, references, test scores, transcript. *Deadline:* March 15.

Contact: Scholarship Committee
Italian Catholic Federation Inc.
ICF Central Council Office, 675 Hegenberger Road, Suite 230
Oakland, CA 94621
Phone: 510-633-9058
Fax: 510-633-9758

JUNIOR ACHIEVEMENT http://www.ja.org

HUGH B. SWEENY ACHIEVEMENT AWARD

Award recognizes graduating seniors who demonstrate extraordinary impact on a community through entrepreneurship and similar initiatives. Must have completed JA Company Program or JA Economics.

Award: Scholarship for use in freshman year; not renewable. *Number:* 1. *Amount:* up to $5000.

Eligibility Requirements: Applicant must be high school student; planning to enroll or expecting to enroll full-time at a four-year institution or university and must have an interest in entrepreneurship or leadership. Applicant or parent of applicant must be member of Junior Achievement. Applicant must have 3.0 GPA or higher. Available to U.S. citizens.

Application Requirements: Application, essay, financial need analysis, references. *Deadline:* February 1.

Contact: Denise Terry, Scholarship Coordinator
Junior Achievement
One Education Way
Colorado Springs, CO 80906-4477
Phone: 719-540-6134
Fax: 719-540-6175
E-mail: dterry@ja.org

JUNIOR ACHIEVEMENT JOE FRANCOMANO SCHOLARSHIP

Renewable award to high school seniors who have demonstrated academic achievement, leadership skills, and financial need. May be used at any accredited post secondary educational institution for any field of study resulting in a baccalaureate degree. Must have completed JA Company Program or JA Economics.

Award: Scholarship for use in freshman year; renewable. *Number:* 1. *Amount:* $5000.

Eligibility Requirements: Applicant must be high school student; planning to enroll or expecting to enroll full-time at a four-year institution or university and must have an interest in leadership. Applicant or parent of applicant must be member of Junior Achievement. Applicant must have 3.0 GPA or higher. Available to U.S. and Canadian citizens.

Application Requirements: Application, essay, financial need analysis, references, transcript. *Deadline:* February 1.

Contact: Denise Terry, Scholarship Coordinator
Junior Achievement
One Education Way
Colorado Springs, CO 80906-4477
Phone: 719-540-6134
Fax: 719-540-6175
E-mail: dterry@ja.org

JUNIOR ACHIEVEMENT OFFICE DEPOT SCHOLARSHIP

One-time award to high school graduating seniors seeking a degree from an accredited postsecondary educational institution. Must demonstrate academic achievement and leadership skills. Must have completed a JA program. Minimum 3.0 GPA required. Must write a 500 words or less essay on "How important is diversity in today's corporate environment? Why?".

Award: Scholarship for use in freshman year; not renewable. *Number:* 7. *Amount:* $10,000.

Eligibility Requirements: Applicant must be high school student; planning to enroll or expecting to enroll full-time at a four-year institution or university and must have an interest in leadership. Applicant or parent of applicant must be member of Junior Achievement. Applicant must have 3.0 GPA or higher. Available to U.S. and Canadian citizens.

Application Requirements: Application, essay, financial need analysis, references, test scores, transcript. *Deadline:* February 27.

Contact: Denise Terry, Scholarship Coordinator
Junior Achievement
One Education Way
Colorado Springs, CO 80906-4477
Phone: 719-540-6134
Fax: 719-540-6175
E-mail: dterry@ja.org

KAPPA ALPHA THETA FOUNDATION http://www.kappaalphathetafoundation.org

KAPPA ALPHA THETA FOUNDATION MERIT BASED SCHOLARSHIP PROGRAM

Scholarships to either graduate or undergraduate members of the foundation. Merit-based and applicants are scored in four categories - academics, fraternity activities, campus and/or community activities, and references.

Award: Scholarship for use in freshman, sophomore, junior, senior, graduate, or postgraduate years; not renewable. *Number:* 150–175. *Amount:* $1000–$10,000.

Eligibility Requirements: Applicant must be enrolled or expecting to enroll full-time at a four-year institution or university and female. Available to U.S. and non-U.S. citizens.

Application Requirements: Application, resume, references, transcript. *Deadline:* February 1.

Contact: Cindy Thoennes, Coordinator of Programs
Kappa Alpha Theta Foundation
8740 Founders Road
Indianapolis, IN 46268
Phone: 317-876-1870 Ext. 119
Fax: 317-876-1925
E-mail: cthoennes@kappaalphatheta.org

KAPPA ALPHA THETA FOUNDATION NAMED ENDOWMENT GRANT PROGRAM

The program was established to provide funds for undergraduate and alumna members of the fraternity for leadership training and non-degree educational opportunities. Individual Thetas, collegiate or alumna undergraduate, and college and alumnae chapters may apply for grant.

Award: Grant for use in freshman, sophomore, junior, or senior years; not renewable. *Number:* up to 50. *Amount:* $100–$5000.

Eligibility Requirements: Applicant must be enrolled or expecting to enroll full- or part-time at a four-year institution or university and female. Available to U.S. and non-U.S. citizens.

Application Requirements: Application, resume, references, budget, proposal, narrative. *Deadline:* continuous.

Contact: Cindy Thoennes, Coordinator of Programs
Kappa Alpha Theta Foundation
8740 Founders Road
Indianapolis, IN 46268
Phone: 317-876-1870 Ext. 119
Fax: 317-876-1925
E-mail: cthoennes@kappaalphatheta.org

KNIGHTS OF COLUMBUS http://www.kofc.org

FOURTH DEGREE PRO DEO AND PRO PATRIA (CANADA)

Renewable scholarships for members of Canadian Knights of Columbus councils and their children who are entering first year of study for baccalaureate degree. Based on academic excellence. Award not limited to Fourth Degree members.

Award: Scholarship for use in freshman year; renewable. *Number:* varies. *Amount:* $1500.

Eligibility Requirements: Applicant must be Roman Catholic; Canadian citizen and enrolled or expecting to enroll full-time at a four-year institution or university. Applicant or parent of applicant must be member of Knights of Columbus. Applicant must have 3.0 GPA or higher.

Application Requirements: Application, autobiography, references, test scores, transcript. *Deadline:* May 1.

Contact: Donald Barry, Director of Scholarship Aid
Knights of Columbus
PO Box 1670
New Haven, CT 06507-0901
Phone: 203-752-4332
Fax: 203-752-4103

FOURTH DEGREE PRO DEO AND PRO PATRIA SCHOLARSHIPS

Award available to students entering freshman year at a Catholic university or college in United States. Applicant must be a member or child of a member of Knights of Columbus or Columbian Squires. Scholarships are awarded on the basis of academic excellence. Minimum 3.0 GPA required.

Award: Scholarship for use in freshman, sophomore, junior, or senior years; renewable. *Number:* varies. *Amount:* $1500.

Eligibility Requirements: Applicant must be Roman Catholic and enrolled or expecting to enroll full-time at a four-year institution or university. Applicant or parent of applicant must be member of Columbian Squires or Knights of Columbus. Applicant must have 3.0 GPA or higher. Available to U.S. and Canadian citizens.

Application Requirements: Application, autobiography, essay, references, test scores, transcript. *Deadline:* May 1.

Contact: Rev. Donald Barry, Director of Scholarship Aid
Knights of Columbus
PO Box 1670
New Haven, CT 06507-0901
Phone: 203-752-4332
Fax: 203-752-4103

FRANCIS P. MATTHEWS AND JOHN E. SWIFT EDUCATIONAL TRUST SCHOLARSHIPS

Available to dependent children of Knights of Columbus who died or became permanently and totally disabled while in military service during a time of conflict, from a cause connected with military service, or as the result of criminal violence while in the performance of their duties as full-time law enforcement officers or firemen. The scholarship is awarded at a Catholic college and includes the amount not covered by other financial aid for tuition, room, board, books and fees.

Award: Scholarship for use in freshman, sophomore, junior, or senior years; renewable. *Number:* varies. *Amount:* varies.

Eligibility Requirements: Applicant must be Roman Catholic and enrolled or expecting to enroll full-time at a four-year institution or university. Applicant or parent of applicant must be member of Knights of Columbus. Applicant or parent of applicant must have employment or volunteer experience in police/firefighting. Applicant must have 2.5 GPA or higher. Available to U.S. citizens. Applicant or parent must meet one or more of the following requirements: general military experience; retired from active duty; disabled or killed as a result of military service; prisoner of war; or missing in action.

Application Requirements: Application, proof of parent's military service or employment in law enforcement services. *Deadline:* March 1.

Contact: Donald Barry, Director of Scholarship Aid
Knights of Columbus
PO Box 1670
New Haven, CT 06507-0901
Phone: 203-752-4332
Fax: 203-752-4103

JOHN W. MCDEVITT (FOURTH DEGREE) SCHOLARSHIPS

Scholarship for students entering freshman year at a Catholic college or university in United States. Applicant must submit Pro Deo and Pro Patria Scholarship application. Must be a member or wife, son, or daughter of a member of the Knights of Columbus. Minimum 3.0 GPA required.

Award: Scholarship for use in freshman year; renewable. *Number:* varies. *Amount:* $1500.

Eligibility Requirements: Applicant must be Roman Catholic and enrolled or expecting to enroll full-time at a four-year institution or university. Applicant or parent of applicant must be member of Knights of Columbus. Applicant must have 3.0 GPA or higher. Available to U.S. citizens.

Knights of Columbus (continued)

Application Requirements: Application, autobiography, references, test scores, transcript. *Deadline:* March 1.

Contact: Donald Barry, Director of Scholarship Aid
Knights of Columbus
PO Box 1670
New Haven, CT 06507-0901
Phone: 203-752-4332
Fax: 203-752-4103

PERCY J. JOHNSON ENDOWED SCHOLARSHIPS

Renewable scholarship for young men entering freshman year at a Catholic college or university. Applicants must submit Pro Deo and Pro Patria Scholarship application and a copy of Student Aid Report (SAR). Must be a member or a son of a member of the Knights of Columbus. Must also rank in upper third of class or have 3.0 GPA.

Award: Scholarship for use in freshman year; renewable. *Number:* varies. *Amount:* $1500.

Eligibility Requirements: Applicant must be Roman Catholic; enrolled or expecting to enroll full-time at a four-year institution or university and male. Applicant or parent of applicant must be member of Knights of Columbus. Applicant must have 3.0 GPA or higher. Available to U.S. citizens.

Application Requirements: Application, autobiography, financial need analysis, references, test scores, transcript. *Deadline:* March 1.

Contact: Rev. Donald Barry, Director of Scholarship Aid
Knights of Columbus
PO Box 1670
New Haven, CT 06507-0901
Phone: 203-752-4332
Fax: 203-752-4103

LADIES AUXILIARY OF THE FLEET RESERVE ASSOCIATION http://www.fra.org

ALLIE MAE ODEN MEMORIAL SCHOLARSHIP

Scholarships are given to the children/grandchildren of members of the FRA or LA FRA. Selections are based on financial need, academic standing, character, and leadership qualities. Must be sponsored by a FRA member in good standing.

Award: Scholarship for use in freshman, sophomore, junior, senior, graduate, or postgraduate years; not renewable. *Number:* varies. *Amount:* $1500.

Eligibility Requirements: Applicant must be enrolled or expecting to enroll full-time at a two-year or four-year institution or university. Applicant or parent of applicant must be member of Fleet Reserve Association/Auxiliary. Available to U.S. citizens. Applicant or parent must meet one or more of the following requirements: Coast Guard, Marine Corps, or Navy experience; retired from active duty; disabled or killed as a result of military service; prisoner of war; or missing in action.

Application Requirements: Application, essay, references, transcript. *Deadline:* April 15.

Contact: Ruth Boggs, Scholarship Chairman
Ladies Auxiliary of the Fleet Reserve Association
125 North West Street
Alexandria, VA 22314-2754
Phone: 209-295-4567
E-mail: oboggs@teknett

LADIES AUXILIARY OF THE FLEET RESERVE ASSOCIATION-NATIONAL PRESIDENT'S SCHOLARSHIP

Scholarships are given to children/grandchildren of U.S. Navy, Marine Corps and Coast Guard personnel active Fleet Reserve, Fleet Marine Corps Reserve and Coast Guard Reserve, retired with pay or deceased. Selections are based on financial need, academic standing, character, and leadership qualities. Must be sponsored by a FRA member in good standing.

Award: Scholarship for use in freshman, sophomore, junior, or senior years; not renewable. *Number:* 1. *Amount:* $1500.

Eligibility Requirements: Applicant must be enrolled or expecting to enroll full-time at a four-year institution or university. Applicant or parent of applicant must be member of Fleet Reserve Association/Auxiliary. Available to U.S. citizens. Applicant or parent must meet one or more of the following requirements: Coast Guard, Marine Corps, or Navy experience; retired from active duty; disabled or killed as a result of military service; prisoner of war; or missing in action.

Application Requirements: Application, essay, references, transcript. *Deadline:* April 15.

Contact: Ruth Boggs, National Scholarship Chair
Ladies Auxiliary of the Fleet Reserve Association
PO Box 3459
Pahrump, NV 89041-3459
Phone: 775-751-3309
E-mail: oboggs@teknett

LADIES AUXILIARY OF THE FLEET RESERVE ASSOCIATION SCHOLARSHIP

Scholarships are given to the daughters/granddaughters of U.S. Navy, Marine Corps, and Coast Guard personnel, active Fleet Reserve, Fleet Marine Corps Reserve, and Coast Guard Reserve, retired with pay or deceased. Selections are based on financial need, academic standing, character, and leadership qualities. Must be sponsored by a FRA member in good standing.

Award: Scholarship for use in freshman, sophomore, junior, or senior years; not renewable. *Number:* varies. *Amount:* $1500.

Eligibility Requirements: Applicant must be enrolled or expecting to enroll full-time at a four-year institution or university and female. Applicant or parent of applicant must be member of Fleet Reserve Association/Auxiliary. Available to U.S. citizens. Applicant or parent must meet one or more of the following requirements: Coast Guard, Marine Corps, or Navy experience; retired from active duty; disabled or killed as a result of military service; prisoner of war; or missing in action.

Application Requirements: Application, essay, references, transcript. *Deadline:* April 15.

Contact: Ruth Boggs, National Scholarship Chair
Ladies Auxiliary of the Fleet Reserve Association
PO Box 3459
Pahrump, NV 89041-3459
Phone: 775-751-3309

SAM ROSE MEMORIAL SCHOLARSHIP

Scholarships are given to the child/grandchild of a deceased FRA member or persons who were eligible to be FRA members at the time of death. Selections are based on financial need, academic standing, character, and leadership qualities. Must be sponsored by a FRA member in good standing.

Award: Scholarship for use in freshman, sophomore, junior, or senior years; not renewable. *Number:* varies. *Amount:* $1500.

Eligibility Requirements: Applicant must be enrolled or expecting to enroll full-time at a four-year institution or university. Applicant or parent of applicant must be member of Fleet Reserve Association/Auxiliary. Available to U.S. citizens. Applicant or parent must meet one or more of the following requirements: Coast Guard, Marine Corps, or Navy experience; retired from active duty; disabled or killed as a result of military service; prisoner of war; or missing in action.

Application Requirements: Application, essay, references, transcript. *Deadline:* April 15.

Contact: Ruth Boggs, National Scholarship Chair
Ladies Auxiliary of the Fleet Reserve Association
PO Box 3459
Pahrump, NV 89041-3459
Phone: 775-751-3309
E-mail: oboggs@teknett

LADIES AUXILIARY TO THE VETERANS OF FOREIGN WARS http://www.ladiesauxvfw.org

JUNIOR GIRLS SCHOLARSHIP PROGRAM

One-time awards available to female high school students under age 17 who have been members of Junior Girls Unit of Ladies Auxiliary for one year. Awards based on scholastic aptitude, participation in Junior Girls Unit, and school activities.

Award: Scholarship for use in freshman year; not renewable. *Number:* up to 2. *Amount:* $5000–$10,000.

Eligibility Requirements: Applicant must be high school student; age 13-16; planning to enroll or expecting to enroll full-time at a two-year or four-year or technical institution; single female and must have an interest in leadership. Applicant or parent of applicant must be member of Veterans of Foreign Wars or Auxiliary. Available to U.S. citizens.

Application Requirements: Application, applicant must enter a contest, references, transcript. *Deadline:* March 11.

Contact: Judith Millick, Administrator of Programs
Ladies Auxiliary to the Veterans of Foreign Wars
406 West 34th Street, Tenth Floor
Kansas City, MO 64111
Phone: 816-561-8655 Ext. 19
Fax: 816-931-4753
E-mail: jmillick@ladiesauxvfw.org

LINCOLN COMMUNITY FOUNDATION http://www.lcf.org

P.G. RICHARDSON MASONIC MEMORIAL SCHOLARSHIP

Scholarship for graduating high school seniors who have a family member belonging to Custer Lodge Number 148 A.F. & A.M. Must be Nebraska resident.

Award: Scholarship for use in freshman year; not renewable. *Number:* 1. *Amount:* $500–$2000.

Eligibility Requirements: Applicant must be enrolled or expecting to enroll full-time at a two-year or four-year or technical institution or university and resident of Nebraska. Applicant or parent of applicant must be member of Freemasons. Applicant must have 2.5 GPA or higher. Available to U.S. citizens.

Application Requirements: Application, references, test scores, transcript. *Deadline:* March 6.

Contact: Doug Sadler, Masonic Scholarship Chairman
Lincoln Community Foundation
611 South N Street
Broken Bow, NE 68822

MILITARY ORDER OF THE STARS AND BARS http://www.scv.org

SONS OF CONFEDERATE VETERANS STAND WATIE SCHOLARSHIP

Applicants must be a sophomore, junior, or senior at an accredited degree-granting junior college or four-year college or university. Awards shall be made annually, and the total amount of the scholarship money to be awarded each year shall not exceed $1000. Applicants must be a member in good standing in one of the following organizations: Sons of Confederate Veterans, Children of the Confederacy, or United Daughters of the Confederacy.

Award: Scholarship for use in sophomore, junior, or senior years; not renewable. *Number:* 1–6. *Amount:* $1000.

Eligibility Requirements: Applicant must be enrolled or expecting to enroll full-time at a two-year or four-year institution or university. Applicant or parent of applicant must be member of Children of the Confederacy, Sons of Confederate Veterans, or United Daughters of the Confederacy. Applicant must have 3.0 GPA or higher. Available to U.S. and non-U.S. citizens.

Application Requirements: Application, resume, references, transcript, membership proof. *Deadline:* continuous.

Contact: Mr. M. Dann Hayes, Chair, Scholarship Committee
Military Order of the Stars and Bars
PO Box 59
Columbia, TN 38402-0059
Phone: 641-269-4834
E-mail: iowa_rebel@yahoo.com

MINNESOTA AFL-CIO http://www.mnaflcio.org

BILL PETERSON SCHOLARSHIP

Scholarship available to an union member, spouse, or dependent to attend a postsecondary institution. Must have participated in, or made a donation to the Bill Peterson Golf Tournament. See Web site for additional information: http://www.mnaflcio.org.

Award: Scholarship for use in freshman, sophomore, junior, or senior years; not renewable. *Number:* 20. *Amount:* $1000.

Eligibility Requirements: Applicant must be enrolled or expecting to enroll full-time at a four-year institution or university; resident of Minnesota; studying in Minnesota and must have an interest in golf. Applicant or parent of applicant must be member of AFL-CIO. Available to U.S. citizens.

Application Requirements: Application, essay. *Deadline:* April 30.

Contact: Computer Information Specialist
Minnesota AFL-CIO
175 Aurora Avenue
St. Paul, MN 55103
Phone: 651-227-7647
Fax: 651-227-3801

MARTIN DUFFY ADULT LEARNER SCHOLARSHIP AWARD

Scholarship available for union members affiliated with the Minnesota AFL-CIO or the Minnesota Joint Council 32. May be used at any postsecondary institution in Minnesota. Information available on Web site at http://www.mnaflcio.org.

Award: Scholarship for use in freshman, sophomore, junior, or senior years; not renewable. *Number:* 4. *Amount:* $500.

Eligibility Requirements: Applicant must be enrolled or expecting to enroll full-time at a four-year institution or university; resident of Minnesota and studying in Minnesota. Applicant or parent of applicant must be member of AFL-CIO. Available to U.S. citizens.

Application Requirements: Application. *Deadline:* April 30.

Contact: Computer Information Specialist
Minnesota AFL-CIO
175 Aurora Avenue
St. Paul, MN 55103
Phone: 651-227-7647
Fax: 651-227-3801

MINNESOTA AFL-CIO SCHOLARSHIPS

Applicant must be attending a college or university located in Minnesota. Must have a parent or legal guardian, who has held a one year membership in a local union which is an affiliate of the Minnesota AFL-CIO. Winners are selected by lot. Academic eligibility based on a straight "B" average or better. See Web site: http://www.mnaflcio.org for information and application.

Award: Scholarship for use in freshman year; not renewable. *Number:* up to 5. *Amount:* $1000.

Eligibility Requirements: Applicant must be high school student; planning to enroll or expecting to enroll full-time at a two-year or four-year or technical institution or university and studying in Minnesota. Applicant or parent of applicant must be member of AFL-CIO. Applicant must have 3.0 GPA or higher. Available to U.S. citizens.

Application Requirements: Application, transcript. *Deadline:* April 30.

Contact: Computer Information Specialist
Minnesota AFL-CIO
175 Aurora Avenue
St. Paul, MN 55103
Phone: 651-227-7647
Fax: 651-227-3801

MINNESOTA COMMUNITY FOUNDATION http://www.mncommunityfoundation.org

JOSIP AND AGNETE TEMALI SCHOLARSHIP (BIG BROTHERS/BIG SISTERS)

Scholarship intended to help finance the postsecondary education of a graduating high school senior who: has been an active program participant or volunteer in Big Brothers Big Sisters of the Greater Twin Cities during the two years immediately preceding application; is a United States citizen; and expects to attend an accredited public college, university or technical college in Minnesota as a full-time student upon graduation from high school.

Award: Scholarship for use in freshman year; renewable. *Number:* varies. *Amount:* $4000.

Eligibility Requirements: Applicant must be high school student; planning to enroll or expecting to enroll full- or part-time at a two-year or four-year or technical institution or university; resident of Minnesota and studying in Minnesota. Applicant or parent of applicant must be member of Big Brothers/Big Sisters. Applicant must have 2.5 GPA or higher. Available to U.S. citizens.

Minnesota Community Foundation (continued)

Application Requirements: Application, references, transcript. *Deadline:* April 16.

Contact: Donna Paulson, Administrative Assistant
Minnesota Community Foundation
55 Fifth Street East, Suite 600
St. Paul, MN 55101-1797
Phone: 651-325-4212
E-mail: dkp@mncommunityfoundation.org

NAAS-USA FUND http://www.naas.org

NAAS AWARDS

Merit-based scholarships available for tuition, room, board, books, and academically-related supplies. Applicants must be high school seniors or equivalent home-school seniors. Application periods are September 15 to May 1. Required 2.0 GPA. Electronic applications available to NAAS subscribers; no fees for NAAS subscribers.

Award: Scholarship for use in freshman year; renewable. *Number:* 10–14. *Amount:* $200–$10,000.

Eligibility Requirements: Applicant must be high school student and planning to enroll or expecting to enroll full-time at a four-year institution or university. Applicant or parent of applicant must be member of National Academy of American Scholars. Available to U.S. and non-U.S. citizens.

Application Requirements: Application, self-addressed stamped envelope. *Fee:* $3. *Deadline:* May 1.

Contact: K. France, Program Director
NAAS-USA Fund
2248 Meridian Boulevard, Suite H
Minden, NV 89423
Phone: 800-725-7849
E-mail: staff@naas.org

NATIONAL AGRICULTURAL AVIATION ASSOCIATION http://www.agaviation.org

WNAAA ANNUAL SCHOLARSHIP ESSAY CONTEST

Awards two prizes of $1000 and $2000 to entrants who are members of NAAA or to children, grandchildren, sons-in-law, daughters-in-law, or spouse of any NAAA operator. Must be high school graduate and enrolled in continuing education during the year of entry. Essays judged on content, theme development, clarity, originality, and proper grammar.

Award: Prize for use in freshman, sophomore, junior, senior, graduate, or postgraduate years; not renewable. *Number:* 2. *Amount:* $1000–$2000.

Eligibility Requirements: Applicant must be enrolled or expecting to enroll full- or part-time at a two-year or four-year or technical institution or university. Applicant or parent of applicant must be member of National Agricultural Aviation Association. Available to U.S. citizens.

Application Requirements: Application, applicant must enter a contest, autobiography, essay, photo, one copy of the manuscript. *Deadline:* August 15.

Contact: Scholarship Chairman
National Agricultural Aviation Association
4142 57th Avenue, SE
Medina, ND 58467
Phone: 701-486-3414
E-mail: medfly@daktel.com

NATIONAL ALLIANCE OF POSTAL AND FEDERAL EMPLOYEES (NAPFE) http://www.napfe.com

ASHBY B. CARTER MEMORIAL SCHOLARSHIP FUND FOUNDERS AWARD

Scholarships available to high school seniors. Must be a U.S. citizen. Applicant must be a dependent of NAPFE Labor Union member with a minimum three year membership. Applicant must take the SAT on or before March 1 of the year they apply for award.

Award: Scholarship for use in freshman year; not renewable. *Number:* 3. *Amount:* $2000–$5000.

Eligibility Requirements: Applicant must be high school student; age 17-18 and planning to enroll or expecting to enroll full-time at a four-year institution or university. Applicant or parent of applicant must be member of National Alliance of Postal and Federal Employees. Available to U.S. citizens.

Application Requirements: Application, photo, references, self-addressed stamped envelope, test scores, transcript. *Deadline:* April 1.

Contact: Melissa Jeffries-Stewart, Director
National Alliance of Postal and Federal Employees (NAPFE)
1628 11th Street, NW
Washington, DC 20001
Phone: 202-939-6325 Ext. 239
Fax: 202-939-6389
E-mail: headquarters@napfe.org

NATIONAL ASSOCIATION FOR THE ADVANCEMENT OF COLORED PEOPLE http://www.naacp.org

AGNES JONES JACKSON SCHOLARSHIP

Scholarship for undergraduate and graduate students who have been members of the NAACP for at least one year, or fully paid life members. Undergraduates must have 2.5 GPA and graduate students must have 3.0 GPA.

Award: Scholarship for use in freshman, sophomore, junior, senior, or graduate years; not renewable. *Number:* 1. *Amount:* $1500–$2500.

Eligibility Requirements: Applicant must be American Indian/Alaska Native, Asian/Pacific Islander, Black (non-Hispanic), or Hispanic; age 24 or under and enrolled or expecting to enroll full- or part-time at a two-year or four-year institution or university. Applicant or parent of applicant must be member of National Association for the Advancement of Colored People. Applicant must have 2.5 GPA or higher. Available to U.S. citizens.

Application Requirements: Application, financial need analysis, references, transcript, evidence of NAACP membership. *Deadline:* April 30.

Contact: Victor Goode, Attorney
National Association for the Advancement of Colored People
4805 Mount Hope Drive
Baltimore, MD 21215-3297
Phone: 410-580-5760
Fax: 410-585-1329
E-mail: info@naacp.org

ROY WILKINS SCHOLARSHIP

One-time award for a freshman enrolled full-time in an accredited U.S. college. Must be U.S. citizen and have minimum 2.5 GPA. NAACP membership and participation is preferable.

Award: Scholarship for use in freshman year; not renewable. *Number:* 1. *Amount:* $500–$1000.

Eligibility Requirements: Applicant must be American Indian/Alaska Native, Asian/Pacific Islander, Black (non-Hispanic), or Hispanic; high school student and planning to enroll or expecting to enroll full-time at a two-year or four-year institution or university. Applicant or parent of applicant must be member of National Association for the Advancement of Colored People. Applicant must have 2.5 GPA or higher. Available to U.S. citizens.

Application Requirements: Application, financial need analysis, references, transcript. *Deadline:* April 30.

Contact: Victor Goode, Attorney
National Association for the Advancement of Colored People
4805 Mount Hope Drive
Baltimore, MD 21215-3297
Phone: 410-580-5760
Fax: 410-585-1329
E-mail: info@naacp.org

NATIONAL ASSOCIATION FOR THE SELF-EMPLOYED http://www.nase.org

NASE FUTURE ENTREPRENEUR SCHOLARSHIP

Scholarship of $12,000 given to undergraduate and young micro-business owner in any field of study. May renew for a $4000 scholarship each additional year for up to three consecutive years of undergraduate work for a maximum award of $24,000. Applicant must be a member of NASE.

Award: Scholarship for use in freshman, sophomore, junior, or senior years; not renewable. *Number:* 1. *Amount:* up to $12,000.

Eligibility Requirements: Applicant must be enrolled or expecting to enroll full-time at a four-year institution or university and must have an interest in entrepreneurship. Applicant or parent of applicant must be member of National Association for the Self-Employed. Available to U.S. citizens.

Application Requirements: Application, financial need analysis. *Deadline:* April 25.

Contact: Maureen Petron, Affairs Associate
National Association for the Self-Employed
DFW Airport
PO Box 612067
Dallas, TX 75261-2067
Phone: 202-466-2100
Fax: 202-466-2123
E-mail: mpetron@nase.org

NASE SCHOLARSHIPS

Scholarship of $4000 for high school students or college undergraduates enrolled in full-time program of study. Total number of available awards varies. Must be NASE members between the ages of 16 and 24.

Award: Scholarship for use in freshman, sophomore, junior, or senior years; not renewable. *Number:* varies. *Amount:* $4000.

Eligibility Requirements: Applicant must be age 16-24; enrolled or expecting to enroll full-time at a four-year institution or university and must have an interest in leadership. Applicant or parent of applicant must be member of National Association for the Self-Employed. Available to U.S. citizens.

Application Requirements: Application, financial need analysis, resume, references. *Deadline:* May 15.

Contact: Maureen Petron, Affairs Associate
National Association for the Self-Employed
DFW Airport
PO Box 612067
Dallas, TX 75261-2067
Phone: 202-466-2100
Fax: 202-466-2123
E-mail: mpetron@nase.org

NATIONAL ASSOCIATION OF ENERGY SERVICE COMPANIES http://www.aesc.net

ASSOCIATION OF ENERGY SERVICE COMPANIES SCHOLARSHIP PROGRAM

Applicant must be the legal dependent of an employee of an AESC member company, or an employee. Dependents of company officers are not eligible. Must submit application to local AESC chapter chairman. Application must include ACT or SAT test scores.

Award: Scholarship for use in freshman, sophomore, junior, senior, or graduate years; renewable. *Number:* 150–200. *Amount:* $1000.

Eligibility Requirements: Applicant must be enrolled or expecting to enroll full-time at a two-year or four-year or technical institution or university. Applicant or parent of applicant must be member of Association of Energy Service Companies. Available to U.S. and non-U.S. citizens.

Application Requirements: Application, essay, test scores, transcript. *Deadline:* March 14.

Contact: Nikki James, Administrative Assistant
National Association of Energy Service Companies
10200 Richmond Avenue, Suite 275
Houston, TX 77042
Phone: 800-692-0771
Fax: 713-781-7542
E-mail: njames@aesc.net

NATIONAL ASSOCIATION OF LETTER CARRIERS http://www.nalc.org

COSTAS G. LEMONOPOULOS SCHOLARSHIP

Scholarships to children of NALC members attending public, four-year colleges or universities supported by the state of Florida or St. Petersburg Junior College. Scholarships are renewable one time.

Award: Scholarship for use in freshman, sophomore, junior, or senior years; renewable. *Number:* 1–20. *Amount:* varies.

Eligibility Requirements: Applicant must be enrolled or expecting to enroll full-time at a two-year or four-year institution or university and studying in Florida. Applicant or parent of applicant must be member of National Association of Letter Carriers. Available to U.S. citizens.

Application Requirements: Application, references, transcript. *Deadline:* June 1.

Contact: Ann Porch, Membership Committee
National Association of Letter Carriers
100 Indiana Avenue, NW
Washington, DC 20001-2144
Phone: 202-393-4695
Fax: 202-737-1540
E-mail: nalcinf@nalc.org

JOHN T. DONELON SCHOLARSHIP

Scholarship for sons and daughters of NALC members who are high school seniors when making application. The $1000 scholarship will be renewable for four years.

Award: Scholarship for use in freshman year; renewable. *Number:* 5. *Amount:* $1000.

Eligibility Requirements: Applicant must be high school student and planning to enroll or expecting to enroll full-time at a four-year institution or university. Applicant or parent of applicant must be member of National Association of Letter Carriers. Available to U.S. citizens.

Application Requirements: Application, references, transcript. *Deadline:* December 31.

Contact: Ann Porch, Membership Committee
National Association of Letter Carriers
100 Indiana Avenue, NW
Washington, DC 20001-2144
Phone: 202-393-4695
Fax: 202-737-1540
E-mail: nalcinf@nalc.org

National Association of Letter Carriers (continued)

UNION PLUS SCHOLARSHIP PROGRAM

One-time cash award available for undergraduate and graduate study programs. Scholarship ranges from $500 to $4000. Three awards are granted. Must be children of members of NALC.

Award: Scholarship for use in freshman year; not renewable. *Number:* 3. *Amount:* $500–$4000.

Eligibility Requirements: Applicant must be high school student and planning to enroll or expecting to enroll full-time at a four-year institution or university. Applicant or parent of applicant must be member of National Association of Letter Carriers. Available to U.S. citizens.

Application Requirements: Application, references, transcript. *Deadline:* January 31.

Contact: Ann Porch, Membership Committee
National Association of Letter Carriers
100 Indiana Avenue, NW
Washington, DC 20001-2144
Phone: 202-393-4695
Fax: 202-737-1540
E-mail: nalcinf@nalc.org

WILLIAM C. DOHERTY SCHOLARSHIP FUND

Five scholarships of $4000 each are awarded to children of members in NALC. Renewable for three consecutive years thereafter providing the winner maintains satisfactory grades. Applicant must be a high school senior when making application.

Award: Scholarship for use in freshman year; renewable. *Number:* 5. *Amount:* $4000.

Eligibility Requirements: Applicant must be high school student and planning to enroll or expecting to enroll full-time at a four-year institution or university. Applicant or parent of applicant must be member of National Association of Letter Carriers. Available to U.S. citizens.

Application Requirements: Application, test scores, transcript. *Deadline:* December 31.

Contact: Ann Porch, Membership Committee
National Association of Letter Carriers
100 Indiana Avenue, NW
Washington, DC 20001-2144
Phone: 202-393-4695
Fax: 202-737-1540
E-mail: nalcinf@nalc.org

NATIONAL ASSOCIATION OF SECONDARY SCHOOL PRINCIPALS http://www.nhs.us

NATIONAL HONOR SOCIETY SCHOLARSHIPS

One-time award to high school seniors who are National Honor Society members for use at an accredited two- or four-year college or university in the U.S. Application fee $6. Contact school counselor or NHS chapter adviser. Minimum 3.0 GPA.

Award: Scholarship for use in freshman year; not renewable. *Number:* 200. *Amount:* $1000–$10,000.

Eligibility Requirements: Applicant must be high school student and planning to enroll or expecting to enroll full-time at a two-year or four-year institution or university. Applicant or parent of applicant must be member of National Honor Society. Applicant must have 3.0 GPA or higher. Available to U.S. and non-U.S. citizens.

Application Requirements: Application, essay, references, test scores, transcript. *Fee:* $6. *Deadline:* January 18.

Contact: Wanda Carroll, Program Manager
National Association of Secondary School Principals
1904 Association Drive
Reston, VA 20191-1537
Phone: 703-860-0200
Fax: 703-476-5432
E-mail: carrollw@principals.org

NATIONAL BETA CLUB http://www.betaclub.org

NATIONAL BETA CLUB SCHOLARSHIP

Applicant must be in twelfth grade and a member of the National Beta Club. Must be nominated by school chapter of the National Beta Club, therefore, applications will not be sent to the individual students. Renewable and nonrenewable awards available. Contact school Beta Club sponsor for more information.

Award: Scholarship for use in freshman year; renewable. *Number:* 213. *Amount:* $1000–$15,000.

Eligibility Requirements: Applicant must be high school student and planning to enroll or expecting to enroll full-time at a two-year or four-year institution or university. Applicant or parent of applicant must be member of National Beta Club. Available to U.S. citizens.

Application Requirements: Application, essay, references, test scores, transcript. *Fee:* $10. *Deadline:* December 10.

Contact: Joan Burnett, Administrative Assistant
National Beta Club
151 Beta Club Way
Spartanburg, SC 29306-3012
Phone: 864-583-4553
E-mail: jburnett@betaclub.org

NATIONAL BICYCLE LEAGUE (NBL) http://www.nbl.org

BOB WARNICKE MEMORIAL SCHOLARSHIP PROGRAM

Scholarship assists students and their families in meeting the costs of undergraduate or trade school education. Applicant must be a high school senior, graduate or attending a postsecondary school at the time of application, or accepted and plan to attend an accredited postsecondary school as a full-time or part-time student for the complete award year. Must be an active member or official of the National Bicycle League.

Award: Scholarship for use in freshman year; not renewable. *Number:* varies. *Amount:* varies.

Eligibility Requirements: Applicant must be enrolled or expecting to enroll full- or part-time at a two-year or four-year or technical institution or university. Applicant or parent of applicant must be member of National Bicycle League. Available to U.S. citizens.

Application Requirements: Application, photo, references, transcript, acceptance letter from the school. *Deadline:* December 15.

Contact: Scholarship Committee
National Bicycle League (NBL)
3958 Brown Park Drive, Suite D
Hilliard, OH 43026
Phone: 800-886-2691

NATIONAL FFA ORGANIZATION http://www.ffa.org

NATIONAL FFA COLLEGE AND VOCATIONAL/TECHNICAL SCHOOL SCHOLARSHIP PROGRAM

Scholarship to high school seniors planning to enroll in a full-time course of study at an accredited vocational/technical school, college or university. A smaller number of awards are available to currently enrolled undergraduates. Most of the awards require that the applicant be an FFA member. However some awards are available to high school seniors who are not FFA members.

Award: Scholarship for use in freshman year; not renewable. *Number:* 1750. *Amount:* $1000–$15,000.

Eligibility Requirements: Applicant must be enrolled or expecting to enroll full-time at a four-year institution or university. Applicant or parent of applicant must be member of Future Farmers of America. Available to U.S. citizens.

Application Requirements: Application. *Deadline:* February 15.

Contact: Scholarship Program Coordinator
National FFA Organization
6060 FFA Drive, PO Box 68960
Indianapolis, IN 46268-0960
Phone: 317-802-4321
Fax: 317-802-5321
E-mail: scholarships@ffa.org

NATIONAL FOSTER PARENT ASSOCIATION http://www.nfpaonline.org

NATIONAL FOSTER PARENT ASSOCIATION YOUTH SCHOLARSHIP

Award for high school senior who will be entering first year of college, comparable education, or training program. Six $1000 awards, three for foster children currently in foster care with an NFPA member family, and one each for birth and adopted children of foster parents. NFPA family membership required ($35 membership fee).

Award: Scholarship for use in freshman year; not renewable. *Number:* 6. *Amount:* $1000.

Eligibility Requirements: Applicant must be high school student and planning to enroll or expecting to enroll full- or part-time at a two-year or four-year or technical institution or university. Applicant or parent of applicant must be member of National Foster Parent Association. Available to U.S. citizens.

Application Requirements: Application, autobiography, essay, references, test scores, transcript. *Deadline:* March 31.

Contact: Karen Jorgenson, Executive Director
National Foster Parent Association
7512 Stanich Avenue, Suite 6
Gig Harbor, WA 98335
Phone: 253-853-4000
Fax: 253-853-4001
E-mail: info@nfpaonline.org

NATIONAL FRATERNAL SOCIETY OF THE DEAF http://www.nfsd.com

NATIONAL FRATERNAL SOCIETY OF THE DEAF SCHOLARSHIPS

Provides scholarship to cover room and board, tuition and/or fees. Applicant or parent must be member of the NFSD for one full year. Applicant must be in a postsecondary program or ready to enter one as a full-time student.

Award: Scholarship for use in freshman, sophomore, junior, senior, graduate, or postgraduate years; not renewable. *Number:* 5–10. *Amount:* $1000.

Eligibility Requirements: Applicant must be enrolled or expecting to enroll full-time at a two-year or four-year institution or university. Applicant or parent of applicant must be member of National Fraternal Society of the Deaf. Available to U.S. citizens.

Application Requirements: Application, photo, references, transcript. *Deadline:* July 1.

Contact: Scholarship Information
National Fraternal Society of the Deaf
1118 South Sixth Street
Springfield, IL 62703
Phone: 217-789-7429
Fax: 217-789-7489
E-mail: thefrat@nfsd.com

NATIONAL JUNIOR ANGUS ASSOCIATION http://www.angusfoundation.org

ANGUS FOUNDATION SCHOLARSHIPS

Applicants must have at one time been a National Junior Angus Association member and currently be a junior, regular or life member of the association. Must have applied to undergraduate studies in any field. Applicants must have a minimum 2.0 GPA. See Web site for further information and to download application.

Award: Scholarship for use in freshman, sophomore, junior, or senior years; not renewable. *Number:* 20. *Amount:* $1000–$5000.

Eligibility Requirements: Applicant must be age 25 or under and enrolled or expecting to enroll full-time at a two-year or four-year or technical institution or university. Applicant or parent of applicant must be member of American Angus Association. Available to U.S. citizens.

Application Requirements: Application, references, transcript. *Deadline:* May 1.

Contact: Milford Jenkins, President
National Junior Angus Association
3201 Frederick Avenue
St. Joseph, MO 64506
Phone: 816-383-5100
Fax: 816-233-9703
E-mail: mjenkins@angusfoundation.org

NATIONAL ORDER OF OMEGA http://www.orderofomega.org

FOUNDERS SCHOLARSHIP

Scholarship of $1000 available to juniors or seniors displaying leadership and service to their Order of Omega chapter.

Award: Scholarship for use in junior or senior years; not renewable. *Number:* 1. *Amount:* $1000.

Eligibility Requirements: Applicant must be enrolled or expecting to enroll full-time at a four-year institution or university and must have an interest in leadership. Applicant or parent of applicant must be member of Order of Omega. Available to U.S. and Canadian citizens.

Application Requirements: Application, essay, photo, references, transcript. *Deadline:* November 16.

Contact: Scholarship Committee
National Order of Omega
300 East Border Street
Arlington, TX 76010-1656

NATIONAL RIFLE ASSOCIATION http://www.nrafoundation.org

JEANNE E. BRAY MEMORIAL SCHOLARSHIP PROGRAM

Renewable scholarship of $2000 for a maximum of four years for undergraduate students enrolled full-time in accredited colleges or universities. Must have a minimum GPA of 2.5.

Award: Scholarship for use in freshman, sophomore, junior, or senior years; renewable. *Number:* 1. *Amount:* $2000.

Eligibility Requirements: Applicant must be enrolled or expecting to enroll full-time at a two-year or four-year institution or university. Applicant or parent of applicant must be member of National Rifle Association. Applicant must have 2.5 GPA or higher. Available to U.S. citizens.

Application Requirements: Application, essay, references, test scores, transcript, proof of acceptance to college or university, referral on letterhead signed by agency official documenting qualifying parent. *Deadline:* November 15.

Contact: Sandy Elkin, Grants Manager
National Rifle Association
11250 Waples Mill Road
Fairfax, VA 22030
Phone: 703-267-1131
Fax: 703-267-1083
E-mail: selkin@nrahqn.org

NATIONAL SOCIETY DAUGHTERS OF THE AMERICAN REVOLUTION http://www.dar.org

NATIONAL SOCIETY DAUGHTERS OF THE AMERICAN REVOLUTION LILLIAN AND ARTHUR DUNN SCHOLARSHIP

A $2000 scholarship awarded for up to four years to well-qualified, deserving sons and daughters of members of the NSDAR. Outstanding recipients will be considered for an additional period of up to four years of study. Must include DAR member number.

Award: Scholarship for use in freshman, sophomore, junior, or senior years; renewable. *Number:* varies. *Amount:* $2000.

Eligibility Requirements: Applicant must be enrolled or expecting to enroll full-time at a four-year institution or university. Applicant or parent of applicant must be member of Daughters of the American Revolution. Available to U.S. citizens.

National Society Daughters of the American Revolution (continued)

Application Requirements: Application, financial need analysis, references, self-addressed stamped envelope, transcript, letter of sponsorship. *Deadline:* February 15.

Contact: Eric Weisz, Manager, Office of the Reporter General
National Society Daughters of the American Revolution
1776 D Street, NW
Washington, DC 20006-5303
Phone: 202-628-1776
Fax: 202-879-3348
E-mail: nsdarscholarships@dar.org

NATIONAL SOCIETY OF COLLEGIATE SCHOLARS (NSCS) http://www.nscs.org

NSCS INTEGRITY SCHOLARSHIP

Three $1000 scholarships, one each to the three members who demonstrate a true commitment to integrity through a series of short answer questions describing a time when their integrity has been challenged. Must be working towards an undergraduate or graduate degree.

Award: Scholarship for use in freshman, sophomore, junior, senior, or graduate years; not renewable. *Number:* 3. *Amount:* $1000.

Eligibility Requirements: Applicant must be enrolled or expecting to enroll full- or part-time at a four-year institution or university. Applicant or parent of applicant must be member of National Society of Collegiate Scholars. Available to U.S. and non-U.S. citizens.

Application Requirements: Application. *Deadline:* March 21.

Contact: Stephen Loflin, Executive Director
National Society of Collegiate Scholars (NSCS)
11 Dupont Circle NW, Suite 650
Washington, DC 20036
Phone: 202-965-9000
Fax: 800-784-1015
E-mail: nscs@nscs.org

NSCS MERIT AWARD

Fifty merit awards to outstanding new NSCS members around the country. Student is chosen based upon how they exemplify the mission of NSCS.

Award: Scholarship for use in freshman, sophomore, junior, senior, graduate, or postgraduate years; not renewable. *Number:* 50. *Amount:* $1000.

Eligibility Requirements: Applicant must be enrolled or expecting to enroll full- or part-time at a two-year or four-year or technical institution or university. Applicant or parent of applicant must be member of National Society of Collegiate Scholars. Available to U.S. and non-U.S. citizens.

Application Requirements: Application. *Deadline:* July 31.

Contact: Stephen Loflin, Executive Director
National Society of Collegiate Scholars (NSCS)
11 Dupont Circle NW, Suite 650
Washington, DC 20036
Phone: 202-965-9000
Fax: 800-784-1015
E-mail: nscs@nscs.org

NSCS SCHOLAR ABROAD SCHOLARSHIP

Scholarship for active NSCS member who has been accepted to and enrolled in an accredited study abroad program. One $5000 scholarship is awarded each fall and spring semester and one $2500 scholarship is awarded for the summer term.

Award: Scholarship for use in freshman, sophomore, junior, senior, graduate, or postgraduate years; not renewable. *Number:* 2. *Amount:* $2500–$5000.

Eligibility Requirements: Applicant must be enrolled or expecting to enroll full-time at a two-year or four-year or technical institution or university. Applicant or parent of applicant must be member of National Society of Collegiate Scholars. Available to U.S. and non-U.S. citizens.

Application Requirements: Application. *Deadline:* May 6.

Contact: Stephen Loflin, Executive Director
National Society of Collegiate Scholars (NSCS)
11 Dupont Circle NW, Suite 650
Washington, DC 20036
Phone: 202-965-9000
Fax: 800-784-1015
E-mail: nscs@nscs.org

NATIONAL SOCIETY OF HIGH SCHOOL SCHOLARS http://www.nshss.org

ABERCROMBIE & FITCH GLOBAL DIVERSITY & LEADERSHIP SCHOLAR AWARDS

Ten scholarships of $1000 to high school seniors who are members of NSHSS. Must submit written response to the question posed by A&F regarding diversity and inclusion.

Award: Scholarship for use in freshman year; not renewable. *Number:* 10. *Amount:* $1000.

Eligibility Requirements: Applicant must be high school student and planning to enroll or expecting to enroll full-time at a four-year institution or university. Applicant or parent of applicant must be member of National Society of High School Scholars. Available to U.S. and non-U.S. citizens.

Application Requirements: Application, photo, resume, references, transcript. *Deadline:* April 30.

Contact: Dr. Susan Thurman, Scholarship Director
National Society of High School Scholars
1936 N Druid Hills Road
Atlanta, GA 30319
Phone: 866-343-1800
E-mail: susan.thurman@nshss.org

CLAES NOBEL ACADEMIC SCHOLARSHIPS FOR NSHSS MEMBERS

Scholarship of $5000 to current high school seniors who are members of NSHSS. Award is based upon community service, leadership, academic performance, and school and extracurricular activities. Must complete an online application form. Deadline varies.

Award: Scholarship for use in freshman year; not renewable. *Number:* 5–10. *Amount:* $5000.

Eligibility Requirements: Applicant must be high school student; planning to enroll or expecting to enroll full- or part-time at a four-year institution or university and must have an interest in leadership. Applicant or parent of applicant must be member of National Society of High School Scholars. Applicant or parent of applicant must have employment or volunteer experience in community service. Available to U.S. and non-U.S. citizens.

Application Requirements: Application, essay, transcript. *Deadline:* varies.

Contact: Susan Thurman, Scholarship Director
National Society of High School Scholars
1936 North Druid Hills Road
Atlanta, GA 30319
Phone: 866-343-1800
Fax: 866-282-4634
E-mail: information@nshss.org

GRIFFITH COLLEGE SCHOLARS SCHOLARSHIPS FOR NSHSS MEMBERS

Five $1000 scholarships awarded to NSHSS members who are part- and full-time students. May be used at any college or university.

Award: Scholarship for use in freshman year; not renewable. *Number:* 5. *Amount:* $1000.

Eligibility Requirements: Applicant must be high school student and planning to enroll or expecting to enroll full- or part-time at a four-year institution or university. Applicant or parent of applicant must be member of National Society of High School Scholars. Available to U.S. and non-U.S. citizens.

Application Requirements: Application, photo, resume, references, transcript. *Deadline:* April 30.

Contact: Susan Thurman, Scholarship Director
National Society of High School Scholars
1936 North Druid Hills Road
Atlanta, GA 30319
Phone: 866-343-1800
Fax: 866-282-4634
E-mail: information@nshss.org

KAPLAN TEST PREP AND ADMISSION SCHOLARSHIPS FOR NSHSS MEMBERS

Two $1000 scholarships awarded to students for use at a college of their choice. Available for students enrolled in both full or part-time study.

Award: Scholarship for use in freshman year; not renewable. *Number:* 2. *Amount:* $1000.

Eligibility Requirements: Applicant must be high school student and planning to enroll or expecting to enroll full- or part-time at a four-year institution or university. Applicant or parent of applicant must be member of National Society of High School Scholars. Available to U.S. and non-U.S. citizens.

Application Requirements: Application, photo, resume, references, transcript. *Deadline:* April 30.

Contact: Susan Thurman, Scholarship Director
National Society of High School Scholars
1936 North Druid Hills Road
Atlanta, GA 30319
Phone: 866-343-1800
Fax: 866-282-4634
E-mail: information@nshss.org

NATIONAL SCHOLAR AWARDS FOR NSHSS MEMBERS

Scholarship of $1000 for undergraduate study. Applicant must be a member of NSHSS.

Award: Scholarship for use in freshman year; not renewable. *Number:* 10–30. *Amount:* $1000.

Eligibility Requirements: Applicant must be high school student and planning to enroll or expecting to enroll full- or part-time at a two-year or four-year or technical institution or university. Applicant or parent of applicant must be member of National Society of High School Scholars. Available to U.S. and non-U.S. citizens.

Application Requirements: Application, photo, resume, references, transcript. *Deadline:* November 30.

Contact: Susan Thurman, Scholarship Director
National Society of High School Scholars
1936 North Druid Hills Road
Atlanta, GA 30319
Phone: 866-343-1800
Fax: 866-282-4634
E-mail: information@nshss.org

PRESIDENTIAL CLASSROOM PUBLIC SERVICE SCHOLARSHIPS FOR NSHSS MEMBERS

Award of $750 to be used by the applicant for college expenses at any postsecondary institution of the recipients choice. Applicant must be a graduating high school senior and member of NSHSS.

Award: Scholarship for use in freshman year; not renewable. *Number:* 1. *Amount:* $750.

Eligibility Requirements: Applicant must be high school student and planning to enroll or expecting to enroll full- or part-time at a four-year institution or university. Applicant or parent of applicant must be member of National Society of High School Scholars. Available to U.S. and non-U.S. citizens.

Application Requirements: Application, essay, photo, resume, transcript. *Deadline:* August 1.

Contact: Susan Thurman, Scholarship Director
National Society of High School Scholars
1936 North Druid Hills Road
Atlanta, GA 30319
Phone: 866-343-1800
Fax: 866-282-4634
E-mail: information@nshss.org

NATIONAL UNION OF PUBLIC AND GENERAL EMPLOYEES http://www.nupge.ca

SCHOLARSHIP FOR ABORIGINAL CANADIANS

Award for aboriginal Canadian students who plan to enter the first year of a Canadian college or university and who are children or foster children of a member of the NUPGE. Must write a 750 to 1000 words essay on: "The importance of quality public services in enhancing the quality of life of Aboriginal Canadians".

Award: Scholarship for use in freshman year; not renewable. *Number:* 1. *Amount:* $1500.

Eligibility Requirements: Applicant must be of Canadian heritage and Canadian citizen; American Indian/Alaska Native; high school student; planning to enroll or expecting to enroll full-time at a four-year institution or university and studying in Alberta, British Columbia, Manitoba, New Brunswick, Newfoundland, North West Territories, Nova Scotia, Ontario, Prince Edward Island, Saskatchewan, or Yukon. Applicant or parent of applicant must be member of National Union of Public and General Employees.

Application Requirements: Application, applicant must enter a contest, essay. *Deadline:* June 30.

Contact: Louise Trepanier, Scholarship Committee
National Union of Public and General Employees
15 Auriga Drive
Nepean, ON K2E 1B7
Canada
Phone: 613-228-9800
Fax: 613-228-9801
E-mail: ltrepanier@nupge.ca

SCHOLARSHIP FOR VISIBLE MINORITIES

Award for first year Canadian students who are, by race or color, in a visible minority and who are children or foster children of a member of the NUPGE. Must write a 750 to 1000 words essay on: "The importance of quality public services in enhancing the quality of life of visible minorities".

Award: Scholarship for use in freshman year; not renewable. *Number:* 1. *Amount:* $1500.

Eligibility Requirements: Applicant must be Canadian citizen; American Indian/Alaska Native, Asian/Pacific Islander, Black (non-Hispanic), or Hispanic; high school student; planning to enroll or expecting to enroll full-time at a four-year institution or university and studying in Alberta, British Columbia, Manitoba, New Brunswick, Newfoundland, North West Territories, Nova Scotia, Ontario, Prince Edward Island, Saskatchewan, or Yukon. Applicant or parent of applicant must be member of National Union of Public and General Employees.

Application Requirements: Application, applicant must enter a contest, essay. *Deadline:* June 30.

Contact: Louise Trepanier, Scholarship Committee
National Union of Public and General Employees
15 Auriga Drive
Nepean, ON K2E 1B7
Canada
Phone: 613-228-9800
Fax: 613-228-9801
E-mail: ltrepanier@nupge.ca

TERRY FOX MEMORIAL SCHOLARSHIP

Award for Canadian students with disabilities who plan to enter the first year of a Canadian college or university and who are the children or foster children of a member of the NUPGE. Must write a 750 to 1000 words essay on: "The importance of quality public services in enhancing the quality of life of people with disabilities".

Award: Scholarship for use in freshman year; not renewable. *Number:* 1. *Amount:* $1500.

Eligibility Requirements: Applicant must be Canadian citizen; high school student; planning to enroll or expecting to enroll full-time at a four-year institution or university and studying in Alberta, British Columbia, Manitoba, New Brunswick, Newfoundland, North West Territories, Nova Scotia, Ontario, Prince Edward Island, Saskatchewan, or Yukon. Applicant or parent of applicant must be member of National Union of Public and General Employees. Applicant must be hearing impaired, learning disabled, physically disabled, or visually impaired.

National Union of Public and General Employees (continued)

Application Requirements: Application, applicant must enter a contest, essay. *Deadline:* June 30.

Contact: Louise Trepanier, Scholarship Committee
National Union of Public and General Employees
15 Auriga Drive
Nepean, ON K2E 1B7
Canada
Phone: 613-228-9800
Fax: 613-228-9801
E-mail: ltrepanier@nupge.ca

TOMMY DOUGLAS SCHOLARSHIP

Award for first year students at a Canadian college or university who are children or foster children of members of NUPGE. Must write an essay on the topic: "How Tommy Douglas contributed to making Canada a more just and equitable society".

Award: Scholarship for use in freshman year; not renewable. *Number:* 1. *Amount:* $1500.

Eligibility Requirements: Applicant must be Canadian citizen; high school student; planning to enroll or expecting to enroll full-time at a four-year institution or university and studying in Alberta, British Columbia, Manitoba, New Brunswick, Newfoundland, North West Territories, Nova Scotia, Ontario, Prince Edward Island, Saskatchewan, or Yukon. Applicant or parent of applicant must be member of National Union of Public and General Employees.

Application Requirements: Application, applicant must enter a contest, essay. *Deadline:* June 30.

Contact: Louise Trepanier, Scholarship Committee
National Union of Public and General Employees
15 Auriga Drive
Nepean, ON K2E 1B7
Canada
Phone: 613-228-9800
Fax: 613-228-9801
E-mail: ltrepanier@nupge.ca

NEW YORK STATE GRANGE http://www.nysgrange.com

CAROLINE KARK AWARD

Award available to a Grange member who is preparing for a career working with the deaf, or a deaf individual who is furthering his or her education beyond high school. The recipient must be a New York State resident. The award is based on funds available.

Award: Scholarship for use in freshman year; not renewable. *Number:* varies. *Amount:* varies.

Eligibility Requirements: Applicant must be high school student; planning to enroll or expecting to enroll full- or part-time at a four-year institution or university and resident of New York. Applicant or parent of applicant must be member of Grange Association. Applicant must be hearing impaired. Available to U.S. citizens.

Application Requirements: Application. *Deadline:* April 15.

Contact: Program Manager
New York State Grange
100 Grange Place
Cortland, NY 13045
Phone: 607-756-7553
Fax: 607-756-7757
E-mail: nysgrange@nysgrange.com

SUSAN W. FREESTONE EDUCATION AWARD

Grants for members of Junior Grange and Subordinate Grange in New York State. Students must enroll in an approved two or four-year college in New York State. Second grants available with reapplication.

Award: Scholarship for use in freshman year; renewable. *Number:* 1. *Amount:* $1000.

Eligibility Requirements: Applicant must be high school student; planning to enroll or expecting to enroll full-time at a two-year or four-year institution; resident of New York and studying in New York. Applicant or parent of applicant must be member of Grange Association. Applicant must have 2.5 GPA or higher. Available to U.S. citizens.

Application Requirements: Application, financial need analysis, references, self-addressed stamped envelope, transcript. *Deadline:* April 15.

Contact: Scholarship Committee
New York State Grange
100 Grange Place
Cortland, NY 13045
Phone: 607-756-7553
Fax: 607-756-7757
E-mail: nysgrange@nysgrange.com

NEW YORK STATE SOCIETY OF PROFESSIONAL ENGINEERS http://www.nysspe.org

NYSSPE-PAST OFFICERS' SCHOLARSHIP

Scholarship of $1000 is awarded to the child of a NYSSPE member and is based on academic achievement. Minimum GPA of 3.5.

Award: Scholarship for use in freshman, sophomore, junior, or senior years; not renewable. *Number:* 1. *Amount:* $1000.

Eligibility Requirements: Applicant must be enrolled or expecting to enroll full-time at a four-year institution or university. Applicant or parent of applicant must be member of New York State Society of Professional Engineers. Applicant must have 3.5 GPA or higher. Available to U.S. citizens.

Application Requirements: Application, essay, references, test scores, transcript. *Deadline:* December 1.

Contact: Director of Programs
New York State Society of Professional Engineers
RPI Technology Park, 385 Jordan Road
Troy, NY 12180
Phone: 518-283-7490
E-mail: jamiller@nysspe.org

NON COMMISSIONED OFFICERS ASSOCIATION (NCOA) http://www.ncoausa.org

BETSY ROSS EDUCATIONAL FUND

Awards to assist in defraying the cost of taking a course at a local business or technical school. Must be NCOA auxiliary division members who wish to prepare themselves for employment or improve on employable skills.

Award: Grant for use in freshman year; not renewable. *Number:* 24. *Amount:* $250.

Eligibility Requirements: Applicant must be high school student and planning to enroll or expecting to enroll full- or part-time at a technical institution. Applicant or parent of applicant must be member of Non Commissioned Officers Association. Available to U.S. and non-U.S. citizens.

Application Requirements: Application. *Deadline:* varies.

Contact: Tina Kish, Scholarship Fund Administrator
Non Commissioned Officers Association (NCOA)
10635 IH 35 North
San Antonio, TX 78233
Phone: 210-653-6161 Ext. 261
Fax: 210-637-3337
E-mail: tkish@ncoausa.org

NON-COMMISSIONED OFFICERS ASSOCIATION SCHOLARSHIPS

Awards for children and spouses of members of the association. Must be full-time students. Children of members must be under the age of 25 to receive initial grant. Applicants must maintain 3.0 GPA for renewal.

Award: Scholarship for use in freshman, sophomore, junior, or senior years; renewable. *Number:* 16. *Amount:* $900–$1000.

Eligibility Requirements: Applicant must be enrolled or expecting to enroll full-time at a four-year institution or university. Applicant or parent of applicant must be member of Non Commissioned Officers Association. Applicant must have 3.0 GPA or higher. Available to U.S. and non-U.S. citizens. Applicant or parent must meet one or more of the following requirements: Army experience; retired from active duty; disabled or killed as a result of military service; prisoner of war; or missing in action.

Application Requirements: Application, autobiography, essay, references, test scores, transcript. *Deadline:* March 31.

Contact: Tina Kish, Scholarship Fund Administrator
Non Commissioned Officers Association (NCOA)
10635 IH 35 North
San Antonio, TX 78233
Phone: 210-653-6161 Ext. 261
Fax: 210-637-3337
E-mail: tkish@ncoausa.org

NORTHEASTERN LOGGERS' ASSOCIATION INC. http://www.northernlogger.com

NORTHEASTERN LOGGERS' ASSOCIATION SCHOLARSHIPS

Scholarships available to those whose family belongs to the Northeastern Loggers' Association or whose family member is an employee of the Industrial and Associate Members of the Northeastern Loggers' Association. Must submit paper on topic of "What it means to grow up in the forest industry."

Award: Scholarship for use in freshman, sophomore, junior, or senior years; not renewable. *Number:* 8. *Amount:* $500–$1000.

Eligibility Requirements: Applicant must be enrolled or expecting to enroll full-time at a two-year or four-year or technical institution or university. Applicant or parent of applicant must be member of Northeastern Loggers Association. Available to U.S. and non-U.S. citizens.

Application Requirements: Application, applicant must enter a contest, essay, transcript. *Deadline:* March 31.

Contact: Mona Lincoln, Director, Training and Safety
Northeastern Loggers' Association Inc.
PO Box 69
Old Forge, NY 13420-0069
Phone: 315-369-3078
Fax: 315-369-3736
E-mail: mona@northernlogger.com

NORTH EAST ROOFING EDUCATIONAL FOUNDATION http://www.nerca.org

NORTH EAST ROOFING EDUCATIONAL FOUNDATION SCHOLARSHIP

Applicants must be a member of NERCA, their employees, or their respective immediate family. Immediate family is defined as self, spouse, or child. The child may be natural, legally adopted or a stepchild. Also must be a high school senior or graduate who plans to enroll in a full-time undergraduate course of study at an accredited two-year or four-year college, university, or vocational-technical school.

Award: Scholarship for use in freshman, sophomore, junior, or senior years; not renewable. *Number:* 11. *Amount:* up to $2000.

Eligibility Requirements: Applicant must be enrolled or expecting to enroll full-time at a two-year or four-year or technical institution or university. Applicant or parent of applicant must be member of North East Roofing Contractors Association. Available to U.S. and Canadian citizens.

Application Requirements: Application, references, self-addressed stamped envelope, transcript. *Deadline:* May 1.

Contact: Patsy Sweeney, Clerk
North East Roofing Educational Foundation
150 Grossman Drive Street, Suite 313
Braintree, MA 02184
Phone: 781-849-0555
Fax: 781-849-3223
E-mail: info@nerca.org

OFFICE AND PROFESSIONAL EMPLOYEES INTERNATIONAL UNION http://www.opeiu.org

OFFICE AND PROFESSIONAL EMPLOYEES INTERNATIONAL UNION HOWARD COUGHLIN MEMORIAL SCHOLARSHIP FUND

Scholarship of twelve full-time awards of $6000 and six part-time awards of $2400 is given to undergraduate students. Applicants should be a member or associate member of the Union.

Award: Scholarship for use in freshman, sophomore, junior, or senior years; not renewable. *Number:* 18. *Amount:* $2400–$6000.

Eligibility Requirements: Applicant must be enrolled or expecting to enroll full- or part-time at a two-year or four-year or technical institution or university. Applicant or parent of applicant must be member of Office and Professional Employees International Union. Available to U.S. citizens.

Application Requirements: Application, transcript, SAT/CAT scores. *Deadline:* March 31.

Contact: Nancy Wohlforth, Secretary and Treasurer
Office and Professional Employees International Union
1660 L Street, NW, Suite 801
Washington, DC 20036
Phone: 202-393-4464
Fax: 202-347-0649
E-mail: opeiu@opeiudc.org

OHIO CIVIL SERVICE EMPLOYEES ASSOCIATION http://www.ocsea.org

LES BEST SCHOLARSHIP

Scholarships worth up to $1000 will be awarded to eligible union members, spouses and their dependent children. For more details see Web site: http://www.ocsea.org.

Award: Scholarship for use in freshman, sophomore, junior, or senior years; not renewable. *Number:* 9. *Amount:* $250–$1000.

Eligibility Requirements: Applicant must be high school student; planning to enroll or expecting to enroll full- or part-time at a two-year or four-year or technical institution or university and resident of Ohio. Applicant or parent of applicant must be member of Ohio Civil Service Employee Association. Available to U.S. citizens.

Application Requirements: Application, essay, references, transcript, proof of enrollment. *Deadline:* April 30.

Contact: Customer Service Representative
Ohio Civil Service Employees Association
390 Worthington Road, Suite A
Westerville, OH 43082-8331
Phone: 614-865-4740
Fax: 614-865-4777

OHIO 4-H http://www.ohio4h.org

ALL AMERICAN YOUTH HORSE SHOW FOUNDATION 4-H SCHOLARSHIP

Scholarship for high school seniors and current 4-H horse members planning to enroll in the fall at any accredited postsecondary institution in any course of study. One award of $1500 will be granted.

Award: Scholarship for use in freshman year; not renewable. *Number:* 1. *Amount:* $1500.

Eligibility Requirements: Applicant must be high school student and planning to enroll or expecting to enroll full- or part-time at a two-year or four-year institution or university. Applicant or parent of applicant must be member of National 4-H. Available to U.S. citizens.

Application Requirements: Application, essay, resume, references, transcript. *Deadline:* November 8.

Contact: Ryan Schmiesing, Interim Assistant Director
Ohio 4-H
4-H Centre, 2201 Fred Taylor Drive
Columbus, OH 43210
Phone: 614-292-4444
Fax: 614-292-5937
E-mail: schmiesing.3@cfaes.osu.edu

KATHRYN BEICH 4-H SCHOLARSHIP

One $500 scholarship is awarded. Applicants must be high school seniors and current 4-H members planning to enroll in the fall at any accredited postsecondary institution in any course of study.

Award: Scholarship for use in freshman year; not renewable. *Number:* 1. *Amount:* $500.

Eligibility Requirements: Applicant must be high school student and planning to enroll or expecting to enroll full- or part-time at a two-year or four-year institution or university. Applicant or parent of applicant must be member of National 4-H. Available to U.S. citizens.

Ohio 4-H (continued)

Application Requirements: Application, essay, resume, references, transcript. *Deadline:* November 8.

Contact: Allen Auck, Extension Associate-Events and Activities
Ohio 4-H
4-H Centre, 2201 Fred Taylor Drive
Columbus, OH 43210
Phone: 614-292-8148
Fax: 614-292-5937
E-mail: auck.1@osu.edu

MARY E. BORDER OHIO SCHOLARSHIP

Applicants must be high school seniors and current 4-H members planning to enroll in the fall at any accredited postsecondary institution in any course of study. Two $1000 scholarships are awarded.

Award: Scholarship for use in freshman year; not renewable. *Number:* 2. *Amount:* $1000.

Eligibility Requirements: Applicant must be high school student and planning to enroll or expecting to enroll full- or part-time at a two-year or four-year institution or university. Applicant or parent of applicant must be member of National 4-H. Available to U.S. citizens.

Application Requirements: Application, essay, resume, references, transcript. *Deadline:* November 8.

Contact: Ryan Schmiesing, Interim Assistant Director
Ohio 4-H
4-H Centre, 2201 Fred Taylor Drive
Columbus, OH 43210
Phone: 614-292-4444
Fax: 614-292-5937
E-mail: schmiesing.3@cfaes.osu.edu

OKLAHOMA ALUMNI & ASSOCIATES OF FHA, HERO AND FCCLA INC. http://www.okfccla.net

OKLAHOMA ALUMNI & ASSOCIATES OF FHA, HERO AND FCCLA INC. SCHOLARSHIP

One-time award for FCCLA members who will be pursuing a postsecondary education. Must be a resident of Oklahoma. Scholarship value is $1000. Two scholarships are granted.

Award: Scholarship for use in freshman year; not renewable. *Number:* 2. *Amount:* $1000.

Eligibility Requirements: Applicant must be high school student; planning to enroll or expecting to enroll full-time at a two-year or four-year or technical institution or university and resident of Oklahoma. Applicant or parent of applicant must be member of Family, Career and Community Leaders of America. Applicant must have 3.0 GPA or higher. Available to U.S. citizens.

Application Requirements: Application, essay, references, transcript. *Deadline:* March 1.

Contact: Denise Morris, State FCCLA Adviser
Oklahoma Alumni & Associates of FHA, HERO and FCCLA Inc.
1500 West Seventh Avenue
Stillwater, OK 74074
Phone: 405-743-5467
Fax: 405-743-6809
E-mail: dmorr@okcareertech.org

OREGON STUDENT ASSISTANCE COMMISSION http://www.osac.state.or.us

AFSCME: AMERICAN FEDERATION OF STATE, COUNTY, AND MUNICIPAL EMPLOYEES LOCAL 1724 SCHOLARSHIP

Award for active, laid-off, retired, or disabled members in good standing or spouses (including life partners and their children), natural children, stepchildren, or grandchildren of active, laid-off retired, disabled, or deceased members in good standing. Qualifying members must have been active in AFSCME Local 1724 one year or more as of March 1 of the year in which the scholarship application is filed, or a member one year or more preceding the date of layoff, death, disability.

Award: Scholarship for use in freshman, sophomore, junior, senior, or graduate years; not renewable. *Number:* varies. *Amount:* varies.

Eligibility Requirements: Applicant must be enrolled or expecting to enroll full- or part-time at a four-year institution or university and resident of Oregon. Applicant or parent of applicant must be member of American Federation of State, County, and Municipal Employees. Available to U.S. citizens.

Application Requirements: Application, essay, financial need analysis, references, transcript, activity chart. *Deadline:* March 1.

Contact: Director of Grant Programs
Oregon Student Assistance Commission
1500 Valley River Drive, Suite 100
Eugene, OR 97401-7020
Phone: 800-452-8807 Ext. 7395

AFSCME: AMERICAN FEDERATION OF STATE, COUNTY, AND MUNICIPAL EMPLOYEES LOCAL 75 SCHOLARSHIP

One-time award for active, laid-off, retired, or disabled members in good standing or spouses (including life partners and their children), natural children, or grandchildren of active, laid-off, retired, disabled, or deceased members in good standing. Qualifying members must have been active in AFSCME Local 1724 one year or more as of the March 1 scholarship deadline or have been a member one year or more preceding the date of layoff, death, disability, or retirement.

Award: Scholarship for use in freshman, sophomore, junior, senior, or graduate years; not renewable. *Number:* varies. *Amount:* varies.

Eligibility Requirements: Applicant must be enrolled or expecting to enroll full- or part-time at a two-year or four-year institution or university and resident of Oregon. Applicant or parent of applicant must be member of American Federation of State, County, and Municipal Employees. Available to U.S. citizens.

Application Requirements: Application, essay, financial need analysis, transcript, activity chart. *Deadline:* March 1.

Contact: Director of Grant Programs
Oregon Student Assistance Commission
1500 Valley River Drive, Suite 100
Eugene, OR 97401-7020
Phone: 800-452-8807 Ext. 7395

INTERNATIONAL BROTHERHOOD OF ELECTRICAL WORKERS LOCAL 280 SCHOLARSHIP

One-time award available for children or grandchildren of active or retired members of IBEW Local 280. Must be a resident of Oregon. Not based on financial need.

Award: Scholarship for use in freshman, sophomore, junior, or senior years; not renewable. *Number:* up to 4. *Amount:* varies.

Eligibility Requirements: Applicant must be enrolled or expecting to enroll full-time at a four-year institution and resident of Oregon. Applicant or parent of applicant must be member of International Brotherhood of Electrical Workers. Available to U.S. citizens.

Application Requirements: Application, essay, transcript, activities chart. *Deadline:* March 1.

Contact: Director of Grant Programs
Oregon Student Assistance Commission
1500 Valley River Drive, Suite 100
Eugene, OR 97401-7020
Phone: 800-452-8807 Ext. 7395

INTERNATIONAL UNION OF OPERATING ENGINEERS LOCAL 701 SCHOLARSHIP

One-time award available for graduating high school seniors who are children of Local 701 members. Not based on financial need.

Award: Scholarship for use in freshman year; not renewable. *Number:* up to 2. *Amount:* varies.

Eligibility Requirements: Applicant must be enrolled or expecting to enroll full-time at a four-year institution and resident of Oregon. Applicant or parent of applicant must be member of International Union of Operating Engineers. Available to U.S. citizens.

Application Requirements: Application, essay, transcript, activities chart. *Deadline:* March 1.

Contact: Director of Grant Programs
Oregon Student Assistance Commission
1500 Valley River Drive, Suite 100
Eugene, OR 97401-7020
Phone: 800-452-8807 Ext. 7395

NORTHWEST AUTOMATIC VENDING ASSOCIATION SCHOLARSHIP

One-time award to graduating high school seniors who are either children (natural, adopted, or step) or grandchildren of members or associate members of Northwest Automatic Vending Association.

Award: Scholarship for use in freshman year; not renewable. *Number:* varies. *Amount:* varies.

Eligibility Requirements: Applicant must be high school student and planning to enroll or expecting to enroll full-time at a four-year institution or university. Applicant or parent of applicant must be member of Northwest Automatic Vending Association. Available to U.S. citizens.

Application Requirements: Application, essay, financial need analysis, transcript, activities chart. *Deadline:* March 1.

Contact: Director of Grant Programs
Oregon Student Assistance Commission
1500 Valley River Drive, Suite 100
Eugene, OR 97401-7020
Phone: 800-452-8807 Ext. 7395

OREGON AFL-CIO SCHOLARSHIP

One-time award for graduating Oregon high school seniors. Must write essay. Preference given to applicants from union families. Visit Web site http://www.osac.state.or.us for details.

Award: Scholarship for use in freshman year; not renewable. *Number:* varies. *Amount:* varies.

Eligibility Requirements: Applicant must be high school student; planning to enroll or expecting to enroll full- or part-time at a two-year or four-year or technical institution or university and resident of Oregon. Applicant or parent of applicant must be member of AFL-CIO. Available to U.S. citizens.

Application Requirements: Application, essay, financial need analysis, test scores, transcript, activity chart. *Deadline:* March 1.

Contact: Director of Grant Programs
Oregon Student Assistance Commission
1500 Valley River Drive, Suite 100
Eugene, OR 97401-7020
Phone: 800-452-8807 Ext. 7395

OREGON METRO FEDERAL CREDIT UNION SCHOLARSHIP

One-time award. Scholarship available to graduates of Oregon high schools who are Oregon Metro Federal Credit Union members. Preference given to graduating high school senior and applicant who plans to attend an Oregon college.

Award: Scholarship for use in freshman year; not renewable. *Number:* 5. *Amount:* varies.

Eligibility Requirements: Applicant must be enrolled or expecting to enroll full-time at a four-year institution; resident of Oregon and studying in Oregon. Applicant or parent of applicant must be member of Oregon Metro Federal Credit Union. Available to U.S. citizens.

Application Requirements: Application, essay, financial need analysis, references, transcript, activity chart, name of credit union in place of work-site in membership section. *Deadline:* March 1.

Contact: Director of Grant Programs
Oregon Student Assistance Commission
1500 Valley River Drive, Suite 100
Eugene, OR 97401-7020
Phone: 800-452-8807 Ext. 7395

OREGON PUBLISHING COMPANY/HILLIARD SCHOLARSHIP

Available for graduating high school seniors who are members of the Prospective Gents Club of the Bridge Builders organization. Must be in the process of completing requirements for Bridge Builders "Rites of Passage Program." Automatically renewable upon volunteer service to Bridge Builders Program.

Award: Scholarship for use in freshman year; renewable. *Number:* varies. *Amount:* varies.

Eligibility Requirements: Applicant must be high school student; planning to enroll or expecting to enroll full-time at a four-year institution and resident of Oregon. Available to U.S. citizens.

Application Requirements: Application, essay, financial need analysis, references, transcript, activity chart. *Deadline:* March 1.

Contact: Director of Grant Programs
Oregon Student Assistance Commission
1500 Valley River Drive, Suite 100
Eugene, OR 97401-7020
Phone: 800-452-8807 Ext. 7395

OREGON STATE FISCAL ASSOCIATION SCHOLARSHIP

One-time award for OSFA members or their children. Member must enroll at least half-time and must study public administration, finance, economics, or related fields. Children of members must enroll full-time and may enter any program of study. Must be enrolled in an Oregon college.

Award: Scholarship for use in freshman, sophomore, junior, senior, or graduate years; renewable. *Number:* varies. *Amount:* varies.

Eligibility Requirements: Applicant must be enrolled or expecting to enroll full- or part-time at a two-year or four-year institution; resident of Oregon and studying in Oregon. Applicant or parent of applicant must be member of Oregon State Fiscal Association. Available to U.S. citizens.

Application Requirements: Application, essay, financial need analysis, references, transcript, activity chart. *Deadline:* March 1.

Contact: Director of Grant Programs
Oregon Student Assistance Commission
1500 Valley River Drive, Suite 100
Eugene, OR 97401-7020
Phone: 800-452-8807 Ext. 7395

TEAMSTERS CLYDE C. CROSBY/JOSEPH M. EDGAR MEMORIAL SCHOLARSHIP

One-time scholarship available for Oregon resident who is a graduating high school senior with a minimum 3.0 cumulative GPA and is a child, or dependent stepchild of an active, retired, disabled, or deceased member of local union affiliated with Teamsters 37. Member must have been active for at least one year. Award may be received for a maximum of twelve quarters.

Award: Scholarship for use in freshman, sophomore, junior, or senior years; renewable. *Number:* varies. *Amount:* varies.

Eligibility Requirements: Applicant must be high school student; planning to enroll or expecting to enroll full-time at a four-year institution and resident of Oregon. Applicant or parent of applicant must be member of Teamsters. Applicant must have 3.0 GPA or higher. Available to U.S. citizens.

Application Requirements: Application, essay, financial need analysis, transcript, activity chart. *Deadline:* March 1.

Contact: Director of Grant Programs
Oregon Student Assistance Commission
1500 Valley River Drive, Suite 100
Eugene, OR 97401-7020
Phone: 800-452-8807 Ext. 7395

TEAMSTERS COUNCIL 37 FEDERAL CREDIT UNION SCHOLARSHIP

One-time award for members or dependents of Council 37 credit union who are active in local affiliated with the Joint Council of Teamsters 37 for one year. Applicant must have a cumulative GPA between 2.0 and 3.0 and enroll at least half-time. Additional essay topic: "The Importance of Preserving the Right to Strike in a Free Enterprise System".

Award: Scholarship for use in freshman, sophomore, junior, or senior years; not renewable. *Number:* varies. *Amount:* varies.

Eligibility Requirements: Applicant must be enrolled or expecting to enroll full- or part-time at a two-year or four-year institution and resident of Oregon. Applicant or parent of applicant must be member of Teamsters. Available to U.S. citizens.

Oregon Student Assistance Commission (continued)

Application Requirements: Application, essay, financial need analysis, references, transcript, activity chart. *Deadline:* March 1.

Contact: Director of Grant Programs
Oregon Student Assistance Commission
1500 Valley River Drive, Suite 100
Eugene, OR 97401-7020
Phone: 800-452-8807 Ext. 7395

TEAMSTERS LOCAL 305 SCHOLARSHIP

Graduating high school seniors who are children or dependent stepchildren of active, retired, disabled, or deceased members of Local 305 of the Joint Council of Teamsters 37. Members must have been active at least one year. Not based on financial need.

Award: Scholarship for use in freshman, sophomore, junior, or senior years; renewable. *Number:* 2. *Amount:* varies.

Eligibility Requirements: Applicant must be enrolled or expecting to enroll full-time at a four-year institution and resident of Oregon. Applicant or parent of applicant must be member of Teamsters. Available to U.S. citizens.

Application Requirements: Application, essay, transcript, activities chart. *Deadline:* March 1.

Contact: Director of Grant Programs
Oregon Student Assistance Commission
1500 Valley River Drive, Suite 100
Eugene, OR 97401-7020
Phone: 800-452-8807 Ext. 7395

PENNSYLVANIA AFL-CIO http://www.paaflcio.org

PA AFL-CIO UNIONISM IN AMERICA ESSAY CONTEST

Contest consists of three categories: high school seniors, students currently attending an accredited postsecondary institution, and affiliated members attending an accredited postsecondary institution. Must be a U.S. citizen.

Award: Prize for use in freshman, sophomore, junior, or senior years; not renewable. *Number:* 9. *Amount:* $500–$2000.

Eligibility Requirements: Applicant must be enrolled or expecting to enroll full-time at a two-year or four-year or technical institution or university. Applicant or parent of applicant must be member of AFL-CIO. Available to U.S. citizens.

Application Requirements: Application, applicant must enter a contest, references, hard copy, CD copy of essay. *Deadline:* January 31.

Contact: Carl Dillinger, Education Director
Pennsylvania AFL-CIO
231 State Street
Harrisburg, PA 17101-1110
Phone: 717-231-2843
Fax: 717-238-8541
E-mail: cdillinger@paaflcio.org

PENNSYLVANIA FEDERATION OF DEMOCRATIC WOMEN INC. http://www.pfdw.org

PENNSYLVANIA FEDERATION OF DEMOCRATIC WOMEN INC. ANNUAL SCHOLARSHIP AWARDS

Award of $1000 for any female resident of Pennsylvania who is a junior at an accredited college or university and is a registered Democrat. Applicants must possess a Democratic Party family background or be an active participant in activities of the Democratic Party.

Award: Scholarship for use in senior year; not renewable. *Number:* 5–6. *Amount:* $1000.

Eligibility Requirements: Applicant must be enrolled or expecting to enroll full-time at a four-year institution or university; female and resident of Pennsylvania. Applicant or parent of applicant must be member of Democratic Party. Available to U.S. citizens.

Application Requirements: Application, essay, financial need analysis, references, transcript. *Deadline:* May 1.

Contact: Bonita Hannis, Scholarship Chair
Pennsylvania Federation of Democratic Women Inc.
36 Betts Lane
Lock Haven, PA 17745
Phone: 570-769-7175
E-mail: behannis@kcnet.org

PENNSYLVANIA YOUTH FOUNDATION http://www.pagrandlodge.org/pmyf

PENNSYLVANIA MASONIC YOUTH FOUNDATION EDUCATIONAL ENDOWMENT FUND SCHOLARSHIPS

Grants for children, stepchildren, grandchildren, siblings, or dependents of members in good standing of a Pennsylvania Masonic Lodge, or members in good standing of a PA Masonic-sponsored youth group. Applicants must be high school graduates or high school seniors pursuing a college education. Minimum GPA 3.0.

Award: Grant for use in freshman, sophomore, junior, or senior years; renewable. *Number:* varies. *Amount:* $1000–$3000.

Eligibility Requirements: Applicant must be enrolled or expecting to enroll full-time at a two-year or four-year or technical institution or university. Applicant or parent of applicant must be member of Freemasons. Applicant must have 3.0 GPA or higher. Available to U.S. and non-U.S. citizens.

Application Requirements: Application, essay, financial need analysis, transcript, proof of relationship to a PA Masonic or membership in a PA Masonic-sponsored youth group. *Deadline:* March 15.

Contact: Amy Nace, Executive Assistant
Pennsylvania Youth Foundation
1244 Bainbridge Road
Elizabethtown, PA 17022-9423
Phone: 717-367-1536 Ext. 2
Fax: 717-367-0616
E-mail: pmyf@pagrandlodge.org

PHILIPINO-AMERICAN ASSOCIATION OF NEW ENGLAND http://www.pamas.org

PAMAS RESTRICTED SCHOLARSHIP AWARD

Award of $500 for any sons or daughters of PAMAS members who are currently active in PAMAS projects and activities. Must be of Filipino descent, a resident of New England, a high school senior at the time of award, and have college acceptance letter from accredited institution. Minimum of 3.3 GPA required. For application details visit: http://www.pamas.org.

Award: Scholarship for use in freshman year; not renewable. *Number:* 1. *Amount:* $500.

Eligibility Requirements: Applicant must be Asian/Pacific Islander; high school student; planning to enroll or expecting to enroll full-time at a four-year institution or university and resident of Connecticut, Maine, Massachusetts, New Hampshire, Rhode Island, or Vermont. Applicant or parent of applicant must be member of Philipino-American Association. Available to U.S. citizens.

Application Requirements: Application, essay, references, transcript, college acceptance letter. *Deadline:* May 31.

Contact: Amanda Kalb, First Vice President
Philipino-American Association of New England
Quincy Post Office
PO Box 690372
Quincy, MA 02269-0372
Phone: 617-471-3513
E-mail: balic2ss@comcast.net

PHI SIGMA KAPPA INTERNATIONAL HEADQUARTERS http://www.phisigmakappa.org

WENDEROTH UNDERGRADUATE SCHOLARSHIP

Available to sophomores and juniors on the basis of academic criteria. Must submit an essay and letter of recommendation along with the application.

Award: Scholarship for use in sophomore or junior years; not renewable. *Number:* 1–4. *Amount:* $1750–$4000.

Eligibility Requirements: Applicant must be enrolled or expecting to enroll full-time at a four-year institution or university. Applicant or parent of applicant must be member of Phi Sigma Kappa. Available to U.S. and non-U.S. citizens.

Application Requirements: Application, essay, photo, resume, references, transcript. *Deadline:* January 31.

Contact: Michael Carey, Executive Director
Phi Sigma Kappa International Headquarters
2925 East 96th Street
Indianapolis, IN 46240
Phone: 317-573-5420
Fax: 317-573-5430
E-mail: michael@phisigmakappa.org

ZETA SCHOLARSHIP

Scholarships are available following a generous gift to the Phi Sigma Kappa Foundation from the Zeta Alumni Association. Phi Sig or a child of a Phi Sig having minimum 3.0 GPA are eligible to apply.

Award: Scholarship for use in freshman, sophomore, junior, senior, or graduate years; not renewable. *Number:* 2. *Amount:* $2500.

Eligibility Requirements: Applicant must be enrolled or expecting to enroll full-time at a four-year institution or university. Applicant or parent of applicant must be member of Phi Sigma Kappa. Applicant must have 3.0 GPA or higher. Available to U.S. citizens.

Application Requirements: Application, photo, resume, references, test scores, transcript. *Deadline:* January 31.

Contact: Scholarship Program Coordinator
Phi Sigma Kappa International Headquarters
2925 East 96th Street
Indianapolis, IN 46240
Phone: 317-573-5420
Fax: 317-573-5430

PHI SIGMA PI NATIONAL HONOR FRATERNITY http://www.phisigmapi.org

RICHARD CECIL TODD AND CLAUDA PENNOCK TODD TRIPOD SCHOLARSHIP

Scholarship to promote the future academic opportunity of brothers (members) of the fraternity, who have excelled in embodying the ideals of scholarship, leadership, and fellowship. One-time award for full-time student, sophomore level or higher, with minimum 3.0 GPA.

Award: Scholarship for use in sophomore, junior, or senior years; not renewable. *Number:* 1. *Amount:* up to $1500.

Eligibility Requirements: Applicant must be enrolled or expecting to enroll full-time at a two-year or four-year or technical institution or university and must have an interest in leadership. Applicant must have 3.0 GPA or higher. Available to U.S. and non-U.S. citizens.

Application Requirements: Application, autobiography, essay, references, transcript. *Deadline:* April 15.

Contact: Suzanne Schaffer, Executive Director
Phi Sigma Pi National Honor Fraternity
2119 Ambassador Circle
Lancaster, PA 17603
Phone: 717-299-4710
Fax: 717-390-3054
E-mail: schaffer@phisigmapi.org

POLISH NATIONAL ALLIANCE http://www.pna-znp.org

POLISH NATIONAL ALLIANCE SCHOLARSHIP AWARD

The program is awarded to Polish National Alliance members only. Must be a member for at least three years. Must currently be enrolled full-time in an accredited college as an undergraduate sophomore, junior or senior. Applicants with 3.0 GPA or greater preferred, but not required. Application URL: http://www.pna-znp.org/content/educationaldept/scholarshipapp.pdf.

Award: Scholarship for use in sophomore, junior, or senior years; renewable. *Number:* 250. *Amount:* $500.

Eligibility Requirements: Applicant must be of Polish heritage and enrolled or expecting to enroll full-time at a four-year institution or university. Applicant or parent of applicant must be member of Polish National Alliance. Applicant must have 3.0 GPA or higher. Available to U.S. citizens.

Application Requirements: Photo, test scores, transcript, completed applications signed by the lodge president or secretary. *Deadline:* April 15.

Contact: Teresa N. Abick, Chairperson, Educational Department
Polish National Alliance
6100 North Cicero Avenue
Chicago, IL 60646
Phone: 773-286-0500
Fax: 773-286-4937
E-mail: teresa.abick@pna-znp.org

PONY OF THE AMERICAS CLUB http://www.poac.org

PONY OF THE AMERICAS SCHOLARSHIP

Two to four renewable awards that may be used for any year or any institution but must be for full-time undergraduate study. Application and transcript required. Award restricted to those who have interest in animal or agricultural competition and active involvement in Pony of the Americas.

Award: Scholarship for use in freshman, sophomore, junior, or senior years; renewable. *Number:* 2–4. *Amount:* $500–$1000.

Eligibility Requirements: Applicant must be enrolled or expecting to enroll full-time at a two-year or four-year or technical institution or university and must have an interest in animal/agricultural competition. Applicant or parent of applicant must be member of Pony of the Americas Club. Available to U.S. and non-U.S. citizens.

Application Requirements: Application, autobiography, essay, references, transcript. *Deadline:* June 1.

Contact: Lynda Corn, Scholarship Administrator
Pony of the Americas Club
3828 South Emerson Avenue
Indianapolis, IN 46203
Phone: 317-788-0107
Fax: 317-788-8974
E-mail: lyndac@poac.org

PROFESSIONAL BOWLERS ASSOCIATION http://www.pba.com

PROFESSIONAL BOWLERS ASSOCIATION BILLY WELU MEMORIAL SCHOLARSHIP

One-time award available to a currently enrolled student who demonstrates outstanding academic and bowling achievement. Must be a member of USBC. Must have minimum 2.5 GPA.

Award: Scholarship for use in freshman, sophomore, junior, or senior years; not renewable. *Number:* 1. *Amount:* $1000.

Eligibility Requirements: Applicant must be enrolled or expecting to enroll full- or part-time at a four-year institution or university and must have an interest in bowling. Applicant or parent of applicant must be member of Young American Bowling Alliance. Applicant must have 2.5 GPA or higher. Available to U.S. citizens.

Application Requirements: Application, essay, references, transcript. *Deadline:* May 31.

Contact: Scholarship Administrator
Professional Bowlers Association
719 Second Avenue, Suite 701
Seattle, WA 98104
Phone: 206-332-9688
Fax: 206-332-9722

PROFESSIONAL HORSEMEN'S SCHOLARSHIP FUND INC. http://www.nationalpha.com

PROFESSIONAL HORSEMEN'S SCHOLARSHIP FUND

Scholarship provides financial assistance from a fund established for children of professional members or professional members of more than two years who are enrolled in an approved school for the advancement of their education beyond the elementary level.

Award: Scholarship for use in freshman, sophomore, junior, or senior years; renewable. *Number:* 10–15. *Amount:* $1000–$1500.

Eligibility Requirements: Applicant must be enrolled or expecting to enroll full-time at a two-year or four-year or technical institution or university. Applicant or parent of applicant must be member of Professional Horsemen Association. Available to U.S. citizens.

Professional Horsemen's Scholarship Fund Inc. (continued)

Application Requirements: Application, autobiography, financial need analysis, references, transcript. *Deadline:* July 1.

Contact: Mrs. Frank Grenci, Scholarship Committee
Professional Horsemen's Scholarship Fund Inc.
20 Via del Corso
Palm Beach Gardens, FL 33418
Phone: 561-694-6893
Fax: 561-694-2254
E-mail: foxhill33@aol.com

PROJECT BEST SCHOLARSHIP FUND http://www.projectbest.com

PROJECT BEST SCHOLARSHIP

One-time award of $1000 to $2000 for employees or children or spouses of employees working for a company or labor union in the construction industry that is affiliated with Project BEST. Must be residents of West Virginia, Pennsylvania, or Ohio and attend a West Virginia or Ohio postsecondary institution. Must be U.S. citizens.

Award: Scholarship for use in freshman, sophomore, junior, senior, or graduate years; renewable. *Number:* 11–22. *Amount:* $1000–$2000.

Eligibility Requirements: Applicant must be enrolled or expecting to enroll full-time at a two-year or four-year institution or university; resident of Ohio, Pennsylvania, or West Virginia and studying in Ohio or West Virginia. Applicant or parent of applicant must be member of AFL-CIO. Applicant or parent of applicant must have employment or volunteer experience in construction. Available to U.S. citizens.

Application Requirements: Application. *Deadline:* continuous.

Contact: Mary Jo Klempa, Director
Project BEST Scholarship Fund
21 Armory Drive
Wheeling, WV 26003
Phone: 304-242-0520
Fax: 304-242-7261
E-mail: best2003@swave.net

PUEBLO OF ISLETA, DEPARTMENT OF EDUCATION http://www.isletapueblo.com

HIGHER EDUCATION SUPPLEMENTAL SCHOLARSHIP ISLETA PUEBLO HIGHER EDUCATION DEPARTMENT

Applicants must be students seeking a postsecondary degree. The degree granting institution must be a nationally accredited vocational or postsecondary institution offering a certificate, associate, bachelors, master's or doctorate degree. Enrolled tribal members of the Isleta Pueblo may apply for this scholarship if they also apply for additional scholarships from different sources. Deadlines: April 1 for summer, November 1 for spring and July 1 for fall.

Award: Scholarship for use in freshman, sophomore, junior, senior, graduate, or postgraduate years; renewable. *Number:* varies. *Amount:* varies.

Eligibility Requirements: Applicant must be American Indian/Alaska Native and enrolled or expecting to enroll full- or part-time at a two-year or four-year or technical institution or university. Applicant or parent of applicant must be member of Ice Skating Institute. Available to U.S. citizens.

Application Requirements: Application, financial need analysis, transcript, certificate of Indian blood, class schedule. *Deadline:* varies.

Contact: Higher Education Director
Pueblo of Isleta, Department of Education
PO Box 1270
Isleta, NM 87022
Phone: 505-869-2680
Fax: 505-869-7690
E-mail: isletahighered@yahoo.com

RAILWAY SUPPLY INSTITUTE http://www.rsiweb.org

RSI UNDERGRADUATE SCHOLARSHIP PROGRAM

Scholarship available to a full-time student enrolled in a four- or five-year program leading to a bachelor's degree. Applicants must be 22 years old or under and be the dependant son, daughter, grandson or granddaughter of a railroad employee, who is a member of one of the mechanical associations listed on the Web site. For application and association list go to http://www.rsiweb.org/scholarship.

Award: Scholarship for use in sophomore, junior, or senior years; not renewable. *Number:* 4. *Amount:* up to $3000.

Eligibility Requirements: Applicant must be age 22 or under and enrolled or expecting to enroll full-time at a four-year institution or university. Applicant or parent of applicant must be member of Mutual Benefit Society. Applicant or parent of applicant must have employment or volunteer experience in railroad industry. Available to U.S. and Canadian citizens.

Application Requirements: Application, essay, resume, references, transcript. *Deadline:* March 17.

Contact: Howard Tom, Executive Director
Railway Supply Institute
29W 140 Butterfield Road, Suite 103-A
Warrenville, IL 60555
Phone: 630-393-0106
Fax: 630-393-0108
E-mail: rsupplya@aol.com

RECORDING FOR THE BLIND & DYSLEXIC http://www.rfbd.org

MARION HUBER LEARNING THROUGH LISTENING AWARDS

Awards presented to RFB&D members who are high school seniors with learning disabilities, in recognition of extraordinary leadership, scholarship, enterprise and service to others. Must have minimum 3.0 GPA.

Award: Prize for use in freshman year; not renewable. *Number:* 6. *Amount:* $2000–$6000.

Eligibility Requirements: Applicant must be high school student; planning to enroll or expecting to enroll full-time at a two-year or four-year institution and must have an interest in leadership. Applicant or parent of applicant must be member of Recording for the Blind and Dyslexic. Applicant or parent of applicant must have employment or volunteer experience in community service. Applicant must be learning disabled. Applicant must have 3.0 GPA or higher. Available to U.S. citizens.

Application Requirements: Application, essay, references, transcript. *Deadline:* March 3.

Contact: Julie Haggith, Strategic Communications Department
Recording for the Blind & Dyslexic
20 Roszel Road
Princeton, NJ 08540
Phone: 609-520-8044
Fax: 609-520-7990
E-mail: jhaggith@rfbd.org

MARY P. OENSLAGER SCHOLASTIC ACHIEVEMENT AWARDS

Award presented to RFB&D members who are college seniors and blind or visually impaired, in recognition of extraordinary leadership, scholarship, enterprise, and service to others.

Award: Prize for use in senior or graduate years; not renewable. *Number:* up to 9. *Amount:* $1000–$6000.

Eligibility Requirements: Applicant must be enrolled or expecting to enroll full-time at a four-year institution or university and must have an interest in leadership. Applicant or parent of applicant must be member of Recording for the Blind and Dyslexic. Applicant or parent of applicant must have employment or volunteer experience in community service. Applicant must be visually impaired. Applicant must have 3.0 GPA or higher. Available to U.S. citizens.

Application Requirements: Application, essay, references, transcript. *Deadline:* April 14.

Contact: Julie Haggith, Strategic Communications Department
Recording for the Blind & Dyslexic
20 Roszel Road
Princeton, NJ 08540
Phone: 609-520-8044
Fax: 609-520-7990
E-mail: jhaggith@rfbd.org

RED ANGUS ASSOCIATION OF AMERICA http://www.redangus.org

DEE SONSTEGARD MEMORIAL SCHOLARSHIP

Scholarship of $500 given to active members of the National Junior Red Angus Association. Must be high school seniors or college underclassmen.

Award: Scholarship for use in freshman or sophomore years; not renewable. *Number:* 2. *Amount:* $500.

Eligibility Requirements: Applicant must be enrolled or expecting to enroll full-time at a two-year or four-year institution or university. Applicant or parent of applicant must be member of National Junior Red Angus Association. Available to U.S. citizens.

Application Requirements: Application, photo, references, transcript. *Deadline:* March 31.

Contact: Betty Grimshaw, Association Administrative Director
Red Angus Association of America
4201 North Interstate 35
Denton, TX 76207-3415
Phone: 940-387-3502
Fax: 940-383-4036
E-mail: betty@redangus.org

FARM AND RANCH CONNECTION SCHOLARSHIP

Scholarship of $500 given to active members of the National Junior Red Angus Association. Must be high school seniors or college underclassmen.

Award: Scholarship for use in freshman or sophomore years; not renewable. *Number:* 1. *Amount:* $500.

Eligibility Requirements: Applicant must be enrolled or expecting to enroll full-time at a two-year or four-year institution or university. Applicant or parent of applicant must be member of National Junior Red Angus Association. Available to U.S. citizens.

Application Requirements: Application, photo, references, transcript. *Deadline:* March 31.

Contact: Betty Grimshaw, Association Administrative Director
Red Angus Association of America
4201 North Interstate 35
Denton, TX 76207-3415
Phone: 940-387-3502
Fax: 940-383-4036
E-mail: betty@redangus.org

4 RAAA/JUNIOR RED ANGUS SCHOLARSHIP

Scholarship of $500 given to active members of the National Junior Red Angus Association. Must be high school seniors or college underclassmen.

Award: Scholarship for use in freshman or sophomore years; not renewable. *Number:* 2. *Amount:* $500.

Eligibility Requirements: Applicant must be enrolled or expecting to enroll full-time at a two-year or four-year institution or university. Applicant or parent of applicant must be member of National Junior Red Angus Association. Available to U.S. citizens.

Application Requirements: Application, photo, references, transcript. *Deadline:* March 31.

Contact: Betty Grimshaw, Association Administrative Director
Red Angus Association of America
4201 North Interstate 35
Denton, TX 76207-3415
Phone: 940-387-3502
Fax: 940-383-4036
E-mail: betty@redangus.org

LEONARD A. LORENZEN MEMORIAL SCHOLARSHIP

Scholarship of $500 given to active members of the National Junior Red Angus Association. Must be high school seniors or college underclassmen.

Award: Scholarship for use in freshman or sophomore years; not renewable. *Number:* 2. *Amount:* $500.

Eligibility Requirements: Applicant must be enrolled or expecting to enroll full-time at a two-year or four-year institution or university. Applicant or parent of applicant must be member of National Junior Red Angus Association. Available to U.S. citizens.

Application Requirements: Application, photo, references, transcript. *Deadline:* March 31.

Contact: Betty Grimshaw, Association Administrative Director
Red Angus Association of America
4201 North Interstate 35
Denton, TX 76207-3415
Phone: 940-387-3502
Fax: 940-383-4036
E-mail: betty@redangus.org

RESERVE OFFICERS ASSOCIATION http://www.roa.org

HENRY J. REILLY MEMORIAL SCHOLARSHIP-HIGH SCHOOL SENIORS AND FIRST YEAR FRESHMEN

One-time award for high school seniors or college freshmen who are U.S. citizens and children or grandchildren of active members of the Reserve Officers Association. Must demonstrate leadership, have minimum 3.0 GPA and 1250 on the SAT. Must submit sponsor verification. College freshmen must submit college transcript.

Award: Scholarship for use in freshman year; not renewable. *Number:* 25–50. *Amount:* $500.

Eligibility Requirements: Applicant must be enrolled or expecting to enroll full-time at a four-year institution or university and must have an interest in leadership. Applicant or parent of applicant must be member of Reserve Officers Association. Applicant must have 3.0 GPA or higher. Available to U.S. citizens. Applicant or parent must meet one or more of the following requirements: general military experience; retired from active duty; disabled or killed as a result of military service; prisoner of war; or missing in action.

Application Requirements: Application, essay, test scores, transcript. *Deadline:* April 10.

Contact: Dennis M. McCarthy, Executive Director
Reserve Officers Association
One Constitution Avenue, NE
Washington, DC 20002-5655
Phone: 202-479-2200
Fax: 202-479-0416
E-mail: mhagen@roa.org

HENRY J. REILLY MEMORIAL UNDERGRADUATE SCHOLARSHIP PROGRAM FOR COLLEGE ATTENDEES

One-time award of $500 for members and children or grandchildren of members of the Reserve Officers Association or its Auxiliary. Must be a U.S. citizen, 26 years old or younger, and enrolled at an accredited four-year institution. Must submit sponsor verification. Minimum 3.0 GPA required. Submit SAT or ACT scores; contact for score requirements.

Award: Scholarship for use in freshman, sophomore, junior, or senior years; not renewable. *Number:* 25–35. *Amount:* $500.

Eligibility Requirements: Applicant must be age 26 or under and enrolled or expecting to enroll full-time at a two-year or four-year institution or university. Applicant or parent of applicant must be member of Reserve Officers Association. Applicant must have 3.0 GPA or higher. Available to U.S. citizens. Applicant or parent must meet one or more of the following requirements: general military experience; retired from active duty; disabled or killed as a result of military service; prisoner of war; or missing in action.

Application Requirements: Application, essay, test scores, transcript, sponsor verification. *Deadline:* April 10.

Contact: Mickey Hagen, Coordinator of Applications
Reserve Officers Association
One Constitution Avenue, NE
Washington, DC 20002-5655
Phone: 202-479-2200
Fax: 202-479-0416
E-mail: mhagen@roa.org

RETAIL, WHOLESALE AND DEPARTMENT STORE UNION http://www.rwdsu.org

ALVIN E. HEAPS MEMORIAL SCHOLARSHIP

Scholarship for RWDSU members or members of an RWDSU family. Applicant must submit 500-word essay on the benefits of union membership. See Web site for application: http://www.rwdsu.info/heapsscholar.htm

Retail, Wholesale and Department Store Union (continued)

Award: Scholarship for use in freshman, sophomore, junior, or senior years; not renewable. *Number:* varies. *Amount:* varies.

Eligibility Requirements: Applicant must be enrolled or expecting to enroll full- or part-time at a two-year or four-year institution or university. Applicant or parent of applicant must be member of Retail, Wholesale and Department Store Union. Available to U.S. citizens.

Application Requirements: Application, essay, transcript. *Deadline:* varies.

Contact: Scholarship Committee
Retail, Wholesale and Department Store Union
30 East 29th Street
New York, NY 10016
Phone: 212-684-5300
Fax: 212-779-2809

RHODE ISLAND FOUNDATION http://www.rifoundation.org

EDWARD LEON DUHAMEL FREEMASONS SCHOLARSHIP

Applicants must be descendants of members of Franklin Lodge or descendants of other Freemasons in Rhode Island. Must be accepted into an accredited postsecondary institution. Must demonstrate scholastic achievement, financial need and good citizenship.

Award: Scholarship for use in freshman, sophomore, junior, or senior years; renewable. *Number:* 2–4. *Amount:* $500–$1000.

Eligibility Requirements: Applicant must be enrolled or expecting to enroll full-time at a four-year institution or university. Applicant or parent of applicant must be member of Freemasons. Available to U.S. citizens.

Application Requirements: Application, essay, financial need analysis, self-addressed stamped envelope, transcript. *Deadline:* May 19.

Contact: Libby Monahan, Funds Administrator
Rhode Island Foundation
One Union Station
Providence, RI 02903
Phone: 401-274-4564 Ext. 3117
Fax: 401-751-7983
E-mail: libbym@rifoundation.org

SCREEN ACTORS GUILD FOUNDATION http://www.sagfoundation.org

SCREEN ACTORS GUILD FOUNDATION/JOHN L. DALES SCHOLARSHIP FUND (STANDARD)

Award for guild members and children of members. Applicant must have been a member in good standing for five years and have $30,000 lifetime gross income in the guild's jurisdiction. The parent of an applicant must have been a member in good standing for ten years and have a $100,000 lifetime gross income in the guild's jurisdiction. Award ranges from $3000 to $4000.

Award: Scholarship for use in freshman, sophomore, junior, senior, or graduate years; not renewable. *Number:* up to 100. *Amount:* $3000–$4000.

Eligibility Requirements: Applicant must be enrolled or expecting to enroll full-time at a two-year or four-year institution or university. Applicant or parent of applicant must be member of Screen Actors' Guild. Available to U.S. citizens.

Application Requirements: Application, essay, financial need analysis, resume, references, test scores, transcript. *Deadline:* March 14.

Contact: Davidson Lloyd, Administrative Director
Screen Actors Guild Foundation
5757 Wilshire Boulevard, Suite 124
Los Angeles, CA 90036-3600
Phone: 323-549-6649
Fax: 323-549-6710
E-mail: dlloyd@sag.org

SCREEN ACTORS GUILD FOUNDATION/JOHN L. DALES SCHOLARSHIP (TRANSITIONAL)

Award for guild members and children of members, studying at accredited colleges or universities. Must be U.S. citizen. Minimum twelve awards are granted annually. Scholarship amount ranges between $3000 and $5000.

Award: Scholarship for use in freshman, sophomore, junior, senior, or graduate years; not renewable. *Number:* 12. *Amount:* $3000–$5000.

Eligibility Requirements: Applicant must be enrolled or expecting to enroll full-time at a two-year or four-year institution or university. Applicant or parent of applicant must be member of Screen Actors' Guild. Available to U.S. citizens.

Application Requirements: Application, essay, financial need analysis, resume, references, test scores, transcript. *Deadline:* March 14.

Contact: Davidson Lloyd, Administrative Director
Screen Actors Guild Foundation
5757 Wilshire Boulevard, Suite 124
Los Angeles, CA 90036-3600
Phone: 323-549-6649
Fax: 323-549-6710
E-mail: dlloyd@sag.org

SECOND BOMBARDMENT ASSOCIATION

SECOND BOMBARDMENT ASSOCIATION SCHOLARSHIP

Award for children of members of the Second Bombardment Wing of the U.S. Air Force. Write for more information. Program is administered by Air Force Aid in Washington, D.C. Documentation must be submitted to them.

Award: Scholarship for use in freshman, sophomore, junior, senior, or graduate years; renewable. *Number:* 2. *Amount:* $1000.

Eligibility Requirements: Applicant must be enrolled or expecting to enroll full-time at a four-year institution or university. Applicant or parent of applicant must be member of Second Bombardment Association. Available to U.S. and non-U.S. citizens. Applicant or parent must meet one or more of the following requirements: Air Force experience; retired from active duty; disabled or killed as a result of military service; prisoner of war; or missing in action.

Application Requirements: Application, financial need analysis, proof of parent's service. *Deadline:* continuous.

Contact: Kemp Martin, Scholarship Chairman
Second Bombardment Association
806 Oak Valley
Houston, TX 77024-3123
Phone: 713-467-5435
Fax: 713-973-1700
E-mail: kmartin1@pdq.net

SEMINOLE TRIBE OF FLORIDA http://www.seminoletribe.com

SEMINOLE TRIBE OF FLORIDA BILLY L. CYPRESS SCHOLARSHIP PROGRAM

Awards full scholarships to applicants who meet membership requirements (must have a membership number). Applicant must belong to Seminole tribe of Florida to be eligible. Must maintain a 2.0 GPA with 12 semester credit hours earned each semester.

Award: Scholarship for use in freshman, sophomore, junior, senior, graduate, or postgraduate years; renewable. *Number:* 75. *Amount:* varies.

Eligibility Requirements: Applicant must be American Indian/Alaska Native and enrolled or expecting to enroll full- or part-time at a two-year or four-year institution or university. Applicant or parent of applicant must be member of Teamsters. Available to U.S. citizens.

Application Requirements: Application, transcript, acceptance letter from university. *Deadline:* varies.

Contact: Linda Iley, Higher Education Adviser
Seminole Tribe of Florida
6300 Stirling Road
Hollywood, FL 33024-2153
Phone: 954-989-6840 Ext. 10540
Fax: 954-233-9545
E-mail: eiley@semtribe.com

SERVICE EMPLOYEES INTERNATIONAL UNION-CALIFORNIA STATE COUNCIL OF SERVICE EMPLOYEES http://www.seiuca.org

CHARLES HARDY MEMORIAL SCHOLARSHIP AWARDS

Renewable $1000 award for California residents. For full-time study only. Must be SEIU members or children of members. For recent affiliates to SEIU, you must have been a member of the association for three years.

Award: Scholarship for use in freshman year; renewable. *Number:* 1–4. *Amount:* $1000.

Eligibility Requirements: Applicant must be high school student; planning to enroll or expecting to enroll full-time at a two-year or four-year institution or university and resident of California. Applicant or parent of applicant must be member of Service Employees International Union. Available to U.S. citizens.

Application Requirements: Application, online test. *Deadline:* April 1.

Contact: Scholarship Committee
Service Employees International Union-California State Council of Service Employees
1313 L Street, NW
Washington, DC 20005
Phone: 800-846-1561

SERVICE EMPLOYEES INTERNATIONAL UNION (SEIU) http://www.seiu.org

SEIU JESSE JACKSON SCHOLARSHIP PROGRAM

Renewable scholarship of $5000 given to a student whose work and aspirations for economic and social justice reflect the values and accomplishments of the Rev. Jackson.

Award: Scholarship for use in freshman, sophomore, junior, or senior years; renewable. *Number:* 1. *Amount:* $5000.

Eligibility Requirements: Applicant must be enrolled or expecting to enroll full-time at a four-year institution or university. Applicant or parent of applicant must be member of Service Employees International Union. Available to U.S. citizens.

Application Requirements: Application, essay. *Deadline:* March 1.

Contact: c/o Scholarship Program Administrators, Inc.
Service Employees International Union (SEIU)
PO Box 23737
Nashville, TN 37202-3737
Phone: 615-320-3149
Fax: 615-320-3151
E-mail: info@spaprog.com

SEIU JOHN GEAGAN SCHOLARSHIP

Scholarship to SEIU members or their children or SEIU local union staff. Priority will be given to those applicants who are not served by traditional education institutions-typically adults who have been in the workforce and have decided to go, or return to, college.

Award: Scholarship for use in freshman, sophomore, junior, or senior years; not renewable. *Number:* 1. *Amount:* $2500.

Eligibility Requirements: Applicant must be enrolled or expecting to enroll full-time at a two-year or four-year or technical institution or university. Applicant or parent of applicant must be member of Service Employees International Union. Available to U.S. citizens.

Application Requirements: Application, essay. *Deadline:* March 1.

Contact: c/o Scholarship Program Administrators, Inc.
Service Employees International Union (SEIU)
PO Box 23737
Nashville, TN 37202-3737
Phone: 615-320-3149
Fax: 615-320-3151
E-mail: info@spaprog.com

SEIU NORA PIORE SCHOLARSHIP PROGRAM

Renewable award of $4375 to SEIU members enrolled full-time in an undergraduate study. Applicant's financial need will be considered during the selection process.

Award: Scholarship for use in freshman, sophomore, junior, or senior years; renewable. *Number:* 1. *Amount:* $4375.

Eligibility Requirements: Applicant must be enrolled or expecting to enroll full-time at a four-year institution or university. Applicant or parent of applicant must be member of Service Employees International Union. Available to U.S. citizens.

Application Requirements: Application. *Deadline:* March 1.

Contact: c/o Scholarship Program Administrators, Inc.
Service Employees International Union (SEIU)
PO Box 23737
Nashville, TN 37202-3737
Phone: 615-320-3149
Fax: 615-320-3151
E-mail: info@spaprog.com

SEIU SCHOLARSHIP PROGRAM

Fifteen $1000 scholarships available in annual installments for up to four years. Applicants must graduate from a high school or GED program by August. Must be enrolled as a full-time college freshman by the fall semester at an accredited, four-year college or university.

Award: Scholarship for use in freshman year; renewable. *Number:* 15. *Amount:* $1000.

Eligibility Requirements: Applicant must be high school student and planning to enroll or expecting to enroll full-time at a four-year institution or university. Applicant or parent of applicant must be member of Service Employees International Union. Available to U.S. citizens.

Application Requirements: Application. *Deadline:* March 1.

Contact: c/o Scholarship Program Administrators, Inc.
Service Employees International Union (SEIU)
PO Box 23737
Nashville, TN 37202-3737
Phone: 615-320-3149
Fax: 615-320-3151
E-mail: info@spaprog.com

SIGMA ALPHA MU http://www.sam.org/default.asp

UNDERGRADUATE ACHIEVEMENT AWARDS

Scholarship for seniors or juniors of undergraduate students enrolled full-time study. Must be member of Sigma Alpha Mu Foundation. Scholarship value varies.

Award: Scholarship for use in junior or senior years; not renewable. *Number:* 2. *Amount:* varies.

Eligibility Requirements: Applicant must be enrolled or expecting to enroll full-time at a four-year institution or university. Applicant or parent of applicant must be member of Sigma Alpha Mu Foundation. Available to U.S. citizens.

Application Requirements: Application, transcript. *Deadline:* March 1.

Contact: Bill Schwartz, Executive Director
Sigma Alpha Mu
9245 North Meridian, Suite 105
Indianapolis, IN 46260
Phone: 317-846-0600
Fax: 317-846-9462
E-mail: bill@sam.org

YOUNG SCHOLARS PROGRAM

Scholarship for candidates achieving a 3.75 GPA (or equivalent) for courses taken in the academic term of the undergraduate study. Must be member of Sigma Alpha Mu Foundation. Deadline varies.

Award: Scholarship for use in freshman, sophomore, junior, or senior years; not renewable. *Number:* varies. *Amount:* $200.

Eligibility Requirements: Applicant must be enrolled or expecting to enroll full-time at a four-year institution or university. Applicant or parent of applicant must be member of Sigma Alpha Mu Foundation. Applicant must have 3.5 GPA or higher. Available to U.S. citizens.

Sigma Alpha Mu (continued)

Application Requirements: Application, transcript. *Deadline:* varies.

Contact: Bill Schwartz, Executive Director
Sigma Alpha Mu
9245 North Meridian, Suite 105
Indianapolis, IN 46260
Phone: 317-846-0600
Fax: 317-846-9462
E-mail: bill@sam.org

SIGMA CHI FOUNDATION http://www.sigmachi.org

GENERAL SCHOLARSHIP GRANTS

Applicants must have completed three semesters (or four quarters) of undergraduate study to be considered for current year awards. Funds are available for tuition/fees payments only.

Award: Scholarship for use in sophomore, junior, or senior years; not renewable. *Number:* varies. *Amount:* varies.

Eligibility Requirements: Applicant must be enrolled or expecting to enroll full-time at a four-year institution or university and male. Applicant or parent of applicant must be member of Sigma Chi Fraternity. Available to U.S. and non-U.S. citizens.

Application Requirements: Application, financial need analysis, references, transcript. *Deadline:* April 13.

Contact: Chadd Montgomery, Associate Director Accountability
Sigma Chi Foundation
1714 Hinman Avenue
PO Box 469
Evanston, IL 60201-0469
Phone: 847-869-3655
Fax: 847-869-4906
E-mail: chadd.montgomery@sigmachi.org

ORDER OF THE SCROLL AWARD

Awarded to undergraduates who have been nominated by fellow chapter members for the outstanding direction of the chapter's educational program. Must be member of Sigma Chi.

Award: Scholarship for use in sophomore, junior, or senior years; not renewable. *Number:* varies. *Amount:* $1000.

Eligibility Requirements: Applicant must be enrolled or expecting to enroll full-time at a four-year institution or university and male. Applicant or parent of applicant must be member of Sigma Chi Fraternity. Available to U.S. and non-U.S. citizens.

Application Requirements: Application, financial need analysis, references, transcript. *Deadline:* April 13.

Contact: Chadd Montgomery, Associate Director Accountability
Sigma Chi Foundation
1714 Hinman Avenue
PO Box 469
Evanston, IL 60201-0469
Phone: 847-869-3655
Fax: 847-869-4906
E-mail: chadd.montgomery@sigmachi.org

SLOVAK GYMNASTIC UNION SOKOL, USA http://www.sokolusa.org

SLOVAK GYMNASTIC UNION SOKOL, USA/MILAN GETTING SCHOLARSHIP

Available to members of SOKOL, U.S.A who have been in good standing for at least three years. Must have plans to attend college. Renewable for a maximum of four years, based upon academic achievement. Minimum GPA 2.5 required.

Award: Scholarship for use in freshman, sophomore, junior, or senior years; renewable. *Number:* 4–8. *Amount:* $500.

Eligibility Requirements: Applicant must be enrolled or expecting to enroll full-time at a four-year institution or university. Applicant or parent of applicant must be member of SOKOL, USA. Applicant must have 2.5 GPA or higher. Available to U.S. citizens.

Application Requirements: Application, references, transcript. *Deadline:* April 15.

Contact: Milan Kovac, Supreme Secretary
Slovak Gymnastic Union SOKOL, USA
276 Prospect Street, PO Box 189
East Orange, NJ 07019
Phone: 973-676-0280
Fax: 973-676-3348
E-mail: sokolusahqs@aol.com

SLOVENIAN WOMEN'S UNION OF AMERICA http://www.swua.org

CONTINUING EDUCATION AWARD

Award of $500 given to 2 applicants to continue or update their education. Applicant must be an active participant of the Slovenian Women's Union for the three years prior to applying for an award.

Award: Scholarship for use in freshman, sophomore, junior, senior, or graduate years; not renewable. *Number:* 2. *Amount:* $500.

Eligibility Requirements: Applicant must be enrolled or expecting to enroll full- or part-time at a two-year or four-year or technical institution or university. Applicant or parent of applicant must be member of Slovenian Women's Union of America. Available to U.S. citizens.

Application Requirements: Application, autobiography, essay, financial need analysis, photo, resume, references, test scores, transcript. *Deadline:* March 1.

Contact: Mary H. Turvey, Director
Slovenian Women's Union of America
52 Oakridge Drive
Marquette, MI 49855
Phone: 906-249-4288
E-mail: mturvey@aol.com

SLOVENIAN WOMEN'S UNION OF AMERICA SCHOLARSHIP PROGRAM

One-time award for full-time study only. Applicant must have been an active participant or member of Slovenian Women's Union for the past three years. Essay, transcripts, letters of recommendation from principal/teacher and SWU branch officer, financial need form, photo, civic and church activities information required. Open to high school seniors.

Award: Scholarship for use in freshman, sophomore, junior, or senior years; not renewable. *Number:* 5. *Amount:* $1000–$2000.

Eligibility Requirements: Applicant must be enrolled or expecting to enroll full-time at a two-year or four-year institution or university. Applicant or parent of applicant must be member of Slovenian Women's Union of America. Available to U.S. citizens.

Application Requirements: Application, autobiography, essay, financial need analysis, photo, resume, references, test scores, transcript. *Deadline:* March 1.

Contact: Mary Turvey, Director
Slovenian Women's Union of America
52 Oakridge Drive
Marquette, MI 49855
Phone: 906-249-4288
E-mail: mturvey@aol.com

SONS OF NORWAY FOUNDATION http://www.sonsofnorway.com

ASTRID G. CATES AND MYRTLE BEINHAUER SCHOLARSHIP FUNDS

Merit and need-based award available to students ages 17 to 22 who are members, children, or grandchildren of members of the Sons of Norway. School transcript required. Financial need is key criterion for award. Minimum 3.0 GPA required.

Award: Scholarship for use in freshman, sophomore, junior, or senior years; not renewable. *Number:* 2–6. *Amount:* $1000–$3000.

Eligibility Requirements: Applicant must be of Norwegian heritage; age 17-22 and enrolled or expecting to enroll full-time at a two-year or four-year institution or university. Applicant or parent of applicant must be member of Mutual Benefit Society. Applicant must have 3.0 GPA or higher. Available to U.S. citizens.

Application Requirements: Application, essay, financial need analysis, references, self-addressed stamped envelope, test scores, transcript. *Deadline:* March 1.

Contact: Scholarship Coordinator
Sons of Norway Foundation
1455 West Lake Street
Minneapolis, MN 55408-2666
Phone: 612-827-3611
Fax: 612-827-0658

SOROPTIMIST INTERNATIONAL OF THE AMERICAS http://www.soroptimist.org

SOROPTIMIST WOMEN'S OPPORTUNITY AWARD

Applicant must be a woman who is the head of household, and pursuing a vocational or an undergraduate degree. Recipients are chosen on the basis of financial need as well as a statement of clear career goals. One-time award of $10,000. Must send a self-addressed stamped business-size envelope with 60 cents postage for information, or download the application from the Web site. Must be a resident of SIA's member countries and territories.

Award: Prize for use in freshman, sophomore, junior, or senior years; not renewable. *Number:* varies. *Amount:* $10,000.

Eligibility Requirements: Applicant must be enrolled or expecting to enroll full- or part-time at a two-year or four-year or technical institution or university and female. Applicant or parent of applicant must be member of Soroptimist Club. Available to U.S. and non-U.S. citizens.

Application Requirements: Application, essay, financial need analysis, references, self-addressed stamped envelope. *Deadline:* December 1.

Contact: Susan Doughty, Scholarship Committee
Soroptimist International of the Americas
1709 Spruce Street
Philadelphia, PA 19103-6103
Phone: 215-893-9300 Ext. 123
Fax: 215-893-5200
E-mail: susan@soroptimist.org

SOUTH CAROLINA STATE EMPLOYEES ASSOCIATION http://www.scsea.com

ANNE A. AGNEW SCHOLARSHIP

Nonrenewable scholarship for full-time study only. Must be a sophomore, junior, senior, graduate or postgraduate student. Application forms are available after January 1 of each year.

Award: Scholarship for use in sophomore, junior, senior, graduate, or postgraduate years; not renewable. *Number:* 3. *Amount:* $1000.

Eligibility Requirements: Applicant must be enrolled or expecting to enroll full-time at a four-year institution or university and resident of South Carolina. Applicant or parent of applicant must be member of South Carolina State Employees Association. Available to U.S. and non-U.S. citizens.

Application Requirements: Application, essay, financial need analysis, transcript. *Deadline:* March 12.

Contact: Broadus Jamerson, Executive Director
South Carolina State Employees Association
PO Box 8447
Columbia, SC 29202
Phone: 803-765-0680
Fax: 803-779-6558
E-mail: scsea@scsea.com

RICHLAND/LEXINGTON SCSEA SCHOLARSHIP

Scholarships available to SCSEA members or their relatives, with priority given to Richland-Lexington Chapter members, spouses and/or children of Chapter members. The awardees must be currently enrolled at a recognized and accredited college, university, trade school or other institution of higher learning and must have completed at least one academic semester/quarter.

Award: Scholarship for use in sophomore, junior, senior, graduate, or postgraduate years; not renewable. *Number:* 3. *Amount:* $750.

Eligibility Requirements: Applicant must be enrolled or expecting to enroll full-time at a two-year or four-year institution or university and resident of South Carolina. Applicant or parent of applicant must be member of Society of Architectural Historians. Available to U.S. citizens.

Application Requirements: Application, essay, transcript. *Deadline:* March 12.

Contact: Broadus Jamerson, Executive Director
South Carolina State Employees Association
PO Box 8447
Columbia, SC 29202
Phone: 803-765-0680
Fax: 803-779-6558
E-mail: scsea@scsea.com

SUPREME COUNCIL OF SES http://www.seslife.org

SUPREME COUNCIL OF SOCIEDADE DO ESPIRITO SANTO SCHOLARSHIP PROGRAM

Applicant must be a member of the SES for a minimum of two years prior to filling date of scholarship and have insurance premiums paid to date. Must be graduating seniors at time of application or have graduated from high school during the current year. Minimum of 3.0 GPA required.

Award: Scholarship for use in freshman year; not renewable. *Number:* 35. *Amount:* $500–$1200.

Eligibility Requirements: Applicant must be enrolled or expecting to enroll full-time at a four-year institution or university. Applicant or parent of applicant must be member of Supreme Council of Sociedade Do Espirito Santo. Applicant must have 3.0 GPA or higher. Available to U.S. citizens.

Application Requirements: Application, essay, resume, references, transcript. *Deadline:* February 15.

Contact: Scholarship Committee
Supreme Council of SES
PO Box 247
Santa Clara, CA 95052-0247

SUPREME GUARDIAN COUNCIL, INTERNATIONAL ORDER OF JOB'S DAUGHTERS http://www.iojd.org

SUPREME GUARDIAN COUNCIL SCHOLARSHIP

Scholarships of $750 to aid Job's Daughters students of outstanding ability whom have a sincerity of purpose. High school seniors, or graduates, junior college, technical school, or college students who are in early graduation programs, are eligible to apply.

Award: Scholarship for use in freshman, sophomore, junior, senior, graduate, or postgraduate years; not renewable. *Number:* varies. *Amount:* $750.

Eligibility Requirements: Applicant must be enrolled or expecting to enroll full- or part-time at a two-year or four-year or technical institution or university and female. Applicant or parent of applicant must be member of Jobs Daughters. Available to U.S. and non-U.S. citizens.

Application Requirements: Application, essay, financial need analysis, references, recommendation from Executive Bethel Guardian Council, achievements outside of Job's Daughters. *Deadline:* April 30.

Contact: Barbara Hill, Scholarship Committee Chairman
Supreme Guardian Council, International Order of Job's Daughters
337 Illinois Street
Pekin, IL 61554-2270
Phone: 309-346-5564
E-mail: dubahill@grics.net

SUSIE HOLMES MEMORIAL SCHOLARSHIP

Scholarships of $1000 awarded to Job's Daughters high school students with a minimum of 2.5 GPA.

Award: Scholarship for use in freshman, sophomore, junior, senior, graduate, or postgraduate years; not renewable. *Number:* 1. *Amount:* $1000.

Eligibility Requirements: Applicant must be enrolled or expecting to enroll full-time at a two-year or four-year or technical institution or university and female. Applicant or parent of applicant must be member of Jobs Daughters. Applicant must have 2.5 GPA or higher. Available to U.S. and non-U.S. citizens.

Supreme Guardian Council, International Order of Job's Daughters (continued)

Application Requirements: Application, essay, references, test scores, transcript. *Deadline:* April 30.

Contact: Barbara Hill, Scholarship Committee Chairman
Supreme Guardian Council, International Order of Job's Daughters
337 Illinois Street
Pekin, IL 61554-2270
Phone: 309-346-5564
E-mail: dubahill@grics.net

TENNESSEE EDUCATION ASSOCIATION http://www.teateachers.org

TEA DON SAHLI-KATHY WOODALL SONS AND DAUGHTERS SCHOLARSHIP

Scholarship is available to a TEA member's child who is a high school senior, undergraduate or graduate student, and is planning to enroll, or is already enrolled, in a Tennessee college.

Award: Scholarship for use in freshman, sophomore, junior, senior, or graduate years; not renewable. *Number:* 1. *Amount:* $1000.

Eligibility Requirements: Applicant must be enrolled or expecting to enroll full-time at a four-year institution or university; resident of Tennessee and studying in Tennessee. Applicant or parent of applicant must be member of Tennessee Education Association. Applicant must have 3.0 GPA or higher. Available to U.S. citizens.

Application Requirements: Application, applicant must enter a contest, essay, financial need analysis, references, transcript, statement of income. *Deadline:* March 1.

Contact: Stephanie Faulkner, Manager of Business Affairs
Tennessee Education Association
801 Second Avenue North
Nashville, TN 37201-1099
Phone: 615-242-8392
Fax: 615-259-4581
E-mail: sfaulkner@tea.nea.org

TEXAS AFL-CIO http://www.texasaflcio.org

TEXAS AFL-CIO SCHOLARSHIP PROGRAM

Award for sons or daughters of affiliated union members. Selection by testing or interview process. One-time awards of $1000. Applicant must be a graduating high school senior and Texas resident.

Award: Scholarship for use in freshman year; not renewable. *Number:* up to 20. *Amount:* $1000.

Eligibility Requirements: Applicant must be high school student; planning to enroll or expecting to enroll full-time at a two-year or four-year institution or university and resident of Texas. Applicant or parent of applicant must be member of AFL-CIO. Available to U.S. citizens.

Application Requirements: Application, essay, financial need analysis, interview, photo, test scores, transcript. *Deadline:* January 31.

Contact: Edward Sills
Texas AFL-CIO
PO Box 12727
Austin, TX 78711
Phone: 512-477-6195
Fax: 512-477-2962
E-mail: ed@texasaflcio.org

TEXAS WOMEN IN LAW ENFORCEMENT http://www.twle.com

VANESSA RUDLOFF SCHOLARSHIP PROGRAM

Scholarships of $1000 awarded to qualified TWLE members and their dependents who are entering or continuing students at an accredited college or university. For details refer to Web Site: http://www.twle.net/.

Award: Scholarship for use in freshman, sophomore, junior, senior, graduate, or postgraduate years; not renewable. *Number:* 4. *Amount:* $1000.

Eligibility Requirements: Applicant must be enrolled or expecting to enroll full- or part-time at a two-year or four-year or technical institution or university. Applicant or parent of applicant must be member of Texas Women in Law Enforcement. Applicant must have 3.0 GPA or higher. Available to U.S. and non-U.S. citizens.

Application Requirements: Application, essay, references. *Deadline:* April 15.

Contact: Glenda Baker, Scholarship Awards Chairperson
Texas Women in Law Enforcement
12605 Rhea Court
Austin, TX 78727
E-mail: gbakerab@aol.com

TKE EDUCATIONAL FOUNDATION http://www.tke.org

ALL-TKE ACADEMIC TEAM RECOGNITION AND JOHN A. COURSON TOP SCHOLAR AWARD

One-time award given to full-time students who are active members of Tau Kappa Epsilon with junior or senior standing. Candidates should be able to maintain excellent academic standing while making positive contributions to chapter, campus, and community. Must have a minimum of 3.0 GPA.

Award: Scholarship for use in junior or senior years; not renewable. *Number:* 10. *Amount:* up to $3250.

Eligibility Requirements: Applicant must be enrolled or expecting to enroll full-time at a four-year institution or university and must have an interest in leadership. Applicant or parent of applicant must be member of Tau Kappa Epsilon. Applicant must have 3.0 GPA or higher. Available to U.S. and Canadian citizens.

Application Requirements: Application, photo, transcript. *Deadline:* February 29.

Contact: Gary A. Reed, President and Chief Executive Officer
TKE Educational Foundation
8645 Founders Road
Indianapolis, IN 46268-1393
Phone: 317-872-6533
Fax: 317-875-8353
E-mail: reedga@tke.org

CANADIAN TKE SCHOLARSHIP

Scholarship available to an undergraduate who has been initiated into a Canadian TKE chapter and has demonstrated leadership qualities within the fraternity and the campus community, while maintaining a good academic record.

Award: Scholarship for use in freshman, sophomore, junior, or senior years; not renewable. *Number:* 1. *Amount:* $250.

Eligibility Requirements: Applicant must be enrolled or expecting to enroll full-time at a four-year institution or university; male and must have an interest in leadership. Applicant or parent of applicant must be member of Tau Kappa Epsilon. Applicant must have 2.5 GPA or higher. Available to U.S. and non-U.S. citizens.

Application Requirements: Application, essay, photo, transcript. *Deadline:* February 28.

Contact: Gary Reed, President and Chief Executive Officer
TKE Educational Foundation
8645 Founders Road
Indianapolis, IN 46268
Phone: 317-872-6533
Fax: 317-875-8353
E-mail: reedga@tke.org

CHARLES WALGREEN JR. SCHOLARSHIP

Award given in recognition of outstanding leadership, as demonstrated by the activities and accomplishments of an individual within the chapter, on campus and in the community, while maintaining a good academic record. All initiated undergraduate members of TKE, in good standing with a cumulative GPA of 3.0 or higher, are eligible to apply.

Award: Scholarship for use in freshman, sophomore, junior, or senior years; not renewable. *Number:* 1. *Amount:* $2500.

Eligibility Requirements: Applicant must be enrolled or expecting to enroll full-time at a four-year institution or university; male and must have an interest in leadership. Applicant or parent of applicant must be member of Tau Kappa Epsilon. Applicant must have 3.0 GPA or higher. Available to U.S. and non-U.S. citizens.

Application Requirements: Application, essay, photo, transcript, narrative summary of how TKE membership has benefited applicant. *Deadline:* February 29.

Contact: Scholarship Committee
TKE Educational Foundation
8645 Founders Road
Indianapolis, IN 46268-1336
Phone: 317-872-6533
Fax: 317-875-8353
E-mail: tef@tke.org

DONALD A. AND JOHN R. FISHER MEMORIAL SCHOLARSHIP

One-time award of $1400 given to an undergraduate member of Tau Kappa Epsilon, who has demonstrated leadership ability within his chapter, campus, or community. Must be a full-time student in good standing with a GPA of 3.0 or higher.

Award: Scholarship for use in freshman, sophomore, junior, or senior years; not renewable. *Number:* 1. *Amount:* $1400.

Eligibility Requirements: Applicant must be enrolled or expecting to enroll full-time at a four-year institution or university and must have an interest in leadership. Applicant or parent of applicant must be member of Tau Kappa Epsilon. Applicant must have 3.0 GPA or higher. Available to U.S. and non-U.S. citizens.

Application Requirements: Application, essay, photo, transcript. *Deadline:* February 29.

Contact: Gary A. Reed, President and Chief Executive Officer
TKE Educational Foundation
8645 Founders Road
Indianapolis, IN 46268-1393
Phone: 317-872-6533
Fax: 317-875-8353
E-mail: reedga@tke.org

DWAYNE R. WOERPEL MEMORIAL LEADERSHIP AWARD

Award available to an undergraduate Tau Kappa Epsilon member who is a full-time student and graduate of the TKE Leadership Academy. Applicants should have demonstrated leadership qualities in service to the Fraternity and to the civic and religious community while maintaining a 3.0 GPA or higher.

Award: Scholarship for use in freshman, sophomore, junior, or senior years; not renewable. *Number:* 1. *Amount:* $700.

Eligibility Requirements: Applicant must be enrolled or expecting to enroll full-time at a four-year institution or university; male and must have an interest in leadership. Applicant or parent of applicant must be member of Tau Kappa Epsilon. Applicant must have 3.0 GPA or higher. Available to U.S. and non-U.S. citizens.

Application Requirements: Application, essay, photo, transcript. *Deadline:* February 29.

Contact: Scholarship Committee
TKE Educational Foundation
8645 Founders Road
Indianapolis, IN 46268-1336
Phone: 317-872-6533
Fax: 317-875-8353
E-mail: tef@tke.org

ELMER AND DORIS SCHMITZ SR. MEMORIAL SCHOLARSHIP

One-time award of $500 given to an undergraduate member of Tau Kappa Epsilon from Wisconsin who has demonstrated leadership ability within his chapter, campus, or community. Must be a full-time student in good standing with a GPA of 2.5 or higher.

Award: Scholarship for use in freshman, sophomore, junior, or senior years; not renewable. *Number:* 1. *Amount:* $500.

Eligibility Requirements: Applicant must be enrolled or expecting to enroll full-time at a four-year institution or university; resident of Wisconsin and must have an interest in leadership. Applicant or parent of applicant must be member of Tau Kappa Epsilon. Applicant must have 2.5 GPA or higher. Available to U.S. and non-U.S. citizens.

Application Requirements: Application, essay, photo, transcript, narrative summary of how TKE membership has benefited applicant. *Deadline:* February 29.

Contact: Gary A. Reed, President and Chief Executive Officer
TKE Educational Foundation
8645 Founders Road
Indianapolis, IN 46268-1393
Phone: 317-872-6533
Fax: 317-875-8353
E-mail: reedga@tke.org

EUGENE C. BEACH MEMORIAL SCHOLARSHIP

One-time award of $400 given to an undergraduate member of Tau Kappa Epsilon who has demonstrated leadership ability within chapter, campus, or community. Must be a full-time student in good standing with a GPA of 3.0 or higher.

Award: Scholarship for use in freshman, sophomore, junior, or senior years; not renewable. *Number:* 1. *Amount:* $400.

Eligibility Requirements: Applicant must be enrolled or expecting to enroll full-time at a four-year institution or university and must have an interest in leadership. Applicant or parent of applicant must be member of Tau Kappa Epsilon. Applicant must have 3.0 GPA or higher. Available to U.S. and non-U.S. citizens.

Application Requirements: Application, essay, photo, transcript, narrative summary of how TKE membership has benefited applicant. *Deadline:* February 29.

Contact: Gary A. Reed, President and Chief Executive Officer
TKE Educational Foundation
8645 Founders Road
Indianapolis, IN 46268-1393
Phone: 317-872-6533
Fax: 317-875-8353
E-mail: reedga@tke.org

J. RUSSEL SALSBURY MEMORIAL SCHOLARSHIP

One-time award of $300 given to an undergraduate member of Tau Kappa Epsilon who has demonstrated leadership ability within his chapter, campus, or community. Must be a full-time student in good standing with a GPA of 3.0 or higher.

Award: Scholarship for use in freshman, sophomore, junior, or senior years; not renewable. *Number:* 1. *Amount:* $300.

Eligibility Requirements: Applicant must be enrolled or expecting to enroll full-time at a four-year institution or university and must have an interest in leadership. Applicant or parent of applicant must be member of Tau Kappa Epsilon. Applicant must have 3.0 GPA or higher. Available to U.S. and non-U.S. citizens.

Application Requirements: Application, essay, photo, transcript. *Deadline:* February 29.

Contact: Gary A. Reed, President and Chief Executive Officer
TKE Educational Foundation
8645 Founders Road
Indianapolis, IN 46268-1393
Phone: 317-872-6533
Fax: 317-875-8353
E-mail: reedga@tke.org

MICHAEL J. MORIN MEMORIAL SCHOLARSHIP

One-time award for any undergraduate member of Tau Kappa Epsilon who has demonstrated leadership capacity within his chapter, on campus or the community. Must have a cumulative GPA of 3.0 or higher and be a full-time student in good standing.

Award: Scholarship for use in freshman, sophomore, junior, or senior years; not renewable. *Number:* 1. *Amount:* $400.

Eligibility Requirements: Applicant must be enrolled or expecting to enroll full-time at a four-year institution or university and must have an interest in leadership. Applicant or parent of applicant must be member of Tau Kappa Epsilon. Applicant must have 3.0 GPA or higher. Available to U.S. and non-U.S. citizens.

TKE Educational Foundation (continued)

Application Requirements: Application, essay, photo, transcript, narrative summary of how TKE membership has benefited applicant. *Deadline:* February 29.

Contact: Scholarship Committee
TKE Educational Foundation
8645 Founders Road
Indianapolis, IN 46268-1336
Phone: 317-872-6553
Fax: 317-875-8353
E-mail: tef@tke.org

MILES GRAY MEMORIAL SCHOLARSHIP

One-time award of $400 given to an undergraduate member of Tau Kappa Epsilon who has demonstrated leadership ability within his chapter, campus, or community. Must be a full-time student in good standing with a GPA of 3.0 or higher.

Award: Scholarship for use in freshman, sophomore, junior, or senior years; not renewable. *Number:* 1. *Amount:* $400.

Eligibility Requirements: Applicant must be enrolled or expecting to enroll full-time at a four-year institution or university and must have an interest in leadership. Applicant or parent of applicant must be member of Tau Kappa Epsilon. Applicant must have 3.0 GPA or higher. Available to U.S. and non-U.S. citizens.

Application Requirements: Application, essay, photo, transcript. *Deadline:* February 29.

Contact: Gary A. Reed, President and Chief Executive Officer
TKE Educational Foundation
8645 Founders Road
Indianapolis, IN 46268-1393
Phone: 317-872-6533
Fax: 317-875-8353
E-mail: reedga@tke.org

RONALD REAGAN LEADERSHIP AWARD

One-time award of $2000 for initiated undergraduate member of Tau Kappa Epsilon, given in recognition of outstanding leadership, as demonstrated by activities and accomplishments within chapter, on campus, and in community. Recipient should attend official fraternity function to accept award.

Award: Scholarship for use in freshman, sophomore, junior, or senior years; not renewable. *Number:* 1. *Amount:* $2000.

Eligibility Requirements: Applicant must be enrolled or expecting to enroll full-time at a four-year institution or university and must have an interest in leadership. Applicant or parent of applicant must be member of Tau Kappa Epsilon. Applicant must have 3.0 GPA or higher. Available to U.S. and non-U.S. citizens.

Application Requirements: Application, essay, photo, transcript, narrative summary of how TKE membership has benefited applicant. *Deadline:* February 29.

Contact: Gary A. Reed, President and Chief Executive Officer
TKE Educational Foundation
8645 Founders Road
Indianapolis, IN 46268-1393
Phone: 317-872-6533
Fax: 317-875-8353
E-mail: reedga@tke.org

T.J. SCHMITZ SCHOLARSHIP

Award for an initiated undergraduate member of TKE. Must be a full-time student in good standing with a minimum cumulative GPA of 3.0. Must have demonstrated leadership capability within chapter, campus, or community.

Award: Scholarship for use in freshman, sophomore, junior, or senior years; not renewable. *Number:* 1. *Amount:* $800.

Eligibility Requirements: Applicant must be enrolled or expecting to enroll full-time at a four-year institution or university; male and must have an interest in leadership. Applicant or parent of applicant must be member of Tau Kappa Epsilon. Applicant must have 3.0 GPA or higher. Available to U.S. and non-U.S. citizens.

Application Requirements: Application, essay, photo, transcript, narrative summary of how TKE membership has benefited applicant. *Deadline:* February 29.

Contact: Gary A. Reed, President and Chief Executive Officer
TKE Educational Foundation
8645 Founders Road
Indianapolis, IN 46268-1393
Phone: 317-872-6533
Fax: 317-875-8353
E-mail: reedga@tke.org

WALLACE MCCAULEY MEMORIAL SCHOLARSHIP

One-time award to undergraduate member of Tau Kappa Epsilon with junior or senior standing. Must have demonstrated understanding of the importance of good alumni relations. Must have excelled in the development, promotion, and execution of programs which increase alumni contact, awareness, and participation in fraternity activities.

Award: Scholarship for use in junior or senior years; not renewable. *Number:* 1. *Amount:* $500.

Eligibility Requirements: Applicant must be enrolled or expecting to enroll full-time at a four-year institution or university and must have an interest in leadership. Applicant or parent of applicant must be member of Tau Kappa Epsilon. Applicant must have 3.0 GPA or higher. Available to U.S. and non-U.S. citizens.

Application Requirements: Application, essay, photo, transcript, narrative summary of how TKE membership has benefited applicant. *Deadline:* February 29.

Contact: Gary A. Reed, President and Chief Executive Officer
TKE Educational Foundation
8645 Founders Road
Indianapolis, IN 46268-1393
Phone: 317-872-6533
Fax: 317-875-8353
E-mail: reedga@tke.org

WILLIAM V. MUSE SCHOLARSHIP

Award of $700 given to an undergraduate member of Tau Kappa Epsilon who has completed at least 30 semester hours of course work. Applicant should demonstrate leadership within chapter and maintain 3.0 GPA. Preference given to members of Epsilon-Upsilon Chapter.

Award: Scholarship for use in freshman, sophomore, junior, or senior years; not renewable. *Number:* 1. *Amount:* $700.

Eligibility Requirements: Applicant must be enrolled or expecting to enroll full-time at a four-year institution or university and must have an interest in leadership. Applicant or parent of applicant must be member of Tau Kappa Epsilon. Applicant must have 3.0 GPA or higher. Available to U.S. and non-U.S. citizens.

Application Requirements: Application, essay, photo, transcript, narrative summary of how TKE membership has benefited applicant. *Deadline:* February 29.

Contact: Gary A. Reed, President and Chief Executive Officer
TKE Educational Foundation
8645 Founders Road
Indianapolis, IN 46268-1393
Phone: 317-872-6533
Fax: 317-875-8353
E-mail: reedga@tke.org

WILLIAM WILSON MEMORIAL SCHOLARSHIP

One-time award given to undergraduate member of Tau Kappa Epsilon with junior or senior standing. Must have demonstrated understanding of the importance of good alumni relations. Must have excelled in the development, promotion, and execution of programs which increase alumni contact, awareness, and participation in fraternity activities.

Award: Scholarship for use in junior or senior years; not renewable. *Number:* 1. *Amount:* $500.

Eligibility Requirements: Applicant must be enrolled or expecting to enroll full-time at a four-year institution or university and must have an interest in leadership. Applicant or parent of applicant must be member of Tau Kappa Epsilon. Applicant must have 3.0 GPA or higher. Available to U.S. and non-U.S. citizens.

Application Requirements: Application, essay, photo, transcript, narrative summary of how TKE membership has benefited applicant. *Deadline:* February 29.

Contact: Gary A. Reed, President and Chief Executive Officer
TKE Educational Foundation
8645 Founders Road
Indianapolis, IN 46268-1393
Phone: 317-872-6533
Fax: 317-875-8353
E-mail: reedga@tke.org

UKRAINIAN FRATERNAL ASSOCIATION

UKRAINIAN FRATERNAL ASSOCIATION IVAN FRANKO SCHOLARSHIP FUND

Awards a senior in high school or a student attending an accredited university or college. Must have been a member of the Ukrainian Fraternal Association for at least two years. Submission of an essay on a topic chosen by the scholarship commission is required. Must submit recommendation.

Award: Scholarship for use in freshman, sophomore, junior, or senior years; not renewable. *Number:* up to 3. *Amount:* $750–$1250.

Eligibility Requirements: Applicant must be of Ukrainian heritage and enrolled or expecting to enroll full-time at a four-year institution or university. Applicant or parent of applicant must be member of Ukrainian Fraternal Association. Available to U.S. and Canadian citizens.

Application Requirements: Application, autobiography, essay, financial need analysis, photo, references, transcript. *Deadline:* May 31.

Contact: Christine Shablovsky, Supreme Secretary
Ukrainian Fraternal Association
371 North Ninth Avenue
Scranton, PA 18504-2005
Phone: 570-342-0937
Fax: 570-347-5649
E-mail: fratrag@aol.com

UKRAINIAN FRATERNAL ASSOCIATION STUDENT AID

Awards students of Ukrainian ancestry who have been a member in good standing of the Ukrainian Fraternal Association for at least two years. Must have completed one year of college and have minimum 2.0 GPA.

Award: Scholarship for use in sophomore, junior, or senior years; not renewable. *Number:* varies. *Amount:* up to $300.

Eligibility Requirements: Applicant must be of Ukrainian heritage and enrolled or expecting to enroll full-time at a four-year institution or university. Applicant or parent of applicant must be member of Ukrainian Fraternal Association. Available to U.S. and Canadian citizens.

Application Requirements: Application, autobiography, photo, references, transcript. *Deadline:* May 31.

Contact: Christina Shablovsky, Supreme Secretary
Ukrainian Fraternal Association
371 North Ninth Avenue
Scranton, PA 18504-2005
Phone: 570-342-0937
Fax: 570-347-5649
E-mail: fratrag@aol.com

UNION PLUS SCHOLARSHIP PROGRAM http://www.unionplus.org

UNION PLUS SCHOLARSHIP PROGRAM

One-time cash award for AFL-CIO union members, their spouses or dependent children. Based upon academic achievement, character, leadership, career goals, social awareness and financial need. Must be from Canada or U.S. including Puerto Rico. Members must download application from Web site http://www.unionplus.org.

Award: Scholarship for use in freshman, sophomore, junior, senior, or graduate years; not renewable. *Number:* 100–120. *Amount:* $500–$4000.

Eligibility Requirements: Applicant must be enrolled or expecting to enroll full- or part-time at a two-year or four-year or technical institution or university. Applicant or parent of applicant must be member of AFL-CIO. Available to U.S. and non-U.S. citizens.

Application Requirements: Application, essay, financial need analysis, references, test scores. *Deadline:* January 31.

Contact: Union Plus Education Program
c/o Union Privilege
PO Box 34800
Washington, DC 20043-4800
E-mail: info@unionprivilege.org

UNITED AGRIBUSINESS LEAGUE http://www.ual.org

UNITED AGRICULTURAL BENEFIT TRUST SCHOLARSHIP

Award available to a student who is a member, or an employee of a member of UAL and/or UABT (or a child of a member or a child of an employee of a member) who is enrolled at an accredited college or university majoring in any field of study.

Award: Scholarship for use in freshman, sophomore, junior, or senior years; renewable. *Number:* 7. *Amount:* $1000–$5000.

Eligibility Requirements: Applicant must be enrolled or expecting to enroll full-time at a two-year or four-year institution or university. Applicant or parent of applicant must be member of United Agribusiness League. Applicant must have 2.5 GPA or higher. Available to U.S. and non-Canadian citizens.

Application Requirements: Application, essay, financial need analysis, resume, references, test scores, transcript. *Deadline:* March 30.

Contact: Christiane Steele, Scholarship Coordinator
United Agribusiness League
54 Corporate Park
Irvine, CA 92606-5105
Phone: 949-975-1424
Fax: 949-975-1573
E-mail: scholarship@ual.org

UNITED COMMUNITY SERVICES FOR WORKING FAMILIES

RONALD LORAH MEMORIAL SCHOLARSHIP

One-time award available to a union member, spouse of a union member, or child of a union member. Must be a resident of Pennsylvania. Must submit essay that is clear, concise, persuasive and show an understanding of unions.

Award: Scholarship for use in freshman, sophomore, junior, senior, graduate, or postgraduate years; not renewable. *Number:* 2. *Amount:* $500–$1000.

Eligibility Requirements: Applicant must be enrolled or expecting to enroll full-time at a two-year or four-year institution or university and resident of Pennsylvania. Applicant or parent of applicant must be member of AFL-CIO. Available to U.S. citizens.

Application Requirements: Application, essay, financial need analysis, transcript. *Deadline:* July 18.

Contact: Ruth Mathews, Executive Director
United Community Services for Working Families
116 North Fifth Street
Reading, PA 19601
Phone: 610-374-3319
Fax: 610-374-6521
E-mail: ruth.mathews@comcast.net

UNITED DAUGHTERS OF THE CONFEDERACY http://www.hqudc.org

ADMIRAL RAPHAEL SEMMES SCHOLARSHIP

Renewable award for undergraduate students who are descendants of an eligible Confederate. Must be enrolled in an accredited college or university. Minimum 3.0 GPA required. Submit letter of endorsement from sponsoring chapter of the United Daughters of the Confederacy.

Award: Scholarship for use in freshman, sophomore, junior, or senior years; renewable. *Number:* 1–2. *Amount:* $800–$1000.

Eligibility Requirements: Applicant must be enrolled or expecting to enroll full-time at a four-year institution or university. Applicant or parent of applicant must be member of United Daughters of the Confederacy. Applicant must have 3.0 GPA or higher. Available to U.S. citizens. Applicant or parent must meet one or more of the following

United Daughters of the Confederacy (continued)

requirements: Air Force, Army, or Navy experience; retired from active duty; disabled or killed as a result of military service; prisoner of war; or missing in action.

Application Requirements: Application, essay, financial need analysis, photo, references, self-addressed stamped envelope, transcript, copy of applicant's birth certificate, copy of confederate ancestor's proof of service. *Deadline:* March 15.

Contact: Deanna Bryant, Second Vice President General
United Daughters of the Confederacy
328 North Boulevard
Richmond, VA 23220-4009
Phone: 804-355-1636
Fax: 804-353-1396
E-mail: hqudc@rcn.com

BARBARA JACKSON SICHEL MEMORIAL SCHOLARSHIP

Renewable award for undergraduate students who are descendant of a Confederate soldier, sailor or marine. Must be enrolled in an accredited college or university. Minimum of 3.0 GPA required. Submit a letter of endorsement from sponsoring Chapter of the United Daughters of the Confederacy.

Award: Scholarship for use in freshman, sophomore, junior, or senior years; renewable. *Number:* 1–2. *Amount:* $800–$1000.

Eligibility Requirements: Applicant must be enrolled or expecting to enroll full-time at a four-year institution or university. Applicant or parent of applicant must be member of United Daughters of the Confederacy. Applicant must have 3.0 GPA or higher. Available to U.S. citizens. Applicant or parent must meet one or more of the following requirements: Air Force, Army, or Navy experience; retired from active duty; disabled or killed as a result of military service; prisoner of war; or missing in action.

Application Requirements: Application, essay, financial need analysis, photo, references, self-addressed stamped envelope, transcript, proof of confederate ancestor's service, copy of applicant's birth certificate. *Deadline:* March 15.

Contact: Deanna Bryant, Second Vice President General
United Daughters of the Confederacy
328 North Boulevard
Richmond, VA 23220-4009
Phone: 804-355-1636
Fax: 804-353-1396
E-mail: hqudc@rcn.com

CHARLOTTE M. F. BENTLEY/NEW YORK CHAPTER 103 SCHOLARSHIP

Renewable award for undergraduate students who are descendant of a Confederate soldier, sailor or marine. Must be enrolled in an accredited college or university. Minimum of 3.0 GPA required. Must be members of United Daughters of the Confederacy and Children of the Confederacy from New York.

Award: Scholarship for use in freshman, sophomore, junior, or senior years; renewable. *Number:* 1–2. *Amount:* $800–$1000.

Eligibility Requirements: Applicant must be enrolled or expecting to enroll full-time at a four-year institution or university and resident of New York. Applicant or parent of applicant must be member of Catholic Workman Fraternal Society or United Daughters of the Confederacy. Applicant must have 3.0 GPA or higher. Available to U.S. citizens. Applicant or parent must meet one or more of the following requirements: Air Force or Navy experience; retired from active duty; disabled or killed as a result of military service; prisoner of war; or missing in action.

Application Requirements: Application, essay, financial need analysis, photo, references, self-addressed stamped envelope, transcript, proof of confederate ancestor's service, copy of applicant's birth certificate. *Deadline:* March 15.

Contact: Deanna Bryant, Second Vice President General
United Daughters of the Confederacy
328 North Boulevard
Richmond, VA 23220-4009
Phone: 804-355-1636
Fax: 804-353-1396
E-mail: hqudc@rcn.com

CODY BACHMAN SCHOLARSHIP

Renewable award for undergraduate students who are descendants of an eligible Confederate. Must be enrolled in an accredited college or university. Minimum 3.0 GPA required. Applicants must be endorsed by the President and the Second Vice President/Education Chairman of Chapter and Division, and by the Second Vice President General.

Award: Scholarship for use in freshman, sophomore, junior, or senior years; renewable. *Number:* 1–2. *Amount:* $800–$1000.

Eligibility Requirements: Applicant must be enrolled or expecting to enroll full-time at a four-year institution or university. Applicant or parent of applicant must be member of United Daughters of the Confederacy. Applicant must have 3.0 GPA or higher. Available to U.S. citizens. Applicant or parent must meet one or more of the following requirements: Air Force, Army, or Navy experience; retired from active duty; disabled or killed as a result of military service; prisoner of war; or missing in action.

Application Requirements: Application, essay, financial need analysis, photo, references, self-addressed stamped envelope, transcript, copy of applicant's birth certificate, copy of confederate ancestor's proof of service. *Deadline:* March 15.

Contact: Deanna Bryant, Second Vice President General
United Daughters of the Confederacy
328 North Boulevard
Richmond, VA 23220-4009
Phone: 804-355-1636
Fax: 804-353-1396
E-mail: hqudc@rcn.com

CORA BELL WESLEY MEMORIAL SCHOLARSHIP

Renewable award for undergraduate students who are descendants of a Confederate soldier, sailor or marine. Must be enrolled in an accredited college or university. Minimum 3.0 GPA required. Submit letter of endorsement from sponsoring chapter of the United Daughters of the Confederacy.

Award: Scholarship for use in freshman, sophomore, junior, or senior years; renewable. *Number:* 1–2. *Amount:* $800–$1000.

Eligibility Requirements: Applicant must be enrolled or expecting to enroll full-time at a four-year institution or university. Applicant or parent of applicant must be member of United Daughters of the Confederacy. Applicant must have 3.0 GPA or higher. Available to U.S. citizens. Applicant or parent must meet one or more of the following requirements: Air Force, Army, or Navy experience; retired from active duty; disabled or killed as a result of military service; prisoner of war; or missing in action.

Application Requirements: Application, essay, financial need analysis, photo, references, self-addressed stamped envelope, transcript, copy of applicant's birth certificate, copy of confederate ancestor's proof of service. *Deadline:* March 15.

Contact: Deanna Bryant, Second Vice President General
United Daughters of the Confederacy
328 North Boulevard
Richmond, VA 23220-4009
Phone: 804-355-1636
Fax: 804-353-1396
E-mail: hqudc@rcn.com

CORNELIA BRANCH STONE SCHOLARSHIP

Renewable award for undergraduate students who are descendants of an eligible Confederate. Must be enrolled in an accredited college or university. Minimum of 3.0 GPA required. Submit a letter of endorsement from sponsoring Chapter of the United Daughters of the Confederacy.

Award: Scholarship for use in freshman, sophomore, junior, or senior years; renewable. *Number:* 1–2. *Amount:* $800–$1000.

Eligibility Requirements: Applicant must be enrolled or expecting to enroll full-time at a four-year institution or university. Applicant or parent of applicant must be member of United Daughters of the Confederacy. Applicant must have 3.0 GPA or higher. Available to U.S. citizens. Applicant or parent must meet one or more of the following requirements: Air Force, Army, or Navy experience; retired from active duty; disabled or killed as a result of military service; prisoner of war; or missing in action.

Application Requirements: Application, essay, financial need analysis, photo, references, self-addressed stamped envelope, transcript, copy of applicant's birth certificate, copy of confederate ancestor's proof of service. *Deadline:* March 15.

Contact: Deanna Bryant, Second Vice President General
United Daughters of the Confederacy
328 North Boulevard
Richmond, VA 23220-4009
Phone: 804-355-1636
Fax: 804-353-1396
E-mail: hqudc@rcn.com

DAVID STEPHEN WYLIE SCHOLARSHIP

Renewable award for undergraduate students who are descendants of a Confederate soldier, sailor or marine. Must be enrolled in an accredited college or university. Minimum 3.0 GPA required. Submit letter of endorsement from sponsoring chapter of the United Daughters of the Confederacy.

Award: Scholarship for use in freshman, sophomore, junior, or senior years; renewable. *Number:* 1–2. *Amount:* $800–$1000.

Eligibility Requirements: Applicant must be enrolled or expecting to enroll full-time at a four-year institution or university. Applicant or parent of applicant must be member of United Daughters of the Confederacy. Applicant must have 3.0 GPA or higher. Available to U.S. citizens. Applicant or parent must meet one or more of the following requirements: Air Force, Army, or Navy experience; retired from active duty; disabled or killed as a result of military service; prisoner of war; or missing in action.

Application Requirements: Application, essay, financial need analysis, photo, references, self-addressed stamped envelope, transcript, copy of applicant's birth certificate, copy of confederate ancestor's proof of service. *Deadline:* March 15.

Contact: Deanna Bryant, Second Vice President General
United Daughters of the Confederacy
328 North Boulevard
Richmond, VA 23220-4009
Phone: 804-355-1636
Fax: 804-353-1396
E-mail: hqudc@rcn.com

DOROTHY WILLIAMS SCHOLARSHIP

Renewable award for undergraduate students who are descendants of a Confederate soldier, sailor or marine. Must be enrolled in an accredited college or university. Minimum 3.0 GPA required. Submit a letter of endorsement from sponsoring chapter of the United Daughters of the Confederacy.

Award: Scholarship for use in freshman, sophomore, junior, or senior years; renewable. *Number:* 1–2. *Amount:* $800–$1000.

Eligibility Requirements: Applicant must be enrolled or expecting to enroll full-time at a four-year institution or university. Applicant or parent of applicant must be member of United Daughters of the Confederacy. Applicant must have 3.0 GPA or higher. Available to U.S. citizens. Applicant or parent must meet one or more of the following requirements: Air Force, Army, or Navy experience; retired from active duty; disabled or killed as a result of military service; prisoner of war; or missing in action.

Application Requirements: Application, essay, financial need analysis, photo, references, self-addressed stamped envelope, transcript, copy of applicant's birth certificate, copy of confederate ancestor's proof of service. *Deadline:* March 15.

Contact: Deanna Bryant, Second Vice President General
United Daughters of the Confederacy
328 North Boulevard
Richmond, VA 23220-4009
Phone: 804-355-1636
Fax: 804-353-1396
E-mail: hqudc@rcn.com

ELIZABETH AND WALLACE KINGSBURY SCHOLARSHIP

Award for full-time undergraduate students who are descendants of a Confederate soldier, studying at an accredited college or university. Must have been a member of the Children of the Confederacy for a minimum of three years. Minimum 3.0 GPA required.

Award: Scholarship for use in freshman, sophomore, junior, or senior years; renewable. *Number:* 1–2. *Amount:* $800–$1000.

Eligibility Requirements: Applicant must be enrolled or expecting to enroll full-time at a four-year institution or university. Applicant or parent of applicant must be member of United Daughters of the Confederacy. Applicant must have 3.0 GPA or higher. Available to U.S. citizens. Applicant or parent must meet one or more of the following requirements: Air Force, Army, or Navy experience; retired from active duty; disabled or killed as a result of military service; prisoner of war; or missing in action.

Application Requirements: Application, essay, financial need analysis, photo, references, self-addressed stamped envelope, transcript, copy of applicant's birth certificate, copy of confederate ancestor's proof of service. *Deadline:* March 15.

Contact: Deanna Bryant, Second Vice President General
United Daughters of the Confederacy
328 North Boulevard
Richmond, VA 23220-4009
Phone: 804-355-1636
Fax: 804-353-1396
E-mail: hqudc@rcn.com

GERTRUDE BOTTS-SAUCIER SCHOLARSHIP

Award for full-time undergraduate students who are descendants of a Confederate soldier, sailor or marine. Must be from Texas, Mississippi or Louisiana. Must be enrolled in an accredited college or university and have a minimum 3.0 GPA. Submit letter of endorsement from sponsoring chapter of the United Daughters of the Confederacy.

Award: Scholarship for use in freshman, sophomore, junior, or senior years; renewable. *Number:* 1–2. *Amount:* $800–$1000.

Eligibility Requirements: Applicant must be enrolled or expecting to enroll full-time at a four-year institution or university and resident of Louisiana, Mississippi, or Texas. Applicant or parent of applicant must be member of United Daughters of the Confederacy. Applicant must have 3.0 GPA or higher. Available to U.S. citizens. Applicant or parent must meet one or more of the following requirements: Air Force, Army, or Navy experience; retired from active duty; disabled or killed as a result of military service; prisoner of war; or missing in action.

Application Requirements: Application, essay, financial need analysis, photo, references, self-addressed stamped envelope, transcript, copy of applicant's birth certificate, copy of confederate ancestor's proof of service. *Deadline:* March 15.

Contact: Deanna Bryant, Second Vice President General
United Daughters of the Confederacy
328 North Boulevard
Richmond, VA 23220-4009
Phone: 804-355-1636
Fax: 804-353-1396
E-mail: hqudc@rcn.com

HECTOR W. CHURCH SCHOLARSHIP

Renewable award for undergraduate student who is a descendant of an eligible Confederate. Must be enrolled in an accredited college or university. Minimum of 3.0 GPA required. Submit letter of endorsement from sponsoring chapter of the United Daughters of the Confederacy.

Award: Scholarship for use in freshman, sophomore, junior, or senior years; renewable. *Number:* 1–5. *Amount:* $800–$1000.

Eligibility Requirements: Applicant must be enrolled or expecting to enroll full-time at a four-year institution or university. Applicant or parent of applicant must be member of United Daughters of the Confederacy. Applicant must have 3.0 GPA or higher. Available to U.S. citizens. Applicant or parent must meet one or more of the following requirements: Air Force, Army, or Navy experience; retired from active duty; disabled or killed as a result of military service; prisoner of war; or missing in action.

Application Requirements: Application, essay, financial need analysis, photo, references, self-addressed stamped envelope, transcript, copy of applicant's birth certificate, copy of confederate ancestor's proof of service. *Deadline:* March 15.

United Daughters of the Confederacy (continued)

Contact: Deanna Bryant, Second Vice President General
United Daughters of the Confederacy
328 North Boulevard
Richmond, VA 23220-4009
Phone: 804-355-1636
Fax: 804-353-1396
E-mail: hqudc@rcn.com

HENRY CLAY DARSEY SCHOLARSHIP

Renewable award for undergraduate students who are descendants of an eligible Confederate. Must be enrolled in an accredited college or university. Minimum 3.0 GPA required. Submit letter of endorsement from sponsoring Chapter of the United Daughters of the Confederacy.

Award: Scholarship for use in freshman, sophomore, junior, or senior years; renewable. *Number:* 1–2. *Amount:* $800–$1000.

Eligibility Requirements: Applicant must be enrolled or expecting to enroll full-time at a four-year institution or university. Applicant or parent of applicant must be member of United Daughters of the Confederacy. Applicant must have 3.0 GPA or higher. Available to U.S. citizens. Applicant or parent must meet one or more of the following requirements: Air Force, Army, or Navy experience; retired from active duty; disabled or killed as a result of military service; prisoner of war; or missing in action.

Application Requirements: Application, essay, financial need analysis, photo, references, self-addressed stamped envelope, transcript, copy of applicant's birth certificate, copy of confederate ancestor's proof of service. *Deadline:* March 15.

Contact: Deanna Bryant, Second Vice President General
United Daughters of the Confederacy
328 North Boulevard
Richmond, VA 23220-4009
Phone: 804-355-1636
Fax: 804-353-1396
E-mail: hqudc@rcn.com

JANET B. SEIPPEL SCHOLARSHIP

Renewable award for undergraduate students who are a descendant of a confederate. Must be enrolled in an accredited college or university. Minimum of 3.0 GPA required. Submit a letter of endorsement from sponsoring chapter of the United Daughters of the Confederacy.

Award: Scholarship for use in freshman, sophomore, junior, or senior years; renewable. *Number:* 1–2. *Amount:* $800–$1000.

Eligibility Requirements: Applicant must be enrolled or expecting to enroll full-time at a four-year institution or university. Applicant or parent of applicant must be member of United Daughters of the Confederacy. Applicant must have 3.0 GPA or higher. Available to U.S. citizens. Applicant or parent must meet one or more of the following requirements: Air Force, Army, or Navy experience; retired from active duty; disabled or killed as a result of military service; prisoner of war; or missing in action.

Application Requirements: Application, essay, financial need analysis, photo, references, self-addressed stamped envelope, transcript, copy of applicant's birth certificate, copy of confederate ancestor's proof of service. *Deadline:* March 15.

Contact: Deanna Bryant, Second Vice President General
United Daughters of the Confederacy
328 North Boulevard
Richmond, VA 23220-4009
Phone: 804-355-1636
Fax: 804-353-1396
E-mail: hqudc@rcn.com

LOLA B. CURRY SCHOLARSHIP

Award for full-time undergraduate students from Alabama who are descendants of a Confederate soldier. Must be enrolled in an accredited college or university in Alabama. Minimum 3.0 GPA required. Submit letter of endorsement from sponsoring chapter of the United Daughters of the Confederacy.

Award: Scholarship for use in freshman, sophomore, junior, or senior years; renewable. *Number:* 1–2. *Amount:* $800–$1000.

Eligibility Requirements: Applicant must be enrolled or expecting to enroll full-time at a four-year institution or university; resident of Alabama and studying in Alabama. Applicant or parent of applicant must be member of United Daughters of the Confederacy. Applicant must have 3.0 GPA or higher. Available to U.S. citizens. Applicant or parent must meet one or more of the following requirements: Air Force, Army, or Navy experience; retired from active duty; disabled or killed as a result of military service; prisoner of war; or missing in action.

Application Requirements: Application, essay, financial need analysis, photo, references, self-addressed stamped envelope, transcript, copy of applicant's birth certificate, copy of confederate ancestor's proof of service. *Deadline:* March 15.

Contact: Deanna Bryant, Second Vice President General
United Daughters of the Confederacy
328 North Boulevard
Richmond, VA 23220-4009
Phone: 804-355-1636
Fax: 804-353-1396
E-mail: hqudc@rcn.com

MAJOR MADISON BELL SCHOLARSHIP

Renewable award for undergraduate student who is a descendant of an eligible Confederate. Must be enrolled in an accredited college or university. Minimum 3.0 GPA required. Applicants must be endorsed by the President and the Second Vice President/Education Chairman of Chapter and Division, and by the Second Vice President General.

Award: Scholarship for use in freshman, sophomore, junior, or senior years; renewable. *Number:* 1–2. *Amount:* $800–$1000.

Eligibility Requirements: Applicant must be enrolled or expecting to enroll full-time at a four-year institution or university. Applicant or parent of applicant must be member of United Daughters of the Confederacy. Applicant must have 3.0 GPA or higher. Available to U.S. citizens. Applicant or parent must meet one or more of the following requirements: Air Force, Army, or Navy experience; retired from active duty; disabled or killed as a result of military service; prisoner of war; or missing in action.

Application Requirements: Application, essay, financial need analysis, photo, references, self-addressed stamped envelope, transcript, copy of applicant's birth certificate, copy of confederate ancestor's proof of service. *Deadline:* March 15.

Contact: Deanna Bryant, Second Vice President General
United Daughters of the Confederacy
328 North Boulevard
Richmond, VA 23220-4009
Phone: 804-355-1636
Fax: 804-353-1396
E-mail: hqudc@rcn.com

MARY B. POPPENHEIM MEMORIAL SCHOLARSHIP

Renewable award for undergraduate student who is a descendant of an eligible Confederate. Must be enrolled in an accredited college or university. Minimum 3.0 GPA required. Submit a letter of endorsement from sponsoring Chapter of the United Daughters of the Confederacy.

Award: Scholarship for use in freshman, sophomore, junior, or senior years; renewable. *Number:* 1–2. *Amount:* $800–$1000.

Eligibility Requirements: Applicant must be enrolled or expecting to enroll full-time at a four-year institution or university. Applicant or parent of applicant must be member of United Daughters of the Confederacy. Applicant must have 3.0 GPA or higher. Available to U.S. citizens. Applicant or parent must meet one or more of the following requirements: Air Force, Army, or Navy experience; retired from active duty; disabled or killed as a result of military service; prisoner of war; or missing in action.

Application Requirements: Application, essay, financial need analysis, photo, references, self-addressed stamped envelope, transcript, copy of applicant's birth certificate, copy of confederate ancestor's proof of service. *Deadline:* March 15.

Contact: Deanna Bryant, Second Vice President General
United Daughters of the Confederacy
328 North Boulevard
Richmond, VA 23220-4009
Phone: 804-355-1636
Fax: 804-353-1396
E-mail: hqudc@rcn.com

MATTHEW FONTAINE MAURY SCHOLARSHIP

Renewable award for undergraduate students who are descendants of an eligible Confederate. Must be enrolled in an accredited college or university. Minimum 3.0 GPA required. Submit letter of endorsement from sponsoring Chapter of the United Daughters of the Confederacy.

Award: Scholarship for use in freshman, sophomore, junior, or senior years; renewable. *Number:* 1–2. *Amount:* $800–$1000.

Eligibility Requirements: Applicant must be enrolled or expecting to enroll full-time at a four-year institution or university. Applicant or parent of applicant must be member of United Daughters of the Confederacy. Applicant must have 3.0 GPA or higher. Available to U.S. citizens. Applicant or parent must meet one or more of the following requirements: Air Force, Army, or Navy experience; retired from active duty; disabled or killed as a result of military service; prisoner of war; or missing in action.

Application Requirements: Application, essay, financial need analysis, photo, references, self-addressed stamped envelope, transcript, copy of applicant's birth certificate, copy of confederate ancestor's proof of service. *Deadline:* March 15.

Contact: Deanna Bryant, Second Vice President General
United Daughters of the Confederacy
328 North Boulevard
Richmond, VA 23220-4009
Phone: 804-355-1636
Fax: 804-353-1396
E-mail: hqudc@rcn.com

MRS. ELLA M. FRANKLIN SCHOLARSHIP

Renewable award for undergraduate students who are descendants of an eligible Confederate. Must be enrolled in an accredited college or university. Minimum 3.0 GPA required. Submit letter of endorsement from sponsoring chapter of the United Daughters of the Confederacy.

Award: Scholarship for use in freshman, sophomore, junior, or senior years; renewable. *Number:* 1–2. *Amount:* $800–$1000.

Eligibility Requirements: Applicant must be enrolled or expecting to enroll full-time at a four-year institution or university. Applicant or parent of applicant must be member of United Daughters of the Confederacy. Applicant must have 3.0 GPA or higher. Available to U.S. citizens. Applicant or parent must meet one or more of the following requirements: Air Force, Army, or Navy experience; retired from active duty; disabled or killed as a result of military service; prisoner of war; or missing in action.

Application Requirements: Application, essay, financial need analysis, photo, references, self-addressed stamped envelope, transcript, copy of applicant's birth certificate, copy of confederate ancestor's proof of service. *Deadline:* March 15.

Contact: Deanna Bryant, Second Vice President General
United Daughters of the Confederacy
328 North Boulevard
Richmond, VA 23220-4009
Phone: 804-355-1636
Fax: 804-353-1396
E-mail: hqudc@rcn.com

MRS. L. H. RAINES MEMORIAL SCHOLARSHIP

Renewable award for undergraduate students who are descendants of eligible Confederates. Must be enrolled in an accredited college or university. Minimum 3.0 GPA required. Submit letter of endorsement from sponsoring chapter of the United Daughters of the Confederacy.

Award: Scholarship for use in freshman, sophomore, junior, or senior years; renewable. *Number:* 1–2. *Amount:* $800–$1000.

Eligibility Requirements: Applicant must be enrolled or expecting to enroll full-time at a four-year institution or university. Applicant or parent of applicant must be member of United Daughters of the Confederacy. Applicant must have 3.0 GPA or higher. Available to U.S. citizens. Applicant or parent must meet one or more of the following requirements: Air Force, Army, or Navy experience; retired from active duty; disabled or killed as a result of military service; prisoner of war; or missing in action.

Application Requirements: Application, essay, financial need analysis, photo, references, self-addressed stamped envelope, transcript, copy of applicant's birth certificate, copy of confederate ancestor's proof of service. *Deadline:* March 15.

Contact: Deanna Bryant, Second Vice President General
United Daughters of the Confederacy
328 North Boulevard
Richmond, VA 23220-4009
Phone: 804-355-1636
Fax: 804-353-1396
E-mail: hqudc@rcn.com

S.A. CUNNINGHAM SCHOLARSHIP

Renewable award for undergraduate students who are descendants of an eligible Confederate. Must be enrolled in an accredited college or university. Minimum 3.0 GPA required. Submit letter of endorsement from sponsoring Chapter of the United Daughters of the Confederacy.

Award: Scholarship for use in freshman, sophomore, junior, or senior years; renewable. *Number:* 1–2. *Amount:* $800–$1000.

Eligibility Requirements: Applicant must be enrolled or expecting to enroll full-time at a four-year institution or university. Applicant or parent of applicant must be member of United Daughters of the Confederacy. Applicant must have 3.0 GPA or higher. Available to U.S. citizens. Applicant or parent must meet one or more of the following requirements: Air Force, Army, or Navy experience; retired from active duty; disabled or killed as a result of military service; prisoner of war; or missing in action.

Application Requirements: Application, essay, financial need analysis, photo, references, self-addressed stamped envelope, transcript, copy of applicant's birth certificate, copy of confederate ancestor's proof of service. *Deadline:* March 15.

Contact: Deanna Bryant, Second Vice President General
United Daughters of the Confederacy
328 North Boulevard
Richmond, VA 23220-4009
Phone: 804-355-1636
Fax: 804-353-1396
E-mail: hqudc@rcn.com

STONEWALL JACKSON SCHOLARSHIP

Renewable award for undergraduate students who are descendants of an eligible Confederate. Must be enrolled in an accredited college or university. Minimum 3.0 GPA required. Submit letter of endorsement from sponsoring Chapter of the United Daughters of the Confederacy.

Award: Scholarship for use in freshman, sophomore, junior, or senior years; renewable. *Number:* 1–2. *Amount:* $800–$1000.

Eligibility Requirements: Applicant must be enrolled or expecting to enroll full-time at a four-year institution or university. Applicant or parent of applicant must be member of United Daughters of the Confederacy. Applicant must have 3.0 GPA or higher. Available to U.S. citizens. Applicant or parent must meet one or more of the following requirements: Air Force, Army, or Navy experience; retired from active duty; disabled or killed as a result of military service; prisoner of war; or missing in action.

Application Requirements: Application, essay, financial need analysis, photo, references, self-addressed stamped envelope, transcript, copy of applicant's birth certificate, copy of confederate ancestor's proof of service. *Deadline:* March 15.

Contact: Deanna Bryant, Second Vice President General
United Daughters of the Confederacy
328 North Boulevard
Richmond, VA 23220-4009
Phone: 804-355-1636
Fax: 804-353-1396
E-mail: hqudc@rcn.com

WINNIE DAVIS-CHILDREN OF THE CONFEDERACY SCHOLARSHIP

Award for full-time undergraduate students who are descendants of a Confederate soldier, enrolled in an accredited college or university. Recipient must be,

United Daughters of the Confederacy (continued)

or have been until age of 18, a participating member of the Children of the Confederacy and approved by the Third Vice President General. Minimum 3.0 GPA required.

Award: Scholarship for use in freshman, sophomore, junior, or senior years; renewable. *Number:* 1–2. *Amount:* $800–$1000.

Eligibility Requirements: Applicant must be age 18 and over and enrolled or expecting to enroll full-time at a four-year institution or university. Applicant or parent of applicant must be member of United Daughters of the Confederacy. Applicant must have 3.0 GPA or higher. Available to U.S. citizens. Applicant or parent must meet one or more of the following requirements: Air Force, Army, or Navy experience; retired from active duty; disabled or killed as a result of military service; prisoner of war; or missing in action.

Application Requirements: Application, essay, financial need analysis, photo, references, self-addressed stamped envelope, transcript, copy of applicant's birth certificate, copy of confederate ancestor's proof of service. *Deadline:* March 15.

Contact: Deanna Bryant, Second Vice President General
United Daughters of the Confederacy
328 North Boulevard
Richmond, VA 23220-4009
Phone: 804-355-1636
Fax: 804-353-1396
E-mail: hqudc@rcn.com

UNITED FOOD AND COMMERCIAL WORKERS INTERNATIONAL UNION http://www.ufcw.org

JAMES A. SUFFRIDGE UNITED FOOD AND COMMERCIAL WORKERS SCHOLARSHIP PROGRAM

Scholarships available to graduating high school seniors and college students during the specific program year. Must be a member of UFCW or unmarried dependent under age 20 of a UFCW member. Scholarship is disbursed over a four-year period of undergraduate study.

Award: Scholarship for use in freshman, sophomore, junior, or senior years; renewable. *Number:* 14. *Amount:* up to $8000.

Eligibility Requirements: Applicant must be enrolled or expecting to enroll full- or part-time at a two-year or four-year or technical institution or university. Applicant or parent of applicant must be member of United Food and Commercial Workers. Available to U.S. citizens.

Application Requirements: Application, transcript. *Deadline:* March 15.

Contact: Field Assistant
United Food and Commercial Workers International Union
1775 K Street, NW
Washington, DC 20006
Phone: 202-223-3111
Fax: 202-466-1587
E-mail: scholarship@ufcw.org

UNITED STATES JUNIOR CHAMBER OF COMMERCE http://www.usjaycees.org

JAYCEE CHARLES R. FORD SCHOLARSHIP

One-time award of $3000 available to active members of Jaycee wishing to return to college to complete his/her formal education. Must be U.S. citizen, possess academic potential and leadership qualities and show financial need. To receive an application, send $10 application fee and self-addressed stamped envelope by February 1.

Award: Scholarship for use in freshman, sophomore, junior, or senior years; not renewable. *Number:* 1. *Amount:* $3000.

Eligibility Requirements: Applicant must be age 18-39; enrolled or expecting to enroll full- or part-time at a two-year or four-year institution or university and must have an interest in leadership. Applicant or parent of applicant must be member of Jaycees. Available to U.S. citizens.

Application Requirements: Application, financial need analysis, self-addressed stamped envelope. *Fee:* $10. *Deadline:* February 1.

Contact: Karen Fitzgerald, Customer Service and Data Processing
United States Junior Chamber of Commerce
PO Box 7
Tulsa, OK 74102-0007
Phone: 918-584-2481
Fax: 918-584-4422
E-mail: customerservice@usjaycees.org

JAYCEE THOMAS WOOD BALDRIDGE SCHOLARSHIP

One-time award of $3000 available to a Jaycee immediate family member or a descendant of a Jaycee member. Must be U.S. citizen, possess academic potential and leadership qualities and show financial need. To receive an application, send $10 application fee and self-addressed stamped envelope by February 1.

Award: Scholarship for use in freshman, sophomore, junior, or senior years; not renewable. *Number:* 1. *Amount:* $3000.

Eligibility Requirements: Applicant must be age 18-39; enrolled or expecting to enroll full- or part-time at a two-year or four-year institution or university and must have an interest in leadership. Applicant or parent of applicant must be member of Jaycees. Available to U.S. citizens.

Application Requirements: Application, financial need analysis, self-addressed stamped envelope. *Fee:* $10. *Deadline:* February 1.

Contact: Karen Fitzgerald, Customer Service and Data Processing
United States Junior Chamber of Commerce
PO Box 7
Tulsa, OK 74102-0007
Phone: 918-584-2481
Fax: 918-584-4422
E-mail: customerservice@usjaycees.org

UNITED STATES NAVAL SEA CADET CORPS http://www.seacadets.org

HARRY AND ROSE HOWELL SCHOLARSHIP

Renewable award for Sea Cadets only. Two Howell Scholarships of $2500 each and one scholarship of $2000. Applicants must be U.S. citizens with a minimum 3.0 GPA.

Award: Scholarship for use in freshman, sophomore, junior, or senior years; renewable. *Number:* 3. *Amount:* $2000–$2500.

Eligibility Requirements: Applicant must be enrolled or expecting to enroll full-time at a two-year or four-year institution or university. Applicant or parent of applicant must be member of Naval Sea Cadet Corps. Applicant must have 3.0 GPA or higher. Available to U.S. citizens.

Application Requirements: Application, financial need analysis, references, test scores, transcript. *Deadline:* May 1.

Contact: M. Ford, Executive Director
United States Naval Sea Cadet Corps
2300 Wilson Boulevard
Arlington, VA 22201-3308
Phone: 703-243-6910
Fax: 703-243-3985
E-mail: mford@navyleague.org

KINGSLEY FOUNDATION AWARDS

One-time award to assist Cadets in continuing their education at an accredited four-year college or university. Must be a member of NSCC for at least two years. Minimum 3.0 GPA required.

Award: Scholarship for use in freshman, sophomore, junior, or senior years; not renewable. *Number:* 5. *Amount:* $1000.

Eligibility Requirements: Applicant must be enrolled or expecting to enroll full-time at a four-year institution or university. Applicant or parent of applicant must be member of Naval Sea Cadet Corps. Applicant must have 3.0 GPA or higher. Available to U.S. citizens.

Application Requirements: Application, financial need analysis, references, test scores, transcript. *Deadline:* May 1.

Contact: M. Ford, Executive Director
United States Naval Sea Cadet Corps
2300 Wilson Boulevard
Arlington, VA 22201-3308
Phone: 703-243-6910
Fax: 703-243-3985
E-mail: mford@navyleague.org

NAVAL SEA CADET CORPS BOARD OF DIRECTORS SCHOLARSHIP

Renewable award up to $1400 is available for Sea Cadets. Award available to U.S. citizens and minimum GPA of 3.0 is required.

Award: Scholarship for use in freshman, sophomore, junior, or senior years; renewable. *Number:* 1. *Amount:* $1200–$1400.

Eligibility Requirements: Applicant must be enrolled or expecting to enroll full-time at a two-year or four-year institution. Applicant or parent of applicant must be member of Naval Sea Cadet Corps. Applicant must have 3.0 GPA or higher. Available to U.S. citizens.

Application Requirements: Application, financial need analysis, references, test scores, transcript. *Deadline:* May 1.

Contact: M. Ford, Executive Director
United States Naval Sea Cadet Corps
2300 Wilson Boulevard
Arlington, VA 22201-3308
Phone: 703-243-6910
Fax: 703-243-3985
E-mail: mford@navyleague.org

NAVAL SEA CADET CORPS SCHOLARSHIP PROGRAM

One-time award to assist Cadets in continuing their education at an accredited four-year college or university. Must be a member of NSCC for at least two years. Minimum 3.0 GPA required.

Award: Scholarship for use in freshman, sophomore, junior, or senior years; not renewable. *Number:* up to 5. *Amount:* $1000.

Eligibility Requirements: Applicant must be enrolled or expecting to enroll full-time at a four-year institution or university. Applicant or parent of applicant must be member of Naval Sea Cadet Corps. Applicant must have 3.0 GPA or higher. Available to U.S. citizens.

Application Requirements: Application, financial need analysis, references, test scores, transcript. *Deadline:* May 1.

Contact: M. Ford, Executive Director
United States Naval Sea Cadet Corps
2300 Wilson Boulevard
Arlington, VA 22201-3308
Phone: 703-243-6910
Fax: 703-243-3985
E-mail: mford@navyleague.org

ROBERT AND HELEN HUTTON SCHOLARSHIP

One renewable award of $1000 is available for Sea Cadets to assist them in continuing their education at an accredited four-year college or university. Minimum 3.0 GPA required.

Award: Scholarship for use in freshman, sophomore, junior, or senior years; renewable. *Number:* 1. *Amount:* $1000.

Eligibility Requirements: Applicant must be enrolled or expecting to enroll full-time at a two-year or four-year institution or university. Applicant or parent of applicant must be member of Naval Sea Cadet Corps. Applicant must have 3.0 GPA or higher. Available to U.S. citizens.

Application Requirements: Application, financial need analysis, references, test scores, transcript. *Deadline:* May 1.

Contact: M. Ford, Executive Director
United States Naval Sea Cadet Corps
2300 Wilson Boulevard
Arlington, VA 22201-3308
Phone: 703-243-6910
Fax: 703-243-3985
E-mail: mford@navyleague.org

STOCKHOLM SCHOLARSHIP PROGRAM

Renewable award for a selected Cadet, to be designated a Stockholm Scholar. Must be a member of NSCC for at least two years. Assistance provided for no more than four consecutive years at an accredited college or university. Minimum 3.0 GPA required.

Award: Scholarship for use in freshman, sophomore, junior, or senior years; renewable. *Number:* 1. *Amount:* $2000–$2500.

Eligibility Requirements: Applicant must be enrolled or expecting to enroll full-time at a four-year institution or university. Applicant or parent of applicant must be member of Naval Sea Cadet Corps. Applicant must have 3.0 GPA or higher. Available to U.S. citizens.

Application Requirements: Application, financial need analysis, references, test scores, transcript. *Deadline:* May 1.

Contact: M. Ford, Executive Director
United States Naval Sea Cadet Corps
2300 Wilson Boulevard
Arlington, VA 22201-3308
Phone: 703-243-6910
Fax: 703-243-3985
E-mail: mford@navyleague.org

UNITED STATES SUBMARINE VETERANS INC. http://www.ussvcf.org

UNITED STATES SUBMARINE VETERANS INC. NATIONAL SCHOLARSHIP PROGRAM

Program requires the sponsor to be a qualified Base Member or Member-at-Large (MAL) in good standing. Must demonstrate financial need, have a minimum 2.5 GPA, and submit an essay. Open to children, stepchildren, and grandchildren of qualified members. Applicants must be between the ages of 17 to 23 and must be unmarried.

Award: Scholarship for use in freshman, sophomore, junior, or senior years; not renewable. *Number:* 2–18. *Amount:* $750–$1500.

Eligibility Requirements: Applicant must be age 17-23; enrolled or expecting to enroll full-time at a two-year or four-year or technical institution or university and single. Applicant or parent of applicant must be member of Veterans of Foreign Wars or Auxiliary. Applicant or parent of applicant must have employment or volunteer experience in seafaring/fishing industry. Applicant must have 2.5 GPA or higher. Available to U.S. citizens. Applicant or parent must meet one or more of the following requirements: Navy experience; retired from active duty; disabled or killed as a result of military service; prisoner of war; or missing in action.

Application Requirements: Application, essay, financial need analysis, references, test scores, transcript. *Deadline:* April 15.

Contact: Paul William Orstad, National Scholarship Chairman
United States Submarine Veterans Inc.
30 Surrey Lane
Norwich, CT 06369-6541
Phone: 860-889-4750
Fax: 860-334-6457
E-mail: hogan343@aol.com

UTILITY WORKERS UNION OF AMERICA http://www.uwua.net

UTILITY WORKERS UNION OF AMERICA SCHOLARSHIP AWARDS PROGRAM

Renewable award for high school juniors who are children of active members of the Utility Workers Union of America. Must take the PSAT National Merit Scholarship Qualifying Test in junior year and plan to enter college in the fall after high school graduation.

Award: Scholarship for use in freshman year; renewable. *Number:* 2. *Amount:* $500–$2000.

Utility Workers Union of America (continued)

Eligibility Requirements: Applicant must be high school student and planning to enroll or expecting to enroll full-time at a four-year institution or university. Applicant or parent of applicant must be member of Utility Workers Union of America. Available to U.S. citizens.

Application Requirements: Application, test scores. *Deadline:* January 31.

Contact: Rosanna Farley, Office Manager
Utility Workers Union of America
815 16th Street, NW
Washington, DC 20006
Phone: 202-974-8200
Fax: 202-974-8201
E-mail: rfarley@aflcio.org

VIETNOW NATIONAL HEADQUARTERS http://www.vietnow.com

VIETNOW NATIONAL SCHOLARSHIP

One-time award available to dependants of members of VietNow only. Applicants' academic achievements, abilities and extracurricular activities will be reviewed. Must be U.S. citizen and under the age of 35.

Award: Scholarship for use in freshman, sophomore, junior, senior, or graduate years; not renewable. *Number:* varies. *Amount:* $500–$1000.

Eligibility Requirements: Applicant must be age 35 or under and enrolled or expecting to enroll full-time at a four-year institution or university. Applicant or parent of applicant must be member of VietNow. Available to U.S. citizens.

Application Requirements: Application, autobiography, essay, test scores, transcript. *Deadline:* April 1.

Contact: Eileen Shoemaker, Executive Assistant
VietNow National Headquarters
1835 Broadway
Rockford, IL 61104
Phone: 815-227-5100
Fax: 815-227-5127
E-mail: vnnatl@inwave.com

WESTERN FRATERNAL LIFE ASSOCIATION http://www.wflains.org

WESTERN FRATERNAL LIFE ASSOCIATION NATIONAL SCHOLARSHIP

Ten national scholarships will be awarded annually for up to $1000 to qualified members attending college or vocational programs. Traditional and non-traditional students are eligible. Must be a WFLA member in good standing for two years prior to the application deadline. A member is an individual who has life insurance or an annuity with WFLA. High school seniors may apply. Members who are qualified for the National Scholarship may also qualify for 3 state scholarships

Award: Scholarship for use in freshman, sophomore, junior, senior, or graduate years; renewable. *Number:* 10. *Amount:* $1000.

Eligibility Requirements: Applicant must be enrolled or expecting to enroll full-time at a two-year or four-year or technical institution or university. Applicant or parent of applicant must be member of Western Fraternal Life Association. Available to U.S. citizens.

Application Requirements: Application, driver's license, essay, references, test scores, transcript. *Deadline:* March 1.

Contact: Linda Grove, Publication Coordinator
Western Fraternal Life Association
1900 First Avenue, NE
Cedar Rapids, IA 52402-5372
Phone: 877-935-2467
Fax: 319-363-8806
E-mail: wflains@wflains.org

WISCONSIN ASSOCIATION FOR FOOD PROTECTION http://www.wafp-wi.org

WAFP MEMORIAL SCHOLARSHIP

Scholarship for a child or dependent of a current or deceased association member, or the applicant may be a WAFP student member. Must have been accepted into an accredited degree program in a university, college, or technical institute.

Award: Scholarship for use in freshman year; not renewable. *Number:* 1. *Amount:* $1000.

Eligibility Requirements: Applicant must be enrolled or expecting to enroll full-time at a four-year or technical institution or university. Applicant or parent of applicant must be member of Wisconsin Association for Food Protection. Available to U.S. and non-U.S. citizens.

Application Requirements: Application, references, transcript. *Deadline:* July 1.

Contact: George Nelson, Chair, Scholarship Committee
Wisconsin Association for Food Protection
PO Box 329
Sun Prairie, WI 53590
Phone: 715-235-4114
E-mail: nelsong@uwstout.edu

WOODMEN OF THE WORLD http://www.denverwoodmen.com

WOODMEN OF THE WORLD SCHOLARSHIP PROGRAM

One-time award for full-time study at a trade/technical school, two-year college, four-year college or university. Applicant must be a member or child of a member by a family rider of Woodmen the World of Denver, Colorado. Applicant must have minimum 2.5 GPA.

Award: Scholarship for use in freshman, sophomore, junior, senior, or graduate years; not renewable. *Number:* 50. *Amount:* $500–$2000.

Eligibility Requirements: Applicant must be enrolled or expecting to enroll full-time at a two-year or four-year or technical institution or university. Applicant or parent of applicant must be member of Woodmen of the World. Applicant must have 2.5 GPA or higher. Available to U.S. citizens.

Application Requirements: Application, essay, photo, transcript. *Deadline:* March 15.

Contact: Jerry Christensen, Fraternal Vice President
Woodmen of the World
8000 East Maplewood Avenue, Suite 105
Greenwood Village, CO 80111
Phone: 303-792-9777
Fax: 303-792-9793
E-mail: fraternal@denverwoodmen.com

WYOMING FARM BUREAU FEDERATION http://www.wyfb.org

KING-LIVINGSTON SCHOLARSHIP

One-time award given to graduates of Wyoming high schools. Must attend a Wyoming junior college or the University of Wyoming. Minimum 2.5 GPA required. Applicant's family must be a current member of the Wyoming Farm Bureau.

Award: Scholarship for use in freshman, sophomore, junior, senior, or graduate years; not renewable. *Number:* 1. *Amount:* $1000.

Eligibility Requirements: Applicant must be enrolled or expecting to enroll full-time at a two-year or four-year institution or university; resident of Wyoming and studying in Wyoming. Applicant or parent of applicant must be member of Wyoming Farm Bureau. Applicant must have 2.5 GPA or higher. Available to U.S. and non-U.S. citizens.

Application Requirements: Application, financial need analysis, photo, resume, references, transcript. *Deadline:* March 1.

Contact: Ellen Westbrook, Executive Secretary
Wyoming Farm Bureau Federation
931 Boulder Drive
Laramie, WY 82070
Phone: 307-721-7719
Fax: 307-721-7790
E-mail: ewestbrook@wyfb.org

WYOMING FARM BUREAU CONTINUING EDUCATION SCHOLARSHIPS

Award to students attending a two-year college in Wyoming or the University of Wyoming. Must be a resident of Wyoming and applicant's family must be a current member of the Wyoming Farm Bureau. Must submit at least two semesters of college grade transcripts. Freshmen must submit first semester grades and proof of enrollment in second semester. Minimum 2.5 GPA.

Award: Scholarship for use in freshman, sophomore, junior, senior, or graduate years; not renewable. *Number:* 3. *Amount:* $500.

Eligibility Requirements: Applicant must be enrolled or expecting to enroll full-time at a two-year or four-year institution or university; resident of Wyoming and studying in Wyoming. Applicant or parent of applicant must be member of Wyoming Farm Bureau. Applicant must have 2.5 GPA or higher. Available to U.S. and non-U.S. citizens.

Application Requirements: Application, financial need analysis, photo, resume, references, test scores, transcript. *Deadline:* March 1.

Contact: Ellen Westbrook, Executive Secretary
Wyoming Farm Bureau Federation
931 Boulder Drive
Laramie, WY 82070
Phone: 307-721-7719
Fax: 307-721-7790
E-mail: ewestbrook@wyfb.org

WYOMING FARM BUREAU FEDERATION SCHOLARSHIPS

Five $500 scholarships will be given to graduates of Wyoming high schools. Eligible candidates must be enrolled in a two-year college in Wyoming or the University of Wyoming and must have a minimum 2.5 GPA. Applicant's family should be current member of the Wyoming Farm Bureau Federation.

Award: Scholarship for use in freshman, sophomore, junior, senior, or graduate years; not renewable. *Number:* 5. *Amount:* $500.

Eligibility Requirements: Applicant must be enrolled or expecting to enroll full-time at a two-year or four-year institution or university; resident of Wyoming and studying in Wyoming. Applicant or parent of applicant must be member of Wyoming Farm Bureau. Applicant must have 2.5 GPA or higher. Available to U.S. and non-U.S. citizens.

Application Requirements: Application, financial need analysis, photo, resume, references, transcript. *Deadline:* March 1.

Contact: Ellen Westbrook, Executive Secretary
Wyoming Farm Bureau Federation
931 Boulder Drive
Laramie, WY 82070
Phone: 307-721-7719
Fax: 307-721-7790
E-mail: ewestbrook@wyfb.org

YOUNG AMERICAN BOWLING ALLIANCE (YABA) http://www.bowl.com

GIFT FOR LIFE SCHOLARSHIP

One-time award for high school students who compete in the sport of bowling. Minimum 2.0 GPA required. Must demonstrate financial need. Must be a member in good standing of YABA.

Award: Scholarship for use in freshman year; not renewable. *Number:* 12. *Amount:* $1000.

Eligibility Requirements: Applicant must be high school student; planning to enroll or expecting to enroll full- or part-time at a four-year institution or university and must have an interest in bowling. Applicant or parent of applicant must be member of Young American Bowling Alliance. Available to U.S. citizens.

Application Requirements: Application, references, transcript. *Deadline:* April 1.

Contact: Scholarship Programs Manager
Young American Bowling Alliance (YABA)
5301 South 76th Street
Greendale, WI 53129
Phone: 800-514-2695 Ext. 3318
E-mail: egocha@bowlinginc.com

PEPSI-COLA YOUTH BOWLING CHAMPIONSHIPS

Awarded to members of the Young American Bowling Alliance. Must win state or provincial tournaments to be eligible for international championships. U.S. citizens abroad may participate through military affiliate. Application fee varies by state. Contact Youth Director at local bowling center.

Award: Scholarship for use in freshman, sophomore, junior, or senior years; not renewable. *Number:* 292. *Amount:* $500–$2000.

Eligibility Requirements: Applicant must be enrolled or expecting to enroll full- or part-time at a two-year or four-year institution or university and must have an interest in bowling. Applicant or parent of applicant must be member of Young American Bowling Alliance. Available to U.S. citizens.

Application Requirements: Application, applicant must enter a contest, references, transcript. *Deadline:* February 28.

Contact: Scholarship Programs Manager
Young American Bowling Alliance (YABA)
5301South 76th Street
Greendale, WI 53129-1192
Phone: 800-514-2695 Ext. 3318

CORPORATE AFFILIATION

ADMINISTRATIVE MANAGEMENT SERVICES (AMS) http://cdnawards.com

CHRYSLER CANADA INC. SCHOLARSHIP PROGRAM

Student must be graduating from high school and enrolling in first year of a three- to four-year degree program. Twelve students are chosen based on academic performance, extracurricular activities, and community service. Maybe be renewable if student maintains a "B" average with full workload. Open to Canadian citizens who are dependents of employees of Chrysler Canada, Inc.

Award: Scholarship for use in freshman year; renewable. *Number:* 12. *Amount:* $1000.

Eligibility Requirements: Applicant must be Canadian citizen; high school student and planning to enroll or expecting to enroll full-time at a four-year institution or university. Applicant or parent of applicant must be affiliated with Daimler Chrysler Canada, Inc.. Applicant or parent of applicant must have employment or volunteer experience in community service. Applicant must have 3.0 GPA or higher.

Application Requirements: Application, autobiography, references, transcript. *Deadline:* April 30.

Contact: Donna Burnett, Scholarship Coordinator
Administrative Management Services (AMS)
829 Norwest Road, Suite 412
Kingston, ON K7P 2N3
Canada
Phone: 613-634-4350
Fax: 613-634-4209
E-mail: djburnett@cogeco.ca

CHRYSLER FINANCIAL SERVICES CANADA INC. SCHOLARSHIP PROGRAM

Scholarship for student graduating from high school and enrolling in first year of a three- to four-year degree program. Two students are chosen based on academic performance, extracurricular activities, and community service. Once in the program they could be eligible for four awards as long as a "B" average is maintained on a full workload. Open to Canadian citizens who are dependents of employees of Chrysler Financial Services Canada, Inc.

Award: Scholarship for use in freshman year; renewable. *Number:* 2. *Amount:* up to $1000.

Eligibility Requirements: Applicant must be Canadian citizen; high school student and planning to enroll or expecting to enroll full-time at a four-year institution or university. Applicant or parent of applicant must be affiliated with Daimler Chrysler Canada, Inc.. Applicant or parent of applicant must have employment or volunteer experience in community service.

Application Requirements: Application, test scores, transcript. *Deadline:* April 30.

Contact: Scholarship Coordinator
Administrative Management Services (AMS)
829 Norwest Road, Suite 412
Kingston, ON K7P 2N3
Canada
Phone: 613-634-4350
Fax: 613-634-4209
E-mail: djburnett@cogeco.ca

SYNCRUDE HIGHER EDUCATION AWARDS PROGRAM

Awards Canadian students enrolled in a program that involves a minimum of two years full-time study. Students could qualify for four awards at the

Administrative Management Services (AMS) (continued)

undergraduate level and two years at the graduate or professional level as long as they are under 25 years of age. Awards may be held at the community college level for a maximum of two years. Must be a dependent of a Syncrude Canada Inc. employee or Northward Development Ltd. employee.

Award: Scholarship for use in freshman, sophomore, junior, senior, or graduate years; renewable. *Number:* varies. *Amount:* $2400.

Eligibility Requirements: Applicant must be Canadian citizen; age 25 or under and enrolled or expecting to enroll full-time at a two-year or technical institution or university. Applicant or parent of applicant must be affiliated with Syncrude Canada, Inc..

Application Requirements: Application, transcript. *Deadline:* November 15.

Contact: Donna Burnett, Awards Coordinator
Administrative Management Services (AMS)
829 Norwest Road, Suite 412
Kingston, ON K7P 2M3
Canada
Phone: 613-634-4350
Fax: 613-634-4209
E-mail: djburnett@cogeco.ca

ALBERTA HERITAGE SCHOLARSHIP FUND/ ALBERTA SCHOLARSHIP PROGRAMS

http://www.alis.gov.ab.ca

ALBERTA HERITAGE SCHOLARSHIP FUND CANA SCHOLARSHIPS

Award to recognize and reward the academic achievements of children of CANA and ACE Construction employees. Must be Alberta residents, have completed one year of undergraduate studies at a designated postsecondary institution in Canada or the United States, be enrolled full-time in their second or subsequent year of study, and have at least one parent employed by CANA or ACE Construction for the last two consecutive years.

Award: Scholarship for use in sophomore, junior, or senior years; not renewable. *Number:* 3. *Amount:* $1000–$1500.

Eligibility Requirements: Applicant must be Canadian citizen; enrolled or expecting to enroll full-time at a two-year or four-year institution or university and resident of Alberta. Applicant or parent of applicant must be affiliated with CANA.

Application Requirements: Application, applicant must enter a contest, transcript. *Deadline:* October 31.

Contact: Scholarship Committee
Alberta Heritage Scholarship Fund/Alberta Scholarship Programs
9940 106th Street, Fourth Floor, Sterling Place
PO Box 28000, Station Main
Edmonton, AB T5J 4R4
Canada
Phone: 780-427-8640
Fax: 780-427-1288
E-mail: scholarships@gov.ab.ca

STREAM-FLO/MASTER FLO SCHOLARSHIPS

Renewable awards of CAN$3000 available to high school students who are sons and daughters of Stream-Flo Industries Ltd., Master Flo Valve Inc., and ERC Industries employees. Selection is based on the highest average obtained on five grade 12 subjects.

Award: Scholarship for use in freshman year; renewable. *Number:* 2.

Eligibility Requirements: Applicant must be high school student; planning to enroll or expecting to enroll full-time at a four-year institution or university and studying in Alberta, British Columbia, or Saskatchewan. Applicant or parent of applicant must be affiliated with Stream-Flo Industries Ltd.. Available to Canadian citizens.

Application Requirements: Application, test scores. *Deadline:* July 31.

Contact: Scholarship Committee
Alberta Heritage Scholarship Fund/Alberta Scholarship Programs
9940 106th Street, Fourth Floor, Sterling Place
PO Box 28000, Station Main
Edmonton, AB T5J 4R4
Canada
Phone: 780-427-8640
Fax: 780-427-1288
E-mail: scholarships@gov.ab.ca

ARMSTRONG WORLD INDUSTRIES INC.

http://www.armstrongfoundation.com

ARMSTRONG FOUNDATION SCHOLARSHIP

Scholarship available to sons and daughters of regular full- or part-time U.S. employees, expatriates, or retirees of Armstrong and its domestic subsidiaries. Applicants must be high school juniors and planning to enter an accredited college or junior college as a full-time student in the United States.

Award: Scholarship for use in freshman year; renewable. *Number:* varies. *Amount:* $2000.

Eligibility Requirements: Applicant must be high school student and planning to enroll or expecting to enroll full-time at a two-year or four-year institution or university. Applicant or parent of applicant must be affiliated with Armstrong World Industries. Available to U.S. citizens.

Application Requirements: Application. *Deadline:* January 31.

Contact: Jan Biagio, Armstrong Foundation Coordinator
Armstrong World Industries Inc.
2500 Columbia Avenue
PO Box 3001
Lancaster, PA 17604-3001
Phone: 717-396-5536
Fax: 717-396-6124
E-mail: foundation@armstrongfoundation.com

BUTLER MANUFACTURING COMPANY

http://www.butlermfg.com

BUTLER MANUFACTURING COMPANY FOUNDATION SCHOLARSHIP PROGRAM

Award for high school seniors who are the children of full-time employees of Butler Manufacturing Company and its subsidiaries. Award is renewable for up to four years. Must enroll full-time and stay in upper half of class.

Award: Scholarship for use in freshman year; renewable. *Number:* 8. *Amount:* $3000.

Eligibility Requirements: Applicant must be high school student and planning to enroll or expecting to enroll full-time at a four-year institution or university. Applicant or parent of applicant must be affiliated with Butler Manufacturing Company. Available to U.S. and Canadian citizens.

Application Requirements: Application, essay, financial need analysis, references, test scores, transcript. *Deadline:* February 15.

Contact: Jill Harmon, Foundation Administrator
Butler Manufacturing Company
1540 Genessee Street
PO Box 419917
Kansas City, MO 64102
Phone: 816-968-3208
Fax: 816-968-6501
E-mail: jcharmon@butlermfg.org

CARGILL

http://www.cargill.com

CARGILL NATIONAL MERIT SCHOLARSHIP PROGRAM FOR SONS AND DAUGHTERS

Scholarships of $1000 for children of Cargill Inc. and Cargill joint venture employees in the United States.

Award: Scholarship for use in freshman year; renewable. *Number:* 10. *Amount:* $1000.

Eligibility Requirements: Applicant must be high school student and planning to enroll or expecting to enroll full-time at a four-year institution or university. Applicant or parent of applicant must be affiliated with Cargill, Inc.. Available to U.S. citizens.

Application Requirements: Application. *Deadline:* February 15.

Contact: Rebecca Oswald, Community Relations Associate
Cargill
PO Box 9300
Minneapolis, MN 55440-9300
Phone: 952-742-6247
Fax: 952-742-7224
E-mail: cargill_scholarships@cargill.com

CARGILL SCHOLARSHIP PROGRAM FOR SONS AND DAUGHTERS

Scholarships of $3000 to high school seniors who are the children of Cargill Inc. and Cargill joint venture employees in the United States.

Award: Scholarship for use in freshman year; not renewable. *Number:* 40. *Amount:* $3000.

Eligibility Requirements: Applicant must be high school student and planning to enroll or expecting to enroll full-time at a four-year institution or university. Applicant or parent of applicant must be affiliated with Cargill, Inc.. Available to U.S. citizens.

Application Requirements: Application, transcript. *Deadline:* February 15.

Contact: Rebecca Oswald, Community Relations Associate
Cargill
PO Box 9300
Minneapolis, MN 55440-9300
Phone: 952-742-6247
Fax: 952-742-7224
E-mail: cargill_scholarships@cargill.com

CENTER FOR SCHOLARSHIP ADMINISTRATION http://www.scholarshipprograms.org

BILL ROGERS BONITZ SCHOLARSHIP

Applicants must be dependent children of active full-time employees of Bonitz of South Carolina Inc., who have been employed continuously for one year prior to January 1 of the year the awards will be made. Must be high school seniors or undergraduate students already enrolled in college. Applicants must have a cumulative GPA of 2.5, and be under the age of 21. Contact the Human Resource Manager at Bonitz of South Carolina for more detailed information on additional criteria.

Award: Scholarship for use in freshman, sophomore, junior, or senior years; renewable. *Number:* 1. *Amount:* up to $3000.

Eligibility Requirements: Applicant must be high school student; age 21 or under and planning to enroll or expecting to enroll full-time at a two-year or four-year or technical institution or university. Applicant or parent of applicant must be affiliated with Bonitz. Applicant must have 2.5 GPA or higher. Available to U.S. citizens.

Application Requirements: Application, essay, financial need analysis, references, transcript. *Deadline:* December 1.

Contact: Scholarship Committee
Center for Scholarship Administration
PO Box 1465
Taylors, SC 29687-0031
Phone: 864-268-3363
Fax: 864-268-7160
E-mail: cfsainc@bellsouth.net

BI-LO JOHN ROHALEY SCHOLARSHIP

Scholarships available to associates of BI-LO who have had a minimum one year of service averaging 15 hours a week. Officers and directors are not eligible. Applicant must be a high school senior or a freshman, sophomore, or junior enrolled in an accredited, two- or four-year college, university, or technical school. Three nonrenewable $2000 scholarships are awarded for the academic year.

Award: Scholarship for use in freshman, sophomore, junior, or senior years; not renewable. *Number:* 3. *Amount:* $2000.

Eligibility Requirements: Applicant must be enrolled or expecting to enroll full- or part-time at a two-year or four-year or technical institution or university. Applicant or parent of applicant must be affiliated with BI-LO. Available to U.S. citizens.

Application Requirements: Application, essay, financial need analysis, references, transcript. *Deadline:* February 15.

Contact: Scholarship Committee
Center for Scholarship Administration
PO Box 1465
Taylors, SC 29687-0031
Phone: 864-268-3363
Fax: 864-268-7160
E-mail: cfsainc@bellsouth.net

CARDINAL LOGISTICS MANAGEMENT INC. SCHOLARSHIP FUND

Renewable scholarships for dependent children of qualified employees of Cardinal Logistics Management Inc. Applicants must be seniors in high school who are planning to attend college as full-time students in the fall. Must have a minimum cumulative 2.5 GPA.

Award: Scholarship for use in freshman year; renewable. *Number:* 1. *Amount:* $2000.

Eligibility Requirements: Applicant must be high school student; age 23 or under; planning to enroll or expecting to enroll full-time at a four-year institution or university and single. Applicant or parent of applicant must be affiliated with Cardinal Logistic Management. Applicant must have 2.5 GPA or higher. Available to U.S. citizens.

Application Requirements: Application, essay, references, transcript. *Deadline:* January 31.

Contact: Scholarship Committee
Center for Scholarship Administration
PO Box 1465
Taylors, SC 29687-0031
Phone: 864-268-3363
Fax: 864-268-7160
E-mail: cfsainc@bellsouth.net

CARRIS REELS SCHOLARSHIP PROGRAM

Nonrenewable scholarships for dependent children of qualified active, retired, disabled, or deceased employees of Carris Financial Corp. The employee/parent must have been continuously employed full-time by Carris for a period of at least two years as of January 1 of the year of application. Applicant must be a senior in high school, a high school graduate, or be a full-time student attending and planning to attend an accredited, postsecondary college or university.

Award: Scholarship for use in freshman, sophomore, junior, or senior years; not renewable. *Number:* varies. *Amount:* up to $4000.

Eligibility Requirements: Applicant must be high school student and planning to enroll or expecting to enroll full-time at a two-year or four-year or technical institution or university. Applicant or parent of applicant must be affiliated with Carris Financial Corporation. Available to U.S. citizens.

Application Requirements: Application, essay, financial need analysis, references, transcript, latest filed federal tax form 1040 (first page only) and their W-2 forms. *Deadline:* January 31.

Contact: Scholarship Committee
Center for Scholarship Administration
PO Box 1465
Taylors, SC 29687-0031
Phone: 864-268-3363
Fax: 864-268-7160
E-mail: cfsainc@bellsouth.net

CONSOLIDATED SYSTEMS: BILL ROGERS SCHOLARSHIP PROGRAM

Applicants must be dependent children of active employees of Consolidated Systems Inc., who are on the hourly payroll and who have had at least one year of continuous employment prior to January 1 of the year the awards are made. Must be high school seniors or undergraduate students already enrolled in a postsecondary institution. Must be under the age of 25 years. Contact the human resource manager for more information.

Award: Scholarship for use in freshman, sophomore, junior, or senior years; renewable. *Number:* 1. *Amount:* $2000.

Eligibility Requirements: Applicant must be high school student; age 25 or under and planning to enroll or expecting to enroll full-time at a two-year or four-year or technical institution or university. Applicant or parent of applicant must be affiliated with Consolidation Systems, Inc.. Available to U.S. citizens.

Center for Scholarship Administration (continued)

Application Requirements: Application, essay, references, transcript. *Deadline:* February 15.

Contact: Scholarship Committee
Center for Scholarship Administration
PO Box 1465
Taylors, SC 29687-0031
Phone: 864-268-3363
Fax: 864-268-7160
E-mail: cfsainc@bellsouth.net

CONSOLIDATED SYSTEMS INC. THOMAS C. MEREDITH JR. SCHOLARSHIP

Applicants must be dependent children of active employees of Consolidated Systems who are on the salaried payroll and who have had at least one year of continuous employment prior to January 1 of the year the awards are made. Applicants must be high school seniors or undergraduate students already enrolled in a college. Awards are renewable. Applicants must be under the age of 25. Contact the human resource manager for more detailed information.

Award: Scholarship for use in freshman, sophomore, junior, or senior years; renewable. *Number:* 1. *Amount:* $2000.

Eligibility Requirements: Applicant must be high school student; age 25 or under and planning to enroll or expecting to enroll full-time at a two-year or four-year or technical institution or university. Applicant or parent of applicant must be affiliated with Consolidation Systems, Inc.. Available to U.S. citizens.

Application Requirements: Application, essay, references, transcript. *Deadline:* February 15.

Contact: Scholarship Committee
Center for Scholarship Administration
PO Box 1465
Taylors, SC 29687-0031
Phone: 864-268-3363
Fax: 864-268-7160
E-mail: cfsainc@bellsouth.net

DAN RIVER FOUNDATION SCHOLARSHIP

Renewable scholarships for dependent children of any active, retired, disabled, or deceased Dan River Inc. employee. Applicants must be seniors in high school or undergraduate students already enrolled in college and must be planning to attend college in the fall. Children of any division or corporate officers of Dan River Inc. or its subsidiaries and children of officers and directors of the Dan River Foundation are not eligible.

Award: Scholarship for use in freshman, sophomore, junior, or senior years; renewable. *Number:* varies. *Amount:* up to $2000.

Eligibility Requirements: Applicant must be high school student and planning to enroll or expecting to enroll full-time at a two-year or four-year institution or university. Applicant or parent of applicant must be affiliated with Dan River, Inc.. Available to U.S. citizens.

Application Requirements: Application, essay, financial need analysis, references, transcript, copy of federal tax form 1040 (first page only) and W-2 forms. *Deadline:* March 31.

Contact: Scholarship Committee
Center for Scholarship Administration
PO Box 1465
Taylors, SC 29687-0031
Phone: 864-268-3363
Fax: 864-268-7160
E-mail: cfsainc@bellsouth.net

DELTA APPAREL INC. SCHOLARSHIP

Renewable scholarships for dependent children of qualified employees of Delta Apparel Inc. Must be either a high school senior planning to enter college in the fall or a student already attending college. Must have a cumulative 2.5 GPA. The recipient's school of choice must be exempt from federal income tax under Section 501 (c) (3) of the Internal Revenue Code.

Award: Scholarship for use in freshman, sophomore, junior, or senior years; renewable. *Number:* varies. *Amount:* $1000.

Eligibility Requirements: Applicant must be high school student and planning to enroll or expecting to enroll full-time at a two-year or four-year or technical institution or university. Applicant or parent of applicant must be affiliated with Delta Apparel, Inc.. Applicant must have 2.5 GPA or higher. Available to U.S. citizens.

Application Requirements: Application, essay, financial need analysis, references, transcript, copy of latest filed federal tax form 1040 (page one only) and latest W-2 forms. *Deadline:* March 31.

Contact: Scholarship Committee
Center for Scholarship Administration
PO Box 1465
Taylors, SC 29687-0031
Phone: 864-268-3363
Fax: 864-268-7160
E-mail: cfsainc@bellsouth.net

FLEXIBLE TECHNOLOGIES INC. SCHOLARSHIP

Renewable scholarships for dependent children of qualified employees of Flexible Technologies Inc. Applicants must be high school seniors and must have a minimum of 800 on the SAT/ACT test and a cumulative "B" average from high school. Funds may not be used to attend summer school. A minimum cumulative GPA of 3.0 is required.

Award: Scholarship for use in freshman year; renewable. *Number:* 2. *Amount:* $2000.

Eligibility Requirements: Applicant must be high school student and planning to enroll or expecting to enroll full-time at a four-year institution or university. Applicant or parent of applicant must be affiliated with Flexible Technologies, Inc.. Applicant must have 3.0 GPA or higher. Available to U.S. and Canadian citizens.

Application Requirements: Application, essay, references, test scores, transcript. *Deadline:* March 31.

Contact: Scholarship Committee
Center for Scholarship Administration
PO Box 1465
Taylors, SC 29687-0031
Phone: 864-268-3363
Fax: 864-268-7160
E-mail: cfsainc@bellsouth.net

LUCILLE P. AND EDWARD C. GILES FOUNDATION SCHOLARSHIP

Renewable scholarships for dependent children or grandchildren of qualified employees of Caraustar Industries Inc. Applicants must be seniors in high school, or high school graduates, or full-time college students, or college graduates planning to attend graduate school, provided they have received less than four years of awards from Giles. Recipients must maintain a cumulative GPA of 2.0 to be considered for renewal.

Award: Scholarship for use in freshman, sophomore, junior, senior, or graduate years; renewable. *Number:* varies. *Amount:* up to $6000.

Eligibility Requirements: Applicant must be enrolled or expecting to enroll full-time at a two-year or four-year or technical institution or university. Applicant or parent of applicant must be affiliated with Caraustar Industries, Inc.. Available to U.S. citizens.

Application Requirements: Application, essay, financial need analysis, references, transcript, copy of parent's latest filed federal tax form 1040 (page one only) and W-2 forms. *Deadline:* February 15.

Contact: Scholarship Committee
Center for Scholarship Administration
PO Box 1465
Taylors, SC 29687-0031
Phone: 864-268-3363
Fax: 864-268-7160
E-mail: cfsainc@bellsouth.net

MAYER SCHOLARSHIP FUND

Scholarship is open to dependent children of full-time active employees of Liberty Hardware Manufacturing Corp. Applicants must be high school seniors or undergraduate students already enrolled in college. Must have a cumulative GPA of 2.5. Two renewable scholarships of up to $2000 are awarded annually.

Award: Scholarship for use in freshman, sophomore, junior, or senior years; renewable. *Number:* 2. *Amount:* up to $2000.

Eligibility Requirements: Applicant must be high school student and planning to enroll or expecting to enroll full-time at a two-year or four-year or technical institution or university. Applicant or parent of applicant must be affiliated with Liberty Hardware Manufacturing Company. Applicant must have 2.5 GPA or higher. Available to U.S. citizens.

Application Requirements: Application, essay, references, transcript, copy of parent's latest filed federal tax form 1040 (page one only) and W-2 forms. *Deadline:* January 31.

Contact: Scholarship Committee
Center for Scholarship Administration
PO Box 1465
Taylors, SC 29687-0031
Phone: 864-268-3363
Fax: 864-268-7160
E-mail: cfsainc@bellsouth.net

MICHELIN NORTH AMERICA DEPENDENT SCHOLARSHIP

Renewable award for qualified employees or dependent children of qualified Michelin North America employees. Applicants must be unmarried and be 23 years old or younger. Must be high school seniors or undergraduate students already attending a college or university and planning to attend college as full-time students in the fall. Must maintain a minimum GPA of 3.0.

Award: Scholarship for use in freshman, sophomore, junior, or senior years; renewable. *Number:* up to 15. *Amount:* $1000–$2500.

Eligibility Requirements: Applicant must be high school student; age 23 or under; planning to enroll or expecting to enroll full-time at a two-year or four-year or technical institution or university and single. Applicant or parent of applicant must be affiliated with Michelin North America. Applicant must have 3.0 GPA or higher. Available to U.S. citizens.

Application Requirements: Application, essay, references, transcript. *Deadline:* March 3.

Contact: Scholarship Committee
Center for Scholarship Administration
PO Box 1465
Taylors, SC 29687-0031
Phone: 864-268-3363
Fax: 864-268-7160
E-mail: cfsainc@bellsouth.net

SONOCO SCHOLARSHIP

Renewable scholarships available for dependent children of qualified employees of Sonoco. The employee/parent must have been continuously employed full-time by Sonoco for a period of at least one year as of January 1 of the year the application is made. Applicant must be a senior in high school, and must be planning to attend college in the fall. Awards four-year scholarship of $2000 to ten selected students.

Award: Scholarship for use in freshman year; renewable. *Number:* 10. *Amount:* $2000.

Eligibility Requirements: Applicant must be high school student and planning to enroll or expecting to enroll full-time at a four-year institution or university. Applicant or parent of applicant must be affiliated with Sonoco. Available to U.S. citizens.

Application Requirements: Application, essay, financial need analysis, references, transcript, copy of parent/employee's federal tax form and W-2 forms. *Deadline:* February 28.

Contact: Scholarship Committee
Center for Scholarship Administration
PO Box 1465
Taylors, SC 29687-0031
Phone: 864-268-3363
Fax: 864-268-7160
E-mail: cfsainc@bellsouth.net

SPARTANBURG STAINLESS PRODUCTS INC. SCHOLARSHIP

Renewable scholarships available to dependent children of qualified full-time employees of Spartanburg Stainless Inc. Must be graduating high school seniors planning to pursue postsecondary studies. Minimum 2.0 GPA required. Contact the human resources manager for more detailed information on additional criteria.

Award: Scholarship for use in freshman year; renewable. *Number:* varies. *Amount:* $1000.

Eligibility Requirements: Applicant must be high school student and planning to enroll or expecting to enroll full-time at a two-year or four-year or technical institution or university. Applicant or parent of applicant must be affiliated with Spartanburg Stainless Products, Inc.. Available to U.S. citizens.

Application Requirements: Application, essay, references, transcript. *Deadline:* March 31.

Contact: Scholarship Committee
Center for Scholarship Administration
PO Box 1465
Taylors, SC 29687-0031
Phone: 864-268-3363
Fax: 864-268-7160
E-mail: cfsainc@bellsouth.net

STRATA MARKETING INC. SCHOLARSHIP PROGRAM

One-time award for dependent children of Strata Marketing Inc. employees. The employee/parent must have been continuously employed full-time by Strata Marketing for a period of at least one year as of January 1 of the year the student is applying for a scholarship. Must be seniors in high school or undergraduate students who have already enrolled in college. Minimum cumulative GPA of 3.0.

Award: Scholarship for use in freshman, sophomore, junior, or senior years; not renewable. *Number:* up to 3. *Amount:* up to $8000.

Eligibility Requirements: Applicant must be high school student; age 25 or under; planning to enroll or expecting to enroll full-time at a four-year institution or university and single. Applicant or parent of applicant must be affiliated with Strata Marketing, Inc.. Applicant must have 3.0 GPA or higher. Available to U.S. citizens.

Application Requirements: Application, essay, references, transcript. *Deadline:* March 15.

Contact: Scholarship Committee
Center for Scholarship Administration
PO Box 1465
Taylors, SC 29687-0031
Phone: 864-268-3363
Fax: 864-268-7160
E-mail: cfsainc@bellsouth.net

SUBWAY OF SOUTH CAROLINA SCHOLARSHIP

Nonrenewable scholarships available to qualified employees or dependent children of qualified employees of Subway of South Carolina. Applicants must be either high school seniors, or freshmen attending an accredited, undergraduate college, university or technical college as full-time students.

Award: Scholarship for use in freshman year; not renewable. *Number:* 1–10. *Amount:* $5000.

Eligibility Requirements: Applicant must be high school student and planning to enroll or expecting to enroll full-time at a two-year or four-year or technical institution or university. Applicant or parent of applicant must be affiliated with Subway. Available to U.S. citizens.

Application Requirements: Application, essay, references, transcript. *Deadline:* January 31.

Contact: Scholarship Committee
Center for Scholarship Administration
PO Box 1465
Taylors, SC 29687-0031
Phone: 864-268-3363
Fax: 864-268-7160
E-mail: cfsainc@bellsouth.net

SUBWAY SCHOLARSHIPS

Nonrenewable scholarships for qualified employees of Subway who have been employed by the company for a minimum of six months prior to January 1 of the current year. Applicants must be either high school seniors or students already attending an accredited college, university, or technical college as full-time undergraduate students. Minimum GPA of 2.75 required.

Award: Scholarship for use in freshman, sophomore, junior, or senior years; not renewable. *Number:* varies. *Amount:* $1000.

Eligibility Requirements: Applicant must be enrolled or expecting to enroll full-time at a two-year or four-year or technical institution or university. Applicant or parent of applicant must be affiliated with Subway. Available to U.S. citizens.

Center for Scholarship Administration (continued)

Application Requirements: Application, essay, references, transcript. *Deadline:* November 30.

Contact: Scholarship Committee
Center for Scholarship Administration
PO Box 1465
Taylors, SC 29687-0031
Phone: 864-268-3363
Fax: 864-268-7160
E-mail: cfsainc@bellsouth.net

TIETEX INTERNATIONAL SCHOLARSHIP

Renewable scholarships for the dependent children of active employees of Tietex International Ltd. who have been continuously employed for a minimum of two years prior to January 1 of the year the awards are made. Applicants must be graduating high school seniors, and have a minimum 2.0 GPA.

Award: Scholarship for use in freshman year; renewable. *Number:* varies. *Amount:* $1500.

Eligibility Requirements: Applicant must be high school student and planning to enroll or expecting to enroll full-time at a four-year institution or university. Applicant or parent of applicant must be affiliated with Teitex International. Available to U.S. citizens.

Application Requirements: Application, essay, references, transcript. *Deadline:* January 31.

Contact: Scholarship Committee
Center for Scholarship Administration
PO Box 1465
Taylors, SC 29687-0031
Phone: 864-268-3363
Fax: 864-268-7160
E-mail: cfsainc@bellsouth.net

TUPPERWARE U.S. INC. SCHOLARSHIP

Nonrenewable scholarships available for the dependent children of qualified associates of Tupperware U.S. Inc. Applicant must be a senior in high school and plan to enter college in the fall. Must have a cumulative GPA of 2.0. Awards up to $10,500 annually.

Award: Scholarship for use in freshman year; not renewable. *Number:* varies. *Amount:* $1000–$10,500.

Eligibility Requirements: Applicant must be high school student and planning to enroll or expecting to enroll full-time at a two-year or four-year or technical institution or university. Applicant or parent of applicant must be affiliated with Tupperware U.S., Inc.. Available to U.S. citizens.

Application Requirements: Application, essay, financial need analysis, references, test scores, transcript, copy of parent's latest filed federal tax form 1040 (page one only) and W-2 forms. *Deadline:* January 31.

Contact: Scholarship Committee
Center for Scholarship Administration
PO Box 1465
Taylors, SC 29687-0031
Phone: 864-268-3363
Fax: 864-268-7160
E-mail: cfsainc@bellsouth.net

WACHOVIA DEPENDENT SCHOLARSHIP

Renewable scholarships available for dependent children of qualified employees of Wachovia. Applicant must be a senior in high school and planning to attend college as a full-time student in the fall. A minimum SAT score of 1500 or an ACT composite score of 21 required. Must have a minimum of 3.0 GPA. Awards up to 125 new scholarships in an amount of up to $4000 per year.

Award: Scholarship for use in freshman year; renewable. *Number:* up to 125. *Amount:* up to $4000.

Eligibility Requirements: Applicant must be high school student; planning to enroll or expecting to enroll full-time at a four-year institution or university and single. Applicant or parent of applicant must be affiliated with Wachovia Bank. Applicant must have 3.0 GPA or higher. Available to U.S. citizens.

Application Requirements: Application, essay, financial need analysis, references, transcript, copies of parent's latest federal tax form 1040 (page one only) and W-2 forms. *Deadline:* March 10.

Contact: Scholarship Committee
Center for Scholarship Administration
PO Box 1465
Taylors, SC 29687-0031
Phone: 864-268-3363
Fax: 864-268-7160
E-mail: cfsainc@bellsouth.net

CHESAPEAKE CORPORATION FOUNDATION

CHESAPEAKE CORPORATION FOUNDATION SCHOLARSHIP PROGRAM FOR CHESAPEAKE EMPLOYEES' CHILDREN

Award of up to $3500 per academic year for up to four years to help finance the college education of outstanding sons and daughters of Chesapeake Corporation employees.

Award: Scholarship for use in freshman year; renewable. *Number:* 2. *Amount:* up to $3500.

Eligibility Requirements: Applicant must be high school student and planning to enroll or expecting to enroll full-time at a four-year institution or university. Applicant or parent of applicant must be affiliated with Chesapeake Corporation. Available to U.S. and non-U.S. citizens.

Application Requirements: Application, autobiography, test scores, transcript. *Deadline:* November 14.

Contact: Debra Hodges, Secretary
Chesapeake Corporation Foundation
PO Box 2350
Richmond, VA 23218
Phone: 804-697-1000
Fax: 804-697-1195
E-mail: debra.hodges@cskcorp.com

CHICK-FIL-A INC. http://www.chick-fil-a.com

CHICK-FIL-A LEADERSHIP SCHOLARSHIP

Scholarships available to current employees of Chick-fil-A restaurants. Must show proof of enrollment in technical school, two- or four-year college or university. Must demonstrate solid work ethic, be actively involved in school or community activities, and possess strong leadership abilities. Must apply with approval of a Unit Operator accompanied by their letter of recommendation. Letter of recommendation from non-work-related individual also required

Award: Scholarship for use in freshman, sophomore, junior, or senior years; not renewable. *Number:* up to 1400. *Amount:* $1000.

Eligibility Requirements: Applicant must be enrolled or expecting to enroll full- or part-time at a two-year or four-year or technical institution or university. Applicant or parent of applicant must be affiliated with Chick-Fil-A, Inc.. Applicant or parent of applicant must have employment or volunteer experience in food service. Available to U.S. citizens.

Application Requirements: Application, references, transcript, letter of acceptance. *Deadline:* continuous.

Contact: Scholarship Coordinator
Chick-fil-A Inc.
5200 Buffington Road
Atlanta, GA 30349-2998
Phone: 404-765-8038

S. TRUETT CATHY SCHOLAR AWARDS

This award is given to the top twenty-five Chick-fil-A Leadership Scholarship recipients each year. Scholarship amount is $1000.

Award: Scholarship for use in freshman, sophomore, junior, or senior years; not renewable. *Number:* up to 25. *Amount:* up to $1000.

Eligibility Requirements: Applicant must be enrolled or expecting to enroll full- or part-time at a two-year or four-year or technical institution or university. Applicant or parent of applicant must be affiliated with Chick-Fil-A, Inc.. Available to U.S. citizens.

Application Requirements: Application, references, transcript, unit operator approval, proof of enrollment. *Deadline:* continuous.

Contact: Scholarship Coordinator
Chick-fil-A Inc.
5200 Buffington Road
Atlanta, GA 30349-2998
Phone: 404-765-8038

CLARA ABBOTT FOUNDATION http://clara.abbott.com

CLARA ABBOTT SCHOLARSHIP PROGRAM

Scholarships for the children of Abbott Laboratories employees and retirees. Must be under 24 years of age and planning to attend an accredited undergraduate program. Must reapply each year. Must submit completed application, copies of W2 and IRS 1040 form, and student's most recent grade report. Awards based on financial need. Need to maintain a 2.0/4.0 cumulative grade point average in order to be eligible to reapply for a scholarship next year.

Award: Scholarship for use in freshman, sophomore, junior, or senior years; not renewable. *Number:* up to 4000. *Amount:* $500–$5000.

Eligibility Requirements: Applicant must be age 17-24 and enrolled or expecting to enroll full- or part-time at a two-year or four-year or technical institution or university. Applicant or parent of applicant must be affiliated with Abbott Laboratories. Available to U.S. and non-U.S. citizens.

Application Requirements: Application, financial need analysis, transcript, copy of W-2 forms, copy of 1040 forms, FAFSA. *Deadline:* March 15.

Contact: Scholarship Management Services, Division of Scholarship America
Clara Abbott Foundation
1 Scholarship Way, PO Box 297
St. Peter, MN 56082
Phone: 866-931-0419
E-mail: claraabbott@scholarshipamerica.org

CLEVELAND SCHOLARSHIP PROGRAMS http://www.cspohio.org

CSP MANAGED FUNDS-HITACHI MEDICAL SYSTEMS AMERICA INC. ROBERT A. SCHLUETER MEMORIAL SCHOLARSHIP

Scholarship to sons or daughters of a full-time employee of Hitachi Medical Systems America. Applicants may be graduating high school seniors or high school graduates not currently enrolled in college or college undergraduates.

Award: Scholarship for use in freshman, sophomore, junior, or senior years; renewable. *Number:* 1. *Amount:* $2000.

Eligibility Requirements: Applicant must be enrolled or expecting to enroll full-time at a two-year or four-year or technical institution or university. Applicant or parent of applicant must be affiliated with Hitachi Medical Systems America, Inc.. Applicant must have 2.5 GPA or higher. Available to U.S. citizens.

Application Requirements: Application, transcript. *Deadline:* varies.

Contact: Latasha Williams, Senior Manager of Programs
Cleveland Scholarship Programs
200 Public Square, Suite 3820
Cleveland, OH 44114
Phone: 216-241-5587
Fax: 216-241-6184
E-mail: lwilliams@cspohio.org

CSP MANAGED FUNDS-MRI ALAN R. SCHONBERG SCHOLARSHIP

Student applicants must be sons or daughters of employees or franchise owners who have been with Management Recruiters International for two years as of the application cut-off date. The student selected to receive the award must be either a graduating high school senior planning to enter college directly after high school or a current college undergraduate.

Award: Scholarship for use in freshman, sophomore, junior, or senior years; not renewable. *Number:* 5. *Amount:* $3000.

Eligibility Requirements: Applicant must be enrolled or expecting to enroll full-time at a two-year or four-year institution or university. Applicant or parent of applicant must be affiliated with Management Recruiters International, Inc.. Applicant must have 3.0 GPA or higher. Available to U.S. citizens.

Application Requirements: Application, essay, references, test scores, transcript. *Deadline:* June 15.

Contact: Latasha Williams, Senior Manager of Programs
Cleveland Scholarship Programs
200 Public Square, Suite 3820
Cleveland, OH 44114
Phone: 216-241-5587
Fax: 216-241-6184
E-mail: lwilliams@cspohio.org

CSP MANAGED FUNDS-OGLEBAY NORTON COMPANY EMPLOYEE SCHOLARSHIP

Award to assist graduating high school seniors or current college students who are sons and daughters of full-time employees of Oglebay Norton Company and its subsidiaries. Must have at least 3.0 GPA.

Award: Scholarship for use in freshman, sophomore, junior, or senior years; renewable. *Number:* 4. *Amount:* $1000.

Eligibility Requirements: Applicant must be enrolled or expecting to enroll full-time at a two-year or four-year institution or university. Applicant or parent of applicant must be affiliated with Oglebay Norton Company. Applicant must have 3.0 GPA or higher. Available to U.S. citizens.

Application Requirements: Application. *Deadline:* April 21.

Contact: Latasha Williams, Senior Manager of Programs
Cleveland Scholarship Programs
200 Public Square, Suite 3820
Cleveland, OH 44114
Phone: 216-241-5587
Fax: 216-241-6184
E-mail: lwilliams@cspohio.org

COMMUNITY FOUNDATION FOR GREATER ATLANTA INC. http://www.atlcf.org

RUSSELL CORPORATION SCHOLARSHIP

Scholarship to support dependents of Russell Corporation employees in their pursuit of an undergraduate degree. Must maintain a minimum GPA of 3.0. Parents of applicants must be full-time employees of Russell Corporation for a minimum of two years.

Award: Scholarship for use in freshman, sophomore, junior, or senior years; renewable. *Number:* 2. *Amount:* $5000.

Eligibility Requirements: Applicant must be enrolled or expecting to enroll full-time at a four-year institution or university. Applicant or parent of applicant must be affiliated with Russell Corporation. Applicant must have 3.0 GPA or higher. Available to U.S. citizens.

Application Requirements: Application, essay, financial need analysis, references, transcript. *Deadline:* March 26.

Contact: Kristina Morris, Program Associate
Community Foundation for Greater Atlanta Inc.
50 Hurt Plaza, Suite 449
Atlanta, GA 30303
Phone: 404-688-5525
Fax: 404-688-3060
E-mail: scholarships@atlcf.org

COMMUNITY FOUNDATION OF WESTERN MASSACHUSETTS http://www.communityfoundation.org

DEERFIELD PLASTICS/BARKER FAMILY SCHOLARSHIP

Scholarship for the children of employees of the former Deerfield Plastics. Award value ranges from $1500 to $3000. Must be a resident of Kentucky or Massachusetts.

Award: Scholarship for use in freshman, sophomore, junior, senior, or graduate years; not renewable. *Number:* 1. *Amount:* $1500–$3000.

Eligibility Requirements: Applicant must be enrolled or expecting to enroll full- or part-time at a two-year or four-year institution or university and resident of Kentucky or Massachusetts. Applicant or parent of applicant must be affiliated with Deerfield Plastics. Available to U.S. citizens.

Community Foundation of Western Massachusetts (continued)

Application Requirements: Application, financial need analysis, transcript, Student Aid Report (SAR). *Deadline:* March 31.

Contact: Dorothy Theriaque, Education Associate
Community Foundation of Western Massachusetts
1500 Main Street, PO Box 15769
Springfield, MA 01115
Phone: 413-732-2858
Fax: 413-733-8565
E-mail: dtheriaque@communityfoundation.org

DEMOLAY FOUNDATION INCORPORATED http://www.demolay.org

FRANK S. LAND SCHOLARSHIP

Scholarship awarded to members of DeMolay International, who have not yet reached the age of 21, to assist in financing their education. Must be U.S. resident.

Award: Scholarship for use in freshman, sophomore, junior, or senior years; not renewable. *Number:* 10–15. *Amount:* $800.

Eligibility Requirements: Applicant must be age 21 or under; enrolled or expecting to enroll full-time at a two-year or four-year institution or university and male. Applicant or parent of applicant must be affiliated with DeMolay. Available to U.S. citizens.

Application Requirements: Application, references, self-addressed stamped envelope, transcript. *Deadline:* April 1.

Contact: Jeffrey Kitsmiller, Executive Director
DeMolay Foundation Incorporated
10200 NW Ambassador Drive
Kansas City, MO 64153
Phone: 800-336-6529
Fax: 816-891-9062
E-mail: admin@demolay.org

DONALDSON COMPANY http://www.donaldson.com

DONALDSON COMPANY INC. SCHOLARSHIP PROGRAM

Scholarships for children of U.S. employees of Donaldson Company Inc. Any form of accredited postsecondary education is eligible. The amount of the award can range from $1000 to $3000 for each year of full-time study and may be renewed for up to a total of four years. The number of scholarships awarded is limited to a maximum of 25 percent of the number of applicants.

Award: Scholarship for use in freshman, sophomore, junior, or senior years; renewable. *Number:* varies. *Amount:* $1000–$3000.

Eligibility Requirements: Applicant must be enrolled or expecting to enroll full-time at a two-year or four-year institution or university. Applicant or parent of applicant must be affiliated with Donaldson Company. Available to U.S. citizens.

Application Requirements: Application, essay, financial need analysis, references, transcript. *Deadline:* March 15.

Contact: Norm Linnell, Vice President, General Counsel and Secretary
Donaldson Company
PO Box 1299
Minneapolis, MN 55440
Phone: 952-887-3631
Fax: 952-887-3005
E-mail: norm.linnell@donaldson.com

DUKE ENERGY CORPORATION http://www.duke-energy.com

DUKE ENERGY SCHOLARS PROGRAM

The scholarship is for undergraduate study at accredited, two-year technical schools or community colleges and/or four-year colleges or universities in the United States and Canada who are children of eligible employees and retirees of Duke Energy and its subsidiaries. Recipients selected by five-member outside committee.

Award: Scholarship for use in freshman, sophomore, junior, or senior years; renewable. *Number:* 15. *Amount:* $1000–$5000.

Eligibility Requirements: Applicant must be enrolled or expecting to enroll full-time at a two-year or four-year or technical institution or university. Applicant or parent of applicant must be affiliated with Duke Energy Corporation. Available to U.S. and Canadian citizens.

Application Requirements: Application, autobiography, essay, financial need analysis, references, test scores, transcript. *Deadline:* December 1.

Contact: Celia Beam, Scholarship Administrator
Duke Energy Corporation
526 South Church Street
PO Box 1244
Charlotte, NC 28202-1904
Phone: 704-382-5544
Fax: 704-382-3553
E-mail: chbeam@duke-energy.com

FEDERATION OF AMERICAN CONSUMERS AND TRAVELERS http://www.usafact.org

FEDERATION OF AMERICAN CONSUMERS AND TRAVELERS IN-SCHOOL SCHOLARSHIP

FACT scholarships are offered in four categories for current high school seniors, persons who graduated from high school, four or more years ago and now plan to go to a university or college, for students currently enrolled in a college or university, and for trade or technical school aspirants. Scholarships range in amount from $2500 to $10,000. Members of FACT, their children and grandchildren are eligible to apply.

Award: Scholarship for use in freshman, sophomore, junior, or senior years; not renewable. *Number:* varies. *Amount:* $2500–$10,000.

Eligibility Requirements: Applicant must be enrolled or expecting to enroll full-time at a two-year or four-year institution or university. Applicant or parent of applicant must be affiliated with Connecticut Union of Telephone Workers. Available to U.S. citizens.

Application Requirements: Application, essay, resume, references, test scores, transcript. *Deadline:* January 15.

Contact: Vicki Rolens, Scholarship Coordinator and Managing Director
Federation of American Consumers and Travelers
PO Box 104
Edwardsville, IL 62025
Phone: 800-872-3228
Fax: 618-656-5369
E-mail: vrolens@usafact.org

FEDERATION OF AMERICAN CONSUMERS AND TRAVELERS SECOND CHANCE SCHOLARSHIP

FACT scholarships are offered in four categories: (1) for current high school seniors: (2) for persons who graduated from high school four or more years ago and now plan to go to a university or college; (3) for students currently enrolled in a college or university, and (4) for trade or technical school aspirants. Scholarships range in size from $2500 to $10,000. Members of FACT, their children and grandchildren are eligible to apply.

Award: Scholarship for use in freshman, sophomore, junior, or senior years; not renewable. *Number:* varies. *Amount:* $2500–$10,000.

Eligibility Requirements: Applicant must be enrolled or expecting to enroll full- or part-time at a two-year or four-year or technical institution or university. Applicant or parent of applicant must be affiliated with Connecticut Union of Telephone Workers. Available to U.S. citizens.

Application Requirements: Application, essay, resume, references, test scores, transcript. *Deadline:* January 15.

Contact: Vicki Rolens, Scholarship Coordinator and Managing Director
Federation of American Consumers and Travelers
PO Box 104
Edwardsville, IL 62025
Phone: 800-872-3228
Fax: 618-656-5369
E-mail: vrolens@usafact.org

GANNETT FOUNDATION http://www.gannettfoundation.org

GANNETT FOUNDATION/MADELYN P. JENNINGS SCHOLARSHIP AWARD

One-time awards for high school students whose parents are current full-time Gannett Company employees. Must be planning to attend a 4-year college or university for full-time study in the fall after graduation. Students must meet all requirements for participation in the National Merit Scholarship Program and take the PSAT/NMSQT in their junior year of high school.

Award: Scholarship for use in freshman year; not renewable. *Number:* 12. *Amount:* $3000.

Eligibility Requirements: Applicant must be high school student and planning to enroll or expecting to enroll full-time at a four-year institution or university. Applicant or parent of applicant must be affiliated with Gannett Company, Inc.. Available to U.S. citizens.

Application Requirements: Application, test scores. *Deadline:* March 1.

Contact: Collette Horton, Benefits Representative
Gannett Foundation
7950 Jones Branch Drive
McLean, VA 22107
Phone: 800-828-4414 Ext. 6254
Fax: 703-854-2006
E-mail: cnhorton@gannett.com

GATEWAY PRESS INC. OF LOUISVILLE

http://www.gatewaypressinc.com

GATEWAY PRESS SCHOLARSHIP

Scholarship for graduating high school seniors whose parents have been employees of Gateway Press Inc. for a minimum of 5 years. Applicant must be accepted at a college or university and maintain a minimum GPA of 2.25.

Award: Scholarship for use in freshman year; renewable. *Number:* varies. *Amount:* up to $3000.

Eligibility Requirements: Applicant must be high school student and planning to enroll or expecting to enroll full-time at a four-year institution or university. Applicant or parent of applicant must be affiliated with Gateway Press Inc.. Available to U.S. citizens.

Application Requirements: Application, references, transcript. *Deadline:* January 1.

Contact: Chris Georgehead, Human Resources Manager
Gateway Press Inc. of Louisville
4500 Robards Lane
Louisville, KY 40218
Phone: 502-454-0431
Fax: 502-459-7930
E-mail: kit@gatewaypressinc.com

GRACO INC.

http://www.graco.com

GRACO EXCELLENCE SCHOLARSHIP

Three awards of $7500 (one for athletic achievement) for children of Graco employees with at least one year of company service. Award based on academics, financial need, and tuition costs. Must be under 25 years of age.

Award: Scholarship for use in freshman, sophomore, junior, senior, or graduate years; renewable. *Number:* 3. *Amount:* $7500.

Eligibility Requirements: Applicant must be age 25 or under; enrolled or expecting to enroll full-time at a two-year or four-year or technical institution or university and must have an interest in athletics/sports. Applicant or parent of applicant must be affiliated with Graco, Inc.. Available to U.S. and non-U.S. citizens.

Application Requirements: Application, financial need analysis, test scores, transcript. *Deadline:* March 15.

Contact: Kristin Ridley, Grants Administration Manager
Graco Inc.
PO Box 1441
Minneapolis, MN 55440-1441
Phone: 612-623-6684
Fax: 612-623-6944

GRACO INC. SCHOLARSHIP PROGRAM

Renewable award for children of Graco employees under 26 years of age pursuing undergraduate or graduate education. Awards are based upon academics, financial need, and tuition costs. Submit transcripts, test scores, and financial need analysis with application.

Award: Scholarship for use in freshman, sophomore, junior, senior, or graduate years; renewable. *Number:* varies. *Amount:* $3500–$5000.

Eligibility Requirements: Applicant must be age 26 or under and enrolled or expecting to enroll full-time at a two-year or four-year or technical institution or university. Applicant or parent of applicant must be affiliated with Graco, Inc.. Available to U.S. and non-U.S. citizens.

Application Requirements: Application, financial need analysis, test scores, transcript. *Deadline:* March 15.

Contact: Kristin Ridley, Grants Administration Manager
Graco Inc.
PO Box 1441
Minneapolis, MN 55440-1441
Phone: 612-623-6684
Fax: 612-623-6944

GREATER SAINT LOUIS COMMUNITY FOUNDATION

http://www.gstlcf.org

ST. ANTHONY'S MEDICAL CENTER NORBERT SIEGFRIED HEALTH PROFESSIONS SCHOLARSHIP

Scholarship open to dependent children of the Medical Center's full time and regular part time staff, who demonstrate financial need. For use at a regionally accredited four-year Missouri college or university or at any of Southern Illinois University's five campuses.

Award: Scholarship for use in freshman, sophomore, junior, or senior years; renewable. *Number:* varies. *Amount:* $2000–$10,000.

Eligibility Requirements: Applicant must be enrolled or expecting to enroll full-time at a four-year institution or university and studying in Illinois or Missouri. Applicant or parent of applicant must be affiliated with St. Anthony"s Medical Center, St. Louis, MO. Applicant must have 3.0 GPA or higher. Available to U.S. citizens.

Application Requirements: Application, essay, financial need analysis, references, transcript, FAFSA, Student Aid Report (SAR). *Deadline:* April 15.

Contact: Amy Murphy, Donor Services and Scholarship Officer
Greater Saint Louis Community Foundation
319 North Fourth Street, Suite 300
St. Louis, MO 63102-1906
Phone: 314-588-8200 Ext. 132
Fax: 314-588-8088
E-mail: amurphy@gstlcf.org

HERMAN O. WEST FOUNDATION

http://www.westpharma.com

HERMAN O. WEST FOUNDATION SCHOLARSHIP PROGRAM

Awards up to seven scholarships per year to high school seniors who will be attending college in the fall after graduation. The scholarship may only be applied toward tuition cost up to $2500 per year for up to four years. Available only to children of active employees.

Award: Scholarship for use in freshman year; renewable. *Number:* 1–7. *Amount:* $2500.

Eligibility Requirements: Applicant must be high school student and planning to enroll or expecting to enroll full-time at a four-year institution or university. Applicant or parent of applicant must be affiliated with West Pharmaceuticals. Available to U.S. citizens.

Application Requirements: Application, essay, references, test scores, transcript. *Deadline:* February 28.

Contact: Maureen Goebel, Administrator
Herman O. West Foundation
101 Gordon Drive
Lionville, PA 19341
Phone: 610-594-2945
Fax: 610-594-3011
E-mail: maureen.goebel@westpharma.com

HORMEL FOODS CORPORATION

http://www.hormelfoods.com

HORMEL FOODS CHARITABLE TRUST SCHOLARSHIP

College scholarships worth $2000. Must apply in junior year of high school. Scholarships are renewable for up to four years. Must be the child of a Hormel Food employee or retiree. Must submit PSAT scores.

Award: Scholarship for use in freshman year; renewable. *Number:* 15. *Amount:* $2000.

Eligibility Requirements: Applicant must be high school student and planning to enroll or expecting to enroll full-time at a four-year institution or university. Applicant or parent of applicant must be affiliated with Hormel Foods Corporation. Available to U.S. citizens.

Hormel Foods Corporation (continued)

Application Requirements: Application, test scores, PSAT scores. *Deadline:* January 10.

Contact: Julie Craven, Vice President Corporate Communications
Hormel Foods Corporation
One Hormel Place
Austin, MN 55912-3680
Phone: 507-437-5345
Fax: 507-434-6721

HUMANA FOUNDATION http://www.humanafoundation.com

HUMANA FOUNDATION SCHOLARSHIP PROGRAM

Applicants must be under 25 years of age and a United States citizen. Must be a dependent of a Humana employee.

Award: Scholarship for use in freshman, sophomore, or junior years; not renewable. *Number:* up to 75. *Amount:* $1500–$3000.

Eligibility Requirements: Applicant must be age 25 or under and enrolled or expecting to enroll full-time at a two-year or four-year institution. Applicant or parent of applicant must be affiliated with Humana Foundation. Available to U.S. citizens.

Application Requirements: Application, references, transcript. *Deadline:* February 14.

Contact: Charles Jackson, Program Manager
Humana Foundation
500 West Main Street, Room 208
Louisville, KY 40202
Phone: 502-580-1245
Fax: 502-580-1256
E-mail: cjackson@humana.com

JOHNSON CONTROLS INC. http://www.johnsoncontrols.com

JOHNSON CONTROLS FOUNDATION SCHOLARSHIP PROGRAM

Available to high school seniors who are children of Johnson Controls, Inc. employees. 20 one-time awards of $2000 and 25 renewable scholarships of $2000 a year for up to four years.

Award: Scholarship for use in freshman year; renewable. *Number:* up to 45. *Amount:* $2000.

Eligibility Requirements: Applicant must be high school student and planning to enroll or expecting to enroll full-time at a four-year institution or university. Applicant or parent of applicant must be affiliated with Johnson Controls, Inc.. Applicant must have 3.0 GPA or higher. Available to U.S. citizens.

Application Requirements: Application, transcript. *Deadline:* March 3.

Contact: Marlene Griffith, Human Resources Administration Coordinator
Johnson Controls Inc.
5757 North Green Bay Avenue, X-34
Milwaukee, WI 53209
Phone: 414-524-2425
Fax: 414-524-2299

KOHLER COMPANY http://www.kohler.com

KOHLER COMPANY COLLEGE SCHOLARSHIP

Renewable award for college-bound children of Kohler and its U.S. and Canadian subsidiary employees. High school students who are Kohler employees are also eligible. Scholarships are $2500 per year. Scholarships are accepted from December 1 to February 15.

Award: Scholarship for use in freshman, sophomore, junior, or senior years; renewable. *Number:* 21. *Amount:* $2500.

Eligibility Requirements: Applicant must be enrolled or expecting to enroll full-time at a four-year institution or university. Applicant or parent of applicant must be affiliated with Kohler Company. Available to U.S. and Canadian citizens.

Application Requirements: Application, references, test scores, transcript. *Deadline:* February 15.

Contact: Lynn Kulow, Charitable Contributions & Research Manager
Kohler Company
444 Highland Drive
Kohler, WI 53044
Phone: 920-457-4441
Fax: 920-459-1889
E-mail: lynn.kulow@kohler.com

LINCOLN COMMUNITY FOUNDATION http://www.lcf.org

GEORGE L. WATTERS/NEBRASKA PETROLEUM MARKETERS ASSOCIATION SCHOLARSHIP

Multiple scholarships are available to current high school seniors who are the sons, daughters or grandchildren of any Nebraska Petroleum Marketer and Convenience Store Association member or of a full- or part-time employee. Must demonstrate academic achievement, leadership qualities, and have expressed a desire and intent to continue education leading to a degree.

Award: Scholarship for use in freshman year; not renewable. *Number:* varies. *Amount:* $1000.

Eligibility Requirements: Applicant must be high school student; planning to enroll or expecting to enroll full-time at a four-year institution or university; resident of Nebraska; studying in Nebraska and must have an interest in leadership. Applicant or parent of applicant must be affiliated with Nebraska Petroleum Marketers Association. Applicant must have 3.0 GPA or higher. Available to U.S. citizens.

Application Requirements: Application, references, transcript. *Deadline:* March 1.

Contact: Grafton and Associates Certified Public Accountants
Lincoln Community Foundation
8101 O Street, Suite 200
Lincoln, NE 68510

THOMAS C. WOODS, JR. MEMORIAL SCHOLARSHIP

Scholarships for graduating seniors or former graduates of any high school in the following counties in Nebraska: Adams, Butler, Cass, Clay, Fillmore, Gage, Hamilton, Jefferson, Johnson, Lancaster, Nemaha, Nucholls, Otoe, Pawnee, Polk, Richardson, Saline, Saunders, Seward, Thayer, Webster, and York. Applicants must be qualified dependents of current ALLTEL employees. Minimum 2.5 GPA required.

Award: Scholarship for use in freshman, sophomore, junior, or senior years; renewable. *Number:* varies. *Amount:* $500–$2000.

Eligibility Requirements: Applicant must be enrolled or expecting to enroll full-time at a two-year or four-year institution or university; resident of Nebraska and studying in Nebraska. Applicant or parent of applicant must be affiliated with ALLTEL. Applicant must have 2.5 GPA or higher. Available to U.S. citizens.

Application Requirements: Application, essay, financial need analysis, test scores. *Deadline:* April 17.

Contact: Sonya Brakeman, Grants/Scholarships Coordinator
Lincoln Community Foundation
215 Centennial Mall South, Suite 100
Lincoln, NE 68508
Phone: 402-474-2345
Fax: 402-476-8532
E-mail: sonyab@lcf.org

MAINE COMMUNITY FOUNDATION INC. http://www.mainecf.org

CMP GROUP SCHOLARSHIP FUND

Three or more $1000–$5000 awards will be made annually to dependants of CMP Group and its affiliate employees or retirees who reside within the company's service area. Must be high school senior graduating from a Maine secondary school.

Award: Scholarship for use in freshman year; not renewable. *Number:* 3. *Amount:* $1000–$5000.

Eligibility Requirements: Applicant must be high school student; planning to enroll or expecting to enroll full-time at a two-year or four-year or technical institution or university and resident of Maine. Applicant or parent of applicant must be affiliated with CPM Group. Available to U.S. citizens.

Application Requirements: Application, essay, financial need analysis, references, transcript. *Deadline:* May 1.

Contact: Jean Warren, Scholarship Coordinator
Maine Community Foundation Inc.
245 Main Street
Ellsworth, ME 04605-1613
Phone: 207-667-9735
Fax: 207-667-0447
E-mail: jwarren@mainecf.org

LAWRENCE AND LOUISE ROBBINS SCHOLARSHIP FUND

Scholarship for employees or retirees of the Robbins Lumber Company of Searsmont or their children/grandchildren to pursue postsecondary education. Recipients will be selected on the basis of academic achievement, personal aspirations, and contributions to school and the community.

Award: Scholarship for use in freshman, sophomore, junior, or senior years; renewable. *Number:* 2–20. *Amount:* varies.

Eligibility Requirements: Applicant must be high school student and planning to enroll or expecting to enroll full-time at a four-year institution or university. Applicant or parent of applicant must be affiliated with Robbins Lumber Company. Available to U.S. and non-U.S. citizens.

Application Requirements: Application, essay, transcript. *Deadline:* April 15.

Contact: Catherine Jollisse, Controller
Maine Community Foundation Inc.
Robbins Lumber Inc., PO Box 9
Searsmont, ME 04973
Phone: 207-342-5221
Fax: 207-342-5201

MINNESOTA COMMUNITY FOUNDATION http://www.mncommunityfoundation.org

CEMSTONE COMPANIES SCHOLARSHIP

Scholarship to FT employees of Cemstone Company and their dependents. Two or more awards of at least $2000 are awarded.

Award: Scholarship for use in freshman, sophomore, junior, senior, or graduate years; not renewable. *Number:* 2. *Amount:* $2000.

Eligibility Requirements: Applicant must be enrolled or expecting to enroll full- or part-time at a two-year or four-year or technical institution or university. Applicant or parent of applicant must be affiliated with Cemstone Company. Available to U.S. citizens.

Application Requirements: Application, transcript. *Deadline:* May 1.

Contact: Donna Paulson, Administrative Assistant
Minnesota Community Foundation
55 Fifth Street East, Suite 600
St. Paul, MN 55101-1797
Phone: 651-325-4212
E-mail: dkp@mncommunityfoundation.org

J.C. AND L.A. DUKE SCHOLARSHIP

Awards 50 or more renewable scholarships ranging from $1500 to $2000 each year to legal dependents of active, disabled, retired or deceased persons employed by 3M for a minimum of two years prior to January 1 of the year in which the student graduates from high school.

Award: Scholarship for use in freshman year; renewable. *Number:* 50. *Amount:* $1500–$2000.

Eligibility Requirements: Applicant must be high school student and planning to enroll or expecting to enroll full- or part-time at a four-year institution or university. Applicant or parent of applicant must be affiliated with 3M Corporation. Available to U.S. citizens.

Application Requirements: Application, transcript, income of parents, IRS Form 1040. *Deadline:* March 1.

Contact: Donna Paulson, Administrative Assistant
Minnesota Community Foundation
55 Fifth Street East, Suite 600
St. Paul, MN 55101-1797
Phone: 651-325-4212
E-mail: dkp@mncommunityfoundation.org

PAUL AND FERN YOCUM SCHOLARSHIP

Scholarship to dependent children of FT Yocum Oil employees.

Award: Scholarship for use in freshman, sophomore, junior, senior, or graduate years; not renewable. *Number:* 3. *Amount:* $1000.

Eligibility Requirements: Applicant must be enrolled or expecting to enroll full- or part-time at a four-year institution or university. Applicant or parent of applicant must be affiliated with Yocum Oil Company. Available to U.S. and non-Canadian citizens.

Application Requirements: Application. *Deadline:* April 15.

Contact: Donna Paulson, Administrative Assistant
Minnesota Community Foundation
55 Fifth Street East, Suite 600
St. Paul, MN 55101-1797
Phone: 651-325-4212
E-mail: dkp@mncommunityfoundation.org

YOUNG AMERICA CORPORATION SCHOLARSHIP

Scholarship to employees or dependent children or grandchildren of active Young America employees with a minimum of one year of active employment as of the application deadline, enrolling in an undergraduate course of study. Five awards of $1000 are awarded annually.

Award: Scholarship for use in freshman, sophomore, junior, or senior years; not renewable. *Number:* 5. *Amount:* $1000.

Eligibility Requirements: Applicant must be enrolled or expecting to enroll full- or part-time at a four-year institution or university. Applicant or parent of applicant must be affiliated with Young America Corporation. Available to U.S. citizens.

Application Requirements: Application, resume, references, transcript. *Deadline:* June 15.

Contact: Donna Paulson, Administrative Assistant
Minnesota Community Foundation
55 Fifth Street East, Suite 600
St. Paul, MN 55101-1797
Phone: 651-325-4212
E-mail: dkp@mncommunityfoundation.org

NEW HAMPSHIRE FOOD INDUSTRIES EDUCATION FOUNDATION http://www.grocers.org

NEW HAMPSHIRE FOOD INDUSTRY SCHOLARSHIPS

Awards are $1000 each. The purpose is to assist students who are employees or children of employees working for New Hampshire Grocers Association member firms (either retailer or supplier).

Award: Scholarship for use in freshman, sophomore, junior, or senior years; renewable. *Number:* up to 35. *Amount:* $1000.

Eligibility Requirements: Applicant must be enrolled or expecting to enroll full- or part-time at a two-year or four-year or technical institution or university and resident of New Hampshire. Applicant or parent of applicant must be affiliated with New Hampshire Grocers Association member companies. Available to U.S. citizens.

Application Requirements: Application, essay, references, test scores, transcript. *Deadline:* April 1.

Contact: Mr. John M. Dumais, Secretary and Treasurer
New Hampshire Food Industries Education Foundation
110 Stark Street
Manchester, NH 03101-1977
Phone: 603-669-9333 Ext. 110
Fax: 603-623-1137
E-mail: scholarships@grocers.org

OREGON STUDENT ASSISTANCE COMMISSION http://www.osac.state.or.us

ALBINA FUEL COMPANY SCHOLARSHIP

One-time award. Scholarship available to a dependent child of a current Albina Fuel Company employee. The employee must have been employed for at least one full year as of October 1 prior to the scholarship deadline.

Award: Scholarship for use in freshman, sophomore, junior, or senior years; not renewable. *Number:* varies. *Amount:* varies.

Eligibility Requirements: Applicant must be enrolled or expecting to enroll full-time at a four-year institution and resident of Oregon or Washington. Applicant or parent of applicant must be affiliated with Albina Fuel Company. Available to U.S. citizens.

Application Requirements: Application, essay, transcript, activity chart. *Deadline:* March 1.

Contact: Director of Grant Programs
Oregon Student Assistance Commission
1500 Valley River Drive, Suite 100
Eugene, OR 97401-7020
Phone: 800-452-8807 Ext. 7395

A. VICTOR ROSENFELD SCHOLARSHIP

Award for children of employees of Calbag Metals of Portland, Oregon who have worked for that company for three years prior to the March 1 scholarship deadline.

Award: Scholarship for use in freshman, sophomore, junior, or senior years; renewable. *Number:* varies. *Amount:* varies.

Eligibility Requirements: Applicant must be enrolled or expecting to enroll full-time at a four-year institution and resident of Oregon. Applicant or parent of applicant must be affiliated with Calbag Metals. Available to U.S. citizens.

Application Requirements: Application, essay, financial need analysis, references, transcript, activity chart. *Deadline:* March 1.

Contact: Director of Grant Programs
Oregon Student Assistance Commission
1500 Valley River Drive, Suite 100
Eugene, OR 97401-7020
Phone: 800-452-8807 Ext. 7395

BANK OF THE CASCADES SCHOLARSHIP

Award for current employees or natural, adopted, or step children between the ages of 17 and 25 of the Bank of the Cascades. Children must be high school graduates with minimum 3.0 GPA. Employees must have been continuously employed at Bank of the Cascades for one year at no fewer than 20 hours per week as of the March 1 scholarship deadline. For use at Oregon colleges only. Children of Bank of the Cascades officers are not eligible.

Award: Scholarship for use in freshman, sophomore, junior, or senior years; renewable. *Number:* varies. *Amount:* varies.

Eligibility Requirements: Applicant must be age 17-25; enrolled or expecting to enroll full-time at a four-year institution; resident of Oregon and studying in Oregon. Applicant or parent of applicant must be affiliated with Bank of the Cascades. Applicant must have 3.0 GPA or higher. Available to U.S. citizens.

Application Requirements: Application, essay, financial need analysis, transcript, activities chart. *Deadline:* March 1.

Contact: Director of Grant Programs
Oregon Student Assistance Commission
1500 Valley River Drive, Suite 100
Eugene, OR 97401-7020
Phone: 800-452-8807 Ext. 7395

BLUE HERON PAPER EMPLOYEE DEPENDENTS SCHOLARSHIP

Renewable award to children, grandchildren, or legal dependents of active Blue Heron Paper employees. Must be employed by Blue Heron Paper one year as of the March 1 scholarship deadline. Must be 22 or younger, exception to age extended by years served to maximum of 26 if entered U.S. Armed Forces directly from high school.

Award: Scholarship for use in freshman, sophomore, junior, or senior years; renewable. *Number:* varies. *Amount:* varies.

Eligibility Requirements: Applicant must be age 22 or under; enrolled or expecting to enroll full-time at a four-year institution and resident of Oregon. Applicant or parent of applicant must be affiliated with Blue Heron Paper. Available to U.S. citizens.

Application Requirements: Application, essay, references, transcript, activity chart. *Deadline:* March 1.

Contact: Director of Grant Programs
Oregon Student Assistance Commission
1500 Valley River Drive, Suite 100
Eugene, OR 97401-7020
Phone: 800-452-8807 Ext. 7395

DAN KONNIE MEMORIAL DEPENDENTS SCHOLARSHIP

Renewable award for graduating high school seniors who are children of Swanson Brothers Lumber Co. employees. Must be an Oregon resident and enrolled only in Oregon public college.

Award: Scholarship for use in freshman year; renewable. *Number:* varies. *Amount:* varies.

Eligibility Requirements: Applicant must be high school student; planning to enroll or expecting to enroll full-time at a four-year institution; resident of Oregon and studying in Oregon. Applicant or parent of applicant must be affiliated with Swanson Brothers Lumber Company. Available to U.S. citizens.

Application Requirements: Application, essay, references, transcript, activity chart. *Deadline:* March 1.

Contact: Director of Grant Programs
Oregon Student Assistance Commission
1500 Valley River Drive, Suite 100
Eugene, OR 97401-7020
Phone: 800-452-8807 Ext. 7395

ESSEX GENERAL CONSTRUCTION SCHOLARSHIP

Award for employee or natural, adopted, or step children between the ages of 17 and 25 of current employees of Essex General Construction. Employee (parent or legal guardian of applicant) must have been continuously employed at Essex one year or more at no fewer than 20 hours per week as of the March 1. Must reapply each year for up to four years.

Award: Scholarship for use in freshman, sophomore, junior, or senior years; renewable. *Number:* 1. *Amount:* $5000.

Eligibility Requirements: Applicant must be age 17-25; enrolled or expecting to enroll full-time at a four-year institution and resident of Oregon. Applicant or parent of applicant must be affiliated with Essex General Construction. Available to U.S. citizens.

Application Requirements: Application, essay, financial need analysis, transcript, activities chart. *Deadline:* March 1.

Contact: Director of Grant Programs
Oregon Student Assistance Commission
1500 Valley River Drive, Suite 100
Eugene, OR 97401-7020
Phone: 800-452-8807 Ext. 7395

FORD SONS AND DAUGHTERS OF EMPLOYEES OF ROSEBURG FOREST PRODUCTS COMPANY SCHOLARSHIP

Renewable award for legal dependents of employees of Roseburg Forest Products Co. Must be twenty one years of age or younger. Qualifying parents must have been employed for a minimum of eighteen months prior to the March 1 deadline. All recipients must be planning to enroll in a full-time, undergraduate course of study leading to a baccalaureate degree or certificate in a technical program, at an eligible institution.

Award: Scholarship for use in freshman, sophomore, junior, or senior years; renewable. *Number:* varies. *Amount:* varies.

Eligibility Requirements: Applicant must be age 21 or under; enrolled or expecting to enroll full-time at a two-year or four-year institution and resident of Oregon. Applicant or parent of applicant must be affiliated with Roseburg Forest Products. Available to U.S. citizens.

Application Requirements: Application, essay, references, transcript, activity chart. *Deadline:* March 1.

Contact: Director of Grant Programs
Oregon Student Assistance Commission
1500 Valley River Drive, Suite 100
Eugene, OR 97401-7020
Phone: 800-452-8807 Ext. 7395

GLENN JACKSON SCHOLARS SCHOLARSHIPS (OCF)

Award for graduating high school seniors who are dependents of employees or retirees of Oregon Department of Transportation or Parks and Recreation Department. Employees must have worked in their department at least three years as of the March 1 scholarship deadline. Award for maximum twelve undergraduate quarters or six quarters at a two-year institution. Visit Web site http://www.osac.state.or.us for more details.

Award: Scholarship for use in freshman, sophomore, junior, or senior years; renewable. *Number:* varies. *Amount:* varies.

Eligibility Requirements: Applicant must be high school student; planning to enroll or expecting to enroll full- or part-time at a four-year institution and resident of Oregon. Applicant or parent of applicant must be affiliated with Oregon Department of Transportation Parks and Recreation. Available to U.S. citizens.

Application Requirements: Application, essay, financial need analysis, references, transcript, activity chart. *Deadline:* March 1.

Contact: Director of Grant Programs
Oregon Student Assistance Commission
1500 Valley River Drive, Suite 100
Eugene, OR 97401-7020
Phone: 800-452-8807 Ext. 7395

MCGARRY MACHINE INC. SCHOLARSHIP

One-time award for employees or dependents of employees of McGarry Machine who are high school graduates or GED recipients enrolling at least half-time in college. Contact Web site http://www.osac.state.or.us for further information.

Award: Scholarship for use in freshman, sophomore, junior, senior, or graduate years; renewable. *Number:* varies. *Amount:* varies.

Eligibility Requirements: Applicant must be enrolled or expecting to enroll full- or part-time at a four-year institution or university and resident of Oregon. Applicant or parent of applicant must be affiliated with McGarry Machine, Inc.. Available to U.S. citizens.

Application Requirements: Application, essay, references, transcript, activity chart. *Deadline:* March 1.

Contact: Director of Grant Programs
Oregon Student Assistance Commission
1500 Valley River Drive, Suite 100
Eugene, OR 97401-7020
Phone: 800-452-8807 Ext. 7395

OREGON TRUCKING ASSOCIATION SAFETY COUNCIL SCHOLARSHIP

One-time award available to a child of an Oregon Trucking Association member, or child of employee of member. Applicants must be Oregon residents who are graduating high school seniors from an Oregon high school.

Award: Scholarship for use in freshman year; not renewable. *Number:* 4. *Amount:* varies.

Eligibility Requirements: Applicant must be high school student; planning to enroll or expecting to enroll full-time at a four-year institution and resident of Oregon. Applicant or parent of applicant must be affiliated with Oregon Trucking Association. Available to U.S. citizens.

Application Requirements: Application, essay, financial need analysis, references, transcript, activity chart. *Deadline:* March 1.

Contact: Director of Grant Programs
Oregon Student Assistance Commission
1500 Valley River Drive, Suite 100
Eugene, OR 97401-7020
Phone: 800-452-8807 Ext. 7395

PACIFICSOURCE SCHOLARSHIP

Award for high school graduates or GED recipients between the ages of 17 to 25 who are the natural, adopted, or step children of PacificSource employees. Employee must have been continuously employed at PacificSource for at least two years at no fewer than 20 hours per week. Children of PacificSource officers are not eligible to participate. Must reapply each year for up to four years.

Award: Scholarship for use in freshman, sophomore, junior, or senior years; renewable. *Number:* varies. *Amount:* varies.

Eligibility Requirements: Applicant must be age 17-25; enrolled or expecting to enroll full-time at a four-year institution or university and resident of Oregon. Applicant or parent of applicant must be affiliated with PacificSource. Applicant must have 3.0 GPA or higher. Available to U.S. citizens.

Application Requirements: Application, essay, transcript, activities chart. *Deadline:* March 1.

Contact: Director of Grant Programs
Oregon Student Assistance Commission
1500 Valley River Drive, Suite 100
Eugene, OR 97401-7020
Phone: 800-452-8807 Ext. 7395

REED'S FUEL AND TRUCKING COMPANY SCHOLARSHIP

Award for employees and dependents of Reed's. Employees who have been employed one year as of the March 1 scholarship deadline. Must attend a college or a university in Oregon and have minimum cumulative 2.5 GPA. Employees may enroll part-time. Dependents must enroll full-time.

Award: Scholarship for use in freshman, sophomore, junior, or senior years; renewable. *Number:* varies. *Amount:* varies.

Eligibility Requirements: Applicant must be enrolled or expecting to enroll full- or part-time at a two-year or four-year institution or university; resident of Oregon and studying in Oregon. Applicant or parent of applicant must be affiliated with Reeds Fuel and Trucking Company. Applicant must have 2.5 GPA or higher. Available to U.S. citizens.

Application Requirements: Application, essay, references, transcript, activity chart. *Deadline:* March 1.

Contact: Director of Grant Programs
Oregon Student Assistance Commission
1500 Valley River Drive, Suite 100
Eugene, OR 97401-7020
Phone: 800-452-8807 Ext. 7395

RICHARD F. BRENTANO MEMORIAL SCHOLARSHIP

One-time award for legal dependents of Waste Control Systems Inc., and subsidiaries. Employees must be employed at least one year as of the March 1 scholarship deadline. Must be 24 years old or less, 26 years old for dependents entering U.S. Armed Forces directly from high school.

Award: Scholarship for use in freshman, sophomore, junior, or senior years; not renewable. *Number:* varies. *Amount:* varies.

Eligibility Requirements: Applicant must be age 24 or under; enrolled or expecting to enroll full-time at a four-year institution and resident of Oregon. Applicant or parent of applicant must be affiliated with Waste Control Systems, Inc.. Available to U.S. citizens.

Application Requirements: Application, essay, references, transcript, activity chart. *Deadline:* March 1.

Contact: Director of Grant Programs
Oregon Student Assistance Commission
1500 Valley River Drive, Suite 100
Eugene, OR 97401-7020
Phone: 800-452-8807 Ext. 7395

ROBERT D. FORSTER SCHOLARSHIP

One scholarship available to a dependent child of a Walsh Construction Co. employee who has completed 1000 hours or more in each of three consecutive fiscal years. Award may be received for a maximum of twelve quarters of undergraduate study and may only be used at four-year colleges.

Award: Scholarship for use in freshman, sophomore, junior, or senior years; renewable. *Number:* varies. *Amount:* varies.

Eligibility Requirements: Applicant must be enrolled or expecting to enroll full-time at a four-year institution and resident of California, Oregon, or Washington. Applicant or parent of applicant must be affiliated with Walsh Construction Company. Available to U.S. citizens.

Oregon Student Assistance Commission (continued)

Application Requirements: Application, essay, financial need analysis, references, transcript, activity chart. *Deadline:* March 1.

Contact: Director of Grant Programs
Oregon Student Assistance Commission
1500 Valley River Drive, Suite 100
Eugene, OR 97401-7020
Phone: 800-452-8807 Ext. 7395

ROGER W. EMMONS MEMORIAL SCHOLARSHIP

Scholarship available to a graduating Oregon high school senior who is a child or grandchild of an employee (for at least three years) of member of the Oregon Refuse and Recycling Association.

Award: Scholarship for use in freshman year; renewable. *Number:* varies. *Amount:* varies.

Eligibility Requirements: Applicant must be high school student; planning to enroll or expecting to enroll full-time at a four-year institution and resident of Oregon. Applicant or parent of applicant must be affiliated with Oregon Refuse and Recycling Association. Available to U.S. citizens.

Application Requirements: Application, essay, references, transcript, activity chart. *Deadline:* March 1.

Contact: Director of Grant Programs
Oregon Student Assistance Commission
1500 Valley River Drive, Suite 100
Eugene, OR 97401-7020
Phone: 800-452-8807 Ext. 7395

SP NEWSPRINT COMPANY, NEWBERG MILL, EMPLOYEE DEPENDENTS SCHOLARSHIP

One-time award available to children, grandchildren, legal dependents (22 years old and under) of active SP Newsprint Co. Age limit extended by years served to maximum age of 26 for those entering armed services directly from high school. Employees must be employed by the company more than one year.

Award: Scholarship for use in freshman, sophomore, junior, or senior years; not renewable. *Number:* varies. *Amount:* varies.

Eligibility Requirements: Applicant must be age 22 or under; enrolled or expecting to enroll full-time at a two-year or four-year institution and resident of Oregon. Applicant or parent of applicant must be affiliated with SP Newsprint Company. Available to U.S. citizens.

Application Requirements: Application, essay, financial need analysis, references, transcript, activity chart. *Deadline:* March 1.

Contact: Director of Grant Programs
Oregon Student Assistance Commission
1500 Valley River Drive, Suite 100
Eugene, OR 97401-7020
Phone: 800-452-8807 Ext. 7395

STIMSON LUMBER COMPANY SCHOLARSHIP

Award for dependents of Stimson employees who are graduating seniors from accredited high school. One-year-only scholarships available for two- or four-year colleges. Candidates for renewable scholarships must attend four-year colleges. Minimum 2.7 cumulative GPA required.

Award: Scholarship for use in freshman year; renewable. *Number:* varies. *Amount:* varies.

Eligibility Requirements: Applicant must be enrolled or expecting to enroll full-time at a two-year or four-year institution and resident of Oregon. Applicant or parent of applicant must be affiliated with Stimson Lumber Company. Available to U.S. citizens.

Application Requirements: Application, essay, financial need analysis, references, transcript, activity chart. *Deadline:* March 1.

Contact: Director of Grant Programs
Oregon Student Assistance Commission
1500 Valley River Drive, Suite 100
Eugene, OR 97401-7020
Phone: 800-452-8807 Ext. 7395

TAYLOR MADE LABELS SCHOLARSHIP

Award available to a children, grandchildren or legal dependent of an active employee of Taylor Made Label Company. Employee must have been employed by Taylor Made for a minimum of one year as of the March 1 scholarship deadline. Must be 22 or younger.

Award: Scholarship for use in freshman, sophomore, junior, or senior years; renewable. *Number:* varies. *Amount:* varies.

Eligibility Requirements: Applicant must be age 22 or under; enrolled or expecting to enroll full-time at a four-year institution and resident of Oregon. Applicant or parent of applicant must be affiliated with Taylor Made Label Company. Available to U.S. citizens.

Application Requirements: Application, essay, financial need analysis, references, transcript, activity chart. *Deadline:* March 1.

Contact: Director of Grant Programs
Oregon Student Assistance Commission
1500 Valley River Drive, Suite 100
Eugene, OR 97401-7020
Phone: 800-452-8807 Ext. 7395

WALTER DAVIES SCHOLARSHIP

Award for current U.S. Bancorp employees or employees' natural or adopted children. Must be Oregon high school graduates.

Award: Scholarship for use in freshman, sophomore, junior, or senior years; renewable. *Number:* varies. *Amount:* varies.

Eligibility Requirements: Applicant must be enrolled or expecting to enroll full-time at a four-year institution and resident of Oregon. Applicant or parent of applicant must be affiliated with U.S. Bancorp. Available to U.S. citizens.

Application Requirements: Application, essay, financial need analysis, references, transcript, activity chart. *Deadline:* March 1.

Contact: Director of Grant Programs
Oregon Student Assistance Commission
1500 Valley River Drive, Suite 100
Eugene, OR 97401-7020
Phone: 800-452-8807 Ext. 7395

WILLETT AND MARGUERITE LAKE SCHOLARSHIP

Scholarship awards children, stepchildren and grandchildren of current employees of Bonita Pioneer Packaging Company who have been employed by the company for two years. Open to high school seniors and undergraduates. Must be Oregon resident.

Award: Scholarship for use in freshman, sophomore, junior, senior, or graduate years; renewable. *Number:* varies. *Amount:* varies.

Eligibility Requirements: Applicant must be enrolled or expecting to enroll full-time at a four-year institution or university and resident of Oregon. Applicant or parent of applicant must be affiliated with Bonita Pioneer Packaging Company. Available to U.S. citizens.

Application Requirements: Application, essay, financial need analysis, transcript, activity chart. *Deadline:* March 1.

Contact: Director of Grant Programs
Oregon Student Assistance Commission
1500 Valley River Drive, Suite 100
Eugene, OR 97401-7020
Phone: 800-452-8807 Ext. 7395

WOODARD FAMILY SCHOLARSHIP

Scholarships are available to employees and children of employees of Kimwood Corporation and Middlefield Estates. Applicants must have graduated from a U.S. high school. Awards may be used at Oregon colleges only, and may be received for a maximum of twelve quarters of undergraduate study.

Award: Scholarship for use in freshman, sophomore, junior, or senior years; renewable. *Number:* varies. *Amount:* varies.

Eligibility Requirements: Applicant must be enrolled or expecting to enroll full-time at a two-year or four-year institution; resident of Oregon and studying in Oregon. Applicant or parent of applicant must be affiliated with Kimwood Corporation or Middlefield Village. Available to U.S. citizens.

Application Requirements: Application, essay, financial need analysis, references, transcript. *Deadline:* March 1.

Contact: Director of Grant Programs
Oregon Student Assistance Commission
1500 Valley River Drive, Suite 100
Eugene, OR 97401-7020
Phone: 800-452-8807 Ext. 7395

RHODE ISLAND FOUNDATION http://www.rifoundation.org

A.T. CROSS SCHOLARSHIP

Scholarships ranging from $1000 to $3000 for new applicants and from $300 to $2000 for renewals are available to children of full-time employees of A.T. Cross Company. Must be Rhode Island residents.

Award: Scholarship for use in freshman, sophomore, junior, or senior years; renewable. *Number:* varies. *Amount:* $1000–$3000.

Eligibility Requirements: Applicant must be enrolled or expecting to enroll full-time at a four-year institution or university and resident of Rhode Island. Applicant or parent of applicant must be affiliated with A.T. Cross. Available to U.S. citizens.

Application Requirements: Application, essay, financial need analysis, references, self-addressed stamped envelope, transcript. *Deadline:* May 12.

Contact: Libby Monahan, Funds Administrator
Rhode Island Foundation
One Union Station
Providence, RI 02903
Phone: 401-274-4564 Ext. 3117
Fax: 401-751-7983
E-mail: libbym@rifoundation.org

SAN DIEGO FOUNDATION http://www.sdfoundation.org

CLUB AT MORNINGSIDE SCHOLARSHIP

Scholarships to employees, full or part-time, employed by The Club at Morningside for a minimum of two consecutive years on a seasonal or year-round basis. Open to graduating high school seniors, students already in school, or those planning to attend an accredited two- or four-year college or university, graduate school, or licensed trade/vocational school in the United States. Minimum 2.5 GPA required.

Award: Scholarship for use in freshman, sophomore, junior, or senior years; not renewable. *Number:* varies. *Amount:* varies.

Eligibility Requirements: Applicant must be enrolled or expecting to enroll full-time at a two-year or four-year or technical institution or university and resident of California. Applicant or parent of applicant must be affiliated with Club at Morningside. Applicant must have 2.5 GPA or higher. Available to U.S. citizens.

Application Requirements: Application, financial need analysis, references, transcript. *Deadline:* January 26.

Contact: Shryl Helvie, Scholarship Coordinator
San Diego Foundation
2508 Historic Decatur Road, Suite 200
San Diego, CA 92106
Phone: 619-814-1307
Fax: 619-239-1710
E-mail: shryl@sdfoundation.org

REMINGTON CLUB SCHOLARSHIP

Scholarship to employees and the children of employees at The Remington Club. Applicants must plan to attend an accredited two- or four-year college or university, or licensed trade/vocational school in the United States. Must have a commitment to their community as demonstrated by their involvement in extracurricular activities, community service, sports, or work experience. May be renewable for up to four years provided the recipient maintains positive academic and citizenship standing.

Award: Scholarship for use in freshman year; renewable. *Number:* varies. *Amount:* $1000–$4000.

Eligibility Requirements: Applicant must be high school student; planning to enroll or expecting to enroll full-time at a two-year or four-year or technical institution or university and resident of California. Applicant or parent of applicant must be affiliated with Remington Club. Applicant must have 2.5 GPA or higher. Available to U.S. citizens.

Application Requirements: Application, references, transcript, personal statement, copy of tax return. *Deadline:* January 26.

Contact: Shryl Helvie, Scholarship Coordinator
San Diego Foundation
2508 Historic Decatur Road, Suite 200
San Diego, CA 92106
Phone: 619-814-1307
Fax: 619-239-1710
E-mail: shryl@sdfoundation.org

THEODORE R. AND VIVIAN M. JOHNSON SCHOLARSHIP FOUNDATION INC. http://www.johnsonscholarships.org

THEODORE R. AND VIVIAN M. JOHNSON SCHOLARSHIP PROGRAM FOR CHILDREN OF UPS EMPLOYEES OR UPS RETIREES

The children of United Parcel Service employees or retirees who live in Florida are eligible for scholarship funds to attend college or vocational school in Florida. Awards are for undergraduate study only and ranges from $1000 to $10,000. Community college students and vocational school students may receive a maximum of $5000 per year.

Award: Scholarship for use in freshman year; renewable. *Number:* 1–50. *Amount:* $1000–$10,000.

Eligibility Requirements: Applicant must be high school student; planning to enroll or expecting to enroll full-time at a two-year or four-year institution or university; resident of Florida and studying in Florida. Applicant or parent of applicant must be affiliated with UPS-United Parcel Service. Available to U.S. and non-U.S. citizens.

Application Requirements: Application, financial need analysis, transcript. *Deadline:* April 15.

Contact: Sharon Wood, Office and Grants Administrator
Theodore R. and Vivian M. Johnson Scholarship Foundation Inc.
505 South Flagler Drive, Suite 1460
West Palm Beach, FL 33401
Phone: 561-659-2005
Fax: 561-659-1054
E-mail: wood@jsf.bz

TRIANGLE COMMUNITY FOUNDATION http://www.trianglecf.org

GEORGE AND MARY NEWTON SCHOLARSHIP

One scholarship per year is granted to a child of a Newton Instrument Company employee. Must demonstrate academic achievement and financial aid, and be a graduating senior from a Granville County high school.

Award: Scholarship for use in freshman year; renewable. *Number:* 5. *Amount:* $500–$20,000.

Eligibility Requirements: Applicant must be high school student and planning to enroll or expecting to enroll full- or part-time at a four-year institution or university. Applicant or parent of applicant must be affiliated with Newton Instrument Company. Available to U.S. and non-U.S. citizens.

Application Requirements: Application, transcript. *Deadline:* March 15.

Contact: Linda Depo, Philanthropic Services Associate
Triangle Community Foundation
4813 Emperor Boulevard, Suite 130
Durham, NC 27703
Phone: 919-474-8370
Fax: 919-941-9208
E-mail: linda@trianglecf.org

UNITED NEGRO COLLEGE FUND http://www.uncf.org

KFC SCHOLARS PROGRAM

Award for KFC corporate or franchise employee who has at least one year of work experience with KFC and who wishes to pursue a bachelor's degree in business management, computer sciences, restaurant management or liberal arts at a UNCF institution. Must have a 2.5 GPA, be an employee in good standing, and have an unmet financial need.

United Negro College Fund (continued)

Award: Scholarship for use in freshman year; renewable. *Number:* 1. *Amount:* varies.

Eligibility Requirements: Applicant must be enrolled or expecting to enroll full- or part-time at a four-year institution or university. Applicant or parent of applicant must be affiliated with Kentucky Fried Chicken. Applicant must have 2.5 GPA or higher. Available to U.S. citizens.

Application Requirements: Application, essay, transcript. *Deadline:* June 30.

Contact: Director, Program Services
United Negro College Fund
8260 Willow Oaks Corporate Drive
PO Box 10444
Fairfax, VA 22031-8044
Phone: 800-331-2244
E-mail: rebecca.bennett@uncf.org

LEON JACKSON JR. SCHOLARSHIP

Award for current UNCF employees who desire to return to school to complete their associate, undergraduate, or graduate education. Please see Web site for more information: http://www.uncf.org.

Award: Scholarship for use in freshman, sophomore, junior, senior, or graduate years; renewable. *Number:* up to 2. *Amount:* $2500.

Eligibility Requirements: Applicant must be Black (non-Hispanic) and enrolled or expecting to enroll full- or part-time at a two-year or four-year institution or university. Applicant or parent of applicant must be affiliated with United Negro College Fund. Applicant must have 2.5 GPA or higher. Available to U.S. citizens.

Application Requirements: Application, essay, financial need analysis, references, transcript, FAFSA, Student Aid Report (SAR). *Deadline:* May 31.

Contact: Director, Program Services
United Negro College Fund
8260 Willow Oaks Corporate Drive
PO Box 10444
Fairfax, VA 22031-8044
Phone: 800-331-2244
E-mail: rebecca.bennett@uncf.org

VERIZON FOUNDATION http://foundation.verizon.com

VERIZON FOUNDATION SCHOLARSHIP

Award up to 250 four-year scholarships to high school seniors who are children of Verizon employees in the United States, and are planning to attend a four-year college or university. Deadline varies.

Award: Scholarship for use in freshman year; renewable. *Number:* up to 250. *Amount:* $5000–$20,000.

Eligibility Requirements: Applicant must be high school student and planning to enroll or expecting to enroll full- or part-time at a four-year institution or university. Applicant or parent of applicant must be affiliated with Verizon. Available to U.S. citizens.

Application Requirements: Application. *Deadline:* varies.

Contact: Scholarship Committee
Verizon Foundation
One Verizon Way
Basking Ridge, NJ 07920
Phone: 800-360-7955
Fax: 908-630-2660
E-mail: veriizon.foundation@verizon.com

WAL-MART FOUNDATION http://www.walmartfoundation.org

WAL-MART ASSOCIATE SCHOLARSHIPS

Awards for college-bound graduating high school seniors, those receiving a home-school diploma, or receiving a GED equivalency who work for Wal-Mart at least 1 continuous year. Based on ACT or SAT scores (minimum 18 ACT or 800 SAT score) and can prove financial need by required documents. One-time award of up to $2000. For use at an accredited two- or four-year U.S. institution.

Award: Scholarship for use in freshman year; not renewable. *Number:* 150–300. *Amount:* up to $2000.

Eligibility Requirements: Applicant must be high school student and planning to enroll or expecting to enroll full-time at a two-year or four-year institution or university. Applicant or parent of applicant must be affiliated with Wal-Mart Foundation. Available to U.S. citizens.

Application Requirements: Application, financial need analysis, test scores, transcript, federal income tax return. *Deadline:* continuous.

Contact: Scholarship Program Administrators, Inc.
Wal-Mart Foundation
PO Box 22492
Nashville, TN 37202
Phone: 866-851-3372
Fax: 615-523-7100

WAL-MART HIGHER REACH SCHOLARSHIP

Applicants must be a full-time or part-time Wal-Mart Stores Associate. Must have been employed by Wal-Mart Stores for at least one continuous year. Must have been out of high school for at least one year or a GED equivalency certificate. Award is based on financial need and job performance (meet/exceed expectations on most recent Associate Evaluation). Applications available online at https://www.scholarshipadministrators.net. Access key: WALMT.

Award: Scholarship for use in freshman, sophomore, junior, senior, or graduate years; not renewable. *Number:* varies. *Amount:* $500–$2000.

Eligibility Requirements: Applicant must be enrolled or expecting to enroll full- or part-time at a two-year or four-year institution or university. Applicant or parent of applicant must be affiliated with Wal-Mart Foundation. Available to U.S. citizens.

Application Requirements: Application, essay, financial need analysis, references, test scores, transcript, job performance appraisal. *Deadline:* January 12.

Contact: Scholarship Program Administrators, Inc.
Wal-Mart Foundation
PO Box 22492
Nashville, TN 37202
Phone: 866-851-3372
Fax: 615-523-7100

WALTON FAMILY FOUNDATION SCHOLARSHIP

Award for high-school seniors, or those receiving a home-school diploma, or receiving a GED-equivalency who are children of a Wal-Mart associate who has been employed as a full-time associate. A $10,000 undergraduate scholarship is payable over four years. Minimum of 22 (ACT) or 1030 (SAT) score and can prove financial need by required documents. Application available online at https://www.scholarshipadministrators.net/EmailRequestForm.asp. Access key: WFFS.

Award: Scholarship for use in freshman year; renewable. *Number:* 100–120. *Amount:* up to $2500.

Eligibility Requirements: Applicant must be high school student and planning to enroll or expecting to enroll full-time at a two-year or four-year institution or university. Applicant or parent of applicant must be affiliated with Wal-Mart Foundation. Available to U.S. citizens.

Application Requirements: Application, financial need analysis, test scores, transcript, federal income tax return. *Deadline:* February 1.

Contact: Scholarship Program Administrators, Inc.
Wal-Mart Foundation
PO Box 22492
Nashville, TN 37202
Phone: 866-851-3372
Fax: 615-523-7100

WEYERHAEUSER COMPANY FOUNDATION http://www.weyerhaeuser.com

WEYERHAEUSER COMPANY FOUNDATION SCHOLARSHIPS

Renewable awards for children of Weyerhaeuser Company employees. Must be in senior year in high school. Thirty scholarships to four-year institutions and 20 scholarships to community colleges or vocational/technical schools are awarded each year.

Award: Scholarship for use in freshman year; renewable. *Number:* 50. *Amount:* $1000–$4000.

Eligibility Requirements: Applicant must be high school student and planning to enroll or expecting to enroll full-time at a two-year or four-year or technical institution. Applicant or parent of applicant must be affiliated with Weyerhauser Company. Available to U.S. and Canadian citizens.

Application Requirements: Application. *Deadline:* January 15.

Contact: Program Manager
Weyerhaeuser Company Foundation
CH 1K36, PO Box 9777
Federal Way, WA 98063-9777
Phone: 253-924-3159
Fax: 253-924-3658

WILLITS FOUNDATION

WILLITS FOUNDATION SCHOLARSHIP PROGRAM

Renewable awards for children of full-time employees of C. R. Bard Inc. Children of Bard officers are not eligible. Must be pursuing, or planning to pursue, full-time postsecondary studies in the year in which the application is made.

Award: Scholarship for use in freshman, sophomore, junior, or senior years; renewable. *Number:* 10–15. *Amount:* $1000–$5000.

Eligibility Requirements: Applicant must be enrolled or expecting to enroll full-time at a four-year institution or university. Applicant or parent of applicant must be affiliated with C.R. Bard, Inc. Available to U.S. and Canadian citizens.

Application Requirements: Application, essay, photo, references, test scores, transcript. *Deadline:* March 1.

Contact: Linda Hrevnack, Program Manager
Willits Foundation
730 Central Avenue
Murray Hill, NJ 07974
Phone: 908-277-8182
Fax: 908-277-8098

EMPLOYMENT/VOLUNTEER EXPERIENCE

ADMINISTRATIVE MANAGEMENT SERVICES (AMS) http://cdnawards.com

CHRYSLER CANADA INC. SCHOLARSHIP PROGRAM

• *See page 571*

CHRYSLER FINANCIAL SERVICES CANADA INC. SCHOLARSHIP PROGRAM

• *See page 571*

A.F. & H.G. MCNEELY FOUNDATION http://www.axaonline.com/axafoundation

AXA ACHIEVEMENT SCHOLARSHIP

One high school senior from each state, the District of Colombia, and Puerto Rico are selected to receive this one-time award of $10,000. From the 52 state winners, 10 are selected as national winners and receive an additional $15,000, plus a laptop computer and offer of an internship with AXA.

Award: Scholarship for use in freshman year; not renewable. *Number:* 52. *Amount:* $10,000–$25,000.

Eligibility Requirements: Applicant must be high school student and planning to enroll or expecting to enroll full-time at a two-year or four-year institution or university. Applicant or parent of applicant must have employment or volunteer experience in community service. Available to U.S. citizens.

Application Requirements: Application, essay, references, transcript. *Deadline:* December 15.

Contact: Scholarship Committee
A.F. & H.G. McNeely Foundation
1290 Avenue of the Americas
New York, NY 10104
Phone: 507-931-0437
Fax: 507-931-9168
E-mail: axaachievement@scholarship.org

AIR TRAFFIC CONTROL ASSOCIATION INC. http://www.atca.org

BUCKINGHAM MEMORIAL SCHOLARSHIP

Scholarships granted to children of air traffic control specialists pursuing a bachelor's degree or higher in any course of study. Must be the child, natural or by adoption, of a person serving, or having served as an air traffic control specialist, be it with the U.S. government, U.S. military, or in a private facility in the United States.

Award: Scholarship for use in freshman, sophomore, junior, senior, or graduate years; not renewable. *Number:* 2–4. *Amount:* $1000–$2500.

Eligibility Requirements: Applicant must be enrolled or expecting to enroll full- or part-time at a four-year institution or university. Applicant or parent of applicant must have employment or volunteer experience in air traffic controller field. Available to U.S. citizens.

Application Requirements: Application, autobiography, essay, financial need analysis, references, transcript. *Deadline:* May 1.

Contact: Miguel Vazquez, Director
Air Traffic Control Association Inc.
1101 King Street, Suite 300
Alexandria, VA 22201
Phone: 703-522-5717
Fax: 703-527-7251
E-mail: info@atca.org

ALABAMA COMMISSION ON HIGHER EDUCATION http://www.ache.alabama.gov

POLICE OFFICERS AND FIREFIGHTERS SURVIVORS EDUCATION ASSISTANCE PROGRAM-ALABAMA

Provides tuition, fees, books, and supplies to dependents of full-time police officers and firefighters killed in the line of duty. Must attend any Alabama public college as an undergraduate. Must be Alabama resident.

Award: Scholarship for use in freshman, sophomore, junior, or senior years; renewable. *Number:* 15–30. *Amount:* $2000–$5000.

Eligibility Requirements: Applicant must be enrolled or expecting to enroll full-time at a two-year or four-year or technical institution or university; single; resident of Alabama and studying in Alabama. Applicant or parent of applicant must have employment or volunteer experience in police/firefighting. Available to U.S. citizens.

Application Requirements: Application. *Deadline:* continuous.

Contact: William Wall, Associate Executive Director for Student Assistance
Alabama Commission on Higher Education
100 North Union Street, PO Box 302000
Montgomery, AL 36104-3758
Phone: 334-242-2273
Fax: 334-242-0268
E-mail: wwall@ache.state.al.us

ALBERTA HERITAGE SCHOLARSHIP FUND/ ALBERTA SCHOLARSHIP PROGRAMS http://www.alis.gov.ab.ca

ALBERTA HERITAGE SCHOLARSHIP FUND HAL HARRISON MEMORIAL SCHOLARSHIP

Awards a 12th-grade student with high marks, who is enrolled full-time at a postsecondary institution. Must have one parent who is a member in Alberta Volunteer Fire Fighters Association in good standing. Must be a resident of Alberta, Canada. Must be ranked in upper third of class or have a minimum GPA of 3.0.

Award: Scholarship for use in freshman year; not renewable. *Number:* 1. *Amount:* $186.

Eligibility Requirements: Applicant must be Canadian citizen; high school student; planning to enroll or expecting to enroll full-time at a two-year or four-year or technical institution or university and resident of Alberta. Applicant or parent of applicant must have employment or volunteer experience in police/firefighting. Applicant must have 3.0 GPA or higher.

Alberta Heritage Scholarship Fund/Alberta Scholarship Programs (continued)

Application Requirements: Application, transcript. *Deadline:* June 1.

Contact: Scholarship Committee
Alberta Heritage Scholarship Fund/Alberta Scholarship Programs
9940 106th Street, Fourth Floor, Sterling Place
PO Box 28000, Station Main
Edmonton, AB T5J 4R4
Canada
Phone: 780-427-8640
Fax: 780-427-1288
E-mail: scholarships@gov.ab.ca

AMERICAN ASSOCIATION OF SCHOOL ADMINISTRATORS/DISCOVER SCHOLARSHIPPROGRAM http://www.aasa.org

DISCOVER SCHOLARSHIP PROGRAM

Applicants should be current high school juniors with minimum 2.75 GPA. Must plan to further education beyond high school in any accredited certification, licensing, or training program or institution of higher education. Must demonstrate accomplishments in community service and leadership.

Award: Scholarship for use in freshman year; not renewable. *Number:* up to 10. *Amount:* up to $30,000.

Eligibility Requirements: Applicant must be high school student; planning to enroll or expecting to enroll full- or part-time at a two-year or four-year or technical institution or university and must have an interest in leadership. Applicant or parent of applicant must have employment or volunteer experience in community service. Available to U.S. citizens.

Application Requirements: Application, essay, references, transcript. *Deadline:* January 31.

Contact: Kathy Foster, Program Coordinator
American Association of School Administrators/Discover ScholarshipProgram
PO Box 9338
Arlington, VA 22219
Phone: 866-756-7932
E-mail: kfoster@aasa.org

AMERICAN ASSOCIATION OF STATE TROOPERS INC. http://www.statetroopers.org

AMERICAN ASSOCIATION OF STATE TROOPERS SCHOLARSHIP

Scholarships to children of AAST members. For a dependent to be eligible, the parent must have been a member of AAST for one year prior to the scholarship application deadline.

Award: Scholarship for use in freshman, sophomore, junior, or senior years; renewable. *Number:* 4. *Amount:* $500–$1500.

Eligibility Requirements: Applicant must be enrolled or expecting to enroll full- or part-time at a two-year or four-year institution or university. Applicant or parent of applicant must have employment or volunteer experience in police/firefighting. Applicant must have 2.5 GPA or higher. Available to U.S. citizens.

Application Requirements: Application, essay, photo, transcript, proof of enrollment for the current academic year. *Deadline:* July 31.

Contact: Ken Howes, Executive Director
American Association of State Troopers Inc.
1949 Raymond Diehl Road
Tallahassee, FL 32308
Phone: 850-385-7904 Ext. 202
Fax: 850-385-8697
E-mail: ken@statetroopers.org

AMERICAN CANCER SOCIETY, FLORIDA DIVISION INC. http://www.cancer.org

AMERICAN CANCER SOCIETY, FLORIDA DIVISION R.O.C.K. COLLEGE SCHOLARSHIP PROGRAM

Applicants must have had a personal diagnosis of cancer, be a Florida resident between the ages of 18 and 21, and plan to attend college in Florida. Must have Minimum 2.5 GPA score. Awards will be based on financial need, scholarship, leadership, and community service.

Award: Scholarship for use in freshman, sophomore, junior, or senior years; renewable. *Number:* 150–175. *Amount:* up to $3000.

Eligibility Requirements: Applicant must be age 18-21; enrolled or expecting to enroll full- or part-time at a two-year or four-year or technical institution or university; resident of Florida; studying in Florida and must have an interest in leadership. Applicant or parent of applicant must have employment or volunteer experience in community service. Applicant must be physically disabled. Applicant must have 2.5 GPA or higher. Available to U.S. citizens.

Application Requirements: Application, essay, financial need analysis, interview, resume, references, transcript, SAT and/or ACT scores. *Deadline:* April 10.

Contact: Anna Torrens, Director of Childhood Cancer Programs
American Cancer Society, Florida Division Inc.
3709 West Jetton Avenue
Tampa, FL 33629
Phone: 800-444-1410 Ext. 4405
E-mail: anna.torrens@cancer.org

AMERICAN FOREIGN SERVICE ASSOCIATION http://www.afsa.org

AMERICAN FOREIGN SERVICE ASSOCIATION (AFSA)/AAFSW MERIT AWARD PROGRAM

• *See page 511*

AMERICAN FOREIGN SERVICE ASSOCIATION (AFSA) FINANCIAL AID AWARD PROGRAM

• *See page 511*

AMERICAN LEGION AUXILIARY DEPARTMENT OF CONNECTICUT http://www.ct.legion.org

AMERICAN LEGION AUXILIARY DEPARTMENT OF CONNECTICUT MEMORIAL EDUCATIONAL GRANT

• *See page 511*

AMERICAN LEGION AUXILIARY DEPARTMENT OF MAINE http://www.mainelegion.org

AMERICAN LEGION AUXILIARY DEPARTMENT OF MAINE NATIONAL PRESIDENT'S SCHOLARSHIP

Scholarships to children of veterans who served in the Armed Forces during the eligibility dates for The American Legion. One $2500, one $2000, and one $1000 scholarship will be awarded. Applicant must complete 50 hours of community service during his/her high school years.

Award: Scholarship for use in freshman year; not renewable. *Number:* 3. *Amount:* $1000–$2500.

Eligibility Requirements: Applicant must be high school student; planning to enroll or expecting to enroll full-time at a four-year institution or university and resident of Maine. Applicant or parent of applicant must have employment or volunteer experience in community service. Available to U.S. citizens. Applicant or parent must meet one or more of the following requirements: general military experience; retired from active duty; disabled or killed as a result of military service; prisoner of war; or missing in action.

Application Requirements: Application, essay, references, test scores, transcript. *Deadline:* March 1.

Contact: Mary Wells, Education Chairman
American Legion Auxiliary Department of Maine
21 Limerock Street
PO Box 434
Rockland, ME 04841
Phone: 207-532-6007
E-mail: aladeptsecme@verizon.net

AMERICAN LEGION AUXILIARY DEPARTMENT OF MASSACHUSETTS

AMERICAN LEGION AUXILIARY DEPARTMENT OF MASSACHUSETTS DEPARTMENT PRESIDENT'S SCHOLARSHIP

Awarded to children of veterans who served in the armed forces during the eligibility dates specified by the legion. The applicant must complete 50 hours of community service during high school years to be eligible for this scholarship.

Award: Scholarship for use in freshman, sophomore, junior, or senior years; not renewable. *Number:* 12. *Amount:* $200–$750.

Eligibility Requirements: Applicant must be age 16-22; enrolled or expecting to enroll full-time at a two-year or four-year institution or university; resident of Massachusetts and studying in Massachusetts. Applicant or parent of applicant must have employment or volunteer experience in community service. Available to U.S. citizens. Applicant or parent must meet one or more of the following requirements: general military experience; retired from active duty; disabled or killed as a result of military service; prisoner of war; or missing in action.

Application Requirements: Application. *Deadline:* March 1.

Contact: Beverly Monaco, Secretary and Treasurer
American Legion Auxiliary Department of Massachusetts
546-2 State House
Boston, MA 02133-1044
Phone: 617-727-2958
Fax: 617-727-0741

AMERICAN LEGION AUXILIARY DEPARTMENT OF MISSOURI

AMERICAN LEGION AUXILIARY DEPARTMENT OF MISSOURI NATIONAL PRESIDENT'S SCHOLARSHIP

• *See page 513*

AMERICAN LEGION AUXILIARY DEPARTMENT OF NORTH DAKOTA http://www.ndlegion.org

AMERICAN LEGION AUXILIARY DEPARTMENT OF NORTH DAKOTA NATIONAL PRESIDENT'S SCHOLARSHIP

Three division scholarships for children of veterans who served in the Armed Forces during eligible dates for American Legion membership. Must be U.S. citizen and a high school senior with a minimum 2.5 GPA. Must be entered by local American Legion Auxiliary Unit.

Award: Scholarship for use in freshman year; not renewable. *Number:* 3. *Amount:* $1000–$2500.

Eligibility Requirements: Applicant must be high school student; planning to enroll or expecting to enroll full-time at a four-year institution or university; resident of North Dakota and studying in North Dakota. Applicant or parent of applicant must have employment or volunteer experience in community service. Applicant must have 2.5 GPA or higher. Available to U.S. citizens. Applicant or parent must meet one or more of the following requirements: general military experience; retired from active duty; disabled or killed as a result of military service; prisoner of war; or missing in action.

Application Requirements: Application, essay, financial need analysis, references, test scores, transcript, proof of 50 hours voluntary service. *Deadline:* March 1.

Contact: Myrna Runholm, Department Secretary
American Legion Auxiliary Department of North Dakota
PO Box 1060
Jamestown, ND 58402-1060
Phone: 701-253-5992
Fax: 701-952-5993
E-mail: ala-hq@ndlegion.org

AMERICAN LEGION AUXILIARY DEPARTMENT OF TENNESSEE

AMERICAN LEGION AUXILIARY DEPARTMENT OF TENNESSEE VARA GRAY SCHOLARSHIP-GENERAL

One-time award for high school senior who is the child of a veteran. Must be Tennessee resident and single. Must have completed 50 hours of voluntary community service. Award must be used within one year.

Award: Scholarship for use in freshman year; not renewable. *Number:* 3. *Amount:* $500.

Eligibility Requirements: Applicant must be high school student; planning to enroll or expecting to enroll full-time at a two-year or four-year institution or university; single and resident of Tennessee. Applicant or parent of applicant must have employment or volunteer experience in community service. Available to U.S. citizens. Applicant or parent must meet one or more of the following requirements: general military experience; retired from active duty; disabled or killed as a result of military service; prisoner of war; or missing in action.

Application Requirements: Application, essay, financial need analysis, references, test scores, transcript. *Deadline:* March 10.

Contact: Sue Milliken, Department Secretary and Treasurer
American Legion Auxiliary Department of Tennessee
104 Point East Drive
Nashville, TN 37216
Phone: 615-226-8648
Fax: 615-226-8649
E-mail: alatn@bellsouth.net

AMERICAN LEGION AUXILIARY NATIONAL HEADQUARTERS http://www.legion-aux.org

AMERICAN LEGION AUXILIARY GIRL SCOUT ACHIEVEMENT AWARD

• *See page 516*

AMERICAN LEGION DEPARTMENT OF VERMONT http://www.legionvthq.com

AMERICAN LEGION EAGLE SCOUT OF THE YEAR

• *See page 521*

AMERICAN LEGION NATIONAL HEADQUARTERS http://www.legion.org

AMERICAN LEGION NATIONAL HEADQUARTERS EAGLE SCOUT OF THE YEAR

• *See page 522*

AMERICAN POSTAL WORKERS UNION http://www.apwu.org

E.C. HALLBECK SCHOLARSHIP FUND

• *See page 522*

VOCATIONAL SCHOLARSHIP PROGRAM

• *See page 522*

AMERICAN QUARTER HORSE FOUNDATION (AQHF) http://www.aqha.com/foundation

EXCELLENCE IN EQUINE/AGRICULTURAL INVOLVEMENT SCHOLARSHIP

• *See page 522*

FARM AND RANCH HERITAGE SCHOLARSHIP

• *See page 523*

NEBRASKA QUARTER HORSE YOUTH SCHOLARSHIP

• *See page 523*

AMERICAN ROAD & TRANSPORTATION BUILDERS ASSOCIATION-TRANSPORTATION DEVELOPMENT FOUNDATION (ARTBA-TDF) http://www.artba.org

ARTBA-TDF HIGHWAY WORKERS MEMORIAL SCHOLARSHIP PROGRAM

The ARTBA-TDF Highway Worker Memorial Scholarship Program provides financial assistance to help the sons, daughters or legally adopted children of highway workers killed or permanently disabled in the line of duty pursue post-high school education. Minimum 2.5 GPA required.

Award: Scholarship for use in freshman, sophomore, junior, or senior years; not renewable. *Number:* varies. *Amount:* $1000–$2000.

Eligibility Requirements: Applicant must be enrolled or expecting to enroll full- or part-time at a two-year or four-year or technical institution or university. Applicant or parent of applicant must have employment or volunteer experience in roadway work. Applicant must have 2.5 GPA or higher. Available to U.S. citizens.

American Road & Transportation Builders Association-Transportation Development Foundation (ARTBA-TDF) (continued)

Application Requirements: Application, essay, financial need analysis, photo, references, transcript, copy of current year's federal tax return, copy of parents' current year federal tax return. *Deadline:* March 20.

Contact: Rhonda Britton, Scholarship and Awards Manager
American Road & Transportation Builders Association-Transportation Development Foundation (ARTBA-TDF)
1219 28th Street, NW
Washington, DC 20007
Phone: 202-289-4434
E-mail: rbritton@artba.org

AMERICAN TRAFFIC SAFETY SERVICES FOUNDATION http://www.atssa.com

ROADWAY WORKER MEMORIAL SCHOLARSHIP PROGRAM

One-time scholarship providing financial assistance for post-high school education to the children of roadway workers killed or permanently disabled in work zones, including mobile operations and the installation of roadway safety features or to the parents or legal guardians of such children.

Award: Scholarship for use in freshman, sophomore, junior, or senior years; not renewable. *Number:* 2–5. *Amount:* $2000–$3000.

Eligibility Requirements: Applicant must be enrolled or expecting to enroll full- or part-time at a two-year or four-year or technical institution or university. Applicant or parent of applicant must have employment or volunteer experience in roadway work. Available to U.S. citizens.

Application Requirements: Application, essay, financial need analysis, resume, references, transcript, 200-word statement. *Deadline:* February 15.

Contact: Foundation Director
American Traffic Safety Services Foundation
15 Riverside Parkway, Suite 100
Fredericksburg, VA 22406
Phone: 540-368-1701
Fax: 540-368-1717

ARIZONA HIGHER EDUCATION LOAN AUTHORITY http://www.ahela.org

AHELA COMMUNITY LEADERS SCHOLARSHIP

This scholarship is to increase access to higher education for community-minded and involved students. AHELA wants to encourage students to be involved and active in their community, as well as support students as they pursue the education and skills necessary to be successful leaders. Scholarship winners will be selected based on community activities and involvement, academic achievement, and financial need.

Award: Scholarship for use in freshman, sophomore, junior, or senior years; not renewable. *Number:* 4. *Amount:* $1000.

Eligibility Requirements: Applicant must be enrolled or expecting to enroll full-time at a two-year or four-year institution or university; studying in Arizona and must have an interest in leadership. Applicant or parent of applicant must have employment or volunteer experience in community service. Applicant must have 2.5 GPA or higher. Available to U.S. citizens.

Application Requirements: Application, driver's license, essay. *Deadline:* March 5.

Contact: Dana Macke-Redford, Manager, Marketing, Scholarship and Outreach
Arizona Higher Education Loan Authority
2141 East Broadway Road, Suite 202
Tempe, AZ 85282
Phone: 480-383-8707 Ext. 207
E-mail: dredford@ahela.org

ARKANSAS DEPARTMENT OF HIGHER EDUCATION http://www.adhe.edu

LAW ENFORCEMENT OFFICERS' DEPENDENTS SCHOLARSHIP-ARKANSAS

Scholarship for dependents, under 23 years old, of Arkansas law-enforcement officers killed or permanently disabled in the line of duty. Renewable award is a waiver of tuition, fees, and room at two- or four-year Arkansas institution. Submit birth certificate, death certificate, and claims commission report of findings of fact. Proof of disability from State Claims Commission may also be submitted.

Award: Scholarship for use in freshman, sophomore, junior, or senior years; renewable. *Number:* 27–32. *Amount:* $2000–$2500.

Eligibility Requirements: Applicant must be age 23 or under; enrolled or expecting to enroll full- or part-time at a two-year or four-year or technical institution or university; resident of Arkansas and studying in Arkansas. Applicant or parent of applicant must have employment or volunteer experience in police/firefighting. Available to U.S. citizens.

Application Requirements: Application. *Deadline:* continuous.

Contact: Tara Smith, Director of Financial Aid
Arkansas Department of Higher Education
114 East Capitol Avenue
Little Rock, AR 72201-3818
Phone: 501-371-2000
Fax: 501-371-2001
E-mail: taras@adhe.edu

A.W. BODINE-SUNKIST GROWERS INC. http://www.sunkist.com

A.W. BODINE-SUNKIST MEMORIAL SCHOLARSHIP

Renewable award for undergraduate study for applicants whose family derives most of its income from the agriculture industry in Arizona or California. Award is based on minimum 2.7 GPA and financial need.

Award: Scholarship for use in freshman, sophomore, junior, or senior years; renewable. *Number:* 20. *Amount:* $2000.

Eligibility Requirements: Applicant must be enrolled or expecting to enroll full-time at a two-year or four-year institution or university and resident of Arizona or California. Applicant or parent of applicant must have employment or volunteer experience in agriculture. Available to U.S. citizens.

Application Requirements: Application, essay, financial need analysis, resume, references, test scores, transcript. *Deadline:* April 30.

Contact: Claire Smith, Scholarship Administrator
A.W. Bodine-Sunkist Growers Inc.
PO Box 7888
Van Nuys, CA 91409-7888
Phone: 818-986-4800
Fax: 818-379-7511

BEST BUY CHILDREN FOUNDATION http://www.bestbuy.com/scholarships

BEST BUY SCHOLARSHIPS

$1500 scholarships available to students based on outstanding community service and academic achievement. Must be entering an accredited U.S. university, college, or technical school in the fall immediately following high school graduation.

Award: Scholarship for use in freshman or postgraduate years; not renewable. *Number:* 1551. *Amount:* $1500.

Eligibility Requirements: Applicant must be high school student and planning to enroll or expecting to enroll full-time at a two-year or four-year or technical institution or university. Applicant or parent of applicant must have employment or volunteer experience in community service. Available to U.S. citizens.

Application Requirements: Application, references, transcript. *Deadline:* February 15.

Contact: Scholarship Committee
Best Buy Children Foundation
PO Box 9448
Minneapolis, MN 55440
Phone: 888-237-8289
E-mail: communityrelations@bestbuy.com

BOETTCHER FOUNDATION http://www.boettcherfoundation.org

BOETTCHER FOUNDATION SCHOLARSHIPS

Merit-based scholarship available to graduating seniors in the state of Colorado. Selection based on class rank (top 5 percent), test scores, leadership, and service.

Renewable for four years and can be used at any Colorado university or college. Includes full tuition and fees, living stipend of $2800 per year, and a stipend for books.

Award: Scholarship for use in freshman, sophomore, junior, or senior years; renewable. *Number:* 40. *Amount:* $40,000–$50,000.

Eligibility Requirements: Applicant must be high school student; planning to enroll or expecting to enroll full-time at a four-year institution or university; resident of Colorado; studying in Colorado and must have an interest in leadership. Applicant or parent of applicant must have employment or volunteer experience in community service. Applicant must have 3.5 GPA or higher. Available to U.S. citizens.

Application Requirements: Application, essay, interview, references, test scores, transcript. *Deadline:* November 1.

Contact: Molly Smith, Scholarship Program Coordinator
Boettcher Foundation
600 17th Street, Suite 2210 S
Denver, CO 80202-5422
Phone: 303-285-6207
Fax: 303-534-1943
E-mail: scholarships@boettcherfoundation.org

BOY SCOUTS OF AMERICA-MUSKINGUM VALLEY COUNCIL http://www.learning-for-life.org

YOUNG AMERICAN AWARD

Award for young adults between the ages of 15 and 25, who have achieved excellence in the fields of art, athletics, business, education, government, humanities, literature, music, religion, science, or service. Applicant must have been involved in service to their community, state, or country that adds to the quality of life. Must be participant of the Learning for Life Exploring program.

Award: Prize for use in freshman year; not renewable. *Number:* 5. *Amount:* $7500.

Eligibility Requirements: Applicant must be high school student; age 15-25 and planning to enroll or expecting to enroll full-time at a four-year institution or university. Applicant or parent of applicant must have employment or volunteer experience in community service. Available to U.S. and non-U.S. citizens.

Application Requirements: Application, applicant must enter a contest, references, transcript. *Deadline:* December 1.

Contact: Bill Rogers, Associate Director
Boy Scouts of America-Muskingum Valley Council
1325 West Walnut Hill Lane
PO Box 152079
Irving, TX 75015-2079
Phone: 972-580-2433
Fax: 972-580-2137
E-mail: brogers@lflmail.org

CALIFORNIA CORRECTIONAL PEACE OFFICERS ASSOCIATION http://www.ccpoa.org

CALIFORNIA CORRECTIONAL PEACE OFFICERS ASSOCIATION JOE HARPER SCHOLARSHIP

Scholarship program for immediate relatives of current, retired, or deceased correctional peace officers working the toughest beat in the state. Must be or must have been members in good standing of CCPOA. Applicant must be a high school senior with minimum 3.0 GPA or currently enrolled college student.

Award: Scholarship for use in freshman, sophomore, junior, senior, or graduate years; not renewable. *Number:* 100–200. *Amount:* $500–$1000.

Eligibility Requirements: Applicant must be enrolled or expecting to enroll full- or part-time at a two-year or four-year or technical institution or university and resident of California. Applicant or parent of applicant must have employment or volunteer experience in police/firefighting. Applicant must have 3.0 GPA or higher. Available to U.S. citizens.

Application Requirements: Application, essay, financial need analysis, photo, references, test scores, transcript, copies of federal income tax return from the previous year. *Deadline:* April 30.

Contact: Marcia Bartlett, CCPOA Membership Committee
California Correctional Peace Officers Association
755 Riverpoint Drive, Suite 200
West Sacramento, CA 95605-1634
Phone: 916-372-6060
Fax: 916-372-6623
E-mail: marcia.bartlett@ccpoa.org

CALIFORNIA STATE PARENT-TEACHER ASSOCIATION http://www.capta.org

CONTINUING EDUCATION-PTA VOLUNTEERS SCHOLARSHIP

• *See page 526*

GRADUATING HIGH SCHOOL SENIOR SCHOLARSHIP

Available to high school seniors graduating between January 1 and June 30 of the current academic year from high schools in California with a PTA/PTSA unit in good standing. Must be a California resident. Must have volunteered in the school and community volunteer service.

Award: Scholarship for use in freshman year; renewable. *Number:* varies. *Amount:* $500.

Eligibility Requirements: Applicant must be high school student; planning to enroll or expecting to enroll full-time at a two-year or four-year or technical institution or university and resident of California. Applicant or parent of applicant must have employment or volunteer experience in community service. Available to U.S. citizens.

Application Requirements: Application, essay, references, transcript, copy of current PTA/PTSA membership card. *Deadline:* February 1.

Contact: Becky Reece, Scholarship and Award Chairman
California State Parent-Teacher Association
930 Georgia Street
Los Angeles, CA 90015-1322
Phone: 213-620-1100
Fax: 213-620-1411
E-mail: info@capta.org

CALIFORNIA STUDENT AID COMMISSION http://www.csac.ca.gov

LAW ENFORCEMENT PERSONNEL DEPENDENTS SCHOLARSHIP

Provides college grants to needy dependents of California law enforcement officers, officers and employees of the Department of Corrections and Department of Youth Authority, and firefighters killed or disabled in the line of duty.

Award: Grant for use in freshman, sophomore, junior, or senior years; renewable. *Number:* varies. *Amount:* $100–$11,259.

Eligibility Requirements: Applicant must be enrolled or expecting to enroll full- or part-time at a two-year or four-year institution or university; resident of California and studying in California. Applicant or parent of applicant must have employment or volunteer experience in police/firefighting. Available to U.S. citizens.

Application Requirements: Application, financial need analysis, transcript, birth certificate, death certificate of parents or spouse, police report. *Deadline:* continuous.

Contact: Catalina Mistler, Chief, Program Administration & Services Division
California Student Aid Commission
PO Box 419026
Rancho Cordova, CA 95741-9026
Phone: 916-526-7268
Fax: 916-526-8002
E-mail: studentsupport@csac.ca.gov

CALIFORNIA TABLE GRAPE COMMISSION http://www.freshcaliforniagrapes.com

CALIFORNIA TABLE GRAPE FARM WORKERS SCHOLARSHIP PROGRAM

Applicants must be high school graduates who plan to attend any college or university in California. The applicant, a parent, or a legal guardian must have

California Table Grape Commission (continued)

worked in the California table grape harvest during the last season. School activities, personal references, and financial need are considered. Must be a U.S. citizen.

Award: Scholarship for use in freshman year; not renewable. *Number:* 3. *Amount:* $16,000.

Eligibility Requirements: Applicant must be enrolled or expecting to enroll full-time at a four-year institution or university and studying in California. Applicant or parent of applicant must have employment or volunteer experience in agriculture. Available to U.S. citizens.

Application Requirements: Application, essay, references, test scores, transcript. *Deadline:* March 19.

Contact: Scholarship Coordinator
California Table Grape Commission
392 West Fallbrook, Suite 101
Fresno, CA 93711-6150
Phone: 559-447-8350
Fax: 559-447-9184

CALIFORNIA TEACHERS ASSOCIATION (CTA) http://www.cta.org

CALIFORNIA TEACHERS ASSOCIATION SCHOLARSHIP FOR MEMBERS

• *See page 526*

CALIFORNIA WINE GRAPE GROWERS FOUNDATION http://www.cawg.org/cwggf

CALIFORNIA WINE GRAPE GROWERS FOUNDATION SCHOLARSHIP

Scholarship for high school seniors whose parents or legal guardians are vineyard employees of wine grape growers. Recipients may study the subject of their choice at any campus of the University of California system, the California State University system, or the California Community College system.

Award: Scholarship for use in freshman year; not renewable. *Number:* 1–6. *Amount:* $1000–$4000.

Eligibility Requirements: Applicant must be high school student; planning to enroll or expecting to enroll full-time at a two-year or four-year institution or university; resident of California and studying in California. Applicant or parent of applicant must have employment or volunteer experience in agriculture. Applicant must have 2.5 GPA or higher. Available to U.S. citizens.

Application Requirements: Application, essay, references, test scores, transcript. *Deadline:* April 1.

Contact: Carolee Williams, Assistant Executive Director
California Wine Grape Growers Foundation
601 University Avenue, Suite 135
Sacramento, CA 95825
Phone: 916-924-5370
Fax: 916-924-5374
E-mail: carolee@cawg.org

CAP FOUNDATION http://www.ronbrown.org

RON BROWN SCHOLAR PROGRAM

The program seeks to identify African-American high school seniors who will make significant contributions to the society. Applicants must excel academically, show exceptional leadership potential, participate in community service activities, and demonstrate financial need. Must be a U.S. citizen or hold permanent resident visa. Must plan to attend a four-year college or university. Deadlines: November 1 and January 9.

Award: Scholarship for use in freshman year; renewable. *Number:* 10–20. *Amount:* $10,000–$40,000.

Eligibility Requirements: Applicant must be Black (non-Hispanic); high school student; planning to enroll or expecting to enroll full-time at a four-year institution or university and must have an interest in leadership. Applicant or parent of applicant must have employment or volunteer experience in community service. Available to U.S. citizens.

Application Requirements: Application, essay, financial need analysis, interview, photo, references, test scores, transcript. *Deadline:* varies.

Contact: Ms. Cathy Ames, Executive Assistant
CAP Foundation
1160 Pepsi Place, Suite 206
Charlottesville, VA 22901
Phone: 434-964-1588
Fax: 434-964-1589
E-mail: franh@ronbrown.org

CENTER FOR EDUCATION SOLUTIONS http://www.cesresources.org

A. PATRICK CHARNON SCHOLARSHIP

Scholarship of $1500 for students admitted to or enrolled in a full-time undergraduate program of study in an accredited four-year college or university in the United States. Awarded to students who value tolerance, compassion and respect for all people in their communities, and who have demonstrated their commitments to these values by their actions. Recipients may reapply each year for up to four years.

Award: Scholarship for use in freshman, sophomore, junior, or senior years; not renewable. *Number:* varies. *Amount:* $1500.

Eligibility Requirements: Applicant must be enrolled or expecting to enroll full-time at a four-year institution or university. Applicant or parent of applicant must have employment or volunteer experience in community service. Available to U.S. citizens.

Application Requirements: Application, essay, references. *Deadline:* varies.

Contact: Scholarship Committee
Center for Education Solutions
PO Box 208
San Francisco, CA 94104-0208
Phone: 925-934-7304
E-mail: scholarship@cesresources.org

CENTER FOR SCHOLARSHIP ADMINISTRATION http://www.scholarshipprograms.org

GREENVILLE AREA PERSONNEL ASSOCIATION WALTER L. MARTIN MEMORIAL SCHOLARSHIP PROGRAM

• *See page 527*

CENTRAL SCHOLARSHIP BUREAU http://www.centralsb.org

DALY SCHOLARSHIP AT CENTRAL SCHOLARSHIP BUREAU

Scholarship of up to $5000 awarded to Maryland residents who are educators (teachers or administrators) and their children. Verification of employment in education is required. Scholarships are for full-time undergraduate students, or full- or part-time graduate students.

Award: Scholarship for use in freshman, sophomore, junior, senior, or graduate years; renewable. *Number:* up to 2. *Amount:* $2500–$5000.

Eligibility Requirements: Applicant must be enrolled or expecting to enroll full- or part-time at a four-year institution or university and resident of Maryland. Applicant or parent of applicant must have employment or volunteer experience in teaching/education. Available to U.S. citizens.

Application Requirements: Application, essay, financial need analysis, interview, transcript. *Deadline:* May 31.

Contact: Roberta Goldman, Program Director
Central Scholarship Bureau
1700 Reisterstown Road, Suite 220
Baltimore, MD 21208-2903
Phone: 410-415-5558
Fax: 410-415-5501
E-mail: rgoldman@centralsb.org

CHAIRSCHOLARS FOUNDATION INC. http://www.chairscholars.org

CHAIRSCHOLARS FOUNDATION INC. SCHOLARSHIPS

Award for students who are severely physically challenged. Applicants may be high school seniors or college freshmen. Must be outstanding citizen with history of public service. Minimum 3.5 GPA required. Ten to twelve renewable awards of $5000 are granted. Must be under 21 years of age.

Award: Scholarship for use in freshman year; renewable. *Number:* 15–20. *Amount:* up to $5000.

Eligibility Requirements: Applicant must be age 21 or under and enrolled or expecting to enroll full-time at a two-year or four-year institution or university. Applicant or parent of applicant must have employment or volunteer experience in community service. Applicant must be physically disabled. Applicant must have 3.5 GPA or higher. Available to U.S. citizens.

Application Requirements: Application, autobiography, essay, financial need analysis, photo, portfolio, resume, references, self-addressed stamped envelope, test scores, transcript, parent's tax return from previous year. *Deadline:* February 28.

Contact: Caroll Vick, Program Director
Chairscholars Foundation Inc.
16101 Carencia Lane
Odessa, FL 33556
Phone: 813-920-2737
E-mail: hugokeim@earthlink.net

CHICK-FIL-A INC. http://www.chick-fil-a.com

CHICK-FIL-A LEADERSHIP SCHOLARSHIP

• *See page 576*

COCA-COLA SCHOLARS FOUNDATION INC. http://www.coca-colascholars.org

COCA-COLA TWO-YEAR COLLEGES SCHOLARSHIP

Nonrenewable awards based on community involvement, leadership, and academic performance. Must pursue a two-year degree. Each institution may nominate up to two applicants. Minimum 2.5 GPA is required.

Award: Scholarship for use in freshman or sophomore years; not renewable. *Number:* 350. *Amount:* $1000.

Eligibility Requirements: Applicant must be enrolled or expecting to enroll full- or part-time at a two-year institution and must have an interest in leadership. Applicant or parent of applicant must have employment or volunteer experience in community service. Applicant must have 2.5 GPA or higher. Available to U.S. citizens.

Application Requirements: Application, essay, nomination from institution. *Deadline:* May 31.

Contact: Ryan Rodriguez, Program Facilitator
Coca-Cola Scholars Foundation Inc.
PO Box 442
Atlanta, GA 30301-0442
Phone: 800-306-2653
Fax: 404-733-5439
E-mail: scholars@na.ko.com

COLLEGEBOUND FOUNDATION http://www.collegeboundfoundation.org

BALTIMORE JUNIOR ASSOCIATION OF COMMERCE (BJAC) SCHOLARSHIP

Award for Baltimore City public high school graduates. Must have participated in verifiable community service activities, and submit a one-page typed essay describing in detail the community service activities participated in and the importance of these activities. Minimum GPA of 3.0 is required.

Award: Scholarship for use in freshman year; not renewable. *Number:* 1. *Amount:* $1000.

Eligibility Requirements: Applicant must be high school student; planning to enroll or expecting to enroll full-time at a two-year or four-year institution or university and resident of Maryland. Applicant or parent of applicant must have employment or volunteer experience in community service. Applicant must have 3.0 GPA or higher. Available to U.S. citizens.

Application Requirements: Application, essay, financial need analysis, transcript, financial aid award letters, SAR. *Deadline:* March 1.

Contact: Jamie Crouse, Scholarship Program Administrator
CollegeBound Foundation
300 Water Street, Suite 300
Baltimore, MD 21202
Phone: 410-783-2905 Ext. 207
Fax: 410-727-5786
E-mail: jcrouse@collegeboundfoundation.org

BALTIMORE ROTARY SERVICE ABOVE SELF AWARD PROGRAM

One time scholarship awards ranging from $1000 to $1500 for high school graduates who possess a minimum GPA of 2.5. Must have verifiable community service. For more information visit Web site: http://www.collegeboundfoundation.org.

Award: Scholarship for use in freshman year; not renewable. *Number:* 4. *Amount:* $1000–$1500.

Eligibility Requirements: Applicant must be high school student and planning to enroll or expecting to enroll full-time at a two-year or four-year institution or university. Applicant or parent of applicant must have employment or volunteer experience in community service. Applicant must have 2.5 GPA or higher. Available to U.S. citizens.

Application Requirements: Application, essay, financial need analysis, references, transcript, financial aid award letters, SAR. *Deadline:* March 1.

Contact: Jamie Crouse, Scholarship Program Administrator
CollegeBound Foundation
300 Water Street, Suite 300
Baltimore, MD 21202
Phone: 410-783-2905 Ext. 207
Fax: 410-727-5786
E-mail: jcrouse@collegeboundfoundation.org

GREEN FAMILY BOOK AWARD

One-time award of $800 for a high school graduate who possess a minimum GPA of 3.0. Must have verifiable community service and demonstrate financial need. Must submit an essay (250-500 words) describing "a significant experience, achievement or risk that you have taken and its impact on you".

Award: Scholarship for use in freshman year; not renewable. *Number:* 1. *Amount:* $800.

Eligibility Requirements: Applicant must be high school student and planning to enroll or expecting to enroll full-time at a two-year or four-year institution or university. Applicant or parent of applicant must have employment or volunteer experience in community service. Applicant must have 3.0 GPA or higher. Available to U.S. citizens.

Application Requirements: Application, essay, financial need analysis, transcript, financial aid award letters, SAR. *Deadline:* March 1.

Contact: Jamie Crouse, Scholarship Program Administrator
CollegeBound Foundation
300 Water Street, Suite 300
Baltimore, MD 21202
Phone: 410-783-2905 Ext. 207
Fax: 410-727-5786
E-mail: jcrouse@collegeboundfoundation.org

JANE AND CLARENCE SPILMAN SCHOLARSHIP

Award for Baltimore City public high school graduates with at least 3.0 GPA. Must have verifiable community service. Must attend Bowie State University, Coppin State University, Frostburg State University, Morgan State University, St. Mary's College of Maryland, Towson University, University of Maryland College Park, University of Maryland Eastern Shore, or Villa Julie College.

Award: Scholarship for use in freshman year; renewable. *Number:* 1. *Amount:* $1500.

Eligibility Requirements: Applicant must be high school student; planning to enroll or expecting to enroll full-time at a two-year or four-year institution or university; resident of Maryland and studying in Maryland. Applicant or parent of applicant must have employment or volunteer experience in community service. Applicant must have 3.0 GPA or higher. Available to U.S. citizens.

CollegeBound Foundation (continued)

Application Requirements: Application, essay, financial need analysis, references, transcript, financial aid award letters, SAR. *Deadline:* March 1.

Contact: Jamie Crouse, Scholarship Program Administrator
CollegeBound Foundation
300 Water Street, Suite 300
Baltimore, MD 21202
Phone: 410-783-2905 Ext. 207
Fax: 410-727-5786
E-mail: jcrouse@collegeboundfoundation.org

COLLEGE FOUNDATION OF NORTH CAROLINA INC. http://www.cfnc.org

LATINO DIAMANTE SCHOLARSHIP FUND

Awards high school seniors recognizing their contributions to the community, leadership qualities, and the achievements among Hispanics in North Carolina. Graduating high school seniors who plan to enroll at North Carolina institutions of higher education can apply for this scholarship. Must maintain a GPA of at least 2.5.

Award: Scholarship for use in freshman year; not renewable. *Number:* 2. *Amount:* $500.

Eligibility Requirements: Applicant must be Hispanic; high school student; planning to enroll or expecting to enroll full- or part-time at a two-year or four-year institution or university; resident of North Carolina; studying in North Carolina and must have an interest in leadership. Applicant or parent of applicant must have employment or volunteer experience in community service. Applicant must have 2.5 GPA or higher. Available to U.S. citizens.

Application Requirements: Application, essay, references, transcript. *Deadline:* August 15.

Contact: Scholarship Committee
College Foundation of North Carolina Inc.
Diamante Inc., 106 Lochwood East Drive
Cary, NC 27518
Phone: 919-852-0075
E-mail: scholarships@diamanteinc.org

NORTH CAROLINA BAR ASSOCIATION SCHOLARSHIP

Award is available to natural or adopted children of a North Carolina law enforcement officer who was killed or permanently disabled in the line of duty. Recipient must be enrolled or accepted for admission in a college, vocational training school or other educational institution approved by the scholarship committee of the young lawyers division of the North Carolina Bar Association.

Award: Scholarship for use in freshman, sophomore, junior, senior, or graduate years; renewable. *Number:* varies. *Amount:* $2000.

Eligibility Requirements: Applicant must be enrolled or expecting to enroll full- or part-time at a two-year or four-year or technical institution or university and resident of North Carolina. Applicant or parent of applicant must have employment or volunteer experience in police/firefighting. Available to U.S. citizens.

Application Requirements: Application, transcript. *Deadline:* April 1.

Contact: Jacquelyn Terrell-Fountain, Scholarship Committee
College Foundation of North Carolina Inc.
PO Box 3688
Cary, NC 27519
Phone: 800-662-7407
E-mail: jtfount@mail.ncbar.org

COMCAST LEADERS AND ACHIEVERS SCHOLARSHIP PROGRAM http://www.comcast.com

COMCAST LEADERS AND ACHIEVERS SCHOLARSHIP

Nominees must be full-time high school seniors, must demonstrate a strong commitment to community service and display leadership abilities. Minimum 2.8 GPA required. Must be nominated by their high school principal. Employees of Comcast, its subsidiaries and affiliates, and their families, are not eligible. E-mail for nomination form: comcast@spaprog.com.

Award: Scholarship for use in freshman year; not renewable. *Number:* varies. *Amount:* $1000.

Eligibility Requirements: Applicant must be high school student and planning to enroll or expecting to enroll full-time at a two-year or four-year institution or university. Applicant or parent of applicant must have employment or volunteer experience in community service. Applicant must have 3.0 GPA or higher. Available to U.S. and non-U.S. citizens.

Application Requirements: *Deadline:* January 29.

Contact: Executive Director
Comcast Leaders and Achievers Scholarship Program
1500 Market Street, East Tower, 33rd Floor
Philadelphia, PA 19102
Phone: 866-851-4274
E-mail: comcast@spaprog.com

COMMERCE BANK http://www.commerceonline.com

AMERICAN DREAM SCHOLARSHIPS

Nonrenewable scholarships awarded to graduating high school seniors who reside in a county served by Commerce Bank. Must be planning to enroll in full-time programs at accredited 2- or 4-year colleges or vocational-technical schools in the United States. Recipients are selected on the basis of demonstrated academic achievement and community service. Financial need is not a factor. See Web site for eligible counties and application: http://www.commerceonline.com/americandream.

Award: Scholarship for use in freshman year; not renewable. *Number:* 225. *Amount:* $1000.

Eligibility Requirements: Applicant must be high school student; planning to enroll or expecting to enroll full-time at a two-year or four-year or technical institution or university; resident of Connecticut, Delaware, District of Columbia, Florida, Maryland, New Jersey, New York, Pennsylvania, or Virginia and must have an interest in leadership. Applicant or parent of applicant must have employment or volunteer experience in community service. Applicant must have 3.0 GPA or higher. Available to U.S. citizens.

Application Requirements: Application. *Deadline:* December 15.

Contact: Scholarship Management Services, Division of Scholarship America
Commerce Bank
1 Scholarship Way, PO Box 297
St. Peter, MN 56082
Phone: 800-537-4180

"CASH FOR COLLEGE" SCHOLARSHIP

Award available to graduating high school seniors who have demonstrated exceptional community service and plan to enroll in a full-time course of study at an accredited two- or four-year college or university or vocational-technical school in the United States. Must reside within Commerce Bank's service area in one of the following Pennsylvania counties: Berks, Cumberland, Dauphin, Lebanon, Lancaster, or York. Submission of two essays is required. See Web site for details and application: http://www.commercepc.com/inside_commerce/scholarship.cfm.

Award: Scholarship for use in freshman year; not renewable. *Number:* 1. *Amount:* $2500.

Eligibility Requirements: Applicant must be high school student; planning to enroll or expecting to enroll full-time at a two-year or four-year or technical institution or university and resident of Pennsylvania. Applicant or parent of applicant must have employment or volunteer experience in community service. Available to U.S. citizens.

Application Requirements: Application, essay, transcript. *Deadline:* March 7.

Contact: Scholarship Committee
Commerce Bank
3801 Paxton Street
Harrisburg, PA 17111

COMMUNITY BANKER ASSOCIATION OF ILLINOIS http://www.cbai.com

COMMUNITY BANKER ASSOCIATION OF ILLINOIS CHILDREN OF COMMUNITY BANKING SCHOLARSHIP WILLIAM C. HARRIS MEMORIAL SCHOLARSHIP

• *See page 528*

COMMUNITY FOUNDATION OF WESTERN MASSACHUSETTS http://www.communityfoundation.org

HORACE HILL SCHOLARSHIP

• *See page 528*

CONCERT ARTISTS GUILD http://www.concertartists.org

CONCERT ARTISTS GUILD COMPETITION

Award for young professional-level classical musicians. Suggested age for instrumentalists and ensembles is under 30, and for singers, under 35. Concert Artists Guild presents and manages prize-winning artists. Winner receives $5000 and a management contract. Runners-up receive management contracts. Submit two tapes. Application fee is $75. Visit Web site for deadline information.

Award: Prize for use in freshman, sophomore, junior, senior, graduate, or postgraduate years; not renewable. *Number:* varies. *Amount:* $5000.

Eligibility Requirements: Applicant must be age 35 or under; enrolled or expecting to enroll full- or part-time at a two-year or four-year or technical institution or university and must have an interest in music. Applicant or parent of applicant must have employment or volunteer experience in fine arts. Available to U.S. and non-U.S. citizens.

Application Requirements: Application, applicant must enter a contest, 2 CDs. *Fee:* $75. *Deadline:* March 1.

Contact: Amy Frawley, Competition Manager
Concert Artists Guild
850 Seventh Avenue, Suite 1205
New York, NY 10019-5230
Phone: 212-333-5200 Ext. 14
Fax: 212-977-7149
E-mail: caguild@concertartists.org

CONGRESSIONAL HISPANIC CAUCUS INSTITUTE http://www.chciyouth.org

CONGRESSIONAL HISPANIC CAUCUS INSTITUTE SCHOLARSHIP AWARDS

One-time award for Latino students who have a history of public service-oriented activities. Provides scholarship of $5000 to attend a four-year or graduate level institution, $1000 to attend a two-year community college. Must be enrolled full-time. See Web site at http://www.chci.org for further information.

Award: Scholarship for use in freshman, sophomore, junior, senior, or graduate years; not renewable. *Number:* 111. *Amount:* $1000–$5000.

Eligibility Requirements: Applicant must be Hispanic and enrolled or expecting to enroll full-time at a two-year or four-year institution or university. Applicant or parent of applicant must have employment or volunteer experience in community service. Available to U.S. citizens.

Application Requirements: Application, essay, resume, references, transcript. *Deadline:* January 31.

Contact: Salvador Hernandez, Programs Coordinator
Congressional Hispanic Caucus Institute
911 Second Street, NE
Washington, DC 20002
Phone: 202-543-1771
Fax: 202-546-2143
E-mail: shernandez@chci.org

DAYTON FOUNDATION http://www.daytonfoundation.org

BRIGHTWELL FAMILY MEMORIAL SCHOLARSHIP

Scholarship awarded to a high school senior who is a child or grandchild of current or retired full-time Dayton firefighter. Must be an Ohio resident.

Award: Scholarship for use in freshman year; not renewable. *Number:* up to 2. *Amount:* up to $1000.

Eligibility Requirements: Applicant must be high school student; planning to enroll or expecting to enroll full-time at a four-year institution or university and resident of Ohio. Applicant or parent of applicant must have employment or volunteer experience in fire service. Applicant must have 3.0 GPA or higher. Available to U.S. citizens.

Application Requirements: Application, essay, financial need analysis, references, transcript. *Deadline:* March 28.

Contact: Diane Timmons, Vice President, Grants and Programs
Dayton Foundation
2300 Kettering Tower
Dayton, OH 45423
Phone: 937-225-9966
E-mail: dtimmons@daytonfoundation.org

DELAWARE HIGHER EDUCATION COMMISSION http://www.doe.k12.de.us

AGENDA FOR DELAWARE WOMEN TRAILBLAZER SCHOLARSHIP

Award for women legal residents of Delaware who are U.S. citizens or eligible non-citizens. Must enroll in a public or private nonprofit college in Delaware as an undergraduate student. Must have a cumulative GPA of 2.5 or higher. Award based 50 percent on financial need, 50 percent on community and school activities, vision, participation, and leadership.

Award: Scholarship for use in freshman, sophomore, junior, or senior years; renewable. *Number:* 2. *Amount:* $2500.

Eligibility Requirements: Applicant must be enrolled or expecting to enroll full-time at a four-year institution or university; female; resident of Delaware; studying in Delaware and must have an interest in leadership. Applicant or parent of applicant must have employment or volunteer experience in community service. Applicant must have 2.5 GPA or higher. Available to U.S. citizens.

Application Requirements: Application, financial need analysis, FAFSA, Student Aid Report (SAR). *Deadline:* April 11.

Contact: Carylin Brinkley, Program Administrator
Delaware Higher Education Commission
Carvel State Office Building, 820 North French Street, Fifth Floor
Wilmington, DE 19801-3509
Phone: 302-577-5240
Fax: 302-577-6765
E-mail: cbrinkley@doe.k12.de.us

EDUCATIONAL BENEFITS FOR CHILDREN OF DECEASED VETERANS AND OTHERS AWARD

Award for children between the ages of 16 and 24 of deceased/MIA/POW veterans or state police officers. Must have been a resident of Delaware for 3 or more years prior to the date of application. If the applicant's parent is a member of the armed forces, the parent must have been a resident of Delaware at the time of death or declaration of missing in action or prisoner of war status. Award will not exceed tuition and fees at a Delaware public college.

Award: Grant for use in freshman, sophomore, junior, or senior years; renewable. *Number:* varies. *Amount:* varies.

Eligibility Requirements: Applicant must be age 16-24; enrolled or expecting to enroll full-time at a two-year or four-year institution or university and resident of Delaware. Applicant or parent of applicant must have employment or volunteer experience in police/firefighting. Available to U.S. citizens. Applicant or parent must meet one or more of the following requirements: general military experience; retired from active duty; disabled or killed as a result of military service; prisoner of war; or missing in action.

Application Requirements: Application, verification of service-related death. *Deadline:* continuous.

Contact: Carvel State Office Building
Delaware Higher Education Commission
820 North French
Wilmington, DE 19801
Phone: 302-577-5240
Fax: 302-577-6765

DELTA DELTA DELTA FOUNDATION http://www.tridelta.org

DELTA DELTA DELTA UNDERGRADUATE SCHOLARSHIP

• *See page 530*

DENVER HISPANIC CHAMBER OF COMMERCE EDUCATION FOUNDATION http://www.dhcc.com/default.asp

HISPANIC YOUTH SCHOLARSHIP PROGRAM

Award of $1000 scholarships to selected recipients including high school seniors through working adults. Must be a resident of Colorado. Must maintain a minimum of 3.0 GPA. Recipients are required to fulfill 10 hours of community service during year of funding.

Award: Scholarship for use in freshman year; not renewable. *Number:* varies. *Amount:* $1000.

Eligibility Requirements: Applicant must be Hispanic; enrolled or expecting to enroll full-time at a two-year or four-year institution or university and resident of Colorado. Applicant or parent of applicant must have employment or volunteer experience in community service. Applicant must have 3.0 GPA or higher. Available to U.S. citizens.

Application Requirements: Application, essay, financial need analysis, references. *Deadline:* May 18.

Contact: Scholarship Selection Committee
Denver Hispanic Chamber of Commerce Education Foundation
924 West Colfax, Suite 201
Denver, CO 80204
Phone: 303-534-7783
Fax: 303-595-8977

DEVRY INC. http://www.devry.edu

GIRL SCOUT GOLD AWARD SCHOLARSHIP-HIGH SCHOOL GRADUATE

• *See page 531*

DISABLED AMERICAN VETERANS http://www.dav.org

JESSE BROWN MEMORIAL YOUTH SCHOLARSHIP PROGRAM

Scholarship awarded annually to outstanding youth volunteers who are active in Department of Veterans Affairs Voluntary Services (VAVS) programs and activities.

Award: Scholarship for use in freshman, sophomore, junior, senior, graduate, or postgraduate years; renewable. *Number:* 12. *Amount:* $5000–$15,000.

Eligibility Requirements: Applicant must be age 21 or under and enrolled or expecting to enroll full-time at a two-year or four-year or technical institution or university. Applicant or parent of applicant must have employment or volunteer experience in community service or helping handicapped. Available to U.S. citizens.

Application Requirements: Application, essay. *Deadline:* varies.

Contact: Edward Hartman, National Director of Voluntary Services
Disabled American Veterans
807 Maine Avenue, SW
Washington, DC 20024
Phone: 202-554-3501
Fax: 202-554-3581
E-mail: ehartman@davmail.org

EAST LOS ANGELES COMMUNITY UNION (TELACU) EDUCATION FOUNDATION http://www.telacu.com

LINC TELACU SCHOLARSHIP PROGRAM

Scholarships available to low-income applicants from the Greater East Side of Los Angeles. Must be U.S. citizen or permanent resident. Must be a resident of one of the following communities: East Los Angeles, Bell Gardens, Commerce, Huntington Park, Montebello, Monterey Park, Pico Rivera, Santa Ana, South Gate, and the City of Los Angeles. Must be the first generation in their family to achieve a college degree. Must have a record of community service. Further restriction see Web site.

Award: Scholarship for use in freshman, sophomore, junior, senior, or graduate years; not renewable. *Number:* up to 600. *Amount:* $500–$5000.

Eligibility Requirements: Applicant must be enrolled or expecting to enroll full-time at a two-year or four-year institution or university and resident of California. Applicant or parent of applicant must have employment or volunteer experience in community service. Applicant must have 2.5 GPA or higher. Available to U.S. citizens.

Application Requirements: Application, essay, financial need analysis, interview, resume, references, transcript. *Deadline:* March 29.

Contact: Daniel Garcia, Scholarship Program Coordinator
East Los Angeles Community Union (TELACU) Education Foundation
5400 East Olympic Boulevard, Suite 300
Los Angeles, CA 90022
Phone: 323-721-1655
Fax: 323-724-3372
E-mail: dgarcia@telacu.com

EXPLOSIVE ORDNANCE DISPOSAL MEMORIAL COMMITTEE http://www.eodmemorial.org

EXPLOSIVE ORDNANCE DISPOSAL MEMORIAL SCHOLARSHIP

Award based on academic merit, community involvement, and financial need for the children and spouses of military Explosive Ordnance Disposal technicians. This scholarship is for students enrolled or planning to enroll full-time as an undergraduate in a U.S. accredited two year, four year, or vocational school. Applications are only available on the Web site at http://www.eodmemorial.org.

Award: Scholarship for use in freshman, sophomore, junior, or senior years; not renewable. *Number:* 25–75. *Amount:* $1900–$2500.

Eligibility Requirements: Applicant must be enrolled or expecting to enroll full-time at a two-year or four-year or technical institution or university. Applicant or parent of applicant must have employment or volunteer experience in explosive ordnance disposal. Available to U.S. citizens. Applicant or parent must meet one or more of the following requirements: general military experience; retired from active duty; disabled or killed as a result of military service; prisoner of war; or missing in action.

Application Requirements: Application, financial need analysis, transcript. *Deadline:* March 1.

Contact: Mary McKinley, Administrator
Explosive Ordnance Disposal Memorial Committee
PO Box 594
Niceville, FL 32588
Phone: 850-729-2401
Fax: 850-729-2401
E-mail: admin@eodmemorial.org

FEDERAL EMPLOYEE EDUCATION AND ASSISTANCE FUND http://www.feea.org

FEEA/NARFE SCHOLARSHIP

• *See page 532*

FEEA SCHOLARSHIPS

One-time award ranging from $500 to $2500 for students enrolled or plan to enroll in an accredited postsecondary school. High school seniors can also apply. Employee applicants may be part-time students, but dependents must be full-time. Must be a current civilian federal or postal employee with at least three years of federal service, or a dependent family member. Minimum 3.0 GPA required.

Award: Scholarship for use in freshman, sophomore, junior, senior, or graduate years; not renewable. *Number:* 400–500. *Amount:* $500–$1500.

Eligibility Requirements: Applicant must be enrolled or expecting to enroll full- or part-time at a two-year or four-year or technical institution or university. Applicant or parent of applicant must have employment or volunteer experience in federal/postal service. Applicant must have 3.0 GPA or higher. Available to U.S. citizens.

Application Requirements: Application, essay, references, self-addressed stamped envelope, test scores, transcript. *Deadline:* March 28.

Contact: Scholarships Committee
Federal Employee Education and Assistance Fund
8441 West Bowles Avenue, Suite 200
Littleton, CO 80123-9501
Phone: 303-933-7580
Fax: 303-933-7587

FINANCE AUTHORITY OF MAINE http://www.famemaine.com

TUITION WAIVER PROGRAMS

Provides tuition waivers for children and spouses of EMS personnel, firefighters, and law enforcement officers who have been killed in the line of duty and for students who were foster children under the custody of the Department of Human Services when they graduated from high school. Waivers valid at the University of Maine System, the Maine Technical College System, and Maine Maritime Academy. Applicant must reside and study in Maine.

Award: Grant for use in freshman, sophomore, junior, or senior years; renewable. *Number:* up to 30. *Amount:* varies.

Eligibility Requirements: Applicant must be enrolled or expecting to enroll full- or part-time at a four-year institution or university; resident of Maine and studying in Maine. Applicant or parent of applicant must have employment or volunteer experience in police/firefighting. Available to U.S. citizens.

Application Requirements: Application, letter from the Department of Human Services documenting that applicant is in their custody and residing in foster care at the time of graduation from high school or its equivalent. *Deadline:* continuous.

Contact: Lisa Bongiovanni, Manager, Operations
Finance Authority of Maine
Five Community Drive
PO Box 949
Augusta, ME 04332-0949
Phone: 207-623-3263
Fax: 207-623-0095
E-mail: education@famemaine.com

FIRST COMMAND EDUCATIONAL FOUNDATION http://www.firstcommand.org

FIRST COMMAND EDUCATIONAL FOUNDATION SCHOLARSHIP

Scholarship awarded to students seeking associate, undergraduate, or graduate degrees. Also available to those seeking professional certification or attending vocational school. Details announced in October of each year.

Award: Scholarship for use in freshman, sophomore, junior, senior, or graduate years; not renewable. *Number:* varies. *Amount:* $5000–$10,000.

Eligibility Requirements: Applicant must be enrolled or expecting to enroll full-time at a four-year institution or university. Applicant or parent of applicant must have employment or volunteer experience in community service. Available to U.S. citizens.

Application Requirements: Application, essay. *Deadline:* varies.

Contact: Pam Elliott, Scholarship Coordinator
First Command Educational Foundation
One FirstComm Plaza
Ft Worth, TX 76109-4999
Phone: 817-569-2940
Fax: 817-569-2970
E-mail: pelliott@firstcommand.org

FRATERNAL ORDER OF POLICE ASSOCIATES OF OHIO INC. http://www.fopaohio.org

FRATERNAL ORDER OF POLICE ASSOCIATES, STATE LODGE OF OHIO INC., SCHOLARSHIP FUND

Scholarship available to a graduating high school senior whose parent or guardian is a member in good standing of the Fraternal Order of Police, State Lodge of Ohio Inc. The amount of each scholarship will be up to $4000 payable over a four-year period. A one-time award of $500 will be given to the first runner-up. Scholarships will be awarded on the basis of scholastic merit, economic need and goals in life.

Award: Scholarship for use in freshman year; not renewable. *Number:* 1–4. *Amount:* $500–$1000.

Eligibility Requirements: Applicant must be high school student; planning to enroll or expecting to enroll full-time at a four-year institution or university and resident of Ohio. Applicant or parent of applicant must have employment or volunteer experience in police/firefighting. Applicant must have 2.5 GPA or higher. Available to U.S. citizens.

Application Requirements: Application, financial need analysis, photo, references, transcript, proof of guardianship. *Deadline:* May 1.

Contact: Mr. Michael J. Esposito, Scholarship Assistance
Fraternal Order of Police Associates of Ohio Inc.
PO Box 14564
Cincinnati, OH 45250-0564
Phone: 513-684-4755
E-mail: mje@fopaohio.org

GEORGIA STUDENT FINANCE COMMISSION http://www.gsfc.org

GEORGIA PUBLIC SAFETY MEMORIAL GRANT/LAW ENFORCEMENT PERSONNEL DEPARTMENT GRANT

Award for children of Georgia law enforcement officers, prison guards, or fire fighters killed or permanently disabled in the line of duty. Must attend an accredited postsecondary Georgia school. Complete the Law Enforcement Personnel Dependents application.

Award: Grant for use in freshman, sophomore, junior, or senior years; renewable. *Number:* 20–40. *Amount:* $2000.

Eligibility Requirements: Applicant must be enrolled or expecting to enroll full-time at a two-year or four-year or technical institution or university; resident of Georgia and studying in Georgia. Applicant or parent of applicant must have employment or volunteer experience in police/firefighting. Available to U.S. citizens.

Application Requirements: Application, selective service registration. *Deadline:* continuous.

Contact: Tracy Irleand, Vice President
Georgia Student Finance Commission
2082 East Exchange Place, Suite 100
Tucker, GA 30084
Phone: 770-724-9000
E-mail: tracyi@gsfc.org

GLORIA BARRON PRIZE FOR YOUNG HEROES http://www.barronprize.org

GLORIA BARRON PRIZE FOR YOUNG HEROES

Award honors young people ages 8 to 18 who have shown leadership and courage in public service to people or to the planet. Must be nominated by a responsible adult who is not a relative. Award is to be applied to higher education or a service project. For further information and nomination forms, see Web site at http://www.barronprize.org.

Award: Prize for use in freshman year; not renewable. *Number:* 1–10. *Amount:* up to $2000.

Eligibility Requirements: Applicant must be age 8-18; enrolled or expecting to enroll full- or part-time at a two-year or four-year or technical institution or university and must have an interest in leadership. Applicant or parent of applicant must have employment or volunteer experience in community service. Available to U.S. and Canadian citizens.

Application Requirements: Application, essay, photo, nomination form, references form. *Deadline:* April 30.

Contact: Barbara Ann Richman, Executive Director
Gloria Barron Prize for Young Heroes
545 Pearl Street
Boulder, CO 80302
E-mail: ba_richman@barronprize.org

GOLDEN KEY INTERNATIONAL HONOUR SOCIETY http://www.goldenkey.org

GOLDEN KEY SERVICE AWARD

One award totaling $500, disbursed as $250 to the recipient and $250 to the charity of the recipient's choice. Undergraduate and graduate members who were enrolled as students during the previous academic year are eligible.

Award: Scholarship for use in sophomore, junior, senior, or graduate years; not renewable. *Number:* 1. *Amount:* $500.

Eligibility Requirements: Applicant must be enrolled or expecting to enroll full- or part-time at a four-year institution or university. Applicant or parent of applicant must have employment or volunteer experience in community service. Available to Canadian and non-U.S. citizens.

Golden Key International Honour Society (continued)

Application Requirements: Application, essay, references, cover page from the online registration, statement of project. *Deadline:* March 3.

Contact: Tony Kearney, Director
Golden Key International Honour Society
621 North Avenue, NE, Suite C-100
Atlanta, GA 30308
Phone: 404-377-2400
Fax: 678-420-6757
E-mail: scholarships@goldenkey.org

GRAND LODGE OF IOWA, AF AND AM http://www.gl-iowa.org

GRAND LODGE OF IOWA MASONIC SCHOLARSHIP PROGRAM

Scholarships are awarded based on scholastics, school and community activity, and leadership. Applicants are selected to be interviewed based on their written application. Recipients are selected based on those interviews.

Award: Scholarship for use in freshman year; not renewable. *Number:* 60–70. *Amount:* $2000.

Eligibility Requirements: Applicant must be high school student; planning to enroll or expecting to enroll full-time at a two-year or four-year institution or university; resident of Iowa and must have an interest in leadership. Applicant or parent of applicant must have employment or volunteer experience in community service. Available to U.S. and non-U.S. citizens.

Application Requirements: Application, autobiography, interview, references, transcript. *Deadline:* February 1.

Contact: William Crawford, Grand Secretary
Grand Lodge of Iowa, AF and AM
PO Box 279
Cedar Rapids, IA 52406-0279
Phone: 319-365-1438
Fax: 319-365-1439
E-mail: gs@gl-iowa.org

GREATER KANAWHA VALLEY FOUNDATION http://www.tgkvf.org

SCPA SCHOLARSHIP FUND

Renewable award for West Virginia residents who are full-time students with minimum 2.5 GPA. Applicant must have parent who is employed or has been previously employed by the coal industry in southern West Virginia. Scholarships are awarded on a financial need basis and may be awarded for one or more years.

Award: Scholarship for use in freshman, sophomore, junior, or senior years; renewable. *Number:* up to 10. *Amount:* $1000.

Eligibility Requirements: Applicant must be enrolled or expecting to enroll full-time at a four-year institution or university and resident of West Virginia. Applicant or parent of applicant must have employment or volunteer experience in coal industry. Applicant must have 2.5 GPA or higher. Available to U.S. citizens.

Application Requirements: Application, essay, financial need analysis, references, self-addressed stamped envelope, test scores, transcript. *Deadline:* January 12.

Contact: Susan Hoover, Scholarship Coordinator
Greater Kanawha Valley Foundation
PO Box 3041
Charleston, WV 25331
Phone: 304-346-3620
Fax: 304-346-3640

WEST VIRGINIA GOLF ASSOCIATION FUND

Award of $1000 available to students at any accredited West Virginia college or university. This fund is open to individuals who meet the following criteria: (1) have played golf in WV as an amateur for recreation or competition or (2) have been or are presently employed in WV as a caddie, groundskeeper, bag boy, etc. Must also include a reference by a coach, golf professional or employer and an essay explaining how the game of golf has made an impact in applicant's life. Scholarships are awarded with a commitment of one year. May apply for two Foundation scholarships but will only be chosen for one.

Award: Scholarship for use in freshman, sophomore, junior, senior, or graduate years; not renewable. *Number:* 2. *Amount:* $1000.

Eligibility Requirements: Applicant must be enrolled or expecting to enroll full-time at a two-year or four-year or technical institution or university; resident of West Virginia and studying in West Virginia. Applicant or parent of applicant must have employment or volunteer experience in private club/caddying. Applicant must have 2.5 GPA or higher. Available to U.S. citizens.

Application Requirements: Application, applicant must enter a contest, essay, references, transcript. *Deadline:* January 12.

Contact: Susan Hoover, Scholarship Coordinator
Greater Kanawha Valley Foundation
PO Box 3041
Charleston, WV 25331
Phone: 304-346-3620
Fax: 304-346-3640

GREATER WASHINGTON URBAN LEAGUE http://www.gwul.org

SAFEWAY/GREATER WASHINGTON URBAN LEAGUE SCHOLARSHIP

Award to graduating high school students who reside in the service area of the League. Applicants must complete an essay on a subject selected by the sponsors and must have completed 90 percent of their school district's community service requirement. Minimum GPA of 2.7 required.

Award: Scholarship for use in freshman year; not renewable. *Number:* 6. *Amount:* $3000.

Eligibility Requirements: Applicant must be high school student; planning to enroll or expecting to enroll full-time at a four-year institution or university and resident of District of Columbia. Applicant or parent of applicant must have employment or volunteer experience in community service. Available to U.S. citizens.

Application Requirements: Application, applicant must enter a contest, essay, test scores. *Deadline:* February 12.

Contact: Audrey Epperson, Director of Education
Greater Washington Urban League
2901 14th Street, NW
Washington, DC 20009
Phone: 202-265-8200
Fax: 202-387-7019
E-mail: epperson@gwulparentcenter.org

GUARDIAN LIFE INSURANCE COMPANY OF AMERICA http://www.girlsgoingplaces.com

GIRLS GOING PLACES ENTREPRENEURSHIP AWARD PROGRAM

Rewards enterprising female students between the ages of 12 and 18 who demonstrate budding entrepreneurship, are taking the first steps toward financial independence, and making a difference in their school and community.

Award: Grant for use in freshman year; renewable. *Number:* 15. *Amount:* $1000–$10,000.

Eligibility Requirements: Applicant must be high school student; age 12-18; planning to enroll or expecting to enroll full-time at a technical institution; single female and must have an interest in entrepreneurship. Applicant or parent of applicant must have employment or volunteer experience in community service. Applicant must have 3.5 GPA or higher. Available to U.S. citizens.

Application Requirements: Application, essay, references. *Deadline:* varies.

Contact: Maureen Charles, Marketing Specialist
Guardian Life Insurance Company of America
Seven Hanover Square, H26-J
New York, NY 10004
Phone: 212-598-1559
Fax: 212-919-2586
E-mail: maureen_charles@glic.com

HARNESS HORSE YOUTH FOUNDATION http://www.hhyf.org

CHARLES BRADLEY MEMORIAL SCHOLARSHIP

One-time award for full-time undergraduates between the ages of 18 and 24. Open to children of licensed pari-mutuel harness racing officials. Minimum 2.5 GPA required. Must be U.S. or Canadian citizens.

Award: Scholarship for use in freshman, sophomore, junior, or senior years; not renewable. *Number:* 1–3. *Amount:* $250–$500.

Eligibility Requirements: Applicant must be age 18-24 and enrolled or expecting to enroll full-time at a two-year or four-year or technical institution or university. Applicant or parent of applicant must have employment or volunteer experience in harness racing. Applicant must have 2.5 GPA or higher. Available to U.S. and Canadian citizens.

Application Requirements: Application, essay, references, transcript, page 1 of parents' IRS form. *Deadline:* April 30.

Contact: Ellen Taylor, Executive Director
Harness Horse Youth Foundation
16575 Carey Road
Westfield, IN 46074
Phone: 317-867-5877
Fax: 317-867-5896
E-mail: ellen@hhyf.org

CURT GREENE MEMORIAL SCHOLARSHIP

One-time award with preference given to those under age 24, who have a passion for harness racing. Based on merit, need, and horsemanship or racing experience. Minimum 2.5 GPA required. Available for study in any field. May reapply.

Award: Scholarship for use in freshman, sophomore, junior, or senior years; not renewable. *Number:* 1–2. *Amount:* $2500.

Eligibility Requirements: Applicant must be age 18-24 and enrolled or expecting to enroll full-time at a two-year or four-year or technical institution or university. Applicant or parent of applicant must have employment or volunteer experience in harness racing. Applicant must have 2.5 GPA or higher. Available to U.S. and Canadian citizens.

Application Requirements: Application, essay, references, transcript, page 1 of parents' IRS form. *Deadline:* April 30.

Contact: Ellen Taylor, Executive Director
Harness Horse Youth Foundation
16575 Carey Road
Westfield, IN 46074
Phone: 317-867-5877
Fax: 317-867-5896
E-mail: ellen@hhyf.org

HARNESS TRACKS OF AMERICA INC. http://www.harnesstracks.com

HARNESS TRACKS OF AMERICA SCHOLARSHIP

One-time, merit-based award of $5000 for students actively involved in harness racing or the children of licensed drivers, trainers, breeders, or caretakers, living or deceased. Based on financial need, academic merit, and active harness racing involvement by applicant or family member. High school seniors may apply for the following school year award.

Award: Scholarship for use in freshman, sophomore, junior, senior, or graduate years; not renewable. *Number:* 5. *Amount:* $5000.

Eligibility Requirements: Applicant must be enrolled or expecting to enroll full-time at a two-year or four-year or technical institution or university. Applicant or parent of applicant must have employment or volunteer experience in harness racing. Available to U.S. and non-U.S. citizens.

Application Requirements: Application, essay, financial need analysis, transcript, IRS 1040 of parents and/or applicant. *Deadline:* June 15.

Contact: Editorial Coordinator
Harness Tracks of America Inc.
4640 East Sunrise Drive, Suite 200
Tucson, AZ 85718
Phone: 520-529-2525
Fax: 520-529-3235
E-mail: info@harnesstracks.com

HERB KOHL EDUCATIONAL FOUNDATION INC. http://www.kohleducation.org

HERB KOHL EXCELLENCE SCHOLARSHIP PROGRAM

Scholarships of $1000 to Wisconsin high school graduates awarded annually. Applicants must be Wisconsin residents. Recipients are chosen for their demonstrated academic potential, outstanding leadership, citizenship, community service, integrity and other special talents.

Award: Scholarship for use in freshman year; not renewable. *Number:* 100. *Amount:* $1000.

Eligibility Requirements: Applicant must be high school student; planning to enroll or expecting to enroll full-time at a two-year or four-year or technical institution or university; resident of Wisconsin and must have an interest in leadership. Applicant or parent of applicant must have employment or volunteer experience in community service. Available to U.S. citizens.

Application Requirements: Application, essay, references, transcript. *Deadline:* November 16.

Contact: Scholarship Committee
Herb Kohl Educational Foundation Inc.
Wisconsin Parents Association
PO Box 2502
Madison, WI 53701-2502
Phone: 608-283-3131

HISPANIC ANNUAL SALUTE http://www.hispanicannualsalute.org

HISPANIC ANNUAL SALUTE SCHOLARSHIP

Scholarships of $2000 are awarded to graduating high school seniors. Program is intended to help foster a strong Hispanic presence within colleges and universities that will ultimately lead to active community leadership and volunteerism. Applicant must maintain a minimum GPA of 2.5.

Award: Scholarship for use in freshman year; not renewable. *Number:* 10. *Amount:* $2000.

Eligibility Requirements: Applicant must be Hispanic; high school student and planning to enroll or expecting to enroll full-time at a four-year institution or university. Applicant or parent of applicant must have employment or volunteer experience in community service. Applicant must have 2.5 GPA or higher. Available to U.S. citizens.

Application Requirements: Application, essay, references, test scores. *Deadline:* December 4.

Contact: Dan Sandos, President
Hispanic Annual Salute
PO Box 40720
Denver, CO 80204
Phone: 303-699-0715
Fax: 303-627-4205
E-mail: dcsandos@aol.com

HITACHI FOUNDATION http://www.hitachifoundation.org

YOSHIYAMA AWARD FOR EXEMPLARY SERVICE TO THE COMMUNITY

Prizes for high school seniors based on their community service activities. Must be nominated by someone familiar with their service. Submit nomination form, letter of nomination, and two supporting letters.

Award: Prize for use in freshman year; not renewable. *Number:* 8–10. *Amount:* $5000.

Eligibility Requirements: Applicant must be high school student and planning to enroll or expecting to enroll full-time at a four-year institution or university. Applicant or parent of applicant must have employment or volunteer experience in community service. Available to U.S. citizens.

Application Requirements: References, nomination form, letter of nomination. *Deadline:* April 1.

Contact: Assistant Coordinator
Hitachi Foundation
1509 22nd Street, NW
Washington, DC 20037-1098
Phone: 202-457-0588
Fax: 202-296-1098

HOSPITAL CENTRAL SERVICES INC. http://www.giveapint.org

HOSPITAL CENTRAL SERVICES STUDENT VOLUNTEER SCHOLARSHIP

Award to a graduating high school senior. Must have completed a minimum of 135 hours of volunteer service to the Blood Center in no less than a two calendar year period. Minimum 2.5 GPA required. Children of employees of Hospital Central Services or its affiliates are not eligible.

Award: Scholarship for use in freshman year; not renewable. *Number:* up to 2. *Amount:* $1000.

Eligibility Requirements: Applicant must be high school student and planning to enroll or expecting to enroll full- or part-time at a two-year or four-year institution or university. Applicant or parent of applicant must have employment or volunteer experience in community service. Applicant must have 2.5 GPA or higher. Available to U.S. citizens.

Application Requirements: Application, references, test scores, transcript. *Deadline:* March 31.

Contact: Sandra D. Thomas, Director of Development and Customer Service
Hospital Central Services Inc.
1465 Valley Center Parkway
Bethlehem, PA 18017
Phone: 610-691-5850 Ext. 292

IDAHO STATE BOARD OF EDUCATION http://www.boardofed.idaho.gov

PUBLIC SAFETY OFFICER DEPENDENT SCHOLARSHIP

Scholarship for dependents of full-time Idaho public safety officers who were killed or disabled in the line of duty. Recipients will attend an Idaho postsecondary institution with a full waiver of fees. Scholarship value is $500.

Award: Scholarship for use in freshman year; renewable. *Number:* varies. *Amount:* up to $500.

Eligibility Requirements: Applicant must be enrolled or expecting to enroll full- or part-time at a two-year or four-year institution or university; resident of Idaho and studying in Idaho. Applicant or parent of applicant must have employment or volunteer experience in police/firefighting. Available to U.S. citizens. Applicant or parent must meet one or more of the following requirements: general military experience; retired from active duty; disabled or killed as a result of military service; prisoner of war; or missing in action.

Application Requirements: Application. *Deadline:* January 15.

Contact: Dana Kelly, Program Manager
Idaho State Board of Education
PO Box 83720
Boise, ID 83720-0037
Phone: 208-332-1574
E-mail: dana.kelly@osbe.idaho.gov

ILLINOIS STUDENT ASSISTANCE COMMISSION (ISAC) http://www.collegezone.org

GRANT PROGRAM FOR DEPENDENTS OF POLICE, FIRE, OR CORRECTIONAL OFFICERS

Awards available to Illinois residents who are dependents of police, fire, and correctional officers killed or disabled in line of duty. Provides for tuition and fees at approved Illinois institutions. Number of grants and individual dollar amount awarded vary.

Award: Grant for use in freshman, sophomore, junior, senior, graduate, or postgraduate years; renewable. *Number:* varies. *Amount:* varies.

Eligibility Requirements: Applicant must be enrolled or expecting to enroll full- or part-time at a two-year or four-year or technical institution or university; resident of Illinois and studying in Illinois. Applicant or parent of applicant must have employment or volunteer experience in police/firefighting. Available to U.S. citizens.

Application Requirements: Application, proof of status. *Deadline:* varies.

Contact: College Zone Counselor
Illinois Student Assistance Commission (ISAC)
1755 Lake Cook Road
Deerfield, IL 60015-5209
Phone: 800-899-4722
E-mail: collegezone@isac.org

INDEPENDENT COLLEGE FUND OF MARYLAND (I-FUND) http://www.i-fundinfo.org

MARYLAND SCHOLARS

Scholarship awarded to permanent residents of Maryland. Must have at least 3.0 GPA. Preference given to students with a history of volunteerism and/or community involvement.

Award: Scholarship for use in freshman, sophomore, junior, or senior years; renewable. *Number:* 1. *Amount:* $1000.

Eligibility Requirements: Applicant must be enrolled or expecting to enroll full- or part-time at a four-year institution or university and resident of Maryland. Applicant or parent of applicant must have employment or volunteer experience in community service. Applicant must have 3.0 GPA or higher. Available to U.S. citizens.

Application Requirements: Application, financial need analysis, thank you letters. *Deadline:* varies.

Contact: Lori Subotich, Director of Programs and Scholarships
Independent College Fund of Maryland (I-Fund)
3225 Ellerslie Avenue, Suite C160
Baltimore, MD 21218-3519
Phone: 443-997-5700
Fax: 443-997-2740
E-mail: lsubot@jhmi.edu

INTERNATIONAL ASSOCIATION OF FIRE FIGHTERS http://www.iaff.org

W.H. "HOWIE" MCCLENNAN SCHOLARSHIP

Sons, daughters, or legally adopted children of IAFF members killed in the line of duty who are planning to attend an institution of higher learning can apply. Award of $2500 for each year. Renewable up to four years. Applicant must have a GPA of 2.0

Award: Scholarship for use in freshman year; renewable. *Number:* 20–25. *Amount:* $2500.

Eligibility Requirements: Applicant must be enrolled or expecting to enroll full- or part-time at a two-year or four-year or technical institution. Applicant or parent of applicant must have employment or volunteer experience in police/firefighting. Available to U.S. citizens.

Application Requirements: Application, essay, financial need analysis, references, transcript. *Deadline:* February 1.

Contact: Office of the McClennan Scholarship General President
International Association of Fire Fighters
1750 New York Avenue, NW
Washington, DC 20006-5395
Phone: 202-737-8484
Fax: 202-737-8418

INTERNATIONAL FEDERATION OF PROFESSIONAL AND TECHNICAL ENGINEERS http://www.ifpte.org

INTERNATIONAL FEDERATION OF PROFESSIONAL AND TECHNICAL ENGINEERS ANNUAL SCHOLARSHIP

• *See page 537*

INTERNATIONAL ORGANIZATION OF MASTERS, MATES AND PILOTS HEALTH AND BENEFIT PLAN http://www.bridgedeck.org

M.M. & P. HEALTH AND BENEFIT PLAN SCHOLARSHIP PROGRAM

Scholarships available to dependent children (under 23 years of age) of parents who meet the eligibility requirements set forth by the MM&P Health and Benefit Plan. Selection of winners will be based on test scores, high school record, extracurricular activities, leadership qualities, recommendations, and students' own statements.

Award: Scholarship for use in freshman, sophomore, junior, or senior years; renewable. *Number:* 6. *Amount:* up to $5000.

Eligibility Requirements: Applicant must be age 23 or under; enrolled or expecting to enroll full-time at a four-year institution or university and single. Applicant or parent of applicant must have employment or volunteer experience in seafaring/fishing industry. Available to U.S. citizens.

Application Requirements: Application, test scores. *Deadline:* November 30.

Contact: Mary Ellen Beach, Scholarship Committee
International Organization of Masters, Mates and Pilots Health and Benefit Plan
700 Maritime Boulevard, Suite B
Linthicum Heights, MD 21090-1941
Phone: 410-850-8624
Fax: 410-850-8655
E-mail: communications@bridgedeck.org

JACKIE ROBINSON FOUNDATION http://www.jackierobinson.org

JACKIE ROBINSON SCHOLARSHIP

Scholarship for graduating high school seniors accepted to accredited four-year colleges or universities. Must be a minority student, United States citizen, and demonstrate leadership potential and financial need. See Web site for additional details.

Award: Scholarship for use in freshman year; renewable. *Number:* varies. *Amount:* up to $7500.

Eligibility Requirements: Applicant must be American Indian/Alaska Native, Asian/Pacific Islander, Black (non-Hispanic), or Hispanic; high school student; planning to enroll or expecting to enroll full-time at a four-year institution or university and must have an interest in leadership. Applicant or parent of applicant must have employment or volunteer experience in community service. Available to U.S. citizens.

Application Requirements: Application, essay, financial need analysis, references, test scores, transcript. *Deadline:* March 31.

Contact: Scholarship Application
Jackie Robinson Foundation
75 Varick Street, 2nd Floor
New York, NY 10013
Phone: 212-290-8600
Fax: 212-290-8081
E-mail: scholarships@jackierobinson.org

JOHN EDGAR THOMSON FOUNDATION

JOHN EDGAR THOMSON FOUNDATION GRANTS

Must be the daughter of a deceased railroad employee. Employee (mother/father) must have been actively employed at time of death. Recipients of disability, sick leave, workman's compensation are considered eligible. Monthly grant is available until the age of 22, as long as recipient is in college full-time, earning at least 12 credits. Termination at age 22 or upon graduation, whichever comes first. Recipient must remain unmarried. Based upon financial need. Must submit birth certificate.

Award: Grant for use in freshman, sophomore, junior, or senior years; renewable. *Number:* 144. *Amount:* $500–$4400.

Eligibility Requirements: Applicant must be age 22 or under; enrolled or expecting to enroll full-time at a two-year or four-year or technical institution or university and single female. Applicant or parent of applicant must have employment or volunteer experience in railroad industry. Available to U.S. citizens.

Application Requirements: Application, financial need analysis, interview, photo, references, transcript, birth certificate. *Deadline:* varies.

Contact: Sheila Cohen, Director
John Edgar Thomson Foundation
201 South 18th Street, Suite 318
Philadelphia, PA 19103
Phone: 215-545-6083
Fax: 215-545-6083

J. WOOD PLATT CADDIE SCHOLARSHIP TRUST http://www.gapgolf.org

J. WOOD PLATT CADDIE SCHOLARSHIP TRUST

Renewable award for high school seniors or college undergraduates who have caddied at least one year at a member club of the Golf Association of Philadelphia. Submit transcript and financial need analysis with application. Interview required.

Award: Scholarship for use in freshman, sophomore, junior, senior, or graduate years; renewable. *Number:* 250–300. *Amount:* $400–$7000.

Eligibility Requirements: Applicant must be enrolled or expecting to enroll full-time at a two-year or four-year institution or university. Applicant or parent of applicant must have employment or volunteer experience in private club/caddying. Available to U.S. and non-U.S. citizens.

Application Requirements: Application, financial need analysis, interview, references, test scores, transcript. *Deadline:* April 25.

Contact: Robert Caucci, Program Administrator
J. Wood Platt Caddie Scholarship Trust
PO Box 808
Southeastern, PA 19399-0808
Phone: 610-687-2340 Ext. 21
Fax: 610-687-2082

KE ALI'I PAUAHI FOUNDATION http://www.pauahi.org

CHARLES COCKETT 'OHANA SCHOLARSHIP

Scholarship requirements include a minimum GPA of 2.0, demonstrated commitment to making a difference in the community, and participation in school activities. Must submit Student Aid Report (SAR) and essay describing involvement in community service, including organizations, number or hours and length of volunteer service.

Award: Scholarship for use in freshman, sophomore, junior, senior, or graduate years; not renewable. *Number:* 2. *Amount:* up to $500.

Eligibility Requirements: Applicant must be enrolled or expecting to enroll full-time at a four-year institution or university. Applicant or parent of applicant must have employment or volunteer experience in community service. Available to U.S. citizens.

Application Requirements: Application, essay, financial need analysis, references, transcript, Student Aid Report (SAR), college acceptance letter. *Deadline:* May 2.

Contact: Elizabeth Stevenson, Development Manager
Ke Ali'i Pauahi Foundation
567 South King Street, Suite 160
Honolulu, HI 96813
Phone: 808-534-3966
Fax: 808-534-3890
E-mail: scholarships@pauahi.org

DANIEL KAHIKINA AND MILLIE AKAKA SCHOLARSHIP

Educational scholarships for undergraduate or graduate students demonstrating financial need. Minimum GPA of 3.2 required. Recipients are strongly encouraged to provide a minimum of 10 hours of community service to the Council for Native Hawaiian Advancement.

Award: Scholarship for use in freshman, sophomore, junior, senior, or graduate years; not renewable. *Number:* up to 1. *Amount:* up to $1600.

Eligibility Requirements: Applicant must be enrolled or expecting to enroll full-time at a two-year or four-year institution or university; resident of Hawaii and must have an interest in Hawaiian language/culture. Applicant or parent of applicant must have employment or volunteer experience in community service. Available to U.S. citizens.

Application Requirements: Application, financial need analysis, references, transcript, college acceptance letter, printed signature confirmation page, copy of SAR. *Deadline:* May 2.

Contact: Elizabeth Stevenson, Development Manager
Ke Ali'i Pauahi Foundation
567 South King Street, Suite 160
Honolulu, HI 96813
Phone: 808-534-3966
Fax: 808-534-3890
E-mail: scholarships@pauahi.org

KAMEHAMEHA SCHOOLS ALUMNI ASSOCIATION-MAUI REGION SCHOLARSHIP

Scholarship available to assist students who are residents of the island of Maui and did not graduate from Kamehameha Schools in pursing a postsecondary education. Applicants must demonstrate academic achievement or excellence, service to the community, financial need.

Award: Scholarship for use in freshman, sophomore, junior, senior, or graduate years; not renewable. *Number:* varies. *Amount:* varies.

Eligibility Requirements: Applicant must be enrolled or expecting to enroll full-time at a four-year institution or university and resident of

Ke Ali'i Pauahi Foundation (continued)

Hawaii. Applicant or parent of applicant must have employment or volunteer experience in community service. Available to U.S. citizens.

Application Requirements: Application, financial need analysis, references, transcript, Student Aid Report (SAR), college acceptance letter. *Deadline:* May 2.

Contact: Elizabeth Stevenson, Development Manager
Ke Ali'i Pauahi Foundation
567 South King Street, Suite 160
Honolulu, HI 96813
Phone: 808-534-3966
Fax: 808-534-3890
E-mail: scholarships@pauahi.org

KAMEHAMEHA SCHOOLS CLASS OF 1970 SCHOLARSHIP

Scholarship recognizes a student who has demonstrated exceptional service to the community with the intent to support their ongoing education and to encourage continued service in support of Hawaiian communities. Required minimum GPA of 2.0. Preference will be given to an immediate family member of a KS Class of 1970 graduate.

Award: Scholarship for use in freshman, sophomore, junior, senior, or graduate years; not renewable. *Number:* 1. *Amount:* $2000.

Eligibility Requirements: Applicant must be enrolled or expecting to enroll full-time at a four-year institution or university and resident of Hawaii. Applicant or parent of applicant must have employment or volunteer experience in community service. Available to U.S. citizens.

Application Requirements: Application, essay, financial need analysis, transcript, Student Aid Report (SAR), college acceptance letter. *Deadline:* May 2.

Contact: Elizabeth Stevenson, Development Manager
Ke Ali'i Pauahi Foundation
567 South King Street, Suite 160
Honolulu, HI 96813
Phone: 808-534-3966
Fax: 808-534-3890
E-mail: scholarships@pauahi.org

KAMEHAMEHA SCHOOLS CLASS OF 1960 GRANT

Grant recognizes a Hawaii resident who has demonstrated scholastic excellence, provided service to the community, demonstrated good character, and demonstrated an intent to utilize special skills in order to benefit the Hawaiian community. Preference will be given to an immediate family member of a KS Class of 1960 graduate.

Award: Grant for use in freshman, sophomore, junior, senior, or graduate years; not renewable. *Number:* varies. *Amount:* $1200.

Eligibility Requirements: Applicant must be enrolled or expecting to enroll full-time at a four-year institution or university and resident of Hawaii. Applicant or parent of applicant must have employment or volunteer experience in community service. Available to U.S. citizens.

Application Requirements: Application, financial need analysis, transcript, Student Aid Report (SAR), college acceptance letter. *Deadline:* May 2.

Contact: Elizabeth Stevenson, Development Manager
Ke Ali'i Pauahi Foundation
567 South King Street, Suite 160
Honolulu, HI 96813
Phone: 808-534-3966
Fax: 808-534-3890
E-mail: scholarships@pauahi.org

KNIGHTS OF COLUMBUS http://www.kofc.org

FRANCIS P. MATTHEWS AND JOHN E. SWIFT EDUCATIONAL TRUST SCHOLARSHIPS

• *See page 539*

LOWE'S COMPANIES INC. http://www.lowes.com

LOWE'S EDUCATIONAL SCHOLARSHIP

$1000–$15,000 scholarships available to all high school seniors who plan to attend any accredited 2-year or 4-year college or university within the United States. Selection based upon leadership skills, community service, and academic achievement.

Award: Scholarship for use in freshman year; not renewable. *Number:* up to 375. *Amount:* $1000–$15,000.

Eligibility Requirements: Applicant must be high school student; planning to enroll or expecting to enroll full- or part-time at a two-year or four-year or technical institution or university and must have an interest in leadership. Applicant or parent of applicant must have employment or volunteer experience in community service. Available to U.S. citizens.

Application Requirements: Application, resume. *Deadline:* March 15.

Contact: Scholarship Committee
Lowe's Companies Inc.
1000 Lowes Boulevard
Mooresville, NC 28117
Phone: 704-758-1000
Fax: 336-658-6937

MAGIC JOHNSON FOUNDATION INC. http://www.magicjohnson.org

TAYLOR MICHAELS SCHOLARSHIP FUND

Scholarship to provide support for deserving minority high school students who exemplify a strong potential for academic achievement but face social-economic conditions that hinder them from reaching their full potential. Must have strong community service involvement.

Award: Scholarship for use in freshman year; renewable. *Number:* varies. *Amount:* $1000–$5000.

Eligibility Requirements: Applicant must be American Indian/Alaska Native, Asian/Pacific Islander, Black (non-Hispanic), or Hispanic; high school student and planning to enroll or expecting to enroll full-time at a four-year institution or university. Applicant or parent of applicant must have employment or volunteer experience in community service. Applicant must have 2.5 GPA or higher. Available to U.S. and non-U.S. citizens.

Application Requirements: Application, essay, references, transcript. *Deadline:* February 5.

Contact: Scholarship Coordinator
Magic Johnson Foundation Inc.
9100 Wilshire Boulevard, Suite 700, East Tower
Beverly Hills, CA 90212
Phone: 310-246-4400

MARYLAND HIGHER EDUCATION COMMISSION http://www.mhec.state.md.us

EDWARD T. CONROY MEMORIAL SCHOLARSHIP PROGRAM

Scholarship for dependents of deceased or 100 percent disabled U.S. Armed Forces personnel; the son, daughter, or surviving spouse of a victim of the September 11, 2001 terrorist attacks who died as a result of the attacks on the World Trade Center in New York City, the attack on the Pentagon in Virginia, or the crash of United Airlines Flight 93 in Pennsylvania; a POW/MIA of the Vietnam Conflict or his/her son or daughter; the son, daughter or surviving spouse (who has not remarried) of a state or local public safety employee or volunteer who died in the line of duty; or a state or local public safety employee or volunteer who was 100 percent disabled in the line of duty. Must be Maryland resident at time of disability. Submit applicable VA certification. Must be at least 16 years of age and attend Maryland institution.

Award: Scholarship for use in freshman, sophomore, junior, senior, or graduate years; renewable. *Number:* up to 70. *Amount:* $7200–$9000.

Eligibility Requirements: Applicant must be age 16-24; enrolled or expecting to enroll full- or part-time at a two-year or four-year institution or university; resident of Maryland and studying in Maryland. Applicant or parent of applicant must have employment or volunteer experience in police/firefighting. Available to U.S. citizens. Applicant or parent must meet one or more of the following requirements: general military experience; retired from active duty; disabled or killed as a result of military service; prisoner of war; or missing in action.

Application Requirements: Application, birth and death certificate, and disability papers. *Deadline:* July 15.

Contact: Linda Asplin, Office of Student Financial Assistance
Maryland Higher Education Commission
839 Bestgate Road, Suite 400
Annapolis, MD 21401-3013
Phone: 410-260-4563
Fax: 410-260-3203
E-mail: lasplin@mhec.state.md.us

MASSACHUSETTS OFFICE OF STUDENT FINANCIAL ASSISTANCE http://www.osfa.mass.edu

MASSACHUSETTS PUBLIC SERVICE GRANT PROGRAM

Scholarships for children and/or spouses of deceased members of fire, police, and corrections departments, who were killed in the line of duty. Awards Massachusetts residents attending Massachusetts institutions. Applicant should have not received a prior bachelor's degree or its equivalent.

Award: Grant for use in freshman, sophomore, junior, or senior years; not renewable. *Number:* varies. *Amount:* varies.

Eligibility Requirements: Applicant must be enrolled or expecting to enroll full-time at a four-year institution or university and resident of Massachusetts. Applicant or parent of applicant must have employment or volunteer experience in police/firefighting. Available to U.S. and non-U.S. citizens. Applicant or parent must meet one or more of the following requirements: general military experience; retired from active duty; disabled or killed as a result of military service; prisoner of war; or missing in action.

Application Requirements: Application, financial need analysis, copy of birth certificate, copy of veteran's death certificate. *Deadline:* May 1.

Contact: Alison Leary, Director of Scholarships and Grants
Massachusetts Office of Student Financial Assistance
454 Broadway, Suite 200
Revere, MA 02151
Phone: 617-727-9420
Fax: 617-727-0667
E-mail: osfa@osfa.mass.edu

MINNESOTA DEPARTMENT OF MILITARY AFFAIRS http://www.minnesotanationalguard.org

LEADERSHIP, EXCELLENCE AND DEDICATED SERVICE SCHOLARSHIP

Scholarship provides a maximum of thirty $1000 to selected high school seniors who become a member of the Minnesota National Guard and complete the application process. The award recognizes demonstrated leadership, community services and potential for success in the Minnesota National Guard.

Award: Scholarship for use in freshman year; not renewable. *Number:* up to 30. *Amount:* $1000.

Eligibility Requirements: Applicant must be high school student; planning to enroll or expecting to enroll full- or part-time at a two-year or four-year or technical institution or university; resident of Minnesota and must have an interest in leadership. Applicant or parent of applicant must have employment or volunteer experience in community service. Available to U.S. citizens. Applicant or parent must meet one or more of the following requirements: Air Force National Guard or Army National Guard experience; retired from active duty; disabled or killed as a result of military service; prisoner of war; or missing in action.

Application Requirements: Essay, resume, references, transcript. *Deadline:* March 15.

Contact: Barbara O'Reilly, Education Services Officer
Minnesota Department of Military Affairs
20 West 12th Street, Veterans Services Building
St. Paul, MN 55155-2098
Phone: 651-282-4508
E-mail: barbara.oreilly@mn.ngb.army.mil

MINNESOTA HIGHER EDUCATION SERVICES OFFICE http://www.getreadyforcollege.org

SAFETY OFFICERS' SURVIVOR GRANT PROGRAM

Grant for eligible survivors of Minnesota public safety officers killed in the line of duty. Safety officers who have been permanently or totally disabled in the line of duty are also eligible. Must be used at a Minnesota institution participating in State Grant Program. Write for details. Must submit proof of death or disability and Public Safety Officers Benefit Fund Certificate. Must apply each year. Can be renewed for four years.

Award: Grant for use in freshman, sophomore, junior, or senior years; renewable. *Number:* 1. *Amount:* up to $9438.

Eligibility Requirements: Applicant must be age 23 or under; enrolled or expecting to enroll full- or part-time at a two-year or four-year or technical institution or university; resident of Minnesota and studying in Minnesota. Applicant or parent of applicant must have employment or volunteer experience in police/firefighting. Available to U.S. citizens.

Application Requirements: Application, proof of death or disability. *Deadline:* continuous.

Contact: Ginny Dodds, Manager
Minnesota Higher Education Services Office
1450 Energy Park Drive, Suite 350
St. Paul, MN 55108-5227
Phone: 651-642-0567
Fax: 651-642-0675
E-mail: ginny.dodds@state.mn.us

NATIONAL ASSOCIATION FOR CAMPUS ACTIVITIES http://www.naca.org

LORI RHETT MEMORIAL SCHOLARSHIP

Scholarships will be given to undergraduate or graduate students with a cumulative GPA of 2.5 or better at the time of the application and during the academic term in which the scholarship is awarded. Must demonstrate significant leadership skill and ability while holding a significant leadership position on campus. Applicants must have made contributions via volunteer involvement, either on or off campus.

Award: Scholarship for use in freshman, sophomore, junior, senior, or graduate years; not renewable. *Number:* 1. *Amount:* $250–$300.

Eligibility Requirements: Applicant must be enrolled or expecting to enroll full- or part-time at a two-year or four-year institution or university; studying in Alaska, Idaho, Montana, Oregon, or Washington and must have an interest in leadership. Applicant or parent of applicant must have employment or volunteer experience in community service. Applicant must have 2.5 GPA or higher. Available to U.S. citizens.

Application Requirements: Application, resume, references, transcript. *Deadline:* June 30.

Contact: Dionne Ellison, Administrative Assistant
National Association for Campus Activities
13 Harbison Way
Columbia, SC 29212-3401
Phone: 803-732-6222 Ext. 131
Fax: 803-749-1047
E-mail: dionnee@naca.org

NATIONAL ASSOCIATION FOR CAMPUS ACTIVITIES EAST COAST UNDERGRADUATE SCHOLARSHIP FOR STUDENT LEADERS

Scholarship for undergraduate students who are in good standing at the time of the application and during the academic term in which the scholarship is awarded. Applicants must maintain a 2.5 GPA, demonstrate leadership skills and abilities while holding a significant leadership position on campus or in community, and have made significant contributions via volunteer involvement. Eligible students must be attending a college or university within the NACA East Coast Region.

Award: Scholarship for use in freshman, sophomore, junior, or senior years; not renewable. *Number:* up to 2. *Amount:* $250–$300.

Eligibility Requirements: Applicant must be enrolled or expecting to enroll full- or part-time at a two-year or four-year institution or university; studying in Delaware, District of Columbia, Maryland, New Jersey, New York, or Pennsylvania and must have an interest in leadership. Applicant or parent of applicant must have employment or volunteer experience in community service. Applicant must have 2.5 GPA or higher. Available to U.S. citizens.

National Association for Campus Activities (continued)

Application Requirements: Application, essay, resume, references, transcript, current enrollment form. *Deadline:* March 31.

Contact: Dionne Ellison, Administrative Assistant
National Association for Campus Activities
13 Harbison Way
Columbia, SC 29212-3401
Phone: 803-732-6222 Ext. 131
Fax: 803-749-1047
E-mail: dionnee@naca.org

NATIONAL ASSOCIATION FOR CAMPUS ACTIVITIES SOUTHEAST REGION STUDENT LEADERSHIP SCHOLARSHIP

Scholarships will be given to full-time undergraduate students in good standing at the time of the application and during the academic term in which the scholarship is awarded. Must demonstrate significant leadership skill and ability while holding a significant leadership position on campus. Applicants must have made contributions via volunteer involvement, either on or off campus. Must be enrolled in a college/university in the NACA Southeast Region.

Award: Scholarship for use in freshman, sophomore, junior, or senior years; not renewable. *Number:* up to 4. *Amount:* $250–$300.

Eligibility Requirements: Applicant must be enrolled or expecting to enroll full-time at a two-year or four-year institution or university; studying in Alabama, Florida, Georgia, Mississippi, North Carolina, Puerto Rico, South Carolina, Tennessee, or Virginia and must have an interest in leadership. Applicant or parent of applicant must have employment or volunteer experience in community service. Available to U.S. citizens.

Application Requirements: Application, essay, resume, references, transcript, enrollment form. *Deadline:* March 31.

Contact: Dionne Ellison, Administrative Assistant
National Association for Campus Activities
13 Harbison Way
Columbia, SC 29212-3401
Phone: 803-732-6222 Ext. 131
Fax: 803-749-1047
E-mail: dionnee@naca.org

NATIONAL ASSOCIATION FOR CAMPUS ACTIVITIES WISCONSIN REGION STUDENT LEADERSHIP SCHOLARSHIP

Scholarships will be awarded to undergraduate or graduate students in good standing and enrolled in the equivalent of at least six academic credits at the time of the application and during the academic term in which the scholarship is awarded. Must be currently enrolled in or received a degree from a college or university within the NACA Wisconsin Region or Michigan (area code 906) and demonstrated leadership skill and significant service to their campus community.

Award: Scholarship for use in freshman, sophomore, junior, senior, or graduate years; not renewable. *Number:* 1. *Amount:* $250–$300.

Eligibility Requirements: Applicant must be enrolled or expecting to enroll full- or part-time at a two-year or four-year institution or university; studying in Michigan or Wisconsin and must have an interest in leadership. Applicant or parent of applicant must have employment or volunteer experience in community service. Available to U.S. citizens.

Application Requirements: Application, essay, resume, references, transcript. *Deadline:* January 15.

Contact: Dionne Ellison, Administrative Assistant
National Association for Campus Activities
13 Harbison Way
Columbia, SC 29212-3401
Phone: 803-732-6222 Ext. 131
Fax: 803-749-1047
E-mail: dionnee@naca.org

SCHOLARSHIPS FOR STUDENT LEADERS

Scholarships will be awarded to undergraduate students in good standing at the time of the application and who, during the academic term in which the scholarship is awarded, hold a significant leadership position on their campus. Must make significant contributions to their campus communities and demonstrate leadership skills and abilities.

Award: Scholarship for use in freshman, sophomore, junior, or senior years; not renewable. *Number:* up to 6. *Amount:* $250–$300.

Eligibility Requirements: Applicant must be enrolled or expecting to enroll full- or part-time at a two-year or four-year institution or university and must have an interest in leadership. Applicant or parent of applicant must have employment or volunteer experience in community service. Available to U.S. and non-U.S. citizens.

Application Requirements: Application, resume, references, transcript, current enrollment form. *Deadline:* November 1.

Contact: Dionne Ellison, Administrative Assistant
National Association for Campus Activities
13 Harbison Way
Columbia, SC 29212-3401
Phone: 803-732-6222 Ext. 131
Fax: 803-749-1047
E-mail: dionnee@naca.org

NATIONAL BURGLAR AND FIRE ALARM ASSOCIATION http://www.alarm.org

NBFAA YOUTH SCHOLARSHIP PROGRAM

One-time award for high school seniors entering postsecondary education, who are deserving sons or daughters of police and fire officials. The number of awards granted varies annually.

Award: Scholarship for use in freshman year; not renewable. *Number:* varies. *Amount:* $500–$10,000.

Eligibility Requirements: Applicant must be high school student; age 15-20; planning to enroll or expecting to enroll full-time at a four-year institution or university and resident of California, Connecticut, Georgia, Indiana, Kentucky, Louisiana, Maryland, Minnesota, New Jersey, New York, North Carolina, Pennsylvania, Tennessee, Virginia, or Washington. Applicant or parent of applicant must have employment or volunteer experience in police/firefighting. Available to U.S. citizens.

Application Requirements: Application, essay, test scores, transcript. *Deadline:* March 30.

Contact: Georjia Calaway, Marketing Coordinator
National Burglar and Fire Alarm Association
8380 Colesville Road, Suite 750
Silver Spring, MD 20910
Phone: 301-585-1855 Ext. 133
Fax: 301-585-1866
E-mail: georjiac@alarm.org

NATIONAL FEDERATION OF THE BLIND http://www.nfb.org

CHARLES AND MELVA T. OWEN MEMORIAL SCHOLARSHIP

Award for legally blind students in a degree program who are not pursuing a degree in religious studies. Must submit letter from the NFB state officer with whom they have discussed their application. Minimum 3.5 GPA required. Based on financial need, community service, and academic excellence.

Award: Scholarship for use in freshman, sophomore, junior, or senior years; not renewable. *Number:* 1. *Amount:* $10,000.

Eligibility Requirements: Applicant must be enrolled or expecting to enroll full-time at a four-year institution or university. Applicant or parent of applicant must have employment or volunteer experience in community service. Applicant must be visually impaired. Applicant must have 3.5 GPA or higher. Available to U.S. and non-U.S. citizens.

Application Requirements: Application, autobiography, essay, financial need analysis, references, test scores, transcript, letter from NFB state officer. *Deadline:* March 31.

Contact: Anil Lewis, Chairman, Scholarship Committee
National Federation of the Blind
315 West Ponce De Leon Avenue
Decatur, GA 30030
Phone: 404-371-1000
E-mail: alewis@nfbga.org

E. U. PARKER SCHOLARSHIP

Award for students who are legally blind and pursuing postsecondary education at a U.S. institution. Must submit recommendation from state officer of the NFB. Awards based on academic excellence, service to the community, and financial need.

Award: Scholarship for use in freshman, sophomore, junior, or senior years; not renewable. *Number:* 1. *Amount:* $3000.

Eligibility Requirements: Applicant must be enrolled or expecting to enroll full-time at a four-year institution or university. Applicant or parent of applicant must have employment or volunteer experience in community service. Applicant must be visually impaired. Available to U.S. and non-U.S. citizens.

Application Requirements: Application, autobiography, essay, financial need analysis, references, test scores, transcript, letter from state officer of the NFB. *Deadline:* March 31.

Contact: Anil Lewis, Chairman, Scholarship Committee
National Federation of the Blind
315 West Ponce De Leon Avenue
Decatur, GA 30030
Phone: 404-371-1000
E-mail: alewis@nfbga.org

HERMIONE GRANT CALHOUN SCHOLARSHIP

Award for full-time female undergraduate and graduate students, who are legally blind. Must submit a letter from state officer of NFB with whom they have discussed their application. Award based on academic excellence, service to the community, and financial need.

Award: Scholarship for use in freshman, sophomore, junior, senior, or graduate years; not renewable. *Number:* 1. *Amount:* $3000.

Eligibility Requirements: Applicant must be enrolled or expecting to enroll full-time at a four-year institution or university and female. Applicant or parent of applicant must have employment or volunteer experience in community service. Applicant must be visually impaired. Applicant must have 2.5 GPA or higher. Available to U.S. and non-U.S. citizens.

Application Requirements: Application, autobiography, essay, financial need analysis, references, test scores, transcript, letter from NFB state officer. *Deadline:* March 31.

Contact: Anil Lewis, Chairman, Scholarship Committee
National Federation of the Blind
315 West Ponce De Leon Avenue
Decatur, GA 30030
Phone: 404-371-1000
E-mail: alewis@nfbga.org

JENNICA FERGUSON MEMORIAL SCHOLARSHIP

One-time award for legally blind students pursuing full-time secondary education in the United States. Applicant must send a letter from a state officer of the NFB with whom they have discussed their application. Award is based on academic excellence, financial need and service to the community.

Award: Scholarship for use in freshman, sophomore, junior, or senior years; not renewable. *Number:* 1. *Amount:* $5000.

Eligibility Requirements: Applicant must be enrolled or expecting to enroll full-time at a two-year or four-year institution or university. Applicant or parent of applicant must have employment or volunteer experience in community service. Applicant must be visually impaired. Available to U.S. and non-U.S. citizens.

Application Requirements: Application, essay, financial need analysis, references, test scores, transcript, letter from state officer of the NFB. *Deadline:* March 31.

Contact: Anil Lewis, Chairman, Scholarship Committee
National Federation of the Blind
315 West Ponce De Leon Avenue
Decatur, GA 30030
Phone: 404-371-1000
E-mail: alewis@nfbga.org

KENNETH JERNIGAN SCHOLARSHIP

One-time, $12,000 award for full-time postsecondary students who are legally blind. Applicants must submit recommendation from state officer of NFB. Minimum GPA of 3.5 required.

Award: Scholarship for use in freshman, sophomore, junior, or senior years; not renewable. *Number:* 1. *Amount:* $12,000.

Eligibility Requirements: Applicant must be enrolled or expecting to enroll full-time at a four-year institution or university. Applicant or parent of applicant must have employment or volunteer experience in community service. Applicant must be visually impaired. Applicant must have 3.5 GPA or higher. Available to U.S. and non-U.S. citizens.

Application Requirements: Application, autobiography, essay, financial need analysis, references, transcript. *Deadline:* March 31.

Contact: Anil Lewis, Chairman, Scholarship Committee
National Federation of the Blind
315 West Ponce De Leon Avenue
Decatur, GA 30030
Phone: 404-371-1000
E-mail: alewis@nfbga.org

KUCHLER-KILLIAN MEMORIAL SCHOLARSHIP

$3000 award for legally blind full-time students. Applicants must submit a letter from a state officer of NFB with whom they have discussed their application. Award is based upon financial need, community service, and academic excellence. May reapply each year.

Award: Scholarship for use in freshman, sophomore, junior, or senior years; not renewable. *Number:* 1. *Amount:* $3000.

Eligibility Requirements: Applicant must be enrolled or expecting to enroll full-time at a four-year institution or university. Applicant or parent of applicant must have employment or volunteer experience in community service. Applicant must be visually impaired. Available to U.S. and non-U.S. citizens.

Application Requirements: Application, autobiography, essay, financial need analysis, references, test scores, transcript, letter from a state officer of NFB. *Deadline:* March 31.

Contact: Anil Lewis, Chairman, Scholarship Committee
National Federation of the Blind
315 West Ponce De Leon Avenue
Decatur, GA 30030
Phone: 404-371-1000
E-mail: alewis@nfbga.org

NATIONAL FEDERATION OF THE BLIND SCHOLARSHIPS

Award for legally blind students pursuing postsecondary education in the United States. Must submit recommendation from state officer of the NFB. Awards based on academic excellence, service to the community, and financial need. One award given to a person working full-time and attending or planning to attend a part-time course of study to broaden opportunities in work.

Award: Scholarship for use in freshman, sophomore, junior, or senior years; not renewable. *Number:* 17. *Amount:* $3000–$7000.

Eligibility Requirements: Applicant must be enrolled or expecting to enroll full- or part-time at a four-year institution or university. Applicant or parent of applicant must have employment or volunteer experience in community service. Applicant must be visually impaired. Available to U.S. and non-U.S. citizens.

Application Requirements: Application, essay, financial need analysis, references, transcript, letter from state officer of the NFB. *Deadline:* March 31.

Contact: Anil Lewis, Chairman, Scholarship Committee
National Federation of the Blind
315 West Ponce De Leon Avenue
Atlanta, GA 30030
Phone: 404-371-1000
E-mail: scholarships@nfb.org

NATIONAL SOCIETY OF HIGH SCHOOL SCHOLARS http://www.nshss.org

CLAES NOBEL ACADEMIC SCHOLARSHIPS FOR NSHSS MEMBERS

• *See page 546*

ROBERT P. SHEPPARD LEADERSHIP AWARD FOR NSHSS MEMBERS

Scholarship of $1000 awarded to an NSHSS member demonstrating outstanding dedication to community service and initiative in volunteer activities.

Award: Scholarship for use in freshman year; not renewable. *Number:* 1. *Amount:* $1000.

Eligibility Requirements: Applicant must be high school student and planning to enroll or expecting to enroll full- or part-time at a four-year institution or university. Applicant or parent of applicant must have employment or volunteer experience in community service. Available to U.S. and non-U.S. citizens.

National Society of High School Scholars (continued)

Application Requirements: Application, references, transcript. *Deadline:* February 21.

Contact: Susan Thurman, Scholarship Director
National Society of High School Scholars
1936 North Druid Hills Road
Atlanta, GA 30319
Phone: 866-343-1800
Fax: 866-282-4634
E-mail: information@nshss.org

NATSO FOUNDATION http://www.natso.com

BILL MOON SCHOLARSHIP

Available to employees or dependents of NATSO-affiliated truck stops/travel plazas. Visit Web site at http://www.natsofoundation.org for additional information.

Award: Scholarship for use in freshman, sophomore, junior, senior, or graduate years; not renewable. *Number:* 13. *Amount:* $2500.

Eligibility Requirements: Applicant must be enrolled or expecting to enroll full- or part-time at a two-year or four-year institution or university. Applicant or parent of applicant must have employment or volunteer experience in transportation industry. Available to U.S. and non-U.S. citizens.

Application Requirements: Application, essay, financial need analysis, references, transcript, signature from employer. *Deadline:* April 14.

Contact: Sharon Corigliano, Executive Director
NATSO Foundation
1737 King Street, Suite 200
Alexandria, VA 22314
Phone: 703-549-2100 Ext. 8561
Fax: 703-684-9667
E-mail: scorigliano@natso.com

NETAID FOUNDATION/MERCY CORPS http://www.globalactionawards.org

GLOBAL ACTION AWARDS

Awards honor high school students who have taken outstanding actions to fight global poverty. Honorees receive $5000 for their education or a charity of their choice. College freshman who completed their project while in a U.S. high school may apply.

Award: Scholarship for use in freshman year; not renewable. *Number:* 5. *Amount:* $5000.

Eligibility Requirements: Applicant must be high school student; planning to enroll or expecting to enroll full-time at a four-year institution and must have an interest in leadership. Applicant or parent of applicant must have employment or volunteer experience in community service. Available to U.S. citizens.

Application Requirements: Application, references, projects. *Deadline:* varies.

Contact: Suzanne Guthrie, Manager, Education and Youth Programs
NetAid Foundation/Mercy Corps
75 Broad Street, Suite 2410
New York, NY 10004
Phone: 212-537-0518
Fax: 212-537-0501
E-mail: gaa@nyc.mercycorps.org

NEW JERSEY HIGHER EDUCATION STUDENT ASSISTANCE AUTHORITY http://www.hesaa.org

LAW ENFORCEMENT OFFICER MEMORIAL SCHOLARSHIP

Scholarships for full-time undergraduate study at approved New Jersey institutions for the dependent children of New Jersey law enforcement officers killed in the line of duty. Value of scholarship will be established annually. Deadline varies.

Award: Scholarship for use in freshman, sophomore, junior, or senior years; renewable. *Number:* varies. *Amount:* varies.

Eligibility Requirements: Applicant must be enrolled or expecting to enroll full-time at a four-year institution or university; resident of New Jersey and studying in New Jersey. Applicant or parent of applicant must have employment or volunteer experience in police/firefighting. Available to U.S. citizens.

Application Requirements: Application. *Deadline:* varies.

Contact: Carol Muka, Assistant Director of Grants and Scholarships
New Jersey Higher Education Student Assistance Authority
PO Box 540
Trenton, NJ 08625
Phone: 800-792-8670 Ext. 3266
Fax: 609-588-2228
E-mail: cmuka@hesaa.org

SURVIVOR TUITION BENEFITS PROGRAM

The scholarship provides tuition fees for spouses and dependents of law enforcement officers, fire, or emergency services personnel killed in the line of duty. Eligible recipients may attend any independent institution in the state; however, the annual value of the grant cannot exceed the highest tuition charged at a New Jersey public institution.

Award: Scholarship for use in freshman, sophomore, junior, or senior years; renewable. *Number:* varies. *Amount:* varies.

Eligibility Requirements: Applicant must be enrolled or expecting to enroll full- or part-time at a two-year or four-year institution or university; resident of New Jersey and studying in New Jersey. Applicant or parent of applicant must have employment or volunteer experience in police/firefighting. Available to U.S. citizens.

Application Requirements: Application. *Deadline:* varies.

Contact: Carol Muka, Scholarship Coordinator
New Jersey Higher Education Student Assistance Authority
PO Box 540
Trenton, NJ 08625
Phone: 800-792-8670 Ext. 3266
Fax: 609-588-2228
E-mail: cmuka@hesaa.org

NEW JERSEY STATE GOLF ASSOCIATION http://www.njsga.org

NEW JERSEY STATE GOLF ASSOCIATION CADDIE SCHOLARSHIP

Applicants for this scholarship must reside in New Jersey, have a minimum 2.5 GPA, and have been for at least one year at a member club of the New Jersey State Golf Association. Scholarship award is based on grades, test scores, references, and financial need. Award renewable for undergraduate use.

Award: Scholarship for use in freshman, sophomore, junior, or senior years; renewable. *Number:* 241. *Amount:* $2000–$4000.

Eligibility Requirements: Applicant must be enrolled or expecting to enroll full-time at a four-year institution or university and resident of New Jersey. Applicant or parent of applicant must have employment or volunteer experience in private club/caddying. Applicant must have 2.5 GPA or higher. Available to U.S. citizens.

Application Requirements: Application, financial need analysis, references, test scores, transcript. *Deadline:* May 1.

Contact: Jay Petersen, Education Director
New Jersey State Golf Association
PO Box 6947
Freehold, NJ 07728
Phone: 732-780-4822
Fax: 732-780-4822
E-mail: j.o.petersen@att.net

NEW YORK STATE HIGHER EDUCATION SERVICES CORPORATION http://www.hesc.com

NEW YORK MEMORIAL SCHOLARSHIPS FOR FAMILIES OF DECEASED POLICE OFFICERS, FIRE FIGHTERS AND PEACE OFFICERS

Renewable scholarship for families of New York police officers, peace officers, emergency medical service workers or firefighters who died in the line of duty. Provides up to the cost of SUNY educational expenses.

Award: Scholarship for use in freshman, sophomore, junior, or senior years; renewable. *Number:* varies. *Amount:* varies.

Eligibility Requirements: Applicant must be enrolled or expecting to enroll full-time at a four-year institution or university; resident of New

York and studying in New York. Applicant or parent of applicant must have employment or volunteer experience in police/firefighting. Available to U.S. citizens.

Application Requirements: Application, financial need analysis, transcript. *Deadline:* May 1.

Contact: Adrienne Day, Associate HESC Information Representative
New York State Higher Education Services Corporation
99 Washington Avenue, Room 1320
Albany, NY 12255
Phone: 518-474-2991
Fax: 518-474-2839
E-mail: aday@hesc.com

NORTH CAROLINA BAR ASSOCIATION http://www.ncbar.org

NORTH CAROLINA BAR ASSOCIATION YOUNG LAWYERS DIVISION SCHOLARSHIP

Renewable award for children of North Carolina law enforcement officers killed or permanently disabled in the line of duty, studying full-time in accredited colleges or universities. Must be resident of North Carolina and under 26 years of age. The number of awards and the dollar value of the award varies annually.

Award: Scholarship for use in freshman, sophomore, junior, senior, graduate, or postgraduate years; renewable. *Number:* varies. *Amount:* varies.

Eligibility Requirements: Applicant must be age 26 or under; enrolled or expecting to enroll full-time at a two-year or four-year or technical institution or university and resident of North Carolina. Applicant or parent of applicant must have employment or volunteer experience in police/firefighting. Available to U.S. citizens.

Application Requirements: Application, essay, financial need analysis, photo, test scores, transcript, verification letter from law enforcement agency. *Deadline:* April 3.

Contact: Jacquelyn Terrell-Fountain, Assistant Director of Sections, YLD Staff Liaison
North Carolina Bar Association
PO Box 3688
Cary, NC 27519
Phone: 919-677-0561
Fax: 919-677-0761
E-mail: jterrell@ncbar.org

OHIO BOARD OF REGENTS http://www.regents.ohio.gov

OHIO SAFETY OFFICERS COLLEGE MEMORIAL FUND

Renewable award covering up to full tuition is available to children and surviving spouses of peace officers and fire fighters killed in the line of duty in any state. Children must be under 26 years of age. Dollar value of each award varies. Must be an Ohio resident and enroll full-time or part-time at an Ohio college or university.

Award: Scholarship for use in freshman, sophomore, junior, or senior years; renewable. *Number:* 50–65. *Amount:* varies.

Eligibility Requirements: Applicant must be age 26 or under; enrolled or expecting to enroll full- or part-time at a two-year or four-year institution or university; resident of Ohio and studying in Ohio. Applicant or parent of applicant must have employment or volunteer experience in police/firefighting. Available to U.S. citizens.

Application Requirements: *Deadline:* continuous.

Contact: Barbara Thoma, Program Administrator
Ohio Board of Regents
30 East Broad Street, 36th Floor
Columbus, OH 43215-3414
Phone: 614-752-9535
Fax: 614-752-5903
E-mail: bthoma@regents.state.oh.us

OREGON STUDENT ASSISTANCE COMMISSION http://www.osac.state.or.us

BANDON SUBMARINE CABLE COUNCIL SCHOLARSHIP

Renewable award to high school graduates who have not matriculated as postsecondary students. Preference to members or dependent children of members of the Bandon Submarine Cable Council; any commercial fisherman or family member; any postsecondary student residing in Clatsop, Coos, Curry, Lane, Lincoln, or Tillamook County; any postsecondary student in Oregon. Must indicate name of vessel in worksite section.

Award: Scholarship for use in freshman, sophomore, junior, or senior years; renewable. *Number:* varies. *Amount:* varies.

Eligibility Requirements: Applicant must be enrolled or expecting to enroll full-time at a four-year institution and resident of Oregon. Applicant or parent of applicant must have employment or volunteer experience in seafaring/fishing industry. Available to U.S. citizens.

Application Requirements: Application, essay, financial need analysis, transcript, activities chart. *Deadline:* March 1.

Contact: Director of Grant Programs
Oregon Student Assistance Commission
1500 Valley River Drive, Suite 100
Eugene, OR 97401-7020
Phone: 800-452-8807 Ext. 7395

JOSE D. GARCIA MIGRANT EDUCATION SCHOLARSHIP

One-time award for U.S. citizens or permanent residents in Oregon Migrant Education program. Must be high school graduates or GED recipients enrolling at least half-time in freshman year undergraduate study. Must enter parent names in membership section of application.

Award: Scholarship for use in freshman year; not renewable. *Number:* varies. *Amount:* varies.

Eligibility Requirements: Applicant must be enrolled or expecting to enroll full- or part-time at a four-year institution or university and resident of Oregon. Applicant or parent of applicant must have employment or volunteer experience in migrant work. Available to U.S. citizens.

Application Requirements: Application, essay, financial need analysis, transcript, activity chart. *Deadline:* March 1.

Contact: Director of Grant Programs
Oregon Student Assistance Commission
1500 Valley River Drive, Suite 100
Eugene, OR 97401-7020
Phone: 800-452-8807 Ext. 7395

OREGON DUNGENESS CRAB COMMISSION SCHOLARSHIP

One scholarship available to children, stepchildren, or legal dependents of licensed Oregon Dungeness Crab fishermen or crew, graduating as high school senior. One-time award. Indicate name of vessel in worksite.

Award: Scholarship for use in freshman year; not renewable. *Number:* 1. *Amount:* varies.

Eligibility Requirements: Applicant must be high school student; planning to enroll or expecting to enroll full-time at a four-year institution and resident of Oregon. Applicant or parent of applicant must have employment or volunteer experience in seafaring/fishing industry. Available to U.S. citizens.

Application Requirements: Application, essay, financial need analysis, transcript, activity chart, name of vessel in place of work-site in membership section. *Deadline:* March 1.

Contact: Director of Grant Programs
Oregon Student Assistance Commission
1500 Valley River Drive, Suite 100
Eugene, OR 97401-7020
Phone: 800-452-8807 Ext. 7395

OREGON OCCUPATIONAL SAFETY AND HEALTH DIVISION WORKERS MEMORIAL SCHOLARSHIP

Available to Oregon residents who are high school graduates or GED recipients, and either who are the dependents or spouses of an Oregon worker who was killed or permanently disabled on the job. Submit essay of 500 words.

Award: Scholarship for use in freshman, sophomore, junior, senior, or graduate years; renewable. *Number:* varies. *Amount:* varies.

Eligibility Requirements: Applicant must be enrolled or expecting to enroll full-time at a four-year institution or university and resident of Oregon. Applicant or parent of applicant must have employment or volunteer experience in occupational health and safety. Available to U.S. citizens.

Oregon Student Assistance Commission (continued)

Application Requirements: Application, essay, financial need analysis, test scores, transcript, social security number or workers compensation claim. *Deadline:* March 1.

Contact: Director of Grant Programs
Oregon Student Assistance Commission
1500 Valley River Drive, Suite 100
Eugene, OR 97401-7020
Phone: 800-452-8807 Ext. 7395

OREGON SALMON COMMISSION SCHOLARSHIP

One-time award open to graduating high school seniors. Must be a dependent of a licensed Oregon salmon fisherman. Must be a resident of Oregon. Should place name of vessel in place of worksite in membership section of application.

Award: Scholarship for use in freshman year; not renewable. *Number:* varies. *Amount:* varies.

Eligibility Requirements: Applicant must be enrolled or expecting to enroll full-time at a four-year institution and resident of Oregon. Applicant or parent of applicant must have employment or volunteer experience in seafaring/fishing industry. Available to U.S. citizens.

Application Requirements: Application, essay, financial need analysis, transcript, activity chart. *Deadline:* March 1.

Contact: Director of Grant Programs
Oregon Student Assistance Commission
1500 Valley River Drive, Suite 100
Eugene, OR 97401-7020
Phone: 800-452-8807 Ext. 7395

OREGON TRAWL COMMISSION SCHOLARSHIP

Award for graduating high school seniors and college students who are dependents of licensed Oregon Trawl fishermen or crew. Visit Web site: http://www.osac.state.or.us for more details.

Award: Scholarship for use in freshman, sophomore, junior, or senior years; renewable. *Number:* varies. *Amount:* varies.

Eligibility Requirements: Applicant must be enrolled or expecting to enroll full-time at a four-year institution and resident of Oregon. Applicant or parent of applicant must have employment or volunteer experience in seafaring/fishing industry. Available to U.S. citizens.

Application Requirements: Application, essay, financial need analysis, references, transcript, activity chart. *Deadline:* March 1.

Contact: Director of Grant Programs
Oregon Student Assistance Commission
1500 Valley River Drive, Suite 100
Eugene, OR 97401-7020
Phone: 800-452-8807 Ext. 7395

PENDLETON POSTAL WORKERS SCHOLARSHIP

One-time award for graduating high school seniors who are children or grandchildren of active, retired or deceased members of Pendleton APWU Local 110, at least one year preceding as of the March 1 scholarship deadline. Contact for application requirements and deadlines. Essay required "What has the labor movement accomplished historically for working people?".

Award: Scholarship for use in freshman year; not renewable. *Number:* varies. *Amount:* varies.

Eligibility Requirements: Applicant must be high school student; planning to enroll or expecting to enroll full-time at a four-year institution and resident of Oregon. Applicant or parent of applicant must have employment or volunteer experience in federal/postal service. Available to U.S. citizens.

Application Requirements: Application, essay, references, transcript, activity chart. *Deadline:* March 1.

Contact: Director of Grant Programs
Oregon Student Assistance Commission
1500 Valley River Drive, Suite 100
Eugene, OR 97401-7020
Phone: 800-452-8807 Ext. 7395

PACERS FOUNDATION INC. http://www.pacersfoundation.org

PACERS TEAMUP SCHOLARSHIP

Scholarship is awarded to Indiana high school seniors for their first year of undergraduate study at any accredited four-year college or university or two-year college or junior college. Primary selection criteria is student involvement in community service.

Award: Scholarship for use in freshman year; not renewable. *Number:* 5. *Amount:* $2000.

Eligibility Requirements: Applicant must be enrolled or expecting to enroll full-time at a two-year or four-year institution or university and resident of Indiana. Applicant or parent of applicant must have employment or volunteer experience in community service. Available to U.S. citizens.

Application Requirements: Application, essay, references, transcript. *Deadline:* March 1.

Contact: Jami Marsh, Executive Director
Pacers Foundation Inc.
125 South Pennsylvania Street
Indianapolis, IN 46204
Phone: 317-917-2856
E-mail: foundation@pacers.com

PENNSYLVANIA BURGLAR AND FIRE ALARM ASSOCIATION http://www.pbfaa.com

PENNSYLVANIA BURGLAR AND FIRE ALARM ASSOCIATION YOUTH SCHOLARSHIP PROGRAM

Non-renewable scholarships available to sons and daughters of active Pennsylvania police and fire personnel, and volunteer fire department personnel for full-time study at a two- or four-year college, or university. Must be a senior attending a Pennsylvania high school. Scholarship amount in the range of $500 to $6500.

Award: Scholarship for use in freshman year; not renewable. *Number:* 6–8. *Amount:* $500–$6500.

Eligibility Requirements: Applicant must be high school student; planning to enroll or expecting to enroll full-time at a two-year or four-year institution or university and resident of Pennsylvania. Applicant or parent of applicant must have employment or volunteer experience in police/firefighting. Available to U.S. citizens.

Application Requirements: Application, essay, resume, test scores, transcript. *Deadline:* March 1.

Contact: Dale Eller, Executive Director
Pennsylvania Burglar and Fire Alarm Association
3718 West Lake Road
Erie, PA 16505
Phone: 814-838-3093
Fax: 814-838-5127
E-mail: info@pbfaa.com

PENNSYLVANIA HIGHER EDUCATION ASSISTANCE AGENCY http://www.pheaa.org

POSTSECONDARY EDUCATION GRATUITY PROGRAM

The program offers waiver of tuition and fees for children of Pennsylvania police officers, firefighters, rescue or ambulance squad members, corrections facility employees, or National Guard members who died in line of duty after January 1, 1976.

Award: Grant for use in freshman, sophomore, junior, or senior years; renewable. *Number:* varies. *Amount:* varies.

Eligibility Requirements: Applicant must be age 25 or under; enrolled or expecting to enroll full-time at a two-year or four-year institution or university; resident of Pennsylvania and studying in Pennsylvania. Applicant or parent of applicant must have employment or volunteer experience in police/firefighting. Available to U.S. citizens. Applicant or parent must meet one or more of the following requirements: Air Force National Guard or Army National Guard experience; retired from active duty; disabled or killed as a result of military service; prisoner of war; or missing in action.

Application Requirements: Application. *Deadline:* August 1.

Contact: Keith New, Vice President, Public Relations
Pennsylvania Higher Education Assistance Agency
1200 North Seventh Street
Harrisburg, PA 17102-1444
Phone: 717-720-2509
Fax: 717-720-3903
E-mail: knew@pheaa.org

PHOENIX SUNS CHARITIES/SUN STUDENTS SCHOLARSHIP http://www.suns.com

QWEST LEADERSHIP CHALLENGE

Student must be a member of the varsity basketball team and volunteer in a community outreach program. Upon completion of 30 volunteer hours for a nonprofit or educational organization, each participating school will receive a check for $250 to be donated to its nonprofit organization of choice. In addition, two student-athletes will be chosen to receive $5000 scholarships.

Award: Scholarship for use in junior or senior years; not renewable. *Number:* 2. *Amount:* up to $5000.

Eligibility Requirements: Applicant must be enrolled or expecting to enroll full-time at a four-year institution or university; resident of Arizona and must have an interest in athletics/sports. Applicant or parent of applicant must have employment or volunteer experience in community service. Available to U.S. citizens.

Application Requirements: Application. *Deadline:* continuous.

Contact: Partnership Activation
Phoenix Suns Charities/Sun Students Scholarship
PO Box 1369
Phoenix, AZ 85001
Phone: 602-379-7987
E-mail: dpreuss@suns.com

SUN STUDENT COLLEGE SCHOLARSHIP PROGRAM

Applicants must be seniors preparing to graduate from a high school in Arizona. Eligible applicants must have a minimum 2.5 GPA. Must provide evidence of regular involvement in charitable activities or volunteer service in school, church, or community organizations. Fifteen $2000 scholarships and one $5000 scholarship will be awarded.

Award: Scholarship for use in freshman year; not renewable. *Number:* 1–16. *Amount:* $2000–$5000.

Eligibility Requirements: Applicant must be high school student; planning to enroll or expecting to enroll full- or part-time at a two-year or four-year institution or university and resident of Arizona. Applicant or parent of applicant must have employment or volunteer experience in community service. Applicant must have 2.5 GPA or higher. Available to U.S. citizens.

Application Requirements: Application, essay, references, transcript. *Deadline:* February 15.

Contact: Janell Jakubowski, Administrative Assistant
Phoenix Suns Charities/Sun Students Scholarship
PO Box 1369
Phoenix, AZ 85001
Phone: 602-379-7767
Fax: 602-379-7922
E-mail: jornelas@suns.com

PNY TECHNOLOGIES http://www.pny.com

SENIORS HELPING SENIORS

A challenge for high school seniors in teams of 1 to 5 persons to conceive and perform a project that will enhance the lives of senior citizens within their community using PNY products. Each team member of the winning project will receive a $2500 scholarship. See Web site for entry form and complete rules: http://www.2pny.com/education/howtoenter.html.

Award: Scholarship for use in freshman year; not renewable. *Number:* 1–5. *Amount:* $2500.

Eligibility Requirements: Applicant must be high school student and planning to enroll or expecting to enroll full-time at a two-year or four-year or technical institution or university. Applicant or parent of applicant must have employment or volunteer experience in community service. Available to U.S. citizens.

Application Requirements: Application, applicant must enter a contest, essay, photo, self-addressed stamped envelope. *Deadline:* December 31.

Contact: Margaret Salleroli, Senior Marketing Communications Manager
PNY Technologies
PO Box 5416
Parsippany, NJ 07054
Phone: 800-769-0143
E-mail: shs@pny.com

PROJECT BEST SCHOLARSHIP FUND http://www.projectbest.com

PROJECT BEST SCHOLARSHIP

• *See page 554*

PUEBLO OF SAN JUAN, DEPARTMENT OF EDUCATION http://www.sanjuaned.org

OHKAY OWINGEH TRIBAL SCHOLARSHIP OF THE PUEBLO OF SAN JUAN

Scholarship for residents of New Mexico enrolled either full-time or part-time in accredited colleges or universities. Minimum GPA of 2.0 required. Must complete required number of hours of community service in the San Juan Pueblo. Up to thirty scholarships are granted and the value of the award ranges from $300 to $600. Deadline varies.

Award: Scholarship for use in freshman, sophomore, junior, or senior years; renewable. *Number:* 1–30. *Amount:* $300–$600.

Eligibility Requirements: Applicant must be American Indian/Alaska Native; enrolled or expecting to enroll full- or part-time at a two-year or four-year or technical institution or university and resident of New Mexico. Applicant or parent of applicant must have employment or volunteer experience in community service. Available to U.S. citizens.

Application Requirements: Application, transcript, letter of acceptance. *Deadline:* varies.

Contact: Adam Garcia, Education Coordinator
Pueblo of San Juan, Department of Education
State Highway 74, Day School Street
PO Box 1269
Ohkay Owingeh, NM 87566
Phone: 505-852-3477
Fax: 505-852-3030
E-mail: wevog68@valornet.com

POP'AY SCHOLARSHIP

Scholarship for members of Pueblo of San Juan tribe pursuing their first associate or baccalaureate degree. Must complete a minimum of 20 hours of community service within the San Juan Pueblo. Scholarship value is $2500. Seventeen awards are granted. Deadlines: December 30 for spring, April 30 for summer, and June 30 for fall.

Award: Scholarship for use in freshman, sophomore, junior, or senior years; renewable. *Number:* up to 17. *Amount:* $2500.

Eligibility Requirements: Applicant must be American Indian/Alaska Native; enrolled or expecting to enroll full-time at a two-year or four-year institution or university and resident of New Mexico. Applicant or parent of applicant must have employment or volunteer experience in community service. Available to U.S. citizens.

Application Requirements: Application, transcript, letter of acceptance. *Deadline:* varies.

Contact: Adam Garcia, Education Coordinator
Pueblo of San Juan, Department of Education
State Highway 74, Day School Street
PO Box 1269
Ohkay Owingeh, NM 87566
Phone: 505-852-3477
Fax: 505-852-3030
E-mail: wevog68@valornet.com

RAILWAY SUPPLY INSTITUTE http://www.rsiweb.org

RSI UNDERGRADUATE SCHOLARSHIP PROGRAM

• *See page 554*

RAISE THE NATION FOUNDATION http://www.raisethenation.org

RAISE THE NATION STUDENT LOAN GRANT

Grant is awarded to professional single parent women with outstanding student loan debt who contribute to their community through volunteer work. Community service hours will be determined/decided when you receive an award.

Award: Grant for use in freshman, sophomore, junior, senior, graduate, or postgraduate years; renewable. *Number:* 1–50. *Amount:* $100–$5000.

Eligibility Requirements: Applicant must be age 18-99; enrolled or expecting to enroll full- or part-time at a two-year or four-year or technical institution or university and single female. Applicant or parent of applicant must have employment or volunteer experience in community service. Available to U.S. citizens.

Application Requirements: Application, autobiography, essay, financial need analysis, transcript. *Fee:* $20. *Deadline:* varies.

Contact: Michelle McMullen, Executive Director
Raise the Nation Foundation
PO Box 8058
Albuquerque, NM 87198
Phone: 505-265-1201
E-mail: suppoetdesk@raisethenation.org

RECORDING FOR THE BLIND & DYSLEXIC http://www.rfbd.org

MARION HUBER LEARNING THROUGH LISTENING AWARDS

• *See page 554*

MARY P. OENSLAGER SCHOLASTIC ACHIEVEMENT AWARDS

• *See page 554*

RHODE ISLAND FOUNDATION http://www.rifoundation.org

RHODE ISLAND FOUNDATION ASSOCIATION OF FORMER LEGISLATORS SCHOLARSHIP

One-time award of $1500 for graduating high school seniors who are Rhode Island residents. Must have a history of substantial voluntary involvement in community service. Must be accepted into an accredited post-secondary institution and should be able to demonstrate financial need.

Award: Scholarship for use in freshman year; not renewable. *Number:* 4–5. *Amount:* $1500.

Eligibility Requirements: Applicant must be high school student; planning to enroll or expecting to enroll full-time at a four-year institution or university and resident of Rhode Island. Applicant or parent of applicant must have employment or volunteer experience in community service. Available to U.S. citizens.

Application Requirements: Application, essay, financial need analysis, references, self-addressed stamped envelope, test scores, transcript. *Deadline:* June 4.

Contact: Libby Monahan, Funds Administrator
Rhode Island Foundation
One Union Station
Providence, RI 02903
Phone: 401-274-4564 Ext. 3117
Fax: 401-751-7983
E-mail: libbym@rifoundation.org

ST. CLAIRE REGIONAL MEDICAL CENTER http://www.st-claire.org

SR. MARY JEANNETTE WESS, S.N.D. SCHOLARSHIP

Scholarships available for undergraduates in their junior or senior year of study, or graduate students. Must have graduated from an eastern Kentucky high school in one of the following counties: Bath, Carter, Elliott, Fleming, Lewis, Magoffin, Menifee, Montgomery, Morgan, Rowan, or Wolfe. Must demonstrate academic achievement, leadership, service, and financial need.

Award: Scholarship for use in junior, senior, or graduate years; renewable. *Number:* 2. *Amount:* $750.

Eligibility Requirements: Applicant must be enrolled or expecting to enroll full-time at a four-year institution or university; resident of Kentucky and must have an interest in leadership. Applicant or parent of applicant must have employment or volunteer experience in community service. Available to U.S. and non-U.S. citizens.

Application Requirements: Application, financial need analysis, references, self-addressed stamped envelope, transcript. *Deadline:* varies.

Contact: Tom Lewis, Director of Development
St. Claire Regional Medical Center
222 Medical Circle
Morehead, KY 40351
Phone: 606-783-6511
Fax: 606-783-6795
E-mail: telewis@st-claire.org

SAMUEL HUNTINGTON FUND http://www.nationalgridus.com/education

SAMUEL HUNTINGTON PUBLIC SERVICE AWARD

Award provides a $10,000 stipend to a graduating college senior to perform a one-year public service project anywhere in the world immediately following graduation. Written proposals of 100 words or less are requested with application. Project may encompass any activity that furthers the public good. Awards will be based on quality of proposal, academic record, and other personal achievements. Semi-finalists will be interviewed.

Award: Grant for use in senior year; not renewable. *Number:* 1–3. *Amount:* $10,000.

Eligibility Requirements: Applicant must be enrolled or expecting to enroll full-time at a four-year institution or university. Applicant or parent of applicant must have employment or volunteer experience in community service. Available to U.S. and non-U.S. citizens.

Application Requirements: Application, essay, financial need analysis, resume, references, transcript. *Deadline:* February 15.

Contact: Amy Stacy, Executive Assistant
Samuel Huntington Fund
25 Research Drive
Westborough, MA 01582
Phone: 508-389-3390
Fax: 508-389-2605
E-mail: amy.stacy@us.ngrid.com

SAN DIEGO FOUNDATION http://www.sdfoundation.org

DRINKWATER FAMILY SCHOLARSHIP

Scholarship to graduating high school seniors who will be the first in their family to attend an accredited four-year university in the United States. Must have minimum GPA of 3.25, a demonstrated financial need, and be actively involved in serving their community as shown by their participation in extracurricular or church activities, or community service. Scholarship may be used for tuition, books and fees.

Award: Scholarship for use in freshman year; not renewable. *Number:* varies. *Amount:* varies.

Eligibility Requirements: Applicant must be high school student; planning to enroll or expecting to enroll full-time at an institution or university and resident of California. Applicant or parent of applicant must have employment or volunteer experience in community service. Available to U.S. citizens.

Application Requirements: Application, references, transcript, personal statement, copy of tax return. *Deadline:* January 26.

Contact: Shryl Helvie, Scholarship Coordinator
San Diego Foundation
2508 Historic Decatur Road, Suite 200
San Diego, CA 92106
Phone: 619-814-1307
Fax: 619-239-1710
E-mail: shryl@sdfoundation.org

HARVEY L. SIMMONS MEMORIAL SCHOLARSHIP

Scholarship to graduating high school seniors who will attend an accredited two-year college or four-year university in the United States. Applicants must demonstrate financial need, and a commitment to serving their community through their involvement in community service, church or extracurricular activities. Preference given to applicants who have participated in high school sports for at least three years, two at the varsity level, and are intending to play at the college level.

Award: Scholarship for use in freshman year; not renewable. *Number:* 2. *Amount:* $500.

Eligibility Requirements: Applicant must be high school student; planning to enroll or expecting to enroll full-time at a two-year or four-year institution or university and resident of California. Applicant or parent of applicant must have employment or volunteer experience in community service. Available to U.S. citizens.

Application Requirements: Application, references, transcript, personal statement, copy of tax return. *Deadline:* January 26.

Contact: Shryl Helvie, Scholarship Coordinator
San Diego Foundation
2508 Historic Decatur Road, Suite 200
San Diego, CA 92106
Phone: 619-814-1307
Fax: 619-239-1710
E-mail: shryl@sdfoundation.org

LESLIE JANE HAHN MEMORIAL SCHOLARSHIP

Scholarship to graduating high school senior girls from a public school who will be attending an accredited four-year college or university in the United States. Applicants must have at least a 3.75 GPA and a demonstrated financial need. Must also have a history of active involvement in athletics, other extracurricular activities, community service or work experience.

Award: Scholarship for use in freshman, sophomore, junior, or senior years; renewable. *Number:* 1. *Amount:* $3000.

Eligibility Requirements: Applicant must be enrolled or expecting to enroll full-time at a four-year institution or university; female; resident of California and must have an interest in athletics/sports. Applicant or parent of applicant must have employment or volunteer experience in community service. Available to U.S. citizens.

Application Requirements: Application, financial need analysis, references, transcript, personal statement, copy of tax return. *Deadline:* January 26.

Contact: Shryl Helvie, Scholarship Coordinator
San Diego Foundation
2508 Historic Decatur Road, Suite 200
San Diego, CA 92106
Phone: 619-814-1307
Fax: 619-239-1710
E-mail: shryl@sdfoundation.org

SAN DIEGO PATHWAYS TO COLLEGE SCHOLARSHIP

Scholarship to graduating high school seniors who are attending a four-year university in the state of California. Must be legal residents of San Diego County. Applicants must have a minimum 3.0 GPA and a demonstrated financial need. Also, students must be actively involved in extracurricular activities, community service, religious activities, work experience, or athletics.

Award: Scholarship for use in freshman year; not renewable. *Number:* 25. *Amount:* $1000–$10,000.

Eligibility Requirements: Applicant must be high school student; planning to enroll or expecting to enroll full-time at a four-year institution or university; resident of California and studying in California. Applicant or parent of applicant must have employment or volunteer experience in community service. Applicant must have 3.0 GPA or higher. Available to U.S. citizens.

Application Requirements: Application, financial need analysis, references, transcript, personal statement, copy of tax return. *Deadline:* January 26.

Contact: Shryl Helvie, Scholarship Coordinator
San Diego Foundation
2508 Historic Decatur Road, Suite 200
San Diego, CA 92106
Phone: 619-814-1307
Fax: 619-239-1710
E-mail: shryl@sdfoundation.org

USA FREESTYLE MARTIAL ARTS SCHOLARSHIP

Scholarship to students who are currently attending or have attended USA Freestyle Martial Arts for at least two years. Applicants must have a minimum 2.5 GPA and either be graduating high school seniors or current college students who plan to attend an accredited two- or four-year college or university, or licensed trade/vocational school in the United States. Applicants must be committed to their communities as demonstrated by their involvement in community service.

Award: Scholarship for use in freshman, sophomore, junior, or senior years; not renewable. *Number:* 2. *Amount:* $1000–$3000.

Eligibility Requirements: Applicant must be enrolled or expecting to enroll full-time at a two-year or four-year or technical institution or university; resident of California and must have an interest in athletics/sports. Applicant or parent of applicant must have employment or volunteer experience in community service. Applicant must have 2.5 GPA or higher. Available to U.S. citizens.

Application Requirements: Application, financial need analysis, references, transcript, personal statement, copy of tax return. *Deadline:* January 26.

Contact: Shryl Helvie, Scholarship Coordinator
San Diego Foundation
2508 Historic Decatur Road, Suite 200
San Diego, CA 92106
Phone: 619-814-1307
Fax: 619-239-1710
E-mail: shryl@sdfoundation.org

SCHOLARSHIP WORKSHOP LLC — http://www.scholarshipworkshop.com

RAGINS/BRASWELL NATIONAL SCHOLARSHIP

Scholarship available to high school seniors, undergraduate, and graduate students who attend The Scholarship Workshop presentation or an online class given by Marianne Ragins. Award is based on use of techniques taught in the workshop or class, application, essay, leadership, extracurricular activities, achievements, and community responsibility. See Web site: http://www.scholarshipworkshop.com. Scholarship amounts vary.

Award: Scholarship for use in freshman, sophomore, junior, senior, or graduate years; not renewable. *Number:* 1–3. *Amount:* varies.

Eligibility Requirements: Applicant must be enrolled or expecting to enroll full-time at a four-year institution or university and must have an interest in leadership. Applicant or parent of applicant must have employment or volunteer experience in community service. Available to U.S. citizens.

Application Requirements: Application, essay. *Deadline:* April 30.

Contact: Scholarship Coordinator
Scholarship Workshop LLC
PO Box 176
Centreville, VA 20122
Phone: 703-579-4245
Fax: 703-579-4245
E-mail: scholars@scholarshipworkshop.com

SKILLSUSA — http://www.skillsusa.org

SKILLSUSA ALUMNI AND FRIENDS MERIT SCHOLARSHIP

Scholarship of up to $1000 recognizes qualities of leadership, commitment to community service, improving the image of career and technical education, and improving the image of his/her chosen occupation.

Award: Scholarship for use in freshman, sophomore, junior, senior, graduate, or postgraduate years; not renewable. *Number:* 1. *Amount:* $500–$1000.

Eligibility Requirements: Applicant must be enrolled or expecting to enroll full-time at a two-year or four-year or technical institution or university and must have an interest in leadership. Applicant or parent of applicant must have employment or volunteer experience in community service. Available to U.S. citizens.

Application Requirements: Application, references. *Deadline:* May 15.

Contact: Karen Perrino, Associate Director
SkillsUSA
PO Box 3000
Leesburg, VA 20177-0300
Phone: 703-737-0610
Fax: 703-777-8999
E-mail: kperrino@skillsusa.org

STATE FARM COMPANIES/YOUTH SERVICE AMERICA http://ysa.org

HARRIS WOFFORD AWARDS

Awards recognize extraordinary achievements in three categories: youth (ages 12 to 25), organization (nonprofit, corporate, foundation), and media (organization or individual) for actively contributing towards, "Making service and service-learning the common expectation and common experience of every young person."

Award: Grant for use in freshman, sophomore, junior, senior, graduate, or postgraduate years; not renewable. *Number:* up to 3. *Amount:* $500–$1000.

Eligibility Requirements: Applicant must be age 12-25 and enrolled or expecting to enroll full- or part-time at a two-year or four-year or technical institution or university. Applicant or parent of applicant must have employment or volunteer experience in community service. Available to U.S. citizens.

Application Requirements: Application. *Deadline:* October 19.

Contact: Julie Mancuso, Grant Manager
State Farm Companies/Youth Service America
1101 15th Street, NW, Suite 200
Washington, DC 20005
Phone: 202-296-2992 Ext. 111
Fax: 202-296-4030
E-mail: jmancuso@ysa.org

STONEWALL COMMUNITY FOUNDATION http://www.stonewallfoundation.org

HARRY BARTEL MEMORIAL SCHOLARSHIP FUND

Gay male students who are 23 years or younger with a record of community service can apply for this scholarship. Deadline varies.

Award: Scholarship for use in freshman, sophomore, junior, senior, graduate, or postgraduate years; not renewable. *Number:* varies. *Amount:* varies.

Eligibility Requirements: Applicant must be age 23 or under; enrolled or expecting to enroll full-time at a two-year or four-year or technical institution or university; male and must have an interest in LGBT issues. Applicant or parent of applicant must have employment or volunteer experience in community service. Available to U.S. citizens.

Application Requirements: Application. *Deadline:* varies.

Contact: Roz Lee, Program Director
Stonewall Community Foundation
119 West 24th Street, Seventh Floor
New York, NY 10011
Phone: 212-367-1155
Fax: 212-367-1157
E-mail: stonewall@stonewallfoundation.org

TENNESSEE STUDENT ASSISTANCE CORPORATION http://www.collegepaystn.com

DEPENDENT CHILDREN SCHOLARSHIP PROGRAM

Scholarship aid for Tennessee residents who are dependent children of a Tennessee law enforcement officer, fireman, or an emergency medical service technician who has been killed or totally and permanently disabled while performing duties within the scope of such employment. The scholarship awarded to full-time undergraduate students for a maximum of four academic years or the period required for the completion of the program of study.

Award: Scholarship for use in freshman, sophomore, junior, or senior years; renewable. *Number:* up to 30. *Amount:* varies.

Eligibility Requirements: Applicant must be enrolled or expecting to enroll full-time at a two-year or four-year institution or university and resident of Tennessee. Applicant or parent of applicant must have employment or volunteer experience in police/firefighting. Available to U.S. citizens.

Application Requirements: Application, FAFSA. *Deadline:* July 15.

Contact: Scholarship Committee
Tennessee Student Assistance Corporation
404 James Robertson Parkway, Suite 1510, Parkway Towers
Nashville, TN 37243-0820
Phone: 615-741-1346
Fax: 615-741-6101

TERRY FOX HUMANITARIAN AWARD PROGRAM http://www.terryfox.org

TERRY FOX HUMANITARIAN AWARD

Award granted to Canadian students entering postsecondary education. Criteria includes commitment to voluntary humanitarian work, courage in overcoming obstacles, excellence in academics, fitness and amateur sports. Value of award is CAN$7000 awarded annually for maximum of four years. Must be no older than age 25.

Award: Scholarship for use in freshman, sophomore, junior, or senior years; renewable. *Number:* up to 20.

Eligibility Requirements: Applicant must be Canadian citizen; age 25 or under; enrolled or expecting to enroll full-time at a two-year or four-year institution or university and must have an interest in athletics/sports. Applicant or parent of applicant must have employment or volunteer experience in community service.

Application Requirements: Application, references, self-addressed stamped envelope, transcript. *Deadline:* February 1.

Contact: W. Davis, Executive Director
Terry Fox Humanitarian Award Program
Simon Fraser University, 8888 University Drive
Burnaby, BC V5A 1S6
Canada
Phone: 604-291-3057
Fax: 604-291-3311
E-mail: terryfox@sfu.ca

TEXAS RESTAURANT ASSOCIATION http://www.restaurantville.com

W. PRICE JR. MEMORIAL SCHOLARSHIP

Scholarships of $5000 for recipients attending a four-year university, culinary academy, or graduate program, and $2000 for recipients attending a two-year college. Applicant must be employed by an ARA member in good standing, must have an overall B grade average, and must submit an essay summarizing how their experience in the food service industry has affected their career goals.

Award: Scholarship for use in freshman, sophomore, junior, or senior years; not renewable. *Number:* 4. *Amount:* $2000–$5000.

Eligibility Requirements: Applicant must be enrolled or expecting to enroll full-time at a two-year or four-year institution or university. Applicant or parent of applicant must have employment or volunteer experience in food service. Available to U.S. citizens.

Application Requirements: Application, references, transcript. *Deadline:* February 1.

Contact: Susan Petty, Scholarship Coordinator
Texas Restaurant Association
PO Box 1429
Austin, TX 78767-1429
Phone: 512-457-4100
Fax: 512-472-2777
E-mail: spetty@tramail.org

TUITION EXCHANGE INC. http://www.tuitionexchange.org

TUITION EXCHANGE SCHOLARSHIPS

The Tuition Exchange is an association of 540 colleges and universities awarding over 3700 full or substantial scholarships each year for children and other family members of faculty and staff employed at participating institutions. Students must maintain a cumulative 2.300 GPA. Application procedures and deadlines vary by school. Contact Tuition Exchange Liaison Officer at home institution for details.

Award: Scholarship for use in freshman, sophomore, junior, senior, graduate, or postgraduate years; renewable. *Number:* 3400–4000. *Amount:* $10,000–$21,000.

Eligibility Requirements: Applicant must be enrolled or expecting to enroll full-time at a two-year or four-year institution or university. Applicant or parent of applicant must have employment or volunteer experience in teaching/education. Available to U.S. and non-U.S. citizens.

Application Requirements: Application. *Deadline:* continuous.

Contact: Robert L. Norris, President
Tuition Exchange Inc.
1743 Connecticut Avenue, NW
Washington, DC 20009-1108
Phone: 202-518-0135
Fax: 202-518-0137
E-mail: rnorris@tuitionexchange.org

TWO TEN FOOTWEAR FOUNDATION http://www.twoten.org

TWO/TEN FOOTWEAR FOUNDATION SCHOLARSHIP

Renewable, merit and need-based award available to students who have 500 hours work experience in footwear, leather, or allied industries during year of application, or have a parent employed in one of these fields for at least two years. Must have proof of employment and maintain 2.5 GPA.

Award: Scholarship for use in freshman year; renewable. *Number:* 200–250. *Amount:* $210–$3000.

Eligibility Requirements: Applicant must be enrolled or expecting to enroll full- or part-time at a four-year institution or university. Applicant or parent of applicant must have employment or volunteer experience in leather/footwear industry. Applicant must have 2.5 GPA or higher. Available to U.S. citizens.

Application Requirements: Application, essay, financial need analysis, references, transcript. *Deadline:* February 15.

Contact: Phyllis Molta, Director of Scholarship
Two Ten Footwear Foundation
1466 Main Street
Waltham, MA 02451-1623
Phone: 781-736-1503
Fax: 781-736-1555
E-mail: scholarship@twoten.org

UNITED STATES SUBMARINE VETERANS INC. http://www.ussvcf.org

UNITED STATES SUBMARINE VETERANS INC. NATIONAL SCHOLARSHIP PROGRAM

• *See page 569*

WESTERN GOLF ASSOCIATION-EVANS SCHOLARS FOUNDATION http://www.evansscholarsfoundation.com

CHICK EVANS CADDIE SCHOLARSHIP

Full tuition and housing awards renewable up to four years available to high school seniors who have worked at least two years as a caddy at a Western Golf Association member club. Must demonstrate need, outstanding character, and at least a B average in college preparatory courses. Limited to use at universities where Evans Foundation maintains a Scholarship House, where recipients are required to reside. See Web site for complete list.

Award: Scholarship for use in freshman year; renewable. *Number:* up to 200. *Amount:* varies.

Eligibility Requirements: Applicant must be high school student; planning to enroll or expecting to enroll full-time at a four-year institution or university and studying in Colorado, Illinois, Indiana, Kansas, Michigan, Minnesota, Missouri, Ohio, Oregon, Pennsylvania, Washington, or Wisconsin. Applicant or parent of applicant must have employment or volunteer experience in private club/caddying. Available to U.S. and non-U.S. citizens.

Application Requirements: Application, essay, financial need analysis, interview, references, test scores, transcript. *Deadline:* September 30.

Contact: Scholarship Committee
Western Golf Association-Evans Scholars Foundation
One Briar Road
Golf, IL 60029
Phone: 847-724-4600
Fax: 847-724-7133
E-mail: evansscholars@wgaesf.com

WILLIAM G. AND MARIE SELBY FOUNDATION http://www.selbyfdn.org

SELBY SCHOLAR PROGRAM

Scholarships awarded up to $6500 annually, not to exceed 1/3 of individual's financial need. Renewable for four years if student is full-time undergraduate at accredited college or university. Must demonstrate values of leadership and service to the community. Must reside in Sarasota, Manatee, Charlotte, and Desoto counties in Florida.

Award: Scholarship for use in freshman, sophomore, junior, or senior years; renewable. *Number:* 35. *Amount:* up to $6500.

Eligibility Requirements: Applicant must be enrolled or expecting to enroll full-time at a four-year institution or university; resident of Florida and must have an interest in leadership. Applicant or parent of applicant must have employment or volunteer experience in community service. Applicant must have 3.0 GPA or higher. Available to U.S. citizens.

Application Requirements: Application, essay, financial need analysis, interview, references, test scores, transcript. *Deadline:* April 1.

Contact: Jan Noah, Grants Manager
William G. and Marie Selby Foundation
1800 Second Street, Suite 750
Sarasota, FL 34236
Phone: 941-957-0442
Fax: 941-957-3135
E-mail: jnoah@selbyfdn.org

YOUNG AMERICAN BOWLING ALLIANCE (YABA) http://www.bowl.com

USBC ANNUAL ZEB SCHOLARSHIP

Scholarship awarded to a USBC Youth member who achieves academic success and gives back to the community through service. Candidates must have a current GPA of 2.0 or better.

Award: Scholarship for use in freshman year; not renewable. *Number:* 1. *Amount:* $2500.

Eligibility Requirements: Applicant must be high school student; planning to enroll or expecting to enroll full- or part-time at a four-year institution or university and must have an interest in bowling. Applicant or parent of applicant must have employment or volunteer experience in community service. Available to U.S. citizens.

Application Requirements: Application, references, transcript. *Deadline:* April 1.

Contact: Ed Gocha, Scholarship Programs Manager
Young American Bowling Alliance (YABA)
5301 South 76th Street
Greendale, WI 53129-1192
Phone: 800-514-2695
Fax: 414-423-3014
E-mail: smart@bowlinginc.com

YOUTH FOUNDATION INC. http://www.foundationcenter.org/grantmaker/youthfdn/index.html

ALEXANDER AND MAUDE HADDEN SCHOLARSHIP

Youth Foundation offers exceptional students with financial need an award of $2500 to $4000 per year which is renewable for four years at the foundation's discretion. Minimum GPA of 3.5 required, community service and extra curricular activities expected. Must write Foundation for information and application request form.

Award: Scholarship for use in freshman, sophomore, junior, or senior years; renewable. *Number:* varies. *Amount:* $2500–$4000.

Eligibility Requirements: Applicant must be enrolled or expecting to enroll full- or part-time at a four-year institution or university. Applicant or parent of applicant must have employment or volunteer experience in community service. Applicant must have 3.5 GPA or higher. Available to U.S. citizens.

Youth Foundation Inc. (continued)

Application Requirements: Application, essay, test scores, transcript. *Deadline:* February 29.

Contact: Scholarship Committee
Youth Foundation Inc.
36 West 44th Street
New York, NY 10036
Phone: 212-840-6291

ZONTA INTERNATIONAL FOUNDATION http://www.zonta.org

YOUNG WOMEN IN PUBLIC AFFAIRS AWARD

One-time award for pre-college women with a commitment to the volunteer sector and evidence of volunteer leadership achievements. Must be 16 to 20 years of age with a career interest in public affairs, public policy and community organizations. Further information and application available at Web site: http://www.zonta.org.

Award: Scholarship for use in freshman year; not renewable. *Number:* up to 5. *Amount:* $500–$1000.

Eligibility Requirements: Applicant must be high school student; age 16-20; planning to enroll or expecting to enroll full-time at a four-year institution or university and female. Applicant or parent of applicant must have employment or volunteer experience in community service. Available to U.S. and non-U.S. citizens.

Application Requirements: Application, references. *Deadline:* varies.

Contact: Ana Ubides, Program Coordinator
Zonta International Foundation
557 West Randolph Street
Chicago, IL 60661
Phone: 312-930-5848
Fax: 312-930-0951
E-mail: zontaintl@zonta.org

IMPAIRMENT

ALEXANDER GRAHAM BELL ASSOCIATION FOR THE DEAF AND HARD OF HEARING http://www.agbell.org

AG BELL COLLEGE SCHOLARSHIP PROGRAM

Available to students with pre-lingual hearing loss who attend a mainstream and accredited college or university on a full-time basis. Specific eligibility criteria, submission guidelines, deadline and application available on AG Bell Web site at http://www.agbell.org.

Award: Scholarship for use in freshman, sophomore, junior, senior, or graduate years; not renewable. *Number:* 5–20. *Amount:* $1000–$10,000.

Eligibility Requirements: Applicant must be enrolled or expecting to enroll full-time at a four-year institution or university. Applicant must be hearing impaired. Available to U.S. and non-U.S. citizens.

Application Requirements: Application, essay, references, transcript, unaided audiogram or mapping report. *Deadline:* varies.

Contact: Scholarship Coordinator
Alexander Graham Bell Association for the Deaf and Hard of Hearing
3417 Volta Place, NW
Washington, DC 20007
Phone: 202-337-5220
E-mail: financialaid@agbell.org

DEAF AND HARD OF HEARING SECTION SCHOLARSHIP FUND

Award to undergraduate born with profound or severe hearing loss (of at least 60 dB), or who experienced hearing loss before acquiring language. Must be accepted or enrolled in a college or university that primarily enrolls students with normal hearing as a full-time student and must use spoken communication as primary mode of communication. Must be member of AG Bell and member of the DHHS. Must submit audiogram and letters of recommendation.

Award: Scholarship for use in freshman, sophomore, junior, or senior years; not renewable. *Number:* 2. *Amount:* $1000.

Eligibility Requirements: Applicant must be enrolled or expecting to enroll full-time at a four-year institution or university. Applicant must be hearing impaired. Available to U.S. citizens.

Application Requirements: Application, references, transcript, current audiological report. *Deadline:* March 1.

Contact: Financial Aid and Scholarship Programs
Alexander Graham Bell Association for the Deaf and Hard of Hearing
3417 Volta Place, NW
Washington, DC 20007-2778
Phone: 202-337-5220
Fax: 202-337-8314
E-mail: financialaid@agbell.org

FEDERATION OF JEWISH WOMEN'S ORGANIZATION SCHOLARSHIP

Award available to undergraduate born with profound or severe hearing loss (of at least 60 dB), or who experienced hearing loss before acquiring language. Must be accepted or enrolled in a mainstream college or university as a full-time student and must use spoken communication as primary mode of communication. Must submit audio-gram and letters of recommendation. Application is available at Web site: http://www.agbell.org.

Award: Scholarship for use in freshman, sophomore, junior, or senior years; not renewable. *Number:* 1. *Amount:* $2000.

Eligibility Requirements: Applicant must be enrolled or expecting to enroll full-time at a four-year institution or university. Applicant must be hearing impaired. Available to U.S. citizens.

Application Requirements: Application, references, transcript, current audiological report. *Deadline:* March 1.

Contact: Financial Aid and Scholarship Programs
Alexander Graham Bell Association for the Deaf and Hard of Hearing
3417 Volta Place, NW
Washington, DC 20007-2778
Phone: 202-337-5220
Fax: 202-337-8314
E-mail: financialaid@agbell.org

AMERICAN ACADEMY OF ALLERGY, ASTHMA AND IMMUNOLOGY http://www.aaaai.org

AWARD OF EXCELLENCE ASTHMA SCHOLARSHIP PROGRAM

One-time award to high school seniors with asthma who are furthering their education in a postsecondary school. Must demonstrate academic excellence. Must be a U.S. or Canadian citizen. Application deadline generally the first week of January. Only online applications will be accepted. Visit Web site: http://www.aaaai.org for updated information.

Award: Scholarship for use in freshman year; not renewable. *Number:* 60. *Amount:* varies.

Eligibility Requirements: Applicant must be high school student and planning to enroll or expecting to enroll full-time at a two-year or four-year or technical institution or university. Applicant must be physically disabled. Available to U.S. and Canadian citizens.

Application Requirements: Application, essay, references, transcript, verification from physician on severity of asthma. *Deadline:* January 11.

Contact: John Augustyniak, Executive Director
American Academy of Allergy, Asthma and Immunology
555 East Wells Street, Suite 1100
Milwaukee, WI 53202-3823
Phone: 414-272-6071
Fax: 414-272-6070
E-mail: jaugustyniak@aaaai.org

AMERICAN CANCER SOCIETY, FLORIDA DIVISION INC. http://www.cancer.org

AMERICAN CANCER SOCIETY, FLORIDA DIVISION R.O.C.K. COLLEGE SCHOLARSHIP PROGRAM

• *See page 588*

AMERICAN CANCER SOCIETY INC.-GREAT LAKES DIVISION http://www.cancer.org/scholarships

COLLEGE SCHOLARSHIPS FOR CANCER SURVIVORS

Scholarships for Michigan and Indiana residents who have had a diagnosis of cancer before the age of 21. Applicant must be under 21 at time of application. To be used for undergraduate degrees at any accredited Michigan or Indiana college or university. Deadline: mid-April. Open to U.S. citizens only.

Award: Scholarship for use in freshman, sophomore, junior, or senior years; renewable. *Number:* 1. *Amount:* $1000.

Eligibility Requirements: Applicant must be age 21 or under; enrolled or expecting to enroll full-time at a two-year or four-year or technical institution or university; resident of Indiana or Michigan and studying in Indiana or Michigan. Applicant must be physically disabled. Available to U.S. citizens.

Application Requirements: Application, essay, financial need analysis, references, test scores, transcript, letter from physician verifying cancer diagnosis. *Deadline:* varies.

Contact: Katie Wilson, Project Coordinator
American Cancer Society Inc.-Great Lakes Division
1755 Abbey Road
East Lansing, MI 48823
Phone: 800-723-0360
Fax: 517-664-1497
E-mail: kathleen.wilson@cancer.org

AMERICAN COUNCIL OF THE BLIND http://www.acb.org

AMERICAN COUNCIL OF THE BLIND SCHOLARSHIPS

Merit-based award available to undergraduate students who are legally blind in both eyes. Submit certificate of legal blindness and proof of acceptance at an accredited postsecondary institution.

Award: Scholarship for use in freshman, sophomore, junior, or senior years; renewable. *Number:* 16–20. *Amount:* $1000–$2500.

Eligibility Requirements: Applicant must be enrolled or expecting to enroll full- or part-time at a four-year institution or university. Applicant must be visually impaired. Applicant must have 3.5 GPA or higher. Available to U.S. citizens.

Application Requirements: Application, autobiography, essay, references, transcript, evidence of legal blindness, proof of post-secondary school acceptance. *Deadline:* March 1.

Contact: Tatricia Castillo, Scholarship Coordinator
American Council of the Blind
1155 15th Street, NW, Suite 1004
Washington, DC 20005
Phone: 202-467-5081
Fax: 202-467-5085
E-mail: tcastillo@acp.org

AMERICAN FOUNDATION FOR THE BLIND http://www.afb.org

FERDINAND TORRES SCHOLARSHIP

Awards one scholarship of $2500 to a full-time undergraduate or graduate student who presents evidence of economic need. To be eligible the applicant must reside in the U.S., but need not be a citizen of the U.S. Preference will be given to applicants residing in the New York City metropolitan area and new immigrants to the U.S. Must submit proof of legal blindness. For additional information and application requirements, visit: www.afb.org/scholarships.asp.

Award: Scholarship for use in freshman, sophomore, junior, senior, or graduate years; not renewable. *Number:* 1. *Amount:* $2500.

Eligibility Requirements: Applicant must be enrolled or expecting to enroll full-time at a two-year or four-year institution or university. Applicant must be visually impaired. Available to U.S. and non-U.S. citizens.

Application Requirements: Application, essay, financial need analysis, references, transcript, proof of acceptance in an accredited full-time undergraduate or graduate program, proof of legal blindness. *Deadline:* March 31.

Contact: Dawn Bodrogi, Information Center and Library Coordinator
American Foundation for the Blind
11 Penn Plaza, Suite 300
New York, NY 10001
Phone: 212-502-7661
Fax: 212-502-7771
E-mail: dbodrogi@afb.net

GUIDE DOGS FOR THE BLIND DORTHEA AND ROLAND BOHDE PERSONAL ACHIEVEMENT SCHOLARSHIP

Scholarship provides one award of $1000 to a full-time undergraduate student in any field of study. Must submit proof of legal blindness from an optometrist, ophthalmologist, or state or private agency for the blind.

Award: Scholarship for use in freshman, sophomore, junior, or senior years; renewable. *Number:* 1. *Amount:* $1000.

Eligibility Requirements: Applicant must be enrolled or expecting to enroll full-time at a four-year institution or university. Applicant must be visually impaired. Available to U.S. citizens.

Application Requirements: Application, essay, references, transcript, proof of legal blindness, proof of citizenship, proof of acceptance in an accredited full-time undergraduate program. *Deadline:* March 31.

Contact: Dawn Bodrogi, Information Center and Library Coordinator
American Foundation for the Blind
11 Penn Plaza, Suite 300
New York, NY 10001
Phone: 212-502-7661
Fax: 212-502-7771
E-mail: dbodrogi@afb.net

ASHLEY FOUNDATION http://www.theashleyfoundation.org

ASHLEY TAMBURRI SCHOLARSHIP

Scholarship for a cancer survivor or individual currently diagnosed with cancer. An active cancer patient does not have to be receiving treatment to qualify. The cancer may be in remission or deemed cured. Applicant must be a senior, attending a high school in a county served by the Foundation as of the beginning of that current academic year. Students attending a high school in Carroll, Frederick, Howard, Montgomery, or Washington County, Maryland are eligible to apply.

Award: Scholarship for use in freshman year; renewable. *Number:* varies. *Amount:* up to $1000.

Eligibility Requirements: Applicant must be high school student; planning to enroll or expecting to enroll full-time at a four-year institution or university and resident of Maryland. Applicant must be physically disabled. Available to U.S. citizens.

Application Requirements: Application, essay, references. *Deadline:* March 31.

Contact: Lori Maze, Community Liaison
Ashley Foundation
22 South Market Street, Suite 17
PO Box 672
New Market, MD 21774
Phone: 301-694-6414
E-mail: info@theashleyfoundation.org

ASSOCIATION FOR EDUCATION AND REHABILITATION OF THE BLIND AND VISUALLY IMPAIRED http://www.aerbvi.org

WILLIAM AND DOROTHY FERREL SCHOLARSHIP

Nonrenewable scholarship given in even years for postsecondary education leading to career in services for blind or visually impaired. Applicant must submit proof of legal blindness or visual field impairment of 20 percent or less.

Award: Scholarship for use in freshman, sophomore, junior, or senior years; not renewable. *Number:* 2. *Amount:* $1000.

Eligibility Requirements: Applicant must be enrolled or expecting to enroll full- or part-time at a two-year or four-year or technical institution or university. Applicant must be visually impaired. Available to U.S. and non-U.S. citizens.

Association for Education and Rehabilitation of the Blind and Visually Impaired (continued)

Application Requirements: Application, proof of legal blindness. *Deadline:* February 15.

Contact: Scholarship Coordinator
Association for Education and Rehabilitation of the Blind and Visually Impaired
1703 North Beauregard Street, Suite 440
Alexandria, VA 22311-1717
Phone: 703-671-4500 Ext. 201
E-mail: bsherr@aerbvi.org

ASSOCIATION OF BLIND CITIZENS http://www.blindcitizens.org

REGGIE JOHNSON MEMORIAL SCHOLARSHIP

Award for high school or college student who is legally blind. High school or college transcript, certificate of legal blindness, or a letter from ophthalmologist required. Must submit two letters of reference and a disk copy of your biographical sketch.

Award: Scholarship for use in freshman, sophomore, junior, senior, graduate, or postgraduate years; not renewable. *Number:* 1–8. *Amount:* $1000–$2000.

Eligibility Requirements: Applicant must be enrolled or expecting to enroll full-time at a two-year or four-year institution or university. Applicant must be visually impaired. Available to U.S. citizens.

Application Requirements: Application, autobiography, references, transcript, certificate of legal blindness or a letter from an ophthalmologist. *Deadline:* April 15.

Contact: John Oliveira, President
Association of Blind Citizens
PO Box 246
Holbrook, MA 02343
Phone: 781-961-1023
Fax: 781-961-0004
E-mail: president@blindcitizens.org

BILL MCADAM SCHOLARSHIP FUND

BILL MCADAM SCHOLARSHIP FUND

Scholarship for a person with hemophilia, including their spouse, partner, child or sibling, planning to attend an accredited college, university, trade, or technical school.

Award: Scholarship for use in freshman, sophomore, junior, senior, graduate, or postgraduate years; not renewable. *Number:* 1. *Amount:* $2000.

Eligibility Requirements: Applicant must be enrolled or expecting to enroll full- or part-time at a two-year or four-year or technical institution or university. Applicant must be physically disabled. Available to U.S. citizens.

Application Requirements: Application. *Deadline:* May 15.

Contact: Scholarship Coordinator
Bill McAdam Scholarship Fund
22226 Doxtator
Dearborn, MI 48128
Phone: 313-563-1412
E-mail: mcmcadam@comcast.net

CALIFORNIA COUNCIL OF THE BLIND http://www.ccbnet.org

CALIFORNIA COUNCIL OF THE BLIND SCHOLARSHIPS

Scholarships available to blind student applicants who are California residents entering or continuing studies at an accredited California college, university, or vocational training school. Must be a full-time student registered for at least twelve units for the entire academic year. Applications must be typed and all blanks must be filled to be considered for scholarship. Applications available at Web site: http://www.ccbnet.org.

Award: Scholarship for use in freshman, sophomore, junior, senior, graduate, or postgraduate years; renewable. *Number:* up to 20. *Amount:* $375–$2500.

Eligibility Requirements: Applicant must be enrolled or expecting to enroll full-time at a two-year or four-year or technical institution or university; resident of California and studying in California. Applicant must be visually impaired. Available to U.S. and non-U.S. citizens.

Application Requirements: Application, interview, references, transcript, proof of blindness. *Deadline:* June 15.

Contact: Colette Davis, Scholarship Chair
California Council of the Blind
2879 East Alden Place
Anaheim, CA 92806
Phone: 714-630-8098
Fax: 714-666-2494

CHAIRSCHOLARS FOUNDATION INC. http://www.chairscholars.org

CHAIRSCHOLARS FOUNDATION INC. SCHOLARSHIPS

• *See page 592*

CHRISTIAN RECORD SERVICES INC. http://www.christianrecord.org

CHRISTIAN RECORD SERVICES INC. SCHOLARSHIPS

One-time award for legally blind or blind college undergraduates. Submit application, essay-autobiography, photo, references, and financial information by April 1.

Award: Scholarship for use in freshman, sophomore, junior, or senior years; renewable. *Number:* 7–10. *Amount:* $250–$500.

Eligibility Requirements: Applicant must be enrolled or expecting to enroll full-time at a four-year institution or university. Applicant must be visually impaired. Available to U.S. citizens.

Application Requirements: Application, autobiography, essay, financial need analysis, photo, references. *Deadline:* April 1.

Contact: Shelly Kittleson, Assistant to Treasurer
Christian Record Services Inc.
4444 South 52nd Street
Lincoln, NE 68516-1302
Phone: 402-488-0981 Ext. 213
Fax: 402-488-7582
E-mail: info@christianrecord.org

COALITION OF TEXANS WITH DISABILITIES http://www.cotwd.org

KENNY MURGIA MEMORIAL SCHOLARSHIP

Awarded annually to a high school senior who has demonstrated activism on disability issues. This program also provides for a part-time paid internship for a college student with disabilities at CTD's Austin office.

Award: Scholarship for use in freshman year; not renewable. *Number:* 1. *Amount:* $1000.

Eligibility Requirements: Applicant must be high school student; planning to enroll or expecting to enroll full-time at a four-year institution or university and resident of Texas. Applicant must be hearing impaired, learning disabled, physically disabled, or visually impaired. Available to U.S. citizens.

Application Requirements: Application, references, transcript. *Deadline:* May 31.

Contact: Jodi Park, Director of Projects and Communications
Coalition of Texans with Disabilities
316 West 12th Street, Suite 405
Austin, TX 78701
Phone: 512-478-3366
Fax: 512-478-3370
E-mail: cotwd@cotwd.org

COLLEGEBOUND FOUNDATION http://www.collegeboundfoundation.org

ERICA LYNNE DURANT MEMORIAL SCHOLARSHIP

One-time scholarship award of $500 for a physically challenged or learning disabled student. Must provide proof of disability from a licensed professional. See Web site for application: http://www. collegeboundfoundation.org.

Award: Scholarship for use in freshman year; not renewable. *Number:* 1. *Amount:* $500.

Eligibility Requirements: Applicant must be high school student; planning to enroll or expecting to enroll full-time at a two-year or four-year institution or university; resident of Maryland and studying in Maryland. Applicant must be learning disabled or physically disabled. Available to U.S. citizens.

Application Requirements: Application, essay, financial need analysis, interview, references, transcript, financial aid award letters, SAR. *Deadline:* March 1.

Contact: Jamie Crouse, Scholarship Program Administrator
CollegeBound Foundation
300 Water Street, Suite 300
Baltimore, MD 21202
Phone: 410-783-2905 Ext. 207
Fax: 410-727-5786
E-mail: jcrouse@collegeboundfoundation.org

COLLEGE WOMEN'S ASSOCIATION OF JAPAN http://www.cwaj.org

SCHOLARSHIP FOR THE VISUALLY IMPAIRED TO STUDY ABROAD

Scholarship for visually impaired Japanese nationals or permanent residents of Japan who have been accepted into an undergraduate or graduate degree program at an accredited English-speaking university or research institution. Former recipients of CWAJ awards and members of CWAJ are ineligible. Award value is JPY3 million. Deadline on or between November 1 and November 30.

Award: Scholarship for use in junior, senior, or postgraduate years; not renewable. *Number:* 1.

Eligibility Requirements: Applicant must be of Japanese heritage and Japanese citizen and enrolled or expecting to enroll full-time at a four-year institution or university. Applicant must be visually impaired. Available to citizens of countries other than the U.S. or Canada.

Application Requirements: Application, essay, references, test scores, transcript, certificate of disability. *Fee:* $8. *Deadline:* varies.

Contact: Scholarship Committee
College Women's Association of Japan
2-24-13-1202 Kami-Osaki, Shinagawa-ku
Tokyo 141-0021
Japan
Phone: 81 03 3491 2091
Fax: 81 03 3491 2092
E-mail: scholarship@cwaj.org

SCHOLARSHIP FOR THE VISUALLY IMPAIRED TO STUDY IN JAPAN

Scholarship for visually impaired Japanese or permanent resident students for graduate or undergraduate study in Japan. Former recipients of CWAJ awards and members of CWAJ are ineligible. Award Value is JPY2.0 million. Deadline on or between November 1 and November 30.

Award: Scholarship for use in junior, senior, or graduate years; not renewable. *Number:* 1.

Eligibility Requirements: Applicant must be of Japanese heritage and Japanese citizen and enrolled or expecting to enroll full-time at a four-year institution or university. Applicant must be visually impaired. Available to citizens of countries other than the U.S. or Canada.

Application Requirements: Application, essay, references, self-addressed stamped envelope, transcript, certificate of disability. *Fee:* $8. *Deadline:* November 30.

Contact: Scholarship Committee
College Women's Association of Japan
2-24-13-1202 Kami-Osaki, Shinagawa-ku
Tokyo 141-0021
Japan
Phone: 81 03 3491 2091
Fax: 81 03 3491 2092
E-mail: scholarship@cwaj.org

COMMITTEE OF TEN THOUSAND http://www.cott1.org

RACHEL WARNER SCHOLARSHIP

Scholarship for persons with any bleeding disorder. For educational use, both undergraduate and graduate studies. Scholarship amount and the number of available awards varies.

Award: Scholarship for use in freshman, sophomore, junior, senior, or graduate years; not renewable. *Number:* varies. *Amount:* up to $1000.

Eligibility Requirements: Applicant must be enrolled or expecting to enroll full- or part-time at a two-year or four-year or technical institution or university. Applicant must be physically disabled. Available to U.S. citizens.

Application Requirements: Application, essay, references. *Deadline:* May 1.

Contact: Scholarship Coordinator
Committee of Ten Thousand
236 Massachusetts Avenue, NE, Suite 609
Washington, DC 20002
Phone: 800-488-2688
Fax: 202-543-6720
E-mail: cott-dc@earthlink.net

COUNCIL FOR INTERNATIONAL EDUCATIONAL EXCHANGE http://www.ciee.org

ROBERT B. BAILEY III MINORITY SCHOLARSHIPS FOR EDUCATION ABROAD

One-time award for students from underrepresented groups in study abroad participating in Council for International Educational Exchange (CIEE)-administered overseas program. Deadlines: April 1 and November 1. Applicant must be self-identified as belonging to an underrepresented group in study abroad.

Award: Scholarship for use in freshman, sophomore, junior, or senior years; not renewable. *Number:* 15. *Amount:* $500–$2000.

Eligibility Requirements: Applicant must be American Indian/Alaska Native, Asian/Pacific Islander, Black (non-Hispanic), or Hispanic and enrolled or expecting to enroll full-time at a four-year institution or university. Applicant must be hearing impaired, learning disabled, physically disabled, or visually impaired. Applicant must have 3.5 GPA or higher. Available to U.S. citizens.

Application Requirements: Application, essay, financial need analysis, references, transcript. *Deadline:* varies.

Contact: Chris Wilson, Grant Programs Manager
Council for International Educational Exchange
300 Fore Street
Portland, ME 04101
Phone: 800-448-9944 Ext. 4117
Fax: 207-553-4299
E-mail: scholarships@ciee.org

COURAGE CENTER, VOCATIONAL SERVICES DEPARTMENT http://www.courage.org

SCHOLARSHIP FOR PEOPLE WITH DISABILITIES

Award provides financial assistance to students with sensory or physical disabilities. May reapply each year. Applicant must be pursuing educational goals or technical expertise beyond high school. Must be U.S. citizen and resident of Minnesota, or participate in Courage Center Services. Indication of extracurricular work and volunteer history must be submitted along with application form.

Award: Scholarship for use in freshman, sophomore, junior, or senior years; not renewable. *Number:* 15–19. *Amount:* $500–$1000.

Eligibility Requirements: Applicant must be enrolled or expecting to enroll full-time at a two-year or four-year or technical institution or university and resident of Minnesota. Applicant must be hearing impaired, physically disabled, or visually impaired. Available to U.S. citizens.

Application Requirements: Application, essay, financial need analysis, interview. *Deadline:* May 31.

Contact: Nancy Robinow, Administrative Assistant
Courage Center, Vocational Services Department
3915 Golden Valley Road
Golden Valley, MN 55422-4298
Phone: 763-520-0553
Fax: 763-520-0861
E-mail: nrobinow@courage.org

CYSTIC FIBROSIS SCHOLARSHIP FOUNDATION

http://www.cfscholarship.org

CYSTIC FIBROSIS SCHOLARSHIP

One-time $1000 to $10,000 scholarships for young adults with cystic fibrosis to be used to further their education after high school. Awards may be used for tuition, books, and fees. Students may reapply in subsequent years.

Award: Scholarship for use in freshman, sophomore, junior, or senior years; not renewable. *Number:* 40–50. *Amount:* $1000–$10,000.

Eligibility Requirements: Applicant must be enrolled or expecting to enroll full-time at a two-year or four-year or technical institution or university. Applicant must be physically disabled. Available to U.S. citizens.

Application Requirements: Application, essay, financial need analysis, references, test scores, transcript. *Deadline:* March 21.

Contact: Mary K. Bottorff, President
Cystic Fibrosis Scholarship Foundation
2814 Grant Street
Evanston, IL 60201
Phone: 847-328-0127
Fax: 847-328-0127
E-mail: mkbcfsf@aol.com

DISABLEDPERSON INC. COLLEGE SCHOLARSHIP

http://www.disabledperson.com

DISABLEDPERSON INC. COLLEGE SCHOLARSHIP AWARD

Essay contest for disabled persons who are enrolled as full-time students in a two- or four-year accredited college or university. Length of the essay must not exceed 1000 words.

Award: Prize for use in freshman, sophomore, junior, or senior years; not renewable. *Number:* up to 1. *Amount:* up to $750.

Eligibility Requirements: Applicant must be enrolled or expecting to enroll full-time at a two-year or four-year institution or university and must have an interest in writing. Applicant must be hearing impaired, learning disabled, physically disabled, or visually impaired. Available to U.S. citizens.

Application Requirements: Application, applicant must enter a contest, essay, transcript, proof of disability. *Deadline:* varies.

Contact: Diana Corso, Executive Director
disABLEDperson Inc. College Scholarship
PO Box 230636
Encinitas, CA 92023-0636
Phone: 760-420-1269
Fax: 760-753-2954
E-mail: disabledpersons@aol.com

EAR FOUNDATION MINNIE PEARL SCHOLARSHIP PROGRAM

http://www.earfoundation.org

MINNIE PEARL SCHOLARSHIP PROGRAM

Renewable scholarship for full-time college students with a severe to profound bilateral hearing loss. Initially, recipients must be high school seniors with at least a 3.0 GPA. Renewals based upon maintenance of GPA.

Award: Scholarship for use in freshman year; renewable. *Number:* 1–5. *Amount:* $2500.

Eligibility Requirements: Applicant must be high school student and planning to enroll or expecting to enroll full-time at a two-year or four-year or technical institution or university. Applicant must be hearing impaired. Applicant must have 3.0 GPA or higher. Available to U.S. citizens.

Application Requirements: Application, essay, photo, references, self-addressed stamped envelope, transcript. *Deadline:* February 15.

Contact: Amy Nielsen, Scholarship Coordinator
Ear Foundation Minnie Pearl Scholarship Program
955 Woodland Street
Nashville, TN 37203
Phone: 615-627-2724
Fax: 615-627-2728
E-mail: amy@earfoundation.org

EASTERN AMPUTEE GOLF ASSOCIATION

http://www.eaga.org

EASTERN AMPUTEE GOLF ASSOCIATION SCHOLARSHIP FUND

Six $1000 college scholarships are available to any EAGA amputee member and/or a member of his or her family. Award recipients do not need to be in attendance. Award covers each of the four school years depending on when applications are accepted. Award recipient must maintain a 2.0 GPA.

Award: Scholarship for use in freshman, sophomore, junior, or senior years; renewable. *Number:* 6. *Amount:* $1000.

Eligibility Requirements: Applicant must be enrolled or expecting to enroll full-time at a four-year institution or university. Applicant must be physically disabled. Available to U.S. and Canadian citizens.

Application Requirements: Application, autobiography, essay, financial need analysis, resume, transcript, SAR. *Deadline:* June 25.

Contact: Bob Buck, Secretary
Eastern Amputee Golf Association
2015 Amherst Drive
Bethlehem, PA 18015-5606
Phone: 888-868-0992
Fax: 610-867-9295
E-mail: info@eaga.org

EDMONTON COMMUNITY FOUNDATION

http://www.DollarsForLearners.com

CHARMAINE LETOURNEAU SCHOLARSHIP

Annual award to a deaf or hard of hearing person who will attend an academic or training program at a qualified postsecondary institution. Must be resident of Alberta at time of application. The amount of the award varies each year.

Award: Prize for use in freshman, sophomore, junior, senior, or graduate years; renewable. *Number:* 1. *Amount:* $1200.

Eligibility Requirements: Applicant must be Canadian citizen; enrolled or expecting to enroll full-time at a four-year institution or university; resident of Alberta and studying in Alberta. Applicant must be hearing impaired.

Application Requirements: Application, financial need analysis, references, transcript, personal letter, medical documentation of hearing loss. *Deadline:* May 31.

Contact: Craig Stumpf-Allen, Associate Director, Scholarships
Edmonton Community Foundation
9910-103 Street, NW
Edmonton, AB T5K 2V7
Canada
Phone: 780-426-0015
Fax: 780-425-0121
E-mail: info@dollarsforlearners.com

EPILEPSY FOUNDATION OF IDAHO

http://www.epilepsyidaho.org

GREGORY W. GILE MEMORIAL SCHOLARSHIP PROGRAM

Scholarship of $1000 to $1500 awarded to a graduate of an Idaho high school who is entering or continuing school and pursuing an academic or vocational undergraduate degree or certificate. Must be a resident of Idaho.

Award: Scholarship for use in freshman, sophomore, junior, or senior years; not renewable. *Number:* 1. *Amount:* $1000–$1500.

Eligibility Requirements: Applicant must be enrolled or expecting to enroll full-time at a two-year or four-year or technical institution or university and resident of Idaho. Applicant must be physically disabled. Available to U.S. citizens.

Application Requirements: Application, essay, references, doctor's statement. *Deadline:* March 15.

Contact: David Blackwell, Executive Director
Epilepsy Foundation of Idaho
310 West Idaho Street
Boise, ID 83702
Phone: 208-344-4340 Ext. 12
Fax: 208-343-0093
E-mail: efid@epilepsyidaho.org

MARK MUSIC MEMORIAL SCHOLARSHIP

One-time award of $500 to promote educational opportunities for Idaho residents with epilepsy. Applicant must be a high school graduate or hold an equivalent certificate, and be either entering or continuing school and pursuing an academic or vocational undergraduate degree or certificate.

Award: Scholarship for use in freshman, sophomore, junior, or senior years; not renewable. *Number:* 1. *Amount:* $500.

Eligibility Requirements: Applicant must be enrolled or expecting to enroll full-time at a two-year or four-year or technical institution or university and resident of Idaho. Applicant must be physically disabled. Available to U.S. citizens.

Application Requirements: Application, essay, references, doctor's statement. *Deadline:* March 15.

Contact: Executive Director
Epilepsy Foundation of Idaho
310 West Idaho Street
Boise, ID 83702

FACTOR SUPPORT NETWORK http://www.factorsupport.com

MIKE HYLTON AND RON NIEDERMAN MEMORIAL SCHOLARSHIPS

One-time scholarship for men with hemophilia or von Willebrand Disease and their immediate family members. Must be attending or entering a college, university, trade or technical school, either full-time or part-time. Only U.S. residents are eligible.

Award: Scholarship for use in freshman, sophomore, junior, or senior years; not renewable. *Number:* 5. *Amount:* $1000.

Eligibility Requirements: Applicant must be enrolled or expecting to enroll full- or part-time at a two-year or four-year or technical institution or university and male. Applicant must be physically disabled. Available to U.S. citizens.

Application Requirements: Application, essay, references, proof of diagnosis from physician. *Deadline:* April 30.

Contact: Scholarship Committee
Factor Support Network
900 Avenida Acaso, Suite A
Camarillo, CA 93012-8749
Fax: 805-482-6324
E-mail: scholarships@factorsupport.com

MILLIE GONZALEZ MEMORIAL SCHOLARSHIP

Scholarship for women with hemophilia or von Willebrand Disease who are attending or entering a college, university, trade or technical school, either full-time or part-time. Must be U.S. resident.

Award: Scholarship for use in freshman, sophomore, junior, senior, or graduate years; not renewable. *Number:* 2. *Amount:* $1000.

Eligibility Requirements: Applicant must be enrolled or expecting to enroll full- or part-time at a two-year or four-year or technical institution or university and female. Applicant must be physically disabled. Available to U.S. citizens.

Application Requirements: Application, essay, references, proof of diagnosis from physician. *Deadline:* April 30.

Contact: Scholarship Committee
Factor Support Network
900 Avenida Acaso, Suite A
Camarillo, CA 93012-8749
Fax: 805-482-6324
E-mail: scholarships@factorsupport.com

GREAT LAKES HEMOPHILIA FOUNDATION http://www.glhf.org

GLHF INDIVIDUAL CLASS SCHOLARSHIP

Scholarship available to members of the Wisconsin bleeding disorder community, individuals with a bleeding disorder and their immediate families. Provides funding assistance for tuition and enrollment fees relevant to continuing education in a non-traditional or non-degree format.

Award: Scholarship for use in freshman, sophomore, junior, or senior years; not renewable. *Number:* 1. *Amount:* up to $500.

Eligibility Requirements: Applicant must be enrolled or expecting to enroll full- or part-time at a two-year or four-year or technical institution or university and resident of Wisconsin. Applicant must be physically disabled. Available to U.S. citizens.

Application Requirements: Application, essay, references, transcript. *Deadline:* varies.

Contact: Karin Koppen, Program Services Coordinator
Great Lakes Hemophilia Foundation
638 North 18 Street, Suite 108
Milwaukee, WI 53233
Phone: 414-257-0200
Fax: 414-257-1225
E-mail: kkoppen@glhf.org

GREAT LAKES HEMOPHILIA FOUNDATION EDUCATION SCHOLARSHIP

This scholarship not only targets the traditional college and vocational students, but also looks at retraining adults with bleeding disorders who are finding it difficult to function in their chosen field because of health complications. It also targets parents of children with bleeding disorders who through career advancement can better meet the financial needs of caring for their child.

Award: Scholarship for use in freshman, sophomore, junior, senior, graduate, or postgraduate years; not renewable. *Number:* 5–6. *Amount:* $500–$2000.

Eligibility Requirements: Applicant must be enrolled or expecting to enroll full- or part-time at a two-year or four-year or technical institution or university and resident of Wisconsin. Applicant must be physically disabled. Available to U.S. citizens.

Application Requirements: Application, essay, references, transcript. *Deadline:* May 1.

Contact: Karin Koppen, Program Services Coordinator
Great Lakes Hemophilia Foundation
638 North 18 Street, Suite 108
Milwaukee, WI 53233
Phone: 414-257-0200
Fax: 414-257-1225
E-mail: kkoppen@glhf.org

HEMOPHILIA FEDERATION OF AMERICA http://www.hemophiliaed.org

ARTISTIC ENCOURAGEMENT GRANT

Grant available for an individual with hemophilia or von Willebrand (VWD). Award may be used for mounting an exhibition of applicant's artistic work, publishing a story/ book or animation, writing a play, holding a recital, or any kind of creative endeavor.

Award: Grant for use in freshman, sophomore, junior, senior, graduate, or postgraduate years; not renewable. *Number:* 1. *Amount:* $1500.

Eligibility Requirements: Applicant must be enrolled or expecting to enroll full- or part-time at a two-year or four-year or technical institution or university and must have an interest in art, theater, or writing. Applicant must be physically disabled. Available to U.S. citizens.

Application Requirements: Application, essay, financial need analysis, portfolio, references, brief summary of project, timeline. *Deadline:* April 30.

Contact: Scholarship Committee
Hemophilia Federation of America
1405 West Pinhook Road, Suite 101
Lafayette, LA 70503
Phone: 337-261-9787
E-mail: info@hemophiliafed.org

HEMOPHILIA FEDERATION OF AMERICA EDUCATIONAL SCHOLARSHIP

One-time scholarship for persons with hemophilia, attending either full-time or part-time in any accredited two- or four-year college, university, or vocation/ technical school in the United States.

Award: Scholarship for use in freshman, sophomore, junior, or senior years; not renewable. *Number:* 1–3. *Amount:* $1500.

Eligibility Requirements: Applicant must be enrolled or expecting to enroll full- or part-time at a two-year or four-year or technical institution or university. Applicant must be physically disabled. Available to U.S. citizens.

Hemophilia Federation of America (continued)

Application Requirements: Application, essay, financial need analysis, references. *Deadline:* April 30.

Contact: Scholarship Committee
Hemophilia Federation of America
1405 West Pinhook Road, Suite 101
Lafayette, LA 70503
Phone: 337-261-9787
E-mail: info@hemophiliafed.org

HEMOPHILIA FOUNDATION OF MICHIGAN http://www.hfmich.org

HEMOPHILIA FOUNDATION OF MICHIGAN ACADEMIC SCHOLARSHIP

Scholarship for individuals or immediate family members, with hemophilia or other inherited bleeding disorder and residing in Michigan. Must be pursuing education in accredited colleges or universities in the United States.

Award: Scholarship for use in freshman, sophomore, junior, or senior years; not renewable. *Number:* 3. *Amount:* $1500–$2000.

Eligibility Requirements: Applicant must be enrolled or expecting to enroll full- or part-time at a two-year or four-year or technical institution or university. Applicant must be physically disabled. Available to U.S. citizens.

Application Requirements: Application. *Deadline:* March 14.

Contact: Academic Scholarship Committee
Hemophilia Foundation of Michigan
1921 West Michigan
Ypsilanti, MI 48197
Phone: 734-544-0015
E-mail: hfm@hfmich.org

HEMOPHILIA FOUNDATION OF SOUTHERN CALIFORNIA http://www.hemosocal.org

CHRISTOPHER MARK PITKIN MEMORIAL SCHOLARSHIP

Scholarship open to all members of the hemophilia community, including spouses and siblings. Applicants must be pursuing a college or technical/trade school education.

Award: Scholarship for use in freshman, sophomore, junior, or senior years; not renewable. *Number:* 2. *Amount:* $500–$1000.

Eligibility Requirements: Applicant must be enrolled or expecting to enroll full- or part-time at a two-year or four-year or technical institution or university. Applicant must be physically disabled. Available to U.S. citizens.

Application Requirements: Application, references. *Deadline:* July 25.

Contact: Scholarship Coordinator
Hemophilia Foundation of Southern California
6720 Melrose Avenue
Hollywood, CA 90038
Phone: 323-525-0440
E-mail: ofcmgr@hemosocal.org

HEMOPHILIA HEALTH SERVICES http://www.hemophiliahealth.com

HEMOPHILIA HEALTH SERVICES MEMORIAL SCHOLARSHIP

Award to U.S. citizens with hemophilia and related bleeding disorders. Applicants must be high school seniors, college freshmen, sophomores, or juniors. Also eligible to apply are college seniors who are planning to attend graduate school, or students who are already enrolled in graduate school.

Award: Scholarship for use in freshman, sophomore, junior, senior, graduate, or postgraduate years; not renewable. *Number:* 7–10. *Amount:* $1500–$2000.

Eligibility Requirements: Applicant must be enrolled or expecting to enroll full-time at a four-year institution or university. Applicant must be physically disabled. Available to U.S. citizens.

Application Requirements: Application, essay, financial need analysis, references, test scores, transcript, physician certification form. *Deadline:* May 1.

Contact: Sally Johnson, Manager Operations Support
Hemophilia Health Services
c/o Scholarship Program Administrators, Inc.
PO Box 23737
Nashville, TN 37202-3737
Phone: 615-850-5175
Fax: 615-352-2588
E-mail: scholarship@hemophiliahealth.com

IDAHO STATE BOARD OF EDUCATION http://www.boardofed.idaho.gov

IDAHO MINORITY AND "AT RISK" STUDENT SCHOLARSHIP

Renewable award for Idaho residents who are disabled or members of a minority group and have financial need. Must attend one of eight postsecondary institutions in the state for undergraduate study. Deadlines vary by institution. Must be a U.S. citizen and be a graduate of an Idaho high school. Contact college financial aid office. The awards range up to $3000 a year for a maximum of four years.

Award: Scholarship for use in freshman, sophomore, junior, or senior years; renewable. *Number:* 35–40. *Amount:* up to $3000.

Eligibility Requirements: Applicant must be American Indian/Alaska Native, Asian/Pacific Islander, Black (non-Hispanic), or Hispanic; enrolled or expecting to enroll full-time at a two-year or four-year or technical institution or university; resident of Idaho and studying in Idaho. Applicant must be hearing impaired, physically disabled, or visually impaired. Available to U.S. citizens.

Application Requirements: Application, financial need analysis, transcript. *Deadline:* varies.

Contact: Dana Kelly, Program Manager
Idaho State Board of Education
PO Box 83720
Boise, ID 83720-0037
Phone: 208-332-1574
E-mail: dana.kelly@osbe.idaho.gov

ILLINOIS COUNCIL OF THE BLIND http://www.icbonline.org

FLOYD CARGILL SCHOLARSHIP

Award for a visually impaired Illinois resident attending or planning to attend an Illinois college. One-time award of $750.

Award: Scholarship for use in freshman, sophomore, junior, or senior years; not renewable. *Number:* 1. *Amount:* $750.

Eligibility Requirements: Applicant must be enrolled or expecting to enroll full-time at a two-year or four-year or technical institution or university; resident of Illinois and studying in Illinois. Applicant must be visually impaired. Applicant must have 2.5 GPA or higher. Available to U.S. citizens.

Application Requirements: Application, autobiography, references, test scores, transcript. *Deadline:* June 15.

Contact: Maggie Uorich, Office Manager
Illinois Council of the Blind
PO Box 1336
Springfield, IL 62705-1336
Phone: 217-523-4967
E-mail: icb@icbonline.org

IMMUNE DEFICIENCY FOUNDATION http://www.primaryimmune.org

IMMUNE DEFICIENCY FOUNDATION SCHOLARSHIP

One-time award available to individuals diagnosed with a primary immune deficiency disease. Must submit medical verification of diagnosis. Available for study at the undergraduate level at any postsecondary institution. Must be U.S. citizen.

Award: Scholarship for use in freshman, sophomore, junior, or senior years; not renewable. *Number:* 30–40. *Amount:* $750–$2000.

Eligibility Requirements: Applicant must be enrolled or expecting to enroll full- or part-time at a two-year or four-year or technical institution or university. Applicant must be physically disabled. Available to U.S. citizens.

Application Requirements: Application, autobiography, essay, financial need analysis, references, medical verification of diagnosis. *Deadline:* March 31.

Contact: Diana Gill, Director of Patient Programs
Immune Deficiency Foundation
40 West Chesapeake Avenue, Suite 308
Towson, MD 21204
Phone: 800-296-4433 Ext. 2545
Fax: 410-321-9165
E-mail: dgill@primaryimmune.org

IOWA DIVISION OF VOCATIONAL REHABILITATION SERVICES http://www.ivrs.iowa.gov

IOWA VOCATIONAL REHABILITATION

Provides vocational rehabilitation services to individuals with disabilities who need these services in order to maintain, retain, or obtain employment compatible with their disabilities. Must be Iowa resident.

Award: Grant for use in freshman, sophomore, junior, senior, graduate, or postgraduate years; renewable. *Number:* 4000. *Amount:* $4000.

Eligibility Requirements: Applicant must be enrolled or expecting to enroll full- or part-time at a two-year or four-year or technical institution or university and resident of Iowa. Applicant must be hearing impaired, learning disabled, physically disabled, or visually impaired. Available to U.S. and non-U.S. citizens.

Application Requirements: Application, interview. *Deadline:* varies.

Contact: Ralph Childers, Policy and Workforce Initiatives Coordinator
Iowa Division of Vocational Rehabilitation Services
510 East 12th Street
Des Moines, IA 50319
Phone: 515-281-4151
Fax: 515-281-4703
E-mail: ralph.childers@iowa.gov

JAY'S WORLD CHILDHOOD CANCER FOUNDATION http://www.jaysworld.org

JAY'S WORLD CHILDHOOD CANCER FOUNDATION SCHOLARSHIP

Scholarship for a student either cured of cancer, in remission, or able to attend college while undergoing treatment. Must be a graduating high school senior and a New York State resident.

Award: Scholarship for use in freshman year; not renewable. *Number:* varies. *Amount:* varies.

Eligibility Requirements: Applicant must be high school student; planning to enroll or expecting to enroll full- or part-time at a four-year institution or university and resident of New York. Applicant must be physically disabled. Available to U.S. citizens.

Application Requirements: Application, references, transcript, current 1040 tax form, letter from the oncologist. *Deadline:* April 15.

Contact: Jason Napolitano, President
Jay's World Childhood Cancer Foundation
825 East Gate Boulevard, Suite 100
PO Box 173
Garden City, NY 11530
Phone: 516-297-5328
E-mail: info@jaysworld.org

JEWISH GUILD FOR THE BLIND http://www.jgb.org

GUILDSCHOLAR AWARD

Annual scholarship program for college-bound high school students who are legally blind. Applications will be accepted from students at the end of the junior year.

Award: Scholarship for use in freshman year; not renewable. *Number:* up to 15. *Amount:* up to $15,000.

Eligibility Requirements: Applicant must be high school student and planning to enroll or expecting to enroll full-time at a four-year institution or university. Applicant must be visually impaired. Applicant must have 3.0 GPA or higher. Available to U.S. citizens.

Application Requirements: Application, essay, references, test scores, transcript, proof of legal blindness, proof of U.S. citizenship or legal residency, personal statement. *Deadline:* July 1.

Contact: Gordon Rovins, Director of Special Programs
Jewish Guild for the Blind
15 West 65th Street
New York, NY 10023
Phone: 212-769-7801
Fax: 212-769-6266
E-mail: rovinsg@jgb.org

KENTUCKY DEPARTMENT OF VOCATIONAL REHABILITATION http://ovr.ky.gov

KENTUCKY OFFICE OF VOCATIONAL REHABILITATION

Grant provides services necessary to secure employment. Eligible individual must possess physical or mental impairment that results in a substantial impediment to employment; benefit from vocational rehabilitation services in terms of an employment outcome; and require vocational rehabilitation services to prepare for, enter, or retain employment.

Award: Grant for use in freshman, sophomore, junior, senior, graduate, or postgraduate years; renewable. *Number:* varies. *Amount:* varies.

Eligibility Requirements: Applicant must be enrolled or expecting to enroll full- or part-time at a two-year or four-year or technical institution or university. Applicant must be learning disabled or physically disabled. Available to U.S. citizens.

Application Requirements: Application, financial need analysis, interview, transcript, proof of disability. *Deadline:* continuous.

Contact: Charles Tuckett, Program Administrator
Kentucky Department of Vocational Rehabilitation
209 Saint Clair Street
Frankfort, KY 40601
Phone: 502-595-3423
Fax: 502-564-6745
E-mail: marianu.spencer@mail.state.ky.us

LAWRENCE MADEIROS MEMORIAL SCHOLARSHIP http://www.adirondackspintacular.com

LAWRENCE MADEIROS MEMORIAL SCHOLARSHIP

Award to a high school student with bleeding disorder or other chronic disorder. Applicant must have applied to and been accepted at an accredited college or university and must be graduating high school in the year of the scholarship award.

Award: Scholarship for use in freshman year; not renewable. *Number:* 1. *Amount:* $1000.

Eligibility Requirements: Applicant must be high school student and planning to enroll or expecting to enroll full- or part-time at a two-year or four-year institution or university. Applicant must be physically disabled. Available to U.S. citizens.

Application Requirements: Application, interview. *Deadline:* June 1.

Contact: Carol Madeiros, Scholarship Committee
Lawrence Madeiros Memorial Scholarship
PO Box 11
Mayfield, NY 12117
Phone: 518-661-6005
Fax: 518-863-6126
E-mail: carol@adirondackspintacular.com

LIGHTHOUSE INTERNATIONAL http://www.lighthouse.org

SCHOLARSHIP AWARDS

One-time award designed to reward excellence, recognize accomplishments, and to help students who are blind or partially sighted achieve their career goals. There are 4 categories: college bound, undergraduate, graduate, adult undergraduate II. Students must be legally blind, U.S. citizens, enrolled in an accredited program of study. Applicants must be a resident of and attend school in New England, New York, New Jersey, Pennsylvania, Delaware, Maryland or Washington, DC.

Award: Prize for use in freshman, sophomore, junior, senior, or graduate years; not renewable. *Number:* up to 4. *Amount:* up to $5000.

Lighthouse International (continued)

Eligibility Requirements: Applicant must be enrolled or expecting to enroll full-time at a two-year or four-year institution or university; resident of Connecticut, Delaware, District of Columbia, Florida, Maine, Maryland, Massachusetts, New Hampshire, New Jersey, New York, North Carolina, Pennsylvania, Rhode Island, Vermont, or West Virginia and studying in Connecticut, Delaware, District of Columbia, Florida, Maine, Maryland, Massachusetts, New Hampshire, New Jersey, New York, North Carolina, or Pennsylvania. Applicant must be visually impaired. Available to U.S. citizens.

Application Requirements: Application, essay, references, transcript, proof of U.S. citizenship, proof of legal blindness. *Deadline:* March 28.

Contact: Rowena Saunders, Vice President of Volunteer Services
Lighthouse International
111 East 59th Street
New York, NY 10022-1202
Phone: 212-821-9405
Fax: 212-821-9707
E-mail: rsaunders@lighthouse.org

LILLY REINTEGRATION PROGRAMS http://www.reintegration.com

LILLY REINTEGRATION SCHOLARSHIP

Scholarships available to students diagnosed with schizophrenia, bi-polar, schizophreniform, or a schizoaffective disorder. Must be currently receiving medical treatment for the disease, including medications and psychiatric follow-up. Must also be U.S. citizen and actively involved in rehabilitative or reintegration efforts. Applicants must be at least 18 years of age.

Award: Scholarship for use in freshman, sophomore, junior, senior, graduate, or postgraduate years; not renewable. *Number:* 70–100. *Amount:* $2500–$5000.

Eligibility Requirements: Applicant must be age 18 and over and enrolled or expecting to enroll full- or part-time at a two-year or four-year or technical institution or university. Applicant must be physically disabled. Available to U.S. citizens.

Application Requirements: Application, essay, references, transcript. *Deadline:* January 25.

Contact: Lilly Secretariat
Lilly Reintegration Programs
310 Busse Highway, PO Box 327
Park Ridge, IL 60068-3251
Phone: 800-809-8202
E-mail: lillyscholarships@reintegration.com

MOBILITY INTERNATIONAL USA http://www.miusa.org

US COSTA RICA DISABILITY RIGHTS EXCHANGE PROGRAM

A grant of $2000 is available for graduate or undergraduate students within the age 18 and 24. Only students having any kind of disability are eligible. A non refundable application fee of $20 is required.

Award: Grant for use in freshman, sophomore, junior, senior, or graduate years; not renewable. *Number:* 12. *Amount:* $2000.

Eligibility Requirements: Applicant must be age 18-24 and enrolled or expecting to enroll full- or part-time at a two-year or four-year or technical institution or university. Applicant must be hearing impaired, learning disabled, physically disabled, or visually impaired. Available to U.S. citizens.

Application Requirements: Application, references. *Fee:* $20. *Deadline:* March 28.

Contact: Jamie Kinsel, Program Assistant
Mobility International USA
132 East Broadway, Suite 343
Eugene, OR 97401
Phone: 541-343-1284
Fax: 541-343-6812
E-mail: jkinsel@miusa.org

NATIONAL CENTER FOR LEARNING DISABILITIES INC. http://www.ld.org

ANNE FORD SCHOLARSHIP

Award of $10,000 given to a high school senior of high merit with an identified learning disability who is pursuing a college degree. The ideal candidate is a person who has faced the challenges of having a learning disability and who, through perseverance and academic endeavor, has created a life of purpose and achievement.

Award: Scholarship for use in freshman, sophomore, junior, or senior years; not renewable. *Number:* 1. *Amount:* $10,000.

Eligibility Requirements: Applicant must be high school student and planning to enroll or expecting to enroll full-time at a four-year institution or university. Applicant must be learning disabled. Applicant must have 3.0 GPA or higher. Available to U.S. citizens.

Application Requirements: Application, essay, financial need analysis, references, test scores, transcript. *Deadline:* December 31.

Contact: Katie Reilly, Coordinator
National Center for Learning Disabilities Inc.
381 Park Avenue South, Suite 1401
New York, NY 10016-8806
Phone: 212-545-7510 Ext. 233
Fax: 212-545-9665

NATIONAL COUNCIL OF JEWISH WOMEN NEW YORK SECTION http://www.ncjwny.org

JACKSON-STRICKS SCHOLARSHIP

Scholarship provides financial aid to a physically challenged person for academic study or vocational training that leads to independent living.

Award: Scholarship for use in freshman, sophomore, junior, senior, or graduate years; not renewable. *Number:* varies. *Amount:* varies.

Eligibility Requirements: Applicant must be enrolled or expecting to enroll full- or part-time at a two-year or four-year institution or university and resident of New York. Applicant must be physically disabled. Available to U.S. citizens.

Application Requirements: Application, essay, references, transcript. *Deadline:* April 18.

Contact: Scholarship Committee
National Council of Jewish Women New York Section
820 Second Avenue
New York, NY 10017
Phone: 212-687-5030
Fax: 212-687-5032

NATIONAL FEDERATION OF THE BLIND http://www.nfb.org

CHARLES AND MELVA T. OWEN MEMORIAL SCHOLARSHIP
• *See page 604*

E. U. PARKER SCHOLARSHIP
• *See page 604*

HERMIONE GRANT CALHOUN SCHOLARSHIP
• *See page 605*

JENNICA FERGUSON MEMORIAL SCHOLARSHIP
• *See page 605*

KENNETH JERNIGAN SCHOLARSHIP
• *See page 605*

KUCHLER-KILLIAN MEMORIAL SCHOLARSHIP
• *See page 605*

NATIONAL FEDERATION OF THE BLIND SCHOLARSHIPS
• *See page 605*

NATIONAL FEDERATION OF THE BLIND OF CALIFORNIA http://www.nfbcal.org

GERALD DRAKE MEMORIAL SCHOLARSHIP

One-time award for legally blind students pursuing an undergraduate or graduate degree. Must be a California resident and full-time student.

Award: Scholarship for use in freshman, sophomore, junior, senior, or graduate years; not renewable. *Number:* up to 5. *Amount:* $1500.

Eligibility Requirements: Applicant must be enrolled or expecting to enroll full-time at a four-year institution or university and resident of California. Applicant must be visually impaired. Available to U.S. and non-U.S. citizens.

Application Requirements: Application. *Deadline:* March 31.

Contact: Robert Stigile, President
National Federation of the Blind of California
5530 Corbin Avenue, Suite 313
Tarzana, CA 91356
Phone: 818-342-6524
Fax: 818-344-7930
E-mail: nfbcal@yahoo.com

JULIE LANDUCCI SCHOLARSHIP

Award for legally blind students pursuing an undergraduate or graduate degree. Must be a California resident and full-time student. Award available to U.S. citizens.

Award: Scholarship for use in freshman, sophomore, junior, senior, or graduate years; renewable. *Number:* 1. *Amount:* up to $2000.

Eligibility Requirements: Applicant must be enrolled or expecting to enroll full-time at a four-year institution or university and resident of California. Applicant must be visually impaired. Available to U.S. citizens.

Application Requirements: Application. *Deadline:* March 31.

Contact: Robert Stigile, President
National Federation of the Blind of California
5530 Corbin Avenue, Suite 313
Tarzana, CA 91356
Phone: 818-342-6524
Fax: 818-344-7930
E-mail: nfbcal@yahoo.com

LA VYRL "PINKY" JOHNSON MEMORIAL SCHOLARSHIP

One-time award up to $2000 for legally blind students pursuing an undergraduate or graduate degree. Must be a California resident and full-time student.

Award: Scholarship for use in freshman, sophomore, junior, senior, or graduate years; renewable. *Number:* 1. *Amount:* $2000.

Eligibility Requirements: Applicant must be enrolled or expecting to enroll full-time at a four-year institution or university and resident of California. Applicant must be visually impaired. Available to U.S. citizens.

Application Requirements: Application. *Deadline:* March 31.

Contact: Robert Stigile, President
National Federation of the Blind of California
5530 Corbin Avenue, Suite 313
Tarzana, CA 91356
Phone: 818-342-6524
Fax: 818-344-7930
E-mail: nfbcal@yahoo.com

LAWRENCE "MUZZY" MARCELINO MEMORIAL SCHOLARSHIP

Scholarship provides financial assistance for graduate or undergraduate education to blind students in California. Any legally blind student may apply for a scholarship but must attend the convention of the National Federation of the Blind of California. Selection is based first on academic merit and second on financial need.

Award: Scholarship for use in freshman, sophomore, junior, senior, or graduate years; renewable. *Number:* up to 4. *Amount:* $1500.

Eligibility Requirements: Applicant must be enrolled or expecting to enroll full-time at a four-year institution or university and resident of California. Applicant must be visually impaired. Available to U.S. citizens.

Application Requirements: Application. *Deadline:* March 15.

Contact: Robert Stigile, President
National Federation of the Blind of California
5530 Corbin Avenue, Suite 313
Tarzana, CA 91356
Phone: 818-342-6524
Fax: 818-344-7930
E-mail: nfbcal@yahoo.com

NATIONAL FEDERATION OF THE BLIND OF CALIFORNIA MERIT SCHOLARSHIPS

Scholarships to qualified blind students pursuing undergraduate or graduate studies in order to achieve an academic degree. This opportunity is also available to high school seniors preparing to enter undergraduate programs.

Award: Scholarship for use in freshman, sophomore, junior, senior, or graduate years; renewable. *Number:* up to 5. *Amount:* $1000.

Eligibility Requirements: Applicant must be enrolled or expecting to enroll full-time at a four-year institution or university and resident of California. Applicant must be visually impaired. Available to U.S. citizens.

Application Requirements: Application. *Deadline:* March 15.

Contact: Robert Stigile, President
National Federation of the Blind of California
5530 Corbin Avenue, Suite 313
Tarzana, CA 91356
Phone: 818-342-6524
Fax: 818-344-7930
E-mail: nfbcal@yahoo.com

NATIONAL FEDERATION OF THE BLIND OF CONNECTICUT http://www.nfbct.org

C. RODNEY DEMAREST MEMORIAL SCHOLARSHIP

Scholarship of $3000 awarded for graduating high school senior or college student residing or attending school full-time in Connecticut. Applicant must be legally blind.

Award: Scholarship for use in freshman, sophomore, junior, or senior years; not renewable. *Number:* 1. *Amount:* $3000.

Eligibility Requirements: Applicant must be enrolled or expecting to enroll full-time at a two-year or four-year or technical institution or university; resident of Connecticut and studying in Connecticut. Applicant must be visually impaired. Available to U.S. citizens.

Application Requirements: Application, references, transcript, state officer letter. *Deadline:* September 15.

Contact: Scholarship Committee
National Federation of the Blind of Connecticut
477 Connecticut Boulevard, Suite 217
East Hartford, CT 06108
Phone: 860-289-1971
Fax: 860-291-2795
E-mail: info@nfbct.org

DORIS E. HIGLEY MEMORIAL SCHOLARSHIP

Scholarship of $6000 awarded for graduating high school senior or college student residing or attending school full-time in Connecticut. Applicant must be legally blind.

Award: Scholarship for use in freshman, sophomore, junior, or senior years; not renewable. *Number:* 1. *Amount:* $6000.

Eligibility Requirements: Applicant must be enrolled or expecting to enroll full-time at a two-year or four-year or technical institution or university; resident of Connecticut and studying in Connecticut. Applicant must be visually impaired. Available to U.S. citizens.

National Federation of the Blind of Connecticut (continued)

Application Requirements: Application, references, transcript, state officer letter. *Deadline:* September 15.

Contact: Scholarship Committee
National Federation of the Blind of Connecticut
477 Connecticut Boulevard, Suite 217
East Hartford, CT 06108
Phone: 860-289-1971
Fax: 860-291-2795
E-mail: info@nfbct.org

HOWARD E. MAY MEMORIAL SCHOLARSHIP

Scholarship of $6000 awarded for graduating high school senior or college student residing or attending school full-time in Connecticut. Applicant must be legally blind.

Award: Scholarship for use in freshman, sophomore, junior, or senior years; not renewable. *Number:* 1. *Amount:* $6000.

Eligibility Requirements: Applicant must be enrolled or expecting to enroll full-time at a two-year or four-year or technical institution or university; resident of Connecticut and studying in Connecticut. Applicant must be visually impaired. Available to U.S. citizens.

Application Requirements: Application, references, transcript, state officer letter. *Deadline:* September 15.

Contact: Scholarship Committee
National Federation of the Blind of Connecticut
477 Connecticut Boulevard, Suite 217
East Hartford, CT 06108
Phone: 860-289-1971
Fax: 860-291-2795
E-mail: info@nfbct.org

MARY MAIN MEMORIAL SCHOLARSHIP

Scholarship of $4000 awarded for graduating high school senior or college student residing or attending school full-time in Connecticut. Applicant must be legally blind.

Award: Scholarship for use in freshman, sophomore, junior, or senior years; not renewable. *Number:* 1. *Amount:* $4000.

Eligibility Requirements: Applicant must be enrolled or expecting to enroll full-time at a two-year or four-year or technical institution or university; resident of Connecticut and studying in Connecticut. Applicant must be visually impaired. Available to U.S. citizens.

Application Requirements: Application, references, transcript, state officer letter. *Deadline:* September 15.

Contact: Scholarship Committee
National Federation of the Blind of Connecticut
477 Connecticut Boulevard, Suite 217
East Hartford, CT 06108
Phone: 860-289-1971
Fax: 860-291-2795
E-mail: info@nfbct.org

NATIONAL FEDERATION OF THE BLIND OF MISSOURI
http://www.nfbmo.org

NATIONAL FEDERATION OF THE BLIND OF MISSOURI SCHOLARSHIPS TO LEGALLY BLIND STUDENTS

Awards are based on achievement, commitment to community, and financial need. Recipients must be legally blind. Amount of money each year available for program will vary.

Award: Scholarship for use in freshman, sophomore, junior, senior, graduate, or postgraduate years; not renewable. *Number:* up to 2. *Amount:* $500–$1500.

Eligibility Requirements: Applicant must be enrolled or expecting to enroll full- or part-time at a two-year or four-year or technical institution or university. Applicant must be visually impaired. Available to U.S. citizens.

Application Requirements: Application, autobiography, essay, financial need analysis, interview, references, transcript. *Deadline:* February 1.

Contact: Gary Wunder, President
National Federation of the Blind of Missouri
3910 Tropical Lane
Columbia, MO 65202
Phone: 573-874-1774
Fax: 573-442-5617
E-mail: president@nfbmo.org

NATIONAL HEMOPHILIA FOUNDATION
http://www.hemophilia.org

KEVIN CHILD SCHOLARSHIP

Scholarship for a person with hemophilia or von Willebrand disease. Must be a high school senior planning to attend college, university, or vocational school, or a college student already pursuing postsecondary education.

Award: Scholarship for use in freshman year; not renewable. *Number:* 1. *Amount:* $500–$1000.

Eligibility Requirements: Applicant must be high school student and planning to enroll or expecting to enroll full- or part-time at a two-year or four-year or technical institution or university. Applicant must be physically disabled. Available to U.S. citizens.

Application Requirements: Application. *Deadline:* June 27.

Contact: Renee LaBrew, Department of Finance, Administration and MIS
National Hemophilia Foundation
116 West 32nd Street, 11th Floor
New York, NY 10001-3212
Phone: 212-328-3700

NATIONAL KIDNEY FOUNDATION OF INDIANA INC.
http://www.kidneyindiana.org

LARRY SMOCK SCHOLARSHIP

Scholarship provides financial assistance for kidney dialysis and transplant patients to pursue post-secondary education. Applicant must be resident of Indiana over the age of 18. Must have a high school diploma or its equivalent.

Award: Scholarship for use in freshman, sophomore, junior, or senior years; renewable. *Number:* 2–6. *Amount:* $500–$1000.

Eligibility Requirements: Applicant must be age 18 and over; enrolled or expecting to enroll full- or part-time at a two-year or four-year or technical institution or university and resident of Indiana. Applicant must be physically disabled. Available to U.S. citizens.

Application Requirements: Application, references, transcript. *Deadline:* March 2.

Contact: Marilyn Winn, Program Director
National Kidney Foundation of Indiana Inc.
911 86th Street, Suite 100
Indianapolis, IN 46240-1840
Phone: 317-722-5640
Fax: 317-722-5650
E-mail: nkfi@myvine.com

NATIONAL MULTIPLE SCLEROSIS SOCIETY–MID AMERICA CHAPTER
http://www.msmidamerica.org

NATIONAL MULTIPLE SCLEROSIS SOCIETY MID AMERICA CHAPTER SCHOLARSHIP

Scholarships available from $1000 to $3000 to high school seniors and graduates (or GED) with MS, or who are children of people with MS. Must be attending a postsecondary school for the first time.

Award: Scholarship for use in freshman, sophomore, junior, or senior years; not renewable. *Number:* 100. *Amount:* $1000–$3000.

Eligibility Requirements: Applicant must be enrolled or expecting to enroll full- or part-time at a two-year or four-year or technical institution or university. Applicant must be physically disabled. Available to U.S. citizens.

Application Requirements: Application, autobiography, essay, financial need analysis, references, test scores, transcript. *Deadline:* January 15.

Contact: Director of Programs
National Multiple Sclerosis Society–Mid America Chapter
5442 Martway
Mission, KS 66205
Phone: 913-432-3926
Fax: 913-432-6912
E-mail: info@nmsskc.org

NATIONAL PKU NEWS http://www.pkunews.org

ROBERT GUTHRIE PKU SCHOLARSHIP AND AWARDS

Scholarship for persons with phenylketonuria (PKU) who are on a special diet for PKU treatment. Award is for full-time or part-time study at any accredited U.S. institution. Up to 12 scholarships of between $500 and $3500 are granted.

Award: Scholarship for use in freshman, sophomore, junior, senior, graduate, or postgraduate years; not renewable. *Number:* 6–12. *Amount:* $500–$3500.

Eligibility Requirements: Applicant must be enrolled or expecting to enroll full- or part-time at a two-year or four-year or technical institution or university. Applicant must be physically disabled. Available to U.S. and non-U.S. citizens.

Application Requirements: Application, autobiography, essay, photo, resume, references, test scores, transcript. *Deadline:* November 1.

Contact: Virginia Schuett, Director
National PKU News
6869 Woodlawn Avenue NE, Suite 116
Seattle, WA 98115-5469
Phone: 206-525-8140
Fax: 206-525-5023
E-mail: schuett@pkunews.org

NATIONAL UNION OF PUBLIC AND GENERAL EMPLOYEES http://www.nupge.ca

TERRY FOX MEMORIAL SCHOLARSHIP

• *See page 547*

NEW YORK STATE GRANGE http://www.nysgrange.com

CAROLINE KARK AWARD

• *See page 548*

NORTH CAROLINA DIVISION OF SERVICES FOR THE BLIND http://www.ncdhhs.gov

NORTH CAROLINA DIVISION OF SERVICES FOR THE BLIND REHABILITATION SERVICES

Financial assistance is available for North Carolina residents who are blind or visually impaired and who require vocational rehabilitation to help find employment. Tuition and other assistance provided based on need. Open to U.S. citizens and legal residents of United States. Applicants goal must be to work after receiving vocational services. To apply, contact the local DSB office and apply for vocational rehabilitation services.

Award: Scholarship for use in freshman, sophomore, junior, or senior years; renewable. *Number:* varies. *Amount:* varies.

Eligibility Requirements: Applicant must be enrolled or expecting to enroll full-time at a two-year or four-year or technical institution or university and resident of North Carolina. Applicant must be visually impaired. Available to U.S. citizens.

Application Requirements: Application, financial need analysis, interview, proof of eligibility. *Deadline:* continuous.

Contact: JoAnn Strader, Chief of Rehabilitation Field Services
North Carolina Division of Services for the Blind
2601 Mail Service Center
Raleigh, NC 27699-2601
Phone: 919-733-9700
Fax: 919-715-8771
E-mail: joann.strader@ncmail.net

NORTH CAROLINA DIVISION OF VOCATIONAL REHABILITATION SERVICES http://www.dhhs.state.nc.us

TRAINING SUPPORT FOR YOUTH WITH DISABILITIES

Public service program that helps persons with disabilities obtain jobs. To qualify, student must have a mental or physical disability that is an impediment to employment. Each program is designed individually for the student. Assistance is based on need and type of program in which the student enrolls.

Award: Grant for use in freshman, sophomore, junior, or senior years; renewable. *Number:* varies. *Amount:* $2400.

Eligibility Requirements: Applicant must be enrolled or expecting to enroll full- or part-time at a two-year or four-year or technical institution or university and resident of North Carolina. Applicant must be hearing impaired, learning disabled, physically disabled, or visually impaired. Available to U.S. citizens.

Application Requirements: Application, financial need analysis, interview, test scores, transcript. *Deadline:* continuous.

Contact: Alma Taylor, Program Specialist for Transition
North Carolina Division of Vocational Rehabilitation Services
2801 Mail Service Center
Raleigh, NC 27699-2801
Phone: 919-855-3572
Fax: 919-715-0616
E-mail: alma.taylor@ncmail.net

NUFACTOR http://www.nufactor.com

ERIC DOSTIE MEMORIAL COLLEGE SCHOLARSHIP

Scholarship for persons or family members with hemophilia or other bleeding disorder, enrolled full-time in an accredited college. Must be a U.S. citizen.

Award: Scholarship for use in freshman, sophomore, junior, senior, or graduate years; not renewable. *Number:* 10. *Amount:* $1000.

Eligibility Requirements: Applicant must be enrolled or expecting to enroll full-time at a two-year or four-year institution or university. Applicant must be physically disabled. Applicant must have 2.5 GPA or higher. Available to U.S. citizens.

Application Requirements: Application, essay, photo, references, test scores, transcript, request application after November 1. *Deadline:* March 1.

Contact: Scholarship Coordinator
NuFACTOR
41093 County Center Drive, Suite B
Temecula, CA 92591
Phone: 800-323-6832
Fax: 951-296-2565

OPTIMIST INTERNATIONAL FOUNDATION http://www.optimist.org

COMMUNICATIONS CONTEST FOR THE DEAF AND HARD OF HEARING

College scholarship (district level) for young people through grade twelve in the U.S. and Canada, to CEGEP in Quebec and grade thirteen in the Caribbean. Students interested in participating in the contest must submit the results of an audiogram conducted no longer than twenty four months prior to the date of the contest from a qualified audiologist. Must be certified to have a hearing loss of forty decibels or more and supported by the audiogram to be eligible to compete.

Award: Scholarship for use in freshman, sophomore, junior, senior, or graduate years; not renewable. *Number:* 15–53. *Amount:* up to $1500.

Eligibility Requirements: Applicant must be enrolled or expecting to enroll full- or part-time at a two-year or four-year or technical institution or university. Applicant must be hearing impaired. Available to U.S. and Canadian citizens.

Optimist International Foundation (continued)

Application Requirements: Application, applicant must enter a contest, self-addressed stamped envelope, speech/presentation, audiogram. *Deadline:* varies.

Contact: Danielle Baugher, International Programs Manager
Optimist International Foundation
4494 Lindell Boulevard
St. Louis, MO 63108
Phone: 800-500-8130
Fax: 314-371-6006
E-mail: programs@optimist.org

OREGON COMMUNITY FOUNDATION http://www.ocf1.org

HARRY LUDWIG SCHOLARSHIP FUND

Scholarship for visually impaired students, for use in the pursuit of a postsecondary education at a college or university. For full-time students only.

Award: Scholarship for use in freshman, sophomore, junior, or senior years; not renewable. *Number:* 1. *Amount:* $500.

Eligibility Requirements: Applicant must be enrolled or expecting to enroll full-time at a four-year institution or university. Applicant must be visually impaired. Available to U.S. citizens.

Application Requirements: Application, references. *Deadline:* March 1.

Contact: Dianne Causey, Program Associate for Scholarships and Grants
Oregon Community Foundation
1221 Yamhill, SW, Suite 100
Portland, OR 97205
Phone: 503-227-6846
Fax: 503-274-7771
E-mail: diannec@ocf1.org

OREGON STUDENT ASSISTANCE COMMISSION http://www.osac.state.or.us

HARRY LUDWIG MEMORIAL SCHOLARSHIP

Award for visually-impaired Oregon residents planning to enroll full-time in undergraduate or graduate studies. Must document visual impairment with a letter from a physician. Must enroll in an Oregon college.

Award: Scholarship for use in freshman, sophomore, junior, senior, or graduate years; renewable. *Number:* varies. *Amount:* varies.

Eligibility Requirements: Applicant must be enrolled or expecting to enroll full-time at a two-year or four-year institution or university; resident of Oregon and studying in Oregon. Applicant must be visually impaired. Available to U.S. citizens.

Application Requirements: Application, essay, financial need analysis, references, transcript, documentation of visual impairment. *Deadline:* March 1.

Contact: Director of Grant Programs
Oregon Student Assistance Commission
1500 Valley River Drive, Suite 100
Eugene, OR 97401-7020
Phone: 800-452-8807 Ext. 7395

PATIENT ADVOCATE FOUNDATION http://www.patientadvocate.org

CHERYL GRIMMEL AWARD

Scholarship of $3000 will be given for a survivor of a life threatening, chronic, or debilitating disease. Applicant must maintain an overall 3.0 GPA.

Award: Scholarship for use in freshman, sophomore, junior, senior, or graduate years; renewable. *Number:* 1. *Amount:* $3000.

Eligibility Requirements: Applicant must be enrolled or expecting to enroll full-time at a two-year or four-year institution or university. Applicant must be physically disabled. Applicant must have 3.0 GPA or higher. Available to U.S. citizens.

Application Requirements: Application, essay, financial need analysis, references, transcript. *Deadline:* April 14.

Contact: Ruth Anne Reed, Vice President of Human Resource Programs
Patient Advocate Foundation
700 Thimble Shoals Boulevard, Suite 200
Newport News, VA 23606
Phone: 800-532-5274
Fax: 757-952-2475
E-mail: ruthar@patientadvocate.org

MONICA BAILES AWARD

Award of $3000 for a survivor of a life threatening, chronic or debilitating disease. Applicant must maintain an overall 3.0 GPA.

Award: Scholarship for use in freshman, sophomore, junior, senior, or graduate years; renewable. *Number:* 1. *Amount:* $3000.

Eligibility Requirements: Applicant must be enrolled or expecting to enroll full-time at a two-year or four-year institution or university. Applicant must be physically disabled. Applicant must have 3.0 GPA or higher. Available to U.S. citizens.

Application Requirements: Application, essay, financial need analysis, references, transcript, written documentation from physician. *Deadline:* April 14.

Contact: Ruth Anne Reed, Vice President of Human Resource Programs
Patient Advocate Foundation
700 Thimble Shoals Boulevard, Suite 200
Newport News, VA 23606
Phone: 800-532-5274
Fax: 757-952-2475
E-mail: ruthar@patientadvocate.org

P. BUCKLEY MOSS SOCIETY http://www.mosssociety.org

ANNE AND MATT HARBISON SCHOLARSHIP

Scholarship of $1500 to one high school senior with a certified language-related learning difference who is pursuing postsecondary education.

Award: Scholarship for use in freshman, sophomore, junior, or senior years; renewable. *Number:* 1. *Amount:* $1500.

Eligibility Requirements: Applicant must be enrolled or expecting to enroll full- or part-time at a four-year institution or university. Applicant must be learning disabled. Available to U.S. citizens.

Application Requirements: Application, transcript. *Deadline:* March 31.

Contact: Scholarship Committee
P. Buckley Moss Society
20 Stoneridge Drive, Suite 102
Waynesboro, VA 22980
Phone: 540-943-5678

PFIZER http://www.epilepsy-scholarship.com

PFIZER EPILEPSY SCHOLARSHIP AWARD

Award for students with epilepsy who excel academically and in extracurricular activities. Must be pursuing an undergraduate degree or be a college senior entering first year of graduate school. Must be under the care of a physician for epilepsy to qualify.

Award: Scholarship for use in freshman, sophomore, junior, senior, or graduate years; not renewable. *Number:* 25. *Amount:* up to $3000.

Eligibility Requirements: Applicant must be enrolled or expecting to enroll full- or part-time at a two-year or four-year or technical institution or university. Applicant must be physically disabled. Available to U.S. citizens.

Application Requirements: Application, essay, references, test scores, transcript. *Deadline:* March 1.

Contact: Mary Drach, Coordinator
Pfizer
c/o The Eden Communications Group
515 Valley Street, Suite 200
Maplewood, NJ 07040
Phone: 973-275-6500 Ext. 6556
E-mail: marydrach@edencom.com

RECORDING FOR THE BLIND & DYSLEXIC http://www.rfbd.org

MARION HUBER LEARNING THROUGH LISTENING AWARDS

• *See page 554*

MARY P. OENSLAGER SCHOLASTIC ACHIEVEMENT AWARDS

• *See page 554*

SAN DIEGO FOUNDATION http://www.sdfoundation.org

RUBINSTEIN CROHN'S AND COLITIS SCHOLARSHIP

Scholarship provides financial assistance to graduating high school seniors or students already enrolled at an institution of higher education who have been diagnosed with Crohn's and Colitis. Applicants must have a minimum 3.0 GPA and plan to attend an accredited two-year college or four-year university in the U.S. Scholarship may be renewable for up to four years provided recipients maintain full-time enrollment, a 3.0 cumulative GPA and positive record of citizenship.

Award: Scholarship for use in freshman year; renewable. *Number:* 1. *Amount:* $1000.

Eligibility Requirements: Applicant must be enrolled or expecting to enroll full-time at a two-year or four-year institution or university and resident of California. Applicant must be physically disabled. Applicant must have 3.0 GPA or higher. Available to U.S. citizens.

Application Requirements: Application, essay, references, transcript, personal statement, copy of tax return. *Deadline:* January 26.

Contact: Shryl Helvie, Scholarship Coordinator
San Diego Foundation
2508 Historic Decatur Road, Suite 200
San Diego, CA 92106
Phone: 619-814-1307
Fax: 619-239-1710
E-mail: shryl@sdfoundation.org

SERTOMA INTERNATIONAL http://www.sertoma.org

SERTOMA SCHOLARSHIP FOR DEAF OR HARD OF HEARING STUDENT

Applicants must have a minimum 40dB bilateral hearing loss as evidenced on audiogram by a SRT of 40dB or greater in both ears. Must have a minimum 3.2 unweighted GPA or be at least 85 percent in all courses.

Award: Scholarship for use in freshman, sophomore, junior, or senior years; not renewable. *Number:* 40. *Amount:* $1000.

Eligibility Requirements: Applicant must be enrolled or expecting to enroll full-time at a four-year institution or university. Applicant must be hearing impaired. Available to U.S. citizens.

Application Requirements: Application, essay, references, transcript, proof of hearing loss. *Deadline:* May 1.

Contact: Amy Ellington, Director of Finance
Sertoma International
1912 East Meyer Boulevard
Kansas City, MO 64132-1174
Phone: 816-333-8300
Fax: 816-333-4320
E-mail: aellington@sertomahq.org

SEVENSECURE http://www.novoseven-us.com

SEVENSECURE ADULT EDUCATION GRANTS

Provides grants to adults aged 23 and over with either hemophilia with inhibitors or FVII deficiency who would like to take courses or get more training to help improve their career or transition to a new one. Applications are accepted throughout the year. One award per eligible patient per year.

Award: Grant for use in freshman, sophomore, junior, senior, or graduate years; not renewable. *Number:* varies. *Amount:* up to $2500.

Eligibility Requirements: Applicant must be age 23 and over and enrolled or expecting to enroll full-time at a four-year institution or university. Applicant must be physically disabled. Available to U.S. citizens.

Application Requirements: Application. *Deadline:* continuous.

Contact: Scholarship Coordinator
SevenSECURE
PO Box 18648
Louisville, KY 40261
Phone: 877-668-6777

SICKLE CELL DISEASE ASSOCIATION OF AMERICA/ CONNECTICUT CHAPTER INC. http://www.sicklecellct.org

I. H. MCLENDON MEMORIAL SCHOLARSHIP

One-time scholarship to graduating high school seniors with sickle cell disease in Connecticut who will enter college, university, or technical training. Minimum 3.0 GPA required.

Award: Scholarship for use in freshman year; not renewable. *Number:* 1. *Amount:* $1000.

Eligibility Requirements: Applicant must be high school student; planning to enroll or expecting to enroll full- or part-time at a two-year or four-year or technical institution or university and resident of Connecticut. Applicant must be physically disabled. Applicant must have 3.0 GPA or higher. Available to U.S. citizens.

Application Requirements: Application, autobiography, interview, references, self-addressed stamped envelope, transcript, letter from physician attesting to existence of sickle cell disease. *Deadline:* April 30.

Contact: Samuel Byrd, Program Assistant
Sickle Cell Disease Association of America/Connecticut Chapter Inc.
Gengras Ambulatory Center, 114 Woodland Street, Suite 2101
Hartford, CT 06105-1299
Phone: 860-714-5540
Fax: 860-714-8007
E-mail: scdaa@iconn.net

SICKLE CELL DISEASE ASSOCIATION OF AMERICA INC. http://www.sicklecelldisease.org

KERMIT B. NASH, JR. ACADEMIC SCHOLARSHIP

One award for a total of $5000 per academic year for up to four years. Award will be disbursed per semester based on academic status. Must be graduating high school seniors with Sickle Cell Disease attending four-year accredited college. Minimum of 3.0 GPA required. Must be a U.S. citizen or permanent resident.

Award: Scholarship for use in freshman year; renewable. *Number:* 1. *Amount:* $5000–$20,000.

Eligibility Requirements: Applicant must be high school student and planning to enroll or expecting to enroll full-time at a four-year institution. Applicant must be physically disabled. Applicant must have 3.0 GPA or higher. Available to U.S. citizens.

Application Requirements: Application, essay, interview, photo, references, self-addressed stamped envelope, test scores, transcript. *Deadline:* May 31.

Contact: Lawrence Manning, Office Manager
Sickle Cell Disease Association of America Inc.
231 East Baltimore Street, Suite 800
Baltimore, MD 21202
Phone: 410-528-1555
Fax: 410-528-1495
E-mail: scdaa@sicklecelldisease.org

SIR EDWARD YOUDE MEMORIAL FUND COUNCIL http://www.sfaa.gov.hk

SIR EDWARD YOUDE MEMORIAL OVERSEAS SCHOLARSHIP FOR DISABLED STUDENTS

Scholarship for financing outstanding disabled Hong Kong students for overseas undergraduate or postgraduate studies. Must be permanent residents of Hong Kong. Must have received at least five to seven years of continuous education. Must belong to one of the following categories of disabilities: total blindness/severe low vision, profound/severe hearing impairment and physically handicapped. Award value is HK$262,000. Refer to Web Site: http://www.sfaa.gov.hk/eng/scholar/seym5.htm.

Award: Scholarship for use in freshman, sophomore, junior, senior, graduate, or postgraduate years; not renewable. *Number:* 1.

Sir Edward Youde Memorial Fund Council (continued)

Eligibility Requirements: Applicant must be Chinese citizen and enrolled or expecting to enroll full-time at a four-year institution or university. Applicant must be hearing impaired, physically disabled, or visually impaired. Available to citizens of countries other than the U.S. or Canada.

Application Requirements: Application, autobiography, essay, interview, photo, resume, references, test scores, transcript. *Deadline:* varies.

Contact: Elsa Sit, Council Secretariat
Sir Edward Youde Memorial Fund Council
Room 1217, 12/F, 303 Cheung Sha Wan Road
Kowloon
Hong Kong
Phone: 852 2150 6103
Fax: 852 2511 2720
E-mail: sgl3@sfaa.gov.hk

SISTER KENNY REHABILITATION INSTITUTE http://www.allina.com/ahs/ski.nsf

INTERNATIONAL ART SHOW FOR ARTISTS WITH DISABILITIES

One-time award for artwork submitted by artists of any age with visual, hearing, physical, or learning impairment. Contact Sister Kenny Rehabilitation Institute for show information. This is a one-time prize, not an academic scholarship.

Award: Prize for use in freshman, sophomore, junior, senior, or graduate years; not renewable. *Number:* 25–70. *Amount:* $25–$500.

Eligibility Requirements: Applicant must be enrolled or expecting to enroll full- or part-time at a four-year institution or university and must have an interest in art. Applicant must be hearing impaired, learning disabled, physically disabled, or visually impaired. Available to U.S. and non-U.S. citizens.

Application Requirements: Application, applicant must enter a contest. *Deadline:* March 17.

Contact: Laura Swift, Administrative Assistant
Sister Kenny Rehabilitation Institute
800 East 28th Street
Minneapolis, MN 55407-3799
Phone: 612-863-4466
Fax: 612-863-8942
E-mail: laura.swift@allina.com

SPINA BIFIDA ASSOCIATION OF AMERICA http://www.sbaa.org

SBAA ONE-YEAR SCHOLARSHIP

Scholarship available for a student with spina bifida who has applied for, enrolled in, or accepted by a junior college, approved trade, vocational or business school. Applicant must be high school graduate or possess a GED.

Award: Scholarship for use in freshman year; not renewable. *Number:* up to 5. *Amount:* $2000.

Eligibility Requirements: Applicant must be enrolled or expecting to enroll full-time at a four-year or technical institution or university. Applicant must be physically disabled. Available to U.S. citizens.

Application Requirements: Application, transcript, physician's statement of disability. *Deadline:* March 2.

Contact: Caroline Alston, Director of Programs
Spina Bifida Association of America
4590 MacArthur Boulevard, Suite 250
Washington, DC 20007-4226
Phone: 202-944-3285
Fax: 202-944-3295
E-mail: sbaa@sbaa.org

SPINA BIFIDA ASSOCIATION OF AMERICA EDUCATIONAL SCHOLARSHIP

One-time award to enhance opportunities for persons born with spina bifida to achieve their full potential through higher education. Minimum 2.5 GPA required. Must submit doctor's statement of disability and acceptance letter from college/university/school.

Award: Scholarship for use in freshman, sophomore, junior, or senior years; not renewable. *Number:* varies. *Amount:* $1000.

Eligibility Requirements: Applicant must be enrolled or expecting to enroll full-time at a four-year or technical institution or university. Applicant must be physically disabled. Applicant must have 2.5 GPA or higher. Available to U.S. citizens.

Application Requirements: Application, essay, financial need analysis, references, test scores, transcript, statement of disability. *Deadline:* March 2.

Contact: Caroline Alston, Director of Programs
Spina Bifida Association of America
4590 MacArthur Boulevard, Suite 250
Washington, DC 20007-4226
Phone: 202-944-3285
Fax: 202-944-3295
E-mail: sbaa@sbaa.org

SPINA BIFIDA ASSOCIATION OF AMERICA FOUR-YEAR SCHOLARSHIP FUND

Renewable award for a young person born with spina bifida to achieve full potential through higher education, and attend a four-year college otherwise outside of their family's financial reach. Open to U.S. citizens.

Award: Scholarship for use in freshman, sophomore, junior, or senior years; renewable. *Number:* 1. *Amount:* $5000.

Eligibility Requirements: Applicant must be enrolled or expecting to enroll full-time at a four-year institution or university. Applicant must be physically disabled. Available to U.S. citizens.

Application Requirements: Application, essay, financial need analysis, references, test scores, transcript, physician's statement of disability. *Deadline:* March 2.

Contact: Caroline Alston, Director of Programs
Spina Bifida Association of America
4590 MacArthur Boulevard, Suite 250
Washington, DC 20007-4226
Phone: 202-944-3285
Fax: 202-944-3295
E-mail: sbaa@sbaa.org

STEPHEN T. MARCHELLO SCHOLARSHIP FOUNDATION http://www.stmfoundation.org

A LEGACY OF HOPE SCHOLARSHIPS FOR SURVIVORS OF CHILDHOOD CANCER

Scholarship of up to $10,000 per year for four years of postsecondary undergraduate education. Applicant must be a survivor of childhood cancer. Must submit a letter from doctor, clinic, or hospital where cancer treatment was received. Residents of CO, AZ, CA, and MT are eligible. Must be U.S. citizen. Minimum 2.5 GPA required.

Award: Scholarship for use in freshman year; renewable. *Number:* 1–6. *Amount:* $1000–$10,000.

Eligibility Requirements: Applicant must be high school student; planning to enroll or expecting to enroll full- or part-time at a two-year or four-year or technical institution or university and resident of Arizona, California, Colorado, or Montana. Applicant must be physically disabled. Applicant must have 2.5 GPA or higher. Available to U.S. citizens.

Application Requirements: Application, essay, references, self-addressed stamped envelope, test scores, transcript. *Deadline:* March 15.

Contact: Franci Marchello, President
Stephen T. Marchello Scholarship Foundation
1170 East Long Place
Centennial, CO 80122
Phone: 303-886-5018
Fax: 303-886-5018
E-mail: fmarchello@earthlink.net

TRAVELERS PROTECTIVE ASSOCIATION OF AMERICA http://www.tpahq.org

TRAVELERS PROTECTIVE ASSOCIATION SCHOLARSHIP TRUST FOR THE HEARING IMPAIRED

Scholarships are awarded to deaf or hearing-impaired persons of any age, race, or religion for specialized education, mechanical devices, or medical or specialized treatment. Based on financial need.

Award: Scholarship for use in freshman, sophomore, junior, senior, graduate, or postgraduate years; not renewable. *Number:* varies. *Amount:* $200–$600.

Eligibility Requirements: Applicant must be enrolled or expecting to enroll full- or part-time at a two-year or four-year or technical institution or university. Applicant must be hearing impaired. Available to U.S. citizens.

Application Requirements: Application, financial need analysis, photo. *Deadline:* March 1.

Contact: B. K. Schulte, Executive Secretary
Travelers Protective Association of America
3755 Lindell Boulevard
St. Louis, MO 63108
Phone: 314-371-0533
Fax: 314-371-0537

UCB INC. http://www.crohnsandme.com

UCB CROHN'S SCHOLARSHIP PROGRAM

Awards thirty one-time scholarships of up to $10,000 each to people diagnosed with Crohn's disease who are entering college, are currently enrolled in college, or to adults of any age returning to school. Students of all ages are welcome to apply, and the scholarship can be used for a two-year, four-year, trade or specialty school.

Award: Scholarship for use in freshman, sophomore, junior, senior, or graduate years; not renewable. *Number:* up to 30. *Amount:* up to $10,000.

Eligibility Requirements: Applicant must be enrolled or expecting to enroll full- or part-time at a two-year or four-year or technical institution or university. Applicant must be physically disabled. Available to U.S. citizens.

Application Requirements: Application, autobiography, essay, photo, references, self-addressed stamped envelope, test scores, transcript, medical certificate. *Deadline:* April 18.

Contact: Scholarship Committee
UCB Inc.
c/o S&R Communications Group, 2511 Old Cornwallis Road, Suite 200
Durham, NC 27713
Phone: 800-234-8770
E-mail: ucbcrohnsscholarship@srcomgroup.com

ULMAN CANCER FUND FOR YOUNG ADULTS http://www.ulmanfund.org

MATT STAUFFER MEMORIAL SCHOLARSHIP

Supports the financial needs of college students who are battling or have overcome cancer who display financial need.

Award: Scholarship for use in freshman, sophomore, junior, or senior years; not renewable. *Number:* 3–8. *Amount:* $1000.

Eligibility Requirements: Applicant must be age 15-40 and enrolled or expecting to enroll full- or part-time at a two-year or four-year or technical institution or university. Applicant must be physically disabled. Available to U.S. and non-U.S. citizens.

Application Requirements: Application, autobiography, essay, financial need analysis, references, medical history. *Deadline:* May 10.

Contact: Kathryn Lalumiere, Scholarship Program Coordinator
Ulman Cancer Fund for Young Adults
4725 Dorsey Hall Drive, Suite A, PO Box 505
Ellicott City, MD 21042

UNITED NEGRO COLLEGE FUND http://www.uncf.org

YOUTH EMPOWERMENT SCHOLARSHIP

One-time non-renewable scholarship for junior college students. Award amount varies. Deadline January 2.

Award: Scholarship for use in junior year; not renewable. *Number:* 1. *Amount:* varies.

Eligibility Requirements: Applicant must be enrolled or expecting to enroll part-time at a four-year institution. Applicant must be physically disabled. Available to citizens of countries other than the U.S. or Canada. Applicant or parent must meet one or more of the following requirements: Marine Corps experience; retired from active duty; disabled or killed as a result of military service; prisoner of war; or missing in action.

Application Requirements: Application, financial need analysis. *Deadline:* January 2.

Contact: Director, Program Services
United Negro College Fund
8260 Willow Oaks Corporate Drive
PO Box 10444
Fairfax, VA 22031-8044
Phone: 800-331-2244
E-mail: rebecca.bennett@uncf.org

UNITED STATES ASSOCIATION FOR BLIND ATHLETES http://www.usaba.org

ARTHUR E. AND HELEN COPELAND SCHOLARSHIPS

Scholarship for a full-time college student who is blind or visually impaired. All applicants must be current members of USABA.

Award: Scholarship for use in freshman, sophomore, junior, or senior years; not renewable. *Number:* 1–2. *Amount:* $500.

Eligibility Requirements: Applicant must be enrolled or expecting to enroll full-time at a four-year institution or university. Applicant must be visually impaired. Available to U.S. citizens.

Application Requirements: Application, autobiography, references, transcript, proof of acceptance. *Deadline:* October 1.

Contact: Mark Lucas, Executive Director
United States Association for Blind Athletes
33 North Institute Street
Colorado Springs, CO 80903
Phone: 719-630-0422 Ext. 13
Fax: 719-630-0616
E-mail: mlucas@usaba.org

WISCONSIN HIGHER EDUCATIONAL AIDS BOARD http://www.heab.state.wi.us

HANDICAPPED STUDENT GRANT-WISCONSIN

One-time award available to residents of Wisconsin who have severe or profound hearing or visual impairment. Must be enrolled at least half-time at a nonprofit institution. If the handicap prevents the student from attending a Wisconsin school, the award may be used out-of-state in a specialized college. Refer to Web site for further details: http://www.heab.state.wi.us.

Award: Grant for use in freshman, sophomore, junior, or senior years; not renewable. *Number:* varies. *Amount:* $250–$1800.

Eligibility Requirements: Applicant must be enrolled or expecting to enroll full- or part-time at a four-year institution or university and resident of Wisconsin. Applicant must be hearing impaired or visually impaired. Available to U.S. citizens.

Application Requirements: Application, financial need analysis. *Deadline:* continuous.

Contact: Sandy Thomas, Program Coordinator
Wisconsin Higher Educational Aids Board
PO Box 7885
Madison, WI 53707-7885
Phone: 608-266-0888
Fax: 608-267-2808
E-mail: sandy.thomas@heab.state.wi.us

WYETH PHARMACEUTICALS, INC. http://www.wyeth.com

SOOZIE COURTER "SHARING A BRIGHTER TOMORROW" HEMOPHILIA SCHOLARSHIP PROGRAM

Scholarship for students with hemophilia A or B. Must be a high school senior, or recipient of a GED, or currently enrolled in an accredited junior college, college (undergraduate or graduate) or vocational school. Fund includes sixteen $5000 undergraduate scholarships, two $7500 graduate scholarships, and two $2500 vocational scholarships. See Web site for details and application: http://www.hemophiliavillage.com.

Award: Scholarship for use in freshman, sophomore, junior, senior, or graduate years; not renewable. *Number:* 20. *Amount:* $2500–$7500.

Wyeth Pharmaceuticals, Inc. (continued)

Eligibility Requirements: Applicant must be enrolled or expecting to enroll full-time at a two-year or four-year or technical institution or university. Applicant must be physically disabled. Available to U.S. citizens.

Application Requirements: Application. *Deadline:* April 4.

Contact: Wyeth Hemophilia Hotline
Philadelphia, PA 19101
Phone: 888-999-2349

MILITARY SERVICE: AIR FORCE

AEROSPACE EDUCATION FOUNDATION http://www.afa.org

SPOUSE SCHOLARSHIP

Awards to spouses of Air Force active duty, Air National Guard, or Air Force Reserve members during the spring semester. Spouses who are military members are not eligible. Minimum 3.5 GPA required. Undergraduate students must be enrolled with a minimum of 6 credit hours when the scholarship is awarded in May. Graduate and post-graduate students must be enrolled in a minimum of 3 credit hours.

Award: Scholarship for use in freshman, sophomore, junior, senior, graduate, or postgraduate years; not renewable. *Number:* 8. *Amount:* $2500.

Eligibility Requirements: Applicant must be enrolled or expecting to enroll full- or part-time at a two-year or four-year or technical institution or university. Applicant must have 3.5 GPA or higher. Available to U.S. citizens. Applicant or parent must meet one or more of the following requirements: Air Force or Air Force National Guard experience; retired from active duty; disabled or killed as a result of military service; prisoner of war; or missing in action.

Application Requirements: Application, essay, references, transcript, college acceptance letter. *Deadline:* April 30.

Contact: Program Assistance
Aerospace Education Foundation
1501 Lee Highway
Arlington, VA 22209
Phone: 800-291-8480
Fax: 703-247-5853
E-mail: mmakinen@afa.org

AIR FORCE AID SOCIETY http://www.afas.org

GENERAL HENRY H. ARNOLD EDUCATION GRANT PROGRAM

Renewable grants awarded to selected sons and daughters of active duty, Title 10 AGR/Reserve, Title 32 AGR performing full-time active duty, retired reserve and deceased Air Force members; spouses (stateside) of active members and Title 10 AGR/Reservist; and surviving spouses of deceased personnel for their undergraduate studies. Dependent children must be unmarried and under the age of 23. High school seniors may apply. Minimum 2.0 GPA is required.

Award: Grant for use in freshman, sophomore, junior, or senior years; renewable. *Number:* 3000–4000. *Amount:* $2000.

Eligibility Requirements: Applicant must be enrolled or expecting to enroll full-time at a two-year or four-year or technical institution or university. Available to U.S. citizens. Applicant or parent must meet one or more of the following requirements: Air Force or Air Force National Guard experience; retired from active duty; disabled or killed as a result of military service; prisoner of war; or missing in action.

Application Requirements: Application, financial need analysis, transcript, program's own financial forms, USAF military orders (member/parent), ID cards (applicant and member parent). *Deadline:* March 7.

Contact: Education Assistance Department
Air Force Aid Society
241 18th Street South, Suite 202
Arlington, VA 22202-3409
Phone: 703-607-3072
Fax: 703-607-3022
E-mail: ed@afas-hq.org

AIR FORCE RESERVE OFFICER TRAINING CORPS http://www.afrotc.com

AFROTC HBCU SCHOLARSHIP PROGRAM

Up to $15,000 awarded to student studying at a historically black college or university (HBCU). Please refer to Web site for more information: http://www.afrotc.com/scholarships/incolschol/minority/hbcu.php.

Award: Scholarship for use in freshman, sophomore, junior, or senior years; not renewable. *Number:* up to 15. *Amount:* up to $15,000.

Eligibility Requirements: Applicant must be enrolled or expecting to enroll full-time at a four-year institution or university. Available to U.S. citizens. Applicant must have served in the Air Force or Air Force National Guard.

Application Requirements: Application. *Deadline:* varies.

Contact: Elmarko Magee, Chief of Advertising
Air Force Reserve Officer Training Corps
551 East Maxwell Boulevard
Maxwell AFB, AL 36112
Phone: 866-423-7682

AFROTC HSI SCHOLARSHIP PROGRAM

$15,000 scholarships to students at colleges and universities defined as Hispanic Serving Institutions by the United States Department of Education. Student must already be enrolled in school to receive award.

Award: Scholarship for use in freshman, sophomore, junior, or senior years; not renewable. *Number:* up to 15. *Amount:* $15,000.

Eligibility Requirements: Applicant must be enrolled or expecting to enroll full-time at a four-year institution or university. Available to U.S. citizens. Applicant must have served in the Air Force or Air Force National Guard.

Application Requirements: Application. *Deadline:* varies.

Contact: Elmarko Magee, Chief of Advertising
Air Force Reserve Officer Training Corps
551 East Maxwell Boulevard
Maxwell Air Force Base, AL 36112-6106
Phone: 334-953-2278
Fax: 334-953-6167
E-mail: elmarko.magee@maxwell.af.mil

AIR FORCE ROTC COLLEGE SCHOLARSHIP

Scholarship program provides three- and four-year scholarships in three different types to high school seniors. All scholarship cadets receive a nontaxable monthly allowance (stipend) during the academic year. For more details refer to Web Site: http://www.afrotc.com/scholarships/hsschol/types.php.

Award: Scholarship for use in freshman, sophomore, junior, or senior years; renewable. *Number:* 2000–4000. *Amount:* $9000–$15,000.

Eligibility Requirements: Applicant must be age 17-30 and enrolled or expecting to enroll full-time at a two-year or four-year institution or university. Applicant must have 3.0 GPA or higher. Available to U.S. citizens. Applicant or parent must meet one or more of the following requirements: Air Force experience; retired from active duty; disabled or killed as a result of military service; prisoner of war; or missing in action.

Application Requirements: Application, interview, test scores, transcript. *Deadline:* December 1.

Contact: Ty Christian, Chief Air Force ROTC Advertising Manager
Air Force Reserve Officer Training Corps
551 East Maxwell Boulevard
Maxwell Air Force Base, AL 36112-6106
Phone: 334-953-2278
Fax: 334-953-4384
E-mail: ty.christian@maxwell.af.mil

AIRMEN MEMORIAL FOUNDATION/AIR FORCE SERGEANTS ASSOCIATION http://www.afsahq.org

AIR FORCE SERGEANTS ASSOCIATION SCHOLARSHIP

Scholarships awarded to dependent youth of Air Force Sergeants Association/Auxiliary members. Must be under the age of 23, be enrolled or accepted as an undergraduate in an accredited college or university, have minimum combined score of 1650 on SAT 1 or 24 on ACT, and a minimum GPA of 3.5.

Award: Scholarship for use in freshman, sophomore, junior, or senior years; not renewable. *Number:* up to 30. *Amount:* $500–$3000.

Eligibility Requirements: Applicant must be age 23 or under and enrolled or expecting to enroll full-time at a four-year institution or university. Applicant must have 3.5 GPA or higher. Available to U.S. and non-U.S. citizens. Applicant or parent must meet one or more of the following requirements: Air Force or Air Force National Guard experience; retired from active duty; disabled or killed as a result of military service; prisoner of war; or missing in action.

Application Requirements: Application, essay, references, transcript. *Deadline:* March 31.

Contact: Melanie Shirley, Scholarship Coordinator
Airmen Memorial Foundation/
Air Force Sergeants Association
5211 Auth Road
Suitland, MD 20746
Phone: 301-899-3500
Fax: 301-899-8136
E-mail: staff@afsahq.org

AIRMEN MEMORIAL FOUNDATION SCHOLARSHIP

Scholarship for full-time undergraduate studies of dependent children of Air Force, Air Force Reserve Command and Air National Guard members in active duty, retired or veteran status. Must be under age of 23, have minimum combined score of 1650 on SAT 1 or 24 on ACT, and a minimum GPA of 3.5.

Award: Scholarship for use in freshman, sophomore, junior, or senior years; not renewable. *Number:* 20. *Amount:* $500–$2000.

Eligibility Requirements: Applicant must be age 23 or under and enrolled or expecting to enroll full-time at a four-year institution or university. Applicant must have 3.5 GPA or higher. Available to U.S. and non-U.S. citizens. Applicant or parent must meet one or more of the following requirements: Air Force or Air Force National Guard experience; retired from active duty; disabled or killed as a result of military service; prisoner of war; or missing in action.

Application Requirements: Application, essay, references, transcript. *Deadline:* March 31.

Contact: Melanie Shirley, Scholarship Coordinator
Airmen Memorial Foundation/
Air Force Sergeants Association
5211 Auth Road
Suitland, MD 20746
Phone: 301-899-3500
Fax: 301-899-8136
E-mail: staff@afsahq.org

CHIEF MASTER SERGEANTS OF THE AIR FORCE SCHOLARSHIP PROGRAM

Scholarship to financially assist the full-time undergraduate studies of dependent children of Air Force, Air Force Reserve Command and Air National Guard enlisted members in active duty, retired or veteran status. Must be under age twenty-three and participate in the Airmen Memorial Foundation Scholarship Program. Must have minimum combined score of 1650 on SAT 1 or 24 on ACT, and a minimum GPA of 3.5.

Award: Scholarship for use in freshman, sophomore, junior, or senior years; not renewable. *Number:* up to 30. *Amount:* $500–$3000.

Eligibility Requirements: Applicant must be age 23 or under and enrolled or expecting to enroll full-time at a four-year institution or university. Applicant must have 3.5 GPA or higher. Available to U.S. and non-U.S. citizens. Applicant or parent must meet one or more of the following requirements: Air Force or Air Force National Guard experience; retired from active duty; disabled or killed as a result of military service; prisoner of war; or missing in action.

Application Requirements: Application, essay, references, transcript. *Deadline:* March 31.

Contact: Melanie Shirley, Scholarship Coordinator
Airmen Memorial Foundation/
Air Force Sergeants Association
5211 Auth Road
Suitland, MD 20746
Phone: 301-899-3500
Fax: 301-899-8136
E-mail: staff@afsahq.org

DEPARTMENT OF VETERANS AFFAIRS (VA) http://www.gibill.va.gov

MONTGOMERY GI BILL (SELECTED RESERVE)

Educational assistance program for members of the selected reserve of the Army, Navy, Air Force, Marine Corps and Coast Guard, as well as the Army and Air National Guard. Available to all reservists and National Guard personnel who commit to a six-year obligation, and remain in the Reserve or Guard during the six years. Award is renewable. Monthly benefit is $309 for up to thirty-six months for full-time.

Award: Scholarship for use in freshman, sophomore, junior, senior, or postgraduate years; renewable. *Number:* varies. *Amount:* up to $3708.

Eligibility Requirements: Applicant must be enrolled or expecting to enroll full- or part-time at a two-year or four-year or technical institution or university. Available to U.S. citizens. Applicant or parent must meet one or more of the following requirements: general military experience; retired from active duty; disabled or killed as a result of military service; prisoner of war; or missing in action.

Application Requirements: Application, proof of military service of six years in the reserve or guard. *Deadline:* continuous.

Contact: Keith Wilson, Director, Education Service
Department of Veterans Affairs (VA)
810 Vermont Avenue, NW
Washington, DC 20420
Phone: 202-273-7132
E-mail: co225a@vba.va.gov

FOUNDATION OF THE FIRST CAVALRY DIVISION ASSOCIATION http://www.1cda.org

FOUNDATION OF THE 1ST CAVALRY DIVISION ASSOCIATION (IA DRANG) SCHOLARSHIP

Award for children and grandchildren of soldiers of 1st Cavalry Division, U.S. Air Force Forward Air Controllers and A1E pilots, and war correspondents who served in designated qualifying units which were involved in battles of the Ia Drang Valley during the period of November 3-19, 1965. Include self-addressed stamped envelope. More information on www.1cda.org.

Award: Scholarship for use in freshman, sophomore, junior, senior, graduate, or postgraduate years; renewable. *Number:* varies. *Amount:* up to $1000.

Eligibility Requirements: Applicant must be enrolled or expecting to enroll full-time at a two-year or four-year institution or university. Available to U.S. citizens. Applicant or parent must meet one or more of the following requirements: Air Force or Army experience; retired from active duty; disabled or killed as a result of military service; prisoner of war; or missing in action.

Application Requirements: Application, self-addressed stamped envelope, birth certificate, proof of father or grandfather's participation in specified units and battles, proof of registration for Selective Service for males. *Deadline:* continuous.

Contact: Lorinda Davison, Office Manager
Foundation of the First Cavalry Division Association
302 North Main Street
Copperas Cove, TX 76522-1703
Phone: 254-547-6537
Fax: 254-547-8853
E-mail: firstcav@1cda.org

INDIANA DEPARTMENT OF VETERANS AFFAIRS http://www.in.gov/dva

RESIDENT TUITION FOR ACTIVE DUTY MILITARY PERSONNEL

Applicant must be a nonresident of Indiana serving on active duty and stationed in Indiana and attending any state-supported college or university. Dependents remain eligible for the duration of their enrollment, even if the active duty person is no longer in Indiana. Entitlement is to the resident tuition rate.

Award: Grant for use in freshman, sophomore, junior, senior, graduate, or postgraduate years; renewable. *Number:* varies. *Amount:* varies.

Eligibility Requirements: Applicant must be enrolled or expecting to enroll full- or part-time at a two-year or four-year or technical institution or university and studying in Indiana. Available to U.S. citizens. Applicant or parent must meet one or more of the following requirements: Air Force, Army, Marine Corps, or Navy experience; retired from active duty; disabled or killed as a result of military service; prisoner of war; or missing in action.

Application Requirements: Application. *Deadline:* continuous.

Contact: Jon Brinkley, State Service Officer
Indiana Department of Veterans Affairs
302 West Washington Street, Room E-120
Indianapolis, IN 46204-2738
Phone: 317-232-3910
Fax: 317-232-7721
E-mail: jbrinkley@dva.in.gov

SECOND BOMBARDMENT ASSOCIATION

SECOND BOMBARDMENT ASSOCIATION SCHOLARSHIP
• See page 556

UNITED DAUGHTERS OF THE CONFEDERACY http://www.hqudc.org

ADMIRAL RAPHAEL SEMMES SCHOLARSHIP
• See page 563

BARBARA JACKSON SICHEL MEMORIAL SCHOLARSHIP
• See page 564

CHARLOTTE M. F. BENTLEY/NEW YORK CHAPTER 103 SCHOLARSHIP
• See page 564

CODY BACHMAN SCHOLARSHIP
• See page 564

CORA BELL WESLEY MEMORIAL SCHOLARSHIP
• See page 564

CORNELIA BRANCH STONE SCHOLARSHIP
• See page 564

DAVID STEPHEN WYLIE SCHOLARSHIP
• See page 565

DOROTHY WILLIAMS SCHOLARSHIP
• See page 565

ELIZABETH AND WALLACE KINGSBURY SCHOLARSHIP
• See page 565

GERTRUDE BOTTS-SAUCIER SCHOLARSHIP
• See page 565

HECTOR W. CHURCH SCHOLARSHIP
• See page 565

HENRY CLAY DARSEY SCHOLARSHIP
• See page 566

JANET B. SEIPPEL SCHOLARSHIP
• See page 566

LOLA B. CURRY SCHOLARSHIP
• See page 566

MAJOR MADISON BELL SCHOLARSHIP
• See page 566

MARY B. POPPENHEIM MEMORIAL SCHOLARSHIP
• See page 566

MATTHEW FONTAINE MAURY SCHOLARSHIP
• See page 567

MRS. ELLA M. FRANKLIN SCHOLARSHIP
• See page 567

MRS. L. H. RAINES MEMORIAL SCHOLARSHIP
• See page 567

S.A. CUNNINGHAM SCHOLARSHIP
• See page 567

STONEWALL JACKSON SCHOLARSHIP
• See page 567

WINNIE DAVIS-CHILDREN OF THE CONFEDERACY SCHOLARSHIP
• See page 567

WISCONSIN DEPARTMENT OF VETERANS AFFAIRS http://www.dva.state.wi.us

VETERANS EDUCATION (VETED) REIMBURSEMENT GRANT

Open only to Wisconsin veterans enrolled at approved schools for undergraduate study. Benefit is based on length of time serving on active duty in the armed forces (active duty for training does not apply). Pre-application due no later than 30 days after the start of semester. Application deadline no later than 60 days after the course completion. Veterans may be reimbursed up to 100 percent of tuition and fees.

Award: Grant for use in freshman, sophomore, junior, or senior years; renewable. *Number:* varies. *Amount:* up to $3594.

Eligibility Requirements: Applicant must be enrolled or expecting to enroll full- or part-time at a two-year or four-year or technical institution or university and resident of Wisconsin. Available to U.S. citizens. Applicant or parent must meet one or more of the following requirements: Air Force, Army, Coast Guard, Marine Corps, or Navy experience; retired from active duty; disabled or killed as a result of military service; prisoner of war; or missing in action.

Application Requirements: Application. *Deadline:* varies.

Contact: Ms. Leslie Busby-Amegashie, Analyst
Wisconsin Department of Veterans Affairs
PO Box 7843
Madison, WI 53707-7843
Phone: 800-947-8387

MILITARY SERVICE: AIR FORCE NATIONAL GUARD

AEROSPACE EDUCATION FOUNDATION http://www.afa.org

SPOUSE SCHOLARSHIP
• *See page 630*

AIR FORCE AID SOCIETY http://www.afas.org

GENERAL HENRY H. ARNOLD EDUCATION GRANT PROGRAM
• *See page 630*

AIR FORCE RESERVE OFFICER TRAINING CORPS http://www.afrotc.com

AFROTC HBCU SCHOLARSHIP PROGRAM
• *See page 630*

AFROTC HSI SCHOLARSHIP PROGRAM
• *See page 630*

AIRMEN MEMORIAL FOUNDATION/AIR FORCE SERGEANTS ASSOCIATION http://www.afsahq.org

AIR FORCE SERGEANTS ASSOCIATION SCHOLARSHIP
• *See page 631*

AIRMEN MEMORIAL FOUNDATION SCHOLARSHIP
• *See page 631*

CHIEF MASTER SERGEANTS OF THE AIR FORCE SCHOLARSHIP PROGRAM
• *See page 631*

ALABAMA COMMISSION ON HIGHER EDUCATION http://www.ache.alabama.gov

ALABAMA NATIONAL GUARD EDUCATIONAL ASSISTANCE PROGRAM

Renewable award aids Alabama residents who are members of the Alabama National Guard and are enrolled in an accredited college in Alabama. Forms must be signed by a representative of the Alabama Military Department and financial aid officer. Recipient must be in a degree-seeking program.

Award: Scholarship for use in freshman, sophomore, junior, or senior years; renewable. *Number:* varies. *Amount:* up to $1000.

Eligibility Requirements: Applicant must be enrolled or expecting to enroll full- or part-time at a two-year or four-year or technical institution or university; resident of Alabama and studying in Alabama. Available to U.S. citizens. Applicant or parent must meet one or more of the following requirements: Air Force National Guard or Army National Guard experience; retired from active duty; disabled or killed as a result of military service; prisoner of war; or missing in action.

Application Requirements: Application. *Deadline:* continuous.

Contact: William Wall, Associate Executive Director for Student Assistance
Alabama Commission on Higher Education
100 North Union Street, PO Box 302000
Montgomery, AL 36104-3758
Phone: 334-242-2271
Fax: 334-242-0268
E-mail: wwall@ache.state.al.us

AMERICAN LEGION DEPARTMENT OF TENNESSEE http://www.tennesseelegion.org

JROTC SCHOLARSHIP

One scholarship of $2000 available to a Tennessee JROTC cadet who has been awarded either The American Legion General Military Excellence, or The American Legion Scholastic Award Medal. JROTC Senior Instructor must provide the recommendation for the award. Information and recommendation forms are provided each JROTC Unit in Tennessee. Must be U.S. citizen.

Award: Scholarship for use in freshman year; not renewable. *Number:* 1. *Amount:* $2000.

Eligibility Requirements: Applicant must be high school student; planning to enroll or expecting to enroll full- or part-time at a four-year institution or university; resident of Tennessee and studying in Tennessee. Available to U.S. citizens. Applicant must have served in the Air Force National Guard or Army National Guard.

Application Requirements: Application. *Deadline:* May 15.

Contact: Darlene Burgess, Executive Assistant
American Legion Department of Tennessee
215 Eighth Avenue, North
Nashville, TN 37203
Phone: 615-254-0568
Fax: 615-255-1551
E-mail: tnleg1@bellsouth.net

DELAWARE NATIONAL GUARD http://www.delawarenationalguard.com

STATE TUITION ASSISTANCE

Award providing tuition assistance for any member of the Air or Army National Guard attending a Delaware two-year or four-year college. Awards are renewable. Applicant's minimum GPA must be 2.0.

Award: Scholarship for use in freshman, sophomore, junior, or senior years; renewable. *Number:* 1–300. *Amount:* up to $10,000.

Eligibility Requirements: Applicant must be enrolled or expecting to enroll full- or part-time at a two-year or four-year institution or university and studying in Delaware. Applicant must have 2.5 GPA or higher. Available to U.S. citizens. Applicant or parent must meet one or more of the following requirements: Air Force National Guard or Army National Guard experience; retired from active duty; disabled or killed as a result of military service; prisoner of war; or missing in action.

Application Requirements: Application, transcript. *Deadline:* varies.

Contact: Robert Csizmadia, State Tuition Assistance Manager
Delaware National Guard
1st Regiment Road
Wilmington, DE 19808-2191
Phone: 302-326-7012
Fax: 302-326-7029
E-mail: robert.csizmadi@de.ngb.army.mil

DEPARTMENT OF VETERANS AFFAIRS (VA) http://www.gibill.va.gov

MONTGOMERY GI BILL (SELECTED RESERVE)
• *See page 631*

RESERVE EDUCATION ASSISTANCE PROGRAM

The program provides educational assistance to members of National Guard and reserve components. Selected Reserve and Individual Ready Reserve (IRR) who are called or ordered to active duty service in response to a war or national emergency as declared by the president or Congress are eligible. For further information see Web site: http://www.GIBILL.va.gov.

Award: Scholarship for use in freshman, sophomore, junior, senior, graduate, or postgraduate years; renewable. *Number:* 1. *Amount:* $215–$860.

Eligibility Requirements: Applicant must be enrolled or expecting to enroll full- or part-time at a two-year or four-year or technical institution or university. Available to U.S. citizens. Applicant or parent must meet one

Department of Veterans Affairs (VA) (continued)

or more of the following requirements: general military experience; retired from active duty; disabled or killed as a result of military service; prisoner of war; or missing in action.

Application Requirements: Application. *Deadline:* continuous.

Contact: Keith Wilson, Director, Education Service
Department of Veterans Affairs (VA)
810 Vermont Avenue, NW
Washington, DC 20420
Phone: 202-273-7132
E-mail: co225a@vba.va.gov

ENLISTED ASSOCIATION OF THE NATIONAL GUARD OF NEW JERSEY http://www.eang-nj.org

CSM VINCENT BALDASSARI MEMORIAL SCHOLARSHIP PROGRAM

Scholarships open to the legal children of New Jersey National Guard Members who are also members of the Enlisted Association. Also open to any drilling guardsperson who is a member of the Enlisted Association. Along with application, submit proof of parent's membership and a letter stating the reason for applying and future intents.

Award: Scholarship for use in freshman, sophomore, junior, senior, graduate, or postgraduate years; not renewable. *Number:* 5. *Amount:* $1000.

Eligibility Requirements: Applicant must be enrolled or expecting to enroll full- or part-time at a two-year or four-year or technical institution or university and resident of New Jersey. Available to U.S. and non-U.S. citizens. Applicant or parent must meet one or more of the following requirements: Air Force National Guard or Army National Guard experience; retired from active duty; disabled or killed as a result of military service; prisoner of war; or missing in action.

Application Requirements: Application, essay, photo, references, transcript. *Deadline:* May 15.

Contact: Michael Amoroso, Scholarship Committee Chairman
Enlisted Association of the National Guard of New Jersey
3650 Saylors Pond Road
Fort Dix, NJ 08640
Phone: 609-562-0754
Fax: 609-562-0731
E-mail: michael.c@us.army.mil

USAA SCHOLARSHIP

Scholarship of $1000 open to any drilling guardsperson (need not be a member of the EANGNJ).

Award: Scholarship for use in freshman, sophomore, junior, senior, graduate, or postgraduate years; not renewable. *Number:* 1. *Amount:* $1000.

Eligibility Requirements: Applicant must be enrolled or expecting to enroll full- or part-time at a two-year or four-year or technical institution or university. Available to U.S. and non-U.S. citizens. Applicant or parent must meet one or more of the following requirements: Air Force National Guard or Army National Guard experience; retired from active duty; disabled or killed as a result of military service; prisoner of war; or missing in action.

Application Requirements: Application, essay, photo, transcript. *Deadline:* May 15.

Contact: Michael Amoroso, Scholarship Committee Chairman
Enlisted Association of the National Guard of New Jersey
3650 Saylors Pond Road
Fort Dix, NJ 08640
Phone: 609-562-0754
Fax: 609-562-0731
E-mail: michael.c@us.army.mil

ILLINOIS STUDENT ASSISTANCE COMMISSION (ISAC) http://www.collegezone.org

ILLINOIS NATIONAL GUARD GRANT PROGRAM

Active duty members of the Illinois National Guard, or who are within 12 months of discharge, and who have completed one full year of service are eligible. May be used for study at Illinois two- or four-year public colleges for a maximum of the equivalent of four academic years of full-time enrollment. Deadlines: October 1 of the academic year for full year, March 1 for second/third term, or June 15 for the summer term.

Award: Grant for use in freshman, sophomore, junior, senior, or graduate years; renewable. *Number:* varies. *Amount:* varies.

Eligibility Requirements: Applicant must be enrolled or expecting to enroll full- or part-time at a two-year or four-year institution or university; resident of Illinois and studying in Illinois. Available to U.S. citizens. Applicant or parent must meet one or more of the following requirements: Air Force National Guard or Army National Guard experience; retired from active duty; disabled or killed as a result of military service; prisoner of war; or missing in action.

Application Requirements: Application, documentation of service. *Deadline:* varies.

Contact: College Zone Counselor
Illinois Student Assistance Commission (ISAC)
1755 Lake Cook Road
Deerfield, IL 60015-5209
Phone: 800-899-4722
E-mail: collegezone@isac.org

INDIANA DEPARTMENT OF VETERANS AFFAIRS http://www.in.gov/dva

NATIONAL GUARD SCHOLARSHIP EXTENSION PROGRAM

A scholarship extension applicant is eligible for a tuition scholarship under Indiana Code 21-13-5-4 for a period not to exceed the period of scholarship extension the applicant served on active duty as a member of the National Guard (mobilized and deployed). Must apply not later than one (1) year after the applicant ceases to be a member of the Indiana National Guard. Applicant should apply through the education officer of their last unit of assignment.

Award: Grant for use in freshman, sophomore, junior, or senior years; renewable. *Number:* varies. *Amount:* varies.

Eligibility Requirements: Applicant must be enrolled or expecting to enroll full- or part-time at a two-year or four-year or technical institution or university and studying in Indiana. Available to U.S. citizens. Applicant must have served in the Air Force National Guard or Army National Guard.

Application Requirements: Application. *Deadline:* continuous.

Contact: Pamela Moody, National Guard Education Officer
Indiana Department of Veterans Affairs
302 West Washington Street, Suite E120
Indianapolis, IN 46204
Phone: 317-964-7017
Fax: 317-232-7721
E-mail: pamela.moody@in.ngb.army.mil

NATIONAL GUARD TUITION SUPPLEMENT PROGRAM

Applicant must be a member of the Indiana National Guard, in active drilling status, who has not been AWOL during the last 12 months, does not possess a bachelor's degree, possesses the requisite academic qualifications, meets the requirements of the state-supported college or university, and meets all National Guard requirements.

Award: Grant for use in freshman, sophomore, junior, or senior years; renewable. *Number:* varies. *Amount:* varies.

Eligibility Requirements: Applicant must be enrolled or expecting to enroll full- or part-time at a two-year or four-year or technical institution or university and studying in Indiana. Available to U.S. citizens. Applicant must have served in the Air Force National Guard or Army National Guard.

Application Requirements: Application, FAFSA. *Deadline:* continuous.

Contact: Jon Brinkley, State Service Officer
Indiana Department of Veterans Affairs
302 West Washington Street, Room E-120
Indianapolis, IN 46204-2738
Phone: 317-232-3910
Fax: 317-232-7721
E-mail: jbrinkley@dva.in.gov

TUITION AND FEE REMISSION FOR CHILDREN AND SPOUSES OF NATIONAL GUARD MEMBERS

Award to an individual whose father, mother or spouse was a member of the Indiana National Guard and suffered a service-connected death while serving on state active duty (which includes mobilized and deployed for federal active duty). The student must be eligible to pay the resident tuition rate at the state-supported college or university and must possess the requisite academic qualifications.

Award: Grant for use in freshman, sophomore, junior, or senior years; renewable. *Number:* varies. *Amount:* varies.

Eligibility Requirements: Applicant must be enrolled or expecting to enroll full- or part-time at a two-year or four-year or technical institution or university and studying in Indiana. Available to U.S. citizens. Applicant or parent must meet one or more of the following requirements: Air Force National Guard or Army National Guard experience; retired from active duty; disabled or killed as a result of military service; prisoner of war; or missing in action.

Application Requirements: Application, FAFSA. *Deadline:* continuous.

Contact: R. Martin Umbarger, Adjutant General
Indiana Department of Veterans Affairs
2002 South Holt Road
Indianapolis, IN 46241
Phone: 317-247-3559
Fax: 317-247-3540
E-mail: r.martin.umbarger@in.ngb.army.mil

IOWA COLLEGE STUDENT AID COMMISSION http://www.iowacollegeaid.gov

IOWA NATIONAL GUARD EDUCATION ASSISTANCE PROGRAM

Program provides postsecondary tuition assistance to members of Iowa National Guard Units. Must study at a postsecondary institution in Iowa. Contact the office for additional information.

Award: Grant for use in freshman, sophomore, junior, or senior years; not renewable. *Number:* varies. *Amount:* $1200–$6420.

Eligibility Requirements: Applicant must be enrolled or expecting to enroll full- or part-time at a two-year or four-year or technical institution or university; resident of Iowa and studying in Iowa. Available to U.S. citizens. Applicant or parent must meet one or more of the following requirements: Air Force National Guard or Army National Guard experience; retired from active duty; disabled or killed as a result of military service; prisoner of war; or missing in action.

Application Requirements: Application. *Deadline:* continuous.

Contact: Julie Leeper, Director, Program Administration
Iowa College Student Aid Commission
200 Tenth Street, Fourth Floor
Des Moines, IA 50309-3609
Phone: 515-725-3420
Fax: 515-725-3401
E-mail: julie.leeper@iowa.gov

LOUISIANA NATIONAL GUARD-STATE OF LOUISIANA, JOINT TASK FORCE LA http://www.la.ngb.army.mil

LOUISIANA NATIONAL GUARD STATE TUITION EXEMPTION PROGRAM

Renewable award for college undergraduates to receive tuition exemption upon satisfactory performance in the Louisiana National Guard. Applicant must attend a state-funded institution in Louisiana, be a resident and registered voter in Louisiana, meet the academic and residency requirements of the university attended, and provide documentation of Louisiana National Guard enlistment. The exemption can be used for up to 15 semesters. Minimum 2.5 GPA required.

Award: Scholarship for use in freshman, sophomore, junior, or senior years; renewable. *Number:* varies. *Amount:* varies.

Eligibility Requirements: Applicant must be enrolled or expecting to enroll full- or part-time at a two-year or four-year or technical institution or university; resident of Louisiana and studying in Louisiana. Applicant must have 2.5 GPA or higher. Available to U.S. citizens. Applicant or parent must meet one or more of the following requirements: Air Force National Guard or Army National Guard experience; retired from active duty; disabled or killed as a result of military service; prisoner of war; or missing in action.

Application Requirements: Application, test scores, transcript. *Deadline:* continuous.

Contact: Jona M. Hughes, Education Services Officer
Louisiana National Guard-State of Louisiana, Joint Task Force LA
Building 35, Jackson Barracks, JI-PD
New Orleans, LA 70146-0330
Phone: 504-278-8531 Ext. 8304
Fax: 504-278-8025
E-mail: hughesj@la-arng.ngb.army.mil

MINNESOTA DEPARTMENT OF MILITARY AFFAIRS http://www.minnesotanationalguard.org

LEADERSHIP, EXCELLENCE AND DEDICATED SERVICE SCHOLARSHIP

• *See page 603*

NATIONAL GUARD ASSOCIATION OF COLORADO EDUCATION FOUNDATION http://www.ngaco.org

NATIONAL GUARD ASSOCIATION OF COLORADO (NGACO) EDUCATION FOUNDATION INC. SCHOLARSHIP

Scholarships for current members of the Colorado National Guard. Applicants must be enrolled as full or part-time at a college, university, trade or business school. Deadlines: June 30 for the fall semester and November 30 for the spring semester.

Award: Scholarship for use in freshman, sophomore, junior, senior, graduate, or postgraduate years; not renewable. *Number:* up to 40. *Amount:* up to $1000.

Eligibility Requirements: Applicant must be enrolled or expecting to enroll full- or part-time at a two-year or four-year or technical institution or university and resident of Colorado. Available to U.S. citizens. Applicant must have served in the Air Force National Guard or Army National Guard.

Application Requirements: Application, essay, references, transcript. *Deadline:* varies.

Contact: Dave Sprenkle, President
National Guard Association of Colorado Education Foundation
6848 South Revere Parkway, Suite 2-234
Centennial, CO 80112-6703
Phone: 303-353-3555
E-mail: dave.sprenkle@merrick.com

NORTH CAROLINA NATIONAL GUARD http://www.nc.ngb.army.mil

NORTH CAROLINA NATIONAL GUARD TUITION ASSISTANCE PROGRAM

Scholarship for members of the North Carolina Air and Army National Guard who will remain in the service for two years following the period for which assistance is provided. Must reapply for each academic period. For use at approved North Carolina institutions.

Award: Grant for use in freshman, sophomore, junior, senior, or graduate years; not renewable. *Number:* varies. *Amount:* up to $2000.

Eligibility Requirements: Applicant must be enrolled or expecting to enroll full- or part-time at a two-year or four-year or technical institution or university; resident of North Carolina and studying in North Carolina.

North Carolina National Guard (continued)

Available to U.S. citizens. Applicant or parent must meet one or more of the following requirements: Air Force National Guard or Army National Guard experience; retired from active duty; disabled or killed as a result of military service; prisoner of war; or missing in action.

Application Requirements: Application. *Deadline:* varies.

Contact: Anne Gildhouse, Education Services Officer
North Carolina National Guard
Claude T. Bowers Military Center, 4105 Reedy Creek Road
Raleigh, NC 27607-6410
Phone: 919-664-6000
Fax: 919-664-6520
E-mail: anne.gildhouse@nc.ngb.army.mil

OHIO NATIONAL GUARD http://www.ongsp.org

OHIO NATIONAL GUARD SCHOLARSHIP PROGRAM

Scholarships are for undergraduate studies at an approved Ohio post-secondary institution. Applicants must enlist for six years of Selective Service Reserve Duty in the Ohio National Guard. Scholarship pays 100% instructional and general fees for public institutions and an average of cost of public schools is available for private schools. May reapply up to four years. Deadlines: July 1, November 1, February 1, April 1.

Award: Scholarship for use in freshman, sophomore, junior, or senior years; not renewable. *Number:* up to 3500. *Amount:* up to $3911.

Eligibility Requirements: Applicant must be enrolled or expecting to enroll full- or part-time at a two-year or four-year or technical institution or university; resident of Ohio and studying in Ohio. Available to U.S. citizens. Applicant or parent must meet one or more of the following requirements: Air Force National Guard or Army National Guard experience; retired from active duty; disabled or killed as a result of military service; prisoner of war; or missing in action.

Application Requirements: Application. *Deadline:* varies.

Contact: Toni Davis, Grants Administrator
Ohio National Guard
2825 West Dublin Granville Road
Columbus, OH 43235-2789
Phone: 614-336-7143
Fax: 614-336-7318
E-mail: toni.davis@tagoh.gov

PENNSYLVANIA HIGHER EDUCATION ASSISTANCE AGENCY http://www.pheaa.org

POSTSECONDARY EDUCATION GRATUITY PROGRAM

• *See page 608*

STATE OF GEORGIA http://www.gsfc.org

GEORGIA NATIONAL GUARD SERVICE CANCELABLE LOAN PROGRAM

Forgivable loans will be awarded to residents of Georgia maintaining good military standing as an eligible member of the Georgia National Guard who are enrolled at least half-time in an undergraduate degree program at an eligible college, university or technical school within the state of Georgia.

Award: Forgivable loan for use in freshman, sophomore, junior, or senior years; not renewable. *Number:* 200–250. *Amount:* $150–$1821.

Eligibility Requirements: Applicant must be enrolled or expecting to enroll full- or part-time at a two-year or four-year or technical institution or university; resident of Georgia and studying in Georgia. Available to U.S. citizens. Applicant or parent must meet one or more of the following requirements: Air Force National Guard or Army National Guard experience; retired from active duty; disabled or killed as a result of military service; prisoner of war; or missing in action.

Application Requirements: Application, financial need analysis. *Deadline:* June 4.

Contact: Peggy Matthews, Manager, GSFA Origination
State of Georgia
2082 East Exchange Place, Suite 230
Tucker, GA 30084
Phone: 770-724-9230
Fax: 770-724-9225
E-mail: peggy@gsfc.org

STATE STUDENT ASSISTANCE COMMISSION OF INDIANA (SSACI) http://www.in.gov/ssaci

INDIANA NATIONAL GUARD SUPPLEMENTAL GRANT

The award is a supplement to the Indiana Higher Education Grant program. Applicants must be members of the Indiana National Guard. All Guard paperwork must be completed prior to the start of each semester. The FAFSA must be received by March 10. Award covers certain tuition and fees at select public colleges.

Award: Grant for use in freshman, sophomore, junior, or senior years; not renewable. *Number:* 503–925. *Amount:* $20–$7110.

Eligibility Requirements: Applicant must be enrolled or expecting to enroll full- or part-time at a two-year or four-year institution or university; resident of Indiana and studying in Indiana. Available to U.S. citizens. Applicant or parent must meet one or more of the following requirements: Air Force National Guard or Army National Guard experience; retired from active duty; disabled or killed as a result of military service; prisoner of war; or missing in action.

Application Requirements: Application. *Deadline:* March 10.

Contact: Kathryn Moore, Grants Counselor
State Student Assistance Commission of Indiana (SSACI)
150 West Market Street, Suite 500
Indianapolis, IN 46204-2805
Phone: 317-232-2350
Fax: 317-232-2360
E-mail: kmoore@ssaci.in.gov

TEXAS HIGHER EDUCATION COORDINATING BOARD http://www.collegefortexans.com

TEXAS NATIONAL GUARD TUITION ASSISTANCE PROGRAM

Provides exemption from the payment of tuition to certain members of the Texas National Guard, Texas Air Guard or the State Guard. Must be Texas resident and attend school in Texas. Deadline varies.

Award: Scholarship for use in freshman, sophomore, junior, or senior years; renewable. *Number:* varies. *Amount:* varies.

Eligibility Requirements: Applicant must be enrolled or expecting to enroll full- or part-time at a four-year institution or university; resident of Texas and studying in Texas. Available to U.S. citizens. Applicant or parent must meet one or more of the following requirements: Air Force National Guard or Army National Guard experience; retired from active duty; disabled or killed as a result of military service; prisoner of war; or missing in action.

Application Requirements: Application. *Deadline:* varies.

Contact: State Adjutant General's Office
Texas Higher Education Coordinating Board
PO Box 5218
Austin, TX 78763-5218
Phone: 512-465-5515
E-mail: education.office@tx.ngb.army.mil

MILITARY SERVICE: ARMY

AMERICAN LEGION AUXILIARY DEPARTMENT OF CALIFORNIA http://www.calegionaux.org

AMERICAN LEGION AUXILIARY DEPARTMENT OF CALIFORNIA JUNIOR SCHOLARSHIP

• *See page 511*

AMERICAN LEGION AUXILIARY DEPARTMENT OF KENTUCKY http://www.kylegion.org

AMERICAN LEGION AUXILIARY DEPARTMENT OF KENTUCKY LAURA BLACKBURN MEMORIAL SCHOLARSHIP

Scholarship to the child, grandchild, or great grandchild of a veteran who served in the Armed Forces. Applicant must be a Kentucky resident.

Award: Scholarship for use in freshman year; not renewable. *Number:* 1. *Amount:* $1000.

Eligibility Requirements: Applicant must be high school student; planning to enroll or expecting to enroll full-time at a four-year institution or university and resident of Kentucky. Available to U.S. citizens. Applicant or parent must meet one or more of the following requirements: Army experience; retired from active duty; disabled or killed as a result of military service; prisoner of war; or missing in action.

Application Requirements: Application, financial need analysis, transcript. *Deadline:* March 31.

Contact: Betty Cook, Secretary and Treasurer
American Legion Auxiliary Department of Kentucky
PO Box 189
Greensburg, KY 42743
Phone: 270-932-7533
Fax: 270-932-7672
E-mail: secretarykyala@aol.com

AMERICAN LEGION AUXILIARY DEPARTMENT OF MARYLAND http://www.alamd.org

AMERICAN LEGION AUXILIARY DEPARTMENT OF MARYLAND CHILDREN AND YOUTH SCHOLARSHIPS

One scholarship of $2000 for undergraduate student enrolled in full-time study at an accredited college or university. Must be U.S. citizen, Maryland resident, and child of a military veteran.

Award: Scholarship for use in freshman, sophomore, junior, or senior years; renewable. *Number:* 1. *Amount:* $2000.

Eligibility Requirements: Applicant must be enrolled or expecting to enroll full-time at a four-year institution or university and resident of Maryland. Available to U.S. citizens. Applicant or parent must meet one or more of the following requirements: Army experience; retired from active duty; disabled or killed as a result of military service; prisoner of war; or missing in action.

Application Requirements: Application, financial need analysis, references, transcript. *Deadline:* May 1.

Contact: Meredith Beeg, Vice President
American Legion Auxiliary Department of Maryland
1589 Sulphur Spring Road, Suite 105
Baltimore, MD 21227
Phone: 410-242-9519
Fax: 410-242-9553
E-mail: hq@alamd.org

AMERICAN LEGION DEPARTMENT OF NEW JERSEY http://www.njamericanlegion.org

LUTERMAN SCHOLARSHIP

• *See page 520*

STUTZ SCHOLARSHIP

• *See page 520*

ARMY OFFICERS' WIVES CLUB OF GREATER WASHINGTON AREA http://www.fmthriftshop.org

ARMY OFFICERS WIVES CLUB OF THE GREATER WASHINGTON AREA SCHOLARSHIP

Scholarship for high school seniors, college students or children or spouses of U.S. Army personnel. Scholarship awards are based on scholastic merit and community involvement.

Award: Scholarship for use in freshman, sophomore, junior, or senior years; not renewable. *Number:* 1–3. *Amount:* $100–$500.

Eligibility Requirements: Applicant must be age 22 or under and enrolled or expecting to enroll full-time at a four-year institution or university. Available to U.S. citizens. Applicant or parent must meet one or more of the following requirements: Army experience; retired from active duty; disabled or killed as a result of military service; prisoner of war; or missing in action.

Application Requirements: Application, essay, references, self-addressed stamped envelope, transcript, military dependent ID card. *Deadline:* March 31.

Contact: Janis Waller, Scholarship Committee Chair
Army Officers' Wives Club of Greater Washington Area
12025 William & Mary Circle
Woodbridge, VA 22192-1634

DEPARTMENT OF THE ARMY http://www.goarmy.com/rotc

ARMY ROTC TWO-YEAR, THREE-YEAR AND FOUR-YEAR SCHOLARSHIPS FOR ACTIVE DUTY ARMY ENLISTED PERSONNEL

Award for freshman, sophomore, and junior year for use at a four-year institution for Army enlisted personnel. Merit considered. Must also be member of the school's ROTC program. Must pass physical and have completed two years of active duty. Applicant must be at least seventeen years of age by college enrollment and under thirty-one years of age in the year of graduation. Submit recommendations from Commanding Officer and Field Grade Commander. Include DODMERB Physical Forms and DA Form 2A.

Award: Scholarship for use in freshman, sophomore, junior, or senior years; not renewable. *Number:* 200. *Amount:* up to $10,000.

Eligibility Requirements: Applicant must be age 17-30 and enrolled or expecting to enroll full-time at a four-year institution or university. Applicant must have 2.5 GPA or higher. Available to U.S. citizens. Applicant or parent must meet one or more of the following requirements: Army or Army National Guard experience; retired from active duty; disabled or killed as a result of military service; prisoner of war; or missing in action.

Application Requirements: Application, essay, photo, references, test scores, transcript, DA Form 2A, DODMERB physical, APFT, GT. *Deadline:* April 1.

Contact: Linda Matthews, Scholarship Management Branch
Department of the Army
U.S. Army Cadet Command, 55 Patch Road, Building 56
Fort Monroe, VA 23651-1052
Phone: 757-788-4559
Fax: 757-788-4643
E-mail: linda.matthews@usacc.army.mil

TWO-, THREE-, FOUR-YEAR ARMY ROTC GREEN TO GOLD SCHOLARSHIP PROGRAM

One-time award for selected active duty enlisted members of the Army entering college for the first time, and those who have completed 1 or 2 years of college. Must join school's ROTC program, pass physical, and APFT. U.S. citizens only. Must be at least 17 years of age by college enrollment and under 31 years of age at time of graduation.

Award: Scholarship for use in freshman, sophomore, or junior years; not renewable. *Number:* 190–200. *Amount:* $10,000–$27,000.

Eligibility Requirements: Applicant must be age 17-31 and enrolled or expecting to enroll full-time at a four-year institution or university. Applicant must have 2.5 GPA or higher. Available to U.S. citizens. Applicant must have served in the Army.

Application Requirements: Application, financial need analysis, interview, photo, references, test scores, transcript. *Deadline:* April 1.

Contact: Joycelyn Bryant, Military Personnel Technician Green to Gold Coordinator
Department of the Army
U.S. Army Cadet Command, 55 Patch Road, Building 56
Fort Monroe, VA 23651-1052
Phone: 757-788-3341
Fax: 757-788-4643
E-mail: joycelyn.bryant@usacc.army.mil

TWO-, THREE-, FOUR-YEAR CAMPUS-BASED SCHOLARSHIPS

One-time award for college freshmen, sophomores, or juniors or students with BA who need two years to obtain graduate degree. Must be a member of school's ROTC program. Must pass physical. Minimum 2.5 GPA required. Professor of military science must submit application. Applicant must be at least 17 when

Department of the Army (continued)

enrolled in college and under thirty-one years of age in the year of graduation. Must be U.S. citizen/national at time of award. Open year-round.

Award: Scholarship for use in freshman, sophomore, junior, or graduate years; not renewable. *Number:* 1920. *Amount:* $10,000.

Eligibility Requirements: Applicant must be age 17-30 and enrolled or expecting to enroll full-time at a four-year institution or university. Applicant must have 2.5 GPA or higher. Available to U.S. citizens. Applicant or parent must meet one or more of the following requirements: Army or Army National Guard experience; retired from active duty; disabled or killed as a result of military service; prisoner of war; or missing in action.

Application Requirements: Application, interview, test scores, transcript. *Deadline:* continuous.

Contact: Mr. Joseph O'Donnell, Scholarship Management Branch
Department of the Army
U.S. Army Cadet Command, 55 Patch Road, Building 56
Fort Monroe, VA 23651-1052
Phone: 757-788-2994
Fax: 757-788-4643
E-mail: joseph.odonnell@usacc.army.mil

U.S. ARMY ROTC FOUR-YEAR COLLEGE SCHOLARSHIP

One-time award for students entering college for the first time, or freshmen in a documented five-year degree program. Must join school's ROTC program, pass physical, and submit teacher evaluations. Must be a U.S. citizen and have a qualifying SAT or ACT score. Applicant must be at least seventeen years of age by college enrollment and under thirty-one years of age in the year of graduation. Online application available.

Award: Scholarship for use in freshman or sophomore years; not renewable. *Number:* 700–5000. *Amount:* $5000–$35,000.

Eligibility Requirements: Applicant must be age 17-31 and enrolled or expecting to enroll full-time at a four-year institution. Applicant must have 2.5 GPA or higher. Available to U.S. citizens. Applicant must have served in the Army or Army National Guard.

Application Requirements: Application, essay, interview, references, test scores, transcript. *Deadline:* January 10.

Contact: Jennifer Crewe, Lead, Scholarship Branch
Department of the Army
U.S. Army Cadet Command, 55 Patch Road, Building 56
Fort Monroe, VA 23651-1052
Phone: 757-788-4563
Fax: 757-788-4643
E-mail: jennifer.crewe@usacc.army.mil

U.S. ARMY ROTC FOUR-YEAR HISTORICALLY BLACK COLLEGE/ UNIVERSITY SCHOLARSHIP

One-time award for students attending college for the first time Must attend a historically black college or university and must join school's ROTC program. Must pass physical. Must have a qualifying SAT or ACT score and minimum GPA of 2.5. Applicant must be at least 17 by college enrollment and under thirty-one years of age in the year of graduation. Must be a U.S. citizen/national at time of award. Application available online.

Award: Scholarship for use in freshman year; not renewable. *Number:* 79. *Amount:* up to $10,000.

Eligibility Requirements: Applicant must be Black (non-Hispanic); age 17-30 and enrolled or expecting to enroll full-time at a four-year institution or university. Applicant must have 2.5 GPA or higher. Available to U.S. citizens. Applicant or parent must meet one or more of the following requirements: Army or Army National Guard experience; retired from active duty; disabled or killed as a result of military service; prisoner of war; or missing in action.

Application Requirements: Application, essay, interview, references, test scores, transcript. *Deadline:* January 10.

Contact: Jennifer Crewe, Lead, Scholarship Branch
Department of the Army
U.S. Army Cadet Command, 55 Patch Road, Building 56
Fort Monroe, VA 23651-1052
Phone: 757-788-4563
Fax: 757-788-4643
E-mail: jennifer.crewe@usacc.army.mil

DEPARTMENT OF VETERANS AFFAIRS (VA) http://www.gibill.va.gov

MONTGOMERY GI BILL (SELECTED RESERVE)

• *See page 632*

11TH ARMORED CAVALRY VETERANS OF VIETNAM AND CAMBODIA http://www.11thcavnam.com

11ACVVC SCHOLARSHIP PROGRAM

Applications will be accepted for undergraduate studies from children or stepchildren of current members of the 11ACVVC in good standing. Priority given to children of Vietnam War Blackhorse Troopers Killed In Action (KIA) or Died of Wounds.

Award: Scholarship for use in freshman, sophomore, junior, or senior years; not renewable. *Number:* 27. *Amount:* $3000.

Eligibility Requirements: Applicant must be age 26 or under and enrolled or expecting to enroll full- or part-time at a four-year institution or university. Available to U.S. citizens. Applicant or parent must meet one or more of the following requirements: Army experience; retired from active duty; disabled or killed as a result of military service; prisoner of war; or missing in action.

Application Requirements: Application, references, transcript. *Deadline:* May 15.

Contact: Gene Johnson, Scholarship Committee Chairman
11th Armored Cavalry Veterans of Vietnam and Cambodia
PO Box 296
Milam, TX 75959
Phone: 409-625-1736
E-mail: gene677@aol.com

FIRST INFANTRY DIVISION FOUNDATION http://www.bigredone.org

LIEUTENANT GENERAL CLARENCE R. HUEBNER SCHOLARSHIP PROGRAM

Award for undergraduate study for children and grandchildren of veterans of the First Infantry Division, U.S. Army. Essay, letter of acceptance, proof of registration with selective service (if male), and proof of parent's or grandparent's service required. Must be high school senior to apply. Send self-addressed stamped envelope for essay topic and details.

Award: Scholarship for use in freshman, sophomore, junior, or senior years; renewable. *Number:* 3–6. *Amount:* $1000–$4000.

Eligibility Requirements: Applicant must be enrolled or expecting to enroll full-time at a four-year institution or university. Available to U.S. citizens. Applicant or parent must meet one or more of the following requirements: Army experience; retired from active duty; disabled or killed as a result of military service; prisoner of war; or missing in action.

Application Requirements: Application, essay, references, self-addressed stamped envelope, test scores, transcript, letter of acceptance, proof of parent's or grandparent's service with the First Infantry Division. *Deadline:* June 1.

Contact: Scholarship Committee
First Infantry Division Foundation
1933 Morris Road
Blue Bell, PA 19422

FOUNDATION OF THE FIRST CAVALRY DIVISION ASSOCIATION http://www.1cda.org

FOUNDATION OF THE 1ST CAVALRY DIVISION ASSOCIATION (IA DRANG) SCHOLARSHIP

• *See page 632*

INDIANA DEPARTMENT OF VETERANS AFFAIRS http://www.in.gov/dva

RESIDENT TUITION FOR ACTIVE DUTY MILITARY PERSONNEL

• *See page 632*

NON COMMISSIONED OFFICERS ASSOCIATION (NCOA) http://www.ncoausa.org

NON-COMMISSIONED OFFICERS ASSOCIATION SCHOLARSHIPS

• *See page 548*

101ST AIRBORNE DIVISION ASSOCIATION http://www.screamingeagle.org

101ST AIRBORNE DIVISION ASSOCIATION CHAPPIE HALL SCHOLARSHIP PROGRAM

The major factors to be considered in the evaluation and rating of applicants are eligibility, career objectives, academic record, financial need, and insight gained from the letter requesting consideration, and letters of recommendation. Applicant's parents, grandparents, or spouse, living or deceased must have/had membership with 101st Airborne Division. Dollar amount and total number of awards varies.

Award: Scholarship for use in freshman, sophomore, junior, senior, graduate, or postgraduate years; renewable. *Number:* up to 11. *Amount:* $1000.

Eligibility Requirements: Applicant must be enrolled or expecting to enroll full-time at a two-year or four-year or technical institution or university. Applicant must have 2.5 GPA or higher. Available to U.S. and non-U.S. citizens. Applicant or parent must meet one or more of the following requirements: Army experience; retired from active duty; disabled or killed as a result of military service; prisoner of war; or missing in action.

Application Requirements: Application, autobiography, financial need analysis, photo, references, test scores, transcript. *Deadline:* May 31.

Contact: Sam Bass, Executive Secretary-Treasurer
101st Airborne Division Association
PO Box 929
Fort Campbell, KY 42223-0929
Phone: 270-439-0445
Fax: 270-439-6645
E-mail: sambass101@comcast.net

SOCIETY OF DAUGHTERS OF THE UNITED STATES ARMY

SOCIETY OF DAUGHTERS OF THE UNITED STATES ARMY SCHOLARSHIPS

Applicants must be daughter or granddaughter (step or adopted) of a career warrant or commissioned officer in the U.S. Army who: (1) is currently on active duty; (2) retired from active duty after at least 20 years of service; (3) was medically retired before 20 years of active service; (4) died while on active duty; (5) died after retiring from active duty.

Award: Scholarship for use in freshman, sophomore, or junior years; renewable. *Number:* 13. *Amount:* $1000.

Eligibility Requirements: Applicant must be enrolled or expecting to enroll full-time at a two-year or four-year or technical institution or university; female and must have an interest in leadership. Applicant must have 3.0 GPA or higher. Available to U.S. citizens. Applicant or parent must meet one or more of the following requirements: Army or Army National Guard experience; retired from active duty; disabled or killed as a result of military service; prisoner of war; or missing in action.

Application Requirements: Application, essay, resume, references, self-addressed stamped envelope, test scores, transcript, proof of service of qualifying service member (state relationship to member), SASE. *Deadline:* March 1.

Contact: Mary P. Maroney, Chairperson, Memorial and Scholarship Funds
Society of Daughters of the United States Army
11804 Grey Birch Place
Reston, VA 20191
Phone: 703-476-6443

UNITED DAUGHTERS OF THE CONFEDERACY http://www.hqudc.org

ADMIRAL RAPHAEL SEMMES SCHOLARSHIP

• *See page 563*

BARBARA JACKSON SICHEL MEMORIAL SCHOLARSHIP

• *See page 564*

CODY BACHMAN SCHOLARSHIP

• *See page 564*

CORA BELL WESLEY MEMORIAL SCHOLARSHIP

• *See page 564*

CORNELIA BRANCH STONE SCHOLARSHIP

• *See page 564*

DAVID STEPHEN WYLIE SCHOLARSHIP

• *See page 565*

DOROTHY WILLIAMS SCHOLARSHIP

• *See page 565*

ELIZABETH AND WALLACE KINGSBURY SCHOLARSHIP

• *See page 565*

GERTRUDE BOTTS-SAUCIER SCHOLARSHIP

• *See page 565*

HECTOR W. CHURCH SCHOLARSHIP

• *See page 565*

HENRY CLAY DARSEY SCHOLARSHIP

• *See page 566*

JANET B. SEIPPEL SCHOLARSHIP

• *See page 566*

LOLA B. CURRY SCHOLARSHIP

• *See page 566*

MAJOR MADISON BELL SCHOLARSHIP

• *See page 566*

MARY B. POPPENHEIM MEMORIAL SCHOLARSHIP

• *See page 566*

MATTHEW FONTAINE MAURY SCHOLARSHIP

• *See page 567*

MRS. ELLA M. FRANKLIN SCHOLARSHIP

• *See page 567*

MRS. L. H. RAINES MEMORIAL SCHOLARSHIP

• *See page 567*

S.A. CUNNINGHAM SCHOLARSHIP

• *See page 567*

STONEWALL JACKSON SCHOLARSHIP

• *See page 567*

WINNIE DAVIS-CHILDREN OF THE CONFEDERACY SCHOLARSHIP

• *See page 567*

V.E.T.S.-VICTORY ENSURED THROUGH SERVICE

V.E.T.S. ANNUAL SCHOLARSHIP

Scholarships for graduating high school seniors, junior college students, continuing college or university students, graduate students, and vocational school students. Applicants must be a veteran, or a spouse, child, grandchild of a veteran and be a U.S. citizen. Must have maintained a 3.0 GPA with no failing grades in any subject. Amount awarded is usually $500, but Board of Directors can grant special scholarships up to $1500 based on need and qualifications.

Award: Scholarship for use in freshman, sophomore, junior, senior, graduate, or postgraduate years; not renewable. *Number:* 6. *Amount:* $500–$1500.

Eligibility Requirements: Applicant must be enrolled or expecting to enroll full-time at a two-year or four-year or technical institution or university and resident of Arizona or California. Applicant must have 3.0 GPA or higher. Available to U.S. citizens. Applicant or parent must meet one or more of the following requirements: Army or Army National Guard experience; retired from active duty; disabled or killed as a result of military service; prisoner of war; or missing in action.

V.E.T.S.-Victory Ensured Through Service (continued)

Application Requirements: Application, financial need analysis, photo, references, test scores, transcript, DD Form 214 or military discharge "Honorable". *Deadline:* April 1.

Contact: Candace Filek, Scholarship Chair
V.E.T.S.-Victory Ensured Through Service
8698 Midview Drive
Palo Cedro, CA 96073
Phone: 530-547-3776

WISCONSIN DEPARTMENT OF VETERANS AFFAIRS http://www.dva.state.wi.us

VETERANS EDUCATION (VETED) REIMBURSEMENT GRANT
• *See page 633*

WOMEN'S ARMY CORPS VETERANS ASSOCIATION http://www.armywomen.org

WOMEN'S ARMY CORPS VETERANS' ASSOCIATION SCHOLARSHIP

Scholarship to graduating high school senior showing academic promise. Must be a child, grandchild, niece or nephew of an Army servicewoman. Minimum cumulative GPA of 3.5 required. Applicants must plan to enroll in a degree program as a full-time student at an accredited college or university in the United States.

Award: Scholarship for use in freshman year; not renewable. *Number:* 1. *Amount:* $1500.

Eligibility Requirements: Applicant must be high school student and planning to enroll or expecting to enroll full-time at a four-year institution or university. Applicant must have 3.5 GPA or higher. Available to U.S. citizens. Applicant or parent must meet one or more of the following requirements: Army experience; retired from active duty; disabled or killed as a result of military service; prisoner of war; or missing in action.

Application Requirements: Application, autobiography, references, transcript, documentation of sponsor's military service. *Deadline:* May 1.

Contact: Eldora Engebretson, Scholarship Committee
Women's Army Corps Veterans Association
PO Box 5577
Fort McClellan, AL 36205-5577
Phone: 623-566-9299
E-mail: info@armywomen.org

MILITARY SERVICE: ARMY NATIONAL GUARD

ALABAMA COMMISSION ON HIGHER EDUCATION http://www.ache.alabama.gov

ALABAMA NATIONAL GUARD EDUCATIONAL ASSISTANCE PROGRAM
• *See page 633*

AMERICAN LEGION DEPARTMENT OF TENNESSEE http://www.tennesseelegion.org

JROTC SCHOLARSHIP
• *See page 633*

CONNECTICUT ARMY NATIONAL GUARD http://www.ct.ngb.army.mil

CONNECTICUT ARMY NATIONAL GUARD 100% TUITION WAIVER

Program is for any active member of the Connecticut Army National Guard in good standing. Must be a resident of Connecticut attending any Connecticut state (public) university, community-technical college or regional vocational-technical school. The total number of available awards is unlimited.

Award: Scholarship for use in freshman, sophomore, junior, or senior years; not renewable. *Number:* varies. *Amount:* $16,000.

Eligibility Requirements: Applicant must be age 17-65; enrolled or expecting to enroll full- or part-time at a two-year or four-year or technical institution or university; resident of Connecticut and studying in Connecticut. Available to U.S. and non-U.S. citizens. Applicant or parent must meet one or more of the following requirements: Army National Guard experience; retired from active duty; disabled or killed as a result of military service; prisoner of war; or missing in action.

Application Requirements: Application. *Deadline:* July 1.

Contact: Capt. Jeremy Lingenfelser, Education Services Officer
Connecticut Army National Guard
360 Broad Street
Hartford, CT 06105-3795
Phone: 860-524-4816
Fax: 860-524-4904
E-mail: education@ct.ngb.army.mil

DELAWARE NATIONAL GUARD http://www.delawarenationalguard.com

STATE TUITION ASSISTANCE
• *See page 633*

DEPARTMENT OF THE ARMY http://www.goarmy.com/rotc

ARMY ROTC TWO-YEAR, THREE-YEAR AND FOUR-YEAR SCHOLARSHIPS FOR ACTIVE DUTY ARMY ENLISTED PERSONNEL
• *See page 637*

TWO-, THREE-, FOUR-YEAR CAMPUS-BASED SCHOLARSHIPS
• *See page 637*

U.S. ARMY ROTC FOUR-YEAR COLLEGE SCHOLARSHIP
• *See page 638*

U.S. ARMY ROTC FOUR-YEAR HISTORICALLY BLACK COLLEGE/ UNIVERSITY SCHOLARSHIP
• *See page 638*

U.S. ARMY ROTC GUARANTEED RESERVE FORCES DUTY (GRFD), (ARNG/USAR) AND DEDICATED ARNG SCHOLARSHIPS

One-time award for college sophomores and juniors, or two-year graduate degree students. Must be a member of school's ROTC program. Must pass physical. Minimum 2.5 GPA required. Applicant must be at least seventeen years of age when enrolled in college and under thirty-one years of age in the year of graduation. Must be a U.S. citizen/national at the time of award.

Award: Scholarship for use in sophomore, junior, or graduate years; not renewable. *Number:* 2700. *Amount:* up to $10,000.

Eligibility Requirements: Applicant must be age 17-30 and enrolled or expecting to enroll full-time at a four-year institution or university. Applicant must have 2.5 GPA or higher. Available to U.S. citizens. Applicant or parent must meet one or more of the following requirements: Army National Guard experience; retired from active duty; disabled or killed as a result of military service; prisoner of war; or missing in action.

Application Requirements: Application, interview, transcript. *Deadline:* March 15.

Contact: Maj. David Eldridge, Program Manager
Department of the Army
U.S. Army Cadet Command, 55 Patch Road, Building 56
Fort Monroe, VA 23651-1052
Phone: 757-788-4551
Fax: 757-788-4643
E-mail: david.eldridge@usacc.army.mil

U.S. ARMY ROTC MILITARY JUNIOR COLLEGE (MJC) SCHOLARSHIP

One-time award for high school graduates who wish to attend a two-year military junior college. Must serve simultaneously in the Army National Guard or Reserve and qualify for the ROTC Advanced Course. Must have a minimum GPA of 2.5. Must be a U.S. citizen/national at time of award. Must also be eighteen years of age by October 1 and under twenty-seven years of age on June 30 in the year of graduation. On-line application available. Must be used at one of five military junior colleges. See Professor of Military Science at college for application.

Award: Scholarship for use in freshman year; not renewable. *Number:* 300. *Amount:* up to $10,000.

Eligibility Requirements: Applicant must be age 18-26 and enrolled or expecting to enroll full-time at a two-year institution. Applicant must have 2.5 GPA or higher. Available to U.S. citizens. Applicant or parent must meet one or more of the following requirements: Army National Guard experience; retired from active duty; disabled or killed as a result of military service; prisoner of war; or missing in action.

Application Requirements: Application, essay, interview, references, test scores, transcript. *Deadline:* August 25.

Contact: Maj. David Eldridge, Program Manager
Department of the Army
U.S. Army Cadet Command, 55 Patch Road, Building 56
Fort Monroe, VA 23651-1052
Phone: 757-788-4551
Fax: 757-788-4643
E-mail: david.eldridge@usacc.army.mil

DEPARTMENT OF VETERANS AFFAIRS (VA) http://www.gibill.va.gov

MONTGOMERY GI BILL (SELECTED RESERVE)
• *See page 632*

RESERVE EDUCATION ASSISTANCE PROGRAM
• *See page 634*

ENLISTED ASSOCIATION OF THE NATIONAL GUARD OF NEW JERSEY http://www.eang-nj.org

CSM VINCENT BALDASSARI MEMORIAL SCHOLARSHIP PROGRAM
• *See page 634*

USAA SCHOLARSHIP
• *See page 634*

ILLINOIS STUDENT ASSISTANCE COMMISSION (ISAC) http://www.collegezone.org

ILLINOIS NATIONAL GUARD GRANT PROGRAM
• *See page 634*

INDIANA DEPARTMENT OF VETERANS AFFAIRS http://www.in.gov/dva

NATIONAL GUARD SCHOLARSHIP EXTENSION PROGRAM
• *See page 634*

NATIONAL GUARD TUITION SUPPLEMENT PROGRAM
• *See page 635*

TUITION AND FEE REMISSION FOR CHILDREN AND SPOUSES OF NATIONAL GUARD MEMBERS
• *See page 635*

IOWA COLLEGE STUDENT AID COMMISSION http://www.iowacollegeaid.gov

IOWA NATIONAL GUARD EDUCATION ASSISTANCE PROGRAM
• *See page 635*

LOUISIANA NATIONAL GUARD-STATE OF LOUISIANA, JOINT TASK FORCE LA http://www.la.ngb.army.mil

LOUISIANA NATIONAL GUARD STATE TUITION EXEMPTION PROGRAM
• *See page 635*

MINNESOTA DEPARTMENT OF MILITARY AFFAIRS http://www.minnesotanationalguard.org

LEADERSHIP, EXCELLENCE AND DEDICATED SERVICE SCHOLARSHIP
• *See page 603*

NATIONAL GUARD ASSOCIATION OF COLORADO EDUCATION FOUNDATION http://www.ngaco.org

NATIONAL GUARD ASSOCIATION OF COLORADO (NGACO) EDUCATION FOUNDATION INC. SCHOLARSHIP
• *See page 635*

NORTH CAROLINA NATIONAL GUARD http://www.nc.ngb.army.mil

NORTH CAROLINA NATIONAL GUARD TUITION ASSISTANCE PROGRAM
• *See page 636*

OHIO NATIONAL GUARD http://www.ongsp.org

OHIO NATIONAL GUARD SCHOLARSHIP PROGRAM
• *See page 636*

PENNSYLVANIA HIGHER EDUCATION ASSISTANCE AGENCY http://www.pheaa.org

POSTSECONDARY EDUCATION GRATUITY PROGRAM
• *See page 608*

SOCIETY OF DAUGHTERS OF THE UNITED STATES ARMY

SOCIETY OF DAUGHTERS OF THE UNITED STATES ARMY SCHOLARSHIPS
• *See page 639*

STATE OF GEORGIA http://www.gsfc.org

GEORGIA NATIONAL GUARD SERVICE CANCELABLE LOAN PROGRAM
• *See page 636*

STATE STUDENT ASSISTANCE COMMISSION OF INDIANA (SSACI) http://www.in.gov/ssaci

INDIANA NATIONAL GUARD SUPPLEMENTAL GRANT
• *See page 636*

TEXAS HIGHER EDUCATION COORDINATING BOARD http://www.collegefortexans.com

TEXAS NATIONAL GUARD TUITION ASSISTANCE PROGRAM
• *See page 636*

V.E.T.S.-VICTORY ENSURED THROUGH SERVICE

V.E.T.S. ANNUAL SCHOLARSHIP
• *See page 639*

MILITARY SERVICE: COAST GUARD

DEPARTMENT OF VETERANS AFFAIRS (VA) http://www.gibill.va.gov

MONTGOMERY GI BILL (SELECTED RESERVE)
• *See page 632*

FLEET RESERVE ASSOCIATION http://www.fra.org

FLEET RESERVE ASSOCIATION SCHOLARSHIP
• *See page 532*

OLIVER AND ESTHER R. HOWARD SCHOLARSHIP
• *See page 532*

SCHUYLER S. PYLE AWARD
• *See page 533*

STANLEY A. DORAN MEMORIAL SCHOLARSHIP

Award for dependent children of members in good standing of the Fleet Reserve Association or of a member in good standing at time of death. Minimum 3.0 GPA required.

Award: Scholarship for use in freshman, sophomore, junior, or senior years; not renewable. *Number:* 1. *Amount:* up to $3000.

Eligibility Requirements: Applicant must be enrolled or expecting to enroll full-time at a two-year or four-year institution or university. Applicant must have 3.0 GPA or higher. Available to U.S. citizens. Applicant or parent must meet one or more of the following

Fleet Reserve Association (continued)

requirements: Coast Guard, Marine Corps, or Navy experience; retired from active duty; disabled or killed as a result of military service; prisoner of war; or missing in action.

Application Requirements: Application, essay, financial need analysis, references, test scores, transcript. *Deadline:* April 15.

Contact: Scholarship Administrator
Fleet Reserve Association
125 North West Street
Alexandria, VA 22314-2754

LADIES AUXILIARY OF THE FLEET RESERVE ASSOCIATION http://www.fra.org

ALLIE MAE ODEN MEMORIAL SCHOLARSHIP

• *See page 540*

LADIES AUXILIARY OF THE FLEET RESERVE ASSOCIATION-NATIONAL PRESIDENT'S SCHOLARSHIP

• *See page 540*

LADIES AUXILIARY OF THE FLEET RESERVE ASSOCIATION SCHOLARSHIP

• *See page 540*

SAM ROSE MEMORIAL SCHOLARSHIP

• *See page 540*

TAILHOOK EDUCATIONAL FOUNDATION http://www.tailhook.org

TAILHOOK EDUCATIONAL FOUNDATION SCHOLARSHIP

Applicant must be a high school graduate and the natural, step or adopted son or daughter of a current or former Naval Aviator, Naval Flight Officer or Naval Air-crewman. Individuals or children of individuals serving or having served on board a U.S. Navy Aircraft Carrier in ship's company or the Air Wing also eligible.

Award: Scholarship for use in freshman, sophomore, junior, or senior years; renewable. *Number:* 50. *Amount:* $2000–$10,000.

Eligibility Requirements: Applicant must be enrolled or expecting to enroll full-time at a two-year or four-year institution or university. Applicant must have 3.0 GPA or higher. Available to U.S. citizens. Applicant or parent must meet one or more of the following requirements: Coast Guard, Marine Corps, or Navy experience; retired from active duty; disabled or killed as a result of military service; prisoner of war; or missing in action.

Application Requirements: Application, driver's license, essay, references, self-addressed stamped envelope, test scores, transcript, proof of eligibility. *Deadline:* March 15.

Contact: Marc Ostertag, Executive Director of Education
Tailhook Educational Foundation
PO Box 26626
San Diego, CA 92196
Phone: 800-269-8267
Fax: 858-578-8839
E-mail: tag@tailhook.net

WISCONSIN DEPARTMENT OF VETERANS AFFAIRS http://www.dva.state.wi.us

VETERANS EDUCATION (VETED) REIMBURSEMENT GRANT

• *See page 633*

MILITARY SERVICE: GENERAL

ALABAMA DEPARTMENT OF VETERANS AFFAIRS http://www.va.alabama.gov

ALABAMA G.I. DEPENDENTS SCHOLARSHIP PROGRAM

Full scholarship for dependents of Alabama disabled, prisoner-of-war, or missing-in-action veterans. Child or stepchild must initiate training before 26th birthday; age 30 deadline may apply in certain situations. No age deadline for spouses or widows.

Award: Scholarship for use in freshman, sophomore, junior, or senior years; renewable. *Number:* varies. *Amount:* varies.

Eligibility Requirements: Applicant must be age 30 or under; enrolled or expecting to enroll full- or part-time at a four-year institution or university; resident of Alabama and studying in Alabama. Available to U.S. and non-U.S. citizens. Applicant or parent must meet one or more of the following requirements: general military experience; retired from active duty; disabled or killed as a result of military service; prisoner of war; or missing in action.

Application Requirements: Application. *Deadline:* varies.

Contact: Willie E. Moore, Scholarship Administrator
Alabama Department of Veterans Affairs
PO Box 1509
Montgomery, AL 36102-1509
Phone: 334-242-5077
Fax: 334-242-5102
E-mail: wmoore@va.state.al.us

AMERICAN LEGION AUXILIARY DEPARTMENT OF ALABAMA

AMERICAN LEGION AUXILIARY DEPARTMENT OF ALABAMA SCHOLARSHIP PROGRAM

Merit-based scholarships for Alabama residents, preferably ages 17 to 25, who are children or grandchildren of veterans of World War I, World War II, Korea, Vietnam, Operation Desert Storm, Beirut, Grenada, or Panama. Submit proof of relationship and service record. Renewable awards of $850 each. Must send self-addressed stamped envelope for application.

Award: Scholarship for use in freshman, sophomore, junior, or senior years; renewable. *Number:* up to 40. *Amount:* $850.

Eligibility Requirements: Applicant must be age 17-25; enrolled or expecting to enroll full-time at a four-year institution or university and resident of Alabama. Applicant must have 3.5 GPA or higher. Available to U.S. citizens. Applicant or parent must meet one or more of the following requirements: general military experience; retired from active duty; disabled or killed as a result of military service; prisoner of war; or missing in action.

Application Requirements: Application, financial need analysis, photo, references, self-addressed stamped envelope, test scores, transcript, birth certificate, service record. *Deadline:* April 1.

Contact: Anita Barber, Education and Scholarship Chairperson
American Legion Auxiliary Department of Alabama
120 North Jackson Street
Montgomery, AL 36104-3811
Phone: 334-262-1176
Fax: 334-262-1176
E-mail: americanlegionaux1@juno.com

AMERICAN LEGION AUXILIARY DEPARTMENT OF ARKANSAS http://www.arlegion.org

AMERICAN LEGION AUXILIARY DEPARTMENT OF ARKANSAS ACADEMIC SCHOLARSHIP

One-time award of $500 for Arkansas residents who are the children of veterans who served during eligibility dates for membership. Must attend school in Arkansas. Open to high school seniors.

Award: Scholarship for use in freshman year; not renewable. *Number:* 1. *Amount:* $500.

Eligibility Requirements: Applicant must be high school student; planning to enroll or expecting to enroll full-time at a four-year institution or university; resident of Arkansas and studying in Arkansas. Available to U.S. citizens. Applicant or parent must meet one or more of the following requirements: general military experience; retired from active duty; disabled or killed as a result of military service; prisoner of war; or missing in action.

Application Requirements: Application, essay, financial need analysis, references, self-addressed stamped envelope, test scores, transcript, copy of veteran discharge papers, branch of service, dates of service, DD Form 214. *Deadline:* March 1.

Contact: Department Secretary
American Legion Auxiliary Department of Arkansas
1415 West Seventh Street
Little Rock, AR 72201
Phone: 501-374-5836
Fax: 501-372-0855
E-mail: arkaux@juno.com

AMERICAN LEGION AUXILIARY DEPARTMENT OF COLORADO http://www.coloradolegion.org

AMERICAN LEGION AUXILIARY DEPARTMENT OF COLORADO DEPARTMENT PRESIDENT'S SCHOLARSHIP FOR JUNIOR MEMBER

Open to children, spouses, grandchildren, and great-grandchildren of veterans, and veterans who served in the Armed Forces during eligibility dates for membership in the American Legion. Applicants must be Colorado residents who have been accepted by an accredited school in Colorado.

Award: Scholarship for use in freshman year; not renewable. *Number:* 1–2. *Amount:* up to $500.

Eligibility Requirements: Applicant must be high school student; planning to enroll or expecting to enroll full- or part-time at a four-year institution or university; resident of Colorado and studying in Colorado. Available to U.S. citizens. Applicant or parent must meet one or more of the following requirements: general military experience; retired from active duty; disabled or killed as a result of military service; prisoner of war; or missing in action.

Application Requirements: Application, essay, references, transcript. *Deadline:* April 15.

Contact: Jean Lennie, Department Secretary and Treasurer
American Legion Auxiliary Department of Colorado
7465 East First Avenue, Suite D
Denver, CO 80230
Phone: 303-367-5388
Fax: 303-367-0688
E-mail: ala@coloradolegion.org

AMERICAN LEGION AUXILIARY DEPARTMENT OF CONNECTICUT http://www.ct.legion.org

AMERICAN LEGION AUXILIARY DEPARTMENT OF CONNECTICUT MEMORIAL EDUCATIONAL GRANT

• *See page 511*

AMERICAN LEGION AUXILIARY DEPARTMENT OF CONNECTICUT PAST PRESIDENTS' PARLEY MEMORIAL EDUCATION GRANT

• *See page 511*

AMERICAN LEGION AUXILIARY DEPARTMENT OF FLORIDA http://www.alafl.org

AMERICAN LEGION AUXILIARY DEPARTMENT OF FLORIDA DEPARTMENT SCHOLARSHIPS

Scholarship for children of veterans who were honorably discharged. Must be Florida resident attending an institution within Florida for full-time undergraduate study. Minimum 2.5 GPA. Must submit copy of parent's military discharge.

Award: Scholarship for use in freshman, sophomore, junior, or senior years; renewable. *Number:* 16–22. *Amount:* $500–$1000.

Eligibility Requirements: Applicant must be enrolled or expecting to enroll full-time at a two-year or four-year or technical institution or university; resident of Florida and studying in Florida. Applicant must have 2.5 GPA or higher. Available to U.S. citizens. Applicant or parent must meet one or more of the following requirements: general military experience; retired from active duty; disabled or killed as a result of military service; prisoner of war; or missing in action.

Application Requirements: Application, financial need analysis, references, transcript, proof of discharge from armed services. *Deadline:* March 1.

Contact: Robin Briere, Department Secretary and Treasurer
American Legion Auxiliary Department of Florida
PO Box 547917
Orlando, FL 32854-7917
Phone: 407-293-7411
Fax: 407-299-6522
E-mail: contact@alafl.org

AMERICAN LEGION AUXILIARY DEPARTMENT OF FLORIDA MEMORIAL SCHOLARSHIP

• *See page 512*

AMERICAN LEGION AUXILIARY DEPARTMENT OF FLORIDA NATIONAL PRESIDENTS' SCHOLARSHIP

Nonrenewable scholarship for children of veterans who served in the Armed Forces during eligibility dates for American Legion membership. Must be a high school senior and have completed 50 hours of community service.

Award: Scholarship for use in freshman year; not renewable. *Number:* 3–15. *Amount:* $500–$2500.

Eligibility Requirements: Applicant must be high school student and planning to enroll or expecting to enroll full-time at a four-year institution or university. Available to U.S. citizens. Applicant or parent must meet one or more of the following requirements: general military experience; retired from active duty; disabled or killed as a result of military service; prisoner of war; or missing in action.

Application Requirements: Application, essay, references. *Deadline:* March 15.

Contact: Robin Briere, Department Secretary and Treasurer
American Legion Auxiliary Department of Florida
PO Box 547917
Orlando, FL 32854-7917
Phone: 407-293-7411
Fax: 407-299-6522
E-mail: contact@alafl.org

AMERICAN LEGION AUXILIARY DEPARTMENT OF IDAHO

AMERICAN LEGION AUXILIARY DEPARTMENT OF IDAHO NATIONAL PRESIDENT'S SCHOLARSHIP

Undergraduate scholarship for children of veterans who served in the armed forces during WWI, WWII, Korean or Vietnam Wars, Grenada and Lebanon, Panama, Persian Gulf. Must be a high school senior and Idaho resident. Must be entered by local American Legion Auxiliary Unit. One-time award of $2000 to $2500.

Award: Scholarship for use in freshman year; not renewable. *Number:* up to 15. *Amount:* $2000–$2500.

Eligibility Requirements: Applicant must be high school student; planning to enroll or expecting to enroll full-time at a two-year or four-year or technical institution or university and resident of Idaho. Available to U.S. citizens. Applicant or parent must meet one or more of the following requirements: general military experience; retired from active duty; disabled or killed as a result of military service; prisoner of war; or missing in action.

Application Requirements: Application, essay, references, self-addressed stamped envelope, transcript. *Deadline:* March 1.

Contact: Mary Chase, Secretary
American Legion Auxiliary Department of Idaho
905 South Warren Street
Boise, ID 83706-3825
Phone: 208-342-7066
Fax: 208-342-7066
E-mail: idalegionaux@msn.com

AMERICAN LEGION AUXILIARY DEPARTMENT OF INDIANA http://www.amlegauxin.org

AMERICAN LEGION AUXILIARY DEPARTMENT OF INDIANA EDNA M. BURCUS MEMORIAL SCHOLARSHIP

One-time award for child, grandchild, or great-grandchild of veteran who served during American Legion eligibility dates. Must be Indiana resident and graduating high school senior enrolled as full-time undergraduate at an accredited Indiana institution.

Award: Scholarship for use in freshman year; not renewable. *Number:* 3. *Amount:* $500.

Eligibility Requirements: Applicant must be high school student; planning to enroll or expecting to enroll full-time at a two-year or four-year institution or university; resident of Indiana and studying in Indiana. Available to U.S. citizens. Applicant or parent must meet one or more of the following requirements: general military experience; retired from active duty; disabled or killed as a result of military service; prisoner of war; or missing in action.

Application Requirements: Application, essay, financial need analysis, self-addressed stamped envelope. *Deadline:* April 1.

Contact: Judy Otey, Department Secretary and Treasurer
American Legion Auxiliary Department of Indiana
777 North Meridian, Room 107
Indianapolis, IN 46204
Phone: 317-630-1390
Fax: 317-630-1277
E-mail: ala777@sbcglobal.net

AMERICAN LEGION AUXILIARY DEPARTMENT OF IOWA http://www.ialegion.org

AMERICAN LEGION AUXILIARY DEPARTMENT OF IOWA CHILDREN OF VETERANS SCHOLARSHIP

One-time award available to a high school senior, child of a veteran who served in the armed forces during eligibility dates for American Legion membership. Must be U.S. citizen and Iowa resident enrolled at an Iowa institution.

Award: Scholarship for use in freshman year; not renewable. *Number:* 10. *Amount:* $300.

Eligibility Requirements: Applicant must be high school student; planning to enroll or expecting to enroll full- or part-time at a four-year institution or university; resident of Iowa and studying in Iowa. Available to U.S. citizens. Applicant or parent must meet one or more of the following requirements: general military experience; retired from active duty; disabled or killed as a result of military service; prisoner of war; or missing in action.

Application Requirements: Application, autobiography, essay, financial need analysis, photo, references, self-addressed stamped envelope, test scores, transcript. *Deadline:* June 1.

Contact: Marlene Valentine, Secretary and Treasurer
American Legion Auxiliary Department of Iowa
720 Lyon Street
Des Moines, IA 50309
Phone: 515-282-7987
Fax: 515-282-7583
E-mail: alasectreas@ialegion.org

AMERICAN LEGION AUXILIARY DEPARTMENT OF KENTUCKY http://www.kylegion.org

AMERICAN LEGION AUXILIARY DEPARTMENT OF KENTUCKY MARY BARRETT MARSHALL SCHOLARSHIP

Scholarship to the daughter or grand daughter of a veteran in The American Legion. Applicant must attend a Kentucky college, and demonstrate financial need.

Award: Scholarship for use in freshman year; not renewable. *Number:* 1. *Amount:* $1000.

Eligibility Requirements: Applicant must be high school student; planning to enroll or expecting to enroll full-time at a four-year institution or university; female and studying in Kentucky. Available to U.S. citizens. Applicant or parent must meet one or more of the following requirements: general military experience; retired from active duty; disabled or killed as a result of military service; prisoner of war; or missing in action.

Application Requirements: Application, financial need analysis, transcript. *Deadline:* April 1.

Contact: Betty Cook, Secretary and Treasurer
American Legion Auxiliary Department of Kentucky
PO Box 189
Greensburg, KY 42743
Phone: 270-932-7533
Fax: 270-932-7672
E-mail: secretarykyala@aol.com

AMERICAN LEGION AUXILIARY DEPARTMENT OF MAINE http://www.mainelegion.org

AMERICAN LEGION AUXILIARY DEPARTMENT OF MAINE DANIEL E. LAMBERT MEMORIAL SCHOLARSHIP

Scholarships to assist young men and women in continuing their education beyond high school. Must demonstrate financial need, must be a resident of the State of Maine, U.S. citizen, and parent must be a veteran.

Award: Scholarship for use in freshman year; not renewable. *Number:* up to 2. *Amount:* $1000.

Eligibility Requirements: Applicant must be high school student; planning to enroll or expecting to enroll full-time at a four-year institution or university and resident of Maine. Available to U.S. citizens. Applicant or parent must meet one or more of the following requirements: general military experience; retired from active duty; disabled or killed as a result of military service; prisoner of war; or missing in action.

Application Requirements: Application, financial need analysis. *Deadline:* May 1.

Contact: Mary Wells, Education Chairman
American Legion Auxiliary Department of Maine
21 Limerock Street
PO Box 434
Rockland, ME 04841
Phone: 207-532-6007
E-mail: aladeptsecme@verizon.net

AMERICAN LEGION AUXILIARY DEPARTMENT OF MAINE NATIONAL PRESIDENT'S SCHOLARSHIP

• *See page 588*

AMERICAN LEGION AUXILIARY DEPARTMENT OF MARYLAND http://www.alamd.org

AMERICAN LEGION AUXILIARY DEPARTMENT OF MARYLAND NATIONAL PRESIDENT'S SCHOLARSHIP

• *See page 512*

AMERICAN LEGION AUXILIARY DEPARTMENT OF MARYLAND SCHOLARSHIP FOR NON-TRADITIONAL STUDENTS

• *See page 512*

AMERICAN LEGION AUXILIARY DEPARTMENT OF MARYLAND SPIRIT OF YOUTH SCHOLARSHIP FOR JUNIOR MEMBERS

• *See page 512*

AMERICAN LEGION AUXILIARY DEPARTMENT OF MASSACHUSETTS

AMERICAN LEGION AUXILIARY DEPARTMENT OF MASSACHUSETTS DEPARTMENT PRESIDENT'S SCHOLARSHIP

• *See page 589*

AMERICAN LEGION AUXILIARY DEPARTMENT OF MASSACHUSETTS PAST PRESIDENTS' PARLEY SCHOLARSHIP

One-time awards of $200 to $750 for residents of Massachusetts who are children of living or deceased veterans. Must be between the ages of 16 to 22 years and enrolled full-time at a Massachusetts institution.

Award: Scholarship for use in freshman, sophomore, junior, or senior years; not renewable. *Number:* 1. *Amount:* $200–$750.

Eligibility Requirements: Applicant must be age 16-22; enrolled or expecting to enroll full-time at a two-year or four-year institution or university; resident of Massachusetts and studying in Massachusetts. Available to U.S. citizens. Applicant or parent must meet one or more of the following requirements: general military experience; retired from active duty; disabled or killed as a result of military service; prisoner of war; or missing in action.

Application Requirements: Application. *Deadline:* March 1.

Contact: Beverly Monaco, Secretary and Treasurer
American Legion Auxiliary Department of Massachusetts
546-2 State House
Boston, MA 02133-1044
Phone: 617-727-2958
Fax: 617-727-0741

AMERICAN LEGION AUXILIARY DEPARTMENT OF MICHIGAN http://www.michalaux.org

AMERICAN LEGION AUXILIARY DEPARTMENT OF MICHIGAN MEMORIAL SCHOLARSHIP

Scholarship for daughter, granddaughter, and great-granddaughter of any honorably discharged or deceased veteran of U.S. wars or conflicts. Must be Michigan resident for minimum of one year, female between 16 and 21 years, and attend college in Michigan. Must include copy of discharge and copy of parent or guardian's IRS 1040 form.

Award: Scholarship for use in freshman or sophomore years; not renewable. *Number:* 10–35. *Amount:* up to $500.

Eligibility Requirements: Applicant must be age 16-21; enrolled or expecting to enroll full-time at a two-year or four-year or technical institution or university; female; resident of Michigan and studying in Michigan. Available to U.S. citizens. Applicant or parent must meet one or more of the following requirements: general military experience; retired from active duty; disabled or killed as a result of military service; prisoner of war; or missing in action.

Application Requirements: Application, financial need analysis, references, transcript, discharge papers. *Deadline:* March 15.

Contact: Scholarship Coordinator
American Legion Auxiliary Department of Michigan
212 North Verlinden Avenue
Lansing, MI 48915
Phone: 517-371-4720 Ext. 19
Fax: 517-371-2401
E-mail: michalaux@voyager.net

AMERICAN LEGION AUXILIARY DEPARTMENT OF MICHIGAN NATIONAL PRESIDENT'S SCHOLARSHIP

One-time scholarship for son or daughter of veterans, who were in armed forces during the eligibility dates for American Legion membership. Must be high school senior in Michigan. Only one candidate per unit. Applicant must complete 50 hours of volunteer service in the community. Must submit essay of no more than 1000 words on a specified topic.

Award: Scholarship for use in freshman year; not renewable. *Number:* 10–15. *Amount:* $1000–$2500.

Eligibility Requirements: Applicant must be high school student; planning to enroll or expecting to enroll full-time at a two-year or four-year institution or university and resident of Michigan. Available to U.S. citizens. Applicant or parent must meet one or more of the following requirements: general military experience; retired from active duty; disabled or killed as a result of military service; prisoner of war; or missing in action.

Application Requirements: Application, essay, financial need analysis, references, test scores, transcript, original article (1000-word maximum). *Deadline:* March 1.

Contact: Scholarship Coordinator
American Legion Auxiliary Department of Michigan
212 North Verlinden Avenue
Lansing, MI 48915
Phone: 517-371-4720 Ext. 19
Fax: 517-371-2401
E-mail: michalaux@voyager.net

AMERICAN LEGION AUXILIARY DEPARTMENT OF MICHIGAN SCHOLARSHIP FOR NON-TRADITIONAL STUDENT

Applicant must be a dependent of a veteran. Must be one of the following: nontraditional student returning to classroom after some period of time in which their education was interrupted, student over the age of 22 attending college for the first time to pursue a degree, or student over the age of 22 attending a trade or vocational school. Applicants must be Michigan residents only and attend Michigan institution. Judging based on: need-25 points, character/leadership-25 points, scholastic standing-25 points, initiative/goal-25 points.

Award: Scholarship for use in sophomore, junior, or senior years; not renewable. *Number:* up to 5. *Amount:* up to $1000.

Eligibility Requirements: Applicant must be age 23 and over; enrolled or expecting to enroll full-time at a two-year or four-year or technical institution or university; resident of Michigan and studying in Michigan. Available to U.S. citizens. Applicant or parent must meet one or more of the following requirements: general military experience; retired from active duty; disabled or killed as a result of military service; prisoner of war; or missing in action.

Application Requirements: Application, financial need analysis, transcript. *Deadline:* March 1.

Contact: Leisa Eldred, Scholarship Coordinator
American Legion Auxiliary Department of Michigan
212 North Verlinden Avenue
Lansing, MI 48915
Phone: 517-371-4720 Ext. 19
Fax: 517-371-2401
E-mail: michalaux@voyager.net

AMERICAN LEGION AUXILIARY DEPARTMENT OF MINNESOTA http://www.mnlegion.org

AMERICAN LEGION AUXILIARY DEPARTMENT OF MINNESOTA SCHOLARSHIPS

Seven $1000 awards for the sons, daughters, grandsons, or granddaughters of veterans who served in the Armed Forces during specific eligibility dates. Must be a Minnesota resident, a high school senior or graduate, in need of financial assistance, of good character, having a good scholastic record and at least a C average. Must be planning to attend a Minnesota post secondary institution.

Award: Scholarship for use in freshman, sophomore, junior, or senior years; not renewable. *Number:* up to 7. *Amount:* $1000.

Eligibility Requirements: Applicant must be enrolled or expecting to enroll full-time at a two-year or four-year or technical institution or university; resident of Minnesota and studying in Minnesota. Available to U.S. citizens. Applicant or parent must meet one or more of the following requirements: general military experience; retired from active duty; disabled or killed as a result of military service; prisoner of war; or missing in action.

Application Requirements: Application, essay, financial need analysis, references, transcript. *Deadline:* March 15.

Contact: Eleanor Johnson, Executive Secretary
American Legion Auxiliary Department of Minnesota
State Veterans Service Building, 20 West 12th Street, Room 314
St. Paul, MN 55155
Phone: 651-224-7634
Fax: 651-224-5243

AMERICAN LEGION AUXILIARY DEPARTMENT OF MISSOURI

AMERICAN LEGION AUXILIARY DEPARTMENT OF MISSOURI LELA MURPHY SCHOLARSHIP

• *See page 513*

AMERICAN LEGION AUXILIARY DEPARTMENT OF MISSOURI NATIONAL PRESIDENT'S SCHOLARSHIP

• *See page 513*

AMERICAN LEGION AUXILIARY DEPARTMENT OF NEBRASKA http://www.nebraskalegionaux.net

AMERICAN LEGION AUXILIARY DEPARTMENT OF NEBRASKA PRESIDENT'S SCHOLARSHIP FOR JUNIOR MEMBERS

• *See page 513*

AMERICAN LEGION AUXILIARY DEPARTMENT OF NEBRASKA PRESIDENT'S SCHOLARSHIPS

One-time award for Nebraska high school students who had entered into the national competition and did not win. Must be child of a veteran. Must rank in the upper third of class or have minimum 3.0 GPA.

American Legion Auxiliary Department of Nebraska (continued)

Award: Scholarship for use in freshman year; not renewable. *Number:* 1. *Amount:* $200.

Eligibility Requirements: Applicant must be high school student; planning to enroll or expecting to enroll full-time at a four-year institution or university and resident of Nebraska. Applicant must have 3.0 GPA or higher. Available to U.S. citizens. Applicant or parent must meet one or more of the following requirements: general military experience; retired from active duty; disabled or killed as a result of military service; prisoner of war; or missing in action.

Application Requirements: Application, essay, financial need analysis, references, test scores, transcript, letter of acceptance, proof of enrollment. *Deadline:* March 15.

Contact: Jackie O'Neill, Department Secretary
American Legion Auxiliary Department of Nebraska
PO Box 5227
Lincoln, NE 68505-0227
Phone: 402-466-1808
Fax: 402-466-0182
E-mail: neaux@alltel.net

AMERICAN LEGION AUXILIARY DEPARTMENT OF NEBRASKA ROBERTA MARIE STRETCH MEMORIAL SCHOLARSHIP

One-time award for Nebraska residents who are children or grandchildren of veterans. Must be enrolled in an undergraduate or graduate program at a four-year institution. Preference given to former Nebraska Girls State citizens. Must rank in upper third of class or have a minimum 3.0 GPA.

Award: Scholarship for use in freshman, sophomore, junior, senior, or graduate years; not renewable. *Number:* 1. *Amount:* $400.

Eligibility Requirements: Applicant must be enrolled or expecting to enroll full-time at a two-year or four-year institution or university and resident of Nebraska. Applicant must have 3.0 GPA or higher. Available to U.S. citizens. Applicant or parent must meet one or more of the following requirements: general military experience; retired from active duty; disabled or killed as a result of military service; prisoner of war; or missing in action.

Application Requirements: Application, essay, financial need analysis, references, test scores, transcript, letter of acceptance, proof of enrollment. *Deadline:* March 15.

Contact: Jackie O'Neill, Department Secretary
American Legion Auxiliary Department of Nebraska
PO Box 5227
Lincoln, NE 68505-0227
Phone: 402-466-1808
Fax: 402-466-0182
E-mail: neaux@alltel.net

AMERICAN LEGION AUXILIARY DEPARTMENT OF NEBRASKA RUBY PAUL CAMPAIGN FUND SCHOLARSHIP

• *See page 513*

AMERICAN LEGION AUXILIARY DEPARTMENT OF NEBRASKA STUDENT AID GRANTS

One-time award for veteran or veteran's child in financial need. Must be a Nebraska resident of at least five years. Must be accepted or enrolled at an institution of higher learning. If in school, must rank in upper third of class or have a minimum 3.0 GPA.

Award: Grant for use in freshman, sophomore, junior, or senior years; not renewable. *Number:* 1–30. *Amount:* $200–$300.

Eligibility Requirements: Applicant must be enrolled or expecting to enroll full-time at a two-year or four-year or technical institution or university and resident of Nebraska. Applicant must have 3.0 GPA or higher. Available to U.S. citizens. Applicant or parent must meet one or more of the following requirements: general military experience; retired from active duty; disabled or killed as a result of military service; prisoner of war; or missing in action.

Application Requirements: Application, essay, financial need analysis, references, test scores, transcript, letter of acceptance, proof of enrollment. *Deadline:* March 15.

Contact: Department Secretary
American Legion Auxiliary Department of Nebraska
PO Box 5227
Lincoln, NE 68505-0227
Phone: 402-466-1808
Fax: 402-466-0182
E-mail: neaux@alltel.net

AMERICAN LEGION AUXILIARY DEPARTMENT OF NORTH DAKOTA

http://www.ndlegion.org

AMERICAN LEGION AUXILIARY DEPARTMENT OF NORTH DAKOTA NATIONAL PRESIDENT'S SCHOLARSHIP

• *See page 589*

AMERICAN LEGION AUXILIARY DEPARTMENT OF OHIO

AMERICAN LEGION AUXILIARY DEPARTMENT OF OHIO CONTINUING EDUCATION FUND

One-time award for Ohio residents who are the children or grandchildren of veterans, living or deceased, honorably discharged during eligibility dates for American Legion membership. Awards are for undergraduate use, based on need. Freshmen not eligible. Application must be signed by a unit representative.

Award: Scholarship for use in sophomore, junior, or senior years; not renewable. *Number:* 15. *Amount:* $200.

Eligibility Requirements: Applicant must be enrolled or expecting to enroll full-time at a two-year or four-year institution or university and resident of Ohio. Available to U.S. citizens. Applicant or parent must meet one or more of the following requirements: general military experience; retired from active duty; disabled or killed as a result of military service; prisoner of war; or missing in action.

Application Requirements: Application, financial need analysis, transcript. *Deadline:* November 1.

Contact: Heather Amspaugh, Scholarship Coordinator
American Legion Auxiliary Department of Ohio
PO Box 2760
Zanesville, OH 43702-2760
Phone: 740-452-8245
Fax: 740-452-2620
E-mail: hamspaugh@rrohio.com

AMERICAN LEGION AUXILIARY DEPARTMENT OF OHIO DEPARTMENT PRESIDENT'S SCHOLARSHIP

Scholarship for children or grandchildren of veterans who served in Armed Forces during eligibility dates for American Legion membership. Must be high school senior, ages 16 to 18, Ohio resident, and U.S. citizen. Award for full-time undergraduate study. One-time award of $1000 to $1500.

Award: Scholarship for use in freshman year; not renewable. *Number:* 2. *Amount:* $1000–$1500.

Eligibility Requirements: Applicant must be high school student; age 16-18; planning to enroll or expecting to enroll full-time at a two-year or four-year institution or university and resident of Ohio. Available to U.S. citizens. Applicant or parent must meet one or more of the following requirements: general military experience; retired from active duty; disabled or killed as a result of military service; prisoner of war; or missing in action.

Application Requirements: Application, essay, financial need analysis, references, transcript. *Deadline:* March 1.

Contact: Department Scholarship Coordinator
American Legion Auxiliary Department of Ohio
PO Box 2760
Zanesville, OH 43702-2760
Phone: 740-452-8245
Fax: 740-452-2620

AMERICAN LEGION AUXILIARY DEPARTMENT OF OREGON

AMERICAN LEGION AUXILIARY DEPARTMENT OF OREGON DEPARTMENT GRANTS

One-time award for educational use in the state of Oregon. Must be a resident of Oregon who is the child or widow of a veteran or the wife of a disabled veteran.

Award: Grant for use in freshman, sophomore, junior, or senior years; not renewable. *Number:* 2. *Amount:* $1000.

Eligibility Requirements: Applicant must be enrolled or expecting to enroll full- or part-time at a two-year or four-year or technical institution or university; resident of Oregon and studying in Oregon. Available to U.S. citizens. Applicant or parent must meet one or more of the following requirements: general military experience; retired from active duty; disabled or killed as a result of military service; prisoner of war; or missing in action.

Application Requirements: Application, essay, financial need analysis, interview, references, test scores, transcript. *Deadline:* March 10.

Contact: Pat Calhoun-Floren, Secretary
American Legion Auxiliary Department of Oregon
PO Box 1730
Wilsonville, OR 97070
Phone: 503-682-3162
Fax: 503-685-5008
E-mail: pcalhoun@pcez.com

AMERICAN LEGION AUXILIARY DEPARTMENT OF OREGON NATIONAL PRESIDENT'S SCHOLARSHIP

One-time award for children of veterans who served in the Armed Forces during eligibility dates for American Legion membership. Must be high school senior and Oregon resident. Must be entered by a local American Legion auxiliary unit. Three scholarships of varying amounts.

Award: Scholarship for use in freshman year; not renewable. *Number:* 3. *Amount:* up to $2500.

Eligibility Requirements: Applicant must be high school student; planning to enroll or expecting to enroll full- or part-time at a four-year institution or university and resident of Oregon. Available to U.S. citizens. Applicant or parent must meet one or more of the following requirements: general military experience; retired from active duty; disabled or killed as a result of military service; prisoner of war; or missing in action.

Application Requirements: Application, essay, financial need analysis, interview, references, transcript. *Deadline:* March 1.

Contact: Pat Calhoun-Floren, Secretary
American Legion Auxiliary Department of Oregon
PO Box 1730
Wilsonville, OR 97070
Phone: 503-682-3162
Fax: 503-685-5008

AMERICAN LEGION AUXILIARY DEPARTMENT OF OREGON SPIRIT OF YOUTH SCHOLARSHIP

• *See page 514*

AMERICAN LEGION AUXILIARY DEPARTMENT OF SOUTH DAKOTA

AMERICAN LEGION AUXILIARY DEPARTMENT OF SOUTH DAKOTA COLLEGE SCHOLARSHIPS

• *See page 514*

AMERICAN LEGION AUXILIARY DEPARTMENT OF SOUTH DAKOTA SENIOR SCHOLARSHIP

• *See page 514*

AMERICAN LEGION AUXILIARY DEPARTMENT OF SOUTH DAKOTA THELMA FOSTER SCHOLARSHIP FOR SENIOR AUXILIARY MEMBERS

• *See page 514*

AMERICAN LEGION AUXILIARY DEPARTMENT OF SOUTH DAKOTA THELMA FOSTER SCHOLARSHIPS FOR JUNIOR AUXILIARY MEMBERS

• *See page 514*

AMERICAN LEGION AUXILIARY DEPARTMENT OF SOUTH DAKOTA VOCATIONAL SCHOLARSHIP

• *See page 515*

AMERICAN LEGION AUXILIARY DEPARTMENT OF TENNESSEE

AMERICAN LEGION AUXILIARY DEPARTMENT OF TENNESSEE VARA GRAY SCHOLARSHIP-GENERAL

• *See page 589*

AMERICAN LEGION AUXILIARY DEPARTMENT OF TEXAS

http://www.alatexas.org

AMERICAN LEGION AUXILIARY DEPARTMENT OF TEXAS GENERAL EDUCATION SCHOLARSHIP

Scholarships available for Texas residents. Must be a child of a veteran who served in the Armed Forces during eligibility dates. Some additional criteria used for selection are recommendations, academics, and finances.

Award: Scholarship for use in freshman, sophomore, junior, senior, graduate, or postgraduate years; not renewable. *Number:* up to 10. *Amount:* $500.

Eligibility Requirements: Applicant must be enrolled or expecting to enroll full-time at a two-year or four-year or technical institution or university and resident of Texas. Available to U.S. citizens. Applicant or parent must meet one or more of the following requirements: general military experience; retired from active duty; disabled or killed as a result of military service; prisoner of war; or missing in action.

Application Requirements: Application, financial need analysis, photo, resume, references, transcript, letter stating qualifications and intentions. *Deadline:* May 1.

Contact: Paula Raney, Department Secretary
American Legion Auxiliary Department of Texas
PO Box 140407
Austin, TX 78714-2902
Phone: 512-476-7278
Fax: 512-482-8391
E-mail: alatexas@txlegion.org

AMERICAN LEGION AUXILIARY DEPARTMENT OF UTAH

http://www.legion-aux.org

AMERICAN LEGION AUXILIARY DEPARTMENT OF UTAH NATIONAL PRESIDENT'S SCHOLARSHIP

• *See page 515*

AMERICAN LEGION AUXILIARY DEPARTMENT OF WASHINGTON

http://www.walegion-aux.org

AMERICAN LEGION AUXILIARY DEPARTMENT OF WASHINGTON GIFT SCHOLARSHIPS

Scholarship for a child of an incapacitated or deceased veteran. Award is for high school seniors and should be used within twelve months of receipt. Submit statement of military service of veteran parent through which applicant is eligible. One-time award of $400 for residents of Washington.

Award: Scholarship for use in freshman year; not renewable. *Number:* 2. *Amount:* $400.

Eligibility Requirements: Applicant must be high school student; age 20 or under; planning to enroll or expecting to enroll full- or part-time at a two-year or four-year or technical institution or university and resident of Washington. Available to U.S. citizens. Applicant or parent must meet one or more of the following requirements: general military experience; retired from active duty; disabled or killed as a result of military service; prisoner of war; or missing in action.

Application Requirements: Application, essay, references, transcript. *Deadline:* April 1.

Contact: Nicole Ross, News Department Secretary
American Legion Auxiliary Department of Washington
3600 Ruddell Road
Lacey, WA 98503
Phone: 360-456-5995
Fax: 360-491-7442
E-mail: alawash@qwest.net

AMERICAN LEGION AUXILIARY DEPARTMENT OF WISCONSIN http://www.amlegionauxwi.org

AMERICAN LEGION AUXILIARY DEPARTMENT OF WISCONSIN DELLA VAN DEUREN MEMORIAL SCHOLARSHIP

• *See page 515*

AMERICAN LEGION AUXILIARY DEPARTMENT OF WISCONSIN H.S. AND ANGELINE LEWIS SCHOLARSHIPS

• *See page 515*

AMERICAN LEGION AUXILIARY DEPARTMENT OF WISCONSIN MERIT AND MEMORIAL SCHOLARSHIPS

• *See page 515*

AMERICAN LEGION AUXILIARY DEPARTMENT OF WISCONSIN PAST PRESIDENTS' PARLEY HEALTH CAREER SCHOLARSHIPS

• *See page 516*

AMERICAN LEGION AUXILIARY DEPARTMENT OF WISCONSIN PRESIDENT'S SCHOLARSHIPS

• *See page 516*

AMERICAN LEGION AUXILIARY NATIONAL HEADQUARTERS http://www.legion-aux.org

AMERICAN LEGION AUXILIARY NATIONAL PRESIDENT'S SCHOLARSHIPS

One-time scholarship for high school children of veterans who served in the Armed Forces during the eligibility dates for The American Legion.

Award: Scholarship for use in freshman year; not renewable. *Number:* 15. *Amount:* $1000–$2500.

Eligibility Requirements: Applicant must be high school student and planning to enroll or expecting to enroll full-time at a four-year institution or university. Available to U.S. citizens. Applicant or parent must meet one or more of the following requirements: general military experience; retired from active duty; disabled or killed as a result of military service; prisoner of war; or missing in action.

Application Requirements: Application, essay, references, self-addressed stamped envelope, test scores, transcript. *Deadline:* March 1.

Contact: Maria Potts, Program Coordinator
American Legion Auxiliary National Headquarters
777 North Meridian Street, Third Floor
Indianapolis, IN 46204
Phone: 317-955-3845
Fax: 317-955-3884
E-mail: mpotts@legion-aux.org

AMERICAN LEGION AUXILIARY NON-TRADITIONAL STUDENTS SCHOLARSHIPS

• *See page 516*

SAMSUNG AMERICAN LEGION AUXILIARY SCHOLARSHIP

$1000–$20,000 one-time scholarship for high school juniors who are direct descendants or legally adopted children of a U.S. wartime veteran who served on active duty during specificied periods of war. Deadline varies.

Award: Scholarship for use in freshman, sophomore, junior, or senior years; not renewable. *Number:* up to 98. *Amount:* $1000–$20,000.

Eligibility Requirements: Applicant must be enrolled or expecting to enroll full-time at a four-year institution or university. Available to U.S. citizens. Applicant or parent must meet one or more of the following requirements: general military experience; retired from active duty; disabled or killed as a result of military service; prisoner of war; or missing in action.

Application Requirements: Application, financial need analysis, references, test scores, transcript. *Deadline:* varies.

Contact: Maria Potts, Program Coordinator
American Legion Auxiliary National Headquarters
777 North Meridian Street, Third Floor
Indianapolis, IN 46204
Phone: 317-955-3845
Fax: 317-955-3884
E-mail: mpotts@legion-aux.org

AMERICAN LEGION DEPARTMENT OF ARKANSAS http://www.arklegion.homestead.com

AMERICAN LEGION DEPARTMENT OF ARKANSAS COUDRET SCHOLARSHIP AWARD

• *See page 517*

AMERICAN LEGION DEPARTMENT OF IDAHO http://idlegion.home.mindspring.com

AMERICAN LEGION DEPARTMENT OF IDAHO SCHOLARSHIP

• *See page 517*

AMERICAN LEGION DEPARTMENT OF KANSAS http://www.ksamlegion.org

ALBERT M. LAPPIN SCHOLARSHIP

• *See page 518*

CHARLES W. AND ANNETTE HILL SCHOLARSHIP

• *See page 518*

HUGH A. SMITH SCHOLARSHIP FUND

• *See page 518*

ROSEDALE POST 346 SCHOLARSHIP

• *See page 518*

TED AND NORA ANDERSON SCHOLARSHIPS

• *See page 519*

AMERICAN LEGION DEPARTMENT OF MAINE http://www.mainelegion.org

AMERICAN LEGION DEPARTMENT OF MAINE CHILDREN AND YOUTH SCHOLARSHIP

Scholarships available to high school seniors, college students, and veterans who are residents of Maine. Must be in upper half of high school class. One-time award of $500.

Award: Scholarship for use in freshman, sophomore, junior, senior, or graduate years; not renewable. *Number:* 7. *Amount:* $500.

Eligibility Requirements: Applicant must be enrolled or expecting to enroll full-time at a two-year or four-year or technical institution or university and resident of Maine. Available to U.S. citizens. Applicant or parent must meet one or more of the following requirements: general military experience; retired from active duty; disabled or killed as a result of military service; prisoner of war; or missing in action.

Application Requirements: Application, essay, financial need analysis, references, transcript. *Deadline:* May 1.

Contact: Scholarship Committee
American Legion, Department of Maine
54 South Upper Narrows Lane
Winthrop, ME 04364
Phone: 207-873-3229
Fax: 207-872-0501

DANIEL E. LAMBERT MEMORIAL SCHOLARSHIP

One-time award for undergraduate and graduate student whose parents are veterans. Award is based on financial need and good character. Must be U.S. citizen. Applicant must show evidence of being enrolled, or attending accredited college or vocational technical school. Scholarship value is from $500 to $1000.

Award: Scholarship for use in freshman, sophomore, junior, senior, or graduate years; not renewable. *Number:* 1–2. *Amount:* $500–$1000.

Eligibility Requirements: Applicant must be enrolled or expecting to enroll full-time at a two-year or four-year or technical institution or university and resident of Maine. Available to U.S. citizens. Applicant or parent must meet one or more of the following requirements: general military experience; retired from active duty; disabled or killed as a result of military service; prisoner of war; or missing in action.

Application Requirements: Application, references. *Deadline:* May 1.

Contact: Department Adjutant
American Legion, Department of Maine
21 College Avenue
PO Box 900
Waterville, ME 04903-0900
Phone: 207-873-3229
Fax: 207-872-0501
E-mail: legionme@me.acadia.net

JAMES V. DAY SCHOLARSHIP

• *See page 519*

AMERICAN LEGION DEPARTMENT OF MARYLAND http://www.mdlegion.org

AMERICAN LEGION DEPARTMENT OF MARYLAND GENERAL SCHOLARSHIP FUND

Nonrenewable scholarship for veterans or children of veterans who served in the Armed Forces during dates of eligibility for American Legion membership. Merit-based award. Application available on Web site: http://mdlegion.org.

Award: Scholarship for use in freshman, sophomore, junior, or senior years; not renewable. *Number:* up to 3. *Amount:* up to $500.

Eligibility Requirements: Applicant must be enrolled or expecting to enroll full-time at a four-year institution or university and resident of Maryland. Available to U.S. citizens. Applicant or parent must meet one or more of the following requirements: general military experience; retired from active duty; disabled or killed as a result of military service; prisoner of war; or missing in action.

Application Requirements: Application, essay, financial need analysis, transcript. *Deadline:* April 1.

Contact: Thomas Davis, Department Adjutant
American Legion, Department of Maryland
101 North Gay, Room E
Baltimore, MD 21202
Phone: 410-752-1405
Fax: 410-752-3822
E-mail: tom@mdlegion.org

AMERICAN LEGION DEPARTMENT OF MICHIGAN http://www.michiganlegion.org

GUY M. WILSON SCHOLARSHIPS

Scholarship for undergraduate use at a Michigan college. Must be resident of Michigan and the son or daughter of a veteran, living or deceased. Must submit copy of veteran's honorable discharge. Must have minimum 2.5 GPA. Total number of awards given vary each year depending upon the number of applications received. Applicants have to refer the Web site for the deadline.

Award: Scholarship for use in freshman year; not renewable. *Number:* 11. *Amount:* $500.

Eligibility Requirements: Applicant must be high school student; planning to enroll or expecting to enroll full- or part-time at a two-year or four-year institution or university; resident of Michigan and studying in Michigan. Applicant must have 2.5 GPA or higher. Available to U.S. citizens. Applicant or parent must meet one or more of the following requirements: general military experience; retired from active duty; disabled or killed as a result of military service; prisoner of war; or missing in action.

Application Requirements: Application, essay, financial need analysis, test scores, transcript. *Deadline:* varies.

Contact: Deanna Clark, Department Administrative Assistant for Programs
American Legion Department of Michigan
212 North Verlinden Avenue
Lansing, MI 48915
Phone: 517-371-4720 Ext. 11
Fax: 517-371-2401
E-mail: programs@michiganlegion.org

WILLIAM D. AND JEWELL W. BREWER SCHOLARSHIP TRUSTS

One-time award for residents of Michigan who are the sons or daughters of veterans, living or deceased. Must submit copy of veteran's honorable discharge. Several scholarships of $500 each. Must have minimum 2.5 GPA. Scholarship can be applied to any college or university within the United States.

Award: Scholarship for use in freshman, sophomore, junior, or senior years; not renewable. *Number:* 4. *Amount:* $500.

Eligibility Requirements: Applicant must be enrolled or expecting to enroll full- or part-time at a two-year or four-year institution or university and resident of Michigan. Applicant must have 2.5 GPA or higher. Available to U.S. citizens. Applicant or parent must meet one or more of the following requirements: general military experience; retired from active duty; disabled or killed as a result of military service; prisoner of war; or missing in action.

Application Requirements: Application, essay, financial need analysis, test scores, transcript. *Deadline:* varies.

Contact: Deanna Clark, Department Administrative Assistant for Programs
American Legion Department of Michigan
212 North Verlinden Avenue
Lansing, MI 48915
Phone: 517-371-4720 Ext. 11
Fax: 517-371-2401
E-mail: programs@michiganlegion.org

AMERICAN LEGION DEPARTMENT OF MINNESOTA http://www.mnlegion.org

AMERICAN LEGION DEPARTMENT OF MINNESOTA MEMORIAL SCHOLARSHIP

• *See page 519*

MINNESOTA LEGIONNAIRES INSURANCE TRUST SCHOLARSHIP

• *See page 519*

AMERICAN LEGION DEPARTMENT OF MISSOURI http://www.missourilegion.org

CHARLES L. BACON MEMORIAL SCHOLARSHIP

• *See page 519*

LILLIE LOIS FORD SCHOLARSHIP FUND

Two awards of $1000 each are given each year to one boy and one girl. Applicant must have attended a full session of Missouri Boys/Girls State or Missouri Cadet Patrol Academy. Must be a Missouri resident below age 21, attending an accredited college/university as a full-time student. Must be an unmarried descendant of a veteran having served at least 90 days on active duty in the Army, Air Force, Navy, Marine Corps or Coast Guard of the United States.

Award: Scholarship for use in freshman year; not renewable. *Number:* 2. *Amount:* $1000.

Eligibility Requirements: Applicant must be high school student; age 21 or under; planning to enroll or expecting to enroll full-time at a two-year or four-year institution or university; single and resident of Missouri. Available to U.S. citizens. Applicant or parent must meet one or more of the following requirements: general military experience; retired from active duty; disabled or killed as a result of military service; prisoner of war; or missing in action.

Application Requirements: Application, financial need analysis, test scores, copy of the veteran's discharge certificate. *Deadline:* April 20.

Contact: John Doane, Chairman, Education and Scholarship Committee
American Legion, Department of Missouri
PO Box 179
Jefferson City, MO 65102-0179
Phone: 417-924-8186

AMERICAN LEGION DEPARTMENT OF NEBRASKA http://www.nebraskalegion.net

MAYNARD JENSEN AMERICAN LEGION MEMORIAL SCHOLARSHIP

• *See page 520*

AMERICAN LEGION DEPARTMENT OF NORTH DAKOTA http://www.ndlegion.org

HATTIE TEDROW MEMORIAL FUND SCHOLARSHIP

Applicants must be legal residents of North Dakota, high school seniors, and direct descendents of a veteran with honorable service in the U.S. military. The student will have two years from the date of graduation from high school to use his/her award.

American Legion Department of North Dakota (continued)

Award: Scholarship for use in freshman year; not renewable. *Number:* varies. *Amount:* varies.

Eligibility Requirements: Applicant must be high school student; planning to enroll or expecting to enroll full-time at a two-year or four-year institution or university and resident of North Dakota. Available to U.S. citizens. Applicant or parent must meet one or more of the following requirements: general military experience; retired from active duty; disabled or killed as a result of military service; prisoner of war; or missing in action.

Application Requirements: Application, self-addressed stamped envelope, test scores. *Deadline:* April 15.

Contact: Terri Bryant, Program Coordinator
American Legion Department of North Dakota
405 West Main Avenue
PO Box 5057
West Fargo, ND 58078-2666
Phone: 701-293-3120
Fax: 701-293-9951
E-mail: programs@ndlegion.org

AMERICAN LEGION DEPARTMENT OF OHIO http://www.ohiolegion.com

OHIO AMERICAN LEGION SCHOLARSHIPS

• *See page 520*

AMERICAN LEGION DEPARTMENT OF VERMONT http://www.legionvthq.com

AMERICAN LEGION DEPARTMENT OF VERMONT HIGH SCHOOL ORATORICAL CONTEST

Students in grades 9 to 12 are eligible to compete. Must attend an accredited Vermont high school. Must be a U.S. citizen. Selection based on oration.

Award: Prize for use in freshman year; not renewable. *Number:* 1. *Amount:* $2000.

Eligibility Requirements: Applicant must be high school student; planning to enroll or expecting to enroll full- or part-time at a four-year institution or university; resident of Vermont and must have an interest in public speaking. Available to U.S. citizens. Applicant or parent must meet one or more of the following requirements: general military experience; retired from active duty; disabled or killed as a result of military service; prisoner of war; or missing in action.

Application Requirements: Applicant must enter a contest. *Deadline:* January 1.

Contact: Ronald Aldrich, Chairman
American Legion Department of Vermont
126 State Street
Montpelier, VT 05601
E-mail: alvthq@verizon.net

AMERICAN LEGION DEPARTMENT OF WASHINGTON http://www.walegion.org

AMERICAN LEGION DEPARTMENT OF WASHINGTON CHILDREN AND YOUTH SCHOLARSHIPS

• *See page 521*

AMERICAN LEGION DEPARTMENT OF WEST VIRGINIA http://www.wvlegion.org

SONS OF THE AMERICAN LEGION WILLIAM F. "BILL" JOHNSON MEMORIAL SCHOLARSHIP

• *See page 521*

AMERICAN LEGION NATIONAL HEADQUARTERS http://www.legion.org

AMERICAN LEGION LEGACY SCHOLARSHIP

Scholarship for child/children, or legally adopted child/children of active duty U.S. military, National Guard, and Reserve personnel, who were federalized and died on active duty on or after September 11, 2001. Must be a high school senior or high school graduate. For undergraduate study at a U.S. school of higher education.

Award: Scholarship for use in freshman year; renewable. *Number:* varies. *Amount:* up to $20,000.

Eligibility Requirements: Applicant must be enrolled or expecting to enroll full-time at a four-year institution or university. Available to U.S. citizens. Applicant or parent must meet one or more of the following requirements: general military experience; retired from active duty; disabled or killed as a result of military service; prisoner of war; or missing in action.

Application Requirements: Application, financial need analysis, test scores, transcript, photocopy of veteran's certificate of death. *Deadline:* April 15.

Contact: Robert Caudell, Assistant Director
American Legion National Headquarters
PO Box 1055
Indianapolis, IN 46206-1055
Phone: 317-630-1212
Fax: 317-630-1369
E-mail: rcaudell@legion.org

SAMSUNG AMERICAN LEGION SCHOLARSHIP

Scholarship for high school juniors who participate in and complete either an American Legion boys state or American Legion auxiliary girls state program, and be a direct descendant or a legally adopted child of a U.S. wartime veteran. For undergraduate study only and may be used for: tuition, books, fees, and room and board.

Award: Scholarship for use in freshman year; renewable. *Number:* 98. *Amount:* $5000–$20,000.

Eligibility Requirements: Applicant must be high school student and planning to enroll or expecting to enroll full-time at a four-year institution or university. Available to U.S. citizens. Applicant or parent must meet one or more of the following requirements: general military experience; retired from active duty; disabled or killed as a result of military service; prisoner of war; or missing in action.

Application Requirements: Application, essay, financial need analysis, references, test scores. *Deadline:* varies.

Contact: Robert Caudell, Assistant Director
American Legion National Headquarters
PO Box 1055
Indianapolis, IN 46206-1055
Phone: 317-630-1212
Fax: 317-630-1369
E-mail: rcaudell@legion.org

AMERICAN MILITARY RETIREES ASSOCIATION http://www.amra1973.org

SERGEANT MAJOR DOUGLAS R. DRUM MEMORIAL SCHOLARSHIP FUND

One-time award limited to the member, dependents, spouse, children, or grandchildren of members of the American Military Retirees' Association. May be used only for tuition, books, room and board. Must be U.S. citizen. Scholarship is awarded in August.

Award: Scholarship for use in freshman, sophomore, junior, or senior years; not renewable. *Number:* 1–24. *Amount:* $1000–$5000.

Eligibility Requirements: Applicant must be enrolled or expecting to enroll full-time at a two-year or four-year or technical institution or university. Available to U.S. citizens. Applicant or parent must meet one or more of the following requirements: general military experience; retired from active duty; disabled or killed as a result of military service; prisoner of war; or missing in action.

Application Requirements: Application, autobiography, essay, photo, references, test scores, transcript. *Deadline:* April 4.

Contact: Bernard Dillon, Committee Chairperson
American Military Retirees Association
5436 Peru Street, Suite 1
Plattsburgh, NY 12901
Phone: 518-563-9479
Fax: 518-324-5204
E-mail: info@amra1973.org

AMVETS AUXILIARY http://www.amvetsaux.org

AMVETS NATIONAL LADIES AUXILIARY SCHOLARSHIP

• *See page 524*

AMVETS DEPARTMENT OF ILLINOIS http://www.ilamvets.org

ILLINOIS AMVETS LADIES AUXILIARY MEMORIAL SCHOLARSHIP

Applicant must be an Illinois student and a child of an honorably discharged veteran who served after September 15, 1940. Must submit ACT scores, IRS 1040 form, high school rank and grades.

Award: Scholarship for use in freshman year; not renewable. *Number:* 1–3. *Amount:* $500.

Eligibility Requirements: Applicant must be high school student; planning to enroll or expecting to enroll full-time at a two-year or four-year or technical institution or university and resident of Illinois. Available to U.S. citizens. Applicant or parent must meet one or more of the following requirements: general military experience; retired from active duty; disabled or killed as a result of military service; prisoner of war; or missing in action.

Application Requirements: Application, financial need analysis, test scores, transcript, IRS 1040 form. *Deadline:* March 1.

Contact: Sara Van Dyke, Scholarship Director
AMVETS Department of Illinois
2200 South Sixth Street
Springfield, IL 62703-3496
Phone: 217-528-4713
Fax: 217-528-9896
E-mail: scholarship@amvetsillinois.com

ILLINOIS AMVETS LADIES AUXILIARY WORCHID SCHOLARSHIPS

Applicant must be an Illinois student and the child of an honorably discharged, deceased veteran who served after September 15, 1940. Must submit ACT score and IRS 1040 form.

Award: Scholarship for use in freshman year; not renewable. *Number:* 1–3. *Amount:* $500.

Eligibility Requirements: Applicant must be high school student; age 17-18; planning to enroll or expecting to enroll full-time at a two-year or four-year or technical institution or university and resident of Illinois. Available to U.S. citizens. Applicant or parent must meet one or more of the following requirements: general military experience; retired from active duty; disabled or killed as a result of military service; prisoner of war; or missing in action.

Application Requirements: Application, financial need analysis, test scores, transcript, IRS 1040 form. *Deadline:* March 1.

Contact: Sara Van Dyke, Scholarship Director
AMVETS Department of Illinois
2200 South Sixth Street
Springfield, IL 62703-3496
Phone: 217-528-4713
Fax: 217-528-9896
E-mail: scholarship@amvetsillinois.com

ILLINOIS AMVETS SERVICE FOUNDATION SCHOLARSHIP AWARD

Nonrenewable awards of $3000 available annually. Must submit ACT scores and IRS 1040 form. Must be the child or grandchild of an honorably discharged veteran who served after September 15, 1940, or is currently serving in the military.

Award: Scholarship for use in freshman, sophomore, junior, or senior years; not renewable. *Number:* 30–50. *Amount:* $3000.

Eligibility Requirements: Applicant must be age 17-18; enrolled or expecting to enroll full-time at a two-year or four-year or technical institution or university and resident of Illinois. Available to U.S. citizens. Applicant or parent must meet one or more of the following requirements: general military experience; retired from active duty; disabled or killed as a result of military service; prisoner of war; or missing in action.

Application Requirements: Application, financial need analysis, test scores, transcript, IRS 1040 form. *Deadline:* March 1.

Contact: Sara Van Dyke, Scholarship Director
AMVETS Department of Illinois
2200 South Sixth Street
Springfield, IL 62703-3496
Phone: 217-528-4713
Fax: 217-528-9896
E-mail: scholarship@amvetsillinois.com

ILLINOIS AMVETS TRADE SCHOOL SCHOLARSHIP

Applicant must be an Illinois student who has been accepted in a pre-approved trade school program. Must be a child or grandchild of a veteran who served after September 15th, 1940 and was honorably discharged or is presently serving in the military.

Award: Scholarship for use in freshman or sophomore years; renewable. *Number:* 1–2. *Amount:* up to $3000.

Eligibility Requirements: Applicant must be age 17-18; enrolled or expecting to enroll full-time at a technical institution and resident of Illinois. Available to U.S. citizens. Applicant or parent must meet one or more of the following requirements: general military experience; retired from active duty; disabled or killed as a result of military service; prisoner of war; or missing in action.

Application Requirements: Application, acceptance letter. *Deadline:* March 1.

Contact: Sara Van Dyke, Scholarship Director
AMVETS Department of Illinois
2200 South Sixth Street
Springfield, IL 62703-3496
Phone: 217-528-4713
Fax: 217-528-9896
E-mail: scholarship@amvetsillinois.com

ARKANSAS DEPARTMENT OF HIGHER EDUCATION http://www.adhe.edu

MILITARY DEPENDENT'S SCHOLARSHIP PROGRAM-ARKANSAS

Renewable waiver of tuition, fees, room and board undergraduate students seeking a bachelor's degree or certificate of completion at any public college, university or technical school in Arkansas who qualify as a spouse or dependent child of an Arkansas resident who has been declared to be missing in action, killed in action, a POW, or killed on ordnance delivery, or a veteran who has been declared to be 100% totally and permanently disabled during, or as a result of, active military service.

Award: Scholarship for use in freshman, sophomore, junior, or senior years; renewable. *Number:* 1. *Amount:* up to $2500.

Eligibility Requirements: Applicant must be enrolled or expecting to enroll full-time at a two-year or four-year or technical institution or university; resident of Arkansas and studying in Arkansas. Available to U.S. citizens. Applicant or parent must meet one or more of the following requirements: general military experience; retired from active duty; disabled or killed as a result of military service; prisoner of war; or missing in action.

Application Requirements: Application, references, report of casualty. *Deadline:* continuous.

Contact: Tara Smith, Director of Financial Aid
Arkansas Department of Higher Education
114 East Capitol Avenue
Little Rock, AR 72201-3818
Phone: 501-371-2000
Fax: 501-371-2001
E-mail: taras@adhe.edu

BLINDED VETERANS ASSOCIATION http://www.bva.org

KATHERN F. GRUBER SCHOLARSHIP

Award for undergraduate or graduate study is available to dependent children and spouses of legally blind veterans. The veteran's blindness may be either service or non-service connected. High school seniors may apply. Applicant must be enrolled or accepted for admission as a full-time student in an accredited institution of higher learning, business, secretarial, or vocational school. Three awards of $2000 each and three awards of $1000 each are given.

Blinded Veterans Association (continued)

Award: Scholarship for use in freshman, sophomore, junior, senior, or graduate years; renewable. *Number:* 6. *Amount:* $1000–$2000.

Eligibility Requirements: Applicant must be enrolled or expecting to enroll full-time at a two-year or four-year or technical institution or university. Available to U.S. citizens. Applicant or parent must meet one or more of the following requirements: general military experience; retired from active duty; disabled or killed as a result of military service; prisoner of war; or missing in action.

Application Requirements: Application, essay, references, transcript. *Deadline:* April 16.

Contact: Keleeba Scott, Scholarship Coordinator
Blinded Veterans Association
477 H Street, NW
Washington, DC 20001-2694
Phone: 202-371-8880
Fax: 202-371-8258
E-mail: kscott@bva.org

COLLEGE FOUNDATION OF NORTH CAROLINA INC. http://www.cfnc.org

NORTH CAROLINA VETERANS SCHOLARSHIPS

Scholarship assists children of certain deceased or disabled veterans, or children of veterans who were listed as POW/MIA. Veteran must have been a legal resident of North Carolina at time of entry into service, or child must have been born in North Carolina and resided there continuously. Applications can be obtained through the http://www.NCNeighbors.com Web site or by sending a request and a self-addressed stamped envelope to NCVVI.

Award: Scholarship for use in freshman, sophomore, junior, senior, or graduate years; not renewable. *Number:* varies. *Amount:* $1500–$4500.

Eligibility Requirements: Applicant must be enrolled or expecting to enroll full- or part-time at a four-year institution or university and resident of North Carolina. Available to U.S. citizens. Applicant or parent must meet one or more of the following requirements: general military experience; retired from active duty; disabled or killed as a result of military service; prisoner of war; or missing in action.

Application Requirements: Application, essay, self-addressed stamped envelope, transcript, copy of the Department of Defense Form DD214 to document Vietnam service, copy of the applicant's birth certificate and/or marriage license, a personal statement, and a list of current activities and awards. *Deadline:* February 28.

Contact: Scholarship Coordinator
College Foundation of North Carolina Inc.
PO Box 17082
Raleigh, NC 27619

COMMANDER WILLIAM S. STUHR SCHOLARSHIP FUND FOR MILITARY SONS AND DAUGHTERS

COMMANDER WILLIAM S. STUHR SCHOLARSHIP FUND FOR MILITARY SONS AND DAUGHTERS

Scholarship to high school seniors and dependents of active duty or retired career officer/enlisted person. Must be in upper ten percent of class. One award given for each branch of service, including the Reserves and the National Guard.

Award: Scholarship for use in freshman year; not renewable. *Number:* up to 6. *Amount:* up to $1125.

Eligibility Requirements: Applicant must be high school student and planning to enroll or expecting to enroll full-time at a four-year institution or university. Applicant must have 3.5 GPA or higher. Available to U.S. citizens. Applicant or parent must meet one or more of the following requirements: general military experience; retired from active duty; disabled or killed as a result of military service; prisoner of war; or missing in action.

Application Requirements: Application, autobiography, essay, financial need analysis, photo, references, self-addressed stamped envelope, test scores, transcript, copy of military ID card. *Deadline:* March 1.

Contact: Mr. James Pollan, Executive Director and Trustee
Commander William S. Stuhr Scholarship Fund for Military Sons and Daughters
3292 Thompson Bridge Road, Suite 120
Gainesville, GA 30506
E-mail: stuhrstudents@earthlink.net

DATATEL INC. http://www.datatel.com/dsf

ANGELFIRE SCHOLARSHIP

For any student who is a 1964 to 1975 Vietnam veteran, or spouse or child of same. Available to refugees from Cambodia, Laos, or Vietnam. Also available to military personnel who have served or are serving in Operations Desert Storm, Enduring Freedom, and Iraqi Freedom. Applicant must attend a Datatel client institution. School list can be found at www.datatel.com/dsf. Completed on-line applications and 2 letters of recommendation must be submitted electronically by January 31.

Award: Scholarship for use in freshman, sophomore, junior, senior, graduate, or postgraduate years; not renewable. *Number:* 15–30. *Amount:* $1700.

Eligibility Requirements: Applicant must be enrolled or expecting to enroll full- or part-time at a two-year or four-year or technical institution or university. Available to U.S. and non-U.S. citizens. Applicant or parent must meet one or more of the following requirements: general military experience; retired from active duty; disabled or killed as a result of military service; prisoner of war; or missing in action.

Application Requirements: Application, essay, references, transcript. *Deadline:* January 31.

Contact: Stacey Fessler, Project Leader
Datatel Inc.
4375 Fair Lakes Court
Fairfax, VA 22033
Phone: 800-486-4332
E-mail: scholars@datatel.com

DAUGHTERS OF THE CINCINNATI http://www.daughters1894.org

DAUGHTERS OF THE CINCINNATI SCHOLARSHIP

Need and merit-based award available to graduating high school seniors. Minimum GPA of 3.0 required. Must be daughter of commissioned officer in regular Army, Navy, Coast Guard, Air Force, Marines (active, retired, or deceased). Must submit parent's rank and branch of service.

Award: Scholarship for use in freshman year; renewable. *Number:* up to 10. *Amount:* $1000–$3000.

Eligibility Requirements: Applicant must be high school student; planning to enroll or expecting to enroll full-time at a two-year or four-year institution or university and female. Applicant must have 3.0 GPA or higher. Available to U.S. citizens. Applicant or parent must meet one or more of the following requirements: general military experience; retired from active duty; disabled or killed as a result of military service; prisoner of war; or missing in action.

Application Requirements: Application, essay, financial need analysis, references, test scores, transcript. *Deadline:* March 15.

Contact: Jose Ramon Gonzalez, Scholarship Administrator
Daughters of the Cincinnati
20 West 44th Street, Room 508
New York, NY 10036
Phone: 212-991-9945
E-mail: scholsrships@daughters1894.org

DEFENSE COMMISSARY AGENCY http://www.militaryscholar.org

SCHOLARSHIPS FOR MILITARY CHILDREN

One-time award to unmarried dependants of military personnel for full-time undergraduate study at a four-year institution. Must be 23 years of age. Minimum 3.0 GPA required. Further information and applications available at Web site http://www.militaryscholar.org.

Award: Scholarship for use in freshman, sophomore, or junior years; not renewable. *Number:* 500. *Amount:* $1500.

Eligibility Requirements: Applicant must be age 23 or under; enrolled or expecting to enroll full-time at a four-year institution or university and single. Applicant must have 3.0 GPA or higher. Available to U.S. citizens. Applicant or parent must meet one or more of the following requirements: general military experience; retired from active duty; disabled or killed as a result of military service; prisoner of war; or missing in action.

Application Requirements: Application, essay, transcript. *Deadline:* February 20.

Contact: Mr. Bernard Cote, Scholarship Coordinator
Defense Commissary Agency
307 Provincetown Road
Cherry Hill, NJ 08134
Phone: 856-573-9400
E-mail: militaryscholar@scholarshipmanagers.com

DELAWARE HIGHER EDUCATION COMMISSION http://www.doe.k12.de.us

EDUCATIONAL BENEFITS FOR CHILDREN OF DECEASED VETERANS AND OTHERS AWARD

• *See page 595*

DEPARTMENT OF VETERANS AFFAIRS (VA) http://www.gibill.va.gov

MONTGOMERY GI BILL (ACTIVE DUTY) CHAPTER 30

Award provides up to thirty-six months of education benefits to eligible veterans for college, business school, technical courses, vocational courses, correspondence courses, apprenticeships/job training, or flight training. Must be an eligible veteran with an Honorable Discharge and have high school diploma or GED before applying for benefits.

Award: Scholarship for use in freshman, sophomore, junior, senior, or graduate years; renewable. *Number:* varies. *Amount:* $1101–$37,224.

Eligibility Requirements: Applicant must be enrolled or expecting to enroll full- or part-time at a two-year or four-year or technical institution or university. Available to U.S. citizens. Applicant or parent must meet one or more of the following requirements: general military experience; retired from active duty; disabled or killed as a result of military service; prisoner of war; or missing in action.

Application Requirements: Application, proof of active military service of at least 2 years. *Deadline:* continuous.

Contact: Keith Wilson, Director, Education Service
Department of Veterans Affairs (VA)
810 Vermont Avenue, NW
Washington, DC 20420
Phone: 202-273-7132
E-mail: co225a@vba.va.gov

MONTGOMERY GI BILL (SELECTED RESERVE)

• *See page 632*

RESERVE EDUCATION ASSISTANCE PROGRAM

• *See page 634*

SURVIVORS AND DEPENDENTS EDUCATIONAL ASSISTANCE (CHAPTER 35)-VA

Monthly $860 benefits for up to 45 months. Must be spouses or children under age 26 of current veterans missing in action or of deceased or totally and permanently disabled (service-related) service persons. For more information visit the following Web site: http://www.gibill.va.gov.

Award: Scholarship for use in freshman, sophomore, junior, or senior years; renewable. *Number:* 10,733. *Amount:* up to $10,320.

Eligibility Requirements: Applicant must be age 25 or under and enrolled or expecting to enroll full- or part-time at a two-year or four-year or technical institution or university. Available to U.S. and non-U.S. citizens. Applicant or parent must meet one or more of the following requirements: general military experience; retired from active duty; disabled or killed as a result of military service; prisoner of war; or missing in action.

Application Requirements: Application, proof of parent or spouse's qualifying service. *Deadline:* continuous.

Contact: Keith Wilson, Director, Education Service
Department of Veterans Affairs (VA)
810 Vermont Avenue, NW
Washington, DC 20420
Phone: 202-273-7132
E-mail: co225a@vba.va.gov

DEVRY INC. http://www.devry.edu

DEVRY/KELLER MILITARY SERVICE GRANT

Grant is available to students called to active duty at a time which necessitates the interruption of studies during a term. The grant is available only to those students who resume their studies following their active duty service. Upon resuming their studies, students must provide written documentation of active duty service. The grant is to be used during the first term the student resumes. For details visit http://finance.devry.edu/devrygrants_scholarships.html#military.

Award: Grant for use in freshman, sophomore, junior, senior, or graduate years; not renewable. *Number:* varies. *Amount:* varies.

Eligibility Requirements: Applicant must be enrolled or expecting to enroll full- or part-time at an institution or university. Available to U.S. citizens. Applicant or parent must meet one or more of the following requirements: general military experience; retired from active duty; disabled or killed as a result of military service; prisoner of war; or missing in action.

Application Requirements: Documentation of active duty service. *Deadline:* varies.

Contact: Thonie Simpson, National High School Program Manager
DeVry Inc.
One Tower Lane
Oak Brook Terrace, IL 60181-4624
Phone: 630-706-3122
Fax: 630-574-1696
E-mail: scholarships@devry.edu

EXPLOSIVE ORDNANCE DISPOSAL MEMORIAL COMMITTEE http://www.eodmemorial.org

EXPLOSIVE ORDNANCE DISPOSAL MEMORIAL SCHOLARSHIP

• *See page 596*

FLORIDA DEPARTMENT OF EDUCATION http://www.floridastudentfinancialaid.org

SCHOLARSHIPS FOR CHILDREN & SPOUSES OF DECEASED OR DISABLED VETERANS OR SERVICEMEMBERS

Renewable scholarships for children and spouses of deceased or disabled veterans and service members. Children must be between the ages of 16 and 22, and attend an eligible Florida public, nonpublic postsecondary institution or enrolled part-time. Must ensure that the Florida Department of Veterans Affairs certifies the applicants eligibility. Must maintain GPA of 2.0.

Award: Scholarship for use in freshman, sophomore, junior, or senior years; renewable. *Number:* varies. *Amount:* varies.

Eligibility Requirements: Applicant must be age 16-22; enrolled or expecting to enroll full- or part-time at a two-year or four-year or technical institution or university; resident of Florida and studying in Florida. Available to U.S. citizens. Applicant or parent must meet one or more of the following requirements: general military experience; retired from active duty; disabled or killed as a result of military service; prisoner of war; or missing in action.

Application Requirements: Application, financial need analysis. *Deadline:* April 1.

Contact: State Programs Director
Florida Department of Education
Office of Student Financial Assistance, 1940 North
Tallahassee, FL 32303-4759
Phone: 850-410-5180
Fax: 850-487-6244

FOUNDATION OF THE FIRST CAVALRY DIVISION ASSOCIATION http://www.1cda.org

FOUNDATION OF THE 1ST CAVALRY DIVISION ASSOCIATION SCHOLARSHIP

Several scholarships for children of the 1st Cavalry Division soldiers who died or have been declared permanently and totally (100%) disabled from combat with the 1st Cavalry Division. Show proof of relationship, death or disability of parent, and acceptance at higher education institution. Include self-addressed stamped envelope.

Award: Scholarship for use in freshman, sophomore, junior, senior, graduate, or postgraduate years; renewable. *Number:* varies. *Amount:* up to $1000.

Eligibility Requirements: Applicant must be enrolled or expecting to enroll full- or part-time at a two-year or four-year institution or university. Available to U.S. citizens. Applicant or parent must meet one or more of the following requirements: general military experience; retired from active duty; disabled or killed as a result of military service; prisoner of war; or missing in action.

Application Requirements: Application, self-addressed stamped envelope, transcript, birth certificate, proof of service with the division, proof of disability or death of parent due to service with the 1st Cavalry Division in combat. *Deadline:* varies.

Contact: Lorinda Davison, Office Manager
Foundation of the First Cavalry Division Association
302 North Main Street
Copperas Cove, TX 76522-1703
Phone: 254-547-6537
Fax: 254-547-8853
E-mail: firstcav@1cda.org

IDAHO STATE BOARD OF EDUCATION http://www.boardofed.idaho.gov

FREEDOM SCHOLARSHIP

Scholarship for children of Idaho citizens determined by the federal government to have been prisoners of war, missing in action, or killed in action or died of injuries or wounds sustained in action in southeast Asia, including Korea, or who shall become so hereafter, in any area of armed conflicts. Applicant must attend an Idaho public college or university and meet all requirements for regular admission. The award value and the number of awards granted varies.

Award: Scholarship for use in freshman, sophomore, junior, senior, graduate, or postgraduate years; not renewable. *Number:* varies. *Amount:* varies.

Eligibility Requirements: Applicant must be enrolled or expecting to enroll full- or part-time at a two-year or four-year or technical institution or university; resident of Idaho and studying in Idaho. Available to U.S. citizens. Applicant or parent must meet one or more of the following requirements: general military experience; retired from active duty; disabled or killed as a result of military service; prisoner of war; or missing in action.

Application Requirements: Application. *Deadline:* January 15.

Contact: Dana Kelly, Program Manager
Idaho State Board of Education
PO Box 83720
Boise, ID 83720-0037
Phone: 208-332-1574
E-mail: dana.kelly@osbe.idaho.gov

PUBLIC SAFETY OFFICER DEPENDENT SCHOLARSHIP

• *See page 600*

ILLINOIS DEPARTMENT OF VETERANS AFFAIRS http://www.state.il.us/agency/dva

MIA/POW SCHOLARSHIPS

One-time award for spouse, child, or step-child of veterans who are missing in action or were a prisoner of war. Must be enrolled at a state-supported school in Illinois. Candidate must be U.S. citizen. Must apply and be accepted before beginning of school. Also for children and spouses of veterans who are determined to be 100 percent disabled as established by the Veterans Administration. Scholarship value and the number of awards granted varies.

Award: Scholarship for use in freshman, sophomore, junior, senior, or graduate years; renewable. *Number:* varies. *Amount:* varies.

Eligibility Requirements: Applicant must be enrolled or expecting to enroll full- or part-time at a two-year or four-year institution or university; resident of Illinois and studying in Illinois. Available to U.S. citizens. Applicant or parent must meet one or more of the following requirements: general military experience; retired from active duty; disabled or killed as a result of military service; prisoner of war; or missing in action.

Application Requirements: Application. *Deadline:* continuous.

Contact: Ms. Tracy Mahan, Grants Section
Illinois Department of Veterans Affairs
833 South Spring Street
Springfield, IL 62794-9432
Phone: 217-782-3564
Fax: 217-782-4161

VETERANS' CHILDREN EDUCATIONAL OPPORTUNITIES

$250 award for each child aged 10 to 18 of a veteran who died or became totally disabled as a result of service during World War I, World War II, Korean, or Vietnam War. Must be Illinois resident studying in Illinois. Death must be service-connected. Disability must be rated 100 percent for two or more years.

Award: Grant for use in freshman year; not renewable. *Number:* varies. *Amount:* $250.

Eligibility Requirements: Applicant must be age 10-18; enrolled or expecting to enroll full- or part-time at a two-year or four-year institution or university; resident of Illinois and studying in Illinois. Available to U.S. citizens. Applicant or parent must meet one or more of the following requirements: general military experience; retired from active duty; disabled or killed as a result of military service; prisoner of war; or missing in action.

Application Requirements: Application. *Deadline:* June 30.

Contact: Tracy Mahan, Grants Section
Illinois Department of Veterans Affairs
833 South Spring Street
Springfield, IL 62794-9432
Phone: 217-782-3564
Fax: 217-782-4161

ILLINOIS STUDENT ASSISTANCE COMMISSION (ISAC) http://www.collegezone.org

ILLINOIS VETERAN GRANT PROGRAM-IVG

Awards qualified veterans and pays eligible tuition and fees for study in Illinois public universities or community colleges. Program eligibility units are based on the enrolled hours for a particular term, not the dollar amount of the benefits paid. Applications are available at college financial aid office and can be submitted any time during the academic year for which assistance is being requested.

Award: Grant for use in freshman, sophomore, junior, senior, or graduate years; renewable. *Number:* 11,000–13,000. *Amount:* $1400–$1600.

Eligibility Requirements: Applicant must be enrolled or expecting to enroll full- or part-time at a two-year or four-year institution or university; resident of Illinois and studying in Illinois. Available to U.S. citizens. Applicant or parent must meet one or more of the following requirements: general military experience; retired from active duty; disabled or killed as a result of military service; prisoner of war; or missing in action.

Application Requirements: Application. *Deadline:* continuous.

Contact: College Zone Counselor
Illinois Student Assistance Commission (ISAC)
1755 Lake Cook Road
Deerfield, IL 60015-5209
Phone: 800-899-4722
E-mail: collegezone@isac.org

INDIANA DEPARTMENT OF VETERANS AFFAIRS http://www.in.gov/dva

CHILD OF DISABLED VETERAN GRANT OR PURPLE HEART RECIPIENT GRANT

Free tuition at Indiana state-supported colleges or universities for children of disabled veterans or Purple Heart recipients. Must submit form DD214 or service record. Covers tuition and mandatory fees.

Award: Grant for use in freshman, sophomore, junior, senior, graduate, or postgraduate years; renewable. *Number:* varies. *Amount:* varies.

Eligibility Requirements: Applicant must be enrolled or expecting to enroll full- or part-time at a two-year or four-year institution or university; resident of Indiana and studying in Indiana. Available to U.S. citizens. Applicant or parent must meet one or more of the following requirements: general military experience; retired from active duty; disabled or killed as a result of military service; prisoner of war; or missing in action.

Application Requirements: Application, FAFSA. *Deadline:* continuous.

Contact: Jon Brinkley, State Service Officer
Indiana Department of Veterans Affairs
302 West Washington Street, Room E-120
Indianapolis, IN 46204-2738
Phone: 317-232-3910
Fax: 317-232-7721
E-mail: jbrinkley@dva.in.gov

DEPARTMENT OF VETERANS AFFAIRS FREE TUITION FOR CHILDREN OF POW/MIA'S IN VIETNAM

Renewable award for residents of Indiana who are the children of veterans declared missing in action or prisoner-of-war after January 1, 1960. Provides tuition at Indiana state-supported institutions for undergraduate study.

Award: Grant for use in freshman, sophomore, junior, senior, graduate, or postgraduate years; renewable. *Number:* varies. *Amount:* varies.

Eligibility Requirements: Applicant must be age 24 or under; enrolled or expecting to enroll full- or part-time at a two-year or four-year institution or university; resident of Indiana and studying in Indiana. Available to U.S. citizens. Applicant or parent must meet one or more of the following requirements: general military experience; retired from active duty; disabled or killed as a result of military service; prisoner of war; or missing in action.

Application Requirements: Application. *Deadline:* continuous.

Contact: Jon Brinkley, State Service Officer
Indiana Department of Veterans Affairs
302 West Washington Street, Room E-120
Indianapolis, IN 46204-2738
Phone: 317-232-3910
Fax: 317-232-7721
E-mail: jbrinkley@dva.in.gov

KANSAS COMMISSION ON VETERANS AFFAIRS http://www.kcva.org

KANSAS EDUCATIONAL BENEFITS FOR CHILDREN OF MIA, POW, AND DECEASED VETERANS OF THE VIETNAM WAR

Scholarship awarded to students who are children of veterans. Must show proof of parent's status as missing in action, prisoner-of-war, or killed in action in the Vietnam War. Kansas residence required of veteran at time of entry to service. Must attend a state-supported postsecondary school.

Award: Scholarship for use in freshman, sophomore, junior, or senior years; not renewable. *Number:* 1. *Amount:* varies.

Eligibility Requirements: Applicant must be enrolled or expecting to enroll full-time at a two-year or four-year or technical institution or university and studying in Kansas. Available to U.S. citizens. Applicant or parent must meet one or more of the following requirements: general military experience; retired from active duty; disabled or killed as a result of military service; prisoner of war; or missing in action.

Application Requirements: Application, birth certificate, school acceptance letter, military discharge of veteran. *Deadline:* varies.

Contact: Wayne Bollig, Program Director
Kansas Commission on Veterans Affairs
700 Jackson, SW, Suite 701
Topeka, KS 66603-3743
Phone: 785-296-3976
Fax: 785-296-1462
E-mail: wbollig@kcva.org

KNIGHTS OF COLUMBUS http://www.kofc.org

FRANCIS P. MATTHEWS AND JOHN E. SWIFT EDUCATIONAL TRUST SCHOLARSHIPS

• *See page 539*

LOUISIANA DEPARTMENT OF VETERANS AFFAIRS http://www.vetaffairs.com

LOUISIANA DEPARTMENT OF VETERANS AFFAIRS STATE AID PROGRAM

Tuition exemption at any state-supported college, university, or technical institute in Louisiana for children (dependents between the ages of 18-25) of veterans that are rated 90% or above service connected disabled by the U.S. Department of Veterans Affairs. Tuition exemption also available for the surviving spouse and children (dependents between the ages of 18-25) of veterans who died on active duty, in line of duty, or where death was the result of a disability incurred in or aggravated by military service. For residents of Louisiana.

Award: Scholarship for use in freshman, sophomore, junior, senior, graduate, or postgraduate years; not renewable. *Number:* varies. *Amount:* varies.

Eligibility Requirements: Applicant must be age 18-25; enrolled or expecting to enroll full-time at a two-year or four-year or technical institution or university; resident of Louisiana and studying in Louisiana. Available to U.S. citizens. Applicant or parent must meet one or more of the following requirements: general military experience; retired from active duty; disabled or killed as a result of military service; prisoner of war; or missing in action.

Application Requirements: Application. *Deadline:* continuous.

Contact: Richard Blackwell, Veterans Affairs Regional Manager
Louisiana Department of Veterans Affairs
PO Box 94095
Capitol Station
Baton Rouge, LA 70804-4095
Phone: 225-922-0500 Ext. 203
Fax: 225-922-0511
E-mail: rblackwell@vetaffairs.com

MAINE BUREAU OF VETERANS SERVICES http://www.state.me.us

VETERANS DEPENDENTS EDUCATIONAL BENEFITS-MAINE

Tuition waiver award for dependents or spouses of veterans who were prisoners of war, missing in action, or permanently disabled as a result of service. Veteran must have been Maine resident at service entry for five years preceding application. For use at Maine University system, Community colleges and Maine Maritime. Must be high school graduate. Must submit birth certificate and proof of VA disability of veteran.

Award: Scholarship for use in freshman, sophomore, junior, or senior years; not renewable. *Number:* varies. *Amount:* varies.

Eligibility Requirements: Applicant must be age 21-22; enrolled or expecting to enroll full- or part-time at a two-year or technical institution or university; resident of Maine and studying in Maine. Available to U.S. and non-U.S. citizens. Applicant or parent must meet one or more of the following requirements: general military experience; retired from active duty; disabled or killed as a result of military service; prisoner of war; or missing in action.

Maine Bureau of Veterans Services (continued)

Application Requirements: Application, birth certificate, proof of VA disability of veteran. *Deadline:* continuous.

Contact: Peter W. Ogden, Director
Maine Bureau of Veterans Services
State House, Station 117
Augusta, ME 04333-0117
Phone: 207-626-4464
Fax: 207-626-4471
E-mail: mainebzs@maine.gov

MARYLAND HIGHER EDUCATION COMMISSION http://www.mhec.state.md.us

EDWARD T. CONROY MEMORIAL SCHOLARSHIP PROGRAM

• *See page 602*

VETERANS OF THE AFGHANISTAN AND IRAQ CONFLICTS SCHOLARSHIP PROGRAM

Provides financial assistance to Maryland resident U.S. Armed Forces personnel who served in Afghanistan or Iraq Conflicts and their children or spouses who are attending Maryland institutions.

Award: Scholarship for use in freshman, sophomore, junior, or senior years; renewable. *Number:* 75. *Amount:* $8850.

Eligibility Requirements: Applicant must be enrolled or expecting to enroll full- or part-time at a two-year or four-year institution or university; resident of Maryland and studying in Maryland. Available to U.S. citizens. Applicant or parent must meet one or more of the following requirements: general military experience; retired from active duty; disabled or killed as a result of military service; prisoner of war; or missing in action.

Application Requirements: Application, financial need analysis, birth certificate/marriage certificate, documentation of military order. *Deadline:* March 1.

Contact: Linda Asplin, Program Administrator
Maryland Higher Education Commission
839 Bestgate Road, Suite 400
Annapolis, MD 21401-3013
Phone: 410-260-4563
Fax: 410-260-3203
E-mail: lasplin@mhec.state.md.us

MASSACHUSETTS OFFICE OF STUDENT FINANCIAL ASSISTANCE http://www.osfa.mass.edu

MASSACHUSETTS PUBLIC SERVICE GRANT PROGRAM

• *See page 603*

MICHIGAN BUREAU OF STUDENT FINANCIAL ASSISTANCE http://www.michigan.gov/studentaid

CHILDREN OF VETERANS TUITION GRANT

Awards available for students who are children of a disabled or deceased Michigan veteran. Must be enrolled at least half-time in a degree-granting Michigan public or private nonprofit institution. Must be a U.S. citizen or permanent resident and must be residing in Michigan.

Award: Grant for use in freshman, sophomore, junior, or senior years; renewable. *Number:* varies. *Amount:* up to $2800.

Eligibility Requirements: Applicant must be age 17-25; enrolled or expecting to enroll full- or part-time at a two-year or four-year institution or university; resident of Michigan and studying in Michigan. Available to U.S. citizens. Applicant or parent must meet one or more of the following requirements: general military experience; retired from active duty; disabled or killed as a result of military service; prisoner of war; or missing in action.

Application Requirements: Application. *Deadline:* varies.

Contact: Scholarship and Grant Director
Michigan Bureau of Student Financial Assistance
PO Box 30462
Lansing, MI 48909-7962
Phone: 888-447-2687
E-mail: osg@michigan.gov

MICHIGAN VETERANS TRUST FUND http://www.michigan.gov/dmva

MICHIGAN VETERANS TRUST FUND TUITION GRANT PROGRAM

Provides grants for the emergency needs of veterans, tuition grants to dependents of disabled and deceased veterans, and emergency education loans to veterans and their children. Tuition grants are available to sons and daughters of totally disabled or deceased service-connected veterans attending Michigan institutions of higher education. Refer to Web Site: http://www.michigan.gov/textonly/0,2964,7-153-10366_10871-44121—,00.html for details.

Award: Grant for use in freshman, sophomore, junior, or senior years; renewable. *Number:* varies. *Amount:* up to $2800.

Eligibility Requirements: Applicant must be age 17-25; enrolled or expecting to enroll full-time at a two-year or four-year or technical institution or university; resident of Michigan and studying in Michigan. Available to U.S. citizens. Applicant or parent must meet one or more of the following requirements: general military experience; retired from active duty; disabled or killed as a result of military service; prisoner of war; or missing in action.

Application Requirements: Application. *Deadline:* continuous.

Contact: Mary Kay Bitten, Scholarship Committee
Michigan Veterans Trust Fund
3423 North, Martin Luther King Jr. Boulevard
Lansing, MI 48909-7962
Phone: 517-335-1636
Fax: 517-335-1631

MILITARY BENEFIT ASSOCIATION http://www.militarybenefit.org

MILITARY BENEFIT ASSOCIATION SCHOLARSHIP

Scholarship to the dependent children of members of the Military Benefit Association. They must maintain a minimum of 2.5 GPA. Applicants must have a high school degree or GED and plan to enroll in a full-time undergraduate course of study at an accredited two- or four-year college, university or vocational-technical school by fall of the year in which the award is granted.

Award: Scholarship for use in freshman, sophomore, junior, or senior years; not renewable. *Number:* up to 5. *Amount:* $2000.

Eligibility Requirements: Applicant must be enrolled or expecting to enroll full-time at a two-year or four-year or technical institution or university. Applicant must have 2.5 GPA or higher. Available to U.S. citizens. Applicant or parent must meet one or more of the following requirements: general military experience; retired from active duty; disabled or killed as a result of military service; prisoner of war; or missing in action.

Application Requirements: Application, transcript. *Deadline:* February 15.

Contact: David Howell, Scholarship Coordinator
Military Benefit Association
14605 Avion Parkway
PO Box 221110
Chantilly, VA 20153-1110
Phone: 800-336-0100 Ext. 314
Fax: 703-938-2536
E-mail: memberservices@militarybenefit.org

MILITARY OFFICERS ASSOCIATION OF AMERICA (MOAA) http://www.moaa.org

GENERAL JOHN RATAY EDUCATIONAL FUND GRANTS

Grants available to the children of the surviving spouse of retired officers. Must be under 24 years old and the child of a deceased retired officer who was a member of MOAA. For more details and an application go to Web site: http://www.moaa.org/education.

Award: Grant for use in freshman, sophomore, junior, or senior years; not renewable. *Number:* 10. *Amount:* $4000.

Eligibility Requirements: Applicant must be age 24 or under and enrolled or expecting to enroll full-time at a two-year or four-year institution or university. Applicant must have 3.0 GPA or higher. Available to U.S. citizens. Applicant or parent must meet one or more of the following requirements: general military experience; retired from active duty; disabled or killed as a result of military service; prisoner of war; or missing in action.

Application Requirements: Application, financial need analysis, test scores, transcript, lists of high school and college activities. *Deadline:* March 3.

Contact: Laurie Wavering, Program Manager
Military Officers Association of America (MOAA)
201 North Washington Street
Alexandria, VA 22314-2529
Phone: 800-234-6622
Fax: 703-838-5819
E-mail: edassist@moaa.org

MOAA AMERICAN PATRIOT SCHOLARSHIP

Scholarships are available to a student under the age of 24 and who are children of MOAA members and children of active-duty, reserve, National Guard, or enlisted personnel whose military parent has died on active service are eligible to apply. For more information and to access the online application go to Web site: http://www.moaa.org/education.

Award: Scholarship for use in freshman, sophomore, junior, or senior years; not renewable. *Number:* up to 60. *Amount:* $2500–$5000.

Eligibility Requirements: Applicant must be age 24 or under and enrolled or expecting to enroll full-time at a two-year or four-year institution or university. Available to U.S. citizens. Applicant or parent must meet one or more of the following requirements: general military experience; retired from active duty; disabled or killed as a result of military service; prisoner of war; or missing in action.

Application Requirements: Application, test scores, transcript, list of high school and college activities. *Deadline:* March 3.

Contact: Laurie Wavering, Program Manager
Military Officers Association of America (MOAA)
201 North Washington Street
Alexandria, VA 22314-2529
Phone: 800-234-6622
Fax: 703-838-5819
E-mail: edassist@moaa.org

MOAA BASE/POST SCHOLARSHIP

Recipients are randomly selected from dependent sons and daughters of active duty officers, members of the Drill and Reserve, National Guard, and enlisted military personnel. Eligible applicants will be under the age of 24. For more details and an application go to Web site: http://www.moaa.org/education.

Award: Scholarship for use in freshman, sophomore, junior, or senior years; not renewable. *Number:* 25. *Amount:* $1000.

Eligibility Requirements: Applicant must be age 24 or under and enrolled or expecting to enroll full-time at a two-year or four-year institution or university. Available to U.S. citizens. Applicant or parent must meet one or more of the following requirements: general military experience; retired from active duty; disabled or killed as a result of military service; prisoner of war; or missing in action.

Application Requirements: Application, service parent's Leave and Earning Statement (LES). *Deadline:* March 3.

Contact: Laurie Wavering, Program Manager
Military Officers Association of America (MOAA)
201 North Washington Street
Alexandria, VA 22314-2529
Phone: 800-234-6622
Fax: 703-838-5819
E-mail: edassist@moaa.org

MILITARY ORDER OF THE PURPLE HEART http://www.purpleheart.org

MILITARY ORDER OF THE PURPLE HEART SCHOLARSHIP

Scholarship for Military Order of the Purple Heart recipients/spouses or children, stepchildren, adopted children or grandchildren. Must submit $10 application fee, essay, high school/college transcript, and proof of receipt of Purple Heart or membership in order. Must be U.S. citizen and high school graduate with minimum GPA of 2.75 and accepted or enrolled as a full-time student at a U.S. college, university of trade school at the time the scholarship is awarded.

Award: Scholarship for use in freshman, sophomore, junior, senior, or graduate years; not renewable. *Number:* up to 50. *Amount:* $3000.

Eligibility Requirements: Applicant must be enrolled or expecting to enroll full-time at a two-year or four-year or technical institution or university. Applicant must have 3.0 GPA or higher. Available to U.S. citizens. Applicant or parent must meet one or more of the following requirements: general military experience; retired from active duty; disabled or killed as a result of military service; prisoner of war; or missing in action.

Application Requirements: Application, essay, references, transcript, Purple Heart or MOPH membership proof. *Fee:* $10. *Deadline:* February 19.

Contact: Mr. Stewart Mckeown, Scholarship Coordinator
Military Order of the Purple Heart
5413-B Backlick Road
Springfield, VA 22151-3960
Phone: 703-642-5360
Fax: 703-642-2054
E-mail: info@purpleheart.org

MINNESOTA HIGHER EDUCATION SERVICES OFFICE http://www.getreadyforcollege.org

MINNESOTA GI BILL PROGRAM

Provides financial assistance to eligible Minnesota veterans and non-veterans who have served 5 or more years cumulatively as a member of the National Guard or Reserves, and served on or after September 11, 2001. Surviving spouses and children of service members who have died or have a total and permanent disability and who served on or after September 11, 2001 may also be eligible. Full-time students may receive up to $1000 per term, and part-time students up to $500 per term. Maximum lifetime benefit is $10,000.

Award: Scholarship for use in freshman, sophomore, junior, senior, graduate, or postgraduate years; renewable. *Number:* varies. *Amount:* up to $1000.

Eligibility Requirements: Applicant must be enrolled or expecting to enroll full- or part-time at a two-year or four-year or technical institution or university; resident of Minnesota and studying in Minnesota. Available to U.S. and non-U.S. citizens. Applicant or parent must meet one or more of the following requirements: general military experience; retired from active duty; disabled or killed as a result of military service; prisoner of war; or missing in action.

Application Requirements: Application, financial need analysis, military records. *Deadline:* continuous.

Contact: Grant Staff
Minnesota Higher Education Services Office
1450 Energy Park Drive
St. Paul, MN 55108
Phone: 651-642-0567
Fax: 651-642-0675

MINNESOTA STATE VETERANS' DEPENDENTS ASSISTANCE PROGRAM

Tuition assistance to dependents of persons considered to be prisoner-of-war or missing in action after August 1, 1958. Must be Minnesota resident attending Minnesota two- or four-year school.

Award: Scholarship for use in freshman, sophomore, junior, or senior years; renewable. *Number:* varies. *Amount:* varies.

Eligibility Requirements: Applicant must be enrolled or expecting to enroll full- or part-time at a two-year or four-year institution; resident of Minnesota and studying in Minnesota. Available to U.S. citizens. Applicant or parent must meet one or more of the following requirements: general military experience; retired from active duty; disabled or killed as a result of military service; prisoner of war; or missing in action.

Application Requirements: Application. *Deadline:* continuous.

Contact: Ginny Dodds, Manager
Minnesota Higher Education Services Office
1450 Energy Park Drive, Suite 350
St. Paul, MN 55108-5227
Phone: 651-642-0567
Fax: 651-642-0675
E-mail: ginny.dodds@state.mn.us

NATIONAL MILITARY FAMILY ASSOCIATION http://www.nmfa.org

NMFA JOANNE HOLBROOK PATTON MILITARY SPOUSE SCHOLARSHIPS

Scholarships ranging from $500 to $1000 are awarded to spouses of Uniformed Services members (active duty, National Guard and Reserve, retirees, and survivors) to obtain professional certification or to attend postsecondary or graduate school. Award number varies.

Award: Scholarship for use in freshman, sophomore, junior, senior, or graduate years; not renewable. *Number:* varies. *Amount:* $500–$1000.

Eligibility Requirements: Applicant must be enrolled or expecting to enroll full- or part-time at a two-year or four-year or technical institution or university and married. Available to U.S. citizens. Applicant or parent must meet one or more of the following requirements: general military experience; retired from active duty; disabled or killed as a result of military service; prisoner of war; or missing in action.

Application Requirements: Application, copy of current Uniformed Services ID card/ DEERS card (back and front), other proof of status as a military spouse or surviving spouse. *Deadline:* March 15.

Contact: Jo Koeniger, Deputy Director, Development
National Military Family Association
2500 North Van Dorn Street, Suite 102
Alexandria, VA 22302-1601
Phone: 703-931-6632
Fax: 703-931-4600
E-mail: families@nmfa.org

NEW HAMPSHIRE CHARITABLE FOUNDATION http://www.nhcf.org

ADULT STUDENT AID PROGRAM

Award for New Hampshire residents who are at least 24 years old, or who have served in the military, are wards of the court, have not been claimed by their parents for two consecutive years, are married, or who have dependent children. Application deadlines are August 15, December 15, and May 15. Application fee is $15. Further information and application available at Web site http://www.nhcf.org.

Award: Grant for use in freshman, sophomore, junior, or senior years; not renewable. *Number:* 100–200. *Amount:* $100–$1500.

Eligibility Requirements: Applicant must be age 24 and over; enrolled or expecting to enroll full- or part-time at a two-year or four-year or technical institution or university; married and resident of New Hampshire. Available to U.S. citizens. Applicant or parent must meet one or more of the following requirements: general military experience; retired from active duty; disabled or killed as a result of military service; prisoner of war; or missing in action.

Application Requirements: Application, financial need analysis, resume, references, transcript. *Fee:* $15. *Deadline:* varies.

Contact: Judith Burrows, Director, Student Aid
New Hampshire Charitable Foundation
37 Pleasant Street
Concord, NH 03301-4005
Phone: 603-225-6641 Ext. 224
E-mail: jb@nhcf.org

NEW HAMPSHIRE POSTSECONDARY EDUCATION COMMISSION http://www.nh.gov/postsecondary

SCHOLARSHIPS FOR ORPHANS OF VETERANS-NEW HAMPSHIRE

Scholarship to provide financial assistance (room, board, books and supplies) to children of parents) who served in World War II, Korean Conflict, Vietnam (Southeast Asian Conflict) or the Gulf Wars, or any other operation for which the armed forces expeditionary medal or theater of operations service medal was awarded to the veteran.

Award: Scholarship for use in freshman, sophomore, junior, or senior years; renewable. *Number:* 1–10. *Amount:* up to $2500.

Eligibility Requirements: Applicant must be age 16-25; enrolled or expecting to enroll full-time at a two-year or four-year institution or university; resident of New Hampshire and studying in New Hampshire. Available to U.S. citizens. Applicant or parent must meet one or more of the following requirements: general military experience; retired from active duty; disabled or killed as a result of military service; prisoner of war; or missing in action.

Application Requirements: Application. *Deadline:* varies.

Contact: Judith Knapp, Coordinator of Financial Aid Programs
New Hampshire Postsecondary Education Commission
Three Barrell Court, Suite 300
Concord, NH 03301-8543
Phone: 603-271-2555 Ext. 352
Fax: 603-271-2696
E-mail: jknapp@pec.state.nh.us

NEW JERSEY DEPARTMENT OF MILITARY AND VETERANS AFFAIRS http://www.state.nj.us/military

NEW JERSEY WAR ORPHANS TUITION ASSISTANCE

$500 scholarship to children of those service personnel who died while in the military or due to service-connected disabilities, or who are officially listed as missing in action by the U.S. Department of Defense. Must be a resident of New Jersey for at least one year immediately preceding the filing of the application and be between the ages of 16 and 21 at the time of application.

Award: Scholarship for use in freshman, sophomore, junior, or senior years; renewable. *Number:* varies. *Amount:* $500.

Eligibility Requirements: Applicant must be age 16-21; enrolled or expecting to enroll full-time at a four-year institution or university and resident of New Jersey. Available to U.S. citizens. Applicant or parent must meet one or more of the following requirements: general military experience; retired from active duty; disabled or killed as a result of military service; prisoner of war; or missing in action.

Application Requirements: Application, transcript. *Deadline:* varies.

Contact: Patricia Richter, Grants Manager
New Jersey Department of Military and Veterans Affairs
PO Box 340
Trenton, NJ 08625-0340
Phone: 609-530-6854
Fax: 609-530-6970
E-mail: patricia.richter@njdmava.state.nj.us

POW-MIA TUITION BENEFIT PROGRAM

Free undergraduate college tuition provided to any child born or adopted before or during the period of time his or her parent was officially declared a prisoner of war or person missing in action after January 1, 1960. The POW-MIA must have been a New Jersey resident at the time he or she entered the service. Child of veteran must attend either a public or private institution in New Jersey. A copy of DD 1300 must be furnished with the application. Minimum 2.5 GPA required.

Award: Scholarship for use in freshman, sophomore, junior, or senior years; renewable. *Number:* varies. *Amount:* varies.

Eligibility Requirements: Applicant must be enrolled or expecting to enroll full-time at a two-year or four-year or technical institution or university; resident of New Jersey and studying in New Jersey. Applicant must have 2.5 GPA or higher. Available to U.S. citizens. Applicant or parent must meet one or more of the following requirements: general military experience; retired from active duty; disabled or killed as a result of military service; prisoner of war; or missing in action.

Application Requirements: Application, transcript, copy of DD 1300. *Deadline:* varies.

Contact: Patricia Richter, Grants Manager
New Jersey Department of Military and Veterans Affairs
PO Box 340
Trenton, NJ 08625-0340
Phone: 609-530-6854
Fax: 609-530-6970
E-mail: patricia.richter@njdmava.state.nj.us

VETERANS TUITION CREDIT PROGRAM-NEW JERSEY

Award for New Jersey resident veterans who served in the armed forces between December 31, 1960, and May 7, 1975. Must have been a New Jersey resident at time of induction or discharge or for two years immediately prior to application.

Award: Scholarship for use in freshman, sophomore, junior, or senior years; renewable. *Number:* varies. *Amount:* $200–$400.

Eligibility Requirements: Applicant must be enrolled or expecting to enroll full- or part-time at a two-year or four-year or technical institution or university and resident of New Jersey. Available to U.S. citizens.

Applicant or parent must meet one or more of the following requirements: general military experience; retired from active duty; disabled or killed as a result of military service; prisoner of war; or missing in action.

Application Requirements: Application. *Deadline:* varies.

Contact: Patricia Richter, Grants Manager
New Jersey Department of Military and Veterans Affairs
PO Box 340
Trenton, NJ 08625-0340
Phone: 609-530-6854
Fax: 609-530-6970
E-mail: patricia.richter@njdmava.state.nj.us

NEW MEXICO COMMISSION ON HIGHER EDUCATION http://www.hed.state.nm.us

VIETNAM VETERANS' SCHOLARSHIP PROGRAM

Renewable scholarship program created to provide aid for Vietnam veterans who are undergraduate and graduate students attending public postsecondary institutions or select private colleges in New Mexico. Private colleges include: College of Santa Fe, St. John's College and College of the Southwest.

Award: Scholarship for use in freshman, sophomore, junior, senior, or graduate years; renewable. *Number:* 1. *Amount:* varies.

Eligibility Requirements: Applicant must be enrolled or expecting to enroll full-time at a two-year or four-year institution; resident of New Mexico and studying in New Mexico. Available to U.S. citizens. Applicant or parent must meet one or more of the following requirements: general military experience; retired from active duty; disabled or killed as a result of military service; prisoner of war; or missing in action.

Application Requirements: Application, certification by the NM Veteran's commission. *Deadline:* varies.

Contact: Tashina Banks Moore, Interim Director of Financial Aid
New Mexico Commission on Higher Education
1068 Cerrillos Road
Santa Fe, NM 87505
Phone: 505-476-6549
Fax: 505-476-6511
E-mail: tashina.banks-moore@state.nm.us

NEW MEXICO VETERANS SERVICE COMMISSION http://www.dvs.state.nm.us

CHILDREN OF DECEASED VETERANS SCHOLARSHIP-NEW MEXICO

Award for New Mexico residents who are children of veterans killed or disabled as a result of service, prisoner of war, or veterans missing in action. Must be between ages 16 and 26. For use at New Mexico schools for undergraduate study. Must submit parent's death certificate and DD form 214.

Award: Scholarship for use in freshman, sophomore, junior, or senior years; renewable. *Number:* varies. *Amount:* $300.

Eligibility Requirements: Applicant must be age 16-26; enrolled or expecting to enroll full- or part-time at a two-year or four-year institution or university; resident of New Mexico and studying in New Mexico. Available to U.S. citizens. Applicant or parent must meet one or more of the following requirements: general military experience; retired from active duty; disabled or killed as a result of military service; prisoner of war; or missing in action.

Application Requirements: Application, transcript, death certificate or notice of casualty, DD form 214. *Deadline:* continuous.

Contact: Alan Martinez, Director, State Benefits Division
New Mexico Veterans Service Commission
Bataan Memorial Building
407 Galisteo, Room 142
Santa Fe, NM 87504
Phone: 505-827-6300
Fax: 505-827-6372
E-mail: alan.martinez@state.nm.us

NEW MEXICO VIETNAM VETERAN SCHOLARSHIP

Award for Vietnam veterans who have been New Mexico residents for a minimum of ten years and are attending state-funded postsecondary schools. Must have been awarded the Vietnam Campaign medal. Must submit DD 214 and discharge papers.

Award: Scholarship for use in freshman, sophomore, junior, or senior years; renewable. *Number:* 115. *Amount:* $3500–$4000.

Eligibility Requirements: Applicant must be enrolled or expecting to enroll full- or part-time at a two-year or four-year or technical institution or university; resident of New Mexico and studying in New Mexico. Available to U.S. citizens. Applicant or parent must meet one or more of the following requirements: general military experience; retired from active duty; disabled or killed as a result of military service; prisoner of war; or missing in action.

Application Requirements: Application, copy of DD Form 214. *Deadline:* continuous.

Contact: Alan Martinez, Director, State Benefits Division
New Mexico Veterans Service Commission
Bataan Memorial Building
407 Galisteo, Room 142
Santa Fe, NM 87504
Phone: 505-827-6300
Fax: 505-827-6372
E-mail: alan.martinez@state.nm.us

NEW YORK STATE HIGHER EDUCATION SERVICES CORPORATION http://www.hesc.com

NEW YORK VIETNAM/PERSIAN GULF/AFGHANISTAN VETERANS TUITION AWARDS

Scholarship for veterans who served in Vietnam, the Persian Gulf, or Afghanistan. Must be a New York resident attending a New York institution. Must establish eligibility by September 1.

Award: Scholarship for use in freshman, sophomore, junior, or senior years; renewable. *Number:* varies. *Amount:* $500–$1000.

Eligibility Requirements: Applicant must be enrolled or expecting to enroll full- or part-time at a two-year or four-year or technical institution or university; resident of New York and studying in New York. Available to U.S. citizens. Applicant or parent must meet one or more of the following requirements: general military experience; retired from active duty; disabled or killed as a result of military service; prisoner of war; or missing in action.

Application Requirements: Application, financial need analysis, transcript. *Deadline:* May 1.

Contact: Adrienne Day, Associate HESC Information Representative
New York State Higher Education Services Corporation
99 Washington Avenue, Room 1320
Albany, NY 12255
Phone: 518-474-2991
Fax: 518-474-2839
E-mail: aday@hesc.com

REGENTS AWARD FOR CHILD OF VETERAN

Award for students whose parent, as a result of service in U.S. Armed Forces during war or national emergency, died; suffered a 40 percent or more disability; or is classified as missing in action or a prisoner of war. Veteran must be current New York State resident or have been so at time of death. Student must be a New York resident, attending, or planning to attend, college in New York State. Must establish eligibility before applying for payment.

Award: Scholarship for use in freshman, sophomore, junior, or senior years; not renewable. *Number:* varies. *Amount:* $450.

Eligibility Requirements: Applicant must be enrolled or expecting to enroll full-time at a two-year or four-year institution or university; resident of New York and studying in New York. Available to U.S. citizens. Applicant or parent must meet one or more of the following requirements: general military experience; retired from active duty; disabled or killed as a result of military service; prisoner of war; or missing in action.

Application Requirements: Application, proof of eligibility. *Deadline:* May 1.

Contact: Rita McGivern, Student Information
New York State Higher Education Services Corporation
99 Washington Avenue, Room 1320
Albany, NY 12255
E-mail: rmcgivern@hesc.com

NORTH CAROLINA DIVISION OF VETERANS AFFAIRS http://www.doa.state.nc.us/vets/va.htm

NORTH CAROLINA VETERANS SCHOLARSHIPS CLASS I-A

Scholarships for children of certain deceased, disabled or POW/MIA veterans. Award value is $4500 per nine-month academic year in private colleges and junior colleges. No limit on number awarded each year.

Award: Scholarship for use in freshman, sophomore, junior, or senior years; renewable. *Number:* varies. *Amount:* $4500.

Eligibility Requirements: Applicant must be enrolled or expecting to enroll full-time at a two-year or four-year or technical institution or university; resident of North Carolina and studying in North Carolina. Available to U.S. citizens. Applicant or parent must meet one or more of the following requirements: general military experience; retired from active duty; disabled or killed as a result of military service; prisoner of war; or missing in action.

Application Requirements: Application, financial need analysis, interview, transcript. *Deadline:* continuous.

Contact: Charles Smith, Assistant Secretary
North Carolina Division of Veterans Affairs
325 North Salisbury Street
Raleigh, NC 27603
Phone: 919-733-3851
Fax: 919-733-2834
E-mail: charlie.smith@ncmail.net

NORTH CAROLINA VETERANS SCHOLARSHIPS CLASS I-B

Awards for children of veterans rated by USDVA as 100 percent disabled due to wartime service as defined in the law, and currently or at time of death drawing compensation for such disability. Parent must have been a North Carolina resident at time of entry into service. Duration of the scholarship is four academic years (8 semesters) if used within 8 years. No limit on number awarded each year.

Award: Scholarship for use in freshman, sophomore, junior, or senior years; renewable. *Number:* varies. *Amount:* $1500.

Eligibility Requirements: Applicant must be enrolled or expecting to enroll full- or part-time at a two-year or four-year or technical institution or university; resident of North Carolina and studying in North Carolina. Available to U.S. citizens. Applicant or parent must meet one or more of the following requirements: general military experience; retired from active duty; disabled or killed as a result of military service; prisoner of war; or missing in action.

Application Requirements: Application, financial need analysis, interview, transcript. *Deadline:* continuous.

Contact: Charles Smith, Assistant Secretary
North Carolina Division of Veterans Affairs
325 North Salisbury Street
Raleigh, NC 27603
Phone: 919-733-3851
Fax: 919-733-2834
E-mail: charlie.smith@ncmail.net

NORTH CAROLINA VETERANS SCHOLARSHIPS CLASS II

Awards for children of veterans rated by USDVA as much as 20 percent but less than 100 percent disabled due to wartime service as defined in the law, or awarded Purple Heart Medal for wounds received. Parent must have been a North Carolina resident at time of entry into service. Duration of the scholarship is four academic years (8 semesters) if used within 8 years. Free tuition and exemption from certain mandatory fees as set forth in the law in Public, Community and Technical Colleges.

Award: Scholarship for use in freshman, sophomore, junior, or senior years; renewable. *Number:* up to 100. *Amount:* $4500.

Eligibility Requirements: Applicant must be enrolled or expecting to enroll full- or part-time at a two-year or four-year or technical institution or university; resident of North Carolina and studying in North Carolina. Available to U.S. citizens. Applicant or parent must meet one or more of the following requirements: general military experience; retired from active duty; disabled or killed as a result of military service; prisoner of war; or missing in action.

Application Requirements: Application, financial need analysis, interview, transcript. *Deadline:* March 1.

Contact: Charles Smith, Assistant Secretary
North Carolina Division of Veterans Affairs
325 North Salisbury Street
Raleigh, NC 27603
Phone: 919-733-3851
Fax: 919-733-2834
E-mail: charlie.smith@ncmail.net

NORTH CAROLINA VETERANS SCHOLARSHIPS CLASS III

Awards for children of a deceased war veteran, who was honorably discharged and who does not qualify under any other provision within this synopsis or veteran who served in a combat zone or waters adjacent to a combat zone and received a campaign badge or medal and who does not qualify under any other provision within this synopsis. Duration of the scholarship is four academic years (8 semesters) if used within 8 years.

Award: Scholarship for use in freshman, sophomore, junior, or senior years; renewable. *Number:* up to 100. *Amount:* $4500.

Eligibility Requirements: Applicant must be enrolled or expecting to enroll full- or part-time at a two-year or four-year or technical institution or university; resident of North Carolina and studying in North Carolina. Available to U.S. citizens. Applicant or parent must meet one or more of the following requirements: general military experience; retired from active duty; disabled or killed as a result of military service; prisoner of war; or missing in action.

Application Requirements: Application, financial need analysis, interview, transcript. *Deadline:* March 1.

Contact: Charles Smith, Assistant Secretary
North Carolina Division of Veterans Affairs
325 North Salisbury Street
Raleigh, NC 27603
Phone: 919-733-3851
Fax: 919-733-2834
E-mail: charlie.smith@ncmail.net

NORTH CAROLINA VETERANS SCHOLARSHIPS CLASS IV

Awards for children of veterans, who were prisoner of war or missing in action. Duration of the scholarship is four academic years (8 semesters) if used within 8 years. No limit on number awarded each year. Award value is $4500 per nine-month academic year in private colleges and junior colleges.

Award: Scholarship for use in freshman, sophomore, junior, or senior years; renewable. *Number:* varies. *Amount:* $4500.

Eligibility Requirements: Applicant must be enrolled or expecting to enroll full- or part-time at a two-year or four-year or technical institution or university; resident of North Carolina and studying in North Carolina. Available to U.S. citizens. Applicant or parent must meet one or more of the following requirements: general military experience; retired from active duty; disabled or killed as a result of military service; prisoner of war; or missing in action.

Application Requirements: Application, financial need analysis, interview, transcript. *Deadline:* continuous.

Contact: Charles Smith, Assistant Secretary
North Carolina Division of Veterans Affairs
325 North Salisbury Street
Raleigh, NC 27603
Phone: 919-733-3851
Fax: 919-733-2834
E-mail: charlie.smith@ncmail.net

OHIO BOARD OF REGENTS http://www.regents.ohio.gov

OHIO MISSING IN ACTION AND PRISONERS OF WAR ORPHANS SCHOLARSHIP

Renewable award aids children of Vietnam conflict servicemen who have been classified as missing in action or prisoner of war. Applicants must be under the age of 25 and be enrolled full-time at an Ohio college. Full tuition awards. Dollar value of each award varies.

Award: Scholarship for use in freshman, sophomore, junior, or senior years; renewable. *Number:* 1–5. *Amount:* varies.

Eligibility Requirements: Applicant must be age 25 or under; enrolled or expecting to enroll full-time at a four-year institution or university; resident of Ohio and studying in Ohio. Available to U.S. citizens.

Applicant or parent must meet one or more of the following requirements: general military experience; retired from active duty; disabled or killed as a result of military service; prisoner of war; or missing in action.

Application Requirements: Application. *Deadline:* July 1.

Contact: Jathiya Abdullah-Simmons, Program Administrator
Ohio Board of Regents
30 East Broad Street, 36th Floor
Columbus, OH 43215-3414
Phone: 614-752-9528
Fax: 614-752-5903
E-mail: jabdullah-simmons@regents.state.oh.us

OHIO WAR ORPHANS SCHOLARSHIP

Aids Ohio residents attending an eligible college in Ohio. Must be between the ages of 16 to 25, the child of a disabled or deceased veteran, and enrolled full-time. Renewable up to five years. Amount of award varies. Must include Form DD214.

Award: Scholarship for use in freshman, sophomore, junior, or senior years; renewable. *Number:* 300–450. *Amount:* varies.

Eligibility Requirements: Applicant must be age 16-25; enrolled or expecting to enroll full-time at a two-year or four-year institution or university; resident of Ohio and studying in Ohio. Available to U.S. citizens. Applicant or parent must meet one or more of the following requirements: general military experience; retired from active duty; disabled or killed as a result of military service; prisoner of war; or missing in action.

Application Requirements: Application. *Deadline:* July 1.

Contact: Jathiya Abdullah-Simmons, Program Administrator
Ohio Board of Regents
30 East Broad Street, 36th Floor
Columbus, OH 43215-3414
Phone: 614-752-9528
Fax: 614-752-5903
E-mail: jabdullah-simmons@regents.state.oh.us

OREGON DEPARTMENT OF VETERANS AFFAIRS http://www.oregon.gov/odva

OREGON VETERANS' EDUCATION AID

To be eligible, veteran must have served in U.S. armed forces 90 days and been discharged under honorable conditions. Must be U.S. citizen and Oregon resident. Korean War veteran or received campaign or expeditionary medal or ribbon awarded by U.S. armed forces for services after June 30, 1958. Full-time students receive $50 per month, and part-time students receive $35 per month.

Award: Grant for use in freshman, sophomore, junior, senior, graduate, or postgraduate years; not renewable. *Number:* up to 100. *Amount:* $420–$600.

Eligibility Requirements: Applicant must be enrolled or expecting to enroll full- or part-time at a two-year or four-year or technical institution or university; resident of Oregon and studying in Oregon. Available to U.S. citizens. Applicant or parent must meet one or more of the following requirements: general military experience; retired from active duty; disabled or killed as a result of military service; prisoner of war; or missing in action.

Application Requirements: Application, certified copy of DD Form 214. *Deadline:* continuous.

Contact: Loriann Sheridan, Educational Aid Coordinator
Oregon Department of Veterans Affairs
700 Summer Street, NE
Salem, OR 97301-1289
Phone: 503-373-2085
Fax: 503-373-2393
E-mail: sheridl@odva.state.or.us

OREGON STUDENT ASSISTANCE COMMISSION http://www.osac.state.or.us

AMERICAN EX-PRISONER OF WAR SCHOLARSHIPS: PETER CONNACHER MEMORIAL SCHOLARSHIP

Renewable award for American prisoners-of-war and their descendants. Written proof of prisoner-of-war status and discharge papers from the U.S. Armed Forces must accompany application. Statement of relationship between applicant and former prisoner-of-war is required. See Web site at http://www.osac.state.or.us for details.

Award: Scholarship for use in freshman, sophomore, junior, or senior years; renewable. *Number:* varies. *Amount:* varies.

Eligibility Requirements: Applicant must be enrolled or expecting to enroll full-time at a two-year or four-year institution and resident of Oregon. Available to U.S. citizens. Applicant or parent must meet one or more of the following requirements: general military experience; retired from active duty; disabled or killed as a result of military service; prisoner of war; or missing in action.

Application Requirements: Application, essay, financial need analysis, transcript, activities chart. *Deadline:* March 1.

Contact: Director of Grant Programs
Oregon Student Assistance Commission
1500 Valley River Drive, Suite 100
Eugene, OR 97401-7020
Phone: 800-452-8807 Ext. 7395

MARIA JACKSON/GENERAL GEORGE A. WHITE SCHOLARSHIP

Available to Oregon residents who served or whose parents serve or have served in the U.S. Armed Forces and resided in Oregon at time of enlistment. Must have at least 3.75 GPA and submit documentation of service. For use at Oregon colleges only. U.S. Bank employees, their children, and near relatives are not eligible.

Award: Scholarship for use in freshman, sophomore, junior, senior, or graduate years; not renewable. *Number:* 54. *Amount:* varies.

Eligibility Requirements: Applicant must be enrolled or expecting to enroll full-time at a four-year institution or university; resident of Oregon and studying in Oregon. Available to U.S. citizens. Applicant or parent must meet one or more of the following requirements: general military experience; retired from active duty; disabled or killed as a result of military service; prisoner of war; or missing in action.

Application Requirements: Application, essay, financial need analysis, test scores, transcript, proof of service (DD93, DD214, or discharge papers). *Deadline:* March 1.

Contact: Director of Grant Programs
Oregon Student Assistance Commission
1500 Valley River Drive, Suite 100
Eugene, OR 97401-7020
Phone: 800-452-8807 Ext. 7395

PARALYZED VETERANS OF AMERICA-SPINAL CORD RESEARCH FOUNDATION http://www.pva.org

PARALYZED VETERANS OF AMERICA EDUCATIONAL SCHOLARSHIP PROGRAM

Open to PVA members, their spouses and unmarried children, under 24 years of age, to obtain a postsecondary education. Applicants must be U.S. citizens accepted or enrolled as full-time students in a degree program. For details and application visit Web site: http://www.pva.org.

Award: Scholarship for use in freshman, sophomore, junior, or senior years; renewable. *Number:* 10–20. *Amount:* $500–$1000.

Eligibility Requirements: Applicant must be age 24 or under and enrolled or expecting to enroll full- or part-time at a four-year institution or university. Available to U.S. citizens. Applicant or parent must meet one or more of the following requirements: general military experience; retired from active duty; disabled or killed as a result of military service; prisoner of war; or missing in action.

Application Requirements: Application, references, transcript, personal statement, verification of enrollment. *Deadline:* June 30.

Contact: Patricia Rollins, Member Services Coordinator
Paralyzed Veterans of America-Spinal Cord Research Foundation
801 Eighteenth Street, NW
Washington, DC 20006-3517
Phone: 800-424-8200 Ext. 619
E-mail: trishr@pva.org

PENNSYLVANIA HIGHER EDUCATION ASSISTANCE AGENCY http://www.pheaa.org

ARMED FORCES LOAN FORGIVENESS PROGRAM

Loan forgiveness for non-residents of Pennsylvania who served in Armed Forces in an active duty status after September 11, 2001. Must be a student who either left a PA approved institution of postsecondary education due to call to active duty, or was living in PA at time of enlistment, or enlisted in military immediately after attending a PA approved institution of postsecondary education. Number of loans forgiven varies.

Award: Forgivable loan for use in freshman, sophomore, junior, or senior years; not renewable. *Number:* varies. *Amount:* up to $2500.

Eligibility Requirements: Applicant must be enrolled or expecting to enroll full- or part-time at a two-year or four-year or technical institution or university. Available to U.S. citizens. Applicant or parent must meet one or more of the following requirements: general military experience; retired from active duty; disabled or killed as a result of military service; prisoner of war; or missing in action.

Application Requirements: Application. *Deadline:* December 31.

Contact: Keith New, Vice President, Public Relations
Pennsylvania Higher Education Assistance Agency
1200 North Seventh Street
Harrisburg, PA 17102-1444
Phone: 717-720-2509
Fax: 717-720-3903
E-mail: knew@pheaa.org

RESERVE OFFICERS ASSOCIATION http://www.roa.org

HENRY J. REILLY MEMORIAL SCHOLARSHIP-HIGH SCHOOL SENIORS AND FIRST YEAR FRESHMEN

• *See page 555*

HENRY J. REILLY MEMORIAL UNDERGRADUATE SCHOLARSHIP PROGRAM FOR COLLEGE ATTENDEES

• *See page 555*

RETIRED ENLISTED ASSOCIATION http://www.trea.org

RETIRED ENLISTED ASSOCIATION SCHOLARSHIP

One-time award for dependent children or grandchildren of a TREA member or TREA auxiliary member in good standing.

Award: Scholarship for use in freshman, sophomore, junior, senior, graduate, or postgraduate years; not renewable. *Number:* varies. *Amount:* $1000–$1500.

Eligibility Requirements: Applicant must be enrolled or expecting to enroll full-time at a two-year or four-year or technical institution or university. Available to U.S. citizens. Applicant or parent must meet one or more of the following requirements: general military experience; retired from active duty; disabled or killed as a result of military service; prisoner of war; or missing in action.

Application Requirements: Application, essay, financial need analysis, photo, references, test scores, transcript, copy of IRS tax forms. *Deadline:* April 30.

Contact: Donnell Minnis, Executive Assistant
Retired Enlisted Association
c/o National Scholarship Committee, 1111 South Abilene Court
Aurora, CO 80012-4909
Phone: 303-752-0660
Fax: 303-752-0835
E-mail: execasst@trea.org

STATE OF WYOMING, ADMINISTERED BY UNIVERSITY OF WYOMING http://www.uwyo.edu/scholarships

VIETNAM VETERANS AWARD-WYOMING

Scholarship available to Wyoming residents who served in the armed forces between August 5, 1964 and May 7, 1975, and received a Vietnam service medal.

Award: Scholarship for use in freshman, sophomore, junior, or senior years; renewable. *Number:* varies. *Amount:* varies.

Eligibility Requirements: Applicant must be enrolled or expecting to enroll full- or part-time at a two-year or four-year institution or university and resident of Wyoming. Available to U.S. citizens. Applicant or parent must meet one or more of the following requirements: general military experience; retired from active duty; disabled or killed as a result of military service; prisoner of war; or missing in action.

Application Requirements: Application. *Deadline:* continuous.

Contact: Tammy Mack, Assistant Director, Scholarships
State of Wyoming, Administered by University of Wyoming
Student Financial Aid Department 3335, 1000 East University Avenue
Laramie, WY 82071-3335
Phone: 307-766-2117
Fax: 307-766-3800
E-mail: finaid@uwyo.edu

37TH DIVISION VETERANS ASSOCIATION http://www.37thdva.org

37TH DIVISION VETERANS ASSOCIATION SCHOLARSHIP

Scholarships are awarded annually to a son or a daughter of a 37th Division veteran who served in World War I, World War II, or the Korean War. Applicants must display financial need and academic excellence.

Award: Scholarship for use in freshman, sophomore, junior, senior, or graduate years; not renewable. *Number:* varies. *Amount:* varies.

Eligibility Requirements: Applicant must be enrolled or expecting to enroll full- or part-time at a two-year or four-year institution or university. Available to U.S. citizens. Applicant or parent must meet one or more of the following requirements: general military experience; retired from active duty; disabled or killed as a result of military service; prisoner of war; or missing in action.

Application Requirements: Application, financial need analysis, references. *Deadline:* April 1.

Contact: Cyril Sedlacko, Secretary and Treasurer
37th Division Veterans Association
35 East Chestnut Street, Suite 425, Fourth Floor
Columbus, OH 43215
Phone: 614-228-3788
Fax: 614-228-3793
E-mail: ops@37thdva.org

VA MORTGAGE CENTER http://www.vamortgagecenter.com

MILITARY EDUCATION SCHOLARSHIP

Scholarships for all ROTC program students or active duty military looking to return to college. To compete, applicants must submit a two to three page essay on "Why I Choose to Serve". For more information, please see Web site: http://www.vamortgagecenter.com/guidelines.html.

Award: Scholarship for use in freshman, sophomore, junior, senior, graduate, or postgraduate years; not renewable. *Number:* 5. *Amount:* $1500.

Eligibility Requirements: Applicant must be enrolled or expecting to enroll full- or part-time at a two-year or four-year or technical institution or university. Available to U.S. citizens. Applicant or parent must meet one or more of the following requirements: general military experience; retired from active duty; disabled or killed as a result of military service; prisoner of war; or missing in action.

Application Requirements: Application, essay. *Deadline:* May 12.

Contact: Mr. Nathan Long, Chief Executive Officer
VA Mortgage Center
2101 Chapel Plaza Court, Suite 107
Columbia, MO 65203
Phone: 800-405-6682
E-mail: customer_service@vamortgagecenter.com

VETERANS OF FOREIGN WARS OF THE UNITED STATES http://www.vfw.org

VFW MILITARY FAMILY SCHOLARSHIP

Scholarship program provides 25 $3000 scholarships annually to VFW members who are currently serving in uniform or have been discharged within the 36 months before the deadline. Scholarships will be awarded to five members from each branch of service (Army, Navy, Marine Corps, Air Force and Coast Guard) during the first quarter of the year following the deadline.

Award: Scholarship for use in freshman, sophomore, junior, senior, graduate, or postgraduate years; not renewable. *Number:* 25. *Amount:* $3000.

Eligibility Requirements: Applicant must be enrolled or expecting to enroll full- or part-time at a two-year or four-year or technical institution or university. Available to U.S. citizens. Applicant or parent must meet one or more of the following requirements: general military experience; retired from active duty; disabled or killed as a result of military service; prisoner of war; or missing in action.

Application Requirements: Application, supporting documentation. *Deadline:* December 31.

Contact: Kris Harmer, Secretary
Veterans of Foreign Wars of the United States
406 West 34th Street, VFW Building
Kansas City, MO 64111
Phone: 816-968-1117
Fax: 816-968-1149
E-mail: kharmer@vfw.org

VIRGINIA DEPARTMENT OF VETERANS SERVICES http://www.dvs.virginia.gov

VIRGINIA MILITARY SURVIVORS AND DEPENDENTS EDUCATION PROGRAM

Scholarships for post-secondary students between ages 16 and 19 to attend Virginia state-supported institutions. Must be child or surviving child of veteran who has either been permanently or totally disabled due to war or other armed conflict; died as a result of war or other armed conflict; or been listed as a POW or MIA. Parent must also meet Virginia residency requirements.

Award: Scholarship for use in freshman, sophomore, junior, senior, or graduate years; renewable. *Number:* varies. *Amount:* varies.

Eligibility Requirements: Applicant must be age 16-19; enrolled or expecting to enroll full-time at a two-year or four-year or technical institution or university; resident of Virginia and studying in Virginia. Available to U.S. citizens. Applicant or parent must meet one or more of the following requirements: general military experience; retired from active duty; disabled or killed as a result of military service; prisoner of war; or missing in action.

Application Requirements: Application, references. *Deadline:* varies.

Contact: Doris Sullivan, Coordinator
Virginia Department of Veterans Services
Poff Federal Building, 270 Franklin Road, SW, Room 503
Roanoke, VA 24011-2215
Phone: 540-857-7101 Ext. 213
Fax: 540-857-7573

MILITARY SERVICE: MARINES

DEPARTMENT OF VETERANS AFFAIRS (VA) http://www.gibill.va.gov

MONTGOMERY GI BILL (SELECTED RESERVE)

• *See page 632*

FIRST MARINE DIVISION ASSOCIATION http://www.1stmarinedivisionassociation.org

FIRST MARINE DIVISION ASSOCIATION SCHOLARSHIP FUND

Scholarship to assist dependents of deceased or 100 percent permanently disabled veterans of service with the 1st Marine Division in furthering their education towards a bachelor's degree. Awarded to full-time, undergraduate students who are attending an accredited college, university, or higher technical trade school, up to a maximum of four years.

Award: Scholarship for use in freshman, sophomore, junior, or senior years; not renewable. *Number:* varies. *Amount:* up to $1750.

Eligibility Requirements: Applicant must be age 22 or under; enrolled or expecting to enroll full-time at a four-year or technical institution or university and single. Available to U.S. citizens. Applicant or parent must meet one or more of the following requirements: Marine Corps experience; retired from active duty; disabled or killed as a result of military service; prisoner of war; or missing in action.

Application Requirements: Application, essay, photo, transcript, social security number, birth certificate, proof of parent's death. *Deadline:* continuous.

Contact: Col. Len Hayes, Executive Director
First Marine Division Association
410 Pier View Way
Oceanside, CA 92054
Phone: 760-967-8561
Fax: 760-967-8567
E-mail: oldbreed@sbcglobal.net

FLEET RESERVE ASSOCIATION http://www.fra.org

COLONEL HAZEL ELIZABETH BENN U.S.M.C. SCHOLARSHIP

Scholarship available for freshman or sophomore undergraduate education for an unmarried dependent child of a Fleet Reserve Association member in good standing who served or is now serving in the United States Navy with an enlisted medical rating, serving with the United States Marine Corps.

Award: Scholarship for use in freshman or sophomore years; not renewable. *Number:* varies. *Amount:* up to $2000.

Eligibility Requirements: Applicant must be enrolled or expecting to enroll full-time at a four-year institution or university and single. Available to U.S. citizens. Applicant or parent must meet one or more of the following requirements: Marine Corps or Navy experience; retired from active duty; disabled or killed as a result of military service; prisoner of war; or missing in action.

Application Requirements: Application, essay, financial need analysis, references, transcript. *Deadline:* April 15.

Contact: Vince Cuthie Sr., Scholarship Administrator
Fleet Reserve Association
125 North West Street
Alexandria, VA 22314-2754
Phone: 703-683-1400
E-mail: fra@fra.org

FLEET RESERVE ASSOCIATION SCHOLARSHIP

• *See page 532*

OLIVER AND ESTHER R. HOWARD SCHOLARSHIP

• *See page 532*

SCHUYLER S. PYLE AWARD

• *See page 533*

STANLEY A. DORAN MEMORIAL SCHOLARSHIP

• *See page 641*

INDIANA DEPARTMENT OF VETERANS AFFAIRS http://www.in.gov/dva

RESIDENT TUITION FOR ACTIVE DUTY MILITARY PERSONNEL

• *See page 632*

LADIES AUXILIARY OF THE FLEET RESERVE ASSOCIATION http://www.fra.org

ALLIE MAE ODEN MEMORIAL SCHOLARSHIP

• *See page 540*

LADIES AUXILIARY OF THE FLEET RESERVE ASSOCIATION-NATIONAL PRESIDENT'S SCHOLARSHIP

• *See page 540*

LADIES AUXILIARY OF THE FLEET RESERVE ASSOCIATION SCHOLARSHIP

• *See page 540*

SAM ROSE MEMORIAL SCHOLARSHIP

• *See page 540*

MARINE CORPS SCHOLARSHIP FOUNDATION INC. http://www.mcsf.org

MARINE CORPS SCHOLARSHIP FOUNDATION

Available to undergraduate dependent children of current or former Marine Corps members whose family income does not exceed $77,000. Must submit proof of parent's service. Send for applications in the winter.

Marine Corps Scholarship Foundation Inc. (continued)

Award: Scholarship for use in freshman, sophomore, junior, or senior years; renewable. *Number:* 1000. *Amount:* $1000–$10,000.

Eligibility Requirements: Applicant must be enrolled or expecting to enroll full- or part-time at a two-year or four-year or technical institution or university. Available to U.S. citizens. Applicant or parent must meet one or more of the following requirements: Marine Corps experience; retired from active duty; disabled or killed as a result of military service; prisoner of war; or missing in action.

Application Requirements: Application, essay, financial need analysis, transcript. *Deadline:* varies.

Contact: June Hering, Scholarship Program Director
Marine Corps Scholarship Foundation Inc.
PO Box 3008
Princeton, NJ 08543-3008
Phone: 800-292-7777
Fax: 609-452-2259
E-mail: mcsf@marine-scholars.org

MARINE CORPS TANKERS ASSOCIATION INC. http://mcta.webexone.com

MARINE CORPS TANKERS ASSOCIATION, JOHN CORNELIUS/MAX ENGLISH SCHOLARSHIP

Award for Marine tankers or former Marine tankers, or dependents of Marines who served in a tank unit and are on active duty, retired, reserve or have been honorably discharged. Applicant must be a high school graduate or planning to graduate in June. May be enrolled in college, undergraduate or graduate or have previously attended college. Must be a member of MCTA or intends to join in the future.

Award: Scholarship for use in freshman, sophomore, junior, senior, or graduate years; not renewable. *Number:* 10. *Amount:* up to $2000.

Eligibility Requirements: Applicant must be enrolled or expecting to enroll full-time at a two-year or four-year or technical institution or university. Available to U.S. citizens. Applicant or parent must meet one or more of the following requirements: Marine Corps experience; retired from active duty; disabled or killed as a result of military service; prisoner of war; or missing in action.

Application Requirements: Application, essay, photo, references, test scores, transcript. *Deadline:* March 15.

Contact: Phil Morell, Scholarship Chair
Marine Corps Tankers Association Inc.
1112 Alpine Heights Road
Alpine, CA 91901-2814
Phone: 619-445-8423
Fax: 619-445-8423
E-mail: mpmorell@cox.net

NAVY-MARINE CORPS RELIEF SOCIETY http://www.nmcrs.org/education

ADMIRAL MIKE BOORDA SCHOLARSHIP PROGRAM

Scholarship for undergraduate students enrolled full-time in accredited colleges or universities. Must be 22 years of age or younger. Minimum 2.0 GPA required.

Award: Scholarship for use in freshman, sophomore, junior, or senior years; not renewable. *Number:* 1. *Amount:* $2000.

Eligibility Requirements: Applicant must be age 22 or under; enrolled or expecting to enroll full-time at a two-year or four-year or technical institution or university and single. Available to U.S. citizens. Applicant or parent must meet one or more of the following requirements: Marine Corps or Navy experience; retired from active duty; disabled or killed as a result of military service; prisoner of war; or missing in action.

Application Requirements: Application, financial need analysis, copy of military ID/orders. *Deadline:* May 1.

Contact: Mary Gaebel Laeske, Director, Education Programs
Navy-Marine Corps Relief Society
875 North Randolph Street, Suite 225
Arlington, VA 22203
Phone: 703-696-4960
E-mail: education@hq.nmcrs.org

NAVY-MARINE CORPS RELIEF SOCIETY-CHILDREN OF DECEASED SERVICE MEMBER WHO DIED AFTER RETIREMENT

Nonrenewable award for students enrolled full-time in accredited colleges or universities. Must have minimum 2.0 GPA.

Award: Scholarship for use in freshman, sophomore, junior, or senior years; not renewable. *Number:* 1. *Amount:* up to $3000.

Eligibility Requirements: Applicant must be age 22 or under; enrolled or expecting to enroll full-time at a two-year or four-year or technical institution or university and single. Available to U.S. citizens. Applicant or parent must meet one or more of the following requirements: Marine Corps or Navy experience; retired from active duty; disabled or killed as a result of military service; prisoner of war; or missing in action.

Application Requirements: Application, financial need analysis, copy of military ID card, DD 214, death certificate. *Deadline:* March 1.

Contact: Mary Gaebel Laeske, Director, Education Programs
Navy-Marine Corps Relief Society
875 North Randolph Street, Suite 225
Arlington, VA 22203
Phone: 703-696-4960
E-mail: education@hq.nmcrs.org

NAVY-MARINE CORPS RELIEF SOCIETY-SURVIVING CHILDREN OF DECEASED SERVICE MEMBER SCHOLARSHIP PROGRAM

Scholarship for full-time undergraduate students enrolled in accredited colleges or universities. Must be 22 years of age or younger. Must have minimum 2.0 GPA.

Award: Scholarship for use in freshman, sophomore, junior, or senior years; not renewable. *Number:* 1. *Amount:* $500–$3000.

Eligibility Requirements: Applicant must be age 22 or under; enrolled or expecting to enroll full-time at a two-year or four-year or technical institution or university and single. Available to U.S. citizens. Applicant or parent must meet one or more of the following requirements: Marine Corps or Navy experience; retired from active duty; disabled or killed as a result of military service; prisoner of war; or missing in action.

Application Requirements: Application, financial need analysis. *Deadline:* March 1.

Contact: Mary Gaebel Laeske, Director, Education Programs
Navy-Marine Corps Relief Society
875 North Randolph Street, Suite 225
Arlington, VA 22203
Phone: 703-696-4960
E-mail: education@hq.nmcrs.org

USS TENNESSEE SCHOLARSHIP FUND

Scholarship for undergraduate students enrolled full-time in accredited colleges or universities. Must be within 22 years of age. Must have minimum 2.0 GPA.

Award: Scholarship for use in freshman, sophomore, junior, or senior years; not renewable. *Number:* 1. *Amount:* up to $2000.

Eligibility Requirements: Applicant must be age 22 or under; enrolled or expecting to enroll full-time at a two-year or four-year or technical institution or university and single. Available to U.S. citizens. Applicant or parent must meet one or more of the following requirements: Marine Corps or Navy experience; retired from active duty; disabled or killed as a result of military service; prisoner of war; or missing in action.

Application Requirements: Application, financial need analysis, copy of military ID, proof of service in Tennessee. *Deadline:* March 1.

Contact: Mary Gaebel Laeske, Director, Education Programs
Navy-Marine Corps Relief Society
875 North Randolph Street, Suite 225
Arlington, VA 22203
Phone: 703-696-4960
E-mail: education@hq.nmcrs.org

SECOND MARINE DIVISION ASSOCIATION http://www.2marine.com

SECOND MARINE DIVISION ASSOCIATION MEMORIAL SCHOLARSHIP FUND

Renewable award for students who are unmarried sons, daughters or grandchildren of former or current members of Second Marine Division or attached units. Must submit proof of parent's service. Family adjusted gross income must not exceed $57,000. Award is merit-based. Minimum 2.5 GPA required.

Award: Scholarship for use in freshman, sophomore, junior, or senior years; renewable. *Number:* 37. *Amount:* $1000.

Eligibility Requirements: Applicant must be enrolled or expecting to enroll full-time at a two-year or four-year or technical institution or university and single. Applicant must have 2.5 GPA or higher. Available to U.S. and non-U.S. citizens. Applicant or parent must meet one or more of the following requirements: Marine Corps experience; retired from active duty; disabled or killed as a result of military service; prisoner of war; or missing in action.

Application Requirements: Application, financial need analysis, references, self-addressed stamped envelope, transcript. *Deadline:* April 1.

Contact: Peter Grimes, Executive Director
Second Marine Division Association
PO Box 8180
Camp LeJeune, NC 28547-8180
Phone: 910-451-3167
E-mail: peter.grimes@usmc.mil

TAILHOOK EDUCATIONAL FOUNDATION http://www.tailhook.org

TAILHOOK EDUCATIONAL FOUNDATION SCHOLARSHIP
• *See page 642*

THIRD MARINE DIVISION ASSOCIATION INC. http://www.caltrap.com

THIRD MARINE DIVISION ASSOCIATION MEMORIAL SCHOLARSHIP FUND

Scholarship for dependents of Third Marine Division personnel (Marine or Navy) deceased or 100 percent service-connected disabled veterans; and two-year members of the Association, living or dead. For further details visit Web site: http://www.caltrap.com. Total number of awards varies.

Award: Scholarship for use in freshman, sophomore, junior, or senior years; renewable. *Number:* varies. *Amount:* $500–$1500.

Eligibility Requirements: Applicant must be age 16-23; enrolled or expecting to enroll full-time at a two-year or four-year or technical institution or university and single. Available to U.S. citizens. Applicant or parent must meet one or more of the following requirements: Marine Corps or Navy experience; retired from active duty; disabled or killed as a result of military service; prisoner of war; or missing in action.

Application Requirements: Application, financial need analysis, photo, transcript, birth certificate/adoption order (if applicable). *Deadline:* April 15.

Contact: James G. Kyser III, Secretary
Third Marine Division Association Inc.
PO Box 254
Chalfont, PA 18914-0254
Phone: 703-670-8227
E-mail: supertop@aol.com

UNITED NEGRO COLLEGE FUND http://www.uncf.org

YOUTH EMPOWERMENT SCHOLARSHIP
• *See page 629*

WISCONSIN DEPARTMENT OF VETERANS AFFAIRS http://www.dva.state.wi.us

VETERANS EDUCATION (VETED) REIMBURSEMENT GRANT
• *See page 633*

MILITARY SERVICE: NAVY

ANCHOR SCHOLARSHIP FOUNDATION http://www.anchorscholarship.com

ANCHOR SCHOLARSHIP FOUNDATION PROGRAM

Applicant must be dependent child or spouse of US Navy service member (active or retired), who has served at least six years after 1975, under the administrative control of Commander, Naval Surface Force, U.S. Atlantic or Pacific Fleets. To obtain application, applicant must submit military sponsor's full name and rank/rate, list of duty stations, home-ports, ship hull numbers and dates on board. Selection is based upon academics, extracurricular activities, character and financial report.

Award: Scholarship for use in freshman, sophomore, junior, or senior years; renewable. *Number:* 25–40. *Amount:* $1000–$3000.

Eligibility Requirements: Applicant must be enrolled or expecting to enroll full-time at a four-year institution or university. Available to U.S. citizens. Applicant or parent must meet one or more of the following requirements: Navy experience; retired from active duty; disabled or killed as a result of military service; prisoner of war; or missing in action.

Application Requirements: Application, essay, financial need analysis, references, self-addressed stamped envelope, test scores, transcript. *Deadline:* March 15.

Contact: Marilyn Warner, Secretary/Treasurer
Anchor Scholarship Foundation
PO Box 9535
Norfolk, VA 23505-0535
Phone: 757-374-3769
E-mail: admin@anchorscholarship.com

DEPARTMENT OF VETERANS AFFAIRS (VA) http://www.gibill.va.gov

MONTGOMERY GI BILL (SELECTED RESERVE)
• *See page 632*

DOLPHIN SCHOLARSHIP FOUNDATION http://www.dolphinscholarship.org

DOLPHIN SCHOLARSHIPS

Renewable award for undergraduate students. Applicant's parent/stepparent must meet one of the following requirements: be current/former member of the U.S. Navy who qualified in submarines and served in the Submarine Force for at least eight years; current or former member of the Navy who served in submarine support activities for at least ten years; or Navy member who died while on active duty in the Submarine Force. Must be single, under age 24.

Award: Scholarship for use in freshman, sophomore, junior, or senior years; renewable. *Number:* 30–35. *Amount:* up to $3250.

Eligibility Requirements: Applicant must be age 24 or under; enrolled or expecting to enroll full-time at a four-year institution or university and single. Available to U.S. citizens. Applicant or parent must meet one or more of the following requirements: Navy experience; retired from active duty; disabled or killed as a result of military service; prisoner of war; or missing in action.

Application Requirements: Application, essay, financial need analysis, references, self-addressed stamped envelope, test scores, transcript. *Deadline:* March 15.

Contact: Tomi Roeske, Scholarship Administrator
Dolphin Scholarship Foundation
5040 Virginia Beach Boulevard, Suite 104A
Virginia Beach, VA 23462
Phone: 757-671-3200 Ext. 111
Fax: 757-671-3330
E-mail: scholars@dolphinscholarship.org

FLEET RESERVE ASSOCIATION http://www.fra.org

COLONEL HAZEL ELIZABETH BENN U.S.M.C. SCHOLARSHIP
• *See page 663*

FLEET RESERVE ASSOCIATION SCHOLARSHIP
• *See page 532*

Fleet Reserve Association (continued)

OLIVER AND ESTHER R. HOWARD SCHOLARSHIP

• *See page 532*

SCHUYLER S. PYLE AWARD

• *See page 533*

STANLEY A. DORAN MEMORIAL SCHOLARSHIP

• *See page 641*

GAMEWARDENS OF VIETNAM ASSOCIATION INC. http://www.tf116.org

GAMEWARDENS OF VIETNAM SCHOLARSHIP

Scholarship for entering freshman who is a descendant of a U.S. Navy man or woman who worked with TF-116 in Vietnam. One-time award, but applicant may reapply.

Award: Scholarship for use in freshman year; not renewable. *Number:* 1–3. *Amount:* $500.

Eligibility Requirements: Applicant must be high school student; age 16-21 and planning to enroll or expecting to enroll full-time at a two-year or four-year or technical institution or university. Applicant must have 2.5 GPA or higher. Available to U.S. and non-U.S. citizens. Applicant or parent must meet one or more of the following requirements: Navy experience; retired from active duty; disabled or killed as a result of military service; prisoner of war; or missing in action.

Application Requirements: Application, resume, references, test scores, transcript. *Deadline:* April 1.

Contact: David Ajax, Scholarship Coordinator
Gamewardens of Vietnam Association Inc.
6630 Perry Court
Arvada, CO 80003
Phone: 303-426-6385
Fax: 303-426-6186
E-mail: dpajax@comcast.net

INDIANA DEPARTMENT OF VETERANS AFFAIRS http://www.in.gov/dva

RESIDENT TUITION FOR ACTIVE DUTY MILITARY PERSONNEL

• *See page 632*

LADIES AUXILIARY OF THE FLEET RESERVE ASSOCIATION http://www.fra.org

ALLIE MAE ODEN MEMORIAL SCHOLARSHIP

• *See page 540*

LADIES AUXILIARY OF THE FLEET RESERVE ASSOCIATION-NATIONAL PRESIDENT'S SCHOLARSHIP

• *See page 540*

LADIES AUXILIARY OF THE FLEET RESERVE ASSOCIATION SCHOLARSHIP

• *See page 540*

SAM ROSE MEMORIAL SCHOLARSHIP

• *See page 540*

NAVAL RESERVE ASSOCIATION http://www.navy-reserve.org

NAVAL RESERVE ASSOCIATION SCHOLARSHIP PROGRAM

Award is given to children of active members of the association. Must be U.S. citizens and under the age of 24. Must be enrolled in or accepted for full-time enrollment at an accredited college, university or a fully-accredited technical school.

Award: Scholarship for use in freshman, sophomore, junior, or senior years; not renewable. *Number:* varies. *Amount:* $1000–$5000.

Eligibility Requirements: Applicant must be age 24 or under and enrolled or expecting to enroll full-time at a two-year or four-year or technical institution or university. Available to U.S. citizens. Applicant or parent must meet one or more of the following requirements: Navy experience; retired from active duty; disabled or killed as a result of military service; prisoner of war; or missing in action.

Application Requirements: Application, autobiography, essay, financial need analysis, references, test scores, transcript. *Deadline:* May 1.

Contact: Mr. Bob Lyman, Chief Financial Officer
Naval Reserve Association
1619 King Street
Alexandria, VA 22314
Phone: 703-548-5800
Fax: 703-683-3647
E-mail: cfo@navy-reserve.org

NAVAL SPECIAL WARFARE FOUNDATION http://www.nswfoundation.org

AGRON SEAL SCHOLARSHIP

Scholarship for academic study at any accredited college or university for an associate or bachelors degree. The applicant can be either a current high school student or an existing college student. The recipient must maintain a GPA of 3.2 or higher in their college courses to continue to receive the grant. Only active duty SEALs, their current spouse, and immediate children are eligible.

Award: Scholarship for use in freshman, sophomore, junior, or senior years; renewable. *Number:* varies. *Amount:* up to $1000.

Eligibility Requirements: Applicant must be enrolled or expecting to enroll full- or part-time at a four-year institution or university. Available to U.S. citizens. Applicant or parent must meet one or more of the following requirements: Navy experience; retired from active duty; disabled or killed as a result of military service; prisoner of war; or missing in action.

Application Requirements: Application, essay, photo, test scores, transcript, proof of active duty or parent/spouse's active duty. *Deadline:* March 19.

Contact: Robert Rieve, President and Chief Executive Officer
Naval Special Warfare Foundation
PO Box 5965
Virginia Beach, VA 23471
Phone: 757-363-7490
Fax: 757-363-7491
E-mail: info@nswfoundation.org

HAD RICHARDS UDT-SEAL MEMORIAL SCHOLARSHIP

One-time award for dependent children of UDT-SEAL association members. Freshmen given priority. Applicant may not be older than 22. Must be U.S. citizen.

Award: Scholarship for use in freshman, sophomore, junior, or senior years; not renewable. *Number:* varies. *Amount:* varies.

Eligibility Requirements: Applicant must be age 22 or under and enrolled or expecting to enroll full-time at a four-year institution or university. Available to U.S. citizens. Applicant or parent must meet one or more of the following requirements: Navy experience; retired from active duty; disabled or killed as a result of military service; prisoner of war; or missing in action.

Application Requirements: Application, essay, photo, test scores, transcript, proof of active duty or parent/spouse's active duty. *Deadline:* March 19.

Contact: Robert Rieve, Executive Director
Naval Special Warfare Foundation
PO Box 5965
Virginia Beach, VA 23471
Phone: 757-363-7490
Fax: 757-363-7491
E-mail: info@nswfoundation.org

NAVAL SPECIAL WARFARE SCHOLARSHIP

Awards given to active duty SEAL's, SWCC's, and other active duty military serving in a Naval Special Warfare command or their spouses and dependents.

Award: Scholarship for use in freshman, sophomore, junior, or senior years; not renewable. *Number:* varies. *Amount:* varies.

Eligibility Requirements: Applicant must be enrolled or expecting to enroll full- or part-time at a four-year institution or university. Available to U.S. citizens. Applicant or parent must meet one or more of the following requirements: Navy experience; retired from active duty; disabled or killed as a result of military service; prisoner of war; or missing in action.

Application Requirements: Application, financial need analysis, transcript, proof of active duty or parent/spouses active duty. *Deadline:* March 19.

Contact: Robert Rieve, Executive Director
Naval Special Warfare Foundation
PO Box 5965
Virginia Beach, VA 23471
Phone: 757-363-7490
Fax: 757-363-7491
E-mail: info@nswfoundation.org

UDT-SEAL SCHOLARSHIP

Award for dependent children of UDT-SEAL association members. Freshmen given priority. Applicant may not be older than 22. Must be U.S. citizen.

Award: Scholarship for use in freshman, sophomore, junior, or senior years; not renewable. *Number:* varies. *Amount:* varies.

Eligibility Requirements: Applicant must be age 22 or under and enrolled or expecting to enroll full-time at a four-year institution or university. Available to U.S. citizens. Applicant or parent must meet one or more of the following requirements: Navy experience; retired from active duty; disabled or killed as a result of military service; prisoner of war; or missing in action.

Application Requirements: Application, essay, photo, test scores, transcript, proof of active duty or parent/spouse's active duty. *Deadline:* March 19.

Contact: Robert Rieve, Executive Director
Naval Special Warfare Foundation
PO Box 5965
Virginia Beach, VA 23471
Phone: 757-363-7490
Fax: 757-363-7491
E-mail: info@nswfoundation.org

NAVY-MARINE CORPS RELIEF SOCIETY http://www.nmcrs.org/education

ADMIRAL MIKE BOORDA SCHOLARSHIP PROGRAM
• *See page 664*

NAVY-MARINE CORPS RELIEF SOCIETY-CHILDREN OF DECEASED SERVICE MEMBER WHO DIED AFTER RETIREMENT
• *See page 664*

NAVY-MARINE CORPS RELIEF SOCIETY-SURVIVING CHILDREN OF DECEASED SERVICE MEMBER SCHOLARSHIP PROGRAM
• *See page 664*

USS TENNESSEE SCHOLARSHIP FUND
• *See page 664*

SEABEE MEMORIAL SCHOLARSHIP ASSOCIATION INC. http://www.seabee.org

SEABEE MEMORIAL ASSOCIATION SCHOLARSHIP

Award available to children or grandchildren of current or former members of the Naval Construction Force (Seabees) or Naval Civil Engineer Corps. Not available for graduate study or to great-grandchildren of Seabees.

Award: Scholarship for use in freshman, sophomore, junior, or senior years; renewable. *Number:* up to 94. *Amount:* up to $1500.

Eligibility Requirements: Applicant must be enrolled or expecting to enroll full-time at a four-year institution or university. Available to U.S. citizens. Applicant or parent must meet one or more of the following requirements: Navy experience; retired from active duty; disabled or killed as a result of military service; prisoner of war; or missing in action.

Application Requirements: Application, essay, financial need analysis, test scores, transcript. *Deadline:* April 15.

Contact: Sheryl Chiogioji, Administrative Assistant
Seabee Memorial Scholarship Association Inc.
PO Box 6574
Silver Spring, MD 20916
Phone: 301-570-2850
Fax: 301-570-2873
E-mail: smsa@erols.com

TAILHOOK EDUCATIONAL FOUNDATION http://www.tailhook.org

TAILHOOK EDUCATIONAL FOUNDATION SCHOLARSHIP
• *See page 642*

THIRD MARINE DIVISION ASSOCIATION INC. http://www.caltrap.com

THIRD MARINE DIVISION ASSOCIATION MEMORIAL SCHOLARSHIP FUND
• *See page 665*

UNITED DAUGHTERS OF THE CONFEDERACY http://www.hqudc.org

ADMIRAL RAPHAEL SEMMES SCHOLARSHIP
• *See page 563*

BARBARA JACKSON SICHEL MEMORIAL SCHOLARSHIP
• *See page 564*

CHARLOTTE M. F. BENTLEY/NEW YORK CHAPTER 103 SCHOLARSHIP
• *See page 564*

CODY BACHMAN SCHOLARSHIP
• *See page 564*

CORA BELL WESLEY MEMORIAL SCHOLARSHIP
• *See page 564*

CORNELIA BRANCH STONE SCHOLARSHIP
• *See page 564*

DAVID STEPHEN WYLIE SCHOLARSHIP
• *See page 565*

DOROTHY WILLIAMS SCHOLARSHIP
• *See page 565*

ELIZABETH AND WALLACE KINGSBURY SCHOLARSHIP
• *See page 565*

GERTRUDE BOTTS-SAUCIER SCHOLARSHIP
• *See page 565*

HECTOR W. CHURCH SCHOLARSHIP
• *See page 565*

HENRY CLAY DARSEY SCHOLARSHIP
• *See page 566*

JANET B. SEIPPEL SCHOLARSHIP
• *See page 566*

LOLA B. CURRY SCHOLARSHIP
• *See page 566*

MAJOR MADISON BELL SCHOLARSHIP
• *See page 566*

MARY B. POPPENHEIM MEMORIAL SCHOLARSHIP
• *See page 566*

MATTHEW FONTAINE MAURY SCHOLARSHIP
• *See page 567*

MRS. ELLA M. FRANKLIN SCHOLARSHIP
• *See page 567*

MRS. L. H. RAINES MEMORIAL SCHOLARSHIP
• *See page 567*

S.A. CUNNINGHAM SCHOLARSHIP
• *See page 567*

STONEWALL JACKSON SCHOLARSHIP
• *See page 567*

WINNIE DAVIS-CHILDREN OF THE CONFEDERACY SCHOLARSHIP
• *See page 567*

UNITED STATES SUBMARINE VETERANS INC. http://www.ussvcf.org

UNITED STATES SUBMARINE VETERANS INC. NATIONAL SCHOLARSHIP PROGRAM

• *See page 569*

WINGS OVER AMERICA SCHOLARSHIP FOUNDATION http://www.wingsoveramerica.us

WINGS OVER AMERICA SCHOLARSHIP

Applicant must be graduates of an accredited high school or the equivalent home school or institution and must plan to attend an accredited academic institution.

Award: Scholarship for use in freshman year; not renewable. *Number:* varies. *Amount:* $1000.

Eligibility Requirements: Applicant must be high school student; age 23 and over and planning to enroll or expecting to enroll full- or part-time at a two-year or four-year institution or university. Available to U.S. citizens. Applicant or parent must meet one or more of the following requirements: Navy experience; retired from active duty; disabled or killed as a result of military service; prisoner of war; or missing in action.

Application Requirements: Application, essay. *Deadline:* April 1.

Contact: Susan Hunter, Scholarship Committee
Wings Over America Scholarship Foundation
5040 Virginia Beach Boulevard, Suite 104A
Virginia Beach, VA 23462
Phone: 757-671-3200
Fax: 757-671-3330
E-mail: info@wingsoveramerica.us

WISCONSIN DEPARTMENT OF VETERANS AFFAIRS http://www.dva.state.wi.us

VETERANS EDUCATION (VETED) REIMBURSEMENT GRANT

• *See page 633*

NATIONAL OR ETHNIC BACKGROUND

ACTORS THEATRE OF LOUISVILLE http://www.actorstheatre.org

NATIONAL TEN-MINUTE PLAY CONTEST

Writers submit short plays (10 pages or less) that have not received an equity production, which are considered for the annual Apprentice Showcase (to be eligible, characters in the play must be appropriate for actors aged 20 to 30), the Humana Festival of new American plays, and the $1000 Heideman Award. Must be U.S. citizen.

Award: Prize for use in freshman, sophomore, junior, senior, graduate, or postgraduate years; not renewable. *Number:* 1. *Amount:* $1000.

Eligibility Requirements: Applicant must be U.S. Colonial citizen; enrolled or expecting to enroll full- or part-time at a two-year or four-year or technical institution or university and must have an interest in theater or writing. Available to U.S. citizens.

Application Requirements: Application, applicant must enter a contest, 10-page play. *Deadline:* November 1.

Contact: Ms. Adrien-Alice Hansel, New Play Development Director
Actors Theatre of Louisville
316 West Main Street
Louisville, KY 40202-4218
Phone: 502-584-1265 Ext. 3031
Fax: 502-561-3300
E-mail: ahansel@actorstheatre.org

ADMINISTRATIVE MANAGEMENT SERVICES (AMS) http://cdnawards.com

CHRYSLER CANADA INC. SCHOLARSHIP PROGRAM

• *See page 571*

CHRYSLER FINANCIAL SERVICES CANADA INC. SCHOLARSHIP PROGRAM

• *See page 571*

SYNCRUDE HIGHER EDUCATION AWARDS PROGRAM

• *See page 571*

ALABAMA INDIAN AFFAIRS COMMISSION http://www.aiac.state.al.us

AIAC SCHOLARSHIP

Scholarship for state or federally recognized Indian tribe. Must have a tribal roll card. Must be a resident of the state of Alabama. Must attend a school in the state of Alabama, unless program is not offered in an Alabama school.

Award: Scholarship for use in freshman, sophomore, junior, senior, or graduate years; not renewable. *Number:* varies. *Amount:* $500.

Eligibility Requirements: Applicant must be American Indian/Alaska Native; enrolled or expecting to enroll full-time at a four-year institution or university; resident of Alabama and studying in Alabama. Available to U.S. citizens.

Application Requirements: Application, tribal certification, letter of acceptance from school of choice. *Deadline:* May 1.

Contact: Eloise Josey, Executive Director
Alabama Indian Affairs Commission
771 South Lawrence Street, Suite 106
Montgomery, AL 36104
Phone: 334-242-2831
Fax: 334-240-3408
E-mail: aiac@mindspring.com

ALBERTA HERITAGE SCHOLARSHIP FUND/ ALBERTA SCHOLARSHIP PROGRAMS http://www.alis.gov.ab.ca

ADULT HIGH SCHOOL EQUIVALENCY SCHOLARSHIPS

Awards to recognize and reward the academic achievement of mature students in the attainment of high school equivalency and provide an incentive for students to continue their education at the postsecondary level. Applicants must be residents of Alberta, have been out of high school for a minimum of three years prior to commencing a high school equivalency program, and be enrolled full-time in a high school equivalency program.

Award: Scholarship for use in freshman year; not renewable. *Number:* up to 200. *Amount:* $500.

Eligibility Requirements: Applicant must be Canadian citizen; enrolled or expecting to enroll full-time at a two-year or four-year or technical institution or university; resident of Alberta and studying in Alberta. Applicant must have 3.0 GPA or higher.

Application Requirements: Application, nomination. *Deadline:* September 1.

Contact: Scholarship Committee
Alberta Heritage Scholarship Fund/Alberta Scholarship Programs
9940 106th Street, Fourth Floor, PO Box 28000, Station Main
Edmonton, AB T5J 4R4
Canada
Phone: 780-427-8640
Fax: 780-422-4516
E-mail: scholarships@gov.ab.ca

ALBERTA BLUE CROSS 50TH ANNIVERSARY SCHOLARSHIPS FOR ABORIGINAL STUDENTS

Award for three outstanding aboriginal students, to encourage further studies at the postsecondary level. Must be registered Indian, Inuit or Metis, be residents of Alberta and entering their first year of postsecondary study at an accredited Alberta postsecondary institution. Selected on the basis of academic results of the top five grade 12 courses of a minimum 5 credit value.

Award: Scholarship for use in freshman year; not renewable. *Number:* 3.

Eligibility Requirements: Applicant must be American Indian/Alaska Native; high school student; planning to enroll or expecting to enroll full-time at a two-year or four-year or technical institution or university; resident of Alberta and studying in Alberta. Available to Canadian citizens.

Application Requirements: Application. *Deadline:* June 1.

Contact: Scholarship Committee
Alberta Heritage Scholarship Fund/Alberta Scholarship Programs
9940 106th Street, Fourth Floor, Sterling Place
PO Box 28000, Station Main
Edmonton, AB T5J 4R4
Canada
Phone: 780-427-8640
Fax: 780-427-1288
E-mail: scholarships@gov.ab.ca

ALBERTA HERITAGE SCHOLARSHIP FUND ALBERTA PRESS COUNCIL SCHOLARSHIP

Award of CAN$500 to CAN$1500 to assist residents of Alberta currently attending high school and planning to enroll full-time in a post-secondary program. Selection based on a 1,000-word essay on a pre-determined topic. Essays are judged on creativity, style and content. See Web site for current topic.

Award: Scholarship for use in freshman year; not renewable. *Number:* 2.

Eligibility Requirements: Applicant must be Canadian citizen; high school student; planning to enroll or expecting to enroll full-time at a two-year or four-year or technical institution or university; resident of Alberta and must have an interest in writing.

Application Requirements: Application, applicant must enter a contest, essay. *Deadline:* February 28.

Contact: Scholarship Committee
Alberta Heritage Scholarship Fund/Alberta Scholarship Programs
9940 106th Street, Fourth Floor, Sterling Place
PO Box 28000, Station Main
Edmonton, AB T5J 4R4
Canada
Phone: 780-427-8640
Fax: 780-427-1288
E-mail: scholarships@gov.ab.ca

ALBERTA HERITAGE SCHOLARSHIP FUND CANA SCHOLARSHIPS

• *See page 572*

ALBERTA HERITAGE SCHOLARSHIP FUND HAL HARRISON MEMORIAL SCHOLARSHIP

• *See page 587*

ALEXANDER RUTHERFORD SCHOLARSHIPS FOR HIGH SCHOOL ACHIEVEMENT

Award of up to CAN$2500 available to high school students who are residents of Alberta and plan to enroll or are enrolled in a full-time postsecondary program of at least one semester. Awarded on the basis of achieving an 80 percent average on five designated subjects in grades 10, 11 and 12.

Award: Scholarship for use in freshman year; not renewable. *Number:* 10,000.

Eligibility Requirements: Applicant must be Canadian citizen; high school student; planning to enroll or expecting to enroll full-time at a two-year or four-year or technical institution or university and resident of Alberta.

Application Requirements: Application, transcript. *Deadline:* varies.

Contact: Scholarship Committee
Alberta Heritage Scholarship Fund/Alberta Scholarship Programs
9940 106th Street, Fourth Floor, Sterling Place
PO Box 28000, Station Main
Edmonton, AB T5J 4R4
Canada
Phone: 780-427-8640
Fax: 780-427-1288
E-mail: scholarships@gov.ab.ca

CHARLES S. NOBLE JUNIOR "A" HOCKEY SCHOLARSHIPS

Award to reward the athletic and academic excellence of junior "A" hockey players and to provide an incentive and means for these players to continue their postsecondary education. Must be Alberta residents and enrolled full-time at a postsecondary institution in Alberta. Must have maintained a minimum GPA of 2.0. Interested applicants should contact their team coach or manager.

Award: Scholarship for use in freshman, sophomore, junior, or senior years; not renewable. *Number:* 10. *Amount:* $2000.

Eligibility Requirements: Applicant must be Canadian citizen; enrolled or expecting to enroll full-time at a two-year or four-year or technical institution or university; resident of Alberta; studying in Alberta and must have an interest in athletics/sports.

Application Requirements: Application, essay, transcript. *Deadline:* December 1.

Contact: Scholarship Committee
Alberta Heritage Scholarship Fund/Alberta Scholarship Programs
9940 106th Street, Fourth Floor, Sterling Place
PO Box 28000, Station Main
Edmonton, AB T5J 4R4
Canada
Phone: 780-427-8640
Fax: 780-427-1288
E-mail: scholarships@gov.ab.ca

CHARLES S. NOBLE JUNIOR FOOTBALL SCHOLARSHIPS

Scholarship awarded to reward the athletic and academic excellence of junior football players at universities, colleges, and technical institutes in Alberta. Must be Alberta residents and enrolled full-time in an undergraduate, professional, or graduate program at a university, college, or technical institute in Alberta. Must be a playing member on an Alberta junior football team. Must have maintained a minimum GPA of 2.0 in their previous semester. Interested applicants should contact their team coach or manager.

Award: Scholarship for use in freshman, sophomore, junior, senior, or graduate years; not renewable. *Number:* 30. *Amount:* up to $1000.

Eligibility Requirements: Applicant must be Canadian citizen; enrolled or expecting to enroll full-time at a two-year or four-year or technical institution or university; resident of Alberta; studying in Alberta and must have an interest in athletics/sports.

Application Requirements: Application, test scores, transcript. *Deadline:* October 1.

Contact: Scholarship Committee
Alberta Heritage Scholarship Fund/Alberta Scholarship Programs
9940 106th Street, Fourth Floor, Sterling Place
PO Box 28000, Station Main
Edmonton, AB T5J 4R4
Canada
Phone: 780-427-8640
Fax: 780-427-1288
E-mail: scholarships@gov.ab.ca

DR. ERNEST AND MINNIE MEHL SCHOLARSHIP

Award to encourage students to pursue a postsecondary education, and to recognize and reward exceptional academic achievement at the senior high school level. Applicants must be Canadian citizens or landed immigrants who have completed their grade twelve in Alberta at a school that follows the Alberta education curriculum. Applicants must be continuing their studies at a degree granting postsecondary institution in Canada. University transfer programs are acceptable.

Award: Scholarship for use in freshman, sophomore, junior, or senior years; not renewable. *Number:* 1. *Amount:* $3500.

Eligibility Requirements: Applicant must be Canadian citizen; high school student; planning to enroll or expecting to enroll full-time at a two-year or four-year or technical institution or university and resident of Alberta.

Application Requirements: Application, financial need analysis, transcript. *Deadline:* June 1.

Alberta Heritage Scholarship Fund/Alberta Scholarship Programs (continued)

Contact: Scholarship Committee
Alberta Heritage Scholarship Fund/Alberta Scholarship Programs
9940 106th Street, Fourth Floor, Sterling Place
PO Box 28000, Station Main
Edmonton, AB T5J 4R4
Canada
Phone: 780-427-8640
Fax: 780-427-1288
E-mail: scholarships@gov.ab.ca

GRANT MACEWAN UNITED WORLD COLLEGE SCHOLARSHIPS

Award to reward Alberta's best grade eleven students with a chance to complete their high school at one of the twelve United World Colleges located throughout the world. Applicants must be Alberta residents and be between the ages of 16 and 17 and a half. Applicants are normally in the process of completing their grade eleven. Scholarship is based on a student's academic record, breadth of study, personal accomplishments, community involvement, and interest in the goals of the United World Colleges.

Award: Scholarship for use in freshman year; renewable. *Number:* 8. *Amount:* varies.

Eligibility Requirements: Applicant must be Canadian citizen; high school student; age 16-17; planning to enroll or expecting to enroll full-time at a four-year institution or university and resident of Alberta.

Application Requirements: Application, essay, interview, references, transcript. *Deadline:* February 15.

Contact: Scholarship Committee
Alberta Heritage Scholarship Fund/Alberta Scholarship Programs
9940 106th Street, Fourth Floor, Sterling Place
PO Box 28000, Station Main
Edmonton, AB T5J 4R4
Canada
Phone: 780-427-8640
Fax: 780-427-1288
E-mail: scholarships@gov.ab.ca

INTERNATIONAL EDUCATION AWARDS-UKRAINE

Award to recognize the accomplishments of intern, co-op, practicum, apprenticeship, and research students. Must be a postsecondary student or an apprenticeship student taking a practicum, internship, co-op, apprenticeship program, or a student conducting research (one-term). Recipient will be selected based on demonstrated past accomplishments and potential for improving relations between Ukraine and Alberta.

Award: Scholarship for use in freshman, sophomore, junior, or senior years; not renewable. *Number:* 5. *Amount:* $5000.

Eligibility Requirements: Applicant must be Canadian or Ukrainian citizen; enrolled or expecting to enroll full-time at a two-year or four-year or technical institution or university and studying in Alberta. Available to Canadian and non-U.S. citizens.

Application Requirements: Application. *Deadline:* February 1.

Contact: Scholarship Committee
Alberta Heritage Scholarship Fund/Alberta Scholarship Programs
9940 106th Street, Fourth Floor, Sterling Place
PO Box 28000, Station Main
Edmonton, AB T5J 4R4
Canada
Phone: 780-427-8640
Fax: 780-427-1288
E-mail: scholarships@gov.ab.ca

JIMMIE CONDON ATHLETIC SCHOLARSHIPS

Award of CAN$1800 available to Alberta residents enrolled full-time in an undergraduate, professional, or graduate program at a university, college, or technical institute in Alberta. Must be a member of a designated sports team or a Provincial Disabled Athletic Team recognized by the Alberta Athlete Development Program, and must be nominated by coach.

Award: Scholarship for use in freshman, sophomore, junior, senior, or graduate years; not renewable. *Number:* 2000.

Eligibility Requirements: Applicant must be Canadian citizen; enrolled or expecting to enroll full-time at a two-year or four-year or technical institution or university; resident of Alberta; studying in Alberta and must have an interest in athletics/sports.

Application Requirements: Application. *Deadline:* November 1.

Contact: Scholarship Committee
Alberta Heritage Scholarship Fund/Alberta Scholarship Programs
9940 106th Street, Fourth Floor, Sterling Place
PO Box 28000, Station Main
Edmonton, AB T5J 4R4
Canada
Phone: 780-427-8640
Fax: 780-427-1288
E-mail: scholarships@gov.ab.ca

LAURENCE DECORE STUDENT LEADERSHIP AWARDS

Awards of CAN$500 for postsecondary students who have demonstrated outstanding dedication and leadership to fellow students and to their community. Must be Alberta residents who are currently enrolled in a minimum of three full courses at a designated Alberta postsecondary institution. Selected on the basis of involvement in either student government or student societies, clubs, or organizations.

Award: Scholarship for use in freshman, sophomore, junior, or senior years; not renewable. *Number:* 100.

Eligibility Requirements: Applicant must be Canadian citizen; enrolled or expecting to enroll full-time at a two-year or four-year or technical institution or university; resident of Alberta; studying in Alberta and must have an interest in leadership.

Application Requirements: Application, nomination from school. *Deadline:* March 1.

Contact: Scholarship Committee
Alberta Heritage Scholarship Fund/Alberta Scholarship Programs
9940 106th Street, Fourth Floor, Sterling Place
PO Box 28000, Station Main
Edmonton, AB T5J 4R4
Canada
Phone: 780-427-8640
Fax: 780-427-1288
E-mail: scholarships@gov.ab.ca

LOUISE MCKINNEY POSTSECONDARY SCHOLARSHIPS

Student awards of up to CAN$2500 to residents of Alberta and plan to enroll at a university, college, or technical institute in the second or subsequent year of full-time study. Alberta students studying outside the province because their program of study is not offered in Alberta will be considered for a scholarship if their class standing is in the top two percent of their program.

Award: Scholarship for use in sophomore, junior, senior, or graduate years; not renewable. *Number:* 950.

Eligibility Requirements: Applicant must be Canadian citizen; enrolled or expecting to enroll full-time at a two-year or four-year institution or university and resident of Alberta.

Application Requirements: Application, test scores, transcript. *Deadline:* varies.

Contact: Scholarship Committee
Alberta Heritage Scholarship Fund/Alberta Scholarship Programs
9940 106th Street, Fourth Floor, Sterling Place
PO Box 28000, Station Main
Edmonton, AB T5J 4R4
Canada
Phone: 780-427-8640
Fax: 780-427-1288
E-mail: scholarships@gov.ab.ca

NORTHERN ALBERTA DEVELOPMENT COUNCIL BURSARY

Awards to increase the number of trained professionals in Northern Alberta and to encourage students from Northern Alberta to obtain a postsecondary education. Must be residents of Alberta, and planning to enroll in a full-time postsecondary program. Applicants must also be within two years of completion of their postsecondary program. Students must live and work for one year in Northern Alberta.

Award: Scholarship for use in freshman, sophomore, junior, senior, or graduate years; not renewable. *Number:* 125. *Amount:* $1750.

Eligibility Requirements: Applicant must be Canadian citizen; enrolled or expecting to enroll full-time at a two-year or four-year or technical institution or university; resident of Alberta and studying in Alberta.

Application Requirements: Application, essay, financial need analysis, transcript. *Deadline:* February 1.

Contact: Scholarship Committee
Alberta Heritage Scholarship Fund/Alberta Scholarship Programs
9940 106th Street, Fourth Floor, Sterling Place
PO Box 28000, Station Main
Edmonton, AB T5J 4R4
Canada
Phone: 780-427-8640
Fax: 780-427-1288
E-mail: scholarships@gov.ab.ca

PERSONS CASE SCHOLARSHIPS

Awards to assist students whose studies will ultimately contribute to the advancement of women, or who are studying in fields where members of their gender are traditionally few in number. Applicants must be residents of Alberta and enrolled full-time at a postsecondary institution in Alberta. Students studying out-of-province may be considered for this award if their program of study is not available in Alberta.

Award: Scholarship for use in freshman, sophomore, junior, or senior years; not renewable. *Number:* 5–10. *Amount:* up to $5000.

Eligibility Requirements: Applicant must be Canadian citizen; enrolled or expecting to enroll full-time at a two-year or four-year or technical institution or university; female and resident of Alberta. Applicant must have 3.0 GPA or higher.

Application Requirements: Application, essay, financial need analysis, resume, transcript. *Deadline:* September 30.

Contact: Scholarship Committee
Alberta Heritage Scholarship Fund/Alberta Scholarship Programs
9940 106th Street, Fourth Floor, Sterling Place
PO Box 28000, Station Main
Edmonton, AB T5J 4R4
Canada
Phone: 780-427-8640
Fax: 780-427-1288
E-mail: scholarships@gov.ab.ca

QUEEN ELIZABETH II GOLDEN JUBILEE CITIZENSHIP MEDAL

Award of CAN$5000, a medal, and letter of commendation from the Lieutenant Governor to recognize the eight most outstanding students among those receiving a Premiers Citizenship award in recognition of the Queen's Golden Jubilee. Available to high school students. Must be nominated.

Award: Prize for use in freshman year; not renewable. *Number:* 8.

Eligibility Requirements: Applicant must be Canadian citizen; high school student; planning to enroll or expecting to enroll full-time at a four-year institution or university and resident of Alberta.

Application Requirements: Proof of winning the Premiers Citizenship Award. *Deadline:* June 15.

Contact: Scholarship Committee
Alberta Heritage Scholarship Fund/Alberta Scholarship Programs
9940 106th Street, Fourth Floor, Sterling Place
PO Box 28000, Station Main
Edmonton, AB T5J 4R4
Canada
Phone: 780-427-8640
Fax: 780-427-1288
E-mail: scholarships@gov.ab.ca

RUTHERFORD SCHOLARS

Recipients are selected on the basis of results obtained on Diploma Examinations in English 30, or Franþais 30, Social Studies 30 and three other subjects. Averages normally are in the 98.0 to 98.8 per cent range. Only the first writing of the diploma exam will be considered. No application is required. Recipients are selected from all Alexander Rutherford Scholarship applications received before August 1. Amount of award is CAN$1500.

Award: Scholarship for use in freshman year; not renewable. *Number:* 10.

Eligibility Requirements: Applicant must be Canadian citizen; high school student; planning to enroll or expecting to enroll full-time at a four-year institution or university and resident of Alberta.

Application Requirements: Test scores, transcript. *Deadline:* August 1.

Contact: Scholarship Committee
Alberta Heritage Scholarship Fund/Alberta Scholarship Programs
9940 106th Street, Fourth Floor, Sterling Place
PO Box 28000, Station Main
Edmonton, AB T5J 4R4
Canada
Phone: 780-427-8640
Fax: 780-427-1288
E-mail: scholarships@gov.ab.ca

ALBUQUERQUE COMMUNITY FOUNDATION http://www.albuquerquefoundation.org

NOTAH BEGAY III SCHOLARSHIP PROGRAM FOR NATIVE AMERICAN SCHOLAR ATHLETES

The program requires the applicant to attend an accredited, not-for-profit educational institution in the United States. Total number of awards and the dollar value varies, must have played in varsity level sports in high school, and must maintain a 3.0 GPA. Deadline varies.

Award: Scholarship for use in freshman, sophomore, junior, or senior years; not renewable. *Number:* varies. *Amount:* varies.

Eligibility Requirements: Applicant must be American Indian/Alaska Native; enrolled or expecting to enroll full-time at a two-year or four-year institution or university; resident of New Mexico and must have an interest in athletics/sports. Applicant must have 3.0 GPA or higher. Available to U.S. citizens.

Application Requirements: Application, essay, financial need analysis, resume, references, test scores, transcript, proof of tribal enrollment or certificate of Indian blood (minimum 25 percent). *Deadline:* varies.

Contact: Nancy Johnson, Program Director
Albuquerque Community Foundation
PO Box 36960
Albuquerque, NM 87176-6960
Phone: 505-883-6240
E-mail: foundation@albuquerquefoundation.org

AMERICAN BAPTIST FINANCIAL AID PROGRAM http://www.abc-usa.org

AMERICAN BAPTIST FINANCIAL AID PROGRAM NATIVE AMERICAN GRANTS

Renewable award of $1000 to $2000 for Native Americans who are members of an American Baptist Church/USA congregation. Must be a U.S. citizen. Must be attending an accredited educational institution in the United States.

Award: Grant for use in freshman, sophomore, junior, senior, or graduate years; renewable. *Number:* 1–5. *Amount:* $1000–$2000.

Eligibility Requirements: Applicant must be Baptist; American Indian/Alaska Native and enrolled or expecting to enroll full-time at a four-year institution or university. Available to U.S. citizens.

Application Requirements: Application, financial need analysis, references. *Deadline:* May 31.

Contact: Lynne Eckman, Director of Financial Aid
American Baptist Financial Aid Program
PO Box 851
Valley Forge, PA 19482-0851
Phone: 610-768-2067
Fax: 610-768-2470
E-mail: lynne.eckman@abc-usa.org

AMERICAN INDIAN EDUCATION FOUNDATION http://www.aiefprograms.org

AMERICAN INDIAN EDUCATION FOUNDATION SCHOLARSHIP

AIEF provides tuition and living expenses for American Indian students. Scholarships are awarded based on student's history of volunteerism, their commitment to return to their community, and an ACT score of at least 14.

Award: Scholarship for use in freshman, sophomore, junior, or senior years; not renewable. *Number:* 150. *Amount:* $2000.

Eligibility Requirements: Applicant must be American Indian/Alaska Native and enrolled or expecting to enroll full-time at a two-year or four-year or technical institution or university. Available to U.S. and non-U.S. citizens.

Application Requirements: Application, essay, ACT score. *Deadline:* April 4.

Contact: Lyn Tysdal, Program Manager
American Indian Education Foundation
2401 Eglin Street, Rapid City
Rapid City, SD 57703
Phone: 866-866-8642
Fax: 605-342-4113
E-mail: ltysdal@nrc1.org

AMERICAN INDIAN GRADUATE CENTER http://www.aigcs.org

ACCENTURE AMERICAN INDIAN SCHOLARSHIP

Scholarships awarded to Alaskan Native undergraduate and graduate students. Must be U.S. citizen and have minimum 3.0 GPA.

Award: Scholarship for use in freshman, sophomore, junior, senior, or graduate years; renewable. *Number:* up to 5. *Amount:* $2000–$20,000.

Eligibility Requirements: Applicant must be American Indian/Alaska Native and enrolled or expecting to enroll full-time at a four-year institution or university. Applicant must have 3.0 GPA or higher. Available to U.S. citizens.

Application Requirements: Application, essay, financial need analysis, tribal eligibility certificate. *Deadline:* varies.

Contact: Marveline Vallo, Program Assistant
American Indian Graduate Center
4520 Montgomery Boulevard, NE, Suite 1B
Albuquerque, NM 87109
Phone: 505-881-4584 Ext. 108
Fax: 505-884-0427
E-mail: marveline@aigcs.org

GATES MILLENNIUM SCHOLARS PROGRAM

Award enables American-Indian/Alaska native students to complete an undergraduate and graduate education. Must be entering a U.S. accredited college or university as a full-time student. Minimum 3.3 GPA required. Must demonstrate leadership abilities. Must meet federal Pell Grant eligibility criteria. Visit Web site at http://www.gmsp.org.

Award: Scholarship for use in freshman, sophomore, junior, senior, or graduate years; renewable. *Number:* 150. *Amount:* $500–$20,000.

Eligibility Requirements: Applicant must be American Indian/Alaska Native; enrolled or expecting to enroll full-time at a two-year or four-year institution or university and must have an interest in leadership. Available to U.S. citizens.

Application Requirements: Application, financial need analysis, references, nomination packet. *Deadline:* January 16.

Contact: Christa Moya, GMS Representative
American Indian Graduate Center
4520 Montgomery Boulevard, NE, Suite 1B
Albuquerque, NM 87109
Phone: 866-884-7007
Fax: 505-884-8683
E-mail: christa@aigcs.org

WELLS FARGO SCHOLARSHIP FOR NATIVE AMERICAN COLLEGE STUDENTS

Scholarships of up to $2000 awarded to Alaskan Native undergraduate and graduate students. Must maintain a minimum 3.0 GPA.

Award: Scholarship for use in freshman, sophomore, junior, senior, or graduate years; renewable. *Number:* up to 10. *Amount:* up to $2000.

Eligibility Requirements: Applicant must be American Indian/Alaska Native and enrolled or expecting to enroll full-time at a four-year institution or university. Applicant must have 3.0 GPA or higher. Available to U.S. citizens.

Application Requirements: Application, essay, financial need analysis, tribal eligibility certificate. *Deadline:* varies.

Contact: Marveline Vallo, Program Assistant
American Indian Graduate Center
4520 Montgomery Boulevard, NE, Suite 1B
Albuquerque, NM 87109
Phone: 505-881-4584 Ext. 108
Fax: 505-884-0427
E-mail: marveline@aigcs.org

AMERICAN INSTITUTE FOR FOREIGN STUDY http://www.aifsabroad.com

AIFS DIVERSITY SCHOLARSHIPS

Two scholarships for 50% of the program fee and round trip airfare are awarded, one per semester. Three runner-up scholarships of $2000 each are also awarded each semester. Applicants must submit the scholarship application materials in addition to the AIFS study abroad application and the required application fee of $95. Deadlines: April 15 for fall, October 1 for spring. Refer to Web site for details: http://www.aifsabroad.com.

Award: Scholarship for use in freshman, sophomore, junior, or senior years; not renewable. *Number:* 4. *Amount:* $2000–$8000.

Eligibility Requirements: Applicant must be American Indian/Alaska Native, Asian/Pacific Islander, Black (non-Hispanic), or Hispanic; age 17 and over; enrolled or expecting to enroll full-time at a two-year or four-year institution or university and must have an interest in international exchange or leadership. Applicant must have 3.0 GPA or higher. Available to U.S. and non-U.S. citizens.

Application Requirements: Application, essay, photo, references, transcript. *Fee:* $95. *Deadline:* varies.

Contact: David Mauro, Admissions Counselor
American Institute for Foreign Study
River Plaza, Nine West Broad Street
Stamford, CT 06902-3788
Phone: 800-727-2437 Ext. 5163
Fax: 203-399-5463
E-mail: dmauro@aifs.com

AIFS-HACU SCHOLARSHIPS

Scholarships to outstanding Hispanic students to study abroad with AIFS. Available to students attending HACU member schools. Students will receive scholarships of up to 50% of the full program fee. Students must meet all standard AIFS eligibility requirements. Deadlines: April 15 for fall, October 1 for spring, March 15 for summer.

Award: Scholarship for use in freshman, sophomore, junior, or senior years; not renewable. *Number:* varies. *Amount:* $6000–$8000.

Eligibility Requirements: Applicant must be Hispanic; age 17 and over; enrolled or expecting to enroll full-time at a two-year or four-year institution or university and must have an interest in international exchange. Applicant must have 3.0 GPA or higher. Available to U.S. and non-U.S. citizens.

Application Requirements: Application, essay, photo, references, transcript. *Fee:* $95. *Deadline:* varies.

Contact: David Mauro, Admissions Counselor
American Institute for Foreign Study
River Plaza, Nine West Broad Street
Stamford, CT 06902-3788
Phone: 800-727-2437 Ext. 5163
Fax: 203-399-5463
E-mail: dmauro@aifs.com

AIFS SUMMER DIVERSITYABROAD.COM SCHOLARSHIP

Scholarships are available for students studying abroad in the summer on any program offered by a DiversityAbroad.com member organization. African-American, Asian-American, Hispanic/Latino and Native-American students are strongly encouraged to apply. Visit http://www.aifsabroad.com/scholarships.asp#diversityabroad for more information.

Award: Scholarship for use in freshman, sophomore, junior, or senior years; not renewable. *Number:* 5. *Amount:* $2000.

Eligibility Requirements: Applicant must be American Indian/Alaska Native, Asian/Pacific Islander, Black (non-Hispanic), or Hispanic; enrolled or expecting to enroll full-time at a two-year or four-year institution or university and must have an interest in international exchange. Applicant must have 2.5 GPA or higher. Available to U.S. citizens.

Application Requirements: Application, essay, photo, resume, references, transcript. *Fee:* $95. *Deadline:* April 15.

Contact: David Mauro, Admissions Counselor
American Institute for Foreign Study
River Plaza, Nine West Broad Street
Stamford, CT 06902-3788
Phone: 800-727-2437 Ext. 5163
Fax: 203-399-5463
E-mail: dmauro@aifs.com

DIVERSITY SCHOLARSHIPS

Applications will be accepted from African-American, Asian American, Native American, Hispanic American and Pacific Islanders, who are currently enrolled as undergraduates at a U.S. institution applying to an AIFS study abroad program. Applicants must demonstrate leadership ability, academic accomplishment, and meet program requirements. One full scholarship and three runners-up scholarships are awarded each semester.

Award: Scholarship for use in freshman, sophomore, junior, or senior years; not renewable. *Number:* 2. *Amount:* $5000–$7000.

Eligibility Requirements: Applicant must be American Indian/Alaska Native, Asian/Pacific Islander, Black (non-Hispanic), or Hispanic; age 17 and over; enrolled or expecting to enroll full-time at a two-year or four-year institution or university and must have an interest in leadership. Applicant must have 3.0 GPA or higher. Available to U.S. and non-U.S. citizens.

Application Requirements: Application, essay, photo, references, transcript. *Fee:* $95. *Deadline:* varies.

Contact: David Mauro, Admissions Counselor
American Institute for Foreign Study
Nine West Broad Street, River Plaza
Stamford, CT 06902-3788
Phone: 800-727-2437 Ext. 5163
Fax: 203-399-5463
E-mail: dmauro@aifs.com

AMERICAN INSTITUTE OF CERTIFIED PUBLIC ACCOUNTANTS http://www.aicpa.org

SCHOLARSHIP FOR MINORITY ACCOUNTING STUDENTS

This program provides financial awards to minority students who show significant potential to become Certified Public Accountants. Applicants must be full-time declared undergraduate accounting majors or full-time declared graduate accounting, finance or tax majors. Applicants must have a major GPA of 3.3 and have completed at least 30 semester hours (or equivalent) of coursework, including at least six semester hours in accounting.

Award: Scholarship for use in freshman, sophomore, junior, senior, graduate, or postgraduate years; renewable. *Number:* varies. *Amount:* $1500–$5000.

Eligibility Requirements: Applicant must be American Indian/Alaska Native, Asian/Pacific Islander, Black (non-Hispanic), or Hispanic and enrolled or expecting to enroll full-time at a four-year institution or university. Available to U.S. and non-U.S. citizens.

Application Requirements: Application, essay, financial need analysis, references, test scores, transcript, copy of acceptance letter. *Deadline:* June 1.

Contact: Elizabeth DeBragga, Coordinator of Diversity, Work/Life and Women's Initiatives
American Institute of Certified Public Accountants
Palladian One, 220 Leigh Farm Road
Durham, NC 27707
Phone: 919-402-4931
E-mail: MIC_Programs@aicpa.org

ARAB AMERICAN INSTITUTE FOUNDATION http://www.aaiusa.org

HELEN ABBOTT COMMUNITY SERVICE AWARDS

Maximum of two $1000 prizes for college students and one $500 grant to a high school student whose devotion to community service, selfless acts of care, and interest in improving the quality of life for others reflect the life of the Awards' namesake. Must be U.S. citizen and be of Arab descent.

Award: Prize for use in freshman, sophomore, junior, or senior years; not renewable. *Number:* up to 3. *Amount:* $500–$1000.

Eligibility Requirements: Applicant must be of Arab heritage and enrolled or expecting to enroll full- or part-time at a four-year institution or university. Available to U.S. citizens.

Application Requirements: Application, essay, resume, transcript. *Deadline:* March 14.

Contact: Sabeen Altaf, Program Manager
Arab American Institute Foundation
1600 K Street NW, Suite 601
Washington, DC 20006
Phone: 202-429-9210
Fax: 202-429-9214
E-mail: saltaf@aaiusa.org

RAYMOND JALLOW AWARDS FOR PUBLIC SERVICE

Two $500 grants are given annually to students and adults who are actively involved in, or plan to participate, in public service. Must be currently enrolled at a college or university, be a U.S. citizen under the age of 30, and be of Arab descent.

Award: Prize for use in freshman, sophomore, junior, senior, graduate, or postgraduate years; not renewable. *Number:* 2. *Amount:* $500.

Eligibility Requirements: Applicant must be of Arab heritage; age 30 or under and enrolled or expecting to enroll full- or part-time at a two-year or four-year or technical institution or university. Available to U.S. citizens.

Application Requirements: Application, essay, resume, references. *Deadline:* March 14.

Contact: Sabeen Altaf, Program Manager
Arab American Institute Foundation
1600 K Street NW, Suite 601
Washington, DC 20006
Phone: 202-429-9210
Fax: 202-429-9214
E-mail: saltaf@aaiusa.org

ARMENIAN RELIEF SOCIETY OF EASTERN USA INC.-REGIONAL OFFICE http://www.arseastus.org

ARMENIAN RELIEF SOCIETY UNDERGRADUATE SCHOLARSHIP

Applicant must be an undergraduate student of Armenian heritage attending an accredited four-year college or university in the United States. Award for full-time students only. Must be U.S. or Canadian citizen. High school students may not apply.

Award: Scholarship for use in freshman, sophomore, junior, or senior years; not renewable. *Number:* varies. *Amount:* $13,000–$15,000.

Eligibility Requirements: Applicant must be of Armenian heritage and enrolled or expecting to enroll full-time at a four-year institution or university. Available to U.S. and Canadian citizens.

Application Requirements: Application, financial need analysis, references, self-addressed stamped envelope, transcript. *Deadline:* April 1.

Contact: Scholarship Committee
Armenian Relief Society of Eastern USA Inc.-Regional Office
80 Bigelow Avenue, Suite 200
Watertown, MA 02472
Phone: 617-926-3801
Fax: 617-924-7238
E-mail: arseastus@aol.com

ARMENIAN STUDENTS ASSOCIATION OF AMERICA INC. http://www.asainc.org

ARMENIAN STUDENTS ASSOCIATION OF AMERICA INC. SCHOLARSHIPS

One-time award for students of Armenian descent. Must be an undergraduate in sophomore, junior, or senior years, or graduate student, attending an accredited U.S. institution. Award based on need, merit, and character. Application fee: $15.

Award: Scholarship for use in sophomore, junior, senior, or graduate years; not renewable. *Number:* 30. *Amount:* $1000–$3500.

Eligibility Requirements: Applicant must be of Armenian heritage and enrolled or expecting to enroll full-time at a four-year institution or university. Available to U.S. citizens.

Application Requirements: Application, essay, financial need analysis, references, transcript, proof of tuition costs and enrollment. *Fee:* $15. *Deadline:* March 15.

Contact: Nathalie Yaghoobian, Scholarship Administrator
Armenian Students Association of America Inc.
333 Atlantic Avenue
Warwick, RI 02888
Phone: 401-461-6114
Fax: 401-461-6112
E-mail: headasa.com@aol.com

ASIAN PROFESSIONAL EXTENSION INC. http://www.apex-ny.org

APEX SCHOLARSHIP

Scholarship to students based on academic excellence, personal essays, letters of recommendation, extracurricular activities/volunteer service, and financial need. Two winners will receive scholarships of $500 and $1000. Deadline varies.

Award: Scholarship for use in freshman, sophomore, junior, senior, or graduate years; not renewable. *Number:* 2. *Amount:* $500–$1000.

Eligibility Requirements: Applicant must be American Indian/Alaska Native or Asian/Pacific Islander and enrolled or expecting to enroll full- or part-time at a four-year institution or university. Available to U.S. citizens.

Application Requirements: Application, applicant must enter a contest, essay, financial need analysis, references, transcript. *Deadline:* varies.

Contact: Trang Le-Chan, Deputy Director of Programs
Asian Professional Extension Inc.
352 Seventh Avenue, Suite 201
New York, NY 10001
Phone: 212-748-1225 Ext. 101
Fax: 212-748-1250
E-mail: trang.le-chan@apex-ny.org

ASIAN REPORTER http://www.arfoundation.net

ASIAN REPORTER SCHOLARSHIP

Scholarship available to graduating high school student or currently enrolled college student of Asian descent. Must be a resident of Washington or Oregon and attend school full-time in either state. Minimum 3.5 GPA required. Must demonstrate financial need, and involvement in community or school-related activities.

Award: Scholarship for use in freshman, sophomore, junior, or senior years; renewable. *Number:* 4. *Amount:* $500–$2000.

Eligibility Requirements: Applicant must be Asian/Pacific Islander; enrolled or expecting to enroll full-time at a four-year institution or university; resident of Oregon or Washington and studying in Oregon or Washington. Applicant must have 3.5 GPA or higher. Available to U.S. citizens.

Application Requirements: Application, driver's license, essay, financial need analysis, photo, references, transcript. *Deadline:* February 28.

Contact: Jason Lim, Program Director
Asian Reporter
922 North Killingsworth Street, Suite 1A
Portland, OR 97217
Phone: 503-283-0595
Fax: 503-283-4445
E-mail: arfoundation@asianreporter.com

ASSOCIATION ON AMERICAN INDIAN AFFAIRS (AAIA) http://www.indian-affairs.org

ADOLPH VAN PELT SPECIAL FUND FOR INDIAN SCHOLARSHIPS

Scholarship is open to undergraduate students pursuing a bachelors degree in any curriculum. Must be an American Indian. See www.indian-affairs.org for specific details.

Award: Scholarship for use in freshman, sophomore, junior, or senior years; not renewable. *Number:* varies. *Amount:* up to $1500.

Eligibility Requirements: Applicant must be American Indian/Alaska Native and enrolled or expecting to enroll full-time at a two-year or four-year institution or university. Available to U.S. citizens.

Application Requirements: Application, essay, financial need analysis, references, transcript. *Deadline:* July 1.

Contact: Lisa Wyzlic, Director of Scholarship Programs
Association on American Indian Affairs (AAIA)
966 Hungerford Drive, Suite 12-B
Rockville, MD 20850
Phone: 240-314-7155
Fax: 240-314-7155
E-mail: lw.aaia@verizon.net

ALLOGAN SLAGLE MEMORIAL SCHOLARSHIP

Scholarship to American Indian undergraduate students who are members of tribes that are not federally recognized. See www.indian-affairs.org for specific details.

Award: Scholarship for use in freshman, sophomore, junior, or senior years; not renewable. *Number:* varies. *Amount:* $1500.

Eligibility Requirements: Applicant must be American Indian/Alaska Native and enrolled or expecting to enroll full-time at a two-year or four-year institution or university. Available to U.S. citizens.

Application Requirements: Application, essay, financial need analysis, references, transcript. *Deadline:* July 1.

Contact: Lisa Wyzlic, Director of Scholarship Programs
Association on American Indian Affairs (AAIA)
966 Hungerford Drive, Suite 12-B
Rockville, MD 20850
Phone: 240-314-7155
Fax: 240-314-7159
E-mail: lw.aaia@verizon.net

DAVID RISLING EMERGENCY AID SCHOLARSHIP

Scholarship is for acute temporary needs for undergraduate students. Must be an American Indian. Tuition, books and computers are not considered emergencies. See our Web site at www.indian-affairs.org for details.

Award: Scholarship for use in freshman, sophomore, junior, or senior years; not renewable. *Number:* varies. *Amount:* $100–$400.

Eligibility Requirements: Applicant must be American Indian/Alaska Native and enrolled or expecting to enroll full-time at a two-year or four-year institution or university. Available to U.S. citizens.

Application Requirements: Application, essay, financial need analysis, references, transcript. *Deadline:* varies.

Contact: Lisa Wyzlic, Director of Scholarship Programs
Association on American Indian Affairs (AAIA)
966 Hungerford Drive, Suite 12-B
Rockville, MD 20850
Phone: 240-314-7155
Fax: 240-314-7159
E-mail: lw.aaia@verizon.net

DISPLACED HOMEMAKER SCHOLARSHIP

This scholarship is for men and women who would not otherwise be able to complete their educational goals due to family responsibilities. Must be an American Indian. See www.indian-affairs.org for specific details.

Award: Scholarship for use in freshman, sophomore, junior, or senior years; not renewable. *Number:* varies. *Amount:* $1500.

Eligibility Requirements: Applicant must be American Indian/Alaska Native and enrolled or expecting to enroll full-time at a two-year or four-year institution or university. Available to U.S. citizens.

Application Requirements: Application, essay, financial need analysis, references, transcript. *Deadline:* July 1.

Contact: Lisa Wyzlic, Director of Scholarship Programs
Association on American Indian Affairs (AAIA)
966 Hungerford Drive, Suite 12-B
Rockville, MD 20850
Phone: 240-314-7155
Fax: 240-314-7159
E-mail: lw.aaia@verizon.net

AUSTRALIAN FEDERATION OF UNIVERSITY WOMEN-SA http://www.flinders.edu.au

PADNENDADLU UNDERGRADUATE BURSARIES

Bursary open to indigenous Australian women undergraduates in each of the South Australian universities. Applicants must be undertaking subjects for the final year of their bachelor degree, or undertaking an honors year. Scholarship amount is $700 per institution.

Award: Scholarship for use in senior year; renewable. *Number:* varies. *Amount:* $700.

Eligibility Requirements: Applicant must be of Australian heritage; enrolled or expecting to enroll full-time at a four-year institution or university and female. Available to U.S. and non-U.S. citizens.

Application Requirements: Application, financial need analysis, resume, transcript. *Deadline:* March 1.

Contact: Rachel Spencer, Trustee
Australian Federation of University Women-SA
PO Box 634
Adelaide SA 5001
Australia
Phone: 61 08 8201 3986
E-mail: rachel.spencer@flinders.edu.au

BLACKFEET NATION HIGHER EDUCATION PROGRAM

BLACKFEET NATION HIGHER EDUCATION GRANT

Grants of up to $3000 will be awarded to students who are enrolled members of the Blackfeet Tribe and actively pursuing an undergraduate degree. Must submit a certification of Blackfeet blood.

Award: Grant for use in freshman, sophomore, junior, or senior years; renewable. *Number:* 150. *Amount:* up to $3000.

Eligibility Requirements: Applicant must be American Indian/Alaska Native and enrolled or expecting to enroll full-time at a two-year or four-year institution or university. Available to U.S. citizens.

Application Requirements: Application, essay, financial need analysis, transcript, certification of Blackfeet blood. *Deadline:* March 1.

Contact: Conrad LaFromboise, Director
Blackfeet Nation Higher Education Program
PO Box 850
Browning, MT 59417
Phone: 406-338-7539
Fax: 406-338-7530
E-mail: bhep@blackfeetnation.com

BUREAU OF INDIAN AFFAIRS OFFICE OF INDIAN EDUCATION PROGRAMS http://www.oiep.bia.edu

BUREAU OF INDIAN EDUCATION GRANT PROGRAM

Grants are provided to supplement financial assistance to eligible American Indian/Alaska Native students entering college seeking a baccalaureate degree. A student must be a member of, or at least one-quarter degree Indian blood descendent of a member of an American Indian tribe who are eligible for the special programs and services provided by the United States through the Bureau of Indian Affairs to Indians because of their status as Indians.

Award: Grant for use in freshman year; not renewable. *Number:* varies. *Amount:* varies.

Eligibility Requirements: Applicant must be American Indian/Alaska Native; high school student and planning to enroll or expecting to enroll full-time at a two-year or four-year institution or university. Available to U.S. citizens.

Application Requirements: Application, references, test scores, transcript. *Deadline:* varies.

Contact: Paulina Bell, Office Automation Assistant
Bureau of Indian Affairs Office of Indian Education Programs
1849 C Street, NW, MS 3609-MIB
Washington, DC 20240-0001
Phone: 202-208-6123
Fax: 202-208-3312

CABRILLO CIVIC CLUBS OF CALIFORNIA INC. http://www.cabrillocivicclubs.org

CABRILLO CIVIC CLUBS OF CALIFORNIA SCHOLARSHIP

Applicants must be graduating California high school seniors of Portuguese heritage and American citizenship, with an overall 3.5 GPA.

Award: Scholarship for use in freshman year; not renewable. *Number:* 75–100. *Amount:* $500.

Eligibility Requirements: Applicant must be of Portuguese heritage; high school student; planning to enroll or expecting to enroll full-time at a technical institution and resident of California. Applicant must have 3.5 GPA or higher. Available to U.S. citizens.

Application Requirements: Application, autobiography, photo, resume, references, self-addressed stamped envelope, transcript. *Deadline:* March 15.

Contact: Breck L. Austin, Scholarship Chairperson
Cabrillo Civic Clubs of California Inc.
2174 South Coast Highway
Oceanside, CA 92054
E-mail: shampoobla@sbcglobal.net

CANADA MILLENNIUM SCHOLARSHIP FOUNDATION http://www.millenniumscholarships.ca

CANADA MILLENNIUM EXCELLENCE AWARD PROGRAM

Entrance and in-course awards for postsecondary study in Canada recognizing community involvement, leadership, innovation, and academics.

Award: Scholarship for use in freshman, sophomore, junior, or senior years; renewable. *Number:* 1–2300. *Amount:* $2000–$4000.

Eligibility Requirements: Applicant must be Canadian citizen and enrolled or expecting to enroll full-time at a two-year or four-year or technical institution or university. Applicant must have 3.0 GPA or higher.

Application Requirements: Application, autobiography, financial need analysis, interview, photo, references, transcript. *Deadline:* varies.

Contact: Maria Modafferi, Information Officer
Canada Millennium Scholarship Foundation
1000 Sherbrooke Street, West, Suite 800
Montreal Quebec, QC H3A 3R2
Canada
Phone: 514-284-7230
Fax: 514-985-5987
E-mail: millennium.foundation@bm-ms.org

CAP FOUNDATION http://www.ronbrown.org

RON BROWN SCHOLAR PROGRAM

• *See page 592*

CENTRAL COUNCIL, TLINGIT AND HAIDA INDIAN TRIBES OF ALASKA http://www.hied.org

ALUMNI STUDENT ASSISTANCE PROGRAM

The program provides annual scholarship awards to all enrolled Tlingit or Haida tribal members regardless of service area, community affiliation, origination, residence, tribal compact, or signatory status.

Award: Scholarship for use in freshman, sophomore, junior, senior, graduate, or postgraduate years; not renewable. *Number:* 1–100. *Amount:* $300–$500.

Eligibility Requirements: Applicant must be American Indian/Alaska Native and enrolled or expecting to enroll full-time at a two-year or four-year institution or university. Applicant must have 2.5 GPA or higher. Available to U.S. citizens.

Central Council, Tlingit and Haida Indian Tribes of Alaska (continued)

Application Requirements: Application, essay, financial need analysis, references, transcript, tribal enrollment certification form, letter of admission. *Deadline:* September 15.

Contact: Miss. Leslie Rae Isturis, Education Specialist
Central Council, Tlingit and Haida Indian Tribes of Alaska
3239 Hospital Drive
Juneau, AK 99801
Phone: 907-463-7375
Fax: 907-463-7173
E-mail: listuris@ccthita.org

COLLEGE STUDENT ASSISTANCE PROGRAM

A federally funded program which authorizes a program of assistance, by educational grants, to Indians seeking higher education. Awards available only to enrolled T&H members. Minimum 2.0 GPA required.

Award: Scholarship for use in freshman, sophomore, junior, senior, graduate, or postgraduate years; renewable. *Number:* 1–200. *Amount:* up to $2000.

Eligibility Requirements: Applicant must be American Indian/Alaska Native and enrolled or expecting to enroll full-time at a two-year or four-year institution or university. Available to U.S. citizens.

Application Requirements: Application, test scores, transcript, letter of admission. *Deadline:* May 15.

Contact: Miss. Leslie Rae Isturis, Education Specialist
Central Council, Tlingit and Haida Indian Tribes of Alaska
3239 Hospital Drive
Juneau, AK 99801
Phone: 907-463-7375
Fax: 907-463-7173
E-mail: listuris@ccthita.org

CENTRAL SCHOLARSHIP BUREAU http://www.centralsb.org

LESSANS FAMILY SCHOLARSHIP

Scholarship available for Jewish students from Maryland who attend undergraduate colleges, universities or vocational schools full-time. Students can attend any accredited U.S. college or university. Awards are based on need and merit. The scholarship committee determines award amounts.

Award: Scholarship for use in freshman, sophomore, junior, or senior years; renewable. *Number:* 12–20. *Amount:* $1000.

Eligibility Requirements: Applicant must be Jewish; of Jewish heritage; enrolled or expecting to enroll full-time at a two-year or four-year institution or university and resident of Maryland. Applicant must have 3.0 GPA or higher. Available to U.S. citizens.

Application Requirements: Essay, financial need analysis, interview, transcript, CSB online application. *Deadline:* May 31.

Contact: Roberta Goldman, Program Director
Central Scholarship Bureau
1700 Reisterstown Road, Suite 220
Baltimore, MD 21208-2903
Phone: 410-415-5558
Fax: 410-415-5501
E-mail: rgoldman@centralsb.org

CHEROKEE NATION OF OKLAHOMA http://www.cherokee.org

CHEROKEE NATION HIGHER EDUCATION SCHOLARSHIP

A supplementary program that provides financial assistance to Cherokee Nation Members only. It is a need-based program which provides assistance in seeking a bachelor's degree.

Award: Scholarship for use in freshman, sophomore, junior, or senior years; renewable. *Number:* up to 2800. *Amount:* $100–$1000.

Eligibility Requirements: Applicant must be American Indian/Alaska Native and enrolled or expecting to enroll full-time at a four-year institution or university. Applicant must have 2.5 GPA or higher. Available to U.S. citizens.

Application Requirements: Test scores, transcript, written request for application. *Deadline:* June 13.

Contact: Nita Wilson, Higher Education Specialist
Cherokee Nation of Oklahoma
PO Box 948
Tahlequah, OK 74465
Phone: 918-458-6195
E-mail: nwilson@cherokee.org

CHICANA/LATINA FOUNDATION http://www.chicanalatina.org

SCHOLARSHIPS FOR LATINA STUDENTS

Scholarships are awarded to female Latina students enrolled in two-year, four-year or graduate levels. Applicants must be from the nine counties of Northern California.

Award: Scholarship for use in freshman, sophomore, junior, senior, or graduate years; not renewable. *Number:* 15–20. *Amount:* $1500.

Eligibility Requirements: Applicant must be of Hispanic heritage; enrolled or expecting to enroll full-time at a two-year or four-year institution or university; female and resident of California. Applicant must have 2.5 GPA or higher. Available to U.S. citizens.

Application Requirements: Application, essay, interview, references, transcript. *Deadline:* March 17.

Contact: Claudia Leon, Program Coordinator
Chicana/Latina Foundation
1419 Burlingame Avenue, Suite N
Burlingame, CA 94010
Phone: 650-373-1085
Fax: 650-373-1090
E-mail: claudia@chicanalatina.org

CHINESE AMERICAN ASSOCIATION OF MINNESOTA http://www.caam.org

CHINESE AMERICAN ASSOCIATION OF MINNESOTA (CAAM) SCHOLARSHIPS

Merit and need scholarships of $1000 each are available for college and graduate students of Chinese descent and a resident of Minnesota. Applicants will be evaluated on their academic records, leadership qualities, and community service.

Award: Scholarship for use in freshman, sophomore, junior, senior, or graduate years; not renewable. *Number:* varies. *Amount:* $1000.

Eligibility Requirements: Applicant must be of Chinese heritage; Asian/Pacific Islander; enrolled or expecting to enroll full-time at a two-year or four-year or technical institution or university and resident of Minnesota. Available to U.S. citizens.

Application Requirements: Application, financial need analysis, references, SAT score. *Deadline:* November 15.

Contact: Scholarship Committee
Chinese American Association of Minnesota
PO Box 582584
Minneapolis, MN 55458-2584

CIRI FOUNDATION (TCF) http://www.thecirifoundation.org

CAREER UPGRADE GRANTS

Awards applicant who are accepted or enrolled part-time in a course of study that directly contributes toward potential employment or employment upgrade. May reapply each quarter until grant cap is reached. Must be a CIRI original enrollee or descendant. Deadlines: March 31, June 30, September 30, and December 1.

Award: Grant for use in freshman, sophomore, junior, senior, graduate, or postgraduate years; not renewable. *Number:* varies. *Amount:* up to $4500.

Eligibility Requirements: Applicant must be American Indian/Alaska Native and enrolled or expecting to enroll part-time at a two-year or four-year institution or university. Applicant must have 2.5 GPA or higher. Available to U.S. and non-U.S. citizens.

Application Requirements: Application, essay, references, transcript, proof of eligibility, birth certificate or adoption decree. *Deadline:* varies.

Contact: Susan Anderson, President and Chief Executive Officer
CIRI Foundation (TCF)
3600 San Jeronimo Drive, Suite 256
Anchorage, AK 99508-2870
Phone: 907-793-3575
Fax: 907-793-3585
E-mail: tcf@thecirifoundation.org

CIRI FOUNDATION ACHIEVEMENT ANNUAL SCHOLARSHIPS

Merit scholarships for applicants with exceptional academic promise. Annual award includes two academic semesters. Must be Alaska Native student only, CIRI original enrollee, or descendant. Should have a cumulative 3.0 GPA or better.

Award: Scholarship for use in freshman, sophomore, junior, senior, or graduate years; not renewable. *Number:* varies. *Amount:* up to $8000.

Eligibility Requirements: Applicant must be American Indian/Alaska Native and enrolled or expecting to enroll full-time at a four-year institution or university. Applicant must have 3.0 GPA or higher. Available to U.S. and non-U.S. citizens.

Application Requirements: Application, essay, references, transcript, proof of eligibility, birth certificate or adoption decree. *Deadline:* June 1.

Contact: Susan Anderson, President and Chief Executive Officer
CIRI Foundation (TCF)
3600 San Jeronimo Drive, Suite 256
Anchorage, AK 99508-2870
Phone: 907-793-3575
Fax: 907-793-3585
E-mail: tcf@thecirifoundation.org

CIRI FOUNDATION EXCELLENCE ANNUAL SCHOLARSHIPS

Merit scholarships for outstanding academic and community services experience. Annual award includes two academic semesters. Must be Alaska Native student only, CIRI original enrollee or descendant. Should have a cumulative 3.7 GPA or better.

Award: Scholarship for use in freshman, sophomore, junior, senior, or graduate years; not renewable. *Number:* varies. *Amount:* up to $10,000.

Eligibility Requirements: Applicant must be American Indian/Alaska Native and enrolled or expecting to enroll full-time at a four-year institution or university. Available to U.S. and non-U.S. citizens.

Application Requirements: Application, essay, references, transcript, proof of eligibility, birth certificate or adoption decree. *Deadline:* June 1.

Contact: Susan Anderson, President and Chief Executive Officer
CIRI Foundation (TCF)
3600 San Jeronimo Drive, Suite 256
Anchorage, AK 99508-2870
Phone: 907-793-3575
Fax: 907-793-3585
E-mail: tcf@thecirifoundation.org

CIRI FOUNDATION GENERAL SEMESTER SCHOLARSHIP

Merit scholarships for applicants with academic promise. Award of $2500 maximum based on stated need. Must be Alaska Native student only, CIRI original enrollee or descendant. Deadlines: June 1 and December 1.

Award: Scholarship for use in freshman, sophomore, junior, senior, or graduate years; not renewable. *Number:* varies. *Amount:* up to $2500.

Eligibility Requirements: Applicant must be American Indian/Alaska Native and enrolled or expecting to enroll full-time at a two-year or four-year institution or university. Applicant must have 2.5 GPA or higher. Available to U.S. and non-U.S. citizens.

Application Requirements: Application, essay, references, transcript, proof of eligibility, birth certificate or adoption decree. *Deadline:* varies.

Contact: Susan Anderson, President and Chief Executive Officer
CIRI Foundation (TCF)
3600 San Jeronimo Drive, Suite 256
Anchorage, AK 99508-2870
Phone: 907-793-3575
Fax: 907-793-3585
E-mail: tcf@thecirifoundation.org

CIRI FOUNDATION SPECIAL EXCELLENCE SCHOLARSHIP

Awards a scholarship of $20,000. Must be enrolled full-time in a four-year undergraduate or graduate degree program. Applicant must be Alaska Native original enrollees or descendants of Cook Inlet Region Inc. Must have a cumulative GPA of 3.7 or better. Preference given to study in fields of business, education, math, sciences, health services, and engineering.

Award: Scholarship for use in freshman, sophomore, junior, senior, or graduate years; not renewable. *Number:* 1. *Amount:* $20,000.

Eligibility Requirements: Applicant must be American Indian/Alaska Native and enrolled or expecting to enroll full-time at a four-year institution or university. Available to U.S. and non-U.S. citizens.

Application Requirements: Application, essay, references, transcript, proof of eligibility, birth certificate or adoption decree. *Deadline:* June 1.

Contact: Susan Anderson, President and Chief Executive Officer
CIRI Foundation (TCF)
3600 San Jeronimo Drive, Suite 256
Anchorage, AK 99508-2870
Phone: 907-793-3575
Fax: 907-793-3585
E-mail: tcf@thecirifoundation.org

CULTURAL FELLOWSHIP GRANTS

Awards applicants who are accepted or enrolled in a seminar or conference that is accredited, authorized, or approved by the CIRI Foundation. May reapply each quarter until grant cap is reached and may reapply the following year. Must be Alaska Native student, CIRI original enrollee, or descendant. Must have studies in Alaska Native arts and cultures, including visual or performing arts, communications, languages, history. Deadlines: March 31, June 30, September 30, and December 1.

Award: Grant for use in freshman, sophomore, junior, senior, graduate, or postgraduate years; not renewable. *Number:* varies. *Amount:* $500.

Eligibility Requirements: Applicant must be American Indian/Alaska Native; age 18 and over; enrolled or expecting to enroll full- or part-time at a two-year or four-year institution or university and resident of Alaska. Applicant must have 2.5 GPA or higher. Available to U.S. and non-U.S. citizens.

Application Requirements: Application, essay, references, transcript, proof of eligibility, birth certificate or adoption decree. *Deadline:* varies.

Contact: Susan Anderson, President and Chief Executive Officer
CIRI Foundation (TCF)
3600 San Jeronimo Drive, Suite 256
Anchorage, AK 99508-2870
Phone: 907-793-3575
Fax: 907-793-3585
E-mail: tcf@thecirifoundation.org

GENERAL FELLOWSHIP GRANTS

Awards applicants who are accepted or enrolled in a seminar or conference that is accredited, authorized, or approved by the CIRI Foundation. Also funds for special employment-related non-credit workshops or seminars. Must be Alaska Native student, CIRI original enrollee, or descendant. Deadlines: March 31, June 30, September 30, and December 1.

Award: Grant for use in freshman, sophomore, junior, senior, graduate, or postgraduate years; not renewable. *Number:* varies. *Amount:* up to $500.

Eligibility Requirements: Applicant must be American Indian/Alaska Native; age 18 and over and enrolled or expecting to enroll full- or part-time at a two-year or four-year or technical institution or university. Applicant must have 2.5 GPA or higher. Available to U.S. and non-U.S. citizens.

CIRI Foundation (TCF) (continued)

Application Requirements: Application, essay, references, transcript, proof of eligibility, birth certificate or adoption decree. *Deadline:* varies.

Contact: Susan Anderson, President and Chief Executive Officer
CIRI Foundation (TCF)
3600 San Jeronimo Drive, Suite 256
Anchorage, AK 99508-2870
Phone: 907-793-3575
Fax: 907-793-3585
E-mail: tcf@thecirifoundation.org

HOWARD ROCK FOUNDATION SCHOLARSHIP PROGRAM

Scholarships are available to undergraduate and graduate students, who are Alaska Native original enrollees of an ANCSA regional and/or village corporation, a direct lineal descendant, or a member of a tribal or other organization. Preference is given to junior and senior standing students. Affiliated regional and/or village corporations must be current members of Alaska Village Initiatives. Must have a minimum GPA of 2.5 for undergraduates and 3.0 for graduates.

Award: Scholarship for use in freshman, sophomore, junior, senior, or graduate years; not renewable. *Number:* 3. *Amount:* $2500–$5000.

Eligibility Requirements: Applicant must be American Indian/Alaska Native and enrolled or expecting to enroll full-time at a four-year institution or university. Available to U.S. and Canadian citizens.

Application Requirements: Application, essay, financial need analysis, photo, references, transcript, proof of eligibility, statement of purpose. *Deadline:* June 1.

Contact: Susan Anderson, President and Chief Executive Officer
CIRI Foundation (TCF)
3600 San Jeronimo Drive, Suite 256
Anchorage, AK 99508-2870
Phone: 907-793-3575
Fax: 907-793-3585
E-mail: tcf@thecirifoundation.org

NINILCHIK NATIVE ASSOCIATION INC. SCHOLARSHIP AND GRANT PROGRAM

Scholarship is for eligible Alaska Natives who are original enrollees or descendants of Ninilchik Native Association Inc. Must be a full-time student. Must have a cumulative 2.5 GPA or better. Deadlines: June 1 and December 1.

Award: Scholarship for use in freshman, sophomore, junior, senior, or graduate years; renewable. *Number:* 1. *Amount:* $1000–$2000.

Eligibility Requirements: Applicant must be American Indian/Alaska Native and enrolled or expecting to enroll full-time at a two-year or four-year or technical institution or university. Applicant must have 2.5 GPA or higher. Available to U.S. citizens.

Application Requirements: Application, essay, photo, references, test scores, transcript. *Deadline:* varies.

Contact: Scholarship Committee
CIRI Foundation (TCF)
3600 San Jeronimo Drive, Suite 256
Anchorage, AK 99508-2870
Phone: 907-793-3575
Fax: 907-793-3585
E-mail: tcf@thecirifoundation.org

SALAMATOF NATIVE ASSOCIATION INC. SCHOLARSHIP PROGRAM

Two annual scholarships or education grants are awarded to qualified applicants. Alaska Native original enrollees of SNAI and their lineal descendants and spouses may apply.

Award: Scholarship for use in freshman, sophomore, junior, senior, or graduate years; not renewable. *Number:* 2. *Amount:* varies.

Eligibility Requirements: Applicant must be American Indian/Alaska Native and enrolled or expecting to enroll full-time at a four-year institution or university. Applicant must have 2.5 GPA or higher. Available to U.S. and non-U.S. citizens.

Application Requirements: Application, essay, transcript, proof of eligibility, birth certificate or adoption degree. *Deadline:* June 1.

Contact: Susan Anderson, President and Chief Executive Officer
CIRI Foundation (TCF)
3600 San Jeronimo Drive, Suite 256
Anchorage, AK 99508-2870
Phone: 907-793-3575
Fax: 907-793-3585
E-mail: tcf@thecirifoundation.org

TYONEK NATIVE CORPORATION SCHOLARSHIP AND GRANT FUND

Award to encourage Alaska Native student to prepare for professional career after high school. Applicant must be accepted or enrolled full-time in an accredited or otherwise approved postsecondary college, university, or technical skills education program. Must be Alaska Native original enrollee to Tyonek Native Corporation or the Native Village of Tyonek, or lineal descendant.

Award: Scholarship for use in freshman, sophomore, junior, senior, or graduate years; not renewable. *Number:* varies. *Amount:* varies.

Eligibility Requirements: Applicant must be American Indian/Alaska Native and enrolled or expecting to enroll full-time at a two-year or four-year or technical institution or university. Available to U.S. and non-U.S. citizens.

Application Requirements: Application, essay, references, transcript, proof of eligibility, birth certificate or adoption decree. *Deadline:* varies.

Contact: Susan Anderson, President and Chief Executive Officer
CIRI Foundation (TCF)
3600 San Jeronimo Drive, Suite 256
Anchorage, AK 99508-2870
Phone: 907-793-3575
Fax: 907-793-3585
E-mail: tcf@thecirifoundation.org

VOCATIONAL TRAINING GRANTS

Awards applicants who are accepted or enrolled part- or full-time in a technical skills certificate or degree program such as (but not limited to) craft/trade, automotive technology, office occupations and computer technology, which prepares the student for employment. Must be a CIRI original enrollee, or descendant. Deadlines: March 31, June 30, September 30, and December 1.

Award: Grant for use in freshman, sophomore, junior, senior, graduate, or postgraduate years; not renewable. *Number:* varies. *Amount:* up to $4500.

Eligibility Requirements: Applicant must be American Indian/Alaska Native; age 18 and over and enrolled or expecting to enroll full- or part-time at a two-year or four-year or technical institution or university. Applicant must have 2.5 GPA or higher. Available to U.S. and non-U.S. citizens.

Application Requirements: Application, essay, references, transcript, proof of eligibility, birth certificate or adoption decree. *Deadline:* varies.

Contact: Susan Anderson, President and Chief Executive Officer
CIRI Foundation (TCF)
3600 San Jeronimo Drive, Suite 256
Anchorage, AK 99508-2870
Phone: 907-793-3575
Fax: 907-793-3585
E-mail: tcf@thecirifoundation.org

CITIZEN POTAWATOMI NATION http://www.potawatomi.org

CITIZEN POTAWATOMI NATION TRIBAL SCHOLARSHIP

Provides financial assistance for payment of tuition for members of the Citizen Potawatomi Nation. Minimum 2.0 GPA required. Deadlines: December 1 for spring, August 1 for fall, June 1 for summer. Award amount varies from $750 to $1500.

Award: Scholarship for use in freshman, sophomore, junior, senior, or graduate years; renewable. *Number:* varies. *Amount:* $750–$1500.

Eligibility Requirements: Applicant must be American Indian/Alaska Native and enrolled or expecting to enroll full- or part-time at a two-year or four-year or technical institution or university. Available to U.S. citizens.

Application Requirements: Application, financial need analysis, test scores, transcript. *Deadline:* varies.

Contact: Charles Clark, Director, Tribal Rolls
Citizen Potawatomi Nation
1601 South Gordon Cooper Drive
Shawnee, OK 74801-8699
Phone: 800-880-9880
Fax: 405-878-4653
E-mail: cclark@potawatomi.org

COLLEGE FOUNDATION OF NORTH CAROLINA INC. http://www.cfnc.org

LATINO DIAMANTE SCHOLARSHIP FUND

• *See page 594*

NORTH CAROLINA HISPANIC COLLEGE FUND SCHOLARSHIP

Four-year renewable scholarship for Hispanic students. Must have graduated from a North Carolina high school within the past 2 years, have a four-year cumulative GPA of 2.5, and be accepted into a two- or four-year college or university. Preference is given to full-time students but part-time students may apply. Preference will be given to foreign-born applicants or native-born children of foreign-born parents. Applications are available online at http://www.thencshp.org/nchcf.

Award: Scholarship for use in freshman, sophomore, junior, or senior years; renewable. *Number:* varies. *Amount:* $500–$2500.

Eligibility Requirements: Applicant must be Hispanic; enrolled or expecting to enroll full- or part-time at a two-year or four-year institution or university and resident of North Carolina. Applicant must have 2.5 GPA or higher. Available to U.S. and non-U.S. citizens.

Application Requirements: Application, transcript. *Deadline:* continuous.

Contact: Scholarship Committee
College Foundation of North Carolina Inc.
PO Box 1557
Apex, NC 27502-3557
Phone: 919-654-4516
E-mail: mailbox@thenchsp.org

COLLEGE WOMEN'S ASSOCIATION OF JAPAN http://www.cwaj.org

SCHOLARSHIP FOR THE VISUALLY IMPAIRED TO STUDY ABROAD

• *See page 617*

SCHOLARSHIP FOR THE VISUALLY IMPAIRED TO STUDY IN JAPAN

• *See page 617*

COMMUNITY FOUNDATION OF WESTERN MASSACHUSETTS http://www.communityfoundation.org

PUTNAM SCHOLARSHIP FUND

Provides scholarships for African-American and Latino students who attend college. See the Web site for further details on how to complete the application process.

Award: Scholarship for use in freshman, sophomore, junior, or senior years; renewable. *Number:* up to 7. *Amount:* $1500–$2000.

Eligibility Requirements: Applicant must be Black (non-Hispanic) or Hispanic; enrolled or expecting to enroll full- or part-time at a two-year or four-year institution or university and resident of Connecticut or Massachusetts. Available to U.S. citizens.

Application Requirements: Application, references, transcript, pastoral letter of reference from any denomination, Student Aid Report (SAR). *Deadline:* March 31.

Contact: Dorothy Theriaque, Education Associate
Community Foundation of Western Massachusetts
1500 Main Street, PO Box 15769
Springfield, MA 01115
Phone: 413-732-2858
Fax: 413-733-8565
E-mail: dtheriaque@communityfoundation.org

CONFEDERATED TRIBES OF GRAND RONDE http://www.grandronde.org

ADULT VOCATIONAL TRAINING COMPETITIVE SCHOLARSHIP

Available to any enrolled member of the Confederated Tribes of Grand Ronde. Four $6000 full-time and one $3000 part-time awards are given each year. Intended for programs of study two years or less in length.

Award: Scholarship for use in freshman or sophomore years; renewable. *Number:* 5. *Amount:* $3000–$6000.

Eligibility Requirements: Applicant must be American Indian/Alaska Native and enrolled or expecting to enroll full- or part-time at a two-year or technical institution. Available to U.S. and non-U.S. citizens.

Application Requirements: Application, essay, references, transcript, verification of tribal enrollment. *Deadline:* April 30.

Contact: Luhui Whitebear, Tribal Scholarship Coordinator
Confederated Tribes of Grand Ronde
9615 Grand Ronde Road
Grand Ronde, OR 97347
Phone: 800-422-0232 Ext. 2275
Fax: 503-879-2286
E-mail: education@grandronde.org

UNDERGRADUATE COMPETETIVE SCHOLARSHIP

Available to any enrolled member of the Confederated Tribes of Grand Ronde. Ten $3000, two $4500, and three $6000 full-time awards, and two $3000 part-time awards are given each year. Renewable for twelve terms/eight semesters of continuous study. Scholarship may be used at community colleges for transfer credits.

Award: Scholarship for use in freshman, sophomore, junior, or senior years; renewable. *Number:* 17. *Amount:* $3000–$6000.

Eligibility Requirements: Applicant must be American Indian/Alaska Native and enrolled or expecting to enroll full- or part-time at a two-year or four-year institution or university. Available to U.S. and non-U.S. citizens.

Application Requirements: Application, essay, references, transcript, verification of tribal enrollment. *Deadline:* April 30.

Contact: Luhui Whitebear, Tribal Scholarship Coordinator
Confederated Tribes of Grand Ronde
9615 Grand Ronde Road
Grand Ronde, OR 97347
Phone: 800-422-0232 Ext. 2275
Fax: 503-879-2286
E-mail: education@grandronde.org

CONGRESSIONAL HISPANIC CAUCUS INSTITUTE http://www.chciyouth.org

CONGRESSIONAL HISPANIC CAUCUS INSTITUTE SCHOLARSHIP AWARDS

• *See page 595*

CORPORATION FOR OHIO APPALACHIAN DEVELOPMENT (COAD) http://www.coadinc.org

DAVID V. STIVISON APPALACHIAN SCHOLARSHIP FUND

Provides financial assistance to students who are residents in the Corporation for Ohio Appalachian Development's (COAD) service area and want to attend college, but lack the required resources. Individual income must not exceed $19,600. See Web site for application information: http://www.coadinc.org/Main.php?page=scholarships-info.

Award: Scholarship for use in freshman, sophomore, junior, or senior years; not renewable. *Number:* 12. *Amount:* $500–$1500.

Eligibility Requirements: Applicant must be American Indian/Alaska Native; enrolled or expecting to enroll full-time at a two-year or four-year institution or university and resident of Ohio. Available to U.S. citizens.

Corporation for Ohio Appalachian Development (COAD) (continued)

Application Requirements: Application, financial need analysis, transcript. *Deadline:* March 1.

Contact: Allyssa Mefford, Operations Manager
Corporation for Ohio Appalachian Development (COAD)
One Pinchot Lane
PO Box 787
Athens, OH 45701-0787
Phone: 740-594-8499
Fax: 740-592-5994
E-mail: amefford@coadinc.org

COUNCIL FOR INTERNATIONAL EDUCATIONAL EXCHANGE http://www.ciee.org

ROBERT B. BAILEY III MINORITY SCHOLARSHIPS FOR EDUCATION ABROAD

• *See page 617*

COUNCIL OF ENERGY RESOURCE TRIBES (CERT) EDUCATION FUND INC. http://www.certredearth.com

COUNCIL OF ENERGY RESOURCES TRIBES EDUCATION FUND SCHOLARSHIP

Renewable scholarship for full-time Native American students. Award applicable to any accredited two- or four-year institution including trade or technical school. Applicant must submit application, transcript, recommendations, and certificate proving Native American heritage. Financial need will be taken into account. Must be accepted and have completed the six weeks T program at the University of New Mexico to be eligible for the scholarship.

Award: Scholarship for use in freshman, sophomore, junior, senior, or graduate years; renewable. *Number:* 50. *Amount:* $1000.

Eligibility Requirements: Applicant must be American Indian/Alaska Native and enrolled or expecting to enroll full-time at a four-year institution or university. Applicant must have 2.5 GPA or higher. Available to U.S. and Canadian citizens.

Application Requirements: Application, financial need analysis, references, transcript, certificate of Indian blood. *Deadline:* February 14.

Contact: Mr. Clint LeBeau, Program Assistant
Council of Energy Resource Tribes (CERT) Education Fund Inc.
695 South Colorado Boulevard, Suite 10
Denver, CO 80246
Phone: 303-282-7576 Ext. 16
Fax: 303-282-7584
E-mail: clebeau@certredearth.com

CROATIAN SCHOLARSHIP FUND http://www.croatianscholarship.org

CROATIAN SCHOLARSHIP FUND SCHOLARSHIP PROGRAM

Scholarship for students of Croation heritage. Award based on academic achivement and financial need. Must demonstrate appropriate degree selection. Scholarships are awarded depending on availability of funds and number of applicants.

Award: Scholarship for use in freshman, sophomore, junior, or senior years; renewable. *Number:* varies. *Amount:* $1200–$1500.

Eligibility Requirements: Applicant must be of Croatian/Serbian heritage; age 18-25 and enrolled or expecting to enroll full-time at a four-year institution or university. Applicant must have 3.5 GPA or higher. Available to U.S. and non-U.S. citizens.

Application Requirements: Application, autobiography, financial need analysis, photo, references, test scores, transcript. *Deadline:* April 15.

Contact: Vesna Brekalo, Scholarship Liaison
Croatian Scholarship Fund
31 Mesa Vista Court
San Ramon, CA 94583
Phone: 925-556-6263
Fax: 925-556-6263
E-mail: vbrekalo@msn.com

DANIEL KOVACH SCHOLARSHIP FOUNDATION http://www.collegescholarships.org

MINORITY SCHOLARSHIP

Scholarship of $1000 awarded to a minority college student who currently attending full-time in post-secondary education both undergraduate and graduate. Must be a U.S. citizen. Minimum 3.0 GPA required.

Award: Scholarship for use in freshman, sophomore, junior, senior, or graduate years; not renewable. *Number:* 1. *Amount:* $1000.

Eligibility Requirements: Applicant must be American Indian/Alaska Native, Asian/Pacific Islander, Black (non-Hispanic), or Hispanic and enrolled or expecting to enroll full-time at a four-year institution or university. Applicant must have 3.0 GPA or higher. Available to U.S. citizens.

Application Requirements: Application, essay, test scores, transcript. *Deadline:* December 24.

Contact: Daniel Kovach, Scholarship Committee
Daniel Kovach Scholarship Foundation
5506 Red Robin Road
Raleigh, NC 27613
Phone: 919-630-4895
E-mail: danielkovach@gmail.com

DAUGHTERS OF PENELOPE FOUNDATION

ALEXANDRA APOSTOLIDES SONENFELD SCHOLARSHIP

• *See page 529*

JOANNE V. HOLOGGITAS, PHD SCHOLARSHIP

• *See page 529*

KOTTIS FAMILY SCHOLARSHIP

• *See page 529*

MARY M. VERGES SCHOLARSHIP

• *See page 529*

PAST GRAND PRESIDENTS SCHOLARSHIP

• *See page 529*

DENVER HISPANIC CHAMBER OF COMMERCE EDUCATION FOUNDATION http://www.dhcc.com/default.asp

HISPANIC YOUTH SCHOLARSHIP PROGRAM

• *See page 596*

DEPARTMENT OF THE ARMY http://www.goarmy.com/rotc

U.S. ARMY ROTC FOUR-YEAR HISTORICALLY BLACK COLLEGE/ UNIVERSITY SCHOLARSHIP

• *See page 638*

DIVERSITY CITY MEDIA http://www.blacknews.com

BLACKNEWS.COM SCHOLARSHIP ESSAY CONTEST

Scholarship of $500 awarded to an African-American student for the best essay submitted. Must be a U.S. citizen.

Award: Scholarship for use in freshman, sophomore, junior, or senior years; not renewable. *Number:* up to 4. *Amount:* $500.

Eligibility Requirements: Applicant must be Black (non-Hispanic); enrolled or expecting to enroll full- or part-time at a two-year or four-year or technical institution or university and must have an interest in writing. Available to U.S. citizens.

Application Requirements: Application, applicant must enter a contest, essay. *Deadline:* April 31.

Contact: Dante Lee, President and Chief Executive Officer
Diversity City Media
750-Q Cross Pointe Road, Suite 203
Columbus, OH 43230
Phone: 866-910-6277
E-mail: scholarship@blacknews.com

DOGRIB TREATY 11 SCHOLARSHIP COMMITTEE http://www.tlicho.com

BHP BILLITON UNIVERSITY SCHOLARSHIPS

Award for undergraduate, master's or PhD degree students of Dogrib ancestry. Applicants should be a member of Tilcho Citizens band. Must be enrolled full-time in a Canadian university degree program and be interested and active in community affairs. Scholarship value is $5000.

Award: Scholarship for use in freshman, sophomore, junior, senior, graduate, or postgraduate years; not renewable. *Number:* 4. *Amount:* $5000.

Eligibility Requirements: Applicant must be Canadian citizen; American Indian/Alaska Native and enrolled or expecting to enroll full-time at a two-year or four-year or technical institution or university.

Application Requirements: Application, references, transcript. *Deadline:* July 15.

Contact: Joe Beaverho, Program Manager
Dogrib Treaty 11 Scholarship Committee
PO Box 5
Behchoko, NT X0E 0Y0
Canada
Phone: 867-392-3000 Ext. 269
Fax: 867-392-3001
E-mail: jbeaverho@dogrib.net

DIAVIK DIAMONDS INC. SCHOLARSHIPS FOR COLLEGE STUDENTS

Scholarship for students enrolled full-time in a Canadian college diploma program. Must be of Dogrib ancestry. Must be interested and active in community affairs. Applicants should be a member of Tilcho Citizens band. Scholarship value is $3000.

Award: Scholarship for use in freshman or sophomore years; not renewable. *Number:* 10. *Amount:* $3000.

Eligibility Requirements: Applicant must be Canadian citizen; American Indian/Alaska Native and enrolled or expecting to enroll full-time at a technical institution.

Application Requirements: Application, essay, references, transcript. *Deadline:* varies.

Contact: Joe Beaverho, Program Manager
Dogrib Treaty 11 Scholarship Committee
PO Box 5
Behchoko, NT X0E 0Y0
Canada
Phone: 867-392-3000 Ext. 269
Fax: 867-392-3001
E-mail: jbeaverho@dogrib.net

EDGAR ALLEN POE LITERARY SOCIETY http://www.ravens.org

DISTINGUISHED RAVEN FAC MEMORIAL SCHOLARSHIP

Scholarship provides educational assistance to the descendants of those Lao/Hmong who served alongside the Ravens in defense of their country.

Award: Scholarship for use in freshman, sophomore, junior, or senior years; not renewable. *Number:* 1. *Amount:* $1000.

Eligibility Requirements: Applicant must be Asian/Pacific Islander and enrolled or expecting to enroll full-time at a two-year or four-year institution or university. Available to U.S. and non-U.S. citizens.

Application Requirements: Application, essay, references, transcript. *Deadline:* February 29.

Contact: James McKinley, Administrator
Edgar Allen Poe Literary Society
2944 Mountain Top Drive
West Blocton, AL 35184
Phone: 205-938-1516
E-mail: jamesleemac@aol.com

EDMONTON COMMUNITY FOUNDATION http://www.DollarsForLearners.com

BELCOURT BROSSEAU METIS AWARDS

Scholarship for Metis Albertans in an academic or vocational training program at a qualified postsecondary institution in Alberta. Priority will be given to students who are entering the first year of a postsecondary program for the first time. Students pursuing studies at the graduate level are not eligible.

Award: Prize for use in freshman, sophomore, junior, or senior years; renewable. *Number:* up to 140. *Amount:* $2000–$9000.

Eligibility Requirements: Applicant must be Canadian citizen; enrolled or expecting to enroll full-time at a two-year or four-year institution or university; resident of Alberta and studying in Alberta.

Application Requirements: Application, financial need analysis, references, transcript, personal letter, proof of Metis status. *Deadline:* March 31.

Contact: Craig Stumpf-Allen, Associate Director, Scholarships
Edmonton Community Foundation
9910-103 Street, NW
Edmonton, AB T5K 2V7
Canada
Phone: 780-426-0015
Fax: 780-425-0121
E-mail: info@dollarsforlearners.com

CHARMAINE LETOURNEAU SCHOLARSHIP

• *See page 618*

YOUTH FORMERLY IN CARE BURSARY

Scholarship funds awarded to disadvantaged young people to support their postsecondary education and training. Supports students who are residents of Alberta and who have spent a minimum of two years in the care and/or guardianship of Alberta Children's Services. Students considering part-time studies may be considered for an award.

Award: Grant for use in freshman, sophomore, junior, or senior years; renewable. *Number:* 1. *Amount:* $1000.

Eligibility Requirements: Applicant must be Canadian citizen; enrolled or expecting to enroll full- or part-time at a four-year institution or university and resident of Alberta.

Application Requirements: Application, financial need analysis, references, transcript, personal letter. *Deadline:* May 15.

Contact: Craig Stumpf-Allen, Associate Director, Scholarships
Edmonton Community Foundation
9910-103 Street, NW
Edmonton, AB T5K 2V7
Canada
Phone: 780-426-0015
Fax: 780-425-0121
E-mail: info@dollarsforlearners.com

FIRST CATHOLIC SLOVAK LADIES ASSOCIATION http://www.fcsla.org

FIRST CATHOLIC SLOVAK LADIES ASSOCIATION FRATERNAL SCHOLARSHIP AWARD

Must be FCSLA member in good standing for at least three years. Must attend accredited college in the United States or Canada in undergraduate or graduate degree program. Must submit certified copy of college acceptance. Award value is $1250 for undergraduates and $1750 for graduates.

Award: Scholarship for use in freshman, sophomore, junior, senior, or graduate years; not renewable. *Number:* 133. *Amount:* $1250–$1750.

Eligibility Requirements: Applicant must be of Slavic/Czech heritage and enrolled or expecting to enroll full-time at a two-year or four-year institution or university. Available to U.S. and Canadian citizens.

Application Requirements: Application, autobiography, essay, photo, references, test scores, transcript. *Deadline:* March 1.

Contact: Dorothy Szumski, Director of Fraternal Scholarships
First Catholic Slovak Ladies Association
24950 Chagrin Boulevard
Beachwood, OH 44122
Phone: 216-464-8015 Ext. 134
Fax: 216-464-9260
E-mail: info@fcsla.com

FLORIDA DEPARTMENT OF EDUCATION http://www.floridastudentfinancialaid.org

JOSE MARTI SCHOLARSHIP CHALLENGE GRANT FUND

Award available to Hispanic-American students who were born in, or whose parent was born in a Hispanic country. Must have lived in Florida for one year, be enrolled full-time in Florida at an eligible school, and have a GPA of 3.0 or above. Must be U.S. citizen or eligible non-citizen. FAFSA must be processed by May 15.

Award: Scholarship for use in freshman, sophomore, junior, senior, or graduate years; renewable. *Number:* varies. *Amount:* $2000.

Eligibility Requirements: Applicant must be of Hispanic heritage; enrolled or expecting to enroll full-time at a two-year or four-year or technical institution or university; resident of Florida and studying in Florida. Applicant must have 3.0 GPA or higher. Available to U.S. citizens.

Application Requirements: Application, financial need analysis. *Deadline:* April 1.

Contact: Theresa Antworth, Director State Scholarships and Grants
Florida Department of Education
Office of Student Financial Assistance, 1940 North Monroe Street, Suite 70
Tallahassee, FL 32303-4759
Phone: 850-410-5185
Fax: 850-487-6244
E-mail: theresa.antworth@fldoe.org

ROSEWOOD FAMILY SCHOLARSHIP FUND

Renewable award for eligible minority students to enable them to attend a Florida public postsecondary institution on a full-time basis. Preference given to direct descendants of African-American Rosewood families affected by the incidents of January 1923. Must be Black, Hispanic, Asian, Pacific Islander, American Indian, or Alaska Native. Must not have previously received a baccalaureate degree.

Award: Scholarship for use in freshman, sophomore, junior, or senior years; renewable. *Number:* up to 25. *Amount:* up to $4000.

Eligibility Requirements: Applicant must be American Indian/Alaska Native, Asian/Pacific Islander, Black (non-Hispanic), or Hispanic; enrolled or expecting to enroll full-time at a two-year or four-year or technical institution or university and studying in Florida. Available to U.S. citizens.

Application Requirements: Application, financial need analysis. *Deadline:* April 1.

Contact: Theresa Antworth, Director State Scholarships and Grants
Florida Department of Education
Office of Student Financial Assistance, 1940 North Monroe Street, Suite 70
Tallahassee, FL 32303-4759
Phone: 850-410-5185
Fax: 850-487-6244
E-mail: theresa.antworth@fldoe.org

FONDO FUTURO http://www.fondofuturo.com

FONDO FUTURO SCHOLARSHIP

Scholarship program's mission is to support Hispanic higher education and increase the number of Hispanic students attending college, graduate school, training programs, and continuing education programs. Scholarship information and application are at: http://www.fondofuturo.com.

Award: Scholarship for use in freshman, sophomore, junior, senior, graduate, or postgraduate years; not renewable. *Number:* 1–5. *Amount:* $1000.

Eligibility Requirements: Applicant must be Hispanic and enrolled or expecting to enroll full- or part-time at a two-year or four-year or technical institution or university. Available to U.S. and non-U.S. citizens.

Application Requirements: Application. *Deadline:* varies.

Contact: Luis Betanzo, Account Executive
Fondo Futuro
1126 16th Street, NW
Washington, DC 20036
Phone: 202-558-0005
Fax: 202-637-8801
E-mail: fondofuturo@fondo.us.com

GENERAL BOARD OF GLOBAL MINISTRIES http://www.gbgm-umc.org

NATIONAL LEADERSHIP DEVELOPMENT GRANTS

Award for racial and ethnic minority members of the United Methodist Church who are pursuing undergraduate study. Must be U.S. citizen, resident alien, or reside in U.S. as a refugee.

Award: Grant for use in freshman, sophomore, junior, or senior years; renewable. *Number:* 5–10. *Amount:* $1000–$4000.

Eligibility Requirements: Applicant must be Methodist; American Indian/Alaska Native, Asian/Pacific Islander, Black (non-Hispanic), or Hispanic and enrolled or expecting to enroll full-time at a two-year or four-year or technical institution or university. Available to U.S. citizens.

Application Requirements: Application, essay, financial need analysis, photo, references, transcript. *Deadline:* May 31.

Contact: Lisa Katzenstein Gomez, Administrator
General Board of Global Ministries
475 Riverside Drive, Room 1351
New York, NY 10115
Phone: 212-870-3787
Fax: 212-870-3932
E-mail: scholars@gbgm-umc.org

GENERAL BOARD OF HIGHER EDUCATION AND MINISTRY http://www.gbhem.org

BISHOP JOSEPH B. BETHEA SCHOLARSHIP

Undergraduate scholarship for full-time African American students. Must be a member of the Southeastern Jurisdiction Black Methodists for Church Renewal (SEJBMCR) and an active, full member of a United Methodist Church for at least one year prior to applying. Must be U.S. citizen or permanent resident, maintain a GPA of 2.8, and demonstrate financial need.

Award: Scholarship for use in freshman, sophomore, junior, or senior years; not renewable. *Number:* varies. *Amount:* varies.

Eligibility Requirements: Applicant must be Methodist; Black (non-Hispanic) and enrolled or expecting to enroll full-time at a four-year institution or university. Available to U.S. citizens.

Application Requirements: Application, essay, resume, references, transcript. *Deadline:* May 1.

Contact: Scholarship Committee
General Board of Higher Education and Ministry
The United Methodist Church, 1001 Nineteenth Avenue South
PO Box 340007
Nashville, TN 37202
Phone: 615-340-7344
Fax: 615-340-7367
E-mail: sddm@gbhem.org

ETHNIC MINORITY SCHOLARSHIP

Undergraduate award for U.S. citizens who are Native American, Asian, African American, Hispanic or Pacific Islanders. Must maintain a GPA of 2.5 or higher, and be a full and active member of a United Methodist Church for at least one year.

Award: Scholarship for use in freshman, sophomore, junior, or senior years; not renewable. *Number:* varies. *Amount:* varies.

Eligibility Requirements: Applicant must be Methodist; American Indian/Alaska Native, Asian/Pacific Islander, Black (non-Hispanic), or Hispanic and enrolled or expecting to enroll full-time at a four-year institution or university. Applicant must have 2.5 GPA or higher. Available to U.S. citizens.

Application Requirements: Application, essay, resume, references, transcript. *Deadline:* May 1.

Contact: Scholarship Committee
General Board of Higher Education and Ministry
The United Methodist Church, 1001 Nineteenth Avenue South
PO Box 340007
Nashville, TN 37202
Phone: 615-340-7344
Fax: 615-340-7367
E-mail: sddm@gbhem.org

HANA SCHOLARSHIP

$3000 to $5000 award for full-time college junior, senior, or graduate student of Hispanic, Asian, Native American/Alaskan Indian, or Pacific Islander parentage.

Must be an active, full member of the United Methodist Church for at least three years prior to application. Undergraduates must have GPA of 2.85, graduate students must have 3.0 GPA. Must demonstrate leadership ability within UMC.

Award: Scholarship for use in junior, senior, or graduate years; not renewable. *Number:* varies. *Amount:* $3000–$5000.

Eligibility Requirements: Applicant must be Methodist; American Indian/Alaska Native, Asian/Pacific Islander, or Hispanic; enrolled or expecting to enroll full-time at a four-year institution or university and must have an interest in leadership. Available to U.S. citizens.

Application Requirements: Application, essay, resume, references, transcript, leadership development plan. *Deadline:* April 1.

Contact: Scholarship Committee
General Board of Higher Education and Ministry
The United Methodist Church, 1001 Nineteenth Avenue South
PO Box 340007
Nashville, TN 37202
Phone: 615-340-7344
Fax: 615-340-7367
E-mail: sddm@gbhem.org

HBCU-CENTRAL.COM http://www.hbcu-central.com

HBCU-CENTRAL.COM MINORITY SCHOLARSHIP PROGRAM

Scholarship to minorities attending a historically Black college or university. Must attend or be enrolled into an HBCU. Selection based on quality of content in the online registration, and financial need.

Award: Scholarship for use in freshman, sophomore, junior, or senior years; not renewable. *Number:* varies. *Amount:* $1000.

Eligibility Requirements: Applicant must be American Indian/Alaska Native, Asian/Pacific Islander, Black (non-Hispanic), or Hispanic and enrolled or expecting to enroll full-time at a four-year institution or university. Available to U.S. citizens.

Application Requirements: Application, autobiography, essay, financial need analysis, interview, resume, transcript. *Deadline:* September 1.

Contact: William Moss III, President
HBCU-Central.com
750 Cross Pointe Road, Suite Q
Columbus, OH 43230
Phone: 614-284-3007
Fax: 215-893-5398
E-mail: wrmoss@hbcuconnect.com

HEBREW IMMIGRANT AID SOCIETY http://www.hias.org

HEBREW IMMIGRANT AID SOCIETY SCHOLARSHIP AWARDS COMPETITION

• *See page 535*

HELLENIC TIMES SCHOLARSHIP FUND http://www.htsf.org

HELLENIC TIMES SCHOLARSHIP FUND

One-time award to students of Greek/Hellenic descent. Must be between the ages of 17 and 25. For use in any year of undergraduate education. Employees of the Hellenic Times and their families are not eligible.

Award: Scholarship for use in freshman, sophomore, junior, or senior years; not renewable. *Number:* 30–40. *Amount:* $500–$10,000.

Eligibility Requirements: Applicant must be of Greek heritage; age 17-25 and enrolled or expecting to enroll full-time at a two-year or four-year or technical institution or university. Available to U.S. and non-U.S. citizens.

Application Requirements: Application, financial need analysis, resume, references, transcript. *Deadline:* February 19.

Contact: Nick Katsoris, President of Scholarship Fund
Hellenic Times Scholarship Fund
823 11th Avenue, Fifth Floor
New York, NY 10019-3535
Phone: 212-986-6881
Fax: 212-977-3662
E-mail: htsfund@aol.com

HELLENIC UNIVERSITY CLUB OF PHILADELPHIA http://www.hucphila.org

ANDREW G. CHRESSANTHIS MEMORIAL SCHOLARSHIP

$2000 scholarship for a full-time student enrolled in a degree program at an accredited four-year college or university.Must be a U.S. citizen of Greek descent and a resident of particular counties in NJ or PA.

Award: Scholarship for use in freshman, sophomore, junior, or senior years; not renewable. *Number:* varies. *Amount:* up to $2000.

Eligibility Requirements: Applicant must be of Greek heritage; enrolled or expecting to enroll full-time at a four-year institution or university and resident of New Jersey or Pennsylvania. Available to U.S. citizens.

Application Requirements: Application, financial need analysis, transcript. *Deadline:* April 21.

Contact: Zoe Tripolitis, Scholarship Chairman
Hellenic University Club of Philadelphia
PO Box 42199
Philadelphia, PA 19101-2199
Phone: 215-483-7440
E-mail: hucphila@yahoo.com

CHRISTOPHER DEMETRIS SCHOLARSHIP

$1200 scholarship for a full-time student enrolled in a degree program at an accredited four-year college or university. High school seniors accepted for enrollment in such a degree program may also apply. Must be a U.S. citizen of Greek descent and a resident of particular counties in NJ or PA.

Award: Scholarship for use in freshman, sophomore, junior, or senior years; not renewable. *Number:* varies. *Amount:* up to $1200.

Eligibility Requirements: Applicant must be of Greek heritage; enrolled or expecting to enroll full-time at a four-year institution or university and resident of New Jersey or Pennsylvania. Available to U.S. citizens.

Application Requirements: Application, financial need analysis, transcript. *Deadline:* April 21.

Contact: Zoe Tripolitis, Scholarship Chairman
Hellenic University Club of Philadelphia
PO Box 42199
Philadelphia, PA 19101-2199
Phone: 215-483-7440
E-mail: hucphila@yahoo.com

DORIZAS MEMORIAL SCHOLARSHIP

$3000 award for a full-time student enrolled in a degree program at an accredited four-year college or university. Must be a U.S. citizen of Greek descent and a resident of particular counties in NJ or PA.

Award: Scholarship for use in freshman, sophomore, junior, or senior years; not renewable. *Number:* varies. *Amount:* up to $3000.

Eligibility Requirements: Applicant must be of Greek heritage; enrolled or expecting to enroll full-time at a four-year institution or university and resident of New Jersey or Pennsylvania. Available to U.S. citizens.

Application Requirements: Application, financial need analysis, transcript. *Deadline:* April 21.

Contact: Zoe Tripolitis, Scholarship Chairman
Hellenic University Club of Philadelphia
PO Box 42199
Philadelphia, PA 19101-2199
Phone: 215-483-7440
E-mail: hucphila@yahoo.com

DR. NICHOLAS PADIS MEMORIAL GRADUATE SCHOLARSHIP

$5000 scholarship for a qualifying senior undergraduate or graduate student pursuing a full-time degree at an accredited university or professional school. Must be a U.S. citizen of Greek descent and a resident of particular counties in NJ or PA. Academic excellence is the primary consideration for this scholarship.

Award: Scholarship for use in senior or graduate years; not renewable. *Number:* up to 1. *Amount:* up to $5000.

Eligibility Requirements: Applicant must be of Greek heritage; enrolled or expecting to enroll full-time at a four-year institution or university and resident of New Jersey or Pennsylvania. Available to U.S. citizens.

Hellenic University Club of Philadelphia (continued)

Application Requirements: Application, financial need analysis, transcript. *Deadline:* April 21.

Contact: Zoe Tripolitis, Scholarship Chairman
Hellenic University Club of Philadelphia
PO Box 42199
Philadelphia, PA 19101-2199
Phone: 215-483-7440
E-mail: hucphila@yahoo.com

FOUNDERS SCHOLARSHIP

$3000 award for a full-time student enrolled in a degree program at an accredited four-year college or university.Must be a U.S. citizen of Greek descent and a resident of particular counties in NJ or PA.

Award: Scholarship for use in freshman, sophomore, junior, or senior years; not renewable. *Number:* varies. *Amount:* up to $3000.

Eligibility Requirements: Applicant must be of Greek heritage; enrolled or expecting to enroll full-time at a four-year institution or university and resident of New Jersey or Pennsylvania. Available to U.S. citizens.

Application Requirements: Application, financial need analysis, transcript. *Deadline:* April 21.

Contact: Zoe Tripolitis, Scholarship Chairman
Hellenic University Club of Philadelphia
PO Box 42199
Philadelphia, PA 19101-2199
Phone: 215-483-7440
E-mail: hucphila@yahoo.com

JAMES COSMOS MEMORIAL SCHOLARSHIP

Scholarship of up to $1000 for students enrolled full-time in a degree program at an accredited four-year college or university. High school seniors accepted for enrollment in such a degree program may also apply. Must be a U.S. citizen of Greek descent and a resident of particular counties in NJ or PA.

Award: Scholarship for use in freshman, sophomore, junior, or senior years; not renewable. *Number:* varies. *Amount:* $1000.

Eligibility Requirements: Applicant must be of Greek heritage; enrolled or expecting to enroll full-time at a four-year institution or university and resident of New Jersey or Pennsylvania. Available to U.S. citizens.

Application Requirements: Application, financial need analysis. *Deadline:* April 20.

Contact: Zoe Tripolitis, Scholarship Chairman
Hellenic University Club of Philadelphia
PO Box 42199
Philadelphia, PA 19101-2199
Phone: 215-483-7440
E-mail: hucphila@yahoo.com

PAIDEIA SCHOLARSHIP

• *See page 535*

HENRY SACHS FOUNDATION http://www.sachsfoundation.org

SACHS FOUNDATION SCHOLARSHIPS

Award to undergraduate students based on performance, financial need, and applicant's area of study and life goals. Must be African-American and a resident of Colorado. Minimum 3.5 GPA required.

Award: Scholarship for use in freshman year; renewable. *Number:* up to 50. *Amount:* up to $4000.

Eligibility Requirements: Applicant must be Black (non-Hispanic); high school student; planning to enroll or expecting to enroll full-time at a four-year institution or university and resident of Colorado. Applicant must have 3.5 GPA or higher. Available to U.S. citizens.

Application Requirements: Application, financial need analysis, photo. *Deadline:* March 1.

Contact: Lisa Harris, Secretary and Treasurer
Henry Sachs Foundation
90 South Cascade Avenue, Suite 1410
Colorado Springs, CO 80903
Phone: 719-633-2353
E-mail: info@sachsfoundation.org

HISPANIC ANNUAL SALUTE http://www.hispanicannualsalute.org

HISPANIC ANNUAL SALUTE SCHOLARSHIP

• *See page 599*

HISPANIC ASSOCIATION OF COLLEGES AND UNIVERSITIES (HACU) http://www.hacu.net

HISPANIC ASSOCIATION OF COLLEGES AND UNIVERSITIES SCHOLARSHIP PROGRAMS

The scholarship programs are sponsored by corporate and federal organizations. To be eligible, students must attend a HACU member college or university and meet all additional criteria. Visit Web site: https://scholarships.hacu.net/applications/applicants/ for details.

Award: Scholarship for use in freshman, sophomore, junior, senior, or graduate years; not renewable. *Number:* up to 200. *Amount:* $500–$3000.

Eligibility Requirements: Applicant must be Hispanic and enrolled or expecting to enroll full-time at a two-year or four-year institution or university. Applicant must have 3.0 GPA or higher. Available to U.S. citizens.

Application Requirements: Application, essay, financial need analysis, resume, transcript, enrollment certification form. *Deadline:* May 25.

Contact: Laura Castillo, Scholarship Coordinator
Hispanic Association of Colleges and Universities (HACU)
High Point Tower, 8415 Datapoint Drive, Suite 400
San Antonio, TX 78229
Phone: 210-692-3805
Fax: 210-692-0823
E-mail: scholarship@hacu.net

HISPANIC COLLEGE FUND INC. http://www.hispanicfund.org

FIRST IN MY FAMILY SCHOLARSHIP PROGRAM

One-time scholarship open to full-time undergraduates of Hispanic descent who are the first in their family to attend college. Must be a U.S. citizen residing in the United States or Puerto Rico and have a minimum 3.0 GPA.

Award: Scholarship for use in freshman, sophomore, junior, or senior years; not renewable. *Number:* 100–200. *Amount:* $500–$5000.

Eligibility Requirements: Applicant must be Hispanic and enrolled or expecting to enroll full-time at a two-year or four-year or technical institution or university. Applicant must have 3.0 GPA or higher. Available to U.S. citizens.

Application Requirements: Application, essay, financial need analysis, resume, references, test scores, transcript, college acceptance letter, copy of taxes, Student Aid Report (SAR). *Deadline:* March 15.

Contact: Fernando Barrueta, Chief Executive Officer
Hispanic College Fund Inc.
1301 K Street, NW, Suite 450-A West
Washington, DC 20005
Phone: 202-296-5400
Fax: 202-296-3774
E-mail: hcf-info@hispanicfund.org

HILTON FAMILY DIVERSITY SCHOLARSHIP PROGRAM

Scholarships to deserving Hispanic students attending any four-year college or university within the United States. Must maintain minimum GPA of 3.0.

Award: Scholarship for use in freshman, sophomore, junior, or senior years; renewable. *Number:* 10. *Amount:* up to $2500.

Eligibility Requirements: Applicant must be Hispanic and enrolled or expecting to enroll full-time at a two-year or four-year institution or university. Applicant must have 3.0 GPA or higher. Available to U.S. citizens.

Application Requirements: Application, essay, references, proof of family income, citizenship proof. *Deadline:* March 15.

Contact: Fernando Barrueta, Chief Executive Officer
Hispanic College Fund Inc.
1301 K Street, NW, Suite 450-A West
Washington, DC 20005
Phone: 202-296-5400
Fax: 202-296-3774
E-mail: hcf-info@hispanicfund.org

HISPANIC COLLEGE FUND SCHOLARSHIP PROGRAM

Scholarships to U.S. citizens or permanent residents who are Hispanic or of Hispanic descent. Must be studying at an accredited university in the United States or Puerto Rico and enrolled full-time as an undergraduate for the upcoming academic year. Must maintain GPA of 3.0.

Award: Scholarship for use in freshman, sophomore, junior, or senior years; renewable. *Number:* 600–750. *Amount:* $500–$5000.

Eligibility Requirements: Applicant must be Hispanic and enrolled or expecting to enroll full-time at a two-year or four-year institution or university. Applicant must have 3.0 GPA or higher. Available to U.S. citizens.

Application Requirements: Application, essay, financial need analysis, resume, references, transcript, copy of tax return, Student Aid Report (SAR), proof of citizenship status. *Deadline:* March 15.

Contact: Fernando Barrueta, Chief Executive Officer
Hispanic College Fund Inc.
1301 K Street, NW, Suite 450-A West
Washington, DC 20005
Phone: 202-296-5400
Fax: 202-296-3774
E-mail: hcf-info@hispanicfund.org

HISPANIC METROPOLITAN CHAMBER SCHOLARSHIPS http://www.hmccoregon.com

HISPANIC METROPOLITAN CHAMBER SCHOLARSHIPS

Scholarships to encourage Hispanics to pursue higher education. Applicant must have a minimum 2.75 GPA. For full-time study only. The award is available only to Hispanic students from Oregon and Southwest Washington.

Award: Scholarship for use in freshman, sophomore, junior, or senior years; renewable. *Number:* up to 55. *Amount:* $1000–$5000.

Eligibility Requirements: Applicant must be Hispanic; enrolled or expecting to enroll full- or part-time at a four-year institution or university and resident of Oregon or Washington. Available to U.S. citizens.

Application Requirements: Application, essay, transcript. *Deadline:* February 2.

Contact: MaryAnn Potter, Scholarship Committee
Hispanic Metropolitan Chamber Scholarships
PO Box 1837
Portland, OR 97207
Phone: 503-222-0280
Fax: 503-243-5597
E-mail: hmcc@qwest.net

HISPANIC SCHOLARSHIP FUND http://www.hsf.net

COLLEGE SCHOLARSHIP PROGRAM

Merit-based award for U.S. citizens or permanent residents of Hispanic heritage with plans to enroll full-time in a degree-seeking program at a U.S. accredited institution in the upcoming academic year. Applicants must have a minimum 3.0 GPA. Must include official transcript and SAR.

Award: Scholarship for use in freshman, sophomore, junior, senior, graduate, or postgraduate years; not renewable. *Number:* 2900–3500. *Amount:* $2500–$5000.

Eligibility Requirements: Applicant must be of Hispanic, Latin American/Caribbean, Mexican, Nicaraguan, or Spanish heritage and enrolled or expecting to enroll full-time at a two-year or four-year institution or university. Applicant must have 3.0 GPA or higher. Available to U.S. citizens.

Application Requirements: Application, essay, financial need analysis, references, transcript, Student Aid Report (SAR). *Deadline:* March 15.

Contact: Scholarship Administrator
Hispanic Scholarship Fund
55 Second Street, Suite 1500
San Francisco, CA 94105
Phone: 877-473-4636
Fax: 415-808-2302
E-mail: scholar1@hsf.net

GATES MILLENNIUM SCHOLARS PROGRAM

Award enables Hispanic-American students to complete an undergraduate or graduate education. Applicant may be pursuing undergraduate studies in any discipline; graduate studies limited to fields of mathematics, science, engineering, education, or library science. Must be entering a U.S. accredited college or university as a full-time degree-seeking student. Minimum 3.3 GPA required. Must demonstrate leadership abilities and significant financial need.

Award: Scholarship for use in freshman, sophomore, junior, senior, or graduate years; renewable. *Number:* 1000. *Amount:* varies.

Eligibility Requirements: Applicant must be American Indian/Alaska Native, Asian/Pacific Islander, Black (non-Hispanic), or Hispanic and enrolled or expecting to enroll full-time at a four-year institution or university. Available to U.S. and non-Canadian citizens.

Application Requirements: Application, financial need analysis. *Deadline:* January 11.

Contact: GMS Representative
Hispanic Scholarship Fund
55 Second Street, Suite 1500
San Francisco, CA 94105
Phone: 877-473-4636
Fax: 415-808-2302
E-mail: gmsinfo@hsf.net

HSF/FORD MOTOR COMPANY FUND SCHOLARSHIP PROGRAM

Scholarship to assist graduating high school seniors of Hispanic heritage nationwide who are seeking a bachelor's degree. Minimum 3.0 GPA required.

Award: Scholarship for use in freshman year; not renewable. *Number:* up to 30. *Amount:* $2500.

Eligibility Requirements: Applicant must be of Hispanic, Latin American/Caribbean, Mexican, Nicaraguan, or Spanish heritage; high school student and planning to enroll or expecting to enroll full-time at a four-year institution or university. Applicant must have 3.0 GPA or higher. Available to U.S. citizens.

Application Requirements: Application, essay, financial need analysis, references, transcript. *Deadline:* March 15.

Contact: John Schmucker, Scholarship Coordinator
Hispanic Scholarship Fund
55 Second Street, Suite 1500
San Francisco, CA 94105
Phone: 877-473-4636
E-mail: highschool@hsf.net

HSF/IDT HOPE HIGH SCHOOL SCHOLARSHIP PROGRAM

Renewable award to assist students of Hispanic heritage in New York City and Newark metropolitan areas who are seeking a bachelor's degree. Must be a high school senior graduating from a school in one of the following counties within the New York City metropolitan area: Bronx, Kings, New York, Queens, and Richmond; or in the following counties within the Newark metropolitan area: Bergen, Essex, Hudson, Hunterdon, Middlesex, Passaic, and Somerset. Minimum 3.0 GPA required. Award amount may be up to $10,600 over four years.

Award: Scholarship for use in freshman year; renewable. *Number:* up to 8. *Amount:* $2650.

Eligibility Requirements: Applicant must be of Hispanic, Latin American/Caribbean, Mexican, Nicaraguan, or Spanish heritage; high school student; planning to enroll or expecting to enroll full-time at a four-year institution or university and resident of New Jersey or New York. Applicant must have 3.0 GPA or higher. Available to U.S. citizens.

Hispanic Scholarship Fund (continued)

Application Requirements: Application, essay, financial need analysis, references, transcript. *Deadline:* March 15.

Contact: John Schmucker, Scholarship Coordinator
Hispanic Scholarship Fund
55 Second Street, Suite 1500
San Francisco, CA 94105
Phone: 877-473-4636
E-mail: highschool@hsf.net

HOPI TRIBE

BIA HIGHER EDUCATION GRANT

Grant provides financial support for eligible Hopi individuals pursuing postsecondary education. Minimum 2.5 CGPA required. Deadlines: July 1 for fall, and December 1 for spring.

Award: Grant for use in freshman, sophomore, junior, senior, graduate, or postgraduate years; not renewable. *Number:* 1–130. *Amount:* $50–$2500.

Eligibility Requirements: Applicant must be American Indian/Alaska Native and enrolled or expecting to enroll full-time at a two-year or four-year institution or university. Applicant must have 2.5 GPA or higher. Available to U.S. citizens.

Application Requirements: Application, financial need analysis, test scores, transcript, verification of Hopi Indian blood. *Deadline:* varies.

Contact: Theresa Lomakema, Financial Aid Processor/Monitor
Hopi Tribe
PO Box 123
Kykotsmovi, AZ 86039-0123
Phone: 928-734-3533
Fax: 928-734-9575
E-mail: info@hopi.nsn.us

HOPI EDUCATION AWARD

Grant provides financial support for eligible Hopi individuals pursuing postsecondary education. Minimum 2.5 CGPA required. Deadlines: April 1 for summer, July 1 for fall, and December 1 for spring.

Award: Scholarship for use in freshman, sophomore, junior, senior, graduate, or postgraduate years; renewable. *Number:* 1–400. *Amount:* $50–$2500.

Eligibility Requirements: Applicant must be American Indian/Alaska Native and enrolled or expecting to enroll full- or part-time at a two-year or four-year institution or university. Applicant must have 2.5 GPA or higher. Available to U.S. citizens.

Application Requirements: Application, financial need analysis, test scores, transcript, verification of Hopi Indian blood. *Deadline:* varies.

Contact: Theresa Lomakema, Financial Aid Processor/Monitor
Hopi Tribe
PO Box 123
Kykotsmovi, AZ 86039-0123
Phone: 928-734-3533
Fax: 928-734-9575
E-mail: info@hopi.nsn.us

HOPI SCHOLARSHIP

Scholarship awarded to eligible Hopi students on the basis of academic merit. Entering freshmen must be in the top 10 percent of their graduating class or score a minimum composite score of 930 on the SAT or a minimum of 21 on the ACT. Undergraduates must maintain a minimum 3.0 GPA for all undergraduate course work and other graduate, post graduate, and professional degree students must maintain a minimum 3.2 GPA for all graduate course work.

Award: Scholarship for use in freshman, sophomore, junior, senior, graduate, or postgraduate years; not renewable. *Number:* 25. *Amount:* up to $2500.

Eligibility Requirements: Applicant must be American Indian/Alaska Native and enrolled or expecting to enroll full-time at a four-year institution or university. Applicant must have 3.0 GPA or higher. Available to U.S. citizens.

Application Requirements: Application, financial need analysis, test scores, transcript, FAFSA. *Deadline:* varies.

Contact: Theresa Lomakema, Financial Aid Processor/Monitor
Hopi Tribe
PO Box 123
Kykotsmovi, AZ 86039-0123
Phone: 928-734-3533
Fax: 928-734-9575
E-mail: info@hopi.nsn.us

HTGSP GRANT AND TUITION/BOOK SCHOLARSHIP

Scholarship available to Hopi students pursuing post secondary education for reasons of personal growth, career enhancement/change, and/or continuing education for part-time students. Minimum cumulative GPA (CGPA) for undergraduates is 2.00; graduates, postgraduates, and professional degree students must be in good academic standing as defined by their university.

Award: Scholarship for use in freshman, sophomore, junior, senior, graduate, or postgraduate years; not renewable. *Number:* 30–50. *Amount:* up to $2500.

Eligibility Requirements: Applicant must be American Indian/Alaska Native and enrolled or expecting to enroll full- or part-time at a four-year institution or university. Available to U.S. citizens.

Application Requirements: Application, financial need analysis, test scores, transcript, FAFSA, Hopi enrollment form. *Deadline:* varies.

Contact: Theresa Lomakema, Financial Aid Processor/Monitor
Hopi Tribe
PO Box 123
Kykotsmovi, AZ 86039-0123
Phone: 928-734-3533
Fax: 928-734-9575
E-mail: info@hopi.nsn.us

TRIBAL PRIORITY AWARD

Scholarship provides financial support for eligible Hopi individuals pursuing postsecondary education. Minimum 3.0 GPA required.

Award: Scholarship for use in junior, senior, graduate, or postgraduate years; not renewable. *Number:* 1–5. *Amount:* $2500–$15,000.

Eligibility Requirements: Applicant must be American Indian/Alaska Native and enrolled or expecting to enroll full-time at a two-year or four-year institution or university. Applicant must have 3.0 GPA or higher. Available to U.S. citizens.

Application Requirements: Application, financial need analysis, interview, references, test scores, transcript, verification of Hopi Indian blood. *Deadline:* varies.

Contact: Theresa Lomakema, Financial Aid Processor/Monitor
Hopi Tribe
PO Box 123
Kykotsmovi, AZ 86039-0123
Phone: 928-734-3533
Fax: 928-734-9575
E-mail: info@hopi.nsn.us

HOUSTON COMMUNITY SERVICES

AZTECA SCHOLARSHIP

Scholarships are awarded annually to a male and a female high school senior planning to attend a university or a college as first-time, first-year students. Must be Texas resident.

Award: Scholarship for use in freshman year; not renewable. *Number:* 2. *Amount:* $500.

Eligibility Requirements: Applicant must be of Mexican heritage; Hispanic; high school student; planning to enroll or expecting to enroll full-time at a two-year or four-year institution or university and resident of Texas. Available to U.S. citizens.

Application Requirements: Application, essay, photo, transcript, income tax report, letter of acceptance. *Deadline:* March 28.

Contact: Edward Castillo, Coordinator
Houston Community Services
Centro Aztlan, 5115 Harrisburg Boulevard
Houston, TX 77011
Phone: 713-926-8771
E-mail: hcsaztlan@sbcglobal.net

HUGH FULTON BYAS MEMORIAL FUNDS INC.

HUGH FULTON BYAS MEMORIAL GRANT

Grant is awarded only to the U.K. citizens. Available only for college students. Dollar value of awards and number of available awards varies.

Award: Grant for use in sophomore, junior, senior, or graduate years; renewable. *Number:* varies. *Amount:* varies.

Eligibility Requirements: Applicant must be English, Scottish, or Welsh citizen and enrolled or expecting to enroll full-time at a four-year institution or university. Available to citizens of countries other than the U.S. or Canada.

Application Requirements: Application, document of U.K. passport. *Deadline:* varies.

Contact: Linda Maffei, Administrator
Hugh Fulton Byas Memorial Funds Inc.
261 Bradley Street
New Haven, CT 06511
Phone: 203-777-8356
Fax: 203-562-6288
E-mail: byasmfund@gmail.com

IDAHO STATE BOARD OF EDUCATION http://www.boardofed.idaho.gov

IDAHO MINORITY AND "AT RISK" STUDENT SCHOLARSHIP

• *See page 620*

INDIAN AMERICAN CULTURAL ASSOCIATION http://www.iasf.org

INDIAN AMERICAN SCHOLARSHIP FUND

Scholarships for descendents of families who are from modern-day India and are graduating from public or private high schools in Georgia. They must be enrolled in four-year colleges or universities. There are both academic and need-based awards available through this program.

Award: Scholarship for use in freshman year; renewable. *Number:* 3. *Amount:* $500–$5000.

Eligibility Requirements: Applicant must be of Indian heritage; Asian/Pacific Islander; high school student; planning to enroll or expecting to enroll full-time at a four-year institution or university and resident of Georgia. Applicant must have 3.0 GPA or higher. Available to U.S. citizens.

Application Requirements: Application, essay, financial need analysis, resume, test scores, transcript, IRS 1040 form. *Deadline:* varies.

Contact: Rajesh Kurup, Scholarship Coordinator
Indian American Cultural Association
2407 Waterford Cove
Decatur, GA 30126
E-mail: rajnina@mindspring.com

INTERNATIONAL ORDER OF THE KING'S DAUGHTERS AND SONS http://www.iokds.org

INTERNATIONAL ORDER OF THE KING'S DAUGHTERS AND SONS NORTH AMERICAN INDIAN SCHOLARSHIP

Scholarships available for Native American students. Proof of reservation registration, college acceptance letter, and financial aid office address required. Merit-based award. Send self-addressed stamped envelope. Must maintain minimum 2.5 GPA.

Award: Scholarship for use in freshman, sophomore, junior, or senior years; renewable. *Number:* 45–60. *Amount:* $500–$650.

Eligibility Requirements: Applicant must be American Indian/Alaska Native and enrolled or expecting to enroll full-time at a two-year or four-year or technical institution or university. Applicant must have 2.5 GPA or higher. Available to U.S. and Canadian citizens.

Application Requirements: Application, essay, financial need analysis, references, self-addressed stamped envelope, transcript, written documentation of reservation registration. *Deadline:* varies.

Contact: Director, North American Indian Department
International Order of the King's Daughters and Sons
PO Box 1017
Chautauqua, NY 14722-1040
Phone: 716-357-4951

INTERNATIONAL UNION OF BRICKLAYERS AND ALLIED CRAFTWORKERS http://www.bacweb.org

CANADIAN BATES SCHOLARSHIP PROGRAM

• *See page 537*

INTER-TRIBAL COUNCIL OF MICHIGAN INC. http://www.itcmi.org

MICHIGAN INDIAN TUITION WAIVER

Renewable award provides free tuition for Native-American of 1/4 or more blood degree who attend a Michigan public college or university. Must be a Michigan resident for at least one year. The tuition waiver program covers full-time, part-time or summer school student attending a public, state, community, junior college, public college, or public university. Deadline: continuous.

Award: Scholarship for use in freshman, sophomore, junior, senior, graduate, or postgraduate years; renewable. *Number:* varies. *Amount:* varies.

Eligibility Requirements: Applicant must be American Indian/Alaska Native; enrolled or expecting to enroll full- or part-time at a two-year or four-year or technical institution or university; resident of Michigan and studying in Michigan. Available to U.S. citizens.

Application Requirements: Application, driver's license, transcript, tribal certification, proof of residency. *Deadline:* continuous.

Contact: Christin McKerchie, Executive Assistant to Programs
Inter-Tribal Council of Michigan Inc.
2956 Ashmun Street, Suite A
Sault Ste. Marie, MI 49783
Phone: 906-632-6896 Ext. 136
Fax: 906-632-6878

INTERTRIBAL TIMBER COUNCIL http://www.itcnet.org

DICK FRENCH MEMORIAL SCHOLARSHIP PROGRAM

Program to assist Native American/Native Alaskan undergraduate or graduate student enrolled full-time at an accredited two- or four-year college or university.

Award: Scholarship for use in freshman, sophomore, junior, senior, or graduate years; not renewable. *Number:* 1. *Amount:* $500.

Eligibility Requirements: Applicant must be American Indian/Alaska Native and enrolled or expecting to enroll full-time at a two-year or four-year institution or university. Available to U.S. citizens.

Application Requirements: Application, references, transcript, federal tax records. *Deadline:* April 1.

Contact: Education Committee
Intertribal Timber Council
1112 21st Avenue, NE, Suite 4
Portland, OR 97232-2114
Phone: 503-282-4296
Fax: 503-282-1274
E-mail: itc1@teleport.com

IOWA COLLEGE FOUNDATION (ICF) http://www.iowacollegefoundation.org

IOWA COLLEGE FOUNDATION MINORITY SCHOLARSHIPS

Scholarships of $5000 to incoming minority students. Must be a resident of Iowa.

Award: Scholarship for use in freshman year; not renewable. *Number:* 20. *Amount:* $5000.

Eligibility Requirements: Applicant must be American Indian/Alaska Native, Asian/Pacific Islander, Black (non-Hispanic), or Hispanic; high school student; planning to enroll or expecting to enroll full- or part-time at a four-year institution or university and resident of Iowa. Available to U.S. citizens.

Iowa College Foundation (ICF) (continued)

Application Requirements: Application. *Deadline:* April 11.

Contact: Jack Jones, President
Iowa College Foundation (ICF)
505 Fifth Avenue, Suite 1034
Des Moines, IA 50309
Phone: 515-282-0473
Fax: 515-282-9508
E-mail: jack@iaicu-icf.edu

ITALIAN-AMERICAN CHAMBER OF COMMERCE MIDWEST http://www.italianchamber.us

ITALIAN-AMERICAN CHAMBER OF COMMERCE OF CHICAGO SCHOLARSHIP

One-time awards for Illinois residents of Italian descent. Available to high school seniors and college students for use at a four-year institution. Applicants must have a 3.5 GPA. Must reside in Cook, Du Page, Kane, Lake, McHenry, or Will counties of Illinois. Must submit a letter including a biographical account of themselves and two letters of recommendation, one from a teacher and one from their counselor.

Award: Scholarship for use in freshman, sophomore, junior, or senior years; not renewable. *Number:* 1. *Amount:* up to $1000.

Eligibility Requirements: Applicant must be of Italian heritage; enrolled or expecting to enroll full-time at a four-year institution and resident of Illinois. Applicant must have 3.5 GPA or higher. Available to U.S. and non-U.S. citizens.

Application Requirements: Application, autobiography, essay, photo, references, self-addressed stamped envelope, transcript. *Deadline:* May 31.

Contact: Frank Pugno, Scholarship Chairman
Italian-American Chamber of Commerce Midwest
30 South Michigan Avenue, Suite 504
Chicago, IL 60603
Phone: 312-553-9137 Ext. 13
Fax: 312-553-9142
E-mail: info.chicago@italchambers.net

JACKIE ROBINSON FOUNDATION http://www.jackierobinson.org

JACKIE ROBINSON SCHOLARSHIP

• *See page 601*

JEWISH FOUNDATION FOR EDUCATION OF WOMEN http://www.jfew.org

JFEW/UJA FEDERATION ROSE BILLER SCHOLARSHIPS

Students applying for these scholarships must be Jewish, permanent residents of and attending colleges or graduate or professional schools in New York City or the counties of Nassau, Suffolk or Westchester. Scholarships will not be granted to medical, dental or law students.

Award: Scholarship for use in freshman, sophomore, junior, senior, or graduate years; renewable. *Number:* varies. *Amount:* up to $5000.

Eligibility Requirements: Applicant must be Jewish; of Jewish heritage; enrolled or expecting to enroll full-time at a four-year institution or university; resident of New York and studying in New York. Available to U.S. citizens.

Application Requirements: Application, financial need analysis. *Deadline:* June 16.

Contact: Leonard Petlakh, Assistant Executive Director
Jewish Foundation for Education of Women
135 East 64th Street
New York, NY 10065
Phone: 212-288-3931
Fax: 212-288-5798
E-mail: info@jfew.org

KAISER PERMANENTE http://xnet.kp.org/hr/ca/kpapan

KAISER PERMANENTE ASIAN PACIFIC AMERICAN NETWORK SCHOLARSHIP PROGRAM

Award for graduating high school senior planning to attend college, university, trade or technical school. Must reside in Southern California and be of Asian descent. Minimum 3.25 GPA required.

Award: Scholarship for use in freshman year; not renewable. *Number:* 6. *Amount:* $1000–$2000.

Eligibility Requirements: Applicant must be Asian/Pacific Islander; high school student; planning to enroll or expecting to enroll full- or part-time at a two-year or four-year or technical institution or university and resident of California. Available to U.S. citizens.

Application Requirements: Application, essay, references, self-addressed stamped envelope, transcript. *Deadline:* April 15.

Contact: Pauline Tsai, Scholarship Committee
Kaiser Permanente
PO Box 950
Pasadena, CA 91102-0950
E-mail: pauline.b.tsai@kp.org

KANSAS BOARD OF REGENTS http://www.kansasregents.org

KANSAS ETHNIC MINORITY SCHOLARSHIP

Scholarship program designed to assist financially needy, academically competitive students who are identified as members of any of the following ethnic/racial groups: African-American, American Indian or Alaskan Native, Asian or Pacific Islander, or Hispanic. Priority is given to applicants who are freshman. For more details refer to Web site: http://www.kansasregents.org/financial_aid/minority.html.

Award: Scholarship for use in freshman, sophomore, junior, or senior years; renewable. *Number:* varies. *Amount:* up to $1850.

Eligibility Requirements: Applicant must be American Indian/Alaska Native, Asian/Pacific Islander, Black (non-Hispanic), or Hispanic; enrolled or expecting to enroll full-time at a two-year or four-year institution or university and studying in Kansas. Applicant must have 3.0 GPA or higher. Available to U.S. citizens.

Application Requirements: Application, financial need analysis, test scores. *Fee:* $10. *Deadline:* May 1.

Contact: Diane Lindeman, Director of Student Financial Assistance
Kansas Board of Regents
1000 Jackson, SW, Suite 520
Topeka, KS 66612-1368
Phone: 785-296-3517
Fax: 785-296-0983
E-mail: dlindeman@ksbor.org

KIMBO FOUNDATION http://www.kimbofoundation.org

KIMBO FOUNDATION SCHOLARSHIP

Scholarship available to Korean-American students only. Full time study only. Application deadline varies every year.

Award: Scholarship for use in freshman, sophomore, junior, senior, graduate, or postgraduate years; not renewable. *Number:* 30–50. *Amount:* $1500.

Eligibility Requirements: Applicant must be of Korean heritage; Asian/Pacific Islander and enrolled or expecting to enroll full-time at a two-year or four-year or technical institution or university. Available to citizens of countries other than the U.S. or Canada.

Application Requirements: Application, essay, references, transcript, copy of household income tax return. *Deadline:* varies.

Contact: Jennifer Chung, Program Coordinator
Kimbo Foundation
430 Shotwell Street
San Francisco, CA 94110
Phone: 415-285-4100
Fax: 415-285-4103
E-mail: info@kimbofoundation.org

KNIGHTS OF COLUMBUS http://www.kofc.org

FOURTH DEGREE PRO DEO AND PRO PATRIA (CANADA)

• *See page 539*

KONIAG EDUCATION FOUNDATION http://www.koniageducation.org

GLENN GODFREY MEMORIAL SCHOLARSHIP

Scholarship for sophomore, junior, or seniors in their undergraduate study. Applicants must be Alaska Native shareholders or descendants (may be adopted) of the Koniag Region. Must have and maintain a minimum cumulative GPA of 2.5.

Award: Scholarship for use in sophomore, junior, or senior years; not renewable. *Number:* 1. *Amount:* up to $5000.

Eligibility Requirements: Applicant must be American Indian/Alaska Native and enrolled or expecting to enroll full-time at a four-year institution or university. Applicant must have 2.5 GPA or higher. Available to U.S. citizens.

Application Requirements: Application, essay, interview, photo, resume, references, transcript, birth certificate (for descendants only). *Deadline:* varies.

Contact: Tyan Hayes, Executive Director
Koniag Education Foundation
6927 Old Seward Highway, Suite 103
Anchorage, AK 99518
Phone: 907-562-9093
Fax: 907-562-9023

KONIAG EDUCATION CAREER DEVELOPMENT GRANT

Applicants must be Alaska Native shareholders or descendents (may be adopted) of the Koniag Region. Applicants must be accepted or enrolled in a career development course and able to demonstrate how the training will assist the student in gaining employment or job security and/or advancement. Awards up to $1000.

Award: Grant for use in freshman year; not renewable. *Number:* 1. *Amount:* $1000.

Eligibility Requirements: Applicant must be American Indian/Alaska Native and enrolled or expecting to enroll part-time at a technical institution. Available to U.S. and non-Canadian citizens.

Application Requirements: Application, autobiography, resume. *Deadline:* varies.

Contact: Tyan Hayes, Executive Director
Koniag Education Foundation
6927 Old Seward Highway, Suite 103
Anchorage, AK 99518
Phone: 907-562-9093
Fax: 907-562-9023

KONIAG EDUCATION FOUNDATION ACADEMIC/GRADUATE SCHOLARSHIP

Scholarships to honor students who excel academically, and who show the potential to succeed in college studies. Applicants must be Alaska Native shareholders or descendents (may be adopted) of the Koniag Region. Deadlines: March 15 for summer term, June 1 for fall/spring terms.

Award: Scholarship for use in freshman, sophomore, junior, senior, graduate, or postgraduate years; not renewable. *Number:* 130–170. *Amount:* $500–$2500.

Eligibility Requirements: Applicant must be American Indian/Alaska Native and enrolled or expecting to enroll full- or part-time at a two-year or four-year or technical institution or university. Applicant must have 3.0 GPA or higher. Available to U.S. citizens.

Application Requirements: Application, autobiography, essay, financial need analysis, photo, references, transcript, proof of eligibility from Koniag Inc. *Deadline:* varies.

Contact: Tyan Hayes, Executive Director
Koniag Education Foundation
6927 Old Seward Highway, Suite 103
Anchorage, AK 99518
Phone: 907-562-9093
Fax: 907-562-9023

KONIAG EDUCATION FOUNDATION COLLEGE/UNIVERSITY BASIC SCHOLARSHIP

Scholarship to honor students who show the potential to succeed in college studies. Applicants must be Alaska Native shareholders or descendants (may be adopted) of the Koniag Region. Must maintain a minimum cumulative GPA of 2.0 or equivalent scores. Awarded up to $1000 a year. Deadlines: March 15 for summer term, June 1 for fall/spring terms.

Award: Scholarship for use in freshman, sophomore, junior, senior, graduate, or postgraduate years; not renewable. *Number:* varies. *Amount:* up to $1000.

Eligibility Requirements: Applicant must be American Indian/Alaska Native and enrolled or expecting to enroll full- or part-time at a two-year or four-year or technical institution or university. Available to U.S. citizens.

Application Requirements: Application, essay, references, transcript. *Deadline:* varies.

Contact: Tyan Hayes, Executive Director
Koniag Education Foundation
6927 Old Seward Highway, Suite 103
Anchorage, AK 99518
Phone: 907-562-9093
Fax: 907-562-9023

KOREAN AMERICAN SCHOLARSHIP FOUNDATION http://www.kasf.org

KOREAN-AMERICAN SCHOLARSHIP FOUNDATION EASTERN REGION SCHOLARSHIPS

Scholarships available to Korean-American and Korean students enrolled in a full-time undergraduate or graduate program in the United States. Selection based on financial need, academic achievement, school activities, and community services. Each applicant must submit an application to the respective KASF region. For more details and an application see Web site: http://www.kasf.org.

Award: Scholarship for use in freshman, sophomore, junior, senior, or graduate years; not renewable. *Number:* varies. *Amount:* $1000.

Eligibility Requirements: Applicant must be of Korean heritage; Asian/Pacific Islander; enrolled or expecting to enroll full-time at a four-year institution or university and studying in Delaware, District of Columbia, Kentucky, Maryland, North Carolina, Pennsylvania, Virginia, or West Virginia. Available to U.S. and non-U.S. citizens.

Application Requirements: Application, essay, financial need analysis, photo, references, self-addressed stamped envelope, transcript. *Deadline:* May 31.

Contact: Dr. Brandon Yi, Scholarship Committee
Korean American Scholarship Foundation
803 Russell Avenue, Suite 2C
Reston, VA 20879
E-mail: eastern@kasf.org

KOREAN-AMERICAN SCHOLARSHIP FOUNDATION NORTHEASTERN REGION SCHOLARSHIPS

Scholarships available to Korean-American and Korean students enrolled in a full-time undergraduate or graduate program in the United States. Selection based on financial need, academic achievement, school activities, and community services. Each applicant must submit an application to the respective KASF region. For more details and an application see Web site: http://www.kasf.org.

Award: Scholarship for use in freshman, sophomore, junior, senior, graduate, or postgraduate years; not renewable. *Number:* 60. *Amount:* $1000–$2500.

Eligibility Requirements: Applicant must be of Korean heritage; Asian/Pacific Islander; enrolled or expecting to enroll full-time at a

Korean American Scholarship Foundation (continued)

four-year institution or university and studying in Connecticut, Maine, Massachusetts, New Hampshire, New Jersey, New York, Rhode Island, or Vermont. Available to U.S. citizens.

Application Requirements: Application, essay, financial need analysis, photo, references, transcript. *Deadline:* June 23.

Contact: Mr. William Y. Kim, Scholarship Committee Chairman
Korean American Scholarship Foundation
51 West Overlook
Port Washington, NY 11050
Phone: 516-883-1142
Fax: 516-883-1964
E-mail: kim.william@gmail.com

KOREAN-AMERICAN SCHOLARSHIP FOUNDATION SOUTHERN REGION SCHOLARSHIPS

Scholarships available to Korean-American and Korean students enrolled in a full-time undergraduate or graduate program in the United States. Selection based on financial need, academic achievement, school activities, and community services. Each applicant must submit an application to the respective KASF region. For more details and an application see Web site: http://www.kasf.org.

Award: Scholarship for use in freshman, sophomore, junior, senior, or graduate years; not renewable. *Number:* up to 45. *Amount:* $1000.

Eligibility Requirements: Applicant must be of Korean heritage; Asian/Pacific Islander; enrolled or expecting to enroll full-time at a four-year institution or university and studying in Alabama, Arkansas, Florida, Georgia, Louisiana, Mississippi, North Carolina, Oklahoma, South Carolina, Tennessee, or Texas. Available to U.S. citizens.

Application Requirements: Application, essay, financial need analysis, photo, references, transcript. *Deadline:* June 10.

Contact: Dr. Sam Sook Chung, Scholarship Committee
Korean American Scholarship Foundation
2989 Preston Drive
Rex, GA 30273
Phone: 770-968-6768
E-mail: samsookchung@hotmail.com

KOREAN-AMERICAN SCHOLARSHIP FOUNDATION WESTERN REGION SCHOLARSHIPS

Scholarships available to Korean-American and Korean students enrolled in a full-time undergraduate or graduate program in the United States. Selection based on financial need, academic achievement, school activities, and community services. Each applicant must submit an application to the respective KASF region. For more details and an application see Web site: http://www.kasf.org.

Award: Scholarship for use in freshman, sophomore, junior, senior, or graduate years; not renewable. *Number:* varies. *Amount:* $2000.

Eligibility Requirements: Applicant must be of Korean heritage; Asian/Pacific Islander; enrolled or expecting to enroll full-time at a four-year institution or university and studying in Alaska, Arizona, California, Colorado, Hawaii, Idaho, Montana, Nevada, New Mexico, Oregon, Utah, or Washington. Applicant must have 3.0 GPA or higher. Available to U.S. citizens.

Application Requirements: Application, essay, financial need analysis, photo, references, transcript. *Deadline:* May 31.

Contact: KASF Western Regional Chapter
Korean American Scholarship Foundation
3435 Wilshire Boulevard, Suite 2450B
Los Angeles, CA 90010
Phone: 213-380-5273
Fax: 213-380-5273
E-mail: western@kasf.org

KOSCIUSZKO FOUNDATION http://www.kosciuszkofoundation.org

MASSACHUSETTS FEDERATION OF POLISH WOMEN'S CLUBS SCHOLARSHIPS

Nonrenewable award for sophomores, juniors, and seniors attending an accredited four-year college or university. Preference given to MFPWC members and children or grandchildren of members. In the event that no members apply, the scholarship may be awarded to residents of Massachusetts or New England. Must submit proof of Polish ancestry. Minimum 3.0 GPA required.

Award: Scholarship for use in sophomore, junior, or senior years; not renewable. *Number:* 3. *Amount:* $1250.

Eligibility Requirements: Applicant must be of Polish heritage; enrolled or expecting to enroll full-time at a four-year institution or university and resident of Massachusetts. Applicant must have 3.0 GPA or higher. Available to U.S. and non-Canadian citizens.

Application Requirements: Application, essay, financial need analysis, photo, references, transcript, proof of Polish ancestry. *Fee:* $35. *Deadline:* January 15.

Contact: Ms. Addy Tymczyszyn, Grants Department
Kosciuszko Foundation
15 East 65th Street
New York, NY 10021-6595
Phone: 212-734-2130 Ext. 210
Fax: 212-628-4552
E-mail: thekfaddy@aol.com

POLISH AMERICAN CLUB OF NORTH JERSEY SCHOLARSHIPS

Scholarships of $500 to $2000 awarded to qualified students for full-time undergraduate and graduate studies at accredited colleges and universities in the United States. The scholarship is renewable. U.S. citizens of Polish descent and Polish citizens with permanent residency status in the United States with minimum GPA of 3.0 are eligible.

Award: Scholarship for use in freshman, sophomore, junior, senior, or graduate years; renewable. *Number:* varies. *Amount:* $500–$2000.

Eligibility Requirements: Applicant must be of Polish heritage and enrolled or expecting to enroll full-time at a four-year institution or university. Applicant must have 3.0 GPA or higher. Available to U.S. and non-Canadian citizens.

Application Requirements: Application, photo, references, transcript, proof of Polish ancestry. *Fee:* $35. *Deadline:* January 15.

Contact: Addy Tymczyszyn, Director of Scholarships and Grants for Americans
Kosciuszko Foundation
15 East 65th Street
New York, NY 10021-6595
Phone: 212-734-2130 Ext. 210
Fax: 212-628-4552
E-mail: thekfaddy@aol.com

POLISH NATIONAL ALLIANCE OF BROOKLYN USA INC. SCHOLARSHIPS

Scholarships of $2000 available to qualified undergraduate students for full-time studies at accredited colleges and universities in the United States. U.S. citizens of Polish descent and Polish citizens with permanent residency status in the United States with minimum GPA of 3.0 are eligible.

Award: Scholarship for use in freshman, sophomore, junior, or senior years; not renewable. *Number:* 2–3. *Amount:* $2000.

Eligibility Requirements: Applicant must be of Polish heritage and enrolled or expecting to enroll full-time at a four-year institution or university. Applicant must have 3.0 GPA or higher. Available to U.S. and non-Canadian citizens.

Application Requirements: Application, photo, references, transcript, proof of Polish ancestry. *Fee:* $35. *Deadline:* January 15.

Contact: Addy Tymczyszyn, Director of Scholarships and Grants for Americans
Kosciuszko Foundation
15 East 65th Street
New York, NY 10021-6595
Phone: 212-734-2130 Ext. 210
Fax: 212-628-4552
E-mail: thekfaddy@aol.com

LATIN AMERICAN EDUCATIONAL FOUNDATION http://www.laef.org

LATIN AMERICAN EDUCATIONAL FOUNDATION SCHOLARSHIPS

Scholarship for Colorado residents of Hispanic heritage. Applicant should be accepted in an accredited college, university or vocational school. Must maintain a minimum GPA of 3.0.

Award: Scholarship for use in freshman, sophomore, junior, senior, or graduate years; not renewable. *Number:* varies. *Amount:* varies.

Eligibility Requirements: Applicant must be Hispanic and enrolled or expecting to enroll full-time at a four-year institution or university. Applicant must have 3.0 GPA or higher. Available to U.S. citizens.

Application Requirements: Application, essay, financial need analysis, interview, references, transcript. *Deadline:* March 1.

Contact: Scholarship Selection Committee
Latin American Educational Foundation
561 Santa Fe Drive
Denver, CO 80204

LEAGUE OF UNITED LATIN AMERICAN CITIZENS NATIONAL EDUCATIONAL SERVICE CENTERS INC. http://www.lnesc.org

LULAC NATIONAL SCHOLARSHIP FUND

Awards scholarships to Hispanic students who are enrolled or planning to enroll in accredited colleges or universities in the United States. Applicants must be U.S. citizens or legal residents. Scholarships may be used for the payment of tuition, academic fees, room, board and the purchase of required educational materials. For additional information visit Web site: http://www.lnesc.org to see a list of participating councils or send a self-addressed stamped envelope.

Award: Scholarship for use in freshman, sophomore, junior, or senior years; not renewable. *Number:* 1000. *Amount:* $250–$2000.

Eligibility Requirements: Applicant must be Hispanic and enrolled or expecting to enroll full-time at a two-year or four-year institution or university. Available to U.S. citizens.

Application Requirements: Application, autobiography, essay, financial need analysis, interview, references, self-addressed stamped envelope, test scores, transcript. *Deadline:* March 31.

Contact: Scholarship Coordinator
League of United Latin American Citizens National Educational Service Centers Inc.
2000 L Street, NW, Suite 610
Washington, DC 20036
Phone: 202-835-9646
Fax: 202-835-9685

LOS PADRES FOUNDATION http://www.lospadresfoundation.com

COLLEGE TUITION ASSISTANCE PROGRAM

Program for eligible students who are the first family member to attend college. Must be a legal resident or citizen of the U.S. and a resident of New York or New Jersey. Must have a 3.0 GPA. For further information, refer to Web site http://www.lospadresfoundation.com.

Award: Scholarship for use in freshman year; renewable. *Number:* 25–30. *Amount:* $2000–$3000.

Eligibility Requirements: Applicant must be Hispanic; high school student; planning to enroll or expecting to enroll full-time at a two-year or four-year institution or university and resident of New Jersey or New York. Applicant must have 3.0 GPA or higher. Available to U.S. citizens.

Application Requirements: Application, essay, financial need analysis, references, transcript. *Deadline:* June 1.

Contact: Scholarship Committee
Los Padres Foundation
PO Box 8421
McLean, VA 22106-0421
Phone: 877-843-7555
Fax: 866-810-1361
E-mail: lpfadmin@lospadresfoundation.com

SECOND CHANCE SCHOLARSHIPS

Scholarships granted to Puerto Rican/Latinos students who wish to return to college, trade school or apprenticeship program. Must be a resident of New York or New Jersey. Must demonstrate financial need. For further information, refer to Web site http://www.lospadresfoundation.com.

Award: Scholarship for use in freshman year; renewable. *Number:* 1–5. *Amount:* $2000.

Eligibility Requirements: Applicant must be of Hispanic heritage; high school student; planning to enroll or expecting to enroll full-time at a two-year or four-year or technical institution or university and resident of New Jersey or New York. Available to U.S. citizens.

Application Requirements: Application, essay, financial need analysis, interview, photo, references, transcript. *Deadline:* January 20.

Contact: Scholarship Committee
Los Padres Foundation
PO Box 8421
McLean, VA 22106-0421
Phone: 877-843-7555
Fax: 866-810-1361
E-mail: lpfadmin@lospadresfoundation.com

MAGIC JOHNSON FOUNDATION INC. http://www.magicjohnson.org

TAYLOR MICHAELS SCHOLARSHIP FUND

• *See page 602*

MENNONITE EDUCATION AGENCY http://www.mennoniteeducation.org

RACIAL/ETHNIC LEADERSHIP EDUCATION (RELE)

One-time grant for underrepresented minorities (especially people of color) who are not part of a recognized associate group in the Mennonite Church.

Award: Grant for use in freshman, sophomore, junior, or senior years; not renewable. *Number:* 6. *Amount:* $500.

Eligibility Requirements: Applicant must be American Indian/Alaska Native, Asian/Pacific Islander, Black (non-Hispanic), or Hispanic and enrolled or expecting to enroll full- or part-time at a two-year or four-year institution or university. Available to U.S. citizens.

Application Requirements: Application, financial need analysis, references. *Deadline:* continuous.

Contact: Carlos Romero, Executive Director
Mennonite Education Agency
63846 County Road 35, Suite 1
Goshen, IN 46528-9621
Phone: 574-642-3164
Fax: 574-642-4863
E-mail: info@mennoniteeducation.org

MENOMINEE INDIAN TRIBE OF WISCONSIN http://www.menominee-nsn.gov

MENOMINEE INDIAN TRIBE ADULT VOCATIONAL TRAINING PROGRAM

Renewable award for enrolled Menominee tribal members to use at vocational or technical schools. Must be at least 1/4 Menominee and show proof of Indian blood. Must complete financial aid form. Deadlines: March 1 and November 1.

Award: Grant for use in freshman or sophomore years; renewable. *Number:* 50–70. *Amount:* $100–$2200.

Eligibility Requirements: Applicant must be American Indian/Alaska Native and enrolled or expecting to enroll full- or part-time at a technical institution. Available to U.S. citizens.

Application Requirements: Application, financial need analysis, proof of Indian blood. *Deadline:* varies.

Contact: Virginia Nuske, Education Director
Menominee Indian Tribe of Wisconsin
PO Box 910
Keshena, WI 54135
Phone: 715-799-5110
Fax: 715-799-5102
E-mail: vnuske@mitw.org

MENOMINEE INDIAN TRIBE OF WISCONSIN HIGHER EDUCATION GRANTS

Renewable award for enrolled Menominee tribal member to use at a two- or four-year college or university. Must be at least 1/4 Menominee and show proof of Indian blood. Must complete financial aid form.

Award: Grant for use in freshman, sophomore, junior, or senior years; renewable. *Number:* 136. *Amount:* $100–$2200.

Eligibility Requirements: Applicant must be American Indian/Alaska Native and enrolled or expecting to enroll full- or part-time at a two-year or four-year institution or university. Available to U.S. citizens.

Menominee Indian Tribe of Wisconsin (continued)

Application Requirements: Application, financial need analysis, proof of Indian blood. *Deadline:* continuous.

Contact: Virginia Nuske, Education Director
Menominee Indian Tribe of Wisconsin
PO Box 910
Keshena, WI 54135
Phone: 715-799-5110
Fax: 715-799-5102
E-mail: vnuske@mitw.org

MINNESOTA HIGHER EDUCATION SERVICES OFFICE http://www.getreadyforcollege.org

MINNESOTA INDIAN SCHOLARSHIP

Scholarship for Minnesota residents who are one fourth or more American Indian ancestry and attending an eligible Minnesota postsecondary institution. Maximum award is $4000 for undergraduates and $6000 for graduates. Scholarships are limited to 3 years for certificate or AA/AS programs, 5 years for bachelor's degree programs, and 5 years for graduate programs. Applicants must maintain satisfactory academic progress, not be in default on student loans, and show need for a Pell or State Grant.

Award: Scholarship for use in freshman, sophomore, junior, senior, or graduate years; renewable. *Number:* 550. *Amount:* up to $6000.

Eligibility Requirements: Applicant must be American Indian/Alaska Native; enrolled or expecting to enroll full- or part-time at a two-year or four-year or technical institution or university; resident of Minnesota and studying in Minnesota. Available to U.S. citizens.

Application Requirements: Application, American Indian ancestry proof. *Deadline:* varies.

Contact: Grant Staff
Minnesota Higher Education Services Office
1450 Energy Park Drive, Suite 350
St. Paul, MN 55108
Phone: 651-642-0567 Ext. 1
Fax: 651-642-0675
E-mail: sandy.bowes@state.mn.us

MINNESOTA INDIAN SCHOLARSHIP OFFICE http://www.mheso.state.mn.us

MINNESOTA INDIAN SCHOLARSHIP PROGRAM

Applicant must be one quarter Native-American and a resident of Minnesota. Must re-apply for scholarship annually.

Award: Scholarship for use in freshman, sophomore, junior, senior, or graduate years; renewable. *Number:* 6–700. *Amount:* $4000–$6000.

Eligibility Requirements: Applicant must be American Indian/Alaska Native; enrolled or expecting to enroll full-time at a two-year or four-year or technical institution or university; resident of Minnesota and studying in Minnesota. Available to U.S. citizens.

Application Requirements: Application, financial need analysis. *Deadline:* July 1.

Contact: Yvonne Novack, Director
Minnesota Indian Scholarship Office
1500 Highway 36W
Roseville, MN 55113-4266
Phone: 800-657-3927
E-mail: cfl.indianeducation@state.mn.us

MISSOURI STATE DEPARTMENT OF ELEMENTARY/ SECONDARY EDUCATION http://www.dese.mo.gov

MINORITY TEACHING SCHOLARSHIP

Renewable scholarship of $3000 for up to four years for an undergraduate study. Applicant must be a Missouri resident. Number of awards varies.

Award: Scholarship for use in freshman, sophomore, junior, or senior years; renewable. *Number:* varies. *Amount:* $3000.

Eligibility Requirements: Applicant must be American Indian/Alaska Native, Asian/Pacific Islander, Black (non-Hispanic), or Hispanic; enrolled or expecting to enroll full- or part-time at a four-year institution or university and resident of Missouri. Applicant must have 3.0 GPA or higher. Available to U.S. citizens.

Application Requirements: Application, financial need analysis, references, transcript. *Deadline:* February 15.

Contact: Laura Harrison, Administrative Assistant
Missouri State Department of Elementary/Secondary Education
205 Jefferson Street, Seventh Floor
PO Box 480
Jefferson City, MO 65102
Phone: 573-751-1668
Fax: 573-526-3580
E-mail: laura.harrison@dese.mo.gov

MONGOLIA SOCIETY INC. http://www.mongoliasociety.org

DR. GOMBOJAB HANGIN MEMORIAL SCHOLARSHIP

One-time award for students of Mongolian heritage only. Must have permanent residency in Mongolia, the People's Republic of China, or the former Soviet Union. Award is for tuition at U.S. institutions. Upon conclusion of award year, recipient must write a report of his or her activities. Application requests must be in English and the application must be filled out in English. Write for application.

Award: Scholarship for use in freshman, sophomore, junior, senior, or graduate years; not renewable. *Number:* 1. *Amount:* up to $2400.

Eligibility Requirements: Applicant must be of Mongolian heritage and Chinese, Mongolian, or Russian citizen; Asian/Pacific Islander and enrolled or expecting to enroll full-time at a two-year or four-year or technical institution or university. Available to U.S. and non-U.S. citizens.

Application Requirements: Application, references, curriculum vitae, copy of ID card and passport. *Deadline:* January 1.

Contact: Susie Drost, Treasurer
Mongolia Society Inc.
Indiana University, 322 Goodbody Hall, 1011 East Third Street
Bloomington, IN 47405-7005
Phone: 815-855-4078
Fax: 815-855-7500
E-mail: monsoc@indiana.edu

NAACP LEGAL DEFENSE AND EDUCATIONAL FUND INC. http://www.naacpldf.org

HERBERT LEHMAN SCHOLARSHIP PROGRAM

Renewable award for successful African-American high school seniors and freshmen to attend a four-year college on a full-time basis. Candidates are required to be U.S. citizens and must have outstanding potential as evidenced by their high school academic records, test scores, and personal essays.

Award: Scholarship for use in freshman, sophomore, junior, or senior years; renewable. *Number:* 25–30. *Amount:* $2000.

Eligibility Requirements: Applicant must be Black (non-Hispanic) and enrolled or expecting to enroll full-time at a four-year institution or university. Available to U.S. citizens.

Application Requirements: Application, essay, photo, references, test scores, transcript. *Deadline:* April 30.

Contact: Michael Bagley, Program Director
NAACP Legal Defense and Educational Fund Inc.
99 Hudson Street, Suite 1600
New York, NY 10013
Phone: 212-965-2225
Fax: 212-219-1595

NANA (NORTHWEST ALASKA NATIVE ASSOCIATION) REGIONAL CORPORATION http://www.nana.com

ROBERT AQQALUK NEWLIN SR. MEMORIAL TRUST SCHOLARSHIP

Scholarship for NANA shareholders, descendants of NANA shareholders, or dependents of NANA shareholders or their descendants. Applicant must be enrolled or accepted for admittance at a postsecondary educational institution or vocational school.

Award: Scholarship for use in freshman, sophomore, junior, or senior years; not renewable. *Number:* 250–400. *Amount:* $1000–$2000.

Eligibility Requirements: Applicant must be American Indian/Alaska Native and enrolled or expecting to enroll full- or part-time at a two-year or four-year or technical institution or university. Available to U.S. citizens.

Application Requirements: Application, financial need analysis, references, transcript, college acceptance letter, enrollment proof. *Deadline:* varies.

Contact: Erica Nelson, Education Director
NANA (Northwest Alaska Native Association) Regional Corporation
PO Box 509
Kotzebue, AK 99752
Phone: 907-442-1607
Fax: 907-442-2289
E-mail: erica.nelson@nana.org

NATIONAL ASSOCIATION FOR CAMPUS ACTIVITIES http://www.naca.org

MULTICULTURAL SCHOLARSHIP PROGRAM

Scholarships will be given to applicants identified as African-American, Latina/Latino, Native-American, Asian-American or Pacific Islander ethnic minorities. A letter of recommendation affirming his/her ethnic minority status, his/her financial need, and that he/she will be in the campus activity field at least one year following the program for which a scholarship is being sought, should accompany applications.

Award: Scholarship for use in freshman, sophomore, junior, senior, or graduate years; not renewable. *Number:* up to 4. *Amount:* $250–$300.

Eligibility Requirements: Applicant must be American Indian/Alaska Native, Asian/Pacific Islander, Black (non-Hispanic), or Hispanic; enrolled or expecting to enroll full- or part-time at a two-year or four-year institution or university and must have an interest in leadership. Available to U.S. and non-U.S. citizens.

Application Requirements: Application, essay, financial need analysis, references. *Deadline:* May 1.

Contact: Dionne Ellison, Administrative Assistant
National Association for Campus Activities
13 Harbison Way
Columbia, SC 29212-3401
Phone: 803-732-6222 Ext. 131
Fax: 803-749-1047
E-mail: dionnee@naca.org

NATIONAL ASSOCIATION FOR THE ADVANCEMENT OF COLORED PEOPLE http://www.naacp.org

AGNES JONES JACKSON SCHOLARSHIP

• *See page 542*

ROY WILKINS SCHOLARSHIP

• *See page 543*

NATIONAL ASSOCIATION OF COLORED WOMEN'S CLUBS http://www.nacwc.org

HALLIE Q. BROWN SCHOLARSHIP

One-time $1000–$2000 scholarship for high school graduates who have completed at least one semester in a postsecondary accredited institution with a minimum "C" average.

Award: Scholarship for use in freshman year; not renewable. *Number:* 4–6. *Amount:* $1000–$2000.

Eligibility Requirements: Applicant must be Black (non-Hispanic); high school student and planning to enroll or expecting to enroll full-time at a two-year or four-year institution or university. Available to U.S. citizens.

Application Requirements: Application, references, transcript. *Deadline:* March 30.

Contact: Dr. Gerldine Jenkins, Program Coordinator
National Association of Colored Women's Clubs
Program Coordinator
Washington, DC 20009
Phone: 202-667-4080
Fax: 202-667-2574

NATIONAL ASSOCIATION OF NEGRO BUSINESS AND PROFESSIONAL WOMEN'S CLUBS INC. http://www.nanbpwc.org

NATIONAL SCHOLARSHIP

Scholarship for African-American graduating high school seniors with a minimum 3.0 GPA. Must submit 300-word essay on the topic "Why Education is Important to Me".

Award: Scholarship for use in freshman year; not renewable. *Number:* 6–8. *Amount:* $500–$1000.

Eligibility Requirements: Applicant must be Black (non-Hispanic); high school student and planning to enroll or expecting to enroll full-time at a four-year institution or university. Applicant must have 3.0 GPA or higher. Available to U.S. citizens.

Application Requirements: Application, essay, references, test scores, transcript. *Deadline:* March 1.

Contact: Twyla Whitby, National Director of Education Scholarship Program
National Association of Negro Business and Professional Women's Clubs Inc.
1806 New Hampshire Avenue, NW
Washington, DC 20009-3298
Phone: 202-483-4206
E-mail: info@nanbpwc.org

NATIONAL ITALIAN AMERICAN FOUNDATION http://www.niaf.org

EMANUELE AND EMILIA INGLESE MEMORIAL SCHOLARSHIP

Scholarship available to Italian American undergraduate students who trace their lineage to the Lombardy region, and who are the first generation of their family to attend college. Applicants must have a 3.0 or higher GPA and financial need. Applicants must be enrolled in an accredited institution of higher education and be a United States citizen or a permanent resident alien.

Award: Scholarship for use in freshman, sophomore, junior, or senior years; not renewable. *Number:* 1. *Amount:* $2500.

Eligibility Requirements: Applicant must be of Italian heritage and enrolled or expecting to enroll full- or part-time at a two-year or four-year or technical institution or university. Applicant must have 3.0 GPA or higher. Available to U.S. citizens.

Application Requirements: Application, transcript. *Deadline:* March 7.

Contact: Elissa Ruffino, Director of Communications and Public Relations
National Italian American Foundation
1860 19th Street, NW
Washington, DC 20009
Phone: 202-939-3106 Ext. 135
E-mail: elissa@niaf.org

NATIONAL ITALIAN AMERICAN FOUNDATION CATEGORY I SCHOLARSHIP

Award available to Italian-American students who have outstanding potential and high academic achievements. Minimum 3.5 GPA required. Must be a U.S. citizen and be enrolled in an accredited institution of higher education. Application can only be submitted online. For further information, deadlines, and online application visit Web site: http://www.niaf.org/scholarships/index.asp.

Award: Scholarship for use in freshman, sophomore, junior, senior, graduate, or postgraduate years; not renewable. *Number:* varies. *Amount:* $2500–$10,000.

Eligibility Requirements: Applicant must be of Italian heritage and enrolled or expecting to enroll full- or part-time at a four-year institution or university. Applicant must have 3.5 GPA or higher. Available to U.S. citizens.

National Italian American Foundation (continued)

Application Requirements: Application, essay, references, transcript. *Deadline:* March 7.

Contact: Miss. Molly Conti, Program Assistant, Education and Culture Programs
National Italian American Foundation
1860 19th Street, NW
Washington, DC 20009
Phone: 202-939-3119
Fax: 202-483-2618
E-mail: mconti@niaf.org

NATIONAL SOCIETY DAUGHTERS OF THE AMERICAN REVOLUTION http://www.dar.org

NATIONAL SOCIETY DAUGHTERS OF THE AMERICAN REVOLUTION AMERICAN INDIAN SCHOLARSHIP

One-time scholarship available to Native Americans. All awards are judged based on financial need and academic achievement. Undergraduate students are given preference. GPA of 2.75 or higher is required. Deadlines: April 1 for fall term and October 1 for spring term.

Award: Scholarship for use in freshman, sophomore, junior, senior, or graduate years; not renewable. *Number:* varies. *Amount:* $500.

Eligibility Requirements: Applicant must be American Indian/Alaska Native and enrolled or expecting to enroll full-time at a two-year or four-year or technical institution or university. Available to U.S. citizens.

Application Requirements: Application, self-addressed stamped envelope, proof of American Indian blood. *Deadline:* varies.

Contact: Eric Weisz, Manager, Office of the Reporter General
National Society Daughters of the American Revolution
1776 D Street, NW
Washington, DC 20006-5303
Phone: 202-628-1776
Fax: 202-879-3348
E-mail: nsdarscholarships@dar.org

NATIONAL SOCIETY DAUGHTERS OF THE AMERICAN REVOLUTION FRANCES CRAWFORD MARVIN AMERICAN INDIAN SCHOLARSHIP

Nonrenewable award available for a Native American to attend any two- or four-year college or university. Must demonstrate financial need, academic achievement, and have a 3.0 GPA or higher. Must submit a self-addressed stamped envelope to be considered.

Award: Scholarship for use in freshman, sophomore, junior, or senior years; not renewable. *Number:* 1. *Amount:* varies.

Eligibility Requirements: Applicant must be American Indian/Alaska Native and enrolled or expecting to enroll full-time at a two-year or four-year institution or university. Applicant must have 3.0 GPA or higher. Available to U.S. citizens.

Application Requirements: Application, financial need analysis, self-addressed stamped envelope, transcript, letter or proof papers. *Deadline:* February 1.

Contact: Eric Weisz, Manager, Office of the Reporter General
National Society Daughters of the American Revolution
1776 D Street, NW
Washington, DC 20006-5303
Phone: 202-628-1776
Fax: 202-879-3348
E-mail: nsdarscholarships@dar.org

NATIONAL UNION OF PUBLIC AND GENERAL EMPLOYEES http://www.nupge.ca

SCHOLARSHIP FOR ABORIGINAL CANADIANS

• *See page 547*

SCHOLARSHIP FOR VISIBLE MINORITIES

• *See page 547*

TERRY FOX MEMORIAL SCHOLARSHIP

• *See page 547*

TOMMY DOUGLAS SCHOLARSHIP

• *See page 548*

NATIONAL WELSH-AMERICAN FOUNDATION http://www.wales-usa.org

EXCHANGE SCHOLARSHIP

Limited to colleges/universities in Wales only. Applicant must have a Welsh background through birth and be willing to promote Welsh-American relations both here and abroad. Requested to consider becoming a member of NWAF upon completion of study. Required to complete four-year college study in United States. Applicant must be 21 years of age or older.

Award: Scholarship for use in freshman, sophomore, junior, senior, or graduate years; not renewable. *Number:* 1. *Amount:* $5000.

Eligibility Requirements: Applicant must be of Welsh heritage; age 21 and over and enrolled or expecting to enroll full-time at a four-year institution or university. Available to U.S. citizens.

Application Requirements: Application, autobiography, references, test scores. *Deadline:* March 1.

Contact: Donna Lloyd-Kolkin, Scholarship Committee
National Welsh-American Foundation
143 Sunny Hillside Road
Benton, PA 17814-7822
Phone: 570-925-6923
Fax: 570-925-6735
E-mail: nwaf@epix.net

NATIVE VISION FUND http://www.nativevision.org

NATIVE VISION

Scholarship available to any American Indian high school senior who has been accepted to college.

Award: Scholarship for use in freshman year; not renewable. *Number:* 2. *Amount:* $5000.

Eligibility Requirements: Applicant must be American Indian/Alaska Native; high school student and planning to enroll or expecting to enroll full-time at a four-year institution or university. Applicant must have 3.0 GPA or higher. Available to U.S. and non-U.S. citizens.

Application Requirements: Application, essay, references, transcript. *Deadline:* May 1.

Contact: Marlena Hammen, Scholarship Coordinator
Native Vision Fund
621 North Washington Street
Baltimore, MD 21205
Phone: 410-955-6931
Fax: 410-955-2010
E-mail: mhammen@jhsph.edu

NEW YORK STATE HIGHER EDUCATION SERVICES CORPORATION http://www.hesc.com

NEW YORK STATE AID TO NATIVE AMERICANS

Award for enrolled members of a New York State tribe and their children who are attending or planning to attend a New York State college and who are New York State residents. Deadlines: July 15 for the fall semester, December 31 for the spring semester, and May 20 for summer session.

Award: Scholarship for use in freshman, sophomore, junior, or senior years; renewable. *Number:* varies. *Amount:* $85–$2000.

Eligibility Requirements: Applicant must be American Indian/Alaska Native; enrolled or expecting to enroll full- or part-time at a two-year or four-year or technical institution or university; resident of New York and studying in New York. Available to U.S. citizens.

Application Requirements: Application, financial need analysis, references, transcript. *Deadline:* varies.

Contact: Native American Education Unit
New York State Higher Education Services Corporation
EBA Room 475
Albany, NY 12234
Phone: 518-474-0537

NEXTGEN NETWORK INC. http://www.nextgennetwork.com

DONNA JAMISON LAGO MEMORIAL SCHOLARSHIP

Awards to assist with future educational expenses of African-American, U.S. citizens. The essay competition is open to those who would complete their studies in that current year. Applicants must be seeking acceptance to an accredited U.S. college or university. The essay competition encourages high school seniors to think critically about important issues that affect their lives.

Award: Scholarship for use in freshman year; not renewable. *Number:* 9. *Amount:* $500–$2500.

Eligibility Requirements: Applicant must be Black (non-Hispanic); high school student; planning to enroll or expecting to enroll full-time at a two-year or four-year institution or university and must have an interest in writing. Available to U.S. citizens.

Application Requirements: Application, applicant must enter a contest, autobiography, essay, photo, references. *Deadline:* May 30.

Contact: Mr. K.J. Mburu, Scholarship Committee
NextGen Network Inc.
1010 Wisconsin Avenue, NW, Suite 430
Washington, DC 20007
Phone: 202-686-9260 Ext. 101
Fax: 202-944-3322
E-mail: info@nextgennetwork.com

NISEI STUDENT RELOCATION COMMEMORATIVE FUND http://www.nsrcfund.org

NISEI STUDENT RELOCATION COMMEMORATIVE FUND

Scholarships are made available to graduating high school seniors who are SE Asian refugees or children of refugees. Scholarship value is $1000. Deadline varies.

Award: Scholarship for use in freshman year; not renewable. *Number:* up to 5. *Amount:* up to $1000.

Eligibility Requirements: Applicant must be Asian/Pacific Islander; high school student and planning to enroll or expecting to enroll full-time at a two-year or four-year or technical institution or university. Available to U.S. citizens.

Application Requirements: Application, autobiography, essay, financial need analysis, references, test scores, transcript. *Deadline:* varies.

Contact: Jean Hibino, Executive Secretary
Nisei Student Relocation Commemorative Fund
19 Scenic Drive
Portland, CT 06480
E-mail: jeanhibino@aol.com

NORTHERN CHEYENNE TRIBAL EDUCATION DEPARTMENT

HIGHER EDUCATION SCHOLARSHIP PROGRAM

Scholarships will be provided for enrolled Northern Cheyenne Tribal members who meet the requirements listed in the higher education guidelines. Must be U.S. citizen enrolled in a postsecondary institution. Minimum 2.0 GPA required.

Award: Scholarship for use in freshman, sophomore, junior, or senior years; renewable. *Number:* 72. *Amount:* $50–$6000.

Eligibility Requirements: Applicant must be American Indian/Alaska Native and enrolled or expecting to enroll full- or part-time at a two-year or four-year institution or university. Available to U.S. citizens.

Application Requirements: Application, essay, financial need analysis, references, test scores, transcript. *Deadline:* March 1.

Contact: Norma Bixby, Director
Northern Cheyenne Tribal Education Department
PO Box 307
Lame Deer, MT 59043
Phone: 406-477-6602
Fax: 406-477-8150
E-mail: norma@rangeweb.net

OFFICE OF NAVAJO NATION SCHOLARSHIP AND FINANCIAL ASSISTANCE http://www.onnsfa.org

CHIEF MANUELITO SCHOLARSHIP PROGRAM

Award programs established to recognize and award undergraduate students with high test scores and GPA of 3.0. Priorities to Navajo Nation applicants. Must be enrolled as a full-time undergraduate and pursue a degree program leading to a baccalaureate. For further details visit Web Site: http://www.onnsfa.org/docs/polproc.pdf.

Award: Scholarship for use in freshman, sophomore, junior, or senior years; not renewable. *Number:* 1. *Amount:* $7000.

Eligibility Requirements: Applicant must be American Indian/Alaska Native and enrolled or expecting to enroll full-time at a two-year or four-year institution or university. Applicant must have 3.0 GPA or higher. Available to U.S. citizens.

Application Requirements: Application, financial need analysis, test scores, transcript. *Deadline:* April 1.

Contact: Maxine Damon Sr., Financial Aid Counselor
Office of Navajo Nation Scholarship and Financial Assistance
PO Box 1870
Window Rock, AZ 86515-1870
Phone: 800-243-2956
Fax: 928-871-6561
E-mail: maxinedamon@navajo.org

ONEIDA TRIBE OF INDIANS OF WISCONSIN http://www.oneidanation.org

ONEIDA HIGHER EDUCATION GRANT PROGRAM

Renewable award available to enrolled members of the Oneida Tribe of Indians of Wisconsin, who are accepted into an accredited postsecondary institution within the United States. Have a high school diploma, HSED or GED.

Award: Grant for use in freshman, sophomore, junior, senior, graduate, or postgraduate years; renewable. *Number:* 1000. *Amount:* up to $20,000.

Eligibility Requirements: Applicant must be American Indian/Alaska Native; enrolled or expecting to enroll full- or part-time at a four-year or technical institution or university and resident of Wisconsin. Applicant must have 3.0 GPA or higher. Available to U.S. citizens.

Application Requirements: Application, financial need analysis, Oneida tribal enrollment. *Deadline:* April 15.

Contact: Cheryl Van Den Berg, Higher Education Director
Oneida Tribe of Indians of Wisconsin
PO Box 365
Oneida, WI 54155
Phone: 800-236-2214 Ext. 4033
Fax: 920-869-4039
E-mail: cvanden2@oneidanation.org

OREGON NATIVE AMERICAN CHAMBER OF COMMERCE SCHOLARSHIP http://www.onacc.org

OREGON NATIVE AMERICAN CHAMBER OF COMMERCE SCHOLARSHIP

Scholarships available to Native American students studying in Oregon. Must verify Native American status and be actively involved in the Native American community.

Award: Scholarship for use in freshman, sophomore, junior, or senior years; not renewable. *Number:* 1. *Amount:* $1000.

Eligibility Requirements: Applicant must be American Indian/Alaska Native; enrolled or expecting to enroll full- or part-time at a four-year institution or university and studying in Oregon. Available to U.S. and Canadian citizens.

Application Requirements: Application, transcript, proof of Native American descent. *Deadline:* varies.

Contact: Kelly Anne Ilagan, Secretary
Oregon Native American Chamber of Commerce Scholarship
PO Box 82068
Portland, OR 97282
Phone: 503-654-2138
E-mail: kellyanne@onacc.org

OREGON STUDENT ASSISTANCE COMMISSION http://www.osac.state.or.us

VERL AND DOROTHY MILLER NATIVE AMERICAN VOCATIONAL SCHOLARSHIP

Scholarship available to students of Native American ancestry. Must plan to enroll full-time in trade or vocational study at eligible institutions. Must submit certification of tribal enrollment or Indian ancestry.

Award: Scholarship for use in freshman or sophomore years; renewable. *Number:* varies. *Amount:* varies.

Oregon Student Assistance Commission (continued)

Eligibility Requirements: Applicant must be American Indian/Alaska Native; enrolled or expecting to enroll full-time at a two-year or four-year or technical institution and resident of Oregon. Available to U.S. citizens.

Application Requirements: Application, essay, financial need analysis, transcript, certification of Native American ancestry, tribal enrollment card, Johnson O'Malley student eligibility form, letter from tribe stating blood quantum. *Deadline:* March 1.

Contact: Director of Grant Programs
Oregon Student Assistance Commission
1500 Valley River Drive, Suite 100
Eugene, OR 97401-7020
Phone: 800-452-8807 Ext. 7395

ORGANIZATION OF CHINESE AMERICANS

http://www.ocanatl.org

GATES MILLENNIUM SCHOLARS

Award enables Asian Pacific Islander American students to complete an undergraduate and graduate education. Must be entering a U.S. accredited college or university as a full-time degree-seeking student. Minimum 3.3 GPA required. Must demonstrate leadership abilities. Must meet federal Pell Grant eligibility criteria. Visit Web site at http://www.gmsp.org.

Award: Scholarship for use in freshman, sophomore, junior, senior, or graduate years; renewable. *Number:* 1000. *Amount:* varies.

Eligibility Requirements: Applicant must be Asian/Pacific Islander and enrolled or expecting to enroll full-time at a four-year institution or university. Available to U.S. citizens.

Application Requirements: Application, essay, financial need analysis, test scores, transcript, nomination packet. *Deadline:* January 11.

Contact: Kara Sukumoto, Outreach Coordinator
Organization of Chinese Americans
1900 L Street, NW, Suite 210
Washington, DC 20036
Phone: 202-530-8894 Ext. 2
Fax: 202-530-0643
E-mail: gmsoutreach@apiasf.com

OCA-AXA ACHIEVEMENT SCHOLARSHIP

A college achievement scholarship for Asian Pacific Americans entering their first year of college. For full-time study only. Must have an minimum GPA of 3.0.

Award: Scholarship for use in freshman year; not renewable. *Number:* 10. *Amount:* $2000.

Eligibility Requirements: Applicant must be Asian/Pacific Islander; high school student and planning to enroll or expecting to enroll full-time at a two-year or four-year institution or university. Applicant must have 3.0 GPA or higher. Available to U.S. citizens.

Application Requirements: Application, essay, financial need analysis, self-addressed stamped envelope, transcript. *Deadline:* April 18.

Contact: Scholarship Coordinator
Organization of Chinese Americans
1001 Connecticut Avenue, NW, Suite 601
Washington, DC 20036
Phone: 202-223-5500
Fax: 202-296-0540
E-mail: oca@ocanational.org

OCA/UPS FOUNDATION GOLD MOUNTAIN SCHOLARSHIP

Scholarships for Asian Pacific Americans who are the first person in their immediate family to attend college. Must be entering first year of college in the upcoming fall. Winners attend OCA National Convention.

Award: Scholarship for use in freshman year; not renewable. *Number:* 12. *Amount:* $2000.

Eligibility Requirements: Applicant must be Asian/Pacific Islander; high school student and planning to enroll or expecting to enroll full-time at a two-year or four-year institution or university. Applicant must have 3.0 GPA or higher. Available to U.S. citizens.

Application Requirements: Application, essay, financial need analysis, resume, self-addressed stamped envelope, transcript. *Deadline:* April 18.

Contact: Scholarship Coordinator
Organization of Chinese Americans
1001 Connecticut Avenue, NW, Suite 601
Washington, DC 20036
Phone: 202-223-5500
Fax: 202-296-0540
E-mail: oca@ocanational.org

OCA-VERIZON SCHOLARSHIP

Scholarships for Asian Pacific Americans who are financially disadvantaged and will be entering their first year of college. For full-time study only.

Award: Scholarship for use in freshman year; not renewable. *Number:* 20–25. *Amount:* $1500–$2000.

Eligibility Requirements: Applicant must be Asian/Pacific Islander; high school student and planning to enroll or expecting to enroll full-time at a two-year or four-year institution or university. Applicant must have 3.0 GPA or higher. Available to U.S. citizens.

Application Requirements: Application, essay, financial need analysis, self-addressed stamped envelope, transcript. *Deadline:* April 18.

Contact: Scholarship Coordinator
Organization of Chinese Americans
1001 Connecticut Avenue, NW, Suite 601
Washington, DC 20036
Phone: 202-223-5500
E-mail: oca@ocanatl.org

OSAGE SCHOLARSHIP FUND

MAE LASSLEY OSAGE SCHOLARSHIP FUND

Renewable awards to Osage Indian Tribe members who are members of the Roman Catholic Church. Must attend an accredited college or university as an undergraduate or graduate student on a full-time basis. Minimum 2.5 GPA required.

Award: Scholarship for use in freshman, sophomore, junior, senior, or graduate years; renewable. *Number:* 12–20. *Amount:* $500–$1000.

Eligibility Requirements: Applicant must be Roman Catholic; American Indian/Alaska Native and enrolled or expecting to enroll full-time at a two-year or four-year institution or university. Applicant must have 2.5 GPA or higher. Available to U.S. citizens.

Application Requirements: Application, financial need analysis, references, transcript, CDIB card. *Deadline:* April 15.

Contact: Scholarship Committee
Osage Scholarship Fund
PO Box 690240
Tulsa, OK 74169
Phone: 918-294-1904 Ext. 4928
Fax: 918-294-0920

OSAGE TRIBAL EDUCATION COMMITTEE

OSAGE TRIBAL EDUCATION COMMITTEE SCHOLARSHIP

Available for Osage Tribal members only. 150 to 250 renewable scholarship awards. Spring Deadline: December 31; Fall Deadline: July 1; Summer Deadline: May 1.

Award: Scholarship for use in freshman, sophomore, junior, or senior years; renewable. *Number:* 150–250. *Amount:* $200.

Eligibility Requirements: Applicant must be American Indian/Alaska Native and enrolled or expecting to enroll full- or part-time at a two-year or four-year or technical institution or university. Applicant must have 2.5 GPA or higher. Available to U.S. and non-U.S. citizens.

Application Requirements: Application, essay, photo, references, transcript. *Deadline:* varies.

Contact: Cheryl Lewis, Business Manager
Osage Tribal Education Committee
4149 Highline Boulevard, Suite 380
Oklahoma City, OK 73108
Phone: 405-605-6051 Ext. 304
Fax: 405-605-6057

OSAGE TRIBAL EDUCATION DEPARTMENT http://www.osagetribe.com/education

OSAGE HIGHER EDUCATION SCHOLARSHIP

Award available only to those who have proof of Osage Indian descent. Must submit proof of financial need. Deadlines: July 1 for fall, December 31 for spring, May 1 for summer.

Award: Scholarship for use in freshman, sophomore, junior, senior, graduate, or postgraduate years; renewable. *Number:* up to 1000. *Amount:* $1200–$2100.

Eligibility Requirements: Applicant must be American Indian/Alaska Native and enrolled or expecting to enroll full- or part-time at a two-year or four-year institution or university. Available to U.S. citizens.

Application Requirements: Application, financial need analysis, transcript, verification of enrollment, Osage Indian descent proof, copy of CDIB card, copy of membership card. *Deadline:* varies.

Contact: Jennifer Holding, Scholarship Coordinator
Osage Tribal Education Department
HC 66, PO Box 900
Hominy, OK 74035
Phone: 800-390-6724
Fax: 918-287-5567
E-mail: jholding@osagetribe.org

PETER AND ALICE KOOMRUIAN FUND

PETER AND ALICE KOOMRUIAN ARMENIAN EDUCATION FUND

Award for students of Armenian descent to pursue postsecondary studies in any field at any accredited college or university in the U.S. Submit student identification and letter of enrollment. Must rank in upper third of class or have minimum GPA of 3.0.

Award: Scholarship for use in freshman, sophomore, junior, senior, graduate, or postgraduate years; not renewable. *Number:* 5–20. *Amount:* $1000–$2250.

Eligibility Requirements: Applicant must be of Armenian heritage and enrolled or expecting to enroll full-time at a two-year or four-year institution or university. Applicant must have 3.0 GPA or higher. Available to U.S. and non-U.S. citizens.

Application Requirements: Application, photo, references, self-addressed stamped envelope, transcript, school ID, current enrollment letter. *Deadline:* April 15.

Contact: Mr. Terenik Koujakian, Awards Committee Member
Peter and Alice Koomruian Fund
15915 Ventura Boulevard, Suite P-1
Encino, CA 91436
Phone: 818-990-7454
E-mail: terenikkoujakian@hotmail.com

PETER DOCTOR MEMORIAL INDIAN SCHOLARSHIP FOUNDATION INC.

PETER DOCTOR MEMORIAL IROQUOIS SCHOLARSHIP

One-time award available to enrolled New York state Iroquois Indian students. Must be a full-time student at the sophomore level or above.

Award: Scholarship for use in sophomore, junior, senior, or graduate years; not renewable. *Number:* varies. *Amount:* $700–$1500.

Eligibility Requirements: Applicant must be American Indian/Alaska Native; enrolled or expecting to enroll full-time at a two-year or four-year or technical institution or university and resident of New York. Available to U.S. citizens.

Application Requirements: Application, autobiography, financial need analysis, references, tribal certification. *Deadline:* May 31.

Contact: Clara Hill, Treasurer
Peter Doctor Memorial Indian Scholarship Foundation Inc.
PO Box 431
Basom, NY 14013
Phone: 716-542-2025
E-mail: cehill@wnynet.net

PHILIPINO-AMERICAN ASSOCIATION OF NEW ENGLAND http://www.pamas.org

BLESSED LEON OF OUR LADY OF THE ROSARY AWARD

Award for any Filipino-American high school student. Must be of Filipino descent, and have a minimum GPA of 3.3. Application details URL: http://www.pamas.org.

Award: Scholarship for use in freshman year; not renewable. *Number:* 1. *Amount:* $250.

Eligibility Requirements: Applicant must be Asian/Pacific Islander; high school student; planning to enroll or expecting to enroll full-time at a two-year or four-year or technical institution or university and resident of Connecticut, Maine, Massachusetts, New Hampshire, Rhode Island, or Vermont. Available to U.S. citizens.

Application Requirements: Application, essay, references, transcript, college acceptance letter. *Deadline:* May 31.

Contact: Amanda Kalb, First Vice President
Philipino-American Association of New England
Quincy Post Office
PO Box 690372
Quincy, MA 02269-0372
Phone: 617-471-3513
E-mail: balic2ss@comcast.net

PAMAS RESTRICTED SCHOLARSHIP AWARD

• *See page 552*

RAVENSCROFT FAMILY AWARD

Award for any Filipino-American high school student, who is active in the Filipino community. Must be of Filipino descent, a resident of New England, and have a minimum GPA of 3.3. Application details URL: http://www.pamas.org.

Award: Scholarship for use in freshman year; not renewable. *Number:* 1. *Amount:* $250.

Eligibility Requirements: Applicant must be Asian/Pacific Islander; high school student; planning to enroll or expecting to enroll full-time at a four-year institution or university and resident of Connecticut, Maine, Massachusetts, New Hampshire, Rhode Island, or Vermont. Available to U.S. citizens.

Application Requirements: Application, essay, references, transcript, college acceptance letter. *Deadline:* May 31.

Contact: Amanda Kalb, First Vice President
Philipino-American Association of New England
Quincy Post Office
PO Box 690372
Quincy, MA 02269-0372
Phone: 617-471-3513
E-mail: balic2ss@comcast.net

POLISH HERITAGE ASSOCIATION OF MARYLAND http://www.pha-md.org

DR KENNETH AND NANCY WILLIAMS SCHOLARSHIP

Scholarship available for study towards a baccalaureate degree in a college or university in the United States. Must be of Polish descent (at least two Polish grandparents), resident of Maryland, and a U.S. citizen.

Award: Scholarship for use in freshman, sophomore, junior, or senior years; not renewable. *Number:* 1. *Amount:* up to $1000.

Eligibility Requirements: Applicant must be of Polish heritage; enrolled or expecting to enroll full-time at a two-year or four-year institution or university and resident of Maryland. Available to U.S. citizens.

Application Requirements: Application, financial need analysis, references, transcript. *Deadline:* March 31.

Contact: Thomas Hollowak, Scholarship Committee Chair
Polish Heritage Association of Maryland
Seven Dendron Court
Parkville, MD 21234
Phone: 410-837-4268
E-mail: thollowak@ubalt.edu

POLISH HERITAGE SCHOLARSHIP

Scholarships given to individuals of Polish descent (at least two Polish grandparents) who demonstrates academic excellence, financial need, and promotes their Polish Heritage. Must be a legal Maryland resident. Scholarship value is $1500.

Polish Heritage Association of Maryland (continued)

Award: Scholarship for use in freshman, sophomore, junior, or senior years; not renewable. *Number:* 1. *Amount:* up to $1500.

Eligibility Requirements: Applicant must be of Polish heritage; enrolled or expecting to enroll full-time at a two-year or four-year institution or university and resident of Maryland. Applicant must have 3.0 GPA or higher. Available to U.S. citizens.

Application Requirements: Application, essay, financial need analysis, interview, photo, references, transcript. *Deadline:* March 31.

Contact: Thomas Hollowak, Scholarship Chair
Polish Heritage Association of Maryland
Seven Dendron Court
Baltimore, MD 21234
Phone: 410-837-4268
Fax: 410-668-2513
E-mail: thollowalk@ubmail.ubalt.edu

POLISH NATIONAL ALLIANCE http://www.pna-znp.org

POLISH NATIONAL ALLIANCE SCHOLARSHIP AWARD

• *See page 553*

POLISH WOMEN'S ALLIANCE http://www.pwaa.org

POLISH WOMEN'S ALLIANCE SCHOLARSHIP

Scholarships are given to members of the Polish Women's Alliance of America who have been in good standing for five years. May apply during their sophomore and junior year of full-time undergraduate study. Awards are given on the junior and senior year level of undergraduate study. For details visit Web Site: http://www.pwaa.org.

Award: Scholarship for use in sophomore, junior, or senior years; renewable. *Number:* 5. *Amount:* $1000.

Eligibility Requirements: Applicant must be of Polish heritage and enrolled or expecting to enroll full-time at a four-year institution or university. Available to U.S. citizens.

Application Requirements: Application, essay, photo, transcript. *Deadline:* March 15.

Contact: Sharon Zago, Vice President and Scholarship Chairman
Polish Women's Alliance
6643 North Northwest Highway
Chicago, IL 60068
Phone: 847-384-1208
E-mail: vpres@pwaa.org

PORTUGUESE FOUNDATION INC. http://www.pfict.org

PORTUGUESE FOUNDATION SCHOLARSHIP PROGRAM

Scholarships of $4000 to four deserving students. Student must be of Portuguese ancestry, resident of Connecticut, U.S. citizen or a permanent resident, applying for, or currently in college, full-time student in an undergraduate degree conferring program or a part-time student in a master's or doctorate program.

Award: Scholarship for use in freshman, sophomore, junior, senior, or graduate years; not renewable. *Number:* 4. *Amount:* $4000.

Eligibility Requirements: Applicant must be of Portuguese heritage; enrolled or expecting to enroll full- or part-time at a four-year institution or university and resident of Connecticut. Applicant must have 2.5 GPA or higher. Available to U.S. citizens.

Application Requirements: Application, essay, financial need analysis, references, test scores, transcript, FAFSA, copy of recent federal income tax return. *Deadline:* March 15.

Contact: John Bairos, President
Portuguese Foundation Inc.
PO Box 331441
Hartford, CT 06133-1441
Phone: 860-614-8614
E-mail: info@pfict.org

PRESBYTERIAN CHURCH (USA) http://www.pcusa.org/financialaid

NATIVE AMERICAN EDUCATION GRANT

Grants awarded to Native Americans and Alaska Natives for full-time postsecondary education. Preference will be given to active members of the Presbyterian Church (USA). Must be U.S. citizen or permanent resident.

Award: Grant for use in junior or senior years; renewable. *Number:* 75. *Amount:* $200–$3000.

Eligibility Requirements: Applicant must be American Indian/Alaska Native and enrolled or expecting to enroll full-time at a four-year institution or university. Applicant must have 2.5 GPA or higher. Available to U.S. citizens.

Application Requirements: Application, financial need analysis, references, transcript, copy of the tribal membership card. *Deadline:* June 15.

Contact: Frances Cook, Associate, Financial Aid for Studies
Presbyterian Church (USA)
100 Witherspoon Street
Louisville, KY 40202-1396
Phone: 888-728-7228 Ext. 5776
Fax: 502-569-8766
E-mail: frances.cook@ctr.pcusa.org

NATIVE AMERICAN EDUCATION GRANTS

Award to assist members of any tribe with their education. Students receive funding beginning with their postsecondary education and grants are awarded through a doctoral degree.

Award: Grant for use in freshman, sophomore, junior, senior, graduate, or postgraduate years; renewable. *Number:* 10–125. *Amount:* $500–$1500.

Eligibility Requirements: Applicant must be American Indian/Alaska Native and enrolled or expecting to enroll full-time at a two-year or four-year or technical institution or university. Applicant must have 2.5 GPA or higher. Available to U.S. citizens.

Application Requirements: Application, essay, financial need analysis, test scores, transcript, tribal membership. *Deadline:* June 15.

Contact: Frances Cook, Associate
Presbyterian Church (USA)
100 Witherspoon Street
Louisville, KY 40202-1396
Phone: 502-569-5776
Fax: 502-569-8766
E-mail: frances.cook@pcusa.org

PUEBLO OF ISLETA, DEPARTMENT OF EDUCATION http://www.isletapueblo.com

HIGHER EDUCATION SUPPLEMENTAL SCHOLARSHIP ISLETA PUEBLO HIGHER EDUCATION DEPARTMENT

• *See page 554*

PUEBLO OF SAN JUAN, DEPARTMENT OF EDUCATION http://www.sanjuaned.org

OHKAY OWINGEH TRIBAL SCHOLARSHIP OF THE PUEBLO OF SAN JUAN

• *See page 609*

POP'AY SCHOLARSHIP

• *See page 609*

RYU FAMILY FOUNDATION INC.

SEOL BONG SCHOLARSHIP

One-time award to support and advance education and research. Must be Korean residing in DE, PA, NJ, NY, CT, VT, RI, NH, MA or ME. Minimum 3.5 GPA required.

Award: Scholarship for use in freshman, sophomore, junior, senior, or graduate years; not renewable. *Number:* 25. *Amount:* $1500–$2000.

Eligibility Requirements: Applicant must be of Korean heritage; Asian/Pacific Islander; enrolled or expecting to enroll full-time at a four-year institution or university; resident of Connecticut, Delaware, Maine, Massachusetts, New Hampshire, New Jersey, New York, Pennsylvania, Rhode Island, or Vermont and studying in Connecticut,

Delaware, Maine, Massachusetts, New Hampshire, New Jersey, New York, Pennsylvania, Rhode Island, or Vermont. Applicant must have 3.5 GPA or higher. Available to U.S. and non-Canadian citizens.

Application Requirements: Application, essay, photo, references, test scores, transcript. *Deadline:* November 15.

Contact: Jenny Kang, Scholarship Secretary
Ryu Family Foundation Inc.
186 Parish Drive
Wayne, NJ 07470
Phone: 973-692-9696
Fax: 973-692-0999
E-mail: jennyk@toplineus.com

SAINT ANDREW'S SOCIETY OF THE STATE OF NEW YORK http://www.standrewsny.org

ST. ANDREWS SCHOLARSHIP

Scholarship for senior undergraduate students who will obtain a bachelor's degree from an accredited college or university in the spring and can demonstrate the significance of studying in Scotland. Proof of application to their selected school will be required for finalists. Applicant must be of Scottish descent.

Award: Scholarship for use in senior year; not renewable. *Number:* 2. *Amount:* up to $15,000.

Eligibility Requirements: Applicant must be of Scottish heritage and enrolled or expecting to enroll full-time at a four-year institution or university. Applicant must have 2.5 GPA or higher. Available to U.S. citizens.

Application Requirements: Application. *Deadline:* December 15.

Contact: Brigid Franklin, Office Manager
Saint Andrew's Society of the State of New York
150 East 55th Street
New York, NY 10022
Phone: 212-223-4248
Fax: 212-223-0748
E-mail: office@standrewsny.org

ST. ANDREW'S SOCIETY OF WASHINGTON, DC http://www.saintandrewsociety.org

DONALD MALCOLM MACARTHUR SCHOLARSHIP

One-time award is available for U.S. students to study in Scotland or students from Scotland to study in the United States. Special attention will be given to applicants whose work would demonstrably contribute to enhanced knowledge of Scottish history or culture. Must be a college junior, senior, or graduate student to apply. Need for financial assistance and academic record considered. Visit Web site for details and application: http://www.thecapitalscot.com/standrew/scholarships.html.

Award: Scholarship for use in junior, senior, or graduate years; not renewable. *Number:* 1. *Amount:* up to $2500.

Eligibility Requirements: Applicant must be of Scottish heritage; enrolled or expecting to enroll full-time at a four-year institution or university and resident of Delaware, District of Columbia, Maryland, New Jersey, North Carolina, Pennsylvania, Virginia, or Wisconsin. Available to U.S. and non-U.S. citizens.

Application Requirements: Application, essay, financial need analysis, interview, references, self-addressed stamped envelope. *Deadline:* April 30.

Contact: T.J. Holland, Chairman, Scholarship Committee
St. Andrew's Society of Washington, DC
1443 Laurel Hill Road
Vienna, VA 22182-1711
E-mail: tjholland@wmalumni.com

SALVADORAN AMERICAN LEADERSHIP AND EDUCATIONAL FUND http://www.salef.org

FULFILLING OUR DREAMS SCHOLARSHIP FUND

Up to 60 scholarships ranging from $500 to $2500 will be awarded to students who come from a Latino heritage. Must have a 2.5 GPA. See Web site for more details: http://www.salef.org.

Award: Scholarship for use in freshman, sophomore, junior, senior, graduate, or postgraduate years; not renewable. *Number:* 50–60. *Amount:* $500–$2500.

Eligibility Requirements: Applicant must be of Hispanic or Latin American/Caribbean heritage; enrolled or expecting to enroll full- or part-time at a two-year or four-year institution or university; resident of California and studying in California. Applicant must have 2.5 GPA or higher. Available to U.S. and non-U.S. citizens.

Application Requirements: Application, essay, financial need analysis, interview, photo, resume, references, self-addressed stamped envelope, test scores, transcript. *Deadline:* June 30.

Contact: Mayra Soriano, Educational and Youth Programs Manager
Salvadoran American Leadership and Educational Fund
1625 West Olympic Boulevard, Suite 718
Los Angeles, CA 90015
Phone: 213-480-1052
Fax: 213-487-2530
E-mail: msoriano@salef.org

SAN DIEGO FOUNDATION http://www.sdfoundation.org

SAN DIEGO FIRE VICTIMS SCHOLARSHIP-LATINO FUND

Scholarship to graduating Latino high school seniors and current Latino college students who lost their homes in the 2003 wildfires and plan to attend an accredited two-year college, four-year university, or licensed trade or vocational school in the state of California. Must be legal residents of San Diego County. Minimum 2.0 GPA required. Preference will be given to students who are attending a public institution. Scholarship may be renewable for up to two years provided recipients continue to meet the terms of the scholarship. Deadline varies.

Award: Scholarship for use in freshman, sophomore, junior, or senior years; renewable. *Number:* 5. *Amount:* $500–$2500.

Eligibility Requirements: Applicant must be Hispanic; enrolled or expecting to enroll full-time at a two-year or four-year or technical institution or university; resident of California and studying in California. Available to U.S. citizens.

Application Requirements: Application, financial need analysis, references, transcript, personal statement, copy of tax return, formal documentation. *Deadline:* varies.

Contact: Shryl Helvie, Scholarship Coordinator
San Diego Foundation
2508 Historic Decatur Road, Suite 200
San Diego, CA 92106
Phone: 619-814-1307
Fax: 619-239-1710
E-mail: shryl@sdfoundation.org

SANTO DOMINGO SCHOLARSHIP PROGRAM

SANTO DOMINGO SCHOLARSHIP

Fourth degree Santo Domingo-enrolled with tribe. Letter of acceptance from high school or college. For any tribal member to have the opportunity to get an undergraduate degree. 2.0 GPA required. If full time 12 credits or more must be completed each semester. Amount is need based. Supported by Bureau of Indian Affairs. Deadlines: March 1 for Fall; November 1 for Spring.

Award: Scholarship for use in freshman, sophomore, junior, or senior years; renewable. *Number:* varies. *Amount:* varies.

Eligibility Requirements: Applicant must be American Indian/Alaska Native and enrolled or expecting to enroll full- or part-time at a two-year or four-year or technical institution. Available to U.S. citizens.

Application Requirements: Application, references, transcript, certificate of Indian blood. *Deadline:* varies.

Contact: Maria Lovato, Education Secretary
Santo Domingo Scholarship Program
PO Box 99
Santo Domingo, NM 87052
Phone: 505-465-2214
Fax: 505-465-2688
E-mail: kewaeduc@yahoo.com

SEMINOLE TRIBE OF FLORIDA http://www.seminoletribe.com

SEMINOLE TRIBE OF FLORIDA BILLY L. CYPRESS SCHOLARSHIP PROGRAM

• *See page 556*

SENECA NATION OF INDIANS http://www.sni.org

SENECA NATION HIGHER EDUCATION PROGRAM

Renewable award for enrolled Senecas of the Cattaraugus and Allegany Indian reservations who are in need of financial assistance. Application deadlines: July 1 for fall; December 1 for spring; May 1 for summer. Must be degree seeking and enrolled in a two-year college, four-year college or university. Must have GPA of 2.0.

Award: Scholarship for use in freshman, sophomore, junior, senior, graduate, or postgraduate years; renewable. *Number:* varies. *Amount:* \$6000–\$11,000.

Eligibility Requirements: Applicant must be American Indian/Alaska Native and enrolled or expecting to enroll full-time at a two-year or four-year institution or university. Available to U.S. citizens.

Application Requirements: Application, essay, financial need analysis, references, transcript, tribal certification. *Deadline:* varies.

Contact: Debra Hoag, Higher Education Coordinator
Seneca Nation of Indians
PO Box 231
Salamanca, NY 14779
Phone: 716-945-1790 Ext. 3103
Fax: 716-945-7170
E-mail: dhoag@sni.org

SIR EDWARD YOUDE MEMORIAL FUND COUNCIL http://www.sfaa.gov.hk

SIR EDWARD YOUDE MEMORIAL OVERSEAS SCHOLARSHIP FOR DISABLED STUDENTS

• *See page 627*

SIR EDWARD YOUDE MEMORIAL SCHOLARSHIPS FOR OVERSEAS STUDIES

Fellowships are for financing outstanding Hong Kong students for overseas undergraduate studies. They are expected to contribute significantly to the development of Hong Kong upon graduation. Must be permanent residents of Hong Kong. Must have received at least five years of continuous education in Hong Kong. Award value is HK\$262,000. For further details refer: http://www.sfaa.gov.hk/eng/scholar/seym3.htm.

Award: Scholarship for use in freshman, sophomore, junior, or senior years; renewable. *Number:* varies.

Eligibility Requirements: Applicant must be Chinese citizen and enrolled or expecting to enroll full-time at a four-year institution or university. Available to citizens of countries other than the U.S. or Canada.

Application Requirements: Application, autobiography, essay, interview, photo, resume, references, test scores, transcript. *Deadline:* varies.

Contact: Elsa Sit, Council Secretariat
Sir Edward Youde Memorial Fund Council
Room 1217, 12/F, 303 Cheung Sha Wan Road
Kowloon
Hong Kong
Phone: 852 2150 6103
Fax: 852 2511 2720
E-mail: sgl3@sfaa.gov.hk

SONS OF ITALY FOUNDATION http://www.osia.org

SONS OF ITALY NATIONAL LEADERSHIP GRANTS COMPETITION GENERAL SCHOLARSHIPS

Scholarships for undergraduate or graduate students who are U.S. citizens of Italian descent. Must demonstrate academic excellence. For more details see Web site http://www.osia.org.

Award: Scholarship for use in freshman, sophomore, junior, senior, graduate, or postgraduate years; not renewable. *Number:* 8–14. *Amount:* \$5000–\$25,000.

Eligibility Requirements: Applicant must be of Italian heritage and enrolled or expecting to enroll full-time at a four-year institution or university. Available to U.S. citizens.

Application Requirements: Application, autobiography, essay, resume, references, self-addressed stamped envelope, test scores, transcript. *Fee:* \$30. *Deadline:* February 28.

Contact: Margaret O'Rourke, Scholarship Coordinator
Sons of Italy Foundation
219 E Street, NE
Washington, DC 20002
Phone: 202-547-2900
Fax: 202-546-8168
E-mail: scholarships@osia.org

SONS OF ITALY NATIONAL LEADERSHIP GRANTS COMPETITION HENRY SALVATORI SCHOLARSHIPS

Scholarships for college-bound high school seniors who demonstrate exceptional leadership, distinguished scholarship, and a deep understanding and respect for the principles upon which our nation was founded: liberty, freedom, and equality. Must be a U.S. citizen of Italian descent. For more details see Web site: http://www.osia.org.

Award: Scholarship for use in freshman year; not renewable. *Number:* up to 1. *Amount:* up to \$5000.

Eligibility Requirements: Applicant must be of Italian heritage; high school student and planning to enroll or expecting to enroll full-time at a four-year institution or university. Available to U.S. citizens.

Application Requirements: Application, autobiography, essay, resume, references, self-addressed stamped envelope, test scores, transcript. *Fee:* \$30. *Deadline:* February 28.

Contact: Margaret O'Rourke, Scholarship Coordinator
Sons of Italy Foundation
219 E Street, NE
Washington, DC 20002
Phone: 202-547-2900
Fax: 202-546-8168
E-mail: scholarships@osia.org

SONS OF NORWAY FOUNDATION http://www.sonsofnorway.com

ASTRID G. CATES AND MYRTLE BEINHAUER SCHOLARSHIP FUNDS

• *See page 558*

STATE OF NORTH DAKOTA http://www.ndus.nodak.edu

NORTH DAKOTA INDIAN SCHOLARSHIP PROGRAM

Award of \$500 to \$2000 per year to assist American Indian students who are North Dakota residents in obtaining a college education. Must have been accepted for admission at an institution of higher learning or state vocational education program within North Dakota. For full-time study only. Based upon scholastic ability and unmet financial need. Minimum 2.0 GPA required.

Award: Scholarship for use in freshman, sophomore, junior, senior, or graduate years; renewable. *Number:* 150–175. *Amount:* \$500–\$2000.

Eligibility Requirements: Applicant must be American Indian/Alaska Native; enrolled or expecting to enroll full-time at a two-year or four-year institution or university; resident of North Dakota and studying in North Dakota. Available to U.S. citizens.

Application Requirements: Application, financial need analysis, transcript, proof of tribal enrollment, budget. *Deadline:* July 15.

Contact: Rhonda Schauer, Coordinator of American Indian Higher Education
State of North Dakota
919 South Seventh Street, Suite 300
Bismarck, ND 58504-5881
Phone: 701-328-9661
E-mail: rhonda.schauer@ndus.nodak.edu

STEVEN KNEZEVICH TRUST

STEVEN KNEZEVICH GRANT

One-time grant for students of Serbian descent. Award not restricted to citizens of the United States. Amount of award varies. Applicants must be attending an accredited institution of higher learning. Grant will be applied toward student's spring semester. To receive additional information and the application itself, applicant must send SASE, along with proof of Serbian descent.

Award: Grant for use in freshman, sophomore, junior, senior, or graduate years; not renewable. *Number:* varies. *Amount:* varies.

Eligibility Requirements: Applicant must be of Croatian/Serbian heritage and enrolled or expecting to enroll full- or part-time at a two-year or four-year or technical institution or university. Available to U.S. and non-U.S. citizens.

Application Requirements: Application, self-addressed stamped envelope, transcript, proof of Serbian heritage. *Deadline:* November 30.

Contact: Stanley Hack, Trustee
Steven Knezevich Trust
9830 North Courtland Drive
Mequon, WI 53092-6052
Phone: 262-241-5663
Fax: 262-241-5645
E-mail: jbrodkey@hotmail.com

STRAIGHTFORWARD MEDIA http://www.straightforwardmedia.com

STRAIGHTFORWARD MEDIA MINORITY SCHOLARSHIP

Scholarship for minority students who are currently enrolled in or planning to enroll in postsecondary education.

Award: Scholarship for use in freshman, sophomore, junior, or senior years; not renewable. *Number:* 4. *Amount:* $500.

Eligibility Requirements: Applicant must be American Indian/Alaska Native, Asian/Pacific Islander, Black (non-Hispanic), or Hispanic and enrolled or expecting to enroll full- or part-time at a two-year or four-year institution or university. Available to U.S. and non-U.S. citizens.

Application Requirements: Application. *Deadline:* varies.

Contact: Scholarship Committee
StraightForward Media
2040 West Main Street, Suite 104
Rapid City, SD 57701
Phone: 605-348-3042
Fax: 605-348-3043

SWEDISH INSTITUTE/SVENSKA INSTITUTET http://www.si.se

VISBY PROGRAM: HIGHER EDUCATION AND RESEARCH

Scholarships to pursue studies in Sweden are available to citizens of Belarus, Russia and Ukraine. For more details see Web site: http://www.sweden.se/templates/cs/Article____5065.aspx.

Award: Scholarship for use in freshman, sophomore, junior, senior, or graduate years; not renewable. *Number:* varies. *Amount:* varies.

Eligibility Requirements: Applicant must be of Latvian, Lithuanian, Polish, Russian, or Ukrainian heritage and enrolled or expecting to enroll full-time at a four-year institution or university. Available to citizens of countries other than the U.S. or Canada.

Application Requirements: Application. *Deadline:* February 8.

Contact: Olle Wastberg, Director General
Swedish Institute/Svenska Institutet
Skeppsbron 2
PO Box 7434
Stockholm SE-103 91
Sweden
Phone: 46 8 453 78 00
Fax: 46 8 20 72 48
E-mail: grant@si.se

SWISS BENEVOLENT SOCIETY OF CHICAGO http://www.sbschicago.org

SWISS BENEVOLENT SOCIETY OF CHICAGO SCHOLARSHIPS

Scholarship for undergraduate college students of Swiss descent, having permanent residence in Illinois or Southern Wisconsin. Must have 3.3 GPA. High school students need a 26 on ACT or 1050 on SAT.

Award: Scholarship for use in freshman, sophomore, junior, or senior years; renewable. *Number:* 30. *Amount:* $750–$2500.

Eligibility Requirements: Applicant must be of Swiss heritage; enrolled or expecting to enroll full-time at a four-year institution or university and resident of Illinois or Wisconsin. Available to U.S. citizens.

Application Requirements: Application, essay, self-addressed stamped envelope, test scores, transcript. *Deadline:* April 1.

Contact: Franziska Lys, Chair
Swiss Benevolent Society of Chicago
PO Box 2137
Chicago, IL 60690-2137
Phone: 847-491-8298
E-mail: education@sbschicago.org

SWISS BENEVOLENT SOCIETY OF NEW YORK http://www.sbsny.org

MEDICUS STUDENT EXCHANGE

One-time award to students of Swiss nationality or parentage. Open to U.S. residents for study in Switzerland and to Swiss residents for study in the U.S. Must be proficient in foreign language of instruction.

Award: Grant for use in junior, senior, or graduate years; not renewable. *Number:* 1–10. *Amount:* $2000–$10,000.

Eligibility Requirements: Applicant must be of Swiss heritage; enrolled or expecting to enroll full-time at a four-year institution or university and must have an interest in foreign language. Applicant must have 3.5 GPA or higher. Available to U.S. and non-Canadian citizens.

Application Requirements: Application, references, test scores, transcript. *Deadline:* March 31.

Contact: Swiss Benevolent Society of New York, Scholarship Committee
Swiss Benevolent Society of New York
500 Fifth Avenue, Room 1800
New York, NY 10110
Phone: 212-246-0655
Fax: 212-246-1366

PELLEGRINI SCHOLARSHIP GRANTS

Award to students who have a minimum 3.0 GPA and show financial need. Must submit proof of Swiss nationality or descent. Must be a permanent resident of Connecticut, Delaware, New Jersey, New York, or Pennsylvania.

Award: Scholarship for use in freshman, sophomore, junior, senior, or graduate years; renewable. *Number:* 50. *Amount:* $500–$5000.

Eligibility Requirements: Applicant must be of Swiss heritage; enrolled or expecting to enroll full-time at a two-year or four-year or technical institution or university and resident of Connecticut, Delaware, New Jersey, New York, or Pennsylvania. Applicant must have 3.0 GPA or higher. Available to U.S. citizens.

Application Requirements: Application, financial need analysis, references, test scores, transcript, copies of tax return. *Deadline:* March 31.

Contact: Swiss Benevolent Society of New York, Scholarship Committee
Swiss Benevolent Society of New York
500 Fifth Avenue, Room 1800
New York, NY 10110
Phone: 212-246-0655
Fax: 212-246-1366

TERRY FOX HUMANITARIAN AWARD PROGRAM http://www.terryfox.org

TERRY FOX HUMANITARIAN AWARD

• *See page 612*

TEXAS BLACK BAPTIST SCHOLARSHIP COMMITTEE http://www.bgct.org

TEXAS BLACK BAPTIST SCHOLARSHIP

Renewable award for Texas residents attending a Baptist educational institution in Texas. Must be of African-American descent with a minimum 2.0 GPA. Must be a member in good standing of a Baptist church.

Award: Scholarship for use in freshman, sophomore, junior, or senior years; renewable. *Number:* varies. *Amount:* $1600.

Eligibility Requirements: Applicant must be Baptist; Black (non-Hispanic); age 18 and over; enrolled or expecting to enroll full- or part-time at a two-year or four-year institution or university; resident of Texas and studying in Texas. Available to U.S. citizens.

Texas Black Baptist Scholarship Committee (continued)

Application Requirements: Application, autobiography, financial need analysis, interview, photo, portfolio, resume, references, test scores, transcript. *Deadline:* continuous.

Contact: Charlie Singleton, Director
Texas Black Baptist Scholarship Committee
African American Ministries, 333 North Washington, Suite 340
Dallas, TX 75246-1798
Phone: 214-828-5130
Fax: 214-828-5284
E-mail: charlie.singleton@bgct.org

UKRAINIAN FRATERNAL ASSOCIATION

UKRAINIAN FRATERNAL ASSOCIATION EUGENE R. AND ELINOR R. KOTUR SCHOLARSHIP TRUST FUND

Award for students of Ukrainian ancestry who are enrolled in selected colleges and universities. Must be sophomore, junior, or senior.

Award: Scholarship for use in sophomore, junior, senior, or graduate years; renewable. *Number:* 1–3. *Amount:* up to $3000.

Eligibility Requirements: Applicant must be of Ukrainian heritage and enrolled or expecting to enroll full-time at a four-year institution or university. Available to U.S. and Canadian citizens.

Application Requirements: Application, autobiography, photo, references, transcript. *Deadline:* May 31.

Contact: Christina Shablovsky, Supreme Secretary
Ukrainian Fraternal Association
371 North Ninth Avenue
Scranton, PA 18504-2005
Phone: 570-342-0937
Fax: 570-342-5649
E-mail: fratrag@aol.com

UKRAINIAN FRATERNAL ASSOCIATION IVAN FRANKO SCHOLARSHIP FUND

• *See page 563*

UKRAINIAN FRATERNAL ASSOCIATION STUDENT AID

• *See page 563*

UNICO NATIONAL INC. http://www.unico.org

ALPHONSE A. MIELE SCHOLARSHIP

Scholarship available to a graduating high school senior. Must reside and attend high school within the corporate limits or adjoining suburbs of a city wherein an active chapter of UNICO National is located. Application must be signed by student's principal and properly certified by sponsoring chapter president and chapter secretary. Must have letter of endorsement from president or scholarship chairperson of sponsoring chapter.

Award: Scholarship for use in freshman year; not renewable. *Number:* 1. *Amount:* up to $1500.

Eligibility Requirements: Applicant must be of Italian heritage; high school student and planning to enroll or expecting to enroll full-time at a four-year institution or university. Available to U.S. citizens.

Application Requirements: Application, financial need analysis, references, transcript. *Deadline:* varies.

Contact: Ann Tichenor, Secretary
UNICO National Inc.
271 U.S. Highway 46 West, Suite A-108
Fairfield, NJ 07004
Phone: 973-808-0035
Fax: 973-808-0043

MAJOR DON S. GENTILE SCHOLARSHIP

Annual awards for students of Italian origin who are enrolled at a postsecondary institution. Due date and number of awards varies.

Award: Scholarship for use in freshman year; not renewable. *Number:* varies. *Amount:* $1500.

Eligibility Requirements: Applicant must be of Italian heritage; high school student and planning to enroll or expecting to enroll full-time at a two-year or four-year or technical institution or university. Available to U.S. citizens.

Application Requirements: Application, financial need analysis, references, transcript. *Deadline:* varies.

Contact: Ann Tichenor, Secretary
UNICO National Inc.
271 U.S. Highway 46 West, Suite A-108
Fairfield, NJ 07004
Phone: 973-808-0035
Fax: 973-808-0043

WILLIAM C. DAVINI SCHOLARSHIP

Scholarship available to a graduating high school senior of Italian descent. Applicant must reside and attend high school within the corporate limits or adjoining suburbs of a city wherein an active chapter of UNICO National is located. Application must be signed by student's principal and properly certified by sponsoring chapter president and chapter secretary. Must have letter of endorsement from president or scholarship chairperson of sponsoring chapter.

Award: Scholarship for use in freshman year; not renewable. *Number:* 1. *Amount:* $1500.

Eligibility Requirements: Applicant must be of Italian heritage; high school student and planning to enroll or expecting to enroll full-time at a four-year institution or university. Available to U.S. citizens.

Application Requirements: Application, financial need analysis, references, transcript. *Deadline:* varies.

Contact: Ann Tichenor, Secretary
UNICO National Inc.
271 U.S. Highway 46 West, Suite A-108
Fairfield, NJ 07004
Phone: 973-808-0035
Fax: 973-808-0043

UNITED METHODIST CHURCH http://www.gbhem.org

UNITED METHODIST CHURCH ETHNIC SCHOLARSHIP

Awards for minority students pursuing undergraduate degree. Must have been certified members of the United Methodist Church for one year. Proof of membership and pastor's statement required. One-time award but applicant may re-apply each year. Minimum 2.5 GPA required.

Award: Scholarship for use in freshman, sophomore, junior, or senior years; not renewable. *Number:* varies. *Amount:* varies.

Eligibility Requirements: Applicant must be Methodist; American Indian/Alaska Native, Asian/Pacific Islander, Black (non-Hispanic), or Hispanic and enrolled or expecting to enroll full-time at a two-year or four-year institution or university. Applicant must have 2.5 GPA or higher. Available to U.S. citizens.

Application Requirements: Application, essay, references, transcript, membership proof, pastor's statement. *Deadline:* May 1.

Contact: Patti J. Zimmerman, Scholarships Administrator
United Methodist Church
PO Box 340007
Nashville, TN 37203-0007
Phone: 615-340-7344
E-mail: pzimmer@gbhem.org

UNITED METHODIST CHURCH HISPANIC, ASIAN, AND NATIVE AMERICAN SCHOLARSHIP

Award for members of United Methodist Church who are Hispanic, Asian, Native-American, or Pacific Islander college juniors, seniors, or graduate students. Proof of membership and pastor's letter required. Minimum 2.85 GPA.

Award: Scholarship for use in freshman, sophomore, junior, senior, or graduate years; not renewable. *Number:* varies. *Amount:* varies.

Eligibility Requirements: Applicant must be Methodist; American Indian/Alaska Native, Asian/Pacific Islander, or Hispanic and enrolled or expecting to enroll full-time at a four-year institution or university. Available to U.S. citizens.

Application Requirements: Application, essay, references, transcript, membership proof, pastor's letter. *Deadline:* April 1.

Contact: Patti J. Zimmerman, Scholarships Administrator
United Methodist Church
PO Box 340007
Nashville, TN 37203-0007
Phone: 615-340-7344
E-mail: pzimmer@gbhem.org

UNITED METHODIST YOUTH ORGANIZATION http://www.gbod.org/youngpeople

RICHARD S. SMITH SCHOLARSHIP

Open to racial/ethnic minority youth only. Must be a United Methodist Youth who has been active in local church for at least one year prior to application. Must be a graduating senior in high school (who maintained at least a "C" average) entering the first year of undergraduate study and be pursuing a "church-related" career.

Award: Scholarship for use in freshman year; not renewable. *Number:* up to 2. *Amount:* up to $2300.

Eligibility Requirements: Applicant must be Methodist; American Indian/Alaska Native, Asian/Pacific Islander, Black (non-Hispanic), or Hispanic; high school student and planning to enroll or expecting to enroll full-time at a two-year or four-year or technical institution or university. Available to U.S. citizens.

Application Requirements: Application, essay, financial need analysis, references, transcript, certification of church membership by pastor. *Deadline:* June 1.

Contact: Grants Coordinator
United Methodist Youth Organization
PO Box 340003
Nashville, TN 37203-0003
Phone: 877-899-2780 Ext. 7184
Fax: 615-340-7063
E-mail: youngpeople@gbod.org

UNITED NEGRO COLLEGE FUND http://www.uncf.org

ABBINGTON, VALLANTEEN SCHOLARSHIP

Scholarship of $5000 to high school students who plan to attend a UNCF member college or university. Applicant must be a resident of Missouri. Scholarship is renewed annually. Minimum 3.0 GPA in high school. GPA requirement increases to 3.3 after the sophomore year and 3.5 after the junior year. Please visit Web site for more information: http://www.uncf.org.

Award: Scholarship for use in freshman year; renewable. *Number:* varies. *Amount:* $5000.

Eligibility Requirements: Applicant must be Black (non-Hispanic); high school student; planning to enroll or expecting to enroll full- or part-time at a four-year institution or university and resident of Missouri. Available to U.S. citizens.

Application Requirements: Application, financial need analysis, FAFSA, Student Aid Report (SAR). *Deadline:* varies.

Contact: William Dunham, Program Services
United Negro College Fund
8260 Willow Oaks Corporate Drive
Fairfax, VA 22031
Phone: 703-205-3486

BANK OF AMERICA SCHOLARSHIP

Scholarship supports UNCF students attending a UNCF college or university located in any of the Bank of America core states. Minimum 3.0 GPA required. Prospective applicants should complete the student profile found at Web site: http://www.uncf.org.

Award: Scholarship for use in freshman, sophomore, junior, or senior years; not renewable. *Number:* 1. *Amount:* $1000.

Eligibility Requirements: Applicant must be Black (non-Hispanic); enrolled or expecting to enroll full-time at a four-year institution or university and studying in Florida, Georgia, North Carolina, South Carolina, or Texas. Applicant must have 3.0 GPA or higher. Available to U.S. and non-U.S. citizens.

Application Requirements: Application, essay, references, transcript. *Deadline:* November 25.

Contact: Director, Program Services
United Negro College Fund
8260 Willow Oaks Corporate Drive
PO Box 10444
Fairfax, VA 22031-8044
Phone: 800-331-2244
E-mail: rebecca.bennett@uncf.org

BILDNER FAMILY FOUNDATION SCHOLARSHIP

Scholarship open to New Jersey residents attending a UNCF member college or university. Must have minimum 2.5 GPA. Prospective applicants should complete the Student Profile found at Web site: http://www.uncf.org.

Award: Scholarship for use in freshman, sophomore, junior, or senior years; not renewable. *Number:* varies. *Amount:* $1000–$2500.

Eligibility Requirements: Applicant must be Black (non-Hispanic); enrolled or expecting to enroll full- or part-time at a four-year institution or university and resident of New Jersey. Applicant must have 2.5 GPA or higher. Available to U.S. citizens.

Application Requirements: Application. *Deadline:* continuous.

Contact: Director, Program Services
United Negro College Fund
8260 Willow Oaks Corporate Drive
PO Box 10444
Fairfax, VA 22031-8044
Phone: 800-331-2244
E-mail: rebecca.bennett@uncf.org

BRITTON FUND SCHOLARSHIP PROGRAM

Scholarships available to students from Northern Ohio enrolled in a UNCF member college or university with a minimum GPA of 2.5. The scholarship value varies based on need.

Award: Scholarship for use in freshman, sophomore, junior, senior, or graduate years; not renewable. *Number:* 1. *Amount:* varies.

Eligibility Requirements: Applicant must be Black (non-Hispanic); enrolled or expecting to enroll full-time at a four-year institution or university and resident of Ohio. Applicant must have 2.5 GPA or higher. Available to U.S. citizens.

Application Requirements: Application, financial need analysis, FAFSA, Student Aid Report (SAR). *Deadline:* varies.

Contact: Director, Program Services
United Negro College Fund
8260 Willow Oaks Corporate Drive
PO Box 10444
Fairfax, VA 22031-8044
Phone: 800-331-2244
E-mail: rebecca.bennett@uncf.org

CAROLYN BAILEY THOMAS SCHOLARSHIP

Need-based scholarship for students enrolled in UNCF member colleges and universities with a minimum GPA of 3.0. The scholarship value varies.

Award: Scholarship for use in freshman, sophomore, junior, or senior years; renewable. *Number:* varies. *Amount:* varies.

Eligibility Requirements: Applicant must be Black (non-Hispanic) and enrolled or expecting to enroll full- or part-time at a four-year institution or university. Applicant must have 3.0 GPA or higher. Available to U.S. and non-U.S. citizens.

Application Requirements: Application, financial need analysis, FAFSA. *Deadline:* varies.

Contact: Director, Program Services
United Negro College Fund
8260 Willow Oaks Corporate Drive
PO Box 10444
Fairfax, VA 22031-8044
Phone: 800-331-2244
E-mail: rebecca.bennett@uncf.org

CASIMIR, DOMINIQUE AND JAQUES SCHOLARSHIP

The scholarship is available for two male and female undergraduate sophomore or juniors from the state of Texas. Should have minimum GPA of 2.5 and the scholarship value is $1500.

Award: Scholarship for use in sophomore or junior years; renewable. *Number:* 4. *Amount:* $1500.

Eligibility Requirements: Applicant must be Black (non-Hispanic); enrolled or expecting to enroll full-time at a four-year institution or university and resident of Texas. Applicant must have 2.5 GPA or higher. Available to U.S. citizens.

United Negro College Fund (continued)

Application Requirements: Application, financial need analysis, FAFSA, Student Aid Report (SAR). *Deadline:* varies.

Contact: Director, Program Services
United Negro College Fund
8260 Willow Oaks Corporate Drive
PO Box 10444
Fairfax, VA 22031-8044
Phone: 800-331-2244
E-mail: rebecca.bennett@uncf.org

CHICAGO INTER-ALUMNI COUNCIL SCHOLARSHIP

Scholarship for Chicago high school students. The top three candidates raising the most funds for the pageant receive scholarships to attend a UNCF member college or university. The scholarship value varies and is applicable to Illinois residents with minimum GPA of 2.5.

Award: Scholarship for use in freshman year; not renewable. *Number:* 3. *Amount:* varies.

Eligibility Requirements: Applicant must be Black (non-Hispanic); high school student; planning to enroll or expecting to enroll full-time at a four-year institution or university and resident of Illinois. Applicant must have 2.5 GPA or higher. Available to U.S. citizens.

Application Requirements: Application, financial need analysis, FAFSA, Student Aid Report (SAR). *Deadline:* varies.

Contact: Director, Program Services
United Negro College Fund
8260 Willow Oaks Corporate Drive
PO Box 10444
Fairfax, VA 22031-8044
Phone: 800-331-2244
E-mail: rebecca.bennett@uncf.org

CHICAGO PUBLIC SCHOOLS UNCF CAMPAIGN

Scholarship open to students who have attended Chicago public schools with minimum 2.5 GPA. The scholarship pays tuition and fees for four years.

Award: Scholarship for use in freshman year; renewable. *Number:* varies. *Amount:* varies.

Eligibility Requirements: Applicant must be Black (non-Hispanic); enrolled or expecting to enroll full-time at a four-year institution or university and resident of Illinois. Applicant must have 2.5 GPA or higher. Available to U.S. citizens.

Application Requirements: Application, financial need analysis, FAFSA, Student Aid Report (SAR). *Deadline:* varies.

Contact: Director, Program Services
United Negro College Fund
8260 Willow Oaks Corporate Drive
PO Box 10444
Fairfax, VA 22031-8044
Phone: 800-331-2244
E-mail: rebecca.bennett@uncf.org

CLEVELAND MUNICIPAL SCHOOL SCHOLARSHIP

Scholarship awarded to seniors who meet requirements and are graduating from a Cleveland district high school with minimum GPA of 2.5. The scholarship value varies.

Award: Scholarship for use in freshman year; renewable. *Number:* 1. *Amount:* varies.

Eligibility Requirements: Applicant must be Black (non-Hispanic); high school student; planning to enroll or expecting to enroll full-time at a four-year institution or university and resident of Ohio. Applicant must have 2.5 GPA or higher. Available to U.S. citizens.

Application Requirements: Application, financial need analysis, FAFSA, Student Aid Report (SAR). *Deadline:* varies.

Contact: Director, Program Services
United Negro College Fund
8260 Willow Oaks Corporate Drive
PO Box 10444
Fairfax, VA 22031-8044
Phone: 800-331-2244
E-mail: rebecca.bennett@uncf.org

CLOROX COMPANY FOUNDATION SCHOLARSHIP

Scholarship awarded each year to five recipients from the San Francisco Bay, attending UNCF member colleges or universities. Must be a resident of California with minimum GPA of 2.5. The scholarship value is $2000.

Award: Scholarship for use in freshman, sophomore, junior, senior, or graduate years; not renewable. *Number:* 5. *Amount:* $2000.

Eligibility Requirements: Applicant must be Black (non-Hispanic); enrolled or expecting to enroll full-time at a four-year institution or university and resident of California. Applicant must have 2.5 GPA or higher. Available to U.S. citizens.

Application Requirements: Application, financial need analysis, FAFSA, Student Aid Report (SAR). *Deadline:* varies.

Contact: Director, Program Services
United Negro College Fund
8260 Willow Oaks Corporate Drive
PO Box 10444
Fairfax, VA 22031-8044
Phone: 800-331-2244
E-mail: rebecca.bennett@uncf.org

COSTCO SCHOLARSHIP

Renewable scholarship of $5000 for students from Washington and Oregon attending UNCF member colleges and universities. Minimum 2.5 GPA required. Prospective applicants should complete the student profile found at Web site: http://www.uncf.org.

Award: Scholarship for use in freshman, sophomore, junior, or senior years; renewable. *Number:* 1. *Amount:* $5000.

Eligibility Requirements: Applicant must be Black (non-Hispanic); enrolled or expecting to enroll full- or part-time at a four-year institution or university and resident of Oregon or Washington. Applicant must have 2.5 GPA or higher. Available to U.S. citizens.

Application Requirements: Application. *Deadline:* continuous.

Contact: William Dunham, Program Services
United Negro College Fund
8260 Willow Oaks Corporate Drive
Fairfax, VA 22031-4511
Phone: 703-205-3486

DALLAS INDEPENDENT SCHOOL DISTRICT SCHOLARSHIP

Applicant must be a high school senior from the Dallas Independent School District with minimum GPA of 2.5. The scholarship value is up to $2500. Must attend a UNCF member college/university or any other Historically Black College or University.

Award: Scholarship for use in freshman year; not renewable. *Number:* varies. *Amount:* up to $2500.

Eligibility Requirements: Applicant must be Black (non-Hispanic); high school student; planning to enroll or expecting to enroll full-time at a four-year institution or university and resident of Texas. Applicant must have 2.5 GPA or higher. Available to U.S. citizens.

Application Requirements: Application, essay, financial need analysis, FAFSA. *Deadline:* May 9.

Contact: Dr. Kendall Beck, Scholarship Coordinator
United Negro College Fund
2538 South Ervay
Dallas, TX 75215
Phone: 972-925-4893

DALLAS METROPLEX COUNCIL OF BLACK ALUMNI ASSOCIATION SCHOLARSHIP

Need-based scholarship offered by the Dallas Metroplex Council of Black Alumni Association. Should have minimum GPA of 2.5 and the scholarship value varies.

Award: Scholarship for use in freshman, sophomore, junior, senior, or graduate years; renewable. *Number:* 1. *Amount:* varies.

Eligibility Requirements: Applicant must be Black (non-Hispanic) and enrolled or expecting to enroll full- or part-time at a four-year institution or university. Applicant must have 2.5 GPA or higher. Available to U.S. and non-U.S. citizens.

Application Requirements: Application, financial need analysis, FAFSA, Student Aid Report (SAR). *Deadline:* varies.

Contact: Director, Program Services
United Negro College Fund
8260 Willow Oaks Corporate Drive
PO Box 10444
Fairfax, VA 22031-8044
Phone: 800-331-2244
E-mail: rebecca.bennett@uncf.org

DAVENPORT FORTE PEDESTAL FUND

Scholarship of $10000 for students who graduates from the Detroit Public Schools system. Applicant must be a first semester freshman. Must have a minimum of 2.7 GPA.

Award: Scholarship for use in freshman year; not renewable. *Number:* 1. *Amount:* $10,000.

Eligibility Requirements: Applicant must be Black (non-Hispanic); enrolled or expecting to enroll full-time at a four-year institution or university and resident of Michigan. Available to U.S. citizens.

Application Requirements: Application, financial need analysis, FAFSA, Student Aid Report (SAR). *Deadline:* varies.

Contact: Director, Program Services
United Negro College Fund
8260 Willow Oaks Corporate Drive
PO Box 10444
Fairfax, VA 22031-8044
Phone: 800-331-2244
E-mail: rebecca.bennett@uncf.org

DENIS D'AMORE SCHOLARSHIP

Scholarship is open to students from Massachusetts. Must have a minimum GPA of 2.5 and the scholarship value is $2000. Award for both full-time and part-time students.

Award: Scholarship for use in freshman, sophomore, junior, senior, or graduate years; not renewable. *Number:* varies. *Amount:* $2000.

Eligibility Requirements: Applicant must be Black (non-Hispanic); enrolled or expecting to enroll full- or part-time at a four-year institution or university and resident of Massachusetts. Applicant must have 2.5 GPA or higher. Available to U.S. citizens.

Application Requirements: Application, financial need analysis, FAFSA, Student Aid Report (SAR). *Deadline:* varies.

Contact: Director, Program Services
United Negro College Fund
8260 Willow Oaks Corporate Drive
PO Box 10444
Fairfax, VA 22031-8044
Phone: 800-331-2244
E-mail: rebecca.bennett@uncf.org

EUNICE WALKER JOHNSON ENDOWED SCHOLARSHIP

Award available to all students who attend UNCF member colleges and universities and Selma University. Must have a 3.0 GPA and the scholarship value up to $5000.

Award: Scholarship for use in freshman, sophomore, junior, or senior years; renewable. *Number:* varies. *Amount:* up to $5000.

Eligibility Requirements: Applicant must be Black (non-Hispanic) and enrolled or expecting to enroll full- or part-time at a four-year institution or university. Applicant must have 3.0 GPA or higher. Available to U.S. and non-U.S. citizens.

Application Requirements: Application, financial need analysis, FAFSA. *Deadline:* December 1.

Contact: Director, Program Services
United Negro College Fund
8260 Willow Oaks Corporate Drive
PO Box 10444
Fairfax, VA 22031-8044
Phone: 800-331-2244
E-mail: rebecca.bennett@uncf.org

EVELYN LEVINA WRIGHT SCHOLARSHIP

Scholarship of $3500 is awarded to a resident of the Philadelphia, Pennsylvania, Wilmington, Delaware, or Camden, New Jersey area. Must have a minimum GPA of 2.5.

Award: Scholarship for use in freshman, sophomore, junior, or senior years; renewable. *Number:* 1. *Amount:* $3500.

Eligibility Requirements: Applicant must be Black (non-Hispanic); enrolled or expecting to enroll full- or part-time at a four-year institution or university and resident of Delaware, New Jersey, or Pennsylvania. Applicant must have 2.5 GPA or higher. Available to U.S. citizens.

Application Requirements: Application, financial need analysis, FAFSA. *Deadline:* varies.

Contact: Director, Program Services
United Negro College Fund
8260 Willow Oaks Corporate Drive
PO Box 10444
Fairfax, VA 22031-8044
Phone: 800-331-2244
E-mail: rebecca.bennett@uncf.org

FIFTH/THIRD SCHOLARS PROGRAM

Scholarship awards students who are residents of Dayton, Columbus, or Cincinnati, Ohio. Student must attend a UNCF member college or university. Must have a minimum GPA of 2.5 and the scholarship value varies based on need.

Award: Scholarship for use in freshman, sophomore, junior, senior, or graduate years; renewable. *Number:* varies. *Amount:* varies.

Eligibility Requirements: Applicant must be Black (non-Hispanic); enrolled or expecting to enroll full- or part-time at a four-year institution or university and resident of Ohio. Applicant must have 2.5 GPA or higher. Available to U.S. citizens.

Application Requirements: Application, financial need analysis, FAFSA, Student Aid Report (SAR). *Deadline:* varies.

Contact: Director, Program Services
United Negro College Fund
8260 Willow Oaks Corporate Drive
PO Box 10444
Fairfax, VA 22031-8044
Phone: 800-331-2244
E-mail: rebecca.bennett@uncf.org

FORT WORTH INDEPENDENT SCHOOL DISTRICT SCHOLARSHIP

Scholarship awarded to graduating high school senior from the Fort Worth Independent School District. Applicant must submit 250 to 500 word essay addressing: "Why it is important to attend a Historically Black College or University". Please visit Web site for more information: http://www.uncf.org.

Award: Scholarship for use in freshman year; not renewable. *Number:* varies. *Amount:* up to $2500.

Eligibility Requirements: Applicant must be Black (non-Hispanic); high school student; planning to enroll or expecting to enroll full- or part-time at a four-year institution or university and resident of Texas. Applicant must have 2.5 GPA or higher. Available to U.S. citizens.

United Negro College Fund (continued)

Application Requirements: Application, essay, financial need analysis, FAFSA, Student Aid Report (SAR). *Deadline:* May 4.

Contact: Director, Program Services
United Negro College Fund
8260 Willow Oaks Corporate Drive
PO Box 10444
Fairfax, VA 22031-8044
Phone: 800-331-2244
E-mail: rebecca.bennett@uncf.org

GATES MILLENNIUM SCHOLARS PROGRAM (GATES FOUNDATION)

Award enables African-American students to complete an undergraduate and graduate education. Must be entering a U.S. accredited college or university as full-time degree-seeking students. Minimum 3.3 GPA required. Must demonstrate leadership abilities. Must meet federal Pell Grant eligibility criteria.

Award: Scholarship for use in freshman, sophomore, junior, senior, or graduate years; renewable. *Number:* varies. *Amount:* $1000.

Eligibility Requirements: Applicant must be Black (non-Hispanic) and enrolled or expecting to enroll full-time at a four-year institution or university. Available to U.S. and non-U.S. citizens.

Application Requirements: Application, financial need analysis, nomination packet. *Deadline:* January 12.

Contact: Director, Program Services
United Negro College Fund
8260 Willow Oaks Corporate Drive
PO Box 10444
Fairfax, VA 22031-8044
Phone: 800-331-2244
E-mail: rebecca.bennett@uncf.org

GHEENS FOUNDATION SCHOLARSHIP

Scholarship supports students from Kentucky. For use in one of the following universities: Clark Atlanta University, Morehouse College, Morris Brown College, Spelman College, Tuskegee University, Howard University, Florida A&M, Southern University, Tennessee State or Prairie View University.

Award: Scholarship for use in freshman, sophomore, junior, senior, or graduate years; not renewable. *Number:* varies. *Amount:* up to $2000.

Eligibility Requirements: Applicant must be Black (non-Hispanic); enrolled or expecting to enroll full- or part-time at a four-year institution or university; resident of Kentucky and studying in Alabama, District of Columbia, Florida, Georgia, Louisiana, Tennessee, or Texas. Applicant must have 2.5 GPA or higher. Available to U.S. citizens.

Application Requirements: Application, financial need analysis, transcript. *Deadline:* varies.

Contact: Director, Program Services
United Negro College Fund
8260 Willow Oaks Corporate Drive
PO Box 10444
Fairfax, VA 22031-8044
Phone: 800-331-2244
E-mail: rebecca.bennett@uncf.org

HOUGHTON-MIFFLIN COMPANY FELLOWS PROGRAM

Scholarship is awarded to undergraduate junior after completion of paid internship to introduce selected students to careers in the publishing industry. Must attend a UNCF member college or university. Minimum 3.0 GPA required. Prospective applicants should complete the Student Profile found at Web site: http://www.uncf.org.

Award: Scholarship for use in junior year; not renewable. *Number:* varies. *Amount:* $3700.

Eligibility Requirements: Applicant must be Black (non-Hispanic) and enrolled or expecting to enroll full-time at a four-year institution or university. Applicant must have 3.0 GPA or higher. Available to U.S. citizens.

Application Requirements: Application, financial need analysis. *Deadline:* varies.

Contact: Director, Program Services
United Negro College Fund
8260 Willow Oaks Corporate Drive
PO Box 10444
Fairfax, VA 22031-8044
Phone: 800-331-2244
E-mail: rebecca.bennett@uncf.org

JOHN W. ANDERSON FOUNDATION SCHOLARSHIP

Need-based scholarship for students from Indiana attending UNCF member colleges and universities. Prospective applicants should complete the Student Profile found at Web site: http://www.uncf.org.

Award: Scholarship for use in freshman, sophomore, junior, or senior years; not renewable. *Number:* 1. *Amount:* up to $3000.

Eligibility Requirements: Applicant must be Black (non-Hispanic); enrolled or expecting to enroll full- or part-time at a four-year institution or university and resident of Indiana. Applicant must have 2.5 GPA or higher. Available to U.S. citizens.

Application Requirements: Application, financial need analysis. *Deadline:* continuous.

Contact: Director, Program Services
United Negro College Fund
8260 Willow Oaks Corporate Drive
PO Box 10444
Fairfax, VA 22031-8044
Phone: 800-331-2244
E-mail: rebecca.bennett@uncf.org

JOSEPH A. TOWLES AFRICAN STUDY ABROAD SCHOLARSHIP

Award to students who have been accepted into a study abroad program in Africa. Must have 3.0 GPA. Visit Web site for more information: http://www.uncf.org.

Award: Scholarship for use in sophomore, junior, or senior years; renewable. *Number:* varies. *Amount:* up to $10,000.

Eligibility Requirements: Applicant must be Black (non-Hispanic) and enrolled or expecting to enroll full- or part-time at a four-year institution or university. Applicant must have 3.0 GPA or higher. Available to U.S. and non-U.S. citizens.

Application Requirements: Application, financial need analysis, FAFSA, Student Aid Report (SAR). *Deadline:* April 30.

Contact: Director, Program Services
United Negro College Fund
8260 Willow Oaks Corporate Drive
PO Box 10444
Fairfax, VA 22031-8044
Phone: 800-331-2244
E-mail: rebecca.bennett@uncf.org

KANSAS CITY INITIATIVE SCHOLARSHIP

Award for a minority student in the Kansas City metropolitan area, who plans to attend a UNCF member college or university or the University of Missouri at Kansas City. The entering freshman must have a GPA of at least a 3.0 and the upperclassman must have a GPA of 2.5.

Award: Scholarship for use in freshman, sophomore, junior, or senior years; renewable. *Number:* varies. *Amount:* $2500–$5000.

Eligibility Requirements: Applicant must be Black (non-Hispanic); enrolled or expecting to enroll full- or part-time at a four-year institution or university and resident of Kansas or Missouri. Available to U.S. citizens.

Application Requirements: Application, financial need analysis, FAFSA, Student Aid Report (SAR). *Deadline:* varies.

Contact: Director, Program Services
United Negro College Fund
8260 Willow Oaks Corporate Drive
PO Box 10444
Fairfax, VA 22031-8044
Phone: 800-331-2244
E-mail: rebecca.bennett@uncf.org

KROGER/PEPSI SCHOLARSHIP

Student must be a resident of the Kroger Great Lakes marketing area (lower peninsula of Michigan, central and northern Ohio and northern West Virginia).

Must be a high school senior planning to attend a UNCF institution or a four-year fully accredited institution of higher learning.

Award: Scholarship for use in freshman year; not renewable. *Number:* varies. *Amount:* $5000.

Eligibility Requirements: Applicant must be Black (non-Hispanic); high school student; planning to enroll or expecting to enroll full- or part-time at a four-year institution or university and resident of Michigan, Ohio, or West Virginia. Applicant must have 2.5 GPA or higher. Available to U.S. citizens.

Application Requirements: Application, essay, financial need analysis, photo, references, transcript, FAFSA. *Deadline:* May 18.

Contact: Director, Program Services
United Negro College Fund
8260 Willow Oaks Corporate Drive
PO Box 10444
Fairfax, VA 22031-8044
Phone: 800-331-2244
E-mail: rebecca.bennett@uncf.org

KROGER SCHOLARSHIP

Awards for students residing in targeted Kroger retail store locations (GA, AL, SC, TN) who will be attending a UNCF participating college or university.

Award: Scholarship for use in freshman, sophomore, junior, or senior years; not renewable. *Number:* varies. *Amount:* up to $5000.

Eligibility Requirements: Applicant must be Black (non-Hispanic); enrolled or expecting to enroll full- or part-time at a four-year institution or university and resident of Alabama, Georgia, South Carolina, or Tennessee. Applicant must have 2.5 GPA or higher. Available to U.S. citizens.

Application Requirements: Application, financial need analysis, FAFSA, Student Aid Report (SAR). *Deadline:* April 1.

Contact: Director, Program Services
United Negro College Fund
8260 Willow Oaks Corporate Drive
PO Box 10444
Fairfax, VA 22031-8044
Phone: 800-331-2244
E-mail: rebecca.bennett@uncf.org

KUNTZ FOUNDATION SCHOLARSHIP

Need-based scholarship for students attending a UNCF member college or university. Minimum 2.5 GPA required. Prospective applicants should complete the Student Profile found at Web site: http://www.uncf.org.

Award: Scholarship for use in freshman, sophomore, junior, or senior years; not renewable. *Number:* 1. *Amount:* $500.

Eligibility Requirements: Applicant must be Black (non-Hispanic) and enrolled or expecting to enroll full- or part-time at a four-year institution or university. Applicant must have 2.5 GPA or higher. Available to U.S. citizens.

Application Requirements: Application, financial need analysis. *Deadline:* continuous.

Contact: Director, Program Services
United Negro College Fund
8260 Willow Oaks Corporate Drive
PO Box 10444
Fairfax, VA 22031-8044
Phone: 800-331-2244
E-mail: rebecca.bennett@uncf.org

LEON JACKSON JR. SCHOLARSHIP

• See page 586

LIMITED INC. AND INTIMATE BRANDS INC. SCHOLARSHIP

Scholarships awarded to students attending a UNCF member college or university. Minimum 2.5 GPA required. Prospective applicants should complete the Student Profile found at Web site: http://www.uncf.org.

Award: Scholarship for use in freshman, sophomore, junior, or senior years; not renewable. *Number:* 1. *Amount:* $500.

Eligibility Requirements: Applicant must be Black (non-Hispanic); enrolled or expecting to enroll full- or part-time at a four-year institution or university and resident of Ohio. Applicant must have 2.5 GPA or higher. Available to U.S. citizens.

Application Requirements: Application, financial need analysis. *Deadline:* continuous.

Contact: Director, Program Services
United Negro College Fund
8260 Willow Oaks Corporate Drive
PO Box 10444
Fairfax, VA 22031-8044
Phone: 800-331-2244
E-mail: rebecca.bennett@uncf.org

MARTIN LUTHER KING JR. CHILDREN'S CHOIR SCHOLARSHIP

Scholarship for students who were part of a class action suit. The recipients receive a one-time award and may attend any college or university of their choice. Should have minimum of 2.5 GPA and the value of scholarship is $1000.

Award: Scholarship for use in freshman, sophomore, junior, or senior years; not renewable. *Number:* varies. *Amount:* $1000.

Eligibility Requirements: Applicant must be Black (non-Hispanic) and enrolled or expecting to enroll full- or part-time at a four-year institution or university. Applicant must have 2.5 GPA or higher. Available to U.S. and non-U.S. citizens.

Application Requirements: Application, financial need analysis. *Deadline:* varies.

Contact: Director, Program Services
United Negro College Fund
8260 Willow Oaks Corporate Drive
PO Box 10444
Fairfax, VA 22031-8044
Phone: 800-331-2244
E-mail: rebecca.bennett@uncf.org

MINNESOTA STUDENT AID PROGRAM

Scholarship is awarded to students from Minnesota who are attending a UNCF member college or university with a unmet financial need. Number of award varies and students with Minimum GPA of 2.5 are eligible.

Award: Scholarship for use in freshman, sophomore, junior, or senior years; renewable. *Number:* varies. *Amount:* up to $3000.

Eligibility Requirements: Applicant must be Black (non-Hispanic); enrolled or expecting to enroll full- or part-time at a four-year institution or university and resident of Minnesota. Applicant must have 2.5 GPA or higher. Available to U.S. citizens.

Application Requirements: Application, financial need analysis. *Deadline:* varies.

Contact: Director, Program Services
United Negro College Fund
8260 Willow Oaks Corporate Drive
PO Box 10444
Fairfax, VA 22031-8044
Phone: 800-331-2244
E-mail: rebecca.bennett@uncf.org

NEW JERSEY MAYOR'S TASK FORCE SCHOLARSHIP

Awards available for African American students who live in one of the New Jersey Task Force participating cities. Must attend a historically black college or university, or a UNCF member institution. Requirements may vary for each city. Check Web site for details. http://www.uncf.org.

Award: Scholarship for use in freshman, sophomore, junior, or senior years; renewable. *Number:* varies. *Amount:* $1350.

Eligibility Requirements: Applicant must be American Indian/Alaska Native or Black (non-Hispanic); enrolled or expecting to enroll full- or part-time at a four-year institution or university and resident of New Jersey. Applicant must have 2.5 GPA or higher. Available to U.S. citizens.

United Negro College Fund (continued)

Application Requirements: Application, essay, financial need analysis, photo, references, transcript, FAFSA, Student Aid Report (SAR). *Deadline:* varies.

Contact: Director, Program Services
United Negro College Fund
8260 Willow Oaks Corporate Drive
PO Box 10444
Fairfax, VA 22031-8044
Phone: 800-331-2244
E-mail: rebecca.bennett@uncf.org

PENNSYLVANIA STATE EMPLOYEES SCHOLARSHIP FUND

Scholarships for UNCF students from Pennsylvania. Funds may be used for tuition, room and board, books, or to repay federal student loans. Minimum 2.5 GPA required. Prospective applicants should complete the Student Profile found at Web site: http://www.uncf.org.

Award: Scholarship for use in freshman, sophomore, junior, or senior years; not renewable. *Number:* 20. *Amount:* up to $4000.

Eligibility Requirements: Applicant must be Black (non-Hispanic); enrolled or expecting to enroll full-time at a four-year institution or university and resident of Pennsylvania. Applicant must have 2.5 GPA or higher. Available to U.S. citizens.

Application Requirements: Application, financial need analysis. *Deadline:* July 14.

Contact: Director, Program Services
United Negro College Fund
8260 Willow Oaks Corporate Drive
PO Box 10444
Fairfax, VA 22031-8044
Phone: 800-331-2244
E-mail: rebecca.bennett@uncf.org

RICHMOND SCHOLARSHIP

Scholarships available to students who reside in Central Virginia. Minimum 2.5 GPA required. Must attend a UNCF member college or university. Details on Web site at http://www.uncf.org.

Award: Scholarship for use in freshman, sophomore, junior, or senior years; renewable. *Number:* varies. *Amount:* up to $2000.

Eligibility Requirements: Applicant must be Black (non-Hispanic); enrolled or expecting to enroll full- or part-time at a four-year institution or university and resident of Virginia. Applicant must have 2.5 GPA or higher. Available to U.S. citizens.

Application Requirements: Application, financial need analysis, FAFSA, Student Aid Report (SAR). *Deadline:* varies.

Contact: Director, Program Services
United Negro College Fund
8260 Willow Oaks Corporate Drive
PO Box 10444
Fairfax, VA 22031-8044
Phone: 800-331-2244
E-mail: rebecca.bennett@uncf.org

RONALD MCDONALD'S CHICAGOLAND SCHOLARSHIP

Scholarships awarded to students attending a UNCF member college or university. Scholarship value is $3000. Must maintain minimum GPA of 2.5 and is applicable for four years of study.

Award: Scholarship for use in freshman, sophomore, junior, or senior years; renewable. *Number:* varies. *Amount:* $3000.

Eligibility Requirements: Applicant must be Black (non-Hispanic) and enrolled or expecting to enroll full-time at a four-year institution or university. Applicant must have 2.5 GPA or higher. Available to U.S. citizens.

Application Requirements: Application, financial need analysis. *Deadline:* continuous.

Contact: Director, Program Services
United Negro College Fund
8260 Willow Oaks Corporate Drive
PO Box 10444
Fairfax, VA 22031-8044
Phone: 800-331-2244
E-mail: rebecca.bennett@uncf.org

RONALD MCDONALD'S HOUSE CHARITIES SCHOLARSHIP-OHIO

Scholarships available for African American students residing in Ohio. Must attend a UNCF member college or university. Must have a minimum 2.5 GPA. Information on Web site at http://www.uncf.org.

Award: Scholarship for use in freshman, sophomore, junior, or senior years; renewable. *Number:* varies. *Amount:* varies.

Eligibility Requirements: Applicant must be Black (non-Hispanic); enrolled or expecting to enroll full- or part-time at a two-year or four-year institution or university and resident of Ohio. Applicant must have 2.5 GPA or higher. Available to U.S. citizens.

Application Requirements: Application, financial need analysis, FAFSA, Student Aid Report (SAR). *Deadline:* varies.

Contact: Director, Program Services
United Negro College Fund
8260 Willow Oaks Corporate Drive
PO Box 10444
Fairfax, VA 22031-8044
Phone: 800-331-2244
E-mail: rebecca.bennett@uncf.org

ST. PETERSBURG GOLF CLASSIC SCHOLARSHIP

Each year two men and two women students from the Tampa Bay, Florida area are chosen to receive this scholarship. Visit Web site for more information: http://www.uncf.org.

Award: Scholarship for use in freshman, sophomore, junior, or senior years; renewable. *Number:* 4. *Amount:* up to $5000.

Eligibility Requirements: Applicant must be Black (non-Hispanic); enrolled or expecting to enroll full- or part-time at a four-year institution or university and resident of Florida. Applicant must have 2.5 GPA or higher. Available to U.S. citizens.

Application Requirements: Application, financial need analysis, FAFSA, Student Aid Report (SAR). *Deadline:* varies.

Contact: Director, Program Services
United Negro College Fund
8260 Willow Oaks Corporate Drive
PO Box 10444
Fairfax, VA 22031-8044
Phone: 800-331-2244
E-mail: rebecca.bennett@uncf.org

SALLIE MAE FUND AMERICAN DREAM SCHOLARSHIP

Awards from $500 to $5000 to African-American students with financial need and enrolled in a two- or four-year title IV eligible, accredited college or university. Open to incoming freshmen as well as current undergraduate students. Please visit Web site for more information: http://www.uncf.org.

Award: Scholarship for use in freshman, sophomore, junior, or senior years; renewable. *Number:* varies. *Amount:* $500–$5000.

Eligibility Requirements: Applicant must be Black (non-Hispanic) and enrolled or expecting to enroll full-time at a two-year or four-year institution or university. Applicant must have 2.5 GPA or higher. Available to U.S. citizens.

Application Requirements: Application, essay, financial need analysis, references, transcript, FAFSA, Student Aid Report (SAR). *Deadline:* April 15.

Contact: Director, Program Services
United Negro College Fund
8260 Willow Oaks Corporate Drive
PO Box 10444
Fairfax, VA 22031-8044
Phone: 800-331-2244
E-mail: rebecca.bennett@uncf.org

SAN JOSE MERCURY NEWS SCHOLARSHIP

Award for both full-time and part-time student from Silicon Valley, CA. Must have 2.5 GPA and attend a UNCF Member College or University.

Award: Scholarship for use in freshman, sophomore, junior, or senior years; renewable. *Number:* 1. *Amount:* $2000.

Eligibility Requirements: Applicant must be Black (non-Hispanic); enrolled or expecting to enroll full- or part-time at a four-year institution or university and resident of California. Applicant must have 2.5 GPA or higher. Available to U.S. citizens.

Application Requirements: Application, financial need analysis, FAFSA, Student Aid Report (SAR). *Deadline:* varies.

Contact: Director, Program Services
United Negro College Fund
8260 Willow Oaks Corporate Drive
PO Box 10444
Fairfax, VA 22031-8044
Phone: 800-331-2244
E-mail: rebecca.bennett@uncf.org

SHELL/EQUILON UNCF CLEVELAND SCHOLARSHIP FUND

Awards Ohio residents who are attending a UNCF member college or university. Must have minimum 2.5 GPA and attend a UNCF member college or university.

Award: Scholarship for use in freshman, sophomore, junior, or senior years; renewable. *Number:* varies. *Amount:* $3000.

Eligibility Requirements: Applicant must be Black (non-Hispanic); enrolled or expecting to enroll full- or part-time at a four-year institution or university and resident of Ohio. Applicant must have 2.5 GPA or higher. Available to U.S. citizens.

Application Requirements: Application, financial need analysis, FAFSA, Student Aid Report (SAR). *Deadline:* varies.

Contact: Director, Program Services
United Negro College Fund
8260 Willow Oaks Corporate Drive
PO Box 10444
Fairfax, VA 22031-8044
Phone: 800-331-2244
E-mail: rebecca.bennett@uncf.org

SIRAGUSA FOUNDATION SCHOLARSHIP

Scholarships available to students attending a UNCF member college or university. Minimum 2.5 GPA required. Prospective applicants should complete the student profile found at Web site: http://www.uncf.org.

Award: Scholarship for use in freshman, sophomore, junior, or senior years; not renewable. *Number:* 1. *Amount:* $2000.

Eligibility Requirements: Applicant must be Black (non-Hispanic) and enrolled or expecting to enroll full-time at a four-year institution or university. Applicant must have 2.5 GPA or higher. Available to U.S. and non-U.S. citizens.

Application Requirements: Application, financial need analysis. *Deadline:* continuous.

Contact: Director, Program Services
United Negro College Fund
8260 Willow Oaks Corporate Drive
PO Box 10444
Fairfax, VA 22031-8044
Phone: 800-331-2244
E-mail: rebecca.bennett@uncf.org

STERLING BANK SCHOLARSHIP

Scholarship available to students attending UNCF member colleges or universities. Minimum 2.5 GPA required. Prospective applicants should complete the Student Profile found at Web site: http://www.uncf.org.

Award: Scholarship for use in freshman, sophomore, junior, or senior years; not renewable. *Number:* 1. *Amount:* up to $1000.

Eligibility Requirements: Applicant must be Black (non-Hispanic) and enrolled or expecting to enroll full- or part-time at a four-year institution or university. Applicant must have 2.5 GPA or higher. Available to U.S. citizens.

Application Requirements: Application, financial need analysis. *Deadline:* continuous.

Contact: Director, Program Services
United Negro College Fund
8260 Willow Oaks Corporate Drive
PO Box 10444
Fairfax, VA 22031-8044
Phone: 800-331-2244
E-mail: rebecca.bennett@uncf.org

TJX FOUNDATION SCHOLARSHIP

Award available to Massachusetts residents who live near TJ Maxx stores. Must have 2.5 GPA. Please visit Web site for more information: http://www.uncf.org.

Award: Scholarship for use in freshman, sophomore, junior, or senior years; renewable. *Number:* varies. *Amount:* $1000.

Eligibility Requirements: Applicant must be Black (non-Hispanic); enrolled or expecting to enroll full- or part-time at a four-year institution or university and resident of Massachusetts. Applicant must have 2.5 GPA or higher. Available to U.S. citizens.

Application Requirements: Application, financial need analysis, FAFSA, Student Aid Report (SAR). *Deadline:* varies.

Contact: Director, Program Services
United Negro College Fund
8260 Willow Oaks Corporate Drive
PO Box 10444
Fairfax, VA 22031-8044
Phone: 800-331-2244
E-mail: rebecca.bennett@uncf.org

TRULL FOUNDATION SCHOLARSHIP

Need-based scholarship to students attending a UNCF member college or university. Minimum 2.5 GPA required. Prospective applicants should complete the student profile found at Web site: http://www.uncf.org.

Award: Scholarship for use in freshman, sophomore, junior, or senior years; not renewable. *Number:* varies. *Amount:* varies.

Eligibility Requirements: Applicant must be Black (non-Hispanic) and enrolled or expecting to enroll full-time at a four-year institution or university. Applicant must have 2.5 GPA or higher. Available to U.S. citizens.

Application Requirements: Application, financial need analysis. *Deadline:* continuous.

Contact: Director, Program Services
United Negro College Fund
8260 Willow Oaks Corporate Drive
PO Box 10444
Fairfax, VA 22031-8044
Phone: 800-331-2244
E-mail: rebecca.bennett@uncf.org

UNION BANK OF CALIFORNIA

Scholarship available to all California students who attend a UNCF member college or university. Minimum 2.5 GPA required. Prospective applicants should complete the Student Profile found at Web site: http://www.uncf.org.

Award: Scholarship for use in freshman, sophomore, junior, or senior years; not renewable. *Number:* 1. *Amount:* varies.

Eligibility Requirements: Applicant must be Black (non-Hispanic); enrolled or expecting to enroll full- or part-time at a four-year institution or university and resident of California. Applicant must have 2.5 GPA or higher. Available to U.S. citizens.

United Negro College Fund (continued)

Application Requirements: Application, financial need analysis. *Deadline:* continuous.

Contact: Director, Program Services
United Negro College Fund
8260 Willow Oaks Corporate Drive
PO Box 10444
Fairfax, VA 22031-8044
Phone: 800-331-2244
E-mail: rebecca.bennett@uncf.org

UNITED INSURANCE SCHOLARSHIP

Students or the parents of students applying for this award must have a policy with United Insurance Company. Visit Web site for more information: http://www.uncf.org.

Award: Scholarship for use in freshman, sophomore, junior, or senior years; renewable. *Number:* varies. *Amount:* $5000.

Eligibility Requirements: Applicant must be Black (non-Hispanic) and enrolled or expecting to enroll full- or part-time at a four-year institution or university. Applicant must have 2.5 GPA or higher. Available to U.S. and Canadian citizens.

Application Requirements: Application, financial need analysis, FAFSA, Student Aid Report (SAR). *Deadline:* August 31.

Contact: Director, Program Services
United Negro College Fund
8260 Willow Oaks Corporate Drive
PO Box 10444
Fairfax, VA 22031-8044
Phone: 800-331-2244
E-mail: rebecca.bennett@uncf.org

UNITED PARCEL SERVICE FOUNDATION SCHOLARSHIP

Award provides students with financial support for tuition and other education costs. Based on need amount varies. Please visit Web site for more information: http://www.uncf.org.

Award: Scholarship for use in freshman, sophomore, junior, or senior years; renewable. *Number:* varies. *Amount:* varies.

Eligibility Requirements: Applicant must be Black (non-Hispanic) and enrolled or expecting to enroll full-time at a four-year institution or university. Applicant must have 2.5 GPA or higher. Available to U.S. citizens.

Application Requirements: Application, financial need analysis, FAFSA, Student Aid Report (SAR). *Deadline:* varies.

Contact: Director, Program Services
United Negro College Fund
8260 Willow Oaks Corporate Drive
PO Box 10444
Fairfax, VA 22031-8044
Phone: 800-331-2244
E-mail: rebecca.bennett@uncf.org

UNITED WAY OF NEW ORLEANS EMERGENCY ASSISTANCE FUND

Award providing emergency assistance for students at Dillard University and Xavier University in Louisiana. For both full-time and part-time students. Deadline varies.

Award: Scholarship for use in freshman, sophomore, junior, or senior years; renewable. *Number:* varies. *Amount:* up to $2500.

Eligibility Requirements: Applicant must be Black (non-Hispanic); enrolled or expecting to enroll full- or part-time at a four-year institution or university; resident of Louisiana and studying in Louisiana. Applicant must have 2.5 GPA or higher. Available to U.S. citizens.

Application Requirements: Application, financial need analysis, FAFSA, Student Aid Report (SAR). *Deadline:* varies.

Contact: Director, Program Services
United Negro College Fund
8260 Willow Oaks Corporate Drive
PO Box 10444
Fairfax, VA 22031-8044
Phone: 800-331-2244
E-mail: rebecca.bennett@uncf.org

UNITED WAY OF WESTCHESTER AND PUTNAM INC./ UNCF EMERGENCY ASSISTANCE FUND

Award providing emergency assistance for students from the Westchester/Putnam, NY area. A 2.5 GPA is required if attending a UNCF school, or 2.0 if attending Mercy College or Westchester Community College. Students are only eligible to receive emergency assistance for two consecutive semesters. Visit Web site for more information: http://www.uncf.org.

Award: Scholarship for use in freshman, sophomore, junior, or senior years; not renewable. *Number:* varies. *Amount:* up to $5000.

Eligibility Requirements: Applicant must be Black (non-Hispanic) or Hispanic; enrolled or expecting to enroll full- or part-time at a four-year institution or university; resident of New York and studying in New York. Available to U.S. citizens.

Application Requirements: Application, financial need analysis, FAFSA, Student Aid Report (SAR). *Deadline:* August 31.

Contact: Director, Program Services
United Negro College Fund
8260 Willow Oaks Corporate Drive
PO Box 10444
Fairfax, VA 22031-8044
Phone: 800-331-2244
E-mail: rebecca.bennett@uncf.org

VERIZON FOUNDATION SCHOLARSHIP

Scholarships for students who reside within the Mid-Atlantic and Northeast Regions and attending a UNCF member college or university. Minimum 2.5 GPA required. Prospective applicants should complete the student profile found at Web site: http://www.uncf.org.

Award: Scholarship for use in freshman, sophomore, junior, or senior years; not renewable. *Number:* 1. *Amount:* $2000–$4000.

Eligibility Requirements: Applicant must be Black (non-Hispanic); enrolled or expecting to enroll full-time at a four-year institution or university and resident of Connecticut, Delaware, Maine, Maryland, Massachusetts, New Hampshire, New Jersey, New York, Pennsylvania, Rhode Island, or Vermont. Applicant must have 2.5 GPA or higher. Available to U.S. citizens.

Application Requirements: Application, financial need analysis. *Deadline:* varies.

Contact: Director, Program Services
United Negro College Fund
8260 Willow Oaks Corporate Drive
PO Box 10444
Fairfax, VA 22031-8044
Phone: 800-331-2244
E-mail: rebecca.bennett@uncf.org

V103/WAOK UNCF EMERGENCY ASSISTANCE SCHOLARSHIP FUND

Scholarship is open to graduating seniors in their final semester at Clark Atlanta University, Morehouse College, Spelman College or Interdenominational Theological Center. Must be enrolled full-time with at least 2.5 GPA. Prospective applicants should complete the student profile found at Web site: http://www.uncf.org.

Award: Scholarship for use in senior year; not renewable. *Number:* varies. *Amount:* varies.

Eligibility Requirements: Applicant must be Black (non-Hispanic); enrolled or expecting to enroll full-time at a four-year institution or university and studying in Georgia. Applicant must have 2.5 GPA or higher. Available to U.S. citizens.

Application Requirements: Application, financial need analysis. *Deadline:* varies.

Contact: Director, Program Services
United Negro College Fund
8260 Willow Oaks Corporate Drive
PO Box 10444
Fairfax, VA 22031-8044
Phone: 800-331-2244
E-mail: rebecca.bennett@uncf.org

WHIRLPOOL FOUNDATION SCHOLARSHIP

Renewable award for students participating in Whirlpool's INROADS program in LaPorte, IN; Benton Harbor, MI; and LaVerne, TN. Must have 3.0 GPA.

Award: Scholarship for use in freshman, sophomore, junior, or senior years; renewable. *Number:* varies. *Amount:* $2500.

Eligibility Requirements: Applicant must be Black (non-Hispanic); enrolled or expecting to enroll full-time at a four-year institution or university and resident of Indiana, Michigan, or Tennessee. Applicant must have 3.0 GPA or higher. Available to U.S. citizens.

Application Requirements: Application, financial need analysis, FAFSA, Student Aid Report (SAR). *Deadline:* varies.

Contact: Director, Program Services
United Negro College Fund
8260 Willow Oaks Corporate Drive
PO Box 10444
Fairfax, VA 22031-8044
Phone: 800-331-2244
E-mail: rebecca.bennett@uncf.org

WISCONSIN STUDENT AID

Award for African-American Wisconsin residents. For both full-time and part-time study. Must have 2.5 GPA. Please visit Web site for more information: http://www.uncf.org.

Award: Scholarship for use in freshman, sophomore, junior, or senior years; renewable. *Number:* varies. *Amount:* up to $2500.

Eligibility Requirements: Applicant must be Black (non-Hispanic); enrolled or expecting to enroll full- or part-time at a four-year institution or university and resident of Wisconsin. Applicant must have 2.5 GPA or higher. Available to U.S. citizens.

Application Requirements: Application, financial need analysis, FAFSA, Student Aid Report (SAR). *Deadline:* varies.

Contact: Director, Program Services
United Negro College Fund
8260 Willow Oaks Corporate Drive
PO Box 10444
Fairfax, VA 22031-8044
Phone: 800-331-2244
E-mail: rebecca.bennett@uncf.org

UNITED SOUTH AND EASTERN TRIBES INC. http://www.usetinc.org

UNITED SOUTH AND EASTERN TRIBES SCHOLARSHIP FUND

One-time scholarship for Native American students who are members of United South and Eastern Tribes, enrolled or accepted in a postsecondary educational institution.

Award: Scholarship for use in freshman, sophomore, junior, or senior years; not renewable. *Number:* 4–8. *Amount:* $500.

Eligibility Requirements: Applicant must be Indian citizen; American Indian/Alaska Native and enrolled or expecting to enroll full- or part-time at a four-year institution or university.

Application Requirements: Application, essay, financial need analysis, transcript, proof of tribal enrollment. *Deadline:* April 30.

Contact: Theresa Embry, Executive Assistant to Director
United South and Eastern Tribes Inc.
711 Stewarts Ferry Pike, Suite 100
Nashville, TN 37214-2634
Phone: 615-872-7900
Fax: 615-872-7417

UNITED STATES HISPANIC LEADERSHIP INSTITUTE http://www.ushli.org

DR. JUAN ANDRADE, JR. SCHOLARSHIP

Scholarship for young Hispanic leaders. Applicants must be enrolled or accepted for enrollment as a full-time student in a four-year institution in the United States or U.S. territories, and demonstrate a verifiable need for financial support. At least one parent must be of Hispanic ancestry.

Award: Scholarship for use in freshman, sophomore, junior, or senior years; not renewable. *Number:* 30. *Amount:* $500–$1000.

Eligibility Requirements: Applicant must be Hispanic and enrolled or expecting to enroll full-time at a two-year or four-year institution or university. Available to U.S. citizens.

Application Requirements: Application, autobiography, essay, photo, resume, references, transcript. *Deadline:* January 11.

Contact: Isabel Reyes, Scholarship Coordinator
United States Hispanic Leadership Institute
431 South Dearborn Street, Suite 1203
Chicago, IL 60605
Phone: 312-427-8683
Fax: 312-427-5183
E-mail: ireyes@ushli.org

URBAN LEAGUE OF RHODE ISLAND INC. http://www.ulri.org

URBAN LEAGUE OF RHODE ISLAND SCHOLARSHIP

Scholarship offered to minority students who are Rhode Island residents seeking postsecondary education. Priority is given to recent high school graduates.

Award: Scholarship for use in freshman, sophomore, junior, or senior years; not renewable. *Number:* varies. *Amount:* varies.

Eligibility Requirements: Applicant must be American Indian/Alaska Native, Asian/Pacific Islander, Black (non-Hispanic), or Hispanic; enrolled or expecting to enroll full-time at a two-year or four-year or technical institution or university and resident of Rhode Island. Available to U.S. citizens.

Application Requirements: Application, financial need analysis, interview, references, transcript. *Deadline:* April 30.

Contact: Marcia Ranglin' Vassell, Associate Director
Urban League of Rhode Island Inc.
246 Prairie Avenue
Providence, RI 02905
Phone: 401-351-5000
Fax: 401-454-1946
E-mail: education@ulri.org

VIKKI CARR SCHOLARSHIP FOUNDATION http://www.vikkicarr.net/scholarship_foundation.htm

VIKKI CARR SCHOLARSHIPS

Scholarship awarded for high school senior entering the first year of college. Applicant must be of Mexican-American descent and Texas resident.

Award: Scholarship for use in freshman year; not renewable. *Number:* varies. *Amount:* varies.

Eligibility Requirements: Applicant must be Hispanic; high school student; planning to enroll or expecting to enroll full- or part-time at a two-year or four-year institution and resident of Texas. Available to U.S. citizens.

Application Requirements: Application, essay, financial need analysis, photo, test scores, transcript. *Deadline:* March 1.

Contact: Scholarship Committee
Vikki Carr Scholarship Foundation
PO Box 780968
San Antonio, TX 78278
E-mail: vicarent@aol.com

WASHINGTON HIGHER EDUCATION COORDINATING BOARD http://www.hecb.wa.gov

AMERICAN INDIAN ENDOWED SCHOLARSHIP

Awarded to financially needy undergraduate and graduate students with close social and cultural ties with a Native-American community. Must be Washington resident, enrolled full-time at Washington school.

Award: Scholarship for use in freshman, sophomore, junior, senior, or graduate years; renewable. *Number:* 17. *Amount:* $500–$2000.

Eligibility Requirements: Applicant must be American Indian/Alaska Native; enrolled or expecting to enroll full-time at a two-year or four-year or technical institution or university; resident of Washington and studying in Washington. Available to U.S. citizens.

Application Requirements: Application, financial need analysis. *Deadline:* February 1.

Contact: Ann Lee, Program Manager
Washington Higher Education Coordinating Board
917 Lakeridge Way, PO Box 43430
Olympia, WA 98504-3430
Phone: 360-755-7843
Fax: 360-704-6243
E-mail: annl@hecb.wa.gov

WHITE EARTH TRIBAL COUNCIL http://www.whiteearth.com

WHITE EARTH SCHOLARSHIP PROGRAM

Renewable scholarship for students who are enrolled in postsecondary institutions. Must have a GPA of 2.5. Must be U.S. citizen.

Award: Scholarship for use in freshman, sophomore, junior, senior, graduate, or postgraduate years; renewable. *Number:* 200. *Amount:* $3000.

Eligibility Requirements: Applicant must be American Indian/Alaska Native and enrolled or expecting to enroll full- or part-time at a two-year or four-year or technical institution or university. Applicant must have 2.5 GPA or higher. Available to U.S. citizens.

Application Requirements: Application, financial need analysis, transcript. *Deadline:* May 31.

Contact: Leslie Nessman, Scholarship Manager
White Earth Tribal Council
PO Box 418
White Earth, MN 56591-0418
Phone: 218-983-3285
Fax: 218-983-4299

WILLIAM E. DOCTER EDUCATIONAL FUND/ST. MARY ARMENIAN CHURCH http://www.wedfund.org

WILLIAM ERVANT DOCTER EDUCATIONAL FUND

Grant up to $2000 available to worthy students regardless of age, gender, or level of education or training. Funds given to American citizens of Armenian ancestry to pursue studies and training in the United States or Canada.

Award: Grant for use in freshman, sophomore, junior, senior, graduate, or postgraduate years; not renewable. *Number:* 20. *Amount:* $1000–$2000.

Eligibility Requirements: Applicant must be of Armenian heritage and enrolled or expecting to enroll full- or part-time at a two-year or four-year or technical institution or university. Available to U.S. citizens.

Application Requirements: Application, essay, financial need analysis, test scores, transcript, proof of US citizenship. *Deadline:* June 30.

Contact: Edward Alexander, Scholarship Committee Chairman
William E. Docter Educational Fund/St. Mary Armenian Church
PO Box 39224
Washington, DC 20016
Fax: 202-364-1441
E-mail: wedfund@aol.com

WISCONSIN HIGHER EDUCATIONAL AIDS BOARD http://www.heab.state.wi.us

MINORITY UNDERGRADUATE RETENTION GRANT-WISCONSIN

The grant provides financial assistance to African-American, Native-American, Hispanic, and former citizens of Laos, Vietnam, and Cambodia, for study in Wisconsin. Must be Wisconsin resident, enrolled at least half-time in Wisconsin Technical College System schools, non-profit independent colleges and universities, and tribal colleges. Refer to Web site for further details: http://www.heab.state.wi.us.

Award: Grant for use in sophomore, junior, senior, or graduate years; not renewable. *Number:* varies. *Amount:* $250–$2500.

Eligibility Requirements: Applicant must be American Indian/Alaska Native, Asian/Pacific Islander, Black (non-Hispanic), or Hispanic; enrolled or expecting to enroll full- or part-time at a two-year or four-year or technical institution or university; resident of Wisconsin and studying in Wisconsin. Available to U.S. and non-U.S. citizens.

Application Requirements: Application, financial need analysis. *Deadline:* continuous.

Contact: Mary Lou Kuzdas, Program Coordinator
Wisconsin Higher Educational Aids Board
PO Box 7885
Madison, WI 53707-7885
Phone: 608-267-2212
Fax: 608-267-2808
E-mail: mary.kuzdas@heab.state.wi.us

WISCONSIN NATIVE AMERICAN/INDIAN STUDENT ASSISTANCE GRANT

Grants for Wisconsin residents who are at least one-quarter American Indian. Must be attending a college or university within the state. Refer to Web site for further details: http://www.heab.state.wi.us.

Award: Grant for use in freshman, sophomore, junior, senior, graduate, or postgraduate years; not renewable. *Number:* varies. *Amount:* $250–$1100.

Eligibility Requirements: Applicant must be American Indian/Alaska Native; enrolled or expecting to enroll full- or part-time at a two-year or four-year or technical institution or university; resident of Wisconsin and studying in Wisconsin. Available to U.S. citizens.

Application Requirements: Application, financial need analysis. *Deadline:* continuous.

Contact: Sandra Thomas, Program Coordinator
Wisconsin Higher Educational Aids Board
PO Box 7885
Madison, WI 53707-7885
Phone: 608-266-0888
Fax: 608-267-2808
E-mail: sandy.thomas@heab.state.wi.us

WOMEN OF THE EVANGELICAL LUTHERAN CHURCH IN AMERICA http://www.womenoftheelca.org

AMELIA KEMP SCHOLARSHIP

Scholarship for ELCA women who are of an ethnic minority in undergraduate, graduate, professional, or vocational courses of study. Must be at least 21 years old and hold membership in the ELCA. Must have experienced an interruption of two or more years in education since the completion of high school.

Award: Scholarship for use in freshman, sophomore, junior, senior, or graduate years; not renewable. *Number:* 1. *Amount:* up to $1000.

Eligibility Requirements: Applicant must be Lutheran; American Indian/Alaska Native, Asian/Pacific Islander, Black (non-Hispanic), or Hispanic; age 21 and over; enrolled or expecting to enroll full- or part-time at a two-year or four-year or technical institution or university and female. Available to U.S. citizens.

Application Requirements: Application, resume, references, transcript. *Deadline:* February 15.

Contact: Emily Hansen, Scholarship Committee
Women of the Evangelical Lutheran Church in America
8765 West Higgins Road
Chicago, IL 60631-4189
Phone: 800-638-3522 Ext. 2736
Fax: 773-380-2419
E-mail: womenelca@elca.org

YEMENI AMERICAN ASSOCIATION

YEMENI AMERICAN ASSOCIATION SCHOLARSHIPS

One-time scholarship of $1000 for high school seniors of Yemeni heritage. Up to ten awards are granted annually. Deadline varies.

Award: Scholarship for use in freshman year; not renewable. *Number:* up to 10. *Amount:* $1000.

Eligibility Requirements: Applicant must be Muslim faith; Arab citizen; high school student and planning to enroll or expecting to enroll full- or part-time at a two-year or four-year institution or university. Available to U.S. citizens.

Application Requirements: Application, transcript. *Deadline:* varies.

Contact: Scholarship Committee
Yemeni American Association
PO Box 4148
Dearborn, MI 48126
Phone: 313-841-4200

YMCA BLACK ACHIEVERS SCHOLARSHIP http://www.ymcaofcentralky.org

YMCA BLACK ACHIEVERS SCHOLARSHIP

Need-based scholarships awarded to deserving African-American students. Dollar value and number of available awards varies, and application deadline varies.

Award: Scholarship for use in freshman, sophomore, junior, or senior years; not renewable. *Number:* varies. *Amount:* varies.

Eligibility Requirements: Applicant must be Black (non-Hispanic) and enrolled or expecting to enroll full- or part-time at a two-year or four-year or technical institution or university. Available to U.S. citizens.

Application Requirements: Application, financial need analysis. *Deadline:* varies.

Contact: Jill Wilson, Director, Black Achievers
YMCA Black Achievers Scholarship
Central Kentucky YMCA, 644 Georgetown Street
Lexington, KY 40508
Phone: 859-226-0393 Ext. 15
Fax: 859-226-0385
E-mail: jwilson@ymcaofcentralky.org

YOUTH OPPORTUNITIES FOUNDATION

YOUTH OPPORTUNITIES FOUNDATION SCHOLARSHIPS

Scholarships for Hispanic/Latino high school students that rank in the top 10 percent of their class and score at least 1000 on the SATs. AP classes, leadership skills and community activities will be weighed toward consideration. Must be California resident. At least one parent must be of Hispanic descent. Students must write to foundation for an application.

Award: Scholarship for use in freshman year; not renewable. *Number:* 100. *Amount:* $100–$500.

Eligibility Requirements: Applicant must be Hispanic; high school student; planning to enroll or expecting to enroll full-time at a two-year or four-year institution or university; resident of California and must have an interest in leadership. Available to U.S. citizens.

Application Requirements: Application, photo, references, test scores, transcript. *Deadline:* March 31.

Contact: Felix Castro, Executive Director
Youth Opportunities Foundation
8820 South Sepulveda Boulevard, Suite 208
PO Box 45762
Los Angeles, CA 90045
Phone: 310-670-7664
Fax: 310-670-5238
E-mail: yofgrants@aol.com

RELIGIOUS AFFILIATION

AMERICAN BAPTIST FINANCIAL AID PROGRAM http://www.abc-usa.org

AMERICAN BAPTIST FINANCIAL AID PROGRAM NATIVE AMERICAN GRANTS

• *See page 671*

AMERICAN BAPTIST SCHOLARSHIPS

One-time award for undergraduates who are members of an American Baptist Church. Must be attending an accredited college or university in the United States or Puerto Rico. If attending an ABC-related school, the scholarship amount is $2000 for the year. If not ABC-related, the amount is $1000. Minimum GPA of 2.75 required.

Award: Scholarship for use in freshman, sophomore, junior, or senior years; not renewable. *Number:* 1–5. *Amount:* $1000–$2000.

Eligibility Requirements: Applicant must be Baptist and enrolled or expecting to enroll full-time at a four-year institution or university. Available to U.S. citizens.

Application Requirements: Application, financial need analysis, references. *Deadline:* May 31.

Contact: Lynne Eckman, Director of Financial Aid
American Baptist Financial Aid Program
PO Box 851
Valley Forge, PA 19482-0851
Phone: 610-768-2067
Fax: 610-768-2470
E-mail: lynne.eckman@abc-usa.org

AMERICAN SEPHARDI FOUNDATION http://www.americansephardifederation.org

BROOME AND ALLEN BOYS CAMP AND SCHOLARSHIP FUND

The Broome and Allen Scholarship is awarded to students of Sephardic origin or those working in Sephardic studies. Both graduate and undergraduate degree candidates as well as those doing research projects will be considered. It is awarded for one year and must be renewed for successive years. Enclose copy of tax returns with application.

Award: Scholarship for use in freshman, sophomore, junior, senior, or graduate years; not renewable. *Number:* 20–60. *Amount:* $500–$2000.

Eligibility Requirements: Applicant must be Jewish and enrolled or expecting to enroll full- or part-time at a two-year or four-year or technical institution or university. Available to U.S. and non-U.S. citizens.

Application Requirements: Application, essay, financial need analysis, references, transcript, copy of tax returns. *Deadline:* May 15.

Contact: Ms. Ellen Cohen, Membership and Outreach Coordinator
American Sephardi Foundation
15 West 16th Street
New York, NY 10011
Phone: 212-294-8350 Ext. 4
Fax: 212-294-8348
E-mail: ecohen@asf.cjh.org

BANK OF AMERICA

WILLIAM HEATH EDUCATION SCHOLARSHIP FOR MINISTERS, PRIESTS AND MISSIONARIES

• *See page 478*

CATHOLIC AID ASSOCIATION http://www.catholicaid.org

CATHOLIC AID ASSOCIATION POST HIGH SCHOOL TUITION SCHOLARSHIP

Scholarship requires applicants to be an association member for at least two years. Applicants receive $300 if they attend a non-Catholic college, university, community college, business school or technical school, and will receive $500 if they attend a Catholic college or university. Must be entering first or second year of post-high school education, as part of a degree or certificate program.

Award: Scholarship for use in freshman or sophomore years; not renewable. *Number:* 200. *Amount:* $300–$500.

Eligibility Requirements: Applicant must be Roman Catholic and enrolled or expecting to enroll full-time at a two-year or four-year or technical institution or university. Available to U.S. citizens.

Application Requirements: Application, essay. *Deadline:* February 15.

Contact: Cassandra Voyda, Administrative Assistant
Catholic Aid Association
3499 North Lexington Avenue
St. Paul, MN 55126-8098
Phone: 651-490-0170
Fax: 651-766-1007
E-mail: cvoyda@catholicaid.org

CENTRAL SCHOLARSHIP BUREAU http://www.centralsb.org

LESSANS FAMILY SCHOLARSHIP

• *See page 676*

COMMUNITY FOUNDATION OF WESTERN MASSACHUSETTS http://www.communityfoundation.org

KIMBER RICHTER FAMILY SCHOLARSHIP

Scholarship is given to a student of the Bahai faith who attends or plans to attend college. For more information or application visit http://www.communityfoundation.org.

Award: Scholarship for use in freshman, sophomore, junior, or senior years; renewable. *Number:* 1. *Amount:* up to $500.

Eligibility Requirements: Applicant must be Baha'i faith; enrolled or expecting to enroll full- or part-time at a four-year institution and resident of Massachusetts. Available to U.S. citizens.

Application Requirements: Application, financial need analysis, transcript, Student Aid Report (SAR). *Deadline:* March 31.

Contact: Dorothy Theriaque, Education Associate
Community Foundation of Western Massachusetts
1500 Main Street, PO Box 15769
Springfield, MA 01115
Phone: 413-732-2858
Fax: 413-733-8565
E-mail: dtheriaque@communityfoundation.org

EASTERN ORTHODOX COMMITTEE ON SCOUTING http://www.eocs.org

EASTERN ORTHODOX COMMITTEE ON SCOUTING SCHOLARSHIPS

• *See page 531*

FADEL EDUCATIONAL FOUNDATION INC. http://www.fadelfoundation.org

ANNUAL AWARD PROGRAM

Grants of $400 to $2000 awarded on the basis of merit, financial need, and the potential of an applicant to positively impact Muslims' lives in the United States.

Award: Grant for use in freshman, sophomore, junior, senior, graduate, or postgraduate years; renewable. *Number:* 20–45. *Amount:* $400–$2000.

Eligibility Requirements: Applicant must be Muslim faith and enrolled or expecting to enroll full- or part-time at a two-year or four-year or technical institution or university. Available to U.S. citizens.

Application Requirements: Application, essay, financial need analysis, references, test scores, transcript. *Deadline:* March 23.

Contact: Hossam E. Fadel, President
Fadel Educational Foundation Inc.
PO Box 212135
Augusta, GA 30917-2135
Phone: 317-223-8632
Fax: 866-705-9495
E-mail: afadel@bww.com

FIRST PRESBYTERIAN CHURCH http://www.firstchurchtulsa.org

CLARENCE WARREN SCHOLARSHIP FUND

Scholarship for undergraduate study for student in financial need. Must be member of the First Presbyterian Church; preference given to members of the First Presbyterian Church, Tulsa, OK.

Award: Scholarship for use in freshman, sophomore, junior, or senior years; not renewable. *Number:* varies. *Amount:* $500–$2000.

Eligibility Requirements: Applicant must be Presbyterian and enrolled or expecting to enroll full-time at a four-year institution or university. Available to U.S. and non-U.S. citizens.

Application Requirements: Application, financial need analysis, interview, references, transcript. *Deadline:* April 15.

Contact: Tonye Briscoe, Facilities and Benefits Coordinator
First Presbyterian Church
706 South Boston Avenue
Tulsa, OK 74119-1629
Phone: 918-584-4701
Fax: 918-584-5233
E-mail: tbriscoe@firstchurchtulsa.org

CYDNA ANN HUFFSTETLER MEMORIAL TRUST FUND

Award for First Presbyterian Church member to attend an accredited university, college or vocational school. For full-time study only.

Award: Scholarship for use in freshman, sophomore, junior, senior, graduate, or postgraduate years; not renewable. *Number:* varies. *Amount:* $500–$1000.

Eligibility Requirements: Applicant must be Presbyterian and enrolled or expecting to enroll full-time at a two-year or four-year or technical institution or university. Available to U.S. and non-U.S. citizens.

Application Requirements: Application, financial need analysis, interview, references, transcript. *Deadline:* April 15.

Contact: Tonye Briscoe, Facilities and Benefits Coordinator
First Presbyterian Church
706 South Boston Avenue
Tulsa, OK 74119-1629
Phone: 918-584-4701
Fax: 918-584-5233
E-mail: tbriscoe@firstchurchtulsa.org

ETHEL FRANCIS CRATE SCHOLARSHIP FUND

Scholarships for students who are members of the Presbyterian Church and who are in their junior or senior year of college. Must demonstrate financial need. Preference given to members of the First Presbyterian Church, Tulsa, OK.

Award: Scholarship for use in junior or senior years; not renewable. *Number:* varies. *Amount:* $500–$2000.

Eligibility Requirements: Applicant must be Presbyterian and enrolled or expecting to enroll full-time at a four-year institution or university. Available to U.S. and non-U.S. citizens.

Application Requirements: Application, financial need analysis, interview, references, transcript. *Deadline:* April 15.

Contact: Tonye Briscoe, Facilities and Benefits Coordinator
First Presbyterian Church
706 South Boston Avenue
Tulsa, OK 74119-1629
Phone: 918-584-4701
Fax: 918-584-5233
E-mail: tbriscoe@firstchurchtulsa.org

FOUNDATION FOR CHRISTIAN COLLEGE LEADERS http://www.collegechristianleader.com

FOUNDATION FOR COLLEGE CHRISTIAN LEADERS SCHOLARSHIP

Applicant must be accepted to or currently enrolled in an undergraduate degree program. Candidate must demonstrate Christian leadership. Combined income of parents and student must be less than $60,000. Minimum 3.0 GPA required.

Award: Scholarship for use in freshman, sophomore, junior, senior, or graduate years; not renewable. *Number:* varies. *Amount:* varies.

Eligibility Requirements: Applicant must be Christian; enrolled or expecting to enroll full- or part-time at a four-year institution or university and must have an interest in leadership. Applicant must have 3.0 GPA or higher. Available to U.S. citizens.

Application Requirements: Application, financial need analysis, interview, references, leadership assessment form, cover sheet. *Deadline:* May 7.

Contact: Scholarship Committee
Foundation for Christian College Leaders
2658 Del Mar Heights Road
PO Box 266
Del Mar, CA 92014
Phone: 858-481-0848
Fax: 858-481-0848
E-mail: lmhays@aol.com

GENERAL BOARD OF GLOBAL MINISTRIES http://www.gbgm-umc.org

NATIONAL LEADERSHIP DEVELOPMENT GRANTS

• *See page 682*

GENERAL BOARD OF HIGHER EDUCATION AND MINISTRY http://www.gbhem.org

BISHOP JOSEPH B. BETHEA SCHOLARSHIP

• *See page 682*

ETHNIC MINORITY SCHOLARSHIP

• *See page 682*

GIFT OF HOPE: 21ST CENTURY SCHOLARS PROGRAM

$1000 scholarship to United Methodist undergraduate students who are full-time, active members of UMC for at least three years prior to applying. Must demonstrate leadership in the United Methodist Church and be enrolled in a full-time degree program at a regionally accredited U.S. institution. Cumulative GPA of 3.0 or higher required.

Award: Scholarship for use in freshman, sophomore, junior, or senior years; not renewable. *Number:* varies. *Amount:* $1000.

Eligibility Requirements: Applicant must be Methodist; enrolled or expecting to enroll full-time at a four-year institution or university and must have an interest in leadership. Applicant must have 3.0 GPA or higher. Available to U.S. citizens.

Application Requirements: Application, essay, resume, references, transcript. *Deadline:* May 1.

Contact: Scholarship Committee
General Board of Higher Education and Ministry
The United Methodist Church, 1001 Nineteenth Avenue South
PO Box 340007
Nashville, TN 37202
Phone: 615-340-7344
Fax: 615-340-7367
E-mail: sddm@gbhem.org

HANA SCHOLARSHIP

• *See page 682*

HELEN AND ALLEN BROWN SCHOLARSHIP

Scholarship for outstanding high school graduates and undergraduate college students who are members of the Nashville District of the Tennessee Annual Conference of UMC or members of the New Orleans District of the Louisiana Annual Conference of UMC. Must have been full and active members of The United Methodist Church for at least three years and maintain a GPA of 3.0.

Award: Scholarship for use in freshman, sophomore, junior, or senior years; not renewable. *Number:* varies. *Amount:* varies.

Eligibility Requirements: Applicant must be Methodist and enrolled or expecting to enroll full-time at a four-year institution or university. Applicant must have 3.0 GPA or higher. Available to U.S. citizens.

Application Requirements: Application, essay, resume, references, transcript. *Deadline:* May 1.

Contact: Scholarship Committee
General Board of Higher Education and Ministry
Clark Memorial United Methodist Church, 1014 14th Avenue North
Nashville, TN 37208

ITALIAN CATHOLIC FEDERATION INC. http://www.icf.org

ITALIAN CATHOLIC FEDERATION FIRST YEAR SCHOLARSHIP

• *See page 538*

JEWISH FOUNDATION FOR EDUCATION OF WOMEN http://www.jfew.org

JFEW/UJA FEDERATION ROSE BILLER SCHOLARSHIPS

• *See page 688*

JEWISH VOCATIONAL SERVICE-LOS ANGELES http://www.jvsla.org

JEWISH VOCATIONAL SERVICE SCHOLARSHIP FUND

Need-based scholarships to support Jewish students from Los Angeles County in their pursuit of college, graduate, and vocational education. Applicants must be Jewish, permanent residents of Los Angeles, maintain a minimum 2.7 GPA and demonstrate verifiable financial need.

Award: Scholarship for use in freshman, sophomore, junior, senior, or graduate years; renewable. *Number:* 1. *Amount:* $500–$5000.

Eligibility Requirements: Applicant must be Jewish; enrolled or expecting to enroll full-time at a two-year or four-year or technical institution or university and resident of California. Available to U.S. citizens.

Application Requirements: Application, essay, financial need analysis, resume, references, test scores, transcript, FAFSA, Student Aid Report (SAR). *Deadline:* March 14.

Contact: Cathy Kersh, Scholarship Program Manager
Jewish Vocational Service-Los Angeles
6505 Wilshire Boulevard, Suite 200
Los Angeles, CA 90048
Phone: 323-761-8888 Ext. 8868
Fax: 323-761-8575
E-mail: scholarship@jvsla.org

KNIGHTS OF COLUMBUS http://www.kofc.org

FOURTH DEGREE PRO DEO AND PRO PATRIA (CANADA)

• *See page 539*

FOURTH DEGREE PRO DEO AND PRO PATRIA SCHOLARSHIPS

• *See page 539*

FRANCIS P. MATTHEWS AND JOHN E. SWIFT EDUCATIONAL TRUST SCHOLARSHIPS

• *See page 539*

JOHN W. MCDEVITT (FOURTH DEGREE) SCHOLARSHIPS

• *See page 539*

PERCY J. JOHNSON ENDOWED SCHOLARSHIPS

• *See page 540*

LINCOLN COMMUNITY FOUNDATION http://www.lcf.org

WILLIAM B. AND VIRGINIA S. ROLOFSON SCHOLARSHIP

Applicants must be a current graduating senior or a first year college student and be a member of St. Luke United Methodist Church in Lincoln, Nebraska. Applicants must attend a two- or four-year college or university in Nebraska, must be first year college students. Preference will be given to those applicants under the age of 25 but all students are welcome to apply.

Award: Scholarship for use in freshman year; renewable. *Number:* 1. *Amount:* $500.

Eligibility Requirements: Applicant must be Methodist; enrolled or expecting to enroll full-time at a two-year or four-year institution or university; resident of Nebraska and studying in Nebraska. Available to U.S. citizens.

Application Requirements: Application, financial need analysis, references, test scores, transcript. *Deadline:* April 30.

Contact: Sonya Brakeman, Grants/Scholarships Coordinator
Lincoln Community Foundation
215 Centennial Mall South, Suite 100
Lincoln, NE 68508
Phone: 402-474-2345
Fax: 402-476-8532
E-mail: sonyab@lcf.org

MELLON NEW ENGLAND http://www.mellon.com

HENRY FRANCIS BARROWS SCHOLARSHIP

Award for Protestant males only. Must be a resident of Massachusetts and applying to a non-Catholic U.S. institution of higher learning. Eligible applicant must be recommended by educational institution. Not for graduate study programs.

Mellon New England (continued)

Award: Scholarship for use in freshman, sophomore, junior, or senior years; not renewable. *Number:* varies. *Amount:* up to $2000.

Eligibility Requirements: Applicant must be Protestant; enrolled or expecting to enroll full-time at a two-year or four-year or technical institution or university; male and resident of Massachusetts. Available to U.S. citizens.

Application Requirements: Application, essay, transcript. *Deadline:* April 15.

Contact: Sandra Brown-McMullen, Vice President
Mellon New England
1 Boston Place, 024-0084
Boston, MA 02108
Phone: 617-722-3891
E-mail: brown-mcmullen.s@mellon.com

MORRIS J. AND BETTY KAPLUN FOUNDATION http://www.kaplunfoundation.org

MORRIS J. AND BETTY KAPLUN FOUNDATION ANNUAL ESSAY CONTEST

Prize up to $1800 will be awarded to the first place contest winner for essay on a topic related to Jewish heritage, culture, or values. Additional awards for five finalists. Essay must be between 250-1000 words. Open to students in grades 7-12. See Web site for specific essay questions and additional details: http://www.kaplunfoundation.org/.

Award: Prize for use in freshman year; not renewable. *Number:* 12–18. *Amount:* $750–$1800.

Eligibility Requirements: Applicant must be Jewish; high school student; planning to enroll or expecting to enroll full- or part-time at a four-year institution or university and must have an interest in Jewish culture or writing. Available to U.S. and non-U.S. citizens.

Application Requirements: Applicant must enter a contest, essay. *Deadline:* March 17.

Contact: Eve Seligson, Essay Contest Committee
Morris J. and Betty Kaplun Foundation
PO Box 234428
Great Neck, NY 11023
Phone: 212-966-5020
Fax: 212-966-6205

OSAGE SCHOLARSHIP FUND

MAE LASSLEY OSAGE SCHOLARSHIP FUND

• *See page 696*

PRESBYTERIAN CHURCH (USA) http://www.pcusa.org/financialaid

NATIONAL PRESBYTERIAN COLLEGE SCHOLARSHIP

Scholarships between $200 and $1400 available to incoming undergraduate enrolled in full-time programs in colleges associated with the Presbyterian Church (U.S.A.). Applicants must have a minimum GPA of 3.0 and be residents of the U.S. for a minimum of two years and demonstrate financial need.

Award: Scholarship for use in freshman, sophomore, junior, or senior years; renewable. *Number:* 250. *Amount:* $200–$1400.

Eligibility Requirements: Applicant must be Presbyterian and enrolled or expecting to enroll full-time at a four-year institution or university. Applicant must have 3.0 GPA or higher. Available to U.S. citizens.

Application Requirements: Application, autobiography, essay, financial need analysis, resume, references, test scores, transcript. *Deadline:* January 31.

Contact: Ms. Laura Bryan, Program Assistant
Presbyterian Church (USA)
100 Witherspoon Street
Louisville, KY 40202-1396
Phone: 888-728-7228 Ext. 5735
Fax: 502-569-8776
E-mail: laura.bryan@pcusa.org

STUDENT OPPORTUNITY SCHOLARSHIP

Designed to assist undergraduate students with their junior and senior year of college. Preference will be given to the member of Presbyterian Church USA. Must be a resident of the U.S. for a minimum of two years.

Award: Scholarship for use in junior or senior years; renewable. *Number:* 100. *Amount:* $200–$2000.

Eligibility Requirements: Applicant must be Presbyterian and enrolled or expecting to enroll full-time at a four-year institution or university. Applicant must have 2.5 GPA or higher. Available to U.S. citizens.

Application Requirements: Application, essay, financial need analysis, resume, references, transcript. *Deadline:* June 15.

Contact: Mrs. Frances Cook, Associate
Presbyterian Church (USA)
100 Witherspoon Street
Louisville, KY 40202-1396
Phone: 888-728-7228 Ext. 5776
Fax: 502-569-8766
E-mail: frances.cook@pcusa.org

SYNOD OF THE COVENANT http://www.synodofthecovenant.org

CECA ETHNIC SCHOLARSHIP

Scholarship will be awarded for full- or part-time study toward baccalaureate degree or certification at colleges, universities, and vocational schools. Award also available for full-time students enrolled in master's degree programs for church vocations at approved Presbyterian theological institutions. Priority will be given to Presbyterian applicants from the states of Michigan and Ohio. Applicants must maintain a minimum 2.0 GPA. Deadlines: February 1 and September 1.

Award: Scholarship for use in freshman, sophomore, junior, senior, or graduate years; not renewable. *Number:* 30. *Amount:* $400–$800.

Eligibility Requirements: Applicant must be Presbyterian; enrolled or expecting to enroll full- or part-time at a four-year institution or university and resident of Michigan or Ohio. Available to U.S. and non-U.S. citizens.

Application Requirements: Application, financial need analysis, test scores, transcript, verification enrollment letter. *Deadline:* varies.

Contact: Ms. Janet Chapman, Executive Assistant
Synod of the Covenant
Attn: CECA Ethnic Scholarship Committee
1911 Indian Wood Circle, Suite B
Maumee, OH 43537
Phone: 419-754-4050
Fax: 419-754-4051
E-mail: j.chapman@synodofthecovenant.org

TEXAS BLACK BAPTIST SCHOLARSHIP COMMITTEE http://www.bgct.org

TEXAS BLACK BAPTIST SCHOLARSHIP

• *See page 701*

UNITARIAN UNIVERSALIST ASSOCIATION http://www.uua.org

CHILDREN OF UNITARIAN UNIVERSALIST MINISTERS

Non-renewable scholarship available to children of Unitarian Universalist Ministers to defray undergraduate college expenses. Dollar value and number of awards varies. Priority is given to applicants whose family income does not exceed $50,000.

Award: Scholarship for use in freshman, sophomore, junior, or senior years; not renewable. *Number:* varies. *Amount:* varies.

Eligibility Requirements: Applicant must be Unitarian Universalist and enrolled or expecting to enroll full- or part-time at a four-year institution or university. Available to U.S. citizens.

Application Requirements: Application. *Deadline:* July 31.

Contact: Ms. Hillary Goodridge, Program Director
Unitarian Universalist Association
PO Box 301149
Boston, MA 02130
Phone: 617-971-9600
Fax: 617-971-0029
E-mail: uufp@aol.com

JOSEPH SUMNER SMITH SCHOLARSHIP

Funds are available for Unitarian Universalist (UU) students attending Anitoch (including satellite and nonresidential campuses) and Harvard. While there is no restriction on the course of studies the student may elect to pursue, nor any restrictions on choice of career, student interested in pursuing the ministry after graduation are especially urged to apply.

Award: Scholarship for use in freshman, sophomore, junior, senior, or graduate years; not renewable. *Number:* varies. *Amount:* $500–$1000.

Eligibility Requirements: Applicant must be Unitarian Universalist and enrolled or expecting to enroll full- or part-time at a two-year or four-year or technical institution or university. Available to U.S. citizens.

Application Requirements: Application. *Deadline:* April 30.

Contact: Ms. Hillary Goodridge, Program Director
Unitarian Universalist Association
PO Box 301149
Boston, MA 02130
Phone: 617-971-9600
Fax: 617-971-0029
E-mail: uufp@aol.com

UNITED METHODIST CHURCH http://www.gbhem.org

J. A. KNOWLES MEMORIAL SCHOLARSHIP

One-time award for Texas residents attending a United Methodist institution in Texas. Must have been United Methodist Church member for at least one year. Must be U.S. citizens or permanent residents. Minimum 2.5 GPA required.

Award: Scholarship for use in freshman, sophomore, junior, senior, or graduate years; not renewable. *Number:* varies. *Amount:* varies.

Eligibility Requirements: Applicant must be Methodist; enrolled or expecting to enroll full-time at a two-year or four-year institution or university; resident of Texas and studying in Texas. Applicant must have 2.5 GPA or higher. Available to U.S. citizens.

Application Requirements: Application, essay, references, transcript. *Deadline:* May 15.

Contact: Scholarships Administrator
United Methodist Church
PO Box 340007
Nashville, TN 37203-0007
Phone: 615-340-7344
E-mail: pzimmer@gbhem.org

UNITED METHODIST CHURCH ETHNIC SCHOLARSHIP

• *See page 702*

UNITED METHODIST CHURCH HISPANIC, ASIAN, AND NATIVE AMERICAN SCHOLARSHIP

• *See page 702*

UNITED METHODIST YOUTH ORGANIZATION http://www.gbod.org/youngpeople

DAVID W. SELF SCHOLARSHIP

Must be a United Methodist Youth who has been active in local church for at least one year prior to application. Must be a graduating senior in high school (who maintained at least a "C" average) entering the first year of undergraduate study. Must be pursuing a "church-related" career and should have maintained at least a "C" average throughout high school.

Award: Scholarship for use in freshman year; not renewable. *Number:* up to 5. *Amount:* up to $2500.

Eligibility Requirements: Applicant must be Methodist; high school student and planning to enroll or expecting to enroll full-time at a four-year institution or university. Available to U.S. citizens.

Application Requirements: Application, essay, financial need analysis, transcript, certification of church membership. *Deadline:* June 1.

Contact: Grants Coordinator
United Methodist Youth Organization
PO Box 340003
Nashville, TN 37203-0003
Phone: 877-899-2780 Ext. 7184
Fax: 615-340-7063
E-mail: youngpeople@gbod.org

RICHARD S. SMITH SCHOLARSHIP

• *See page 703*

WOMAN'S MISSIONARY UNION FOUNDATION http://www.wmufoundation.com

WOMAN'S MISSIONARY UNION SCHOLARSHIP PROGRAM

The program is primarily for Baptist young women with high scholastic accomplishments and service through Baptist organizations. Must have an interest in Christian women's leadership development or missionary service. Preference is given for WMU/Acteen membership in a Baptist church. The total number of available awards and dollar amount varies.

Award: Scholarship for use in freshman, sophomore, junior, senior, graduate, or postgraduate years; renewable. *Number:* 5–10. *Amount:* $500–$1500.

Eligibility Requirements: Applicant must be Baptist; enrolled or expecting to enroll full-time at a two-year or four-year institution or university and female. Available to U.S. and non-U.S. citizens.

Application Requirements: Application, references, transcript, WMU endorsements. *Deadline:* March 1.

Contact: Linda Lucas, Administrative Assistant
Woman's Missionary Union Foundation
PO Box 11346
Birmingham, AL 35202-1346
Phone: 205-408-5525
Fax: 205-408-5508
E-mail: llucas@wmu.org

WOMEN OF THE EVANGELICAL LUTHERAN CHURCH IN AMERICA http://www.womenoftheelca.org

AMELIA KEMP SCHOLARSHIP

• *See page 712*

BELMER/FLORA PRINCE SCHOLARSHIP

Scholarship for women who have experienced an interruption of two or more years in education since the completion of high school. Must be member of ELCA and be at least 21 years old.

Award: Scholarship for use in freshman, sophomore, junior, senior, or graduate years; not renewable. *Number:* 2. *Amount:* up to $1000.

Eligibility Requirements: Applicant must be Lutheran; age 21 and over; enrolled or expecting to enroll full- or part-time at a two-year or four-year or technical institution or university and female. Available to U.S. citizens.

Application Requirements: Application, resume, references, transcript. *Deadline:* February 15.

Contact: Emily Hansen, Scholarship Committee
Women of the Evangelical Lutheran Church in America
8765 West Higgins Road
Chicago, IL 60631-4189
Phone: 800-638-3522 Ext. 2736
Fax: 773-380-2419
E-mail: womenelca@elca.org

YEMENI AMERICAN ASSOCIATION

YEMENI AMERICAN ASSOCIATION SCHOLARSHIPS

• *See page 712*

RESIDENCE

ABBIE SARGENT MEMORIAL SCHOLARSHIP INC. http://www.nhfarmbureau.org

ABBIE SARGENT MEMORIAL SCHOLARSHIP

Up to three awards between $400 and $500 will be provided to deserving New Hampshire residents, planning to attend an institution of higher learning. Must be a U.S. citizen.

Award: Scholarship for use in freshman, sophomore, junior, senior, graduate, or postgraduate years; not renewable. *Number:* 1–3. *Amount:* $400–$500.

Eligibility Requirements: Applicant must be enrolled or expecting to enroll full- or part-time at a two-year or four-year or technical institution or university and resident of New Hampshire. Available to U.S. citizens.

Application Requirements: Application, autobiography, financial need analysis, photo, references, transcript. *Deadline:* March 15.

Contact: Melanie Phelps, Treasurer
Abbie Sargent Memorial Scholarship Inc.
295 Sheep Davis Road
Concord, NH 03301
Phone: 603-224-1934
Fax: 603-228-8432
E-mail: melaniep@nhfarmbureau.org

AIKEN ELECTRIC COOPERATIVE INC. http://www.aikenco-op.org

TRUSTEE SCHOLARSHIP

Scholarship awarded to high school graduating senior in the cooperative service area. Award based on need and academic performance. The primary residence of the applicant must have an account with either Aiken Electric Cooperative Inc. or Aikenelectric.net.

Award: Scholarship for use in freshman year; not renewable. *Number:* 1. *Amount:* up to $1000.

Eligibility Requirements: Applicant must be high school student; planning to enroll or expecting to enroll full-time at a two-year or four-year institution or university and resident of South Carolina. Available to U.S. citizens.

Application Requirements: Application, essay, financial need analysis. *Deadline:* January 12.

Contact: Marilyn Gerrity, Manager, Marketing and Strategic Services
Aiken Electric Cooperative Inc.
2790 Wagener Road
PO Box 417
Aiken, SC 29802
Phone: 803-649-6245
Fax: 803-641-8310
E-mail: aec@aikenco-op.org

ALABAMA COMMISSION ON HIGHER EDUCATION http://www.ache.alabama.gov

ALABAMA NATIONAL GUARD EDUCATIONAL ASSISTANCE PROGRAM

• *See page 633*

ALABAMA STUDENT ASSISTANCE PROGRAM

Scholarship award of $300 to $2500 per academic year given to undergraduate students residing in the state of Alabama and attending a college or university in Alabama.

Award: Scholarship for use in freshman, sophomore, junior, or senior years; not renewable. *Number:* varies. *Amount:* $300–$2500.

Eligibility Requirements: Applicant must be enrolled or expecting to enroll full- or part-time at a four-year institution or university; resident of Alabama and studying in Alabama. Available to U.S. citizens.

Application Requirements: Application. *Deadline:* continuous.

Contact: Cheryl Newton, Scholarship Coordinator
Alabama Commission on Higher Education
100 North Union Street
PO Box 302000
Montgomery, AL 36130-2000
Phone: 334-242-2273
Fax: 334-242-0268
E-mail: cheryl.newton@ache.alabama.gov

ALABAMA STUDENT GRANT PROGRAM

Nonrenewable awards available to Alabama residents for undergraduate study at certain independent colleges within the state. Both full and half-time students are eligible. Deadlines: September 15, January 15, and February 15.

Award: Grant for use in freshman, sophomore, junior, or senior years; not renewable. *Number:* varies. *Amount:* up to $1200.

Eligibility Requirements: Applicant must be enrolled or expecting to enroll full- or part-time at a four-year institution or university; resident of Alabama and studying in Alabama. Available to U.S. citizens.

Application Requirements: Application. *Deadline:* varies.

Contact: William Wall, Associate Executive Director for Student Assistance
Alabama Commission on Higher Education
100 North Union Street, PO Box 302000
Montgomery, AL 36130-2000
Phone: 334-242-2271
Fax: 334-242-0268
E-mail: wwall@ache.state.al.us

POLICE OFFICERS AND FIREFIGHTERS SURVIVORS EDUCATION ASSISTANCE PROGRAM-ALABAMA

• *See page 587*

ALABAMA DEPARTMENT OF VETERANS AFFAIRS http://www.va.alabama.gov

ALABAMA G.I. DEPENDENTS SCHOLARSHIP PROGRAM

• *See page 642*

ALABAMA INDIAN AFFAIRS COMMISSION http://www.aiac.state.al.us

AIAC SCHOLARSHIP

• *See page 668*

ALASKA STATE DEPARTMENT OF EDUCATION http://www.eed.state.ak.us

GEAR UP ALASKA SCHOLARSHIP

Scholarship provides up to $7000 each year for up to four years of undergraduate study (up to $3500 each year for half-time study). Applicant must be an Alaska high school senior or have an Alaska diploma or GED. Must be under age 22.

Award: Scholarship for use in freshman, sophomore, junior, or senior years; not renewable. *Number:* varies. *Amount:* $3500–$7000.

Eligibility Requirements: Applicant must be age 22 or under; enrolled or expecting to enroll full- or part-time at a two-year or four-year institution or university and resident of Alaska. Available to U.S. citizens.

Application Requirements: Application, financial need analysis, references, transcript. *Deadline:* May 31.

Contact: Amy Gaisford, Scholarship Coordinator
Alaska State Department of Education
801 West 10th Street, Suite 200
PO Box 110505
Juneau, AK 99811-0500
Phone: 907-465-2800
Fax: 907-465-5316
E-mail: customer_service@acpe.state.ak.us

ALBERTA AGRICULTURE FOOD AND RURAL DEVELOPMENT 4-H BRANCH http://www.4h.ab.ca

ALBERTA AGRICULTURE FOOD AND RURAL DEVELOPMENT 4-H SCHOLARSHIP PROGRAM

• *See page 509*

ALBERTA HERITAGE SCHOLARSHIP FUND/ ALBERTA SCHOLARSHIP PROGRAMS

http://www.alis.gov.ab.ca

ADULT HIGH SCHOOL EQUIVALENCY SCHOLARSHIPS

• *See page 668*

ALBERTA BLUE CROSS 50TH ANNIVERSARY SCHOLARSHIPS FOR ABORIGINAL STUDENTS

• *See page 668*

ALBERTA CENTENNIAL PREMIER'S SCHOLARSHIPS-ALBERTA

Award to commemorate the province of Alberta's centennial. Twenty-five awards for each province and territory in Canada have been established. Must be Canadian citizens or permanent residents of Canada and Alberta residents. Awards students entering any level of postsecondary study at any university, college, technical institute, or apprenticeship program in Canada.

Award: Scholarship for use in freshman, sophomore, junior, or senior years; not renewable. *Number:* 25. *Amount:* $2005.

Eligibility Requirements: Applicant must be high school student; planning to enroll or expecting to enroll full-time at a two-year or four-year or technical institution or university and resident of Alberta. Available to Canadian citizens.

Application Requirements: Nomination from high school counselors. *Deadline:* June 15.

Contact: Scholarship Committee
Alberta Heritage Scholarship Fund/Alberta Scholarship Programs
9940 106th Street, Fourth Floor, Sterling Place
PO Box 28000, Station Main
Edmonton, AB T5J 4R4
Canada
Phone: 780-427-8640
Fax: 780-427-1288
E-mail: scholarships@gov.ab.ca

ALBERTA CENTENNIAL PREMIER'S SCHOLARSHIPS-CANADA

Award to commemorate the province of Alberta's centennial, and twenty-five awards for each province and territory in Canada have been established. Must be Canadian citizens or permanent residents of Canada. Awards students entering any level of postsecondary study at any university, college, technical institute, or apprenticeship program in Canada. Each province and territory will be responsible for selecting recipients.

Award: Scholarship for use in freshman, sophomore, junior, or senior years; not renewable. *Number:* 25. *Amount:* $2005.

Eligibility Requirements: Applicant must be enrolled or expecting to enroll full-time at a two-year or four-year or technical institution or university and resident of Alberta, British Columbia, Manitoba, New Brunswick, Newfoundland, North West Territories, Nova Scotia, Ontario, Prince Edward Island, Quebec, Saskatchewan, or Yukon. Available to Canadian citizens.

Application Requirements: Application, financial need analysis. *Deadline:* varies.

Contact: Scholarship Committee
Alberta Heritage Scholarship Fund/Alberta Scholarship Programs
9940 106th Street, Fourth Floor, Sterling Place
PO Box 28000, Station Main
Edmonton, AB T5J 4R4
Canada
Phone: 780-427-8640
Fax: 780-427-1288
E-mail: scholarships@gov.ab.ca

ALBERTA HERITAGE SCHOLARSHIP FUND ALBERTA PRESS COUNCIL SCHOLARSHIP

• *See page 669*

ALBERTA HERITAGE SCHOLARSHIP FUND CANA SCHOLARSHIPS

• *See page 572*

ALBERTA HERITAGE SCHOLARSHIP FUND HAL HARRISON MEMORIAL SCHOLARSHIP

• *See page 587*

ALBERTA OPPORTUNITIES BURSARY

Award to offset the rising costs of postsecondary education and related student debt loads. Must be high school or postsecondary student and be enrolled in first or second year of full-time postsecondary studies at a participating institution and qualify for an Alberta student loan of at least $4000. No separate application for this bursary. If the candidate receive the Alberta Opportunities Bursary, the student loan will be reduced by the amount of grant received.

Award: Scholarship for use in freshman or sophomore years; not renewable. *Number:* varies. *Amount:* $500–$1500.

Eligibility Requirements: Applicant must be enrolled or expecting to enroll full-time at a two-year or four-year or technical institution or university; resident of Alberta and studying in Alberta. Available to Canadian citizens.

Application Requirements: Proof of received Alberta Opportunities Bursary loan. *Deadline:* continuous.

Contact: Scholarship Committee
Alberta Heritage Scholarship Fund/Alberta Scholarship Programs
9940 106th Street, Fourth Floor, Sterling Place
PO Box 28000, Station Main
Edmonton, AB T5J 4R4
Canada
Phone: 780-427-8640
Fax: 780-427-1288
E-mail: scholarships@gov.ab.ca

ALEXANDER RUTHERFORD SCHOLARSHIPS FOR HIGH SCHOOL ACHIEVEMENT

• *See page 669*

BOYS AND GIRLS CLUB OF ALBERTA SCHOLARSHIPS

• *See page 509*

CANADA MILLENNIUM BURSARY

Award to help Alberta's students in highest financial need access this bursary and reduce their debt load. Must be enrolled full-time at a Canadian postsecondary institution and must be attending their second or subsequent year of undergraduate study or any year of a professional program. Students do not need to apply for this scholarship separately. Eligibility will be based on original applications for financial assistance and confirmation of academic progress by students postsecondary institution.

Award: Scholarship for use in sophomore, junior, or senior years; not renewable. *Number:* varies. *Amount:* $2250–$3000.

Eligibility Requirements: Applicant must be enrolled or expecting to enroll full-time at a four-year or technical institution or university and resident of Alberta. Available to Canadian citizens.

Application Requirements: Financial need analysis. *Deadline:* continuous.

Contact: Scholarship Committee
Alberta Heritage Scholarship Fund/Alberta Scholarship Programs
9940 106th Street, Fourth Floor, Sterling Place
PO Box 28000, Station Main
Edmonton, AB T5J 4R4
Canada
Phone: 780-427-8640
Fax: 780-427-1288
E-mail: scholarships@gov.ab.ca

CENTRAL ALBERTA RURAL ELECTRIFICATION ASSOCIATION SCHOLARSHIP

Award to recognize the academic accomplishments of the children of members of the Central Alberta Rural Electrification Association and to assist and encourage their higher education. Must be Alberta residents entering the first year of a postsecondary program that is a minimum of two years in length. Scholarship based on academic achievement on the top five grade 12 courses.

Award: Scholarship for use in freshman year; not renewable. *Number:* 2.

Alberta Heritage Scholarship Fund/Alberta Scholarship Programs (continued)

Eligibility Requirements: Applicant must be high school student; planning to enroll or expecting to enroll full-time at a two-year or four-year or technical institution or university and resident of Alberta. Available to Canadian citizens.

Application Requirements: Application, essay, references, test scores. *Deadline:* July 1.

Contact: Scholarship Committee
Alberta Heritage Scholarship Fund/Alberta Scholarship Programs
9940 106th Street, Fourth Floor, Sterling Place
PO Box 28000, Station Main
Edmonton, AB T5J 4R4
Canada
Phone: 780-427-8640
Fax: 780-427-1288
E-mail: scholarships@gov.ab.ca

CHARLES S. NOBLE JUNIOR "A" HOCKEY SCHOLARSHIPS

• *See page 669*

CHARLES S. NOBLE JUNIOR FOOTBALL SCHOLARSHIPS

• *See page 669*

DR. ERNEST AND MINNIE MEHL SCHOLARSHIP

• *See page 669*

EARL AND COUNTESS OF WESSEX-WORLD CHAMPIONSHIPS IN ATHLETICS SCHOLARSHIPS

Award to recognize the top male and female Alberta students who have excelled in track and field, have a strong academic record, and plan to continue their studies at the postsecondary level in Alberta. Must be Canadian citizens or landed immigrants and residents of Alberta. Must have completed grade twelve in Alberta in the same year they apply for the scholarship. Must be planning on continuing their studies at a postsecondary institution in Alberta.

Award: Scholarship for use in freshman year; not renewable. *Number:* 2. *Amount:* $3000.

Eligibility Requirements: Applicant must be high school student; planning to enroll or expecting to enroll full-time at a two-year or four-year or technical institution or university; resident of Alberta; studying in Alberta and must have an interest in athletics/sports. Available to Canadian citizens.

Application Requirements: Application, transcript. *Deadline:* October 1.

Contact: Scholarship Committee
Alberta Heritage Scholarship Fund/Alberta Scholarship Programs
9940 106th Street, Fourth Floor, Sterling Place
PO Box 28000, Station Main
Edmonton, AB T5J 4R4
Canada
Phone: 780-427-8640
Fax: 780-427-1288
E-mail: scholarships@gov.ab.ca

GRANT MACEWAN UNITED WORLD COLLEGE SCHOLARSHIPS

• *See page 670*

INTERNATIONAL EDUCATION AWARDS-UKRAINE

• *See page 670*

JIMMIE CONDON ATHLETIC SCHOLARSHIPS

• *See page 670*

LAURENCE DECORE STUDENT LEADERSHIP AWARDS

• *See page 670*

LOUISE MCKINNEY POSTSECONDARY SCHOLARSHIPS

• *See page 670*

NEW APPRENTICESHIP SCHOLARSHIPS

A $1000 scholarship available for apprentices in a trade and trainees in a designated occupation, to encourage recipients to complete their apprenticeship or occupational training programs. Must be a Canadian citizen or landed immigrant and Alberta resident. For more details see Web site: http://www.alis.gov.ab.ca.

Award: Scholarship for use in freshman year; not renewable. *Number:* 170. *Amount:* $1000.

Eligibility Requirements: Applicant must be enrolled or expecting to enroll full-time at a technical institution and resident of Alberta. Available to Canadian citizens.

Application Requirements: Application. *Deadline:* July 31.

Contact: Scholarship Committee
Alberta Heritage Scholarship Fund/Alberta Scholarship Programs
9940 106th Street, Fourth Floor, Sterling Place
PO Box 28000, Station Main
Edmonton, AB T5J 4R4
Canada
Phone: 780-427-8640
Fax: 780-427-1288
E-mail: scholarships@gov.ab.ca

NORTHERN ALBERTA DEVELOPMENT COUNCIL BURSARY

• *See page 670*

NORTHERN ALBERTA DEVELOPMENT COUNCIL BURSARY PARTNERSHIP PROGRAM

Award is intended to attract graduates to live and work in Northern Alberta. Bursary recipients must live and work in Northern Alberta within six months of graduation. The return service obligation is one full-time month (or equivalent) for every $250 of bursary funds received. Students who do not work in the north will be required to repay the bursary. Must be enrolled full-time in a postsecondary program at an institution recognized by Alberta Advanced Education.

Award: Forgivable loan for use in freshman, sophomore, junior, or senior years; not renewable. *Number:* varies. *Amount:* $1750.

Eligibility Requirements: Applicant must be enrolled or expecting to enroll full-time at a two-year or four-year or technical institution or university; resident of Alberta and studying in Alberta. Available to Canadian citizens.

Application Requirements: Application. *Deadline:* February 1.

Contact: Scholarship Committee
Alberta Heritage Scholarship Fund/Alberta Scholarship Programs
9940 106th Street, Fourth Floor, Sterling Place
PO Box 28000, Station Main
Edmonton, AB T5J 4R4
Canada
Phone: 780-427-8640
Fax: 780-427-1288
E-mail: scholarships@gov.ab.ca

NORTHERN STUDENT SUPPLEMENT

Award for northern Alberta students with a high financial need to enter postsecondary programs. Residents of Northern Alberta may be eligible for this supplement. Must be first time, first- or second-year postsecondary students, and must be attending an educational institution participating in the Alberta Opportunities Bursary (AOB) program.

Award: Grant for use in freshman or sophomore years; not renewable. *Number:* varies. *Amount:* $500–$1500.

Eligibility Requirements: Applicant must be enrolled or expecting to enroll full-time at a two-year or four-year or technical institution or university; resident of Alberta and studying in Alberta. Available to Canadian citizens.

Application Requirements: Application, financial need analysis. *Deadline:* continuous.

Contact: Scholarship Committee
Alberta Heritage Scholarship Fund/Alberta Scholarship Programs
9940 106th Street, Fourth Floor, Sterling Place
PO Box 28000, Station Main
Edmonton, AB T5J 4R4
Canada
Phone: 780-427-8640
Fax: 780-427-1288
E-mail: scholarships@gov.ab.ca

PERSONS CASE SCHOLARSHIPS

• *See page 671*

PRAIRIE BASEBALL ACADEMY SCHOLARSHIPS

The scholarship rewards athletic and academic excellence of baseball players, and provides an incentive and means for these players to continue with their postsecondary education. Must be Alberta residents and enrolled full-time at a postsecondary institution in Alberta. Applicants must be a participant in the Prairie Baseball Academy and must have achieved a minimum GPA of 2.0 in their previous semester.

Award: Scholarship for use in freshman, sophomore, junior, or senior years; not renewable. *Number:* 20–50. *Amount:* $500–$2500.

Eligibility Requirements: Applicant must be enrolled or expecting to enroll full-time at a two-year or four-year or technical institution or university; resident of Alberta; studying in Alberta and must have an interest in athletics/sports. Available to Canadian citizens.

Application Requirements: Application, references. *Deadline:* October 15.

Contact: Scholarship Committee
Alberta Heritage Scholarship Fund/Alberta Scholarship Programs
9940 106th Street, Fourth Floor, Sterling Place
PO Box 28000, Station Main
Edmonton, AB T5J 4R4
Canada
Phone: 780-427-8640
Fax: 780-427-1288
E-mail: scholarships@gov.ab.ca

QUEEN ELIZABETH II GOLDEN JUBILEE CITIZENSHIP MEDAL

• *See page 671*

REGISTERED APPRENTICESHIP PROGRAM SCHOLARSHIPS

Award to recognize the accomplishments of Alberta high school students taking the registered apprenticeship program, and to encourage recipients to continue their apprenticeship training after completing high school. Must be a Canadian citizen or landed immigrant, and a resident of Alberta; must have completed the requirements for high school graduation between August 1 and July 31 of the current year and be registered as an Alberta apprentice in a trade while still attending high school.

Award: Scholarship for use in freshman year; not renewable. *Number:* 1. *Amount:* $1000.

Eligibility Requirements: Applicant must be enrolled or expecting to enroll full-time at a two-year or four-year or technical institution or university and resident of Alberta. Available to Canadian citizens.

Application Requirements: Application, essay, references. *Deadline:* February 28.

Contact: Scholarship Committee
Alberta Heritage Scholarship Fund/Alberta Scholarship Programs
9940 106th Street, Fourth Floor, Sterling Place
PO Box 28000, Station Main
Edmonton, AB T5J 4R4
Canada
Phone: 780-427-8640
Fax: 780-427-1288
E-mail: scholarships@gov.ab.ca

RUTHERFORD SCHOLARS

• *See page 671*

STREAM-FLO/MASTER FLO SCHOLARSHIPS

• *See page 572*

ALBUQUERQUE COMMUNITY FOUNDATION http://www.albuquerquefoundation.org

NEW MEXICO MANUFACTURED HOUSING SCHOLARSHIP PROGRAM

The scholarship is to be used for study in a four-year college or university. The total number of available awards and the dollar value of each award varies. Deadline varies. Refer to Web site for details and application: http://www.albuquerquefoundation.org.

Award: Scholarship for use in freshman year; not renewable. *Number:* up to 2. *Amount:* $1000.

Eligibility Requirements: Applicant must be high school student; planning to enroll or expecting to enroll full-time at a four-year institution or university; resident of New Mexico and studying in New Mexico. Applicant must have 3.0 GPA or higher. Available to U.S. citizens.

Application Requirements: Application, financial need analysis, resume, references, test scores, transcript. *Deadline:* varies.

Contact: Nancy Johnson, Program Director
Albuquerque Community Foundation
PO Box 36960
Albuquerque, NM 87176-6960
Phone: 505-883-6240
E-mail: foundation@albuquerquefoundation.org

NOTAH BEGAY III SCHOLARSHIP PROGRAM FOR NATIVE AMERICAN SCHOLAR ATHLETES

• *See page 671*

SUSSMAN-MILLER EDUCATIONAL ASSISTANCE FUND

The program provides financial aid to enable students to continue with an undergraduate program. This is a "gap" program based on financial need. Must be resident of New Mexico. Minimum 3.0 GPA required. Deadline varies. The fund requests not to write or call for information. Please visit Web site: http://www.albuquerquefoundation.org for complete information.

Award: Scholarship for use in freshman, sophomore, junior, or senior years; renewable. *Number:* 29. *Amount:* $500–$3100.

Eligibility Requirements: Applicant must be enrolled or expecting to enroll full-time at a four-year institution or university and resident of New Mexico. Applicant must have 3.0 GPA or higher. Available to U.S. citizens.

Application Requirements: Application, autobiography, essay, financial need analysis, resume, references, test scores, transcript. *Deadline:* varies.

Contact: Nancy Johnson, Program Director
Albuquerque Community Foundation
PO Box 36960
Albuquerque, NM 87176-6960
Phone: 505-883-6240
E-mail: foundation@albuquerquefoundation.org

ALERT SCHOLARSHIP http://www.alertmagazine.org

ALERT SCHOLARSHIP

Scholarship of $500 for the best essay on drug and alcohol abuse. Applicant must be high school student living in Washington, Idaho, Montana, Wyoming, Colorado, North Dakota, or South Dakota. Minimum 2.5 GPA required. For further details visit Web site: http://www.alertmagazine.org/ScholarshipRequirements.htm.

Award: Scholarship for use in freshman year; not renewable. *Number:* 16. *Amount:* $500.

Eligibility Requirements: Applicant must be high school student; planning to enroll or expecting to enroll full- or part-time at a four-year institution or university; resident of Colorado, Idaho, Montana, North Dakota, South Dakota, Washington, or Wyoming and must have an interest in writing. Applicant must have 2.5 GPA or higher. Available to U.S. citizens.

Application Requirements: Applicant must enter a contest, essay, photo, transcript. *Deadline:* continuous.

Contact: Jolene Smith, Editor
Alert Scholarship
3085 North Cole, Suite 105
PO Box 4833
Boise, ID 83711
Phone: 208-375-7911
Fax: 208-376-0770
E-mail: alertmagazine@aol.com

ALEXANDER FOUNDATION http://www.thealexanderfoundation.org

SCHOLARSHIP GRANT PROGRAM

Scholarships provides financial assistance to undergraduate or graduate students accepted or enrolled in Colorado institution of higher education. Applicants must be gay, lesbian, bisexual, or transgendered and reside in Colorado. Must demonstrate financial need.

Alexander Foundation (continued)

Award: Scholarship for use in freshman, sophomore, junior, senior, or graduate years; not renewable. *Number:* varies. *Amount:* varies.

Eligibility Requirements: Applicant must be enrolled or expecting to enroll full- or part-time at a four-year institution or university; resident of Colorado; studying in Colorado and must have an interest in LGBT issues. Available to U.S. citizens.

Application Requirements: Application, essay, financial need analysis, references, transcript. *Deadline:* April 15.

Contact: Scholarship Committee
Alexander Foundation
PO Box 1995
Denver, CO 80201-1995
Phone: 303-331-7733
Fax: 303-331-1953
E-mail: infoalexander@thealexanderfoundation.org

AMERICAN CANCER SOCIETY, FLORIDA DIVISION INC. http://www.cancer.org

AMERICAN CANCER SOCIETY, FLORIDA DIVISION R.O.C.K. COLLEGE SCHOLARSHIP PROGRAM

• *See page 588*

AMERICAN CANCER SOCIETY INC.-GREAT LAKES DIVISION http://www.cancer.org/scholarships

COLLEGE SCHOLARSHIPS FOR CANCER SURVIVORS

• *See page 615*

AMERICAN LEGION AUXILIARY DEPARTMENT OF ALABAMA

AMERICAN LEGION AUXILIARY DEPARTMENT OF ALABAMA SCHOLARSHIP PROGRAM

• *See page 642*

AMERICAN LEGION AUXILIARY DEPARTMENT OF ARKANSAS http://www.arlegion.org

AMERICAN LEGION AUXILIARY DEPARTMENT OF ARKANSAS ACADEMIC SCHOLARSHIP

• *See page 642*

AMERICAN LEGION AUXILIARY DEPARTMENT OF CALIFORNIA http://www.calegionaux.org

AMERICAN LEGION AUXILIARY DEPARTMENT OF CALIFORNIA CONTINUING/RE-ENTRY STUDENT SCHOLARSHIP

Awarded to undergraduate students. Must be a continuing or re-entry college student and attend a California college or university.

Award: Scholarship for use in freshman, sophomore, junior, or senior years; not renewable. *Number:* 2–3. *Amount:* $500–$1000.

Eligibility Requirements: Applicant must be enrolled or expecting to enroll full- or part-time at a two-year or four-year institution or university; resident of California and studying in California. Available to U.S. citizens.

Application Requirements: Application. *Deadline:* March 16.

Contact: Theresa Jacob, Secretary/Treasurer
American Legion Auxiliary Department of California
401 Van Ness Avenue, Room 113
San Francisco, CA 94102
Phone: 415-862-5092
Fax: 415-861-8365
E-mail: calegionaux@calegionaux.org

AMERICAN LEGION AUXILIARY DEPARTMENT OF CALIFORNIA GENERAL SCHOLARSHIP

Award ranges from $500 to $1000 for high school senior or graduate of an accredited high school who has not been able to begin college due to circumstances of illness or finance. Student must attend a California college or university. Deadline March 16.

Award: Scholarship for use in freshman, sophomore, junior, or senior years; not renewable. *Number:* varies. *Amount:* $500–$1000.

Eligibility Requirements: Applicant must be enrolled or expecting to enroll full- or part-time at a two-year or four-year institution or university; resident of California and studying in California. Available to U.S. citizens.

Application Requirements: Application. *Deadline:* March 16.

Contact: Theresa Jacob, Secretary/Treasurer
American Legion Auxiliary Department of California
401 Van Ness Avenue, Room 113
San Francisco, CA 94102
Phone: 415-862-5092
Fax: 415-861-8365
E-mail: calegionaux@calegionaux.org

AMERICAN LEGION AUXILIARY DEPARTMENT OF CALIFORNIA JUNIOR SCHOLARSHIP

• *See page 511*

AMERICAN LEGION AUXILIARY DEPARTMENT OF COLORADO http://www.coloradolegion.org

AMERICAN LEGION AUXILIARY DEPARTMENT OF COLORADO DEPARTMENT PRESIDENT'S SCHOLARSHIP FOR JUNIOR MEMBER

• *See page 643*

AMERICAN LEGION AUXILIARY DEPARTMENT OF CONNECTICUT http://www.ct.legion.org

AMERICAN LEGION AUXILIARY DEPARTMENT OF CONNECTICUT PAST PRESIDENTS' PARLEY MEMORIAL EDUCATION GRANT

• *See page 511*

AMERICAN LEGION AUXILIARY DEPARTMENT OF FLORIDA http://www.alafl.org

AMERICAN LEGION AUXILIARY DEPARTMENT OF FLORIDA DEPARTMENT SCHOLARSHIPS

• *See page 643*

AMERICAN LEGION AUXILIARY DEPARTMENT OF FLORIDA MEMORIAL SCHOLARSHIP

• *See page 512*

AMERICAN LEGION AUXILIARY DEPARTMENT OF IDAHO

AMERICAN LEGION AUXILIARY DEPARTMENT OF IDAHO NATIONAL PRESIDENT'S SCHOLARSHIP

• *See page 643*

AMERICAN LEGION AUXILIARY DEPARTMENT OF INDIANA http://www.amlegauxin.org

AMERICAN LEGION AUXILIARY DEPARTMENT OF INDIANA EDNA M. BURCUS MEMORIAL SCHOLARSHIP

• *See page 644*

AMERICAN LEGION AUXILIARY DEPARTMENT OF INDIANA HOOSIER SCHOOLHOUSE SCHOLARSHIP

One-time award for Indiana residents who are high school seniors planning to continue their education. Award is primarily based on need.

Award: Scholarship for use in freshman year; not renewable. *Number:* 2. *Amount:* $500.

Eligibility Requirements: Applicant must be high school student; planning to enroll or expecting to enroll full-time at a two-year or four-year institution or university; resident of Indiana and studying in Indiana. Available to U.S. citizens.

Application Requirements: Application, financial need analysis, self-addressed stamped envelope, transcript. *Deadline:* varies.

Contact: Judy Otey, Department Secretary and Treasurer
American Legion Auxiliary Department of Indiana
777 North Meridian, Room 107
Indianapolis, IN 46204
Phone: 317-630-1390
Fax: 317-630-1277
E-mail: ala777@sbcglobal.net

AMERICAN LEGION AUXILIARY DEPARTMENT OF IOWA http://www.ialegion.org

AMERICAN LEGION AUXILIARY DEPARTMENT OF IOWA CHILDREN OF VETERANS SCHOLARSHIP

• *See page 644*

AMERICAN LEGION AUXILIARY DEPARTMENT OF KENTUCKY http://www.kylegion.org

AMERICAN LEGION AUXILIARY DEPARTMENT OF KENTUCKY LAURA BLACKBURN MEMORIAL SCHOLARSHIP

• *See page 637*

AMERICAN LEGION AUXILIARY DEPARTMENT OF KENTUCKY MARY BARRETT MARSHALL SCHOLARSHIP

• *See page 644*

AMERICAN LEGION AUXILIARY DEPARTMENT OF MAINE http://www.mainelegion.org

AMERICAN LEGION AUXILIARY DEPARTMENT OF MAINE DANIEL E. LAMBERT MEMORIAL SCHOLARSHIP

• *See page 644*

AMERICAN LEGION AUXILIARY DEPARTMENT OF MAINE NATIONAL PRESIDENT'S SCHOLARSHIP

• *See page 588*

AMERICAN LEGION AUXILIARY DEPARTMENT OF MARYLAND http://www.alamd.org

AMERICAN LEGION AUXILIARY DEPARTMENT OF MARYLAND CHILDREN AND YOUTH SCHOLARSHIPS

• *See page 637*

AMERICAN LEGION AUXILIARY DEPARTMENT OF MASSACHUSETTS

AMERICAN LEGION AUXILIARY DEPARTMENT OF MASSACHUSETTS DEPARTMENT PRESIDENT'S SCHOLARSHIP

• *See page 589*

AMERICAN LEGION AUXILIARY DEPARTMENT OF MASSACHUSETTS PAST PRESIDENTS' PARLEY SCHOLARSHIP

• *See page 644*

AMERICAN LEGION AUXILIARY DEPARTMENT OF MICHIGAN http://www.michalaux.org

AMERICAN LEGION AUXILIARY DEPARTMENT OF MICHIGAN MEMORIAL SCHOLARSHIP

• *See page 645*

AMERICAN LEGION AUXILIARY DEPARTMENT OF MICHIGAN NATIONAL PRESIDENT'S SCHOLARSHIP

• *See page 645*

AMERICAN LEGION AUXILIARY DEPARTMENT OF MICHIGAN SCHOLARSHIP FOR NON-TRADITIONAL STUDENT

• *See page 645*

AMERICAN LEGION AUXILIARY DEPARTMENT OF MINNESOTA http://www.mnlegion.org

AMERICAN LEGION AUXILIARY DEPARTMENT OF MINNESOTA SCHOLARSHIPS

• *See page 645*

AMERICAN LEGION AUXILIARY DEPARTMENT OF MISSOURI

AMERICAN LEGION AUXILIARY DEPARTMENT OF MISSOURI LELA MURPHY SCHOLARSHIP

• *See page 513*

AMERICAN LEGION AUXILIARY DEPARTMENT OF MISSOURI NATIONAL PRESIDENT'S SCHOLARSHIP

• *See page 513*

AMERICAN LEGION AUXILIARY DEPARTMENT OF NEBRASKA http://www.nebraskalegionaux.net

AMERICAN LEGION AUXILIARY DEPARTMENT OF NEBRASKA PRESIDENT'S SCHOLARSHIP FOR JUNIOR MEMBERS

• *See page 513*

AMERICAN LEGION AUXILIARY DEPARTMENT OF NEBRASKA PRESIDENT'S SCHOLARSHIPS

• *See page 645*

AMERICAN LEGION AUXILIARY DEPARTMENT OF NEBRASKA ROBERTA MARIE STRETCH MEMORIAL SCHOLARSHIP

• *See page 646*

AMERICAN LEGION AUXILIARY DEPARTMENT OF NEBRASKA RUBY PAUL CAMPAIGN FUND SCHOLARSHIP

• *See page 513*

AMERICAN LEGION AUXILIARY DEPARTMENT OF NEBRASKA STUDENT AID GRANTS

• *See page 646*

AMERICAN LEGION AUXILIARY DEPARTMENT OF NORTH DAKOTA http://www.ndlegion.org

AMERICAN LEGION AUXILIARY DEPARTMENT OF NORTH DAKOTA NATIONAL PRESIDENT'S SCHOLARSHIP

• *See page 589*

AMERICAN LEGION AUXILIARY DEPARTMENT OF NORTH DAKOTA SCHOLARSHIPS

One-time award for North Dakota residents who are already attending a North Dakota institution of higher learning. Contact local or nearest American Legion Auxiliary Unit for more information. Must be a U.S. citizen.

Award: Scholarship for use in sophomore, junior, senior, or graduate years; not renewable. *Number:* 3. *Amount:* $400.

Eligibility Requirements: Applicant must be enrolled or expecting to enroll full-time at a two-year or four-year or technical institution or university; resident of North Dakota and studying in North Dakota. Available to U.S. citizens.

Application Requirements: Application, autobiography, essay, financial need analysis, references, self-addressed stamped envelope, test scores, transcript. *Deadline:* January 15.

Contact: Myrna Runholm, Department Secretary
American Legion Auxiliary Department of North Dakota
PO Box 1060
Jamestown, ND 58402-1060
Phone: 701-253-5992
E-mail: ala-hq@ndlegion.org

AMERICAN LEGION AUXILIARY DEPARTMENT OF OHIO

AMERICAN LEGION AUXILIARY DEPARTMENT OF OHIO CONTINUING EDUCATION FUND

• *See page 646*

AMERICAN LEGION AUXILIARY DEPARTMENT OF OHIO DEPARTMENT PRESIDENT'S SCHOLARSHIP

• *See page 646*

AMERICAN LEGION AUXILIARY DEPARTMENT OF OREGON

AMERICAN LEGION AUXILIARY DEPARTMENT OF OREGON DEPARTMENT GRANTS

• *See page 647*

AMERICAN LEGION AUXILIARY DEPARTMENT OF OREGON NATIONAL PRESIDENT'S SCHOLARSHIP

• *See page 647*

AMERICAN LEGION AUXILIARY DEPARTMENT OF OREGON SPIRIT OF YOUTH SCHOLARSHIP

• *See page 514*

AMERICAN LEGION AUXILIARY DEPARTMENT OF PENNSYLVANIA http://www.pa-legion.com

AMERICAN LEGION AUXILIARY DEPARTMENT OF PENNSYLVANIA PAST DEPARTMENT PRESIDENTS' MEMORIAL SCHOLARSHIP

Renewable award of $400 given each year to high school seniors. Must be residents of Pennsylvania.

Award: Scholarship for use in freshman year; renewable. *Number:* 1. *Amount:* $400.

Eligibility Requirements: Applicant must be high school student; planning to enroll or expecting to enroll full-time at a four-year institution or university and resident of Pennsylvania. Available to U.S. citizens.

Application Requirements: Application. *Deadline:* March 15.

Contact: Colleen Watson, Executive Secretary and Treasurer
American Legion Auxiliary Department of Pennsylvania
PO Box 1285
Camp Hill, PA 17001-1285
Phone: 717-763-7545
Fax: 717-763-0617
E-mail: paalad@hotmail.com

AMERICAN LEGION AUXILIARY DEPARTMENT OF PENNSYLVANIA SCHOLARSHIP FOR DEPENDENTS OF DISABLED OR DECEASED VETERANS

Renewable award of $600 to high school seniors who are residents of Pennsylvania. Applicants must enroll in full-time studies.

Award: Scholarship for use in freshman year; renewable. *Number:* 1. *Amount:* $600.

Eligibility Requirements: Applicant must be high school student; planning to enroll or expecting to enroll full-time at a four-year institution or university and resident of Pennsylvania. Available to U.S. citizens.

Application Requirements: Application. *Deadline:* March 15.

Contact: Colleen Watson, Executive Secretary and Treasurer
American Legion Auxiliary Department of Pennsylvania
PO Box 1285
Camp Hill, PA 17001-1285
Phone: 717-763-7545
Fax: 717-763-0617
E-mail: paalad@hotmail.com

AMERICAN LEGION AUXILIARY DEPARTMENT OF PENNSYLVANIA SCHOLARSHIP FOR DEPENDENTS OF LIVING VETERANS

Renewable award of $600 for high school seniors who are residents of Pennsylvania. Applicants must enroll in a program of full-time study.

Award: Scholarship for use in freshman year; renewable. *Number:* 1. *Amount:* $600.

Eligibility Requirements: Applicant must be high school student; planning to enroll or expecting to enroll full-time at a four-year institution or university and resident of Pennsylvania. Available to U.S. citizens.

Application Requirements: Application. *Deadline:* March 15.

Contact: Colleen Watson, Executive Secretary and Treasurer
American Legion Auxiliary Department of Pennsylvania
PO Box 1285
Camp Hill, PA 17001-1285
Phone: 717-763-7545
Fax: 717-763-0617
E-mail: paalad@hotmail.com

AMERICAN LEGION AUXILIARY DEPARTMENT OF SOUTH DAKOTA

AMERICAN LEGION AUXILIARY DEPARTMENT OF SOUTH DAKOTA COLLEGE SCHOLARSHIPS

• *See page 514*

AMERICAN LEGION AUXILIARY DEPARTMENT OF SOUTH DAKOTA SENIOR SCHOLARSHIP

• *See page 514*

AMERICAN LEGION AUXILIARY DEPARTMENT OF SOUTH DAKOTA VOCATIONAL SCHOLARSHIP

• *See page 515*

AMERICAN LEGION AUXILIARY DEPARTMENT OF TENNESSEE

AMERICAN LEGION AUXILIARY DEPARTMENT OF TENNESSEE VARA GRAY SCHOLARSHIP-GENERAL

• *See page 589*

AMERICAN LEGION AUXILIARY DEPARTMENT OF TEXAS http://www.alatexas.org

AMERICAN LEGION AUXILIARY DEPARTMENT OF TEXAS GENERAL EDUCATION SCHOLARSHIP

• *See page 647*

AMERICAN LEGION AUXILIARY DEPARTMENT OF UTAH http://www.legion-aux.org

AMERICAN LEGION AUXILIARY DEPARTMENT OF UTAH NATIONAL PRESIDENT'S SCHOLARSHIP

• *See page 515*

AMERICAN LEGION AUXILIARY DEPARTMENT OF WASHINGTON http://www.walegion-aux.org

AMERICAN LEGION AUXILIARY DEPARTMENT OF WASHINGTON GIFT SCHOLARSHIPS

• *See page 647*

AMERICAN LEGION AUXILIARY DEPARTMENT OF WASHINGTON SUSAN BURDETT SCHOLARSHIP

Applicant must be a former citizen of Evergreen Girls State. Must be obtained and processed through a Washington State American Legion Auxiliary Unit. One-time award of $300.

Award: Scholarship for use in freshman, sophomore, junior, or senior years; not renewable. *Number:* 1. *Amount:* $300.

Eligibility Requirements: Applicant must be enrolled or expecting to enroll full- or part-time at a two-year or four-year institution or university; female and resident of Washington. Available to U.S. citizens.

Application Requirements: Application, essay, references, transcript. *Deadline:* April 1.

Contact: Nicole Ross, News Department Secretary
American Legion Auxiliary Department of Washington
3600 Ruddell Road
Lacey, WA 98503
Phone: 360-456-5995
Fax: 360-491-7442
E-mail: alawash@qwest.net

AMERICAN LEGION AUXILIARY DEPARTMENT OF WISCONSIN http://www.amlegionauxwi.org

AMERICAN LEGION AUXILIARY DEPARTMENT OF WISCONSIN DELLA VAN DEUREN MEMORIAL SCHOLARSHIP

• *See page 515*

AMERICAN LEGION AUXILIARY DEPARTMENT OF WISCONSIN H.S. AND ANGELINE LEWIS SCHOLARSHIPS

• *See page 515*

AMERICAN LEGION AUXILIARY DEPARTMENT OF WISCONSIN MERIT AND MEMORIAL SCHOLARSHIPS

• *See page 515*

AMERICAN LEGION AUXILIARY DEPARTMENT OF WISCONSIN PAST PRESIDENTS' PARLEY HEALTH CAREER SCHOLARSHIPS

• *See page 516*

AMERICAN LEGION AUXILIARY DEPARTMENT OF WISCONSIN PRESIDENT'S SCHOLARSHIPS

• *See page 516*

AMERICAN LEGION DEPARTMENT OF ARIZONA http://www.azlegion.org

AMERICAN LEGION DEPARTMENT OF ARIZONA HIGH SCHOOL ORATORICAL CONTEST

Each student must present an 8 to 10 minute prepared oration on any part of the U.S. Constitution without any notes, podiums, or coaching. The student will then be asked to do a 3 to 5 minute oration on one of four possible topics. Which one of the four topics will not be be known in advance, so students must be prepared to respond to any of the four. Open to students in grade 9 to 12.

Award: Prize for use in freshman year; not renewable. *Number:* 10. *Amount:* $150–$1500.

Eligibility Requirements: Applicant must be high school student; age 20 or under; planning to enroll or expecting to enroll full-time at a four-year institution or university; resident of Arizona and must have an interest in public speaking. Available to U.S. citizens.

Application Requirements: Application, applicant must enter a contest. *Deadline:* January 15.

Contact: Jim Burke, Department Oratorical Chairman
American Legion Department of Arizona
4701 North 19th Avenue, Suite 200
Phoenix, AZ 85015-3799
Phone: 602-264-7706
Fax: 602-264-0029

AMERICAN LEGION DEPARTMENT OF ARKANSAS http://www.arklegion.homestead.com

AMERICAN LEGION DEPARTMENT OF ARKANSAS COUDRET SCHOLARSHIP AWARD

• *See page 517*

AMERICAN LEGION DEPARTMENT OF ARKANSAS HIGH SCHOOL ORATORICAL CONTEST

Oratorical contest open to students in ninth to twelfth grades of any accredited Arkansas high school. Begins with finalists at the post level and proceeds through area and district levels to national contest.

Award: Prize for use in freshman year; not renewable. *Number:* 4. *Amount:* $1250–$3500.

Eligibility Requirements: Applicant must be high school student; age 19 or under; planning to enroll or expecting to enroll full-time at a four-year institution or university; resident of Arkansas and must have an interest in public speaking. Applicant must have 2.5 GPA or higher. Available to U.S. citizens.

Application Requirements: Application, applicant must enter a contest, photo, references. *Deadline:* December 15.

Contact: William Winchell, Department Adjutant
American Legion Department of Arkansas
PO Box 3280
Little Rock, AR 72203-3280
Phone: 501-375-1104
Fax: 501-375-4236
E-mail: alegion@swbell.net

AMERICAN LEGION DEPARTMENT OF HAWAII http://www.legion.org

AMERICAN LEGION DEPARTMENT OF HAWAII HIGH SCHOOL ORATORICAL CONTEST

Oratorical contest open to students in ninth to twelfth grades of any accredited Hawaii high school. Must be under 20 years of age. Speech contests begin in January at post level and continue on to the national competition. Contact local American Legion Post or department for deadlines and application details.

Award: Prize for use in freshman year; not renewable. *Number:* 1–3. *Amount:* up to $1500.

Eligibility Requirements: Applicant must be high school student; age 20 or under; planning to enroll or expecting to enroll full-time at a four-year institution or university and resident of Hawaii. Available to U.S. citizens.

Application Requirements: Application, applicant must enter a contest. *Deadline:* varies.

Contact: Bernard K.Y. Lee, Department Adjutant and Oratorical Contest Chairman
American Legion Department of Hawaii
612 McCully Street
Honolulu, HI 96826-3935
Phone: 808-946-6383
Fax: 808-947-3957
E-mail: aldepthi@hawaii.rr.com

AMERICAN LEGION DEPARTMENT OF IDAHO http://idlegion.home.mindspring.com

AMERICAN LEGION DEPARTMENT OF IDAHO SCHOLARSHIP

• *See page 517*

AMERICAN LEGION DEPARTMENT OF ILLINOIS http://www.illegion.org

AMERICAN ESSAY CONTEST SCHOLARSHIP

• *See page 517*

AMERICAN LEGION DEPARTMENT OF ILLINOIS BOY SCOUT/EXPLORER SCHOLARSHIP

• *See page 517*

AMERICAN LEGION DEPARTMENT OF ILLINOIS HIGH SCHOOL ORATORICAL CONTEST

Multilevel oratorical contest with winners advancing to the next level. Open to students in 9th to 12th grades of any accredited Illinois high school. Seniors must be in attendance as of January 1. Must contact local American Legion post or department headquarters for complete information and applications, which will be available in the fall.

Award: Prize for use in freshman year; not renewable. *Number:* up to 130. *Amount:* $75–$1600.

Eligibility Requirements: Applicant must be high school student; planning to enroll or expecting to enroll full- or part-time at a four-year institution or university; resident of Illinois and must have an interest in public speaking. Available to U.S. citizens.

Application Requirements: Application, applicant must enter a contest. *Deadline:* varies.

Contact: Bill Bechtel, Assistant Adjutant
American Legion Department of Illinois
PO Box 2910
Bloomington, IL 61702
Phone: 309-663-0361
Fax: 309-663-5783

AMERICAN LEGION DEPARTMENT OF ILLINOIS SCHOLARSHIPS

• *See page 517*

AMERICAN LEGION DEPARTMENT OF INDIANA http://www.indlegion.org

AMERICAN LEGION DEPARTMENT OF INDIANA, AMERICANISM AND GOVERNMENT TEST

Study guides are provided to high schools. Students take a test and write an essay. Two students from each grade (10 to 12) are selected as state winners.

Award: Scholarship for use in freshman year; not renewable. *Number:* 6. *Amount:* $1000.

Eligibility Requirements: Applicant must be high school student; planning to enroll or expecting to enroll full-time at a four-year institution or university and resident of Indiana. Available to U.S. citizens.

American Legion Department of Indiana (continued)

Application Requirements: Applicant must enter a contest, essay, test scores. *Deadline:* December 1.

Contact: Susan Long, Program Coordinator
American Legion Department of Indiana
777 North Meridan Street, Room 104
Indianapolis, IN 46204
Phone: 317-630-1264
Fax: 317-237-9891
E-mail: slong@indlegion.org

AMERICAN LEGION DEPARTMENT OF INDIANA HIGH SCHOOL ORATORICAL CONTEST

Oratorical contest open to students in grades nine to twelve of any accredited Indiana high school. Speech contests begin in November at post level and continue on to national competition. Contact local American Legion post for application details.

Award: Scholarship for use in freshman, sophomore, junior, senior, graduate, or postgraduate years; not renewable. *Number:* 4–8. *Amount:* $200–$4200.

Eligibility Requirements: Applicant must be high school student; age 19 or under; planning to enroll or expecting to enroll full- or part-time at a two-year or four-year or technical institution or university; resident of Indiana and must have an interest in public speaking. Available to U.S. citizens.

Application Requirements: Application, applicant must enter a contest. *Deadline:* December 1.

Contact: Susan Long, Program Coordinator
American Legion Department of Indiana
777 North Meridan Street, Room 104
Indianapolis, IN 46204
Phone: 317-630-1264
Fax: 317-237-9891
E-mail: slong@indlegion.org

FRANK W. MCHALE MEMORIAL SCHOLARSHIPS

One-time award for Indiana high school juniors who recently participated in the Boys State Program. Must be nominated by Boys State official. Write for more information and deadline.

Award: Scholarship for use in freshman year; not renewable. *Number:* 3. *Amount:* $1000–$1500.

Eligibility Requirements: Applicant must be high school student; planning to enroll or expecting to enroll full- or part-time at a four-year institution or university; male; resident of Indiana and must have an interest in leadership. Available to U.S. citizens.

Application Requirements: Application, participation in the Boys State Program, nomination from Boys State official. *Deadline:* June 13.

Contact: Susan Long, Program Coordinator
American Legion Department of Indiana
777 North Meridan Street, Room 104
Indianapolis, IN 46204-1189
Phone: 317-630-1264
Fax: 317-237-9891
E-mail: slong@indlegion.org

AMERICAN LEGION DEPARTMENT OF IOWA http://www.ialegion.org

AMERICAN LEGION DEPARTMENT OF IOWA EAGLE SCOUT OF THE YEAR SCHOLARSHIP

• *See page 518*

AMERICAN LEGION DEPARTMENT OF IOWA HIGH SCHOOL ORATORICAL CONTEST

All contestants in the department of Iowa American Legion High School Oratorical Contest shall be citizens or lawful permanent residents of the United States. The department of Iowa American Legion High School Oratorical Contest shall consist of one contestant from each of the three area contests. The area contest shall consist of one contestant from each district in the designated Area.

Award: Prize for use in freshman year; not renewable. *Number:* up to 3. *Amount:* $1000–$2000.

Eligibility Requirements: Applicant must be high school student; planning to enroll or expecting to enroll full-time at a two-year or four-year institution or university; resident of Iowa and must have an interest in public speaking. Available to U.S. citizens.

Application Requirements: Application, applicant must enter a contest. *Deadline:* varies.

Contact: Kathy Nees, Program Director, Youth Programs
American Legion Department of Iowa
720 Lyon Street
Des Moines, IA 50309
Phone: 515-282-5068
Fax: 515-282-7583
E-mail: knees@ialegion.org

AMERICAN LEGION DEPARTMENT OF IOWA OUTSTANDING SENIOR BASEBALL PLAYER

One-time award for Iowa residents who participated in the American Legion Senior Baseball Program and display outstanding sportsmanship, athletic ability, and proven academic achievements. Must be recommended by Baseball Committee.

Award: Scholarship for use in freshman year; not renewable. *Number:* 1. *Amount:* $750–$1500.

Eligibility Requirements: Applicant must be high school student; age 15-18; planning to enroll or expecting to enroll full-time at a two-year or four-year institution or university; resident of Iowa and must have an interest in athletics/sports. Available to U.S. citizens.

Application Requirements: Application, applicant must enter a contest, references. *Deadline:* July 15.

Contact: Kathy Nees, Program Director, Youth Programs
American Legion Department of Iowa
720 Lyon Street
Des Moines, IA 50309
Phone: 515-282-5068
Fax: 515-282-7583
E-mail: knees@ialegion.org

AMERICAN LEGION DEPARTMENT OF KANSAS http://www.ksamlegion.org

ALBERT M. LAPPIN SCHOLARSHIP

• *See page 518*

CHARLES W. AND ANNETTE HILL SCHOLARSHIP

• *See page 518*

DR. CLICK COWGER BASEBALL SCHOLARSHIP

Scholarship available to a high school senior or college freshman or sophomore enrolled in a Kansas institution. Applicant may intend to enroll in a junior college, university or trade school in Kansas only. Must be a male and should play or has played Kansas American Legion baseball. Must be an average or a better student scholastically.

Award: Scholarship for use in freshman or sophomore years; not renewable. *Number:* 1. *Amount:* $500.

Eligibility Requirements: Applicant must be enrolled or expecting to enroll full-time at a two-year or four-year or technical institution or university; male; resident of Kansas; studying in Kansas and must have an interest in athletics/sports. Available to U.S. citizens.

Application Requirements: Application, financial need analysis, photo, references, transcript. *Deadline:* July 15.

Contact: Jim Gravenstein, Chairman, Scholarship Committee
American Legion Department of Kansas
1314 Topeka Boulevard, SW
Topeka, KS 66612
Phone: 785-232-9315
Fax: 785-232-1399

HUGH A. SMITH SCHOLARSHIP FUND

• *See page 518*

PAUL FLAHERTY ATHLETIC SCHOLARSHIP

Scholarship available to high school seniors, college level freshmen or sophomores enrolled or intending to enroll in an approved junior college, college, university, or trade school. Must have participated in any form of high school athletics. Must be an average or a better student scholastically.

Award: Scholarship for use in freshman or sophomore years; not renewable. *Number:* 1. *Amount:* $250.

Eligibility Requirements: Applicant must be enrolled or expecting to enroll full-time at a two-year or four-year or technical institution or university; studying in Kansas and must have an interest in athletics/sports. Available to U.S. citizens.

Application Requirements: Application, financial need analysis, photo, references, transcript, latest 1040 income statement of supporting parents. *Deadline:* July 15.

Contact: Jim Gravenstein, Chairman, Scholarship Committee
American Legion Department of Kansas
1314 Topeka Boulevard, SW
Topeka, KS 66612
Phone: 785-232-9513
Fax: 785-232-1399

ROSEDALE POST 346 SCHOLARSHIP

• ***See page 518***

TED AND NORA ANDERSON SCHOLARSHIPS

• ***See page 519***

AMERICAN LEGION DEPARTMENT OF MAINE

http://www.mainelegion.org

AMERICAN LEGION DEPARTMENT OF MAINE CHILDREN AND YOUTH SCHOLARSHIP

• ***See page 648***

DANIEL E. LAMBERT MEMORIAL SCHOLARSHIP

• ***See page 648***

JAMES V. DAY SCHOLARSHIP

• ***See page 519***

AMERICAN LEGION DEPARTMENT OF MARYLAND

http://www.mdlegion.org

AMERICAN LEGION DEPARTMENT OF MARYLAND GENERAL SCHOLARSHIP

Scholarship of $500 for Maryland high school students. Must plan on attending a two-year or four-year college or university in the state of Maryland. Nonrenewable award. Based on financial need and citizenship. Applications available on Web site: http://mdlegion.org.

Award: Scholarship for use in freshman year; not renewable. *Number:* up to 3. *Amount:* up to $500.

Eligibility Requirements: Applicant must be high school student; age 19 or under; planning to enroll or expecting to enroll full-time at a two-year or four-year institution or university; resident of Maryland and studying in Maryland. Available to U.S. citizens.

Application Requirements: Application, essay, financial need analysis, transcript. *Deadline:* April 1.

Contact: Thomas Davis, Department Adjutant
American Legion Department of Maryland
101 North Gay, Room E
Baltimore, MD 21202
Phone: 410-752-1405
Fax: 410-752-3822
E-mail: tom@mdlegion.org

AMERICAN LEGION DEPARTMENT OF MARYLAND GENERAL SCHOLARSHIP FUND

• ***See page 649***

AMERICAN LEGION DEPARTMENT OF MICHIGAN

http://www.michiganlegion.org

AMERICAN LEGION DEPARTMENT OF MICHIGAN HIGH SCHOOL ORATORICAL CONTEST

Oratorical contest open to students in ninth to twelfth grades of any accredited Michigan high school or state accredited home school. Five one-time awards of varying amounts.

Award: Prize for use in freshman year; not renewable. *Number:* 5. *Amount:* $800–$1500.

Eligibility Requirements: Applicant must be high school student; age 20 or under; planning to enroll or expecting to enroll full- or part-time at a two-year or four-year institution or university; resident of Michigan and must have an interest in public speaking. Available to U.S. citizens.

Application Requirements: Application, applicant must enter a contest, essay. *Deadline:* varies.

Contact: Deanna Clark, Department Administrative Assistant for Programs
American Legion Department of Michigan
212 North Verlinden Avenue
Lansing, MI 48915
Phone: 517-371-4720 Ext. 11
Fax: 517-371-2401
E-mail: programs@michiganlegion.org

GUY M. WILSON SCHOLARSHIPS

• ***See page 649***

WILLIAM D. AND JEWELL W. BREWER SCHOLARSHIP TRUSTS

• ***See page 649***

AMERICAN LEGION DEPARTMENT OF MINNESOTA

http://www.mnlegion.org

AMERICAN LEGION DEPARTMENT OF MINNESOTA HIGH SCHOOL ORATORICAL CONTEST

Oratorical contest open to students in ninth to twelfth grades of any accredited Minnesota high school. Speech contests begin in January at post level and continue on to the national competition. Contact local American Legion Post for application details.

Award: Prize for use in freshman year; not renewable. *Number:* 4. *Amount:* $500–$1200.

Eligibility Requirements: Applicant must be high school student; planning to enroll or expecting to enroll full- or part-time at a two-year or four-year or technical institution or university; resident of Minnesota and must have an interest in public speaking. Available to U.S. citizens.

Application Requirements: Application, applicant must enter a contest. *Deadline:* December 31.

Contact: Jennifer Kelley, Program Coordinator
American Legion Department of Minnesota
20 West 12th Street, Room 300A
St. Paul, MN 55155
Phone: 651-291-1800
Fax: 651-291-1057
E-mail: department@mnlegion.org

AMERICAN LEGION DEPARTMENT OF MINNESOTA MEMORIAL SCHOLARSHIP

• ***See page 519***

MINNESOTA LEGIONNAIRES INSURANCE TRUST SCHOLARSHIP

• ***See page 519***

AMERICAN LEGION DEPARTMENT OF MISSOURI

http://www.missourilegion.org

CHARLES L. BACON MEMORIAL SCHOLARSHIP

• ***See page 519***

LILLIE LOIS FORD SCHOLARSHIP FUND

• ***See page 649***

AMERICAN LEGION DEPARTMENT OF MONTANA

http://www.mtlegion.org

AMERICAN LEGION DEPARTMENT OF MONTANA HIGH SCHOOL ORATORICAL CONTEST

Applicants participate in a statewide memorized oratorical contest on the U.S. Constitution. Four places are awarded. Must be a Montana high school student. Contact state adjutant American Legion Department of Montana for further details. Each state winner who competes in the first round of the national contest will receive a $1000 scholarship. Participants in the second round who do not advance to the national final round will receive an additional $1000 scholarship.

Award: Scholarship for use in freshman year; not renewable. *Number:* 1–4. *Amount:* $300–$2000.

Eligibility Requirements: Applicant must be high school student; planning to enroll or expecting to enroll full-time at a two-year or

American Legion Department of Montana (continued)

four-year or technical institution or university; resident of Montana and must have an interest in public speaking. Available to U.S. citizens.

Application Requirements: Application, applicant must enter a contest. *Deadline:* continuous.

Contact: Gary White, State Adjutant
American Legion Department of Montana
PO Box 6075
Helena, MT 59604
Phone: 406-324-3989
Fax: 406-324-3991
E-mail: amlegmt@in-tch.com

AMERICAN LEGION DEPARTMENT OF NEBRASKA http://www.nebraskalegion.net

AMERICAN LEGION BASEBALL SCHOLARSHIP-NEBRASKA AMERICAN LEGION BASEBALL PLAYER OF THE YEAR

Any Team Manager or Head Coach of an American Legion Post-affiliated team may nominate one player for consideration for this award. Application, letters of recommendation, and certification form must be completed, postmarked, and mailed to the state's Department Headquarters no later than July 15. Three letters of testimony must be attached to the nomination form.

Award: Scholarship for use in freshman year; not renewable. *Number:* 1. *Amount:* $600–$750.

Eligibility Requirements: Applicant must be high school student; planning to enroll or expecting to enroll full- or part-time at a two-year or four-year or technical institution or university; resident of Nebraska and must have an interest in athletics/sports. Available to U.S. citizens.

Application Requirements: Application, photo, references. *Deadline:* July 15.

Contact: Mr. Jody Moeller, Activities Director
American Legion Department of Nebraska
PO Box 5205
Lincoln, NE 68505-0205
Phone: 402-464-6338
Fax: 402-464-6330
E-mail: actdirlegion@alltel.net

AMERICAN LEGION DEPARTMENT OF NEBRASKA HIGH SCHOOL ORATORICAL CONTEST

Local high school winners advance to District. Fifteen District Winners advance to Area contest. Area contestants awarded $100. Four Area winners advance to State contest. State prizes range from $200 to $1000. State winner advances to National contest. National prizes range from $14,000 to $18,000.

Award: Prize for use in freshman year; not renewable. *Number:* 4–19. *Amount:* $100–$1000.

Eligibility Requirements: Applicant must be high school student; planning to enroll or expecting to enroll full- or part-time at a two-year or four-year or technical institution or university; resident of Nebraska and must have an interest in public speaking. Available to U.S. citizens.

Application Requirements: Applicant must enter a contest, 8- to 10-minute prepared oration on some aspect the U.S. Constitution, a discourse on an assigned topic lasting 3 to 5 minutes. *Deadline:* varies.

Contact: Jody Moeller, Activities Director
American Legion Department of Nebraska
PO Box 5205
Lincoln, NE 68505-0205
Phone: 402-464-6338
Fax: 402-464-6880
E-mail: actdirlegion@alltel.net

AMERICAN LEGION DEPARTMENT OF NEBRASKA JIM HURLBERT MEMORIAL BASEBALL SCHOLARSHIP

Award to a Nebraska American Legion Baseball player in last year of eligibility and/or graduating senior. One applicant nominated by each Senior American Legion Baseball team. Student must attend a postsecondary educational institution within the state of Nebraska, and must have maintained a GPA in the upper half of his/her graduating class.

Award: Scholarship for use in freshman year; not renewable. *Number:* up to 4. *Amount:* up to $500.

Eligibility Requirements: Applicant must be high school student; planning to enroll or expecting to enroll full- or part-time at a two-year or four-year or technical institution or university; resident of Nebraska; studying in Nebraska and must have an interest in athletics/sports. Applicant must have 2.5 GPA or higher. Available to U.S. citizens.

Application Requirements: Application, financial need analysis, references, transcript. *Deadline:* June 15.

Contact: Mr. Jody Moeller, Activities Director
American Legion Department of Nebraska
PO Box 5205
Lincoln, NE 68505-0205
Phone: 402-464-6338
Fax: 402-464-6330
E-mail: actdirlegion@alltel.net

EAGLE SCOUT OF THE YEAR SCHOLARSHIP

• *See page 520*

MAYNARD JENSEN AMERICAN LEGION MEMORIAL SCHOLARSHIP

• *See page 520*

AMERICAN LEGION DEPARTMENT OF NEW YORK http://www.ny.legion.org

AMERICAN LEGION DEPARTMENT OF NEW YORK HIGH SCHOOL ORATORICAL CONTEST

Oratorical contest open to students under 20 years in 9th-12th grades of any accredited New York high school. Speech contests begin in November at post levels and continue to national competition. Must be U.S. citizen or permanent resident. Payments are made directly to college and are awarded over a four-year period. Deadline varies.

Award: Scholarship for use in freshman year; not renewable. *Number:* varies. *Amount:* $2000–$6000.

Eligibility Requirements: Applicant must be high school student; age 20 or under; planning to enroll or expecting to enroll full-time at a four-year institution or university; resident of New York and must have an interest in public speaking. Available to U.S. citizens.

Application Requirements: Application, applicant must enter a contest. *Deadline:* varies.

Contact: Richard Pedro, Department Adjutant
American Legion Department of New York
112 State Street, Suite 400
Albany, NY 12207
Phone: 518-463-2215
Fax: 518-427-8443
E-mail: newyork@legion.org

AMERICAN LEGION DEPARTMENT OF NORTH CAROLINA http://www.nclegion.org

AMERICAN LEGION DEPARTMENT OF NORTH CAROLINA HIGH SCHOOL ORATORICAL CONTEST

Objective of the program is to develop a deeper knowledge and appreciation of the U.S. Constitution, develop leadership qualities, the ability to think and speak clearly and intelligently, and prepare for acceptance of duties, responsibilities, rights, and privileges of American citizenship. Open to North Carolina high school students. Must be U.S. citizen or lawful permanent resident.

Award: Scholarship for use in freshman year; renewable. *Number:* 5. *Amount:* $500–$2000.

Eligibility Requirements: Applicant must be high school student; age 20 or under; planning to enroll or expecting to enroll full- or part-time at a two-year or four-year or technical institution or university; resident of North Carolina and must have an interest in public speaking. Available to U.S. citizens.

Application Requirements: Application, applicant must enter a contest. *Deadline:* varies.

Contact: Debra Rose, Department Executive Secretary
American Legion Department of North Carolina
4 North Blount Street, PO Box 26657
Raleigh, NC 27611-6657
Phone: 919-832-7506
Fax: 919-832-6428
E-mail: drose-nclegion@nc.rr.com

AMERICAN LEGION DEPARTMENT OF NORTH DAKOTA http://www.ndlegion.org

AMERICAN LEGION DEPARTMENT OF NORTH DAKOTA NATIONAL HIGH SCHOOL ORATORICAL CONTEST

Oratorical contest for high school students in grades nine to twelve. Contestants must prepare to speak on the topic of the U.S. Constitution. Must graduate from an accredited North Dakota high school. Contest begins at the local level and continues to the national level. Several one-time awards of $100 to $2000.

Award: Prize for use in freshman year; not renewable. *Number:* 38. *Amount:* $100–$2000.

Eligibility Requirements: Applicant must be high school student; planning to enroll or expecting to enroll full-time at a four-year institution or university; resident of North Dakota and must have an interest in public speaking. Available to U.S. citizens.

Application Requirements: Application, applicant must enter a contest. *Deadline:* November 30.

Contact: Terri Bryant, Program Coordinator
American Legion Department of North Dakota
405 West Main Avenue
PO Box 5057
West Fargo, ND 58078-2666
Phone: 701-293-3120
Fax: 701-293-9951
E-mail: programs@ndlegion.org

HATTIE TEDROW MEMORIAL FUND SCHOLARSHIP

• *See page 649*

NORTH DAKOTA CARING CITIZEN SCHOLARSHIP

One-time award for North Dakota high school juniors who participated in the Boys State Program. Must be nominated by Boys State official. Must demonstrate care and concern for fellow students.

Award: Scholarship for use in freshman year; not renewable. *Number:* varies. *Amount:* varies.

Eligibility Requirements: Applicant must be high school student; planning to enroll or expecting to enroll full-time at a two-year or four-year or technical institution or university; male and resident of North Dakota. Available to U.S. citizens.

Application Requirements: Application, references, nomination. *Deadline:* varies.

Contact: Terri Bryant, Program Coordinator
American Legion Department of North Dakota
405 West Main Avenue
PO Box 5057
West Fargo, ND 58078-2666
Phone: 701-293-3120
Fax: 701-293-9951
E-mail: programs@ndlegion.org

AMERICAN LEGION DEPARTMENT OF OREGON

AMERICAN LEGION DEPARTMENT OF OREGON HIGH SCHOOL ORATORICAL CONTEST

Students give two orations, one prepared and one extemporaneous on an assigned topic pertaining to the Constitution of the United States of America. Awards are given at Post, District, and State level with the state winner advancing to the National level contest. Open to students enrolled in high schools within the state of Oregon.

Award: Scholarship for use in freshman year; not renewable. *Number:* up to 4. *Amount:* $200–$500.

Eligibility Requirements: Applicant must be high school student; planning to enroll or expecting to enroll full-time at a four-year institution or university; resident of Oregon and must have an interest in public speaking. Available to U.S. citizens.

Application Requirements: Application, applicant must enter a contest. *Deadline:* December 1.

Contact: Barry Snyder, Adjutant
American Legion Department of Oregon
PO Box 1730
Wilsonville, OR 97070-1730
Phone: 503-685-5006
Fax: 503-685-5008
E-mail: orlegion@aol.com

AMERICAN LEGION DEPARTMENT OF PENNSYLVANIA http://www.pa-legion.com

AMERICAN LEGION DEPARTMENT OF PENNSYLVANIA HIGH SCHOOL ORATORICAL CONTEST

Oratorical contest open to students in 9th-12th grades of any accredited Pennsylvania high school. Speech contests begin in January at post level and continue on to national competition. Contact local American Legion post for deadlines and application details. Three one-time awards ranging from $7500 for first place, second place $5000, and third place $4000.

Award: Prize for use in freshman year; not renewable. *Number:* 3. *Amount:* $4000–$7500.

Eligibility Requirements: Applicant must be high school student; planning to enroll or expecting to enroll full-time at a two-year or four-year or technical institution or university; resident of Pennsylvania and must have an interest in public speaking. Available to U.S. citizens.

Application Requirements: Application, applicant must enter a contest. *Deadline:* varies.

Contact: Colleen Washinger, Executive Secretary
American Legion Department of Pennsylvania
PO Box 2324
Harrisburg, PA 17105-2324
Phone: 717-730-9100
Fax: 717-975-2836
E-mail: hq@pa-legion.com

JOSEPH P. GAVENONIS COLLEGE SCHOLARSHIP (PLAN I)

• *See page 521*

AMERICAN LEGION DEPARTMENT OF SOUTH DAKOTA http://www.sdlegion.org

AMERICAN LEGION DEPARTMENT OF SOUTH DAKOTA HIGH SCHOOL ORATORICAL CONTEST

Provide an 8 to 10 minute oration on some phase of the U.S. Constitution. Be prepared to speak extemporaneously for 3 to 5 minutes on specified articles or amendments. Compete at Local, District, and State levels. State winner goes on to National Contest and opportunity to win $18,000 in scholarships. Contact local American Legion post for contest dates.

Award: Prize for use in freshman, sophomore, junior, or senior years; not renewable. *Number:* 1–4. *Amount:* $200–$1000.

Eligibility Requirements: Applicant must be enrolled or expecting to enroll full-time at a two-year or four-year or technical institution or university; resident of South Dakota and must have an interest in public speaking. Available to U.S. citizens.

Application Requirements: Applicant must enter a contest, oration. *Deadline:* varies.

Contact: Ronald Boyd, Department Adjutant
American Legion Department of South Dakota
PO Box 67
Watertown, SD 57201-0067
Phone: 605-886-3604
Fax: 605-886-2870
E-mail: sdlegion@dailypost.com

AMERICAN LEGION DEPARTMENT OF TENNESSEE http://www.tennesseelegion.org

AMERICAN LEGION DEPARTMENT OF TENNESSEE EAGLE SCOUT OF THE YEAR

• *See page 521*

AMERICAN LEGION DEPARTMENT OF TENNESSEE HIGH SCHOOL ORATORICAL CONTEST

Scholarship for graduating Tennessee high school seniors enrolled either part-time or full-time in accredited colleges or universities.

Award: Scholarship for use in freshman year; not renewable. *Number:* 1–3. *Amount:* $1000–$4000.

Eligibility Requirements: Applicant must be high school student; planning to enroll or expecting to enroll full- or part-time at a two-year or four-year institution or university; resident of Tennessee and must have an interest in public speaking. Available to U.S. citizens.

Application Requirements: Applicant must enter a contest. *Deadline:* varies.

Contact: Darlene Burgess, Executive Assistant
American Legion Department of Tennessee
215 Eighth Avenue, North
Nashville, TN 37203
Phone: 615-254-0568
Fax: 615-255-1551
E-mail: tnleg1@bellsouth.net

JROTC SCHOLARSHIP

• *See page 633*

AMERICAN LEGION DEPARTMENT OF TEXAS http://www.txlegion.org

AMERICAN LEGION DEPARTMENT OF TEXAS HIGH SCHOOL ORATORICAL CONTEST

Scholarships will be given to the winners of oratorical contests. Contestants must be in high school with plans to further their education in a postsecondary institution. The winner of first place will be certified to national headquarters as the Texas representative in the quarter finals and the department will award a $2000 scholarship to the college of the applicant's choice. The department champion will receive additional scholarships each time he/she advances to the next level.

Award: Prize for use in freshman year; not renewable. *Number:* up to 20. *Amount:* $500–$2000.

Eligibility Requirements: Applicant must be high school student; age 20 or under; planning to enroll or expecting to enroll full-time at a two-year or four-year or technical institution or university; resident of Texas and must have an interest in public speaking. Available to U.S. citizens.

Application Requirements: Application, applicant must enter a contest, essay, interview, copy of prepared oration. *Deadline:* varies.

Contact: Robert Squyres, Director of Internal Affairs
American Legion Department of Texas
3401 Ed Bluestein Boulevard
Austin, TX 78721-2902
Phone: 512-472-4138
Fax: 512-472-0603
E-mail: programs@txlegion.org

AMERICAN LEGION DEPARTMENT OF VERMONT http://www.legionvthq.com

AMERICAN LEGION DEPARTMENT OF VERMONT DEPARTMENT SCHOLARSHIPS

Awards for high school seniors who attend a Vermont high school or similar school in an adjoining state whose parents are legal residents of Vermont, or reside in an adjoining state and attend a Vermont secondary school.

Award: Scholarship for use in freshman year; not renewable. *Number:* up to 12. *Amount:* $500–$1500.

Eligibility Requirements: Applicant must be high school student; planning to enroll or expecting to enroll full- or part-time at a two-year or four-year or technical institution or university and resident of New Hampshire, New York, or Vermont. Available to U.S. citizens.

Application Requirements: Application, essay, financial need analysis, references, transcript. *Deadline:* April 1.

Contact: Richard Farmer, Chairman
American Legion Department of Vermont
PO Box 396
Montpelier, VT 05601-0396
Phone: 802-223-7131
Fax: 802-223-0318
E-mail: alvthq@verizon.net

AMERICAN LEGION DEPARTMENT OF VERMONT HIGH SCHOOL ORATORICAL CONTEST

• *See page 650*

AMERICAN LEGION EAGLE SCOUT OF THE YEAR

• *See page 521*

AMERICAN LEGION DEPARTMENT OF VIRGINIA http://www.valegion.org

AMERICAN LEGION DEPARTMENT OF VIRGINIA HIGH SCHOOL ORATORICAL CONTEST

Three one-time awards of up to $1100. Oratorical contest open to applicants who are winners of the Virginia department oratorical contest and who attend high school in Virginia. Competitors must demonstrate their knowledge of the U.S. Constitution. Must be students in ninth to twelfth grades at accredited Virginia high schools.

Award: Prize for use in freshman year; not renewable. *Number:* 3. *Amount:* $600–$1100.

Eligibility Requirements: Applicant must be high school student; age 20 or under; planning to enroll or expecting to enroll full-time at a four-year institution or university and resident of Virginia. Available to U.S. citizens.

Application Requirements: Application, applicant must enter a contest. *Deadline:* December 1.

Contact: Dale Chapman, Adjutant
American Legion Department of Virginia
1708 Commonwealth Avenue
Richmond, VA 23230
Phone: 804-353-6606
Fax: 804-358-1940
E-mail: eeccleston@valegion.org

AMERICAN LEGION DEPARTMENT OF WASHINGTON http://www.walegion.org

AMERICAN LEGION DEPARTMENT OF WASHINGTON CHILDREN AND YOUTH SCHOLARSHIPS

• *See page 521*

AMERICAN LEGION DEPARTMENT OF WEST VIRGINIA http://www.wvlegion.org

AMERICAN LEGION DEPARTMENT OF WEST VIRGINIA BOARD OF REGENTS SCHOLARSHIP

One-time prize awarded annually to the winner of the West Virginia American Legion state oratorical contest. Must be in ninth to twelfth grade of an accredited West Virginia high school to compete. For use at a West Virginia institution only.

Award: Scholarship for use in freshman year; not renewable. *Number:* 1. *Amount:* up to $1500.

Eligibility Requirements: Applicant must be high school student; planning to enroll or expecting to enroll full-time at a four-year institution or university; resident of West Virginia; studying in West Virginia and must have an interest in public speaking. Available to U.S. citizens.

Application Requirements: Application, applicant must enter a contest. *Deadline:* January 1.

Contact: Miles Epling, State Adjutant
American Legion Department of West Virginia
2016 Kanawha Boulevard East, PO Box 3191
Charleston, WV 25332-3191
Phone: 304-343-7591
Fax: 304-343-7592
E-mail: wvlegion@suddenlinkmail.com

AMERICAN LEGION DEPARTMENT OF WEST VIRGINIA HIGH SCHOOL ORATORICAL CONTEST

Oratorical contest open to students in ninth to twelfth grades of any accredited West Virginia high school. Speech contests begin in January at post level and continue on to national competition. Contact local American Legion Post for deadlines and application details.

Award: Scholarship for use in freshman year; not renewable. *Number:* 25–39. *Amount:* $150–$500.

Eligibility Requirements: Applicant must be high school student; planning to enroll or expecting to enroll full-time at a four-year institution or university; resident of West Virginia and must have an interest in public speaking. Available to U.S. citizens.

Application Requirements: Application, applicant must enter a contest. *Deadline:* January 1.

Contact: Miles Epling, State Adjutant
American Legion Department of West Virginia
2016 Kanawha Boulevard East, PO Box 3191
Charleston, WV 25332-3191
Phone: 304-343-7591
Fax: 304-343-7592
E-mail: wvlegion@suddenlinkmail.com

SONS OF THE AMERICAN LEGION WILLIAM F. "BILL" JOHNSON MEMORIAL SCHOLARSHIP

• *See page 521*

AMERICAN QUARTER HORSE FOUNDATION (AQHF) http://www.aqha.com/foundation

DR. GERALD O'CONNOR MICHIGAN SCHOLARSHIP

• *See page 522*

INDIANA QUARTER HORSE YOUTH SCHOLARSHIP

• *See page 523*

JOAN CAIN FLORIDA QUARTER HORSE YOUTH SCHOLARSHIP

• *See page 523*

NEBRASKA QUARTER HORSE YOUTH SCHOLARSHIP

• *See page 523*

RAY MELTON MEMORIAL VIRGINIA QUARTER HORSE YOUTH SCHOLARSHIP

• *See page 523*

SWAYZE WOODRUFF MEMORIAL MID-SOUTH SCHOLARSHIP

• *See page 524*

AMERICAN SAVINGS FOUNDATION http://www.asfdn.org

AMERICAN SAVINGS FOUNDATION SCHOLARSHIPS

Scholarship awards range from $500 to $3000 for students entering any year of a two- or four-year undergraduate program or technical/vocational program at an accredited institution. Applicant must be a Connecticut resident. Minimum 2.5 GPA required.

Award: Scholarship for use in freshman, sophomore, junior, or senior years; renewable. *Number:* varies. *Amount:* $500–$3000.

Eligibility Requirements: Applicant must be enrolled or expecting to enroll full- or part-time at a two-year or four-year or technical institution or university and resident of Connecticut. Applicant must have 2.5 GPA or higher. Available to U.S. citizens.

Application Requirements: Application, financial need analysis, references, transcript. *Deadline:* March 31.

Contact: Maria Falvo, Senior Program Officer, Scholarships
American Savings Foundation
185 Main Street
New Britain, CT 06051
Phone: 860-827-2572
Fax: 860-832-4582
E-mail: mfalvo@asfdn.org

AMERICAN SWEDISH INSTITUTE http://www.americanswedishinst.org

LILLY LORENZEN SCHOLARSHIP

One-time award for a Minnesota resident, or a student attending a school in Minnesota. Must have working knowledge of Swedish and present a creditable plan for study in Sweden. Must be a U.S. citizen.

Award: Scholarship for use in freshman, sophomore, junior, senior, graduate, or postgraduate years; not renewable. *Number:* 1. *Amount:* $1500–$2500.

Eligibility Requirements: Applicant must be enrolled or expecting to enroll full- or part-time at a two-year or four-year or technical institution or university; resident of Minnesota; studying in Minnesota and must have an interest in Scandinavian language. Available to U.S. citizens.

Application Requirements: Application, interview, transcript. *Deadline:* May 1.

Contact: Nina Clark, Education Programs Coordinator
American Swedish Institute
2600 Park Avenue
Minneapolis, MN 55407-1090
Phone: 612-870-3374
Fax: 612-871-8682
E-mail: ninac@americanswedishinst.org

AMVETS DEPARTMENT OF ILLINOIS http://www.ilamvets.org

ILLINOIS AMVETS JUNIOR ROTC SCHOLARSHIPS

Four-year scholarship of $3000 per year for students who have taken the ACT or SAT tests. Preference will be given to children or grandchildren of veterans.

Award: Scholarship for use in freshman, sophomore, junior, or senior years; renewable. *Number:* varies. *Amount:* up to $3000.

Eligibility Requirements: Applicant must be enrolled or expecting to enroll full-time at a four-year institution or university and resident of Illinois. Available to U.S. citizens.

Application Requirements: Application, test scores. *Deadline:* March 1.

Contact: Crystal Bales, Program Director
AMVETS Department of Illinois
State Headquarters, 2200 South Sixth Street
Springfield, IL 62703
Phone: 217-528-4713 Ext. 207
Fax: 217-528-9896
E-mail: crystal@ilamvets.org

ILLINOIS AMVETS LADIES AUXILIARY MEMORIAL SCHOLARSHIP

• *See page 651*

ILLINOIS AMVETS LADIES AUXILIARY WORCHID SCHOLARSHIPS

• *See page 651*

ILLINOIS AMVETS SERVICE FOUNDATION SCHOLARSHIP AWARD

• *See page 651*

ILLINOIS AMVETS TRADE SCHOOL SCHOLARSHIP

• *See page 651*

ARIZONA COMMISSION FOR POSTSECONDARY EDUCATION http://www.azhighered.gov

ARIZONA PRIVATE POSTSECONDARY EDUCATION STUDENT FINANCIAL ASSISTANCE PROGRAM

Provides grants to financially needy Arizona Community College graduates, to attend a private postsecondary baccalaureate degree-granting institution.

Arizona Commission for Postsecondary Education (continued)

Award: Forgivable loan for use in junior or senior years; renewable. *Number:* varies. *Amount:* $1000–$2000.

Eligibility Requirements: Applicant must be enrolled or expecting to enroll full-time at a four-year institution or university; resident of Arizona and studying in Arizona. Applicant must have 2.5 GPA or higher. Available to U.S. citizens.

Application Requirements: Application, financial need analysis, transcript, promissory note. *Deadline:* June 30.

Contact: Mila Zaporteza, Business Manager
Arizona Commission for Postsecondary Education
2020 North Central Avenue, Suite 650
Phoenix, AZ 85004-4503
Phone: 602-258-2435 Ext. 102
Fax: 602-258-2483
E-mail: mila@azhighered.gov

LEVERAGING EDUCATIONAL ASSISTANCE PARTNERSHIP

Grants to financially needy students, who enroll in and attend postsecondary education or training in Arizona schools. Program was formerly known as the State Student Incentive Grant or SSIG Program.

Award: Grant for use in freshman, sophomore, junior, senior, or graduate years; not renewable. *Number:* varies. *Amount:* $100–$2500.

Eligibility Requirements: Applicant must be enrolled or expecting to enroll full- or part-time at a two-year or four-year or technical institution or university; resident of Arizona and studying in Arizona. Available to U.S. citizens.

Application Requirements: Application, financial need analysis, transcript. *Deadline:* April 30.

Contact: Mila A. Zaporteza, Business Manager and LEAP Financial Aid Manager
Arizona Commission for Postsecondary Education
2020 North Central Avenue, Suite 650
Phoenix, AZ 85004-4503
Phone: 602-258-2435 Ext. 102
Fax: 602-258-2483
E-mail: mila@azhighered.gov

POSTSECONDARY EDUCATION GRANT PROGRAM

Awards of up to $2000 to Arizona residents studying in Arizona. May be renewed annually for a maximum of four calendar years. Minimum 2.5 GPA required. Deadline June 30.

Award: Forgivable loan for use in freshman, sophomore, junior, or senior years; renewable. *Number:* varies. *Amount:* $1000–$2000.

Eligibility Requirements: Applicant must be enrolled or expecting to enroll full- or part-time at a four-year institution or university; resident of Arizona and studying in Arizona. Applicant must have 2.5 GPA or higher. Available to U.S. citizens.

Application Requirements: Application, driver's license, transcript, promissory note. *Deadline:* June 30.

Contact: Dr. April Osborn, Executive Director
Arizona Commission for Postsecondary Education
2020 North Central Avenue, Suite 650
Phoenix, AZ 85004-4503
Phone: 602-258-2435
Fax: 602-258-2483
E-mail: aosborn@azhighered.gov

ARIZONA HIGHER EDUCATION LOAN AUTHORITY http://www.ahela.org

AHELA CARES SCHOLARSHIP

This scholarship is to increase access to higher education for low-income or disadvantaged youth. Applicants must be from a family with income less than or equal to $30,000. Scholarship winners will be selected based on financial need and a short essay.

Award: Scholarship for use in freshman, sophomore, junior, or senior years; not renewable. *Number:* 2. *Amount:* $2000.

Eligibility Requirements: Applicant must be enrolled or expecting to enroll full-time at a two-year or four-year institution or university and studying in Arizona. Applicant must have 2.5 GPA or higher. Available to U.S. citizens.

Application Requirements: Application, driver's license, essay. *Deadline:* March 5.

Contact: Dana Macke-Redford, Manager, Marketing, Scholarship and Outreach
Arizona Higher Education Loan Authority
2141 East Broadway Road, Suite 202
Tempe, AZ 85282
Phone: 480-383-8707 Ext. 207
E-mail: dredford@ahela.org

AHELA COMMUNITY LEADERS SCHOLARSHIP

• *See page 590*

ARIZONA PRIVATE SCHOOL ASSOCIATION http://www.arizonapsa.org

ARIZONA PRIVATE SCHOOL ASSOCIATION SCHOLARSHIP

Scholarships are for graduating students from Arizona and the high school determines the recipients of the awards. Each spring the Arizona Private School Association awards two $1000 Scholarships to every private high school in Arizona.

Award: Scholarship for use in freshman year; not renewable. *Number:* 600. *Amount:* $1000.

Eligibility Requirements: Applicant must be high school student; planning to enroll or expecting to enroll full-time at a four-year institution or university and resident of Arizona. Available to U.S. citizens.

Application Requirements: Application, essay. *Deadline:* April 30.

Contact: Fred Lockhart, Executive Director
Arizona Private School Association
202 East McDowell Road, Suite 273
Phoenix, AZ 85004
Phone: 602-254-5199
Fax: 602-254-5073
E-mail: apsa@eschelon.com

ARIZONA STATE DEPARTMENT OF EDUCATION http://www.ade.az.gov

ROBERT C. BYRD HONORS SCHOLARSHIP-ARIZONA

A program for high school graduates who show academic excellence and the promise of continued success in postsecondary education. A Byrd Scholar receives $1500 for each academic year for a maximum of four years to be applied toward undergraduate study at any accredited college or university in the United States. The number of scholarships awarded each year is subject to change due to funding.

Award: Scholarship for use in freshman year; renewable. *Number:* 50–150. *Amount:* $1500.

Eligibility Requirements: Applicant must be high school student; planning to enroll or expecting to enroll full-time at a four-year institution or university and resident of Arizona. Available to U.S. citizens.

Application Requirements: Application, transcript. *Deadline:* March 24.

Contact: Julene Gaftard, Program and Project Coordinator
Arizona State Department of Education
1535 West Jefferson
Phoenix, AZ 85007
Phone: 602-542-3710
Fax: 602-364-1532
E-mail: byrd@azed.gov

ARKANSAS DEPARTMENT OF HIGHER EDUCATION http://www.adhe.edu

ARKANSAS ACADEMIC CHALLENGE SCHOLARSHIP PROGRAM

Awards for Arkansas residents who are graduating high school seniors to study at an Arkansas institution. Must have at least a 2.75 GPA, meet minimum ACT composite score standards, and have financial need. Renewable up to three additional years.

Award: Scholarship for use in freshman, sophomore, junior, or senior years; renewable. *Number:* 7000–10,000. *Amount:* $2500–$3500.

Eligibility Requirements: Applicant must be enrolled or expecting to enroll full-time at a two-year or four-year institution or university; resident of Arkansas and studying in Arkansas. Available to U.S. citizens.

Application Requirements: Application, financial need analysis, test scores, transcript. *Deadline:* June 1.

Contact: Tara Smith, Director of Financial Aid
Arkansas Department of Higher Education
114 East Capitol Avenue
Little Rock, AR 72201-3818
Phone: 501-371-2000
Fax: 501-371-2001
E-mail: finaid@adhe.arknet.edu

GOVERNOR'S SCHOLARS-ARKANSAS

Awards for outstanding Arkansas high school seniors. Must be an Arkansas resident and have a high school GPA of at least 3.5 or have scored at least 27 on the ACT. Award is $4000 per year for four years of full-time undergraduate study. Applicants who attain 32 or above on ACT, 1410 or above on SAT and have an academic 3.5 GPA, or are selected as National Merit or National Achievement finalists may receive an award equal to tuition, mandatory fees, room, and board up to $10,000 per year at any Arkansas institution.

Award: Scholarship for use in freshman, sophomore, junior, or senior years; renewable. *Number:* up to 375. *Amount:* $4000–$10,000.

Eligibility Requirements: Applicant must be enrolled or expecting to enroll full-time at a two-year or four-year institution or university; resident of Arkansas and studying in Arkansas. Applicant must have 3.5 GPA or higher. Available to U.S. citizens.

Application Requirements: Application, test scores, transcript. *Deadline:* February 1.

Contact: Tara Smith, Director of Financial Aid
Arkansas Department of Higher Education
114 East Capitol Avenue
Little Rock, AR 72201-3818
Phone: 501-371-2000
Fax: 501-371-2001
E-mail: taras@adhe.edu

LAW ENFORCEMENT OFFICERS' DEPENDENTS SCHOLARSHIP-ARKANSAS

• *See page 590*

MILITARY DEPENDENT'S SCHOLARSHIP PROGRAM-ARKANSAS

• *See page 651*

SECOND EFFORT SCHOLARSHIP

Awarded to those scholars who achieved one of the 10 highest scores on the Arkansas High School Diploma Test (GED). Must be at least age 18 and not have graduated from high school. Students do not apply for this award, they are contacted by the Arkansas Department of Higher Education.

Award: Scholarship for use in freshman year; renewable. *Number:* 10. *Amount:* up to $1000.

Eligibility Requirements: Applicant must be high school student; age 18 and over; planning to enroll or expecting to enroll full- or part-time at a four-year institution or university; resident of Arkansas and studying in Arkansas. Applicant must have 2.5 GPA or higher. Available to U.S. citizens.

Application Requirements: Application. *Deadline:* varies.

Contact: Tara Smith, Director of Financial Aid
Arkansas Department of Higher Education
114 East Capitol Avenue
Little Rock, AR 72201-3818
Phone: 501-371-2000
Fax: 501-371-2001
E-mail: taras@adhe.edu

ARKANSAS SINGLE PARENT SCHOLARSHIP FUND — http://www.aspsf.org

ARKANSAS SINGLE PARENT SCHOLARSHIP

Scholarships for economically disadvantaged single parents who reside in Arkansas to pursue higher education. Must have custodial care of one or more children under the age of 18 and must not have previously earned a diploma or degree from a four-year institution of higher learning. Award value varies. Cleveland county residents are not eligible to apply.

Award: Scholarship for use in freshman, sophomore, junior, or senior years; renewable. *Number:* varies. *Amount:* $600.

Eligibility Requirements: Applicant must be enrolled or expecting to enroll full- or part-time at a two-year or four-year institution or university; single and resident of Arkansas. Available to U.S. citizens.

Application Requirements: Application, essay, financial need analysis, transcript. *Deadline:* varies.

Contact: Ralph H. Nesson, Executive Director
Arkansas Single Parent Scholarship Fund
614 East Emma Avenue, Suite 119
Springdale, AR 72764
Phone: 479-927-1402
Fax: 479-751-1110
E-mail: rnesson@jtlshop.jonesnet.org

ARKANSAS STATE DEPARTMENT OF EDUCATION — http://arkansased.org

ROBERT C. BYRD HONORS SCHOLARSHIP-ARKANSAS

Applicant must be a graduate of a public or private school or receive a recognized equivalent of a high school diploma. Must be a resident of Arkansas. Must be admitted to an institution of higher education, demonstrate outstanding academic achievement and show promise of continued academic achievement. Award is $1500 for each academic year for a maximum of four years.

Award: Scholarship for use in freshman year; renewable. *Number:* 62. *Amount:* $1500.

Eligibility Requirements: Applicant must be high school student; planning to enroll or expecting to enroll full-time at a two-year or four-year or technical institution or university and resident of Arkansas. Available to U.S. citizens.

Application Requirements: Application, transcript. *Deadline:* February 16.

Contact: Margaret Amps, Program Coordinator
Arkansas State Department of Education
Four Capitol Mall
Little Rock, AR 72201
Phone: 501-682-4396
E-mail: margaret.amps@arkansas.gov

ARKANSAS STUDENT LOAN AUTHORITY — http://www.asla.info

R. PRESTON WOODRUFF JR. SCHOLARSHIP

Scholarship provides a minimum of twenty $1000 scholarships each year to potential college students in Arkansas. Each year, one of the twenty scholarships drawn will be renewable for four years.

Award: Scholarship for use in freshman, sophomore, junior, senior, or graduate years; renewable. *Number:* 20. *Amount:* $1000.

Eligibility Requirements: Applicant must be enrolled or expecting to enroll full- or part-time at a two-year or four-year or technical institution or university; resident of Arkansas and studying in Arkansas. Available to U.S. citizens.

Application Requirements: Application. *Deadline:* April 1.

Contact: Teresa Boothe, Student Outreach Counselor
Arkansas Student Loan Authority
3801 Woodland Heights, Suite 200
Little Rock, AR 72212
Phone: 800-443-6030
E-mail: tboothe@asla.info

ARRL FOUNDATION INC. — http://www.arrl.org

ALBERT H. HIX W8AH MEMORIAL SCHOLARSHIP

One-time award available to general class or higher class amateur radio operators. Preference is given to the residents of West Virginia section or the Roanoke Division, or those attending postsecondary school in West Virginia section. Minimum GPA of 3.0 required.

Award: Scholarship for use in freshman, sophomore, junior, or senior years; not renewable. *Number:* 1. *Amount:* $500.

Eligibility Requirements: Applicant must be enrolled or expecting to enroll full-time at a two-year or four-year or technical institution or

ARRL Foundation Inc. (continued)

university; resident of North Carolina, South Carolina, or West Virginia and must have an interest in amateur radio. Applicant must have 3.0 GPA or higher. Available to U.S. citizens.

Application Requirements: Application, test scores, transcript. *Deadline:* February 1.

Contact: Mary M. Hobart, Secretary
ARRL Foundation Inc.
225 Main Street
Newington, CT 06111-1494
Phone: 860-594-0397
Fax: 860-594-0259
E-mail: k1mmh@arrl.org

ALBUQUERQUE AMATEUR RADIO CLUB/TOBY CROSS SCHOLARSHIP

Scholarship of $500 for students working on undergraduate degree. Must be a licensed amateur radio operator. Residents of New Mexico preferred. Must supply one-page essay on role of amateur radio in their life.

Award: Scholarship for use in freshman, sophomore, junior, or senior years; not renewable. *Number:* 1. *Amount:* $500.

Eligibility Requirements: Applicant must be enrolled or expecting to enroll full-time at a four-year institution or university; resident of New Mexico and must have an interest in amateur radio. Available to U.S. citizens.

Application Requirements: Application, essay, transcript. *Deadline:* February 1.

Contact: Mary M. Hobart, Secretary
ARRL Foundation Inc.
225 Main Street
Newington, CT 06111-4845
Phone: 860-594-0397
Fax: 860-594-0259
E-mail: K1mmh@arrl.org

CENTRAL ARIZONA DX ASSOCIATION SCHOLARSHIP

Award available to amateur radio operators with a technician license. Preference given to residents of Arizona. Graduating high school students will be considered before current college students. Must have 3.2 GPA or above.

Award: Scholarship for use in freshman year; not renewable. *Number:* 1. *Amount:* $500.

Eligibility Requirements: Applicant must be high school student; planning to enroll or expecting to enroll full-time at a two-year or four-year institution or university; resident of Arizona and must have an interest in amateur radio.

Application Requirements: Application, transcript. *Deadline:* February 1.

Contact: Mary M. Hobart, Secretary
ARRL Foundation Inc.
225 Main Street
Newington, CT 06111-1494
Phone: 860-594-0397
Fax: 860-594-0259
E-mail: k1mmh@arrl.org

CHARLES CLARKE CORDLE MEMORIAL SCHOLARSHIP

One-time award for licensed amateur radio operators. Preference given to residents of Georgia and Alabama. Must be a attending school in Georgia or Alabama. Must have minimum GPA of 2.5.

Award: Scholarship for use in freshman, sophomore, junior, or senior years; not renewable. *Number:* 1. *Amount:* $1000.

Eligibility Requirements: Applicant must be enrolled or expecting to enroll full-time at a four-year institution or university; resident of Alabama or Georgia; studying in Alabama or Georgia and must have an interest in amateur radio. Applicant must have 2.5 GPA or higher. Available to U.S. citizens.

Application Requirements: Application, transcript. *Deadline:* February 1.

Contact: Mary M. Hobart, Secretary
ARRL Foundation Inc.
225 Main Street
Newington, CT 06111-1494
Phone: 860-594-0397
Fax: 860-594-0259
E-mail: k1mmh@arrl.org

CHICAGO FM CLUB SCHOLARSHIPS

Multiple awards available to amateur radio operators with technician license. Preference given to residents of FCC Ninth Call District (Indiana, Illinois, Wisconsin). Student in post-secondary course of study at accredited 2- or 4-year college or trade school is eligible. Must be U.S. citizen or within 3 months of citizenship.

Award: Scholarship for use in freshman, sophomore, junior, or senior years; not renewable. *Number:* varies. *Amount:* $500.

Eligibility Requirements: Applicant must be enrolled or expecting to enroll full-time at a two-year or four-year or technical institution or university; resident of Illinois, Indiana, or Wisconsin and must have an interest in amateur radio. Available to U.S. citizens.

Application Requirements: Application, transcript. *Deadline:* February 1.

Contact: Mary M. Hobart, Secretary
ARRL Foundation Inc.
225 Main Street
Newington, CT 06111-1494
Phone: 860-594-0397
Fax: 860-594-0259
E-mail: k1mmh@arrl.org

FRANCIS WALTON MEMORIAL SCHOLARSHIP

One or more $500 scholarships available to student radio operators with 5 WPM certification. Preference to Illinois resident or resident of ARRL Central Division (IL, IN, WI). Must be pursuing a baccalaureate or higher degree at a regionally accredited institution.

Award: Scholarship for use in freshman, sophomore, junior, senior, or graduate years; not renewable. *Number:* 1. *Amount:* $500.

Eligibility Requirements: Applicant must be enrolled or expecting to enroll full-time at a four-year institution or university; resident of Illinois, Indiana, or Wisconsin and must have an interest in amateur radio. Available to U.S. citizens.

Application Requirements: Application, transcript. *Deadline:* February 1.

Contact: Mary M. Hobart, Secretary
ARRL Foundation Inc.
225 Main Street
Newington, CT 06111-1494
Phone: 860-594-0397
Fax: 860-594-0259
E-mail: k1mmh@arrl.org

IRARC MEMORIAL JOSEPH P. RUBINO WA4MMD SCHOLARSHIP

• See page 525

MARY LOU BROWN SCHOLARSHIP

Multiple awards available to amateur radio operators with general license. Preference given to residents of Alaska, Idaho, Montana, Oregon, and Washington pursuing baccalaureate or higher course of study. GPA of 3.0 or higher required. Must demonstrate interest in promoting Amateur Radio Service.

Award: Scholarship for use in freshman, sophomore, junior, senior, or graduate years; not renewable. *Number:* varies. *Amount:* $2500.

Eligibility Requirements: Applicant must be enrolled or expecting to enroll full-time at a four-year institution or university; resident of Arkansas, Idaho, Montana, Oregon, or Washington and must have an interest in amateur radio. Applicant must have 3.0 GPA or higher. Available to U.S. citizens.

Application Requirements: Application, transcript. *Deadline:* February 1.

Contact: Mary M. Hobart, Secretary
ARRL Foundation Inc.
225 Main Street
Newington, CT 06111-1494
Phone: 860-594-0397
Fax: 860-594-0259
E-mail: k1mmh@arrl.org

NEW ENGLAND FEMARA SCHOLARSHIPS

One-time award of $1000 available to students licensed as amateur radio operator technicians. Multiple Awards per year. Preference is given to the residents of Vermont, Maine, New Hampshire, Rhode Island, Massachusetts, or Connecticut.

Award: Scholarship for use in freshman, sophomore, junior, or senior years; not renewable. *Number:* varies. *Amount:* $1000.

Eligibility Requirements: Applicant must be enrolled or expecting to enroll full-time at a four-year institution or university; resident of Connecticut, Maine, New Hampshire, Rhode Island, or Vermont and must have an interest in amateur radio. Available to U.S. citizens.

Application Requirements: Application, transcript. *Deadline:* February 1.

Contact: Mary M. Hobart, Secretary
ARRL Foundation Inc.
225 Main Street
Newington, CT 06111-4845
Phone: 860-594-0397
Fax: 860-594-0259
E-mail: k1mmh@arrl.org

SIX METER CLUB OF CHICAGO SCHOLARSHIP

For licensed amateur radio operators. Preference is given to Illinois residents pursuing an undergraduate study. Applicants from Indiana and Wisconsin will be considered if none from Illinois selected.

Award: Scholarship for use in freshman, sophomore, junior, or senior years; not renewable. *Number:* 1. *Amount:* $500.

Eligibility Requirements: Applicant must be enrolled or expecting to enroll full-time at a two-year or four-year or technical institution or university; resident of Illinois, Indiana, or Wisconsin; studying in Illinois and must have an interest in amateur radio. Available to U.S. citizens.

Application Requirements: Application, transcript. *Deadline:* February 1.

Contact: Mary M. Hobart, Secretary
ARRL Foundation Inc.
225 Main Street
Newington, CT 06111-1494
Phone: 860-594-0397
Fax: 860-594-0259
E-mail: k1mmh@arrl.org

TOM AND JUDITH COMSTOCK SCHOLARSHIP

One-time award of $2000 for high school seniors. Preference given to residents of Texas and Oklahoma. Must be licensed amateur radio operator. Must be accepted at a two- or four-year institution.

Award: Scholarship for use in freshman year; not renewable. *Number:* 1. *Amount:* $2000.

Eligibility Requirements: Applicant must be high school student; planning to enroll or expecting to enroll full-time at a two-year or four-year institution or university; resident of Oklahoma or Texas and must have an interest in amateur radio. Available to U.S. citizens.

Application Requirements: Application, transcript. *Deadline:* February 1.

Contact: Mary M. Hobart, Secretary
ARRL Foundation Inc.
225 Main Street
Newington, CT 06111-1494
Phone: 860-594-0397
Fax: 860-594-0259
E-mail: k1mmh@arrl.org

YANKEE CLIPPER CONTEST CLUB INC. YOUTH SCHOLARSHIP

One-time award available to general class or higher licensed amateur radio operators. Must reside or attend college within the 175-mile radius of YCCC Center. Qualifying area includes all of Massachusetts, Rhode Island, Connecticut, and Long Island, NY, most of Vermont and New Hampshire, portions of Maine, eastern New York, and extreme north-eastern sections of Pennsylvania and New Jersey.

Award: Scholarship for use in freshman, sophomore, junior, or senior years; not renewable. *Number:* 1. *Amount:* $1000.

Eligibility Requirements: Applicant must be enrolled or expecting to enroll full-time at a two-year or four-year institution or university; resident of Connecticut, Maine, Massachusetts, New Hampshire, New Jersey, New York, Pennsylvania, Rhode Island, or Vermont and must have an interest in amateur radio. Available to U.S. citizens.

Application Requirements: Application, transcript. *Deadline:* February 1.

Contact: Mary M. Hobart, Secretary
ARRL Foundation Inc.
225 Main Street
Newington, CT 06111
Phone: 860-594-0397
Fax: 860-594-0259
E-mail: k1mmh@arrl.org

YOU'VE GOT A FRIEND IN PENNSYLVANIA SCHOLARSHIP

• *See page 525*

ASAP/UNION BANK & TRUST COMPANY-LINCOLN JOURNAL STAR'S NEWSPAPERS IN EDUCATION http://www.asapubt.com

"WE HAVE MONEY TO LEARN" SCHOLARSHIPS

Scholarships for Nebraska high school seniors who will be attending a Nebraska postsecondary institution on a full-time basis. Applications are considered for selection based on several criteria including ACT, GPA, essay, class rank, and school and community involvement.

Award: Scholarship for use in freshman year; not renewable. *Number:* 24. *Amount:* $500.

Eligibility Requirements: Applicant must be high school student; planning to enroll or expecting to enroll full-time at a two-year or four-year institution or university; resident of Nebraska and studying in Nebraska. Applicant must have 3.0 GPA or higher. Available to U.S. citizens.

Application Requirements: Application, essay, photo, resume, test scores, parental/guardian signature. *Deadline:* March 15.

Contact: Mark Schilmoeller, Director and Vice President
ASAP/Union Bank & Trust Company-Lincoln Journal Star's Newspapers in Education
121 South 13th Street, Suite 102
Lincoln, NE 68508
Phone: 402-458-2322
Fax: 402-458-2322
E-mail: mark.schilmoeller@nelnet.net

ASHLEY FOUNDATION http://www.theashleyfoundation.org

ASHLEY TAMBURRI SCHOLARSHIP

• *See page 615*

ASIAN REPORTER http://www.arfoundation.net

ASIAN REPORTER SCHOLARSHIP

• *See page 674*

A.W. BODINE-SUNKIST GROWERS INC. http://www.sunkist.com

A.W. BODINE-SUNKIST MEMORIAL SCHOLARSHIP

• *See page 590*

BARKING FOUNDATION http://www.barkingfoundation.org

BARKING FOUNDATION GRANTS

One-time award of $3000 available to Maine residents. Minimum GPA of 3.5 is desirable. Only first 300 completed applications will be accepted. Essay, financial information, and transcripts required. Available to full- and part-time students. Scholarships vary in number from year to year.

Award: Grant for use in freshman, sophomore, junior, senior, graduate, or postgraduate years; not renewable. *Number:* up to 25. *Amount:* $3000.

Barking Foundation (continued)

Eligibility Requirements: Applicant must be enrolled or expecting to enroll full- or part-time at a four-year institution or university and resident of Maine. Applicant must have 3.5 GPA or higher. Available to U.S. citizens.

Application Requirements: Application, essay, financial need analysis, references, transcript, copy of SAR. *Deadline:* February 15.

Contact: Stephanie Leonard, Administrator
Barking Foundation
PO Box 855
Bangor, ME 04402
Phone: 207-990-2910
Fax: 207-990-2975
E-mail: info@barkingfoundation.org

BIG Y FOODS INC. http://www.bigy.com

BIG Y SCHOLARSHIPS

Awards for customers or dependents of customers of Big Y Foods. Big Y trade area covers Norfolk county, western and central Massachusetts, and Connecticut. Also awards for Big Y employees and dependents of employees. Awards are based on academic excellence. Grades, board scores and two letters of recommendation required.

Award: Scholarship for use in freshman, sophomore, junior, senior, or graduate years; not renewable. *Number:* 300–350. *Amount:* $500–$2000.

Eligibility Requirements: Applicant must be enrolled or expecting to enroll full- or part-time at a two-year or four-year or technical institution or university; resident of Connecticut or Massachusetts and studying in Connecticut or Massachusetts. Available to U.S. and non-U.S. citizens.

Application Requirements: Application, resume, references, test scores, transcript. *Deadline:* February 1.

Contact: Missy Lajoie, Scholarship Committee
Big Y Foods Inc.
PO Box 7840
Springfield, MA 01102-7840
Phone: 413-504-4047
Fax: 413-504-6509
E-mail: wecare@bigy.com

BLUE GRASS ENERGY http://www.bgenergy.com

BLUE GRASS ENERGY ACADEMIC SCHOLARSHIP

Scholarships for Kentucky high school seniors whose parents or guardians are members of Blue Grass Energy residing in the service area. Must have minimum GPA of 3.0 and have demonstrated academic achievement and financial need. For application and information, visit Web site: http://www.bgenergy.com.

Award: Scholarship for use in freshman year; not renewable. *Number:* 10. *Amount:* $1000.

Eligibility Requirements: Applicant must be high school student; planning to enroll or expecting to enroll full-time at a four-year institution or university and resident of Kentucky. Applicant must have 3.0 GPA or higher. Available to U.S. and non-U.S. citizens.

Application Requirements: Application, financial need analysis, transcript, handwritten request for scholarship. *Deadline:* March 31.

Contact: Magen Howard, Communications Adviser
Blue Grass Energy
PO Box 990
Nicholasville, KY 40340-0990
Phone: 859-885-2104
Fax: 859-885-2854
E-mail: magenh@bgenergy.com

BOETTCHER FOUNDATION http://www.boettcherfoundation.org

BOETTCHER FOUNDATION SCHOLARSHIPS

• *See page 590*

BOYS AND GIRLS CLUBS OF CHICAGO http://www.bgcc.org

BOYS AND GIRLS CLUBS OF CHICAGO SCHOLARSHIPS

• *See page 525*

BOYS AND GIRLS CLUBS OF GREATER SAN DIEGO http://www.sdyouth.org

BOYS AND GIRLS CLUBS FOUNDATION SCHOLARSHIP

• *See page 526*

BRITISH COLUMBIA MINISTRY OF ADVANCED EDUCATION http://www.studentaidbc.ca

IRVING K. BARBER BRITISH COLUMBIA SCHOLARSHIP PROGRAM (FOR STUDY IN BRITISH COLUMBIA)

Scholarship to students who, after completing two years at a British Columbia public community college, university college or institute, must transfer to another public postsecondary institution in British Columbia to complete their degree. Students must demonstrate merit as well as exceptional involvement in their institution and community. Must have a GPA of at least 3.5. For more details, visit: http://www.aved.gov.bc.ca/studentaidbc/specialprograms/irvingkbarber/bc_scholarship.htm.

Award: Scholarship for use in junior or senior years; not renewable. *Number:* up to 150. *Amount:* up to $5000.

Eligibility Requirements: Applicant must be enrolled or expecting to enroll full-time at a four-year institution or university and studying in British Columbia. Applicant must have 3.5 GPA or higher. Available to Canadian citizens.

Application Requirements: Application, essay, references, test scores, transcript. *Deadline:* March 31.

Contact: Victoria Thibeau, Loan Remission and Management Unit
British Columbia Ministry of Advanced Education
Station Prov Government, First Floor
PO Box 9173
Victoria, BC V8W 9H7
Canada
Phone: 250-387-6100
E-mail: victoria.thibeau@gov.bc.ca

BUFFALO AFL-CIO COUNCIL http://www.wnyalf.org

AFL-CIO COUNCIL OF BUFFALO SCHOLARSHIP WNY ALF SCHOLARSHIP

• *See page 526*

CABRILLO CIVIC CLUBS OF CALIFORNIA INC. http://www.cabrillocivicclubs.org

CABRILLO CIVIC CLUBS OF CALIFORNIA SCHOLARSHIP

• *See page 675*

CALIFORNIA COMMUNITY COLLEGES http://www.cccco.edu

COOPERATIVE AGENCIES RESOURCES FOR EDUCATION PROGRAM

Renewable award available to California resident attending a two-year California community college. Must have no more than 70 degree-applicable units, currently receive CALWORKS/TANF, and have at least one child under fourteen years of age. Must be in EOPS, single head of household, and 18 or older. Contact local college EOPS-CARE office.

Award: Grant for use in freshman or sophomore years; renewable. *Number:* 10,000–11,000. *Amount:* varies.

Eligibility Requirements: Applicant must be age 18 and over; enrolled or expecting to enroll full-time at a two-year institution; single; resident of California and studying in California. Available to U.S. citizens.

Application Requirements: Application, financial need analysis, test scores, transcript. *Deadline:* varies.

Contact: Cheryl Fong, CARE Coordinator
California Community Colleges
1102 Q Street
Sacramento, CA 95814-6511
Phone: 916-323-5954
Fax: 916-327-8232
E-mail: cfong@cccco.edu

CALIFORNIA CORRECTIONAL PEACE OFFICERS ASSOCIATION http://www.ccpoa.org

CALIFORNIA CORRECTIONAL PEACE OFFICERS ASSOCIATION JOE HARPER SCHOLARSHIP

• *See page 591*

CALIFORNIA COUNCIL OF THE BLIND http://www.ccbnet.org

CALIFORNIA COUNCIL OF THE BLIND SCHOLARSHIPS

• *See page 616*

CALIFORNIA GRANGE FOUNDATION http://www.californiagrange.org

CALIFORNIA GRANGE FOUNDATION SCHOLARSHIP

• *See page 526*

CALIFORNIA JUNIOR MISS SCHOLARSHIP PROGRAM http://www.ajm.org

CALIFORNIA JUNIOR MISS SCHOLARSHIP PROGRAM

Scholarship program to recognize and reward outstanding high school junior females in the areas of academics, leadership, athletics, public speaking, and the performing arts. Must be single, U.S. citizen, and resident of California. Minimum 3.0 GPA required.

Award: Scholarship for use in freshman year; not renewable. *Number:* 25. *Amount:* $500–$10,000.

Eligibility Requirements: Applicant must be high school student; age 15-17; planning to enroll or expecting to enroll full-time at a four-year institution or university; single female; resident of California and must have an interest in beauty pageant, leadership, or public speaking. Applicant must have 3.0 GPA or higher. Available to U.S. citizens.

Application Requirements: Application, essay, interview, test scores, transcript. *Deadline:* varies.

Contact: Joan McDonald, Chairman
California Junior Miss Scholarship Program
385 Via Montanosa
Encinitas, CA 92024
Phone: 760-420-4177
E-mail: jmcdonald@bellmicro.com

CALIFORNIA MASONIC FOUNDATION http://www.freemason.org/index.php

CALIFORNIA MASONIC FOUNDATION SCHOLARSHIP AWARDS

Scholarships range from $1000 to $10,000; most are renewable annually. An interview is a part of the selection process. Must be a U.S. citizen and a resident of California for at least one year. Must be a high school senior. Must have a minimum GPA of 3.0 and plan to attend an accredited two- or four-year institution as a full-time undergraduate freshman in the fall following high school graduation.

Award: Scholarship for use in freshman year; renewable. *Number:* up to 57. *Amount:* $1000–$10,000.

Eligibility Requirements: Applicant must be high school student; planning to enroll or expecting to enroll full-time at a two-year or four-year institution or university and resident of California. Applicant must have 3.0 GPA or higher. Available to U.S. citizens.

Application Requirements: Application, essay, financial need analysis, interview, references, self-addressed stamped envelope, test scores, transcript. *Deadline:* February 15.

Contact: Jeff Reyes, Director Scholarships
California Masonic Foundation
1111 California Street
San Francisco, CA 94108-2284
Phone: 415-292-9112
E-mail: dismail@freemason.org

CALIFORNIA STATE PARENT-TEACHER ASSOCIATION http://www.capta.org

CONTINUING EDUCATION-PTA VOLUNTEERS SCHOLARSHIP

• *See page 526*

GRADUATING HIGH SCHOOL SENIOR SCHOLARSHIP

• *See page 591*

CALIFORNIA STUDENT AID COMMISSION http://www.csac.ca.gov

CAL GRANT C

Award for California residents who are enrolled in a short-term vocational training program. Program must lead to a recognized degree or certificate. Course length must be a minimum of 4 months and no longer than 24 months. Students must be attending an approved California institution and show financial need.

Award: Grant for use in freshman or sophomore years; renewable. *Number:* up to 7761. *Amount:* $576–$3168.

Eligibility Requirements: Applicant must be enrolled or expecting to enroll full- or part-time at a two-year or technical institution; resident of California and studying in California. Available to U.S. citizens.

Application Requirements: Application, financial need analysis, GPA verification. *Deadline:* March 2.

Contact: Catalina Mistler, Chief, Program Administration & Services Division
California Student Aid Commission
PO Box 419026
Rancho Cordova, CA 95741-9026
Phone: 916-526-7268
Fax: 916-526-8002
E-mail: studentsupport@csac.ca.gov

COMPETITIVE CAL GRANT A

Award for California residents who are not recent high school graduates attending an approved college or university within the state. Must show financial need and meet minimum 3.0 GPA requirement.

Award: Grant for use in freshman, sophomore, junior, or senior years; renewable. *Number:* 22,500. *Amount:* $2772–$6636.

Eligibility Requirements: Applicant must be enrolled or expecting to enroll full- or part-time at a two-year or four-year institution or university; resident of California and studying in California. Applicant must have 3.0 GPA or higher. Available to U.S. citizens.

Application Requirements: Application, financial need analysis, GPA verification. *Deadline:* March 2.

Contact: Catalina Mistler, Chief, Program Administration & Services Division
California Student Aid Commission
PO Box 419026
Rancho Cordova, CA 95741-9026
Phone: 916-526-7268
Fax: 916-526-8002
E-mail: studentsupport@csac.ca.gov

ENTITLEMENT CAL GRANT B

Provide grant funds for access costs for low-income students in an amount not to exceed $1551. Must be California residents and enroll in an undergraduate academic program of not less than one academic year at a qualifying postsecondary institution. Must show financial need and meet the minimum 2.0 GPA requirement.

Award: Grant for use in freshman, sophomore, junior, or senior years; renewable. *Number:* varies. *Amount:* $700–$1551.

Eligibility Requirements: Applicant must be age 23 or under; enrolled or expecting to enroll full- or part-time at a two-year or four-year or technical institution or university; resident of California and studying in California. Available to U.S. citizens.

Application Requirements: Application, financial need analysis. *Deadline:* March 2.

Contact: Catalina Mistler, Chief, Program Administration & Services Division
California Student Aid Commission
PO Box 419026
Rancho Cordova, CA 95741-9026
Phone: 916-526-7268
Fax: 916-526-8002
E-mail: studentsupport@csac.ca.gov

California Student Aid Commission (continued)

LAW ENFORCEMENT PERSONNEL DEPENDENTS SCHOLARSHIP

• *See page 591*

ROBERT C. BYRD HONORS SCHOLARSHIP-CALIFORNIA

Federally funded award is available to California high school seniors. Students are awarded based on outstanding academic merit. Students must be nominated by their high school. Recipients must maintain satisfactory academic progress.

Award: Scholarship for use in freshman year; renewable. *Number:* 700–800. *Amount:* up to $1500.

Eligibility Requirements: Applicant must be high school student; planning to enroll or expecting to enroll full-time at a two-year or four-year institution or university and resident of California. Applicant must have 3.5 GPA or higher. Available to U.S. citizens.

Application Requirements: Application, financial need analysis, test scores, GPA/test score verification form. *Deadline:* April 30.

Contact: Catalina Mistler, Chief, Program Administration & Services Division
California Student Aid Commission
PO Box 419026
Rancho Cordova, CA 95741-9026
Phone: 916-526-7268
Fax: 916-526-8002
E-mail: studentsupport@csac.ca.gov

CALIFORNIA TABLE GRAPE COMMISSION http://www.freshcaliforniagrapes.com

CALIFORNIA TABLE GRAPE FARM WORKERS SCHOLARSHIP PROGRAM

• *See page 591*

CALIFORNIA TEACHERS ASSOCIATION (CTA) http://www.cta.org

CALIFORNIA TEACHERS ASSOCIATION SCHOLARSHIP FOR MEMBERS

• *See page 526*

CALIFORNIA WINE GRAPE GROWERS FOUNDATION http://www.cawg.org/cwggf

CALIFORNIA WINE GRAPE GROWERS FOUNDATION SCHOLARSHIP

• *See page 592*

CANADA ICELAND FOUNDATION INC. SCHOLARSHIPS http://www.logberg.com

CANADA ICELAND FOUNDATION SCHOLARSHIP PROGRAM

One scholarship of $500, to be awarded annually. To be offered to a university student studying towards a degree in any Canadian university.

Award: Scholarship for use in freshman, sophomore, junior, senior, or graduate years; not renewable. *Number:* 1. *Amount:* $500.

Eligibility Requirements: Applicant must be enrolled or expecting to enroll full-time at an institution or university; studying in Alberta, British Columbia, Manitoba, New Brunswick, Newfoundland, Nova Scotia, Ontario, Quebec, or Saskatchewan and must have an interest in leadership. Available to Canadian citizens.

Application Requirements: Application, references, test scores, transcript. *Deadline:* varies.

Contact: Karen Bowman, Administrative Assistant
Canada Iceland Foundation Inc. Scholarships
100-283 Portage Avenue, The Sterling Building
Winnipeg, MB R3B 2B5
Canada
Phone: 204-284-5686
Fax: 204-284-7099
E-mail: karen@lh-inc.ca

CAREER COLLEGES AND SCHOOLS OF TEXAS http://www.colleges-schools.org

CAREER COLLEGES AND SCHOOLS OF TEXAS SCHOLARSHIP PROGRAM

One-time award available to graduating high school seniors who plan to attend a Texas trade or technical institution. Must be a Texas resident. Criteria selection, which is determined independently by each school's guidance counselors, may be based on academic excellence, financial need, or student leadership. Must be U.S. citizen. Deadline: continuous.

Award: Scholarship for use in freshman year; not renewable. *Number:* up to 6000. *Amount:* $1000.

Eligibility Requirements: Applicant must be high school student; planning to enroll or expecting to enroll full- or part-time at a technical institution; resident of Texas; studying in Texas and must have an interest in leadership. Available to U.S. citizens.

Application Requirements: Application. *Deadline:* continuous.

Contact: Bob Aguirre, Scholarship Chairman
Career Colleges and Schools of Texas
5700 Cromo Drive
El Paso, TX 79912
Phone: 915-842-0422 Ext. 1108
Fax: 915-585-2584
E-mail: bob.aguirre@ibcelpaso.edu

CARMEL MUSIC SOCIETY http://www.carmelmusic.org

CARMEL MUSIC SOCIETY COMPETITION

Open competition to pianists between the ages of 18 and 30. Competition will provide an opportunity for young instrumentalists across Western states to compete for a grand prize of $4000, which includes an opportunity to perform in the subscription series. Second place winner will receive $2000 and third place winner will receive $1500. Other finalists will each receive $500.

Award: Prize for use in freshman, sophomore, junior, senior, graduate, or postgraduate years; not renewable. *Number:* 3. *Amount:* $500–$4000.

Eligibility Requirements: Applicant must be age 18-30; enrolled or expecting to enroll full-time at a two-year or four-year or technical institution or university; resident of California, Oregon, or Washington and must have an interest in music. Available to U.S. citizens.

Application Requirements: Application, applicant must enter a contest, driver's license, resume, transcript, six high-quality CDs of the program to be performed for the competition, copies of the repertoire selections. *Fee:* $40. *Deadline:* February 11.

Contact: Competition Chair
Carmel Music Society
PO Box 22783
Carmel, CA 93922
Phone: 831-625-9938
Fax: 831-625-6823
E-mail: carmelmusic@sbcglobal.net

CENTER FOR SCHOLARSHIP ADMINISTRATION http://www.scholarshipprograms.org

KITTIE M. FAIREY EDUCATIONAL FUND SCHOLARSHIPS

Renewable scholarships are for graduating high school seniors residing in South Carolina. Scholarships provide funding for half tuition and room and board (for boarding students).

Award: Scholarship for use in freshman, sophomore, junior, or senior years; renewable. *Number:* varies. *Amount:* varies.

Eligibility Requirements: Applicant must be high school student; planning to enroll or expecting to enroll full-time at a two-year or four-year institution or university and resident of South Carolina. Applicant must have 3.0 GPA or higher. Available to U.S. citizens.

Application Requirements: Application, essay, references, transcript. *Deadline:* December 1.

Contact: Scholarship Committee
Center for Scholarship Administration
PO Box 1465
Taylors, SC 29687-0031
Phone: 864-268-3363
Fax: 864-268-7160
E-mail: cfsainc@bellsouth.net

SOUTH CAROLINA JUNIOR GOLF FOUNDATION SCHOLARSHIP

Scholarships available to student residents of South Carolina who have a competitive or recreational interest in golf. Must be high school seniors at a South Carolina high school or undergraduates already attending college in South Carolina. Must have and maintain a 2.75 cumulative GPA. Awards will be renewable for up to three years. The recipient's school of choice must be exempt from federal income tax under Section 501 (c) (3) of the Internal Revenue Code.

Award: Scholarship for use in freshman, sophomore, junior, or senior years; renewable. *Number:* varies. *Amount:* $2500.

Eligibility Requirements: Applicant must be high school student; planning to enroll or expecting to enroll full-time at a four-year institution or university; resident of South Carolina and must have an interest in golf. Available to U.S. citizens.

Application Requirements: Application, essay, financial need analysis, references, transcript, copy of parent/employee's federal tax form and W-2 forms. *Deadline:* November 30.

Contact: Scholarship Committee
Center for Scholarship Administration
PO Box 1465
Taylors, SC 29687-0031
Phone: 864-268-3363
Fax: 864-268-7160
E-mail: cfsainc@bellsouth.net

CENTRAL NATIONAL BANK & TRUST COMPANY OF ENID TRUSTEE http://www.onecentralsource.us/trust_services.html

MAY T. HENRY SCHOLARSHIP FOUNDATION

A $1000 scholarship renewed annually for four years. Awarded to any student enrolled in an Oklahoma state-supported college, university or tech school. Based on need, scholastic performance and personal traits valued by May T. Henry. Minimum 3.0 GPA required.

Award: Scholarship for use in freshman, sophomore, junior, senior, graduate, or postgraduate years; renewable. *Number:* varies. *Amount:* $1000.

Eligibility Requirements: Applicant must be enrolled or expecting to enroll full-time at a two-year or four-year or technical institution or university and studying in Oklahoma. Applicant must have 3.0 GPA or higher. Available to U.S. and non-U.S. citizens.

Application Requirements: Application, essay, financial need analysis, references, test scores, transcript. *Deadline:* April 1.

Contact: Trust Department
Central National Bank & Trust Company of Enid Trustee
PO Box 3448
Enid, OK 73702-3448
Phone: 580-213-1612
Fax: 580-249-5926
E-mail: waholt@cnb-enid.com

CENTRAL SCHOLARSHIP BUREAU http://www.centralsb.org

CENTRAL SCHOLARSHIP BUREAU GRANTS

A limited number of grants are available each year on a competitive basis. Selection criteria is a combination of merit and demonstrated need.

Award: Grant for use in freshman, sophomore, junior, senior, or graduate years; renewable. *Number:* 20–30. *Amount:* $1000–$3000.

Eligibility Requirements: Applicant must be enrolled or expecting to enroll full-time at a two-year or four-year or technical institution or university and resident of Maryland. Applicant must have 3.0 GPA or higher. Available to U.S. citizens.

Application Requirements: Essay, financial need analysis, interview, transcript, CSB online application. *Deadline:* May 31.

Contact: Roberta Goldman, Program Director
Central Scholarship Bureau
1700 Reisterstown Road, Suite 220
Baltimore, MD 21208-2903
Phone: 410-415-5558
Fax: 410-415-5501
E-mail: rgoldman@centralsb.org

DALY SCHOLARSHIP AT CENTRAL SCHOLARSHIP BUREAU

• *See page 592*

LESSANS FAMILY SCHOLARSHIP

• *See page 676*

MARY RUBIN AND BENJAMIN M. RUBIN SCHOLARSHIP FUND

Renewable scholarship for tuition only to women who are attending a college, university, or other institution of higher learning. Must be a resident of Maryland. Have a GPA of 3.0 or better and meet the financial requirements. Contact for application or download from Web site: http://www.centralsb.org.

Award: Scholarship for use in sophomore, junior, senior, graduate, or postgraduate years; renewable. *Number:* 20–35. *Amount:* $500–$2500.

Eligibility Requirements: Applicant must be enrolled or expecting to enroll full- or part-time at a two-year or four-year or technical institution or university; female and resident of Maryland. Applicant must have 3.0 GPA or higher. Available to U.S. citizens.

Application Requirements: Application, essay, financial need analysis, references, transcript. *Deadline:* May 31.

Contact: Roberta Goldman, Program Director
Central Scholarship Bureau
1700 Reisterstown Road, Suite 220
Baltimore, MD 21208-2903
Phone: 410-415-5558
Fax: 410-415-5501
E-mail: rgoldman@centralsb.org

MEYERHOFF MARYLAND SCHOLARS PROGRAM AT CENTRAL SCHOLARSHIP BUREAU

Scholarships of up to $7000 a year will be awarded to middle income Maryland residents who are undergraduates at Maryland public colleges and universities. If the recipient graduates within four years with a cumulative GPA of 3.0 or higher, an additional $7000 grant will be awarded to apply toward student loan debt.

Award: Scholarship for use in sophomore year; renewable. *Number:* varies. *Amount:* up to $7000.

Eligibility Requirements: Applicant must be enrolled or expecting to enroll full-time at a four-year institution or university and resident of Maryland. Applicant must have 3.0 GPA or higher. Available to U.S. citizens.

Application Requirements: Application, essay, financial need analysis, interview, transcript. *Deadline:* May 31.

Contact: Roberta Goldman, Program Director
Central Scholarship Bureau
1700 Reisterstown Road, Suite 220
Baltimore, MD 21208-2903
Phone: 410-415-5558
Fax: 410-415-5501
E-mail: rgoldman@centralsb.org

SHOE CITY-WB54/WB50 SCHOLARSHIP

Scholarship for high school seniors who are permanent residents of Maryland or Washington D.C. Four $1500 awards are granted annually.

Award: Scholarship for use in freshman year; not renewable. *Number:* 4. *Amount:* up to $1500.

Eligibility Requirements: Applicant must be high school student; planning to enroll or expecting to enroll full-time at a four-year institution or university and resident of Maryland or Washington. Available to U.S. citizens.

Application Requirements: Essay, financial need analysis, interview, references, test scores, transcript, CSB online application. *Deadline:* May 31.

Contact: Roberta Goldman, Program Director
Central Scholarship Bureau
1700 Reisterstown Road, Suite 220
Baltimore, MD 21208-2903
Phone: 410-415-5558
Fax: 410-415-5501
E-mail: rgoldman@centralsb.org

STRAUS SCHOLARSHIP PROGRAM FOR UNDERGRADUATE EDUCATION

Scholarship provides assistance to Maryland residents who are full-time undergraduate students in their sophomore, junior, or senior years at an accredited college or university. Renewable grants of up to $5000 each per year

Central Scholarship Bureau (continued)

will be awarded. If the recipient graduates within four years with a cumulative GPA of 3.0 or higher, an additional $5000 grant will be awarded to apply toward student loan debt.

Award: Scholarship for use in sophomore, junior, or senior years; renewable. *Number:* 5–8. *Amount:* up to $5000.

Eligibility Requirements: Applicant must be enrolled or expecting to enroll full-time at a four-year institution or university and resident of Maryland. Applicant must have 3.0 GPA or higher. Available to U.S. citizens.

Application Requirements: Essay, financial need analysis, interview, transcript, CSB online application. *Deadline:* May 31.

Contact: Roberta Goldman, Program Director
Central Scholarship Bureau
1700 Reisterstown Road, Suite 220
Baltimore, MD 21208-2903
Phone: 410-415-5558
Fax: 410-415-5501
E-mail: rgoldman@centralsb.org

CHICANA/LATINA FOUNDATION http://www.chicanalatina.org

SCHOLARSHIPS FOR LATINA STUDENTS

• *See page 676*

CHINESE AMERICAN ASSOCIATION OF MINNESOTA http://www.caam.org

CHINESE AMERICAN ASSOCIATION OF MINNESOTA (CAAM) SCHOLARSHIPS

• *See page 676*

CIRI FOUNDATION (TCF) http://www.thecirifoundation.org

CULTURAL FELLOWSHIP GRANTS

• *See page 677*

CIVIL SERVICE EMPLOYEES INSURANCE COMPANY http://www.cseinsurance.com

YOUTH AUTOMOBILE SAFETY SCHOLARSHIP ESSAY COMPETITION FOR CHILDREN OF PUBLIC EMPLOYEES

Applicants must be residents of California, Arizona, Utah, or Nevada with minimum 3.0 GPA. Awards are for children of full-time or retired public employees. Letter of acceptance required.

Award: Scholarship for use in freshman year; not renewable. *Number:* 1–10. *Amount:* $500–$1000.

Eligibility Requirements: Applicant must be high school student; planning to enroll or expecting to enroll full-time at a two-year or four-year or technical institution or university and resident of Arizona, California, Nevada, or Utah. Applicant must have 3.0 GPA or higher. Available to U.S. citizens.

Application Requirements: Application, applicant must enter a contest, essay, references, transcript. *Deadline:* April 7.

Contact: Robert Pick, Product Development Supervisor
Civil Service Employees Insurance Company
PO Box 8041
Walnut Creek, CA 94956-8041
Phone: 925-817-6496
Fax: 925-817-6489
E-mail: rpick@cse-insurance.com

CLEVELAND SCHOLARSHIP PROGRAMS http://www.cspohio.org

CSP ADULT ACCESS SCHOLARSHIP

Scholarship for students pursuing first associates or bachelors degree in an eligible two- or four-year program. Individuals already having a bachelors degree are not eligible. Applicants must be a resident of Ashtabula, Cuyahoga, Geauga, Lake, Lorain, Mahoning, Medina, Portage, Stark, Summit or Trumbull County.

Award: Scholarship for use in freshman, sophomore, junior, or senior years; not renewable. *Number:* 1. *Amount:* $500–$1000.

Eligibility Requirements: Applicant must be age 19 and over; enrolled or expecting to enroll full- or part-time at a two-year or four-year institution or university and resident of Ohio. Applicant must have 2.5 GPA or higher. Available to U.S. citizens.

Application Requirements: Application, financial need analysis, transcript. *Deadline:* October 19.

Contact: Scholarship Committee
Cleveland Scholarship Programs
BP Tower, 200 Public Square, Suite 3820
Cleveland, OH 44114
Phone: 216-241-5587
Fax: 216-241-6184
E-mail: alp@cspohio.org

CSP CERTIFIED PROFESSIONALS SCHOLARSHIP

Award to students pursuing a non-degree certificate or license in a vocational or technical program. Individuals who have already obtained a bachelors degree are not eligible. Applicants must be a resident of Ashtabula, Cuyahoga, Geauga, Lake, Lorain, Mahoning, Medina, Portage, Stark, Summit or Trumbull County. Minimum 2.0 GPA required.

Award: Scholarship for use in freshman or sophomore years; not renewable. *Number:* 1. *Amount:* $500–$1000.

Eligibility Requirements: Applicant must be age 19 and over; enrolled or expecting to enroll full- or part-time at a technical institution and resident of Ohio. Available to U.S. citizens.

Application Requirements: Application, essay, transcript, FAFSA. *Deadline:* October 19.

Contact: Latasha Williams, Senior Manager of Programs
Cleveland Scholarship Programs
200 Public Square, Suite 3820
Cleveland, OH 44114
Phone: 216-241-5587
Fax: 216-241-6184
E-mail: lwilliams@cspohio.org

CSP FINALIST SCHOLARSHIPS FOR HIGH SCHOOL SENIORS

Scholarship to students attending a high school serviced by a CSP Advisor. Winners are selected based on recommendations by the CSP advisor and students must also meet CSP criteria for academic performance (high school grades, SAT/ACT test scores and financial need) to receive the grant.

Award: Scholarship for use in freshman year; renewable. *Number:* 1. *Amount:* $500.

Eligibility Requirements: Applicant must be high school student; planning to enroll or expecting to enroll full- or part-time at a four-year institution or university and resident of Ohio. Available to U.S. citizens.

Application Requirements: Application, financial need analysis, transcript. *Deadline:* varies.

Contact: Latasha Williams, Senior Manager of Programs
Cleveland Scholarship Programs
200 Public Square, Suite 3820
Cleveland, OH 44114
Phone: 216-241-5587
Fax: 216-241-6184
E-mail: lwilliams@cspohio.org

CSP MANAGED FUNDS-OHIO TRANSFER COUNCIL DAVID GALL MEMORIAL SCHOLARSHIP

Five one-year, non-renewable $2000 scholarships to students presently enrolled with a minimum overall cumulative GPA of 3.0 during their undergraduate course work.

Award: Scholarship for use in freshman, sophomore, junior, or senior years; not renewable. *Number:* 5. *Amount:* $2000.

Eligibility Requirements: Applicant must be enrolled or expecting to enroll full-time at a four-year institution or university; resident of Ohio and studying in Ohio. Applicant must have 3.0 GPA or higher. Available to U.S. citizens.

Application Requirements: Application, essay, references, transcript, copy of class schedule, financial aid award letter. *Deadline:* June 30.

Contact: Latasha Williams, Senior Manager of Programs
Cleveland Scholarship Programs
200 Public Square, Suite 3820
Cleveland, OH 44114
Phone: 216-241-5587
Fax: 216-241-6184
E-mail: lwilliams@cspohio.org

COALITION OF TEXANS WITH DISABILITIES http://www.cotwd.org

KENNY MURGIA MEMORIAL SCHOLARSHIP

• *See page 616*

COLLEGEBOUND FOUNDATION http://www.collegeboundfoundation.org

ANDERSON-BELL FAMILY COLLEGE CARE PACKAGE AWARD

Award available for a first-generation college student who graduated from a Baltimore City public school. Requires a minimum cumulative GPA of 2.0. Award includes dorm room furnishings and supplies. Finalist must be available for an interview.

Award: Prize for use in freshman, sophomore, junior, or senior years; renewable. *Number:* 1. *Amount:* varies.

Eligibility Requirements: Applicant must be high school student; planning to enroll or expecting to enroll full- or part-time at a two-year or four-year institution and resident of Maryland. Available to U.S. citizens.

Application Requirements: Application, essay, interview, references. *Deadline:* March 1.

Contact: Jamie Crouse, Scholarship Program Administrator
CollegeBound Foundation
300 Water Street, Suite 300
Baltimore, MD 21202
Phone: 410-783-2905 Ext. 207
Fax: 410-727-5786
E-mail: jcrouse@collegeboundfoundation.org

BALTIMORE JUNIOR ASSOCIATION OF COMMERCE (BJAC) SCHOLARSHIP

• *See page 593*

CARMEN V. D'ANNA MEMORIAL SCHOLARSHIP OF THE MARS SUPERMARKET EDUCATIONAL FUND

Must be a senior in a Baltimore City Public High School entering a Maryland State college or university for the first time. Must demonstrate financial need and exhibit a strong desire to achieve. Submit a typed one-page essay describing why a college education is important to you.

Award: Scholarship for use in freshman, sophomore, junior, or senior years; renewable. *Number:* 1. *Amount:* up to $10,000.

Eligibility Requirements: Applicant must be high school student; planning to enroll or expecting to enroll full-time at a two-year or four-year institution or university; resident of Maryland and studying in Maryland. Available to U.S. citizens.

Application Requirements: Application, essay, financial need analysis, resume, transcript. *Deadline:* March 1.

Contact: Jamie Crouse, Scholarship Program Administrator
CollegeBound Foundation
300 Water Street, Suite 300
Baltimore, MD 21202
Phone: 410-783-2905 Ext. 207
Fax: 410-727-5786
E-mail: jcrouse@collegeboundfoundation.org

COLLEGEBOUND FOUNDATION LAST DOLLAR GRANT

A need-based award for Baltimore City public high school graduates whose expected family contribution and financial aid package total less than the cost to attend college. Grant value is up to $3000 per year, renewable for up to five years of college or the maximum amount of $15,000.

Award: Grant for use in freshman, sophomore, junior, or senior years; renewable. *Number:* 90–250. *Amount:* up to $3000.

Eligibility Requirements: Applicant must be high school student; planning to enroll or expecting to enroll full-time at a four-year institution or university; resident of Maryland and studying in Maryland. Available to U.S. citizens.

Application Requirements: Application, financial need analysis, transcript, acceptance letter. *Deadline:* March 1.

Contact: Jamie Crouse, Scholarship Program Administrator
CollegeBound Foundation
300 Water Street, Suite 300
Baltimore, MD 21202
Phone: 410-783-2905 Ext. 207
Fax: 410-727-5786
E-mail: jcrouse@collegeboundfoundation.org

COX EDUCATION FUND

Award for Baltimore City public high school graduates. Applicant should be a valedictorian in high school graduating class, be ranked in the top ten of class while applying for award, and attend two- or four-year college or university.

Award: Scholarship for use in freshman year; not renewable. *Number:* 4. *Amount:* $300.

Eligibility Requirements: Applicant must be high school student; planning to enroll or expecting to enroll full-time at a two-year or four-year institution or university and resident of Maryland. Available to U.S. citizens.

Application Requirements: Application, financial need analysis, references, transcript, financial aid award letters, SAR. *Deadline:* March 1.

Contact: Jamie Crouse, Scholarship Program Administrator
CollegeBound Foundation
300 Water Street, Suite 300
Baltimore, MD 21202
Phone: 410-783-2905 Ext. 207
Fax: 410-727-5786
E-mail: jcrouse@collegeboundfoundation.org

ERICA LYNNE DURANT MEMORIAL SCHOLARSHIP

• *See page 616*

EXCHANGE CLUB OF BALTIMORE SCHOLARSHIP

Award for Baltimore City public high school graduates. Minimum GPA of 3.0 and SAT score of 1000 is required. Must have verifiable community service. Submit a typed one-page essay describing your personal and professional goals and your expectations for college.

Award: Scholarship for use in freshman year; not renewable. *Number:* 5. *Amount:* $1000–$2000.

Eligibility Requirements: Applicant must be high school student; planning to enroll or expecting to enroll full-time at a two-year or four-year institution or university and resident of Maryland. Applicant must have 3.0 GPA or higher. Available to U.S. citizens.

Application Requirements: Application, essay, financial need analysis, references, transcript, financial aid award letters, SAR. *Deadline:* March 1.

Contact: Jamie Crouse, Scholarship Program Administrator
CollegeBound Foundation
300 Water Street, Suite 300
Baltimore, MD 21202
Phone: 410-783-2905 Ext. 207
Fax: 410-727-5786
E-mail: jcrouse@collegeboundfoundation.org

HY ZOLET STUDENT ATHLETE SCHOLARSHIP

Scholarship available to a high school athlete with a minimum cumulative GPA of 2.5. Must furnish at least two letters verifying participation in high school athletics. Must submit SAT (critical reading and math) scores, and a one-page essay indicating why you should receive this award.

Award: Scholarship for use in freshman, sophomore, junior, or senior years; renewable. *Number:* 4. *Amount:* $1000.

Eligibility Requirements: Applicant must be high school student; planning to enroll or expecting to enroll full-time at a four-year institution or university; resident of Maryland and must have an interest in athletics/sports. Applicant must have 2.5 GPA or higher. Available to U.S. citizens.

CollegeBound Foundation (continued)

Application Requirements: Application, essay, references, test scores, transcript. *Deadline:* March 1.

Contact: Jamie Crouse, Scholarship Program Administrator
CollegeBound Foundation
300 Water Street, Suite 300
Baltimore, MD 21202
Phone: 410-783-2905 Ext. 207
Fax: 410-727-5786
E-mail: jcrouse@collegeboundfoundation.org

JANE AND CLARENCE SPILMAN SCHOLARSHIP

• *See page 593*

KENNETH HOFFMAN SCHOLARSHIP

Scholarship for students who have verifiable community service, an SAT (critical reading and math)) score of 1000, and high school GPA of 3.0. Must attend Bowie State University, Coppin State University, Frostburg State University, Morgan State University, St. Mary's College of Maryland, Towson University, University of Maryland College Park, University of Maryland Eastern Shore, or Villa Julie College.

Award: Scholarship for use in freshman year; renewable. *Number:* 1. *Amount:* $1500.

Eligibility Requirements: Applicant must be high school student; planning to enroll or expecting to enroll full-time at a two-year or four-year institution or university and studying in Maryland. Applicant must have 3.0 GPA or higher. Available to U.S. citizens.

Application Requirements: Application, financial need analysis, references, transcript, financial aid award letters, SAR. *Deadline:* March 1.

Contact: Jamie Crouse, Scholarship Program Administrator
CollegeBound Foundation
300 Water Street, Suite 300
Baltimore, MD 21202
Phone: 410-783-2905 Ext. 207
Fax: 410-727-5786
E-mail: jcrouse@collegeboundfoundation.org

LESLIE MOORE FOUNDATION SCHOLARSHIP

Three awards for students from Baltimore City public high schools and two from other county schools. Must have GPA of at least 2.0 and verifiable community service. See Web site for application: http://www.collegeboundfoundation.org.

Award: Scholarship for use in freshman, sophomore, junior, or senior years; renewable. *Number:* 5. *Amount:* $2500.

Eligibility Requirements: Applicant must be enrolled or expecting to enroll full-time at a two-year or four-year institution and resident of Maryland. Available to U.S. citizens.

Application Requirements: Application, essay, financial need analysis, interview, references, transcript, financial aid award letters, SAR. *Deadline:* March 1.

Contact: Jamie Crouse, Scholarship Program Administrator
CollegeBound Foundation
300 Water Street, Suite 300
Baltimore, MD 21202
Phone: 410-783-2905 Ext. 207
Fax: 410-727-5786
E-mail: jcrouse@collegeboundfoundation.org

SCARBOROUGH-SCHEELER SCHOLARSHIP

Scholarship for students with a cumulative high school GPA of at least 2.5. Must demonstrate financial need. Submit an essay (500-1000 words) describing your college expectations. Must plan on attending Goucher College, McDaniel College, Towson University or University of Maryland College Park.

Award: Scholarship for use in freshman, sophomore, junior, or senior years; renewable. *Number:* 1. *Amount:* $1000.

Eligibility Requirements: Applicant must be high school student; planning to enroll or expecting to enroll full-time at a four-year institution or university; resident of Maryland and studying in Maryland. Applicant must have 2.5 GPA or higher. Available to U.S. citizens.

Application Requirements: Application, essay, financial need analysis, references, transcript. *Deadline:* March 1.

Contact: Jamie Crouse, Scholarship Program Administrator
CollegeBound Foundation
300 Water Street, Suite 300
Baltimore, MD 21202
Phone: 410-783-2905 Ext. 207
Fax: 410-727-5786
E-mail: jcrouse@collegeboundfoundation.org

COLLEGE FOUNDATION OF NORTH CAROLINA INC. http://www.cfnc.org

CRUMLEY AND ASSOCIATES-CRIB TO COLLEGE SCHOLARSHIP

Scholarship will provide financial assistance and laptop computers to five outstanding North Carolina high school seniors. Applicants must be a graduating senior at a North Carolina high school and enroll at an accredited four-year college or university or an accredited two-year technical school or community college. Must maintain a minimum GPA of 3.0. Application is available only on the company Web site at http://www.crumleyandassociates.com/crib-to-college.php and must be completed online only.

Award: Scholarship for use in freshman year; not renewable. *Number:* 5. *Amount:* $1000.

Eligibility Requirements: Applicant must be high school student; planning to enroll or expecting to enroll full-time at a two-year or four-year or technical institution or university and resident of North Carolina. Applicant must have 3.0 GPA or higher. Available to U.S. citizens.

Application Requirements: Application, essay, references, test scores, transcript. *Deadline:* March 15.

Contact: Stephen Keaney, Scholarship Committee
College Foundation of North Carolina Inc.
Crumley and Associates, 2400 Freeman Mill Road, Suite 300
Greensboro, NC 27406
Phone: 336-333-0044
E-mail: smkeaney@crumleyandassociates.com

FEDERAL SUPPLEMENTAL EDUCATIONAL OPPORTUNITY GRANT PROGRAM

Applicant must have exceptional financial need to qualify for this award. Amount of financial need is determined by the educational institution the student attends. Available only to undergraduate students. Recipient must be a U.S. citizen or permanent resident. Priority is given to a students who receive Federal Pell Grants.

Award: Grant for use in freshman, sophomore, junior, or senior years; not renewable. *Number:* varies. *Amount:* $100–$4400.

Eligibility Requirements: Applicant must be enrolled or expecting to enroll full-time at a four-year institution or university and resident of North Carolina. Available to U.S. citizens.

Application Requirements: Application, financial need analysis, transcript. *Deadline:* continuous.

Contact: Federal Student Aid Information Center
College Foundation of North Carolina Inc.
PO Box 84
Washington, DC 20044
Phone: 800-433-3243

GOLDEN LEAF SCHOLARSHIP-FOUR YEAR UNIVERSITY PROGRAM

Renewable scholarship for current high school seniors and current community college students planning to enter North Carolina public four-year university, and currently enrolled students at NC public four-year universities. Must be a permanent resident of a rural NC county that is economically distressed and/or tobacco crop-dependent.

Award: Scholarship for use in freshman, sophomore, junior, or senior years; not renewable. *Number:* 580. *Amount:* $3000.

Eligibility Requirements: Applicant must be enrolled or expecting to enroll full-time at a four-year institution or university; resident of North Carolina and studying in North Carolina. Available to U.S. citizens.

Application Requirements: Application, financial need analysis, transcript. *Deadline:* March 17.

Contact: Scholarship Coordinator
College Foundation of North Carolina Inc.
PO Box 13663
RTP, NC 27709-3663
Phone: 866-866-2362
Fax: 919-248-4687
E-mail: programinformation@cfnc.org

GOLDEN LEAF SCHOLARS PROGRAM-TWO-YEAR COLLEGES

Need- and merit-based scholarships of up to $750 per semester, including summer session for curriculum students, and up to $250 per semester for occupational education students. Student must be a permanent resident of one of the seventy-three eligible counties and be enrolled at one of the fifty-eight member institutions of the North Carolina community college system. Must demonstrate a need under federal TRIO formula.

Award: Scholarship for use in freshman or sophomore years; not renewable. *Number:* varies. *Amount:* $500–$1500.

Eligibility Requirements: Applicant must be enrolled or expecting to enroll part-time at a two-year institution; resident of North Carolina and studying in North Carolina. Available to U.S. citizens.

Application Requirements: Application, financial need analysis, transcript, waiver form. *Deadline:* varies.

Contact: Scholarship Coordinator
College Foundation of North Carolina Inc.
2917 Highwoods Boulevard
PO Box 41966
Raleigh, NC 27604
Phone: 866-866-2362
Fax: 919-248-4687
E-mail: programinformation@cfnc.org

LATINO DIAMANTE SCHOLARSHIP FUND

• *See page 594*

NORTH CAROLINA BAR ASSOCIATION SCHOLARSHIP

• *See page 594*

NORTH CAROLINA 4-H DEVELOPMENT FUND SCHOLARSHIPS

Scholarship for a resident of North Carolina, enrolling as an undergraduate in a four-year accredited North Carolina college or university or a junior or community college in the state, provided the program of study selected is transferable to a four-year college. Must demonstrate an aptitude for college work through SAT scores. For some of the awards, financial need is a prerequisite. Some awards have geographic restrictions to regions of the state. Some scholarships are renewable.

Award: Scholarship for use in freshman, sophomore, junior, or senior years; renewable. *Number:* varies. *Amount:* $500–$2500.

Eligibility Requirements: Applicant must be enrolled or expecting to enroll full-time at a two-year or four-year institution or university; resident of North Carolina and studying in North Carolina. Available to U.S. citizens.

Application Requirements: Application, financial need analysis, test scores, transcript. *Deadline:* continuous.

Contact: Scholarship Committee
College Foundation of North Carolina Inc.
PO Box 41966
Raleigh, NC 27629-1966
Phone: 919-515-2801
E-mail: programinformation@cfnc.org

NORTH CAROLINA HISPANIC COLLEGE FUND SCHOLARSHIP

• *See page 679*

NORTH CAROLINA STUDENT INCENTIVE GRANT

Grant available for North Carolina resident who is enrolled or accepted for enrollment on a full-time basis at a North Carolina postsecondary institution. Should not be enrolled in a program designed primarily for career preparation in a religious vocation. Must be a U.S. citizen and maintain satisfactory academic progress. Available to undergraduates who demonstrate substantial financial need.

Award: Grant for use in freshman, sophomore, junior, or senior years; not renewable. *Number:* varies. *Amount:* $700.

Eligibility Requirements: Applicant must be enrolled or expecting to enroll full-time at a four-year institution or university; resident of North Carolina and studying in North Carolina. Available to U.S. citizens.

Application Requirements: Financial need analysis. *Deadline:* March 15.

Contact: Scholarship Committee
College Foundation of North Carolina Inc.
PO Box 41966
Raleigh, NC 27629-1966
Phone: 888-234-6400
Fax: 919-821-3139
E-mail: programinformation@cfnc.org

NORTH CAROLINA VETERANS SCHOLARSHIPS

• *See page 652*

STATE EMPLOYEES ASSOCIATION OF NORTH CAROLINA (SEANC) SCHOLARSHIPS

Scholarships available to SEANC members, their spouses and dependents seeking postsecondary education. Awarded in three categories: based on academic merit, financial need, and awards for SEANC members only. Applicants can request for application or more information at http://www.seanc.org/.

Award: Scholarship for use in freshman, sophomore, junior, or senior years; not renewable. *Number:* 2. *Amount:* $500–$1000.

Eligibility Requirements: Applicant must be enrolled or expecting to enroll full-time at a two-year or four-year or technical institution or university and resident of North Carolina. Available to U.S. citizens.

Application Requirements: Application, financial need analysis, test scores, transcript. *Deadline:* April 15.

Contact: Scholarship Committee
College Foundation of North Carolina Inc.
PO Box 41966
Raleigh, NC 27629-1966
Phone: 888-234-6400
E-mail: programinformation@cfnc.org

UNIVERSITY OF NORTH CAROLINA NEED BASED GRANT

Grants available for eligible students attending one of the 16 campuses of the University of North Carolina. Students must be enrolled in at least 6 credit hours at one of the 16 constituent institutions of The University of North Carolina. Award amounts vary, based on legislative appropriations.

Award: Grant for use in freshman, sophomore, junior, or senior years; not renewable. *Number:* varies. *Amount:* varies.

Eligibility Requirements: Applicant must be enrolled or expecting to enroll full- or part-time at a four-year institution or university; resident of North Carolina and studying in North Carolina. Available to U.S. citizens.

Application Requirements: Financial need analysis. *Deadline:* continuous.

Contact: Scholarship Coordinator
College Foundation of North Carolina Inc.
2917 Highwoods Boulevard
PO Box 41966
Raleigh, NC 27604
Phone: 866-866-2362
Fax: 919-248-4687
E-mail: programinformation@cfnc.org

COLLEGE IN COLORADO http://www.collegeincolorado.org

COLORADO HIGH SCHOOL ACTIVITIES ASSOCIATION (CHSAA) SCHOLARSHIP

Students attending a CHSAA event or participating in CHSAA sponsored activities are eligible for the CHSAA scholarship. Three $1000 CHSAA scholarships are available to Colorado students.

Award: Scholarship for use in freshman year; not renewable. *Number:* 3. *Amount:* $1000.

Eligibility Requirements: Applicant must be enrolled or expecting to enroll full- or part-time at a four-year institution or university and resident of Colorado. Available to U.S. citizens.

College in Colorado (continued)

Application Requirements: Application. *Deadline:* May 30.

Contact: Shelby Burnette, Outreach Coordinator
College in Colorado
1801 Broadway, Suite 360
Denver, CO 80202
Phone: 720-264-8570
E-mail: shelby.burnette@cic.state.co.us

COLORADO SPORTS HALL OF FAME SCHOLARSHIP

Scholarship awarded to students in high school who excel in football.

Award: Scholarship for use in freshman year; not renewable. *Number:* varies. *Amount:* $1000.

Eligibility Requirements: Applicant must be enrolled or expecting to enroll full- or part-time at a two-year or four-year institution; resident of Colorado and must have an interest in athletics/sports. Available to U.S. citizens.

Application Requirements: Application. *Deadline:* varies.

Contact: Bridget Redfern, Scholarship Committee
College in Colorado
1801 Broadway, Suite 360
Denver, CO 80202
Phone: 720-264-8571
Fax: 303-296-1637
E-mail: bridget.redfern@cic.state.co.us

COLLEGE SUCCESS FOUNDATION http://www.collegesuccessfoundation.org

GOVERNORS SCHOLARSHIP PROGRAM

Scholarship award amounts range from $1000 to $5000 depending on each student's financial need. Scholarships can be used up to five years until completion of the student's program of study. Students must be enroll full time and maintain satisfactory academic progress in order to renew scholarships each year. Minimum 2.0 GPA required.

Award: Scholarship for use in freshman year; renewable. *Number:* 30. *Amount:* $1000–$5000.

Eligibility Requirements: Applicant must be high school student; planning to enroll or expecting to enroll full-time at a four-year institution or university; resident of Washington and studying in Washington. Available to U.S. citizens.

Application Requirements: Application, references, FAFSA. *Deadline:* March 4.

Contact: Erica Meier, Director, Human Resources and Operations
College Success Foundation
1605 NW Sammamish Road, Suite 100
Issaquah, WA 98027
Phone: 425-416-2000
Fax: 425-416-2001
E-mail: info@collegesuccessfoundation.org

WASHINGTON STATE ACHIEVERS PROGRAM SCHOLARSHIP

Scholarship amounts will be established annually for students attending public community colleges, public four-year and independent institutions. Scholarships averages approximately between $5000 to $10,000.

Award: Scholarship for use in freshman year; not renewable. *Number:* 600. *Amount:* $5000–$10,000.

Eligibility Requirements: Applicant must be high school student; planning to enroll or expecting to enroll full-time at a two-year or four-year or technical institution or university; resident of Washington and studying in Washington. Available to U.S. citizens.

Application Requirements: Application, financial need analysis. *Deadline:* varies.

Contact: Erica Meier, Director, Human Resources and Operations
College Success Foundation
1605 NW Sammamish Road, Suite 100
Issaquah, WA 98027
Phone: 425-416-2000
Fax: 425-416-2001
E-mail: info@collegesuccessfoundation.org

COLLEGE SUCCESS NETWORK http://www.collegesuccessnetwork.org

NEW MEXICO FINISH LINE SCHOLARSHIP

Awards range from $300 to $1000. Scholarship is for the academically proven New Mexico college student who has completed at least one semester of undergraduate coursework. Must have at least 3.0 GPA.

Award: Scholarship for use in freshman, sophomore, junior, or senior years; renewable. *Number:* 1. *Amount:* $300–$1000.

Eligibility Requirements: Applicant must be enrolled or expecting to enroll full- or part-time at a four-year institution or university; resident of New Mexico and studying in New Mexico. Applicant must have 3.0 GPA or higher. Available to U.S. citizens.

Application Requirements: Application, essay, self-addressed stamped envelope, transcript, financial aid award letter. *Deadline:* October 15.

Contact: Sharon Oizumi, Interim Executive Director
College Success Network
5850 Eubank Boulevard, NE, Suite B32
Albuquerque, NM 87111
Phone: 505-821-2100
Fax: 505-821-2042
E-mail: info@collegesuccessnetwork.org

COLORADO COMMISSION ON HIGHER EDUCATION http://www.state.co.us/cche

COLORADO LEVERAGING EDUCATIONAL ASSISTANCE PARTNERSHIP (CLEAP)

Scholarship of up to $5000 awarded for undergraduate student enrolled at least half time. Applicant must be a U.S citizen and Colorado resident.

Award: Scholarship for use in freshman, sophomore, junior, or senior years; not renewable. *Number:* varies. *Amount:* up to $5000.

Eligibility Requirements: Applicant must be enrolled or expecting to enroll full- or part-time at a two-year or four-year or technical institution or university and resident of Colorado. Available to U.S. citizens.

Application Requirements: Application. *Deadline:* varies.

Contact: Tobin Bliss, Financial Aid Director
Colorado Commission on Higher Education
1380 Lawrence Street, Suite 1200
Denver, CO 80204-2059
Phone: 303-866-2723
E-mail: tobin.bliss@cche.state.co.us

COLORADO STUDENT GRANT

Grants for Colorado residents attending eligible public, private, or vocational institutions within the state. Application deadlines vary by institution. Renewable award for undergraduates. Contact the financial aid office at the college/institution for application and more information.

Award: Grant for use in freshman, sophomore, junior, or senior years; renewable. *Number:* varies. *Amount:* $1500–$5000.

Eligibility Requirements: Applicant must be enrolled or expecting to enroll full- or part-time at a two-year or four-year or technical institution or university; resident of Colorado and studying in Colorado. Available to U.S. citizens.

Application Requirements: Application, financial need analysis. *Deadline:* varies.

Contact: Tobin Bliss, Financial Aid Director
Colorado Commission on Higher Education
1380 Lawrence Street, Suite 1200
Denver, CO 80204-2059
Phone: 303-866-2723
E-mail: tobin.bliss@cche.state.co.us

COLORADO UNDERGRADUATE MERIT SCHOLARSHIPS

Renewable awards for students who are Colorado residents attending Colorado state-supported institutions at the undergraduate level. Must demonstrate superior scholarship or talent. Contact college financial aid office for complete information and deadlines.

Award: Scholarship for use in freshman, sophomore, junior, or senior years; renewable. *Number:* 10,823. *Amount:* $1230.

Eligibility Requirements: Applicant must be enrolled or expecting to enroll full- or part-time at a two-year or four-year or technical institution or university; resident of Colorado and studying in Colorado. Applicant must have 3.0 GPA or higher. Available to U.S. citizens.

Application Requirements: Application, test scores, transcript. *Deadline:* varies.

Contact: Tobin Bliss, Financial Aid Director
Colorado Commission on Higher Education
1380 Lawrence Street, Suite 1200
Denver, CO 80204-2059
Phone: 303-866-2723
E-mail: tobin.bliss@cche.state.co.us

GOVERNOR'S OPPORTUNITY SCHOLARSHIP

Scholarship available for the most needy first-time freshman whose parents' adjusted gross income is less than $26,000. Must be U.S. citizen or permanent legal resident. Work-study is part of the program.

Award: Scholarship for use in freshman year; renewable. *Number:* 250. *Amount:* up to $10,700.

Eligibility Requirements: Applicant must be high school student; planning to enroll or expecting to enroll full-time at a two-year or four-year or technical institution or university; resident of Colorado and studying in Colorado. Available to U.S. citizens.

Application Requirements: Application, financial need analysis, test scores, transcript. *Deadline:* continuous.

Contact: Tobin Bliss, Financial Aid Director
Colorado Commission on Higher Education
1380 Lawrence Street, Suite 1200
Denver, CO 80204-2059
Phone: 303-866-2723
E-mail: tobin.bliss@cche.state.co.us

COLORADO COUNCIL ON HIGH SCHOOL/ COLLEGE RELATIONS http://www.coloradocouncil.org

COLORADO COUNCIL VOLUNTEERISM/COMMUNITY SERVICE SCHOLARSHIP

Awarded to a graduating high school senior. Applicant must have a minimum GPA 2.5. Award value is $1500.

Award: Scholarship for use in freshman year; not renewable. *Number:* 16. *Amount:* $1500.

Eligibility Requirements: Applicant must be high school student; planning to enroll or expecting to enroll full-time at a two-year or four-year institution or university and resident of Colorado. Applicant must have 2.5 GPA or higher. Available to U.S. citizens.

Application Requirements: Application, essay, references, transcript. *Deadline:* January 30.

Contact: Mark Thompson, Counselor
Colorado Council on High School/College Relations
600 17th Street, Suite 2210 South
Denver, CO 80202
Phone: 970-264-2231 Ext. 226
E-mail: mthompson@pagosa.k12.co.us

COLORADO EDUCATIONAL SERVICES AND DEVELOPMENT ASSOCIATION http://www.cesda.org

CESDA DIVERSITY SCHOLARSHIPS

Award for underrepresented, economically, and disadvantaged high school seniors planning to pursue undergraduate studies at a Colorado college or university. Must be Colorado resident. Applicant must be a first generation student, or member of an underrepresented ethnic or racial minority, and/or show financial need. Minimum 2.8 GPA required.

Award: Scholarship for use in freshman, sophomore, junior, or senior years; not renewable. *Number:* 6. *Amount:* $1000.

Eligibility Requirements: Applicant must be enrolled or expecting to enroll full- or part-time at a two-year or four-year institution or university; resident of Colorado and studying in Colorado. Available to U.S. citizens.

Application Requirements: Application, financial need analysis, transcript. *Deadline:* March 31.

Contact: Ximena Quintana, Scholarship Committee
Colorado Educational Services and Development Association
2960 North Speer Boulevard
Denver, CO 80211
Phone: 720-423-2907
E-mail: xquintana@denverscholarship.org

COLORADO MASONS BENEVOLENT FUND ASSOCIATION http://www.coloradofreemasons.org

COLORADO MASONS BENEVOLENT FUND SCHOLARSHIPS

Applicants must be graduating seniors from a Colorado public high school accepted at a Colorado postsecondary institution. The maximum grant is $7000 renewable over four years. Obtain scholarship materials and specific requirements from high school counselor.

Award: Scholarship for use in freshman year; renewable. *Number:* 10–14. *Amount:* up to $7000.

Eligibility Requirements: Applicant must be high school student; planning to enroll or expecting to enroll full-time at a two-year or four-year or technical institution or university; resident of Colorado and studying in Colorado. Available to U.S. citizens.

Application Requirements: Application, essay, financial need analysis, interview, references, transcript. *Deadline:* March 7.

Contact: Ron Kadera, Scholarship Administrator
Colorado Masons Benevolent Fund Association
1130 Panorama Drive
Colorado Springs, CO 80904
Phone: 719-471-9587
Fax: 719-471-9157
E-mail: scholarships@coloradofreemasons.org

COLORADO STATE GRANGE LEADERSHIP AND SCHOLARSHIP FOUNDATION http://www.coloradogrange.org

COLORADO STATE GRANGE SCHOLARSHIPS

• *See page 528*

COMMERCE BANK http://www.commerceonline.com

AMERICAN DREAM SCHOLARSHIPS

• *See page 594*

"CASH FOR COLLEGE" SCHOLARSHIP

• *See page 594*

COMMUNITY BANKER ASSOCIATION OF ILLINOIS http://www.cbai.com

COMMUNITY BANKER ASSOCIATION OF ILLINOIS ANNUAL SCHOLARSHIP PROGRAM

Open to Illinois high school seniors who are sponsored by a CBAI member bank. Student bank employees, immediate families of bank employees, board members, stockholders, CBAI employees, and judges are ineligible. For more details see Web site: http://www.cbai.com.

Award: Scholarship for use in freshman year; not renewable. *Number:* up to 13. *Amount:* $1000–$4000.

Eligibility Requirements: Applicant must be high school student; planning to enroll or expecting to enroll full-time at a four-year institution or university and resident of Illinois. Available to U.S. citizens.

Application Requirements: Application, essay. *Deadline:* February 11.

Contact: Andrea Cusick, Senior Vice President of Communications
Community Banker Association of Illinois
901 Community Drive
Springfield, IL 62703-5184
Phone: 217-529-2265
Fax: 217-585-8738
E-mail: cbaicom@cbai.com

COMMUNITY BANKER ASSOCIATION OF ILLINOIS CHILDREN OF COMMUNITY BANKING SCHOLARSHIP WILLIAM C. HARRIS MEMORIAL SCHOLARSHIP

• *See page 528*

COMMUNITY BANKERS ASSOCIATION OF GEORGIA http://www.cbaofga.com

JULIAN AND JAN HESTER MEMORIAL SCHOLARSHIP

Scholarship available to Georgia high school seniors who will be entering a Georgia two- or four-year college or university, or a program at a technical institution. Recipients will be named on the basis of merit, and family financial need is not considered. Application must be sponsored by a local community bank, and must include an essay on community banking and what it represents.

Award: Scholarship for use in freshman year; not renewable. *Number:* 4. *Amount:* $1000.

Eligibility Requirements: Applicant must be high school student; planning to enroll or expecting to enroll full-time at a two-year or four-year or technical institution or university; resident of Georgia and studying in Georgia. Available to U.S. citizens.

Application Requirements: Application, references, test scores, transcript. *Deadline:* March 30.

Contact: Lauren Dismuke, Public Relations and Marketing Coordinator
Community Bankers Association of Georgia
1900 The Exchange, Suite 600
Atlanta, GA 30339
Phone: 770-541-4490
Fax: 770-541-4496
E-mail: lauren@cbaofga.com

COMMUNITY FOUNDATION FOR GREATER ATLANTA INC. http://www.atlcf.org

GEORGE AND PEARL STRICKLAND SCHOLARSHIP

For undergraduate or graduate students with financial need pursuing degrees at Atlanta University Center Colleges. For complete eligibility requirements and for an application, please visit www.atlcf.org.

Award: Scholarship for use in freshman, sophomore, junior, or senior years; not renewable. *Number:* up to 20. *Amount:* $1000–$2000.

Eligibility Requirements: Applicant must be enrolled or expecting to enroll full- or part-time at a four-year institution or university; resident of Georgia and studying in Georgia. Available to U.S. citizens.

Application Requirements: Application, driver's license, essay, references, transcript. *Deadline:* March 26.

Contact: Kristina Morris, Program Associate
Community Foundation for Greater Atlanta Inc.
50 Hurt Plaza, Suite 449
Atlanta, GA 30303
Phone: 404-688-5525
Fax: 404-688-3060
E-mail: scholarships@atlcf.org

NANCY PENN LYONS SCHOLARSHIP FUND

Award for graduating high school seniors with financial need living in Georgia who have been accepted for enrollment at prestigious or out-of-state universities. Please visit the Web site (www.atlcf.org) for complete eligibility requirements.

Award: Scholarship for use in freshman year; renewable. *Number:* 1–5. *Amount:* $5000.

Eligibility Requirements: Applicant must be high school student; planning to enroll or expecting to enroll full-time at a four-year institution or university and resident of Georgia. Applicant must have 3.0 GPA or higher. Available to U.S. citizens.

Application Requirements: Application, essay, financial need analysis, references, test scores, transcript. *Deadline:* April 19.

Contact: Kristina Morris, Program Associate
Community Foundation for Greater Atlanta Inc.
50 Hurt Plaza, Suite 449
Atlanta, GA 30303
Phone: 404-688-5525
Fax: 404-688-3060
E-mail: scholarships@atlcf.org

COMMUNITY FOUNDATION FOR PALM BEACH AND MARTIN COUNTIES http://www.yourcommunityfoundation.org

COMMUNITY FOUNDATION SCHOLARSHIP PROGRAM

Award ranges between $750 and $2500 per year. Applicant must be a full-time student and graduating high school senior in Palm Beach or Martin County.

Award: Scholarship for use in freshman year; renewable. *Number:* up to 50. *Amount:* $750–$2500.

Eligibility Requirements: Applicant must be high school student; planning to enroll or expecting to enroll full-time at a four-year institution or university and resident of Florida. Available to U.S. citizens.

Application Requirements: Application, financial need analysis, interview, transcript. *Deadline:* February 1.

Contact: Carolyn Jenco, Development Associate and Scholarship Coordinator
Community Foundation for Palm Beach and Martin Counties
700 South Dixie Highway, Suite 200
West Palm Beach, FL 33401
Phone: 561-659-6800
E-mail: info@cfpbmc.org

COMMUNITY FOUNDATION OF WESTERN MASSACHUSETTS http://www.communityfoundation.org

CHRISTINE MITUS ROSE MEMORIAL SCHOLARSHIP

Scholarship available to Massachusetts students who have had a parent die; preference to those who have had a parent die of cancer.

Award: Scholarship for use in freshman, sophomore, junior, or senior years; not renewable. *Number:* 1. *Amount:* up to $500.

Eligibility Requirements: Applicant must be enrolled or expecting to enroll full-time at a four-year institution or university and resident of Massachusetts. Available to U.S. citizens.

Application Requirements: Application, financial need analysis, transcript, Student Aid Report (SAR). *Deadline:* March 31.

Contact: Dorothy Theriaque, Education Associate
Community Foundation of Western Massachusetts
1500 Main Street, PO Box 15769
Springfield, MA 01115
Phone: 413-732-2858
Fax: 413-733-8565
E-mail: dtheriaque@communityfoundation.org

DEERFIELD PLASTICS/BARKER FAMILY SCHOLARSHIP

• *See page 577*

FIRST NATIONAL BANK OF AMHERST CENTENNIAL EDUCATIONAL SCHOLARSHIP

Scholarships available for graduating seniors from Amherst Regional High School, Hopkins Academy, Northampton High School, Amherst College, Hampshire College, and the University of Massachusetts-Amherst.

Award: Scholarship for use in freshman year; renewable. *Number:* 1. *Amount:* $315–$350.

Eligibility Requirements: Applicant must be enrolled or expecting to enroll full- or part-time at a two-year or four-year or technical institution or university; resident of Massachusetts and studying in Massachusetts. Available to U.S. citizens.

Application Requirements: Application, financial need analysis, transcript, Student Aid Report (SAR). *Deadline:* March 31.

Contact: Dorothy Theriaque, Education Associate
Community Foundation of Western Massachusetts
1500 Main Street, PO Box 15769
Springfield, MA 01115
Phone: 413-732-2858
Fax: 413-733-8565
E-mail: dtheriaque@communityfoundation.org

FRED K. LANE SCHOLARSHIP

Available for graduating high school seniors who are past or current members (individual or family) or employees of the Orchards Golf Club, South Hadley, MA.

Award: Scholarship for use in freshman year; not renewable. *Number:* 1. *Amount:* up to $1000.

Eligibility Requirements: Applicant must be high school student; planning to enroll or expecting to enroll full-time at a four-year institution or university and resident of Massachusetts. Available to U.S. citizens.

Application Requirements: Application, financial need analysis, transcript, Student Aid Report (SAR). *Deadline:* March 31.

Contact: Dorothy Theriaque, Education Associate
Community Foundation of Western Massachusetts
1500 Main Street, PO Box 15769
Springfield, MA 01115
Phone: 413-732-2858
Fax: 413-733-8565
E-mail: dtheriaque@communityfoundation.org

KIMBER RICHTER FAMILY SCHOLARSHIP

• *See page 714*

MASSMUTUAL RENEWABLE SCHOLARS PROGRAM

Awards previous recipients of the MassMutual scholarship program pursuing undergraduate study, who have exhausted their original MassMutual scholarship award and have maintained a cumulative 3.0 GPA.

Award: Scholarship for use in freshman, sophomore, junior, or senior years; renewable. *Number:* 10. *Amount:* $5000.

Eligibility Requirements: Applicant must be enrolled or expecting to enroll full- or part-time at a two-year or four-year institution or university and resident of Connecticut or Massachusetts. Applicant must have 3.0 GPA or higher. Available to U.S. citizens.

Application Requirements: Application, financial need analysis, transcript. *Deadline:* March 31.

Contact: Dorothy Theriaque, Education Associate
Community Foundation of Western Massachusetts
1500 Main Street, Tower Square, Suite 2300
PO Box 15769
Springfield, MA 01115
Phone: 413-732-2858
Fax: 413-733-8565
E-mail: scholar@communityfoundation.org

PUTNAM SCHOLARSHIP FUND

• *See page 679*

CONNECTICUT ARMY NATIONAL GUARD http://www.ct.ngb.army.mil

CONNECTICUT ARMY NATIONAL GUARD 100% TUITION WAIVER

• *See page 640*

CONNECTICUT DEPARTMENT OF HIGHER EDUCATION http://www.ctdhe.org

CAPITOL SCHOLARSHIP PROGRAM

Award for Connecticut residents attending eligible institutions in Connecticut or in a state with reciprocity with Connecticut (Massachusetts, Maine, New Hampshire, Pennsylvania, Rhode Island, Vermont, or Washington, D.C). Must be U.S. citizen or permanent resident alien who is a high school senior or graduate. Must rank in top 20% of class or score at least 1800 on SAT. Must show financial need.

Award: Scholarship for use in freshman, sophomore, junior, or senior years; renewable. *Number:* 4500. *Amount:* $500–$3000.

Eligibility Requirements: Applicant must be enrolled or expecting to enroll full- or part-time at a two-year or four-year or technical institution or university; resident of Connecticut and studying in Connecticut, District of Columbia, Maine, Massachusetts, New Hampshire, Pennsylvania, Rhode Island, or Vermont. Applicant must have 3.5 GPA or higher. Available to U.S. citizens.

Application Requirements: Application, financial need analysis, test scores, FAFSA. *Deadline:* February 15.

Contact: Associate Director
Connecticut Department of Higher Education
61 Woodland Street
Hartford, CT 06105-2326
Phone: 860-947-1855
Fax: 860-947-1311
E-mail: mfrench@ctdhe.org

CONNECTICUT AID TO PUBLIC COLLEGE STUDENTS GRANT

Award for Connecticut residents attending public colleges or universities within the state. Renewable awards based on financial need. Application deadline varies by institution. Apply at college financial aid office.

Award: Grant for use in freshman, sophomore, junior, or senior years; renewable. *Number:* varies. *Amount:* varies.

Eligibility Requirements: Applicant must be enrolled or expecting to enroll full- or part-time at a two-year or four-year institution or university; resident of Connecticut and studying in Connecticut. Available to U.S. citizens.

Application Requirements: Application, financial need analysis, FAFSA. *Deadline:* varies.

Contact: Associate Director
Connecticut Department of Higher Education
61 Woodland Street
Hartford, CT 06105-2326
Phone: 860-947-1855
Fax: 860-947-1311
E-mail: mfrench@ctdhe.org

CONNECTICUT INDEPENDENT COLLEGE STUDENT GRANTS

Award for Connecticut residents attending an independent college or university within the state on at least a half-time basis. Renewable awards based on financial need. Application deadline varies by institution. Apply at college financial aid office.

Award: Grant for use in freshman, sophomore, junior, or senior years; renewable. *Number:* varies. *Amount:* up to $8500.

Eligibility Requirements: Applicant must be enrolled or expecting to enroll full- or part-time at a two-year or four-year institution or university; resident of Connecticut and studying in Connecticut. Available to U.S. citizens.

Application Requirements: Application, financial need analysis, FAFSA. *Deadline:* varies.

Contact: Associate Director
Connecticut Department of Higher Education
61 Woodland Street
Hartford, CT 06105-2326
Phone: 860-947-1855
Fax: 860-947-1311
E-mail: mfrench@ctdhe.org

ROBERT C. BYRD HONORS SCHOLARSHIP-CONNECTICUT

Renewable scholarship for Connecticut high school seniors in the top 2% of their class or scoring 2100 or above on the SAT. Acceptance letter from college required. File applications through high school guidance office.

Award: Scholarship for use in freshman year; renewable. *Number:* 1–80. *Amount:* $1500.

Eligibility Requirements: Applicant must be high school student; planning to enroll or expecting to enroll full-time at a two-year or four-year institution or university and resident of Connecticut. Available to U.S. citizens.

Application Requirements: Application, test scores. *Deadline:* April 1.

Contact: Associate Director
Connecticut Department of Higher Education
61 Woodland Street
Hartford, CT 06105-2326
Phone: 860-947-1855
Fax: 860-947-1311
E-mail: mfrench@ctdhe.org

CONNECTICUT STUDENT LOAN FOUNDATION http://www.cslf.com

VINCENT J. MAIOCCO SCHOLARSHIP

Award to provide access to postsecondary education. Must have received a Federal Stafford Loan guaranteed by CSLF, must be a United States citizen and Connecticut resident since the time of high school graduation, and must have successfully completed his or her first year of study at a four-year degree granting institution within the United States.

Award: Scholarship for use in sophomore, junior, or senior years; not renewable. *Number:* varies. *Amount:* varies.

Eligibility Requirements: Applicant must be enrolled or expecting to enroll full-time at a four-year institution or university and resident of Connecticut. Available to U.S. citizens.

Application Requirements: Application, essay, transcript, financial aid award letter. *Deadline:* varies.

Contact: Melissa Trombley, Executive Manager
Connecticut Student Loan Foundation
525 Brook Street, PO Box 1009
Rocky Hill, CT 06067
Phone: 800-237-9721 Ext. 204
Fax: 860-257-1743
E-mail: mtrombl@mail.cslf.org

CORPORATION FOR OHIO APPALACHIAN DEVELOPMENT (COAD) http://www.coadinc.org

DAVID V. STIVISON APPALACHIAN SCHOLARSHIP FUND

• *See page 679*

COURAGE CENTER, VOCATIONAL SERVICES DEPARTMENT http://www.courage.org

SCHOLARSHIP FOR PEOPLE WITH DISABILITIES

• *See page 617*

DALLAS ARCHITECTURAL FOUNDATION-HKS/ JOHN HUMPHRIES MINORITY SCHOLARSHIP http://www.dallasfoundation.org

CHUCK FULGHAM SCHOLARSHIP FUND

Scholarship for adult graduate of a literacy program needing financial assistance to pursue a college education at a regionally accredited college or university, or a high school graduate with a demonstrated enthusiasm in the humanities and a GPA of 3.0 or lower. Must be resident of Texas, preference given to Dallas county residents.

Award: Scholarship for use in freshman, sophomore, junior, or senior years; not renewable. *Number:* 1–2. *Amount:* up to $2500.

Eligibility Requirements: Applicant must be enrolled or expecting to enroll full-time at a two-year or four-year institution or university and resident of Texas. Applicant must have 3.0 GPA or higher. Available to U.S. citizens.

Application Requirements: Application, essay, financial need analysis, references, transcript. *Deadline:* April 1.

Contact: Cathy McNally, Program Manager
Dallas Architectural Foundation-HKS/John Humphries Minority Scholarship
900 Jackson Street, Suite 150
Dallas, TX 75202
Phone: 214-741-9898
Fax: 214-741-9848
E-mail: cmcnally@dallasfoundation.org

DANIELS FUND http://www.danielsfund.org

DANIELS SCHOLARSHIPS

Scholarship to graduating high school seniors from Colorado, New Mexico, Utah, and Wyoming for use at any two- or four-year accredited college or university in the United States. Must intend to complete bachelor's degree. Students entering dual-degree programs allowing them to earn their undergraduate and graduate degrees in five years are also eligible.

Award: Scholarship for use in freshman year; not renewable. *Number:* 250. *Amount:* varies.

Eligibility Requirements: Applicant must be high school student; planning to enroll or expecting to enroll full-time at a two-year or four-year institution or university and resident of Colorado, New Mexico, Utah, or Wyoming. Available to U.S. citizens.

Application Requirements: Application. *Deadline:* October 1.

Contact: Miguel Lovato, Manager
Daniels Fund
101 Monroe Street
Denver, CO 80206
Phone: 303-393-7220
Fax: 303-393-7339
E-mail: contact@danielsfund.org

DAVIS-ROBERTS SCHOLARSHIP FUND INC.

DAVIS-ROBERTS SCHOLARSHIPS

• *See page 530*

DAYTON FOUNDATION http://www.daytonfoundation.org

BRIGHTWELL FAMILY MEMORIAL SCHOLARSHIP

• *See page 595*

DAYTON SUPERIOR CORPORATION SCHOLARSHIP

$2500 award for Ohio resident who is the child of a full-time, regular employee of Dayton Superior Corporation, its affiliates or subsidiaries. Available to freshman only.

Award: Scholarship for use in freshman year; not renewable. *Number:* up to 6. *Amount:* up to $2500.

Eligibility Requirements: Applicant must be high school student; planning to enroll or expecting to enroll full-time at a four-year institution or university and resident of Ohio. Available to U.S. citizens.

Application Requirements: Application, financial need analysis, transcript. *Deadline:* March 14.

Contact: Douglas Good, Scholarship Coordinator
Dayton Foundation
721 Richard Street
Miamisburg, OH 45342
Phone: 937-866-0711 Ext. 260
E-mail: douggood@daytonsuperior.com

DELAWARE HIGHER EDUCATION COMMISSION http://www.doe.k12.de.us

AGENDA FOR DELAWARE WOMEN TRAILBLAZER SCHOLARSHIP

• *See page 595*

DIAMOND STATE SCHOLARSHIP

Award for legal residents of Delaware who are U.S. citizens or eligible non-citizens. Must be enrolled as a full-time student in a degree program at a nonprofit, regionally accredited institution. Minimum 3.0 GPA required. High school seniors should rank in upper quarter of class and have a combined score of at least 1800 on the SAT.

Award: Scholarship for use in freshman year; renewable. *Number:* 50. *Amount:* $1250.

Eligibility Requirements: Applicant must be high school student; planning to enroll or expecting to enroll full-time at a four-year institution or university and resident of Delaware. Applicant must have 3.0 GPA or higher. Available to U.S. citizens.

Application Requirements: Application, essay, test scores, transcript. *Deadline:* March 28.

Contact: Carylin Brinkley, Program Administrator
Delaware Higher Education Commission
Carvel State Office Building, 820 North French Street, Fifth Floor
Wilmington, DE 19801-3509
Phone: 302-577-5240
Fax: 302-577-6765
E-mail: cbrinkley@doe.k12.de.us

EDUCATIONAL BENEFITS FOR CHILDREN OF DECEASED VETERANS AND OTHERS AWARD

• *See page 595*

FIRST STATE MANUFACTURED HOUSING ASSOCIATION SCHOLARSHIP

Award for legal residents of Delaware who are high school seniors or former graduates seeking to further their education. Must have been a resident of a manufactured home for at least one year prior to the application. Evaluated on scholastic record, financial need, essay, and recommendations. Award for any type of accredited two- or four-year degree program, or for any accredited training, licensing, or certification program.

Award: Scholarship for use in freshman, sophomore, junior, or senior years; renewable. *Number:* up to 2. *Amount:* up to $2000.

Eligibility Requirements: Applicant must be enrolled or expecting to enroll full- or part-time at a two-year or four-year or technical institution or university and resident of Delaware. Available to U.S. citizens.

Application Requirements: Application, essay, financial need analysis, references, transcript, FAFSA. *Deadline:* March 7.

Contact: Carylin Brinkley, Program Administrator
Delaware Higher Education Commission
Carvel State Office Building, 820 North French Street, Fifth Floor
Wilmington, DE 19801-3509
Phone: 302-577-5240
Fax: 302-577-6765
E-mail: cbrinkley@doe.k12.de.us

GOVERNOR'S WORKFORCE DEVELOPMENT GRANT

Grants for part-time undergraduate students attending Delaware College of Art and Design, Delaware State University, Delaware Technical and Community College, Goldey-Beacom College, University of Delaware, Wesley College, Widener University (Delaware Campus), or Wilmington College. Must be at least 18 years old, a resident of Delaware, and employed by a company in Delaware that contributes to the Blue Collar Training Fund Program.

Award: Grant for use in freshman, sophomore, junior, or senior years; renewable. *Number:* 40. *Amount:* $2000.

Eligibility Requirements: Applicant must be age 18 and over; enrolled or expecting to enroll full- or part-time at a two-year or four-year institution or university; resident of Delaware and studying in Delaware. Available to U.S. and non-U.S. citizens.

Application Requirements: Application. *Deadline:* varies.

Contact: Carylin Brinkley, Program Administrator
Delaware Higher Education Commission
Carvel State Office Building, 820 North French Street, Fifth Floor
Wilmington, DE 19801-3509
Phone: 302-577-5240
Fax: 302-577-6765
E-mail: cbrinkley@doe.k12.de.us

LEGISLATIVE ESSAY SCHOLARSHIP

Award for legal residents of Delaware who are U.S. citizens or eligible non-citizens. Must be high school seniors in public or private schools or in home school programs who plans to enroll full-time at a nonprofit, regionally accredited college. Must submit an essay on topic: "Pluribus Unum: Is this motto adopted in 1782 relevant to our country today?".

Award: Prize for use in freshman year; not renewable. *Number:* up to 62. *Amount:* $1000–$10,000.

Eligibility Requirements: Applicant must be high school student; planning to enroll or expecting to enroll full- or part-time at a two-year or four-year or technical institution or university and resident of Delaware. Available to U.S. citizens.

Application Requirements: Application, applicant must enter a contest, essay. *Deadline:* November 30.

Contact: Carylin Brinkley, Program Administrator
Delaware Higher Education Commission
Carvel State Office Building, 820 North French Street, Fifth Floor
Wilmington, DE 19801-3509
Phone: 302-577-5240
Fax: 302-577-6765
E-mail: cbrinkley@doe.k12.de.us

ROBERT C. BYRD HONORS SCHOLARSHIP-DELAWARE

Award for legal residents of Delaware who are U.S. citizens or eligible non-citizens. For high school seniors who rank in upper quarter of class or GED recipients with a minimum score of 300 and a combined score of at least 1800 on the SAT. Minimum 3.5 GPA required. Must be enrolled at least half-time at a nonprofit, regionally accredited institution.

Award: Scholarship for use in freshman year; renewable. *Number:* 20. *Amount:* $1500.

Eligibility Requirements: Applicant must be high school student; planning to enroll or expecting to enroll full-time at a two-year or four-year institution or university and resident of Delaware. Applicant must have 3.5 GPA or higher. Available to U.S. citizens.

Application Requirements: Application, essay, test scores, transcript. *Deadline:* March 28.

Contact: Carylin Brinkley, Program Administrator
Delaware Higher Education Commission
Carvel State Office Building, 820 North French Street, Fifth Floor
Wilmington, DE 19801-3509
Phone: 302-577-5240
Fax: 302-577-6765
E-mail: cbrinkley@doe.k12.de.us

SCHOLARSHIP INCENTIVE PROGRAM-DELAWARE

Award for legal residents of Delaware who are U.S. citizens or eligible non-citizens. Must demonstrate substantial financial need and enroll full-time in an undergraduate degree program at a nonprofit, regionally accredited institution in Delaware or Pennsylvania. Minimum 2.5 GPA required.

Award: Grant for use in freshman, sophomore, junior, senior, or graduate years; not renewable. *Number:* 1000–1300. *Amount:* $700–$2200.

Eligibility Requirements: Applicant must be enrolled or expecting to enroll full-time at a two-year or four-year institution or university; resident of Delaware and studying in Delaware or Pennsylvania. Applicant must have 2.5 GPA or higher. Available to U.S. citizens.

Application Requirements: Application, financial need analysis, transcript, FAFSA. *Deadline:* April 15.

Contact: Carylin Brinkley, Program Administrator
Delaware Higher Education Commission
Carvel State Office Building, 820 North French Street, Fifth Floor
Wilmington, DE 19801-3509
Phone: 302-577-5240
Fax: 302-577-6765
E-mail: cbrinkley@doe.k12.de.us

DELAWARE NATIONAL GUARD http://www.delawarenationalguard.com

STATE TUITION ASSISTANCE

• *See page 633*

DEMOCRATIC WOMEN'S CLUB OF FLORIDA INC. http://www.democratic-women.org

DEMOCRATIC WOMEN'S CLUB OF FLORIDA SCHOLARSHIP

Scholarship to high school seniors attending schools in Florida. Award value is $1000. Minimum 3.0 GPA required.

Award: Scholarship for use in freshman year; not renewable. *Number:* 1. *Amount:* $1000.

Eligibility Requirements: Applicant must be high school student; age 18 and over; planning to enroll or expecting to enroll full-time at a four-year

Democratic Women's Club of Florida Inc. (continued)

institution or university; resident of Florida and studying in Florida. Applicant must have 3.0 GPA or higher. Available to U.S. citizens.

Application Requirements: Application, essay, financial need analysis, references, transcript, copy of voter registration card. *Deadline:* varies.

Contact: Janie Holman, President
Democratic Women's Club of Florida Inc.
117 NE Surfside Avenue
Port St. Lucie, FL 34983
Phone: 321-639-4717
E-mail: president@democratic-women.org

DENVER FOUNDATION http://www.denverfoundation.org

REISHER FAMILY SCHOLARSHIP FUND

Scholarships awarded to Colorado residents who attend Metropolitan State College, the University of Northern Colorado, and the University of Colorado at Denver. Sophomores or transferring juniors who do not have sufficient funding to otherwise complete their degrees are eligible to apply. Must have at least a 3.0 GPA.

Award: Scholarship for use in sophomore or junior years; not renewable. *Number:* varies. *Amount:* varies.

Eligibility Requirements: Applicant must be enrolled or expecting to enroll full-time at a four-year institution or university; resident of Colorado and studying in Colorado. Applicant must have 3.0 GPA or higher. Available to U.S. citizens.

Application Requirements: Application. *Deadline:* varies.

Contact: Karla Bieniulis, Scholarship Committee
Denver Foundation
55 Madison Street, Eighth Floor
Denver, CO 80206
Phone: 303-300-1790 Ext. 103
Fax: 303-300-6547
E-mail: info@denverfoundation.org

DENVER HISPANIC CHAMBER OF COMMERCE EDUCATION FOUNDATION http://www.dhcc.com/default.asp

HISPANIC YOUTH SCHOLARSHIP PROGRAM

• *See page 596*

DEVRY INC. http://www.devry.edu

DEVRY HIGH SCHOOL COMMUNITY SCHOLARS AWARD

Award to high school graduates. Amount of $1000 per semester to students, valued up to $9000. Must be in top 50 percent of class or have a GPA of 2.7. Nominations must be received by July 1 and students have one year from high school graduation to apply and start.

Award: Scholarship for use in freshman year; renewable. *Number:* varies. *Amount:* $2000–$9000.

Eligibility Requirements: Applicant must be high school student; planning to enroll or expecting to enroll full-time at an institution or university and studying in Ohio or Pennsylvania. Applicant must have 2.5 GPA or higher. Available to U.S. and Canadian citizens.

Application Requirements: Application, interview, references, test scores, transcript. *Deadline:* July 1.

Contact: Thonie Simpson, National High School Program Manager
DeVry Inc.
One Tower Lane
Oak Brook Terrace, IL 60181-4624
Phone: 630-706-3122
Fax: 630-574-1696
E-mail: scholarships@devry.edu

DISTRICT OF COLUMBIA PUBLIC SCHOOLS http://www.k12.dc.us

ROBERT C. BYRD HONORS SCHOLARSHIP-DISTRICT OF COLUMBIA

Federally funded, state administered program to recognize exceptionally able high school seniors who show promise of continued excellence in postsecondary education. Must be a U.S. citizen and permanent resident of District of Columbia and be accepted at an accredited institution of higher education in the United States. Minimum 3.2 GPA required. Must be school's nominee. Renewable based on maintenance of satisfactory academic standing.

Award: Scholarship for use in freshman year; renewable. *Number:* 10. *Amount:* $1500.

Eligibility Requirements: Applicant must be high school student; planning to enroll or expecting to enroll full-time at a four-year institution or university and resident of District of Columbia. Available to U.S. citizens.

Application Requirements: Application, interview, test scores, transcript, 250-word essay on life goals, nominee form. *Deadline:* March 30.

Contact: Claudia Nichols, Director of Student Affairs
District of Columbia Public Schools
825 North Capitol Street, NE, Sixth Floor
Washington, DC 20002
Phone: 202-442-5110
Fax: 202-442-5094
E-mail: claudia.nichols@dc.gov

DISTRICT OF COLUMBIA STATE EDUCATION OFFICE http://www.osse.dc.gov

DC LEVERAGING EDUCATIONAL ASSISTANCE PARTNERSHIP PROGRAM (LEAP)

$250 to $1500 grant available to District of Columbia residents enrolled in undergraduate program. Must attend an eligible college at least half-time.

Award: Grant for use in freshman, sophomore, junior, or senior years; renewable. *Number:* 2274–2300. *Amount:* $250–$1500.

Eligibility Requirements: Applicant must be enrolled or expecting to enroll full- or part-time at a two-year or four-year or technical institution or university and resident of District of Columbia. Available to U.S. citizens.

Application Requirements: Application, financial need analysis, transcript, Student Aid Report (SAR), FAFSA. *Deadline:* June 30.

Contact: Mr. Deborah Gist, Superintendent
District of Columbia State Education Office
51 N Street NE, 7th Floor
Washington, DC 20002
Phone: 202-727-3471
Fax: 202-727-2019
E-mail: deborah.gist@dc.gov

DC TUITION ASSISTANCE GRANT PROGRAM

Grant pays the difference between in-state and out-of-state tuition and fees at any public college or university in the United States up to $10,000 per year. It also pays up to $2500 per year of tuition and fees at private colleges and universities in the Washington metropolitan area, and at historically black colleges and universities throughout the United States. Students must be enrolled in a degree-granting program at an eligible institution, and live in the District of Columbia.

Award: Grant for use in freshman, sophomore, junior, or senior years; renewable. *Number:* up to 7000. *Amount:* $2500–$10,000.

Eligibility Requirements: Applicant must be age 24 or under; enrolled or expecting to enroll full- or part-time at a two-year or four-year or technical institution or university and resident of District of Columbia. Available to U.S. citizens.

Application Requirements: Application, transcript, Student Aid Report (SAR), current utility bill, D-40 tax return. *Deadline:* June 30.

Contact: Mr. Deborah Gist, Superintendent
District of Columbia State Education Office
51 N Street NE, 7th Floor
Washington, DC 20002
Phone: 202-727-3471
Fax: 202-727-2019
E-mail: deborah.gist@dc.gov

DISTRICT OF COLUMBIA ADOPTION SCHOLARSHIP

Grant designed for adopted individuals who are wards of the District, lost their parents in the September 11 event. Applicants must show proof of adoption, current postsecondary enrollment status, and social security number. Must be U.S. citizen. Grant value is up to $10,000.

Award: Grant for use in freshman, sophomore, junior, or senior years; not renewable. *Number:* varies. *Amount:* up to $10,000.

Eligibility Requirements: Applicant must be age 24 or under; enrolled or expecting to enroll full-time at a two-year or four-year or technical institution or university and resident of District of Columbia. Available to U.S. citizens.

Application Requirements: Application, proof of adoption, enrollment verification. *Deadline:* June 30.

Contact: Mr. Deborah Gist, Superintendent
District of Columbia State Education Office
51 N Street NE, 7th Floor
Washington, DC 20002
Phone: 202-727-3471
Fax: 202-727-2019
E-mail: deborah.gist@dc.gov

DIXIE BOYS BASEBALL http://www.dixie.org

DIXIE BOYS BASEBALL SCHOLARSHIP PROGRAM

Eleven scholarships are presented annually to deserving high school seniors who have participated in the Dixie Boys Baseball Program. Citizenship, scholarship, residency in a state with Dixie Baseball Programs and financial need are considered in determining the awards.

Award: Scholarship for use in freshman year; not renewable. *Number:* 11. *Amount:* $1500.

Eligibility Requirements: Applicant must be high school student; planning to enroll or expecting to enroll full-time at a two-year or four-year institution or university; male; resident of Alabama, Arkansas, Florida, Georgia, Louisiana, Mississippi, North Carolina, South Carolina, Tennessee, Texas, or Virginia and must have an interest in athletics/sports. Available to U.S. citizens.

Application Requirements: Application, financial need analysis, photo, references. *Deadline:* April 1.

Contact: James Sandy Jones, Commissioner
Dixie Boys Baseball
PO Box 877
Marshall, TX 75671
Phone: 334-793-3331

DIXIE YOUTH SCHOLARSHIP PROGRAM

Scholarships are presented annually to deserving high school seniors who participated in the Dixie Youth Baseball program while age 12 and under. Financial need is considered. Scholarship value is $2000.

Award: Scholarship for use in freshman year; not renewable. *Number:* up to 70. *Amount:* $2000.

Eligibility Requirements: Applicant must be high school student; planning to enroll or expecting to enroll full-time at a two-year or four-year or technical institution or university; resident of Alabama, Arkansas, Florida, Georgia, Louisiana, Mississippi, North Carolina, South Carolina, Tennessee, Texas, or Virginia and must have an interest in athletics/sports. Available to U.S. citizens.

Application Requirements: Application, essay, financial need analysis, photo, references, transcript, 1040 form. *Deadline:* March 1.

Contact: Scholarship Chairman
Dixie Boys Baseball
PO Box 877
Marshall, TX 75671-0877
E-mail: dyb@dixie.org

DOC HURLEY SCHOLARSHIP FOUNDATION INC. http://www.docscholar.org

DOC HURLEY SCHOLARSHIP

Scholarship of $2000 to $10,000 awarded for graduating senior from eligible Greater Hartford area high school. Number of awards varies.

Award: Scholarship for use in freshman year; not renewable. *Number:* varies. *Amount:* $2000–$10,000.

Eligibility Requirements: Applicant must be high school student; planning to enroll or expecting to enroll full-time at a four-year institution or university and resident of Connecticut. Available to U.S. citizens.

Application Requirements: Application, essay, financial need analysis, references, test scores, transcript, Student Aid Report (SAR). *Deadline:* March 21.

Contact: Scholarship Committee
Doc Hurley Scholarship Foundation Inc.
103 Woodland Street
Hartford, CT 06105
Phone: 860-549-5012
Fax: 860-549-5955
E-mail: dhsf@docscholar.org

DON'T MESS WITH TEXAS http://www.dontmesswithtexas.org

DON'T MESS WITH TEXAS SCHOLARSHIP PROGRAM

Scholarship for Texas graduating high school seniors who plan to attend accredited two- or four-year colleges or public or private universities in Texas.

Award: Scholarship for use in freshman year; not renewable. *Number:* 2–3. *Amount:* $1000–$3000.

Eligibility Requirements: Applicant must be high school student; planning to enroll or expecting to enroll full- or part-time at a two-year or four-year institution or university; resident of Texas and studying in Texas. Available to U.S. and non-U.S. citizens.

Application Requirements: Application, essay, references. *Deadline:* April 4.

Contact: Michael Roberts, Scholarship Committee
Don't Mess With Texas
1717 West Sixth Street, Suite 400
Austin, TX 78703
Phone: 512-476-4368
Fax: 512-476-4392
E-mail: scholarship@dontmesswithtexas.org

EAST BAY FOOTBALL OFFICIALS ASSOCIATION http://www.ebfoa.org

EAST BAY FOOTBALL OFFICIALS ASSOCIATION COLLEGE SCHOLARSHIP

Scholarship for high school seniors who currently participate in one of the football programs served by the East Bay Football Officials Association. Must be a resident of California, achieve at least a 3.0 GPA and have plans to attend any accredited two or four-year institution.

Award: Scholarship for use in freshman year; renewable. *Number:* 3–4. *Amount:* up to $1000.

Eligibility Requirements: Applicant must be high school student; planning to enroll or expecting to enroll full-time at a two-year or four-year institution or university; resident of California and must have an interest in athletics/sports. Applicant must have 3.0 GPA or higher. Available to U.S. citizens.

Application Requirements: Application, essay, references, transcript. *Deadline:* October 31.

Contact: Sam Moriana, Program Coordinator
East Bay Football Officials Association
21 Chatham Pointe
Alameda, CA 94502
Phone: 510-521-4121
E-mail: smoriana@comcast.net

EAST LOS ANGELES COMMUNITY UNION (TELACU) EDUCATION FOUNDATION http://www.telacu.com

LINC TELACU SCHOLARSHIP PROGRAM

• *See page 596*

EDMONTON COMMUNITY FOUNDATION http://www.DollarsForLearners.com

BELCOURT BROSSEAU METIS AWARDS

• *See page 681*

CHARMAINE LETOURNEAU SCHOLARSHIP

• *See page 618*

Edmonton Community Foundation (continued)

YOUTH FORMERLY IN CARE BURSARY

• *See page 681*

EDMUND F. MAXWELL FOUNDATION http://www.maxwell.org

EDMUND F. MAXWELL FOUNDATION SCHOLARSHIP

Scholarships awarded to residents of Western Washington to attend accredited independent colleges or universities. Awards up to $5000 per year based on need, merit, citizenship, and activities. Renewable for up to four years if academic progress is suitable and financial need is unchanged.

Award: Scholarship for use in freshman year; renewable. *Number:* 110. *Amount:* up to $5000.

Eligibility Requirements: Applicant must be enrolled or expecting to enroll full-time at a four-year institution or university and resident of Washington. Available to U.S. and non-U.S. citizens.

Application Requirements: Application, essay, financial need analysis, test scores, transcript, employment history. *Deadline:* April 30.

Contact: Jane Thomas, Administrator
Edmund F. Maxwell Foundation
PO Box 22537
Seattle, WA 98122
Phone: 206-303-4402
Fax: 206-303-4419
E-mail: admin@maxwell.org

ENLISTED ASSOCIATION OF THE NATIONAL GUARD OF NEW JERSEY http://www.eang-nj.org

CSM VINCENT BALDASSARI MEMORIAL SCHOLARSHIP PROGRAM

• *See page 634*

EPILEPSY FOUNDATION OF IDAHO http://www.epilepsyidaho.org

GREGORY W. GILE MEMORIAL SCHOLARSHIP PROGRAM

• *See page 618*

MARK MUSIC MEMORIAL SCHOLARSHIP

• *See page 618*

ESSAYJOLT.COM http://www.essayjolt.com

ESSAYJOLT SCHOLARSHIP

Essay contest open to high school juniors and seniors who may be citizens of any country, but must live in New Jersey. Essays are judged on originality, insight, and quality of writing by an independent panel of writers and editors. Only one winner is selected. See Web site for current essay question and guidelines: http://www.essayjolt.com.

Award: Prize for use in freshman year; not renewable. *Number:* 1. *Amount:* $500.

Eligibility Requirements: Applicant must be high school student; planning to enroll or expecting to enroll full- or part-time at a two-year or four-year or technical institution or university; resident of New Jersey and must have an interest in writing. Available to U.S. and non-U.S. citizens.

Application Requirements: Applicant must enter a contest, essay. *Deadline:* varies.

Contact: Meg Hartmann, Director
EssayJolt.com
1308 Centennial Avenue, Suite 243
Piscataway, NJ 08854
Phone: 917-575-3165
E-mail: scholarship@essayjolt.com

EVERLY SCHOLARSHIP FUND INC.

EVERLY SCHOLARSHIP

Renewable award for undergraduates attending an accredited institution full-time. Must be New Jersey residents. Minimum 3.0 GPA required and minimum SAT score of 1100.

Award: Scholarship for use in senior year; renewable. *Number:* varies. *Amount:* $2500.

Eligibility Requirements: Applicant must be enrolled or expecting to enroll full-time at a four-year institution or university and resident of New Jersey. Applicant must have 3.0 GPA or higher. Available to U.S. citizens.

Application Requirements: Application, autobiography, essay, financial need analysis, interview, references, test scores, transcript. *Deadline:* May 1.

Contact: John R. Lolio, Jr., President
Everly Scholarship Fund Inc.
4300 Haddonfield Road, Suite 311
Pennsauken, NJ 08109
Phone: 856-661-2094
Fax: 856-662-0165
E-mail: jlolio@sskrplaw.com

FINANCE AUTHORITY OF MAINE http://www.famemaine.com

ROBERT C. BYRD HONORS SCHOLARSHIP-MAINE

Merit-based, renewable scholarship of up to $1500 annually for graduating high school seniors. Must have a minimum of 3.0 GPA. Must be a resident of Maine. Superior academic performance is the primary criterion. For application, see Web site: http://www.famemaine.com.

Award: Scholarship for use in freshman year; renewable. *Number:* up to 30. *Amount:* up to $1500.

Eligibility Requirements: Applicant must be high school student; planning to enroll or expecting to enroll full-time at a two-year or four-year or technical institution or university and resident of Maine. Applicant must have 3.0 GPA or higher. Available to U.S. citizens.

Application Requirements: Application, essay, transcript, high school profile. *Deadline:* May 1.

Contact: Lisa Bongiovanni, Manager, Operations
Finance Authority of Maine
Five Community Drive
PO Box 949
Augusta, ME 04332-0949
Phone: 207-623-3263
Fax: 207-623-0095
E-mail: education@famemaine.com

STATE OF MAINE GRANT PROGRAM

Scholarship for residents of Maine, attending an eligible school in Connecticut, Maine, Massachusetts, New Hampshire, Pennsylvania, Rhode Island, Washington, D.C., or Vermont. Award based on need. Must apply annually. Complete free application for Federal Student Aid to apply. One-time award of $600 to $1450 for undergraduate study. For further information see Web site: http://www.famemaine.com.

Award: Grant for use in freshman, sophomore, junior, or senior years; not renewable. *Number:* up to 13,000. *Amount:* $600–$1450.

Eligibility Requirements: Applicant must be enrolled or expecting to enroll full- or part-time at a two-year or four-year or technical institution or university; resident of Maine and studying in Connecticut, District of Columbia, Maine, Massachusetts, New Hampshire, Pennsylvania, Rhode Island, or Vermont. Available to U.S. citizens.

Application Requirements: Application, financial need analysis, FAFSA. *Deadline:* May 1.

Contact: Lisa Bongiovanni, Manager, Operations
Finance Authority of Maine
Five Community Drive
PO Box 949
Augusta, ME 04332-0949
Phone: 207-623-3263
Fax: 207-623-0095
E-mail: education@famemaine.com

TUITION WAIVER PROGRAMS

• *See page 597*

FLORIDA ASSOCIATION FOR MEDIA IN EDUCATION http://www.floridamedia.org

INTELLECTUAL FREEDOM STUDENT SCHOLARSHIP

Scholarship in the amount of $1000 is awarded annually to a graduating senior from a high school in Florida. Only students whose library media specialists are members of FAME are eligible. Essays written by senior students will be submitted to the FAME Intellectual Freedom Committee.

Award: Scholarship for use in freshman year; not renewable. *Number:* 1. *Amount:* $1000.

Eligibility Requirements: Applicant must be high school student; planning to enroll or expecting to enroll full-time at a two-year or four-year or technical institution or university and resident of Florida. Available to U.S. citizens.

Application Requirements: Application, essay. *Deadline:* March 15.

Contact: Larry Bodkin, Executive Director
Florida Association for Media in Education
2563 Capital Medical Boulevard
Tallahassee, FL 32308
Phone: 850-531-8350
Fax: 850-531-8344
E-mail: lbodkin@floridamedia.org

FLORIDA ASSOCIATION OF POSTSECONDARY SCHOOLS AND COLLEGES http://www.FAPSC.org

FLORIDA ASSOCIATION OF POST-SECONDARY SCHOOLS AND COLLEGES SCHOLARSHIP PROGRAM

Awards full and partial scholarship to students either graduating from high school or receiving GED in the current school year from private career schools in Florida. Must be a resident of Florida. Minimum 2.0 GPA required.

Award: Scholarship for use in freshman year; not renewable. *Number:* 225–600. *Amount:* $1000–$5000.

Eligibility Requirements: Applicant must be high school student; planning to enroll or expecting to enroll full-time at a two-year or four-year or technical institution or university; resident of Florida and studying in Florida. Available to U.S. citizens.

Application Requirements: Application, essay, references, transcript. *Deadline:* March 7.

Contact: Wanda Taylor, Deputy Executive Director of Membership Services
Florida Association of Postsecondary Schools and Colleges
150 South Monroe Street, Suite 303
Tallahassee, FL 32301
Phone: 850-577-3139
Fax: 850-577-3133
E-mail: scholarship@fapsc.org

FLORIDA DEPARTMENT OF EDUCATION http://www.floridastudentfinancialaid.org

ACCESS TO BETTER LEARNING AND EDUCATION GRANT

Grant program provides tuition assistance to Florida undergraduate students enrolled in degree programs at eligible private Florida colleges or universities. Must be U.S. citizen or eligible non-citizen and must meet Florida residency requirements. Participating institution determines application procedures, deadlines, and student eligibility.

Award: Grant for use in freshman, sophomore, junior, or senior years; renewable. *Number:* varies. *Amount:* varies.

Eligibility Requirements: Applicant must be enrolled or expecting to enroll full-time at a four-year institution or university; resident of Florida and studying in Florida. Available to U.S. citizens.

Application Requirements: Application. *Deadline:* varies.

Contact: Theresa Antworth, Director State Scholarships and Grants
Florida Department of Education
Office of Student Financial Assistance, 1940 North Monroe Street, Suite 70
Tallahassee, FL 32303-4759
Phone: 850-410-5185
Fax: 850-487-6244
E-mail: theresa.antworth@fldoe.org

ETHICS IN BUSINESS SCHOLARSHIP

Scholarship program provides assistance to undergraduate college students, who enroll at community colleges and eligible independent postsecondary educational institutions. Scholarships are funded by private and state contributions. Awards are dependent on private, matching funds.

Award: Scholarship for use in freshman, sophomore, junior, or senior years; not renewable. *Number:* varies. *Amount:* varies.

Eligibility Requirements: Applicant must be enrolled or expecting to enroll full-time at a two-year or four-year institution or university and studying in Florida. Available to U.S. citizens.

Application Requirements: Application. *Deadline:* varies.

Contact: Theresa Antworth, Director State Scholarships and Grants
Florida Department of Education
Office of Student Financial Assistance, 1940 North Monroe Street, Suite 70
Tallahassee, FL 32303-4759
Phone: 850-410-5185
Fax: 850-487-6244
E-mail: theresa.antworth@fldoe.org

FIRST GENERATION MATCHING GRANT PROGRAM

Need-based grants to Florida resident undergraduate students who are enrolled in state universities in Florida and whose parents have not earned baccalaureate degrees. Available state funds are contingent upon matching contributions from private sources on a dollar-for-dollar basis.

Award: Grant for use in freshman, sophomore, junior, or senior years; renewable. *Number:* varies. *Amount:* varies.

Eligibility Requirements: Applicant must be enrolled or expecting to enroll full- or part-time at an institution or university; resident of Florida and studying in Florida. Available to U.S. citizens.

Application Requirements: Application, financial need analysis. *Deadline:* varies.

Contact: Theresa Antworth, Director State Scholarships and Grants
Florida Department of Education
Office of Student Financial Assistance, 1940 North Monroe Street, Suite 70
Tallahassee, FL 32303-4759
Phone: 850-410-5185
Fax: 850-487-6244
E-mail: theresa.antworth@fldoe.org

FLORIDA POSTSECONDARY STUDENT ASSISTANCE GRANT

Scholarships to degree-seeking, resident, undergraduate students who demonstrate substantial financial need and are enrolled in eligible degree-granting private colleges and universities not eligible under the Florida Private Student Assistance Grant. FSAG is a decentralized program, and each participating institution determines application procedures, deadlines, student eligibility. Number of awards varies.

Award: Grant for use in freshman, sophomore, junior, or senior years; renewable. *Number:* varies. *Amount:* $200–$1808.

Eligibility Requirements: Applicant must be enrolled or expecting to enroll full-time at a two-year or four-year institution or university; resident of Florida and studying in Florida. Available to U.S. citizens.

Application Requirements: Application, financial need analysis. *Deadline:* varies.

Contact: Theresa Antworth, Director State Scholarships and Grants
Florida Department of Education
Office of Student Financial Assistance, 1940 North Monroe Street, Suite 70
Tallahassee, FL 32303-4759
Phone: 850-410-5185
Fax: 850-487-6244
E-mail: theresa.antworth@fldoe.org

FLORIDA PRIVATE STUDENT ASSISTANCE GRANT

Grants for Florida residents who are U.S. citizens or eligible non-citizens attending eligible private, nonprofit, four-year colleges and universities in Florida. Must be a full-time student and demonstrate substantial financial need. For renewal, must have earned a minimum cumulative GPA of 2.0 at the last institution attended.

Award: Grant for use in freshman, sophomore, junior, or senior years; renewable. *Number:* varies. *Amount:* $200.

Eligibility Requirements: Applicant must be enrolled or expecting to enroll full-time at a four-year institution or university; resident of Florida and studying in Florida. Available to U.S. citizens.

Florida Department of Education (continued)

Application Requirements: Application, financial need analysis. *Deadline:* varies.

Contact: Theresa Antworth, Director State Scholarships and Grants
Florida Department of Education
Office of Student Financial Assistance, 1940 North Monroe Street, Suite 70
Tallahassee, FL 32303-4759
Phone: 850-410-5185
Fax: 850-487-6244
E-mail: theresa.antworth@fldoe.org

FLORIDA PUBLIC STUDENT ASSISTANCE GRANT

Grants for Florida residents, U.S. citizens or eligible non-citizens who attend state universities and public community colleges. For renewal, must have earned a minimum cumulative GPA of 2.0 at the last institution attended. Students with documented disabilities are able to qualify for part-time status.

Award: Grant for use in freshman, sophomore, junior, or senior years; renewable. *Number:* varies. *Amount:* $200.

Eligibility Requirements: Applicant must be enrolled or expecting to enroll full- or part-time at a two-year or four-year institution or university; resident of Florida and studying in Florida. Available to U.S. citizens.

Application Requirements: Application, financial need analysis. *Deadline:* varies.

Contact: Theresa Antworth, Director State Scholarships and Grants
Florida Department of Education
Office of Student Financial Assistance, 1940 North Monroe Street, Suite 70
Tallahassee, FL 32303-4759
Phone: 850-410-5185
Fax: 850-487-6244
E-mail: theresa.antworth@fldoe.org

FLORIDA WORK EXPERIENCE PROGRAM

Need-based program providing eligible Florida students work experiences that will complement and reinforce their educational and career goals. Must maintain GPA of 2.0. Postsecondary institution will determine applicant's eligibility, number of hours to be worked per week, and the award amount.

Award: Grant for use in freshman, sophomore, junior, or senior years; renewable. *Number:* varies. *Amount:* varies.

Eligibility Requirements: Applicant must be enrolled or expecting to enroll full- or part-time at a two-year or four-year institution or university; resident of Florida and studying in Florida. Available to U.S. citizens.

Application Requirements: Application, financial need analysis. *Deadline:* varies.

Contact: Elizabeth Farney, Scholarship Committee
Florida Department of Education
150 W University Boulevard
Melbourne, FL 32901

JOSE MARTI SCHOLARSHIP CHALLENGE GRANT FUND

• *See page 682*

MARY MCLEOD BETHUNE SCHOLARSHIP

Renewable award to Florida students with a GPA of 3.0 or above, who will attend Bethune-Cookman College, Edward Waters College, Florida A&M University, or Florida Memorial University. Must not have previously received a baccalaureate degree. Must demonstrate financial need as specified by the institution.

Award: Scholarship for use in freshman, sophomore, junior, or senior years; renewable. *Number:* varies. *Amount:* $3000.

Eligibility Requirements: Applicant must be enrolled or expecting to enroll full-time at a two-year or four-year institution or university; resident of Florida and studying in Florida. Applicant must have 3.0 GPA or higher. Available to U.S. citizens.

Application Requirements: Application, financial need analysis. *Deadline:* October 5.

Contact: Theresa Antworth, Director State Scholarships and Grants
Florida Department of Education
Office of Student Financial Assistance, 1940 North Monroe Street, Suite 70
Tallahassee, FL 32303-4759
Phone: 850-410-5185
Fax: 850-487-6244
E-mail: theresa.antworth@fldoe.org

ROBERT C. BYRD HONORS SCHOLARSHIP-FLORIDA

One applicant per high school may be nominated by the Florida high school principal or designee by May 15. Must be U.S. citizen or eligible non-citizen and Florida resident. Application must be submitted in the same year as graduation. Must meet selective service system registration requirements. May attend any postsecondary accredited institution.

Award: Scholarship for use in freshman, sophomore, junior, or senior years; renewable. *Number:* 1400. *Amount:* $1500.

Eligibility Requirements: Applicant must be high school student; planning to enroll or expecting to enroll full-time at a technical institution and resident of Florida. Available to U.S. citizens.

Application Requirements: Application, references, test scores, transcript. *Deadline:* April 15.

Contact: Theresa Antworth, Director State Scholarships and Grants
Florida Department of Education
Office of Student Financial Assistance, 1940 North Monroe Street, Suite 70
Tallahassee, FL 32303-4759
Phone: 850-410-5185
Fax: 850-487-6244
E-mail: theresa.antworth@fldoe.org

ROSEWOOD FAMILY SCHOLARSHIP FUND

• *See page 682*

SCHOLARSHIPS FOR CHILDREN & SPOUSES OF DECEASED OR DISABLED VETERANS OR SERVICEMEMBERS

• *See page 653*

WILLIAM L. BOYD IV FLORIDA RESIDENT ACCESS GRANT

Renewable awards to Florida undergraduate students attending an eligible private, nonprofit Florida college or university. Postsecondary institution will determine applicant's eligibility. Renewal applicant must have earned a minimum institutional GPA of 2.0.

Award: Grant for use in freshman, sophomore, junior, or senior years; renewable. *Number:* varies. *Amount:* $3000.

Eligibility Requirements: Applicant must be enrolled or expecting to enroll full-time at a four-year institution or university; resident of Florida and studying in Florida. Available to U.S. citizens.

Application Requirements: Application. *Deadline:* varies.

Contact: Theresa Antworth, Director State Scholarships and Grants
Florida Department of Education
Office of Student Financial Assistance, 1940 North Monroe Street, Suite 70
Tallahassee, FL 32303-4759
Phone: 850-410-5185
Fax: 850-487-6244
E-mail: theresa.antworth@fldoe.org

FLORIDA LAND TITLE ASSOCIATION

http://www.flta.org

JOHN STARR THORNTON JR. MEMORIAL SCHOLARSHIPS

• *See page 533*

MARJORIE S. SCHWARTZ MEMORIAL SCHOLARSHIPS

• *See page 533*

SAM D. MANSFIELD MEMORIAL SCHOLARSHIPS

• *See page 533*

FLORIDA PTA/PTSA http://www.floridapta.org

FLORIDA PTA/PTSA ANNUAL SCHOLARSHIP

Renewable scholarship of $1000 awarded to students enrolled full-time in their undergraduate study. Must maintain minimum 3.0 GPA.

Award: Scholarship for use in freshman, sophomore, junior, or senior years; renewable. *Number:* 2–3. *Amount:* $1000.

Eligibility Requirements: Applicant must be enrolled or expecting to enroll full-time at a four-year institution or university and resident of Florida. Applicant must have 3.0 GPA or higher. Available to U.S. citizens.

Application Requirements: Application, essay, references. *Deadline:* March 1.

Contact: Janice Bailey, Executive Director
Florida PTA/PTSA
1747 Orlando Central Parkway
Orlando, FL 32809
Phone: 407-855-7604
Fax: 407-240-9577
E-mail: janice@floridapta.org

FLORIDA PTA/PTSA COMMUNITY/JUNIOR COLLEGE SCHOLARSHIP

One time award of $1000 to high school students who enrolled in in a community or junior college. Must be a resident of Florida for at least 2 years. Must be a U.S. citizen and have at least a two-year attendance in a Florida PTA / PTSA high school. Minimum 2.5 GPA or higher.

Award: Scholarship for use in freshman year; not renewable. *Number:* 1–2. *Amount:* $1000.

Eligibility Requirements: Applicant must be enrolled or expecting to enroll full-time at a two-year institution and resident of Florida. Applicant must have 2.5 GPA or higher. Available to U.S. citizens.

Application Requirements: Application, essay, references, proof of enrollment. *Deadline:* March 1.

Contact: Janice Bailey, Executive Director
Florida PTA/PTSA
1747 Orlando Central Parkway
Orlando, FL 32809
Phone: 407-855-7604
Fax: 407-240-9577
E-mail: janice@floridapta.org

FLORIDA PTA/PTSA VOCATIONAL/TECHNICAL SCHOLARSHIP

Scholarship of $1000 is awarded to graduating senior enrolled full time in a vocational/technical institution within the state of Florida. Must have at least a two-year attendance in a Florida PTA/PTSA high school. Minimum GPA is 2.0.

Award: Scholarship for use in freshman year; not renewable. *Number:* 3. *Amount:* $1000.

Eligibility Requirements: Applicant must be high school student; planning to enroll or expecting to enroll full-time at a two-year or technical institution; resident of Florida and studying in Florida. Available to U.S. citizens.

Application Requirements: Application, essay, references, proof of enrollment. *Deadline:* March 1.

Contact: Janice Bailey, Executive Director
Florida PTA/PTSA
1747 Orlando Central Parkway
Orlando, FL 32809
Phone: 407-855-7604
Fax: 407-240-9577
E-mail: janice@floridapta.org

FLORIDA SOCIETY, SONS OF THE AMERICAN REVOLUTION http://www.patriot-web.com/essay

GEORGE S. AND STELLA M. KNIGHT ESSAY CONTEST

Award for the best essay about an event, person, philosophy, or ideal associated with the American Revolution, the Declaration of Independence, or the framing of the U.S. Constitution. Must be a resident of Florida and U.S. citizen or legal resident. State winner may enter the national contest. For more information, see Web site: http://www.patriot-web.com/essay/.

Award: Prize for use in sophomore, junior, or senior years; not renewable. *Number:* 3. *Amount:* $250–$1000.

Eligibility Requirements: Applicant must be enrolled or expecting to enroll full- or part-time at a two-year or four-year or technical institution or university; resident of Florida and must have an interest in writing. Available to U.S. citizens.

Application Requirements: Applicant must enter a contest, essay. *Deadline:* January 31.

Contact: Kevin Yarnell, Scholarship Chairman
Florida Society, Sons of the American Revolution
7507 Summer Bridge Drive
Tampa, FL 33634-2260
Phone: 813-767-0270
E-mail: kayarnell@hotmail.com

FLORIDA WOMEN'S STATE GOLF ASSOCIATION http://www.fwsga.org

FLORIDA WOMEN'S STATE GOLF ASSOCIATION JUNIOR GIRLS' SCHOLARSHIP FUND

The FWSGA Scholarship Fund assists in paying for the education of young women to whom golf is meaningful. Applicants must be Florida residents, play golf, maintain a 3.0 GPA, attend a Florida college or university, and have a need for financial assistance.

Award: Scholarship for use in freshman year; renewable. *Number:* 1. *Amount:* $5000.

Eligibility Requirements: Applicant must be high school student; planning to enroll or expecting to enroll full-time at a two-year or four-year institution or university; female; resident of Florida; studying in Florida and must have an interest in golf. Applicant must have 3.0 GPA or higher. Available to U.S. citizens.

Application Requirements: Application, financial need analysis, interview, references, test scores, transcript. *Deadline:* April 1.

Contact: Kelly Thormahlen, Executive Director
Florida Women's State Golf Association
8875 Hidden River Parkway, Suite 110
Tampa, FL 33637
Phone: 813-864-2130
Fax: 813-864-2129
E-mail: info@fwsga.org

FRANK M. DOYLE FOUNDATION INC. http://www.frankmdoyle.org

FRANK M. DOYLE FOUNDATION SCHOLARSHIP

Scholarships for graduating seniors or graduates (G.E.D. is acceptable) of the Huntington Beach Union High School District, or graduates or students of Huntington Beach Adult High School, or Graduates or current/previous students of the following community colleges in Southern California: Orange Coast, Golden West, Coastline, Irvine Valley, Fullerton, Cypress, Santa Ana, Saddleback, or Santiago Canyon. See Web site for details.

Award: Scholarship for use in freshman, sophomore, junior, or senior years; not renewable. *Number:* varies. *Amount:* varies.

Eligibility Requirements: Applicant must be enrolled or expecting to enroll full- or part-time at a four-year institution or university; resident of California and studying in California. Available to U.S. citizens.

Application Requirements: Application, essay, references, transcript, Student Aid Report (SAR). *Deadline:* March 1.

Contact: Scholarship Committee
Frank M. Doyle Foundation Inc.
3732 Lakeside Drive, Suite 202A
Reno, NV 89509-5238
Phone: 775-329-1972
Fax: 775-329-8917
E-mail: fmdfoundation@aol.com

FRATERNAL ORDER OF POLICE ASSOCIATES OF OHIO INC. http://www.fopaohio.org

FRATERNAL ORDER OF POLICE ASSOCIATES, STATE LODGE OF OHIO INC., SCHOLARSHIP FUND

• *See page 597*

FRESH START SCHOLARSHIP FOUNDATION INC. http://www.wwb.org/freshstart.html

FRESH START SCHOLARSHIP

Scholarship offering a "fresh start" to women who are returning to school after a hiatus of two years to better their life and opportunities. Must be entering an undergraduate program in Delaware.

Award: Scholarship for use in freshman, sophomore, junior, or senior years; not renewable. *Number:* up to 10. *Amount:* $750–$2000.

Eligibility Requirements: Applicant must be age 20 and over; enrolled or expecting to enroll full- or part-time at a two-year or four-year institution or university; female and studying in Delaware. Available to U.S. citizens.

Application Requirements: Application, essay, financial need analysis, references, transcript. *Deadline:* May 30.

Contact: Barbara Buckley, Scholarship Chair
Fresh Start Scholarship Foundation Inc.
PO Box 7784
Wilmington, DE 19803
Phone: 302-656-4411
Fax: 610-347-0438
E-mail: fsscholar@comcast.net

FRIENDS OF 440 SCHOLARSHIP FUND INC. http://www.440scholarship.org

FRIENDS OF 440 SCHOLARSHIP

Scholarships to students who are dependents or descendants of workers who were injured or killed in the course and scope of their employment and who are eligible to receive benefits under the Florida Workers' Compensation system, or are dependents or descendants of those primarily engaged in the administration of the Florida Workers' Compensation Law.

Award: Scholarship for use in freshman, sophomore, junior, or senior years; not renewable. *Number:* 1. *Amount:* up to $6000.

Eligibility Requirements: Applicant must be enrolled or expecting to enroll full- or part-time at a four-year institution or university and resident of Florida. Available to U.S. and non-U.S. citizens.

Application Requirements: Application, transcript, copy of tax return. *Deadline:* December 31.

Contact: Richard Sadow, President
Friends of 440 Scholarship Fund Inc.
80 SW Eighth Street, Suite 1910
Miami, FL 33130
Phone: 305-539-9000
Fax: 305-530-0033

FULFILLMENT FUND http://www.fulfillment.org

BRIGHT FUTURE SCHOLARSHIP

Los Angeles students who participated in the Fulfillment Fund's high school program for two years before graduation are eligible for scholarships awarded to students who excel academically and make significant contributions to their community. Available for both full- and part-time study.

Award: Scholarship for use in freshman, sophomore, junior, or senior years; not renewable. *Number:* varies. *Amount:* $15,000.

Eligibility Requirements: Applicant must be enrolled or expecting to enroll full- or part-time at a four-year institution or university and resident of California. Available to U.S. citizens.

Application Requirements: Application. *Deadline:* varies.

Contact: Darcine Thomas, Community Outreach Manager
Fulfillment Fund
6100 Wilshire Boulevard, Suite 600
Los Angeles, CA 90048
Phone: 323-900-8753

FULFILLMENT FUND POST-SECONDARY SCHOLARSHIPS

Los Angeles students who participated in the Fulfillment Fund's high school program for two years before graduation are eligible for an award of $1000 to $1500. For both full- and part-time study.

Award: Scholarship for use in freshman, sophomore, junior, or senior years; not renewable. *Number:* 1. *Amount:* $1000–$1500.

Eligibility Requirements: Applicant must be enrolled or expecting to enroll full- or part-time at a two-year or four-year institution or university and resident of California. Available to U.S. citizens.

Application Requirements: Application. *Deadline:* varies.

Contact: Darcine Thomas, Community Outreach Manager
Fulfillment Fund
6100 Wilshire Boulevard, Suite 600
Los Angeles, CA 90048
Phone: 323-900-8753

FULFILLMENT FUND SCHOLARSHIPS

Award is for undergraduates. Serving students in seven partner high schools, Fremont, Hamilton, Locke, Los Angeles, Manual Arts, Crenshaw and Wilson. Only students who participated in the Fulfillment Fund High School Program for at least two years are eligible to apply for the scholarship.

Award: Scholarship for use in freshman, sophomore, junior, or senior years; not renewable. *Number:* varies. *Amount:* $1000–$1500.

Eligibility Requirements: Applicant must be enrolled or expecting to enroll full- or part-time at a four-year institution or university and resident of California. Available to U.S. citizens.

Application Requirements: Application. *Deadline:* varies.

Contact: Darcine Thomas, Community Outreach Manager
Fulfillment Fund
6100 Wilshire Boulevard, Suite 600
Los Angeles, CA 90048
Phone: 323-900-8753

JANA WARING GREER SCHOLARSHIP

Los Angeles students who participated in the Fulfillment Fund's high school program for two years before graduation are eligible to apply for scholarship of $15,000 to assist them with tuition, books, supplies and other expenses at a post-secondary institution.

Award: Scholarship for use in freshman, sophomore, junior, or senior years; not renewable. *Number:* varies. *Amount:* $15,000.

Eligibility Requirements: Applicant must be enrolled or expecting to enroll full- or part-time at a four-year institution or university and resident of California. Available to U.S. citizens.

Application Requirements: Application. *Deadline:* varies.

Contact: Darcine Thomas, Community Outreach Manager
Fulfillment Fund
6100 Wilshire Boulevard, Suite 600
Los Angeles, CA 90048
Phone: 323-900-8753

GALLUP ORGANIZATION/CORNHUSKER STATE GAMES http://www.cornhuskerstategames.com

GALLUP CSG SCHOLARSHIP PROGRAM

One-time award for Nebraska students who are participants in the Cornhusker State Games. For use at a Nebraska postsecondary institution.

Award: Scholarship for use in freshman, sophomore, junior, senior, graduate, or postgraduate years; not renewable. *Number:* 5. *Amount:* $1000.

Eligibility Requirements: Applicant must be enrolled or expecting to enroll full- or part-time at a two-year or four-year or technical institution or university; resident of Nebraska and studying in Nebraska. Available to U.S. citizens.

Application Requirements: Application, applicant must enter a contest, essay, transcript. *Deadline:* June 20.

Contact: Tami McLaughlin, Director of Administration
Gallup Organization/Cornhusker State Games
4903 North 57th Street
PO Box 29366
Lincoln, NE 68529
Phone: 402-471-2544
Fax: 402-471-9712
E-mail: info@cornhuskerstategames.com

GENERAL FEDERATION OF WOMEN'S CLUBS OF MASSACHUSETTS http://www.gfwcma.org

GENERAL FEDERATION OF WOMEN'S CLUBS OF MASSACHUSETTS STUDY ABROAD SCHOLARSHIP

Scholarship for undergraduate or graduate students to study abroad. Applicant must submit personal statement and letter of endorsement from the president of the sponsoring General Federation of Women's Clubs of Massachusetts. Must be resident of Massachusetts.

Award: Scholarship for use in freshman, sophomore, junior, senior, or graduate years; not renewable. *Number:* 1. *Amount:* $800.

Eligibility Requirements: Applicant must be enrolled or expecting to enroll full-time at a four-year institution or university and resident of Massachusetts. Available to U.S. citizens.

Application Requirements: Application, essay, interview, references, self-addressed stamped envelope, transcript. *Deadline:* March 1.

Contact: Marta DiBenedetto, Scholarship Chairperson
General Federation of Women's Clubs of Massachusetts
PO Box 679, 245 Dutton Road
Sudbury, MA 01776-0679
Phone: 978-444-9105
E-mail: marta_dibenedetto@nylim.com

GENERAL FEDERATION OF WOMEN'S CLUBS OF VERMONT

BARBARA JEAN BARKER MEMORIAL SCHOLARSHIP FOR A DISPLACED HOMEMAKER

Applicants must be Vermont residents who have been homemakers (primarily) for at least fifteen years and have lost their main means of support through death, divorce, separation, spouse's long-time illness, or spouse's long-time unemployment. Provides one to three scholarships ranging from $500 to $1500.

Award: Grant for use in freshman, sophomore, junior, senior, or graduate years; not renewable. *Number:* 1–3. *Amount:* $500–$1500.

Eligibility Requirements: Applicant must be age 35 and over; enrolled or expecting to enroll full- or part-time at a two-year or four-year or technical institution or university; female and resident of Vermont. Available to U.S. citizens.

Application Requirements: Application, autobiography, financial need analysis, interview, references. *Deadline:* March 15.

Contact: Betty Haggerty, Chairman
General Federation of Women's Clubs of Vermont
16 Taylor Street
Bellows Falls, VT 05101
Phone: 802-463-4159
E-mail: hubett@hotmail.com

GEORGE SNOW SCHOLARSHIP FUND http://snow.accrisoft.com

GEORGE SNOW SCHOLARSHIP FUND/FEMINIST SCHOLARSHIP

Scholarships available to graduating Florida high school seniors entering their first year of college. Students applying for this scholarship can attend any accredited college, university, vocational/technical school they wish, anywhere in the country and major in any subject.

Award: Scholarship for use in freshman year; not renewable. *Number:* varies. *Amount:* varies.

Eligibility Requirements: Applicant must be high school student; planning to enroll or expecting to enroll full- or part-time at a two-year or four-year or technical institution or university and resident of Florida. Available to U.S. and non-U.S. citizens.

Application Requirements: Application, interview, transcript, IRS 1040 forms, FAFSA. *Deadline:* February 1.

Contact: Scholarship Coordinator
George Snow Scholarship Fund
Citibank Building, 998 South Federal Highway, Suite 203
Boca Raton, FL 33432
Phone: 561-347-6799
E-mail: info@scholarship.org

GEORGIA STUDENT FINANCE COMMISSION http://www.gsfc.org

GEORGIA LEVERAGING EDUCATIONAL ASSISTANCE PARTNERSHIP GRANT PROGRAM

Awards based on financial need. Recipients must be eligible for the Federal Pell Grant. Renewable award for Georgia residents enrolled in a state postsecondary institution. Must be U.S. citizen.

Award: Grant for use in freshman, sophomore, junior, or senior years; renewable. *Number:* 2500–3000. *Amount:* $300–$2000.

Eligibility Requirements: Applicant must be enrolled or expecting to enroll full- or part-time at a two-year or four-year or technical institution or university; resident of Georgia and studying in Georgia. Available to U.S. citizens.

Application Requirements: Application, financial need analysis. *Deadline:* continuous.

Contact: Tracy Ireland, Vice President
Georgia Student Finance Commission
2082 East Exchange Place, Suite 100
Tucker, GA 30084
Phone: 770-724-9000
E-mail: tracyi@gsfc.org

GEORGIA PUBLIC SAFETY MEMORIAL GRANT/LAW ENFORCEMENT PERSONNEL DEPARTMENT GRANT

• *See page 597*

GEORGIA TUITION EQUALIZATION GRANT (GTEG)

Award for Georgia residents pursuing undergraduate study at an accredited two- or four-year Georgia private institution. Also available to residents of Georgia who live near the State borders to attend certain four-year public colleges out-of-state.

Award: Grant for use in freshman, sophomore, junior, or senior years; renewable. *Number:* 1–35,000. *Amount:* $1100.

Eligibility Requirements: Applicant must be enrolled or expecting to enroll full-time at a two-year or four-year institution or university; resident of Georgia and studying in Alabama, Florida, Georgia, or Tennessee. Available to U.S. citizens.

Application Requirements: Application, social security number. *Deadline:* continuous.

Contact: Tracy Ireland, Vice President
Georgia Student Finance Commission
2082 East Exchange Place, Suite 100
Tucker, GA 30084
Phone: 770-724-9000
E-mail: tracyi@gsfc.org

GOVERNOR'S SCHOLARSHIP-GEORGIA

Award to assist students selected as Georgia STAR students, or valedictorians. For use at two- and four-year colleges and universities in Georgia. Recipients are selected as entering freshmen. Renewable award of up to $900. Minimum 3.0 GPA required.

Award: Scholarship for use in freshman year; renewable. *Number:* 1000–2000. *Amount:* up to $900.

Eligibility Requirements: Applicant must be high school student; planning to enroll or expecting to enroll full-time at a two-year or four-year institution or university; resident of Georgia and studying in Georgia. Applicant must have 3.0 GPA or higher. Available to U.S. citizens.

Application Requirements: Application, transcript. *Deadline:* continuous.

Contact: Tracy Ireland, Vice President
Georgia Student Finance Commission
2082 East Exchange Place, Suite 100
Tucker, GA 30084
Phone: 770-724-9000
E-mail: tracyi@gsfc.org

HOPE—HELPING OUTSTANDING PUPILS EDUCATIONALLY

Scholarship and Grant program for Georgia residents who are college undergraduates to attend an accredited two or four-year Georgia institution. Tuition and fees may be covered at public college or $3000 per year at private colleges. Minimum 3.0 GPA required. Renewable if student maintains grades. Write for deadlines.

Georgia Student Finance Commission (continued)

Award: Scholarship for use in freshman, sophomore, junior, or senior years; renewable. *Number:* 200,000–210,000. *Amount:* $300–$5000.

Eligibility Requirements: Applicant must be enrolled or expecting to enroll full- or part-time at a two-year or four-year institution or university; resident of Georgia and studying in Georgia. Applicant must have 3.0 GPA or higher. Available to U.S. citizens.

Application Requirements: Application, transcript. *Deadline:* continuous.

Contact: Tracy Ireland, Vice President
Georgia Student Finance Commission
2082 East Exchange Place, Suite 100
Tucker, GA 30084
Phone: 770-724-9000
E-mail: tracyi@gsfc.org

ROBERT C. BYRD HONORS SCHOLARSHIP-GEORGIA

Complete the application provided by the Georgia Department of Education. Renewable awards for outstanding graduating Georgia high school seniors to be used for full-time undergraduate study at eligible U.S. institution. Must a legal resident of Georgia and a U.S. citizen.

Award: Scholarship for use in freshman year; renewable. *Number:* 600–720. *Amount:* up to $1500.

Eligibility Requirements: Applicant must be high school student; planning to enroll or expecting to enroll full-time at a two-year or four-year institution or university and resident of Georgia. Applicant must have 3.0 GPA or higher. Available to U.S. citizens.

Application Requirements: Application, transcript. *Deadline:* February 1.

Contact: Tracy Ireland, Vice President
Georgia Student Finance Commission
2082 East Exchange Place, Suite 100
Tucker, GA 30084
Phone: 770-724-9000
E-mail: tracyi@gsfc.org

GIRL SCOUTS OF CONNECTICUT http://www.gsofct.org

EMILY CHAISON GOLD AWARD SCHOLARSHIP

• *See page 533*

GRAND LODGE OF IOWA, AF AND AM http://www.gl-iowa.org

GRAND LODGE OF IOWA MASONIC SCHOLARSHIP PROGRAM

• *See page 598*

GRANGE INSURANCE ASSOCIATION http://www.grange.com

GRANGE INSURANCE GROUP SCHOLARSHIP

Scholarships to current GIG policyholder/ member (or children or grandchildren of GIG policyholder) in California, Colorado, Idaho, Oregon, Washington or Wyoming. See Web site at http://www.grange.com for further details.

Award: Scholarship for use in freshman, sophomore, junior, senior, graduate, or postgraduate years; renewable. *Number:* 25–28. *Amount:* $1000–$1500.

Eligibility Requirements: Applicant must be enrolled or expecting to enroll full- or part-time at a two-year or four-year or technical institution or university and resident of California, Colorado, Idaho, Oregon, Washington, or Wyoming. Available to U.S. citizens.

Application Requirements: Application, autobiography, essay, financial need analysis, references, transcript. *Deadline:* April 15.

Contact: Scholarship Committee
Grange Insurance Association
PO Box 21089
Seattle, WA 98111-3089
Phone: 800-247-2643 Ext. 2200

GREATER KANAWHA VALLEY FOUNDATION http://www.tgkvf.org

KID'S CHANCE OF WEST VIRGINIA SCHOLARSHIP

Award of $1000 awarded to children (between the ages of 16 and 25) of a parents) injured in a WV work-related accident. Preference shall be given to students with financial need, academic performance, leadership abilities, demonstrated and potential contributions to school and community who are pursuing any field of study in any accredited trade, vocational school, college, or university. May apply for two Foundation scholarships but will only be chosen for one.

Award: Scholarship for use in freshman, sophomore, junior, senior, or graduate years; renewable. *Number:* 2. *Amount:* $1000.

Eligibility Requirements: Applicant must be age 16-25; enrolled or expecting to enroll full-time at a two-year or four-year or technical institution or university; resident of West Virginia and must have an interest in leadership. Applicant must have 2.5 GPA or higher. Available to U.S. citizens.

Application Requirements: Application, essay, financial need analysis, references, transcript. *Deadline:* January 12.

Contact: Susan Hoover, Scholarship Coordinator
Greater Kanawha Valley Foundation
PO Box 3041
Charleston, WV 25331
Phone: 304-346-3620
Fax: 304-346-3640

NORMAN S. AND BETTY M. FITZHUGH FUND

Award of $500 available to West Virginia residents who demonstrate academic excellence and financial need to attend any accredited college or university. Scholarships are awarded for one or more years. May apply for two Foundation scholarships but will only be chosen for one.

Award: Scholarship for use in freshman, sophomore, junior, senior, or graduate years; renewable. *Number:* 1. *Amount:* $500.

Eligibility Requirements: Applicant must be enrolled or expecting to enroll full-time at a two-year or four-year or technical institution or university and resident of West Virginia. Applicant must have 2.5 GPA or higher. Available to U.S. citizens.

Application Requirements: Application, essay, financial need analysis, references, transcript. *Deadline:* January 12.

Contact: Susan Hoover, Scholarship Coordinator
Greater Kanawha Valley Foundation
PO Box 3041
Charleston, WV 25331
Phone: 304-346-3620
Fax: 304-346-3640

RUTH ANN JOHNSON SCHOLARSHIP

Award of $1000 available to West Virginia residents who demonstrate academic excellence and financial need to attend any accredited college or university in any state or county. Scholarships are awarded for one or more years. May apply for two Foundation scholarships but will only be chosen for one.

Award: Scholarship for use in freshman, sophomore, junior, or senior years; renewable. *Number:* 54. *Amount:* $1000.

Eligibility Requirements: Applicant must be enrolled or expecting to enroll full-time at a four-year institution or university and resident of West Virginia. Applicant must have 2.5 GPA or higher. Available to U.S. and Canadian citizens.

Application Requirements: Application, essay, financial need analysis, references, transcript. *Deadline:* January 12.

Contact: Susan Hoover, Scholarship Coordinator
Greater Kanawha Valley Foundation
PO Box 3041
Charleston, WV 25331
Phone: 304-346-3620
Fax: 304-346-3640

SCPA SCHOLARSHIP FUND

• *See page 598*

WEST VIRGINIA GOLF ASSOCIATION FUND

• *See page 598*

W. P. BLACK SCHOLARSHIP FUND

Renewable award for West Virginia residents who demonstrate academic excellence and financial need and who are enrolled in an undergraduate program in any accredited college or university. May apply for two Foundation scholarships but will only be chosen for one.

Award: Scholarship for use in freshman, sophomore, junior, or senior years; renewable. *Number:* 102. *Amount:* $1000.

Eligibility Requirements: Applicant must be enrolled or expecting to enroll full-time at a four-year institution or university and resident of West Virginia. Applicant must have 2.5 GPA or higher. Available to U.S. citizens.

Application Requirements: Application, essay, financial need analysis, references, self-addressed stamped envelope, test scores, transcript. *Deadline:* January 12.

Contact: Susan Hoover, Scholarship Coordinator
Greater Kanawha Valley Foundation
PO Box 3041
Charleston, WV 25331
Phone: 304-346-3620
Fax: 304-346-3640

GREATER SAINT LOUIS COMMUNITY FOUNDATION http://www.gstlcf.org

ST. ANTHONY'S MEDICAL CENTER NORBERT SIEGFRIED HEALTH PROFESSIONS SCHOLARSHIP

• *See page 579*

GREATER WASHINGTON URBAN LEAGUE http://www.gwul.org

SAFEWAY/GREATER WASHINGTON URBAN LEAGUE SCHOLARSHIP

• *See page 598*

GREAT LAKES HEMOPHILIA FOUNDATION http://www.glhf.org

GLHF INDIVIDUAL CLASS SCHOLARSHIP

• *See page 619*

GREAT LAKES HEMOPHILIA FOUNDATION EDUCATION SCHOLARSHIP

• *See page 619*

GREENHOUSE PARTNERS http://www.greenhousescholars.org

GREENHOUSE SCHOLARS

Renewable scholarship for under-resourced, high-performing high school seniors planning to attend a four-year accredited institution. Includes mentorship, community network, peer support, and summer symposium. Open to Colorado residents with minimum 3.5 GPA and excellent leadership skills.

Award: Scholarship for use in freshman year; renewable. *Number:* 30–50. *Amount:* $1000–$5000.

Eligibility Requirements: Applicant must be high school student; planning to enroll or expecting to enroll full-time at a four-year institution or university; resident of Colorado and must have an interest in leadership. Applicant must have 3.5 GPA or higher. Available to U.S. citizens.

Application Requirements: Application, essay, financial need analysis, interview, references, transcript. *Deadline:* January 28.

Contact: Ben Mustin, Vice President
Greenhouse Partners
1011 Walnut Street, Third Floor
Boulder, CO 80302
Phone: 303-464-7811
Fax: 303-464-7796
E-mail: scholars@greenhousepartners.com

HARTFORD WHALERS BOOSTER CLUB http://www.whalerwatch.com

HARTFORD WHALERS BOOSTER CLUB SCHOLARSHIP

Scholarship for graduating high-school seniors who have played high school hockey and intend to play collegiate hockey. Must be a Connecticut resident.

Award: Scholarship for use in freshman year; not renewable. *Number:* 1. *Amount:* up to $1000.

Eligibility Requirements: Applicant must be high school student; planning to enroll or expecting to enroll full- or part-time at a four-year institution or university; resident of Connecticut and must have an interest in athletics/sports. Available to U.S. citizens.

Application Requirements: Application, resume, references, transcript, brief description of career goals. *Deadline:* March 20.

Contact: Alan Victor, President
Hartford Whalers Booster Club
PO Box 273
Hartford, CT 06141
Phone: 860-225-0265
Fax: 860-257-8331
E-mail: alan_m_victor@sbcglobal.net

HAWAII COMMUNITY FOUNDATION http://www.hawaiicommunityfoundation.org

HAWAII COMMUNITY FOUNDATION SCHOLARSHIPS

The foundation offers postsecondary scholarships to residents of Hawaii. The average amount is $1400. GPA should be 2.75. Visit the Web site at http://www.communityfoundation.org for more information.

Award: Scholarship for use in freshman, sophomore, junior, senior, or graduate years; not renewable. *Number:* 2200. *Amount:* $1400.

Eligibility Requirements: Applicant must be enrolled or expecting to enroll full-time at a two-year or four-year or technical institution or university and resident of Hawaii. Available to U.S. citizens.

Application Requirements: Application, financial need analysis. *Deadline:* March 1.

Contact: Judy Oliveira, Scholarship Officer
Hawaii Community Foundation
1164 Bishop Street, Suite 800
Honolulu, HI 96813
Phone: 808-566-5505
E-mail: scholarships@hcf-hawaii.org

HAWAII DEPARTMENT OF EDUCATION http://doe.k12.hi.us

ROBERT C. BYRD HONORS SCHOLARSHIP-HAWAII

Scholarship is available to students planning to attend college. The scholarship is federally funded, state-administered and recognizes exceptional high school seniors who show promise of continued excellence in the post-secondary educational system. Must have a minimum GPA of 3.3 and 1270 SAT. Applicant must be a legal resident of the State of Hawaii. Hawaii residents who are attending high school in another state are eligible to apply.

Award: Scholarship for use in freshman year; renewable. *Number:* 28. *Amount:* $1500.

Eligibility Requirements: Applicant must be high school student; planning to enroll or expecting to enroll full-time at a four-year institution or university and resident of Hawaii. Available to U.S. citizens.

Application Requirements: Application, transcript. *Deadline:* March 13.

Contact: Deanna Helber, Education Specialist
Hawaii Department of Education
641 18th Avenue, Building V, Room 201
Honolulu, HI 96816-4444
Phone: 808-735-6222
Fax: 808-733-9890
E-mail: dee_helber@notes.k12.hi.us

HAWAII EDUCATION ASSOCIATION http://www.heaed.com

HAWAII EDUCATION ASSOCIATION HIGH SCHOOL STUDENT SCHOLARSHIP

• *See page 535*

HAWAII SCHOOLS FEDERAL CREDIT UNION http://www.hawaiischoolsfcu.org

EDWIN KUNIYUKI MEMORIAL SCHOLARSHIP

Annual scholarship for an incoming college freshman in recognition of academic excellence. Applicant must be Hawaii Schools Federal Credit Union member for one year prior to scholarship application.

Award: Scholarship for use in freshman year; not renewable. *Number:* 1. *Amount:* $1000.

Eligibility Requirements: Applicant must be high school student; planning to enroll or expecting to enroll full-time at a two-year or four-year or technical institution or university and resident of Hawaii. Applicant must have 3.0 GPA or higher. Available to U.S. citizens.

Application Requirements: Application, essay, references, transcript. *Deadline:* February 28.

Contact: Kristy Garan, Administrative Assistant
Hawaii Schools Federal Credit Union
233 Vineyard Street
Honolulu, HI 96813
Phone: 808-521-0302
Fax: 808-791-6229
E-mail: kgaran@hawaiischoolsfcu.org

HAWAII STATE POSTSECONDARY EDUCATION COMMISSION

HAWAII STATE STUDENT INCENTIVE GRANT

Grants are given to residents of Hawaii who are enrolled in a participating Hawaiian state school. Funds are for undergraduate tuition only. Applicants must submit a financial need analysis.

Award: Grant for use in freshman, sophomore, junior, or senior years; renewable. *Number:* 470. *Amount:* $200–$2000.

Eligibility Requirements: Applicant must be enrolled or expecting to enroll full- or part-time at a two-year or four-year or technical institution or university; resident of Hawaii and studying in Hawaii. Available to U.S. citizens.

Application Requirements: Application, financial need analysis. *Deadline:* continuous.

Contact: Janine Oyama, Financial Aid Specialist
Hawaii State Postsecondary Education Commission
University of Hawaii
Honolulu, HI 96822
Phone: 808-956-6066

HEART OF A MARINE FOUNDATION http://www.heartofamarine.org

LANCE CORPORAL PHILLIP E. FRANK MEMORIAL SCHOLARSHIP

Scholarships available to graduating high school seniors who are residents of New Jersey and Illinois in an effort to encourage youth who exemplify the spirit of "The Heart of a Marine" ideal, which is honor, patriotism, loyalty, respect and concern for others. There is no GPA requirement; character is what counts the most. Discharged military personnel continuing their education are also eligible. See Web site for application and additional information: http://www.heartofamarine.org.

Award: Scholarship for use in freshman, sophomore, junior, or senior years; not renewable. *Number:* 2. *Amount:* $500–$750.

Eligibility Requirements: Applicant must be enrolled or expecting to enroll full-time at a two-year or four-year or technical institution or university and resident of Illinois or New Jersey. Available to U.S. citizens.

Application Requirements: Application, driver's license, essay, photo, references. *Deadline:* May 1.

Contact: Georgette Frank, Executive Director
Heart of a Marine Foundation
PO Box 1732
Elk Grove Village, IL 60007
E-mail: theheartofamarine@comcast.net

HELLENIC UNIVERSITY CLUB OF PHILADELPHIA http://www.hucphila.org

ANDREW G. CHRESSANTHIS MEMORIAL SCHOLARSHIP

• *See page 683*

CHRISTOPHER DEMETRIS SCHOLARSHIP

• *See page 683*

DORIZAS MEMORIAL SCHOLARSHIP

• *See page 683*

DR. NICHOLAS PADIS MEMORIAL GRADUATE SCHOLARSHIP

• *See page 683*

FOUNDERS SCHOLARSHIP

• *See page 684*

JAMES COSMOS MEMORIAL SCHOLARSHIP

• *See page 684*

PAIDEIA SCHOLARSHIP

• *See page 535*

HENRY SACHS FOUNDATION http://www.sachsfoundation.org

SACHS FOUNDATION SCHOLARSHIPS

• *See page 684*

HERBERT HOOVER PRESIDENTIAL LIBRARY ASSOCIATION http://www.hooverassociation.org

HERBERT HOOVER UNCOMMON STUDENT AWARD

Only juniors in an Iowa high school or home school program may apply. Grades and test scores are not evaluated. Applicants are chosen on the basis of submitted project proposals. Those chosen to complete their project and make a presentation receive $750. Three are chosen for $5000 award.

Award: Scholarship for use in freshman year; not renewable. *Number:* 15. *Amount:* $1000–$5000.

Eligibility Requirements: Applicant must be high school student; planning to enroll or expecting to enroll full-time at a four-year institution or university and resident of Iowa. Available to U.S. citizens.

Application Requirements: Application, references, project proposal. *Deadline:* March 31.

Contact: Patricia Hand, Manager of Academic Programs
Herbert Hoover Presidential Library Association
302 Parkside Drive, PO Box 696
West Branch, IA 52358
Phone: 800-828-0475
Fax: 319-643-2391
E-mail: scholarship@hooverassociation.org

HERB KOHL EDUCATIONAL FOUNDATION INC. http://www.kohleducation.org

HERB KOHL EXCELLENCE SCHOLARSHIP PROGRAM

• *See page 599*

HERSCHEL C. PRICE EDUCATIONAL FOUNDATION

HERSCHEL C. PRICE EDUCATIONAL FOUNDATION SCHOLARSHIPS

Scholarships open to undergraduates, graduates and high school seniors. Must be a U.S. citizen, and either a resident of West Virginia, or attend a West Virginia college. Based on academic achievement and financial need. Deadlines: April 1 for fall term and October 1 for spring term.

Award: Scholarship for use in freshman, sophomore, junior, senior, or graduate years; not renewable. *Number:* 200–300. *Amount:* $500–$5000.

Eligibility Requirements: Applicant must be enrolled or expecting to enroll full- or part-time at a two-year or four-year institution or university and resident of West Virginia. Available to U.S. citizens.

Application Requirements: Application, financial need analysis, interview, test scores, transcript. *Deadline:* varies.

Contact: Jonna Hughes, Trustee and Director
Herschel C. Price Educational Foundation
PO Box 412
Huntington, WV 25708-0412
Phone: 304-529-3852

HISPANIC METROPOLITAN CHAMBER SCHOLARSHIPS http://www.hmccoregon.com

HISPANIC METROPOLITAN CHAMBER SCHOLARSHIPS

• *See page 685*

HISPANIC SCHOLARSHIP FUND http://www.hsf.net

HSF/IDT HOPE HIGH SCHOOL SCHOLARSHIP PROGRAM

• *See page 685*

HORIZONS FOUNDATION http://www.horizonsfoundation.org

MARKOWSKI-LEACH SCHOLARSHIP

Scholarship of $1250 awarded to a student who attends San Francisco State University, Stanford University, or University of California, and self-identifies as lesbian or gay. Recipient is chosen based on demonstrated potential as a positive role model for the LGBT community through service, education, or employment. Graduate students and undergraduates in their junior or senior year are eligible to apply.

Award: Scholarship for use in freshman, sophomore, junior, senior, or graduate years; renewable. *Number:* 1. *Amount:* $1250.

Eligibility Requirements: Applicant must be enrolled or expecting to enroll full-time at a two-year or four-year or technical institution or university; studying in California and must have an interest in LGBT issues. Applicant must have 2.5 GPA or higher. Available to U.S. and Canadian citizens.

Application Requirements: Application, essay, references. *Deadline:* April 1.

Contact: Director
Horizons Foundation
870 Market Street, Suite 728
San Francisco, CA 94102
Phone: 415-398-2333
Fax: 415-398-4733

HOUSTON COMMUNITY SERVICES

AZTECA SCHOLARSHIP

• *See page 686*

HUMANE SOCIETY OF THE UNITED STATES http://www.hsus.org

SHAW-WORTH MEMORIAL SCHOLARSHIP

Scholarship for a New England high school senior, who has made a meaningful contribution to animal protection over a significant amount of time. Passive liking of animals or the desire to enter an animal care field does not justify the award.

Award: Scholarship for use in freshman year; not renewable. *Number:* 1. *Amount:* $2000.

Eligibility Requirements: Applicant must be high school student; planning to enroll or expecting to enroll full-time at a four-year institution or university and resident of Connecticut, Maine, Massachusetts, New Hampshire, Rhode Island, or Vermont. Available to U.S. citizens.

Application Requirements: Essay, references. *Deadline:* March 17.

Contact: Administrator
Humane Society of the United States
PO Box 619
Jacksonville, VT 05342-0619
Phone: 802-368-2790
Fax: 802-368-2756

IDAHO POWER COMPANY http://www.idahopower.com

IDAHO POWER SCHOLARSHIP FOR ACADEMIC EXCELLENCE

Scholarship of $1000 for graduating high school students of Idaho. Applicants must have a minimum 3.75 unweighted GPA. Must be enrolled at an accredited Idaho or Oregon college, university or vocational-technical school. Recipients may renew their scholarship annually, up to three times.

Award: Scholarship for use in freshman year; renewable. *Number:* 5. *Amount:* $1000.

Eligibility Requirements: Applicant must be high school student; planning to enroll or expecting to enroll full-time at a two-year or four-year or technical institution or university; resident of Idaho and studying in Idaho or Oregon. Available to U.S. citizens.

Application Requirements: Application, essay, resume, references, test scores, transcript. *Deadline:* June 15.

Contact: Scholarship Program Administrator
Idaho Power Company
PO Box 1000
Pocatello, ID 83204

IDAHO STATE BOARD OF EDUCATION http://www.boardofed.idaho.gov

FREEDOM SCHOLARSHIP

• *See page 654*

IDAHO GOVERNOR'S CUP SCHOLARSHIP

Renewable scholarship available to Idaho residents enrolled full-time in an undergraduate academic or vocational-technical program at an eligible Idaho public or private college or university. Minimum GPA: 2.8. Merit-based award. Must be a high school senior and U.S. citizen to apply.

Award: Scholarship for use in freshman year; renewable. *Number:* up to 12. *Amount:* $3000.

Eligibility Requirements: Applicant must be high school student; planning to enroll or expecting to enroll full-time at a two-year or four-year or technical institution or university; resident of Idaho and studying in Idaho. Available to U.S. citizens.

Application Requirements: Application, applicant must enter a contest, essay, portfolio, references, test scores, transcript. *Deadline:* January 15.

Contact: Dana Kelly, Program Manager, Student Affairs
Idaho State Board of Education
PO Box 83720
Boise, ID 83720-0037
Phone: 208-332-1574
Fax: 208-334-2632
E-mail: dana.kelly@osbe.idaho.gov

IDAHO MINORITY AND "AT RISK" STUDENT SCHOLARSHIP

• *See page 620*

IDAHO PROMISE CATEGORY A SCHOLARSHIP PROGRAM

Renewable award available to Idaho residents who are graduating high school seniors. Must attend an approved Idaho institution of higher education on full-time basis. Must have a cumulative GPA of 3.5 or above and an ACT score of 28 or above.

Award: Scholarship for use in freshman year; renewable. *Number:* 25. *Amount:* $3000.

Eligibility Requirements: Applicant must be high school student; planning to enroll or expecting to enroll full-time at a two-year or four-year or technical institution or university; resident of Idaho and studying in Idaho. Applicant must have 3.5 GPA or higher. Available to U.S. citizens.

Idaho State Board of Education (continued)

Application Requirements: Application, applicant must enter a contest, test scores. *Deadline:* January 15.

Contact: Dana Kelly, Program Manager, Student Affairs
Idaho State Board of Education
PO Box 83720
Boise, ID 83720-0037
Phone: 208-332-1574
Fax: 208-334-2632
E-mail: dana.kelly@osbe.idaho.gov

IDAHO PROMISE CATEGORY B SCHOLARSHIP PROGRAM

Available to Idaho residents entering college for the first time prior to the age of 22. Must have completed high school or its equivalent in Idaho and have a minimum GPA of 3.0 or an ACT score of 20 or higher. Scholarship limited to two years or four semesters.

Award: Scholarship for use in freshman year; renewable. *Number:* varies. *Amount:* $500.

Eligibility Requirements: Applicant must be high school student; age 22 or under; planning to enroll or expecting to enroll full-time at a two-year or four-year or technical institution or university; resident of Idaho and studying in Idaho. Applicant must have 3.0 GPA or higher. Available to U.S. citizens.

Application Requirements: Application, transcript. *Deadline:* continuous.

Contact: Lynn Humphrey, Manager, Student Aid Programs
Idaho State Board of Education
PO Box 83720
Boise, ID 83720-0037
Phone: 208-334-2270
Fax: 208-334-2632

LEVERAGING EDUCATIONAL ASSISTANCE STATE PARTNERSHIP PROGRAM (LEAP)

One-time award assists students attending participating Idaho trade schools, colleges, and universities majoring in any field except theology or divinity. Must be U.S. citizen or permanent resident, and show financial need. Deadlines vary by institution.

Award: Grant for use in freshman, sophomore, junior, senior, or graduate years; not renewable. *Number:* varies. *Amount:* $400–$5000.

Eligibility Requirements: Applicant must be enrolled or expecting to enroll full- or part-time at a two-year or four-year or technical institution or university; resident of Idaho and studying in Idaho. Available to U.S. citizens.

Application Requirements: Application, financial need analysis, self-addressed stamped envelope. *Deadline:* varies.

Contact: Lynn Humphrey, Manager, Student Aid Programs
Idaho State Board of Education
PO Box 83720
Boise, ID 83720-0037
Phone: 208-334-2270
Fax: 208-334-2632

PUBLIC SAFETY OFFICER DEPENDENT SCHOLARSHIP

• *See page 600*

ROBERT C. BYRD HONORS SCHOLARSHIP-IDAHO

Renewable scholarships available to Idaho residents based on outstanding academic achievement. Students must apply as high school seniors.

Award: Scholarship for use in freshman year; renewable. *Number:* 90. *Amount:* up to $1500.

Eligibility Requirements: Applicant must be high school student; planning to enroll or expecting to enroll full-time at a four-year institution or university and resident of Idaho. Applicant must have 3.5 GPA or higher. Available to U.S. citizens.

Application Requirements: Application, references, test scores, transcript. *Deadline:* January 15.

Contact: Dana Kelly, Manager, Student Affairs Programs
Idaho State Board of Education
PO Box 83720
Boise, ID 83720-0037
Phone: 208-334-2270
Fax: 208-334-2632
E-mail: dana.kelly@osbe.idaho.gov

ILLINOIS COUNCIL OF THE BLIND http://www.icbonline.org

FLOYD CARGILL SCHOLARSHIP

• *See page 620*

ILLINOIS DEPARTMENT OF VETERANS AFFAIRS http://www.state.il.us/agency/dva

MIA/POW SCHOLARSHIPS

• *See page 654*

VETERANS' CHILDREN EDUCATIONAL OPPORTUNITIES

• *See page 654*

ILLINOIS EDUCATION FOUNDATION http://www.iledfoundation.org

DANIEL M. KERRANE, JR. FOUNDATION SCHOLARSHIP

Scholarship awards educational expenses required to attend community college, in addition to many affiliated schools and programs. Applicants must have a minimum GPA of 2.0.

Award: Scholarship for use in freshman, sophomore, junior, or senior years; renewable. *Number:* up to 30. *Amount:* $400–$1500.

Eligibility Requirements: Applicant must be enrolled or expecting to enroll full-time at a four-year institution or university; resident of Illinois and studying in Illinois. Available to U.S. citizens.

Application Requirements: Application, essay, references. *Deadline:* May 31.

Contact: William Collins, Scholarship Chairman
Illinois Education Foundation
226 West Jackson Boulevard, Suite 426
Chicago, IL 60606
Phone: 312-920-9605
Fax: 312-920-9607
E-mail: info@iledfoundation.org

ILLINOIS EDUCATION FOUNDATION SIGNATURE SCHOLARSHIPS

Scholarship awards educational expenses required to attend community college, in addition to many affiliated schools and programs. Applicant should have a minimum GPA of 2.0. Must be currently a high school senior.

Award: Scholarship for use in freshman year; not renewable. *Number:* up to 30. *Amount:* $400–$1500.

Eligibility Requirements: Applicant must be high school student; planning to enroll or expecting to enroll full-time at a two-year or technical institution and resident of Illinois. Available to U.S. citizens.

Application Requirements: Application, essay, references, test scores, transcript. *Deadline:* May 31.

Contact: William Collins, Scholarship Chairman
Illinois Education Foundation
226 West Jackson Boulevard, Suite 426
Chicago, IL 60606
Phone: 312-920-9605
Fax: 312-920-9607
E-mail: info@iledfoundation.org

ILLINOIS STUDENT ASSISTANCE COMMISSION (ISAC)

http://www.collegezone.org

GRANT PROGRAM FOR DEPENDENTS OF POLICE, FIRE, OR CORRECTIONAL OFFICERS

• *See page 600*

HIGHER EDUCATION LICENSE PLATE PROGRAM-HELP

Need-based grants for students who are Illinois residents and attend approved Illinois colleges. May be eligible to receive the grant for the equivalent of 10 semesters of full-time enrollment. Number of grants made through this program and the individual dollar amount awarded varies.

Award: Grant for use in freshman, sophomore, junior, or senior years; not renewable. *Number:* varies. *Amount:* varies.

Eligibility Requirements: Applicant must be enrolled or expecting to enroll full- or part-time at a two-year or four-year institution or university; resident of Illinois and studying in Illinois. Available to U.S. citizens.

Application Requirements: Application, financial need analysis, FAFSA. *Deadline:* varies.

Contact: College Zone Counselor
Illinois Student Assistance Commission (ISAC)
1755 Lake Cook Road
Deerfield, IL 60015-5209
Phone: 800-899-4722
E-mail: collegezone@isac.org

ILLINOIS COLLEGE SAVINGS BOND BONUS INCENTIVE GRANT PROGRAM

Program offers Illinois college savings bond holders a grant for each year of bond maturity payable upon bond redemption if at least 70 percent of proceeds are used to attend college in Illinois. The amount of grant will depend on the amount of the bond, ranging from a $40 to $440 grant per $5000 of the bond. Applications are accepted between August 1 and May 30 of the academic year in which the bonds matured, or in the academic year immediately following maturity.

Award: Grant for use in freshman, sophomore, junior, senior, graduate, or postgraduate years; not renewable. *Number:* varies.

Eligibility Requirements: Applicant must be enrolled or expecting to enroll full- or part-time at a two-year or four-year or technical institution or university and studying in Illinois. Available to U.S. citizens.

Application Requirements: Application. *Deadline:* varies.

Contact: College Zone Counselor
Illinois Student Assistance Commission (ISAC)
1755 Lake Cook Road
Deerfield, IL 60015-5209
Phone: 800-899-4722
E-mail: collegezone@isac.org

ILLINOIS GENERAL ASSEMBLY SCHOLARSHIP

Scholarships available for Illinois students enrolled at an Illinois four-year state-supported college. Must contact the general assembly member for eligibility criteria. Deadline varies.

Award: Scholarship for use in freshman, sophomore, junior, or senior years; not renewable. *Number:* varies. *Amount:* varies.

Eligibility Requirements: Applicant must be enrolled or expecting to enroll full- or part-time at a four-year institution or university; resident of Illinois and studying in Illinois. Available to U.S. citizens.

Application Requirements: Application. *Deadline:* varies.

Contact: College Zone Counselor
Illinois Student Assistance Commission (ISAC)
1755 Lake Cook Road
Deerfield, IL 60015-5209
Phone: 800-899-4722
E-mail: collegezone@isac.org

ILLINOIS MONETARY AWARD PROGRAM

Awards to Illinois residents enrolled in a minimum of 3 hours per term in a degree program at an approved Illinois institution. See Web site for complete list of participating schools. Must demonstrate financial need, based on the information provided on the Free Application for Federal Student Aid. Number of grants and the individual dollar amount awarded vary. Deadlines: August 15 and September 30.

Award: Grant for use in freshman, sophomore, junior, or senior years; renewable. *Number:* 146,853. *Amount:* $2365.

Eligibility Requirements: Applicant must be enrolled or expecting to enroll full- or part-time at a two-year or four-year or technical institution or university; resident of Illinois and studying in Illinois. Available to U.S. citizens.

Application Requirements: Financial need analysis, FAFSA online. *Deadline:* varies.

Contact: College Zone Counselor
Illinois Student Assistance Commission (ISAC)
1755 Lake Cook Road
Deerfield, IL 60015-5209
Phone: 800-899-4722
E-mail: collegezone@isac.org

ILLINOIS NATIONAL GUARD GRANT PROGRAM

• *See page 634*

ILLINOIS STUDENT-TO-STUDENT PROGRAM OF MATCHING GRANTS

Grant is available to undergraduates at participating state-supported colleges. Number of grants and the individual dollar amount awarded vary. Contact financial aid office at the institution.

Award: Grant for use in freshman, sophomore, junior, or senior years; not renewable. *Number:* varies. *Amount:* $300–$1000.

Eligibility Requirements: Applicant must be enrolled or expecting to enroll full- or part-time at a two-year or four-year institution or university; resident of Illinois and studying in Illinois. Available to U.S. citizens.

Application Requirements: Application, financial need analysis. *Deadline:* varies.

Contact: College Zone Counselor
Illinois Student Assistance Commission (ISAC)
1755 Lake Cook Road
Deerfield, IL 60015-5209
Phone: 800-899-4722
E-mail: collegezone@isac.org

ILLINOIS VETERAN GRANT PROGRAM-IVG

• *See page 654*

MERIT RECOGNITION SCHOLARSHIP (MRS) PROGRAM

One-time awards available to Illinois residents for use at Illinois institutions. Must be ranked in the top 5 percent of high school class or have scored among the top 5 percent on the ACT, SAT, or Prairie State Achievement Exam. Number of scholarships granted varies.

Award: Scholarship for use in freshman year; not renewable. *Number:* varies. *Amount:* up to $1000.

Eligibility Requirements: Applicant must be high school student; planning to enroll or expecting to enroll full- or part-time at a two-year or four-year institution or university; resident of Illinois and studying in Illinois. Applicant must have 3.5 GPA or higher. Available to U.S. citizens.

Application Requirements: Application, transcript. *Deadline:* June 15.

Contact: College Zone Counselor
Illinois Student Assistance Commission (ISAC)
1755 Lake Cook Road
Deerfield, IL 60015-5209
Phone: 800-899-4722
E-mail: collegezone@isac.org

ROBERT C. BYRD HONORS SCHOLARSHIP-ILLINOIS

Scholarship for Illinois residents and graduating high school seniors accepted on a full-time basis as an undergraduate student at an Illinois college or university. The award is up to $1500 per year, for a maximum of four years. Minimum 3.5 GPA required. Students are automatically considered for this scholarship if they meet the eligibility requirements. High school counselors submit information to selection process.

Award: Scholarship for use in freshman year; renewable. *Number:* varies. *Amount:* up to $1500.

Eligibility Requirements: Applicant must be high school student; planning to enroll or expecting to enroll full-time at a two-year or four-year institution or university; resident of Illinois and studying in Illinois. Applicant must have 3.5 GPA or higher. Available to U.S. citizens.

Illinois Student Assistance Commission (ISAC) (continued)

Application Requirements: Application, test scores, transcript. *Deadline:* July 15.

Contact: College Zone Counselor
Illinois Student Assistance Commission (ISAC)
1755 Lake Cook Road
Deerfield, IL 60015-5209
Phone: 800-899-4722
Fax: 847-831-8549
E-mail: collegezone@isac.org

SILAS PURNELL ILLINOIS INCENTIVE FOR ACCESS PROGRAM

Students whose information provided on the FAFSA results in a calculated zero expected family contribution when they are college freshmen may be eligible to receive a grant of up to $500. Must be a U.S. citizen and an Illinois resident studying at a participating Illinois institution. See Web site for complete list of schools and additional requirements.

Award: Grant for use in freshman year; not renewable. *Number:* varies. *Amount:* up to $500.

Eligibility Requirements: Applicant must be high school student; planning to enroll or expecting to enroll full- or part-time at a two-year or four-year or technical institution or university; resident of Illinois and studying in Illinois. Available to U.S. citizens.

Application Requirements: Financial need analysis, FAFSA. *Deadline:* July 1.

Contact: College Zone Counselor
Illinois Student Assistance Commission (ISAC)
1755 Lake Cook Road
Deerfield, IL 60015-5209
Phone: 800-899-4722
E-mail: collegezone@isac.org

INDEPENDENT COLLEGE FUND OF MARYLAND (I-FUND) http://www.i-fundinfo.org

LEADERSHIP SCHOLARSHIPS

Annual scholarship available to an outstanding student for study at one of the Independent Colleges of Maryland. A $25,000 Challenge Grant from UPS is matched dollar for dollar, with the goal of providing one $5000 scholarship for each independent college in Maryland.

Award: Scholarship for use in junior or senior years; not renewable. *Number:* 1. *Amount:* $5000.

Eligibility Requirements: Applicant must be enrolled or expecting to enroll full- or part-time at a four-year institution or university; studying in Maryland and must have an interest in leadership. Available to U.S. citizens.

Application Requirements: Application. *Deadline:* varies.

Contact: Lori Subotich, Director of Programs and Scholarships
Independent College Fund of Maryland (I-Fund)
3225 Ellerslie Avenue, Suite C160
Baltimore, MD 21218-3519
Phone: 443-997-5700
Fax: 443-997-2740
E-mail: lsubot@jhmi.edu

MARYLAND SCHOLARS

• *See page 600*

T. ROWE PRICE FOUNDATION SCHOLARSHIPS

Award of $3000 to students who exhibit outstanding leadership qualities on campus and/or in the community. Must be permanent residents of Maryland and have at least 3.0 GPA.

Award: Scholarship for use in freshman, sophomore, junior, or senior years; not renewable. *Number:* 1. *Amount:* $3000.

Eligibility Requirements: Applicant must be enrolled or expecting to enroll full-time at a four-year institution or university; resident of Maryland and must have an interest in leadership. Applicant must have 3.0 GPA or higher. Available to U.S. citizens.

Application Requirements: Application, financial need analysis, thank you letters. *Deadline:* varies.

Contact: Lori Subotich, Director of Programs and Scholarships
Independent College Fund of Maryland (I-Fund)
3225 Ellerslie Avenue, Suite C160
Baltimore, MD 21218-3519
Phone: 443-997-5700
Fax: 443-997-2740
E-mail: lsubot@jhmi.edu

INDIANA DEPARTMENT OF VETERANS AFFAIRS http://www.in.gov/dva

CHILD OF DISABLED VETERAN GRANT OR PURPLE HEART RECIPIENT GRANT

• *See page 655*

DEPARTMENT OF VETERANS AFFAIRS FREE TUITION FOR CHILDREN OF POW/MIA'S IN VIETNAM

• *See page 655*

NATIONAL GUARD SCHOLARSHIP EXTENSION PROGRAM

• *See page 634*

NATIONAL GUARD TUITION SUPPLEMENT PROGRAM

• *See page 635*

RESIDENT TUITION FOR ACTIVE DUTY MILITARY PERSONNEL

• *See page 632*

TUITION AND FEE REMISSION FOR CHILDREN AND SPOUSES OF NATIONAL GUARD MEMBERS

• *See page 635*

INDIANA FARM BUREAU INSURANCE http://www.infarmbureau.com

EXCEL AWARDS

All Indiana high school students are eligible to participate, including private school and home-schooled students. A first, second, and third place winner will be named in each of the six awards competition categories.

Award: Prize for use in freshman year; not renewable. *Number:* 18. *Amount:* $2000–$3000.

Eligibility Requirements: Applicant must be high school student; planning to enroll or expecting to enroll full-time at a four-year institution or university and resident of Indiana. Available to U.S. citizens.

Application Requirements: Application, applicant must enter a contest, presentation on the topic. *Deadline:* January 1.

Contact: Pam Sites, Special Markets Coordinator
Indiana Farm Bureau Insurance
PO Box 1250
Indianapolis, IN 46202-1250
Phone: 317-692-7748

INDIAN AMERICAN CULTURAL ASSOCIATION http://www.iasf.org

INDIAN AMERICAN SCHOLARSHIP FUND

• *See page 687*

INTER-COUNTY ENERGY http://www.intercountyenergy.net

INTER-COUNTY ENERGY SCHOLARSHIP

Scholarship available for Kentucky high school senior who is a child of a resident of the Inter-County Energy service area and an active member of the cooperative. Student must plan to enroll in a postsecondary institution: two- or four-year college, university, or trade/technical institution. Must submit a brief biography. Write or call for application.

Award: Scholarship for use in freshman year; not renewable. *Number:* 6. *Amount:* up to $1000.

Eligibility Requirements: Applicant must be high school student; planning to enroll or expecting to enroll full-time at a four-year institution or university and resident of Kentucky. Available to U.S. citizens.

Application Requirements: Application, autobiography, financial need analysis, references, transcript. *Deadline:* April 8.

Contact: Lori Statom, Customer Services Assistant
Inter-County Energy
PO Box 87
Danville, KY 40423-0087
Phone: 859-236-4561
Fax: 859-236-5012
E-mail: lori@intercountyenergy.net

KENTUCKY WOMEN IN RURAL ELECTRIFICATION SCHOLARSHIP

Scholarship for Kentucky student whose family is served by a Kentucky rural electric cooperative. The student must have at least 60 credit hours at the beginning of the fall college term. The student must attend a Kentucky college or university.

Award: Scholarship for use in junior or senior years; not renewable. *Number:* varies. *Amount:* up to $1000.

Eligibility Requirements: Applicant must be enrolled or expecting to enroll full- or part-time at a four-year institution or university; female; resident of Kentucky and studying in Kentucky. Available to U.S. citizens.

Application Requirements: Application, financial need analysis, references. *Deadline:* June 15.

Contact: Ellie Hobgood, Administrative Assistant
Inter-County Energy
PO Box 32170
Louisville, KY 40232
Phone: 502-451-2430
Fax: 502-459-3209

INTER-TRIBAL COUNCIL OF MICHIGAN INC. http://www.itcmi.org

MICHIGAN INDIAN TUITION WAIVER

• *See page 687*

IOWA COLLEGE FOUNDATION (ICF) http://www.iowacollegefoundation.org

IOWA COLLEGE FOUNDATION MINORITY SCHOLARSHIPS

• *See page 687*

IOWA COLLEGE STUDENT AID COMMISSION http://www.iowacollegeaid.gov

ALL IOWA OPPORTUNITY SCHOLARSHIP

Students attending eligible Iowa colleges and universities may receive awards of up to $6420. Minimum 2.5 GPA. Priority will be given to students who participated in the Federal TRIO Programs, graduated from alternative high schools, and to homeless youth. Applicant must enroll within 2 academic years of graduating from high school. Maximum individual awards cannot exceed more than the resident tuition rate at Iowa Regent Universities.

Award: Scholarship for use in freshman or sophomore years; renewable. *Number:* 179. *Amount:* up to $6420.

Eligibility Requirements: Applicant must be enrolled or expecting to enroll full- or part-time at a two-year or four-year institution or university; resident of Iowa and studying in Iowa. Applicant must have 2.5 GPA or higher. Available to U.S. citizens.

Application Requirements: Application, financial need analysis. *Deadline:* May 1.

Contact: Julie Leeper, Director, Program Administration
Iowa College Student Aid Commission
200 Tenth Street, Floor 4
Des Moines, IA 50309-3609
Phone: 515-725-3420
Fax: 515-725-3401
E-mail: julie.leeper@iowa.gov

GOVERNOR TERRY E. BRANSTAD IOWA STATE FAIR SCHOLARSHIP

Awards up to four scholarships ranging from $500 to $1000 to students graduating from an Iowa high school. Must actively participate at the Iowa State fair. For more details see Web site: http://www.iowacollegeaid.org.

Award: Scholarship for use in freshman year; not renewable. *Number:* up to 4. *Amount:* $500–$1000.

Eligibility Requirements: Applicant must be high school student; planning to enroll or expecting to enroll full- or part-time at a four-year institution or university; resident of Iowa and studying in Iowa. Available to U.S. citizens.

Application Requirements: Application, essay, financial need analysis, references, transcript. *Deadline:* May 1.

Contact: Misty Thompson, Program Planner
Iowa College Student Aid Commission
200 Tenth Street, Fourth Floor
Des Moines, IA 50309-3609
Phone: 515-725-3424
Fax: 515-725-3401
E-mail: misty.thompson@iowa.gov

IOWA GRANTS

Statewide need-based program to assist high-need Iowa residents. Recipients must demonstrate a high level of financial need to receive awards ranging from $100 to $1000. Awards are prorated for students enrolled for less than full-time. Awards must be used at Iowa postsecondary institutions.

Award: Grant for use in freshman, sophomore, junior, or senior years; not renewable. *Number:* 2100. *Amount:* $100–$1000.

Eligibility Requirements: Applicant must be enrolled or expecting to enroll full- or part-time at a two-year or four-year or technical institution or university; resident of Iowa and studying in Iowa. Available to U.S. citizens.

Application Requirements: Application, financial need analysis. *Deadline:* continuous.

Contact: Julie Leeper, Director, Program Administration
Iowa College Student Aid Commission
200 Tenth Street, Fourth Floor
Des Moines, IA 50309-3609
Phone: 515-725-3420
Fax: 515-725-3401
E-mail: julie.leeper@iowa.gov

IOWA NATIONAL GUARD EDUCATION ASSISTANCE PROGRAM

• *See page 635*

IOWA TUITION GRANT PROGRAM

Program assists students who attend independent postsecondary institutions in Iowa. Iowa residents currently enrolled, or planning to enroll, for at least 3 semester hours at one of the eligible Iowa postsecondary institutions may apply. Awards currently range from $100 to $4000. Grants may not exceed the difference between independent college and university tuition fees and the average tuition fees at the three public Regent universities.

Award: Grant for use in freshman, sophomore, junior, or senior years; not renewable. *Number:* 17,200. *Amount:* $100–$4000.

Eligibility Requirements: Applicant must be enrolled or expecting to enroll full- or part-time at a four-year institution or university; resident of Iowa and studying in Iowa. Available to U.S. citizens.

Application Requirements: Application, financial need analysis. *Deadline:* July 1.

Contact: Julie Leeper, Director, Program Administration
Iowa College Student Aid Commission
200 Tenth Street, Fourth Floor
Des Moines, IA 50309-3609
Phone: 515-725-3420
E-mail: julie.leeper@iowa.gov

IOWA VOCATIONAL-TECHNICAL TUITION GRANT PROGRAM

Program provides need-based financial assistance to Iowa residents enrolled in career education (vocational-technical), and career option programs at Iowa area community colleges. Grants range from $150 to $1200, depending on the length of the program, financial need, and available funds.

Award: Grant for use in freshman or sophomore years; not renewable. *Number:* 2100. *Amount:* $150–$1200.

Eligibility Requirements: Applicant must be enrolled or expecting to enroll full- or part-time at a technical institution; resident of Iowa and studying in Iowa. Available to U.S. citizens.

Iowa College Student Aid Commission (continued)

Application Requirements: Application, financial need analysis. *Deadline:* July 1.

Contact: Julie Leeper, Director, Program Administration
Iowa College Student Aid Commission
200 Tenth Street, Fourth Floor
Des Moines, IA 50309-3609
Phone: 515-725-3420
Fax: 515-725-3401
E-mail: julie.leeper@iowa.gov

ROBERT C. BYRD HONORS SCHOLARSHIP-IOWA

Scholarships up to $1500 are awarded to exceptionally able Iowa high school seniors who show promise of continued academic excellence. Must have a minimum of a 28 ACT or 1240 SAT, a 3.5 GPA and rank in the top 10 percent of the student's high school graduating class. For more details see Web site: http://www.iowacollegeaid.org.

Award: Scholarship for use in freshman year; renewable. *Number:* up to 70. *Amount:* up to $1500.

Eligibility Requirements: Applicant must be high school student; planning to enroll or expecting to enroll full-time at a four-year institution or university and resident of Iowa. Applicant must have 3.5 GPA or higher. Available to U.S. citizens.

Application Requirements: Application, test scores, transcript. *Deadline:* February 1.

Contact: Misty Thompson, Program Planner
Iowa College Student Aid Commission
200 Tenth Street, Fourth Floor
Des Moines, IA 50309-3609
Phone: 515-725-3424
Fax: 515-725-3401
E-mail: misty.thompson@iowa.gov

STATE OF IOWA SCHOLARSHIP PROGRAM

Program provides recognition and financial honorarium to Iowa's academically talented high school seniors. Must be used at an Iowa postsecondary institution. Minimum 3.5 GPA required.

Award: Scholarship for use in freshman year; not renewable. *Number:* up to 1700. *Amount:* varies.

Eligibility Requirements: Applicant must be high school student; planning to enroll or expecting to enroll full-time at a two-year or four-year or technical institution or university; resident of Iowa and studying in Iowa. Applicant must have 3.5 GPA or higher. Available to U.S. citizens.

Application Requirements: Application, test scores. *Deadline:* November 1.

Contact: Misty Thompson, Program Planner
Iowa College Student Aid Commission
200 Tenth Street, Fourth Floor
Des Moines, IA 50309-3609
Phone: 515-725-3424
Fax: 515-725-3401
E-mail: misty.thompson@iowa.gov

IOWA DIVISION OF VOCATIONAL REHABILITATION SERVICES http://www.ivrs.iowa.gov

IOWA VOCATIONAL REHABILITATION

• *See page 621*

ITALIAN-AMERICAN CHAMBER OF COMMERCE MIDWEST http://www.italianchamber.us

ITALIAN-AMERICAN CHAMBER OF COMMERCE OF CHICAGO SCHOLARSHIP

• *See page 688*

ITALIAN CATHOLIC FEDERATION INC. http://www.icf.org

ITALIAN CATHOLIC FEDERATION FIRST YEAR SCHOLARSHIP

• *See page 538*

JACKSON ENERGY COOPERATIVE http://www.jacksonenergy.com

JACKSON ENERGY SCHOLARSHIP

Scholarships are awarded to winners in an essay contest. Must be at least a senior in a Kentucky high school and no more than 21 years of age. Parents or legal guardian must be a cooperative member, but not an employee of Jackson Energy.

Award: Scholarship for use in freshman, sophomore, junior, or senior years; not renewable. *Number:* 8. *Amount:* $1000.

Eligibility Requirements: Applicant must be age 21 or under; enrolled or expecting to enroll full-time at a two-year or four-year or technical institution or university and resident of Kentucky. Available to U.S. citizens.

Application Requirements: Application, applicant must enter a contest, essay. *Deadline:* March 1.

Contact: Karen Combs, Director of Public Relations
Jackson Energy Cooperative
115 Jackson Energy lane
McKee, KY 40447
Phone: 606-364-1000
Fax: 606-364-1011
E-mail: karencombs@jacksonenergy.com

JAMES F. BYRNES FOUNDATION http://www.byrnesscholars.org

JAMES F. BYRNES SCHOLARSHIP

Renewable award for residents of South Carolina ages 17-22 with one or both parents deceased. Must show financial need; a satisfactory scholastic record; and qualities of character, ability, and enterprise. Award is for undergraduate study. Results of SAT must be provided. Information available on Web site: http://www.byrnesscholars.org.

Award: Scholarship for use in freshman or sophomore years; renewable. *Number:* 10–20. *Amount:* up to $3250.

Eligibility Requirements: Applicant must be age 17-22; enrolled or expecting to enroll full-time at a four-year institution and resident of South Carolina. Available to U.S. citizens.

Application Requirements: Application, autobiography, financial need analysis, interview, photo, references, test scores, transcript. *Deadline:* February 15.

Contact: Kenya White, Executive Secretary
James F. Byrnes Foundation
PO Box 6781
Columbia, SC 29260-6781
Phone: 803-254-9325
Fax: 803-254-9354
E-mail: info@byrnesscholars.org

JAY'S WORLD CHILDHOOD CANCER FOUNDATION http://www.jaysworld.org

JAY'S WORLD CHILDHOOD CANCER FOUNDATION SCHOLARSHIP

• *See page 621*

J. CRAIG AND PAGE T. SMITH SCHOLARSHIP FOUNDATION http://www.jcraigsmithfoundation.org

FIRST IN FAMILY SCHOLARSHIP

Scholarships are available for graduating Alabama high school seniors. Must be planning to enroll in an Alabama institution in fall and pursue a four-year degree. Students who apply must want to give back to their community by volunteer and civic work. Special consideration will be given to applicants who would be the first in either their mother's or father's family (or both) to attend college.

Award: Scholarship for use in freshman year; renewable. *Number:* 10. *Amount:* $12,500–$15,000.

Eligibility Requirements: Applicant must be high school student; planning to enroll or expecting to enroll full-time at a four-year institution or university; resident of Alabama and studying in Alabama. Applicant must have 2.5 GPA or higher. Available to U.S. citizens.

Application Requirements: Application, essay, financial need analysis, references, test scores, transcript. *Deadline:* January 15.

Contact: Ahrian Tyler, Administrator/Chairman of the Board
J. Craig and Page T. Smith Scholarship Foundation
505 20th Street North, Suite 1800
Birmingham, AL 35203
Phone: 205-250-6669
Fax: 205-328-7234
E-mail: ahrian@jcraigsmithfoundation.org

JEWISH FOUNDATION FOR EDUCATION OF WOMEN http://www.jfew.org

JFEW/UJA FEDERATION ROSE BILLER SCHOLARSHIPS

• *See page 688*

JEWISH VOCATIONAL SERVICE-LOS ANGELES http://www.jvsla.org

JEWISH VOCATIONAL SERVICE SCHOLARSHIP FUND

• *See page 715*

KAISER PERMANENTE http://xnet.kp.org/hr/ca/kpapan

KAISER PERMANENTE ASIAN PACIFIC AMERICAN NETWORK SCHOLARSHIP PROGRAM

• *See page 688*

KANSAS BOARD OF REGENTS http://www.kansasregents.org

KANSAS ETHNIC MINORITY SCHOLARSHIP

• *See page 688*

KANSAS COMMISSION ON VETERANS AFFAIRS http://www.kcva.org

KANSAS EDUCATIONAL BENEFITS FOR CHILDREN OF MIA, POW, AND DECEASED VETERANS OF THE VIETNAM WAR

• *See page 655*

KE ALI'I PAUAHI FOUNDATION http://www.pauahi.org

ANNE H. MYERS SCHOLARSHIP

Scholarship to support the education of a Hawaii resident enrolled full-time in an accredited college in a degree-seeking program. Must have a successful record of academic achievement.

Award: Scholarship for use in freshman, sophomore, junior, senior, or graduate years; not renewable. *Number:* 1. *Amount:* up to $600.

Eligibility Requirements: Applicant must be enrolled or expecting to enroll full-time at a two-year or four-year institution or university and resident of Hawaii. Available to U.S. citizens.

Application Requirements: Application, essay, financial need analysis, references, transcript, college acceptance letter, copy of SAR. *Deadline:* May 2.

Contact: Elizabeth Stevenson, Development Manager
Ke Ali'i Pauahi Foundation
567 South King Street, Suite 160
Honolulu, HI 96813
Phone: 808-534-3966
Fax: 808-534-3890
E-mail: scholarships@pauahi.org

DANIEL KAHIKINA AND MILLIE AKAKA SCHOLARSHIP

• *See page 601*

JALENE KANANI BELL 'OHANA SCHOLARSHIP

Scholarship open to part-time or full-time undergraduate or graduate students who are Hawaii residents with a GPA of 2.5 or above. Must have demonstrated interest in the Hawaiian language, culture, and history.

Award: Scholarship for use in freshman, sophomore, junior, senior, or graduate years; not renewable. *Number:* 1. *Amount:* $1000.

Eligibility Requirements: Applicant must be enrolled or expecting to enroll full- or part-time at a four-year institution or university; resident of Hawaii and must have an interest in Hawaiian language/culture. Applicant must have 2.5 GPA or higher. Available to U.S. citizens.

Application Requirements: Application, references, transcript, Student Aid Report (SAR), college acceptance letter. *Deadline:* May 2.

Contact: Elizabeth Stevenson, Development Manager
Ke Ali'i Pauahi Foundation
567 South King Street, Suite 160
Honolulu, HI 96813
Phone: 808-534-3966
Fax: 808-534-3890
E-mail: scholarships@pauahi.org

KAMEHAMEHA SCHOOLS ALUMNI ASSOCIATION-MAUI REGION SCHOLARSHIP

• *See page 601*

KAMEHAMEHA SCHOOLS CLASS OF 1956 GRANT

Grant to assist at least one male and one female student who demonstrate financial need and have a minimum 2.5 GPA. Applicants must show an interest in Hawaiian language, culture and history, and demonstrate a commitment to contribute to the greater community.

Award: Grant for use in freshman, sophomore, junior, senior, or graduate years; not renewable. *Number:* 2. *Amount:* $600.

Eligibility Requirements: Applicant must be enrolled or expecting to enroll full-time at a four-year institution or university; resident of Hawaii and must have an interest in Hawaiian language/culture. Available to U.S. citizens.

Application Requirements: Application, financial need analysis, references, transcript, Student Aid Report (SAR), college acceptance letter. *Deadline:* May 2.

Contact: Elizabeth Stevenson, Development Manager
Ke Ali'i Pauahi Foundation
567 South King Street, Suite 160
Honolulu, HI 96813
Phone: 808-534-3966
Fax: 808-534-3890
E-mail: scholarships@pauahi.org

KAMEHAMEHA SCHOOLS CLASS OF 1974 SCHOLARSHIP

Scholarship will provide support to students enrolled at a postsecondary institution, including non-traditional programs such as Hawaiian culture or self-improvement seminars. Applicants must have a minimum GPA of 2.8 and demonstrate financial need. Preference will be given to family members of Kamehameha Schools Class of 1974.

Award: Scholarship for use in freshman, sophomore, junior, senior, or graduate years; not renewable. *Number:* varies. *Amount:* $1200.

Eligibility Requirements: Applicant must be enrolled or expecting to enroll full-time at a two-year or four-year institution or university; resident of Hawaii and must have an interest in Hawaiian language/culture. Available to U.S. citizens.

Application Requirements: Application, financial need analysis, references, transcript, Student Aid Report (SAR), college acceptance letter. *Deadline:* May 2.

Contact: Elizabeth Stevenson, Development Manager
Ke Ali'i Pauahi Foundation
567 South King Street, Suite 160
Honolulu, HI 96813
Phone: 808-534-3966
Fax: 808-534-3890
E-mail: scholarships@pauahi.org

KAMEHAMEHA SCHOOLS CLASS OF 1970 SCHOLARSHIP

• *See page 602*

KAMEHAMEHA SCHOOLS CLASS OF 1972 SCHOLARSHIP

Scholarship to assist Kamehameha Schools Class of 1972 graduates, and their children and grandchildren with a minimum GPA of 2.8, to earn an undergraduate or graduate degree. May also be awarded to assist individuals whose lives have been impacted by challenging circumstances, such as death of a significant family member, domestic violence, sexual abuse, poverty, or major illness.

Award: Scholarship for use in freshman, sophomore, junior, senior, or graduate years; not renewable. *Number:* varies. *Amount:* $1100.

Eligibility Requirements: Applicant must be enrolled or expecting to enroll full-time at a four-year institution or university and resident of Hawaii. Available to U.S. citizens.

Ke Ali'i Pauahi Foundation (continued)

Application Requirements: Application, financial need analysis, references, transcript, Student Aid Report (SAR), college acceptance letter. *Deadline:* May 2.

Contact: Elizabeth Stevenson, Development Manager
Ke Ali'i Pauahi Foundation
567 South King Street, Suite 160
Honolulu, HI 96813
Phone: 808-534-3966
Fax: 808-534-3890
E-mail: scholarships@pauahi.org

KAMEHAMEHA SCHOOLS CLASS OF 1960 GRANT

• *See page 602*

KENERGY CORPORATION http://www.kenergycorp.com

KENERGY SCHOLARSHIP

Student must be a member owner of Kenergy, or must have his/her primary residence with a parent or legal guardian who receives electric service from Kenergy. Must be accompanied by his/her parent(s) or legal guardians to the Kenergy Annual Membership Meeting in Henderson, Kentucky where the student may register for scholarship drawings.

Award: Scholarship for use in freshman, sophomore, junior, senior, or graduate years; not renewable. *Number:* up to 20. *Amount:* $500.

Eligibility Requirements: Applicant must be enrolled or expecting to enroll full-time at a two-year or four-year or technical institution or university and resident of Kentucky. Available to U.S. and non-U.S. citizens.

Application Requirements: Application, transcript. *Deadline:* varies.

Contact: Beverly Hooper, Scholarship Coordinator
Kenergy Corporation
6402 Old Corydon Road, PO Box 18
Henderson, KY 42420
Phone: 270-826-3991 Ext. 3811
Fax: 270-826-3999
E-mail: bhooper@kenergycorp.com

KENTUCKY ASSOCIATION OF ELECTRIC COOPERATIVES INC. http://www.kaec.org

WOMEN IN RURAL ELECTRIFICATION (WIRE) SCHOLARSHIP

Scholarship to students whose family is served by a Kentucky Rural Electric Cooperative. Student must have at least 60 credit hours at the beginning of the fall semester and must attend a Kentucky college or university. Scholarships will be awarded based on academic achievements, extracurricular activities, career goals, recommendations from professors and community leaders, and financial need.

Award: Scholarship for use in junior or senior years; not renewable. *Number:* up to 3. *Amount:* $1000.

Eligibility Requirements: Applicant must be enrolled or expecting to enroll full-time at a four-year institution or university; resident of Kentucky and studying in Kentucky. Available to U.S. citizens.

Application Requirements: Application, financial need analysis, references, transcript, proof of work experience. *Deadline:* June 16.

Contact: Ellie Hobgood, Administrative Assistant
Kentucky Association of Electric Cooperatives Inc.
4515 Bishop Lane
Louisville, KY 40218
Phone: 502-451-2430
Fax: 502-459-1611

KENTUCKY DEPARTMENT OF EDUCATION http://www.education.ky.gov

ROBERT C. BYRD HONORS SCHOLARSHIP-KENTUCKY

Scholarship available to high school seniors who show past high achievement and potential for continued academic success. Must have applied for admission or have been accepted for enrollment at a public or private nonprofit postsecondary school. Must be a Kentucky resident.

Award: Scholarship for use in freshman, sophomore, junior, or senior years; renewable. *Number:* varies. *Amount:* up to $1500.

Eligibility Requirements: Applicant must be high school student; planning to enroll or expecting to enroll full-time at a two-year or four-year institution or university and resident of Kentucky. Applicant must have 3.5 GPA or higher. Available to U.S. citizens.

Application Requirements: Application, test scores. *Deadline:* March 14.

Contact: Donna Melton, Scholarship Committee
Kentucky Department of Education
500 Mero Street, 17th Floor
Frankfort, KY 40601
Phone: 502-564-1479
E-mail: dmelton@kde.state.ky.us

KENTUCKY DEPARTMENT OF VETERANS AFFAIRS http://www.veterans.ky.gov

DEPARTMENT OF VETERANS AFFAIRS TUITION WAIVER-KY KRS 164-507

Scholarship available to college students who are residents of Kentucky under the age of 26.

Award: Scholarship for use in freshman, sophomore, junior, or senior years; not renewable. *Number:* 350. *Amount:* varies.

Eligibility Requirements: Applicant must be age 26 or under; enrolled or expecting to enroll full-time at a two-year or four-year institution or university and resident of Kentucky. Available to U.S. citizens.

Application Requirements: Application. *Deadline:* varies.

Contact: Barbara Sipek, Administrative Specialist
Kentucky Department of Veterans Affairs
321 West Main Street, Suite 390
Louisville, KY 40213-9095
Phone: 502-595-4447
Fax: 502-595-4448
E-mail: barbaraa.sipek@ky.gov

KENTUCKY HIGHER EDUCATION ASSISTANCE AUTHORITY (KHEAA) http://www.kheaa.com

COLLEGE ACCESS PROGRAM (CAP) GRANT

Award for U.S. citizen and Kentucky resident with no previous college degree. Applicants seeking degrees in religion are not eligible. Must demonstrate financial need and submit Free Application for Federal Student Aid. Expected family contribution (EFC) towards the students educational expenses cannot exceed $3850.

Award: Grant for use in freshman, sophomore, junior, or senior years; not renewable. *Number:* 35,000–40,000. *Amount:* up to $1900.

Eligibility Requirements: Applicant must be enrolled or expecting to enroll full- or part-time at a two-year or four-year or technical institution or university; resident of Kentucky and studying in Kentucky. Available to U.S. citizens.

Application Requirements: Application, financial need analysis, FAFSA. *Deadline:* March 15.

Contact: Michael D. Morgan, Program Coordinator
Kentucky Higher Education Assistance Authority (KHEAA)
PO Box 798
Frankfort, KY 40602-0798
Phone: 502-696-7394
Fax: 502-696-7373
E-mail: mmorgan@kheaa.com

EDUCATION AT WORK SCHOLARSHIP

Scholarships available for Kentucky residents enrolled in a Kentucky postsecondary institution. Must have received services from the State Office for the Blind, Office of Employment and Training, Office of Career and Technical Education, Office of Vocational Rehabilitation, or Kentucky Adult Education in the past three years. Must submit an application, two character references, and an essay of under 600 words.

Award: Scholarship for use in freshman, sophomore, junior, or senior years; not renewable. *Number:* 20–36. *Amount:* $1000.

Eligibility Requirements: Applicant must be enrolled or expecting to enroll full- or part-time at a two-year or four-year or technical institution or university; resident of Kentucky and studying in Kentucky. Available to U.S. citizens.

Application Requirements: Application, essay, references. *Deadline:* continuous.

Contact: Wynee Hecker, Program Coordinator
Kentucky Higher Education Assistance Authority (KHEAA)
500 Mero Street, Second Floor
Frankfort, KY 40601
Phone: 502-564-6606 Ext. 128
E-mail: wyneej.hecker@ky.gov

KENTUCKY EDUCATIONAL EXCELLENCE SCHOLARSHIP (KEES)

Annual award based on GPA and highest ACT or SAT score received at the time of high school graduation. Awards are renewable, if required cumulative GPA is maintained at a Kentucky postsecondary school. Must be a Kentucky resident, and a graduate of a Kentucky high school.

Award: Scholarship for use in freshman year; renewable. *Number:* 60,000–65,000. *Amount:* varies.

Eligibility Requirements: Applicant must be high school student; planning to enroll or expecting to enroll full- or part-time at a two-year or four-year or technical institution or university; resident of Kentucky and studying in Kentucky. Applicant must have 2.5 GPA or higher. Available to U.S. citizens.

Application Requirements: Application, test scores, transcript. *Deadline:* continuous.

Contact: Linda Renschler, Director
Kentucky Higher Education Assistance Authority (KHEAA)
PO Box 798
Frankfort, KY 40602-0798
Phone: 502-696-7400
Fax: 502-696-7373
E-mail: lrenschler@kheaa.com

KENTUCKY TUITION GRANT (KTG)

Grants available to Kentucky residents who are full-time undergraduates at an independent college within the state. Must not be enrolled in a religion program. Based on financial need. Must submit FAFSA.

Award: Grant for use in freshman, sophomore, junior, or senior years; not renewable. *Number:* 10,000–12,000. *Amount:* $200–$3000.

Eligibility Requirements: Applicant must be enrolled or expecting to enroll full-time at a two-year or four-year institution or university; resident of Kentucky and studying in Kentucky. Available to U.S. citizens.

Application Requirements: Application, financial need analysis, FAFSA. *Deadline:* March 15.

Contact: Tim Phelps, Student Aid Branch Manager
Kentucky Higher Education Assistance Authority (KHEAA)
PO Box 798
Frankfort, KY 40602-0798
Phone: 502-696-7393
Fax: 502-696-7496
E-mail: tphelps@kheaa.com

KENTUCKY TOUCHSTONE ENERGY COOPERATIVES http://www.ekpc.coop

TOUCHSTONE ENERGY ALL "A" CLASSIC SCHOLARSHIP

Award of $1000 for senior student in good standing at a Kentucky high school which is a member of the All Classic. Applicant must be a U.S. citizen and must plan to attend a postsecondary institution in Kentucky in the upcoming year as a full-time student and be drug free.

Award: Scholarship for use in freshman year; not renewable. *Number:* 12. *Amount:* $1000.

Eligibility Requirements: Applicant must be high school student; planning to enroll or expecting to enroll full-time at a two-year or four-year or technical institution or university; resident of Kentucky and studying in Kentucky. Available to U.S. citizens.

Application Requirements: Application, essay, photo, references, transcript. *Deadline:* December 3.

Contact: David Cowden, Chairperson, Scholarship Committee
Kentucky Touchstone Energy Cooperatives
1320 Lincoln Road
Lewisport, KY 42351
Phone: 859-744-4812
E-mail: allaclassic@alltel.net

KOREAN AMERICAN SCHOLARSHIP FOUNDATION http://www.kasf.org

KOREAN-AMERICAN SCHOLARSHIP FOUNDATION EASTERN REGION SCHOLARSHIPS

• *See page 689*

KOREAN-AMERICAN SCHOLARSHIP FOUNDATION NORTHEASTERN REGION SCHOLARSHIPS

• *See page 689*

KOREAN-AMERICAN SCHOLARSHIP FOUNDATION SOUTHERN REGION SCHOLARSHIPS

• *See page 690*

KOREAN-AMERICAN SCHOLARSHIP FOUNDATION WESTERN REGION SCHOLARSHIPS

• *See page 690*

KOSCIUSZKO FOUNDATION http://www.kosciuszkofoundation.org

MASSACHUSETTS FEDERATION OF POLISH WOMEN'S CLUBS SCHOLARSHIPS

• *See page 690*

LEE-JACKSON EDUCATIONAL FOUNDATION http://www.lee-jackson.org

LEE-JACKSON EDUCATIONAL FOUNDATION SCHOLARSHIP COMPETITION

Essay contest for junior and senior Virginia high school students. Must demonstrate appreciation for the exemplary character and soldierly virtues of Generals Robert E. Lee and Thomas J. "Stonewall" Jackson. Three one-time awards of $1000 in each of Virginia's eight regions. A bonus scholarship of $1000 will be awarded to the author of the best essay in each of the eight regions. An additional award of $8000 will go to the essay judged the best in the state.

Award: Scholarship for use in freshman, sophomore, junior, or senior years; not renewable. *Number:* 27. *Amount:* $1000–$10,000.

Eligibility Requirements: Applicant must be high school student; planning to enroll or expecting to enroll full-time at a four-year institution or university; resident of Virginia and must have an interest in writing. Available to U.S. citizens.

Application Requirements: Application, applicant must enter a contest, essay, transcript. *Deadline:* December 21.

Contact: Stephanie Leech, Administrator
Lee-Jackson Educational Foundation
PO Box 8121
Charlottesville, VA 22906
Phone: 434-977-1861
E-mail: salp_leech@yahoo.com

LIGHTHOUSE INTERNATIONAL http://www.lighthouse.org

SCHOLARSHIP AWARDS

• *See page 621*

LINCOLN COMMUNITY FOUNDATION http://www.lcf.org

BRENDA BROWN DESATNICK MEMORIAL SCHOLARSHIP

Applicants must be a former graduate of any high school in the United States. Must plan to attend any qualified, regionally accredited two- or four-year college or university. Preference will be given to women over the age of 25 who reside in Lincoln/Lancaster County in Nebraska. Applicants must show interest in becoming self-supporting and independent and demonstrate financial need. No criteria related to field of study.

Award: Scholarship for use in freshman, sophomore, junior, senior, graduate, or postgraduate years; not renewable. *Number:* 1. *Amount:* $500–$800.

Eligibility Requirements: Applicant must be enrolled or expecting to enroll full-time at a two-year or four-year institution or university; female and resident of Nebraska. Available to U.S. citizens.

Lincoln Community Foundation (continued)

Application Requirements: Application, essay, financial need analysis, references. *Deadline:* June 1.

Contact: Sonya Brakeman, Grants/Scholarships Coordinator
Lincoln Community Foundation
215 Centennial Mall South, Suite 100
Lincoln, NE 68508
Phone: 402-474-2345
Fax: 402-476-8532
E-mail: sonyab@lcf.org

GEORGE L. WATTERS/NEBRASKA PETROLEUM MARKETERS ASSOCIATION SCHOLARSHIP

• *See page 580*

HARRY RICHARDSON-CEDARS SCHOLARSHIP

Scholarship for individuals with a GED or have been a recipient of any service offered by Cedars Youth Services in Lincoln, Nebraska. Applicants must demonstrate financial need and ability to complete coursework. Recipients must be high school graduating seniors or first year college students.

Award: Scholarship for use in freshman, sophomore, junior, or senior years; not renewable. *Number:* 1. *Amount:* $1000.

Eligibility Requirements: Applicant must be enrolled or expecting to enroll full-time at a two-year or four-year institution or university and resident of Nebraska. Available to U.S. citizens.

Application Requirements: Application, essay, references. *Deadline:* April 1.

Contact: Sonya Brakeman, Grants/Scholarships Coordinator
Lincoln Community Foundation
215 Centennial Mall South, Suite 100
Lincoln, NE 68508
Phone: 402-474-2345
Fax: 402-476-8532
E-mail: sonyab@lcf.org

JENNINGS AND BEULAH HAGGERTY SCHOLARSHIP

Scholarship for graduating seniors from public or private high schools in Lincoln, NE area. Must be in the top third of graduating class, and enroll in a two- or four-year institution in Nebraska. Must demonstrate financial need and academic achievement.

Award: Scholarship for use in freshman year; not renewable. *Number:* 10–20. *Amount:* $500–$1000.

Eligibility Requirements: Applicant must be high school student; planning to enroll or expecting to enroll full-time at a two-year or four-year or technical institution or university; resident of Nebraska and studying in Nebraska. Applicant must have 3.0 GPA or higher. Available to U.S. citizens.

Application Requirements: Application, essay, financial need analysis, interview, references, test scores, transcript. *Deadline:* July 1.

Contact: Sonya Brakeman, Grants/Scholarships Coordinator
Lincoln Community Foundation
215 Centennial Mall South, Suite 100
Lincoln, NE 68508
Phone: 402-474-2345
Fax: 402-476-8532
E-mail: sonyab@lcf.org

NEBRASKA RURAL SCHOOLS SCHOLARSHIP

Multi-scholarships available to current high school seniors or graduates of a rural high school in Nebraska who rank in the top ten percent of their high school graduating class, or are college students with a 3.5 GPA or better. Applicants attending a university, college or community college in Nebraska are eligible to apply. See Web site for application: http://www.lcf.org.

Award: Scholarship for use in freshman, sophomore, junior, or senior years; renewable. *Number:* 4. *Amount:* $500–$2000.

Eligibility Requirements: Applicant must be enrolled or expecting to enroll full-time at a four-year institution or university; resident of Nebraska and studying in Nebraska. Applicant must have 3.5 GPA or higher. Available to U.S. citizens.

Application Requirements: Application, essay, financial need analysis, test scores, transcript. *Deadline:* August 1.

Contact: Sonya Brakeman, Grants/Scholarships Coordinator
Lincoln Community Foundation
215 Centennial Mall South, Suite 100
Lincoln, NE 68508
Phone: 402-474-2345
Fax: 402-476-8532
E-mail: sonyab@lcf.org

NORMAN AND RUTH GOOD EDUCATIONAL ENDOWMENT

Multi-scholarships available to current college students attending private colleges in Nebraska with junior or senior standing. Must have a 3.5 GPA or better. See Web site for application: http://www.lcf.org.

Award: Scholarship for use in junior or senior years; renewable. *Number:* 10–15. *Amount:* $500–$2000.

Eligibility Requirements: Applicant must be enrolled or expecting to enroll full-time at a four-year institution or university and studying in Nebraska. Applicant must have 3.5 GPA or higher. Available to U.S. citizens.

Application Requirements: Application, test scores, transcript. *Deadline:* April 15.

Contact: Sonya Brakeman, Grants/Scholarships Coordinator
Lincoln Community Foundation
215 Centennial Mall South, Suite 100
Lincoln, NE 68508
Phone: 402-474-2345
Fax: 402-476-8532
E-mail: sonyab@lcf.org

P.G. RICHARDSON MASONIC MEMORIAL SCHOLARSHIP

• *See page 541*

THOMAS C. WOODS, JR. MEMORIAL SCHOLARSHIP

• *See page 580*

WHITE MEMORIAL SCHOLARSHIP

Applicants must be current graduating seniors or former graduates of any high school in Nebraska. Preference will be given to those students graduating from high schools in Lincoln, Lyons or Fairbury high schools in Nebraska. Applicants must demonstrate financial need. Preference will be given to first year college students. Scholarship may be renewed for a period of up to four years provided the applicant continues to meet the criteria.

Award: Scholarship for use in freshman year; renewable. *Number:* 3. *Amount:* $500–$1000.

Eligibility Requirements: Applicant must be high school student; planning to enroll or expecting to enroll full-time at a two-year or four-year institution or university and resident of Nebraska. Available to U.S. citizens.

Application Requirements: Application, essay, financial need analysis, test scores, transcript. *Deadline:* March 15.

Contact: Sonya Brakeman, Grants/Scholarships Coordinator
Lincoln Community Foundation
215 Centennial Mall South, Suite 100
Lincoln, NE 68508
Phone: 402-474-2345
Fax: 402-476-8532
E-mail: sonyab@lcf.org

WILLIAM B. AND VIRGINIA S. ROLOFSON SCHOLARSHIP

• *See page 715*

LOS ALAMOS NATIONAL LABORATORY FOUNDATION

http://www.lanlfoundation.org

LOS ALAMOS EMPLOYEES' SCHOLARSHIP

Scholarship supports students in Northern New Mexico who are pursuing undergraduate degrees in fields that will serve the region. Financial need, diversity, and regional representation are integral components of the selections process. Applicant should be a permanent resident of Northern New Mexico with at least a 3.25 cumulative GPA and 19 ACT or 930 SAT score.

Award: Scholarship for use in freshman, sophomore, junior, or senior years; renewable. *Number:* 50. *Amount:* $1000–$30,000.

Eligibility Requirements: Applicant must be enrolled or expecting to enroll full- or part-time at a two-year or four-year institution or university and resident of New Mexico. Available to U.S. and non-U.S. citizens.

Application Requirements: Application, essay, photo, references, test scores, transcript. *Deadline:* January 22.

Contact: Tony Fox, Program Officer
Los Alamos National Laboratory Foundation
1302 Calle de la Merced, Suite A
Espanola, NM 87532
Phone: 505-753-8890 Ext. 16
Fax: 505-753-8915
E-mail: tfox@lanlfoundation.org

LOS ANGELES PHILHARMONIC http://www.laphil.com

BRONISLAW KAPER AWARDS FOR YOUNG ARTISTS

Competition for young musicians under the age of 18, or a senior in high school. This award is not for post-secondary students. Offers cash prizes. The instrumental category alternates annually between piano and strings. Must be a California resident. Visit Web site at http://www.laphil.com for deadlines.

Award: Prize for use in freshman year; not renewable. *Number:* 4. *Amount:* $500–$2500.

Eligibility Requirements: Applicant must be high school student; age 18 or under; planning to enroll or expecting to enroll full- or part-time at a four-year institution or university; resident of California and must have an interest in music. Available to U.S. citizens.

Application Requirements: Application, applicant must enter a contest, audition. *Deadline:* varies.

Contact: Karl Montezirgen, Program Manager
Los Angeles Philharmonic
151 South Grand Avenue
Los Angeles, CA 90012
Phone: 213-972-0705
Fax: 213-972-7650
E-mail: education@laphil.org

LOS PADRES FOUNDATION http://www.lospadresfoundation.com

COLLEGE TUITION ASSISTANCE PROGRAM

• *See page 691*

SECOND CHANCE SCHOLARSHIPS

• *See page 691*

LOUISIANA DEPARTMENT OF VETERANS AFFAIRS http://www.vetaffairs.com

LOUISIANA DEPARTMENT OF VETERANS AFFAIRS STATE AID PROGRAM

• *See page 655*

LOUISIANA NATIONAL GUARD-STATE OF LOUISIANA, JOINT TASK FORCE LA http://www.la.ngb.army.mil

LOUISIANA NATIONAL GUARD STATE TUITION EXEMPTION PROGRAM

• *See page 635*

LOUISIANA OFFICE OF STUDENT FINANCIAL ASSISTANCE http://www.osfa.state.la.us

LEVERAGING EDUCATIONAL ASSISTANCE PROGRAM (LEAP)

Apply by completing the FAFSA each year. Eligibility is determined by the institution the student attends. Must be a resident of Louisiana and must be attending an institution in Louisiana.

Award: Grant for use in freshman, sophomore, junior, or senior years; renewable. *Number:* 3000–4000. *Amount:* $200–$2000.

Eligibility Requirements: Applicant must be enrolled or expecting to enroll full- or part-time at a two-year or four-year or technical institution or university; resident of Louisiana and studying in Louisiana. Available to U.S. citizens.

Application Requirements: Application, financial need analysis. *Deadline:* July 1.

Contact: Public Information
Louisiana Office of Student Financial Assistance
PO Box 91202
Baton Rouge, LA 70821-9202
Phone: 800-259-5626 Ext. 1012
Fax: 225-922-0790
E-mail: custserv@osfa.state.la.us

TOPS HONORS AWARD

Award is fully state funded. Unit core curriculum is 17.5. GPA requirement 3.0. The weighted average public tuition would be approximately $1338(In addition $400 would be provided). The award is renewable up to eight semesters.

Award: Scholarship for use in freshman, sophomore, junior, or senior years; renewable. *Number:* varies. *Amount:* up to $1738.

Eligibility Requirements: Applicant must be high school student; planning to enroll or expecting to enroll full-time at a two-year or four-year or technical institution or university; resident of Louisiana and studying in Louisiana. Applicant must have 3.0 GPA or higher. Available to U.S. citizens.

Application Requirements: Application, test scores. *Deadline:* July 1.

Contact: Public Information
Louisiana Office of Student Financial Assistance
PO Box 91202
Baton Rouge, LA 70821-9202
Phone: 800-259-5626 Ext. 1012
Fax: 225-922-0790
E-mail: custserv@osfa.state.la.us

TOPS PERFORMANCE AWARD

Award is fully state funded. Unit core curriculum is 17.5. GPA requirement is 3.0. The weighted average public tuition would be approximately $1338. The award is renewable up to eight semesters. Must be a Louisiana resident.

Award: Scholarship for use in freshman, sophomore, junior, or senior years; renewable. *Number:* varies. *Amount:* up to $1338.

Eligibility Requirements: Applicant must be high school student; planning to enroll or expecting to enroll full-time at a two-year or four-year or technical institution or university; resident of Louisiana and studying in Louisiana. Applicant must have 3.0 GPA or higher. Available to U.S. citizens.

Application Requirements: Application, test scores. *Deadline:* July 1.

Contact: Public Information
Louisiana Office of Student Financial Assistance
PO Box 91202
Baton Rouge, LA 70821-9202
Phone: 800-259-5626 Ext. 1012
Fax: 225-922-0790
E-mail: custserv@osfa.state.la.us

TOPS TECH AWARD

Program awards an amount equal to tuition for up to two years of technical training at a Louisiana postsecondary institution that offers a vocational or technical education certificate or diploma program, or a non-academic degree program. Must have a 2.5 high school GPA based on TOPS Tech core curriculum, an ACT score of 17, and complete the TOPS-Tech core curriculum. Must be a Louisiana resident.

Award: Scholarship for use in freshman or sophomore years; renewable. *Number:* varies. *Amount:* $879–$1679.

Eligibility Requirements: Applicant must be enrolled or expecting to enroll full-time at a technical institution; resident of Louisiana and studying in Louisiana. Applicant must have 2.5 GPA or higher. Available to U.S. citizens.

Louisiana Office of Student Financial Assistance (continued)

Application Requirements: Application, test scores, FAFSA, ACT score. *Deadline:* July 1.

Contact: Public Information
Louisiana Office of Student Financial Assistance
PO Box 91202
Baton Rouge, LA 70821-9202
Phone: 800-259-5626 Ext. 1012
Fax: 225-922-0790
E-mail: custserv@osfa.state.la.us

TUITION OPPORTUNITY PROGRAM FOR STUDENTS

Program awards an amount equal to tuition fee to students attending a Louisiana public institution, or an amount equal to the weighted average public tuition fee to students attending a LAICU private institution. Must have a minimum high school GPA of 2.5 based on the TOPS core curriculum, the prior year's state average ACT score, and complete a 17.5 unit core curriculum. Must be a Louisiana resident. Number of awards given varies each year.

Award: Scholarship for use in freshman, sophomore, junior, or senior years; renewable. *Number:* varies. *Amount:* $879–$4434.

Eligibility Requirements: Applicant must be enrolled or expecting to enroll full-time at a two-year or four-year institution or university; resident of Louisiana and studying in Louisiana. Applicant must have 2.5 GPA or higher. Available to U.S. citizens.

Application Requirements: Application, test scores, ACT scores, completion of a 17.5 unit core curriculum. *Deadline:* July 1.

Contact: Public Information
Louisiana Office of Student Financial Assistance
PO Box 91202
Baton Rouge, LA 70821-9202
Phone: 800-259-5626 Ext. 1012
Fax: 225-922-0790
E-mail: custserv@osfa.state.la.us

LOUISIANA STATE DEPARTMENT OF EDUCATION http://www.doe.state.la.us

ROBERT C. BYRD HONORS SCHOLARSHIP-LOUISIANA

Applicant must have earned a high school diploma or equivalent (GED) in Louisiana in the same academic year in which the scholarship is to be awarded. Minimum 3.5 GPA required. Must be a U.S. citizen and legal resident of Louisiana. Total number of awards vary each year.

Award: Scholarship for use in freshman, sophomore, junior, or senior years; renewable. *Number:* 110. *Amount:* up to $6000.

Eligibility Requirements: Applicant must be enrolled or expecting to enroll full-time at a four-year institution or university and resident of Louisiana. Applicant must have 3.5 GPA or higher. Available to U.S. citizens.

Application Requirements: Application, essay, test scores, transcript, selective service form. *Deadline:* March 10.

Contact: Melissa Hollins, Scholarship Coordinator
Louisiana State Department of Education
PO Box 94064
Baton Rouge, LA 70804
Phone: 225-342-2098
E-mail: melissa.hollins@la.gov

MAINE BUREAU OF VETERANS SERVICES http://www.state.me.us

VETERANS DEPENDENTS EDUCATIONAL BENEFITS-MAINE

• *See page 655*

MAINE COMMUNITY COLLEGE SYSTEM http://www.mccs.me.edu

EARLY COLLEGE FOR ME

Scholarship for high school students who have not made plans for college but are academically capable of success in college. Recipients are selected by their school principal or director. Students must be entering a Maine Community College. Refer to Web site: http://www.mccs.me.edu/scholarships.html.

Award: Scholarship for use in freshman year; renewable. *Number:* 200. *Amount:* $2000.

Eligibility Requirements: Applicant must be high school student; planning to enroll or expecting to enroll full-time at a two-year or four-year institution or university; resident of Maine and studying in Maine. Available to U.S. citizens.

Application Requirements: Application, financial need analysis, references, transcript. *Deadline:* varies.

Contact: Charles P. Collins, State Director, Center for Career Development
Maine Community College System
323 State Street
Augusta, ME 04330
Phone: 207-767-5210 Ext. 4115
Fax: 207-629-4048
E-mail: ccollins@mccs.me.edu

OSHER SCHOLARSHIP

Scholarships to students who are Maine residents not currently enrolled in a program at any college or university, have accumulated no more than 24 college credits and qualify for and are accepted into the Associate in Arts in liberal/general studies program.

Award: Scholarship for use in freshman year; not renewable. *Number:* varies. *Amount:* up to $468.

Eligibility Requirements: Applicant must be enrolled or expecting to enroll full-time at a two-year or technical institution; resident of Maine and studying in Maine. Available to U.S. citizens.

Application Requirements: Application. *Deadline:* varies.

Contact: Scholarship Committee
Maine Community College System
323 State Street
Augusta, ME 04330
Phone: 207-629-4000
Fax: 207-629-4048
E-mail: info@mccs.me.edu

MAINE COMMUNITY FOUNDATION INC. http://www.mainecf.org

CHALLENGER MEMORIAL SCHOLARSHIP FUND

Renewable scholarship, granted on the basis of established Maine residency, academic or artistic talents, aspirations, leadership skills, and financial need. Scholarships will range up to ten percent of the receiving scholar's stated tuition.

Award: Scholarship for use in freshman year; renewable. *Number:* varies. *Amount:* varies.

Eligibility Requirements: Applicant must be high school student; planning to enroll or expecting to enroll full-time at a two-year or four-year institution or university and resident of Maine. Available to U.S. citizens.

Application Requirements: Application, essay, financial need analysis, transcript. *Deadline:* May 1.

Contact: Amy Pollien, Program Administrator
Maine Community Foundation Inc.
245 Main Street
Ellsworth, ME 04605
Phone: 207-667-9735
Fax: 207-667-9735
E-mail: apollien@mainecf.org

CMP GROUP SCHOLARSHIP FUND

• *See page 580*

ISLAND INSTITUTE SCHOLARSHIP FUND

Scholarship offers renewable scholarship support to students from Maine's 14 year-round un-bridged island communities who are attending postsecondary education at a two- or four-year institution.

Award: Scholarship for use in freshman, sophomore, junior, or senior years; renewable. *Number:* 2–30. *Amount:* $2500–$5000.

Eligibility Requirements: Applicant must be enrolled or expecting to enroll full-time at a two-year or four-year institution and resident of Maine. Available to U.S. citizens.

Application Requirements: Application, essay, financial need analysis, photo, references, transcript. *Deadline:* April 1.

Contact: Amy Pollien, Program Administrator
Maine Community Foundation Inc.
245 Main Street
Ellsworth, ME 04605-1613
Phone: 207-667-9735
Fax: 207-667-0447
E-mail: info@mainecf.org

JOSEPH W. MAYO ALS SCHOLARSHIP FUND

Annual award to students who are spouses, children, stepchildren, grandchildren, and domestic partners of ALS patients. Must attend a postsecondary institution and be a graduate of high school or GED program in Maine.

Award: Scholarship for use in junior or senior years; not renewable. *Number:* 1. *Amount:* varies.

Eligibility Requirements: Applicant must be enrolled or expecting to enroll full-time at a two-year or four-year institution or university and resident of Maine. Available to U.S. citizens.

Application Requirements: Application, essay. *Deadline:* May 1.

Contact: Joseph Pietroski, President
Maine Community Foundation Inc.
132 State Street, PO Box 735
Augusta, ME 04332-0735
Phone: 207-622-6131
Fax: 207-622-0314

MAINE COMMUNITY FOUNDATION SCHOLARSHIP PROGRAMS

Various scholarships available for Maine residents attending secondary, postsecondary, and graduate programs. Restrictions and application requirements vary based on specific scholarship. See Web site for details. Deadline varies (generally March or April).

Award: Scholarship for use in freshman, sophomore, junior, senior, or graduate years; not renewable. *Number:* 150–700. *Amount:* $500–$5000.

Eligibility Requirements: Applicant must be enrolled or expecting to enroll full- or part-time at a two-year or four-year or technical institution or university and resident of Maine. Applicant must have 3.0 GPA or higher. Available to U.S. citizens.

Application Requirements: Application. *Deadline:* varies.

Contact: Ms. Amy Pollien, Grants Administration
Maine Community Foundation Inc.
245 Main Street
Ellsworth, ME 04605
Phone: 207-667-9735
E-mail: apollien@mainecf.org

RICE SCHOLARSHIP FUND

Scholarship support for students who have resided a substantial part of their formative years on one of the off-shore islands of Maine in the area from Seguin to Eastport, and who are attending accredited degree-granting colleges or vocational training schools. Recipients will be selected based on financial need and community service.

Award: Scholarship for use in freshman, sophomore, junior, or senior years; renewable. *Number:* 10–20. *Amount:* varies.

Eligibility Requirements: Applicant must be enrolled or expecting to enroll full-time at a two-year or four-year or technical institution or university and resident of Maine. Available to U.S. citizens.

Application Requirements: Application, essay, financial need analysis, references, transcript. *Deadline:* May 1.

Contact: Scholarship Coordinator
Maine Community Foundation Inc.
245 Main Street
Ellsworth, ME 04605-1613
Phone: 207-667-9735
Fax: 207-667-0447
E-mail: info@mainecf.org

SENATOR GEORGE J. MITCHELL SCHOLARSHIP FUND

Scholarship for legal Maine residents who are graduating seniors from a public high school in Maine. Must plan to attend a four-year or two-year degree program at an accredited college or university. Award of up to $5,000 ($1250 per year) for students pursuing a four-year degree and $2,500 for students pursuing a two-year degree.

Award: Scholarship for use in freshman year; not renewable. *Number:* 1. *Amount:* up to $1250.

Eligibility Requirements: Applicant must be high school student; planning to enroll or expecting to enroll full-time at a four-year institution or university and resident of Maine. Available to U.S. citizens.

Application Requirements: Application, essay, financial need analysis, references, transcript. *Deadline:* May 1.

Contact: Patty Higgins, Director of Scholarship Programs
Maine Community Foundation Inc.
Mitchell Institute, 22 Monument Square, Suite 200
Portland, ME 04101
Phone: 207-773-7700 Ext. 102
Fax: 207-773-1133
E-mail: info@mitchellinstitute.org

MAINE EDUCATION SERVICES

http://www.mesfoundation.com

MAINE LEGISLATIVE MEMORIAL SCHOLARSHIP

One-time awards for students going to a two- or four-year degree-granting Maine school. Scholarships are available to graduating high school seniors or full/part-time postsecondary students accepted or enrolled in a Maine college. Graduate students are also eligible.

Award: Scholarship for use in freshman, sophomore, junior, senior, graduate, or postgraduate years; not renewable. *Number:* up to 16. *Amount:* up to $1000.

Eligibility Requirements: Applicant must be enrolled or expecting to enroll full- or part-time at a two-year or four-year or technical institution or university; resident of Maine and studying in Maine. Available to U.S. citizens.

Application Requirements: Application, essay, financial need analysis, references, transcript. *Deadline:* April 18.

Contact: Kim Benjamin, Vice President of Operations
Maine Education Services
131 Presumpscot Street
Portland, ME 04103
Phone: 207-791-3600
Fax: 207-791-3616

MAINE MASONIC AID FOR CONTINUING EDUCATION

Scholarships for $1000 each are available for 12 adults pursuing higher education. May be full or part-time students. Students must meet federal criteria for an independent student. In addition, they must have exceptional financial need, have a serious educational plan, and contribute to the community.

Award: Scholarship for use in freshman, sophomore, junior, senior, graduate, or postgraduate years; not renewable. *Number:* up to 12. *Amount:* up to $1000.

Eligibility Requirements: Applicant must be enrolled or expecting to enroll full- or part-time at a two-year or four-year or technical institution or university and resident of Maine. Available to U.S. citizens.

Application Requirements: Application, essay, references. *Deadline:* April 18.

Contact: Kim Benjamin, Vice President of Operations
Maine Education Services
131 Presumpscot Street
Portland, ME 04103
Phone: 207-791-3600
Fax: 207-791-3616

MAINE STATE CHAMBER OF COMMERCE SCHOLARSHIP-ADULT LEARNER

One $1500 scholarship is given to an adult learner planning to pursue an education at a two-year, four-year degree granting college. Preference may be to a student attending a Maine college and seeking a degree in a business- or education-related field. Awards are based on an adult being 23 years or older and having legal dependents other than a spouse.

Award: Scholarship for use in freshman, sophomore, junior, or senior years; not renewable. *Number:* up to 1. *Amount:* up to $1500.

Eligibility Requirements: Applicant must be age 23 and over; enrolled or expecting to enroll full- or part-time at a two-year or four-year or technical institution or university and resident of Maine. Available to U.S. citizens.

Maine Education Services (continued)

Application Requirements: Application, essay, financial need analysis, references, transcript. *Deadline:* April 18.

Contact: Kim Benjamin, Vice President of Operations
Maine Education Services
131 Presumpscot Street
Portland, ME 04103
Phone: 207-791-3600
Fax: 207-791-3616

MAINE STATE SOCIETY FOUNDATION OF WASHINGTON, DC INC. http://www.mainestatesociety.org

MAINE STATE SOCIETY FOUNDATION SCHOLARSHIP

Scholarship(s) awarded to full-time students enrolled in undergraduate courses at a four-year degree-granting, nonprofit institution in Maine. Must be Maine resident. All inquiries must be accompanied by a self-addressed stamped envelope. Applicant must be 25 or younger.

Award: Scholarship for use in sophomore, junior, or senior years; not renewable. *Number:* 5–10. *Amount:* $1000–$2500.

Eligibility Requirements: Applicant must be age 25 or under; enrolled or expecting to enroll full-time at a four-year institution; resident of Maine and studying in Maine. Applicant must have 3.0 GPA or higher. Available to U.S. citizens.

Application Requirements: Application, autobiography, essay, self-addressed stamped envelope, transcript. *Deadline:* April 15.

Contact: Hugh Dwelley, Director
Maine State Society Foundation of Washington, DC Inc.
10340 Democracy Lane, Room 105
Fairfax, VA 22030-2936
Phone: 703-352-0846
E-mail: hldwelley@aol.com

MARYLAND HIGHER EDUCATION COMMISSION http://www.mhec.state.md.us

DELEGATE SCHOLARSHIP PROGRAM-MARYLAND

Delegate scholarships help Maryland residents attending Maryland degree-granting institutions, certain career schools, or nursing diploma schools. May attend out-of-state institution if Maryland Higher Education Commission deems major to be unique and not offered at a Maryland institution. Free Application for Federal Student Aid may be required. Students interested in this program should apply by contacting their legislative district delegate.

Award: Scholarship for use in freshman, sophomore, junior, senior, or graduate years; not renewable. *Number:* up to 3500. *Amount:* $200–$8650.

Eligibility Requirements: Applicant must be enrolled or expecting to enroll full- or part-time at a two-year or four-year or technical institution or university; resident of Maryland and studying in Maryland. Available to U.S. citizens.

Application Requirements: Application, FAFSA. *Deadline:* continuous.

Contact: Office of Student Financial Assistance
Maryland Higher Education Commission
839 Bestgate Road, Suite 400
Annapolis, MD 21401-3013
Phone: 800-974-1024
Fax: 410-260-3200
E-mail: osfamail@mhec.state.md.us

DISTINGUISHED SCHOLAR AWARD-MARYLAND

Renewable award for Maryland students enrolled full-time at Maryland institutions. National Merit Scholar Finalists automatically offered award. Others may qualify for the award in satisfying criteria of a minimum 3.7 GPA or in combination with high test scores, or for Talent in Arts competition in categories of music, drama, dance, or visual arts. Must maintain annual 3.0 GPA in college for award to be renewed.

Award: Scholarship for use in freshman, sophomore, junior, or senior years; renewable. *Number:* up to 1400. *Amount:* up to $3000.

Eligibility Requirements: Applicant must be high school student; planning to enroll or expecting to enroll full-time at a two-year or four-year institution or university; resident of Maryland and studying in Maryland. Available to U.S. citizens.

Application Requirements: Application, test scores, transcript. *Deadline:* varies.

Contact: Tamika McKelvin, Program Administrator
Maryland Higher Education Commission
839 Bestgate Road, Suite 400
Annapolis, MD 21401-3013
Phone: 410-260-4546
Fax: 410-260-3200
E-mail: tmckelvi@mhec.state.md.us

DISTINGUISHED SCHOLAR COMMUNITY COLLEGE TRANSFER PROGRAM

Scholarship available for Maryland residents who have completed 60 credit hours or an associate's degree at a Maryland community college and are transferring to a Maryland four-year institution.

Award: Scholarship for use in freshman or sophomore years; renewable. *Number:* 50. *Amount:* $3000.

Eligibility Requirements: Applicant must be enrolled or expecting to enroll full-time at a two-year institution; resident of Maryland and studying in Maryland. Available to U.S. citizens.

Application Requirements: Application, transcript. *Deadline:* March 1.

Contact: Elizabeth Urbanski, Associate Director
Maryland Higher Education Commission
839 Bestgate Road, Suite 400
Annapolis, MD 21401-3013
Phone: 410-260-4561
Fax: 410-260-3202
E-mail: eurbansk@mhec.state.md.us

EDWARD T. CONROY MEMORIAL SCHOLARSHIP PROGRAM

• *See page 602*

HOWARD P. RAWLINGS EDUCATIONAL EXCELLENCE AWARDS GUARANTEED ACCESS GRANT

Award for Maryland resident enrolling full-time in an undergraduate program at a Maryland institution. Must be under 21 at time of first award and begin college within one year of completing high school in Maryland with a minimum 2.5 GPA. Must have an annual family income less than 130 percent of the federal poverty level guideline.

Award: Grant for use in freshman, sophomore, junior, or senior years; renewable. *Number:* up to 1000. *Amount:* $400–$14,800.

Eligibility Requirements: Applicant must be age 21 or under; enrolled or expecting to enroll full-time at a two-year or four-year institution or university; resident of Maryland and studying in Maryland. Applicant must have 2.5 GPA or higher. Available to U.S. citizens.

Application Requirements: Application, financial need analysis, transcript. *Deadline:* March 1.

Contact: Theresa Lowe, Office of Student Financial Assistance
Maryland Higher Education Commission
839 Bestgate Road, Suite 400
Annapolis, MD 21401-3013
Phone: 410-260-4555
Fax: 410-260-3200
E-mail: osfamail@mhec.state.md.us

J.F. TOLBERT MEMORIAL STUDENT GRANT PROGRAM

Awards of $500 granted to Maryland residents attending a private career school in Maryland. The scholarship deadline continues.

Award: Grant for use in freshman or sophomore years; not renewable. *Number:* 400. *Amount:* $500.

Eligibility Requirements: Applicant must be enrolled or expecting to enroll full-time at a technical institution; resident of Maryland and studying in Maryland. Available to U.S. citizens.

Application Requirements: Application, financial need analysis. *Deadline:* continuous.

Contact: Glenda Hamlet, Office of Student Financial Assistance
Maryland Higher Education Commission
839 Bestgate Road, Suite 400
Annapolis, MD 21401-3013
Phone: 800-974-1024
Fax: 410-260-3200
E-mail: osfamail@mhec.state.md.us

PART-TIME GRANT PROGRAM-MARYLAND

Funds provided to Maryland colleges and universities. Eligible students must be enrolled on a part-time basis (6 to 11 credits) in an undergraduate degree program. Must demonstrate financial need and also be Maryland resident. Contact financial aid office at institution for more information.

Award: Grant for use in freshman, sophomore, junior, or senior years; renewable. *Number:* 1800–9000. *Amount:* $200–$1500.

Eligibility Requirements: Applicant must be enrolled or expecting to enroll part-time at a two-year or four-year institution or university; resident of Maryland and studying in Maryland. Available to U.S. citizens.

Application Requirements: Application, financial need analysis. *Deadline:* March 1.

Contact: Elizabeth Urbanski, Associate Director
Maryland Higher Education Commission
839 Bestgate Road, Suite 400
Annapolis, MD 21401-3013
Phone: 410-260-4561
Fax: 410-260-3202
E-mail: eurbansk@mhec.state.md.us

SENATORIAL SCHOLARSHIPS-MARYLAND

Renewable award for Maryland residents attending a Maryland degree-granting institution, nursing diploma school, or certain private career schools. May be used out-of-state only if Maryland Higher Education Commission deems major to be unique and not offered at Maryland institution. The scholarship value is $400 to $7000.

Award: Scholarship for use in freshman, sophomore, junior, senior, or graduate years; renewable. *Number:* up to 7000. *Amount:* $400–$7000.

Eligibility Requirements: Applicant must be enrolled or expecting to enroll full- or part-time at a two-year or four-year or technical institution or university; resident of Maryland and studying in Maryland. Available to U.S. citizens.

Application Requirements: Application, financial need analysis, test scores. *Deadline:* March 1.

Contact: Glenda Hamlet, Office of Student Financial Assistance
Maryland Higher Education Commission
839 Bestgate Road, Suite 400
Annapolis, MD 21401-3013
Phone: 800-974-1024
Fax: 410-260-3200
E-mail: osfamail@mhec.state.md.us

TUITION WAIVER FOR FOSTER CARE RECIPIENTS

Applicant must be a high school graduate or GED recipient and under the age of 21. Must either have resided in a foster care home in Maryland at the time of high school graduation or GED reception, or until 14th birthday, and been adopted after 14th birthday. Applicant, if status approved, will be exempt from paying tuition and mandatory fees at a public college in Maryland.

Award: Grant for use in freshman, sophomore, junior, senior, or graduate years; renewable. *Number:* varies. *Amount:* varies.

Eligibility Requirements: Applicant must be age 21 or under; enrolled or expecting to enroll full- or part-time at a two-year or four-year institution or university; resident of Maryland and studying in Maryland. Available to U.S. citizens.

Application Requirements: Application, financial need analysis, must inquire at financial aid office of schools. *Deadline:* March 1.

Contact: Elizabeth Urbanski, Associate Director
Maryland Higher Education Commission
839 Bestgate Road, Suite 400
Annapolis, MD 21401-3013
Phone: 410-260-4561
Fax: 410-260-3202
E-mail: eurbansk@mhec.state.md.us

VETERANS OF THE AFGHANISTAN AND IRAQ CONFLICTS SCHOLARSHIP PROGRAM

• *See page 656*

WORKFORCE SHORTAGE STUDENT ASSISTANCE GRANT PROGRAM

Scholarship of $4000 available to students who will be required to major in specific areas and will be obligated to serve in the state of Maryland after completion of degree.

Award: Scholarship for use in freshman, sophomore, junior, senior, or graduate years; renewable. *Number:* 1300. *Amount:* $4000.

Eligibility Requirements: Applicant must be enrolled or expecting to enroll full- or part-time at a two-year or four-year institution or university; resident of Maryland and studying in Maryland. Available to U.S. citizens.

Application Requirements: Application, essay, financial need analysis, resume, references, transcript, certain majors require additional documentation. *Deadline:* July 1.

Contact: Elizabeth Urbanski, Associate Director
Maryland Higher Education Commission
839 Bestgate Road, Suite 400
Annapolis, MD 21401-3013
Phone: 410-260-4561
Fax: 410-260-3202
E-mail: eurbansk@mhec.state.md.us

MARYLAND STATE DEPARTMENT OF EDUCATION http://www.marylandpublicschools.org

ROBERT C. BYRD HONORS SCHOLARSHIP-MARYLAND

Scholarship amount varies each year, ranging from $1000 to $1500. Amount received is based on the total cost of attendance at each institution of higher education. Awarded on merit basis. Students in the top 1 percent of their graduating class may be nominated by the principal or headmaster. Must be admitted to an institution of higher education as full-time student and be Maryland resident.

Award: Scholarship for use in freshman year; renewable. *Number:* varies. *Amount:* $1000–$1500.

Eligibility Requirements: Applicant must be high school student; planning to enroll or expecting to enroll full-time at a four-year institution or university and resident of Maryland. Available to U.S. citizens.

Application Requirements: Application. *Deadline:* varies.

Contact: William Cappe, Scholarship Coordinator
Maryland State Department of Education
200 West Baltimore Street
Baltimore, MD 21201
Phone: 888-246-0016
E-mail: wcappe@msde.state.md.us

MASSACHUSETTS AFL-CIO http://www.massaflcio.org

MASSACHUSETTS AFL-CIO SCHOLARSHIP

Scholarships to union members, their children/stepchildren, grandchildren, nieces, nephews, and non-union Massachusetts's high school seniors.

Award: Scholarship for use in freshman year; not renewable. *Number:* 100–150. *Amount:* $250–$12,000.

Eligibility Requirements: Applicant must be high school student; planning to enroll or expecting to enroll full-time at a four-year institution or university; resident of Massachusetts and studying in Massachusetts. Available to U.S. citizens.

Massachusetts AFL-CIO (continued)

Application Requirements: Application. *Deadline:* December 21.

Contact: Jackie Bergantino, Scholarship Administrator
Massachusetts AFL-CIO
389 Main Street, Suite 101
Malden, MA 02148
Phone: 781-324-8230
Fax: 781-324-8225
E-mail: jbergantino@massaflcio.org

MASSACHUSETTS DEPARTMENT OF EDUCATION http://www.doe.mass.edu

ROBERT C. BYRD HONORS SCHOLARSHIP-MASSACHUSETTS

Scholarship for high school senior who is a resident of Massachusetts for at least one year prior to the beginning of the academic year he/she will enter college. Must have applied or been accepted to an accredited institution of higher education and be a U.S. citizen, national or permanent resident.

Award: Scholarship for use in freshman year; renewable. *Number:* varies. *Amount:* $1500.

Eligibility Requirements: Applicant must be high school student; planning to enroll or expecting to enroll full-time at a four-year institution or university and resident of Massachusetts. Applicant must have 3.5 GPA or higher. Available to U.S. citizens.

Application Requirements: Application, transcript. *Deadline:* June 1.

Contact: Sally Teixeira, Scholarship Coordinator
Massachusetts Department of Education
350 Main Street
Malden, MA 02148-5023
Phone: 781-338-6304
E-mail: steixeira@doe.mass.edu

MASSACHUSETTS OFFICE OF STUDENT FINANCIAL ASSISTANCE http://www.osfa.mass.edu

AGNES M. LINDSAY SCHOLARSHIP

Scholarships for students with demonstrated financial need who are from rural areas of Massachusetts and attend public institutions of higher education in Massachusetts. Deadline varies.

Award: Scholarship for use in freshman, sophomore, junior, or senior years; not renewable. *Number:* varies. *Amount:* varies.

Eligibility Requirements: Applicant must be enrolled or expecting to enroll full-time at a two-year or four-year institution or university; resident of Massachusetts and studying in Massachusetts. Available to U.S. citizens.

Application Requirements: Application, financial need analysis. *Deadline:* varies.

Contact: Robert Brun, Director of Scholarships and Grants
Massachusetts Office of Student Financial Assistance
454 Broadway, Suite 200
Revere, MA 02151
Phone: 617-727-9420
Fax: 617-727-0667
E-mail: osfa@osfa.mass.edu

CHRISTIAN A. HERTER MEMORIAL SCHOLARSHIP

Renewable award for Massachusetts residents who are in the tenth and eleventh grades, and whose socio-economic backgrounds and environment may inhibit their ability to attain educational goals. Must exhibit severe personal or family-related difficulties, medical problems, or have overcome a personal obstacle. Provides up to 50 percent of the student's calculated need, as determined by federal methodology, at the college of their choice within the continental United States.

Award: Scholarship for use in freshman year; renewable. *Number:* 25. *Amount:* up to $15,000.

Eligibility Requirements: Applicant must be high school student; planning to enroll or expecting to enroll full-time at a two-year or four-year or technical institution or university and resident of Massachusetts. Applicant must have 2.5 GPA or higher. Available to U.S. citizens.

Application Requirements: Application, autobiography, financial need analysis, interview, references. *Deadline:* March 14.

Contact: Robert Brun, Director of Scholarships and Grants
Massachusetts Office of Student Financial Assistance
454 Broadway, Suite 200
Revere, MA 02151
Phone: 617-727-9420
Fax: 617-727-0667
E-mail: osfa@osfa.mass.edu

DSS ADOPTED CHILDREN TUITION WAIVER

Need-based tuition waiver for Massachusetts residents who are full-time undergraduate students. Must attend a Massachusetts public institution of higher education and be under 24 years of age. File the FAFSA after January 1. Contact school financial aid office for more information.

Award: Scholarship for use in freshman, sophomore, junior, or senior years; renewable. *Number:* varies. *Amount:* varies.

Eligibility Requirements: Applicant must be age 24 or under; enrolled or expecting to enroll full-time at a two-year or four-year institution and resident of Massachusetts. Available to U.S. and non-Canadian citizens.

Application Requirements: Application, financial need analysis, FAFSA. *Deadline:* varies.

Contact: Robert Brun, Director of Scholarships and Grants
Massachusetts Office of Student Financial Assistance
454 Broadway, Suite 200
Revere, MA 02151
Phone: 617-727-9420
Fax: 617-727-0667
E-mail: osfa@osfa.mass.edu

JOHN AND ABIGAIL ADAMS SCHOLARSHIP

Scholarship to reward and inspire student achievement, attract more high-performing students to Massachusetts public higher education, and provide families of college-bound students with financial assistance. Must be a U.S. citizen or an eligible non-citizen. There is no application process for the scholarship. Students who are eligible will be notified in the fall of their senior year in high school.

Award: Scholarship for use in freshman year; not renewable. *Number:* varies. *Amount:* varies.

Eligibility Requirements: Applicant must be high school student; planning to enroll or expecting to enroll full-time at a two-year or four-year institution or university; resident of Massachusetts and studying in Massachusetts. Applicant must have 3.0 GPA or higher. Available to U.S. citizens.

Application Requirements: *Deadline:* varies.

Contact: Robert Brun, Director of Scholarships and Grants
Massachusetts Office of Student Financial Assistance
454 Broadway, Suite 200
Revere, MA 02151
Phone: 617-727-9420
Fax: 617-727-0667
E-mail: osfa@osfa.mass.edu

MASSACHUSETTS ASSISTANCE FOR STUDENT SUCCESS PROGRAM

Provides need-based financial assistance to Massachusetts residents to attend undergraduate postsecondary institutions in Connecticut, Maine, Massachusetts, New Hampshire, Pennsylvania, Rhode Island, Vermont, and District of Columbia. High school seniors may apply. Expected Family Contribution (EFC) should be $3850. Timely filing of FAFSA required.

Award: Grant for use in freshman, sophomore, junior, or senior years; not renewable. *Number:* 25,000–30,000. *Amount:* $300–$2400.

Eligibility Requirements: Applicant must be enrolled or expecting to enroll full-time at a two-year or four-year or technical institution or university; resident of Massachusetts and studying in Connecticut, District of Columbia, Maine, Massachusetts, New Hampshire, Pennsylvania, Rhode Island, or Vermont. Available to U.S. citizens.

Application Requirements: Financial need analysis, FAFSA. *Deadline:* May 1.

Contact: Robert Brun, Director of Scholarships and Grants
Massachusetts Office of Student Financial Assistance
454 Broadway, Suite 200
Revere, MA 02151
Phone: 617-727-9420
Fax: 617-727-0667
E-mail: osfa@osfa.mass.edu

MASSACHUSETTS CASH GRANT PROGRAM

A need-based grant to assist with mandatory fees and non-state supported tuition. This supplemental award is available to Massachusetts residents, who are undergraduates at public two-year, four-year colleges and universities in Massachusetts. Must file FAFSA before May 1. Contact college financial aid office for information.

Award: Grant for use in freshman, sophomore, junior, or senior years; not renewable. *Number:* varies. *Amount:* varies.

Eligibility Requirements: Applicant must be enrolled or expecting to enroll full-time at a two-year or four-year institution or university and resident of Massachusetts. Available to U.S. citizens.

Application Requirements: Application, financial need analysis, FAFSA. *Deadline:* continuous.

Contact: Robert Brun, Director of Scholarships and Grants
Massachusetts Office of Student Financial Assistance
454 Broadway, Suite 200
Revere, MA 02151
Phone: 617-727-9420
Fax: 617-727-0667
E-mail: osfa@osfa.mass.edu

MASSACHUSETTS GILBERT MATCHING STUDENT GRANT PROGRAM

Grants for permanent Massachusetts residents attending an independent, regionally accredited Massachusetts school or school of nursing full time. Must be U.S. citizen and permanent legal resident of Massachusetts. File the Free Application for Federal Student Aid after January 1. Contact college financial aid office for complete details and deadlines.

Award: Grant for use in freshman, sophomore, junior, or senior years; not renewable. *Number:* varies. *Amount:* $200–$2500.

Eligibility Requirements: Applicant must be enrolled or expecting to enroll full-time at a four-year institution or university; resident of Massachusetts and studying in Massachusetts. Available to U.S. citizens.

Application Requirements: Financial need analysis, FAFSA. *Deadline:* varies.

Contact: Robert Brun, Director of Scholarships and Grants
Massachusetts Office of Student Financial Assistance
454 Broadway, Suite 200
Revere, MA 02151
Phone: 617-727-9420
Fax: 617-727-0667
E-mail: rbrun@osfa.mass.edu

MASSACHUSETTS PART-TIME GRANT PROGRAM

Award for permanent Massachusetts residents who have enrolled part-time for at least one year in a state-approved postsecondary school. The recipient must not have a bachelor's degree. FAFSA must be filed before May 1. Contact college financial aid office for further information.

Award: Grant for use in freshman, sophomore, junior, or senior years; not renewable. *Number:* 200. *Amount:* $200–$1150.

Eligibility Requirements: Applicant must be enrolled or expecting to enroll part-time at a two-year or four-year or technical institution or university and resident of Massachusetts. Available to U.S. citizens.

Application Requirements: Application, financial need analysis, FAFSA. *Deadline:* varies.

Contact: Robert Brun, Director of Scholarships and Grants
Massachusetts Office of Student Financial Assistance
454 Broadway, Suite 200
Revere, MA 02151
Phone: 617-727-9420
Fax: 617-727-0667
E-mail: osfa@osfa.mass.edu

MASSACHUSETTS PUBLIC SERVICE GRANT PROGRAM

• *See page 603*

PAUL TSONGAS SCHOLARSHIP PROGRAM

Scholarship to recognize achievement and reward Massachusetts students, who have graduated from high school within three years with a GPA of 3.75 and a SAT score of at least 1200, and who also meet the one year residency requirement for tuition classification at the state colleges.

Award: Scholarship for use in freshman, sophomore, junior, or senior years; renewable. *Number:* varies. *Amount:* varies.

Eligibility Requirements: Applicant must be enrolled or expecting to enroll full-time at a two-year or four-year institution or university; resident of Massachusetts and studying in Massachusetts. Available to U.S. citizens.

Application Requirements: Application, test scores. *Deadline:* varies.

Contact: Robert Brun, Director of Scholarships and Grants
Massachusetts Office of Student Financial Assistance
454 Broadway, Suite 200
Revere, MA 02151
Phone: 617-727-9420
Fax: 617-727-0667
E-mail: osfa@osfa.mass.edu

MCCURRY FOUNDATION INC.

http://www.mccurryfoundation.org

MCCURRY FOUNDATION SCHOLARSHIP

Scholarship open to all public high school seniors, with preference given to applicants from Clay, Duval, Nassau, and St. Johns Counties, Florida and from Glynn County, Georgia. Scholarship emphasizes leadership, work ethic, and academic excellence. A minimum GPA of 3.0 is required and family income cannot exceed a maximum of $75,000 (AGI).

Award: Scholarship for use in freshman year; renewable. *Number:* varies. *Amount:* varies.

Eligibility Requirements: Applicant must be high school student; planning to enroll or expecting to enroll full-time at a two-year or four-year or technical institution or university; resident of Florida or Georgia and must have an interest in leadership. Applicant must have 3.0 GPA or higher. Available to U.S. and non-U.S. citizens.

Application Requirements: Application, essay, financial need analysis, interview, resume, references, transcript, report card, tax return. *Deadline:* February 15.

Contact: Scholarship Selection Committee
McCurry Foundation Inc.
11645 Beach Boulevard, Suite 200
Jacksonville, FL 32246
Phone: 904-645-6555

MCKELVEY FOUNDATION

http://www.mckelveyfoundation.org

MCKELVEY SCHOLARSHIP-FIRST GENERATION EDUCATION

Applicant must attend a partnering high school in NY, PA, or WV and be a first generation to attend college. Awards will be granted up to $3000 per year for all four years. Applicant should maintain a GPA of 2.5.

Award: Scholarship for use in freshman year; renewable. *Number:* varies. *Amount:* up to $3000.

Eligibility Requirements: Applicant must be high school student; planning to enroll or expecting to enroll full- or part-time at a four-year institution and studying in New York, Pennsylvania, or West Virginia. Applicant must have 2.5 GPA or higher. Available to U.S. citizens.

Application Requirements: Application, financial need analysis. *Deadline:* December 1.

Contact: Scholarship Committee
McKelvey Foundation
200 Park Avenue, 44th Floor
New York, NY 10166
Phone: 212-847-7236
E-mail: info@mckelveyfoundation.org

MELLON NEW ENGLAND http://www.mellon.com

CHARLES C. ELY EDUCATIONAL FUND

Award for men who are residents of Massachusetts. Academic performance, character and financial need will be considered. Eligible applicant must be recommended by educational institution. Not for graduate study programs.

Award: Scholarship for use in freshman, sophomore, junior, or senior years; not renewable. *Number:* varies. *Amount:* up to $2000.

Eligibility Requirements: Applicant must be enrolled or expecting to enroll full-time at a two-year or four-year or technical institution or university; male and resident of Massachusetts. Available to U.S. citizens.

Application Requirements: Application, essay, transcript. *Deadline:* April 15.

Contact: Sandra Brown-McMullen, Vice President
Mellon New England
1 Boston Place, 024-0084
Boston, MA 02108
Phone: 617-722-3891
E-mail: brown-mcmullen.s@mellon.com

HENRY FRANCIS BARROWS SCHOLARSHIP

• *See page 715*

MICHIGAN BUREAU OF STUDENT FINANCIAL ASSISTANCE http://www.michigan.gov/studentaid

CHILDREN OF VETERANS TUITION GRANT

• *See page 656*

MICHIGAN ADULT PART-TIME GRANT

Grant is intended for financially needy, independent undergraduates who have been out of high school for at least two years. Must be Michigan resident.

Award: Grant for use in freshman, sophomore, junior, or senior years; renewable. *Number:* varies. *Amount:* up to $600.

Eligibility Requirements: Applicant must be enrolled or expecting to enroll part-time at a two-year or four-year institution or university; resident of Michigan and studying in Michigan. Available to U.S. citizens.

Application Requirements: Financial need analysis. *Deadline:* March 1.

Contact: Scholarship and Grant Director
Michigan Bureau of Student Financial Assistance
PO Box 30462
Lansing, MI 48909-7962
Phone: 888-447-2687
E-mail: osg@michigan.gov

MICHIGAN COMPETITIVE SCHOLARSHIP

Renewable award of $1300 for for Michigan resident to pursue undergraduate study at a Michigan institution. Awards limited to tuition. Must maintain at least a 2.0 grade point average and meet the college's academic progress requirements. Must file Free Application for Federal Student Aid.

Award: Scholarship for use in freshman, sophomore, junior, or senior years; renewable. *Number:* varies. *Amount:* $100–$1300.

Eligibility Requirements: Applicant must be enrolled or expecting to enroll full- or part-time at a two-year or four-year institution or university; resident of Michigan and studying in Michigan. Available to U.S. citizens.

Application Requirements: Application, financial need analysis, test scores. *Deadline:* March 1.

Contact: Scholarship and Grant Director
Michigan Bureau of Student Financial Assistance
PO Box 30466
Lansing, MI 48909-7962
Phone: 888-447-2687
E-mail: osg@michigan.gov

MICHIGAN EDUCATIONAL OPPORTUNITY GRANT

Need-based program for Michigan residents who are at least half-time undergraduates attending public Michigan colleges. Must maintain good academic standing. Award of up to $1000.

Award: Grant for use in freshman, sophomore, junior, or senior years; renewable. *Number:* varies. *Amount:* up to $1000.

Eligibility Requirements: Applicant must be enrolled or expecting to enroll full- or part-time at an institution or university; resident of Michigan and studying in Michigan. Available to U.S. citizens.

Application Requirements: Financial need analysis. *Deadline:* March 1.

Contact: Scholarship and Grant Director
Michigan Bureau of Student Financial Assistance
PO Box 30462
Lansing, MI 48909-7962
Phone: 888-447-2687
E-mail: osg@michigan.gov

MICHIGAN PROMISE SCHOLARSHIP

Scholarship available for students who have taken the state's assessment test. Students who meet or exceed test standards may receive $1000 during each of their first two years of college and another $2000 after completing two years with at least a 2.5 GPA. Students who do not meet or exceed state standards may receive $4000 after completing two years of postsecondary study with at least a 2.5 GPA. Must be a Michigan resident enrolled at an approved Michigan postsecondary institution.

Award: Scholarship for use in freshman, sophomore, or junior years; not renewable. *Number:* varies. *Amount:* up to $4000.

Eligibility Requirements: Applicant must be enrolled or expecting to enroll full- or part-time at a two-year or four-year or technical institution or university; resident of Michigan and studying in Michigan. Applicant must have 2.5 GPA or higher. Available to U.S. citizens.

Application Requirements: Test scores. *Deadline:* continuous.

Contact: Scholarship and Grant Director
Michigan Bureau of Student Financial Assistance
PO Box 30462
Lansing, MI 48909-7962
Phone: 888-447-2687
E-mail: osg@michigan.gov

MICHIGAN TUITION GRANT

Need-based program. Students must be Michigan residents and attend a Michigan private, nonprofit, degree-granting college. Must file the Free Application for Federal Student Aid and meet the college's academic progress requirements.

Award: Grant for use in freshman, sophomore, junior, senior, or graduate years; renewable. *Number:* varies. *Amount:* $100–$2100.

Eligibility Requirements: Applicant must be enrolled or expecting to enroll full- or part-time at a two-year or four-year institution or university; resident of Michigan and studying in Michigan. Available to U.S. citizens.

Application Requirements: Financial need analysis. *Deadline:* March 1.

Contact: Scholarship and Grant Director
Michigan Bureau of Student Financial Assistance
PO Box 30462
Lansing, MI 48909-7962
Phone: 888-447-2687
E-mail: osg@michigan.gov

TUITION INCENTIVE PROGRAM

Award for Michigan residents who receive or have received Medicaid for required period of time through the Department of Human Services. Scholarship provides two years tuition towards an associate degree at a Michigan college or university and $2000 total assistance for third and fourth years. Must apply before graduating from high school or earning a general education development diploma.

Award: Grant for use in freshman, sophomore, junior, or senior years; renewable. *Number:* varies. *Amount:* varies.

Eligibility Requirements: Applicant must be enrolled or expecting to enroll full- or part-time at a two-year or four-year institution or university; resident of Michigan and studying in Michigan. Available to U.S. citizens.

Application Requirements: Application, Medicaid eligibility for specified period of time. *Deadline:* continuous.

Contact: Scholarship and Grant Director
Michigan Bureau of Student Financial Assistance
PO Box 30462
Lansing, MI 48909-7962
Phone: 888-447-2687
E-mail: osg@michigan.gov

MICHIGAN VETERANS TRUST FUND http://www.michigan.gov/dmva

MICHIGAN VETERANS TRUST FUND TUITION GRANT PROGRAM

• *See page 656*

MIDWESTERN HIGHER EDUCATION COMPACT http://www.mhec.org

MIDWEST STUDENT EXCHANGE PROGRAM

Over 140 colleges and universities in Kansas, Michigan, Minnesota, Missouri, Nebraska, North Dakota, and Wisconsin participate in the MSEP tuition reciprocity program. It is not a scholarship, but for qualified students, provides a discount on out-of-state tuition for courses of study not avialable in a student's home state. Requirements vary by institution. See Web site for details: http://www.mhec.org.

Award: Grant for use in freshman, sophomore, junior, senior, graduate, or postgraduate years; renewable. *Number:* varies. *Amount:* varies.

Eligibility Requirements: Applicant must be enrolled or expecting to enroll full- or part-time at a two-year or four-year or technical institution or university; resident of Kansas, Michigan, Minnesota, Missouri, Nebraska, North Dakota, or Wisconsin and studying in Kansas, Michigan, Minnesota, Missouri, Nebraska, North Dakota, or Wisconsin. Available to U.S. citizens.

Application Requirements: Application. *Deadline:* varies.

Contact: Ms. Jennifer Dahlquist, Director of Student Access
Midwestern Higher Education Compact
1300 South Second Street, Suite 130
Minneapolis, MN 55454-1079
Phone: 612-626-1602
Fax: 612-626-8290
E-mail: jenniferd@mhec.org

MINNESOTA AFL-CIO http://www.mnaflcio.org

BILL PETERSON SCHOLARSHIP

• *See page 541*

MARTIN DUFFY ADULT LEARNER SCHOLARSHIP AWARD

• *See page 541*

MINNESOTA AFL-CIO SCHOLARSHIPS

• *See page 541*

MINNESOTA COMMUNITY FOUNDATION http://www.mncommunityfoundation.org

COSS FAMILY FOUNDATION SCHOLARSHIP

Scholarship for graduating high school seniors located in Ramsey or Dakota counties in Minnesota and Meade, Pennington, Hyde, Hand or Buffalo counties in South Dakota. Must demonstrate financial need.

Award: Scholarship for use in freshman year; renewable. *Number:* 20. *Amount:* $3000.

Eligibility Requirements: Applicant must be high school student; planning to enroll or expecting to enroll full- or part-time at a four-year institution or university and resident of Minnesota or South Dakota. Available to U.S. citizens.

Application Requirements: Application, transcript. *Deadline:* March 1.

Contact: Donna Paulson, Administrative Assistant
Minnesota Community Foundation
55 Fifth Street East, Suite 600
St. Paul, MN 55101-1797
Phone: 651-325-4212
E-mail: dkp@mncommunityfoundation.org

JANE RING AND SUE RING-JARVI GIRLS'/WOMEN'S HOCKEY FUND

Two non-renewable scholarships of $2000 awarded to students who have demonstrated leadership ability together with athletic and academic achievement. Applicant must be a senior female student graduating from a high school in Minnesota.

Award: Scholarship for use in freshman year; not renewable. *Number:* 2. *Amount:* $2000.

Eligibility Requirements: Applicant must be high school student; planning to enroll or expecting to enroll full- or part-time at a four-year institution or university; female; resident of Minnesota and must have an interest in athletics/sports or leadership. Applicant must have 3.0 GPA or higher. Available to U.S. citizens.

Application Requirements: Application, references, transcript. *Deadline:* April 20.

Contact: Donna Paulson, Administrative Assistant
Minnesota Community Foundation
55 Fifth Street East, Suite 600
St. Paul, MN 55101-1797
Phone: 651-325-4212
E-mail: dkp@mncommunityfoundation.org

JOSIP AND AGNETE TEMALI SCHOLARSHIP (BIG BROTHERS/BIG SISTERS)

• *See page 541*

RICHARD W. TANNER SCHOLARSHIP

Scholarship for students in junior or senior year in college. Must be a Minnesota resident or have significant ties to a Minnesota Tribe.

Award: Scholarship for use in junior or senior years; not renewable. *Number:* 1. *Amount:* $1000.

Eligibility Requirements: Applicant must be enrolled or expecting to enroll full- or part-time at a four-year institution or university and resident of Minnesota. Available to U.S. citizens.

Application Requirements: Application, essay, financial need analysis, references, transcript, proof of tribal enrollment. *Deadline:* July 1.

Contact: Donna Paulson, Administrative Assistant
Minnesota Community Foundation
55 Fifth Street East, Suite 600
St. Paul, MN 55101-1797
Phone: 651-325-4212
E-mail: dkp@mncommunityfoundation.org

TWO FEATHERS ENDOWMENT SCHOLARSHIP

Scholarship of $1000 to a Minnesota resident or students with significant ties to a Minnesota Tribe.

Award: Scholarship for use in freshman, sophomore, junior, or senior years; not renewable. *Number:* varies. *Amount:* $1000.

Eligibility Requirements: Applicant must be enrolled or expecting to enroll full- or part-time at a four-year institution or university and resident of Minnesota. Available to U.S. citizens.

Application Requirements: Application, essay, resume, references, transcript. *Deadline:* July 1.

Contact: Dayonna Knutson, Program Assistant
Phone: 651-325-4252
E-mail: dlk@mncommunityfoundation.org

WILLIAM C. AND CORINNE J. DIETRICH AWARD

Scholarship for a graduating senior at a Minnesota public high school. Available for both full- or part-time study.

Award: Scholarship for use in freshman year; not renewable. *Number:* 1. *Amount:* $20,000.

Eligibility Requirements: Applicant must be high school student; planning to enroll or expecting to enroll full- or part-time at a four-year institution or university and resident of Minnesota. Available to U.S. and non-Canadian citizens.

Minnesota Community Foundation (continued)

Application Requirements: Application, transcript. *Deadline:* April 1.

Contact: Donna Paulson, Administrative Assistant
Minnesota Community Foundation
55 Fifth Street East, Suite 600
St. Paul, MN 55101-1797
Phone: 651-325-4212
E-mail: dkp@mncommunityfoundation.org

MINNESOTA DEPARTMENT OF MILITARY AFFAIRS http://www.minnesotanationalguard.org

LEADERSHIP, EXCELLENCE AND DEDICATED SERVICE SCHOLARSHIP

• *See page 603*

MINNESOTA GAY/LESBIAN/BISEXUAL/ TRANSGENDER EDUCATIONAL FUND http://www.pfundonline.org

MINNESOTA GAY/LESBIAN/BISEXUAL/TRANSGENDER SCHOLARSHIP FUND

Scholarship available for gay, lesbian, bisexual, or transgender identified students, or students from GLBT families. Must be a legal resident of the state of Minnesota or attending a qualified Minnesota academic institution. Former winners of this fund are not eligible. For more details, visit: http://www.pfundonline.org/scholarships.html.

Award: Scholarship for use in freshman, sophomore, junior, or senior years; not renewable. *Number:* 20–30. *Amount:* $1500–$5000.

Eligibility Requirements: Applicant must be enrolled or expecting to enroll full- or part-time at a two-year or four-year or technical institution or university; resident of Minnesota; studying in Minnesota and must have an interest in LGBT issues. Available to U.S. and non-U.S. citizens.

Application Requirements: Application, essay, photo, references, transcript, confidentiality statement. *Deadline:* February 1.

Contact: Alfomso Wenker, Programs Manager
Minnesota Gay/Lesbian/Bisexual/Transgender Educational Fund
c/o Philanthrofund Foundation
1409 Willow Street, Suite 210
Minneapolis, MN 55403
Phone: 612-870-1806
Fax: 612-871-6587
E-mail: awenker@pfundonline.org

MINNESOTA HIGHER EDUCATION SERVICES OFFICE http://www.getreadyforcollege.org

MINNESOTA ACADEMIC EXCELLENCE SCHOLARSHIP

Students must demonstrate outstanding ability, achievement, and potential in one of the following subjects: English or creative writing, fine arts, foreign language, math, science, or social science. Implementation depends on the availability of funds, which are to come from the sale of special collegiate license plates. Apply directly to college. Must be a Minnesota resident and study in Minnesota. At public institutions, the scholarship may cover up to the full price of tuition and fees for one academic year. At private institutions, the scholarship may cover either the actual tuition and fees charged by that school, or the tuition and fees in comparable public institutions whichever is less.

Award: Scholarship for use in freshman, sophomore, junior, or senior years; renewable. *Number:* varies. *Amount:* varies.

Eligibility Requirements: Applicant must be enrolled or expecting to enroll full-time at a four-year institution or university; resident of Minnesota; studying in Minnesota and must have an interest in art, English language, foreign language, or writing. Available to U.S. citizens.

Application Requirements: Application, transcript. *Deadline:* varies.

Contact: Ginny Dodds, Manager
Minnesota Higher Education Services Office
1450 Energy Park Drive, Suite 350
St. Paul, MN 55108-5227
Phone: 651-642-0567
Fax: 651-642-0675
E-mail: ginny.dodds@state.mn.us

MINNESOTA ACHIEVE SCHOLARSHIP

Minnesota residents who complete one of four sets of rigorous programs of study while in high school or in a home-school setting may be eligible to receive a one-time scholarship of $1200. Student must have graduated from a Minnesota high school and completed, with a grade of C or above, all of the required courses. Must have a household adjusted gross income of less than $75,000. Scholarships are available to eligible students up to 4 years after high school graduation.

Award: Scholarship for use in freshman, sophomore, junior, or senior years; not renewable. *Number:* varies. *Amount:* up to $1200.

Eligibility Requirements: Applicant must be enrolled or expecting to enroll full- or part-time at a two-year or four-year or technical institution or university; resident of Minnesota and studying in Minnesota. Available to U.S. and non-U.S. citizens.

Application Requirements: Application, financial need analysis, test scores, transcript. *Deadline:* varies.

Contact: Grant Staff
Minnesota Higher Education Services Office
1450 Energy Park Drive
St. Paul, MN 55108
Phone: 651-642-0567
Fax: 651-642-0675

MINNESOTA GI BILL PROGRAM

• *See page 657*

MINNESOTA INDIAN SCHOLARSHIP

• *See page 692*

MINNESOTA RECIPROCAL AGREEMENT

Renewable tuition waiver for Minnesota residents. Waives all or part of non-resident tuition surcharge at public institutions in Iowa, Kansas, Michigan, Missouri, Nebraska, North Dakota, South Dakota, and Wisconsin. Deadline: last day of academic term.

Award: Scholarship for use in freshman, sophomore, junior, senior, graduate, or postgraduate years; renewable. *Number:* varies. *Amount:* varies.

Eligibility Requirements: Applicant must be enrolled or expecting to enroll full- or part-time at a two-year or four-year or technical institution or university; resident of Minnesota and studying in Iowa, Kansas, Michigan, Missouri, Nebraska, North Dakota, South Dakota, or Wisconsin. Available to U.S. citizens.

Application Requirements: Application. *Deadline:* varies.

Contact: Ginny Dodds, Manager
Minnesota Higher Education Services Office
1450 Energy Park Drive, Suite 350
St. Paul, MN 55108-5227
Phone: 651-642-0567
Fax: 651-642-0675
E-mail: ginny.dodds@state.mn.us

MINNESOTA STATE GRANT PROGRAM

Need-based grant program available for Minnesota residents attending Minnesota colleges. Student covers 46% of cost with remainder covered by Pell Grant, parent contribution and state grant. Students apply with FAFSA and college administers the program on campus.

Award: Grant for use in freshman, sophomore, junior, or senior years; renewable. *Number:* 71,000–81,000. *Amount:* $100–$8372.

Eligibility Requirements: Applicant must be age 17 and over; enrolled or expecting to enroll full- or part-time at a two-year or four-year or technical institution or university; resident of Minnesota and studying in Minnesota. Available to U.S. citizens.

Application Requirements: Application, financial need analysis. *Deadline:* varies.

Contact: Grant Staff
Minnesota Higher Education Services Office
1450 Energy Park Drive, Suite 350
St. Paul, MN 55108
Phone: 651-642-0567 Ext. 1

MINNESOTA STATE VETERANS' DEPENDENTS ASSISTANCE PROGRAM

• *See page 657*

POSTSECONDARY CHILD CARE GRANT PROGRAM-MINNESOTA

Grant available for students not receiving MFIP. Based on financial need. Cannot exceed actual child care costs or maximum award chart (based on income). Must be Minnesota resident. For use at Minnesota two- or four-year school, including public technical colleges.

Award: Grant for use in freshman, sophomore, junior, or senior years; renewable. *Number:* varies. *Amount:* $100–$2600.

Eligibility Requirements: Applicant must be enrolled or expecting to enroll full- or part-time at a two-year or four-year or technical institution or university; resident of Minnesota and studying in Minnesota. Available to U.S. citizens.

Application Requirements: Application, financial need analysis. *Deadline:* continuous.

Contact: Ginny Dodds, Manager
Minnesota Higher Education Services Office
1450 Energy Park Drive, Suite 350
St. Paul, MN 55108-5227
Phone: 651-642-0567
Fax: 651-642-0675
E-mail: ginny.dodds@state.mn.us

SAFETY OFFICERS' SURVIVOR GRANT PROGRAM

• *See page 603*

MINNESOTA INDIAN SCHOLARSHIP OFFICE http://www.mheso.state.mn.us

MINNESOTA INDIAN SCHOLARSHIP PROGRAM

• *See page 692*

MISSISSIPPI STATE STUDENT FINANCIAL AID http://www.ihl.state.ms.us

HIGHER EDUCATION LEGISLATIVE PLAN (HELP)

Eligible applicant must be resident of Mississippi and be freshman and/or sophomore student who graduated from high school within the immediate past two years. Must demonstrate need as determined by the results of the FAFSA: documenting an average family adjusted gross income of $36,500 or less over the prior two years. Must be enrolled full-time at a Mississippi college or university, have a GPA of 2.5 and have scored 20 on the ACT.

Award: Scholarship for use in freshman or sophomore years; renewable. *Number:* varies. *Amount:* varies.

Eligibility Requirements: Applicant must be enrolled or expecting to enroll full-time at a four-year institution or university; resident of Mississippi and studying in Mississippi. Applicant must have 2.5 GPA or higher. Available to U.S. citizens.

Application Requirements: Application, financial need analysis, test scores, transcript, FAFSA. *Deadline:* March 31.

Contact: Mary Covington, Assistant Director, State Student Financial Aid
Mississippi State Student Financial Aid
3825 Ridgewood Road
Jackson, MS 39211-6453
Phone: 800-327-2980
E-mail: sfa@ihl.state.ms.us

MISSISSIPPI EMINENT SCHOLARS GRANT

Award for an entering freshmen or as a renewal for sophomore, junior or senior. who are residents of Mississippi. Applicants must achieve a GPA of 3.5 and must have scored 29 on the ACT. Must enroll full-time at an eligible Mississippi college or university.

Award: Grant for use in freshman, sophomore, junior, or senior years; renewable. *Number:* varies. *Amount:* up to $2500.

Eligibility Requirements: Applicant must be enrolled or expecting to enroll full-time at a two-year or four-year institution or university; resident of Mississippi and studying in Mississippi. Applicant must have 3.5 GPA or higher. Available to U.S. citizens.

Application Requirements: Application, test scores, transcript. *Deadline:* September 15.

Contact: Mary Covington, Assistant Director, State Student Financial Aid
Mississippi State Student Financial Aid
3825 Ridgewood Road
Jackson, MS 39211-6453
Phone: 800-327-2980
E-mail: sfa@ihl.state.ms.us

MISSISSIPPI LEVERAGING EDUCATIONAL ASSISTANCE PARTNERSHIP (LEAP)

Award for Mississippi residents enrolled for full-time study at a Mississippi college or university. Based on financial need. Contact college financial aid office. Award value and deadline varies.

Award: Grant for use in freshman, sophomore, junior, or senior years; renewable. *Number:* varies. *Amount:* varies.

Eligibility Requirements: Applicant must be enrolled or expecting to enroll full-time at a two-year or four-year institution or university; resident of Mississippi and studying in Mississippi. Available to U.S. citizens.

Application Requirements: Application, financial need analysis, FAFSA. *Deadline:* varies.

Contact: Mary Covington, Assistant Director, State Student Financial Aid
Mississippi State Student Financial Aid
3825 Ridgewood Road
Jackson, MS 39211-6453
Phone: 800-327-2980
E-mail: sfa@ihl.state.ms.us

MISSISSIPPI RESIDENT TUITION ASSISTANCE GRANT

Must be a resident of Mississippi enrolled full-time at an eligible Mississippi college or university. Must maintain a minimum 2.5 GPA each semester. MTAG awards may be up to $500 per academic year for freshman and sophomores and $1000 per academic year for juniors and seniors.

Award: Grant for use in freshman, sophomore, junior, or senior years; renewable. *Number:* varies. *Amount:* $500–$1000.

Eligibility Requirements: Applicant must be enrolled or expecting to enroll full-time at a two-year or four-year institution or university; resident of Mississippi and studying in Mississippi. Applicant must have 2.5 GPA or higher. Available to U.S. citizens.

Application Requirements: Application, test scores, transcript. *Deadline:* September 15.

Contact: Mary Covington, Assistant Director, State Student Financial Aid
Mississippi State Student Financial Aid
3825 Ridgewood Road
Jackson, MS 39211-6453
Phone: 800-327-2980
E-mail: sfa@ihl.state.ms.us

NISSAN SCHOLARSHIP

Renewable award for Mississippi residents attending a Mississippi institution. Must be graduating from a Mississippi high school in the current year. The scholarship will pay full tuition and a book allowance. Minimum GPA of 2.0 as well as an ACT composite of at least 20 or combined SAT scores of 940 or better. Must demonstrate financial need and leadership abilities.

Award: Scholarship for use in freshman year; renewable. *Number:* varies. *Amount:* varies.

Eligibility Requirements: Applicant must be high school student; planning to enroll or expecting to enroll full-time at a two-year or four-year institution or university; resident of Mississippi and studying in Mississippi. Available to U.S. citizens.

Mississippi State Student Financial Aid (continued)

Application Requirements: Application, essay, financial need analysis, references, test scores, transcript. *Deadline:* March 1.

Contact: Mary Covington, Assistant Director, State Student Financial Aid
Mississippi State Student Financial Aid
3825 Ridgewood Road
Jackson, MS 39211-6453
Phone: 800-327-2980
E-mail: sfa@ihl.state.ms.us

MISSOURI CONSERVATION AGENTS ASSOCIATION SCHOLARSHIP http://www.moagent.com

MISSOURI CONSERVATION AGENTS ASSOCIATION SCHOLARSHIP

Scholarship of up to $500 per student per year for full-time undergraduate students who reside in the state of Missouri. The applicant must be a U.S. citizen.

Award: Scholarship for use in freshman, sophomore, junior, or senior years; not renewable. *Number:* varies. *Amount:* up to $500.

Eligibility Requirements: Applicant must be enrolled or expecting to enroll full-time at a four-year or technical institution or university and resident of Missouri. Applicant must have 2.5 GPA or higher. Available to U.S. citizens.

Application Requirements: Essay, transcript. *Deadline:* February 1.

Contact: Brian Ham, Scholarship Committee
Missouri Conservation Agents Association Scholarship
PO Box 1072
Kirksville, MO 63501
Phone: 573-896-8628

MISSOURI DEPARTMENT OF ELEMENTARY AND SECONDARY EDUCATION http://www.dese.mo.gov

ROBERT C. BYRD HONORS SCHOLARSHIP-MISSOURI

Award for high school seniors who are residents of Missouri. Amount of the award each year depends on the amount the state is allotted by the U.S. Department of Education. Maximum amount awarded per student is $1500. Students must rank in top 10 percent of high school class and score in top 10 percent on ACT.

Award: Scholarship for use in freshman year; renewable. *Number:* 100–150. *Amount:* up to $1500.

Eligibility Requirements: Applicant must be high school student; planning to enroll or expecting to enroll full-time at a four-year institution or university and resident of Missouri. Available to U.S. citizens.

Application Requirements: Application, test scores, transcript. *Deadline:* April 15.

Contact: Laura Harrison, Administrative Assistant II
Missouri Department of Elementary and Secondary Education
PO Box 480
Jefferson City, MO 65102-0480
Phone: 573-751-1668
Fax: 573-526-3580
E-mail: laura.harrison@dese.mo.gov

MISSOURI DEPARTMENT OF HIGHER EDUCATION http://www.dhe.mo.gov

CHARLES GALLAGHER STUDENT ASSISTANCE PROGRAM

Program providing need-based grants for U.S. citizens who are Missouri residents to access Missouri postsecondary education. Must be a full-time undergraduate student and working toward a first baccalaureate degree. Must maintain satisfactory academic progress as defined by the school.

Award: Grant for use in freshman, sophomore, junior, or senior years; not renewable. *Number:* varies. *Amount:* $1500.

Eligibility Requirements: Applicant must be enrolled or expecting to enroll full-time at a two-year or four-year or technical institution or university; resident of Missouri and studying in Missouri. Available to U.S. citizens.

Application Requirements: Financial need analysis, FAFSA. *Deadline:* April 1.

Contact: Information Center
Missouri Department of Higher Education
3515 Amazonas Drive
Jefferson City, MO 65109-5717
Phone: 800-473-6757 Ext. 1
Fax: 573-751-6635
E-mail: info@dhe.mo.gov

MARGUERITE ROSS BARNETT MEMORIAL SCHOLARSHIP

Scholarship was established for students who are employed while attending school part-time. Must be enrolled at least half-time but less than full-time at a participating Missouri postsecondary school, be employed and compensated for at least 20 hours per week, be 18 years of age, be a Missouri resident and a U.S. citizen or an eligible non-citizen.

Award: Scholarship for use in freshman, sophomore, junior, or senior years; renewable. *Number:* varies. *Amount:* varies.

Eligibility Requirements: Applicant must be age 18 and over; enrolled or expecting to enroll part-time at a two-year or four-year or technical institution or university; resident of Missouri and studying in Missouri. Available to U.S. and non-U.S. citizens.

Application Requirements: Application, financial need analysis. *Deadline:* varies.

Contact: Information Center
Missouri Department of Higher Education
3515 Amazonas Drive
Jefferson City, MO 65109-5717
Phone: 800-473-6757 Ext. 1
Fax: 573-751-6635
E-mail: info@dhe.mo.gov

MISSOURI COLLEGE GUARANTEE PROGRAM

Grant is based on demonstrated financial need, as well as high school and college academic achievement. Must have a high school GPA of 2.5 or higher, be enrolled full-time at a participating Missouri postsecondary school, be a Missouri resident and a U.S. citizen. Must have participated in high school extracurricular activities.

Award: Scholarship for use in freshman, sophomore, junior, or senior years; not renewable. *Number:* varies. *Amount:* varies.

Eligibility Requirements: Applicant must be enrolled or expecting to enroll full-time at a two-year or four-year institution or university; resident of Missouri and studying in Missouri. Applicant must have 2.5 GPA or higher. Available to U.S. citizens.

Application Requirements: Financial need analysis, test scores, FAFSA. *Deadline:* varies.

Contact: Information Center
Missouri Department of Higher Education
3515 Amazonas Drive
Jefferson City, MO 65109-5717
Phone: 800-473-6757 Ext. 1
Fax: 573-751-6635
E-mail: info@dhe.mo.gov

MISSOURI HIGHER EDUCATION ACADEMIC SCHOLARSHIP (BRIGHT FLIGHT)

Program encourages top-ranked high school seniors to attend approved Missouri postsecondary schools. Must be a Missouri resident and a U.S. citizen. Must have a composite score on the ACT or the SAT in the top three percent of all Missouri students taking those tests. Annual scholarship of $2000 is awarded in two payments of $1000 each semester.

Award: Scholarship for use in freshman year; renewable. *Number:* varies. *Amount:* $2000.

Eligibility Requirements: Applicant must be high school student; planning to enroll or expecting to enroll full-time at a two-year or four-year or technical institution or university; resident of Missouri and studying in Missouri. Available to U.S. citizens.

Application Requirements: Test scores. *Deadline:* varies.

Contact: Information Center
Missouri Department of Higher Education
3515 Amazonas Drive
Jefferson City, MO 65109-5717
Phone: 800-473-6757 Ext. 1
Fax: 573-751-6635
E-mail: info@dhe.mo.gov

MISSOURI STATE DEPARTMENT OF ELEMENTARY/ SECONDARY EDUCATION http://www.dese.mo.gov

MINORITY TEACHING SCHOLARSHIP

• *See page 692*

TEACHER EDUCATION SCHOLARSHIP

The scholarship is a competitive, one-time, nonrenewable award of $2000 to be used in one academic year. Applicants must be a Missouri resident and a high school senior or student enrolled full-time at a community or four-year college or university in Missouri.

Award: Scholarship for use in freshman, sophomore, junior, or senior years; not renewable. *Number:* up to 240. *Amount:* up to $2000.

Eligibility Requirements: Applicant must be enrolled or expecting to enroll full-time at a two-year or four-year institution or university; resident of Missouri and studying in Missouri. Available to U.S. citizens.

Application Requirements: Application, applicant must enter a contest, essay, resume, references, test scores, transcript. *Deadline:* February 15.

Contact: Ms. Laura Harrison, Administrative Assistant
Missouri State Department of Elementary/Secondary Education
PO Box 480
Jefferson City, MO 65102-0480
Phone: 573-751-1668
Fax: 573-526-3580
E-mail: laura.harrison@dese.mo.gov

MITCHELL INSTITUTE http://www.mitchellinstitute.org

MITCHELL SCHOLARSHIP

Awards scholarship to graduating senior from every public high school in Maine. The scholarship award is in the amount of up to $5000 ($1250 per year) for students who are pursuing a four-year degree and $2500 for students pursuing a two-year degree. One scholarship per county in the amount of $6000 ($1500 per year) is awarded with a preference to a first-generation college student.

Award: Scholarship for use in freshman year; renewable. *Number:* 130. *Amount:* $1250–$1500.

Eligibility Requirements: Applicant must be high school student; planning to enroll or expecting to enroll full- or part-time at a two-year or four-year or technical institution or university and resident of Maine. Available to U.S. citizens.

Application Requirements: Application, essay, financial need analysis, photo, references, transcript. *Deadline:* April 1.

Contact: Patricia Higgins, Director of Scholarship Programs
Mitchell Institute
22 Monument Square, Suite 200
Portland, ME 04101
Phone: 207-773-7700
Fax: 207-773-1133
E-mail: phiggins@mitchellinstitute.org

MLGPA FOUNDATION http://www.equalitymaine.org

JOEL ABROMSON MEMORIAL FOUNDATION

One-time award for full-time postsecondary study available to winner of essay contest. Open to Maine residents only. Contact for essay topic and complete information. SASE.

Award: Scholarship for use in freshman year; not renewable. *Number:* 2. *Amount:* $500–$1000.

Eligibility Requirements: Applicant must be high school student; planning to enroll or expecting to enroll full-time at a two-year or four-year or technical institution or university and resident of Maine. Available to U.S. citizens.

Application Requirements: Application, applicant must enter a contest, essay, references, self-addressed stamped envelope, copy of acceptance letter to institution of higher learning. *Deadline:* April 15.

Contact: Betsy Smith, Executive Director
MLGPA Foundation
PO Box 1951
Portland, ME 04104
Phone: 207-761-3732
Fax: 207-761-3752
E-mail: info@equalitymaine.org

MONTANA GUARANTEED STUDENT LOAN PROGRAM, OFFICE OF COMMISSIONER OF HIGHER EDUCATION http://www.mgslp.state.mt.us

MONTANA HIGHER EDUCATION OPPORTUNITY GRANT

This grant is awarded based on need to undergraduate students attending either part-time or full-time who are residents of Montana and attending participating Montana schools. Awards are limited to the most needy students. A specific major or program of study is not required. This grant does not need to be repaid, and students may apply each year. Apply by filing FAFSA by March 1 and contacting the financial aid office at the admitting college.

Award: Grant for use in freshman, sophomore, junior, or senior years; not renewable. *Number:* up to 800. *Amount:* $400–$600.

Eligibility Requirements: Applicant must be enrolled or expecting to enroll full- or part-time at a two-year or four-year institution or university; resident of Montana and studying in Montana. Available to U.S. citizens.

Application Requirements: Application, financial need analysis, resume, FAFSA. *Deadline:* March 1.

Contact: Jamie Dushin, Budget Analyst
Montana Guaranteed Student Loan Program, Office of Commissioner of Higher Education
PO Box 203101
Helena, MT 59620-3101
Phone: 406-444-0638
Fax: 406-444-1869
E-mail: jdushin@mgslp.state.mt.us

MONTANA TUITION ASSISTANCE PROGRAM-BAKER GRANT

Need-based grant for Montana residents attending participating Montana schools who have earned at least $2575 during the previous calendar year. Must be enrolled full time. Grant does not need to be repaid. Award covers the first undergraduate degree or certificate. Apply by filing FAFSA by March 1 and contacting the financial aid office at the admitting college.

Award: Grant for use in freshman, sophomore, junior, or senior years; not renewable. *Number:* 1000–3000. *Amount:* $100–$1000.

Eligibility Requirements: Applicant must be enrolled or expecting to enroll full-time at a two-year or four-year institution or university; resident of Montana and studying in Montana. Available to U.S. citizens.

Application Requirements: Application, financial need analysis, resume, FAFSA. *Deadline:* March 1.

Contact: Jamie Dushin, Budget Analyst
Montana Guaranteed Student Loan Program, Office of Commissioner of Higher Education
PO Box 203101
Helena, MT 59620-3101
Phone: 406-444-0638
Fax: 406-444-1869
E-mail: jdushin@mgslp.state.mt.us

MONTANA UNIVERSITY SYSTEM HONOR SCHOLARSHIP

Scholarship will be awarded annually to high school seniors graduating from accredited Montana high schools. The MUS Honor Scholarship is a four year renewable scholarship that waives the tuition and registration fee at one of the Montana University System campuses or one of the three community colleges (Flathead Valley in Kalispell, Miles in Miles City or Dawson in Glendive). The scholarship must be used within 9 months after high school graduation. Applicant should have a GPA of 3.4.

Award: Scholarship for use in freshman year; renewable. *Number:* up to 200. *Amount:* up to $4020.

Montana Guaranteed Student Loan Program, Office of Commissioner of Higher Education (continued)

Eligibility Requirements: Applicant must be high school student; planning to enroll or expecting to enroll full-time at a four-year institution or university; resident of Montana and studying in Montana. Available to U.S. citizens.

Application Requirements: Application, test scores, transcript, college acceptance letter. *Deadline:* February 15.

Contact: Janice Kirkpatrick, Grant and Scholarship Coordinator
Montana Guaranteed Student Loan Program, Office of Commissioner of Higher Education
PO Box 203101
Helena, MT 59620-3101
Phone: 406-444-0638
Fax: 406-444-1869
E-mail: jkirkpatrick@mgslp.state.mt.us

MONTANA STATE OFFICE OF PUBLIC INSTRUCTION http://www.opi.mt.gov

ROBERT C. BYRD HONORS SCHOLARSHIP-MONTANA

The scholarship is available to graduating seniors and graduates of GED programs who will be entering college as freshmen. Minimum 3.6 GPA required. Award restricted to Montana residents. Scholarship value is $1500.

Award: Scholarship for use in freshman year; renewable. *Number:* 22–23. *Amount:* $1500.

Eligibility Requirements: Applicant must be high school student; planning to enroll or expecting to enroll full- or part-time at a four-year institution or university and resident of Montana. Available to U.S. citizens.

Application Requirements: Application, essay, test scores, transcript. *Deadline:* March 2.

Contact: Carol Gneckow, Program Specialist
Montana State Office of Public Instruction
PO Box 202501
Helena, MT 59620-2501
Phone: 406-444-3095
Fax: 406-444-1373
E-mail: cgneckow@mt.gov

UNITED STATES SENATE YOUTH PROGRAM-THE WILLIAM RANDOLPH HEARST FOUNDATION

Two high school juniors or seniors from Montana have a week long orientation in Washington, D.C. on the operation of the United States Senate and other components of the federal government. Potential awardees compete for the scholarship by taking a 50-point test, then the top ten applicants answer 5 to 7 questions in a video presentation. Must be currently serving in a high school government office. See Web site for specific details.

Award: Scholarship for use in freshman year; not renewable. *Number:* 2. *Amount:* $5000.

Eligibility Requirements: Applicant must be high school student; planning to enroll or expecting to enroll full- or part-time at a four-year institution or university and resident of Montana. Available to U.S. citizens.

Application Requirements: Application, applicant must enter a contest, interview, test scores, video presentation. *Deadline:* October 12.

Contact: Carol Gneckow, Program Specialist
Montana State Office of Public Instruction
PO Box 202501
Helena, MT 59620-2501
Phone: 406-444-3095
Fax: 406-444-1373
E-mail: cgneckow@mt.gov

MOUNT VERNON URBAN RENEWAL AGENCY http://www.ci.mount-vernon.ny.us

THOMAS E. SHARPE MEMORIAL EDUCATIONAL ASSISTANCE PROGRAM

Awards offered only to the low and moderate income residents of the city of Mount Vernon for the purpose of pursuing higher education at a vocational/technical school or college.

Award: Grant for use in freshman, sophomore, junior, or senior years; renewable. *Number:* up to 150. *Amount:* varies.

Eligibility Requirements: Applicant must be enrolled or expecting to enroll full-time at a two-year or four-year or technical institution or university and resident of New York. Applicant must have 2.5 GPA or higher. Available to U.S. citizens.

Application Requirements: Application, driver's license, essay, financial need analysis, transcript, proof of residence. *Deadline:* July 1.

Contact: Mary E. Fleming, Director, Scholarship Programs
Mount Vernon Urban Renewal Agency
Department of Planning, One Roosevelt Square, City Hall
Mount Vernon, NY 10550
Phone: 914-699-7230 Ext. 110
Fax: 914-699-1435
E-mail: mfleming@ci.mount-vernon.ny.us

NATIONAL ASSOCIATION FOR CAMPUS ACTIVITIES http://www.naca.org

LORI RHETT MEMORIAL SCHOLARSHIP

• *See page 603*

NATIONAL ASSOCIATION FOR CAMPUS ACTIVITIES EAST COAST UNDERGRADUATE SCHOLARSHIP FOR STUDENT LEADERS

• *See page 603*

NATIONAL ASSOCIATION FOR CAMPUS ACTIVITIES SOUTHEAST REGION STUDENT LEADERSHIP SCHOLARSHIP

• *See page 604*

NATIONAL ASSOCIATION FOR CAMPUS ACTIVITIES WISCONSIN REGION STUDENT LEADERSHIP SCHOLARSHIP

• *See page 604*

TESS CALDARELLI MEMORIAL SCHOLARSHIP

Scholarship available to undergraduate or graduate students with a minimum 3.0 GPA. Must demonstrate significant leadership skills and hold a significant position on campus. Must attend school in the NACA Great Lakes Region. The scholarship is to be used for educational purposes, such as tuition, fees and books or for professional development purposes.

Award: Scholarship for use in freshman, sophomore, junior, senior, or graduate years; not renewable. *Number:* varies. *Amount:* $250–$300.

Eligibility Requirements: Applicant must be enrolled or expecting to enroll full- or part-time at a two-year or four-year institution or university; studying in Kentucky, Michigan, Ohio, Pennsylvania, or West Virginia and must have an interest in leadership. Applicant must have 3.0 GPA or higher. Available to U.S. citizens.

Application Requirements: Application, resume, references, transcript. *Deadline:* November 1.

Contact: Dionne Ellison, Administrative Assistant
National Association for Campus Activities
13 Harbison Way
Columbia, SC 29212-3401
Phone: 803-732-6222 Ext. 131
Fax: 803-749-1047
E-mail: dionnee@naca.org

ZAGUNIS STUDENT LEADERS SCHOLARSHIP

Scholarships will be awarded to undergraduate or graduate students maintaining a cumulative GPA of 3.0 or better at the time of the application and during the academic term in which the scholarship is awarded. Applicants should demonstrate leadership skills and abilities while holding a significant leadership position on campus. Applicants must submit two letters of recommendation and a description of the applicant's leadership activities, skills, abilities and accomplishments. Must be enrolled in a college/university in the NACA Great Lakes Region.

Award: Scholarship for use in freshman, sophomore, junior, senior, or graduate years; not renewable. *Number:* 1. *Amount:* $300.

Eligibility Requirements: Applicant must be enrolled or expecting to enroll full- or part-time at a two-year or four-year institution or university; studying in Kentucky, Michigan, Ohio, Pennsylvania, or West Virginia and must have an interest in leadership. Applicant must have 3.0 GPA or higher. Available to U.S. citizens.

Application Requirements: Application, resume, references, transcript, current enrollment form. *Deadline:* November 1.

Contact: Dionne Ellison, Administrative Assistant
National Association for Campus Activities
13 Harbison Way
Columbia, SC 29212-3401
Phone: 803-732-6222 Ext. 131
Fax: 803-749-1047
E-mail: dionnee@naca.org

NATIONAL ASSOCIATION OF LETTER CARRIERS http://www.nalc.org

COSTAS G. LEMONOPOULOS SCHOLARSHIP

• See page 543

NATIONAL ASSOCIATION TO ADVANCE FAT ACCEPTANCE (NEW ENGLAND CHAPTER) http://www.naafa.org

NEW ENGLAND CHAPTER-NATIONAL ASSOCIATION TO ADVANCE FAT ACCEPTANCE SCHOLARSHIP

Scholarship for New England high school seniors who are overweight. Essay required with application. Must have a minimum GPA of 2.5. Must be single, and pursue study in Connecticut, Maine, Massachusetts, New Hampshire, Rhode Island, or Vermont.

Award: Scholarship for use in freshman year; not renewable. *Number:* 2. *Amount:* $500.

Eligibility Requirements: Applicant must be high school student; planning to enroll or expecting to enroll full-time at a two-year or four-year or technical institution or university; single; resident of Connecticut, Maine, Massachusetts, New Hampshire, Rhode Island, or Vermont and studying in Connecticut, Maine, Massachusetts, New Hampshire, Rhode Island, or Vermont. Applicant must have 2.5 GPA or higher. Available to U.S. citizens.

Application Requirements: Application, autobiography, essay, photo, references, self-addressed stamped envelope, transcript. *Deadline:* May 1.

Contact: Roni Krinsky, Chairperson, Scholarship Committee
National Association to Advance Fat Acceptance (New England Chapter)
PO Box 51820
Boston, MA 02205-1820
Phone: 781-986-2232
Fax: 617-782-8460
E-mail: ronikrink@aol.com

NATIONAL BURGLAR AND FIRE ALARM ASSOCIATION http://www.alarm.org

NBFAA YOUTH SCHOLARSHIP PROGRAM

• See page 604

NATIONAL COUNCIL OF JEWISH WOMEN NEW YORK SECTION http://www.ncjwny.org

JACKSON-STRICKS SCHOLARSHIP

• See page 622

NATIONAL DEFENSE TRANSPORTATION ASSOCIATION-SCOTT ST. LOUIS CHAPTER http://www.ndtascottstlouis.org

NATIONAL DEFENSE TRANSPORTATION ASSOCIATION, SCOTT AIR FORCE BASE-ST. LOUIS AREA CHAPTER SCHOLARSHIP

Three scholarships of $2000 each are open to any high school students in Illinois and Missouri that meet the eligibility criteria. One scholarship of $2000 is available for eligible college students enrolled in a degree program. An additional $2000 scholarship is set aside for immediate family members of active NDTA Scott/St. Louis Chapter members. Minimum 3.0 GPA required. College applicants must be a full-time student in the following states: CO, IA, IL, IN, KS, MI, MN, MO, MT, ND, NE, SD, WI, or WY.

Award: Scholarship for use in freshman, sophomore, junior, or senior years; not renewable. *Number:* 5. *Amount:* $2000.

Eligibility Requirements: Applicant must be enrolled or expecting to enroll full-time at a two-year or four-year institution or university; resident of Illinois or Missouri and studying in Colorado, Illinois, Indiana, Iowa, Kansas, Michigan, Minnesota, Missouri, Montana, Nebraska, North Dakota, or South Dakota. Applicant must have 3.0 GPA or higher. Available to U.S. citizens.

Application Requirements: Application, essay, references, test scores, transcript. *Deadline:* March 1.

Contact: Mr. Michael Carnes, Scholarship Committee
National Defense Transportation Association-Scott St. Louis Chapter
1716 Corporate Crossing, Suite 1
O'Fallon, IL 62269
Phone: 618-628-4208 Ext. 252
Fax: 618-628-4790
E-mail: mcarnes@csc.com

NATIONAL FEDERATION OF THE BLIND OF CALIFORNIA http://www.nfbcal.org

GERALD DRAKE MEMORIAL SCHOLARSHIP

• See page 622

JULIE LANDUCCI SCHOLARSHIP

• See page 623

LA VYRL "PINKY" JOHNSON MEMORIAL SCHOLARSHIP

• See page 623

LAWRENCE "MUZZY" MARCELINO MEMORIAL SCHOLARSHIP

• See page 623

NATIONAL FEDERATION OF THE BLIND OF CALIFORNIA MERIT SCHOLARSHIPS

• See page 623

NATIONAL FEDERATION OF THE BLIND OF CONNECTICUT http://www.nfbct.org

C. RODNEY DEMAREST MEMORIAL SCHOLARSHIP

• See page 623

DORIS E. HIGLEY MEMORIAL SCHOLARSHIP

• See page 623

HOWARD E. MAY MEMORIAL SCHOLARSHIP

• See page 624

MARY MAIN MEMORIAL SCHOLARSHIP

• See page 624

NATIONAL GUARD ASSOCIATION OF COLORADO EDUCATION FOUNDATION http://www.ngaco.org

NATIONAL GUARD ASSOCIATION OF COLORADO (NGACO) EDUCATION FOUNDATION INC. SCHOLARSHIP

• See page 635

NATIONAL KIDNEY FOUNDATION OF INDIANA INC. http://www.kidneyindiana.org

LARRY SMOCK SCHOLARSHIP

• See page 624

NATIONAL UNION OF PUBLIC AND GENERAL EMPLOYEES http://www.nupge.ca

SCHOLARSHIP FOR ABORIGINAL CANADIANS

• See page 547

SCHOLARSHIP FOR VISIBLE MINORITIES

• See page 547

TERRY FOX MEMORIAL SCHOLARSHIP

• See page 547

TOMMY DOUGLAS SCHOLARSHIP

• See page 548

NEBRASKA DEPARTMENT OF EDUCATION http://www.nde.state.ne.us/byrd

ROBERT C. BYRD HONORS SCHOLARSHIP-NEBRASKA

Award for high school seniors, renewable for up to four years. Must be U.S. citizen and Nebraska resident. Awards designed to promote student excellence and achievement, and to recognize able students who show promise of continued excellence. Funded scholars must submit renewal application each year. Renewal based on continuing eligibility requirements. Must have minimum ACT score of 30.

Award: Scholarship for use in freshman year; renewable. *Number:* 40–45. *Amount:* $1500.

Eligibility Requirements: Applicant must be high school student; planning to enroll or expecting to enroll full-time at a four-year institution or university and resident of Nebraska. Available to U.S. citizens.

Application Requirements: Application, test scores, transcript. *Deadline:* March 15.

Contact: Mardi North, Robert C. Byrd Scholarship Information
Nebraska Department of Education
301 Centennial Mall South, PO Box 94987
Lincoln, NE 68509-4987
Phone: 402-471-3962
Fax: 402-471-8850
E-mail: mardi.north@nde.ne.gov

NEGRO EDUCATIONAL EMERGENCY DRIVE http://www.needld.org

UNMET NEED PROGRAM GRANTS

Scholarship provides last dollar funding to lower-income students that still have a need for aid after all federal, state, local and private scholarships and grants have been secured. Must be a U.S. citizen, graduating senior, resident of a participating county in Western PA, and have a minimum 2.0 GPA.

Award: Grant for use in freshman, sophomore, junior, or senior years; not renewable. *Number:* 1000–3500. *Amount:* varies.

Eligibility Requirements: Applicant must be enrolled or expecting to enroll full- or part-time at a two-year or four-year or technical institution or university and resident of Pennsylvania. Available to U.S. citizens.

Application Requirements: Application, financial need analysis. *Deadline:* May 31.

Contact: Arlene Tyler Holland, Student Services Manager
Negro Educational Emergency Drive
Warner Centre, 332 5th Avenue, First floor
Pittsburgh, PA 15222
Phone: 412-566-2760
Fax: 412-471-6643
E-mail: atyler@needld.org

NEVADA DEPARTMENT OF EDUCATION http://www.doe.nv.gov

NEVADA STUDENT INCENTIVE GRANT

Grants awarded to undergraduate and graduate students who are Nevada residents pursuing their first degree. Recipients must be enrolled at least halftime and have financial need. Awards may range from $200 to $4000. High school students may not apply.

Award: Grant for use in freshman, sophomore, junior, senior, or graduate years; not renewable. *Number:* 400–800. *Amount:* $200–$4000.

Eligibility Requirements: Applicant must be enrolled or expecting to enroll full- or part-time at a two-year or four-year or technical institution or university; resident of Nevada and studying in Nevada. Available to U.S. citizens.

Application Requirements: Application, financial need analysis. *Deadline:* continuous.

Contact: Bill Arensdorf, Director
Nevada Department of Education
700 East Fifth Street
Carson City, NV 89701
Phone: 775-687-9200
Fax: 775-687-9113
E-mail: warensdorf@doe.nv.gov

ROBERT C. BYRD HONORS SCHOLARSHIP-NEVADA

Award for senior graduating from public or private Nevada high school. Must be Nevada resident. Renewable award of $1500. No application necessary. Nevada scholars are chosen from a database supplied by ACT and SAT. SAT scores of 1100 and above qualify as initial application. ACT score is automatically submitted for a score of 25 or greater. GPA must be 3.5 or higher.

Award: Scholarship for use in freshman year; renewable. *Number:* 40–60. *Amount:* $1500.

Eligibility Requirements: Applicant must be high school student; planning to enroll or expecting to enroll full-time at a four-year institution or university; resident of Nevada and studying in Nevada. Applicant must have 3.5 GPA or higher. Available to U.S. citizens.

Application Requirements: Test scores, transcript. *Deadline:* continuous.

Contact: Bill Arensdorf, Director
Nevada Department of Education
700 East Fifth Street
Carson City, NV 89701
Phone: 775-687-9200
Fax: 775-687-9113
E-mail: warensdorf@doe.nv.gov

NEVADA OFFICE OF THE STATE TREASURER http://www.nevadatreasurer.gov

GOVERNOR GUINN MILLENNIUM SCHOLARSHIP

Scholarship for high school graduates with a diploma from a Nevada public or private high school in the graduating class of the year 2000 or later. Must complete high school with at least 3.25 GPA.

Award: Scholarship for use in freshman, sophomore, junior, or senior years; not renewable. *Number:* 1. *Amount:* $10,000.

Eligibility Requirements: Applicant must be enrolled or expecting to enroll full-time at a two-year or four-year institution or university and resident of Nevada. Available to U.S. citizens.

Application Requirements: Application. *Deadline:* varies.

Contact: Reba Coombs, Executive Director
Nevada Office of the State Treasurer
555 East Washington Avenue, Suite 4600
Las Vegas, NV 89101
Phone: 702-486-3383
Fax: 702-486-3246
E-mail: info@nevadatreasurer.gov

NEW ENGLAND BOARD OF HIGHER EDUCATION http://www.nebhe.org

NEW ENGLAND REGIONAL STUDENT PROGRAM

Scholarship for residents of New England. Students pay reduced out-of-state tuition at public colleges or universities in other New England states when enrolling in certain majors not offered at public institutions in home state.

Award: Scholarship for use in freshman, sophomore, junior, senior, or graduate years; renewable. *Number:* 8000. *Amount:* varies.

Eligibility Requirements: Applicant must be enrolled or expecting to enroll full- or part-time at a two-year or four-year institution or university and resident of Connecticut, Maine, Massachusetts, New Hampshire, Rhode Island, or Vermont. Available to U.S. citizens.

Application Requirements: College application. *Deadline:* continuous.

Contact: Wendy Lindsay, Senior Director of Regional Student Program
New England Board of Higher Education
45 Temple Place
Boston, MA 02111-1305
Phone: 617-357-9620 Ext. 111
Fax: 617-338-1577
E-mail: tuitionbreak@nebhe.org

NEW HAMPSHIRE CHARITABLE FOUNDATION http://www.nhcf.org

ADULT STUDENT AID PROGRAM

• *See page 658*

CAREER AID TO TECHNOLOGY STUDENTS PROGRAM

Awards for New Hampshire residents enrolled in any accredited vocational or technical program that does not lead to a four-year baccalaureate degree. Must be financially needy and planning to enroll at least half time. See Web site at http://www.nhcf.org for further information and application.

Award: Grant for use in freshman or sophomore years; not renewable. *Number:* varies. *Amount:* $100–$2500.

Eligibility Requirements: Applicant must be age 17-24; enrolled or expecting to enroll full- or part-time at a two-year or technical institution and resident of New Hampshire. Available to U.S. citizens.

Application Requirements: Application, financial need analysis, transcript. *Deadline:* June 27.

Contact: CATS Program
New Hampshire Charitable Foundation
37 Pleasant Street
Concord, NH 03301-4005
Phone: 800-464-6641

FISHER CATS SCHOLAR ATHLETES

Award available for students who are graduating from high school. A maximum of 10 athletes will be awarded $2500.

Award: Scholarship for use in freshman year; not renewable. *Number:* 10. *Amount:* up to $2500.

Eligibility Requirements: Applicant must be high school student; planning to enroll or expecting to enroll full-time at a two-year or four-year or technical institution; resident of New Hampshire and must have an interest in athletics/sports. Available to U.S. citizens.

Application Requirements: Application, financial need analysis, resume, transcript. *Deadline:* March 31.

Contact: Judith Burrows, Director, Student Aid
New Hampshire Charitable Foundation
37 Pleasant Street
Concord, NH 03301-4005
Phone: 603-225-6641 Ext. 224
E-mail: jb@nhcf.org

NEW HAMPSHIRE DEPARTMENT OF EDUCATION http://www.state.nh.us/doe/

ROBERT C. BYRD HONORS SCHOLARSHIP-NEW HAMPSHIRE

Scholarships awarded to graduates of approved New Hampshire secondary schools based on academic achievement. Contact department for application deadlines. May be funded through four years of college if recipient maintains high academic achievement. Must be high school senior to apply and must submit letters of recommendation. Award is offered in senior year of high school. Minimum 3.0 GPA required.

Award: Scholarship for use in freshman year; renewable. *Number:* 26–30. *Amount:* $1500.

Eligibility Requirements: Applicant must be high school student; planning to enroll or expecting to enroll full- or part-time at a two-year or four-year institution or university and resident of New Hampshire. Applicant must have 3.0 GPA or higher. Available to U.S. citizens.

Application Requirements: Application, essay, portfolio, references, test scores, transcript. *Deadline:* varies.

Contact: Patricia Butler, Administrative Assistant
New Hampshire Department of Education
101 Pleasant Street
Concord, NH 03301-3860
Phone: 603-271-3144
Fax: 603-271-1953
E-mail: pbutler@ed.state.nh.us

NEW HAMPSHIRE FOOD INDUSTRIES EDUCATION FOUNDATION http://www.grocers.org

NEW HAMPSHIRE FOOD INDUSTRY SCHOLARSHIPS

• *See page 581*

NEW HAMPSHIRE POSTSECONDARY EDUCATION COMMISSION http://www.nh.gov/postsecondary

LEVERAGED INCENTIVE GRANT PROGRAM

Grants to provide assistance on the basis of merit and need to full-time undergraduate New Hampshire students at New Hampshire accredited institutions. Must be a New Hampshire resident, and demonstrate financial need as determined by the federal formula and by merit as determined by the institution. Must be a sophomore, junior or senior undergraduate student.

Award: Grant for use in sophomore, junior, or senior years; not renewable. *Number:* varies. *Amount:* $250–$7500.

Eligibility Requirements: Applicant must be enrolled or expecting to enroll full-time at a two-year or four-year or technical institution or university; resident of New Hampshire and studying in New Hampshire. Available to U.S. citizens.

Application Requirements: Application, financial need analysis. *Deadline:* varies.

Contact: Judith Knapp, Coordinator of Financial Aid Programs
New Hampshire Postsecondary Education Commission
Three Barrell Court, Suite 300
Concord, NH 03301-8543
Phone: 603-271-2555 Ext. 352
Fax: 603-271-2696
E-mail: jknapp@pec.state.nh.us

NEW HAMPSHIRE INCENTIVE PROGRAM (NHIP)

Grants to provide financial assistance to New Hampshire students attending eligible institutions in New England. Must demonstrate financial need. May be a part- or full-time undergraduate student with no previous bachelor's degree.

Award: Grant for use in freshman, sophomore, junior, or senior years; renewable. *Number:* 4300–4500. *Amount:* $125–$1000.

Eligibility Requirements: Applicant must be enrolled or expecting to enroll full- or part-time at a four-year institution or university; resident of New Hampshire and studying in Connecticut, Maine, Massachusetts, New Hampshire, Rhode Island, or Vermont. Available to U.S. citizens.

Application Requirements: Application, financial need analysis, FAFSA. *Deadline:* May 1.

Contact: Judith Knapp, Coordinator of Financial Aid Programs
New Hampshire Postsecondary Education Commission
Three Barrell Court, Suite 300
Concord, NH 03301-8543
Phone: 603-271-2555 Ext. 352
Fax: 603-271-2696
E-mail: jknapp@pec.state.nh.us

SCHOLARSHIPS FOR ORPHANS OF VETERANS-NEW HAMPSHIRE

• *See page 658*

UNIQUE SCHOLARSHIP

Grant available to New Hampshire residents enrolled at a New Hampshire institution of higher education. Must demonstrate financial need. Contact financial aid office for more information. High school students not considered.

Award: Grant for use in freshman, sophomore, junior, or senior years; renewable. *Number:* 500. *Amount:* $1500.

New Hampshire Postsecondary Education Commission (continued)

Eligibility Requirements: Applicant must be enrolled or expecting to enroll full-time at a two-year or four-year or technical institution or university; resident of New Hampshire and studying in New Hampshire. Available to U.S. citizens.

Application Requirements: Application, financial need analysis, FAFSA. *Deadline:* May 1.

Contact: Judith Knapp, Coordinator of Financial Aid Programs
New Hampshire Postsecondary Education Commission
Three Barrell Court, Suite 300
Concord, NH 03301-8543
Phone: 603-271-2555 Ext. 352
Fax: 603-271-2696
E-mail: jknapp@pec.state.nh.us

NEW JERSEY DEPARTMENT OF EDUCATION http://www.state.nj.us

ROBERT C. BYRD HONORS SCHOLARSHIP-NEW JERSEY

Award for outstanding graduating high school seniors who have been accepted for full-time study at a U.S. college or university. Must have a minimum 3.5 GPA. Award is renewable for up to four years. Must be legal resident of New Jersey and U.S. citizen.

Award: Scholarship for use in freshman year; renewable. *Number:* varies. *Amount:* $1500.

Eligibility Requirements: Applicant must be high school student; planning to enroll or expecting to enroll full-time at a four-year institution or university and resident of New Jersey. Applicant must have 3.5 GPA or higher. Available to U.S. citizens.

Application Requirements: Application. *Deadline:* April 4.

Contact: Sue Sliker, Program Administrator
New Jersey Department of Education
PO Box 500
Trenton, NJ 08625-0500
Phone: 609-777-0800

NEW JERSEY DEPARTMENT OF MILITARY AND VETERANS AFFAIRS http://www.state.nj.us/military

NEW JERSEY WAR ORPHANS TUITION ASSISTANCE

• *See page 658*

POW-MIA TUITION BENEFIT PROGRAM

• *See page 658*

VETERANS TUITION CREDIT PROGRAM-NEW JERSEY

• *See page 658*

NEW JERSEY HIGHER EDUCATION STUDENT ASSISTANCE AUTHORITY http://www.hesaa.org

DANA CHRISTMAS SCHOLARSHIP FOR HEROISM

Honors young New Jersey residents for acts of heroism. Scholarship is a nonrenewable award of up to $10,000 for 5 students. This scholarship may be used for undergraduate or graduate study. Deadline varies.

Award: Scholarship for use in freshman, sophomore, junior, senior, or graduate years; not renewable. *Number:* up to 5. *Amount:* up to $10,000.

Eligibility Requirements: Applicant must be age 21 or under; enrolled or expecting to enroll full- or part-time at a two-year or four-year or technical institution or university and resident of New Jersey. Available to U.S. citizens.

Application Requirements: Application. *Deadline:* varies.

Contact: Gisele Joachim, Director, Financial Aid Services
New Jersey Higher Education Student Assistance Authority
4 Quakerbridge Plaza, PO Box 540
Trenton, NJ 08625
Phone: 800-792-8670 Ext. 2349
Fax: 609-588-7389
E-mail: gjoachim@hesaa.org

EDWARD J. BLOUSTEIN DISTINGUISHED SCHOLARS

Renewable scholarship for students who are placed in top 10 percent of their classes and have a minimum combined SAT score of 1260, or ranked first, second or third in their classes as of end of junior year. Must be New Jersey resident and must attend a New Jersey two-year college, four-year college or university, or approved programs at proprietary institutions. Secondary schools must forward to HESAA, the names and class standings for all nominees. Award value up to $1000 and deadline varies.

Award: Scholarship for use in freshman, sophomore, junior, senior, or graduate years; renewable. *Number:* varies. *Amount:* up to $1000.

Eligibility Requirements: Applicant must be enrolled or expecting to enroll full-time at a two-year or four-year institution or university; resident of New Jersey and studying in New Jersey. Available to U.S. citizens.

Application Requirements: Application, test scores, nomination by high school. *Deadline:* varies.

Contact: Carol Muka, Assistant Director of Grants and Scholarships
New Jersey Higher Education Student Assistance Authority
PO Box 540
Trenton, NJ 08625
Phone: 800-792-8670 Ext. 3266
Fax: 609-588-2228
E-mail: cmuka@hesaa.org

LAW ENFORCEMENT OFFICER MEMORIAL SCHOLARSHIP

• *See page 606*

NEW JERSEY STUDENT TUITION ASSISTANCE REWARD SCHOLARSHIP II

Scholarship for high school graduates who plan to pursue a baccalaureate degree at a New Jersey four-year public institution. Scholarship will cover the cost of tuition and approved fees for up to 18 credits per semester when combined with other state, federal and institutional aid. Deadline varies.

Award: Scholarship for use in freshman year; renewable. *Number:* varies. *Amount:* $2000.

Eligibility Requirements: Applicant must be enrolled or expecting to enroll full-time at a four-year institution or university; resident of New Jersey and studying in New Jersey. Applicant must have 3.0 GPA or higher. Available to U.S. citizens.

Application Requirements: Application, FAFSA. *Deadline:* varies.

Contact: Cathleen Lewis, Assistant Director, Client Services
New Jersey Higher Education Student Assistance Authority
Fourth Quaker Bridge Plaza
PO Box 540
Trenton, NJ 08625-0540
Phone: 609-588-3280
Fax: 609-588-2228
E-mail: clewis@hesaa.org

NEW JERSEY WORLD TRADE CENTER SCHOLARSHIP

Scholarship was established by the legislature to aid the dependent children and surviving spouses of New Jersey residents who were killed in the terrorist attacks, or who are missing and officially presumed dead as a direct result of the attacks; applies to instate and out-of-state institutions for students seeking undergraduate degrees. Deadlines: March 1 for fall, October 1 for spring.

Award: Scholarship for use in freshman, sophomore, junior, or senior years; renewable. *Number:* varies. *Amount:* up to $6500.

Eligibility Requirements: Applicant must be enrolled or expecting to enroll full-time at a four-year institution or university and resident of New Jersey. Available to U.S. citizens.

Application Requirements: Application. *Deadline:* varies.

Contact: Giselle Joachim, Director of Financial Aid Services
New Jersey Higher Education Student Assistance Authority
PO Box 540
Trenton, NJ 08625
Phone: 800-792-8670 Ext. 2349
Fax: 609-588-7389
E-mail: gjoachim@hesaa.org

NJ STUDENT TUITION ASSISTANCE REWARD SCHOLARSHIP

Scholarship for students who graduate in the top 20 percent of their high school class. Recipients may be awarded up to five semesters of tuition (up to 15 credits per term) and approved fees at one of New Jersey's nineteen county colleges.

Award: Scholarship for use in freshman, sophomore, junior, or senior years; renewable. *Number:* varies. *Amount:* $2500–$7500.

Eligibility Requirements: Applicant must be enrolled or expecting to enroll full-time at a two-year or four-year institution or university;

resident of New Jersey and studying in New Jersey. Applicant must have 3.0 GPA or higher. Available to U.S. citizens.

Application Requirements: Application, transcript. *Deadline:* varies.

Contact: Carol Muka, Assistant Director of Grants and Scholarships
New Jersey Higher Education Student Assistance Authority
PO Box 540
Trenton, NJ 08625
Phone: 800-792-8670 Ext. 3266
Fax: 609-588-2228
E-mail: cmuka@hessa.org

OUTSTANDING SCHOLAR RECRUITMENT PROGRAM

Awards students who meet the eligibility criteria and who are enrolled as first-time freshmen at participating New Jersey institutions receive annual scholarship awards of up to $7500.

Award: Scholarship for use in freshman, sophomore, junior, or senior years; renewable. *Number:* varies. *Amount:* $2500–$7500.

Eligibility Requirements: Applicant must be enrolled or expecting to enroll full-time at a four-year institution or university; resident of New Jersey and studying in New Jersey. Available to U.S. citizens.

Application Requirements: Application. *Deadline:* varies.

Contact: Carol Muka, Assistant Director of Grants and Scholarships
New Jersey Higher Education Student Assistance Authority
PO Box 540
Trenton, NJ 08625
Phone: 800-792-8670 Ext. 3266
Fax: 609-588-2228
E-mail: cmuka@hesaa.org

PART-TIME TUITION AID GRANT (TAG) FOR COUNTY COLLEGES

Provides financial aid to eligible part-time undergraduate students enrolled for 9 to 11 credits at participating New Jersey community colleges. Deadlines: March 1 for spring and October 1 for fall.

Award: Grant for use in freshman, sophomore, junior, or senior years; not renewable. *Number:* varies. *Amount:* $419–$628.

Eligibility Requirements: Applicant must be enrolled or expecting to enroll part-time at a two-year or four-year institution or university; resident of New Jersey and studying in New Jersey. Available to U.S. citizens.

Application Requirements: Application, financial need analysis. *Deadline:* varies.

Contact: Sherri Fox, Acting Director of Grants and Scholarships
New Jersey Higher Education Student Assistance Authority
PO Box 540
Trenton, NJ 08625
Phone: 800-792-8670
Fax: 609-588-2228

SURVIVOR TUITION BENEFITS PROGRAM

• *See page 606*

TUITION AID GRANT

The program provides tuition fees to eligible undergraduate students attending participating in-state institutions. Deadlines: March 1 for fall, October 1 for spring.

Award: Grant for use in freshman, sophomore, junior, or senior years; not renewable. *Number:* varies. *Amount:* $868–$7272.

Eligibility Requirements: Applicant must be enrolled or expecting to enroll full-time at a two-year or four-year institution or university; resident of New Jersey and studying in New Jersey. Available to U.S. citizens.

Application Requirements: Application, financial need analysis. *Deadline:* varies.

Contact: Sherri Fox, Acting Director of Grants and Scholarships
New Jersey Higher Education Student Assistance Authority
PO Box 540
Trenton, NJ 08625
Phone: 800-792-8670
Fax: 609-588-2228

URBAN SCHOLARS

Renewable scholarship to high achieving students attending public secondary schools in the urban and economically distressed areas of New Jersey. Students must rank in the top 10 percent of their class and have a GPA of at least 3.0 at the end of their junior year. Must be New Jersey resident and attend a New Jersey two-year college, four-year college or university, or approved programs at proprietary institutions. Students do not apply directly for scholarship consideration. Deadline varies.

Award: Scholarship for use in freshman, sophomore, junior, or senior years; renewable. *Number:* varies. *Amount:* up to $1000.

Eligibility Requirements: Applicant must be enrolled or expecting to enroll full-time at a two-year or four-year institution or university; resident of New Jersey and studying in New Jersey. Applicant must have 3.0 GPA or higher. Available to U.S. citizens.

Application Requirements: Application, test scores, nomination by school. *Deadline:* varies.

Contact: Carol Muka, Assistant Director of Grants and Scholarships
New Jersey Higher Education Student Assistance Authority
PO Box 540
Trenton, NJ 08625
Phone: 800-792-8670 Ext. 3266
Fax: 609-588-2228
E-mail: cmuka@hesaa.org

NEW JERSEY STATE GOLF ASSOCIATION http://www.njsga.org

NEW JERSEY STATE GOLF ASSOCIATION CADDIE SCHOLARSHIP

• *See page 606*

NEW JERSEY VIETNAM VETERANS MEMORIAL FOUNDATION http://www.njvvmf.org

NEW JERSEY VIETNAM VETERANS' MEMORIAL FOUNDATION SCHOLARSHIP

One-time scholarship for graduating high school seniors of New Jersey. For full-time study only.

Award: Scholarship for use in freshman year; not renewable. *Number:* 2. *Amount:* $2500.

Eligibility Requirements: Applicant must be high school student; planning to enroll or expecting to enroll full-time at a two-year or four-year institution or university and resident of New Jersey. Available to U.S. citizens.

Application Requirements: Application, essay, acceptance letter. *Deadline:* April 18.

Contact: Lynn Duane, Administrative Assistant
New Jersey Vietnam Veterans Memorial Foundation
One Memorial Lane, PO Box 648
Holmdel, NJ 07733
Phone: 732-335-0033
Fax: 732-335-1107
E-mail: lduane@njvvmf.org

NEW MEXICO COMMISSION ON HIGHER EDUCATION http://www.hed.state.nm.us

COLLEGE AFFORDABILITY GRANT

Grant available to New Mexico students with financial need who do not qualify for other state grants and scholarships, to attend and complete educational programs at a New Mexico public college or university. Student must have unmet need after all other financial aid has been awarded. Student may not be receiving any other state grants or scholarships. Renewable upon satisfactory academic progress.

Award: Grant for use in freshman, sophomore, junior, or senior years; renewable. *Number:* varies. *Amount:* $1000.

Eligibility Requirements: Applicant must be enrolled or expecting to enroll full- or part-time at a two-year or four-year institution or university; resident of New Mexico and studying in New Mexico. Available to U.S. citizens.

New Mexico Commission on Higher Education (continued)

Application Requirements: Application, financial need analysis, FAFSA. *Deadline:* continuous.

Contact: Tashina Banks Moore, Interim Director of Financial Aid
New Mexico Commission on Higher Education
1068 Cerrillos Road
Santa Fe, NM 87505
Phone: 505-476-6549
Fax: 505-476-6511
E-mail: tashina.banks-moore@state.nm.us

LEGISLATIVE ENDOWMENT SCHOLARSHIPS

Renewable scholarships to provide aid for undergraduate students with substantial financial need who are attending public postsecondary institutions in New Mexico. Four-year schools may award up to $2500 per academic year, two-year schools may award up to $1000 per academic year. Deadlines varies.

Award: Scholarship for use in freshman, sophomore, junior, or senior years; renewable. *Number:* varies. *Amount:* $1000–$2500.

Eligibility Requirements: Applicant must be enrolled or expecting to enroll full- or part-time at a two-year or four-year institution or university; resident of New Mexico and studying in New Mexico. Available to U.S. citizens.

Application Requirements: Application, financial need analysis, FAFSA. *Deadline:* varies.

Contact: Tashina Banks Moore, Interim Director of Financial Aid
New Mexico Commission on Higher Education
1068 Cerrillos Road
Santa Fe, NM 87505
Phone: 505-476-6549
Fax: 505-476-6511
E-mail: tashina.banks-moore@state.nm.us

LEGISLATIVE LOTTERY SCHOLARSHIP

Renewable Scholarship for New Mexico high school graduates or GED recipients who plan to attend an eligible New Mexico public college or university. Must be enrolled full-time and maintain 2.5 GPA.

Award: Scholarship for use in freshman year; renewable. *Number:* 1. *Amount:* varies.

Eligibility Requirements: Applicant must be high school student; planning to enroll or expecting to enroll full-time at a four-year institution or university; resident of New Mexico and studying in New Mexico. Applicant must have 2.5 GPA or higher. Available to U.S. citizens.

Application Requirements: Application, FAFSA. *Deadline:* varies.

Contact: Tashina Banks Moore, Interim Director of Financial Aid
New Mexico Commission on Higher Education
1068 Cerrillos Road
Santa Fe, NM 87505
Phone: 505-476-6549
Fax: 505-476-6511
E-mail: tashina.banks-moore@state.nm.us

NEW MEXICO COMPETITIVE SCHOLARSHIP

Scholarships for non-residents or non-citizens of the United States to encourage out-of-state students who have demonstrated high academic achievement in high school to enroll in public four-year universities in New Mexico. Renewable for up to four years. For details visit: http://fin.hed.state.nm.us.

Award: Scholarship for use in freshman year; renewable. *Number:* varies. *Amount:* varies.

Eligibility Requirements: Applicant must be high school student; planning to enroll or expecting to enroll full-time at a four-year institution or university and studying in New Mexico. Available to Canadian and non-U.S. citizens.

Application Requirements: Application, essay, references, test scores. *Deadline:* varies.

Contact: Tashina Banks Moore, Interim Director of Financial Aid
New Mexico Commission on Higher Education
1068 Cerrillos Road
Santa Fe, NM 87505
Phone: 505-476-6549
Fax: 505-476-6511
E-mail: tashina.banks-moore@state.nm.us

NEW MEXICO SCHOLARS' PROGRAM

Renewable award program created to encourage New Mexico high school students to attend public postsecondary institutions or the following private colleges in New Mexico: College of Santa Fe, St. John's College, College of the Southwest. For details visit: http://fin.hed.state.nm.us.

Award: Scholarship for use in freshman year; renewable. *Number:* 1. *Amount:* varies.

Eligibility Requirements: Applicant must be high school student; age 21 or under; planning to enroll or expecting to enroll full-time at a two-year or four-year institution; resident of New Mexico and studying in New Mexico. Available to U.S. citizens.

Application Requirements: Application, financial need analysis, test scores, FAFSA. *Deadline:* varies.

Contact: Tashina Banks Moore, Interim Director of Financial Aid
New Mexico Commission on Higher Education
1068 Cerrillos Road
Santa Fe, NM 87505
Phone: 505-476-6549
Fax: 505-476-6511
E-mail: tashina.banks-moore@state.nm.us

NEW MEXICO STUDENT INCENTIVE GRANT

Grant created to provide aid for undergraduate students with substantial financial need who are attending public colleges or universities or the following eligible colleges in New Mexico: College of Santa Fe, St. John's College, College of the Southwest, Institute of American Indian Art, Crownpoint Institute of Technology, Dine College and Southwestern Indian Polytechnic Institute. Part-time students are eligible for pro-rated awards.

Award: Grant for use in freshman, sophomore, junior, or senior years; not renewable. *Number:* varies. *Amount:* $200–$2500.

Eligibility Requirements: Applicant must be enrolled or expecting to enroll full- or part-time at a two-year or four-year or technical institution or university; resident of New Mexico and studying in New Mexico. Available to U.S. citizens.

Application Requirements: Application, financial need analysis, FAFSA. *Deadline:* varies.

Contact: Tashina Banks Moore, Interim Director of Financial Aid
New Mexico Commission on Higher Education
1068 Cerrillos Road
Santa Fe, NM 87505
Phone: 505-476-6549
Fax: 505-476-6511
E-mail: tashina.banks-moore@state.nm.us

VIETNAM VETERANS' SCHOLARSHIP PROGRAM

• *See page 659*

NEW MEXICO STATE DEPARTMENT OF EDUCATION

http://www.ped.state.nm.us

ROBERT C. BYRD HONORS SCHOLARSHIP-NEW MEXICO

Award for outstanding graduating high school seniors from either a public or private high school in New Mexico who have been accepted for full-time study at a U.S. college or university. Must have a minimum of 3.5 GPA and either a score of 27 on the ACT or 1220 on the SAT.

Award: Scholarship for use in freshman year; renewable. *Number:* 1–44. *Amount:* $1500.

Eligibility Requirements: Applicant must be high school student; planning to enroll or expecting to enroll full-time at a four-year institution or university and resident of New Mexico. Applicant must have 3.5 GPA or higher. Available to U.S. citizens.

Application Requirements: Application, test scores, transcript. *Deadline:* March 30.

Contact: Jenna Jaquez, Assistant Program Coordinator
New Mexico State Department of Education
120 South Federal Place, Room 206
Santa Fe, NM 87501
Phone: 505-827-1421
E-mail: jenna.jaquez@state.nm.us

NEW MEXICO VETERANS SERVICE COMMISSION http://www.dvs.state.nm.us

CHILDREN OF DECEASED VETERANS SCHOLARSHIP-NEW MEXICO

• *See page 659*

NEW MEXICO VIETNAM VETERAN SCHOLARSHIP

• *See page 659*

NEW YORK LOTTERY http://www.nylottery.org

NEW YORK LOTTERY LEADERS OF TOMORROW (LOT) SCHOLARSHIP

Scholarship to one eligible graduating senior from every participating public and private high school in New York State is awarded a $1250, four-year college scholarship. Scholarships can only be used toward the cost of tuition.

Award: Scholarship for use in freshman year; renewable. *Number:* varies. *Amount:* $1250.

Eligibility Requirements: Applicant must be high school student; planning to enroll or expecting to enroll full-time at a four-year institution; resident of New York and studying in New York. Applicant must have 3.0 GPA or higher. Available to U.S. citizens.

Application Requirements: Application, essay, transcript. *Deadline:* March 26.

Contact: Scholarship Coordinator
New York Lottery
One Broadway Center, PO Box 7540
Schenectady, NY 12301-7540
Phone: 518-525-2686
Fax: 518-525-2689
E-mail: lotscholar@lottery.state.ny.us

NEW YORK STATE EDUCATION DEPARTMENT http://www.highered.nysed.gov

ROBERT C. BYRD HONORS SCHOLARSHIP-NEW YORK

Award for outstanding high school seniors accepted to U.S. college or university. Based on SAT score and high school average. Minimum 1875 combined SAT score from one sitting. Must be legal resident of New York and a U.S. citizen. Renewable for up to four years.

Award: Scholarship for use in freshman year; renewable. *Number:* 400. *Amount:* $1500.

Eligibility Requirements: Applicant must be high school student; planning to enroll or expecting to enroll full-time at a two-year or four-year institution or university and resident of New York. Available to U.S. citizens.

Application Requirements: Application. *Deadline:* March 1.

Contact: Lewis Hall, Supervisor
New York State Education Department
89 Washington Avenue, Room 1078 EBA
Albany, NY 12234
Phone: 518-486-1319
Fax: 518-486-5346
E-mail: scholar@mail.nysed.gov

SCHOLARSHIP FOR ACADEMIC EXCELLENCE

Renewable award for New York residents. Scholarship winners must attend a college or university in New York. 2000 scholarships are for $1500 and 6000 are for $500. The selection criteria used are based on Regents test scores or rank in class or local exam. Must be U.S. citizen or permanent resident.

Award: Scholarship for use in freshman year; renewable. *Number:* up to 8000. *Amount:* $500–$1500.

Eligibility Requirements: Applicant must be high school student; planning to enroll or expecting to enroll full-time at a two-year or four-year institution or university; resident of New York and studying in New York. Available to U.S. citizens.

Application Requirements: Application. *Deadline:* December 19.

Contact: Lewis Hall, Supervisor
New York State Education Department
89 Washington Avenue, Room 1078 EBA
Albany, NY 12234
Phone: 518-486-1319
Fax: 518-486-5346
E-mail: scholar@mail.nysed.gov

NEW YORK STATE GRANGE http://www.nysgrange.com

CAROLINE KARK AWARD

• *See page 548*

SUSAN W. FREESTONE EDUCATION AWARD

• *See page 548*

NEW YORK STATE HIGHER EDUCATION SERVICES CORPORATION http://www.hesc.com

NEW YORK AID FOR PART-TIME STUDY (APTS)

Renewable scholarship provides tuition assistance to part-time undergraduate students who are New York residents, meet income eligibility requirements and are attending New York accredited institutions. Deadline varies. Must be U.S. citizen.

Award: Grant for use in freshman, sophomore, junior, or senior years; renewable. *Number:* varies. *Amount:* up to $2000.

Eligibility Requirements: Applicant must be enrolled or expecting to enroll part-time at a two-year or four-year institution or university; resident of New York and studying in New York. Available to U.S. citizens.

Application Requirements: Application, financial need analysis. *Deadline:* varies.

Contact: Student Information
New York State Higher Education Services Corporation
99 Washington Avenue, Room 1320
Albany, NY 12255
Phone: 518-473-3887
Fax: 518-474-2839

NEW YORK MEMORIAL SCHOLARSHIPS FOR FAMILIES OF DECEASED POLICE OFFICERS, FIRE FIGHTERS AND PEACE OFFICERS

• *See page 606*

NEW YORK STATE AID TO NATIVE AMERICANS

• *See page 694*

NEW YORK STATE TUITION ASSISTANCE PROGRAM

Award for New York state residents attending a New York postsecondary institution. Must be full-time student in approved program with tuition over $200 per year. Must show financial need and not be in default in any other state program. Renewable award of $500 to $5000 dependent on family income and tuition charged.

Award: Grant for use in freshman, sophomore, junior, or senior years; renewable. *Number:* 350,000–360,000. *Amount:* $500–$5000.

Eligibility Requirements: Applicant must be enrolled or expecting to enroll full-time at a two-year or four-year institution or university; resident of New York and studying in New York. Available to U.S. citizens.

Application Requirements: Application, financial need analysis. *Deadline:* May 1.

Contact: Student Information
New York State Higher Education Services Corporation
99 Washington Avenue, Room 1320
Albany, NY 12255

NEW YORK VIETNAM/PERSIAN GULF/AFGHANISTAN VETERANS TUITION AWARDS

• *See page 659*

REGENTS AWARD FOR CHILD OF VETERAN

• *See page 659*

REGENTS PROFESSIONAL OPPORTUNITY SCHOLARSHIPS

Award for New York State residents pursuing career in certain licensed professions. Must attend New York State college. Priority given to economically disadvantaged members of minority group underrepresented in chosen profession and graduates of SEEK, College Discovery, EOP, and HEOP. Must work in

New York State Higher Education Services Corporation (continued)

New York State in chosen profession one year for each annual payment. Scholarships are awarded to undergraduate or graduate students, depending on the program.

Award: Scholarship for use in freshman, sophomore, junior, senior, graduate, or postgraduate years; not renewable. *Number:* 220. *Amount:* $1000–$5000.

Eligibility Requirements: Applicant must be enrolled or expecting to enroll full-time at a two-year or four-year institution or university; resident of New York and studying in New York. Available to U.S. citizens.

Application Requirements: Application. *Deadline:* May 3.

Contact: Scholarship Coordinator
New York State Higher Education Services Corporation
Education Building Addition Room 1071
Albany, NY 12234
Phone: 518-486-1319

SCHOLARSHIPS FOR ACADEMIC EXCELLENCE

Renewable awards of up to $1500 for academically outstanding New York State high school graduates planning to attend an approved postsecondary institution in New York State. For full-time study only. Contact high school guidance counselor to apply.

Award: Scholarship for use in freshman, sophomore, junior, or senior years; renewable. *Number:* 8000. *Amount:* $500–$1500.

Eligibility Requirements: Applicant must be high school student; planning to enroll or expecting to enroll full-time at a four-year institution or university; resident of New York and studying in New York. Available to U.S. citizens.

Application Requirements: Application. *Deadline:* varies.

Contact: Rita McGivern, Student Information
New York State Higher Education Services Corporation
99 Washington Avenue, Room 1320
Albany, NY 12255
E-mail: rmcgivern@hesc.com

WORLD TRADE CENTER MEMORIAL SCHOLARSHIP

Renewable awards of up to the cost of educational expenses at a State University of New York four-year college. Available to the children, spouses and financial dependents of victims who died or were severely disabled as a result of the September 11, 2001 terrorist attacks on the U.S. and the rescue and recovery efforts.

Award: Scholarship for use in freshman, sophomore, junior, or senior years; renewable. *Number:* varies. *Amount:* varies.

Eligibility Requirements: Applicant must be enrolled or expecting to enroll full-time at a four-year institution or university; resident of New York and studying in New York. Available to U.S. citizens.

Application Requirements: Application, financial need analysis, references, transcript. *Deadline:* May 1.

Contact: Scholarship Unit
New York State Higher Education Services Corporation
99 Washington Avenue, Room 1320
Albany, NY 12255
Phone: 518-402-6494

NORTH CAROLINA ASSOCIATION OF EDUCATORS http://www.ncae.org

NORTH CAROLINA ASSOCIATION OF EDUCATORS MARTIN LUTHER KING JR. SCHOLARSHIP

One-time award for high school seniors who are North Carolina residents to attend a postsecondary institution. Must be a U.S. citizen. Based upon financial need, GPA, and essay. Must have a GPA of at least 4.0 on a 5.0 scale or a 3.0 on a 4.0 scale.

Award: Scholarship for use in freshman year; not renewable. *Number:* 3–4. *Amount:* $500–$1000.

Eligibility Requirements: Applicant must be high school student; planning to enroll or expecting to enroll full-time at a four-year institution or university and resident of North Carolina. Available to U.S. citizens.

Application Requirements: Application, essay, financial need analysis, references, transcript. *Deadline:* February 1.

Contact: Dee Leach, Scholarship Coordinator
North Carolina Association of Educators
PO Box 27347
Raleigh, NC 27611
Phone: 800-662-7924
E-mail: dee.leach@ncae.org

NORTH CAROLINA BAR ASSOCIATION http://www.ncbar.org

NORTH CAROLINA BAR ASSOCIATION YOUNG LAWYERS DIVISION SCHOLARSHIP

• *See page 607*

NORTH CAROLINA DIVISION OF SERVICES FOR THE BLIND http://www.ncdhhs.gov

NORTH CAROLINA DIVISION OF SERVICES FOR THE BLIND REHABILITATION SERVICES

• *See page 625*

NORTH CAROLINA DIVISION OF VETERANS AFFAIRS http://www.doa.state.nc.us/vets/va.htm

NORTH CAROLINA VETERANS SCHOLARSHIPS CLASS I-A

• *See page 660*

NORTH CAROLINA VETERANS SCHOLARSHIPS CLASS I-B

• *See page 660*

NORTH CAROLINA VETERANS SCHOLARSHIPS CLASS II

• *See page 660*

NORTH CAROLINA VETERANS SCHOLARSHIPS CLASS III

• *See page 660*

NORTH CAROLINA VETERANS SCHOLARSHIPS CLASS IV

• *See page 660*

NORTH CAROLINA DIVISION OF VOCATIONAL REHABILITATION SERVICES http://www.dhhs.state.nc.us

TRAINING SUPPORT FOR YOUTH WITH DISABILITIES

• *See page 625*

NORTH CAROLINA NATIONAL GUARD http://www.nc.ngb.army.mil

NORTH CAROLINA NATIONAL GUARD TUITION ASSISTANCE PROGRAM

• *See page 636*

NORTH CAROLINA STATE EDUCATION ASSISTANCE AUTHORITY http://www.ncseaa.edu

AUBREY LEE BROOKS SCHOLARSHIPS

Renewable award for high school seniors who are residents of designated North Carolina counties and are planning to attend North Carolina State University, the University of North Carolina at Chapel Hill or the University of North Carolina at Greensboro. Scholarship is renewable, provided the recipient has continued financial need, remains enrolled full time at an eligible institution. Minimum GPA 2.75 required. Write for further details or visit Web site: http://www.cfnc.org.

Award: Scholarship for use in freshman year; renewable. *Number:* 17–19. *Amount:* up to $8000.

Eligibility Requirements: Applicant must be high school student; planning to enroll or expecting to enroll full-time at a four-year institution or university; resident of North Carolina and studying in North Carolina. Applicant must have 3.0 GPA or higher. Available to U.S. and non-Canadian citizens.

Application Requirements: Application, essay, financial need analysis, interview, photo, references, test scores, transcript. *Deadline:* February 1.

Contact: Bill Carswell, Manager of Scholarship and Grant Division
North Carolina State Education Assistance Authority
PO Box 14103
Research Triangle Park, NC 27709
Phone: 919-549-8614
Fax: 919-549-4687
E-mail: carswellb@ncseaa.edu

JAGANNATHAN SCHOLARSHIP

Available to graduating high school seniors who plan to enroll as college freshmen in a full-time degree program at one of the constituent institutions of The University of North Carolina. Applicant must be resident of North Carolina. Applicant must document financial need.

Award: Scholarship for use in freshman year; renewable. *Number:* varies. *Amount:* up to $3500.

Eligibility Requirements: Applicant must be enrolled or expecting to enroll full-time at a four-year institution or university; resident of North Carolina and studying in North Carolina. Applicant must have 3.0 GPA or higher. Available to U.S. citizens.

Application Requirements: Application, financial need analysis. *Deadline:* February 15.

Contact: Bill Carswell, Manager of Scholarship and Grant Division
North Carolina State Education Assistance Authority
PO Box 13663
Research Triangle Park, NC 27709
Phone: 919-549-8614
Fax: 919-248-4687
E-mail: carswellb@ncseaa.edu

NORTH CAROLINA COMMUNITY COLLEGE GRANT PROGRAM

Annual award for North Carolina residents enrolled at least part-time in a North Carolina community college curriculum program. Priority given to those enrolled in college transferable curriculum programs, persons seeking new job skills, women in non-traditional curricula, and those participating in an ABE, GED, or high school diploma program. Contact financial aid office of institution the student attends for information and deadline. Must complete Free Application for Federal Student Aid.

Award: Grant for use in freshman or sophomore years; renewable. *Number:* varies. *Amount:* $683.

Eligibility Requirements: Applicant must be enrolled or expecting to enroll full- or part-time at a two-year or technical institution; resident of North Carolina and studying in North Carolina. Available to U.S. citizens.

Application Requirements: Application, financial need analysis, FAFSA. *Deadline:* varies.

Contact: Bill Carswell, Manager, Scholarship and Grants Division
North Carolina State Education Assistance Authority
PO Box 14103
Research Triangle Park, NC 27709
Phone: 919-549-8614
Fax: 919-248-4687
E-mail: carswellb@ncseaa.edu

NORTH CAROLINA LEGISLATIVE TUITION GRANT PROGRAM (NCLTG)

Renewable aid for North Carolina residents attending approved private colleges or universities within the state. Must be enrolled full or part-time in an undergraduate program not leading to a religious vocation. Contact college financial aid office for deadlines.

Award: Grant for use in freshman, sophomore, junior, or senior years; renewable. *Number:* varies. *Amount:* $1950.

Eligibility Requirements: Applicant must be enrolled or expecting to enroll full- or part-time at a two-year or four-year institution or university; resident of North Carolina and studying in North Carolina. Available to U.S. citizens.

Application Requirements: Application. *Deadline:* varies.

Contact: Bill Carswell, Manager of Scholarship and Grant Division
North Carolina State Education Assistance Authority
PO Box 13663
Research Triangle Park, NC 27709
Phone: 919-549-8614
Fax: 919-248-4687
E-mail: carswellb@ncseaa.edu

STATE CONTRACTUAL SCHOLARSHIP FUND PROGRAM-NORTH CAROLINA

Renewable award for North Carolina residents already attending an approved private college or university in the state and pursuing an undergraduate degree. Must have financial need. Contact college financial aid office for deadline and information. May not be enrolled in a program leading to a religious vocation.

Award: Scholarship for use in freshman, sophomore, junior, or senior years; renewable. *Number:* varies. *Amount:* up to $1350.

Eligibility Requirements: Applicant must be enrolled or expecting to enroll full- or part-time at a four-year institution or university; resident of North Carolina and studying in North Carolina. Available to U.S. citizens.

Application Requirements: Application, financial need analysis. *Deadline:* varies.

Contact: Bill Carswell, Manager of Scholarship and Grant Division
North Carolina State Education Assistance Authority
PO Box 13663
Research Triangle Park, NC 27709
Phone: 919-549-8614
Fax: 919-248-4687
E-mail: carswellb@ncseaa.edu

UNIVERSITY OF NORTH CAROLINA NEED-BASED GRANT

Applicants must be enrolled in at least 6 credit hours at one of sixteen UNC system universities. Eligibility based on need; award varies, consideration for grant automatic when FAFSA is filed. Late applications may be denied due to insufficient funds.

Award: Grant for use in freshman, sophomore, junior, or senior years; renewable. *Number:* varies. *Amount:* varies.

Eligibility Requirements: Applicant must be enrolled or expecting to enroll full- or part-time at an institution or university; resident of North Carolina and studying in North Carolina. Available to U.S. citizens.

Application Requirements: Application, financial need analysis, FAFSA. *Deadline:* varies.

Contact: Bill Carswell, Manager of Scholarship and Grant Division
North Carolina State Education Assistance Authority
PO Box 13663
Research Triangle Park, NC 27709
Phone: 919-549-8614
Fax: 919-248-4687
E-mail: carswellb@ncseaa.edu

NORTH DAKOTA DEPARTMENT OF PUBLIC INSTRUCTION http://www.dpi.state.nd.us

ROBERT C. BYRD HONORS SCHOLARSHIP-NORTH DAKOTA

Awards to high school graduates who have been accepted for enrollment at institutions of higher education (IHEs), have demonstrated outstanding academic achievement, and show promise of continued academic excellence. For details refer to Web site: http://www.ed.gov/programs/iduesbyrd/eligibility.html.

Award: Scholarship for use in freshman, sophomore, junior, or senior years; renewable. *Number:* 10–12. *Amount:* $1500.

Eligibility Requirements: Applicant must be enrolled or expecting to enroll full-time at a two-year or four-year or technical institution or university and resident of North Dakota. Available to U.S. citizens.

North Dakota Department of Public Instruction (continued)

Application Requirements: Application, essay, references, test scores, transcript, college acceptance letter. *Deadline:* April 31.

Contact: Heidi Bergland, Scholarship Contact
North Dakota Department of Public Instruction
600 East Boulevard Avenue, Department 201
Bismarck, ND 58505-0440
Phone: 707-328-2317
Fax: 701-328-4770
E-mail: hbergland@state.nd.us

OHIO ASSOCIATION FOR ADULT AND CONTINUING EDUCATION http://www.oaace.org

LIFELONG LEARNING SCHOLARSHIP

Scholarship available for a Ohio resident student with Ohio high school equivalence diploma or high school diploma, who is currently enrolled in any adult education program or has been enrolled within the last twelve months. Must enroll in postsecondary education or training within six months of receiving scholarship. Number of awards granted varies.

Award: Scholarship for use in freshman year; not renewable. *Number:* varies. *Amount:* $1500.

Eligibility Requirements: Applicant must be high school student; planning to enroll or expecting to enroll full-time at a four-year institution or university and resident of Ohio. Available to U.S. citizens.

Application Requirements: Application, references. *Deadline:* March 1.

Contact: Chairman, Scholarship Committee
Ohio Association for Adult and Continuing Education
1601 West Fifth Avenue
PO Box 103
Columbus, OH 43212-2310
Phone: 866-996-2223
Fax: 740-435-0212
E-mail: awards@oaace.org

LINDA LUCA MEMORIAL GED SCHOLARSHIP

Scholarship available for a Ohio resident student who scored in the top 100 of GED scores for the year. Must enroll in postsecondary education or training within six months of receiving scholarship. Scholarship value: $1500.

Award: Scholarship for use in freshman year; not renewable. *Number:* varies. *Amount:* $1500.

Eligibility Requirements: Applicant must be high school student; planning to enroll or expecting to enroll full-time at a four-year institution or university and resident of Ohio. Available to U.S. citizens.

Application Requirements: Application, references. *Deadline:* varies.

Contact: Chairman, Scholarship Committee
Ohio Association for Adult and Continuing Education
1601 West Fifth Avenue
PO Box 103
Columbus, OH 43212-2310
Phone: 866-996-2223
Fax: 740-435-0212
E-mail: awards@oaace.org

OAACE MEMBER SCHOLARSHIP

Scholarship for Ohio resident and member of OAACE. Should enroll in postsecondary education or professional development training within six months of receiving scholarship.

Award: Scholarship for use in freshman year; not renewable. *Number:* varies. *Amount:* $2000.

Eligibility Requirements: Applicant must be high school student; planning to enroll or expecting to enroll full-time at a four-year institution or university and resident of Ohio. Available to U.S. citizens.

Application Requirements: Application, references. *Deadline:* March 1.

Contact: Chairman, Scholarship Committee
Ohio Association for Adult and Continuing Education
1601 West Fifth Avenue
PO Box 103
Columbus, OH 43212-2310
Phone: 866-996-2223
Fax: 740-435-0212
E-mail: awards@oaace.org

OHIO ASSOCIATION OF CAREER COLLEGES AND SCHOOLS http://www.members.aol.com/oaccs

LEGISLATIVE SCHOLARSHIP

One-time scholarship for graduating high school seniors enrolling in accredited colleges or universities. Must be Ohio high school student. The scholarship amount and the number of scholarships granted varies.

Award: Scholarship for use in freshman year; not renewable. *Number:* varies. *Amount:* varies.

Eligibility Requirements: Applicant must be high school student; planning to enroll or expecting to enroll full-time at a two-year or four-year or technical institution or university and resident of Ohio. Available to U.S. and non-U.S. citizens.

Application Requirements: Application, references, transcript. *Deadline:* March 30.

Contact: Max Lerner, Executive Director
Ohio Association of Career Colleges and Schools
1857 Northwest Boulevard
Columbus, OH 43212
Phone: 614-487-8180
Fax: 614-487-8190
E-mail: oaccs@aol.com

OHIO ASSOCIATION OF COLLEGIATE REGISTRARS AND ADMISSIONS OFFICERS http://www.oacrao.ohiou.edu

LEADERSHIP AND SERVICE SCHOLARSHIP

Nonrenewable $500 scholarship to students currently enrolled in an accredited/chartered high school, joint vocational school or recognized home school in the State of Ohio. Must be U.S. citizen or have been classified as a permanent resident. Must have a minimum cumulative GPA of 2.75 (4.0 scale), 3.44 (5.0 scale), or 4.12 (6.0 scale) at the end of the junior year. Refer to Web site: http://www.oacrao.ohiou.edu/scholarship/scholarapp.pdf for details.

Award: Scholarship for use in freshman year; not renewable. *Number:* varies. *Amount:* $500.

Eligibility Requirements: Applicant must be high school student; planning to enroll or expecting to enroll full- or part-time at a four-year institution or university; resident of Ohio and studying in Ohio. Available to U.S. citizens.

Application Requirements: Application, references, personal statement. *Deadline:* February 26.

Contact: Stacey Jones, Scholarship Committee Chair
Ohio Association of Collegiate Registrars and Admissions Officers
The Ohio State University, 1800 Cannon Drive, 730 Lincoln Tower
Columbus, OH 43210-1288
Phone: 740-826-8211
E-mail: sjones@capital.edu

OHIO BOARD OF REGENTS http://www.regents.ohio.gov

OHIO ACADEMIC SCHOLARSHIP PROGRAM

Award for academically outstanding Ohio residents planning to attend an approved Ohio college. Must be a high school senior intending to enroll full-time. Award is renewable for up to four years. Must rank in upper quarter of class or have a minimum GPA of 3.5.

Award: Scholarship for use in freshman year; renewable. *Number:* 1000. *Amount:* $2205.

Eligibility Requirements: Applicant must be high school student; planning to enroll or expecting to enroll full-time at a two-year or four-year institution; resident of Ohio and studying in Ohio. Applicant must have 3.5 GPA or higher. Available to U.S. citizens.

Application Requirements: Application, test scores, transcript. *Deadline:* February 23.

Contact: Jathiya Abdullah-Simmons, Program Administrator
Ohio Board of Regents
30 East Broad Street, 36th Floor
Columbus, OH 43215-3414
Phone: 614-752-9528
Fax: 614-752-5903
E-mail: jabdullah-simmons@regents.state.oh.us

OHIO INSTRUCTIONAL GRANT

Award for low- and middle-income Ohio residents attending an approved college or school in Ohio or Pennsylvania. Must be enrolled full-time and have financial need. May be used for any course of study except theology.

Award: Grant for use in freshman, sophomore, junior, or senior years; renewable. *Number:* varies. *Amount:* $78–$5466.

Eligibility Requirements: Applicant must be enrolled or expecting to enroll full-time at a two-year or four-year institution or university; resident of Ohio and studying in Ohio or Pennsylvania. Available to U.S. citizens.

Application Requirements: Application, financial need analysis. *Deadline:* October 1.

Contact: Tamika Braswell, Program Administrator
Ohio Board of Regents
30 East Broad Street, 36th Floor
Columbus, OH 43215-3414
Phone: 614-728-8862
Fax: 614-752-5903
E-mail: tbraswell@regents.state.oh.us

OHIO MISSING IN ACTION AND PRISONERS OF WAR ORPHANS SCHOLARSHIP

• *See page 660*

OHIO SAFETY OFFICERS COLLEGE MEMORIAL FUND

• *See page 607*

OHIO STUDENT CHOICE GRANT PROGRAM

Renewable award available to Ohio residents attending private colleges within the state. Must be enrolled full-time in a bachelor's degree program. Do not apply to state. Check with financial aid office of private, non-profit college.

Award: Grant for use in freshman, sophomore, junior, or senior years; renewable. *Number:* varies. *Amount:* up to $660.

Eligibility Requirements: Applicant must be enrolled or expecting to enroll full-time at a four-year institution or university; resident of Ohio and studying in Ohio. Available to U.S. citizens.

Application Requirements: *Deadline:* continuous.

Contact: Barbara Thoma, Program Administrator
Ohio Board of Regents
30 East Broad Street, 36th Floor
Columbus, OH 43215-3414
Phone: 614-752-9535
Fax: 614-752-5903
E-mail: bthoma@regents.state.oh.us

OHIO WAR ORPHANS SCHOLARSHIP

• *See page 661*

STUDENT WORKFORCE DEVELOPMENT GRANT PROGRAM

Provides tuition assistance to Ohio students pursuing full-time study in eligible Ohio private career schools. Must not have been enrolled prior to July 1, 2000.

Award: Grant for use in freshman, sophomore, junior, or senior years; renewable. *Number:* 1. *Amount:* $300.

Eligibility Requirements: Applicant must be enrolled or expecting to enroll full-time at a four-year institution or university; resident of Ohio and studying in Ohio. Available to U.S. citizens.

Application Requirements: *Deadline:* varies.

Contact: Barbara Thoma, Program Administrator
Ohio Board of Regents
30 East Broad Street, 36th Floor
Columbus, OH 43215-3414
Phone: 614-752-9535
Fax: 614-752-5903
E-mail: bthoma@regents.state.oh.us

OHIO CIVIL SERVICE EMPLOYEES ASSOCIATION http://www.ocsea.org

LES BEST SCHOLARSHIP

• *See page 549*

OHIO DEPARTMENT OF EDUCATION http://www.ode.state.oh.us

ROBERT C. BYRD HONORS SCHOLARSHIP-OHIO

Renewable award for graduating Ohio high school seniors who demonstrate outstanding academic achievement. Each Ohio high school receives applications by January of each year. School can submit one application for every 200 students in the senior class.

Award: Scholarship for use in freshman, sophomore, junior, or senior years; renewable. *Number:* varies. *Amount:* up to $1500.

Eligibility Requirements: Applicant must be high school student; planning to enroll or expecting to enroll full-time at a two-year or four-year institution or university; resident of Ohio and studying in Ohio. Applicant must have 3.5 GPA or higher. Available to U.S. citizens.

Application Requirements: Application, test scores. *Deadline:* varies.

Contact: Mark Lynskey, Program Administrator
Ohio Department of Education
25 South Front Street, Second Floor
Columbus, OH 43215
Phone: 614-466-2650
E-mail: mark.lynskey@ode.state.oh.us

OHIO NATIONAL GUARD http://www.ongsp.org

OHIO NATIONAL GUARD SCHOLARSHIP PROGRAM

• *See page 636*

OKLAHOMA ALUMNI & ASSOCIATES OF FHA, HERO AND FCCLA INC. http://www.okfccla.net

OKLAHOMA ALUMNI & ASSOCIATES OF FHA, HERO AND FCCLA INC. SCHOLARSHIP

• *See page 550*

OKLAHOMA STATE DEPARTMENT OF EDUCATION http://www.sde.state.ok.us

ROBERT C. BYRD HONORS SCHOLARSHIP-OKLAHOMA

Scholarships available to high school seniors. Applicants must be U.S. citizens or national, or be permanent residents of the United States. Must be legal residents of Oklahoma. Must have a minimum ACT composite score of 32 and/or a minimum SAT combined score of 1420 and/or 2130 or a minimum GED score of 700. Application URL: http://www.sde.state.ok.us/pro/Byrd/application.pdf.

Award: Scholarship for use in freshman year; not renewable. *Number:* 10. *Amount:* $1500.

Eligibility Requirements: Applicant must be high school student; planning to enroll or expecting to enroll full-time at a four-year institution or university and resident of Oklahoma. Available to U.S. citizens.

Application Requirements: Application, essay, references, transcript. *Deadline:* April 11.

Contact: Certification Specialist
Oklahoma State Department of Education
2500 North Lincoln Boulevard, Suite 212
Oklahoma City, OK 73105-4599
Phone: 405-521-2808

OKLAHOMA STATE REGENTS FOR HIGHER EDUCATION http://www.okhighered.org

ACADEMIC SCHOLARS PROGRAM

Awards for students of high academic ability to attend institutions in Oklahoma. Renewable up to four years. ACT or SAT scores must fall between 99.5 and 100th percentiles, or applicant must be designated as a National Merit scholar or finalist. Oklahoma public institutions can also select institutional nominees.

Award: Scholarship for use in freshman year; renewable. *Number:* varies. *Amount:* $1800–$5500.

Oklahoma State Regents for Higher Education (continued)

Eligibility Requirements: Applicant must be high school student; planning to enroll or expecting to enroll full-time at a two-year or four-year institution or university and studying in Oklahoma. Available to U.S. citizens.

Application Requirements: Application, test scores, transcript. *Deadline:* continuous.

Contact: Scholarship Programs Coordinator
Oklahoma State Regents for Higher Education
PO Box 108850
Oklahoma City, OK 73101-8850
Phone: 800-858-1840
Fax: 405-225-9230
E-mail: studentinfo@osrhe.edu

HEARTLAND SCHOLARSHIP FUND

Renewable award for dependent children of individuals killed as a result of the 1995 Oklahoma City bombing, or a surviving dependent child who was injured in the Alfred P. Murrah Federal Building day care center as a result of the bombing. The awards are applicable to the cost of tuition, fees, special fees, books and room and board. The award is for undergraduate study anywhere in the United States, and for graduate study at an Oklahoma institution.

Award: Scholarship for use in freshman, sophomore, junior, senior, or graduate years; renewable. *Number:* varies. *Amount:* $3500–$5500.

Eligibility Requirements: Applicant must be enrolled or expecting to enroll full-time at a two-year or four-year institution or university and resident of Oklahoma. Available to U.S. and non-U.S. citizens.

Application Requirements: Application. *Deadline:* continuous.

Contact: Scholarship Programs Coordinator
Oklahoma State Regents for Higher Education
PO Box 108850
Oklahoma City, OK 73101-8850
Phone: 405-225-9131
Fax: 405-225-9230
E-mail: studentinfo@osrhe.edu

OKLAHOMA TUITION AID GRANT

Award for Oklahoma residents enrolled at an Oklahoma institution at least part time each semester in a degree program. May be enrolled in two- or four-year or approved vocational-technical institution. Award for students attending public institutions or private colleges. Application is made through FAFSA.

Award: Grant for use in freshman, sophomore, junior, or senior years; renewable. *Number:* varies. *Amount:* $1000–$1300.

Eligibility Requirements: Applicant must be enrolled or expecting to enroll full- or part-time at a two-year or four-year or technical institution or university; resident of Oklahoma and studying in Oklahoma. Available to U.S. citizens.

Application Requirements: Application, financial need analysis, FAFSA. *Deadline:* varies.

Contact: Alicia Harris, Scholarship Programs Coordinator
Oklahoma State Regents for Higher Education
PO Box 3020
Oklahoma City, OK 73101-3020
Phone: 405-225-9131
Fax: 405-225-9230
E-mail: aharris@osrhe.edu

REGIONAL UNIVERSITY BACCALAUREATE SCHOLARSHIP

Renewable award for Oklahoma residents attending one of 11 participating Oklahoma public universities. Must have an ACT composite score of at least 30 or be a National Merit semifinalist or commended student. In addition to the award amount, each recipient will receive a resident tuition waiver from the institution. Must maintain a 3.25 GPA. Deadlines vary depending upon the institution attended.

Award: Scholarship for use in freshman, sophomore, junior, or senior years; renewable. *Number:* varies. *Amount:* $3000.

Eligibility Requirements: Applicant must be enrolled or expecting to enroll full-time at an institution or university; resident of Oklahoma and studying in Oklahoma. Available to U.S. citizens.

Application Requirements: Application. *Deadline:* varies.

Contact: Alicia Harris, Scholarship Programs Coordinator
Oklahoma State Regents for Higher Education
PO Box 108850
Oklahoma City, OK 73101-8850
Phone: 405-225-9131
Fax: 405-225-9230
E-mail: aharris@osrhe.edu

WILLIAM P. WILLIS SCHOLARSHIP

Renewable award for low-income Oklahoma residents attending an Oklahoma institution. Must be a full-time undergraduate. Deadline varies.

Award: Scholarship for use in freshman, sophomore, junior, or senior years; renewable. *Number:* 32. *Amount:* $2000–$3000.

Eligibility Requirements: Applicant must be enrolled or expecting to enroll full-time at a two-year or four-year institution or university; resident of Oklahoma and studying in Oklahoma. Available to U.S. citizens.

Application Requirements: Application. *Deadline:* varies.

Contact: Scholarship Programs Coordinator
Oklahoma State Regents for Higher Education
PO Box 108850
Oklahoma City, OK 73101-8850
Phone: 405-225-9131
Fax: 405-225-9230
E-mail: studentinfo@osrhe.edu

ONEIDA TRIBE OF INDIANS OF WISCONSIN http://www.oneidanation.org

ONEIDA HIGHER EDUCATION GRANT PROGRAM

• *See page 695*

OREGON COLLECTORS ASSOCIATION (ORCA) SCHOLARSHIP FUND http://www.orcascholarshipfund.com

OREGON COLLECTORS ASSOCIATION BOB HASSON MEMORIAL SCHOLARSHIP FUND

Scholarship available to Oregon high school seniors for use as full-time students at an Oregon accredited public or private two- or four-year college, university, or trade school. Must submit fictional essay on "the proper use of credit in the 21st century." Applicants may not be children/grandchildren of owners or officers of collection agencies in Oregon.

Award: Scholarship for use in freshman year; not renewable. *Number:* 3. *Amount:* $1500–$3000.

Eligibility Requirements: Applicant must be high school student; planning to enroll or expecting to enroll full-time at a two-year or four-year or technical institution or university; resident of Oregon and studying in Oregon. Available to U.S. citizens.

Application Requirements: Application, applicant must enter a contest, essay. *Deadline:* March 1.

Contact: Doug Jones, Scholarship Committee
Oregon Collectors Association (ORCA) Scholarship Fund
3012 NE 111th Circle
Vancouver, WA 98686
Phone: 503-963-1201
E-mail: dcj@pandhbilling.com

OREGON COMMUNITY FOUNDATION http://www.ocf1.org

ERNEST ALAN AND BARBARA PARK MEYER SCHOLARSHIP FUND

Scholarship for Oregon high school graduates for use in the pursuit of a postsecondary education (undergraduate or graduate) at a nonprofit two- or four-year college or university.

Award: Scholarship for use in freshman, sophomore, junior, senior, or graduate years; not renewable. *Number:* up to 35. *Amount:* $1500.

Eligibility Requirements: Applicant must be enrolled or expecting to enroll full-time at a two-year or four-year or technical institution or university and resident of Oregon. Available to U.S. citizens.

Application Requirements: Application, references. *Deadline:* March 1.

Contact: Dianne Causey, Program Associate for Scholarships and Grants
Oregon Community Foundation
1221 Yamhill, SW, Suite 100
Portland, OR 97205
Phone: 503-227-6846
Fax: 503-274-7771
E-mail: diannec@ocf1.org

FRIENDS OF BILL RUTHERFORD EDUCATION FUND

Scholarship for Oregon high school graduates or GED recipients who are dependent children of individuals holding statewide elected office or currently serving in the Oregon State Legislature. Students must be enrolled full-time in a two- or four-year college or university.

Award: Scholarship for use in freshman, sophomore, junior, or senior years; not renewable. *Number:* 1. *Amount:* $1000.

Eligibility Requirements: Applicant must be enrolled or expecting to enroll full-time at a two-year or four-year institution or university and resident of Oregon. Available to U.S. citizens.

Application Requirements: Application, references. *Deadline:* March 1.

Contact: Dianne Causey, Program Associate for Scholarships and Grants
Oregon Community Foundation
1221 Yamhill, SW, Suite 100
Portland, OR 97205
Phone: 503-227-6846
Fax: 503-274-7771
E-mail: diannec@ocf1.org

MARY E. HORSTKOTTE SCHOLARSHIP FUND

Award available for academically talented and financially needy students for use in the pursuit of a postsecondary education. Must be Oregon resident. For both full-time and part-time study.

Award: Scholarship for use in freshman, sophomore, junior, or senior years; not renewable. *Number:* 1. *Amount:* $2000.

Eligibility Requirements: Applicant must be enrolled or expecting to enroll full- or part-time at a two-year or four-year or technical institution or university and resident of Oregon. Available to U.S. citizens.

Application Requirements: Application, references. *Deadline:* March 1.

Contact: Dianne Causey, Program Associate for Scholarships and Grants
Oregon Community Foundation
1221 Yamhill, SW, Suite 100
Portland, OR 97205
Phone: 503-227-6846
Fax: 503-274-7771
E-mail: diannec@ocf1.org

RUBE AND MINAH LESLIE EDUCATIONAL FUND

Scholarship for Oregon residents for the pursuit of a postsecondary education. Selection is based on financial need. Award for both full-time and part-time study.

Award: Scholarship for use in freshman, sophomore, junior, or senior years; not renewable. *Number:* 1. *Amount:* $2000.

Eligibility Requirements: Applicant must be enrolled or expecting to enroll full- or part-time at a four-year institution or university and resident of Oregon. Available to U.S. citizens.

Application Requirements: Application, financial need analysis. *Deadline:* March 1.

Contact: Dianne Causey, Program Associate for Scholarships and Grants
Oregon Community Foundation
1221 Yamhill, SW, Suite 100
Portland, OR 97205
Phone: 503-227-6846
Fax: 503-274-7771
E-mail: diannec@ocf1.org

WILLIAM L. AND DELLA WAGGONER SCHOLARSHIP FUND

Scholarship for undergraduates of any Oregon high school who show academic potential and financial need, for use in the pursuit of a postsecondary education.

Award: Scholarship for use in freshman, sophomore, junior, or senior years; not renewable. *Number:* up to 30. *Amount:* $2000.

Eligibility Requirements: Applicant must be enrolled or expecting to enroll full-time at a four-year institution or university and resident of Oregon. Available to U.S. citizens.

Application Requirements: Application, references. *Deadline:* March 1.

Contact: Dianne Causey, Program Associate for Scholarships and Grants
Oregon Community Foundation
1221 Yamhill, SW, Suite 100
Portland, OR 97205
Phone: 503-227-6846
Fax: 503-274-7771
E-mail: diannec@ocf1.org

OREGON DEPARTMENT OF VETERANS AFFAIRS http://www.oregon.gov/odva

OREGON VETERANS' EDUCATION AID

• *See page 661*

OREGON NATIVE AMERICAN CHAMBER OF COMMERCE SCHOLARSHIP http://www.onacc.org

OREGON NATIVE AMERICAN CHAMBER OF COMMERCE SCHOLARSHIP

• *See page 695*

OREGON STUDENT ASSISTANCE COMMISSION http://www.osac.state.or.us

AFSCME: AMERICAN FEDERATION OF STATE, COUNTY, AND MUNICIPAL EMPLOYEES LOCAL 1724 SCHOLARSHIP

• *See page 550*

AFSCME: AMERICAN FEDERATION OF STATE, COUNTY, AND MUNICIPAL EMPLOYEES LOCAL 75 SCHOLARSHIP

• *See page 550*

ALBINA FUEL COMPANY SCHOLARSHIP

• *See page 582*

AMERICAN EX-PRISONER OF WAR SCHOLARSHIPS: PETER CONNACHER MEMORIAL SCHOLARSHIP

• *See page 661*

A. VICTOR ROSENFELD SCHOLARSHIP

• *See page 582*

BANDON SUBMARINE CABLE COUNCIL SCHOLARSHIP

• *See page 607*

BANK OF THE CASCADES SCHOLARSHIP

• *See page 582*

BENJAMIN FRANKLIN/EDITH GREEN SCHOLARSHIP

One-time award open to graduating Oregon high school seniors. Must attend a four-year public Oregon college. See Web site at http://www.osac.state.or.us for more information.

Award: Scholarship for use in freshman year; not renewable. *Number:* varies. *Amount:* varies.

Eligibility Requirements: Applicant must be high school student; planning to enroll or expecting to enroll full-time at a four-year institution; resident of Oregon and studying in Oregon. Available to U.S. citizens.

Application Requirements: Application, essay, financial need analysis, transcript, activity chart. *Deadline:* March 1.

Contact: Director of Grant Programs
Oregon Student Assistance Commission
1500 Valley River Drive, Suite 100
Eugene, OR 97401-7020
Phone: 800-452-8807 Ext. 7395

BEN SELLING SCHOLARSHIP

Award for Oregon residents enrolling as sophomores or higher in college. College GPA 3.5 or higher required. Apply/compete annually. Must be U.S. citizen or permanent resident. Wells Fargo employees, their children or near relatives must provide complete disclosure of employment status to receive this award.

Award: Scholarship for use in sophomore, junior, or senior years; not renewable. *Number:* varies. *Amount:* varies.

Oregon Student Assistance Commission (continued)

Eligibility Requirements: Applicant must be enrolled or expecting to enroll full-time at a two-year or four-year institution and resident of Oregon. Applicant must have 3.5 GPA or higher. Available to U.S. citizens.

Application Requirements: Application, essay, financial need analysis, references, transcript, activity chart. *Deadline:* March 1.

Contact: Director of Grant Programs
Oregon Student Assistance Commission
1500 Valley River Drive, Suite 100
Eugene, OR 97401-7020
Phone: 800-452-8807 Ext. 7395

BLUE HERON PAPER EMPLOYEE DEPENDENTS SCHOLARSHIP

• *See page 582*

CHILDREN, ADULT, AND FAMILY SERVICES SCHOLARSHIP

Award for graduating high school seniors currently in foster care or participating in Independent Living Program (ILP) or GED recipients or continuing college students formerly in foster care. Only for Oregon public colleges. Visit Web site: http://www.osac.state.or.us for more details.

Award: Scholarship for use in freshman, sophomore, junior, senior, or graduate years; renewable. *Number:* varies. *Amount:* varies.

Eligibility Requirements: Applicant must be enrolled or expecting to enroll full-time at a two-year or four-year institution or university; resident of Oregon and studying in Oregon. Available to U.S. citizens.

Application Requirements: Application, essay, financial need analysis, references, transcript, activity chart. *Deadline:* March 1.

Contact: Director of Grant Programs
Oregon Student Assistance Commission
1500 Valley River Drive, Suite 100
Eugene, OR 97401-7020
Phone: 800-452-8807 Ext. 7395

DAN KONNIE MEMORIAL DEPENDENTS SCHOLARSHIP

• *See page 582*

DOROTHY CAMPBELL MEMORIAL SCHOLARSHIP

Renewable award for female Oregon high school graduates with a minimum 2.75 GPA. Must submit essay describing strong, continuing interest in golf and the contribution that sport has made to applicant's development.

Award: Scholarship for use in freshman, sophomore, junior, or senior years; renewable. *Number:* varies. *Amount:* varies.

Eligibility Requirements: Applicant must be enrolled or expecting to enroll full-time at a four-year institution; female; resident of Oregon; studying in Oregon and must have an interest in golf. Available to U.S. citizens.

Application Requirements: Application, essay, financial need analysis, transcript, activity chart. *Deadline:* March 1.

Contact: Director of Grant Programs
Oregon Student Assistance Commission
1500 Valley River Drive, Suite 100
Eugene, OR 97401-7020
Phone: 800-452-8807 Ext. 7395

ESSEX GENERAL CONSTRUCTION SCHOLARSHIP

• *See page 582*

FORD OPPORTUNITY PROGRAM

Automatically renewable. Awards 90% of unmet financial need to residents of Oregon or Siskiyou County, CA, who are single heads of household with custody of a dependent child or children. Must be planning to earn a bachelor's degree. Only for use at Oregon or California colleges. Must have minimum cumulative GPA of 3.00. If minimum requirements are not met, special recommendation form required (see high school counselor or contact OSAC).

Award: Scholarship for use in freshman, sophomore, junior, or senior years; renewable. *Number:* varies. *Amount:* varies.

Eligibility Requirements: Applicant must be enrolled or expecting to enroll full-time at a two-year or four-year institution or university; single; resident of California or Oregon and studying in California or Oregon. Applicant must have 3.0 GPA or higher. Available to U.S. citizens.

Application Requirements: Application, essay, financial need analysis, interview, transcript, activities chart. *Deadline:* March 1.

Contact: Ford Family Foundation Scholarship Office
Oregon Student Assistance Commission
440 East Broadway, Suite 200
Eugene, OR 97401
Phone: 877-864-2872
E-mail: fordscholarships@tfff.org

FORD RESTART PROGRAM

Award to support nontraditional adult students who wish to begin or continue education at the postsecondary level. Must be at least 25 years of age by March 1 of the application year. Be residents of Oregon or Siskiyou County, California. Have a high school diploma or GED certificate. Must not previously have earned a bachelors degree. Program meets 90 percent of the recipients unmet financial need. A Restart Reference Form is required and must be submitted with the application.

Award: Scholarship for use in freshman, sophomore, junior, or senior years; renewable. *Number:* varies. *Amount:* varies.

Eligibility Requirements: Applicant must be age 25 and over; enrolled or expecting to enroll full-time at a two-year or four-year or technical institution; resident of Oregon and studying in Oregon. Available to U.S. citizens.

Application Requirements: Application, essay, financial need analysis, interview, transcript, activity chart, reference form. *Deadline:* March 1.

Contact: Scholarship Office
Oregon Student Assistance Commission
440 East Broadway, Suite 200
Eugene, OR 97401
Phone: 877-864-2872

FORD SCHOLARS PROGRAM

Automatically renewable. Awards 90% of unmet financial need to residents of Oregon or Siskiyou County, CA, who are graduating high school seniors or students at the point of transferring from a community college to a four year college. Must have minimum cumulative GPA of 3.00, planning to earn a bachelor's degree. If minimum requirements are not met, special recommendation form required (see high school counselor or contact OSAC).

Award: Scholarship for use in freshman, sophomore, junior, or senior years; renewable. *Number:* varies. *Amount:* varies.

Eligibility Requirements: Applicant must be enrolled or expecting to enroll full-time at a two-year or four-year institution or university; resident of California or Oregon and studying in Oregon. Applicant must have 3.0 GPA or higher. Available to U.S. citizens.

Application Requirements: Application, essay, financial need analysis, interview, test scores, transcript, activities chart. *Deadline:* March 1.

Contact: Ford Family Foundation Scholarship Office
Oregon Student Assistance Commission
440 East Broadway, Suite 200
Eugene, OR 97401
Phone: 877-864-2872
E-mail: fordscholarships@tfff.org

FORD SONS AND DAUGHTERS OF EMPLOYEES OF ROSEBURG FOREST PRODUCTS COMPANY SCHOLARSHIP

• *See page 582*

GLENN JACKSON SCHOLARS SCHOLARSHIPS (OCF)

• *See page 583*

HARRY LUDWIG MEMORIAL SCHOLARSHIP

• *See page 626*

IDA M. CRAWFORD SCHOLARSHIP

One-time scholarship awarded to graduates of accredited Oregon high school seniors with a cumulative GPA of 3.5. Not available to applicants majoring in law, medicine, theology, teaching, or music. U.S. Bancorp employees, their children or near relatives, are not eligible. Must supply proof of birth in the contiguous United States.

Award: Scholarship for use in freshman year; not renewable. *Number:* varies. *Amount:* varies.

Eligibility Requirements: Applicant must be high school student; planning to enroll or expecting to enroll full-time at a four-year institution and resident of Oregon. Applicant must have 3.5 GPA or higher. Available to U.S. citizens.

Application Requirements: Application, essay, financial need analysis, transcript, activities chart, copy of birth certificate. *Deadline:* March 1.

Contact: Director of Grant Programs
Oregon Student Assistance Commission
1500 Valley River Drive, Suite 100
Eugene, OR 97401-7020
Phone: 800-452-8807 Ext. 7395

INTERNATIONAL BROTHERHOOD OF ELECTRICAL WORKERS LOCAL 280 SCHOLARSHIP

• *See page 550*

INTERNATIONAL UNION OF OPERATING ENGINEERS LOCAL 701 SCHOLARSHIP

• *See page 550*

IRMGARD SCHULZ SCHOLARSHIP

Award for graduating seniors of a U.S. public high school with first preference going to applicants from high schools in Josephine County, Oregon. Second preference is for applicants who are orphans or from foster or single-parent homes. Prior-year recipients may reapply annually.

Award: Scholarship for use in freshman, sophomore, junior, senior, or graduate years; not renewable. *Number:* up to 22. *Amount:* varies.

Eligibility Requirements: Applicant must be high school student; planning to enroll or expecting to enroll full-time at a four-year institution or university and resident of Oregon. Available to U.S. citizens.

Application Requirements: Application, essay, financial need analysis, transcript, activities chart. *Deadline:* March 1.

Contact: Director of Grant Programs
Oregon Student Assistance Commission
1500 Valley River Drive, Suite 100
Eugene, OR 97401-7020
Phone: 800-452-8807 Ext. 7395

JEROME B. STEINBACH SCHOLARSHIP

Award for Oregon residents enrolled in Oregon institution as sophomore or above with minimum 3.5 GPA. Award for undergraduate study only. U.S. Bancorp employees, their children, or near relatives are not eligible. Must submit proof of U.S. birth.

Award: Scholarship for use in sophomore, junior, or senior years; renewable. *Number:* 93. *Amount:* varies.

Eligibility Requirements: Applicant must be enrolled or expecting to enroll full-time at a four-year institution or university; resident of Oregon and studying in Oregon. Applicant must have 3.5 GPA or higher. Available to U.S. citizens.

Application Requirements: Application, essay, financial need analysis, transcript, proof of U.S. birth. *Deadline:* varies.

Contact: Director of Grant Programs
Oregon Student Assistance Commission
1500 Valley River Drive, Suite 100
Eugene, OR 97401-7020
Phone: 800-452-8807 Ext. 7395

JOSE D. GARCIA MIGRANT EDUCATION SCHOLARSHIP

• *See page 607*

MARIA JACKSON/GENERAL GEORGE A. WHITE SCHOLARSHIP

• *See page 661*

MCGARRY MACHINE INC. SCHOLARSHIP

• *See page 583*

OREGON AFL-CIO SCHOLARSHIP

• *See page 551*

OREGON COLLECTORS ASSOCIATION BOB HASSON MEMORIAL SCHOLARSHIP

One-time award for graduating Oregon high school seniors enrolling in Oregon colleges within twelve months of graduation. Children or grandchildren of owners and officers of collection agencies registered in Oregon are not eligible. Awards based on a three to four page fictional essay with topic: The Proper Use of Credit in the 21st Century. See Web site: www.orcascholarshipfund.com for further information.

Award: Scholarship for use in freshman year; not renewable. *Number:* varies. *Amount:* $1500–$3000.

Eligibility Requirements: Applicant must be high school student; planning to enroll or expecting to enroll full-time at a two-year or four-year institution; resident of Oregon and studying in Oregon. Available to U.S. citizens.

Application Requirements: Application, applicant must enter a contest, essay, financial need analysis, test scores, transcript, activity chart. *Deadline:* March 1.

Contact: Scholarship Coordinator
Oregon Student Assistance Commission
PO Box 42409
Portland, OR 97242

OREGON DUNGENESS CRAB COMMISSION SCHOLARSHIP

• *See page 607*

OREGON METRO FEDERAL CREDIT UNION SCHOLARSHIP

• *See page 551*

OREGON OCCUPATIONAL SAFETY AND HEALTH DIVISION WORKERS MEMORIAL SCHOLARSHIP

• *See page 607*

OREGON PUBLISHING COMPANY/HILLIARD SCHOLARSHIP

• *See page 551*

OREGON SALMON COMMISSION SCHOLARSHIP

• *See page 608*

OREGON SCHOLARSHIP FUND COMMUNITY COLLEGE STUDENT AWARD

Scholarship open to Oregon residents enrolled or planning to enroll in Oregon community college programs. May apply for one additional year.

Award: Scholarship for use in freshman or sophomore years; renewable. *Number:* varies. *Amount:* varies.

Eligibility Requirements: Applicant must be enrolled or expecting to enroll full-time at a two-year institution; resident of Oregon and studying in Oregon. Available to U.S. citizens.

Application Requirements: Application, essay, financial need analysis, transcript, activity chart. *Deadline:* March 1.

Contact: Director of Grant Programs
Oregon Student Assistance Commission
1500 Valley River Drive, Suite 100
Eugene, OR 97401-7020
Phone: 800-452-8807 Ext. 7395

OREGON SCHOLARSHIP FUND TRANSFER STUDENT AWARD

Award open to Oregon residents who are currently enrolled in their second year at a community college and are planning to transfer to a four-year college in Oregon. Prior recipients may apply for one additional year.

Award: Scholarship for use in sophomore or junior years; renewable. *Number:* varies. *Amount:* varies.

Eligibility Requirements: Applicant must be enrolled or expecting to enroll full-time at a two-year or four-year institution; resident of Oregon and studying in Oregon. Available to U.S. citizens.

Application Requirements: Application, essay, financial need analysis, transcript, activity chart. *Deadline:* March 1.

Contact: Director of Grant Programs
Oregon Student Assistance Commission
1500 Valley River Drive, Suite 100
Eugene, OR 97401-7020
Phone: 800-452-8807 Ext. 7395

OREGON STATE FISCAL ASSOCIATION SCHOLARSHIP

• *See page 551*

OREGON STUDENT ASSISTANCE COMMISSION EMPLOYEE AND DEPENDENT SCHOLARSHIP

Award for current permanent employees of the OSAC, who are past initial trial service or legally dependent children of current permanent employees at the time of the March 1 scholarship deadline or legally dependent children of an

Oregon Student Assistance Commission (continued)

employee who retires, is permanently disabled, or deceased directly from employment at OSAC. Dependents must enroll full-time and employees must enroll at least half-time. May reapply each year for up to four years.

Award: Scholarship for use in freshman, sophomore, junior, or senior years; not renewable. *Number:* 1. *Amount:* varies.

Eligibility Requirements: Applicant must be enrolled or expecting to enroll full- or part-time at a four-year institution and resident of Oregon. Available to U.S. citizens.

Application Requirements: Application, essay, transcript, activities chart. *Deadline:* March 1.

Contact: Director of Grant Programs
Oregon Student Assistance Commission
1500 Valley River Drive, Suite 100
Eugene, OR 97401-7020
Phone: 800-452-8807 Ext. 7395

OREGON TRAWL COMMISSION SCHOLARSHIP

• *See page 608*

OREGON TRUCKING ASSOCIATION SAFETY COUNCIL SCHOLARSHIP

• *See page 583*

PACIFIC NW FEDERAL CREDIT UNION SCHOLARSHIP

One scholarship available to graduating high school senior who is a member of Pacific North West Federal Credit Union. Must submit an essay on "Why is My Credit Union an important consumer choice?". Dependents of Pacific NW Federal Credit Union employees and credit union elected, appointed officials are not eligible.

Award: Scholarship for use in freshman year; not renewable. *Number:* 1. *Amount:* varies.

Eligibility Requirements: Applicant must be high school student; planning to enroll or expecting to enroll full-time at a four-year institution and resident of Oregon. Available to U.S. citizens.

Application Requirements: Application, essay, references, transcript. *Deadline:* March 1.

Contact: Director of Grant Programs
Oregon Student Assistance Commission
1500 Valley River Drive, Suite 100
Eugene, OR 97401-7020
Phone: 800-452-8807 Ext. 7395

PACIFICSOURCE SCHOLARSHIP

• *See page 583*

PENDLETON POSTAL WORKERS SCHOLARSHIP

• *See page 608*

PETER CROSSLEY MEMORIAL SCHOLARSHIP

Award for graduating seniors of an Oregon public alternative high school. Must submit essay on "How I Faced Challenges and Overcame Obstacles to Graduate from High School." Must enroll at least half time. See Web site: http://www.osac.state.or.us for more information.

Award: Scholarship for use in freshman, sophomore, junior, or senior years; renewable. *Number:* varies. *Amount:* varies.

Eligibility Requirements: Applicant must be high school student; planning to enroll or expecting to enroll full- or part-time at a four-year institution and resident of Oregon. Available to U.S. citizens.

Application Requirements: Application, essay, financial need analysis, transcript, activity chart. *Deadline:* March 1.

Contact: Director of Grant Programs
Oregon Student Assistance Commission
1500 Valley River Drive, Suite 100
Eugene, OR 97401-7020
Phone: 800-452-8807 Ext. 7395

PORTLAND WOMEN'S CLUB SCHOLARSHIP

Renewable award open to graduates of any Oregon high school. Must have a minimum 3.0 cumulative GPA. Preference for female students.

Award: Scholarship for use in freshman, sophomore, junior, or senior years; renewable. *Number:* varies. *Amount:* varies.

Eligibility Requirements: Applicant must be enrolled or expecting to enroll full-time at a four-year institution and resident of Oregon. Applicant must have 3.0 GPA or higher. Available to U.S. citizens.

Application Requirements: Application, essay, financial need analysis, transcript, activity chart. *Deadline:* March 1.

Contact: Director of Grant Programs
Oregon Student Assistance Commission
1500 Valley River Drive, Suite 100
Eugene, OR 97401-7020
Phone: 800-452-8807 Ext. 7395

REED'S FUEL AND TRUCKING COMPANY SCHOLARSHIP

• *See page 583*

RICHARD F. BRENTANO MEMORIAL SCHOLARSHIP

• *See page 583*

ROBERT C. BYRD FEDERAL HONORS PROGRAM-OREGON

Automatically renewable award available to Oregon high school seniors with a minimum GPA of 3.85 or minimum GED score of 3300, and ACT scores of at least 29 or SAT combined math and critical reading scores of 1300. 75 new awards each year, 15 per Congressional District. See OSAC Web site: www.getcollegefunds.org for more information.

Award: Scholarship for use in freshman, sophomore, junior, or senior years; renewable. *Number:* 75. *Amount:* $1500.

Eligibility Requirements: Applicant must be high school student; planning to enroll or expecting to enroll full-time at a two-year or four-year or technical institution or university and resident of Oregon. Available to U.S. citizens.

Application Requirements: Application, essay, test scores, transcript, activities chart. *Deadline:* March 1.

Contact: Director of Grant Programs
Oregon Student Assistance Commission
1500 Valley River Drive, Suite 100
Eugene, OR 97401-2148
Phone: 541-687-7395

ROBERT D. FORSTER SCHOLARSHIP

• *See page 583*

ROGER W. EMMONS MEMORIAL SCHOLARSHIP

• *See page 584*

SP NEWSPRINT COMPANY, NEWBERG MILL, EMPLOYEE DEPENDENTS SCHOLARSHIP

• *See page 584*

STIMSON LUMBER COMPANY SCHOLARSHIP

• *See page 584*

TAYLOR MADE LABELS SCHOLARSHIP

• *See page 584*

TEAMSTERS CLYDE C. CROSBY/JOSEPH M. EDGAR MEMORIAL SCHOLARSHIP

• *See page 551*

TEAMSTERS COUNCIL 37 FEDERAL CREDIT UNION SCHOLARSHIP

• *See page 551*

TEAMSTERS LOCAL 305 SCHOLARSHIP

• *See page 552*

TYKESON FAMILY SCHOLARSHIP

Renewable award available to children aged 23 years and under of full-time employees who have been employed for at least two years prior to March 1 of application deadline. Companies included are: Bend Cable Communications LLC, Central Oregon Cable Advertising LLC, or Tykeson/Associates Enterprises. Must attend an Oregon college. See Web site: http://www.osac.state.or.us for more information.

Award: Scholarship for use in freshman, sophomore, junior, or senior years; renewable. *Number:* varies. *Amount:* varies.

Eligibility Requirements: Applicant must be age 23 or under; enrolled or expecting to enroll full-time at a four-year institution; resident of Oregon and studying in Oregon. Available to U.S. citizens.

Application Requirements: Application, essay, financial need analysis, references, transcript, activity chart. *Deadline:* March 1.

Contact: Director of Grant Programs
Oregon Student Assistance Commission
1500 Valley River Drive, Suite 100
Eugene, OR 97401-7020
Phone: 800-452-8807 Ext. 7395

UMATILLA ELECTRIC COOPERATIVE SCHOLARSHIP

Applicant may be either high school graduate (including home-school graduate) or GED recipient. Applicant or applicant's parents/legal guardians must be active members of the Umatilla Electric Cooperative (UEC) and be receiving service from UEC at their primary residence. Married applicants with UEC membership in a spouse's name are eligible. Indicate name of qualifying UEC member in membership section.

Award: Scholarship for use in freshman, sophomore, junior, or senior years; renewable. *Number:* varies. *Amount:* varies.

Eligibility Requirements: Applicant must be enrolled or expecting to enroll full-time at a four-year institution and resident of Oregon. Available to U.S. citizens.

Application Requirements: Application, essay, financial need analysis, references, transcript, activity chart. *Deadline:* March 1.

Contact: Director of Grant Programs
Oregon Student Assistance Commission
1500 Valley River Drive, Suite 100
Eugene, OR 97401-7020
Phone: 800-452-8807 Ext. 7395

VERL AND DOROTHY MILLER NATIVE AMERICAN VOCATIONAL SCHOLARSHIP

• *See page 695*

WALTER DAVIES SCHOLARSHIP

• *See page 584*

WILLETT AND MARGUERITE LAKE SCHOLARSHIP

• *See page 584*

WILLIAM D. AND RUTH D. ROY SCHOLARSHIP

Scholarships available for Oregon high school graduates, home scholars, and GED recipients. Preference given to engineering majors attending Portland State University of Oregon State University. Minimum 2.75 GPA required.

Award: Scholarship for use in freshman, sophomore, junior, or senior years; renewable. *Number:* up to 14. *Amount:* varies.

Eligibility Requirements: Applicant must be enrolled or expecting to enroll full-time at a four-year institution or university and resident of Oregon. Available to U.S. citizens.

Application Requirements: Application, essay, financial need analysis, transcript, activities chart. *Deadline:* March 1.

Contact: Director of Grant Programs
Oregon Student Assistance Commission
1500 Valley River Drive, Suite 100
Eugene, OR 97401-7020
Phone: 800-452-8807 Ext. 7395

WOODARD FAMILY SCHOLARSHIP

• *See page 584*

OWEN ELECTRIC COOPERATIVE http://www.owenelectric.com

OWEN ELECTRIC COOPERATIVE SCHOLARSHIP PROGRAM

Scholarships available to college juniors and seniors who are enrolled full-time at a four-year college or university. Parents of applicant must have an active Owen Electric account in good standing. If applicant has not earned 60 hours at time of application, must provide additional transcript upon completion of 60 hours. Must submit 400- to 700-word essay. For essay topics, application, and additional information visit Web site: http://www.owenelectric.com.

Award: Scholarship for use in junior or senior years; not renewable. *Number:* 12. *Amount:* $2000.

Eligibility Requirements: Applicant must be enrolled or expecting to enroll full-time at a four-year institution or university and resident of Kentucky. Applicant must have 3.0 GPA or higher. Available to U.S. citizens.

Application Requirements: Application, applicant must enter a contest, essay, references, transcript. *Deadline:* February 1.

Contact: Brian Linder, Manager of Key Accounts
Owen Electric Cooperative
8205 Highway 127 North
PO Box 400
Owenton, KY 40359-0400
Phone: 502-484-3471 Ext. 3542
Fax: 502-484-2661
E-mail: blinder@owenelectric.com

PACERS FOUNDATION INC. http://www.pacersfoundation.org

PACERS TEAMUP SCHOLARSHIP

• *See page 608*

PARENTS, FAMILIES, AND FRIENDS OF LESBIANS AND GAYS-ATLANTA http://www.pflagatl.org

PFLAG SCHOLARSHIP AWARDS PROGRAM

Scholarship to recognize outstanding lesbian, gay, bisexual, and transgender (LGBT) individuals; encourage continuing education for self-identified LGBT individuals; and foster a positive image of LGBT people in society. For more details on eligibility and terms, see Web site: http://www.pflagatl.org/scholarships.htm.

Award: Scholarship for use in freshman, sophomore, junior, or senior years; not renewable. *Number:* 5–10. *Amount:* $500–$3000.

Eligibility Requirements: Applicant must be age 16 and over; enrolled or expecting to enroll full- or part-time at a two-year or four-year or technical institution or university; resident of Georgia; studying in Georgia and must have an interest in LGBT issues. Available to U.S. and non-U.S. citizens.

Application Requirements: Application, autobiography, essay, financial need analysis, references, test scores, transcript. *Deadline:* March 31.

Contact: Scholarship Program Coordinator
Parents, Families, and Friends of Lesbians and Gays-Atlanta
PO Box 450393
Atlanta, GA 31145-0393
Phone: 770-662-6475
E-mail: pflagatlschols@netscape.net

PENNSYLVANIA BURGLAR AND FIRE ALARM ASSOCIATION http://www.pbfaa.com

PENNSYLVANIA BURGLAR AND FIRE ALARM ASSOCIATION YOUTH SCHOLARSHIP PROGRAM

• *See page 608*

PENNSYLVANIA FEDERATION OF DEMOCRATIC WOMEN INC. http://www.pfdw.org

PENNSYLVANIA FEDERATION OF DEMOCRATIC WOMEN INC. ANNUAL SCHOLARSHIP AWARDS

• *See page 552*

PENNSYLVANIA HIGHER EDUCATION ASSISTANCE AGENCY http://www.pheaa.org

PENNSYLVANIA STATE GRANTS

Award for Pennsylvania residents attending an approved postsecondary institution as undergraduates in a program of at least two years duration. Renewable for up to eight semesters if applicants show continued need and academic progress. Must submit FAFSA. Number of awards granted varies annually. Scholarship value is $3500 to $4500. Deadlines: May 1 and August 1.

Award: Grant for use in freshman, sophomore, junior, or senior years; renewable. *Number:* varies. *Amount:* $3500–$4500.

Eligibility Requirements: Applicant must be enrolled or expecting to enroll full- or part-time at a two-year or four-year or technical institution or university and resident of Pennsylvania. Available to U.S. citizens.

Pennsylvania Higher Education Assistance Agency (continued)

Application Requirements: Financial need analysis, FAFSA. *Deadline:* varies.

Contact: Keith New, Director of Communications and Press Office
Pennsylvania Higher Education Assistance Agency
1200 North Seventh Street
Harrisburg, PA 17102-1444
Phone: 717-720-2509
Fax: 717-720-3903

POSTSECONDARY EDUCATION GRATUITY PROGRAM

• *See page 608*

ROBERT C. BYRD HONORS SCHOLARSHIP-PENNSYLVANIA

Awards Pennsylvania residents who are graduating high school seniors. Must rank in the top 5 percent of graduating class, have at least a 3.5 GPA and score 1150 or above on the SAT, 25 or above on the ACT, or 355 or above on the GED. Renewable award and the amount granted varies. Applicants are expected to be a full-time freshman student enrolled at an eligible institution of higher education, following high school graduation.

Award: Scholarship for use in freshman year; renewable. *Number:* varies. *Amount:* $1500.

Eligibility Requirements: Applicant must be high school student; planning to enroll or expecting to enroll full-time at a four-year institution or university and resident of Pennsylvania. Applicant must have 3.5 GPA or higher. Available to U.S. citizens.

Application Requirements: Application, references, test scores, transcript, letter of acceptance. *Deadline:* May 1.

Contact: Keith R. New, Director of Communications and Press Office
Pennsylvania Higher Education Assistance Agency
1200 North Seventh Street
Harrisburg, PA 17102
Phone: 717-720-2509
Fax: 717-720-3903

PETER DOCTOR MEMORIAL INDIAN SCHOLARSHIP FOUNDATION INC.

PETER DOCTOR MEMORIAL IROQUOIS SCHOLARSHIP

• *See page 697*

PHILIPINO-AMERICAN ASSOCIATION OF NEW ENGLAND http://www.pamas.org

BLESSED LEON OF OUR LADY OF THE ROSARY AWARD

• *See page 697*

PAMAS RESTRICTED SCHOLARSHIP AWARD

• *See page 552*

RAVENSCROFT FAMILY AWARD

• *See page 697*

PHOENIX SUNS CHARITIES/SUN STUDENTS SCHOLARSHIP http://www.suns.com

QWEST LEADERSHIP CHALLENGE

• *See page 609*

SUN STUDENT COLLEGE SCHOLARSHIP PROGRAM

• *See page 609*

PINE TREE STATE 4-H CLUB FOUNDATION/4-H POSTSECONDARY SCHOLARSHIP http://www.umaine.edu

PARKER-LOVEJOY SCHOLARSHIP

One-time scholarship of $1000 is available to a graduating high school senior. Applicants must be residents of Maine.

Award: Scholarship for use in freshman year; not renewable. *Number:* 1. *Amount:* $1000.

Eligibility Requirements: Applicant must be high school student; planning to enroll or expecting to enroll full-time at a two-year or four-year institution or university and resident of Maine. Available to U.S. citizens.

Application Requirements: Application. *Deadline:* March 14.

Contact: Angela Martin, Administrative Assistant
Pine Tree State 4-H Club Foundation/4-H Postsecondary Scholarship
c/o University of Maine, 5714 Libby Hall
Orono, ME 04469-5717
Phone: 207-581-3739
Fax: 207-581-1387
E-mail: amartin@umext.maine.edu

WAYNE S. RICH SCHOLARSHIP

Scholarship for an outstanding Maine or New Hampshire 4-H member for postsecondary study. Awarded to a Maine student in odd numbered years and a New Hampshire student in even numbered years.

Award: Scholarship for use in freshman year; not renewable. *Number:* 1. *Amount:* up to $1000.

Eligibility Requirements: Applicant must be high school student; planning to enroll or expecting to enroll full-time at a two-year or four-year institution or university and resident of Maine or New Hampshire. Available to U.S. citizens.

Application Requirements: Application. *Deadline:* March 14.

Contact: Angela Martin, Administrative Assistant
Pine Tree State 4-H Club Foundation/4-H Postsecondary Scholarship
c/o University of Maine, 5714 Libby Hall
Orono, ME 04469-5717
Phone: 207-581-3739
Fax: 207-581-1387
E-mail: amartin@umext.maine.edu

PITON FOUNDATION http://www.piton.org

CHARTER FUND SCHOLARSHIP

Award available for first year of an accredited trade school, two-year, or four-year college. Must be a high school senior and resident of Colorado.

Award: Scholarship for use in freshman year; not renewable. *Number:* 100. *Amount:* $500–$2500.

Eligibility Requirements: Applicant must be high school student; planning to enroll or expecting to enroll full- or part-time at a two-year or four-year or technical institution or university and resident of Colorado. Available to U.S. citizens.

Application Requirements: Application, financial need analysis. *Deadline:* May 2.

Contact: Jeanette Montoya, Grant Selection Committee
Piton Foundation
370 17th Street, Suite 5300
Denver, CO 80202
Phone: 303-572-1727
Fax: 303-628-3837
E-mail: info@piton.org

POLISH HERITAGE ASSOCIATION OF MARYLAND http://www.pha-md.org

DR KENNETH AND NANCY WILLIAMS SCHOLARSHIP

• *See page 697*

POLISH HERITAGE SCHOLARSHIP

• *See page 697*

PORTUGUESE FOUNDATION INC. http://www.pfict.org

PORTUGUESE FOUNDATION SCHOLARSHIP PROGRAM

• *See page 698*

POTLATCH FOUNDATION FOR HIGHER EDUCATION SCHOLARSHIP http://www.potlatchcorp.com

POTLATCH FOUNDATION FOR HIGHER EDUCATION SCHOLARSHIP

Award for undergraduate studies. Scholarship recipients may pursue two-year or four-year courses of instruction leading to a bachelor's degree, professional or technical degree, or any other course of instruction. Must maintain a cumulative GPA of 2.0 or higher. Refer to Web Site: http://www.potlatchcorp.com/scholarship/NewApplicant.asp for details.

Award: Scholarship for use in freshman, sophomore, junior, or senior years; renewable. *Number:* 50–80. *Amount:* $1400.

Eligibility Requirements: Applicant must be enrolled or expecting to enroll full-time at a two-year or four-year or technical institution or university and resident of Arkansas, Idaho, Michigan, or Minnesota. Available to U.S. citizens.

Application Requirements: Application, transcript. *Deadline:* February 15.

Contact: Sharon Pegau, Corporate Programs and Board Administrator
Potlatch Foundation For Higher Education Scholarship
601 West Riverside Avenue, Suite 1100
Spokane, WA 99201
Phone: 509-835-1515
Fax: 509-835-1566
E-mail: foundation@potlatchcorp.com

PRIDE FOUNDATION http://www.pridefoundation.org

PRIDE FOUNDATION/GREATER SEATTLE BUSINESS ASSOCIATION SCHOLARSHIPS

Scholarships up to $10,000 awarded to support college, creative or vocational training. Forty different scholarships totaling more than $350,000 available, but only one application is required. Open to residents of Washington, Oregon, Idaho, Montana, and Alaska who demonstrate commitment to human and civil rights for all people. LGBT students and allies (straight and supportive of LGBT issues), children of LGBT families, and students of color are particularly encouraged to apply. Successful applicants demonstrate the potential to be good leaders and role models.

Award: Scholarship for use in freshman, sophomore, junior, senior, graduate, or postgraduate years; not renewable. *Number:* 90–100. *Amount:* $500–$10,000.

Eligibility Requirements: Applicant must be enrolled or expecting to enroll full- or part-time at a two-year or four-year or technical institution or university; resident of Alaska, Idaho, Montana, Oregon, or Washington and must have an interest in LGBT issues. Available to U.S. citizens.

Application Requirements: Application, essay, financial need analysis, interview, references, transcript. *Deadline:* January 25.

Contact: Randy Brians, Scholarship Manager
Pride Foundation
1122 East Pike
PO Box 1001
Seattle, WA 98122-3934
Phone: 206-323-3318
Fax: 206-323-1017
E-mail: scholarships@pridefoundation.org

PROJECT BEST SCHOLARSHIP FUND http://www.projectbest.com

PROJECT BEST SCHOLARSHIP

• *See page 554*

PUEBLO OF SAN JUAN, DEPARTMENT OF EDUCATION http://www.sanjuaned.org

OHKAY OWINGEH TRIBAL SCHOLARSHIP OF THE PUEBLO OF SAN JUAN

• *See page 609*

POP'AY SCHOLARSHIP

• *See page 609*

RHODE ISLAND FOUNDATION http://www.rifoundation.org

ALDO FREDA LEGISLATIVE PAGES SCHOLARSHIP

One-time scholarship of $1000 awarded to support Rhode Island Legislative Pages to further the education in a college or university. Must show scholastic achievement and good citizenship. Must be accepted into a full-time accredited postsecondary institution or graduate program. Must be a Rhode Island resident and a citizen of the United States.

Award: Scholarship for use in freshman, sophomore, junior, senior, or graduate years; not renewable. *Number:* 2–3. *Amount:* $1000.

Eligibility Requirements: Applicant must be enrolled or expecting to enroll full- or part-time at a two-year or four-year institution or university and resident of Rhode Island. Available to U.S. citizens.

Application Requirements: Application, essay, financial need analysis, references, transcript. *Deadline:* April 4.

Contact: Libby Monahan, Funds Administrator
Rhode Island Foundation
One Union Station
Providence, RI 02903
Phone: 401-274-4564 Ext. 3117
Fax: 401-751-7983
E-mail: libbym@rifoundation.org

A.T. CROSS SCHOLARSHIP

• *See page 585*

BRUCE AND MARJORIE SUNDLUN SCHOLARSHIP

Scholarships for low-income single parents seeking to upgrade their career skills. Preference given to single parents previously receiving state support, and also for those previously incarcerated. Must be a Rhode Island resident and must attend school in the state.

Award: Scholarship for use in freshman, sophomore, junior, or senior years; not renewable. *Number:* 3–5. *Amount:* up to $1000.

Eligibility Requirements: Applicant must be enrolled or expecting to enroll full- or part-time at a two-year or four-year or technical institution or university; resident of Rhode Island and studying in Rhode Island. Available to U.S. and non-U.S. citizens.

Application Requirements: Application, essay, financial need analysis, references, self-addressed stamped envelope, transcript. *Deadline:* June 13.

Contact: Libby Monahan, Funds Administrator
Rhode Island Foundation
One Union Station
Providence, RI 02903
Phone: 401-274-4564 Ext. 3117
Fax: 401-751-7983
E-mail: libbym@rifoundation.org

DAVID M. GOLDEN MEMORIAL SCHOLARSHIP

Scholarship awarded to benefit college-bound Rhode Island high school graduates, whose parents did not have the benefit of attending college. Must be enrolled in an accredited nonprofit postsecondary institution offering either a two- or a four-year college degree. Must demonstrate financial need.

Award: Scholarship for use in freshman, sophomore, junior, or senior years; renewable. *Number:* varies. *Amount:* varies.

Eligibility Requirements: Applicant must be enrolled or expecting to enroll full-time at a two-year or four-year institution or university and resident of Rhode Island. Available to U.S. citizens.

Application Requirements: Application, essay, references, self-addressed stamped envelope, transcript. *Deadline:* May 8.

Contact: Libby Monahan, Funds Administrator
Rhode Island Foundation
One Union Station
Providence, RI 02903
Phone: 401-274-4564 Ext. 3117
Fax: 401-751-7983
E-mail: libbym@rifoundation.org

LILY AND CATELLO SORRENTINO MEMORIAL SCHOLARSHIP

Scholarships for Rhode Island residents. Applicant must be 45 years or older wishing to attend college or university in Rhode Island (only students attending non-parochial schools). Must demonstrate financial need. Preference to first-time applicants.

Award: Scholarship for use in freshman, sophomore, junior, or senior years; not renewable. *Number:* varies. *Amount:* $350–$1000.

Eligibility Requirements: Applicant must be age 45 and over; enrolled or expecting to enroll full- or part-time at a four-year institution or university; resident of Rhode Island and studying in Rhode Island. Available to U.S. citizens.

Rhode Island Foundation (continued)

Application Requirements: Application, financial need analysis, self-addressed stamped envelope, transcript. *Deadline:* May 15.

Contact: Libby Monahan, Funds Administrator
Rhode Island Foundation
One Union Station
Providence, RI 02903
Phone: 401-274-4564 Ext. 3117
Fax: 401-751-7983
E-mail: libbym@rifoundation.org

MICHAEL P. METCALF MEMORIAL SCHOLARSHIP

One-time award of up to $5000 awarded to encourage personal growth through travel, study, and public service programs for college sophomores and juniors. Must be a Rhode Island resident. The scholarship is for educational enrichment outside the classroom; therefore, the awards are not to be used for school tuition. Those selected must submit a final project in writing, perhaps another medium used to communicate the value of the experience in furthering their long-term goals.

Award: Scholarship for use in freshman, sophomore, or junior years; not renewable. *Number:* varies. *Amount:* up to $5000.

Eligibility Requirements: Applicant must be enrolled or expecting to enroll full-time at a four-year institution or university and resident of Rhode Island. Available to U.S. citizens.

Application Requirements: Application, financial need analysis, references, transcript, description of enrichment experience, supporting documentation concerning the proposed experience, 3 forms of proof of Rhode Island residency. *Deadline:* January 11.

Contact: Libby Monahan, Funds Administrator
Rhode Island Foundation
One Union Station
Providence, RI 02903
Phone: 401-274-4564 Ext. 3117
Fax: 401-751-7983
E-mail: libbym@rifoundation.org

RHODE ISLAND COMMISSION ON WOMEN/FREDA GOLDMAN EDUCATION AWARD

Applicant must meet the following criteria: either preparing for a nontraditional job or career through an educational program; or returning to the labor market in need of training to sharpen your skills; or be an ex-offender wishing to undertake vocational or career education and training; or be a displaced homemaker and/or single mother wishing to further their education. Must be enrolled or registered in an educational or job skills training program. Must be a woman living in Rhode Island.

Award: Scholarship for use in freshman, sophomore, junior, or senior years; renewable. *Number:* varies. *Amount:* varies.

Eligibility Requirements: Applicant must be enrolled or expecting to enroll full- or part-time at a four-year institution or university; female and resident of Rhode Island. Available to U.S. citizens.

Application Requirements: Application, essay, references, self-addressed stamped envelope, transcript. *Deadline:* June 12.

Contact: Libby Monahan, Funds Administrator
Rhode Island Foundation
One Union Station
Providence, RI 02903
Phone: 401-274-4564 Ext. 3117
Fax: 401-751-7983
E-mail: libbym@rifoundation.org

RHODE ISLAND FOUNDATION ASSOCIATION OF FORMER LEGISLATORS SCHOLARSHIP

• ***See page 610***

RHODE ISLAND HIGHER EDUCATION ASSISTANCE AUTHORITY http://www.riheaa.org

COLLEGE BOUND FUND ACADEMIC PROMISE SCHOLARSHIP

Award to graduating high school seniors. Eligibility based on financial need and SAT/ACT scores. Must maintain specified GPA each year for renewal. Must be Rhode Island resident and attend college full-time. Must complete the FAFSA. GPA required: first year is 2.5, second year is 2.62, third year is 2.75.

Award: Scholarship for use in freshman, sophomore, junior, or senior years; renewable. *Number:* 100. *Amount:* $2500.

Eligibility Requirements: Applicant must be high school student; planning to enroll or expecting to enroll full-time at a two-year or four-year or technical institution or university and resident of Rhode Island. Available to U.S. citizens.

Application Requirements: Application, financial need analysis, test scores. *Deadline:* March 1.

Contact: Ms. Mary Ann Welch, Director of Program Administration
Rhode Island Higher Education Assistance Authority
560 Jefferson Boulevard
Warwick, RI 02886
Phone: 401-736-1171
Fax: 401-736-1178
E-mail: mawelch@riheaa.org

RHODE ISLAND STATE GRANT PROGRAM

Grants for residents of Rhode Island attending an approved school in United States. Based on need. Renewable for up to four years if in good academic standing.

Award: Grant for use in freshman, sophomore, junior, or senior years; renewable. *Number:* 10,000–12,900. *Amount:* $300–$1400.

Eligibility Requirements: Applicant must be enrolled or expecting to enroll full- or part-time at a two-year or four-year or technical institution or university and resident of Rhode Island. Available to U.S. citizens.

Application Requirements: Application, financial need analysis. *Deadline:* March 1.

Contact: Ms. Mary Ann Welch, Director of Program Administration
Rhode Island Higher Education Assistance Authority
560 Jefferson Boulevard
Warwick, RI 02886
Phone: 401-736-1171
Fax: 401-736-1178
E-mail: mawelch@riheaa.org

ROCKY MOUNTAIN COAL MINING INSTITUTE http://www.rmcmi.org

ROCKY MOUNTAIN COAL MINING INSTITUTE TECHNICAL SCHOLARSHIP

Scholarship for a first year student at a two-year technical/trade school in good standing at the time of selection. Must be U.S. citizen and a legal resident of one of the Rocky Mountain Coal Mining Institute member states.

Award: Scholarship for use in freshman year; not renewable. *Number:* varies. *Amount:* $1000.

Eligibility Requirements: Applicant must be enrolled or expecting to enroll full-time at a technical institution and resident of Arizona, Colorado, Montana, New Mexico, North Dakota, Texas, Utah, or Wyoming. Available to U.S. citizens.

Application Requirements: Application. *Deadline:* February 1.

Contact: Beth Coen, Executive Director
Rocky Mountain Coal Mining Institute
8057 South Yukon Way
Littleton, CO 80128-5510
Phone: 303-948-3300
E-mail: mail@rmcmi.org

RONALD SIMON FAMILY FOUNDATION http://www.rmsff.org

SIMON SCHOLARS COLLEGE SCHOLARSHIP PROGRAM

Scholarships are given to high school seniors in Atlanta, GA or Decab County or Santa Fe and Albuquerque, NM or Orange county and Garden Grove, CA. Deadlines vary for each region. For more details visit Web site: http://www.rmsff.org.

Award: Scholarship for use in freshman year; not renewable. *Number:* 60–70. *Amount:* $32,000.

Eligibility Requirements: Applicant must be high school student; planning to enroll or expecting to enroll full-time at a four-year institution or university and studying in California, Georgia, or New Mexico. Available to U.S. citizens.

Application Requirements: Application. *Deadline:* varies.

Contact: Megan Woodmanse, Scholarship Chairman
Ronald Simon Family Foundation
620 Newport Center Drive, 12th Floor
Newport Beach, CA 92660
Phone: 949-270-3638
Fax: 949-729-8072
E-mail: mwoodmanse@rmsff.org

ROOTHBERT FUND INC. http://www.roothbertfund.org

ROOTHBERT FUND INC. SCHOLARSHIP

Scholarships are open to all in the United States regardless of sex, age, color, nationality or religious background. Provide SASE when requesting an application.

Award: Scholarship for use in freshman, sophomore, junior, senior, or graduate years; renewable. *Number:* 20. *Amount:* $2000–$3000.

Eligibility Requirements: Applicant must be enrolled or expecting to enroll full-time at a two-year or four-year or technical institution or university and studying in Connecticut, Delaware, District of Columbia, Maryland, Massachusetts, New Hampshire, New Jersey, New York, Ohio, Pennsylvania, Rhode Island, or Virginia. Available to U.S. citizens.

Application Requirements: Application, autobiography, essay, financial need analysis, interview, photo, references, self-addressed stamped envelope, test scores, transcript. *Deadline:* February 1.

Contact: Percy Preston Jr., Office Manager
Roothbert Fund Inc.
475 Riverside Drive, Room 252
New York, NY 10115
Phone: 212-870-3116

R.O.S.E. FUND http://www.rosefund.org

R.O.S.E. FUND SCHOLARSHIP PROGRAM

Scholarship of up to $10,000 per year (depending on student's other financial aid). May be applied to tuition and books at any college/university in New England.

Award: Scholarship for use in freshman, sophomore, junior, or senior years; renewable. *Number:* 10. *Amount:* $500–$10,000.

Eligibility Requirements: Applicant must be enrolled or expecting to enroll full- or part-time at a two-year or four-year institution or university; female and studying in Connecticut, Maine, Massachusetts, New Hampshire, New Jersey, New York, Pennsylvania, Rhode Island, or Vermont. Applicant must have 2.5 GPA or higher. Available to U.S. citizens.

Application Requirements: Application, autobiography, interview, references, test scores, transcript. *Deadline:* June 30.

Contact: Jone Victoria, Director of Programs and Events
R.O.S.E. Fund
175 Federal Street, Suite 455
Boston, MA 02110
Phone: 617-482-5400
Fax: 617-482-3443
E-mail: jvictoria@rosefund.org

RYU FAMILY FOUNDATION INC.

SEOL BONG SCHOLARSHIP

• *See page 698*

ST. ANDREW'S SOCIETY OF WASHINGTON, DC http://www.saintandrewsociety.org

DONALD MALCOLM MACARTHUR SCHOLARSHIP

• *See page 699*

ST. CLAIRE REGIONAL MEDICAL CENTER http://www.st-claire.org

SR. MARY JEANNETTE WESS, S.N.D. SCHOLARSHIP

• *See page 610*

ST. PETERSBURG TIMES FUND INC. http://sptimes.com

ST. PETERSBURG TIMES BARNES SCHOLARSHIP

Four high school seniors from the St. Petersburg Times' audience area are selected each year and each are awarded up to $15,000 annually for four years to attend any nationally accredited college or university. Criteria for scholarship include high academic achievement, financial need, evidence of having overcome significant obstacles in life, and community service.

Award: Scholarship for use in freshman year; renewable. *Number:* 4. *Amount:* up to $15,000.

Eligibility Requirements: Applicant must be high school student; planning to enroll or expecting to enroll full- or part-time at a four-year institution or university and resident of Florida. Available to U.S. citizens.

Application Requirements: Application, applicant must enter a contest, financial need analysis. *Deadline:* October 15.

Contact: Nancy Waclawek, Director
St. Petersburg Times Fund Inc.
PO Box 1121
St. Petersburg, FL 33731
Phone: 727-893-8780
Fax: 727-892-2257
E-mail: waclawek@sptimes.com

SALT RIVER ELECTRIC COOPERATIVE CORPORATION http://www.srelectric.com

SALT RIVER ELECTRIC SCHOLARSHIP PROGRAM

Scholarships available to Kentucky high school seniors who reside in Salt River Electric Service area or the primary residence of their parents/guardian is in the service area. Must be enrolled or plan to enroll in a postsecondary institution. Minimum GPA of 2.5 required. Must demonstrate financial need. Must submit a 500-word essay on a topic chosen from the list on the Web site. Application and additional information available on Web site: http://www.srelectric.com

Award: Scholarship for use in freshman year; not renewable. *Number:* 4. *Amount:* $1000.

Eligibility Requirements: Applicant must be high school student; planning to enroll or expecting to enroll full- or part-time at a two-year or four-year or technical institution or university and resident of Kentucky. Applicant must have 2.5 GPA or higher. Available to U.S. citizens.

Application Requirements: Application, essay, financial need analysis, photo, transcript. *Deadline:* April 4.

Contact: Nicky Rapier, Scholarship Coordinator
Salt River Electric Cooperative Corporation
111 West Brashear Avenue
Bardstown, KY 40004
Phone: 502-348-3931
Fax: 502-348-1993
E-mail: nickyr@srelectric.com

SALVADORAN AMERICAN LEADERSHIP AND EDUCATIONAL FUND http://www.salef.org

FULFILLING OUR DREAMS SCHOLARSHIP FUND

• *See page 699*

SAN DIEGO FOUNDATION http://www.sdfoundation.org

CLUB AT MORNINGSIDE SCHOLARSHIP

• *See page 585*

DRINKWATER FAMILY SCHOLARSHIP

• *See page 610*

HARVEY L. SIMMONS MEMORIAL SCHOLARSHIP

• *See page 610*

JOSEPH C. LARSON ENTREPRENEURIAL SCHOLARSHIP

Scholarship to graduating high school seniors who will attend an accredited four-year university or students who have successfully completed at least one full academic year toward their undergraduate degree at an accredited four-year university in the United States. Students who can demonstrate their interest in entrepreneurial endeavors through the creation of their own business or consulting venue, will be given special consideration.

Award: Scholarship for use in freshman, sophomore, junior, or senior years; not renewable. *Number:* 3. *Amount:* $2500.

San Diego Foundation (continued)

Eligibility Requirements: Applicant must be enrolled or expecting to enroll full-time at an institution or university; resident of California and must have an interest in entrepreneurship. Applicant must have 3.0 GPA or higher. Available to U.S. citizens.

Application Requirements: Application, essay, financial need analysis, references, transcript, personal statement, copy of tax return. *Deadline:* January 26.

Contact: Shryl Helvie, Scholarship Coordinator
San Diego Foundation
2508 Historic Decatur Road, Suite 200
San Diego, CA 92106
Phone: 619-814-1307
Fax: 619-239-1710
E-mail: shryl@sdfoundation.org

JULIE ALLEN WORLD CLASSROOM SCHOLARSHIP

Scholarship to undergraduate students already enrolled at the University of San Diego, University of California, San Diego, or San Diego State University with a minimum 2.5 GPA and a demonstrated financial need. Applicants must be planning to study abroad for a minimum of one semester in a second- or third-world country whose culture, language and customs are different from their own. For more details visit: http://www.sdfoundation.org/scholarships/allen.shtml.

Award: Scholarship for use in freshman, sophomore, junior, or senior years; not renewable. *Number:* 1. *Amount:* $1000.

Eligibility Requirements: Applicant must be enrolled or expecting to enroll full-time at an institution or university; resident of California and must have an interest in international exchange. Applicant must have 2.5 GPA or higher. Available to U.S. and non-U.S. citizens.

Application Requirements: Application, essay, references, transcript, personal statement, copy of tax return. *Deadline:* January 26.

Contact: Shryl Helvie, Scholarship Coordinator
San Diego Foundation
2508 Historic Decatur Road, Suite 200
San Diego, CA 92106
Phone: 619-814-1307
Fax: 619-239-1710
E-mail: shryl@sdfoundation.org

LESLIE JANE HAHN MEMORIAL SCHOLARSHIP

• See page 611

LOUISE A. BRODERICK SAN DIEGO COUNTY SCHOLARSHIP

Scholarship to single parents with dependent children who are re-entering college or are already enrolled in college. Applicants must have a minimum 2.0 GPA, demonstrated financial need, and plan to attend a two-year community college, four-year university, or trade and vocational school. This scholarship may be renewable for up to four years dependent upon the recipient maintaining a positive academic (minimum 2.0 GPA) and citizenship record.

Award: Scholarship for use in freshman, sophomore, junior, or senior years; renewable. *Number:* 2. *Amount:* $2000.

Eligibility Requirements: Applicant must be enrolled or expecting to enroll full-time at a two-year or four-year or technical institution or university and resident of California. Available to U.S. citizens.

Application Requirements: Application, financial need analysis, references, transcript, personal statement, copy of tax return. *Deadline:* January 26.

Contact: Shryl Helvie, Scholarship Coordinator
San Diego Foundation
2508 Historic Decatur Road, Suite 200
San Diego, CA 92106
Phone: 619-814-1307
Fax: 619-239-1710
E-mail: shryl@sdfoundation.org

RANDY WILLIAMS SCHOLARSHIP

Scholarship to graduating high school seniors who have participated in high school and/or club competitive swimming programs and plan to attend an accredited two-year college, four-year university or licensed trade/vocational school in the United States. Preference given to applicants planning to attend school outside of San Diego County. Minimum 2.5 GPA required. For more details visit: http://www.sdfoundation.org/scholarships/randy.shtml.

Award: Scholarship for use in freshman year; renewable. *Number:* 1. *Amount:* $1000.

Eligibility Requirements: Applicant must be high school student; planning to enroll or expecting to enroll full-time at a two-year or four-year or technical institution or university; resident of California and must have an interest in athletics/sports. Applicant must have 2.5 GPA or higher. Available to U.S. citizens.

Application Requirements: Application, essay, references, transcript, personal statement. *Deadline:* January 26.

Contact: Shryl Helvie, Scholarship Coordinator
San Diego Foundation
2508 Historic Decatur Road, Suite 200
San Diego, CA 92106
Phone: 619-814-1307
Fax: 619-239-1710
E-mail: shryl@sdfoundation.org

REMINGTON CLUB SCHOLARSHIP

• See page 585

RUBINSTEIN CROHN'S AND COLITIS SCHOLARSHIP

• See page 627

SAN DIEGO FIRE VICTIMS SCHOLARSHIP-GENERAL FUND

Scholarship is open to graduating high school seniors and current college students who lost their homes in the 2003 wildfires and plan to attend an accredited two-year college, four-year university, or licensed trade or vocational school in the United States. Must be legal residents of San Diego County. Scholarship may be renewable for up to two years provided recipients continue to meet the terms of the scholarship and maintain a positive academic and citizenship record.

Award: Scholarship for use in freshman, sophomore, junior, or senior years; renewable. *Number:* 5. *Amount:* $500–$2500.

Eligibility Requirements: Applicant must be enrolled or expecting to enroll full-time at a two-year or four-year or technical institution or university and resident of California. Applicant must have 2.5 GPA or higher. Available to U.S. citizens.

Application Requirements: Application, references, transcript, personal statement, copy of tax return, formal documentation. *Deadline:* January 26.

Contact: Shryl Helvie, Scholarship Coordinator
San Diego Foundation
2508 Historic Decatur Road, Suite 200
San Diego, CA 92106
Phone: 619-814-1307
Fax: 619-239-1710
E-mail: shryl@sdfoundation.org

SAN DIEGO FIRE VICTIMS SCHOLARSHIP-LATINO FUND

• See page 699

SAN DIEGO PATHWAYS TO COLLEGE SCHOLARSHIP

• See page 611

USA FREESTYLE MARTIAL ARTS SCHOLARSHIP

• See page 611

WILLIAM AND LUCILLE ASH SCHOLARSHIP

Scholarship fund is to provide financial assistance to adult re-entry students. Applicants must have a minimum 3.0 GPA, demonstrated financial need, and be attending an accredited two- or 4-year college or university, or licensed trade/vocational school in the state of California. Students must be employed (minimum part-time). Scholarship may be renewable for up to four years provided recipients maintain a positive academic and citizenship record.

Award: Scholarship for use in freshman, sophomore, junior, or senior years; renewable. *Number:* 3. *Amount:* $1000–$5000.

Eligibility Requirements: Applicant must be enrolled or expecting to enroll full-time at a two-year or four-year or technical institution or university; resident of California and studying in California. Applicant must have 3.0 GPA or higher. Available to U.S. citizens.

Application Requirements: Application, financial need analysis, references, transcript, personal statement, copy of tax return. *Deadline:* January 26.

Contact: Shryl Helvie, Scholarship Coordinator
San Diego Foundation
2508 Historic Decatur Road, Suite 200
San Diego, CA 92106
Phone: 619-814-1307
Fax: 619-239-1710
E-mail: shryl@sdfoundation.org

SAN FRANCISCO FOUNDATION http://www.sff.org

JOSEPH HENRY JACKSON LITERARY AWARD

Award presented annually to an author of an unpublished work in progress: fiction, nonfiction, prose, or poetry. Must be residents of and currently living in northern California or the state of Nevada for three consecutive years and be between 20 to 35 years of age. Award values from $2000 to $3000. Submit manuscript.

Award: Prize for use in freshman, sophomore, junior, senior, graduate, or postgraduate years; not renewable. *Number:* 3. *Amount:* $2000–$3000.

Eligibility Requirements: Applicant must be age 20-35; enrolled or expecting to enroll full- or part-time at a two-year or four-year institution or university; resident of California or Nevada and must have an interest in writing. Available to U.S. citizens.

Application Requirements: Application, applicant must enter a contest, self-addressed stamped envelope, manuscript. *Deadline:* March 31.

Contact: Awards Coordinator
San Francisco Foundation
225 Bush Street, Suite 500
San Francisco, CA 94104-4224
Phone: 415-733-8500
E-mail: rec@sff.org

SERVICE EMPLOYEES INTERNATIONAL UNION-CALIFORNIA STATE COUNCIL OF SERVICE EMPLOYEES http://www.seiuca.org

CHARLES HARDY MEMORIAL SCHOLARSHIP AWARDS

• *See page 557*

SHELBY ENERGY COOPERATIVE http://www.shelbyenergy.com

SHELBY ENERGY COOPERATIVE SCHOLARSHIPS

Scholarships for high school seniors in Kentucky, whose parents or guardians are Shelby Energy members. Award based on financial need, academic excellence, community and school involvement, and essay.

Award: Scholarship for use in freshman year; not renewable. *Number:* 6. *Amount:* $1000.

Eligibility Requirements: Applicant must be high school student; planning to enroll or expecting to enroll full-time at a four-year institution or university and resident of Kentucky. Available to U.S. citizens.

Application Requirements: Application, financial need analysis. *Deadline:* April 5.

Contact: Teresa Atha, Marketing Department
Shelby Energy Cooperative
620 Old Finchville Road
Shelbyville, KY 40065
Phone: 502-633-4420
Fax: 502-633-2387
E-mail: shelbyenergy@shelbyenergy.com

SICKLE CELL DISEASE ASSOCIATION OF AMERICA/ CONNECTICUT CHAPTER INC. http://www.sicklecellct.org

I. H. MCLENDON MEMORIAL SCHOLARSHIP

• *See page 627*

SYBIL FONG SAM SCHOLARSHIP ESSAY CONTEST

The program provides three scholarships to graduating high school seniors based upon submission of an essay on a pre-selected topic. Minimum 3.0 GPA required. Must be a Connecticut resident.

Award: Scholarship for use in freshman year; not renewable. *Number:* 3. *Amount:* $200–$500.

Eligibility Requirements: Applicant must be high school student; planning to enroll or expecting to enroll full- or part-time at a two-year or four-year or technical institution or university; resident of Connecticut and must have an interest in writing. Applicant must have 3.0 GPA or higher. Available to U.S. citizens.

Application Requirements: Application, applicant must enter a contest, essay, references, transcript. *Deadline:* April 30.

Contact: Samuel Byrd, Program Assistant
Sickle Cell Disease Association of America/Connecticut Chapter Inc.
Gengras Ambulatory Center, 114 Woodland Street, Suite 2101
Hartford, CT 06105-1299
Phone: 860-714-5540
Fax: 860-714-8007
E-mail: scdaa@iconn.net

SIMON YOUTH FOUNDATION http://www.simonyouth.scholarshipamerica.org

SIMON YOUTH FOUNDATION COMMUNITY SCHOLARSHIP PROGRAM

Scholarship available to any high school senior living in a community that hosts a Simon property. Must be planning to enroll in a full-time undergraduate course of study at an accredited two- or four-year college, university, or vocational/technical school.

Award: Scholarship for use in freshman year; not renewable. *Number:* 100–200. *Amount:* $1500–$2500.

Eligibility Requirements: Applicant must be high school student; planning to enroll or expecting to enroll full-time at a two-year or four-year or technical institution or university and resident of Arizona, California, Florida, Indiana, Kansas, Louisiana, Missouri, Ohio, Pennsylvania, Texas, or Washington. Available to U.S. citizens.

Application Requirements: Application, financial need analysis, test scores, transcript. *Deadline:* varies.

Contact: Scholarship America
Simon Youth Foundation
PO Box 297
Saint Peter, MN 56082
Phone: 800-537-4180

SIMON YOUTH FOUNDATION EDUCATIONAL RESOURCE CENTRE SCHOLARSHIP PROGRAM

Scholarship for graduating Education Resource Centre students. Must be planning to enroll in a full-time undergraduate course of study at an accredited two- or four-year college, university, or vocational/technical school.

Award: Scholarship for use in freshman year; renewable. *Number:* varies. *Amount:* $1500–$2500.

Eligibility Requirements: Applicant must be high school student; planning to enroll or expecting to enroll full- or part-time at a two-year or four-year or technical institution or university and resident of Arizona, California, Florida, Indiana, Kansas, Louisiana, Missouri, Ohio, Pennsylvania, Texas, or Washington. Available to U.S. citizens.

Application Requirements: Application, test scores, transcript. *Deadline:* February 28.

Contact: Marlene Johnson, Program Manager, Scholarship Management Services
Simon Youth Foundation
Scholarship America, 1 Scholarship Way
PO Box 297
St. Peter, MN 56082
Phone: 507-931-1682

SOUTH CAROLINA COMMISSION ON HIGHER EDUCATION http://www.che.sc.gov

PALMETTO FELLOWS SCHOLARSHIP PROGRAM

Renewable award for qualified high school seniors in South Carolina to attend a four-year South Carolina institution. The scholarship must be applied directly towards the cost of attendance, less any other gift aid received.

Award: Scholarship for use in freshman year; renewable. *Number:* 4846. *Amount:* $6700–$7500.

South Carolina Commission on Higher Education (continued)

Eligibility Requirements: Applicant must be high school student; planning to enroll or expecting to enroll full-time at a four-year institution or university; resident of South Carolina and studying in South Carolina. Applicant must have 3.5 GPA or higher. Available to U.S. citizens.

Application Requirements: Application, test scores, transcript. *Deadline:* December 15.

Contact: Dr. Karen Woodfaulk, Director of Student Services
South Carolina Commission on Higher Education
1333 Main Street, Suite 200
Columbia, SC 29201
Phone: 803-737-2244
Fax: 803-737-3610
E-mail: kwoodfaulk@che.sc.gov

SOUTH CAROLINA HOPE SCHOLARSHIP

A merit-based scholarship for eligible first-time entering freshman attending a four-year South Carolina institution. Minimum GPA of 3.0 required. Must be a resident of South Carolina.

Award: Scholarship for use in freshman year; not renewable. *Number:* 2605. *Amount:* $2800.

Eligibility Requirements: Applicant must be high school student; planning to enroll or expecting to enroll full-time at a four-year institution or university; resident of South Carolina and studying in South Carolina. Applicant must have 3.0 GPA or higher. Available to U.S. citizens.

Application Requirements: Transcript. *Deadline:* continuous.

Contact: Gerrick Hampton, Scholarship Coordinator
South Carolina Commission on Higher Education
1333 Main Street, Suite 200
Columbia, SC 29201
Phone: 803-737-4544
Fax: 803-737-3610
E-mail: ghampton@che.sc.gov

SOUTH CAROLINA NEED-BASED GRANTS PROGRAM

Award based on FAFSA. A student may receive up to $2500 annually for full-time and up to $1250 annually for part-time study. The grant must be applied directly towards the cost of college attendance for a maximum of eight full-time equivalent terms.

Award: Grant for use in freshman, sophomore, junior, senior, or graduate years; renewable. *Number:* 1–26,730. *Amount:* $1250–$2500.

Eligibility Requirements: Applicant must be enrolled or expecting to enroll full- or part-time at a two-year or four-year or technical institution or university; resident of South Carolina and studying in South Carolina. Available to U.S. citizens.

Application Requirements: Application, financial need analysis. *Deadline:* continuous.

Contact: Dr. Karen Woodfaulk, Director of Student Service
South Carolina Commission on Higher Education
1333 Main Street, Suite 200
Columbia, SC 29201
Phone: 803-737-2244
Fax: 803-737-2297
E-mail: kwoodfaulk@che.sc.gov

SOUTH CAROLINA DEPARTMENT OF EDUCATION http://www.ed.sc.gov

ROBERT C. BYRD HONORS SCHOLARSHIP-SOUTH CAROLINA

Renewable award for a graduating high school senior from South Carolina, who will be attending a two- or four-year institution. Applicants should be superior students who demonstrate academic achievement and show promise of continued success at a postsecondary institution. Interested applicants should contact their high school counselors after the first week of December for an application.

Award: Scholarship for use in freshman year; renewable. *Number:* varies. *Amount:* varies.

Eligibility Requirements: Applicant must be high school student; planning to enroll or expecting to enroll full-time at a two-year or four-year institution or university and resident of South Carolina. Applicant must have 3.5 GPA or higher. Available to U.S. citizens.

Application Requirements: Application, test scores, ACT or SAT scores. *Deadline:* varies.

Contact: Beth Cope, Program Coordinator
South Carolina Department of Education
1424 Senate Street
Columbia, SC 29201
Phone: 803-734-8116
Fax: 803-734-4387
E-mail: bcope@sde.state.sc.us

SOUTH CAROLINA STATE EMPLOYEES ASSOCIATION http://www.scsea.com

ANNE A. AGNEW SCHOLARSHIP

• *See page 559*

RICHLAND/LEXINGTON SCSEA SCHOLARSHIP

• *See page 559*

SOUTH CAROLINA TUITION GRANTS COMMISSION http://www.sctuitiongrants.com

SOUTH CAROLINA TUITION GRANTS PROGRAM

Award assists South Carolina residents attending one of twenty-one approved South Carolina independent colleges. Freshmen must be in upper 3/4 of high school class or have SAT score of at least 900 or ACT of 19 or 2.0 final GAP on SC uniform grading scale. Upper-class students must complete 24 semester hours per year to be eligible.

Award: Grant for use in freshman, sophomore, junior, or senior years; renewable. *Number:* up to 12,000. *Amount:* $100–$3100.

Eligibility Requirements: Applicant must be enrolled or expecting to enroll full-time at a two-year or four-year institution or university; resident of South Carolina and studying in South Carolina. Available to U.S. citizens.

Application Requirements: Application, financial need analysis, test scores, transcript, FAFSA. *Deadline:* June 30.

Contact: Toni Cave, Financial Aid Counselor
South Carolina Tuition Grants Commission
101 Business Park Boulevard, Suite 2100
Columbia, SC 29203-9498
Phone: 803-896-1120
Fax: 803-896-1126
E-mail: toni@sctuitiongrants.org

SOUTH DAKOTA BOARD OF REGENTS http://www.sdbor.edu

SOUTH DAKOTA BOARD OF REGENTS MARLIN R. SCARBOROUGH MEMORIAL SCHOLARSHIP

One-time merit-based award for a student who is a junior at a South Dakota university. Must be nominated by the university and must have community service and leadership experience. Minimum 3.5 GPA required. Application deadline varies.

Award: Scholarship for use in junior year; not renewable. *Number:* 1. *Amount:* $1000.

Eligibility Requirements: Applicant must be enrolled or expecting to enroll full-time at an institution or university; resident of South Dakota; studying in South Dakota and must have an interest in leadership. Applicant must have 3.5 GPA or higher. Available to U.S. citizens.

Application Requirements: Application, essay. *Deadline:* varies.

Contact: Janelle Toman, Director of Institutional Research
South Dakota Board of Regents
306 East Capitol Avenue, Suite 200
Pierre, SD 57501-2545
Phone: 605-773-3455
Fax: 605-773-2422
E-mail: info@sdbor.edu

SOUTH DAKOTA OPPORTUNITY SCHOLARSHIP

Renewable scholarship may be worth up to $5000 over four years to students who take a rigorous college-prep curriculum while in high school and stay in the state for their postsecondary education.

Award: Scholarship for use in freshman year; renewable. *Number:* 1000. *Amount:* $1000.

Eligibility Requirements: Applicant must be high school student; planning to enroll or expecting to enroll full-time at a two-year or four-year or technical institution or university; resident of South Dakota and studying in South Dakota. Applicant must have 3.0 GPA or higher. Available to U.S. citizens.

Application Requirements: Application, test scores, transcript. *Deadline:* September 1.

Contact: Janelle Toman, Scholarship Committee
South Dakota Board of Regents
306 East Capitol, Suite 200
Pierre, SD 57501-2545
Phone: 605-773-3455
Fax: 605-773-2422
E-mail: info@sdbor.edu

SOUTH DAKOTA DEPARTMENT OF EDUCATION http://doe.sd.gov/scholarships/byrd/index.asp

ROBERT C. BYRD HONORS SCHOLARSHIP-SOUTH DAKOTA

For South Dakota residents in their senior year of high school. Must have a minimum 3.5 GPA and a minimum ACT score of 30 or above. Awards are renewable up to four years. Contact high school guidance office for more details.

Award: Scholarship for use in freshman year; renewable. *Number:* 15–25. *Amount:* $1500.

Eligibility Requirements: Applicant must be high school student; planning to enroll or expecting to enroll full-time at a two-year or four-year or technical institution or university and resident of South Dakota. Applicant must have 3.5 GPA or higher. Available to U.S. citizens.

Application Requirements: Application, references, test scores, transcript. *Deadline:* May 1.

Contact: Mark Gageby, Management Analyst
South Dakota Department of Education
700 Governors Drive
Pierre, SD 57501-2291
Phone: 605-773-3248
Fax: 605-773-6139
E-mail: mark.gageby@state.sd.us

SOUTH FLORIDA FAIR AND PALM BEACH COUNTY EXPOSITIONS INC. http://www.southfloridafair.com

SOUTH FLORIDA FAIR COLLEGE SCHOLARSHIP

Renewable award of up to $4000 for students who might not otherwise have an opportunity to pursue a college education. Must be a permanent resident of Florida.

Award: Scholarship for use in freshman, sophomore, junior, or senior years; renewable. *Number:* 10. *Amount:* $1000–$4000.

Eligibility Requirements: Applicant must be enrolled or expecting to enroll full- or part-time at a four-year institution or university and resident of Florida. Available to U.S. and non-U.S. citizens.

Application Requirements: Application, essay, references, self-addressed stamped envelope, test scores, transcript. *Deadline:* October 15.

Contact: Scholarship Committee
South Florida Fair and Palm Beach County Expositions Inc.
PO Box 210367
West Palm Beach, FL 33421-0367
Phone: 561-790-5245

SOUTH KENTUCKY RURAL ELECTRIC COOPERATIVE CORPORATION http://www.skrecc.com

WOMEN IN RURAL ELECTRIFICATION (WIRE) SCHOLARSHIPS

Scholarship available to Kentucky students who are juniors or seniors in a Kentucky college or university and have 60 credit hours by fall semester. Immediate family of student must be served by one of the state's 24 rural electric distribution cooperatives. Awards based on academic achievement, extracurricular activities, career goals, recommendations.

Award: Scholarship for use in junior or senior years; not renewable. *Number:* 3. *Amount:* $1000.

Eligibility Requirements: Applicant must be enrolled or expecting to enroll full- or part-time at a four-year institution or university; resident of Kentucky and studying in Kentucky. Available to U.S. citizens.

Application Requirements: Application. *Deadline:* June 15.

Contact: Ellie Hobgood, Scholarship Coordinator
South Kentucky Rural Electric Cooperative Corporation
PO Box 32170
Louisville, KY 40232
Phone: 800-264-5112

STATE COUNCIL OF HIGHER EDUCATION FOR VIRGINIA http://www.schev.edu

COLLEGE SCHOLARSHIP ASSISTANCE PROGRAM

Need-based scholarship for undergraduate study by a Virginia resident at a participating Virginia two- or four-year college, or university. Contact financial aid office at the participating Virginia public or nonprofit private institution.

Award: Grant for use in freshman, sophomore, junior, or senior years; renewable. *Number:* varies. *Amount:* $400–$5000.

Eligibility Requirements: Applicant must be enrolled or expecting to enroll full- or part-time at a two-year or four-year institution or university; resident of Virginia and studying in Virginia. Available to U.S. citizens.

Application Requirements: Application, financial need analysis, FAFSA. *Deadline:* varies.

Contact: Lee Andes, Assistant Director for Financial Aid
State Council of Higher Education for Virginia
James Monroe Building, 101 North 14th Street, 10th Floor
Richmond, VA 23219
Phone: 804-225-2614
E-mail: leeandes@schev.edu

VIRGINIA COMMONWEALTH AWARD

Need-based award for undergraduate or graduate study at a Virginia public two- or four-year college, or university. Undergraduates must be Virginia residents. The application and awards process are administered by the financial aid office at the Virginia public institution where student is enrolled. Dollar value of each award varies. Contact financial aid office for application and deadlines.

Award: Grant for use in freshman, sophomore, junior, senior, or graduate years; renewable. *Number:* varies. *Amount:* varies.

Eligibility Requirements: Applicant must be enrolled or expecting to enroll full- or part-time at a two-year or four-year institution or university; resident of Virginia and studying in Virginia. Available to U.S. citizens.

Application Requirements: Application, financial need analysis, FAFSA. *Deadline:* varies.

Contact: Lee Andes, Assistant Director for Financial Aid
State Council of Higher Education for Virginia
James Monroe Building, 101 North 14th Street, 10th Floor
Richmond, VA 23219
Phone: 804-225-2614
E-mail: leeandes@schev.edu

VIRGINIA GUARANTEED ASSISTANCE PROGRAM

Awards to undergraduate students proportional to their need, up to full tuition, fees and book allowance. Must be a graduate of a Virginia high school, not home-schooled. High school GPA of 2.5 required. Must be enrolled full-time in a Virginia two- or four-year institution and demonstrate financial need. Must maintain minimum college GPA of 2.0 for renewal awards.

Award: Scholarship for use in freshman, sophomore, junior, or senior years; renewable. *Number:* varies. *Amount:* varies.

Eligibility Requirements: Applicant must be enrolled or expecting to enroll full-time at a two-year or four-year institution or university; resident of Virginia and studying in Virginia. Applicant must have 2.5 GPA or higher. Available to U.S. citizens.

State Council of Higher Education for Virginia (continued)

Application Requirements: Application, financial need analysis, transcript, FAFSA. *Deadline:* varies.

Contact: Lee Andes, Assistant Director for Financial Aid
State Council of Higher Education for Virginia
James Monroe Building, 101 North 14th Street, 10th Floor
Richmond, VA 23219
Phone: 804-225-2614
E-mail: leeandes@schev.edu

VIRGINIA TUITION ASSISTANCE GRANT PROGRAM (PRIVATE INSTITUTIONS)

Renewable awards of approximately $3200 annually each for undergraduate and $1900 for graduate and first professional degree students attending an approved private, nonprofit college within Virginia. Must be a Virginia resident and be enrolled full-time. Not to be used for religious study. Information and application available from participating Virginia colleges financial aid office.

Award: Grant for use in freshman, sophomore, junior, senior, or graduate years; renewable. *Number:* 18,600. *Amount:* $1900–$3200.

Eligibility Requirements: Applicant must be enrolled or expecting to enroll full-time at a four-year institution or university; resident of Virginia and studying in Virginia. Available to U.S. citizens.

Application Requirements: Application. *Deadline:* July 31.

Contact: Lee Andes, Assistant Director for Financial Aid
State Council of Higher Education for Virginia
James Monroe Building, 101 North 14th Street, 10th Floor
Richmond, VA 23219
Phone: 804-225-2614
E-mail: leeandes@schev.edu

STATE OF GEORGIA http://www.gsfc.org

GEORGIA NATIONAL GUARD SERVICE CANCELABLE LOAN PROGRAM

• *See page 636*

STATE OF NEBRASKA COORDINATING COMMISSION FOR POSTSECONDARY EDUCATION http://www.ccpe.state.ne.us

NEBRASKA STATE GRANT

Available to undergraduates attending a participating postsecondary institution in Nebraska. Available to Pell Grant recipients only. Nebraska residency required. Awards determined by each participating institution. Contact financial aid office at institution for application and additional information.

Award: Grant for use in freshman, sophomore, junior, or senior years; not renewable. *Number:* varies. *Amount:* $100–$1500.

Eligibility Requirements: Applicant must be enrolled or expecting to enroll full- or part-time at a two-year or four-year or technical institution or university; resident of Nebraska and studying in Nebraska. Available to U.S. citizens.

Application Requirements: Application, financial need analysis. *Deadline:* continuous.

Contact: J. Ritchie Morrow, Financial Aid Coordinator
State of Nebraska Coordinating Commission for Postsecondary Education
140 North Eighth Street, Suite 300, PO Box 95005
Lincoln, NE 68509-5005
Phone: 402-471-0032
Fax: 402-471-2886
E-mail: rmorrow@ccpe.st.ne.us

STATE OF NORTH DAKOTA http://www.ndus.nodak.edu

NORTH DAKOTA INDIAN SCHOLARSHIP PROGRAM

• *See page 700*

NORTH DAKOTA SCHOLARS PROGRAM

Provides scholarships equal to cost of tuition at the public colleges in North Dakota for North Dakota residents. Must score at or above the 95th percentile on ACT and rank in top twenty percent of high school graduation class. Must take ACT in fall. For high school seniors with a minimum 3.5 GPA. Deadline: October or June ACT test date.

Award: Scholarship for use in freshman year; renewable. *Number:* 45–50. *Amount:* $5000.

Eligibility Requirements: Applicant must be high school student; planning to enroll or expecting to enroll full-time at a two-year or four-year institution or university; resident of North Dakota and studying in North Dakota. Applicant must have 3.5 GPA or higher. Available to U.S. citizens.

Application Requirements: Application, references, test scores, transcript. *Deadline:* varies.

Contact: Peggy Wipf, Director of Financial Aid
State of North Dakota
600 East Boulevard Avenue, Department 215
Bismarck, ND 58505-0230
Phone: 701-328-4114
E-mail: peggy.wipf@ndus.nodak.edu

NORTH DAKOTA STATE STUDENT INCENTIVE GRANT PROGRAM

Aids North Dakota residents attending an approved college or university in North Dakota. Must be enrolled in a program of at least nine months in length. Must be a U.S. citizen.

Award: Grant for use in freshman, sophomore, junior, or senior years; renewable. *Number:* 3500–3700. *Amount:* $800.

Eligibility Requirements: Applicant must be enrolled or expecting to enroll full-time at a two-year or four-year institution or university; resident of North Dakota and studying in North Dakota. Available to U.S. citizens.

Application Requirements: Application, financial need analysis. *Deadline:* March 15.

Contact: Peggy Wipf, Director of Financial Aid
State of North Dakota
600 East Boulevard Avenue, Department 215
Bismarck, ND 58505-0230
Phone: 701-328-4114

STATE OF WYOMING, ADMINISTERED BY UNIVERSITY OF WYOMING http://www.uwyo.edu/scholarships

VIETNAM VETERANS AWARD-WYOMING

• *See page 662*

STATE STUDENT ASSISTANCE COMMISSION OF INDIANA (SSACI) http://www.in.gov/ssaci

FRANK O'BANNON GRANT PROGRAM

A need-based, tuition-restricted program for students attending Indiana public, private, or proprietary institutions seeking a first undergraduate degree. Students (and parents of dependent students) who are U.S. citizens and Indiana residents must file the FAFSA yearly by the March 10 deadline.

Award: Grant for use in freshman, sophomore, junior, or senior years; not renewable. *Number:* 48,408–70,239. *Amount:* $200–$10,992.

Eligibility Requirements: Applicant must be enrolled or expecting to enroll full-time at a two-year or four-year or technical institution or university; resident of Indiana and studying in Indiana. Available to U.S. citizens.

Application Requirements: Application, financial need analysis, FAFSA. *Deadline:* March 10.

Contact: Grants Counselor
State Student Assistance Commission of Indiana (SSACI)
150 West Market Street, Suite 500
Indianapolis, IN 46204-2805
Phone: 317-232-2350
Fax: 317-232-3260
E-mail: grants@ssaci.state.in.us

HOOSIER SCHOLAR AWARD

A $500 nonrenewable award. Based on the size of the senior class, one to three scholars are selected by the guidance counselor's) of each accredited high school in Indiana. The award is based on academic merit and may be used for any educational expense at an eligible Indiana institution of higher education.

Award: Scholarship for use in freshman year; not renewable. *Number:* 666–840. *Amount:* $500.

Eligibility Requirements: Applicant must be high school student; planning to enroll or expecting to enroll full-time at a two-year or four-year institution or university; resident of Indiana and studying in Indiana. Applicant must have 3.5 GPA or higher. Available to U.S. citizens.

Application Requirements: Application, references. *Deadline:* March 10.

Contact: Ada Sparkman, Program Coordinator
State Student Assistance Commission of Indiana (SSACI)
150 West Market Street, Suite 500
Indianapolis, IN 46204-2805
Phone: 317-232-2350
Fax: 317-232-3260

INDIANA NATIONAL GUARD SUPPLEMENTAL GRANT

• *See page 636*

PART-TIME GRANT PROGRAM

Program is designed to encourage part-time undergraduates to start and complete their associate or baccalaureate degrees or certificates by subsidizing part-time tuition costs. It is a term-based award that is based on need. State residency requirements must be met and a FAFSA must be filed. Eligibility is determined at the institutional level subject to approval by SSACI.

Award: Grant for use in freshman, sophomore, junior, or senior years; not renewable. *Number:* 4680–6700. *Amount:* $20–$4000.

Eligibility Requirements: Applicant must be enrolled or expecting to enroll part-time at a two-year or four-year or technical institution or university; resident of Indiana and studying in Indiana. Available to U.S. citizens.

Application Requirements: Application, financial need analysis. *Deadline:* continuous.

Contact: Grants Counselor
State Student Assistance Commission of Indiana (SSACI)
150 West Market Street, Suite 500
Indianapolis, IN 46204-2805
Phone: 317-232-2350
Fax: 317-232-3260
E-mail: grants@ssaci.state.in.us

ROBERT C. BYRD HONORS SCHOLARSHIP-INDIANA

Scholarship is designed to recognize academic achievement and requires a minimum SAT score of 1300 or ACT score of 31, or recent GED score of 65. The scholarship is awarded equally among Indiana's congressional districts. The amount of the scholarship varies depending upon federal funding and is automatically renewed if the institution's satisfactory academic progress requirements are met.

Award: Scholarship for use in freshman, sophomore, junior, or senior years; renewable. *Number:* 550–570. *Amount:* $1500.

Eligibility Requirements: Applicant must be enrolled or expecting to enroll full-time at a two-year or four-year institution or university and resident of Indiana. Applicant must have 3.5 GPA or higher. Available to U.S. citizens.

Application Requirements: Application, test scores, transcript. *Deadline:* April 24.

Contact: Yvonne Heflin, Director, Special Programs
State Student Assistance Commission of Indiana (SSACI)
150 West Market Street, Suite 500
Indianapolis, IN 46204-2805
Phone: 317-232-2350
Fax: 317-232-3260

TWENTY-FIRST CENTURY SCHOLARS GEAR UP SUMMER SCHOLARSHIP

Grant of up to $3000 that pays for summer school tuition and regularly assessed course fees (does not cover other costs such as textbooks or room and board).

Award: Scholarship for use in freshman, sophomore, junior, or senior years; not renewable. *Number:* 1. *Amount:* up to $3000.

Eligibility Requirements: Applicant must be enrolled or expecting to enroll full-time at a two-year or four-year institution or university; resident of Indiana and studying in Indiana. Available to U.S. citizens.

Application Requirements: Application, must be in twenty-first century scholars program, high school diploma. *Deadline:* varies.

Contact: Coordinator, Office of Twenty-First Century Scholars
State Student Assistance Commission of Indiana (SSACI)
150 West Market Street, Suite 500
Indianapolis, IN 46204
Phone: 317-234-1394
E-mail: 21stscholars@ssaci.in.gov

STEPHEN T. MARCHELLO SCHOLARSHIP FOUNDATION http://www.stmfoundation.org

A LEGACY OF HOPE SCHOLARSHIPS FOR SURVIVORS OF CHILDHOOD CANCER

• *See page 628*

SWISS BENEVOLENT SOCIETY OF CHICAGO http://www.sbschicago.org

SWISS BENEVOLENT SOCIETY OF CHICAGO SCHOLARSHIPS

• *See page 701*

SWISS BENEVOLENT SOCIETY OF NEW YORK http://www.sbsny.org

PELLEGRINI SCHOLARSHIP GRANTS

• *See page 701*

SYNOD OF THE COVENANT http://www.synodofthecovenant.org

CECA ETHNIC SCHOLARSHIP

• *See page 716*

TENNESSEE EDUCATION ASSOCIATION http://www.teateachers.org

TEA DON SAHLI-KATHY WOODALL SONS AND DAUGHTERS SCHOLARSHIP

• *See page 560*

TENNESSEE STUDENT ASSISTANCE CORPORATION http://www.collegepaystn.com

ASPIRE AWARD

$1500 supplement to the Tennessee HOPE scholarship. Must meet Tennessee HOPE Scholarship requirements and student's parents must have an Adjusted Gross Income on their federal tax return of $36,000 or less.

Award: Scholarship for use in freshman, sophomore, junior, or senior years; renewable. *Number:* varies. *Amount:* up to $1500.

Eligibility Requirements: Applicant must be enrolled or expecting to enroll full- or part-time at a two-year or four-year institution or university; resident of Tennessee and studying in Tennessee. Applicant must have 3.0 GPA or higher. Available to U.S. citizens.

Application Requirements: Application, financial need analysis. *Deadline:* September 1.

Contact: Robert Biggers, Program Administrator
Tennessee Student Assistance Corporation
404 James Robertson Parkway, Suite 1510
Nashville, TN 37243-0820
Phone: 800-342-1663
Fax: 615-741-6101
E-mail: tsac.aidinfo@state.tn.us

DEPENDENT CHILDREN SCHOLARSHIP PROGRAM

• *See page 612*

NED MCWHERTER SCHOLARS PROGRAM

Award for Tennessee high school seniors with high academic ability. Must have minimum high school GPA of 3.5 and a score of 29 on the ACT or SAT equivalent. Must attend a college or university in Tennessee and be a permanent U.S. citizen.

Award: Scholarship for use in freshman, sophomore, junior, or senior years; renewable. *Number:* up to 180. *Amount:* up to $6000.

Eligibility Requirements: Applicant must be enrolled or expecting to enroll full-time at a two-year or four-year or technical institution or

Tennessee Student Assistance Corporation (continued)

university; resident of Tennessee and studying in Tennessee. Applicant must have 3.5 GPA or higher. Available to U.S. citizens.

Application Requirements: Application, test scores, transcript. *Deadline:* February 15.

Contact: Kathy Stripling, Scholarship Coordinator
Tennessee Student Assistance Corporation
404 James Robertson Parkway, Suite 1510, Parkway Towers
Nashville, TN 37243-0820
Phone: 615-741-1346
Fax: 615-741-6101
E-mail: kathy.stripling@state.tn.us

ROBERT C. BYRD HONORS SCHOLARSHIP-TENNESSEE

Award available to outstanding Tennessee residents graduating from high school. Minimum GPA of 3.5 required. May also qualify with a 3.0 GPA and 24 ACT or 1090 SAT. Renewable up to four years. Those with GED Test score of 570 or above also may apply.

Award: Scholarship for use in freshman, sophomore, junior, or senior years; renewable. *Number:* up to 535. *Amount:* up to $1500.

Eligibility Requirements: Applicant must be enrolled or expecting to enroll full-time at a two-year or four-year institution or university and resident of Tennessee. Available to U.S. citizens.

Application Requirements: Application, test scores, transcript. *Deadline:* March 1.

Contact: Kathy Stripling, Scholarship Coordinator
Tennessee Student Assistance Corporation
404 James Robertson Parkway, Suite 1510, Parkway Towers
Nashville, TN 37243-0820
Phone: 615-741-1346
Fax: 615-741-6101
E-mail: kathy.stripling@state.tn.us

TENNESSEE EDUCATION LOTTERY SCHOLARSHIP PROGRAM GENERAL ASSEMBLY MERIT SCHOLARSHIP

Scholarship of $1000 per semester. Entering freshmen must have 3.75 GPA and 29 ACT (1280 SAT). Must be a U.S. citizen and be a resident of Tennessee.

Award: Scholarship for use in freshman, sophomore, junior, or senior years; renewable. *Number:* varies. *Amount:* up to $2000.

Eligibility Requirements: Applicant must be enrolled or expecting to enroll full- or part-time at a two-year or four-year institution or university; resident of Tennessee and studying in Tennessee. Available to U.S. citizens.

Application Requirements: Application. *Deadline:* September 1.

Contact: Robert Biggers, Program Administrator
Tennessee Student Assistance Corporation
404 James Robertson Parkway, Suite 1510
Nashville, TN 37243-0820
Phone: 800-342-1663
Fax: 615-741-6101
E-mail: tsac.aidinfo@state.tn.us

TENNESSEE EDUCATION LOTTERY SCHOLARSHIP PROGRAM TENNESSEE HOPE ACCESS GRANT

Non-renewable award of $2650 for students at four-year colleges or $1700 for students at two-year colleges. Entering freshmen must have a minimum GPA of 2.75 and parents income must be $36,000 or less. Recipients will be eligible for Tennessee HOPE Scholarship by meeting HOPE Scholarship renewal criteria.

Award: Scholarship for use in freshman, sophomore, junior, or senior years; not renewable. *Number:* varies. *Amount:* $1700–$2650.

Eligibility Requirements: Applicant must be enrolled or expecting to enroll full- or part-time at a two-year or four-year institution or university; resident of Tennessee and studying in Tennessee. Available to U.S. citizens.

Application Requirements: Application, financial need analysis. *Deadline:* September 1.

Contact: Robert Biggers, Program Administrator
Tennessee Student Assistance Corporation
404 James Robertson Parkway, Suite 1510
Nashville, TN 37243-0820
Phone: 800-342-1663
Fax: 615-741-6101
E-mail: tsac.aidinfo@state.tn.us

TENNESSEE EDUCATION LOTTERY SCHOLARSHIP PROGRAM TENNESSEE HOPE SCHOLARSHIP

Award amount is $4000 for 4-year institutions; $2000 for 2-year institutions. Must be a Tennessee resident attending a Tennessee institution. Number of awards varies.

Award: Scholarship for use in freshman, sophomore, junior, or senior years; renewable. *Number:* varies. *Amount:* $2000–$4000.

Eligibility Requirements: Applicant must be enrolled or expecting to enroll full- or part-time at a two-year or four-year institution or university; resident of Tennessee and studying in Tennessee. Applicant must have 3.0 GPA or higher. Available to U.S. citizens.

Application Requirements: Application. *Deadline:* September 1.

Contact: Robert Biggers, Program Administrator
Tennessee Student Assistance Corporation
404 James Robertson Parkway, Suite 1510
Nashville, TN 37243-0820
Phone: 800-342-1663
Fax: 615-741-6101
E-mail: tsac.aidinfo@state.tn.us

TENNESSEE EDUCATION LOTTERY SCHOLARSHIP PROGRAM WILDER-NAIFEH TECHNICAL SKILLS GRANT

Award up to $2000 for students enrolled in Tennessee Technology Centers. Cannot be prior recipient of Tennessee HOPE Scholarship.

Award: Scholarship for use in freshman or sophomore years; renewable. *Number:* varies. *Amount:* up to $2000.

Eligibility Requirements: Applicant must be enrolled or expecting to enroll full- or part-time at a technical institution; resident of Tennessee and studying in Tennessee. Available to U.S. citizens.

Application Requirements: Application. *Deadline:* varies.

Contact: Robert Biggers, Program Administrator
Tennessee Student Assistance Corporation
404 James Robertson Parkway, Suite 1510
Nashville, TN 37243-0820
Phone: 800-342-1663
Fax: 615-741-6101
E-mail: tsac.aidinfo@state.tn.us

TENNESSEE STUDENT ASSISTANCE AWARD PROGRAM

Award to assist Tennessee residents attending an approved college or university within the state. Complete a Free Application for Federal Student Aid form. FAFSA must be processed by May 1 for priority consideration.

Award: Grant for use in freshman, sophomore, junior, or senior years; renewable. *Number:* 26,000. *Amount:* $100–$2130.

Eligibility Requirements: Applicant must be enrolled or expecting to enroll full- or part-time at a two-year or four-year or technical institution or university; resident of Tennessee and studying in Tennessee. Available to U.S. citizens.

Application Requirements: Application, financial need analysis, FAFSA. *Deadline:* May 1.

Contact: Naomi Derryberry, Grant and Scholarship Administrator
Tennessee Student Assistance Corporation
404 James Robertson Parkway, Suite 1950, Parkway Towers
Nashville, TN 37243-0820
Phone: 615-741-1346
Fax: 615-741-6101
E-mail: naomi.derryberry@state.tn.us

TERRY FOUNDATION http://www.terryfoundation.org

TERRY FOUNDATION SCHOLARSHIP

Scholarships to Texas high school seniors who have been admitted to the universities affiliated with the foundation: University of Texas at Austin, Texas

A&M University at College Station, University of Houston, Texas State University - San Marcos, University of Texas at San Antonio and University of Texas at Dallas.

Award: Scholarship for use in freshman year; renewable. *Number:* 208–650. *Amount:* $19,000–$76,000.

Eligibility Requirements: Applicant must be high school student; planning to enroll or expecting to enroll full-time at a four-year institution or university; resident of Texas; studying in Texas and must have an interest in leadership. Applicant must have 2.5 GPA or higher. Available to U.S. citizens.

Application Requirements: Application, essay, financial need analysis, interview, references, transcript. *Deadline:* January 12.

Contact: Ms. Beth Freeman, Scholarship Committee
Terry Foundation
3104 Edloe, Suite 205
Houston, TX 77027
Phone: 713-552-0002
Fax: 713-650-8729
E-mail: beth.freeman@terryfoundation.org

TEXAS AFL-CIO http://www.texasaflcio.org

TEXAS AFL-CIO SCHOLARSHIP PROGRAM

• *See page 560*

TEXAS BLACK BAPTIST SCHOLARSHIP COMMITTEE http://www.bgct.org

TEXAS BLACK BAPTIST SCHOLARSHIP

• *See page 701*

TEXAS CHRISTIAN UNIVERSITY NEELY SCHOOL OF BUSINESS ENTREPRENEURSHIP PROGRAM http://www.nep.tcu.edu

TCU TEXAS YOUTH ENTREPRENEUR OF THE YEAR AWARDS

Award available to currently enrolled Texas high school students who are Texas residents and started and managed a business while in high school. Must submit description of currently-operating business they founded. Finalists must attend TCU Young Entrepreneurs Days and individually participate in interviews. Award may be applied to any college, but is doubled if the student attends TCU. Information and application available on Web site: http://www.tcuyeya.org.

Award: Scholarship for use in freshman year; not renewable. *Number:* 6. *Amount:* $1000–$5000.

Eligibility Requirements: Applicant must be high school student; age 14-19; planning to enroll or expecting to enroll full- or part-time at a two-year or four-year or technical institution or university; resident of Texas and must have an interest in entrepreneurship. Available to U.S. citizens.

Application Requirements: Application, interview, references, description of business started and managed by applicant. *Deadline:* November 1.

Contact: Sheryl Doll, Program Director
Texas Christian University Neely School of Business Entrepreneurship Program
PO Box 298530
Fort Worth, TX 76129
Phone: 817-257-5078
Fax: 817-257-5775
E-mail: s.doll@tcu.edu

TEXAS 4-H YOUTH DEVELOPMENT FOUNDATION http://texas4-h.tamu.edu

TEXAS 4-H OPPORTUNITY SCHOLARSHIP

Renewable award for Texas 4-H members to attend a Texas college or university. Minimum GPA of 2.5 required. Must attend full-time.

Award: Scholarship for use in freshman, sophomore, junior, or senior years; renewable. *Number:* 225. *Amount:* $1500–$15,000.

Eligibility Requirements: Applicant must be enrolled or expecting to enroll full-time at a two-year or four-year or technical institution; resident of Texas; studying in Texas and must have an interest in animal/agricultural competition. Applicant must have 2.5 GPA or higher. Available to U.S. citizens.

Application Requirements: Application, essay, financial need analysis, interview, references, test scores, transcript. *Deadline:* varies.

Contact: Jim Reeves, Executive Director
Texas 4-H Youth Development Foundation
Texas A&M University
7607 Eastmark Drive, Suite 101
College Station, TX 77840-2473
Phone: 979-845-1213
Fax: 979-845-6495
E-mail: jereeves@ag.tamu.edu

TEXAS HIGHER EDUCATION COORDINATING BOARD http://www.collegefortexans.com

TEXAS NATIONAL GUARD TUITION ASSISTANCE PROGRAM

• *See page 636*

TOWARD EXCELLENCE ACCESS AND SUCCESS (TEXAS GRANT)

Renewable aid for students enrolled in a public or private nonprofit, trade school, college or university in Texas. Must be a resident of Texas and have minimum 2.5 GPA. Based on need. Amount of award is determined by the financial aid office of each school. Deadlines vary. Contact the college/university financial aid office for application information.

Award: Grant for use in freshman, sophomore, junior, or senior years; renewable. *Number:* varies. *Amount:* $1670–$4750.

Eligibility Requirements: Applicant must be enrolled or expecting to enroll full- or part-time at a two-year or four-year or technical institution or university; resident of Texas and studying in Texas. Applicant must have 2.5 GPA or higher. Available to U.S. citizens.

Application Requirements: Financial need analysis, transcript. *Deadline:* varies.

Contact: Financial Aid Office
Texas Higher Education Coordinating Board
PO Box 12788
Austin, TX 78711-2788
Phone: 512-427-6101
Fax: 512-427-6127
E-mail: grantinfo@thecb.state.tx.us

TUITION EQUALIZATION GRANT (TEG) PROGRAM

Renewable award for Texas residents enrolled full-time at an independent college or university within the state. Based on financial need. Maintain an overall college GPA of at least 2.5. Deadlines vary by institution. Must not be receiving athletic scholarship. Contact college/university financial aid office for application information. Nonresidents who are National Merit Finalists may also receive awards.

Award: Grant for use in freshman, sophomore, junior, senior, or graduate years; renewable. *Number:* 30,000. *Amount:* $2900.

Eligibility Requirements: Applicant must be enrolled or expecting to enroll full-time at a two-year or four-year institution or university; resident of Texas and studying in Texas. Applicant must have 2.5 GPA or higher. Available to U.S. citizens.

Application Requirements: Financial need analysis, FAFSA. *Deadline:* varies.

Contact: Financial Aid Office
Texas Higher Education Coordinating Board
PO Box 12788
Austin, TX 78711-2788
Phone: 512-427-6101
Fax: 512-427-6127
E-mail: grantinfo@thecb.state.tx.us

TEXAS TENNIS FOUNDATION http://www.texastennisfoundation.com

TEXAS TENNIS FOUNDATION SCHOLARSHIPS AND ENDOWMENTS

College scholarships for highly recommended students residing in Texas, with an interest in tennis. Financial need is considered. Must be between the ages of 17 and 19. Refer to Web Site for details: http://www.texastennisfoundation.com/web90/scholarships/tenniscampsscholarships.asp.

Texas Tennis Foundation (continued)

Award: Scholarship for use in freshman, sophomore, junior, or senior years; not renewable. *Number:* 10. *Amount:* $1000.

Eligibility Requirements: Applicant must be age 17-19; enrolled or expecting to enroll full-time at a two-year or four-year or technical institution or university; resident of Texas and must have an interest in athletics/sports. Available to U.S. citizens.

Application Requirements: Application, essay, financial need analysis, photo, references, test scores, transcript, copy of parent or guardian's federal tax return. *Deadline:* April 15.

Contact: Ken McAllister, Executive Director
Texas Tennis Foundation
8105 Exchange Drive
Austin, TX 78754-4788
Phone: 512-443-1334 Ext. 201
Fax: 512-443-4748
E-mail: kmcallister@texas.usta.com

THEODORE R. AND VIVIAN M. JOHNSON SCHOLARSHIP FOUNDATION INC. http://www.johnsonscholarships.org

THEODORE R. AND VIVIAN M. JOHNSON SCHOLARSHIP PROGRAM FOR CHILDREN OF UPS EMPLOYEES OR UPS RETIREES

• *See page 585*

TIDEWATER SCHOLARSHIP FOUNDATION http://www.accesscollege.org

ACCESS SCHOLARSHIP/LAST DOLLAR AWARD

A renewable scholarship of $500 to $1000 for the undergraduates participating in Norfolk, Portsmouth, and Virginia Beach, Virginia secure scholarships and financial aid for college.

Award: Scholarship for use in freshman year; renewable. *Number:* varies. *Amount:* $500–$1000.

Eligibility Requirements: Applicant must be high school student; planning to enroll or expecting to enroll full-time at a two-year or four-year institution or university and resident of Virginia. Applicant must have 2.5 GPA or higher. Available to U.S. citizens.

Application Requirements: Application, financial need analysis. *Deadline:* May 1.

Contact: Bonnie Sutton, President and Chief Executive Officer
Tidewater Scholarship Foundation
7300 Newport Avenue, Suite 500
Norfolk, VA 23505
Phone: 757-962-6113
Fax: 757-962-7314
E-mail: bsutton@accesscollege.org

TIGER WOODS FOUNDATION http://www.tigerwoodsfoundation.org

ALFRED "TUP" HOLMES MEMORIAL SCHOLARSHIP

Given yearly to one worthy Atlanta metropolitan area graduating high school senior who has displayed high moral character while demonstrating leadership potential and academic excellence. Must be U.S. citizen. Minimum 3.0 GPA required.

Award: Scholarship for use in freshman year; not renewable. *Number:* 1. *Amount:* $2500.

Eligibility Requirements: Applicant must be high school student; planning to enroll or expecting to enroll full-time at a two-year or four-year institution or university and resident of Georgia. Applicant must have 3.0 GPA or higher. Available to U.S. citizens.

Application Requirements: Application, essay, references, test scores, transcript. *Deadline:* April 1.

Contact: Michelle Kim, Scholarship and Grant Coordinator
Tiger Woods Foundation
121 Innovation, Suite 150
Irvine, CA 92617
Phone: 949-725-3003
Fax: 949-725-3002
E-mail: grants@tigerwoodsfoundation.org

TKE EDUCATIONAL FOUNDATION http://www.tke.org

ELMER AND DORIS SCHMITZ SR. MEMORIAL SCHOLARSHIP

• *See page 561*

TOWNSHIP OFFICIALS OF ILLINOIS http://www.toi.org

TOWNSHIP OFFICIALS OF ILLINOIS SCHOLARSHIP FUND

The scholarships are awarded to graduating Illinois high school seniors who have a B average or above, have demonstrated an active interest in school activities, who have submitted an essay on "The Importance of Township Government," high school transcript, and letters of recommendation. Students must attend Illinois institutions, either four-year or junior colleges. Must be full-time student.

Award: Scholarship for use in freshman year; not renewable. *Number:* 6. *Amount:* $2000.

Eligibility Requirements: Applicant must be high school student; planning to enroll or expecting to enroll full-time at a two-year or four-year institution or university; resident of Illinois and studying in Illinois. Applicant must have 3.0 GPA or higher. Available to U.S. citizens.

Application Requirements: Application, essay, interview, references, test scores, transcript. *Deadline:* March 1.

Contact: Bryan Smith, Editor and Executive Director
Township Officials of Illinois
408 South Fifth Street
Springfield, IL 62701-1804
Phone: 217-744-2212
Fax: 217-744-7419
E-mail: bryantoi@toi.org

TRIANGLE COMMUNITY FOUNDATION http://www.trianglecf.org

GLAXO SMITH KLINE OPPORTUNITIES SCHOLARSHIP

Renewable award for any type of education or training program. Must be a legal resident of the United States with a permanent residence in Durham, Orange, Wake. No income limitations. For further information see Web site at http://www.tranglecf.org.

Award: Scholarship for use in freshman, sophomore, junior, senior, or graduate years; renewable. *Number:* 1–5. *Amount:* $5000–$20,000.

Eligibility Requirements: Applicant must be enrolled or expecting to enroll full-time at a two-year or four-year institution or university; resident of North Carolina and studying in North Carolina. Available to U.S. citizens.

Application Requirements: Application, autobiography, essay, financial need analysis, references, test scores, transcript, proof of U.S. citizenship. *Deadline:* March 15.

Contact: Libby Long, Scholarships and Special Projects Coordinator
Triangle Community Foundation
324 BlackWell Street, Suite 1220
Durham, NC 27701
Phone: 919-474-8370 Ext. 134
Fax: 919-949-9208
E-mail: libby@trianglecf.org

UNITED COMMUNITY SERVICES FOR WORKING FAMILIES

RONALD LORAH MEMORIAL SCHOLARSHIP

• *See page 563*

UNITED DAUGHTERS OF THE CONFEDERACY http://www.hqudc.org

CHARLOTTE M. F. BENTLEY/NEW YORK CHAPTER 103 SCHOLARSHIP

• *See page 564*

GERTRUDE BOTTS-SAUCIER SCHOLARSHIP

• *See page 565*

LOLA B. CURRY SCHOLARSHIP

• *See page 566*

UNITED METHODIST CHURCH http://www.gbhem.org

J. A. KNOWLES MEMORIAL SCHOLARSHIP
• *See page 717*

UNITED NEGRO COLLEGE FUND http://www.uncf.org

ABBINGTON, VALLANTEEN SCHOLARSHIP
• *See page 703*

BANK OF AMERICA SCHOLARSHIP
• *See page 703*

BILDNER FAMILY FOUNDATION SCHOLARSHIP
• *See page 703*

BRITTON FUND SCHOLARSHIP PROGRAM
• *See page 703*

CASIMIR, DOMINIQUE AND JAQUES SCHOLARSHIP
• *See page 703*

CHICAGO INTER-ALUMNI COUNCIL SCHOLARSHIP
• *See page 704*

CHICAGO PUBLIC SCHOOLS UNCF CAMPAIGN
• *See page 704*

CLEVELAND MUNICIPAL SCHOOL SCHOLARSHIP
• *See page 704*

CLOROX COMPANY FOUNDATION SCHOLARSHIP
• *See page 704*

COSTCO SCHOLARSHIP
• *See page 704*

DALLAS INDEPENDENT SCHOOL DISTRICT SCHOLARSHIP
• *See page 704*

DAVENPORT FORTE PEDESTAL FUND
• *See page 705*

DENIS D'AMORE SCHOLARSHIP
• *See page 705*

EVELYN LEVINA WRIGHT SCHOLARSHIP
• *See page 705*

FIFTH/THIRD SCHOLARS PROGRAM
• *See page 705*

FORT WORTH INDEPENDENT SCHOOL DISTRICT SCHOLARSHIP
• *See page 705*

GHEENS FOUNDATION SCHOLARSHIP
• *See page 706*

JOHN W. ANDERSON FOUNDATION SCHOLARSHIP
• *See page 706*

KANSAS CITY INITIATIVE SCHOLARSHIP
• *See page 706*

KROGER/PEPSI SCHOLARSHIP
• *See page 706*

KROGER SCHOLARSHIP
• *See page 707*

LIMITED INC. AND INTIMATE BRANDS INC. SCHOLARSHIP
• *See page 707*

MINNESOTA STUDENT AID PROGRAM
• *See page 707*

NEW JERSEY MAYOR'S TASK FORCE SCHOLARSHIP
• *See page 707*

PENNSYLVANIA STATE EMPLOYEES SCHOLARSHIP FUND
• *See page 708*

RICHMOND SCHOLARSHIP
• *See page 708*

RONALD MCDONALD'S HOUSE CHARITIES SCHOLARSHIP-OHIO
• *See page 708*

ST. PETERSBURG GOLF CLASSIC SCHOLARSHIP
• *See page 708*

SAN JOSE MERCURY NEWS SCHOLARSHIP
• *See page 709*

SHELL/EQUILON UNCF CLEVELAND SCHOLARSHIP FUND
• *See page 709*

TJX FOUNDATION SCHOLARSHIP
• *See page 709*

UNION BANK OF CALIFORNIA
• *See page 709*

UNITED WAY OF NEW ORLEANS EMERGENCY ASSISTANCE FUND
• *See page 710*

UNITED WAY OF WESTCHESTER AND PUTNAM INC./ UNCF EMERGENCY ASSISTANCE FUND
• *See page 710*

VERIZON FOUNDATION SCHOLARSHIP
• *See page 710*

V103/WAOK UNCF EMERGENCY ASSISTANCE SCHOLARSHIP FUND
• *See page 710*

WHIRLPOOL FOUNDATION SCHOLARSHIP
• *See page 711*

WISCONSIN STUDENT AID
• *See page 711*

UNIVERSITY AVIATION ASSOCIATION http://www.uaa.aero

CHICAGO AREA BUSINESS AVIATION ASSOCIATION SCHOLARSHIP

One-time awards of $2500. Must be a U.S. citizen. Minimum GPA of 2.5. Priority given to Chicagoland residents followed by Illinois residents.

Award: Scholarship for use in freshman, sophomore, junior, senior, graduate, or postgraduate years; not renewable. *Number:* 6. *Amount:* $2500.

Eligibility Requirements: Applicant must be enrolled or expecting to enroll full-time at a two-year or four-year or technical institution or university and resident of Illinois. Applicant must have 2.5 GPA or higher. Available to U.S. citizens.

Application Requirements: Application, essay, references. *Deadline:* April 20.

Contact: David A. NewMyer, Department Chair, Aviation Management and Flight
University Aviation Association
Southern Illinois University at Carbondale, College of Applied Sciences and Arts, 1365 Douglas Drive
Carbondale, IL 62901-6623
Phone: 618-453-8898
Fax: 618-453-7286
E-mail: newmyer@siu.edu

UNIVERSITY OF NEW MEXICO http://www.unm.edu

BRIDGE TO SUCCESS SCHOLARSHIP

Scholarship to the students who reside in New Mexico and are U.S. citizens. Applicant must be a graduate from a New Mexico public (or accredited private) high school or be a GED recipient. Must have a minimum high school GPA of 2.5 or GED score 530. Deadline varies for fall it is June 30 and for spring it is November 30.

Award: Scholarship for use in freshman year; not renewable. *Number:* varies. *Amount:* varies.

Eligibility Requirements: Applicant must be high school student; planning to enroll or expecting to enroll full-time at a four-year institution or university and resident of New Mexico. Applicant must have 2.5 GPA or higher. Available to U.S. citizens.

University of New Mexico (continued)

Application Requirements: Application, transcript, proof of enrollment. *Deadline:* continuous.

Contact: Robert Romero, Financial Aid Adviser
University of New Mexico
Mesa Vista Hall, Room 3019
Albuquerque, NM 87131
Phone: 505-277-6090
Fax: 505-277-5325
E-mail: schol@unm.edu

NM LOTTERY SUCCESS SCHOLARSHIP

Scholarship to the residents of New Mexico. Applicant must be graduate from a New Mexico public (or accredited private) high school or receive a GED. Must enroll full-time in a baccalaureate degree program.

Award: Scholarship for use in freshman year; renewable. *Number:* varies. *Amount:* varies.

Eligibility Requirements: Applicant must be enrolled or expecting to enroll full-time at a four-year institution or university and resident of New Mexico. Applicant must have 2.5 GPA or higher. Available to U.S. citizens.

Application Requirements: Application, resume, transcript. *Deadline:* varies.

Contact: Robert Romero, Financial Aid Adviser
University of New Mexico
Mesa Vista Hall, Room 3019
Albuquerque, NM 87131
Phone: 505-277-6090
Fax: 505-277-5325
E-mail: schol@unm.edu

URBAN LEAGUE OF RHODE ISLAND INC. http://www.ulri.org

URBAN LEAGUE OF RHODE ISLAND SCHOLARSHIP

• *See page 711*

UTAH HIGHER EDUCATION ASSISTANCE AUTHORITY http://www.uheaa.org

UTAH CENTENNIAL OPPORTUNITY PROGRAM FOR EDUCATION

Award available to students with substantial financial need for use at any of the participating Utah institutions. The student must be a Utah resident. Contact the financial aid office of the participating institution for requirements and deadlines.

Award: Grant for use in freshman, sophomore, junior, or senior years; not renewable. *Number:* up to 5183. *Amount:* $300–$5000.

Eligibility Requirements: Applicant must be enrolled or expecting to enroll full- or part-time at a two-year or four-year or technical institution or university; resident of Utah and studying in Utah. Available to U.S. citizens.

Application Requirements: Financial need analysis, FAFSA. *Deadline:* continuous.

Contact: Ms. Lynda Reid, Student Aid Specialist III
Utah Higher Education Assistance Authority
60 South 400 West
The Board of Regents Building, The Gateway
Salt Lake City, UT 84101-1284
Phone: 801-321-7207
Fax: 801-366-7168
E-mail: lreid@utahsbr.edu

UTAH LEVERAGING EDUCATIONAL ASSISTANCE PARTNERSHIP

Award available to Utah resident students with substantial financial need for use at any of the participating Utah institutions. Contact the financial aid office of the participating institution for requirements and deadlines.

Award: Grant for use in freshman, sophomore, junior, or senior years; not renewable. *Number:* up to 3894. *Amount:* $300–$2500.

Eligibility Requirements: Applicant must be enrolled or expecting to enroll full- or part-time at a two-year or four-year or technical institution or university; resident of Utah and studying in Utah. Available to U.S. citizens.

Application Requirements: Financial need analysis, FAFSA. *Deadline:* continuous.

Contact: Ms. Lynda Reid, Student Aid Specialist III
Utah Higher Education Assistance Authority
60 South 400 West
The Board of Regents Building, The Gateway
Salt Lake City, UT 84101-1284
Phone: 801-321-7207
Fax: 801-366-7168
E-mail: lreid@utahsbr.edu

UTAH STATE BOARD OF REGENTS http://www.utahsbr.edu

NEW CENTURY SCHOLARSHIP

Scholarship for qualified high school graduates of Utah. Must attend Utah state-operated college. Award depends on number of hours student enrolled. Please contact for further eligibility requirements. Eligible recipients receive an award equal to 75 percent of tuition for 60 credit hours toward the completion of a bachelor's degree. For more details see Web site.

Award: Scholarship for use in freshman, sophomore, junior, or senior years; renewable. *Number:* 1. *Amount:* $564–$2166.

Eligibility Requirements: Applicant must be enrolled or expecting to enroll full- or part-time at a four-year institution or university; resident of Utah and studying in Utah. Available to U.S. citizens.

Application Requirements: Application, transcript, GPA/copy of enrollment verification from an eligible Utah 4-year institution, verification from registrar of completion of requirements for associate's degree. *Deadline:* continuous.

Contact: Charles Downer, Compliance Officer
Utah State Board of Regents
Board of Regents Building, The Gateway, 60 South 400 West
Salt Lake City, UT 84101-1284
Phone: 801-321-7221
Fax: 801-366-8470
E-mail: cdowner@utahsbr.edu

VERMONT STUDENT ASSISTANCE CORPORATION http://services.vsac.org

VERMONT INCENTIVE GRANTS

Renewable grants for Vermont residents based on financial need. Must meet needs test. Must be college undergraduate or graduate student enrolled full-time at an approved post secondary institution. Only available to U.S. citizens or permanent residents.

Award: Grant for use in freshman, sophomore, junior, senior, or graduate years; renewable. *Number:* varies. *Amount:* $500–$10,600.

Eligibility Requirements: Applicant must be enrolled or expecting to enroll full-time at a two-year or four-year or technical institution or university and resident of Vermont. Available to U.S. citizens.

Application Requirements: Application, financial need analysis, FAFSA. *Deadline:* continuous.

Contact: Grant Program
Vermont Student Assistance Corporation
PO Box 2000
Winooski, VT 05404-2000
Phone: 802-655-9602
Fax: 802-654-3765

VERMONT NON-DEGREE STUDENT GRANT PROGRAM

Need-based, renewable grants for Vermont residents enrolled in non-degree programs in a college, vocational school, or high school adult program, that will improve employability or encourage further study. Award amounts vary.

Award: Grant for use in freshman, sophomore, junior, or senior years; renewable. *Number:* varies. *Amount:* varies.

Eligibility Requirements: Applicant must be enrolled or expecting to enroll full- or part-time at a two-year or four-year or technical institution or university and resident of Vermont. Available to U.S. citizens.

Application Requirements: Application, financial need analysis. *Deadline:* continuous.

Contact: Grant Program Department
Vermont Student Assistance Corporation
10 East Allen Street
PO Box 2000
Winooski, VT 05404-2000
Phone: 802-655-9602
Fax: 802-654-3765

VERMONT PART-TIME STUDENT GRANTS

For undergraduates carrying less than twelve credits per semester who have not received a bachelors degree. Must be Vermont resident. Based on financial need. Complete Vermont Financial Aid Packet to apply. May be used at any approved post-secondary institution.

Award: Grant for use in freshman, sophomore, junior, or senior years; renewable. *Number:* varies. *Amount:* $250–$7950.

Eligibility Requirements: Applicant must be enrolled or expecting to enroll part-time at a four-year institution or university and resident of Vermont. Available to U.S. citizens.

Application Requirements: Application, financial need analysis. *Deadline:* continuous.

Contact: Grant Program
Vermont Student Assistance Corporation
PO Box 2000
Winooski, VT 05404-2000
Phone: 802-655-9602
Fax: 802-654-3765

V.E.T.S.-VICTORY ENSURED THROUGH SERVICE

V.E.T.S. ANNUAL SCHOLARSHIP

• *See page 639*

VIKKI CARR SCHOLARSHIP FOUNDATION http://www.vikkicarr.net/scholarship_foundation.htm

VIKKI CARR SCHOLARSHIPS

• *See page 711*

VIRGINIA BUSINESS AND PROFESSIONAL WOMEN'S FOUNDATION http://www.vabpwfoundation.org

BUENA M. CHESSHIR MEMORIAL WOMEN'S EDUCATIONAL SCHOLARSHIP

One-time award assists mature women seeking to complete or enhance their education. Its purposes are helping women who are employed or seeking employment, increasing the number of women qualified for promotion, and helping women achieve economic self-sufficiency. Award may be used for tuition, fees, books, transportation, living expenses, or dependent care. Must be a Virginia resident and studying in Virginia.

Award: Scholarship for use in freshman, sophomore, junior, senior, or graduate years; not renewable. *Number:* 1–10. *Amount:* $100–$1000.

Eligibility Requirements: Applicant must be age 25 and over; enrolled or expecting to enroll full- or part-time at a two-year or four-year institution or university; female; resident of Virginia and studying in Virginia. Available to U.S. citizens.

Application Requirements: Application, essay, financial need analysis, references, transcript. *Deadline:* April 1.

Contact: Julia Kroos, Chair and Trustee
Virginia Business and Professional Women's Foundation
PO Box 4842
McLean, VA 22103-4842
Phone: 703-450-5108
E-mail: info@vabpwfoundation.org

NETTIE TUCKER YOWELL SCHOLARSHIP

One-time award offered to Virginia high school seniors who have been accepted for enrollment as freshman in a Virginia college or university for the fall semester following graduation. Scholarship recipients must attend a Virginia college or university to receive funds, which are disbursed directly to the college or university. Minimum 3.0 GPA required.

Award: Scholarship for use in freshman year; not renewable. *Number:* 1–10. *Amount:* $250–$1000.

Eligibility Requirements: Applicant must be high school student; planning to enroll or expecting to enroll full-time at a four-year institution or university; resident of Virginia and studying in Virginia. Applicant must have 3.0 GPA or higher. Available to U.S. citizens.

Application Requirements: Application, essay, financial need analysis, references, test scores, transcript. *Deadline:* April 1.

Contact: Julia Kroos, Chair and Trustee
Virginia Business and Professional Women's Foundation
PO Box 4842
McLean, VA 22103-4842
Phone: 703-450-5108
E-mail: info@vabpwfoundation.org

VIRGINIA CONGRESS OF PARENTS AND TEACHERS http://www.vapta.org

CITIZENSHIP ESSAY PROJECT

Essay contest with prizes awarded in two age categories: grades 6-8 and grades 9-12. Only students enrolled in a Virginia school that is a PTA or PTSA school may apply. See Web site for essay topic and application details. Specific criteria varies by grade level.

Award: Prize for use in freshman year; not renewable. *Number:* 6. *Amount:* $250–$1000.

Eligibility Requirements: Applicant must be high school student; planning to enroll or expecting to enroll full-time at a four-year institution or university; resident of Virginia and must have an interest in writing. Available to U.S. citizens.

Application Requirements: Application, essay. *Deadline:* February 1.

Contact: Scholarship Chair
Virginia Congress of Parents and Teachers
1027 Wilmer Avenue
Richmond, VA 23227-2419
Phone: 434-264-1234
E-mail: info@vapta.org

VIRGINIA DEPARTMENT OF EDUCATION http://www.pen.k12.va.us

GRANVILLE P. MEADE SCHOLARSHIP

High school seniors only are eligible to apply for this scholarship. Students are selected based upon GPA, standardized test scores, letters of recommendations, extra curricular activities, and financial need.

Award: Scholarship for use in freshman year; renewable. *Number:* 5. *Amount:* $2000.

Eligibility Requirements: Applicant must be high school student; planning to enroll or expecting to enroll full-time at a two-year or four-year institution or university and resident of Virginia. Available to U.S. citizens.

Application Requirements: Application, essay, financial need analysis, references, test scores, transcript. *Deadline:* March 16.

Contact: Joseph Wharff, School Counseling Specialist
Virginia Department of Education
101 North 14th Street, James Monroe Building
PO Box 2120
Richmond, VA 23218-2120
Phone: 804-786-9377
Fax: 804-786-1597
E-mail: joseph.wharff@doe.virginia.gov

ROBERT C. BYRD HONORS SCHOLARSHIP-VIRGINIA

High school seniors are the only students eligible to apply for the scholarships. Students are selected based upon GPA, standardized test scores, letters of recommendation, extracurricular activities, and community involvement.

Award: Scholarship for use in freshman year; renewable. *Number:* 100–150. *Amount:* $750–$1500.

Eligibility Requirements: Applicant must be high school student; planning to enroll or expecting to enroll full-time at a two-year or four-year institution or university and resident of Virginia. Available to U.S. citizens.

Virginia Department of Education (continued)

Application Requirements: Application, references, test scores, transcript. *Deadline:* April 6.

Contact: Joseph Wharff, School Counseling Specialist
Virginia Department of Education
101 North 14th Street, James Monroe Building
PO Box 2120
Richmond, VA 23218-2120
Phone: 804-786-9377
Fax: 804-786-1597
E-mail: joseph.wharff@doe.virginia.gov

VIRGINIA DEPARTMENT OF VETERANS SERVICES http://www.dvs.virginia.gov

VIRGINIA MILITARY SURVIVORS AND DEPENDENTS EDUCATION PROGRAM

• *See page 663*

VIRGINIA SOCIETY OF CERTIFIED PUBLIC ACCOUNTANTS EDUCATION FOUNDATION http://www.cpastudentzone.com

GOODMAN & COMPANY ANNUAL SCHOLARSHIP

Scholarship for student currently enrolled in an accredited Virginia college or university who has demonstrated academic excellence and financial need.

Award: Scholarship for use in freshman, sophomore, junior, or senior years; not renewable. *Number:* 1. *Amount:* $2500.

Eligibility Requirements: Applicant must be enrolled or expecting to enroll full- or part-time at a four-year institution or university and studying in Virginia. Applicant must have 3.0 GPA or higher. Available to U.S. citizens.

Application Requirements: Application, essay, resume, references, transcript. *Deadline:* January 10.

Contact: Tracey Zink, Community Relations Coordinator
Virginia Society of Certified Public Accountants Education Foundation
PO Box 4620
Glen Allen, VA 23058-4620
Phone: 800-733-8272
Fax: 804-273-1741
E-mail: tzink@vscpa.com

WASHINGTON HIGHER EDUCATION COORDINATING BOARD http://www.hecb.wa.gov

AMERICAN INDIAN ENDOWED SCHOLARSHIP

• *See page 712*

EDUCATIONAL OPPORTUNITY GRANT

Annual grants of $2500 to encourage financially needy, placebound students to complete bachelor's degree. Must be unable to continue education due to family or work commitments, health concerns, financial needs or other similar factors. Must be Washington residents, and have completed two years of college. Grants can only be used at eligible four-year colleges in Washington. Applications are accepted from the beginning of April through the following months until funds are depleted.

Award: Grant for use in junior or senior years; renewable. *Number:* varies. *Amount:* $2500.

Eligibility Requirements: Applicant must be enrolled or expecting to enroll full-time at a four-year institution; resident of Washington and studying in Washington. Available to U.S. citizens.

Application Requirements: Application, financial need analysis. *Deadline:* continuous.

Contact: Educational Opportunity Grant
Washington Higher Education Coordinating Board
917 Lakeridge Way, PO Box 43430
Olympia, WA 98504-3430
Phone: 888-535-0747 Ext. 6
Fax: 360-753-7808
E-mail: eog@hecb.wa.gov

PASSPORT TO COLLEGE PROMISE SCHOLARSHIP

Scholarship to encourage Washington residents who are former foster care youth to prepare for and succeed in college. Recipients must have spent at least one year in foster care after their 16th birthday.

Award: Scholarship for use in freshman, sophomore, junior, or senior years; renewable. *Number:* 1–150. *Amount:* $1–$6900.

Eligibility Requirements: Applicant must be age 17-26; enrolled or expecting to enroll full- or part-time at a two-year or four-year or technical institution or university and resident of Washington. Available to U.S. citizens.

Application Requirements: Application, financial need analysis, consent form. *Deadline:* continuous.

Contact: Ms. Dawn Cypriano-McAferty, Program Manager
Washington Higher Education Coordinating Board
917 Lakeridge Way, SW
Olympia, WA 98504-3430
Phone: 360-753-7800
Fax: 360-704-6246
E-mail: passporttocollege@hecb.wa.gov

ROBERT C. BYRD HONORS SCHOLARSHIP-WASHINGTON

Scholarship for high school seniors who demonstrate outstanding academic achievement and show promise of continued academic excellence. Must be Washington residents.

Award: Scholarship for use in freshman, sophomore, junior, or senior years; not renewable. *Number:* varies. *Amount:* $1500–$6000.

Eligibility Requirements: Applicant must be high school student; planning to enroll or expecting to enroll full-time at a four-year institution or university and resident of Washington. Available to U.S. citizens.

Application Requirements: Application, transcript. *Deadline:* varies.

Contact: Tony May, Office of the Superintendent of Public Instruction
Washington Higher Education Coordinating Board
PO Box 47200
Olympia, WA 98504-7200
Phone: 360-725-6231

STATE NEED GRANT

The program helps Washington's lowest-income undergraduate students to pursue degrees, hone skills, or retrain for new careers. Students with family incomes equal to or less than 50 percent of the state median are eligible for up to 100 percent of the maximum grant. Students with family incomes between 51 percent and 65 percent of the state median are eligible for up to 75 percent of the maximum grant.

Award: Grant for use in freshman, sophomore, junior, or senior years; renewable. *Number:* 55,000. *Amount:* varies.

Eligibility Requirements: Applicant must be enrolled or expecting to enroll full- or part-time at a two-year or four-year institution or university; resident of Washington and studying in Washington. Available to U.S. citizens.

Application Requirements: Application, financial need analysis, FAFSA. *Deadline:* continuous.

Contact: Kristin Ritter, Administrative Assistant
Washington Higher Education Coordinating Board
917 Lakeridge Way
PO Box 43430
Olympia, WA 98504-3430
Phone: 360-753-7850
Fax: 360-753-6250
E-mail: kristinr@hecb.wa.gov

WASHINGTON AWARD FOR VOCATIONAL EXCELLENCE (WAVE)

Award to honor vocational students from the districts of Washington. Grants for up to two years of undergraduate resident tuition. Must be enrolled in Washington high school, skills center, or technical college at time of application. Must complete 360 hours in single vocational program in high school or one year at technical college. Contact principal or guidance counselor for more information.

Award: Grant for use in freshman, sophomore, junior, or senior years; renewable. *Number:* varies. *Amount:* up to $6300.

Eligibility Requirements: Applicant must be enrolled or expecting to enroll full-time at a two-year or four-year or technical institution or university; resident of Washington and studying in Washington. Available to U.S. citizens.

Application Requirements: Application. *Deadline:* February 16.

Contact: Scholarship Coordinator
Washington Higher Education Coordinating Board
917 Lakeridge Way, PO Box 43430
Olympia, WA 98504-3430
Phone: 360-753-7843
Fax: 360-753-7808
E-mail: ddonahoo@wtb.wa.gov

WASHINGTON SCHOLARS PROGRAM

Awards high school students from the legislative districts of Washington. Must be enrolled in college or university in Washington. Scholarships equal up to four years of full-time resident undergraduate tuition and fees. Student must not be pursuing a degree in theology. Contact principal or guidance counselor for more information.

Award: Grant for use in freshman year; renewable. *Number:* 147. *Amount:* $2676–$6290.

Eligibility Requirements: Applicant must be high school student; planning to enroll or expecting to enroll full- or part-time at a four-year institution or university; resident of Washington and studying in Washington. Available to U.S. citizens.

Application Requirements: Application. *Deadline:* January 1.

Contact: Ann Lee, Program Manager
Washington Higher Education Coordinating Board
917 Lakeridge Way, PO Box 43430
Olympia, WA 98504-3430
Phone: 360-753-7843
Fax: 360-704-6243
E-mail: annl@hecb.wa.gov

WASHINGTON HOSPITAL HEALTHCARE SYSTEM http://www.whhs.com

WASHINGTON HOSPITAL EMPLOYEE ASSOCIATION SCHOLARSHIP

Scholarship for a dependent of a Washington Hospital Employee. Must be a graduating senior, community college student, transferring community college student, or a student attending a four-year institution.

Award: Scholarship for use in freshman, sophomore, junior, or senior years; not renewable. *Number:* 1. *Amount:* $2000.

Eligibility Requirements: Applicant must be enrolled or expecting to enroll full- or part-time at a two-year or four-year or technical institution or university and resident of California. Available to U.S. citizens.

Application Requirements: Application, autobiography, essay, references, test scores, transcript. *Deadline:* March 5.

Contact: Scholarship Chair, c/o Personnel Department
Washington Hospital Healthcare System
2500 Mowry Avenue
Fremont, CA 94538
Phone: 510-818-6220

WASHINGTON STATE PARENT TEACHER ASSOCIATION SCHOLARSHIPS FOUNDATION http://www.wastatepta.org

WASHINGTON STATE PARENT TEACHER ASSOCIATION SCHOLARSHIPS FOUNDATION

One-time scholarships for students who have graduated from a public high school in the state of Washington, and who greatly need financial help to begin full-time postsecondary education.

Award: Scholarship for use in freshman year; not renewable. *Number:* 60–80. *Amount:* $1000–$2000.

Eligibility Requirements: Applicant must be high school student; planning to enroll or expecting to enroll full-time at a four-year institution or university and resident of Washington. Available to U.S. citizens.

Application Requirements: Application, essay, financial need analysis, references, transcript. *Deadline:* March 31.

Contact: Jean Carpenter, Executive Director
Washington State Parent Teacher Association Scholarships Foundation
2003 65th Avenue West
Tacoma, WA 98466-6215
Phone: 253-565-2153
Fax: 253-565-7753
E-mail: jcarpenter@wastatepta.org

WATERBURY FOUNDATION http://www.conncf.org

FERRIS P. ELLIS CREATIVE WRITING SCHOLARSHIP

To enable high-school students residing in the Foundation's service area to participate in a summer program in creative writing.

Award: Scholarship for use in freshman year; not renewable. *Number:* 1–3. *Amount:* varies.

Eligibility Requirements: Applicant must be high school student; planning to enroll or expecting to enroll full- or part-time at a four-year institution or university; resident of Connecticut; studying in Connecticut and must have an interest in writing. Available to U.S. citizens.

Application Requirements: Application, essay, financial need analysis, transcript. *Deadline:* March 1.

Contact: Josh Carey, Program Officer
Waterbury Foundation
43 Field Street
Waterbury, CT 06702-1216
Phone: 203-753-1315
Fax: 203-756-3054
E-mail: jcarey@conncf.org

REGIONAL AND RESTRICTED SCHOLARSHIP AWARD PROGRAM

Supports accredited college or university study for residents of the Connecticut community twenty-one town service area. In addition, a variety of restricted award programs are based on specific fund criteria (residency, school, course of study, etc). Scholarships are awarded on a competitive basis with consideration given to academic record, extracurricular activities, work experience, financial need, reference letter, and an essay.

Award: Scholarship for use in freshman, sophomore, junior, or senior years; renewable. *Number:* 200–250. *Amount:* $250–$5000.

Eligibility Requirements: Applicant must be enrolled or expecting to enroll full- or part-time at a two-year or four-year institution or university and resident of Connecticut. Applicant must have 2.5 GPA or higher. Available to U.S. citizens.

Waterbury Foundation (continued)

Application Requirements: Application, essay, financial need analysis, references, transcript. *Deadline:* March 1.

Contact: Josh Carey, Program Officer
Waterbury Foundation
43 Field Street
Waterbury, CT 06702-1216
Phone: 203-753-1315
Fax: 203-756-3054
E-mail: jcarey@conncf.org

WATSON-BROWN FOUNDATION INC. http://www.watson-brown.org

WATSON-BROWN FOUNDATION SCHOLARSHIP

Scholarships for students from Georgia or South Carolina who attend four- year, accredited U.S. colleges and universities. Annual scholarships are awarded on two levels: $3000 and $5000.

Award: Scholarship for use in freshman, sophomore, junior, or senior years; renewable. *Number:* 260–1000. *Amount:* $3000–$5000.

Eligibility Requirements: Applicant must be enrolled or expecting to enroll full-time at a four-year institution or university and resident of Georgia or South Carolina. Available to U.S. citizens.

Application Requirements: Application, essay, financial need analysis, references, transcript, IRS Form 1040. *Deadline:* February 15.

Contact: Sarah Katherine McNeil, Director, Scholarships and Alumni Relations
Watson-Brown Foundation Inc.
310 Tom Watson Way
Thomson, GA 30824
Phone: 866-923-6863
E-mail: skmcneil@watson-brown.org

WESTERN GOLF ASSOCIATION-EVANS SCHOLARS FOUNDATION http://www.evansscholarsfoundation.com

CHICK EVANS CADDIE SCHOLARSHIP

• *See page 613*

WESTERN INTERSTATE COMMISSION FOR HIGHER EDUCATION http://www.wiche.edu/sep

WESTERN UNDERGRADUATE EXCHANGE (WUE) PROGRAM

Students in designated states can enroll in two- and four-year undergraduate programs at public institutions in participating states and pay 150 percent of resident tuition. Applicants apply directly to the admissions office at participating institution. Applicants must indicate that they want to be considered for the "WUE tuition discount".

Award: Scholarship for use in freshman, sophomore, junior, or senior years; renewable. *Number:* varies. *Amount:* varies.

Eligibility Requirements: Applicant must be enrolled or expecting to enroll full-time at a two-year or four-year institution; resident of Alaska, Arizona, California, Colorado, Hawaii, Idaho, Montana, Nevada, New Mexico, North Dakota, Oregon, South Dakota, Utah, Washington, or Wyoming and studying in Alaska, Arizona, California, Colorado, Hawaii, Idaho, Montana, Nevada, New Mexico, North Dakota, Oregon, or South Dakota. Available to U.S. citizens.

Application Requirements: Application. *Deadline:* varies.

Contact: Ms. Laura Ewing, Administrative Assistant, Student Exchange
Western Interstate Commission for Higher Education
3035 Center Green Drive
Boulder, CO 80301
Phone: 303-541-0270
E-mail: info-sep@wiche.edu

WEST VIRGINIA HIGHER EDUCATION POLICY COMMISSION-OFFICE OF FINANCIAL AID AND OUTREACH SERVICES http://wvhepcnew.wvnet.edu/

ROBERT C. BYRD HONORS SCHOLARSHIP-WEST VIRGINIA

Award for West Virginia residents who have demonstrated outstanding academic achievement. Must be a graduating high school senior. May apply for renewal consideration for a total of four years of assistance. For full-time study only.

Award: Scholarship for use in freshman year; renewable. *Number:* 36. *Amount:* $1500.

Eligibility Requirements: Applicant must be high school student; planning to enroll or expecting to enroll full-time at a two-year or four-year or technical institution or university and resident of West Virginia. Applicant must have 3.5 GPA or higher. Available to U.S. citizens.

Application Requirements: Application, test scores, transcript, letter of acceptance from a college/university. *Deadline:* March 1.

Contact: Darlene Elmore, Scholarship Coordinator
West Virginia Higher Education Policy Commission-Office of Financial Aid and Outreach Services
1018 Kanawha Boulevard, East, Suite 700
Charleston, WV 25301
E-mail: elmore@hepc.wvnet.edu

WEST VIRGINIA HIGHER EDUCATION GRANT PROGRAM

Award available for West Virginia resident for one year immediately preceding the date of application, high school graduate or the equivalent, demonstrate financial need, and enroll as a full-time undergraduate at an approved university or college located in West Virginia or Pennsylvania.

Award: Grant for use in freshman year; not renewable. *Number:* 10,755–11,000. *Amount:* $375–$3542.

Eligibility Requirements: Applicant must be high school student; planning to enroll or expecting to enroll full-time at a four-year institution or university; resident of West Virginia and studying in Pennsylvania or West Virginia. Available to U.S. citizens.

Application Requirements: Application, financial need analysis, references, test scores, transcript. *Deadline:* March 1.

Contact: Judy Smith, Senior Project Coordinator
West Virginia Higher Education Policy Commission-Office of Financial Aid and Outreach Services
1018 Kanawha Boulevard East, Suite 700
Charleston, WV 25301-2827
Phone: 304-558-4618
Fax: 304-558-4622
E-mail: kee@hepc.wvnet.edu

WILLIAM D. SQUIRES EDUCATIONAL FOUNDATION INC. http://www.wmd-squires-foundation.org

WILLIAM D. SQUIRES SCHOLARSHIP

Scholarship for graduating seniors from Ohio planning to pursue a degree, certificate, or diploma full-time at an accredited college, university, technical, or business school. Minimum 3.2 GPA required.

Award: Scholarship for use in senior year; renewable. *Number:* varies. *Amount:* $3000.

Eligibility Requirements: Applicant must be enrolled or expecting to enroll full-time at a two-year or four-year or technical institution or university; resident of Ohio and studying in Ohio. Available to U.S. citizens.

Application Requirements: Application, essay, references, transcript. *Deadline:* April 5.

Contact: Scholarship Committee
William D. Squires Educational Foundation Inc.
PO Box 2940
Jupiter, FL 33468-2940
Phone: 561-741-7751
E-mail: wmdsquires@comcast.net

WILLIAM F. COOPER SCHOLARSHIP TRUST http://www.wachoviascholars.com

WILLIAM F. COOPER SCHOLARSHIP

Scholarship to provide financial assistance to women living within the state of Georgia for undergraduate studies. Cannot be used for law, theology or medicine fields of study. Nursing is an approved area of study. For more details visit Web site: http://www.wachoviascholars.com.

Award: Scholarship for use in freshman, sophomore, junior, or senior years; renewable. *Number:* varies. *Amount:* $1000.

Eligibility Requirements: Applicant must be enrolled or expecting to enroll full- or part-time at a four-year institution or university; female and resident of Georgia. Available to U.S. citizens.

Application Requirements: Application, financial need analysis, references, test scores, transcript, federal tax form 1040, W-2 forms. *Deadline:* April 1.

Contact: Sally King, Program Coordinator
William F. Cooper Scholarship Trust
4320-G Wade Hampton Boulevard
Taylors, SC 29687
Phone: 800-576-5135
Fax: 864-268-7160
E-mail: sallyking@bellsouth.net

WILLIAM G. AND MARIE SELBY FOUNDATION http://www.selbyfdn.org

SELBY SCHOLAR PROGRAM

• *See page 613*

WISCONSIN DEPARTMENT OF VETERANS AFFAIRS http://www.dva.state.wi.us

VETERANS EDUCATION (VETED) REIMBURSEMENT GRANT

• *See page 633*

WISCONSIN HIGHER EDUCATIONAL AIDS BOARD http://www.heab.state.wi.us

HANDICAPPED STUDENT GRANT-WISCONSIN

• *See page 629*

MINORITY UNDERGRADUATE RETENTION GRANT-WISCONSIN

• *See page 712*

TALENT INCENTIVE PROGRAM GRANT

Grant assists residents of Wisconsin who are attending a nonprofit institution in Wisconsin, and who have substantial financial need. Must meet income criteria, be considered economically and educationally disadvantaged, and be enrolled at least half-time. Refer to Web site for further details: http://www.heab.state.wi.us.

Award: Grant for use in freshman, sophomore, junior, or senior years; renewable. *Number:* varies. *Amount:* $250–$1800.

Eligibility Requirements: Applicant must be enrolled or expecting to enroll full- or part-time at a two-year or four-year institution or university; resident of Wisconsin and studying in Wisconsin. Available to U.S. citizens.

Application Requirements: Application, financial need analysis, nomination. *Deadline:* continuous.

Contact: John Whitt, Program Coordinator
Wisconsin Higher Educational Aids Board
PO Box 7885
Madison, WI 53707-7885
Phone: 608-266-1665
Fax: 608-267-2808
E-mail: john.whitt@heab.state.wi.us

WISCONSIN ACADEMIC EXCELLENCE SCHOLARSHIP

Renewable award for high school seniors with the highest GPA in graduating class. Must be a Wisconsin resident. Award covers tuition for up to four years. Must maintain 3.0 GPA for renewal. Scholarship value is $2250. Must attend a nonprofit Wisconsin institution full-time. Refer to Web site for further details: http://www.heab.state.wi.us.

Award: Scholarship for use in freshman year; renewable. *Number:* varies. *Amount:* up to $2250.

Eligibility Requirements: Applicant must be high school student; planning to enroll or expecting to enroll full-time at a two-year or four-year or technical institution or university; resident of Wisconsin and studying in Wisconsin. Applicant must have 3.0 GPA or higher. Available to U.S. citizens.

Application Requirements: Application, test scores, transcript. *Deadline:* continuous.

Contact: Alice Winters, Program Coordinator
Wisconsin Higher Educational Aids Board
PO Box 7885
Madison, WI 53707-7885
Phone: 608-267-2213
Fax: 608-267-2808
E-mail: alice.winters@heab.state.wi.us

WISCONSIN HIGHER EDUCATION GRANTS (WHEG)

Grants for residents of Wisconsin enrolled at least half-time in degree or certificate programs at University of Wisconsin or Wisconsin Technical College. Must show financial need. Refer to Web site for further details: http://www.heab.state.wi.us.

Award: Grant for use in freshman, sophomore, junior, or senior years; not renewable. *Number:* varies. *Amount:* $250–$3000.

Eligibility Requirements: Applicant must be enrolled or expecting to enroll full- or part-time at a two-year or four-year or technical institution or university; resident of Wisconsin and studying in Wisconsin. Available to U.S. citizens.

Application Requirements: Application, financial need analysis. *Deadline:* continuous.

Contact: Sandra Thomas, Program Coordinator
Wisconsin Higher Educational Aids Board
PO Box 7885
Madison, WI 53707-7885
Phone: 608-266-0888
Fax: 608-267-2808
E-mail: sandy.thomas@heab.state.wi.us

WISCONSIN NATIVE AMERICAN/INDIAN STUDENT ASSISTANCE GRANT

• *See page 712*

WISCONSIN SCHOOL COUNSELORS ASSOCIATION http://www.wscaweb.com

WSCA/TCF BANK SCHOLARSHIP PROGRAM

Scholarship available to high school seniors in Wisconsin who plan to attend a postsecondary institution in the fall.

Award: Scholarship for use in freshman year; not renewable. *Number:* 4. *Amount:* $1000.

Eligibility Requirements: Applicant must be high school student; planning to enroll or expecting to enroll full-time at a two-year or four-year institution or university and resident of Wisconsin. Available to U.S. citizens.

Application Requirements: Application, essay, self-addressed stamped envelope. *Deadline:* December 1.

Contact: Kevin Formolo, Scholarship Committee
Wisconsin School Counselors Association
3128 South 12th Street
Sheboygan, WI 53081
Phone: 920-803-7842

WYOMING DEPARTMENT OF EDUCATION

DOUVAS MEMORIAL SCHOLARSHIP

Available to Wyoming residents who are first-generation Americans. Must be between 18 and 22 years old. Must be used at any Wyoming public institution of higher education for study in freshman year.

Award: Scholarship for use in freshman year; not renewable. *Number:* 1. *Amount:* $500.

Eligibility Requirements: Applicant must be age 18-22; enrolled or expecting to enroll full- or part-time at a two-year or four-year institution or university; resident of Wyoming and studying in Wyoming. Available to U.S. citizens.

Wyoming Department of Education (continued)

Application Requirements: Application. *Deadline:* March 24.

Contact: Gerry Maas, Director, Health and Safety
Wyoming Department of Education
2300 Capitol Avenue, Hathaway Building, 2nd Floor
Cheyenne, WY 82002-0050
Phone: 307-777-6282
Fax: 307-777-6234
E-mail: gmaas@educ.state.wy.us

HATHAWAY SCHOLARSHIP

Scholarship for Wyoming students to pursue postsecondary education within the state. Award ranges from $1000 to $1600. Deadline varies.

Award: Scholarship for use in freshman, sophomore, junior, or senior years; not renewable. *Number:* 1. *Amount:* $1000–$1600.

Eligibility Requirements: Applicant must be enrolled or expecting to enroll full-time at a two-year or four-year institution or university; resident of Wyoming and studying in Wyoming. Available to U.S. citizens.

Application Requirements: Application. *Deadline:* varies.

Contact: Kay Post, Director
Wyoming Department of Education
2020 Grand Avenue, Suite 500
Laramie, WY 82070
Phone: 307-777-5599
E-mail: kpost@educ.state.wy.us

ROBERT C. BYRD HONORS SCHOLARSHIP-WYOMING

Award available to Wyoming residents who show outstanding academic ability. Must attend an accredited postsecondary institution, have a minimum 3.8 GPA, and be a high school senior. Renewable award of $1500. Applications are mailed to all high school counselors in the spring.

Award: Scholarship for use in freshman year; renewable. *Number:* 11. *Amount:* $1500.

Eligibility Requirements: Applicant must be high school student; planning to enroll or expecting to enroll full-time at a two-year or four-year institution or university and resident of Wyoming. Applicant must have 3.5 GPA or higher. Available to U.S. citizens.

Application Requirements: Application, essay, test scores, transcript, nomination. *Deadline:* April 18.

Contact: D. Leeds Pickering, Scholarship Committee
Wyoming Department of Education
Hathaway Building, Second Floor
Cheyenne, WY 82002-0050

WYOMING FARM BUREAU FEDERATION

http://www.wyfb.org

KING-LIVINGSTON SCHOLARSHIP

• *See page 570*

WYOMING FARM BUREAU CONTINUING EDUCATION SCHOLARSHIPS

• *See page 570*

WYOMING FARM BUREAU FEDERATION SCHOLARSHIPS

• *See page 571*

YOUTH OPPORTUNITIES FOUNDATION

YOUTH OPPORTUNITIES FOUNDATION SCHOLARSHIPS

• *See page 713*

ZINCH.COM

http://www.zinch.com

ZINCH.COM CALIFORNIA SCHOLARSHIP

The program awards outstanding high school students who currently reside in California. Scholarships ranges from $1000 to $5000. To apply, a high school student needs to fill out a zinch.com profile. Both the need of student and merit of student are considered. Winners are chosen based on the student's zinch.com profile. A minimum 2.0 GPA required.

Award: Scholarship for use in freshman year; renewable. *Number:* 1–8. *Amount:* $1000–$5000.

Eligibility Requirements: Applicant must be high school student; planning to enroll or expecting to enroll full- or part-time at a four-year institution or university and resident of California. Available to U.S. citizens.

Application Requirements: Application. *Deadline:* May 25.

Contact: Mick Hagen, CEO
Zinch.com
42 North University Avenue, Suite 210
Provo, UT 84601
Phone: 801-830-2048
Fax: 801-356-0293
E-mail: mickey@zinch.com

ZINCH.COM NEW YORK SCHOLARSHIP

The program awards outstanding high school students who live in the State of New York. Scholarships ranges from $1000 to $5000. To apply, a high school student needs to fill out a zinch.com profile. Both the need of student and merit of student are considered. Winners are chosen based on the student's zinch.com profile. Must maintain a minimum GPA of 2.0.

Award: Scholarship for use in freshman year; renewable. *Number:* 1–8. *Amount:* $1000–$5000.

Eligibility Requirements: Applicant must be high school student; planning to enroll or expecting to enroll full- or part-time at a four-year institution or university and resident of New York. Available to U.S. citizens.

Application Requirements: Application. *Deadline:* May 25.

Contact: Mick Hagen, CEO
Zinch.com
42 North University Avenue, Suite 210
Provo, UT 84601
Phone: 801-830-2048
Fax: 801-356-0293
E-mail: mickey@zinch.com

ZINCH.COM UTAH SCHOLARSHIP

The program awards outstanding high school students who live in the State of Utah. Scholarships ranges from $1000 to $5000. To apply, a high school student needs to fill out a zinch.com profile. Both the need and merit of student are considered. Winners are chosen based on the student's zinch.com profile. Must maintain a minimum GPA of 2.0.

Award: Scholarship for use in freshman year; renewable. *Number:* 1–8. *Amount:* $1000–$5000.

Eligibility Requirements: Applicant must be high school student; planning to enroll or expecting to enroll full- or part-time at a four-year institution or university and resident of Utah. Available to U.S. citizens.

Application Requirements: Application. *Deadline:* May 25.

Contact: Mick Hagen, CEO
Zinch.com
42 North University Avenue, Suite 210
Provo, UT 84601
Phone: 801-830-2048
Fax: 801-356-0293
E-mail: mickey@zinch.com

TALENT/INTEREST AREA

ACTORS THEATRE OF LOUISVILLE

http://www.actorstheatre.org

NATIONAL TEN-MINUTE PLAY CONTEST

• *See page 668*

AKADEMOS INC.

http://www.textbookx.com

TEXTBOOKX.COM SCHOLARSHIP

Students must write an essay and reference one book on the assigned topic. Essay must be between 250 and 750 words. One grand prize winner is selected and two runners-up. See Web site for current essay topic: http://www.textbookx.com/scholarship.

Award: Scholarship for use in freshman, sophomore, junior, senior, graduate, or postgraduate years; renewable. *Number:* 3. *Amount:* $250–$2000.

Eligibility Requirements: Applicant must be enrolled or expecting to enroll full- or part-time at a two-year or four-year or technical institution or university and must have an interest in writing. Available to U.S. and non-U.S. citizens.

Application Requirements: Application, applicant must enter a contest, essay. *Deadline:* October 31.

Contact: Sarah Jensen, Marketing Manager
Akademos Inc.
25 Van Zant Street
Norwalk, CT 06855
Phone: 203-866-0190
Fax: 203-866-0199

ALBERTA HERITAGE SCHOLARSHIP FUND/ ALBERTA SCHOLARSHIP PROGRAMS http://www.alis.gov.ab.ca

ALBERTA HERITAGE SCHOLARSHIP FUND ALBERTA PRESS COUNCIL SCHOLARSHIP
• *See page 669*

CHARLES S. NOBLE JUNIOR "A" HOCKEY SCHOLARSHIPS
• *See page 669*

CHARLES S. NOBLE JUNIOR FOOTBALL SCHOLARSHIPS
• *See page 669*

EARL AND COUNTESS OF WESSEX-WORLD CHAMPIONSHIPS IN ATHLETICS SCHOLARSHIPS
• *See page 720*

JIMMIE CONDON ATHLETIC SCHOLARSHIPS
• *See page 670*

LAURENCE DECORE STUDENT LEADERSHIP AWARDS
• *See page 670*

PRAIRIE BASEBALL ACADEMY SCHOLARSHIPS
• *See page 721*

ALBUQUERQUE COMMUNITY FOUNDATION http://www.albuquerquefoundation.org

NOTAH BEGAY III SCHOLARSHIP PROGRAM FOR NATIVE AMERICAN SCHOLAR ATHLETES
• *See page 671*

ALERT SCHOLARSHIP http://www.alertmagazine.org

ALERT SCHOLARSHIP
• *See page 721*

ALEXANDER FOUNDATION http://www.thealexanderfoundation.org

SCHOLARSHIP GRANT PROGRAM
• *See page 721*

AMERICAN ASSOCIATION OF SCHOOL ADMINISTRATORS/DISCOVER SCHOLARSHIPPROGRAM http://www.aasa.org

DISCOVER SCHOLARSHIP PROGRAM
• *See page 588*

AMERICAN BOWLING CONGRESS http://www.bowl.com

CHUCK HALL STAR OF TOMORROW SCHOLARSHIP
• *See page 510*

AMERICAN CANCER SOCIETY, FLORIDA DIVISION INC. http://www.cancer.org

AMERICAN CANCER SOCIETY, FLORIDA DIVISION R.O.C.K. COLLEGE SCHOLARSHIP PROGRAM
• *See page 588*

AMERICAN FOREIGN SERVICE ASSOCIATION http://www.afsa.org

AMERICAN FOREIGN SERVICE ASSOCIATION (AFSA)/AAFSW MERIT AWARD PROGRAM
• *See page 511*

AMERICAN INDIAN GRADUATE CENTER http://www.aigcs.org

GATES MILLENNIUM SCHOLARS PROGRAM
• *See page 672*

AMERICAN INSTITUTE FOR FOREIGN STUDY http://www.aifsabroad.com

AIFS AFFILIATE SCHOLARSHIPS

Students from colleges and universities that participate in the AIFS Affiliates program are eligible. Application fee: $95. For more details, visit http://www.aifsabroad.com/scholarships.asp.

Award: Scholarship for use in freshman, sophomore, junior, or senior years; not renewable. *Number:* varies. *Amount:* varies.

Eligibility Requirements: Applicant must be enrolled or expecting to enroll full-time at a two-year or four-year institution or university and must have an interest in international exchange. Available to U.S. and non-U.S. citizens.

Application Requirements: Application, essay, photo, references, transcript. *Fee:* $95. *Deadline:* varies.

Contact: David Mauro, Admissions Counselor
American Institute for Foreign Study
River Plaza, Nine West Broad Street
Stamford, CT 06902-3788
Phone: 800-727-2437 Ext. 5163
Fax: 203-399-5463
E-mail: dmauro@aifs.com

AIFS DIVERSITY SCHOLARSHIPS
• *See page 672*

AIFS GILMAN SCHOLARSHIP BONUS-$500 SCHOLARSHIPS

Award of $500 to each student who receives a Benjamin A. Gilman International Scholarship and uses it toward an AIFS program. More information about Benjamin A. Gilman International Scholarships is available at www.iie.org/gilman.

Award: Scholarship for use in freshman, sophomore, junior, or senior years; not renewable. *Number:* varies. *Amount:* $500.

Eligibility Requirements: Applicant must be age 17 and over; enrolled or expecting to enroll full-time at a four-year institution or university and must have an interest in international exchange. Available to U.S. and non-U.S. citizens.

Application Requirements: Application, essay, photo, references, transcript. *Fee:* $95. *Deadline:* varies.

Contact: David Mauro, Admissions Counselor
American Institute for Foreign Study
River Plaza, Nine West Broad Street
Stamford, CT 06902-3788
Phone: 800-727-2437 Ext. 5163
Fax: 203-399-5463
E-mail: dmauro@aifs.com

AIFS-HACU SCHOLARSHIPS
• *See page 672*

AIFS INTERNATIONAL SCHOLARSHIPS

Awards available to undergraduates on an AIFS study abroad program. Applicants must demonstrate leadership potential, have a minimum 3.0 cumulative GPA, and meet program requirements. The program application fee is $95. Deadlines: April 15 for fall, October 1 for spring, March 15 for summer.

Award: Scholarship for use in freshman, sophomore, junior, or senior years; not renewable. *Number:* 40. *Amount:* $500–$1000.

Eligibility Requirements: Applicant must be age 17 and over; enrolled or expecting to enroll full-time at a two-year or four-year institution or university and must have an interest in international exchange. Applicant must have 3.0 GPA or higher. Available to U.S. and non-U.S. citizens.

American Institute for Foreign Study (continued)

Application Requirements: Application, essay, photo, references, transcript. *Fee:* $95. *Deadline:* varies.

Contact: David Mauro, Admissions Counselor
American Institute for Foreign Study
River Plaza, Nine West Broad Street
Stamford, CT 06902-3788
Phone: 800-727-2437 Ext. 5163
Fax: 203-399-5463
E-mail: dmauro@aifs.com

AIFS STUDY AGAIN SCHOLARSHIPS

Students who studied abroad on an AIFS summer program will receive a $1000 scholarship to study abroad on an AIFS semester or academic year catalog program, or a $500 scholarship toward a summer catalog program. Students who studied abroad on an AIFS semester or academic year program will receive a $500 scholarship toward a summer catalog program or a $1000 scholarship toward a semester program in a different academic year. Deadlines: April 15 for fall, October 15 for spring, March 15 for summer.

Award: Scholarship for use in freshman, sophomore, junior, or senior years; not renewable. *Number:* varies. *Amount:* $500–$1000.

Eligibility Requirements: Applicant must be age 17 and over; enrolled or expecting to enroll full-time at a two-year or four-year institution or university and must have an interest in international exchange. Available to U.S. and non-U.S. citizens.

Application Requirements: Application, essay, photo, references, transcript. *Fee:* $95. *Deadline:* April 15.

Contact: David Mauro, Admissions Counselor
American Institute for Foreign Study
River Plaza, Nine West Broad Street
Stamford, CT 06902-3788
Phone: 800-727-2437 Ext. 5163
Fax: 203-399-5463
E-mail: dmauro@aifs.com

AIFS SUMMER DIVERSITYABROAD.COM SCHOLARSHIP

• *See page 672*

AMERICAN INSTITUTE FOR FOREIGN STUDY INTERNATIONAL SCHOLARSHIPS, FALL SEMESTER

Awards are available to undergraduates on an AIFS study abroad program. Applicants must demonstrate leadership potential, have a minimum 3.0 cumulative GPA, and meet program requirements. Must submit program and scholarship applications by April 15 for fall semester. The program application fee is $95.

Award: Scholarship for use in freshman, sophomore, junior, or senior years; not renewable. *Number:* up to 40. *Amount:* up to $1000.

Eligibility Requirements: Applicant must be age 17 and over; enrolled or expecting to enroll full-time at a two-year or four-year institution or university and must have an interest in leadership. Applicant must have 3.0 GPA or higher. Available to U.S. and non-U.S. citizens.

Application Requirements: Application, essay, photo, references, transcript. *Fee:* $95. *Deadline:* April 15.

Contact: David Mauro, Admissions Counselor
American Institute for Foreign Study
Nine West Broad Street, River Plaza
Stamford, CT 06902-3788
Phone: 800-727-2437 Ext. 5163
Fax: 203-399-5463
E-mail: dmauro@aifs.com

DIVERSITY SCHOLARSHIPS

• *See page 673*

AMERICAN JEWISH LEAGUE FOR ISRAEL http://www.americanjewishleague.org

AMERICAN JEWISH LEAGUE FOR ISRAEL SCHOLARSHIP PROGRAM

Scholarship provides support with tuition for a full year of study (September to May) at one of seven Israeli universities, Bar Ilan, Ben Gurion, Haifa, Hebrew, Tel Aviv, Technion, and Weizmann, Interdisciplinary Center at Herzliya. Additional information is available on Web site: http://www.americanjewishleague.org/ScholarshipInformation.html.

Award: Scholarship for use in freshman, sophomore, junior, senior, graduate, or postgraduate years; not renewable. *Number:* 3–15. *Amount:* $2000.

Eligibility Requirements: Applicant must be enrolled or expecting to enroll full-time at a four-year institution or university and must have an interest in Jewish culture. Available to U.S. citizens.

Application Requirements: Application, references, transcript, personal and academic aspirations. *Deadline:* May 1.

Contact: Dr. Martin Kalmanson, University Scholarship Fund
American Jewish League for Israel
400 North Flagler Drive PHD4
West Palm Beach, FL 33401
Phone: 561-659-0402
Fax: 561-659-0402
E-mail: ajlimlk@aol.com

AMERICAN LEGION DEPARTMENT OF ARIZONA http://www.azlegion.org

AMERICAN LEGION DEPARTMENT OF ARIZONA HIGH SCHOOL ORATORICAL CONTEST

• *See page 725*

AMERICAN LEGION DEPARTMENT OF ARKANSAS http://www.arklegion.homestead.com

AMERICAN LEGION DEPARTMENT OF ARKANSAS HIGH SCHOOL ORATORICAL CONTEST

• *See page 725*

AMERICAN LEGION DEPARTMENT OF ILLINOIS http://www.illegion.org

AMERICAN ESSAY CONTEST SCHOLARSHIP

• *See page 517*

AMERICAN LEGION DEPARTMENT OF ILLINOIS HIGH SCHOOL ORATORICAL CONTEST

• *See page 725*

AMERICAN LEGION DEPARTMENT OF INDIANA http://www.indlegion.org

AMERICAN LEGION DEPARTMENT OF INDIANA HIGH SCHOOL ORATORICAL CONTEST

• *See page 726*

FRANK W. MCHALE MEMORIAL SCHOLARSHIPS

• *See page 726*

AMERICAN LEGION DEPARTMENT OF IOWA http://www.ialegion.org

AMERICAN LEGION DEPARTMENT OF IOWA HIGH SCHOOL ORATORICAL CONTEST

• *See page 726*

AMERICAN LEGION DEPARTMENT OF IOWA OUTSTANDING SENIOR BASEBALL PLAYER

• *See page 726*

AMERICAN LEGION DEPARTMENT OF KANSAS http://www.ksamlegion.org

AMERICAN LEGION DEPARTMENT OF KANSAS HIGH SCHOOL ORATORICAL CONTEST

Awards a total of $2400 ($1500, $500, $250, and $150) in scholarships to the top four winners in each state. The state winner's school receives $500. The top three contestants in the nation are awarded scholarships totaling $48,000 ($18,000, $16,000, and $14,000).

Award: Prize for use in freshman year; not renewable. *Number:* 4. *Amount:* $150–$18,000.

Eligibility Requirements: Applicant must be high school student; planning to enroll or expecting to enroll full-time at a four-year institution or university and must have an interest in public speaking. Available to U.S. citizens.

Application Requirements: Application, applicant must enter a contest. *Deadline:* varies.

Contact: Ralph Snyder, Oratorical Contest Committee
American Legion Department of Kansas
1314 Topeka Boulevard, SW
Topeka, KS 66612
Phone: 785-232-9315
Fax: 785-232-1399

DR. CLICK COWGER BASEBALL SCHOLARSHIP
• *See page 726*

PAUL FLAHERTY ATHLETIC SCHOLARSHIP
• *See page 726*

AMERICAN LEGION DEPARTMENT OF MICHIGAN http://www.michiganlegion.org

AMERICAN LEGION DEPARTMENT OF MICHIGAN HIGH SCHOOL ORATORICAL CONTEST
• *See page 727*

AMERICAN LEGION DEPARTMENT OF MINNESOTA http://www.mnlegion.org

AMERICAN LEGION DEPARTMENT OF MINNESOTA HIGH SCHOOL ORATORICAL CONTEST
• *See page 727*

AMERICAN LEGION DEPARTMENT OF MONTANA http://www.mtlegion.org

AMERICAN LEGION DEPARTMENT OF MONTANA HIGH SCHOOL ORATORICAL CONTEST
• *See page 727*

AMERICAN LEGION DEPARTMENT OF NEBRASKA http://www.nebraskalegion.net

AMERICAN LEGION BASEBALL SCHOLARSHIP-NEBRASKA AMERICAN LEGION BASEBALL PLAYER OF THE YEAR
• *See page 728*

AMERICAN LEGION DEPARTMENT OF NEBRASKA HIGH SCHOOL ORATORICAL CONTEST
• *See page 728*

AMERICAN LEGION DEPARTMENT OF NEBRASKA JIM HURLBERT MEMORIAL BASEBALL SCHOLARSHIP
• *See page 728*

AMERICAN LEGION DEPARTMENT OF NEW JERSEY http://www.njamericanlegion.org

AMERICAN LEGION DEPARTMENT OF NEW JERSEY HIGH SCHOOL ORATORICAL CONTEST

Award to promote and coordinate the Oratorical Contest Program at the Department, District, County and Post Levels. High School Oratorical Contest is to develop a deeper knowledge and understanding of the constitution of the United States.

Award: Prize for use in freshman year; not renewable. *Number:* 5. *Amount:* $1000–$4000.

Eligibility Requirements: Applicant must be high school student; planning to enroll or expecting to enroll full-time at a four-year institution or university and must have an interest in public speaking. Available to U.S. citizens.

Application Requirements: Application, applicant must enter a contest. *Deadline:* March 8.

Contact: Raymond Zawacki, Department Adjutant
American Legion Department of New Jersey
135 West Hanover Street
Trenton, NJ 08618
Phone: 609-695-5418
Fax: 609-394-1532
E-mail: ray@njamericanlegion.org

AMERICAN LEGION DEPARTMENT OF NEW YORK http://www.ny.legion.org

AMERICAN LEGION DEPARTMENT OF NEW YORK HIGH SCHOOL ORATORICAL CONTEST
• *See page 728*

AMERICAN LEGION DEPARTMENT OF NORTH CAROLINA http://www.nclegion.org

AMERICAN LEGION DEPARTMENT OF NORTH CAROLINA HIGH SCHOOL ORATORICAL CONTEST
• *See page 728*

AMERICAN LEGION DEPARTMENT OF NORTH DAKOTA http://www.ndlegion.org

AMERICAN LEGION DEPARTMENT OF NORTH DAKOTA NATIONAL HIGH SCHOOL ORATORICAL CONTEST
• *See page 729*

AMERICAN LEGION DEPARTMENT OF OREGON

AMERICAN LEGION DEPARTMENT OF OREGON HIGH SCHOOL ORATORICAL CONTEST
• *See page 729*

AMERICAN LEGION DEPARTMENT OF PENNSYLVANIA http://www.pa-legion.com

AMERICAN LEGION DEPARTMENT OF PENNSYLVANIA HIGH SCHOOL ORATORICAL CONTEST
• *See page 729*

AMERICAN LEGION DEPARTMENT OF SOUTH DAKOTA http://www.sdlegion.org

AMERICAN LEGION DEPARTMENT OF SOUTH DAKOTA HIGH SCHOOL ORATORICAL CONTEST
• *See page 729*

AMERICAN LEGION DEPARTMENT OF TENNESSEE http://www.tennesseelegion.org

AMERICAN LEGION DEPARTMENT OF TENNESSEE HIGH SCHOOL ORATORICAL CONTEST
• *See page 730*

AMERICAN LEGION DEPARTMENT OF TEXAS http://www.txlegion.org

AMERICAN LEGION DEPARTMENT OF TEXAS HIGH SCHOOL ORATORICAL CONTEST
• *See page 730*

AMERICAN LEGION DEPARTMENT OF VERMONT http://www.legionvthq.com

AMERICAN LEGION DEPARTMENT OF VERMONT HIGH SCHOOL ORATORICAL CONTEST
• *See page 650*

AMERICAN LEGION DEPARTMENT OF WEST VIRGINIA http://www.wvlegion.org

AMERICAN LEGION DEPARTMENT OF WEST VIRGINIA BOARD OF REGENTS SCHOLARSHIP
• *See page 730*

AMERICAN LEGION DEPARTMENT OF WEST VIRGINIA HIGH SCHOOL ORATORICAL CONTEST
• *See page 731*

AMERICAN LEGION NATIONAL HEADQUARTERS http://www.legion.org

AMERICAN LEGION NATIONAL HIGH SCHOOL ORATORICAL CONTEST

Scholarship up to $18,000 will be presented to the 3 finalists in the final round of the national contest. Students currently in high school are eligible to apply for this contest.

Award: Scholarship for use in freshman, sophomore, junior, senior, or graduate years; not renewable. *Number:* 54. *Amount:* $1500–$18,000.

Eligibility Requirements: Applicant must be enrolled or expecting to enroll full-time at a two-year or four-year institution or university and must have an interest in public speaking. Available to U.S. citizens.

Application Requirements: Application. *Deadline:* December 1.

Contact: Robert Caudell, Assistant Director
American Legion National Headquarters
PO Box 1055
Indianapolis, IN 46206-1055
Phone: 317-630-1212
Fax: 317-630-1369
E-mail: rcaudell@legion.org

AMERICAN MORGAN HORSE INSTITUTE http://www.morganhorse.com

AMERICAN MORGAN HORSE INSTITUTE EDUCATIONAL SCHOLARSHIPS

Selection is based on the ability and aptitude for serious study, community service, leadership, and financial need. Must be actively involved with registered Morgan Horses Association. Application deadline varies every year. For information and application go to http://www.morganhorse.com.

Award: Scholarship for use in freshman year; not renewable. *Number:* 5. *Amount:* $3000.

Eligibility Requirements: Applicant must be enrolled or expecting to enroll full- or part-time at a two-year or four-year or technical institution or university and must have an interest in animal/agricultural competition. Available to U.S. and non-U.S. citizens.

Application Requirements: Application, essay, photo, references, transcript. *Deadline:* varies.

Contact: Sally Wadhams, Development Officer
American Morgan Horse Institute
122 Bostwick Road
PO Box 837
Shelburne, VT 05482-0519
Phone: 802-985-8477
Fax: 802-985-8430
E-mail: amhioffice@aol.com

AMERICAN MORGAN HORSE INSTITUTE GRAND PRIX DRESSAGE AWARD

Award available to riders of registered Morgan horses who reach a certain proficiency at the Grand Prix dressage level. For information and application go to http://www.morganhorse.com. The application deadline varies every year.

Award: Scholarship for use in freshman, sophomore, junior, senior, graduate, or postgraduate years; not renewable. *Number:* 1. *Amount:* $2500.

Eligibility Requirements: Applicant must be enrolled or expecting to enroll full- or part-time at a two-year or four-year or technical institution or university and must have an interest in animal/agricultural competition. Available to U.S. and non-U.S. citizens.

Application Requirements: Application, essay, photo, references, transcript, copy of horse's USDF report. *Deadline:* varies.

Contact: Sally Wadhams, Development Officer
American Morgan Horse Institute
122 Bostwick Road
PO Box 837
Shelburne, VT 05482-0519
Phone: 802-985-8477
Fax: 802-985-8430
E-mail: amhioffice@aol.com

AMERICAN MORGAN HORSE INSTITUTE GRAYWOOD YOUTH HORSEMANSHIP GRANT

Provides a youth who is an active member of the American Morgan Horse Association (AMHA) or an AMHA youth group with the opportunity to further his/her practical study of Morgan horses. For information and application go to http://www.morganhorse.com.

Award: Grant for use in freshman year; not renewable. *Number:* up to 2. *Amount:* $250–$500.

Eligibility Requirements: Applicant must be age 13-21; enrolled or expecting to enroll full- or part-time at a two-year or four-year or technical institution or university and must have an interest in animal/agricultural competition. Available to U.S. and non-U.S. citizens.

Application Requirements: Application, essay, photo, references, transcript. *Deadline:* February 1.

Contact: Sally Wadhams, Development Officer
American Morgan Horse Institute
122 Bostwick Road
PO Box 837
Shelburne, VT 05482-0519
Phone: 802-985-8477
Fax: 802-985-8430
E-mail: amhioffice@aol.com

AMERICAN MORGAN HORSE INSTITUTE VAN SCHAIK DRESSAGE SCHOLARSHIP

Awarded to an individual wishing to further their proficiency in classically ridden dressage on a registered Morgan horse. For information and application go to http://www.morganhorse.com.

Award: Scholarship for use in freshman, sophomore, junior, senior, graduate, or postgraduate years; not renewable. *Number:* 1. *Amount:* $1000.

Eligibility Requirements: Applicant must be enrolled or expecting to enroll full- or part-time at a two-year or four-year or technical institution or university and must have an interest in animal/agricultural competition. Available to U.S. and non-U.S. citizens.

Application Requirements: Application, essay, photo, references, narrative. *Deadline:* February 1.

Contact: Sally Wadhams, Development Officer
American Morgan Horse Institute
122 Bostwick Road
PO Box 837
Shelburne, VT 05482-0519
Phone: 802-985-8477
Fax: 802-985-8430
E-mail: amhioffice@aol.com

AMERICAN MUSEUM OF NATURAL HISTORY http://www.research.amnh.org

YOUNG NATURALIST AWARDS

Essay contest open to students in grades 7-12 who are currently enrolled in a public, private, parochial, or home school in the United States, Canada, the U.S. territories, or a U.S.-sponsored school abroad. Essays must be based on an original scientific investigation conducted by the student. See Web site for guidelines: http://www.amnh.org/nationalcenter/youngnaturalistawards/read.html

Award: Prize for use in freshman year; not renewable. *Number:* 1. *Amount:* varies.

Eligibility Requirements: Applicant must be high school student; planning to enroll or expecting to enroll part-time at a four-year institution or university and must have an interest in writing. Available to Canadian citizens.

Application Requirements: Application, essay, photo. *Deadline:* March 1.

Contact: Maria Dickson, Manager, Fellowships
American Museum of Natural History
Central Park West, 79th Street
New York, NY 10024-5192
Phone: 212-769-5017
Fax: 212-769-5257
E-mail: grants@amnh.org

AMERICAN NATIONAL CATTLE WOMEN INC. http://www.nationalbeefambassador.org

NATIONAL BEEF AMBASSADOR PROGRAM

Award's purpose is to train young spokespersons in the beef industry. Applicant must be fully prepared to answer questions and debate focusing on topic related to beef consumption and distribution, as well as social factors related to the industry. The prize value is from $500 to $2500. Details and tools for preparation are available on the Web site: http://www.ancw.org.

Award: Prize for use in freshman, sophomore, junior, or senior years; not renewable. *Number:* 1–3. *Amount:* $500–$2500.

Eligibility Requirements: Applicant must be age 17-20; enrolled or expecting to enroll full- or part-time at a two-year or four-year institution or university and must have an interest in public speaking. Available to U.S. citizens.

Application Requirements: Applicant must enter a contest, interview. *Deadline:* varies.

Contact: Carol Abrahamzon, Project Manager
American National Cattle Women Inc.
PO Box 3881
Englewood, CO 80155
E-mail: cabrahamzon@beef.org

AMERICAN QUARTER HORSE FOUNDATION (AQHF) http://www.aqha.com/foundation

DR. GERALD O'CONNOR MICHIGAN SCHOLARSHIP

• *See page 522*

SWAYZE WOODRUFF MEMORIAL MID-SOUTH SCHOLARSHIP

• *See page 524*

AMERICAN SHEEP INDUSTRY ASSOCIATION/ NATIONAL MAKE IT YOURSELF WITH WOOL http://www.sheepusa.org

NATIONAL "MAKE IT WITH WOOL" COMPETITION

Awards available for entrants ages 13 to 24 years. Must enter at state level with home-constructed garment of at least 60 percent wool. Applicant must model garment. Entry fee is $10.

Award: Prize for use in freshman, sophomore, junior, senior, or graduate years; not renewable. *Number:* 2–4. *Amount:* up to $1000.

Eligibility Requirements: Applicant must be age 13-24; enrolled or expecting to enroll full- or part-time at a two-year or four-year or technical institution or university and must have an interest in sewing. Available to U.S. citizens.

Application Requirements: Application, applicant must enter a contest, self-addressed stamped envelope, sample of fabric (5x5). *Fee:* $10. *Deadline:* November 1.

Contact: Marie Lehfeldt, Coordinator
American Sheep Industry Association/National Make It Yourself With Wool
PO Box 175
Lavina, MT 59046
Phone: 406-636-2731
Fax: 406-636-2731

AMERICAN STRING TEACHERS ASSOCIATION http://www.astaweb.com

NATIONAL SOLO COMPETITION

Twenty-six individual awards. Instrument categories are violin, viola, cello, double bass, classical guitar, and harp. Applicants competing in Junior Division must be under age 19. Senior Division competitors must be ages 19 to 25. Application fee is $75. Visit Web site for application forms. Applicant must be a member of ASTA.

Award: Prize for use in freshman, sophomore, junior, senior, or graduate years; not renewable. *Number:* 26. *Amount:* varies.

Eligibility Requirements: Applicant must be age 19-25; enrolled or expecting to enroll full- or part-time at a two-year or four-year or technical institution or university and must have an interest in music. Available to U.S. and Canadian citizens.

Application Requirements: Application, applicant must enter a contest, proof of age, proof of membership. *Fee:* $75. *Deadline:* varies.

Contact: Laura Kobayashi, Committee Chair
American String Teachers Association
4153 Chain Bridge Road
Fairfax, VA 22030
Phone: 703-279-2113
Fax: 703-279-2114
E-mail: lkobayas@myway.com

AMERICAN SWEDISH INSTITUTE http://www.americanswedishinst.org

LILLY LORENZEN SCHOLARSHIP

• *See page 731*

MALMBERG SCHOLARSHIP FOR STUDY IN SWEDEN

Award for a U.S. resident interested in Sweden and Swedish America. Applicant must be either a student enrolled in a degree-granting program at an accredited college or university, or a qualified scholar engaged in study or research whose work can be enhanced by study in Sweden. Scholarships are usually granted for a full academic year term (nine months), but can be for study periods of shorter duration.

Award: Scholarship for use in senior, graduate, or postgraduate years; not renewable. *Number:* up to 1. *Amount:* up to $10,000.

Eligibility Requirements: Applicant must be age 18 and over; enrolled or expecting to enroll full-time at a four-year institution or university and must have an interest in Scandinavian language. Available to U.S. citizens.

Application Requirements: Application, essay, resume, references, letter of invitation from host institution. *Deadline:* November 15.

Contact: Nina Clark, Education Programs Coordinator
American Swedish Institute
2600 Park Avenue
Minneapolis, MN 55104
Phone: 612-871-3374
Fax: 612-871-8682
E-mail: ninac@americanswedishinst.org

AMERICAN THEATRE ORGAN SOCIETY INC. http://www.atos.org

AMERICAN THEATRE ORGAN SOCIETY ORGAN PERFORMANCE SCHOLARSHIP

Renewable awards available to students between the ages of 13 to 27. Must have a talent in music and have an interest in theater organ performance studies (not for general music studies). There are two categories for this scholarship Category A: Organ students studying with professional theatre organ instructors. Category B: Theatre organ students furthering their musical education by working toward a college organ performance degree.

Award: Scholarship for use in freshman, sophomore, junior, or senior years; renewable. *Number:* 11. *Amount:* $500–$1000.

Eligibility Requirements: Applicant must be age 13-27; enrolled or expecting to enroll full- or part-time at a four-year institution or university and must have an interest in music. Available to U.S. and non-U.S. citizens.

Application Requirements: Application, essay. *Deadline:* April 15.

Contact: Carlton B. Smith, Chairperson, Scholarship Program
American Theatre Organ Society Inc.
2175 North Irwin Street
Indianapolis, IN 46219-2220
Phone: 317-356-1270
Fax: 317-322-9379
E-mail: smith@atos.org

AMERICAN WATER SKI EDUCATIONAL FOUNDATION http://www.waterskihalloffame.com

AMERICAN WATER SKI EDUCATIONAL FOUNDATION SCHOLARSHIP

• *See page 524*

AMERICA'S JUNIOR MISS SCHOLARSHIP PROGRAM http://www.ajm.org

AMERICA'S JUNIOR MISS SCHOLARSHIP PROGRAM

Awards are given to contestants in local, regional, and national levels of competition. Must be female, high school juniors or seniors, U.S. citizens, and legal residents of the county and state of competition. Contestants are evaluated on scholastic, interview, talent, fitness, and poise. The number of awards and their amount vary from year to year.

Award: Scholarship for use in freshman year; not renewable. *Number:* varies. *Amount:* varies.

Eligibility Requirements: Applicant must be high school student; age 16-18; planning to enroll or expecting to enroll full-time at a two-year or four-year institution or university; single female and must have an interest in beauty pageant. Available to U.S. citizens.

Application Requirements: Application, applicant must enter a contest, test scores, transcript, birth certificate, certificate of health. *Deadline:* varies.

Contact: National Field Director
America's Junior Miss Scholarship Program
751 Government Street
Mobile, AL 36602
Phone: 251-438-3621
Fax: 251-431-0063
E-mail: nicole@ajm.org

APPALACHIAN CENTER AND APPALACHIAN STUDIES ASSOCIATION http://www.appalachianstudies.org

WEATHERFORD AWARD

One-time award given to the best work of fiction, non-fiction, book, poetry, or short piece about the Appalachian South published in the most recent calendar year. Two awards will be given: one for non-fiction; one for fiction and poetry. Seven copies of the nominated work must be sent to the chair of the award committee.

Award: Prize for use in freshman, sophomore, junior, senior, graduate, or postgraduate years; not renewable. *Number:* 2. *Amount:* up to $500.

Eligibility Requirements: Applicant must be enrolled or expecting to enroll full- or part-time at a two-year or four-year or technical institution or university and must have an interest in writing. Available to U.S. and non-U.S. citizens.

Application Requirements: Application, nomination, 7 copies of the book. *Deadline:* December 31.

Contact: Gordon McKinney, Chair, Award Committee
Appalachian Center and Appalachian Studies Association
PO Box 2166
Berea, KY 40404
Phone: 859-985-3000
Fax: 859-985-3642
E-mail: gordon_mckinney@berea.edu

APPALOOSA HORSE CLUB-APPALOOSA YOUTH PROGRAM http://www.appaloosa.com

APPALOOSA YOUTH EDUCATIONAL SCHOLARSHIPS

• *See page 524*

ARIZONA HIGHER EDUCATION LOAN AUTHORITY http://www.ahela.org

AHELA COMMUNITY LEADERS SCHOLARSHIP

• *See page 590*

ARRL FOUNDATION INC. http://www.arrl.org

ALBERT H. HIX W8AH MEMORIAL SCHOLARSHIP

• *See page 733*

ALBUQUERQUE AMATEUR RADIO CLUB/TOBY CROSS SCHOLARSHIP

• *See page 734*

ARRL FOUNDATION GENERAL FUND SCHOLARSHIPS

Available to students who are amateur radio operators. Students can be licensed in any class of operators. Nonrenewable award for use in undergraduate years. Multiple awards per year..

Award: Scholarship for use in freshman, sophomore, junior, or senior years; not renewable. *Number:* varies. *Amount:* $1000.

Eligibility Requirements: Applicant must be enrolled or expecting to enroll full-time at a four-year institution or university and must have an interest in amateur radio. Available to U.S. citizens.

Application Requirements: Application, transcript. *Deadline:* February 1.

Contact: Mary M. Hobart, Secretary
ARRL Foundation Inc.
225 Main Street
Newington, CT 06111-1494
Phone: 860-594-0397
Fax: 860-594-0259
E-mail: k1mmh@arrl.org

CENTRAL ARIZONA DX ASSOCIATION SCHOLARSHIP

• *See page 734*

CHARLES CLARKE CORDLE MEMORIAL SCHOLARSHIP

• *See page 734*

CHICAGO FM CLUB SCHOLARSHIPS

• *See page 734*

FRANCIS WALTON MEMORIAL SCHOLARSHIP

• *See page 734*

IRARC MEMORIAL JOSEPH P. RUBINO WA4MMD SCHOLARSHIP

• *See page 525*

K2TEO MARTIN J. GREEN SR. MEMORIAL SCHOLARSHIP

Available to students with a general amateur license for radio operation. Preference given to students from a ham family. Nonrenewable award for use in undergraduate years.

Award: Scholarship for use in freshman, sophomore, junior, or senior years; not renewable. *Number:* 1. *Amount:* $1000.

Eligibility Requirements: Applicant must be enrolled or expecting to enroll full-time at a four-year institution or university and must have an interest in amateur radio. Available to U.S. citizens.

Application Requirements: Application, transcript. *Deadline:* February 1.

Contact: Mary M. Hobart, Secretary
ARRL Foundation Inc.
225 Main Street
Newington, CT 06111-1494
Phone: 860-594-0397
Fax: 860-594-0259
E-mail: k1mmh@arrl.org

MARY LOU BROWN SCHOLARSHIP

• *See page 734*

NEW ENGLAND FEMARA SCHOLARSHIPS

• *See page 735*

SIX METER CLUB OF CHICAGO SCHOLARSHIP

• *See page 735*

TOM AND JUDITH COMSTOCK SCHOLARSHIP

• *See page 735*

YANKEE CLIPPER CONTEST CLUB INC. YOUTH SCHOLARSHIP

• *See page 735*

YOU'VE GOT A FRIEND IN PENNSYLVANIA SCHOLARSHIP

• *See page 525*

ARTIST-BLACKSMITH'S ASSOCIATION OF NORTH AMERICA INC. http://www.abana.org

ARTIST'S-BLACKSMITH'S ASSOCIATION OF NORTH AMERICA INC AFFILIATE VISITING ARTIST GRANT PROGRAM

Grant provide financial support to ABANA Affiliates sponsoring visiting artists for educational purposes such as conferences or workshops. Deadlines: January 2, April 1, July 1 or October 1.

Award: Grant for use in freshman, sophomore, junior, senior, graduate, or postgraduate years; not renewable. *Number:* 8. *Amount:* $600.

Eligibility Requirements: Applicant must be enrolled or expecting to enroll part-time at a two-year or four-year or technical institution or university and must have an interest in art. Available to U.S. and non-U.S. citizens.

Application Requirements: Application, essay, financial need analysis, photo, resume. *Deadline:* varies.

Contact: Heather Hutton, Central Office Administrator
Artist-Blacksmith's Association of North America Inc.
PO Box 3425
Knoxville, TN 37927-3425
Phone: 865-546-7733
Fax: 865-546-9964
E-mail: abana@abana.org

AUTHOR SERVICES INC. http://www.writersofthefuture.com

L. RON HUBBARD'S ILLUSTRATORS OF THE FUTURE CONTEST

An ongoing competition for new and amateur artists judged by professional artists. Eligible submissions consist of three science fiction or fantasy illustrations. Prize amount ranges from $500 to $5000. Quarterly deadlines: December 31, March 31, June 30 and September 30. All entrants retain rights to artwork.

Award: Prize for use in freshman, sophomore, junior, senior, graduate, or postgraduate years; not renewable. *Number:* up to 12. *Amount:* $500–$5000.

Eligibility Requirements: Applicant must be enrolled or expecting to enroll full- or part-time at a two-year or four-year or technical institution or university and must have an interest in art. Available to U.S. and non-U.S. citizens.

Application Requirements: Applicant must enter a contest, self-addressed stamped envelope, 3 illustrations. *Deadline:* varies.

Contact: Contest Administrator
Author Services Inc.
PO Box 3190
Los Angeles, CA 90078
Phone: 323-466-3310
Fax: 323-466-6474
E-mail: contests@authorservicesinc.com

L. RON HUBBARD'S WRITERS OF THE FUTURE CONTEST

An ongoing competition for new and amateur writers judged by professional writers. Eligible submissions are short stories and novelettes of science fiction or fantasy. Deadline varies and prize amount ranges from $500 to $5000.

Award: Prize for use in freshman, sophomore, junior, senior, graduate, or postgraduate years; not renewable. *Number:* up to 12. *Amount:* $500–$5000.

Eligibility Requirements: Applicant must be enrolled or expecting to enroll full- or part-time at a two-year or four-year or technical institution or university and must have an interest in writing. Available to U.S. and non-U.S. citizens.

Application Requirements: Applicant must enter a contest, self-addressed stamped envelope, copy of the manuscript. *Deadline:* varies.

Contact: Contest Administrator
Author Services Inc.
PO Box 1630
Los Angeles, CA 90078
Phone: 323-466-3310
Fax: 323-466-6474
E-mail: contests@authorservicesinc.com

AYN RAND INSTITUTE http://www.aynrand.org

ANNUAL ESSAY CONTEST ON AYN RAND'S "ATLAS SHRUGGED"

Forty-nine awards totaling $114,000 for essays demonstrating an outstanding grasp of the philosophical meaning of "Atlas Shrugged." Students must be enrolled in either an undergraduate or graduate program at the time of submission. Essays should be between 1,000 to 1,200 words in length. Winners will be announced on November 27. For complete rules and guidelines, visit Web site: www.aynrand.org/contests.

Award: Prize for use in freshman, sophomore, junior, senior, graduate, or postgraduate years; not renewable. *Number:* 49. *Amount:* $50–$10,000.

Eligibility Requirements: Applicant must be enrolled or expecting to enroll full- or part-time at a two-year or four-year or technical institution or university and must have an interest in writing. Available to U.S. and non-U.S. citizens.

Application Requirements: Applicant must enter a contest, essay. *Deadline:* September 17.

Contact: Meg Sullivan, Essay Contest Coordinator
Ayn Rand Institute
2121 Alton Parkway, Suite 250
Irvine, CA 92606-4926
Phone: 949-222-6550 Ext. 247
Fax: 949-222-6558
E-mail: essay@aynrand.org

ANNUAL ESSAY CONTEST ON AYN RAND'S NOVELETTE, "ANTHEM"

Entrant must be in the 9th or 10th grade. Essays will be judged on both style and content. Winning essays must demonstrate an outstanding grasp of the philosophical meaning of Ayn Rand's novelette, "Anthem." For complete rules and guidelines visit Web site: http://www.aynrand.org/contests.

Award: Prize for use in freshman or sophomore years; not renewable. *Number:* 235. *Amount:* $30–$2000.

Eligibility Requirements: Applicant must be high school student; planning to enroll or expecting to enroll full- or part-time at a four-year institution or university and must have an interest in writing. Available to U.S. and non-U.S. citizens.

Application Requirements: Applicant must enter a contest, essay. *Deadline:* March 20.

Contact: Meg Sullivan, Essay Contest Coordinator
Ayn Rand Institute
2121 Alton Parkway, Suite 250
Irvine, CA 92606-4926
Phone: 949-222-6550 Ext. 247
Fax: 949-222-6558
E-mail: essay@aynrand.org

ANNUAL ESSAY CONTEST ON AYN RAND'S NOVEL, "THE FOUNTAINHEAD"

Prizes totaling $43,500 awarded to 11th and 12th grades for essays on Ayn Rand's novel "The Fountainhead". Essays should be between 800 and 1600 words. For complete rules and guidelines, refer to Web site: http://www.aynrand.org/contests.

Award: Prize for use in freshman year; not renewable. *Number:* 235. *Amount:* $50–$10,000.

Eligibility Requirements: Applicant must be high school student; planning to enroll or expecting to enroll full- or part-time at a four-year institution or university and must have an interest in writing. Available to U.S. and non-U.S. citizens.

Application Requirements: Applicant must enter a contest, essay. *Deadline:* April 25.

Contact: Meg Sullivan, Essay Contest Coordinator
Ayn Rand Institute
2121 Alton Parkway, Suite 250
Irvine, CA 92606-4926
Phone: 949-222-6550 Ext. 247
Fax: 949-222-6558
E-mail: essay@aynrand.org

BABE RUTH LEAGUE. INC. http://www.baberuthleague.org

BABE RUTH SCHOLARSHIP PROGRAM

Program to provide assistance to individuals who plan on furthering their education beyond high school. Outstanding student athletes will receive $1000 each towards their college tuition.

Award: Scholarship for use in freshman year; not renewable. *Number:* 1. *Amount:* $1000.

Eligibility Requirements: Applicant must be high school student; planning to enroll or expecting to enroll full- or part-time at a four-year institution or university and must have an interest in athletics/sports. Available to U.S. citizens.

Application Requirements: Application, references, transcript. *Deadline:* September 1.

Contact: Rosemary Schoellkopf, Scholarship Committee
Babe Ruth League. Inc.
1770 Brunswick Pike
PO Box 5000
Trenton, NJ 08638
Phone: 800-880-3142
Fax: 609-695-2505
E-mail: info@baberuthleague.org

BILL DICKEY SCHOLARSHIP ASSOCIATION http://www.nmjgsa.org

BDSA SCHOLARSHIPS

One-time and renewable awards available. Awards are based on academic achievement, entrance exam scores, financial need, references, evidence of community service, and golfing ability. High school seniors or younger who are not already in the association's database may see Web site to enter profile for eligibility, and for application.

Award: Scholarship for use in freshman year; renewable. *Number:* varies. *Amount:* $1000.

Eligibility Requirements: Applicant must be high school student; planning to enroll or expecting to enroll full- or part-time at a four-year institution or university and must have an interest in golf. Available to U.S. citizens.

Application Requirements: Application, financial need analysis, references. *Deadline:* April 21.

Contact: Andrea Bourdeaux, Executive Director
Bill Dickey Scholarship Association
1140 East Washington Street, Suite 103
Phoenix, AZ 85034
Phone: 602-258-7851
Fax: 602-258-3412
E-mail: andrea@bdscholar.org

BOETTCHER FOUNDATION http://www.boettcherfoundation.org

BOETTCHER FOUNDATION SCHOLARSHIPS

• *See page 590*

BOOKS AND SCHOLARSHIPS http://www.booksandscholarships.com

ELWOOD GRIMES LITERARY SCHOLARSHIP

Literary scholarship available to students attending an accredited four-year college or university in the U.S. at least half-time. Must submit an essay of less than 500 words on the book specified on the scholarship Web site: http://www.booksandscholarships.com

Award: Scholarship for use in freshman, sophomore, junior, senior, or graduate years; not renewable. *Number:* 3. *Amount:* $1000–$5000.

Eligibility Requirements: Applicant must be enrolled or expecting to enroll full- or part-time at a four-year institution or university and must have an interest in writing. Available to U.S. citizens.

Application Requirements: Application, applicant must enter a contest, essay, transcript. *Deadline:* September 30.

Contact: Gary Grimes, Scholarship Administrator
Books and Scholarships
4525 Cherry Forest Circle
Louisville, KY 40245
E-mail: gcgrimes@bellsouth.net

BOYS AND GIRLS CLUBS OF AMERICA http://www.bgca.org

BOYS AND GIRLS CLUBS OF AMERICA NATIONAL YOUTH OF THE YEAR AWARD

• *See page 525*

CALIFORNIA JUNIOR MISS SCHOLARSHIP PROGRAM http://www.ajm.org

CALIFORNIA JUNIOR MISS SCHOLARSHIP PROGRAM

• *See page 737*

CANADA ICELAND FOUNDATION INC. SCHOLARSHIPS http://www.logberg.com

CANADA ICELAND FOUNDATION SCHOLARSHIP PROGRAM

• *See page 738*

CAP FOUNDATION http://www.ronbrown.org

RON BROWN SCHOLAR PROGRAM

• *See page 592*

CAREER COLLEGES AND SCHOOLS OF TEXAS http://www.colleges-schools.org

CAREER COLLEGES AND SCHOOLS OF TEXAS SCHOLARSHIP PROGRAM

• *See page 738*

CARGILL http://www.cargill.com

CARGILL COMMUNITY SCHOLARSHIP PROGRAM

One-time scholarships administered by the National FFA Organization. Each award is valued at $1000, and also enables the recipient's high school to become eligible for a $200 library grant. Award based upon academic performance and leadership in school and community activities. Applicants must be U.S. high school students who live in or near Cargill communities. Students are required to obtain a signature on their applications from a employee at a local Cargill facility or subsidiary.

Award: Scholarship for use in freshman year; not renewable. *Number:* 350. *Amount:* $1000.

Eligibility Requirements: Applicant must be high school student; planning to enroll or expecting to enroll full-time at a two-year or four-year institution or university and must have an interest in leadership. Available to U.S. citizens.

Application Requirements: Application. *Deadline:* February 15.

Contact: Rebecca Oswald, Community Relations Associate
Cargill
PO Box 9300
Minneapolis, MN 55440-9300
Phone: 952-742-6247
Fax: 952-742-7224
E-mail: cargill_scholarships@cargill.com

CARMEL MUSIC SOCIETY http://www.carmelmusic.org

CARMEL MUSIC SOCIETY COMPETITION

• *See page 738*

CENTER FOR LESBIAN AND GAY STUDIES (C.L.A.G.S.) http://www.clags.org

SYLVIA RIVERA AWARD IN TRANSGENDER STUDIES

Award given for the best book or article to appear on transgender studies during the current year. Applications may be submitted by the author or by nomination.

Award: Prize for use in freshman, sophomore, junior, senior, graduate, or postgraduate years; not renewable. *Number:* 1. *Amount:* $1000.

Eligibility Requirements: Applicant must be enrolled or expecting to enroll full- or part-time at a two-year or four-year institution or university and must have an interest in LGBT issues or writing. Available to U.S. and non-U.S. citizens.

Application Requirements: Application, 6 copies of the article or 6 copies of the first chapter or first 20 pages for books, cover sheet, details about the publication, contact details. *Deadline:* June 1.

Contact: Naz Qazi, Fellowship Membership Coordinator
Center for Lesbian and Gay Studies (C.L.A.G.S.)
365 Fifth Avenue, Room 7115
New York, NY 10016
Phone: 212-817-1955
Fax: 212-817-1567
E-mail: clags@gc.cuny.edu

CENTER FOR SCHOLARSHIP ADMINISTRATION http://www.scholarshipprograms.org

SOUTH CAROLINA JUNIOR GOLF FOUNDATION SCHOLARSHIP

• *See page 738*

CHRISTOPHERS http://www.christophers.org

POSTER CONTEST FOR HIGH SCHOOL STUDENTS

Contest invites students in grades nine through twelve to interpret the theme: "You can make a difference." Posters must include this statement and illustrate the idea that one person can change the world for the better. Judging is based on overall impact, content, originality and artistic merit. More information can be found at http://www.christophers.org.

Award: Prize for use in freshman year; not renewable. *Number:* up to 8. *Amount:* $100–$1000.

Eligibility Requirements: Applicant must be high school student; planning to enroll or expecting to enroll full- or part-time at a four-year institution or university and must have an interest in art. Available to U.S. and non-U.S. citizens.

Application Requirements: Application, applicant must enter a contest, poster. *Deadline:* January 8.

Contact: David Dicerto, Youth Coordinator
Christophers
5 Hanover Square, 11th Floor
New York, NY 10014
Phone: 212-759-4050
Fax: 212-838-5073
E-mail: youth@christophers.org

VIDEO CONTEST FOR COLLEGE STUDENTS

Contest requires college students to use any style or format to express the following theme: "One person can make a difference." Entries can be up to 5 minutes in length and must be submitted in standard, full-sized VHS format. Entries will be judged on content, artistic and technical proficiency, and adherence to contest rules. More information is available at http://www.christophers.org.

Award: Prize for use in freshman, sophomore, junior, senior, or graduate years; not renewable. *Number:* 8. *Amount:* $100–$3000.

Eligibility Requirements: Applicant must be enrolled or expecting to enroll full- or part-time at a two-year or four-year or technical institution or university and must have an interest in art. Available to U.S. and non-U.S. citizens.

Application Requirements: Application, applicant must enter a contest, VHS tape or DVD. *Deadline:* June 6.

Contact: David Dicerto, Youth Coordinator
Christophers
5 Hanover Square, 11th Floor
New York, NY 10014
Phone: 212-759-4050
Fax: 212-838-5073
E-mail: youth@christophers.org

COCA-COLA SCHOLARS FOUNDATION INC. http://www.coca-colascholars.org

COCA-COLA TWO-YEAR COLLEGES SCHOLARSHIP

• *See page 593*

C.O.L.A.G.E. (CHILDREN OF LESBIANS AND GAYS EVERYWHERE) http://www.colage.org

LEE DUBIN SCHOLARSHIP FUND

The scholarship is available to the sons and daughters of LGBT parents attending college, who have a demonstrated ability in and commitment to affecting change in the LGBT community, including working against homophobia, and increasing positive awareness of LGBT families. Must maintain a minimum GPA of 2.0.

Award: Scholarship for use in freshman, sophomore, junior, or senior years; renewable. *Number:* 3–5. *Amount:* $500–$1000.

Eligibility Requirements: Applicant must be enrolled or expecting to enroll full- or part-time at a two-year or four-year or technical institution or university and must have an interest in leadership or LGBT issues. Available to U.S. citizens.

Application Requirements: Application, essay, financial need analysis, transcript, proof of enrollment. *Deadline:* April 20.

Contact: Scholarship Committee
C.O.L.A.G.E. (Children of Lesbians and Gays Everywhere)
1550 Bryant Street, Suite 830
San Francisco, CA 94103
Phone: 415-861-5437
E-mail: colage@colage.org

COLLEGEBOUND FOUNDATION http://www.collegeboundfoundation.org

HY ZOLET STUDENT ATHLETE SCHOLARSHIP

• *See page 741*

COLLEGEFINANCIALAIDINFORMATION.COM http://www.easyaid.com

FRANK O'NEILL MEMORIAL SCHOLARSHIP

One-time award available to applicants attending or aspiring to attend a university, college, trade school, technical institute, vocational training, or other postsecondary education program. Must submit essay explaining educational goals and financial need.

Award: Scholarship for use in freshman, sophomore, junior, senior, or graduate years; not renewable. *Number:* 2. *Amount:* $1000.

Eligibility Requirements: Applicant must be enrolled or expecting to enroll full- or part-time at a two-year or four-year or technical institution or university and must have an interest in writing. Available to U.S. and non-U.S. citizens.

Application Requirements: Application, essay. *Deadline:* December 31.

Contact: Geoff Anderla, Owner
CollegeFinancialAidInformation.com
11200 West Wisconsin Avenue, Suite 9
Youngtown, AZ 85363
Phone: 623-972-4282
E-mail: questions@easyaid.com

COLLEGE FOUNDATION OF NORTH CAROLINA INC. http://www.cfnc.org

LATINO DIAMANTE SCHOLARSHIP FUND

• *See page 594*

COLLEGE IN COLORADO http://www.collegeincolorado.org

COLORADO SPORTS HALL OF FAME SCHOLARSHIP

• *See page 744*

COLLEGEWEEKLIVE.COM http://www.collegeweeklive.com

COLLEGEWEEKLIVE.COM SCHOLARSHIP

$1500 scholarship to high school students demonstrating excellence in writing ability, creativity and originality.

CollegeWeekLive.com (continued)

Award: Scholarship for use in freshman year; not renewable. *Number:* up to 3. *Amount:* $1500.

Eligibility Requirements: Applicant must be high school student; planning to enroll or expecting to enroll full- or part-time at a two-year or four-year or technical institution or university and must have an interest in writing. Available to U.S. citizens.

Application Requirements: Application, essay. *Deadline:* varies.

Contact: Lori Grandstaff, Scholarship Management Coordinator
CollegeWeekLive.com
2950 Halcyon Lane, Suite 501
Jacksonville, FL 32223
Phone: 904-854-6750 Ext. 11
Fax: 904-854-6751
E-mail: lori@scholarshipexperts.com

COLORADO STATE GRANGE LEADERSHIP AND SCHOLARSHIP FOUNDATION http://www.coloradogrange.org

COLORADO STATE GRANGE SCHOLARSHIPS

• *See page 528*

COLUMBIA 300 http://www.columbia300.com

COLUMBIA 300 JOHN JOWDY SCHOLARSHIP

Renewable scholarship for graduating high school seniors who are actively involved in the sport of bowling. Must have minimum GPA of 3.0.

Award: Scholarship for use in freshman year; renewable. *Number:* 1. *Amount:* $500.

Eligibility Requirements: Applicant must be high school student; planning to enroll or expecting to enroll full- or part-time at a four-year institution or university and must have an interest in bowling. Applicant must have 3.0 GPA or higher. Available to U.S. citizens.

Application Requirements: Application. *Deadline:* April 1.

Contact: Dale Garner, Scholarship Committee
Columbia 300
PO Box 13430
San Antonio, TX 78213
Phone: 800-531-5920

COLUMBIA UNIVERSITY, DEPARTMENT OF MUSIC http://www.music.columbia.edu

JOSEPH H. BEARNS PRIZE IN MUSIC

This prize is open to U.S. citizens between 18 and 25 years of age on January 1st of the competition year, and offers prizes for both short form and long form works of music in order to encourage talented young composers.

Award: Prize for use in freshman, sophomore, junior, or senior years; renewable. *Number:* 2. *Amount:* $2000–$3000.

Eligibility Requirements: Applicant must be age 18-25; enrolled or expecting to enroll full- or part-time at a two-year or four-year or technical institution or university and must have an interest in music. Available to U.S. citizens.

Application Requirements: Applicant must enter a contest, self-addressed stamped envelope, music score, information regarding prior studies, social security number. *Deadline:* March 17.

Contact: Department, Music
Columbia University, Department of Music
621 Dodge Hall, MC No. 1813, 2960 Broadway
New York, NY 10027
Phone: 212-854-3825
Fax: 212-854-8191

COMMERCE BANK http://www.commerceonline.com

AMERICAN DREAM SCHOLARSHIPS

• *See page 594*

CONCERT ARTISTS GUILD http://www.concertartists.org

CONCERT ARTISTS GUILD COMPETITION

• *See page 595*

CONCORD REVIEW http://www.tcr.org

RALPH WALDO EMERSON PRIZE

Prize awarded to high school students who have submitted an essay to the journal. Essay must be between 4,000 to 6,000 words with Turabian endnotes and bibliography. Pages must not be formatted. Essay may focus on any historical topic. Submission fee of $40. Please refer to Web site for further details: http://www.tcr.org.

Award: Prize for use in freshman year; not renewable. *Number:* up to 5. *Amount:* $500.

Eligibility Requirements: Applicant must be high school student; planning to enroll or expecting to enroll full- or part-time at a four-year institution or university and must have an interest in writing. Available to U.S. and non-U.S. citizens.

Application Requirements: Applicant must enter a contest, essay, self-addressed stamped envelope. *Fee:* $40. *Deadline:* continuous.

Contact: Will Fitzhugh, Founder and President
Concord Review
730 Boston Road, Suite 24
Sudbury, MA 01776
Phone: 978-443-0022
E-mail: fitzhugh@tcr.org

CONTEMPORARY RECORD SOCIETY http://www.crsnews.org

CONTEMPORARY RECORD SOCIETY NATIONAL COMPETITION FOR PERFORMING ARTISTS

Applicant may submit one performance tape of varied length with each application. May use any number of instrumentalists and voices. First prize is commercial distribution of winner's recording. Application fee is $50. Submit self-addressed stamped envelope for application.

Award: Prize for use in freshman, sophomore, junior, senior, graduate, or postgraduate years; not renewable. *Number:* 1. *Amount:* $2000–$6000.

Eligibility Requirements: Applicant must be enrolled or expecting to enroll full- or part-time at a two-year or four-year or technical institution or university and must have an interest in music/singing. Available to U.S. and non-U.S. citizens.

Application Requirements: Application, applicant must enter a contest, autobiography, resume, references, self-addressed stamped envelope. *Fee:* $50. *Deadline:* March 10.

Contact: Jack Shusterman, Artist Representative
Contemporary Record Society
724 Winchester Road
Broomall, PA 19008
Phone: 610-544-5920
Fax: 610-544-5921
E-mail: crsnews@verizon.net

NATIONAL COMPETITION FOR COMPOSERS' RECORDINGS

Must submit a work that is non-published and not commercially recorded. First prize is a recording grant. Limit of nine performers and twenty-five minutes. Send self-addressed stamped envelope with $4 postage if applicant wants work returned. Application fee is $50.

Award: Prize for use in freshman, sophomore, junior, senior, graduate, or postgraduate years; not renewable. *Number:* 1. *Amount:* $2000–$6000.

Eligibility Requirements: Applicant must be enrolled or expecting to enroll full- or part-time at a two-year or four-year or technical institution or university and must have an interest in music/singing. Available to U.S. and non-U.S. citizens.

Application Requirements: Application, applicant must enter a contest, autobiography, resume, references, self-addressed stamped envelope. *Fee:* $50. *Deadline:* March 10.

Contact: Jack Shusterman, Artist Representative
Contemporary Record Society
724 Winchester Road
Broomall, PA 19008
Phone: 610-544-5920
Fax: 610-544-5921
E-mail: crsnews@verizon.net

CROSSLITES http://www.crosslites.com

CROSSLITES SCHOLARSHIP AWARD

Scholarship contest is open to high school, college and graduate school students. There are no minimum GPA, SAT, ACT, GMAT, GRE, or any other test score requirements.

Award: Prize for use in freshman, sophomore, junior, senior, or graduate years; not renewable. *Number:* 3. *Amount:* $300–$1500.

Eligibility Requirements: Applicant must be enrolled or expecting to enroll full- or part-time at a two-year or four-year or technical institution or university and must have an interest in writing. Available to U.S. and non-U.S. citizens.

Application Requirements: Application, applicant must enter a contest, essay. *Deadline:* January 3.

Contact: Samuel Certo, Scholarship Committee
CrossLites
1000 Holt Avenue
Winter Park, FL 32789

DANIEL KOVACH SCHOLARSHIP FOUNDATION http://www.collegescholarships.org

BLOGGING SCHOLARSHIP

Scholarship of $10,000 awarded annually to a student who maintains a weblog and is enrolled full-time in post-secondary education in the United States. Must be a U.S. citizen.

Award: Scholarship for use in freshman, sophomore, junior, or senior years; not renewable. *Number:* up to 3. *Amount:* $1000–$10,000.

Eligibility Requirements: Applicant must be enrolled or expecting to enroll full-time at a four-year institution or university and must have an interest in writing. Available to U.S. citizens.

Application Requirements: Application, applicant must enter a contest, essay. *Deadline:* October 6.

Contact: Daniel Kovach, Scholarship Committee
Daniel Kovach Scholarship Foundation
5506 Red Robin Road
Raleigh, NC 27613
Phone: 919-630-4895
E-mail: danielkovach@gmail.com

DELAWARE HIGHER EDUCATION COMMISSION http://www.doe.k12.de.us

AGENDA FOR DELAWARE WOMEN TRAILBLAZER SCHOLARSHIP

• *See page 595*

DELTA TAU DELTA EDUCATIONAL FUND http://www.deltfoundation.org

NED H. GUSTAFSON/KEVIN R. JOHNS SCHOLARSHIP

• *See page 531*

DEVRY INC. http://www.devry.edu

DEVRY UNIVERSITY FIRST SCHOLAR AWARD

Award to high school graduates and GED recipients. Must be a registered participant in any regional FIRST Robotics Competition. Must have an ACT composite score of 19 or SAT combined math and verbal/critical reading score of at least 900. Must submit letter of recommendation from FIRST team advisor. Deadline: one year from high school graduation to apply and start.

Award: Scholarship for use in freshman year; renewable. *Number:* 1. *Amount:* $2000–$9000.

Eligibility Requirements: Applicant must be high school student; planning to enroll or expecting to enroll full-time at an institution or university and must have an interest in science. Available to U.S. and Canadian citizens.

Application Requirements: Application, essay, references, test scores, transcript. *Deadline:* varies.

Contact: Thonie Simpson, National High School Program Manager
DeVry Inc.
One Tower Lane
Oak Brook Terrace, IL 60181-4624
Phone: 630-706-3122
Fax: 630-574-1696
E-mail: scholarships@devry.edu

DIET-LIVE POETS SOCIETY http://www.highschoolpoetrycontest.com

NATIONAL HIGH SCHOOL POETRY CONTEST/EASTERDAY POETRY AWARD

Award to encourage the youth of America in the pursuit of literary exploration and excellence, and to help provide a venue in which American High School students may share their poetic works. All U.S. high school students are eligible to enter this contest.

Award: Scholarship for use in freshman year; not renewable. *Number:* 1–11. *Amount:* $100–$1000.

Eligibility Requirements: Applicant must be high school student; planning to enroll or expecting to enroll full-time at a two-year or four-year institution or university and must have an interest in English language or writing. Available to U.S. citizens.

Application Requirements: Applicant must enter a contest, self-addressed stamped envelope, poem of 20 lines or less. *Deadline:* March 31.

Contact: Mr. D. Edwards, Editor
DIET-Live Poets Society
PO Box 8841
Turnersville, NJ 08012
E-mail: lpsnj@comcast.net

DISABLEDPERSON INC. COLLEGE SCHOLARSHIP http://www.disabledperson.com

DISABLEDPERSON INC. COLLEGE SCHOLARSHIP AWARD

• *See page 618*

DIVERSITY CITY MEDIA http://www.blacknews.com

BLACKNEWS.COM SCHOLARSHIP ESSAY CONTEST

• *See page 680*

DIXIE BOYS BASEBALL http://www.dixie.org

DIXIE BOYS BASEBALL SCHOLARSHIP PROGRAM

• *See page 751*

DIXIE YOUTH SCHOLARSHIP PROGRAM

• *See page 751*

DUPONT IN COOPERATION WITH GENERAL LEARNING COMMUNICATIONS http://www.thechallenge.dupont.com

DUPONT CHALLENGE SCIENCE ESSAY AWARDS PROGRAM

Student science and technology prize program in the United States and Canada. Students must submit an essay of 700 to 1000 words discussing a scientific or technological development, event, or theory that has captured their interest. For students in grades 7-12. Must mail all entries in a 9 x 12-inch envelope. For more details go to Web site: http://www.thechallenge.dupont.com.

Award: Prize for use in freshman year; not renewable. *Number:* 100. *Amount:* $100–$3000.

Eligibility Requirements: Applicant must be high school student; age 12-19; planning to enroll or expecting to enroll full- or part-time at a four-year institution or university and must have an interest in writing. Available to U.S. and Canadian citizens.

DuPont in Cooperation with General Learning Communications (continued)

Application Requirements: Applicant must enter a contest, essay, official entry form. *Deadline:* January 31.

Contact: Carole Rubenstein, Editorial Director
DuPont in Cooperation with General Learning Communications
900 Skokie Boulevard, Suite 200
Northbrook, IL 60062-4028
Phone: 847-205-3000
Fax: 847-564-8197
E-mail: c.rubenstein@glcomm.com

EAST BAY FOOTBALL OFFICIALS ASSOCIATION http://www.ebfoa.org

EAST BAY FOOTBALL OFFICIALS ASSOCIATION COLLEGE SCHOLARSHIP

• *See page 751*

ELDER & LEEMAUR PUBLISHERS http://www.elpublishers.com

AUTHORS OF TOMORROW SCHOLARSHIP

Scholarship is available to current undergraduate students in any field of study and any student in either junior or senior high school.

Award: Scholarship for use in freshman, sophomore, junior, or senior years; not renewable. *Number:* varies. *Amount:* up to $10,000.

Eligibility Requirements: Applicant must be enrolled or expecting to enroll full- or part-time at a four-year institution or university and must have an interest in writing. Available to U.S. citizens.

Application Requirements: Application, essay. *Deadline:* December 1.

Contact: Joni Hara, Public Relations Assistant
Elder & Leemaur Publishers
115 Garfield Street, Suite 5432
Sumas, WA 98295
Phone: 604-263-3540
E-mail: joni@elpublishers.com

ELIE WIESEL FOUNDATION FOR HUMANITY http://www.eliewieselfoundation.org

ELIE WIESEL PRIZE IN ETHICS ESSAY CONTEST

Scholarship for full-time junior or senior at a four-year accredited college or university in the United States. Up to five awards are granted.

Award: Prize for use in junior or senior years; not renewable. *Number:* up to 5. *Amount:* $500–$5000.

Eligibility Requirements: Applicant must be enrolled or expecting to enroll full-time at a four-year institution or university and must have an interest in writing. Available to U.S. and non-U.S. citizens.

Application Requirements: Application, applicant must enter a contest, essay, self-addressed stamped envelope, student entry form, faculty sponsor form. *Deadline:* December 1.

Contact: Essay Contest Coordinator
NY 10022
Phone: 212-490-7788
Fax: 212-490-6006

ELKS NATIONAL FOUNDATION http://www.elks.org/enf

ELKS MOST VALUABLE STUDENT CONTEST

Five hundred awards ranging from $1000 to $15,000 per year, renewable for four years, are allocated nationally by state quota for graduating high school seniors. Based on scholarship, leadership, and financial need. Must be a U.S. citizen pursuing a 4-year degree at a U.S. college or university. For full-time study only.

Award: Scholarship for use in freshman year; renewable. *Number:* 500. *Amount:* $1000–$15,000.

Eligibility Requirements: Applicant must be high school student; planning to enroll or expecting to enroll full-time at a four-year institution or university and must have an interest in leadership. Applicant must have 2.5 GPA or higher. Available to U.S. citizens.

Application Requirements: Application, applicant must enter a contest, essay, financial need analysis, references, self-addressed stamped envelope, test scores, transcript. *Deadline:* varies.

Contact: Ms. Jeannine Kunz, Program Coordinator
Elks National Foundation
2750 North Lakeview Avenue
Chicago, IL 60614-2256
Phone: 773-755-4732
Fax: 773-755-4733
E-mail: scholarship@elks.org

ESSAYJOLT.COM http://www.essayjolt.com

ESSAYJOLT SCHOLARSHIP

• *See page 752*

FINANCIAL SERVICE CENTERS OF AMERICA INC. http://www.fisca.org

FINANCIAL SERVICE CENTERS OF AMERICA SCHOLARSHIP FUND

Cash grants of at least $2000 to two students from each of the 5 geographic regions across the country. Criteria is based on academic achievement, financial need, leadership skills in schools and the community, and an essay written expressly for the competition. Applicant must be single.

Award: Grant for use in freshman year; not renewable. *Number:* 10–22. *Amount:* $2000.

Eligibility Requirements: Applicant must be high school student; planning to enroll or expecting to enroll full-time at a two-year or four-year institution or university; single and must have an interest in leadership. Available to U.S. citizens.

Application Requirements: Application, applicant must enter a contest, essay, financial need analysis, photo, references, transcript. *Deadline:* April 5.

Contact: Henry Shyne, Executive Director
Financial Service Centers of America Inc.
21 Main Street, First Floor, Court Plaza South, East Wing
PO Box 647
Hackensack, NJ 07602
Phone: 201-487-0412
Fax: 201-487-3954
E-mail: hshyne@fisca.org

FLEET RESERVE ASSOCIATION http://www.fra.org

FLEET RESERVE ASSOCIATION SCHOLARSHIP

• *See page 532*

SCHUYLER S. PYLE AWARD

• *See page 533*

FLORIDA SOCIETY, SONS OF THE AMERICAN REVOLUTION http://www.patriot-web.com/essay

GEORGE S. AND STELLA M. KNIGHT ESSAY CONTEST

• *See page 755*

FLORIDA WOMEN'S STATE GOLF ASSOCIATION http://www.fwsga.org

FLORIDA WOMEN'S STATE GOLF ASSOCIATION JUNIOR GIRLS' SCHOLARSHIP FUND

• *See page 755*

FOREST ROBERTS THEATRE http://www.nmu.edu

MILDRED AND ALBERT PANOWSKI PLAYWRITING AWARD

Prize designed to encourage and stimulate artistic growth among playwrights. Winner receives a cash prize and a world premiere of their play.

Award: Prize for use in freshman, sophomore, junior, senior, graduate, or postgraduate years; not renewable. *Number:* 1. *Amount:* $2000.

Eligibility Requirements: Applicant must be enrolled or expecting to enroll full- or part-time at a two-year or four-year or technical institution or university and must have an interest in theater or writing. Available to U.S. and non-U.S. citizens.

Application Requirements: Application, applicant must enter a contest, self-addressed stamped envelope, manuscript in English. *Deadline:* October 31.

Contact: Matt Hudson, Playwriting Award Coordinator
Forest Roberts Theatre
Northern Michigan University, 1401 Presque Isle Avenue
Marquette, MI 49855-5364
Phone: 906-227-2559
Fax: 906-227-2567

FORT COLLINS SYMPHONY ASSOCIATION http://www.fcsymphony.org

ADELINE ROSENBERG MEMORIAL PRIZE

$4000 to $6000 prize for senior division (25 years or under) instrumental competitions held in odd-numbered years. Piano competitions held in even-numbered years. Auditions required. Must submit proof of age, perform a standard concerto, and be recommended by music teacher. Send self-addressed stamped envelope for application.

Award: Prize for use in freshman, sophomore, junior, senior, graduate, or postgraduate years; not renewable. *Number:* 2. *Amount:* $4000–$6000.

Eligibility Requirements: Applicant must be age 25 or under; enrolled or expecting to enroll full- or part-time at a four-year institution or university and must have an interest in music. Available to U.S. and non-U.S. citizens.

Application Requirements: Application, applicant must enter a contest, autobiography, references, self-addressed stamped envelope, proof of age. *Fee:* $50. *Deadline:* March 21.

Contact: Carol Kauffman, Office Manager
Fort Collins Symphony Association
214 South College Avenue
PO Box 1963
Fort Collins, CO 80524
Phone: 970-482-4823
Fax: 970-482-4858
E-mail: yac@fcsymphony.org

FORT COLLINS SYMPHONY ASSOCIATION YOUNG ARTIST COMPETITION, JUNIOR DIVISION

Junior division (between 12 and 18 years of age on day of competition) piano and instrumental competition held every year. Auditions required. Limited to the first twenty applicants and two alternates per division. Must submit verification of age. Applicant must perform one movement of a standard concerto and be recommended by music teacher. Send self-addressed stamped envelope for application. Fee of $35.

Award: Prize for use in freshman, sophomore, junior, or senior years; not renewable. *Number:* 4. *Amount:* $300–$500.

Eligibility Requirements: Applicant must be age 12-18; enrolled or expecting to enroll full- or part-time at a four-year institution or university and must have an interest in art. Available to U.S. and non-U.S. citizens.

Application Requirements: Application, applicant must enter a contest, autobiography, references, self-addressed stamped envelope, proof of age. *Fee:* $40. *Deadline:* March 21.

Contact: Carol Kauffman, Office Manager
Fort Collins Symphony Association
214 South College Avenue
PO Box 1963
Fort Collins, CO 80524
Phone: 970-482-4823
Fax: 970-482-4858
E-mail: yac@fcsymphony.org

FOUNDATION FOR CHRISTIAN COLLEGE LEADERS http://www.collegechristianleader.com

FOUNDATION FOR COLLEGE CHRISTIAN LEADERS SCHOLARSHIP

• *See page 714*

FREEDOM FROM RELIGION FOUNDATION http://www.ffrf.org

FREEDOM FROM RELIGION FOUNDATION COLLEGE ESSAY CONTEST

Any currently enrolled college student may submit college essays. Essays should be typed, double-spaced 4-5 pages with standard margins. Contestants must choose an original title for essay. Each contestant must include a paragraph biography giving campus and permanent addresses, phone numbers, and emails. The scholarship value varies. The essay topic and specific guidelines are posted in February. For more information visit: http://www.ffrf.org/

Award: Scholarship for use in freshman, sophomore, junior, or senior years; not renewable. *Number:* 3. *Amount:* $100–$2000.

Eligibility Requirements: Applicant must be enrolled or expecting to enroll full-time at a two-year or four-year institution or university and must have an interest in writing. Available to U.S. and Canadian citizens.

Application Requirements: Applicant must enter a contest, essay. *Deadline:* July 1.

Contact: Program Coordinator
Freedom From Religion Foundation
PO Box 750
Madison, WI 53701

FREEDOM FROM RELIGION FOUNDATION HIGH SCHOOL ESSAY CONTEST

High-school essay submitted must have an original title. Each entrant must include a paragraph biography giving campus and permanent addresses, phone numbers and emails. First prize winner will receive $2000, second place $1000, third place $500, honorable mentions $100. The essay topic and specific guidelines are posted in February. For more information visit: http://www.ffrf.org/.

Award: Prize for use in freshman year; not renewable. *Number:* 3. *Amount:* $100–$2000.

Eligibility Requirements: Applicant must be high school student; planning to enroll or expecting to enroll full-time at a two-year or four-year or technical institution or university and must have an interest in writing. Available to U.S. and Canadian citizens.

Application Requirements: Applicant must enter a contest, essay. *Deadline:* June 1.

Contact: Essay Competition Coordinator
Freedom From Religion Foundation
PO Box 750
Madison, WI 53701

GENERAL BOARD OF HIGHER EDUCATION AND MINISTRY http://www.gbhem.org

GIFT OF HOPE: 21ST CENTURY SCHOLARS PROGRAM

• *See page 715*

HANA SCHOLARSHIP

• *See page 682*

GEORGE T. WELCH TRUST http://www.bakerboyer.com

EDUCATION EXCHANGE COLLEGE GRANT PROGRAM

Awards range from four $1000 to thirty $5000 scholarships. Must be U.S. citizens and provide written acceptance to an accredited four-year college by May 15 of the award year.

Award: Grant for use in freshman year; not renewable. *Number:* 34. *Amount:* $1000–$5000.

Eligibility Requirements: Applicant must be high school student; planning to enroll or expecting to enroll full-time at a four-year institution or university and must have an interest in leadership. Available to U.S. citizens.

Application Requirements: Application, essay, references, transcript, acceptance letter to a four-year institution, copy of first two pages of parent or guardian's federal income tax return. *Deadline:* March 15.

Contact: Scholarship Committee
George T. Welch Trust
Education Exchange, PO Box 559
Morris Plains, NJ 07950

GERMAN ACADEMIC EXCHANGE SERVICE (DAAD) http://www.daad.org

DAAD STUDY SCHOLARSHIP

One of DAAD's flagship competitive scholarship awarded for study at all public universities in Germany. Open to students of all fields. Applicable to one year of study and extendable for the pursuit of a master's degree at a German institution.

Award: Scholarship for use in senior, graduate, or postgraduate years; renewable. *Number:* varies. *Amount:* varies.

Eligibility Requirements: Applicant must be enrolled or expecting to enroll full-time at a four-year institution or university and must have an interest in German language/culture. Available to U.S. and non-U.S. citizens.

Application Requirements: Application, applicant must enter a contest, resume, transcript, proposal, DAAD German language certificate. *Deadline:* November 15.

Contact: Jane Fu, Information Officer
German Academic Exchange Service (DAAD)
871 United Nations Plaza
New York, NY 10017
Phone: 212-758-3223
Fax: 212-755-5780
E-mail: daadny@daad.org

GLAMOUR http://www.glamour.com

TOP 10 COLLEGE WOMEN COMPETITION

Female students with leadership experience on and off campus, excellence in field of study, and inspiring goals can apply for this competition. Winners will be awarded $3000 along with a trip to New York City. Must be a junior studying full-time with a minimum GPA of 3.0. in either the United States or Canada. Non-U.S. citizens may apply if attending U.S. postsecondary institutions.

Award: Prize for use in junior year; not renewable. *Number:* 10. *Amount:* $3000.

Eligibility Requirements: Applicant must be enrolled or expecting to enroll full-time at a four-year institution or university; female and must have an interest in leadership. Applicant must have 3.0 GPA or higher. Available to U.S. and non-U.S. citizens.

Application Requirements: Application, essay, photo, references, transcript. *Deadline:* February 2.

Contact: Lynda Laux-Bachand, Reader Services Editor
Glamour
Four Times Square, 16th Floor
New York, NY 10036-6593
Phone: 212-286-6667
Fax: 212-286-6922

GLENN MILLER BIRTHPLACE SOCIETY http://www.glennmiller.org

GLENN MILLER INSTRUMENTAL SCHOLARSHIP

One-time awards for high school seniors and college freshmen. Scholarships are awarded as competition prizes and must be used for any education-related expenses. Must submit 10-minute, high-quality audio tape of pieces selected for competition or those of similar style. Applicant is responsible for travel to and lodging during the competition.

Award: Scholarship for use in freshman year; not renewable. *Number:* 3. *Amount:* $1000–$4000.

Eligibility Requirements: Applicant must be high school student; planning to enroll or expecting to enroll full-time at a four-year institution or university and must have an interest in music/singing. Available to U.S. and non-U.S. citizens.

Application Requirements: Application, applicant must enter a contest, essay, performance tape or CD. *Deadline:* March 15.

Contact: Arlene Leonard, Secretary
Glenn Miller Birthplace Society
107 East Main Street, PO Box 61
Clarinda, IA 51632-0061
Phone: 712-542-2461
Fax: 712-542-2461
E-mail: gmbs@heartland.net

JACK PULLAN MEMORIAL SCHOLARSHIP

One scholarship for a male or female vocalist, awarded as competition prize and, to be used for any education-related expenses. Must submit 10 minute, high-quality audio tape of pieces selected for competition or those of similar style. Applicant is responsible for travel to and lodging during the competition. One-time award for high school seniors and college freshmen. More information on http://www.glennmiller.org/scholar.htm.

Award: Scholarship for use in freshman year; not renewable. *Number:* 1. *Amount:* $1000.

Eligibility Requirements: Applicant must be high school student; planning to enroll or expecting to enroll full-time at a four-year institution or university and must have an interest in music/singing. Available to U.S. and non-U.S. citizens.

Application Requirements: Application, applicant must enter a contest, essay, performance tape. *Deadline:* March 15.

Contact: Arlene Leonard, Secretary
Glenn Miller Birthplace Society
107 East Main Street, PO Box 61
Clarinda, IA 51632-0061
Phone: 712-542-2461
Fax: 712-542-2461
E-mail: gmbs@heartland.net

RALPH BREWSTER VOCAL SCHOLARSHIP

One scholarship for a male or female vocalist, awarded as competition prize and, to be used for any education-related expenses. Must submit 10 minute, high-quality audio tape of pieces selected for competition or those of similar style. Applicant is responsible for travel to and lodging during the competition. One-time award for high school seniors and college freshmen.

Award: Scholarship for use in freshman year; not renewable. *Number:* 1. *Amount:* $2000.

Eligibility Requirements: Applicant must be high school student; planning to enroll or expecting to enroll full-time at a four-year institution or university and must have an interest in music/singing. Available to U.S. and non-U.S. citizens.

Application Requirements: Application, applicant must enter a contest, essay, performance tape of competition or concert quality (up to 5 minutes duration). *Deadline:* March 15.

Contact: Arlene Leonard, Secretary
Glenn Miller Birthplace Society
107 East Main Street, PO Box 61
Clarinda, IA 51632-0061
Phone: 712-542-2461
Fax: 712-542-2461
E-mail: gmbs@heartland.net

GLORIA BARRON PRIZE FOR YOUNG HEROES http://www.barronprize.org

GLORIA BARRON PRIZE FOR YOUNG HEROES

• *See page 597*

GOLDEN KEY INTERNATIONAL HONOUR SOCIETY http://www.goldenkey.org

INTERNATIONAL STUDENT LEADERS AWARD

• *See page 534*

GRACO INC. http://www.graco.com

GRACO EXCELLENCE SCHOLARSHIP

• *See page 579*

GRAND LODGE OF IOWA, AF AND AM http://www.gl-iowa.org

GRAND LODGE OF IOWA MASONIC SCHOLARSHIP PROGRAM

• *See page 598*

GREATER KANAWHA VALLEY FOUNDATION http://www.tgkvf.org

KID'S CHANCE OF WEST VIRGINIA SCHOLARSHIP

• *See page 758*

GREENHOUSE PARTNERS http://www.greenhousescholars.org

GREENHOUSE SCHOLARS

• *See page 759*

GUARDIAN LIFE INSURANCE COMPANY OF AMERICA http://www.girlsgoingplaces.com

GIRLS GOING PLACES ENTREPRENEURSHIP AWARD PROGRAM

• *See page 598*

HARTFORD WHALERS BOOSTER CLUB http://www.whalerwatch.com

HARTFORD WHALERS BOOSTER CLUB SCHOLARSHIP

• *See page 759*

HEMOPHILIA FEDERATION OF AMERICA http://www.hemophiliaed.org

ARTISTIC ENCOURAGEMENT GRANT

• *See page 619*

HERB KOHL EDUCATIONAL FOUNDATION INC. http://www.kohleducation.org

HERB KOHL EXCELLENCE SCHOLARSHIP PROGRAM

• *See page 599*

HOLLAND & KNIGHT CHARITABLE FOUNDATION HOLOCAUST REMEMBRANCE PROJECT http://www.foundation.hklaw.com

HOLOCAUST REMEMBRANCE PROJECT ESSAY CONTEST

Contest open to all students age 19 and under who are currently enrolled as high school students, and are residents of either the United States or Mexico, or who are United States citizens living abroad. Submit essay on any aspect of the Holocaust using relevant research sources and addressing key points indicated in the instructions. Prizes for winning essays include scholarships. Essay must be submitted online. For information see Web site: http://holocaust.hklaw.com

Award: Prize for use in freshman year; not renewable. *Number:* 30. *Amount:* $300–$10,000.

Eligibility Requirements: Applicant must be high school student; age 19 or under; planning to enroll or expecting to enroll full- or part-time at a four-year institution or university and must have an interest in writing. Available to U.S. citizens.

Application Requirements: Application, essay. *Deadline:* April 30.

Contact: Scholarship Committee
Holland & Knight Charitable Foundation Holocaust Remembrance Project
PO Box 2877
Tampa, FL 33601-2877
Phone: 866-452-2737
E-mail: holocaust@hklaw.com

HORIZONS FOUNDATION http://www.horizonsfoundation.org

MARKOWSKI-LEACH SCHOLARSHIP

• *See page 761*

HOSTESS COMMITTEE SCHOLARSHIPS/MISS AMERICA PAGEANT http://www.missamerica.org

MISS AMERICA ORGANIZATION COMPETITION SCHOLARSHIPS

Scholarship competition open to 70 contestants, each serving as state representative. Women will be judged in Private Interview, Swimsuit, Evening Wear and Talent competition. Other awards may be based on points assessed by judges during competitions. Upon reaching the National level, award values range from $2000 to $50,000. Additional awards not affecting the competition can be won with values from $1000 to $10,000.

Award: Prize for use in freshman, sophomore, junior, senior, or graduate years; not renewable. *Number:* 70. *Amount:* $2000–$50,000.

Eligibility Requirements: Applicant must be age 17-24; enrolled or expecting to enroll full- or part-time at a two-year or four-year or technical institution or university; female and must have an interest in beauty pageant. Available to U.S. citizens.

Application Requirements: Application, applicant must enter a contest. *Deadline:* varies.

Contact: Doreen Lindell Gordon, Controller and Scholarship Administrator
Hostess Committee Scholarships/Miss America Pageant
Two Miss America Way, Suite 1000
Atlantic City, NJ 08401
Phone: 609-345-7571 Ext. 27
Fax: 609-653-8740
E-mail: doreen@missamerica.org

MISS STATE SCHOLAR

Award available only to pageant participants at the state level. Candidates evaluated strictly on academics.

Award: Scholarship for use in freshman, sophomore, junior, senior, or graduate years; not renewable. *Number:* up to 51. *Amount:* up to $1000.

Eligibility Requirements: Applicant must be enrolled or expecting to enroll full-time at a two-year or four-year institution or university; female and must have an interest in beauty pageant. Available to U.S. citizens.

Application Requirements: Application, transcript. *Deadline:* varies.

Contact: Doreen Lindell Gordon, Controller and Scholarship Administrator
Hostess Committee Scholarships/Miss America Pageant
Two Miss America Way, Suite 1000
Atlantic City, NJ 08401
Phone: 609-345-7571 Ext. 27
Fax: 609-653-8740
E-mail: doreen@missamerica.org

HUMANIST MAGAZINE http://www.thehumanist.org

HUMANIST ESSAY CONTEST

Contest is open to students residing in the United States or Canada who are enrolled in grades 9-12. Essays should be 1,500 to 2,500 words, written in English, single-spaced.

Award: Prize for use in freshman year; not renewable. *Number:* 3. *Amount:* $1000.

Eligibility Requirements: Applicant must be high school student; planning to enroll or expecting to enroll full- or part-time at a two-year or four-year or technical institution or university and must have an interest in writing. Available to U.S. citizens.

Application Requirements: Application, applicant must enter a contest, essay. *Deadline:* March 3.

Contact: Scholarship Committee
Humanist Magazine
1777 T Street, NW
Washington, DC 20009-7125
Phone: 800-837-3792
E-mail: contest@thehumanist.org

INDEPENDENT COLLEGE FUND OF MARYLAND (I-FUND) http://www.i-fundinfo.org

LEADERSHIP SCHOLARSHIPS

• *See page 764*

Independent College Fund of Maryland (I-Fund) (continued)

T. ROWE PRICE FOUNDATION SCHOLARSHIPS
• *See page 764*

JACKIE ROBINSON FOUNDATION http://www.jackierobinson.org

JACKIE ROBINSON SCHOLARSHIP
• *See page 601*

JANE AUSTEN SOCIETY OF NORTH AMERICA http://www.jasna.org

JANE AUSTEN SOCIETY OF NORTH AMERICA ESSAY CONTEST

Essay contest with three divisions: high school, college undergraduate, and graduate students. First prize in each division is free trip to conference or cash equivalent of $500. Must submit essay of 1,200 to 2,000 words that contains personal, original insight into Jane Austen's artistry, ideas, and values, and is not primarily a research paper. Essay topic is posted each winter on the Web site: http://www.jasna.org.

Award: Prize for use in freshman, sophomore, junior, senior, graduate, or postgraduate years; not renewable. *Number:* 9. *Amount:* $500.

Eligibility Requirements: Applicant must be enrolled or expecting to enroll full- or part-time at a two-year or four-year institution or university and must have an interest in English language or writing. Available to U.S. and non-U.S. citizens.

Application Requirements: Application, applicant must enter a contest, essay, references. *Deadline:* May 1.

Contact: Barbara Sullivan, Contest Chair
Jane Austen Society of North America
1360 Pronghorn Court
Cheyenne, WY 82009
Phone: 307-635-5736
Fax: 307-638-0564
E-mail: janebrs@starband.net

JAPANESE GOVERNMENT/THE MONBUSHO SCHOLARSHIP PROGRAM http://www.la.us.emb-japan.go.jp

VOCATIONAL SCHOOL STUDENT SCHOLARSHIPS

Award open to students enrolled in vocational schools in Japan. Study involves one year of language training and two years of vocational school. All vocational training will be in Japanese. Scholarship comprises transportation, accommodations, medical expenses, and monthly and arrival allowances.

Award: Scholarship for use in freshman or sophomore years; not renewable. *Number:* varies. *Amount:* varies.

Eligibility Requirements: Applicant must be age 17-20; enrolled or expecting to enroll full-time at a technical institution and must have an interest in Japanese language. Available to U.S. citizens.

Application Requirements: Application, essay, interview, photo, references, transcript, medical certificate, certificate of enrollment. *Deadline:* varies.

Contact: Jean Do, Scholarship Coordinator
Japanese Government/The Monbusho Scholarship Program
350 South Grand Avenue, Suite 1700
Los Angeles, CA 90071
Phone: 213-617-6700 Ext. 338
Fax: 213-617-6728
E-mail: info@la-cgjapan.org

JUNIOR ACHIEVEMENT http://www.ja.org

HUGH B. SWEENY ACHIEVEMENT AWARD
• *See page 538*

JUNIOR ACHIEVEMENT JOE FRANCOMANO SCHOLARSHIP
• *See page 538*

JUNIOR ACHIEVEMENT OFFICE DEPOT SCHOLARSHIP
• *See page 538*

KARMEL SCHOLARSHIP http://www.karenandmelody.com

KARMEL SCHOLARSHIP

Scholarship to encourage students to write or create something that will express their views on a topic related to GLBT issues.

Award: Scholarship for use in freshman, sophomore, junior, senior, or graduate years; not renewable. *Number:* 2. *Amount:* $300–$400.

Eligibility Requirements: Applicant must be enrolled or expecting to enroll full- or part-time at a two-year or four-year or technical institution or university and must have an interest in art, LGBT issues, music/singing, or writing. Available to U.S. and non-U.S. citizens.

Application Requirements: Application, applicant must enter a contest, essay. *Deadline:* March 31.

Contact: Scholarship Committee
KarMel Scholarship
PO Box 70382
Sunnyvale, CA 94086
E-mail: karen@karenandmelody.com

KE ALI'I PAUAHI FOUNDATION http://www.pauahi.org

CHOY-KEE 'OHANA SCHOLARSHIP

Scholarship recognizes the academic achievements and efforts of worthy students with a minimum GPA of 3.0 who are pursuing a postsecondary education. Must submit essay addressing what the biggest problem in Hawai'i is and potential solutions.

Award: Scholarship for use in freshman, sophomore, junior, senior, or graduate years; not renewable. *Number:* 1. *Amount:* up to $1000.

Eligibility Requirements: Applicant must be enrolled or expecting to enroll full-time at a two-year or four-year institution or university and must have an interest in Hawaiian language/culture. Applicant must have 3.0 GPA or higher. Available to U.S. citizens.

Application Requirements: Application, essay, references, Student Aid Report (SAR), college acceptance letter. *Deadline:* May 2.

Contact: Elizabeth Stevenson, Development Manager
Ke Ali'i Pauahi Foundation
567 South King Street, Suite 160
Honolulu, HI 96813
Phone: 808-534-3966
Fax: 808-534-3890
E-mail: scholarships@pauahi.org

DANIEL KAHIKINA AND MILLIE AKAKA SCHOLARSHIP
• *See page 601*

DWAYNE "NAKILA" STEELE SCHOLARSHIP

Scholarship supports students who demonstrate a desire to work in the area of perpetuating the Hawaiian language upon graduation. Requirements include demonstrated interest in the Hawaiian language, culture, and history, in addition to a commitment to contribute to the greater community and demonstrated financial need.

Award: Scholarship for use in freshman, sophomore, junior, senior, or graduate years; not renewable. *Number:* 1. *Amount:* up to $900.

Eligibility Requirements: Applicant must be enrolled or expecting to enroll full-time at a four-year institution or university and must have an interest in Hawaiian language/culture. Available to U.S. citizens.

Application Requirements: Application, financial need analysis, references, transcript, Student Aid Report (SAR), college acceptance letter. *Deadline:* May 2.

Contact: Elizabeth Stevenson, Development Manager
Ke Ali'i Pauahi Foundation
567 South King Street, Suite 160
Honolulu, HI 96813
Phone: 808-534-3966
Fax: 808-534-3890
E-mail: scholarships@pauahi.org

JALENE KANANI BELL 'OHANA SCHOLARSHIP
• *See page 767*

KAMEHAMEHA SCHOOLS CLASS OF 1956 GRANT
• *See page 767*

KAMEHAMEHA SCHOOLS CLASS OF 1974 SCHOLARSHIP

• *See page 767*

KNIGHTS OF PYTHIAS http://www.pythias.org

KNIGHTS OF PYTHIAS POSTER CONTEST

Poster contest open to all high school students in the U.S. and Canada. Contestants must submit an original drawing. Eight winners are chosen. The winners are not required to attend institution of higher education.

Award: Prize for use in freshman year; not renewable. *Number:* 8. *Amount:* $100–$1000.

Eligibility Requirements: Applicant must be high school student; planning to enroll or expecting to enroll full- or part-time at a four-year institution or university and must have an interest in art. Available to U.S. and Canadian citizens.

Application Requirements: Applicant must enter a contest. *Deadline:* April 30.

Contact: Alfred Saltzman, Supreme Secretary
Knights of Pythias
Office of Supreme Lodge
59 Coddington Street, Suite 202
Quincy, MA 02169-4150
Phone: 617-472-8800
Fax: 617-376-0363
E-mail: kop@earthlink.net

KOSCIUSZKO FOUNDATION http://www.kosciuszkofoundation.org

MARCELLA SEMBRICH VOICE COMPETITION

The competition encourages young singers to study the repertoire of Polish composers. Three prizes awarded: $2000, $1250 and $750. Open to all singers who are at least 18 years old and preparing for professional careers. Must be U.S. citizens or international full-time students with a valid student visa.

Award: Prize for use in freshman, sophomore, junior, senior, or graduate years; not renewable. *Number:* 3. *Amount:* $750–$2000.

Eligibility Requirements: Applicant must be age 18 and over; enrolled or expecting to enroll full- or part-time at a four-year institution or university and must have an interest in music/singing. Available to U.S. and non-Canadian citizens.

Application Requirements: Application, applicant must enter a contest, photo, references, 2 cassette tapes. *Fee:* $35. *Deadline:* January 18.

Contact: Mr. Thomas Pniewski, Director of Cultural Programs
Kosciuszko Foundation
15 East 65th Street
New York, NY 10021-6595
Phone: 212-734-2130
Fax: 212-628-4552
E-mail: tompkf@aol.com

KURT WEILL FOUNDATION FOR MUSIC http://www.kwf.org

KURT WEILL FOUNDATION FOR MUSIC GRANTS PROGRAM

One-time awards for projects that perpetuate the artistic legacy of Kurt Weill. These can include performance of works by Kurt Weill or scholarly research directly related to Weill or his wife Lotte Lenya.

Award: Grant for use in freshman, sophomore, junior, senior, graduate, or postgraduate years; not renewable. *Number:* varies. *Amount:* varies.

Eligibility Requirements: Applicant must be enrolled or expecting to enroll full- or part-time at a two-year or four-year or technical institution or university and must have an interest in music/singing. Available to U.S. and non-U.S. citizens.

Application Requirements: Application, applicant must enter a contest. *Deadline:* November 1.

Contact: Carolyn Weber, Director
Kurt Weill Foundation for Music
Seven East 20th Street
New York, NY 10003-1106
Phone: 212-505-5240
E-mail: kwfinfo@kwf.org

LOTTE LENYA COMPETITION FOR SINGERS

The competition recognizes excellence in the performance of music for the theater, including opera, operetta, and American musical theater. Applicants should contact the foundation for more information.

Award: Prize for use in freshman, sophomore, junior, senior, graduate, or postgraduate years; not renewable. *Number:* varies. *Amount:* varies.

Eligibility Requirements: Applicant must be age 19-32; enrolled or expecting to enroll full- or part-time at a two-year or four-year or technical institution or university and must have an interest in music/singing or theater. Available to U.S. and non-U.S. citizens.

Application Requirements: Application, applicant must enter a contest, audition. *Deadline:* varies.

Contact: Carolyn Weber, Director
Kurt Weill Foundation for Music
Seven East 20th Street
New York, NY 10003-1106
Phone: 212-505-5240
Fax: 212-353-9663
E-mail: cweber@kwf.org

LADIES AUXILIARY TO THE VETERANS OF FOREIGN WARS http://www.ladiesauxvfw.org

JUNIOR GIRLS SCHOLARSHIP PROGRAM

• *See page 540*

YOUNG AMERICAN CREATIVE PATRIOTIC ART AWARDS PROGRAM

One-time awards for high school students in grades 9 through 12. Must submit an original work of art expressing their patriotism. First place state-level winners go on to national competition. Three awards of varying amounts. Must reside in same state as sponsoring organization.

Award: Scholarship for use in freshman year; not renewable. *Number:* up to 4. *Amount:* $1500–$10,000.

Eligibility Requirements: Applicant must be high school student; planning to enroll or expecting to enroll full-time at a two-year or four-year or technical institution; single and must have an interest in art. Available to U.S. citizens.

Application Requirements: Application, applicant must enter a contest, references. *Deadline:* March 31.

Contact: Judith Millick, Administrator of Programs
Ladies Auxiliary to the Veterans of Foreign Wars
406 West 34th Street
Kansas City, MO 64111
Phone: 816-561-8655
Fax: 816-931-4753
E-mail: jmillick@ladiesauxvfw.org

LEE-JACKSON EDUCATIONAL FOUNDATION http://www.lee-jackson.org

LEE-JACKSON EDUCATIONAL FOUNDATION SCHOLARSHIP COMPETITION

• *See page 769*

LESBIAN, BISEXUAL, GAY AND TRANSGENDERED UNITED EMPLOYEES (LEAGUE) AT AT&T FOUNDATION http://www.leaguefoundation.org

LEAGUE FOUNDATION ACADEMIC SCHOLARSHIP

Scholarship awarded to graduating high school seniors who are gay, lesbian, bisexual, or transgender. Must have a 3.0 GPA. Application information can be found at www.leaguefoundation.org.

Award: Scholarship for use in freshman year; not renewable. *Number:* 3–7. *Amount:* $1500–$2500.

Lesbian, Bisexual, Gay and Transgendered United Employees (LEAGUE) at AT&T Foundation (continued)

Eligibility Requirements: Applicant must be high school student; planning to enroll or expecting to enroll full-time at a two-year or four-year or technical institution or university and must have an interest in LGBT issues. Applicant must have 3.0 GPA or higher. Available to U.S. citizens.

Application Requirements: Application, essay, references, test scores, transcript, college or university acceptance letter. *Deadline:* April 30.

Contact: Charles Eader, Executive Director
Lesbian, Bisexual, Gay and Transgendered United Employees (LEAGUE) at AT&T Foundation
One AT&T Way, Room 4B214J
Bedminster, NJ 07921
Phone: 908-234-7484
Fax: 908-532-1079
E-mail: info@leaguefoundation.org

LIEDERKRANZ FOUNDATION http://www.liederkranznycity.org

LIEDERKRANZ FOUNDATION SCHOLARSHIP AWARD FOR VOICE

Nonrenewable awards for voice for both full-and part-time study. Those studying general voice must be between ages 18 to 45 years old while those studying Wagnerian voice must be between ages 25 to 45 years old. Application fee: $50. Applications not available before August and September.

Award: Prize for use in freshman, sophomore, junior, senior, or graduate years; not renewable. *Number:* 14–18. *Amount:* $1000–$8000.

Eligibility Requirements: Applicant must be age 18-45; enrolled or expecting to enroll full- or part-time at a four-year institution or university and must have an interest in music/singing. Available to U.S. and non-U.S. citizens.

Application Requirements: Application, applicant must enter a contest, driver's license, self-addressed stamped envelope, proof of age. *Fee:* $50. *Deadline:* November 15.

Contact: Manager
Liederkranz Foundation
Six East 87th Street
New York, NY 10128
Phone: 212-534-0880
Fax: 212-828-5372
E-mail: contactus@liederkranznycity.org

LINCOLN COMMUNITY FOUNDATION http://www.lcf.org

GEORGE L. WATTERS/NEBRASKA PETROLEUM MARKETERS ASSOCIATION SCHOLARSHIP

• *See page 580*

LIQUITEX ARTIST MATERIALS PURCHASE AWARD PROGRAM http://www.liquitex.com

LIQUITEX EXCELLENCE IN ART PURCHASE AWARD PROGRAM-SECONDARY CATEGORY

Prizes up to $500 in cash plus $250 in Liquitex products will be awarded to the best art submissions. Submissions should be made in 35mm slides. Void in Quebec or where prohibited by law. For more details see Web site: http://www.liquitex.com.

Award: Prize for use in freshman, sophomore, junior, senior, graduate, or postgraduate years; not renewable. *Number:* 3. *Amount:* $500–$750.

Eligibility Requirements: Applicant must be enrolled or expecting to enroll full- or part-time at a two-year or four-year or technical institution or university and must have an interest in art. Available to U.S. and Canadian citizens.

Application Requirements: Application, applicant must enter a contest, 35mm color slides of artwork. *Deadline:* January 15.

Contact: Mrs. Renee Hile, Vice President Marketing
Liquitex Artist Materials Purchase Award Program
11 Constitution Avenue
PO Box 1396
Piscataway, NJ 08855-1396
Phone: 732-562-0770
Fax: 732-562-0941

LOS ANGELES PHILHARMONIC http://www.laphil.com

BRONISLAW KAPER AWARDS FOR YOUNG ARTISTS

• *See page 771*

LOWE'S COMPANIES INC. http://www.lowes.com

LOWE'S EDUCATIONAL SCHOLARSHIP

• *See page 602*

MARTIN D. ANDREWS SCHOLARSHIP http://mdascholarship.tripod.com

MARTIN D. ANDREWS MEMORIAL SCHOLARSHIP FUND

One-time award for student seeking undergraduate or graduate degree. Recipient must have been in a Drum Corp for at least three years. Must submit essay and two recommendations. Must be U.S. citizen.

Award: Scholarship for use in freshman, sophomore, junior, senior, or graduate years; not renewable. *Number:* 2–5. *Amount:* $300–$1000.

Eligibility Requirements: Applicant must be enrolled or expecting to enroll full- or part-time at a two-year or four-year institution or university and must have an interest in drum corps. Available to U.S. citizens.

Application Requirements: Application, essay, references. *Deadline:* April 1.

Contact: Peter D. Andrews, Scholarship Committee
Martin D. Andrews Scholarship
2069 Perkins Street
Bristol, CT 06010
Phone: 860-673-2929
E-mail: mdascholarship@musician.org

MCCURRY FOUNDATION INC. http://www.mccurryfoundation.org

MCCURRY FOUNDATION SCHOLARSHIP

• *See page 777*

MCKELVEY FOUNDATION http://www.mckelveyfoundation.org

MCKELVEY FOUNDATION ENTREPRENEURIAL SCHOLARSHIP

Award available for high school students who own a business with at least one employee and sales revenue. Award value is up to $10,000 per year to attend any four-year college or university within the United States.

Award: Scholarship for use in freshman, sophomore, junior, or senior years; not renewable. *Number:* varies. *Amount:* up to $10,000.

Eligibility Requirements: Applicant must be enrolled or expecting to enroll full- or part-time at a four-year institution or university and must have an interest in entrepreneurship. Available to U.S. citizens.

Application Requirements: Application, financial need analysis. *Deadline:* January 25.

Contact: Scholarship Committee
McKelvey Foundation
200 Park Avenue, 44th Floor
New York, NY 10166
Phone: 212-847-7236
E-mail: info@mckelveyfoundation.org

MINNESOTA AFL-CIO http://www.mnaflcio.org

BILL PETERSON SCHOLARSHIP

• *See page 541*

MINNESOTA COMMUNITY FOUNDATION http://www.mncommunityfoundation.org

JANE RING AND SUE RING-JARVI GIRLS'/WOMEN'S HOCKEY FUND

• *See page 779*

MINNESOTA DEPARTMENT OF MILITARY AFFAIRS http://www.minnesotanationalguard.org

LEADERSHIP, EXCELLENCE AND DEDICATED SERVICE SCHOLARSHIP

• *See page 603*

MINNESOTA GAY/LESBIAN/BISEXUAL/TRANSGENDER EDUCATIONAL FUND http://www.pfundonline.org

MINNESOTA GAY/LESBIAN/BISEXUAL/TRANSGENDER SCHOLARSHIP FUND

• *See page 780*

MINNESOTA HIGHER EDUCATION SERVICES OFFICE http://www.getreadyforcollege.org

MINNESOTA ACADEMIC EXCELLENCE SCHOLARSHIP

• *See page 780*

MISS AMERICAN COED PAGEANTS INC. http://www.gocoed.com

MISS AMERICAN COED PAGEANT

Awards available for girls aged 3 to 22. Must be single and maintain a 3.0 GPA where applicable. Prizes are awarded by age groups. Winners of state competitions may compete at the national level. Application fee would vary for each state between $25 to $35 and will be refunded if not accepted into competition. Deadline varies each year.

Award: Prize for use in freshman year; not renewable. *Number:* up to 52. *Amount:* $150–$3000.

Eligibility Requirements: Applicant must be age 3-22; enrolled or expecting to enroll full- or part-time at a two-year or four-year institution; single female and must have an interest in beauty pageant. Applicant must have 3.0 GPA or higher. Available to U.S. citizens.

Application Requirements: Application, applicant must enter a contest, transcript. *Deadline:* varies.

Contact: George Scarborough, National Director
Miss American Coed Pageants Inc.
3695 Wimbledon Drive
Pensacola, FL 32504-4555
Phone: 850-432-0069
Fax: 850-469-8841
E-mail: amerteen@aol.com

MORRIS J. AND BETTY KAPLUN FOUNDATION http://www.kaplunfoundation.org

MORRIS J. AND BETTY KAPLUN FOUNDATION ANNUAL ESSAY CONTEST

• *See page 716*

NATIONAL AMATEUR BASEBALL FEDERATION (NABF) http://www.nabf.com

NATIONAL AMATEUR BASEBALL FEDERATION SCHOLARSHIP FUND

Scholarships are awarded to candidates who are enrolled in an accredited college or university. Applicant must be a bona fide participant in a federation event and be sponsored by an NABF-franchised member association. Self-nominated candidates are not eligible for this scholarship award.

Award: Scholarship for use in freshman, sophomore, junior, or senior years; not renewable. *Number:* varies. *Amount:* varies.

Eligibility Requirements: Applicant must be enrolled or expecting to enroll full-time at a two-year or four-year or technical institution or university and must have an interest in athletics/sports. Available to U.S. citizens.

Application Requirements: Application, essay, references, transcript, letter of acceptance. *Deadline:* November 15.

Contact: Awards Committee Chairman
National Amateur Baseball Federation (NABF)
PO Box 705
Bowie, MD 20718

NATIONAL ASSOCIATION FOR CAMPUS ACTIVITIES http://www.naca.org

LORI RHETT MEMORIAL SCHOLARSHIP

• *See page 603*

MULTICULTURAL SCHOLARSHIP PROGRAM

• *See page 693*

NATIONAL ASSOCIATION FOR CAMPUS ACTIVITIES EAST COAST UNDERGRADUATE SCHOLARSHIP FOR STUDENT LEADERS

• *See page 603*

NATIONAL ASSOCIATION FOR CAMPUS ACTIVITIES REGIONAL COUNCIL STUDENT LEADER SCHOLARSHIPS

Scholarships will be given to undergraduate students in good standing at the time of the application and during the academic term in which the scholarship is awarded. Must demonstrate significant leadership skill and ability while holding a significant leadership position on campus. The scholarship value and the number of awards granted varies.

Award: Scholarship for use in freshman, sophomore, junior, or senior years; not renewable. *Number:* up to 7. *Amount:* $250–$300.

Eligibility Requirements: Applicant must be enrolled or expecting to enroll full- or part-time at a four-year institution or university and must have an interest in leadership. Available to U.S. and non-U.S. citizens.

Application Requirements: Application, essay, resume, references, transcript. *Deadline:* May 1.

Contact: Dionne Ellison, Administrative Assistant
National Association for Campus Activities
13 Harbison Way
Columbia, SC 29212-3401
Phone: 803-732-6222 Ext. 131
Fax: 803-749-1047
E-mail: dionnee@naca.org

NATIONAL ASSOCIATION FOR CAMPUS ACTIVITIES SOUTHEAST REGION STUDENT LEADERSHIP SCHOLARSHIP

• *See page 604*

NATIONAL ASSOCIATION FOR CAMPUS ACTIVITIES WISCONSIN REGION STUDENT LEADERSHIP SCHOLARSHIP

• *See page 604*

SCHOLARSHIPS FOR STUDENT LEADERS

• *See page 604*

TESS CALDARELLI MEMORIAL SCHOLARSHIP

• *See page 784*

ZAGUNIS STUDENT LEADERS SCHOLARSHIP

• *See page 784*

NATIONAL ASSOCIATION FOR THE SELF-EMPLOYED http://www.nase.org

NASE FUTURE ENTREPRENEUR SCHOLARSHIP

• *See page 543*

NASE SCHOLARSHIPS

• *See page 543*

NATIONAL ASSOCIATION OF SECONDARY SCHOOL PRINCIPALS http://www.nhs.us

PRINCIPAL'S LEADERSHIP AWARD

One-time award available only to high school seniors for use at an accredited two- or four-year college or university. Selection based on leadership and school or community involvement. Contact school counselor or principal. Citizens of countries other than the U.S. may only apply if attending a United States overseas institution. Minimum 3.0 GPA. Application fee: $6.

National Association of Secondary School Principals (continued)

Award: Scholarship for use in freshman year; not renewable. *Number:* 100. *Amount:* $1000.

Eligibility Requirements: Applicant must be high school student; planning to enroll or expecting to enroll full-time at a two-year or four-year institution or university and must have an interest in leadership. Applicant must have 3.0 GPA or higher. Available to U.S. and non-U.S. citizens.

Application Requirements: Application, essay, references, test scores, transcript. *Fee:* $6. *Deadline:* December 7.

Contact: Wanda Carroll, Program Manager
National Association of Secondary School Principals
1904 Association Drive
Reston, VA 20191-1537
Phone: 703-860-0200
Fax: 703-476-5432
E-mail: carrollw@principals.org

NATIONAL COUNCIL OF TEACHERS OF ENGLISH (NCTE) http://www.ncte.org

ACHIEVEMENT AWARDS IN WRITING

Writing contest to encourage high school students in their writing and to recognize publicly some of the best student writers in the nation.

Award: Prize for use in freshman year; not renewable. *Number:* varies. *Amount:* varies.

Eligibility Requirements: Applicant must be high school student; planning to enroll or expecting to enroll full- or part-time at a four-year institution or university and must have an interest in writing. Available to U.S. citizens.

Application Requirements: Application, essay, best writing sample, two written compositions. *Deadline:* February 1.

Contact: Scholarship Coordinator
National Council of Teachers of English (NCTE)
1111 West Kenyon Road
Urbana, IL 61801-1096
E-mail: aa@ncte.org

NATIONAL FEDERATION OF STATE POETRY SOCIETIES (NFSPS) http://www.nfsps.com

NATIONAL FEDERATION OF STATE POETRY SOCIETIES SCHOLARSHIP AWARDS-COLLEGE/UNIVERSITY LEVEL POETRY COMPETITION

Must submit application and ten original poems, forty-line per-poem limit. Manuscript must be titled. For more information, visit the Web site.

Award: Scholarship for use in freshman, sophomore, junior, or senior years; not renewable. *Number:* 2. *Amount:* $500.

Eligibility Requirements: Applicant must be enrolled or expecting to enroll full-time at a two-year or four-year institution or university and must have an interest in writing. Available to U.S. citizens.

Application Requirements: Application, applicant must enter a contest, must be notarized. *Deadline:* February 1.

Contact: Colwell Snell, Chairman
National Federation of State Poetry Societies (NFSPS)
3444 South Dover Terrace, PO Box 520698
Salt Lake City, UT 84152-0698
Phone: 801-484-3113
E-mail: sbsenior@juno.com

NATIONAL FOUNDATION FOR ADVANCEMENT IN THE ARTS http://www.youngARTS.org

YOUNGARTS

One-time award for high school seniors 17 to 18 years old who show talent in dance, film and video, jazz, music, photography, theater, visual arts, voice, and/or writing. Must submit portfolio, videotape or audiotape, along with application fee. Must be citizens or permanent residents of the U.S., except for the music/jazz discipline, which accepts international applicants.

Award: Prize for use in freshman year; not renewable. *Number:* up to 15. *Amount:* $100–$10,000.

Eligibility Requirements: Applicant must be high school student; age 17-18; planning to enroll or expecting to enroll full- or part-time at a two-year or four-year or technical institution or university and must have an interest in art, music/singing, photography/photogrammetry/filmmaking, theater, or writing. Available to U.S. citizens.

Application Requirements: Application, applicant must enter a contest, portfolio. *Fee:* $25. *Deadline:* October 1.

Contact: Carla Hill, Programs Department
National Foundation for Advancement in the Arts
444 Brickell Avenue, Suite R14
Miami, FL 33133
Phone: 800-970-2787
Fax: 305-377-1149
E-mail: nfaa@nfaa.org

NATIONAL ORDER OF OMEGA http://www.orderofomega.org

FOUNDERS SCHOLARSHIP

• *See page 545*

NATIONAL SOCIETY OF COLLEGIATE SCHOLARS (NSCS) http://www.nscs.org

NSCS EXEMPLARY SCHOLAR AWARD

Scholarship of $500 to outstanding undergraduates among the NSCS members, for their high academic achievement as well as additional scholarly pursuits outside of the classroom.

Award: Scholarship for use in freshman, sophomore, junior, or senior years; not renewable. *Number:* 1. *Amount:* $500.

Eligibility Requirements: Applicant must be enrolled or expecting to enroll full- or part-time at a four-year institution or university and must have an interest in leadership. Available to U.S. and non-U.S. citizens.

Application Requirements: Application. *Deadline:* January 6.

Contact: Stephen Loflin, Executive Director
National Society of Collegiate Scholars (NSCS)
11 Dupont Circle NW, Suite 650
Washington, DC 20036
Phone: 202-965-9000
Fax: 800-784-1015
E-mail: nscs@nscs.org

NATIONAL SOCIETY OF HIGH SCHOOL SCHOLARS http://www.nshss.org

CLAES NOBEL ACADEMIC SCHOLARSHIPS FOR NSHSS MEMBERS

• *See page 546*

NATIONAL SOCIETY OF THE SONS OF THE AMERICAN REVOLUTION http://www.sar.org

JOSEPH S. RUMBAUGH HISTORICAL ORATION CONTEST

Prize ranging from $1000 to $3000 is awarded to a sophomore, junior, or senior. The oration must be original and not less than five minutes or more than six minutes in length.

Award: Prize for use in sophomore, junior, or senior years; not renewable. *Number:* 1–3. *Amount:* $1000–$3000.

Eligibility Requirements: Applicant must be enrolled or expecting to enroll full-time at a two-year or four-year or technical institution or university and must have an interest in public speaking. Available to U.S. and non-U.S. citizens.

Application Requirements: Application, applicant must enter a contest. *Deadline:* June 15.

Contact: Lawrence Mckinley, National Chairman
National Society of the Sons of the American Revolution
12158 Holly Knoll Circle
Great Fall, VA 22066
E-mail: dustoff@bellatlantic.net

NETAID FOUNDATION/MERCY CORPS http://www.globalactionawards.org

GLOBAL ACTION AWARDS

• *See page 606*

NEW HAMPSHIRE CHARITABLE FOUNDATION http://www.nhcf.org

FISHER CATS SCHOLAR ATHLETES

• *See page 787*

NEXTGEN NETWORK INC. http://www.nextgennetwork.com

DONNA JAMISON LAGO MEMORIAL SCHOLARSHIP

• *See page 694*

NIMROD INTERNATIONAL JOURNAL OF PROSE AND POETRY http://www.utulsa.edu/nimrod

KATHERINE ANNE PORTER PRIZE FOR FICTION

Awards the winners of fiction writing contest. A first place prize of $2000 and a second place prize of $1000 will be awarded for fiction. The award includes publication in Nimrod. Entry fee is $20, which includes one year subscription to Nimrod. For further details visit Web site: http://www.utulsa.edu/nimrod.

Award: Prize for use in freshman, sophomore, junior, senior, graduate, or postgraduate years; not renewable. *Number:* 2. *Amount:* $1000–$2000.

Eligibility Requirements: Applicant must be enrolled or expecting to enroll full- or part-time at a two-year or four-year or technical institution or university and must have an interest in writing. Available to U.S. citizens.

Application Requirements: Application, applicant must enter a contest, essay, manuscript (story). *Fee:* $20. *Deadline:* April 30.

Contact: Francine Ringold, Editor-in-Chief
Nimrod International Journal of Prose and Poetry
800 South Tucker Drive
Tulsa, OK 74104-3189
Phone: 918-631-3080
Fax: 918-631-3033
E-mail: nimrod@utulsa.edu

PABLO NERUDA PRIZE FOR POETRY

Awards the winners of poetry writing contest. A first place prize of $2000 and a second place prize of $1000 will be awarded. The award includes publication of the poetry in Nimrod. Entry fee is $20, which includes one year subscription to Nimrod.

Award: Prize for use in freshman, sophomore, junior, senior, graduate, or postgraduate years; not renewable. *Number:* 2. *Amount:* $1000–$2000.

Eligibility Requirements: Applicant must be enrolled or expecting to enroll full- or part-time at a two-year or four-year or technical institution or university and must have an interest in writing. Available to U.S. citizens.

Application Requirements: Application, applicant must enter a contest, essay, manuscript (poetry). *Fee:* $20. *Deadline:* April 30.

Contact: Francine Ringold, Editor-in-Chief
Nimrod International Journal of Prose and Poetry
800 South Tucker Drive
Tulsa, OK 74104-3189
Phone: 918-631-3080
Fax: 918-631-3033
E-mail: nimrod@utulsa.edu

OP LOFTBED COMPANY http://www.oploftbed.com/

OP LOFTBED $500 SCHOLARSHIP AWARD

Scholarship is awarded to the student whose answers to the application questions on the OP Loftbed Web site were the most creative and amusing. Must be a U.S. citizen who is enrolled in a college or university in the U.S. Submit entry on Web site: http://www.oploftbed.com.

Award: Scholarship for use in freshman, sophomore, junior, senior, graduate, or postgraduate years; not renewable. *Number:* 1. *Amount:* $500.

Eligibility Requirements: Applicant must be enrolled or expecting to enroll full- or part-time at a two-year or four-year or technical institution or university and must have an interest in writing. Available to U.S. citizens.

Application Requirements: Application, applicant must enter a contest, essay. *Deadline:* July 31.

Contact: Program Coordinator
OP Loftbed Company
PO Box 573
Thomasville, NC 27361-0573
Phone: 866-567-5638

OPTIMIST INTERNATIONAL FOUNDATION http://www.optimist.org

OPTIMIST INTERNATIONAL ESSAY CONTEST

Essay contest for students under age 19 as of December 31 of the current school year. Club winners advance to the District contest to compete for a $650 college scholarship. Each district winner is automatically entered into the International essay contest where scholarships are awarded as follows: first place: $6000; second place: $3750; and third place: $2250.

Award: Scholarship for use in freshman, sophomore, junior, senior, or graduate years; not renewable. *Number:* 50–56. *Amount:* $650–$6000.

Eligibility Requirements: Applicant must be age 19 or under; enrolled or expecting to enroll full- or part-time at a two-year or four-year or technical institution or university and must have an interest in writing. Available to U.S. and Canadian citizens.

Application Requirements: Application, applicant must enter a contest, essay, self-addressed stamped envelope, birth certificate. *Deadline:* varies.

Contact: Danielle Baugher, International Programs Manager
Optimist International Foundation
4494 Lindell Boulevard
St. Louis, MO 63108
Phone: 800-500-8130
Fax: 314-371-6006
E-mail: programs@optimist.org

OPTIMIST INTERNATIONAL ORATORICAL CONTEST

Contest for youth to gain experience in public speaking and to provide them with the opportunity to compete for college scholarships. Students must first compete at the Club level. Club winners are then entered into the Zone/Regional contest and those winners compete in the district contest. District scholarships range from $500 to $1500.

Award: Scholarship for use in freshman or sophomore years; not renewable. *Number:* up to 106. *Amount:* $500–$1500.

Eligibility Requirements: Applicant must be age 16 or under; enrolled or expecting to enroll full- or part-time at a two-year or four-year institution or university and must have an interest in public speaking. Available to U.S. and Canadian citizens.

Application Requirements: Application, applicant must enter a contest, self-addressed stamped envelope, birth certificate, speech. *Deadline:* varies.

Contact: Danielle Baugher, International Programs Manager
Optimist International Foundation
4494 Lindell Boulevard
St. Louis, MO 63108
Phone: 800-500-8130
Fax: 314-371-6006
E-mail: programs@optimist.org

OREGON COMMUNITY FOUNDATION http://www.ocf1.org

DOROTHY S. CAMPBELL MEMORIAL SCHOLARSHIP FUND

Scholarship for female graduates of Oregon high schools with a strong and continuing interest in the game of golf. For use in the pursuit of a postsecondary education at a four-year college or university in Oregon.

Award: Scholarship for use in freshman, sophomore, junior, or senior years; not renewable. *Number:* 1. *Amount:* $1000.

Eligibility Requirements: Applicant must be enrolled or expecting to enroll full-time at a four-year institution or university; female and must have an interest in golf. Available to U.S. citizens.

Oregon Community Foundation (continued)

Application Requirements: Application, references. *Deadline:* March 1.

Contact: Dianne Causey, Program Associate for Scholarships and Grants
Oregon Community Foundation
1221 Yamhill, SW, Suite 100
Portland, OR 97205
Phone: 503-227-6846
Fax: 503-274-7771
E-mail: diannec@ocf1.org

OREGON STUDENT ASSISTANCE COMMISSION http://www.osac.state.or.us

DOROTHY CAMPBELL MEMORIAL SCHOLARSHIP

• *See page 798*

OUR WORLD UNDERWATER SCHOLARSHIP SOCIETY http://www.owuscholarship.org

OUR WORLD UNDERWATER SCHOLARSHIPS

Annual award for individual planning to pursue a career in a water-related discipline through practical exposure to various fields and leaders of underwater endeavors. Scuba experience required. Must be at least 21 but not yet 25. Scholarship value is $20,000.

Award: Scholarship for use in freshman, sophomore, junior, senior, or graduate years; not renewable. *Number:* 1. *Amount:* $20,000.

Eligibility Requirements: Applicant must be age 21-24; enrolled or expecting to enroll full-time at a two-year or four-year or technical institution or university and must have an interest in scuba diving. Available to U.S. and non-U.S. citizens.

Application Requirements: Application, autobiography, essay, interview, resume, references, transcript, diver certification. *Fee:* $25. *Deadline:* December 31.

Contact: Scholarship Application Coordinator
Our World Underwater Scholarship Society
PO Box 4428
Chicago, IL 60680-4428
Phone: 800-969-6690
Fax: 630-969-6690
E-mail: info@owuscholarship.org

PARENTS, FAMILIES, AND FRIENDS OF LESBIANS AND GAYS-ATLANTA http://www.pflagatl.org

PFLAG SCHOLARSHIP AWARDS PROGRAM

• *See page 801*

PENGUIN PUTNAM INC. http://www.penguin.com

SIGNET CLASSIC SCHOLARSHIP ESSAY CONTEST

Contest is open to high school juniors and seniors. Students should submit a two- to three-page double-spaced essay answering one of three possible questions on a designated novel. Entries must be submitted by a high school English teacher.

Award: Scholarship for use in freshman year; not renewable. *Number:* 5. *Amount:* $1000.

Eligibility Requirements: Applicant must be high school student; planning to enroll or expecting to enroll full- or part-time at a four-year institution or university and must have an interest in writing. Available to U.S. citizens.

Application Requirements: Applicant must enter a contest, essay, references. *Deadline:* April 15.

Contact: Kamahue Budkle, Academic Marketing Assistant
Penguin Putnam Inc.
375 Hudson Street
New York, NY 10014
Phone: 212-366-2377
Fax: 212-366-2933
E-mail: academic@penguin.com

PHILLIPS FOUNDATION http://www.thephillipsfoundation.org

RONALD REAGAN COLLEGE LEADERS SCHOLARSHIP PROGRAM

The program offers renewable scholarships to college juniors and seniors who demonstrate leadership on behalf of freedom, American values, and constitutional principles. Winners will receive a scholarship for their junior year and may apply for renewal before their senior year.

Award: Scholarship for use in sophomore or junior years; renewable. *Number:* up to 100. *Amount:* $1000–$10,000.

Eligibility Requirements: Applicant must be enrolled or expecting to enroll full-time at a four-year institution and must have an interest in leadership. Available to U.S. citizens.

Application Requirements: Application, essay, resume, references, proof of full-time enrollment in good standing. *Deadline:* January 15.

Contact: John Farley, Secretary
Phillips Foundation
One Massachusetts Avenue, NW, Suite 620
Washington, DC 20001
Phone: 202-250-3887
E-mail: jfarley@thephillipsfoundation.org

PHI SIGMA PI NATIONAL HONOR FRATERNITY http://www.phisigmapi.org

RICHARD CECIL TODD AND CLAUDA PENNOCK TODD TRIPOD SCHOLARSHIP

• *See page 553*

PHOENIX SUNS CHARITIES/SUN STUDENTS SCHOLARSHIP http://www.suns.com

QWEST LEADERSHIP CHALLENGE

• *See page 609*

PIRATE'S ALLEY FAULKNER SOCIETY http://www.wordsandmusic.org

WILLIAM FAULKNER-WILLIAM WISDOM CREATIVE WRITING COMPETITION

Prizes for unpublished manuscripts written in English. One prize awarded in each category: $7500, novel; $2500, novella; $2000 novel-in-progress; $1500, short story; $1000, essay; $750, poem; $750 high school short story-student author, $250 sponsoring teacher. Manuscripts will not be returned and must be mailed, not emailed or faxed, accompanied by entry fee ranging from $10 for high school category to $35 for novel.

Award: Prize for use in freshman, sophomore, junior, senior, graduate, or postgraduate years; not renewable. *Number:* 7. *Amount:* $250–$7500.

Eligibility Requirements: Applicant must be enrolled or expecting to enroll full- or part-time at a two-year or four-year or technical institution or university and must have an interest in English language or writing. Available to U.S. and non-U.S. citizens.

Application Requirements: Application, applicant must enter a contest, manuscript. *Fee:* $10. *Deadline:* April 1.

Contact: Rosemary James, Writing Competition Coordinator
Pirate's Alley Faulkner Society
624 Pirate's Alley
New Orleans, LA 70116-3254
Phone: 504-586-1609
Fax: 504-522-9725
E-mail: faulkhouse@aol.com

PONY OF THE AMERICAS CLUB http://www.poac.org

PONY OF THE AMERICAS SCHOLARSHIP

• *See page 553*

PRIDE FOUNDATION http://www.pridefoundation.org

PRIDE FOUNDATION/GREATER SEATTLE BUSINESS ASSOCIATION SCHOLARSHIPS

• *See page 803*

PRO BOWLERS ASSOCIATION http://www.pba.com

BILLY WELU BOWLING SCHOLARSHIP

Scholarship awarded annually, recognizing exemplary qualities in male and female college students who compete in the sport of bowling. Winner will receive $1000. Candidates must be amateur bowlers who are currently in college (preceding the application deadline) and maintain at least a 2.5 GPA or equivalent.

Award: Scholarship for use in freshman, sophomore, junior, or senior years; not renewable. *Number:* 1. *Amount:* $1000.

Eligibility Requirements: Applicant must be enrolled or expecting to enroll full-time at a two-year or four-year institution or university and must have an interest in bowling. Applicant must have 2.5 GPA or higher. Available to U.S. citizens.

Application Requirements: Application, essay, transcript. *Deadline:* May 31.

Contact: Karen Day, Controller
Pro Bowlers Association
719 Second Avenue, Suite 701
Seattle, WA 98104
Phone: 206-332-9688
Fax: 206-332-9722
E-mail: karen.day@pba.com

PROFESSIONAL BOWLERS ASSOCIATION http://www.pba.com

PROFESSIONAL BOWLERS ASSOCIATION BILLY WELU MEMORIAL SCHOLARSHIP

• See page 553

RECORDING FOR THE BLIND & DYSLEXIC http://www.rfbd.org

MARION HUBER LEARNING THROUGH LISTENING AWARDS

• See page 554

MARY P. OENSLAGER SCHOLASTIC ACHIEVEMENT AWARDS

• See page 554

RESERVE OFFICERS ASSOCIATION http://www.roa.org

HENRY J. REILLY MEMORIAL SCHOLARSHIP-HIGH SCHOOL SENIORS AND FIRST YEAR FRESHMEN

• See page 555

ST. CLAIRE REGIONAL MEDICAL CENTER http://www.st-claire.org

SR. MARY JEANNETTE WESS, S.N.D. SCHOLARSHIP

• See page 610

SAN DIEGO FOUNDATION http://www.sdfoundation.org

JOSEPH C. LARSON ENTREPRENEURIAL SCHOLARSHIP

• See page 805

JULIE ALLEN WORLD CLASSROOM SCHOLARSHIP

• See page 806

LESLIE JANE HAHN MEMORIAL SCHOLARSHIP

• See page 611

RANDY WILLIAMS SCHOLARSHIP

• See page 806

USA FREESTYLE MARTIAL ARTS SCHOLARSHIP

• See page 611

SAN FRANCISCO FOUNDATION http://www.sff.org

JAMES DUVAL PHELAN LITERARY AWARD

Award presented annually to an author of an unpublished work in progress: fiction, nonfiction, prose, poetry, or drama. Must have been born in California, but need not be a current resident. Must be between 20 to 35 years of age. Submit manuscript.

Award: Prize for use in freshman, sophomore, junior, senior, graduate, or postgraduate years; not renewable. *Number:* 3. *Amount:* $2000–$3000.

Eligibility Requirements: Applicant must be age 20-35; enrolled or expecting to enroll full- or part-time at a two-year or four-year institution or university and must have an interest in writing. Available to U.S. citizens.

Application Requirements: Application, applicant must enter a contest, self-addressed stamped envelope, manuscript. *Deadline:* March 31.

Contact: Awards Coordinator
San Francisco Foundation
225 Bush Street, Suite 500
San Francisco, CA 94104-4224
Phone: 415-733-8500
E-mail: rec@sff.org

JOSEPH HENRY JACKSON LITERARY AWARD

• See page 807

SCHOLARSHIP WORKSHOP LLC http://www.scholarshipworkshop.com

"LEADING THE FUTURE II" SCHOLARSHIP

Scholarship designed to elevate students' consciousness about their future and their role in helping others once they receive a college degree and become established in a community. It is open to U.S. residents who are high school seniors or college undergraduates at any level. Students must visit http://www.scholarshipworkshop.com to get additional information and to download an application.

Award: Scholarship for use in freshman, sophomore, junior, or senior years; not renewable. *Number:* 1–3. *Amount:* varies.

Eligibility Requirements: Applicant must be enrolled or expecting to enroll full-time at a four-year institution or university and must have an interest in leadership. Available to U.S. citizens.

Application Requirements: Application, essay. *Deadline:* March 1.

Contact: Scholarship Coordinator
Scholarship Workshop LLC
PO Box 176
Centreville, VA 20122
Phone: 703-579-4245
Fax: 703-579-4245
E-mail: scholars@scholarshipworkshop.com

RAGINS/BRASWELL NATIONAL SCHOLARSHIP

• See page 611

SCIENCE SERVICE INC. http://www.societyforscience.org

INTEL INTERNATIONAL SCIENCE AND ENGINEERING FAIR

Culminating event in a series of local, regional, and state science fairs. Students in ninth through twelfth grades must compete at local fairs in order to be nominated for international competition. Awards include scholarships. Visit Web site for more information: http://www.sciserv.org.

Award: Prize for use in freshman year; not renewable. *Number:* 1. *Amount:* $500–$50,000.

Eligibility Requirements: Applicant must be high school student; planning to enroll or expecting to enroll full-time at a four-year institution or university and must have an interest in science. Available to U.S. and non-U.S. citizens.

Application Requirements: Application, applicant must enter a contest, essay, interview. *Deadline:* varies.

Contact: Michelle Glidden, Scholarship Committee
Science Service Inc.
1719 North Street, NW
Washington, DC 20036
Phone: 202-785-2255
Fax: 202-785-1243

INTEL SCIENCE TALENT SEARCH

Science competition for high school seniors. Students must submit an individually researched project. Forty finalists will be chosen to attend Science Talent Institute in Washington, DC to exhibit their project and compete for $100,000 four-year scholarship. For more information, visit Web site: http://www.sciserv.org.

Award: Scholarship for use in freshman year; not renewable. *Number:* 40. *Amount:* $5000.

Science Service Inc. (continued)

Eligibility Requirements: Applicant must be high school student; planning to enroll or expecting to enroll full-time at a two-year or four-year institution or university and must have an interest in science. Available to U.S. and non-U.S. citizens.

Application Requirements: Application, applicant must enter a contest, essay, references, test scores, transcript. *Deadline:* December 1.

Contact: Michelle Glidden, Scholarship Committee
Science Service Inc.
1719 North Street, NW
Washington, DC 20036
Phone: 202-785-2255
Fax: 202-785-1243

SEVENTEEN MAGAZINE http://www.seventeen.com

SEVENTEEN MAGAZINE FICTION CONTEST

Enter by submitting an original short story of no longer than 2000 words. Submissions must be typed, double-spaced, on one side of each sheet of paper, and must not have been previously published in any form, with the exception of school publications. All entries must include the full name, age, home and e-mail addresses, telephone number, date of birth, and signature in the top right hand corner of each page of every story you send. Multiple entries are permitted.

Award: Prize for use in freshman, sophomore, junior, senior, graduate, or postgraduate years; not renewable. *Number:* 8. *Amount:* $100–$2500.

Eligibility Requirements: Applicant must be age 13-21; enrolled or expecting to enroll full- or part-time at a two-year or four-year or technical institution or university and must have an interest in writing. Available to U.S. citizens.

Application Requirements: Applicant must enter a contest, essay, photo, copy of story. *Deadline:* December 31.

Contact: Fiction Contest Coordinator
Seventeen Magazine
300 West 57th Street, 17th Floor
New York, NY 10019
Phone: 917-934-6500
Fax: 917-934-6574

SICKLE CELL DISEASE ASSOCIATION OF AMERICA/ CONNECTICUT CHAPTER INC. http://www.sicklecellct.org

SYBIL FONG SAM SCHOLARSHIP ESSAY CONTEST

• *See page 807*

SINFONIA FOUNDATION http://www.sinfonia.org

SINFONIA EDUCATIONAL FOUNDATION SCHOLARSHIP

Award to assist the collegiate members and chapters of Sinfonia in their endeavors. Must be a collegiate member for at least two years. Should submit an essay on "How the work of Phi Mu Alpha Sinfonia is integral in creating a philanthropic culture that benefits the common good of society".

Award: Scholarship for use in sophomore, junior, senior, or graduate years; not renewable. *Number:* 2. *Amount:* $2500–$5000.

Eligibility Requirements: Applicant must be enrolled or expecting to enroll full- or part-time at a four-year institution or university and must have an interest in music. Available to U.S. citizens.

Application Requirements: Application, essay, photo, references, transcript, name and address of hometown newspaper. *Deadline:* May 1.

Contact: Matthew Garber, Director of Development
Sinfonia Foundation
10600 Old State Road
Evansville, IN 47711
Phone: 812-867-2433 Ext. 110
Fax: 812-867-0633
E-mail: garber@sinfonia.org

SISTER KENNY REHABILITATION INSTITUTE http://www.allina.com/ahs/ski.nsf

INTERNATIONAL ART SHOW FOR ARTISTS WITH DISABILITIES

• *See page 628*

SKILLSUSA http://www.skillsusa.org

INTERNATIONAL SKILLSUSA DEGREE SCHOLARSHIP

Scholarship for students who successfully receive their degree. To qualify, all candidates must submit a letter of application for the scholarship within 45 days of receipt of the degree. The scholarship candidate must include with the application copies of receipts for lodging, meals, travel, and preparation of the presentation.

Award: Scholarship for use in senior year; not renewable. *Number:* 1. *Amount:* up to $1000.

Eligibility Requirements: Applicant must be enrolled or expecting to enroll full-time at a four-year institution or university and must have an interest in leadership. Available to U.S. citizens.

Application Requirements: Application, references, copies of receipts for lodging, meals, travel, and preparation of the presentation. *Deadline:* May 1.

Contact: Karen Perrino, Associate Director
SkillsUSA
PO Box 3000
Leesburg, VA 20177-0300
Phone: 703-737-0610
Fax: 703-777-8999
E-mail: kperrino@skillsusa.org

NTHS SKILLSUSA SCHOLARSHIP

NTHS will award two $1000 scholarships to SkillsUSA members at the SkillsUSA national leadership conference. One scholarship will be awarded to a high school member, and one scholarship will be awarded to a college/ postsecondary member. Students must be active, dues-paying members of both SkillsUSA and NTHS.

Award: Scholarship for use in freshman, sophomore, junior, or senior years; not renewable. *Number:* 2. *Amount:* $1000.

Eligibility Requirements: Applicant must be enrolled or expecting to enroll full-time at a two-year or four-year or technical institution or university and must have an interest in leadership. Available to U.S. citizens.

Application Requirements: Application, references. *Deadline:* March 1.

Contact: Karen Perrino, Associate Director
SkillsUSA
PO Box 3000
Leesburg, VA 20177-0300
Phone: 703-737-0610
Fax: 703-777-8999
E-mail: kperrino@skillsusa.org

SKILLSUSA ALUMNI AND FRIENDS MERIT SCHOLARSHIP

• *See page 611*

SOCIETY OF DAUGHTERS OF THE UNITED STATES ARMY

SOCIETY OF DAUGHTERS OF THE UNITED STATES ARMY SCHOLARSHIPS

• *See page 639*

SOUTH DAKOTA BOARD OF REGENTS http://www.sdbor.edu

SOUTH DAKOTA BOARD OF REGENTS MARLIN R. SCARBOROUGH MEMORIAL SCHOLARSHIP

• *See page 808*

SOUTHERN TEXAS PGA http://www.stpga.com

DICK FORESTER COLLEGE SCHOLARSHIP

One-time award of $4000 to promote the attainment of higher education goals of youth who have demonstrated a high level of achievement during high school or college. Must demonstrate financial need, and have shown an interest in the game of golf.

Award: Scholarship for use in freshman, sophomore, junior, senior, graduate, or postgraduate years; not renewable. *Number:* 1. *Amount:* $4000.

Eligibility Requirements: Applicant must be enrolled or expecting to enroll full-time at a two-year or four-year institution or university and must have an interest in golf. Available to U.S. citizens.

Application Requirements: Application, financial need analysis, test scores, transcript. *Deadline:* April 4.

Contact: Steve Termeer, Scholarship Committee Chairperson
Southern Texas PGA
21604 Cypresswood Drive
Spring, TX 77373
Phone: 832-442-2404
Fax: 832-442-2403
E-mail: stexas@pgahq.com

SPINSTER'S INK http://www.spinstersink.com

SPINSTER'S INK YOUNG FEMINIST SCHOLARSHIP

Scholarship for young women in their last year of high school. Must submit an essay on what feminism means to them and the winning essay receives a $1000 scholarship to the school of their choice and the opportunity to spend one week at a writer's retreat.

Award: Scholarship for use in freshman year; not renewable. *Number:* varies. *Amount:* $1000.

Eligibility Requirements: Applicant must be high school student; planning to enroll or expecting to enroll full- or part-time at a two-year or four-year institution or university; female and must have an interest in writing. Available to U.S. citizens.

Application Requirements: Application, essay. *Deadline:* varies.

Contact: Scholarship Committee
Spinster's Ink
PO Box 242
Midway, FL 32343
Phone: 800-301-6860
E-mail: info@spinstersink.com

STONEWALL COMMUNITY FOUNDATION http://www.stonewallfoundation.org

GENE AND JOHN ATHLETIC SCHOLARSHIP

Scholarship of $2500 to $5000 for LGBT student athletes looking to continue their education while pursuing athletics.

Award: Scholarship for use in freshman, sophomore, junior, senior, graduate, or postgraduate years; not renewable. *Number:* 1–3. *Amount:* $2500–$5000.

Eligibility Requirements: Applicant must be enrolled or expecting to enroll full-time at a two-year or four-year or technical institution or university and must have an interest in athletics/sports or LGBT issues. Available to U.S. and Canadian citizens.

Application Requirements: Application, essay, references. *Deadline:* July 31.

Contact: Roz Lee, Program Director
Stonewall Community Foundation
119 West 24th Street, Seventh Floor
New York, NY 10011
Phone: 212-367-1155
Fax: 212-367-1157
E-mail: stonewall@stonewallfoundation.org

HARRY BARTEL MEMORIAL SCHOLARSHIP FUND

• *See page 612*

TRAUB-DICKER RAINBOW SCHOLARSHIP

Non-renewable scholarships available to lesbian-identified students. Must be graduating high school seniors planning to attend a recognized college, or already matriculated college students in any year of study, including graduate school.

Award: Scholarship for use in freshman, sophomore, junior, senior, or graduate years; not renewable. *Number:* 3. *Amount:* $3000.

Eligibility Requirements: Applicant must be enrolled or expecting to enroll full- or part-time at a four-year institution or university; female and must have an interest in LGBT issues. Available to U.S. citizens.

Application Requirements: Application, essay, references. *Deadline:* April 15.

Contact: Roz Lee, Program Director
Stonewall Community Foundation
119 West 24th Street, Seventh Floor
New York, NY 10011
Phone: 212-367-1155
Fax: 212-367-1157
E-mail: stonewall@stonewallfoundation.org

SUPERCOLLEGE.COM http://www.supercollege.com

SUPERCOLLEGE.COM SCHOLARSHIP

An award for outstanding high school, college or graduate students. Based on academic and extracurricular achievement, leadership, and integrity. May study any major and attend or plan to attend any accredited college or university in the United States. No paper applications accepted. Applications are only available online at http://www.supercollege.com.

Award: Scholarship for use in freshman, sophomore, junior, senior, graduate, or postgraduate years; not renewable. *Number:* 1–5. *Amount:* $500–$2500.

Eligibility Requirements: Applicant must be enrolled or expecting to enroll full-time at a two-year or four-year or technical institution or university and must have an interest in leadership. Available to U.S. citizens.

Application Requirements: Application, essay. *Deadline:* July 31.

Contact: Scholarship Coordinator
SuperCollege.com
3286 Oak Court
Belmont, CA 94022
Phone: 650-618-2221
E-mail: supercollege@supercollege.com

SWISS BENEVOLENT SOCIETY OF NEW YORK http://www.sbsny.org

MEDICUS STUDENT EXCHANGE

• *See page 701*

TERRY FOUNDATION http://www.terryfoundation.org

TERRY FOUNDATION SCHOLARSHIP

• *See page 812*

TERRY FOX HUMANITARIAN AWARD PROGRAM http://www.terryfox.org

TERRY FOX HUMANITARIAN AWARD

• *See page 612*

TEXAS CHRISTIAN UNIVERSITY NEELY SCHOOL OF BUSINESS ENTREPRENEURSHIP PROGRAM http://www.nep.tcu.edu

TCU TEXAS YOUTH ENTREPRENEUR OF THE YEAR AWARDS

• *See page 813*

TEXAS 4-H YOUTH DEVELOPMENT FOUNDATION http://texas4-h.tamu.edu

TEXAS 4-H OPPORTUNITY SCHOLARSHIP

• *See page 813*

TEXAS TENNIS FOUNDATION http://www.texastennisfoundation.com

TEXAS TENNIS FOUNDATION SCHOLARSHIPS AND ENDOWMENTS

• *See page 813*

TKE EDUCATIONAL FOUNDATION http://www.tke.org

ALL-TKE ACADEMIC TEAM RECOGNITION AND JOHN A. COURSON TOP SCHOLAR AWARD

• *See page 560*

CANADIAN TKE SCHOLARSHIP

• *See page 560*

TKE Educational Foundation (continued)

CHARLES WALGREEN JR. SCHOLARSHIP
• See page 560

DONALD A. AND JOHN R. FISHER MEMORIAL SCHOLARSHIP
• See page 561

DWAYNE R. WOERPEL MEMORIAL LEADERSHIP AWARD
• See page 561

ELMER AND DORIS SCHMITZ SR. MEMORIAL SCHOLARSHIP
• See page 561

EUGENE C. BEACH MEMORIAL SCHOLARSHIP
• See page 561

J. RUSSEL SALSBURY MEMORIAL SCHOLARSHIP
• See page 561

MICHAEL J. MORIN MEMORIAL SCHOLARSHIP
• See page 561

MILES GRAY MEMORIAL SCHOLARSHIP
• See page 562

RONALD REAGAN LEADERSHIP AWARD
• See page 562

T.J. SCHMITZ SCHOLARSHIP
• See page 562

WALLACE MCCAULEY MEMORIAL SCHOLARSHIP
• See page 562

WILLIAM V. MUSE SCHOLARSHIP
• See page 562

WILLIAM WILSON MEMORIAL SCHOLARSHIP
• See page 562

TOSHIBA/NSTA http://www.exploravision.org

EXPLORAVISION SCIENCE COMPETITION

Competition for students in grades K-12 who enter as small teams by grade level and work on a science project. In each group, first place team members are each awarded a savings bond worth $10,000 at maturity, second place, a $5000 savings bond. Deadline varies.

Award: Prize for use in freshman year; not renewable. *Number:* varies. *Amount:* $5000–$10,000.

Eligibility Requirements: Applicant must be enrolled or expecting to enroll full- or part-time at a four-year institution or university and must have an interest in science. Available to U.S. citizens.

Application Requirements: Application, applicant must enter a contest. *Deadline:* varies.

Contact: Paloma Olbes, Media Contact
Toshiba/NSTA
c/o Dobbin/Bolgla Associates
156 Fifth Avenue, Fifth Floor
New York, NY 10010
Phone: 212-388-1400
E-mail: polbes@dba-pr.com

TOURO SYNAGOGUE FOUNDATION http://www.tourosynagogue.org

AARON AND RITA SLOM SCHOLARSHIP FUND FOR FREEDOM AND DIVERSITY

Scholarship available for high school seniors who plan to enroll in an institute of higher learning for a minimum of 6 credits. Entries should include an interpretative work focusing on the historic "George Washington Letter to the Congregation" in context with the present time. Text of the letter is available on the Web site. Submissions may be in the form of an essay, story, poem, film, video, or computer presentation. Applications, guidelines, resource materials are available on Web site: http://www.tourosynagogue.org.

Award: Scholarship for use in freshman year; not renewable. *Number:* 2. *Amount:* $1000.

Eligibility Requirements: Applicant must be high school student; planning to enroll or expecting to enroll full- or part-time at a four-year institution or university and must have an interest in writing. Available to U.S. citizens.

Application Requirements: Application, interpretative work based on historic George Washington letter. *Deadline:* March 30.

Contact: Scholarship Committee
Touro Synagogue Foundation
85 Touro Street
Newport, RI 02840
Phone: 401-847-4794 Ext. 31
Fax: 401-845-6790

UNITED NATIONS ASSOCIATION OF THE UNITED STATES OF AMERICA http://www.unausa.org

NATIONAL HIGH SCHOOL ESSAY CONTEST

Essay contest is open to all US students in grades 9-12. Essays should be no longer than 1500 words, typed and double-spaced.

Award: Prize for use in freshman year; not renewable. *Number:* 3. *Amount:* $750–$3000.

Eligibility Requirements: Applicant must be high school student; planning to enroll or expecting to enroll full- or part-time at a four-year institution or university and must have an interest in writing. Available to U.S. citizens.

Application Requirements: Application, applicant must enter a contest, essay. *Deadline:* January 3.

Contact: Scholarship Committee
United Nations Association of the United States of America
801 Second Avenue
New York, NY 10017
Phone: 212-907-1300
Fax: 212-682-9185
E-mail: unahq@unausa.org

UNITED STATES JUNIOR CHAMBER OF COMMERCE http://www.usjaycees.org

JAYCEE CHARLES R. FORD SCHOLARSHIP
• See page 568

JAYCEE THOMAS WOOD BALDRIDGE SCHOLARSHIP
• See page 568

JAYCEE WAR MEMORIAL FUND SCHOLARSHIP

$1000 scholarship for students who are U.S. citizens, possess academic potential and leadership qualities, and show financial need. Minimum 2.5 GPA required. To receive an application, send $10 application fee and stamped, self-addressed envelope by February 1.

Award: Scholarship for use in freshman, sophomore, junior, or senior years; not renewable. *Number:* 10. *Amount:* $1000.

Eligibility Requirements: Applicant must be enrolled or expecting to enroll full-time at a two-year or four-year or technical institution or university and must have an interest in leadership. Applicant must have 2.5 GPA or higher. Available to U.S. citizens.

Application Requirements: Application, financial need analysis, self-addressed stamped envelope, transcript. *Fee:* $10. *Deadline:* February 1.

Contact: Karen Fitzgerald, Customer Service and Data Processing
United States Junior Chamber of Commerce
PO Box 7
Tulsa, OK 74102-0007
Phone: 918-584-2481
Fax: 918-584-4422
E-mail: customerservice@usjaycees.org

USA BADMINTON REGION 1 http://www.northeastbadminton.net

BADMINTON SCHOLARSHIP PROGRAM

Scholarship awarded to a collegiate varsity badminton player exhibiting outstanding achievement, participation, and performance during the badminton playing season. Award is restricted to residents of the northeast region of the United States.

Award: Scholarship for use in freshman, sophomore, junior, or senior years; renewable. *Number:* 1. *Amount:* $1000.

Eligibility Requirements: Applicant must be enrolled or expecting to enroll full-time at a four-year institution or university and must have an interest in athletics/sports. Available to U.S. citizens.

Application Requirements: Application, applicant must enter a contest, references, coaches letter, NCAA team verification. *Deadline:* continuous.

Contact: Eric Miller, Scholarship Program Coordinator
USA Badminton Region 1
125 Prospect Street
Phoenixville, PA 19460
Phone: 610-999-5960
E-mail: eric@usbadminton.net

USA FILM FESTIVAL http://www.usafilmfestival.com

FAMILY AWARD

Award of $500 for the best film or video art at an international level. Some part of the film should be produced in USA. Application fee would be $40 before February 1st and $50 after February 1st.

Award: Prize for use in freshman, sophomore, junior, senior, graduate, or postgraduate years; not renewable. *Number:* 1. *Amount:* $500.

Eligibility Requirements: Applicant must be enrolled or expecting to enroll full- or part-time at a two-year or four-year or technical institution or university and must have an interest in photography/photogrammetry/filmmaking. Available to U.S. and non-U.S. citizens.

Application Requirements: Application, applicant must enter a contest, film/video art. *Deadline:* March 1.

Contact: Ann Alexander, Director of Operations
USA Film Festival
6116 North Central Expressway, Suite 105
Dallas, TX 75206
Phone: 214-821-6300
Fax: 214-821-6364
E-mail: usafilmfestival@aol.com

GRAND PRIZE

Award of $1000 for the best film or video art at an international level. Categories include fiction, non-fiction, experimental and animation. Some part of the film should be produced in USA. Application fee would be $40 before February 1st and $50 after February 1st.

Award: Prize for use in freshman, sophomore, junior, senior, graduate, or postgraduate years; not renewable. *Number:* 4. *Amount:* $1000.

Eligibility Requirements: Applicant must be enrolled or expecting to enroll full- or part-time at a two-year or four-year or technical institution or university and must have an interest in photography/photogrammetry/filmmaking. Available to U.S. and non-U.S. citizens.

Application Requirements: Application, applicant must enter a contest, film/video art. *Deadline:* March 1.

Contact: Ann Alexander, Director of Operations
USA Film Festival
6116 North Central Expressway, Suite 105
Dallas, TX 75206
Phone: 214-821-6300
Fax: 214-821-6364
E-mail: usafilmfestival@aol.com

SPECIAL JURY AWARD

Award of $250 for the best film or video art at an international level. Some part of the film should be produced in USA. Application fee would be $40 before February 1st and $50 after February 1st.

Award: Prize for use in freshman, sophomore, junior, senior, graduate, or postgraduate years; not renewable. *Number:* varies. *Amount:* $250.

Eligibility Requirements: Applicant must be enrolled or expecting to enroll full- or part-time at a two-year or four-year or technical institution or university and must have an interest in photography/photogrammetry/filmmaking. Available to U.S. and non-U.S. citizens.

Application Requirements: Application, applicant must enter a contest, film/video art. *Deadline:* March 1.

Contact: Ann Alexander, Director of Operations
USA Film Festival
6116 North Central Expressway, Suite 105
Dallas, TX 75206
Phone: 214-821-6300
Fax: 214-821-6364
E-mail: usafilmfestival@aol.com

STUDENT AWARD

Award of $500 for the best film or video art at an international level. Some part of the film should be produced in USA. Application fee would be $40 before February 1st and $50 after February 1st.

Award: Prize for use in freshman, sophomore, junior, senior, graduate, or postgraduate years; not renewable. *Number:* 1. *Amount:* $500.

Eligibility Requirements: Applicant must be enrolled or expecting to enroll full- or part-time at a two-year or four-year or technical institution or university and must have an interest in photography/photogrammetry/filmmaking. Available to U.S. and non-U.S. citizens.

Application Requirements: Application, applicant must enter a contest, film/video art. *Deadline:* March 1.

Contact: Ann Alexander, Director of Operations
USA Film Festival
6116 North Central Expressway, Suite 105
Dallas, TX 75206
Phone: 214-821-6300
Fax: 214-821-6364
E-mail: usafilmfestival@aol.com

TEXAS AWARD

Award of $500 for the best film or video art at an international level. Some part of the film should be produced in Texas, USA. Application fee would be $40 before February 1st and $50 after February 1st.

Award: Prize for use in freshman, sophomore, junior, senior, graduate, or postgraduate years; not renewable. *Number:* 1. *Amount:* $500.

Eligibility Requirements: Applicant must be enrolled or expecting to enroll full- or part-time at a four-year or technical institution or university and must have an interest in photography/photogrammetry/filmmaking. Available to U.S. and non-U.S. citizens.

Application Requirements: Application, applicant must enter a contest, film/video art. *Deadline:* March 1.

Contact: Ann Alexander, Director of Operations
USA Film Festival
6116 North Central Expressway, Suite 105
Dallas, TX 75206
Phone: 214-821-6300
Fax: 214-821-6364
E-mail: usafilmfestival@aol.com

USA TODAY/GOT MILK? http://www.bodybymilk.com

SCHOLAR ATHLETE MILK MUSTACHE OF THE YEAR AWARDS

One-time award for senior high school athletes who also achieve in academics, community service, and leadership. Open to legal residents of the 48 contiguous United States and District of Columbia. Residents of Hawaii, Alaska, and Puerto Rico are not eligible. Must submit essay of 75 words or less on how drinking milk has been a part of their life and training regimen. Application only through Web site: http//www.sammyapplication.com.

Award: Scholarship for use in freshman year; not renewable. *Number:* 25. *Amount:* $7500.

Eligibility Requirements: Applicant must be high school student; planning to enroll or expecting to enroll full-time at a four-year institution or university and must have an interest in athletics/sports. Available to U.S. citizens.

USA Today/Got Milk? (continued)

Application Requirements: Application, essay, photo, references, transcript. *Deadline:* March 7.

Contact: Debbie McMahon, Scholarship Committee
USA Today/Got Milk?
6701 Democracy Boulevard, Suite 300
Bethesda, MD 20817
Phone: 800-828-4414 Ext. 5418
E-mail: dmcmahon@usatoday.com

VETERANS OF FOREIGN WARS OF THE UNITED STATES http://www.vfw.org

PATRIOT'S PEN

Nationwide essay contest that gives students in grades six, seven and eight the opportunity to write essays expressing their views on democracy.

Award: Prize for use in freshman year; renewable. *Number:* up to 44. *Amount:* $1000–$10,000.

Eligibility Requirements: Applicant must be high school student; planning to enroll or expecting to enroll full-time at a four-year institution or university and must have an interest in writing. Available to U.S. citizens.

Application Requirements: Application, applicant must enter a contest, essay. *Deadline:* November 1.

Contact: Kris Harmer, Secretary
Veterans of Foreign Wars of the United States
406 West 34th Street, VFW Building
Kansas City, MO 64111
Phone: 816-968-1117
Fax: 816-968-1149
E-mail: kharmer@vfw.org

VOICE OF DEMOCRACY PROGRAM

Student must be sponsored by a local VFW Post. Student submits a three to five minute audio essay on a contest theme (changes each year). Open to high school students (9th to 12th grade). Award available for all levels of postsecondary study in an American institution. Open to permanent U.S. residents only. Competition starts at local level. No entries are to be submitted to the National Headquarters. Visit Web site http://www.vfw.org for more information.

Award: Prize for use in freshman year; not renewable. *Number:* 59. *Amount:* $1000–$30,000.

Eligibility Requirements: Applicant must be high school student; age 19 or under; planning to enroll or expecting to enroll full- or part-time at a four-year institution or university and must have an interest in public speaking or writing. Available to U.S. and non-U.S. citizens.

Application Requirements: Application, applicant must enter a contest, essay, audio cassette tape. *Deadline:* November 1.

Contact: Kris Harmer, Secretary
Veterans of Foreign Wars of the United States
406 West 34th Street, VFW Building
Kansas City, MO 64111
Phone: 816-968-1117
Fax: 816-968-1149
E-mail: kharmer@vfw.org

VIRGINIA CONGRESS OF PARENTS AND TEACHERS http://www.vapta.org

CITIZENSHIP ESSAY PROJECT

• *See page 817*

VSA ARTS http://www.vsarts.org

VSA ARTS PLAYWRIGHT DISCOVERY AWARD

One-time award for students in grades 6 to 12, with and without disabilities. One-act script must explore the experience of living with a disability. One script is selected for production and one is selected for a staged reading at the John F. Kennedy Center for the Performing Arts. A jury of theater professionals selects the winning scripts, and award recipients receive monetary awards and a trip to Washington, D.C. to view the reading or production.

Award: Scholarship for use in freshman year; not renewable. *Number:* 1. *Amount:* $2000.

Eligibility Requirements: Applicant must be high school student; planning to enroll or expecting to enroll full- or part-time at a four-year institution or university and must have an interest in theater or writing. Available to U.S. citizens.

Application Requirements: Application, applicant must enter a contest, autobiography, 2 copies of typed script. *Deadline:* April 11.

Contact: Liz McCloskey, Performing Arts Manager
VSA arts
818 Connecticut Avenue, NW, Suite 600
Washington, DC 20006
Phone: 800-933-8721
Fax: 202-429-0868
E-mail: info@vsarts.org

WALTER W. NAUMBURG FOUNDATION http://www.naumburg.org

INTERNATIONAL VIOLONCELLO COMPETITION

Prizes of $2500 to $7500 awarded to violoncellists between the ages of 17 and 31. Application fee is $125.

Award: Prize for use in freshman, sophomore, junior, senior, graduate, or postgraduate years; not renewable. *Number:* 3. *Amount:* $2500–$7500.

Eligibility Requirements: Applicant must be age 17-31; enrolled or expecting to enroll full- or part-time at a two-year or four-year or technical institution or university and must have an interest in music. Available to U.S. and non-U.S. citizens.

Application Requirements: Application, applicant must enter a contest, references, self-addressed stamped envelope, applicant's audio track (CD) of no less than 30 minutes. *Fee:* $125. *Deadline:* March 1.

Contact: Lucy Mann, Executive Director
Walter W. Naumburg Foundation
120 Claremont Avenue
New York, NY 10027-4698
Phone: 212-362-9877
Fax: 212-362-9877
E-mail: luciamann@aol.com

WATERBURY FOUNDATION http://www.conncf.org

FERRIS P. ELLIS CREATIVE WRITING SCHOLARSHIP

• *See page 819*

WILLIAM G. AND MARIE SELBY FOUNDATION http://www.selbyfdn.org

SELBY SCHOLAR PROGRAM

• *See page 613*

WILLIAM RANDOLPH HEARST FOUNDATION http://www.hearstfdn.org

UNITED STATES SENATE YOUTH PROGRAM

Scholarship for high school juniors and seniors holding elected student offices. Two students selected from each state. Selection process will vary by state. Contact school principal or state department of education for information. Deadlines: early fall of each year for most states, but specific date will vary by state. Program is open to citizens and permanent residents of the United States Department of Defense schools overseas and the District of Columbia (not the territories).

Award: Scholarship for use in freshman year; not renewable. *Number:* 104. *Amount:* $5000.

Eligibility Requirements: Applicant must be high school student; planning to enroll or expecting to enroll full-time at a technical institution and must have an interest in leadership. Available to U.S. citizens.

Application Requirements: Application procedures will vary by state. *Deadline:* varies.

Contact: Rayne Guilford, Program Director
William Randolph Hearst Foundation
90 New Montgomery Street, Suite 1212
San Francisco, CA 94105-4504
Phone: 800-841-7048
Fax: 415-243-0760
E-mail: ussyp@hearstfdn.org

WOMEN'S BASKETBALL COACHES ASSOCIATION http://www.wbca.org

WBCA SCHOLARSHIP AWARD

One-time award for two women's basketball players who have demonstrated outstanding commitment to the sport of women's basketball and to academic excellence. Minimum 3.5 GPA required. Must be nominated by the head coach of women's basketball who is WBCA member.

Award: Scholarship for use in freshman, sophomore, junior, senior, or graduate years; not renewable. *Number:* up to 2. *Amount:* up to $1000.

Eligibility Requirements: Applicant must be enrolled or expecting to enroll full- or part-time at a four-year institution or university; female and must have an interest in athletics/sports. Applicant must have 3.5 GPA or higher. Available to U.S. and non-U.S. citizens.

Application Requirements: Application, references, statistics. *Deadline:* February 15.

Contact: Betty Jaynes, Consultant
Women's Basketball Coaches Association
4646 Lawrenceville Highway
Lilburn, GA 30047-3620
Phone: 770-279-8027 Ext. 102
Fax: 770-279-6290
E-mail: bettyj@wbca.org

WOMEN'S INTERNATIONAL BOWLING CONGRESS http://www.bowl.com

ALBERTA E. CROWE STAR OF TOMORROW AWARD

Nonrenewable award for a U.S. or Canadian female college student who competes in the sport of bowling. Must be a current USBC member in good standing, and under 21 years of age. Minimum 2.5 GPA required.

Award: Scholarship for use in sophomore, junior, or senior years; not renewable. *Number:* 1. *Amount:* $6000.

Eligibility Requirements: Applicant must be age 21 or under; enrolled or expecting to enroll full-time at a four-year institution or university; female and must have an interest in bowling. Applicant must have 2.5 GPA or higher. Available to U.S. and non-U.S. citizens.

Application Requirements: Application, essay, references, transcript. *Deadline:* October 1.

Contact: Ed Gocha, Manager
Women's International Bowling Congress
5301 South 76th Street
Greendale, WI 53129-1192
Phone: 800-514-2695 Ext. 3343
Fax: 414-421-3013
E-mail: readsmart@bowl.com

WOMEN'S WESTERN GOLF FOUNDATION http://www.wwga.org/foundation.htm

WOMEN'S WESTERN GOLF FOUNDATION SCHOLARSHIP

Scholarships for female high school seniors for use at a four-year college or university. Based on academic record, financial need, character, and involvement in golf. Golf skill not a criteria. Must continue to have financial need. Award is $2000 per student per year. Must be 17 to 18 years of age.

Award: Scholarship for use in freshman year; renewable. *Number:* up to 70. *Amount:* $2000.

Eligibility Requirements: Applicant must be high school student; age 17-18; planning to enroll or expecting to enroll full-time at a four-year institution or university; female and must have an interest in golf. Applicant must have 3.0 GPA or higher. Available to U.S. citizens.

Application Requirements: Application, self-addressed stamped envelope. *Deadline:* March 1.

Contact: Richard Willis, Scholarship Chairman
Women's Western Golf Foundation
393 Ramsay Road
Deerfield, IL 60015
Phone: 847-945-0451
E-mail: wwgasfw@aol.com

WRITER'S DIGEST http://www.writersdigest.com

WRITER'S DIGEST ANNUAL WRITING COMPETITION

Annual writing competition. Only original, unpublished entries in any of the ten categories accepted. Send self-addressed stamped envelope for guidelines and entry form. Application fee: $15.

Award: Prize for use in freshman, sophomore, junior, senior, or graduate years; not renewable. *Number:* 100. *Amount:* $25–$3000.

Eligibility Requirements: Applicant must be enrolled or expecting to enroll full- or part-time at a two-year or four-year or technical institution or university and must have an interest in writing. Available to U.S. and non-U.S. citizens.

Application Requirements: Application, applicant must enter a contest, self-addressed stamped envelope. *Fee:* $15. *Deadline:* May 1.

Contact: Joan Gay, Customer Service Representative
Writer's Digest
4700 East Galbraith Road
Cincinnati, OH 45236
Phone: 513-531-2690
Fax: 513-531-0798
E-mail: competitions@fwpubs.com

WRITER'S DIGEST POPULAR FICTION AWARDS

Writing contest accepts as many manuscripts as the applicant likes in each of the following categories: romance, mystery/crime fiction, sci-fi/fantasy, thriller/suspense and horror. Manuscripts must not be more than 4,000 words.

Award: Prize for use in freshman, sophomore, junior, senior, graduate, or postgraduate years; not renewable. *Number:* 6. *Amount:* $500–$2500.

Eligibility Requirements: Applicant must be enrolled or expecting to enroll full- or part-time at a two-year or four-year or technical institution or university and must have an interest in writing. Available to U.S. and non-U.S. citizens.

Application Requirements: Application, applicant must enter a contest, self-addressed stamped envelope, manuscript. *Fee:* $12. *Deadline:* November 1.

Contact: Terri Boes, Customer Service Representative
Writer's Digest
4700 East Galbraith Road
Cincinnati, OH 45236
Phone: 513-531-2690 Ext. 1328
Fax: 513-531-0798
E-mail: competitions@fwpubs.com

WRITER'S DIGEST SELF-PUBLISHED BOOK AWARDS

Awards open to self-published books for which the author has paid full cost. Send self-addressed stamped envelope for guidelines and entry form. Application fee: $100.

Award: Prize for use in freshman, sophomore, junior, senior, graduate, or postgraduate years; not renewable. *Number:* 10. *Amount:* $1000–$3000.

Eligibility Requirements: Applicant must be enrolled or expecting to enroll full- or part-time at a two-year or four-year or technical institution or university and must have an interest in writing. Available to U.S. and non-U.S. citizens.

Application Requirements: Application, applicant must enter a contest, self-addressed stamped envelope. *Fee:* $100. *Deadline:* May 1.

Contact: Joan Gay, Customer Service Representative
Writer's Digest
4700 East Galbraith Road
Cincinnati, OH 45236
Phone: 513-531-2690 Ext. 1328
Fax: 513-531-0798
E-mail: competitions@fwpubs.com

YOUNG AMERICAN BOWLING ALLIANCE (YABA) http://www.bowl.com

GIFT FOR LIFE SCHOLARSHIP

• *See page 571*

Young American Bowling Alliance (YABA) (continued)

PEPSI-COLA YOUTH BOWLING CHAMPIONSHIPS

• *See page 571*

USBC ALBERTA E. CROWE STAR OF TOMORROW AWARD

Award given to recognize star qualities in a female high school or college student who competes in the sport of bowling. Applicants must be current USBC Youth or USBC members in good standing and currently competing in certified events.

Award: Prize for use in freshman, sophomore, junior, or senior years; not renewable. *Number:* 1. *Amount:* $6000.

Eligibility Requirements: Applicant must be enrolled or expecting to enroll full-time at a two-year or four-year institution or university; female and must have an interest in bowling. Applicant must have 2.5 GPA or higher. Available to U.S. citizens.

Application Requirements: Application, applicant must enter a contest, references, transcript. *Deadline:* October 1.

Contact: Ed Gocha, Scholarship Programs Manager
Young American Bowling Alliance (YABA)
5301 South 76th Street
Greendale, WI 53129-1192
Phone: 800-514-2695
Fax: 414-423-3014
E-mail: smart@bowlinginc.com

USBC ANNUAL ZEB SCHOLARSHIP

• *See page 613*

USBC CHUCK HALL STAR OF TOMORROW SCHOLARSHIP

Scholarship is given to recognize star qualities in a male high school senior or college student who competes in the sport of bowling. Applicant must be a current USBC Youth or USBC member in good standing and currently compete in certified events.

Award: Scholarship for use in freshman, sophomore, junior, or senior years; renewable. *Number:* 1. *Amount:* $6000.

Eligibility Requirements: Applicant must be enrolled or expecting to enroll full-time at a two-year or four-year institution or university; male and must have an interest in bowling. Applicant must have 2.5 GPA or higher. Available to U.S. citizens.

Application Requirements: Application, references, transcript. *Deadline:* October 1.

Contact: Ed Gocha, Scholarship Programs Manager
Young American Bowling Alliance (YABA)
5301 South 76th Street
Greendale, WI 53129-1192
Phone: 800-514-2695
Fax: 414-423-3014
E-mail: smart@bowlinginc.com

USBC EARL ANTHONY MEMORIAL SCHOLARSHIPS

Scholarship given to recognize male and/or female bowlers for their community involvement and academic achievements, both in high school and college. Candidates must be enrolled in their senior year of high school or presently attending college and be current members of USBC in good standing.

Award: Scholarship for use in freshman, sophomore, junior, or senior years; not renewable. *Number:* 5. *Amount:* $5000.

Eligibility Requirements: Applicant must be enrolled or expecting to enroll full- or part-time at a two-year or four-year institution or university and must have an interest in bowling. Applicant must have 2.5 GPA or higher. Available to U.S. citizens.

Application Requirements: Application, references, transcript. *Deadline:* May 1.

Contact: Ed Gocha, Scholarship Programs Manager
Young American Bowling Alliance (YABA)
5301 South 76th Street
Greendale, WI 53129-1192
Phone: 800-514-2695
Fax: 414-423-3014
E-mail: smart@bowlinginc.com

USBC MALE AND FEMALE YOUTH LEADERS OF THE YEAR SCHOLARSHIP

Scholarship presented to one male and one female Youth Leader who has demonstrated outstanding skills in organizing, administering and promoting youth bowling at the local and/or state level.

Award: Scholarship for use in freshman year; not renewable. *Number:* 2. *Amount:* $1500.

Eligibility Requirements: Applicant must be high school student; planning to enroll or expecting to enroll full- or part-time at a four-year institution or university and must have an interest in bowling. Available to U.S. citizens.

Application Requirements: Application, references, transcript. *Deadline:* November 1.

Contact: Ed Gocha, Scholarship Programs Manager
Young American Bowling Alliance (YABA)
5301 South 76th Street
Greendale, WI 53129-1192
Phone: 800-514-2695
Fax: 414-423-3014
E-mail: smart@bowlinginc.com

YOUTH OPPORTUNITIES FOUNDATION

YOUTH OPPORTUNITIES FOUNDATION SCHOLARSHIPS

• *See page 713*

ZINCH.COM http://www.zinch.com

ZINCH.COM "STUDENT GOVERNMENT" SCHOLARSHIP

The program awards outstanding high school students who are members of the high school student government or student council. Scholarships ranges from $1000 to $5000. To apply, a high school student needs to fill out a zinch.com profile. Both the need of student and merit of student are considered. Winners are chosen based on the student's zinch.com profile. A minimum 2.0 GPA is required.

Award: Scholarship for use in freshman year; renewable. *Number:* 1–8. *Amount:* $1000–$5000.

Eligibility Requirements: Applicant must be high school student; planning to enroll or expecting to enroll full- or part-time at a four-year institution or university and must have an interest in leadership. Available to U.S. and non-U.S. citizens.

Application Requirements: Application. *Deadline:* May 25.

Contact: Mick Hagen, CEO
Zinch.com
42 North University Avenue, Suite 210
Provo, UT 84601
Phone: 801-830-2048
Fax: 801-356-0293
E-mail: mickey@zinch.com

Miscellaneous Criteria

ALFRED G. AND ELMA M. MILOTTE SCHOLARSHIP FUND http://www.milotte.org

ALFRED G. AND ELMA M. MILOTTE SCHOLARSHIP

Grant of up to $4000 to high school graduate or students holding the GED. Applicants must have been accepted at a trade school, art school, two-year or four-year college or university for undergraduate or graduate studies.

Award: Scholarship for use in freshman, sophomore, junior, senior, or graduate years; not renewable. *Number:* varies. *Amount:* up to $4000.

Eligibility Requirements: Applicant must be enrolled or expecting to enroll full- or part-time at a two-year or four-year or technical institution or university. Applicant must have 3.0 GPA or higher. Available to U.S. citizens.

Application Requirements: Application, references, transcript, samples of work expressing applicant's observations of the natural world. *Deadline:* March 1.

Contact: Sean Ferguson, Assistant Vice President
Alfred G. and Elma M. Milotte Scholarship Fund
Bank of America Trust Services, 715 Peachtree Street, Eighth Floor
Atlanta, GA 30308
Phone: 800-832-9071
Fax: 800-552-3182
E-mail: info@milotte.org

ALL-INK.COM PRINTER SUPPLIES ONLINE http://www.all-ink.com

ALL-INK.COM COLLEGE SCHOLARSHIP PROGRAM

One-time award for any level of postsecondary education. Minimum 2.5 GPA. Must apply online only at Web site http://www.all-ink.com. Recipients selected annually.

Award: Scholarship for use in freshman, sophomore, junior, senior, graduate, or postgraduate years; not renewable. *Number:* 5–10. *Amount:* $1000–$5000.

Eligibility Requirements: Applicant must be enrolled or expecting to enroll full-time at a two-year or four-year or technical institution or university. Applicant must have 2.5 GPA or higher. Available to U.S. and non-U.S. citizens.

Application Requirements: Application, applicant must enter a contest, essay. *Deadline:* December 31.

Contact: Aaron M. Gale, President
All-Ink.com Printer Supplies Online
1460 North Main Street, Suite 2
Spanish Fork, UT 84660
Phone: 801-794-0123
Fax: 801-794-0124
E-mail: scholarship@all-ink.com

ALPHA KAPPA ALPHA http://www.akaeaf.org

AKA EDUCATIONAL ADVANCEMENT FOUNDATION UNMET FINANCIAL NEED SCHOLARSHIP

Scholarship for students who have completed a minimum of one year in a degree-granting institution and need financial aid to continue their studies in such an institution. May also be a student in a non-institutional based program that may or may not grant degrees, and must submit a course of study outline. Must have a minimum GPA of 2.5.

Award: Scholarship for use in sophomore, junior, senior, or graduate years; not renewable. *Number:* varies. *Amount:* $750–$2000.

Eligibility Requirements: Applicant must be enrolled or expecting to enroll full-time at a four-year institution or university. Applicant must have 2.5 GPA or higher. Available to U.S. and non-U.S. citizens.

Application Requirements: Application, references. *Deadline:* varies.

Contact: Andrea Kerr, Program Coordinator
Alpha Kappa Alpha
5656 South Stony Island Avenue
Chicago, IL 60637
Phone: 773-947-0026 Ext. 8
E-mail: akaeaf@akaeaf.net

ALPHA LAMBDA DELTA http://www.nationalald.org

JO ANNE J. TROW SCHOLARSHIPS

One-time award for initiated members of Alpha Lambda Delta. Minimum 3.5 GPA required. Must be nominated by chapter.

Award: Scholarship for use in junior year; not renewable. *Number:* up to 35. *Amount:* $1000–$3000.

Eligibility Requirements: Applicant must be enrolled or expecting to enroll full-time at a four-year institution or university. Applicant must have 3.5 GPA or higher. Available to U.S. and non-U.S. citizens.

Application Requirements: Application, essay, references, transcript. *Deadline:* April 1.

Contact: Glenda Earwood, Executive Director
Alpha Lambda Delta
PO Box 4403
Macon, GA 31208-4403
Phone: 478-744-9595
Fax: 478-744-9929
E-mail: glenda@nationalald.org

AMERICAN FIRE SPRINKLER ASSOCIATION http://www.afsascholarship.org

AFSA SCHOLARSHIP CONTEST

One-time award for high school seniors. Must submit essay, application, and recommendation and must take an online test. Visit web site for essay topic and application.

Award: Scholarship for use in freshman year; not renewable. *Number:* 10. *Amount:* $2000.

Eligibility Requirements: Applicant must be high school student and planning to enroll or expecting to enroll full-time at a two-year or four-year or technical institution or university. Available to U.S. citizens.

Application Requirements: Applicant must enter a contest, online test. *Deadline:* August 28.

Contact: D'Arcy Montalvo, Public Relations Manager
American Fire Sprinkler Association
9696 Skillman Street, Suite 300
Dallas, TX 75243
Phone: 214-349-5965
Fax: 214-343-8898
E-mail: dmontalvo@firesprinkler.org

AMERICAN INSTITUTE FOR FOREIGN STUDY http://www.aifsabroad.com

STUDY AGAIN SCHOLARSHIPS

Scholarships for AIFS alumni. AIFS summer program students will receive a $1500 scholarship to study abroad on an AIFS semester or academic year program. AIFS semester or academic year program students will receive a $500 scholarship towards a four or five week summer program, or a $750 scholarship towards a summer program of six weeks or more.

Award: Scholarship for use in freshman, sophomore, junior, or senior years; not renewable. *Number:* up to 15. *Amount:* $500–$1500.

American Institute for Foreign Study (continued)

Eligibility Requirements: Applicant must be enrolled or expecting to enroll full-time at a two-year or four-year institution or university. Applicant must have 2.5 GPA or higher. Available to U.S. and non-U.S. citizens.

Application Requirements: Application, essay, photo, references, transcript. *Fee:* $95. *Deadline:* varies.

Contact: David Mauro, Admissions Counselor
American Institute for Foreign Study
9 West Broad Street, River Plaza
Stamford, CT 06902-3788
Phone: 800-727-2437 Ext. 5163
Fax: 203-399-5463
E-mail: dmauro@aifs.com

AMERICAN INSTITUTE OF CERTIFIED PUBLIC ACCOUNTANTS http://www.aicpa.org

AICPA/ACCOUNTEMPS STUDENT SCHOLARSHIP

This program provides financial assistance to students who are currently majoring in accounting, finance, or information systems to encourage them to consider careers in accounting and business. Eligible applicants will have an overall and major GPA of at least 3.0 and be enrolled as a full-time undergraduate or graduate student at an accredited college/university.

Award: Scholarship for use in freshman, sophomore, junior, senior, graduate, or postgraduate years; not renewable. *Number:* up to 5. *Amount:* up to $2500.

Eligibility Requirements: Applicant must be enrolled or expecting to enroll full-time at a two-year or four-year institution or university. Applicant must have 3.0 GPA or higher. Available to U.S. and non-U.S. citizens.

Application Requirements: Application, essay, references, test scores, transcript. *Deadline:* April 1.

Contact: Danielle Grant, Coordinator of Education and Recruitment
American Institute of Certified Public Accountants
Palladian One, 220 Leigh Farm Road
Durham, NC 27707
Phone: 919-402-4014
E-mail: educat@aicpa.org

ANYCOLLEGE.COM http://www.anycollege.com

ANYCOLLEGE.COM SCHOLARSHIP

Four $2000 scholarships awarded annually by random drawing. All students planning to attend an accredited college or university are eligible to apply. Deadlines: March 31, June 30, September 30, and December 31.

Award: Scholarship for use in freshman year; renewable. *Number:* 4. *Amount:* $2000.

Eligibility Requirements: Applicant must be high school student and planning to enroll or expecting to enroll full-time at a two-year or four-year institution or university. Available to U.S. and non-U.S. citizens.

Application Requirements: Application, applicant must enter a contest. *Deadline:* varies.

Contact: Cory Klinnert, Director of Marketing
AnyCollege.com
403 Center Avenue, Suite 704
Moorhead, MN 56560
Phone: 218-284-9933
Fax: 218-284-3394
E-mail: cklinnert@anycollege.com

BANK OF AMERICA STUDENT BANKING GROUP http://www.bankofamerica.com

BANK OF AMERICA FINANCIAL AID SWEEPSTAKES

Scholarship available to legal residents of the United States, including the District of Columbia, 13 years of age or older who are full-time high school seniors or college students (attending a high school or accredited college or university within the U.S).

Award: Scholarship for use in freshman, sophomore, junior, or senior years; not renewable. *Number:* 5. *Amount:* $1000.

Eligibility Requirements: Applicant must be age 13 and over and enrolled or expecting to enroll full-time at a two-year or four-year institution or university. Available to U.S. citizens.

Application Requirements: Application, transcript. *Deadline:* July 20.

Contact: Program Manager
Bank of America Student Banking Group
PO Box 515210
Los Angeles, CA 90051-6510
Phone: 213-345-2244

BARBIZON INTERNATIONAL LLC http://www.barbizonscholarship.com

BARBIZON COLLEGE TUITION SCHOLARSHIP

Scholarship for full college tuition is awarded every other year by random drawing. Entry forms are available at high schools throughout the United States. For more details, visit web site: http://www.barbizonscholarship.com.

Award: Scholarship for use in freshman, sophomore, junior, or senior years; not renewable. *Number:* 1. *Amount:* up to $100,000.

Eligibility Requirements: Applicant must be enrolled or expecting to enroll full-time at a four-year institution or university. Available to U.S. citizens.

Application Requirements: Application, applicant must enter a contest. *Deadline:* December 1.

Contact: Wendy Cleveland, Vice President of Marketing
Barbizon International LLC
3111 North University Drive, Suite 1002
Coral Springs, FL 33065
Phone: 954-345-4140
Fax: 954-345-8055
E-mail: wendy@barbizonmodeling.com

BRICKFISH http://www.brickfish.com

BATTLE OF THE FANS PRIZE

$100 to $5000 prize for U.S. residents 18 years or older at the time of entry. Requires Internet access for entry.

Award: Scholarship for use in freshman, sophomore, junior, senior, graduate, or postgraduate years; not renewable. *Number:* 2–54. *Amount:* $100–$5000.

Eligibility Requirements: Applicant must be age 18 and over and enrolled or expecting to enroll full- or part-time at a two-year or four-year or technical institution or university. Available to U.S. citizens.

Application Requirements: Applicant must enter a contest, photo or video demonstrating being a Super Fan. *Deadline:* March 26.

Contact: Chris Hall, Senior Director
Brickfish
6165 Greenwich Drive, Suite 320
San Diego, CA 92122
Phone: 858-587-2530 Ext. 434
Fax: 858-875-6688
E-mail: membersupport@brickfish.com

BRICKFISH SCHOLARSHIPS

Scholarships for Brickfish.com members who are at least 14 years of age or older.

Award: Scholarship for use in freshman, sophomore, junior, senior, graduate, or postgraduate years; not renewable. *Number:* 5–30. *Amount:* $100–$1000.

Eligibility Requirements: Applicant must be age 14 and over and enrolled or expecting to enroll full- or part-time at a two-year or four-year or technical institution or university. Available to U.S. and Canadian citizens.

Application Requirements: Application, applicant must enter a contest. *Deadline:* varies.

Contact: Chris Hall, Senior Director
Brickfish
6165 Greenwich Drive, Suite 320
San Diego, CA 92122
Phone: 858-587-2530 Ext. 434
E-mail: membersupport@brickfish.com

$1,000 VIDEO ESSAY CONTEST

Contest open to anyone who has access to the Internet, who is 14 years of age or older at the time of entry, and is a member of Brickfish.com community.

Award: Prize for use in freshman, sophomore, junior, senior, graduate, or postgraduate years; not renewable. *Number:* 2. *Amount:* $250–$1000.

Eligibility Requirements: Applicant must be age 14 and over and enrolled or expecting to enroll full- or part-time at a two-year or four-year or technical institution or university. Available to U.S. and non-U.S. citizens.

Application Requirements: Applicant must enter a contest, video essay. *Deadline:* March 31.

Contact: Chris Hall, Senior Director
Brickfish
6165 Greenwich Drive, Suite 320
San Diego, CA 92122
Phone: 858-587-2530 Ext. 434
Fax: 858-875-6688
E-mail: membersupport@brickfish.com

BRIDGESTONE FIRESTONE http://www.bfor.com

SAFETY SCHOLARS VIDEO CONTEST SCHOLARSHIP

Three $5000 college scholarships for the most compelling and effective videos that drive home life-saving messages on auto and tire safety. Must be between the ages of 16 and 21, possess a valid driver's license, and be enrolled as a full-time student in an accredited secondary, college level, or trade school.

Award: Scholarship for use in freshman, sophomore, junior, or senior years; not renewable. *Number:* 3. *Amount:* $5000.

Eligibility Requirements: Applicant must be age 16-21 and enrolled or expecting to enroll full-time at a four-year institution. Available to U.S. citizens.

Application Requirements: Applicant must enter a contest, driver's license, 25- or 55-second video about auto safety. *Deadline:* June 24.

Contact: Miss. Ashley Charlton, Assistant Account Executive
Bridgestone Firestone
209 Seventh Avenue, North
Nashville, TN 37219
Phone: 615-780-3383
E-mail: ashley.charlton@dvl.com

CANADA MILLENNIUM SCHOLARSHIP FOUNDATION http://www.millenniumscholarships.ca

CANADA MILLENNIUM EXCELLENCE AWARD PROGRAM

• *See page 675*

CAREER COLLEGE FOUNDATION http://www.imagine-america.org

IMAGINE AMERICA SCHOLARSHIP

One-time award available to graduating high school seniors. Must attend an accredited private postsecondary institution. Must be nominated by school counselor or principal. See Web site: http://www.careercollegefoundation.com. Contact the guidance counselor at high school.

Award: Scholarship for use in freshman year; not renewable. *Number:* up to 8500. *Amount:* $1000.

Eligibility Requirements: Applicant must be high school student; age 17-18 and planning to enroll or expecting to enroll full-time at a two-year or four-year or technical institution. Applicant must have 2.5 GPA or higher. Available to U.S. citizens.

Application Requirements: Financial need analysis, nomination. *Deadline:* December 31.

Contact: Chris Carroll, Foundation Staff Member
Career College Foundation
10 G Street, NE, Suite 750
Washington, DC 20002-4213
Phone: 202-336-6812
Fax: 202-408-8102
E-mail: chrisc@imagine-america.org

CARPE DIEM FOUNDATION OF ILLINOIS http://www.carpediemfoundation.org

CARPE DIEM FOUNDATION OF ILLINOIS SCHOLARSHIP COMPETITION

Renewable awards for U.S. citizens studying full-time at accredited U.S. educational institutions, including music conservatories, schools of design, and academies of the arts. For undergraduate study only. Merit based. Priority is given to students whose parents are or have been employed in education; local, state, or federal government; social service or public health; the administration of justice; the fine arts. Must maintain a B average and demonstrate commitment to public service.

Award: Scholarship for use in freshman, sophomore, junior, or senior years; renewable. *Number:* 10–15. *Amount:* $2500–$5000.

Eligibility Requirements: Applicant must be enrolled or expecting to enroll full-time at a four-year institution or university. Applicant must have 3.0 GPA or higher. Available to U.S. citizens.

Application Requirements: Application, essay, references, self-addressed stamped envelope, test scores, transcript, portfolio, CD, tape (if arts or music candidate). *Fee:* $10. *Deadline:* May 13.

Contact: Gordon V. Levine, Executive Director
Carpe Diem Foundation of Illinois
PO Box 3194
Chicago, IL 60690-3194
Phone: 312-263-3416
E-mail: glevine@carpediemfoundation.org

CENTER FOR SCHOLARSHIP ADMINISTRATION http://www.scholarshipprograms.org

NARUSE ACADEMIC SCHOLARSHIP FUND

Renewable four-year scholarship offered to students who are eligible dependent employees of AFL Telecommunications who have been continuously employed for a period of at least one year prior to the year the student is applying for the award. Must be high school seniors or home-schooled students, have a cumulative GPA of 3.0, and attend an accredited four-year college or university offering a bachelor's degree.

Award: Scholarship for use in freshman year; renewable. *Number:* varies. *Amount:* $2000.

Eligibility Requirements: Applicant must be high school student and planning to enroll or expecting to enroll full-time at a four-year institution or university. Applicant must have 3.0 GPA or higher. Available to U.S. citizens.

Application Requirements: Application, essay, references, test scores, transcript. *Deadline:* March 7.

Contact: Scholarship Program Coordinator
Center for Scholarship Administration
PO Box 1465
Taylors, SC 29687
Phone: 864-268-3363
E-mail: ljenkinscsa@bellsouth.net

COCA-COLA SCHOLARS FOUNDATION INC. http://www.coca-colascholars.org

COCA-COLA SCHOLARS PROGRAM

Renewable scholarship for graduating high school seniors enrolled either full-time or part-time in accredited colleges or universities. Minimum 3.0 GPA required. 250 awards are granted annually.

Award: Scholarship for use in freshman year; renewable. *Number:* 250. *Amount:* $10,000–$20,000.

Eligibility Requirements: Applicant must be high school student and planning to enroll or expecting to enroll full- or part-time at a two-year or

Coca-Cola Scholars Foundation Inc. (continued)

four-year or technical institution or university. Applicant must have 3.0 GPA or higher. Available to U.S. citizens.

Application Requirements: Application, essay, interview, references, test scores, transcript. *Deadline:* varies.

Contact: Mark Davis, President
Coca-Cola Scholars Foundation Inc.
PO Box 442
Atlanta, GA 30301-0442
Phone: 800-306-2653
Fax: 404-733-5439
E-mail: scholars@na.ko.com

CODA INTERNATIONAL http://www.coda-international.org

MILLIE BROTHER ANNUAL SCHOLARSHIP FOR CHILDREN OF DEAF ADULTS

Scholarship awarded to any higher education student who is the hearing child of deaf parents. One-time award based on transcripts, letters of reference, and an essay.

Award: Scholarship for use in freshman, sophomore, junior, or senior years; not renewable. *Number:* 2. *Amount:* up to $3000.

Eligibility Requirements: Applicant must be enrolled or expecting to enroll full-time at a two-year or four-year institution or university. Available to U.S. and non-U.S. citizens.

Application Requirements: Application, essay, references, self-addressed stamped envelope, transcript. *Deadline:* May 2.

Contact: Dr. Robert J. Hoffmeister, Chair, Scholarship
CODA International
Boston University, 6 Commonwealth Avenue
Boston, MA 02215
Phone: 617-353-3205
Fax: 617-353-3292
E-mail: rhoff@bu.edu

COLLEGE FOUNDATION OF NORTH CAROLINA INC. http://www.cfnc.org

NORTH CAROLINA EDUCATION AND TRAINING VOUCHER PROGRAM

Four-year scholarship for foster youth and former foster youth. You must have been accepted into or be enrolled in a degree, certificate or other accredited program at a college, university, technical or vocational school and show progress towards a degree or certificate. Must be a U.S. citizen or qualified non-citizen. Must have an active email account to complete the application form.

Award: Scholarship for use in freshman, sophomore, junior, or senior years; not renewable. *Number:* varies. *Amount:* up to $5000.

Eligibility Requirements: Applicant must be age 18-20 and enrolled or expecting to enroll full-time at a two-year or four-year institution or university. Available to U.S. and non-U.S. citizens.

Application Requirements: Application, essay. *Deadline:* continuous.

Contact: Scholarship Committee
College Foundation of North Carolina Inc.
PO Box 41966
Raleigh, NC 27629-1966
Phone: 888-234-6400
E-mail: etv@statevoucher.org

COLLEGE IN COLORADO http://www.collegeincolorado.org

GET SCHOOLED! SCHOLARSHIP

Entrants must be legal residents of the United States and a student between the ages of 13-18 residing in Colorado. Residency is subject to verification under Colorado law. One entry per student. Amount ranges from $400 to $850.

Award: Scholarship for use in freshman year; not renewable. *Number:* varies. *Amount:* $400–$850.

Eligibility Requirements: Applicant must be age 13-18 and enrolled or expecting to enroll full- or part-time at a four-year institution or university. Available to U.S. citizens.

Application Requirements: Application, essay. *Deadline:* varies.

Contact: Scholarship Committee
College in Colorado
1801 Broadway, Suite 360
Denver, CO 80202

COLLEGE INSIDER RESOURCES http://www.ezcir.com

COLLEGE INSIDER RADIO SCHOLARSHIP

Scholarship for both high school and college students in the U.S. as well as international students. High school students must have a 2.0 GPA, and college students must have 2.5 GPA. This is a need/merit based scholarship awarded monthly.

Award: Scholarship for use in freshman, sophomore, junior, senior, graduate, or postgraduate years; renewable. *Number:* 1–3. *Amount:* $500–$1000.

Eligibility Requirements: Applicant must be enrolled or expecting to enroll full-time at a two-year or four-year institution or university. Available to U.S. and non-U.S. citizens.

Application Requirements: Application, essay, financial need analysis. *Deadline:* continuous.

Contact: Mr. Cliff deQuilettes, CEO
Phone: 406-670-3866
E-mail: cliff@ezcir.com

COLLEGE INSIDER SCHOLARSHIP PROGRAM

Scholarship offered to undergraduate students with a minimum GPA of 2.5. International students attending college in the United States are also eligible. Refer to Web site for additional information: http://www.ezcir.com/college_request.asp.

Award: Scholarship for use in freshman, sophomore, junior, or senior years; renewable. *Number:* 1. *Amount:* $1000.

Eligibility Requirements: Applicant must be age 13 and over and enrolled or expecting to enroll full-time at a two-year or four-year or technical institution or university. Available to U.S. and non-U.S. citizens.

Application Requirements: Application. *Deadline:* varies.

Contact: Mr. Cliff deQuilettes, CEO
Phone: 406-652-8900
E-mail: cliff@ezcir.com

COLLEGEPROWLER INC. http://www.collegeprowler.com

COLLEGE PROWLER MONTHLY SCHOLARSHIP

Scholarship for a current high school or college student. Must submit a college application essay that is their original work. Must be a legal resident of the United States or an international student with valid visa. Awards $1000 along with ten free College Prowler guidebooks every month. Winners will be notified by e-mail and posted online at http://www.collegeprowler.com.

Award: Scholarship for use in freshman, sophomore, junior, senior, or graduate years; not renewable. *Number:* 12. *Amount:* $1000.

Eligibility Requirements: Applicant must be enrolled or expecting to enroll full-time at a two-year or four-year or technical institution or university. Available to U.S. citizens.

Application Requirements: Applicant must enter a contest, essay. *Deadline:* continuous.

Contact: Heather Estes, Director of Business Development
CollegeProwler Inc.
5001 Baum Boulevard, Suite 750
Pittsburgh, PA 15213
Phone: 412-697-1392
Fax: 412-697-1396
E-mail: heather@collegeprowler.com

COMMON KNOWLEDGE SCHOLARSHIP FOUNDATION http://www.cksf.org

AMERICAN HEROES SCHOLARSHIP–U.S. MILITARY

Scholarship quiz rewards students for demonstrating what they know about the U.S. Armed Forces. For more information about this scholarship, please visit: http://www.cksf.org/cksf.cfm?Page=Home&Subpage=MilitaryChallenge.

Award: Scholarship for use in freshman, sophomore, junior, senior, graduate, or postgraduate years; not renewable. *Number:* 1. *Amount:* up to $250.

Eligibility Requirements: Applicant must be enrolled or expecting to enroll full- or part-time at a two-year or four-year or technical institution or university. Available to U.S. citizens.

Application Requirements: Applicant must enter a contest. *Deadline:* varies.

Contact: Mr. Daryl Hulce, President
Common Knowledge Scholarship Foundation
PO Box 290361
Davie, FL 33329-0361
Phone: 954-262-8553
Fax: 954-262-2847
E-mail: hulce@cksf.org

AUTISM AWARENESS SCHOLARSHIP

Scholarship for students who are quizzed on what they know about autism and associated speech, language and communication disorders. For more information about this scholarship, please visit: http://www.cksf.org/cksf.cfm?Page=Home&Subpage=AutismChallenge.

Award: Scholarship for use in freshman, sophomore, junior, senior, graduate, or postgraduate years; not renewable. *Number:* 1. *Amount:* up to $250.

Eligibility Requirements: Applicant must be enrolled or expecting to enroll full- or part-time at a two-year or four-year or technical institution or university. Available to U.S. citizens.

Application Requirements: Applicant must enter a contest. *Deadline:* varies.

Contact: Mr. Daryl Hulce, President
Common Knowledge Scholarship Foundation
PO Box 290361
Davie, FL 33329-0361
Phone: 954-262-8553
Fax: 954-262-2847
E-mail: hulce@cksf.org

BIBLE SCHOLARSHIP–BOOK OF GENESIS

Scholarship rewards students for demonstrating what they know about the Bible.For more information about this scholarship, please refer to this Web site: http://www.cksf.org/cksf.cfm?Page=Home&Subpage=Biblical.

Award: Scholarship for use in freshman, sophomore, junior, senior, graduate, or postgraduate years; not renewable. *Number:* 1. *Amount:* up to $250.

Eligibility Requirements: Applicant must be enrolled or expecting to enroll full- or part-time at a two-year or four-year or technical institution or university. Available to U.S. citizens.

Application Requirements: Applicant must enter a contest. *Deadline:* varies.

Contact: Mr. Daryl Hulce, President
Common Knowledge Scholarship Foundation
PO Box 290361
Davie, FL 33329-0361
Phone: 954-262-8553
Fax: 954-262-2847
E-mail: hulce@cksf.org

BLACK HISTORY SCHOLARSHIP

Scholarship challenges participants by quizzing them on important historical facts that define the African American experience and achievements in the U.S. For more information about this scholarship, please visit: http://www.cksf.org/cksf.cfm?Page=Home&Subpage=BlackHistory.

Award: Scholarship for use in freshman, sophomore, junior, senior, graduate, or postgraduate years; not renewable. *Number:* 1. *Amount:* up to $250.

Eligibility Requirements: Applicant must be enrolled or expecting to enroll full- or part-time at a two-year or four-year or technical institution or university. Available to U.S. citizens.

Application Requirements: Application, applicant must enter a contest. *Deadline:* varies.

Contact: Mr. Daryl Hulce, President
Common Knowledge Scholarship Foundation
PO Box 290361
Davie, FL 33329-0361
Phone: 954-262-8553
Fax: 954-262-2847
E-mail: hulce@cksf.org

CKSF MOVIE SCHOLARSHIP

Scholarship quiz rewards students for their knowledge of popular movie facts. For more information about this scholarship, please visit the following Web site: http://www.cksf.org/CKSF.cfm?Page=CKSF_AvailableScholarships.

Award: Scholarship for use in freshman, sophomore, junior, senior, graduate, or postgraduate years; not renewable. *Number:* 1. *Amount:* up to $250.

Eligibility Requirements: Applicant must be enrolled or expecting to enroll full- or part-time at a two-year or four-year or technical institution or university. Available to U.S. citizens.

Application Requirements: Application, applicant must enter a contest. *Deadline:* varies.

Contact: Mr. Daryl Hulce, President
Common Knowledge Scholarship Foundation
PO Box 290361
Davie, FL 33329-0361
Phone: 954-262-8553
Fax: 954-262-2847
E-mail: hulce@cksf.org

COMMON KNOWLEDGE MOVIE SCHOLARSHIPS

Students should register at the CKSF Web site, and then take a series of multiple-choice quizzes. Each question is worth 500 points, and one point is deducted for every second it takes to complete each question. The person with the most points at the end of the competition is the scholarship winner.

Award: Scholarship for use in freshman, sophomore, junior, senior, or graduate years; not renewable. *Number:* 2. *Amount:* $250.

Eligibility Requirements: Applicant must be age 14 and over and enrolled or expecting to enroll full- or part-time at a two-year or four-year institution or university. Available to U.S. citizens.

Application Requirements: Applicant must enter a contest, online registration. *Deadline:* continuous.

Contact: Mr. Daryl Hulce, President
Common Knowledge Scholarship Foundation
PO Box 290361
Davie, FL 33329-0361
Phone: 954-262-8553
Fax: 954-262-2847
E-mail: hulce@cksf.org

CRIMINAL JUSTICE SCHOLARSHIP

Scholarship for participants who register and compete by taking online multiple-choice quizzes at the CKSF website. The quizzes will consist of 15-25 questions based on knowledge about various law enforcement agencies. Available to high school students, college students, and parents.

Award: Forgivable loan for use in freshman, sophomore, junior, senior, graduate, or postgraduate years; not renewable. *Number:* 1. *Amount:* up to $250.

Eligibility Requirements: Applicant must be enrolled or expecting to enroll full- or part-time at a two-year or four-year or technical institution or university. Available to U.S. citizens.

Common Knowledge Scholarship Foundation (continued)

Application Requirements: Applicant must enter a contest. *Deadline:* varies.

Contact: Mr. Daryl Hulce, President
Common Knowledge Scholarship Foundation
PO Box 290361
Davie, FL 33329-0361
Phone: 954-262-8553
Fax: 954-262-2847
E-mail: hulce@cksf.org

FAMILY COMMON KNOWLEDGE SCHOLARSHIP

Scholarship quiz competition designed to have generations of family members work together to answer the quiz questions. For more information about this scholarship, please visit: http://www.cksf.org/cksf.cfm?Page=Home&Subpage=FamilyProgram.

Award: Scholarship for use in freshman, sophomore, junior, senior, graduate, or postgraduate years; not renewable. *Number:* 1. *Amount:* up to $250.

Eligibility Requirements: Applicant must be enrolled or expecting to enroll full- or part-time at a two-year or four-year or technical institution or university. Available to U.S. citizens.

Application Requirements: Applicant must enter a contest. *Deadline:* varies.

Contact: Mr. Daryl Hulce, President
Common Knowledge Scholarship Foundation
PO Box 290361
Davie, FL 33329-0361
Phone: 954-262-8553
Fax: 954-262-2847
E-mail: hulce@cksf.org

FBI COMMON KNOWLEDGE CHALLENGE

Scholarship quiz educates participants about the mission, goals, history, and inner workings of the Federal Bureau of Investigation. Participants will understand what it means to work for the FBI and have knowledge of how to choose the agency as a career path. For more information visit: http://www.cksf.org/cksf.cfm?Page=Home&Subpage=FBIProgram.

Award: Prize for use in freshman, sophomore, junior, senior, graduate, or postgraduate years; not renewable. *Number:* 1. *Amount:* $250.

Eligibility Requirements: Applicant must be enrolled or expecting to enroll full- or part-time at a four-year institution or university. Available to U.S. citizens.

Application Requirements: Applicant must enter a contest. *Deadline:* varies.

Contact: Mr. Daryl Hulce, President
Common Knowledge Scholarship Foundation
PO Box 290361
Davie, FL 33329-0361
Phone: 954-262-8553
Fax: 954-262-2847
E-mail: hulce@cksf.org

HIGH SCHOOL INTERNET CHALLENGE

The program tests students' knowledge on both academic and common knowledge topics. Open to students in grades nine to twelve. For more information and online registration, check the following web site: http://www.cksf.org. Deadline varies.

Award: Prize for use in freshman year; not renewable. *Number:* 1. *Amount:* $100–$500.

Eligibility Requirements: Applicant must be high school student; age 15-19 and planning to enroll or expecting to enroll full- or part-time at a four-year institution or university. Available to U.S. citizens.

Application Requirements: Applicant must enter a contest. *Deadline:* varies.

Contact: Mr. Daryl Hulce, President
Common Knowledge Scholarship Foundation
PO Box 290361
Davie, FL 33329-0361
Phone: 954-262-8553
Fax: 954-262-2847
E-mail: hulce@cksf.org

JIM CRAMER'S STAY MAD FOR LIFE SCHOLARSHIP

Scholarship for students who take online quizzes on saving and investing strategies outlined by Jim Cramer. For more information about this scholarship, please visit: http://www.cksf.org/cksf.cfm?Page=Home&Subpage=CramerChallenge.

Award: Scholarship for use in freshman, sophomore, junior, senior, graduate, or postgraduate years; not renewable. *Number:* 1. *Amount:* up to $250.

Eligibility Requirements: Applicant must be enrolled or expecting to enroll full- or part-time at a two-year or four-year or technical institution or university. Available to U.S. citizens.

Application Requirements: Applicant must enter a contest. *Deadline:* varies.

Contact: Mr. Daryl Hulce, President
Common Knowledge Scholarship Foundation
PO Box 290361
Davie, FL 33329-0361
Phone: 954-262-8553
Fax: 954-262-2847
E-mail: hulce@cksf.org

MUSEUM SCHOLARSHIP

Scholarship quiz for students discovering facts about the Louvre Museum in France. For more information about this scholarship, please visit: http://www.cksf.org/cksf.cfm?Page=Home&Subpage=MuseeduLouvre.

Award: Scholarship for use in freshman, sophomore, junior, senior, graduate, or postgraduate years; not renewable. *Number:* 1. *Amount:* up to $250.

Eligibility Requirements: Applicant must be enrolled or expecting to enroll full- or part-time at a two-year or four-year or technical institution or university. Available to U.S. citizens.

Application Requirements: Applicant must enter a contest. *Deadline:* varies.

Contact: Mr. Daryl Hulce, President
Common Knowledge Scholarship Foundation
PO Box 290361
Davie, FL 33329-0361
Phone: 954-262-8553
Fax: 954-262-2847
E-mail: hulce@cksf.org

NATIONAL LITERATURE SCHOLARSHIP–HAMLET

Scholarship quiz challenges students on facts about Shakespeare's Hamlet. For more information about this scholarship, please visit: http://www.cksf.org/cksf.cfm?Page=Home&Subpage=LiteratureHamlet

Award: Scholarship for use in freshman, sophomore, junior, senior, graduate, or postgraduate years; not renewable. *Number:* 1. *Amount:* up to $250.

Eligibility Requirements: Applicant must be enrolled or expecting to enroll full- or part-time at a two-year or four-year or technical institution or university. Available to U.S. citizens.

Application Requirements: Applicant must enter a contest. *Deadline:* varies.

Contact: Mr. Daryl Hulce, President
Common Knowledge Scholarship Foundation
PO Box 290361
Davie, FL 33329-0361
Phone: 954-262-8553
Fax: 954-262-2847
E-mail: hulce@cksf.org

NFL SCHOLARSHIP

Awards of $250 for high school students, college students, and parents. Participants register with the Common Knowledge Scholarship Foundation and compete for scholarship money by taking online multiple-choice quizzes at the CKSF Web site. For more information, please refer to Web site: http://www.cksf.org/cksf.cfm?Page=Home&Subpage=NFLScholarship.

Award: Scholarship for use in freshman, sophomore, junior, senior, graduate, or postgraduate years; not renewable. *Number:* 1. *Amount:* up to $250.

Eligibility Requirements: Applicant must be enrolled or expecting to enroll full- or part-time at a two-year or four-year or technical institution or university. Available to U.S. citizens.

Application Requirements: Applicant must enter a contest. *Deadline:* varies.

Contact: Mr. Daryl Hulce, President
Common Knowledge Scholarship Foundation
PO Box 290361
Davie, FL 33329-0361
Phone: 954-262-8553
Fax: 954-262-2847
E-mail: hulce@cksf.org

PHYSICIAN ASSISTANT SCHOLARSHIP

Award tests students' knowledge of core courses associated with the physician assistant curriculum. For more information about this scholarship, please visit this Web site:
http://www.cksf.org/cksf.cfm?Page=Home&Subpage=PhysicianAssistant.

Award: Scholarship for use in freshman, sophomore, junior, senior, or postgraduate years; not renewable. *Number:* 1. *Amount:* up to $250.

Eligibility Requirements: Applicant must be enrolled or expecting to enroll full- or part-time at a two-year or four-year or technical institution or university. Available to U.S. citizens.

Application Requirements: Applicant must enter a contest. *Deadline:* varies.

Contact: Mr. Daryl Hulce, President
Common Knowledge Scholarship Foundation
PO Box 290361
Davie, FL 33329-0361
Phone: 954-262-8553
Fax: 954-262-2847
E-mail: hulce@cksf.org

THINK GREEN SCHOLARSHIP

Scholarship competition to reward students for demonstrating what they know about environment and conservation. For more information about this scholarship, please visit:
http://www.cksf.org/CKSF.cfm?Page=CKSF_AvailableScholarships.

Award: Scholarship for use in freshman, sophomore, junior, senior, graduate, or postgraduate years; not renewable. *Number:* 1. *Amount:* up to $250.

Eligibility Requirements: Applicant must be enrolled or expecting to enroll full- or part-time at a two-year or four-year or technical institution or university. Available to U.S. citizens.

Application Requirements: Applicant must enter a contest. *Deadline:* varies.

Contact: Mr. Daryl Hulce, President
Common Knowledge Scholarship Foundation
PO Box 290361
Davie, FL 33329-0361
Phone: 954-262-8553
Fax: 954-262-2847
E-mail: hulce@cksf.org

COMMUNITY FOUNDATION FOR GREATER ATLANTA INC. http://www.atlcf.org

DREAMS2 SCHOLARSHIP

Scholarship designed to provide scholarship opportunities for deserving students who want to pursue their education. Minimum 2.0 GPA, maximum 3.0 GPA required. For complete eligibility requirements or to download an application, please visit http://www.atlcf.org

Award: Scholarship for use in freshman, sophomore, junior, or senior years; not renewable. *Number:* up to 6. *Amount:* $2000.

Eligibility Requirements: Applicant must be enrolled or expecting to enroll full-time at a two-year or four-year or technical institution or university. Available to U.S. and non-U.S. citizens.

Application Requirements: Application, essay, references, transcript. *Deadline:* March 26.

Contact: Kristina Morris, Program Associate
Community Foundation for Greater Atlanta Inc.
50 Hurt Plaza, Suite 449
Atlanta, GA 30303
Phone: 404-688-5525
Fax: 404-688-3060
E-mail: scholarships@atlcf.org

CONGRESSIONAL BLACK CAUCUS SPOUSES PROGRAM http://www.cbcfinc.org

CONGRESSIONAL BLACK CAUCUS SPOUSES EDUCATION SCHOLARSHIP FUND

Award made to students who reside or attend school in a Congressional district represented by an African-American member of Congress. Awards scholarships to academically talented and highly motivated students who intend to pursue full-time undergraduate, graduate or doctoral degrees. Minimum 2.5 GPA required. Contact the Congressional office in the appropriate district for information and applications.

Award: Scholarship for use in freshman, sophomore, junior, senior, or graduate years; renewable. *Number:* 200. *Amount:* $500–$4000.

Eligibility Requirements: Applicant must be enrolled or expecting to enroll full-time at a two-year or four-year or technical institution or university. Applicant must have 2.5 GPA or higher. Available to U.S. citizens.

Application Requirements: Application, essay, financial need analysis, photo, references, transcript. *Deadline:* May 1.

Contact: Janet Carter, Scholarship Coordinator
Congressional Black Caucus Spouses Program
1720 Massachusetts Avenue, NW
Washington, DC 20036
Phone: 202-263-2840
Fax: 202-263-0844
E-mail: jcarter@cbcfinc.org

COUNCIL FOR INTERNATIONAL EDUCATIONAL EXCHANGE http://www.ciee.org

BOWMAN TRAVEL GRANT

The grant is awarded only to eligible students participating in a life study or volunteer programs in less traditional destinations. Recipients must be attending a CIEE member or academic consortium member institution. Recipients receive awards to be used as partial reimbursement for travel costs to program destination. Deadlines: April 1 and November 1.

Award: Grant for use in freshman, sophomore, junior, or senior years; not renewable. *Number:* 20–30. *Amount:* $500–$1000.

Eligibility Requirements: Applicant must be enrolled or expecting to enroll full-time at a two-year or four-year or technical institution or university. Applicant must have 3.5 GPA or higher. Available to U.S. citizens.

Council for International Educational Exchange (continued)

Application Requirements: Application, applicant must enter a contest, essay, financial need analysis, references, transcript. *Deadline:* varies.

Contact: Chris Wilson, Grant Programs Manager
Council for International Educational Exchange
300 Fore Street
Portland, ME 04101
Phone: 800-448-9944 Ext. 4117
Fax: 207-553-4299
E-mail: scholarships@ciee.org

DANIEL KOVACH SCHOLARSHIP FOUNDATION http://www.collegescholarships.org

POLITICAL BLOGGING SCHOLARSHIP

Scholarship of $2000 awarded annually to students currently enrolled full-time in post-secondary education. Applicant must maintain a political weblog. Must be a U.S. citizen. Minimum 3.0 GPA required.

Award: Scholarship for use in freshman, sophomore, junior, or senior years; not renewable. *Number:* 1. *Amount:* $2000.

Eligibility Requirements: Applicant must be enrolled or expecting to enroll full-time at a four-year institution or university. Applicant must have 3.0 GPA or higher. Available to U.S. citizens.

Application Requirements: Application, applicant must enter a contest. *Deadline:* February 21.

Contact: Daniel Kovach, Scholarship Committee
Daniel Kovach Scholarship Foundation
5506 Red Robin Road
Raleigh, NC 27613
Phone: 919-630-4895
E-mail: danielkovach@gmail.com

WEB DESIGN SCHOLARSHIP

Web design contest for students enrolled full-time at a post-secondary institution. Applicant must be a U.S. citizen.

Award: Scholarship for use in freshman, sophomore, junior, or senior years; not renewable. *Number:* 1. *Amount:* $5000.

Eligibility Requirements: Applicant must be enrolled or expecting to enroll full-time at a four-year institution or university. Available to U.S. citizens.

Application Requirements: Application, applicant must enter a contest, Web design. *Deadline:* August 18.

Contact: Daniel Kovach, Scholarship Committee
Daniel Kovach Scholarship Foundation
5506 Red Robin Road
Raleigh, NC 27613
Phone: 919-630-4895
E-mail: danielkovach@gmail.com

WOMEN'S SCHOLARSHIP

Scholarship of $1000 awarded annually to female students currently attending full time study in post-secondary education both undergraduate and graduate. Minimum 3.0 GPA required.

Award: Scholarship for use in freshman, sophomore, junior, senior, or graduate years; not renewable. *Number:* 1. *Amount:* $1000.

Eligibility Requirements: Applicant must be enrolled or expecting to enroll full-time at a four-year institution or university and female. Applicant must have 3.0 GPA or higher. Available to U.S. citizens.

Application Requirements: Application, essay. *Deadline:* December 24.

Contact: Daniel Kovach, Scholarship Committee
Daniel Kovach Scholarship Foundation
5506 Red Robin Road
Raleigh, NC 27613
Phone: 919-630-4895
E-mail: danielkovach@gmail.com

DATATEL INC. http://www.datatel.com/dsf

DATATEL SCHOLARS FOUNDATION SCHOLARSHIP

One-time award for students attending institutions which use Datatel administrative software. Available for students currently attending at least 6 credits. Completed online applications, including two letters of recommendation must be submitted electronically.

Award: Scholarship for use in freshman, sophomore, junior, senior, graduate, or postgraduate years; not renewable. *Number:* up to 270. *Amount:* $1000–$2400.

Eligibility Requirements: Applicant must be enrolled or expecting to enroll full- or part-time at a two-year or four-year or technical institution or university. Available to U.S. and non-U.S. citizens.

Application Requirements: Application, essay, references, transcript. *Deadline:* January 31.

Contact: Stacey Fessler, Project Leader
Datatel Inc.
4375 Fair Lakes Court
Fairfax, VA 22033
Phone: 800-486-4332
E-mail: scholars@datatel.com

RUSS GRIFFITH MEMORIAL SCHOLARSHIP

For any student who has returned to higher education after an absence of five years or more. One-time award for students attending institutions which use Datatel administrative software. Must be currently enrolled in courses totaling at least 6 credits. Completed online applications, including two letters of recommendation must be submitted electronically.

Award: Scholarship for use in freshman, sophomore, junior, senior, graduate, or postgraduate years; not renewable. *Number:* 50. *Amount:* $2000.

Eligibility Requirements: Applicant must be enrolled or expecting to enroll full- or part-time at a two-year or four-year or technical institution or university. Available to U.S. and non-U.S. citizens.

Application Requirements: Application, essay, references, transcript. *Deadline:* January 31.

Contact: Stacey Fessler, Project Leader
Datatel Inc.
4375 Fair Lakes Court
Fairfax, VA 22033
Phone: 800-486-4332
E-mail: scholars@datatel.com

DEVRY INC. http://www.devry.edu

DEVRY COMMUNITY COLLEGE SCHOLARSHIPS

Award to community college graduates who earned an associate degree from a regionally accredited or public community or junior college with a minimum GPA of 3.3.

Award: Scholarship for use in junior or senior years; renewable. *Number:* varies. *Amount:* $3000.

Eligibility Requirements: Applicant must be enrolled or expecting to enroll full-time at a four-year institution or university. Available to U.S. citizens.

Application Requirements: Application, interview, transcript. *Deadline:* varies.

Contact: Thonie Simpson, National High School Program Manager
DeVry Inc.
One Tower Lane
Oak Brook Terrace, IL 60181-4624
Phone: 630-706-3122
Fax: 630-574-1696
E-mail: scholarships@devry.edu

DEVRY DEAN'S SCHOLARSHIPS

Awards to high school seniors or GED recipients who have SAT scores of 1100 or higher, or ACT scores of 24 or higher; Canada-Composite CPT of 430 or higher for Canadians. There is no separate scholarship application.

Award: Scholarship for use in freshman year; renewable. *Number:* varies. *Amount:* $1500–$13,500.

Eligibility Requirements: Applicant must be high school student and planning to enroll or expecting to enroll full-time at a four-year institution or university. Available to U.S. and Canadian citizens.

Application Requirements: Application, interview, test scores, transcript. *Deadline:* varies.

Contact: Thonie Simpson, National High School Program Manager
DeVry Inc.
One Tower Lane
Oak Brook Terrace, IL 60181-4624
Phone: 630-706-3122
Fax: 630-574-1696
E-mail: scholarships@devry.edu

DEVRY HIGH SCHOOL COMMUNITY SCHOLARS AWARD
• *See page 750*

EAST BAY COLLEGE FUND http://www.eastbaycollegefund.org

GREAT EXPECTATIONS AWARD

Program provides renewable scholarships, mentoring, college counseling, and life skills training. Must have at least 3.0 cumulative GPA.

Award: Scholarship for use in freshman, sophomore, junior, or senior years; renewable. *Number:* 17. *Amount:* $4000–$16,000.

Eligibility Requirements: Applicant must be enrolled or expecting to enroll full-time at a four-year institution or university. Applicant must have 3.0 GPA or higher. Available to U.S. citizens.

Application Requirements: Application, essay, financial need analysis, references, test scores, transcript. *Deadline:* March 5.

Contact: Susan Keiter, College Counselor
East Bay College Fund
6114 LaSalle Avenue, Suite 314
Oakland, CA 94611
Phone: 510-444-1545
E-mail: info@eastbaycollegefund.org

E-COLLEGEDEGREE.COM http://e-collegedegree.com

E-COLLEGEDEGREE.COM ONLINE EDUCATION SCHOLARSHIP AWARD

The award is to be used for online education. Application must be submitted online. Visit Web site for more information and application: http://www.e-collegedegree.com.

Award: Scholarship for use in freshman, sophomore, junior, senior, graduate, or postgraduate years; renewable. *Number:* 1. *Amount:* $1000.

Eligibility Requirements: Applicant must be age 18 and over and enrolled or expecting to enroll full- or part-time at a two-year or four-year or technical institution or university. Available to U.S. citizens.

Application Requirements: Application, applicant must enter a contest, essay. *Deadline:* December 31.

Contact: Chris Lee, Site Manager
e-CollegeDegree.com
9109 West 101st Terrace
Overland Park, KS 66212
Phone: 913-341-6949
E-mail: scholarship@e-collegedegree.com

EDUCAID, WACHOVIA CORPORATION http://www.wachovia.com

EDUCAID GIMME FIVE SCHOLARSHIP SWEEPSTAKES

Awards twelve high school seniors for their first year at an accredited college or trade school. The scholarships are not based on grades or financial need, so every eligible high school senior who enters has an equal chance of winning. Apply online at the following web site: http://www.educaid.com.

Award: Prize for use in freshman year; not renewable. *Number:* 12. *Amount:* $5000.

Eligibility Requirements: Applicant must be enrolled or expecting to enroll full-time at a two-year or four-year or technical institution or university. Available to U.S. citizens.

Application Requirements: Application, self-addressed stamped envelope. *Deadline:* March 31.

Contact: Scholarship Committee
Educaid, Wachovia Corporation
PO Box 13667
Sacramento, CA 95853-3667
Phone: 877-689-0763

EDUCATION IS FREEDOM FOUNDATION http://www.educationisfreedom.com

EDUCATION IS FREEDOM NATIONAL SCHOLARSHIP

Applicants for this renewable scholarship must be high school seniors planning full-time undergraduate study at a two- or four-year college or university. Selection criteria are based on financial need, leadership and activities, work history, and candidate appraisal. Application available online at: http://www.educationisfreedom.com.

Award: Scholarship for use in freshman year; renewable. *Number:* up to 225. *Amount:* $2000.

Eligibility Requirements: Applicant must be high school student and planning to enroll or expecting to enroll full-time at a two-year or four-year institution or university. Applicant must have 3.0 GPA or higher. Available to U.S. citizens.

Application Requirements: Application, financial need analysis, references, transcript. *Deadline:* April 15.

Contact: Barb Weber, Director of Operations
Education is Freedom Foundation
4711 North Haskell Avenue
Saint Peter, MN 56082

EPSILON SIGMA ALPHA FOUNDATION http://www.esaintl.com

EPSILON SIGMA ALPHA FOUNDATION SCHOLARSHIPS

Awards for various fields of study. Must have at least 3.0 GPA. Applications must be sent to the Epsilon Sigma Alpha designated state counselor. See Web site at http://www.esaintl.com/esaf for further information, application forms and a list of state counselors.

Award: Scholarship for use in freshman, sophomore, junior, senior, or graduate years; not renewable. *Number:* 100–150. *Amount:* $500–$1500.

Eligibility Requirements: Applicant must be enrolled or expecting to enroll full- or part-time at a two-year or four-year or technical institution or university. Applicant must have 3.0 GPA or higher. Available to U.S. and non-U.S. citizens.

Application Requirements: Application, essay, references, transcript. *Fee:* $5. *Deadline:* February 1.

Contact: Scholarship Chairman
Epsilon Sigma Alpha Foundation
PO Box 270517
Fort Collins, CO 80527
Phone: 541-476-4617
Fax: 970-223-4456
E-mail: orcycler@vsisp.net

EXECUTIVE WOMEN INTERNATIONAL http://www.executivewomen.org

ADULT STUDENTS IN SCHOLASTIC TRANSITION

Scholarship for adult students at transitional points in their lives. Applicants may be single parents, individuals just entering the workforce, or displaced homemakers. Applications are available on the organization's web site: http://www.executivewomen.org.

Award: Scholarship for use in junior, senior, graduate, or postgraduate years; not renewable. *Number:* 100–150. *Amount:* $1000–$2000.

Eligibility Requirements: Applicant must be enrolled or expecting to enroll full-time at a two-year or four-year or technical institution or university. Available to U.S. and non-U.S. citizens.

Executive Women International (continued)

Application Requirements: Application, tax information. *Deadline:* varies.

Contact: Office Administrator
Executive Women International
515 South 700 East, Suite 2A
Salt Lake City, UT 84102
Phone: 801-355-2800

EXECUTIVE WOMEN INTERNATIONAL SCHOLARSHIP PROGRAM

Competitive award to high school juniors planning careers in any business or professional field of study which requires a four-year college degree. Award is renewable based on continuing eligibility. All awards are given through local chapters of the EWI. Applicant must apply through nearest chapter and live within 50 miles. Student must have a sponsoring teacher and school to be considered. For more details visit Web site: http://www.executivewomen.org.

Award: Scholarship for use in freshman year; renewable. *Number:* 75–100. *Amount:* $1000–$10,000.

Eligibility Requirements: Applicant must be high school student and planning to enroll or expecting to enroll full-time at a four-year institution or university. Applicant must have 2.5 GPA or higher. Available to U.S. and non-U.S. citizens.

Application Requirements: Application, autobiography, interview, references, transcript. *Deadline:* varies.

Contact: Misty Hudson, Education Manager
Executive Women International
515 South 700 East, Suite 2A
Salt Lake City, UT 84102
Phone: 801-355-2800
Fax: 801-355-2852
E-mail: misty@executivewomen.org

FOUNDATION FOR INDEPENDENT HIGHER EDUCATION http://www.fihe.org

HSBC FIRST OPPORTUNITY PARTNERS SCHOLARSHIPS

Award targets the students with multiple at-risk factors as identified by financial aid officers in FIHE colleges. For undergraguate students with at least 2.4 GPA after the first semester of the freshman year. Deadline varies.

Award: Scholarship for use in freshman, sophomore, junior, or senior years; renewable. *Number:* 1. *Amount:* $5000.

Eligibility Requirements: Applicant must be enrolled or expecting to enroll full-time at a four-year institution or university. Available to U.S. citizens.

Application Requirements: Application, financial need analysis. *Deadline:* varies.

Contact: William Hamm, President
Foundation for Independent Higher Education
1920 North Street, NW, Suite 210
Washington, DC 20036
Phone: 202-367-0333
Fax: 202-367-0334
E-mail: info@fihe.org

UPS SCHOLARSHIP PROGRAM

Scholarship program for undergraduate students attending FIHE-affiliated colleges. Deadline varies.

Award: Scholarship for use in freshman, sophomore, junior, or senior years; not renewable. *Number:* 1. *Amount:* $2850.

Eligibility Requirements: Applicant must be enrolled or expecting to enroll full- or part-time at a four-year institution or university. Available to U.S. and non-U.S. citizens.

Application Requirements: Application. *Deadline:* varies.

Contact: William Hamm, President
Foundation for Independent Higher Education
1920 North Street, NW, Suite 210
Washington, DC 20036
Phone: 202-367-0333
Fax: 202-367-0334
E-mail: info@fihe.org

FOUNDATION FOR OUTDOOR ADVERTISING RESEARCH AND EDUCATION (FOARE) http://www.oaaa.org

FOARE SCHOLARSHIP PROGRAM

One-time award of $2000 for 6 students. High school seniors, undergraduates, and graduate students enrolled in or accepted to an accredited institution are eligible to apply. Selections are based on financial need, academic performance, and career goals.

Award: Scholarship for use in freshman, sophomore, junior, senior, or graduate years; not renewable. *Number:* 6. *Amount:* $2000.

Eligibility Requirements: Applicant must be enrolled or expecting to enroll full-time at a four-year institution or university. Available to U.S. citizens.

Application Requirements: Application, essay, financial need analysis, transcript. *Deadline:* June 15.

Contact: Scholarship Program
Foundation for Outdoor Advertising Research and Education (FOARE)
c/o Thomas M. Smith & Associates, 4601 Tilden Street, NW
Washington, DC 20016
Phone: 202-364-7130
E-mail: tmfsmith@starpower.net

FREEMAN FOUNDATION/INSTITUTE OF INTERNATIONAL EDUCATION http://www.iie.org/Freeman-ASIA

FREEMAN AWARDS FOR STUDY IN ASIA

Program offers awards to qualifying U.S. students needing financial support to study abroad in East/Southeast Asia. Must have applied or have been accepted to a study abroad based program in Cambodia, China, Hong Kong, Indonesia, Japan, Korea, Laos, Macao, Malaysia, Mongolia, Philippines, Singapore, Taiwan, Thailand, or Vietnam. Program must award academic credits through home campus or other U.S. accredited college or university.

Award: Grant for use in freshman, sophomore, junior, or senior years; not renewable. *Number:* varies. *Amount:* $3000–$7000.

Eligibility Requirements: Applicant must be enrolled or expecting to enroll full-time at a two-year or four-year institution or university. Available to U.S. citizens.

Application Requirements: Application, essay, financial need analysis, application certified by the applicant's Study Abroad Adviser and Financial Aid Adviser on their U.S. home campus. *Deadline:* varies.

Contact: Program Coordinator
Freeman Foundation/Institute of International Education
809 United Nations Plaza
New York, NY 10017-3580
Phone: 212-984-5542
Fax: 212-984-5325
E-mail: freeman-asia@iie.org

GEORGE T. WELCH TRUST http://www.bakerboyer.com

JOHN O. HENDRICKS MEMORIAL SCHOLARSHIP

Grants payable to students after completion of first quarter or semester. Must be enrolled full-time. Must maintain a minimum GPA of 2.0. Must reapply. The budget form must be completed and cover the entire school year.

Award: Scholarship for use in freshman, sophomore, junior, or senior years; not renewable. *Number:* varies. *Amount:* varies.

Eligibility Requirements: Applicant must be enrolled or expecting to enroll full-time at a four-year institution or university. Available to U.S. citizens.

Application Requirements: Application, responsibility shown in one or more of the following areas: community, school, home, church. *Deadline:* April 13.

Contact: Ted Cohan, Trust Portfolio Manager
George T. Welch Trust
Baker Boyer Bank, Investment Management & Trust Services
7 West Main, PO Box 1796
Walla Walla, WA 99362
Phone: 509-526-1204
Fax: 509-522-3136
E-mail: cohant@bakerboyer.com

MILTON-FREEWATER AREA FOUNDATION SCHOLARSHIPS

Grants for all four years of undergraduate work. Entering freshman must maintain a GPA of 2.5, and all students must maintain a minimum GPA of 2.0. Must reapply. The budget form must be completed and cover the entire school year.

Award: Scholarship for use in freshman, sophomore, junior, senior, or graduate years; not renewable. *Number:* varies. *Amount:* varies.

Eligibility Requirements: Applicant must be enrolled or expecting to enroll full-time at a two-year or four-year institution or university. Available to U.S. citizens.

Application Requirements: Application. *Deadline:* April 13.

Contact: Scholarship Committee
George T. Welch Trust
Baker Boyer Bank, Wealth Management Services, PO Box 1796
Walla Walla, WA 99362

GUERNSEY-MUSKINGUM ELECTRIC COOPERATIVE INC. http://www.gmenergy.com

HIGH SCHOOL SENIOR SCHOLARSHIP

Two $1000 scholarships, two $500 scholarships, two $300 scholarships, and two $200 scholarships are available to a student graduating from high school whose parent or legal guardian receives electric service from Guernsey-Muskingum Electric Cooperative.

Award: Scholarship for use in freshman year; not renewable. *Number:* 8. *Amount:* $200–$1000.

Eligibility Requirements: Applicant must be high school student and planning to enroll or expecting to enroll full-time at a two-year or four-year institution or university. Applicant must have 3.0 GPA or higher. Available to U.S. citizens.

Application Requirements: Application, interview, references, transcript. *Deadline:* February 1.

Contact: Brian Bennett, Manager, Member Services
Guernsey-Muskingum Electric Cooperative Inc.
17 South Liberty Street
New Concord, OH 43762
Phone: 740-826-7661
Fax: 740-826-7171
E-mail: mailbox@gmenergy.com

HELPING HANDS FOUNDATION http://www.helpinghandsbookscholarship.com

HELPING HANDS BOOK SCHOLARSHIP PROGRAM

The grant assists students with the high cost of textbooks and study materials. Awards are open to individuals of ages 16 and up, planning to attend or currently attending a two- or four-year college or university or a technical/vocational institution. Application fee is $5. Scholarship value is from $100 to $1000. Deadline varies.

Award: Grant for use in freshman, sophomore, junior, senior, or graduate years; not renewable. *Number:* 20–50. *Amount:* $100–$1000.

Eligibility Requirements: Applicant must be age 16 and over and enrolled or expecting to enroll full- or part-time at a two-year or four-year or technical institution or university. Available to U.S. and non-U.S. citizens.

Application Requirements: Application, essay, self-addressed stamped envelope, transcript. *Fee:* $5. *Deadline:* varies.

Contact: Scholarship Director
Helping Hands Foundation
4480-H South Cobb Drive, PO Box 435
Smyrna, GA 30080

HEMOPHILIA FEDERATION OF AMERICA http://www.hemophiliaed.org

PARENT CONTINUING EDUCATION SCHOLARSHIP

Scholarship for a parent of a school-age child with a blood clotting disorder. For use in furthering the parent's own education. Previous scholarship recipients are encouraged to reapply.

Award: Scholarship for use in freshman or sophomore years; not renewable. *Number:* 2. *Amount:* $1500.

Eligibility Requirements: Applicant must be enrolled or expecting to enroll full- or part-time at a technical institution. Available to U.S. citizens.

Application Requirements: Application, essay, financial need analysis, references. *Deadline:* April 30.

Contact: Sandy Aultman, Scholarship Coordinator
Hemophilia Federation of America
1045 West Pinhook Road, Suite 101
Lafayette, LA 70503
Phone: 337-261-9787
Fax: 337-261-1787

SIBLING CONTINUING EDUCATION SCHOLARSHIP

Scholarship for the sibling of a school-age child with a blood clotting disorder. For use in furthering the sibling's own education. Previous scholarship recipients may reapply.

Award: Scholarship for use in freshman year; not renewable. *Number:* 3. *Amount:* $1500.

Eligibility Requirements: Applicant must be high school student and planning to enroll or expecting to enroll full- or part-time at a four-year institution or university. Available to U.S. citizens.

Application Requirements: Application, essay, financial need analysis, references. *Deadline:* April 30.

Contact: Scholarship Committee
Hemophilia Federation of America
1405 West Pinhook Road, Suite 101
Lafayette, LA 70503
Phone: 337-261-9787
E-mail: info@hemophiliafed.org

HENKEL CONSUMER ADHESIVES INC. http://www.ducktapeclub.com

DUCK BRAND DUCT TAPE "STUCK AT PROM" SCHOLARSHIP CONTEST

Contest is open to residents of the United States and Canada. Must be 14 years or older. First place winners receive a $3000 college scholarship each and $3000 for the high school hosting the winning couple's prom. The second place winners will each receive a $2000 college scholarship, with the high school receiving $2000. The third place couple will each win a $1000 college scholarship and the high school will receive $1000.

Award: Prize for use in freshman, sophomore, junior, or senior years; not renewable. *Number:* 3. *Amount:* $1000–$3000.

Eligibility Requirements: Applicant must be age 14 and over and enrolled or expecting to enroll full- or part-time at a two-year or four-year or technical institution or university. Available to U.S. and Canadian citizens.

Application Requirements: Application, applicant must enter a contest, photo, entry form, release form. *Deadline:* June 11.

Contact: Michelle Heffner, Digital Marketing Communications Manager
Henkel Consumer Adhesives Inc.
32150 Just Imagine Drive
Avon, OH 44011-1355
Phone: 440-937-7000

HORATIO ALGER ASSOCIATION OF DISTINGUISHED AMERICANS http://www.horatioalger.org

HORATIO ALGER ASSOCIATION SCHOLARSHIP PROGRAMS

The association provides financial assistance to students in the United States who have exhibited integrity and perseverance in overcoming personal adversity and who aspire to pursue higher education. Scholarship award for full-time students under 19 years of age seeking undergraduate degree. Minimum 2.0 GPA required.

Award: Scholarship for use in freshman year; not renewable. *Number:* 1200. *Amount:* $2500–$20,000.

Eligibility Requirements: Applicant must be high school student; age 19 or under and planning to enroll or expecting to enroll full-time at a four-year institution or university. Available to U.S. citizens.

Application Requirements: Application, essay, financial need analysis, references. *Deadline:* October 31.

Contact: Frank Smith, Manager, Educational Programs
Horatio Alger Association of Distinguished Americans
99 Canal Center Plaza, Suite 320
Alexandria, VA 22314
Phone: 703-684-9444
Fax: 703-684-9445

HUGH FULTON BYAS MEMORIAL FUNDS INC.

HUGH FULTON BYAS MEMORIAL GRANT

• *See page 687*

INDEPENDENT INSTITUTE http://www.independent.org

SIR JOHN M. TEMPLETON FELLOWSHIPS ESSAY CONTEST

Essay contest for junior higher education faculty and students. Student applicants must be born on or after May 2, 1972. Student applicants may be pursuing any degree including associates, undergraduate, postgraduate or doctoral.

Award: Prize for use in freshman, sophomore, junior, senior, graduate, or postgraduate years; not renewable. *Number:* 6. *Amount:* $1000–$10,000.

Eligibility Requirements: Applicant must be age 35 or under and enrolled or expecting to enroll full- or part-time at a two-year or four-year institution or university. Available to U.S. and non-U.S. citizens.

Application Requirements: Application, applicant must enter a contest, essay. *Deadline:* May 1.

Contact: Carl Close, Academic Affairs Director
Independent Institute
100 Swan Way, Suite 200
Oakland, CA 94621-1428
Phone: 510-632-1366
Fax: 510-568-6040
E-mail: cclose@independent.org

INTEREXCHANGE FOUNDATION http://www.interexchange.org

CHRISTIANSON GRANT

A total of 8 scholarships awarded every year. Two $10,000, two $5000 and four $2500 scholarships are awarded to undergraduate students. Applicants should be between the ages of 18 and 28. Deadlines: March 15 and October 15.

Award: Grant for use in freshman, sophomore, junior, or senior years; not renewable. *Number:* 8. *Amount:* $2500–$10,000.

Eligibility Requirements: Applicant must be age 18-28 and enrolled or expecting to enroll full- or part-time at a two-year or four-year or technical institution or university. Available to U.S. citizens.

Application Requirements: Application, essay, interview, resume, references. *Fee:* $25. *Deadline:* varies.

Contact: Myisha Battle, Foundation Coordinator
InterExchange Foundation
161 Sixth Avenue
New York, NY 10013
Phone: 917-305-5471
Fax: 212-924-0575
E-mail: grants@interexchange.org

WORKING ABROAD GRANT

Grant open to applicants who have been accepted to an InterExchange Working Abroad program. Awards cover program fees plus up to $2000 toward transportation, insurance, and living expenses.

Award: Grant for use in freshman, sophomore, junior, or senior years; not renewable. *Number:* 5–8. *Amount:* $2000–$4000.

Eligibility Requirements: Applicant must be age 18-28 and enrolled or expecting to enroll full- or part-time at a two-year or four-year or technical institution or university. Available to U.S. citizens.

Application Requirements: Application, essay, interview, resume, references. *Fee:* $25. *Deadline:* continuous.

Contact: Myisha Battle, Foundation Coordinator
InterExchange Foundation
161 Sixth Avenue
New York, NY 10013
Phone: 917-305-5471
Fax: 212-924-0575
E-mail: grants@interexchange.org

JACK KENT COOKE FOUNDATION http://www.jackkentcookefoundation.org

JACK KENT COOKE FOUNDATION UNDERGRADUATE TRANSFER SCHOLARSHIP PROGRAM

Scholarships to students and recent alumni from community college to complete their bachelor's degrees at accredited four-year colleges or universities in the United States or abroad. Candidates must be nominated by a faculty representative from their community college.

Award: Scholarship for use in freshman, sophomore, junior, or senior years; renewable. *Number:* 50. *Amount:* $30,000.

Eligibility Requirements: Applicant must be enrolled or expecting to enroll full-time at a four-year institution or university. Applicant must have 3.5 GPA or higher. Available to U.S. and non-U.S. citizens.

Application Requirements: Application, essay, financial need analysis, references, transcript. *Deadline:* February 1.

Contact: Gaby Ruess, Scholarship Committee
Jack Kent Cooke Foundation
44325 Woodridge Parkway
Lansdowne, VA 20176
Phone: 800-498-6478
E-mail: jkc-u@act.org

JEANNETTE RANKIN FOUNDATION INC. http://www.rankinfoundation.org

JEANNETTE RANKIN FOUNDATION AWARDS

Applicants must be low-income women, age 35 or older, who are U.S. citizens pursuing a technical/vocational education, an associate's degree, or a first-time bachelor's degree at a regionally accredited college. Applications are available from November to February.

Award: Scholarship for use in freshman, sophomore, junior, or senior years; renewable. *Number:* 80. *Amount:* $2000.

Eligibility Requirements: Applicant must be age 35 and over; enrolled or expecting to enroll full- or part-time at a two-year or four-year or technical institution or university and female. Available to U.S. citizens.

Application Requirements: Application, essay, financial need analysis, references, self-addressed stamped envelope, transcript. *Deadline:* March 1.

Contact: Andrea Anderson, Program Coordinator
Jeannette Rankin Foundation Inc.
PO Box 6653
Athens, GA 30604-6653
Phone: 706-208-1211
E-mail: info@rankinfoundation.org

JOHN GYLES EDUCATION AWARDS http://www.johngyleseducationcenter.com

JOHN GYLES EDUCATION AWARDS

Financial assistance available to students enrolled full-time at (or accepted to) a college or university program as an undergraduate or graduate student in any area of postsecondary study. High school seniors, and others, may apply pending acceptance. Applicants must have a minimum GPA of 2.7 (or similar grade assessment) and must have U.S. or Canadian citizenship.

Award: Scholarship for use in freshman, sophomore, junior, senior, or graduate years; renewable. *Number:* up to 15. *Amount:* up to $3000.

Eligibility Requirements: Applicant must be enrolled or expecting to enroll full-time at a two-year or four-year institution or university. Available to U.S. and Canadian citizens.

Application Requirements: Application. *Deadline:* June 1.

Contact: R. James Cougle, Administrator
John Gyles Education Awards
259-103 Brunswick Street, PO Box 4808
Fredericton, NB E3B 5G4
Canada

KE ALI'I PAUAHI FOUNDATION http://www.pauahi.org

KAMEHAMEHA SCHOOLS CLASS OF 1952 "NA HOALOHA O KAMEHAMEHA" SCHOLARSHIP

Scholarship to assist students pursuing a certificate or degree from an accredited vocational/business school or a two- or four-year post-secondary institution. Must demonstrate financial need. Minimum 2.0 GPA required. Preference given to students of Hawaiian ancestry.

Award: Scholarship for use in freshman, sophomore, junior, or senior years; not renewable. *Number:* varies. *Amount:* up to $1000.

Eligibility Requirements: Applicant must be enrolled or expecting to enroll full-time at a two-year or four-year or technical institution or university. Available to U.S. citizens.

Application Requirements: Application, financial need analysis, references, transcript, SAR, college acceptance letter. *Deadline:* May 2.

Contact: Elizabeth Stevenson, Development Manager
Ke Ali'i Pauahi Foundation
567 South King Street, Suite 160
Honolulu, HI 96813
Phone: 808-534-3966
Fax: 808-534-3890
E-mail: scholarships@pauahi.org

KAMEHAMEHA SCHOOLS CLASS OF 1973 "PROUD TO BE 73" SCHOLARSHIP

Provides scholarships to students pursuing college, vocational school, cultural training/knowledge classes, and professional/personal advancement seminars. Preference will be given to those of Hawaiian ancestry and Kamehameha Schools Class of 1973 graduates or their family members.

Award: Scholarship for use in freshman, sophomore, junior, senior, or graduate years; not renewable. *Number:* 4. *Amount:* $300.

Eligibility Requirements: Applicant must be enrolled or expecting to enroll full-time at a two-year or four-year or technical institution or university. Available to U.S. citizens.

Application Requirements: Application, financial need analysis, references, transcript, SAR, college acceptance letter. *Deadline:* May 2.

Contact: Elizabeth Stevenson, Development Manager
Ke Ali'i Pauahi Foundation
567 South King Street, Suite 160
Honolulu, HI 96813
Phone: 808-534-3966
Fax: 808-534-3890
E-mail: scholarships@pauahi.org

KAMEHAMEHA SCHOOLS CLASS OF 1968 "KA POLI O KAIONA" SCHOLARSHIP

Scholarships for students pursuing a two-year, four-year, or graduate degree from an accredited post-secondary institution. Minimum 2.8 GPA required. Must demonstrate financial need. Preference will be given to family members of Kamehameha Schools Class of 1968 graduates and those of Hawaiian ancestry.

Award: Scholarship for use in freshman, sophomore, junior, senior, or graduate years; not renewable. *Number:* 1. *Amount:* $1300.

Eligibility Requirements: Applicant must be enrolled or expecting to enroll full-time at a two-year or four-year institution or university. Available to U.S. citizens.

Application Requirements: Application, essay, financial need analysis, references, transcript, SAR, college acceptance letter. *Deadline:* May 2.

Contact: Elizabeth Stevenson, Development Manager
Ke Ali'i Pauahi Foundation
567 South King Street, Suite 160
Honolulu, HI 96813
Phone: 808-534-3966
Fax: 808-534-3890
E-mail: scholarships@pauahi.org

KENNEDY FOUNDATION http://www.columbinecorp.com/kennedyfoundation

KENNEDY FOUNDATION SCHOLARSHIPS

Renewable scholarships for current high school students for up to four years of undergraduate study. Renewal contingent upon academic performance. Must maintain a GPA of 2.5. Send self-addressed stamped envelope for application. See Web site for details: http://www.columbinecorp.com/kennedyfoundation.

Award: Scholarship for use in freshman year; renewable. *Number:* 8–14. *Amount:* $2000.

Eligibility Requirements: Applicant must be high school student and planning to enroll or expecting to enroll full-time at a two-year or four-year institution or university. Applicant must have 2.5 GPA or higher. Available to U.S. citizens.

Application Requirements: Application, self-addressed stamped envelope, test scores, transcript. *Deadline:* June 30.

Contact: Jonathan Kennedy, Vice President
Kennedy Foundation
PO Box 27296
Denver, CO 80227

LEOPOLD SCHEPP FOUNDATION http://www.scheppfoundation.org

LEOPOLD SCHEPP SCHOLARSHIP

Scholarship for undergraduates under 30 years of age and graduate students under 40 years of age at the time of application. Applicants must have a minimum GPA of 3.0. High school seniors are not eligible. All applicants must either be enrolled in college or have completed at least one year of college at the time of issuing the application. Must be citizens or permanent residents of the United States. Deadline varies.

Award: Scholarship for use in sophomore, junior, senior, or graduate years; renewable. *Number:* 1. *Amount:* up to $8500.

Eligibility Requirements: Applicant must be age 30-40 and enrolled or expecting to enroll full-time at a four-year institution or university. Applicant must have 3.0 GPA or higher. Available to U.S. citizens.

Leopold Schepp Foundation (continued)

Application Requirements: Application, financial need analysis, interview, references, transcript. *Deadline:* varies.

Contact: Scholarship Committee
Leopold Schepp Foundation
551 Fifth Avenue, Suite 3000
New York, NY 10176
Phone: 212-692-0191

MENNONITE WOMEN http://www.mennonitewomenusa.org

INTERNATIONAL WOMEN'S FUND

Scholarship for women from developing countries for postsecondary studies. Must submit letter of recommendations or reference from the church.

Award: Scholarship for use in freshman, sophomore, junior, senior, graduate, or postgraduate years; renewable. *Number:* 12. *Amount:* $500–$1000.

Eligibility Requirements: Applicant must be enrolled or expecting to enroll full- or part-time at a two-year or four-year institution or university and female. Available to citizens of countries other than the U.S. or Canada.

Application Requirements: Application, references. *Deadline:* September 1.

Contact: Rhoda Keener, Program Director
Mennonite Women
722 Main Street
PO Box 347
Newton, KS 67114
Phone: 717-532-9723
Fax: 316-283-0454
E-mail: office@mennonitewomenusa.org

METAVUE CORPORATION http://www.metavue.com

DR. ROBERT RUFFLO SCIENCES PAPER CONTEST

Scholarship fund awards two scholarships a year to high school and college students enrolled in accredited schools in the United States, must be enrolled at an accredited high school, two-year, four-year college or university, or be enrolled in a graduate-level program. Must be a legal resident of the United States or hold a valid student visa. For details refer to Web Site: http://www.metavue.com/Scholarships/mvcp_Scholarship.asp?id=4.

Award: Scholarship for use in freshman, sophomore, junior, senior, or graduate years; not renewable. *Number:* 2. *Amount:* $500.

Eligibility Requirements: Applicant must be enrolled or expecting to enroll full-time at a two-year or four-year institution or university. Applicant must have 3.0 GPA or higher. Available to U.S. and non-U.S. citizens.

Application Requirements: Application, applicant must enter a contest, essay. *Deadline:* June 15.

Contact: Michael Rufflo, Scholarship Committee
Metavue Corporation
1110 Surrey Drive
Sun Prairie, WI 53590
Phone: 608-577-0642
Fax: 512-685-4074
E-mail: rufflo@metavue.com

MICHAEL AND SUSAN DELL FOUNDATION http://www.msdf.org

DELL SCHOLARS PROGRAM

250 scholarships offered annually to high school students participating in approved college readiness programs. Must have a minimum 2.4 GPA and should be participating in a MSDF-approved college readiness program for a minimum of two years prior to application.

Award: Scholarship for use in freshman year; not renewable. *Number:* 250. *Amount:* varies.

Eligibility Requirements: Applicant must be high school student and planning to enroll or expecting to enroll full- or part-time at a two-year or four-year or technical institution or university. Available to U.S. citizens.

Application Requirements: Application, references, transcript. *Deadline:* January 15.

Contact: Scholarship Committee
Michael and Susan Dell Foundation
PO Box 163867
Austin, TX 78716
Phone: 512-329-0799

NAAS-USA FUND http://www.naas.org

NAAS II NATIONAL AWARDS

One renewable scholarship of $500 to $3000 available for tuition, room, board, books, and academic supplies. Applicant must be college freshman or sophomore attending an American college/university. U.S. citizenship is not required. Must be under the age of 25. Applicants that request an application by mail must enclose a $3 handling fee and a self-addressed stamped envelope. Electronic application available to NAAS subscribers at http://www.naas.org; no fees for NAAS subscribers.

Award: Scholarship for use in freshman or sophomore years; renewable. *Number:* 1. *Amount:* $500–$3000.

Eligibility Requirements: Applicant must be age 25 or under and enrolled or expecting to enroll full-time at a four-year institution or university. Available to U.S. and non-U.S. citizens.

Application Requirements: Application, self-addressed stamped envelope. *Deadline:* May 1.

Contact: K. France, Program Director
NAAS-USA Fund
2248 Meridian Boulevard, Suite H
Minden, NV 89423
Phone: 800-725-7849
E-mail: staff@naas.org

NATIONAL ASSOCIATION OF RAILWAY BUSINESS WOMEN http://www.narbw.org

NARBW SCHOLARSHIP

Scholarship awarded to the members of NARBW and their relatives. The number of awards varies every year. Applications are judged on scholastic ability, ambition and potential, and financial need.

Award: Scholarship for use in freshman, sophomore, junior, or senior years; not renewable. *Number:* varies. *Amount:* $500–$1000.

Eligibility Requirements: Applicant must be enrolled or expecting to enroll full-time at a two-year or four-year or technical institution or university and female. Available to U.S. citizens.

Application Requirements: Application, financial need analysis. *Deadline:* varies.

Contact: Scholarship Chairman
National Association of Railway Business Women
2631 Daleton Boulevard NE
Roanoke, VA 24012
E-mail: narbwinfo@narbw.org

NATIONAL HONOR ROLL http://www.nationalhonorroll.org

NATIONAL HONOR ROLL AWARD FOR ACADEMIC ACHIEVEMENT

Scholarships of $1000 awarded to students in grades 8 through 12 for tuition at an accredited college, university, or technical school. Applicant should be a resident of United States. Deadline varies.

Award: Grant for use in freshman year; not renewable. *Number:* 25. *Amount:* $1000.

Eligibility Requirements: Applicant must be high school student; age 14-19 and planning to enroll or expecting to enroll full-time at a two-year or four-year institution or university. Available to U.S. citizens.

Application Requirements: Application, essay. *Deadline:* varies.

Contact: Program Coordinator
National Honor Roll
2020 Pennsylvania Avenue, NW, Suite 8000
Washington, DC 20006
Phone: 516-872-3979

NATIONAL JUNIOR ANGUS ASSOCIATION http://www.angusfoundation.org

AMERICAN ANGUS AUXILIARY SCHOLARSHIP

Scholarship available to graduating high school senior. Can apply only in one state. Any unmarried girl or unmarried boy recommended by a state or regional Auxiliary is eligible.

Award: Scholarship for use in freshman year; not renewable. *Number:* up to 55. *Amount:* $850–$1200.

Eligibility Requirements: Applicant must be high school student; planning to enroll or expecting to enroll full-time at a four-year institution or university and single. Available to U.S. citizens.

Application Requirements: Application, applicant must enter a contest, autobiography, photo, references. *Deadline:* May 1.

Contact: Michelle Rieff, Chairman
National Junior Angus Association
PO Box 923
Bentonville, AR
Phone: 479-795-2584
Fax: 479-271-1128
E-mail: michellerieff@aol.com

NATIONAL RIFLE ASSOCIATION http://www.nrafoundation.org

NRA YOUTH EDUCATIONAL SUMMIT (YES) SCHOLARSHIPS

Awards for Youth Educational Summit participants based on the initial application, on-site debate, and degree of participation during the week-long event. Must be graduating high school seniors enrolled in undergraduate program. Must have a minimum GPA of 3.0.

Award: Scholarship for use in freshman year; not renewable. *Number:* 1–6. *Amount:* $1000–$10,000.

Eligibility Requirements: Applicant must be high school student and planning to enroll or expecting to enroll full- or part-time at a two-year or four-year or technical institution or university. Applicant must have 3.0 GPA or higher. Available to U.S. citizens.

Application Requirements: Application, applicant must enter a contest, essay, references, transcript. *Deadline:* March 1.

Contact: Event Services Manager
National Rifle Association
11250 Waples Mill Road
Fairfax, VA 22030
Phone: 703-267-1354
E-mail: fnra@nrahq.org

NAVAL SERVICE TRAINING COMMAND/NROTC http://www.nrotc.navy.mil/colleges.cfm

NROTC SCHOLARSHIP PROGRAM

Scholarships are based on merit and are awarded through a highly competitive national selection process. NROTC scholarships pay for college tuition, fees, uniforms, a book stipend, a monthly allowance and other financial benefits. Room and board expenses are not covered. Scholarship nominees must be medically qualified.

Award: Scholarship for use in freshman, sophomore, junior, or senior years; not renewable. *Number:* up to 2000. *Amount:* varies.

Eligibility Requirements: Applicant must be age 17-23 and enrolled or expecting to enroll full-time at a four-year institution or university. Available to U.S. citizens.

Application Requirements: Application, essay, interview, references, test scores, transcript. *Deadline:* January 31.

Contact: NROTC Scholarship Selection Office (OD2A)
Naval Service Training Command/NROTC
250 Dallas Street, Suite A
Pensacola, FL 32508-5268
Phone: 800-628-7682
Fax: 850-452-2486
E-mail: pnsc_nrotc.scholarship@navy.mil

NAVY COUNSELORS ASSOCIATION http://www.usnca.org

NAVY COUNSELORS ASSOCIATION EDUCATIONAL SCHOLARSHIP

The program awards at least one scholarship to a deserving student who is currently enrolled in, or accepted to, an undergraduate-level college, university or vocational tech program. Scholarship nominations must be from immediate family members of NCA members.

Award: Scholarship for use in freshman, sophomore, junior, or senior years; not renewable. *Number:* 1–4. *Amount:* varies.

Eligibility Requirements: Applicant must be enrolled or expecting to enroll full- or part-time at a four-year institution or university. Applicant must have 3.0 GPA or higher. Available to U.S. citizens.

Application Requirements: Application, essay, references, transcript. *Deadline:* April 30.

Contact: Joseph Mack, President
Navy Counselors Association
National Headquarters
PO Box 15233
Norfolk, VA 23511-0233
Phone: 901-874-3194
Fax: 901-874-2055
E-mail: president@usnca.org

NEEDHAM AND COMPANY WTC SCHOLARSHIP FUND http://www.needhamco.com

NEEDHAM AND COMPANY SEPTEMBER 11TH SCHOLARSHIP FUND

Scholarship going to those individuals who had a pre-September 11th gross income of less than $125,000. Must be currently accepted or attending an accredited university or college. Recipients decided on a case-by-case basis. Fund designed to benefit the children of the victims who lost their lives at the World Trade Center.

Award: Scholarship for use in freshman, sophomore, junior, or senior years; not renewable. *Number:* 8–15. *Amount:* $7000–$10,000.

Eligibility Requirements: Applicant must be enrolled or expecting to enroll full-time at a four-year institution or university. Available to U.S. citizens.

Application Requirements: Application, financial need analysis. *Deadline:* continuous.

Contact: Joseph J. Turano, Secretary and Treasurer
Needham and Company WTC Scholarship Fund
445 Park Avenue
New York, NY 10022
Phone: 212-705-0314
E-mail: jturano@needhamco.com

NEXT STEP PUBLISHING http://www.nextstepmag.com

NEXT STEP MAGAZINE WIN FREE COLLEGE TUITION

One-time award for one year of free tuition, up to $20,000, to one randomly selected winner. Students must register at http://www.nextstepmagazine.com

Award: Scholarship for use in freshman, sophomore, junior, or senior years; not renewable. *Number:* 1. *Amount:* up to $20,000.

Eligibility Requirements: Applicant must be age 14 and over and enrolled or expecting to enroll full- or part-time at a two-year or four-year or technical institution or university. Available to U.S. and Canadian citizens.

Application Requirements: Online registration. *Deadline:* June 20.

Contact: Shelly Stuart, Webmaster
Next Step Publishing
86 West Main Street
Victor, NY 14564
Phone: 585-742-1260
Fax: 585-742-1263
E-mail: shelly@nextstepmag.com

OFFICE OF PERSONNEL MANAGEMENT http://www.sfs.opm.gov

SCHOLARSHIP FOR SERVICE (SFS) PROGRAM

This program provides scholarships that fully fund the typical costs that students pay for books, tuition, and room and board while attending an approved institution of higher learning. Participants receive stipends of up to $8000 for undergraduate and $12,000 for graduate students.

Award: Scholarship for use in freshman, sophomore, junior, senior, or graduate years; renewable. *Number:* 1. *Amount:* $8000–$12,000.

Eligibility Requirements: Applicant must be enrolled or expecting to enroll full-time at a four-year institution or university. Available to U.S. citizens.

Application Requirements: Application. *Deadline:* varies.

Contact: Kathy Roberson, Program Manager
Office of Personnel Management
1900 East Street, NW
Washington, DC 20415
Phone: 202-606-1800
E-mail: sfs@opm.gov

OREGON POLICE CORPS http://www.portlandonline.com

OREGON POLICE CORPS SCHOLARSHIP

Scholarships available for undergraduate juniors and seniors and graduate students, or for reimbursement of educational expenses for college graduates. Must agree to commit to four years of employment at a participating law enforcement agency. Check Web site for details: http://www.oregonpolicecorps.com.

Award: Scholarship for use in junior, senior, or graduate years; not renewable. *Number:* 10. *Amount:* up to $30,000.

Eligibility Requirements: Applicant must be enrolled or expecting to enroll full-time at a four-year institution or university. Available to U.S. citizens.

Application Requirements: Application, driver's license, essay, interview, resume, references. *Deadline:* continuous.

Contact: Tim Evans, Scholarship Coordinator
Oregon Police Corps
1120 Fifth Avenue, SW, Room 404
Portland, OR 97204
Phone: 888-735-4259
E-mail: tevans@police.ci.portland.or.us

ORPHAN FOUNDATION OF AMERICA http://www.orphan.org

OFA NATIONAL SCHOLARSHIP/CASEY FAMILY SCHOLARS

Award of up to $10,000 to young people, under the age of 25, who have spent at least twelve months in foster care and were not subsequently adopted. Scholarships were awarded for the pursuit of postsecondary education, including vocational/technical training, and are renewable each year based on satisfactory progress and financial need.

Award: Scholarship for use in freshman, sophomore, junior, senior, graduate, or postgraduate years; renewable. *Number:* 350. *Amount:* up to $10,000.

Eligibility Requirements: Applicant must be age 25 or under and enrolled or expecting to enroll full- or part-time at a two-year or four-year or technical institution or university. Available to U.S. citizens.

Application Requirements: Application, essay, financial need analysis, references, transcript, foster care verification, parents' death certificates. *Deadline:* March 31.

Contact: Tina Raheem, Scholarship Coordinator
Orphan Foundation of America
21351 Gentry Drive, Suite 130
Sterling, VA 20166
Phone: 571-203-0270
Fax: 571-203-0273
E-mail: scholarship@orphan.org

OUTSTANDING STUDENTS OF AMERICA http://www.outstandingstudentsofamerica.com

OUTSTANDING STUDENTS OF AMERICA SCHOLARSHIP

Awards of $1000 each are payable to the college of the recipient's choice. Students must be high school seniors, participate in community/school activities, and maintain a minimum GPA of 3.0. For details refer to Web site: http://www.outstandingstudentsofamerica.com/.

Award: Scholarship for use in freshman year; not renewable. *Number:* varies. *Amount:* $1000.

Eligibility Requirements: Applicant must be high school student and planning to enroll or expecting to enroll full- or part-time at a four-year institution or university. Applicant must have 3.0 GPA or higher. Available to U.S. citizens.

Application Requirements: Application, self-addressed stamped envelope. *Deadline:* October 1.

Contact: Michael Layson, President
Outstanding Students of America
3047 Sagefield Road
Tuscaloosa, AL 35405
Phone: 205-344-6322
Fax: 205-344-6322
E-mail: info@outstandingstudentsofamerica.com

PADGETT BUSINESS SERVICES FOUNDATION http://www.smallbizpros.com

PADGETT BUSINESS SERVICES FOUNDATION SCHOLARSHIP PROGRAM

Scholarship awards to the dependents of small business owners throughout the United States and Canada. Must be a dependent of a business owner who employs fewer than 20 people, owns at least 10 percent of the stock or capital in the business, and is active in the day-to-day operations of the business. For more details, visit the Web site: http://www.smallbizpros.com.

Award: Scholarship for use in freshman year; not renewable. *Number:* 65–75. *Amount:* $500.

Eligibility Requirements: Applicant must be high school student and planning to enroll or expecting to enroll full-time at a two-year or four-year or technical institution or university. Available to U.S. and Canadian citizens.

Application Requirements: Application, essay, test scores, transcript, school activities. *Deadline:* March 1.

Contact: Heather Stokley, Administrator
Padgett Business Services Foundation
160 Hawthorne Park
Athens, GA 30606
Phone: 800-723-4388
Fax: 800-548-1040
E-mail: hstokley@smallbizpros.com

PAPERCHECK.COM http://www.papercheck.com

PAPERCHECK.COM CHARLES SHAFAE' SCHOLARSHIP FUND

Awards two $500 scholarships each year to winners of the Papercheck essay contest. Must be enrolled at an accredited four-year college or university. Must maintain a cumulative GPA of at least 3.2. Scholarship guidelines available at http://www.papercheck.com.

Award: Scholarship for use in freshman, sophomore, junior, or senior years; not renewable. *Number:* 2. *Amount:* $500.

Eligibility Requirements: Applicant must be enrolled or expecting to enroll full-time at a four-year institution or university. Applicant must have 3.0 GPA or higher. Available to U.S. and non-U.S. citizens.

Application Requirements: Application, applicant must enter a contest, essay. *Deadline:* varies.

Contact: Darren Shafae, Scholarship Coordinator
Papercheck.com
PO Box 642
Half Moon Bay, CA 94019
Phone: 650-712-9440
E-mail: scholarships@papercheck.com

PARENT RELOCATION COUNCIL http://www.parentrelocationcouncil.com

PARENT RELOCATION COUNCIL SCHOLARSHIP

Scholarship to assist students who have demonstrated success in overcoming difficulties during their family's relocation. Students must have relocated to or within a service area of the Parent Relocation Council within the past five years. Minimum 2.5 GPA required.

Award: Scholarship for use in freshman year; not renewable. *Number:* 1. *Amount:* $500–$2500.

Eligibility Requirements: Applicant must be high school student and planning to enroll or expecting to enroll full-time at a two-year or four-year or technical institution or university. Applicant must have 2.5 GPA or higher. Available to U.S. citizens.

Application Requirements: Application, essay. *Deadline:* May 31.

Contact: Claudia Montesano, Scholarship Coordinator
Parent Relocation Council
30 Corporate Park, Suite 410
Irvine, CA 92606
Phone: 949-553-4202 Ext. 46
Fax: 949-553-4211
E-mail: cmontesano@oc-cf.org

PATIENT ADVOCATE FOUNDATION http://www.patientadvocate.org

SCHOLARSHIPS FOR SURVIVORS

Scholarships to provide support to patients seeking to initiate or complete a course of study that has been interrupted or delayed by a diagnosis of cancer or another critical or life threatening illness. Five awards of $3000 available to U.S. citizens. Minimum 3.0 GPA required.

Award: Scholarship for use in freshman, sophomore, junior, senior, graduate, or postgraduate years; renewable. *Number:* up to 5. *Amount:* up to $3000.

Eligibility Requirements: Applicant must be enrolled or expecting to enroll full-time at a two-year or four-year institution or university. Applicant must have 3.0 GPA or higher. Available to U.S. citizens.

Application Requirements: Application, essay, financial need analysis, references, transcript, physician letter. *Deadline:* April 14.

Contact: Ruth Anne Reed, Vice President of Human Resource Programs
Patient Advocate Foundation
700 Thimble Shoals Boulevard, Suite 200
Newport News, VA 23606
Phone: 800-532-5274
Fax: 757-952-2475
E-mail: scholarship@patientadvocate.org

PATRICK KERR SKATEBOARD SCHOLARSHIP FUND http://www.skateboardscholarship.org

PATRICK KERR SKATEBOARD SCHOLARSHIP

Scholarship for high school senior accepted in a full-time undergraduate course of study at an accredited two- or four-year college/university. One individual will receive a $5000 scholarship and three individuals will receive a $1000 scholarship. Applicant must be a skateboarder and U.S. citizen. Minimum 2.5 GPA required.

Award: Scholarship for use in freshman year; not renewable. *Number:* 4. *Amount:* $1000–$5000.

Eligibility Requirements: Applicant must be high school student and planning to enroll or expecting to enroll full-time at a two-year or four-year institution or university. Applicant must have 2.5 GPA or higher. Available to U.S. citizens.

Application Requirements: Application, essay, references, transcript. *Deadline:* April 20.

Contact: Patrick Kerr, Scholarship Committee
Patrick Kerr Skateboard Scholarship Fund
PO Box 2054
Jenkintown, PA 19046
Phone: 215-663-9329
Fax: 215-663-5897
E-mail: info@skateboardscholarship.org

PETERSON'S, A NELNET COMPANY http://www.petersons.com

PETERSON'S UNDERGRADUATE STUDENT NETWORKS SCHOLARSHIP

Sweepstakes award of $5000 is open to all high school students who are legal residents of the United States. Must be at least 13 years old and be able to verify secondary school enrollment or enrollment in a secondary-level home schooling program at the date of entry. To enter, complete the Regional Colleges survey at http://www.petersons.com/studentnetworks. Only one survey may be completed per person.

Award: Scholarship for use in freshman year; not renewable. *Number:* 1. *Amount:* $5000.

Eligibility Requirements: Applicant must be high school student; age 13-18 and planning to enroll or expecting to enroll full- or part-time at a two-year or four-year or technical institution or university. Available to U.S. citizens.

Application Requirements: Application. *Deadline:* December 31.

Contact: Scholarship Committee
Peterson's, a Nelnet company
2000 Lenox Drive, Suite 300
Lawrenceville, NJ 08648
Phone: 609-896-1800
Fax: 609-896-4535

PHI BETA SIGMA FRATERNITY INC. http://www.pbs1914.org

PHI BETA SIGMA FRATERNITY NATIONAL PROGRAM OF EDUCATION

Scholarships are awarded to both graduate and undergraduate students. Applicants must have minimum 3.0 GPA.

Award: Scholarship for use in freshman, sophomore, junior, senior, or graduate years; not renewable. *Number:* varies. *Amount:* varies.

Eligibility Requirements: Applicant must be enrolled or expecting to enroll full-time at a four-year institution or university and male. Applicant must have 3.0 GPA or higher. Available to U.S. citizens.

Application Requirements: Application, essay, photo, resume, references, transcript. *Deadline:* June 15.

Contact: Emile Pitre, Chairman
Phi Beta Sigma Fraternity Inc.
2 Belmonte Circle, SW
Atlanta, GA 30311
Phone: 404-759-6827
E-mail: mikewhines@aol.com

PROGRESSIVEU.ORG http://www.progressiveu.org

BLOGGING FOR PROGRESS

Participants must maintain a blog at the ProgressiveU website during contest period in order to be eligible. Winners are based on total accumulated points as of the last day of entry period with points awarded for each blog entry and comment accepted for posting to the Web site and for each read of a participants blog entries by members and visitors. Participants also have opportunities to earn bonus points towards the scholarship throughout the semester by participating in various programs.

Award: Scholarship for use in freshman, sophomore, junior, senior, or graduate years; not renewable. *Number:* 3–6. *Amount:* $500–$1000.

Eligibility Requirements: Applicant must be age 16 and over and enrolled or expecting to enroll full- or part-time at a two-year or four-year or technical institution or university. Available to U.S. citizens.

Application Requirements: Application, applicant must enter a contest. *Deadline:* April 15.

Contact: Mrs. Fallon Glenn, Director of Public Relations
ProgressiveU.org
2300 Rebsamen Park Road, Suite A107
Little Rock, AR 72202
Phone: 501-542-4465
E-mail: fallon@progressiveu.org

PRUDENT PUBLISHING COMPANY INC. http://www.gallerycollection.com

2ND ANNUAL CREATE-A-GREETING-CARD $10,000 SCHOLARSHIP CONTEST

$10,000 scholarship for high school, college, and university students to create a greeting card cover using original photos, artwork and computer graphics. The winning design will be made into a greeting card. Must be at least 14 years of age.

Award: Scholarship for use in freshman, sophomore, junior, senior, graduate, or postgraduate years; not renewable. *Number:* 1. *Amount:* $10,000.

Eligibility Requirements: Applicant must be age 14 and over and enrolled or expecting to enroll full- or part-time at a two-year or four-year or technical institution or university. Available to U.S. citizens.

Application Requirements: Application, applicant must enter a contest, greeting card design. *Deadline:* January 15.

Contact: Scholarship Administrator
Prudent Publishing Company Inc.
65 Challenger Road
Ridgefield Park, NJ 07660
Phone: 201-641-7900
E-mail: scholarshipadmin@gallerycollection.com

PUSH FOR EXCELLENCE http://www.pushexcel.org

ORA LEE SANDERS SCHOLARSHIP

U.S. Citizens who will be freshmen, sophomore, juniors or seniors are eligible. The scholarship is renewable up to 4 years based upon GPA. Full time study with minimum 2.5 GPA.

Award: Scholarship for use in freshman, sophomore, junior, or senior years; renewable. *Number:* varies. *Amount:* $1000.

Eligibility Requirements: Applicant must be enrolled or expecting to enroll full-time at a four-year institution or university. Applicant must have 2.5 GPA or higher. Available to U.S. citizens.

Application Requirements: Application, essay, references, self-addressed stamped envelope, transcript, proof of current enrollment or acceptance in a college or university. *Deadline:* April 30.

Contact: Scholarship Committee
Push for Excellence
930 East 50th Street
Chicago, IL 60615
Phone: 773-373-3366
E-mail: info@pushexcel.org

RAISE THE NATION FOUNDATION http://www.raisethenation.org

RAISE THE NATION CHILD OF A SINGLE PARENT SCHOLARSHIP

Scholarship to reduce the financial burden of paying for college faced by children of single parent women. Applicant must be claimed by their mother as a dependent child (under 24 years of age) and entering or currently enrolled in a postsecondary course of study.

Award: Scholarship for use in freshman, sophomore, junior, or senior years; renewable. *Number:* 1–50. *Amount:* $100–$5000.

Eligibility Requirements: Applicant must be age 17-23 and enrolled or expecting to enroll full- or part-time at a two-year or four-year or technical institution or university. Available to U.S. citizens.

Application Requirements: Application, autobiography, essay, financial need analysis, proof of single parent status (tax form 1040), proof of acceptance or enrollment into a postsecondary degree program. *Fee:* $20. *Deadline:* varies.

Contact: Michelle McMullen, Executive Director
Raise the Nation Foundation
PO Box 8058
Albuquerque, NM 87198
Phone: 505-265-1201
E-mail: suppoetdesk@raisethenation.org

RAISE THE NATION CONTINUING EDUCATION SCHOLARSHIP

Scholarship available to single parent women who would like to go to school or continue with their education, but have been denied sufficient resources. Applicant must be accepted or currently enrolled in a postsecondary course of study to qualify for this scholarship.

Award: Scholarship for use in freshman, sophomore, junior, or senior years; renewable. *Number:* 1–50. *Amount:* $100–$5000.

Eligibility Requirements: Applicant must be age 18-99; enrolled or expecting to enroll full- or part-time at a two-year or four-year or technical institution or university and single female. Available to U.S. citizens.

Application Requirements: Application, autobiography, essay, financial need analysis, proof of enrollment or acceptance into a postsecondary program, proof of single parent status (tax form 1040). *Fee:* $20. *Deadline:* varies.

Contact: Michelle McMullen, Executive Director
Raise the Nation Foundation
PO Box 8058
Albuquerque, NM 87198
Phone: 505-265-1201
E-mail: suppoetdesk@raisethenation.org

RESOURCE CENTER

HEATHER JOY MEMORIAL SCHOLARSHIP

One-time award given to students in honor of Heather Joy, who lost her young life due to financial needs. Available to part- or full-time students enrolled in technical school, college, or university. Recipient selection will be based on a 250-word original essay and referral letters.

Award: Scholarship for use in freshman, sophomore, junior, senior, graduate, or postgraduate years; not renewable. *Number:* 1–10. *Amount:* $50–$1000.

Eligibility Requirements: Applicant must be enrolled or expecting to enroll full- or part-time at a two-year or four-year or technical institution or university. Available to U.S. and non-U.S. citizens.

Application Requirements: Application, essay, references, self-addressed stamped envelope, transcript. *Fee:* $5. *Deadline:* varies.

Contact: Dee Blaha, Owner
Resource Center
16362 Wilson Boulevard
Masaryktown, FL 34604-7335
Phone: 352-799-1381
E-mail: dblaha1@tampabay.rr.com

ROPAGE GROUP LLC http://www.patricias-scholarship.org

PATRICIA M. MCNAMARA MEMORIAL SCHOLARSHIP

Scholarship open to students who are already attending college or will be attending college within a year of the deadline. Students must utilize the online form to submit the scholarship application and essay. For more details, see Web site: http://www.patricias-scholarship.org.

Award: Scholarship for use in freshman, sophomore, junior, or senior years; not renewable. *Number:* 1. *Amount:* $1000.

Eligibility Requirements: Applicant must be enrolled or expecting to enroll full- or part-time at a two-year or four-year or technical institution or university. Available to U.S. and non-U.S. citizens.

Application Requirements: Application, essay. *Deadline:* varies.

Contact: Scholarship Committee
Ropage Group LLC
8877 North 107th Avenue, Suite 302, PO Box 287
Peoria, AZ 85345
E-mail: questions@patricias-scholarship.org

SABERTEC LLC/BLADE YOUR RIDE http://www.bladeyourride.com

BLADE YOUR RIDE SCHOLARSHIP PROGRAM

Scholarship for students enrolled in a full time bachelor's degree program or master's degree program. Applicant should maintain a GPA of 3.0.

Award: Scholarship for use in freshman, sophomore, junior, senior, or graduate years; not renewable. *Number:* 3. *Amount:* $5000–$15,000.

Eligibility Requirements: Applicant must be enrolled or expecting to enroll full-time at a four-year institution or university. Applicant must have 3.0 GPA or higher. Available to U.S. and non-U.S. citizens.

Application Requirements: Application, resume, references, transcript, creative talents Webcast. *Deadline:* June 30.

Contact: Ashley Fontaine, Scholarship Committee
Sabertec LLC/Blade Your Ride
3801 North Capital of Texas Highway E240D-B7
Austin, TX 78746
Phone: 512-703-8255
E-mail: ashley@bladeyourride.com

SALLIE MAE FUND http://www.thesalliemaefund.org

SALLIE MAE FUND UNMET NEED SCHOLARSHIP PROGRAM

Open to families with a combined income of $30,000 or less, this program is intended to supplement financial aid packages that fall more than $1000 short of students' financial need. Open to U.S. citizens and permanent residents who are accepted or enrolled as full-time undergraduate students. Students must have minimum 2.5 GPA.

Award: Scholarship for use in freshman, sophomore, junior, or senior years; not renewable. *Number:* varies. *Amount:* $1000–$3800.

Eligibility Requirements: Applicant must be enrolled or expecting to enroll full-time at a four-year institution or university. Applicant must have 2.5 GPA or higher. Available to U.S. citizens.

Application Requirements: Application, test scores, transcript. *Deadline:* May 31.

Contact: Scholarship Committee
Sallie Mae Fund
One Scholarship Way, PO Box 297
Saint Peter, MN 56082
Phone: 507-931-1682

SALLIE MAE 911 EDUCATION FUND LOAN RELIEF

Funds individuals or spouses, same-sex partners, or co-borrowers of those killed or declared totally and permanently disabled in the 9/11 terrorist attacks, and who are borrowers of loan owned or serviced by Sallie Mae. Applicant can also be an estate administrator who has held an education loan.

Award: Forgivable loan for use in sophomore, junior, or senior years; not renewable. *Number:* varies. *Amount:* up to $5000.

Eligibility Requirements: Applicant must be enrolled or expecting to enroll full- or part-time at a two-year or four-year or technical institution or university. Available to U.S. citizens.

Application Requirements: Application, supporting documents. *Deadline:* continuous.

Contact: Laura Gemery, Scholarship Committee
Sallie Mae Fund
12061 Bluemont Way
Reston, VA 20190
Phone: 703-810-3000
Fax: 703-984-5042

SALLIE MAE 911 EDUCATION FUND SCHOLARSHIP PROGRAM

Scholarship program open to children of those who were killed or permanently disabled as a result of the 9/11 terrorist attacks who are enrolled as full-time undergraduate students at approved accredited institutions. May be renewed on an annual academic basis subject to satisfactory academic progress. Applications available at the following Web site: http://www.thesalliemaefund.org/smfnew/pdf/911application.pdf.

Award: Scholarship for use in freshman, sophomore, junior, or senior years; renewable. *Number:* up to 335. *Amount:* up to $2500.

Eligibility Requirements: Applicant must be enrolled or expecting to enroll full-time at a two-year or four-year institution or university. Available to U.S. citizens.

Application Requirements: Application, financial need analysis, proof of death or disability of parent. *Deadline:* May 15.

Contact: Laura Gemery, Scholarship Committee
Sallie Mae Fund
12061 Bluemont Way
Reston, VA 20190
Phone: 703-810-3000
Fax: 703-984-5042

SCHOLARSHIPEXPERTS.COM http://www.scholarshipexperts.com/apply.htx

SCHOLARSHIPEXPERTS.COM SCHOLARSHIP PROGRAM

All scholarship programs are open to U.S. students who are 13 years of age and older, and who are currently enrolled or plan to enroll in an accredited post-secondary institution of higher education. Five separate scholarship programs are offered with varying deadlines throughout the year. Students must submit a short essay. See Web site for specific essay questions, deadlines, and online application: http://www.scholarshipexperts.com/apply.htx

Award: Scholarship for use in freshman, sophomore, junior, senior, graduate, or postgraduate years; not renewable. *Number:* 21. *Amount:* $1000–$5000.

Eligibility Requirements: Applicant must be age 13 and over and enrolled or expecting to enroll full- or part-time at a two-year or four-year or technical institution or university. Available to U.S. citizens.

Application Requirements: Application, essay. *Deadline:* varies.

Contact: Scholarship Committee
ScholarshipExperts.com
2950 Halcyon Lane, Suite 501
Jacksonville, FL 32223
Phone: 904-854-6750
Fax: 904-854-6751
E-mail: members@scholarshipexperts.com

SIEMENS FOUNDATION/SIEMENS-WESTINGHOUSE SCHOLARSHIP http://www.siemens-foundation.org

SIEMENS AWARDS FOR ADVANCED PLACEMENT

$2000 scholarships for students from each state who have earned the greatest number of AP grades of 5 in eight exams. Each state potentially has two winners, one male and one female.

Award: Prize for use in freshman year; not renewable. *Number:* 102. *Amount:* $2000–$5000.

Eligibility Requirements: Applicant must be high school student and planning to enroll or expecting to enroll full-time at a four-year institution or university. Available to U.S. citizens.

Application Requirements: Application. *Deadline:* varies.

Contact: Scholarship Committee
Siemens Foundation/Siemens-Westinghouse Scholarship
170 Wood Avenue South
Iselin, NJ 08830
Phone: 877-822-5233
Fax: 732-603-5890
E-mail: foundation.us@siemens.com

SIR EDWARD YOUDE MEMORIAL FUND COUNCIL http://www.sfaa.gov.hk

SIR EDWARD YOUDE MEMORIAL SCHOLARSHIPS FOR OVERSEAS STUDIES

• *See page 700*

SPENDONLIFE.COM http://students.spendonlife.com

SPENDONLIFE COLLEGE SCHOLARSHIP

$500 to $5000 scholarship program offers financial assistance for college students who are unable to obtain student loans due to a negative credit history. Awards are based on financial need and participation in the application process.

Award: Scholarship for use in freshman, sophomore, junior, senior, graduate, or postgraduate years; not renewable. *Number:* 2–10. *Amount:* $500–$5000.

Eligibility Requirements: Applicant must be enrolled or expecting to enroll full-time at a two-year or four-year institution or university. Available to U.S. citizens.

Application Requirements: Application, essay. *Deadline:* May 15.

Contact: Keith Lauren, Scholarship Administrator
SPENDonLIFE.com
8144 Walnut Hill Lane, Suite 510
Dallas, TX 75231
Phone: 469-916-1700 Ext. 269
E-mail: scholarship@spendonlife.com

STATE DEPARTMENT FEDERAL CREDIT UNION ANNUAL SCHOLARSHIP PROGRAM http://www.sdfcu.org

STATE DEPARTMENT FEDERAL CREDIT UNION ANNUAL SCHOLARSHIP PROGRAM

Scholarships available to members who are currently enrolled in a degree program and have completed 12 credit hours of coursework at an accredited college or university. Must have an account in good standing in their name with SDFCU, have a minimum 2.5 GPA, submit official cumulative transcripts, and describe need for financial assistance to continue their education.

Award: Scholarship for use in freshman, sophomore, junior, or senior years; renewable. *Number:* varies. *Amount:* varies.

Eligibility Requirements: Applicant must be enrolled or expecting to enroll full-time at a four-year institution or university. Applicant must have 2.5 GPA or higher. Available to U.S. citizens.

Application Requirements: Application, applicant must enter a contest, financial need analysis, transcript, personal statement. *Deadline:* April 11.

Contact: Scholarship Coordinator
State Department Federal Credit Union Annual Scholarship Program
1630 King Street
Alexandria, VA 22314
Phone: 703-706-5019
E-mail: sdfcu@sdfcu.org

STEPHEN PHILLIPS MEMORIAL SCHOLARSHIP FUND http://www.phillips-scholarship.org

STEPHEN PHILLIPS MEMORIAL SCHOLARSHIP FUND

Award open to full-time undergraduate students with financial need who display academic excellence, strong citizenship and character, and a desire to make a meaningful contribution to society. For more details see Web site: http://www.phillips-scholarship.org.

Award: Scholarship for use in freshman, sophomore, junior, or senior years; renewable. *Number:* 150–200. *Amount:* $3000–$10,000.

Eligibility Requirements: Applicant must be enrolled or expecting to enroll full-time at a two-year or four-year institution or university. Applicant must have 3.0 GPA or higher. Available to U.S. citizens.

Application Requirements: Application, essay, financial need analysis, references, test scores, transcript. *Deadline:* May 1.

Contact: Karen Emery, Scholarship Coordinator
Stephen Phillips Memorial Scholarship Fund
PO Box 870
Salem, MA 01970
Phone: 978-744-2111
Fax: 978-744-0456
E-mail: kemery@spscholars.org

STRAIGHTFORWARD MEDIA http://www.straightforwardmedia.com

DALE E. FRIDELL MEMORIAL SCHOLARSHIP

Scholarships are open to anyone aspiring to attend a university, college, trade school, technical institute, vocational training, or other postsecondary education program. Eligible students may not have already been awarded a full tuition scholarship or waiver from another source. International students are welcome to apply.

Award: Scholarship for use in freshman, sophomore, junior, senior, or graduate years; not renewable. *Number:* 1. *Amount:* $1000.

Eligibility Requirements: Applicant must be enrolled or expecting to enroll full- or part-time at a two-year or four-year or technical institution or university. Available to U.S. and non-U.S. citizens.

Application Requirements: Essay. *Deadline:* varies.

Contact: Scholarship Committee
StraightForward Media
2040 West Main Street, Suite 104
Rapid City, SD 57701
Phone: 605-348-3042
Fax: 605-348-3043

GET OUT OF DEBT SCHOLARSHIP

Annual award to help students hampered by debt to continue their studies. Must be attending or planning to attend a college, trade school, technical institute, vocational program or other postsecondary education program.

Award: Scholarship for use in freshman, sophomore, junior, senior, graduate, or postgraduate years; not renewable. *Number:* 1–4. *Amount:* $500.

Eligibility Requirements: Applicant must be enrolled or expecting to enroll full- or part-time at a two-year or four-year or technical institution or university. Available to U.S. and non-U.S. citizens.

Application Requirements: Essay. *Deadline:* varies.

Contact: Scholarship Committee
StraightForward Media
2040 West Main Street, Suite 104
Rapid City, SD 57701
Phone: 605-348-3042
Fax: 605-348-3043

MESOTHELIOMA MEMORIAL SCHOLARSHIP

Open to all students attending or planning to attend a postsecondary educational program, including 2- or 4-year college or university, vocational school, continuing education, ministry training, and job skills training. Refer to Web site for details: http://www.straightforwardmedia.com/meso/mesothelioma-memorial.php.

Award: Scholarship for use in freshman, sophomore, junior, senior, graduate, or postgraduate years; not renewable. *Number:* 1–4. *Amount:* $500.

Eligibility Requirements: Applicant must be enrolled or expecting to enroll full- or part-time at a two-year or four-year or technical institution or university. Available to U.S. and non-U.S. citizens.

Application Requirements: Essay. *Deadline:* varies.

Contact: Scholarship Committee
StraightForward Media
2040 West Main Street, Suite 104
Rapid City, SD 57701
Phone: 605-348-3042
Fax: 605-348-3043

STUDENT INSIGHTS http://www.student-view.com

STUDENT-VIEW SCHOLARSHIP PROGRAM

Scholarship available by random drawing from the pool of entrants who respond to an online survey from Student Insights marketing organization. Parental permission to participate required for applicants under age 18.

Award: Scholarship for use in freshman year; not renewable. *Number:* 1–9. *Amount:* $500–$3000.

Eligibility Requirements: Applicant must be high school student; planning to enroll or expecting to enroll full-time at a two-year or four-year or technical institution or university and single. Available to U.S. citizens.

Application Requirements: Application. *Deadline:* April 22.

Contact: Program Coordinator
Student Insights
136 Justice Drive
Valencia, PA 16059
Phone: 724-612-3685
E-mail: contact@studentinsights.com

SUNSHINE LADY FOUNDATION INC. http://www.sunshinelady.org

WOMEN'S INDEPENDENCE SCHOLARSHIP PROGRAM

Scholarship of $250 to $5000 to enable female survivors of domestic violence (partner abuse) to return to school to gain skills necessary to become independent and self-sufficient. Requires sponsorship by nonprofit domestic violence service agency. First priority candidates are single mothers with young children. Must be U.S. citizens or permanent legal residents with critical financial need. Deadline varies.

Award: Scholarship for use in freshman, sophomore, junior, senior, or graduate years; renewable. *Number:* 500–600. *Amount:* $250–$5000.

Eligibility Requirements: Applicant must be enrolled or expecting to enroll full- or part-time at a two-year or four-year or technical institution or university and female. Available to U.S. citizens.

Application Requirements: Application, essay, financial need analysis, references. *Deadline:* varies.

Contact: Nancy Soward, Program Director
Sunshine Lady Foundation Inc.
4900 Randall Parkway, Suite H
Wilmington, NC 28403
Phone: 910-397-7742 Ext. 101
Fax: 910-397-0023
E-mail: nancy@sunshinelady.org

SUNTRUST BANK http://www.suntrusteducation.com

OFF TO COLLEGE SCHOLARSHIP SWEEPSTAKES AWARD

Award of $100 to a high school senior planning to attend college in the fall. Must complete an online entry form by accessing the Web site: http://www.offtocollege.info.

Award: Scholarship for use in freshman year; not renewable. *Number:* 15. *Amount:* $1000.

Eligibility Requirements: Applicant must be high school student and planning to enroll or expecting to enroll full- or part-time at a two-year or four-year institution or university. Available to U.S. citizens.

Application Requirements: Application. *Deadline:* continuous.

Contact: Joy Blauvelt, Scholarship Coordinator
SunTrust Bank
1001 Semmes Avenue
PO Box 27172
Richmond, VA 23224
Phone: 800-552-3006
Fax: 804-319-4823

TALBOTS CHARITABLE FOUNDATION http://www.talbots.com/

TALBOTS WOMEN'S SCHOLARSHIP FUND

One-time scholarship for women who earned their high school diploma or GED at least 10 years ago, and who are now seeking an undergraduate college degree.

Award: Scholarship for use in freshman, sophomore, junior, or senior years; not renewable. *Number:* 5–50. *Amount:* $1000–$10,000.

Eligibility Requirements: Applicant must be enrolled or expecting to enroll full- or part-time at a two-year or four-year or technical institution or university and female. Available to U.S. citizens.

Application Requirements: Application, essay, financial need analysis, references, transcript. *Deadline:* January 3.

Contact: Genny Miller, Program Manager, Scholarship America
Talbots Charitable Foundation
1 Scholarship Way, PO Box 297
Saint Peter, MN 56082
Phone: 507-931-0452
Fax: 507-931-9278
E-mail: gmiller@scholarshipamerica.org

TALL CLUBS INTERNATIONAL FOUNDATION INC, AND TALL CLUBS INTERNATIONAL INC. http://www.tall.org

KAE SUMNER EINFELDT SCHOLARSHIP

Females 5'10" or males 6'2" (minimum heights) are eligible to apply for the scholarship. Interested individuals should contact their local Tall Clubs Chapter. Canadian and U.S. winners are selected from finalists submitted by each local chapter.

Award: Scholarship for use in freshman year; not renewable. *Number:* 4–6. *Amount:* $1000.

Eligibility Requirements: Applicant must be high school student; age 17-21 and planning to enroll or expecting to enroll full- or part-time at a four-year institution or university. Available to U.S. and Canadian citizens.

Application Requirements: Application, essay, photo, references, transcript, verification of height. *Deadline:* April 1.

Contact: Shiela Koster, Director
Tall Clubs International Foundation Inc, and Tall Clubs International Inc.
9837 Forbes Avenue
North Ridge, CA 91343
Phone: 818-895-2665
Fax: 818-892-6126
E-mail: bskoster@aol.com

TEXAS FEDERATION OF BUSINESS AND PROFESSIONAL WOMEN'S FOUNDATION http://www.bpwtx.org/foundation.asp

GILDA MURRAY SCHOLARSHIP

Scholarship of $500 awarded to members of BPW/Texas, age 25 or older, to obtain education or training at an accredited college or university, technology institution, or training center. The number of awards varies.

Award: Scholarship for use in freshman, sophomore, junior, or senior years; not renewable. *Number:* varies. *Amount:* $500.

Eligibility Requirements: Applicant must be age 25 and over and enrolled or expecting to enroll full- or part-time at a four-year or technical institution or university. Available to U.S. and non-U.S. citizens.

Application Requirements: Application, essay, references, regular attendance at LO meetings, active participation on at least one BPW committee. *Deadline:* May 1.

Contact: Jerrie Schubert, Executive Director
Texas Federation of Business and Professional Women's Foundation
803 Forest Ridge Drive, Suite 104
Bedford, TX 76022
Phone: 817-283-0862
Fax: 817-283-0872
E-mail: bpwtx@sbcglobal.net

TEXAS MUTUAL INSURANCE COMPANY http://www.texasmutual.com

TEXAS MUTUAL INSURANCE COMPANY SCHOLARSHIP PROGRAM

A scholarship program open to qualified family members of policyholder employees who died from on-the-job injuries or accidents, policyholder employees who qualify for lifetime income benefits pursuant to the Texas Workers Compensation Act, and family members of injured employees who qualify for lifetime income benefits.

Award: Scholarship for use in freshman, sophomore, junior, or senior years; renewable. *Number:* 11. *Amount:* up to $4000.

Eligibility Requirements: Applicant must be age 17 and over and enrolled or expecting to enroll full- or part-time at a two-year or four-year or technical institution. Applicant must have 2.5 GPA or higher. Available to U.S. and non-U.S. citizens.

Application Requirements: Application, financial need analysis, references, test scores, transcript, fee bill, death certificate of family member, acceptance letter for freshmen. *Deadline:* varies.

Contact: Doris Limon, Administrative Assistant
Texas Mutual Insurance Company
6210 East Highway 290
PO Box 12058
Austin, TX 78723-1098
Phone: 800-859-5995 Ext. 3820
Fax: 512-224-3999
E-mail: dlimon@texasmutual.com

TG http://www.tgslc.org

CHARLEY WOOTAN GRANT PROGRAM

Grants available to high school seniors or graduates, including GED recipients, who plan to enroll or are already enrolled at least half-time in an undergraduate course of study. Must be a U.S. citizen or permanant resident, demonstrate

TG (continued)

financial need, and be eligible to receive Title IV federal financial aid funding. Only the first 5,000 applications submitted will be considered. See Web site for details: http://www.aie.org/wootan.

Award: Grant for use in freshman, sophomore, junior, or senior years; not renewable. *Number:* varies. *Amount:* $1000–$4245.

Eligibility Requirements: Applicant must be enrolled or expecting to enroll full- or part-time at a two-year or four-year or technical institution or university. Available to U.S. citizens.

Application Requirements: Application, financial need analysis, transcript. *Deadline:* May 5.

Contact: Grant Program Manager
TG
301 Sundance Parkway
PO Box 83100
Round Rock, TX 78683-3100
Phone: 800-537-4180
E-mail: wootan@scholarshipamerica.org

THETA DELTA CHI EDUCATIONAL FOUNDATION INC. http://www.tdx.org

THETA DELTA CHI EDUCATIONAL FOUNDATION INC. SCHOLARSHIP

Scholarships for undergraduate or graduate students enrolled in an accredited institution. Awards are based on candidate's history of service to the fraternity, scholastic achievement, and need. See Web site for application and additional information: http://www.tdx.org/scholarship/scholarship.html.

Award: Scholarship for use in freshman, sophomore, junior, senior, or graduate years; renewable. *Number:* 15. *Amount:* $1000–$5000.

Eligibility Requirements: Applicant must be enrolled or expecting to enroll full-time at a four-year institution or university. Available to U.S. and non-U.S. citizens.

Application Requirements: Application, financial need analysis, references, transcript. *Deadline:* May 15.

Contact: William McClung, Executive Director
Theta Delta Chi Educational Foundation Inc.
214 Lewis Wharf
Boston, MA 02110-3927
Phone: 617-742-8886
Fax: 617-742-8868
E-mail: execdir@tdx.org

THURGOOD MARSHALL SCHOLARSHIP FUND http://www.thurgoodmarshallfund.org

THURGOOD MARSHALL SCHOLARSHIP

Merit scholarships for students attending one of 45 member HBCUs (historically black colleges, universities) including 5 member law schools. Must maintain an average GPA of 3.0 to renew, demonstrate financial need, and be a U.S. citizen. Apply through member HBCU's campus scholarship coordinator. For further details refer to Web site: http://www.thurgoodmarshallfund.org.

Award: Scholarship for use in freshman, sophomore, junior, senior, or graduate years; renewable. *Number:* varies. *Amount:* up to $4400.

Eligibility Requirements: Applicant must be enrolled or expecting to enroll full-time at a four-year institution or university. Applicant must have 3.0 GPA or higher. Available to U.S. citizens.

Application Requirements: Application, essay, financial need analysis, interview, photo, resume, references, test scores, transcript. *Deadline:* March 15.

Contact: Sophia Rogers, Scholarship Manager
Thurgood Marshall Scholarship Fund
80 Maiden Lane, Suite 2204
New York, NY 10038
Phone: 212-573-8888
Fax: 212-573-8497
E-mail: srogers@tmcfund.org

TRIANGLE EDUCATION FOUNDATION http://www.triangle.org

MORTIN SCHOLARSHIP

One-time award of $2500 annually for an active member of the Triangle Fraternity. Awarded based on a combination of need, grades and participation in campus and Triangle Activities. Minimum 3.0 GPA. Further information available at Web site http://www.triangle.org.

Award: Scholarship for use in freshman, sophomore, junior, or senior years; not renewable. *Number:* 1. *Amount:* up to $2500.

Eligibility Requirements: Applicant must be enrolled or expecting to enroll full-time at a four-year institution or university and male. Applicant must have 3.0 GPA or higher. Available to U.S. and non-U.S. citizens.

Application Requirements: Application, essay, financial need analysis, references, self-addressed stamped envelope, transcript. *Deadline:* February 15.

Contact: Scott Bova, President
Triangle Education Foundation
120 South Center Street
Plainfield, IN 46168-1214
Phone: 317-705-9803
Fax: 317-837-9642
E-mail: sbova@triangle.org

PETER AND BARBARA BYE SCHOLARSHIP

Scholarship for a Triangle Fraternity member for undergraduate study. Preference given to applicants from Cornell University Triangle chapter. Applicant must have a minimum GPA of 2.7. Additional information on Web site: http://www.triangle.org.

Award: Scholarship for use in freshman, sophomore, junior, or senior years; not renewable. *Number:* 1. *Amount:* up to $2000.

Eligibility Requirements: Applicant must be enrolled or expecting to enroll full- or part-time at a four-year institution or university and male. Available to U.S. and non-U.S. citizens.

Application Requirements: Application, financial need analysis, references, transcript. *Deadline:* February 15.

Contact: Scott Bova, President
Triangle Education Foundation
120 South Center Street
Plainfield, IN 46168-1214
Phone: 317-705-9803
Fax: 317-837-9642
E-mail: sbova@triangle.org

TROY STUDIOS http://www.cenimar.com

EXCELLENCE IN PREDICTING THE FUTURE AWARD

Two scholarship contests, open to students worldwide, with prizes awarded on alternate months. Participants must sign up for a free online account at: http://cenimar.com/contest/award.jsp. Players who make the best trades during the contest period win the prize, or, in the case of a tie, share the prize.

Award: Prize for use in freshman, sophomore, junior, senior, graduate, or postgraduate years; renewable. *Number:* 30–42. *Amount:* $100–$400.

Eligibility Requirements: Applicant must be enrolled or expecting to enroll full- or part-time at a two-year or four-year or technical institution or university. Available to U.S. and non-U.S. citizens.

Application Requirements: Applicant must enter a contest, electronic application. *Deadline:* varies.

Contact: George Troy, Owner
Troy Studios
5543 Saint Francis Circle West
Loomis, CA 95650
Phone: 916-632-8760
Fax: 916-632-9083
E-mail: support@cenimar.com

TWIN TOWERS ORPHAN FUND http://www.ttof.org

TWIN TOWERS ORPHAN FUND

Fund offers assistance to children who lost one or both parents in the terrorist attacks on September 11, 2001. Long-term education program established to provide higher education needs to children until they complete their uninterrupted studies, or reach age of majority. Visit Web site for additional information: http://www.ttof.org.

Award: Scholarship for use in freshman, sophomore, junior, senior, or graduate years; renewable. *Number:* varies. *Amount:* $5000–$7000.

Eligibility Requirements: Applicant must be enrolled or expecting to enroll full- or part-time at a two-year or four-year or technical institution or university. Available to U.S. and non-U.S. citizens.

Application Requirements: Application, financial need analysis, references, birth certificate, parent's death certificate, marriage license. *Deadline:* varies.

Contact: Karlene Boss, Case Manager
Twin Towers Orphan Fund
4800 Easton Drive, Suite 109
Bakersfield, CA 93309
Phone: 661-633-9076
Fax: 661-760-8981
E-mail: ttof2@ttof.org

TWO TEN FOOTWEAR FOUNDATION http://www.twoten.org

TWO TEN SUPER SCHOLARSHIPS

Scholarship available for candidates who meet the Two Ten scholarship criteria and exhibit extraordinary financial need. Super scholarship worth up to $15,000 per year and renewable for four years of undergraduate study. Should have minimum 2.5 GPA.

Award: Scholarship for use in freshman, sophomore, junior, or senior years; renewable. *Number:* 1. *Amount:* up to $15,000.

Eligibility Requirements: Applicant must be enrolled or expecting to enroll full-time at a four-year institution or university. Applicant must have 2.5 GPA or higher. Available to U.S. citizens.

Application Requirements: Application, essay, financial need analysis, references, transcript. *Deadline:* February 15.

Contact: Phyllis Molta, Director of Scholarship
Two Ten Footwear Foundation
1466 Main Street
Waltham, MA 02451-1623
Phone: 781-736-1503
Fax: 781-736-1555
E-mail: scholarship@twoten.org

ULMAN CANCER FUND FOR YOUNG ADULTS http://www.ulmanfund.org

MARILYN YETSO MEMORIAL SCHOLARSHIP

Provides support for the financial needs of college students who have a parent with cancer or who have lost a parent to cancer. Currently attending, or accepted to, a two- or four-year college, university or vocational program (including graduate and professional schools).

Award: Scholarship for use in freshman, sophomore, junior, or senior years; not renewable. *Number:* 1–2. *Amount:* $1000.

Eligibility Requirements: Applicant must be age 15-35 and enrolled or expecting to enroll full- or part-time at a two-year or four-year or technical institution or university. Available to U.S. and non-U.S. citizens.

Application Requirements: Application, autobiography, essay, financial need analysis, references, self-addressed stamped envelope, parent's medical history. *Deadline:* May 10.

Contact: Fay Baker, Scholarship Coordinator
Ulman Cancer Fund for Young Adults
4725 Dorsey Hall Drive, Suite A
PO Box 505
Ellicott City, MD 21042
Phone: 410-964-0202
Fax: 410-964-0402
E-mail: scholarship@ulmanfund.org

UNITED AGRIBUSINESS LEAGUE http://www.ual.org

UNITED AGRIBUSINESS LEAGUE SCHOLARSHIP PROGRAM

Award available to a student who is a member, or an employee of a member of UAL and/or UABT (or a child of a member or a child of an employee of a member) who is enrolled at an accredited college or university majoring in any field of study.

Award: Scholarship for use in freshman, sophomore, junior, senior, or graduate years; renewable. *Number:* 10–15. *Amount:* $1000–$5000.

Eligibility Requirements: Applicant must be enrolled or expecting to enroll full-time at a two-year or four-year institution or university. Applicant must have 2.5 GPA or higher. Available to U.S. and non-U.S. citizens.

Application Requirements: Application, essay, financial need analysis, resume, references, test scores, transcript. *Deadline:* March 30.

Contact: Christiane Steele, Scholarship Coordinator
United Agribusiness League
54 Corporate Park
Irvine, CA 92606-5105
Phone: 949-975-1424
Fax: 949-975-1573
E-mail: scholarship@ual.org

UNITED NEGRO COLLEGE FUND http://www.uncf.org

KECK FOUNDATION SCHOLARSHIP

Scholarship is available to any students attending UNCF colleges and universities whose families have suffered a financial hardship as a result of the September 11 tragedy.

Award: Scholarship for use in freshman, sophomore, junior, or senior years; renewable. *Number:* varies. *Amount:* $2000–$5000.

Eligibility Requirements: Applicant must be enrolled or expecting to enroll full- or part-time at a four-year institution or university. Applicant must have 2.5 GPA or higher. Available to U.S. citizens.

Application Requirements: Application. *Deadline:* varies.

Contact: Director, Program Services
United Negro College Fund
8260 Willow Oaks Corporate Drive
PO Box 10444
Fairfax, VA 22031-8044
Phone: 800-331-2244
E-mail: rebecca.bennett@uncf.org

UNITED STATES ACHIEVEMENT ACADEMY http://www.usaa-academy.com

DR. GEORGE A. STEVENS FOUNDER'S AWARD

One $10,000 scholarship cash grant to enhance the intellectual and personal growth of students who demonstrate a genuine interest in learning. Award must be used for educational purposes. Must maintain a minimum GPA of 3.0.

Award: Grant for use in freshman year; not renewable. *Number:* 1. *Amount:* $10,000.

Eligibility Requirements: Applicant must be high school student and planning to enroll or expecting to enroll full-time at a four-year institution or university. Applicant must have 3.0 GPA or higher. Available to U.S. and non-U.S. citizens.

Application Requirements: Application. *Deadline:* June 1.

Contact: Scholarship Committee
United States Achievement Academy
2528 Palumbo Drive
Lexington, KY 40509
Phone: 859-269-5674
Fax: 859-268-9068
E-mail: usaa@usaa-academy.com

NATIONAL SCHOLARSHIP CASH GRANT

The Foundation awards 400 national scholarship cash grants of $1500. All scholarship winners are determined by an independent selection committee. Winners are selected based on GPA, school activities, SAT scores (if applicable), honors and awards.

Award: Grant for use in freshman year; not renewable. *Number:* 400. *Amount:* $1500.

United States Achievement Academy (continued)

Eligibility Requirements: Applicant must be high school student and planning to enroll or expecting to enroll full-time at a four-year institution or university. Applicant must have 3.0 GPA or higher. Available to U.S. and non-U.S. citizens.

Application Requirements: Application. *Deadline:* June 1.

Contact: Scholarship Committee
United States Achievement Academy
2528 Palumbo Drive
Lexington, KY 40509
Phone: 859-269-5674
Fax: 859-268-9068
E-mail: usaa@usaa-academy.com

UNITED STATES-INDONESIA SOCIETY http://www.usindo.org

UNITED STATES-INDONESIA SOCIETY TRAVEL GRANTS

Grants are provided to fund travel to Indonesia or the United States for American and Indonesian students and professors to conduct research, language training or other independent study/research. Must have a minimum 3.0 GPA.

Award: Grant for use in freshman, sophomore, junior, senior, graduate, or postgraduate years; not renewable. *Number:* 1–15. *Amount:* $1000–$2000.

Eligibility Requirements: Applicant must be enrolled or expecting to enroll full- or part-time at a four-year institution or university. Applicant must have 3.0 GPA or higher. Available to U.S. and non-Canadian citizens.

Application Requirements: Application, resume, references, transcript, basic budget. *Deadline:* continuous.

Contact: Thomas Spooner, Educational Officer
United States-Indonesia Society
1625 Massachusetts Avenue, NW, Suite 550
Washington, DC 20036-2260
Phone: 202-232-1400
Fax: 202-232-7300
E-mail: tspooner@usindo.org

UNITED TRANSPORTATION UNION INSURANCE ASSOCIATION http://www.utuia.org

UTUIA SCHOLARSHIP

Scholarships of $500 awarded to undergraduate students. Applicant must be at least a high school senior or equivalent, age 25 or under, be a UTU or UTUIA insured member, the child or grandchild of a UTU or UTUIA insured member, or the child of a deceased UTU or UTUIA-insured member.

Award: Scholarship for use in freshman, sophomore, junior, or senior years; renewable. *Number:* 50. *Amount:* $500.

Eligibility Requirements: Applicant must be age 25 or under and enrolled or expecting to enroll full-time at a four-year institution or university. Available to U.S. citizens.

Application Requirements: Application. *Deadline:* March 31.

Contact: Scholarship Committee
United Transportation Union Insurance Association
14600 Detroit Avenue
Cleveland, OH 44107-4250
Phone: 216-228-9400

U.S. BANK INTERNET SCHOLARSHIP PROGRAM http://www.usbank.com

U.S. BANK INTERNET SCHOLARSHIP PROGRAM

One-time award for high school seniors who are planning to enroll full-time in an accredited two- or four-year college or university. Must apply online at Web site: http://www.usbank.com/studentbanking. Application available October to February. Please do not send any requests for application to address.

Award: Scholarship for use in freshman year; not renewable. *Number:* up to 30. *Amount:* up to $1000.

Eligibility Requirements: Applicant must be high school student and planning to enroll or expecting to enroll full-time at a two-year or four-year institution or university. Available to U.S. citizens.

Application Requirements: Application. *Deadline:* February 28.

Contact: Mary Ennis, Scholarship Coordinator
U.S. Bank Internet Scholarship Program
2322 East Sprague Avenue
Spokane, WA 99202
Phone: 800-242-1200
Fax: 888-329-8775
E-mail: mary.ennis@usbank.com

VHMNETWORK LLC http://www.vhmnetwork.com

ONLINE-DEGREE-SCHOLARSHIP

Advertising-based scholarship available twice a year to students age 18 and older for tuition, books, rent, or additional expenses. See Web site for details: http://www.Online-Degree-Scholarships.com.

Award: Scholarship for use in freshman, sophomore, junior, senior, graduate, or postgraduate years; not renewable. *Number:* 2. *Amount:* $2000.

Eligibility Requirements: Applicant must be age 18 and over and enrolled or expecting to enroll full- or part-time at a two-year or four-year or technical institution or university. Available to U.S. citizens.

Application Requirements: Application. *Deadline:* varies.

Contact: Michael Derilavova, President
VHMnetwork LLC
419 Lafayette Street, 2nd Floor
New York, NY 10003
Phone: 646-723-4353 Ext. 4444
Fax: 212-228-6636
E-mail: michael@vhmnetwork.com

WAL-MART FOUNDATION http://www.walmartfoundation.org

SAM WALTON COMMUNITY SCHOLARSHIP

Award for high school seniors not affiliated with Wal-Mart stores. Based on academic merit, financial need, and school or community work activities. Should be a permanent legal resident of the United States for at least one year. For use at an accredited two- or four-year U.S. institution. Applications available online at https://www.scholarshipadministrators.net, Access key: SWCS. Applicants may apply beginning November 1.

Award: Scholarship for use in freshman year; not renewable. *Number:* 2900–3400. *Amount:* $1000.

Eligibility Requirements: Applicant must be high school student and planning to enroll or expecting to enroll full-time at a two-year or four-year institution or university. Applicant must have 3.0 GPA or higher. Available to U.S. citizens.

Application Requirements: Application, essay, financial need analysis, test scores, transcript. *Deadline:* January 12.

Contact: Scholarship Program Administrators, Inc.
Wal-Mart Foundation
PO Box 22117
Nashville, TN 37202-2117
Phone: 866-851-3372
Fax: 615-523-7100

WOMEN'S JEWELRY ASSOCIATION http://www.womensjewelry.org

WJA MEMBER GRANT

Grants are generally up to $500 and can be used by members to pay for any aspect of further education during the year. For more information please visit Web site: http://www.womensjewelry.org/.

Award: Grant for use in freshman, sophomore, junior, senior, graduate, or postgraduate years; not renewable. *Number:* 1. *Amount:* up to $500.

Eligibility Requirements: Applicant must be enrolled or expecting to enroll full- or part-time at a two-year or four-year or technical institution or university and female. Available to U.S. and non-U.S. citizens.

Application Requirements: Application, essay. *Deadline:* January 1.

Contact: Scholarship Committee
Women's Jewelry Association
7000 West Southwest Highway, Suite 202
Chicago Ridge, IL 60415
Phone: 708-361-6266
Fax: 708-361-6166
E-mail: info@womensjewelry.org

ZETA PHI BETA SORORITY INC. NATIONAL EDUCATIONAL FOUNDATION http://www.zphib1920.org

GENERAL UNDERGRADUATE SCHOLARSHIP

Scholarships available for undergraduate students. Awarded for full-time study for one academic year. Check Web site for information and application: http://www.zphib1920.org.

Award: Scholarship for use in freshman, sophomore, junior, or senior years; not renewable. *Number:* 1. *Amount:* $500–$1000.

Eligibility Requirements: Applicant must be enrolled or expecting to enroll full-time at a four-year institution or university. Available to U.S. citizens.

Application Requirements: Application, essay, references, transcript, enrollment proof. *Deadline:* February 1.

Contact: Cheryl Williams, National Second Vice President
Zeta Phi Beta Sorority Inc. National Educational Foundation
1734 New Hampshire Avenue, NW
Washington, DC 20009-2595
Fax: 318-631-4028
E-mail: 2ndanti@zphib1920.org

ZINCH.COM http://www.zinch.com

ZINCH.COM GENERAL SCHOLARSHIP

The program awards outstanding high school students with scholarships ranging from $1000 to $5000. Both the financial need and merit of the student are considered. Winners are chosen based on the student's zinch.com profile. Must maintain a GPA of at least 2.0. Must apply at this Web site: http://www.zinch.com/scholarships.

Award: Scholarship for use in freshman year; renewable. *Number:* 1–8. *Amount:* $1000–$5000.

Eligibility Requirements: Applicant must be high school student and planning to enroll or expecting to enroll full- or part-time at a four-year institution or university. Available to U.S. and non-U.S. citizens.

Application Requirements: Application. *Deadline:* May 25.

Contact: Mr. Mick Hagen, CEO
Zinch.com
42 North University Avenue, Suite 210
Provo, UT 84604
Phone: 801-830-2048
Fax: 801-356-0293
E-mail: mickey@zinch.com

Indexes

Award Name

Sponsor

Academic Fields/ Career Goals

American Studies

Animal/Veterinary Sciences

Anthropology

Applied Sciences

Archaeology

Architecture

Area/Ethnic Studies

Art History

Arts

Asian Studies

Audiology

Aviation/Aerospace

Behavioral Science

Biology

Business/Consumer Services

Campus Activities

Canadian Studies

Chemical Engineering

Child and Family Studies

Civil Engineering

Classics

Communications

Computer Science/Data Processing

Construction Engineering/Management

Cosmetology

Criminal Justice/Criminology

Culinary Arts

Dental Health/Services

Drafting

Earth Science

Economics

Education

Electrical Engineering/Electronics

Energy and Power Engineering

Engineering/Technology

Engineering-Related Technologies

Entomology

Environmental Health

Environmental Science

European Studies

Fashion Design

Filmmaking/Video

Fire Sciences

Flexography

Food Science/Nutrition

Food Service/Hospitality

Foreign Language

Funeral Services/Mortuary Science

Gemology

Geography

German Studies

Graphics/Graphic Arts/Printing

Health Administration

Health and Medical Sciences

Health Information Management/ Technology

Heating, Air-Conditioning, and Refrigeration Mechanics

Historic Preservation and Conservation

History

Home Economics

Horticulture/Floriculture

Hospitality Management

Human Resources

Humanities

Hydrology

Industrial Design

Insurance and Actuarial Science

Interior Design

International Migration

International Studies

Journalism

Landscape Architecture

Law Enforcement/Police Administration

Law/Legal Services

Library and Information Sciences

Literature/English/Writing

Marine Biology

Marine/Ocean Engineering

Materials Science, Engineering, and Metallurgy

Mathematics

Mechanical Engineering

Meteorology/Atmospheric Science

Military and Defense Studies

Museum Studies

Music

Natural Resources

Natural Sciences

Neurobiology

Nuclear Science

Nursing

Occupational Safety and Health

Oceanography

Oncology

Optometry

Osteopathy

Paper and Pulp Engineering

Peace and Conflict Studies

Performing Arts

Pharmacy

Philosophy

Photojournalism/Photography

Physical Sciences and Math

Political Science

Psychology

Public Health

Public Policy and Administration

Radiology

Real Estate

Recreation, Parks, Leisure Studies

Religion/Theology

Science, Technology, and Society

Social Sciences

Social Services

Special Education

Sports-Related/Exercise Science

Surveying; Surveying Technology, Cartography, or Geographic Information Science

Therapy/Rehabilitation

Trade/Technical Specialties

Transportation

Travel/Tourism

TV/Radio Broadcasting

Urban and Regional Planning

Women's Studies

Civic, Professional, Social, or Union Affiliation

Corporate Affiliation

Employment/Volunteer Experience

Fine Arts

Food Service

Government/Politics

Harness Racing

Helping Handicapped

Hospitality/Hotel Administration/Operations

Human Services

Journalism/Broadcasting

Leather/Footwear Industry

Library Work

Mentoring/Advising

Migrant Work

Nursing

Occupational Health and Safety

Physical Therapy/Rehabilitation

Police/Firefighting

Private Club/Caddying

Railroad Industry

Roadway Work

Seafaring/Fishing Industry

Teaching/Education

Transportation Industry

Travel and Tourism Industry

U.S. Government Foreign Service

Impairment

Military Service

Air Force

Air Force National Guard

Army

Army National Guard

Coast Guard

General

Marine Corps

Navy

Nationality or Ethnic Heritage

American Indian/Alaska Native

Arab

Armenian

Asian/Pacific Islander

Australian

Black, Non-Hispanic

Canadian

Chinese

Croatian/Serbian

English

Former Soviet Union

Greek

Hispanic

Indian

Italian

Japanese

Jewish

Korean

Latin American/Caribbean

Latvian

Lithuanian

Mexican

Mongolian

New Zealander

Nicaraguan

Norwegian

Polish

Portuguese

Russian

Scottish

Slavic/Czech

Spanish

Swiss

Ukrainian

Welsh

Religious Affiliation

Residence

Alabama

Alaska

Alberta

Arizona

Arkansas

British Columbia

Delaware

District of Columbia

Florida

Georgia

Hawaii

Idaho

Illinois

Indiana

Iowa

Kansas

Kentucky

Louisiana

Maine

Manitoba

Maryland

Massachusetts

Michigan

Minnesota

Mississippi

Missouri

Montana

Nebraska

Nevada

New Brunswick

New Hampshire

New Jersey

New Mexico

New York

Newfoundland

North Carolina

North Dakota

North West Territories

Nova Scotia

Ohio

Oklahoma

Ontario

Oregon

Pennsylvania

Prince Edward Island

Puerto Rico

Quebec

Rhode Island

Saskatchewan

South Carolina

South Dakota

Tennessee

Texas

Utah

Vermont

Virginia

Washington

West Virginia

Wisconsin

Wyoming

Yukon

Location of Study

Colorado

Connecticut

Delaware

District of Columbia

Florida

Georgia

Hawaii

Idaho

Illinois

Indiana

Iowa

Kansas

Kentucky

Louisiana

Maine

Manitoba

Maryland

Massachusetts

Michigan

Minnesota

Mississippi

Missouri

Montana

Nebraska

North Dakota

North West Territories

Nova Scotia

Ohio

Oklahoma

Ontario

Oregon

Pennsylvania

Utah

Vermont

Virginia

Washington

West Virginia

Wisconsin

Wyoming

Yukon

Talent/Interest Area

LGBT Issues

Music

Music/Singing

Photography/Photogrammetry/ Filmmaking

Polish Language

Public Speaking

Scandinavian Language

Science

Scuba diving

Sewing

Spanish Language

Theater

Wildlife Conservation/Animal Rescue

Writing

NOTES

NOTES

NOTES

NOTES

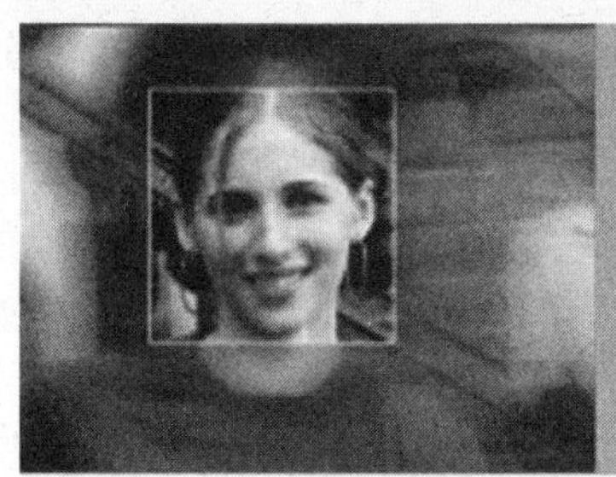

Peterson's
Book Satisfaction Survey

Give Us Your Feedback

Thank you for choosing Peterson's as your source for personalized solutions for your education and career achievement. Please take a few minutes to answer the following questions. Your answers will go a long way in helping us to produce the most user-friendly and comprehensive resources to meet your individual needs.

When completed, please tear out this page and mail it to us at:

Publishing Department
Peterson's, a Nelnet company
2000 Lenox Drive
Lawrenceville, NJ 08648

You can also complete this survey online at **www.petersons.com/booksurvey.**

1. What is the ISBN of the book you have purchased? (The ISBN can be found on the book's back cover in the lower right-hand corner.) ____________________

2. Where did you purchase this book?

- ❑ Retailer, such as Barnes & Noble
- ❑ Online reseller, such as Amazon.com
- ❑ Petersons.com
- ❑ Other (please specify) ____________________

3. If you purchased this book on Petersons.com, please rate the following aspects of your online purchasing experience on a scale of 4 to 1 (4 = Excellent and 1 = Poor).

	4	3	2	1
Comprehensiveness of Peterson's Online Bookstore page	❑	❑	❑	❑
Overall online customer experience	❑	❑	❑	❑

4. Which category best describes you?

- ❑ High school student
- ❑ Parent of high school student
- ❑ College student
- ❑ Graduate/professional student
- ❑ Returning adult student
- ❑ Teacher
- ❑ Counselor
- ❑ Working professional/military
- ❑ Other (please specify) ____________________

5. Rate your overall satisfaction with this book.

Extremely Satisfied	Satisfied	Not Satisfied
❑	❑	❑

6. Rate each of the following aspects of this book on a scale of 4 to 1 (4 = Excellent and 1 = Poor).

	4	3	2	1
Comprehensiveness of the information	❑	❑	❑	❑
Accuracy of the information	❑	❑	❑	❑
Usability	❑	❑	❑	❑
Cover design	❑	❑	❑	❑
Book layout	❑	❑	❑	❑
Special features *(e.g., CD, flashcards, charts, etc.)*	❑	❑	❑	❑
Value for the money	❑	❑	❑	❑

7. This book was recommended by:

❑ Guidance counselor
❑ Parent/guardian
❑ Family member/relative
❑ Friend
❑ Teacher
❑ Not recommended by anyone—I found the book on my own
❑ Other (please specify) ______________________________

8. Would you recommend this book to others?

Yes	Not Sure	No
❑	❑	❑

9. Please provide any additional comments.

____

____

____

____

____

Remember, you can tear out this page and mail it to us at:

Publishing Department
Peterson's, a Nelnet company
2000 Lenox Drive
Lawrenceville, NJ 08648

or you can complete the survey online at **www.petersons.com/booksurvey.**

Your feedback is important to us at Peterson's, and we thank you for your time!

If you would like us to keep in touch with you about new products and services, please include your e-mail address here: ______________________________